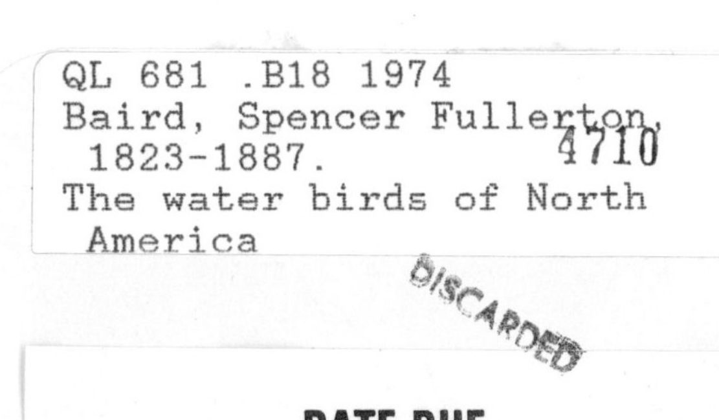

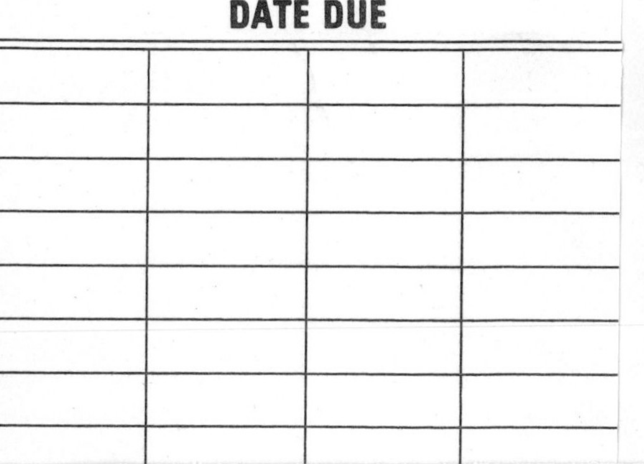

COLORADO
MOUNTAIN
COLLEGE

NATURAL SCIENCES IN AMERICA

THE WATER BIRDS OF NORTH AMERICA

S[pencer] F[ullerton] Baird
T[homas] M. Brewer
R[obert] Ridgway

Volumes I and II

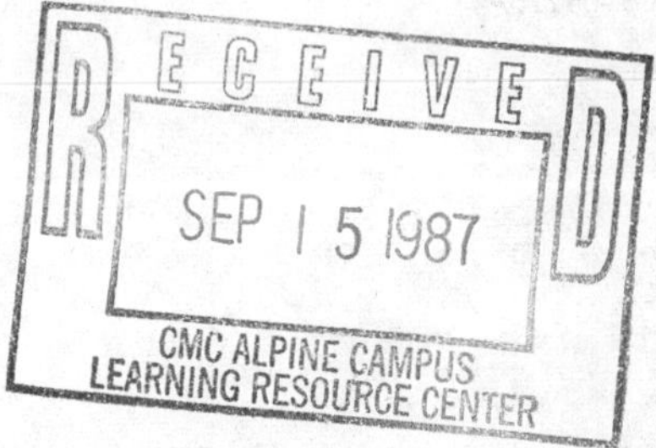

ARNO PRESS
A New York Times Company
New York, N. Y. • 1974

Reprint Edition 1974 by Arno Press Inc.

Reprinted from copies in the University
of Illinois Library

NATURAL SCIENCES IN AMERICA
ISBN for complete set: 0-405-05700-8
See last pages of this volume for titles.

Manufactured in the United States of America

Publisher's Note: The illustrations in this book have been reduced by 10%.

Library of Congress Cataloging in Publication Data

Baird, Spencer Fullerton, 1823-1887.
The water birds of North America.

(Natural sciences in America)
Reprint of the 1884 ed. published by Little, Brown, Boston, which was issued as v. 12-13 of Memoirs of the Museum of Comparative Zoology, Harvard College.
1. Water-birds--North America. I. Brewer, Thomas Mayo, 1814-1880, joint author. II. Ridgway, Robert, 1850-1929, joint author. III. Title. IV. Series. V. Series: Harvard University. Museum of Comparative Zoology. Memoirs, v. 12-13.
QL681.B18 1974 598.2'97 73-17800
ISBN 0-405-05716-4

THE WATER BIRDS

OF

NORTH AMERICA.

VOL. I.

Memoirs of the Museum of Comparative Zoölogy
AT HARVARD COLLEGE.
VOL. XII.

THE WATER BIRDS OF NORTH AMERICA.

BY

S. F. BAIRD, T. M. BREWER,
AND
R. RIDGWAY.

ISSUED IN CONTINUATION OF THE
PUBLICATIONS OF THE GEOLOGICAL SURVEY OF CALIFORNIA.
J. D. WHITNEY, STATE GEOLOGIST.

VOLUME I.

BOSTON:
LITTLE, BROWN, AND COMPANY.
1884.

UNIVERSITY
JOHN WILSON & SON
UNIVERSITY PRESS
1639
CAMBRIDGE, MASS.

CONTENTS.

INTRODUCTION.

As this work will in all probability fall into the hands of those who have not seen the ornithological volume issued as a part of the Publications of the State Geological Survey of California, it is proper that the origin and connection of these two contributions to this branch of American natural history should be here explained.

The Act authorizing a geological survey of the State of California, which became a law in 1860, required of the State Geologist, in addition to the topographical and geological work usually expected on such a survey, "a full and complete description of the botanical and zoological productions of California." In accordance with this requirement, the efforts of the head of the Survey were, from the time of the beginning of the work, directed toward the collection of such material as would be of value for use in the preparation of Reports in the various departments of the natural history of California and the adjacent regions of the Pacific coast. The establishment of a State museum of geology and natural history was also contemplated — although not provided for — in the Act authorizing the Survey, as supplementary to the preparation of such Reports on the various branches of science as should make possible the study of geology, botany, and zoology in the schools and colleges of California and the adjacent States and Territories.

The Survey as thus organized went on without interruption until 1868, when appropriations were withheld for two years; but the work was not brought to an absolute stoppage, all the materials having been left in the hands of the State Geologist, without any direction as to what was to be done with them, and also without any appropriation of money to pay either for the care and preservation of collections then on hand, or for the continuation of publications at that time actually in progress.

Nevertheless the work did go on; and among the volumes completed during the stoppage of the Survey was one on which considerable progress had been made at the time the appropriations were suspended. This volume belonged to the

Natural History Series, and was devoted to a description of the Land Birds occurring west of the Rocky Mountains and north of Mexico, having been selected as the volume most suitable to succeed those of Geology and Palæontology already published, partly because it was thought that the subject would prove popularly attractive, and partly because circumstances favored its being more rapidly completed than the other volumes of the Natural History Series possibly could be.

For the volume of Land Birds published in 1870 by the California Survey, the biographical portion was chiefly drawn from the notes of Dr. J. G. Cooper, Zoologist of the Survey; and by mutual consent these notes were placed in the hands of Professor Baird, at that time in charge of the Natural History Department of the Smithsonian Institution, in order that they might be worked up at the place where a more copious supply of materials and greater facilities for such an undertaking existed than at any other scientific centre in this country.

The result was the publication, in 1870, of a volume entitled: "Ornithology. Volume I. The Land Birds." It was illustrated by nearly eight hundred woodcuts, each species (except in the case of the *Raptores*) being represented by a head of life size, introduced with the text, and intended to be colored by hand, and each genus by a full-length figure, together with numerous diagrams giving the details of wings, claws, and such other parts as are of special value in generic determination.

During the preparation of this ornithological volume of the California series of Reports, it was agreed between the State Geologist and Professor Baird that the illustrations of that volume should be used by him in a work of larger scope, including the Land Birds of all North America; and this plan was carried out, the result being the well-known work, in three volumes, entitled "A History of North American Birds: Land Birds," by Messrs. Baird, Brewer, and Ridgway. This work — completed in 1875 — followed closely the California volume in its general style, appearance, and manner of illustration; the principal exception to this being that the heads were placed together at the end of each volume, and printed by the chromolithographic process, instead of being colored by hand. For these volumes between seven and eight hundred illustrations were furnished by the California Survey without charge — Professor Baird having promised, in return for this favor, that the portion of the Ornithology remaining to be completed and published as a part of the California Report should include all the Water Birds of the continent north of Mexico. The propriety of this stipulation must be evident to all, since it was clear that, after the appearance of the work of Messrs. Baird, Brewer, and Ridgway, there would be only the most limited demand for the much less comprehensive one previously issued by the California Survey.

As it turned out, however, this stipulation was not one of so much practical importance as had been expected, since the cost of the publication of the "Land Birds of North America" was so great that the publishers of that work would have been unwilling to continue it at their own risk and expense — and, in fact, did decline to do so, when, after the stoppage of the California Survey, the present work was offered to them for publication by joint consent of the authors and the former State Geologist of California. The latter, however, having devoted himself, subsequently to the second and final stoppage of the Survey in 1874, to a continuation — chiefly at his own risk and expense — of the publication of the material left in a more or less fragmentary condition in his hands, finally concluded to take up the unfinished volumes of Ornithology; and, with the generous co-operation of the Director of the Museum of Comparative Zoology, now presents them to the public, as forming at the same time a portion of the series of Memoirs of that institution, and a continuation of the Reports of the Geological Survey of California.

As in the previously published volumes of the North American Birds, the technical or descriptive portion of the present division of that work has been prepared by Messrs. Baird and Ridgway; and the latter has had the opportunity of making, during the printing, such additions and corrections as were rendered necessary by the fact that several years have elapsed since the manuscript was originally prepared for publication. The biographical portion of the volumes devoted to the Water Birds is from the pen of Dr. T. M. Brewer — who, however, did not live to see the beginning of the printing of this, the final, portion of a work on which he had bestowed so much labor. The task of revising his not entirely completed manuscript has fallen upon the undersigned, who has endeavored to do the best he could with it, especially as regards the occasionally somewhat uncertain orthography of the names of persons and places. In this he has had the assistance of Mr. J. A. Allen, of the Museum of Comparative Zoology.

The illustrations of this volume were, with few and unimportant exceptions, drawn upon the wood by Mr. Edwin L. Sheppard, of Philadelphia, and engraved by Mr. Hobart H. Nichols, of Washington. The coloring of the heads was done under the direction of Mrs. F. H. Russell, of Brookline, Mass., from patterns prepared by Mr. Ridgway.

J. D. WHITNEY.

CAMBRIDGE, MASS., March 31, 1884.

SYNOPSIS

OF

NORTH AMERICAN ORDERS OF WATER BIRDS.

A. Legs lengthened, the tibiæ usually denuded for a considerable distance above the knee. Toes not fully webbed, except in *Recurvirostra* and *Phœnicopterus*. **(Waders.)**

I. **HERODIONES.** Neck and legs much lengthened. Hind toe much lengthened, and inserted at the same level as the anterior toes (shorter and slightly elevated in *Ciconiidæ*). Habits altricial[1] and young dasypædic.[2] Palate desmognathous. Carotids double.

II. **LIMICOLÆ.** Neck and legs usually elongated (the latter sometimes excessively so), the tibiæ usually more or less naked below. Hind toe short or rudimentary, sometimes absent, and inserted above the level of the anterior toes. Habits præcocial,[3] and young dasypædic. Palate schizognathous. Carotids double.

III. **ALECTORIDES.** Hind toe small and elevated (but neck much lengthened and bill strong and hard) in *Gruidæ;* lengthened and incumbent in *Aramidæ* and *Rallidæ*. Wings comparatively short and rounded, and body compressed (except in *Gruidæ*). Habits præcocial, and young dasypædic. Palate schizognathous. Carotids double.

IV. **PHŒNICOPTERI.** Neck and legs excessively elongated, the anterior toes webbed, and the tibiæ naked for the greater part of their length. Hind toe small and elevated, or wholly absent. Bill of very peculiar form, being greatly thickened and abruptly bent downward from the middle portion, the tomia provided with lamellæ, as in the *Anseres*. Habits præcocial and young dasypædic, Palate saurognathous. Carotids double, but the left much reduced in size.

B. Legs short, the tibiæ wholly or mostly feathered. Anterior toes distinctly (usually fully) webbed, or else broadly lobed and provided with broad flat nails (*Podicipidæ*). **(Swimmers.)**

V. **ANSERES.** Bill broad and depressed (nearly cylindrical in *Merginæ*), the tip provided with a distinct nail or unguis, and the tomia with vertical lamellæ or strainers (more tooth-like in *Merginæ*). Habits præcocial, young dasypædic. Palate saurognathous. Carotids double.

[1] Altricial birds are those whose young are hatched in a blind and helpless condition, and are reared in the nest until able to fly.

[2] Young birds which are covered with down when hatched are said to be dasypædic ; *e. g.*, chicks of the Domestic Fowl and other gallinaceous birds, ducklings, etc.

[3] Præcocial birds are those whose young are capable of running about as soon as hatched, and although led and otherwise cared for by the parents, are not fed by them ; *e. g.*, the young of the Domestic Fowl Ducks, Geese, etc.

VI. **STEGANOPODES.** Hind toe lengthened and incumbered, and united to the inner toe by a complete web (small only in *Tachypetidæ*). Bill extremely variable, but usually with a more or less extensible naked gular sac between the mandibular rami. Nostrils obsolete. Habits altricial, young dasypædic in *Tachypetidæ*, *Phalacrocoracidæ*, *Plotidæ*, and *Phaëthontidæ*, gymnopædic[1] in *Pelecanidæ* and *Sulidæ*. Palate saurognathous. Carotids double.

VII. **LONGIPENNES.** Hind toe small or rudimentary, and elevated, sometimes almost obsolete; anterior toes fully webbed. Bill more or less compressed (nearly cylindrical only in some *Stercorariidæ*), the nostrils linear, never tubular. Habits altricial, young dasypædic. Palate schizognathous. Carotids double. Eggs, two or more, colored.

VIII. **TUBINARES.** Hind toe absent or very rudimentary; anterior toes fully webbed. Bill variable, but usually nearly cylindrical or compressed (rarely depressed), the terminal portion strongly hooked. Nostrils tubular. Habits altricial, young dasypædic. Palate schizognathous. Carotids double. Eggs, never more than one, white.

IX. **PYGOPODES.** Legs inserted far backward, the tarsi extremely compressed. Anterior toes fully webbed or else strongly lobed and with broad flat nails (*Podicipidæ*). Bill extremely variable. Habits præcocial in *Podicipidæ* and *Colymbidæ*, altricial in *Alcidæ*; young dasypædic. Palate schizognathous. Carotids double, except in *Podicipidæ* and some *Alcidæ* (*e. g.*, genus *Alle*).

The above arrangement is not strictly natural, but the division of Water Birds into "Waders" and "Swimmers" is adopted for the convenience of the student. The Orders most nearly related are the *Herodiones* and *Steganopodes*, *Limicolæ* and *Alectorides*, *Phœnicopteri* and *Anseres*, and *Longipennes* and *Tubinares*. Of the *Pygopodes* (which as here defined is certainly not a properly limited group) the *Alcidæ* present many points of true relationship to the *Tubinares* and *Longipennes*, while the latter are not far removed from the *Limicolæ*. The *Podicipidæ* also appear to resemble in some respects (perhaps only teleological) the *Steganopodes*.

1 Young birds are gymnopædic when naked or very incompletely covered with down when hatched; *e. g.*, the young of all Passeres, Woodpeckers, Pigeons, etc.

THE

WATER BIRDS

OF

NORTH AMERICA.

ORDER HERODIONES.[1]

ALTRICIAL GRALLATORES.

CHAR. Altricial Grallatores, with the hallux lengthened, and nearly or quite incumbent; in habits more or less arboreal (generally nesting on trees, while all are "Perchers"). Palate desmognathous. Carotids double.

The above brief diagnosis is sufficient to succinctly characterize this eminently natural group of birds. The *Herodiones,* which include the Boatbills (*Cancromidæ*), Herons (*Ardeidæ*), Storks (*Ciconiidæ*), Ibises (*Ibididæ*), and Spoonbills (*Plataleidæ*), with perhaps, but not certainly, some other minor groups, are at once distinguished from the Præcocial Grallatores (*Limicolæ, Alectorides,* and *Phœnicopteri*) by their altricial nature, the young being completely helpless at birth, and having to be reared in the nest, instead of being at once capable of active movement and able to shift for themselves, although they *follow* their parents for a considerable time. There are also important peculiarities of the osteological and anatomical structure, which alone are sufficient to demonstrate the fact that this group is not intimately related to other Waders, their general exterior resemblance to them being one of analogy and not of affinity. According to Huxley (P. Z. S. 1867, 461), the osteological characters of this group are as follows: There are no basipterygoid processes; the palatines are usually united for a greater or less distance behind the posterior nares, and are destitute of a vertical plate depending from their junction; the maxillo-palatines large and spongy; the sternum broad, and with two to four posterior notches. The relation between the phalanges is the same as in the "*Chenomorphæ*" (= *Anatidæ*) and "*Amphimorphæ*" (= *Phœnicopteri*).

The Water Birds most nearly related structurally to the present group are the *Steganopodes,* — Pelicans, Cormorants, Gannets, and their allies, — which are likewise both desmognathous and altricial; and what is an important fact in

[1] An analysis of the Orders of Water Birds is given on pages x, xi.

this connection is the circumstance that, besides being altricial, they are, with very few exceptions, also decidedly arboreal, most of them even placing their nests on trees. They are all swimmers, however, instead of being strictly or in part waders.

Without discussing further the characters which distinguish this "order," we proceed to define the families into which it seems most naturally divisible.

Synopsis of the American Herodionine Families.

A. Pterylæ very narrow, interspersed with "powder-down" tracts. Hallux perfectly incumbent; inner edge of middle claw distinctly pectinated. (*Herodiones ardeiformes*, = *Herodii*, SUNDEV. Meth. Nat. Av. Disp. Tent. 1872, 122.)

1. **Cancromidæ.** Four pairs of powder-down tracts. Bill greatly depressed and excessively dilated laterally, the lateral outlines much bowed; gonys excessively short, not longer than the width of the mandibular rami.

2. **Ardeidæ.** Two to three pairs of powder-down tracts. Bill compressed, elongate-conical, the lateral outlines straight or even a little concave; the vertical outlines nearly straight, slightly convex terminally; gonys lengthened, several times longer than the width of the mandibular rami.

B. Pterylæ broad, without powder-down tracts. Hallux elevated at the base above the base of the anterior toes; inner edge of middle claw not pectinated; *claws resting upon a horny, crescentic "shoe."* (*Herodiones ciconiiformes*, = *Pelargi*, SUNDEV. Meth. Nat. Av. Disp. Tent. 1872, 123.)

a. Sides of the maxilla without any trace of lateral groove. Skull holorhinal. Angle of the mandible truncated. *Pectoralis major* muscle in two easily separable layers. No *accessory femoro-caudal* muscle; *semitendinosus* muscle tendinous for its distal half; *biceps cubiti* and *tensor patagii longus* muscles unconnected. (GARROD, P. Z. S. 1875, 301.)

3. **Ciconiidæ.** Bill elongate-conical, either straight or curved a little up or down at the end.

b. Sides of the maxilla with a deep, narrow groove, extending uninterruptedly from the nasal fossæ to the extreme tip of the bill. Skull schizorhinal. Angle of the mandible produced and decurved. *Pectoralis major* muscle simple (not separable into distinct layers); *accessory femoro-caudal* muscle well developed; *semitendinosus* muscle muscular throughout; *biceps cubiti* and *tensor patagii longus* muscles connected by a small muscular "belly." (GARROD.)

4. **Ibididæ.** Bill slender, attenuated terminally, nearly cylindrical or somewhat compressed, conspicuously decurved, or arched above.

5. **Plataleidæ.** Bill very broad, excessively depressed and greatly expanded terminally, much narrowed across the middle portion, the extreme tip only much decurved.

In addition to the above well-defined families, all of which have American representatives, while one (*Cancromidæ*) is peculiarly American, there are several others which probably belong to the *Herodiones*, but which, excepting the *Eurypygidæ* (Sun Bitterns), are peculiar to the Old World, and may therefore be passed by without further notice.

FAMILY ARDEIDÆ. — THE HERONS.

CHAR. Altricial waders having the bill compressed, pointed, all the outlines nearly straight; the lores and orbits naked; the rest of the head (except, sometimes, the malar region, or part of the throat) feathered, the occiput frequently with ornamental plumes. Lower part of the neck, back, or scapulars, frequently with ornamental plumes. Plumage generally handsome and variegated. Two to three pairs of powder-down tracts. Other characters variable.

The Herons are among the most widely diffused of birds, one species, our common Night Heron (*Nycticorax griseus*), being nearly or quite cosmopolitan. Many of the Old World forms have not been examined in the present connection, but there is good reason for believing that the number of sub-families here recognized as represented in America can be consistently increased.

Sub-family **Ardeinæ**. Outer toe equal to, or decidedly longer than, the inner. Claws usually short, generally strongly curved. Three pairs of powder-down tracts. Rectrices lengthened, stiffish, twelve in number (except in *Zebrilus*).

Sub-family **Botaurinæ**. Outer toe decidedly shorter than the inner. Claws long, slender, slightly curved. Two pairs only of powder-down tracts. Rectrices very short, soft, only ten in number.

Synopsis of American Genera.[1]

a. SUB-FAMILY ARDEINÆ. — THE TRUE HERONS.

A. *Rectrices twelve; tibiæ with the lower portion more or less naked.*

a. Pectoral and inguinal powder-down tracts widely separated.

§. *Malar region completely feathered* (except in *Pilherodius*, where anterior part is bare). *Bill shorter than the tarsus and middle toe* (usually shorter than, or about equal to, the tarsus).

1. **Ardea**. Size very large. *Adult* with scapular plumes elongated, narrowly-lanceolate, and with compact webs; *in the breeding season*, the occiput with two long, slender, compact-webbed, pendant plumes. Color mainly plumbeous- or slate-blue (rarely — *e. g.* white phase of *A. occidentalis* — wholly pure white). Culmen shorter than the middle toe.

2. **Herodias**. Size large, but smaller than the species of the preceding genus. *Adult* with the scapular plumes greatly elongated, reaching far beyond the end of the tail, the shafts thick and rigid, the webs decomposed, hair-like, and distant. Color entirely pure white.

3. **Garzetta**. Size small. *Adult* with occipital, jugular, and scapular plumes, the latter reaching to or a little beyond the end of the tail; the shafts moderately rigid, and recurved terminally; the webs decomposed, with long, hair-like, but not distant fibres Other plumes varying in structure, according to the species. Color entirely pure white.

4 **Dichromanassa**. Size medium. *Adult* with the feathers of the entire head and neck, excepting the throat and foreneck, elongated, linear, lanceolate, and stiffish, most elongated on the occiput and jugulum. Scapular plumes extending beyond end of tail; the shafts rigid, the webs decomposed, with rather close, hair-like fibrillæ. Color wholly pure white, or plumbeous, with or without reddish neck. Tarsus twice as long as middle toe.

5. **Hydranassa**. Size medium. *Adult* with an occipital tuft of several elongated, lanceolate white feathers. Jugular feathers broadly lanceolate, with distinct outlines. Scapular plumes hair-like, extending a little beyond the tail. Color mainly plumbeous, with lower parts and rump white. Bill longer than tarsus.

6. **Florida**. Size small. *Adult* with scapular plumes elongated, extending to or beyond end of tail, linear-lanceolate, with compact webs; jugular plumes similar; occipital plumes hair-like, a few of them much elongated. Color pure white, with bluish tips to outer primaries, dark slate-blue with maroon-colored head and neck, or variously "patched" with blue and white.

7. **Butorides**. Size small. *Adult* with scapular plumes elongated, compact-webbed, lanceolate, but with rounded tips. Feathers of the pileum elongated, lanceolate. Jugular plumes broad, blended. Culmen longer than tarsus; middle toe almost equal to tarsus. Color much variegated.

[1] The genera enclosed in brackets are extralimital.

8. [**Syrigma.**] Size medium. *Adult* with several elongated, narrow, compact-webbed, round-tipped, somewhat rigid and slightly recurved plumes on lower part of occiput. Jugular feathers soft, broad, blended. No scapular plumes. Culmen about equal to middle toe. Color much variegated, the tail and lower parts white.

9. [**Pilherodius.**] Size medium. Orbits and anterior part of malar region naked. Occiput with two extremely elongated linear, compact-webbed plumes. Jugular plumes broad, blended. No scapular plumes. Color white, the crown and occiput black. Middle toe shorter than culmen ; culmen shorter than tarsus.

10. **Nycticorax.** Size medium. *Adult* with several extremely elongated linear, compact-webbed occipital plumes. No scapular plumes. Jugular feathers broad, blended. Culmen about equal to tarsus ; tarsus slightly longer than middle toe. Lateral outlines of bill concave ; gonys nearly straight. Adult and young exceedingly different in plumage.

11. **Nyctherodius.** Size medium. *Adult* with several extremely elongated linear, compact-webbed occipital plumes. Scapular plumes elongated, narrow, round-tipped, the webs somewhat decomposed. Jugular feathers broad, blended. Culmen much shorter than tarsus (a little longer than middle toe) ; tarsus much longer than middle toe. Color much variegated. Lateral outlines of the bill straight ; gonys very convex. Adult and young exceedingly different in plumage.

§§. *Malar region entirely naked. Bill longer than tarsus and middle toe.*

12. [**Agamia.**] Size medium. Bill extremely elongated, narrow, and compressed. *Adult* with greatly elongated, broadly lanceolate, acute occipital plumes ; lower back with similar, but more loosely webbed, plumes overhanging rump. Sides of neck with recurved, sickle-shaped, narrow, and acute plumes. Jugular feathers broad, blended. Tarsus nearly twice middle toe.

b. Pectoral and inguinal powder-down tracts united into a continuous strip.

13. [**Tigrisoma.**] Malar region and throat naked, the latter with or without a medial feathered strip. *Tarsus with hexagonal scutellæ in front.* Outer toe longer than inner ; claws short, strongly curved. Plumage much variegated ; feathers of neck loose, "fluffy."

B. *Rectrices ten. Tibiæ with the lower portion completely feathered. Pectoral and inguinal powder-down tracts widely separated. Malar region completely feathered.*

14. [**Zebrilus.**] Size very small (among the smallest of Herons). Plumage exceedingly lax and "fluffy." Bill and feet very small. Culmen about equal to tarsus, both longer than middle toe ; outer toe longest. Plumage dull, with transverse undulations of dusky and light fulvous.

b. SUB-FAMILY BOTAURINÆ. — THE BITTERNS.

15. **Botaurus.** Size medium, or rather large. Sexes similar ; young similar to adult.

16. **Ardetta.** Size extremely small (the smallest of Herons). Sexes dissimilar (in all species ?) ; young slightly different from adult.

GENUS **ARDEA**, LINNÆUS.

Ardea, LINN. S. N. I. 1735; ed. 12, I. 1766, 233 (type, *A. cinerea*, LINN.).
Audubonia, BONAP. Consp. II. 1855, 113 (type, *Ardea occidentalis*, AUD.).

CHAR. Herons of largest size (of Stork-like stature), the adults distinguished by lengthened, narrowly-lanceolate, acute jugular and scapular plumes (the former rather rigid, the latter overhanging the wings and rump) ; a tuft of broad feathers on each side the breast (having a different color from adjacent parts), and, *in the breeding season*, by the presence of two or three extremely lengthened, narrow, pendant, occipital plumes.

Culmen almost straight ; gonys ascending, more or less convex, about equal in length to the mandibular rami ; upper and lower outlines of the bill parallel for the basal half. Mental apex anterior to half-way between point of bill and anterior angle of the eye ; frontal apex a little posterior to the nostrils and slightly anterior to the malar apex.[1] Middle toe more than half the tarsus, and about equal to bare portion of tibia; outer toe reaching to about the middle of the penultimate phalanx of the middle toe; inner toe decidedly shorter, reaching only to the second articulation of the middle toe; hallux a little longer than the basal phalanx of the outer toe; claws rather short,

A. herodias

strongly curved. Front of tarsus with broad, transverse scutellæ, in single series, for upper half. Pileum crested, the feathers of the crown and occiput being elongated, lanceolate, and decurved. Primaries reaching decidedly beyond tertials. Second, third, and fourth quills nearly equal, and longest; first longer than fifth; inner webs of outer three slightly sinuated near ends.

Synopsis of the American Species.[2]

COM. CHAR. Above bluish-plumbeous, the penicillate scapular plumes more hoary; remiges and rectrices slate-color. Lower parts longitudinally striped with black and white. *Young* without any plumes, and with the colors much duller, the pattern badly defined.

A. *Tibiæ and border of the wing purplish-cinnamon or rufous.*

1. **A. occidentalis.** Pileum and occipital plumes, with rest of head, white; forehead streaked with black. *Sometimes whole plumage pure white!* Culmen, 6.40–6.75; tarsus, 8.00–8.75; wing, 19.00–21.00. *Hab.* Florida to Southern Illinois; Cuba; Jamaica.
2. **A. Wardi.** Similar to *A. occidentalis*, the white phase apparently undistinguishable, but colored phase combining the head-pattern of *A. herodias* with light-colored under-parts and large size of "*Würdemanni.*" Culmen, 6.50–7.00; tarsus, 8.50–9.00; wing, 20.00–20.50. *Hab.* Southwestern Florida.
3. **A. herodias.** Pileum and occipital plumes black; forehead and central feathers of the crown white; culmen, 4.30–6.25; tarsus, 6.00–8.25; wing, 17.90–20.00. *Hab.* North America in general; Middle America; Galapagos; Venezuela; West Indies.

1 The terms "mental apex," "malar apex," and "frontal apex" are here employed to denote the apices, or points, of the feathering of the head at the base of the bill.

2 Of the exotic species properly referable to this genus, we have seen only *A. purpurea*, Linn. (European). This seems to be strictly congeneric as to details of form, except that the claws are much lengthened; but it has a very different system of coloration.

B. *Tibiæ and border of the wing white.*

4. **A. cinerea.** Pileum and occipital plumes black; forehead and centre of crown white (as in *A. herodias*). Neck cinereous. Culmen, 4.80; tarsus, 6.00–6.25; wing, 18.50. *Hab.* Europe, etc. Accidental in Southern Greenland.

[5. **A. cocoi.**[1]] Entire pileum (including forehead, etc.) and occipital plumes black. Neck white. Culmen, 5.85–6.75; tarsus, 7.20–8.00; wing, 18.50–19.50. *Hab.* South America.

Ardea occidentalis.

THE GREAT WHITE HERON; WÜRDEMANN'S HERON.

a. *White phase.*

Ardea occidentalis, AUD. Orn. Biog. III. 1835, 542; V. 1839, 596; Synop. 1839, 264; B. Am. VI. 1843, 110, pl. 308. — COUES, Key, 1872, 267; Check List, 1873, no. 451; 2d ed. 1882, no. 656. — SCL. & SALV. Nom. Neotr. 1873, 125. — RIDGW. Bull. U. S. Geol. & Geog. Survey Terr. IV. no. 1, 1878, 227 (critical). — RIDGW. Nom. N. Am. B. 1881, no. 486.

Audubonia occidentalis, BONAP. Consp. II. 1855, 113. — BAIRD, B. N. Am. 1858, 670; Cat. N. Am. B. 1859, no. 489.

b. *Colored phase.*

Ardea Würdemannii, BAIRD, B. N. Am. 1858, 669; ed. 1860, pl. 86; Cat. N. Am. B. 1859, no. 488. — COUES, Key, 1872, 267; Check List, 1873, no. 450.

HAB. The "Austroriparian" region[2] of eastern North America, from Florida to Southern Illinois (Wabash River); Jamaica.

SP. CHAR. (*a. White phase,* = *occidentalis*, AUD.). *Adult:* Entire plumage pure white. "Bill yellow, the upper mandible dusky green at the base; loral space yellowish-green; orbital space light blue; iris bright yellow. Tibia and hind part of tarsus yellow; fore part of tibia [tarsus?] olivaceous; sides of latter greenish yellow; claws light brown" (AUDUBON, *l. c.*).[3] *Young:* Similar in color to the adult, but destitute of any plumes.

[1] ARDEA COCOI, Linn.

Ardea cocoi, LINN. S. N. I, 1766, 237. — BONAP. Consp. II. 1855, 110. — GRAY, Hand-list, III. 1871, 27, no. 10103. — SCL. & SALV. Nom. Neotr. 1873, 125. — BOUCARD, Cat. Av. 1876, 49, no. 1372. — RIDGW. Bull. U. S. Geol. & Geog. Survey Terr. IV. no. 1, 1878, 244 (critical).

Ardea fuscicollis, VIEILL. Nouv. Dict. XIV. 1817, 410.

Ardea soco, VIEILL. t. c. 423 (ex Lath.).

? *Ardea major*, FRASER, P. Z S. 1843, 116 (Chili).

Ardea plumbea, MERREM. Ersch. Gruber's Encycl. V. 1820, 177. — REICHENOW, J. F. O. 1877, 264.

Ardea maguari, SPIX, Av. Bras. II. 1825, 171.

Ardea palliata, "Illig." WAGL. Syst. Av. 1827, Ardea sp. 2.

[2] From the fact of this species having been observed at Mount Carmel, Illinois, on several occasions, it is inferred that its range may comprehend the Austroriparian region, or Louisianian fauna in general, although probably nowhere common, except in parts of Florida.

[3] The following measurements are given by Audubon: —

♂: "Length to end of tail, 54 inches; to end of wings, 54; to end of claws, 70; extent of wings, 83;

b. Blue phase (= "*Würdemanni*," Baird).

Adult: Entire head, including occipital crest, pure white; the forehead streaked with black (the feathers edged with black, the median stripe being white). Abdomen and crissum pure white, the former sparsely streaked with black (these streaks on the inner edge of the feathers, and broader anteriorly); crissum immaculate. Neck deep violaceous-drab (darker and more violaceous than in *A. herodias*, and ending almost abruptly against the white of the head); the throat with a narrow series of black and rufous dashes on a white ground; plumes of the lower neck white, most of them edged with black, but the longer without grayish tinge. Lateral jugular tufts blue-black, with

wide median stripes of pure white. Upper parts exactly as in *A. herodias*, except that the lower wing-coverts have conspicuous median streaks of white, while the edge of the wing from the carpus back is *white*, tinged with rufous, instead of *wholly rufous*. Tibial feathers paler rufous than in *A. herodias*, growing almost white next the body on the inner side. Naked tibiæ *yellow;* under side of toes *yellow;* rest of legs and feet *yellowish-olive*. *Young:* Similar to young of *A. herodias*, but lesser wing-coverts widely tipped with bright ferruginous, producing thereby a conspicuous spotting of this color; all the lower wing-coverts, large and small, with a large, terminal, wedge-shaped spot of white. Forehead and crown dusky slate-color, most of the feathers with whitish shafts; occipital plumes all whitish at the base, only the ends being dusky.

Wing, 21.00; tail, 8.00; culmen, 6.45; depth of bill (through middle of nostrils), 1.15; naked portion of tibia, 5.50; tarsus, 8.00; middle toe, 4.80. [Type, No. 8690, South Florida.]

The specimen described above as the young of *A.* "*Würdemanni*" is a very young bird, with the downy filaments still adhering to the tips of all the feathers of the crown, and with the remiges only half grown out. It is much larger than any specimens of *A. herodias* of corresponding age, the culmen measuring 5.15, the tibia 5.00, the tarsus 7.80, and the middle toe 4.60. The plumage is even more different: In the young of *A. herodias*, the dusky of the crown includes the entire upper half of the head, the occiput being wholly blackish and the cheeks slaty; in the specimen under consideration the cheeks are entirely white, like the throat, and the occipital feathers white, tipped with dusky, thus restricting the continuous dusky to the forehead and crown. The conspicuous white spots on the wing-coverts agree with the similar but smaller markings seen in the adult of *A.* "*Würdemanni*," but wanting in all ages and stages of *A. herodias*.

The identity of *Ardea Würdemanni*, Baird, with *A. occidentalis*, Audubon, although not proven, is inferred from a number of circumstances and coincidences in the history of each, which, together

wing from flexure, 19; tail, 7; bill along the back, 6¾; along the edges, 8¾; bare part of tibia, 6; tarsus, 8½; middle toe, 4 10/12; its claw, 10/12. Weight, 9½ lbs."

♀: "Length to end of tail, 50; to end of wings, 50; to end of claws, 65; extent of wings, 75; wing from flexure, 18¾; tail, 6¾; bill along the back, 5 10/12; along the edges, 7¾; its depth at base, 1 5/12; tarsus, 7½; middle toe, 4¼; its claw, 9/12. Weight, 7¼ lbs." — Aud.

with their entire similarity of size and form, render it extremely probable that the case of *Ardea rufa*, Boddaert, and *A.* "*Pealei*," Bonaparte, is repeated in the present instance; these two supposed species in all probability being, as has been incontestably proven with *rufa* and "*Pealei*," "dichromatic" phases of the same species. The facts bearing directly upon the case have already been given at length elsewhere,[1] and are too voluminous to reproduce here.

The Great White Heron, so far as we are aware, has a residence restricted to Florida and the West India Islands. It was first met with by Mr. Audubon at Indian Key, Florida, in April, 1832. Although generally unmolested by man at that time, he found it shy, and extremely difficult to procure. Sometimes it would rise when at the distance of half a mile, and fly out of sight; and it was impossible to approach one while perched or standing in the water. He found it a constant resident on the Florida Keys, and more abundant there during the breeding season than anywhere else. It was rare as far eastward as Cape Florida. It has, however, been seen in Southern Illinois, and may have a more extended distribution. It pairs early in March, but many did not lay their eggs until the middle of April. Their nests were usually found at considerable distance from each other, although many were found on the same keys. They were generally only a few feet above high-water mark, were quite large, averaging about three feet in diameter, built of sticks, without any lining, quite flat, and several inches thick. He was informed that incubation lasted about thirty days. Both birds sit, the female being the most assiduous, with their legs stretched out before them. The young, from ten days to a month old, showed no signs of a crest, and were pure white, with a tinge of cream-color; and even those that had been kept more than a year exhibited nothing of the kind. It is described as quite sedate, and less animated than the *herodias*. It walks with firmness and great elegance, collects in flocks at its breeding grounds, sometimes a hundred or more being seen together, betaking themselves to the mud-flats and sandbars at a distance from the keys, on which they roost and breed. It is diurnal in its habits, as our observations appeared to show. While on the banks it stands motionless, waiting until its prey comes near; and then it strikes it and swallows it alive, or when large beats it on the water or shakes it violently. It remains on its feeding-ground until driven off by the tide. When roosting it stands on one foot, the other being lifted up, draws in its long neck, and places its head under its wing. When surprised it leaves its perch with a rough croaking sound, and flies directly to a great distance, but never inland. Its flight is said to be firm, regular, and greatly protracted. It propels itself by regular slow flaps, the head being drawn in after it has proceeded a few yards, and its legs extended behind. It occasionally rises high in the air, where it sails in wide circles, and rarely re-alights without performing this circling flight.

Mr. Audubon carried several of these herons, taken when quite young, alive with him to Charleston. Two that had been allowed the liberty of the deck killed and devoured the young of other and smaller species; and when placed in a coop with young of the *herodias*, would have killed the latter if they had not been separated. Two others, which had been kept in confinement on Indian Key, he found with their bills very much broken by the force with which they struck at the fish thrown to them on the rock of their enclosure. They never evinced the least animosity towards one another, but would on every occasion seek to attack and kill those of other

[1] See Bulletin of the U. S. Geol. & Geog. Survey of the Territories, Vol. IV. No. 1 (Feb. 5, 1878), pp. 229–236, and Bulletin of the Nuttall Ornithological Club, Vol. VII. No. 1 (January, 1882), pp. 1–6.

species. Four reached Charleston alive, and were kept some time by Dr. Bachman, Dr. Gibbes, and Dr. Wilson. These proved to be troublesome pets, devouring such quantities of fish that it was difficult to provide for them. They would strike at and kill chickens, ducks, and grown fowl, and in one instance stabbed through and pinned to the wooden steps of the veranda a sleeping cat. They even pursued and threatened the children; and it became necessary to destroy them.

Dr. Bryant met with this Heron in Florida in only two places. One of these was on the headwaters of the St. Sebastian, where it was breeding in company with the Wood Ibis; the other was on a small island in Lake Jessup, without any other birds. The attachment of this species to its breeding-place was strikingly shown at this island. About a month before Dr. Bryant's visit a dense tangled growth of coarse marsh grasses and bushes, with which it was covered, had been accidentally set on fire, and many of the birds and the majority of the nests destroyed. At the time of his visit the latter had been rebuilt, and the birds were again sitting on their eggs. In the few nests which had not been destroyed, and in most instances had been blackened by the fire, the young were already hatched and nearly half grown. He found it breeding on many of the Keys. Two nests were rarely seen near each other, and only in one instance did he find two within twenty feet of one another. They did not seem to object to the company of other species, as he found one on the same bush with a nest of a Great Blue Heron; and at Sandy Key, near Cape Sable, he found several pairs breeding on the cacti, which were growing amidst trees covered with the nests of the Louisiana Heron. He never saw more than five or six individuals feeding near each other, and regarded it as much more solitary than the *herodias*, as the latter is than other species, and as by far the wildest bird of its genus with which he was acquainted. As he found many of its young nearly fledged by the 20th of April, and as at that time none at the Keys were less than half grown, and all older than the young of the *herodias*, he thinks it must commence laying by the 1st of February.

According to Mr. March, this species occurs occasionally in Jamaica, but is rare on that island. It may always be readily recognized by its superior size, the absence of occipital plumes, and by the lengthened feathers of the back of the head. It is regarded as a straggler. Mr. Audubon states that the eggs are always three in number, measure two and three quarters inches in length, and one and two thirds inches in breadth, and have a rather thick shell of a uniform plain light bluish-green color. An egg in my collection (No. 285) collected by Mr. Audubon in 1832, is of a slightly oblong oval shape, and nearly equally rounded at either end. Its color is somewhat faded, but seems to have been a light wash of Prussian blue mingled with rather more than the usual proportion of green than in most of the eggs of the Heron family. It measures 2.75 inches in length, and 1.90 inches in breadth, having the same length, but a greater breadth, than in the measurements given by Mr. Audubon.

The bird known as *A. Würdemanni*, which Mr. Ridgway regards as merely the colored phase of this species, is even more rare than the white form called *occidentalis*. Its habits may be safely presumed to be not essentially different from those of either of these two species. So far as known, its residence seems to be confined to Southern Florida and to the West India Islands. It is enumerated by Mr. March as one of the birds of Jamaica, where the fishermen and the gunners on the coast regard it as the male of the *herodias* in its summer plumage. Mr. March's observations led him to the conclusion that the two are entirely distinct species. Eggs of this species collected by Mr. Maynard in Southern Florida are more rounded than the eggs of most of the Heron family, and have the same uniform color of light greenish Prussian blue. They measure 2.23 inches in length by 1.85 inches in breadth.

Mr. N. B. Moore deems it highly probable that the birds now standing as *A. Würdemanni* may prove to be only a rare and elegant variety of *herodias.* He was led to this conclusion by examining, at a distance of about a hundred yards, a flock of Herons which seemed to him to correspond with the description of this rare variety, and yet to be rather varieties of, than a species differing from, the true *herodias.* We abridge his account: Seated in shade of a bunch of "saw-grass," near a pond about half a mile from Sarasota Bay, Feb. 20, 1874, he saw a Great Blue Heron descend and perch on a bush. By the aid of a spy-glass he was able to see, on what seemed to be a true *A. herodias,* an occipital white plume nearly four inches in length. In a few minutes three others appeared; one had a head that was pure white in every part, and occipital plumes of the same color, six or seven inches long.

He spent the remainder of the day watching their movements, and at about sundown the strange birds rose and flew away towards the north without coming within the reach of his gun or nearer than about eighty yards. During five hours of observation he saw it in every position and under every possible direction of sunbeam and shadow. The head was entirely a pure white, as were also the occipital streamers. The lower parts appeared to be whiter than those of its adult companion. The upper parts of shoulders, back, and lanceolate plumes seemed rather lighter and more silvery than those of the other. The tibial feathers in both were rufous, and both had black at the lower neck where uncovered at the carpus. The upper parts of the neck in both were washed in cinnamon, and both had the neck below an ashy lilac. Had he seen it by itself or in any other company than *A. herodias,* he would have unhesitatingly regarded it as an elegant specimen of *A. Würdemanni.*

Applying what he considers a never-failing test — the habits of Herons in general when in company with those of their own species — Mr. Moore was sure that this bird was an *A. herodias.*[1] At this season this bird, the most unsocial of all the Herons, will admit to the same pond, to feed in sight of it, one or more of its kind; but its disposition to tease and harass all but its mate is occasionally exhibited, and occurred repeatedly here. These appeared to be migrants moving north. One was a young bird of the first year. None of the others attempted to annoy it until it chanced to pierce a siren, when the master bird, in the true dress of an *herodias,* rushed at it and caused it to liberate its prey. The one with a white head when pursued seemed to act as if in deference to its companion, and to approach it, though not very near. On being teased it seemed to submit, as if well acquainted with its oppressor. These Herons came from the south, were evidently strangers, and moved on toward the north. The young bird was the last to leave, but soon followed its companions.

Ardea Wardi.

WARD'S GREAT BLUE HERON.

Ardea Wardi, RIDGW. Bull. Nutt. Orn. Club, Vol. VII. No. 1, January, 1882, p. 5 (Oyster Bay, Southwestern Florida).

SP. CHAR. Colored phase exactly like *A. Würdemanni* (= dark phase of *A. occidentalis?*), but with the head colored as in *A. herodias.* Differing from *herodias* in much larger size (culmen,

[1] Mr. Moore's observations in respect to this matter do not correspond at all with the experience of others. His inferences are doubtless incorrect, and the birds he saw were in all probability *A. "Würdemanni"* and *A. Wardi.* — R. R.

6.50–7.00 inches; tarsus, 8.50–9.00 inches), lighter general coloration, and (in dried skin) light brown instead of black legs. Dichromatic; the white phase being indistinguishable from that of *A. occidentalis* (?).

Adult ♂ (No. 82,329, U. S. Nat. Mus., Oyster Bay, Florida, March, 1881; Charles W. Ward): Head white, with the sides of the crown and entire occiput (including the lengthened plumes) deep black; neck lavender-gray (much lighter than in the type of *Würdemanni*), the fore-neck white, thickly streaked with black for the lower two thirds; jugular plumes chiefly white, their lengthened tapering portion entirely so. Upper surface uniform bluish plumbeous, the lengthened scapular plumes hoary whitish or pale silvery gray. Upper breast uniform black; abdomen and lower breast white, rather indistinctly streaked with dark gray; anal region mixed black and white, in longitudinal dashes (the black rather predominating); crissum immaculate pure white. Tibiæ uniform light cinnamon; edge of the wing (especially near the bend) deeper cinnamon, but this much mixed with white toward the bases of the quills; lining of the wing, axillars, sides, and flanks, uniform plumbeous. Bill, apparently, entirely olivaceous-yellow; naked portion of tibiæ very pale brown (evidently yellowish or flesh-colored in life); tarsi light brown (olivaceous in life?), darker in front; toes light brown. Wing, 20.50; culmen, 6.75; depth of bill through nostril, 1.10; tarsus, 8.75; middle toe, 5.10; naked portion of tibiæ, 5.50.

Mr. W. H. Collins, of Detroit, who kindly presented the specimen described above to the National Museum, has sent measurements of two other specimens, one in his own possession, the other mounted for Mr. Ward. As may be seen below, they agree closely in dimensions with the type, their measurements being, respectively, wing, 20.00–20.50; culmen, 6.50–7.00; depth of bill through nostril, 1.25; tarsus, 8.75–9.00; middle toe, 5.25–5.45; naked portion of tibia, 5.75–6.00.

The following facts in relation to this apparently distinct species or race of large Heron is substantially the same as that printed in the original account cited above. The specimens described were obtained by Mr. Charles W. Ward, of Pontiac, Michigan, who spent several weeks at the breeding-grounds of the bird in question, and was thus enabled to make many very interesting observations on its habits, etc. Mr. Ward's memoranda, which are especially interesting in connection with the question of *Ardea occidentalis*, Aud., and *A. Würdemanni*, Baird, are as follows: —

"My observations of the Herons during the past season do not correspond with those of Mr. N. B. Moore, as recorded on page 232 of your article,[1] in regard to their feeding habits. I found them generally living in communities, roosting, nesting, and feeding together, like Pigeons, and often observed flocks of the Little White, Reddish, and other Egrets, feeding together like Teal Ducks. Two specimens of *A. occidentalis* were seen feeding quietly within twenty feet of one of the Herons procured by me [*A. Wardi*, nobis]. They were feeding on a mud-bar at low tide. I was once concealed in the low brush near a small pool watching three Louisiana Egrets chasing minnows, when two of them making for the same minnow squared off for a knock-down, while the third coolly appropriated the prize, leaving the combatants situated like complainant and defendant at the close of a lawsuit. In all my observations of the Herons I have seen nothing to lead to a conclusion that one of these birds held any particular antipathy against its own species while feeding. In the many squabbles between Herons on their feeding-grounds, the encounters occurred quite as often between different species as members of the same species. It may be that during the breeding season they are more friendly than at other times. In order that you may understand my opportunities for observing these birds, I inclose a rough map of Mound Key and surroundings, my camping-place from January 20 till April 10. As you will see by the figures marked . . . . it was in the midst of their feeding-grounds, these places being mud- and sand-bars, bare at low tide. Regarding the Reddish Egret, among many thousands of them I saw only one in the pure white plumage,

[1] Cf. Bull. U. S. Geol. Geog. Survey Terr. Vol. IV. No. 1, pp. 231, 232.

and no white young; but one of my dark specimens has white feathers on the head and in the tail, while one of the secondary quills has the outer web chiefly white. My companion of last winter's Florida trip reports that he saw no Reddish Egrets with white except on the secondaries.

"Regarding the large Herons [i. e. *A. Wardi*], I am much inclined to think them a geographical variety . . . the specimens being very uniform in color. . . . I examined some thirty nests at least, fifteen of which contained young, all being dark colored, *with one exception.* These birds are common in Southwestern Florida, and their nests are frequently found along the coast. From all the information at my command, connected with my own observations, I am almost convinced that the bird in question is separate and distinct from *A. occidentalis* and *A. Würdemanni*, and the fact that Audubon found the former in immense numbers among the mangrove islands of Eastern Florida is strong evidence that he happened in the vicinity of one of their rookeries. As you will observe by examining the diagram of my camping-place, and noting the rookeries of large Herons, . . . these birds were quite common in that vicinity; while I saw only a few specimens of *A. occidentalis.* The white bird found in the nest with the blue might have come there from an adjoining empty nest, some thirty or forty feet distant, as it could easily have done, being nearly full-grown. This surmise is strengthened by the circumstance that I saw a large white Heron on the island marked '*,' and my companion killed a similar, if not the same, specimen on the large island marked '2,' which he threw away, supposing it to be a common White Egret [*Herodias egretta*]. These I now believe to have been *A. occidentalis;* the other [*H. egretta*] was then laying its eggs, while the description of *A. occidentalis* corresponds to my recollection of the bird he killed. At the time, I was not familiar with the description of *A. occidentalis.*

"In the Little Blue Heron [*Florida cærulea*] and Reddish Egret [*Dichromanassa rufa*], where dichromatism appears to be an established fact, each species presents different phases and mixtures of both colors, especially the Little Blue, which shows almost every variety of curious markings of blue and white; while in the Reddish Egret, one specimen shows white on the head, tail, and wings, and others reported by Mr. Adams show white on the wings.

"As before said, I believe the bird to be a geographical variation of *A. herodias*, residing permanently and breeding in South Florida. I think that further search and observation will develop more evidence concerning *A. occidentalis* and *A. Würdemanni*, which may result in confirming your theory of their being one and the same species. You will pardon my opposing your opinion; but my convictions are so strong, that only the finding of white birds with blue young, and more cases of blue parents with white young, or adults showing mixtures of both phases, would overcome them."

Assuming that the large white birds observed by Mr. Ward were really a white phase of the dark-colored birds obtained by him, which were so numerous in the locality, it certainly appears strange that so few of the former were seen. The case of the Reddish Egret which he cites, affords, however, an exact parallel, and it is now considered established beyond question that "Peale's Egret" (*Ardea Pealei*, BONAP., — a pure white bird) is merely a white phase of this species. As to the comparative rarity of these large white birds, in the locality where observed by Mr. Ward, militating against any theory of their specific identity with the dark-colored birds, it should be remembered that in the case of nearly every dichromatic species of bird this condition is more or less variable with locality. A pertinent example may be cited in the case of *Demiegretta sacra*, a Heron of wide distribution in the Far East.

This species inhabits a considerable number of islands in the Polynesian group, and it has been noticed and recorded by naturalists who have visited that region, that on some islands all or nearly all the birds of this species are dark-colored, on others all or nearly all are white, while on others still there may be a more equal proportion of the two phases. It may be remarked that the two phases in this species are even more distinct in coloration than in the case of *Dichromanassa rufa*, the colored phase being darker than in the latter species. Upon the whole, even admitting the possibility of the white young bird seen by Mr. Ward having of its own volition taken up its abode in a nest containing dark-colored young, I am strongly inclined to believe that it belonged to the same species with the latter, the question of its parentage (*i.e.*, whether its parents were white or dark-colored birds) being a comparatively unimportant consideration, as affecting the main question. But in adopting the view of their specific identity, a problem arises which in the light of our present knowledge appears unsolvable, and which may be briefly stated thus: —

The large "blue" Herons obtained by Mr. Ward are, in every respect as regards size and proportions, identical with *Ardea occidentalis*, AUD., and *A. Würdemanni*, BAIRD; in coloration they agree exactly with the latter, except only in the pattern of the head and tint of the neck, which are precisely as in *A. herodias*. The bird in question is apparently "dichromatic," having a white phase; hence, assuming that *A. occidentalis* and *A. Würdemanni* are dichromatic phases of one species, it necessarily follows that white individuals of the bird in question would be *absolutely indistinguishable from white examples of A. occidentalis!* Still, in view of the fact that the colored phase differs from *A. Würdemanni* in its most essential feature of coloration, *i.e.* the pattern of the head-markings, it seems impossible to unite them, unless it can be shown that the type of *A. Würdemanni* does not represent the perfect colored phase of that species.[1] There are hence several hypotheses which might be plausibly argued upon theoretical grounds, and which may be stated as follows: (1) That *A. occidentalis, A. Würdemanni, A. Wardi*, and *A. herodias* all belong to a single species, which reaches its extremes of variation in the first- and last-named; (2) That these names include three distinct races or species: *A. herodias*, which is never white; *A. occidentalis*, which is dichromatic (having separate white and colored phases), and *A. Wardi*, also dichromatic, its white phase indistinguishable from that of *A. occidentalis*, and its colored phase distinguishable from that of the same species (*A. Würdemanni*) by the different pattern and color of the head and neck alone; and (3) that there are two species, *A. occidentalis* and *A. herodias*, which in Florida hybridize on an extensive scale, producing the intermediate specimens which have been distinguished as *A. Würdemanni* and *A. Wardi*.

Of these hypotheses I have, after careful consideration of them all, concluded to adopt the second, as being most consistent with known facts, and have accordingly proposed for the bird in question the name given above.

Ardea herodias.

THE GREAT BLUE HERON.

Ardea herodias, LINN. S. N. I. 1758, 143, ed. 12, I. 1766, 237. — WILS. Am. Orn. VIII. 1814, 28, pl. 65, fig. 5. — SW. & RICH. F. B. A. II. 1831, 373. — NUTT. Man. II. 1834, 42. — AUD. Orn. Biog.

[1] After many careful examinations of the type specimen, I am led to the conclusion that it does represent the perfect colored phase, since no combination or division of the markings of *A. herodias* and *A. occidentalis* — or, in other words, no partial development of the head-pattern of the former — would give the peculiar markings which distinguish *A. Würdemanni.*

II. 1835, 87; V. 1839, 599, pl. 211; Synop. 1839, 265; B. Am. VI. 1843, 122, pl. 369. — BAIRD, B. N. Am. 1858, 668; Cat. N. Am. B. 1859, no. 487. — COUES, Key, 1872, 267; Check List, 1873, no. 449; 2d ed. 1882, no. 655; Birds N. W. 1874, 517. — RIDGW. Nom. N. Am. B. 1881, no. 487.

Ardea Hudsonias, LINN. S. N. I. 1766, 238.

HAB. The whole of North and Middle America, excepting Arctic districts; north to Hudson's Bay, "Fur Countries," and Sitka; south to New Granada, Venezuela, and the Galapagos; Bermudas, and throughout the West Indies.

SP. CHAR. *Adult:* Length, about 42.00–50.00; extent, 72.00; weight, 5 to 8 pounds. Forehead and central feathers of the crown pure white; sides of crown and whole of the occiput, including the long plumes, blue-black. Chin, throat, and malar region pure white. Neck lavender-gray, fading gradually above into the white of cheeks and throat. Foreneck with a narrow medial series of black and ferruginous dashes mixed with white; lower neck-plumes pale lavender-gray. Lateral jugular tufts uniform blue-black; breast and abdomen black, almost uni-

form laterally, but the middle feathers with broad medial stripes of white. Crissum white, the feathers sometimes edged with rufous. Tibial feathers deep chestnut-rufous, not growing conspicuously paler toward the body. Upper parts fine slate-blue, the dorsal and scapular plumes paler, more pearl-gray, — the lightness of the tint proportionate to the length of the plume; remiges black, the inner secondaries growing gradually more slaty, so that the innermost are scarcely darker than the tertials. Tail deep slate-blue, a shade darker than the tertials. Entire border of the wing, from the armpit to the metacarpo-phalangeal joint, rich purplish-rufous, scarcely mixed anywhere with white, and much the widest at the bend. Bill olive above, the culmen blackish; lower mandible wax-yellow, brighter terminally (sometimes wholly yellow); iris bright yellow; bare loral space cobalt-blue in spring, olive-greenish or yellowish after breeding season. *Legs and feet dusky-black throughout. Young:* Above slate-gray (less bluish than in the adult), destitute of any penicillate plumes; anterior lesser wing-coverts bordered terminally with light rufous; border of the wing (broadly) white, more or less tinged with rufous, especially at and near the bend, where this color prevails. Entire pileum, including all the occipital feathers, blackish-slate, with a narrow median crest of more elongated darker-colored feathers, with pale fulvous shaft-streaks. Cheeks dark grayish; malar region, chin, and throat only, pure white. Neck dull gray, sometimes tinged with rufous, some of the feathers with indistinctly lighter shaft-streaks; foreneck with a narrow longitudinal series of black, rufous, and whitish dashes, much as in the adult. Breast and abdomen broadly striped with dark cinereous and white, in nearly equal amount (sometimes suffused with rufous). Tibiæ very pale rufous, sometimes almost white; crissum white. Upper mandible black, paler, or horn-color, along the tomium; lower, pale pea-green, deepening into clear horn-yellow on terminal half; eyelids and horizontal space on lore light apple-green; iris gamboge-yellow; tibiæ and soles of toes, apple-green; rest of legs and feet black.[1]

Wing, 17.90–20.00; tail, 7.30–8.00; culmen, 4.30–6.00; depth of bill, through middle of nostril, 0.85–1.10; naked portion of tibia, 3.50–5.00; tarsus, 6.00–8.00; middle toe, 3.50–4.50. [Extremes of 17 adult specimens.]

Geographical and Individual Variations. So far as is indicated by the rather scant material before me (17 adult specimens), there is little, if any, variation in proportions or colors which can be considered strictly geographical. Especially is this so with regard to dimensions and relative measurements of different parts in an individual, — a fact which is clearly shown by the carefully-made measurements of the whole series. The typical style, indeed, prevails with such uniformity, that of seventeen specimens only four differ in any noteworthy respect from the average style. These "aberrant" examples are the following: —

No. 68300, from Florida, is decidedly the largest in the whole series, its general size almost equalling that of *A. occidentalis.* The bill also approaches quite nearly to that of the latter species, both in size and form. In colors, however, it is true *herodias*, so far as essential characters are concerned, the head-pattern being exactly as in typical specimens of that species; the abdomen with black largely prevailing, etc. The only obvious difference from ordinary specimens of the species consists in the peculiar plumage of the neck, which at first sight appears to be white throughout. A close examination, however, reveals the fact that the feathers are very much worn or abraded, and that wherever they are least so a lavender-gray tinge is distinctly visible! Now, if we examine closely the neck plumage of typical *A. herodias*, we find that it is only the *surface* which has this lavender-gray color, the concealed portion of the feathers being *whitish;* so that the white appearance of the neck in this specimen is thus readily accounted for. As probably indicating a tendency to albinism, it may be remarked that there are in this specimen many pure white feathers mixed through the rump and upper tail-coverts.[2]

The most important specimen of all, since its peculiarities are real, and not merely apparent, is No. 8065, from Mexico, also an adult. This example represents the opposite extreme in size from that just noticed, being much the smallest in the whole series. As to plumage, it is typical *A. herodias.* The shades of color are very deep and dark throughout, however, though not more so than 4524, from Cape Flattery, W. T., which almost exactly resembles it in this respect. The neck of this specimen is of precisely the same shade as that of *A. occidentalis* ("*Würdemanni*"). The chief peculiarity of this specimen is that the bill is throughout of a clear bright yellow, whereas in true *herodias* only part of the lower mandible is of this color, the upper being mainly dusky. Should this latter character, taken together with the very small size, prove constant in Mexican adult specimens, they may rank as a geographical race, for which the term "*Ardea Lessoni,*" Bonap., would probably have to be employed.

The Cape Flattery specimen alluded to above agrees exactly with the Mexican specimen as to colors, but its proportions are very peculiar. Thus, while the wing is above the average length and the tail up to the maximum, the bill is considerably below the average, being smallest of all except that of the Mexican specimen; the tibia and tarsus represent the minimum length, while the middle toe is shorter than that of any other in the entire series!

The only other specimen in the collection worth mentioning in this connection is No. 33134, Cape Saint Lucas. This specimen, also an adult, is remarkable simply on account of its *very light colors.* There is an unusual predominance of white on the breast and jugulum, and the colors generally (excepting, of course, the black) are two or three shades lighter than in the average. Its measurements come near the maximum. In these peculiarities, however, we see only the result of an extremely dry and hot climate, the bleaching effect of which is plainly visible in all the birds of brown or grayish plumage in that region of continued droughts, which embraces, besides

[1] Notes taken from fresh specimen [No. 84, 578, Nat. Mus., ♀ *juv.*, Mount Carmel, Illinois, Sept. 26, 1870. Length, 42.00; expanse, 68.50].

[2] Since the above was written, a re-examination of the specimen proves it to be *A. Wardi!* The first inspection was made several years previous to the discovery of the latter species.

the peninsula of Lower California, the whole of the desert region of the Southwestern United States and Western Mexico.

Younger specimens (probably in the second year), of which No. 12670, is a fair example, have the forehead dusky-slate, there being only a few white feathers in the crown; the cheeks strongly tinged with buff. The specimen alluded to is equally dark with that from Cape Flattery, W. T., and that from Mexico.

SEASONAL VARIATIONS. Although the plumage of this species is essentially the same throughout the year, there are certain differences depending on the season which are worthy of note. In the spring, or at the commencement of the breeding season, the bill, except on the culmen, is almost entirely yellow (generally a wax-yellow, brighter on the lower mandible); and the bare orbital space cobalt-blue, while from the occiput grow two long, slender, pendant, black plumes. After the young are hatched, these plumes are dropped, the bare skin around the eye has changed to a yellowish-green hue, and the upper mandible become almost wholly dusky blackish-olive, with only the tomia and lower mandible yellowish. Of some twenty specimens killed June 11, 1877, at the Little Cypress Swamp, of Knox Co., Indiana, none had the white occipital plumes, while the bill and orbits were colored as last stated above. These birds were all shot at their breeding grounds, where were about one hundred and fifty occupied nests, mostly containing full-grown young. A male killed at Washington, D. C., April 9, 1875, and consequently in perfect plumage, had the bill and soft parts colored as follows: — Bill dull wax-yellow, brighter on the lower mandible; bare orbital space cobalt-blue; iris bright chrome-yellow; legs black, the tibiæ inclining to brownish; soles of toes dull grayish naples-yellow. A female obtained in spring at Mount Carmel, Ill., was similarly colored.

The Great Blue Heron — one of the most eminently characteristic birds of North America — is found, in varying abundance, throughout the continent, south of the more northern regions, from the Pacific to the Atlantic coast; it is also found in several of the West India Islands and in Central America. Richardson regarded it as only an accidental straggler in the Fur Region; but Captain Blakiston notes it as a regular summer visitant, and as breeding on the Saskatchewan. It was found by M. Bourgeau, in July, 1858, breeding on one of the tributaries of the north branch of the Saskatchewan. There were several nests in a poplar grove, situated in a large ravine near a lake; they were all about fifty feet from the ground. One nest, containing six eggs, was taken. This bird was found at Sitka by Bischoff, where it was rare; and it is included by Mr. R. Browne in his list of the birds of Vancouver. In California, Dr. Cooper speaks of it as everywhere common about the shores and marshes, almost forming one of the characteristic features of the landscape of that region. It is resident, not even migrating from the Columbia River, though wandering to a considerable distance for food. It visits the islands along the coast, and occasionally stands to feed on the floating kelp at some distance from the shore. He found its nest with fresh eggs about April 24, near San Diego. The nests were built in oak trees, up dry ravines, at some distance from the water. Sometimes there were two or three nests in the same tree. At Santa Barbara, he found them in lofty poplars, three miles from the shore. They were loosely constructed of coarse sticks, laid flat. The eggs, four in number, measured from 2.60 to 2.68 inches in length, and 1.78 to 1.80 in breadth. The birds made no attempt to defend their nest, but flew around uttering a low croaking.

It usually fishes in the early morning and in the evening, often wading up to its tarsal joint in the water, standing motionless, watching until its prey comes near, and then seizing it by a very rapid stroke of the bill, and swallowing it head downward. It also feeds on meadow mice, frogs, small birds, grasshoppers, etc. Its flight is rapid and easy, and when migrating is sometimes very high; but it usually keeps near the ground or water. It is at all times very vigilant, and difficult of approach.

When wounded it defends itself with its bill, and can inflict a dangerous wound. In flying, it doubles back the neck between the wings, and allows the legs to stick out straight behind. It has been known to collect in flocks of two hundred or more, near the Columbia, when the herring were entering the bay in August. It is said to be quite eatable when young, if properly cleaned.

Captain Bendire mentions this species as a very common summer resident throughout the lower Harney Valley, in Eastern Oregon. It breeds on one of the small islands in Malheur Lake in great numbers, in company with the Double-crested Cormorant and the White Pelican. Its nests were placed on greasewood bushes, from two to four feet from the ground, nearly every bush containing a nest. They were all flat structures, built of such materials as were close at hand — dry sticks and reeds, with a little swamp-grass for a lining. The usual number of eggs was five. The measurement of the largest egg was 2.73×1.96; of the smallest, 2.40×1.82; and the average, 2.65×1.80. The first laid eggs in a set were usually of a lighter or faded color. The female began to lay about the 20th of April. The young for the first two weeks were nearly destitute of feathers, and made a hissing noise when disturbed. They sit close together in a circle on their nests, with their heads all turned toward its centre. When one of their colonies is disturbed, the old birds at once depart, without any manifestation of concern.

This Heron is also known occasionally to breed on precipitous and rocky sides of streams, where other opportunities are not present, making use of projecting ledges of rocks instead of trees or bushes.

Mr. Salvin notes the occurrence of this Heron near the Lake of Dueñas, in Guatemala; it was seen fishing on the River Guacalate; he also met with it frequenting the lagoons on the Pacific coast of that Republic, and mentions its great shyness. Professor Newton cites this Heron as occurring in St. Croix in March and April, and again in August, 1857. Mr. E. Newton had no doubt that it breeds on the island, as it was observed there on the 10th of June. According to Dr. Gundlach, it breeds in Cuba; and on the authority of Mr. Richard Hill and Mr. March, in Jamaica. Mr. Dresser found it common in Tamaulipas, Mexico, all the year, excepting only the two coldest months; and Dr. Berlandier, in his manuscript notes, mentions its occurrence in Eastern Mexico from November to the end of February, and as abundant throughout the entire State of Tamaulipas.

Major Wedderburn gives this species as resident in the Bermudas, many arriving in autumn, and a few remaining throughout the year. In 1846 a nest of this bird containing two eggs was found among the mangrove-trees in Hungry Bay, and the Rev. H. B. Tristram is said to have kept one alive in his garden, at the parsonage on Ireland Island, which was once seen to seize a Ground-dove and swallow it entire. Mr. Hardis, however, regards it as entirely migratory in Bermuda; first seen about the 19th of September, continuing to arrive in October, when it becomes common, and occasionally met with from that period to April; it then disappears for the summer months. During the violent gale of October, 1848, a number sought refuge in the Bermudas, appearing on all parts of the coast, and landing in a state of such great exhaustion that five were taken alive. In arriving it was seen to keep close to the surface of the water.

Professor Verrill found this Heron breeding in the interior of Maine, a hundred miles or more from the coast; and Mr. Boardman informs us that it is found in New Brunswick and Nova Scotia, as far to the north as the Gulf of St. Lawrence. According to the observations of Mr. Giraud, it is common on all the salt-marshes of Long Island, where it confines itself almost entirely to the wet and miry flats in the vicinity of the beach. In its habits it is diurnal as well as nocturnal. It may be observed by day wading out on the shoals, collecting crabs and various species of shell-fish, and at other times standing in the water up to its knees, with its bill poised ready to strike its prey. It is then especially shy, intently observing everything that is passing within a wide circle. Yet even this bird, vigilant as it is, may be enticed by decoys within gunshot; and by many its flesh is very highly esteemed.

It will venture even more fearlessly forth at night in quest of food, always standing in the same motionless posture, with bill ready poised for the coming of its prey. While in this position its plumage is parted, exposing a portion of the breast, which is said to be furnished with a downy substance emitting a phosphorescent light. By some this is called the bird's lantern, and is said to be serviceable to it while fishing, both by attracting its prey, and by showing it where to strike. Even in dead specimens this luminous substance is said to give out a pale glow, not unlike that produced by decaying wood.

This Heron was met with by Mr. J. A. Allen in September, in the Valley of Great Salt Lake, where it was quite common. Mr. Ridgway also found it an abundant species in the wooded valley of the Truckee River, and breeding in numbers on all the rocky islands in Pyramid Lake. Several of its nests, containing from three to four young each, were found on the large island. These were very bulky, but well made, composed of sticks, and placed on the tops of the greasewood bushes (*Obione*), about five feet from the ground. Those on the "Pyramid" were placed among the rocks, at varying heights above the water. Among the marshes around Great Salt Lake, and in the *tule* lagoons near Sacramento, he also found it abundant.

Wilson found this Heron breeding in the gloomy solitudes of the tallest cedar-swamps in the lower parts of New Jersey, where, if undisturbed, it continues many years in succession. The young are hatched about the middle of May, and are unable to fly until they are as large as their parents. It breeds but once in a season. The noise which this Heron makes when disturbed in its breeding-place is said sometimes to resemble the honking of a goose; at other times it is a hoarse, hollow grunting sound, like that of a hog, but louder.

Like the common Heron of Europe, which it closely resembles in many other respects, this bird is of solitary habit, excepting during the breeding season, going in pairs only from March to August; the rest of the year leading a solitary life. Furious battles are said to take place between the males at the beginning of the pairing season.

Mr. N. B. Moore has supplied some very interesting observations upon the habits of this species, tracing the history of a pair from the first labor of making a nest, through the periods of egg-laying, incubation, and rearing their young. They were observed at the nest with a field-glass, and were first seen Feb. 5. One was carrying sticks to a certain willow growing in a pond. The other was standing in a part of the tree near the top, or fifteen feet from the mud below. This was the female, and a few sticks were placed near her. The sticks, broken from the blasted willow-tops, were brought by the male. He generally alighted with them a little higher than she. The latter reached up her bill, took them, and placed them on the pile, each in its proper place. The work was so carried on to its completion — the male acting as procurer of materials, his mate as architect. During these labors, the female seems by far the more impatient to advance the business. She takes the stick from him and lays it in its place; and if he stops, and seems loath to leave her side, she motions him to leave, though no sound is heard, and away he goes for another stick. The sticks were carried, not across the bill, but pointing out before it, in a line with it. Neither the eggs nor the young, until the latter are able to use their bills well for defence, are ever left by both birds at once. Copulation takes place in the nest.

Both parents incubate, and both bring food to the young. After these are able to strike with their bills, the old birds spend little time with them, or even in sight. The eagerness and the dash of the bill of a hungry nestling, as well as its powerful gripe, are interesting peculiarities. The struggle between the young Heron and the parent seems like a wrestling-match, the former standing up almost as high as the latter, the tree swaying to and fro, and both birds staggering upon the nest, to such an extent that the mother is occasionally compelled to step off and stand on one of the branches, to avoid falling. This struggle occurs when all the food has been given, and the mother is seeking to extricate her bill from that of her young. On one occasion Mr. Moore saw one of the parents, after having fed its young, pick up a good-sized eel from the nest, deliberately swallow it, and then fly away.

This species is never known to run, or even to walk briskly; and it never rakes the bottom for its food. It is sometimes seen in the water watching for its prey at two o'clock in the morning. It often feeds on sirens, eating the posterior portion only of the larger ones. In very cold winters many more are seen in Florida than in milder seasons. After swallowing a good-sized fish, it drinks by dipping its bill into the water from one to five times. The larger the fish, the more water it drinks. Mr. Moore has seen one take a large fish that lay flirting its tail, and fly two hundred yards before laying it on the sand. On being approached the bird again carried it off as before. In catching fish this Heron usually strikes its prey through the body. Now and then it is said to strike at a fish so large and strong as to endanger its own life. Audubon was a witness to an incident of this kind, where a Heron, on the Florida coast, after striking a fish, was dragged several yards, and was able to disengage itself only after a severe struggle. This species is said to take three years in attaining maturity; and even after that period it gains in size and weight. When first hatched it has a very grotesque appearance: the legs, neck, and bill seem disproportionately long, and it is nearly bare. It is soon covered with a silky down of dark gray color.

In Florida the number of its eggs is nearly uniformly three; but farther north the number increases to four or five, and in a few instances to six. The egg resembles, in its rounded oval shape and in its color, the eggs of most of the Heron family. This color is uniform and unspotted, and is a faint wash of a greenish Prussian blue. The eggs vary somewhat in size, and some are more oblong in shape than others; eggs from Florida are noticeably smaller than those from Massachusetts. Three in my cabinet exhibit the following measurements: No. 60, from Grand Menan, 2.50 × 1.80 inches; No. 61, from Naushon, Mass., 2.50 × 1.70; and No. 977, from Cape Charles, Va., 2.57 × 1.80 inches.

Ardea cinerea.

THE COMMON HERON OF EUROPE.

Ardea cinerea, LINN. Faun. Suec. 1746, 59; S. N. I. 1766, 236. — FABR. Faun. Groenl. 1780, 106 (Greenland). — GMEL. S. N. I. ii. 1788, 627. — NAUM. Vög. Deutschl. IX. 1838, 24, pl. 220. — GOULD, B. Eur. 1837, pl. 273. — BONAP. Consp. II. 1855, 111. — KEYS. & BLAS. Wirb. Eur. 1840, 79. — MACGILL. Man. Brit. Orn. II. 1842, 128. — GRAY, Cat. Brit. B. 1863, 145. — REINH. Ibis, 1861, 9 (Nenortalik, Greenland). — RIDGW. Nom. N. Am. B. 1881, no. 488. — COUES, Check List, 2d ed. 1882, no. 657.

Ardea major, LINN. S. N. I. 1766, 236.

Ardea rhenana, SANDER. Naturf. XIII. 1779, 195.
Ardea Johannæ, GMEL. S. N. I. ii. 1788, 629.
Ardea cineracea, BREHM, Vög. Deutschl. 1831, 580.
Ardea vulgaris, BECHST. Orn. Tasch. 1803, 255.
Ardea brag, GEOFF. Jacq. Voy. Ind. IV. 1844, 85.
Ardea leucophæa, GOULD, P. Z. S. 1848, 58.
Ardea cinerea major, minor, media, et brachyrhyncha, BREHM, Verz. Samml. C. L. Brehm's, 1866, 12 (*Reichenow.*).

Hab. Palæarctic region, south to Australia ; accidental in Southern Greenland.

SP. CHAR. *Adult:* Forehead and centre of pileum pure white ; sides of crown and occipital plumes deep black ; rest of head wholly white. Neck light cinereous, with a very faint lavender tinge, gradually fading into the white of the head ; the front part with a narrow longitudinal series

of black dashes on a white ground. Upper parts bluish-gray, the penicillate plumes of the back and scapulars much lighter or pale pearl-gray. Border of the wing pure white ; anteaxillar tufts deep blue-black. Sides and flanks uniform pale blue-gray. Medial lower parts white, heavily striped laterally with blue-black. Tibiæ and crissum pure white. Bill yellow, usually with the culmen brownish terminally ; bare loral space green ; iris yellow ; feet dull green ; tibiæ yellow. (MACGILLIVRAY.) *Juv.:* Pileum deep ash-gray ; occipital plumes black. Neck ash-gray, the front with a narrow longitudinal series of black and rufous dashes, mixed with white, the former predominating. Upper parts uniform slate-gray, destitute of penicillate plumes. Malar region, chin, and throat white. Anteaxillar tufts white, tipped with a rusty tinge. Edge of the wing and entire lower parts wholly white, tinged with buff.

Wing, 18.50 ; tail, 8.00 ; culmen, 4.80 ; depth of bill through middle of nostril, 0.85 ; bare tibia, 3.25 ; tarsus, 6.25 ; middle toe, 3.80. [No. 57006 ; Europe.]

The Common or Gray Heron of Europe has small claim to a place in the fauna of North America. Two specimens are recorded as having been known in Greenland,— one, seen in August, 1765, by the missionary Stach ; the other, a young bird found dead near Nenortalik in 1856. It is a familiar European species, as also one of the most numerous of this peculiar and well-marked family.

Formerly, before falconry had become one of the lost arts, it was the typical Heron of olden times, and occupied an important place in the sporting world. The localities in which it bred were forbidden ground, except to the servants of royalty; the bird itself was exclusively royal game, and penal enactments preserved it for royal sport. But now that it must depend upon itself for safety, it has become shy, watchful, and solitary, and during the winter seldom more than one is seen at the same time and in the same place. In the spring, however, numbers collect together, and resort anew to the favorite wood in which, for years in succession, they have spent the breeding season. At this time their habits are said to resemble those of the Rook; and, like that bird, the Heron builds on high trees — generally large oaks — and associates in such great numbers that Pennant counted more than eighty nests of this species upon one oak at Cressy Hall — an estate then belonging to the Heron family. In some instances it has been known to build on precipitous rocks near the coast, and at others on the ground amongst reeds and rushes. The nest is usually of large size, formed of sticks, and often lined with wool.

The usual number of eggs in the nest of this Heron is said to be four or five, and incubation lasts about four weeks. The parents sit on the eggs by turns, the sitting bird being supplied with food by its mate. When the young are hatched, both parents assist in the supply of food. If the heronry is visited during the breeding season, the old birds betray great anxiety, sailing in circles high above the trees. It feeds the young with fish and reptiles, occasionally with small mammalia also. It is assiduous in collecting food during the breeding season, but at other times it usually fishes only late in the evening or very early in the morning, sitting the whole day perched on the branch of a large tree.

It stands motionless in the water when fishing, the head drawn back toward the shoulders, ready to strike with its sharp beak the approaching prey. When a large eel has been secured, it is often disabled by beating it on the ground. Mr. Dana states that in the Orkney and Shetland Islands, where this Heron is very plentiful, it always selects the lee side of the island for its fishing operations.

Mr. Yarrell states that this Heron is said to be very long lived. It was in former years held in great esteem as an article of food. The heronries are occupied for breeding purposes from spring until August. During the winter a few stragglers only are seen, who seem to be left to pay occasional visits to maintain the right of occupation. Occasionally furious battles take place between the Rooks and the Herons for the possession of particular trees.

This Heron is a summer visitant of Scandinavia, going occasionally as far north as the Faroe Islands and Iceland, from which it straggles to the south coast of Greenland. It is found in Russia and Siberia, and thence southward over the whole European continent. It is said to be specially abundant in Holland. In its migrations it is found in most of the islands of the Mediterranean, and winters in North Africa. It has been traced to the Island of Madeira, and is even said to visit the Cape of Good Hope. It has been found in the countries about the Caucasus, is said to inhabit India, China, and Japan, and is included by Horsfield among the birds of Java.

The eggs are of a uniform pale sea-green color, and are of a rounded oval form, 2.25 inches in length by 1.75 inches in breadth.

GENUS **HERODIAS**, BOIE.

Herodias, BOIE, Isis, 1822. Type, *Ardea egretta*, LINN.

GEN. CHAR. White Herons of large size, and without plumes, except in the breeding season, when ornamented simply (in most species [1]) by a long train of straight feathers, with thick shafts, and long, sparse, decomposed, slender barbs, which grow from the dorsal region and overhang the tail. Bill moderately slender, the upper and lower outlines almost parallel to near the end, where gently curved, the culmen more abruptly so than the gonys, though the curve is quite gradual. Mental apex reaching a point about midway between the tip of the bill and the eye ; malar apex decidedly anterior to the frontal apex, and extending to beneath the posterior end of the nostrils. Toes very long, the middle one about two thirds the tarsus, the hallux much less than one half the former. Tibiæ bare for about one half their length, or for about the length of the middle toe.

H. egretta.

Anterior scutellæ of tarsus large, distinct, and nearly quadrate. Nuptial plumes confined to the anterior part of the back, whence spring numerous long, straight, and thick shafts, reaching, when fully developed, to considerably beyond the end of the tail ; each stem having along each side very long, slender, and distant fibrillæ. Tail even, of twelve broad feathers. Lower nape well feathered. Plumage entirely pure white at all stages and seasons.

This genus, like *Ardea*, *Garzetta*, etc., is nearly cosmopolitan, being wanting only in the islands of the South Pacific and in the colder latitudes of other regions. It comprises but a single American species, which has a more extensive range than any other of the American Herons, excepting only *Nyctiardea grisea nævia*,[2] its regular habitat extending from the United States to Chili and Patagonia. In their immature stage and in winter plumage, the several Old World species closely resemble the American species, as well as one another. But it is believed that in full dress the following distinctions will be found to hold good in the forms which we have been able to compare. Gray's *Hand-list* (vol. III. pp. 27, 28) recognizes the following species : (1) *H. alba*, L., of Europe, Africa, India, and Australia ; (2) *H. egretta*, GMEL., of America ; (3) *H. intermedia*, V.

[1] An Old World species (*H. plumiferus*, GOULD) has long jugular feathers with decomposed webs.

[2] It is an unsettled question, however, whether the Night Heron of Chili, Patagonia, etc., may not be a distinct race (*N. grisea obscura* ; see page 56).

HASSELQ., of Java, India, Japan, New South Wales, and Tasmania; (4) *H. timorensis*, CUV., of Timor; and (5) *H. brevipes*, VERR. & DESM., from New Caledonia. To which of these the fourth species of the following synopsis belongs, I am at present unable to determine.

Synopsis of Species.

A. *Jugular plumes slightly lengthened, with broad and undecomposed webs.*

a. With light-colored legs and feet, and the bill usually principally dusky.

1. **H. alba.**[1] Plumes of the train reaching to only about 2–3 inches beyond the tail; bill chiefly dusky in the breeding plumage; legs and feet chiefly light flesh-colored, with the larger scutellæ more brownish. Wing, 16.00–18.30; culmen, 4.75–6.00; tarsus, 6.50–7.90; middle toe, 3.60–4.60. *Hab.* Europe and other parts of Old World.

b. With deep black legs and feet, the bill usually mostly yellow.

2. **H. syrmatophorus.**[2] With a short train, like *H. alba*, but bill wholly yellow, and the legs and feet deep black (except tibiæ, which are pale dull yellow), as in *H. egretta.* Wing, 14.50; culmen, 4.50; tarsus, 6.25; middle toe, 3.65. *Hab.* Australia.

3. **H. egretta.** Bill usually chiefly yellow, with more or less of the terminal portion black; sometimes, however, with the manilla wholly black or entirely yellow; tibiæ black. Train extending usually 6 inches or more beyond the tail. Wing, 14.10–16.80; culmen, 4.20–4.90; tarsus, 5.50–6.80; middle toe, 3.50–4.30. *Hab.* Warmer parts of America.

B. *Jugular plumes similar to those of the dorsal train, only smaller.*

4. **H. plumiferus.**[3] Bill with about the terminal half of both mandibles black, the basal portion pale-colored (yellow in life?); legs and feet deep black. Wing, 12.50; culmen, 3.10; tarsus, 4.80; middle toe, 3. *Hab.* China (No. 85747 U. S. Nat. Mus.; ♂ ad., Woo Sung, China, May 23, 1881; Shanghai Museum); Australia (GOULD).

Herodias egretta.

THE AMERICAN EGRET.

La Grande Aigrette d'Amérique, BUFF. Pl. Enl. 1770–86, pl. 925.
Great White Heron, LATH. Synop. III. 1785, 91.
Great Egret, LATH. t. c. 89 (based on Pl. Enl. 925).
Ardea egretta, GMEL. S. N. I. 1788, 629, no. 34 (based on Pl. Enl. 925, and Lath., l. c.). — WILS. Am. Orn. VII. 1813, 106, pl. 61, fig. 4. — NUTT. Man. II. 1834, 47. — AUD. Orn. Biog. IV. 1838, 600, pl. 386; Synop. 1839, 265; B. Am. VI. 1843, 132, pl. 370. — COUES, Key, 1872, 267; Check List, 1873, no. 452; Birds N. W. 1874, 519.
Herodias egretta, GRAY, Gen. B. III. 1849. — BAIRD, B. N. Am. 1858, 666; Cat. N. Am. B. 1859, no. 486. — COUES, Check List, ed. 2, 1882, no. 658.
Herodias alba, var. *egretta*, RIDGW. Am. Lyc. N. Y. Jan. 1874, 386.
Herodias alba egretta, RIDGW. Bull. Essex Inst. Oct. 1874, 171; Nom. N. Am. B. 1881, no. 489.

[1] HERODIAS ALBA, Linn. European Egret.
Ardea alba, LINN. S. N. ed. 10, I. 1758, 144; ed. 12, I. 1766, 239.
Herodias alba. AUCT.
Ardea egrettoides, S. G. GMEL. Reise, II. 193, pl. 24.
Erodius Victoriæ, MACGILL. Man. N. H. Orn. II. 131.
Herodias candida, BREHM, Vög. Deutschl. 584.

[2] HERODIAS SYRMATOPHORUS, Gould. Australian Egret.
Herodias syrmatophorus, GOULD, B. Austr. VI. 1848, pl. 56.

It is somewhat doubtful whether this bird can be separated from *H. egretta.* A Floridian specimen of the latter is in *all respects* identical, except as to size, the measurements being, wing, 15.50; culmen, 4.50; tarsus, 6.00; and middle toe, 3.85, — certainly not as great a difference as occurs between specimens of either *H. alba* or *H. egretta.*

[3] HERODIAS PLUMIFERUS, Gould. Plumed Egret.
Herodias plumiferus, GOULD, P. Z. S. 1847, 221; B. Austr. VI. 1848, pl. 57.

Herodias egretta, var. *californica*, BAIRD, B. N. Am. 1858, 667; Cat. N. Am. B. 1859, no. 486 *a*.
Ardea leuce, "ILLIGER," LICHT. Verz. Doubl. 1823, no. 793.
Ardea alba, subspec. *galatea*, REICHENOW, J. f. O. 1877, 272.

HAB. The whole of temperate and tropical America, from Nova Scotia, Canada West, Minnesota, and Oregon, to Chili and Patagonia; throughout the West Indies.

SP. CHAR. Length, about 37.00–39.00; extent, about 55.00–57.00; wing, 14.10–16.80; tail, 5.60–7.30; culmen, 4.20–4.90; depth of bill, .70–.80; tarsus, 5.50–6.80; middle toe, 3.50–4.30; naked portion of tibia, 3.50–4.50; weight, about 2¼ lbs. Color entirely pure white at all seasons and at all ages. Bill and lores rich chrome-yellow (the latter sometimes tinged with light green), the culmen usually black near the tip, sometimes nearly the entire maxilla black; iris naples-yellow; legs and feet entirely deep black.

Having specimens before us from all parts of its range, we are unable to detect in this species any variations of a geographical nature. The chief difference between individuals consists in the

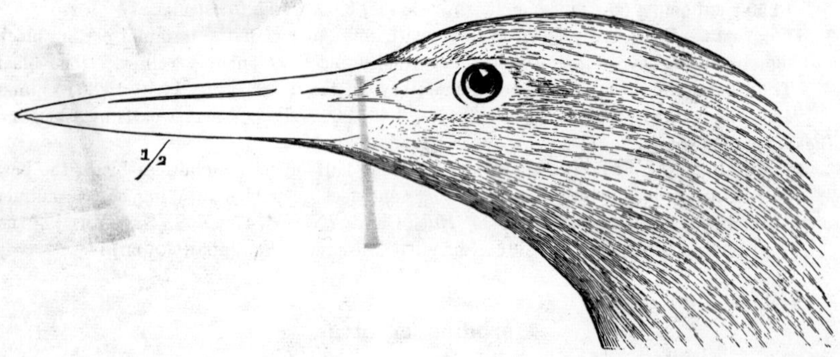

amount of black on the maxilla, this being sometimes almost *nil*, while again the maxilla may be entirely black. That this variation has no relation to season is shown by the fact that in a considerable series shot from one "rookery" in Florida, and all bearing the nuptial train, the extremes are presented by different individuals, others being variously intermediate.

The American Egret may be easily enough distinguished from that of Europe (*H. alba*) by its smaller size, jet-black instead of pale flesh-colored legs, brighter yellow bill, etc.; but I have thus far been unsuccessful in my search for characters which will serve always to distinguish the Australian Egret from *H. egretta*. Australian specimens agree with the latter in black legs and feet (though the tibiæ are said to be pale dull yellow), yellow bill, and smaller size. A single specimen in nuptial plumage has the train short, like *H. alba;* but a Florida example of *H. egretta* differs in no respect whatever, that I can see, except measurements; and in this respect the discrepancy is much less than between examples of *H. egretta* shot at the same time in the same locality! Following are the measurements of the two specimens in question:—

No. 71567, *H. syrmatophorus,*	14.50	4.50	6.25	3.65	New South Wales.
No. 73524, *H. egretta,*	15.50	4.50	6.00	3.85	Florida.

It is possible, however, that a larger series of *H. syrmatophorus* than the one which I have been able to examine might show differences which have as yet escaped my notice.

The Great White Egret of America has an extended distribution, breeding throughout North America as far as New Jersey, on the Atlantic coast, in the interior as far north as Southern Illinois, and throughout South America, almost to Patagonia. It is a great wanderer, and stragglers have been met with from the Straits of Magellan to Nova Scotia, and from the Atlantic to the Pacific, where it is found as far to the north as the Columbia River, and probably beyond. In midsummer it wanders to

Lake Michigan and others of the larger lakes. Mr. Salvin found it common in Central America, both on the Atlantic and the Pacific coasts. It was much more solitary in its habits than the *candidissima*. Mr. G. C. Taylor also met with it at Tigre Island, in Honduras, where it was not uncommon. It is an occasional visitant, both in the spring and in the fall, to Bermuda. Léotaud speaks of it as a very common species in Trinidad, where it was principally found on the banks of the sea, or of rivers influenced by the tides. It is said to hunt for fish in the daytime, and also to feed on soft mollusks. It reposes on the branches of the mangrove-trees in a state of continued immobility. It is found usually singly, or not more than two or three together. Although very shy in its wild state, it is readily reconciled to captivity. Confined in a courtyard or a garden, it becomes a very attractive ornament. The brilliant whiteness of its plumage, the gracefulness of its movements, the elegance of its plumes, and the dignity of its carriage, combine to make it very attractive. It will watch for a rat or a mouse with complete immobility, when suddenly, and with a surprising rapidity of movement, it seizes its prey. It devours everything it meets with, sparing neither insect nor reptile. If another of this species is put in the same enclosure, a furious contest is sure to ensue, which not unfrequently ends in the crippling of one of the combatants. They strike furious blows at each other with their beaks, but these are usually warded off. In the struggle they interlace their feet and wings, and not unfrequently one of the wings gets broken: this ends the contest.

The Egret is a resident of Trinidad, breeds there, and never leaves the island. It is given by Dr. Gundlach as breeding in Cuba, and by Mr. Gosse and Mr. March as a resident in Jamaica; and it is found in other West India Islands. Mr. C. W. Wyatt mentions meeting with this species on the Lake of Paturia, in Colombia, S. A. Dr. Burmeister records it as found everywhere throughout the La Plata region in South America, on the banks of the rivers and among the lagoons, or among the reeds in marshy ground from the Banda Oriental as far as the Andes. Specimens were taken by Dr. Cunningham (Ibis, 1867) near Port Ordway, in the Straits of Magellan.

During the summer this species straggles along our entire Atlantic coast, and even into the interior. Mr. Boardman informs me that it not only occasionally is taken in the neighborhood of Calais, but that individuals have been shot as far up the Bay of Fundy as Windsor, Nova Scotia. Several instances are on record of its having been taken in Massachusetts. Mr. Allen reports two taken near Hudson by Mr. Jillson in 1867; these were in immature plumage. Several others were seen at the same time. A male in full plumage was taken at Ashland, in May, several years since, and another near Lynn by Mr. Vickary. Mr. H. A. Purdie records the capture of a fine specimen in Westford in the summer of 1873. In the summer of 1869 an example of this species was shot on the Onion or Winooski River, in Vermont. Though rare in the interior, it is yet found in suitable localities. Professor Kumlien informs me that in the months of August and September it is to be seen every year, fishing on the edge of Lake Koskonong, Wisconsin. New Jersey is the most northern point on the Atlantic coast where it has been known to breed. On Long Island, according to Giraud, it is not a frequent visitor. Occasionally one may be seen, during the summer months, on the marshes or meadows, or wading about on the shoals in pursuit of small fish, on which it feeds, as well as frogs and lizards. The largest number ever in sight at one time is five. These were seen on Coney Island, and were extremely shy and vigilant, eluding all attempts to secure them. In Wilson's time, or about 1810, this Heron bred in considerable numbers in the extensive cedar-swamps in the lower part of New Jersey, where their nests were built in societies on trees. The young made their first appearance in the marshes in August, in parties of twenty or thirty, and were frequently shot. The old birds were too shy to be often secured. Their food, as shown by the remains found in their stomach, consists of frogs, lizards, small fish, insects, seeds of a species of *nymphœa,* water-snakes, mice, moles, and other kinds of vermin.

Audubon met with this species abundantly in Florida, where it is resident throughout the year. It is found along the Gulf coast to Mexico; but is rarely met with inland, and usually not more than fifty miles from the coast, and then always near some large river. It frequents, for purposes of reproduction, low, marshy districts covered with large trees, the margin of streams, ponds, or bayous, or gloomy swamps covered with water. In a few instances Mr. Audubon met with its nests in low trees, and on sandy islands at a short distance from the mainland. Early in December Mr. Audubon found this Heron congregated together in vast numbers, apparently for the purpose of mating, in East Florida. He describes the courtship of the males as very curious and interesting. Their throats swelling out in the manner of Cormorants, emitting gurgling sounds, they strutted round the females, raising their long plumes almost erect, and pacing majestically before the objects of their selection. Conflicts now and then took place, but they were not so frequent as he had been led to suppose. These performances were continued from day to day for nearly a week, occupying the warmer portion of the day.

The flight of this Heron is well sustained and vigorous. On foot its movements are graceful, its step measured, its long neck being gracefully retracted and curved. Its long and silky train makes its appearance a few weeks previous to the love season, and continues to grow and to increase in beauty until incubation has commenced. After this period it begins to deteriorate, and disappears about the time the young bird leaves the nest.

Those that migrate northward leave Florida about the first of March; but none reach New Jersey before the middle of May. In Florida the young are full grown by the 8th of May; in New Jersey, not before the 1st of August: in the former State two broods are raised in a season.

Regarding the supposed California form of the White Egret as identical with the eastern *egretta,* I can find no mention of any peculiar characteristics differing from those found on the Southern Atlantic or the Gulf coast. Dr. Cooper has found the Californian birds abundant in the southern part of that State throughout the year. Being without doubt the bird referred to by Dr. Newberry as the *Ardea occidentalis,* it is found in the summer as far north as the Columbia River. It in all probability breeds throughout this extended range, chiefly in swampy woods near the sea. Dr. Cooper met with a large number in June, in a grove near the mouth of the Santa Margarita River. He also met with it in May near Santa Barbara, and has procured examples also near Fort Mojave.

Mr. Ridgway mentions having met with this bird once, in June, near Sacramento; and on several occasions in the vicinity of Pyramid Lake, in the months of December and May.

Captain Bendire informs me, January, 1875, that a large heronry of this species exists in the neighborhood of Fort Harney, about seventy-five miles south of Canyon City, Grant County, Oregon.

The nests of this Egret vary greatly in position: some are found on the tops of lofty cypress trees from one hundred to one hundred and fifty feet from the ground, others on low mangroves not six feet above the water, and others in intermediate positions. The nest is always a large flat structure, composed of sticks loosely put together. It usually overhangs the water, and is resorted to year after year by the same pair. When the nest is on a tall tree, the young remain in it or on the branches until they are able to fly; but when it is near the water or ground, they leave much sooner.

The number of eggs in a nest in Florida, according to Audubon, is invariably three. According to Wilson, in New Jersey the number is four or five. Audubon gives their size as two and a quarter inches in length and one and five eighths in breadth, and their color a pale blue, which soon fades. Two eggs in my collection, obtained in Florida by Dr. Bryant, measure, one 2.30 × 1.52 inches; the other 2.28 × 1.60 inches. They are oval in shape, nearly equal at either end, and their color is that uniform unspotted washing or faint shading of greenish Prussian blue, common to all our herons, the two bitterns alone excepted.

Genus **GARZETTA**, Kaup.

Garzetta, Kaup, Nat. Syst. Eur. Thierw. 1829, 76. Bonap. Consp. II. 1855, 118 (type, *Ardea garzetta*, Linn.).

Gen. Char. Small white Herons, crested at all ages and seasons, and in the nuptial season adorned with jugular and dorsal plumes. Bill slender, very little compressed, the culmen decidedly but ascending; the lower edge of the mandibular rami straight or appreciably concave. Mental curved for the terminal half, somewhat depressed for the basal half; the gonys nearly straight,

G. candidissima.

apices falling far short of reaching half-way from the middle of the eye to the point of the bill; malar apices reaching just as far as the frontal apices, and falling far short of the posterior end of the nostrils. Toes short, the middle one but little more than one half the tarsus, the hallux about one half its length; bare portion of tibia nearly three fourths as long as the tarsus. Tarsal scutellæ as in *Herodias*.

Nuptial plumes adorning the occiput, jugulum, and back; these, in the American species, all of similar structure, having decomposed webs; but in the Old World species, those of the occiput and jugulum narrow and with compact webs. Dorsal plumes (in all species) reaching but little beyond the tail, and strongly recurved at ends.

Of the extralimital species of this genus we have only *G. nivea*, GMEL., of Europe at hand for comparison. This species bears a close general resemblance to *G. candidissima*, being of nearly the same size, and having exactly similar scapular plumes. The jugular plumes, however, are acicular and somewhat rigid, instead of hairlike, with decomposed webs; while the occipital plumes are entirely different, there being two very long, narrow feathers springing from the occiput, very much like those of the species of *Ardea*. The differences between the two species are more precisely expressed in the following table: –

COM. CHAR. Plumage wholly pure white at all ages and seasons. Dorsal plumes reaching to about the end of the tail, their shafts rigid and more or less strongly recurved at ends, the webs decomposed, with the fibrillæ hairlike, and rather widely separated.

1. **G. candidissima.** Occipital crest composed of numerous elongated feathers with their webs decomposed and hairlike; jugular plumes similar. Bill black, yellow at base; iris and eyelids yellow; tibiæ and tarsi black, the lower part of the latter, with toes, yellow. Culmen, 2.08–3.55; tarsus, 3.30–4.40; wing, 8.20–10.50. *Hab.* Warmer parts of America.
2. **G. nivea.**[1] Occipital crest composed of two or three long, slender, decurved or pendant plumes, with compact webs; jugular plumes acicular, somewhat rigid. Bill black, the base light green; tibia and upper half of tarsi black; lower half of latter, with toes, greenish-yellow. Culmen, 3.25–3.75; tarsus, 3.60–4.00; wing, 10.75. *Hab.* Europe and parts of Asia and Africa.
3. **G. immaculata.**[2] Similar to *G. nivea*, but without occipital crest, and with the toes blackish. Culmen, 3.70; tarsus, 3.75. *Hab.* Australia.

Garzetta candidissima.

THE SNOWY HERON.

Ardea nivea, JACQ. Beitr. 1784, 18, no. 13 (not of S. G. Gmel. 1770–1774). — LATH. Ind. Orn. II. 1790, 696 (part).

Little White Heron, LATH. Synop. III. 1785, 93.

Little Egret, LATH. Synop. III. 1785, 90 (part; includes also *G. nivea*).

Ardea candidissima, GMEL. S. N. I. ii. 1788, 633, no. 45. — WILS. Am. Orn. VII. 1813, 120, pl. 62, fig. 4. — NUTT. Man. II. 1834, 49. — AUD. Orn. Biog. III. 1835, 317; V. 1839, 606, pl. 242; Synop. 1839, 267; Birds Am. VI. 1843, 163, pl. 374. — COUES, Key, 1872, 267; Check List, 1873, 89, no. 453; Birds N. W. 1874, 521. — REICHENOW, J. f. O. 1877, 273.

Garzetta candidissima, BONAP. Consp. II. 1855, 119. — BAIRD, Birds N. Am. 1858, 665; Cat. N. Am. B. 1859, no. 485. — RIDGW. Nom. N. Am. B. 1881, no. 490. — COUES, Check List, 2d ed. 1882, no. 659.

Ardea oula, GMEL. S. N. I. ii. 1788, 633 (Chili).

Ardea thula, LATH. Ind. Orn. II. 1791, 688.

Ardea carolinensis, ORD. ed. Wils. VII. 1825, 125.

Ardea lactea, "CUV." Less. Traité, I. 1831, 575 (Cayenne).

HAB. The whole of temperate and tropical America, from the northern United States to Chili and Buenos Ayres; summer or autumnal visitant only at the northern and southern extremes of its range. West Indies.

SP. CHAR. Length, about 20.00–24.00; expanse of wings, about 36.00–40.00; wing, 8.20–10.50; tail, 3.00–4.80; culmen, 2.08–3.65; depth of bill, .40–.55; tarsus, 3.15–4.50; middle

[1] GARZETTA NIVEA, Gmel. The Little Egret of Europe.
Ardea garzetta, LINN. S. N. I. 1766, 237. — NAUM. Vög. Deutschl. IX. 1838, 101, pl. 223.
Egretta garzetta, MACGILL. Hist. Brit. B. IV. 1852, 471 (Little White Egret).
Ardea nivea, S. G. GMEL. Nov. Comm. Petrop. XV. 458, pl. 17.
Herodias nivea, BREHM, Vög. Deutschl. p. 587.
Herodias jubata, BREHM, Vög. Deutschl. p. 586.

[2] GARZETTA IMMACULATA, Gould. Australian Little Egret.
Herodias immaculata, GOULD, B. Australia, vol. VI. 1848, pl. 58.

toe, 2.20–3.20; bare portion of tibia, 1.70–2.75; weight, about 10-14 ounces. Color entirely pure white, at all ages and seasons. Bill black, the basal portion of the lower mandible (sometimes one-half) yellow, or light colored; lores, iris, and eyelids, yellow; tibiæ and tarsi black, the lower posterior portion of the latter, with the toes, yellow; claws blackish.

Nuptial plumes slender shafted and loose fibred, those of the back reaching to or slightly beyond the end of the tail, and, normally, recurved terminally; those of the occiput sometimes exceeding the bill in length; those of the jugulum slightly less developed. In the young these are all absent, except on the occiput, where they are but slightly developed; in the adults the occipital plumes appear to be permanent, the others assumed only during the breeding season.

In this extensively distributed species there is a wide range of variation in size, and, to a less extent, in proportions; specimens from the Pacific coast of California and Mexico averaging considerably larger than those from the eastern United States, while those from northeastern South America are still smaller than the latter. There is not a sufficient amount of material available to determine whether this variation is strictly geographical, or whether other differences constantly accompany these variations. It seems to be a general rule among the birds of this family to vary in the same way, however.

As a rule, specimens from Lower California average a little larger, and those from Demerara considerably smaller, than examples from other localities. Examples from Chili are intermediate in size between Demerara specimens and others from the eastern United States. In the full dress, the bill is deep black, with the extreme base and the lores yellow; the tarsus deep black, the toes yellowish (bright yellow or orange in life), in more or less marked contrast. Winter specimens, however, even if possessing the plumes, have more or less of the basal portion of the lower mandible yellow, but are not otherwise obviously different. Among individuals, even from the same locality, there is a great range of variation in size and proportions; there is also a considerable individual variation in the color of the feet, the yellow being as a rule confined to the toes, but sometimes occupying a greater or less extent of the lower part of the tarsus.

Between specimens of the same stage from the eastern United States, the West Indies, Lower California, Demerara, Chili, and Brazil, we can detect no differences other than those of an individual nature except the very slight geographical one of size, alluded to above.[1]

The Snowy Egret is one of the most abundant, as well as one of the most widely distributed, of its family. It is found on both the Pacific and the Atlantic coasts, wandering on both shores several hundred miles farther north than it is known to breed. On the Atlantic a few are supposed to be summer residents as far north as Long Island. From thence southward it is found along the entire Gulf coast, and the shores of both oceans, throughout a very large extent of South America,

[1] Since the above was written we have noticed very nearly the extremes of size in a series of these birds from Florida, collected at the same place and at the same time.

including the West India Islands, Mexico, and Central America. It is also found distributed through the interior as far north as Oregon and the Great Lakes. Mr. Salvin found it quite common on the Atlantic coast of Central America, and states that it also occasionally visited the Lake of Dueñas in the interior. When observed it was usually in companies. On the coast of Honduras he visited one of the breeding places of this species, but the nests were mostly deserted, as all the young birds of those still inhabited were able to run along the branches and make their escape. The nests were composed entirely of sticks, and placed near the end of a horizontal bough. He also found this species abundant on the Pacific coast of Guatemala. It occasionally visits Bermuda, both in the spring and in the fall. Léotaud speaks of it as a very common, and once a very abundant, bird in Trinidad, where it frequents the borders of the sea and the vicinity of streams and marshes affected by the influences of the tides. Its habits are said to be very similar to those of the larger *egretta*. Its numbers were rapidly diminishing, and it promised soon to become an extinct species in that island. It is given by Dr. Gundlach as an abundant species in Cuba, where it is resident, and breeds in large communities. In Jamaica, according to Gosse, it is not so common, and occurs chiefly as a visitant in midwinter. Mr. March mentions it as of frequent occurrence. Mr. C. W. Wyatt found it in Colombia, S. A., on the borders of Lake Paturia. Dr. Burmeister found it throughout the region of the La Plata even more numerous than the *Herodias egretta*, especially in the more westerly portions.

This species is found in the summer months as far to the northeast as Calais, Me., and a few straggle up the Bay of Fundy, even to the extreme eastern arm of that bay at Windsor, N. S. J. Matthew Jones states that it has been recently (1868) captured on the sea-coast of that province, near Halifax. A specimen was taken at Windsor, N. S., in the summer of 1872.

On Long Island, according to Giraud, it occurs during the summer months, but is not abundant. Yet it is by no means uncommon, and is well known to most of the gunners. It is said to frequent the salt marshes in small parties, and may be seen wading about over the mud-flats and sand-bars, or in the shallow water, in search of small crabs, lizards, and worms, which, with several species of aquatic plants, constitute its principal food. The Snowy Heron always feeds by day; and when wading about in search of its favorite food, or while making short excursions, it is rendered so conspicuous by the snowy whiteness of its plumage, that it seldom passes unobserved by the gunners. It visits Long Island late in the spring, and may be seen on the salt marshes until late in the autumn, though it usually migrates southwards in the last of September. It is not positively known to breed on any part of Long Island.

In August, 1863, Mr. Dresser saw large flocks of this Heron visiting the lagoons near Matamoras, in such large numbers that on one occasion he killed thirteen at one discharge. In the spring of 1864 he noticed several near San Antonio, and found a few breeding on Galveston Island in June, and received one from Fort Stockton.

Dr. Cooper speaks of it as common, at all seasons, along the southern coast of California. In summer it migrates to the summits of the Sierra Nevada, to Lake Tahoe, and probably throughout California and Oregon. He has always found it very shy, more so even than the larger white one. About the end of April it migrates to some extent from the southern parts of the State in large flocks, but he has met with it in July near San Pedro, when he supposed that it was nesting in the mountains, or some other retired places, in the vicinity.

About the middle of May, Wilson visited an extensive breeding place of this Heron among the red cedars of Summer's Beach, on the coast of Cape May. The place was sheltered from the Atlantic by a range of sand-hills, and on its land side was a fresh-water marsh. The cedars were not high, but were so closely crowded together as to render it difficult to penetrate through them. Some trees contained three, others four nests, built wholly of sticks. The eggs, usually three in number, measured $1\frac{3}{4}$ inches by $1\frac{1}{4}$. The birds rose, without clamor, in vast numbers, and alighted on the tops of the trees around. Wilson adds that this Heron was seen at all times during the summer among the salt marshes, searching for food, or passing in flocks from one part of the bay to the other. It often made excursions up the rivers and inlets, but returned regularly in the evening to the cedars to roost. He also found the same species early in June on the Mississippi as far up as Fort Adams, among the creeks and inundated woods.

According to Audubon, it is a resident throughout the year in Florida and in Louisiana. It is very sensitive to cold, and does not remain in severe weather near Charleston, nor return there in the spring before the 18th of March. It reaches New Jersey the first week in May. In its migrations it flies, both by night and by day, in loose flocks of from twenty to a hundred, sometimes in lines, but usually in a straggling manner. It is silent, and flies at a height rarely more than a hundred yards. Its flight seems undetermined, yet is well sustained. In the breeding season it has been observed to exhibit the most singular movements, now and then tumbling over and over, in the manner of the Tumbler Pigeon. It breeds in large communities, is very social, and does not disturb such birds as seek to breed in its neighborhood. Several nests are sometimes built in the same tree, and occasionally so low that a person can easily see into them. Where it has been disturbed it breeds in taller trees, but very rarely in high ones. The nest is usually over water. The structure is rather small, is built of dry sticks, and has a shallow cavity. The eggs are usually three, measure $1\frac{11}{16}$ inches in length, and $1\frac{1}{4}$ in breadth, and are broadly elliptical in form. Audubon states that while in the Carolinas, in the month of April, this bird resorts to the borders of the salt-water marshes, and feeds principally on shrimps. At the time the shrimps are ascending the Mississippi River this Heron is frequently seen standing on floating logs busily engaged in picking them up. At later periods it feeds on small fry, crabs, snails, aquatic insects, small lizards, and young frogs.

This Heron, more than any other kind, is what Mr. N. B. Moore designates as a *scraper*, or *raker*, because it uses its legs and claws to start from their hiding-places such animals as it wishes to seize for food — namely, crawfish, tadpoles, suckers, aquatic insects, etc. In this movement it far surpasses all other species, and manages its legs with greater adroitness and rapidity. On Feb. 18, 1873, he watched a flock of seventy making their meal, being himself concealed within a few steps. In the same pond were a number of the *egretta*, and a few of other kinds. Scarcely one of this species obtained any food without raking for it, numbers being thus engaged at the same time. The use of the foot was so rapid as to cause the whole body to quiver. The scrapers will thus work sometimes in water so deep as to reach their bellies, and at times in water only an inch or two deep. Each species has its own peculiar mode of managing its feet.

On April 27, 1867, Mr. Moore visited a heronry in Louisiana, where this species and the Little Blue Heron were breeding in close proximity. He climbed to a tree-top, where he could look down upon many nests. In seventy belonging to this species he found, in ten five eggs in each, in a large majority four eggs in each, while some had only one egg.

During the summer, in Louisiana, the young of this species resort to commons and dry pastures, to feed on insects of many kinds. Mr. Moore has seen a flock of a dozen hovering pretty close together above a shoal of minnows in the bay, settling down with their legs hanging and dangling near the water, and attempting to seize them by reaching down their bills. In the confusion of wings, legs, and necks so near together, it was impossible to tell whether they took any fish, but he presumes that they did. He has found their eggs from the 10th to the 25th of April, and a second brood on the 1st of June. Two eggs of this Heron, in my collection, taken by Dr. Bryant in Florida, have an oval shape, are equally rounded at either end, and are of a uniform light greenish-blue tint. There is just a shade more of green tinting the Prussian blue in this than in the other kinds of Heron. One egg measures 1.87 inches in length by 1.36 inches in breadth; the other is 1.80 inches long by 1.30 inches in breadth. The egg is more oblong than that of the *cærulea*, but is more rounded than that of the *ludoviciana*.

Genus **DICHROMANASSA**, Ridgway.

< "*Demiegretta*" (nec Blyth), Baird, B. N. Am. 1858, 660 (part).
= *Dichromanassa*, Ridgw. Bull. U. S. Geol. & Geog. Survey, Terr. IV. no. 1, Feb. 5, 1878, 246. Type, *Ardea rufa*, Bodd.
< *Erodius*, Reichenow, Jour. für Orn. 1877, 268 (includes *Hydranassa, Herodius, Leptherodius*, and *Garzetta*).

Gen. Chars. Medium sized Herons, of uniform white or plumbeous plumage, with (adult) or without (young) cinnamon-colored head and neck; the form slender, the toes very short, and the legs very long; the adults with the entire head and neck (except throat and foreneck) covered with long, narrowly lanceolate, compact-webbed feathers, which on the occiput form an ample crest, the feathers of which are very narrowly lanceolate and decurved.

Bill much longer than the middle toe (about two thirds the tarsus), the upper and lower outlines almost precisely similar in contour, being nearly parallel along the middle portion, where slightly approximated; the terminal portion of both culmen and gonys gently and about equally curved. Mental apex extending to a little more than one third the distance from the middle of the eye to the tip of the bill, or to about even with the anterior end of the nostril; malar apex about even with that of the frontal feathers. Toes very short, the middle one less than half the tarsus, the hallux less than half the middle toe; bare portion of tibia more than half as long as tarsus; scutellation of tarsus, etc., as in *Herodias, Garzetta*, and allied genera.

Plumes of the adult consisting of a more or less lengthened train of fastigiate, stiff-shafted feathers, with long, loose, and straight plumules, and extending beyond the tail; in addition to this train, the scapulars and the feathers of the whole head and neck, except the throat and foreneck, are long and narrow, distinctly lanceolate, and acuminate, with compact webs, and on the occiput are developed into an ample decurved crest.

Affinities. — This genus is perhaps most nearly allied to *Demiegretta*, Blyth,[1] with which it agrees quite closely in the form of the bill, and also, to a considerable extent, in coloration. *Demiegretta*, however, is at once distinguished by its extremely short tarsus (much shorter than the bill, instead of nearly a third longer!), which is altogether more abbreviated than in any American genus of this group, in proportion to the other dimensions. The plumes also are entirely different, there being none on the neck, with the exception of the jugulum, while those of the back are slenderly lanceolate, with compact webs, almost exactly as in *Florida cærulea*.

[1] Type, *Ardea jugularis*, Blyth, Notes on the Fauna of the Nicobar Islands, Journ. Asiatic Soc. Bengal, xv. 1846, 376, = *Herodias concolor*, Bonap. Consp. ii. 1855, 121, = *Ardea sacra*, Gmel. This Heron also is dichromatic, having a pure-white phase as in *Dichromanassa rufa*, the normal plumage being uniform dark plumbeous or slate.

The very great difference in form between *Demiegretta* and the present genus may be more clearly shown by the statement that while the bill and wing, as well as the general bulk, are nearly the same in the two, *Demiegretta* has the tarsus about 2.75 instead of 5.80 inches long, the middle toe 2.10 instead of 2.80, and the bare portion of the tibia 1.20 instead of 3.50! It will thus be seen

D. rufa.

that the proportions are entirely different in the two forms. The bill of *Demiegretta* is also very much more obtuse than that of *Dichromanassa.*

Demiegretta novæ-hollandiæ (Lath.) is of more slender build than the type-species, and is scarcely strictly congeneric; but it is otherwise similar, especially in the character of the plumage. The bill is more slender, approaching in form that of *Hydranassa,* but still different; the legs are also more elongated, but are decidedly less so than in the genus under consideration.

Dichromanassa rufa.

THE REDDISH EGRET; PEALE'S EGRET.

a. Colored phase.

L'Aigrette rousse, de la Louisiane, BUFF. Pl. Enl. 1777-1784, pl. 902 (adult).

Ardea rufa, BODD. Tabl. P. E. 1783, 54 (based on Pl. Enl. 902). — COUES, Key, 1872, 268; Check List, 1873, no. 455. — REICHENOW, J. f. O. 1877, 269.

Demiegretta rufa, BAIRD, Birds N. Am. 1858, 662; Cat. N. Am. B. 1859, no. 483.

Dichromanassa rufa, RIDGW. Bull. U. S. Geol. & Geog. Surv. Terr. IV. no. 1, 1878, 236 (in text). — COUES, Check List, 2d ed. 1882, no. 661.

Reddish Egret, LATH. Synop. III. 1785, 88 (quotes Pl. Enl. 902).

Ardea rufescens, GMEL. S. N. I. ii. 1788, 628, no. 33 (based on Pl. Enl. 902). — AUD. Orn. Biog. III. 1835, 411; V. 1839, 604, pl. 256; Birds Am. VI. 1843, 139, pl. 371 (adult; both phases).

Ardea cubensis, "GUNDL. MSS." LEMB. Aves de Cuba, 1850, 84, pl. 13, fig. 1 (young).

Ardea rufa, var. *Pealei,* REICHENOW, J. f. O. 1877, 270.

b. White phase.

Ardea Pealei, BONAP. Am. Lyc. N. Y. II. 1826, 154. — NUTT. Man. II. 1834, 49.

Demiegretta Pealei, BAIRD, B. N. Am. 1858, 661; Cat. N. Am. B. 1859, no. 182.

HAB. Warm-temperate and tropical North America, south to Guatemala; in the United States, apparently restricted to the Eastern Province, but in Mexico occurring on both coasts; north to Southern Illinois; Jamaica; Cuba.

SP. CHAR. Length, about 27.00–32.00; expanse, about 45.00–50.00; weight, about 1½ lbs. (AUDUBON). Wing, 11.90–13.60; tail, 4.10–5.00; culmen, 3.30–4.00; depth of bill, .55–.70; tarsus, 4.90–5.75; middle toe, 2.50–2.85; bare portion of tibia, 2.60–3.75. Colors uniform or unvaried.

Colored phase.

Adult: Plumage in general uniform plumbeous, darker on the back, a little lighter beneath; entire head and neck rich vinaceous-cinnamon, ending abruptly below; the penicillate tips of some of the longer feathers, particularly on the occiput, lighter; train similar to the back anteriorly, but passing into a more brownish tint towards the end, the tips sometimes whitish. Terminal half of the bill black; basal half, including the lores and eyelids, pale flesh-color; iris yellow or white; legs and feet ultramarine-blue, the scutellæ and claws black (AUDUBON).

Young: No train on the back, and no lanceolate feathers on head or neck, except sometimes (in older individuals) on the occiput or jugulum. Prevailing color dull bluish-ashy, tinged here and there with reddish-cinnamon, principally on the throat and jugulum.

A specimen from Mazatlan (No. 52,832, ♂ Nat. Mus.) is the most richly-colored one we have seen. In this the train and back have a very decided lilac-purple tinge, the former without any trace of the usual brownish cast, and the tips of the longer plumes scarcely whitish. The jugular, occipital, and medial plumes of the most delicate light pinkish-vinaceous, deeper and more purplish beneath the surface. No. 39,329 has the malar region on the right side mostly white; there are likewise a few white feathers over the lore on the left side, while the anterior part of the forehead is distinctly pearl bluish.

White phase.

Adult: Plumage entirely pure white, the plumes exactly as in the adult of the colored phase. Iris white; color of bill, lores, and eyelids in life also similar, but legs and feet "dark olive-green, the soles greenish-yellow" (AUDUBON).

Young: Entirely pure white, and destitute of the plumes and train of the adult.

The evidence proving the specific identity of *Ardea rufa*, BODD., and *A. Pealei*, BONAP., has been discussed in full by Dr. Brewer in the *American Sportsman* (West Meriden, Conn.) for Feb. 6, 1875, 294. This matter being far too complicated for discussion here, the reader is referred to Dr. Brewer's article, as above, or, as being perhaps more easy of access, a reprint of it by Mr. Ridgway, in his remarks upon the relation between *Ardea occidentalis*, AUD., and *A. Würdemanni*, BAIRD, in the Bulletin of the U. S. Geol. & Geog. Survey of the Territories (Department of the Interior, Washington, published Feb 5, 1878), Vol. IV., No. 1, pp. 229–232. For the benefit of those, however, who may not be able to consult either publication, we will state briefly that in

Florida, where *A. Pealei* and *A. rufa* breed abundantly, both forms have been found in the *same nest*, attended by parents either both reddish, both white, or one in each of these stages of plumage; other circumstances at the same time leading irresistibly to the conclusion that the two phases are

White phase, = *D. "Pealei."*

not only not specifically distinct, but that they have nothing to do with either sex, age, or season. The same condition of "dichromatism" exists also in several Old World species of this family, and probably also in the American *Ardea occidentalis*, AUD.

While accepting the identity of the two forms, *rufa* and *Pealei*, as one and the same specifically, notwithstanding the incongruities of their plumage, it will be convenient in giving its history as that of one species, at the same time to distinguish the white form as Peale's Egret, and the blue-and-russet one as the Reddish Egret, or *rufa*. Peale's Egret is an extremely southern bird to the United States, occurring only in Florida and on the Gulf coast to Mexico. It is found in several West India islands, on the Mexican coast, in Central America, and the northern parts of South America, in the last of which its distribution is not ascertained. It is common in Cuba, where it breeds abundantly, and from whence I have received its eggs from Dr. Gundlach. It is not given by either Gosse or March as a bird of Jamaica. Mr. Dresser mentions it, on the authority of Dr. Heermann, as not uncommon near San Antonio, Texas, and throughout the eastern part of that State during the summer months.

Mr. Salvin met with it on the Pacific coast of Guatemala, where it was very generally, though nowhere very commonly, met with among the mud-flats that surround the salt-pools in the neighborhood of Chiapam. Mr. G. C. Taylor mentions it as plentiful in all suitable localities in Honduras. In the Bay of Fonseca he noticed large trees overhanging the water, that seemed nearly covered with birds of this form. Audubon regarded it as the young of the Russet Egret, supposing that in its third summer the white bird would put on the plumage of that bird. The two forms are now regarded as distinctly permanent; and it is impossible to separate from Audubon's account of the *rufescens* that which may be peculiar to the white-plumaged bird. It is not probable that there exist any very material differences in the habits of the two forms. It is very evident from Audubon's account that they breed together in the same heronries, and that they permit no other kind to frequent the same settlement. This, however, is not always the case. The eggs of the white *Pealei* are much smaller than are those of the blue-and-russet form.

Mr. Audubon states that the young when just hatched are nearly naked, and are of a dark color, there being only a few scanty tufts of long, soft down. When the feathers begin to appear, they are white. The young are fed by regurgitation, grow fast, and soon become noisy. When about a month old they sit upright on their nest, and soon crawl out into the branches. Becoming sensible of danger, they hide among the foliage whenever a boat approaches, or seek the interior of the Keys, where it is very difficult to follow them. They do not fly until they are at least seven weeks old; and even then do not venture to leave the island on which they were reared. Mr. Audubon caught several young birds of this form and kept them alive. They fed freely, and became tolerably docile. They were supplied with pieces of green turtle, and some of them reached Charleston in good health. One was kept alive for nearly two years by Rev. Dr. Bachman. It was allowed to walk at large in the garden and poultry-yard, ate an enormous amount of fish and all kinds of garbage, contenting itself, when other food was scarce, with the entrails of fowls; and it even fed freely on moistened corn-meal or mush. It caught insects with great dexterity, was gentle and familiar, and a favorite in the kitchen, living to be twenty-two months old, and retaining its white plumage to the last. This was a male bird.

Two eggs of this Egret, collected in Cuba by Dr. Gundlach, are of a rounded oval shape, equal at either end, and in color are of a very pale wash of Prussian blue very slightly tinged with green. One measures 1.90 inches in length by 1.50 inches in breadth; the other 2.00 inches by 1.50.

The russet form, known as *rufa*, is also confined to the extreme southern border of the United States. It is abundant in Florida, occurs along the Gulf coast to Mexico, and is common in the southern part of Texas. It breeds in Cuba and in several others of the West Indian Islands. It has been met with on the Pacific coast of Guatemala, but has not, that I am aware, been traced farther north on the Pacific. Mr. Dresser states, on the authority of Dr. Heermann, that it occurs in the summer months near San Antonio, and also in the more eastern parts of Texas. Mr. March includes it in his list of the birds of Jamaica, where it is mentioned as rare. It is also included by Dr. Gundlach in his list of the birds of Cuba, and marked as having been found breeding there. Mr. Salvin found it in company with its kindred, the *D. Pealei*, on the mud-flats near Chiapam, on the Pacific coast of Guatemala. It was the more abundant of the two forms.

According to Audubon, this Egret is a constant resident on the Florida Keys, to which it is so partial at all seasons that it never leaves them. Some individuals were observed by him as far east as Cape Florida, and westward along the Gulf of Mexico. He never saw it in other than salt water, and was not aware that it ever feeds in fresh. It is more plump than most of the Herons, but possesses all the gracefulness of its tribe. In walking it lifts its feet high, and usually proceeds at a quiet pace. It alights with ease on trees, and can walk about on the larger branches. It is rarely seen to feed on the edges of the water, but resorts to the shallows of extensive mud or sand flats. There companies of twenty or thirty, or even more, may be seen wading up to the knee-joint in pursuit of prey, usually standing in silence, awaiting the approach of the object, and then striking at it. The prey is either swallowed immediately, or, if too large, taken to the shore and beaten, and then torn in pieces. It usually remains on the flats, thus feeding, until the advancing tide compels it to retire to the land. This account of its habits differs from the observations, referred to below, of Mr. Moore.

The flight of this species is said to be more elevated and regular than that of the smaller Herons. It is peculiarly graceful during the mating season, especially when one unmated male is pursuing another. It is said to pass through the air with great celerity, turning and cutting about in curious curves and zigzags, the pursuing bird frequently erecting its beautiful crest and uttering a cry at the moment it is about to give a thrust at the other. When travelling to and from their feeding-grounds, it propels itself with the usual regular flapping, and in the customary manner of flight of other Herons. On approaching a landing-place, it performs several circumvolutions, as if to satisfy itself that all is safe before alighting. It is much more shy and wary than the smaller Herons; and after the breeding season is over it is almost impossible to shoot one, except when it is taken by surprise, or when flying overhead among the mangroves.

Audubon regarded the two forms as identical, and mentions finding them in what he regarded their mature and their immature conditions, breeding together. At this time, in passing and repassing they are said to utter peculiar rough sounds which it is impossible to describe. He states that their nests are placed for the most part on the southwestern sides of the mangroves immediately bordering the Keys. They are rarely near together, and never on trees at a distance from the water. Some are placed on the tops of the mangroves, others only a foot or two above high-water mark. The nest is quite flat, is large for the bird, and formed of dry sticks interspersed with grass and leaves. The eggs are usually three in number, average an inch and three quarters in length, and one and three eighths in breadth, having an elliptical form, and are of a uniform pale sea-green color; they are excellent eating. Both birds incubate, as is the case with all Herons.

In its habits it seems to be as strictly marine as the Great White Heron. When wounded, it strikes with its bill, scratches with its claws, and, throwing itself on its back, emits its rough and harsh notes, keeping its crest erected and expanded, and its feathers swollen.

Mr. N. B. Moore, of Manatee, Florida, is of the opinion that Peale's Egret and the Reddish Egret are identical as species. He does not think, with Audubon, that the white form is the young bird and the reddish the adult, but that old and young may be white like the *Pealei*, blue and reddish like the *rufescens*, or may exist in a pied form. On the 13th of July he found a nest, where the parents were in the plumage of *rufescens*, one of the young pure white, the other a blue or gray bird. The nest was in a mangrove tree on a wet Key, and was the only Heron's nest there. Both parents were seen. The young were taken, and the attempt was made to keep them alive in order to watch their change of plumage; but it was not successful. Except in the color of the down, the young birds were alike in many respects — *e.g.* the bluish-ash color of the skin, the proportions and color of the eyes, etc.

Mr. Moore has twice met with specimens of pied, or white and blue varieties of this species, and feels quite positive that the white bird is an unchanging variety of the Reddish Egret, and that the pied varieties are equally permanent in their plumage. The young bird in the white plumage remains the same for at least twenty-two months, as is proved by the one kept by Dr. Bachman.

The fact that Dr. Gambel has seen the young of the *rufescens* in purple plumage, while it does controvert Audubon's views that the young are always white, by no means necessarily shows that none of the young are white, or that a large portion may not be so.

Mr. Moore refers to the peculiar petulance displayed by all Herons while feeding, and which is only manifested towards their own species. Several Herons, each of different species, will feed quietly near one another; but let another approach, and before it is within a hundred yards it will be at once pursued, and the attempt made to drive it away; and the pursuer and pursued will always be of the same species. But if the approaching bird is of a species different from any of those feeding, it may descend among them without being disturbed. In this petulance to one of its own species a Heron never makes any mistake. Even the small Blue Heron, whose young are for a year as white as the White Egret, never mistakes the latter for one of its own kind. It is this habit of attacking only birds of its own species that first led Mr. Moore to regard the *rufa* and the *Pealei* as identical; for the purple chase the white, and the white pursue the purple, but they never tease any other species.

These birds use their legs and toes to scrape the oozy bottom, or among the plants, in order to uncover their hidden prey. It is a mode peculiar to this species, and not to be mistaken for that of any other; but both of the two varieties perform this act in the same manner, and their unity of action in other respects is said to be very conspicuous. No other Heron is so awkward, impetuous, and clumsy a fisher. In clear water it gives chase to its prey with expanded wings, which are flirted up and down, or are held open, as it runs or hops, sometimes out of the water, sometimes turning entirely round. In all these wild and awkward movements the two forms exactly imitate each other. In size, too, they are exactly the same. As chasers the two forms are not only alike, but are superior to all others of the family. They pursue their prey — which is almost exclusively fishes — by hasty steps, hops, and doublings. Instead of being shy and suspicious, as Audubon states, they are, according to Mr. Moore, almost as unsuspicious as the Green Heron. This bird breeds in company both with its own and with other species, such as *egretta, candidissima, ludoviciana, virescens,* etc. If, when wounded, it falls into the water, it can swim readily. So far as Mr. Moore's experience goes, the proportion in numbers of the white to the blue is as one to eight.

Two eggs of this species, obtained by Mr. Audubon in 1832 on the Florida Keys, are of a rounded oval shape, are larger than the eggs of the *Pealei,* and the shell is thicker and rougher. They have the uniform greenish-blue shading common to the eggs of all our true Herons, — a washing of Prussian blue with a slight tinge of green. One (No. 98) measures 2.14 inches in length, by 1.65 inches in breadth. The other (784) measures 2.20 inches by 1.66.

Genus **HYDRANASSA**, Baird.

< "*Demiegretta*" (nec Blyth), Baird, B. N. Am. 1858, 660 (part).

= *Hydranassa*, Baird, B. N. Am. 1858, 660, in text. Type, *Ardea ludoviciana*, Wils.,=*A. tricolor*, Müller.

< *Erodius*, Reichenow, J. f. O. 1877, 268 (includes *Dichromanassa, Lepterodius, Herodius,* and *Garzetta*).

Gen. Char. Small Herons of variegated colors, white beneath, plumbeous above, the bill equal to or longer than the tarsus, and very slender. Bill long and slender, but little compressed; the upper and lower outlines appreciably concave about the middle, the gonys almost straight and but slightly ascending, the culmen gently convex towards the end. Mental apex reaching less than one third the distance from the middle of the eye to the point of the bill, but, at the same time, about as far forward as the anterior end of the nostril; malar apex reaching about as far forward as the frontal feathers. Tarsus long, about equal to the bill; middle toe about two thirds the length of the tarsus, the hallux about half as long as the latter; bare portion of the tibia decidedly shorter than the middle toe. *Adult*, with feathers of the neck, except throat, distinctly lanceolate, with compact webs; the occiput with a small pendant crest of several elongated, broadly lanceolate white feathers; feathers of the anterior portion of the back and scapulars also lanceolate; rump covered by a more or less elongated train of lengthened fastigiate feathers with loosened webs, the plumulæ slender, long, and soft.

Hydranassa tricolor ludoviciana.

THE LOUISIANA HERON.

Héron bleuâtre à ventre blanc, de Cayenne, BUFF. Pl. Enl. 1770–84, pl. 350 (adult).
Ardea tricolor, MÜLLER, S. N. Suppl. 1776, 111 (based on Pl. Enl. 350).
Hydranassa tricolor, COUES' Key, 2d ed. 1882, no. 660.
Ardea leucogaster, BODD. Tabl. P. E. 1784 (based on Pl. Enl. 350). — GMEL. S. N. I. ii. 1788, 628. — REICHENOW, J. f. O. 1877, 269.
Demi Egret, LATH. Synop. III. 1785, 88 (quotes Pl. Enl. 350, etc.).
Heron brun, de Cayenne, BUFF. Pl. Enl. 1770–84, pl. 858 (Young).
Brown Heron, LATH. Synop. Suppl. ii. 1801, 304, no. 17 (quotes Pl. Enl. 858).
Ardea fusca, LATH. Ind. Orn. II. 1790, 700, no. 83 (based on the preceding).
Ardea ludoviciana, WILS. Am. Orn. VIII. 1814, 13, pl. xvi. fig. 1 (nec Linn. 1766, = *Butorides virescens*). — NUTT. Man. II. 1834, 51. — AUD. Orn. Biog. III. 1835, 136; V. 1839, 605, pl. 217; Synop. 1839, 266; Birds Am. VI. 1843, 156, pl. 373 (adult).
Demiegretta ludoviciana, BAIRD, B. N. Am. 1858, 663; Cat. N. Am. B. 1859, no. 484.
Ardea leucogastra, Subspec. *ludoviciana*, REICHENOW, J. f. O. 1877, 269.
Hydranassa tricolor ludoviciana, RIDGW. Nom. N. Am. B. 1881, no. 492.
Egretta ruficollis, GOSSE, B. Jam. 1847, 338; Illustr. B. Jam. pl. 93 (Young).
Herodias leucophrymna, "LICHT." BONAP. Comp. II. Jan. 1855, 124.
Ardea leucogastra, var. *leucophrymna*, COUES, Key, 1872, 268; Check List, 1873, no. 454. — CORY, Birds Bahama Isl. 1880, 168.
Ardea cyanirostris, CORY, Birds Bahama Isl. 1880, 168, plate (Inagua, Bahamas; adult in breeding dress!).

HAB. Warm-temperate eastern North America, Middle America, and West Indies. North, casually, to Indiana, and New Jersey. In Mexico, found on both coasts. Cape St. Lucas.

SP. CHAR. Length, about 24.00–28.00; expanse, about 36.00; wing, 8.35–10.80; tail, 3.00–4.10; culmen, 3.30–4.15; depth of bill, .45–.55; tarsus, 3.20–4.15; middle toe, 2.20–2.70; bare portion of tibia, 1.90–2.70; weight, about 1 lb. (AUDUBON).

Adult: Prevailing color above, including the head and neck, plumbeous-blue, with a glaucous

cast to the lanceolate feathers, and darker on the head and upper part of the neck than on the wings. Lanceolate feathers of the occiput and upper part of the nape rich maroon-purplish, from which springs a crest of several feathers of similar form but much more elongated, and white in color; lanceolate feathers of the jugulum mixed maroon-purple and plumbeous-blue, the former prevailing laterally, the latter medially; chin and upper part of throat pure white; rest of the throat bright cinnamon-rufous (the feathers white beneath the surface), this gradually becoming narrower and finally broken up at about the middle of the foreneck, whence continued downward in a series of mixed touches of white, rufous, and plumbeous; rest of the lower parts, including the whole lining of the wing, and also the rump (the latter concealed by the train), pure white. Upper parts nearly uniform plumbeous-blue, except the train, which is light drab, paler towards the extremity of the feathers. *In the breeding season,* the terminal third, or more, of the bill black, "the rest sky-blue, shading into lilac at the base, the latter color extending to the eye; legs slate-color; iris red" (CORY). *At other seasons,* "bill brownish black on the greater part of the upper mandible, and on the sides of the lower mandible towards the point; the rest yellow, as is the bare space before and around the eye; iris bright red; feet light yellowish green, the anterior scutellæ dusky, as are the claws" (AUDUBON).

Young: Head and neck light cinnamon-rufous, the feathers plumbeous beneath the surface, the pileum overlaid with plumbeous, and nape tinged with the same; chin, throat, and malar region uniform white; foreneck white, with a median longitudinal series of cinnamon-colored streaks, these more broken posteriorly, where the white is much wider. Entire lower parts (including axillars and lining of the wing), with entire rump and upper tail-coverts, uniform white. Upper parts uniform bluish-plumbeous, the wing-coverts widely tipped with light cinnamon-rufous, and the back more or less tinged with the same. Occipital feathers slightly elongated, forming an inconspicuous pendant crest, the feathers similar in color to those of adjacent parts; no dorsal plumes. Bill mostly yellow, the culmen and terminal third of upper mandible blackish; "legs deep greenish olive" (AUDUBON).

Demerara specimens, representing the true *H. tricolor*, are very much smaller than more northern examples. They are also decidedly darker, the neck being in some specimens plumbeous-black, in others dark plumbeous, and the ferruginous of the throat very deep.

The Louisiana Heron is common on our southern Atlantic coast from the Chesapeake to the Florida Keys, and is found from thence to Central America in abundance. It is common on the Pacific coast of Guatemala, but has not been met with farther north than Mazatlan. It straggles along the Atlantic coast as far north at least as Long Island. Giraud includes it among his birds of Long Island, but states it to be only a very rare and accidental visitant. A single specimen, shot at Patchogue in the summer of 1836, was the only individual of this species known to have been procured in that vicinity. Mr. Lawrence includes it among his list of birds found near New York City. Mr. Turnbull states that it has been occasionally obtained on the coast of New Jersey. Wilson speaks of it as sometimes found on the swampy river shores of South Carolina, but more frequently along the borders of the Mississippi, particularly below New Orleans. Mr. Dresser speaks of it as common at Matamoras, and also near San Antonio. He also received it from Fort Stockton, taken there in the summer. At San Antonio he obtained one so late in the season as to render it not improbable that some remain through the winter. In June, 1864, he found a number breeding on Galveston Island. They build a heavy nest, either on the ground or in the low bushes. The number of the eggs was four. In Florida, Mr. Boardman found it breeding invariably upon low bushes, and always in company with the *candidissima.* Mr. Salvin states that he found this Heron common about the lagoons that line the whole Pacific coast of Guatemala, but he met with none in the interior. It is given by Dr. Gundlach as breeding in Cuba, and is described as a new species by Gosse, among the birds of Jamaica, under the name of *Egretta ruficollis;* but he only met with a few specimens, though he regarded it as undoubtedly a permanent resident in the island. Mr. March speaks of it as one of the most common birds of the island, where it is known as the Red-necked Gaulin.

Audubon characterizes it as among the most delicate in form, beautiful in plumage, and graceful in movements, of its family. Its measured step is so light that it leaves no impression on the sand. It feeds on insects, fish, snails, lizards, and the like, and nothing escapes its notice, its quick eye instantly detecting any object available for food, from a small fly on a blade of grass, to the minnow in the wave.

It is said to be a constant resident in the southern part of Florida, seldom rambling far from its haunts in the winter season, and at that period rarely seen beyond Savannah, to the east. To the west, it extends to the broad, sedgy flats that border the mouths of the Mississippi, along the whole Gulf of Mexico, and farther south. In the spring it is found abundantly in the Carolinas, and even as far east as Maryland, and up the Mississippi River as far as Natchez. It is never found inland farther than forty miles from the sea. It is eminently a social bird, and moves about in company with the White Egret or the Blue Heron. It frequently associates with the larger species, and breeds in the same places with the White Heron, the Night Heron, and the Yellow-crowned Heron. More frequently, however, it keeps by itself, assembling in immense numbers to breed, and resorting to particular spots for that purpose.

Mr. Audubon states that he found this species extremely abundant in January at St. Augustine; but after a hard frost of a few days all had disappeared, the other Herons remaining, apparently unaffected by the cold: it returned again, however, when the thermometer rose to 80°, and was in full spring plumage by the end of February. Though timid, it is much less shy than most of the other species, and is more easily procured; and on account of its apparent insensibility to danger is called, in Lower Louisiana, *Egrette folle.*

The flight of this Heron is described as light, rather irregular, swifter than that of any other species, and capable of being considerably protracted. It moves in long files, widely separated, in an undulating manner, and with constant flappings. When proceeding to or from their roosting-places, or when on their migrations, this species passes as high over the country as any of the other Herons. On being shot at, it seldom flies to a great distance; and its attachment to a particular place is such, that you are sure to find it there during its stay. If one of its number is wounded, it sympathizes with its companion, and keeps about in the manner of the Gulls and Terns, and a number may in this manner be obtained.

On the 29th of April, in visiting one of the Florida Keys, Mr. Audubon came upon one of the breeding-places of this Heron. The southern exposures of the island were overgrown with low trees and bushes, matted together with smilax and other vines, intermingled with which were several kinds of cactus. Among the branches were several hundred nests of this species, so low and so close that several would be within reach at once. The birds made loud and bitter complaints at being disturbed. The nests were formed of small dry sticks crossing each other in various ways. They were flat, had but little lining, and each nest contained three eggs; and this number Mr. Audubon thinks is never exceeded. He gives as the measurement, a length of one inch and six and a half twelfths, and a breadth of an inch and a quarter. The period of incubation is twenty-one days; and he expresses the opinion that but one brood is raised in a season. The notes of the young bird are extremely plaintive, and resemble the syllables *wiee-wiee-wiee.* When taken by the hand, the young bird defends itself to the utmost. Several were caught and kept in confinement on the vessel; they fed on any garbage thrown to them by the sailors. Mr. Audubon found this species breeding as far to the eastward as Charleston, S. C. During the summer and autumn, after the old birds have separated from their young, it is frequently seen among the rice-fields feeding along the ditches, and at this season is extremely unsuspicious and easily approached. It acquires its full plumage the second year, but continues to increase in size for several years. The flesh of the young bird is said to afford good eating. Its food consists of small fry, water insects, slugs, snails, leeches, and aquatic lizards.

According to Mr. Moore, it is a true *scraper* or *raker;* but, like the Reddish Egret, resorts to this practice much less frequently than the *candidissima.* It saunters about at times in the waters of the Bay, near the shores, on sandbars, and in the fresh ponds, in an awkward and heedless manner. There is less dash and impetuosity in its style of fishing, or seeking its prey, than in that of the Reddish Egret, although it runs through the clear water of the Bay, with its wings expanded, and sometimes flapping, suddenly wheeling, and halting to keep its eyes on the flying fish. At other times — imitating the little Green Heron — having noticed some object near the surface, a yard or more distant, it lowers its head, doubles up its neck, draws its head back to its shoulders, holds its bill in a line with its back, which is parallel to the surface of the water, and creeping along by very slow steps till within striking distance, thrusts its bill forward suddenly at the object. This is a very common practice, either in the Bay or in fresh ponds, and only this bird and the Green Heron adopt this catlike mode of creeping, crouching, and springing upon their prey.

Eggs of this species in my collection, obtained by Dr. Bryant in Florida, measure 1.80 inches in length by 1.32 in breadth. They are oval in shape, one end but just perceptibly more obtuse than the other. Their color is Prussian blue, with a slight shading of green, and of a deeper tint than most of the eggs of this family.

Mr. Moore thinks that this bird has at least two broods in a season, as he has found fresh eggs laid April 10, May 10, and June 1. On the 30th of March, 1874, he found a nest of this species containing six eggs, and on April 15 it had five young and one egg.

Genus **FLORIDA**, Baird.

Florida, Baird, B. N. Am. 1858, 671. Type, *Ardea cœrulea*, Linn.

F. cœrulea.

Gen. Char. Small Herons, dark plumbeous, with maroon-colored necks; pure white, with bluish tips to some of the primaries; or with the plumage variously intermediate between these extremes. Bill slender, acute, appreciably curved toward the tip, the culmen somewhat depressed just above the anterior end of the nostril; lower edge of the mandibular rami slightly concave, the gonys nearly straight, but ascending; anterior point of the malar feathers reaching just about as far forward as that of the frontal feathers, and very far posterior to the posterior end of the nostril; anterior point of chin feathers almost directly beneath the anterior end of the nostril, and a little over two thirds the distance from the middle of the eye to the point of the bill. Toes long, the middle one two thirds, or more, as long as the tarsus, the hallux a little less than half its length; bare portion of tibia considerably less than the middle toe. Tarsal scutellæ as in *Garzetta* and *Herodias*.

Nuptial plumes (occipital, jugular, and scapular) long, slenderly lanceolate, the webs rather compact, especially those of the dorsal region; those of the back reaching, when fully developed, far beyond the tail.

Florida cærulea.

THE LITTLE BLUE HERON.

Ardea cærulea, CATESBY, Carolina, I. 1731, pl. 76 (blue adult).
Héron bleuâtre de Cayenne, BUFF. Pl. Enl. 1770–84, pl. 349 (blue adult).
Ardea cærulea, LINN. S. N. ed. 10, 1758, 143, no. 13 (*ex* Brown, Jam. 478; Catesby, *l.c.*), I. 1766, 238, no. 17. — WILS. Am. Orn. VII. 1813, 117, pl. 62. — NUTT. Man. II. 1834, 58. — AUD. Orn. Biog. IV. 1838, 58, pl. 307; Synop. 1839, 266; B. Am. VI. 1843, 148, pl. 372. — COUES, Key, 1872, 268; Check List, 1873, no. 456.
Florida cærulea, BAIRD, Birds N. Am. 1858, 671; Cat. N. Am. B. 1859, no. 490. — RIDGW. Nom. N. Am. B. 1881, no. 493. — COUES, Check List, 2d ed. 1882, no. 662.
Blue Heron, var. A., LATH. Synop. III. 1785, 79 (blue adult. Quotes Pl. Enl. 349).
Ardea cærulescens, LATH. Ind. Orn. II. 1790, 690, no. 49 (based on the above).
Le Crabier bleu à cou brun, BUFF. Ois. VII. 399 (blue adult).
Blue Heron, LATH. Synop. III. 1785, 78 (quotes *Ardea cærulea*, LINN.).
? *Little White Heron*, var. B., LATH. Synop. III. 1785, 94 (Mexico. Probably young white bird).
Ardea ardesiacea, LESS. Traité, I. 1831, 575 (Cayenne. Individual in pied plumage).
Herodias Poucheti, BONAP. Consp. II. 1855, 123 (blue adult).
"*Egretta nivea*," GOSSE, Birds Jam. 1847, 334; Illustr. B. Jam. pl. 90 (young white bird).
Ardea cærulea, var. *alba*, REICHENOW, J. f. O. July, 1877, 264 (white phase).
Ardea cærulea, var. *cyanopus*, REICHENOW, l.c. (intermediate, or pied, phase. *Ex Ardea cyanopus*, GMEL. S. N. I. ii. 1788, 644).
Ardea mexicana cinerea, BRISS. Orn. V. 1760, 404 (intermediate phase).
Ardea americana cinerea, BRISS. t.c. 406.
Ardea cancrophagus brasiliensis, BRISS. t.c. 479.
Ardea chalybea, STEPHENS, Shaw's Gen. Zool. XI. ii. 1819, 582.

HAB. Warm-temperate eastern North America, the whole of the West Indies and Middle America, and northern South America; north to Massachusetts, Illinois, Kansas, etc.; south to New Granada and Guiana.

SP. CHAR. Length, about 20.00–25.00 inches; expanse, 40.00–42.00; wing, 9.00–10.60; tail, 3.60–4.70; culmen, 2.70–3.30; depth of bill, .45–.55; tarsus, 3.15–4.00; middle toe, 2.35–2.60; bare portion of tibia, 2.00–2.90. Weight, about 11–16 ounces.

White phase.

Adult: Prevailing color white, with the ends of several outer primaries plumbeous, the plumage tinged here and there (in quantity varying with the individual) with delicate pale bluish pearl-gray. Colors of the soft parts as in the blue adult. *Young:* Similar to the adult, but with the plumes absent or but slightly developed. Bill pale lilaceous, becoming gradually black on terminal third; legs and feet uniform pea-green, lighter and brighter than in the blue phase; iris Naples yellow.[1]

[1] Fresh colors of a specimen killed August 6, near Washington, D. C.

Blue phase.

Adult: Head and neck rich purplish-maroon, with a glaucous cast, the feathers more chestnut beneath the surface; rest of the plumage uniform dark bluish-plumbeous, the plumes with a glaucous cast, the maroon and plumbeous gradually blended. *In breeding season*, bill ultramarine-blue at the base, the end black; lores and eyelids ultramarine-blue; iris pale yellow; tibiæ, tarsi,

and toes black (AUDUBON). *In autumn*, bill light plumbeous on the basal half, the terminal half black; lores and eyelids very pale dull greenish; iris sulphur yellow; legs and feet uniform pea-green, darker at the joints.[1] *Young:* Similar in color to the adult, but with less developed plumes, or with none at all; the head and neck more plumbeous.

Pied, or intermediate, phase.

The plumage mixed white and plumbeous, in proportion varying with the individual, forming a series connecting unbrokenly the two extremes described above.

Many specimens show an irregular admixture of blue and white in the plumage; but seldom, so far as we have observed, is there any of the maroon color, seen on the head and neck in the perfect plumage; these parts being, in particolored birds, usually tinged with a pearly-gray or bluish. The comparative amount of the blue and white varies, of course, with the individual. A male from Florida (No. 84591), apparently adult, though not in full breeding plumage, appears at first sight to be entirely pure white, with the exception of the usual blue on the ends of the primaries. A close inspection, however, shows that the feathers of the pileum and nape, as well as those of the whole back and anterior lesser wing-coverts, are more or less strongly tinged, *mostly beneath the surface*, with pale pearl-blue or glaucous; this tinge, particularly on the dorsal region, partaking of the character of minute, more or less densely-sprinkled, dots.

No. 60319, from Porto Rico, an adult with perfectly developed plumes, is white, the pileum, nape, and back washed with pearl-blue, the long back-plumes deeper blue, with the terminal third or more white, finely and sparsely sprinkled with blue. Several of the slender occipital plumes are maroon-purple. One of the secondaries, on each side, has the outer web nearly uniform blue, and the inner web sprinkled with the same.

No. 39650, from the same locality, is pure white, with the long dorsal plumes and many of the feathers of the back uniform dark plumbeous-blue, the head and neck purplish-blue, the throat and foreneck white. There is scarcely a trace of blue on the ends of the primaries; but as these are much abraded terminally, it is probable that the spots of this color are worn off.

No. 72892, Jacksonville, Florida, has the plumage pied blue and white, in irregular blotches and patches, the two colors nearly equal in extent.

No. 70687 Demerara, is mostly blue, with the throat and foreneck medially, some of the jugular plumes, and a few of the wing coverts, white, the latter mostly finely sprinkled with bluish. In this specimen the white of the throat is almost as abruptly defined and conspicuous as in adult *Hydranassa tricolor*.

[1] From a fresh specimen, killed August 6, near Washington, D. C.

No. 3040, ♂ adult, Liberty Co., Georgia, has the normal blue plumage, except that three of the secondaries on each side, and several of the feathers of the base of the wing near its junction with the body (mostly concealed by the overhanging scapulars), are pure white. It is a noteworthy fact that in this specimen these white feathers are greatly abraded, while the rest of the plumage, including the immediately adjacent remiges, have the fresh texture of new feathers. It is also a circumstance of importance that on the two sides of this specimen, as well as of all other particolored examples which we have seen, the pattern is symmetrical; that is, the two colors correspond in their distribution and pattern on the two opposite sides, there not being that asymmetry of pattern almost always seen in albinescent birds.

Specimens from Demerara are rather smaller than others, but the difference is very slight (not nearly so great as in the case of *Hydranassa tricolor* and *Garzetta candidissima*), while, so far as we can see, there is no constant difference in coloration.

Nearly, if not quite, all specimens in the white plumage have a more or less perceptible tinge of pearl-blue on the pileum. Many adults have a well-defined plumbeous-blue stripe down the throat and foreneck.

That the young of this species is not always white, and the adult invariably plumbeous, as has generally been supposed, is conclusively proven by the series we have been enabled to examine; the true state of the case being that the white and blue plumages, usually supposed to represent respectively the young and adult stages, are in reality "dichromatic" phases. The case, although parallel in its nature to that of *Dichromanassa rufa*, differs, however, in the circumstance that the white phase is seldom perfectly developed, while intermediate specimens are very much more numerous.

Audubon thus describes the successive changes of plumage in this species, as understood by him:[1] —

"The young bird is at first almost destitute of feathers, but scantily covered with yellowish-white down. When fully fledged, its bill and legs are greenish-black, and its plumage pure white, or slightly tinged with cream color, the tips of the three outer primaries light grayish-blue. Of this color the bird remains until the breeding season, when, however, some individuals exhibit a few straggling pale-blue feathers. When they have entered on their second year, these young birds become spotted with deeper blue on some parts of the body, or on the head and neck, thus appearing singularly patched with that color and pure white; the former increasing with the age of the bird in so remarkable a manner, that you may see specimens with portions even of the pendant feathers of their head and shoulders so marked. And these are produced by full moultings; by which I mean the unexpected appearance, as it were, of feathers growing out of the skin of the bird colored entirely blue, as is the case in many of our land birds. In all these stages of plumage, and from the first spring after birth, the young birds breed with others, as is equally the case with *Ardea rufescens.* You may see a pure white individual paired with one of a full blue color, or with one patched with blue and white."

The Blue Egret is a Southern species, much more abundant in the Gulf States than farther north, yet breeding along the Atlantic States as far north as New Jersey, and straggling, in midsummer, even as far eastward as Massachusetts. It is found throughout Mexico, Central America, and in the more northern portions of South America, as far south as the Mercedes River and the Rio Negro. It is also found in nearly or quite all the West India Islands, and is a visitant of Bermuda both in the spring and in the fall.

This bird was found at Coban in Guatemala by Mr. Salvin, and is also spoken of as common near Omoa by Mr. Leyland. Mr. E. C. Taylor mentions it as abundant in Trinidad, especially near the mouth of the Caroni River. He afterward found it common at Porto Rico. Léotaud also speaks of it as common in Trinidad — in fact, the most common of the Egret Herons found there. It frequents the borders of the sea, and the banks of the rivers near their outlets. This species is said to seek its

[1] Birds of America, VI. p. 152.

food throughout the day, from morning until night, and this consists of fish, worms, crustacea, and the like. It is always to be seen in flocks of various ages and plumages, presenting a singular sight, some being entirely blue, others wholly white, and again others presenting a singular combination of both colors very irregularly distributed. Towards night the whole flock repairs to a tree, usually the same one, to pass the night. This bird can be accustomed to captivity, but only with difficulty. It is a resident species in Trinidad, and perhaps in all the West India Islands. It is abundant in Cuba, where it breeds. It is also resident and breeds in Jamaica; but, according to Gosse, is not very abundant on that island. Mr. C. W. Wyatt mentions finding it in Colombia, South America, near the Lake of Paturia, and Dr. Burmeister found it common on the shores of the Rio Negro and the Mercedes River.

This Heron has been found breeding in all favorable districts intermediate between Florida and New Jersey, on the coast, and a few wander into the interior. Mr. Brewster met with a single individual in Western Virginia. During the summer it wanders along the Atlantic coast. Well-attested instances are known in which several examples have been taken in Massachusetts; usually these occur in the fall. It is said to be rare on the shores of Long Island. It occurs along the Gulf coast from Florida to Mexico, and thence southward, probably to Brazil. Mr. Dresser found it very common near Matamoras during the summer. He did not find it frequenting the lagoons, but generally met with it on the Rio Grande, either close under the banks, or perched on some old log in the stream. He noticed a few near San Antonio, and also on the Brazos and Colorado rivers.

Gosse speaks of this species as less suspicious than most of its tribe, frequently allowing the beholder to stand and admire it without alarm. Its motions are deliberate and slow while watching for prey, yet in the act of seizing as sudden as the lightning flash. It feeds principally on small crabs, which are usually found much changed in the stomach by the process of digestion. In others he has found quantities of small eel-like fish and insects. An individual that fell wounded into deep water, although one foot was disabled, swam vigorously for several yards, keeping in an upright posture.

Wilson mentions finding this species breeding among the cedars near the sea-beach at Cape May, in company with the Snowy, the Night, and the Green Herons. He shot two specimens in May, and found their nests; these were composed of small sticks, were built in the tops of red cedars, and contained five eggs each. Although only found, in the Atlantic States, in the neighborhood of the sea, this bird seemed particularly fond of freshwater bogs or the edges of salt-marshes. These it often frequented, wading in search of tadpoles, lizards, mud-worms, and various insects. In pursuit of these, it moves actively, sometimes making a run at its prey. It is very silent, intent, and watchful. In the winter it is confined within narrow limits along our southern coast. In most parts of Florida it is a constant resident, some going northward in the summer to breed, others leaving in the winter for Texas and Mexico. About New Orleans the migrants appear, moving north, in March. They never leave the shores of rivers and estuaries. On the Mississippi few are found above Natchez. They return southward in September. In Florida, Mr. Audubon found this species associating with the *egretta* and the *ludoviciana*, roosting with them in the thick evergreen bushes which cover the central portions of the islands. It spends the day principally on the head-waters of the rivers and the freshwater lakes of the interior, preferring the soft mud-banks, where small crabs are abundant. In fishing, this bird, instead of patiently watching the approach of its prey, like the larger species, moves briskly through the water, striking here and there in rapid succession. When it has obtained enough, it retires to some quiet retreat, and there remains in repose until its hunger returns. In this state it is usually well on its guard against the approach of danger. Just before sunset it may always be seen again searching for food. When satisfied, it usually rises to the height of fifty or sixty yards in the air, and then flies in a straight line to its roosting-place. Very few were seen on the St. John in the winter, but on several occasions some were met with on small ponds in the pine-barrens, attracted there by the large number of frogs. Its flight is said to be very similar to that of the *ludoviciana*. When just about to alight, it descends with circular sailing, but otherwise flies, with constant flappings, in a direct line; during adverse winds it flies very low. Except when breeding, it is very shy and vigilant; but when engaged in incubation it appears to lay aside all its usual watchfulness.

Mr. Audubon regarded it as strictly diurnal in its habits. Mr. Moore is very positive that the statement made by Mr. Audubon in reference to the habits of this bird — namely, that where fish are plentiful on the shallows near the shore it will run briskly through the water, striking here and there, capturing several in succession — is very incorrect as applied to this bird, though true of the *ludoviciana*, the *candidissima*, and the *rufa*. It is not known even when very young, at an age when all birds are rather impetuous feeders, to run, or even walk briskly through the water; it never forgets to move slowly. Such acts of indiscretion and greediness have never been detected in the manners or motions of this Heron. Only when suddenly alarmed will it lay aside its calm and dignified demeanor, and then manifest the utmost confusion, awkwardness, and embarrassment.

This species is more disposed to fly about, with its neck stretched forward to its full length, using it as a front rudder to assist its legs — the true rudder — in guiding its course. This Heron is not a *scraper* or *raker;* and although it often feeds in close proximity to the *candidissima*, does not, so far as known, imitate its manner of procuring food.

In Florida it breeds as early as the first of March — a full month earlier than in Louisiana, and two months sooner than in New Jersey. In the Florida Keys it places its nest upon the tops of the tangled cactus; in Louisiana, on low bushes of the water-willow; and in its more northern abodes, on the tops of cedars. Wherever found, it is almost always sure to be in company with other species. The heronries in the southern portions of the country are often of astonishing size. The nest, in whatever situation it may be placed, is always formed of dry sticks intermixed with the leaves of various trees, grass, or moss. It is nearly flat, and without regular lining. In Florida, the number of eggs is three, rarely four, and never five, and their average size is said to be 1.75 inches in length by 1.25 in breadth. They are about the size of the eggs of the *candidissima*, and of the same color, but are more elongated.

Two eggs of this bird (No. 117), taken by Dr. Bachman from a nest near Charleston, S. C., measure, one 1.80 inches in length by 1.20 in breadth, the other 1.81 inches by 1.30. They are of an elongated oval shape, more so than those of any other Herons, and the greenish tinge of Prussian blue with which they are uniformly washed is also deeper than is usual in the egg of a Heron.

Mr. Moore states that at Sarasota Bay the eggs of this species are laid from April 10th to May 15th — not agreeing with Mr. Audubon in point of time.

GENUS **BUTORIDES**, BLYTH.

Butorides, "BLYTH, 1849," BONAP. Consp. II. 1855, 128 (type, *Ardea javanica*, HORSF.).
Oniscus, CABAN. J. f. O. IV. 1856, 343 (type, *Ardea virescens*, LINN.).

GEN. CHAR. Small Herons, of darkish, more or less variegated, colors, the pileum and occiput crested. Bill[1] rather stout, decidedly longer than the tarsus. Mental apex reaching to a little less than half way (in *B. brunnescens* exactly half way) from the middle of the eye to the point of the bill, and to decidedly beyond the anterior end of the nostril; malar apex about even with the frontal, and decidedly posterior to the hinder end of the nostril (in *B. brunnescens* this point falls considerably short of the frontal one). Middle toe very nearly or quite equal to the tarsus (equal to it in *B. javanicus*, a little shorter in the American forms, the difference being most marked in *B. virescens*); outer toe scarcely or not at all longer than the inner (except in *B. brunnescens*);

B. virescens.

hallux about half the length of the middle toe; bare portion of tibia equal to or shorter than the hallux.

Pileum with a full crest of broadly lanceolate, compact-webbed feathers, these longer and more narrowly lanceolate on the occiput. Scapulars and interscapulars elongated and lanceolate in the adult, but not reaching the end of the tail (very much as in *Ardea*).

It will be observed, from the terms of the above diagnosis, that the species of this genus vary somewhat in the minor details of external form; the differences are so slight, however, that they are evidently of not more than specific importance. As stated above, *B. javanica* differs from the American species in the contour of the bill, the culmen being slightly depressed about the middle portion, as in *Dichromanassa rufa*. It should also be noted, however, that the several American

[1] There is a decided difference in the form of the bill between the type of this genus, *Ardea javanica*, HORSFIELD, and the four American species, it being in the former almost exactly as in *Dichromanassa rufa*, in all its outlines and proportions, although it is, of course, very much smaller. All the other characters, however, even the system of coloration, correspond so entirely with those of the American forms that the latter may be all considered typical. The generic characters are therefore modified, as to the bill, so as to include all. *B. patruelis*, PEALE, from Tahiti, is quite similar in form to *B. javanica*.

species differ quite as much among themselves in certain respects. Upon the whole, this genus may be considered one of the most strongly marked in the entire group.

Leaving out *B. plumbea*,[1] of the Galapagos, of which we have seen only an immature example, the three remaining American species of this genus may be distinguished as follows : —

COM. CHAR. Neck uniform chestnut or ash-gray, with an anterior longitudinal series of white and rufous stripes. Lanceolate feathers of the pileum glossy greenish black ; wing-coverts conspicuously bordered with rusty or whitish. *Young* with the colors duller, and the pattern indistinct.

A. Neck chestnut or rufous.

1. **B. brunnescens.**[2] Head and neck, except pileum, uniform chestnut-rufous ; wing-coverts very narrowly edged with rufous. *Young:* nearly uniform rusty brownish. Wing, 6.40–

[1] BUTORIDES PLUMBEA (Sundevall).

Ardea plumbea, SUNDEV. P. Z. S. Feb. 7, 1871, 125, 127 (James I., Galapagos).

Butorides plumbeus, SCL. & SALV. Nom. Neotr. 1873, 125. — SALVIN, Trans. Zool. Soc. IX. ix. 1875, 497.

Ardea Sundevalli, REICHENOW, J. f. O. July, 1877, 253 (s. g. *Butorides*).

Young ♀, transition pl. (nearly adult): Whole pileum uniform greenish black, slightly glossy. Upper parts in general dark brownish slate, the scapular plumes in certain lights appearing glaucous with white shafts, in other lights slightly metallic bottle-greenish. Remiges bluish plumbeous, decidedly glaucous. Wing-coverts (new feathers, adult plumage), dark slaty, with bottle-green gloss, narrowly edged with light rusty. Chin and throat white, sparsely marked with dusky. Sides and fore part of the neck dusky, like the nape, but tinged with purplish brown, the foreneck marked with longitudinal streaks of white and light rusty. Remaining lower parts uniform dark brownish slate. Lining of the wings dusky, narrowly streaked with fulvous white.

Wing, 6.90 ; tail, 2.70 ; culmen, 2.50 ; depth of bill, through nostril, .50 ; tarsus, 1.95 ; middle toe, 1.75 ; bare part of tibia, .45.

[Described from a specimen in Mus. SALVIN & GODMAN ; Indefatigable I., Galapagos, Aug. 25, 1868. Length, 18.00 ; extent, 26.00. Iris orange yellow.]

[2] BUTORIDES BRUNNESCENS. The Brown Heron.

Ardea brunnescens, "GUNDL. MSS." LEMB. Aves de Cuba, 1850, 84, pl. 12. — REICHENOW, J. f. O. 1877, 255 (s. g. *Butorides*).

Butorides brunnescens, BAIRD, Birds N. Am. 1858, 677 (in text); Cat. N. Am. B. 1859, no. 494.

SP. CHAR. Length, about 19.00–20.000 ; extent, 27.0 ; wing, 6.40–7. 00; tail, 2.50–3.00 ; culmen, 2.20–2.75 ; depth of bill, .45 ; tarsus, 1.85–2.30 ; middle toe, 1.70 ; bare portion of tibia, .50. *Adult:* "The top of the head and long glossy occipital feathers are dark glossy green ; the scapulars and inter-

B. brunnescens, juv.

scapulars pale green, washed with bluish gray, having light gray shafts ; the wing-coverts very narrowly edged with rufous ; the entire neck and long feathers extending over the breast bright brownish chestnut, paler on the chin ; abdomen dark plumbeous ash, tinged with rufous on the sides. The wing measures

7.00; culmen, 2.20–2.75; depth at base, .45 (in young); tarsus, 1.85–2.35; middle toe, 1.70 (in young). *Hab.* Cuba.

2. **B. virescens.** Foreneck striped with whitish, and side of head with a narrow rictal stripe of the same. *Young:* Striped beneath, with rusty whitish and dusky. Wing, 6.30–8.00; culmen, 2.00–2.55; depth of bill through base, .40-.60; tarsus, 1.75–2.15; middle toe, 1.65–1.95. *Hab.* Temperate North America, West Indies, Middle America, and northern South America.

B. Neck ash-gray.

3. **B. striata.**[1] Similar to *B. virescens*, but neck fine ash-gray in adult, dull grayish in the young, instead of chestnut or rufous. Wing, 6.55–7.10; tail, 2.50–3.10; culmen, 2.20–2.55; depth of bill, .42–.45; tarsus, 1.90–2.10; middle toe, 1.70–1.85. *Hab.* South America in general.

Butorides virescens.

THE GREEN HERON.

Ardea stellaris minima, CATESBY, Carolina, I. 1754, pl. 80 (adult).

Ardea virescens, LINN. S. N. ed. 10, 1758, 144, no. 15 (based, in part, on the above); ed. 12, 1766, I. 238, no. 20. — WILS. Am. Orn. VII. 1813, 97, pl. 61. — NUTT. Man. II. 1834, 63. — AUD. Orn. Biog. IV. 1838, 247, pl. 333; Synop. 1839, 264; Birds Am. VI. 1843, 105, pl. 367. — COUES,

about 7 inches; tail, 3; tarsus, 2⅓; bill, 2¾. [G. N. Lawrence, in Am. Lyc. N. Y. VII. 1860, p. 271. Mr. Lawrence adds: "It scarcely differs from *B. virescens*, of which it is a remarkable representative, but unmistakably distinct. The plumage generally is darker than in *virescens*. In the appearance of their upper parts the two species closely resemble each other, but *virescens* has the chin and a central line down the throat and neck, also a stripe on the side of the head, white; these parts in *brunnescens* are uniform in color, with no trace of white. This species is also without the light edgings to the wing-coverts and smaller quills so conspicuous in *virescens*."]

Young (No. 33081, Cuba; Dr. Gundlach.): Pileum and occipital crest dull black, with a slight bottle-green gloss; rest of head and neck dull ferruginous, the malar and post-ocular regions streaked with black, the central line of the throat and foreneck with indistinct dusky streaks and narrower ones of light buff. Lower parts dull brown, tinged with light rusty; under-surface of wings uniform dull slate. Upper parts dull greenish brown, the back and scapulars uniform, the wings and tail glossed with bottle-green, all the coverts bordered with ferruginous; primary-coverts and primaries uniform slate without trace of whitish tips; secondaries and tail uniform dark metallic bottle-green. Wing, 6.40; tail, 2.50; culmen, 2.20; depth of bill, .45; tarsus, 1.85; middle toe, 1.70; bare part of tibia, .50.

This is apparently a very distinct species, differing from its allies, not only in colors, but in strongly-marked peculiarities of form. We have never seen the adult, the only specimen in the National Museum being an excellently mounted full-grown young bird of the year, presented by Dr. Gundlach.

[1] BUTORIDES STRIATA (Linn.).

Crabier, de Cayenne, BUFF. Pl. Enl. 908 (adult).

Ardea striata, LINN. S. N. I. 1758, 144; ed. 12, I. 1766, 238. — REICHENOW, J. f. O. 1877, 253 (s. g. *Butorides*).

Cancroma grisea, BODD. Tabl. P. E. 1783, no. 908.

Ardea grisea, LÉOT. Ois. Trinidad, p. 421.

Butorides grisea, CASS. Proc. Philad. Acad. 1860, 196 (Cartagena, Colombia). — BOUC. Cat. Av. 1876, 51, no. 1428.

Ardea fuscicollis, VIEILL. Nouv. Dict. XIV. 1817, 410.

Ardea cyanura, VIEILL. t. c. 421; Enc. Méth. 1120.

Butorides cyanurus, BONAP. Consp. II. 1855, 128. — SCL. & SALV. P. Z. S. 1868, 145 (Conchitas, Buenos Ayres); Nom. Neotr. 1873, 125.

Ardea scapularis, "ILLIG." LICHT. Verz. Doubl. 1823, 77. — BURM. Th. Bras. iii. 1856, 411. — FINSCH. P. Z. S. 1870, 589 (Trinidad).

Egretta scapularis, SW. Anim. Menag. 1838, 333 (Brazil).

Butorides scapularis, BP. Consp. ii. 1855, 128. — SCL. & SALV. P. Z. S. 1866, 199 (Ucayali, E. Peru).

Butorides scapulatus, SCL. & SALV. P. Z. S. 1873, 305 (E. Peru).

Key, 1872, 268; Check List, 1873, no. 457; Birds N. W. 1874, 522. — REICHENOW, J. f. O. 1877, 255.

Butorides virescens, BONAP. Consp. II. 1855, 128. — BAIRD, Birds N. Am. 1858, 676; Cat. N. Am. B. 1859, no. 493. — RIDGW. Nom. N. Am. B. 1881, no. 494. — COUES, Check List, 2d ed. 1882, no. 663.

Crabier de la Louisiane, BUFF. Pl. Enl. 1770–84, pl. 909 (adult).

Crabier tacheté, de la Martinique, BUFF. Pl. Enl. 912 (young).

Green Heron, LATH. Synop. III. 1785, 68.

Louisiana Heron, LATH. t.c. 81.

Ardea ludoviciana, GMEL. S. N. I. ii. 1788, 630, no. 39 (based on Pl. Enl. 909).

? *Blue Heron*, var. *B.*, LATH. Synop. III. 1785, 75 (Queen Charlotte's Sound).

Ardea chloroptera, BODD. Tabl. P. E. 1783, pl. 909.

Cancroma maculata, BODD. t.c. pl. 912.

? *Ardea virgata*, GMEL. S. N. I. ii. 1788, 643.

HAB. The whole of temperate North America, West Indies, Middle America, and northern South America, to Venezuela; north to Canada West and Oregon; abundant both in the Pacific States and Eastern Province, but apparently wanting in the Middle Province; Bermudas.

SP. CHAR. *Adult:* Entire pileum, including occipital crest, glossy dark metallic bottle-green; rest of the head and neck, except throat and foreneck, rich chestnut, varying from a cinnamon shade to a fine purplish maroon; bare orbital space bordered posteriorly with greenish black, from

the lower part of which projects backward, from the rictus, a short stripe of the same; below this, along the upper edge of the malar region, a narrow stripe of white, the lower malar feathers being mixed black and rufous, forming another stripe; throat and foreneck, from chin to jugulum, white, marked with broad longitudinal dashes of dusky. Lower parts ash-gray, the lining of the wing somewhat spotted, and distinctly bordered, outwardly, with creamy white. Scapular plumes glaucous-plumbeous, with a green reflection in certain lights, the shafts white. Wing-coverts and rectrices brilliant metallic bottle-green, the former distinctly bordered, narrowly, with fulvous-white; these borders on the lesser-coverts, more rusty or fulvous; rectrices immaculate bottle-green; remiges and primary-coverts plumbeous, with a green reflection, the inner primaries and adjoining secondaries with narrow crescentic tips of white, the coverts with terminal deltoid spots of the same. Bill deep black, the lower mandible sometimes partly yellowish or greenish; lores and orbits varying from olive-green to bright yellow; iris gamboge-yellow; legs and feet olive-green or olive-yellow, the scutellæ more greenish; claws horn-color. *Young:* Pileum, including crest, as in the adult, but usually streaked with dark rusty anteriorly; sides of the head and neck dull dark rusty, indistinctly streaked with light ochraceous, or buff; lower parts white, tinged with buff, and striped with dusky. Back, scapulars, and rump uniform dull dusky-green, some of the feathers indistinctly bordered with rusty; wings and tail as in the adult, but light borders to larger wing-coverts more ochraceous, and the two or three middle rows marked with medial wedge-shaped dashes of the same. Bill lighter-colored than in the adult, dull greenish prevailing, only the culmen dusky, the lower mandible mostly pale yellowish; legs and feet dull greenish yellow or olivaceous.

Length, about 15.00–19.00; expanse, 25.00–27.00. Weight, 6½ ounces (AUDUBON). Wing, 6.30–8.00; tail, 2.40–3.40; culmen, 2.00–2.55; depth of bill, .40–.60; tarsus, 1.75–2.15; middle toe, 1.65–1.95; bare portion of tibia, .70–.90.

The range of individual variation in this species is very considerable, so far as dimensions are concerned; but the careful measurement of a large series of specimens tends to prove that the variation in this respect is a purely individual one. The largest specimen in a series of about forty is one from the Isthmus of Tehuantepec, Mexico, and the smallest is from Porto Rico.[1] As to colors, the darkest and richest-plumaged example in the whole series is No. 25979, Rockford, Illinois, in which the abdomen is so strongly washed with dark rusty as not to offer any marked contrast to the maroon of the jugulum; the colors elsewhere are quite normal, though a little darker and richer than usual. In specimens which have the feathers more advanced in age, the lanceolate plumes of the back lose the chalky or glaucous cast which distinguishes these feathers when the plumage is more recently acquired, and assume a more or less uniform bronzy hue. The palest-colored adult specimen is No. 49534, Sacramento, California (June 10), which has the neck light cinnamon-rufous, instead of rich purplish chestnut or maroon, the lower parts very pale ash-gray, the remiges and primary-coverts very conspicuously tipped with crescentic marks of pure white, and the plumage generally pale and dull. Another specimen killed at the same locality was similar. The peculiarities presented by these birds, however, appear to be the result of a simple bleaching, caused by the excessively dry and hot climate which prevails continuously in that locality for one half the year; while the white tips to the remiges and primary-coverts are no doubt remnants of the immature plumage, since they may be seen, though generally they are smaller, in specimens which otherwise have assumed the adult livery. Excepting the examples above noted, no variations worthy of the least mention can be detected in the series before us.

The Green Heron is a common and abundant species throughout the United States, from Maine to Oregon, and in the interior extends its migrations into Canada, being found, according to Mr. McIlwraith, near Hamilton, where, however, it is quite rare. It occurs near Niagara Falls, as I have its eggs from Drummondville, Ontario. Mr. Boardman informs us that it is common along the more western portion of the coast of Maine. It is found at Calais, although not common there. It is quite rare in New Brunswick, but abundant throughout the United States, in favorable localities, both on the Atlantic and the Pacific coasts. It is resident in all the West India Islands and in Central America, and is a frequent visitant of the Bermudas. It is also found in the northern regions of South America. Mr. J. A. Allen met with it in Western Kansas, near Fort Hays. Mr. Ridgway observed it in the vicinity of Sacramento City, where it was quite common among the willows bordering the sloughs, and around the stagnant ponds; he did not notice it in the interior. Mr. Dresser found it quite common, breeding on all the large rivers in the southwestern portion of Texas. Dr. Cooper mentions it as common in California throughout the summer, and probably in Oregon also. A few winter in the southern portion of the former State, but most of them migrate farther south, returning northward about the middle of April. This bird chiefly frequents the banks of such running streams as are wooded, and the borders of ponds, and when startled, it usually flies along the stream

[1] The extreme measurements are as follows: —

	Largest.	Smallest.
Wing:	57877, from Tehuantepec, 8.00;	60329, from Porto Rico, 6.30.
Tail:	" " " 3.30;	73069, " " " 2.40.
Culmen:	55570, Ft. Macon, N. C., 2.55;	73069 & 60329, " " 2.08.
Tarsus:	7068, Salt Creek, Kansas, 2.15, and 31887, Manzanillo Bay, W. Mex., 2.15	60329, " " 1.75.
Middle toe:	71221, City of Mexico, 1.95;	60329, 1.55.

silently and slowly, at times uttering a guttural croaking scream, generally alighting again at a short distance. If it hides in a tree, it sits so quietly that it can only with difficulty be distinguished from the foliage. It is generally unsuspicious, and easily shot. It usually feeds in the twilight, is sluggish, and rests in the day. Its food consists of insects, aquatic larvæ, crustacea, and small fishes; although sometimes catching larger ones, which it then breaks in pieces.

Mr. Salvin found it quite common in Guatemala, both on all the rivers along the coast, among the mangrove swamps, and in the interior. About the Lake of Dueñas it was the most common species of Heron. It is mentioned by the Newtons as very common in St. Croix, where it is especially tyrannized over by the *Tyrannus dominicensis.* Being of a mild and inoffensive disposition, it only protests against these attacks by a few loud and hoarse croaks, and then drops into the nearest covert for shelter. The common Humming-bird of the island, *Eulampis chlorolæmus*, also gives chase to it, and compels it to change the direction of its flight. This bird breeds in St. Croix from March to July, and has two broods in the year. The nest is generally placed in a tall tree, near dwelling-houses; for this bird seems to seek the society and protection of man. The stomach of one that had been shot was found to contain five lizards, one of them of good size, one large cricket, with the remains of beetles. The young in the down were black. Mr. E. C. Taylor found that this species was common in Trinidad, and also in all the other West India Islands he visited. Léotaud states that it is frequently met with in Trinidad, where it keeps itself among the reeds that cover the overflowed places, and, at other times, among the mangrove trees. Its food, for which it searches in the night, is generally the same as that of the larger Herons. Whenever observed in the daytime, it seemed to be plunged into a profound sleep. It is a resident of Trinidad, and breeds there.

In Jamaica this bird is known as the Crab-catcher. According to Gosse, it is found on that island wherever there is running water, and most abundantly where the streams expand into broad reedy pools. It is described as perfectly solitary in its habits, and usually too wary to allow a near approach. When wounded so as to be unable to fly, it seeks to escape by running, which it does very swiftly, its neck at the time projecting horizontally, and at intervals it utters a low cluck. Its ordinary call is a loud scream, harsh and guttural.

According to Giraud, this Heron is not so abundant on Long Island as it is in many places in the interior. It arrives about the middle of April, and frequents low and marshy situations. It hunts by day as well as by night, and shows a great deal of address in taking its prey, feeding on frogs, lizards, and various small reptiles such as are found in low boggy grounds. It visits the neighboring mill-ponds and creeks, is a dexterous fisher, and at times darts down after small eels, with which it mounts in the air. Occasionally, as if for amusement, this Heron drops its prey — catching it again, however, before it reaches the ground.

Wilson states that this Heron builds its nest as early as the 20th of April, usually in single pairs, but sometimes in companies. This we have never known it to do. It is frequently seen in company with the Night Heron, and, at the South, with other species; but it must be very unusual for two pairs of this bird to be found nesting in company. The nest is fixed among the branches of trees, is constructed of small sticks lined with finer twigs, and is of considerable size, and very loosely put together. The young do not leave the nest until they are able to fly, and, until late in the autumn, are to be seen in the meadows and marshes.

A few of this species winter in Florida and Lower Louisiana, where some also reside all the year; but the majority retire southwards, beyond our limits. These return in the early spring, in flocks of from twenty to fifty. Their migrations are made at night; in the fall, however, they fly singly, or in small flocks. In the suburbs of Charleston, and in the neighborhood of other Southern cities, this Heron is known to build its nest close to houses, and even to raise its brood on the trees of a garden.

Mr. Moore confirms the statement of Mr. Audubon, that a few of this species remain in Florida during the winter. On the Sarasota some were seen throughout most of the winter; and as this species always frequents close and tangled woods, if the spot is supplied with water and affords abundant food, it may exist in considerable numbers, and yet escape notice.

This Heron has its own peculiar manner of searching for its food, which in some respects differs from that of all the other kinds. It fishes from the shore or from a log, root, snag, or shelving rock, preferring not to wade into the water or to stand in it; still, on seeing a tempting morsel, it will quit its point of observation and walk into the water towards it. Its approach at such times is peculiar; though the Louisiana Heron seems occasionally to copy its style, except that the latter is constantly in the water at the time of fishing. The Green Heron, however, on seeing a fish, crouches low on its legs, draws back its head, crooks its neck, creeps slyly along, laying its tarsi almost down on the rock or the ground, carries the bill level with the top of the back, and when near enough darts the bill forward towards it, sometimes with such force as to topple forward a step or two. It seldom immerses its head in fishing, is always disposed to steal upon its prey in a sly, cat-like, crouching manner, remaining quite motionless for a long time, and often advancing so slowly and stealthily that even a keen-eyed observer would hardly perceive the motion. Its antipathy to and jealousy of its own species at the feeding-grounds is decided. Its eggs are found from the 18th of April to the 1st of June; there are rarely more than four in a nest.

Two eggs of this species, from Lake Koskonong, Wisconsin, in my collection (No. 1965) measure, one, 1.45 by 1.20 inches; the other, 1.40 by 1.12 inches. They are of oval form, slightly rounded, and equal at either end. Their color is like that of the Heron family — a light wash of Prussian blue strongly tinged with green, rather brighter than in other kinds, and of a lighter shade.

Genus **NYCTICORAX**, Stephens.

Nycticorax, Stephens, Shaw's Gen. Zool. XI. xi. 1819, 608 (type, *Ardea nycticorax*, Linn.).
Nyctiardea, Swains. Classif. B. ii. 1837, 354 (same type).

Gen. Char. Medium-sized herons of very short thick build, large, thick heads, and short tarsi. The plumage exceedingly different in the adult and young, but the sexes similar. Adults with two or three exceedingly long thread-like, white occipital plumes.

Bill very stout, the depth through the base being more than one fourth the culmen; the latter nearly straight for the basal two thirds, then gently curved to the tip; lower edge of the mandibular rami nearly straight; gonys nearly straight, very slightly ascending; maxillary tomium decidedly concave, with a very convex outline just forward of the rictus. Mental apex reaching more than half way from the centre of the eye to the point of the bill, and to beyond the anterior end of the nostril; malar apex falling a little short of the frontal apex. Tarsi a little longer than the middle toe, its *scutellæ hexagonal in front;* lateral toes nearly equal, but the outer the longer; hallux less than half the middle toe; bare portion of tibia shorter than the hallux. Inner webs of two outer primaries distinctly emarginated near the end. Tail of twelve broad, moderately hard feathers, as in the typical Herons.

In "Hand-list of Birds," Vol. III. p. 33, Dr. G. R. Gray enumerates three Old World species besides *N.* "*nycticorax*" (*griseus*). These are, "*caledonica*, GM.," New Caledonia; "*? manillensis*, VIG.," Philippines and Solomon Islands, and "*crassirostris*, VIG.," Island of Bonin. These perhaps represent races of one species, although we have seen only the first named. *N. caledonicus*

N. griseus nœvius.

is strictly congeneric with *N. griseus*, with which it agrees very closely in the details of form, in size, in general system of coloration, and in the character of the occipital plumes. As to coloration, the pattern is the same, except that the greenish black of the back and scapulars is wanting, while that of the pileum extends quite to the bill, there being, therefore, no white frontlet. The cinereous of *N. griseus*, however, is entirely replaced by a fine cinnamon-rufous, which gives the two birds quite a different aspect. In the young plumage they are more similar, though still readily distinguishable.

Nycticorax griseus nævius.

THE AMERICAN BLACK-CROWNED NIGHT HERON.

Botaurus nævius, BRISS. Orn. V. 1760, 462.
Ardea nævia, BODD. Tabl. P. E. 1783, 51 bis (ex Pl. Enl. 939.)
Nyctiardea grisea, var. *nævia*, ALLEN, Bull. Mus. Comp. Zool. III. 1872, 182. — COUES, Key, 1872, 269; Check List, 1873, no. 458; B. N. W. 1874, 523.
Nyctiardea grisea nævia, RIDGW. Nom. N. Am. B. 1881, no. 495. — COUES, Check List, 2d ed. 1882, no. 664.
Ardea hoactli, GMEL. S. N. I. 1788, 630.
Ardea cana, GMEL. t. c. 643.
Ardea Gardeni, GMEL. t. c. 645, no. 81 (based on the *Gardenian Heron* of Penn. and Lath.).
Nyctiardea Gardeni, BAIRD, Birds N. Am. 1858, 678; Cat. N. Am. B. 1859, no. 495.
Ardea discolor, NUTT. Mass. Orn. II. 1834, 54.
Nycticorax americanus, BONAP. Comp. List, 1838, 48.
Nycticorax vulgaris, D'ORB. Ois. Cuba, 1839, 208.
Nycticorax griseus (part), REICHENOW, J. f. O. 1877, 237.

HAB. The whole of temperate and tropical America, from British America to Chili and the Falkland Islands. Part of the West Indies; Bermudas.

SP. CHAR. *Adult:* Pileum, scapulars, and interscapulars, glossy blackish bottle-green; forehead, postocular, malar, and gular regions, and medial lower parts, white; lateral lower parts and neck, except in front, pale ash-gray, with a slight lilaceous tinge; wings, rump, upper tail-coverts and tail, deeper ash-gray. Occipital plumes pure white. Bill black; lores and orbits yellowish green; iris bright red; legs and feet yellow; claws brown. [AUDUBON.] *Young, second year:*

Similar to the adult, but scapulars and interscapulars cinereous, like the wings, and the white of the forehead obscured by the blackish of the crown; the colors generally more sombre, with neck and lower parts more decidedly ashy. *Young, first year:* Above, grayish brown, with more or less of a cinnamon cast, especially on the remiges, each feather marked with a medial tear-shaped, or wedge-shaped stripe of white, the remiges with small white terminal spots; rectrices plain ash-gray. Sides of the head and neck, and entire lower parts, striped longitudinally with grayish brown and dull white; chin and throat plain white medially. Bill light apple-green, the upper half of the maxilla blackish, the mandible with a tinge of the same near the end; lores light apple-green; eyelids similar, but brighter — more yellowish, their inner edge black; iris dark chrome-yellow or dull orange; legs and feet light yellowish apple-green; claws grayish horn-color.[1]

Length about 24.00–26.00; expanse, 44.00. Weight, 1 lb. 14 oz. (AUDUBON). Wing, 11.00–12–80; tail, 4.20–5.30; culmen, 2.80–3.10; depth of bill, .70–.85; tarsus, 3.10–3.40; middle toe, 2.65–3.10; bare portion of tibia, .90–1.40.[2]

The series of specimens at hand is unfortunately too small to justify an opinion as to whether the American Night Herons are really separable as a geographical race from those of the Old World, or whether there are two races in America. Authors recognize a *N. obscurus* from the southern part of South America, but ten specimens from that region compared with thirteen from Northern America certainly do not indicate any constant difference, notwithstanding a certain proportion (in this case four of the eight specimens before us, or one half) are more or less darker, though only a small proportion of them are very much darker; while of the other four, two are as light-colored as the very palest of northern ones, the others being about like the average. There being no other differences beyond the slightly larger *average* size of the southern birds (especially noticeable in those from the high districts of Peru and Chili), we are hardly inclined, for the present, at least, to recognize a var. *obscurus*, but, on the other hand, to look upon the latter as the expression of a tendency to partial melanism affecting this species in certain localities of the regions indicated, this tendency, moreover, perhaps affecting only some individuals in such localities.

[1] From a specimen killed August 13, 1879, near Washington, D. C.

[2] Extremes of thirteen examples from North and Middle America.

With five adult examples for comparison, we have been equally unsuccessful in discovering differences between European birds of this species and those from America, beyond the slightly smaller size of the former, there being no difference whatever, that we can see, in plumage. We have not, however, seen among European specimens those dark-colored examples which occur now and then in America.

A nearly adult specimen from the Sandwich Islands (No. 41951; Waimea Kaui; V. KNUDSEN), is very similar in colors to No. 49040 (typical *obscurus*) from Chili; it is smaller, however, and lighter-colored beneath; it is also more adult, and, besides possessing the occipital plumes, has the forehead distinctly white. A young bird from the same locality (No. 41952) agrees strictly with American specimens of the same age.

A young specimen from Lake Titicaca (24278, M. C. Z.) differs from North American examples in darker colors.

The following table of measurements, giving the extremes in each series, may serve to show the difference in size between specimens of this species from various countries, as indicated by the series before us: —

No. of spec's.	Country.	Wing.	Tail.	Culmen.	Depth of bill.	Tarsus.	Middle-toe.
14	North and Middle America,	11.00–12.80	4.20–5.30	2.80–3.10	.70–.85	3.10–3.40	2.65–3.10
8	Chili and Peru,	12.30–13.56	5.50–6.00	2.70–2.90	.70–.80	3.20–3.30	2.70–3.00
2	Brazil and Paraguay,	11.25–11.75	4.70–4.80	2.60–2.70	. . .	3.10–3.20	2.70
1	Sandwich Islands,	11.00	4.40	2.85	.75	2.75	2.55
1	Manilla,	10.80	4.30	2.75	.75	3.00	. . .
1	Kooloo Valley, India,	11.50	4.80	2.85	. . .	. . .	2.75
1	South Africa,	10.80	4.10	2.40	.70	2.75	2.50

The Night Heron — "Quâ-bird," or "Quâk," as this Heron is called in different parts of the country — is distributed over the entire continent, from the Arctic Circle, on the extreme northwest, to the opposite extreme of South America. And if we regard our American bird as clearly a race of, and hardly varying from, the European bird, it must claim to be cosmopolitan in the largest sense, since it is known to occur in nearly all parts of the globe. It is resident throughout Central America, and breeds in all portions where the situation is favorable. It was found breeding at Belize and at Omoa by Mr. Leyland. Mr. G. C. Taylor mentions its presence at Fonseca Bay, in Honduras. It was found at Parana, among the reeds of the lagoons, and on the islands of the river, by Dr. Burmeister; and Captain C. C. Abbott, in his paper on the Birds of the Falkland Islands ("Ibis," 1861), states that when he was in Hope Place, in December, 1859, he visited one of the breeding-places of this Heron. The places selected for laying were the tufts of grass near a freshwater pond, the whole of one side of which was covered with them. In some of the nests, which were composed of a few coarse sticks, were young birds half grown; in others eggs, three in number, some fresh, others with largely developed embryos. There could not have been less than a hundred pairs on the spot, and they were so tame and unsuspicious that they had evidently never been disturbed.

In Europe the Night Heron has apparently less of a northern range than the American form. It is rare in England, where less than a dozen stragglers are known to have been taken since 1782, when the first recorded specimen was procured; and it is still more rare in Ireland and in Scotland. It is found, more or less abundantly, in the warmer parts of Europe, Asia, and in Africa throughout the entire region, even as far as the Cape of Good Hope. It is said to inhabit Nepal, as also the country about Calcutta, and to be found in China and Japan.

The Night Heron is found abundantly, and breeds, in most of the West India Islands, especially in Cuba, Jamaica, and Trinidad. In the latter it is very abundant in all the inundated lands, in company with the other kinds of Heron, and its food is the same. During the day it perches in the mangrove trees, waiting for the sun to set before it goes in quest of its prey. In Jamaica, according to Gosse, though common, it is much more frequently heard than seen; and its loud and hoarse *quok*, heard in the dark solitudes, is often a source of great alarm to the superstitious negro. In floating down the larger streams, especially those margined by overhanging mangroves, it may be frequently seen, seated on some high branch which commands a wide prospect; but no sooner does a canoe approach, than, spreading its wings, it sails heavily off, with its customary outcry. It is vigilant and suspicious, and by no means easily shot. "It is," adds Mr. Gosse, "a noble bird. Its commanding height, erect attitude, stout-built frame, fiery eye, powerful beak, hanging crest, and handsome plumage, give it an imposing aspect." Crabs and other crustacea form its principal diet. If when wounded it falls into water, it can swim well and rapidly, with head erect, and its body not more immersed than that of a duck. The young Night Heron in its spotted plumage is known in Jamaica as the Guinea-hen Quok. It is a common fall and winter visitant of Bermuda.

Mr. Ridgway found it quite common in the vicinity of Sacramento City, as well as on the banks of the Carson and Truckee rivers, and in the neighborhood of Great Salt Lake. Mr. J. A. Allen met with it near Fort Hays, in Western Kansas; and in September he found it tolerably common in the valley of Great Salt Lake. According to Mr. Gosse, it breeds in large communities in Southern Wisconsin, on islands in the lakes; the nest is usually on low trees a few feet from the ground. Mr. Nelson also found this species breeding in the almost impenetrable wild rice swamps of Lake Michigan, in apparently improbable locations. He saw in Grass Lake — a widening of Fox River — over fifty nests placed in the midst of particularly dense bunches of rice, the stiff last-year's stalks of which, converging near the roots, formed a convenient base for their support. The nests were all well-built structures, composed of small pieces of dead rice-stalks from two to ten inches in length. They averaged from twelve to fifteen inches in diameter; and so firmly were they built, that he could stand on them without doing them any perceptible injury.

Dr. J. G. Cooper states that the Night Heron is common in California throughout the year, migrating in the summer at least as far to the north as the Columbia. It is found chiefly in the freshwater marshes. He saw one of its breeding-places at Santa Cruz, in a small grove of negundo trees, surrounded by cultivated fields and near a house. The nests were about the size of those of the Crow, and built in the usual loose manner; about the 1st of June they were observed to contain young. A number of Crows and Owls were on the watch for any luckless young bird they could manage to steal away in the absence of its parents. The old birds were very watchful during his visit, and flew around overhead.

This species appears to be pretty universally distributed over the United States, occurring in isolated colonies in situations where food is abundant. It was found in numbers throughout Texas by Mr. Dresser; and Mr. Boardman informs us that its heronries are met with on the coast and in the interior of Maine, although the species is not abundant in the neighborhood of Calais. According to Giraud, it visits Long Island in the early part of April, and remains there until quite late in the autumn; and that writer was informed that it has been occasionally met with in the depth of winter. It inhabits the overgrown margins of watercourses and ponds, seldom ventures abroad by daylight, and at such times is rarely seen, unless met with by accident. At twilight it is seen flying over the marshes and following the streams, reconnoitring for food, which consists of fishes, frogs, mice, and lizards. When roaming about at night it utters a peculiar guttural sound, from which it derives the name, by which it is generally known by gunners, of Quawk.

Mr. W. E. Endicott, in the first volume of the "Naturalist," gives an account of a heronry visited by him in Norfolk County, Mass., in a cedar swamp, wet and difficult of access. This was first noticed in 1862, attention having been drawn to it by the whiteness of the ground, caused by the surrounding excrements. The young birds were fed from the adjacent ponds and river, their food being in large part herrings. The nests were always built against the trunks of the trees, six or eight feet from the tops. Sometimes as many as four nests might be seen in a single cedar. The eggs were usually four in number, occasionally six, and even seven. The young are covered with down, and are at first quite helpless; but soon gain strength enough to climb to the upper branches, where they are fed by their parents until nearly full grown. Two broods were often reared in a season, and it was no uncommon thing to see four or five of the first brood sitting on the tree-top, while the nest below contained as many more of the younger brood, both sets being fed by their parents. They are clumsy climbers, and yet difficult to dislodge. When one falls to the ground it usually sets off at full speed, croaking unceasingly as it runs. Dr. Charles C. Abbott, writing to the "Naturalist" (III. p. 377), records an interesting instance in which a family of five birds of this species spent the winter months in a yard within the limits of the city of Trenton, New Jersey. The place was near the river, and retained much of its natural wildness. This little colony remained during the daytime in the large pines in the yard, visiting, after sundown, a little pond and spring-brook, from which they obtained a supply of frogs and fish. They occasionally visited the Delaware River, and seemed quite indifferent to the near presence of man. Major Wedderburn states that this species, in the immature plumage only, becomes common in Bermuda in the month of September, and so continues through the winter, until March. The birds were found chiefly in mangrove trees, on the borders of ponds.

The Night Heron is not common north of the forty-second parallel, and is found only in a few scattered and isolated colonies. It has been stated that it does not occur in the Fur Country; but this is not strictly correct: it is known to have been found in a single locality. Donald Gunn states that it is seen in great numbers at Shoal Lake, where it makes its nest, in all instances, on the ground among the reeds, and in a manner similar to that of the Grebes. Audubon states that it is not found in the interior; but this is not without many exceptions.

In the summers of 1834 and 1835 we visited the once celebrated heronry of this bird in the swampy woods near Fresh Pond, Cambridge. It occupied many acres, and previous to the draining of that region was almost inaccessible. At the time of these visits most of the nests contained eggs, and the birds were sitting. Each one, as it left the nest, uttered a loud *quawk*, while a few remained and hovered over our heads, but in silence. The nests were in the highest trees, and never less than twenty feet from the ground. In no instance that we remember were there more than four eggs in a nest. Subsequently we received four young birds taken from one of these nests; they were about a week old, covered with a thin down, and unable to stand. They were easily tamed, fed readily, and grew very fast. They were fed with different kinds of food — principally with liver, occasionally with mice, rats, frogs, and other reptiles. Once only were they given fragments of snakes; but as that killed three of them, and nearly destroyed the survivor, this diet was avoided. The last lived in confinement nearly two years, and proved a very interesting pet. He lived in the society of the poultry, but would not permit their near approach, his loud guttural croak always deterring them from coming too near. He was not afraid of the family; and though he did not like to be handled, would never run away to avoid it, but would come at call, even from a distance, evincing disappointment when no food was given him. The following illustrates his tenacity to first impressions. He was once caught wandering off to a neighboring spring for frogs, and driven back to the barnyard. In his path was a cart — an obstacle which it was necessary to go round — while beyond it was a pile of rubbish, over which he half flew. This was repeated three or four times. Afterward, the cart and the rubbish having been removed, the bird, when driven home from his wanderings, persisted in making a circuit around the spot where the cart had formerly stood, and in giving a flying leap over the place where once the pile had previously made this necessary. This amusing performance he would always go through with, and he was occasionally made to repeat it for the entertainment of visitors. Once in a while he would stray off into Stony Brook, at a point where it flowed past several houses, and would fish for himself. On one occasion, his hoarse gurgling cries created an alarm in the settlement, and the river was searched at midnight for the supposed drowning individual; and our pet was in some danger of its own life before the real cause of the alarm had been ascertained. It readily endured the cold of one winter; but an unusually severe night in the second winter killed the bird before it had assumed its mature plumage.

Three eggs of this species, taken by Mr. Harold Herrick in a heronry at Chettam, N. J., are almost exactly oval in shape, equally tapering at either end, and uniformly washed with a bright, light greenish blue — a light wash of Prussian blue with green shadings. These three eggs measure, respectively, 2.32 by 1.53 inches; 2.10 by 1.48 inches; and 2.00 inches by 1.44, — showing a remarkable variation in size. These were taken May 30, 1873.

GENUS **NYCTHERODIUS**, REICHENBACH.

Nyctherodius, REICHENB. Handb. Orn. (Naturl. Syst. Vög. in Systema Avium), 1851, p. xvi. (type, *Ardea violacea*, LINN.).

Nycticorax, BOIE (part), Isis, 1826, 979 (type, *Ardea violacea*, LINN.).

GEN. CHAR. Medium-sized Herons, of short, thick build; the bill extremely thick and stout, with both outlines strongly convex; the legs long and slender; the dorsal plumes much elongated and very narrow, reaching beyond the tail; the occiput (in adult) with several extremely long, linear white feathers. Habits nocturnal.

Bill short and very stout, the culmen curved regularly from the base, the gonys decidedly convex and very much ascending;[1] maxillary tomium almost perfectly straight throughout, but appreciably concave anteriorly, with a barely perceptible convexity toward the base; mandibular tomium nearly straight, but perceptibly concave anteriorly.[2] Mental apex less than half way from centre of eye to end of bill, and about even with anterior end of nostril; apex of malar region a little posterior to the frontal apex. Tarsi long and slender, exceeding the middle toe by more than

[1] The lower outline of the bill is, in fact, more decidedly convex than the upper.

[2] We find considerable variation among individuals in respect to these outlines: thus, a specimen (♀ adult, No. 2759, Mus. R.R.) from Illinois has the mandibular tomium exactly straight to near the end, where it gradually ascends to the tip, thereby producing a very slight subterminal concavity; in No. 2758, another adult ♀ from the same locality, it is decidedly *convex* in the middle portion; while in an adult ♂, from Mazatlan (No. 58811), it is decidedly *concave* at the same place, — so much so, in fact, that a space is left between it and the upper tomium, on each side, when the bill is closed tight! These discrepancies, however, do not affect the general form of the bill, which is eminently characteristic.

half the length of the latter ; outer toe decidedly longer than inner ; hallux slightly longer than the first phalanx of the middle toe ; bare portion of tibia as long as the outer toe ; tarsal scutellæ with a tendency to form transverse plates on the upper half, in front ; claws exceedingly short, strongly curved, and blunt. Inner webs of two outer primaries emarginated near the end ; tail of

N. violaceus.

twelve broad, moderately hard feathers ; interscapular plumes greatly elongated (extending beyond the tail), narrow, the plumulæ threadlike and soft, and separated outwardly. Occipital plumes linear, flattened, longer than the head and bill, when fully developed, half a dozen or more in number, and graduated in length.

Nyctherodius violaceus.

THE WHITE-CROWNED NIGHT HERON.

Ardea stellaris cristata americana, CATESBY, Carolina, 1754, pl. 79 (adult).
Bihoreau, de Cayenne, BUFF. Pl. Enl. 1770–84, pl. 899 (adult).
Ardea violacea, LINN. S. N. ed. 10, I. 1758, 143, no. 12 (ex Catesby, l.c.) ; ed. 12, I. 1766, 238, no. 16. — WILS. Am. Orn. VIII. 1814, 26, pl. 65. — NUTT. Man. II. 1834, 52. — AUD. Orn. Biog. IV. 1838, 290, pl. 336 ; Synop. 1839, 262 ; Birds Am. VI. 1843, 89, pl. 364 (adult and young).
Nyctiardea violacea, SWAINS. Classif. B. II. 1837, 354. — COUES, Key, 1872, 269 ; Check List, 1873, no. 459.
Nyctherodius violaceus, REICHENB. Syst. Av. 1851, p. xvi. — BAIRD, Birds N. Am. 1858, 679 ; Cat. N. Am. B. 1859, no. 496. — RIDGW. Nom. N. Am. B. 1881, no. 496. — COUES, Check List, 2d ed. 1882, no. 665 (*Nycterodius*).
Cayenne Night Heron, LATH. Synop. III. 1785, 56 (quotes Pl. Enl. 899).
Yellow-crowned Night Heron, LATH. t.c. 80.
Ardea cayennensis, GMEL. S. N. I. ii. 1788, 626, no. 31 (based on Pl. Enl. 899).
Ardea sexsetacea, VIEILL. Enc. Meth. III. 1823, 1130 (Reichenow).
Ardea callocephala, WAGL. Syst. Av. 1827, Ardea, sp. 34 (Reichenow).

HAB. Warm-temperate Eastern North America, West Indies, Middle America, and Northern South America, breeding north to Southern Illinois and Indiana. On Atlantic coast north to Pennsylvania (rare). West to Colorado, south to Western Ecuador and the Amazonian region. Bermudas.

Sp. Char. *Adult:* Forehead, middle of the crown, and long occipital plumes, with a large longitudinal patch from the rictus to the ears, pure white;[1] rest of the head deep black. Plumage in general, clear plumbeous-blue, or cinereous, lighter beneath (the degree of blueness probably depending on the age of the bird); all the feathers of the upper surface marked with a medial stripe of black; the secondaries and rectrices dark plumbeous, bordered with a lighter shade of

the same; primaries plain bluish plumbeous. Bill deep black, the lower basal portion of the mandible, in some specimens, greenish yellow; lores and eyelids greenish yellow; iris pale orange; legs dull yellowish green, the large scutellæ and the claws dusky.[2]

Young: Above, dark sooty grayish brown, sometimes of a slightly olive cast, the feathers of the pileum and wings (in youngest individuals the entire upper surface ?) marked with medial streaks of white or pale buff; these streaks assuming on the wing-coverts a narrowly cuneate form. Lower parts soiled whitish, striped with brownish gray. "Bill greenish black, the lower and basal part of the lower mandible greenish yellow, as are the eyelids and bare space before the eye. Iris pale orange. Legs and feet dull yellowish green, the scutella and scales in front, as well as the claws, dusky" (Audubon). Length, about 23.00–25.00; expanse, 40.00–45.00; weight, 1 lb. 7 oz. to 1 lb. 9 oz. (Audubon). Wing, 10.50–12.65; tail, 4.20–5.10; culmen, 2.50–3.00; depth of bill, .70–.92; tarsus, 3.10–4.20; middle toe, 2.20–2.55; bare portion of tibia, 1.60–2.40.

The variation among different individuals of this species consists mainly in the absence or presence of the ochraceous stain on the forehead (and, if present, its amount), and in the degree of blueness in the plumbeous coloring of the general plumage. The most purely colored specimen I

[1] In living and freshly killed specimens the forehead is a delicate creamy sulphur-yellow color; but this fades perceptibly in a very short time after death, and finally disappears entirely. Audubon ("Birds of America," Vol. VI. p. 91) says, however, that this is characteristic of the breeding season, and "disappears at the approach of autumn, when the bird might with all propriety be named the White-crowned Heron." In view of the fact that this beautiful yellow color is seldom if ever to be seen in dried skins, the term "yellow-crowned" is a decided misnomer; and since it is thus calculated to mislead the student, we prefer the name "white-crowned," and have, for the reasons stated, adopted the latter in this work. In many skins the white of the forehead is tinged more or less with ochraceous- or cinnamon-brown; but this is without much doubt an actual stain caused by contact with the slimy coating on the under side of leaves of aquatic plants.

[2] In an adult female shot from the nest, at Wheatland, Indiana, April 27, 1881, the bill and naked lores were wholly slate-black, the eyelids similar, but tinged with green anteriorly; iris Mars-orange; legs pale olive-buff, the large scutellæ of tarsus and toes deep brownish. In the adult male in spring, according to Audubon, the soft parts are colored as follows: "Bill black. Iris reddish-orange; margins of eyelids and bare space in front of the eye dull yellowish green. Tibia, upper part of the tarsus, its hind part and the soles, bright yellow; the scutella and scales, the fore part of the tarsus, the toes, and the claws, black."

have seen is an adult female from Mount. Carmel, Illinois. This specimen was shot from the nest, and a perfectly developed egg taken from the ovary; consequently there can be no doubt as to the sex. In this specimen the plumbeous is throughout of a clear, fine grayish-blue tinge; the rectrices, even, are dark bluish plumbeous (with a faint green reflection in certain lights), and are distinctly bordered with plumbeous-blue. This fine example is nearly matched by No. 17148, National Museum, from the Tortugas, Florida (spring of 1860). The opposite extreme is nearly represented by another adult female, but probably a younger bird, from the same locality, and obtained at about the same time and under nearly the same circumstances. In this specimen the plumbeous is everywhere much less bluish, and on the back and lesser wing-coverts is even very much obscured by a smoky tinge; the black stripes of the back and wings show a very strong bottle-green reflection, which is not the case with other specimens examined; the rectrices are absolutely uniform slaty plumbeous, without paler edges. The head is marked and colored as usual in fully adult specimens, and the forehead has a slight tinge of ochraceous anteriorly. A specimen from Fort Brown, Texas (3836, March 10), is almost precisely similar.

An adult, in nuptial plumage (No. 67919), from the Talamanca district, Costa Rica, differs from other specimens in full plumage in having several blue-black feathers in the middle of the crown. This specimen is also remarkable for its large size.

Some specimens, apparently in their second year, resemble adults in full plumage, except that they lack the scapular and occipital plumes, and that the black of the head, especially underneath, is mixed with white feathers. Nos. 28062 and 67920 represent this stage. As a proof that the brown tinge on the crown of this species has nothing to do with season or sex, but that, on the contrary, if not an entirely accidental stain from foreign substances, it is rather a mark of immaturity, it may be stated that both these immature specimens have the ferruginous stain very strongly marked, it being in the former specimen deeper than I have ever seen it in any adult, and so dark in places as to appear of a dark sepia- or snuff-brown tinge.

A younger stage of plumage than the above, and one which perhaps illustrates *a change in color of the feathers themselves, without an actual moult*, is represented by No. 11892 (Tortugas, April 5). In this, all the well-defined stripes and streaks of the first stage have become obliterated, but at the same time the sombre colors of this age are retained. The upper parts, *including the scapular plumes, which are not only present, but well developed*,[1] are of a dark oily, sooty, brownish-gray, with a faint green reflection in certain lights; many of the feathers darker medially (especially the wing-coverts and scapular plumes), the wing-coverts having well-defined pale margins. The forehead and middle of the crown are rich brown, of a shade between cinnamon and sepia; the occiput uniform blue-black; the malar region and throat streaked with blue-black and white. The lower parts much as in the first plumage, but the stripes more indistinct. There are no occipital plumes.

From the above, we may reasonably infer that the assumption of the perfect adult plumage is a very gradual process, and not accomplished at a single, nor solely by several moults; but that after each moult a gradual change in the colors of the feathers takes place, — a fact which is certainly established with regard to many birds. Those specimens in which the plumbeous is of a clear, fine bluish cast are therefore to be considered the oldest individuals, and the more sombre ones younger.

In the Galapagos Islands is found a *Nyctherodius* which is said to be distinct from the common species. This form we have seen only in the immature plumage, a description of which is given below.[2]

[1] It is probable that the species breeds in this plumage.

[2] NYCTHERODIUS PAUPER (Scl. & Salv.).

"*Nycticorax violaceus*," DARWIN, Zool. Beag. III. Birds, 1841, 128 (Galapagos).

"*Ardea violacea*," SUNDEV. P. Z. S. 1871, 125 (Galapagos).

Nycticorax pauper, SCL. & SALV. P. Z. S. May 12, 1870, 323, 327 (Galapagos). — SALVIN, Trans. Zool. Soc. IX. ix. 1875, 498.

Young ♂, transition plumage: Head chiefly black, uniform on the sides of the pileum and occiput, the centre of the latter mixed with elongated light-brown feathers having darker mesial stripes. Stripe on side of the head, from the rictus over the ear, light tawny brown; malar region blue-black, with a few narrow whitish streaks; chin and throat more heavily streaked with white. Upper parts in general,

In the adult plumage, this species is probably considerably darker than *N. violaceus*, with the black stripes of the upper parts less distinct, perhaps obsolete.

The Yellow-crowned Heron is a southern species, not known to breed north of the Carolinas on the Atlantic coast, though occasionally wandering much farther north, both on the Atlantic coast and in the interior. It is found along the whole Gulf coast to Mexico, occurs both on the eastern and the western coasts of Mexico and of Central America, and has been received from South America. On the Pacific coast it has not been taken, to our knowledge, so far north as California, though abundant on the Marias and Socorro Islands and the corresponding coast. It is found in and breeds in several of the West India Islands. Professor Newton mentions it as occurring, but as not very common, in St. Croix, where it inhabits the mangrove swamps in the daytime, but leaves them at night to feed in the interior of the island. It is presumed to be resident and to breed in that island, but this has not been positively ascertained. Mr. E. C. Taylor found it abundant in the Oropuche lagoon, in Trinidad, but he did not meet with any elsewhere on that island. Léotaud also speaks of this Heron as being quite common in Trinidad, where it is both resident and known to breed. Its food, for which it searches in the night, is not different from that of other Herons. During the daytime it keeps itself closely concealed among the mangrove trees, which fill all the inlets from the sea. At times this bird is very fat, and is then quite good eating. Unlike the Night Heron, it can never be reconciled to captivity, but always retains its wild and untamable character. It is mentioned by Dr. Gundlach as a common resident species in Cuba, where he obtained its eggs. It is not given by Mr. Gosse, who probably confounded it with the *Gardeni*, as among the birds of Jamaica, but is mentioned by Mr. March as of frequent occurrence on that island. It is known as the Guinea-hen Quok, by which term Mr. Gosse supposed the young of the *Gardeni* to be designated. Mr. Salvin states that specimens of this bird were among the skins collected by Mr. Leyland in Honduras; and he afterward reported that he himself found it not uncommon on the Pacific sea-coast of Guatemala. It is an occasional visitant of Bermuda, both in spring and in fall. It is of rare and accidental occurrence along the Atlantic coast, even as far as Massachusetts. Mr. N. Vickary, of Lynn, obtained a fine specimen that had been killed within the limits of that city in October, 1862. Mr. George N. Lawrence includes it in his list of birds obtained near New York City; and Mr. Giraud states that it occasionally extends its visits as far north as Long Island. It is there of entirely nocturnal habit, keeping hidden in the marshes during the day, and feeding chiefly at night. Professor F. H. Snow records the capture of an adult female Yellow-crowned Night Heron and three young birds at Neosho Falls, Kansas, by Colonel N. S. Goss. The female was in full breeding plumage. One was also taken by Mrs. Maxwell, in Colorado. Mr. Dresser found it more abundant in Southwestern Texas than the common Night Heron, but none were seen about Matamoras until August. Mr. Wil-

dark brownish slate, becoming gradually glaucous-plumbeous on the tertials, remiges, rump, upper tail-coverts, and tail; elongated scapular plumes dark plumbeous, without black mesial stripe; wing-coverts narrowly edged with light fulvous or creamy buff; border of the wing fulvous-white, spotted along the inner edge with dark plumbeous. Neck brownish slate, the foreneck longitudinally striped with pale ochraceous; remaining lower parts similar, but more profusely streaked with light ochraceous and white. Under-surface of the wings nearly uniform plumbeous.

Wing, 10.40; tail, 4.50; culmen, 2.60; depth of bill through nostril, .80; tarsus, 3.40; middle toe, 2.30; bare portion of tibia, 1.50.

[Described from the type in Mus. Salvin & Godman; Indefatigable I. Galapagos, Aug. 30, 1878; Dr. A. Habel. Length, 21.00; extent, 38.00. Iris, orange; bill, black; legs and feet, green.]

son states that it is abundant, and that it breeds in the Bermudas; but in this he was misinformed. Major Wedderburn notes it as only of rare and occasional occurrence there, and only mentions three instances as coming within his knowledge: two of the birds were killed in April, and one in September.

Wilson states that a specimen was shot on the Schuylkill, near Philadelphia, and that it frequently extends its migrations into Virginia. He found it inhabiting the lower parts of South Carolina, Georgia, and Louisiana in the summer season, reposing during the day among low swampy woods, and feeding only at night. It builds in societies, making nests of sticks in the branches of low trees. It was not numerous, and its solitary mode of life was the cause of its being little known. It appeared to have a strong attachment for the vicinity of the ocean, and to feed on fish, crabs, and lizards — principally the former.

Audubon remarks that it is wholly migratory within the United States, arriving only about the end of March, and leaving in the middle of October. In some parts of the Southern States it is said to be quite abundant, while in others it is rarely met with. In some portions of Florida it breeds in great numbers. On his visit to Texas he saw a few of this species on an island in Baie Blanche, and again on Galveston Island, where it was plentiful. On the Mississippi it is rare above Natchez, but a few straggle farther up the river. He does not regard it as entirely nocturnal, as he has seen it searching for food at all hours of the day; and while at Galveston he has frequently seen a large flock similarly occupied. It is probable that this only occurs when the bird is feeding its young. I have noticed the same exceptional conduct by day on the part of the Night Heron, at the same season, when it loads itself with a supply for its young, feeding them by regurgitating the contents of its gullet.

Mr. Audubon satisfied himself that this bird performs its migratory movements in the night, having seen it come down from a height in the air, after sunrise, for rest and food. Its flight is slow and less protracted than that of the Night Heron. When surprised on its perch, it rises perpendicularly a short distance and flies off in a straight line. When on the ground, it is less elegant in its movements than most of the other Herons. Its pace is less sedate, its movements in seizing its prey less rapid, and it feeds more in the manner of the domestic fowl. Its food is very varied, consisting of snails, fish, small snakes, crabs, crays, lizards, leeches, small quadrupeds, young birds, etc. He adds that one which had been killed by Mr. Edward Harris, on the island of Terre Blanche, about four o'clock in the afternoon, when opened the next morning was found to have swallowed a young terrapin, and that this was still alive when liberated. The nest of this Heron is placed in either a high or low situation, according to the nature of the place selected for its breeding-ground. In the interior of swampy woods nests were found on the tops of the loftiest cypresses, as well as on low bushes, but not so close together as with other Herons; in the Florida Keys they were seen either on the tops of the mangroves or on their lower branches, just above the water. In the Carolinas this bird builds on low bushes on the edge of swamps, the nest being, like that of the other Herons, formed of dry sticks loosely put together, lined with a few weeds and fibrous roots. The eggs are three in number, and never more. The young do not remain in the nest until able to fly, but even leave the tree or bush to follow their parents to the shore. When alarmed, they can scramble off with considerable agility and hide. This bird breeds in Florida six weeks sooner than in South Carolina, two broods being usually raised in both sections. The slender plumes on the back of the head commonly fall off after incubation has commenced. When wounded, it defends itself vigorously with its claws and bill, and can inflict severe scratches.

The eggs of this species are in size and shape not unlike those of the Night Heron — an oblong oval. Their shade of greenish blue is lighter and duller, and the proportion of green is less marked. They vary considerably in size. Two in my collection, taken by Dr. Bryant in Florida, measure, one, 2.10 by 1.49 inches, the other, 1.94 by 1.44 inches, averaging 2.02 by 1.46 inches. According to Mr. Moore, the number of eggs in a set is not limited to three, as stated by Audubon. That author mentions that in Louisiana, in May, 1867, he found five eggs in a nest, and in the following year one with even six, and others with five or four. In Florida, April 28, he found one with five and another with four eggs. Mr. Moore discredits the statement that this Heron has two broods in a season, and does not believe the account given by Audubon of its moving from one heronry to another in order to nest and breed.

Mr. Ridgway found this Heron breeding very abundantly at Monteur's Pond, in Knox Co., Indiana, where it was much the most numerous species of the family. Many dozens of pairs had their nests in tall sweet-gum and other trees, in a very wet piece of "bottoms," along one edge of the pond. A female was shot from her nest, and in her oviduct was found an egg ready for ejection. A few hours afterward another female was shot from the same nest! In the similar wet bottoms of Coffee Creek, in Wabash Co., Illinois, quite a colony of these birds was also found nesting, the nests being placed at various heights in white oak and other trees.

GENUS **BOTAURUS**, STEPHENS.

Botaurus, STEPHENS, Shaw's Gen. Zool. XI. ii. 1819, 592 (type, *Ardea stellaris*, LINN.).
Butor, SWAINS. Classif. B. II. 1837, 354 (same type).

GEN. CHAR. — Medium-sized, or rather large, Herons, with the plumage much mottled or striped with different shades of brown and ochraceous (the plumage essentially the same in both

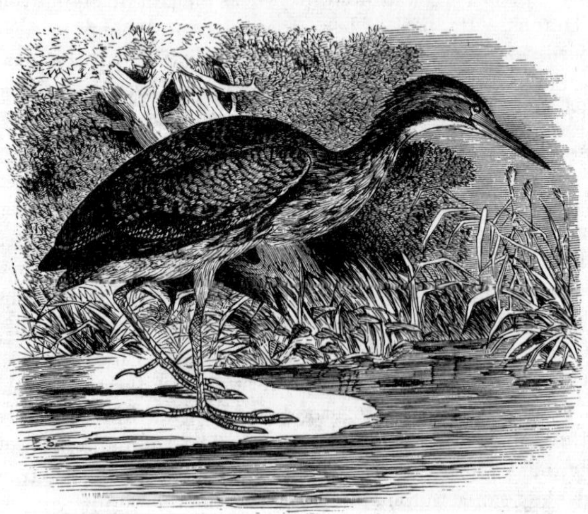

B. lentiginosus.

sexes and at all seasons); the plumage, particularly of the lower neck in front, exceedingly soft and full, and destitute of any ornamental plumes; the bill comparatively small and short (shorter than the middle toe); the tibiæ almost completely feathered, and the claws very long and but slightly curved. Tail, of ten short, soft feathers, slightly rounded or nearly even.

Bill gradually tapering from the base to the point, the upper outline more convex than the lower, the gonys very slightly convex and gently ascending, the lower edge of the maxillary rami perfectly straight; mental apex extending forward about half way from the centre of the eye to the point of the bill, and slightly in advance of the anterior end of the nostril; malar apex falling far short of that of the frontal feathers. Toes very long, the middle one considerably exceeding the bill and almost equalling the tarsus; *inner toe decidedly longer than the outer;* hallux about half the middle toe; claws very long (that of the hallux nearly equal to its digit), and but slightly curved; bare portion of the tibia shorter than the hallux. Tarsi with large regular scutellæ in front.

Only two American species are known, both very distinct. They may be distinguished by the following points of difference: —

B. lentiginosus. Nape and sides of the neck plain ochraceous, or only minutely freckled; wing-coverts minutely speckled with different shades of ochraceous or rusty. A blackish or dull grayish stripe on the side of the neck. Lower parts distinctly striped. Wing, 9.80–12.00; culmen, 2.50–3.20; depth of bill through nostril, .50–.65; tarsus, 3.10–3.85; middle toe, 2.90–3.60. HAB. — North America; south to Guatemala, Cuba, and Jamaica; Bermudas; occasional in British Islands.

B. pinnatus.[1] Nape and sides of neck transversely rayed or barred with blackish; wing-coverts coarsely variegated, in irregular, somewhat "herring-bone" pattern with blackish. No black or grayish stripe on side of neck. Lower parts nearly unvariegated. Wing, 10.10; culmen, 3.25; depth of bill through nostril, .70; tarsus, 3.75; middle toe, 3.75. HAB. — Tropical America, north to Nicaragua.

Botaurus lentiginosus.

THE AMERICAN BITTERN.

Ardea stellaris canadensis, EDWARDS, Nat. Hist. pl. 136.
Le Butor de la Baye de Hudson, EDWARDS, l. c.
Botaurus Freti-Hudsonis, BRISS. Orn. V. 1760, 450, pl. 37, fig. 1.
Ardea stellaris, Varietas, FORST. Philos. Trans. LXII. 1772, 410, no. 38 (Severn R.).
Bittern, Var. A., LATH. Synop. III. 1785, 58.
Ardea stellaris, B., LATH. Ind. Orn. II. 1790, 680, no. 18 B. (ex Edwards, pl. 136).
Ardea mugitans, BARTR. Travels, 1792, ——.
Botaurus mugitans, COUES, Check List, 2d ed. 1882, no. 666.
Ardea lentiginosa, MONTAGUE, Orn. Dict. Suppl. 1813. — SW. & RICH. F. B. A. II. 1831, 374. — NUTT. Man. II. 1834, 60. — AUD. Synop. 1839, 263; Birds Am. VI. 1843, 94, pl. 365.
Botaurus lentiginosus, STEPHENS, Shaw's Gen. Zool. XII. 1819, 596. — BAIRD, Birds N. Am. 1858, 674; Cat. N. Am. B. 1859, no. 492. — REICHENOW, J. f. O. 1877, 248. — RIDGW. Nom. N. Am. B. 1881, no. 497.
Ardea hudsonias, MERREM, Ersch. Grub. Ency. V. 1820, 175.
Ardea minor, WILS. Am. Orn. VIII. 1814, 35, pl. 65, fig. 3.
Botaurus minor, BOIE, Isis, 1826, 979. — COUES, Key, 1872, 269; Check List, 1873, no. 460; Birds N. W. 1874, 523.
Butor americanus, SWAINS. Classif. B. II. 1837, 354.
Ardea mokoko, VIEILL. Nouv. Dict. XIV. 1817, 440.
Botaurus adspersus, "CAB.," BONAP. Consp. II. 1857, 156.

[1] BOTAURUS PINNATUS, Licht.
Ardea pinnata, "LICHT.," WAGL. Isis, 1829, 663.
Botaurus pinnatus, GRAY, Gen. B. III. 557.
Ardea brasiliensis, MAX. Beitr. 1832, 642.

Hab. — The whole of temperate and tropical North America, north to latitude about 60°, south to Guatemala. Cuba; Jamaica; Bermudas. Occasional in Europe (18 British records!).

Sp. Char. — *Adult:* Ground-color of the plumage ochraceous-buff; but this densely mottled and finely sprinkled above with reddish brown and blackish, the latter color prevailing on the dorsal and scapular regions, where the feathers have lighter edges, the buff prevailing on the wing-coverts, where the variegation consists of a finer and sparser sprinkling of the dusky and brown; on the tertials and ends of the secondaries, the reddish (a sort of cinnamon shade) forms the ground-color, and is thickly sprinkled with irregular dusky dottings and zigzags; pectoral tufts nearly uniform dark brown, the feathers with broad lateral borders of clear yellowish ochraceous. Pileum, rusty brown, darker anteriorly, changing gradually backward into the greenish olive-gray of the nape; sides of the head and neck yellowish ochraceous; a malar stripe of dark ferruginous, changing posteriorly into a very conspicuous stripe of blue-black (or in some specimens dull

grayish) down each side of the neck; chin and throat white, with a very narrow medial dusky streak, suffused with ochraceous; foreneck pale buff, with sharply defined stripes of cinnamon-brown edged with a black line; lower parts pale buff, with narrower brownish stripes; tibiæ and crissum plain light creamy buff; primary-coverts and primaries dark slate, tipped with pale reddish ochraceous, finely, but not densely, sprinkled with dusky. Upper mandible olivaceous-black, the tomium (broadly) lemon-yellow; lower mandible pale lemon-yellow, deeper basally, with a stripe of dusky brownish along the posterior part of the tomium; lores and eyelids lemon-yellow, the former divided longitudinally by a median stripe of dusky olive, from the eye to the base of the upper mandible; iris clear, light sulphur-yellow next the pupil, shading exteriorly into orange-brownish, this encircled narrowly with black; legs and feet bright yellowish green; claws pale brown, dusky toward points.[1] *Young:* Similar to the adult, but more reddish, the mottling coarser, and with a tendency to form ragged transverse bars, especially on the posterior upper parts.

Length, about 24.00–28.00; expanse, 37.00–45.00; weight about 1½ lbs. (Audubon); wing, 9.80–12.00; tail, 3.10–4.40; culmen, 2.50–3.20; depth of bill, .50–.65; tarsus, 3.10–3.85; middle toe, 2.90–3.60; bare portion of tibia, 1.00–1.35.[2]

In the large collection of specimens of this species which we have been able to examine and compare are certain variations of plumage and proportions, which appear, however, to be chiefly, if not entirely, of an individual and seasonal character. The most apparent difference as to colors consists of a more reddish shade to the plumage in autumnal birds, while those obtained in the spring or summer are characterized by a more grayish aspect. There is also another noticeable difference between specimens, namely, in the distinctness of the black or dusky stripe along the side of the upper neck. This is usually a deep glossy black; but in many individuals it is

[1] Colors of fresh specimens (♂ and ♀) killed along the Truckee River, Nevada, Nov. 18, and Dec. 11, 1867.

[2] From measurements of twenty-five *adult* specimens!

grayish, and in some even almost obsolete. I cannot determine, however, that this difference is sexual or seasonal, or dependent on locality; it is probably simply an individual variation.

The Common Bittern of North America has a very extended distribution, and one almost co-extensive with the northern continent itself. It is found from Texas to the Arctic regions, and from the Atlantic to the Pacific, and breeds wherever it is found. It is generally, but not universally, distributed, and does not occur in regions unsuited for its residence.

Hearne, in his "Journey to the Northern Ocean," speaks of this bird as being common at Fort York (Hudson's Bay) in summer, but as being seldom met with so far north as Churchill River. It is always found frequenting marshes and swampy places, as also the banks of such rivers as abound with reeds and long grass. It generally feeds on the insects that are bred in the water, and probably on small frogs and tadpoles; and though seldom very fat, is generally considered good eating. It is by no means numerous, even at Fort York, nor, in fact, even in the most southern parts of the Bay that Hearne visited. Richardson speaks of it as a common bird in the marshes and willow thickets of the interior of the Fur Country as far north as the 58th parallel. Its loud booming note is said exactly to resemble that of the Common Bittern of Europe; this may be heard every summer evening, and also frequently in the day. When disturbed or alarmed, it utters a hollow croaking cry. Captain Blakiston did not meet with it on the plains of the Saskatchewan, although he was told that it was not uncommon in the interior. Mr. Mossay met with it on the coast of Hudson's Bay; and Mr. Ross cites its range on the Mackenzie River as extending even to the Arctic Ocean, where its presence must be very rare.

Mr. Boardman informs us that this bird is quite common in the vicinity of Calaìs, where it breeds abundantly. It is usually found on high, or rather on dry, ground, where it makes only a very slight nest. The young birds hide in the long grass; and it is not an uncommon occurrence for mowers when at work to take off their heads. Mr. W. E. Endicott writes to the "Naturalist" (I. p. 325) that the statement that this bird builds in bushes, in the manner of Herons, is not in accordance with his experience. He has never met with its nest, either on low trees or in bushes. So far as he knows, it does not make any nest at all; but all the eggs that he has ever found have been laid on the bare ground among thick tufts of dwarf laurel on the Fowl-meadows that skirt the upper parts of the Neponset River. He has never found this bird in communities, and has never been able to discover more than a single nest in a field of ten acres, though he has searched diligently. That the Bittern, when it nests on the uplands, or on ground constantly dry and secure from inundations, may have, as mentioned by Mr. Boardman, a very scanty nest, or even no nest at all, as was observed by Mr. Endicott, is probable; but it is not universally true. The Bittern in the West builds almost universally a substantial, and sometimes considerably elevated nest, always on the ground; but the portion on which the eggs are laid is considerably above the level of the ground. This is undoubtedly due to the fact that it is forced to nest in places either naturally swampy, or which in rainy seasons are liable to be flooded to the depth of several inches. Experience has doubtless taught the bird that the bare earth, or even a scanty supply of dry rubbish, is not enough in such localities; and thus we find it breeding in the marshes of Lake Koskonong, in the open ground, never among trees or in bushes, and always keeping its eggs as dry as the Least Bittern; the nest, or, more properly speaking, the upper part of the mound on which the eggs are laid, being always dry. It is not at all gregarious in the breeding season.

On Long Island, the Bittern is generally known by the name of the "Indian Pullet," being reputed to have been one of the favorite birds of the Indians. It is more commonly known as the "Look-up," from its habit, when standing on the marshes, of elevating its head. It does not move about much by day, although it is not strictly nocturnal, but is sometimes seen flying low over the meadows, in pursuit of short-tailed or meadow mice, which are frequently taken whole from its stomach. It also feeds on fish, frogs, lizards, etc. Late in the season its flesh is held in high esteem. It can rarely be procured in any great number, and only when the marshes are overflowed by unusually high tides. According to Giraud, it is hunted in boats, much after the manner adopted in the pursuit of the Rail. On ordinary occasions it is a difficult bird to flush. The instant it becomes aware that it has attracted the attention of the fowler, it lowers its head, runs quickly through the grass, and when again seen, is usually in a different direction from that taken by its pursuer, whose movements it closely watches. When thus pursued it seldom exposes more than its head. When wounded it makes a vigorous resistance, erects the feathers on the head and neck, extends its wings, opens its bill, and puts on a fierce expression. It will attack a dog, or even his master; and when defending itself directs its sharp bill at its assailant's eye. It never associates with any other species of Heron, and does not appear fond of the society of its own kind. It is distributed over the marshes either singly or in pairs, and is nowhere abundant.

Mr. Batty writes that he has taken mice from the stomachs of several; and from one a large field-mouse which had apparently but just been devoured. The mouse was whole, and had been swallowed head-first. This bird feeds during the day, but is more nocturnal than diurnal in its habits. When wounded it drops its wings, raises the feathers of the neck in a circle around the head, and then strikes out fiercely with its sharp bill. Mr. Batty has met with individuals about Fire Island as late as the last of November.

It is an autumnal visitant of Bermuda, where, as Major Wedderburn states, it is to be met with in all the marshes from October until December, and occasionally in March. In some seasons it is quite rare. In illustration of its omnivorous habits, Mr. Hurdis mentions that in the stomach of one shot in the Pembroke Marshes were found an eel six inches long, a mouse, a dragon-fly, a grasshopper, and a portion of a small golden carp.

Mr. Dresser found this a common resident species in Southern Texas. Mr. J. A. Allen mentions it as tolerably common in the Valley of Great Salt Lake, in September; and Mr. Ridgway constantly found it in all marshy situations in the interior. Specimens were killed in the latter part of September, in Thousand Spring Valley, in the northeastern portion of Nevada. Mr. Salvin met with it in Guatemala both at Dueñas and at Coban. It is also given by Mr. R. Browne in his list of the birds of Vancouver. According to Wilson, it was known on the New Jersey sea-coast as the *Dunkadoo*, in supposed imitation of its booming cries. But neither Wilson, Audubon, nor Nuttall knew anything as to its nesting; and evidently never saw its egg, their descriptions of which are quite incorrect.

Wilson states that when come upon suddenly, it rises with a callow cry, and may then be easily shot; and Audubon refers to its liability to be paralyzed with fear when surprised, so that it may even be knocked down with a stick; but Mr. Everett Smith, of Portland, in a paper exhibiting complete familiarity with the habits of this species, regards these results as less due to the timidity of the Bittern than to its unsuspicious and gentle nature.

Wilson states that this bird has no booming cry corresponding with that of the

European species. This is a mistake. The cry of our bird is one quite as remarkable, though said by some writers — but not by Richardson — to be quite different. During my residence in Cambridge, in the spring and early summer, its singular, resonant cries could be heard at quite a distance, issuing from the Fresh Pond meadows early in the evening, and even on cloudy days. They seemed to be uttered in a deep choking tone, and have been well compared to the syllables *pomp-ău-gōr*. Dr. Bachman describes it as a hoarse croaking note, sounding as if the bird's throat were filled with water. By many these sounds are thought closely to resemble the noise made by driving a stake in boggy soil; and hence the Bittern is popularly known as the "Stake-driver," and also as the "Post-driver."

It is an occasional visitant to Great Britain, where some five or six instances of its capture have been recorded.

According to the observations of Captain Bendire, the number of eggs in its nest varies from five to seven. I have never met with more than four. Eggs in my collection (No. 783), procured by Mr. Kumlien in Wisconsin, are of a rounded oval shape equally obtuse at either end, and of a uniform brownish-drab color, neither spotted nor having any tinge of green or olive in their shadings, as stated by some writers. They range from 1.90 to 1.95 inches in length, and from 1.45 to 1.50 in breadth. These eggs vary but little in size, shape, or color, and are hardly "pointed at one end," as described by Yarrell.

Genus **ARDETTA**, Gray.

Ardeola, Bonap. Synopsis, 1828 (teste Gray, Gen. & Subg. 1855, 113). Type, *Ardea exilis*, Gmel. (Not of Boie, 1822 !)

Ardetta, Gray, List of Genera, App. 1842, 13. Type, *Ardea minuta*, Linn.

Erodiscus, Gloger, Handb. I. 1842, 410 (same type).

"*Ardeiralla*" (1855), Verreaux (teste Hartl. Orn. Westafr. p. 224). Type, *Ardea Sturmi*, Wagl.

Gen. Char. Extremely small (the smallest of) Herons, or miniature Bitterns; differing from the true Bitterns chiefly in their diminutive size, and in the fact that the sexes differ in color.[1]

A. exilis.

[1] We can find no other difference in form or proportions between *Botaurus* and *Ardetta*. In the sexed specimens of *A. involucris* which we have been able to examine there is no sexual difference of plumage. The sex of the single supposed female, however, may have been incorrectly determined.

COM. CHAR. Prevailing color ochraceous, darker above and paler below. Pileum with a longitudinal space of black; an immaculate pale-colored area covering wing-coverts; front of neck indistinctly striped longitudinally with a deeper shade, upon a whitish ground. Remiges and rectrices uniform dusky, with or without ochraceous tips.

A. *Lower part of tibia naked all round; upper parts nearly uniform brown, or brown and black, without conspicuous stripes.*

1. **A. minuta.**[1] Remiges uniform black. Wing, 5.80–5.90; culmen, 1.70–1.75. *Hab.* Palæarctic Region.
2. **A. exilis.** Remiges narrowly tipped with rufous. Wing, 4.30–5.25; culmen, 1.60–1.90. *Hab.* North, Middle, and northern South America.

B. *Lower part of tibia feathered in front. Upper parts conspicuously striped with black and ochraceous.*

3. **A. involucris.**[2] Remiges broadly tipped with rufous. Wing, 4.85; culmen, 2.00. *Hab.* Southern South America.

Ardetta exilis.

THE AMERICAN LEAST BITTERN.

Little Bittern, PENN. Arct. Zool. II. 1785, 453, no. 359 (part).

Minute Bittern, LATH. Synop. III. 1785, 66 (Jamaica; = ♀ ad.).

Ardea exilis, GMEL. S. N. I. ii. 1788, 645, no. 83 (based on the *Minute Bittern* of LATH. l.c.). — WILS. Am. Orn. VIII. 1814, 37, pl. 65, fig. 4. — NUTT. Man. II. 1834, 66. — AUD. Orn. Biog. III. 1835, 77; V. 1839, 606, pl. 210; Synop. 1839, 263; Birds Am. VI. 1843, 100, pl. 366.

Ardetta exilis, GUNDL. J. f. O. 1856, 345. — BAIRD, B. N. Am. 1858, 673; Cat. N. Am. B. 1859, no. 491. — RIDGW. Nom. N. Am. B. 1881, no. 498. — COUES, Check List, 2d ed. 1882, no. 667.

? *Ardea spadicea*, GMEL. t.c. 641 (Reichenow).

HAB. The whole of temperate North America, north to the British Provinces; West Indies, Middle America, and northern South America, to Brazil. Bermudas.

SP. CHAR. *Adult male:* Pileum, including slight occipital crest, with entire back, scapulars, rump and tail, glossy greenish black, the outer webs of the outer row of scapulars edged with pale buff, forming a narrow longitudinal stripe. Sides of the head and neck bright ochraceous, deepening into reddish chestnut on the nape; chin, throat, and foreneck paler, the first sometimes whitish, with a medial series of dusky and yellowish-buff dashes; the foreneck and jugulum faintly striped with white and pale orange-buff, the latter predominating; on each side the breast a patch of maroon-dusky, the feathers tipped with paler and suffused with blackish, forming tufts of large loose feathers, partly concealed by the large feathers of the jugulum; lower parts whitish, washed with pale creamy-buff. Carpal region, greater wing-coverts, lower webs of tertials and

[1] ARDETTA MINUTA.

Ardea minuta, LINN. S. N. I. 1766, 240. — NAUM. Vög. Deutschl. IX. 1838, 194, pl. 227. — GRAY, Gen. B. III. 556; Cat. Brit. B. 1863, 148.

Botaurus minutus, BOIE, Isis, 1822, 559.

Ardeola minuta, BONAP. Consp. List, 1838, 48.

Ardea danubialis, GMEL. S. N. I. 1788, 637.

Ardea soloniensis, GMEL. l. c.

Botaurus pusillus, BREHM, Vög. Deutschl. 598.

[2] ARDETTA INVOLUCRIS.

Ardea involucris, VIEILL. Enc. Méth. 1823, 1127.

Ardetta involucris, SCL. & SALV. P. Z. S. 1869, 634.

? *Ardea erythromelas*, VIEILL. Enc. Méth. 1121 (based on *Garza roxa y negra*, AZARA, Apunt. III. 182).

Ardeola erythromelas, BONAP. Consp. II. 1855, 134.

Ardea variegata, VIEILL. t.c. 1127 (based on *Garza varia*, AZARA).

tips of primary-coverts, secondaries, and inner primaries, rich cinnamon-rufous; large area, covering middle wing-covert region, pale ochraceous, or buff; remiges and primary-coverts blackish slate, except at tips. "Bill dark olive-brown above, edges of upper mandible and bare frontal space yellow; lower mandible pale yellow, inclining to flesh-color; iris yellow; feet dull greenish yellow; claws brown" (AUDUBON). *Adult female:* Similar to the adult male, but the greenish black replaced by brown (varying from umber-drab to cinnamon, the pileum darker and usually

Adult male.

opaque blackish dusky); the buff stripe along outer border of scapulars much broader and more conspicuous, and the stripes on the foreneck (usually but not always) more distinct. Otherwise exactly like the male. *Young:* Similar to the adult female, but the feathers of the back and scapular region tipped with buff; the stripes on the foreneck also (usually) more distinct.

Length, about 12.00–13.50; expanse, 17.00–18.00. Weight, about $4\frac{3}{4}$ ounces (AUDUBON). Wing, 4.30–5.25; tail, 1.60–2.10; culmen, 1.60–1.90; depth of bill, .28–.35; tarsus, 1.50–1.75; middle toe, 1.40–1.60; bare portion of tibia, .45–.50.[1]

With a considerable series of specimens before us, we can observe no geographical variations other than the slightly smaller size of skins from Demerara and Tehuantepec. As to colors, no tropical examples are brighter than two males from the eastern United States (1549, Carlisle, Pa., and 1090, District of Columbia). The range of individual variation in color is also very slight, though very great as to dimensions.

In a considerable series of Least Bitterns from Guatemala, kindly submitted to us for examination by Mr. Osbert Salvin, there is a single specimen, which, while agreeing very closely in plumage with the adult male of the common North American species, is so different in proportions as to leave little doubt of its specific distinctness. The tarsi and toes are disproportionately shorter than in *A. exilis*, the former measuring only 1.15 and the middle toe 1.12, while the inner toe is just perceptibly longer than the outer, measuring 0.98 against 0.95. The tibiæ are completely feathered, even more so than in *A. involucris*. The other specimens, chiefly from the Lake of Dueñas, are all typical *A. exilis*, mostly young of the year, evidently reared in the locality. Without venturing to name this bird, we give below a full description.[2]

[1] Extremes of twenty-one adult examples.

[2] CHAR. Similar to *A. exilis*, but with the tarsi and toes disproportionately shorter, and the tibiæ completely feathered. *Adult ♂:* Pileum uniform black, with a faint greenish gloss; remainder of the head ochraceous, growing gradually more rufous on the superciliary region; nape bright rufous, becoming nearly chestnut on the lower portion; sides of the neck like the cheeks. Chin and throat immaculate pure white, the lower part of the latter with a very faint wash of pale buff medially; foreneck creamy white, with a narrow mesial stripe of grayish brown. Sides of the breast brownish black, the feathers tipped with light fulvous; remaining lower parts white, tinged with light creamy buff, most distinct laterally; tibiæ deep fulvous; lining of the wings grayish white, purer white anteriorly, where is a spot of mixed ochraceous and dusky on the carpal joint; axillars ash-gray; under-surface of the remiges similar, but deeper. Back and scapulars glossy black, with a faint green reflection, the outer row of interscapular feathers edged exteriorly with light buff, forming, when the feathers are disarranged, a somewhat V-shaped mark, defining the lateral and posterior boundaries of the interscapular region.

The Least Bittern has an extended distribution, being found very nearly throughout the United States, and only not found, so far as we are aware, in the more northerly and eastern portions. It has not been met with by Mr. Boardman near Calais, it is not included by Mr. Verrill as a bird of Oxford County, and is mentioned as rare even in Southern Maine, and is classed as very rare by Mr. Allen, near Springfield, Mass. Like all nocturnal birds, and more especially those species that shelter themselves in the day-time among the rank grass and rushes, it is probably by no means so rare, in many places, as has been supposed. It feeds exclusively in the night-time, and is rarely seen flying during the day. It is not uncommon in eastern Massachusetts, breeding in Fresh Pond marshes, where Mr. Wm. Brewster has met with it both in May and in July. Giraud includes it among the birds of Long Island, where it is usually found hidden in the tall grass and reeds, along the margins of freshwater streams. A few were secured among the salt meadows near Babylon, and on the Hanover Meadow near Pine Brook. It has also been occasionally found on the banks of the Hackensack. Specimens are recorded as having been taken near the city of Brooklyn, and others in a swamp near Fort Hamilton. In the latter place young birds, still unable to fly, were captured. In the Western States it is much more abundant, and in Canada, especially in the neighborhood of the Great Lakes. Mr. McIlwraith mentions it as a common summer resident near Hamilton, and Mr. Kumlien has found it breeding in abundance around Lake Koskonong, in Wisconsin. It appears to be resident in Texas and in Northeastern Mexico. Mr. Dresser met with it, in July and August, in the neighborhood of Matamoras, and occasionally saw it in the vicinity of San Antonio. Mr. Salvin mentions it as found in Guatemala, but whether as a winter visitant or a resident, he does not state. He found it both at Dueñas and at Coban.

It is also found in several of the West India Islands. In Cuba it is given by Dr. Gundlach as a resident throughout the year, and its breeding is inferred. It is mentioned by Gosse as among the birds of Jamaica, where it is not unfrequently seen dodging about the edges of the tall reeds of the morasses, or among the rank sedgy grass that borders the streams. When alarmed, it does not usually fly, but darts into the rushy covert, where the thinness of its form enables it to make its way with ease. When surprised in an open place it crouches, as if expecting to escape observation. In its stomach are found small fishes and crustacea. In Jamaica it is called, according to March, the "Tortoise-shell Bittern." Léotaud names it as one of the birds of Trinidad; but how common it is in that island he was not able to state. It keeps close among the reeds which cover the flooded regions, and is probably quite abundant; although rarely seen, on account of the difficulty of discovering it in the midst of its retreat. It occasionally approaches the edges of narrow watercourses, to fish for the small fry on which it feeds. Its flight is very feeble, and not well sustained. It nests in Trinidad, and has been observed there at all seasons of the year.

Dr. Cooper speaks of it as common among the great fresh marshes of the interior

Rump, upper tail-coverts and tail, uniform plumbeous-black. Anterior and outer lesser wing-coverts, inner secondaries (outer webs) and greater wing-coverts, uniform cinnamon-rufous; posterior, lesser, and all of the middle wing-coverts, light grayish buff (much paler than in *exilis*); tinged with deeper buff, the grayish tints minutely freckled. Primary-coverts and remiges slaty plumbeous, tipped with light cinnamon-rufous.

Wing, 4.60; culmen, 1.68; depth of bill, through nostril, .32; tarsus, 1.15; middle toe, 1.12; inner toe, .98; outer, .95; hallux, .58.

of California. He has met with it along the coast in only a single instance. This was in April, at Santa Barbara. It chiefly frequents the marshes covered with *tule*, or long grass, and is not easily discovered; otherwise we should be probably able to assign it a range as far north as the Columbia River. It is only partially migratory in California. Mr. Ridgway met with a single individual, in May, on the borders of a small stream, among the willows, and not far from Pyramid Lake.

Notwithstanding the impression which prevails, wherever this bird is at all common, that it is unable to sustain a prolonged flight, this idea can hardly be regarded as well founded, as there can be no doubt of the migratory habits of the species. A single specimen is mentioned as captured alive on the rocks of St. David's Head, Bermuda, on the 20th of April, 1853, where it had alighted in its flight to the north; and Major Wedderburn, besides the record of several specimens of this bird taken by him in Bermuda in October and in December, mentions killing one near Boss's Cove, on the 15th of March, while on the wing. With this exception, he was never able to get them to take to wing, they always preferring to run about among the roots of the mangroves, where they could only be found with great difficulty. Wilson speaks of this bird as having been very rarely found on the salt-marshes. A single bird shot near Great Egg Harbor was regarded as something very uncommon. It was seen in the meadows below Philadelphia, on the Delaware and Schuylkill rivers, where it bred every year in the thick tussocks of grass, in swampy places; but neither Wilson nor Audubon seems to have known anything as to its eggs. The latter states that on one occasion he kept a pair alive, feeding them with small fish. They were very expert at catching flies, and would swallow caterpillars and other insects. They were very gentle, and, though they disliked to be handled, made no attempt to strike at any one. They would climb with ease from the floor to the top of the curtain with their feet and claws. At the approach of night they became much more lively. The same author states that this bird breeds in Florida and in the Carolinas. Dr. Holbrook found it also breeding near Charleston. The nest was usually on the ground, and was composed of dried and decayed weeds. The number of eggs, as he states, is three; but his account of them is so incorrect as to throw doubt over his whole description of nesting and eggs. When startled, this bird utters a low cry, like "*quâ;*" but its ordinary cry is a rough croak — a feeble imitation of the note of the Great Blue Heron. Its flight, which by day is apparently so weak, at dusk is quite different. It then may be seen passing steadily along, in the manner of the larger Herons. In the day it can hardly be induced to fly, and it then moves in a confused and uncertain manner. Its food generally consists of snails, slugs, tadpoles, young frogs, water-lizards, and occasionally small shrews and field-mice.

Mr. Nelson speaks of this bird as being a common summer resident everywhere in the marshes and sloughs of Illinois, arriving the 1st of May, and nesting early in June. He has always found its nest supported, at from two to three feet above the water, by the surrounding rushes. It is described as a very frail structure — a thin platform from one to three inches thick, with scarcely depression enough in the centre to prevent the eggs from rolling out. Small dry pieces of reeds are used in building it. The eggs are usually from two to six in number. If approached while on the nest, the female generally steps quietly to one side; but if suddenly surprised, takes to flight. Each nest is usually placed by itself; but, in exceptional cases, six or eight may sometimes be found in close proximity.

Mr. B. F. Goss informs me that the Least Bittern usually constructs a little platform nest a few feet from the ground, on broken-down weeds and grasses, just large enough to hold the eggs, which are usually four in number. There is a coarse cane-like grass growing on the borders of the lakes and rivers of Wisconsin; this is some eight feet in height, and is a favorite breeding-haunt for this bird.

Mr. N. B. Moore writes from Manatee, Florida, that on the 26th of April, 1874, he found this species with already fully grown young ones. The only other Heron having young ones so far advanced at that time was the Great White Egret. It feeds chiefly from a perch over the water, clinging to the upright stems of grasses and sedges, feeding apparently as comfortably thus as when perched on the depressed stems or blades of the same, on the branches of willows, or on other small trees that overhang or dip into the water. It dodges away among the saw-grass and sedges that serve for a hiding-place, clambering with ease along the upright stems, or twisting and turning along the tangled masses of the same in the manner of a Rail.

It has been found breeding in Wisconsin in great abundance by Professor Kumlien, and the nest was always near the ground and usually among reeds, not far from water, and was generally very slight — a mere collection of decayed rushes and coarse grasses, barely enough to keep the eggs from the damp ground. The eggs, usually six or seven in number, are white, with a very slight tinge of greenish. They are of a rounded oval shape, and there is no difference as to size in either end; they are entirely unspotted. Two eggs in my collection, Nos. 114 and 1269, give the extreme of variation — one measuring 1.32 inches in length by 1 inch in breadth, the other 1.25 inches by 1.00.

Family CICONIIDÆ. — The Storks.

Char. Large, Heron-like birds, with the bill much longer than the head, thick through the base, and more or less elongate-conical; the nostrils sub-basal, more or less superior, and bored into the bony substance of the bill, without overhanging or surrounding membrane; maxilla without any lateral groove. Legs covered with small, longitudinally-hexagonal scales; claws short, depressed, their ends broad and convex, resting upon horny, crescentic "shoes;" hallux with its base elevated decidedly above the base of the anterior toes.

The above characters are sufficient to define this family, which is more intimately related to the Ibises (*Ibididæ*) and Spoonbills (*Plataleidæ*) than to the Herons (see page 2). There are two well-marked sub-families, with the following characters: —

Sub-family **Ciconiinæ.** Bill elongate-conical, acute, compressed, the end not decurved, though sometimes recurved. Nostrils rather lateral than superior. Toes very short, the middle one much less than half the tarsus (only a little more than one third); lateral toes nearly equal; claws short, broad, nail-like.

Sub-family **Tantalinæ.** Bill elongated, subconical, subcylindrical, the end attenuated and decurved, with the tip rounded; nostrils decidedly superior; toes long, the middle one, one half or more the length of the tarsus; lateral toes unequal, the outer decidedly longer than the inner; claws moderately lengthened, rather narrow, claw-like.

Synopsis of the American Genera.

Sub-family CICONIINÆ. — The True Storks.

1. **Euxenura.**[1] Bill moderately large, its upper and lower outlines straight throughout; entire head and neck feathered, except the lores and a bare strip along each side of the throat. *Tail abbreviated and deeply forked*, the feathers very rigid, *the lower tail-coverts elongated* (extending beyond the true tail), *and stiffened, so as to resemble true rectrices!* (type, *Ardea maguari*, Gmel.).
2. **Mycteria.** Bill enormously large, the terminal half recurved. Entire head and neck naked, except a longitudinal hairy patch on the occiput. Tail and tail-coverts normal (type, *Mycteria americana*, Gmel. *nec* Linn.[2]).

Sub-family TANTALINÆ. — The Wood Ibises.

3. **Tantalus.**[3] Adult with the whole head and upper half of the neck naked, the skin hard and scurfy; crown covered with a quadrate, or somewhat shield-shaped, smooth horny plate, and skin of nape transversely wrinkled, or corrugated. Nostrils sub-basal; tertials longer than primaries, and with their webs compact or normal (type, *Tantalus loculator*, Linn.).
4. **Pseudotantalus.** Adult with only the fore part of the head naked, the hinder part and entire neck densely feathered; naked skin of fore part of head smooth. Nostrils strictly basal; tertials shorter than primaries, and with their webs somewhat decomposed. Bill, legs, and tail very much longer, and basal outline of the bill of different contour (type, *Tantalus ibis*, Linn.).

The Wood Ibises form a very natural group of about five species, usually included in the single genus *Tantalus*, inhabiting, like their kindred, the Storks, Jabirus, and Adjutants, the warmer

[1] Genus Euxenura, Ridgway.
Ciconia (part), Briss. Orn. V. 1760, 369, no. 3. — Bonap. Consp. II. 1855, 104, et Auct.
Ardea (part), Gmel. S. N. I. ii. 1788, 623.
Euxenura, Ridgw. Bull. U. S. Geol. & Geog. Survey Terr. IV. no. 1, Feb. 5, 1878, 250 (type, *Ardea maguari*, Gmel).

This genus is very decidedly distinct from *Dissoura*, Cabanis (type, *Ardea episcopus*, Bodd.), the only resemblance between them, in addition to the usual Ciconine characters, consisting in the similar form of the tail.

[2] While giving a correct diagnosis of his genus *Mycteria*, with *M. americana* as type, Linnæus (S. N. I. 1766, 233) describes as the latter, in unmistakable terms, the birds afterward named *Ardea maguari* by Gmelin. The references given by Linnæus, however, refer mainly to the true *Mycteria!*

[3] The association of the *Tantalinæ* with the Storks, as has latterly been done by several authors, seems a very proper procedure, even the external structure showing clearly that such are the true affinities of the group. The internal structure affords still more conclusive testimony to this effect, as the following scheme, adapted from Garrod (Proceedings of the Zoological Society of London for 1875, p. 301), may show: —

Ciconiidæ (including *Tantalus*).	Ibididæ (including *Plataleidæ*).
1. Skull holorhinal.	1. Skull schizorhinal.
2. Angle of the mandible truncated.	2. Angle of the mandible produced and recurved.
3. *Pectoralis major* muscle in two layers, — a superficial one, and a deep one, easily separable from the other.	3. *Pectoralis major* muscle simple, not separable into distinct layers.
4. *Accessory femoro-caudal* muscle absent.	4. *Accessory femoro-caudal* muscle well developed.
5. *Semitendinosus* muscle tendinous for its distal half.	5. *Semitendinosus* muscle muscular throughout.
6. "No slip leaves the *biceps cubiti* muscle to join the *tensor patagii longus*."	6. "A small muscular belly is sent from the *biceps cubiti* to the tendon of the *tensor patagii longus* muscle."

Professor Garrod adds to the above tabulation of the diagnostic characters of the *Ciconiidæ* and *Ibididæ*, that "There are many other structural peculiarities, which make it perfectly certain that *Tantalus* is a member of the *Ciconiidæ*, and not an aberrant one, either."

regions of America, Africa, and Asia. Of the five species of *Tantalinæ* admitted by authors, we have seen, in addition to *Tantalus loculator*, only the *T. ibis*, LINN., from Northern and Eastern Africa. This is so different in form and other characters as to seem entitled to separate generic rank; and finding no name already established or available, we have proposed that given above.[1] The Indian Wood Ibis (*T. leucocephalus*, GM.) and all the other Old World species [2] agree closely in structure with the African species (*T. ibis*).

GENUS **MYCTERIA**, LINNÆUS.

Mycteria, LINN. S. N. ed. 10, I. 1758, 140; ed. 12, I. 1766, 232 (type, *M. americana*, GMEL. ex LINN.).

GEN. CHAR. Very large, Stork-like birds, with enormous, somewhat conical and rather recurved beaks, and with head and neck bare of feathers. Bill enormously large, longer than the very long

M. Americana.

[1] Cf. Proc. U. S. Nat. Mus. Vol. V. p. 550.

[2] *T. lacteus*, TEMM., of Java and Sumatra, and *T. longuimembris*, SWINH., of South China (Amoy).

tarsus, much compressed, the lateral outlines elongate-conical, but both curved upward for the terminal half (the gonys most so); depth of the bill at the base equal to about two ninths the length of the culmen; gonys considerably longer than the mandibular rami; nostrils small, longitudinal, in the form of an elongated ellipse, without membrane, but overhung by a sharp projecting bony edge. Legs very long; middle toe a little less than one third the tarsus; lateral toes considerably shorter, the outer a little the longer; hallux about half the length of the inner toe, its articulation elevated decidedly above that of the anterior toes; middle toe united to both the lateral toes at the base by well-developed webs, the outer of which is the larger, these webs extending, narrowly, along each side of the toes for their whole length; claws short, nail-like, or flattened above and with broad rounded ends; bare portion of the tibia much more than one half the tarsus; legs covered everywhere and uniformly with small, longitudinal, hexagonal scales; toes with transverse scutellæ for terminal half. Plumage rather hard and compact above, looser below, the feathers of the posterior parts with their webs somewhat decomposed; upper greater wing-coverts and tertials well developed, long, broad, and compact, the latter extending beyond the tips of the primaries, as well as much beyond the end of the tail; primaries very stiff, their inner webs sinuated near the base.[1] Tail short, a little more than one third as long as the wing, even, the feathers broad, round-ended, and moderately stiff. Occiput and upper part of the nape covered by a patch of rather short and sparse hair-like feathers, the rest of the head and neck bare.

This genus, as defined above, embraces a single species belonging to tropical America, the *M. americana*, GMEL. ex LINN. More or less nearly related Old World genera are *Ephippiorhynchus*, BONAP. (type, *Mycteria senegalensis*, SHAW), *Xenorhynchus*, BONAP. (type, *M. australis*, SHAW), and *Leptoptilos*, LESS. (type, *Ciconia crumenifera*, CUVIER). These I have not been able to examine.

Mycteria americana.

THE JABIRU.

Mycteria americana, LINN. S. N. ed. 10, 1758, 140, no. 1 (part[2]); ed. 12, I. 1766, 232 (part, excl. diagnosis, which = *Euxenura maguari*). — GMEL. S. N. I. 1788, 616. — LATH. Ind. Orn. II. 1790, 670. — BONAP. Consp. II. 1855, 107. — GRAY. Handl. III. 1871, 35, no. 10190. — SCL. & SALV. Nom. Neotr. 1873, 126. — RIDGW. Nom. N. Am. B. 1881, no. 499. — COUES, Check List, 2d ed. 1882, no. 654.

Le Jabiru, de Cayenne, BUFF. Pl. Enl. 1770–84, pl. 817 (adult).

American Jabiru, LATH. Synop. III. i. 1785, 22, pl. 75.

Ciconia mycteria, BURM. Th. Bras. III. 1856, 418.

HAB. Tropical America, south to Buenos Ayres; north, casually, to Southern Texas. No West Indian record.

SP. CHAR. *Adult* (No. 17105, "South America"): Plumage entirely white; bill, legs, and feet, with naked portion of head and neck, black; crop, and lower portion of neck all round, reddish (bright red in life). Wing, 26.00; tail, 9.50; culmen, 12.30; depth of bill at base, 2.50; tarsus, 11.50; middle toe, 4.20; bare portion of tibia, 6.50. *Young, transition plumage* (No. 87485, La Palma, Costa Rica, April 21, 1882; C. C. Nutting): Pileum and occiput clothed with dusky black hair-like feathers, these longest on the occiput, where they form somewhat of a bushy crest; feathered portion of lower neck light brownish gray; rump, upper tail-coverts, and tail, white; rest of upper part soft brownish gray, irregularly mixed with pure white feathers (of the adult livery), these most numerous among the lesser wing-coverts and anterior scapulars; primaries white, tinged with gray at ends. Lower parts entirely white. Bill, all the naked

[1] The wings of the only specimen at present accessible to us are much damaged, so that the wing-formula and the exact character of the outline of the inner webs of the quills cannot be ascertained satisfactorily.

[2] Linnæus's diagnosis, "Magnitudo Ciconiæ, alba, remigibus rectricibusque nigro-purpurascentibus," will not apply at all to this species, but is obviously applicable to *Euxenura maguari* (see page 77). The generic diagnosis, however, applies to *Mycteria*, as do also most of the references cited.

portion of head and neck (except lower portion of the latter), legs, and feet, black; "collar round lower neck bright scarlet; iris brown." Wing, 24.50; tail, 9.50; culmen, 9.75; tarsus, 11.25; middle toe, 4.50.

This species is of accidental occurrence within the limits of the United States. There is but one record of its capture, and that very imperfect. It is said to have occurred near Galveston, Texas. The Jabiru, or American Stork, appears to have much in common, in its manner of life, with the *Ciconiidæ* of the Old World. It is to be met with in portions of Central America and the larger portion of South America, but is of rare occurrence farther north. It is abundant on the seaboard and on the rivers of Demerara, and mention of its presence there is occasionally made by Mr. C. B. Brown in his "Canoe and Camp Life in British Guiana." He speaks of frequently meeting with it, in company with *Ardea cocoi*, and of the peculiar and striking appearance it presents, with its long, stout, up-curved beak, black bare head, and scarlet-banded neck. When wounded and brought to bay, it will inflate the skin of the scarlet-colored portion of its neck like a great bladder. It stands fully five feet in height, and walks with a slow and stately tread. On one occasion he passed near one of the nests of this bird. It was on a lofty tree, and appeared to be a large flat platform, on the edge of which two young Jabirus were standing. It was seemingly in all respects a complete counterpart of the familiar nest of the White Stork of Europe. An egg in the cabinet of Count Turati, of Milan, Italy, is of a rounded oval shape, of a uniform olive-green color, and measures 3.33 inches by 2.20.

Genus **TANTALUS**, Linnæus.

Tantalus, Linn. S. N. ed. 10, I. 1758, 140; ed. 12, I. 1766, 240 (type, *T. loculator*, Linn.).
Tantalides, Reichenb. Hand-b. 1851, p. xiv. Same type. (Not of Wagler, 1832, =*Plegadis*, Kaup.)

Gen. Char. Large, Stork-like birds, with long legs, neck, and beak, the latter attenuated and decurved terminally, much as in the true Ibises. Bill much thickened at the base, both vertically and laterally, much attenuated terminally, where almost abruptly, but not greatly, decurved. Nostrils bored directly into the bony substance of the bill, the maxilla destitute of any trace of a nasal groove. Legs covered with small longitudinally hexagonal scales. Toes long, very slender, the middle one about, or a little more than, half the length of the tarsus, the outer one reaching to the middle of the subterminal phalanx of the middle toe, the inner much shorter, not reaching the subterminal articulation of the middle toe; hallux about equal to the inner toe and claw; bare portion of the tibia longer than the middle toe, the upper third, or more, without scales, and

T. loculator.

smooth; web between inner and middle toes well developed, but smaller than the outer web. Plumage compact above, loose below, the feathers of the neck small, their webs somewhat decomposed. Remiges well developed, the tertials reaching to the end of the primaries, the latter hard, concave beneath, the outer four with their inner webs deeply sinuated at or anterior to the middle portion; second, third, and fourth quills nearly equal, or longest. Tail short (shorter than bill or tarsus), even, of 12 broad, stiff feathers. *Adult*, with the whole head and upper half of the nape bare, covered with a hard, scurfy, and more or less corrugated skin. *Young*, with the whole head and neck, except the chin and forehead, feathered.

Tantalus loculator.

THE WOOD IBIS.

Wood Pelican, CATESBY, Carolina, pl. 81.

Tantalus loculator, LINN. S. N. ed. 10, I. 1758, 140, no. 1 (ex KLEIN, 127; CATESBY, I. 81); ed. 12, 1766, I. 241, no. 1. — WILS. Am. Orn. VIII. 1814, 39, pl. 66, fig. 1. — NUTT. Man. II. 1834, 82. — AUD. Orn. Biog. III. 1835, 128, pl. 216; Synop. 1839, 259; Birds Am. VI. 1843, 64, pl. 361 (adult). — CASS. in Baird's B. N. Am. 1858, 682. — BAIRD, Cat. N. Am. B. 1859, no. 497. — COUES, Key, 1872, 262; Check List, 1873, no. 444; 2d ed. 1882, no. 648; Birds N. W. 1874; 513. — RIDGW. Nom. N. Am. B. 1881, no. 500.

Tantalus plumicollis, SPIX. Av. Bras. pl. 85 (young).

"*Ibis nandasson; I. nandapoa*, VIEILL." (GRAY & BONAP.)

Le Curiaca, de Cayenne, BUFF. Pl. Enl. 1770–84, pl. 868 (adult).

Wood Ibis, PENN. Arct. Zool. II. 1785, 458, no. 360.

Tantalus ichthyophagus, the Gannet, BARTRAM, Travels, 1791, 293.

Hab. The whole of tropical and warm-temperate America; north to New York (casual), Ohio, Indiana, Wisconsin, Colorado, Utah, Nevada, and California; south to Ecuador and Buenos Ayres.

Sp. Char. *Adult:* Head and upper half of the neck naked, and covered with a hard, scurfy skin, of a dusky color; the vertex covered by a somewhat shield-shaped horny plate, of a lighter color, the neck with transverse, somewhat ovate, bark-like, rugose scales. Plumage in general uniform white, the primary-coverts, remiges, and rectrices black, with metallic purple, bronze, and green reflections. "Bill dusky yellowish brown, the edges yellow; sides of the head dark bluish purple, upper part of head horn-color, or dull grayish yellow, the rest of the bare skin of the same

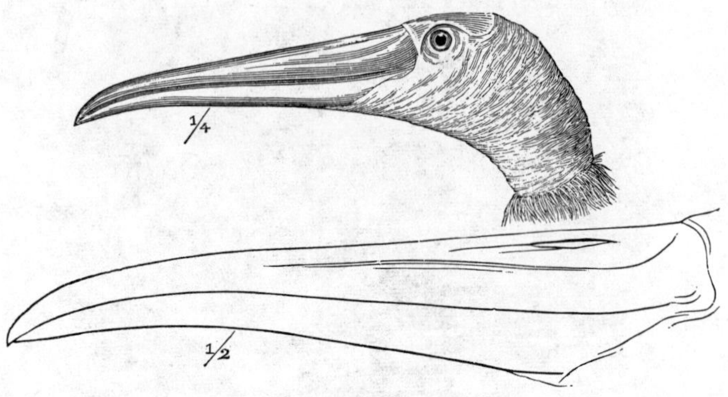

tint, many of the scales anteriorly blue; iris deep brown, at a distance seeming black; tibia and tarsus indigo-blue; toes above black, on the lateral and hind toes, however, many of the scutellæ bluish gray, the webs pale yellowish flesh-color; claws black" (Audubon). *Young:* Head and neck covered with rather scant, somewhat "woolly" feathers, excepting the forehead, anterior part of the crown, lores, anterior portion of malar region, chin, and anterior part of throat, which are covered with a smooth skin. Head and neck grayish brown, darkest on the occiput (where dark sooty), growing gradually paler below. Rest of the plumage as in the adult, but the black feathers of wings and tail less metallic.[1] *Immature:* Head bare and corrugated, as in the adult; neck feathered, as in the young. Wing, 17.60–19.50; tail, 6.10–7.30; culmen, 7.55–9.30; depth of bill through nostril, 1.55–1.90; tarsus, 7.00–8.50; middle toe, 3.85–4.30; bare part of tibia, 5.00–6.25;[2] weight, $11\frac{3}{4}$ lbs.; total length, $44\frac{1}{2}$ inches; extent of wings, 62 inches (Audubon).

Varying accounts have been given of the habits and peculiarities of this remarkable species; and although some of these divergencies have at first appeared irreconcilable with each other, and as if one or the other statement must be utterly erroneous, more recent investigations have done much to explain and harmonize these apparent discords. Bartram, who enjoyed many opportunities for observing the habits of this species in Florida, characterizes it as solitary and indolent, seldom associating in flocks, usually frequenting the banks of the principal rivers and marshes, especially where these are inundated, as well as deserted rice-plantations near the sea-coast. He describes it as a feathered hermit standing listless and alone on the topmost limb of some tall decayed cypress, its neck drawn in

[1] According to Audubon, "the young are dusky gray all over, the quills and tail brownish black; the head all covered with down, excepting just at the base of the bill. After the first moult, the bare space extends over the head and cheeks; the downy feathers of the hind head and neck are dusky; the general color of the plumage is white, the quills and tail as in the adult, but with less gloss."

[2] Ten adults measured.

upon its shoulders, and its enormous bill resting, like a scythe, upon its breast. In this manner the bird is said to pass most of its time, until awakened by the calls of hunger; and it is also mentioned that it is easily approached and shot, and is by many of the inhabitants accounted excellent food. These were Mr. Bartram's observations; and for several of his statements he is severely taken to task by Mr. Audubon.

Dr. Henry Bryant, however, who has since gone over the same ground on the St. John's as Bartram did, and in the same way, remarks, in commenting upon Audubon's criticisms, that the latter should have remembered that the habits of birds vary at different times and in different places, and states that, strange as it may seem when the long period of time that has elapsed is taken into view, his Journal is almost an exact repetition of Bartram's. While in Florida he never saw a *flock* of Wood Ibises except at their breeding-places; and even there, except when they were disturbed, they flew off and returned either singly or in pairs. He did not see them feeding in more than a few instances, and then there was never more than a pair at a time. The stomachs of all those that were killed by Dr. Bryant contained only crayfish, which could not readily be procured in the manner Audubon declares to be its only method of feeding.

The Wood Ibis is found distributed over a large portion of South America, Central America, Mexico, and the southern portions of North America. It is found in all the Gulf States, is most abundant in Florida, straggles into Georgia, South Carolina, Tennessee, and Kentucky, and is not uncommon in Southern Illinois and Missouri, but occurring more rarely in Colorado, Kansas, Nevada, and Utah. Burmeister speaks of it as common on the banks of the Parana River, in small flocks, going from one lagoon to another, rarely seen except when flying. When on the ground it always conceals itself in the reeds, and is hardly ever visible there.

Mr. Salvin mentions it as not uncommon about the large rivers in the forests of the Pacific coast region of Guatemala. It is there known among the Spanish by the name of *Alcatraz*. Mr. Salvin afterward met with it on the Pacific seacoast of Guatemala among the lagoons; and Mr. G. C. Taylor mentions meeting with it in Honduras, near the village of Lamani.

Referring to this species, Mr. C. Barrington Brown, in his work on British Guiana, makes frequent mention of meeting with large birds, called by some, Sowewies, by others, Negroscopes. He found them numerous in that region, and to be seen in large numbers on the sand-beaches of the River Essequibo. He describes their heads and necks as bare of feathers and as covered with a hard black skin divided by furrows into plates. Their white bodies contrasted with their black wings. They were frequently to be seen soaring high up into the heavens, in circles, mounting up higher and higher, until they appeared like mere specks.

In the Mississippi Valley this bird wanders occasionally as far north as Chicago and Racine; in the Red River region of Texas it was observed by Lieutenant M'Cauley as far up as the Staked Plains. It was also seen by Mr. Henshaw at Rush Lake in Utah, where he procured two specimens in October. Mr. Bischoff met with it in Nevada in July.

This bird is said to congregate at times in large numbers high up in the air, where, with hardly any apparent motion, it sweeps in extended circles, in a manner not unlike the graceful movements of the Turkey Vulture, with which bird it is also not unfrequently seen to associate.

Dr. Gundlach includes it among the birds that breed in Cuba; and it probably occurs in most of the West India Islands that afford suitable places of resort. Léotaud states that it occasionally visits Trinidad, where he has often met with it perched upon the large trees that grow on the edges of swampy places, or walking on the borders of pools. He does not give it as a resident of the island, but regarded it as a mere winter visitant, only seen from July to October. He speaks of it as eminently sociable, as being usually seen in small flocks, and of its food as chiefly reptiles.

Mr. Dresser mentions it as of not uncommon occurrence near San Antonio. He was informed by the planters that it breeds on the Brazos and Colorado rivers, Texas. Mr. Boardman informs me that in Florida it is usually known as a "Gannet," from the appearance it presents in the air as it flies. He found it nesting in swamps, in cypress trees, the nests resembling those of Herons. In these this bird roosts throughout the year, when not occupied in incubation.

Dr. Bryant visited two of its breeding-places. The first was in a large cypress swamp at the head-waters of the St. Sebastian. The trees were more than a hundred feet in height, and he could not by any means get access to the nests. The Ibises were breeding in company with the large White Egret. The other breeding-place was in the cypress swamp forming the southern border of Lake Ashby, where there were probably a thousand pairs nesting. Every available spot on the tops of the cypresses had been taken possession of by a pair, and lower down were nests of the Anhingas. No other bird was breeding there except a single pair of Fish-hawks, whose nest was surrounded by those of the Ibis. On first approaching the shore, the birds all rose and flew round in circles, and after a few of them had been killed, flew off; but soon returned, and alighted out of reach among the trees. The nests were all made of small twigs, and seemed to have been occupied for many years. The cavity was quite deep, and carefully lined with long moss. The eggs were three in number, nearly white, when not soiled by the parent bird or stained by the moss. Three specimens, selected by Dr. Bryant, gave the following measurements, — the longest 2.56 by 1.54 inches, the broadest 2.28 by 1.57 inches, and one of average size 2.32 by 1.61 inches. Incubation had commenced by the 1st of April, and many of the young were already hatched. The largest were about the size of a Pigeon, and covered with white down.

Mr. Audubon's observations relative to the habits of this bird led him to some conclusions which are not so general as he supposed, and which the experience of others shows to be not without exceptions. According to him it is rarely met with singly, even after the breeding-season. He states that a number of these birds get together to feed, that they first dance about in the water to render it muddy, and then take advantage of this condition to kill the reptiles and fish in large numbers before eating them. Without discrediting this statement, it is yet apparent that this is by no means its universal, or even its common, course; and much of the food found in its stomach could not have been procured in this way.

He describes its flight as heavy on rising from the ground; its neck is then deeply curved downward, its wings flap heavily, and its legs are not stretched out behind until it has proceeded several yards. It then ascends with great celerity, generally in a spiral direction, in silence, if not alarmed; if frightened, it utters a rough guttural croaking note. It proceeds in a direct flight, with alternate flapping and sailing, the latter being more prolonged. It alights on trees with more ease than the Heron, and either stands erect, or crouches on the branch in the manner of a Wild Turkey. When at rest it places its bill against its breast, while the neck seems to shrink between the shoulders. In this position one may sometimes see fifty on the same tree. In the spring months it collects in large flocks before returning to its breeding-place. When a breeding-place has been once chosen, this is resorted to for many years in succession, and the birds are with difficulty made to abandon it. This Ibis feeds largely on fishes, and also devours frogs, young alligators, wood-rats, various kinds of young birds, crabs, snakes, turtles, and the like. It is very tenacious of life, and if wounded resists vigorously, and is dangerous to approach. It is very tough and oily, and unfit for food.

Mr. Moore states that the Wood Ibis, when feeding, rakes the oozy bottom, or the marine plants, in the manner of several Herons, to startle their prey, crayfish, minnows, sirens, etc. It keeps its long bill in the water, and open two or three inches at the tip, the latter in contact with the mud, at about the depth of the object sought. In this position it walks slowly about, raking the bottom with first one foot, then the other, as each is moved forward to make a step, and just before its weight is thrown upon it. Many of the animals on which the bird feeds are startled from their coverts by this raking, and in their fright take shelter within the open bill of their enemy.

This Ibis feeds both in fresh and in salt water. Mr. Moore counted, on the 28th of February, 114 of this species feeding in one flock in a very shallow and muddy pond, where they were apparently finding many sirens.

Dr. Berlandier states that the Wood Ibis inhabits the coast of the Gulf of Mexico, and is found ten leagues from it about the lakes, and especially in low and marshy places. It occurs in flocks, and is found in summer — in the months of June, July, and August — in the vicinity of Matamoras. It is in appearance a very stupid bird, and is known as the *Tagarates*.

The eggs of this species are of a uniform dull white color, and vary in shape from a rounded oval to a nearly exact oval shape; one end is always a little more obtuse than the other. They average about 2.50 inches in length by 2 inches in breadth. One from Para, collected by John E. Warren, Esq., of Troy, measures 2.78 inches in length by 1.85 in breadth, which does not correspond with Dr. Bryant's measurements.

Family IBIDIDÆ. — The Ibises.

Ibidinæ, Reichenb. Handb. 1851, pp. xiii, xiv (part : includes *Tantalus, Numenius*, and *Pelidna !*)
Ibidinae, Bonap. Consp. II. 1857, 150.
Ibididæ, Ridgw., Bull. U. S. Geol. and Geog. Survey Terr. IV. no. 1, Feb. 5, 1878, 221.

Char. Wading birds of medium to rather large size, the bill much elongated, attenuated, more or less, toward the end, and bent downward, more or less decidedly, in sickle-fashion, like that of the Curlews (*Numenius*). Nostrils sub-basal, latero-superior, with more or less of a membrane above and behind; nasal fossæ continued forward to the very extremity of the maxilla in the form of a deep, narrow, continuous groove. Hallux almost incumbent; claws slender, projecting far beyond the ends of the toes.

The true Ibises form an eminently natural group of wading birds, distinguished from their nearest allies by the above characters. The species are moderately numerous (about twenty-six being known), and are dispersed over the warmer regions of the earth — America possessing a larger number than any other country (nine species, not including several of doubtful validity, or about one third of those known). Of the exotic species, Africa possesses about nine (two of them in common with Southern Europe), Asia five, and Australia two. A very great diversity of form and plumage is to be seen among the various species, some being trim and graceful in their build, and others uncouth, with Vulture-like head and neck — some plain in colors, while others are among the most brilliant of birds. The scarlet plumage of *Eudocimus ruber* is not surpassed in nature for pureness and intensity of color, and the beautiful decomposed tertial plumes of *Ibis æthiopicus* are scarcely excelled in gracefulness. The species of *Molybdophanes, Theristicus,* and *Cercibis,* however, possess but little beauty.

The family is divisible into two well-defined sections, which may be termed sub-families, distinguished mainly by the character of the tarsal scutellation. They may be defined as follows: —

Sub-family **Ibidinæ**. Front of the tarsus covered with hexagonal scales.

Sub-family **Eudociminæ**. Front of the tarsus with large, transverse scutellæ, arranged in a more or less continuous single series.

Both the above sub-families are represented in America, but only the latter in the northern continent. The North American genera may be recognized by the following characters: —

SUB-FAMILY EUDOCIMINÆ.[1] — THE IBISES.

Eudocimus. Head of adult wholly naked anteriorly. Feathers of the pileum short, close, and blended, and those of the neck not distinctly lanceolate. Colors plain white or red, with black wing-tips, in adults, dull gray and white in young.

Plegadis. Head of adult wholly feathered, except the lores; feathers of the pileum distinctly lanceolate and slightly elongated, forming a slightly rounded crest when erected. Colors highly metallic, of varied tints; in adult, metallic greenish, bronze or purple above, plain brown beneath, in young.

GENUS **EUDOCIMUS**, WAGLER.[2]

Eudocimus, WAGL. Isis, 1832, 1232 (type, *Tantalus ruber,* LINN.).
Guara, "JOAN DE LÁET.," REICHENB. Handb. 1851, p. xiv (same type).
"*Paribis,* GEOFFROY."
Leucibis, REICHENB. Handb. 1851, p. xiv (type, *Tantalus alber,* LINN.).

GEN. CHAR. — Bill moderately slender, attenuated toward the end, strongly decurved; bare portion of the tibia equal to or rather shorter than the outer toe; middle toe, with claw, shorter than the tarsus; inner toe (without claw) reaching to or a little beyond the subterminal articulation of the middle toe; outer toe reaching to or beyond the middle of the subterminal phalanx of the middle toe; hallux about equal to the basal phalanx of the inner toe; claws short, moderately curved, that of the middle toe more or less bent outwardly toward the tip, its inner projecting

[1] For a more comprehensive account of the birds of this family, the reader is referred to the following special papers: —

(1) *Review of the Ibidinæ, or Sub-family of the Ibises,* by D. G. Elliot, F.R.S.E., etc., in Proc. Zool. Soc., London, 1877, pp. 477–510.

(2) *Systematische Uebersicht der Schreitvögel* (*Gressores*), etc., von Dr. Ant. Reichenow, in Jour. für Orn., 1877 (the Ibises on pp. 143–146).

[2] Cf. ELLIOT, P. Z. S. 1877, 482; SCL. & SALV., Ibis, Oct. 1878, 449, foot-note. The latter say: "Ibis was applied by Savigny in 1810 to the Sacred Ibis, before Vieillot used it for the former group [i. e. *I. alba* and *I. rubra*], for which, consequently, *Eudocimus* of Wagler is the correct term."

edge convex. Anterior half of the head bare (in the adult) including the forehead, lores, orbital and malar regions, chin, and more or less of the throat; in the young, this bare skin more restricted. Feathers of the head and neck dense but rather soft, with rather distinct outlines, but with somewhat truncated tips. Primaries extending a little beyond the tertials, the second and third quills longest and nearly equal, first a little shorter than the fourth; inner webs of outer four slightly sinuated toward their ends.

Synopsis of Species.

1. **E. ruber.** *Adult:* Ends of several outer primaries glossy blue-black; rest of plumage entirely uniform rich pure scarlet, the shafts of the primaries white, as far as the black tips. Bill dusky or reddish; bare skin of head pinkish, or lake-red; legs and feet red. *Young:* Dark brownish gray, the belly white. Wing, 10.80–11.00; tail, 4.10–4.80; culmen, 6.00–6.50; depth of bill, .70; tarsus, 3.70–3.80; middle toe, 2.55–2.60. *Hab.* Tropical America, on the Atlantic side; accidental (?) in Louisiana and Texas.
2. **E. albus.** Ends of several outer primaries glossy greenish black; rest of plumage entirely pure white. Bill, naked portion of head, legs, and feet, reddish (pale yellowish in dried skins); iris pale blue. *Young:* Uniform grayish brown, the rump, base of tail, and under parts white; head and neck streaked with white and grayish, the former feathered nearly to the bill. Wing, 10.30–11.75; tail, 4.00–5.00; culmen, 4.15–6.30; depth of bill, .60–.72; tarsus, 3.10–4.00; middle toe, 2.15–2.70. *Hab.:* Southern States, north, casually, to Connecticut, Eastern Pennsylvania, Illinois, and Utah; south to Brazil and throughout West Indies.

Eudocimus ruber.

THE SCARLET IBIS.

Tantalus ruber, LINN. S. N. I. 1766, 241, no. 5. — WILSON, Am. Orn. VIII. 1814, 41, pl. lxvi.
Eudocimus ruber, WAGL., Isis, 1832, 1232. — RIDGW. Nom. N. Am. B. 1882, no. 502. — COUES, Check-List, 2d ed. 1882, no. 652.
Scolopax rubra, SCOPOLI, Bemerk. ed. Günth. 1770, 106, no. 130.
Ibis rubra, VIEILL. Nouv. Dict. XVI. 1817, 22. — NUTT. Man. II. 1834, 84. — AUD. Orn. Biog. V. 1839, 62; Synop. 1839, 257; Birds Am. VI. 1843, 53, pl. 359 (adult and young). — CASSIN, in Baird's Birds N. Am. 1858, 683. — BAIRD, Cat. N. Am. B. 1859, no. 498. — COUES, Key, 1872, 264; Check List, 1873, no. 447. — SCL. & SALV. Nom. Neotr. 1873, 126. — BOUCARD, Catal. Av. 1876, 48, no. 1337.

Hab. — Chiefly the northern shores of South America, but also occurs sparingly among the West Indian Islands and on the Gulf Coast of Middle America; accidental (?) in Louisiana and Southern Texas.

SP. CHAR. — *Adult:* Ends of the four outer primaries glossy blue-black, with a steel-blue reflection; rest of the plumage entirely uniform rich pure scarlet, the shafts of the primaries, as far as the black tips, pure white. Bill grayish-black;[1] bare skin of the head pale lake-red or pinkish; legs and feet red. *Young:* Brownish gray, much darker than in *E. albus;* abdomen white.

Length, about 28.00-30.00; expanse, 40.00–45.00; wing, 10.80–11.00; tail, 4.10–4.80; culmen, 6.00–6.50; depth of bill, .70; tarsus, 3.70–3.80; middle toe, 2.55–2.60; bare portion of tibia, 2.00–2.40.

The scarlet color of this splendid bird is probably not exceeded in purity and intensity. It is, in fact, the very perfection of that color. It far surpasses the red of any Passerine bird known to us, even the plumage of the Scarlet Tanager (*Pyranga rubra*) appearing dull and harsh beside it.

The black tips of the primaries do not always end abruptly, but in some specimens this color

[1] Audubon describes the bill as "pale lake." This, however, is not the case with any specimens which we have examined. He also says that the quills are *white* — an evident mistake, the *shafts* of the quills having no doubt been meant.

is continued anteriorly along the edge of the quills for an inch or less, in the form of an irregular spattering or sprinkling.

A nearly adult specimen (No. 70689, Demerara), retaining traces of immaturity in the plumage, differs from the fully mature bird in the following particulars: The feathers of the anterior portion of the throat project forward in a point about .65 of an inch in length, into the bare gular skin, forming an acute angle, as in most specimens of *E. albus*. The plumage in general is continuous pure scarlet, but the head and neck are paler than in perfectly adult specimens, while most of the feathers have a dusky brownish mesial streak. There are also a number of wholly dark brown feathers interspersed over the lower part of the nape and anterior portion of the back. The bill is very light-colored, having been in life apparently of a pale red or pink color.

The Red or Scarlet Ibis is of very doubtful occurrence within the limits of the United States. Wilson was misinformed in regard to its abundance in Carolina, Georgia, and Florida. We are not aware that there is a single well-authenticated instance on record of one having been taken within the limits of our territory. Audubon states that in July, 1821, he saw a flock of three at Bayou Sara, in Louisiana. These were flying in a line, in the manner of the White Ibis, above the tops of the trees, and he had no doubt of their identity. The habits of this species are probably not different from those of the *Ibis alba*, but are not so well known.

The Scarlet Ibis is said by Mr. Gosse to be a not uncommon visitant on the shores of Jamaica, though he never met with it himself. He was informed by Mr. Hill that it was quite common in the winter of 1846–7. Mr. March never met with it, and regarded it as a rare visitant. It was more frequent at the western end of the island. It is not mentioned by Gundlach as occurring in Cuba. It is, however, said by Léotaud to be very common on the Island of Trinidad, where it keeps principally about the banks of rivers, and especially of those which run through swampy places. It is always seen in flocks, and these are generally composed of individuals all of which are about the same age. This bird is a resident of the island, but at times its numbers are largely augmented by the arrival of others from the continent. During these flights this bird moves in single file, one following closely another; and when there is a large number, the line seems almost interminable. It feeds on worms, on soft mollusks, and, at times, on small fishes. It rests at night in the branches of the mangroves; and its brilliant red color forms a striking contrast to the deep green of the foliage. It is easily tamed, becomes reconciled to confinement, and is not only a great ornament to a garden, but makes itself useful by the destruction of hosts of noxious larvæ. This bird will follow closely upon those who are turning up the soil, in order that it may seize upon whatever of this kind is brought to view. The flesh of the young bird is said to be excellent eating; while the brilliant plumage of the adult is much sought for, and a destructive warfare is kept up against it. Its numbers are sensibly diminishing year by year; and it will soon become very rare, if not quite extinct. It was formerly known to nest in Trinidad; but such occurrences have now become quite exceptional.

This bird was found abundant on the Orinoco by Mr. E. C. Taylor, and on the Amazon by Mr. John E. Warren. Mr. Dresser was assured by friends living at Matamoras that the Scarlet Ibis is found there, and at a lagoon near Brownville during the winter. He had no opportunity of verifying the fact; but as this bird is one not easily confounded with any other, he had no doubt of its occurrence, and includes it in his list.

An egg of this species (S. I. No. 15504) obtained at Puerto Cabello by Mr. O. F. Starke, measures 2.10 inches in length by 1.45 in breadth. Its ground color is a grayish white, thinly marked over two thirds of its surface with small blotches of bistre. At the larger end, and around the widest portion, these markings are of greater size and more numerous, and form a large crown, which covers the whole of the obtuse end of the egg. These markings are diversified in their shade, and consist of patches of bistre, intensified in spots.

An egg of this species in my own collection (No. 70), from the Amazon, procured by Mr. W. H. Edwards, is of a slightly oblong oval shape, very nearly equal at either end, and measures 2.41 inches in length by 1.60 in breadth. The ground color is a dull white, with a slight rufous tinge. It is nearly covered — profusely so at the larger end — with irregular blotches of a dull bistre; these are nearly confluent at the extremity, and a few are much deeper than the rest.

Eudocimus albus.

THE WHITE IBIS.

Scolopax alba, LINN. S. N. I. ed. 10, 1758, 145.
Tantalus alber, LINN. S. N. I. 1766, 242.
Tantalus albus, GMEL. S. N. I. 1788, 651. — WILS. Am. Orn. VIII. 1814, 43, pl. 66.
Ibis alba, VIEILL. Nouv. Dict. XVI. 1817, 16. — NUTT. Man. II. 1834, 86. — AUD. Orn. Biog. III. 1835, 178; V. 1839, 593, pl. 222; Synop. 1839, 257; B. Am. VI. 1843, 54, pl. 360. — CASS. in Baird's B. N. Am. 1858, 684. — BAIRD, Cat. N. Am. B. 1859, no. 499. — COUES, Check List, 1873, no. 446.
Eudocimus albus, WAGL. Isis, 1832, 1232. — RIDGW. Nom. N. Am. B. 1881, no. 501. — COUES, Check List, 2d ed. 1882, no. 651.
Tantalus coco, JACQ. Beitr. 1784, 13.
Tantalus griseus, GMEL. S. N. I. 1788, 653 (young).
Eudocimus longirostris, WAGL. Isis, 1829, 760.

HAB. Warm-temperate Eastern North America, West Indies, Middle America, and tropical South America; north to Connecticut, Eastern Pennsylvania, Illinois, and Great Salt Lake, Utah; south to Brazil.

SP. CHAR. *Adult:* Terminal portion (beyond the emargination) of three to five[1] outer primaries, glossy greenish black, with a bright metallic green lustre. Rest of the plumage entirely pure white. Bill, bare skin of the head, legs and feet, bright carmine in the breeding-season; at other times paler, or orange-red; iris fine pearly blue (AUDUBON).[2] End of the bill sometimes

[1] According to Audubon, "There is a curious, though not altogether general, difference between the sexes of this species as to the plumage, — the male has five of its primaries tipped with glossy black for several inches, while the female, which is very little smaller than the male, has only four marked in this manner. On examining more than a hundred individuals of each sex, I found only four exceptions, which occurred in females that were very old birds, and which, as happens in some other species, might perhaps have been undergoing the curious change exhibited by Ducks, Pheasants, and some other birds, the females of which, when old, sometimes assume the livery of the males." This supposed sexual difference we have been unable to verify with the series before us, though it is very possible that some specimens may not have the sex correctly determined.

[2] "Bare parts of the head [in the adult male] light orange-red; bill the same, but towards the tip dusky. Iris of a fine pearly blue. Legs and toes paler than the bill; claws dusky, tipped with horn-color.

"After the first moult, the bill is pale yellowish orange, toward the base greenish; the naked parts of the head are pale orange-yellow, inclining to flesh-color; the eye dark brown; the feet pale blue.

"The change in the coloring of the bill, legs, and feet of this bird, that takes place in the breeding season, is worthy of remark, the bill being then of a deep orange-red, and the legs and feet of a red nearly amounting to carmine. The males at this season have the gular pouch of a rich orange color, and somewhat resembling in shape that of the Frigate Pelican, although proportionally less. During winter these parts are of a dull flesh-color. The irides also lose much of their clear blue, and resume in some degree the umber color of the young birds. I am thus particular in these matters, because it is doubtful if any one else has ever paid attention to them."

blackish. *Young:* Uniform, rather dark, grayish brown, the rump, upper tail-coverts, basal half of tail, and entire lower parts, including axillars and lining of the wing, continuous white; head and neck streaked with dusky or grayish brown on a grayish or dull whitish ground-color. Feathering of the head extending forward almost to the bill.[1]

Length, about 24.00–26.00; expanse, about 40.00; wing, 10.30–11.75; tail, 4.00–5.00; culmen, 4.15–6.30; depth of bill, .60–.72; tarsus, 3.10–4.00; middle toe, 2.15–2.70; bare portion of tibia, 2.00–2.80.

In this species there is a range of individual variation not exceeded by any member of the family; this variation affecting not only size and relative proportions of the different parts, but also characters which have been accorded generic or subgeneric value. Thus, taking two perfectly adult birds from localities geographically near together (Mazatlan and Tehuantepec, Western and Southwestern Mexico), they represent very nearly, if not quite, the extremes of size, especially as regards the bill; one of them (No. 58816, Mazatlan) having this member 6.30 inches in length, while in the other (No. 59773, ♀, Tehuantepec) it measures only 4.70. As to colors, they are identical, both being pure white, with the terminal portion of the *four* outer primaries glossy greenish-black. There is a most remarkable difference, however, between these two examples in the anterior outline of the feathering of the head, which difference may be explained as follows: In the Mazatlan specimen the frontal apex all but comes in contact with the base of the culmen, there being left between a space only about .05 of an inch wide; in the Tehuantepec specimen there is an interval left of .80 of an inch! In the Mazatlan example, the anterior feathers of the throat form a broad angle projecting forward into the bare gular skin for a distance of .60 of an inch; in the Tehuantepec specimen, their anterior outline has exactly the *opposite* form, being regularly and deeply *concave*, so that the bare gular skin has a semicircular or regularly convex posterior outline — exactly as in fully adult specimens of *E. ruber!* In the former of these specimens the malar feathers extend forward to within .25 of an inch of the rictus, or to much beyond the anterior angle of the eye; while in the other they approach to within only about .70 of the rictus, scarcely reaching to below the middle of the eyes.

Other characters in which the Tehuantepec example differs from the one from Mazatlan, consist in the subterminal portion of the bill being black for the space of nearly two inches, and in the distinct serration of the middle portion of the tomia. These extremes of variation are noticeable among skins obtained during the breeding season in Florida, specimens from the same breeding grounds differing as much as the two described above.

Immature specimens show, according to age, all possible stages of plumage intermediate between the pure white adult and gray young.

The White Ibis is a resident only in the more southern portions of the United States, though it not unfrequently occurs as a straggler in various places farther

[1] According to Audubon, "the young birds are at first covered with thick down of a dark gray color."

north, especially on the sea-coast and near the larger rivers of the West. It is abundant throughout Mexico, Central America, and the northern portions of South America. Mr. G. C. Taylor mentions having met with it on the Macaome River in Honduras; and Mr. Salvin speaks of having seen some among the bays on the coast. He afterward mentions having met with it frequently on the sea-coast of Guatemala, among the creeks emptying into the Pacific. Mr. Dresser found it abundant in Northeastern Mexico, near Matamoras. It frequented the town lagoon, where on several occasions he shot four or five before breakfast. He always ate them, and found them excellent — indeed, far superior to the real Curlew, by whose name it was known. In Florida it goes by the name of the "Spanish Curlew."

Mr. Giraud mentions two instances wherein this bird has been met with on the shores of Long Island. One was shot at Raynor South, in the summer of 1836; the other at Moriches, in March, 1843. A single instance only is reported of its having been detected farther north. Mr. Allen met with a few examples of this species in the Valley of Great Salt Lake, in September, and was informed that it is a common summer resident in that neighborhood.

Mr. Audubon found it breeding in immense numbers on a small sandy island about six miles from Cape Sable in Florida. It was in company with the Brown Pelican, four or five species of Herons, both the Gallinules, and other species. It was breeding there in thousands; and on every bush, cactus, or tree on the island he found their nests, so that on one wild plum tree he counted forty-seven of them. The nests of this species measure about fifteen inches in their greatest diameter, and are formed of dry twigs intermixed with fibrous roots and green branches of the trees growing on the island. The interior of each nest is nearly flat, and is finished with leaves of the cane and other plants. This bird is supposed to breed only once in a year, the number of its eggs being three, and they are said to be excellent eating; although they do not look inviting after having been boiled, since the white resembles a livid-colored jelly, and the yolk is of a reddish orange, the former being wonderfully transparent, and not opaque, as is usually the case. The eggs are usually deposited after the 10th of April, and incubation has become pretty general by the 1st of May. The young are, at first, covered by a thick dark gray down, and are fed by regurgitation. They leave the nest when about three weeks old, and stand either on the ground or among the branches, where they are fed by the parents with snakes, small fiddler crabs, and crayfish. The young bird is fully five weeks old before it is able to fly. As soon as it can provide for itself, the parents leave it, and the various individuals may then be seen searching for food separately. The White Ibis, when it is nesting, is very gentle and unwary, unless it has been much disturbed, and will allow itself to be touched while on the nest. The female is silent, but the male manifests its displeasure by uttering sounds which may be imitated by the syllables *croo-croo-croo,* and are not unlike the notes of the White-headed Pigeon. Even the report of a gun does not disturb it at this season, though at other times it is extremely shy and vigilant. While breeding it is said to go to a great distance in search of food for its young, flying in flocks of several hundreds. These excursions take place at periods, determined by the decline of the tides, when all the birds that are not sitting go off twenty or thirty miles to mud-flats, where they collect abundance of food, and return as soon as the tide has begun to rise; this is done by night as well as by day. They do not go singly, however, for on such occasions the entire flock seemed to rise, as if by common consent, from their breeding-ground, and then to form themselves into long lines, and soon disappear. Soon after the turn of the tide they might be seen returning in the same order, and on these occasions they were usually silent. Their flight is described as being rapid and protracted; the advance being made by alternate flapping and sailing. In these movements the flock imitate the leader, each individual following with perfect regularity the motions of the one preceding it. If at this time one is shot, the whole line is broken up, and for a few minutes all is disorder; but soon the former arrangement is resumed, and the flock goes on as before.

A wounded Ibis, if only winged, runs off with great speed; but it never attempts to bite or otherwise to defend itself. At other times than the breeding season this bird will perform wonderful evolutions, in the course of which it sometimes rises to a great height in the air. After thus apparently amusing itself for a while, it will suddenly glide down with astonishing speed. It is apparently as fond as the Wood Ibis of resorting to ponds or bayous that are in the woods; and Mr. Audubon has found it breeding in such situations more than three hundred miles from the sea. This was the case in the State of Mississippi, not far from Natchez, and in the swampy forests around Bayou Sara and Pointe Coupée. When disturbed in these places it flies to the tops of the tallest trees, uttering a hoarse cry, and is usually very shy and difficult of approach. When a wounded Ibis falls into the water, it can swim quite well; but it is unusual for it to do this voluntarily, even to avoid pursuit. Audubon witnessed the escape of one by swimming when chased by an alligator. The bird had fallen broken-winged into the water, and sought protection by hastening to his feet. He kept it alive for some time, feeding it with soaked Indian meal and an occasional crayfish, which latter it received with evident pleasure. On seizing one, the bird beat it sideways on the ground until its claws and legs were broken off, after which the body was swallowed whole. This bird was very fond of lying on its side in the sun and nursing its sore wing. It walked lightly and very gracefully, and became very gentle and tame, following, like a common fowl, those who fed it.

Mr. Lawrence considers this bird as a rare species near New York; Mr. Edward Harris procured it on the Delaware, near Philadelphia; and Mr. Turnbull shot one at Great Egg Harbor, New Jersey, in the summer of 1858. It is rare so far north. Dr. Bryant found it very numerous at Indian River, Florida. Specimens shot April 20 were still in the spring moult. Mr. Turnbull saw a large flock of these birds on the St. John's, near Volusia, but none at Enterprise.

The eggs are of an oblong-oval shape, a little larger and more obtuse at one end, and vary chiefly in size, ranging in length from 2.20 to 2.45 inches, and in breadth from 1.55 to 1.60 inches. Their ground color is a dull clayey white with a greenish tinge, over which are distributed spots, blotches, and longitudinal markings of various shades of reddish brown. In some cases these are few, and scattered over most of the egg, but increasing in size or confluent towards the larger end. In others, these markings are distributed in large and more or less confluent patches over nearly the entire surface. In some eggs the greenish tinge of the ground is much more apparent than in others, but it is always more or less noticeable.

Genus **PLEGADIS**, Kaup.

"*Falcinellus*, Bechst." Auct. (nec Bechstein[1]).
Plegadis, Kaup, Skizz. Entw. Gesch. 1829, 82 (type, *Tantalus falcinellus*, Linn.).
Tantalides, Wagl. Isis, 1832, 1231 (type, *Tantalus falcinellus*, Linn.).

[1] Cf. Salv. & Scl. Ibis, Jan. 1878, p. 112.

GEN. CHAR. Bill shallow through the base, moderately tapering, and gently curved; the base not turgid, and the basal outline of the maxilla deeply concave; bare portion of tibia equal to or longer than outer toe; middle toe about three fourths the tarsus; inner toe reaching past the subterminal articulation of the middle toe; hallux about equal to the basal phalanx of the inner toe. Forehead and orbital, malar, and gular regions completely feathered, the lores only being naked, the feathering on the chin forming an acute angle which advances to as far as the middle of the

P. falcinellus.

nostrils; feathers of the pileum elongated, lanceolate, and distinct, forming, when erected, a sort of full, rounded crest; those of the occiput and nape, and upper half of the neck all round, also distinct and lanceolate. Plumage chiefly metallic green above; the adults with head and upper part of neck chestnut, and lower parts chestnut (*falcinellus* and *guarauna*) or violet-blackish (*Ridgwayi*); the young with head and upper part of neck streaked grayish brown and white, the lower parts grayish brown (*falcinellus* and *guarauna*) or violet-dusky (*Ridgwayi*).

This genus differs conspicuously from *Eudocimus* in the complete feathering of the head[1] (excepting only the lores and the space between the mandibular rami) and in the brilliantly metallic plumage. *P. falcinellus* and *P. guarauna* are exactly alike in the details of form and general coloration; but *P. Ridgwayi* is very different from them in both these respects. Their comparative characters may be thus expressed in a synoptical table: —

A. Legs and feet long and slender, the tarsus with a nearly continuous frontal series of transverse scutellæ. *Adult*, with the neck, back, lesser wing-coverts, and lower parts opaque chestnut. *Young*, with the head and upper part of the neck streaked grayish brown and white, the lower parts plain grayish brown.

1. **P. falcinellus.** Feathers around base of bill, blackish; lores greenish in life. Wing, 10.20–11.85; culmen, 4.30–5.45; tarsus, 2.90–4.30; middle toe, 2.10–2.80. *Hab.* Palæarctic region (warmer portions), Eastern United States and West Indies.
2. **P. guarauna.** Feathers around base of bill whitish; lores lake-red in life. Wing, 9.30–10.80; culmen, 3.75–6.00; tarsus, 3.00–4.40; middle toe, 2.10–2.85. *Hab.* South and Middle America, and Western North America as far north as the Columbia River.

[1] In this feature there is considerable resemblance to *Harpiprion*, which, however, is very different in other respects, and belongs to a different "sub-family" (*Ibidinæ*).

B. Legs and feet comparatively short and stout, the tarsus with the frontal scutellæ more or less irregular and interrupted. *Adult*, with the head and upper portion of neck dark chestnut, the lower neck and lower parts violet-blackish, the lesser wing-coverts metallic green and bronzed purple, the back dark metallic green. *Young*, with the head and upper part of neck streaked with dusky and white, the lower parts dusky, with a violet tinge.

3. **P. Ridgwayi.**[1] Feathers round base of bill dusky chestnut, or dark rusty; lores reddish in life. Wing, 10.15–12.00; culmen, 3.40–5.10; tarsus, 2.70–3.85; middle toe, 1.80–2.30. *Hab.* Vicinity of Lake Titicaca, Peru; Chili.

Plegadis falcinellus.

THE GLOSSY IBIS.

Tantalus falcinellus, LINN. S. N. I. 1766, 241, no. 2 (based on *Numenius rostro arcuato, corpore castaneo, pedibus obscure virentibus*, KRAM. Austr. 350. — *Numenius viridis*, BRISS. Av. 5, p. 326, t. 27, f. 2. — *Falcinellus*, GESN. Av. p. 220, etc.).

Ibis falcinellus, VIEILL. Nouv. Dict. XIV. 1817, 23. — BONAP. Obs. Wils. 1825, no. 199. — NUTT. Man. II. 1834, 88. — AUD. Orn. Biog. IV. 1838, 608, pl. 387; Synop. 1839, 257; B. Am. VI. 1843, 50, pl. 358 (adult).

Plegadis falcinellus, "KAUP," FRITSCH, Vög. Eur. 1869, Taf. 43, fig. 3, p. 378. — RIDGW. Nom. N. Am. B. 1881, no. 503. — COUES, Check List, 2d ed. 1882, no. 649.

Tantalus castaneus, MÜLLER, S. N. Suppl. 1776, 112 (adult).

Courly, d'Italie, BUFF. Pl. Enl. 1770–84, pl. 819 (adult).

Bay Ibis, PENN. Arct. Zool. II. 1785, 460 (adult).

Green Ibis, LATH. Synop. III. i. 1785, 113, sp. 13 (young).

Glossy Ibis, LATH. t. c. 114, sp. 14 (transition pl.).

Tantalus viridis, GMEL. S. N. I. 1788, 648, no. 8 (young).

Tantalus igneus, GMEL. t. c. 649, no. 9 (adult).

Falcinellus igneus, GRAY, Gen. B. ed. 2, 1841, 87. — ELLIOT, P. Z. S. 1877, 503.

"*Ibis noir*, SAVIG. Hist. Myth. de l'Ibis, p. 36, fig. 4, juv." (ELLIOT).

"*Ibis sacra*, TEMM. Man. Orn. 1815, 385" (ELLIOT).

"*Tringa autumnalis*, HASSELQ. It. Pal. deutsche Ausg. p. 306" (ELLIOT).

"*Tantalus mexicanus*," ORD. Jour. Philad. Acad. I. 1817, 52 (not of GMEL.).

Ibis Ordii, BONAP. Consp. List, 1838, 49. — CASS. in Baird's B. N. Am. 1858, 635 (part). — BAIRD, Cat. N. Am. B. 1859, no. 500.

Ibis falcinellus, var. *Ordii*, COUES, Key, 1872, 263; Check List, 1873, no. 445; Birds N. W. 1874, 517.

"*Ibis guarauna*," CABOT, Pr. Boston Soc. II. 1850, 313, 332 (not of LINN.).

"*Numenius longirostris*," GOSSE, B. Jam. 1847, p. 348 (not of WILSON).

Tantalus bengalensis, "LICHT." Bonap. Consp. II. 1855, 158.

Ibis peregrina, "MÜLL." Bonap. t. c. 159.

HAB. Palæarctic region, West Indies, and Eastern United States. Of irregular distribution, and only locally abundant in America.

SP. CHAR. *Adult: Feathers bordering the base of the bill, all round, blackish.* Pileum, cheeks, and chin glossy greenish black, with violet-purple reflections. Hind part of the head, whole neck, anterior part of the back, and anterior half of lesser wing-covert region, rich reddish chestnut, the back darkest. Lower parts, except the crissum, axillars, and lining of the wing, uniform bright reddish chestnut, lighter, brighter, and less purplish than the neck. Remaining upper parts, as well as the lining of the wing, axillars, and crissum, glossy, metallic, dark purple, green, and bronze; the posterior part of the back, posterior scapulars, wing-coverts, tertials, rump, upper tail-coverts, and tail nearly uniform dull violet-purple, changing to bottle-green in certain lights; alulæ,

[1] PLEGADIS RIDGWAYI.

Falcinellus Ridgwayi, ALLEN, Bull. Mus. Comp. Zool. III. July, 1876, 355 (Moho, Conima, and Vilquechico, near Lake Titicaca, Peru). — ELLIOT, P. Z. S. 1877, 506.

"*Ibis falcinellus*, SCL. & SALV. P. Z. S. 1869, 156" (ELLIOT).

? "*Ibis Ordii*," TSCHUDI, Fauna Per. 1844, 298.

? *Ibis brevirostris*, PEALE, Zoöl. Expl. Exp. 1848, 219 (Rimac R., Peru).

primary-coverts, primaries, and lower secondaries brighter bronze-green; upper secondaries more bronzy, with a purple shade in certain lights. Under-surface of wings and tail more burnished, metallic green, bronze, and purple, the tint varying with the inclination to the lights; axillars less

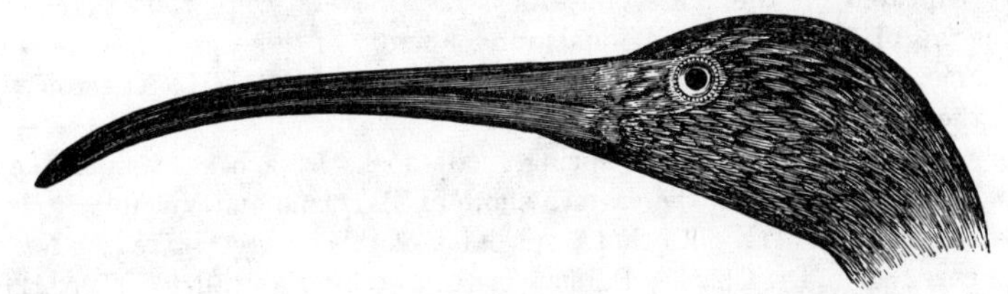

shining, and more violaceous; crissum violet-purple and green, like the rump. Bill black; bare loral space greenish; legs and feet greenish blackish.[1]

Young (changing from first to second plumage): Head and neck distinctly streaked with dusky brown and white, the dusky streaks wider and more blackish on the pileum, the whitish streaks gradually becoming more indistinct below. Entire lower parts plain snuff-brown, with a soft purplish tinge, especially on the breast and tibiæ; crissum, metallic green and violet. Upper parts dark, metallic violet-purple, green, and bronze, the first largely predominating, the last in traces; the back darkest and most uniform, the rump interspersed with bright dark-green feathers. A few dark chestnut feathers interspersed over the anterior portion of the lesser wing-covert region (No. 57003, Greece). *Young (changing from second to third plumage):* In general appearance much like the preceding, but breast, abdomen, and tibiæ mostly reddish chestnut, and the anterior portion of the back and scapulars mixed with many feathers of the same color; head and neck much tinged with chestnut, the streaks indistinct (No. 17493, ♀, Hungary).

[NOTE. — The *Tantalus viridis* of GMELIN (Syst. Nat. II. i. p. 648, no. 8, based on *Green Ibis* of LATHAM, Synopsis, III. i. p. 114, no. 13) seems to be this species in incomplete first plumage, or still retaining the downy covering of the head and neck.]

Length, about 25 inches; expanse, 42; wing, 10.20–11.85; tail, 4.30–4.50; culmen, 4.30–5.45; depth of bill, .50–.60; tarsus, 2.90–4.30; middle toe, 2.10–2.80; bare portion of tibia, 1.70–3.10.

Of this species, there are at present before us four adult specimens, two being from Europe and two from America (Tortugas and Jamaica); between these there is not the slightest difference whatever, beyond the individual discrepancies of size observable in all species of this family.

The young of *P. falcinellus* closely resembles that of *P. guarauna*, but is rather darker colored, the upper parts being much more violaceous, and the lower parts less grayish. There are two specimens in the collection, — those described above.

This species, identical with the well-known Bay or Glossy Ibis of Europe, occurs irregularly in the eastern portion of the United States, and has been known to breed in Florida. It has been found on several occasions as far north as Massachusetts, although nowhere abundant in the States bordering upon the Atlantic. It was first described as a bird of North America by Mr. George Ord, from a specimen obtained at Great Egg Harbor, May 7, 1817. About the same time another specimen was procured near Baltimore, and two others were taken in the District of Columbia. Mr. Audubon states that in the spring of 1837 he saw flocks of this bird in Texas; but it is possible that the birds which he saw there were not of this species. They were apparently only summer residents, associating with the White Ibis, along the grassy margins of the rivers and bayous, going to and returning from their roosting-places in the country. Its flight resembles that of its companion, the White Ibis.

[1] Audubon says: "Bill black; bare part of head grayish blue; iris hazel; feet grayish black, claws brown."

According to Nuttall, specimens were in his day occasionally seen exposed for sale in the market of Boston; and individuals had been at distant intervals shot off Long Island and on the shores of New Jersey. From time to time straggling specimens are captured on the Massachusetts coast. Several were thus taken on Cape Cod in the fall of 1878; and individuals, undoubtedly of this species, were seen during the same season on Prince Edward Island by Mr. Frank L. Tileston; it also occurs in the West India Islands.

At very irregular periods in the spring small flocks have been seen on the coasts of the Middle States and on the eastern shore of Maryland and Virginia. Mr. J. A. Allen states (Am. Nat. III. 637) that a specimen of this bird was taken in Nantucket in September, 1869. Dr. Charles Palmer writes to the "Naturalist" (V. p. 120) that one was obtained by him near Lake Winnepisseogee, in the town of Alton, N. H. It was an old bird in full plumage.

In Europe this species is supposed to be more common in the eastern than in the western portion. The course of its migrations for the summer toward the north of Europe is said to be chiefly in a line from Egypt to Turkey, Hungary, and Poland, and to the southern parts of Russia. It is occasionally seen, on its passage from Northern Africa, in Crete, the Grecian Archipelago, in Sicily, Sardinia, and Genoa. Stragglers are found in Switzerland, France, Holland, and Great Britain; but in all these countries it is a rare bird. In England, though not uncommon, it is always accidental. Yarrell mentions about fifteen instances of its having been taken in England, three in Ireland, and one in Scotland. It has also been known to occur in Denmark; and in Sweden also, although here but very rarely.

Specimens were obtained by Dr. Andrew Smith in Africa as far south as the Cape of Good Hope. It is migratory in Egypt, where it appears to have been once held in high veneration, although it is not the bird commonly known as the Sacred Ibis. It was met with by Messrs. Dickson and Ross at Erzeroom, in the vicinity of the river; and in the Russian expedition it was found in the countries between the Black and the Caspian Seas. It has also been taken near Calcutta, in Thibet, and Nepal. Temminck assigns it to Java, Sunda, and the neighboring islands; and, finally, Mr. Gould states that this species has been found in every part of the vast region of Australia known to him.

In the portions of Europe where this bird is most abundant, it is found to live principally on the banks of rivers and on the shores of lakes, or on muddy flats which are occasionally flooded. It feeds on small reptiles, the fry of fishes, small crustacea, and aquatic insects.

Mr. Dresser mentions this species as having been found by him in great numbers on the lagoons near Matamoras, in the month of August; appearing there somewhat earlier than the White Ibis. He obtained quite a number of specimens, and one was sent to him from Fort Stockton in a collection formed by Mr. P. Duffy.

Although Captain Bendire did not meet with this species in Oregon, he had no doubt that it ranges within the State, as it was found breeding at Quinn River Crossing, in Nevada, only twenty miles from the State line. Lieutenant Wood, U. S. A., procured an example in that locality, July 15, 1875, and on that occasion saw some forty of these birds with young still unable to fly.

Eggs of this species in the Smithsonian Institution (1895) obtained by Dr. Bean at Mecanopy, Florida, are of a rounded oval shape, slightly smaller at one end than at the other, and of a uniform very light shade of Prussian blue. They measure 1.90 inches in length by 1.38 in breadth. Yarrell describes the European egg as being of a very delicate pale blue, and 2 inches in length by 1.50 inches in breadth.

Plegadis guarauna.

THE WHITE-FACED GLOSSY IBIS.

? *Scolopax guarauna,* LINN. S. N. I. 1766, 242, no. 1 (based on *Numenius americanus fuscus,* BRISS. Av. 5, p. 330. — *Guarauna,* MARCGR. Bras. 204).

Falcinellus guarauna, BONAP. Consp. II. 1855, 159. — ELLIOT, P. Z. S. 1877, 505.

Ibis guarauna, WAGL. Syst. Av. 1827, sp. 8. — CASS. in Baird's B. N. Am. ed. 1860, pl. 87, (young). — RIDGW. Am. Nat. 1874, 110, 111 (critical).

Plegadis guarauna, RIDGW. Nom. N. Am. B. 1881, no. 504. — COUES, Check List, 2d ed. 1882, no. 650.

?? *Mexican Ibis,* LATH. Synop. III. i. 1785, 108, no. 5.

?? *Tantalus mexicanus,* GMEL. S. N. I. ii. 1788, 652 (based on *Numenius mexicanus varius,* BRISS. Av. 5, p. 333, no. 7).

"*Ibis falcinellus*" (most quotations from South America).

"*Ibis Ordii*"(quotations from Mexico, Central and South America). — CASS. in Baird's B. N. Am. 1858, 685 (excl. synonymy).

Tantalus chalcopterus, TEMM. Pl. Col. 511 (1830), (adult).

"*Falcinellus igneus,*" SCL. & SALV. Nom. Neotr. 1873, 126 (part).

? *Ibis erythrorhynchus,* GOULD, P. Z. S. Nov. 14, 1837, 127 (Hayti ; young ?).

Ibis thalassinus, RIDGW. Am. Nat. VIII. Feb. 1874, 110, 111 (young in first plumage).

Falcinellus thalassinus, ELLIOT, P. Z. S. 1877, 507.

HAB. Western United States, Middle America, and South America, to Chili and Buenos Ayres, West Indies ? Sandwich Islands ?

SP. CHAR. *Adult : Feathers bordering the base of the bill, all round, whitish,* usually most distinct on the forehead. Pileum dull metallic violet-purple, changing to green, the feathers blackish beneath the surface ; rest of the head cinnamon-brownish, paler on the throat, where lightest anteriorly ; neck cinnamon-chestnut, the feathers blackish beneath the surface, this showing where the feathers are disarranged, and quite conspicuous on the nape, where the dusky has, in certain lights, a faint greenish lustre. Lower neck, entire lower parts (except the crissum, anal region, axillars, and flanks), back, anterior scapulars, and lesser wing-coverts uniform rich chestnut, darker

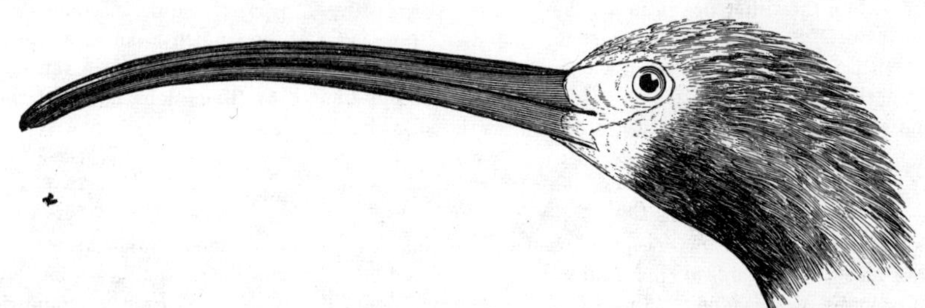

and more purplish above, lighter and more ferruginous or clearer reddish beneath. Rest of the plumage glossy metallic green, bronze, purple, and violet ; the green purest and clearest on the primaries ; the secondaries and greater coverts more bronzy, the middle coverts and posterior half of lesser covert region purplish, changing to dull green ; the crissum and rump mixed green and purple, the green being of a richer, almost grass-green, shade, especially on the rump. Axillars and under wing-coverts bronze-purple ; under-surface of remiges and rectrices very highly burnished. Bill dusky, sometimes tinged with reddish ; lores, eyelids, and naked skin of chin lake-red or pale carmine ; iris crimson ; legs and feet varying from grayish brown to deep lake-red.

Young, second year : Head, neck, and lower parts dull grayish brown, the head and upper part of the neck streaked with white ; back grayish brown with green or purple reflections. Otherwise as in the adult, but metallic colors less brilliant.

Young, first year: Head, neck, and lower parts as in the last, but upper parts and under side of the wing uniform, continuous bronzy green, with little, if any, admixture of purple or violet shades.

No chestnut on the lesser wing-coverts! Bill, pale greenish horn-blue, blackish terminally and dusky basally; iris, "hazel;" legs and feet, deep black (= *F. thalassinus*, RIDGWAY).[1]

Downy young: Bill light yellowish, the base, end, and band around the middle deep black; lores blackish; legs and feet black. Forehead black, bounded posteriorly by a crescentic patch of dull, silvery white, extending from eye to eye, across the posterior portion of the crown; the line of demarcation between the white and black being somewhat mixed or suffused with light rufous. Rest of head, neck, and lower parts covered with soft downy feathers of a uniform brownish gray shade, without any whitish streaks on head or neck. Partially complete plumage of the upper surface entirely uniform, continuous bronze-green, or metallic bottle-green, without the slightest admixture anywhere of purple, blue, or violet.

Length, about 19.00–26.00; expanse, 30.00–40.00; wing, 9.30–10.80; tail, 3.50–5.00; culmen, 3.75–6.00; depth of bill, .50–.60; tarsus, 3.00–4.40; middle toe, 2.10–2.85; bare portion of tibia, 1.50–2.75 [2]

According to Dr. J. C. Merrill (Proc. U. S. Nat. Mus. Vol. I. p. 163), "The young, when first hatched, are clothed in blackish down; the bill is whitish, with dusky base. When nearly fledged, the wings and back have a very marked metallic lustre; the base of bill, with terminal one fourth inch and a two fifths inch median band, black; the intervening portions pinkish white."

In this widely distributed species there is very little variation in colors among specimens of the same age, but the difference in proportions is often very great. A perfectly adult specimen from the vicinity of Santiago, Chili, and one from San Francisco, Cal., are much alike in plumage, except that in the former the crown is darker (being, in fact, decidedly dusky), while the back is of a darker chestnut, with more decided violet-purple reflections. In dimensions, however, they exhibit almost the extremes of measurements, as the following will show: —

Catal. no.	Locality.	Wing.	Culmen.	Tarsus.	Middle Toe.
79928	San Francisco, Cal.	10.80	6.00	4.25	2.75
49042	Santiago, Chili.	9.50	4.15	3.25	2.20

Specimens from the same locality, however, sometimes differ quite as much as those mentioned above; and we are unable to appreciate any geographical differences whatever, examples from Chili, Buenos Ayres, Mexico, and Columbia River being quite identical. A specimen from the Sandwich Islands we refer to this species somewhat doubtfully, it being in immature plumage. It agrees strictly with American examples of the same age in all respects wherein *guarauna* differs from *falcinellus*, even to the reddish color of the bill, lores, and feet. Still, it is possible that perfect adults may show differences from both forms.

This species, known in its mature form as the Bronzed Ibis, and in its immature condition as the Green Ibis, is a common species in Utah, Nevada, and Southwestern Texas, and probably also in New Mexico and Arizona, in localities favorable for its residence and support.

[1] Notes from fresh specimens killed at Oreana, on the Humboldt River, Nevada, Sept. 3, 1867.

[2] Extremes of about forty specimens.

Mr. J. A. Allen met with it in the valley of Great Salt Lake, Utah, in the month of September, where it was known as the Black Snipe. He was told that it was a rather common summer resident, but this had only been the case within a few years. Most of these birds had migrated south before Mr. Allen's arrival, and he found it exceedingly wary, although his party succeeded in procuring seven specimens.

By Mr. Ridgway it was observed in large numbers at Franklin Lake, in August and September; a few had also been seen at Great Salt Lake in May and June. This bird is known to the people of Nevada as the "Black Curlew," and also as the "Black Snipe." In its immature form it was first observed at the Humboldt Marshes in September. It was one of the most abundant water-birds, occurring in flocks of hundreds of individuals. They were generally seen about the margin of the pools. standing in a single line along the edge of the water. At Oreana, forty miles farther up the river, they were seen passing back and forth over the camp by the river, some of the flocks formed with a widely extended front, but more frequently in a V-shaped body. They flew quite low — rarely higher than fifty yards — and quite swiftly. At that distance they seemed of a uniform black color, and resembled the Long-billed Curlew in size and form. Only once was a flock seen to alight. When approached, under cover of the willows, they were found busily engaged in feeding among the aquatic plants, in a slough entirely hemmed in by a dense growth of willows, each individual, as it waded about, uttering a hoarse, low croaking note. Their movements were easy and graceful.

Mr. Cassin refers to this species (Wilkes's Expedition, p. 302) as apparently inhabiting nearly the entire southwestern regions of the continent, from New Mexico and California to Patagonia. It is of frequent occurrence throughout Peru and Chili; and, according to Chilian observers, migrates still farther south. It has been brought in collections from New Mexico and Southern California. Mr. Peale mentions that it was observed in flocks of fifteen or twenty along the banks of fresh-water streams and lakes in Chili, during the month of May. Its flight was quite graceful.

The Bronzed Ibis was first recognized as a bird of North America by Dr. Woodhouse, who procured it on the Rio Zoquette, in Texas, in the expedition to the Zuñi River.

According to the late Dr. Berlandier, this species is found among the swamps on the eastern coast of Mexico; and its habits are described by him as very similar to those of the Green Ibis of Europe. He met with it, although quite rarely, about the lakes near Tamiagua, Tuxpan, and Pueblo Viejo, in the State of Vera Cruz; also in the vicinity of Tampico, Presas, and Soto la Marina, in Tamaulipas, as well as among the swamps produced by the overflow of the Rio Bravo del Norte.

It is undoubtedly to this species that Dr. Kennerly refers, in his notes on the birds observed on the Mexican Boundary Survey. He speaks of it as quite common in June in the vicinity of Santa Cruz, in the State of Sonora, as going in large flocks, and as feeding in the valley of the river in swampy places. It was very tame, and was easily killed.

Dr. James C. Merrill refers to this species as resident in Southwestern Texas, but as much more common in summer than in winter. On the 16th of May, 1877, in company with Mr. G. B. Sennett, he visited a large patch of tule-reeds growing in a shallow lagoon, about ten miles from Fort Brown, in which a large number of this species and several kinds of Herons were breeding. The reeds covered an area of about seventy-five acres, growing in water three or four feet deep. There were occasional irregular spaces free from reeds, but the firm bottom permitted wading without difficulty in any direction. Besides this Ibis, four or five kinds of Herons, as well as several other kinds of birds, were breeding there; and not unfrequently nests of all these different species were placed within a few feet of one another; but in general the different species preferred to form, each for itself, a little nesting group of ten or fifteen pairs. The reeds grew naturally to a height of about six feet above the surface of the water; but they were either beaten down to form a support for the nests, or else dead and partly floating stalks of the previous year were used for that purpose. It was impossible to form any estimate of the number of this species nesting there. As he approached the spot many were seen about the edges of the lagoon, or flying to and from more distant feeding-grounds. On firing a gun a perfect mass of birds arose, with a noise like thunder, from the entire bed of reeds, but they soon settled down again.

Both the nests and the eggs of this Ibis were quite unlike those of any of the Herons, and could be distinguished at a glance. The nests were made of broken bits of dead tules, supported by and attached to broken and upright stalks of living ones. They were well and compactly built, and were usually distinctly cupped, and quite unlike the clumsy platforms of the Herons. Early in May in the following year Dr. Merrill revisited this heronry; but there were no nests and but few birds to be seen: they had evidently moved to some other locality, where there were similar beds of reeds; but he was prevented by sickness from making any farther investigations.

The eggs were found to be nearly always three in number, and at the time of his visit — the middle of May — were far advanced in incubation. Many of the nests contained young of all sizes. By a careful measurement of fifty examples, Dr. Merrill ascertained the average size of the egg of this species to be 1.95 by 1.35, the extremes being 2.20 by 1.49, and 1.73 by 1.29. These eggs are decidedly pointed at the smaller end, and are of a deep bluish-green color.

Family PLATALEIDÆ. — The Spoonbills.

Plataleidæ, Bonap. 1849; Consp. II. 1855, 146.

Char. Large-sized Ibis-like birds, with the bill greatly flattened and expanded terminally. Bill deep through the base (the culmen ascending), but immediately flattened; narrowest across the middle portion, the end widely expanded, the tip rounded and decurved. Nostrils superior, longitudinal, without surrounding or overhanging membrane; nasal fossæ prolonged forward in a narrow, continuous groove to the extreme tip of the bill (as in the Ibises), its course nearly (or in some genera quite) parallel with the lateral outline of the maxilla; approximate surfaces of maxilla and mandible with one or two rows of more or less prominent tooth-like papillæ along each side. Tarsus longer than middle toe, and with small longitudinal hexagonal scales in front; outer toe decidedly longer than inner, its claw reaching to the base of the middle claw; hallux nearly incumbent, about equal to the basal phalanx of the inner toe; bare portion of tibia longer than outer toe; web between inner and middle toes well developed. Wings ample, reaching about to the end of the tail, the primaries a little longer than the tertials. Tail short, even, of twelve stiff, broad, round-ended feathers.

The above diagnosis is sufficient to characterize this well-marked group of birds. The Spoonbills are very intimately related to the Ibises, the only essential differences, so far as external features are concerned, being in the form of the bill.

Seven species of the family are known, only one of these being American; one is African, two Australian, two Palæarctic, and one a native of the Philippine Islands. Three of the six exotic species we have not seen, namely, *Platalea major*, TEMM., SCHLEG. of Japan, *Leucerodius tenuirostris* (TEMM.) of Africa, and *L. luzoniensis* (SCOP.) of the Philippines. The remaining species, however, are now before us, and appear to be each assignable to a distinct genus, the generic characters of each are as follows: —

Genera of Plataleidæ.

A. Bill long and narrow, its greatest breadth not more than one fourth the length of the culmen. Sides and top of the head feathered in the adult. Plumage of the neck normal and compact.

a. Occiput crested; tertials and jugular feathers normal.

1. **Platalea.**[1] Forehead feathered. Tarsus nearly twice the middle toe; bare portion of tibia longer than middle toe.
2. **Spatherodia.**[2] Forehead completely naked. Tarsus much less than twice the middle toe; bare portion of tibia shorter than middle toe.

b. Occiput not crested; tertials with their lower webs decomposed, the fibrillæ long, pendant, hair-like; jugular feathers acicular, stiffish.

3. **Platibis.**[3] Anterior part of forehead bare (also orbital, malar, and gular regions, the posterior outline well defined and nearly vertical). Tarsus nearly twice the length of the middle toe; bare portion of tibia longer than middle toe.

B. Bill rather short, very broad, its greatest breadth about one third the length of the culmen. Sides and top of the head completely naked in the adult. Plumage of the neck short and downy.

4. **Ajaja.** Tarsus but little longer than middle toe; bare portion of tibia shorter than middle toe.

GENUS AJAJA, REICHENBACH.

Ajaja, REICHENB. Handb. 1851, xvi. Type, *Platalea ajaja*, LINN.

GEN. CHAR. Bill much expanded and excessively depressed terminally, the tip decurved, much broader than deep at the base, the middle portion contracted to considerably less than one half the width of the terminal "disk." Nostrils sub-basal, superior, near together, longitudinal, and without adjacent membrane. Head completely bald in the adult (feathered almost to the bill in the young). Legs comparatively short, the tarsus but little longer than the middle toe, covered in front, as well as all round, with small, longitudinal, hexagonal scales. Plumage of the neck short, downy.[4]

[1] *Platalea*, LINN. Syst. Nat. ed. 10, I. 1758, 139; ed. 12, I. 1766, 231. Type, *P. leucerodia*, LINN. (Palæarctic region).

[2] *Spatherodia*, REICHENB. Handb. Sp. Orn. 1851, xvi. Type, *Platalea melanorhyncha*, REICHENB. = *P. regia*, GOULD (P. Z. S. Oct. 24, 1837, 106. — New Cambria, Australia).

[3] *Plateibis*, BONAP. Consp. II. 1855, 149. Type, *Platalea flavipes*, GOULD (P. Z. S. Oct. 24, 1837, 106.— New Cambria, Australia).

[4] A peculiar modification of the trachea further distinguishes the genus *Ajaja* from *Platalea*, according to Professor GARROD (P. Z. S. 1875, p. 299, fig. 2), who describes this organ as "simple, straight, of uniform calibre, and peculiarly short, extending only two thirds the neck, where the uncomplicated syrinx is situated, and the bifurcation of the bronchi occurs." In *Platalea*, on the other hand, the trachea is "convoluted within the thorax," etc. (see YARRELL, Hist. Brit. B. II. p. 504).

The above characters, in addition to those previously given, are sufficient to define this well-marked genus. Only one species is known, the *A. rosea,* whose distribution is coextensive with tropical and sub-tropical America.

A. rosea.

Ajaja rosea.

THE ROSY SPOONBILL.

Platea rosea, Briss. Orn. V. 1760, 356, pl. 30 (adult).
Platalea ajaja, Linn. S. N. ed. 10, 1758, 140, no. 2 (ex Sloane, Jam. II. 316 ; Marcgr. Ray) ; ed. 12, I. 1766, 231, no. 2 (based on *Platea rosea,* Briss. V. 356, t. 30. — *P. incarnata,* Sloane, Jam. II. 316. — *P. brasiliensis, Ajaja dicta,* Marcgr. Bras. 204). — Wils. Am. Orn. VII. 1813, 123, pl. 62 (young, third year). — Nutt. Man. II. 1834, 79. — Aud. Orn. Biog. IV. 1838, 188, 131 ; Synop. 1839, — ; Birds Am. VI. 1843, 72, pl. 362 (adult). — Cass. in Baird's B. N. Am. 1858, 686. — Baird, Cat. N. Am. B. 1859, no. 501. — Coues, Key, 1872, — ; Check List, 1873, no. 448.
Platea mexicana ("Willoughby"), Gamb. Jour. Philad. Acad. I. 1849, 222 ("San Francisco").
Roseate Spoonbill, Penn. Arct. Zool. II. 1785, 440, no. 338.
Ajaja rosea, Reich. "Nat. Syst. 16." — Ridgw. Nom. N. Am. B. 1881, no. 505. — Coues, Check List, 2d ed. 1882, no. 653.

Hab. The whole of tropical and subtropical America, including the West Indies ; south to the Falkland Islands, Patagonia, and Chili, north to the Southern United States.[1]

[1] The *present* northern limit to its range in the United States is not known with precision. We have reliable information of its abundance less than twenty years since in the "American Bottoms," in Illinois, below St. Louis ; but whether it now occurs there at all, we do not know. Its former occurrence on the coast of California as far north as San Francisco, is asserted by Gambel (Jour. Phil. Ac. I. 1849, p. 222).

Sp. Char. *Adult:* Head entirely bare. Neck, back, and breast, white; tail orange-buff, the shafts of the feathers deep pink, the inner webs inclining to pale pink. Rest of the plumage pale rose-pink, the lesser wing-coverts' region, and upper and lower tail-coverts, brilliant, intense carmine. Jugulum with a tuft of light carmine, somewhat twisted, or curled, narrow plumes. Sides of the breast, at base of the wings (concealed by the latter), pale creamy buff. "Bill yellowish gray at the base, mottled with brownish black, in the rest of its extent pale greenish blue, light on the margins; base of margin of lower mandible greenish yellow; iris bright carmine; feet pale lake; claws brownish black; head yellowish green; space around the eye and the gular sac

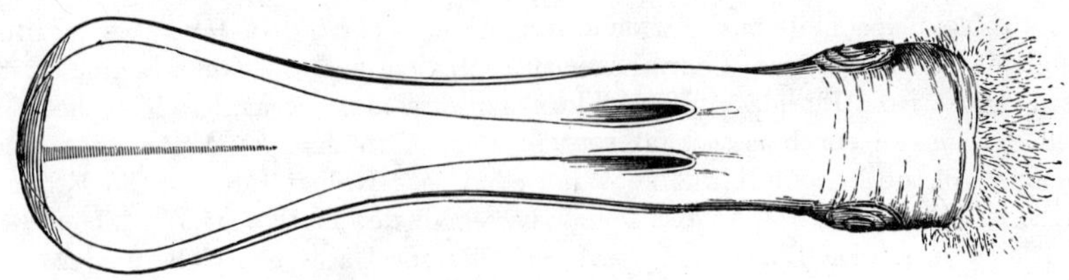

orpiment-orange; a band of black from the lower mandible to the occiput" (Audubon). *Immature:* Like the adult, but lacking the brilliant carmine of the lesser wing-coverts' region, tail-coverts, etc., these portions being pale peach-blossom pink. Tail delicate peach-blossom pink, instead of orange-buff. Nuchal and pectoral colored tufts absent. *Young:* Head completely feathered, except immediately around the base of the bill. Head, neck, back, and anterior lower parts white, in some specimens more or less tinged, especially above,[1] with orange-buff; wings, tail, and posterior part of the body delicate pale peach-blossom pink, the shafts of the remiges and rectrices deeper pink. Outer webs of alulæ, outer primary-coverts, and wide borders to outer primaries (principally on outer webs), clear snuff-brown.

[Note. — We have not seen the young in down, nor when first feathered. The latter is described by Audubon as follows: — "The young, . . . when able to fly, . . . are grayish white. The bill is then quite smooth, of a yellowish-green color, as are the legs and feet, as well as the skin on part of the head. Young birds in their second year have the wings and the lower wing-coverts of a pale roseate tint, the bill more richly colored, and the legs and feet dark brownish red or purplish. At this age they are unadorned with the curling feathers on the breast; but in the third spring the bird is perfect, although it increases in size for several seasons after."]

Length, about 28.00–31.00; expanse, 48.00–53.00; wing, 14.10–15.30; tail, 4.20–5.20; culmen, 6.20–7.15; width of bill, 2.00–2.20; tarsus, 3.75–4.65; middle toe, 2.95–3.35; bare portion of tibia, 2.80–3.20.

All the American Spoonbills examined by us appear to belong to a single species. Mr. W. H. Hudson, however, who resided for a number of years in Buenos Ayres, entertained the belief that there are two species of Spoonbills in that country; and, without at all sharing in this belief, we submit his arguments in its favor, as follows: —

"In reference to the Rose-colored Spoonbills of America, I believe ornithologists have been mistaken in referring them all to one species.

"Whether two or only one species existed was a moot question a century ago; it has been decided that there is but one, the *Platalea ajaja*, and that the paler-plumaged birds, with feathered heads and black eyes, and without the bright wing-spots, the tuft on the breast, horny excrescences on the beak, and other marks, are only immature birds. Now it is quite possible the young of *P. ajaja* resembles the common Rose-colored Spoonbill of Buenos Ayres; but in that country, for one bird with all the characteristic marks of an adult *P. ajaja*, we meet with not less, I am sure, than two or three hundred examples of the paler bird without any trace of such marks.

"This fact of itself might incline one to believe that there are two distinct species, and that the common *Platalea* of Buenos Ayres inhabits the temperate regions south of the range of the true *P. ajaja*.

[1] *Qu.* An accidental stain?

"Other facts confirm me in that opinion. A common Spoonbill was kept tame by a friend of mine seven years, at the end of which time it died without having acquired any of the distinguishing marks of *P. ajaja*.

"I have dissected three examples of the latter species, and observed in them the curiously formed trachea recently described by Mr. Garrod.[1] I have shot perhaps a hundred specimens of the common bird, for they are extremely abundant with us. Of these I have opened about thirty, but in none of them did I find this form of trachea. I am therefore convinced that we have two distinct species of Rose-colored Spoonbill, inhabiting different portions of the continent."

The Roseate Spoonbill has a wide distribution, occurring in favorable localities throughout South America, Central America, Mexico, and the Gulf Region of the United States, from Florida to the Mexican departments. Stragglers have been observed even as far south as the Falkland Islands. Captain C. C. Abbott states that a specimen of the Spoonbill was shot in a pond near Kidney Cove, in the Falkland Islands, in July, 1860; and he also found the remains of another in Whalebone Bay, in the same year. Dr. Burmeister speaks of this species as everywhere present in the La Plata Region, throughout nearly the whole of which it was found frequenting the reeds, on the shores of streams and lagoons. He always found it solitary, and never noticed it in flocks. Mr. C. Barrington Brown mentions finding it common in the inlets of the Cotinga River, in British Guiana. Mr. Salvin notices the procuring of a single individual of this species in Guatemala. It had been shot by an Indian on the borders of Lake Dueñas. Mr. Salvin afterward mentions having met with it occasionally on the Pacific coast of Guatemala, where, not unfrequently, a small flock would fly across the creek, seldom within shot, but often near enough to show their brilliant colors. This species has not, that I am aware, been recorded on the Pacific coast north of Mazatlan; but it is found in several of the West India Islands, and according to Dr. Gundlach it breeds in Cuba. It was not met with by Mr. Gosse in Jamaica, but is given by Mr. Richard Hill as a resident of that island; Mr. March, however, regards it as being of very rare occurrence there. It is given by Léotaud as an occasional visitant to Trinidad, the birds seen there being always in their immature plumage. These visitants usually arrive about the end of June, and leave in the month of October. It is abundant in Southwestern Texas and along the Gulf coast of Mexico. Mr. Dresser speaks of it as common near Matamoras during the summer, and he never visited the lagoon near the town without seeing several. On his journey to San Antonio, in September, he saw a number at different places near the coast; and in June, 1864, he saw two or three on Galveston Island, where it is known under the name of "Flamingo." He was informed that, in former years, it had been known to breed on the island, but that it does so no longer, having been too much disturbed. He received a specimen in a collection from Fort Stockton, where it was obtained on the 3d of August. Occasionally this species wanders up the creeks and rivers flowing into the Gulf, and a specimen was taken as high up on the Mississippi as Natchez. This was the locality of Wilson's type of the species. That author, however, regarded this bird as rare in Florida, while Nuttall thought it common in Jamaica; both these statements have, however, proved to be incorrect. Nuttall records a straggler as having been taken on the banks of the Delaware River; but there is no recent record of such an occurrence.

According to Dr. Berlandier (unpublished MSS.), the Roseate Spoonbill inhabits almost all the eastern coast of Mexico. It is in winter quite common about the lakes of Tampico, Tamiagua, the shores of Panonco, etc., advancing in the summer

[1] P. Z. S. 1875, p. 297.

as far north as Texas. It feeds on fishes and insects, which it hunts in the water. Its common names are "Garza Colorada," "Espatula," etc.

Dr. Henry Bryant, who visited Florida in 1858, states that at the time of his visit the Roseate Spoonbill was breeding in such numbers at Indian River that he has known one person to kill as many as sixty in a single day. The wing-feathers, being largely used in the manufacture of fans, were selling at from one dollar to one and a half for a single pair. He adds that this bird commences breeding at Pelican Island in February, having eggs as early as the middle of that month, the young being nearly fledged by the 1st of April. On the 10th of that month he found one nest containing an egg. All the rest were either empty, or the young were on the point of leaving them. This egg measured 2.56 inches in length, and 1.56 inches in breadth, and was of an elongated oval form, the difference between the two ends being strongly marked. The ground color he gives as white, sprinkled all over with bright rufous spots of different sizes, forming a ring near the large end. Dr. Bryant also met with a few at the Biminis, Bahama, where they were said to breed.

Mr. G. C. Taylor (Ibis, 1862), who visited Florida three years after Dr. Bryant, states that while, only a few years previous to his visit, this species had been very plentiful on Indian River, their number had of late become greatly diminished, owing to the destruction of them for the sake of their wings. He was informed that after breeding on Indian River it moves northwards, and remains during the summer in the salt-marshes about Smyrna. He saw a living bird that had been brought up from Indian River a year previous. It was quite tame, and associated freely with the poultry. While he was staying at Smyrna a person brought with him four young Spoonbills from Indian River which had been taken from their nest a short time previously. There appeared to be no difficulty in rearing them.

Audubon states that it is rarely met with as far north as the Carolinas. Dr. Bachman, during twenty years' observation, knew of but three instances. In one of these he obtained an individual in full plumage ten miles north of Charleston. He found it wintering among the keys near Cape Sable, where it remained until nearly the 1st of March, living chiefly along the watercourses and not far from the coast; they were not seen either wintering or breeding in the interior.

It is to be met with, for the most part, along the marshy or muddy borders of estuaries, the mouths of rivers, on sea islands, or keys partially overgrown with bushes, and still more abundantly along the shores of the salt-water bayous so common within a mile or two of the shore. There the Spoonbill can reside and breed, with almost complete security, in the midst of an abundance of food. It is said to be gregarious at all seasons, and that seldom less than half a dozen may be seen together, unless they have been dispersed by a tempest. At the approach of the breeding-season these small flocks collect together, forming immense collections, after the manner of the Ibis, and resort to their former breeding-places, to which they almost invariably return. Their moult takes place late in May; during this time the young of the previous year conceal themselves among the mangroves, there spending the day, and returning at night to their feeding-grounds, but keeping apart from the old birds, which last have passed through their spring moult early in March. Like the several species of Ibis, this bird is said occasionally to rise suddenly on the wing, and ascend gradually, in a spiral manner, to a great height. It flies with its neck stretched forward to its full length, and its legs and feet extended behind. It moves in the manner of a Heron, with easy flappings, until just as it is about to alight, when it sails over the spot with expanded wing, and comes gradually to the ground. It flies in a confused manner, except when on one of its extended movements.

It is usually found in the company of different Herons, whose vigilance apprises it of any danger. It can usually be approached, when feeding, with proper care. When one is wounded in the wing it usually makes for deep water, and swims for some distance without attempting to dive. If the wing is uninjured, this bird, even though mortally wounded, will fly until it drops dead. It is as nocturnal as the Night Heron, and its principal feeding-time is from near sunset until daylight. In procuring its food the Spoonbill usually wades up to the tibiæ, immerses its bill in the soft mud, with the head, and even the whole neck, beneath the surface, moving its partially opened mandibles to and fro laterally, munching the small fry — insects or shell-fish — before it swallows them. Where many are together, one usually acts as a sentinel. He did not see it feeding in fresh water, though he was told that it does so occasionally.

It can alight on a tree and walk on the large branches with all the facility of a Heron. Its eggs are usually three, and laid about the middle of April, in which his experience differs from that of Dr. Bryant. It builds on the tops of mangroves, placing each nest within a few yards of others. These are formed of sticks of considerable size, and are flat. The eggs are described as measuring 2.63 inches in length by 1.87 in breadth, slightly granulated, equally rounded at both ends, and of a pure white color — evidently the egg of the Brown Pelican, and not corresponding with any egg I have ever seen belonging to this species.

An identified egg in the Smithsonian Collection, obtained by Mr. Edwards in South America, measures 2.60 inches in length by 1.65 inches in breadth. The ground color is a dirty white, marked with small scattering spots of sepia-brown. Two eggs in my own collection (No. 69 and No. 71), from the Amazon River, and collected, one by Mr. John E. Warren, the other by Mr. William H. Edwards, are, as described by Dr. Bryant, of an oblong oval shape, with one end much more tapering than the other. Their ground-color is a dull creamy white, and they are marked with scattering blotches, "69" of dark sepia, "71" of sepia intermingled with fainter blotches of dilute sepia, having a purplish tinge. These measure, one 2.55 by 1.70 inches, the other 2.43 by 1.71 inches.

Three eggs in the Smithsonian Collection (No. 17045), collected in Southern Florida by Professor J. W. P. Jenks, measure respectively 2.65 by 1.80 inches; 2.80 by 1.70 inches; and 2.55 by 1.80 inches. Their ground-color, as in all other cases, is a dull chalky white; the markings are rather sparse, chiefly about the larger end, of different shades of amber-brown. This egg may always be distinguished from that of the White Ibis by its larger size, more rounded smaller ends, and the total absence of green tint in the ground-color. Another egg, No. 17044, given by Captain Bendire, is undistinguishable from No. 17045, measuring 2.65 by 1.80 inches.

ORDER LIMICOLÆ.

PRÆCOCIAL GRALLATORES.

CHAR. Præcocial wading birds, usually of small size, distinguished from the *Alectorides* (Cranes and Rails) by their lengthened, usually pointed, wings, small or rudimentary hind toe, or the latter member entirely wanting.

The very numerous species which together make up this group vary to such great extremes in the details of structure, that the above characters appear the most prominent ones which, in a comprehensive sense, distinguish the *Limicolæ* from the *Alectorides.* It is quite likely, however, that when their internal structure shall have been more extensively studied, more positive characters may be discovered for the trenchant separation of these two "Orders."

It is equally difficult to determine the exact number of Families into which the *Limicolæ* should be divided. It has been customary to allow five — namely, *Hæmatopodidæ* (including *Strepsilas*), *Charadriidæ* (including *Aphriza* and *Anarhynchus*), *Recurvirostridæ, Phalaropodidæ,* and *Scolopacidæ.* As to the three latter families, this division appears perfectly natural; but close study of the first two makes evident the necessity of their sharper definition, by the elimination of certain forms which appear too specialized, or which cannot be conveniently brought within the terms diagnosing either family. Notable examples are *Strepsilas,* usually associated with *Hæmatopus,* but which differs in numerous essential particulars; *Aphriza,* which resembles *Strepsilas* in most respects except the bill, which is like that of the true Plovers; *Anarhynchus,*[1] a very peculiar form, having the bill curved *sideways,* the other characters being Charadrine; and *Œdicnemus,* very large Plover-like birds, somewhat resembling the Bustards. The last-named genus has latterly been raised to family rank by Messrs. Sclater and Salvin; and it seems equally entitled with *Hæmatopus* to such a position. So, also, appear *Strepsilas* and *Anarhynchus,* the only alternative being to consider all, including *Hæmatopus,* of merely sub-family rank.

The following is an attempt to define the principal groups of *Limicolæ* according to their external structure.

A. Bill much longer than the tarsus, excessively compressed, deepest through the middle portion.
Hæmatopodidæ. No hind toe; a well-developed web between outer and middle toes at the base; front of tarsus covered with hexagonal scales. Size very large.

B. Bill about equal to or shorter than the tarsus, moderately compressed, deepest through the base.
Strepsilidæ. A well-developed hind-toe, with a claw; no trace of web between outer and middle toes; front of tarsus covered by a row of transverse scutellæ. Size small.

C. Bill variable, but never longer than the tarsus; more or less depressed in the middle portion; the terminal portion of the culmen being more or less arched; never expanded laterally at the end. Hind toe usually absent.

[1] Cf. "The Ibis," 1869, pp. 304–310, pl. viii.

Charadriidæ. Size large to very small. Bill slender or small, straight, always shorter than the tarsus.

Anarhynchidæ. Size small. Bill slender, *curved to one side*, equal to the tarsus.

Œdicnemidæ. Size very large (much the largest birds of the order). Tarsus nearly three times as long as the middle toe, covered in front with hexagonal scales. Plumage very plain, conspicuously streaked or striped above.

D. Characters much the same as given for section "C," but toes, including the hallux, exceedingly lengthened, the claws also very much lengthened; scutellation of legs much as in the Rallidæ.

Parridæ. Size medium or rather small. Claws very long and compressed, nearly straight, that of the hallux equal to or longer than its digit, linear, and slightly recurved. Bend of the wing (head of metacarpus) armed with a sharp conical horny spur.

E. Bill exceedingly variable, — short or long, straight, slightly recurved, or decidedly decurved, but usually more or less expanded laterally at the end, which is more or less sensitive. Hind toe usually present, rarely absent.

Scolopacidæ. Tarsus rounded in front, where clothed with a single row of transverse scutellæ.

F. Bill subulate (except in *Phalaropus*). Toes either partly webbed, or fringed by a lateral, usually lobed, margin. Plumage peculiarly soft and compact for this order, resembling greatly in this respect that of the *Longipennes*. Tarsi compressed, the anterior edge sharp.

Phalaropodidæ. Size small; tarsi and bill rather short, or but moderately lengthened; toes edged with a lateral, usually scalloped, margin.

Recurvirostridæ. Size large; tarsi and bill very long; toes partly webbed, and without scallopped margin.

FAMILY HÆMATOPODIDÆ. — THE OYSTER CATCHERS.

Hæmatopinæ, "G. R. GRAY, 1840."
Hæmatopodinæ, "G. R. GRAY, 1841;" Handl. III. 1871, 21.
Ostraleginæ, "REICH. 1849."

This family is characterized by the large size of the birds which compose it, their long, extremely compressed, almost knife-like and nearly truncate bill; their robust legs and feet, the former covered in front with hexagonal scales, the latter destitute of a hind toe, and having a well-developed web between the outer and middle toes, at their base. Properly restricted, it includes only the genus *Hæmatopus*, the characters of which are the same as those of the family.

GENUS **HÆMATOPUS**, LINNÆUS.

Hæmatopus, LINN. S. N. ed. 10, 1758, 152; ed. 12, 1766, 257 (type, *H. ostralegus*, LINN.).
Ostralega, BRISS. Orn. V. 1760, 38 (same type).
Melanibyx, REICH. Handb. 1853, p. xii (type, *H. niger*, PALL.).

Synopsis of North American Species.

COM. CHAR. Bill bright red in life (dull reddish or yellowish in dried skins); head, neck, and most of upper parts blackish (in some species entire plumage blackish).

A. *Plumage parti-colored (white and blackish).*

1. **H. ostralegus.** Entire rump white; back and wings black, like the neck and breast; iris

crimson; legs and feet (in life) purplish red. Wing, 9.80–10.25; culmen, 2.85–3.50; tarsus, 2.00–2.20; middle toe, 1.20–1.40. *Hab.* Palæarctic region, New Zealand, etc.

2. **H. palliatus.** Rump brownish slate, like back and wings; iris bright yellow; legs and feet dull fleshy white or pale dull flesh-color. *Young:* Top and sides of head speckled with pale brown; feathers of upper parts broadly margined with dull buff; bill brownish; iris brown. *Downy young:* Above, light brownish gray, faintly mottled with dusky, and marked with two irregular black stripes down the back and one along each side; a post-ocular black streak; lower parts, except foreneck, white. Wing, 9.75–11.00; culmen, 3.00–3.70; tarsus, 2.05–2.55; middle toe, 1.20–1.55. *Hab.* Coasts of America in general, except Pacific coast north of Lower California.

B. *Plumage entirely blackish.*

3. **H. niger.** Entire plumage brownish black, more plumbeous on the head and neck.

a. Wing, 9.60–10.75; culmen, 2.50–2.95; greatest depth of bill, forward of nostril, .45–.52; tarsus, 1.85–2.25; middle toe, 1.30–1.65. *Hab.* Pacific coast of North America. Var. *niger.*

b. Wing, 10.25–10.80; culmen, 2.90–3.00; tarsus, 2.20; middle toe, 1.70–1.75; greatest depth of bill anterior to nostril, .60. *Hab.* Pacific coast of South America. Var. *ater.*[1]

In this species, or race, according to authors, the iris is yellow, eyelids red or orange-red, bill orange-red, and feet flesh-color, or grayish.

H. palliatus.

The *Hæmatopus leucopus* (Garnot), recognized by Sclater and Salvin (*Nomenclator Neotropicalium*, p. 143), is a South American species, with which we are unacquainted. Its habitat is Tierra del Fuego. In the adult of this species the bill is red or orange-red, the iris bright yellow or orange, the eyelids yellow or red, the legs and feet flesh-colored or grayish. In the young, the bill is brownish, the iris brown, the legs and feet grayish. (*Cf.* Scl. & Salv. P. Z. S. 1878, 437, 438; Sharpe, P. Z. S. 1881, 15.)

[1] Hæmatopus niger ater.

Hæmatopus ater, Vieill. Gal. Ois. II. 1825, 88, pl. ccxx. — Cassin, in Baird's B. N. Am. 1858, 700. — Baird, Cat. N. Am. B. 1859, no. 514. — Scl. & Salv. P. Z. S. 1878, 438. — Sharpe, P. Z. S. 1881, 15.

Hæmatopus niger, Cuv. Règ. An. I. 1829, 504 (not of Pallas, 1831).

Hæmatopus Townsendii, Aud. Orn. Biog. V. 1839, 247, pl. 427; Synop. 1839, 229; B. Am. V. 1842, 245, pl. 326.

Hæmatopus ostralegus.

EUROPEAN OYSTER CATCHER.

Hæmatopus ostralegus, LINN. Faun. Suec. 69 ; S. N. ed. 10, 1758, 152 ; ed. 12, 1766, 257. — NAUM. Vög. Deutschl. VII. 1834, 325, pl. 181. — SCHLEG. Rev. Crit. 85. — KEYS. & BLAS. Wirb. Eur. 71. — GRAY, Gen. B. III. 547 ; Cat. Brit. B. 1863, 142. — MACGILL. Hist. Brit. B. IV. 1852, 152. — RIDGW. Nom. N. Am. B. 1881, no. 506. — COUES, Check List, 2d ed. 1882, no. 595 ("*ostrilegus*").

Hæmatopus hypoleucus, PALL. Zoög. Rosso-As. II. 1811, 129.

Hæmatopus longirostris, VIEILL. Enc. Méth. II. 1820, 340. — GOULD. B. Austr. VI. pl. 7.

Hæmatopus picatus, VIGORS, King's Voy. Austr. Alp. 420.

Ostralega pica, BONNAT. Enc. Méth. 1790, 25.

Ostralega europæa, LESS. Traité, 1831, 548.

Hæmatopus australasianus, GOULD, P. Z. S. 1837, 155.

Ostralegus vulgaris, LESS. Rev. Zoöl. 1839, 47.

Ostralegus hæmatopus, MACGILL. Man. II. 59.

Hæmatopus balticus, BREHM, Vög. Deutschl. 563.

Hæmatopus orientalis, BREHM, l. c.

Hæmatopus osculans, SWINH. P. Z. S. 1871, 405.

Pied Oyster Catcher, PENN. Brit. Zoöl. II. 1812, 112, pl. 19.

Oyster Catcher, YARR. Brit. B. ed. 2, II. 496, fig. ; ed. 3, II. 525, fig., et AUCT.

HAB. Sea-coasts of the Palæarctic region, New Zealand, etc. ; occasional in Greenland (REINH. J. f. O. 1854, 425 ; Ibis, 1861–1869. Julianehaab, 1847 ; Godthaab, 1851 ; Nenortalik, three specimens).

SP. CHAR. *Adult:* Head, neck, jugulum, wings, and tail, black, the head and neck somewhat plumbeous in certain lights, the wings and tail slightly brownish. Rest of the plumage, including the entire rump, upper tail-coverts, base of the tail, greater wing-coverts, and lower parts, pure white. Throat sometimes with a white transverse band, and in some specimens other white

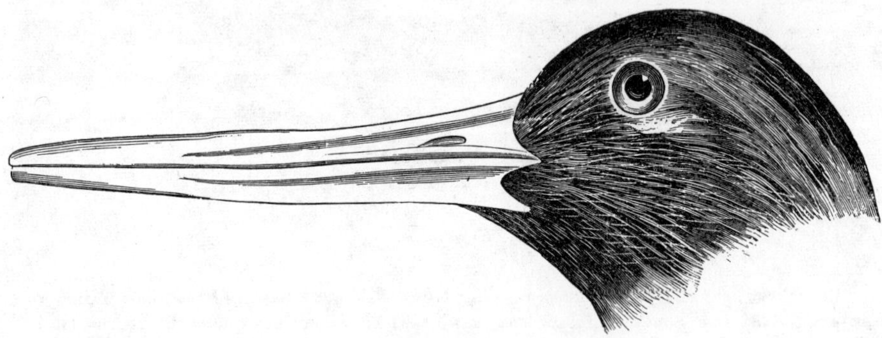

markings about the head.[1] Bill "vermilion, tinged with yellow as far as the end of the nasal groove, the attenuated part dull yellow;" iris crimson, eyelids vermilion; feet "pale lake or purplish red." (MACGILLIVRAY.) *Young:* "General color of the dark parts . . . deep chocolate-brown, the feathers slightly margined with yellowish red; the breast, belly, greater part of the back [*i. e.* rump ?], half of the tail, and its coverts . . . white;" bill "more tinged with orange, but the feet . . . nearly as described above" (MACGILLIVRAY).

[1] According to Macgillivray (*Hist. Brit. B.* IV. p. 155), these variations appear to be of an individual character, "birds at all seasons occurring with the varieties as to the white marks on the neck mentioned above."

The changes of plumage with age are thus described by Macgillivray: "After the first moult the black parts of the plumage are tinged with brown, more especially the quills and tail. There is an obscure half-ring of grayish-white across the fore part of the neck, the tips of the white feathers being black. The legs are pale livid gray, the claws brown, whitish at the base; the iris crimson; and the bill as in the adult, but a little more dusky toward the end. It appears to me that the younger birds only have the white marks on the neck, and that these gradually disappear each successive moult, until in very old birds there exist only faint indications of them, the feathers being merely whitish at the base. The chin, which is slightly mottled with white in the young birds, becomes at length pure black."

The National Museum possesses but a single European specimen of this species, an adult male from Pomerania. Besides this, however, there are two examples (an adult male and female) from Ning Po, China, and one from New Zealand. None of these possess the slightest trace of the white markings described by Macgillivray, the entire neck being glossy black.

The Pied Oyster Catcher from New Zealand and that from China have both been separated from *H. ostralegus*, the former as *H. longirostris*, VIEILLOT, the latter as *H. osculans*, SWINHOE. With the specimens before us, however, we are unable to appreciate any differences beyond slight ones of proportions, the measurements being as follows: —

			Wing.	Culmen.	Depth of bill at base.	Tarsus.	Middle toe.
No. 56899	♂ ad.	Pomerania,	10.25	3.10	.55	2.00	1.40
" 85740	♂ "	Ning Po,	10.00	3.35	.55	2.00	1.30
" 85741	♀ "	"	10.10	2.85	.50	2.15	1.35
" 66276	♀ "	New Zealand,	10.10	3.50	.60	2.10	1.25

The differences of measurements indicated above are not so great as have been found in a larger series of *H. palliatus*, and we are unable to discover any differences of plumage.

The Oyster Catcher of Europe is of occasional occurrence in Iceland and Greenland, and claims, on that account alone, to be included among the birds of our fauna. It is found along the entire Atlantic sea-coast of Europe, is to be seen around the shores of Great Britain, from the Scilly Islands to the Shetland, and is common in Denmark, Sweden, and on the west shores of Norway, from spring to autumn. Pennant states that this species is to be found along the northern shores of Russia and Siberia, where it breeds on the great Arctic flats, and that it even extends its range to Kamtschatka.

This species also inhabits all the coasts of the southern portion of Europe, passing to North Africa by the line of Italy and Sicily. It is included by Temminck among the birds of Japan, and by Reinhardt among those of Greenland, on the strength of three specimens — one sent from Julianehaab in 1847, another from Godthaab in 1851, and a third found in a collection from Nenortalik. Mr. Alfred Newton states that it is more common in the south than in the north of Iceland, and Faber considered it resident throughout the year, as it remained in large flocks during the winter in the south. It is most abundant on the sea-coast, but was found by Herr Preyer on some of the inland waters.

In Great Britain and Ireland it is a common and a well-known species. It appears to prefer the sandy shores of bays and wide inlets bounded with banks of shingle and other localities favorable for the production of the various kinds of mollusks upon which it principally feeds. Its peculiar beak, truncated and wedge-like in its shape, and having a sharp vertical edge, is admirably well adapted for insertion between the two portions of bivalve shells and for forcing them open. The Oyster Catcher is also able with this powerful beak to detach univalve shells and limpets from the surface of rocks, and does this easily and rapidly. Its food appears to be mollusca of all kinds, worms, crustacea, and marine insects.

Mr. Selby speaks of this species as a very handsome bird when seen on the wing, the marked contrast of its pure black and white coloration producing a very striking effect.

The Oyster Catcher can run with great rapidity, and is able both to swim and to dive with ease; and may frequently be seen swimming short distances in search of food. But it seldom or never dives, except when driven to do so by danger, and in order to effect its escape from an enemy.

Although the Oyster Catcher is essentially a shore bird, Yarrell cites quite a number of instances in which it has been found far inland. In one case it was taken at Oatlands, on the Thames, fifty miles from its mouth. Another writer, in the Magazine of Natural History (VI. p. 151), states that in the summer it may always be found along the Don, thirty miles or more from the sea, and that it breeds as high up as Kildrummy. Yarrell states that young birds of this species are readily and frequently tamed, and can easily be made to associate with domestic poultry; he also mentions that a flock of these birds used, some years ago, to run about inside the railing on the grass in front of the Pavilion at Brighton.

In the wild state the birds of this species unite in small flocks towards winter, and are then very shy and difficult of approach. In spring they again separate into pairs, many of these associating and breeding together at particular favorite localities. Montagu mentions that they appeared to be more abundant on some parts of the sandy flat coasts of Lincolnshire than in any other region with which he was acquainted. At a point on that coast called Gibraltar there is an isolated marsh where Oyster Catchers were then known to breed, in such great abundance that a fisherman informed Mr. Montagu that he had collected a bushel of their eggs in a single morning.

The Oyster Catcher makes no nest, but deposits its eggs — usually four in number — on the bare ground, on a shingly beach above high-water mark. They are 2.17 inches in length by 1.50 inches in breadth, and have a yellowish stone ground color, and are spotted and blotched with ashy gray and dark brown.

The female is said to sit upon her eggs about three weeks. During all this time the male keeps a sharp watch, and on the approach of an enemy becomes very clamorous. His mate, warned by this signal of danger, leaves her nest in silence, and after a circuitous flight, joins him in his endeavors to mislead and to decoy away the intruder. The young, when first hatched, are covered with a grayish-brown down.

Hæmatopus palliatus.

AMERICAN OYSTER CATCHER.

Hæmatopus palliatus, TEMM. Man. II. 1820, 532. — AUD. Orn. Biog. III. 1835, 181; V. 580, pl. 223; Synop. 1839, 228; Birds Am. V. 1842, 236, pl. 324. — BAIRD, Birds N. Am. 1858, 699; Cat. N. Am. B. 1859, no. 512. — COUES, Key, 1872, 246; Check List, 1873, no. 404; 2d ed. 1882, no. 596. — RIDGW. Nom. N. Am. B. 1881, no. 507.

"*Hæmatopus ostralegus,*" WILS. Am. Orn. VIII. 1814, 15 pl. lxiv. (nec LINN.).

Hæmatopus arcticus, JARD. ed. Wilson, III. 1832, 35.

? *Hæmatopus* "*brasiliensis,* LICHT." (GRAY, Handl. III. p. 21).

HAB. Sea-coasts of temperate and tropical America, from Nova Scotia and Lower California to Patagonia; Bahamas; Cuba; Tres Marias; Galapagos. Apparently wanting on the Pacific coast of the United States north of Santa Barbara.

SP. CHAR. *Adult:* Head and neck uniform black, with a plumbeous cast in certain lights; back, wings, and tail slate-brown. Rest of the plumage, including the greater wing-coverts, tertials, and basal half of the secondaries, upper tail-coverts, sides of the rump, basal portion of the tail, and the entire lower parts pure white. Bill (in life) rich vermilion, most intense on middle third, basal third more scarlet, the tip yellowish; eyelids rich vermilion; iris bright yellow; legs and feet pale dull fleshy white.[1] *Young:* Head and neck dusky black, the pileum and cheeks speckled with dull fulvous, and the feathers surrounding the base of the bill whitish; upper parts grayish brown, each feather widely margined with pale fulvous or dull buff. Otherwise much like the adult, but upper tail-coverts tipped with buff, bill brownish, iris brown, and feet dull livid grayish. *Downy young:* Head and neck dull light cinereous, finely mottled with darker, and with a narrow postocular line of black; rest of upper parts light fulvous gray, finely mottled with darker, and relieved by two narrow stripes of black, which extend, parallel to one another, from the upper part of the back to the rump. Lower parts, from the jugulum back, immaculate white. Bill dusky, the basal half of the mandible dull orange; iris brown; legs and feet pale dull flesh-color.

Total length, 17 to 21 inches; extent, 32 to 36. Wing, 9.75 to 11.00; culmen, 3.00 to 3.70; tarsus, 2.05 to 2.55; niddle toe, 1.20 to 1.55.

Specimens from nearly all parts of the range of the species have been compared. There is little, if any, variation in colors, but the dimensions vary with the individual. Two Chilian examples have the smallest bill, the culmen measuring respectively 3.00 and 3.25, the greatest depth of the bill, forward of the nostril, being .48. In an example from Isabella Island, Western Mexico, these measurements are 3.10 and .55. In a specimen from Yucatan, the depth of the bill is scarcely .45, the culmen being the same length as in the preceding.

On the Atlantic coast the American Oyster Catcher occurs in more or less abundance, from Massachusetts to Central America. Like the *H. ostralegus* of Europe, it probably wanders inland, especially up the inlets and estuaries of the Carolinas. Wilson mentions having received a stuffed specimen shot from a flock that had been first discovered on a beach near the entrance of Boston Harbor, and in the summer of 1837 a pair of these birds were procured at Marshfield by Daniel Webster and presented to the Boston Natural History Society. It was then no uncommon thing to see specimens of this bird on sale in the Boston market; but this seldom or never occurs now, and the bird for many years, so far as known, has been a stranger to Massachusetts. Mr. Boardman informs me that it is of occasional but rare occurrence in the vicinity of Calais, Me., and that a single specimen has been taken on Grand Menan.

An Oyster Catcher was observed by Mr. Salvin at the mouth of the Nagualete River, and he regarded it as being referable to this species; he also mentions meeting with it on the Pacific coast of Guatemala. Dr. Cooper states that he obtained two specimens of this bird — one at San Diego, the other on Santa Barbara Island, in

[1] Fresh colors of several specimens killed in the breeding-season at Cobb's Island, coast of Virginia.

the months of May and June. The last contained an egg nearly ready for exclusion. The birds were alone, or rather, were associating with the black species only; but not in pairs, as they did. From this Dr. Cooper supposed that it is a mere straggler on the Pacific coast: perhaps more common southward, but it had not been observed by him farther north. He found them among the seaweeds on the rocks, or along the sandy beach, feeding chiefly on small crustacea and mollusca, and very wild. They swallowed small shell-covered animals, either entire or partially broken.

Dr. Bryant mentions finding the Oyster Catcher abundant everywhere throughout the Bahamas, resident and breeding wherever there were sandy or gravelly beaches. It also breeds on the Island of Cuba, from whence we have received undoubted specimens of its eggs.

Léotaud mentions this species as an irregular visitant of Trinidad, where it arrives in small flocks some years, and not at all in others. It usually came in August, and left in October. Mr. Dresser met with a couple in Galveston Bay in June. His boatman called them "Pillwillet," but did not confound them with the Red Willet. He said they were not a common species, but that one or two pairs bred occasionally on the outer island in West Bay. And Dr. Merrill informs us that the Oyster Catcher breeds on Padre and Brazos islands, near the mouth of the Rio Grande.

Mr. H. Durnford ("Ibis," 1878) mentions meeting with several pairs of this species on Tombo Point in Central Patagonia, and evidently nesting, although he failed to discover the eggs: this was in December. He also states that this bird occasionally occurs at the mouth of the Chupat. The fact that it is found in the extreme southern portion of South America is suggestive of its occurrence along the entire coast of that continent; and this is partially confirmed by its presence on the Marias, where Mr. Grayson found it common, as well as on the main coast of Mexico on the Pacific.

Giraud, in his "Birds of Long Island," mentions finding this species a rather scarce bird on Long Island, although during the summer a few may be seen on almost every beach, along the whole extent of its sea-coast. In pairs or in small parties it frequents the sandy beaches or shoals in quest of its food, which consists chiefly of mussels, small crabs, and marine insects. It is apparently confined to the coast, and along that of New Jersey and farther south is more common. Giraud was informed that at low water it visits the oyster-beds, awaiting a favorable opportunity, when the shells open, to thrust in its hard and strong bill and to rob them of their contents. Those seen on Long Island were usually solitary birds, or at most a pair at any time, and were all between Raynor South and Babylon, in which section no oysters are found. They were shy, vigilant, and exceedingly difficult to approach. Their flight is swift, and they have a stately walk. When alarmed this bird utters a sharp whistling note, and runs rapidly along the beach. Should the pursuit be continued, it takes wing, and passes rapidly out of sight. Although its flesh is dark colored and ill-flavored, yet, as it is regarded as a singular as well as a rare bird, it is always sent to the New York market by the Bay-men, by whom it is called the "Flood Gull." Giraud adds that it forms no regular nest, but deposits its eggs — usually three in number — on the sand, leaving them, in fine weather, during the day to be hatched out by the influence of the sun. When wounded, this bird always makes for the water, in which it can both swim and dive well. In autumn it migrates southward, and large numbers are said to winter in Florida, and at that season to collect in flocks; it is, however, said to be rare at St. Augustine.

Wilson found it frequenting the sandy sea-beaches of New Jersey in small parties of two or three pairs together. It was shy, and rarely permitted approach within gunshot, except during the season of breeding. It walked along the shore in a watchful and stately manner, from time to time probing the ground with its bill in search of food. The hard sand to which it resorts was found thickly perforated with oblong holes two or three inches in depth. The fiddler-crab, as well as mussels, sport-fish, and a variety of other shell-fish and sea-insects, with which those shores abound, were its principal food. The inhabitants of Egg Harbor and those of other parts of the coast did not credit its alleged feeding upon oysters, stating that it is never seen in their neighborhood, but confines itself solely to the sands; and this statement Wilson confirms, stating that he has uniformly found it on the smooth beach bordering the ocean; and on the higher dry and level sands, just beyond the reach of tides, and at points where the dry flats are thickly interspersed with drifted shells, he usually found its nests between the middle and the 25th of May. The nest is said to be merely a slight hollow in the sand, and usually contains three eggs, which, when fresh, have a bluish cream-colored ground, marked with large roundish spots of black, and others of a fainter tint. In some eggs this blue tint was wanting, and in these the blotches were larger and of a deep brown. The young were hatched about the 25th of May, and sometimes earlier; Wilson himself found them running about the beach at that period. When I visited the sandy islands off Cape Charles in June, 1852, there were no young birds found, and all the eggs of this species were fresh — a condition probably owing to the fact that their eggs had been previously taken, and no opportunity afforded for their hatching at an earlier period. The young birds are described by Wilson as being at first covered with down of a grayish color, resembling that of the sand, and marked with a streak of blackish brown on the neck, back, and rump, the breast being dusky where in the old birds it is black. Their bills are slightly bent at the tip, and have a hard protuberance, which falls off in a few days after they are hatched. They run along the shore with great ease and swiftness. The female sits on her eggs only during the night or during cold and rainy weather, the heat of the sun and of the sand at other times rendering her presence unnecessary; but she is said to watch the spot with anxiety and fidelity. The young follow the mother from the shell, squat on the sand — from which they are with difficulty distinguished — whenever there is any danger, while both parents make large circuits around the intruder, uttering repeated cries, and practising the common stratagem of counterfeited lameness. Their note is said to be a loud and shrill whistling, like *wheep-wheep-wheō* sharply uttered. A flock of these birds will often rise, descend, and wheel in air with remarkable regularity, as if drilled to the practice; at such times the glittering white of their wings is very conspicuous. This peculiarity is also mentioned by Jardine as having been noticed by him in the European *ostralegus*.

The stomachs of the birds opened by Wilson contained fragments of shell-fish, pieces of crabs and of the great king-crab, with some dark brown marine insects.

Audubon claims to have met with this species in Labrador, and states that he there found several breeding in the month of July. He afterward adds that he saw this bird farther inland in Labrador than in any other part of the country. I am only able to reconcile this statement with the remarkable rarity of this species from Montauk Point to Grand Menan, and with the singular fact that we have no mention by any other author of its appearance on that coast, by supposing that Mr. Audubon was misinformed, or in some way misled in regard to its occurrence farther north.

The eggs of this species vary in length from 2.25 to 2.45 inches, and in breadth from 1.65 to 1.70 inches. Their ground-color is a fawn-colored white, and their markings are of bistre; these are partly rounded spots, and partly irregular confluent blotches, lines, and oblong dashes. The dark-bistre is occasionally washed with the fawn-color of the ground, giving to these markings a diluted, neutral appearance.

Hæmatopus niger.

BLACK OYSTER CATCHER.

Hæmatopus niger, PALL. Zoög. Rosso-As. II. 1831, 131. — BAIRD, Birds N. Am. 1858, 700; Cat. N. Am. B. 1859, no. 513. — COUES, Key, 1872, 246; Check List, 1873, no. 405; 2d ed. 1882, no. 597 — RIDGW. Nom. N. Am. B. 1882, no. 508.

Hæmatopus Bachmani, AUD. Orn. Biog. V. 1839, 245, pl. 427; Synop. 1839, 229; Birds Am. V. 1842, 243, pl. 325. — TOWNS. Narr. 1839, 348.

HAB. Pacific coast of North America, as far south as Lower California; breeding south to Santa Cruz, California. Kurile Islands.

SP. CHAR. *Adult:* Head, neck, and jugulum black, with more or less of a plumbeous cast; rest of the plumage uniform blackish brown. "Bill vermilion, fading to yellow on the worn parts toward the end. Edges of eyelids vermilion; iris yellow. Feet white, slightly tinged with flesh-color; claws yellowish, toward the end dusky" (AUDUBON).

Wing, 9.60–10.75; culmen, 2.50–2.95; greatest depth of bill (forward of nostril), .45–.52; tarsus, 1.85-2.25; middle toe, 1.30–1.65.

There is no very young specimen of *H. niger* in the collection; but a very young example of the southern form (var. *ater*) from Tierra del Fuego (No. 15484) is wholly dusky blackish, each

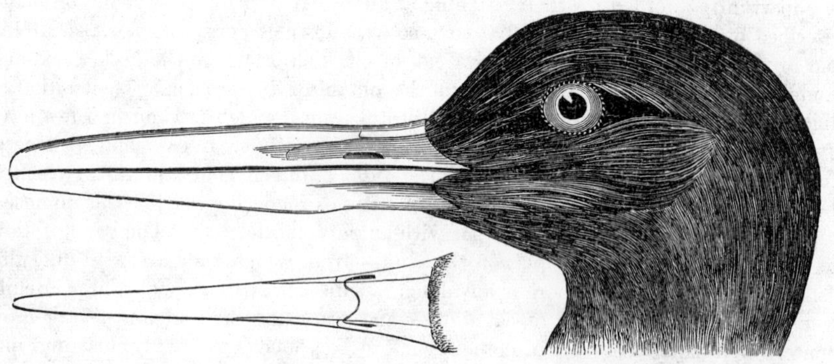

feather, above and below, except on the head and neck, tipped with a narrow bar of pale ochraceous. This character of immaturity is indicated in several of the specimens of *H. niger* in the collection by the presence of a few whitish narrow bars on the abdomen. One example, still younger (No. 28009, Straits of Fuca), has some of the wing-coverts narrowly and indistinctly tipped with ochraceous, and the bill is yellowish horn-color, except on the basal portion.

This species, first made known as a North American bird by Townsend, was called by Audubon Bachman's Oyster Catcher. It had been previously described by Pallas as belonging to Northeastern Asia and the surrounding islands. Mr. Townsend mentions having found it abundant along the whole of our northwest coast, as well as in Regent's Sound. The specimens mentioned by these authors were shot in June, 1836. Other specimens have since been taken in Alaska, at San Miguel Island, Sitka, Kadiak, in California, and elsewhere.

Mr. R. Browne (Ibis, 1868) states that this species, though not a common bird in the southern portion of Vancouver Island, is quite abundant at the northern end, and very plentiful about Queen Charlotte Islands. In March, 1866, while rowing along the narrow sounds among these islands, he often met with it. It was by no means shy, but would sit on the rocks until he could almost touch it; then, uttering a low whistling cry, it would dart off to another skerry, repeating the same manœuvre again and again.

Dr. Cooper regards the Black Oyster Catcher as an eminently characteristic bird of our Pacific coast. He adds that it is more common to the northward than to the south, and that it is particularly partial to rocky coasts and islands, being rarely met with on sand beaches. He found a few on Santa Barbara Island, in May, 1863, and discovered a nest on the 3d of June containing four fresh eggs, supposed to have been a second laying. They were in a slight depression in the gravel, close to the edge of a rocky cliff, against which the waves were dashing almost to its top, and a very slight roll would have sent the water over them. The old birds, unlike the Plovers, showed great solicitude for their eggs, both of them flying round close to him, with a loud whistle, which was their only cry.

Dr. Cooper describes their eggs as measuring from 2.28 to 2.40 inches in length, and from 1.50 to 1.53 inches in breadth. They have a brownish-white ground, sparsely blotched with markings of a light and of a darker brown.

Dr. Cooper thinks that this species does not breed in any of the islands south of Santa Barbara, as he met with none of them during the summer, and saw none along the southern coast. He has noticed this species on the Farallon Islands in June, and believes that this is the bird referred to by Dr. Heermann as *H. Townsendii* of Audubon, inasmuch as this latter has never been seen north of Panama. This last-named species is one that may readily be recognized by its blood-red legs; and Dr. Cooper ventures the suggestion that Townsend really obtained his specimen of it from South America, as it is now known that he did several other species of birds wrongly credited to our coast. Dr. Cooper adds that there appears to be really very little, if any, difference in the habits or cries of the *niger* and those of the *palliatus*, both of which species associate together during the breeding-season.

Mr. Dall mentions this bird as a summer visitor to the Aleutian Islands, and says that it was seen both in Malashka and in the Shumegins. The eggs, partly incubated, were obtained on Range Island, Popoff Strait, June 23, 1872. There were two in one, and one in another, nest, these being mere depressions in the gravel of the beach, with no lining whatever. The birds were exceedingly wary, and kept entirely out of gunshot. When disturbed they uttered a peculiar low whistle, which, once heard, is likely to be remembered; and they have a habit of standing on the beach or rocks a little way apart, and whistling, one calling and the other answering, keeping this up for half an hour at a time. It is one of the most peculiar birds of that region, having a grave, solemn, and stilted gait, and bobbing its head up and down with every step as it moves.

Mr. H. W. Henshaw met with the Black Oyster Catcher in considerable numbers on Santa Cruz Island, and was informed that they occur on other islands of that group, frequenting the little islets that are separated from the main island by narrow channels, and finding these breeding-grounds safe from the intrusion of their enemies. Their short stout legs and feet adapt them for a life among the rocks, and they obtain much of their food among the kelp and seaweed which cover the slippery rocks and shelter various crustaceans and mollusks. Their long, strong, and wedge-like bill is admirably adapted for prying open bivalve shells. On Santa Cruz Island they seemed to obtain a plentiful supply of food by feeding, along the sandy beaches, on objects cast up by the waves or floating on the surface. Their movements appeared rather clumsy, and as if they felt a little out of place. The birds were not at all shy, and permitted Mr. Henshaw to approach them within thirty yards as they wandered along the beach. They were the noisiest of all the feathered tribe frequenting the island, and their harsh and vociferous cries were heard all the day long. After some search he succeeded in finding two nests. One, containing a single fresh-laid egg, was found, June 6, on the extreme point of a high cliff jutting over the sea; the second, obtained a few days later, was on a small islet. The nests were rude affairs, being slight hollows in the pebbly detritus, with bits of stone brought from elsewhere. There was no grass or any lining softer than the stones themselves. In one case the two eggs had been incubated, and were probably all that would have been laid. The eggs were undistinguishable from those of the *palliatus.* Their ground-color was a faint grayish drab, profusely marked with irregular blotches of black. They measured 2.27 by 1.59, 2.29 by 1.48, and 2.18 by 1.52 inches.

Eggs of this species obtained by Mr. Hepburn on Puget Sound average 2.17 by 1.55 inches. Their ground-color is a light olivaceous drab, spotted with rounded markings distributed in a general, but scattered, manner over the entire egg. These spots are of a dark bistre, almost black; and these eggs differ greatly from those of the *palliatus.* From the different aspects presented by the eggs procured by Mr. Hepburn and Mr. Henshaw, it would seem that the eggs of this species must vary, and that while some closely resemble those of the eastern species, others are quite different.

Family STREPSILIDÆ. — The Turnstones.

Strepsilinæ, "G. R. Gray, 1840."
Strepsilidæ, Ridgw. Bull. Ills. State Laborat. Nat. Hist. no. 4, May, 1881, p. 194.
Cinclinæ, "G. R. Gray, 1841;" Handl. III. 1871, 22.

Char. Rather small, Plover-like birds, differing from the true Plovers (*Charadriidæ*) chiefly in the more robust feet, without trace of web between the toes, the well-developed hind toe, and the strong claws; the toes with a lateral margin, forming a broad flat under surface (especially in *Aphriza*); the bill of one genus (*Strepsilas*) peculiar. The two genera may be distinguished by the following characters: —

Strepsilas. Bill compressed and pointed terminally, somewhat upturned at the end, the culmen straight or even slightly concave; tarsus not longer than the bill; tail slightly rounded.

Aphriza. Bill slightly swollen terminally, the terminal portion of the culmen decidedly convex; tarsus decidedly longer than the bill; tail slightly emarginated.

Genus **STREPSILAS,** Illiger.

Morinella, Meyer & Wolf, Taschb. Vög. Deutschl. II. 1810, 383 (type, *Tringa interpres,* Linn.).
Strepsilas, Illiger, Prodromus, 1811 (same type).

Char. Form robust, the head small, neck short, wings long and pointed, feet stout. Bill straight along the culmen (or else slightly concave above), somewhat upturned terminally, compressed toward the end and pointed. Wings reaching beyond the tail, the first primary longest, the tertials not reaching to end of the primaries. Tail slightly rounded. Tarsus decidedly longer than the middle toe, the latter shorter than the bill.

The two species of this genus, both of which are American (one of them exclusively so), may be distinguished as follows: —

COM. CHAR. Lower parts (except jugulum), upper part of rump, upper tail-coverts, and greater wing-coverts, pure white; remainder of plumage dusky, sometimes variegated with white, or white and rufous.

S. interpres.

1. **S. interpres.** Throat always white. *Adult:* Upper parts more or less mixed with rufous, especially in winter plumage, when this color prevails in large patches; head mostly white; jugulum uniform deep black. *Young:* Head mostly dusky; upper parts without rufous, but with ochraceous edgings; jugulum mottled dusky. Wing, about 6.00; culmen, .80–.90; tarsus, 1.00; middle toe, .75. *Hab.* Entirely cosmopolitan, but affecting chiefly the sea-coasts.
2. **S. melanocephalus.** Throat always dusky. *Adult in summer:* Upper parts uniform bronzy brownish black; head, neck, and jugulum, black, with white streaks on forehead and jugulum, and large spot of same on lores. *Adult in winter:* Similar, but head, neck, and jugulum, smoky brownish, and without white markings. *Young:* Similar to the winter plumage, but head, etc., more grayish, the feathers of upper parts bordered terminally with pale buff, or whitish. Wing, 8.80–9.10; culmen, .85–1.00; tarsus, 1.00–1.10; middle toe, .90. *Hab.* Northwest coast of North America.

Strepsilas interpres.

TURNSTONE.

Tringa interpres, LINN. S. N. ed. 10, 1758, I. 148; ed. 12, I. 1766, 248. — WILS. Am. Orn. VII. 1813, 32, pl. lvii.

Strepsilas interpres, ILLIG. Prodr. 1811, 263. — SWAINS. F. B. A. II. 1831, 371. — NUTT. Man. Water Bds. 1834, 30. — AUD. Orn. Biog. IV. 1838, 31, pl. 304; Synop. 1839, 227; Birds Am. V. 1842, 231, pl. 323. — BAIRD, B. N. Am. 1858, 701; Cat. N. Am. B. 1859, no. 515. — COUES, Key, 1872, 246; Check List, 1873, no. 406; 2d ed. 1881, no. 598. — RIDGW. Nom. N. Am. B. 1882, no. 509.

Morinella interpres, STEJN. Proc. U. S. Nat. Mus. Vol. 4, 1882, 32.

Tringa morinellus, LINN. S. N. I. 1766, 249 (= young).

Strepsilas collaris, TEMM. Man. II. 1820, 553.

"*Charadrius cinclus,* PALLAS" (BAIRD, l. c.).

HAB. Sea-coasts of nearly all countries; in America, from Greenland and Alaska to Chili and Brazil; in the interior, more or less common along the shores of the Great Lakes and larger rivers.

SP. CHAR. *Adult:* Chin and throat, a large loral patch, another covering terminal half of the auriculars, border of the pileum, and large transverse patch on each side of the jugulum, white; stripe from the frontlet to the eye, squarish patch beneath the eye, malar stripe, side of the neck, jugulum, and sides of the breast, uniform black, all these markings confluent and sharply defined.

Remainder of the lower parts, upper part of the rump, upper tail-coverts, and ends of secondaries, pure white. *Breeding-plumage:* Upper parts dusky blackish, the wing-coverts lighter, more brownish gray, the feathers showing darker centres; back and scapulars little, if at all, varied with rufous; crown dusky, uniform, or streaked. *Spring (and winter?) plumage:* Upper parts mixed black and bright rufous, the latter color occupying chiefly the middle of the back (longitudinally) and the wing-coverts, the scapulars and tertials mixed black and rufous. Pileum more streaked with white, and markings about the head and neck more sharply defined than in the summer dress. "Bill black; iris hazel; feet deep orange-red, claws black" (AUDUBON). *Young:* Head chiefly mottled grayish, without well-defined markings; black of the jugulum and breast indicated by mottled dusky, occupying the same area, but not sharply defined; upper parts grayish dusky, the feathers bordered terminally with buff or whitish.

Total length about 9 inches; wing, 6.00; tail, 2.50; culmen, .80–.90; tarsus, 1.00; middle toe, .75.

Spring plumage.

The variations noted in a series of more than sixty specimens of this species are chiefly individual and seasonal. Examples are variously intermediate, according to the season, between the two quite distinct stages of plumage described above as the breeding and the winter dress. Unfortunately there are very few specimens from other countries than America, so that we cannot say whether those from different continents differ perceptibly. Two European examples, however, in the winter livery, seem identical with American skins.

The specimens in the dark, dull-colored summer plumage have been erroneously considered as showing a tendency toward the characters of *S. melanocephalus*, or forming the "connecting link" between that species and *S. interpres* — this view being apparently based on geographical considerations, the specimens upon which this opinion was founded coming from the Prybilof Islands. Specimens in the same plumage occur, however, throughout the northern regions, including the Old World, and apparently represent simply the summer dress.

The series of summer specimens from other localities than Alaska, however, is unfortunately very small; and it may possibly prove true, that what we have described above as the breeding-plumage of true *S. interpres* represents really a darker-colored Alaskan race, and that the brighter-colored plumage described as the winter dress is really the full breeding-plumage of true *interpres*. However this may be, the dark Alaskan birds have nothing whatever to do with *S. melanocephalus*, which has not only very different proportions, but also in every stage a conspicuously different pattern of coloration.

The Common Turnstone is one of the most widely distributed and at the same time one of the most abundant of birds. Breeding in great numbers in all the high Arctic regions, and in the northern portions of both continents, it wanders thence southward over all lands. It is found at certain seasons on both the Atlantic and Pacific shores, and also in the interior of North and South America, as far even as the Straits of Magellan. It has been taken in various parts of Europe, Africa, and Asia.

Deriving its name from its singular habit of turning over small stones when searching for food, in quest of the marine insects that lurk underneath them, it is as remarkable in its appearance as in its habits. The singular variety of its colors and the beauty of its plumage render it conspicuous, and cause it to be universally noticed.

Mr. F. Ducane Godman mentions (Ibis, 1866) meeting with this species in the Azores. A few pairs could always be found among the rocks between Santa Cruz and Punta Delgada, on Flores. He obtained several specimens in June, in the full breeding-plumage, and he had no doubt that they were breeding on the small islands near the coast, as they remained there all the year. He afterward met with others in Fayal, near Capellas, and has no doubt that this bird may be found on the coast of the entire group in greater or less numbers. The same writer, in his paper on the migratory birds of Madeira and the Canaries (Ibis, 1871), again expresses his belief that the Turnstone breeds in the Azores, and also on the Canary Islands, where it is not uncommon near the coast.

Dr. J. C. Merrill mentions the presence of this species during the months of May and June along the coast of Southwestern Texas, and was confident that it was breeding there — an opinion strongly corroborated by his procuring examples of females with denuded breast, the almost sure evidence of their having been nesting birds.

Mr. Nelson also speaks of having found the Turnstone as a common migrant along the shores of Lake Michigan, in which neighborhood it arrives about the 15th of May, coming in full bridal plumage and remaining into June. It returns again in August, still in the full breeding-plumage, which it loses about the last of that month. It does not leave that neighborhood until about the 20th of December.

Mr. E. L. Layard, when off Cape St. Francis, Africa, but out of sight of land, observed a flock of four that came off to his vessel. Mr. E. C. Taylor (Ibis, 1878) mentions the procuring by Mr. Fillipponi of three or four examples of this bird in Egypt.

Mr. R. Swinhoe enumerates this species in his list of the birds of Formosa (Ibis, 1863). It comes there in small flocks, and, associating with the Sanderling, departs after a short stay. The same writer, in his paper on the Birds of Hainan, mentions finding large flocks of these birds in the Poochin River on the 5th of March. They sat on the fishing stakes, or ranged themselves in rows on the ropes which ran from one to the other. These birds were all just assuming their summer plumage.

This species has been taken in Senegal, and specimens of it have also been obtained at the Cape of Good Hope. Temminck includes it among the birds of Japan, and mentions having received specimens of it from New Guinea, Sunda, and the Moluccas.

Dr. Middendorff gives it as among the birds of Siberia and Northern Russia, and includes it among those which go to the extreme north. It is found thence throughout Europe southward to Italy, Sicily, Malta, and Africa. Von Baer met with it in Nova Zembla. Professor A. Newton noticed its presence on Spitzbergen, and this was afterward confirmed by Professor A. J. Malmgren (Ibis, 1869), who found a pair on Amsterdam Island. Mr. C. A. Wright mentions it as an irregular and rare visitant of Malta, appearing there in May, August, and September, and once in December. Mr. H. Saunders notices it as appearing regularly in Southern Spain in its migrations. Wheelwright speaks of it as common in the south of Sweden, in the Baltic, and on the Norwegian coast. It goes up far within the Polar Circle. He has found it breeding, and as often sitting on three eggs as on four.

Yarrell states that it frequents the British coast, either singly or in small flocks of four or five in number, from August throughout the winter till May. Dr. Fleming states that it is resident in Zetland, and found there at all seasons. Hewitson mentions its breeding on the coast of Norway. After visiting numerous islands, he was about to land on a flat rock, bare except where, here and there, tufts of grass or stunted juniper were growing, when his attention was attracted by the singular cry of a Turnstone, which had perched itself upon an eminence of the rock, assuring him by its querulous, oft-repeated note and anxious motions, that its nest was there. After a minute search he succeeded in finding the latter placed against a ledge of the rock, and consisting of nothing more than the dropping leaves of the juniper-bush, under a creeping branch of which the eggs, four in number, were snugly concealed, admirably sheltered, and allowing just sufficient room for the bird to cover them. He afterward found several other nests, each containing four eggs. The time of breeding was the middle of June. He describes their eggs as having an olive-green ground, spotted and streaked with ashy blue, and two shades of reddish brown. They measured 1.59 by 1.17 inches.

Professor Alfred Newton mentions that the Turnstone is said by Faber to occur in Iceland, being more common in the south and west than in the north. It arrives about the last week in April, and breeds in Iceland, as Mr. Proctor received its eggs from the northern portion of that island. It usually leaves again in the autumn; but a few remain late in the season, as Faber obtained one Dec. 11, 1820.

In America it occurs throughout the continent, Mr. Charles Darwin finding it, on the voyage of the "Beagle," in the Straits of Magellan, and the various Arctic explorers meeting with it in North Greenland, on Winter Island, at Felix Harbor, and on the coast near Fury Point and Victoria Harbor. Dr. Walker found it breeding early in June in the marshy valleys in Bellot's Strait. Reinhardt includes it among the birds of Greenland. Captain Blakiston met with it at York Factory, Hudson's Bay, in August, and Mr. Ross mentions it as present, but as rare, on the Mackenzie River. Richardson speaks of it as common in the Fur Country, where it reaches its breeding-quarters on the shores of Hudson's Bay and the Arctic Sea, as far north as the 75th parallel, in June, leaving them at the beginning of September. It is common in Bermuda during the winter, and is of irregular occurrence in most, or all, of the West India Islands. Professor Newton met with it in St. Croix in April, 1857, and Mr. E. Newton saw it there, Sept. 8, 1858. Léotaud speaks of it as a migratory visitant of Trinidad, where it never fails to arrive in August, departing in October. It is said to be almost always found alone, flitting along the borders of the sea, sometimes silent, and at other times uttering a soft, peculiar cry, which is not easily described. Certain kinds of shore seem to suit it best; in these it stops to search under the small stones, which it turns over with its bill for the worms, etc., on which it feeds. It is the "Plover" of Trinidad; but its flesh is not held in high esteem. It was taken by Xantus on the Rio Zacatula, in Mexico, and by others in Ecuador, Guiana, the Argentine Republic, Peru, Chili, and in the West Indies.

Mr. Salvin obtained specimens late in April among the islands on the coast of Honduras, and mentions it as common in winter on both coasts of Guatemala. Mr. Dresser noticed a number of these birds quite close to Galveston on the 26th of May, 1864; and afterward, on a second visit, found them as late as June. It is a regular visitant to Massachusetts in its migrations, passing north usually in April, and coming south in September or August. It was quite common on the shore of Lake Koskonong, Wis., about Aug. 15, 1873. Only a single specimen is known to have been taken on the Pacific coast — by Dr. Cooper at the mouth of the Columbia.

In different parts of the United States it is known by various local appellations. It is the "Brant Bird" of Long Island and some parts of New England, and is the "Horse-foot Snipe" of Egg Harbor, where it is so called because it feeds on the spawn of the Horse-foot crab. The young are there known as "Bead Birds." Giraud states that it reaches the shores of Long Island early in April, and leaves for its breeding-places late in May. It returns to the shores of New Jersey and Long Island in September, and there continues until quite late in the fall.

This bird is never seen in large companies, as its habits are rather solitary, and it wanders singly or in small parties along the beach in search of insects and minute shell-fish. Giraud adds that it is usually in fine condition in the fall, and is considered a delicacy. According to Mr. N. B. Moore, many spend the winter in Florida. Although it penetrates far north to breed, and is not known to do so in any part of Florida, it may be seen along the shores of Sarasota Bay during every month in the year. He met with a flock of eleven on the 20th of June, 1870, when their dress was that of winter. After that he saw them almost every day for a month, during which time their plumage remained as we find it in January. As the summer passed on their numbers diminished, either by death or dispersion; and by the time the others had returned from the north — some of whom came in August, and were in very gay plumage — this little band had dwindled down to only one or two. Their plumage was neither worn nor faded, but displayed none of the summer tints, nor did the birds themselves seem feeble. The question arises: Do birds, after they have become old, effete, or barren, prefer to stay in a warm climate?

This species is said by Mr. Moore to alight on the dead branches of mangroves, and on the stumps and stakes which stand in the water near the shore and from two to six feet above it; and there they sit in the manner of the Carolina Dove.

The naturalists of the Wilkes Exploring Expedition appear to have found the Turnstone at home along the sea-coasts of the temperate and tropical regions of the globe. It was common on many of the islands of the Pacific Ocean, north and south of the Equator. None were in full plumage, and all were migrating. In the Kingsmill group, near the Equator, it was seen in large flocks on the 24th of April. Nine were shot at a single discharge; they were exceedingly fat. A specimen was killed at Callao, Peru, in the month of June. One was taken in the Feejee Islands. Dr. Pickering speaks of this bird as having been seen at nearly all the points visited by the Expedition in North and South America, and in the islands of the Pacific Ocean.

In the Smithsonian Collection specimens have been received from Lake Winnipeg, Big Island, Fort Rae, Fort Resolution, Fort Anderson, the Lower Anderson River, Plover Bay, Siberia, Nulato, Fort Simpson, etc. It is known to proceed as far to the north to breed as man has yet penetrated, having been recorded by Dr. Bessels as taken at Polaris Bay, and by Mr. Feilding, of the British Expedition of 1875–76, as tolerably common in Smith's Sound and in the most northern regions visited by that Expedition. It was observed as late as Sept. 5, 1875, in lat. 82° 30′ N., and was first noticed on the 5th of June, 1876, in the neighborhood of the winter quarters of the "Alert." By the 12th of August the young broods were able to fly.

The Turnstone is called the "Hebridal Sandpiper" by Pennant and by Hearne, and in parts of England it is known as the "Variegated Plover." Its habits are peculiar, and differ in several respects from the manners of most Waders, resembling rather those of the Sanderling. It feeds on the smaller crustaceans and the soft-bodied animals which inhabit thin shells, turning over the stones on the beach in search of them, or hunting among the sea-weed for its food. If not disturbed it usually remains longer in one place than most Waders. When on the wing it is said to utter a loud twittering note. It can be readily reconciled to confinement, and will feed on a variety of food, quite different from that which it seeks in a wild state. Rev. Dr. Bachman once kept a bird of this species alive. It had recovered from a slight wound, when he presented it to a lady who fed it on boiled rice and bread soaked in milk, of both of which it was quite fond. It became perfectly gentle, and fed from the hand of its mistress, frequently bathed in a vessel kept at hand for that purpose, and never attempted to escape, although left quite at liberty to do so. Mr. Audubon, in the neighborhood of St. Augustine, Florida, saw this Turnstone feeding on the oyster-beds, searching for such oysters as had been killed by the heat of the sun, and picking out the contents; it would also strike at such small bivalves as had thin shells, and break them. While on the Florida coast, near Cape Sable, he shot one, in the month of May, which had its stomach filled with the beautiful shells, which on account of their resemblance to grains of rice are commonly called rice-shells.

Mr. MacFarlane met with a flock of about a dozen of these birds at Fort Anderson, June, 1864, and obtained a single specimen. They were seen on the river below the fort. He was informed by the Esquimaux that this species was tolerably numerous on the Arctic coast as well as on the islands in Liverpool Bay. Except on the large island in Franklin Bay, where several of this species were seen in July, 1864, Mr. MacFarlane's party noticed none of these birds, either on the "Barren Grounds," or on any part of the coast visited by them. He afterward met with them on the Lower Anderson, and found two nests, both precisely similar to those of the other Waders, consisting of a few withered leaves placed in a depression in the ground, each containing four eggs.

Mr. H. W. Elliott states that this bird visits the Prybilof Islands, arriving in flocks of thousands about the third week in July, and leaving September 10, but not breeding there. On its arrival it is quite poor; but feeding on the larvæ on the killing-grounds, it rapidly fattens, and often bursts open as it falls to the ground after having been shot. Mr. Elliott met with this bird at sea, eight hundred miles from the nearest land, flying in a northwesterly direction towards the Aleutian Islands.

The eggs of few species of Waders vary more than do those of the Turnstone. They vary in shape from a rounded to an oblong ovoid, in length from 1.60 to 1.72 inches, and in breadth from 1.13 to 1.23 inches, averaging about 1.66 by 1.18. Their ground-colors are a light olive-brown, a cream color, a light drab, and a deep clay-color. The eggs are deeply and boldly marked, chiefly about the larger end, with large splashes and blotches of light-brown, in some washed with a lilac shade, and in others with a tinge of bronze.

Strepsilas melanocephalus.

BLACK TURNSTONE.

Strepsilas melanocephalus, VIGORS, Zoöl. Journ. IV. Jan. 1829, 356; Zoöl. Blossom, 1839, 29. — BAIRD, B. N. Am. 1858, 702; Cat. N. Am. B. 1859, no. 516. — RIDGW. Nom. N. Am. B. 1881, no. 510 (*melanocephala*).

Strepsilas interpres, var. *melanocephalus*, COUES, Key, 1872, 247; Check List. 1873, no. 406*a*.

Strepsilas interpres melanocephalus, COUES, Check List, 2d ed. 1882, no. 599.

HAB. Pacific coast of North America, south to Monterey, California, north to the Aleutian Islands; accidental in India.

SP. CHAR. Head, neck, breast, and upper parts in general, fuliginous dusky, with a faint bronzy green reflection, brightest on the upper parts; posterior lower parts, upper part of the rump, upper tail-coverts and ends of the greater coverts, pure white. *Adult, in breeding-plumage:* Anterior lower parts sooty-black, like the back; lores covered by a large patch of white; a small postocular spot of the same; forehead and auriculars streaked or dashed with white; jugulum speckled and dashed with white, forming a wide band of these markings, more or less interrupted in the middle portion. *Adult and young in winter:* Anterior lower parts and head, smoky brown,

Winter plumage.

much lighter than the back; no trace of white markings about the head or jugulum. *Young in first plumage:* Similar to the winter dress, but breast, etc., more gray, each feather of the upper parts narrowly bordered terminally with light buff or whitish.

Length, about 9 inches; wing, 8.80–9.10; culmen, .85–1.00; tarsus, 1.00–1.10; middle toe, .90.

This very distinct species averages considerably larger than *S. interpres*, while it differs radically in its coloration, the pattern of which is to a certain extent quite different, the dusky on the breast extending much farther back than in that species. The summer dress is in this bird much handsomer than the winter livery, while the reverse appears to be the case with the Common Turnstone.

The Black-headed Turnstone is common along the Pacific coast of North America. A single specimen, exactly this bird, has been received from India. Dr. Cooper states that he has seen a few Turnstones, in black plumage, along the southern part of the California coast during the cooler months, and has found several on the Farallon Islands in June; and they have also been obtained at Monterey and in Puget Sound in August, so that there seems to be no change in their colors with the season. Still Dr. Cooper was inclined to regard these as only immature specimens of *S. interpres*, interrupted, from some cause, in their full development. He was unable to find their eggs, and suspected them of barrenness. Their habits, so far as he was able to observe, seemed similar to those of *S. interpres.* They frequent rocky shores, and are fond of perching on logs, wrecks, etc., where they find small crustacea, barnacles, etc., on which they chiefly feed. This bird is said to fly very swiftly, and as it moves, to utter a shrill whistle, which is its only note. It is also described as being very shy, and associating only in small parties.

At Michaelofsky, Alaska, on the shores of Norton Sound, Mr. E. Adams (Ibis, 1878) met with what was probably this species. A few Turnstones made their appearance, in pairs, on the 31st of May. They frequented the salt-marshes, where he often found them sitting upon logs of driftwood which overhung the water. They fed about the mud, on insects, worms, etc.; but he did not see them near the sea-shore, nor in company with any other species.

Mr. R. Browne mentions meeting with this bird on the sea-shore of Vancouver Island, and quite a number of examples of this species were procured at Sitka, as well as at Kadiak, by Mr. Bischoff. Others were taken by Mr. Bannister at St. Michael's and at Nulato, on the Yukon and at Takehemut by Mr. Dall.

Eggs of this species (Smithsonian Collection, 9, 377) obtained by Mr. Dall from near the Yukon River, June 16, 1868, vary greatly in their size, one measuring 1.58 by 1.15 inches, the other 1.85 by 1.19 inches. They are of an oblong pyriform shape, their ground-color is a drab, strongly tinged with olivaceous, and very generally and profusely marked with fine sprinklings of suffused spots and dottings. In the smaller example these markings are larger and darker.

Genus **APHRIZA**, Audubon.

Aphriza, Aud. Orn. Biog. V. 1839, 249 (type, *Tringa virgata*, Lath.).

Char. Similar to *Strepsilas;* but the bill quite different, and much resembling that of the Plovers (*Charadriidæ*), the terminal portion of the culmen being much arched, the middle portion depressed. Tail slightly emarginate; lateral margin of the toes more distinct than in *Strepsilas*, producing a broader, more sole-like under-surface.

A. virgata.

The single species of this genus has usually been associated with the Plovers; but its affinities appear to be much nearer to *Strepsilas*, with which it agrees very closely except in the characters pointed out above. It differs essentially from all the various forms ranged under the *Charadriidæ* in the completely cleft toes, the large, nearly incumbent hallux, and the generally robust character of the feet, which are even stouter than those of *Strepsilas*.

Aphriza virgata.

THE SURF BIRD.

Tringa virgata, Gmel. S. N. I. 1788, 674. — Lath. Ind. Orn. II. 1790, 735.

Aphriza virgata, Gray, Gen. B. III. 1847, pl. cxlvii. — Cassin, in Baird's B. N. Am. 1858, 698. — Baird, Cat. N. Am. B. 1859, no. 509. — Coues, Key, 1872, 245; Check List, 1873, no. 403; 2d ed. 1882, no. 594. — Ridgw. Nom. N. Am. B. 1881, no. 511.

Tringa borealis, Gmel. S. N. I. 1788, 674.

Aphriza Townsendii, Aud. Orn. Biog. V. 1839, 249, pl. 428; Synop. 1839, 226; B. Am. V. 1842, 228, pl. 322.

Hab. Pacific coast of America, from Alaska to Chili ; Sandwich Islands.

Sp. Char. Bill about as long as the head, rather thick at the base, and shallowest about one third of the distance from the end ; nostrils large, situated in a very distinct longitudinal groove, which occupies the middle two thirds of the bill ; wings long ; tail rather long, emarginate ; legs stout. *Adult in summer:* Head, neck, and dorsal region spotted and streaked with dusky and whitish ; the latter predominating on head, neck, and breast, where the darker markings are in the form of irregular streaks, but on the breast becoming irregular, broad, crescentic bars ; scapulars with large, irregular spots of rufous. Upper tail-coverts, basal half of tail, a broad band across

ends of greater wing-coverts, edges of outer webs of secondaries, tips of primary-coverts (broadly) bases, shafts, and tips (narrowly) of primaries, tip of tail, and lower parts from the breast, back (including most of under-side of wing), pure white ; sides and crissum with angular spots of dusky. "Bill dusky toward the end, orange at the base ; feet bluish green, claws black" (Audubon). *Winter plumage:* Head, neck, and breast, and most of upper parts, plain dusky or brownish slate ; white areas as in the summer plumage. "Iris black ; eyelids black ; legs olive-green ; claws black" (Sharpe, P. Z. S. 1881, 15). *Young:* Much like the winter plumage, but with indistinct white borders to feathers of the upper parts, and the breast, throat, etc., white, with dusky streaks, instead of plain dusky. Differing from the summer plumage in the absence of rufous on upper parts, and in the white margins to wing-coverts.

Wing, about 7.00 ; culmen, .95–1.00 ; tarsus, 1.20 ; middle toe, .90.

Very little is known in regard to the habits or the distribution of this species. It is found on the Sandwich Islands and others of the Pacific Ocean, but is rare on our western coast. A single specimen — a female — was obtained at Cape Disappointment, near the mouth of the Columbia, by Mr. Townsend. He states, in regard to it, that it was sitting on the edge of the steep rocks, the heavy surf frequently dashing its spray over it as it foraged among the retreating waves. It flew with a quick jerking motion of its wings, and alighted again at a short distance. The stomach was strong and muscular, and contained fragments of a small black shell-fish which is found adhering to the rocks in that neighborhood.

Dr. Cooper regards this species as a rather rare visitor to our Pacific coast, though he has seen birds which he supposed to be of this species at the mouth of the Columbia and on Santa Barbara Island ; but they were so wild, he could not get a shot at them. Dr. Heermann obtained a specimen of this bird in the San Francisco market in the winter of 1849, and thinks that he met with others of this species the following June on the Farallon Islands, where they were gathered in small flocks, engaged in picking up marine insects from the rock-bound shores, which were covered with kelp and shell-fish. They did not appear wild. Dr. Cooper did not notice any of them on the Farallon Islands in June, 1864, but did see some of the *Strepsilas melanocephalus*, which resembles this species, and may have been mistaken for it by Dr. Heermann.

Mr. R. Browne includes it in his list of the birds observed by him on Vancouver Island, and four specimens of it were procured by Mr. Bischoff near Sitka. Mr. Henshaw did not meet with any of this species on Santa Cruz Island, and he is of the opinion that none breed in that group. Mr. Gruber procured a fine specimen of this bird at Santa Barbara in spring. Mr. Henshaw regarded it as a rather uncommon species on the coast of California, and as one whose habits are but little known. Nothing has been learned in regard to its nesting. It occurs on the Pacific coast of South America as far as Chili.

FAMILY CHARADRIIDÆ. — THE PLOVERS.

CHAR. Small or medium-sized shore-birds (scarcely waders), with rather short, somewhat Pigeon-like bill, large round head, short neck, long and pointed wings, and moderately lengthened legs, the hind toe usually absent.

The above superficial characters are sufficient to define the family of Plovers, as distinguished from the allied groups. The affinities of the Plovers are with the *Strepsilidæ* (Turnstones) on the one hand, and the *Œdicnemidæ* (Thick-kneed Plovers) on the other; but they seem sufficiently distinct from either, and form, upon the whole, a very well-marked family of the great Limicoline group.

The American genera of *Charadriidæ* (with the exception of *Pluvianellus*, HOMB. & JACQ.,[1] which we have not seen) may be characterized as follows: —

Table of American Genera.

A. Size large (wing more than eight inches); head more or less crested; plumage more or less metallic above.

a. Occiput with a slender recurved crest; a well-developed hind toe, with claw; wing rounded, first quill shorter than fourth.

1. **Vanellus.** Wing unarmed, or with very rudimentary spur; tarsus not more than twice as long as the middle toe.

2. **Belonopterus.**[2] Wing armed with a very prominent curved spur on the head of the metacarpus; tarsus more than twice as long as the middle toe.

b. Occipital feathers lengthened, forming a soft, pendant, rather bushy crest; no trace of hind toe; wing pointed, the first quill longest, or longer than fourth.

3. **Ptiloscelys.**[3] Wing armed with a very minute spur; tarsus more than twice as long as middle toe.

B. Size medium or small (wing less than eight inches); head without crest, and plumage without metallic gloss above.

c. Wing more than six inches; plumage much speckled or spotted above; lower parts chiefly black in summer.

4. **Squatarola.** A well-developed hind toe, without claw.

5. **Charadrius.** No trace of hind toe; otherwise very similar to *Squatarola*, but smaller and more slender.

d. Wing less than six inches; plumage nearly or quite uniform grayish or brownish above (the rump ochraceous in *Oxyechus*), the lower parts chiefly or entirely white at all stages.

[1] Type, *P. sociabilis*, HOMB. & JACQ.

[2] *Belonopterus*, REICH. Handb. 1851, xviii. (type, *Charadrius cayennensis*, GMEL. *Hab.* South America).

[3] *Ptiloscelys*, BONAP. Compt. Rend. XLIII. 1856, 429 (type, *Vanellus resplendens*, TSCHUDI. *Hab.* South America).

d'. Wing unarmed.

e'. No trace of hind toe.

f'. Tail very long (half as long as the wing, or more), extending half its length beyond tips of closed wings; rump and upper tail-coverts pale rufous or ochraceous in the American species.

6. **Oxyechus.** Bill slender, about equal in length to the middle toe; tarsus decidedly less than twice as long as middle toe; rump and upper tail-coverts rufous or ochraceous (except in *O. tricollaris*).

f''. Tail short (less than half as long as the wing), reaching little, if any, beyond ends of closed wings; rump concolor with the back.

7. **Ægialitis.** Bill variable, but usually shorter than middle toe, or, if longer, very slender; tarsus less than twice as long as middle toe.

8. **Ochthodromus.** Bill very large (as long as, or longer than, middle toe), the terminal half of the culmen much arched, the base of the gonys forming a decided angle; tarsus about one and a half times to nearly twice as long as middle toe.

9. **Podasocys.** Bill slender, wide at base, much longer than middle toe; tarsus more than twice as long as middle toe.

10. **Oreophilus.**[1] Bill very slender, depressed, nearly twice as long as middle toe; tarsus nearly twice as long as middle toe. Plumage longitudinally striped above.

e''. A well-developed, though small, hind toe, with curved claw.

11. **Zonibyx.**[2] Size small (wing less than six inches); plumage plain above, except in young.

d''. Wing armed with a conical spur on the head of the metacarpus.

12. **Hoploxypterus.**[3] No trace of hind toe. Size medium; first quill longest; tarsus more than twice as long as middle toe. Plumage white beneath, with black pectoral collar; above ashy, varied with black and white in large, rather longitudinal, patches; legs yellow.

Genus VANELLUS, Brisson.

Vanellus, Schaeff. Briss. Orn. V. 1760, 94 (type, *Tringa vanellus*, Linn.).

Char. Size large (larger than *Squatarola*). Bill slender, about equal in length to the middle toe, which is about half as long as the tarsus; a distinct web between outer and middle toes, at the base; a well-developed hind toe, with a small claw. Wings lengthened, but rounded, the first quill shorter than the sixth; the second, third, and fourth nearly equal, and longest. Tail slightly emarginated. Occiput (of adult) ornamented by an elongated, slender, recurved crest. Plumage of upper parts metallic.

A single species only of this genus occurs in America, this being the common Lapwing or Peewit of Europe (*V. cristatus*), which has been found at several localities of Arctic America, including both Greenland and Alaska. The South American birds usually referred to *Vanellus* belong to two quite distinct genera (*Belonopterus* and *Ptiloscelys*), distinguished by important differences of structure, as tabulated on page 128.

[1] *Oreophilus*, Jard. & Selby, Illustr. Orn. pl. 151 (type, *O. totanirostris*, Jard. & Selby, = *Charadrius ruficollis*, Wagl. *Hab.* Southern South America).

[2] *Zonibyx*, Reich. Handb. 1851, xviii. (type, *Vanellus cinctus*, Less., = *Charadrius modestus*, Licht. *Hab.* Southern South America).

[3] *Hoploxypterus*, Bonap. Compt. Rend. XLIII. 1856, 418 (type, *Charadrius cayanus*, Lath. *Hab.* South America.)

A nearly allied Old World genus, *Hoplopterus*, Bonap. (type, *Charadrius spinosus*, Linn.), differs as follows: First primary shorter than the fourth, as in *Vanellus* and *Belonopterus*; wing-spur larger, and curved; the legs almost stilt-like in length (tarsus nearly thrice the middle toe), and black. There is also a well-developed web between the outer and middle toes, at the base, hardly indicated at all in *Hoploxypterus*.

Vanellus capella.

THE LAPWING.

Tringa vanellus, LINN. S. N. ed. 10, 1758, 148; ed. 12, 1766, 248.
Charadrius vanellus, WAGL. Syst. Av. 1827, no. 47. — NAUM. Vög. Deutschl. IX. 1838, 269, pl. 179.
Vanellus capella, SCHAEFF. Orn. Mus. 1789, 49. — STEJN. Proc. U. S. Nat. Mus. Vol. 4, 1882, 35.
Vanellus vulgaris, BECHST. Orn. Taschenb. II. 1803, 313.
Vanellus cristatus, MEYER, Vög. Deutschl. I. 1810, 10. — MACGILL, Man. II. 55. — KEYS. & BLAS. Wirb. Eur. 69. — GRAY, Gen. B. II. 541; Cat. Brit. B. 1863, 137. — GOULD, Birds Eur. pl. 291. — RIDGW. Nom. N. Am. B. 1881, no. 512. — COUES, Check List, 2d ed. 1882, no. 593.
Vanellus gavia, LEACH, Syst. Cat. 1816, 29. — STEPH. Gen. Zool. XI. 509, pl. 38.
Vanellus bicornis, BREHM, Vög. Deutschl. 557.
The Peewit, or Lapwing, YARR. Brit. B. ed. 2, II. 481, fig.; ed. 3, II. 515, fig.

V. capella.

HAB. Entire Palæarctic region; occasional in Arctic America (Greenland, "REINHARDT, Ibis, 1861, 9;" islands in Norton Sound, Alaska, DALL & BANNISTER, Trans. Chicago Acad. I. 1869, 293).

Adult, breeding-plumage: Pileum, crest, fore-part of the lores and malar region, chin, throat and entire breast, blue-black, faintly glossy. Side of the head and neck white, the nape ashy.

Back, scapulars, and tertials, metallic bottle-green, changing to coppery purple on the outer scapulars; wing-coverts dark purplish blue, changing to greenish, becoming decidedly green on the greater coverts. Remiges dull black, the ends of the outer three primaries, for an inch or more, dull light cinereous, the shafts white. Rump like the back, but less metallic; upper tail-coverts deep rufous. Basal half and top of the tail pure white; subterminal portion dull black, this color decreasing in extent to the outer feathers, finally nearly or quite disappearing on the lateral pair. Lower parts in general pure white, becoming light rufous on the lower tail-coverts. *Winter plumage:* Similar, but with anterior half of lores, broad superciliary stripe, chin, and entire throat, white; white of sides of nape and occiput more or less tinged with buff. Bill blackish; iris brown; legs and feet dull crimson or lake-red (brownish in winter).

Downy young: Top and sides of the head, and entire upper parts, dull light brownish gray mottled with black, the shoulders tinged with light rusty, and the rump with large spots of deep black. Whole nape, chin, throat, and entire lower parts (except jugulum), white, the first tinged with light ashy; jugulum nearly uniform dusky grayish (56885, Saxony).

Wing, 8.50–9.00; tail, 4.00-4.25; culmen, 1.00; tarsus, 2.00; middle toe, 1.00–1.10.

The well-known Lapwing of Europe is one of the most common and familiar of the birds of the western portions of that continent. Its occasional presence in Greenland and other parts of North America gives it a place among our rare and accidental visitants. It is common and indigenous to Ireland and the British Islands, and is abundant, in all suitable localities, as far as the most remote of the Shetland group. It is common in Denmark, and is equally abundant throughout Norway and Sweden; also occurring on the Faröe Islands and in Iceland, and being common throughout the Empire of Russia. It is found in less abundance in France, Spain, Italy, Egypt, and Asia Minor, and has been taken on the plains between the Black and the Caspian seas. Specimens have also been received from India and China; and Temminck includes it among the birds of Japan. In some of its general habits the Lapwing appears to be similar to the Kildeer of our own country. It is known to many as the Lapwing, both from its peculiar slow flapping of the wings as it flies, and the singular manner in which it droops its wings, in affected lameness, when its nest is in danger. It is also called the Peewit, from its frequently repeated note, closely resembling the word *pee-weet*. By the French this note is thought to resemble the word *dix-huit*, and the bird is known to them by this name.

The habits of this species are those of a true Plover. It frequents marshy grounds or the margins of lakes and rivers, wild heaths, and open, uninclosed country. In such localities these birds are very common in Great Britain, and breed in large numbers. Their eggs are regarded as a luxury, and are much sought after in all the districts where this species is common.

When its nest is disturbed, the female runs from the eggs and flies near the ground, but makes no noise. The males, however, are very clamorous, fly about the intruder, and endeavor by various instinctive manœuvres to draw off his attention from their treasures.

In some of the English counties all the most likely grounds are carefully searched once every day, in the season for eggs, by women and children, as well as by dogs trained for the purpose. Yarrell states that in 1839 two hundred dozen of these eggs were sent to the London market from Romney Marsh alone.

The nests of the Lapwing, like those of the whole family of Plovers, are mere depressions in the ground, with a few dried bents lining the bottom. The number of eggs is four, and these have an average of 1.93 inches in length by 1.34 inches in breadth. Their color is dark olive, blotched and spotted with blackish brown.

The young Lapwings, just hatched, are covered with a yellowish fawn-colored down spotted with brownish black, and there is a light-colored collar around the neck. They can run almost as soon as hatched, following the parent bird, who leads them in search of food. They feed on earth-worms, slugs, and insects of various kinds, in all their different stages, and, on account of their usefulness in the destruction of insects, are frequently kept in gardens, where they become quite tame, and are very interesting pets.

In the autumn the Lapwings collect in flocks; and from that time to the end of the winter are excellent eating.

This bird is recorded by Reinhardt as of occasional occurrence in Greenland, and Dall and Bannister met with it in Alaska among the islands in Norton Sound.

Genus SQUATAROLA, Cuvier.

Squatarola, Cuvier, Règ. Anim. I. 1817 (type, *Tringa squatarola*, Linn.).

Char. A rudimentary hind toe. Legs reticulated with elongated hexagons anteriorly, of which there are five or six in a transverse row; fewer behind. First primary longest. Tail slightly rounded.

S. helvetica.

Squatarola helvetica.

THE BLACK-BELLIED PLOVER.

Tringa squatarola, Linn. S. N. ed. 10, 1758, 149; ed. 12, 1766, 252.
Tringa helvetica, Linn. S. N. ed. 12, 1766, 250.
Squatarola helvetica, Cuv. Règ. Anim. 1817. — Brehm, Vög. Deutschl. 1831, 554. — Cass. in Baird's B. N. Am. 1858, 697. — Baird, Cat. N. Am. B. 1859, no. 510. — Coues, Key, 1872, 243; Check List, 1873, no. 395; 2d ed. 1882, no. 580; Birds N. W. 1874, 448. — Ridgw. Nom. N. Am. B. 1881, no. 513.
Charadrius helveticus, Licht. Verz. Doubl. 1823, no. 728. — Nutt. Man. II. 1834, 26. — Aud. Orn. Biog. IV. 1838, 280, pl. 334; Synop. 1839, 221; Birds Am. V. 1842, 199, pl. 315.
Charadrius apricarius, Wilson, Am. Orn. VII. 1813, 41.

Hab. Nearly cosmopolitan, but chiefly the northern hemisphere; breeding in the extreme northern parts of its range, migrating in winter to southern regions, extending, in America, as far as Brazil and New Granada. Bermudas, and throughout the West Indies.

Sp. Char. Bill and legs strong; wings long; a very small rudimentary hind toe. *Summer:* Around the base of the bill to the eyes, neck before and under parts of body, black; upper parts white, nearly pure and unspotted on the forehead ; sides of the neck and rump tinged with ashy, and having irregular transverse spots of brownish black on the back, scapulars, and wing-coverts ; the brownish black frequently predominating on those parts, and the rump also frequently with transverse bars of the same. Lower part of the abdomen, tibia, and under tail-coverts, white.

Summer plumage.

Quills, brownish black, lighter on their inner webs, with a middle portion of their shafts white, and a narrow longitudinal stripe of white frequently on the shorter primaries and secondaries. Tail white, with transverse imperfect narrow bands of black. The black color of the under parts generally with a faint bronzed or coppery lustre, and presenting a scale-like appearance; the brownish black of the upper parts with a greenish lustre. Bill and legs black ; iris brown. *Younger and winter plumage:* Entire upper parts dark brown, with circular and irregular small spots of white, and frequently of yellow, most numerous on the wing-coverts ; upper tail-coverts white. Under parts white, with short longitudinal lines and spots of dark brownish cinereous on the neck

Winter plumage.

and breast ; quills brownish black, with a large longitudinal space of white on their inner webs and also on the outer webs of the shorter primaries. *Young:* Upper parts lighter, and with the white spots more irregular or less rounded ; narrow lines on the neck and breast more numerous.

Total length about 11½ inches ; wing, 7½ ; tail, 3 inches ; culmen, about 1.10 ; tarsus, 1.95 ; middle toe, 1.15.

We can discover no difference between American specimens and those from Europe. In the young and winter plumage there is considerable variation in the distinctness of the yellow wash on the upper parts, the light markings of the upper surface being in some examples entirely of this color, while in others there is scarcely even a tinge of it.

While the coloration of this species bears considerable resemblance to that of the Golden Plovers (*Charadrius*), it may be readily distinguished, in all stages, apart from other marked differences, by the dusky black axillars, these feathers being either smoky gray or pure white in the species of *Charadrius*.

The well-known Beetle-head, or Black-bellied Plover, is eminently cosmopolitan in its distribution, ranging over the northern portions of Asia, Europe, and North America during its periods of reproduction, at other times wandering in an irregular manner, in scattered groups, over Southern Asia, Northern and even Southern Africa, Australia, the West Indies, and Central and South America to Brazil.

Mr. Swinhoe (Ibis, 1863, p. 404) mentions finding this species frequenting the shores and the mouths of the rivers of Formosa during winter. This writer afterward speaks of meeting with it in small flocks, in the same season, on the river mud-flats at Amoy, where they were seen up to February, but not later. One was kept in an aviary at Amoy, but appeared to have undergone no change in plumage as late as the end of May. Mr. Swinhoe also records the procuring of a single specimen on the Island of Hainan; it was shot in the Hungpe Lagoon on the 30th of March. Captain Sperling found this bird common at Zanzibar, where in November he procured it in immature plumage. Dr. Andrew Smith noticed it at Algoa Bay, in South Africa, all through the breeding-season, and brought specimens to England; but as none had the black color on the breast, it is not probable that any were actually breeding. Mr. Blyth has obtained this bird at Calcutta; and Mr. Temminck has received it from Japan in both the summer and winter plumage. Specimens from the Sunda Islands and from New Guinea, though killed at different seasons, were all in the immature or winter plumage. This species is also included by Dr. Horsfield in his list of the birds of Java. Dr. Middendorff mentions this Plover as one of the birds of Siberia, and gives it in his hyperborean list, which includes the birds penetrating to the extreme north. Mr. Saunders (Ibis, 1871) states that this Plover is not uncommon in Southern Spain during its migrations. The first specimens were obtained at Malaga in May. During the winter few were met with, the majority having evidently gone farther south. Mr. Wheelwright obtained old birds of this species on the southern coast of Scania in August, in nearly full summer dress, as well as those of the year, and inferred that they must have bred somewhere on the European continent. He is confident they do not breed at Quickiock, nor have any of its eggs been taken there by Mr. Wolley or by any one else. Still he thinks that they must breed somewhere on the Scandinavian fells, and they were found breeding in 1862 in Finland, by Mr. Tristram. Professor A. Newton described an egg (P. Z. S. 1861) which was taken by Middendorff on the Taimyr River, North Russia, lat. 74°, July 1, 1843; and Mr. Wheelwright received what were said to be the eggs of this species from Greenland, and which resembled those of the European *C. pluvialis*. Messrs. Alston and Brown (Ibis, January, 1873) mention meeting with this species near Archangel, Russia, June 2. In Great Britain, Farrell gives it as a winter visitor, and not a native resident. It occurs at the end of autumn, through the winter, and in the spring, retiring to high northern latitudes during the breeding-season, and re-appearing when that season is over. Specimens in the full black plumage may occasionally be procured in the London market in May. Mr. Selby met with a few of these birds in the Fen Islands in June, but could never detect any young. In the winter this Plover is more common on the shores than inland. It is more abundant in Holland and in France than in Germany, and is also found at Genoa and in Italy generally, passing through Sicily on its way to and from Africa.

In the Appendix to Captain Parry's Second Voyage, Richardson states that this bird was found breeding near the margins of the marshes immediately to the southwest of Fury Point in considerable numbers. Some specimens were also obtained near Felix Harbor. The same writer, in his "Fauna Boreali-Americana," states that it breeds in open ground from Pennsylvania to the northern extremity of the continent. This is a mistake — an error originally of Wilson's, but copied also by Audubon, Nuttall, and Samuels. It does not breed within the limits of the United States, and probably nowhere south of the extreme northern latitudes. Specimens have been received from Hudson's Bay by Captain Blakiston which had been taken there by Mr. Murray. It was found on the Mackenzie by Mr. Ross, where, however, it was rare.

This Plover passes northward through the United States in May, and returns southward in August. It occurs sparingly in various parts of this country irregularly during the intervening winter months from August to May. According to Giraud, it reaches Long Island early in the month of May, and spends but a few days on the sandbars and beaches, then leaving for the north. In the month of August it returns with its young. These are so different in their plumage, that by many gunners they are supposed to be a different bird, and are known as the "Bull-headed Plover" or the "Beetle-headed Plover." They are very shy, but may frequently be enticed within gunshot by imitating their plaintive note. In autumn they are found along the whole sea-coast of Long Island, subsisting on minute shell-fish and marine insects, and becoming very fat. They remain until the latter part of September, when they move southward. Early in the autumn this bird is very abundant about Montauk Point, and during September Giraud met with it throughout his entire route across the hills, but found it most numerous on a large bare spot abounding with grubs, worms, and insects of various kinds, about four miles from the lighthouse.

According to Lewis this bird is best known to sportsmen of the Middle States as the "Old Field," or "Whistling" Plover. It passes through New Jersey early in May, and returns in August.

Those that feed on the uplands on berries and grasshoppers are fat and of a fine flavor; but those frequenting the sea-coast soon acquire a sedgy and unpleasant taste. They naturally fly high, and keep up an incessant whistling, which is easily imitated and made use of as a decoy. This bird is difficult of approach while feeding, and its capture requires much precaution and the use of various stratagems.

So far as it is possible to ascertain, this Plover does not breed in the mountains of Pennsylvania; and the statements of Wilson and Audubon in regard to its breeding habits, and their description of its nests and eggs, must be admitted to have been based on incorrect information. The eggs described by Wilson are probably those of the Willet, and do not at all resemble those of this species; while the eggs described by Audubon are yet more dissimilar, and without much doubt were those of Bartram's Tattler, which, as well as this species, is known as the "Field Plover."

In its winter wanderings this species visits the West Indies, Mexico, Central America, and parts of South America. Early in September, or from the 5th to the 10th, they are found on the Rio Grande, and return on their way north during the latter part of May. Mr. Salvin states that it occurs on the sandy plains of Chiapan, in Guatemala, where it was found intermingled with flocks of *Tringæ*. Léotaud mentions it as a migratory visitant in Trinidad, where it is hardly ever seen by itself, but is usually in the midst of a flock of the *Charadrius virginicus*. It arrives about the end of August, and leaves in October. The Beetle-head not only accompanies the Golden Plover, but the manners of both appear to be identical. They are thus met with together both on the shores and in the savannas, but always in limited numbers.

G. H. White procured it near the City of Mexico; it was obtained in the Bahamas by Dr. Bryant; and in the Bermudas, where it is of rare occurrence, by Lieutenant Wedderburn. It is found in Jamaica and in Cuba from August to April. In Florida, according to Mr. Moore, it is present throughout the year, and is quite common even in the summer months. The summer birds are all in their winter plumage, have no black beneath them except on their axillaries, and no white on their heads, but sober winter gray; none show either by their actions or by the condition of their internal organs any symptoms of breeding. Migrants return the 11th of August, and many spend the winter in Florida.

The Baron Droste Hülskoff, in his "Birds of Borkum," states that this species passes there late in May, and again appears in its southward migrations in August and early in September. He describes it as a fine, lively bird, carrying its head and body erect, and its breast thrown forward. It runs backward in the manner of the Golden Plover; and, before flying, always lifts its wings high above its head. Its flight is peculiarly swift — more so than that of most other shore birds — and it flies off in a straight line, now approaching, and now leaving the ground in easy dips, extending the wings far, and flying with powerful strokes. The call-note of this bird, he adds, is a sharp whistle, *tlj-e-ih*, the final note being very softly sounded. On the wing it repeats this note with long pauses; and when at rest, if another of the same species settles down beside it, the last part of the call-note is repeated back and forth between the two. At sunset they are most uneasy, and fly about, calling continually, late into the night. They are very watchful and shy, carefully avoiding every suspicious-looking mound, and very rarely approaching a place where a sportsman is hid. This is the sentinel of other shore-birds, warning them by its sudden flight and loud alarm-note. On the edge of the water it seeks its food in the foam; and, like the sandpiper, wades up to its belly in the water.

Lord Lilford states that this bird has a curious habit of throwing somersaults in the air, in the same manner as the Tumbler Pigeon and Roller. He noticed this particularly in March, 1857, on the Gulf of Arta.

According to Dr. Cooper's observations, this Plover is not common along the southern coast of California, although some are found there from October to May; but a single specimen was obtained by him on Catalina Island. Farther north in that State it is more abundant in the wet season, and chiefly along the sea-beaches. Occasionally it visits the prairies, and is there known as the Whistling Field Plover.

About the end of August these birds descend to the sea-coast at the mouth of the Columbia River, but are later in their appearance within the limits of California. They there feed on shell-fish, crustacea, and other small marine animals. They are generally very shy and watchful, whistling loudly as they fly, after the manner of the Kildeer. This species was noticed in considerable numbers about Lake Koskonong, Wis., Aug. 15, 1873.

Mr. Nelson mentions it as a not uncommon migrant on Lake Michigan, where it arrives, in full breeding-plumage, about the 15th of May. A few remain during the summer; and although Mr. Nelson conjectures that they may breed, this is not probable. Certainly none of their eggs have ever been detected except in the highest Arctic regions. They return in September, wearing their fall plumage.

Mr. MacFarlane discovered this species breeding on an island in Franklin Bay, on the Arctic coast, July 4. The nest contained four eggs, and was composed of a little withered grass, placed in a depression on the side or face of a very gentle eminence. Both parents were seen, and the male shot. They were at first mistaken for the Golden Plover; but their note and general appearance soon undeceived him. This was the first of the species he had ever seen during his sojourn in the country. While it may exist on the Arctic coast and in the Barren Grounds, he is quite confident that he never met with it before. The eggs in this instance contained partially developed embryos. On the following day, July 5, 1864, another nest, containing four eggs also, in the same stage of development, was secured.

A third nest, with four eggs, was discovered the following night, and a snare was set to secure the parent. The female was taken, but before it was secured, a Snowy Owl devoured the bird and destroyed the eggs.

In regard to the breeding of this Plover, we learn from Middendorff that he observed none of this species on the Boganida earlier than the 25th of May. By the 26th of June the females were sitting there on their nests, which had been formed by collecting together dried leaves and grasses, and in which were four eggs, which he compares in shape with the eggs of the Lapwing and the Dotterel (*Charadrius morinellus*). He gives their average length at 2.10 inches, and their average largest diameter 1.40 inches. They differed very considerably in size, the largest being 2.18 inches in length, and the smallest only 1.87 inches. Nor does the color afford any distinctive mark. The ground-color is sometimes yellowish gray and sometimes brownish yellow, the dark-brown spots being like those of the *Ch. pluvialis*. Middendorff also found this bird breeding on the Byrranga Mountains, in latitude 74°.

Mr. Dresser describes one of the eggs obtained by Middendorff as measuring 2.07 by 1.40 inches, with a ground-color of a dull clay-brown, and bearing markings distributed over the surface, but collecting together at the larger end, blackish brown in color, and irregular in shape. There were also a few underlying purplish shell-markings.

Eggs of this species collected by Mr. MacFarlane in an island in Franklin's Bay, on the Arctic coast, in July, 1864, and in 1865, and numbered 11193, 11196, and 11199, S. I., exhibit certain general resemblances to the egg of the more common Golden Plover (*Ch. virginicus*). They have, however, certain constant differences which do not readily admit of exact description. These three sets, two of four and one of three eggs, differ from the average egg of the *virginicus* in the more nearly equal distribution of the spots over the whole egg. In two of these sets the ground color is of a light greenish drab; in the other the ground is a light rufous drab, without any mixture of green. The spots are of a dark shade of umber or bistre, and the darkness of the shade is quite uniform, and never intensified, as in the eggs of the *virginicus*. They are strongly pyriform in shape, and vary in length from 1.90 inches to 2.30, and in breadth from 1.40 to 1.47 inches. They are longer and broader than the *virginicus*, and their breadth is also proportionally greater.

Messrs. Harvie-Brown and Seebohm, in the summer of 1875, found the Gray Plover breeding on the tundras of the Petchora River, in Northern Russia in Europe, where they procured a rich series of eggs described as intermediate in color between those of the Golden Plover and the Lapwing, and subject to variations, some being much browner, and others more olive, but none so green as the eggs of the Lapwing, nor so orange as those of the Plover. The blotching is in every respect the same, the underlying spots equally indistinct, and the surface spots large, especially at the greater end, but occasionally small and scattered. In size they vary from 1.90 by 1.35 to 2.20 by 1.40 inches.

GENUS **CHARADRIUS**, LINNÆUS.

Charadrius, LINN. S. N. ed. 10, 1758, 150; ed. 12, 1766, 253 (type, *C. apricarius*, LINN.).

CHAR. Similar to *Squatarola*, but without any trace of hind toe. Plumage also very similar, but form rather more slender.

Only two species of *Charadrius* proper are known, one peculiar to the Palæarctic Region, but occurring accidentally in Greenland; the other spread over the remaining portions of the world,

C. dominicus.

including the greater part of America, the islands throughout the Pacific, and the coasts of Asia. They differ chiefly in the color of the axillary feathers and the lining of the wings, as follows:—

1. **C. apricarius.** Axillars and lining of the wing pure white. *Hab.* Palæarctic Region, breeding in Eastern Greenland.
2. **C. dominicus.** Axillars and lining of the wing smoky gray.
   a. Var. *dominicus.* Average dimensions:[1] Wing, 7.09; culmen, .92; tarsus, 1.70; middle toe, .90. *Hab.* North America generally, migrating southward; breeding in the high north (including the coasts and islands of Alaska?).
   b. Var. *fulvus.* Average dimensions:[2] Wing, 6.40; culmen, .92; tarsus, 1.72; middle toe, .90. *Hab.* Pacific Islands and Asia; coast and islands of Alaska in migrations.

Charadrius apricarius.

EUROPEAN GOLDEN PLOVER.

Charadrius apricarius, LINN. S. I. ed. 10, I. 1758, 150; ed. 12, I. 1766, 254. — BREHM, Vög. Deutschl. 1831, 541, pl. 27, fig. 3.

Charadrius pluvialis, LINN. S. N. ed. 10, I. 1758, 151; ed. 12, I. 1766, 254. — KEYS. & BLAS. Wirb. Eur. 1840, 70. — SCHLEG. Rev. crit. 1844, 81. — GRAY, Gen. B. III. 1849, 544; Cat. Brit. B. 1363, 139. — RIDGW. Nom. N. Am. B. 1881, no. 514. — COUES, Check List, 2d ed. 1882, no. 583.

Charadrius auratus, BECHST. Naturg. Deutschl. IV. 1809, 395. — NAUM. Vög. Deutschl. VII. 1834, 138, pl. 173.

Charadrius altifrons, BREHM, t.c. 542.

Pluvialis aurea, MACGILL. Man. II. 1842, 49.

The Golden Plover, AUCT.

HAB. Western Palæarctic Region, migrating to Africa, etc., in winter; breeding in Eastern Greenland (FINSCH).

[1] Twenty-four specimens measured.

[2] Twenty-three specimens measured.

SP. CHAR. Lining of the wing and axillars always pure white; tibiæ naked for only about half the length of the tarsus, or less. *Adult in summer:* Above dusky black, everywhere spotted with bright ochre-yellow, the wings with both the ground-color and the markings paler; primaries, primary-coverts, and alulæ, plain brownish-slate, with a narrow terminal margin of white; about the terminal half of the shafts of the quills also white; tail grayish slate, with rather narrow oblique bars of white, these tinged with yellow on the middle feathers. Entire side of head, up to the upper edge of the lores and auriculars, chin, and foreneck uniform dull black or dusky; this extending downward over the middle of the jugulum, gradually narrowing, until below it forms a stripe only a little more than half an inch wide, but, suddenly expanding, covers the entire lower breast, abdomen, and anal region. Forehead and superciliary stripe white, this continued downward along the edge of the black, gradually widening below, until, where the black becomes narrowest, the white measures nearly one inch in width. Sides of the breast (posterior to and above the white) spotted and barred black and ochre-yellow; crissum mostly white. Bill black; iris dark brown; legs and feet bluish gray (MACGILLIVRAY). *Winter plumage:* Upper parts as in summer, but the yellow markings more golden; black of lower parts, throat, etc., replaced by light grayish, spotted and streaked with darker, the throat and abdomen immaculate white. *Young:* Above spotted dusky and ochre-yellow, much as in the adult; lower parts as in the winter adult, but jugulum and sides of breast strongly suffused with light ochre-yellow. *Downy young:* "Bright golden, varied with black on the head and back, the hind part of the neck bright yellow; a spot under the eye, and under surface of the body pure white" (DRESSER).

Total length about 10.50; extent, 22.00. Wing, about 7.00; culmen, .90; tarsus, 1.50–1.60; middle toe, 1.00.

Except in the pure white axillars and under wing-coverts, there is little in the coloration of this species to distinguish it from the American *C. dominicus* and its Asiatic representative, *C. fulvus.* It is more golden above, however, though some specimens of *C. fulvus* are as much marked with this color.

Charadrius dominicus.

THE AMERICAN GOLDEN PLOVER.

Charadrius dominicus, MÜLLER, Syst. Nat. Suppl. 1776, 116. — CASS. Pr. Ac. Nat. Sci. Philad. 1864, 241. — RIDGW. Nom. N. Am. B. 1881, no. 515. — COUES, Check List, 2d ed. 1882, no. 581.

Charadrius pluvialis, WILSON, Am. Orn. VII. 1813, 71, pl. 50, fig. 5 (nec LINN.). — SWAINS. & RICH. F. B. A. II. 1831, 369. — NUTT. Man. II. 1834, 16. — AUD. Orn. Biog. III. 1835, 623.

Charadrius virginicus, "BORCKHAUSEN and BECHSTEIN," LICHT. Verz. Doubl. 1823, no. 729. — CASSIN, in Baird's B. N. Am. 1858, 690. — BAIRD, Cat. N. Am. B. 1859, no. 503.

Charadrius fulvus, var. *virginicus*, COUES, Key, 1872, 243; Check List, 1874, no. 396, Birds N. W. 1874, 449 (synonymy).

Charadrius marmoratus, WAGL. Syst. Av. 1827, no. 42. — AUD. Orn. Biog. V. 1839, 575, pl. 300; Synop. 1839, 222; Birds Am. V. 1842, 203, pl. 316.

Charadrius fulvus americanus, SCHLEG. Mus. P.-B. Cursores, 1865, 53.

HAB. America in general, from the Arctic coast (including Greenland) to Paraguay and Chili; breeding in the Arctic and Subarctic districts, winter migrant to southern localities.

SP. CHAR. Bill rather short, legs moderate, wings long, no hind toe, tarsus covered before and behind with small circular or hexagonal scales. *Summer plumage:* Upper parts brownish black, with numerous small circular and irregular spots of golden yellow, most numerous on the back and rump, and on the upper tail-coverts, assuming the form of transverse bands generally; also with some spots of ashy white. Entire under parts black, with a brownish or bronzed lustre, under tail-coverts mixed or barred with white. Forehead, border of the black of the neck, under tail-coverts, and tibiæ, white; axillary feathers cinereous; quills dark brown; middle portion of the shafts white, frequently extending slightly to the webs and forming longitudinal stripes on the shorter quills; tail dark brown, with numerous irregular bands of ashy white, and frequently tinged with golden yellow; bill black; legs dark bluish brown. *Winter plumage* (*young and adult*) : Under parts dull ashy, spotted with brownish on the neck and breast, frequently more or less mixed with black ; many spots of the upper parts dull ashy white ; other spots, especially on the rump, golden yellow.

Total length, about 9.50 inches ; wing, 7.00 ; tail, 2.50 ; culmen, .92 ; tarsus, 1.70 ; middle toe, .90.

Specimens vary in the relative amount of the black and golden on the upper parts, in the width of the white on the forehead, and other details of coloration. All the specimens in summer

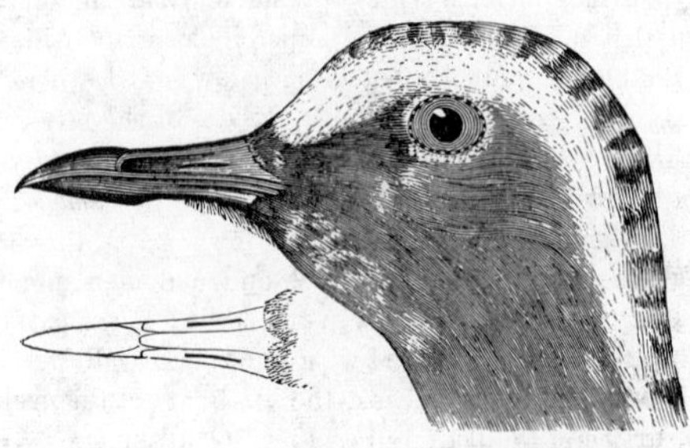

plumage from Alaska, including St. Michael's, Popoff Island, Kadiak, and Sitka, are apparently referable to the American form ; at least we cannot distinguish them from other North American examples in the same plumage, while their measurements are decidedly those of *dominicus*. Twenty-six specimens in all have been examined, these representing almost as many localities, from the Arctic coast to Costa Rica. Careful measurements of this series afford the following results : — *Eleven specimens in summer plumage :* Wing, 6.80–7.35, average, 7.11 ; culmen .85–1.00, average, .91 ; tarsus, 1.60–1.85, average, 1.73 ; middle toe, .85–1.05, average, .91. *Six adults in changing plumage :* Wing, 6.90–7.30, average, 7.12 ; culmen, .90–1.00, average, .96 ; tarsus, 1.65–1.82, average, 1.70 ; middle toe, .80–.95, average, .90. *Seven specimens in winter plumage (mostly young)* : Wing, 6.80–7.20, average, 7.03 ; culmen, .80–1.00, average, .91 ; tarsus, 1.55–1.75, average, 1.66 ; middle toe, .85–.95, average, .87. *Average of the whole series :* Wing, 7.09 ; culmen, .91 ; tarsus, 1.70 ; middle toe, .90.

The Green, or Golden, Plover of North America is, within the limits of the United States, a migratory species exclusively, and is confined, to a large extent, in its flights, to the vicinity of the coast. Straggling parties, in the fall, pass south through the interior ; but these are chiefly birds in an immature plumage. Their migrations in the spring begin, in the more southern States, early in March, and continue through that and the following month. Their movement at this season is more rapid than in the fall, and they make few and short pauses, their flights being made more frequently by interior routes. Audubon, when in New Orleans, March 16, 1821, witnessed an extraordinary flight of these birds near the Lake of St. John. They passed in many thousands in a northeasterly direction. He estimated the number of Plovers destroyed by the sportsmen on that day at forty-eight thousand. These flights took place only just after there had been several very warm days, followed by a strong northeast wind. The birds were not generally in good condition.

The late Dr. Lincecum, of Washington Co., Texas, states in his manuscript notes that all through April the Golden Plover is passing northward throughout Texas. Only very few stop on the prairie and remain all summer, and these do not breed there. They do not, when they are passing north, travel in groups, but fly widely scattered, chirping as they go, and seeming to try to keep in hearing of each other. They appear to travel as much by night as during the day, since their peculiar call, or chirping, is heard during the month of their passage at all hours of the night. They often, when passing, fly at a great elevation. He states that, several minutes before the sun had appeared above the horizon, he has seen it shining brightly on the under-part of their body and wings. They pass southward in early autumn in the same way, travelling wide-scattered, both night and day. He considered it a poor bird for food, never having been so fortunate as to get a fat one.

Their migrations in the fall are more generally noticed, and are more remarkable than those which take place in the spring. They occur with great regularity late in August, when the great body of the migrating flocks move south with so much regularity, and with the accomplishment of such great distances passed over without opportunity for rest, as to excite much interest. A succession of flocks pass through Nova Scotia, striking boldly out to sea, and if the weather is fair, taking a direct line southward; they go to the east of the Bermudas, and if not interfered with by storms, make no stops until the West Indies are reached. They even pass over the first of these in their course. Should an easterly storm prevail about the 24th of August, the birds are driven from their path, and pass in large numbers over the eastern portion of Maine, and subsequently over the southeastern extremity of Massachusetts. In some seasons large numbers suddenly appear on Montauk Point, at the east end of Long Island. Mr. Lawrence states that when they are seen in such numbers it is usually about the 28th of August, not varying more than a day or two from that time, and then only when a southeast storm has driven them out of their regular course over the sea on to the island. Mr. Lawrence was at this point in August, 1858, and a southeast storm began on the 27th of that month. Flocks of these birds were just appearing as he left on that day, and he afterward learned that on the 28th they came in unusual numbers. In these visitations they remain but a short time, the main body moving on south in two or three days. In ordinary seasons only a few flocks pass the Point at the time of their migration. As the result of long observation, Mr. Patrick Gould — Mr. Lawrence's informant — had made out that unless a storm occurred just at the time named, no unusual flight took place, showing that their principal migration is made each year at a fixed period, and is ended within two or three days. Giraud, whose observations of this Plover are confined to their constant and regular migrations, and who took no note of these extraordinary flights, states that in their northern movements in spring they arrive on Long Island in the latter part of April, and soon pass on to more northern regions. They return in the early part of September, and frequent the Plains of Hempstead, Shinnecock Hill, and Montauk, where they feed on a variety of insects. Grasshoppers are their favorite fare, as well as berries. Occasionally he met with these birds along the shores and about the ponds or the low wet meadows; but they generally prefer high and dry land, unincumbered with woods. Hempstead Plains are well adapted to their habits, and in some seasons they are quite abundant on that miniature prairie. To Long Island hunters, and in the New York market, this is known as the "Frost Bird," as it is usually most plentiful during the first frosts of autumn, when it is in fine condition and exceedingly well flavored.

In regard to the appearance of this bird at Bermuda, Major Wedderburn states that during some years large flocks pass over those islands; but he gives the time as September and October, instead of the latter part of August — the usual epoch of its migrations. Except in stormy weather, it does not alight in any great numbers. In 1847 the flight was as early as the 21st of August, and in 1848 a single bird was seen on the 25th of July. On the 9th of March, 1852, one was shot on the north shore — the only instance of its appearing in spring. To this statement Mr. Hurdis adds that this bird only visits Bermuda during its great southern migration, a few being met with by the 1st of September, or, rarely, a few days earlier. As a general rule, it passes over Bermuda in large and numerous flocks between the 10th and 17th of September. If the weather is favorable, the flocks pass on, at a considerable elevation, in a southerly or southeasterly direction, the form of the flight being a leading cluster, from which extend three long lines in single file. They must have come over a distance of eight hundred miles, and have a still longer flight to accomplish before they can reach *terra firma*.

Occasionally hurricanes originate in the West Indies, rage with great violence, and pass to the westward of Bermuda. It is impossible for the Plovers to proceed if they meet one of these terrific storms of wind and rain, and they take refuge in the Bermudas. It is very remarkable that they are always extremely fat, and they are in consequence much sought by the hunters. A few flocks — later arrivals — are met with up to the middle of October. Mr. Hurdis was informed by a friend long resident in Antigua that in September this island is annually visited by countless flocks of this bird. On one occasion, when the weather was stormy, this Plover made its appearance in such multitudes that in St. John's the inhabitants in all directions shot them from their doors and windows, even the boys killing them with sticks and stones. Similar occurrences are narrated as having taken place in Martinique and Barbadoes.

This bird is said to display great activity when on the ground, and it often runs with considerable rapidity before taking wing. It is not so timid as the Black-bellied Plover, and is easily decoyed by imitating its peculiarly mellow note, and is often observed, if thus enticed when passing in a certain direction, to check its course, turn round, and present itself as an easy mark. The stay of this species is short, and as the season advances it passes southward, always moving in flocks and in a very regular manner.

In their wintry wanderings they alternately visit the West Indies, Central and South America, to Paraguay and Chili. Salvin noted their appearance in the open pasture-lands about Dueñas, Guatemala, in the second week of April, where they were always seen in company with flocks of Bartram's Tattler. This bird appears to be of accidental occurrence in Florida, where Mr. Moore saw but two individuals, one in the spring. Professor Alfred Newton refers to their autumnal migrations through St. Croix, where they often appear in large numbers. There they are usually seen after a gale from the south or southwest. From this he infers that they are arrested in their southern migration by the wind, and compelled to defer journeying farther until the weather has changed. To this Mr. Edward Newton adds, that their arrival is hailed with delight by the sportsmen, every one possessing a gun hastening to the pastures on the south side of the island, and there awaiting the long line of these birds as they fly up from the sea without exhibiting the least shyness. They were first noticed by the Newtons, August 31, and as all the birds seen had more or less traces of the black breast of the breeding-plumage, it was supposed that the young birds must have taken a different line from their parents in their migration. In Trinidad, according to Léotaud, this species is a regular migratory visitant, arriving about the end of August and moving south in October, and is always found in flocks of considerable size, frequenting the sea-side, but being even more fond of the interior meadows, and especially of those freshly turned up, where it finds a great abundance of the worms on which it feeds. It is the most regular of the birds of passage, arrives in varying numbers, and is sought after by the local epicures; although Léotaud adds that this supposed excellence of its flesh is more imaginary than real.

On the Pacific coast this bird is comparatively rare. Dr. Cooper never met with it in Southern California, and has only seen a single specimen, shot near San Francisco by Mr. J. Hepburn. Dr. Newberry mentions having noticed it in the northern part of that State in autumn.

In Northeastern Illinois and near the shores of Lake Michigan, Mr. Nelson considers this species a very abundant migrant. It arrives in large flocks early in April, the black of their breeding-plumage only just beginning to mottle their white breasts. They frequent wet prairies until the last of the month, when they leave, a few remaining into May. Returning early in September, they stay until October.

They resort to breed to the most northern portions of the continent, from Greenland to Sitka. Dr. Walker, of the "Fox," mentions meeting with them on the coast of Greenland, near Godthaab, and afterward finding them breeding in the marshy valleys of Bellot's Strait in June. This species is included in Reinhardt's list of the birds of Greenland, on the strength of specimens taken there by Holböll.

Captain Blakiston noted it as only a passing visitor in the more southern parts of British America, and as numerous in autumn on the shores of Hudson's Bay; but it did not appear to be common on the Western plains. Mr. Ross mentioned this Plover as being abundant on the Mackenzie, and Hearne speaks of it as having been called, a century ago, by the Indians of Hudson's Bay, "Hawk's-eye," — a name indicating its watchfulness, when sitting, in preventing a too near approach. He describes its motions when on the wing as swift and irregular, particularly when single or in small flocks. Though never numerous at Churchill River, yet at Fort York, in the fall of 1773, he saw this bird in immense flocks. They were, however, by no means equally plentiful in all years nor in all places. At Fort Albany several barrelsful were annually salted down for winter use. He adds: "This bird during the summer resorts to the remotest northern parts, for I have seen them at Copper River, though in those dreary regions only in pairs. The young leave the nests as soon as hatched, and when but a few days old run very fast. At night or in rainy weather the old ones call them together and cover them with their wings in the same manner as a hen does her chickens."

Richardson in his account states that the breeding-quarters of this species are the Barren Ground, the Arctic coast, and the islands of the Arctic Sea; that they hatch early in June, and retire southward in August. Numbers, however, linger on the muddy shores of Hudson's Bay, and on the sandy beaches of the rivers and lakes of the interior, until the hard frosts of September and October drive them away. At this period they are very fat, and are highly prized by the epicures of the Fur Country.

This Plover appears also to be a common species on the northwestern coast. Bannister gives it as common at St. Michael's. It was procured by Bischoff at Sitka and Kadiak, and is mentioned by Dall as being abundant at Nulato and all along the Yukon River, where it arrives during the latter part of May.

Mr. MacFarlane's Arctic Notes are very full in reference to the nesting and breeding habits of this species. The number of eggs was almost invariably four, but in one instance five were said to have been found. Out of one hundred and fourteen recorded nests, ninety-two contained four eggs. In one instance only one egg, nearly ready to hatch, was found. The nests were noticed throughout the Barren Grounds, from the time of the party's leaving the woods quite up to that of their arrival on the Arctic Ocean. The nests were in all instances mere depressions in the soil, generally lined with a few dry leaves, and were difficult to find, as there was nothing to distinguish them from the soil — which the eggs very closely resemble in color —

and as the female glides from her nest, if approached, even when the intruders are still at a distance. She runs a certain distance, and if she succeeds in enticing the party away, will then take to flight. In a few instances, when the bird was surprised by a near approach before she left, she pretended lameness, and fluttered at their feet. The eggs were found in June, and some even as late as July, and quite fresh. When the ground was covered with newly-fallen snow the nests were more readily recognized. When approached the female usually left her position at a quick pace — between a run and a walk — and in no case was she known to fly up directly from her eggs. In one instance, where the presence of a nest was suspected, but the exact locality of which they were not able to discover, the party withdrew to a distance and watched, when the female, after resorting to various manœuvres to hide the place, at last revealed it by finally settling down upon her eggs.

The eggs of this species have a ground of various shades of drab, differing in several specimens, and varying from a light greenish drab to a very deep shade, unmixed with any other color. Others have a ground of a pale rufous-drab. All are marked with blotches of a deep umber, approaching to blackness. These markings are smaller and more scattered around the pointed end; but are larger and become confluent, with intensified spots, around the obtuse apex. Their average length is about 1.91 inches, and their average breadth 1.31 inches. Their maximum length is 2 inches, their minimum 1.84; their breadth varies from 1.25 to 1.35 inches.

Charadrius dominicus fulvus.

THE PACIFIC GOLDEN PLOVER.

Charadrius fulvus, GMEL. S. N. I. 1788, 687. — COUES, Elliott's Prybilof Islands, 1873, 179 (Prybilof Islands, Alaska).

Charadrius fulvus, a. *fulvus*, COUES, Birds N. W. 1874, 449 (synonymy).

Pluvialis fulvus, BONAP. Compt. Rend. 1856, 417.

Charadrius dominicus fulvus, RIDGW. Proc. U. S. Nat. Mus. Vol. 3, 1880, 198, 221; Nom. N. Am. B. 1881, no. 515 *a*. — COUES, Check List, 2d ed. 1882, no. 582.

Charadrius xanthocheilus, WAGL. Syst. Av. 1827. — CASSIN, U. S. Expl. Exp. 1848, 239.

Charadrius tahitensis, LESS. Man. II. 1828, 321.

Charadrius glaucopsus, FORST. Descr. An. ed. Licht. 1844, 176.

Charadrius longipes, "TEMM. Mus. Lugdun."

Charadrius auratus orientalis, TEMM. & SCHLEG. Fauna Jap. 1845, pl. 62.

Charadrius auratus, SCHRENCK, Reise Amur. 1860, 410.

HAB. Whole of Asia, and islands throughout the Pacific Ocean; Prybilof Islands and coast of Alaska (numerous specimens in National Museum).

CHAR. Similar to *C. dominicus*, but wing much shorter, and color much more golden, the upper surface being almost continuously washed with golden yellow. Average measurements: Wing, 6.40; culmen, .92; tarsus, 1.72; middle toe, .90.

The only American specimens of this form of the Golden Plover, which ranges throughout the islands of the Pacific, besides Southern and Eastern Asia, are from the islands and coasts of Alaska. They are all in the winter plumage, suggesting the probability of their being mere migrants to our shores. The very fine specimens in the collection, obtained chiefly by Messrs. Lucien M. Turner and E. W. Nelson, of the U. S. Signal Service, at St. Michael's, Norton Sound, are perfectly typical of the race, most of them being continuously golden yellow above, relieved only by the black spotting. The jugulum is also deeply tinged with this color. There are no specimens in the summer plumage, from any locality, in the collection, so we are unable to point out the exact differences from the corresponding stage of *C. dominicus*.[1] Altogether we have examined in this

[1] Since the above was written, the National Museum has come into possession of an adult male in changing plumage, from New South Wales (No. 71561, obtained from the New South Wales Museum),

connection upwards of thirty specimens, the greater number being from the Pacific islands. Measurements of a part of this series (other specimens not being available for the purpose) give the following results: — *Seven specimens from Alaska:* Wing, 6.25–6.80, average, 6.49; culmen, .85–.95, average, .89; tarsus, 1.70–1.85, average, 1.76; middle toe, .85–.90, average, .89. *Sixteen specimens from Pacific islands, India, and China:* Wing, 6.10–6.80, average, 6.36; culmen, .85–1.00, average .93; tarsus, 1.55–1.85, average, 1.69; middle toe, .85–.95, average, .91. The average of the whole series is as given above.

In the collection there is one specimen (No. 1853) labelled "*Charadrius pluvialis*," received from Aug. Lefevre, Paris, and supposed to have been obtained in France — although this is not asserted on the original label — which bears, beside the name, only the inscription, "*prenant livrée d'été*." It is typical *fulvus*, having smoky gray axillars, and measuring as follows: Wing, 6.00; culmen, .92; tarsus, 1.70; middle toe, .90. It is an adult in changing plumage.

A single specimen of this Asiatic species was procured by Mr. Elliott on the Prybilof Islands, thus first giving it a place in the fauna of North America.[1] This example was taken on the Island of St. Paul's, May 2, 1873. Mr. Elliott states that a few stragglers land in April or early in May on their way north to breed, but never remain long. They return in greater numbers the latter part of September, and grow fat upon the larvæ generated on the killing-grounds of the fur seal, and leave for the south by the end of October. Numerous specimens taken on the coast of Alaska are in the National Museum. This species is very closely allied to the *virginianus*, so that Drs. Hartlaub and Finsch regard it as very probable that they are identical species.

Mr. Dresser, in his account of this bird, refers to specimens taken in Northeastern Africa on the Red Sea, in Siberia, India, Ceylon, Malacca, Java, Banca, Borneo, Timor, Batchian, Australia, Hainan, Formosa, China, and also to one from the Arctic seas, killed in lat. 69° 30′ N., long. 173° 20′ E., Sept. 3, 1852, and nearer the American than the Asiatic shore. It also occasionally extends its range into Europe, having once been seen at Heligoland and twice at Malta. It will thus be seen either to be a great wanderer or to have quite an extended range.

It is without doubt this bird that is referred to by Pallas as *C. pluvialis*. By that traveller it is spoken of as being rare in the northern parts of Russia, but exceedingly common in Siberia, whence it migrates in the autumn in flocks to more southern localities in company with the Dotterel. It was met with on the banks of small rivers and in cattle pastures. Steller is quoted as having taken it in Kamtschatka in autumn.

Mr. Dresser states that it breeds within the Arctic Circle. Middendorff observed it on the *tundras* of the Taimyr, in lat. 74° N., in full summer plumage. The birds were gathered in large flocks on the 4th of June, and had eggs by the 17th. They assembled on the 2d of August, on Lake Taimyr, to return, and none were seen after

and another, in nearly complete summer dress, from Shanghai, China (No. 85742, April 21, 1881; Shanghai Museum). Upon close comparison of these specimens with examples in corresponding plumage from North America, we cannot see that they differ in the minutest particular as regards coloration. They are, however, decidedly shorter winged, their measurements being, respectively, as follows: —

	Wing.	Culmen.	Tarsus.	Middle Toe.
No. 71561, ♂, New South Wales,	6.30	.95	1.65	1.00
No. 85742, ♂, Shanghai,	6.55	1.02	1.75	.95
Average of *C. dominicus*,	7.09	.91	1.70	.90

[1] Since the above was penned by Dr. Brewer, numerous Alaskan specimens have been received at the U. S. National Museum, collected by Messrs. Turner and Nelson, and others, chiefly at St. Michael's, Norton Sound. — R. R.

the 9th of that month. On the Boganida, lat. 70° N., they arrived May 24, and were not noticed later than August 31. They nested on the barrens of Uldskoj-Ostrog.

According to Mr. Henry Whitely, as quoted by Mr. Dresser, it is by no means a rare bird in Japan, where he obtained three specimens, Sept. 24 and Oct. 3, 1865. In India, according to Dr. Jerdon, it occurs generally in open plains, grassy downs, ploughed fields, and on the edges of rivers and lakes, associating in flocks of varying magnitude, and feeding on beetles and other hard insects, worms, and the like. He speaks of it as having a shrill whistling call, and as flying very rapidly. He also states that many breed in that country — even toward the south, as at Nellore — while others were observed to pass northward to breed, returning in September.

Mr. Holdworth mentions this species as being very common in Ceylon in winter, especially in the north of that island, extending as far south as Columbo. Professor Schlegel refers to more than sixty specimens of this species, collected in nearly every island of the Malay Archipelago, and now in the Leyden Museum.

In Australia, according to Mr. Gould, although nowhere very abundant, this bird is generally dispersed all over the colonies, from Tasmania northward. Several specimens were procured on the banks of the Derwent in Tasmania, and others were observed in small numbers on the flats below Clarence Plains. He also killed examples on an island in Bass's Straits. Its habits, manners, and general economy are said closely to resemble those of the Golden Plover of Europe. It frequents open plains in the neighborhood of marshy lands or the sea-beach, runs with amazing facility, and flies with great rapidity. Indications of the breeding-plumage begin to appear early in the spring. Mr. Gould thinks that none remain to breed in any of the southern parts of Australia.

Dr. E. Gräffe mentions finding this Plover in Tongatabu, one of the Tonga Islands, where it occurred in flocks of from thirty to fifty individuals. They ran in search of food on sand-banks left dry at low water, and when approached within gunshot uttered a shrill *tuli-luli-twi-twi*, and then took to flight. At high-water they frequented the open grassy places on fields and fallows. This species was found all the year round on that island, but was more numerous from October to March, and during the season of migration.

Mr. Layard ("Ibis," 1878, p. 262) mentions its occurrence in New California, where it was found breeding on the islets off Anservata, close to Noumea; and Mr. Blakiston ("Ibis," p. 218) speaks of it as common throughout Japan. Mr. R. Swinhoe ("Ibis," 1874) mentions meeting with this species at Hakodadi in Japan in May. He elsewhere gives the range of this species as throughout China. He procured it between Takoo and Pekin, and states that he found it a common bird near Canton, passing the summer there. He also speaks of finding it in Formosa, where it was common all the year round, breeding in great abundance in marshy plains to the southwest. He also met with it in his excursion to Hainan, and states that it was common in the marsh near the city on the 5th of February. He found it in the dry rice-fields of Paklai, in Western Hainan, on the 21st of March, and abundant among the sweet-potato gardens of Hoitow on the 23d of that month. On the 2d of April, at Kinngehow, he saw these birds on the beach, where they were then beginning to acquire the black underdress of summer.

According to Mr. Swinhoe, its eggs — four in number — are laid in a loose nest of dried grasses and fibres placed in a hollow. They have a yellowish-gray ground, blotched and spotted with deep blackish sepia, and have occasional obsolete purplish gray spots. The eggs do not vary much in their size, are narrowed near one end, and measure 1.50 inches in length by 1.10 in breadth.

Mr. H. Seebohm (Ibis, 1879, p. 153) first met with this species in Siberia, June 5, and secured many specimens as it passed the Koo-rag-i-ka in its migrations. He again met with it on the open *tundra*, beyond the limit of forest-growth, in lat. 69° 30′. The nest was a mere hollow in the ground, lined with broken stalks of reindeer-moss. The eggs, four in number, averaged 1.90 by 1.32. These were taken July 13, and were very much incubated.

Mr. Seebohm shows that Mr. Swinhoe probably erred in stating that this Plover breeds in Formosa, and that he mistook the eggs of *Ægialitis Geoffroyi* for those of this species.

Genus **OXYECHUS**, Reichenbach.

Oxyechus, Reichenb., Av. Syst. 1853, Introd. p. xviii (type, *Charadrius vociferus*, Linn.).

Char. Bill small, slender, about equal to the middle toe (without nail); tarsus nearly twice as long as middle toe; tail long (about two thirds as long as the wings), reaching half its length beyond the ends of the primaries, graduated, the lateral feathers about .75 shorter than the middle pair; rump different in color from the back.

The single North American species of this genus differs conspicuously from the Plovers usually included together under *Ægialitis*, in the broad, lengthened tail, and, so far as coloration is concerned, in the ochraceous rump and the pair of black bands across the breast. It may be remarked, however, that coloration alone is of slight importance as a character in this group.

O. vociferus.

Two Old World species appear to belong here rather than with the true *Ægialitis*, namely, *Charadrius tricollaris*, Vieill., of South Africa, and *Ch. nigrifrons*, Cuvier, of Australia. The former is much like a miniature Kildeer Plover, having two black pectoral bands, like *O. vociferus* (though their relative width is reversed, the posterior one being the broader); the proportions and details of form are quite the same, but the rump and upper tail-coverts are concolor with the back. The Australian species agrees essentially with the above in size and proportions, but has broader and acuminate rectrices, and the tail is more nearly even, while the plumage is handsomer and more varied than in any other species of the group; the scapular region being adorned with a patch of rich maroon chestnut, the upper tail-coverts rufous chestnut, etc.

Oxyechus vociferus.

THE KILDEER PLOVER.

Charadrius vociferus, LINN. S. N. ed. 10, I. 1758, 150 ; ed. 12, I. 1766, 253. — WILS. Am. Orn. VII. 1813, 73, pl. 59, fig. 6. — NUTT. Man. II. 1834, 22. — AUD. Orn. Biog. III. 1835, 191 ; V. 1839, 577, pl. 225 ; Synop. 1839, 222 ; B. Am. V. 1842, 207, pl. 317.

Ægilitis vociferus, BONAP. Comp. List, 1838, 45. — CASSIN in Baird's B. N. Am. 1858, 692. — BAIRD, Cat. N. Am. B. 1859, no. 504. — COUES, Key, 1872, 244 ; Check List, 1874, no. 397 ; 2d ed. 1882, no. 584.

Oxyechus vociferus, REICH. Syst. Av. 1853, pl. xviii. — RIDGW. Nom. N. Am. B. 1881, no. 516.

Charadrius torquatus, LINN. S. N. I. 1766, 255.

Charadrius jamaicensis, GMEL. S. N. I. 1788, 685.

HAB. The whole of temperate North America, migrating in winter into tropical America as far as New Granada ; West Indies in general ; Bermudas ; River Avon, England (fide SCL., Ibis, 1862, 275 ; one specimen taken April, 1857).

SP. CHAR. *Adult:* Pileum and upper parts generally, grayish brown, inclining to umber ; rump and upper tail-coverts ochraceous-rufous, lighter on the latter. Forehead and broad superciliary stripe, throat, nuchal collar, and lower parts, white. Fore part of the crown, loral stripe, continued toward occiput, collar round neck, and band across breast, black. Primaries dusky, the

inner quills marked on outer webs with white. Tail chiefly pale ochraceous-rufous, variegated with white, dusky, and grayish, chiefly toward the end. Bill black ; iris dark brown ; eyelids (in life) orange-red or scarlet ; legs and feet pale pinkish grayish, or pale grayish yellow.

Young: Similar to the adult, but feathers of the upper parts more or less conspicuously margined with pale rusty or fulvous.

Downy Young: Upper parts generally, including pileum, light grayish brown, the two areas of this color bounded all round by black, a wide collar of which crosses the jugulum, and, extending across the nape beneath a broad white collar, completely encircles the neck ; a broad bar of velvety black down the middle of the humeral region, and a narrow, more interrupted stripe of the same down the rump. Forehead, throat, lower parts generally, "hand-wing," and posterior border of the humerus, pure white ; the flanks and crissum more isabella-color ; a narrow black line running from the rictus to the eye.

Total length, about 10 inches ; extent of wings, 20.50 ; wing, 6.50 ; tail, 3.50.

The Killdee, or Kildeer Plover, has a wide distribution throughout the continent, and breeds, wherever it is found, from Central America, Mexico, and Southwestern Texas, to the plains of the Saskatchewan. It is more abundant in some parts of the country than in others, and as a general thing is more numerous in the interior than near the sea-coast. A large proportion are migratory in the winter to the West Indies and Northern South America.

Throughout New England it is found generally distributed, but nowhere common, or only so in very exceptional instances. A few are seen as far eastward as Calais, but only in the fall, and these are evidently accidental visitors. A single specimen is recorded as taken in England. In the interior it is found much farther north than near the coast. Richardson notes its common presence in the Valley of the Saskatchewan, where it arrives about the 20th of April, and where, during its residence, it frequents the gardens and cultivated fields of the trading-posts in quest of its food. It is very familiar, hovering over the heads of intruders, and reiterating its loud, shrill cry. Captain Blakiston noted its first arrival at Fort Carlton, in 1858, on the 19th of April, finding it a bird difficult to approach within shooting distance. M. Bourgeau also obtained specimens, as well as their nests and eggs, on the Saskatchewan.

In Northeastern Illinois, near Lake Michigan, Mr. Nelson regards this species as only a summer resident, arriving the 1st of March and departing in October, although stragglers often appear in the milder days of mid-winter.

In Southeastern Oregon Captain Bendire found it one of the earliest birds to arrive in spring, and generally distributed in summer.

On Long Island, according to Mr. J. H. Batty, the Kildeer remains until quite late in the fall, and is seen again very early in the spring. He does not think, however, that it stays there throughout the winter, although one was procured by him on the 27th of November, 1872, when the ground was frozen hard and all the ponds were covered with ice: its stomach contained common ground-worms.

The Kildeer breeds as far south at least as Mexico. Dr. Berlandier states that it lives in the neighborhood of Matamoras, in the vicinity of swamps, and that it is also found throughout the entire State of Tamaulipas, where it is known as the Tildeo.

Dr. Lincecum states that, in the neighborhood of Long Point, Texas, it remains during winter in large flocks, flies, and feeds, and sounds its peculiar note as much at night, seemingly, as in the day. It occasionally nests about the rocky streamlets on the prairies of that country. He never met with a nest, though he has once been very near to one, the old bird trying by various pretences to allure him away from a certain locality by the side of a rocky stream. It carries its young about with it from their earliest infancy. No bird — as Dr. Lincecum remarks — walks with more ease or more gracefully than the Kildeer, young or old.

Though generally more common in the interior, the Kildeer is occasionally abundant in certain localities near the sea. Dresser found it equally common near the sea-coast, and inland in Texas at almost every pool. This bird breeds in Texas, both in the interior and on the coast, as Mr. Dresser received its eggs from Systerdale taken late in May; and when on Galveston Island, May 26, a German, who was with him, found a young Kildeer in a depression in the ground made by the hoof of a horse.

Major Wedderburn mentions this bird as a winter visitant of Bermuda, where specimens were occasionally obtained from the 12th of November to the 4th of March. Mrs. Hurdis adds that it is principally found in the months of December and January in small flocks; that its note is peculiarly soft and pleasing. It is not seen in the spring.

While a few occasionally winter in the Central Western States, in all the Southern States they are resident throughout the year, and most numerous in the winter. They are also found at this season in Mexico, Central America, and the West Indies. Mr. Salvin observed a flock of these Plovers frequenting the open land near Dueñas during the winter, and occasionally feeding in the cochineal plantations between the rows of nopal. He also found it common in other parts of Guatemala, both in all the highland swamps and in similar localities in the hot district with little elevation, everywhere preferring interior fresh-water marshes to the tide-washed sand-banks of the shore. Mr. Leyland also met with individuals near Omoa, and Mr. G. C. Taylor obtained several specimens on Tigre Island, and afterward on the open part of the plains of Comayagua. Specimens were taken in St. Thomas by Mr. Riise, and Dr. Bryant speaks of it as very common in the Bahamas during winter.

Dr. J. G. Cooper mentions the Kildeer as a constant resident in California wherever water is permanent. It was especially abundant at Los Angeles, December, 1860. Except in its more northern places of abode, it is only partially migratory.

Dr. Cooper also states that this Plover winters in all parts of California south of San Francisco. It migrates during April and May northwards, but a portion remain in summer in all the western part of that State. They prefer gravelly shores of brooks and rivers, but sometimes visit inundated meadows, or even dry and barren plains, where they feed on insects, and probably also on seeds.

They are very noisy, and their note — which to the Spanish ear sounds like *tildeo*, and not *kildeer* — is uttered in a complaining tone whenever any one approaches them. Though by no means timid, they always seem very much distressed by the presence of man, and act as if they had nests at all seasons; and, whether they are actually nesting or not, run before their pursuer, counterfeiting lameness, and apparently trying to excite pity by their melancholy notes. In California they are not generally regarded as good food, being of a strong and musky flavor; but in the autumn, when fat, they are not unfrequently eaten.

Near Fort Hays, in Western Kansas, Mr. J. A. Allen found this species by far the most numerous of the *Grallæ*. He afterward ascertained it to be equally abundant in the northeastern portion of the valley of Great Salt Lake. Mr. Ridgway found it more or less common in the prairies of the southern part of Illinois, and in his Western explorations it was by far the most generally distributed, as well as the most abundant bird of the order in all the fertile portions of the West, and resident in all sections where the streams are not frozen for any length of time during winter.

On Long Island the Kildeer is more numerous than in New England. There, according to Giraud, in summer it prefers the open dry ground; but on the approach of winter it descends to the sea-shore. It is more numerous in the northern portions of that island, which from their higher situation are better adapted than the southern for its residence in the summer. In his pedestrian excursion around that entire island, Giraud met with this Plover occasionally, but found it most abundant in a tract of waste ground near Green Point. The birds were very tame, and had evidently enjoyed undisputed possession of the place for some time. They were collecting worms and various kinds of insects; and he watched their employment without interrupting it.

The Kildeer feeds on worms and various kinds of insects on the uplands, and also frequents shallow pools and brooks in search of such small crustacea as are found in the water. In the fall it is said to follow the ploughman, and pick up the larvæ and other forms of insect life that are turned over in the furrows.

Like most of its race, this Plover passes much of its time on the ground, over which it moves with great rapidity. It can run with such swiftness that — according to Audubon — to run "like a Kildeer" has in some parts of the country passed into a proverbial phrase. This bird is also equally active on the wing, and mounts at pleasure to a great height in the air with a strong and rapid flight, which can be continued for a long distance. Sometimes it skims quite low over the ground, and at other times mounts to a great height; and during the love-season it is said to perform various kinds of evolutions while on the wing.

Its note consists of two syllables, resembling in sound *kill-dee*, rapidly enunciated; and occasionally, when the bird is much excited, only the last syllable is repeated after the first utterance of the double note. Generally it is sounded in a loud, clear tone, and as a signal of alarm. It not unfrequently startles other birds and puts them on their guard, this habit rendering the Kildeer an object of dislike to the hunter. During the summer — especially when it is breeding, and afterward, even when its young are fully grown — the Kildeer is a noisy and restless bird, and is disturbed by the near approach of man. It will often squat until one is close upon it, and will then suddenly fly up or run off, startling the unwary intruder by a loud and clear cry. According to Audubon, during the winter it is an unusually silent bird. At this season it is found dispersed over the cultivated fields in Florida, Georgia, the Carolinas, and other Southern States, diligently searching for food.

It is said to breed in Louisiana in the beginning of April, in the Middle States in May, and on the Saskatchewan in June. Its nest is of very simple construction, and is usually a mere hollow in the ground, without any lining, or with merely a few bits of dry grasses. Occasionally it is said to construct a nest of grass in a bunch of plants, but this is very rarely done. Wilson mentions having seen nests of this species with small fragments of shells forming a rim around the eggs. During incubation the parents alternate in sitting upon their eggs, and do not leave them day or night, differing in a marked manner, in this respect, from the *melodus* and the *Wilsoni*. The young run about the instant they leave the shell. If the nest is approached during incubation, or when the young are in danger, both parents resort to various manœuvres to entice away the intruder: the female droops her wings, utters plaintive notes, and simulates lameness; the male is more demonstrative, and dashes about his head with angry vociferations.

The eggs are usually four in number, never more — so far as known to us — and very rarely less. They are pyriform in shape, being much rounded at one end, and pointed at the other. Their ground, when the egg is fresh, is a rich cream-color, fading into a dull white, over which are profusely spread blotches of varying shape and size, of dark purplish brown, approaching black. These increase in size toward the larger end, and cover a greater proportion of it, but are finer and more scattered elsewhere. They measure 1.65 inches in length by 1.13 inches in their greater breadth.

Genus **ÆGIALITIS**, Boie.

Ægialitis, Boie, Isis, 1822, 558 (type, *Charadrius hiaticula*, Linn.).
Ægialites, Boie, Isis, 1826, 978.
Ægialeus, Reichenb. l. c. (type, *Charadrius semipalmatus*, Bonap.).
Leucopolius, Bonap. Compt. Rend. XLIII. 1856, 417 (type, *Charadrius leucopolius*, Wagl. = *C. marginatus*, Vieill.).
? *Cirripedesmus*, Bonap. Compt. Rend. 1856, 417 (type, *Charadrius cirrhipedesmus*, Wagl. = *Ch. mongolicus*, Pall.).

Char. Similar to *Oxyechus*, but the species of smaller size, with shorter and less graduated tail (less than half as long as the wing), and rump concolor with the back (grayish).

The numerous species of this genus vary greatly among themselves in the details of structure, although there is a general similarity of coloration throughout the group. The American species may be distinguished as follows: —

Æ. nivosa.

A. Nape crossed by a more or less distinct white collar.

a. Bill decidedly shorter than middle toe, very stout (except in *Æ. curonica*), the basal half light colored (orange or yellow) in adults, except in *Æ. curonica.*

a'. A distinct web between base of inner and middle toes.

1. **Æ. semipalmata.** Above, grayish brown; forehead, ring round neck, and lower parts, white. *In summer*, fore part of crown, lores, and broad pectoral collar (continued round back of neck, below the white nuchal collar) black or dusky. *In winter*, these black markings replaced by grayish brown, like the back, etc. *Young*, like winter adults, but bill wholly black, and feathers of upper parts margined terminally with buff. Wing, about 4.50–4.75; culmen, .45–.50; depth of bill at base, .20; tarsus, .95; middle toe, .65–.70. *Hab.* Nearly the whole of America.

a''. No web between base of inner and middle toes.

2. **Æ. hiaticula.** Colors of *Æ. semipalmata*, but pectoral band broader. Wing, about 5.00; culmen, .50–.55; depth of bill at base, .20–.22; tarsus, 1.00; middle toe, .60–.65. *Hab.* Palæarctic Region and portions of Arctic America.

3. **Æ. curonica.** Similar to *Æ. hiaticula*, but smaller and much more slender, especially the bill, which is always black; middle of crown crossed by a more or less distinct whitish bar, immediately behind the black patch. Wing, 4.35–4.70; culmen, .50–.52; depth of bill at base, .15–.18; tarsus, 1.00–1.05; middle toe, .55–.60. *Hab.* Palæarctic Region generally; accidental in California and Alaska?

4. **Æ. meloda.** Above, pale brownish gray; forehead, lores, nuchal collar, and lower parts white. *In summer*, a band across fore part of crown, and one across each side of breast (the latter sometimes connected, so as to form a continuous pectoral band), black or dusky. *In winter*, these black markings replaced by light brownish gray, and the bill almost entirely, or wholly, black. *Young*, like the winter plumage, but feathers of upper surface with distinctly paler terminal margins. Wing, 4.50–4.80; culmen, .45–.50; depth of bill at base, .20–.22; tarsus, .85–1.00; middle toe, .55.

α. var. *meloda.* Black pectoral band wholly or partially interrupted in the middle portion. *Hab.* Atlantic coast of United States.

β. var. *circumcincta.* Black pectoral band entirely continuous. *Hab.* Missouri River Region of United States, straggling eastward.

b. Bill much longer than the middle toe, very slender, wholly black.

5. **Æ. alexandrina.** Above, light brownish gray; forehead, superciliaries, nuchal collar, and lower parts white. *In summer*, fore part of the crown, a transverse patch on each side of breast (and sometimes a loral streak), black or dusky; pileum sometimes (especially in adult males) buffy or rufescent. Bill, legs, and feet, black or dusky.

a. alexandrina.[1] Lores always crossed by a dusky stripe. *In summer,* pileum brownish gray or dull buff. Wing, 4.40; culmen, .55–.60; tarsus, 1.02–1.12; middle toe, .55–.60. *Hab.* Europe, etc.

β. dealbata (?).[2] Lores always with a black streak. *In summer* (and frequently in winter also), pileum bright reddish buff or cinnamon-rufous. Wing, 4.35–4.70; culmen, .68–.78; tarsus, 1.10–1.15; middle toe, .65–.70. *Hab.* Eastern Asia (Hong-Kong, etc.).

γ. nivosa. Lores usually entirely white (never with a continuous or distinct dusky streak). *In summer,* pileum pale brownish gray or grayish buff. Wing, 4.20–4.30; culmen, .60; tarsus, .90–1.05; middle toe, .55–.60. *Hab.* Western America; Yucatan; Cuba (?).

B. Nape without trace of white or dusky collar.

a. Culmen equal to or longer than the middle toe, the bill slender.

6. **Æ. albidipectus.**[3] Breast without trace of either black or grayish band, but tinged, especially on each side, with light cinnamon; the sides of the neck and an indistinct nuchal collar deeper cinnamon; forehead, cheeks, and lower parts, except as described, white; loral stripe, crown, post-ocular streak, and post-auricular spot dusky black. Wing, 4.10; culmen, .60; depth of bill at base, .17; tarsus, 1.10; middle toe, .55. *Hab.* Chili.

7. **Æ. collaris.**[4] Forehead, cheeks, and lower parts pure white, the jugulum with a distinct black transverse band, broadest laterally; distinct loral stripe and anterior half of the crown black; upper parts grayish brown, the feathers margined with paler, and tinged with rufous, especially on the crown, auriculars, and sides of neck. *Young,* with the black on the crown and lores absent or barely indicated, and the jugular band much narrowed, or even interrupted, in the middle portion. Wing, 3.70–4.15; culmen, .60; depth of bill through base, .15–.17; tarsus, 1.00–1.10; middle toe, .50–.55. *Hab.* Tropical America in general, from Paraguay, Buenos Ayres, and Chili to Southern Mexico.

8. **Æ. falklandica.**[5] Forehead, lores, and under parts white, the jugulum crossed by a

[1] ÆGIALITIS ALEXANDRINA (Linn.). The Kentish Plover.
Charadrius alexandrinus, LINN. S. N. ed. 10, I. 1758, 150.
Ægialitis alexandrinus, COLLETT, Christ. Vidensk. Förh. 1881, 4. — STEJN. Proc. U. S. Nat. Mus. Vol. 5, 1882, 35.
Charadrius cantianus, LATH. Ind. Orn. Suppl. 1801, p. lxvi.
Ægialitis cantianus, BOIE, Isis, 1822, 558, et AUCT.
Charadrius albifrons, MEYER, Taschenb. deutsch. Vög. ii. 323.
Charadrius littoralis, BECHST. Naturg. Deutschl. iv. 430, pl. 23.
Ægialitis albigularis, BREHM, Vög. Deutschl. p. 552.

[2] (?) ÆGIALITIS DEALBATA, Swinh. Proc. Zool. Soc. Lond. 1870, 138 (southern coast of China, including Formosa and Hainan).

To this bird I refer, with much hesitation, five specimens of an *Ægialitis* from Hong-Kong Bay, collected by Mr. P. L. Jouy, of the United States National Museum. These birds, while closely resembling *Æ. alexandrina* (vel *cantiana*), are uniformly much larger than European examples of the latter, as indicated by the measurements given above; they are likewise much more richly colored, an adult male collected November 12, and an adult female obtained about the same time, having the entire crown and occiput a soft cinnamon-buff or light cinnamon-rufous, the female having even the whole dorsal region, including the tertials, tinged with this color.

[3] ÆGIALITIS ALBIDIPECTUS, Ridgw. Proc. U. S. Nat. Mus. Vol. 5, 1883, p. 526.

[4] ÆGIALITIS COLLARIS (Vieill.), Azara's Ringed Plover.
Charadrius collaris, VIEILL. Enc. Méth. II. 1823, 334.
Ægialites collaris, SCL. & SALV. P. Z. S. 1869, 252; Nom. Neotr. 1873, 143.
Charadrius Azaræ, LICHT. Verz. Doubl. 1823, 71. — TEMM. Pl. Col. 184.
"*Charadrius larvatus,* LESSON."
Ægialitis gracilis, CABAN. J. f. O. 1872, 158 (Isthmus of Tehuantepec).

[5] ÆGIALITIS FALKLANDICA (Lath.). Falkland Island Ring Plover.
Charadrius falklandicus, LATH. Ind. Orn. ii. 1790, 747.
Ægialites falklandicus, ABBOTT, Ibis, 1861, 155.
"*Charadrius annuligerus,* WAGL. Syst. Av."
"*Charadrius pyrrhocephalus,* LESSON et GARNOT."
Charadrius trifasciatus, LICHT. Verz. Doubl. 1823, 71.
"*Charadrius bifasciatus,* WAGL. Syst. Av. spec. 31."

narrow, the breast by a broader, band of black (or grayish in young and winter dress). *In summer*, band across fore part of crown, auriculars, narrow jugular band, and broad pectoral zone black; pileum and nape usually rufous, more or less mixed with brownish gray centrally (sometimes almost wholly grayish, like back). *In winter*, pileum and nape brownish gray, like the back, and all the black markings replaced by grayish. Wing, 4.75–5.00; culmen, .65–.75; depth of bill at base, .18–.20; tarsus, 1.25; middle toe, .70–.75. *Hab.* Southern South America.

9. **Æ. mongolica.** *In summer*, whole breast and nape clear cinnamon-rufous, and top of head tinged with the same; lores, sub-orbital region, and auriculars black, the former bordered above by a white line, sometimes meeting over the forehead; chin, throat, foreneck, belly, and crissum pure white; upper parts brownish gray. *In winter*, the rufous entirely absent; forehead and lower parts white, the breast crossed by a faint grayish brown bar, darkening into a dusky patch on each side; auriculars and loral streak somewhat dusky. Wing, 5.15–5.40. *Hab.* Asia in general, breeding northward; Choris Peninsula, Alaska.

Ægialitis semipalmata.

THE SEMIPALMATED RING PLOVER.

Tringa hiaticula, WILSON, Am. Orn. VII. 1813, 65, pl. 59, f. 3 (nec LINN).
Charadrius hiaticula, ORD, ed. Wils. VII. 69.
Charadrius semipalmatus, BONAP. Comp. List, 1838, 45.
Ægialites semipalmatus, CABAN. J. f. O. 1856, 425. — CASSIN, in Baird's B. N. Am. 1858, 694. — BAIRD, Cat. N. Am. B. 1859, no. 507. — COUES, Key, 1872, 244; Check List, 1873, no. 399; 2d ed. 1882, No. 586. — RIDGW. Nom. N. Am. B. 1881, no. 517.
Charadrius brevirostris, MAX. Beitr. IV. 769 (Brazil).

HAB. North America in general, breeding in the Arctic and Sub-arctic districts, migrating south in winter throughout the tropical regions, as far as Brazil and Peru. Bermudas; whole of West Indies; Galapagos.

SP. CHAR. Small; wings long, toes connected at base, especially the outer to the middle toe. Front, throat, ring around the neck, and entire under parts, white; a band of deep black across the breast, extending around the back of the neck below the white ring. Band from the base of the bill, under the eye, and wide frontal band above the white band, black. Upper parts ashy brown; quills brownish black, with their shafts white in a middle portion, and occasionally a lanceolate white spot along the shafts of the shorter primaries; shorter tertiaries edged with white; greater coverts tipped with white. Middle feathers of the tail ashy brown, with a wide subterminal band of brownish black, and narrowly tipped with white; two outer tail-feathers white, others intermediate, like the middle, but widely tipped with white. Bill orange-yellow at base, black terminally; legs pale flesh-color. *Female* similar, but rather lighter colored. *Young* with the black replaced by ashy brown, the feathers of the upper parts bordered with paler. *Downy young:* Above, pale grayish brown, mottled with black: a frontal crescent, broad nuchal collar, and entire lower parts white.

Total length, about 7 inches; wing, 4.75; tail, 2.25 inches.

The "Ring Plover" of America is common to the whole of North America, not even excepting its more northern portions. It is apparently as abundant on the shores of the Pacific as of the Atlantic, and during its migrations is common on the margins of the lakes, rivers, and ponds of the interior. It probably breeds in the more northern portions of the United States; but, so far as we are aware, its nest has never been taken within our limits. A few pass the summer on the shores of Lake Koskonong, in Wisconsin, but they are not known to breed there. Audubon is mistaken in saying that they confine themselves in the spring to the sandy beaches of our sea-coasts. They are quite as numerous, and perhaps more so, about the collections of fresh water, in the interior, wherever they can find suitable food.

Dr. Cooper did not find this species common along the southern portion of the California coast. At San Diego he saw only one small flock, on the 2d of May. On the 3d of May, 1854, he found them migrating north of the Columbia River, and is confident that none remain within the United States during the summer. They return in September, and frequent the dry fields, as well as the shore and bays.

In its southern migrations it visits Bermuda, occurring there from the 16th of August to the last of October. It visits all the West India Islands, the Galapagos, and South America, as far at least as Brazil and Peru.

Its northern migrations extend to Greenland. Dr. Walker, of the "Fox," met with it there, and afterward, in June, in the marshy valleys near Bellot's Strait, where it was breeding. It is not mentioned as having been met with by Captain Blakiston on the Saskatchewan, but is recorded as having been taken at York Factory; and Mr. Murray procured it from near Severn House, from Hudson's Bay, and also between there and Lake Winnipeg. Mr. B. R. Ross found it common on the Mackenzie River. A few are known to summer, and probably to breed, on Grand Menan. Richardson states that this species abound during the summer throughout Arctic America, where it breeds in situations similar to those inhabited by the Golden Plover. The natives aver that, on the approach of a storm, this bird has been known to clap its wings and to make a chirruping noise.

Mr. Kennicott met with it in June at Lake Winnipeg, in September at Fort Simpson, and in May at Fort Resolution and on the Yukon River. Mr. B. R. Ross procured specimens at Fort Simpson in May, and Mr. MacFarlane found it breeding on the Arctic coast, June 20, and afterward on the Anderson River. Mr. McDougal met with it in the Gens de Large Mountains, and Mr. R. McDonald in the mountains west of the Lower Mackenzie River.

In Florida, according to Mr. N. B. Moore, the Ring Plover is present during the entire winter, arriving there as early as the 11th of August.

Dr. Bryant found this bird a winter resident in the Bahamas, where it remained from its autumnal flight until its departure in May. Dr. Grayson found a single individual, assigned to this species, on Mare Island, in San Pablo Bay, near San Francisco. Mr. Nelson states that in Illinois the spring migrations of this Plover extend from April 25 to May 30, and its fall movements from July 31 to the end of October. He is suspicious that some breed not much to the north of Chicago; but his opinions require confirmation.

Audubon states that this bird passes the winter along the shores of South Carolina, Georgia, Florida, and the coast of the Gulf of Mexico. Mr. Dresser mentions it as common about the pond-holes near San Antonio in the autumn and spring, but noticed none near Matamoras, and does not speak of it as being seen in winter. It is found during the winter in Mexico, Central America, and in several of the West India Islands. Salvin met with it in Guatemala on the sandy flats near Chiapam. Mr. Léotaud mentions its making its appearance in Trinidad each year, from the last of July to October, and in much larger flocks than the *Wilsonius*. They live in the same manner as the latter do, but not unfrequently forsake the borders of the sea to feed in the moist lands of the interior. At the time of their general departure a few are observed to remain behind and to continue about the edges of marshy pools.

While a few keep in pairs, until joined by their brood, this Plover is generally found in small scattered groups of five to ten associated together, yet each pair by itself. They frequent alike salt-marshes, sandy beaches, and mud-flats left bare by the receding tide. They are found in company with several of the smaller *Tringæ;* and although each bird, while searching for food, appears to be unmindful of the other's presence as long as it is undisturbed, yet if alarmed they rise and join in flocks. They run with great swiftness and grace over the sandy beaches. They are a very silent bird except when their treasures are threatened or when suddenly alarmed. They are unsuspicious to an unusual degree, few Waders more so, and may always be readily approached. The young accompany the parents as soon as hatched, and until nearly grown are sheltered by the mother in the manner of the domestic hen. When first hatched they have a somewhat striking mottled appearance.

On Lake Koskonong, in 1873, this species had reached its greatest abundance by the 15th of August; and Giraud mentions its always arriving in Long Island in the latter part of the same month. It passes northward in its spring migrations early in May. Giraud states that this Plover frequents the same situations with the Semipalmated Sandpiper, in company with which it is often seen gathering its food, and like that bird admitting of a very near approach. When alarmed, it utters a very sharp note. Late in the fall it migrates south.

Audubon states that in their breeding-places birds of this species resort to mountainous mossy lands. In Labrador he met with them in almost every place at which he landed, and found them breeding in all the spots that were adapted for that purpose. On being surprised, when in charge of their young, they would beat the ground with the extremities of their opened wings, as if unable to rise. If pursued, they at first permitted a near approach, and then took to flight, seeking to decoy the intruder from their young, which squatted so closely that it was difficult to distinguish them. If the latter were traced, they ran swiftly off, uttering a plaintive *peep*, which never failed to bring their mothers to their aid.

In that region this bird begins to breed early in June, and young ones about a week old were procured on the 2d of June. The nest of this species is simply a small cavity in the moss, in a place sheltered from the north winds, and open to the full rays of the sun, and usually near the margins of small ponds. The eggs are always four, and placed with the small ends together; they are pyriform in shape — pointed at one end, and obtuse at the other.

Audubon states that by the 12th of August all the individuals that had bred in Labrador had taken their departure, some proceeding by the Atlantic shore, others by the great lakes and rivers. At this period they are sometimes seen in ploughed fields searching for insects and worms. Their usual food consists of small crustacea, mollusks, and the *ova* of marine animals.

This Plover extends its migrations to the shores of the Arctic Sea, and in these more northern localities lines the depression in the sand which serves for its nest with dried grasses. Mr. MacFarlane found its nest made of withered leaves and grasses in a depression on the shore just above high-water mark. This bird was said to be tolerably numerous in that region. Mr. Kennicott found it common on the shores of Lake Winnipeg. It was also found by Mr. Dall to be very common at Nulato, St. Michael's, and near the mouth of the Yukon. There also the eggs were found laid in small depressions, made very smooth and round, and lined with a little dry grass, very carefully put in. The nests observed contained only two eggs each.

Mr. MacFarlane found this species quite common on the shores of the Arctic Sea, at Franklin Bay, at Anderson River, Fort Anderson, and other localities near the coast. The nests were always mere cavities dug in the soil, sometimes with a few withered leaves, and occasionally with no lining whatever. The number of eggs was usually four; in no instance more, but occasionally three or two. The parent bird usually glided from her nest and ran a short distance before flying; sometimes she drooped her wings, and pretended lameness. The nests were near the edge of the sea, near the water of small lakes, and on islands in rivers. Mr. MacFarlane speaks of them as tolerably numerous in that quarter, as well as in the country betwixt the Arctic coast and Fort Good Hope. On his annual July journey to that post, *en route* for Fort Simpson, he has noticed Plovers of this species, together with their young of the season, occupied in feeding and diverting themselves on the shores of the different lakes.

Mr. Ludwig Kumlien mentions the arrival of this bird in the Cumberland waters about the middle of June, and says that it is by no means rare there, breeding on the mossy banks of fresh-water ponds. It migrates southward as soon as the fresh-water ponds are frozen over.

An egg of this species (No. 111) collected in Labrador by Thienemann is of oblong-oval shape, tapering at one end and rounded at the other. The ground-color is a nearly pure drab, and the markings are scattered, isolated, rounded, occasionally irregularly shaped blotches of dark bistre, hardly distinguishable from black. Some are diluted with the ground-color, and are more obscure, having a shading of purplish slate; another (No. 172), also from Labrador, collected by Dr. Trudeau, is more rounded in shape, the blotches being larger, and the deep bistre, in a strong light, shaded with wine-color. Three others (No. 1882) from St. George's Bay, collected by Mr. Drexler, June 26, 1860, correspond with No. 111. These eggs have the following measurements: No. 111, 1.35 inches by .99; No. 172, 1.20 by .98; No. 1882, 1.25 by 1.00, 1.30 by .96, and 1.35 by .99.

Ægialitis hiaticula.

THE EUROPEAN RING PLOVER.

Charadrius hiaticula, LINN. S. N. ed. 10, I. 1758, 150; ed. 12, I. 1766, 253. — NAUM. Vög. Deutschl. VII. 1833, 291, pl. 175. — MACGILL. Man. II. 52. — SCHLEG. Rev. Crit. 83. — GRAY, Gen. III. 544; Cat. Brit. B. 1863, 140.

Ægialitis hiaticula, BOIE, Isis, 1822, 558. — KEYS. & BLAS. Wirb. Eur. 71. — RIDGW. Nom. N. Am. B. 1881, No. 518. — COUES, Check List, 2d ed. 1882, No. 589.

Charadrius torquatus, LEACH, Syst. Cat. 1816, 28.

Ægialitis septentrionalis, BREHM, Vög. Deutschl. 548.

Hiaticula annulata, GRAY, List Gen. B. 1840, 65.

The Ring Dotterel, BEWICK, Brit. B. I. 1797, 334, fig.

Ringed Plover, YARR. Brit. B. ed. 2, II. 465, fig. ed. 3, II. 494, fig. et AUCT.

HAB. The Palæarctic Region, and portions of Arctic America, breeding on western shores of Cumberland Gulf (KUMLIEN).

SP. CHAR. *Adult:* A narrow frontlet, band across fore part of the crown, auriculars, lores, and sub-orbital region, black, all these areas confluent; collar across lower part of the nape, continuous with a broad jugular band, also black. Forehead, postocular patch, nuchal collar, chin, throat, malar region, and lower parts (except as described) pure white. Pileum and upper parts generally, deep brownish gray or grayish brown. Basal half of bill orange-red in life, yellowish or otherwise light colored in the skin; legs and feet orange; iris dark brown; terminal half of bill black. *Young:* The black markings obsolete (replaced by dull grayish) and the feathers of the upper surface bordered with pale buffy. Bill wholly dusky.

Wing, about 5.00; culmen, .50–.55; tarsus, about 1.00; middle toe, .60–.65.

With a close general resemblance to *Æ. semipalmata*, this species may be immediately distinguished by the entire absence of a web between the inner and middle toes, the smaller size of that between the outer and middle toes, the much greater width of the black beneath the eye, and of that across the jugulum. It is also decidedly larger; while there are other differences of coloration.

The four adult examples before us differ very considerably from each other in some points of coloration. A Greenland specimen and two skins from the American shore of Cumberland Gulf have the black jugular collar extending upward over the lower part of the throat, forming there quite a prominent angle, while in a European specimen the anterior border of this jugular collar

forms a straight transverse line; in the latter, on the other hand, the posterior edge of the jugular collar is irregular — decidedly concave in the middle, and convex laterally — while in the American specimens it runs nearly straight across. Whether these differences between the birds of this species from North America and Europe are constant, can only be determined by the examination of more extensive material.

Of the American skins, two adult males collected at the same place and on the same day (head of Cumberland Gulf, June 25, 1878, L. KUMLIEN) differ remarkably from one another in the width of the white frontal band. In No. 76132 this measures only one tenth of an inch in breadth, while in No. 76133 it is three times as wide!; there is a nearly corresponding difference, however, in the extent of the black on the crown, this measuring in the two specimens, respectively, .40 and .30 of an inch.

The present bird, so well known as the Ring Plover of Europe, and until quite recently supposed to have no other claim to a place in our fauna than its rather common presence in Greenland, must now be fully admitted to be a North American species, on other and quite indisputable grounds. An undoubted specimen of it has been taken at Great Slave Lake, and it has since been found breeding within our borders. Professor Newton states that it breeds generally throughout Greenland, and that it is found on Sabine and Clavering islands. It is also said to be abundant on the shores of Possession Bay and Regent's Inlet, and was found by Professor Jorell on the Seven Islands (lat. 80° 45′ N.) — at that time the highest northern range of any shore bird. More recently its claim to be acknowledged as North American, as well as High-Arctic, has been confirmed by Mr. Feilden, of the British Arctic Expedition of 1875–76, and by Mr. Kumlien. The former states (Ibis, October, 1877) that a single example of this species was observed in Smith's Sound, where it was obtained, Aug. 4, 1875, on the beach bordering the Valley of the Twin Glacier, in Buchanan Strait (lat. 78° 48′ N.). It was seen threading its way among the stones and stranded blocks of ice near the water's edge, and was evidently nesting in the neighborhood, as it was a female, and the feathers of the under parts were worn off by incubation. Mr. Kumlien also informs us that this species is apparently more common than even the *semipalmata* in Cumberland. It arrives there about the middle of June, and breeds in the same localities as that species. It is also very common about Disco Island, Greenland, where he procured young birds.

This somewhat cosmopolitan species is found throughout the northern and central portions of Europe, and is particularly common in Great Britain, where it occurs throughout the year. It especially frequents inlets and bays, where it feeds at low water, on the flats along the coast, at points where the ebb of the tide exposes extended surfaces. This bird is also found on the banks of large rivers, and is occasionally met with about the margin of inland sheets of water. As a species it is very abundant, and its habits are described as lively and interesting.

Mr. Yarrell mentions that these birds have been found breeding on the warrens of Beachamwell and at Elveden, and on other warrens and heaths near Thetford in Norfolk, and in several other sandy warrens in Norfolk and in Suffolk, at a considerable distance from the sea. They are said to pair and nest very early in the season. Mr. Salmon found them sitting on their eggs as early as the 30th of March. Like all the birds of this genus, the Ring Plover makes no other nest than a slight cavity in the sand, in which its four eggs are laid; but it sometimes lines or covers this cavity with a number of small stones about the size of peas, upon which the eggs are laid. This very peculiar habit of the species has given rise to the local name, by which it is known in some of the counties of England, of Stonehatch.

When robbed of its eggs, this Plover will lay another set of four; and this it will do three or four times in a season if as often despoiled.

Others of this species deposit their eggs in any accidental depression on a bank of sand, broken shells, or shingle above high-water mark. The parent birds are devoted in their attachment to their young; and when disturbed resort to various devices and expedients to divert attention from their eggs or nestlings. The similarity in color, both of their young and of the eggs, to the surrounding objects is a great source of security, rendering it difficult to distinguish them.

The food of the Ringed Plover consists of insects, worms, and various forms of marine life, thin-shelled crustacea, etc., with which salt-water pools abound. Their note is said to be a shrill whistle.

This species is migratory in the high northern latitudes, in which it breeds, and in which it is found only in the summer, or from March to October. Hewitson found it throughout Norway, and Linnæus met with it in various parts of Lapland in his journey, even as far north as the Lapland Alps. Scoresby, in his Journal, mentions having met with this bird on the east coast of Greenland; and other Arctic explorers have observed it on the west coast of the same island, at Prince Regent's Inlet, and at Hecla Cove. In the interior of Europe it is seen on the banks of rivers. Yarrell states that it occurs as far south as Italy and Sicily, and also in Malta; and specimens have been received from Asia Minor.

The eggs of this Plover measure 1.41 inches in length by 1.06 inches in breadth, and are pyriform in shape; their ground is of a pale buff or cream color, spotted and streaked with lines and blotches of bluish-ash and black.

Ægialitis curonica.

THE LITTLE RINGED PLOVER.

Charadrius curonicus, GMEL. S. N. I. 1788, 692.
Ægialitis curonica, GRAY, Cat. Brit. B. 1863, 141. — HARTING, Handb. Brit. B. 1872, 134. — RIDGW. Nom. N. Am. B. 1881, no. 519. — COUES, Check List, 2d ed. 1882, no. 590.
Charadrius philippinus, LATH. Ind. Orn. II. 1790, 745.
Charadrius fluviatilis, BECHST. Nat. Vög. Deutschl. 1809, 422.
Charadrius minor, MEYER & WOLF, Tasch. Vög. Deutschl. II. 1810, 324.

Ægialites minor, HARTING, P. Z. S. 1871, 117 (Alaska ?).
Charadrius intermedius, MÉNÉTR. Catal. 53.
? *Charadrius zonatus*, SWAINS. B. W. Afr. II. 235, pl. 25.
Ægialitis microrhynchus, RIDGW. Am. Nat. VIII. Feb. 1874, 109 (winter plumage ; "San Francisco, Cal.").
The Little Ringed Plover, YARR. Brit. B. ed. 2, II. p. 473, fig. ed. 3, II. p. 502, fig.

HAB. The Palæarctic Region in general ; Western Africa ; accidental on coast of California (?) and in Alaska (?). Cf. HARTING, P. Z. S. 1871, p. 117.

SP. CHAR. *Adult* ♀ : Lores, auriculars, and beneath the eye, dusky brown, or dull blackish, this color crossing the anterior part of the forehead at the base of the bill ; a broad band of black (about .40 of an inch wide) crossing the anterior part of the crown, from eye to eye, and separated from the black frontlet by a band of white about .15 of an inch wide ; behind this black vertical band a narrow one of ashy white, continued back above the eyes and auriculars to the occiput ; chin, throat, malar region, and cheeks, pure white, confluent with a broad and very distinctly defined white nuchal collar ; a black collar completely encircling the neck, immediately below the white of the throat and nape ; remaining under parts, including under surface of the wing, entirely pure white. Upper parts, including the occiput and posterior part of the crown, brownish gray, lighter on the rump and central upper tail-coverts ; sides of the rump and lateral upper tail-coverts, shaft of the outer primary, terminal margins of the secondaries, outer webs of two outer tail-feathers, with ends of all except the middle pair, white ; inner web of outer tail-feather white, with a dusky sub-terminal spot. Bill small and slender, entirely black, except at the base of the mandible ; iris dark brown ; legs and feet pale-colored, the latter with a small web connecting the outer and middle toes at the base, the inner and middle toes entirely separated. Wing, 4.50 ; culmen, .50 ; tarsus, 1.00 ; middle toe, .55 (No. 56876, Europe ; Schlütter Coll.).

Young (*and winter adult ?*): Similar to the same stage of *Æ. semipalmata*, but cheeks white up to the eye, white of the forehead much less distinctly defined, and grading insensibly into the gray of the crown ; two outer tail-feathers white, the inner webs with a dusky transverse spot near the end. Form much more slender than *Æ. semipalmata*, the bill especially, which is also of entirely different form. Wing, 4.35 ; tail, 2.50 ; culmen, .50 ; greatest depth of bill, .10 ; tarsus, 1.00 ; middle toe, .65. (Type of *Æ.* "*microrhynchus*, RIDGWAY," No. 39523, U. S. Nat. Mus. ; "San Francisco, Cal. ; E. F. LORQUIN.")

Ægialitis meloda.

a. Var. meloda. THE COMMON PIPING PLOVER.

"*Charadrius hiaticula*, var.," WILSON, Am. Orn. V. 1812, 30, pl. 37, f. 2.
Charadrius melodus, ORD. ed. Wils. VII. 1824, 71. — BONAP. Am. Orn. IV. 1832, 74, pl. 24. — NUTT. Man. II. 1834, 18. — AUD. Orn. Biog. III. 1835, 154 ; V. 1839, 578, pl. 220 ; B. Am. V. 1842, 223, pl. 321.
Ægialitis melodus, BONAP. Comp. List, 1838, 45. — CASSIN. in Baird's B. N. Am. 1858, 695. — BAIRD, Cat. N. Am. B. 1859, no. 508. — COUES, Key, 1872, 244 ; Check List, 1873, no. 400 ; 2d ed. 1882, no. 587. — RIDGW. Nom. N. Am. B. 1881, no. 520.
Charadrius Okeni, WAGL. Syst. Av. 1827.

b. Var. circumcincta. THE RINGED PIPING PLOVER.

Ægialitis melodus, var. *circumcinctus*, RIDGW. Am. Nat. VIII. 1874, 109.
Ægialitis meloda, var. *circumcincta*, COUES, Check List, App. p. 133, no. 400*a* ; Birds N. W. 1874, 455.
Ægialites melodus circumcinctus, RIDGW. Nom. N. Am. B. 1881, no. 520*a*. — COUES, Check List, 2d ed. 1882, no. 588.

HAB. The Eastern Province of North America, breeding in the northern portion of its range (British Provinces and more Northern United States), and wintering southward. Bermudas ; Bahamas ; Cuba ; Jamaica. The var. *circumcincta* chiefly restricted to the Missouri River region.

Sp. Char. About the size of *Æ. semipalmata;* bill short, strong. *Adult male:* Forehead ring around the back of the neck, and entire under parts, white ; a band of black in front above the band of white ; band encircling the neck before and behind, but usually interrupted in the middle of the breast, black, immediately below the ring of white on the neck behind. Head above

Æ. meloda.

and upper parts of body light brownish cinereous ; rump and upper tail-coverts lighter, and often nearly white ; quills dark brown, with a large portion of their inner webs and shafts white ; shorter primaries with a large portion of their outer webs white ; tail at base white, and with the outer feathers white ; middle feathers with a wide sub-terminal band of brownish black, and tipped with white. Bill orange at base, tipped with black ; legs orange yellow. *Female :* Similar to the male, but with the dark colors lighter and less in extent. *Young :* No black band in front ; collar around the back of the neck ashy brown.

Total length, about 7 inches ; wing, 4.50 ; tail, 2 inches.

Aside from the geographical variations noted on p. 152, the individual discrepancies in the plumage of this species are quite considerable, involving chiefly the extent and intensity of the

Æ. meloda circumcincta.

black areas. It is quite the rule among specimens from the Atlantic States for the pectoral band to be either decidedly narrower centrally, or altogether interrupted in the middle of the breast ; while in examples from the interior States, especially from the Missouri River region, the pectoral band is, in a large majority of specimens, absolutely continuous, and nearly or quite as wide as in *Æ. semipalmata.*

The common Piping Plover of the Middle and New England States exhibits but very few peculiarities of habits and manners differing from the rest of this group. It is, if anything, a little more shy and distrustful of man, and is less readily approached; but this is probably owing to the intrusions upon its privacy by the throng of summer visitors to places in which this bird was once abundant, and from which it has been forced to depart. From very many of our most frequented beaches in New England and New Jersey this graceful and attractive species has been entirely driven; and in many others where a few still remain their wildness gives them, in all probability, their only chance for existence.

In Wilson's day the Piping Plover was very abundant during the summer on the low sandy shores all along our sea-coast, from Cape May northward; and since then, and until within twenty years past, it was frequently seen on all the beaches of Massachusetts. This bird lives near the edge of the sea, always on sandy beaches, feeding at low water, on the sandy flats, among the sea-weeds of the uncovered rocks, and also on muddy flats. Its food is various forms of minute marine life — worms, crustacea, and the like. It rarely flies while feeding, unless alarmed; but glides along with a peculiar and rapid gait over the surface of the flat sand. At high-tide it resorts to the sandy uplands just above the water; and in these places deposits its eggs in depressions on the bare sand. The eggs — four in number — are so similar to the surrounding objects, that they are not readily recognized; and if approached, the parents resort to simple, but usually successful, artifices to draw away the intruder — simulating lameness, and fluttering near the ground as if disabled. The young are able to run on leaving the shell, and are led by the mother to feed. They also resemble the sandy soil on which they move, and instantly squat if approached, remaining immovable, and will almost allow themselves to be trodden upon rather than by their motion allow their presence to be revealed. During incubation the parents rarely sit upon their eggs, except in the night, or unless the weather is damp; but always keep in the neighborhood, and watch over their treasures with great solicitude.

The notes of this Plover are remarkably musical and pleasing, and its specific name is one not undeserved. Where it can be seen in its natural condition, in a region where it has never been disturbed or made apprehensive by intruders, it is a pleasing object as, gracefully gliding over the sandy flats, and uttering from time to time its soft and plaintive note, it moves rapidly along.

If, when on the nest, this bird be too nearly approached, it immediately endeavors to attract attention by spreading out its wings and tail, dragging itself along as if moving with great difficulty, and at the same time uttering a peculiar squeaking cry. Then, if successful in causing the intruder to abandon the search for the nest, it glides rapidly away, and is soon out of reach.

This species is found along the coast as far to the eastward as Eastport, but becomes quite rare in that neighborhood, and only a few are seen at Grand Menan. Audubon states that he met with it as far north as the Magdalen Islands, where he found it paired and with eggs on the 11th of June, 1833. The same writer mentions having seen these birds breeding in Florida as early as the 3d of May; so that, if he is correct,[1] they are found with more or less abundance along our entire Atlantic coast. Mr. Donald Gunn procured four specimens at Lake Winnipeg. Dr. Gundlach has informed us that he found them breeding, and procured their eggs, in Cuba. They are only partially migratory, leaving our more northern shores in the winter, and are found from October to April on the sandy beaches of the Carolinas and Florida. They move south in the fall in family groups of five or six, and after

[1] Mr. C. B. Cory found this species abundant at the Magdalen Islands in 1878, and Mr. W. A. Stearns has recently reported it as common in Southern Labrador. — J. A. A.

the winter return in pairs. Audubon states that during the winter they are seen in flocks of twenty or thirty, and that they associate with other species, particularly the Turnstones. The same writer asserted that this species never proceeds far inland, even along the sandy margins of our largest rivers; but in this he was mistaken. This Plover is found along the shores of our inland large lakes, especially Lake Ontario; and it occurs both as a resident and as a migrant at Lake Koskonong, in Wisconsin. It is probable that such exceptions as these will be found to be not unfrequent wherever favorable localities exist. Although during its summer residence it seems to prefer to run rather than to fly, yet in its migrations it is capable of extremely rapid as well as protracted journeys — passing through the air by a gliding course, close over the sand in its short flights, but high above the shore in its long passages.

According to Giraud, the Piping Plover is very abundant on the southern shore of Long Island, preferring sandy beaches and shoals, where it feeds on the small bivalve shells which are exposed at low water. It may also be seen near the edge of the surf feeding on the deposit of the receding waves. It makes there no nest other than a slight excavation in the sand. The eggs, four in number, that author describes as being of a pale yellowish or cream-color, speckled with brownish black. When pursued it is said to run rapidly, and if closely followed it takes wing, giving utterance to a note which is more shrill than the ordinarily mellow one which it sounds when not disturbed. In autumn this bird is said to become very fat, and to be then excellent eating. To the fishermen of Long Island it is known as the Beach-bird.

The Piping Plover is thought to be of accidental occurrence in Bermuda, where both Mr. Hardis and Major Wedderburn have noted the occasional presence of stragglers; these were usually seen only after a storm.

Two eggs in my collection (No. 535), from Provincetown, Mass., are of an oval shape, much rounded at one end, and sharply tapering at the other. Their ground is a light fawn-colored drab, over which are sparsely distributed small rounded markings of a dark bistre, intensified almost to blackness. They measure 1.20 inches in length by 1 inch in their greatest breadth. Except in their smaller size and their lighter ground, they are similar to the eggs of Wilson's Plover.

The habitat of var. *circumcinctus* is given by Mr. Ridgway (Am. Nat. VIII. p. 109) as between the Missouri River and the Rocky Mountains. It is, however, found as far eastward as Lake Koskonong, in Southern Wisconsin, and occasionally even along the Atlantic coast. Its habits appear to be identical with those of the *melodus*. Mr. Nelson refers to this species as a very common summer resident on the borders of the lake, where it breeds on the flat pebbly beach between the sand-dunes and the shore. He obtained a perfect egg from an example shot at Waukegan, on the 24th of April; and there were appearances indicating that others were breeding in the neighborhood. Some thirty pairs or more exhibited unmistakable signs of having their nests on the beach at that place within a space of two miles; and he afterward found these birds quite numerous at other points along the shore, although he was unable to discover their nests. They were continually circling about, or standing at a short distance uttering an occasional note of alarm. Dr. Velie procured young of this variety, only a few days old, near the same locality, on the 1st of July. All depart, it is said, about the last of September.

Ægialitis alexandrina nivosa.

THE SNOWY PLOVER.

Ægialitis nivosa, CASSIN, in Baird's B. N. Am. 1858, 696 (San Francisco, Cal.). — BAIRD, Cat. N. Am. B. 1858, no. 509.

Ægialitis cantianus, var. *nivosus*, RIDGW. Am. Nat. VIII. 1874, 109. — COUES, Check List, 1873, App. p. 135, no. 401.

Ægialitis cantianus nivosus, RIDGW. Nom. N. Am. B. 1882, no. 521. — COUES, Check List, 2d ed. 1882, no. 591.

Ægialitis cantianus, COUES, Key, 1872, 245.

HAB. Western Province of North America, both coasts of Middle America, and Western South America as far as Chili ; Cuba ?[1]

SP. CHAR. Bill slender, wholly deep black, as long as the middle toe. *Adult male :* Forehead, superciliary region, indistinct nuchal collar, and entire lower parts, pure white ; a band across the fore part of the crown, auriculars, and transverse patch on each side of the breast, black. Upper

Summer plumage.

parts, rather light brownish gray, the crown and occiput usually tinged with light reddish buff. Primaries, dusky with white shafts, the inner quills marked with white ; inner secondaries almost

[1] *A. tenuirostris*, LAWR. (Ann. Lyc. N. Y. VII. Feb. 1862, p. 455), presumably the same species. The description is as follows : —

"*Female :* Crown, occiput, and back cinereous, the feathers with grayish-white margins ; wing-coverts somewhat darker than the back, the ends of the larger coverts white, forming a transverse bar on the wing ; primaries umber-brown with the inner webs lighter, except at the end, and having the shafts white ; the secondaries are of the same color as the primaries, and tipped with white ; tertiaries paler and largely marked with white ; scapulars ashy brown, lighter on the inner webs, and having both webs crossed with rather obsolete narrow brown bars ; the middle upper tail-coverts are pale ochreous brown, the lateral ones white ; the four central tail-feathers are light ochreous brown at the base, becoming darker toward their ends ; the other tail-feathers are white, those next the central ones being pale ochreous at the end ; front, a line over the eye, cheeks, a collar on the hind neck, and entire under plumage, pure white ; a semi-collar of ashy brown on each side of the upper part of the breast ; bill black, with a small space at the base of the under mandible of dull orange ; irides black ; tarsi and toes purplish black.

"Length about $6\frac{3}{4}$ in. ; wing, $3\frac{7}{8}$; tail, $1\frac{3}{4}$; bill from front, $\frac{5}{8}$; tarsi $\frac{15}{16}$.

"*Habitat*, Cuba.

"This species is allied to *A. melodus*, but is rather smaller ; the bill is longer, depressed at the base, and regularly tapering to the end, where it is comparatively sharp ; in the latter it is quite obtuse and different in form ; there is less white on the quills, with more on the tail, and the tarsi are longer than those of *A. melodus*."

The above description, measurements and all, accords in every respect with the adult female of *Æ. nivosa*, and is probably of a specimen of that species. But a single specimen was captured, this being a female caught with a net while sitting on her three eggs ; the time being July, and the place Guantanamo, on the south coast of the eastern part of the island.

wholly white. Two outer tail-feathers wholly white, the rest growing gradually darker to the inner pair, which are wholly dusky. *Adult female:* Similar to the male, but the black markings less distinct (sometimes nearly obsolete). Bill and eyelids deep black; iris deep brown; legs dull slate-color; toes black; interior of mouth fleshy white. *Young:* More ashy above, the black markings replaced by ashy; feathers of the upper parts indistinctly bordered with whitish.

Winter plumage.

Downy young: Above, pale grayish buff, interrupted by a white nuchal collar, the whole of the colored portion irregularly mottled with black. Forehead, lower parts, and band-wing, white. A distinct postocular streak of dusky.

Total length, 6.25 to 7 inches; extent of wings, 13 to 14.75; wing 4.20–4.30; culmen, .60; tarsus, .90–1.05; middle toe, .55–.60.

Specimens vary chiefly in the depth of the ochraceous tinge to the hood and in the distinctness of the black markings. In some the former feature is so pronounced as to offer a strong contrast of color to the back, while in others, shot from the same flock, there is scarcely a trace of the buff tinge. Some females have the black as distinct as in the males; in others it is almost obsolete.

There can be no question as to the propriety of separating this bird from *Æ. alexandrina* (vel *cantiana*) of Europe, although the relationship is very close. The latter, however, is uniformly larger, with longer tarsi and wings, and has invariably a distinct line of black running from the rictus to the eye across the lores — which mark is rarely even indicated in the American bird, though in a very small percentage it occurs; never so distinct and continuous, however, as in the Old World form.

This species was first described by Mr. Cassin from a single example obtained by Lieutenant Trowbridge on the coast near San Francisco. The extent of its distribution and its specific peculiarities may still be but imperfectly known; it appears, however, to be nearly restricted to the region between the shores of the Pacific and the Rocky Mountains, occurring in South America as far as Chili, and on both shores of Middle America. So far as its habits have become known, they appear to conform to those of all the other members of this family in regard to its food, its manner of flight, its movements on the land, its mode of nesting on the bare sand, and in all its peculiarities of breeding. That it may migrate in the winter to the Pacific coast of Central America is made to appear probable by the fact that Mr. Salvin procured at Chiapam, Guatemala, in September, 1862, a single specimen of a Plover referable to this species; and Messrs. Sclater and Salvin mention its occurrence at Islay, Peru.

Mr. H. W. Henshaw (Lieutenant Wheeler's "Report," 1876, p. 268) found this species abundant on the coast of California. At Santa Barbara it occurred in large numbers, frequenting there only the sandy shores, not following the creeks inland, and never visiting the marshes, though these were within a few yards of its breeding-ground. Its habits seemed to be exactly those of the common Piping Plover, and its notes very similar to those of that bird. Its food consists of all sorts of worms and marine crustacea, which it finds close to the water's edge, following the retreating waves down, and scurrying back as they come rolling in again. On the 7th of July he found two broods of young, which had left the nests but a few hours before. They were clothed in down, and were yet so weak as scarcely to be able to stand. Subsequently he noticed quite a number of nests containing eggs. The spot selected for a breeding-ground was a strip of bare white sand, a hundred yards from the ocean. In every instance but one the eggs were deposited in a slight hollow scratched in the sand, without lining of any sort. In the exceptional case the owners had selected from along the shore little bits of pearly nacre, remnants of broken sea-shells, and upon a smooth lining of this material had placed their treasures. The effect of the richly colored eggs as they lay on their cushion of shining mother-of-pearl is said to have been very pleasing. Mr. Henshaw adds, that so slight was the contrast between the eggs and the drifted sand about them, that they would be difficult enough to find, were it not for the tracks about the nests. As the birds came to relieve their mates in sitting or to bring them food, they alighted near the nest, and thus for a little distance around each one was a series of tracks converging to a common centre, which betrayed their secret. Great was the alarm of the colony as soon as his presence was known. They gathered into little knots, following him at a distance with low sorrowful cries. When her nest was seen to be really discovered, the female would fly close by him and make use of all the arts which birds of this kind know so well how to employ on like occasions. With wings drooping and trailing on the sand, she would move in front till his attention was secured, and would then fall helplessly down, and, burying her breast in the sand, present the very picture of despair and woe, while the male bird and the other pairs expressed their sympathy by loud cries. The full nest complement is said to have been three eggs; and in no instance were more found. He describes them as of a light clay color, marked with numerous blotches and scratchy splashes of black, in size and appearance approaching most closely to those of *Æ. meloda*, but easily to be distinguished by the different style of the spotting. He gives their greatest length as 1.30; their least, 1.22; and their diameter as varying from .89 to .95.

Dr. Cooper speaks of these birds as being quite common along the sandy beaches of the southern part of California, but becoming rather rare near San Francisco, although found north as far as Cape Mendocino. They did not seem to migrate at any particular season, but were found at all times, in small parties, running over the drifted sand or along the edge of the water, catching insects and crustacea. In the spring they are less gregarious, and the females retire to lay their eggs, which are found just above the edge of the highest water-marks, deposited in slight depressions in the sand, sometimes lined with fragments of shells. The eggs are laid from April 15th to July 30th, the latter being probably a second brood. They are large for the size of the bird, measuring 1.22 inches by .92, and have a brownish-white ground, thickly blotched and speckled with blackish-brown marks resembling Turkish letters. In one instance, after an extremely high tide at night, Dr. Cooper found in the early morning four eggs partly hatched in a depression just made in the wet sand, at the very top of the wave-flow. They must have been moved there by the old birds from another nest that morning. Their dampness could hardly have been favorable for their hatching, though soon to be dried by the sun, the heat of which saves these birds much of the trouble of sitting. Dr. Cooper has never heard this bird utter any sound.

Mr. Ridgway characterizes this species as a graceful little Plover, and states that though previously known only from the Pacific Region, he found it very abundant in the neighborhood of the southeastern shore of Great Salt Lake. On the bare mud-flats around the Warm-spring Lake numbers were seen running nimbly and swiftly over the ground, all the while uttering a soft, rather musical, whistling note. All the specimens procured were in the full breeding-plumage.

Mr. E. W. Nelson also mentions meeting with this species on the shores of Salt Lake, near the mouth of the River Jordan. The birds were abundant, and he saw the young — only a few days old — the 1st of August.

The eggs of this species have an average length of 1.18 inches, and a breadth of .95. Their ground is a light fawn-colored drab, over which fine dottings, lines, and irregular markings of a dark bistre are equally distributed, except about the smaller end, which is nearly free from any mark. These eggs were taken near San Francisco by the late Mr. T. Hepburn. The eggs of *Æ. cantianus*, to which this species is now regarded as being very closely allied, are of a slightly more oblong shape, measuring 1.25 inches in length, and .90 in breadth. They have a yellowish stone-colored ground, spotted and streaked with black.

More recent specimens of the eggs of the *nivosa* have a ground-color of a pale grayish buff, with markings in form of small dots and zigzag pencillings of black, and measure 1.25 by .90, and 1.25 by .85 inches.

Ægialitis mongolica.

THE MONGOLIAN PLOVER.

Charadrius mongolus, PALL. Reise, iii. 1776, 700.
Charadrius mongolicus, PALL. Zoogr. Rosso-As. ii. 1831, 136.
Ægialites mongolicus, SWINH. P. Z. S. 1863, 310; 1870, 140. — HARTING, Ibis, 1870, 384; P. Z. S. 1871, 111, 114 (Choris Peninsula, Alaska, summer !), —
Charadrius cirrhipedesmus, WAGL. Syst. Av. 1827, fol. 4. p. 13, no. 18.
Charadrius gularis, WAGL. Syst. Av. 1827. t. c. fol. 5, p. 5, no. 40.
Charadrius sanguineus, LESS. Man. Orn. ii. 1828, 330.
Charadrius ruficollis, "CUVIER & TEMM." PUCH. Rev. Zool. 1851, 282.
Charadrius rufinellus, BLYTH, An. & Mag. N. H. xii. 1843, 169.
Charadrius subrufinus, HODGSON, Zool. Misc. 1844, 86.
Charadrius pyrrhothorax, "TEMM." GOULD, B. Eur. 1837, pl. 299.
Ægialitis pyrrhothorax, KEYS. & BLAS. Wirb. Eur. 1840, 70, et AUCT.
Hiaticula inornata, GOULD, B. Austr. vi. pl. 19.

HAB. Northern Asia in general, west to St. Petersburg, Palestine, and Northeastern Africa, east to Choris Peninsula, Alaska; in winter, migrating south through Southern Asia, Philippines, Malay Archipelago, etc., to Australia.

Adult ♂, in summer (No. 85779, Yokohama, Japan, April 28; P. L. Jouy): Frontlet, lores, and a broad band beneath the eye, involving the auriculars, dull black; a rather narrow frontal band of dull black, anteriorly reaching to the base of the culmen and posteriorly joining the upper anterior margin of the eye; between this and the black loral stripe a narrow stripe of white, reaching to within about .10 of an inch of the anterior angle of the eye; lower eyelid white. Anterior and lateral portions of pileum light reddish buff, the central portion (occiput and posterior part of crown) dull brownish gray; nape and breast clear light reddish cinnamon, paler on the former, and laterally extending, brokenly, along the sides to the flanks; rest of lower parts pure white, that of the throat very abruptly bounded posteriorly against the reddish cinnamon of the breast. Upper parts (except as described) brownish gray, with a slight bronzy lustre in certain lights, the tips of the greater wing-coverts and secondaries, basal portion of outer webs of inner primaries, sides of rump, and tips of upper tail-coverts, white. Bill, legs, and feet, black. Wing, 5.15; tail, 2.00; culmen, .62; tarsus, 1.15; middle toe, .73. *Winter plumage:* "Upper parts light grayish brown; loral streak, ear-coverts, and latero-pectoral patch, more or less marked with brown. A faint brown bar runs across the breast. Forehead, eyebrow, chin, throat, and under parts, white.

Wing hair-brown; lower edge of joint, broad margins and tips to greater coverts, margins to secondaries broadening inwardly, basal halves of outer webs of sixth and remaining primaries, first quill-shaft entirely, the others more or less, white. Upper tail-coverts: central feathers light brown margined with white, the side ones pure white. Tail: first or outer rectrix white, with an oblong longitudinal spot of pale brown on the inner web; second light brown, with white shaft and tip; the rest darker brown, with brown shafts and white tips, the white decreasing on the two centrals. Bill black; legs deep blackish gray; claws black."

"Length of wing, 5.4 inches; tail, 2.5; bill in front, .75; tarsi, 1.18; middle toe (claw, .17), .85." (SWINHOE, P. Z. S. 1870, p. 140.)

GENUS **OCHTHODROMUS**, REICHENBACH.

Ochthodromus, REICHENB. Av. Syst. 1853, Introd. p. xviii (type, *Charadrius Wilsonius*, ORD).

CHAR. Bill large and stout, longer than the middle toe, the terminal half of the culmen strongly convex, and base of the gonys forming a decided angle; basal half of the maxilla depressed decidedly below the level of the terminal half. Tail short, scarcely reaching the tips of the primaries.

The distinctive characters of this well-marked genus consist chiefly in the large head and heavy bill, contrasted with the weak feet and heavy legs. An exotic species, which seems to be strictly congeneric with *O. Wilsonius*, is the *Charadrius Geoffroyi*, WAGL., which agrees minutely in all the details of structure, except that the legs are very decidedly longer. There is also considerable similarity in the style of coloration, especially in the winter plumage; but in summer dress, *O. Geoffroyi* has a rufous, instead of black, jugular band.

America possesses but a single species, *O. Wilsonius*, the type of the genus. This appears in the form of two well-marked geographical races, whose characters are as follows: —

COM. CHAR. Above, brownish gray; forehead and lower parts white. ♂: Fore-part of the crown, lores, and jugular collar, black. ♀: The black replaced by brownish gray or light brownish, paler on the lores.

Var. **Wilsonius.** Sides of the occiput and upper part of nape slightly tinged with buffy ochraceous. Female with the lores nearly white. *Hab.* Coasts of South Atlantic (and Gulf?) States.

Var. **rufinuchus.**[1] Sides of occiput and upper part of nape deep rusty. Female with lores distinctly brownish gray. Colors generally darker in both sexes. *Hab.* West Indies (and other tropical coasts?).

Ochthodromus Wilsonius.

WILSON'S PLOVER.

Charadrius Wilsonius, ORD, ed. Wils. IX. 1825, 77, pl. 73, fig. 5. — NUTT. Man. II. 1834, 21. — AUD. Orn. Biog. III. 1835, 73; V. 1839, 577, pl. 284; Synop. 1839, 223; B. Am. V. 1842, 214, pl. 319.

Ægialites Wilsonius, BONAP. Consp. List, 1838, 45. — COUES, Check List, 2d ed. 1882, no. 585.

Ægialitis Wilsonius, CASS. in Baird's B. N. Am. 1858, 693. — BAIRD, Cat. N. Am. B. 1859, no. 506. — COUES, Key, 1872, 244; Check List, 1873, no. 398.

Ochthodromus Wilsonius, REICH. Syst. Av. 1853, xviii. — RIDGW. Nom. N. Am. B. 1881, no. 522.

? *Charadrius crassirostris*, SPIX, Av. Bras. II. 1825, 77, pl. 94.

HAB. Atlantic sea-coast of temperate North America, and of South America to Brazil; both coasts of Middle America north to Cape St. Lucas; West Indies; Northwestern Peru (TACZAN. P. Z. S. 1877, 330).

[1] OCHTHODROMUS WILSONIUS RUFINUCHUS.

? *Charadrius crassirostris*, SPIX, Av. Bras. II. 1825, 77, pl. 94 (cf. PELZ. Orn. Bras. 1870, 297),

Ægialitis Wilsonius, var. *rufinuchus*, RIDGW. Am. Nat. VIII. Feb. 1874, 109 (Spanishtown, Jamaica).

There is now some doubt whether the characters originally ascribed to this supposed race are constant. In the absence of sufficient material to decide the point, however, we for the present keep it separate.

Sp. Char. *Adult male:* Frontal crescent, extending back on each side of the crown to beyond the eye, ends of greater wing-coverts, shafts of primaries, and entire lower parts, pure white; crescentic patch covering fore part of the crown, lores, and wide band across the jugulum, black; occiput more or less strongly suffused with ochraceous, especially laterally and posteriorly. Upper parts (except as described) uniform brownish gray, the remiges darker. *Adult female:* Similar to the male, but the black replaced by brownish gray, the jugular collar tinged with ochraceous. *Downy young*: Crown and occiput light grayish buff, distinctly but very irregularly marbled or mottled with black; back and rump similar, but more grayish, the mottling coarser and less distinct; arm-wing light buff, mottled with dusky; hand-wing wholly immaculate white. Whole

forehead, lores, superciliaries, side of head, broad nuchal collar, and entire lower parts, white; an irregular but distinct postocular streak of black running into the mottling of the occiput. A large bare space on each side of neck. Bill black; eyelids grayish; iris brown; legs and feet pale grayish flesh-color.

Total length, about 7.75; extent, 16.00; wing, 4.50; culmen, .80; tarsus, 1.25; middle toe, .75.

The geographical variations of this species are not well understood, on account of lack of sufficient material. An adult female from Mazatlan (winter) and two from Cape St. Lucas (December) are uniformly, though slightly, darker than eastern examples; they also have the frontal white very narrow, the brown of the lores continuous, extending (in two specimens, and also in an adult male from Cape St. Lucas) quite broadly across the frontlet, while beneath the eye the brown is very "solid" for a width of .30 of an inch or more. It is possible, however, that these differences may not prove constant.

This Plover, first recognized as a distinct species in 1813, and dedicated to the memory of Wilson by Mr. Ord, is met with, more or less commonly, along our whole Atlantic coast from Long Island to Florida. It also occurs on both coasts of Central America, and probably breeds wherever it is found. Except that one is recorded by Mr. Lindsley as having been taken in Stratford, Conn., so far as I know it has never been traced with certainty to New England. It is quite probable, however, that individuals may occasionally visit the northern shore of Long Island Sound. It also occurs on the Atlantic coast of South America to Brazil. Audubon states that it is found on the shores of the Gulf of Mexico, in all the Southern States, that it breeds there, and that it also spends the winter in the region between Cardina and the mouths of the Mississippi River. That it also occurs in Texas is stated by Dresser, who found it common about the coast during the summer season. He noticed many on Galveston Island during his stay there in May and June, and shot several specimens, but was not able to find their nests or eggs. Dr. Merrill speaks of it as an abundant resident, and as breeding on the coast of Southwestern Texas.

Mr. Salvin met with Wilson's Plover on the coast of Honduras in the latter part of April. It was then breeding, and he discovered two of its nests. He also found that this species was very abundant at Chiapam, in Guatemala, where he met with it in flocks in the company of *Æ. semipalmata.* It occurred also and remained to breed among the bays of Belize. It is also recorded from the northwestern coast of Peru.

According to Léotaud, this Plover is a migratory visitant of the Island of Trinidad, arriving there about the end of July, and leaving in October. It frequents the borders of the sea, running on the sand in quest of the worms on which it feeds. As it takes to flight it usually utters a peculiar cry, which is slightly rolling, and not unpleasant. These birds occur sometimes by themselves, and sometimes mingled with *Tringæ* and other shore-birds; and Dr. Bryant found this an abundant resident species in the Bahamas.

Giraud mentioned this among the birds of Long Island, but as not common there. When observed it was usually in company with the *semipalmata,* with the general characteristics of which its own very closely correspond. Audubon states that while in Florida, near St. Augustine, in the months of December and January, he found this species much more abundant than any other. There were few of the keys having a sandy beach or a rocky shore without one or more pairs. The young birds assembled in the fall and spent the winter months apart from the old ones.

Dr. Coues, who had an excellent opportunity for watching this species in North Carolina, has given (Am. Nat. III. 340) a full and minute account of its habits during the summer months. He regards it as eminently characteristic of the shores of the South Atlantic States. It moves northward along the coast in April, collecting in small flocks of from six to twenty or more, and passing at once to their chosen places, there to explore the sea-beaches and the muddy flats in search of food. They are gentle and unsuspicious. Their note is described as being half a whistle and half a chirp, and as very different from the clear mellow piping of the other species. After a short interval following their first arrival, they separate in pairs and resort to the sand-hills near the coast to breed. When their nest is approached they flit to and fro, near the ground, at a little distance, in anxious groups of three or four, uttering indescribably touching appeals, now alighting, as if in hopes their treasures may remain undiscovered, and then running swiftly along, too frightened for a moment's rest.

Wilson's Plover deposits its eggs in a hollow in the sand about four inches in diameter, but so shallow as to be hardly noticeable as a depression. Sometimes it lays its eggs in a scanty tuft of grass, but in no instance has it been noticed as using any lining for its nests. The number of eggs is said to be invariably three; but that occasionally it may lay four is inferred from finding in the oviduct of a female just killed one egg ready for deposition, and three others in a highly developed state. It begins to lay about the middle of May, but differs as to the time so much that, early in June, eggs quite fresh, others nearly hatched, and newly fledged young, may all be observed. The nestlings are described as being curious-looking and very pretty. They are able to run as soon as they are fairly dry from the egg, and are difficult to find, as they squat so closely to the sand, which they resemble in color.

Their eggs are somewhat like those of the Least Tern, but are larger, and in some other respects different. The variations of the eggs of the Plovers, both in size and shape, are considerable, one measuring 1.45 inches by 1.05, and another only 1.22 inches by 1.00; they also differ very materially in shape from each other. Their ground-color when fresh is described as a pale olive-drab, inclining to a greenish hue in some examples, and to a brownish in others. They are thinly marked all over with brown, so dark as to be almost black, these markings being in irregular, sharply defined spots, small splashes, and fine dots. In some specimens the markings run into fine lines, and in these are the smallest, darkest, most numerous, and most sharply defined. The markings are usually larger and more thickly set on the larger part of the egg. Here and there a few pale obsolete spots are noticed.

Audubon, who probably observed this species in a more northern locality, gives the 1st of June as the date of the first deposition of its egg; and this more nearly corresponds with my own experience. Visiting Cape Charles, June 4, 1852, I met with several nests of this bird, in all of which the eggs were quite fresh.

Audubon describes the flight as rapid, elegant, and protracted. When flying from one sand-beach or island to another, they pass low over the land or water, and as they move give utterance to a clear and soft note. After the breeding-season they form into flocks of twenty or thirty. They do not run quite so rapidly as the Piping Plover, nor are they so shy. They rarely mingle with any other species, and show a decided preference for solitary and unfrequented places. Their food is almost exclusively of a marine character, and consists of minute shell-fish, worms, and small insects. With this food they mingle fine particles of sand. In the fall they become very plump, and afford delicious eating. They are said to feed by night as well as by day, and their peculiarly large eyes seem to adapt them for nocturnal habits.

Mr. Moore, who observed the habits of this bird on Sarasota Bay, Florida, states that out of fourteen nests all but four had three eggs in a set, and these had two. The time of incubation is twenty-four or twenty-five days. The eggs were very rarely found placed with the small ends together. Occasionally an interval of one, two, or three days would pass after the deposition of an egg before another was laid. Eggs were first laid April 8th. No nests were found nearer to one another than twenty yards. One was so near the water and so low as to be flooded at an unusually high tide.

Three eggs of this species in my collection, taken at Cape Charles in 1854 (No. 521), are of an oblong oval shape, rounded at one end and tapering at the other. The ground is a deep drab, and the markings are of bistre intensified to blackness, irregular in shape, some rounded, others longitudinal, larger than in *Æ. meloda*, and with more tendency to coalesce about the larger end. In one, the markings are nearly confined to the obtuse end. The measurements are 1.45 by 1.04 inches; 1.48 by 1.05; and 1.40 by 1.05 inches. The eggs are much more oval in shape than are those of *Æ. meloda*.

GENUS **PODASOCYS**, COUES.

Podasocys, COUES, Pr. Philad. Acad. 1866, 96 (type *Charadrius montanus*, TOWNS.)

CHAR. Bill rather small and slender (much as in *Oxyechus*), but longer than the middle toe; tarsus considerably more than twice as long as the middle toe. Tail short, even, scarcely reaching to the ends of the folded wings. Plumage exceedingly plain.

The genus *Podasocys* is perhaps more nearly related to the Old World *Eudromias* than to any American genus, but may readily be distinguished by the several characters given in the above diagnosis, and in the table on p. 129. At least one Old World species, *Charadrius veredus*, GOULD, seems to be strictly congeneric. We have carefully compared specimens, and can find no difference whatever in the details of structure. The *C. asiaticus*, PALLAS, is said to be a near relation of *C. veredus*, and may also belong to this genus. These two Old World species are characterized by a rufous pectoral band in the summer plumage, while the American species (*P. montanus*) has the jugulum merely shaded with light grayish brown ; but coloration in this group is of little value compared with deviations of structure, the species of *Ægialitis* being a case in point.

Eudromias, the type of which is *Charadrius morinellus*, LINN., differs from *Podasocys* in being of much stouter build, the culmen shorter than the middle toe, the latter nearly half as long as the tarsus, the web between the outer and middle toe much larger, the tertials extending to the ends of the primaries, etc. No American Plover is referable to *Eudromias*, as properly restricted.

Podasocys montanus.

THE MOUNTAIN PLOVER.

Charadrius montanus, TOWNS. Journ. Ac. Nat. Sci. Philad. VII. 1837, 192. — AUD. Orn. Biog. IV. 1838, 362, pl. 350 ; Synop. 1839, 223 ; B. Am. V. 1842, 213, pl. 318.

Ægialitis montanus, CASSIN, in Baird's B. N. Am. 1858, 693. — BAIRD, Cat. N. Am. B. 1859, no. 505.

Podasocys montanus, COUES, Pr. Ac. Nat. Sci. Philad. 1866, 96 ; Check List, 2d ed. 1882, no. 592. — ELLIOT, Illustr. Am. B. II. 1869, pl. 39. — RIDGW. Nom. N. Am. B. 1881, no. 523.

Ægialitis asiaticus, var. *montanus*, COUES, Key, 1872, 245 ; Check List, 1873, no. 402.

Eudromias montanus, COUES, Check List, 1873, App. p. 135, no. 402 ; Birds N. W. 1874, 456.

HAB. Western Province of North America ; accidental in Florida ; no extralimital record.

SP. CHAR. *Adult, breeding plumage:* Wide frontal crescent, superciliary stripe, and entire lower parts white, purest on the forehead, of a more or less soiled tint beneath, the jugulum

Breeding plumage.

shaded with light grayish brown, most distinct laterally where insensibly merging into the color of the upper parts. Fore part of the crown, and stripe from the rictus to the eye (across lores),

Winter plumage.

black. Rest of upper parts, uniform light grayish brown, the remiges and tail dusky ; shafts of primaries, white. *Adult in spring:* Similar to the above, but upper parts and jugulum tinged with light buffy ochraceous. *Adult and young in winter:* More strongly tinged with buff, both above and below, the black markings of the head wanting. *Young, first plumage:* All the feathers of the upper parts distinctly bordered with light buff; whole side of head and neck, and entire jugulum, deep light creamy buff. *Downy Young:* Above brownish buff, mottled with black, this forming a distinct marbling on the crown and occiput, where the ground-color is lighter and clearer buff. Lower parts pale buff, immaculate.

Total length, about 8 inches; wing, 6.00; tail, 2.75; culmen, .80–.90; tarsus, 1.50–1.60; middle toe, .70.

There is considerable individual variation in the extent and distinctness of black on the head in fully adult birds, some specimens having the whole crown black, while in others this color is limited to a crescentic mark just behind the white of the forehead; in some examples the black loral stripe is barely indicated.

The Rocky Mountain Plover, as Mr. Audubon, not very happily, has designated this species, has an extended distribution, from Arizona and Southwestern Texas on the south, to our farthest boundaries on the north, and probably beyond, and from Eastern Kansas and Nebraska to the grassy plains that border the Pacific itself. It is of accidental occurrence in Florida. While in regard to its peculiar specific habits, especially during the breeding-season, much remains to be learned, the last few years have added greatly to our knowledge of its history. It is not entitled to be regarded as a mountain bird, as it confines itself to high and dry level plains, and is never to be met with nearer to mountains than their base.

This bird was first described by Townsend in 1837, and the description of its habits, briefly narrated by Nuttall, was quoted by Audubon in 1842. The former author regarded the species as closely allied to Wilson's Plover. He met with it, only during one or two days, on the central tablelands of the Rocky Mountains, in the plains near the last of the branches of the Platte; and as it was in the month of July, he had no doubt that the bird was breeding in the Subalpine regions. The only individual obtained was seen skulking and running through the artemisia bushes that so generally clothe those arid and dry wastes. After running some time, it would remain perfectly still, as if conscious of the difficulty of distinguishing it from the gray soil on which it stood, and with the color of which its own was so nearly identical. All that were seen were similar to the specimen obtained, but none could be induced, on being flushed, to take wing. He heard from it no note or cry of complaint of any kind, and it apparently sought by silence to conceal its young or its eggs.

We are indebted to Dr. J. G. Cooper ("Am. Nat." III. p. 183) for our first full and accurate account of the habits and distribution of this species. Dr. Cooper mentions meeting with it on his route from Los Angeles, Cal., to Fort Mohave. The birds were running in scattered flocks over the driest tracts, or wheeling in swift columns around the sportsman, their white under parts shining like snowflakes as they turned while on the wing, in the manner of their more aquatic cousins of the seashore. The same writer afterward speaks ("Am. Nat." III. p. 298) of finding this Plover on the plains of the Upper Missouri, in the driest spots and among the villages of the prairie-dog. In Montana Dr. Cooper found it rare along the eastern base of the Rocky Mountains. There also they were usually met with about the prairie-dog villages; but they apparently did not cross the mountains in as large numbers as they do farther south.

Dr. Cooper also states that this species belongs almost exclusively to the vast deserts and plains of the central parts of North America, only visiting the vicinity of the sea-coast in the wet season. They are found in the extensive plains near Los Angeles after the middle of October, but are not known to be there in the summer.

They frequent the dry grassy pastures exclusively, and although but a few rods from the sea-beach, never visit it. They were in large flocks scattered over the plains, and were rather difficult to shoot, except as they chanced to fly near, being very shy if approached when on the ground.

At Fort Mohave Dr. Cooper found a few pairs in March which seemed to have nests on the dry gravelly bluffs. He describes them as being less noisy than the Kildeer, although their cries much resemble those of that bird. In the autumn, when started from the ground, they uttered a low whistle, and flew around in large circles; then, after being joined by stragglers, they re-alighted, but not until they had first carefully examined the vicinity.

Mr. Dresser met with this Plover, during the winter only, in Southwestern Texas. In December, 1863, as he was riding in the open prairie country near San Antonio, he noticed a few individuals; these were generally near the high-roads. In their habits they reminded him very much of the Ring Plover of Europe (*Ægialitis hiaticula*) — running very swiftly, with the head drawn in close to the body. As the winter advanced they became more plentiful, but disappeared in the early spring, none showing themselves later than the beginning of April. They fed on cattle-ticks and beetles of all sorts, and seemed to prefer the barren sand-plains to the grassy parts in the neighborhood of water.

Mr. C. E. Aiken mentions meeting with this species in pairs on the high table-lands of Colorado. Mr. J. A. Allen found the Mountain Plover present, though not abundant, from Eastern Kansas westward. In the vicinity of Fort Hays he noticed it occurring with considerable frequency. During the breeding-season he saw it in isolated pairs, usually in the driest situations, and characterizes it as silent and unsuspicious. Later in the season Mr. Allen mentions meeting with it in small parties composed of one or two broods of young accompanied by their parents; these were observed at intervals throughout the month of July. This species was also often met with in South Park, as well as on the high table-lands which occur at intervals thence to the plains.

Dr. Coues noticed this species on various occasions, and his accounts are generally confirmatory of those previously given by Dr. Cooper. He first mentions meeting with it in his journey from Arizona to the Pacific, and there speaks of it as an unsuspicious and familiar bird, admitting of a very near approach where it was not too often disturbed, running gracefully with the head lowered, often stopping suddenly and drawing itself up to its full height, and watching the intruder with curious eye. Its voice is described as being soft and low, and of a very peculiar tone. More recently, he mentions its occurrence in Dakota, along the parallel of 49° N., where it was breeding in considerable numbers. It was first seen July 1, and was traced thence across the country nearly to the Sweetgrass Hills. Its centre of abundance was about Frenchman's River, where a set of three eggs, with many specimens, both adult and young, were secured. At no time did the birds seem to him wary or suspicious, and when their nests or young were threatened they would hardly retreat even if themselves in danger. On such occasions they utter a low chattering cry very unlike their usual soft mellow whistle, fly low over the ground to a short distance, or run swiftly for a few paces, and then stand motionless, as described by Mr. Nuttall. The chicks are said to be white beneath and curiously variegated in color above, with naked livid spaces about the neck. From the first the young were very difficult to capture alive. The nesting-season is protracted, well-feathered young and fresh eggs occurring at the same period.

In the desert regions of New Mexico west of the Rio Grande, this bird was also found abundant late in June. It was seen in Arizona at various seasons, but not in great numbers. Its food consists principally, if not wholly, of insects, grasshoppers seeming to be its main reliance, with crickets and beetles. In the fall, when food is plenty, the birds are excellent eating.

When forced to fly, this Plover is said to rise rapidly with quick wing-beats, and then to proceed with alternate sailing and flapping. It generally flies low over the ground, and as it alights takes a few mincing steps.

The eggs of this species (S. I. No. 2858) obtained by Dr. Suckley on the North Forks of the Platte, northwest of Fort Kearney, July 15, 1857, do not resemble in their general appearance the eggs of the species of the genus *Ægialitis*. They are a rounded oval in shape, one end being but slightly more pointed than other. The ground-color is a deep brownish drab, nearly uniformly marked with rounded spots of varying size, of deep bistre; these are a little more numerous, and larger about the obtuse end. The eggs measure 1.40 inches in length, and 1.10 in breadth. Specimens of eggs of this species in the Smithsonian Collection from Frenchman's River (No. 17016) have a ground-color of a deep reddish buff, with spots of different shades of brown and black, chiefly the latter. There were three eggs found in the nest, and this seemed to be the complement; they were nearly fresh. The nest was a mere depression on the bare prairie, lined only with a few grass-blades. The eggs measured respectively 1.50 by 1.15, 1.55 by 1.10, and 1.60 by 1.05. Mr. Stevenson describes their nests as being mere depressions in the ground; in one four eggs were found. Mr. J. A. Allen saw newly hatched young, and others full grown, July 27 and 28, in South Park, Colorado.

Family PARRIDÆ. — The Jacanas.

Char. Small-sized Wading-birds, combining the general appearance of Rails and Plovers, but differing from both in the remarkable and excessive elongation of the toes and claws, the latter nearly straight and much compressed, that of the hallux much longer than its digit, and slightly recurved.

The above brief diagnosis is sufficient to distinguish the Jacanas from all other Wading-birds. Their nearest allies appear to be the Plovers, from which they differ chiefly in the character of the feet, as pointed out above. The single American genus *Parra*, Lath., is further characterized by the presence of leaf-like lobes at the base of the bill, and a sharp conical spur projecting from the inside of the bend of the wing, in the possession of which features they present a striking analogy to certain Plovers, as the genera *Lobivanellus*, Strickl., and *Hoplopterus*, Bonap. The genus *Parra*, of which there are several species, all American,[1] is characterized as follows: —

Genus **PARRA**, Linnæus.

Fulica, Linn. S. N. ed. 10, I. 1758, 152 (*F. spinosa* = *Parra jacana*, L. ed. 1766[2]).
Jacana, Briss. Orn. V. 1760, 121 (type, *Parra jacana*, Auct.). (Includes also *Hyd alector*, Wagl., and *Metopodius*, Wagl.)
Parra, Linn. S. N. I. 1766, 259 (type, *P. jacana*, L.).

[1] For a synopsis of the species of this genus, see Sclater "On the American Genus *Parra*," in Proc. Zool. Soc. Lond. 1856, p. 282.

[2] Allowing specific names given in the 10th edition of "Systema Naturæ," against which there appears to be no valid objection, we can see no reason why the common South American Jacana should not be called *P. spinosa*, L., instead of *P. jacana*.

CHAR. Remiges normal; rectrices much abbreviated, very soft, entirely concealed by the tail-coverts; forehead with large leaf-like lobe, free laterally and posteriorly, adhering centrally and anteriorly; rictus ornamented by a smaller lobe (rudimentary in *P. gymnostoma*).

The above characters are chiefly those which distinguish the American genus *Parra* from its Old World allies *Hydrophasianus*,[1] *Metopodius*,[2] and *Hydralector*.[3] I am unable to state in just what essential particulars the two latter differ from *Parra*, never having seen specimens of any species of either form. The first, however, differs very widely in the great development of the rectrices, of which the intermediæ are excessively elongated; in the curious attenuation of the primaries, which are, moreover, of very unequal length, and in the entire absence of lobes about the base of the bill. These characters I have drawn from figures of the single species, *H. chirurgus*, SCOPOLI, not having seen the bird itself.

In addition to the generic characters given above, the following also may be mentioned: —

Bill somewhat Plover-like in form, the basal half with the upper and lower outlines nearly parallel and decidedly approximated, the terminal half of the culmen strongly convex, the gonys nearly straight, and decidedly ascending terminally; nostrils small, horizontal, elliptical, situated about half-way between the anterior angle of the eye and the tip of the bill. Primaries ten, reaching to the tips of the tertials, the three outer quills longest and nearly equal, their inner webs slightly narrowed near the end. Tarsus and bare portion of the tibia covered by a continuous frontal and posterior series of transverse scutellæ, these sometimes fused into continuous sheaths; middle toe (exclusive of its claw) about equal to the tarsus (sometimes a little shorter); outer toe equal to the middle toe, but its claw a little shorter; inner toe a little shorter than the outer, but its claw considerably longer; hallux about equal to the basal phalanx of the middle toe, but its claw reaching nearly, if not quite, to the end of the middle toe.

Parra gymnostoma.

THE MEXICAN JACANA.

Parra gymnostoma, WAGL. Isis, 1831, 517. — SCL. & SALV. Nom. Neotr. 1873, 142. — MERRILL, Bull. Nutt. Orn. Club, I. Nov. 1876, 88 (Fort Brown, Texas); Proc. U. S. Nat. Mus. I. 1878, 167 (Fort Brown). — RIDGW. ib. (synonymy; descriptions); Nom. N. Am. B. 1881, no. 568. — COUES, Check List, 2d ed. 1882, no. 672.

Parra cordifera, LESS. Rev. Zool. 1842, 135 (Acapulco). — DES MURS, Icon. Orn. pl. 42.

HAB. The whole of Central America, from Panama to Northern Mexico; lower Rio Grande Valley of Texas, at Fort Brown (MERRILL, Proc. U. S. Nat. Mus. I. 1878, 167); Cuba.

SP. CHAR. *Adult:* Wing, 4.50–5.40; culmen, 1.15–1.40; tarsus, 1.90–2.35; middle toe, 1.85–

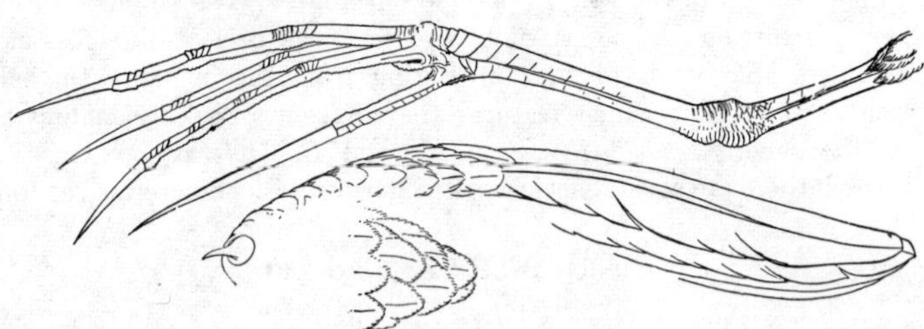

2.25.[4] Head, neck, jugulum, and extreme anterior portion of the back uniform black, with a faint silky green gloss below. Rest of the plumage mainly uniform rich purplish chestnut, with a

[1] "*Hydrophasianus*, WAGL. 1832" (type, *H. chirurgus*, SCOPOLI).

[2] "*Metopodius*, WAGL. 1832" (type, *Parra africana*, LATH., *fide* Gray).

[3] "*Hydralector*, WAGL. 1832" (type, *Parra cristata*, VIEILL., *fide* Gray).

[4] Extremes of thirteen examples.

faint purple gloss, brightest or most rufescent on the wings, more purplish on the back, rump, and upper tail-coverts, and of a rich dark purplish-maroon shade on the breast and sides; anal region, tibiæ, and crissum duller and more grayish. Remiges (except the tertials) pale yellowish pea-green, bordered terminally with dull dusky, this border very narrow, and strictly terminal on the secondaries, but broader, and involving more or less of both edges of the quills on the primaries, where it increases in extent to the outer quill, which has the entire outer web blackish; alulæ and primary coverts dull blackish. Tail-feathers uniform rich chestnut. "Iris dark brown; bill, alar spurs, and frontal leaf, bright yellow; upper base of bill bluish white, the space between it and the nasal leaf bright carmine; feet greenish."[1]

Young: Frontal leaf rudimentary. Pileum grayish brown, bordered on each side by a wide and conspicuous superciliary stripe of buffy white, extending to the occiput; below this stripe, another narrower one of black or dusky, beginning at the posterior angle of the eye and extending along the upper edge of the auriculars to the nape, which is also of this color; remainder of the head, with the entire lower parts, except the sides, continuous buffy white, more strongly tinged with buff across the jugulum. Upper parts in general (except the remiges) light grayish brown, the feathers bordered terminally with rusty buff in the younger stage, but uniform in older individuals; rump more or less tinged with chestnut. Sides and lining of the wing dusky black, but in older examples more or less tinged with chestnut. Remiges as in the adult; rectrices grayish brown.

The downy young is unknown, or at least I have been unable to find any description.

In the considerable series of specimens of this species contained in the collection of the National Museum, notable variations in size and proportions occur among specimens of the same age and sex, but apparently without regard to locality. Cuban specimens do not differ in the least, so far as I can see, from Mexican and Central American examples.

The present species of Jacana was met with by Dr. James C. Merrill near Fort Brown, in Southeastern Texas, early in August, 1876. He saw it on two occasions, on the first of which he had not the means of procuring a specimen, and on the second was unable to obtain the bird he had shot. Very little is known as to the manners and habits of this peculiar family. In its characteristics it seems to combine very many of the characteristics of the Rails and the Plovers; and it may be that its manner of life also partakes of the habits of the two forms so distinct from each other. This species is a common bird of Mexico, probably of a small portion of Northern South America, Central America to Panama, and Cuba, and perhaps other West India Islands.

This species was taken by Sumichrast in Southwestern Mexico, at Santa Efigenia and Zonatepec, in March and April. A set of four eggs of this species, from Cuba, measure 1.22 by .98; 1.20 by 1.00; 1.24 by 1.00; 1.15 by .94. They are of a rounded oval shape, have a ground color of bright drab, and are strikingly marbled over the entire surface with an intersecting net-work of black or very dark-brown waving stripes, blotches, and lines. These markings curve and wind in various ways, always in rounded, never in angular, turns, and the eggs present a very peculiar, unmistakable, and characteristic appearance.

[1] Sumichrast, MS., *fide* Lawr., Bull. U. S. Nat. Mus., No. 4, 1876, p. 50.

FAMILY SCOLOPACIDÆ. — THE SNIPE FAMILY.

The characters of the family *Scolopacidæ* having been given in sufficient detail on p. 108, in the analysis of the families of Limicolæ, it is unnecessary to repeat them here. The Scolopacidæ are among the most widely dispersed of birds, a large proportion of the genera being nearly cosmopolitan. They embrace a very great variety of forms, from the diminutive "Peeps" (*Actodromas* and *Ereunetes*), smaller than a Sparrow, to the large Curlews, of Ibis-like stature and appearance. The bill may be either straight, bent upward, as in the Avocets (*e. g. Limosa* and *Terekia*), or strongly decurved, like a sickle; narrowed at the end, or widely expanded into a paddle-shaped form (*Eurynorhynchus*). The legs may be short and stout (as in *Arquatella, Calidris,* etc.), or of almost Stilt-like length, as in *Micropalama, Totanus,* etc. Between these wide extremes of form, however, there are genera possessing characters intermediate in almost every conceivable degree — so much so as to render it extremely difficult to tabulate the characters of the numerous genera. The following is an attempt at a diagnostic table of the American genera, omitting *Phegornis*, GRAY,[1] of Chili, which we have not been able to examine.

American Genera of Scolopacidæ.

A. Bill longer than the tarsus and middle toe, straight.

B. Bill shorter than the tarsus and middle toe, strongly decurved at the end; wing short, rounded.

C. Bill shorter than the tarsus and middle toe, straight or slightly curved up or down; wing lengthened, pointed.

D. Bill widely expanded laterally at the end.

E. Bill longer than the tarsus and middle toe, strongly decurved.

A. (*Scolopaceæ.*)

a. Tibiæ completely feathered.

1. **Scolopax.** Outer quill longest, broad, like the others.
2. **Philohela.** Outer quill shorter than the sixth, the three outer primaries abruptly much narrower than the rest.

b. Tibiæ partly naked.

3. **Gallinago.** Toes all cleft to the base.
4. **Macrorhamphus.** A well-developed web between anterior toes, at base.

C.[2]

a. Feathers of the forehead not reaching to the nostril; anterior toes all webbed at the base.

5. **Micropalama.** Bill and legs much elongated, the former much compressed, except at end; tarsus twice as long as middle toe; size medium.
6. **Ereunetes.** Bill and legs moderately elongated, or rather short, the former scarcely, if at all, compressed; tarsus much less than twice the middle toe; size small.

b. Feathers of the forehead not reaching to the nostril; anterior toes all cleft to the base.

1.′ A well-developed hind toe.

7. **Tringa.** Tarsus one third its length longer than the middle toe and claw; toes stout, the middle about half as long as the bill; bill stout, straight. Middle tail-feathers not longer than the rest. Size rather large (wing more than 6.00).

[1] Type, *Leptopus Mitchelli*, Fraser.

[2] Section "B" includes only the singular genus *Rhynchæa*, which has representatives in various parts of the Southern Hemisphere, but none in North America.

8. **Arquatella.** Tarsus shorter than the middle toe and claw; toes slender, the middle two thirds to three fourths as long as the bill; bill slender, much compressed, straight, or very slightly decurved at the end; size medium (wing less than 6.00).

9. **Actodromas.** Tarsus about equal to the bill; bill straight, moderately slender; toes slender, the middle one decidedly shorter than the tarsus; size medium to very small.

10. **Pelidna.** Bill very long (nearly as long as the tarsus and middle toe), decidedly decurved terminally; toes slender, the middle one decidedly shorter than the tarsus.

1.″ No hind toe.

11. **Calidris.** Size rather small; bill short, straight, expanded at end.

c. Feathers of forehead not reaching to nostril; a web between outer and middle toes at base (between all in *Symphemia*).

2.′ Gape not extending behind the base of the culmen.

12. **Limosa.** Size large (wing 8.00 or more); bill much longer than tarsus, tapering toward the end, where slightly but decidedly upturned, the lateral groove extending nearly to the tip.

2.″ Gape extending decidedly behind the base of the culmen.

3.′ Lateral groove of the maxilla extending scarcely more than half way to end of bill.

4.′ Back of tarsus covered with transverse scutellæ, as in front.

13. **Totanus.** No web between inner and middle toes; middle toe not more than half as long as tarsus; size medium to large (but wing always less than 8 inches).

14. **Rhyacophilus.** Similar to *Totanus*, but middle toe nearly as long as tarsus.

15. **Symphemia.** A well-developed web between base of inner and middle toes; a large white patch on base of primaries; size large (wing more than 8 inches).

4.″ Back of tarsus covered with small roundish scales.

16. **Heteroscelus.** No web between base of inner and middle toes; size medium (wing less than 8 inches).

3.″ Lateral groove of maxilla extending nearly to tip of bill.

17. **Machetes.** Size large (wing 7 inches or more); tail short (less than half the wing), rounded. *Adult* ♂ with the neck ruffed, and anterior portion of head bare.

18. **Bartramia.** Size large (wing nearly 7 inches); tail lengthened (more than half the wing), graduated. *Adult* ♂ without ruff, the anterior part of the head normally feathered.

19. **Tringoides.** Size small (wing less than 4.50); tail rather lengthened (more than half the wing), graduated.

d. Feathers of the forehead reaching to and partly enclosing the nostril; anterior toes all cleft at the base.

20. **Tryngites.** Size small (a little larger than *Tringoides*); bill small and slender (shorter than the head, about equal to the middle toe), the lateral groove reaching nearly to the tip; gape reaching back of the base of the culmen; middle toe more than half as long as the tarsus; inner webs of quills and under primary-coverts beautifully speckled.

D.

21. **Eurynorhynchus.** Size small (among the smallest of the family); bill widely expanded laterally at the end; otherwise, much as in *Actodromas*.

E.

22. **Numenius.** Size large to very large (wing 8 inches or more); bill long (much longer than tarsus), decidedly decurved or arched.

Genus SCOLOPAX, Linnæus.

Scolopax, Linn. S. N. ed. 10, 1758, 145 ; ed. 12, 1766, 242 (type, *S. rusticola*, Linn.).
Rusticola, Moehr, Av. Gen. 1752, 77 (same type).

Char. Body very robust ; tarsus less than half as long as the bill, and scarcely longer than the middle toe ; tibiæ completely feathered ; primaries normal, the outermost longest, and broad, like the rest.

The above diagnosis is sufficient to distinguish this genus, which embraces the European Woodcock (*S. rusticula*) and two allied Old World species or races,[1] from the genus *Philohela*, of which the American Woodcock (*P. minor*) is the sole representative.

Scolopax rusticula.

THE EUROPEAN WOODCOCK.

Scolopax rusticola, Linn. S. N. ed. 10, 1758, 146 ; ed. 12, 1766, 243.—Naum. Vög. Deutschl. VIII. 1836, 361, pl. 211. — Keys. & Blas. Wirb. Eur. 1840, 78. — Schleg. Rev. crit. 1844, 85. — Gray, Gen. B. III. 1849, 584. — Baird, Am. Jour. Arts & Sci. XLI. 1866, 25 (Newfoundland).

Scolopax rusticula, Whart. Ibis, 1879, 454. — Ridgw. Nom. N. Am. B. 1881, no. 524. — Coues, Check List, 2d ed. 1882, no. 606.

Scolopax major, Leach, Syst. Cat. 1816, 31.

Scolopax pinetorum, Brehm, Vög. Deutschl. 1831, 613, pl. 32, f. 2.

Scolopax sylvestris, Brehm, t. c. 614.

Rusticola sylvestris, Macgill. Man. II. 1840, 105.

Rusticola vulgaris, Vieill. N. D. III. 1816, 348.

Woodcock, Yarr. Brit. B. ed. 2, III. 1845, 1, fig. ed. 3, III. 1, fig. et Auct.

Hab. Palæarctic Region ; occasional in Eastern North America (several records : Loudoun Co., Virginia, Coues, *Forest & Stream*, April 27, 1876, p. 180 ; New Jersey, Coues ; Newfoundland, Baird, Am. Jour. Sci. & Arts, XLI. 1866, 25).

Sp. Char. *Adult :* Above rusty brown, everywhere variegated by lighter transverse spots and dusky lines ; the middle of the back (longitudinally) and the scapulars marked with irregular large black spots or blotches ; scapulars much mixed with light grayish posteriorly, and sides of the interscapular region almost continuously light grayish, forming a pair of well-defined V-shaped

[1] *S. saturata*, Horsfield, of Java, and *S. Rochusseni*, Schlegel, of Africa (Greater Obi).

marks, on each side of the rusty black-spotted area. Rump lighter cinnamon-rusty, narrowly barred with dusky; upper tail-coverts largely tipped with light gray. Tail-feathers black, serrated along the outer edge with rusty, and widely tipped with light gray. Forehead and anterior part of the crown, brownish gray; posterior part of the crown and whole occiput, black, crossed by four transverse narrow bands of light rusty, or ochraceous — two through the black, the other two bounding it anteriorly and posteriorly. A wide loral stripe of blackish brown, running from the rictus to the eye. Chin white. Lower parts in general pale fulvous grayish (nearly white medially), marked with irregular transverse bars of dark brown. Quills dusky, their outer webs marked with triangular spots of light cinnamon, arranged so as to form transverse bands; outer web of exterior quill widely edged with pure white. Bill and feet light horn-color, the former blackish at the end. *Downy Young:* General hue delicate rusty ochraceous, the upper surface marked with large blotch-like areas of deep rusty, these being arranged as follows: an isolated, somewhat wedge-shaped, spot occupying the middle of the forehead; a longitudinal stripe down the middle of the rump; a longitudinal patch covering the occiput and nape, and sending out two lateral branches, the first from the upper part to the eye, the second from the lower part across the neck, where continued, more or less interruptedly, across the jugulum; a dark chestnut (nearly black) stripe from the bill to the eye. The other blotches covering the back, part of the wings, and the anal region.

Wing, nearly 8.00; culmen, about 3.00–3.25; tarsus, 1.50; middle toe, 1.30.

The European Woodcock is of occasional and accidental occurrence in North America, and its appearance quite possibly is more frequent than we are aware of. It is referred to, in one instance, in the "Ibis," as having been included in the Newfoundland collection of mounted birds in the Exposition of 1867.

In Lewis's "American Sportsman" (p. 158), under the heading "Woodcock," reference is made in a footnote to a specimen of a Woodcock sent, about 1860, to Mr. G. D. Wetherill, which weighed fourteen ounces. When received, however, it was too far gone to be preserved; but it was, without much doubt, a bird of this species. Mr. George N. Lawrence cites another similar instance, where a friend of his shot, near Newport, R. I., a large Woodcock, which weighed fourteen ounces; unfortunately it was not preserved. The fact that our Woodcock rarely reaches and never exceeds nine ounces, while the usual weight of the European is fourteen, naturally suggests that in both instances the specimens were examples of the *rusticula.*

We are not, however, restricted to probabilities merely for our evidence of the actual occurrence of this species within our limits. Mr. Lawrence has in his collection the skin of a European Woodcock purchased in the Washington Market of New York, Dec. 6, 1859. It had been brought there with a lot of Quail, on board the boat from Shrewsbury, N. J.

This species appears to be widely distributed over Europe and the western portions of Asia. It resorts in summer to northern regions for purposes of reproduction, and in its migrations visits a wide extent of territory.

A few breed in Great Britain, in various parts of the islands, but a large proportion seen there are migrants from more northern regions. They breed throughout Denmark, Norway, Sweden, Lapland, and Northern Russia, arriving in Scandinavia at the latter end of March or the beginning of April, when they are found on the coast in considerable numbers, but usually depart for the interior on the prevalence of westerly winds. They are common in Western Lapland beyond the Arctic Circle, and are generally and widely dispersed; but are nowhere numerous. The pine-forests are their places of resort in summer. They are not found in Southern Germany in the summer, and breed no farther south than Silesia, and thence northward.

This is a celebrated game-bird in Europe, and especially in Great Britain and Ireland, where, in their fall migrations, the Woodcock arrive in great numbers, and are much sought after by sportsmen. Their large size, their fine flavor, and the interest attending their pursuit, combine to render them attractive objects to the sportsman. The winter visitors to the British Islands usually appear early in October, and remain there until March. It is said that they always arrive in the greatest numbers in hazy weather. They perform their journeys at night; and it is supposed that those which appear in the northern counties of England have made their passage from Norway between sunset and sunrise. If the weather has been calm, the birds exhibit no signs of fatigue on their arrival, and generally come in excellent condition. They fly at a considerable altitude, and usually alight just at dawn of day. The first flight which arrives usually consists exclusively of females; the subsequent and latest one of males. In evidence of the abundance of Woodcock in the eastern counties of England, Yarrell mentions that no less than one hundred and sixty of these birds were shot on the estate of Lord Hastings, in Norfolk, in three days; and instances are on record where two hundred of them have been killed in a single day by one person.

The Woodcock is of nocturnal habits, and reposes in the daytime, remaining hid in dry grassy bottoms, in woods, or among brakes, never moving except when disturbed. Toward night the bird goes by well-known tracks to its feeding-ground. These tracks, or open glades in the woods, are known as "cock-shoots" and "cock-roads;" and in them nets were formerly suspended for the capture of the bird. The common earthworm is the food they most eagerly seek; and in confinement they have been known to consume them in almost incredible quantities. Their mode of feeding, as observed in an aviary in Spain, is thus described by Daniel: "There was a fountain to keep the ground moist, and fresh sod was brought to them, the richest in worms that could be found. The Woodcock stuck its beak into the ground, but never higher than the nostrils, drew the worms out singly, and, raising its bill in the air, it extended upon it the whole length of the worm, and in this way swallowed it smoothly, without any action of the jaws. The whole was performed in an instant, and the bird never once missed its aim."

A small proportion of these birds remain in England through the summer, and are very early breeders. Yarrell states that the young are usually hatched by the end of March or the beginning of April. On the 22d of April, 1838, Mr. Gould exhibited to the Zoological Society two young Woodcocks apparently three weeks old. The nests of this species, so far as known, consist wholly of dead leaves, chiefly of the common fern, loosely laid together, and without any lining. The young run almost from the shell.

It appears to be a well-attested fact that the parent birds of this species, when their young — if not old enough to take care of themselves — are in danger, will take them in their claws and carry them to a place of safety. Yarrell cites several instances in which this curious performance was witnessed. White, in his "Natural History of Selborne," discredits this statement; but it appears to be so well attested by so many trustworthy witnesses that it is unreasonable to doubt its correctness.

The eggs of the Woodcock are said to be usually four in number. Their ground-color is a pale yellowish white, blotched and spotted with ashy gray and two shades of reddish yellow-brown; these markings are most numerous around the larger end. The eggs measure 1.75 inches in length by 1.33 inches in breadth.

Genus PHILOHELA, Gray.

Rusticola, Gray, Genera B. 1840 (nec Moehring, 1752).
Philohela, Gray, List Genera, 1841 (type, *Scolopax minor*, Gmel.).
Microptera, Nutt. Man. II. 1834, 192 (nec Gravenhorst, 1802).

Char. Body very full, and head, bill, and eyes very large. Tibia short, feathered to the joint. Toes cleft to base. Wings short, rounded, the three outer primaries very narrow and much attenuated; the fourth and fifth equal and longest. Tarsi stout, shorter than the middle toe. Hind claw very short, conical, not extending beyond the toe. Tail of twelve feathers.

P minor.

The present genus, embracing a single species, the American Woodcock, is much like *Scolopax*, with the European Woodcock as type, in color and external appearance. The most striking difference is seen in the wings, which are short, rounded; the fourth and fifth primaries longest, and the outer three abruptly attenuated: while in *Scolopax* the wings are long, the first primary longest, and none attenuated.

Philohela minor.

THE AMERICAN WOODCOCK.

Scolopax minor, Gmel. S. N. I. 1788, 661. — Wils. Am. Orn. VI. 1812, 40, pl. 48, fig. 2. — Aud. Orn. Biog. III. 1835, 474, pl. 268.
Rusticola (*Microptera*) *minor*, Nutt. Man. II. 1834, 194.
Philohela minor, Gray, Genera B. 1849. — Cassin, in Baird's B. N. Am. 1858, 709. — Baird, Cat. N. Am. B. 1859, no. 522. — Coues, Key, 1872, 251, fig. 162; Check List, 1873, no. 412; 2d ed. 1882, no. 605; Birds N. W. 1874, 472. — Ridgw. Nom. N. Am. B. 1881, no. 525.
Microptera americana, Aud. Synop. 1839, 250; B. Am. VI. 1843, 15, pl. 352.

Hab. Eastern Province of North America, north to the British Provinces and west to Dakota, Nebraska, and Kansas; breeding throughout its known range; no extra-limital record, except the Bermudas.

Downy young.

Sp. Char. Bill long, compressed, punctulated and (in dried skins) corrugated near the end; upper mandible longer than the under, and fitted to it at the tip; wings moderate, three outer quills very narrow ; tail short; legs moderate ; eyes inserted unusually distant from the bill. *Adult:* Occiput with three transverse bands of black, alternating with three much narrower ones of pale yellowish rufous ; upper parts of body variegated with pale ashy, rufous, or yellowish red of various shades, and black ; large space on front and throat reddish ashy ; line from the eye to the bill, and

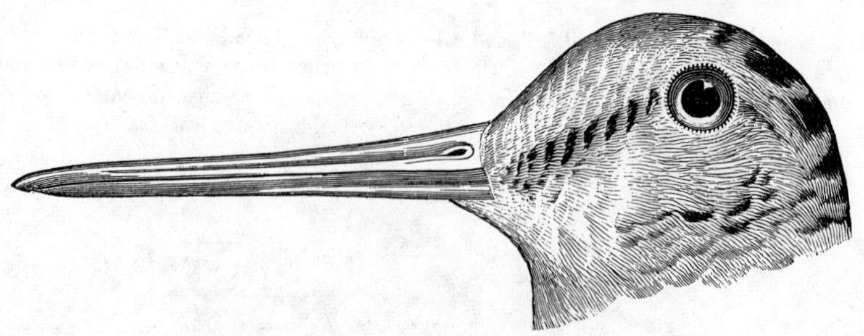

another on the neck below the eye, brownish black ; entire under parts pale grayish rufous, brighter on the sides and under wing-coverts. Quills ashy brown ; tail feathers brownish black, tipped with ashy, darker on the upper surface, paler and frequently white on the under ; bill light brown, paler and yellowish at base ; legs pale reddish.

Downy young: General color light reddish buff or isabella-color, uniform on the lower surface. Line from bill to eye, a large, somewhat elliptical patch covering forehead and fore part of the crown, a patch on the occiput (connected with that on the crown by a narrow isthmus), and a narrow mark behind the eye with an oblique one below it, very dark chestnut ; broad stripe down the rump, also dark chestnut ; stripe down the nape, and various large blotches on the back, wings, etc., rather light snuff-brown.

Total length about 11 inches ; wing, 4.80–5.70; tail, 2.25 ; bill, 2.50 to nearly 3.00 ; tarsus, 1.25 ; middle toe, 1.37.

The American Woodcock — one of the best known and most popular of our game-birds — is found throughout the eastern portion of the continent, from Florida to the Gulf of St. Lawrence on the northeast, and from the Atlantic to Nebraska. It is, however, rare west of the Mississippi. It is abundant at Hamilton, and probably occurs throughout Canada, New Brunswick, and Nova Scotia. Mr. Boardman informs us that it is very common in the vicinity of Calais, where it breeds abundantly, and that it has been known to nest as far north as the river and the banks of the Gulf of St. Lawrence. It breeds in these places in April, even when the ground is still covered with snow. A single specimen has been taken in Bermuda.

On Long Island, according to Giraud, the Woodcock arrives early in March, and begins to build its nest, about the beginning of April, of withered leaves and dry grasses in a very inartistic manner. The eggs are usually four, occasionally five, in number. It is, however, probable that the Woodcock, in favorable seasons, arrives and breeds somewhat earlier on Long Island, as this bird occasionally occurs in Massachusetts in February, and breeds in March. It remains in sheltered localities until quite late in the autumn ; and, near Jamaica, L. I., in wet and springy places, a few have been seen in the months of December and January.

In its habits the Woodcock is nocturnal. It never flies voluntarily by day, but only when forced from its retreats, usually keeping in close and sheltered thickets, and resorting at twilight to its favorite feeding-places. It feeds almost exclusively during the night, as its sight is very imperfect by day. Its eye is remarkably large and handsome, but unfit to bear the glare of the sun, its full and almost amaurotic appearance plainly suggesting the crepuscular habits of the bird. During the greater portion of the day the Woodcock remains closely concealed in marshy thickets or in rank grass; in the early morning or evening, and also on moonlight nights, it seeks its food in open places, but during the day-time in dark and dense coverts.

The favorite places of resort of this species are low marshy grounds, swamps, and meadows with soft bottoms. During very wet seasons it seeks higher land — most generally corn-fields — and searches for food in the soft ploughed ground, where its presence is indicated by the holes made by its bill. In seasons of excessive drought the Woodcock resorts in large numbers to tide-water creeks and the banks of fresh-water rivers; but so averse is it to an excess of water, that after continued or very heavy rains it has been known suddenly to disappear over widely extended tracts of country.

In October and November this bird forsakes its usual feeding-grounds, and resorts to tall swampy woods, small streams overgrown with bushes, and newly cleared lands. Its favorite food consists of larvæ, insects, and, more especially, worms. As the approach of cold weather drives the latter deeper into the ground, the Woodcock resorts to woods and brush-lands, where it gleans a subsistence on insects concealed under the leaves. That is considered by sportsmen as the most favorable season in which to shoot this bird, as it is then larger, fatter, and more free from vermin than at any other time. The best sportsmen contend that the Woodcock should not be shot until the last of September or the first of October, and regard its destruction, when of imperfect flight, as both barbarous in itself, and certain to render the race extinct — at least over portions of the country.

The food of this species consists chiefly of worms, and also of several kinds of larvæ, which it finds under leaves and the *débris* of swampy woods and open bogs. The extreme portion of its bill is well supplied with nerves, and is so extremely sensitive to the touch, that by it the presence of worms in the soft earth at a depth of three inches is readily detected. This is a very voracious bird, and when kept in confinement requires constant attention and a large supply of food. It soon discovers and draws out every worm in the ground; and such as are provided for it are consumed in incredible quantities. It can in time be induced to feed on bread and milk, of which it will also consume an enormous quantity in twenty-four hours. The voracity of this species is evidently one of the occasions of its unsocial character.

For the table the Woodcock is highly esteemed by epicures, and always commands a high price in the markets of our large cities. It is particularly sought for during the early part of the season, although birds taken at that time are much inferior in many respects to those procured later in autumn.

The flight of this species is very peculiar. When flushed in its retreats it rises to the height of the bushes or undergrowth, and quickly drops behind them again; usually running a short distance as soon as it touches the ground. Very little force is required to kill it, but as it presents itself as a mark only for a moment, no other than a practised sportsman will be successful. As it rises, the action of its wings causes a whistling sound. When found in open meadow-land, however, it is comparatively easily shot, as it always gives warning by this whistling sound of its wings, and seldom rises higher than a man's head, skimming over the ground, with a slow and steady flight, to a short distance, when it settles again in the grass. But among bushes and thickets its course is at first indirect and unsteady, and unlike the flight of any other game. Springing rapidly from the ground, it rises perpendicularly until it clears the tops of the trees or bushes: its flight then becomes more steady; but the bird is by that time usually out of reach, or only to be hit by sportsmen of experience and cool judgment.

The call-note of the Woodcock is a short *quack;* but this is not often heard except in the spring, when during the love-season the male is said to have what may be considered as its song. Toward dusk it mounts in the air, uttering peculiar whistling notes, which are continued until a late hour in the evening; and the same are sometimes heard in the early morning. This peculiarity is mentioned by several writers; but the song is by some spoken of as a succession of cries, by others as a series of whistling notes. Lewis mentions it as occurring in the morning, and only occasionally at night. The Woodcock rises in the air by a kind of spiral motion to a considerable height, uttering its notes from time to time, until, having gained a certain elevation, it circles around, in a wild and irregular manner, at the same time making confused and murmuring sounds. It then descends as rapidly as it rose. When it attempts to utter these notes on the ground, it seems to do so with difficulty, throwing its head toward the earth and erecting its tail. These manœuvres and this song are only noticed in spring, and unquestionably are the love-song of the male to his mate.

The Woodcock breeds throughout the Middle and Northern States and the British Provinces. In the winter it generally migrates to the Southern States; but some remain in the more favorable localities in Pennsylvania, New Jersey, and Delaware, and even occasionally as far north as Massachusetts. Their migrations northward begin in February; and some of them pass the summer in the highlands of Georgia, North Carolina, and Tennessee, where they are resident throughout the year, as they are also in the sheltered cedar-swamps of New Jersey, where the springy ground is never completely frozen.

A few Woodcock breed in February and March, but generally this bird begins to lay early in April. The nest is placed on the ground in a retired part of the woods, frequently at the foot of an old stump, and is made of a few withered leaves and dry grasses, thrown together without arrangement or care. The number of eggs is four, or sometimes five. The young Woodcock, when a week or ten days old, is covered with down of a brownish white color. When taken it utters a long, clear, but feeble *peep*, not louder than the cry of a mouse. Its period of incubation is three weeks. The young bird when first hatched is not capable of active movement, and may be very easily caught. This species is said to have frequently two broods in a season. The female exhibits great ingenuity in her endeavors to conceal her young and to draw away intruders, fluttering over the ground, dragging her body heavily along, as if wounded and incapable of flight, and then flying to a short distance, repeating these manœuvres until she has enticed her pursuers sufficiently far, when she suddenly takes wing, and returns to her offspring by a circuitous route.

During the winter months Woodcock are said to resort in incredible numbers to the narrow strip of low land which borders the Mississippi River for a distance of several hundred miles from its mouth. There it is impossible to hunt it in the usual manner, and resort is had to what is called "fire-hunting." The sportsman, armed with a double-barrelled gun, and wearing a broad-brimmed palmetto hat, proceeds on a foggy night to the marshes which are the resort of the Woodcock. A stout negro carries on his head an open vessel supplied with burning pine-knots. The hunter follows the torch-bearer, his eyes being protected from the glare of the light by the hat. The birds are seen sitting about on the ground, staring in dazed bewilderment, and are often killed in great numbers in this illegitimate manner.

The Woodcock is said by Lewis to be known to hunters by various local names in different parts of the country, such as "Mud-Snipe," "Blind Snipe," "Big-headed Snipe," and "Marsh-Plover." Its weight is never more than nine and a half ounces, usually not more than seven, and very rarely as much as eight. The female is the larger bird. The usual weight of the European Woodcock is fourteen ounces.

The egg of the Woodcock is of a rounded oval shape, one end being more tapering than the other; it measures 1.50 inches in length by 1.14 in breadth. The ground is a light buffy cream-color, marked over the entire surface with fine dottings and blotches of sepia-brown, intermingled with shadings of a neutral tint and brown, washed with the buff of the ground, causing these spots to assume an opaque ashy hue.

Genus **GALLINAGO**, Leach.

Gallinago, "Leach, Catal. British Birds, 1816," Gray (type *Scolopax major*, L.).

Char. Lower portion of the tibia bare of feathers, scutellate before and behind, reticulated laterally like the tarsi. Nail of hind toe slender, extending beyond the toe. Bill depressed at the tip. Middle toe longer than tarsus. Tail with twelve to twenty-six feathers. Plumage the same in winter and summer; young like the adult in colors and markings. The more slender body, longer legs, partly naked tibia, and other features, distinguish this genus from *Scolopax* and *Philohela*, and the cleft toes from *Macrorhamphus*.

The species of *Gallinago* are quite numerous, about fifteen being recognized, this number nearly equally divided between America and various portions of the Old World. Of the seven American species, North America claims but two, the common Wilson's Snipe, or, as it is perhaps more popularly known, the "English Snipe," from its very close resemblance to the Common Snipe of Europe, and the latter species, which has been taken in Greenland. With a few ex-

G. Wilsoni.

ceptions, the various species resemble one another very closely in colors and markings — so much so in some cases, that it is necessary to resort to the rectrices in order to discover points of positive difference.

The single species peculiar to North America has usually sixteen rectrices, of which the outer is not notably narrower than the rest; its nearest relative, the European *G. cœlestis*, has usually but fourteen tail-feathers, of which the outer pair are differently marked from those of *G. Wilsoni;* the several South American species possess from fourteen to eighteen rectrices, of which the outer pair are very narrow. The two North American species may be distinguished as follows: —

Com. Char. Tail with a sub-terminal band of rufous, succeeded by a black bar. Pileum black, divided longitudinally by a line of pale buff. Dorsal feathers black, broadly edged exteriorly with pale buff; lining of the wing and sides of the body beneath, sharply barred with slate-color on a pure white ground.

1. **G. cœlestis.** Tail-feathers usually 14. Wing, 5.00–5.30; culmen, 2.80–3.00; tarsus 1.25–1.45; middle toe, 1.15–1.40. *Hab.* Palæarctic Region, occasional in Greenland, accidental in the Bermudas.
2. **G. Wilsoni.** Tail-feathers usually 16. Wing, 4.90–5.30; culmen, 2.50–2.70; tarsus, 1.20–1.30; middle toe, 1.10–1.35. *Hab.* North America, South to Middle America in winter.

Gallinago Wilsoni.

THE AMERICAN, OR WILSON'S, SNIPE.

Scolopax Gallinago, Wilson, Am. Orn. VI. 1812, 18, pl. 47, f. 1 (nec Linn.).
Scolopax Wilsoni, Temm. Pl. Col. V. 1824, livr. lxviii. (in text). — Sw. & Rich. F. B. A. II. 1831, 401. — Nutt. Man. II. 1834, 185. — Aud. Orn. Biog. III. 1835, 322; V. 1839, 583, pl. 243; Synop. 1839, 248, B. Am. V. 1842, 339, pl. 350.
Gallinago Wilsoni, Bonap. Comp. List, 1838, 52. — Cassin, in Baird's B. N. Am. 1858, 710. — Baird, Cat. N. Am. B. 1853, no. 523. — Coues, Key, 1872, 262; Check List, 1873, no. 414; 2d ed. 1882, no. 608; Birds N. W. 1874, 475.
Gallinago gallinaria, var. *Wilsoni*, Ridgw. Ann. Lyc. N. Y. X. 1874, 383.
Gallinago media Wilsoni, Ridgw. Nom. N. Am. B. 1881, no. 526*a*.
Scolopax delicatula, Ord, ed. Wils. IX. 1825, 218.
Scolopax Drummondi, Sw. & Rich. F. B. A. II. 1831, 400. — Nutt. Man. II. 1834, 190. — Aud. Orn. Biog. V. 1839, 319; Synop. 1839, 249; B. Am. VI. 1843, 9.
Scolopax Douglasii, Sw. & Rich. F. B. A. II. 1831, 400. — Nutt. Man. II. 1834, 191.
? Scolopax leucurus, Sw. & Rich. t. c. 501. — Nutt. t. c. 617.

Hab. The whole of North and Middle America, breeding from Northern United States northward, migrating south in winter as far as New Granada; throughout the West Indies; Bermuda; accidental in England.

Sp. Char. Bill long, compressed, flattened and slightly expanded toward the tip, punctulated in its terminal half; wings rather long; legs moderate; tail short. Entire upper parts brownish

black; every feather spotted and widely edged with light rufous, yellowish brown, or ashy white; back and rump transversely barred and spotted with the same; a line from the base of the bill over the top of the head. Throat and neck before, dull reddish ashy; wing-feather marked with dull brownish black; other under parts white, with transverse bars of brownish black on the sides, axillary feathers, under wing-coverts, and under tail-coverts; quills brownish black; outer edge of first primary white; tail glossy brownish black, widely tipped with bright rufous, paler at the tip, and with a sub-terminal narrow band of black; outer feathers of tail paler, frequently nearly white, and barred with black throughout their length. Bill brown (greenish gray in life), paler at base and darker toward the end; legs dark brown (light greenish gray in life).

Total length, about 10.50 to 11.50 inches; extent, 16.50 to 17.50; wing, 5.00 to 5.60; tail, 2.25; bill, 2.50 to 2.60; tarsus, 1.25.

In a very large series of specimens from all parts of the continent north of Panama, no variations are noticeable other than what appear of a purely individual character, and these are seldom very pronounced.

Hardly second even to the famed Woodcock as a game-bird, the common American Snipe has a much more extended range than that species. It is found from the Atlantic to the Pacific, in the winter extending its migrations to Mexico and Central and Northern South America, and in the summer breeding as far north as Whale Cove, on Hudson's Bay, on the east, and Sitka, Kadiak, Fort Yukon, and Fort Anderson on the north and west. It breeds from latitude 42° northward; and a few are occasionally known to nest south of that line, and even in Maryland.

Major Wedderburn states that this bird is more or less common in Bermuda during the autumnal migration, coming in October, and a few remaining until the month of January. In October, 1849, an immense number appeared, and remained a few days. Some are killed from year to year in the months of March, April, and May, in their vernal migrations. Mr. Hurdis states that it was occasionally met with as early as the 13th of September. Mr. Leyland found it common in winter near Omoa. Mr. G. C. Taylor observed it near Comayagua, and has no doubt that it is very common there in the rainy season; and Mr. Salvin met with it in Guatemala. Professor Newton mentions its occurrence in St. Croix in the fall, but not in numbers. It is included by Léotaud among the common birds of the Island of Trinidad, where by many it is regarded as a resident species. The last-named author speaks of it as having the same appearance, the same cry, and the same habits as the common Snipe of Europe. Its flesh is deservedly held in high esteem. It prefers low, moist, and partially inundated meadows, where it is quite common. Hearne, in his "Journey to the Northern Ocean" (p. 425), mentions this Snipe as visiting Hudson's Bay in considerable numbers, but as only very rarely seen north of Whale Cove. Bischoff obtained specimens at Sitka and Kadiak, and Dall found it rare on the Yukon.

Mr. Kennicott saw it breeding at Fort Yukon, May 29. He noticed the male on two occasions perched on the top of a small spruce near its nest, and when startled it flew to other trees, instead of alighting on the ground. It uttered at slight intervals a series of notes a little in the style of the small Virginia Rail, but on a higher key, like *kàk-kak-kak*, and not so rapidly as the Rail. The nest was on a small, nearly naked tussock, surrounded by water, on the edge of a narrow marsh, in the woods, thickly interspersed with large willows. On the land, within a few yards of the nest, was a large thick growth of spruce. The nest was a simple depression, rather deeper than that of *Totanus flavipes*, lined with a little dry grass, and containing three eggs; a fourth was taken from the ovaries of the female.

Captain Bendire mentions the Snipe as present and breeding in Southeastern Oregon, but as not being common there. He met with one on the 15th of February, and also noticed a pair in June, 1876, which were undoubtedly nesting in the marsh from which he started them. Mr. Aiken speaks of it as common in Colorado during the migrations, a few remaining during the winter. In Northeastern Illinois, near Lake Michigan, Mr. Nelson found it a not very rare summer resident, arriving about the 1st of April, nearly all having passed on by the 1st of May. He has found several pairs evidently breeding in the marshes near Waukegan.

Mr. Batty writes us that, while the Snipe returns to Long Island from the north in September, it is most numerous in October, and that it sometimes remains until very late in the season. He killed seven on the 28th of October, 1872, the ground being frozen hard at the time, and having been so for several days. The birds were in high grass, in an elevated part of the meadows. He also states that a few must breed in Connecticut and Massachusetts, as he has seen the young when only a few days old, early in June, near Springfield and New Haven. Mr. Boardman also informs us that he has found the Snipe near St. Stephen's on the 14th of November, when the thermometer stood at 14° above zero.

Mr. J. A. Allen found this species exceedingly abundant in September in the Valley of Great Salt Lake; and Mr. Ridgway speaks of it as a common spring and autumnal bird over all the wet, grassy portions of the interior, both in river valleys and in mountain parks. According to Dr. Cooper, it is abundant in the middle and northern parts of California during winter; but few go to the southern part of the State, on account of its greater dryness. He met with it along the Mojave and Colorado rivers as late as April, and thinks that this bird leaves the lower country about the 1st of May. He saw it about Lake Tahoe in September, and was informed that it breeds there. He also saw this species at Cama, on Prairie Creek, on the eastern border of the Columbia Plains, about the end of September; and Mr. R. Browne also includes this species in his list of the birds found on Vancouver Island.

According to Giraud, this species is known on Long Island as the English Snipe. It arrives on that island early in March, and after spending a short time in the marshy groves in recruiting, it passes on to the north to breed. It returns in September with its young, and during the autumn gets into excellent condition, and is highly prized as game. It is usually found on low, wet meadows and boggy grounds. When flushed it moves off in an irregular manner; but having gone a short distance, its flight becomes more steady. This is a somewhat difficult bird to shoot. It remains in the autumn until the ground becomes frozen, when it passes on to the south. In its migrations it flies high, and at intervals it is said to utter a peculiar cry, which is described as bleating.

A writer in "Doughty's Cabinet" (Vol. I. p. 87) states that near Philadelphia the Snipe season commences in March and continues until the middle of April. The birds are poor on their first arrival, but soon become fat on the rich feeding-grounds in that vicinity, in all the low lands that border the Delaware and the Schuylkill rivers. To shoot Snipe dexterously is a difficult art to acquire, and demands both cool judgment and some deliberation. The sudden and silent manner in which this bird rises from the ground, and the zigzag character of its flight, seem to make calculation almost impossible; and an inexperienced sportsman is apt to fire too soon. In rising, the Snipe usually attains the height of about six feet, and then darts off in this uncertain manner, uttering a peculiar cry; after continuing in this way about twenty yards, it follows a straight course, ascending until it reaches a certain height, when it gradually descends, when near the earth dropping suddenly into the grass.

The true way to hunt the Snipe is said to be with the wind, as they lie closer to the sportsman, and will immediately after rising head the wind, and present a convenient cross-shot. It is also recommended that the shot be reserved until the irregularity of the bird's flight is over, this rarely continuing for more than twenty yards. At times the Snipe is shy, and difficult to approach, springing up beyond the reach of shot; and at other times it is so unsuspicious as not to fly until almost trodden upon. The reasons for this great difference are not satisfactorily explained.

By some it is suggested that the tameness of the birds may be accounted for by supposing that their fatigued and hungry condition renders them tenacious of their good feeding-ground, and reluctant to leave it.

The Snipe is occasionally found in swampy thickets, but more generally in open meadows with a soft bottom. It leaves the Middle States by the end of April, and reaches its breeding-place early in May, where it remains until October. In the fall it is much fatter and more tender than in the spring. Although thus concentrating in rich feeding-grounds, yet the Snipe is by nature a solitary bird, and in its movements to and from its breeding-place it always proceeds singly. It spends its winter in the Southern States, as well as in regions farther south, and congregates in the Carolina rice-fields in immense numbers, and is much more confiding and tame than at the North. It commences its northern migrations in February, reaching Delaware in March, and becoming abundant in Pennsylvania in April. Its stay in any place during its spring migrations varies both in date and length, being controlled by the season and the abundance of its food. This consists largely of worms, larvæ, small insects, and the tender roots of aquatic plants. In confinement this bird will feed greedily upon corn-meal and worms, and can soon be accustomed to a diet of bread and milk.

Lewis ("American Sportsman," p. 184) describes some very singular manœuvres of the Snipe which he witnessed in the spring. At early dawn he saw a pair mount high in the air, beating their wings and sailing around in rapid circles, until they had gained an elevation of a hundred yards or more; then, approaching closely to each other, they whirled around, flapping their wings with great rapidity, and suddenly dropped in mid-air, giving utterance at the same time to a low twittering, or rather a rolling sound, said to be produced by the action of their wings upon the air in their rapid descent. Toward the close of April all these birds that are mated move northward to their breeding-places; but a few remain in the low marshy places of Pennsylvania all summer, and even rear their broods. In May, 1846, as Mr. Lewis was crossing an estate in Maryland, he started up one of this species from the midst of an oat-field; and being attracted by its singular manœuvres, made search for its nest, which was found to contain four eggs. It was placed on a rising piece of ground not far from a marshy meadow.

The Snipe leaves its more northern breeding-places late in September with its young, stopping at favorable localities on the way. It remains several weeks in Pennsylvania and Delaware, and becomes very fat during its stay. In their migrations these birds move with great rapidity, and spread themselves over a wide extent of country in a very short space of time. They are voracious feeders, and obliged to shift their ground with great frequency. From situations where there is a plentiful supply of food, it is hardly possible to drive them entirely away. The Snipe is said to be better eating in the autumn than in the spring.

On Hudson's Bay — according to Hearne — the Snipe does not arrive until the ice of the rivers is broken up, and it retires to the south early in the fall. During its stay it always frequents the marshes near the sea-coast, as well as the shores of the great rivers. In its manner and flight it seemed to him exactly to resemble the European Snipe; but its flesh he considered to be by no means so delicate.

Captain Blakiston noted the arrival of the Snipe in the neighborhood of Fort Carlton as never earlier than May, while the last were seen in the autumn on the Lower Saskatchewan on the 1st of October. At the Red River settlement he found it on the 29th of April, where it arrives even earlier. He noticed that it performed the same aerial evolutions as the European bird, this usually occurring about sunset, but at times continuing an hour and a half later. The noise made on these occasions he compares to rapidly repeated switches of a cane in the air; and this was repeated every half-minute, with occasional longer intervals. The sound lasted about three seconds, and was made as the bird descended rapidly in a vertical direction, being caused apparently by the quill-feathers of the wings. This sometimes took place in the middle of the day, but only during the love-season.

According to Dresser, the Snipe is very common about San Antonio, Texas, during the winter, and was last noticed on the 20th of April, none having been seen during the previous week; according to Mr. Moore, it passes the winter in Florida.

Attention has been called by different writers to the occasional perching of the Snipe on trees, as if something unusual; but it is by no means an uncommon occurrence during the breeding-season, and the bird is said to do this chiefly or wholly when its nest or young are disturbed.

The nest of the Snipe is always on the ground, and is constructed in the most simple manner, it being nothing more than a hollow made in the grass or moss, and lined with a little dry grass or a few feathers. The usual number of the eggs is four, and the young run about as soon as they are hatched. At first they feed on larvæ, small insects, and snails; but at the end of a few weeks their bills have sufficiently hardened to enable them to penetrate into the moist ground and obtain the worms they prefer.

Mr. MacFarlane found the Snipe breeding near Fort Anderson, June 16. The nest was on the ground, and was composed of a few decayed leaves placed in a small hole made in the earth. Another nest was obtained in the same neighborhood, June 29, near a small lake, and was a mere hole in the ground, lined with a small quantity of hay and a few decayed leaves. I have an egg of this species taken from a nest on the Delaware, near Philadelphia, and others from Niagara Falls, Northern New York, Lake Koskonong, Wisconsin, Pictou, Nova Scotia, and Dakota Territory.

The eggs of this species are always four in number, and of a pyriform shape, with one end broadly obtuse and the other rapidly tapering. The ground-color is usually of a light olivaceous brown; in some it is of a light grayish drab, and occasionally a rufous drab. The spots are uniformly of a bright sepia, small and scattered at the smaller apex, but larger, and often confluent, about the other end. The eggs measure 1.50 inches in length and 1.18 in breadth, and are less variable in size than those of most of the Wading-birds.

Gallinago cœlestis.

THE EUROPEAN SNIPE.

Scolopax gallinago, LINN. S. N. ed. 10, 1758, 147; ed. 10, 1766, 244. — NAUM. Vög. Deutschl. VII. 1836, 310, pl. 209. — SCHLEG. Rev. Crit. 86. — MACGILL. Man. II. 103.

Ascolopax gallinago, KEYS. & BLAS. Wirb. Eur. 77.

Scolopax coelestis, FRENZEL, Besch. Vög. Eier Geg. Wittenb. 1801, 58 (cf. STEJNEGER, Proc. U. S. Nat. Mus. Vol. 5, 1882, p. 35).

Gallinago media, LEACH. Syst. Cat. 1816, 31. — STEPH. Gen. Zool. XII. 54. — GRAY, Gen. B. III. 583; Cat. Brit. B. 1863, 173. — RIDGW. Nom. N. Am. B. 1881, no. 526. — COUES, Check List, 2d ed. 1882, no. 607.

Gallinago scolopacinus, BONAP. Comp. List, 1838, 52.

Telmatias septentrionalis, stagnatilis, and *fœrœnsis*, BREHM, Vög. Deutschl.

? *Scolopax Delamotti*, MATTH. in Zoologist, 1852, 3729.

Common Snipe, YARR. Brit. B. ed. 2, III. 25, fig.; ed. 3, III. 31, fig.; et AUCT.

HAB. Palæarctic Region; frequent in Greenland (cf. REINHARDT, "Ibis," 1861, p. 11), and accidental in the Bermudas.

SP. CHAR. Exceedingly similar to *G. Wilsoni*, the difference in coloration scarcely definable. Tail-feathers usually 14 instead of 16, the outer pair with the basal half of the inner web dusky, the terminal half pale creamy-rufous, tipped with white, and crossed by two bars of blackish; the outer web whitish, with about four dusky bars. Lining of the wing mostly white. Wing averaging shorter (5.00–5.30), and bill longer (culmen 2.80–3.00), than in *G. Wilsoni;* tarsi and toes also longer (tarsus, 1.25–1.45; middle toe, 1.15–1.40).

By colors alone it is hardly possible to distinguish this species with certainty from *G. Wilsoni;* the difference in proportions, however, appears quite constant, *G. cœlestis* having the bill decidedly longer, as are also the tarsi and toes, while the wings are shorter.

The difference in the number of tail-feathers appears to be by no means constant (cf. HARTING, "Hand-book Brit. Birds," 1872, pp. 143, 144, footnote).

This species, the Common Snipe of Europe, occurs not unfrequently in Greenland, and occasionally in Bermuda. It has not been, so far as known, detected in North America, though its accidental occurrence may be looked for as quite probable. Its rare appearance in Bermuda, though unchallenged, can only be regarded as an accident. One was said to have been taken by Major Wedderburn, Dec. 24, 1847, and a second on the 29th of the same month. In Greenland, on the other hand, it was so common that Reinhardt has no doubt that it breeds there. This, however, is simply conjectural — no eggs of this species having been obtained in that country.

This species has a pretty general distribution over Europe, appearing in the southern portions during the wintry months, and going to the more northern countries during the season of reproduction.

In the British Islands it is found more or less abundant throughout the year. A limited number continue during the summer, and breed in all parts, from the southern counties of England to the mountains of Scotland, being more numerous in the northern districts. In the fall the numbers are greatly increased by migrants coming from more northern breeding-places.

It is a common species throughout Scandinavia, where it is migratory, only appearing in March, and leaving soon after the close of the breeding-season. Mr. Lloyd, in his "Field-Sports of the North of Europe," states that he found it very numerous in the marshes in the vicinity of Gothenburg. Linnæus, in his "Tour in Lapland," states that on the 14th of May, when near Gefle, he heard the note of the Snipe in the marshes continually. It breeds in extensive morasses and swamps in the mountainous districts of Norway and Sweden, as well as in the smaller bogs of the cultivated districts. From the northern parts of Scandinavia it migrates south in the middle of August; but in the south of Sweden it lingers until October.

In the summer this bird extends its migrations to the Faröe Islands, Iceland, and Greenland, and is also found at the same season in all the northern portions of Russia and Siberia, breeding as far to the south as France, Germany, Holland, Hungary, and Illyria.

In the winter it extends its migrations to Spain, Italy, Sicily, and Malta. This bird is said to be abundant in the marshes about Smyrna, and to be also found in Lower Egypt. It is mentioned by Messrs. Blakiston and Pryer ("Ibis," 1878, p. 222) as common throughout Japan. The birds referred to by Mr. Swinhoe as *G. Wilsoni* ("Ibis," 1875, p. 454) were probably of this species, in their autumnal plumage. They had been received from Hakodadi.

In England, the native Snipes are reinforced by the great flights that take place from Norway and other northern parts of Europe, arriving in the greatest numbers in the beginning of November. They do not remain long in any one situation, but move from place to place; so that it is quite common for the sportsman to find them abundant one day, and that the same place is entirely deserted the next.

Their summer or nuptial plumage is put on about the last of March or the first of April, and the male begins his calls of invitation to his mate. These are always uttered when the bird is on the wing, and are said by Yarrell to consist of piping or clicking notes, often repeated, and accompanied at intervals by a humming or bleating noise. This latter sound is supposed to be produced by a peculiar action of the wings, and is said to be not unlike the cry of a goat, for which reason this bird is known in France by the name of *chèvre volant*. Whenever this sound is heard, the bird is observed always to descend with great velocity and with a tremulous motion of the wings. At this season it is also said to soar to an immense height, remaining long upon the wing, its notes being frequently heard when the bird itself is out of sight. These flights are performed at intervals throughout the day, but are more common toward the evening, and are continued as long as the female is engaged in incubation. Sir Humphry Davy states that the old birds are greatly attached to their offspring, and that if any one approaches the nest, they make a loud and drumming noise over the head of the intruder, as if to divert his attention.

The feeding-ground of this Snipe is in the vicinity of springs and in freshwater meadows. It feeds by thrusting its bill into the thin mud or soft earth up to the base, and drawing it back with great quickness. Yarrell states that the end of the bill of a Snipe, when the bird is living, is smooth, soft, and pulpy, indicating great sensibility. When dry it becomes dimpled like the end of a thimble. If the upper mandible be macerated and the cuticle taken off, the bone laid bare will be found presenting on its external surface numerous elongated hexagonal cells, which furnish space for the expansion, and at the same time protection for minute portions of nerves supplied to them from the fifth pair. In consequence of this provision, the end of the bill becomes a delicate organ of touch, enabling the bird to perceive the presence of its food, even when this lies so deep in the ground as to be entirely out of sight. The food of this Snipe consists of worms, insects, small shells with their inhabitants, etc. Minute seeds are sometimes found in its stomach; but these are supposed to be swallowed accidentally, and when adhering to the glutinous surface of its usual food. A Snipe kept in confinement by Mr. Blyth would eat nothing but earth-worms.

The nests of this Snipe are placed on the ground, and are very inartificial. They are usually among the long grass, by the side of small ponds, or amidst the long heather which grows upon the sides of the hills. Mr. Hewitson met with several of its nests on the Shetland Islands, in the dry heath on the side of a steep hill, at an elevation of a thousand feet above the marshy plain. The nest is always very slight, consisting only of a few bits of dry grass or herbage collected in a depression on the ground, and sometimes upon or under the side of a tuft of grass or bunch of rushes.

The eggs are said to be four in number — occasionally less — having a pale yellowish-white ground, and being marked with elongated blotches of several shades of reddish and yellowish brown; these markings are chiefly about the more obtuse end. The eggs are pyriform in shape, and quite pointed at one end. They measure 1.50 inches in length by 1.08 in breadth.

The young birds are carefully tended, and grow with great rapidity; and before they can fly are larger than their parents.

GENUS **MACRORHAMPHUS**, LEACH.

Macrorhamphus, "LEACH, Cat. Brit. Birds, 1816," GRAY (type, *Scolopax grisea*, GM.).

CHAR. General appearance of *Gallinago*. Tarsi longer than middle toe; a short web between the base of outer and middle toe. Plumage very different in winter and summer; young different from the adult.

The membrane at the base of the toes will at once distinguish this genus from *Gallinago*, though there are other characters involved.

M. griseus.

But a single species of this genus is known; this inhabits the whole of North America, breeding in the northern regions, and occurring more or less frequently in Europe.

The single species of this genus, with its two well-marked geographical races, is characterized as follows: —

1. **M. griseus.** About the size of *Gallinago Wilsoni*, or larger. Bill long, compressed, flattened and expanded toward the end, where (in dried specimens) punctulated and corrugated. Shaft of first primary strong, pure white. Axillars, tail-coverts, and lower part of rump, white, barred, or transversely spotted, with slate-color; upper part of rump white, usually immaculate. Tail slaty or dusky, barred with white (or, in summer adult, with pale cinnamon on the middle feathers). *Adult in summer:* Head, neck, and lower parts light cinnamon (the abdomen sometimes whitish), the foreneck and sides of breast speckled, the sides and crissum barred or speckled with dusky. Upper parts mixed black, light cinnamon, and white, the former prevailing. *Adult in winter:* Belly and anal region white, usually unspotted; rest of the plumage nearly uniform ash-gray, somewhat intermixed with white on the breast and sides; wing-coverts bordered with whitish; a whitish superciliary stripe. *Young, first plumage:* Back, scapulars, and tertials, variegated black and light clay-color, the latter chiefly on the edges of the feathers; lower parts dirty white, soiled with dull buff or pale clay color, especially across the breast; jugulum and sides usually indistinctly speckled with dusky. Total length, about 10.00 to 12.50 inches; extent, 17.50 to 20.25; wing, 5.30–6.00 (5.73); culmen, 2.00–3.00; tarsus, 1.25–1.75 (1.53); middle toe, .90–1.10 (1.00).

a. griseus. Wing, 5.25–5.90 (5.65); culmen, 2.00–2.55 (2.30); tarsus, 1.20–1.55 (1.35); middle toe, .90–1.05 (.95).[1] *Adult in summer:* Abdomen whitish; breast and sides speckled with dusky. *Hab.* Atlantic coast of North America.

β. scolopaceus. Wing, 5.40–6.00 (5.74); culmen, 2.10–3.00 (2.72); tarsus, 1.35–1.75 (1.58); middle toe, .95–1.15 (1.01).[2] *Adult in summer:* Abdomen uniform cinnamon, without markings; breast speckled (usually scantily), and sides barred with dusky. *Hab.* Mississippi Valley and Western Province of North America, from Mexico to Alaska.

[1] Extremes and average of eighteen fully adult specimens.

[2] Extremes and average of forty fully adult specimens.

Macrorhamphus griseus.

a. Griseus. THE GRAY SNIPE; GRAY-BACK; DOWITCHER.

Scolopax grisea, GMEL. S. N. I. 1788, 658 (based on the *Brown Snipe* of PENNANT and LATHAM).
Macrorhamphus griseus, LEACH, Cat. Brit. Mus. 1816, 31. — CASSIN in Baird's B. N. Am. 1858, 712. — BAIRD, Cat. N. Am. B. 1859, no. 524. — COUES, Key, 1872, 253; Check List, 1873, no. 415; 2d ed. 1882, no. 609; Birds N. W. 1874, 476. — RIDGW. Nom. N. Am. B. 1881, no. 527.
Scolopax noveboracensis, GMEL. S. N. I. 1788, 658 (based on the *Red-breasted Snipe* of PENNANT and LATHAM). — WILS. Am. Orn. VII. 1813, 45, pl. 58, fig. 1. — SW. & RICH. F. B. A. II. 1831, 398. — AUD. Orn. Biog. IV. 1838, 288, pl. 399; Synop. 1839, 249; B. Am. VI. 1843, 10, pl. 351.
Scolopax (*Macrorhamphus*) *grisea*, BONAP. Synop. 1828, 330. — NUTT. Man. II. 1834, 181.
Scolopax Paykullii, NILSS. Orn. Suec. II. 106.
Totanus ferrugineicollis, VIEILL. Enc. Méth. III. 1823, 1099 (based on the *Red-breasted Snipe* of PENNANT and LATHAM).

HAB. Atlantic coast of North America (breeding in the region about Hudson's Bay ?).

SP. CHAR. About the size of *Gallinago Wilsoni.* Shaft of first primary strong, pure white; axillars, tail-coverts, and lower part of rump white, barred, or transversely spotted, with slate-color; upper part of rump white, usually immaculate; tail slate-colored or dusky, barred with white (or, in summer adult, with pale cinnamon on middle feathers). *Adult in summer:* Head, neck, and more or less of lower parts, light cinnamon, the abdomen whitish, breast and sides speckled with dusky, the head and neck streaked with the same; upper parts mixed black, light cinnamon, and white, the first prevailing. *Winter plumage:* Belly and anal region white, usually

M. griseus, summer plumage.

unmarked; rest of plumage nearly uniform ash-gray, somewhat mixed with white on breast and sides; a whitish superciliary stripe, and wing-coverts bordered with white. *Young:* Back, scapulars, and tertials, varied with black and light clay-brown, the latter chiefly on edges of the feathers; lower parts dull whitish, soiled with dull buff or clay-color, especially across breast, the jugulum and sides usually indistinctly speckled with dusky. "Bill dark olive; iris reddish hazel; feet light yellowish olive; claws black" (AUDUBON).

Wing, 5.25–5.90 (5.65); culmen, 2.00–2.55 (2.30); tarsus, 1.20–1.55 (1.35); middle toe, .90–1.05 (.95).

b. Scolopaceus. THE RED-BELLIED SNIPE; GREATER LONG-BEAK.

Limosa scolopacea, SAY, Long's Exped. II. 1823, 170.
Macrorhamphus scolopaceus, LAWR. Ann. Lyc. N. Y. V. 1852, 4, pl. 1 (Long Island). — CASS. in Baird's B. N. Am. 1858, 712. — BAIRD, Cat. N. Am. B. 1859, no. 525.
Macrorhamphus griseus, var. *scolopaceus*, COUES, Check List, 1873, no. 415*a*.
Scolopax longirostris, BELL, Ann. Lyc. N. Y. V. 1852, 3.
Macrorhamphus griseus (part), COUES, Key, 1872, 253; B. N. W. 1874, 476.

HAB. North America in general, but chiefly the western portions of the continent; east to the Mississippi Valley, north to Alaska, and south to South America and the West Indies. Occasional along the Atlantic coast of the United States.

CHAR. *Adult in summer:* Similar to *M. griseus*, but abdomen pale cinnamon, like rest of

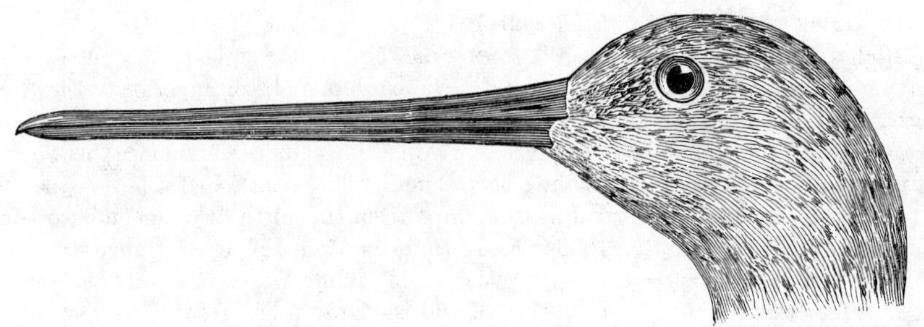

M. griseus scolopaceus, summer plumage.

lower parts, and without markings, the breast scantily speckled and the sides barred with dusky. *Winter plumage and young:* Distinguishable from the corresponding stages of *M. griseus* only (?) by larger size.

Wing, 5.40–6.00 (5.74); culmen, 2.10–3.00 (2.72); tarsus, 1.35–1.75 (1.58); middle toe, .95–1.15 (1.01).

The Red-breasted Snipe appears to be common, at different seasons of the year, in nearly all parts of North America, from the Pacific to the Atlantic shores. During the winter it is found in our Gulf States, in Mexico, in Central and South America, and the West Indies. It breeds, in favorable localities, from lat. 44° N. to the Arctic Ocean. Occasional specimens have been taken in Bermuda.

Mr. Salvin mentions the capture of a single specimen of this bird at San Geronimo, Guatemala; and afterward speaks of finding it common on the Pacific coast of that region, where it frequented the sand-banks. He used always to see it feeding on the open flats, where there was no cover whatever, its habits strongly contrasting in this respect with those of the common Snipe. This bird and the *Scolopax rusticola* of Europe seemed to him to represent two extremes as regards choice of feeding-grounds, the true Snipe occupying an intermediate place in their preference for grass and seeds. It is found along the whole Pacific coast; and though it has not been noticed in the more southern portions of California, it has been taken in Chili, and, on the eastern side, in Brazil. Mr. Dall met with it at Pastolik and at the mouth of the Yukon, where, however, it was not common. Mr. R. Browne mentions it in his list of the birds of Vancouver Island. Dr. Cooper, while he had not met with it in Southern California, found it common in the middle of that State from September to April, frequenting the borders of marshes, ponds, and sand-bars in large flocks, but not so common near the sea-coast. He also found it in the interior among the Cordilleras. Great numbers are brought to the San Francisco market, where they are regarded as among the best of the smaller game-birds.

This Snipe is given by Léotaud as a regular visitant in the Island of Trinidad, coming from July to October. It is usually in flocks, and unmixed with other Waders, but is occasionally accompanied by the Yellowshanks. It is spoken of as keeping principally about the borders of the sea, and also as being frequently found in the marshy grounds not distant from the shore. Its flight is not very rapid, and in taking to wing it does not make any very decided turnings. Its habits, he remarks, are very similar to those of *Micropalama himantopus*.

This species is found in suitable places throughout the interior of the continent, both in the spring and fall migrations. It is more or less common at Lake Koskonong, Wisconsin, where, about Aug. 15, 1873, it was found in unusually large numbers by Mr. Kumlien. It is included by Mr. H. W. Parker in his list of the birds occurring near Grinnell, Ia. Mr. J. A. Allen found it quite common in Great Salt Lake Valley after the 25th of September.

Richardson speaks of it as a species well known throughout the Fur Country, having an extensive breeding-range from the borders of Lake Superior to the Arctic Sea. Individuals killed on the Saskatchewan plains had their crops filled with leeches and fragments of Coleoptera. Reinhardt includes it among the birds of Greenland, a single specimen having been taken at Fiskernaes in 1854.

Mr. Dresser noted the arrival of this Snipe from the north at a lagoon near Matamoras, as early as June 29, 1863. From that time onward it continued to arrive, some migrating farther south, but a considerable number remaining in the neighborhood. He obtained them in both the red and the gray plumage, and they were very numerous both in July and August. They moved in flocks of from ten to thirty, and seemed to be more nearly related to the Sandpiper than to the Snipe in their habits. He invariably found them on the shores of the lagoons, and often in company with the Sandpipers, especially the Stilt Sandpipers; but never in the same localities with Wilson's Snipe.

We are informed by Mr. Boardman that this species probably breeds in the neighborhood of Calais, where it is occasionally seen throughout the summer. In the winter he has found it very numerous in Florida, where it goes in large flocks, and where he once killed thirty at a single shot.

According to Mr. Moore's observations, some of these birds are found in Florida also, throughout the summer, though none of these breed there. Scattered individuals of this species were seen by him on the Sarasota Bay during every month of the year; but those that are thus resident do not assume the summer plumage. Others were noticed there, both when leaving in the spring and arriving in autumn, ten of the latter being seen as early as July 10 in very fine summer plumage. Those that remain throughout the year do not appear at all like these in beauty of coloring, only exhibiting on the wing-coverts and upper parts, here and there, a slight touch of rufous.

This bird has, in a number of instances, been taken in Europe, especially in Great Britain, where six or more specimens have been singly secured. One captured in Sweden was described and figured by Nilsson as a new species. On Long Island Giraud states that this Snipe is known to the hunters by the old provincial name of Dowitcher. It reaches the shores of that island about the close of April, and there resorts to the mud-flats and shoals. At high-tide it retires to the boggy meadows, where it probes the soft ground for worms. The stay of this bird in the spring is short; but about the middle of July it returns with its young, and remains until the end of September. It has a very peculiar whistling note, and one that is easily imitated by hunters, so as to deceive and attract the bird, which is noted for its unsuspicious character. This Snipe is fond of resorting to the freshwater ponds which stand on the low parts of the meadows during the wet season, and such situations are favorable for its capture. Concealed in the rank grass which grows on the salt meadows, the hunter, when he hears the notes of a passing flock, utters a shrill whistle in imitation of their peculiar cry, this being pretty sure to attract the birds. Flying close together and hovering over the flock of decoys, they are easily shot; and it not unfrequently happens that those which escape the first fire return and alight among the dead bodies of their companions, only to share their fate. In dry seasons the scattered flocks feed along the muddy flats, wading in the shoal-water, although seldom to any great depth. Even in these exposed situations but little address is required to approach the bird within shooting distance.

This Snipe is capable of a rapid and protracted flight, which at times is performed at a great elevation. During the dry season, when in search of feeding-grounds, it flies high, and will not be easily decoyed. It is very abundant at Egg Harbor, N. J., where it is known as the Brown Snipe, and also as the Quail Snipe, from its peculiar Quail-like whistle.

In the Atlantic States, according to Lewis ("American Sportsman," p. 241), this Snipe seems to confine itself to the salt-marshes, and there congregates in immense flocks. That author gives the time of its arrival in New Jersey as the first week in May, and that of its return as the middle of July, when it remains until the commencement of cold weather. These birds fly in large flocks, collect in thick masses upon the points to feed, and will suffer a boat to approach near enough to give them a raking fire. They are less wary than most of the shore-birds, and when feeding in company with other species are always the last to take the alarm.

By different explorers this species has been found breeding at various points in the Arctic Region; as, for instance, Fort Yukon, Big Island, Fort Rae, Pastolik, etc. Mr. E. Adams met with it near Michaelaski, Alaska ("Ibis," 1878), where it arrived on the 20th of May, and soon spread over the marshes, singly or in pairs; but the greater number of them frequented the salt-marsh, where they fed about the mud in company with flocks of *Actodromas minutilla* and *Pelidna americana*, the only birds with which they were seen to associate.

Mr. MacFarlane found this species breeding in the Arctic Region, in the vicinity of Fort Anderson. The nests were taken between the 21st of June and the 1st of July, the usual number of eggs in a nest appearing to be four. The nests were placed on the marshy borders of small lakes, and were composed of a few decayed leaves placed in a depression in the mossy ground. In one instance the female was sitting on the nest, and when approached, ascended in the air, uttering shrill and long-continued notes of alarm and annoyance. She was then, after a few minutes, seen to descend in a perpendicular manner to her nest.

The eggs of this species are of a decidedly pyriform shape, and vary considerably in size — namely, from 1.55 to 1.75 inches in length, and from 1.08 to 1.20 in breadth. In some examples the ground is drab, with blended shadings of rufous and olivaceous; in others, the ground is a fawn-colored drab, more slightly olivaceous. The markings are uniformly sepia in color, somewhat intensified about the larger end, and of less size and more scattered at the smaller end.

It is not possible to give an exact account of the distinctive habits of the form called "*scolopaceus*," if it really possesses any that are peculiar to it or distinguishable from those of the preceding. Nor can it be stated with certainty how far, if at all, its distribution differs from that of the more common Red-breasted Snipe. In the dress of the *scolopaceus* this form has been met with both on the Atlantic and on the Pacific coast. It is found in the interior; and, in the winter, has also been met with in Central America. Würdemann secured examples in Florida, and Professor Kumlien has procured birds of this form both in the spring and in the fall, near Lake Koskonong. Lieutenant Warren obtained a single individual on the Missouri River, near Omaha, Nebraska. It has been found very common among the lagoons on the Pacific coast, near San Pedro, in California ("Ibis," 1866, p. 27). It was described as not apparently ever going down to the salt-flats, its habits being given as somewhat similar to those of *Micropalama himantopus,* and therefore inferentially different from those of *M. griseus.*

Mr. Dall mentions the *M. scolopaceus* as common about the mouth of the River Yukon, where the *M. griseus* is spoken of as being very rare up that river. At Nulato this same form is mentioned by Mr. Bannister as being quite common, though not extremely abundant; he found the nest of this Snipe on the 3d of June, and on the 6th secured the parent with the eggs. The nest was a simple hollow in the ground in a grassy hummock, in the centre of a marshy spot, with scarcely any lining whatever; there was nothing in the shape of a nest substantial enough to be removed. The eggs were four in number, and Mr. Bannister describes them as of a brownish color, mottled with a still deeper tint. The female when startled from the nest shuffled off with great rapidity among the grassy hummocks, presenting a very difficult mark to hit. Only one parent bird was seen.

Dr. Cooper states that on the extensive level plains south of Los Angeles he found this species quite abundant during the middle of October, 1865. He also observed that bunches of them, unmixed with any other species, were sold in the town under the name of "Jack Snipe;" while the species commonly known by this name, *Actodromas maculata,* has not, to his knowledge, been met with south of San Francisco. The present species was found frequenting the brackish lagoons and river-banks exclusively, never appearing about the salt-marshes, which are the favorite places of resort of the more northern and eastern form, the *M. griseus.* The birds kept in small flocks, and alighted so close together, that several could be killed at a single shot. They usually fed in water as deep as their long legs and bill would allow them to wade in, probing the bottom.

Mr. George N. Lawrence, in his paper first describing this form, read Jan. 7, 1849, mentions that this bird is found abundantly on the shores of the Gulf of Mexico in winter, that its principal migration is up the Mississippi Valley and farther west, but that it is rare on the Atlantic coast. It is given by the same writer ("Birds of Southern Mexico") as having been taken at San Mateo, Tehuantepec, in August and February. Mr. Lawrence, in his Notes on Cuban Birds (May 21, 1860) also refers to a specimen sent to him by Dr. Gundlach from Cuba. He regards its rarity on our coast, where the *griseus* is so very common, as furnishing further evidence of its distinctness as a species. It makes its appearance quite early in the spring, and is found in the New York market in April, fully three weeks before any of the more common varieties are to be seen. And in this connection I may state that I have received a fine specimen of a female shot on Cape Cod, Mass., as late as November 3, or long after all of the other variety had gone.

Dr. Kennerly, in his Notes on the Birds observed along the Mexican Boundary, speaks of this species as very rare, and as having been only observed occasionally in the valley of the Conalitos River, and once in the Valley of the Peletado. A pair were seen together, and both secured; but no others were obtained.

Eggs in the Smithsonian Collection, marked as having been obtained by Mr. Bannister on the Island of St. Michael's, May 23, 1866, are larger than any eggs of the *griseus* we have ever seen, measuring 1.80 inches in length, by 1.15 inches in breadth. They have a ground of a well-pronounced rufous drab, blotched with much darker markings of a deep shade of sepia brown.

GENUS **MICROPALAMA**, BAIRD.

Hemipalama, BONAP. Synop. 1828, 316 (type, *Tringa himantopus*, BONAP.; nec BONAP. Obs. Wilson, 1825, no. 212, which includes only *Tringa semipalmata*, WILS.).
Micropalama, BAIRD, Birds N. Am. 1858, 726 (type, *Tringa himantopus*, BONAP.).

CHAR. Form slender, the legs very long, the bill long and much compressed, the anterior toes all webbed at the base. Tarsus nearly twice as long as the middle toe, which is a little shorter than the bare portion of the tibiæ, this scutellate before and behind, like the tarsus. Bill slender, straight, about equal to the tarsus, greatly compressed, except at the end, which is decidedly expanded laterally. Tail nearly even, but the central and exterior feathers usually perceptibly longer than the rest. Wings long and pointed.

The present genus, with a basal membrane to all the anterior toes, as in *Ereunetes*, has this a little more deeply emarginate; the bill and legs much longer; the former more curved. The bare portion of tibia is covered before and behind by transverse scutellæ, like the tarsus. The tail is nearly even, with a double emargination. The middle toe is not two thirds the length of the tarsus, but about equal to the bare portion of the tibia. The bill is much pitted at the end in the dry skin.

In many respects this species approaches the Snipes, and its true place is probably very near *Macrorhamphus*. The legs, however, are much longer, and equal to the bill, instead of being much shorter.

Micropalama himantopus.

THE STILT SANDPIPER.

Tringa himantopus, BONAP. Ann. Lyc. N. Y. II. 1826, 157. — SW. & RICH. F. B. A. II. 1831, 380. — AUD. Orn. Biog. IV. 1838, 332, pl. 334; Synop. 1839, 235; B. Am. V. 1842, 271, pl. 334.
Tringa (*Hemipalama*) *himantopus*, BONAP. Specc. Comp. 1827, 61. — NUTT. Man. II. 1834, 138.
Micropalama himantopus, CASS. in Baird's B. N. Am. 1858, 726. — BAIRD, Cat. N. Am. B. 1859, no. 536. — COUES, Key, 1872, 253; Check List, 1873, no. 416; 2d ed. 1882, no. 611; Birds N. W. 1874, 480. — RIDGW. Nom. N. Am. B. 1881, no. 528.
Hemipalama multistrigata, GRAY, Gen. B. III. 1849, 578, pl. 156.
Tringa Douglasii, SW. & RICH. F. B. A. II. 1831, 379, pl. 66.
Tringa (*Hemipalama*) *Douglasii*, NUTT. Man. II. 1834, 141.
Tringa (*Hemipalama*) *Auduboni*, NUTT. t. c. 141.

HAB. Eastern Province of North America, Middle America, and greater part of South America; breeding north of the United States, and visiting the southern localities in winter; Bermudas; West Indies, in general; Brazil; Peru. Not recorded from west of the Rocky Mountains.

SP. CHAR. *Adult, summer plumage:* Above, variegated with black, whitish gray, and pale buff, the first prevailing on the back and scapulars; wings rather dark gray, the feathers edged with

paler; primaries dusky slate; rump grayish, the feathers with darker centres; upper tail-coverts white, the longer ones barred, the anterior ones longitudinally marked with dusky. Middle tail-feathers light gray, the others varied longitudinally with white and pale gray. Pileum dusky, streaked with whitish ; a dark-brown loral stripe, from base of maxilla to the eyes ; auriculars and patch on each side the occiput, light cinnamon-rufous. Lower parts dirty white, the throat and jugulum streaked, other portions transversely barred with dusky. Lining of the wing, and axillars, white, the latter slightly marked with gray. *Adult in winter:* Above, uniform ash-gray, the upper tail-coverts, tail, and wings, only, as in the summer plumage. Superciliary stripe and lower parts white, the jugulum, sides of the neck, and crissum, streaked with gray. *Young:* Back and scapulars blackish, all the feathers widely bordered with buffy white, the middle of the back tinged with rusty ; wing-coverts bordered with pale buff and white ; upper tail-coverts nearly immaculate white. Pileum streaked with dusky, pale buff, and grayish ; nape nearly uniform ash-gray. Lower parts soiled white, the breast and sides more or less strongly suffused with buff, the jugulum, sides of the neck, and flanks, indistinctly streaked with grayish. "Bill black ; iris brown ; feet dull yellowish green, claws black" (AUDUBON).

Wing, about 5.00–5.25 ; culmen, 1-50–1.75 ; tarsus, 1.50–1.75 ; middle toe, .80–.85.

The Stilt Sandpiper, once regarded as a very rare species, has within a few years been found to be far from uncommon in different parts of the country. It has not been met with, that I am aware, on any portion of the Pacific coast north of Central America; a single individual only was observed by Mr. Salvin in Guatemala. This was taken in the interior, near Dueñas, from among a flock of *Actodromas maculata*, in April. According to Major Wedderburn, it occasionally occurs in Bermuda; and Mr. N. B. Moore mentions procuring four specimens of this species on one of the Bahamas as early as August 5. It visits in winter the West Indies and a large part of South America to Brazil and Peru.

In New England — where it has not been recognized as occurring at all till within a few years — it is of irregular appearance in the summer and fall, but is not known to occur in its spring migrations. It has been seen along the coast of Massachusetts, New Hampshire, and Maine, west of Portland;[1] but not in the interior. A single specimen has been taken on Nantucket, and one reported from Cape Cod. It is only occasionally met with, usually singly, or in pairs, and generally in company with *Totanus flavipes*. It is an occasional straggler rather than a regular migrant, and only very rarely known to appear in flocks, or even in family groups, but usually has the air of having wandered off in company with non-kindred species. They evidently move in a due south course, leaving our shores at Buzzard's Bay over the open sea, and some of them reaching the West India Islands early in August. Two instances are recorded of the capture of this bird in Massachusetts as early as July 24; others were taken as late as September 29.

Mr. Lawrence records the obtaining of a single specimen at San Mateo, Mexico, in February, 1869. Professor Snow mentions it as a rare migrant in Kansas, his only record of its occurrence there being three specimens taken near Lawrence in September, 1874, by Mr. William Osburn. Dr. Merrill records it as occurring in the Rio Grande region, on Oct. 13, 1877. Mr. J. Dwight, Jr., mentions meeting with it on the Jersey coast at Squam Beach. Out of ten examples all were single birds except three, showing the straggling character of its movements. Mr. N. T. Lawrence speaks of this species as being not uncommon on the south side of Long Island, where it was seen in parties of from three to five. Two in adult breeding-plumage were taken in July; all the others, in the fall plumage, in September. Mr. George N. Lawrence informs us that on one occasion, at Rockaway, there was a large flight of this species and of *Totanus flavipes*, the latter being the more abundant. Six Stilt Sandpipers were killed at a single shot; he never saw so many together at any other time.

[1] Mr. M. Chamberlain has recently recorded its capture in New Brunswick. — J. A. A.

The Stilt Sandpiper occurs as a migrant in the interior, especially in the spring. Professor Kumlien has procured it in Southern Wisconsin, and the Natural History Society of Boston have received from him several fine specimens in the breeding-plumage. Professor F. H. Snow, of Lawrence, Kansas, informs us that some six or eight specimens were taken in that neighborhood in September, 1874.

Richardson refers to this species as the Douglas Sandpiper, and mentions that it is not uncommon in the Fur Country up to, and probably beyond, the 60th parallel. It frequents the interior in the breeding-season, and resorts to the flat shores of Hudson's Bay in the autumn, previous to taking its departure south. It was found by Mr. MacFarlane breeding on the Arctic coast. This species is said by Léotaud to be a never-failing visitant of Trinidad, where it arrives early in August, and, like nearly all the other migratory Waders, leaves in October. It keeps apart from other species, or only associates with the *Totanus flavipes*, which it is said to resemble in its habits and movements. It is also given, in the list published by Mr. Lawrence, as one of the birds observed by Mr. A. A. Julien, on the Island of Sombrero, West Indies.

According to Giraud, this species, known on Long Island as the Long-legged Sandpiper, is not common there. In all his excursions he only obtained two individuals, both of which proved to be males. These were shot in a large meadow lying on the South Bay, and known as Cedar Island. The first he procured in the latter part of August, 1840; the other in the early part of September in the following year. In both instances the birds were in company with a single Pectoral Sandpiper. The first he shot before it alighted, and had no opportunity to observe its habits. The second alighted among his decoys while he was lying at a salt-pond in the meadow. It walked about with an erect and graceful gait, occasionally stooping to probe the soft mud for worms and minute shellfish, particles of which, on dissection, he found in its stomach. After spending a few minutes within reach of his gun, it became suddenly alarmed, uttered a shrill note, and took wing; as it passed from him he brought it down. An experienced Bay-man, who was on the meadow at the time, informed Mr. Giraud that, in the course of many years' shooting, he had met with only a few stragglers, and had always looked upon them as hybrids. Although somewhat resembling in plumage the Red-breasted Snipe, the two are so unlike in size, that Mr. Giraud regards it as hardly possible that they could ever be mistaken for each other. As he several times found these birds in the New York market — from six to eight on a string — it is very evident that wandering flocks occasionally visit the shores of Long Island.

Mr. Dresser states that shortly after his arrival at Matamoras, while out shooting at the lagoon, he procured a specimen of this Sandpiper, which was then quite new to him. During his stay at Matamoras he shot several more Stilt Sandpipers, meeting with them far oftener as the different kinds of birds of this family began to arrive from the north, and generally finding them in company with the *Macrorhamphus griseus*. When out hunting Snipe, on the 20th of November, 1863, near San Antonio, he shot another of these birds.

Mr. Audubon states that on the 4th of April, 1847, on the Island of Barataria, forty miles from the southwest pass of the Mississippi, he saw a flock of about thirty Long-legged Sandpipers alight, within ten steps of him, near the water. They soon scattered, following the margin of the advancing and retiring waves in search of food, which they procured by probing the wet sand in the manner of the Curlews. They inserted the full length of their bills in the sand, holding it there for some little time, as if engaged in sucking up what they had found. In this way they continued feeding along an extended line of the shore for thirty yards, alternately and simultaneously advancing and retreating with the movement of the water. In about three quarters of an hour they removed a few yards beyond the highest wash of the waves, huddled close together, and began to plume themselves. Suddenly they ceased their occupation, stood still, and several of them uttered a sharp *tweet-tweet*, somewhat like the notes of the Solitary Sandpiper. Soon after this seven other birds of the same species alighted near those he was watching, and began to feed. Fearing that the first flock might join them, and he might lose the opportunity of procuring specimens, he fired into the flock and killed eleven. He afterward saw them on almost every island and bay on his way to Texas, and also procured some on Galveston Island. He describes its flight as being rapid and regular. This Sandpiper moves in compact flocks, and often when about to alight, or after being disturbed, inclines the body to either side, showing alternately the upper and the lower parts. On foot it moves more like a Curlew than a *Tringa*, and is more sedate in its motions than the true Sandpiper. At times, on being approached, it will squat on the ground after the manner of the Esquimaux Curlew. Its flesh is said to be extremely delicate. In the stomachs of those he killed he found small worms, minute shellfish, and vegetable substances, among which were hard seeds of some unknown plant. He found great differences in the color of the plumage of those he killed. He adds that its passage through the United States is very rapid, both in spring and in autumn. A few of these birds are said to spend the winter in Lower Louisiana, but nearly all pass on southward beyond Texas.

Mr. Moore twice met with this species in Florida — once Aug. 4, and again Sept. 17, 1869. Part were in an oozy pool near the Bay of Sarasota; the rest were in a fresh pond. He had an opportunity of witnessing its manner of feeding from a hiding-place near the pond. It was feeding in water that nearly covered its tarsi. It slowly stepped along, carrying its bill immersed nearly up to the base, and sweeping it slowly from side to side, much in the manner of the Roseate Spoonbills, which were at the same moment feeding near by. He noticed no action like that of swallowing at any time, its motions being continuous. This accounts for the black mud found in the stomachs of several kinds of Sandpipers: it is taken in by suction, and with it probably various kinds of animalculæ.

Mr. MacFarlane found this species breeding at Rendezvous Lake, in the Arctic Region, June 27. In situation and composition they are said to be similar to others previously met with. The nest contained four eggs, the female having been shot on leaving it. The contents of the eggs were very slightly developed. This bird was everywhere very rare, except on the Arctic coast at Franklin Bay, where it was found tolerably abundant. At Island Point, July 5, he obtained two young birds in the down, with the female parent. Both parents displayed much courage and ingenuity in defence of their young, two of which were thus enabled to escape. He afterwards, in the same neighborhood, procured other young in the down, with both parents. Another nest, obtained at Langston Harbor in July, 1865, contained four eggs quite fresh. The nest was a mere depression in the ground, lined with a few withered leaves and grasses. Examples of this species were also procured at Fort Resolution by Mr. Kennicott, at Fort Simpson by Mr. B. R. Ross, and at Big Island by Mr. J. Reid.

A set of eggs (S. I. No. 9389) obtained on the Arctic coast by Mr. MacFarlane, June 22, 1863, was in a nest composed of decayed leaves and placed in a hollow partly concealed by tufts of grass. The eggs are three in number, of an oblong pyriform shape, and have a ground-color of a light and bright drab or grayish white, with large rounded and scattered markings of bistre; these markings are larger and more numerous at the obtuse end. The eggs range from 1.47 to 1.50 inches in length, and have a breadth of one inch. Another set (No. 11331), obtained in 1866, have spots that are larger and more confluent about the greater end, and are more rounded in shape, varying between 1.45 and 1.46 inches in length, and in breadth between 1.05 and 1.10 inches.

GENUS **EREUNETES**, ILLIGER.

Ereunetes, ILLIGER, Prodromus, 1811, 262 (type, *E. petrificatus*, ILLIG., = *Tringa pusilla*, LINN.)
Hemipalama, BONAP. Obs. Wils. 1825, no. 212 (same type).
Heteropoda, NUTT. Man. II. 1834, 135 (nec LATREILLE, 1804).

CHAR. Size small; anterior toes webbed at the base; a well-developed hind toe. Bill about as long as or a little longer than the head, straight, somewhat expanded at the end, about as long as the tarsus; middle toe more than half as long as the tarsus; bare portion of tibia nearly equal to the middle toe.

The bill of *Ereunetes* is quite stout and considerably expanded, by which it is readily distinguished from *Actodromas minutilla* independently of the semipalmated feet. The tarsus and middle toe are about equal; the tibia denuded anteriorly for about two thirds the length of tarsus. The basal membrane of toes is more scolloped out interiorly than exteriorly; the notch externally not quite as deep as to the first joint, although the membrane extends beyond the second. There is a tendency to hexagonal subdivision in the bare portion of tibia anteriorly. The tail is doubly emarginate.

But one species is known, the common Semipalmated Sandpiper or "Peep."

Ereunetes pusillus.

THE SEMIPALMATED SANDPIPER.

a. pusillus.

Tringa pusilla, LINN. S. N. I. 1766, 252.
Ereunetes pusillus, CASS. Pr. Ac. Nat. Sci. Philad. XIII. 1860, 195. — COUES, Key, 1872, 254; Check List, 1873, no. 417; 2d ed. 1880, no. 612; Birds N. W. 1874, 481 (part). — RIDGW. Nom. N. Am. B. 1881, no. 541.
Ereunetes petrificatus, ILLIG. Prodr. 1811, 262 (Bahia). — CASS. in Baird's B. N. Am. 1858, 724 (part). — BAIRD, Cat. N. Am. B. 1859, no. 535.
Tringa semipalmata, WILS. Am. Orn. VII. 1813, 131, pl. 63, fig. 3. — SW. & RICH. F. B. A. II. 1831, 381. — AUD. Orn. Biog. V. 1839, 111, pl. 408; Synop. 1839, 236; B. Am. V. 1842, 277, pl. 336.
Tringa (*Heteropoda*) *semipalmata*, NUTT. Man. II. 1834, 136.
Tringa brevirostris, SPIX, Av. Bras. II. 1825, 76, pl. 93.
Tringa Brissoni, LESS. Man. II. 1828, 277.
Heteropoda Mauri, BONAP. Comp. List, 1838, 49.
Hemipalama minor, LEMB. Av. Cuba, 1850, 97.

b. occidentalis.

Ereunetes occidentalis, LAWR. Pr. Philad. Acad. 1864, 107.
Ereunetes pusillus, var. *occidentalis*, COUES, Check List, 1873, no. 417 *a.*
Ereunetes pusillus occidentalis, RIDGW. Nom. N. Am. B. 1881, no. 541 *a.* — COUES, Check List, 2d ed. 1882, no. 613.
Ereunetes pusillus, } AUCT. (citations of western localities).
Ereunetes petrificatus, }

HAB. The whole of North and Middle, and a considerable portion of South, America; throughout the West Indies; Bermuda; south to New Granada and Brazil; breeding chiefly, if not exclusively, north of the United States. The race *occidentalis* is chiefly restricted to the Western Province of North America; the typical *pusillus* entirely confined to the Eastern Province.

Sp. Char. Total length, about 5.75 to 6.50; extent, 11.00 to 12.00; wing, 3.50–4.00; culmen, .68–1.15; tarsus, .80–.95; middle toe, .55–.65.[1] Bill black, becoming greenish olive on basal part of the mandible; iris dark brown; legs and feet greenish olive. Rump slate-color; upper tail-coverts and middle tail-feathers dusky, other rectrices cinereous; wing-coverts and tertials brownish gray with dusky shaft-streaks, the greater coverts tipped with white. Superciliary stripe and lower parts white, the former finely streaked with grayish dusky. Upper parts (except as described) variegated brown, black and rusty in summer adults and young, plain ashy with dusky shaft-streaks in winter plumage.

Summer adult and young: Above brownish, varied with black, rusty, and white (the latter on the terminal borders of the feathers — sometimes almost wanting); beneath white, the jugulum streaked or spotted with dusky in the adult, shaded with grayish buff in young. *Winter plumage:* Above, uniform ashy, finely streaked with dusky; below, pure white.

a. pusillus.

Adult breeding-plumage: Upper surface light grayish brown, the sides of the pileum and edges of some of the scapulars and interscapulars tinged with pale buffy cinnamon, but this sometimes almost wholly absent; pileum heavily streaked, and dorsal region heavily spotted, with black, the latter color occupying the central portion of each feather. A streaked white superciliary stripe, and dusky loral space, the latter usually very distinctly defined along its upper edge, the lower part broken into streaks, which extend backward over the cheeks; auriculars streaked grayish

E. pusillus.

brown. Lower parts pure white, the jugulum and breast tinged with ashy and streaked with dusky. *Winter plumage:* Above brownish gray or cinereous, relieved by dusky shaft-streaks; superciliary stripe and lower parts pure white, the jugulum faintly streaked. *Young:* Similar to the summer adult, but jugulum tinged with pale grayish buff, and without well-defined streaks or spots, the scapulars and interscapulars bordered terminally with white, and the brown usually less rusty. *Downy young:* Forehead dingy white, divided by a mesial line of black; crown light chestnut, marbled posteriorly with black and white; occiput mottled whitish. A distinct loral line of black, forking just before the eye, the upper branch running toward the anterior corner of the eye, the other inclining downward. Throat fulvous-white; other lower parts whitish, nearly pure on the abdomen. Upper parts pale fulvous-brown laterally, black centrally, the whole surface thickly bespangled with fine downy tufts, terminating the down-filaments.

Wing, 3.50–4.00 (3.78); culmen, .68–.92 (.77); tarsus, .80–.95 (.86); middle toe, .55–.65 (.61). [Eighteen summer adults measured.]

b. occidentalis.

Adult breeding-plumage: Upper surface bright rusty cinnamon, the feathers spotted centrally with black, the cinnamon sometimes nearly uniform along the sides of the crown; a white superciliary stripe streaked with dusky grayish, this bordered below by a stripe of light rufous or rusty

[1] Forty-two *adult* specimens measured; the average of this series is as follows: wings, 3.75; culmen, .87; tarsus, .88; middle toe, .60.

on the side of the head, from the bill across the lores, and beneath the eyes over the auriculars; remainder of the head white, streaked, except on the throat (where also sometimes finely flecked) with grayish dusky. Lower parts pure white, the jugulum and breast thickly marked with broad streaks of dusky, these broadest and of triangular form on the sides of the breast; sides marked with sagittate dusky spots. *Adult, winter plumage:* Not distinguishable from typical *pusillus* in

E. pusillus occidentalis.

the same stage, except by greater average length of bill and tarsus. *Young:* similar to young of *E. pusillus*, but with rusty ochraceous prevailing on the dorsal region and pileum. *Downy young:* Similar to the same stage of *E. pusillus*, but the rusty areas of the upper parts more extended and more castaneous.

Wing, 3.60–3.90 (3.74); culmen, .85–1.15 (.95); tarsus, .85–.95 (.89); middle toe, .55–.65 (.60). [Eighteen summer adults measured.]

The range of individual variation, as regards proportions, is probably greater in this species than in any other limicoline bird of its size. The length of the bill, in forty-two adult examples measured, varies from .68 of an inch to 1.15 inches, and the wing from 3.50 to 4.00, the other measurements varying in proportion. The variations are of exactly the same character as in *Macrorhamphus griseus*, the *scolopaceus* type of the latter corresponding to the *occidentalis* form of *Ereunetes*, both being distinguished by a greater average length of bill and tarsus, and an excess of the ferruginous coloring.

The common Semipalmated Sandpiper is found nearly or quite throughout North America. Accepting the form which occurs on the Pacific coast — called by some writers the *occidentalis* — as identical with this, we have for the species a very general distribution. It breeds in the extreme northern portions of the Fur Country; is abundant, both in the spring and fall migrations, along the sea-coasts, and also the banks of rivers and inland lakes. In the winter it is found in the extreme South-western States, in Mexico, Central America, the Bahamas, and some of the West India Islands, and a considerable portion of South America.

Mr. Salvin mentions that a single bird of this species was shot near Dueñas in the month of April, in a flock of *Actodromas maculata*, and that afterward he again found this species very common on the Pacific coast of Guatemala. According to Wedderburn, it occurs in Bermuda during its fall migrations; and from the 1st of August to the beginning of November small flocks are to be seen on most of the sandy bays along the coast. Professor Newton mentions this species as occurring in autumn in St. Croix, frequenting the pastures in flocks of from ten to twenty. Its first arrival was observed by Mr. E. Newton. Léotaud also speaks of it as occurring on the Island of Trinidad, arriving there in July, and leaving in October. It is always seen in flocks, and these are sometimes very numerous, not only frequenting the marshy edges of the sea, but quite as commonly the low damp meadows. Some are said to remain in Trinidad all the year round, and these may be found on the swampy edges of pools from October until July. At this season of the year the heavy rains and the overflowing of the pools compel the birds to seek the borders of the sea, where at other times it is not usual to find them. This species is given by Dr. Gundlach as occurring in Cuba, but only as a visitant.

In Massachusetts this species appears, on its way north, about the last of May, and makes but a very short stay, returning in August, later than the *Actodromas minutilla*, all having left by the middle of September. They are in greatly reduced numbers as compared with former years, when all the beaches and mud-flats appeared alive with the numerous flocks of "Peeps," as they are called — a name also given to the *A. minutilla* and *A. Bonapartii.*

Mr. Dresser met with none of this species near San Antonio, but found it not uncommon near Matamoras, though not so common as the *minutilla.* Audubon, however, mentions it as found in Texas in great numbers in April, and as moving northward with celerity, both along the sea-shore and the larger streams.

Audubon states that he found it dispersed in pairs throughout Labrador, and having nests there in June, though he was not able to find any, the birds squatting on the moss as if they had a nest, and thus effectually misleading his party. He also states that he often saw this species in considerable numbers along the shores of the Ohio and the Mississippi during autumn. At this season they fed on fresh-water insects, worms, and small coleoptera, became very fat, and afforded excellent eating; this, he adds, is rarely the case when they are found along the sea-shore. Their flight is swift and well sustained; and when alarmed, or just before alighting, their evolutions are very graceful.

Mr. Boardman informs us that this species is very abundant in the vicinity of Calais, but does not breed there. It usually arrives early in August, or, in some years, about the last of July. In its season it occurs in nearly every part of North America, congregating in large flocks on the beaches, sand-bars, and low lands along the sea-coast, as well as on the shores of the interior lakes and streams. When feeding, these birds scatter about in small parties; and when surprised, collect together, with a rapid and peculiar movement, in such close bodies that sometimes twenty or thirty may be killed at a single shot. When pursued, they move off in a mass, uttering a peculiar chirping note as they go, by imitating which they may be readily decoyed. On dissection, their stomachs are found filled with minute fragments of animal and vegetable origin.

Individuals and small parties of this species are occasionally met with early in the summer in parts of the country where they are not known to breed. Mr. Allen found a number at Ipswich in June, 1868. They were all in immature plumage, being evidently mere stragglers, and not breeding. Mr. Henshaw mentions seeing a small flock on the sea-shore near Santa Barbara in July. These were all found to be barren birds.

According to the observations of Mr. Moore, this species may be found during the entire summer in Florida, in small groups of not more than fifteen or twenty. They all retain their winter colors, or at best exhibit but slight touches of brown or rufous. It is not easy to account for this continuance of a winter garb throughout the summer in such birds as would assume a different dress were they to resort to their northern habitat to breed. It may be caused by old age, by barrenness, or by disease. It can hardly be because they are unmated, as birds in that condition assume the spring plumage before they migrate. It would be interesting to ascertain if it is inability to propagate which thus arrests the development of the vernal plumage. There were no indications that any of these resident individuals ever breed in Florida.

Captain Bendire mentions this species as abundant, during their migrations, in Southeastern Oregon. A few lingered through the month of May, but did not remain to breed. Mr. C. Hart Merriam regards this species as an occasional summer resident in Connecticut, and in one instance it has been known to breed within the limits of that State. Its nest, with eggs — one of which is in my cabinet — was found July 20, 1877, at Bradford, by Mr. Walter R. Nichols. The bird was not taken, but the egg is not distinguishable from other eggs of this species.

The Western form, occurring on the Pacific coast, does not essentially vary, in habits and peculiarities of nesting, from the other. Dr. Cooper states that it is quite common along the entire Pacific coast, scarcely leaving that region, even in midsummer, but frequenting the shores of muddy bays in large flocks, feeding on the worms, crustacea, and insects left along the edge of the water and on the flats at low tide. Dr. Cooper has obtained it in May and in August as far south as San Pedro, so that possibly it may breed within the State of California. It is found also toward the north in July, visiting the inland fresh-water marshes near the Rocky Mountains. This species associates with other small Sandpipers, and has habits, notes, and flight similar to those of the Eastern bird, from which it cannot be distinguished. This is said to be a rather noisy bird, uttering, when startled, a whistling cry that sounds like *to-wheet.* It is much hunted for the San Francisco market. This was perhaps the species which Mr. Salvin found so common on the Pacific coast of Guatemala.

This bird is mentioned by Mr. Dall as being very common at Sitka and Kadiak, where Bischoff obtained many specimens. It is also abundant at Nulato, and along the sea-shore, and on the Yukon River. Mr. Bannister also mentions it as being very common throughout the spring and summer, and as nesting all over the Island of St. Michael's. All the nests he observed were mere hollows in the ground, with nothing more than a few blades of grass for lining, and were generally placed in some dry tuft of grass, at some distance from the water. The bird, when startled from the nest, would generally fly a little distance and then alight, showing but slight timidity. In the month of May, when in pursuit of Ducks and Geese near St. Michael's, Mr. Bannister saw these little birds all around him, within a distance of a few feet, apparently unmindful of his presence, even when he was shooting at Ducks and Geese as they flew overhead.

Richardson refers to a manuscript left by Hutchins, written about 1770, in which he gives an accurate description of this species, stating also that it arrives on Severn River about the middle of May in large flocks, building early in June a nest of withered grass, and laying four or five black-and-white spotted eggs. Toward autumn it has a chirruping note; in September it retires south.

Mr. MacFarlane found this species breeding very abundantly on the Arctic coast and on the islands in the bays and along the shores of the Arctic Sea. Some were also found nesting in the Barren Grounds west of Franklin Bay. The nests were in most instances mere depressions in the ground, lined with a few grasses and leaves, dry and partially decayed, and were almost always near small pools of salt or brackish water, or inland, near the edge of small ponds. Sometimes the female would glide from her nest, and, pretending to be disabled, would seek to entice away the intruder. If suddenly startled, she would frequently utter disturbed cries. The eggs were usually four in number, and were found from the 20th of June to the 10th of July. At times the nests were hidden in tufts of grass, but not always. When driven from her nest, the female, if unmolested, would almost immediately return. In reference to one nest, procured June 30 on the coast of Franklin Bay,

Mr. MacFarlane writes: "The nest from which these eggs were taken was situated between two small brackish lakes near the sea-shore. One of our party saw the female get off; and when the nest was approached by him she uttered a shrill note of alarm. After searching about for a few minutes, he failed to find the eggs; and he then determined to hide himself, and from his concealment ascertain where the female would alight on her return. In a short time she was seen to return, accompanied by three companions, all of whom looked and moved about; but not discovering anything, seemed to hold a brief consultation, after which they separated, the female to her nest. Another search failed to discover the eggs; and the female again returned with the same birds, who appeared to be in a state of great excitement, judging from the chattering they kept up. After a while they again separated; when the nest was found, and the parent secured. The report of the gun brought the others once more to the spot; but they beat a hasty retreat. The nest was a mere depression in the midst of some hay, and lined with the same and a few withered leaves."

The eggs of this species exhibit great variations in their appearance, in consequence of the differences in the size, the manner of distribution, and the number of the spots. The ground is a light drab, and the markings are of a pure bright sepia. In one set (S. I. No. 11272) of four eggs, the nest — a mere depression in the ground, on the border of a small lake in the midst of marshy ground — was lined with withered grasses. In this set the markings are large, pronounced, and distinct, sparsely distributed around the smaller end, and more numerous and occasionally confluent about the obtuse end. They are pyriform in shape, and the smaller end is very sharply defined. They average 1.25 inches in length, by .86 in breadth. Another set (No. 11271) of four eggs in a nest found placed between two small lakes, and lined with withered grasses and leaves, was obtained in the Barren Grounds, near Fort Anderson. In these eggs the spots are much finer, more numerous about the smaller end, and there very fine, a little larger and more confluent about the larger extremity, and nearly concealing the grayish white or light drab-colored ground. These measure 1.15 inches by .85. Four eggs (No. 11273) found on an island in Franklin Bay, July 4, have markings still more minute and numerous, universally diffused, and more or less confluent over the entire egg, concealing the ground, and having apparently very little resemblance to No. 11272. Four eggs (No. 17041) were found by Mr. L. M. Turner, May 28, 1874, at St. Michael's. Their ground-color is a light grayish buff, thickly spotted with reddish sepia and darker sepia, chiefly on the larger end. Their measurements are as follows: 1.20 by .80 inches; 1.25 by .85; 1.25 by .90; 1.25 by .85.

GENUS **TRINGA**, LINNÆUS.

Tringa, LINN. S. N. ed. 10, 1758, 148; ed. 12, 1766, 247 (type *T. canutus*, LINN.).

CHAR. Body robust; bill and legs short, the former straight, widened terminally, and scarcely longer than the head; tarsus about equal to the bill, or a little shorter; middle toe about two thirds the tarsus. Wings long and pointed, reaching beyond the end of the tail.

The above characters separate at once this genus from *Arquatella*, the one most nearly related, but which has the bill much more compressed, slightly but decidedly decurved toward the end, and much longer than the tarsus; the latter scarcely, if any, longer than the middle toe; the wings shorter, etc. The single species *T. canutus* is the largest of American Sandpipers, and among the largest known species of this group; only one, the *Arquatella crassirostris* (TEMM. & SCHLEG.) of Eastern Asia exceeding it in size.

Tringa canutus.

THE KNOT SANDPIPER.

Tringa canutus, LINN. S. N. ed. 10, 1758, 149; ed. 12, 1766, 251. — CASS. in Baird's B. N. Am. 1858, 715. — BAIRD, Cat. N. Am. B. 1859, no. 526. — COUES, Key, 1872, 256; Check List, 1873, no. 426; ed. 2, 1882, no. 626; Birds N. W. 1874, 490. — RIDGW. Nom. N. Am. B. 1881, 529.

Tringa cinerea, BRÜNN. Orn. Bor. 1764, 53. — GMEL. S. N. I. 1788, 673. — WILSON, Am. Orn. VII. 1813, 36, pl. 57, fig. 2. — SW. & RICH. F. B. A. II. 1831, 387. — NUTT. Man. II. 1834, 125.

Tringa islandica, GMEL. S. N. I. 1788, 682. — AUD. Orn. Biog. IV. 1838, 130, pl. 315; Synop. 1839. 232; B. Am. V. 1842, 254, pl. 328.

Tringa nævia, GMEL. S. N. I. 1788, 681.

Tringa grisea, GMEL. l. c.

? *Tringa australis*, GMEL. t. c. 679.

? *Tringa ferruginea*, BRÜNN. Orn. Bor. 1764, 53.

Tringa rufa, WILSON, Am. Orn. VII. 1813, 43, pl. 57, fig. 5.

Tringa calidris, LINN. S. N. I. 1766, 253.

"*Tringa utopiensis*, MÜLLER."

"*Tringa lornatina*, LICHT."

HAB. Chiefly northern portion of the northern hemisphere, but occasionally visiting the southern hemisphere during winter migrations; chiefly littoral, but occurring also on the larger inland waters. Brazil; Australia; New Zealand.

SP. CHAR. Largest of American Sandpipers (*Tringæ*). Bill straight, rather longer than the head, widened terminally, slightly compressed basally; tarsus about equal to the bill, or a little

Summer plumage.

longer; middle toe about two thirds the tarsus; toes flattened beneath, with a rather wide lateral margin; lower third of the tibia bare, but the tips of the feathers reaching to the joint. Wings long and pointed, extending beyond the tail, which is short, and slightly graduated. *Adult in*

Winter plumage.

summer: Above, mixed black, light gray, and pale rusty, these colors varying in relative extent with the individual, but the grayish usually prevailing; rump and upper tail-coverts white, with narrow bars and spots of blackish. Lower parts, and a distinct superciliary stripe, uniform vinaceous-rufous, or pinkish cinnamon, paler on the middle of the abdomen; crissum, flanks, axillars, and lining of the wing white, usually with spots and bars of dusky. Primaries dusky, with white shafts; tail-feathers plain grayish, edged with whitish, and sometimes with a sub-edging of dusky. *Young:* Above, light ash-gray, darker on the back, each feather bordered with whitish and marked with a sub-edging of dusky; upper tail-coverts white, marked with dusky crescents. Lower parts whitish (nearly pure white on the abdomen), the neck and breast marked with streaks and flecks of dusky, the sides with dim crescentic and irregular spots of the same. An indistinct whitish superciliary stripe. "Bill and feet black; iris dark hazel" (AUDUBON).

Total length, about 10 inches; wing, 6.50; tail, 2.50; bill, from gape, 1.50; tarsus, 1.25.

Adult specimens vary individually in the relative extent of the black, gray, and reddish colors on the upper parts; gray usually predominates in the spring, the black in midsummer. Sometimes (as in No. 10445, ♀, Cape May, New Jersey) there is no rufous whatever on the upper surface. The cinnamon color of the lower parts also varies in intensity.

Two European examples in summer plumage differ from any American ones we have seen, in the great excess of black on the back, where that color nearly uniformly prevails. An immature specimen from Norway, however (No. 56906, Varanger Fiord), is not different from American skins in corresponding plumage.

The Knot is a cosmopolitan species, found throughout the northern hemisphere and apparently more generally distributed over the eastern continent than in the New World. It does not appear to have been detected on the Pacific coast. It visits South America to Brazil, and is also credited to Australia and New Zealand.

Mr. C. A. Wright ("Ibis," 1864) mentions the occurrence of this species at Malta, as attested by a specimen in the University Museum, and also on the authority of Schembri. It is also given by Mr. H. Saunders ("Ibis," 1871) as occurring in Southern Spain, both in autumn and in spring. He has obtained it there in the rufous-plumage in May. Mr. J. H. Gurney ("Ibis," 1868) states that the most southerly examples of this species which have come under his notice were two that were obtained in Walvisch Bay, Africa, Oct. 20 and Nov. 4, 1863. The first of these specimens retained some remains of the breeding-plumage, the second none.

Yarrell speaks of this species as by no means uncommon in Great Britain from autumn, through winter to spring, and says that it remains sometimes as late as the beginning of May, and assumes its breeding-plumage before leaving for the more northern regions in which it breeds. Although one had been shot in Sanda as late as the 15th of June, there is no record of its having been known to breed in the British Islands, and its eggs remained, up to 1856, unknown to British collectors. Mr. Thompson states that it is a regular autumnal visitant of Ireland. At that season it is also found in flocks on the shores of most of the southern and eastern counties of England, the greater portion being young birds of the year. Mr. J. H. Gurney, in a communication to the "Zoloogist," in 1853, states that specimens in the nuptial dress frequently occur on the Norfolk coast of England in the spring, and that in May they were for a few days unusually numerous; also that on the 13th of that month a single hunter of Yarmouth procured seventy-three, nearly all in full summer dress.

Mr. G. D. Rowley ("Ibis," 1864) records the capture of six birds of this species at Brighton, England, in a net, at a single pull; this was on the 19th of September. They were presumed to be all of one family, and it was supposed that they were taken on the day of their arrival from their breeding-grounds.

Nilsson states that this species inhabits the Arctic portions of Sweden and Norway, but makes no mention of its eggs. Mr. Dunn did not meet with this bird in spring and autumn, except on the coast of Scona and in the southern part of Scandinavia.

He ventures the opinion that it occurs in Finland and in the northeastern parts, as it seems to make its first appearance on the eastern coast of Scandinavia. Wheelwright states that it was only seen by him in the south of Scandinavia during the periods of its migrations, and he could learn nothing in reference to its breeding. He received its eggs from Greenland, and describes them as less in size than those of *Gallinago media*, and as resembling them in their markings, although not so dark.

This species is given by Reinhardt as one of the birds of Greenland; and Captain Sabine, in his Memoir on the Birds of that country, states that examples were killed at Hare's Island in June. It is known also to visit Iceland; and that it goes to much higher northern latitudes is attested by the records of most of the Arctic expeditions. Dr. Middendorff includes it in his list of the birds of Siberia, and among those that penetrate to the farthest north. Professor Newton, in his "Notes on the Birds of Iceland," mentions its arrival there late in May; and the opinion of Faber, to which he refers, that it breeds in the uplands of that island, seems to him very probably well founded. But Mr. Fowler, whose attention was particularly called to this bird, could not discover it, and does not believe that it is present on the island during the breeding-season. On the southwest part of the island it is known to be a bird of passage. At the end of May Professor Newton encountered a large flock, which remained about a week, when nearly all of them left; he thinks it quite possible, however, that a few remain behind and breed. I have in my cabinet an egg given me by Canon Tristram as of this species, and taken on islands north of Iceland. It closely resembles the eggs described by Wheelwright, but has a suspicious resemblance to the eggs of *Gallinago media*. In his "Notes on the Birds of Greenland," published in 1875, Professor Newton seems to have changed his views in regard to this bird's breeding in Iceland, expressing the opinion that all pass on farther north. He speaks of it as rare in Southern Greenland, but as often met with in the north, as not breeding below latitude 68° N., remarking that it is thought to nest in the bays of Greenland. Professor Newton adds, that after the breeding-season this bird resorts to the outer islands, and that it was reported as having been found breeding on Melville Peninsula and in great abundance on the Parry Islands. The large flocks of these birds that, in autumn and again in spring, throng the western coasts of Europe and the eastern shores of America, make it more than probable that in its chief breeding-quarters, wherever these may be, it must be very numerous. It has not been met with on the east coast of Greenland, nor in Spitzbergen. It is presumed to breed in countries west and north of Greenland.

Mr. Nelson states that the Knot is another of the maritime species which regularly visits its breeding-grounds by way of the Great Lakes. It is a regular migrant, passing north in May, and returning to the shores of Lake Michigan early in September, where it remains until October.

Mr. L. Kumlien mentions that a small flock of these birds alighted on the schooner's deck in November, after the harbor had been frozen over. He saw none in the spring or summer, but was told that it is quite common in North Greenland, but that it does not nest south of latitude 70° N. There are no accounts of its eggs which can be accepted as authentic.

Mr. Henry W. Feilden, of the Arctic Expedition of 1875–1876, though not so fortunate as to obtain the eggs of this species during his stay in the Polar Regions, found it breeding in some numbers along the shores of Smith's Sound and the north coast of Grinnell Land. It is common throughout the Parry Islands during summer, as Sabine found it in 1820 nesting in great numbers on Melville Island. It was procured by Dr. Anderson, of the "Enterprise," at Cambridge Bay (lat. 69° 10′ N.), in July,

1853. On the 28th of July, 1875, Dr. Coppinger came across a party of six birds, several miles inland from Fort Foulke. They were feeding near a rill, and were very wild; but he secured a male in the full breeding-plumage. August 25, 1875, Mr. Feilden observed several of these birds near the water's edge in Discovery Bay (lat. 81° 44′ N.). The rills and marshes were frozen, and the birds were feeding along the shore on small crustaceans; in pursuit of their prey they ran breast high into the water. They had lost their breeding-plumage. On June 5, 1876, while camped near Knot Harbor, Grinnell Land (lat. 82° 33′ N.), he noted the first arrival of this species. A flock of fourteen or more were circling over a hillside, alighting on bare patches, and feeding eagerly on the buds of the *saxifraga*. Subsequently he met with it in considerable numbers, but always wild and difficult of approach. Their cry was wild, and like that of the Curlew. Immediately after their arrival they began to mate, at this season soaring high in the air like the Common Snipe. When descending from a height they beat their wings behind the back with a rapid motion, producing a loud whirring noise. On the 30th of July, 1876, three of the seamen, walking by the border of a small lake, came upon an old bird accompanied by three nestlings. The old bird proved to be a male. Its stomach and those of the young ones were filled with insects. Dr. Coppinger informed Mr. Feilden that the bird was not uncommon at Thank-God Harbor, and in the first week in August the latter saw family parties at Shift-Rudder Bay (lat. 81° 52′ N.) in the gray autumn plumage. It also bred in the vicinity of Discovery Bay; but no eggs were found there, although the young were obtained in all stages of plumage.

On the American coast this bird occurs, in its migrations, in most of the Atlantic States, and in the winter in the West Indies, and probably on the Gulf coast of Mexico. It breeds in the high Arctic Regions, in the northeastern portions. Sir Edward Parry, in his first voyage, found it breeding in great abundance on the North Georgian Islands; and on his second voyage a single specimen — a young male of the season — was shot on the 17th of August in the Duke of York's Bay. Sir John Richardson also mentions that this species was observed breeding on Melville Peninsula by Captain Lyons, who stated that this bird lays four eggs on a tuft of withered grass, without being at the pains of forming any nest. In the "Fauna Boreali-Americana" the same writer adds that this bird breeds in Hudson's Bay, and down to the fifty-fifth parallel. He describes the eggs as having a light yellowish ground, marked at the larger end with spots of gray and reddish, which form, in a greater or less degree, a zone; but the smaller end is nearly unspotted.

Specimens of this Wader were procured at Nulato, in May, by Mr. Pease, at Sitka by Mr. Bischoff, and at St. Michael's by Mr. Bannister, and also at Unalaklik by Mr. Potter.

Mr. Boardman informs us that it occurs in small flocks in the neighborhood of Calais, Me., but is never very abundant there, being seen only in the spring and fall migrations, and none remaining to breed. It is known there as the Robin Snipe. In Massachusetts this bird is regarded by some hunters as having become less abundant than it was formerly known to be. Mr. William Brewster has met with it in the spring in small flocks of five or six; this was late in May, and it was then rather abundant. It comes regularly in the fall about the middle of August, and thence to the 1st of September.

Mr. Frank H. Tileston, however, informs me that these birds arrive in Barnstable County, Mass., in their migrations northward, with great punctuality, about the 20th of May. They still come in large flocks every year, but rarely stay more than a day or two, passing immediately northward. At Eastham, May 20, 1875, he noted their first arrival that season, in large numbers; by the 22d all had passed on. A fine specimen procured at that time is now in the Collection of the Boston Natural History Society. The birds when in fair condition are regarded as good eating.

The Knot is said to feed principally on aquatic insects and the soft animals inhabiting small bivalve shells. It is also said to be able to swim with great ease. Wilson, who has observed flocks of these birds on the sandy shores of New Jersey, states that their favorite and almost exclusive food seemed to be small, thin, oval bivalve shellfish of a pearly-white color, which lie at a short distance below the surface, and in some places at low-water occur in heaps. These are swallowed whole, and, when loosened by the motion of the waves, are collected by this bird with great ease and dexterity. While doing this the bird follows the flowing and the recession of the waves with great nimbleness, and Wilson adds that it is highly amusing to observe with what adroitness it eludes the tumbling surf while seeming wholly intent on collecting its food. Audubon has seen this species probe the wet sand on the borders of oozy salt-marshes, thrusting in its bill with the same dexterity shown by other species. Its flight is swift, elevated, and well sustained. The aerial evolutions of these birds, on their first arrival in fall, are said to be very beautiful, and they follow each other in their course with incredible celerity.

Dr. Bachman informed Mr. Audubon that the Knot is quite abundant in South Carolina in both of its migrations, but that it is not known there in its breeding-plumage. It is there called the "May-bird," and in the middle districts the "Gray-back." Audubon found it in winter in East Florida; and while in the Bay of Galveston, Texas, in the spring of 1837, he observed groups of Knots arriving there in April, and proceeding eastward.

On Long Island, according to Giraud, it is familiarly known to the hunters both as the "Robin-Snipe" and the "Red-breasted." In the Great South Bay of that island, where there are immense salt-marshes separated by creeks and channels, these birds abound during their spring migrations. They frequent the shoal ponds, which furnish the small shellfish on which they chiefly subsist. There they are easily hunted by sportsmen lying in wait near their favorite haunts, and imitating their peculiar notes so as to bring them within gunshot. At this period of their migration these birds assemble in flocks and pass northward to their breeding-places, returning with their young about the middle of August, and then having a very different plumage from that of spring. They move southward late in September. In its then ashy-gray upper plumage it is the White Robin-Snipe of the Long Island hunters. In the fall it frequents the inner beaches, and is sometimes observed along the surf, collecting the minute marine animals cast on the shore by the waves. It is said to be more timid in the fall than in the spring, frequently passing within hearing of the fowler's whistle without approaching his decoy. This statement of Giraud, in reference to its wariness in the fall, is in remarkable contrast with its almost stupid tameness at the same season, on its first arrival in autumn, as noted by Yarrell. Sir William Jardine also mentions that he once met, in the month of September, on the east side of Holy Island, with a large flock which was so tame as to suffer him to kill as many as he wanted with stones from the beach. Mr. Moore states that this species occurs in Florida during the winter, and that some remain there during the season.

This species, according to Léotaud, visits Trinidad, where, like all the other migratory Waders which visit that island, it arrives in August and leaves in October. It is almost always alone, or very rarely in flocks of three or four, and frequents the borders of the sea. As soon as it alights it immediately begins running with remarkable rapidity. When it stops it crouches for a moment; and this movement occasions its local name of "Crouching-chicken." The number visiting Trinidad is not large.

The Knot is regarded as an excellent bird for the table, and its good qualities have long been known; the name — as is said by Pennant — having been derived from King Canute, or Knut, by whom its excellence was particularly appreciated.

GENUS **ARQUATELLA**, BAIRD.

Arquatella, BAIRD, B. N. Am. 1858, 717 (type *Tringa maritima*, BRÜNN.).

CHAR. Form very compact or robust, the legs especially. Tarsus shorter than the middle toe with claw, the latter two thirds to three fourths as long as the bill, which is slender, much compressed, straight, or very slightly decurved at the end. Size medium (wing less than 6 inches).

By the characters given above, this species may be very readily distinguished from *Tringa*, the nearest ally. The species of *Arquatella* are subject to seasonal changes of plumage which have been very perplexing to ornithologists, the summer and winter dress of the same bird being totally unlike, while that of the young is different still.

Three species of this genus belong to North America. Another species, the *Tringa crassirostris*, TEMM. & SCHLEG., of Japan and other parts of Eastern Asia, may belong to this genus, but we have seen no specimens.

The three species belonging to our fauna may be distinguished as follows: —

COM. CHAR. *Summer dress:* Back and scapulars variegated black, rusty-ochraceous, or buff, and buffy white, the first in the form of sharply defined spots occupying the central portion of each feather, the rusty or buff forming a wide external border, the whitish the tips of the feathers, the latter color sometimes scarcely present or altogether wanting. Rump and upper tail-coverts nearly uniform dusky; wings dusky, the coverts bordered with whitish, the greater coverts tipped with the same, and the inner secondaries chiefly white. Lower parts chiefly white, the breast variegated with dusky, this sometimes forming more or less of an irregular patch. *Winter plumage:* Above nearly uniform plumbeous, the feathers of the back and scapulars darker centrally, and showing faint purplish reflections in certain lights. Jugulum chiefly light plumbeous or grayish, the feathers with whitish borders.

1. **A. maritima**. *Breeding dress:* Pileum streaked with yellowish gray, or grayish white; scapulars and interscapulars irregularly spotted and indented with dull buff, or whitish, and bordered terminally with white; foreneck and jugulum distinctly streaked with dusky, the breast dull grayish, everywhere spotted with darker. *Winter dress:* Back and scapulars sooty black strongly glossed with purplish, the feathers bordered terminally with dark plumbeous gray; jugulum uniform mouse-gray, or brownish plumbeous. *Young, first plumage:* Scapulars, interscapulars, and wing-coverts bordered with pale grayish buff, with little or none of rusty. *Chick:* Above hair-brown, lighter and grayer on the nape, the brown irregularly marbled with black, the wings, back, and rump thickly bespangled with white downy flecks; head grayish white, tinged with fulvous, variously marked with black, the lores having two distinct longitudinal, nearly parallel streaks; lower parts grayish white, without fulvous tinge. *Average measurements of* 13 *adults:* Wing, 5.06; culmen, 1.20; tarsus, .99; middle toe, .90. *Hab.* Northeastern North America, Europe, etc.

2. **A. Couesi**. *Breeding dress:* Pileum streaked with deep rusty; scapulars and interscapulars broadly bordered with bright ferruginous; foreneck and jugulum irregularly clouded with dull pale buff or soiled white and sooty plumbeous, the breast more coarsely clouded, with more or less of a black patch on each side. *Winter dress:* Similar to *A. maritima*, but with the plumbeous borders to dorsal feathers broader and lighter, or more bluish, in tint; jugulum streaked or otherwise varied with white. *Young, first plumage:* Scapulars and interscapulars conspicuously bordered with bright rusty, ochraceous, and whitish; wing-coverts broadly bordered with buffy white or pale buff; breast and sides buffy white, distinctly streaked with dusky. *Chick:* Above bright

rusty fulvous, irregularly marbled with black, the ornamental velvety flecks or papillæ coarser and less pure white than in *A. maritima;* head light fulvous, with markings as in *A. maritima;* lower parts distinctly fulvous laterally. *Average measurements of* 14 *adults:* Wing, 4.86; culmen, 1.13; tarsus, .95; middle toe, .86. *Hab.* Aleutian Islands and contiguous coast of Alaska.

3. **A. ptilocnemis.** *Breeding-dress:* Pileum broadly streaked with ochraceous-buff; scapulars and interscapulars broadly bordered with bright ochraceous-rufous; foreneck and jugulum pure white, sparsely streaked with brownish gray; breast white, streaked anteriorly, and clouded posteriorly, with dusky, the latter forming more or less of a patch on each side. *Winter dress:* In general character similar to the corresponding stage of *A. maritima* and *A. Couesi*, but very much paler, the whole dorsal aspect being light cinereous, the scapulars and interscapulars with small, nearly concealed, central spots, the wing-coverts very broadly edged with pure white; jugulum with white largely predominating. *Young, first plumage:* Similar to *A. Couesi*, but colors throughout much paler, the light borders to the feathers of the dorsal surface broader, the dark centres correspondingly decreased. *Chick:* Similar to that of *A. Couesi*, but paler, the dark streaks on the lores not reaching to the eye. *Average measurements of* 13 *adults:* Wing, 5.16; culmen, 1.33; tarsus, .98; middle toe, .90. *Hab.* Prybilof Islands, Alaska.

Arquatella maritima.

THE PURPLE SANDPIPER.

Tringa maritima, BRÜNN. Orn. Bor. 1764, 54. — GMEL. S. N. I. 1788, 678. — SW. & RICH. F. B. A. II. 1831, 382. — NUTT. Man. II. 1834, 115. — AUD. Orn. Biog. III. 1835, 558, pl. 284; Synop. 1839, 233; B. Am. V. 1842, 261, pl. 330. — CASSIN, in Baird's B. N. Am. 1858, 717. — BAIRD, Cat. N. Am. B. 1859, no. 528. — COUES, Key, 1872, 255; Check List, 1873, no. 423; Birds N. W. 1874, 488.

Arquatella maritima, RIDGW. Bull. Nutt. Orn. Club, V. July, 1880, 162; Nom. N. Am. B. 1881, no. 530. — COUES, Check List, 2d ed. 1882, no. 620.

? *Tringa striata*, LINN. S. N. I. 1766, 248.

Tringa undata, BRÜNN. Orn. Bor. 1764, 55. — GMEL. S. N. I. 1788, 678.

Tringa nigricans, MONT. Linn. Tr. IV. 1796, 40.

Tringa canadensis, LATH. Ind. Orn. Suppl. 1801, lxv.

? *Tringa lincolniensis*, LATH. Ind. Orn. II. 1790, 734.

Tringa arquatella, PALL. Zoog. Rosso-As. II. 1831, 190.

Tringa littoralis, BREHM, Vög. Deutschl. 1831, 652.

HAB. Northeastern portions of North America, breeding in the high north, and migrating southward in winter to the Middle States, the Great Lakes, and the shores of the larger streams in the Mississippi Valley. Bermudas? Also, the northern portions of the Palæarctic Region.

Winter plumage.

SP. CHAR. *Adult, breeding-plumage:* Above, dusky slate, the scapulars and interscapulars nearly black, and faintly glossed, the edge of each feather notched or indented with ochraceous or dull buff, the terminal portion bordered with dull white or pale buff; rump, upper tail-coverts, and middle tail-feathers glossy dusky black, the feathers of the rump sometimes faintly bordered with grayish; remaining rectrices uniform grayish, with white shafts, the shade of gray becoming gradually lighter to the exterior feather. Lesser and middle wing-coverts bordered terminally with grayish white or pale ash ; greater coverts tipped with pure white, forming a distinct bar across the wing ; secondaries narrowly tipped with white and faintly edged with light ashy, the three or four feathers adjoining the tertials mostly white ; primaries with white shafts, the inner quills edged, especially toward the base, with white. Pileum dusky, streaked with pale grayish buff (these streaks sometimes nearly obsolete) ; a conspicuous superciliary stripe of grayish white, streaked with dusky ; a broad grayish-dusky streaked stripe across the lores, from the bill to and beneath the eye, and continued rather indistinctly over the auriculars ; cheeks, lower part of throat, and foreneck grayish white, streaked with grayish dusky ; chin, and sometimes upper part of throat, unstreaked white ; jugulum similarly but more broadly streaked ; breast grayish white or pale ashy, irregularly spotted with dusky, these spots occupying chiefly the central portion of each feather ; remaining lower parts white, the sides irregularly streaked and spotted with grayish ; crissum narrowly streaked with dusky ; axillars and lining of the wing pure white, the latter bordered externally with grayish. "Bill brown, yellow at base ; tarsi and toes dusky yellow ; iris brown." (KUMLIEN, MS.) [Bill and legs dusky in dried skins.[1]] *Winter dress:* Above, uniform smoky plumbeous, the scapulars, interscapulars, rump-feathers, and upper tail-coverts, darker centrally, where glossed with purple ; wings and tail as in the summer plumage. Head and neck uniform smoky plumbeous, darker immediately before the eye, and, to a less extent, on the crown ; the chin and upper part of throat, lower eyelid, and supraloral space, white ; jugulum and breast light smoky plumbeous, squamated with white ; remaining lower parts white, the sides broadly streaked with light brownish gray ; crissum with narrow mesial streaks of dusky. *Young, first plumage:* Above, quite similar to the breeding adult, but the dorsal feathers lacking the lateral ochraceous indentations, and the light borders to the feathers rather more regular, and more creamy in tint, the light borders to the wing-coverts also broader, and pale grayish buff instead of white or pale ashy ; nape and cheeks uniform smoky plumbeous ; lower parts much as in the summer adult. *Downy young:* Above, hair-brown, lighter and more grayish on the nape ; the brown irregularly marbled with black ; the wings, back, and rump thickly bespangled with whitish downy flecks on the tips of the down-tufts. Head pale fulvous, variously marked with black, the crown deep hair-brown, variegated with black. Beneath, entirely grayish-white.

Total length, about 9 inches ; wing, 4.85–5.40 (5.06) ; culmen, 1.10–1.45 (1.20) ; tarsus, .90–1.00 (.99) ; middle toe, .83–.95 (.90). [Extreme and average dimensions of 13 adults.]

The Purple Sandpiper belongs to both continents, and is a bird of somewhat irregular distribution. It is found in high Arctic regions, both in America and on the eastern continent, and yet has been met with in the summer, and apparently breeding, on the Azores. Its occurrence, however, except in high northern regions, is comparatively rare. In North America it appears to be very rare near New York, and entirely unknown on the Atlantic coast south of there. I am informed by Mr. Batty, that although quite uncommon on Long Island, occasional stragglers are found there late in winter or early in spring. A single specimen was procured on Cape Cod, Mass., in full plumage, by Mr. William A. Jeffries, as early as Sept. 6, 1877. Though rare in the interior, its presence on our Great Lakes is not wholly unknown. A fine adult male was obtained near Chicago, on the lake shore, Nov. 7, 1871. It was in company with Sanderlings. This bird was not taken by the British Arctic Expedition of 1875–1876 ; but, according to Dr. Bessels, specimens were procured at Polaris Bay by Captain Hall's party.

It is not given by Dr. Cooper as found on the Pacific coast. Farther north than California, however, it has been met with. It was taken on the Island of St. Michael's by Mr. Bannister, who states that, in October, 1865, he obtained a number of specimens of this species at the Redoubt, where it then appeared to be quite common. In

[1] Audubon says : "Bill deep orange, toward the end dusky ; edges of eyelids gray ; iris orange ; feet light orange, claws dusky."

the succeeding year he had not observed any up to the 1st of October, when he left the country. Mr. Dall procured a single bird of this species a mile or two below Nulato, on the Yukon, and another at Pastolik, but did not find the nest or eggs. He also procured a specimen on St. George's Island, in Behring's Sea, where it was common on the dry uplands and on the hills. Bischoff found this species plentiful at Sitka, and also at Plover Bay, on the Asiatic side of Behring's Straits. Mr. Dall found it a resident of the Aleutian Islands, where it was abundant along the shore throughout the year, in all the islands from Unalashka to the Shumagins. Its nest and eggs he was not able to discover.

This bird visits the Faröe Islands, Iceland, Greenland, Spitzbergen, and Nova Zembla. Von Baer, in his description of the animal life of the last-named place, mentions the Purple Sandpiper as one of the eight species of birds found there. Mr. G. Gillett ("Ibis," 1870) also mentions finding this species on Nova Zembla, where it was very common both in Matthew's Strait and on the eastern coast. One came on board during a storm, and was caught in the hand. When released, it did not offer to fly away, but remained on board two days. Herr von Heuglin also mentions ("Ibis," 1872) that he found this species very common, and generally in pairs, in this same region. In the autumn it occurred in smaller or larger flocks, and often mingled with the *Pelidna cinclus* and the *Tringa minuta.* On the 8th of August he found nestlings still very small, and covered with down. The Messrs. Evans and Sturge found the Purple Sandpiper very abundant at Coal Bay in Spitzbergen, and secured four of its nests. These were on the surface of the high field, and they are said to have been beautiful little structures, built deep in the ground, and lined with stalks of grass and leaves of the dwarf birch (*Betula nana*). They each contained four eggs of an olive-green, handsomely mottled with a purplish-brown, chiefly at the larger end. The writers state that they watched with much interest this elegant little bird as it waded into small pools of snow-water, or ran along the shingle, every now and then raising its wings over its back and exhibiting the delicate tint of the under side, at the same time uttering its loud shrill whistle. Professor Alfred Newton also met with this species on Spitzbergen, where he found it abundant along the coast as far north as Brandywine Bay. Dr. Malmgren informed Professor Newton that on a former voyage he had observed a flock of this bird on the shores of Kobbe Bay as early as May 28. He afterward saw it in the interior of Stor Fiord, and on Bear Island. According to Professor Newton, it is common everywhere in Iceland in the neighborhood of the coast, and is occasionally to be seen inland, where it also breeds. According to Faber, it is a resident of Iceland throughout the year, and is said to hatch its eggs about the middle of June. It is given by Dr. Middendorff as one of the birds of Siberia, and is included in the list of those that go to the Far North.

They are also mentioned by Dr. Reinhardt as occurring in Greenland, and appear to have been observed on all the voyages of Sir Edward Parry. On the first of these they were seen abundant in Davis's Straits and Baffin's Bay; during the second they were noticed on the rocks, at low-water mark, on Winter Island, in June; on the third they were observed at Port Bowen, and on the fourth were found abundant along the shores of Hecla Cove, Sir James C. Ross adding that they were seen in considerable numbers near Fury Point. Richardson states that this species breeds abundantly on Melville Peninsula and on the shores of Hudson's Bay. He describes its eggs as pyriform, 16.50 lines long, and an inch across in its greatest breadth. The ground-color is said to be of a yellowish gray, interspersed with small irregular spots of pale hair-brown, crowded at the obtuse end, and rare at the other.

Mr. Godman met with this species on the Azores. A small flock was usually tc be seen in company with some Turnstones about the rocks near Santa Cruz, in Flores. He was told that in summer they were frequently noticed upon the rough pasture-land, and high up in the mountains. It was the common opinion that they go there only to feed. Mr. Godman had no doubt that they also breed there, as he procured in June a male in full summer or breeding plumage; but his opinions must be regarded as problematical.

In Great Britain, according to Yarrell, the Purple Sandpiper, though well known, is not very numerous. It is found on various parts of the coast, preferring the rocky portions, where it is seen from September, throughout the winter, until April or May. That some which leave do not go far, and that a few remain and breed, is regarded as certain. Some are absent a very short time, young ones returning with them; and on one occasion, on the Farne Islands, Mr. Selby met with a family of this species, the young of which were scarcely able to fly. It is commonly only a winter visitant, and may be seen busily turning over the stones, or searching among the seaweed for the smaller shrimps and sand-hoppers. It also feeds on small crabs, marine insects, and the soft bodies of the smaller shellfish. Mr. Dunn states that it is very numerous in Shetland and the Orkneys in the early spring, collecting there in large flocks. It may be found on the rocks at ebb-tide, watching each retiring wave, running down as the water falls back, picking small shellfish off the stones, and displaying great activity in escaping from the advancing sea. None remain there to breed.

It is said by Wheelwright to breed only in the far north, and never to be seen in Scandinavia except in the autumn, or occasionally in the winter. Sommerfeldt states that it is very common during the summer on the north coast of West Finland. Mr. Wheelwright had received specimens from Iceland and Greenland, but never from Lapland. The Messrs. Godman found it on the islands near Bodöe, in Norway, throughout the summer. The first specimen was obtained May 4. It is occasional in Switzerland and in Italy; and Mr. H. Saunders found it abundant during the winter in Southern Spain.

Mr. Boardman informs me that it is quite common near Calais, Me., in the winter, where it is known as the "Winter Snipe." It is also very abundant about the rocky shores of Grand Menan. It is very irregular in its appearance on the eastern coast of Massachusetts, where in some winters it appears in great numbers, and then again is rarely seen for several years. Mr. Giraud never met with this species, and regarded it as an exceedingly rare bird on the shores of Long Island; occasionally, however, specimens are seen in the New York market which have been taken on the eastern end of that island.

Mr. Kumlien mentions this Wader as the first to arrive at Cumberland, and the last to leave in autumn, coming by the 1st of June, the earliest moment at which they could have found any rocks bare at low-tide. Their arrival took place during a severe snow-storm, and the birds huddled together under the ledges like a flock of Quails in winter. They remained until November, as late as they could find any exposed shore, and were very common. Some are said to remain in the fiords of South Greenland all winter.

They are devoid of fear, and can almost be caught with the hand. They nest on the borders of fresh-water lakes, and at this time nearly desert the sea-shore. When in large flocks they keep up a lively and very pleasant twitter. During the breeding-season the males have a peculiar cry, somewhat resembling that of Bartram's Tattler, but lower, and not so prolonged. When the male utters this note it assumes a dignified strut, raises its wings over its back, and then slowly folds them. The bird is crepuscular in its habits, which in some respects appear to be different from those of most of its family. It is found almost exclusively on rocky shores of the sea, and shuns sandy beaches. It is seldom known to occur far inland. It is a very unsuspicious bird, and when intent on its food seems to be almost entirely regardless of the near presence of man. Its flight is rapid, and can be long sustained in its migrations. This bird is known to hunters as the "Rock Snipe." An egg of this species from Greenland has a ground of a drab color tinged with olivaceous. The egg is pyriform in shape, but is more oval than that of *Arquatella ptilocnemis,* which in some respects it closely resembles. The egg is marked with blotches of sepia-brown, and these are more or less diffused over the entire surface. The eggs in my cabinet — one from Greenland, and others from different localities — average 1.46 inches in length, by 1.10 in their greatest breadth. In some the olivaceous tinge of the ground is much deeper than in others. The spots vary in their number, size, and distribution, in some the smaller end being nearly unspotted.

Arquatella Couesi.

THE ALEUTIAN SANDPIPER.

? *Tringa arquatella,* (part) PALL. Zoog. Rosso-As. II. 1821, 190 (spec. ex Ins Curilica).

Tringa maritima, "BRÜNN." DALL & BANN. Tr. Chicago Acad. I. 1869, 291 (St. Michael's, Alaska). — FINSCH, Abh. Nat. III. 1872, 65 (Alaska).

Tringa (Pelidna) americana, DALL. Pr. Cal. Acad. Sci. Feb. 1873 (Aleutians).

Arquatella Couesi, RIDGW. Bull. Nutt. Orn. Club, V. July, 1880, 160 (Aleutian Islands); Nom. N. Am. B. 1881, no. 531. — COUES, Check List, 2d ed. 1882, no. 621.

SP. CHAR. Similar to *A. maritima,* BRÜNN., but averaging slightly smaller, and the plumage appreciably different at all ages and seasons. *Adult breeding-dress:* Above, fuliginous-slate, the feathers of the pileum broadly edged, those of the dorsal region (including the scapulars) widely bordered, with rusty ochraceous or bright cinnamon (a few of the scapulars and interscapulars tipped with white in some specimens), the central area of each feather nearly black, or much darker than the wings and rump; lesser wing-coverts slightly, and middle coverts broadly, bordered terminally with white; greater coverts widely tipped with white, forming a conspicuous bar across the wing; three or four of the inner secondaries chiefly white, the others, also the inner primaries, narrowly skirted and tipped with white. Rump, upper tail-coverts, and middle tail-feathers, uniform fuliginous-dusky, the remaining rectrices paler, or dull cinereous. A conspicuous whitish superciliary stripe, extending back to the nape, and confluent with the dull whitish of the under side of the head, thus posteriorly bounding a large sooty-brown auricular area; anterior portion of the lores, with the forehead, dull smoky grayish; neck, jugulum, and breast, dirty whitish (sometimes soiled with dingy buff), and clouded or spotted with dull slate, sooty plumbeous, or dusky black, this sometimes forming a large patch on each side of the breast; remaining lower parts pure white, the sides with chain-like series of brownish slaty spots mixed with streaks, the crissum streaked with dusky; lining of the wing pure white, the border brownish gray. Bill, legs, and feet brownish black in the dried skin; iris brown. *In fresh specimens,* "feet, legs, and base of bill dark greenish yellow; terminal two thirds of bill black, or very dark brown" (NELSON, MS.). *Winter plumage:* Above, soft smoky plumbeous, the scapulars and interscapulars glossy purplish dusky centrally, the plumbeous borders to the feathers causing a squamate appearance; head and neck uniform plumbeous, except the throat and a supraloral patch, which are streaked whitish; jugulum squamated with white, the breast similarly but more broadly marked. Wings, etc., as in summer. *Young, first plumage:* Scapulars and interscapulars black, broadly bordered with bright rusty and buffy white, the latter chiefly on the longer and outer scapulars and posterior part of the back; wing-coverts broadly bordered with buffy white; pileum streaked black and ochraceous; jugulum and breast pale buff, or buffy white, streaked with dusky. *Downy young:* Above, bright rusty fulvous, irregularly mottled with black, the back, wings, and rump ornamented by yellowish-white downy flecks or papillæ; head above deep fulvous brown, with a longitudinal stripe of velvety black from the forehead to the occiput, where confluent with a cross band of the same, the lores with two nearly parallel longitudinal streaks of black; there are also other, rather indefinite, black markings, chiefly on the superciliary and occipital regions. Lower parts white, becoming distinctly fulvous laterally.

Wing, 4.50–5.15 (4.86) inches; culmen, .98–1.25 (1.13); tarsus, .88–1.00 (.95) · middle toe, .78–.90 (.86). (Extreme and average measurements of 14 adults.)

HAB. Aleutian Islands and coast of Alaska, north to St. Michael's; west to Commander Islands.

The present species is closely allied to *Arquatella maritima*, BRÜNN., and can with difficulty be distinguished in its winter plumage. A close comparison, however, shows that in this livery *A. Couesi* has decidedly less of the purple gloss to the dorsal region, where the plumbeous borders to the feathers are both broader and paler; the foreneck is also invariably squamated or streaked with white, and not uniformly mouse-gray, as in *maritima*. It is still more nearly related to *A. ptilocnemis*, COUES, of the Prybilof Islands, but averages much smaller, and is always very much darker-colored in every stage of plumage. The three are not only strictly congeneric, but are very probably the descendants of one original stock; but, since no intermediate specimens have been observed in a large series of each kind, they may be considered as having passed the "varietal stage," so that we may treat them as distinct species. Both Mr. Harting and Dr. Coues were wrong in referring *A. ptilocnemis* to the same group as *Pelidna alpina*, which bears only a superficial resemblance in coloration, the details of form being quite different.

While I have been unable to find any name which can be applied to this species, it appears that Pallas refers to it in his description of *Tringa arquatella*, in "Zoög. Rosso-Asiat." II. p. 190, since he says that specimens of his species from the Kurile Islands are marked with rusty yellow, as in the bird under consideration: "Corpus supra plumis fuscis, margine pallidis (*in Curilica ave ferrugineo-luteis*) . . . pectore cinerescens (*in curilica var. lutescens*)." All Alaskan references to *Tringa maritima* of course apply to the present species.

Arquatella ptilocnemis.

THE PRYBILOF SANDPIPER.

Tringa crassirostris, "TEMM. & SCHLEG." DALL, Am. Nat. VIII. 1873, 635 (St. Paul's I. Alaska). — COUES, in Elliott's Alaska, 1873 (not paged); ed. 1875, 182; Check List, 1873, no. 426 bis.

Tringa ptilocnemis, COUES, in Elliott's Alaska, 1873 (not paged); ed. 1875, 182, footnote; Birds N. W. 1874, 491.

Arquatella ptilocnemis, RIDGW. Bull. Nutt. Orn. Club, V. July, 1880, 163; Nom. N. Am. B. 1882, no. 532. — COUES, Check List, 2d ed. 1882, no. 622.

Tringa gracilis, HARTING, P. Z. S. Apr. 1874, 242 (Prybilof Islands).

Black-breasted Sandpiper, COUES, l. c.

HAB. Prybilof Islands, Alaska.

SP. CHAR. Similar to *A. maritima*, but larger, and much lighter colored. *Adult, breeding-plumage:* Back and scapulars light clay-color, or ochraceous, the centre of each feather black, the tips of many of them narrowly whitish; rump and upper tail-coverts dark slate, the feathers indistinctly tipped with plumbeous-gray. Wings plumbeous-gray, the coverts bordered with grayish white, the greater coverts widely tipped with pure white; several (three or four) of the inner secondaries (not tertials) wholly pure white; primaries slate color, with white shafts, the inner ones distinctly edged with white toward the base. Pileum light fulvous, widely streaked with blackish; nape light fulvous, mixed with pale grayish, narrowly and indistinctly streaked. An indistinct loral stripe (this sometimes obsolete), and auriculars, pale grayish fulvous, finely and indistinctly streaked; rest of the head, including a superciliary stripe, and entire lower parts, white, the jugulum usually (in highest plumage) washed with ochraceous, and (always?) streaked with dusky; breast blotched with dusky, the blotches usually coalesced into an irregular large patch, sometimes covering the whole breast; flanks and under tail-coverts marked sparsely with very narrow shaft-streaks of dusky. Inner border of the wing spotted with light grayish, and under primary coverts very pale ash-gray. *Adult, winter plumage:* Wings, rump, tail-coverts, tail, and posterior lower parts as in the summer plumage. Remaining upper parts continuous light ashy plumbeous (many shades lighter than in *A. maritima*), the feathers of the back and the scapulars darker centrally, and with a very faint purplish gloss in certain lights. Head light grayish, darker and almost unbroken on the pileum, lighter and streaked with white elsewhere, the throat white, and but sparsely streaked. Jugulum and breast white, irregularly marked with pale ash-gray.

Young, first plumage: Above, very similar to the summer dress of the adult, but the wing-coverts widely bordered with pale buff; head and neck also very similarly colored. Jugulum pale buff, distinctly marked with short streaks and sagittate marks of dusky gray. *Downy Young:* Above, bright tawny fulvous, irregularly marbled with black, the back and rump bespangled with downy, dot-like flecks of yellowish white; the nape nearly uniform light fulvous grayish; forehead pale buff, with a very narrow medial streak of black, reaching nearly to the bill, and extending posteriorly into the fulvous of the crown and occiput, which is irregularly marbled, longitudinally, with black; a narrow black loral streak reaching about half way to the eye, with a still narrower rictal streak.

Total length, about 9.50 inches; wing, 5.00–5.40; culmen, 1.15–1.45; tarsus, .95–1.00; middle toe, .85–.98.

Although, at first sight, this Sandpiper seems very distinct from *A. maritima* and *A. Couesi*, especially the latter, the apparent differences become greatly reduced upon the careful examination of a large series of specimens. The dimensions, while averaging considerably greater (except as regards the feet), are yet found to inosculate with those of that species, while the difference in plumage, as compared with *A. Couesi*, proves to be solely one of intensity of colors — the lighter tints prevailing in *ptilocnemis*, the darker ones in *Couesi*. The exact correspondence of pattern of coloration between the two extends to every stage of plumage, even including the downy chick. We therefore, all things considered, look upon the present bird as being merely a local insular race of a species of which *A. Couesi* represents the resident form of the coast of Alaska and the Aleutian Chain, and from which *A. maritima* is perhaps not specifically distinct.

For what little we know of the habits of this newly discovered species we are indebted to Mr. Henry W. Elliott, who found a few breeding on the Prybilof Islands. In his brief account of its manner of life he states that it was the only Wader that he found breeding on these islands, with the marked exception, now and then, of a stray pair of *Lobipes hyperboreus*. It is said to make its appearance early in May, and to repair to the dry uplands and mossy hummocks, where it breeds. Its nest is simply a cavity in a bunch of moss, in which the bird deposits its four darkly blotched pyriform eggs, hatching them out within twenty days.

The young come from the shell clothed in a thick yellowish down, with dark-brown markings on the head and back, but taking on the plumage of their parents, and being able to fly as early as the 10th of August; and at that season old and young flock together for the first time, and confine themselves to the sand-beaches and surf-margins about the islands for a few weeks, when they take flight, leaving the islands from about the 1st to the 5th of September, and disappearing until the opening of the new season.

Mr. Elliott describes this bird as a most devoted and fearless parent, and states that he has known it to flutter in feigned distress around by the hour, uttering a low piping note when its nest was too nearly approached. It also makes a sound exactly like our tree-frogs; and before Mr. Elliott had traced the noise to this source, he had searched several weeks, unavailingly, for these reptiles, misled by the call of this bird.

The eggs have the following measurements: 1.60 by 1.10; 1.52 by 1.10; 1.50 by 1.11, and 1.55 by 1.09 inches. They are decidedly pyriform in shape, one end being much more obtuse than the other, the acute ends retreating in a very pronounced manner. The ground-color in all the specimens is of a pure and clear drab, and is very boldly marked with large blotches of sepia brown, intermingled with other markings which are suffused with a wash of a purplish ash. In some instances the sepia markings are dilute, and in others they are intensified almost to blackness. The eggs were taken June 19, 1873, and were then quite fresh.

Genus **ACTODROMAS**, Kaup.

Actodromas, Kaup, Sk. Ent. Eur. Thierw. 1829, 37 (type, *Tringa minuta*, Leisl.).
Heteropygia, Coues, Pr. Philad. Acad. 1861, 190 (type, *Tringa Bonapartei*, Schleg. = *T. fuscicollis*, Vieill.).
Leimonites, Kaup, t. c. (type, *Tringa Temmincki*, Leisl.).
Delopygia, Coues, Pr. Philad. Acad. 1861, 190 (= *Heteropygia*).

Char. Size medium to very small (smallest of the family); form graceful, legs and bill slender, the latter straight, and little, if any, longer than the tarsus. Tarsus decidedly longer than the middle toe with its claws; toes slender, completely cleft. Wings long and pointed, their ends when closed reaching beyond the tip of the tail.

A. maculata.

Although the species of this genus vary greatly in size, they all agree very closely in the details of structure. Besides the American species included in the following synoptical table, there are several Old World *Actodromi*, among which may be named *Tringa minuta*, Leisl., and *T. albescens*, Temm., both nearly allied to, though quite distinct from, our *A. minutilla*. The American species may be distinguished as follows: —

A. Size large (wings more than 5.50).

1. **A. Cooperi.** Tail even, the middle feathers scarcely narrowed at the end, and not projecting notably beyond the rest. Lower parts white, the jugulum, breast, and sides longitudinally flecked with dusky. Above (in adult), brownish gray, the feathers marked centrally with black, producing conspicuous spots on the back and scapulars, streaks elsewhere. Upper tail-coverts white, with irregular sagittate marks of dusky. Wing, 5.80; culmen, 1.25; tarsus, 1.20; middle toe, .80. *Hab.* Long Island.

B. Size medium (wing less than 5.50 and more than 4.00).

2. **A. fuscicollis.** Tail as in *A. Cooperi*, but middle feathers slightly narrower at end and more projecting. Colors of adult as in *A. Cooperi*, but more tinged with light rufous on crown, back, and scapulars. *Young:* Back and scapulars mixed black and rusty, the feathers conspicuously bordered terminally with white; upper tail-coverts white, in marked contrast with the dusky rump; breast light grayish-brown, streaked with dusky, Wing, about 4.90; culmen, .90–1.00; tarsus, .95–1.00; middle toe, .70–.75. *Hab.* Eastern North America; South America in migrations.

3. **A. Bairdi.** Tail as in *A. fuscicollis*. Upper tail-coverts dusky, only the lateral ones whitish. *Adult in summer:* Back and scapulars black, irregularly variegated (spotted and edged) with dull buff. Jugulum white, streaked with dusky. *Adult in winter:* Above, nearly uniform grayish brown, tinged with clay-color; jugulum and sides deeply suffused with clay-color or dirty buff, the former very indistinctly streaked. *Young:* Above, light buffy brown, streaked with dusky, the feathers of the back and the scapulars blackish, conspicuously bordered terminally with dull white; wing-coverts dark grayish, also bordered terminally with white or light buff. Jugulum suffused with buff and indistinctly streaked. Wings, about 4.75–5.00; culmen, about .90; tarsus, .90; middle toe, .70. *Hab.* Western America, from the Arctic Regions to Patagonia; straggler in Eastern North America.

4. **A. maculata.** Middle tail-feathers wedge-shaped at the end and projecting a quarter of an inch or more beyond the rest. Upper tail-coverts dusky, like the rump, the outer feathers whitish, marked with dusky. Jugulum and breast light clay-color, streaked with dusky. *Adult:* Above, without white markings. *Young:* Scapulars bordered terminally with white. Wing, about 5.00; culmen, 1.10; tarsus, 1.00–1.10; middle toe, .90. *Hab.* America in general, breeding in the Arctic Regions.

5. **A. acuminata.** Similar to *A. maculata*, but with the middle tail-feathers still narrower and more pointed, the bill smaller, the jugulum and breast scarcely streaked; lower tail-coverts marked with shaft-streaks of dusky (entirely absent in *maculata*); pileum deep rusty, in strong contrast. *Adult:* Upper parts brownish gray, the feathers marked centrally with blackish; jugulum and breast pale grayish buff, very sparsely streaked; pileum cinnamon-brown, streaked with blackish. *Young:* Above, rusty fulvous, the feathers of the back and the scapulars black centrally, the larger feathers edged terminally with white; pileum bright rusty rufous, in very sharp contrast with a whitish superciliary stripe, and streaked with black; throat immaculate white; jugulum and breast deep rusty ochraceous, the former narrowly streaked anteriorly. Wing, about 5.00; culmen, scarcely 1.00; tarsus, 1.20; middle toe, .85. *Hab.* Australia, etc.; abundant in autumn on coast of Alaska.

C. Size very small (wing less than 4.00).

6. **A. minutilla.** Middle tail-feathers slightly projecting, narrow and somewhat pointed at end in summer, broader and rounded in winter plumage. Upper tail-coverts blackish, the lateral ones white, marked with dusky. *Adult in summer:* Back and scapulars black, the feathers bordered and irregularly barred with rusty ochraceous; tertials bordered with the same. Jugulum dull white, streaked with dusky. *Adult in winter:* Above, uniform brownish gray, the feathers with indistinct dusky mesial streaks, most distinct on the back. Jugulum pale grayish, indistinctly streaked. *Young:* Similar to the adult in summer, but the scapulars and exterior feathers of the back bordered terminally on outer webs with white, and lacking the concealed ochraceous bars. Jugulum very indistinctly streaked, as in the winter plumage. *Hab.* North America, migrating into South America in winter.

Actodromas Cooperi.

COOPER'S SANDPIPER.

Tringa Cooperi, BAIRD, Birds N. Am. 1858, 716 ; ed. 1860, pl. 89, fig. 1. — COUES, Check List, 1873, no. 422 ; Birds N. W. 1874, 491.

Tringa (*Actodromas*) *Cooperi*, COUES, Key, 1872, 255.

Actodromas (*Heteropygia*) *Cooperi*, COUES, Pr. Ac. Nat. Sci. Philad. 1861. 202.

Actodromas Cooperi, RIDGW. Nom. N. Am. B. 1881, no. 535. — COUES, Check List, 2d ed. 1882, no. 618.

HAB. Long Island ; only one specimen known.

SP. CHAR. Nearly as large as *Tringa canutus*, but a typical *Actodromas* in form and coloration. *Adult, summer plumage:* Almost exactly like *A. fuscicollis*, but with a less amount of reddish tinge to the upper parts, and the upper tail-coverts more distinctly marked with dusky. Above, brownish gray, the feathers marked centrally with black, producing rather large, irregularly cuneate spots on the back and scapulars, and longitudinal streaks elsewhere, the latter broadest on the crown, where the ground-color inclines to grayish buff ; a few of the scapulars slightly tinged with light rusty ochraceous ; rump grayish dusky, the feathers bordered with grayish white, and marked with blackish shaft-streaks ; upper tail-coverts white, with irregular sagittate markings of dusky. Wing-

coverts brownish gray, the smaller with darker centres and blackish shafts, the greater distinctly tipped with white ; remiges dusky, the inner primaries edged toward bases, the secondaries toward and around ends, with white ; shafts of the primaries white, becoming brown basally and terminally. Tail light brownish gray, the middle feathers darker terminally, the others indistinctly edged with whitish. Lower parts white, the sides of the head and neck and the jugulum tinged with light rusty buff, and thickly streaked with dusky ; breast, sides, and flanks marked with coarser, irregular, mostly longitudinal specks of dusky, becoming sagittate in form on the flanks ; lower tail-coverts with narrow streaks of dusky. Lining of the wing white, spotted exteriorly and anteriorly with dusky ; under primary coverts pale gray, edged and tipped with white.

Total length, about 9.50 inches ; wing, 5.80 ; culmen, 1.25 ; tarsus, 1.20 ; middle toe, .80.

The relationships of this bird, the type specimen of which still remains unique, are unquestionably with *Actodromas fuscicollis*, from which it could hardly be distinguished, were it not for its much greater size. The plumage is entirely the same, except that there is less of a reddish tinge above, and the upper tail-coverts are more distinctly relieved by V-shaped markings of dusky. It is totally distinct from *T. canutus*, with which it scarcely needs comparison at all, the very different proportions, aside from the differences in coloration, distinguishing it at once.

The history of the manners, habits, and distribution of this rare species continues to remain unknown, and its existence as a veritable species to rest on the evidence of a single specimen. The type, which has thus far remained unique, was taken on the 24th of May, 1833, on Raynor South, Long Island, by William Cooper, and named by Professor Baird in honor of its discoverer. We know nothing as to any individual peculiarities exhibited at the time of its capture, but we may venture the suggestion that its habits probably do not essentially differ from those of the Bonaparte Sandpiper.

Actodromas fuscicollis.

BONAPARTE'S SANDPIPER.

Tringa fuscicollis, VIEILL. Nouv. Dict. XXXIV. 1819, 461 (based on *Chorlito pestorejo pardo*, AZARA, Apunt. III. 1805, 322, Paraguay). — COUES, Birds N. W. 1874, 487.

Tringa Schinzii, BONAP. Synop. 1828, 249; Am. Orn. IV. 1833, 69, pl. 24, fig. 2. — NUTT. Man. II. 1834, 109. — SW. & RICH. F. B. A. II. 1831, 384. — AUD. Orn. Biog. III. 1833, 529, pl. 278; Synop. 1839, 236; B. Am. V. 1842, 275, pl. 335.

Tringa Bonapartei, SCHLEG. Rev. Crit. Ois. Eur. 1844, 89. — CASS. in Baird's B. N. Am. 1858, 722 (part). — BAIRD, Cat. N. Am. B. 1859, no. 533. — COUES, Key, 1872, 255; Check List, 1873, no. 421.

Actodromas Bonapartei, COUES, Check List, 2d ed. 1882, no. 617.

Tringa melanotus, BLAS. List B. Eur. 1862, 19 (nec VIEILL.).

Tringa dorsalis, LICHT. Nomencl. 1854, 92 (fide DRESSER).

Actodromas fuscicollis, RIDGW. Nom. N. Am. B. 1882, no. 536.

HAB. Eastern Province of North America, breeding in the high north; in winter, the whole of Middle America, South America, and the West Indies; Falkland Islands; occasional in Europe.

SP. CHAR. *Adult in summer:* Above, light brownish gray, much tinged, particularly on the crown, back, and inner scapulars, with light rusty buff or ochraceous, all the feathers black centrally, these markings largest and somewhat V-shaped, or sagittate, on the scapulars, streak-like elsewhere, the streaks broadest on the crown and back; rump dusky blackish, the feathers bordered with light gray; upper tail-coverts pure white, in marked contrast, some of the feathers having irregular sagittate, mostly concealed, spots of dusky. Tail brownish gray, the middle feathers blackish, and all slightly edged with whitish. Wing-coverts and tertials brownish gray,

lighter on edges and dusky centrally, the shafts nearly black. Superciliary stripe and entire lower parts pure white; auriculars light buff, indistinctly streaked; sides of head and neck, foreneck, jugulum, and upper part of breast, streaked or dashed with dusky; sides and flanks with larger irregular markings of the same. *Adult in winter:* Wings, rump, upper tail-coverts, and tail as in summer plumage; rest of upper parts continuous brownish gray, relieved by rather indistinct mesial streaks of black; streaks on jugulum, etc., less sharply defined than in the summer plumage. *Young, first plumage:* Back and scapulars black, the feathers bordered terminally with pure white, and laterally with ferruginous, those of the middle of the back also tipped with this color; feathers of the pileum and rump, as well as the tertials, also bordered with rusty; wing-coverts bordered with pale grayish buff. Otherwise as in the winter plumage, but breast, jugulum, etc., suffused with pale fulvous.

Total length, about 7 inches; wing, 4.90; culmen, .90–1.00; tarsus, .95–1.00; middle toe, .70–.75.

Specimens from South America are exactly like northern ones, among which there is the usual amount of individual variation. In midsummer the black of the back and scapulars increases in relative extent, partly by the wearing away of the rusty borders to the feathers, until, in some examples, the dorsal aspect is chiefly black.

The history of the habits and manner of life of the Bonaparte Sandpiper is still but imperfectly known, and the entire range of its distribution is, without doubt, very far from having been fully ascertained. On the Atlantic coast and, to a certain extent, in the interior, it is a migratory visitant, both in the spring and in the fall. During the season of reproduction it visits high Arctic regions, is known to breed in the vicinity of the Arctic coast, and is given by Reinhardt as one of the birds of Greenland. It is stated by Holböll to breed near Julianehaab, where small flocks of old and young were observed by him in August. A very young bird was obtained at Nenortalik in 1835, another in 1840, and three others in 1841.

It is also said to occur and to breed in the extreme southern portions of South America, and to visit the Falkland Islands. During its autumnal migrations it is found in Bermuda, where Major Wedderburn met with it in the fall, and where it was in company with *A. maculata*.

In Massachusetts it also occurs, but is not a very common bird. Mr. William Brewster informs me that in this State, according to his observations, it is not abundant, although its visits are constant, uniform, and regular. It passes north in May, and reappears in its southern migration as early as the 20th of July. It has a very peculiar note, unlike that of any other Sandpiper, which is not in any sense a whistling, but is a low lisping sound, and almost the only cry of a shore-bird which is neither mellow nor whistling. When disturbed, it moves quickly off, repeating this rather low note, which, however, is always distinctly audible above that of the small *Tringæ* with which it associates.

According to Captain C. C. Abbott, this little Sandpiper makes its appearance in the summer on the Falkland Islands, and is known to breed on East Falkland. He met with the young birds, but was not able to find their nests. Mr. H. Durnford also, in his Notes on the Birds of Central Patagonia, speaks of this species as resident. He found it very common in the valleys of both the Sengel and the Sengelen, and always in flocks.

This species, once confounded with distinct European species, was supposed to have a more cosmopolitan distribution than it is now credited with. At present it is thought to be confined to the American continent, occurring along the entire Atlantic sea-coast, and to be met with more sparingly on the banks of interior rivers and lakes.

On Long Island, according to Giraud, it is not a very plentiful species, having never been observed by him in large flocks, although during his excursions he frequently met with small parties distributed along the margins of creeks and pools, feeding in company with the Semipalmated Sandpiper, from which it can always be distinguished by its superior size. It is described as being more watchful than that species, seeming to be more alarmed at the report of a gun, and usually flying to a greater distance. It seldom revisits the place from which it has been driven, although its less timid companion always returns immediately to its feeding-grounds, seemingly as unconcerned as before its flight. Mr. Giraud also states that he has met with this species along the banks of the Hudson River near Poughkeepsie, and on the margins of ponds in the interior counties of New York.

Richardson states that he found this species not unfrequent on the shores of the small lakes which skirt the Saskatchewan Plains. Mr. Audubon met with it at different times in Kentucky, and along the Atlantic shores from Florida to Maine. In the United States he observed it only in the latter part of autumn and in the winter. He procured examples in Labrador at the beginning of August, which were all young birds about to take their departure. He secured also specimens at St. Augustine, in Florida, on the 2d of December. He has always found this species less shy than any other of the same genus; in this respect his observations not according with those of Giraud.

The author of the "Key to North American Birds" met with birds of this species in Labrador, for the first time, July 30. On the 1st of September, when he left that region, it was his belief that they were still as numerous as ever. They were found in great abundance on the rocky shores of that region, where covered with seaweeds and interspersed with muddy flats and shallow pools, in which these birds wade quite up to their breasts, and also in situations where he never found any other kind of Sandpiper — on large masses of rock sloping down abruptly to the water, green and slippery from the continued dashing of the spray. The bird seemed to be very fond of these localities.

Of all the Sandpipers, this is spoken of as the most gentle and unsuspecting, and as being utterly regardless of the near approach of man, not even intermitting its occupation of searching for food, though the observer may be standing within a few feet of it. When startled, it flies off in a very compact flock, uttering a low, soft *tweet*, very different from that of any other Sandpiper. If a part of a flock be killed, the hunter may make equal havoc with his second barrel, as, after a few circlings, those left fly past or alight again on the same spot. This bird flies rapidly, in a rather unsteady manner, alternately showing the under and the upper parts, and may always be recognized, when on the wing, by the conspicuously white upper tail-coverts. It was found associating with the Semipalmated Sandpipers and the Ring Plovers. Those procured were not conspicuously fat.

Mr. N. B. Moore informs us that he met with this species in Florida during the winter months, but that the greater portion seemed to move farther south. The same gentleman in 1876 again observed this species on Fortune Island, one of the Bahamas, where he procured an example as early as the 5th of August.

Mr. Nelson found this bird a rather common migrant on the shores of Lake Michigan, in Illinois. He met with it as late as the 9th of June. Dr. Hoy writes of it as a bird formerly abundant near Racine during its migrations, but as now quite rare; and Mr. R. P. Clarke is quoted as having taken this species late in autumn upon the lake shore near Chicago. Dr. James C. Merrill mentions it as common in Southeastern Texas during the winter.

Mr. L. Kumlien states that this species breeds in Kinguah and Kinguite fiords, and in other suitable localities on both shores of Cumberland Sound. Considerable numbers were observed along the beach near Nuboyant, on the west shore, in July, where they were in all probability breeding.

Mr. MacFarlane was so fortunate as to meet with several nests, with the eggs, of this species on or near the Arctic coast. One of these, taken July 3 on the shore of the Arctic Sea, contained four eggs with very large embryos. Another, found on the following day, contained three eggs. A third, found June 29 on the Barren Grounds, was a mere depression in the ground, lined with a few decayed leaves, containing four eggs with very large embryos. A fourth, obtained on the banks of a small river, was composed of a few decayed leaves, and held four eggs.

Eggs of this species found on the Barren Grounds, near the Arctic coast, by Mr. MacFarlane (S. I. No. 11329), are pyriform in shape, and have a ground-color of a rufous drab marked with bold patches of dark sepia brown, interspersed with spots in which this shade is deepened almost into blackness, and which are collected in confluent groupings around the larger end. These eggs measure 1.35 inches in length by .95 in breadth.

Actodromas Bairdi.

BAIRD'S SANDPIPER.

(?) *Tringa melanotos*, VIEILL. Nouv. Dict. XXXIV. 1819, 462 (based on *Chorlito lomo negro*, AZARA).
Tringa Bonapartii, "SCHLEG." CASS. in Baird's B. N. Am. 1858, 722 (part; nec SCHLEG.).
Tringa maculata, SCHLEG. Mus. P.-B. Scolopaces, 1864, 39 (part).
Actodromas Bairdii, COUES, Pr. Ac. Nat. Sci. Philad. 1861, 194; Check List, 2d ed. 1882, no. 615. — RIDGW. Nom. N. Am. B. 1881, no. 537.
Tringa Bairdii, SCL. P. Z. S. 1867, 332 (Chili). — COUES, Key, 1872, 255; Check List, 1873, no. 419; Birds N. W. 1874, 484.

HAB. America in general, but chiefly the interior of the northern, and the western portion of the southern, continent, ranging from the Arctic coast to Chili and Buenos Ayres; rare in the Eastern Province, and not yet recorded from the Pacific coast of the United States; accidental in South Africa?

SP. CHAR. *Adult in summer:* Above, variegated with black and grayish buff, the former prevailing, in the form of irregular, somewhat diamond-shaped spots on the back and scapulars, the buff occupying most of the border of the feathers, and sending indentations toward the shaft; elsewhere, the black forms distinct streaks, widest on the crown and anterior part of the back; rump and upper tail-coverts dusky-brownish black, feathers bordered with dull clay-color, the exterior ones of the latter chiefly white, with irregular U-shaped markings of dusky. Tail light brownish gray, the middle feather nearly black, all narrowly edged with whitish. Wing-coverts and tertials grayish brown, with lighter edges and darker centres; remiges dull slate. Lower parts white, the sides of the head and neck, the jugulum, and anterior portion of the sides, streaked with dusky. *Adult in winter:* Above, continuous grayish clay-color, the feathers with darker mesial streaks; rump and middle upper tail-coverts dusky, the feathers bordered terminally with dull clay-color; lateral upper tail-coverts brownish white. Beneath, brownish white, the jugulum, breast, sides (anteriorly), and sides of the neck, deeply suffused with clay-color or dull buff. *Young, first plu-*

mage: Above, grayish clay-color, the scapulars and interscapulars blackish centrally, and conspicuously bordered with whitish terminally; the feathers of the crown and nape streaked with dusky. Wing-coverts, rump, etc., much as in the winter plumage; sides of the head and neck, the jugulum, and breast, pale clay-color, rather indistinctly streaked with dusky. Other lower parts white.

Total length, about 7.00 to 7.50 inches; extent, about 15.00; wing, about 4.75; culmen, usually less than 1.00 inch; tarsus, nearly 1.00; middle toe, about .70. Bill black; iris dark brown; legs and feet slate black.

Baird's Sandpiper has been so recently recognized as a species wholly distinct from the Bonaparte Sandpiper, that much remains to be learned in regard to its distribution and other specific peculiarities. Its early history has been more or less blended with that of other species to which it has certain proximate resemblances. It is probable that when sufficient explorations shall have been made to develop a knowledge of its migrations and habits, it will be found to have a much wider distribution than was at first supposed; indeed it is already known to be generally distributed throughout the interior of North America and to the western portions of South America, and it has quite recently been ascertained to be of occasional occurrence on the Atlantic coast. Mr. H. W. Henshaw procured a single specimen, Aug. 27, 1870, on one of the islands in Boston Harbor; and since then Mr. Maynard has obtained some of this species near Ipswich, Mass., and examples have been taken on the same coast by others.

In his "Notes on the Birds of Colorado," Mr. J. A. Allen mentions meeting with this species in that State, not far from Colorado City; and Dr. Woodhouse speaks of seeing birds of this species at different times in various parts of the Indian Territory, as well as in New Mexico, calling them *Tringa Schinzii.* The specimens procured by Dr. Woodhouse near the Pueblo of Zuñi are in the National Museum, and are now known to belong to this species, thus extending its range to the region west of the Rocky Mountains.

It has also been ascertained that three examples, referred to by Mr. Cassin as *Tringa Bonapartei*, really belonged to this species. These were from Omaha, Fort Kearney, and the Yellowstone Region; and it is now known that during the fall migration in the month of August this species is one of the most abundant Sandpipers in Dakota, Idaho, and Montana. It occurs in small flocks along the rivers and small lakes, and also in all other suitable places among the Rocky Mountains. It is not only found among the small saline pools of the prairies, generally near watercourses, but also at times at a distance from any permanent stream. It is described as a very quiet and gentle species, and one that may be approached and secured with ease.

Mr. Henshaw, in his Report on the Birds of Utah and Colorado, states that during its spring and fall migrations, Baird's Sandpiper occurs over most of the interior of North America. Throughout Colorado, New Mexico, and Arizona he found it quite evenly distributed, making its appearance from the north about the latter part of August, and becoming tolerably common in September. He never met with it in large flocks, not more than five or six being generally found together, the number being often swelled by the addition of a few of other species of Waders. These birds are so unsuspicious that he has often walked up to within a dozen feet of a little flock, as they scattered about with hasty steps in search of food. They are not so partial to the vicinity of water as most of the other members of the Wading family, although in general sharing their habits. He not unfrequently met with them about the stock corrals, and even in yards close to the houses.

In the summer of 1872, late in August, Mr. Trippe saw large flocks of this species near the summit of Mount Evans in Colorado, at an elevation of nearly fourteen thousand feet above the sea; they were feeding on grasshoppers.

Mr. Ridgway has also met with this species in Nevada, where he found it rather common during the period of its migrations, associating with various other Sandpipers, particularly with *Actodromas minutilla* and *Ereunetes pusillus.* It has also been noticed on the Pacific coast, as Mr. Dall states that one specimen was obtained by Bischoff at Sitka, and several at Kadiak; and it is not rare on the Yukon. A single specimen was procured on Amak Island, north of the peninsula of Alaska, by Captain Everett Smith.

Mr. J. Edmund Harting, in the "Ibis" (1870, p. 151), states that a single specimen of this species was taken at Walvisch Bay, Africa, Oct. 24, 1863. The finding of this species in Southwestern Africa appears to be not a little remarkable, as it has thus far not been recognized as occurring in Europe. The specimen from Walvisch Bay was found in the collection made there by Mr. C. J. Anderson, and carefully identified.

Mr. Nelson regarded this species as, in his experience, a rather uncommon migrant in Northeastern Illinois, during the middle of May, and again in the last of August and the first of September. It was generally found in small parties or singly, in company with other species of Sandpipers; but it was occasionally seen in large flocks. The same writer, in his Notes on the Birds observed by him on the Humboldt River, near Elko, Nevada, states that several flocks of Baird's Sandpiper were noticed on the small sandbars along the river, and that a single example was obtained.

Dr. James C. Merrill mentions that two specimens, both females, were taken by him on the Lower Rio Grande, March 30, 1876, on a sandbar in the river.

This species was found breeding on the Barren Grounds, June 24, by Mr. MacFarlane. The nest had been made on the ground in a swampy district, between two small lakes, and was composed of a few decayed leaves laid loosely in a small hole or depression, shaded by a tuft of grass. The female bird glided from the nest on being approached, passing closely to him, and then fluttered along, drooping her wings as if wounded, endeavoring thus to lead him away from the nest. This was a rare bird in that quarter. The eggs of this species are usually four in number. One set (S. I. No. 14085) exhibit the following measurements: 1.40 by .99, 1.35 by 1.02, 1.32 by .98, and 1.31 by .98. Their ground-color is a light drab, generally and very uniformly sprinkled with dottings, spots, and a few larger confluent blotches of a bright sepia brown. These are occasionally larger, and a little more numerous at the obtuse end, but generally are distributed with very little difference over the whole surface of the egg.

Actodromas maculata.

THE PECTORAL SANDPIPER.

Tringa maculata, Vieill. Nouv. Dict. XXXIV. 1819, 465. — Cass. in Baird's B. N. Am. 1858, 720. — Baird, Cat. N. Am. B. 1859, no. 531. — Coues, Key, 1872, 255; Check List, 1873, no. 420; Birds N. W. 1874, 486.

Actodromas maculata, Coues, Pr. Ac. Nat. Sci. Philad. 1861, 197, 230; Check List, 2d ed. 1882, no. 616. — Ridgw. Nom. N. Am. B. 1881, no. 534.

Pelidna pectoralis, Bonap. Comp. List, 1838, 50.

Tringa pectoralis, Say, Long's Exp. I. 1823, 171. — Nutt. Man. II. 1834, 111. — Aud. Orn. Biog. III. 1835, 601; V. 1839, 582, pl. 294; Synop. 1839, 232; B. Am. V. 1842, 259, pl. 329.

Tringa dominicensis, Degl. Orn. Eur. II. 1849, 232.

Hab. The whole of North, and the greater part of South, America, ranging south in winter to Southern Brazil and Chili; West Indies in general; Bermudas; frequent in Europe; North China ? (Swinh. "Ibis," 1863, 97). Breeds in Arctic regions.

Sp. Char. *Adult in summer:* Above, light clay-color, the crown, back, scapulars, and tertials washed with light rufous or rusty ochraceous; the feathers black centrally, producing conspicuous streaks, which widen into spots on the scapulars and back; rump and middle upper tail-coverts brownish black; lateral upper tail-coverts white, with dusky shaft-streaks. Middle tail-feathers dusky, edged with lighter; other rectrices pale brownish gray, bordered with white. Wing-coverts light grayish brown, with paler borders and darker centres; a light superciliary stripe, and a darker loral one. Cheeks, sides of the neck, whole jugulum, and breast, pale clay-color or light grayish buff, streaked with dusky; sides sparsely streaked. Remaining lower parts immaculate white. "Basal half of bill dull greenish yellow" (NELSON, MS.). *Adult in winter:* Similar to summer plumage, but the rusty tint above almost or wholly absent, and the black markings less sharply defined. *Young, first plumage:* Quite similar to the summer adult, but the scapulars and outer interscapulars conspicuously tipped externally with white, the breast, etc., more distinctly buff, and rather more narrowly streaked.

Total length, about 9.00 inches; wing, about 5.00; culmen, 1.10; tarsus, 1.00–1.10; middle toe, .90.

The history of this bird is very imperfectly known. During its seasons of migration it is quite abundant, both on the sea-coast and in the interior, about the borders of ponds and the shores of lakes and rivers. As to its distribution during the breeding-season, we have no positive information. Solitary individuals have been observed by Mr. Kumlien about Lake Koskonong during the summer, and at first he supposed they were breeding; but as no nests were found, it is supposed that these individuals were only unmated birds. This species has also been observed in the vicinity of Boston late in July, in company with the *minutilla;* but it is impossible to determine whether the birds thus seen were immature, or such as had thus early completed the duties of incubation. It is comparatively rare on the Pacific coast. A single specimen was collected at Sitka by Bischoff, and Dall speaks of it as not uncommon at Plover Bay, Siberia; but it was not noticed by him on the Aleutian Islands. Dr. Cooper has met with none on the California coast, but states that they have been taken at Puget Sound; and as they visit South America, he thinks that they must occasionally be found on the southern coast of California: but this is purely conjectural. It was taken at Fort Simpson by Mr. B. R. Ross, at Fort Anderson by Mr. MacFarlane, and at Fort Resolution by Mr. Kennicott.

In the winter this bird visits the West Indies, Central America, where it is very abundant, as well as various portions of South America. Mr. Salvin states that about the beginning of April, and toward the end of the dry season, a great portion of the stream is diverted from the River Guacalate and thrown on the open pasture-land near Dueñas, in Guatemala. During this period large numbers of *Scolopacidæ* frequent the inundated region; of these the present species of Wader is by far the most abundant. At this season, as it thus takes its food from fresh water, it is excellent eating. Mr. Edward Newton speaks of having occasionally met with this bird, after September 14, at St. Croix, where he obtained several examples. He did not at any time see more than two of them together. Léotaud gives this species as one of the migratory visitants of Trinidad, whither it goes in August, remaining into October. It is always found in flocks, and frequents the low meadows rather than the sea-shore. It is often seen to crouch on the ground, and is known on the island as the "crouching shore-bird." Not unfrequently, it is seen accompanying a number of the *canutus*, the latter seeming to act as its guides.

Mr. N. B. Moore procured several examples of this species in the Bahamas as early as August 5. In South America its occurrence has been noted even as far south as Patagonia. Mr. H. Durnford ("Ibis," 1877) found it abundant in the Chupat Valley, where he saw large flocks of this bird about the salt lagoon to the north of the village, and also on the sandy flats at the mouth of the river. In their movement and habits they closely resembled the European Dunlin, flying in a body, suddenly wheeling round, displaying alternately their light under-parts and dark backs, and usually raising their wings over their backs before alighting, which they all do at the same moment.

Mr. Boardman informs me that this species is quite common, both in the spring and in the fall, near Calais, where it is seen in company with the Common Snipe, and where it feeds exclusively on the fresh-water marshes and in the uplands. It is distinguished from the Common Snipe by the name of the Jack Snipe. In Massachusetts this is one of the earliest of the migratory Waders, appearing about the middle of July. It is also one of the last to leave, as its migrations continue longer than those of any other bird, or until the middle or the end of October. If it appears at all in its spring migrations, it passes north rapidly, or goes through in the night, and its passage has not been noted. Major Wedderburn speaks of it as more numerous in Bermuda than Bonaparte's Sandpiper. It was not noticed prior to Sept. 20, 1847, on which day two of them were taken. After this the birds became common in all the swampy ponds and bays. On the 9th of October, 1849, they appeared all at once in thousands, particularly at St. George, after a heavy gale of wind. The parade-ground at that place was swarming with them, and one of the officers killed between four and five hundred before breakfast. With the exception of a few stragglers, all were gone by the following day.

According to Mr. Moore, this bird occurs in Florida, but only in the early winter.

Mr. Dresser noted the appearance of the Pectoral Sandpiper near Matamoras in July, 1863. It was not frequenting the salt-water lagoons, but was oftener found on the banks of the Rio Grande, or near small pools after a rain. In April, 1864, he observed several small flocks of four or five about the water-holes near San Antonio, and in May he shot three at Howard's Ranch on the Medina River.

In some seasons, according to Giraud, this species is quite plentiful on the shores of Long Island. It appears generally to have been overlooked by the hunters. In the spring it is not seen there in large numbers, but it apparently hastens on to its breeding-places with but little pause. Returning to Long Island in August, it appears in increased numbers on the necks of land in the immediate vicinity of tide-water, and is also found among the islands in the bay. Although large numbers are sometimes seen occupying the same feeding-grounds, it does not seem to be a social bird, but each one appears to be intent only on providing for its own comfort, and to be entirely regardless of its companions. In feeding, the flock scatters over the bare places which occur on the moist ground frequented by them, and when thus employed, they remain silent. They are by no means wary, and regard the approach of the hunter with indifference. On one occasion, when Mr. Giraud fell in with a large flock, he walked up to within a close shooting distance of the nearest one, appearing to be entirely unnoticed. Although there were upward of fifty in view, yet they were so widely distributed that it was impossible to get two of them in range; nor could he effect this during a hunt, in the course of which he obtained twenty-one birds at as many different shots. At the report of the gun the survivors flew on a short distance, and resumed their previous occupation. During this repeated firing he did not observe a single individual pass beyond the limits of the meadow, which was only a few acres in extent. As this bird flies up when surprised, it presents a fair mark, and if allowed to proceed, flies steadily at a short distance above the ground. It feeds on various kinds of minute insects, and also on the small shellfish which lie near the surface, but at times may be seen boring with its bill to a greater depth. On dissection, particles of plants have been found in its stomach.

Its note is a low whistle, which is not often repeated, except when the bird apprehends danger. This is known as the "Meadow Snipe" on Long Island, and is also called the "Short-neck." It is quite common at Egg Harbor, N. J., in the autumn, and sometimes remains there until November; toward the latter part of the season it is in excellent condition. On the sea-coast of New Jersey it is known as the "Fat-bird." It is found in its migrations in the interior of Pennsylvania, and is there also known as the "Jack Snipe." Stragglers also occur on Long Island in the month of July; but there is no reason to suppose that any breed there. In the autumn its flesh becomes very juicy and finely flavored, and when procured late in the season it is said to be superior to that of any of our shore-birds, and fully equal to any upland game.

This species has been taken several times in Great Britain, where they occur as stragglers only; they were shot in the months of May, September, and October. According to Prince Charles Bonaparte, the Pectoral Sandpiper is found in Brazil and at Montevideo.

Nuttall states that in his day many birds of this species were killed on the shores of Cohasset and other parts of Massachusetts Bay, where they arrived in flocks about the end of August, and remained into September. While there they fed on small coleoptera, larvæ, and the common green *Ulva latissima*, as well as on several species of sea-weed. When startled, they uttered a low plaintive whistle. Like the Snipe, it seems fond of damp meadows and marshes.

Reinhardt includes this bird among those of Greenland on the authority of a specimen taken in 1851, and two in 1859, at Nenortalik. Mr. B. Ross reports this species common on the Mackenzie River.

It is not known to breed so far to the south as Labrador, but makes its first appearance there about the middle of August, in the course of its migrations southward. Wherever found, the "Grass Snipe," as it is called in Massachusetts, is seldom seen on open sandy beaches, preferring low, wet inland meadows. When found near the shore it frequents the muddy flats left bare by the receding tide and the higher salt-marshes. It has more of the habits of the Common Snipe than of the *Tringæ*. As it starts up suddenly from the ground in alarm, its zigzag flight is very Snipe-like, and it is then quite as difficult to shoot as is that bird.

Nothing whatever is known about its breeding, either as to locality or manner. It has been thought that this may take place somewhere along the forty-ninth parallel; this is but a conjecture, not amounting to a probability.

Actodromas acuminata.

THE SHARP-TAILED SANDPIPER.

Totanus acuminatus, HORSF. Linn. Trans. XIII. 1821, 192.
Tringa acuminata, SWINH. P. Z. S. 1863, 315 ; Ibis, 1863, 412. — SCHLEG. Mus. P.-P. Tringæ, 38.
Limnocinclus acuminatus, GRAY, Hand-l. III. 1871, 49.
Actodromas acuminata, RIDGW. Proc. U. S. Nat. Mus. 1881, 199, 222 ; Nom. N. Am. B. 1881, no. 533. — COUES, Check List, 2d ed. 1882, no. 619.
Tringa australis, JARD. Illustr. Orn. II. pl. 91.
Schœniclus australis, GOULD, Birds Austr. VI. pl. 30.
Tringa rufescens, VON MIDDEND. Sibir. Reise, 221 (nec VIEILL.).

HAB. Eastern Asia, migrating south to Australia, and northeastward to coast of Alaska (St. Michael's ; E. W. NELSON).

SP. CHAR. *Adult:* Above, brownish gray, the feathers black centrally ; pileum cinnamon, in marked contrast, and broadly streaked with black ; rump and middle upper tail-coverts brownish black; lateral upper tail-coverts white, streaked with dusky. Middle tail-feathers dusky, edged with whitish; other rectrices deep brownish gray, distinctly bordered with white. A whitish superciliary stripe, sharply defining the cinnamon of the crown; jugulum very pale brownish gray sparsely streaked laterally and anteriorly only; remaining lower parts white, the sides with sparse V-shaped markings, and the lower tail-coverts with streaks of dusky grayish. *Young, first plumage:* Above, chiefly bright rusty ochraceous, the feathers black centrally, the outer scapulars and interscapulars edged terminally with white; whole pileum bright ferruginous, broadly streaked with black, bounded sharply on each side by a white, finely streaked superciliary stripe; rump and middle upper tail-coverts brownish black, the feathers bordered terminally with rusty; outer upper tail-coverts white, with medial streaks of black; middle tail-feathers black, edged laterally with rufous; other rectrices dusky, bordered with rusty whitish. Cheeks whitish, finely streaked with dusky; jugulum, breast, and sides, anteriorly, deep rusty buff, finely streaked anteriorly and laterally with dusky; remaining lower parts, including the throat, white, the lower tail-coverts streaked with dusky. "Iris hazel; bill black at tip, changing to dingy greenish yellow on basal third of lower mandible and base of upper; feet and tarsi dull greenish yellow" (NELSON, MS.).[1]

Wing, 4.90–5.50; culmen, .95–1.00; tarsus, 1.10–1.25; middle toe, .88–.95.

This species resembles very closely the common *A. maculata*, but differs constantly in several respects. As to proportions, the bill is decidedly shorter and more slender, and the tarsus slightly longer, while the wing is about the same length. The middle tail-feathers are narrower and more acuminate. The colors are nearly the same, but the rectrices are darker, the breast almost or quite unspotted centrally and posteriorly, and the crown decidedly rufous.

A specimen from New South Wales, which appears to be this species (No. 15313, U. S. Expl. Exp.), but labelled "*Tringa aurita* (?), LATH.," differs notably from an adult from Australia, received from Mr. J. E. Harting, in the following particulars: The posterior and lateral parts of the breast have coarse, irregular markings of dark brown, many of these markings being V-shaped, others irregularly sagittate or even transverse; these markings are continued, but increased in size along the sides to the crissum, and even the abdomen has a few small markings; the crown is not conspicuously rusty, neither is this color there bounded sharply by the light superciliary stripe. Whether this specimen represents the same species, we are not quite prepared to say, not having sufficient material at hand.

Actodromas minutilla.

THE LEAST SANDPIPER.

Tringa minutilla, VIEILL. Nouv. Dict. XXXIV. 1819, 452. — COUES, Key, 1872, 254; Check List, 1873, no. 418; Birds N. W. 1874, 482.

Actodromas minutilla, BONAP. Compt. Rend. 1856. — RIDGW. Nom. N. Am. B. 1881, no. 538. — COUES, Check List, 2d ed. 1882, no. 614.

Tringa pusilla, WILS. Am. Orn. V. 1813, 32, pl. 37, f. 4 (nec LINN.). — SW. & RICH. F. B. A. II. 1831, 386. — AUD. Orn. Biog. IV. 1838, 180, pl. 320; Synop. 1839, 237; B. Am. V. 1842, 280, pl. 337.

Tringa Wilsonii, NUTT. Man. II. 1834, 121. — CASS. in Baird's B. N. Am. 1858, 721. — BAIRD, Cat. N. Am. B. 1859, no. 532.

Tringa nana, LICHT. Nomencl. 1854, 92.

"*Tringa georgica*, LICHT." (Gray).

HAB. The whole of America, but breeding (so far as known) only north of the United States; accidental in Europe.

SP. CHAR. *Adult, summer plumage:* Back and scapulars black, the feathers bordered and somewhat barred (not continuously, and mostly beneath the surface) with rusty ochraceous, the tips of some of the feathers often whitish; rump and middle upper tail-coverts brownish black; lateral upper tail-coverts white, with wedge-shaped markings of grayish; middle tail-feathers

[1] SWINHOE ("Ibis," 1863, p. 412) says: "Apical half of bill purplish black, basal half olive-brown, with tinge of flesh-color; legs yellowish olive, with black claws."

dusky, with paler edges; other rectrices light brownish gray, with white shafts. Crown light grayish fulvous or ochraceous, heavily streaked with black; wing-coverts brownish gray, with darker centres and paler edges, the shafts blackish; tertials edged with ochraceous; primaries dusky. A light superciliary stripe, and a darker one on side of the head; neck and jugulum very pale grayish fulvous or fulvous-ashy streaked with dusky; sides and crissum narrowly streaked; other lower parts immaculate white. *Adult in winter:* Above, rather dark brownish gray, the feathers with indistinctly darker centres; rump, etc., as in summer plumage. Superciliary stripe and lower parts white, the jugulum light ashy, indistinctly streaked. *Young, first plumage:* Very similar to the summer plumage of the adult, but many of the scapulars and interscapulars tipped with white, these feathers without any bars; wing-coverts bordered with ochraceous. Jugulum suffused with pale fulvous, and obsoletely streaked.[1]

Total length, about 5.50 to 6.50 inches; extent, 11.00 to 12.50; wing, about 3.50 to nearly 4.00; culmen, about .75 to .92; tarsus, .75; middle toe, .60. Bill dull black; iris dark brown; legs and toes dusky.

This abundant and extensively diffused species resembles very closely, both in its small size and in its colors, at all seasons, the equally common and widely distributed Semipalmated Sandpiper, *Ereunetes pusillus.* It may be immediately distinguished, however, by the completely cleft toes, the other species having all the anterior toes webbed at the base.

This common and familiar Sandpiper has an almost universal distribution throughout North America, and in the winter wanders in greater or less numbers into Mexico, Central America, and over a large portion of South America. It breeds as far south as Sable Island, and also in Newfoundland, in Labrador, in Alaska, and in the higher Arctic regions generally. A limited number winter in the Gulf States; but in all the rest of North America this bird appears only in its migrations, passing slowly north in the spring, pausing on its way at every suitable feeding-place, and finally passing out of the United States about the last of May. Within four or five weeks of the final departure of the last stragglers of the movement northward, the advance of the returning host begins to reappear, moving southward. It can hardly be that those which thus early show themselves in New England — some of them early in July — and even in regions much farther south, can have attended to the duties of incubation. Their reappearance thus early can only be satisfactorily explained by the supposition that both the southern and the northern movements are attended by a certain, but probably not a very large, proportion of unmated, immature, or barren birds. These accompany their kindred in their journey north in the spring, linger behind in the rich feeding-places on their way, and being undetained

[1] Some young specimens, apparently of the same age and almost certainly the same species, in the collection differ very strikingly from the above description in the less amount or total absence of rufous above, the feathers having merely narrow ochraceous borders, and scarcely any white on the ends of the feathers; the whole plumage being thus very much duller.

by any domestic cares or responsibilities, begin their southern flight some time before the others, who must wait for the maturity of their broods. Be these conjectures as they may, we find, all over the country, in the interior, on both coasts, even at places surprisingly far from any of their known breeding-places, that this bird is sure to reappear in small numbers in July — this early reappearance remaining as yet unexplained.

Mr. E. Adams ("Ibis," 1878), in his Notes on Birds observed by him on the Sea-coast of Alaska, mentions meeting with this species at Norton Sound as early as the 14th of April, while the snow still covered the greater part of the ground; they were not, however, seen in great numbers until the middle of the following month. They confined themselves almost solely to the salt-marsh and the muddy banks of the river, where it was reached by the tide; at such points they were always to be found, in flocks of from fifty to a hundred, accompanied by a few Dunlins and Brown Snipes. Mr. Adams often sat on a log while they were feeding all around within a foot of him; but on his making the slightest movement, they were gone in an instant, with a whisk and a twitter. Their nests were placed on the higher ground surrounding the marsh; the eggs are described as spotted with shades of olive-green, principally about the large end, and upon a pale brownish ground.

It is quite probable that here and there, in favorable situations, pairs of these birds stop to breed in exceptionally southern latitudes. Mr. Nelson states that on the 5th of June, 1875, he found one of them building its nest near the Calumet River, in Northeastern Illinois; and several of this species were observed by Mr. Rice near Waukegan on the 1st of July, they having, as he felt assured, nested in that vicinity. We are not aware, however, that the eggs or young of this bird have ever been actually taken within the limits of the United States.

Mr. Dall obtained a specimen of this bird at Nulato, May 14, where it is not common. It was more plentiful at the mouth of the Yukon, where its eggs were procured. He met with it also at Popoff Island, one of the Aleutians, June 20, 1872, where it was rather abundant. Mr. Bischoff also obtained it at Sitka.

It is given by Mr. R. Browne as one of the common birds of Vancouver Island. In California, according to Dr. Cooper, it is nearly resident, being absent from the coast only during a part of June and July; it is frequently seen about inland ponds and marshes in the interior. It occurs in immense flocks, during the winter, on the shores of the Pacific in Southern California; and on the same coast, much farther south, about the mouth of the Nagualate River, in Guatemala, Mr. Salvin found it occurring in considerable numbers in the month of March.

Mr. J. A. Allen met with an occasional specimen of this species in the Valley of Salt Lake, in Utah, in the month of September; and Mr. Ridgway also mentions finding it in Utah and Colorado during its migrations.

On the Atlantic coast it is, if anything, even more common and abundant. Along the shores of Hudson's Bay and Davis Straits, throughout Labrador, and on the islands farther south, it is a summer resident from June to the close of its short season. It is abundant, both in the spring and in the fall, along the entire Atlantic coast, a certain proportion remaining all the winter, or from October to April, on the coast of South Carolina, Georgia, Florida, and all the Gulf States, to Mexico, and thence to South America. It is also abundant in the West India Islands, occurring in Cuba, Jamaica, as well as in various other islands, from September to the following May. It visits the Bermudas in its southern migrations, arriving there from the last of July to the first part of November, and being present, at times, in flocks of many hundreds.

According to the observations of Mr. Moore, this species is seen in Florida throughout the year, always in its winter livery, with no indications that it ever breeds there. It is found in company with the *Ereunetes pusillus.*

Professor Newton met with it in St. Croix in the autumn, where it was observed to frequent the pastures as well as the sea-shore; but rarely were more than two seen together. Mr. E. Newton notes its first appearance, August 19. According to Gosse, it does not become numerous in Jamaica before the end of the year, and is then found in the morasses in flocks of about a dozen, running swiftly over the wet soil like other Sandpipers. In the stomachs of these birds were found fragments of shells and comminuted animal matter. Mr. Marsh, however, claims that this bird is resident in Jamaica throughout the year, and that it breeds on the Salinas and on the sandy beaches. This, however, is questioned by Mr. Salvin, and we think on good grounds. The eggs described by Mr. Marsh do not resemble those of this species, either in ground-color or markings; and the character of the nesting, as indicated by him, is not that of this Sandpiper.

Mr. Salvin, as quoted by Mr. Dresser, states that he possesses a specimen of this bird from Costa Rica, and that an example was found near Panama by MacLeannan. Mr. W. S. Wood ascertained it to be very common at Cartagena in November, 1857, and Dr. Habel procured two specimens on one of the Galapagos Islands. Mr. Wallace met with this bird at the mouth of the Amazon, and Natterer secured two specimens in Brazil, one in April at Cuyaba, and the other at Matto Grosso in September. In the department of Vera Cruz it has been taken in the interior, near Orizaba, and also near the City of Mexico. In Guatemala, besides meeting with it on the Pacific coast, Mr. Salvin found it to be a regular winter visitant, arriving in autumn and departing in spring. In the winter it is found only on the shore, and its visits to inland lakes appear to be limited to its passages. In November, 1861, Mr. Salvin found it in the grassy swamps which surround the small Lake of Dueñas, in the highlands of Guatemala, nearly five thousand feet above the sea.

It is mentioned by Léotaud as occurring in Trinidad in the months of August, September, and October, at times in flocks by themselves, but more frequently mingled with flocks of the *Ereunetes pusillus.* In the French West India Islands it is known as the *Petit Maître.*

Mr. Dresser found this species making its appearance at Matamoras as early as the latter part of July, — this affording remarkable evidence of the rapidity of its flight, and confirming the hypothesis that such visitants must be birds that have not raised a brood that season. In the early spring Mr. Dresser met with it near San Antonio.

Dr. Walker met with this species on the coast of Greenland; and in the first part of June following he found it breeding in the marshy valleys near Bellot's Strait.

Mr. Audubon, whilst in Labrador, found this species plentiful, breeding on the moss-clad rocks within a short distance of the sea. When startled from its nest, it would rise on the wing and move off low over the ground with incurved wings and with a slow whirring motion; or, if on the ground, it moves off slowly and limping as if crippled. On the 20th of July, after some search, he found the nest and eggs of this species. The bird flew from the nest more in the manner of the Partridge than of the *Tringæ.* The nest had been formed apparently by the patting of the bird's feet on the crisp moss; and in the slight hollow thus produced were laid a few blades of slender dry grass, bent in a circular manner, the internal diameter being 2.50 inches and its depth 1.25. The eggs, he states, measured .93 by .75 of an inch. Their ground-color was a rich cream-yellow, blotched with very dark umber, the markings larger and more numerous toward the obtuse end; they were quite fresh. The nest was under the lee of a small rock, exposed to all the heat the sun can afford in that high latitude. This pair must have been late in depositing their eggs, as a fortnight later Audubon's party saw young birds almost as large as their parents; and soon after both parents and young were preparing for their departure south.

This species, so very generally distributed, so common everywhere — it being hardly less numerous than the *Ereunetes pusillus* — collects in the fall in immense flocks, and resorts to the great masses of drifting sea-weed on our coasts, frequenting also the shores and sedgy borders of salt ponds, gleaning minute shellfish and marine insects. Although most abundant on the borders of the sea, it is not entirely confined to the shore, but is also found along the margins of the interior lakes and rivers. On the shores of Long Island Giraud speaks of it as very plentiful, and as being, during the month of September, in excellent condition for the table. By some it is considered far superior, both in flavor and in juiciness, to many of our larger shore-birds. Its note is low and lisping; but when alarmed, it moves off in a confused and irregular manner, uttering a shrill twitter sounding like the syllables *peep-peet.* During October it migrates farther south, reappearing early in the spring on the shores of New Jersey and Long Island, where it is seen in numbers during each one of the summer months, although it is not known to breed within the limits of the United States.

Richardson, who described this bird under two specific appellations, speaks of finding it abundant in the autumn, feeding during the recesses of the tide on the extensive mud-flats at the mouths of Nelson and Hayes rivers. He adds that it breeds within the Arctic Circle, arriving there as soon as the snow melts. As early as the 21st of May it was observed on the swampy borders of small lakes in latitude 66°. Its crop was filled with a soft blackish earth and small white worms.

This species was found breeding abundantly at Fort Anderson, on the Barren Grounds, at Lake Rendezvous, and near the Arctic coast, by Mr. MacFarlane. Of the twenty nests, the notes of which we have examined, all but six were taken between the 21st and 30th of June, none being recorded as later than the 3d of July. The number of eggs is generally given as four — in no instance more. The nests were always on the ground, and generally a mere depression, with a lining of a few dry leaves and grasses, and usually near small lakes. The female, as she fluttered off her nest, often imitated the flight of a wounded bird, and if left undisturbed, almost immediately returned to her nest. If persistently interrupted, she kept about the nest, and endeavored by simulated lameness to draw off the intruders, soon becoming quite wary, if shot at.

One set of the eggs of this species, collected near the Arctic coast by Mr. MacFarlane (S. I. No. 9377), measure 1.15 inches by .85. The ground is a light drab, thinly marked with sepia-brown spots, patches of which are suffused with the ground-color, giving them an ashy effect. The markings are more numerous, and of greater size about the larger end. The eggs are decidedly pyriform in shape. Another set (S. I. No. 3324), collected on Sable Island, Nova Scotia, by P. S. Dodd, have a light-drab ground-color; but this is almost entirely concealed by the numerous markings of dark umber brown.

GENUS **PELIDNA**, CUVIER.

Pelidna, CUV. Règ. An. 1817, 490 ; ed. 2, 1829, 526 (type, *Tringa alpina*, LINN.).
Ancylocheilus, KAUP, Sk. Ent. Eur. Thierw. 1829, 50 (type, *Tringa subarquata*, TEMM.).

CHAR. Bill slender, longer than the head, deep through the base, compressed, scarcely or not at all expanded at the tip, and decidedly decurved terminally. Tarsus shorter than the bill, longer than the middle toe. Wings reaching beyond end of tail.

P. alpina.

The genus *Pelidna* includes two well-known Sandpipers, both of which are common to North America and Europe, although one of them, the Curlew Sandpiper (*P. subarquata*) can scarcely be considered as more than a straggler here. The other is represented in the two continents by distinguishable races. The character of the species and races of *Pelidna* are as follows : —

1. **P. alpina.** Upper tail-coverts dusky. *Adult in summer:* Belly black, other lower parts whitish. *Winter plumage:* No black beneath ; above, uniform brownish gray. *Young:* Belly and breast spotted with black.
   a. *Alpina.* Wing, 4.30–4.75 ; culmen, 1.15–1.40 ; tarsus, .85–1.00 ; middle toe, .70–.75. *Hab.* Europe.
   β. *Americana.* Wing, 4.60–4.95 ; culmen, 1.40–1.75 ; tarsus, 1.00–1.15 ; middle toe, .70–.80. *Hab.* North America.
2. **P. subarquata.** Upper tail-coverts white. *Adult in summer:* Beneath, including belly, deep cinnamon-rufous. *Winter plumage:* Beneath, white, obsoletely streaked on the jugulum ; above, brownish gray. *Young:* Belly and breast unspotted. *Hab.* Palæarctic Region ; occasional in Eastern and Northern North America.

Pelidna alpina.

a. Alpina. THE RED-BACKED SANDPIPER; DUNLIN.

Tringa alpina, LINN. S. N. ed. 10, 1758, 149 ; ed. 12, 1766, 249 (based on *Cinclus torquatus*, BRISS. Orn. V. 1760, 216, pl. 19, fig. 2). — NEWT. Man. N. H. Greenl. 1875, 103 (Greenland).
Pelidna alpina, RIDGW. Proc. U. S. Nat. Mus. 1881, 200 ; Nom. N. Am. B. 1882, no. 539. — COUES, Check List, 2d ed. 1882, no. 623.
Tringa cinclus, LINN. S. N. I. 1766, 251 (based on BRISS. Orn. V. 1760, 211, pl. 19, fig. 1).
" *Tringa pusilla*, GMEL. S. N. I. 1788, 663" (GRAY).
Tringa ruficollis, PALL. Reise, III. 1776, 700.
Numenius variabilis, BECHST. Naturg. Deutschl. IV. 141.
Pelidna Schinzii, BREHM. (var. ?) Not of American writers.

β. Americana. THE AMERICAN RED-BACKED SANDPIPER.

Tringa alpina, WILS. Am. Orn. VII. 1813, 25, pl. 56, fig. 2 (nec LINN.) — SW. & RICH. F. B. A. II. 1831, 383. — NUTT. Man. II. 1834, 106. — AUD. Orn. Biog. III. 1835, 580, pl. 290 ; Synop. 1839, 234 ; B. Am. V. 1842, 266.

Tringa alpina, var. *americana,* CASS. in Baird's B. N. Am. 1858, 719. — BAIRD, Cat. N. Am. B. 1859, no. 530. — COUES, Key, 1872, 256 ; Check List, 1873, 424 ; Birds N. W. 1874, 489.

Tringa variabilis, SABINE, Suppl. Parry's First Voy. p. cc.

"*Tringa cinclus,*" WILS. Am. Orn. VII. 1813, 39, pl. 57, fig. 3 (nec LINN.).

Pelidna pacifica, COUES, Pr. Ac. Nat. Sci. Philad. 1861, 189 (in text).

Pelidna alpina americana, RIDGW. Proc. U. S. Nat. Mus. 1881, 200 ; Nom. N. Am. B. 1881, no. 539*a*. — COUES, Check List, 2d ed. 1882, no. 624.

HAB. Of true *alpina,* the Palæarctic Region, accidental in North America (Hudson's Bay : BLAKISTON, "Ibis," 1863, 132). Of *americana,* North America in general, breeding far northward, and straggling to eastern coast of Asia.

SP. CHAR. (*P. americana*). *Adult in summer:* Crown, back, scapulars, rump, and upper tail-coverts, light rufous, the crown streaked, other parts spotted, with black ; wing-coverts brownish gray, the greater broadly tipped with white. Head (except crown), neck, jugulum, and breast, grayish white, streaked with dusky ; abdomen black ; sides, flanks, anal region, crissum, and lining

of the wing, pure white, the sides, flanks, and crissum sparsely streaked. *Adult and young in winter:* Above, entirely plain ash-gray, sometimes with very indistinct dusky shaft-streaks ; indistinct superciliary stripe and lower parts white, the neck and jugulum indistinctly streaked with grayish, the sides, flanks, and crissum sometimes sparsely streaked. *Young:* Back and scapulars black, the feathers broadly bordered with rusty ochraceous, this becoming paler, or even white, on the ends of some of the feathers ; lesser and middle wing-coverts bordered with buff ; rump plain brownish slate ; upper tail-coverts darker, tipped with rusty ; crown light rusty, streaked with black. Head and neck (except crown and throat) dull dingy buff, indistinctly streaked with dusky ; remaining lower parts, including throat, white, the breast and belly with numerous irregularly cordate spots of black, the flanks, crissum, and lining of the wing immaculate. "Bill and feet black ; iris dark brown" (AUDUBON).

Total length, about 8.50 inches ; wing, 4.60–4.95 ; culmen, 1.40–1.75 ; tarsus, 1.00–1.15 ; middle toe, .70–.80.

There is a considerable amount of individual variation in this species, especially noticeable in the extent and continuity of the black abdominal area, the distinctness of the black markings above, and the depth of the rufous tint ; not infrequently the latter is mixed with grayish. In the winter plumage, some examples have the sides and crissum narrowly streaked, while in others these parts are immaculate.

American specimens differ constantly, though slightly, from European ones in their larger size and, in the summer plumage, lighter colors. In three adults of the European bird in summer plumage, the black largely predominates on the dorsal surface, while the ochraceous is much less rusty than in American examples ; the breast is also much more heavily streaked. In the winter plumage, the three specimens before us from Europe are decidedly lighter ash, and quite distinctly streaked above. A young bird from Hungary is much less distinctly spotted beneath than one from Alaska (the only American example in this plumage we are able to compare it with), but is otherwise very similar. The differences between the true *P. alpina* and the American race appear to be quite constant, being verified by all writers who have made actual comparison of specimens. Mr. J. E. Harting, who has made the *Limicolæ* a special study, and who is therefore the best authority on this group of birds, gives his views regarding these representative forms as follows (cf. P. Z. S. 1871, p. 115): —

"On comparing a specimen from New Jersey, in full summer plumage, with one which was shot off the nest in Benbecula (Hebrides), not only are the differences pointed out by Prof. Baird apparent, but it is also observable that the upper portions of the plumage in the American bird are considerably pervaded by bright rufous-brown, whereas in the same parts of the Scottish bird black is the prevailing color. Further, the black of the under parts, which in the Scottish bird extends (as in *Squatarola helvetica*) from the vent almost to the chin, is confined in the American bird (as in *Eudromias morinellus*) to the belly only. Whether this large race of Dunlin, known as *Tringa americana*, is specifically distinct or not, it is not confined to America, as is generally supposed. I have specimens in winter plumage now before me procured by Mr. Swinhoe at Amoy, and others in autumnal plumage shot by myself in this country, which, as regards measurements of bill, wing, and tarsus, correspond in every way with examples from New Jersey. They differ only in color, having been obtained at different seasons of the year. As far as I can judge by the data before me, the smaller bird appears to have a more restricted range, and remains to nest in this country; while the larger bird does not breed with us, but is found on our coasts in spring and autumn, during the migration."

This form, so closely allied to the Common Dunlin or Purre of Europe, has a wide distribution over the continent of North America. It is found in high Arctic regions, and on the shores of the Atlantic, Pacific, and Arctic oceans. Mr. Dall states that it was seen frequently at St. Michael's by Mr. Bannister, and in British Columbia by Mr. Elliott. A number of specimens were obtained at Sitka by Bischoff. Mr. Dall also met with it at Nulato, where it was not uncommon; and it was also abundant at the mouth of the Yukon, where an example of its egg was obtained. Its nest is said to be like that of the *Lobipes hyperboreus*. Mr. R. Browne also includes it among the birds of Vancouver Island. Dr. Cooper is of opinion that it never goes farther on the Californian coast than San Francisco, as he has not met with it on the coast to the south of that place. This bird is, however, very common toward the north from October to May, frequenting chiefly the sandy bars about bays, but not going far into the interior. It is seen in very large flocks, sometimes associating with the other small Sandpipers, from which it is not usually distinguished by hunters.

The American Dunlin — the *Cher-oo-me-nok* of the Esquimaux — is cited by Mr. E. Adams ("Ibis," 1878) as one of the birds observed by him on the shores of Norton Sound, where a few of this species frequented the salt-marsh together with flocks of *Actodromas minutilla*. They built their nests — which consisted merely of a few dry leaves scraped into a slight hollow — on the higher ground surrounding the marsh, and were very often hovering over them and singing a low twittering song. The eggs — four in number — are described as marked with large spots of three shades of brown upon a light olive-green ground, principally about the larger end. The small ends were always placed together in the nest, as is the case with all the Waders.

The Dunlin is included by Reinhardt among the birds of Greenland, where the European species is known to have been taken; and it may be to this that the Greenland examples belong. Professor Newton states that Dr. Paulsen more than once received this species from Greenland, both in the immature and in the autumnal plumage. It probably breeds there, as it is also known to do on Melville Peninsula and on the coast of Davis Strait. Richardson states that it is abundant, and that it breeds on the Arctic coast of America. He also met with it on the Saskatchewan Plain in its passage north, and in autumn on the shores of Hudson's Bay. He describes its eggs as having a ground of an oil-green marked with irregular spots of liver-brown, of different sizes and shades, confluent at the obtuse end. The eggs are said to be 1.28 inches long, and to measure .96 of an inch where broadest, the ends differing greatly in size.

Mr. J. A. Allen mentions finding this species in the eastern portion of Kansas in the earlier part of May. It was quite abundant in the neighborhood of lagoons. Later — during the second week of August — he again met with others of this species at Lake Pass in Colorado. In the following September he again found it quite common in the Valley of Great Salt Lake. Mr. Ridgway states that an individual of this species was shot by one of his party in May on an alkaline pond near Pyramid Lake.

Mr. Boardman informs us that this species occurs, in spring and fall, in the neighborhood of Calais, but he does not think that it is ever abundant. It comes to Massachusetts from the north in October, and remains into November, and is then quite common on the coast. In its spring migrations it passes north late in May. On Long Island this species is known both as the Red-backed Sandpiper and as the Black-breast. According to Giraud, it arrives on the shores of Long Island in the month of April, but soon leaves and passes north, returning in September, at which time it is quite abundant there, and still more so on the coast of New Jersey.

This species associates in flocks, frequenting the shores, sandbars, and muddy flats, feeding on worms and such minute shellfish as abound in localities of this kind. In the month of October it is usually very fat, and is considered excellent eating. The autumnal plumage is so entirely different from the vernal that by hunters this bird is generally regarded at those seasons as representing two different species. The same thing was once true of the European form, the plumage of those two seasons being so unlike as not only to deceive sportsmen, but even ornithologists; hence the common names of Dunlin and Purre, and the two scientific terms *alpina* and *cinclus*. By hunters generally — both in New England and along the shores of Long Island and New Jersey — the autumnal form is known as the "Winter Snipe." In this plumage it closely resembles the winter dress of the Curlew Sandpiper. During the autumn the Red-backed Sandpiper may be found, both on sandy and on muddy shores, along the whole of our central Atlantic coast. It is said to be a restless, active bird, gleaning its food with great dexterity, and seeming to be ever desirous of changing its position. Soon after alighting, the flock collects together, making short excursions over the water, and again settling down at but a short distance from the spot from which they had only just flown. These birds usually crowd so closely together when whirling about in these excursions, that many may be killed at a single shot. Mr. Giraud mentions that on one occasion no less than fifty-two were killed by the discharge of both barrels of a gun into a flock. This is an unusual number; but the killing of ten or twelve at a time is said to be not an uncommon thing.

On the shores of the Atlantic, south of Chesapeake Bay, this species is very abundant in its spring migrations, coming late in April and not leaving until nearly the end of May. In September it reappears, a portion remaining throughout the winter. Many of these birds assume their spring plumage before they leave; probably the greater number of them do so. In their habits they are more like the *maculata* than the other *Tringæ*, and are ranked as Snipe by the hunters, from their preferences as to their feeding-grounds. Mr. Audubon speaks of them as particularly abundant during the winter in Florida; and Messrs. Allen, Maynard, and Boardman have since confirmed this statement. They take their departure from the south about the 1st of April.

The Red-backed Sandpiper passes through the interior, as well as along the coast, in its migrations, pausing on its way to feed on the shores of inland lakes, ponds, and rivers. It has been procured at both seasons by Mr. Kumlien near Lake Koskonong, where, at times, it is quite abundant.

Sabine states that this species was observed in Sir Edward Parry's first voyage; but that it was rare on the coast of Davis Strait and Baffin's Bay and among the islands of the Polar Sea. In the second voyage it was found breeding on Melville Peninsula. And J. C. Ross, in the "Natural History of the Last Arctic Voyage," speaks of this bird as very abundant during the breeding-season, near Felix Harbor, where it builds its nest in the marshes and by the sides of lakes.

Three eggs of this species from South Greenland, taken in June, 1855, measure 1.40 by .98, 1.35 by .98, 1.39 by 1.03. They are pyriform in shape — extremely so — having a ground-color varying from a dirty clayey-white, with a washing of rufous, to a deep clay-color. The eggs are all spotted with large blotches of dark sienna-brown, which occasionally have a purplish tinge, and are irregularly confluent, and more numerous about the larger end than on the other one, where they are few in number, small, and scattered.

The European form of this species, known as the Dunlin or Purre, is entitled to a place in a list of the birds belonging to the fauna of North America, since it is of occasional occurrence in Greenland, where the two forms appear to meet on common ground. It is not probable that the habits of the two forms are otherwise than nearly, if not quite, identical; and as somewhat illustrative of both varieties, we copy, with slight changes, the following graphic summary of their peculiarities, from the pen of Sir William Jardine: "On the coasts of Great Britain the Purre is the most common of the whole race, and may generally be met with, no matter what is the character of the shore. Before they have been much driven about and annoyed, they are also one of the most familiar. During winter the flocks are sometimes immense, and will allow a person to approach very near, looking, and running a few steps, or stretching their wings in preparation for flight, listlessly and in a manner indicative of little alarm; a few shots, however, render them as timorous and wary as they were before careless. In spring they separate into pairs, when some perform a migration to a considerable extent northward, while others retire to the nearer marshes, a few to the shores of inland lakes, and still fewer to the higher inland muirs. Having there performed the duties of incubation, they return again in autumn to the shore, where they may be found in small parties, the amount of the broods; and these gradually congregate as the season advances, and more travellers arrive, until many hundreds are thus joined. Their nests are formed beneath or at the side of any small bush or tuft of grass, very neatly scraped, and with a few straws of grass around the sides. The male is generally in attendance, perched on some near elevation; and on any danger approaching, runs round, uttering at quick intervals his shrill, monotonous whistle. The female, when raised from the nest, flutters off for a few yards, and then assumes the same manner with the male. The young sit and squat among the grass or reeds, and at that time the parents will come within two yards of the person in search of them."

Mr. Macgillivray, as quoted by Audubon, represents the Purre as being seen so constantly in company with the Golden Plover when breeding, that it has obtained the name of "Plover's Page." During the breeding-season it is not seen along the shores. The young leave the nest immediately after exclusion, run about, and when alarmed, conceal themselves by sitting close to the ground and remaining motionless. If, during incubation, a person approaches their retreat, the male — and frequently the female also — flies to meet the intruder, and employs the same artifices for decoying him from the nest or young as the Plover does. When the young are fledged, the birds gather into flocks, often joining those of the Golden Plover, resting at night on the ground in the smoother parts of the heath. When an intruder approaches such a flock, the birds stretch their wings up as if preparing for flight, utter a few low notes, and either stand on the alert or run a few steps. Toward the end of August they betake themselves to the sandy shores. On a large sand ford in Harris, Mr. Macgillivray has, at this season, seen many thousands at once running about with extreme activity in search of food, the place seeming to be a general rendezvous. Mr. Newton states that Dr. Paulsen has more than once received this species from Greenland, both young and in the autumnal plumage. It breeds there, and also on the Melville Peninsula, as well as elsewhere on the coast of Davis Strait.

I have eggs in my collection taken in North Greenland; but whether belonging to this form or to the *americana*, I am not sure. There is no perceptible difference in the eggs of the two species, so far as is known. Greenland specimens, perhaps of the American form, are slightly larger than the average European.

Pelidna subarquata.

THE CURLEW SANDPIPER.

Scolopax subarquata, GÜLD. Nov. Comm. Petrop. XIX. 1775, 471, pl. 18. — GMEL. S. N. I. 1788, 658.
Tringa subarquata, TEMM. Man. I. 1815, 393; II. 1820, 609. — NUTT. Man. II. 1834, 104. — AUD. Orn. Biog. 1835, 444; Synop. 1839, 234; B. Am. V. 1842, 269, pl. 333; CASS. in Baird's B. N. Am. 1858, 718. — BAIRD, Cat. N. Am. B. 1859, no. 529. — COUES, Check List, 1873, no. 425; Birds N. W. 1874, 491.
Pelidna subarquata, RIDGW. Proc. U. S. Nat. Mus. vol. 3, 1881, 200; Nom. N. Am. B. 1881, no. 540.
Tringa (Ancylocheilus) subarquata, BONAP. Cat. Met. 1842, 60. — COUES, Key, 1872, 256.
Ancylochilus subarquatus, COUES, Check List, 2d ed. 1882, no. 625.
Scolopax africanus, GMEL. S. N. I. 1788, 655.
Numenius pygmæus, BECHST. Naturg. Deutschl. IV. 148.
? *Tringa islandica*, RETZ. Fn. Suec. 1800, 192.
? *Tringa ferruginea*, BRÜNN. Orn. Bor. 1764, no. 180.
Trynga falcinella, PALL. Zoog. Rosso-As. II. 1811, 188.
Pelidna macrorhyncha, BREHM, Vög. Deutschl. 1831, 658.
Erolia variegata, VIEILL. Analyse, 1816, 55.
Ærolia varia, VIEILL. Gal. Ois. II. 1834, 89, pl. 231.
"*Scolopax Dethardingii*, SIEMSSEN." (GRAY.)
"*Falcinellus cursorius*, TEMM." (COUES.)

HAB. The Old World in general; occasional in Eastern North America.

SP. CHAR. *Adult, summer plumage:* Back and scapulars variegated with black and rusty; crown rusty, streaked with black. Head, neck, breast, sides, and belly, deep chestnut-rufous; anal region, also upper and lower tail-coverts, white, spotted with black and tinged with rusty; wing-coverts and tertials brownish gray, the greater coverts tipped with white; primaries and middle tail-feathers dark slate-color; rest of the tail ash-gray, the feathers slightly bordered with whitish; axillars immaculate pure white. *Winter plumage:* Above, brownish gray, indistinctly streaked with darker; tail-coverts (above and below) pure white, spotted with black; superciliary stripe and lower parts white, the jugulum indistinctly streaked with grayish.

Young: Back and scapulars dusky black, the feathers bordered laterally with dull light ochraceous, with white terminally; lesser and middle wing-coverts bordered with dull buff; upper tail-coverts white, unspotted. Lores brownish; indistinct superciliary stripe and lower parts white, the jugulum and sides of the breast washed with buff and narrowly streaked with

dusky. "Bill dark olive-green, darker toward point; iris hazel; feet light olive, claws dusky" (AUDUBON).

Total length, about 8.50 to 9.00 inches; wing, 4.80–5.20; culmen, 1.38–1.60; tarsus, 1.10–1.20; middle toe, .70.

In the winter plumage this species is very similar to *P. alpina*, but may be immediately distinguished by the white upper tail-coverts. American specimens are quite identical with European.

The Curlew Sandpiper is of rare occurrence in North America, and has been actually known to have been taken in but few localities and in only a small number of instances. We can therefore only regard it as a straggler. It is one of the rarest of the Sandpipers which visit us. It has been taken in several instances near New York and on Long Island. Three specimens were procured by Mr. George A. Boardman, of St. Stephen, from near St. Andrews, on the St. Croix River. One of these was in the vernal plumage, and two were in the autumnal. So far as I am aware, only two or three instances are on record of its occurrence in New England, — one given by Mr. Maynard, near Ipswich, Mass., one at East Boston, and one near Portland, Me.

It is mentioned by Giraud, in his "Birds of Long Island," as of infrequent occurrence within the limits of the United States, but as having been more frequently observed in the neighborhood of New York than on any other portion of our seacoast. But even he only knew of two or three having been seen in Fulton Market, New York; and Mr. J. G. Bell, the taxidermist, in the course of many years, has purchased seven or eight. Three or four others are known to have been taken on the shores of Long Island.

Audubon states that in the course of his extensive rambles along our coasts he saw only three of this species, which he regards as one of the rarest of its genus. One of Mr. Audubon's specimens was shot on Long Island, near Sandy Hook; the other two at Great Egg Harbor, in New Jersey, in the spring of 1829. No other birds were near, and he approached them without difficulty. They were wading along the shores up to the knees, picking up floating garbage and sand-worms. In their stomachs were fragments of minute shells, slender red-worms, and bits of marine plants. He adds that he has seen several specimens in New York collections, two in Boston, and that Dr. Bachman had also two of this species.

In the eastern hemisphere this bird appears to be very widely diffused, occurring in Europe, Africa, and Asia at different seasons of the year, and according to its migrations. It nowhere seems to occur in great numbers, although in some regions it is now known to be less rare than it was formerly supposed to be.

Dr. Heuglin met with it on the Red Sea from July to September, and in its summer dress; this was between Suakin and Bab-el-Mandeb. Those seen were either solitary individuals, or were in small flocks. In October and November he again met with them on the Somali coast; these were in their winter dress. Mr. T. Ayres ("Ibis," 1878) also mentions procuring an example in the Transvaal; it was in its winter plumage, and was in company with others of the species.

Mr. C. A. Wright speaks of this bird as being common in spring and autumn at Malta. He has also met with it there in June, July, August, and September. Mr. H. Saunders met with it in Southern Spain in May, it being then in its fullest breeding-plumage. Professor Newton states, on the authority of Mr. Proctor, that specimens of this bird have been received from Iceland. Dr. Von Middendorff gives it as one of the birds of Siberia, where it is found on the *tundras* or barrens. Wheelwright speaks of it as rare in Scandinavia, and as only seen on the southern coast during the periods of migration. He shot specimens in their full summer dress on the shores of Scania. This species is supposed to breed on the west coast of Finland, not far from the sea.

According to Yarrell, the Curlew Sandpiper, which was formerly regarded as a very rare visitor to England, is much more common than was supposed, it having probably been confounded with the Dunlin. A few pairs of the species are believed occasionally to breed in that country. Specimens have been shot in the last of May, in the perfection of their summer plumage, in Sandwich; one — also in the breeding-plumage — was shot in Norfolk, and young of this species were taken in the same locality in July.

According to Thompson it is a regular summer visitor to Ireland, and also to certain parts of England; and in September, 1837, more than twenty of this species were exposed for sale on a single day in Leadenhall Market, London.

Nilsson states that this bird visits Sweden, remaining there from spring to autumn; but that it is found only in the eastern part of Scandinavia, and is not known on the western shore. According to Pennant, it visits the shores of the Caspian Sea, Lake Baikal, and the mouth of the Don.

According to Temminck, this species breeds in Holland; and he describes its eggs as being yellowish white, spotted with dark brown. It is said to feed on insects, small crustacea, and worms, which it obtains by probing in the soft sand at the edge of the water.

Messrs. Alston and Harvie-Brown ("Ibis," January, 1873) mention finding full summer-plumaged specimens of this species in the market of Archangel, in Russia, June 18.

It is said to be found in abundance in both its migrations on the coast of Belgium and France, but very rarely straggles inland. Mr. Dresser mentions seeing two large baskets of beautiful specimens of this bird, in full breeding-plumage, in Barcelona, Spain, in May. In winter it visits Africa, ranging southward even as far as the Cape of Good Hope, a few barren birds remaining in North Africa through the summer.

It is also found along all the coasts of Asia, from Asia Minor to China; but writers differ in regard to its abundance in the interior. It is common in Siberia, where it undoubtedly breeds, as Drs. Finsch and Brehm found it breeding in great numbers on the isthmus of the Yalmal Peninsula, near the margins of the lakes on the *tundra*, in latitude 67° 30′. As this was in August, they were too late for eggs, but met with the young in the down — which, however, they failed to secure.

Mr. Kumlien speaks of this species as not uncommon in North Greenland. Eggs were procured at Christianshaab, Greenland, through the kindness of Governor Fencker. It was not observed on any part of Cumberland visited by Mr. Kumlien. Of these two eggs taken in North Greenland, one measured 1.52 inches in length by 1.05 in breadth. Its ground-color is drab, with a distinct shade of olive, and it is thickly marked with blotches of two shades of umber-brown, one quite light, the other much darker; these are most numerous on and around the larger end, and are in a somewhat longitudinal direction, with a tendency also to a spiral course. There are also a few spots of a very dark, almost black, color on the larger end.

The other egg measured 1.47 by 1.04 inches, being of a much more pyriform shape. Its ground-color is a very light greenish drab, with rather sparse markings of a deep umber. These are larger and more confluent about the greater end of the egg, where they are chiefly disposed in a circular ring; but are sparsely distributed over the rest of the surface. About the larger end are a few very dark markings.

Genus **CALIDRIS**, Cuvier.

Calidris, Cuvier, Anat. Comp. V. (in chart), 1805 (type, *Tringa arenaria*, Linn.).

Char. General characters of *Tringa* and *Actodromas*, but hind toe entirely absent. Bill straight, rather longer than the head, slightly expanded or spoon-shaped at end. Toes short, the middle one scarcely two-thirds the tarsus.

The only known species of this genus is nearly cosmopolitan in its range.

C. arenaria.

Calidris arenaria.

THE SANDERLING.

Tringa arenaria, Linn. S. N. I. 1766, 251. — Aud. Orn. Biog. III. 1835, 231; Synop. 1839, 237; B. Am. V. 1842, 287, pl. 338.

Calidris arenaria, Illig. Prodr. 1811, 249. — Sw. & Rich. F. B. A. II. 1831, 366. — Nutt. Man. II. 1834, 4. — Cass. in Baird's B. N. Am. 1858, 723. — Baird, Cat. N. Am. B. 1859, no. 534. — Coues, Key, 1872, 257, fig. 167; Check List, 1873, no. 427; 2d ed. 1882, no. 627; Birds N. W. 1874, 492. — Ridgw. Nom. N. Am. B. 1881, no. 542.

Charadrius calidris, Linn. S. N. I. 1766, 255. — Wilson, Am. Orn. VII. 1813, 68, pl. 59, fig. 4.

Charadrius rubidus, Gmel. S. N. I. 1788, 688. — Wils. Am. Orn. VII. 1813, 129, pl. 58, fig. 3.

Arenaria vulgaris, Bechst. Tasch. Deutschl. II. 462.

Arenaria grisea, Brehm, Vög. Deutschl. 674.

Trynga tridactyla, PALL. Zoog. Rosso-As. II. 1826, 198.
Calidris tringoides, VIEILL. Gal. Ois. II. 1834, 95, pl. 234.
Calidris americana, BREHM, Vög. Deutschl. 1831, 695.
"*Calidris nigellus*, VIEILL."

HAB. Nearly cosmopolitan, but breeding only in the Arctic and Subarctic districts, in America migrating south to Patagonia and Chili. Chiefly littoral, but frequenting also the larger inland waters.

SP. CHAR. No hind toe; front toes moderate or rather long, flattened underneath, distinctly margined with a membrane. Bill straight, rather thick; ridge of upper mandible flattened; nasal groove deep and nearly as long as the upper mandible, not so distinct in the lower; both mandibles widened and flattened at the tip; aperture of the nostril large and covered with a membrane. Wing long; tail short, with the middle feathers longest; under coverts long as the tail; legs moderate; lower third of the tibia naked. Lower parts white, immaculate on the belly, sides, flanks,

axillars, anal region, and crissum; greater wing-coverts broadly tipped with white, and inner primaries white at base of outer webs. *Adult in summer:* Above, light rufous, broken by large spots of black, the feathers mostly tipped with whitish. Head, neck, throat, and jugulum, pale cinnamon-rufous, speckled below and streaked above with blackish. *Adult in winter:* Above, very pale pearl-gray (the lesser wing-coverts darker anteriorly), relieved only by faint darker shaft-streaks of the feathers. Throat and jugulum immaculate pure white. *Adult in spring:* Above, light grayish, with large black spots (streaks on the crown), here and there mixed with rufous; jugulum speckled with dusky on a white ground. *Young:* Above, pale gray, spotted with black and whitish, the latter on tips of the feathers; jugulum immaculate white, faintly tinged with dull buff. "Bill and feet black; iris brown" (AUDUBON).

Total length, about 7.75–8.00 inches; wing, 4.70–5.00; culmen, .95–1.00; tarsus, .90–1.05; middle toe, .55–.60.

In the universality of its distribution the Sanderling is probably not surpassed by any known species. It is found on both the Atlantic and Pacific coast of North America and in the interior. It wanders in fall and winter to the West Indies, Mexico, Central, and over the greater portion of South, America. It is in like manner found in the breeding-season scattered over Northern Europe and Asia, and from August to June it occurs at various periods in Central and Southern Asia and Europe, Africa to Natal, Japan, and on several of the islands lying to the south and southeast of Asia.

This is a bird of the highest Arctic distribution, having been taken by Captain Hall's party, in the "Polaris" Expedition, on the west coast of Greenland. It was also observed by Mr. Feilden, of the Expedition of 1875–1876, in Grinnell Land on the 5th of June, 1876, flying in company with Knots and Turnstones; at this date it was feeding, like the other Waders, on the buds of *Saxifraga oppositifolia*. It was by no means abundant along the coast of that region, but Mr. Feilden observed several pairs in the aggregate, and found one of their nests, containing two eggs, in latitude 82° 33′ N., on the 24th of June, 1876. The nest — from which he killed the male bird — was placed on a gravel ridge, at an altitude of several hundred feet above the sea. The eggs were deposited in a slight depression in the centre of a recumbent plant of Arctic willow, the lining of the nest consisting of a few withered leaves and some of the last year's catkins. On the 8th of August, 1876, along the shores of Robeson Channel, Mr. Feilden saw several parties of young ones — three to four in number — following their parents, and, led by the old birds, searching most diligently for insects. At this date they were in a very interesting stage of plumage, being just able to fly, but retaining some of their down.

The migrations of the Sanderling appear to be made indifferently along the coast or through the interior, both in the Old and in the New World. Wherever there are large bodies of inland water, to the banks of these it is attracted alike in its spring and in its autumnal migrations. It is an abundant visitant along the shores of our own Great Lakes, arriving in full breeding-plumage about the 20th of May, and is seen, according to Mr. Nelson, in flocks of from five to seventy-five along the shore of Lake Michigan until the 10th of June. It returns about the 1st of August, still wearing its breeding-dress which is changed about the last of the month for the more sober colors of winter. It departs about the 20th of October. It is found almost exclusively along the bare sandy beach.

Mr. R. Swinhoe mentions the passage of flocks along the coast of Formosa early in the fall, and their return late in the spring, very few appearing to remain on the shores through the winter. He afterward met with this species at Hungpe Creek, in the Island of Hainan, March 30. On the Red Sea it was met with by Dr. Heuglin, but was not seen there from June to September. It was first noticed, about the end of September, near Ras Belul, on the marshy coast, in small flocks, some being still partly in their summer dress; and in October and November it was very frequent in winter plumage near Zeila, Berbera, Beude, Gam, etc. Specimens have also been procured from India; and Mr. Temminck received them from Japan, from the Sunda Islands, and from New Guinea. Dr. A. Smith obtained specimens in South Africa; and Mr. J. H. Gurney ("Ibis," 1865) mentions the occurrence of this species in the Colony of Natal, also in South Africa, where he found it gregarious on the sea-beach, running about with great activity while feeding, following the waves as they retired, obtaining its food on the very edge of the water, and very rapid in its flight. This bird was observed in the Ionian Islands by Mr. T. L. Powys; and Mr. C. A. Wright ("Ibis," 1864) mentions the capture of a single specimen in Malta, Sept. 24, 1862. It was found by Mr. Saunders abundant in Southern Spain during the autumn and part of the winter, but was not seen by him after the early spring, nor in its breeding-plumage.

The Sanderling, according to Yarrell, is well known on most of the sandy shores of Great Britain and Ireland, where it is found at the water's edge, usually in company with the *Tringa alpina*. It also associates with the smaller Plovers, resembling them in its habits, frequenting the harder part of the sandy shore, and apparently running or flying with equal ease and rapidity. It has been seen as late as June, and as early in the fall as August; but is not known to breed in that country, and its eggs were unknown to Yarrell. Several in full summer livery — says Mr. Heysham — were killed on the coast in the vicinity of Brow-Houses as late as June 4. Others were observed by Mr. Bullock at the northern extremity of Scotland as late as the end of June; but they were believed to go farther north to breed. This species visits the shores of Sweden and Iceland, but breeds — so far as known — still farther north.

Temminck states that the Sanderling is abundant in spring and autumn on the coast of Holland, and that it is found on the shores of France and Italy, occurring occasionally at Nice and Genoa in every stage of plumage; and also in the interior, on the shores of the Black Sea, etc. Dr. Middendorff includes it in his List of the Birds of Siberia, among those that go to the extreme north, and Herr von Heuglin met with flocks of this species in September on Waigat Island, Nova Zembla, mingled with flocks of *Tringa alpina*.

Reinhardt includes the Sanderling among the birds of Greenland, where he found it rare, and breeding on Disco Island. Colonel Sabine, in the Appendix to Parry's "First Voyage," mentions its breeding in considerable numbers on the North Georgian Islands, where several pairs were killed at different periods of the breeding-season. Richardson states that it breeds on the coast of Hudson's Bay as far south as the 55th parallel. Hutchins is quoted as stating that it makes nests of dry grasses in the marshes, and as describing the egg as having a dusky-colored ground spotted with black, incubation commencing in the middle of June. Professor Newton speaks of this species as rare in Greenland, and as said not to breed farther south than latitude 68° N.; but its young have been taken at Godthaab. It was found on the east coast by Graah, and by the German Expedition on Sabine Island. It is also said to have been found breeding in considerable numbers on the Parry Islands.

Mr. Salvin found the Sanderling in considerable numbers on the Pacific coast of Guatemala, and occasionally very abundant; he also met with a few among the bays on the coast of Honduras late in April. Mr. Edward Newton procured a single individual at St. Croix, Sept. 13, 1858. Léotaud includes the Sanderling among the birds of Trinidad, but states that it is only a rare migratory visitant, occurring in small numbers, and only found from August to October. It always stays about the borders of the sea, running over and carefully searching the wet sand and mud for small worms. Mr. Gould states that it is plentiful in Brazil, from whence he has received specimens; and Mr. H. Durnford mentions procuring two out of a flock at Tombo Point, on the coast of Central Patagonia.

The Sanderling passes south along the coast of Massachusetts from the middle of August to the latter part of September, and returns northward in the latter part of May. It reaches Lake Koskonong, Wisconsin, about August 15, and in some seasons is very abundant there. Professor Snow obtained specimens in Kansas in September. It is very common in the spring and fall near Calais, Me. Giraud has never observed it in very large numbers in the spring on the shores of Long Island; but, on its return, it arrives in flocks about the middle of August, and by the 1st of September has become very abundant. It generally prefers the more immediate borders of the ocean, but is often seen occupying, with other small Sandpipers, the shoals and mud-flats in the shallow parts of estuaries. It seems to be eminently sociable, searching for food in company, probing the sand for small bivalve shells and marine worms, or attending the retiring waves in search of shrimps. It is very interesting to watch its active movements as it feeds along the shore, alternately advancing or retreating with the flow of the water. It is naturally very unwary, and is even less suspicious than the rest of the family of *Tringæ*. When a flock is fired into, the survivors rise with a low whistling note, perform a few evolutions, and presently resume their feeding with undiminished confidence. If wounded, it takes to the water, and swims well. Later in the season it becomes very fat, and is excellent eating.

It is very abundant on the shores of the Southern Atlantic States, except during three or four summer months. The greater number of these birds pass north early in May, but a few are seen in June. Some arrive late in August, but most of them in September. After October they become conspicuous by their light color. Up to a short time before their departure they continued in compact flocks, but in May they became more dispersed, and were seen in pairs chasing each other over the sand.

Specimens of this bird were taken in Bermuda by Major Wedderburn from the 4th of September to the 7th of November. According to Mr. Hurdis, it is not known to have occurred there later than the 10th of November. Several individuals of this species were obtained by Mr. J. A. Allen at Ipswich, Mass., in June, 1868; they were in immature plumage, and were mere straggling, unmated birds.

On the Pacific coast the Sanderling was not observed by Dr. Cooper along the southern part of the coast of California, but from San Francisco north it was found numerous in winter; and though a few remain throughout the summer, none are supposed to breed there. Its food on the Pacific coast, and indeed wherever the contents of its stomach have been observed, appears to be slender sea-worms, minute shellfish, crustacea, and fine gravel. Farther north — as Mr. Dall states — it was procured at Sitka by Bischoff, is very common at Nulato, and on the Yukon to the sea, where it arrives early, from May 10th to the 15th, and is one of the last birds to leave in the fall, having been seen by him in October on the edge of the ice. Kennicott found them in the interior, along the beach at Lake Winnipeg in June, where they were in small flocks and numerous. Mr. MacFarlane discovered a nest of this species — the only one at that time known to naturalists — on the Barren Grounds, June 29, 1863. The female was secured, and the nest found to contain four eggs which were quite fresh. The nest is said to have been composed of hay and decayed leaves. It was obtained not far from the Arctic coast, a little east of Anderson River. The two eggs in the Smithsonian Collection (No. 9383) measure, one 1.44 inches in length by .95 in breadth; the other, 1.43 by .99. Their ground-color is a brownish olive, marked with faint spots and small blotches of bistre. These markings are very generally diffused, but are a little more numerous about the larger end. They are of an oblong pyriform shape.

Genus **LIMOSA**, Brisson.

Limosa, Brisson, Orn. 1760 (type, *Scolopax limosa*, L., = *S. ægocephala*, L.).

Char. Bill lengthened, exceeding the tarsus, slender, and curving gently upwards, grooved to near the tip, the tip not attenuated. Tarsus with transverse scutellæ before and behind, reticulated laterally. A short basal membrane between the middle and outer toes. Tail short, even.

Bill much longer than head, nearly equalling tarsi and toes together, curving gently upwards from the base, where it is elevated and compressed, depressed, however, at the end. The grooves on sides of bill and beneath extend nearly to the tip; the tip of the upper mandible is thickened, and extends a little beyond the lower. The gape is slight, not extending beyond the base of the culmen; the feathers on the side of the bill reach forward to about the same point, those on the chin a little farther. Tarsus more than one and one half times the toes, twice the bare part of the tibia; hind toe rather lengthened; outer toe webbed as far as end of first joint, inner toe with only a short basal web. Tail short, even, two-fifths the wings.

In some respects, the bill of this genus resembles that of *Macrorhamphus*, the chief apparent difference being the upward curve of the one and its straightness in the other.

A. Wings without any well-defined white patch.

a. Tail distinctly barred.

1. **L. fedoa**. Prevailing color ochraceous, the head and neck streaked, the remaining upper

parts barred, with brownish dusky; axillars and lining of the wing deep cinnamon-ochre. Wing, 8.50–9.00; culmen, 3.50–5.00; tarsus, 2.75–3.00; middle toe, 1.40. *Hab.* North America.

2. **L. lapponica**. Upper tail-coverts white, spotted with dusky; axillars and lining of wing white, irregularly marked with dusky. *In summer*, head and lower parts cinnamon-color.

L. fedoa.

In winter, head and lower parts whitish, the head and neck streaked, the breast and sides irregularly barred with grayish brown. *Young*, like winter adult, but plumage generally washed with dull light clay-color, the throat and jugulum unstreaked.

a. Lapponica. Rump white, marked with elliptical, acuminate streaks of dusky. Wing, 8.25–8.50; culmen, 2.95–3.80; tarsus, 2.00–2.15; middle toe, 1.10–1.20. *Hab.* Palæarctic Region.

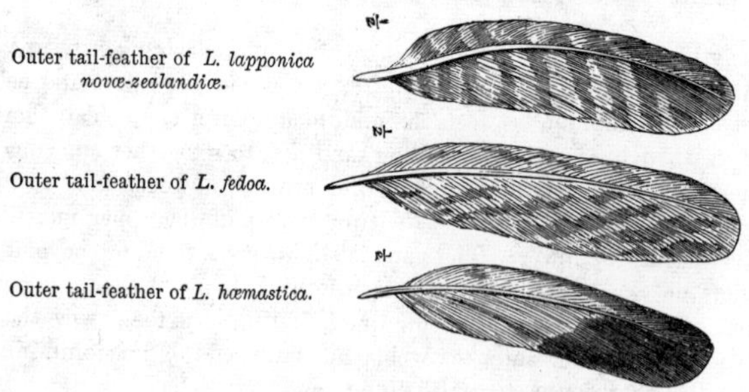

Outer tail-feather of *L. lapponica novæ-zealandiæ.*

Outer tail-feather of *L. fedoa.*

Outer tail-feather of *L. hæmastica.*

β. Novæ-zealandiæ. Rump dusky, the feathers bordered with whitish. Wing, 8.25–9.15; culmen, 3.15–3.55; tarsus, 2.00–2.20; middle toe, 1.10–1.20. *Hab.* Pacific Islands and coasts, from Australia to Alaska.

b. Tail black, with white base and tip, but without bars.

3. **L. hæmastica.** Upper tail-coverts crossed by a wide band of pure white; longer upper tail-coverts, entire rump, and axillars, uniform dusky; lining of wing dusky, spotted with white outwardly. *Summer plumage:* Beneath, chestnut barred with dusky; above, blackish. *Winter plumage:* Beneath, whitish, without markings, the breast and jugulum grayish; above, uniform brownish gray, except rump, upper tail-coverts, and tail. *Young:* Beneath, light grayish clay-color, darker on breast; above, brownish gray, feathers bordered with ochraceous, and somewhat spotted with dusky. Wing, 8.10–8.60; culmen, 2.85–3.45; tarsus, 2.25–2.50; middle toe, 1.15–1.30. *Hab.* America.

B. Wing with two white patches, one at base of inner primaries, the other occupying the greater part of the secondaries.

4. **L. ægocephala.** Upper tail-coverts, rump, and tail much as in *Hudsonica;* axillars and lining of wing pure white. Wing, 8.25; culmen, 3.70; tarsus, 2.85; middle toe, 1.25. *Hab.* Palæarctic Region; Greenland.

Limosa fedoa.

THE MARBLED GODWIT.

Scolopax fedoa, LINN. S. N. I. 1766, 244 (based on *Fedoa americana,* EDW. 137, and *Limosa americana rufa,* BRISS. V. 287). — WILS. Am. Orn. VII. 1813, 30, pl. 56, f. 4.

Limosa fedoa, ORD. ed. WILSON, VII. 1825. — SW. & RICH. F. B. A. II. 1831, 395. — NUTT. Man. II. 1834, 173. — AUD. Orn. Biog. III. 1835, 287; V. 590, pl. 238; Synop. 1839, 246; B. Am. V. 1842, 331, pl. 348. — CASS. in Baird's B. N. Am. 1858, 740. — BAIRD, Cat. N. Am. B. 1859, no. 547. — COUES, Key, 1872, 257; Check List, 1873, no. 428; Birds N. W. 1874, 492.

Limosa fœda, RIDGW. Nom. N. Am. B. 1881, no. 543. — COUES, Check List, 2d ed. 1882, no. 628.

Scolopax marmorata, LATH. Ind. Orn. II. 1790, 720.

"*Limosa americana,* STEPHENS, Shaw's Gen. Zool."

"*Limosa adspersa,* LICHT."

HAB. North America; breeding in the interior of the continent (Missouri Region and northward), wintering southward to Yucatan and Guatemala; Cuba.

SP. CHAR. Bill long, curved upwards; both mandibles grooved; wings long; tail short; legs long; tibia with its lower half naked; toes rather short, margined and flattened underneath; the

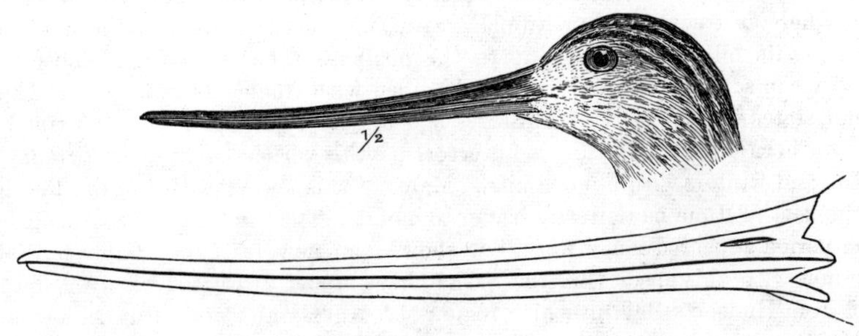

outer and middle toes united by a rather large membrane. Entire upper parts variegated with brownish black and pale reddish, the former disposed in irregular and confluent bands, and the latter in spots and imperfect bands; in many specimens the black color predominating on the back, and the pale red on the rump and upper tail-coverts. Under parts pale rufous, with transverse lines of brownish black on the breast and sides; under wing-coverts and axillaries darker rufous; outer webs of primaries dark brown, inner webs light rufous; secondaries light rufous; tail light rufous, with transverse bars of brownish black. "Bill dull flesh-color in its basal half, the rest blackish brown; iris brown; feet bluish gray" (AUDUBON.)

Total length about 18.00 inches; wing, 9.00; tail, 3.50; bill, 4.00 to 5.00; tarsus, 3 00 inches.[1]

The plumage of this bird in some stages is wonderfully similar to that of *Numenius longirostris;* in fact the resemblance is so great that were it not for the conspicuous generic differences it would be rather difficult to distinguish them specifically. Both have precisely the same tints of color, and also a nearly identical distribution of the markings. The main differences appear to be the following: In *Numenius* the black bars of the upper parts are connected by broad stripes along the middle of the feathers, while in *Limosa* these bars are all isolated and narrower, as well as of a less deep black. The longitudinal streaks on the head and neck are much less conspicuous in *Limosa;* in the latter there is also oftener a tendency to transverse bars on the crissum, and less often to streaks on the foreneck.

The Great Marbled Godwit has been found throughout North America from the Pacific to the Atlantic coast, but is not known to occur north of the Selkirk Settlement, Manitoba, and Hudson's Bay; nor has it yet been traced any nearer than this to the Arctic Circle, and it is not known to occur in any part of Alaska. By our earlier writers it was supposed to be only a bird of transit in the United States; but this is a mistake. It is now known to breed in Northern Ohio, in Wisconsin, Iowa, Minnesota, Kansas, and Nebraska, and also not improbably in Texas and the intervening region. It passes the winter chiefly in the West India Islands, Mexico, Central and South America.

Mr. Leyland found this species common at the Belize; Mr. Salvin met with it on the Pacific coast of Guatemala, and Mr. Henshaw mentions its appearing in large flocks on the Californian coast both in spring and fall. It is also given by Mr. R. Browne in his List of the Birds of Vancouver Island; but it does not appear to have been traced farther north on the Pacific coast than that island, and it is not mentioned by Mr. Dall.

According to Léotaud it visits the Island of Trinidad, arriving there in the month of August and remaining until October. It is always found on the borders of the sea, and is never present in great numbers. It is included by Dr. Gundlach among the birds of Cuba.

Richardson speaks of this species as abounding in the Fur Country, especially in the interior, and mentions it as particularly abundant on the Plains of the Saskatchewan, where it frequents marshy places, walking on the surface of the *sphagna,* and thrusting its bill among them up to the nostrils. The stomachs of those that he killed when so engaged were found to be filled with fragments of leeches. The same author states that in the United States it is a mere bird of passage, wintering beyond our southern limit; but this is an error, as this species — to some extent — both breeds and winters within our limits. Males of this species killed in the Fur Region on the 21st of June had already begun to moult. The plumage of the females at the same period appeared much worn, but showed no new feathers. Captain Blakiston also met with this species on the Saskatchewan, and afterward received specimens of it from Hudson's Bay, in which region Mr. Murray also noticed it occasionally.

Mr. Dresser mentions that in June he noticed a few of these birds near Brownville and Matamoras, but was able to procure only one specimen. Their occurrence in that locality at that period renders it not impossible that a few may breed even in that

[1] A series of ten specimens, including an equal number of males and females, shot by Mr. Franklin Benner, in Minnesota, between June 5th and 20th, was carefully measured, with the following results: *Males*: Total length, 16.50–17.62, average, 17.00; extent, 30.50–31.50, average, 31.10; bill, 3.66–4.00, average, 3.84. *Females:* Total length, 18.12–19.62, average, 19.10; extent, 32.00–33.87, average, 32.82; bill, 4.54–5.06, average, 4.77. (See "Bull. Nutt. Orn. Club," V. Jan. 1880, p. 18.)

southern region. In August they had become more numerous; and about the time of his leaving he saw them daily in the lagoon.

Dr. Cooper states that this species is common through nearly all the year along the southern half of the Californian coast; and it seemed to him probable that it breeds within or near the limits of that State, as the young make their appearance, fully fledged, near San Pedro in July, and remain until the 20th of May, if not later.

According to Giraud it arrives in the month of May on the sea-coast of Long Island, where it is well known to the sportsmen both as the Marlin and as the Great Marbled Godwit. It visits that locality regularly every spring and autumn, but never in abundance. It associates in flocks, and usually passes its time on the shoals and salt-marshes, being exceedingly watchful, and not permitting a near approach; yet whenever any one of its number is wounded, its associates hover around it and utter loud and shrill cries. On such an occasion they crowd together and offer an excellent opportunity for the hunter to secure others. Pelican Bar is said to be a favorable place for procuring this species. Giraud adds that its flesh is tender and juicy, and that it is highly prized as a game-bird by epicures.

This Curlew is not common in Massachusetts, it being much less frequently met with than the smaller species. A few are seen both in their spring migrations and in the fall, in the more easterly portions of Barnstable County. Mr. Boardman informs us that it is found at Grand Menan late in the summer and during its migrations southward.

Wilson, who only observed this bird on the shore of New Jersey, regarded it as exclusively migratory, coming in May and returning in October and November, a few lingering into June. They were known to hunters as the Red Curlew and the Straight-billed Curlew. He characterizes it as shy, cautious, and watchful, yet so strongly attached to its companions, that when one in a flock is wounded, the rest are immediately arrested in their flight, making so many circuits over the spot where it lies fluttering and screaming, that the sportsman often makes great destruction among them. This bird may be enticed within shot by imitating its whistle, but can seldom be otherwise approached. It is found usually among the salt-marshes, and in the fall is very fat.

Nuttall ventured the conjecture — since verified — that some of this species may yet be found to breed in more temperate regions to the West, as well as at the North. In his day this species is said to have appeared about the middle of August in the salt-marshes of Massachusetts, particularly towards the eastern extremity, around Chatham and the Vineyard, their stay being very short. It may be that he mistook for this the *Hudsonian*, which in some seasons is very abundant on this coast. At present, at least, it is only an occasional visitânt, though said in Nuttall's time to assemble in flocks of many hundreds. Verrill speaks of it as rare on the coast of Maine, and it is not given by Boardman in his List of the Birds of Calais, although he has since been informed that it probably breeds in Prince Edward's Island.

Mr. Audubon met with this species in Florida, during winter, on all the large muddy flats of the coast. It was generally seen in flocks of five or six, in company with several other kinds of Waders. Few birds are found more shy or vigilant; but when in large flocks they may occasionally be approached and killed in large numbers. On the last of May, 1832, he saw, on an extensive mud-bar about six miles south of Cape Sable, an immense flock of these birds, amounting to some thousands in number. Four or five shots enabled him to obtain all he desired. Those killed were plump and excellent eating. The next morning the whole flock had moved north. This bird has a regular and quick flight, and when migrating usually moves in extended lines, presenting an irregular front, which undulates and breaks as the flock advances. On such occasions it rarely utters any cries.

According to Mr. Moore, a few of this species remain about Sarasota Bay, Florida, during the summer months, although the larger portion leave for their northern breeding-grounds. Those which remain do not exhibit any symptoms of being mated. Mr. Moore does not credit the statement that this species ever breeds near Charleston: the fact is assumed, rather than proved. The plumage of those that remain in Florida is preserved unchanged.

Three eggs of this species, belonging to the Smithsonian Institution, and obtained in Minnesota, range in length from 2.22 to 2.33 inches, and from 1.56 to 1.60 inches in breadth. Their ground-color is a pale greenish drab. Over the egg are scattered markings in the form of small blotches of olivaceous-umber. These become larger at the greater end of the egg, and intermixed with them are also a few washes of a dilute purplish slate. Three eggs in my own collection — one from Cleveland, Ohio, and two from Northwestern Iowa — do not materially vary. In regard to the nest of this bird we have no direct information.

Limosa lapponica novæ-zealandiæ.

THE PACIFIC GODWIT.

Limosa novæ-zealandiæ, GRAY, Voy. Erebus & Terror, Birds, 1845, 13. — CASS. Orn. U. S. Expl. Exp. 1848, 314 (Rose I., Samoan Group).

Limosa lapponica, var. *novæ-zealandiæ*, GRAY, l. c.

Limosa lapponica novæ-zealandiæ, RIDGW. Proc. U. S. Nat. Mus. Vol. III. 1880, 200; Nom. N. Am. B. 1881, no. 544.

Limosa uropygialis, GOULD, P. Z. S. 1848, 38; Birds Australia, VI. 1848, pl. xxix. — FINSCH & HARTL. Beitr. Fauna Centr. Polyn. 1867, 177. — BAIRD, Trans. Chicago Acad. I. 1869, 320, pl. 32 (Alaska). — DALL & BANNIST. Ib. — COUES, Check List, 2d ed. 1882, no. 631.

Limosa Foxii, PEALE, U. S. Expl. Exped. 1848, 231, pl. lxv.

HAB. Shores and islands of the Pacific Ocean, from Australia to Alaska. Not recorded from the Pacific coast of America south of Alaska, except Lower California (L. BELDING).

SP. CHAR. *Adult in summer:* Back and scapulars dusky, irregularly spotted with whitish and light rufous; wing-coverts light grayish, with dusky shaft-streaks and whitish borders, the anterior

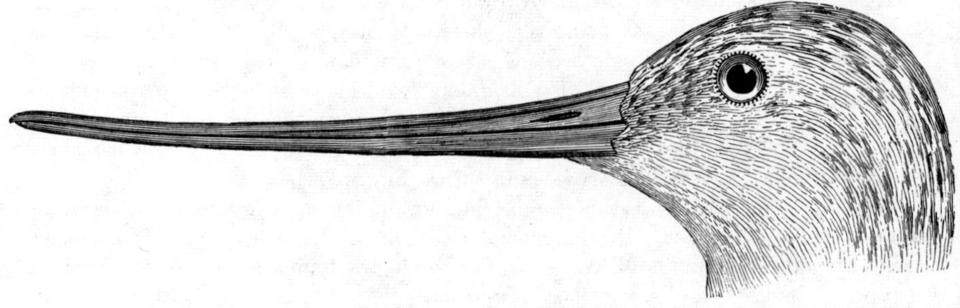

smaller coverts darker and more uniform grayish; primaries and primary-coverts dusky, the inner quills bordered with white. Rump dusky grayish, the feathers bordered with white; upper tail-coverts white, tinged with light cinnamon, and irregularly spotted with dusky; tail grayish, irregularly barred, and narrowly tipped with white. Head, neck, and lower parts, light cinnamon, the crown, nape, and lores streaked with dusky. Axillars and lining of the wing white, irregularly barred and spotted with dusky grayish. *Winter plumage:* Above, plain brownish gray, beneath, plain whitish; rump, upper tail-coverts, tail, axillars, etc., as in summer. *Young:* Above, including wing-coverts, light grayish buff, or pale clay-color, coarsely and irregularly spotted with dusky, the latter chiefly along the centres of the feathers, and showing as conspicuous shaft-streaks on the wing-coverts; lower parts buffy whitish, shaded across the jugulum and breast with deeper grayish buff; in other respects like the adult.

Total length, about 16 inches; wing, 8.25–9.15; culmen, 3.15–3.55; tarsus, 2.00–2.20; middle toe, 1.10–1.20.

There is considerable variation among individuals in the depth and continuity of the cinnamon-color on the lower surface.

The relationship of this form is unquestionably very close to *L. lapponica*, of which it cannot be considered more than a geographical race or sub-species, the differences being very slight, although apparently constant. These consist in the rather paler shade of cinnamon on the lower parts in the summer plumage, and in the grayish instead of distinctly white rump, in all stages of plumage.

Australian examples appear to be quite identical with those from Alaska.

This species is included in the fauna of North America as a summer resident of Alaska Territory, where it was met with by Mr. Dall while engaged on the Telegraph Expedition. Its discovery as a bird of Alaska was one of the most interesting among the results of that survey, as its existence in North America had not been even suspected before it had been thus taken.

So far as had been previously ascertained, its range, during the winter months, had been over Polynesia, Australia, Eastern and Southern Asia, and Japan. In summer it was known to go north to Siberia, where Middendorff found it breeding on the Taimyr River, in latitude 75° N. Specimens from Polynesia were brought home by the United States Exploring Expedition.

Mr. Swinhoe mentions that a pair of this species was observed feeding in company with a large flock of Godwits in the shallows of the creek at Hungpe, on the Island of Hainan, on the 30th of March. They were secured, and proved to be very nearly in full summer plumage. Three days later another example, in the full winter plumage, was obtained on the sandy shores of Hoehow Harbor.

Captain F. W. Hutton ("Ibis," 1871) states that this bird was seen several times on the Chatham Islands, although he did not succeed in obtaining any specimens. These examples were apparently only migratory, leaving the Islands in winter.

In the Proceedings of the Philadelphia Academy, 1858, Mr. Cassin refers to a species of Limosa from Japan, which Mr. Swinhoe states to be probably this one. Both Mr. Swinhoe ("Ibis," 1875) and Messrs. Blakiston and Pryer mention its occurrence in different parts of Japan, especially Yeso and Yokohama. The Messrs. Layard ("Ibis," 1878, p. 262) cite this species as a bird of New Caledonia.

Mr. Dall states that this species was very common at the mouth of the Yukon River, and also on the Pastolik marshes to the north of it. It is the largest Snipe found in the country, being quite as large in body as a Teal, and very excellent eating. He adds that it lays two light-olivaceous and spotted eggs in a rounded depression in a sedge tussock, and that the nest consists of a lining of dry grasses.

Mr. H. W. Elliott met with this species from time to time during his stay on the Prybilof Islands, and speaks of it as only migratory there, and never breeding. It comes in a straggling manner early in May, passing northward with but little delay, and re-appearing toward the end of August in flocks of from a dozen to fifty.

A set of these eggs, two in number, are in the Smithsonian Collection. One of these measures 2.25 inches in length by 1.45 in breadth. The ground-color of one is a deep greenish drab; the markings are scattered in the form of irregular blotches of a dilute umber. The other measures 2.25 by 1.42 inches, and the ground-color is of a pale drab, the markings being much more pronounced than in the other specimen, and more aggregated toward the larger end, as well as more irregular in form, and are of a much deeper shade of umber.

Limosa hæmastica.

THE HUDSONIAN GODWIT.

Scolopax hæmastica, LINN. S. N. ed. 10, I. 1758, 147 (based on Edwards, pl. 138).
Limosa hæmastica, COUES, Bull. Nutt. Orn. Club, 1880, 100; Check List, 2d ed. 1882, no. 629. — RIDGW. Nom. N. Am. B. 1881, no. 545.
Scolopax alba, LINN. S. N. I. 1766, 247 (based on *Fedoa canadensis*, EDW. pl. 139; *Limosa candida*, BRISS. V. 290; *Totanus canadensis*, EDW. pl. 139, f. 1; *Totanus candidus*, BRISS. V. 207).
Scolopax candida, LINN. l. c.
Scolopax lapponica, var. *β*. GMEL. S. N. I. 1788.
Scolopax Hudsonica, LATH. Ind. Orn. II. 1790, 720.
Limosa Hudsonica, SW. & RICH. F. B. A. II. 1831, 396. — NUTT. Man. II. 1834, 175. — AUD. Orn. Biog. III. 1835, 426; V. 592, pl. 258; Synop. 1839, 247; B. Am. V. 1842, 335, pl. 349. — CASSIN, in Baird's B. N. Am. 1858, 741. — BAIRD, Cat. N. Am. B. 1859, no. 548. — COUES, Key, 1872, 258; Check List, 1873, no. 429; Birds N. W. 1874, 494.
Limosa melanura, BONAP. Specc. Comp. 1827, no. 204 (nec LEISL.).
Limosa ægocephala, BONAP. Synop. 1828, 327 (nec LINN.).
Limosa Edwardsi, SW. & RICH. F. B. A. II. 1831, 398.
Limosa australis, GRAY, Cat. Brit. Mus. 1844, 95.

HAB. Eastern North America and the whole of Middle and South America. No West Indian localities recorded except Cuba. Breeds only in the high north.

SP. CHAR. Smaller than *L. fedoa*. *Summer adult:* Above, blackish brown, irregularly spotted and barred with pale ochraceous, the rump plain brownish black; upper tail-coverts immaculate white; wing-coverts and shorter quills plain dark brownish gray; primaries brownish black, their

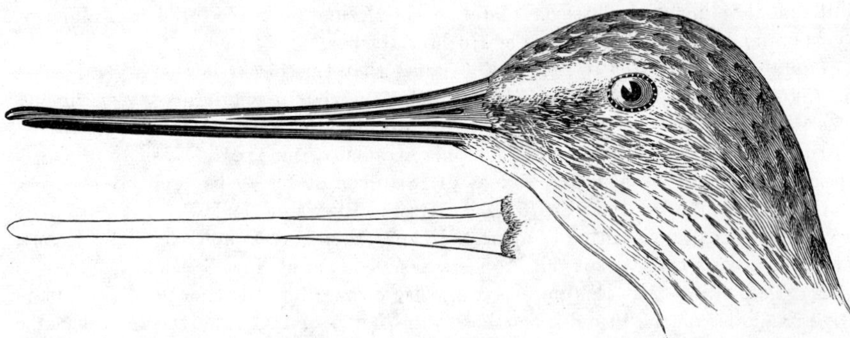

shafts white. Lower parts chestnut-rufous, narrowly barred with brownish black, the feathers of the belly, etc., often tipped with white. Tail black, with the base and tip (narrowly) white. Lining of wings and axillars plain smoky black. *Winter plumage:* Above, plain dull brownish gray; beneath, white, the breast shaded with brownish gray. Other characters as in summer dress. *Young:* Somewhat like the winter plumage, but each feather of dorsal region marked with a subterminal dusky crescent and a narrower terminal one of dull ochraceous; beneath, very pale drab, or dull light buff, the abdomen whitish, and the jugulum more grayish. "Bill grayish yellow, dark brown along the ridge of the upper mandible, and blackish towards the tips of both; iris brown; feet light grayish blue" (AUDUBON).

This species resembles somewhat the European *L. ægocephala*, having the tail marked much the same as in that species. The latter, however, has two white patches on the wing (which in the present bird has no white at all, except the shafts of the primaries), the axillars pure white instead of brownish black. There are also other differences of coloration, while the proportions are quite different, *L. ægocephala* having the bill and legs much longer.

South American specimens are quite identical with northern ones.

Much remains to be ascertained before the history of the habits and distribution of this Godwit can be given with tolerable accuracy or completeness. It appears to have a somewhat irregular distribution over the United States, occurring in some seasons in great abundance in regions where it was not known before, or where, in succeeding years, it has been of only irregular and occasional appearance. In the United States it is only known as migratory, breeding north of the limits of the Union, and in regions farther north than those in which the *fedoa* has been found. Its presence in Patagonia, as also in the Falkland Islands, is equally suggestive of a wide, and perhaps irregular, distribution.

It is not given by Dr. Gundlach as occurring in Cuba; but is mentioned by Léotaud as one of the birds of the Island of Trinidad, where it is spoken of as much more common than the *fedoa,* coming in August, and leaving in October. It is always found in either the immature or the winter plumage, and is only to be met with on the borders of the sea.

Mr. G. C. Taylor mentions finding this species abundant on the shores of Fonseca Bay, where it is in the habit of sitting on the branches of the mangrove-trees which overhang the water. He considered it excellent eating.

Mr. H. Durnford ("Ibis," 1877, p. 43), in his Observations relative to the Birds observed by him in the Valley of the Chupat, in Patagonia, states that during his visit there in November, 1876, a small party of this Godwit was always to be found in the shallow water at the west end of a large lagoon to the north of the village. They were feeding in company with *Tringa maculata* and a species — unidentified — of *Ægialitis*. On the 13th of November he procured two examples.

Mr. C. C. Abbott ("Ibis," 1861) mentions finding flocks of this species at Mare Harbor, Falkland Islands, in the month of May, 1860. He shot two of them at Port Louis on the 20th of that month. Both had the red-barred breast, and were therefore in the winter plumage. He did not notice the presence of this bird in those islands during the winter months; and even when found there in the summer, he has never heard of its eggs having been detected. It was very wary, and difficult to procure.

Hearne, in his book of Arctic travels, published more than a century since, referring to this species as the "Red Godwaite," states that it was then generally known at the more northern settlements on Hudson's Bay as a Plover. He mentions that it visited the shores of that portion of the bay in very large flocks, and usually frequented the marshes and the margins of ponds. It also frequently attended the tide, in the manner of the "Esquimaux Curlew" (*Numenius Hudsonicus*), flying down to the water's edge and feeding on a small fish not much unlike a shrimp; but as the tide advances, retiring to the marshes. The birds were said to fly in such large flocks, and so closely together, that he was often able to kill as many as twelve at one shot. And he further states that a Mr. Anderson, long a resident at Fort York, actually killed seventy-two of this species at one discharge; but this was after they had alighted on the shore. Near Churchill River they were seldom very fat, though in tolerable condition, and they were said to be generally very good eating. They usually weighed from ten to thirteen ounces. The two sexes differ both in color and size, the female being always larger and of a much lighter brown than the male.

This bird retires to the south long before the frosts begin; still, it has been met with as far north as latitude 71° 50′.

This Godwit — Mr. Boardman tells me — is found in the neighborhood of Calais, Me., but is there quite rare. He was informed that a few occur in the summer on Prince Edward's Island, where the species is supposed to breed, and where it has been obtained in its breeding-plumage.

Mr. Ross mentions this bird as occurring — although rarely — on the Mackenzie; and Mr. Murray and Captain Blakiston both procured it on Hudson's Bay.

On the coast of Massachusetts it is of very irregular appearance — at least as to numbers — being in some seasons very common. It is stated by Mr. H. A. Purdie to have been quite abundant on the New England coast in the fall of 1873. A single specimen was obtained at Eastham, Nov. 3, 1878, by Mr. Frank H. Tileston.

This species, in its migrations in spring and fall, also visits the interior lakes and rivers. It is a regular visitant at Lake Koskonong, Wisconsin, where, as Mr. Kumlien informs me, it appeared as early as August 15, in 1873. Mr. Nelson cites it as a not rare migrant in Northern Illinois, where it comes in April and reappears in October.

According to Richardson, this species breeds abundantly on the Barren Ground near the Arctic Sea, where it feeds on insects and shelly mollusca, which it obtains in the small sphagnous lakes. In all its manners and habits it is similar to the Great Marbled Godwit.

According to Giraud, this bird is met with on the shores of Long Island, where, however, it is not so plentiful as the Marbled Godwit. It is known to the hunters of that island as the "Ring-tailed Marlin," and is so called from the white band crossing the tail-feathers. A few are shot every season on those shores, and some are also procured on the more eastern sea-coast. Giraud adds that it is by no means a rare bird in the Middle States, though not abundant. In its habits he regards it as nearly allied with the *fedoa*, with which it sometimes associates.

This species appears to have escaped the notice of Wilson, and to have been but very imperfectly known either to Audubon or to Nuttall. The latter considered it an infrequent visitor to the Eastern and Middle States, and conjectured that it might be more common on our northwestern coast; but this is quite problematical. Two specimens only are recorded by Mr. Dall as having been taken near the mouth of the Yukon River. With this exception, none of our own explorers mention its occurrence on the Pacific shores. Mr. Dall regarded it as quite rare on the Yukon. Mr. E. Adams, however, met with it in Alaska, on the coast of Norton Sound, where, as he states ("Ibis," 1878), a few of these birds frequented the marshes on the river-banks, to which they exclusively confined themselves, living upon the worms found there in abundance. The first seen were feeding in some shallow pools, on the 21st of May. He afterward met with the same species at Port Clarence.

Nuttall did not see more than two or three pairs in the course of a season. These were found on the neighboring coast, near Boston, and were called the "Goose Bird." One pair, obtained about September 8, were very fat and well-flavored, and had been feeding upon *Ulva* and other vegetable matter. He noticed this species in the Boston market from the 6th to the 30th of September.

Audubon regarded this as a very rare species and unknown along the coast south of Maryland. He first met with it in September, 1832, in the Boston market. He afterward received specimens from Pictou, N. S.; and on his way to Labrador, was informed by the inhabitants of the Magdalen Islands that this species breeds in the marshes at the extremity of the principal island. He met with none in Labrador or in Newfoundland, but was informed by Mr. MacCullock that it breeds on Prince Edward's Island, from which the pairs spread along the coast of Nova Scotia, and there remain until very severe weather drives them away.

Mr. MacFarlane found this species breeding in the vicinity of Fort Anderson, on the 9th of June. The nest was on the ground, was composed of a few decayed leaves lying in a small hole scooped in the earth, and contained four eggs. Other nests were found and birds obtained on the Lower Anderson River. They were mere depressions in the ground, lined with withered leaves.

Examples of this species were also taken at Fort Rae, on Great Slave Lake, by Mr. Kennicott; at Moose Fort by Mr. I. McKenzie; on the Anderson River by Mr. B. R. Ross; on Big Island by Mr. Reid; and at Fort Kenzie by Bischoff.

Three of the eggs collected by Mr. MacFarlane are in the Smithsonian Collection. In two of these the ground is of a deep raw-umber color, or an olivaceous drab. There are no well-defined spots, but the apex of the larger end is deeply stained with a dark burnt-umber color. A few very indistinct spots of a paler shade of this tint are visible over the general surface of the eggs. The other egg has a ground-color of a paler umber-drab, and the markings are quite distinct. These are small irregular blotches, longitudinal in their direction, and of a deep burnt-umber tint. The apex of the larger end is covered by a broad patch, in which all the markings, of a very dark umber, almost black, run into each other. These eggs are pyriform in shape, and measure 2.15 by 1.41, 2.12 by 1.39, and 2.22 by 1.40 inches.

Limosa ægocephala.

BLACK-TAILED GODWIT.

Scolopax limosa, LINN. S. N. ed. 10, 1758, 147; ed. 12, 1766, 245.
Scolopax ægocephala, LINN. S. N. I. 1766, 246, no. 16.
Limosa ægocephala, LEACH, Syst. Cat. 1816, 34. — KEYS. & BLAS. Wirb. Eur. 1840, 74. — BONAP. Comp. List, 1838, 52. — GRAY. Gen. B. III. 1849, 570; Cat. Brit. B. 1863, 156. — REINH. Ibis, 1861, 11 (Greenland). — RIDGW. Nom. N. Am. B. 1881, no. 546. — COUES, Check List, 2d ed. 1882, no. 630.
Totanus rufus, BECHST. Naturg. IV. 253.
Limosa melanurus, LEISL. Nacht. zu Bechst. Naturg. 1811–1815, 150, 157. — NAUM. Vög. Deutschl. VIII. 1836, 406, pls. 212, 213. — MACGILL. Man. II. 81.
Scolopax belgica, GMEL. S. N. I. 1788, 663.
Limosa jadreca, LEACH, Syst. Cat. 1816, 32.
Limosa islandica, BREHM, Vög. Deutschl. 1831, 626.
Black-tailed Godwit, YARRELL, Brit. B. ed. 2, II. 634, fig.; ed. 3, II. 681, fig.; et AUCT.

HAB. The Palæarctic Region; accidental in Greenland.

SP. CHAR. *Adult, in summer:* Head, neck, and jugulum, cinnamon, streaked on the first and barred on the last with dusky; remaining lower parts white, the breast and sides barred with dusky. Back and scapulars mixed black, cinnamon, and grayish; wing-coverts, brownish gray; greater coverts widely tipped with white, forming a conspicuous patch; secondaries partly white; primaries dusky, the fifth to the seventh white at the base, forming a second white patch on the wing. Rump, longer upper tail-coverts, and most of the tail dusky; upper tail-coverts (except terminal half of the longer feathers) and base of the tail, immaculate white, this occupying the greater part of the outer rectrices. Axillars and lining of the wing immaculate white. *Winter plumage:* Wings, tail, rump, etc., as in summer; head, neck, back, and scapulars dark brownish gray, the head and neck lighter; jugulum pale gray, without bars; other lower parts white. *Young, first plumage:* "Head dull brown, the feathers edged with rufous-buff; an indistinct light-buff line passing from the base of the bill above and beyond the eye; neck dark buff; back earthy brown, with here and there a dark blackish brown feather, all being edged with dull rufous . . .

elongated inner secondaries dark brown, edged with rufous-buff, and notched with rufous; greater wing-coverts dull earthy gray, broadly tipped with white; median and smaller coverts dull brown, edged and tipped with grayish buff; chin dirty white; sides of head, neck, and breast dark buff; flanks washed with buff" (SHARPE & DRESSER). *Downy young:* "Rusty yellow, marked with

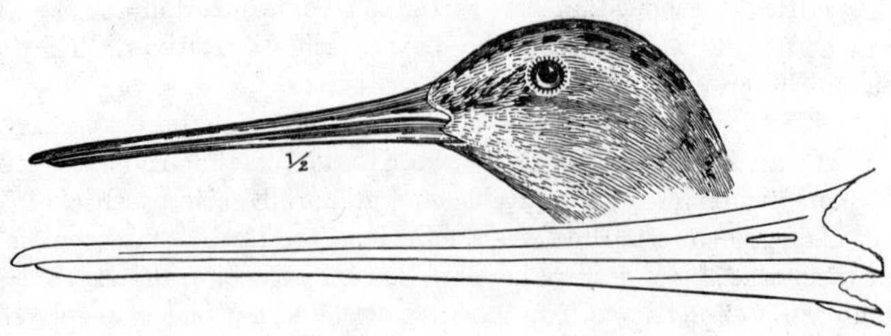

black, especially on crown and rump; a narrow streak through the eye, wing-joints, cheeks, and belly, light yellowish" (SHARPE & DRESSER).

Wing, 8.00–9.80; culmen, 3.70–4.95; tarsus, 2.80–3.80; middle toe, 2.00–2.12.

The Black-tailed Godwit claims a place in the fauna of North America only as an accidental visitant of Greenland. It is an inhabitant of the Old World, breeding only in the more northern portions, but not within high Arctic regions. It is almost exclusively migratory in Great Britain and Ireland, though a few remain there each year and breed.

In England, according to Yarrell, it is most frequently seen in the spring and fall, the first-comers being adult birds on their way to their breeding-grounds in high northern latitudes. In the autumn it is more abundant than in the spring, on account of the large number of young birds of the year going south, for the first time, to their winter-quarters. A few were still known to resort to the marshes of Norfolk and to the fens of Lincolnshire; but these are very rarely permitted to breed unmolested, as the large size, as well as the peculiar action, of this bird when it is breeding, are sure to attract the notice both of the sportsman and the egger. Yarrell was informed in 1855, by the Rev. Richard Lubbock, that this Godwit still breeds occasionally in some of the Norfolk marshes, returning to the same locality year after year, and being found in only two or three situations.

In its flight during the breeding-season it is said to resemble the *Totanus calidris* of Europe; and like that bird it flies, when breeding, around the head of any intruder in the marsh, but in more distant circles, and at a much greater height in the air. It is known in the rural districts of England by the local name of "Shrieker;" but in Yarrell's opinion it does not deserve the name, for its note, though loud, is very far from being inharmonious. It is said to be becoming more and more rare each year in the breeding-season. Its food consists of insects and their larvæ, worms, snails, and various other soft-bodied animals. If disturbed when breeding, it is said to be very clamorous, flying round and uttering a cry which is thought to resemble the syllables *grutto-grutto-grutto;* and by this name it is known by the country folk of Holland. According to Thompson, this bird is seen occasionally in Ireland, and only in the autumn. Examples of it have been obtained in Devonshire, and others at Carlington in Bedfordshire; and Yarrell was informed by Mr. Bond that several specimens have been known to make their appearance in the vicinity of Kingsbury Reservoir, a large sheet of water a few miles north of London. Specimens are also recorded from Cambridgeshire, Northumberland, and from the vicinity of Solway Firth. Living specimens are occasionally brought from Holland to England; and the bird, in a semi-domestic state, is not infrequently confined in walled gardens, where it makes a very interesting and amusing pet. Others are fatted for the market with bread and milk, as is also done with the Ruff; but the Godwit is not equal in flavor to the latter when thus treated.

The Godwit is found during the summer in Denmark; and it also visits, in considerable numbers, various parts of Scandinavia, and especially Lapland, going as far north as Iceland, and occasionally to Greenland. In the more southern countries of the European continent it is exclusively seen in spring and autumn. It is quite common in Spain; and living specimens were sent to the Zoölogical Garden from Tangier, where it was said to be not uncommon, besides others from Tunis and different localities in North Africa. According to Schinz ("Fauna Helvetica"), this bird is occasionally seen, as a migrant, in Switzerland; and not infrequently a pair is supposed to remain and nest, as birds are from time to time taken in their summer plumage. In May it passes north through Italy and Genoa, and returns, reinforced in numbers, in the month of August. It is said to be rare in Sicily, but is more common at Malta, during its migrations. Specimens have been taken in Tripoli; and the Zoölogical Society received a young bird of the year from Trebizond. Hohenacker, a Russian naturalist, mentions this species among the birds obtained by him in the vicinity of the Caucasus; Mr. Hodgson includes it among those found in Nepal, and Mr. Blyth in the list of those occurring at Calcutta. Mr. Temminck also states that it may be found in Japan and on the Isles of Sunda.

According to M. Gerbe, this species has been observed at different seasons in nearly every portion of Europe, Asia, and Africa. In France it is a regular bird of passage in autumn, and again in spring, passing north in March and April, and moving south in September and October. Many of these birds are snared in the spring, between Douai and Cambrai, and kept within gardens enclosed by walls; but the greater number of them perish during the winter for want of suitable food. The same author adds that this species nests in damp meadows, in the grass, or among the reeds. Its eggs are four in number, rounded at one end, pyriform in shape, and quite variable in regard to shades of color. Generally they have a deep olive ground, with points and blotches of a russet, or a pale brown color. Some of these are of a very deep shade, others are very faint. These markings are more numerous, larger, and more confluent about the larger end. M. Gerbe possessed varieties of this egg, some of which had a reddish-white and some a yellowish-white ground; while in others it was of a very pale green color. Some are profusely sprinkled with spots of an intensely deep coloring, and again others are of a uniformly ashy gray, and are entirely unspotted. He gives their greater diameter as varying from 53 to 61 millimetres, and the smaller from 37 to 40.

According to Hewitson, the Black-tailed Godwit begins to lay its eggs early in May. Its nest is composed of dry grass and other vegetables, and is concealed among the coarse herbage of the swamps and low meadows. The eggs, four in number, he describes as of a light olive brown, blotched and spotted with darker brown, their length 2.17 inches and their breadth 1.50 inches, and in form they are decidedly pear-shaped.

In addition, we learn from the observations of Dr. L. Taczanowski, of Warsaw, as quoted by Dresser, that large numbers of this bird breed in marshy localities on the eastern side of the Vistula. In the spring, as soon as the snow disappears, this bird arrives in the marshes, and frequents their edges. It begins to breed early in May, and young are found fully fledged about the middle of June. It breeds in large societies, in damp places covered with a thin herbage, where there are tussocks, or small dry places; and also in scattered pairs in the fields, and in small marshes covered with grass or bushes. In a dry spot the bird makes a depression about three inches deep, lining it neatly and carefully with dry grasses, and depositing four eggs, on which both male and female sit. If an intruder approaches this colony, the birds meet him when at some distance from it, uttering loud cries; and when he is amongst the nests all the birds fly overhead, uttering continual lamentations. Before they have eggs they are very shy, rarely approaching within gunshot; but when the young are hatched they are very courageous, and will come within a few feet of the intruder.

Mr. A. Benzon — also quoted by Mr. Dresser — met with this bird nesting in Denmark, on the west coast of Jutland. He obtained its eggs as early as April 12 and as late as July 4. They were usually deposited early in May.

Genus **TOTANUS**, Bechstein.

Totanus, Bechst. Orn. Taschenb. Deutschl. 1803, 282 (type, *Scolopax totanus*, Linn.). — Naum. Vög. Deutschl. VIII. 53. — Gray, Gen. B. III. 572.

Glottis, Koch, Baier. Zool. 1816, 304 (type, *Totanus glottis*, Bechst., = *nebularius*, Gunn.). — Nilss. Orn. Suec. II. 1817, 55.

Gambetta, Kaup, Sk. Ent. Eur. Thierw. 1829, 54 (type, *Scolopax calidris*, Linn.).

Char. Bill usually slender, and slightly upturned terminally, the lateral groove of the maxilla extending about half way to the tip. No web between the middle and inner toes. Tarsus about twice as long as the middle toe.

Having carefully examined and compared the five species usually referred to the so-called genera *Gambetta*, *Totanus*, and *Glottis*, with their nearest allies, with the view of defining the several generic groups usually recognized, we find that no two species agree exactly in the details of

T. melanoleucus.

structure, and that, therefore, no characters exist which warrant a subdivision of the genus *Totanus* (with *T. stagnatilis* as type), beyond the recognition of *Rhyacophilus* and *Erythroscelus*. The only species agreeing closely with the type of the genus *Totanus* is the American "*Gambetta*" *flavipes* (Gmel.), which differs in having the bill thicker and not at all upturned terminally, and in the much longer primaries, with shorter and broader tertials; the latter in *T. stagnatilis* reaching nearly to the end of the longest quills. "*Gambetta*" *melanoleuca* (Gmel.) is like *flavipes* in regard to the wing; but the bill is much thicker, and decidedly recurved terminally, while it is also longer in proportion to the tarsus. "*Glottis*" *canescens* is very much like *melanoleuca*, but the same characters which separate the latter from *flavipes* are in this more exaggerated; the resemblance, however, being much closer between *canescens* and *melanoleuca* than between the latter and *flavipes*. *T. calidris* (L.) is exactly intermediate in form and proportions between "*Gambetta*" *melanoleuca* and *flavipes*. *Rhyacophilus ochropus* has the bill only as long as the tarsus, instead of very much longer, as in all the foregoing species; but *R. solitarius* and *R. glareola* have it shorter, the latter species (the type of *Rhyacophilus*) differing from the typical species of *Totanus* (*stagnatilis* and *flavipes*) in the longer toes, the middle toe very nearly equalling the bill in length. Upon the whole the Wood Sandpipers (*Rhyacophilus*) and the Redshank (*Erythroscelus fuscus*) seem sufficiently different from the species of *Totanus* to warrant their generic separation, the following being the chief distinctive characters:—

Totanus. Middle toe not more than half as long as the tarsus; bill decidedly shorter than tarsus: 1. *T. stagnatilis*; 2. *T. flavipes*; 3. *T. calidris*; 4. *T. melanoleucus*; 5. *T. glottis*.

Rhyacophilus. Middle toe nearly or quite as long as the tarsus: 1. *R. glareola*; 2. *R. solitarius*; 3. *R. ochropus*.

Erythroscelus. Middle toe about half the tarsus; bill longer than tarsus. Lower parts dusky in adult: 1. *E. fuscus*.

Synopsis of the American Species.

The three American species of *Totanus* may be distinguished as follows, one of them being a mere straggler from Europe:—

A. Size large (wing more than 7 inches); terminal half of bill slightly recurved.

1. **T. nebularius.** Entire rump, upper tail-coverts, and lower parts, pure white, without markings on the crissum; wing-coverts unspotted. Wing, 7.00–7.80; culmen, 2.15–2.20; tarsus, 2.25–2.65; middle toe, 1.12–1.30. *Hab.* Europe; accidental in Florida?
2. **T. melanoleucus.** Rump mottled dusky; upper tail-coverts white, barred with dusky; wing-coverts spotted with white; sides, flanks, and lower tail-coverts irregularly barred with dusky. Wing, 7.40–8.00; culmen, 2.05–2.40; tarsus, 2.35–2.70; middle toe, 1.25–1.50. *Hab.* North America; Central and South America and West Indies in winter.

B. Size small (wing less than 7 inches); bill slender, not recurved terminally.

3. **T. flavipes.** Colors of *T. melanoleucus*. Wing, 6.10–6.65; culmen, 1.30–1.55; tarsus, 2.00–2.15; middle toe, 1.00–1.15. *Hab.* North America, breeding northward; Central and South America and West Indies in winter.

Totanus nebularius.

THE GREENSHANK.

Scolopax nebularius, GUNNERUS, in Leem, Lapp. Beschr. 1767, 251.

Scolopax glottis, LATH. Synop. Suppl. 1787, 292 (nec LINN.).

Totanus glottis, BECHST. Naturg. Deutschl. IV. 1789–1795, 249. — KEYS. & BLAS. Wirb. Eur. 1831, 72. — SCHLEG. Rev. Crit. 92. — GRAY, Gen. B. III. 1849, 573; Cat. Brit. B. 1863, 160. — AUD. Orn. Biog. III. 1835, 483, pl. 269; Synop. 1839, 244; B. Am. V. 1842, 321, pl. 346. — RIDGW. Nom. N. Am. B. 1881, no. 547. — COUES, Check List, 2d ed. 1882, no. 635.

Scolopax canescens, GMEL. S. N. I. 1788, 668.

"*Glottis canescens*, STRICKL." (GRAY).

Scolopax totanus, LINN. S. N. ed. 12, I. 1766, 245 (nec ed. 10, 1758).

Limosa totanus, PALL. Zoogr. Rosso-As. II. 1831, 183.

Totanus fistulans, BECHST. Naturg. IV. 1809, 241.

Totanus griseus, BECHST. t.c. 231.

Glottis chloropus, NILSS. Orn. Suec. II. 1817–1821, 57. — BONAP. Comp. List, 1838, 51. — MACGILL. Man. II. 91.

Totanus chloropus, MEYER & WOLF, Taschb. Vög. Deutschl. II. 1810, 371. — COUES, Key, 1872, 259; Check List, 1873, no. 434.

Glottis natans, KOCH, Baier. Zool. I. 1816, 305 (nec OTTO, 1797).
Glottis floridanus, BONAP. Comp. List, 1838, 51. — CASS. in Baird's B. N. Am. 1858, 730. — BAIRD, Cat. N. Am. B. 1859, no. 538.
Totanus glottoides, VIG. P. Z. S. 1831, 173.
Glottis nivigula, HODGS. in Gray Zool. Misc. II. 1831, 36.
Glottis Vigorsii, GRAY. — *G. Horsfieldi*, GRAY. — *G. Linnei*, MALM.
Greenshank, YARR. Brit. B. ed. 2, II. 618, fig. ; ed. 3, II. 665, fig. ; et AUCT.
Cinereous Godwit, PENN. Brit. Zool. II. 1813, 50, pl. 11.

HAB. The Palæarctic Region, south to Australia; accidental in Eastern North America? (Florida, AUDUBON).

SP. CHAR. *Adult in summer:* Head and neck above, grayish white, widely streaked with dusky; remainder of head and neck, with entire lower parts, pure white; the lores, cheeks, malar region, auriculars, sides of neck and foreneck, finely streaked with dusky; sides of the breast and anterior part of the sides, coarsely and irregularly streaked with dusky, the markings assuming an irregularly sagittate or V-shaped form on the sides. Eyelids, a distinct and rather broad supraloral stripe, chin, throat, abdomen, crissum, and flanks, immaculate white; axillars white, irregularly marked toward ends with grayish; lining of wing white, with irregular sagittate markings of grayish dusky. Back and scapulars dusky blackish, the feathers edged with light ash-gray; wing-coverts nearly uniform brownish slate, the tertials similar, but edged with paler; primaries uniform dark slate; entire rump and upper tail-coverts immaculate pure white, the longer feathers of the latter, however, narrowly zigzagged with dusky. Tail white, narrowly and incompletely barred with grayish dusky. *Winter plumage:* Similar, but nearly uniform grayish above, the feathers bordered with grayish white; foreneck unstreaked. *Young:*[1] Above, light brownish gray, the feathers margined with paler, and with a sub-edging of dusky, in the form of an irregular dusky line near the edge and parallel with the border; these markings changed on the tertials into short zigzag, oblique bars along the edge of both webs. Crown, nape, and lores streaked as in the adult: foreneck, jugulum, and sides immaculate white. "Bill dusky green, black at end; iris brown; feet dull greenish gray" (AUDUBON).

Wing, 7.00–7.80; culmen, 2.15–2.20; tarsus, 2.25–2.65; middle toe, 1.12–1.30.

The only known instance of the occurrence of this species in North America is recorded by Mr. Audubon, by whom three specimens were taken, May 28, 1832, on Sand Key, Florida, near Cape Sable. They were mistaken for Tell-tale Tattlers as they walked about on the bars or in the shallow water, and upon examination were presumed by Audubon to be the Common Greenshank of Europe. They were all males, and probably stragglers. In the "Pacific Railroad Report," Vol. IX., owing to their inferiority in size, these individuals are given as a distinct species; but it is not probable that this claim can be maintained, and we presume that the specimens noted must have been examples of the common European bird, especially as this bird is known to be a great wanderer, having been taken at Trebizond, in Mauritius, and in various parts of Asia, Java, Sunda, the Moluccas, etc. Montagu, in his "Ornithological Dictionary," mentions this species as occurring in North America, stating that one had been seen in the State of New York.

The Greenshank is said not to be anywhere found in large numbers. It is a summer visitant to the British Islands, and more frequent about the time of its spring and fall migrations; a few remaining during the breeding-season, but the greater portion going farther north. These birds are found in the London market, most frequently about the last of April and in May. In Ireland they occur in autumn in small parties or singly. Mr. Selby detected this species breeding in Sutherlandshire, in June, 1834, in various parts of that county — generally in some swampy marsh, or by the margins of the small lakes common in that region. It was very wild and wary, except when it had tender young, at which time, when first disturbed, it would

[1] Described from Audubon's specimen, supposed to have been obtained in Florida.

approach quite near, making a rapid swoop at the head of the intruder. If fired at and missed, it rarely ventures again within range. Mr. Selby obtained one of the young, about a fortnight old, by the aid of a water-dog.

This bird was observed by Hewitson in Norway, where, to his surprise, it was more than once seen seated high above his head, on the top of a tall tree. It breeds as far north as the Arctic Circle, in Lapland. Its note is said to sound like *chio-chio.* Mr. John Wolley obtained several nests and eggs of this bird in Finland. It feeds on small fish, worms, insects, crustacea, and molluscous animals. It visits Russia and breeds in the more northern regions of that country, has been found on the banks of the Rhine, and is a bird of passage in France, Germany, Switzerland, Italy, the islands in the Mediterranean, Asia Minor, etc.

Mr. Macgillivray states that the Greenshank is seen in the Outer Hebrides early in spring, and that it generally departs in October, a few individuals remaining into November. Previous to the breeding-season, and after the young are fledged, it resorts to the shores of the sea, and frequents pools of brackish water and the shallow margins of bays and creeks. It is said to be extremely shy and vigilant, so much so that it can seldom be shot, until after it has deposited its eggs. Many remain in the Hebrides in the summer, and at that season are very easily discovered, as, at the approach of an intruder, even when he is more than a quarter of a mile distant, they rise into the air with clamorous cries, alarming all the birds in their neighborhood, fly round the place of their nests, now wheeling off to a distance, again advancing toward the intruder; then, at intervals, they alight by the edge of the lake, continuing the noise and vibrating their bodies without cessation. Mr. Macgillivray found a nest in one of the Hebrides at a considerable distance from the water; this consisted of a few fragments of heath and some blades of grass placed in a hollow cavity scraped in the turf in an exposed place, and resembled the nest of the Golden Plover, the Common Curlew, and the Lapwing. The eggs, which were placed with their narrow ends together, were four in number, pyriform, larger than those of the Lapwing and smaller than those of the Golden Plover, equally pointed with the latter, but proportionally broader and more rounded at the larger end than either. The dimension of one was 2.00 inches in length by 1.38 in breadth. The ground-color was a pale yellowish green, sprinkled all over with irregular spots of dark brown, intermixed with blotches of light purplish gray, the spots and blotches more numerous on the larger end. Mr. Macgillivray adds, that although these birds may be seen in summer in many parts of the islands, they are yet very rare, pairs being to be met with only at a distance of several miles from each other. This bird is of very rare occurrence in Scotland, except in the Hebrides, making its appearance chiefly in autumn.

Totanus melanoleucus.

TELL-TALE; STONE SNIPE.

Scolopax melanoleuca, GMEL. S. N. I. 1788, 659.

Totanus melanoleucus, VIEILL. Nouv. Dict. VI. 1816, 398. — AUD. Orn. Biog. IV. 1838, 68, pl. 308. — COUES, Key, 1872, 258; Check List, 1873, no. 432; 2d ed. 1882, no. 633; Birds N. W. 1874, 496. — RIDGW. Nom. N. Am. B. 1881, no. 548.

Gambetta melanoleuca, BONAP. Compt. Rend. 1856, 597. — CASS. in Baird's B. N. Am. 1858, 731. — BAIRD, Cat. N. Am. B. no. 539.

Scolopax vociferus, WILS. Am. Orn. VII. 1813, 57, pl. 58, fig. 5.

Totanus vociferus, VIEILL. Nouv. Dict. VI. 1816, 401. — SW. & RICH. F. B. A. II. 1831, 389. — AUD. Synop. 1839, 244; B. Am. V. 1842, 316, pl. 345.

Totanus sasashew, VIEILL. Nouv. Dict. VI. 1816, 412.

Totanus chilensis, PHILIPPI, Wiegm. Archiv, 1851, 264.

HAB. America in general, but breeding only in cold-temperate and subarctic climates of the northern continent; in winter, south to Chili and Buenos Ayres.

SP. CHAR. *Adult, summer plumage:* Above, variegated with slate-black, pale gray, and white, the former predominating, the latter in the form of spots along the edge of the feathers, including the wing-coverts and tertials; crown and nape grayish white, widely streaked with dusky; upper tail-coverts white, irregularly barred with the same; primaries plain blackish slate; tail white, all the feathers barred with dusky, the middle feathers grayish, barred with dusky, the latter some-

times obsolete. Head, neck, and lower parts white, only the abdomen and throat immaculate; lores, cheeks, malar region, auriculars, and neck (all round), streaked with dusky; breast, sides, and flanks, barred or transversely spotted with dusky, the bars more sagittate on the crissum. *Winter plumage:* Above, rather light ash-gray, without the black, but with the white spotting of the summer dress; foreneck and jugulum more narrowly streaked; breast nearly or quite immaculate; and sides and flanks faintly and irregularly marked with grayish. *Young, first plumage:* Similar to the winter dress, but darker and more brownish above, the white spotting tinged with light brownish buff; lower parts similar. Bill black; iris brown; legs and feet deep yellow (tinged with olive in young).

Total length, about 14 inches; wing, 7.50–7.75; culmen, 2.20–2.30; tarsus, 2.50–2.75; middle toe, 1.35–1.50.

In nearly or quite all parts of the United States the "Tell-tale Tattler," as this bird is sometimes called by sportsmen, is known only as a migratory visitant. Wilson speaks of its arriving in the Middle States in April, and of its remaining there until September, and breeding in the marshes. He describes the nest and eggs only from report. In all this he was undoubtedly misinformed; at least it is not now known to remain on any portion of our sea-coast during the summer, and its nest and eggs are still unknown. Mr. Boardman informs me that this bird is found about Calais early in summer, and it is possible that a few may remain and breed; but this is at best very doubtful. It is much the most abundant in the spring and fall.

In Southern Wisconsin, as we are informed by Mr. Kumlien, the Winter Yellow-leg, known there as the "Tell-tale," arrives on the borders of Lake Koskonong in April, and is one of the last birds to leave in the fall. Stragglers are found along the shore throughout the summer. Dr. Hoy, in his "List of the Birds of Wisconsin," states that it nests in all the large marshes of that State. There being very large ones on the borders of Lake Koskonong, this bird may possibly breed among them; but Mr. Kumlien does not think so, as he has not only never noticed it doing so, but has never even found any birds young enough to justify the belief that they were raised near the place. Late in August this bird begins to gather in flocks along the shores of Lake Koskonong, generally in company with the *Totanus flavipes*.

On Long Island, according to Giraud, this species is not so numerous as the *flavipes*. It is there known to the hunters as the "Greater Yellowshanks," arriving in April, about two weeks earlier than the Common Yellowshanks, and, as is the case with the latter, making at that season but a very short visit. It appears to prefer the shores of muddy ponds and creeks, where it collects its food, having apparently, like many other shore-birds, a special fondness for the spawn of the horse-foot crab. It returns from the north in the latter part of August, and remains until cold weather. On the meadows in the vicinity of Oyster Pond Mr. Giraud has met with this bird in November. In the autumn it is in fine condition, and its flesh is then very finely flavored. It does not generally associate in large flocks, but roves about in parties of from five to twelve. Its voice is much stronger than that of the *flavipes*, and consists of fewer notes, imitations of which it will blindly follow. Though more suspicious than the Common Yellowshanks, it can be decoyed if the sportsman is skilful and lies close. This bird is described as having a graceful carriage as it walks over the ground, collecting its food in an elegant and easy manner. It is capable of very rapid flight, and at times mounts high in the air, from which elevation its loud, clear, and familiar notes may often be recognized. In its general habits, as well as in its appearance, it bears a strong resemblance to the *flavipes*. It is more common on the shores of New Jersey than on Long Island, and is said occasionally to breed there; but no good evidence of this has been obtained, and Giraud was unable to find any proof that it ever breeds on Long Island. He never met with it there either in June or in July.

This bird passes north along the coast of Massachusetts about the middle of April, the flight lasting until the middle of May. It returns from the north early in August, and is two or three weeks in passing south.

It is found on the Pacific coast as far north as Vancouver Island, where Mr. R. Browne notes its presence. Dr. Cooper states that it is common throughout California, being usually found, singly or in small families, about marshes — both fresh and salt — during nearly all the year; he did not, however, observe any as far to the south, in July, as San Pedro. One, which he shot at Fort Mojave in January, was of a remarkably small size, though a female; and Dr. Cooper thinks it probable that this smallness is peculiar to all those inhabiting the interior desert regions, and that they may for this reason have been mistaken for the smaller Yellow-legs of the East. Dr. Cooper thinks that this bird breeds, without doubt, in California, although he did not meet with any of its nests along the coast. In the autumn it is found in small families about still waters, feeding on small shells, insects, crustacea, etc.

Mr. Salvin, who observed this species in Guatemala, states that, so far as noticed by him, it seemed to be more solitary in its habits than many of the other Waders. Rarely was more than a single individual seen at a time; and it also appeared to prefer the borders of the lake to the marshy resorts of the other species of Waders.

It is said by Major Wedderburn to visit Bermuda in its southward migrations in the fall. It usually arrives in August, and is more or less common in some seasons. In 1848 quite a number came as early as the 4th of August, in company with the *flavipes* and the smaller Sandpipers. On the 20th of September a large flock was seen moving in a southeasterly direction. It occasionally remains until the 10th of November. In only one instance has it been seen there in the spring; this is said by Mr. Hurdis to have been on the 5th of June, 1852, when a single specimen was taken in full spring plumage.

According to Mr. N. B. Moore, this species, as well as *T. flavipes*, was observed by him during every month of the year on the waters of Sarasota Bay, in Florida. It exhibited no evidence of nesting, nor did its relative, the *flavipes* — which latter is the more numerous, both in the summer and in the winter. On one occasion a flock of twenty-five of the *flavipes* was seen in an oozy lagoon. When the ponds are quite low, in June and July, both species feed in a very curious manner. A mass of black ooze lies just below the surface of the water, on the hard sandy bed. As many as six or eight birds, of one species alone, or of both together, may be seen running at full speed, one behind the other, and sweeping rapidly from side to side, so as to describe a half-circle, with their bills immersed in the water. This is continued for a certain distance, and then the birds all turn round and go back over the same ground, repeating this advance and retreat a second time even. No one can doubt that they are procuring food of some kind, in what the observer mentioned describes as an "impetuous and giddy race;" yet no halt is made either to snatch or swallow anything, neither can they be assisted by their eyes in finding their food. Mr. Moore believes this to consist of the animalculæ which abound in the oozy matter, and that it is taken in by mere suction.

Specimens were collected in August at Moose Factory and at Rupert House by Mr. J. M'Kenzie, and at Sitka and near Fort Kenai by Mr. Bischoff. A single specimen is reported by Mr. Kumlien as having been seen by him on Arctic Island, Cumberland Sound, Sept. 14, 1877.

This species occurs generally in the West Indies. Gundlach includes it in his List of the Birds of Cuba. Gosse mentions obtaining a single individual at Spanishtown on the 21st of March, and was informed by Mr. Hill that in the succeeding month it became exceedingly abundant, so that it was obtained by the market sportsmen in quite extraordinary numbers. According to Léotaud, it visits Trinidad at about the same period, and remains there about the same length of time, as the *flavipes*, to which bird it has a very marked resemblance, and which — when not solitary — it usually accompanies. A few remain during the winter and keep about the pools. It has a very emphatic cry, that sounds like *chin-chin*, by which name it is known in Trinidad. Its flesh is not considered as very good.

Mr. C. W. Wyatt met with it near La Cruz, in Colombia, and it has been found in other portions of South America, as far south as Chili.

Mr. Dresser mentions this bird as being common near San Antonio during the winter season, until the month of April, after which he did not notice it, although it was seen on Galveston Island in June.

This species is supposed to breed in Labrador, where it is said to have been found in great numbers along the shore all through the summer and in the early fall. Though seen in all situations near the water, the favorite localities of this bird seem to be muddy flats laid bare by the tide, and the pools in the adjoining salt-marshes. Richardson found this bird very abundant on the Saskatchewan Plains, but did not discover its nest. He quotes Hutchins as having written that it has four eggs, which are of a dark ground-color, spotted with black, and large for the size of the bird.

It was found on the Amoor River by Schenck, in Siberia by Middendorff, and in the La Plata region by Burmeister — the latter stating that it is everywhere abundant throughout that country on the banks of lakes and rivers.

Audubon says that this species spends the winter along the shores of the estuaries, rivers, ponds, and rice-fields from Maryland to Mexico; and that it is abundant in South Carolina and Florida and on the shores of the Gulf of Mexico, as far as Texas, where he noticed it in considerable numbers, and where it paired in the months of

April and May. It has also been found in the spring and autumn over the whole interior of the country, and quite abundant at those seasons along the entire length of the Mississippi, Ohio, and Missouri rivers, as well as on the Arkansas. This bird congregates in great numbers during the winter in the inland marshes of Florida and along the rivers. Audubon saw them at Eastport as early as the 11th of May, and on the coast of Labrador on the 18th of June. In Newfoundland, on the 11th of August, the young were nearly equal in size to their parents.

Though found at all seasons in the vicinity of salt water, this species seems to prefer fresh-water ponds where the shores are muddy and the water shallow; and in these places it frequently wades to such a depth as to present the appearance of swimming. When just alighted it always holds up its wings, as if doubtful of its footing. It feeds on small fishes, snails, insects, and worms, which it catches and devours with great rapidity. It alights on floating logs on the Mississippi, where it procures shrimps and the fry of fishes.

Audubon found it breeding in Labrador. A female, having been killed, was found to contain a full-formed egg; this was pyriform, 2.25 inches in length, 1.56 inches in breadth, of a pale greenish yellow, and marked with blotches of umber and pale purplish gray. We have had no other knowledge of its eggs than this mention and that of Hutchins, until the Notes of Mr. E. W. Nelson on the Birds of Southeastern Illinois. This writer mentions this bird as not only being a regular migrant to the southern shores of Lake Michigan, but also as breeding in that locality, where it is said to arrive about the middle of April, the greater number going north early in May, returning on the first of September, and then remaining until the last of October. He also met with pairs of this bird in the Calumet marshes; and on observing their actions, became convinced that they were breeding. Mr. Rice, of Evanston, received a set of eggs, which were not identified, but which were attributed to this species. The nest was in a slight depression on the edge of a slough, and was composed of grass-stems and blades. The eggs varied from 1.70 to 1.80 inches in length, and from 1.30 to 1.38 in breadth. The ground-color is described as being a deep grayish white, marked on three eggs with spots of dark brown, and on the other egg with spots and well-defined blotches of a considerably lighter shade of the same color. In addition there were shell-markings and obscure spots of lilac. The markings were abundant over the whole surface, but more numerous about the larger end. This description varies materially from that of Mr. Audubon in regard to the size of the egg.

Totanus flavipes.

YELLOW-LEGS.

Scolopax flavipes, GMEL. S. N. I. 1788, 659. — WILS. Am. Orn. VII. 1813, 55, pl. 58, fig. 4.
Totanus flavipes, VIEILL. Nouv. Dict. VI. 1816, 410. — SW. & RICH. F. B. A. II. 1831, 390. — NUTT. Man. II. 1834, 152. — AUD. Orn. Biog. III. 1835, 573; V. 586, pl. 228; Synop. 1839, 243; B. Am. V. 1842, 313, pl. 344. — COUES, Key, 1872, 259; Check List, 1873, no. 433; 2d ed. 1882, no. 634; Birds N. W. 1874, 497. — RIDGW. Nom. N. Am. B. 1881, no. 549.
Gambetta flavipes, BONAP. Compt. Rend. 1856, 597. — CASS. in Baird's B. N. Am. 1858, 732. — BAIRD, Cat. N. Am. B. 1859, no. 540.
Totanus natator, VIEILL. Nouv. Dict. VI. 1816, 409.
Totanus fuscocapillus, VIEILL. l. c.
" *Totanus leucopyga*, ILLIGER., in Mus. Berol."

HAB. The whole of America, breeding in the cold-temperate and subarctic districts of the northern continent; migrating south in winter to Buenos Ayres and Chili. Much rarer in the Western than in the Eastern Province of North America. Accidental in Europe.

Sp. Char. Very similar to *T. melanoleucus*, but smaller and more slender. Bill rather longer than the head, straight, slender, rather compressed; wing long, pointed; tail short; legs long, lower half of the tibia naked; toes moderate, slender, margined, the outer and middle united at base.

Adult, summer plumage: Above, ashy, mixed with ragged blotches of black, this having a tendency to form regular transverse bars on the secondaries and scapulars. Crown and nape with longitudinal streaks of black on a grayish-white ground; upper tail-coverts pure white, with transverse bars of dusky; tail white, the middle feathers ashy, and all with transverse, rather nar-

rower, bars of ash. Primaries and their coverts plain dusky black. Lower parts white, the jugulum and breast densely streaked with blackish, and the sides marked with more transverse markings of the same color.

Winter plumage: Above, ashy, sometimes nearly unbroken, but generally slightly variegated, especially on the scapulars and wing-coverts, with transverse spots of dusky, and whitish edgings and dots along the margin of the feathers. Streaks almost absent from the head, neck, and jugulum, which are nearly uniform light ashy; the chin, throat, and supraloral stripe white. In other respects like the summer plumage. *Young:* Like the winter adult, but the light markings above more or less tinged with pale brown or dull ochraceous.

Total length about 10.50–11.00 inches; extent, 20.00–21.00; wing, 5.50–6.50; culmen, 1.30–1.55; tarsus, 2.00. Bill black; iris dark brown; legs and feet bright yellow.

This species is exceedingly similar to *T. melanoleucus* in plumage, but differs in the following particulars: in the summer adult the upper parts are more transversely spotted, with a less amount of black, while the lower parts are without well-defined transverse spots or bars of black; in the winter plumage, the head, neck, and jugulum are nearly uniform ashy, instead of distinctly streaked.

The European analogue of *T. flavipes* is the *T. stagnatilis* (Bechst.), the type of the genus. It resembles the American species very closely, but may be immediately distinguished by the rump being wholly pure white, instead of heavily spotted with grayish and dusky. This peculiarity, being shared by several other Palæarctic species, compared with their American allies, presents a very interesting problem bearing upon the question of geographical variation. This curious parallelism was first called attention to by one of the authors of this work in the "American Naturalist" for February, 1874 (p. 108), and the following list of species presented in which it had been noted: —

American (rump dusky spotted).	*European (rump immaculate white).*
Rhyacophilus solitarius,	R. ochropus,
Totanus flavipes,	T. stagnatilis,
Numenius Hudsonicus,	N. phæopus,
Hæmatopus palliatus.	H. ostralegus.

The well-known "Yellow-legs" of Eastern sportsmen has a very abundant distribution throughout all the United States, not excepting the immediate neighborhood of the Pacific; for even there individual examples have been recently reported. It is quite common, in its migrations, beyond the Rocky Mountains. How common it may be in California at any time remains to be ascertained. It is found during the winter in suitable localities throughout Mexico, Central and South America, and the West Indies. Dr. Burmeister mentions finding this species both at Mendoza and at Parana, on the banks of rivers and the shores of lakes. Salvin speaks of meeting with a small flock near Dueñas, in Guatemala, during the early part of the month of April, in company with *Actodromas maculata.* It is included by Gundlach among the birds of Cuba, and by Marsh among those of Jamaica. In the latter island Gosse speaks of finding it always solitary, and wading in shallow water. The stomachs of specimens he procured contained a mass of pulverulent matter which, on being separated in water, was found to contain fragments of insects. According to Professor Newton, this bird occurs, but not plentifully, in St. Croix in the spring and autumn; but it probably does not remain in the island through the winter. He obtained a single specimen, July 26, 1857; and Mr. Edward Newton first met with it Aug. 3, 1858. It is a regular visitant of the Island of Trinidad, coming each year in the month of August, and withdrawing in October. Always in flocks, sometimes of great size, it keeps about the borders of the sea, only leaving them for moist meadows or newly ploughed fields. It requires a soft soil, into which its beak can easily penetrate in quest of worms. In its movements it is said to resemble the Solitary Tattler. After the general departure of this species, a few remain along the edges of pools in swampy tracts. It is much sought after by sportsmen, but its flesh is not of good quality. It feeds largely upon ants and the larvæ of dipterous insects.

It occurs as far, at least, to the south as Patagonia, where Mr. H. Durnford (" Ibis," 1877) mentions finding it common along the banks of the rivers and in the adjacent swamps and pools in the Chupat Valley. He does not indicate it as breeding there; and as his visit only continued from the 1st to the 29th of November, it is probable that it does not do so.

It visits the Bahamas in its migrations; and probably passes through nearly the whole of the interior regions of both North and South America. Captain Bendire notes its abundance in Oregon during its migrations; and Mr. Nelson found it quite numerous in Northeastern Illinois, arriving late in April and returning in September. He has no doubt that a few breed, as he obtained the young, barely able to fly, on the 1st of July, 1874, near Chicago; and since then he has noticed several pairs, during the breeding-season, about the Calumet marshes.

In the summer this species extends its migrations to the extreme Arctic regions. Reinhardt includes it among the birds of Greenland, a single specimen having been received from that region by Pastor Möschler in 1854. Captain Blakiston met with it on the Saskatchewan, obtaining a single specimen near Fort Carlton. Mr. Murray records it as from Hudson's Bay, and Mr. Ross found it abundant on the Mackenzie. Richardson speaks of it as very common in the Fur Countries, where it is seen, either solitary or in pairs, on the banks of every river, lake, or marsh, up to the most northern extremities of the continent. While breeding, it is very impatient of any intrusions, betrays the approach of the sportsman to less vigilant birds by flying round his head, its legs hanging down and wings drooping, uttering its incessant and plaintive cries. Previous to its departure south it collects in small flocks, and stops for a time on the shores of Hudson's Bay. In this locality it was observed by Hearne in 1772, and its habits noted. He speaks of it as the "Spotted Godwait," and states that it visits the Hudson's Bay in considerable numbers, and is even more abundant in the interior, usually frequenting the flat, muddy banks of rivers. In the summer it was generally very poor, but in the autumn it became one mass of fat. Hearne met with this bird in considerable numbers as far north as latitude 71° 54′; and at Fort York he has known it to be shot as late as the latter part of October. At this time it is in its greatest perfection, and is said to be delicious eating.

It is not noted in the ninth volume of the "Pacific Railroad Report" as occurring west of the Missouri, yet Mr. J. A. Allen found it in considerable numbers about the lagoons of Eastern Kansas in the earlier part of May, and afterward in August; he also saw it at Lake Pass, in Colorado, and a few were found in September in the Valley of Great Salt Lake. It was not noticed by Mr. Ridgway in Utah or Nevada; but it has been found very abundant in August and September throughout Dakota and Montana, where it was invariably seen associating with the *melanoleuca*. Both species are there the most unsuspecting of the Waders, so that they may be approached without the slightest difficulty. Mr. L. Belding, in the winter of 1878–1879, procured a specimen on the coast of California.

In the Valley of the Mississippi this species is a regular migrant both in the spring and in the fall. It is much more abundant in its autumnal movement, and much more common, than the *melanoleuca*, coming later and departing earlier than that species. None remain to breed near Lake Koskonong, where, in the fall, they again become very abundant.

It was met with at Fort Resolution from May 5th to the 14th, in 1860, by Mr. R. Kennicott; on the Yukon River, in June, by Mr. Lockhart; at Fort Simpson, from May 15th to the 29th, by Mr. B. R. Ross; at Big Island by Mr. Reid; and was found in great abundance by Mr. MacFarlane at Fort Anderson, on Anderson River, at Horton River, Rendezvous Lake, etc.

On the Atlantic coast it begins to appear, in its migrations southward, in July, and its movements continue through August. It returns in the spring, but comes as late as May 15. In Massachusetts Mr. William Brewster has taken it from July 15 to September 1, and has noted its passing north occasionally as early as the first part of May. A large flock was observed by Mr. Frank B. Tileston near Boston, May 3, 1875. It is quite common near Calais in both these migrations.

On Long Island, according to Giraud, and also on the coast of New Jersey, this species arrives in the early part of May. It is said to associate in flocks, and to frequent the muddy flats which are left bare at the recess of the tide. At high water it resorts to the ponds on the beaches and meadows, where it collects its food, which consists of small shellfish, worms, and insects. Occasionally it may be seen wading into the shallow water in pursuit of small fishes. It is conspicuously gregarious in habit, and is constantly calling upon others to unite with it, its shrill cry betraying its presence to the hunter. It is readily attracted by decoys, answering the fowler's whistle, and, if the sportsman is well concealed, gliding directly up to the decoys, gradually lowering its long legs, which, when it flies, project beyond its tail-feathers. It is much more timid than the Red-breasted Snipe, yet, like that species, when invited by the hunter's whistle, will not infrequently return and receive his second fire. The cry of this species is very shrill, consisting of three or more notes. When wounded in the wing it will run very fast, and will often conceal itself so successfully in the long grass as to escape detection. It is often seen on streams in the interior. Its flesh is not particularly good, yet it meets with a ready sale in the New York market, and large numbers are shot to supply the demand. Giraud mentions one instance in which one hundred and six were killed by the single discharge of a double-barrelled gun into a flock that was sitting along the beach. In the latter part of August the Yellowshank begins to move southward, and in September all have usually retired from the shores of Long Island.

In Bermuda, according to Major Wedderburn, it arrives regularly about the 1st of August in each year, being one of the earliest visitors from the north, and there remains until the end of September. On the 13th of July, 1847, one of this species was caught, in an exhausted state, on the north shore of one of the islands, during a gale from the northwest. On the 28th of July, 1848, a large flock was seen, and a week later the birds had become very numerous.

It is more or less abundant during the winter from South Carolina to Mexico. Mr. Dresser met with it near Matamoras, but it was not common. In the spring of 1864, at San Antonio, he noticed it much oftener than he did at Matamoras, and in April and early in May shot several. He also saw this bird on Galveston Island early in June.

In the opinion of Audubon the Yellowshank is much more abundant in the interior than along the coast. In the early autumn, when the sandbars of the Ohio are uncovered, it may be seen upon them in small flocks, employed in searching for food, wading in the water up to the feathered part of their legs. In the Carolinas they resort to the ricefields, and in Florida to the wet savannahs. He met with a few on the coast of Labrador, but did not find their nests. He was informed by Thomas MacCullock that it breeds in considerable numbers about Pictou; but when in that place, in 1850, I could obtain no corroboration of this statement. Mr. MacCullock described the nest as placed among the grass on the edges of streams and ponds of the interior.

Although this bird has been but once reported on the Southern Pacific shore, yet Mr. Dall states that it was obtained both at Sitka and at Kadiak by Mr. Bischoff. It was not rare at Fort Yukon, where it was found breeding by Lockhart. It was also seen in small numbers at Nulato and near the mouth of the Yukon. Mr. Kennicott, who found it breeding near Fort Resolution, states that it arrives there in the spring among the first birds. He describes its nest as of the simplest kind, it being merely a depression without any lining, at the foot of a small bush, in rather open ground, a rod from the edge of a marsh. Another nest was in an open place among sparse, low bushes — a simple depression, but lined with a few leaves and small sticks. Mr. MacFarlane found the nests of this species, lined with decayed leaves, on the Lower Anderson River; and in some instances they were near the edge of a small lake. Others were taken at Fort Anderson, some as early as June 2. The nests were all mere depressions, with a very scanty lining. The usual number of the eggs was four. In several instances the male bird was seen to perch on trees near the nest, in the manner of the Common Snipe. Some were already hatched by the 19th of June. When the pair had young, they were very noisy, going constantly before the intruder from tree to tree for several hundred yards beyond their nest. The young, even when just hatched, run and hide in the short grass, so as to make it difficult to find them, the parents, in the meanwhile, flying and screaming in the air above.

The eggs of this species obtained by Mr. MacFarlane exhibit some variations in the shading of the ground and in their markings. No. 11397, Nat. Mus., average in measurement 1.68 inches in length and 1.12 in breadth. Their ground-color is a light drab, verging in some into a darker hue, marked with separate rounded blotches of bistre, of a light tint, and washed in a few instances with the ground-color, giving the effect of a light ashy slate. No. 11388, S. I., the ground-color a dull, deep rufous drab; the spots more numerous and confluent, giving to the eggs a very different effect from that usually presented.

Genus **RHYACOPHILUS**, Kaup.

Rhyacophilus, Kaup, Sk. Entw. Europ. Th. 1829, 140 (type, *Tringa glareola*, Linn.).

Char. Similar to *Totanus*, but smaller, and with middle toe nearly as long as tarsus.

There is but one American species of this genus, and the Old World members are by no means numerous — only two, the *R. ochropus* (Linn.) and *R. glareola* (Linn.) being recognized by authori-

R. solitarius.

ties. The latter is the type of the genus, but it resembles the American *R. solitarius* much less than does the former. The three may be distinguished as follows : —

A. Lining of the wing dusky, barred with white.

1. **R. solitarius.** Upper tail-coverts dusky, barred with white ; middle tail-feathers dusky, spotted with white along the edge. Wing, 5.30 ; culmen, 1.15 ; tarsus, 1.30 ; middle toe, 1.00. *Hab.* North America, migrating southward in winter.
2. **R. ochropus.** Upper tail-coverts pure white, nearly or quite immaculate ; middle tail-feathers widely barred with white. Wing, 5.40–5.70 ; culmen, 1.30–1.40 ; tarsus, 1.25–1.40 ; middle toe, .95–1.00. *Hab.* Europe ; accidental in Eastern North America (Nova Scotia).

Lining of the wing white, spotted exteriorly with dusky.

3. **R. glareola.** Upper tail-coverts white, more or less marked with dusky ; middle tail-feathers banded with white. Wing, 4.75–4.90 ; culmen, 1.10–1.15 ; tarsus, 1.40–1.45 ; middle toe, 1.00–1.05. *Hab.* Palæarctic Region.

Rhyacophilus solitarius.

THE SOLITARY SANDPIPER.

Tringa ochropus, var. *β*, Lath. Ind. Orn. II. 1790, 730.
Tringa solitaria, Wils. Am. Orn. VII. 1813, 53, pl. 58, fig. 3.
Totanus solitarius, Aud. Synop. 1839, 242 ; B. Am. V. 1842, 309, pl. 343. — Coues, Key, 1872, 259 ; Check List, 1873, no. 435 ; Birds N. W. 1874, 498.
Rhyacophilus solitarius, Cass. in Baird's B. N. Am. 1858, 733. — Baird, Cat. N. Am. B. 1859, no. 541. — Ridgw. Nom. N. Am. B. 1881, no. 550. — Coues, Check List, 2d ed. 1882, no. 637.
Totanus chloropygius, Vieill. Nouv. Dict. VI. 1816, 401. — Sw. & Rich. F. B. A. II. 1831, 393. — Nutt. Man. II. 1834, 159. — Aud. Orn. Biog. III. 1835, 576 ; V. 1839, 583, pl. 289.
Totanus macroptera, Spix, Av. Bras. II. 1825, 76, 92.
(?) "*Totanus caligatus*, Licht."
"*Totanus guttatus*, Illig."

HAB. The whole of North and Middle America and the greater part of South America, ranging south to Brazil and Peru; breeding throughout temperate North America, but chiefly northward; accidental in Europe.

SP. CHAR. *Adult in summer:* Above, olivaceous slate, rather sparsely speckled with white, the crown and nape indistinctly streaked with the same; outer upper tail-coverts barred with white; primaries and primary-coverts plain slate-black. Tail white (the middle feathers dusky), all the feathers widely barred with dusky, these bars most numerous on outer webs, where extend-

ing to the base of the feathers. Eyelids, supraloral stripe, and lower parts white; the sides of the head, neck (all round), and jugulum streaked with brownish slate; remaining lower parts immaculate. Lining of wing and axillars slate-color, regularly barred with white. *Winter plumage:* Similar to the summer dress, but dark ashy above, less distinctly speckled, and foreneck very indistinctly streaked, or simply washed with ashy. *Young:* Above, grayish brown (lighter and more olivaceous than the adult), thickly speckled with buff; crown and nape plain brownish gray; cheeks and sides of neck nearly uniform gray; foreneck streaked, as in the adult.

Total length, about 8.00–8.50 inches; extent, 15.50–16.50; wing, 5.00–5.40; culmen, 1.15–1.30; tarsus, 1.25–1.30; middle toe, 1.00. Bill greenish brown (in life), dusky terminally; iris brown; legs and feet olive-green in adult, more grayish in young.

It is difficult to reconcile all the various statements in regard to the habits of this species, either with our own observations or with the experience of more recent observers. Audubon speaks of finding it nesting in Louisiana, Wilson of its breeding in the highlands of Pennsylvania, and Giraud considered it a summer resident of Long Island from May to September. How far these statements are reconcilable with fact, or how far they may be erroneous or exceptional, it is not easy to determine. It may be that, like the Common Snipe, this bird occasionally breeds in unusually southern localities. Mr. J. A. Allen met with it at Ipswich, Mass., in June, under circumstances which led him to feel confident that the bird was breeding there. The general rule, however, is that throughout the United States this species is as decidedly migratory as the Winter Yellowleg, and that if it ever nests south of latitude 43°, the instances are rare, exceptional, or caused by peculiar circumstances. It is common, though not abundant, in Massachusetts in spring and fall, although not known to breed in that State. It comes in the spring in the latter part of May, its stay being short, as it almost immediately passes on to its northern breeding-places. It begins to re-appear in midsummer, or about the 15th of July, and is more or less common from that time up to the last of October. Maynard obtained an example at Erroll, N. H., as late as October 31, when the ponds were frozen over; and Mr. William Brewster met with partially grown young in Franconia, N. H., in August.

Major Wedderburn states that this Sandpiper — which reminded him so much, both in appearance and in habits, of *Rhyacophilus glareola* of Europe — is found every year in Bermuda, from the 20th of August to the last of September, where it frequents the swamps filled with stunted trees and bushes. A few stragglers remain into November. One specimen was seen as early as July 25; and in 1850 several were met with, in their spring migrations, as early as the 7th of April. They were generally very shy. Mr. Hurdis mentions that other examples were shot on the 10th and 16th of April of the same year. Mr. Dall noted the presence of this species at Nulato from May 10th to the 18th. Mr. Ross found it near Fort Simpson in the latter part of May. It was also taken at Fort Yukon by Mr. J. McDougal, at Fort Rae by Mr. Clark, and at Big Island by Mr. Reid.

Mr. Henshaw prefers the name of Wood Tattler for this species, as he does not regard it as a solitary bird. He mentions having frequently met with it at the West, in mountainous localities, on the borders of such small ponds as are wholly surrounded by dense forests growing almost to the water's edge. During the migratory season it occurs abundantly on the shores of all the rivers, and in fact frequents every locality which is suited to the wants and tastes of Wading-birds. At these seasons he found it very far from being solitary, and rarely to be seen alone; little companies of six or seven being quite usual, and not infrequently more may be seen together. He did not succeed in finding it breeding, but he has little or no doubt that it actually does so in parts of Utah, Colorado, and even farther south. He states that Mr. Aiken took adult birds near Pueblo, Colorado, late in July, which had undoubtedly spent the summer and were breeding there. Mr. Henshaw procured specimens at different points in Arizona from July 29 to August 24.

This bird winters in Central America, where it is evidently quite common, judging from the number of its skins in all large collections from Guatemala. Mr. Skinner obtained specimens near Coban. It is also found in most of the West India Islands, Gundlach giving it as a visitant of Cuba, and Gosse including it among the birds of Jamaica, where he found it — not seeming particularly solitary — about ponds in pastures and near fresh-water morasses. Its gizzard was filled with fragments of minute water-insects. It is called by him the "Bar-tailed Sandpiper." One of these birds, whose wing had been broken, was kept alive. It had most of the manners of the Kildeer, but frequently held up the wings when running. Another, which had been wounded at Mount Edgcumbe Pond, plunged into the water and swam vigorously.

Professor Newton met with this species on the Island of St. Croix. In its general appearance it reminded him of the Wood Sandpiper of Europe (*Rhyacophilus glareola*), while it has more of the habits and notes of the Green Sandpiper (*R. ochropus*). It was quite common on that island, and arrived about the same time as the *Totanus flavipes*. He obtained one specimen as early as July 26, and Mr. E. Newton one on August 5. In Trinidad, according to Léotaud, it is only a bird of passage, arriving there in August and leaving in October. It is almost always alone, sometimes accompanied by its mate, and occasionally mingled with a flock of other Waders. It is always seen near water, either on the borders of the sea, interior ponds, or where water has softened the soil, thus favoring a search for worms and other food. Its movements are marked by lightness and grace; when it stops it frequently vibrates its head backward and forward, moving its tail at the same time. It flies rapidly, and in flying utters a low cry, as if calling to a companion.

On the Pacific coast it occurs as far north as Alaska, where Mr. Dall met with it at Nulato, sparingly, in the month of May, and where it arrives as early as May 5. In California, Dr. Cooper has not met with this species south of Santa Barbara, Fort Tejon being the most southern locality in which its occurrence has been recorded. It is more common inland and toward the north, frequenting chiefly the banks and gravelly bars along running brooks, and rarely appearing near the sea-coast. The scarcity of clear rivulets in Southern California may be the reason why these birds are not found there, as they go much farther south in the interior in winter. Dr. Cooper has seen them in May on mountain streams in Santa Clara Valley, where they are supposed by him to have had nests.

This species probably does not winter in any portion of the United States, and none are recorded after October. It was found in August by Mr. Dresser on a sand-bank in the Rio Grande, near Matamoras, and none were seen there at any other time. During April he often found them at the small pools and on the banks of the small streams near San Antonio. A single specimen is recorded as having been taken in August in Arizona. Mr. J. A. Allen noticed this species in Eastern Kansas in the early part of May, and found it there quite common. He again met with it during the second week in August at Lake Pass in Colorado, and in September in the Valley of Salt Lake. Mr. Ridgway also met with it occasionally in Utah and Nevada. It arrived in the Truckee Valley May 13, and was noticed in Parley's Park in the Wahsatch Mountains in August. It was much less numerous than *Tringoides macularius*.

In Long Island, according to Giraud, it is not very abundant, yet by no means rare. It is distributed singly or in pairs along such creeks as are reached by the tide; and is also observed about pools and rivulets more remote from the sea. It seldom visits the beach, and is very rarely met with in the salt-marshes on the bays. It often takes up its abode near the habitations of man, preferring his society to that of the numerous species of shore-birds frequenting the seaside. It is not considered game, and is not hunted, and thus becomes quite familiar. When nearly approached it flies but a short distance before it re-alights, to resume its occupation of probing the soft mud for worms and minute shellfish, which abound in its favorite haunts. It also resorts to decayed logs for the purpose of procuring grubs, and from this peculiarity of habit it is by some known as the "Wood Tattler." When surprised it utters a sharp whistling note, raises its wings, and runs nimbly over the miry ground. If closely pursued, it retreats to the opposite side of the pond, arranges its feathers, and soon resumes its usual gentle manners. This bird is very active on the wing, and may sometimes be seen darting after winged insects, which it is very expert in catching; and when flying, its long and gracefully curved wings add greatly to the effect of its neat plumage. It arrives on Long Island in May, and is not seen there after September.

It passes its brief period of reproduction in the extended region north of latitude 44°, but to what extent north is uncertain. Richardson met with a single individual at Great Bear Lake, in latitude 64° 30′, May 14, 1826; and Mr. Dall noticed it at Nulato on about the same parallel. Mr. Ross found it common on the Mackenzie River, and Captain Blakiston observed it on the Saskatchewan Plains. It is found throughout the summer — or from May to September — in the neighborhood of Calais, Me., and Mr. Boardman has no doubt that it breeds there. Yet in the summer of 1873, from May through June — as Mr. Brewster informs us — none of these birds were to be seen in the vicinity of Lake Umbagog; but in the latter part of July, when the migrations southward began, they appeared there in large numbers, apparently having come from a distance. He naturally inferred that few or none breed in that neighborhood.

Wilson states that this species is found in the summer in damp meadows among our highest mountains, from Kentucky to New York, on the mossy margins of mountain springs. He found it unsuspicious, and permitting a near approach without appearing to be in the least alarmed; he had no doubt that these birds regularly bred on Pocano Mountain, near Easton, although he could never find their nests. He notes their resemblance, both in manners and markings, to *R. ochropus,* or the Green Sandpiper of Europe.

Nuttall states that a pair frequented, very familiarly, the small fish-pond in the Botanic Garden in Cambridge, attracted by larvæ that fed on the water-lily. They would trip over the sinking leaves with all the lightness and agility of the Rail.

Mr. Nelson, in his "Notes on the Birds of Northeastern Illinois," speaks of this species as a common migrant, arriving the 1st of May, and remaining until about the 25th, when the majority go farther north. He has several times taken young birds near a prairie slough, which were just able to fly, and has noted the presence of adults throughout the breeding-season, and does not think there can be the slightest doubt that this species breeds in that vicinity, taking its departure southward in August and September. The same writer noticed this Tattler as being common on the banks of the Humboldt, near Elko, Nevada, the young being half-grown. It frequented the sloughs in the meadows, but only a single pair was seen in each.

Early in August, 1878, I noticed a pair of this species with a brood of four young hardly able to fly, near an open reservoir of rain-water, on Appledore, Isles of Shoals. These were too young to have come to that island over the water, the distance being nine miles; and that this brood could have been hatched on that rocky and treeless island seemed very improbable. They were in company with, yet holding aloof from, several pairs of *Tringoides macularius.* My near presence at first appeared greatly to alarm the parents; but they were soon quieted, as I did nothing to disturb them, and they then resumed their search for worms in the black mud on the edge of the water.

Eggs of *T. macularius,* as a general rule, are made to do duty for those of this species. The only egg which I have seen, and have reason to accept as authentic, was one taken in May, 1878, by Mr. Jenness Richardson, near Lake Bombazine, Vermont. The nest was on the ground, and the female parent was shot as she left it. The egg measured 1.37 by .95 inches, the ground-color being a light drab, similar to that of *Ægialitis meloda;* over this were scattered small rounded markings of brown, some of these quite dark, nowhere confluent, and not large enough to be called blotches. At the larger end there were a few faint purplish or lilac discolorations or shell-marks. The egg was elongated pyriform in shape.

Rhyacophilus ochropus.

THE GREEN SANDPIPER.

Tringa ochrophus, LINN. S. N. ed. 10, 1758, 149; ed. 12, 1766, 250.

Totanus ochropus, TEMM. Man. 1815, 420. — NAUM. Vög. Deutschl. VIII. 1836, 59, pl. 197. — KEYS. & BLAS. Wirb. Eur. 73. — BONAP. Comp. List, 1838, 51. — MACGILL. Man. II. 94. — GRAY, Gen. B. III. 573; Cat. Brit. B. 1863, 158.

Rhyacophilus ochropus, RIDGW. Proc. U. S. Nat. Mus. Vol. 3, 1880, 200; Nom. N. Am. B. 1881, no. 551. — COUES, Check List, 2d ed. 1882, no. 636.

Totanus rivalis and *T. leucourus,* BREHM, Vög. Deutschl.

Green Sandpiper, YARR. Brit. B. ed. 2, II. 595, fig.; ed. 3, II. 642, fig.; et AUCT.

HAB. The Palæarctic Region, straying to Eastern North America (Nova Scotia, HARTING).

SP. CHAR. *Adult in summer:* Similar to *R. solitarius,* but upper tail-coverts pure white, without markings; tail white, the middle feathers widely barred, clear across, with dusky, the lateral feathers with only one bar, or immaculate, the others barred only toward ends. Lining of wing and axillars more narrowly barred with white. *Winter plumage:* Similar to *R. solitarius*, except as pointed out above.

The introduction of this well-known European species into the list of American birds rests upon the circumstance of a single stuffed specimen, said to have been killed in Nova Scotia, having come into the possession of J. Edmund Harting, Esq., the well-known authority on the *Limicolæ*. The collection of which it formed a part was received from a responsible dealer direct from Nova Scotia. The skin had evidently been prepared by the same hand as the others of the collection, which were all American species, so that there can be no reason to doubt the authenticity of the ascribed locality. (Cf. Brewer, "Bull. Nutt. Orn. Club," III. Jan. 1878, p. 49.)

The Green Sandpiper, or White-tailed Tattler of Europe, was included by Nuttall as among the birds of North America. It is also given by Richardson in his "Fauna Boreali-Americana," but was not included by Mr. Lawrence in the "Pacific Railroad Report," Vol. IX. Nuttall states that two specimens had been obtained at Hudson's Bay, but he does not mention the name of his informant. It is now restored to the list of North American birds on the authority of J. Edmund Harting, Esq., who in March, 1873, wrote to Professor Baird from London that he had recently received from Mr. H. Whitely, a respectable dealer at Woolwich, a small parcel of North American skins which had been sent to him from Halifax, Nova Scotia, and that among them was an example of this bird. Upon inquiry, he was assured by Mr. Whitely that the skin came to him from Halifax, and that it had been prepared there. Mr. Harting regards this as the first authentic instance of the occurrence of the Green Sandpiper in North America.

According to Yarrell, the habits of this bird are as yet only imperfectly understood. In England it appears to be most plentiful in spring and autumn, a few remaining there to breed, but the greater part going farther north, and probably returning with their young. An occasional specimen of this bird is not infrequently met during the winter months. In some of its habits it resembles our Solitary Tattler, frequenting the sides of shallow streams and the banks of rivers and inland lakes and ponds, not being usually found so near the sea as are the other Sandpipers. When running it spreads and flirts up its tail like the European Redshanks (*T. calidris*). Its food consists of worms and insects. By some it is known as the Whistling Sandpiper, its note — which is a shrill whistle — being thought to sound like *cheet-cheet-cheet.*

Mr. Lubbock informed Yarrell that a pair of this species built its nest in a hollow on the side of a claypit in Norfolk, in the autumn of 1839, and that the bird was common during summer and autumn, upon a small stream near Attleburgh. The same gentleman also stated that he had killed a specimen on the 4th of January, 1837, when there was a deep snow on the ground, and all the Snipes had been driven out of the country by the severity of the weather. He was nearly certain that it remains in England all the year, with the exception of that period in spring and early summer during which it withdraws to rear its young. The 11th of April is the latest time in spring at which he has observed any. A nephew of Mr. Lubbock informed him that on the 23d of July he saw six of this species together, and that they appeared to be two old birds with their four young. This bird is also said to be not uncommon along the whole line of the southern marine counties of England, from Romney Marsh, in Kent, to Sussex, Hampshire, and thence to the Land's End. Mr. Edward Doubleday saw several pairs about small streams in the vicinity of Snowdon in summer; and two pairs were observed near Capel Curig. It is also a summer visitor in Ireland. Mr. Henry Doubleday informed Yarrell that in November, 1840, he shot a Green Sandpiper in the vicinity of Epping. The bird was only slightly wounded, and was kept alive. It was not at all shy, and fed readily on small worms, first dipping them in a pan of water. It would run about the room rapidly, constantly moving its tail up and down like a Wheatear. When flushed it utters a shrill whistle, and generally flies low, skimming over the surface of the water, and following with precision all the bends and angles of the stream.

The Green Sandpiper is said to visit Scandinavia in the spring, and to remain there until August. It is not included among the birds of the Faröe Islands or of Iceland. In the spring and autumn it is very generally distributed over Europe. In France it is esteemed a great delicacy, and is caught by means of limed twigs. It is found in all the countries bordering on the Mediterranean, was taken by Mr. Strickland in Smyrna, and, as Vieillot states, has been seen in Egypt. It is said to be a characteristic summer resident near sheets of water in the wooded districts of Northeastern Germany, but it is never found in open marshes in the breeding-season. It has been known also to breed among the Lower Alps of Southeastern France and throughout the French Pyrenees. It has been found in numbers in winter among the mountains of Abyssinia, and has also been met with even as far south as the Cape Colony. In Asia it appears to be common in Persia, India, Turkestan, Burmah, China, and Japan, and to breed in all the northern portions of that continent. It is said to be very shy and difficult of approach. Its flight is graceful and swift, and it traverses a considerable distance with but few strokes of its wings. It hovers a little just before it alights, and then its wings are more extended than in its flight. It is very peculiar in its mode of nesting, depositing its eggs in old nests situated in trees, and is not known ever to nest on the ground. The details of its breeding-habits were first published in "Cabanis's Journal" (1862, p. 460) by Mr. Hintz, who found its nest for the first time April 26, 1834, in an old one of a *Turdus musicus*. He afterward saw their eggs in old nests of Pigeons, Jays, Shrikes, and other birds, but most commonly in those of the Thrush. Writing in 1862, Mr. Hintz states that none of the nests he had found up to that date were more than three paces from water, some being as low as a foot above the ground, although usually at an elevation of from three to six feet, and in some instances as much as thirty-five. It not infrequently uses the same nest two years in succession. The young, as soon as they are hatched, jump to the ground. It breeds as early as April. In one instance seven eggs of this bird were found in an old nest of a Thrush, most probably laid by two females of this species.

The eggs of the Green Sandpiper are pear-shaped. In some the ground is of a delicate grayish sea-green, over which are sparingly distributed pale purplish-gray shell-markings and dark-brown blotches, the latter being chiefly collected round the larger end. In other examples the spots are smaller, more numerous, and more generally distributed. Six eggs in my cabinet from Eastern Prussia exhibit the following measurements: 1.50 × 1.12; 1.49 × 1.10; 1.51 × 1.11; 1.52 × 1.10; 1.53 × 1.10; 1.51 × 1.08: average, 1.51 × 1.10.

Genus **SYMPHEMIA**, Rafinesque.

Symphemia, Rafinesque, Jour. de Phys. 1819 (type, *Scolopax semipalmata*, Gmel.).
Catoptrophorus, Bonap. Syn. 1828, 323 (same type).

Char. Bill compressed, very thick, the culmen rounded. The lower mandible scarcely grooved the upper grooved to about the middle. Culmen slightly convex; gonys ascending. Bill cleft but little beyond base of culmen. Feathers of sides of both mandibles falling short of the nostrils, the lower rather farther forward. Chin-feathers reaching to middle of nostrils. Bill longer than head; about equal to tarsus, which is more than one and one half times the middle toe. Both toes webbed; the emargination of inner web as far forward as the middle of basal joint of middle toe, the outer

S. semipalmata.

reaching nearly to the end. Bare portion of tibia rather less than middle toe without claw. Tail nearly even, or little rounded, not half the wings.

Symphemia semipalmata.

THE WILLET.

Scolopax semipalmata, GMEL. S. N. I. 1788, 659. — WILS. Am. Orn. VII. 1813, 27, pl. 56, fig. 3.
Totanus semipalmatus, TEMM. Man. Orn. II. 1828, 637. — SW. & RICH. F. B. A. II. 1831, 388, pl. 67. — AUD. Orn. Biog. III. 1835, 510; V. 1839, 585, pl. 274; Synop. 1839, 245; B. Am. V. 1842, 324, pl. 347. — COUES, Key, 1872, 258; Check List, 1873, no. 431; Birds N. W. 1874, 494.
Totanus (*Catoptrophorus*) *semipalmatus*, BONAP. Synop. 1828, 328. — NUTT. Man. II. 1834, 144.
Symphemia semipalmata, HARTL. Rev. Zool. 1845, 342. — CASS. in Baird's B. N. Am. 1858, 729. — BAIRD, Cat. N. Am. B. 1859, no. 537. — RIDGW. Nom. N. Am. B. 1881, no. 552. — COUES, Check List, 2d ed. 1882, no. 632.
Totanus crassirostris, VIEILL. Nouv. Dict. 1816, 406.
Symphemia atlantica, RAFINESQUE, Jour. Phys. lxxxviii. 1819, 417.
Totanus speculiferus, CUVIER, Règ. An. I. 1817, 351.

HAB. Temperate North America, south to Brazil; West Indies. Accidental in Europe.

SP. CHAR. Largest of American Scolopacidæ, except genera *Numenius* and *Limosa*. Primaries black, with nearly the basal half white, producing a very conspicuous patch on the spread wing. *Summer adult:* Above, light brownish gray, streaked on head and neck, and spotted and barred on the back, etc., with blackish; beneath, white, tinged with ashy on foreneck and with buff along sides, the former, with jugulum, spotted with dusky, and the latter barred with the same; upper tail-coverts white; tail ashy, more or less distinctly mottled transversely with a deeper shade of the same; wing-coverts plain ash-gray; axillars and lining of wing plain sooty black. *Winter plumage:* Above, plain ash-gray; beneath, immaculate dull white, the foreneck shaded with grayish. *Young:* Above, brownish gray, the feathers margined with pale ochraceous; sides much tinged with the same, and finely mottled transversely with grayish. Bill black; legs and feet grayish. *In life*, "bill light blue, dusky toward end; iris brown; feet light blue, claws black" (AUDUBON).

Total length, about 15.00–17.00 inches; extent, 25.00–30.00; wing, 8.00–9.00; culmen, 2.30–2.60; tarsus, 2.40–2.85; middle toe, 1.35–1.40.

The Willet is one of the most extensively distributed of all our American birds. It is not only found along the entire Atlantic coast from Nova Scotia to Florida, and along the entire Gulf coast, but is equally abundant on the Pacific and through nearly all the marshy regions of the interior; it also occurs throughout Central and South America as far south as the Pampas, where it breeds in large numbers. Burmeister could find no difference between South American examples of this bird and those from farther north.

Mr. Nelson refers to this species as being a rare summer resident in the marshes and on the wet prairies of Northeastern Illinois, where it arrives the last of April, leaving by the first of October. The same writer afterward found it abundant on the shores of Salt Lake, in company with Avocets, where its clamor made it a perfect nuisance to the sportsman. Captain Bendire also noticed it as an abundant summer resident in Southeastern Oregon, where he procured several sets of its eggs, which began to be laid about the 10th of May. These birds were quite as abundant in the higher mountain valleys, at an altitude of six thousand feet, as they were in the lower regions, apparently frequenting all marshy localities. Dr. Bryant found this to be an abundant species in the Bahamas, where it was also resident, breeding in all suitable localities, and being known as the "Duck Snipe."

On the Pacific coast, according to Dr. Cooper, it is one of the most common of the shore-birds, especially in the southern portions of California and about San Francisco, in the market of which it is plentiful all the year round. Although no nests had been found, there could be no doubt that it breeds abundantly in that State, as Dr. Cooper had met with fledged young at San Pedro early in July. It frequents the marshy ground, both on the coast and in the interior toward the north, but none were seen on the Colorado. According to Dr. Heermann, they are found along Humboldt River. Mr. Ridgway found the Willet in June breeding abundantly on the grassy flats on the southern shores of Great Salt Lake, in company with the Long-billed Curlew. It was found in considerable numbers on the shores of small saline lakes near the Saskatchewan by Richardson, but is not known to range in the summer any farther north than the 56th parallel, occurring only in the interior.

Mr. Salvin speaks of this species as occurring in Guatemala, where it was quite common at Chiapam, as well as on all the lagoons along the entire Pacific coast.

According to Dresser, it was not rare near San Antonio, Texas. He procured examples at the Boca Grande in July and August, and at King's Rancho, between Matamoras and Victoria, in September. He saw several in June on Galveston Island, and an example was sent to him from Fort Stockton.

The Willet is also found in all, or nearly all, the larger West India Islands. It is given by Gundlach as a bird of Cuba. March speaks of it as of irregular occurrence in Jamaica, where it is known as the "Spanish Plover," it being not uncommon there, in some years, during and after the autumnal rains. He never met with this bird in the summer, although he was told that it breeds in Saint Elizabeth. It is referred to by Mr. Gosse, on the authority of Mr. Hill, as abundant on the island in winter. In Trinidad, according to Léotaud, it is known as the "White-wing," and it is said to arrive in that island in August, and to leave in October or before. It is always seen in flocks, and these are sometimes of considerable size. It is not known to leave the borders of the sea. The movements and manners of this species are similar to those of the *Totanus flavipes*, with which it usually associates. Its flesh is not regarded as generally excellent. A single specimen was shot in Bermuda, July 3, 1848.

On the New England coast this bird occurs sparingly from Long Island to Calais, Me., and along the coast of Nova Scotia at least as far as Halifax. I met with it breeding on the small Island of Muskeget, near Nantucket, Mass.; and Mr. Boardman informs me that it occurs in the neighborhood of Calais, Me., and that it undoubtedly breeds there, but that it is not very abundant. Dr. Bryant noticed it breeding on the coast of Nova Scotia near Yarmouth; and I have received its eggs from Mr. Andrew Downes, obtained near Halifax. It is more common on Long Island, on whose shores, according to Mr. Giraud, it arrives about the 1st of May. It is equally common along the coast of New Jersey, Maryland, and Virginia at about the same period. On Long Island it is said to be common, rather than abundant, and it is also far from being so plentiful as it is at Egg Harbor, where it is known to breed. Mr. Giraud was not aware that it had ever been positively ascertained to breed on Long Island; yet as it is known to nest in suitable places along the entire coast from Florida to Halifax, it is hardly probable that this island, with its favoring extent of sea-coast, is an exception. It builds its nest in New Jersey in the latter part of May, in the salt-marshes, among the grass, using for that purpose rushes and coarse herbage.

In Florida, according to Mr. Moore, the full set of four eggs is laid as early as April 25. He never found their smaller ends placed toward one another. These birds have, as he states, the singular habit of alighting on trees during the breeding-season, evidently for the purpose of viewing their nests and eggs. They perch on dead trees or branches which are near the objects of their solicitude, fifteen or twenty feet from the earth, and continuously pour out their notes of apprehension, many joining in the clamor, so that the noise may be heard a half mile or more.

If any one approaches the nest of the Willet during the season of incubation, it is said to rise suddenly from the marsh, to fly wildly around, and to fill the air with its shrill cries, which consist of three notes, repeated with so much force as to be audible for a distance of half a mile; if not disturbed, however, the breeding-season is passed in silence, without any such manifestations of uneasiness. On Muskeget Lake the parent birds withdrew to a distance, and were not seen again, their nest having been discovered and the eggs taken; and on another occasion, where eight or ten nests were found by me on an island near Cape Charles, Va., the birds were silent, and were only noticed as they withdrew from the nests.

The flight of the Willet is swift, and performed with grace and ease. While in general this bird is found in the salt-marshes, it will also at times alight upon bare shoals left exposed by the tide, and may be seen wading breast-deep in the water. It is extremely watchful, and when in an exposed situation very seldom allows a hunter to arrive within shooting distance. Nor is it by any means easily allured by decoys, even though the sportsman be well hidden; and even if the bird approaches and answers the decoy-note, its keen eye will soon enable it to detect the deception, when, quickly changing its course, it darts off like an arrow, and ascends beyond the reach of the fowler. While it rarely associates with others of its kind, it may often be seen feeding in company with Gulls, Sanderlings, and other birds. When flying it is made very conspicuous by the white markings of its wings. It feeds chiefly on worms, aquatic insects, small crabs, and minute shellfish. When in good condition, the flesh of this bird is quite palatable, although not considered a great delicacy; its eggs, however, are very superior food. Audubon was mistaken both as to the absence of this bird from the coast north of Boston and its non-existence in the interior. It is probably rare north of Long Island, but it is often quite abundant at some distance from the coast.

Wilson characterizes it as one of the most noisy of the birds inhabiting the salt-marshes in summer, arriving about the 20th of April, and from that time to the last of July making the vicinity resound almost incessantly with its loud and shrill reiterations of *pill-will-willet.* It begins to lay usually about the 20th of May. At Cape Charles all the eggs I found on the 5th of June were quite fresh. The nests are always on the ground, among the grass of the salt-marshes, and composed of rushes and coarse grass, with only a slight hollow. Wilson states that the nest is gradually increased in size, during the period of laying and sitting, to the height of six inches. The young — which are covered with a gray-colored down — run off soon after they leave the shell, being assisted in their search for food by their mother, while the male bird keeps a continual watch for their safety. The anxiety and affection which the Willets manifest for their young is often quite touching. An intruder into the marshes where they are breeding is at once beset by the birds, who fly around and hover over his head, vociferating with great violence, and uttering a loud clicking note whenever their nest is approached. At times they give out a mournful note expressive of great grief. During the breeding-season the Willet is said to be often much annoyed by the predatory excursions of the Crow, whose visits always create alarm, and are repelled by the united force, who attack and pursue it with great clamor.

According to the observations of Dr. Heermann, the Willet wades in water to a depth equal to the length of its legs, and if wounded swims with great rapidity. Its food he found to consist of the small shells, crabs, etc., with the insects to be found about the marshes. As it is a large bird, and generally well flavored, it is among those shot by the purveyor for market, the first which appear being for sale in August. The young keep in separate flocks, and are easily distinguishable by their pale gray color. They are much better eating than the old birds, and may be found in the market of San Francisco throughout the winter.

The eggs are always four in number. Giraud describes them as being rather more than two inches in length and one and a half in breadth, and very thick at the larger end. In color they are dark olive, blotched with blackish brown, these markings being usually more numerous at the larger end. According to my own observations, the eggs of this species are, without exception, pyriform in shape, quite broad at the larger end, and strongly tapering toward the other extremity, and are very nearly of equal size, but differ in the most marked manner as to their ground-color, and also in the size and distribution of their spots. The ground-color is usually a deep drab, with a slight rufous tinge; occasionally, instead of rufous, the shading is decidedly olivaceous; in a few instances, however, the ground is very light and bright grayish white with a slight tinge of green. The markings are usually of bistre; intermixed with the blotches of a pure shade are others washed over with the shadings of the ground-color, giving them a neutral or slate-colored appearance. One egg (No. 651), collected at Cape Charles, Va., June 5, 1856, measures 2.00 inches by 1.51. It has a dark rufous-drab ground, marked with blotches of bistre. These are scattered and few about the smaller end, but unite in a confluent ring around the larger portion. Another (No. 115) was sent me by Mr. Andrew Downes, from Halifax, Nova Scotia. It measures 2.10 inches by 1.50. Its ground is drab, with a slight olivaceous tinge, and the blotches are more scattered, and nowhere confluent, except on one side near the widest portion of the egg is a remarkable combination of dark blotches, 1.00 inch by 0.61. A third (No. 976), collected at Cape Charles by the Rev. J. N. Jones, measures 2.10 inches by 1.50. Its ground is a light gray — almost white — with a decided bluish tinge. Its spots are small fine dottings of dark bistre. Except in shape, it has no resemblance to the usual egg of the Willet.

Genus **HETEROSCELUS**, Baird.

Heteroscelus, Baird, Birds N. Am. 1858, 734 (type, *Totanus brevipes*, Vieill., = *Scolopax incana*, Gmel.).

Char. Bill longer than head or tarsus, stout, much compressed; commissure straight to near end, where gently decurved; culmen slightly concave in middle portion; nasal groove extending over basal two-thirds of bill. Tarsi short (about equal to middle toe), covered laterally and behind by hexagonal scales, the naked part of tibia covered with similar scales; outer and middle toe con-

H. incanus.

nected by a basal web as far as first joint of the latter, and a rudimentary web between middle and inner toes; hind toe long (nearly one third the tarsus). Tail half as long as wings, nearly even. Plumage perfectly uniform above, without spots or bands of any kind.

This very remarkable Sandpiper differs, in the hexagonal scutellation of the tibia and on the posterior face of the tarsus, from any other of the *Totaneæ*. The bill is stronger than in any American genus, except *Symphemia*, differing mainly from this in the straightness of the bill and greater amount of inflection of the edges. The nasal groove extends farther forward, and the upper jaw is a little more decurved at the end. The gape is a little more deeply cleft. The legs, especially the tarsi, are much shorter; the inner toe only slightly webbed. The claws are short, stout, and unusually curved. The legs have a much roughened appearance.

The single North American species of this genus is one of wide distribution, occurring on the eastern coasts of Asia, and the islands throughout the Pacific Ocean, as well as along the western shores of North America.

Heteroscelus incanus.

THE WANDERING TATTLER.

Scolopax incana, GMEL. S. N. I. 1788, 658.
Totanus incanus, VIEILL. Dict. Deterv. VI. 1816, 400.
Heteroscelus incanus, COUES, Key, 1872, 261; Check List, 1873, no. 440; ed. 2, 1882, no. 642; in Elliott's Alaska, ed. 1875, 187. — RIDGW. Nom. N. Am. B. 1881, no. 553.
Tringa glareola, PALL. Zoog. Rosso-As. II. 1811, 194, pl. 60.
Totanus brevipes, VIEILL. Dict. Deterv. VI. 1816, 400.
Heteroscelus brevipes, CASS. in Baird's B. N. Am. 1858, 734; ed. 1860, pl. 88. — BAIRD, Cat. N. Am. B. 1859, no. 542.
Totanus fuliginosus, GOULD, Voy. Beag. Birds, 1841, 130.
Scolopax undulata, FORST. Descr. An. ed. Licht. 1844, 173.
Totanus pulverulentus, MÜLL. Verh. 1844, 153.
Totanus oceanicus, LESS. Compl. Buff. 1847, 244.
Totanus polynesiæ, PEALE, Voy. Vinc. & Peac. Birds, 1848, 237.
Totanus griseopygius, GOULD, B. Austr. VI. pl. 38.
"*Gambetta brevipes, oceanica, pulverulenta, oceanica, griseopygia*, BONAP."

HAB. The islands and shores of the Pacific Ocean. Of frequent occurrence, during migrations, along the coast of Alaska, and also southward to the Galapagos.

SP. CHAR. Rather larger than *Totanus flavipes*. *Summer adult:* Entire upper parts uniform dark plumbeous; lower parts white, shaded with plumbeous laterally, the foreneck with longitudinal streaks, and other portions with transverse bars, of dusky plumbeous. Lining of wing white, spotted and barred with dark plumbeous; primaries blackish dusky, the shafts brown on the outer and white on the inner surface, that of the first quill, however, white on both sides. *Winter plumage:* Above, plain plumbeous; lower parts white washed with plumbeous along sides and across jugulum. *Young:* Somewhat like the winter plumage, but secondaries, scapulars, and upper tail-coverts indistinctly spotted with white along edges, and the plumbeous of sides, etc., faintly mottled with white.

Wing, 6.50–7.30; culmen, 1.50–1.60; tarsus, 1.25–1.35; middle toe, 1.00–1.05.

The history of the present species is imperfectly known. We have no account of the manner or the locality of its breeding. In North America it seems to be confined to the Pacific shore and islands, and to inhabit by preference the rocky portions of the coast, rather than those that are low, marshy, or sandy. Dr. Cooper writes in reference to this bird, that it seems to differ much in habits from the other members of this family, in that it prefers the rocky shores of the ocean, and in probably never frequenting marshes or inland localities. He has found it only sparingly along the whole southern coast of California, but not on the islands, though the species is so widely distributed throughout the Pacific archipelagoes. He obtained a single specimen at Santa Barbara as late as April 27, and saw another pair — apparently of this species — at San Pedro on the 23d of May; so that probably a few breed along the coast. He also met with it in Monterey in September. This naturalist adds that he has always found it feeding on surf-beaten rocks, among the seaweed, and generally not shy, but when frightened flying off a short distance, with a harsh rattling cry, like the alarm note of the Turnstones. It has also a propensity to hide itself among the rocks, instead of flying, being often difficult to find, even when close at hand. In an account subsequently written, Dr. Cooper mentions, in describing a visit to Monterey, Sept. 10, 1862 ("American Naturalist," IV. 758), having observed a few of the Wandering Tattler, and that they were, as usual, among the rocks along the shore in that neighborhood.

This species is included by Mr. R. Browne among the birds observed by him on Vancouver Island. Mr. Dall states that he procured three specimens of it at Nulato, and Mr. Bischoff two at Sitka; but it is said to be rare on the Yukon River, where, however, one was found by Mr. McDougal. Three were obtained by Dr. Cooper in Shoal Water Bay, W. T., and two by Mr. Elliott on the Prybilof Islands, where it is said by him to be of regular migratory appearance, but not to breed. He adds that it comes regularly every year early in June, and subsequently re-appears toward the end of July, when it may be obtained on the rocky beaches, never visiting the uplands, and being a very shy and quiet bird. A single specimen was also taken at Plover Bay, in Eastern Siberia, September, 1867, by Mr. Bischoff.

Mr. H. W. Henshaw thinks that this bird is well named the "Wandering Tattler," and states that it has a very wide range, being found on the islands of the Pacific generally, and from Alaska to Australia. Santa Cruz Island is the only place where he has enjoyed an opportunity of meeting with it, though, as he is informed, it occurs on other islands also. Captain Forney, of the Coast Survey, secured quite a number on the Island of San Miguel, where this bird occurs in considerable numbers. It is not at all a bird of the sandy shores, but resorts exclusively to rocks covered with seaweed, following the tide as it ebbs and flows, running back and forth, picking up the worms and marine animals, which are found in such localities in abundance. In its motions it is said to simulate exactly the little Spotted Sandpiper, and to have the same curious "tip-up" motion of its body in moments of rest from feeding. It flies with a similar deliberate wing-beat, with pinions slightly decurved, the tips being pointed downward. The voices of the two birds are said to be very different; the notes of this species being very loud and harsh as compared with the smooth whistle of *T. macularius*. Mr. Henshaw found them usually solitary, quite watchful, and full of distrust, though occasionally he found himself within a few feet of one of them, and was able to watch its motions. This was in June; and though the birds were unquestionably paired and breeding, he was not able to obtain even a hint as to their method of nidification.

Genus MACHETES, Cuvier.

Pavoncella, Leach, Cat. M. B. Brit. Mus. 1816 (type, *Tringa pugnax*, L.; cf. Stejneger, Proc. U. S. Nat. Mus. no. 5, 1882, 38).

Machetes, Cuvier, R. Anim. 1817 (same type).

Char. Bill nearly straight, as long as the head or the outer toe. Groove extending nearly to the tip. Bill depressed, broad to the tip, which is scarcely expanded. Gape extending a little farther back than the culmen; the feathers of lower mandibles extending rather farther forward than those of upper; those of chin still farther. Legs slender; tarsus one and one fourth times as

M. pugnax.

long as middle toe, one and one third times the length of bare tibia. A basal web connecting the outer and middle toes to the first joint of the former; inner toe cleft to base. Tail rather long; distinctly barred.

This genus, usually placed among *Tringeæ*, appears to have most affinity with the present section, and in a measure to connect *Tryngites* and *Bartramia*. The bill is more depressed, and rather broader toward the end than usual; but it appears hard and firm, and with little or none of the spoon-shaped expansion at the end. The greater cleft of the mouth, the half webbing of the toes, the bars on the tail, the lengthened tarsi, etc., all seem to indicate the propriety of placing it with *Totaneæ*.

Machetes pugnax.

THE RUFF.

Tringa pugnax, Linn. S. N. I. 1766, 247.

Machetes pugnax, Cuv. Règ. An. I. 1817, 490. — Bonap. Comp. List, 1838, 50. — Naum. Vög. Deutschl. VII. 1834, 502, pls. 190–193. — Macgill. Man. II. 75. — Coues, Bull. Nutt. Orn. Club, Apr. 1880, 100; Check List, 2d ed. 1882, no. 639. — Ridgw. Nom. N. Am. B. 1881, no. 554.

Tringa (*Machetes*) *pugnax*, Nutt. Man. II. 1834, 131.

Philomachus pugnax, Gray, List Gen. 1841, 89; Cat. Brit. B. 1863, 164. — Lawr. Ann. Lyc. N. Y. V. June, 1852, 220 (Long Island). — Cassin, in Baird's B. N. Am. 1858, 737. — Baird, Cat. N. Am. B. 1859, no. 544. — Coues, Key, 1872, 260; Check List, 1873, no. 437.

Pavoncella pugnax, Stejn. Proc. U. S. Nat. Mus. Vol. 5, 1882, p. 38.

Tringa littorea, Linn. S. N. I. 1766, 251.

Tringa rufescens, Bechst. Naturg. IV. 332.

Tringa equestris, LATH. Ind. Orn. II. 1790, 730.
Tringa grenovicensis, LATH. t.c. 731.
Tringa variegata, BRÜNN. Orn. Bor. 54.
Tringa planiceps and *T. alticeps*, BREHM, Vög. Deutschl.
Ruff, YARR. Brit. B. ed. 2, II. 645, fig.; ed. 3, II. 692, fig.; et AUCT.

HAB. The Palæarctic Region, straying to Eastern North America (numerous records).

SP. CHAR. Above, varied with black, buff, and gray, the scapulars and tertials exhibiting these colors in oblique bands. Beneath, white, varied on the jugulum and throat. Primaries dark brown, with greenish reflection above; the inner webs finely mottled toward the base. Outer three tail-feathers plain, the remainder transversely barred. Bill brown; sides of rump white;

Male.

legs yellow. Male in spring dress with the feathers of the neck greatly developed into a ruff; the face covered with reddish papillæ. *Adult male:* Colors indeterminate, probably no two specimens being exactly alike. As a rule, the "cape" and "ruff" are differently colored; thus, of the five examples before us, the cape and ruff are colored in the following manner:—Cape glossy black, buffy white, yellowish ochraceous. Ruff, chestnut-rufous, glossy black streaked with rufous, mottled ferruginous, ochraceous buff, streaked buffy white, and pied with black and pure white. *Adult female:* No ruff; head completely feathered. Plumage transversely banded with black, and

Female.

buff, white, or ferruginous; the abdomen and crissum usually immaculate white. *Young:* Back and scapulars brownish black, feathers bordered with buff or ochraceous; crown ochraceous, streaked with black. Lower parts entirely immaculate, white posteriorly, buffy anteriorly.

Length, about 10.00 inches: wing, 6.40; tail, 2.60; bill, 1.25; tarsus, 1.75; middle toe and claw, 1.40.

The Ruff has been so frequently killed in the Eastern United States as to entitle it to a place among North American birds, although it cannot be said really to belong to our fauna. It is a very curious species, conspicuous for the combats among the males during the breeding-season.

At this time the feathers of the neck are greatly elongated, forming a kind of cape or ruff, and the face is beset with papillæ.

The Ruff is about the size of the Bartram's Tattler or Field Plover, which it otherwise resembles somewhat in color. It has the same mottling of the inner webs of primaries as in *Tryngites rufescens*, though not to so great an extent, this feature not being found in any other North American *Totaneæ*, though seen in *Limosa fedoa*.

The well-known Ruff of Europe claims a place in the North American fauna as a not infrequent straggler within our limits. Several specimens have been from time to time killed on Long Island. More recently other examples have been taken at Grand Menan, all of which were in their winter plumage. Two have been taken in Massachusetts, and others in various portions of New England. In one instance Mr. William Brewster procured a fine specimen near Newburyport, May 20, 1871; it was a female, with her ovaries so far developed as to render it evident that she would have been ready to deposit her eggs within at least two or three weeks.

The most marked peculiarity of this species is the annual appearance of a ruff-like growth of feathers about the neck of the male, from which the bird derives its trivial name. The males, too, differ remarkably in their color — an unusual circumstance among wild birds — and are polygamous. They are also much larger than the females.

This species has an extended distribution, being found at certain seasons throughout Europe, Northern Africa, and in Western Asia. It is only a migrant in Great Britain, making its appearance in April and leaving in the autumn. In Scandinavia the Ruff appears in great numbers on the coast of Scona at the end of April or the beginning of May. It is not known to breed in the southern parts of Scandinavia, although it does abundantly in Denmark. It reaches Lapland the last week in May, where it frequents, on its first coming, the margins of the lakes and rivers. As soon as the grass has grown up, it hides in the extensive and grassy morasses, where it can rarely be forced to show itself on the wing. The old birds migrate south in July, the young lingering until August; by the 15th they have all disappeared.

This species goes as far north as Iceland, visits Russia and Siberia in the summer, and the countries south in their migrations, at which times only are they seen in France, Switzerland, Italy, etc. In a few exceptional cases a pair has occasionally been known to breed in Switzerland. Individuals have also been taken at Malta, at Tunis, Trebizond, in the country about the Caucasus, in Northwestern India, in Nepal, near Calcutta, and throughout Lower Bengal.

Until within comparatively few years the capture of the living birds of this species in England, and the fattening of them for the London market, has been systematically practised by certain persons. Montagu mentions a noted feeder at Spalding whose family had been in this trade more than a century, and who, at the time that author visited him, had eighty-four males and a dozen females in confinement. Of the former there were not two alike. These birds will feed greedily, the moment they are taken, on bread and milk or boiled wheat. The males are very pugnacious, and contend for their food with so much obstinacy that they will not eat unless there are several dishes before them. Their actions in fighting are said to be something like those of a game cock. Although they present a very ferocious appearance when fighting, yet they rarely injure one another.

In the spring the Ruffs assemble on a rising spot of ground, where they contend for the females. Advantage is taken of this by the fowler to capture them alive by means of what is known as a clap-net.

Montagu kept several of these birds in confinement a number of years. In this condition the males took no other notice of the females than to drive them from the food; invariably quarrelling with each other, but taking no notice of other species, and feeding in perfect amity out of the same dish with Land-Rails and other birds confined with them.

When the Rheeves, as the females are called, begin to lay, both they and the Ruffs are least shy, and are easily caught. The females lay their eggs during the first or second week in May, and their young are sometimes hatched out as early as June 3. The nest is usually placed on a slight elevation in moist, swampy places, surrounded by coarse grass, of which material it is chiefly made. The eggs are four in number, have an olive ground-color, and are marked with spots and blotches of umber and liver-brown. They are of an oblong pyriform shape, and measure 1.60 inches in length by 1.09 inches in their greatest breadth. The young, which are prettily spotted when covered with down, soon leave the nest, and are difficult to find without a good dog.

Genus **BARTRAMIA**, Lesson.

Bartramia, Lesson, Traité d'Orn. 1831, 553 (type, *B. laticauda*, Less., = *Tringa longicauda*, Bechst.).
Actidurus, Bonap. Saggio, etc., 1831, 143 (type, *Tringa Bartramia*, Wils., = *Tringa longicauda* Bechst.).
Euliga, Nutt. Man. II. 1834 (same type).

Char. Upper mandible grooved laterally to within the terminal fourth, the lower not quite so far. Culmen concave to near the tip, where it is slightly decurved; gonys straight. Mouth deeply cleft, almost as far back as the anterior canthus. The culmen only about two thirds the commissure, shorter than the head or tarsus, and about equal to middle toe without claw. Feathers extending much farther forward on the upper jaw than on the lower, although those of chin reach nearly to end of nostrils. Tarsus one and one half times middle toe and claw; the bare part of tibia not quite equal to the middle toe above; outer toe united at base as far as first joint; web of inner toe very basal. Tail long, graduated, more than half the wings.

B. longicauda.

Bartramia longicauda.

BARTRAM'S TATTLER; FIELD PLOVER.

Tringa longicauda, Bechst. Vög. Nachtr. übers. Lath. Ind. Orn. 1812, 453.
Tringa Bartramia, Wils. Am. Orn. VII. 1813, 63, pl. 59, fig. 2. — Aud. Synop. 1839, 231; B. Am. V. 1842, 248, pl. 327.
Tringa (Euliga) Bartramia, Nutt. Man. II. 1834, 168.
Totanus Bartramius, Temm. Man. II. 1820, 650. — Sw. & Rich. F. B. A. II. 1831, 391. — Aud. Orn. Biog. IV. 1838, 24, pl. 303.
Actiturus Bartramius, Bonap., Cassin, in Baird's B. N. Am. 1858, 737. — Baird, Cat. N. Am. B. 1859, no. 545. — Coues, Key, 1872, 260: Check List, 1873, no. 438; Birds N. W. 1874, 502.
Actiturus longicaudus, Dresser, B. Eur. pt. 59 and 60.
Bartramius longicaudus, Bp. Rev. et Mag. Zool. XX. 1857, 59.
Bartramia longicauda, Coues, Bull. N. O. C. Apr. 1880, 100; Check List, 2d ed. 1882, no. 640.— Ridgw. Nom. N. Am. B. 1882, no. 555.
Totanus melanopygius, Vieill. Nouv. Dict. VI. 1816, 401.
Totanus campestris, Vieill. t. c. 400.
Totanus variegatus, Vieill. t. c. 317.
Bartramia laticauda, Less. Traité, 1831, 553.

Hab. Eastern North America, migrating to Brazil and Peru, and extending north to Alaska and Nova Scotia. Breeds nearly throughout its North American range. Occasional in Europe.

Sp. Char. Bill about as long as the head, rather wide and flattened at base, slightly curved at the tip; nostril with a large membrane; nasal groove long; wing long; tail long for this group; legs moderate or rather long; lower half of the tibia naked; toes moderate, the outer and middle united by a membrane, inner and middle free to the base; hind toe small. *Adult:* Above, grayish brown, the feathers paler and more ochraceous toward their edges, spotted and barred with black; head and neck (except throat) streaked with blackish; crown blackish, divided by a mesial line of buff; throat, belly, and crissum plain buffy white; axillars pure white and clear dusky slate in regular bars of nearly equal width; tail-feathers (except middle pair) creamy buff, broadly tipped with white, crossed by a broad subterminal black spot, and with a few irregular narrow bars anterior to this; outer webs of primaries plain dusky slate, the inner webs with wide transverse bars of white on the outer quill, on the others broken into a confused mottling. Rump and upper tail-coverts nearly uniform blackish, the outer feathers of the latter with their exterior webs partly white. *Young:* Similar to the adult, but the buff of the head, jugulum, wings, etc., much deeper, the streaks on the foreneck and jugulum much less distinct, and the back plain black, the feathers bordered with buff. "Bill yellowish green, the tip dusky, the edges toward the base yellow; iris dark hazel; legs and tarsi light yellowish gray, toes rather darker, claws brownish black." *Downy young:* Above, coarsely and irregularly mottled with black on a grayish-white ground, tinged with light rusty. Lower parts buffy white, with about three blackish spots on the flanks, one beneath the eye, a smaller one on the lores, about half-way between the bill and the eye, and a large, nearly vertical, one behind the ears.

Total length, about 12 inches; wing, 6.50–7.00; culmen, 1.10–1.15; tarsus, 1.90–2.05; middle toe, .90–1.05.

Bartram's Tattler — or, as it is more generally called by gunners and sportsmen, the Upland or the Field Plover — is more or less abundant in all parts of the United States and in the interior as far north as the Saskatchewan Plains. It breeds from Pennsylvania north, and is more common in the interior than in the higher grounds near the coast. It is also found in Mexico, in Central America, and in South America as far south as the Pampas.

Mr. Salvin, during his stay at Dueñas, in Guatemala, noticed quite a flock of this species, consisting of about eighteen or twenty members, which arrived about the beginning of April at that place. Since they seek dry, open savannas, rather than marshy pools, they fully justify the appellation of Field Plover, their actions and habits closely assimilating them to the *Charadriidæ.* Mr. Salvin afterward met with this bird in April on the coast of Honduras, among the bays. Dr. Burmeister found it common in South America south of Mendoza, on the banks of the River Tunuyan, and could detect no difference between South American and Northern specimens.

Richardson met with this bird on the Saskatchewan Plains, where it was feeding on coleopterous insects. Captain Blakiston also found it common in the same locality, where it breeds during the summer. Mr. J. Lockhart found this Plover breeding as far north as Fort Yukon, June 15, 1862, and snared the female on her nest. Mr. J. Ibbiston also procured specimens in the same neighborhood. Mr. Donald Gunn found it breeding at Selkirk Settlement. Mr. R. McDonald noticed it breeding among the mountains west of the Lower Mackenzie, and Mr. J. M'Dougal met with it in the Gens de Large Mountains, two hundred miles northeast of the Yukon.

The Upland Plover is a great wanderer. In at least three instances stragglers have been taken in England. One of these was obtained near Cambridge in December, 1854, another was afterward procured in Warwickshire, and Mr. John Gould received a specimen of this bird shot near Sydney in Australia. Mr. William Grant records ("Ibis," 1867) the capture of a single specimen in Malta, and Mr. C. A. Wright ("Ibis," 1869) also makes mention of another taken in the same island, Nov. 17, 1865. Mr. Wright adds that almost simultaneously with this occurrence a third example of this species was taken in England near Falmouth, Nov. 14, 1865. Two other instances are named by Temminck of its having been noticed in other parts of Europe.

This species is said by Léotaud to visit Trinidad during the months of August, September, and October, after which it departs for the south. But few visit the island, and these are found in the interior meadows, generally singly.

Mr. Dresser met with this species on his journey from Brownsville to San Antonio, Texas, in September, 1863, and states that on quitting the sandy regions and entering into the grass country he found this species — known there as the Grass Plover — quite abundant. It did not go in flocks, but was scattered singly all over the country. He found it shy and difficult to approach, especially when on foot; but by riding or driving near it, he could always get within shot before it took to flight. When undisturbed it ran about very swiftly, catching insects among the grass, often reminding him of the Stone Curlew of Europe (*Œdicnemus crepitans*). When disturbed it would squat close for a time, and then, if approached, it would rise suddenly and fly off, uttering a clear whistle. In New Orleans — where it is known under the name of "Papabot" — it is much sought after by epicures; and Mr. Dresser thinks with good reason, as he never tasted a better bird. In some instances it was so fat as to burst open on falling to the ground. He observed none during the winter; but in April and May, however, he noticed a few near San Antonio, but these were very shy. Dr. J. C. Merrill, who has carefully studied the habits of this Plover in the Rio Grande region of Southwestern Texas, mentions its arrival there about the second or third week in March, when it becomes very abundant on the grassy prairies. It is in poor condition when it arrives in spring, and soon goes farther north; a few linger, however, until May 10. Some reappear in July, and by the first of September have become abundant, but begin to leave about the middle of that month, few being seen after the first week in October. Their stomachs were usually found filled with snails. In Northern Illinois, where this bird is a very common summer resident, Mr. Nelson states that it arrives early in April and departs in September, frequenting the borders of marshes and uncultivated prairies. At first it is difficult of approach, but it becomes entirely reckless during the breeding-season, when it hovers over the heads of intruders. Not being appreciated as game, it is said to be but little hunted in that part of the country. Dr. Cooper mentions having met with this bird at the western base of Mullan's Pass in Montana, but adds that it is not known to occur west of the mountains. He also saw the young of this species on the plains of the Upper Missouri in June. Mr. J. A. Allen noticed it in Colorado in August. Mr. Ridgway informs me that it is quite abundant on all the prairies of Southern Illinois. He also met with it in July on Kamas Prairie in Utah, where a few were seen in the grassy fields. In Southern Wisconsin, Mr. Kumlien informed me, in 1851 this bird, then very common there, was known as the "Prairie Plover" and also as the "Prairie Snipe," and was much more common on the prairies than in the openings, arriving early in April.

Giraud, in his "Birds of Long Island," mentions finding this species very plentiful on the Shinnecock Hills and on Montauk Point — especially at the latter place. In these hilly districts the capture of this bird by the unmounted sportsman is easier than it would be in a level region, as advantage can be taken of the inequalities of the ground to approach within shooting distance. The customary mode of pursuing it, however, is in a vehicle. In this manner it is more readily approached; and by most hunters its pursuit in any other way than by riding is regarded as hopeless. On the Shinnecock Hills and on Hempstead Plains Giraud found this species quite common, and it is there variously known as the "Upland," the "Field," and the "Grass Plover." It was everywhere very wary and difficult of approach. On the ground it has an erect and graceful gait. When alarmed it runs rapidly for a short distance before taking wing, uttering a whistling note as it rises. Its flight is very rapid, and it frequently goes entirely out of sight before it re-alights. It usually keeps on the dry open ground, feeding on grasshoppers, upon other insects, and on seeds. In the month of August it is generally in very fine condition, and is highly prized as game. When feeding, these birds scatter about, all moving off the instant an alarm is given. They migrate southward in the latter part of August, and perform the journey by night. Some stragglers, however, remain behind until late in September.

The Upland Plover is found in favoring localities in various parts of New England, usually in hilly and uninhabited tracts not far from the coast. Occasionally it is met with in more inland regions, as in elevated and barren districts in New Hampshire, and probably also in Maine. I have found it breeding in Rhode Island near Narragansett Bay, and on high grounds near Carlisle, Pa. In the latter place the nest was a mere depression in a ploughed field, with only a few pieces of decayed grass-stems to keep the eggs from the damp soil.

This species seems to have been only imperfectly known to our earlier ornithological writers. Wilson and Nuttall were unacquainted with its eggs, and Audubon saw them for the first time in my cabinet in 1836. Wilson, who was the first to describe it, met with it near the botanical garden of his friend Bartram, on the banks of the Schuylkill. He mentions that, unlike most of its tribe, it seems to prefer running about in the grass, feeding on beetles and other winged insects, there being usually three or four in company. The bird was extremely watchful, silent, and shy, so that it could only with great difficulty be approached. It was occasionally seen during the months of August and September, and is described as running with great rapidity, sometimes spreading its tail and dropping its wings, in the manner of a bird seeking to attract the intruder away from its nest. It remains as if fixed when it alights, stands very erect, and as it mounts to fly utters two or three sharp whistling notes. It was always remarkably plump. It is probable that much of Wilson's information in regard to the habits and breeding of the Field Plover, attributed by him to the Black-bellied Plover, really belonged to the former, and not to the latter, which is a species not known to breed in any portion of the United States.

Audubon characterizes this bird as the most terrestrial of the Wading tribe, hardly belonging to that family in its habits, but always keeping away from water, and never venturing to wade. In the dry upland plains of Opelousas and Attakapas, in Louisiana, he found it abundant in early spring as well as in autumn, passing through there in the beginning of March, and returning again in the fall. It was equally abundant on all the western prairies, on both sides of the Missouri, arriving there a month later than in Louisiana. The general impression that these birds never associate together in considerable numbers he observed to be not wholly correct, and Mr. Salvin also met with them in quite large flocks in the winter. Audubon also observed them arriving in large bands in the spring in the neighborhood of New Orleans, where they generally remained two weeks, a few continuing until the 15th of May. He noticed that, whether they alighted on fences, trees, and out-houses, or on the ground, they always raised both wings upright to their full extent, and uttered a loud, prolonged, and not unpleasant note. When pursued, they will at times lower their heads and run off rapidly, or, partially extending their wings, run a few steps, and then take to flight, or, moving off sideway, conceal themselves in the grass. When winged they escape by running off rapidly and hiding themselves so that they can rarely be found. In Louisiana they feed chiefly on coleopterous insects, and among these often eat cantharides, and are thus rendered unfit for food. In New England they live chiefly on grasshoppers, crickets, and other insects. In the spring migrations they eat wild strawberries, and their flesh thus acquires a delicious flavor. The flight of this bird is swift and well sustained; its migrations are mostly at night.

In South Carolina, according to Dr. Bachman, this Plover appears, moving south, about the 15th of July — the hottest season of the year — resorts to high grass-lands, remaining there about a month. It is seldom met with there in flocks of more than four or five. It is hunted by riding over the fields in a gig, from which the sportsman can shoot the birds as they rise out of the grass; and this can hardly be done in any other way.

The usual call-note of the Upland Plover, when undisturbed, especially during the breeding-season, is a prolonged and peculiarly soft whistle. This is clear and resonant, and to those familiar with it is readily distinguished from any other. The call-notes vary somewhat in their character, and change as the season progresses, and may be heard during the night when the young brood has appeared. These notes change yet more, and become intensified signals of alarm, when the young are threatened by danger. But under any and all circumstances these cries are peculiar to the species, and are unlike those of any of its tribe.

In Pennsylvania the eggs are hatched out early in June; and there, as elsewhere, only a single brood is raised in one season. The nest is always placed in an open situation; but, notwithstanding this circumstance, it is not easily found without the aid of a good dog trained for the purpose. In 1843, in company with my friend Baird, I searched in vain in an open ploughed field for the nest of a pair we knew must be near. Its site was not found until after the young had gone — only a few days after our first search — the empty egg-shells showing where in the open field it was. The female must have kept closely to the nest, even when we were near her, while her mate was doing his best to delude us. The young are singularly beautiful little balls of soft down, a mottling of white, brown, and black. They are cared for by their parents until nearly grown, and from the shell instinctively hide themselves at the approach of danger.

The eggs of this species — always four in number — vary in length from 1.79 to 1.86 inches, and in breadth from 1.35 to 1.44 inches. Their ground-color is usually a deep pinkish drab, and over this are distributed small roundish spottings of a burnt-sienna tint. These are rather sparsely scattered over the smaller end of the egg, but become more densely aggregated about the larger portion. In others the ground-color is more of a cream-colored drab, without any perceptible shading of pink. In a few the ground is a pale pearly-white color, with a faint shading of cream-color. In these the markings are usually blotches of various shades of a purplish slate, much scattered, and overlain by spottings of a deep sepia, which become confluent at the greater end. The shape of the eggs is a slightly rounded oval, strongly tapering at one end and rounded at the other; their number is uniformly four.

Genus TRINGOIDES, Bonaparte.

Tringoides, Bonap. Saggio di una dist. etc. 1831, 58 (type, *Tringa hypoleucos*, Linn.).
Actitis, Boie, Isis, 1822, 560. Not of Illiger, Prodromus, 1811.

Char. Upper mandible grooved to the terminal fourth; the bill tapering and rather acute. Cleft of mouth only moderate; the culmen about five sixths the commissure. Feathers extending rather farther on side of lower jaw than upper, the former reaching as far as the beginning of the nostrils; those of the chin to about their middle. Bill shorter than the head, straight, equal to the tarsus, which is of the length of middle toe and claw. Bare part of tibia half the tarsus. Outer toe webbed to first joint; inner cleft nearly or quite to the base. Tail much rounded, more than half the wing.

T. macularius.

The Common Sandpiper of Europe (*T. hypoleucus*),[1] the only other known species of the genus, greatly resembles the American Spotted Sandpiper (*T. macularius*), but is entirely unspotted beneath, and otherwise different.

Tringoides macularius.

THE SPOTTED SANDPIPER.

Tringa macularia, LINN. S. N. I. 1766, 249 (based on *Tringa maculata*, EDW. II. 139, pl. 277, fig. 2; *Turdus aquaticus*, BRISS. V. 255). — WILSON, Am. Orn. VII. 1813, 60, pl. 59, fig. 1.
Totanus macularius, TEMM. Man. 1815, 422. — NUTT. Man. II. 1834, 162. — AUD. Orn. Biog. IV. 1838, 81, pl. 310; Synop. 1839, 242; B. Am. V. 1842, 303, pl. 342.
Tringoides macularius, GRAY, Gen. B. III. 1849, 574. — CASS. in Baird's B. N. Am. 1858, 735. — BAIRD, Cat. N. Am. B. 1859, no. 543. — COUES, Key, 1872, 260; Check List, 1873, no. 436; 2d ed. 1882, no. 638; Birds N. W. 1874, 501. — RIDGW. Nom. N. Am. B. 1881, no. 557.
"*Tringa notata*, ILLIGER" (GRAY).
Actitis Wiedi, BONAP. (*fide* GRAY).

HAB. The whole of North and Middle America, and South America as far as Brazil; occasional in Europe; no Greenland record. Breeds throughout temperate North America.

SP. CHAR. Small; bill rather longer than the head, straight, slender; long grooves in both mandibles; wing rather long, pointed; tail medium, rounded; legs rather long, lower third of the tibia naked; toes long, margined, and flattened underneath, outer connected with the middle toe by a large membrane, inner very slightly connected to the middle toe. *Adult:* Upper parts greenish ashy, with a somewhat metallic or bronzed lustre, and with numerous sagittate, lanceolate, and irregular, mostly transverse, spots of brownish black, having the same lustre. Line over the eye and entire under parts white, with numerous circular and oval spots of brownish black over the whole lower surface, smaller on the throat, largest on the abdomen. Primaries plain dusky; tail dark ashy, the outer feathers with dusky and white transverse spots on their terminal portion; axillars immaculate white. *Young:* Above, greenish ashy, the wings with narrow transverse bars of black and ochraceous, most numerous on the coverts. Beneath, white, without any spots, and with an ashy suffusion across the jugulum. *Downy chick:* Above, yellowish gray, with a narrow

[1] TRINGOIDES HYPOLEUCUS. The Common Sandpiper of Europe.
Tringa hypoleucos, LINN. S. N. ed. 10, 1758, 149; ed. 12, I. 1766, 250.
Actitis hypoleucus, BOIE, Isis, 1822, 649. — NAUM. Vög. Deutschl. VIII. 1836, 7, pl. 194. — KEYS. & BLAS. Wirb. Eur. p. 73.
Tringoides hypoleuca, GRAY, List Gen. 1841, 88.
Tringa leucoptera, PALL. Zoogr. II. 1831, 196.
Totanus guinetta, LEACH, Syst. Cat. Br. Mus. 30.
Actitis cinclus, BOIE, Isis, 1826, 327.
Actitis stagnalis, BREHM, Vög. Deutschl. 649.
Common Sandpiper, MONT. Orn. Dict.; BEWICK, YARRELL, et AUCT.

black dorsal stripe from the bill to the tail; a narrow black line through the eye. Beneath, dull white.

Total length, about 7.75 inches; extent, 13.00–14.00; wing, 4.05–4.30; culmen, .90–1.00; tarsus, .90–1.05; middle toe, .70–.80. Mandible and edge of the maxilla pale wax-yellow (in life); rest of bill black; iris dark brown; tarsi and toes pale grayish olive.

The Peet-weet, or Spotted Sandpiper, is one of our most common as well as most widely distributed species. It is found throughout nearly all North America, in the interior and on the shores of both the Pacific and the Atlantic Oceans, breeding wherever found, from Texas to Alaska, and from Florida to Fort Anderson. That it is irregular in its occurrence would appear from the fact that Richardson nowhere met with it in the Fur Region, neither in the interior nor on the sea-coast. It is found in Bermuda and in nearly all the West India Islands, breeding in some of them, and is met with in winter in Mexico, Central America, different parts of South America, and is also of accidental occurrence in Europe.

Major Wedderburn writes that he first met with it in the Bermudas, in immature plumage, July 20, 1847, and that he afterward found it common on all the shores of these islands, where some remain all winter, having been met with rather frequently in April, 1849, few of them having their mature plumage; but they are not known to breed there. In Guatemala, according to Salvin, it is to be met with in the winter months about most of the rivers of that region. It is found principally in the immature plumage. Its range is wide, including both the table-lands and the coast country. Mr. C. W. Wyatt ("Ibis," 1871) mentions meeting with this species on the borders of a stream near Ocaña, in Colombia, S. A. It is given by Dr. Gundlach as a bird of Cuba, and is mentioned by Gosse as a common species in Jamaica, where it haunts the margins and shallows of rocky streams. It arrives there about the end of August, and remains until after the middle of April. Professor Newton mentions it as tolerably common in St. Croix, where it probably remains all the winter. According to the observations of Mr. Edward Newton, it is absent from that island from April 27 to July 27. Mr. E. C. Taylor speaks of it as abundant in Trinidad, in suitable localities, where Léotaud also met with it, but confounded it with the Common Sandpiper (*T. hypoleucus*) of Europe. He states that it is both a migrant and a resident in that island, feeding along the sea-shore and near inland pools, keeping generally by itself, but assembling at night to roost in the branches of the mangroves over the water. It is lively and graceful in manners, and when stopping vibrates its head and tail almost continually. Its flight is described as rapid, and it utters a cry as it moves which gives to it the local name of "Picwit." In August the number of these birds is greatly increased by the arrival of new-comers, which again depart in October.

On Long Island Giraud observed it to be the first of its family to arrive in the spring, appearing there the middle of April, and remaining until quite late in autumn, staying until nearly all the other *Tringæ* had departed. It is a very common species, and from its habit of constantly raising and lowering its tail has in that region the local name of "Teeter." It is not known to associate in large flocks, but is quite solitary in its habits, preferring moist grounds in the vicinity of streams and ponds, and often resorting to the ploughed fields to glean the worms which lie exposed in the furrows. This bird begins to build its nest early in May, using for that purpose straw and dry grasses, placing it on the ground, where it is often found, along the banks of small streams and on the margins of ponds, and not infrequently in exposed parts of pastures, among the stubble. The young run about as soon as hatched, and at first utter low whispering notes, which soon increase in strength, and become hardly distinguishable from the full voice of the parents; and they also at a very early period give the peculiar movements of their tail-feathers for which the species is noted. The flight of this bird is very uneven, being seldom for any considerable distance in a straight line. In the love season it often performs aerial gambols just above the surface of the ground. When wounded it will take to the water and swim beneath the surface with considerable swiftness. In the spring it takes possession, in pairs, of the muddy margins of watercourses, making excursions from thence into the adjoining fields. It is exclusive in habit, never seeking the society of other species.

Mr. J. A. Allen found this species quite common in Eastern Kansas in the early part of May. He afterward noticed it more or less frequently along the streams of Western Kansas, near Fort Hays, and in Colorado he traced it up to the very source of the South Platte, on Mount Lincoln. He also met with it occasionally in the Valley of Great Salt Lake. Dresser obtained in August a single immature specimen near Matamoras, and in September and October found the species abundant near San Antonio. Mr. Ridgway states that, next to the Kildeer, he found this bird the most abundant and generally distributed Wader in the Great Basin. He saw it breeding from an altitude of four thousand feet or less to above seven thousand. At Carson City it arrives about the 29th of April.

Although not met with by Sir John Richardson, this bird has a high northern range, reaching almost to the borders of the Arctic Ocean. Bernard Ross found it abundant along the banks of the Mackenzie; Kennicott mentions it as breeding near Fort Resolution; and in each instance the nests are described as having been mere depressions in the ground, with a few bits of grass or a few dry leaves placed therein. Mr. Dall obtained a few specimens at Nulato from the 16th to the 30th of May; Mr. Bannister found it common on the Island of St. Michael's in the fall; and it was taken by Bischoff at Sitka. Mr. MacFarlane found it breeding and quite common in the neighborhood of Fort Anderson. It is abundant along the Anderson River, and also on the Mackenzie from Fort Good Hope to Fort Simpson. The nests are all spoken of as being mere depressions, scantily lined with leaves and grass; they contained eggs in the latter part of June. Mr. Audubon found it breeding in Labrador on the 17th of June, and by the 29th of July the young were fully fledged.

In favorable seasons the Peet-Weet appears in Massachusetts during the last week in April, and in some seasons nearly a fortnight later. It comes at first in small roving flocks, and for a while moves about in a brief and even sportive manner, flying back and forth along and across the smaller streams, performing strange aerial evolutions, seemingly more for its own enjoyment than in quest of food. As these birds move about — and more especially when they meet other small flocks of their own species — they give utterance to their cheerful and lively whistle, which is loud and shrill, and not unlike the syllables *peet-weet* several times repeated. Toward the close of the refrain the notes are lower and the sound more plaintive. A little later in the season they separate into pairs along the banks of smaller streams, and usually nest in fresh-water meadows or in low uplands not far from water; occasionally they nest on uplands not far from the sea. Sometimes this bird is so familiar as to make its nest within a garden, and not far from the house. In one instance Mr. Nuttall found its eggs in the strawberry beds of a resident of Belmont, Mass., while young and old familiarly fed on the margin of an adjoining duck-pond.

This species has a very characteristic habit of vibrating its tail and moving its head and body, as if balancing itself, the head and tail being alternately depressed and elevated. When excited, and anxious for the safety of its young, this vibratory motion is especially noticeable, and is joined with plaintive cries of *peet-weet-weet.*

The nests of this bird vary in their position and construction. So far as I have noted them, they have been in some small depression in the ground, often sheltered by being placed near a small bush or in a tuft of grass. They are, for the most part, built in the dry open field, never very far from water. Usually they are of very simple structure, being made of dry bent, and answering the purpose of protecting the eggs from the damp ground, but rarely so well interwoven as to bear removal. Mr. Audubon states that the nests of this bird found by him on an island in the Gulf of St. Lawrence were much more bulky, and more neatly constructed, than any seen by him farther south, yet not to be compared with those he had seen in Labrador, where they were concealed under ledges of rocks, and were made of dry moss, raised to the height of several inches, and well finished within with slender grasses and feathers of the Eider Duck. The time of nesting varies three months from Texas to Labrador. On Buffalo Bayou in Texas Audubon found full-grown broods on the 5th of May. In Newfoundland they were only just fledged on the 11th of August.

The young run about with remarkable ease and swiftness almost as soon as they are out of their shell. When danger approaches they immediately, upon an alarm-signal from their parents, run and hide themselves, squatting close to the ground, and there remaining perfectly immovable, resembling a small drab-colored stone with a single streak of black down the middle. If the young bird finds itself discovered, and an attempt is made to take it, it runs with great celerity, uttering the most plaintive cries, and at the same time the parents exhibit symptoms of distress and counterfeit lameness with great skill.

Mr. Bartram informed Wilson that he saw one of these birds defend her young for a considerable time from the attacks of a ground-squirrel. The mother threw herself, with her two young behind her, between them and the land, and at every attempt of the squirrel to seize them raised both her wings in an almost perpendicular position, assuming the most formidable appearance she could, and rushing forward on the squirrel endeavored to drive it back. The young crowded together close behind her, sensible of their perilous situation, moving backward or forward as she advanced or retreated. This lasted some ten minutes, and would have terminated disastrously for the young birds, had not Mr. Bartram interposed for their rescue.

Mr. MacCullock, of Pictou, informed Audubon that having once found the nest of this Sandpiper, and proposing to take it on his return, he marked the place by putting a number of stones in a slanting position over the nest, and so close that it was impossible for the bird to get into it. On his return in the evening, he observed the bird rise from beside the stones in great trepidation, and more than ever anxious to draw him away. On examining the spot, he ascertained that the bird had not only hollowed out a new nest, but had succeeded in abstracting two eggs from the other nest. How she had contrived to remove the eggs he could not conceive, as the stones remained undisturbed.

Audubon states that he has observed this species alight on the branches of trees hanging over watercourses, walking on them deliberately, with their usual elegance of gait and balancing of body and tail. They are also wont to alight on the rails and stakes of fences or walls, and on the tops of haystacks.

The eggs are always four in number, and are of a rounded pyriform shape, varying in length from 1.21 inches to 1.35, and in breadth from .95 to 1.00 inch. Their ground-color varies from a light drab to a dark cream, sometimes tinged with rufous, and occasionally with a muddy clay-color. The markings in some are fine dottings, and in others large and confluent blotches about the larger end. The color of the markings is a rich sepia-brown, with a slight purplish tinge.

Genus **TRYNGITES**, Cabanis.

Tringites, Cab. Journ. für Orn. 1856, 418 (type, *Tringa rufescens*, Vieill.).

Char. Upper mandible grooved to about the terminal fourth ; the lower not quite so far. Culmen and gonys about straight. Mouth deeply cleft more than half way to the eye ; the culmen about two thirds the commissure. Culmen much shorter than the head, and about equal to middle toe without claw. Tarsus about one and one sixth as long as middle toe and claw. Bare part of

T. rufescens.

tibia decidedly shorter than middle toe without claw. Toes cleft to the base, with only a very rudimentary web. Upper jaw feathered to the nostrils ; the side of the lower and beneath feathered much farther, or to the end of the nostrils ; the interspace of the rami entirely filled. Tail somewhat graduated, not half the wing.

Tryngites rufescens.

THE BUFF-BREASTED SANDPIPER.

Tringa rufescens, Vieill. Nouv. Dict. XXXIV. 1819, 470 (Louisiana). — Nutt. Man. II. 1834, 113. — Aud. Orn. Biog. III. 1835, 451, pl. 265 ; Synop. 1839, 235 ; B. Am. V. 1842, 264, pl. 331.

Tryngites rufescens, Caban. J. f. O. 1856, 418 (Cuba). — Cassin, in Baird's B. N. Am. 1858, 739. — Baird, Cat. N. Am. B. 1859, no. 546. — Coues, Key, 1872, 260 ; Check List, 1873, no. 439 ; 2d ed. 1882, no. 641 ; Birds N. W. 1874, 506. — Ridgw. Nom. N. Am. B. 1881, no. 556.

" *Tringa subruficollis*, Vieill." (Gray and Schleg.).

" *Tringa brevirostris*, Lichtenstein" (Gray and Schleg.).

Actidurus nævius, Heerm. Pr. Ac. Nat. Sci. Philad. VII. 1854, 179 ; Pacific R. R. Rep. X. pt. VI. 1859, 20, pl. 6 (Texas).

Hab. North America in general, especially the interior ; breeding chiefly in the interior of British America and the Yukon district ; migrating south to Peru and Uruguay. Frequent in Europe. No West Indian record, except Cuba.

Sp. Char. Bill shorter than the head, straight, compressed, narrow at the point ; nasal groove long ; wings very long, the first quill longest ; tertiaries rather shorter ; tail moderate or longer than usual in this group ; legs rather long, lower third of the tibia naked ; toes free at base, flattened underneath, and slightly margined ; hind toe small. Upper parts pale and dull ochraceous, with an ashy tinge ; every feather with a large central, lanceolate, crescent-shaped, or oblong spot of black, frequently with a glossy green tinge, especially on the back and shorter tertiaries.

Under parts light ochraceous or pale fawn-color, many feathers tipped with white, and paler on the flanks and abdomen, on the breast with partially concealed small spots of black; axillary feathers white. Quills with their outer webs light brown, inner webs ashy white marbled with black and narrowly tipped with white; middle tail-feathers brownish black; outer feathers lighter, with transverse waved lines of black on the terminal half, and tipped with white; under primary-coverts beautifully marbled with black. Bill greenish black; legs greenish yellow. *Young:* Generally

similar, but the upper parts with the black and fawn-color less sharply contrasted, and each feather with a conspicuous terminal border of white. Marbling on inner webs of primaries and on under primary-coverts much more minute and delicate than in the adult. "Bill dull olive-green, dusky toward the point; iris hazel; feet dull yellowish green, claws dusky" (AUDUBON).

Total length, about 7.50 to 8.00 inches; wing, 5.10–5.50; culmen, .75–.80; tarsus, 1.15–1.30; middle toe, .75–.85.

This is a little bird of rather peculiar form and of handsome plumage. Its relationship appears to be to Bartram's Tattler. Both species more habitually frequent plains and other dry localities than any of the true Sandpipers.

Dr. Heermann's type specimen of his *Actidurus nævius* represents the usual adult plumage.

The Buff-breasted Sandpiper is found nearly or quite throughout North America, and its occurrence is not uncommon in the northern and middle portions of South America. It is found both on the Pacific and the Atlantic coasts, is migratory in all parts of the United States, breeds in high Arctic latitudes, and is of occasional appearance in Europe. Its presence on the Atlantic coast, however, is regarded as an infrequent event; but Mr. Boardman mentions it as having been found near Calais, both in the spring and in the fall. It has also been taken at Rye Beach by Mr. Brewster, and in Boston Harbor by Mr. Henshaw; and about the 20th of August a few are usually to be seen in the Boston market.

Mr. Giraud did not consider that it was a common bird on Long Island, although during almost every season a few are noticed along its southern shore. In September this bird is occasionally seen exposed for sale in the markets of New York, together with the Pectoral Sandpiper, from which, however, the Buff-breasted is easily distinguished by the comparative shortness of its bill.

Mr. Giraud also states that in August, 1841, his friend Mr. Brasher observed five of this species together on the shore of Gowanus Bay — a number much larger than is usually seen in one group. They appeared to be very gentle, allowing him to advance within shooting distance without seeming to notice his presence, and three were killed at the first discharge of his gun. The surviving two made a short flight over the water, returning in a few minutes to the shore at a short distance from the point at which they had previously taken wing, thus giving him an opportunity to secure the whole number. When flying from the observer, this bird appears not unlike the Pectoral Sandpiper, on account of the resemblance of the upper plumage of the two species.

Mr. Dresser met with this bird near Matamoras late in August. Visiting the lagoon early one morning, he noticed a flock of Sandpipers near him, on a little grassy place a short distance from the water, and on shooting some of them, found them to be of this species; the next day, on visiting the same place, he was able to procure others. In travelling thence to San Antonio, in September, he found these birds rather common throughout the whole journey; and he often shot them, finding them excellent eating. They were not shy, and went in flocks of from five to twelve in number. They did not resort to the pools, but lived on the small insects found amongst the coarse herbage which often grows some distance from the water. Near Victoria they were very abundant, but after leaving that town he noticed only a few. At San Antonio he saw none, but was informed by Dr. Heermann that they are often found there in the spring and autumn. Dr. Merrill also found this species on the Rio Grande, and mentions its frequenting the same localities and observing the same seasons as the Upland Plover, which it closely resembles in habits, though it is much less shy and suspicious.

This species has not been detected in California, but Dr. Cooper is confident that it occurs there, at least as far south as San Francisco. It is found sparingly north of the Columbia. According to Dr. Heermann, on the interior prairies this species feeds on insects, and utters merely a low *tweet*, two or three times repeated. It runs swiftly and, if alarmed, flies rapidly, making circuitous sweeps before alighting again. This author claims to have found its nest in Texas, made of grasses, placed in a hollow in the ground, and containing four eggs. But as this bird breeds in high northern regions, up to the very borders of the Arctic Ocean, he may have been mistaken in his identification.

It occurs in Cuba, according to Gundlach, as a winter visitant, and probably in other West India islands. It visits Trinidad, where, as Léotaud states, it is known as the Little Yellowleg, and where it makes its appearance in August, departing in October. It comes regularly, but never in great numbers, and it is almost always in company with the *Totanus flavipes*.

During the winter months it appears to be resident in South America as far south as the Plata, where it was procured by Dr. Darwin. Mr. Salvin received an example from Bogota, and Natterer obtained examples in various parts of Brazil between November and March. It is also reported from Peru by Messrs. Salvin and Godman.

It is not of infrequent, although of irregular and accidental, occurrence in Europe. Professor Blasius includes it in his List of the Birds of Heligoland; and Mr. Yarrell records quite a number of instances in which it has been taken in England and Ireland, where it was noticed among flocks of Dunlins and Ring Plovers. Vieillot includes it among the birds of France, on account of one having been taken in Picardy. It was first made known as a species by Vieillot, from a specimen taken in Louisiana, where it had not been noticed by Audubon. It was unknown both to Wilson and to Bonaparte; and the first specimen seen by Audubon was one in possession of the Arctic explorer, Captain James Clark Ross, who had received it from a sailor, by whom it had been procured in the course of one of the numerous inland excursions in the desolate regions from which the party had recently returned. From this Mr. Audubon rightly conjectured that this bird bred within the Arctic Circle. Mr. Bernard Ross mentions having found it on the Mackenzie River, where it was quite rare. A single specimen was noticed by Mr. Frank L. Tileston in Prince Edward's Island, where it was regarded as very uncommon.

Mr. Nelson, in his "Notes on the Birds of Northeastern Illinois," mentions it as a very rare migrant in that region, only one specimen, so far as known, having been taken; this was near Chicago, Sept. 4, 1873. Dr. Hoy speaks of it as common near Racine from September 15 to October 10; but this statement Mr. Nelson seems disposed to question.

Mr. Dall mentions that two specimens of this Sandpiper were obtained on the Yukon, below Nulato, where it was not common. One was obtained at Sitka by Bischoff.

It breeds abundantly in the Anderson River region, where a number of its nests and eggs were found by Mr. MacFarlane; and from his memoranda in reference to the nests and eggs of this species in upward of twenty instances, we gather that the nest is always on the ground, and hardly distinguishable from that of the Golden Plover, being a mere depression in the soil, scantily lined with a few withered leaves and dried grasses. These nests were all obtained on the Barren Grounds between Horton's River and the coast, between the 26th of June and the 9th of July. The eggs in every instance were four in number. Even in July the embryos were not far advanced. When the nest was approached, the female usually made a short low flight to a distance of about twelve yards.

The eggs of this species are conspicuously pyriform in shape, and measure 1.51 inches in length by 1.10 in the greatest breadth. So far as I have noticed them, however much they may vary in certain minor respects, they all present a remarkable uniformity in their general characteristics and appearance. Their ground-color is uniformly an ashy drab, over which are profusely spread rounded markings, splashes, and confluent blotches of deep sepia. The markings are smaller and more rounded in shape around the smaller end, and larger and more confluent about the other. The sepia tint is quite uniform, and the deeper markings are mingled with washes of dilute purplish slate. These markings vary in their shape, size, and character, being in some large splashes, and in others longitudinal, as if made by strokes of a paint-brush. The eggs described are in my own cabinet, and were taken by MacFarlane on the Arctic coast east of Anderson River (No. 1893).

Genus **EURYNORHYNCHUS**, Nilsson.

Eurynorhynchus,[1] Nilss. Orn. Suec. II. 1821, 29 (type, *Platalea pygmæa*, Linn.).

Eurynorhynchus pygmæus.

THE SPOON-BILLED SANDPIPER.

Platalea pygmæa, Linn. S. N. ed. 10, I. 1758, 140; ed. 12, I. 1766, 231 ("Surinam"). — Gmel. S. N. I. 1788, 615 (quotes "Mus. Ad. Fr. 26. Bancr. Guj. 171. *Dwarf Spoonbill*, Lath. Syn. IV. i. p. 17, n. 3").

Eurynorhynchus pygmæus, Pearson, Jour. As. Soc. Beng. V. 1836, 127. — Harting, Ibis, 1869, 427, pl. 12 (critical, with full synonymy; Choris Peninsula, Alaska); P. Z. S. 1879, 111, 114 (same loc.). — Coues, Check List, 2d ed. 1882, 136, no. 884.

Eurinorhynchus pygmæus, Gray, Hand-l. III. 1871, 51. — Ridgw. Nom. N. Am. B. 1881, 85, no. 542 (Point Barrow, Alaska). — Bean, Proc. U. S. Nat. Mus. V. 1882, 165 (Plover Bay, Siberia).

Eurynorhynchus griseus, "Nilss." Temm. Man. ed. 2, II. 1820, 594.

Eurynorhynchus orientalis, Blyth, Ann. Mag. N. H. XIII. 1844, 178, 179.

[1] This name has been variously spelled *Eurinorhynchus, Eurinoryncus, Eurinorinchus, Eurhinorhynchus, Eurinorincus*, etc., but the form given above is the true orthography. See "The Ibis," 1869, p. 427 (footnote).

HAB. In summer, Eastern Siberia, especially along Arctic coast; accidental on shores of Alaska north of Behring's Straits; in winter, "mouths of the Ganges and east coast of Bay of Bengal," and other portions of Southeastern Asia (HARTING).

SP. CHAR. "*Description* (*adult in winter*): Bill black, longer than the head, flat, dilated considerably at the extremity in a rhomboidal shape. Tongue broad and smooth. Forehead, cheeks, throat, and under parts pure white; crown, nape and sides of neck, back, wings, and upper tail-coverts dusky brown, each feather margined more or less with pale gray. Wings long and pointed; shafts of the primaries white; first quill-feather the longest. Tail short, rounded, consisting of twelve feathers, the two middle feathers the longest and darkest in color. Legs and toes black, moderately long, slender, three toes in front, one behind, margined along the sides; a slight membrane connecting the base of the middle and outer toe on each foot. Total length 6.00 inches; bill, 1.00; wing, from carpus, 3.70; tarsus, .90. (Exempl. typ. in Mus. Upsal. *fide auctt. citt.*).

"*Adult in summer* (hitherto undescribed): Bill as above. Head, neck, breast, and back ferruginous; the feathers of the head, nape, and back with dark-brown centres; those of the throat and breast slightly margined with white. Under parts, from the breast downward, becoming gradually whiter toward the tail. Primaries somewhat darker than in winter. Legs and toes black. (Exempl. in Mus. Acad. Oxon.)." — HARTING, "Ibis," 1869, p. 428.

Young (No. 81434, U. S. Nat. Mus. Port Providence, Plover Bay, Siberia; August; Drs. DALL & BEAN): Scapulars and interscapulars black centrally, brownish gray beneath the surface, and broadly bordered terminally with soiled whitish, the anterior feathers, however, both of scapulars and interscapulars margined with rusty; wing brownish gray, the feathers darker centrally, with shafts quite dusky; greater coverts tipped with white, forming a distinct bar across the wing; remiges dusky, the basal portion of secondaries and inner primaries white; pileum dull light grayish, spotted with dull black, the feathers edged with dull rusty; remainder of head, neck, and lower parts soiled white, clouded anteriorly with light grayish brown, but nearly pure white and quite immaculate posteriorly. Bill black; legs and feet blackish brown. Wing, 3.35; culmen, .80; greatest breadth of maxilla, .45; tarsus, .80; middle toe, .60.

The habits and geographical distribution of this very remarkable form are very far from being well understood, though the regions it visits during the breeding-season and in its migrations are a little better known. It was first referred to by Linnæus as having some supposed resemblance to the Spoonbill, and for nearly a century was only known from a unique example in the Museum of Upsala, which was said to have been procured from Surinam; but this was evidently an error. It has since been referred to by Bancroft as a bird of Guiana; but he either followed Linnæus or mistook for it some other species. Lesson gave as its habitat the Arctic Region of both continents, but also stated that an example, shot near Paris, was in one of the museums of that city; and Bonaparte gave it, in his "Geographical List," as a European species. Neither of these statements is now credited, inasmuch as there is no evidence that any example of this species has been taken in Europe.

Professor A. Newton, in an exhaustive paper ("Ibis," 1869, pp. 428–434), assigns to it a place among the Waders, between *Ereunetes petrificatus* and *Tringa subarquata*, and he has with great pains prepared a list of all the examples of the Spoon-billed Sandpiper known to have been taken. The locality of the type-example remains undiscovered. The known localities are Edmondstone's Island, Saugur Sand, 1836; Arracan, in the same year; Calcutta, 1840; mouth of the Ganges, 1840; Amherst in Tenasserim, 1846; three taken in 1856 and twelve in 1859, in Chittagong; and one, the only example known to have been secured in summer plumage, from Behring's Straits. The last-named was taken by the expedition under Captain Moore, and is now in the new Museum of Oxford. Its supposed presence on both shores of Behring's Straits in the breeding-season is the occasion of its being placed in the North American fauna, though Captain Moore's example is given as having come from the northeast corner of Asia (Proc. Zool. Soc. 1859, p. 201).

The Spoon-billed Sandpiper is said to frequent the mud-flats at the mouths of rivers and the sands of the sea-shore, where, in company with various species of *Tringæ*, it procures from the surface of the water an abundant harvest of such food as is always left by a receding tide. Of its nidification nothing is as yet known.

GENUS **NUMENIUS**, BRISSON.

Numenius, BRISS. Orn. V. 1760, 311 (type, *Scolopax arquata*, LINN.).

CHAR. Legs covered anteriorly with transverse scutellæ, laterally and behind with small hexagonal scales. Bill very long, exceeding the tibia, and curved downward for the terminal half; the culmen rounded. Tip of bill expanded laterally and club-shaped. Grooves of bill not reaching beyond the middle. Tertials as long as primaries.

Bill variable in length, always longer than tarsus, sometimes exceeding tarsus and toes. It is nearly straight at the base, then decurving quite rapidly to the tip, where the upper mandible is thickened downward beyond and over the lower. Lateral grooves occupying only the basal half or third of the bill; under mandible not grooved beneath. Cleft of mouth extending but little

N. longirostris.

beyond the base of culmen. Feathers of head extending about the same distance on both mandibles; those of chin to opposite the anterior extremity of the nostrils. Tarsi nearly twice as long as middle toe, rather more than twice the bare part of tibia; covered behind by hexagonal scales larger than the lateral ones. Outer toe webbed for its basal joint; inner for half this distance Tail short, nearly even, not quite half the wings. Tertials as long as the primaries.

Of the genus *Numenius* several species are found in North America, none of them occurring regularly in the Old World, as is the case with so many of the *Tringeæ*.

American Species.

A. Thighs not bristled.

a. *Rump not white.*

1. **N. longirostris.** Wing, 10.00–12.00; culmen, 3.80–8.50; tarsus, 2.25–3.50; middle toe, 1.30–1.55. Lower parts pale cinnamon; axillars deep cinnamon, without distinct bars; crown uniformly streaked, without median stripe. *Hab.* Temperate North America, south to Guatemala, Cuba, Jamaica, and Brazil (?).

2. **N. Hudsonicus.** Wing, 9.00–10.25; culmen, 3.00–4.00; tarsus, 2.25–2.30; middle toe, 1.35–1.40. Lower parts pale buff, the breast marked with linear streaks; inner webs of primaries spotted with buff toward edges; axillars deeper buff, distinctly barred with dusky; crown uniform dusky, divided by a median stripe of pale buff. *Hab.* The whole of America, including West Indies, but breeding only in the colder regions; Greenland.

3. **N. borealis.** Wing, 8.00–8.50; culmen, 2.25–2.50; tarsus, 1.70–1.80; middle toe, 1.00. Very similar to *Hudsonicus*, but breast with V-shaped dusky markings, axillars pale cinnamon, barred with dusky, inner webs of primaries uniform dusky, the whole crown streaked, and without distinct median stripe. *Hab.* Northern and Eastern North America, and Southern South America; no West Indian record; Greenland; occasional in Europe.

b. Rump immaculate white.

4. **N. phæopus.** Wing, 9.30–10.50; culmen, 3.00–3.60; tarsus, 2.30–2.50; middle toe, 1.40. Similar to *Hudsonicus*, but whole rump immaculate white, and axillars white, barred with grayish brown. *Hab.* Palæarctic, African, and Indo-Malayan regions; Greenland.

B. Thighs with elongated bristles, projecting far beyond the feathers.

5. **N. tahitiensis.** Wing, 9.50–10.40; culmen, 2.70–3.70; tarsus, 2.00–2.40; middle toe, 1.35–1.50. Upper tail-coverts and tail ochraceous, the latter regularly barred with dusky brown; crown dark brown, divided longitudinally by a wide medial stripe of buff; axillars pale cinnamon or pinkish buff, widely barred with dark brown. *Hab.* Pacific Islands and coast of Alaska.

Numenius longirostris.

THE LONG-BILLED CURLEW.

Scolopax arquata, var. β, GMEL. S. N. I. 1788, 656.

Numenius arquata, var. B. LATH. Ind. Orn. II. 1790, 710.

Numenius longirostris, WILS. Am. Orn. VIII. 1814, 24, pl. 64, fig. 4. — SW. & RICH. F. B. A. II. 1831, 376. — NUTT. Man. II. 1834, 94. — AUD. Orn. Biog. III. 1835, 240; V. 1839, 587, pl. 231; Synop. 1839, 254; B. Am. VI. 1843, 35, pl. 355. — CASS. in Baird's B. N. Am. 1858, 743. — BAIRD, Cat. N. Am. B. 1859, no. 549. — COUES, Key, 1872, 262; Check List, 1873, no. 441; 2d ed. 1882, no. 643; Birds N. W. 1874, 508. — RIDGW. Nom. N. Am. B. 1881, no. 558.

Numenius rufus, VIEILL. Gal. Ois. II. 1825, 118, pl. 245 (part).

Numenius occidentalis, WOODH. Pr. Ac. Nat. Sci. Philad. VI. 1852, 194; Sitgreaves' Rep. 1853, 98, pl. 6 (=young; Albuquerque, N. M.).

"? *Numenius melanopus*, VIEILL."

"? *Numenius brasiliensis*, MAX."

Young.

HAB. Temperate North America, migrating south to Guatemala. Cuba; Jamaica; Brazil (?).

SP. CHAR. The largest American species of this genus. Bill very long, much curved, upper mandible longer than the under, somewhat knobbed at the tip, wing rather long; legs moderate; toes united at base. Entire upper parts pale rufous, tinged with ashy, every feather with transverse and confluent bands of brownish black, most numerous and predominating on the back and scapulars; secondary quills, under wing-coverts, and axillaries, bright rufous; primaries with their outer webs brownish black and their inner webs rufous, with transverse bands of black. Under parts pale rufous, with longitudinal lines of black on the neck and sides; tail rufous, tinged with ashy, transversely barred with brownish black. Specimens vary to some extent in the shade of the rufous color of the plumage, and very much in the length of the bill. The rufous color is probably more distinct in the young. Total length about 25.00 inches; extent, about 40.00; wing, 10.00–11.00; tail, 4.00; bill, 2.30 (immature individual) to 8.50; tarsus, 2.25. Bill black, becoming dull light lilac-brown on basal half of the mandible; iris brown; legs and feet gray.

Downy young: Very pale ochraceous, with a tinge of sulphur-yellow, rather deeper below than above. Upper parts marbled coarsely and rather irregularly with black. Bill straight, about 1.40 inches long.

The Long-billed Curlew has a general but irregular distribution over North America, from the Gulf of Mexico to Canada, and from the Pacific to the Atlantic. In the Eastern States, though occasionally seen in considerable numbers, it is of uncertain and irregular appearance. It is common on the prairies of the Western States, and is more abundant on the Pacific than on the Atlantic coast. It is not known with certainty ever to visit the Fur Region, nor has it been met with in Alaska, or on the Pacific coast north of Vancouver Island, in which latter place its presence is recorded by Mr. R. Browne.

Dr. Cooper mentions finding the young of this species, common on the Plains of the Upper Missouri, in June. The same writer states that it abounds in California during the cooler months; and as it is to be found in that State in small numbers during May and June, while the young make their appearance in July at San Pedro, he considers it probable that some breed about the lakes in the interior, especially in the northeastern portions of California, where, indeed, this species was noticed by Dr. Newberry in summer. It seems, however, probable that it migrates directly south from its summer resorts to San Pedro, as it is rarely seen at San Francisco before September; after which, however, it remains throughout the winter. Columbia River is about the limit of its northern range along the coast, and it is not common there. In California, as also elsewhere, it frequents dry plains and pastures quite as much as it does the marshes, and flocks may be found throughout the valleys during the winter. It feeds quite as much on grasshoppers and other insects as on worms and small crabs. It is very shy and watchful, especially on the dry and open plains, where artifice is usually necessary to obtain it, and it can often be allured within gunshot by an imitation of its cries, which are usually whistling notes, loud and variable in character. In California this bird is regarded as excellent eating.

Dr. Pickering mentions finding it in Oregon in June, 1841, where large numbers had taken up their residence in the grassy flats and plains, and were undoubtedly breeding. He describes its note as being a sort of whistle, not unlike the word *curlew*, with the last syllable much prolonged, and uttered more quickly, and in a more complaining tone when the bird is flying overhead. In one instance he noticed this bird alighting in the top of a tree during a rain, and frequently repeating its note. Once he saw it attack and chase a Hawk, which retreated quite precipitately. In its habits and general appearance it reminded him of the Cayenne Lapwing as seen in South America; subsequently, in the month of October, Dr. Pickering also met with it in large numbers in California.

Captain Bendire, in his "Notes on the Birds of Eastern Oregon," mentions this species as a common summer resident, breeding abundantly. It often nests in wet and partly flooded meadows. In the spring of 1876 he found three sets partly covered with water. Near Fort Lapwai this bird breeds on high and dry prairies several miles from lake or river. It also breeds in Southern Arizona near Sulphur Springs, thirty miles west of Camp Bowie. The eggs are said to vary greatly in shape, size, and coloration, even in the same nest, averaging 2.60 by 1.74 inches. These birds congregate in large flocks before migrating, and have all left by the 1st of August. They feed chiefly on crickets.

Lieutenant M'Cauley refers to this species as being generally distributed over Kansas, the Indian Territory, and the Red River Region of Texas. He found it breeding in June, and very clamorous when the nests were approached.

Mr. Ridgway also met with Curlews which he had no doubt were of this species, during the spring and summer, along the Truckee River. In the neighborhood of Great Salt Lake they were also more or less abundant during the summer, in all the wet and grassy places. Several young just hatched were caught near the camp on Antelope Island. Mr. J. A. Allen met with a single small colony of these birds in the western portion of Kansas, near Fort Hays. This was late in May, and the birds were evidently breeding.

Mr. Salvin met with occasional specimens about the lagoons of Chiapam, on the Pacific coast. It was usually in company with, but not so numerous as, the *Numenius Hudsonicus.* He also obtained a single specimen at Dueñas, in the interior. On the Atlantic coast it is of comparatively rare occurrence. Mr. Boardman informs me that occasional examples have been taken on the St. Croix River, as far up as Calais; and, as it is not uncommon on Prince Edward's Island, it quite possibly may be met with on the sea-coast of Nova Scotia. It is seen about Calais, but only near the close of summer, in the month of August. At the same season examples have been taken on the Massachusetts coast; and — so far as I am aware — at no other time.

Mr. Boardman has been informed, on good authority, that this bird breeds regularly in considerable numbers on Prince Edward's Island; and this fact accounts for its occasional appearance on the New England coast.

Giraud includes the Long-billed Curlew among the birds of Long Island, where it is occasionally found frequenting the muddy shores of the beaches and marshes, collecting minute shellfish, which, with worms and various insects, constitute its food. When moving about in flocks it is said to fly much after the manner of the Wild Goose, its leader uttering a peculiarly hoarse dull note, which may be easily and effectively imitated, as this bird is proverbial for answering the fowler's call when at a greater distance from his decoy than any other shore-bird. When approaching, and near to the decoys, it spreads its wings and sails slowly up, presenting a fair mark. Its flesh is said to be rank, and the young partake of the same flavor; but this is probably true only of those which feed on the salt-marshes. The birds which are found in the interior, feeding on grasshoppers and berries, are regarded as a great delicacy. This Curlew is noted for its great sympathy with those of its own kind, flocks being often kept within gunshot by the cries of their wounded companions.

Richardson supposed he had good reason for believing that this species frequents the Saskatchewan Plains and the banks of the Columbia. There is said to be a specimen of this Curlew in the Museum of the Hudson's Bay Company; but the locality from which it was procured is not known.

The Long-billed Curlew in its general appearance, and probably also in nearly all its specific habits, bears a very close resemblance to the Common Curlew, *N. arquata,* of Europe; and before Wilson pointed out the difference between them, the two were confounded together. According to Wilson, this Curlew appears in the salt-marshes of New Jersey about the middle of May, and again in September. He inferred — probably incorrectly — that these birds necessarily went north to breed. Their food seemed to consist chiefly of small crabs, for which they very dexterously probe, pulling them out of the holes with their long bills. They also feed on the small sea-snails, so common in the salt-marshes, and on various worms and insects. In the fall they are said to be very fond of the berries of the wild brambles, on which they feed with eagerness, becoming very fat, and are then excellent eating, not having the rank sedgy flavor acquired by those birds which feed exclusively in the marshes. Wilson states that in some cases one or two pairs have been known to remain in the salt-marshes at Cape May all through the summer.

In Major Long's expedition some of this species were observed in the northern part of Illinois (lat. 42° N.), June 15, from which it was naturally inferred that they were breeding there. It is now known that they probably breed in all, or nearly all, the Western States north of the Ohio and west of Lake Erie.

Nuttall observed them on the muddy shores of the Santee, near Charleston, S. C., in January. Audubon afterward ascertained that this Curlew is a constant resident in the Southern States, that it is well known both in summer and winter about Charleston, and that it breeds on the islands on the coast of South Carolina; but he met with none of this species in Labrador or in any place from Eastport to the most northern portion visited by him, and he satisfied himself, from his inquiries among well-informed residents, that none are ever found there.

The Rev. Dr. Bachman found it breeding in South Carolina, where it nested on the ground, forming a very scanty receptacle for its eggs, and placing the nests so closely together that it was almost impossible for a man to walk between them without injuring the eggs.

In South Carolina Audubon observed that this species spent the day in the sea-marshes and returned at the approach of night to the sandy beaches of the sea-shore, where it rested until the morning. He states that the number of these birds that would thus collect for the night sometimes amounted to several thousands. He visited Cole's Island, near Charleston, in order to witness its movements. Just after sunset the birds began to make their appearance, in parties of from three to five, and were by no means shy. As it became darker the number of Curlews increased and the flocks approached in more rapid succession, until they seemed to form a continuous procession, moving in an extended mass at the height of not more than thirty yards, not a sound being heard except the regular flappings of their wings. They flew directly toward their resting place — known as the Bird Banks — and alighted without performing any evolutions. But when the party followed them to these banks — which were small sandy islands — the congregated flocks, amounting to several thousand individuals, all standing close together, rose at once, performed in silence a few evolutions, and re-alighted, as if with one accord, on the extreme margin of the sandbank, close to the breakers. The next morning a little before daylight the party again visited the banks; but as soon as they landed the birds all rose a few yards in the air, and flew off in various directions to their feeding-grounds.

Mr. Moore has met this species in Florida during the summer months, but was not able to obtain any evidence that it breeds there, although regarding it as quite probable that this is the case on the more distant islands along the coast of that State.

The eggs of this species, — which vary considerably in their ground-color and in the distribution of their markings — are pyriform, or a rounded oval pointed at one end. In one (S. I. No. 2910) the ground-color is a pale olive-drab, the markings being very uniformly distributed over the whole surface, and consisting of rather small blotches, longitudinal in direction, and of a burnt-umber tint. In others (S. I. No. 5117) the ground-color is a pearly white, with a shading of cream, covered with large blotches of an ashy lilac, these being overlain by smaller and deeper spots of burnt-umber. These eggs vary from 2.70 to 2.90 inches in length, and from 1.78 to 1.92 inches in breadth.

Numenius Hudsonicus.

THE HUDSONIAN CURLEW.

Scolopax borealis, GMEL. S. N. I. 1788, 654 (nec FORSTER, 1772). — WILS. Am. Orn. VII. 1813, 22, pl. 56, fig. 1.

Numenius borealis, ORD, ed. WILSON, 1825. — BREWER, ed. WILSON, 1840, 473 (excl. syn.).

Numenius Hudsonicus, LATH. Ind. Orn. II. 1790, 712 (based on *Esquimaux Curlew*, Arct. Zool. II. 461, no. 364, pl. 19, and *Hudsonian Curlew*, LATH. Syn. Suppl. VII. 243). — SW. & RICH. F. B. A. II. 1831, 377. — NUTT. Man. II. 1834, 97. — AUD. Orn. Biog. III. 1835, 283; V. 1839, 589, pl. 237; Synop. 1839, 254; B. Am. VI. 1843, 42, pl. 356. — CASS. in Baird's B. N. Am. 1858, 744. — BAIRD, Cat. N. Am. B. 1859, no. 550. — COUES, Key, 1872, 262; Check List, 1873, no. 442; 2d ed. 1882, no. 645; Birds N. W. 1874, 509. — RIDGW. Nom. N. Am. B. 1881, no. 559.

Numenius intermedius, NUTT. Man. II. 1834, 100.

Numenius rufiventris, VIG. Zool. Jour. IV. 1829, 356.

"*Numenius brasiliensis*, MAXIM. et BURM." (SCLATER).

HAB. The whole of America, including the West Indies; breeds in the high north, and winters chiefly south of the United States. Greenland.

SP. CHAR. *Adult:* Crown dark sooty brown, divided longitudinally by a mesial stripe of buff; a narrow dusky stripe on side of head, from bill to anterior angle of the eye, continued back beneath the eye and along upper edge of auriculars, separated from the dusky of the crown by a wide, well-

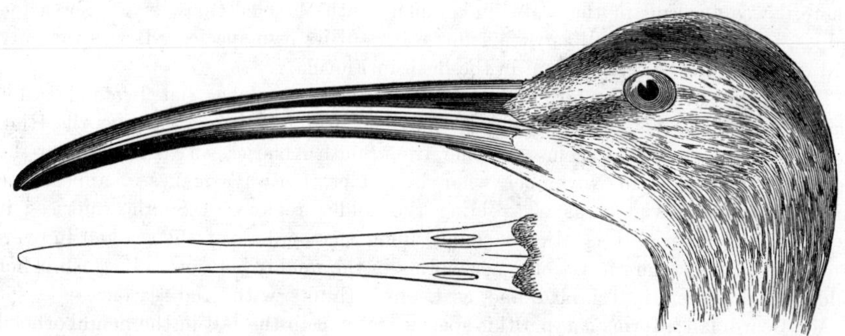

defined superciliary stripe of light buff. Rest of head and neck, and entire lower parts, light buff, the chin, throat, and abdomen immaculate, other portions, including cheeks, entire neck, jugulum, and breast, marked with linear streaks of dark brown; axillars pinkish buff or dilute cinnamon, barred with dark brown. Upper parts spotted with dark sooty brown and light buff, the latter prevailing on the wing-coverts, the former on the back; rump and upper tail-coverts similarly spotted; primaries dusky, the inner quills spotted with buff.

Wing, 9.00–10.25; culmen, 3.00–4.00; tarsus, 2.25–2.30; middle toe, 1.35–1.40.

This species, generally known to sportsmen as the Jack Curlew or Short-billed Curlew, and to ornithologists as the Hudsonian Curlew, is very generally distributed throughout North America, being found both on the Pacific and the Atlantic coast, and from Central America, where it passes the winter months, to the Arctic Ocean, on the borders of which it breeds. In Alaska Mr. Bannister saw it on the Island of St. Michael's, where, however, it was not very common. It was obtained at Sitka by Mr. Bischoff; and Mr. Dall states that it was not rare at the mouth of the Yukon River, where its favorite attitude seemed to be sitting on a high stump or piece of drift-wood, or even an alder-bush when this was large enough, with one of its legs drawn up. Mr. Bernard Ross met with this Curlew in the neighborhood of Great Slave Lake. Professor Reinhardt includes it among the birds of Greenland on the strength of a single specimen — a female — sent from Godthaab by Holböll. The latter mentions having obtained it twice — at Julianehaab and Fiskernaes — and also one specimen from Jakobshavn. It occurs as a migratory visitant in the fall in Bermuda, where it arrives early in August, but is so shy of approach that one can hardly ever get within gunshot of it. It is found only in August and September. Dr. Kjaerbölling mentions ("Naumannia," VI. 308) that he received a specimen of this Curlew from Iceland. Mr. R. Browne speaks of having seen it on Vancouver Island. Dr. Cooper noticed but few of this species on the southern coast of California, and these only in the spring, some remaining in flocks at Santa Barbara as late as May 20, and a few go as far south as San Diego. Though not known to breed south of Hudson's Bay, Dr. Cooper thinks that some may nest among the mountain lakes of California. He adds that, like the Long-billed Curlew, they fly with some approach to a regular order, generally in the form of a V, and in company with most of the other shore-birds, circling high in the air with loud cries when the falling tide begins to lay their feeding-grounds bare. They are also common on the Pacific coast as far south as Guatemala, and Mr. Salvin found them very abundant about the lagoons of Chiapam.

Mr. Moore mentions that on the 22d of March, 1872, a single specimen of this Curlew was brought to him which had been killed on the shore of Sarasota Bay, where it was feeding in the water in company with Marbled Godwits, Red-breasted Snipes, and Willets, as well as with a few others of its own species. It was the only bird of its kind ever seen by him in the flesh in Florida.

It is not mentioned by Dr. Gundlach as occurring in Cuba; but Léotaud states that it is a regular visitant of Trinidad, and that, although known there as the Hudsonian Curlew, it always seems to come from South America. If this were not the case, it would arrive in November, whereas, in fact, it always makes its appearance on that island in August, as if avoiding the colder regions of South America; it departs in October. It is always found along the borders of the sea and in overflowed meadows, where it searches for worms in the muddy bottoms. Its flesh is not held in high esteem in Trinidad, and, as Léotaud thinks, with good reason.

Mr. Boardman informs me that this species is found in the fall in the neighborhood of Calais, but that it is never very common in that neighborhood. In Massachusetts it is quite abundant every year in the fall, coming from the north in irregular, prolonged migrations, from the 25th of August until October. It is not known to occur in the spring in that State, although it may pass through in a prolonged nocturnal flight, since this bird is found on the shores of New Jersey and Long Island late in the month of May. A single specimen was procured by me at the Isles of Shoals on the 15th of August, 1879.

According to Giraud, this Curlew arrives in May on Long Island, where it frequents the marshes and muddy flats, feeding on worms and minute shellfish, but not being so abundant there as are the Long-billed Curlews, with which it sometimes associates. It leaves and passes on to the north early in June, again making its appearance in the salt-marshes of that island in August. It is said sometimes to frequent the uplands, where it feeds on insects and berries of various kinds, becoming very fat, although even then its flesh is not well-flavored. The flight of the Hudsonian Curlew is described as being easy and steady; and it readily obeys the fowler's whistle, generally presenting an excellent mark. This species is remarkable for the manner in which it sympathizes with its wounded companions — a trait also conspicuously displayed by the Long-billed Curlew. Straggling individuals of this species are occasionally observed to linger behind until the early part of November, but in general all have left by the middle of October. They are known to the gunners of Long Island both as the "Short-billed" and as the "Jack" Curlew.

According to Dresser, this species is of occasional occurrence in Southern Texas both in spring and fall; and he procured two specimens which had been shot near San Antonio. It is the least common there of the Curlews.

Hearne, in his "Journey to the Arctic Ocean" — a work published more than a century ago — (p. 424), designates this species as the "Esquimaux Curlew" — a name now given exclusively to the smaller bird, *N. borealis*. He states that at the time of his writing both species were found in great numbers on the coasts of Hudson's Bay during the summer, and that they both breed in all parts of it, as far north as latitude 72°. This bird always keeps near the sea-coast, awaiting the ebbing of the tides, and being frequently found in great numbers at low-water mark, where it feeds on the marine insects which are found in great abundance by the sides of the stones. At high-water it retires to the dry ridges, and awaits the receding of the tide. This bird will answer to a whistle imitating its note. It flies as steadily as a Woodcock, and as it rests long on the wing, presents itself as a mark which can be easily hit. Hearne adds that, at times, this Curlew is regarded as delicious eating.

Audubon did not observe this species in Labrador, and although he made diligent inquiries among intelligent residents, could find no one who knew of its occurrence there. Nevertheless others have met with and secured specimens of a few individuals of this species in that region. This bird is usually very shy, and it is seen in the greatest numbers at the time of the departure of the *borealis*, which species it greatly resembles in its general appearance, habits, and manner of feeding, although having a much louder and harsher voice.

Wilson, although he refers to this species in his description of *Scolopax borealis*, was not aware of the existence of two species of Short-billed Curlews, and it is impossible to determine which one he had in view in his accounts of its habits. It is probable, however, that while his description of the plumage belongs to the larger species, it is the smaller one to which his account of the habits of the Curlew is to be referred. The same is also true of Nuttall's statements, we believing that this species is more exclusively a feeder in the salt-marshes, and that it rarely, if ever, feeds on the uplands in the manner of the *borealis*. Nuttall states that, previous to its departure south in the fall, this species will assemble in large flocks near the sea-beach; and he was informed by a friend that it had been seen in an island in the Piscataqua River in a dense flock of many thousands, thickly covering several acres of ground. Barren birds of this species are found on the Atlantic coast from May to August, but are usually of solitary habit. Audubon states that he has found this bird abundant on the shores of New Jersey in May, where it remains a few weeks, and that he has seen a large flock of these Curlews near Charleston, S. C., in December.

Mr. MacFarlane met with this species breeding on the Barren Grounds, on what is known as the Eskimo Barrens, on the Lower Anderson River. The nests were on the ground, and were usually mere depressions lined with a few withered leaves. The eggs, four in number, were found between the 20th of June and the 10th of July. These nests were found in about 70° north latitude, but were comparatively rare; they were usually placed near small lakes or streams: this, however, was not always the case.

Eggs of this species in the Smithsonian Institution, from Mr. MacFarlane (No. 9428), have a ground-color of a creamy drab. The markings are irregular spots of a dark umber tint, with larger spottings of a slaty brown around the greater end. These measure, one, 2.40 by 1.57 inches; the other, 2.38 by 1.59 inches. Another set (No. 14101) have a similar ground, but the markings are larger, less numerous, and of a paler shade of brown; these measure 2.21 by 1.65 inches.

Numenius borealis.

THE ESKIMO CURLEW.

Scolopax borealis, FORST. Phil. Trans. LXII. 1772, 411, 431 (Albany Fort).
Numenius borealis, LATH. Ind. Orn. II. 1790, 712. — SW. & RICH. F. B. A. II. 1831, 378, pl. 65. — NUTT. Man. II. 1834, 101. — AUD. Orn. Biog. III. 1835, 69; V. 1839, 590, pl. 208; Synop. 1839, 255; B. Am. VI. 1843, 45, pl. 357. — CASS. in Baird's B. N. Am. 1858, 744. — BAIRD, Cat. N. Am. B. 1859, no. 551. — COUES, Key, 1872, 262; Check List, 1873, no. 443; 2d ed. 1882, no. 646; Birds N. W. 1874, 510. — RIDGW. Nom. N. Am. B. 1881, no. 560.
Numenius brevirostris, LICHT. Verz. Doubl. 1823, 75.
Numenius microrhynchus, PHIL. & LANDB. Wiegm. Archiv, 1866, 129 (Chili).

HAB. Eastern Province of North America; breeding in Arctic districts, where extending from the Prybilof Islands (not breeding) to Greenland; migrating south to the extremity of South America (Falkland Islands, Patagonia, Chili, and S. Brazil); no West Indian record, but noted from Bermuda and Trinidad (LÉOTAUD). Occasional in Europe. Not recorded from Western North America.

SP. CHAR. *Adult:* Crown dusky, streaked with buff, but without distinct mesial stripe; a dusky stripe of aggregated streaks on side of head, from bill to and behind the eye; rest of head, neck, and entire lower parts light buff, the cheeks and neck streaked, the breast, sides, flanks, and

crissum with V-shaped markings of dusky brown; axillars and lining of the wing pale cinnamon, the former narrowly barred with dusky. Upper parts spotted dusky and buff, the wing-coverts more grayish brown, with dusky shaft-streaks; primaries, including their inner webs, plain brownish dusky. Rump and upper tail-coverts spotted dusky and light buff. Tail brownish gray, barred with dusky.

Wing, 8.00–8.50 inches; culmen, 2.25–2.50; tarsus, 1.70–1.80; middle toe, 1.00.

In plumage, this little Curlew closely resembles *N. Hudsonicus,* but has the inner webs of the primaries finely and confusedly mottled, instead of being marked with very distinct and regular ochraceous spots; the breast with transverse V-shaped markings instead of linear, longitudinal streaks, while there are other differences, besides the important one of size, which readily distinguish them.

The Smaller Eskimo Curlew, or "Dough-bird," as it is called in New England — in distinction from the larger *Hudsonicus* — has a widely extended distribution over nearly the whole of North and South America. It is included by Reinhardt among the birds of Greenland, and probably correctly, though his evidence was inferential rather than positive. It has been obtained at Fort Yukon by Messrs. McDougal, Lockhart, and Jones, but was found nowhere in Alaska west or south of that point. It has been detected on no part of the Pacific coast, so far as I am aware, although Dr. Heermann speaks of it as common in the San Francisco market. It has not been obtained there by any of the collectors, and Dr. Cooper has no doubt that Dr. Heermann must have had reference to the *Hudsonicus*. It breeds throughout all the northern portions of North America, to the very borders and islands of the Arctic Sea. Several specimens have been taken in Great Britain. Where it passes its winters, or the extent of its wanderings from November to April, is only imperfectly known. It is not given as occurring in St. Croix, Cuba, Jamaica, or St. Domingo. Léotaud mentions the capture of only a single specimen of this species in Trinidad; this was taken in a dry meadow in the month of September. It appears to be equally rare in Central America, where only a single specimen of it is recorded as having been taken — by Mr. R. Owen, at San Geronimo, in Guatemala. It occurs in its migrations on the Gulf-coast of Mexico, but in what number, and for how long a period it is found, is not known with accuracy. Mr. Dresser met with it in spring at San Antonio, where it was more common than the *Hudsonicus*, but not so abundant as the *longirostris*. Dr. Merrill also speaks of this species as being abundant, during its migrations, in the same regions, and he is confident that some spend the winter in the valley of the Lower Rio Grande.

According to the observations of Mr. Nelson, this Curlew passes in considerable numbers through the interior in its migrations. He speaks of it as rather common in Northern Illinois during these movements. It is said to arrive a little later than the *Hudsonicus*, passes north with short delay, and returns about the last of September and in October, frequenting the wet prairies in company with the Golden Plover.

The facts that this species is of such rare occurrence in the West Indies and in Central America; that it is found with so much apparent uncertainty on the Atlantic coast; that its appearance may almost always be explained by the interruption of its flight by storms; and that it is nowhere to be found within our limits during the winter — all this points to South America as its residence during that season. We infer also that its migrations, both in the fall and in the spring, are made in long continuous flights, without any stoppage on the way, except when such is caused by stress of weather, unfavorable winds, fogs, and the like. In this opinion we are strengthened by the fact that this bird may be found on the Amazon and in various other portions of Brazil as early as September, where Natterer procured specimens in considerable numbers. Darwin met with it at Buenos Ayres, and Lichtenstein found it at Montevideo.

We also have the confirmation given by Mr. H. Durnford, in his "Notes on the Birds of Central Patagonia" ("Ibis," 1878, p. 404), where he states that he witnessed the passage of large migratory flocks of this species, from the 8th to the 10th of October, through the valley of the Chupat, in latitude 45° S. They made but a short stay in that valley — two specimens only having been procured — and were not seen again.

In this connection the fact, noted by Dr. Lincecum, is not without interest — that this species, known there as the "Curlew Sandpiper," occurred in his neighborhood in their spring migrations in April. They came in company with the Common Golden Plover, and seemed to feed in the same manner and on the same food. They were found thinly scattered among the Plovers, and were wild and hard to shoot. They were generally very lean. They appeared there about the 4th of April.

Mr. J. A. Allen met with a single stray representative of this species in Western Kansas, near Fort Hays, in May. Dr. Cooper mentions finding this Curlew apparently breeding in the vicinity of Fort Benton, where its young ones were taken by him while they were still in the down; but he saw none on the Columbia Plains.

Mr. Boardman informs me that this species is found in the vicinity of Calais, where it is more abundant than the *Hudsonicus,* although not usually very numerous. It is occasionally found in flocks about the last of August. At this time it is very common in the Bermudas. It is usually much more abundant on the coast of Maine when there have been easterly storms about the 20th of August, and is then seen in remarkable flights; but, except in stormy weather, it is never noticed inland. In some seasons this bird is rare in Massachusetts; in others it is very abundant. It is of very irregular occurrence, and probably is more common when easterly winds prevail during the last third of August.

A single specimen of this Curlew was taken by Mr. H. W. Elliott on the Prybilof Islands in June, 1872.

Richardson states that he found this Curlew frequenting the Barren Lands, within the Arctic Circle, in summer, where it feeds on grubs, fresh-water insects, and the fruit of the *Empetrum nigrum.* He describes its eggs as being of a pyriform shape and of a Siskin-green color clouded with a few large, irregular spots of bright umber-brown. The Copper Indians believe that this bird and some others betray the approach of strangers to the Eskimo. On the 13th of June, 1822, Richardson discovered one of these Curlews sitting on three eggs, on the shore of Point Lake; when he approached the nest, the female bird ran a short distance, crouching close to the ground, and then stopped to observe the fate of her treasures. Hearne, in his "Journey to the Arctic Ocean," refers to this species as being exactly like the larger one in color, shape, and nearly everything else except size. He adds that these two species also differ from others in their manner of life, as they never frequent the water's edge, but always keep among the rocks and dry ridges, feeding on berries and small insects. The flesh of this bird is generally much more highly esteemed by the dwellers on Hudson's Bay than that of the larger species, but it is by no means so numerous in that quarter. Hearne did not meet with this species farther north than Egg River.

Audubon, in his account of this Curlew, confirms the statements made more than a century ago by Hearne, relative to its habits and the way in which they differ from those of the *Hudsonicus.* He was told by Mr. Oakes, of Ipswich, Mass., that during its short stay in that section, in the early autumn, this bird may be met with on the high sandy hills near the sea-shore, where it feeds on grasshoppers and on several kinds of berries. On this food it becomes very fat, is excellent eating, and acquires the name of "Dough-bird" in consequence. He never met with it after leaving Massachusetts, except on one occasion; this was on one of the islands on the coast of South Carolina, at the dawn of a fine day, when a dense flock of this Curlew passed to the southward, near enough to enable him to ascertain the species. On the 29th of July, 1833, these birds made their first appearance in Labrador, near the Harbor of Bras d'Or. They came from the north, and arrived in immense numbers. Flock after flock passed close to his vessel, and directed their course to the sterile mountainous tracts in the neighborhood. Their stay on the coast seemed to be occasioned solely by the density of the fog, and as soon as the weather cleared, they set off in a straight course across the Gulf of St. Lawrence. Wherever there was a spot affording a supply of food, there the Curlews abounded, and were easily approached. By the 12th of August all had left the country. In Labrador Curlews feed chiefly on what is there known as the "Curlew-berry"—a small black fruit growing on a creeping shrub not more than an inch or two high. When in search of feeding-grounds they fly in close masses with remarkable speed, performing beautiful evolutions in the air. While on the wing they emit a soft, whistling note, but are silent when alighted. They run swiftly on the ground, picking up the berries in their way; and when pursued, will squat in the manner of a Snipe, laying neck and head flat on the ground, and when approached, at a single whistle of one of the flock, all immediately scream and fly off, not infrequently realighting on the same spot. These birds continued to arrive in Bras d'Or for several days in flocks of increasing size. This species rises from the ground by a single quick spring, cuts backward and forward and all around in a very curious manner, and occasionally pauses in the air in the manner of a Hawk, remaining stationary, with its head toward the wind, just before it alights. It is more shy in calm and quiet weather than at any other time. In its passage across the Gulf it flies high, in close bodies and at great speed, but not in regular lines. Audubon was informed by old settlers at Bras d'Or that this Curlew passes northward over the same tract about the middle of May.

The Eskimo Curlews are known to migrate through the interior in immense numbers in May. During the second week of that month large flocks of several hundred make their appearance, even while the snow, many feet in depth, still fills the ravines. At this season this Curlew may be found scattered everywhere, dotting the prairie in large, loose flocks.

According to Giraud, this Curlew is found every season on the coast of New Jersey, Long Island, and Rhode Island. It frequents the open ground in the vicinity of the sea-coast, feeding on grasshoppers and other insects, seeds, worms, and berries. It arrives on the shores of Long Island in the latter part of August, and remains until the 1st of November, when it assembles in large flocks and moves off to its winter-quarters. He has shot a few stragglers as late as the 20th of November. It occasionally associates with the Golden Plover, is generally in fine condition in the autumn, and, unlike both the other Curlews, its flesh is finely flavored. In the vicinity of New York it is known by the name of *Futes*. By Southern sportsmen it is known as the "Jack Curlew" and the "Short-billed Curlew." It is said to reach the Middle States from the South early in the spring, remaining only a short time, feeding in the salt-marshes and on the mud-flats. It moves in large flocks, and keeps up a constant whistling during the journey. It has been stated by those who shoot for the Philadelphia market, that a few remain and breed in the marshes about Cape May; but it is more probable that these are only barren stragglers.

On the New Jersey coast it is said to be a very shy bird, and requires great caution to approach. When frightened it flies with great rapidity, and is not easily brought down; but may be much more readily shot as it flies to and from its feeding-grounds, or it may be taken unawares when, unsuspicious of danger, it is feeding with other Waders on bars and points along the creeks. To approach it under such circumstances requires many precautions, as it is easily alarmed. If one is wounded, its companions evince great solicitude for it, and will fly around it for some time; and advantage is often taken of this by the sportsman to obtain others.

Mr. MacFarlane met with this species breeding in great abundance throughout the Barren Grounds up to the Arctic coast, but it was not met with before entering these grounds. The nests — which were found from about June 20 to July 10 — were in every instance mere holes in the ground, lined with a few decayed leaves and having a thin sprinkling of hay in the centre. It was very difficult to detect the nest of this species, as the parent bird glides off long before a near approach, and the eggs closely resemble the grass in their colors. This species was very numerous in the Barrens. The female, soon after leaving her nest, usually ascends into the air in a straight line. The young birds leave the nest as soon as hatched, and when approached, hide themselves in the grass, and can be found only with the greatest difficulty. Some were already hatched by July 12.

The eggs of this species exhibit very great variations in size, colors, and distribution of markings. In No. 9431 (S. I.) the ground is a pale greenish-ash, with large oblique blotches of different shades of sepia, the lighter inclining to a purplish-slaty tint. In No. 14099 (S. I.) the ground is of a deep muddy or clay-colored drab. The markings are chiefly toward the larger end, where they are confluent on the apex, are of an umber tint varying in the depth of the shade. In No. 9432 (S. I.) the ground is a deep olivaceous drab, and the markings, of a very dark sepia-color, are in the form of irregular small blotches, more numerous toward the larger end. In No. 11401 the ground is a light ashy-green color, and the markings are smaller, more numerous, more longitudinal, and of a much lighter shade of sepia. These eggs are of an oblong oval shape, slightly pyriform, one end more rounded than the other, and have an average length of about 2.10 inches, and a breadth at the largest portion of 1.90 inches.

Numenius phæopus.

THE WHIMBREL.

Scolopax phæopus, LINN. S. N. ed. 10, I. 1758, 146 ; ed. 12, I. 1766, 243.

Numenius phæopus, LATH. Ind. Orn. II. 1790, 711. — NAUM. Vög. Deutschl. VIII. 1836, 506. — KEYS. & BLAS. Wirb. Eur. 78. — BONAP. Comp. List, 1838, 49. — MACGILL. Man. II. 78. — GRAY, Gen. B. III. 560 ; Cat. Brit. B. 1863, 154. — DRESSER, Birds Eur. XVII. Apl. 1873, pl. — RIDGW. Nom. N. Am. B. 1881, no. 561. — COUES, Check List, 2d ed. 1882, no. 644.

Numenius minor, LEACH, Syst. Cat. 1816, 32.

Numenius islandicus, BREHM, Vög. Deutschl. 610.

Scolopax borealis, GMEL. S. N. I. 1788, 654 (not of Forster, 1772 !).

Phæopus arquatus, STEPH. Gen. Zool. XII. 36.

Whimbrel, PENN. Brit. Zool. II. 1812, 36, pl. 9. — YARR. Brit. B. ed. 2, II. 583, fig. ; ed. 3, II. 616, fig. ; et AUCT.

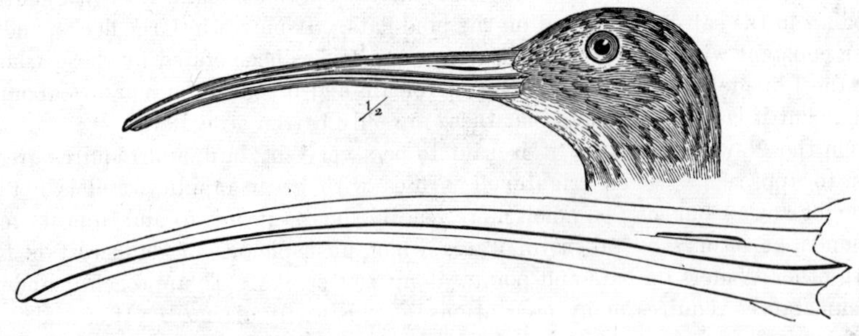

HAB. Palæarctic Region, occasionally visiting Greenland (cf. REINHARDT, "Ibis," 1861, p. 10).

SP. CHAR. *Adult:* Crown snuff-brown or sooty-brown, divided longitudinally by a medial stripe of pale buff ; a dark stripe on side of head, from bill to and behind eye, with a distinct light superciliary stripe above it; remainder of the head, neck, and lower parts generally, buffy white, the chin and throat, abdomen, thighs, and anal region, more nearly white and immaculate; cheeks, neck (all round), jugulum, and breast, distinctly streaked with brown; sides irregularly marked with the same; axillars white, barred with brown. Back and wings grayish brown, irregularly spotted with lighter; primaries dusky, the inner quills slightly spotted. Entire rump immaculate white; upper tail-coverts white, barred with brown. Tail brownish gray, barred with dusky, and tipped with white.

Wing, 9.30–10.50; culmen, 3.00–3.60; tarsus, 2.30–2.50; middle toe, 1.40.

This species bears a strong superficial resemblance to *N. Hudsonicus*, but may be immediately distinguished by the pure white, unspotted, rump.

The "Whimbrel," "Whimbrel Curlew," "Half-Curlew," or "Jack Curlew" — as it is variously called in different parts of Great Britain — is of occasional occurrence in Greenland, and claims a place in our fauna exclusively on that ground. It is found throughout Northern Europe and Asia in its breeding-season, and during the remainder of the year is of uncertain appearance in various portions of the Old World, including Japan and other islands. In all respects, of plumage, haunts, habits, and food, the Whimbrel very closely resembles the Common European Curlew, but is much smaller in size, and nowhere occurs in such numbers. It is met with occasionally on the shores of Great Britain during the winter, but is much more plentiful there in May, and again in September. The larger portion of these birds are migratory, either on their way to more northern regions, where they breed, or returning from the north with their young brood. Only a few breed within the limits of Great Britain, and these almost exclusively in the islands north of Scotland.

According to Thompson this bird is only seen in Ireland in the spring and in the autumn, and at these periods it is also common on the Grampians and in other elevated districts of Scotland. Mr. Selby mentions meeting with this species in the summer of 1834 on the margin of Loch Shin, in Sutherlandshire. Mr. Salmon found it breeding among the Orkney Islands, and states that it nests very early, all its eggs having been hatched by the 3d of June. Yarrell states, on the authority of Dr. Fleming, that this bird also breeds in Shetland, where it is known as the "Tangwhacp," and that the nests are placed on exposed parts of the heath. Mr. Hewitson also found it breeding on two of the Shetland Islands, Yell and Hascosea — where, however, it is rapidly decreasing in numbers. Mr. Dunn, who has several times visited both the Orkney and the Shetland Islands, informed Mr. Yarrell that while the Curlew and the Whimbrel do not associate together, he has found their nests within a gunshot of each other, and that the latter leave those islands as soon as the breeding-season is over.

The Whimbrel is said to feed on insects and worms, and their note to resemble the syllables *telly-telly-tet*, rapidly enunciated. On the continent of Europe, and during the breeding-season, this bird is found throughout Denmark, Scandinavia, and Russia. Mr. Hewitson met with it occasionally in the western part of Norway, and Mr. Dunn informed Mr. Yarrell that a few breed in Lapland as high as latitude 65°. It is also a regular summer visitor to the Faröe Islands and Iceland.

It is not known to breed on the southern coasts of England, yet small flocks have been recorded by Mr. Knox as occurring in Sussex in the months of May and June.

During the winter the Whimbrel is known to extend its migrations as far south as Madeira, and in its journeyings it occurs in Holland, Germany, France, Spain, Italy, and in all the various islands of the Mediterranean. It is more common in Holland than in any other country. It was found by Ménéfriés, a Russian naturalist, on the borders of streams in the region of the Caucasus. It has been met with in various parts of India, and Temminck believes that the specimens from Japan are identical with European birds.

Mr. Dresser regards this bird as one of the most widely distributed of the Waders, inasmuch as it is not only found over the entire Palæarctic Region, but also throughout the Indo-Malayan division, and in Africa as far down as the Cape. In Norway it breeds north of the Fell-range, and in some regions, especially within the Arctic Circle, it is very numerous. It occurs in the extreme northern portions of Scandinavia, but has not been found in Spitzbergen. In Central Russia it is extremely common. It only breeds in the dry steppes in Eastern Europe.

Mr. Dresser states that its extra-limital range includes Siberia, India, China, Australia, and Africa. It has been seen in Kamtschatka and in Eastern Siberia. In Africa it has been taken on the Nile, at Mozambique, in Zanzibar, Madagascar, Mauritius, etc. In South Africa it is rare, but specimens have been obtained even as far south as Capetown.

The presence of this species in Greenland, and its consequent claim to a place in the North American fauna, rests on the authority of Reinhardt, who states ("Ibis," 1861, p. 10) that he has seen, during recent years, five or six specimens from various parts of Greenland, and that he knows of six others that had previously been sent to his father in the years 1831–1835; and he expresses the belief that it will yet be ascertained that this Curlew breeds in Greenland. He is strengthened in this by his conviction that the *Numenius melanorhynchus* of Bonaparte — attributed to Greenland and Iceland (Compt. Rend. XLIII. 1021) — is no other than this species.

The flesh of this bird is said to be excellent eating. The eggs are stated by Yarrell to be four in number. The ground-color is a dark olive-brown, blotched with a still darker brown. They are pyriform in shape, and are very much like those of the *Numenius arquata*, but smaller. They measure 2.34 inches in length by 1.67 inches in breadth.

Mr. Gerbe states that this species passes through France, in its autumnal migrations, in the months of September, October, and November, and returns north again in the months of April and May. In its spring movements it appears either solitary or in small parties of two or three.

Captain Feilden, as quoted by Mr. Dresser, states that it breeds in considerable abundance on the Faröe Islands, from the 25th of May to the 17th of June. The nest is simply a depression in the soil, on the top of some slight elevation in any comparatively dry spot in the marshes, and is usually lined with a few grass bents, or leaves of wild brambles.

According to Mr. Dresser the eggs vary from 2.25 to 2.57 inches in length, and from 1.57 to 1.61 inches in breadth. They are pear-shaped, and vary in color from light olive-brown to dark greenish brown. Most of them are clouded and blotched with dark umber-brown, the spots being more numerous toward the larger end.

Numenius tahitiensis.

THE BRISTLY-THIGHED CURLEW.

Scolopax tahitensis, GMEL. S. N. I. 1788, 656.
Numenius tahitiensis, RIDGW. Nom. N. Am. B. 1881, no. 562.
Numenius taitensis, COUES, Check List, 2d ed. 1882, no. 647.
Numenius femoralis, PEALE, Zool. U. S. Expl. Exp. 1848, 283. — CASS. Orn. U. S. Expl. Exp. 1858, 316, pl. xxxviii. — RIDGW. Am. Nat. July, 1874, 435 (Fort Kenai, Alaska).
Otaheite Curlew, LATH. Synop. III. 1781, 122.
Otahite Curlew, COUES, l. c.

HAB. Islands throughout the Pacific Ocean. Occasional or accidental on the coast of Alaska.

SP. CHAR. *Adult:* Tibial and femoral plumes with their shafts lengthened into long, hair-like bristles; crown dark sooty brown, divided longitudinally by a medial stripe of buff; a stripe of dusky aggregated streaks from bill to and behind the eye; rest of the head, neck, and lower parts, buff, the cheeks, neck, and jugulum streaked with brown, the sides irregularly barred with the same; axillars reddish buff, or dilute cinnamon, widely barred with dark brown. Upper parts sooty brown, coarsely spotted with buff. Rump nearly uniform dark brown; upper tail-coverts and tail ochraceous-buff, the latter regularly barred with brown (the brown bars narrower than the interspaces), the coverts sometimes nearly immaculate, but usually irregularly marked with brown. "Legs and feet dull livid blue; iris hazel; basal half of lower mandible dull dark flesh-color, rest of bill horn-black" (NELSON, MS.).

Total length, about 17.25; extent, 32.50;[1] wing, about 10.50; tail, 4.60; culmen, 3.65; tarsus, 2.20; middle toe, 1.50.

The single Alaskan specimen before us agrees with examples from the Sandwich Islands and Paumotu Group, but, being in more perfect feather, is somewhat deeper colored.

This species was first described by Mr. Peale in 1848 from specimens obtained by the Wilkes Exploring Expedition at Vincennes Island, one of the Paumotu Group, in latitude 16° S., longitude, 144° W. A single male specimen was taken by Mr. Bischoff at Fort Kenai, Alaska, May 18, 1869, and is in the Collection of the Smithsonian Institution. The occurrence of a bird, the habitat of which is presumed to be in the Southwestern Pacific Ocean, and distant some five thousand miles from Alaska, and in a tropical region — a locality so remote and so unlike its natural haunt — can only be regarded as being something purely accidental. The bird is said to bear a general resemblance to the *N. Hudsonicus*, but to be conspicuously distinguishable by the rigid bristles that form the termination of the feathers of the upper portion of the tibiæ. Except a slightly stronger ferruginous tint in the males, the two sexes were not distinguishable. They were abundant on an island of the Paumotu Group named Vincennes by the Expedition, were found in the month of September, and had become exceedingly fat by feeding on the berries of a species of *Canthium*, then very abundant. The birds were rather tame, and when flushed uttered a clear plaintive whistle. Beyond this we have no history of their habits, their manner of breeding not being known.

FAMILY PHALAROPODIDÆ. — THE PHALAROPES.

CHAR. Small birds of Sandpiper-like appearance, but with very full, compact plumage like that of the Coots, Gulls, and Petrels; the tarsus greatly compressed, and the toes partly webbed, as well as fringed by a lateral, sometimes scalloped, margin.

The Phalaropes are small northern birds combining the habits, as well as to a certain extent the appearance, of the Waders and Swimmers. The three known species belong to as many different genera, whose characters are as follows: —

A. Bill flattened, broad, the nostrils sub-basal.

1. **Phalaropus.** Web between outer and middle toes extending to beyond second joint of the latter; lateral membrane of all the toes broad and deeply scalloped.

[1] Fresh measurements of No. 58471, ♂ ad. Fort Kenai, Alaska, May, 18, 1869 (F. BISCHOFF).

B. Bill subulate, the nostrils strictly basal.

2. **Lobipes.** Feet as in *Phalaropus*.
3. **Steganopus.** Web between outer and middle toes not reaching to second joint; lateral membrane to all the toes narrow and scarcely scalloped.

Genus PHALAROPUS, Brisson.

Phalaropus, Briss. Orn. VI. 1760, 12 (type, *Tringa fulicaria*, Vieill.).
"*Crymophilus*, Vieill. 1816" (Cassin).

P. fulicarius.

Char. Bill flattened, broad, the nostrils sub-basal; web between outer and middle toes extending to beyond second joint of the latter; marginal membrane of the toes broad and deeply scalloped.

Phalaropus fulicarius.

THE RED PHALAROPE.

Tringa fulicaria, Linn. S. N. I. 1766, 249 (based on *Phalaropus rufescens*, Briss. Orn. VI. 20; Edwards, pl. 142)

Phalaropus fulicarius, Bonap. Jour. Philad. Acad. IV. 1825, 232. — Sw. & Rich. F. B. A. II. 1831, 407. — Nutt. Man. II. 1834, 236. — Aud. Orn. Biog. III. 1835, 404, pl. 255; Synop. 1839, 239; B. Am. V. 1842, 291, pl. 339. — Cass. in Baird's B. N. Am. 1858, 707. — Baird, Cat. N. Am. B. 1859, no. 521. — Coues, Key, 1872, 248; Check List, 1873, no. 411; 2d ed. 1882, no. 604; B. N. W. 1874, 471. — Ridgw. Nom. N. Am. B. 1882, no. 563.

Phalaropus rufus, Pall. Zoog. Rosso-As. II. 1831, 205, pl. 63.

Phalaropus platyrhynchus, Temm. Man. 1815, 459.

Phalaropus rufescens, Briss. Orn. VI. 1760, 20.

Phalaropus griseus, Leach, Cat. Brit. Mus. 1816, 34.

Hab. Northern portions of the northern hemisphere, breeding in very high latitudes, and migrating southward in winter; chiefly maritime; in America, recorded from as far south as Ohio, Illinois, and Cape St. Lucas.

Sp. Char. *Adult, summer plumage:* Entire lower parts deep purplish cinnamon; sides of head white. Back and scapulars light ochraceous or buff, striped with black; wing-coverts deep bluish plumbeous, the greater widely tipped with pure white; remiges plumbeous-dusky. Lining of the wing white, bordered exteriorly with dusky grayish. *Male*, with the crown and nape streaked, like the back; white on side of head not well defined. *Female*, with the crown uniform plumbeous-black or dark plumbeous, the white on side of the head surrounding the eyes, and abruptly defined, the nape unstreaked cinnamon and plumbeous. *Adult and young in winter:* Head, neck, and lower parts pure white, the occiput and a space partly or completely surrounding the eyes dark plumbeous. Upper parts uniform fine pearl-gray or light bluish plumbeous, the remiges slate-color. *Young, first plumage:* Crown, nape, back, and scapulars dull black, the feathers edged with ochraceous; wing-coverts, rump, and upper tail-coverts plumbeous, the middle coverts bordered with pale buff, the tail-coverts with ochraceous. Head (except crown) and lower parts generally, white; the throat and jugulum suffused with brownish buff. *Downy young:* Above, bright tawny buff, marked with broad irregular stripes of black; superciliary stripes bright tawny buff, separated only by a narrow and sometimes interrupted dusky streak; pileum bright raw-umber brown, bordered exteriorly with black; chin and throat light fulvous-buff, changing to smoky buff on jugulum; rest of lower parts dull whitish.

Total length, about 7.50 inches; wing, about 5.25 to 5.50; culmen, .80 to .95; tarsus, .80 to .85; middle toe, .75 to .80.

In very many respects the habits, movements, and distribution of the Red Phalarope appear to be very nearly identical with those of *Lobipes hyperboreus*. Like that species, it breeds in high Arctic regions, and is even much more decidedly Arctic in its residence during the season of reproduction. It wanders, during the long period that intervenes between these short seasons, irregularly over a large portion of the northern hemisphere, having been traced to Calcutta, where a single specimen was procured, and to Northern Africa, where also one was obtained in January by Mr. Tyrwhitt Blake ("Ibis," 1867). This species is also included by Middendorff among the birds of Siberia, and is given as among those which penetrate to the extreme north. It arrives with the Red-necked Phalarope on the Taimyr River, and the two were equally common there and on the Boganida. In latitude 75° N. the last was seen on the 15th of August, and its fresh eggs were obtained June 17th, and half-fledged young ones July 25th (O. S.). The note of this bird resembles that of the Northern Phalarope (*Lobipes lobatus*), but is even more Finch-like.

In the English Arctic Expedition of 1875–1876 this species was found breeding near the "Alert's" winter-quarters (lat. 82° 37′ N.), and Mr. Feilden obtained a specimen there — a female — on the 30th of June, 1876. During the month of July he also observed a pair on a small fresh-water pond in latitude 82° 30′ N., where they were apparently breeding. The female was larger and brighter-colored than the male. Several other examples were seen in the same neighborhood by various members of the Expedition.

According to Mr. Kumlien, this is the "Whale-bird" and "Bow-head Bird" of whalemen. He met with large flocks of this species at great distances from land; in one instance, on August 4th, in latitude 41°, longitude 68° W. Their numbers increased as he proceeded north, and at a distance of two hundred miles from the Labrador coast he noticed them in a gale in very large flocks. He states that this bird follows the whales, immediately approaching, when one is seen to blow, in quest of the marine animals thus brought to the surface. Whalemen always watch the motions of this bird, as it is well known that it can discern a whale at a much greater distance than they can. A specimen which had been killed on the back of an *Orca gladiator* was brought to Mr. Kumlien by an Eskimo, and its œsophagus was found to be crammed with small crustaceans, which were still alive, though the bird had been killed several hours. This species arrives in Cumberland with the breaking-up of the ice, and is said to have greater powers of flight than either the *L. lobatus* or the *S. Wilsoni*, and to fly much more swiftly.

Prof. Alfred Newton found these birds breeding on Spitzbergen, though he was not able to discover any of their nests. The exploring expedition of the previous year met with one, however, in the beginning of July up the North Fjord of the Sound. Later in the month Professor Duner found a nest with three fresh eggs in Bell Sound. They lay on the ground, without any bedding, among small splinters of stone. Dr. Malmgren met with this species as far north as latitude 80° 10′, and states that it feeds chiefly on a species of nostoc; but the stomachs of those Professor Newton dissected on Rossö contained gnats and their larvæ. Professor Newton also refers to this species as one of the birds of Iceland, where it is well known to the natives. Faber met with three pairs, June 21, 1821, and again, on the 9th of July, with a family party of this species. In 1858 Professor Newton discovered two pairs on a lake in the same district where Faber had found his, but they did not remain to breed. In 1862 he received four eggs, well identified, which had been sent to him from Iceland by a friend.

Wheelwright found this species very rare in Scandinavia; but although he never obtained its eggs, he had no doubt that it breeds on the coast of North Norway and in East and West Finland.

The Red Phalarope is a distinguished swimmer. Sabine, in his memoir on the Birds of Greenland, having met with a flock of four, in latitude 68°, mentions their swimming in the sea among icebergs, several miles from the shore; and Richardson, in his Appendix to "Parry's Second Voyage," states that it was observed in the open sea, out of sight of land, preferring to escape danger by swimming rather than by flying. This bird feeds on the smaller thin-shelled crustacea and on aquatic insects, which it pursues in the water and picks up as they are swimming; and its attitude has been compared to that of a Teal with the head drawn backwards.

This bird is common in the early summer in Greenland. In Parry's Arctic voyages it was also observed to be abundant on the North Georgian Islands, and was found breeding at Igloolik and on Melville Island. It is included in the list of birds given in the zoölogy of Beechey's voyage, but the locality is not given.

Dr. Walker met with a single specimen in Melville Bay, near Cape York. Reinhardt also enumerates it among the birds of Greenland, where it is evidently very abundant during the breeding-season. Captain Blakiston received specimens from Hudson's Bay which were in their summer plumage.

In the summer of 1866 a very remarkable visitation of this bird took place in Great Britain. It appeared in unusually large numbers, and a great many were shot. Mr. J. H. Gurney, in a pamphlet recording this unusual occurrence, states that the first-comers made their appearance on the 20th of August, none being seen after the 8th of October. The greater number of those taken were shot between the 15th and the 25th of September, inclusive. Adult specimens and the young of the year were obtained to the number of not less than two hundred and fifty; they were chiefly taken in the south of England.

Richardson states that he found this species abundant in high northern latitudes, breeding on the North Georgian Islands and on the Melville Peninsula. It was frequently seen by the members of the northern expeditions swimming at a great distance from land. Its eggs — generally four in number — are described as having an oil-green ground, varied by crowded, irregular spots of dark umber-brown, which became confluent toward the obtuse end.

Mr. Batty writes that he has observed this species keeping in its migrations well out to sea, and thinks that it is rarely seen inland. He met with it about the middle of May in the Bay of Fundy, whence it departed for the north shortly after its arrival, returning again in August in countless numbers, keeping, about twelve miles from the land, in the tide-streaks, where it fed on the surface of the water, floating or swimming about in it as small Ducks do.

Giraud considered this Phalarope as of rare occurrence on Long Island, mentioning one specimen known to have been shot at Quoque, and others said to have been taken in that vicinity. It is probably not so rare there as has been supposed. A fine pair in their winter plumage was shot in that neighborhood in October, 1875, by Dr. James C. Merrill, and are now in the collection of the Boston Natural History Society. It is said also to be rare on the coast of New Jersey and on the Atlantic shores generally, although probably more common a short distance out at sea. It occurs as a migrant, in the fall, in the interior, on the Western lakes and rivers; but its appearance is only occasional, and the history of its distribution is but imperfectly known. Audubon met with it on the Ohio, near Louisville, in 1808. It was then late in October, and the birds were in their winter plumage. They seem to have been singularly abundant at that time — so much so, that he shot seventeen at a single discharge. The same author mentions that in September, 1831, — being about sixty miles outside of Nantucket — he passed through an extensive bank of sea-weed, on which hundreds of this species were walking about as unconcernedly as if on land. Their flight he describes as rapid, and not unlike that of the Red-backed Sandpiper (*Pelidna americana*).

Mr. H. W. Elliott noticed this species as being at certain times rather more abundant than *L. lobatus* among the Prybilof Islands; yet he had no reason to believe that it bred there. Like that bird, it was seen by the marshy margins of the lakelets, solitary or paired, but never in flocks. The earliest arrivals occur in June, and it reappears in the greatest number about the 15th of August; by the 5th of October all have left.

Mr. Boardman is quite positive that a few of this species breed on the St. Croix River every season. On one occasion, in company with Mr. Kisder, near Princeton, in the last of June, he came upon some young birds already hatched out and running about, and one of them was killed with a fishing-pole. This was in the neighborhood of Grand Lake, about sixty miles north of Calais, Me.

This bird has not — so far as known — been found abundant on the Pacific coast. Dr. Cooper mentions only a single specimen, which was shot near San Francisco by Mr. Hepburn; but he did not meet with any south of that place.

Mr. Dresser speaks of having received twenty eggs of this bird taken at Egedesminde and Upernavik, Greenland. Some had a pale greenish gray, or sea-green ground color, and were covered with purplish-brown underlying shell-markings and very clearly defined blackish-brown surface spots, which at the larger end were almost confluent. They varied in size from .85 by 1.07 inches to .88 by 1.27 inches.

This species was found breeding on the Arctic coast of North America by Mr. MacFarlane. It was met with in Franklin Bay, on the 4th and 5th of July, and five individuals and two nests were obtained. The nests are said to have been precisely similar to those of *L. lobatus* — mere depressions in the ground, with hardly any lining except a few dry leaves. One nest — found on the 4th — contained three eggs, which were perfectly fresh. The other — taken on the 5th — contained four eggs, in which were but slightly developed embryos.

The eggs of this species found by Mr. MacFarlane on an island in Franklin Bay, on the Arctic coast, measure 1.30 inches in length by .87 of an inch in breadth. Their ground-color is greenish drab, marked with blotches of a varying intensity of sepia-brown, larger, more confluent, and deeper in tint on the obtuse end. The smallest specimens of this egg measure .85 by 1.15, and one egg is .90 in breadth.

Genus LOBIPES, Cuvier.

Lobipes, "Cuv. Règ. Anim. 1817" (type, *Tringa hyperborea*, Linn., = *T. lobata*, Linn.).

Char. Similar to *Phalaropus*, but bill subulate, and the nostrils strictly basal.

L. lobatus.

Lobipes lobatus.

THE NORTHERN PHALAROPE.

Tringa lobata, Linn. S. N. ed. 10, I. 1758, 148 ; ed. 12, I. 1766, 249 (based on Edw. pl. 308).

Tringa hyperborea, Linn. S. N. ed. 12, 1766, 249 (based on Faun. Suec. 179 ; Edw. 143 ; Will. 270 ; Ray, 132. — *Phalaropus cinereus*, Briss. Orn. VI. 15).

Phalaropus hyperboreus (male), Lath. Ind. Orn. II. 1790, 775 (excl. syn. supposed female = *P. fulicarius*). — Nutt. Man. II. 1834, 239. — Aud. Orn. Biog. III. 1835, 118 ; V. 1839, 595, pl. 215. — Cass. in Baird's B. N. Am. 1858, 706. — Baird, Cat. N. Am. B. 1859, no. 520.

Lobipes hyperboreus, Cuv. Règ. Anim. I. ed. 1829, 532. — Aud. Synop. 1839, 240 ; B. Am. V. 1842, 295, pl. 340. — Coues, Key, 1872, 248 ; Check List, 1873, no. 410 ; 2d ed. 1882, no. 603 ; B. N. W. 1874, 469. — Ridgw. Nom. N. Am. B. 1882, no. 564.

Tringa fusca, Gmel. S. N. I. ii. 1788, 675.

Phalaropus ruficollis, Pall. Zoog. Rosso-As. II. 1826, 203.

Phalaropus cinerascens, Pall. t. c. 204.

Phalaropus cinereus, Meyer & Wolf, Tasch. II. 1810, 417.

Phalaropus angustirostris, Naum. Vög. Deutschl. VIII. 1836, 240, pl. 205.

"*Phalaropus australis*, Temm. & Bp." (Schlegel).

Phalaropus Williamsii, Simm. Linn. Trans. VIII. 264.

Hab. Northern portions of the northern hemisphere ; breeding very far north, and not penetrating far within the tropics in winter ; chiefly, but not strictly, maritime. In America, recorded from the following southern localities : Bermudas ; Dueñas, Guatemala ; Isthmus of Tehuantepec.

Sp. Char. *Adult :* Above, dark plumbeous, the back striped with ochraceous ; wings dusky, the greater coverts widely tipped with white ; lower parts chiefly white, the neck with more or less rufous. *Female,* with the sides of the neck and jugulum uniform cinnamon-rufous, the plumbeous above pure and continuous. *Male,* with the rufous confined chiefly to the sides of the neck, the jugulum being mixed white and grayish, tinged with rufous ; plumbeous above duller and less continuous than in the female. *Young, first plumage:* Crown plumbeous-dusky, with or without streaks ; back and scapulars black, distinctly streaked with buff or ochraceous ; wings as in adult, but middle coverts bordered with buff or whitish. Forehead, supra-auricular stripe, lores, and lower parts white, the jugulum and sides of breast sometimes suffused with dull brownish ; auriculars dusky. *Downy young:* Above, bright tawny, the rump with three parallel stripes of black,

enclosing two of lighter fulvous than the ground-color ; crown covered by a triangular patch of mottled darker brown, bounded irregularly with blackish ; a black line over ears, not reaching to the eye ; throat and rest of head light tawny fulvous ; rest of lower parts white, becoming grayish posteriorly.

Total length, about 7.00 inches ; wing, 4.00–4.45 ; culmen, .80–.90 ; tarsus, .75–.85 ; middle toe, .65–.75.

There is no specimen in the Smithsonian Collection representing the winter plumage of this species ; but this stage is thus described by Naumann, in "Die Vögel Deutschlands" (Vol. VIII. pp. 244, 245) : "The winter plumage, which they take after the young plumage, seldom appears in full, and such young birds are yet moulting when another, the spring moulting, sets in. Even old birds are seldom found in full winter plumage, because the autumnal moulting goes on very slowly. The few new feathers which are often found in those killed in late autumn seem to have been overlooked, since a description of them can nowhere be found, although they appear quite different from those of the young, and even of the summer plumage. I have a specimen in which almost the whole plumage has been renewed, and which, therefore, has almost completely taken its winter plumage. It is strikingly different from the other plumages. The forehead, a stripe over the eye extending through the temples, bridles, chin, throat, cheeks (mostly), foreneck, breast, and belly to the tail pure white ; the crown gray, with bluish-white scales with black stripes on shafts ; a little spot before the eye black ; a strip under the eye, somewhat more extended over the auricular region, blackish and whitish gray mingled ; the hind neck light bluish gray, with a few somewhat darker spots ; the sides of the jugulum clouded with pale gray, with a yellowish-brown wash ; upper back, shoulders, and hinder wing-feathers gray, toward the roots of the feathers darkest, approaching blackish brown, with black shafts and broad bluish-white borders, by which the whole gains the appearance of being deep gray, with grayish-white scales. The middle tail-feathers also have dull white borders, and are, besides, like the upper tail-coverts, rump, or lower back, blackish browngray; the latter, however, with only a few light borders to the feathers. All the rest is like the young plumage, but with the wing-coverts somewhat lighter, *in old birds* intermixed with feathers the color of the shoulder-feathers (scapulars)."

Examples vary considerably in the clearness and sharp definition of the colors, even those in the down differing much in this respect, some being pale yellowish, and others deep rusty fulvous ; the latter extreme being represented by a specimen from the region of Hudson's Bay, the former by examples from the Prybilof Islands, Alaska. As, however, several from the latter locality vary among themselves, the difference is perhaps purely individual.

This species, known among writers both as the Gray and as the Red-necked Phalarope — the one name having been suggested by its winter plumage, the other by the bright colors which adorn its summer dress — is common to both continents, breeding in the high Arctic regions of Asia, Europe, and America in the early summer, and from August to the latter part of May wandering irregularly over a large portion of the northern hemisphere.

Mr. R. Swinhoe mentions having procured specimens of this bird in November near Ape's Hill, in Formosa. It was sitting and floating, washing itself in a little stream, and its movements are spoken of as being both pleasing and graceful. At Tamsay, March 14, he procured three others from a flock which was feeding on the shoals of the river; and he afterward met with this species on the Island of Hainan. As he was leaving Hung-pe, four of these birds flew toward the ship and sat floating on the water close to her. He afterward, April 4, on the shore of the Lunchow Peninsula, saw another, which he secured. A single specimen is said ("Ibis," 1867, p. 169) to have been taken by Mr. Wallace in one of the Arru Islands. The naturalists of Perry's Expedition to Japan procured specimens of this bird from the Island of Niphon.

Although a northern bird in its breeding, this species makes its appearance in warmer regions immediately upon the close of its season of reproduction. Mr. Salvin met with four of this species at Dueñas, in Guatemala, in August, 1859. They had apparently but just arrived, and were swimming slowly about on the lake, picking at the weeds, and showing the usual absence of timidity peculiar to these birds.

Middendorff speaks of this species as being abundant in Siberia, and includes it in his list of those birds which penetrate to the extreme north. Von Heuglin found it at the beginning of September on Nova Zembla, already dressed in its autumnal plumage; also on Waygatz Island, where it was gathered in family parties of six or more, on shallow fresh-water pools. Mr. C. W. Shepherd found it breeding in great numbers on the small islands in the Lake of Mý-vatu, in the north of Iceland. The young birds — "tiny little pieces of animated wool" — were very beautiful; and the old birds were so tame that they were caught in the landing-net like butterflies, as they flew around, while the hens sat still, brooding their little ones within a few feet of him.

Professor Newton also mentions finding this bird very common all over Iceland, on all the ponds and lakes, arriving late in May, and at once beginning the duties of nidification. On one occasion, in the month of June, he saw a flock of at least a hundred sitting on the surf, between the breaking waves and the shore.

Although Mr. Wheelwright found this species far more common in Scandinavia than the *fulicarius*, he does not think that they breed anywhere excepting in the Lapland fell-valleys. They breed commonly at Quickiok. The eggs, four in number, he describes as being of a pale olive-green color, and covered with large and small black-brown spots. He found but little difference between the eggs of this species and those of the *fulicarius*, except that the latter are slightly larger.

Yarrell states that this bird is much less rare in England than the Red of the same species; but the latter is more common in the northern islands of Scotland. Mr. Salmon, who visited the Orkneys in the summer of 1831, says of this bird, as quoted by Yarrell: "This beautiful little bird appeared to be very tame; although we shot two pair, those that were swimming about did not take the least notice of the report of the gun; and they seemed to be much attached to each other, for when one of them flew to a short distance, the other directly followed; and while I held a female that was wounded, in my hand, its mate came and fluttered before my face.

After some little difficulty, we were fortunate in finding their nests, which were placed in small tufts of grass, and were about the size of that of a Titlark, but much deeper. They had but just commenced laying, June 13, as we found but one or two eggs in a nest, and their number is four."

Nilsson also mentions this bird visiting Sweden and Norway, and states that a few remain to breed on the margins of fresh-water lakes; but the greater part go farther north. Mr. W. Proctor visited Iceland in the summer of 1837, and states that he found it breeding on little hillocks in the marshes. The young birds left the nest as soon as hatched. On the approach of danger, the old bird runs among the aquatic plants, spreading her wings and counterfeiting lameness. As soon as she has succeeded in attracting the enemy away from her young, she soars upward to a great height, then descends very rapidly, making a noise with her wings, the motions of which in her upward flight are also somewhat remarkable. On returning to the ground she calls her young together with a peculiar cry, and gathers them under her after the manner of the domestic Hen.

This Phalarope is found on the Pacific coast at Vancouver Island, where Mr. R. Browne mentions its presence. Dr. Cooper states that in winter it migrates south of California, not being common beyond Monterey. He procured a single specimen south of San Diego, which had been killed, May 1, by flying against the lighthouse. At Monterey he noticed its arrival, apparently from the mountains, about September 15; and he saw this bird off San Francisco Bay in June, when it may have been nesting among the Coast Ranges.

This species is also mentioned by Reinhardt as occurring in Greenland; and Captain Blakiston received specimens of it from Hudson's Bay and Great Bear Lake; Mr. Ross also found it on the Mackenzie River, although it is not common there.

Major Wedderburn records the taking of two specimens of this bird in Bermuda: one was found dead, March 21, 1848, supposed to have been killed by flying against the iron lighthouse during the night; the other was found the following day, swimming in Hamilton Water, and was killed with a stick. Mr. Hurdis mentions a third, taken March 8, 1852; this one he killed with his walking-stick.

Mr. Boardman informs me that this species is found about Passamaquoddy Bay all the summer, and that it undoubtedly breeds there in the spring and fall. It is generally known as the "Sea Goose," from the peculiar manner in which it sits on the water. Its food appears to be crustacea and marine insects.

Mr. Harold Herrick also states that these birds may be seen in large numbers all the summer on the "Riplings," about eight miles from Grand Menan, where they congregate to feed on the shrimps and animalculæ that drift in the eddies made by the advancing and receding tide. They do not approach the shore except when driven in by storms, but are represented as being very tame.

Richardson states that they breed on all the Arctic coasts of America, and only resort to the shores of Hudson's Bay in the autumn, frequenting shady ponds, in which they swim with ease and elegance, their attitudes resembling those of the Common Teal; and like that bird continually dipping their bills into the water, picking up the small insects which constitute their food.

Giraud, in his "Birds of Long Island," mentions having seen several specimens of this bird that had been procured on the coast of New Jersey, where it is regarded as very rare, as it is also on Long Island. He met with one on the inner beach the latter part of June, in company with a party of small Sandpipers. It was very gentle, and showed no disposition to take wing, even when he came quite near. This proved to be a young male of that year, and its stomach contained particles of shells and sand. This species is infrequent in the middle district, and is rarely seen south of New York. Giraud states, on the authority of Professor Baird, that examples of this Phalarope have twice been taken near Carlisle, Pa.

Specimens of this Phalarope are occasionally taken near Boston, as well as on various other portions of the New England coast; but it does not appear to be common on or near the land. It also occurs as an irregular and infrequent migrant, both in spring and fall, near Lake Koskonong.

A small flock of these birds was seen on the west coast of Greenland, in latitude 71°, in June, on Parry's first voyage; and Ross, in the Appendix to the "Third Voyage," mentions that a small flock alighted under the lee of the ship during a strong breeze, and were so fearless as to approach within a few yards, feeding on small shrimps, which were seen in great numbers. At that time the ship was at least sixty miles from the nearest land. These birds were afterward found breeding on the Whalefish Islands; but none were seen after leaving Greenland.

According to the observations of Mr. L. Kumlien, this species arrives in Cumberland in June in large flocks, but is not so common as *fulicarius;* and he states that he has seen the *lobatus* as far south and farther north, and nearly as far from land as that species; but this is true only of a few individuals. It seems more fond of the shore, breeding plentifully on the islands in Disco Bay. It is less gregarious than *fulicarius,* and prefers small bays to the open sea. This bird alights on the drift-ice, and feeds by jumping into the water after food, where the *fulicarius* would have alighted in the water in the first place.

From the denuded condition of the breasts of the males of this species which have been taken during the breeding-season, there is good reason to believe that, like the Wilson's Phalarope, the males of this species do their full share of the labors of incubation.

Mr. Elliott found a few stray couples breeding upon the Prybilof Islands, nesting around the margins of the ponds; and he secured several newly hatched young birds, which were very pretty and interesting. The down of the head, neck, and upper parts is a rich brownish yellow, variegated with brownish black, the crown being of this color mixed with yellow, with a long stripe extending down the back, flanked with one over each hip, another across the rump, and a shoulder-spot on each side. The under parts are grayish silvery white. When startled or solicitous for the safety of its young, the parent bird utters a succession of sonorous *tweets,* quickly repeated, with long intervals of silence.

Mr. Audubon, who found birds of this species quite numerous in the Bay of Fundy, and afterward met with them in Labrador, regarded them as being somewhat shy. They procured their food on the water, on which they alight like Ducks, and float with all the buoyancy of a Gull. They walk about upon masses of floating seaweed as unconcernedly as if on land. Their notes are said to resemble the syllables *tweet-tweet-tweet,* and are sharp and clear. Their flight is like that of the Common Snipe. At the approach of an enemy they close up their ranks and fly in a body, so that numbers may be killed at one shot. Audubon has met with these birds in large flocks at a distance of more than a hundred miles from land.

In Labrador this Phalarope occurred only in small parties of a few pair, and were always in the immediate vicinity of fresh-water ponds, near which they breed. Their nest is described as a hollow scooped out among the herbage, lined with a few bits of dry grass and moss. The eggs were always four, are said to average 1.19 inches by .88, to be pointed at the smaller end, and with the ground-color of a deep dull buff, irregularly marked with blotches of a dark reddish brown. The birds showed great anxiety for the safety of their eggs, limping or running with extended wings, uttering a feeble and melancholy note. The young leave the nest shortly after they are hatched, and run after their parents over the moss and along the edges of the small ponds. They had all departed by the beginning of August.

Mr. MacFarlane found this species breeding in great abundance in the Arctic regions through which he passed, from the edge of the wooded country to the shores of the Arctic Sea. In more than fifty instances in which he made notes of its nests and eggs, he found the former to be mere depressions in the ground lined with a few dried leaves and grasses, and in almost every instance placed near the edges of small ponds; the number of the eggs was almost invariably four. The nests were seen from the 17th of June until into July, and in several instances perfectly fresh eggs were found as late as July 5. They were tolerably numerous in the wooded country, were also found in the Barrens wherever there were small lakes, and were not less frequently seen at the very edge of the Arctic Sea and on the islands off the coast. Sometimes the birds permitted the near approach of man without any noise or special manifestations of uneasiness; but at other times both parents would make great outcries, and fly from tree to tree in order to draw the intruder away from the nest.

The eggs of this species average 1.10 inches in length by .80 of an inch in breadth. Their ground-color is a greenish drab. The spots are much finer and more numerous than in the eggs of the *fulicarius*, and are of a sepia-brown. They are pyriform in shape, and much smaller than those of the Red Phalarope. Their nests were found by Mr. Lockhart quite common on the Yukon. These eggs, collected in great numbers at various points on both the Yukon and Anderson rivers, exhibit great variations. The ground-color ranges from the darkest olive-green to brownish olive, drab of various shades, to buff, and more rarely to a stone-gray. The spots also vary in size and in their distribution, but are usually very numerous, and often confluent; they vary in their shades from a bistre so dark as to be almost black, to chocolate-brown, and even lighter shades.

Genus **STEGANOPUS**, Vieillot.

Steganopus, Vieill. Enc. Méth. 1823, 1106 (type, *Phalaropus lobatus*, Wils., = *P. Wilsoni*, Sabine).
Holopodius, Bonap. Synop. 1828, 342.

Char. Bill slender and subulate, with strictly basal nostrils, as in *Lobipes;* web between outer and middle toes not reaching to second joint, the lateral membrane of all the toes narrow and scarcely scalloped.

Steganopus Wilsoni.

WILSON'S PHALAROPE.

? *Tringa glacialis*, Gmel. S. N. I. ii. 1788, 675 (based on *Plain Phalarope*, Penn. Arct. Zool. II. 1785, 495, no. 415; Lath. Synop. V. 173).
Phalaropus lobatus, "Linn." Wils. Am. Orn. IX. 1825, 72, pl. 73, fig. 3 (not of Linn.).
Phalaropus Wilsoni, Sabine, App. Frankl. Journ. 1823, 691. — Sw. & Rich. F. B. A. II. 1831, 405, pl. 69. — Nutt. Man. II. 1834, 245. — Aud. Orn. Biog. III. 1835, 400, pl. 254. — Cass. in Baird's B. N. Am. 1858, 705. — Baird, Cat. N. Am. B. 1859, no. 519.
Phalaropus (Holopodius) Wilsoni, Bonap. Synop. 1828, 342, no. 279. — Nutt. Man. II. 1834, 245.
Lobipes Wilsoni, Aud. Synop. 1839, 241; B. Am. V. 1842, 299, pl. 341.
Steganopus Wilsoni, Coues, Ibis, Apr. 1865, 158; Key, 1872, 248; Check List, 1873, no. 409; 2d ed. 1882, no. 602; B. N. W. 1874, 467. — Ridgw. Nom. N. Am. B. 1882, no. 565.

Phalaropus frenatus, VIEILL. Gal. Ois. II. 1825, 178, pl. 271.
Phalaropus stenodactylus, WAGL. Isis, 1831, 523.
Phalaropus fimbriatus, TEMM. Pl. Col. V. pl. 270.
Lobipes incanus, JARD. & SELBY, Ill. Orn. I. pl. 16.
"*Steganopus tricolor*, VIEILL." (COUES).
Lobipes antarcticus, LESS. (*fide* FRAZER, P. Z. S. 1843, 118).

HAB. Temperate North America in general, but chiefly the interior portions; rare along the Atlantic coast, and not recorded from the Pacific slope of California, Oregon, or Washington Territory. North to Eastern Oregon, the Saskatchewan, Nova Scotia, and Maine; south, in migrations, to Brazil and Patagonia (Chupat Valley).

SP. CHAR. *Adult female in summer:* Forehead and crown pale pearl-gray, the former with a blackish line on each side; occiput and nape white, changing to plumbeous gray on the back and scapulars. Stripe on the side of the head (chiefly back of the eye), and continued down the side of the neck, deep black, changing on the lower part of the neck into rich dark chestnut — this extending backward more interruptedly on each side of the interscapular region; outer scapulars marked with a similar stripe. A short stripe above the lores and eyes (not reaching the bill), cheeks, chin, and throat pure white; foreneck and jugulum soft buffy cinnamon, deepest laterally

and posteriorly, and fading gradually into creamy buff on the breast; remaining lower parts white. Wings brownish gray, the coverts and tertials bordered with paler; rump brownish gray, upper tail-coverts pure white. *Adult male in summer:* Smaller and much duller than the female, with the beautiful markings of the latter but faintly indicated. *Adult and young in winter:* Above, continuous light ash-gray; upper tail-coverts, superciliary stripe, and lower parts white, the jugulum and sides of breast tinged faintly with pale ashy. *Young, first plumage:* Crown, back, and scapulars blackish dusky, the feathers bordered conspicuously with buff. Upper tail-coverts, superciliary stripe, and lower parts white, the neck tinged with buff. *Downy young:* Prevailing color bright tawny fulvous, paler beneath, the abdomen nearly white; occiput and nape with a distinct median streak of black, on the former branching laterally into two narrower, somewhat zigzag lines; lower back and rump with three broad black stripes; flanks with a black spot, and caudal region crossed by a wide subterminal bar of the same.

Male: Wing, 4.75–4.80; culmen, 1.25; tarsus, 1.20–1.25; middle toe, .90. *Female:* Wing, 5.20–5.30; culmen, 1.30–1.35; tarsus, 1.30–1.35; middle toe, .90–1.00.

The habits of this exclusively American Phalarope, and to some extent its geographical distribution, have continued, until very recently, to be imperfectly ascertained. It was known to Wilson by only a single specimen, all record of which has been lost. Even Audubon appears to have met with very few of this species, and to have gathered but little information as to its habits. It is now known to be by far more common in the interior than near the coast, to breed in Northern Illinois, Iowa, Wisconsin, Dakota, and Oregon, and thence northward into the British possessions to an unascertained extent. It is also abundant in Utah, but does not appear to have been found on the Pacific coast. During the winter months it occurs in Guatemala and in Mexico, but to what extent we have no certain information.

More recently it has been ascertained to be a common resident in the more southern portions of South America. Mr. H. Durnford, in his account of the birds observed by him in the Chupat Valley of Patagonia, mentions this species as being quite common in that region, where he saw it swimming gracefully in the still pools formed by the eddies of the river, and in nearly all the adjacent stagnant ditches. The birds were usually seen in pairs.

Captain Bendire regards this bird as being moderately common in Eastern Oregon during the breeding-season, at which time it associates with the Willets, which it resembles in its own actions when any one approaches its nesting-place. Mr. Nelson mentions this species as a very common summer resident in the marshes of Northern Illinois, arriving about the middle of May, and remaining until into August. It nests from about the 25th of May until late in June.

Mr. A. L. Kumlien, in "Field and Forest," July, 1876, supplies some interesting notes relative to the very remarkable and eccentric ways of this bird. In its mode of living it is quite different from most Waders; and one very peculiar feature in its habits is that the male attends to the duties of incubation almost entirely alone, while his much more richly dressed mate idly gambols on the shore. Unlike most birds, the female of this species makes the advances to the male during the pairing season, and it is quite common to see two females pursuing one male. Mr. Kumlien has invariably found the naked and wrinkled belly, characteristic of the incubating bird, present in the male, but never in the female. Neither does the female evince the distress shown by the male when the nest is approached, the latter being quite reckless of danger, while his mate will not come within gunshot. The nest is described as being a flat, loosely-constructed affair, built in a tussock of grass, seldom in the immediate vicinity of open water, but usually in the adjoining grassy marshes. In one instance a nest was found, four miles from the nearest sheet of water, in a small slough on a high prairie. Mr. Kumlien speaks of this species as being remarkably quiet and still. The only note he had ever heard it utter was a weak nasal quack repeated six or seven times in quick succession; this is usually done by the male at the time when the nest is approached. The young are conducted to the shore soon after they are hatched, and when surprised will take to the water and swim and dive with great ease. They are fully fledged by the last of July, congregating in considerable flocks at that time.

Professor T. Kumlien wrote me in 1860 that this species, which before that period had been one of the rarest of birds — only two or three having been noticed in as many or more years — had become quite plentiful, moving in large flocks. They arrive May 4, and are at first very shy, but before leaving become as tame as the Least Sandpiper. He often watched their movements from a distance of not more than six or eight feet. From the facts that there was not one male to eight females, that they moved in flocks, and that at the same time the females had eggs full-sized in their ovaries, he was led to suspect that they were polygamous. He has since written me that this species is now found more or less commonly each season near Lake Koskonong. A few remain there to breed, but the greater portion pass through to more northern regions in the latter part of May. The young begin to appear in advance of their parents in August. In the summer of 1873 this species occurred there in unusual numbers. The young birds became very numerous as early as the middle of July, but gradually grew less abundant toward the 15th of August. Mr. Kumlien was of opinion that only a very few of the young birds could have been raised in that immediate vicinity; and it was a particularly noticeable fact that there were few or no old birds to be seen. In one flock of two hundred or more he observed only a single old bird. He conjectured at the time that the parents might be engaged in raising a second brood; but none were seen at any later period in that season. Mr. Kumlien has met with this species every year for more than thirty years. His attention was first called to it by the peculiar manner in which it carries its neck, which bulges out and presents a singular appearance, during the breeding-season, or about the last of May. At this time the birds were fighting, running against one another, and uttering their peculiar grunting notes. They arrive in Wisconsin from the 4th to the middle of May, and leave early in the fall, none having been noticed after the first frost. Those that come to the lake in spring do not all stay. They do not arrive in flocks, like the *Tringæ*, but are more scattered, and select by preference certain places in which they remain. He has never met with them at any great distance from the lake, and has every evidence, except actually finding their nests, that they breed in the marshes not far from it. It is not shy. Before pairing, this bird keeps in small companies, associating with small *Tringæ*, Kildeer, etc. He has never noticed it swimming, except when wounded, and then it swims like a Duck, nodding its head the while. He has never known it to dive, but it often wades up to its belly in the shallow water. Its note — particularly during the breeding-season — is a singular low grunting, which is not easily described. In flying it lifts its wings higher than the Spotted Sandpiper and some of the small *Tringæ*. In the spring of 1873 it was not more numerous than usual, but from the last of June to the last of August it was in unusual numbers, nearly all of them young.

Mr. George O. Welch, of Lynn, Mass., informs me that he has occasionally met with single birds of this species, but regards this as something very unusual. In May, 1874, he procured a fine specimen — a male — in Nahant. It was in its full summer dress, and his attention was called to it by its very singular proceedings. The bird was on the ground at the edge of a small brackish pool, every now and then springing up into the air, and — as was afterward ascertained — catching small dipterous insects. This it did as dexterously and as rapidly as the most expert Fly-catcher. Mr. Batty writes me that it is seen on Long Island occasionally, but that it is very rare there, as well as in Northern New Jersey, where it is called the "Needle-bill Snipe."

Mr. Audubon, in his account of this species, claims to have met with it along the whole eastern coast from Boston to New Jersey; but this probably was a mistake. It is certainly quite a rare bird in that region. Mr. Audubon also states that he saw it in Kentucky, as well as in other parts of the United States. In June, 1829, he received a pair which had just been killed by the fishermen with whom he was staying. These had acted as if nesting, and their appearance seemed also to indicate this; but their nest could not be found. About the same period his son procured two specimens killed on the rocks at the Rapids of the Ohio below Louisville. Late in the summer of 1824 three were obtained near Buffalo Creek on Lake Erie; Edward Harris also procured one near New York, and John Bethune one near Boston. The birds obtained near Lake Erie were feeding around the borders and in the shallows of a pond of small extent. When first seen they were mistaken for Yellowshanks, so much did their movements resemble those of that species. They waded in the water up to their bodies, picking for food right and left, and performing all their movements with vivacity and elegance. They kept closely together, and occasionally raised their wings for a few moments, as if apprehensive of getting into too deep water, and being obliged to fly, and seemed to prefer flying to swimming. They were not heard to utter a note. In their stomachs small worms and fragments of very delicate shells were found. The birds seen at the Rapids of the Ohio flew in the manner of the Common Snipe, proceeding at first in an undulating or zigzag line, but more steadily after reaching a certain elevation.

Mr. Salvin found in the collection of Don Vincente Constancia a specimen of this Phalarope which had been obtained near the City of Guatemala, and Swainson states that it is not uncommon on the borders of the lakes adjoining the City of Mexico, from whence he received specimens of both adult and young. Mr. Dresser mentions that in September, in travelling from Brownville to San Antonio, he saw what he had no doubt was a bird of this species, and on the 4th of July, 1864, he shot a pair on some flooded land near San Antonio. Mr. J. A. Allen found these birds abundant in the Valley of Great Salt Lake, and they continued so into September. He considers this one of the most characteristic species of that region, where it is a summer resident, breeding in great numbers on the islands and shores of Salt Lake. Mr. Ridgway met with the Wilson Phalarope in May at Pyramid Lake in Nevada, and again saw it in June in the ponds near the River Jordan in Utah. It has been noticed in September on the Colorado River; and Dr. Cooper thence infers that this may be the species observed by him during the summer among the lakes of the Cascade Range. This species has been observed about the Upper Missouri in the breeding season, and on the Arkansas River between Forts Larned and Lyons. It has also been met with in the summer in various parts of Minnesota and Dakota.

Richardson states that this Phalarope breeds on the Saskatchewan Plains; but it was not met with by him beyond the 55th parallel, nor were any seen on the coast of Hudson's Bay. He adds that this bird lays two or three eggs among the grass on the margins of small lakes. The eggs are very obtuse at one end and taper much at the other, and have a ground-color intermediate between yellowish gray and cream-yellow, interspersed with roundish spots and a few larger blotches of umber brown, most crowded at the obtuse end. The eggs measured 1.37 inches in length by .94 of an inch in breadth.

Specimens of this Phalarope were shot by Mr. William Brewster at Rye Beach in the summer of 1872. Giraud mentions it as of occasional occurrence at Egg Harbor, New Jersey, as well as on Long Island.

The eggs of this species are pyriform in shape, the ground varying from a light fawn-colored drab to a deep rufous drab. The spots are of a dark bistre, of a varying intensity, and very generally distributed. The specimens in the Smithsonian Collection were procured from different points in Iowa, from Utah and Northern Illinois. My own are from Northern Illinois and from Minnesota. Mr. Kennicott found it breeding in the Calumet marshes in Illinois, near Lake Michigan. Mr. B. F. Goss, who procured the eggs from Minnesota, writes me that it breeds quite commonly on marshes, and generally near water. The nest is almost always on hummocks, quite deeply excavated, and lined with dry grasses. One was found on a platform raised above the shallow water.

FAMILY RECURVIROSTRIDÆ. — THE AVOCETS AND STILTS.

THE *Recurvirostridæ,* in addition to the features already mentioned (see p. 108), are characterized by the excessive length of the legs, with very long slender neck and subulate, elongated bill. The plumage has the same dense, soft character as that of the *Phalaropodidæ, Fulicinæ,* and *Longipennes.*

The three known genera, only two of which occur in America, differ as follows: —

A. Hind toe present.

1. **Recurvirostra.** Anterior toes all webbed; bill recurved.

B. Hind toe wanting.

2. **Cladorhynchus.**[1] Toes all webbed; bill perfectly straight, excessively depressed; tarsus but little if any longer than bill.
3. **Himantopus.** No web between inner and middle toes, and web between outer and middle toes quite small; bill very slightly recurved from the middle, cylindrical or scarcely depressed; tarsus much longer than the bill.

GENUS **RECURVIROSTRA,** LINNÆUS.

Recurvirostra, LINN. Syst. Nat. ed. 10, I. 1758, 151 (type *R. avocetta,* L.).

CHAR. Hind toe rudimentary, but distinct; anterior toes united to the claws by a much emarginated membrane. Bill depressed, decidedly recurved, extended into a fine point, which is slightly decurved. Tail covered by the wings.

R. americana.

The species of Avocet are few in number, there being one peculiar to North America, South America, Australia, and Europe, respectively. The two American species may be distinguished as follows: —

[1] *Cladorhynchus,* G. R. GRAY, Gen. B. III. 1840, 577, pl. 155, fig. 1 (type, *Leptorhynchus pectoralis,* DU BUS).

1. **R. americana.** Outer scapulars, rump, and upper tail-coverts, also part of secondaries and greater wing-coverts, white, at all ages. *Hab.* North and Middle America.

2. **R. andina.**[1] No white whatever on upper parts, except head and neck. *Hab.* Andes of Chili.

Recurvirostra americana.

AMERICAN AVOCET.

Recurvirostra americana, GMEL. S. N. I. 1788, 693. — WILSON, Am. Orn. VII. 1813, 126, pl. 63, fig. 9. — NUTT. Man. II. 1834, 75. — AUD. Orn. Biog. IV. 1838, 168, pl. 318 ; Synop. 1839, 252 ; Birds Am. VI. 1843, 24, pl. 353. — BAIRD, Birds N. Am. 1858, 703 ; Cat. N. Am. B. 1859, no. 517. — COUES, Key, 1872, 147 ; Check List, 1873, no. 407; 2d ed. 1882, no. 600. — RIDGW. Nom. N. Am. B. 1881, no. 566.

Recurvirostra occidentalis, VIG. Zool. Jour. IV. 1829, 356 ; Zool. Voy. Blossom, 1839, 28, pl. 12. — CASSIN, Illustr. B. Cal. Tex. etc. 1855, 232, pl. 40 (= winter plumage !).

HAB. Temperate North America ; north to the Saskatchewan and Great Slave Lake, south (in winter) to Guatemala, Cuba, and Jamaica. Much rarer in the Eastern than in the Western Province.

SP. CHAR. Wings (except secondaries, terminal half of greater coverts, and inner secondaries), inner scapulars, and adjoining feathers of the back, brownish black ; lower parts, rump, outer scapulars, and middle of the back white; tail ashy white or pale ashy. *Adult in summer:* Head, neck, and breast, light cinnamon, becoming white around the bill and fading gradually into the white of the body. Tertials brownish gray. *Adult (and young) in winter:* Head, neck, and

breast, white, more or less tinged with pale bluish gray, especially on crown and nape. *Young:* Primaries slightly tipped with whitish ; scapulars and feathers of back tipped or transversely mottled with pale fulvous or buff. Crown dull grayish ; nape tinged with light rufous. Total length, about 17.00 to 18.75 inches; extent, 30.00 to 36.00 ; Wing, 8.50–9.00 ; culmen, 3.40–3.65 ; tarsus, 3.70–3.80 ; middle toe, 1.60–1.70. Bill deep black ; iris umber-brown ; legs and feet ashy blue.

The intensity of the cinnamon-color on the head and neck varies with the individual ; sometimes there is a dusky gray suffusion around the eye, this being especially characteristic of younger birds.

The American Avocet is a bird of irregular or occasional appearance in various portions of North America, and is found in most of the Southern States in greater or less abundance during the winter months, breeding in numerous localities along the Atlantic coast as far north as Long Island, and also, under favoring circumstances, throughout the interior, at least as far south as Southwestern Texas. It is abundant

[1] *Recurvirostra andina*, PHILIPPI & LANDBECK, Wiegm. Arch. 1863, 131. — HARTING, Ibis, 1874. 257, pl. 9.

in Salt Lake Valley, and to the north as far as the Saskatchewan River. Examples were procured at Fort Rae by Mr. Clarke, at Fort Resolution by Mr. Lockhart, and on Peace River by Mr. Ross.

Mr. Salvin met with it in different parts of Guatemala, finding it common at Chiapam and about the neighboring lagoons on the Pacific coast. The birds of this species which he saw did not have the rust-colored necks and heads of northern specimens, but all were white in these parts.

Only a single example is known to have been taken as far to the northeast as Point Lepreaux, on the Bay of Fundy, and it is a very rare bird in New England. Mr. Ross speaks of it as being very rare on the Mackenzie. Captain Blakiston met with it on the shores of the shallow lakes in the Valley of the Saskatchewan, where he found it feeding on insects and small fresh-water crustacea. Richardson gives a similar account of this bird, having found its stomach filled with fragments of crustacea and gravel. He speaks of it as being very noisy, uttering cries of distress, and flying about the heads of those who invade its haunts.

In Utah it is generally known as the "White Snipe," and was there met with by Mr. Allen, especially in Salt Lake Valley. In September it was still very abundant, and was regarded as being highly characteristic of that region, where it was one of the most common summer residents, breeding on the shores and islands of the lake. Flocks of many thousands of this species were seen at the mouth of the Weber River. Mr. Ridgway also found it abundant in spring and summer about the numerous alkaline ponds and lakes of the Great Basin, breeding in those localities in company with the Stilt (*Himantopus mexicanus*).

Mr. Henshaw also mentions it as a common summer resident in Utah and Colorado, and as still more abundant during the migrations. It lives in summer on the borders of all the lakes and ponds of any considerable size. In seeking food it resorts to the water itself, and not to marshes or bogs. Its long legs are specially adapted to the purposes of wading, and its elongated bill and neck allow it to pick up the insects on the bottom of the shallow pools, or the larvæ that are swimming about. Where it has not been molested it is perfectly tame and unsuspicious, and continues its graceful motions with entire unconcern while subjected to a close scrutiny. But in parts of Utah it had learned to dread man as its enemy, and baffled all his efforts. On the 21st of June it was found in great numbers on some alkaline lakes northwest of Fort Garland, in Southern Colorado. As Mr. Henshaw visited one pond after another, he was met everywhere by troops of the old birds, which flew in wide circles about his head, while the shores resounded with their harsh cries. He shot several; but the others still continued their manœuvrings, merely widening their course. The death of their companions seemed to excite little apprehension, although they occasionally flew close to the body of one which had fallen, or alighted beside it, as if trying to comprehend its fate. Where the water was sufficiently deep to allow of swimming, they alighted freely on the surface, and moved buoyantly about in a graceful and pleasing manner. The crops of those examined were filled with the larvæ of some water insect. A single set of four eggs was found, placed in a slight hollow made for the purpose, and lined with weeds.

Mr. Moore met with a single individual of this species in Florida. It was alone, standing on a sand-spit in a bay near the sea. Its diet had been exclusively fish, sixteen of which were within the throat and œsophagus, and no other food was found. The fish were from seven to fifteen sixteenths of an inch in length.

On Long Island Giraud found this species less frequent than the Stilt, and not generally known to hunters. It frequented shallow pools in the salt-marshes, and was sometimes seen wading breast-deep in pursuit of its food. He found a few breeding near Egg Harbor, N. J., where they are known as "Blue-stockings," from the color of their legs. Their nests were built among thick tufts of grass, usually near a pool of shallow water. In California Dr. Cooper found the Avocet rather rare in the southern part. One which had been killed at San Diego late in November was regarded as a great curiosity. It is more common in the central region of the State in the winter, and is frequently brought to market. Dr. Cooper shot individuals in the Platte Region in August, and thinks that some breed in the northeastern corner of the State of California.

In Wilson's day this bird was called by the inhabitants of Cape May "the Lawyer," from its perpetual clamor. It was found associated with the Stilt on the salt-marshes of New Jersey, on the 20th of May, and was flying around the shallow pools uttering the sharp notes of *click-click-click*, alighting on the marsh or in the water, fluttering its wings, and keeping up a continual cry. A nest was found built among the thick tufts of grass, at a small distance from one of the pools, and was made of small twigs of a seaside shrub, dry grass, and seaweed, and raised to the height of several inches. The eggs, which were four in number, he describes as being of a dull olive color, marked with large irregular blotches of black, and with others of a fainter tint. He adds that this species arrives at Cape May late in April, rears its young, and leaves for the south early in October.

Mr. Audubon found a number of Avocets breeding near Vincennes, Indiana, in June, 1814. Their nests were on an island in a large shallow pond. At his approach the birds kept up a constant noise, remained on the wing, and at times dived through the air toward him. There were three nests with eggs, besides a female with her brood, on the island. He observed that this bird on alighting keeps its wings raised until it has fairly settled. If in the water, it stands a few minutes balancing its head and neck, and then stalks about in search of food, sometimes running for it, and occasionally swimming, or wading up to its breast, with its wings partially raised. In feeding these birds remain separated from each other, although occasionally meeting in their flights, and are silent, but apparently not on unfriendly terms with their fellows. In searching for their food they move their heads to and fro sideways while the bill is passing through the soft mud, and when the water is deep they immerse the whole head and part of the neck. In pursuit of aquatic insects they seize their prey by thrusting the lower mandible beneath it, the other being raised above the surface. This bird is also expert in catching flying insects, which it pursues with partially expanded wings.

On approaching one of the nests on which a female was sitting, the latter scrambled off, running, tumbling, and at last rising on wing, floundering hither and thither over the pool, now lying on the surface as if ready to die, and now limping, as if to invite the intruder to pursue her. All the Avocets left their nests and flew directly at him, except the one with the four young birds, who betook herself to the water and waded off, followed by her brood. The latter swam as well as young ducklings of the same size. The nests were placed in the tallest grass, and were entirely composed of this material, but of another year's growth. The inner nest was five inches wide and lined with fine prairie grass, about two inches in depth, over a bed about an inch and a half thick. The eggs in each instance were four in number.

Audubon describes the Avocet's flight as similar to that of the Stilt, the bird passing through the air as if moving to a great distance, with an easy, swift, continued flight, the legs and neck fully extended. When plunging toward an intruder it moves downward, and passes by the person with the speed of an arrow.

On several occasions Mr. Salvin noticed that the birds of this species seen at Chiapam were swimming, and were most industrious feeders, their bills being constantly at work, and admirably adapted for picking the most minute object from the surface of the water.

Mr. Dresser often saw Avocets at the town-lagoon near Matamoras, generally finding them in families of five or six, some of the young birds being only just able to fly. They were not shy, but came to a shallow part of the lagoon close to the houses, and waded along, moving their heads from side to side with perfect regularity, reminding one of a party of mowers, not going in an even line, but one being slightly behind and to the side of the other. Towards August they had become much more abundant. In May and June, 1864, Mr. Dresser saw several pairs on Galveston Island, and was told that they breed on Bolivar Point, and on the islands outside of the Brazos, and St. Louis Pass.

Mr. Aiken mentions the occurrence of this species in Colorado. Captain Bendire found it an abundant summer resident in the lower valleys of Southeastern Oregon, but not in the higher regions of the Blue Mountains anywhere above an altitude of 4,800 feet. It breeds on Malheur Lake and the swampy shores of Sylvia's River. Mr. Nelson speaks of it as very abundant on Salt Lake, where it frequented the shore by hundreds. One which he had wounded tried to escape by diving and swimming short distances under the water. Dr. Merrill mentions it as being common during the winter in the Rio Grande Region, where a few remained to breed.

Mr. Henshaw saw on Santa Cruz Island, California, several which had paired, and were probably breeding. They lived on the beaches, picking up sea-slugs and small crustaceans from the surface of the water.

Eggs of this species (S. I. No. 13689) found by Mr. Ridgway in an alkaline deposit at Soda Lake, near Carson Desert, June 28, 1868, measure 1.85 by 1.30 inches. Their ground-color is a light rufous drab, over which are profusely distributed blotches of irregular shape and size, the colors being a combination of sepia-brown and bistre. The eggs are oboval in shape, with one end more pointed than the other. Another set (S. I. No. 15444) from Carrington Island, in Great Salt Lake, June, 1869, measure 2.08 by 1.40 inches. Their ground-color is a dark drab, lightly tinged with olivaceous, and spotted with dark blotches exclusively of bistre.

Genus **HIMANTOPUS**, Brisson.

Himantopus, Briss. Orn. V. 1760, 33 (type, *Charadrius himantopus*, Linn.).

Char. Hind toe wanting; outer and middle toes connected at the base by a short web; the inner toe completely separated from the middle. Bill subulate, deeper than broad, slightly upturned toward the end. Legs excessively lengthened, the bare part of the tibia about half as long as the tarsus, which greatly exceeds the bill in length, the latter being nearly twice the length of the middle toe.

The Stilts have much the same range as the Avocets, but the species are more numerous, there being at the present time about seven recognized by authorities. Like *Recurvirostra*, the genus *Himantopus* is represented in America by two very distinct species, the one belonging to North, Central, and Northern South America; the other peculiar to the more southern portions of the Southern Continent. They differ as follows: —

1. **H. mexicanus.** White of the forehead not extending over the crown. Black of the nape continuous with that of the back.

2. **H. brasiliensis.**[1] White of the forehead extending back to and including the occiput. Black of the nape separated from that of the back by a wide white bar across lower part of the nape.

H. mexicanus.

Himantopus mexicanus.

AMERICAN BLACK-NECKED STILT.

Charadrius mexicanus, MÜLLER, S. N. Suppl. 1776, 117.
Himantopus mexicanus, ORD, ed. WILSON, VII. 1824, 52. — BONAP. Comp. List, 1838, 54. — RIDGW. Nom. N. Am. B. 1881, no. 567. — COUES, 2d Check List, 1882, no. 601.
Charadrius himantopus, LATH. Ind. Orn. II. 1790, 741 (part).
Recurvirostra himantopus, WILS. Am. Orn. VII. 1813, 48, pl. 58, fig. 2.

[1] HIMANTOPUS BRASILIENSIS.
? *Himantopus melanurus*, VIEILL. Nouv. Dict. X. 1817, 42 (based on *Zancudo*, AZARA, Apunt. III. 1805, 299 ?).
"*Himantopus nigricollis*," AUCT. (Southern South American references; nec VIEILL.).

H. brasiliensis.

Himantopus brasiliensis, BREHM, Vög. Deutschl. 1831, 684. — SCL. & SALV. P. Z. S. 1873, 454 (fig. of head).
Hab. South Brazil, Buenos Ayres, and Chili.

Himantopus nigricollis, VIEILL. Nouv. Dict. X. 1817, 42. — NUTT. Man. II. 1834, 8. — AUD. Orn. Biog. IV. 1838, 247, pl. 328; Synop. 1839, 253; Birds Am. VI. 1843, 31, pl. 354. — BAIRD, Birds N. Am. 1858, 704; Cat. N. Am. B. 1859, no. 518. — COUES, Key, 1872, 247; Check List, 1873, no. 408; Birds N. W. 1874, 462.

Hypsibates nigricollis, CABAN. in Schomb. Guiana, III. 1847, 758.

Macrotarsus nigricollis, GUNDL. J. f. O. 1856, 422.

Himantopus leucurus, VIEILL. N. D. X. 1817, 42 (Mexico).

HAB. The whole of temperate North America, Middle America, and Northern South America south to Peru and Brazil; Galapagos; West Indies in general, and Bermudas; north, on the Atlantic coast, to Maine. More generally distributed and more abundant in the Western than in the Eastern Province.

SP. CHAR. *Adult male:* Forehead, a large postocular spot, lores, entire lower parts, rump, and upper tail-coverts, white. Remainder of the head, whole nape, back, scapulars, and wings (both surfaces), glossy black, with a greenish-blue reflection. Tail pale grayish. Bill black; iris crimson; legs and feet lake-red or beautiful rose-pink in life, yellowish in the dried skin. *Adult female:*

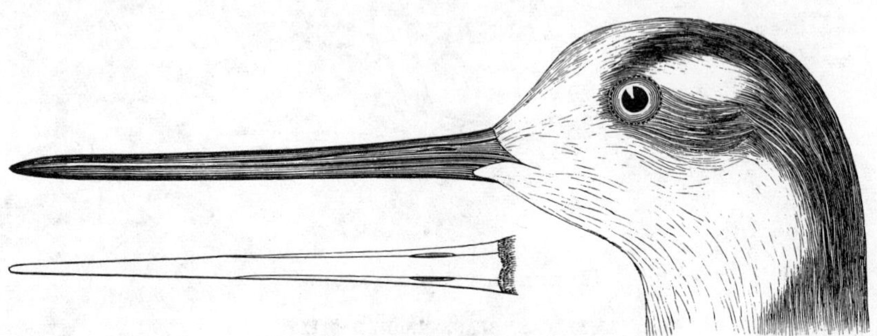

Similar to the male, but back and scapulars brownish slate, and the black of other portions duller. *Young, first plumage:* Similar to the adult female, but the feathers of the back, the scapulars, and tertials bordered with buff or dull whitish, the black of the head and nape finely mottled with the same. *Downy young:* Above light fulvous-grayish, mottled with dusky, the back and rump relieved by several large black blotches. Head, neck, and lower parts fulvous-whitish, the crown, occiput, and nape grayish, the crown with a mesial black streak, the occiput with coarse spots of the same.

Total length, about 14 to 15.50 inches; extent, 27 to 30; wing, 8.50–9.00; culmen, about 2.50; tarsus, 4.00; middle toe, 1.37. Bill deep black; iris rosy carmine; legs and feet fine rose-pink or delicate pale lake-red (in life).

Adult specimens in high breeding-plumage sometimes have the white of the breast, etc., tinged with soft creamy pink.

The Stilt appears to be a common species throughout nearly the whole of the United States, from the Atlantic to the Pacific; more abundant in the Western and Gulf States, and less frequent in the more Northern and Eastern. It occurs occasionally near Calais, but, according to Mr. Boardman, is very rare. Several individual birds have been taken at Grand Menan; and occasional instances of its capture near Boston are known. Mr. Boardman also met with it in Florida, where it was found to be most numerous toward the end of March. It occurs in most of the West India Islands, in Mexico, and in Central and South America. Mr. Salvin found it on the Pacific coast of Guatemala, and also saw a single individual which had been procured near the modern City of Guatemala. Mr. E. Newton mentions the Stilt as being well known by name to most of the inhabitants of St. Croix, although rarely seen. Though not common, it is a regular visitant, and is possibly a resident. According to Léotaud, it is found in Trinidad, and, although not common, is supposed to be resident in that island. Mr. C. W. Wyatt ("Ibis," 1871) mentions finding it wading in the shallows of a lagoon near Cienaga, in Colombia, S. A.

A single example of the Stilt is recorded by Major Wedderburn as having been shot in Bermuda, June 3, 1853. Dr. Berlandier (MSS.) cites this species as inhabiting marshy places on the littoral plains of the Gulf of Mexico, in Texas, Tamaulipas, the vicinity of Tampico, and on the shores of Lake Tamaqua and Tuxpan, in the State of Vera Cruz. It is there known by the trivial name of *Tildillo.*

Dr. Cooper noticed a migrating flock at Fort Mojave, on the 1st of May, 1861; and on the 12th of May, 1863, obtained the first one seen at Santa Barbara. Hence he infers that it always arrives from the south about that time. It is rare on the Pacific coast, but migrates through the interior, and seems to prefer the fresh-water streams and marshes, feeding along their shores. Specimens have been procured near the Rocky Mountains; but it is everywhere rare in California.

According to Giraud, this species is found on Long Island, but is not common; and it is this bird, and not the Avocet, which is the "Lawyer" of hunters. On the sea-coast of New Jersey, where it arrives from the south in the latter part of April, it is more common. Birds of this species associate in small parties, and resort to the shallow ponds on the meadows in the vicinity of the sea-coast, where they wade in pursuit of aquatic insects and minute shellfish. Occasionally a few stragglers may be seen loitering about the pools on the southern shore of Long Island; but these are usually solitary individuals, and such are said to be infrequent. This bird is very rarely exposed for sale in New York markets, and is not known to breed on Long Island.

In Utah, both this species and the Avocet are known as the "White Snipe." Mr. Allen found both species in September, in the valley of the Great Salt Lake, and quite abundant, both species being characteristic of that region, where both are summer residents, and breed on the shores and islands of the lake in great abundance.

Mr. Ridgway met with this bird in the spring and summer months near the alkaline lakes and ponds of the Great Basin, inhabiting the same localities with the Avocet, and being its almost constant companion. In the southeastern portion of Oregon Captain Bendire found it associated with the Avocet, and frequenting the same localities, but not so common. It also breeds in that region.

Mr. Moore writes that he has seen but two pairs of this species, on Sarasota Bay, in Florida, during a residence of two summers, or from February to November in two consecutive years. The first pair seen was June 19, 1870, and the second April 6, 1872; the latter in a pond two miles from the Bay in company with *Totanus flavipes.*

On the coast of Guatemala, as observed by Mr. Salvin, the Stilts were wading about near the shore, pecking at the surface of the water; they were in great numbers, but all in small flocks. Mr. E. Newton, who observed it in a lagoon on the south side of the Island of St. Croix, also mentions its occurring in small flocks of three or four. These were wading mid-leg deep in its shallow water, and were quite regardless of the approach of the boat, but walked slowly about, sometimes picking up insects from the surface of the water, at others dipping their bills into it and, then stopping, with their heads on one side, as if listening, or looking intently into the water. Léotaud speaks of them as usually occurring in pairs in Trinidad, on the borders of partially dried pools. Perched upon their long legs, they move with slow steps, as if measuring the ground, or as if fearful of injuring their long and slender limbs. Their cry is described as being feeble and sad.

Wilson, who had a good opportunity for observing the habits of this bird on the sea-coast of New Jersey, states that it arrives there, about the 25th of April, in small flocks of twenty or thirty, subdividing into smaller parties, associating during the remainder of the season in small companies of two or three pairs. It inhabits the upper portions of the salt-marshes near the uplands, where are numerous shallow pools above all but the highest tides. These pools abound with minute shellfish, aquatic insects, with the larvæ, eggs, and spawn of various forms of marine life; and upon these the Stilt chiefly feeds. A small party of a dozen or more usually make their stay in the thick grass in the vicinity of such localities, and there construct their nests. These are at first slightly formed of a small quantity of dry grass, hardly enough to keep the eggs from the damp ground. As incubation goes on, the nest is increased by the addition of dry twigs, roots of the salt-grass, seaweed, and various other substances, until quite a bulky nest is formed. The eggs are usually four in number, and described by him as of a dark yellowish clay-color, thickly marked with large blotches of black. They are often placed within fifteen or twenty yards of each other, and in the little colony the greatest harmony appears to prevail. While the females are sitting, their mates are usually feeding in the adjoining marshes; but if any person approaches their nests, they all collect in the air, flying with their long legs extended behind them, and keep up a continued yelping note of *click-click-click*. At the same time they droop their wings, stand with their legs half-bent and trembling, as if unable to keep themselves erect, and balancing their bodies with great difficulty. These manœuvres are undoubtedly designed to turn the attention of the intruder from their eggs to themselves. If in wading this bird chances to get into the water beyond its depth, it can swim a short distance as well as the Avocet. It is known to Jersey hunters by the names of "Tilt," "Stilt," and "Longshanks." It occasionally visits the uplands, and wades in fresh-water ponds in search of food, which it scoops up very dexterously with its delicately-formed bill, the extremities of which are soft, and provided with fine nervous membranes, enabling it to detect its food at once. The Stilt raises only a single brood, and departs south early in September.

According to Audubon, a few of this species winter in Louisiana and in Florida, but the greater portion proceed beyond our southern limits. In 1837 this bird made its first appearance near Galveston in April, in small flocks of seven or eight, keeping near the small, shallow, brackish ponds where it sought its food; it is then more shy than while breeding, and utters a whistling cry different from its notes of distress when nesting. It flies in a rapid manner, with regular beats of the wings and with extended neck and legs, and walks with a firm gait, the staggering mentioned by Wilson as noticed when breeding being simulated, and not real. This species is not common along the shores of the Carolinas. Its food is said to consist of insects, small crustacea, worms, the young fry of fishes, and the small Libellulæ.

The Stilt probably breeds in all the Gulf States, in favorable situations. Dresser noticed it at Matamoras in July. On the 2d of June, 1864, he saw two pairs on Galveston Island; and on the 4th of July, after a heavy fall of rain, this bird all at once appeared in abundance in the flooded lands near San Antonio. Dr. Merrill, who had a still better opportunity of observing its habits in the same region, speaks of it as being both common and resident there. It breeds in the marshes in May, making its nests on wet grassy flats, and laying three or four eggs. The nests were platforms of straw and grass, often wet, and barely keeping the eggs out of the water. The average size of the latter was 1.75 by 1.19; the extremes were 1.88 by 1.25, and 1.60 by 1.10.

Two sets of the eggs of this species (S. I. No. 747 and 665) — one from Matamoras, Mexico, procured by Lieutenant Couch, the other by Dr. Würdemann at Calcasieu Pass, La. — measure 1.73 by 1.20 inches, and have a ground-color of dark drab, some with a rufous, others with an olivaceous, tinge. In other examples these shades are more or less intermingled, and they are spotted and blotched with a dark bistre hardly distinguishable from black.

An egg in my cabinet, collected by Mr. N. W. Bishop on the Pampas of South America, belonging to the southern species (*H. brasiliensis*), measures 1.80 by 1.30 inches, but, except in its larger size, is not appreciably different from the eggs of the North American species.

Order ALECTORIDES.

CRANES, RAILS, ETC.

The *Alectorides* are a tolerably well-defined group of birds, related somewhat closely to the *Limicolæ*, but very distinct from the *Herodiones*, to which some of the forms (more especially the *Gruidæ*) bear a teleological resemblance. Typical Families of this Order are the *Gruidæ* (Cranes), *Aramidæ* (Courlans), and *Rallidæ* (Rails), all represented in North America. In addition to these Families, South America possesses several others which have been placed here, but whether rightly or not, we cannot say. These extralimital families are the *Eurypygidæ* (Sun Bitterns), *Heliornithidæ*, *Cariamidæ* (Cariamas), and *Psophiidæ* (Trumpeters).

The typical members of the group are præcocial and ptilopædic.

The Families of this Order which come within the scope of the present work are the following: —

A. Size small or medium ; head normally feathered or with a frontal shield ; middle toe nearly as long as the tarsus ; hallux well developed (nearly as long as the first joint of the middle toe), nearly incumbent. (*Ralli.*)

Rallidæ. Size medium to very small ; outer primary longer than the sixth, very broad ; second nearly or quite equal to the longest. Rectrices almost rudimentary, soft, nearly hidden by the coverts. Bill not curved to one side at tip (usually shorter than the tarsus).

Aramidæ. Size medium or rather large ; outer primary shorter than seventh, the inner web very narrow, except at end ; second quill much shorter than the longest (fifth). Rectrices well developed, firm, twelve in number. Bill curved to one side at tip, equal to or longer than the tarsus ; inner secondaries broad, reaching to end of primaries, their webs partially decomposed.

B. Size large ; head partly naked (except in young), or with ornamental plumes ; middle toe less than half the tarsus ; hallux small, much elevated. (*Grues.*)

Gruidæ. [Characters as above.]

Family RALLIDÆ. — The Rails, Gallinules, and Coots.

Char. Small or medium sized wading or swimming birds, with compressed body, very long toes, which are sometimes (in the Coots) lobed along the edges, short, rounded, concave wings, and very muscular thighs.

The brief diagnosis given above is sufficient to distinguish the Rails, of whatever sub-family, from the Courlans and Cranes, their only near allies. The typical Rails (*Rallinæ*) are of very small to medium size, the typical genus, *Rallus*, being characterized particularly by a lengthened slender bill, while other genera, as *Porzana* and *Crex*, have this member comparatively short and thick. The Coots and Gallinules have the base of the culmen continued upon the forehead, where it widens out into a more or less gibbous or expanded plate or frontal shield. The Coots, however, are peculiar in having the toes fringed with scalloped flaps or lateral lobes.

The three sub-families of *Rallidæ* occurring in North America may be thus distinguished: —

Rallinæ. No frontal process; toes without lateral lobes; size variable; bill sometimes much elongated.

Gallinulinæ. A frontal process, as in *Fulicinæ;* toes without lateral lobes; size large.

Fulicinæ. A frontal process, as in *Gallinulinæ;* toes with a lateral lobed margin; size large.

The several sub-families having thus been defined, the North American genera may be characterized as follows: —

SUB-FAMILY RALLINÆ. — THE TRUE RAILS.

A. Bill slender, equal to or longer than the tarsus.

1. **Rallus.** [Characters as above.]

B. Bill stout, not more than two thirds the tarsus (usually much less).

2. **Porzana.** Middle toe about equal to or slightly longer than tarsus; base of gonys not forming a decided angle; middle of culmen decidedly depressed or concave.
3. **Crex.** Middle toe shorter than tarsus; base of gonys forming a decided angle; middle of culmen scarcely appreciably depressed.

SUB-FAMILY GALLINULINÆ. — THE GALLINULES.

4. **Ionornis.** Nostril small, oval; middle toe shorter than tarsus; toes without trace of lateral membrane; inner posterior face of tarsus with a single row of large quadrate scutellæ.
5. **Gallinula.** Nostril elongated, slit-like; middle toe longer than tarsus; toes with a decided indication of lateral membrane; inner posterior face of tarsus covered with several irregular rows of small hexagonal scales.

SUB-FAMILY FULICINÆ. — THE COOTS.

6. **Fulica.** Nostrils, and proportionate length of toes and tarsus, as in *Gallinula;* toes bordered with a very wide, scalloped, lateral membrane; inner posterior face of tarsus covered with small scales, as in *Gallinula.*[1]

GENUS **RALLUS**, LINNÆUS.

Rallus, LINN. S. N. ed. 10, 1758, 153; ed. 12, 1766, 261 (type, *R. aquaticus*, LINN.).

CHAR. Bill longer than the head, rather slender, compressed; upper mandible slightly curved; nostrils in a long groove, and with a large membrane; wings short; tertiary quills long, frequently longer than the primaries; tail very short; legs moderate; tarsus shorter than the middle toe, and covered on all sides with transverse scales; toes long and rather slender; inner toe rather shorter than the outer; hind toe short and weak.

This genus contains numerous species, inhabiting all the temperate countries of the world, and very similar in their habits, and frequently in appearance. Their long toes enable them to run over and climb amongst aquatic plants with great facility.

[1] A South American genus, *Porphyriops*, PUCHERAN, belonging to the Gallinulinæ, is much like *Gallinula*, but has the lateral margin to the toes more decidedly developed, the gonys very short, and much ascending terminally, the culmen very straight, and the frontal shield small and very pointed.

Synopsis of the North American Species.

Com. Char. Above, olive or ashy, with more or less distinct broad longitudinal stripes of darker; beneath, concolored anteriorly, variegated with bars on the flanks and crissum. Breast more or less reddish; flanks and crissum with brown and white transverse bars; a supraloral light stripe. Wing-coverts usually more rufescent than back.

A. Size large (wing more than 5 inches).

a. Axillars and flanks dusky, with wide white bars (bars about .15 of an inch wide on flanks).

1. **R. elegans.** Back and scapulars ochraceous-olive or yellowish drab, sharply and conspicuously striped with black; breast deep cinnamon. Wing, 5.90–6.80; culmen, 2.10–2.50; least depth of bill, .22–.35; tarsus, 1.90–2.40; middle toe, 1.70–2.10. *Hab.* Fresh-water marshes of Eastern North America.

R. elegans.

b. Axillars and lining of wing dark brown, narrowly barred with white; flanks dark brown distinctly barred with both white and blackish, the bars of the former about .05–.07 of an inch wide.

2. **R. Beldingi.** Above, deep olive-brown, distinctly but not sharply striped with brownish black; breast, etc., rich cinnamon. Wing, 5.70; tail, 2.50; culmen, 2.15; least depth of bill, .30; tarsus, 1.92; middle toe, 1.80. *Hab.* Gulf of California (Espiritu Santo Island).

c. Axillars and flanks brownish gray, with narrow white bars (bars about .10 of an inch wide on flanks).

3. **R. obsoletus.** Back and scapulars grayish olive, indistinctly striped with dusky; breast deep cinnamon. Wing, 6.40–6.60; culmen, 2.25–2.50; least depth of bill, .32–.35; tarsus, 2.10–2.25; middle toe, 2.00–2.15. *Hab.* Salt-water marshes of California.

4. **R. longirostris.** Back and scapulars brownish gray or ashy, obsoletely striped with brown (in Gulf coast specimens distinctly striped with dusky); breast pale buff (in Gulf coast specimens dull cinnamon). Wing, 5.20–6.00; culmen, 2.05–2.50; least depth of bill, .22–.35; tarsus, 1.85–2.10; middle toe, 1.75–2.00. *Hab.* Salt-water marshes of Eastern United States, West Indies, and Northeastern South America.

B. Size small (wing less than 4.50 inches).

5. **R. virginianus.** Similar to *R. elegans*, but rather more deeply colored. *Hab.* North and Middle America.

Rallus elegans.

THE KING RAIL; GREAT RED-BREASTED RAIL.

a. **elegans.**

Rallus crepitans, WILS. Am. Orn. VII. 1813, pl. 62, fig. 2 (fig. but not descr. Not *R. crepitans*, GMEL.). — (?) ALLEN, Bull. Mus. Comp. Zool. III. 1872, 182 (Great Salt Lake, Utah).[1]

Rallus elegans, AUD. Orn. Biog. III. 1835, 27, pl. 203; Synop. 1839, 215; B. Am. V. 1842, 160, pl. 309. — BAIRD, B. N. Am. 1858, 746; Cat. N. Am. B. 1859, no. 552. — COUES, Key, 1872, 273; Check List, 1873, no. 466; 2d ed. 1882, no. 676; Birds N. W. 1874, 535. — RIDGW. Nom. N. Am. B. 1881, no. 569.

b. **tenuirostris.**

Rallus elegans, var. *tenuirostris*, LAWR. Am. Nat. Feb. 1874, 111 (City of Mexico). — RIDGW. Bull. Nutt. Orn. Club, V. no. 3, July, 1880, 139.

HAB. Fresh-water marshes of the Eastern Province of the United States, north, casually, to Massachusetts, Maine, and Canada West, regularly to the Middle States and Northern Illinois; west to Kansas (Great Salt Lake, ALLEN ?[2]). Replaced in the salt-marshes along the Atlantic and Gulf coasts by representative forms of *R. longirostris*.

SP. CHAR. *Adult:* Above, yellowish olive or ochraceous-drab, very conspicuously and sharply striped with black; crown dark brown; a supraloral streak of brownish white, continued to the occiput in a broader stripe of brownish gray; lores and suborbital region brownish gray or dull brownish; chin and throat white; remainder of head and neck, including jugulum and breast,

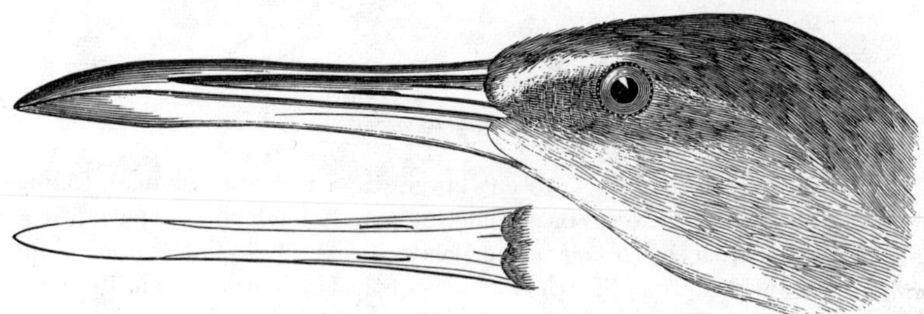

light cinnamon; flanks and sides dark brownish or blackish dusky, barred with white, the white bars averaging about .10–.15 of an inch in width, the interspaces more than twice as wide; crissum mixed dusky and white, the lateral feathers almost immaculate white; middle of the abdomen considerably lighter than the breast, sometimes quite white; axillars and lining of the wing similar to the flanks, but white bars narrower, and less distinct. Wing-coverts rusty brownish, sometimes inclining to chestnut, and not infrequently more or less barred with reddish white; tertials widely striped, like the scapulars; remiges plain umber-brown; rectrices raw-umber, with a dusky medial stripe. "Lower mandible and edges of upper brownish yellow; ridge of upper, and tips of both, deep brown; iris bright red; feet yellowish brown, tinged with olive; claws of the same color" (AUDUBON). *Downy young:* Uniform glossy black; bill dusky, the end, and incomplete wide band near the base (enclosing the nostril), pale yellowish or whitish (in the skin); legs and feet brownish (in skin).

Total length, about 17 inches; wing, 5.90–6.80; culmen, 2.12–2.50; depth of bill in middle, .27–.35; tarsus, 2.20–2.40; middle toe, 1.80–2.10.

The individual variation in this species is very considerable, both as regards coloration and the proportions; but it may always be readily distinguished from the allied forms by the characters

[1] May possibly be *R. obsoletus*.

[2] No specimens seen; may possibly be *obsoletus*.

pointed out in the above synopsis, the very conspicuous, sharply-defined, and broad black stripes above, upon an ochrey-brown or yellowish-olivaceous ground-color, combined with the cinnamon breast and dark flanks, being the prominent distinctive features. The chief variation in colors consists in the degree of ashiness on the side of the head (some examples being distinctly ashy, as in most specimens of *R. longirostris crepitans*), and in the precise shade of the ground-color of the upper parts (which, however, is never ashy).

The only extralimital specimens we have seen are one from the City of Mexico, in the collection of Mr. George N. Lawrence, and one from the Valley of Mexico in the National Museum. These are so different in many respects from the common North American bird as to be entitled to at least sub-specific separation. Compared with true *elegans*, the distinctive characters of the Mexican race are as follows: —

a. **elegans.** Flanks and sides dusky brownish, widely and distinctly barred with pure white. Wing, 5.90–6.80; culmen, 2.12–2.50; least depth of bill, .27–.35; tarsus, 2.20–2.40; middle toe, 1.80–2.10. *Hab.* Fresh-water marshes of Eastern North America.

β. **tenuirostris.** Flanks and sides reddish umber, narrowly and indistinctly barred with reddish white and dilute cinnamon; breast and neck more deeply and uniformly cinnamon than in *elegans.* Wing, 5.90; culmen, 2.00–2.10; least depth of bill, .22; tarsus, 1.80–1.90; middle toe, 1.70. *Hab.* Mexico (Mazatlan and City of Mexico).

The accompanying figure of the bill of *tenuirostris* is taken from the type specimen in Mr. Lawrence's collection.

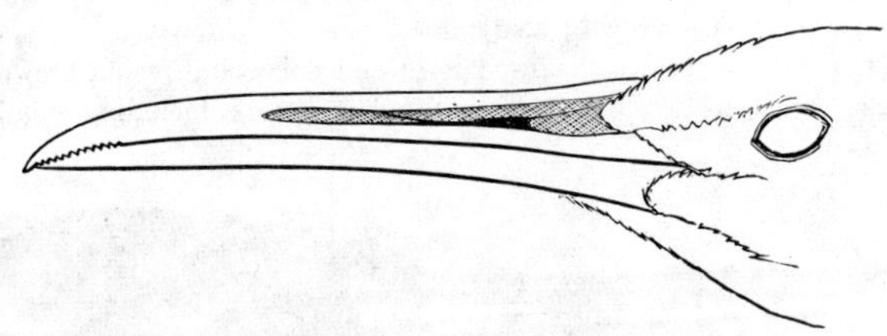

Rallus elegans tenuirostris.

The distinction between the present species and the more common Clapper Rail entirely escaped the notice of Wilson and Nuttall, although the former must unquestionably have met with the *elegans* in the Delaware marshes — in his description of the *crepitans* apparently confounding the manners of the two species. The distinctness of *elegans* as a species and some of its peculiarities were first made known to the public by Mr. Audubon, his attention having been called to the subject by Dr. John Bachman. Although Audubon speaks of having met with a single individual of this species in Kentucky, he seems to have regarded it as an exclusively southern species and as being confined to the fresh-water marshes of the Southern States, and not to have been aware how common it is in the low lands of all the Northwestern States, ranging even as far as Northern Wisconsin and Minnesota. Even now much remains to be learned as to its general abundance in these States, the dates of its appearance and departure.

Mr. Dresser found it pretty common in Southern Texas, on the Brazos and Colorado rivers, and also occasionally on Galveston Island.

Giraud did not meet with any specimens of this Rail in the marshes of Long Island, but mentions the finding a single specimen, taken at Williamsburg, now in the cabinet of Mr. Lawrence; and he regarded it as being extremely rare in that region. Mr. J. H. Batty, however, informs me that he has found stragglers of this species in all parts of Long Island, as well as in the meadows of New Jersey between Jersey City and Newark, where it breeds. He has also taken a single specimen near West Haven, Conn.

Mr. Lewis states that it is well known to the Delaware Rail-shooters as the "King-Rail." It frequents the fresh-water marshes of the interior, and feeds on the same food as the Sora Rail, being often found in the same localities as that bird. He met with it in greater abundance farther south, and rarely noticed it north of the Delaware marshes. Its flesh he regards as very similar to that of the Sora, but as not being quite so delicate, though at times equally juicy and tender. It is found in fresh-water marshes only, according to his experience, and was not met with on the sea-board. It seems to have the same wild skulking habit of the Sora, and its flight is short and labored; when once raised it is easily shot. When wounded it can both swim and dive well, and conceals itself in the water among the reeds. Mr. Lewis shot one in July, on an upland marsh in the midst of a thick wood in Maryland.

Mr. Audubon regarded it as being altogether a fresh-water bird, and confined to the Southern States; and in this first supposition he was undoubtedly correct; for what was supposed to be exceptional in the Pacific coast Rail is only evidence of the distinctness of species; but he was in error in thinking it exclusively southern.

This bird is abundant about Chicago, on Lake Koskonong, Wis., in Minnesota, and in other Western States; and we have no doubt that the Rail referred to by Mr. McIlwraith as breeding about Hamilton, Canada West, is this bird, and not, as he supposed, the *crepitans.* I saw it abundant in the market at Chicago about the 10th of April in an unusually late season. Mr. J. A. Allen met with it in Salt Lake Valley, where he found it very abundant.

Audubon speaks of it as an excessively shy bird, running with celerity, and when caught crying like the Common Fowl. It resides throughout the year in the fresh-water marshes in the interior of South Carolina, Georgia, Florida, Louisiana, and Texas. The same author was informed that this bird is now and then obtained near Philadelphia, where it is considered very rare, and is known as the "King Rail."

In South Carolina, according to Dr. Bachman, although not so numerous as other species, it is not rare in favorable situations. Wherever there are extensive marshes by the side of sluggish streams, this Rail may be found gliding swiftly among the tangled rank grasses and aquatic weeds, or standing on the broad leaves of the water-lily; and there, on some little island of the marsh, it builds its nest. Dr. Bachman states that he has found twenty pairs breeding within a space having a diameter of thirty yards. The nests were placed on the ground and raised to the height of six or eight inches by means of withered weeds and grasses, the number of the eggs being nine or ten. He found a few with eggs about the middle of March, but the greater number of these birds begin to breed about the middle of April. They repair their nests from time to time, and return to them several years in succession. The young — which are at first covered with a black down — leave the nest as soon as they are hatched, and follow their parents along the borders of streams and pools, where they feed on insects, seeds, tadpoles, leeches, and small crayfish. Dr. Bachman several times attempted to domesticate this bird, but failed, probably on account of being unable to obtain a sufficient quantity of suitable food. When grown it feeds on a variety of substances, including seeds and other vegetable productions. In its gizzard were found the seeds of grasses which grow in the places it frequents. On one occasion its stomach was crammed with the seeds of the *Arundo tecta;* and that of another bird contained a quantity of oats which had evidently been picked up on a newly-sown field near the marsh. It is a bird difficult to shoot, as it is not easily raised, and because it confines itself to swampy places, covered with smilax and other briers and thus rendered inaccessible. In seasons of great drought, when the marshes become dry, it has been known entirely to disappear from the neighborhood, retiring to larger and deeper ponds in interior swamps. It has but a single brood in a season, unless the first has been destroyed. Its flight is stronger and more protracted than that of the *crepitans*, but otherwise resembling it. When suddenly flushed, it rises and goes off with a *chuck*, its legs dangling, and proceeds in a straight line for some distance, after which it drops among thick grass and runs off with wonderful speed. Its number is not diminished in winter by any migratory movement.

Mr. Moore mentions as a curious fact in the natural history of this species, as well as in that of *crepitans* and *virginianus*, and the *Porzana carolina*, that it is almost impossible to flush one after the middle of November, in localities where during the two previous months a dozen or more might be put on wing in a few hours. This bird may then be often heard, but not seen, as at other times, to take wing.

Two eggs in my collection (No. 75), obtained in the Calumet marshes, Illinois, by Robert Kennicott, have a ground-color of a dead creamy white; they are marked quite sparsely with small spots and blotches of a prevalent oval shape, some being of a purplish-slate color, but the larger portion being dark purplish brown. One egg measures 1.69 inches in length by 1.29 inches in breadth; the other 1.68 inches by 1.25.

Rallus Beldingi.

BELDING'S RAIL.

Rallus Beldingi, Ridgw. Proc. U. S. Nat. Mus. Vol. 5, 1882, 345.

Hab. Espiritu Santo Island, Gulf of California.

Char. Most resembling *R. elegans*, but darker and richer colored throughout, the sides and flanks with the white bars much narrower, and marked also with very distinct blackish bars. Size smaller. *Adult male* (No. 86419, Espiritu Santo Islands, Lower California, Feb. 1, 1882; L. Belding): Pileum and upper half of nape dark sooty brown or sepia; ground-color of other upper parts deep olive-brown (much as in *R. virginianus* — decidedly darker than in *R. elegans*), broadly striped with brownish black, about as in *R. obsoletus;* wing-coverts dull chestnut-brown, tinged with olive, the exterior feathers more rusty; supraloral stripe light cinnamon, the feathers white at base; lores, continuous with a broad stripe behind the eye, dull grayish brown; under eyelid whitish; malar region, cheeks, entire foreneck, jugulum, and breast rich cinnamon, much deeper than in any of the allied forms; chin white, throat mixed white and cinnamon, the latter on tips of the feathers; entire sides and flanks rather dark hair-brown (less olivaceous than upper parts), rather distinctly barred with blackish and very sharply barred with pure white, the bars of the latter color about .05–.07 of an inch in width; lining of wing dark brown, with very narrow white bars; anterior and middle portion of crissum marked much like the flanks, the lateral and terminal lower tail-coverts pure white. Basal two thirds of the mandible and posterior portion of maxillary tomium deep orange; rest of bill dark horn-brown, the end of the mandible paler; feet dark horn-brown.

Wing, 5.70 inches; tail, 2.50; culmen, 2.15; depth of bill at base, .50; in middle, .30; tarsus, 1.92; middle toe, 1.80.

Compared with specimens of all the allied species and races of the genus, the present bird is instantly distinguishable by the characters pointed out above. In intensity of coloration it most nearly resembles *R. virginianus*, but, apart from its much larger size, presents the following differences of coloration: the side of the head below the eye is chiefly cinnamon, whereas this portion is in *R. virginianus* very distinctly ashy; the breast, etc., are both deeper and redder cinnamon; the ground-color of the sides and flanks much paler (uniform black in *R. virginianus*); the black stripes of the upper parts are both narrower and less sharply defined, while the wings are much less rusty.

Compared with the larger species (*R. longirostris,* with its races, *R. elegans* and *R. obsoletus*), it is difficult to say to which this Rail is most nearly related. None of the forms of *R. longirostris,* however, need close comparison, the darkest-colored race of that species (*R. longirostris saturatus,* from Louisiana) having broader black stripes and a very different (ash-gray) ground-color above; the breast, etc., a very much duller and lighter cinnamon, and the flank-bars broader and on a uniform ground-color. *R. obsoletus* agrees best in the coloration of the upper parts, which, however, in all specimens (including one from San Quentin Bay, on the western side of Lower California) have a lighter, and in some a decidedly grayer, ground-color; but the white flank-bars are much broader, with unicolored interspaces, the breast very conspicuously paler, and the size considerably greater. *R. elegans* has also the breast paler, the ground-color of the upper parts a lighter and much more yellowish olive, and the black stripes much more sharply defined. Upon the whole, I see no other way than to consider the specimen in question as representing a very distinct species or local race, which I take great pleasure in naming after its collector.

[NOTE. — Since the above was written, the National Museum has received two additional specimens, a male and a female, collected by Mr. Belding at La Paz in January, 1883. These agree closely with the type, from Espiritu Santo Island, thus fully establishing the validity of the species.]

Rallus obsoletus.

THE CALIFORNIA CLAPPER RAIL.

? *Rallus elegans,* COOP. & SUCKL. Pacific R. R. Rep. XII. ii. 1860, 246 (Washington Terr.).

Rallus elegans, var. *obsoletus,* RIDGW. Am. Nat. VIII. 1874, 111.—COUES, Check List, App. 1873, 137, no. 466 *a.*

Rallus elegans, b. *obsoletus,* COUES, Birds N. W. 1874, 535.

Rallus obsoletus, RIDGW. Bull. Nutt. Orn. Club, V. no. 3, July, 1880, 139; Nom. N. Am. B. 1881, no. 570.

Rallus longirostris obsoletus, COUES, Check List, 2d ed. 1882, no. 674.

HAB. Salt-marshes of the Pacific coast, south to San Quentin Bay, Lower California, north to Washington Territory (?).

SP. CHAR. *Adult:* Above, grayish olivaceous, indistinctly striped with brownish black; crown and nape brownish dusky; a light brown supraloral stripe; lores and suborbital region dusky brownish; chin and throat white; rest of head and neck, with jugulum and breast, light cinnamon, as in *R. elegans;* flanks and sides grayish brown, with narrow bars of white (bars about .08–.10 of an inch wide, the interspaces .20 to .30); axillars and lining of wing similar, but darker, the white bars narrower; anal region and middle of abdomen plain pale buff; crissum brown or dusky, barred with white, the lateral feathers nearly immaculate white. Wing-coverts umber-brown; remiges plain dusky; rectrices grayish olive, obsoletely dusky centrally. *Downy young:* Uniform glossy black; bill black and whitish (the latter on end and around nostril).

Total length, about 17.00–18.00 inches; wing, 6.40–6.60; culmen, 2.25–2 50; least depth of bill (through middle), .32–.35; tarsus, 2.10–2.25; middle toe, 2.00–2.15.

The Salt-water Marsh-hen of the Pacific coast differs from that of the Atlantic seaboard in the more olivaceous upper parts, with very distinct dusky stripes, and decided cinnamon-color of the breast, in which respects it approaches the Fresh-water species (*R. elegans*), the resemblance to which is so great in the last respect that the bird was originally described as a variety of *R. elegans.* The colors and markings of the flanks, however, as well as its peculiar habitat, prove its relationship to be rather with *R. longirostris.* We here treat it as an independent species, for the reason that it is isolated geographically from any of the races of *R. longirostris,* while it may also always be distinguished by its peculiar colors and proportions.

In the "American Naturalist" for February, 1874, Mr. Ridgway calls attention for the first time to what he then considered a Pacific variety of *R. elegans.* He now regards it as a probably good and distinct species. The type was taken by Dr. Suckley in San Francisco in March, 1857.

Little is known as to its distinctive manners or habits. With regard to this form we have but few notes from any of the writers on the birds of the Pacific coast, and all these were written with the belief that the bird referred to by them was really the *R. elegans.* Dr. Cooper, in his manuscript notes, makes mention of this species as having been met with by himself; and considering it to be the supposed Fresh-water King Rail, he expresses his surprise at finding it by no means confined to the fresh-water marshes. The same writer also mentions having heard the notes of Rails in the Colorado and Mojave valleys; these may possibly have been individuals of the Virginia Rail. The season of the year was the winter and early spring. Since then he has found this species common on the coast, at all seasons of the year, as far north as San Francisco. He found it frequenting indifferently both the salt marshes and the fresh; but it conceals itself so completely, that it can be very rarely obtained, or even seen, except when started by a dog.

Dr. Cooper once found one of these birds concealed in a hole among some rock sand; and instead of making for the marshes, it flew out to sea and settled upon the water. At San Pedro, during the extremely high tides of July, the same observer procured several examples of this species. They were all young birds, but fully grown. They had been driven from the marshy islands by the overflow, and were floating about perched upon pieces of wood, waiting for the waters to subside. They seemed to be perfectly bewildered, and could hardly be induced to take to flight. In another part of his manuscript Dr. Cooper dwells upon the fact — unlooked for by him — that this bird certainly frequents both brackish water and salt-marshes.

Mr. J. A. Allen also makes mention of having met with a Rail, supposed at the time to be *R. elegans,* in the Valley of Great Salt Lake; but this may have been, and probably was, the present species. Whatever it was, he found it very abundant there.

Under the name of *Rallus elegans,* Mr. Henshaw refers to this species as being common in certain marshy spots close to the sea at Santa Barbara, and as retiring during the day into the beds of tall rushes, which serve to screen it from all enemies as well as from the glaring sun. By the first of July the young were out and able to accompany their parents in search of food. These birds began to be active about sunset, heralding the approach of dusk by loud outcries; but they were not entirely quiet during the day, being probably forced to forage more or less at that time in order to satisfy the hunger of their young.

Rallus longirostris.

THE CLAPPER RAIL.

a. longirostris.

Rallus longirostris, Bodd. Tabl. P. E. 1783 (based on *Râle à long bec, de Cayenne,* Buff. Pl. Enl. 849).

Rallus crassirostris, Lawr. Ann. Lyc. N. Y. X. Feb. 1861, in text (Bahia).

b. crepitans.

Rallus crepitans, Gmel. S. N. I. ii. 1788, 713 (based on *Clapper Rail,* Penn. Arct. Zool. II. 1781, no. 407). — Wilson, Am. Orn. VII. 1813, 112 (descr. but not the figure !). — Nutt. Man. II. 1834, 201. — Aud. Orn. Biog. III. 1835, 231, pl. 214; Synop. 1839, 215; B. Am. V. 1842, 165, pl. 310. — Baird, B. N. Am. 1858, 747; Cat. N. Am. B. 1859, no. 553.

Rallus longirostris crepitans, RIDGW. Bull. Nutt. Orn. Club, V. no. 3, July, 1880, 140; Nom. N. Am. B. 1881, no. 571. — COUES, Check List, 2d ed. 1882, no. 673.

Rallus longirostris (nec BODD.), COUES, Key, 1872, 273; Check List, 1873, no. 465; B. N. W. 1874, 536 (excl. syn. pt.).

c. **saturatus.**

Rallus longirostris saturatus, "HENSHAW, MS." RIDGW. Bull. Nutt. Orn. Club, V. no. 3, July, 1880, 140; Nom. N. Am. B. 1882, no. 571 *a*. — COUES, Check List, 2d ed. 1882, no. 675.

d. **caribæus.**

Rallus crepitans and *R. longirostris*, AUCT. (all West Indian references).

Rallus longirostris caribæus, RIDGW. Bull. Nutt. Orn. Club, V. no. 3, July, 1880, 140.

HAB. Salt-water marshes of the Atlantic and Gulf coasts of the United States, north — casually to Massachusetts, regularly to Connecticut; West Indies, and coast of Northern South America, to Brazil. The geographical races limited as follows: *longirostris* to Northern South America (Cayenne to Bahia); *caribæus* to the West Indies; *saturatus* to the Gulf coast of the United States (Louisiana to Florida), and *crepitans* to the Atlantic coast of the United States.

SP. CHAR. *Adult:* Above, olivaceous-gray, or sometimes even ashy, usually very obsoletely striped, sometimes uniform, but, more rarely (more generally in southern specimens), striped with olivaceous or even dusky; crown and nape uniform brown or dusky; a brownish white supraloral stripe; side of the head chiefly grayish (sometimes inclining to ashy), darker on the lores, and

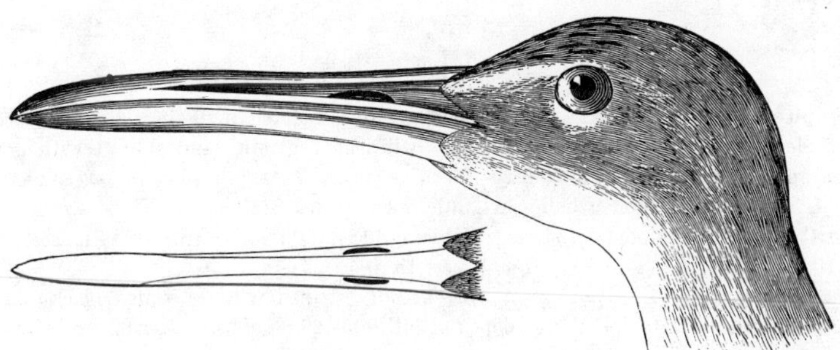

R. longirostris crepitans.

becoming pale cinnamon or buff on the malar region; chin and throat white; rest of the neck, with jugulum and breast, pale cinnamon-buff, olivaceous-buff, or, more rarely, dull cinnamon, tinged with olive; flanks and sides pale olivaceous-gray or brownish slate, barred with white (as in *obsoletus*); axillars and lining of the wing similar, but more narrowly barred with white; anal region and middle of the abdomen plain light buff, grayish, or dusky, barred with white centrally, plain white laterally. Wing-coverts usually more brown than other upper parts; remiges plain umber. *Downy young:* Exactly like that of *R. elegans* and *R. obsoletus*.

Total length, about 14.00–15.00 inches; wing, 5.40–6.00; culmen, 2.10–2.45; least depth of bill (through middle), .22–.28; tarsus, 1.85–2.10; middle toe, 1.70–2.00.

Bill brownish (nearly the color of the supraloral stripe), the upper half of the maxilla dusky; iris raw-umber brown; legs and feet very similar in color to outer webs of primaries (manuscript notes on fresh specimens killed in July on Virginia coast). According to AUDUBON, the fresh colors of specimens examined by him were as follows: "Lower mandible and edges of upper yellowish brown; ridge of upper and tips of both deep brown; iris pale yellow; feet pale livid gray, tinged with orange about the tibio-tarsal joint; claws dusky."

Rallus longirostris is by far the most variable of the North American species of the genus, the variations noted in a large series being plainly local or geographical to a very large degree, but also individual to a considerable extent. Examples from the Atlantic coast of the United States (New York to North Carolina) are the palest-colored, the upper parts being frequently plain grayish, the stripes (olivaceous, not dusky) very faint, or even sometimes quite obsolete; the breast nearly or quite white centrally, with a very decided ash-gray wash across the jugulum. Specimens from Louisiana and Western Florida are quite different, being very darkly colored, the stripes above broad and distinct, dusky black on an ash-gray ground; the breast decided cinnamon, lighter centrally. West Indian skins (of which there is a considerable number before us) are more like those first described above, but have the upper parts distinctly striped with deep olivaceous or raw-umber brown, the breast being colored about the same as in the Atlantic States specimens. It is exceedingly probable that the geographic import of these variations will be confirmed by more extensive series, thus establishing, along with the true *longirostris* (= "*crassirostris*," LAWR.), four well-marked "climatic" races, which may be defined as follows: —

a. **longirostris.** Above, olive-gray, distinctly striped with vandyke-brown; breast deep buff or pale cinnamon. Culmen, 1.90–2.10; least depth of bill, .35–.40; wing, 5.20–5.50; tarsus, 1.75–1.85; middle toe, 1.75. *Hab.* Northern coast of South America (Cayenne to Bahia).

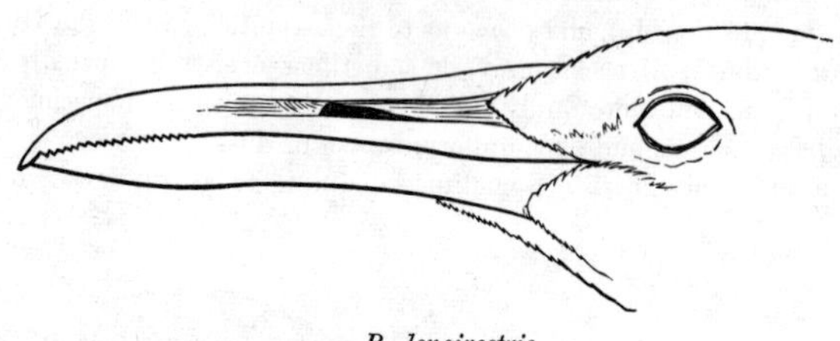

R. longirostris.

b. **crepitans.** Above, ash-gray, the stripes usually obsolete; if distinct, light olivaceous, and not well defined; breast buff, paler (usually whitish) centrally, and shaded with gray across the jugulum. Culmen, 2.10–2.50; least depth of bill, .22–.28; tarsus, 1.85–2.10; middle toe, 1.70–2.00. *Hab.* Salt-water marshes, Atlantic coast United States.

c. **caribæus.** Colors of *longirostris.* Culmen, 2.12–2.50; least depth of bill, .25–.30; tarsus, 1.95–2.10; middle toe, 1.80–1.95. *Hab.* West Indies.

d. **saturatus.** Above, olive-gray or ashy broadly striped with brownish black; breast dull cinnamon. Culmen, 2.10–2.45; least depth of bill, .22–.28; tarsus, 1.95–2.00; middle toe, 1.75–1.80. *Hab.* Louisiana.

The Clapper Rail of the South Atlantic and Gulf Region has a somewhat restricted range within the United States. It is confined to the sea-board, and is found only as far to the north as Long Island Sound, a few, according to Dr. Wood, breeding in Southern Connecticut, but rarely straggling farther north. Along the Atlantic and the Gulf coasts it is seen as far as the Mississippi, and probably beyond to Mexico; but it is not given by Mr. Dresser as a bird of Texas, and I am not aware of any mention of it as having been noticed in Mexico or in Central America. It has not, so far as I am aware, been seen on the Pacific coast, nor anywhere in the interior, excepting that it is mentioned by Mr. McIlwraith as having been found in the vicinity of Hamilton, Ontario; but he probably mistook the *Rallus elegans* for it. It occurs in most of the West India Islands, breeding abundantly in Cuba, Jamaica, Santo Domingo, and other islands, but it is not mentioned as having been noticed in Bermuda.

Professor Newton states that it is found in St. Croix, where it is very local, frequenting a large lagoon in the south of the island, and being there quite numerous and breeding. The birds were very noisy, especially in the evening; and when a gun was fired near their haunts, their outcries could be heard on every side. They were very shy, and not easily shot, as, on being approached, they were seen running across the shallow water, or hopping from root to root of the mangroves, looking like so many rats, and taking refuge among the thickest of the bushes, not showing themselves as long as there was any apparent danger. An adult specimen and a young bird recently hatched were obtained July 21. The stomach of the former contained a portion of a crab and a few shells. The young bird was completely clothed in black down with a greenish gloss.

Léotaud gives this as one of the most common birds of Trinidad, and as being by far the most abundant of the Rails. It is always found among the mangroves, and never leaves the border of the sea. As it moves it always holds its head erect and its tail elevated, fear rather than pride seeming to be the moving cause of these positions. It always seems apprehensive of danger, stopping every moment to watch and to listen, and if seriously threatened concealing itself behind a mangrove-clump, or taking to flight. It then lowers its head, extends its neck horizontally, and starts off with the rapidity of an arrow. When nothing appears to disturb it or to attract its attention, it seems to manifest sportive impulses, uttering its very peculiar rolling cry. Other birds take up and repeat the refrain, until the whole swamp resounds with the clamor, which may be heard to a great distance. This bird will respond readily to a decoy-cry, and is not frightened at the sight of the hunter if the latter keeps motionless; in this way it may be readily obtained. It is much hunted for, as although its flesh is not of the nicest quality, it is considered fairly good.

In many parts of the country this bird is generally known as the "Meadow-hen." It is essentially a southern species, resident throughout the year south of the Potomac, hardly known beyond Long Island, and rare even there. Giraud states that it is, however, abundant on the sea-coast of New Jersey, and that in some seasons it occurs in considerable numbers on the salt-marshes along the south shore of Long Island, which it reaches about the 1st of May, remaining until the latter part of September, and a few continuing even as late as October.

I am, however, informed by Mr. J. H. Batty that, having for some time suspected that this species remains on Long Island during the winter, he obtained positive evidence of the fact in at least one — perhaps exceptional — instance. On the 4th of February, 1873, having been informed that a "Meadow-hen" had been seen on a neighboring creek, he proceeded to the place with his gun and dog, and procured the bird, which proved to be a fine adult male.

This species is said to be confined almost entirely to low wet marshes, hiding in the reeds and rank grass. It can seldom be seen flying, and seems when pursued to depend for escape on its power of running. Its speed is very rapid, and with its thin compressed body it is able to pass through the grass so quickly that it is soon out of sight and danger. In Long Island it breeds in the latter part of May, placing the nest on the meadows, and usually building it so high that it may be readily discovered. This is attributed to the danger from high tides. The eggs are esteemed a great delicacy and are much sought after, the number found in a nest being usually ten, of a pale clay-color, finely dotted with purple. If in making a short excursion in the water this bird becomes suddenly alarmed, it instantly disappears by diving, or, if near the bank, by hiding in the grass. If far from the shore it will cling to the roots of the grass, where it will sometimes remain a surprisingly long while. It is not usually pursued by sportsmen except when the meadows are overflowed by the unusual high tides, which occur after the wind has been blowing heavily from the southeast. Hunters take advantage of these occasions, and pushing a skiff over the sunken meadows, drive the Rails from their retreats, often obtaining them in large numbers. As this bird is slow in its flight and moves in a straight line, it becomes an easy mark when there is nothing to obstruct the sight, and may be very readily taken. Its food consists of small crabs and other minute crustaceans. In the latter part of the season it becomes very fat, acquires a fine flavor, and is highly esteemed by many as food. Mr. Lewis, on the other hand ("American Sportsman," p. 222), maintains that the flesh of this bird is universally insipid, dry, and sedgy. He also speaks of it as being very shy and secret in its habits, and states that he has not met with it except along the salt-marshes of the sea-shore and the mouths of large rivers. He occasionally found it numerous in the brackish fens of Long Island, but has noticed it as being especially abundant along the shores of New Jersey and Delaware. It arrives from the south about the middle of April, and its presence is soon made known by its very peculiar cry or cackle, similar to the well-known notes of the Common Guinea-fowl. Even when these birds are most abundant in the marshes few of them are to be seen.

This bird begins to lay about the close of May; the nest being simple, but artfully contrived for concealment, and having the long grass twisted and plaited over it in the form of an arch, so that when the observer is inexperienced the eggs are effectually concealed. The usual number of these is eight or ten, but there are sometimes as many as fifteen. The egg of this bird is regarded as a great delicacy, and is eagerly sought for. Sometimes the marshes on which this bird breeds are overflowed, in consequence of the long prevalence of easterly gales, and the eggs destroyed in immense numbers. To flush it being almost impossible, the only way to obtain it is to hunt it on the marshes in a light boat during the prevalence of a high tide. The flight of this bird is very similar to that of the Sora Rail, although even more slow and labored, and it is easily brought down when on the wing.

On the coast of the Carolinas this species breeds in great numbers, some remaining nearly all the year; but in winter it occurs in smaller numbers, and occasionally, during the coldest weather, disappears altogether. The number of its eggs is rarely more than seven, and in South Carolina they are laid as early as the 25th of April; but, owing, perhaps, to the nests being so often robbed, fresh eggs are found through June. Two broods are usually raised in one season.

In Jamaica this bird is known as the "Mangrove-hen," it being so named with reference to its appearance, habits, and haunts. It is said by Mr. Hill to ramble about with its callow brood, like a hen and chickens. At low water it visits the uncovered flats, and searches for small crabs. Worms, shell-fish, insects, and crustacea are its animal food, and the seeds and shoots of aquatic plants form the vegetable portion of its nourishment. As this bird has much of the character of the *Gallinaceæ*, and as the young are able to run and feed themselves as soon as they are hatched, these are, when half grown, as helpless on the wing as half-fledged poultry. At this age, when feeding on the shoals, they can be run down with great facility, and are said to be delicious eating.

Wilson states that the eggs of this bird are a great delicacy, far surpassing in his opinion those of the domestic hen. So abundant were the nests of this Rail, according to his observations, that he has known twelve hundred of their eggs to be collected by one man in a single day. Wilson also mentions that on several occasions, when an unusually high tide had flooded the marshes on which these birds were breeding, he has found the dead bodies of the females, who had perished on their nests, strewed along the shore — proving how strong are the ties of maternal affection in this species. He also states that it has a covered pathway through the marshes, under the matted grasses, through which this bird runs in the manner of rats, and by which it escapes observation.

Its cries are said by Audubon to resemble the syllables *căc-căc-căc-căc-că-căhă-càhà*, the first of these notes being extremely loud and rapid, and the later ones lower and protracted. The bird seems to possess the powers of ventriloquism, so that it often appears much nearer than it really is.

In South Carolina, during the month of October and later, it is hunted at high tide, in the same manner as is practised near Philadelphia in hunting the Sora Rail, and many are thus obtained. This can only be done during high water.

Mr. Moore states that he has measured, in one instance, the footprints of the Clapper Rail, made on a smooth sandbar, and found the interval between them, for several steps, nineteen inches. These must have been impressed when the bird was running at its utmost speed. Even then the extent is surprising, when the length of the tarsus is borne in mind, this being only 2.75 inches. The largest stride of a Canada Crane is only 19.50 inches. The interval between the footprints of the Great Blue Heron, in its widest step, is 19.87 inches. An egg with the shell formed was found in one of these birds June 6th; and five young birds, only a few days old, were seen Aug. 4, 1873.

The ground-color of the eggs of this species is usually a pale cream, but much deeper than that of *R. elegans.* The markings are also much more numerous than in those of the latter, but essentially of the same tints — dark purplish brown and a lighter purplish slate. Two eggs in my collection (No. 77), from South Carolina, taken by Dr. Bachman, measure: one 1.60 inches in length by 1.17 in breadth, the other 1.70 by 1.20.

The eggs exhibit great variations in size and shape, the largest measuring 1.80 by 1.10 inches, the smallest 1.50 by 1.05, the most oblong 1.60 by 1.00, etc. The ground-color varies from a pale buff to a dirty white. All are marked — more or less sparsely — with spots and blotches of reddish brown and obscure lilac and slate.

Rallus virginianus.

THE VIRGINIA RAIL; LITTLE RED-BREASTED RAIL.

Rallus virginianus, LINN. S. N. I. 1766, 263 (based on CATESB. 70; BRISS. V. 175). — WILS. Am. Orn. VII. 1813, 109, pl. 62, fig. 1. — NUTT. Man. II. 1834, 205; AUD. Orn. Biog. III. 1835, 41; V. 1839, 573, pl. 205; B. Am. V. 1842, 174, pl. 311. — BAIRD, B. N. Am. 1858, 748; Cat. N. Am. B. 1859, no. 554. — COUES, Key, 1872, 273; Check List, 1873, no. 467; 2d ed. 1882, no. 677; Birds N. W. 1874, 536. — RIDGW. Bull. Nutt. Orn. Club, V. no. 3, 1880, 140; Nom. N. Am. B. 1881, no. 572.

Rallus aquaticus, var. β, LATH. Ind. Orn. II. 1790, 755.

Rallus limicola, VIEILL. Ency. Méth. 1823, 1059.

HAB. The whole of temperate North America as far as the British Provinces, south to Guatemala and Cuba; occasionally winters almost at the northern limit of its range.[1]

SP. CHAR. *Adult:* A miniature of *R. elegans*, but more deeply colored. Above, olivaceous, heavily striped with black; wing-coverts chestnut-rufous; remiges plain dusky; crown and nape dusky, sometimes uniform, usually indistinctly streaked with olive; a brownish-white supraloral line; side of head uniform plumbeous (sometimes obscured with a brownish wash); malar region, foreneck, jugulum, breast, sides, and abdomen, sometimes throat also, cinnamon, the middle of the belly lighter (sometimes whitish); flanks (not sides) and axillars dusky, barred with white; lining of wing dusky, the feathers tipped and bordered with white. *Downy young:* Glossy black; bill scarlet or orange-red in life (whitish or pale yellowish in the skin), slightly marked with blackish in front of the nostril and on base of mandible. *Young (first plumage)*: "Top and sides of head, neck behind, back anteriorly, rump, breast, and sides, dull dead black. Interscapular

[1] A specimen was sent by Captain Bendire to the National Museum from Walla Walla, Washington Territory, which was shot there Jan. 16, 1879, when the snow was more than a foot deep!

region black, with a few of the feathers margined with brownish olive. Wing-coverts and wings nearly as in adult, a little duller and darker, perhaps. Superciliary line obscure ashy. Throat ashy white, finely spotted with black. Central region of lower breast and abdomen, with a few of the feathers on the sides, tinged with white. Anal region and crissum dull reddish chestnut. In my cabinet, from Cambridge, Mass., August, 1875. Several other specimens of corresponding ages agree closely with the one above described. A male, however (Cambridge, Aug. 9, 1875), differs in having a faint reddish wash over the white on the breast and abdomen" (BREWSTER, Bull. Nutt. Orn. Club, Jan. 1879, p. 45).

Total length, about 7.50 inches; wing, 3.90–4.25; culmen, 1.45–1.60; tarsus, 1.30–1.40; middle toe, 1.20–1.40. "Bill dark brown, the lower mandible and edges of upper yellowish brown; iris bright red; feet yellowish brown tinged with olive; claws more dusky" (AUDUBON).

This species is very much like *R. elegans* in miniature, being exceedingly similar to that species in coloration. Close examination, however, reveals several important differences, the more obvious

of which are the following: the whole plumage is darker; the sides of the head more uniformly and distinctly plumbeous; the sides and abdomen are cinnamon, like the breast, instead of being respectively barred, like the flanks, and plain buff or whitish; the lining of the wing is not barred like the flanks, but has dusky and white irregularly mixed, the latter color being on the border and tips of the feathers. There is apparently more of individual variation in this than in any of the larger species, scarcely two examples being closely alike. The chin and throat may be distinctly white, or the cinnamon may extend forward entirely to the bill; some specimens have the lores decidedly dusky, others, clear plumbeous, like the auriculars; the crissum is sometimes plain cinnamon, the concealed bases of the feathers dusky, but oftener is white, tinged with cinnamon. One example (an adult male, No. 84677, U. S. Nat. Mus., Riverdale, Ill., May 3, E. W. NELSON) has the flanks dark brown, with the bars nearly obsolete. No. 7057 (National Museum Collection), from St. Louis, Mo., also an adult male, collected May 6 (W. S. WOOD), has the lower parts dull grayish brown, browner on the breast, almost slaty on the abdomen and tibiæ. There seems to be no geographical variation, however, notwithstanding the extensive range of the species, specimens from Guatemala, Mazatlan, Sonora, California, and Washington Territory being quite identical with others from the Eastern United States.

The Virginia Rail has the most extended distribution of any of this family, being found, at certain seasons, throughout the entire United States, from Florida to the extreme eastern limits of Maine, and from the Atlantic to the Pacific. It occurs in great numbers in Canada, especially in the western portion, and has been found breeding as far north as Big Island by Mr. B. Ross. It is also very abundant in Illinois, Michigan, Wisconsin, and others of the Western and Northwestern States. It is a winter resident of Cuba, but is not known to breed there; nor is it given by either Gosse or Marsh as being found in Jamaica. In Central America it appears to be rare, only a single specimen being on record as noticed there; this is mentioned by Salvin as having been taken at Antigua, in Guatemala, in September, 1859, on one of the cochineal plantations. This species is abundant in the winter months in different parts of Mexico. It was obtained near Matamoras, in August, by Mr. Dresser; and is given by Dr. Heermann as occurring at San Antonio. A single specimen of this bird has been taken in Bermuda. Mr. J. A. Allen found this species very common in the marshes and low lands in the Valley of Great Salt Lake; and Mr. Ridgway mentions having seen two or three individuals in the vicinity of Pyramid Lake, among the sedges on the banks of the sloughs and ponds. It is only partially migratory in the winter, even in places where the winter is quite severe. A specimen was taken by Captain Bendire near Fort Walla Walla, Jan. 3. 1879.

Although Dr. Cooper never obtained any himself, he states that this bird is found throughout the marshes of California, chiefly those of the interior, and as far to the north at least as Cape Flattery. It is undoubtedly resident in California throughout the year, as Dr. Suckley obtained a specimen near the Straits of Fuca in January.

Mr. Boardman informs me that it is found as far east as Calais, and even breeds in that neighborhood, although it is not common. It was once quite abundant in the vicinity of Boston in all our marshes and fresh-water meadows, and more especially on the margins of brooks. In June, 1837, I discovered a nest containing ten eggs within the present limits of Boston, and only a few rods from a recently-constructed railroad track. Mr. Allen included it among the birds of Western Massachusetts, but did not regard it as being of common occurrence there. On May 16, 1859, Mr. Frederick Ware found a nest, with nine eggs, in the Fresh Pond marshes, West Cambridge.

Although found sparingly present, during the breeding-season, along our entire Atlantic coast, from Charleston, S. C., to Eastport, it is far more abundant in the fresh-water meadows of the interior. On Long Island, according to Giraud, it is known to hunters and sportsmen by the name of the "Fresh-water Marsh-hen" or "Mud-hen." It is there only found in low situations, usually selecting the reedy margins of watercourses and rivulets. Giraud also met with it on the low salt-marshes along the sea-coast. In its habits, as well as in its plumage, it bears a greater resemblance to *Rallus elegans* than it does to *R. crepitans*. With all the movements, actions, and manners of the former its own are very much in unison. Hiding, as it does, among reeds and rushes, it escapes observation, except on the part of those who are familiar with its habits.

Like all of this family, the Virginia Rail is very reluctant to take wing, and when pursued by dogs it trusts to its legs until they cease to be sufficient. It runs with great swiftness, and is capable of continuing a very rapid and irregular course through the close grass for some time. Unless followed by a very active dog, it is always able successfully to evade pursuit without exposing itself to the sportsman's gun.

It is not often observed on the water, yet it can swim and dive very well when driven to this element for safety. It seems to prefer wet ground, or water so shallow that it can wade through without being obliged to swim. The food of this species is said to consist of aquatic insects, worms, snails, and the seeds of various kinds of grasses that grow on marshy ground and in the low fresh-water meadows which it frequents. The flesh of this bird is not particularly delicate, yet it is frequently brought to the New York market in the month of April.

Wilson speaks of it as far less numerous than the Common Rail in New Jersey, though frequently seen along the borders of salt-marshes, as well as among the meadows on the banks of the larger rivers. He met with it on the Barrens of Kentucky, but was told by the inhabitants that it was seen in wet places only in the spring, going north during the breeding-season. It feeds less on vegetable and more on animal food than the Common Sora, and on this account its flesh is much inferior to that of this species. In Wilson's time it was known as the "Fresh-water Mud-hen," because it frequented only those parts of the salt-marsh where fresh-water springs rose through the bogs in the salt-marshes. In such places these birds build their nests; and one of these, which was seen by him, is described as being placed in the bottom of a tuft of grass in the midst of an almost impenetrable quagmire, and as composed altogether of old wet grass and rushes. The eggs had been floated out of the nest by an extraordinarily high tide, and lay scattered about. The female still lingered about the spot, and suffered herself to be taken by hand, and during the few hours she was detained laid an egg exactly like the others. Wilson describes the egg as being shaped like that of the Domestic Hen, and as measuring 1.20 inches in length by less than half an inch in breadth; it is of a dirty white or pale cream-color, sprinkled with specks of reddish and pale purple, most numerous near the great end. This bird was supposed to begin to lay early in May, and to raise two broods in a season, as in the month of July Mr. Ord brought to Wilson several young only a few days old, which had been caught on the borders of the Delaware. The parents had shown great solicitude for their safety. The young birds were covered with fine down, and were wholly black, except a white spot on the bill. They had a short piping note. Owing to its secretive habits, this bird can rarely be seen. It stands and runs with its tail erect, which it jerks whenever it moves; it flies only to a short distance, with its legs hanging down. The moment it alights it runs off with great speed.

Nuttall, who heard the notes of the male of this species on the Charles River marshes, describes it as a guttural croaking call, like the noise of a watchman's rattle, sounding like *cut-ă-cut-tee-àh*. The young have a slender cry of *peep-peep;* and the female, when startled, utters a sharp squeaking scream, which seems much nearer than it really is, and sounds like *keek-keek-kek*.

Audubon states that these birds winter in Lower Louisiana, Florida, Georgia, and the Carolinas, remaining in the Western States later in the fall than farther east; but a large proportion retire after the first severe frosts. He met with them on the St. John's River, in New Brunswick — where, however, they are very rare; and he also remarks that he found them breeding in March near New Orleans; in Kentucky in April; and a little later near Vincennes, in Illinois.

Wilson evidently makes a mistake in regard to the breadth of the egg of this species, meaning doubtless an inch, and not half an inch. An egg (No. 210) in my collection, from Calumet marshes, Illinois, identified by Mr. Robert Kennicott, measures 1.28 inches in length by .96 of an inch in breadth; and two (No. 1271) measure each 1.30 inches by exactly 1 inch in breadth. The ground-color in these is a creamy white. The markings are generally very much scattered, except about the larger end, where they are crowded together, but nowhere confluent; these markings are small blotches of a bright brownish red, and there are also slightly larger and fainter ones of a purplish lilac. The markings vary in size in the different eggs. In shape the egg is a rounded oval, one end much more tapering than the other. The usual number of its eggs is nine, never more than this, and very rarely less.

Genus **PORZANA**, Vieillot.

Porzana, Vieill. Analyse, 1816, 61 type, *Rallus porzana*, Linn. — Cass. in Baird's B. N. Am. 1858, 748.

Ortygometra, Leach, Syst. Cat. 1816, 34. — Gray, Gen. B. III. 1846, 593 (type, *Rallus porzana*, Linn.).

Creciscus, Caban. Jour. für Orn. 1856, 428 (type, *Rallus jamaicensis*, Gmel.).

Coturnicops, Bonap. "Compt. Rend. XLIII. 1856, 599" (type, *Fulica noveboracensis*, Gmel.).

CHAR. Bill shorter than the head, compressed, straight; nostrils in a wide groove, with a large membrane; wings moderate; primaries longer than tertials; tail short; legs rather robust, the tarsus about the length of the middle toe; toes long, the inner one slightly shorter than the outer. General form compressed and slender.

This genus contains very numerous species, inhabiting both temperate and tropical regions, frequenting marshes and borders of rivers. In the spring and autumn several species migrate in large numbers.

The genus as here considered probably requires subdivision.

P. carolina.

We have not at hand the required material for defining the exact limits of the genus *Porzana*, so far as its American representatives are concerned. Without, therefore, considering any of the extralimital species, it may suffice to say that of the three which properly belong to North America, one (*P. carolina*) is a very near relative of the type of the genus (*P. maruetta* of Europe and Greenland), while the other two are perhaps sufficiently different to justify generic separation. The species which occur in North America are four in number, including one which is merely a straggler to Greenland from the Palæarctic Region. They may be distinguished as follows: —

A. Above, russet-olive, with black blotches and irregular, partly longitudinal, streaks of white. (*Porzana.*)

1. **P. maruetta.** Neck and breast olive, speckled with white; flanks brown, narrowly and irregularly barred with white. Wing, 4.20–4.40 inches; culmen, .68–.72; tarsus, 1.20–1.30; middle toe, 1.25–1.35. *Hab.* Palæarctic Region; casual in Greenland.

2. **P. carolina.** Neck and breast without white specks; throat blackish, and sides of head and neck plumbeous in adult; throat white, sides of head and neck, with jugulum and breast, fulvous-olive, in young; flanks broadly barred with white and slate-color. Wing, 4.15–4.30 inches; culmen, .75–.90; tarsus, 1.25–1.35; middle toe, 1.30–1.45. *Hab.* North America.

B. Above, ochraceous, with broad black stripes and narrow transverse white bars; secondaries white, forming a conspicuous patch on the extended wing. (*Coturnicops.*)

3. **P. noveboracensis.** Head, neck, and breast ochraceous; flanks dusky, barred with whitish; crissum cinnamon; lining of wing and axillars white. Wing, 3.00–3.60 inches; culmen, .50–.60; tarsus, .95–1.00; middle toe, .90–1.00. *Hab.* Eastern North America.

C. Above, blackish brown, speckled with white. (*Creciscus.*)

4. **P. jamaicensis.** Nape dusky chestnut or sepia-brown; lower parts slate-color or dark plumbeous (the throat sometimes whitish), the posterior portions narrowly barred with white.

a. jamaicensis. Back speckled with white. Wing, 2.95–3.20 inches; culmen, .50–.60; depth of bill through base, .20–.25; tarsus, .85–.90; middle toe, .85–.95. *Hab.* Warm-temperate and tropical America, from the United States to Chili.

β. coturniculus. Back without white specks. Wing, 2.50 inches; culmen, .60; depth of bill through base, .15; tarsus, .75; middle toe, .85. *Hab.* Farallon Islands, coast of California.

Porzana maruetta.

THE EUROPEAN SPOTTED CRAKE.

Rallus porzana, LINN. S. N. ed. 12, I. 1766, 262.
Crex porzana, JENYNS, Man. Brit. Vert. An. 1835, 218. — NAUM. Vög. Deutschl. IX. 1838, 523, pl. 237. — MACGILL. Man. II. 114; Hist. Brit. B. IV. 1852, 535.
Ortygometra porzana, STEPH. Gen. Zool. XII. 223. — BONAP. Comp. List, 1838, 53. — KEYS. & BLAS. Wirb. Eur. 67. — GRAY, Gen. B. III. 593; Cat. Brit. B. 1863, 179. — REINH. Ibis, 1861, 12 (Greenland).
Gallinula maculata, BREHM, Vög. Deutschl. 1831, 698.
Gallinula punctata, BREHM, t. c. 699, pl. 36, fig. 3.
Ortygometra maruetta, LEACH, Syst. Cat. 1816, 34.
Porzana maruetta, GRAY, List Gen. B. 1841, 91. — RIDGW. Proc. U. S. Nat. Mus. Vol. 3, 1880, 201, 222; Nom. N. Am. B. 1881, no. 573. — COUES, Check List, 2d ed. 1882, no. 678.
Spotted Crake, YARR. Brit. B. ed. 2, III. 97, fig.; ed. 3, III. 114, fig.

HAB. Palæarctic Region; occasional in Greenland (cf. REINHARDT, "Ibis," 1861, p. 122).

SP. CHAR. *Adult:* Above, russet-brown, relieved by oblong spots of black and irregular, mostly longitudinal, streaks of white; crown streaked with black, but without a median longitudinal stripe of this color, as in *P. carolina;* a wide superciliary stripe, malar region, chin, and throat, soft mouse-gray; lower half of lores dusky, upper half dull whitish; auriculars, neck, and jugulum light

hair-brown, irregularly speckled with white; abdomen whitish; sides and flanks brown, barred with white: crissum, plain creamy buff. *Young:* Similar to the above, but superciliary stripe finely speckled with white, the malar region, chin, and throat whitish, speckled with brown, the breast and belly washed with pale buff.

Wing, about 4.25–4.50; culmen, .68–.72; tarsus, 1.20–1.30; middle toe, 1.25–1.35. Bill "reddish yellow, brighter at the base," iris reddish brown, feet yellowish green (MACGILLIVRAY).

This species is about the size of the Common "Sora" of North America (*Porzana carolina*), and resembles it very closely in coloration, the upper parts being almost precisely similar. It may be immediately distinguished, however, by the white speckling of the neck and breast, and the streaked crown, characteristic of all stages, and in the adult plumage having no black on the lores or throat.

The "Spotted Crake" of England, or "Porzane Marouette" of the French, is, according to M. Gerbe, a bird common in the greater part of Europe, Asia, and Africa, and more especially in the warmer portions of that region. It is a bird of the old continent, and has no other claim to a place in our fauna than its occasional presence in Greenland. Gerbe says that it is not rare in any part of France, not even the more northerly, where it usually arrives in March, and from which it departs in

September and October, though a few remain later. It is said to be especially common in Italy, in Sicily, and in the southern portion of Russia, but to be very rare in Holland. According to M. Boutelle, as quoted by Gerbe, it breeds in immense numbers in the marshes of Saint-Laurent du Pont, near Grenoble. Its nest is said to be a structure loosely woven of coarse weeds, but so constructed as to be raised or depressed by the rise or fall of water.

The number of the eggs varies from eight to twelve. These are slightly oblong in shape, of a bright clear yellowish brown, covered with numerous very fine points, with scattered blotches of varying size, some small and round, others larger, and varying in shape, but always quite distinct in their coloring. These markings, scattered over most of the egg, but chiefly grouped about its larger end, are of two kinds, one deep violet-gray, others either a reddish or a blackish shade of brown. They are said to measure from 1.34 to 1.38 inches in length, and from .94 to .98 of an inch in breadth.

The bird is said to have habits very similar to those of the European Water Rail, frequenting, like that bird, fresh-water marshes and the margins of water covered with rushes and coarse reeds. It feeds on insects, snails, small reptiles, and aquatic plants. Its flesh in the autumn, when it is fat, is of very fine flavor, and hardly inferior to that of the Land-Rail.

In Great Britain, according to Yarrell, this bird is a summer visitor, arriving in England by the 14th of March, and remaining as late as the 23d of October. In exceptional instances individuals have been taken as late as November, and once even in January. It is, as a species, much less numerous than the Land-Rail, and is more aquatic in its habits. It frequents the sides of streams and lakes, concealing itself among the thick reeds, and seldom leaves its secure position among the luxuriant vegetation of marshy grounds, unless driven out by the aid of a trained dog. Its body is compressible, enabling it to make its way through the thick herbage with facility. Its toes — which are long in proportion to the size of the bird — afford it a firm footing over mud or weeds, and also enable it to swim with ease. It is more abundant in the maritime portions of England than elsewhere, and breeds in considerable numbers in the marshes of Norfolk. It also breeds in other parts of England, where it can find suitable localities, and is more common in the fall than at any other time. It feeds on worms, aquatic insects, and slugs, as well as on soft vegetable substances. When kept in confinement it readily eats bread and milk or worms.

This bird occasionally, but rarely, visits Sweden in the summer. It has been taken at Tunis, and near Smyrna in the winter, and during its migrations in the islands of the Mediterranean.

It breeds in such marshes as are overgrown with reeds and sedges, its nest being built on the wet ground, usually near the edge of the water, and formed of coarse aquatic plants lined on the inside with finer materials. The young are at first covered with a black down, and are said to take to the water with readiness as soon as they are out of the shell. Yarrell describes the egg as being of a pale reddish white, spotted and speckled with a dark reddish brown, and measuring 1.25 inches in length by .87 of an inch in breadth. Three eggs in my own cabinet (No. 1390) — collected in France by Dr. James Trudeau — are oblong and oval in shape, of nearly equal size at either end. The ground-color is a light buff or dark cream-color, with a reddish or a yellowish tinge, spotted irregularly with rounded and scattered markings of a deep brownish red. These are of varying sizes, shapes, and shades, a few as if washed with the ground-color diluted, and exhibit a shade of slate and lavender. They vary in length from 1.30 to 1.35 inches, and in breadth from .94 to .99 of an inch.

Porzana carolina.

THE CAROLINA RAIL; SORA RAIL.

Rallus carolinus, LINN. S. N. I. ed. 10, I. 1758, 153; ed. 12, I. 1766, 263. — SW. & RICH. F. B. A. II. 1831, 403. — AUD. Orn. Biog. III. 1835, 251; V. 1839, 572, pl. 233.

Rallus (*Crex*) *carolinus*, BONAP. Obs. Wils. 1825, no. 230. — NUTT. Man. II. 1834, 209.

Ortygometra carolina, BONAP. Comp. List, 1838, 53. — AUD. Synop. 1839, 213; B. Am. V. 1842, 145, pl. 306.

Porzana carolina, CASS. in Baird's B. N. Am. 1858, 749. — BAIRD, Cat. N. Am. B. 1859, no. 555. — COUES, Key, 1872, 273; Check List, 1873, no. 468; 2d ed. 1882, no. 679; Birds N. W. 1874, 538. — RIDGW. Nom. N. Am. B. 1881, no. 574.

Rallus stolidus, VIEILL. Enc. Méth. 1823, 1071.

HAB. The whole of temperate North America, but most common in the Eastern Province; West Indies in general; whole of Middle America, south to New Granada and Venezuela; accidental in Greenland and Europe; Bermudas (numerous in migrations). Breeds chiefly in the northern part of its range.

SP. CHAR. *Adult:* Above, bright olive-brown, with longitudinal spots of black, some of the feathers edged with white; top of head with a broad longitudinal stripe of black; anterior portion of head, with chin and throat, black; sides of head and neck (except as described), jugulum, and breast light plumbeous; abdomen white; anal region and crissum creamy white or pale

buff; flanks sharply barred with white and slate-color. *Young:* Similar, but lores and superciliary stripe brownish, the chin and throat whitish; rest of neck, with jugulum and breast, light brownish. Bill greenish yellow (more orange, especially at base, in summer adults); iris brown; legs and feet greenish. "*Downy stage* — chick a few days old: Bill short, exceedingly compressed, high at base, rapidly tapering, the tip deflected. The whole body densely covered with dull black down, beyond which are produced abundant long, glossy, black hair-like filaments. Upon the throat is a tuft of stiff, coarse bristle-like feathers of a bright orange-color. These are directed forward, and give the bird a most singular appearance. (From a specimen in my cabinet collected at Cambridge, Mass., June 24, 1874.) This bird, although the only specimen of the kind now at hand, is one of a large brood which was attended by the female parent. Several of the others were distinctly seen and closely examined at the time. All had a similar orange tuft upon the throat." [BREWSTER, in "Bull. Nutt. Orn. Club," January, 1879, p. 48.]

The most abundant and most universally known bird of its genus inhabiting the United States, and variously known as "the Rail," "Sora," or "Ortolan," according to locality. It is especially numerous along the creeks and rivers on the Atlantic during the autumnal migration, when excursions for obtaining it are a favorite amusement of our gunners and sportsmen. It appears to inhabit the entire temperate regions of North America. There is apparently little, if any, geographical variation noticeable in a large series of specimens, and the principal individual variation consists in the extent of the black on the throat, which in some examples extends back as far as the middle of the abdomen.

The Common Sora Rail, so abundant in the eastern portion of the Middle States during its migrations, and so familiar to all the sportsmen of the Delaware, appears to have a very extended distribution. During the winter it is found in favorable localities throughout Central America, Mexico, and the extreme southern portions of the United States, and in the summer it extends its migrations as far north as latitude 62°. It was found at Fort Resolution, Moose Fort, Fort Rae, and on the Red River.

Mr. Salvin states that it is the only Rail found about the Lake of Dueñas, in Guatemala, where it is migratory, leaving that district on the approach of summer. Mr. Skinner also obtained specimens in the district of Vera Paz. A single bird of this species — a female — was taken alive at St. Croix; and this was the only instance of its occurrence which came to the knowledge of Mr. Edward Newton. Léotaud includes this Rail among the visitants of Trinidad, where it is only a bird of passage, arriving in December or January, and leaving in April. It is met with very rarely, and exclusively in overflowed districts and meadow-lands not far from the sea-shore. It is a visitant also of Cuba, where it is not known to breed. It is mentioned by Mr. Gosse as being probably a regular winter visitant of Jamaica, two specimens having been taken there at different times. Mr. March also gives it as a bird of that island, and thinks that it is found there at all seasons and in all waters, fresh or salt. He has never met with its eggs. Both Mr. Brace and Mr. Moore note its presence in the Bahamas in winter.

Its movements and the irregular character of its visits to Bermuda are interesting features in its history. Major J. W. Wedderburn ("Naturalist in Bermuda," p. 45) states that it regularly visits Bermuda, arriving early in September. The first specimen, obtained Sept. 3, 1847, was settling on a branch of a mangrove-tree — a very unusual action for this species, as it very rarely alights on a limb, and this one was four feet from the ground. A few remained throughout the winter. In October, 1849, it arrived in immense numbers, and one was killed January 17, and another April 26. J. L. Hurdis, in some supplementary notes (p. 82) added to Major Wedderburn's paper, states that however heavy and sluggish this bird may appear when disturbed in its marshy retreat, there can be no doubt that it possesses great strength of wing; and the fact that it never fails to visit Bermuda in its great southern migrations is sufficient proof of its powers of flight. A single instance was noted of its being met with as early as August 24. In September it had become rather numerous, but were more abundant in October than at any other time. In some seasons these birds all disappeared about the end of October, while in others a few remained to the 25th of November, and some even beyond that time. In 1849 and the three following years this bird visited Bermuda in its spring migrations, appearing in the latter part of February, and remaining through the months of March and April. Ten specimens were shot and three taken alive. During a southwest gale which prevailed on the 9th of October, 1849, thousands of this bird suddenly appeared in the marshes of Bermuda, and on the 29th of the same month not one of this species was to be seen. The whole immense flight had departed on some unexplained journey. This departure could not have been occasioned by any want of food, for the marshes were abundantly supplied, and the prevailing temperature was between 70° and 80° Fahrenheit. Mr. Hurdis states that this bird is also found in its migrations in the Island of Barbadoes, and thinks that there is little cause to doubt that the rivers and marshes of South America are its southern haunts during the winter months. It is very fat when it arrives in the Bermudas — evidently a provision of nature to sustain it in its long and arduous flight from one region to some distant point, as it probably traverses the Atlantic Ocean for thirty or thirty-five degrees of latitude without food.

Reinhardt retains this species among the birds of Greenland on the strength of a single specimen obtained at Sukkertoppen, Oct. 3, 1823. Sir John Richardson speaks of this species as being common in the Fur Countries, in the summer season, up to the 62d parallel. It is particularly abundant on the shores of the small lakes which skirt the plains of the Saskatchewan.

Mr. Boardman informs me that he has found this Rail in the neighborhood of Calais, Me., where it is known to breed, and where it is much more common than the Virginia Rail. It breeds in all the marshes along the borders of the numerous inlets and rivers on the southern shores of Maine, and I have found it especially abundant on the Sheepscot and Damariscotta rivers. Professor Verrill mentions it as a summer visitant in Oxford County, but as not occurring there in very great numbers. Mr. Allen speaks of it as arriving near Springfield, Mass., in April, remaining until November, breeding and becoming quite common in September and October. The same naturalist also mentions it as common in Great Salt Lake Valley. Mr. Ridgway mentions it as being numerous in the marshes about Pyramid and Great Salt Lakes; and the same was true of Ruby Valley and the vicinity of Parley's Park, and in fact in all the localities of a similar character throughout the entire extent of his route in the Great Basin. Mr. Dresser found this species not uncommon near San Antonio in the months of September, October, and November.

According to the observations of Giraud, it is not common in Long Island, though now and then to be met with along the shrubby banks of creeks, and is also sometimes observed on the salt-marshes. In the vicinity of New York City it is not known to occur in any great numbers, only a few halting in their northern migrations on wet and miry places covered with tall grass and rushes. It is very abundant in the early part of September along the reedy margin of the Hackensack River, where it is hunted in the same manner as the "Clapper Rail." It is exceedingly timid and retiring, seeking seclusion among the rank grass. At low water it can very rarely be detected, as it hides so closely among the tall water-plants; and but for its shrill short notes its presence would not be suspected. In consequence of this peculiarity of its habits, the sportsman's excursions are regulated by the state of the tide, and his visits are timed so as to enable him to be on the spot some time before the tide is in. Seated in a light skiff, aided by a person skilled in the sport, who pushes along the boat and forces the Rails from their places of concealment, he is often enabled to flush and to shoot a large number. The bird is driven from its place of concealment, the rushes no longer affording it any protection, and it is compelled to rise as the boat approaches. As it always springs up at a short distance, and its flight is feeble, it is easily shot. The Sora is very sensitive to cold, and is not to be met with in these marshes after the first sharp frost. In the spring, during its northern migrations, it makes a short stop to recruit in its favorite marshes, but continues its journey with only a very brief delay. Its favorite food is wild-oats, from which its flesh derives a very delicate flavor. In the autumn it becomes very fat, and is then much sought for by epicures. When driven in the fall to warmer shelter by an early frost, it will, on the recurrence of milder weather, often return to its favorite feeding-grounds. It leaves New Jersey early in October.

"Doughty's Cabinet of Natural History" (I. p. 208) gives an interesting account of the manner of hunting this bird on the marshes of the Delaware. Early in August, when the reeds have attained their full growth, the Sora Rail resorts to them in great numbers to feed on the seeds, of which it is very fond. This reed (the *Zizania clavulosa* of Michaux) grows up from the soft muddy shores of the tide-water, where the surface is alternately bare and covered with four or five feet of water, and attains a height of ten feet, covering tracts of many acres in extent, the stalks growing so closely together that a boat, excepting at high water, can hardly make its way through them. The seed of this plant is long and slender, white in color, sweet to the taste, and very nutritious. When the reeds are in fruit the Rails in great numbers take possession of them. At this season a person walking along the banks of the river may hear their cries in every direction. If a stone is thrown among the reeds there is a general outcry and a reiterated *kuk-kuk-kuk*, like the scream of a Guinea-fowl. Any sudden noise produces the same effect. None of the birds, however, can be seen except at high-water; and when the tide is low they keep secreted, and a man may walk where there are hundreds of them without seeing a single one.

On its first arrival this bird is very lean; but as the seeds ripen it rapidly fattens, and from the 20th of September to the middle of October is in excellent condition. The usual mode of shooting it on the Delaware is as already described for the Hackensack River and marshes. The sportsman requires a light skiff, a stout and experienced boatman, and a pole fifteen feet in length, thickened at the lower end. About two hours before high-water the hunter and his companion enter the reeds, and each takes his post, the former standing in the bow, the latter on the stern-seat, pushing the skiff steadily through the reeds. The Rails rise, one by one, as the boat is moved along, and only at a short distance in front of it. Each bird is instantly shot down, the boatman keeping his eye on the spot where the bird fell, directing the boat forward, and collecting the game while the hunter is reloading. In this manner the sport is carried on; the boat being pushed steadily through the reeds, the birds are flushed and shot, the hunter alternately loading and firing, and the assistant pushing the skiff and picking up the fallen game. This is continued until an hour or two after high water, when they are compelled by the fall of the tide to retire. In these excursions it is not uncommon for an active and expert marksman to kill from a hundred to a hundred and fifty Rails in a single tide. As two birds rarely, if ever, rise together, each must be shot singly.

The flight of the Sora Rail among the reeds is usually low, and, shelter being abundant, is rarely extended to more than fifty or a hundred yards. When winged, and uninjured in its legs, it dives and swims with great rapidity, and is seldom seen again. On such occasions it has been found clinging with its feet to the reeds, under the water, or skulking under the floating vegetation with its bill just above the surface. This bird is apparently weak and delicate in everything except its legs; but these possess great vigor; and its body being remarkably thin, it is able to pass readily between the reeds. Though its flight seems feeble, yet it occasionally rises to a considerable height, stretches its legs out behind it, and flies rapidly across the Delaware where it is more than a mile wide.

In Virginia, along the shores of the River James, in the tide-water regions, this Rail is found in the fall in prodigious numbers; and there it is usually taken at night, and in a different manner. A kind of iron grate is fixed on the top of a stout pole, which is placed, like a mast, in a small canoe, and filled with some light combustible. The man who manages the canoe is provided with a paddle ten or twelve feet in length, and, about an hour before high-water, enters the reeds. The space for a considerable extent around is well lighted, the birds are bewildered, and as they appear are knocked down with the paddle. In this manner from twenty to eighty dozen have been killed by three negroes in the short space of three hours.

This Rail is frequently met with at sea between our shores and the West India Islands. Mr. Lewis, in the "American Sportsman," refers to a living example taken on the ship "Michael Angelo," during a voyage from Liverpool, in May, 1851. The nearest land was Cape Sable, three hundred miles distant.

The sensitiveness of this bird to cold, and its immediate departure upon the first severe frost, render its movements variable, and dependent on the season. It usually leaves the Middle States in October, but in favorable seasons remains much later. In 1846 the fall was a remarkably mild one, and the Soras continued abundant on the Delaware River until the last of November.

Captain Bendire mentions this bird as being present in Eastern Oregon during the breeding-season; but how abundantly he was not able to ascertain. He only met with it on four occasions. Mr. Gosse informs me that it breeds in great numbers in the wet marshes of Wisconsin, that its nest is constructed of dry grasses, and that this is sometimes partly arched over, but more frequently under broken-down grasses or weeds. The eggs — as he states — are seven or eight in number, and occasionally even more. A nest found in Lynn, Mass., by Mr. Moon, contained nine eggs, and this is said to be the common number.

Mr. E. W. Nelson, who carefully studied the habits of this Rail in Northern Illinois, gives the 1st of May as the date of its arrival, and October as that of its departure. He states that it nests along the borders of prairie sloughs and marshes, depositing from eight to fourteen eggs, and that its nest may often be discovered at a distance by the appearance of the surrounding grass, the blades of which are in many cases interwoven over the nest, as if to shield the bird from the fierce rays of the sun — felt on the marshes with redoubled force. The nests are sometimes built on solitary tussocks growing in the water, but their usual position is in the soft dense grass growing close to the edge of the slough, and rarely in that which is over eight inches high. The nest is a thick matted platform of soft marsh-grasses, with a slight depression for the eggs.

In Wilson's day the history of this Rail was very imperfectly known, and some of the information in regard to its habits accepted by him as true was without doubt incorrect. This is especially the case in that which relates to its breeding, all of which really had reference to the Virginia Rail, and not to this bird. I believe that this Rail does not breed anywhere south of the 42d parallel, and that it is very rare there, except in the Northwestern States. It breeds from about this parallel to the 62d, in favorable places, from the Atlantic to the Pacific coast. The breeding of this bird was not known to Wilson, Audubon, or Nuttall, and the young and eggs referred to by the first two belong to another species; Dr. Bachman's notice of a nest found on the Hudson has reference, however, to this bird.

The Sora breeds in fresh-water marshes, on small dry or elevated tussocks, and in the middle of tufts of coarse herbage. Its nest is usually a mere collection of decayed rushes and coarse grass loosely aggregated, and not admitting of removal as a nest. The eggs are from seven to twelve in number. Instead of the creamy-white ground of the Virginia Rail, this egg has one of a light drab-color. The markings are spots of a roundish shape, and are all of a uniform dark rufous tint. The form of the egg is also quite different, it being oblong oval, equal at either end, and differing from that of *Rallus virginianus* in all respects, and in so marked a manner as to be at once distinguishable from it. No. 536, from Concord, Mass., measures 1.38 by .88 inches, and is remarkably oblong. Two eggs (No. 1272) obtained by Mr. Goss in Minnesota are much more rounded, and have the larger end more obtuse. These measure, one 1.18 by .90 inches, the other 1.15 by .91 inches.

Porzana noveboracensis.

THE LITTLE YELLOW RAIL.

Fulica noveboracensis, GMEL. S. N. I. ii. 1788, 701.
Ortygometra noveboracensis, STEPHENS, Shaw's Gen. Zool. XII. 1824, 222. — AUD. Synop. 1839, 213; B. Am. V. 1842, 152, pl. 307.
Rallus noveboracensis, BONAP. Specc. Comp. 1827, 212; Am. Orn. IV. 1832, 136, pl. 27, fig. 2. — NUTT. Man. II. 1834, 215. — SW. & RICH. F. B. A. II. 1831, 402. — AUD. Orn. Biog. IV. 1838, 251, pl. 329.
Porzana noveboracensis, CASS. in Baird's B. N. Am. 1858, 750. — BAIRD, Cat. N. Am. B. 1859, no. 557. — COUES, Key, 1872, 274; Check List, 1873, no. 469; 2d ed. 1882, no. 680; Birds N. W. 1874, 539. — RIDGW. Nom. N. Am. B. 1881, no. 575.
Perdix Hudsonica, LATH. Ind. Orn. II. 1790, 655.
Rallus ruficollis, VIEILL. Nouv. Dict. XXVIII. 1819, 556; Gal. Ois. 1834, 168, pl. 266.
"*Porzana jamaicensis* (?)" (error), RIDGW. Orn. 40th Par. Exp. 1877, 613 (Nevada and Utah).[1]

HAB. Eastern North America, north to Hudson's Bay, and Nova Scotia, west to Utah and Nevada. No extralimital record except Cuba and the Bermudas.

SP. CHAR. *Adult:* Yellowish ochraceous, very glossy above, where broadly striped with black, the black intersected by narrow bars of white; belly whitish; flanks dusky, narrowly barred with

white; crissum light cinnamon; axillars, lining of wing, and exposed portion of secondaries, white. "Bill greenish black, with the base dull yellowish orange; iris hazel; feet and claws light flesh-color" (AUDUBON). Total length, about 6.00 inches; wing, 3.00–3.50; culmen, .50–.55; tarsus, .90–1.00; middle toe, .90.

There is a considerable range of individual variation, both in size and markings, even among specimens from the same locality.

The specific habits and distribution of this bird are imperfectly known. It has been found in various localities along the Atlantic coast as far to the eastward as New Brunswick, it is known to breed in Northern Illinois, where its nests and eggs have been taken, and it also occurs on the Pacific coast, probably in at least equal abundance. As it is also found in Southwestern Texas, we naturally infer that it has a very general distribution over the entire United States, from the Gulf shore to Canada, and probably farther north, and from the eastern to the western coasts. That it is anywhere abundant cannot be positively stated, although it might be so, since its small size and skulking habits might prevent its being seen, even when present in considerable numbers.

Mr. Dresser was informed by Dr. Heermann that this bird is not uncommon at Mitchell's Lake, near San Antonio. As when the former visited that locality the

[1] The small Rail referred, with great hesitation, by Mr. Ridgway to *P. jamaicensis*, in his "Ornithology of the Fortieth Parallel," p. 613, was undoubtedly this species, which is the only one showing white along the hinder margin of the wing — a peculiarity noted in the birds observed. The apparently "blackish color" was due to imperfect opportunity of observation.

lake was nearly dried up, he did not succeed in finding it, although told by hunters who resort there that at some seasons it is quite abundant. Mr. Boardman informs me that this Rail occasionally occurs in the neighborhood of Calais, and that one specimen was received by him which had been taken in the Bay of Fundy. He regards its appearance in that section of the country as being a rather uncommon occurrence. It is not known to breed there, and its presence has only been noticed in the fall. It is occasionally noticed also in Massachusetts. A single specimen was taken in Newton by Mr. Maynard, Sept. 8, 1868, in a dry and open field; and I am informed by Mr. Purdie that another was procured in the marshes of Canton, Mass., Oct. 15, 1872.

Mr. Giraud was of opinion, that although the Yellow-breasted Rail is seldom met with on Long Island, it is far from being so rare in that locality as has been supposed. Its habit of skulking among the tall grass and reeds which overgrow certain wet and seldom-frequented marshes, as well as its unwillingness to take wing, explain its supposed scarcity when actually present in abundance.

Richardson, although he did not meet with it in the Arctic Region himself, and could not learn any particulars in regard to its habits or the extent of its migrations, quotes from the manuscript notes of Hutchins a notice of it, written in 1777, mentioning it as an inhabitant of the marshes on the coast of Hudson's Bay, near the efflux of the River Severn, from the middle of May to the end of September. It never flies, he adds, above sixty yards at a time, but runs with great rapidity among the long grass near the shores. In the morning and evening it utters a note which resembles the striking together of a flint and steel. At other times it makes a shrieking noise. He also adds — but in this he is evidently misinformed — that it builds no nest, depositing sixteen *perfectly white eggs* among the grass. Its eggs are known not to be white, and in Illinois its nest resembles the ordinary loosely constructed one of this family.

Dr. Cooper writes that he is indebted to Mr. Mathewson for authority to add this species to the fauna of the Pacific coast. The latter obtained several specimens of it at Martinez in autumn, and afterward other observers met with it in the winter. It seemed to be not uncommon there, and to be a resident species.

The Prince of Musignano obtained a specimen of this bird in the New York market, in February, 1826, and regarded it as an Arctic species. This opinion Mr. Audubon was not inclined to accept, stating it to be a constant resident of Florida, as well as of the lower portion of Louisiana, where he has found it at all seasons; and he regarded its presence in midwinter near New York as accidental. In the neighborhood of New Orleans it is said to be common in all the deserted savannas covered with thick, long grass, among pools of shallow water. There its sharp and curious notes were heard many times in the course of the day. These sounds come upon the ear so as to induce the listener to believe the bird to be much nearer than it really is. In Florida Audubon found this species even more abundant than it was in Louisiana, and he met with it both on the mainland and on several of the Keys — where, as he states, it begins to breed in March. In the neighborhood of New Orleans it is said to breed at the same period. Dr. Bachman has found this bird near Charleston, S. C.; and Mr. Audubon met with it near Vincennes, on the Wabash, in summer, where it had young broods. At Silver Springs, in East Florida, the latter had a good opportunity of observing the habits of this Rail, along the margins of lakes and swampy bayous. He noticed that it followed the margins of the muddy shores with measured steps, until, attracted by some object, it would suddenly jerk its tail upward and disappear for the moment. It was so unsuspicious, that at times he could approach it within a few yards, when it would only rise more erect, gaze at him for a moment, and then resume its occupation. He was told that the best way to obtain a shot at this bird is to lie concealed near an opening, and call it out of cover by imitating its notes; when, being very pugnacious, it comes to the open space and is easily shot. Its flesh is said to be delicate and savory. Its flight is described as being swift, and more protracted than that of most of the Rails.

Mr. Audubon describes the nest of this bird as being similar to that of *Rallus elegans;* but as he mentions that the eggs are white, and that the nest resembles that of the Common Quail, we cannot receive his account as altogether reliable.

Dr. James Trudeau, as quoted by Mr. Audubon, states that this Rail winters in the Southern States, arriving in Louisiana about the end of October or the beginning of November, and that it is common in marshes in the vicinity of woods. It is with difficulty forced to fly, and even when pursued by a dog it will only rise when apparently just on the point of being caught. Some of this species nest in Louisiana; others migrate northward about the beginning of March. Dr. Trudeau has seen them in Salem, N. J., about the end of April, a few remaining there.

Mr. Nuttall mentions that in the meadows of West Cambridge, Mass., and in other wet marsh-lands rarely visited by man, he has occasionally met with this bird. One was brought to him late in autumn that had been surprised while feeding on insects by the margin of a small pool overgrown with the leaves of the water-lily; without attempting either to swim or to fly, it darted nimbly over the floating leaves. When wounded it can swim and dive with great skill. Mr. Ives informed Mr. Nuttall that it is frequently met with, in the fall, in the marshes in the vicinity of Salem, Mass. Mr. Nuttall also mentions that, having spent the night of Oct. 6, 1831, in a lodge on the borders of Fresh Pond, he heard, about sunrise, the Yellow-breasted Rails begin to stir among the reeds. As soon as awake, they called out, in an abrupt and cackling cry, *krèk-krèk, krek, krèk, kuk k'kh.* This note, apparently from young birds, was answered in a lower and soothing tone. These uncouth and guttural notes resembled in sound the croaking of the tree-frog. These birds were probably a migrating brood from the north. By the first of November this cackling ceases, and in all probability the whole have passed farther south.

Three eggs in the Smithsonian Collection (No. 7057), from Winnebago, in Northern Illinois, measure respectively, 1.08 inches by .85, 1.12 by .82, 1.12 by .80. They are of oval shape, one end slightly more tapering than the other. Their ground-color is a very deep buff, and one set of markings — which are almost entirely confined to the larger end — consists of blotches of pale diluted purplish brown; these are overlain by a dense sprinkling of fine dottings of a rusty brown.

Porzana jamaicensis.

THE LITTLE BLACK RAIL.

a. jamaicensis.

Rallus jamaicensis, GMEL. S. N. I. ii. 1788, 718 — AUD. Orn. Biog. IV. 1838, 359, pl. 349.

Ortygometra jamaicensis, "STEPHENS, Shaw's Gen. Zool." — AUD. Synop. 1839, 214; B. Am. V. 1842, 157, pl. 308.

Porzana jamaicensis, CASS. in Baird's B. N. Am. 1858, 749. — BAIRD, Cat. N. Am. B. 1859, no. 556. — COUES, Key, 1872, 247; Check List, 1873, no. 470; 2d ed. 1882, no. 681; Birds N. W. 1874, 539. — RIDGW. Nom. N. Am. B. 1881, no. 576.

Crex pygmæa, BLACKWELL, Brewster's Jour. VI. 1832, 77.

Ortygometra chilensis, BONAP. Compt. Rend. XLIII. 599.

Rallus salinasi, PHILIPPI, Wiegm. Archiv, 1867, 262.

"*Gallinula salinasi*, PHIL. Cat. 1869, 38."

b. coturniculus. — FARALLON RAIL.

Porzana jamaicensis, var. *coturniculus*, "BAIRD MS." — RIDGW. Am. Nat. VIII. Feb. 1874, 111.
Porzana jamaicensis, b. *coturniculus*, COUES, Birds N. W. 1874, 540.
Porzana jamaicensis coturniculus, RIDGW. Proc. U. S. Nat. Mus. Vol. 3, 1881, 202, 222; Nom. N. Am. B. 1881, no. 576 *a.* — COUES, Check List, 2d ed. 1882, no. 682.

HAB. Temperate North America, north to Massachusetts, Northern Illinois (breeding), Kansas, Oregon, and California; south through Western South America to Chili; Cuba; Jamaica; Bermudas. The race *coturniculus* confined to the Farallon Islands, California.

SP. CHAR. Smaller than *P. noveboracensis*, and the smallest of North American *Rallidæ*. *Adult:* Head, neck, and lower parts dark plumbeous or slate-color, darkest, and often nearly black, on the pileum; abdomen and crissum brownish black, marked with transverse bars of white; nape and back dark chestnut or reddish sepia-brown, the other upper parts brownish black, with small dots and irregular transverse bars of white; primaries immaculate dusky, or with small spots of white. *Young:* Similar, but lower parts dull ashy, the throat inclining to white, and the crown tinged with reddish brown. *Downy young:* "Entirely bluish black" (CASSIN). Bill black; iris red; "feet bright yellowish green" (AUDUBON[1]). Total length, about 5.00 inches; wing 2.50–3.20; culmen, .50–.60; tarsus, .85–.90; middle toe, .80–1.00.

P. jamaicensis.

P. jamaicensis coturniculus.

Several Chilian specimens in the collection of the U. S. National Museum appear to be exactly like specimens from the United States. A fine adult from San Francisco, Cal., in Mr. Henshaw's collection, also agrees minutely with eastern specimens and those from Chili, mentioned above; but one (No. 12862) from the Farallon Islands, off the coast of California, differs in so many particulars that Professor Baird has described it as a distinct local race (*P. coturniculus*), with the following distinctive characters: Back without white specks; depth of bill .15 of an inch, instead of .20–.25, the culmen being as long as the maximum in true *P. jamaicensis.* The general size is also smaller.

So far as we are informed, this species — the smallest of our North American Rails — is of infrequent occurrence on the Atlantic coast. It is known to occur from the Delaware marshes about Philadelphia southward; and is said to be more common

[1] In an adult male, killed June 6, 1879, near Washington, D. C., the fresh colors of the "soft parts" were as follows: Bill entirely deep black; iris bright brick-red; legs and feet brown, much the same color as the wing-coverts.

in the West India Islands than with us. Its secretive habits and its extremely small size favor its concealment, and explain its apparently great rarity, without necessarily presuming it to be very uncommon, since it may exist abundantly without its presence being known or suspected. It has been found by Mr. Krider breeding about Philadelphia, and its eggs have been obtained. It is given by Dr. Gundlach as a bird of Cuba, but without positive knowledge as to its breeding on that island. Mr. Gosse states that a specimen of this species was brought to him in Jamaica in April alive and unhurt. It lived in a cage two days, but scarcely ate anything. Although once or twice observed to pick in the mud, in general it would not even walk upon it. It was not at all timid; its motions were very deliberate, it slowly raised its large feet, and then set them down without making even a step. Its neck was usually drawn in short; and then it presented very little of the appearance of a Rail, but rather that of a Passerine bird. When it walked, its neck was more or less extended horizontally, although it occasionally bridled up. When standing still, the throat was often in slight vibration; but there was no flirting or erection of the tail. Mr. Gosse met with these birds on three other occasions. In the latter part of August, in the morasses of Sweet River, several of them flew out from the low rushes at his feet, and fluttering along for a few yards with a very labored flight, dropped into the dense rush again. In the manner of its flight, and in its figure, this bird greatly resembled a chicken. It flies, with its legs hanging inertly down, with feeble and laborious motion, from one tuft of herbage to another, whence it will not emerge until almost trodden on. Mr. Gosse heard it utter no sound; but Robinson, quoted by Mr. Gosse, in describing two of these birds brought to him in October, 1760, says their cry was very low, resembling that of a Coot at a distance. He noticed also their peculiar flight and their mode of squatting. Several, Robinson adds, were killed accidentally by the negroes at work, as the bird is so foolish as to hide its head, cock up its rump, and think itself safe. It is then easily taken alive. The negroes in Clarendon call it the "Cacky-quaw," from its cry. It is also, for the same reason, called the "Kitty-go" and the "Johnny-ho" in Westmoreland. This cry, instead of being limited to three syllables, is said by Mr. March to be like *chi-chi-cro-croo-croo*, several times repeated in sharp, high-toned notes, so as to be audible to a considerable distance.

A single example, agreeing in all respects with others from Jamaica, is stated by Mr. Salvin to have been shot by Mr. Fraser near the Lake of Dueñas, in Guatemala. It is also known to occur in South America as far south as Chili.

Mr. Titian R. Peale informed Audubon that, in July, 1836, he received from Dr. Thomas Rowan an adult and four of its young alive, obtained near Philadelphia. The young died soon after they were received, but the old bird lived four days. They fed sparingly upon Indian meal and water, and soon appeared at home. The old bird proved to be a male — rendering it rather remarkable that he should have allowed himself to be taken by hand in trying to defend his young brood. Mr. Peale had in his museum another specimen, taken many years before, caught in the neighborhood of Philadelphia. Mr. Rowan, supposing the old bird was a female, wrote to Mr. Peale: "The hen flew a few rods, and then flew back to her young in an instant, when they caught her, together with her four young ones." He adds that he has seen the same bird in his meadow every month of the year, and thinks that it is resident, and does not migrate to the south.

Captain Charles Bendire writes me that he observed this Rail, in April, in the vicinity of Lake Malheur, in Southeastern Oregon; and he states later that he has again met with it, and that it unquestionably breeds there.

It has also been taken in the Bermudas. Major Wedderburn met with it in the Pembroke Marsh, Nov. 19, 1847. He saw another in the same place, in October, the following year; a third soon after at the Sluice Ponds; and Mr. Hurdis procured one, Nov. 10, 1852, also at Pembroke Marsh.

It has only recently been credited with a New England residence. Mr. J. H. Batty informs me that he has taken it in Connecticut. He says: "I have never taken but two of this species. I shot them both in a fresh-water marsh, several years ago, at Hazardville, Conn. I had never observed them before that time, nor have I met with them since. They were breeding, as I saw several of their young, and caught one of them, which I examined and let go again. This was in the latter part of June." It has since been recorded by Mr. H. A. Purdie as taken at Saybrook, Conn., on the authority of Mr. J. H. Clark, who wrote him that a neighbor of his, while mowing at that place, July 10, 1876, swung his scythe over a nest of ten eggs on which the bird was sitting, cutting off the bird's head and breaking all but four of the eggs. It has also recently been recorded from Clark's Island, Plymouth Harbor, Mass., where a specimen was obtained in August, 1869.

Mr. Nelson refers to the Little Black Rail as a species of not very rare occurrence in Northern Illinois, where it breeds. During the spring of 1875 he met with three specimens in the Calumet marshes; the first was seen early in May. In the same season, on the 19th of June, Mr. Nelson states that Mr. Frank De Witt, while collecting with him near the Calumet River, was so fortunate as to discover a nest of this species that contained ten freshly laid eggs. The nest had been constructed in a deep cup-shaped depression in a perfectly open situation on the border of a marshy spot, and its only concealment was that furnished by a few straggling *Carices*. It was composed of soft grass-blades, loosely interwoven in a rounded shape. The nest, in its form and manner of construction, was similar to that of a Meadow-lark. Mr. Nelson describes it as having an inside depth of 2.50 inches; inside diameter, 3.25; outside depth, 3.50; outside diameter, 4.50. The eggs are said to be of a creamy white, and to average 1.00 inch by .81, being of a nearly perfect oval, and thinly sprinkled with fine reddish-brown dots, which become larger and more numerous toward the larger end. Minute shell-markings in the form of dots were also visible. Probably in consequence of the small size of the depression in which the nest was inclosed, the eggs were in two layers.

Mr. Henshaw states that this Rail appears to be as numerous in California as in any other part of its habitat. From information given by Mr. Gruber, he judges it to be rather common in the extensive tule swamps of that State. It has also been found by Mr. Gruber on the Farallon Islands. Its small size and skulking habits, as well as the nature of its swampy retreat, render the procuring of specimens difficult. Mr. Mathewson informed Dr. Cooper that he has frequently obtained it at Martinez in the fall and in winter.

Dr. James Trudeau informed Mr. Audubon that this species arrives in Louisiana, in company with the Yellow-breasted Rail, about the end of October, and is very common in marshes in the vicinity of woods. It migrates northward in the beginning of March, and a great number of this species are said to breed in the vicinity of Salem, N. J.

An egg in my collection, obtained by Mr. Ashmead in the neighborhood of Philadelphia, and given me by Mr. Cassin (No. 564), has a ground-color of a light cream or creamy white, over which are generally distributed fine markings or minute specks of a brownish red; these are most numerous at the larger end. The egg is oval in shape, is tapering at one end, and measures 1.00 inch in length by .75 in breadth.

GENUS CREX, BECHSTEIN.

Crex, BECHST. Naturg. Deutschl. IV. 1803, 470 (type, *C. pratensis*, BECHST., = *Rallus crex*, LINN.).

CHAR. Similar to *Porzana*, but larger and of stouter build, the middle toe shorter than the tarsus, the culmen scarcely depressed in the middle portion, and the base of the gonys forming a decided angle.

C. pratensis.

Crex pratensis.

THE CORN-CRAKE.

Rallus crex, LINN. S. N. ed. 10, 1758, 153 ; ed. 12, I. 1766, 261. — DEGL. Orn. Eur. II. 1849, 266.
Gallinula crex, LATH. Ind. Orn. II. 1790, 766.
Crex pratensis, BECHST. Taschenb. Vög. Deutsch. 1803, 337. — NAUM. Vög. Deutschl. IX. 1838, 496, pl. 236. — BONAP. Comp. List, 1838, 53. — KEYS. & BLAS. Wirb. Eur. 1840, 67. — MACGILL. Man. II. 113 ; Hist. Brit. B. IV. 1852, 527. — CASS. Pr. Ac. Nat. Sci. Philad. VII. Jan. 1855, 265 (New Jersey) ; in Baird's B. N. Am. 1858, 751. — BAIRD, Cat. N. Am. B. 1859, no. 558. — COUES, Key, 1872, 274 ; Check List, 1873, no. 471 ; 2d ed. 1882, no. 683. — RIDGW. Nom. N. Am. B. 1881, no. 577.
Crex herbarum and *C. alticeps*, BREHM, Vög. Deutschl. 1831, 694.
The Land-Rail, YARR. Brit. B. ed. 2, III. 92, fig. ; ed. 3, III. 107, fig. ; et AUCT.

HAB. Palæarctic Region, occurring casually or irregularly in Eastern North America ; Greenland ; Bermudas.

SP. CHAR. *Adult:* Above, grayish brown or light drab, conspicuously striped with black ; wings reddish, with indistinct white transverse spots on the larger coverts. Lining of the wing and axillars, soft cinnamon, the former edged with white. Head ash-gray, with an indistinct loral and postocular narrow stripe of very pale drab — the crown like the back ; throat, belly, and anal region, white; foreneck and breast pale drab, tinged with gray; sides and crissum transversely banded with brown and white. *Young:* Similar, but without any gray on the head. *Downy young:* Uniform dark sooty brown, the head blackish; bill uniform dusky, or pale brownish; iris brown; legs and feet "bluish flesh-color" in life (MACGILLIVRAY), pale brownish in dried skins. Total length, about 10.00–10.50; extent, 17.00–18.00; wing, 5.70–6.00; culmen, .85–.90; tarsus, 1.50–1.60; middle toe, 1.30.

The Land-Rail, or Corn-Crake of Europe, is a regular visitant in summer of Greenland, where it breeds, and is thence a straggler to our Eastern Atlantic coast, as far south as Long Island. Its appearance in New England, though probably occasional, has never — that I am aware — been actually detected. It is credited as occurring in Bermuda.

In Great Britain, according to Yarrell, it is a common summer visitor, making its appearance in the southern counties of England during the last ten days of April, but in Yorkshire and farther north, not until the second week in May. It usually leaves the British Islands in October, but single individuals have been met with as late as December and January. It is common in the valleys in Scotland, and abundant on the Orkney and Shetland Islands. It visits Denmark, Sweden, and Norway, going as far north as the Faröe Islands and Iceland. It is abundant over the entire European continent, and has been found in winter in Asia Minor. It is mentioned by Dr. Heineken among the birds of Madeira, and its appearance has been noted in its spring migrations in Malta, Sicily, and Algiers. It is included among the birds of Northern Asia in Pallas's "Zoographia Rosso-Asiatica."

Major Wedderburn states that on the 25th of October, 1847, he shot a single specimen on the Pembroke Marsh, Bermuda. A notice of this "rare occurrence" was sent at the time to the "Zoologist," 1849, and the specimen given to Mr. Yarrell, from whose collection it passed into that of Colonel Drummond.

In Europe this species is said to frequent the long grass of marshy water-meadows near rivers, beds of osiers or reeds, and fields of green grain, where its presence is indicated by its creaking note; and hence one of its names, that of Corn-Crake or Corn-Creak, by which latter name it is known in Ireland. This note can be so nearly imitated by passing the thumb-nail along the teeth of a comb, that the bird can be decoyed within a very short distance by the sound thus produced. This call is the love-note of the male, and is continued until a mate is found. After the season of incubation it is seldom heard. If kept in confinement the Land-Rail, besides this call-note, utters a low guttural sound whenever it is disturbed or suddenly alarmed.

The food of the Corn-Crake is said to consist of slugs, snails, worms, small lizards, and insects, with portions of vegetable matter and a few seeds. Its nest is placed on the ground, and is formed of dry plants. A field of green grain, thick grass, or clover is generally the situation that is chosen. The number of the eggs is said to be from seven to ten; and these, in England, are laid about the middle of June. The young, when first hatched, are covered with down, of a black color, but soon acquire their first feathers, and are able to fly in about six weeks.

It is related by Daniel — as quoted by Yarrell — that in 1808 as some men were mowing grass, upon a little island belonging to the fishing water of Low Bells, on the Tweed, they cut off the head of a Corn-Crake which was sitting on eleven eggs. About twenty yards from the spot they found a Partridge sitting upon eighteen eggs. The mowers took the eggs from the nest of the Corn-Crake and put them in that of the Partridge. Two days later she brought out the entire brood of twenty-nine, all of which were seen running about the island. The Partridge took care of them all, and was observed to gather her large family under her wings without making any distinction between them.

In England many Land-Rails are shot by the sportsmen, and are considered most delicate as articles of food. This bird does not take wing very readily, and flies slowly, with its legs hanging down, seldom going farther than the nearest place of shelter, and is rarely flushed a second time.

Occasionally, when exposed to dangers from which it is unable to escape, this bird will put on the semblance of death. Jesse narrates a striking instance, in which a Corn-Crake had been brought to a gentleman by his dog, to all appearance quite dead. Standing by in silence, he suddenly saw it open an eye. He then took it up: its head again fell, its legs dropped loosely, and it appeared to be quite dead. He then put it in his pocket, and before long he felt it struggling to escape. He took it out, and it was again as apparently lifeless as before. Having laid it upon the ground and retired to a distance, the bird in a few minutes warily raised its head, looked around, and ran off at full speed. Just before these birds take their departure, in the fall, they congregate together in large flocks.

The ground-color of the egg of this species, when fresh, is a pale reddish white, spotted and speckled with ashy gray and a pale red-brown. It measures — according to Yarrell — 1.50 inches in length by 1.13 inches in breadth. An egg in my collection (No. 1389) — given me by Dr. Bachman, and received from Mr. Doubleday — measures 1.50 by 1.10 inches, being oval in shape, one end decidedly tapering. Its ground-color is a light buff with a slightly reddish shade. The markings are few, scattered, and large, nowhere confluent, but larger and more numerous at the obtuse end, and of a rich shade of dark red, with a tendency to brown. It is, in miniature, a fac-simile of the eggs of the common European Gallinule (*Gallinula chloropus*).

Genus **IONORNIS**, Reichenbach.

?[1] *Porphyrula*, Blyth, Cat. B. Asiat. Soc. 1849, 283 (type, *P. chloronotus*, Blyth).
Ionornis, Reichenb. Syst. Av. 1853, p. xxi (type, *Fulica martinica*, Linn.).

I. martinica.

[1] The interrogation-mark here implies the doubt existing as to whether the Indian bird is congeneric with the American species. Should such prove to be the case, which we do not regard probable, our bird would stand as *Porphyrula martinica*.

CHAR. Similar to *Gallinula*, but form more slender, nostrils small and oval, middle toe shorter than the tarsus, and the toes without trace of lateral membrane. Colors very handsome (chiefly opaque blue, purple, and green).

Whether the American species, to which the generic name adopted above is properly applicable, are congeneric with the Old World species (*Porphyrio chloronotus*, BLYTH, nec VIEILL.), which is the type of the genus *Porphyrula*, BLYTH, is at present uncertain. [Cf. D. G. ELLIOT: "The Genus Porphyrio and its Species;" separate pamphlet, from "Stray Feathers," pp. 1–20.]

There are two American species of this genus, which differ in the following particulars:—

I. martinica. Lower parts slaty purple in adult, light buff in young. Wing, 6.80–7.50 inches; culmen, 1.80–1.95; tarsus, 2.20–2.50; middle toe (without claw), 2.25–2.35. *Hab.* Warmer parts of North and South America; West Indies.

I. parva.[1] Lower parts pure white at all ages. Wing, 5.00 inches; culmen, 1.20; tarsus, 1.75; middle toe (*with* claw), 2.50. *Hab.* Northern South America (Cayenne and Amazons).

Ionornis martinica.

THE PURPLE GALLINULE.

Fulica martinica, LINN. S. N. I. 1766, 259.

Gallinula martinica, LATH. Ind. Orn. II. 1790, 769. — NUTT. Man. II. 1834, 221. — AUD. Orn. Biog. IV. 1838, 37, pl. 305; Synop. 1839, 210; B. Am. V. 1842, 128, pl. 303. — CASS. in Baird's B. N. Am. 1858, 753. — BAIRD, Cat. N. Am. B. 1859, no. 561.

Porphyrio martinica, GOSSE, Birds Jam. 1847, 377. — COUES, Key, 1872, 275; Check List, 1873, no. 473.

Ionornis martinica, REICH. Av. Syst. 1853, 21. — RIDGW. Proc. U. S. Nat. Mus. Vol. 3, 1881, 202, 227; Nom. N. Am. B. 1881, no. 578. — COUES, Check List, 2d ed. 1882, no. 685.

Fulica martinicensis, JACQ. Beitr. 1784, 12, pl. iii. — GMEL. S. N. I. ii. 1788, 700.

Fulica flavirostris, GMEL. S. N. I. ii. 1788, 699.

Porphyrio tavona, VIEILL. Gal. Ois. II. 1825, 170.

"*Porphyrio cyanicollis*, VIEILL."

Gallinula porphyrio, WILS. Am. Orn. IX. 1824, 69, pl. 73.

Porphyrio americanus, SWAINS. Classif. B. II. 1837, 357.

Martinico Gallinule, LATH. Synop. III. i. 1785, 255, pl. 83.

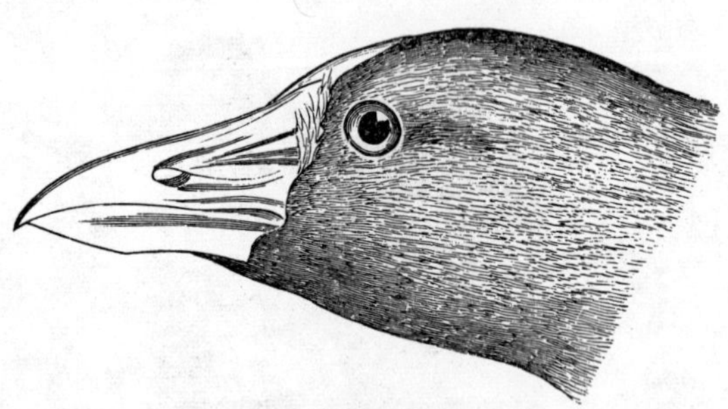

HAB. The whole of tropical and warm-temperate America, south to Brazil; north, casually, to Massachusetts, Maine, New York, Ohio, Wisconsin, Illinois, and Missouri; Bermudas, and throughout West Indies. Not recorded from any part of the Western United States.

[1] IONORNIS PARVA (Bodd.).

La Favorite, de Cayenne, BUFF. Pl. Enl. 897.

Fulica parva, BODD. Tabl. P. E. 1783 (ex Pl. Enl. 897). — *Gallinula parva*, SCHLEG. — *Porphyrio parvus*, SCL. & SALV. P. Z. S. 1868, 460, fig.

Gallinula flavirostris, GMEL. S. N. I. 1788, 699. — *Glaucestes flavirostris*, REICHENB.

Sp. Char. *Adult:* Head, neck, and lower parts slaty bluish purple, darker (sometimes nearly black) on abdomen and tibiæ; crissum pure white; upper parts bright olive-green, changing to bright verditer-blue toward the purple of the lower parts, the sides and lining of wing also greenish blue; wings brighter green than back, and shaded with bright verditer-blue. Frontal shield bright blue in life (greenish or olivaceous in dried skins); bill bright red, tipped with yellow; iris crimson; legs and feet yellowish. *Young:* Above, light fulvous-brown, tinged with greenish on wings; beneath, pale fulvous or buffy, the belly whitish; frontal shield smaller than in adult, dusky (in skins); bill dull yellowish. *Downy young:* "Entirely black" (Audubon). Total length, about 12.50 inches; wing, 7.00–7.50; culmen (including frontal shield), 1.85–1.95; tarsus, 2.25–2.50; middle toe, 2.25–2.35.

Specimens vary remarkably in the size and form of the frontal plate. In 36785, Ceara, Brazil, it is broader than long, and its posterior margin rounded: usually it is longer than broad, and its posterior extremity an angle — sometimes acute. There is also much difference among individuals in the intensity of the colors. All these variations appear, however, to be purely individual, or perhaps partially seasonal, and entirely independent of locality.

The Purple Gallinule is essentially a southern species, and characteristic of the southern districts of the United States, where it is found at all seasons of the year. It is met with from the Carolinas southward along the Southern Atlantic coast, and from Florida to Mexico along the shores of the Gulf. It also occurs in the West India Islands, Mexico, and Central America, and over a large extent of the northern portions of South America. It is a great wanderer, or in its migrations is driven by tempests to distant points, as stragglers have been found along the entire Atlantic coast as far eastward as the Bay of Fundy. A few are said to breed as far north as Charleston, S. C. This bird is an occasional visitant in Bermuda, as also in Missouri, Illinois, Wisconsin, and Ohio. Mr. George A. Boardman informs me that a single instance of the accidental occurrence of this species came under his knowledge in the vicinity of Calais, Me. The bird was found feeding on the flats near that city late in the summer; and Mr. William Brewster also mentions the obtaining a fine specimen on Cape Cod in April, 1870. Mr. Giraud states that this bird is only of rare and occasional occurrence on Long Island. A few instances are mentioned in which it has been found driven out to sea in very stormy weather. In one instance an adult male and female were met with three hundred miles to the south and east of the Belize. These were not found together, but were met with fourteen hours apart. The first alighted on the vessel. The other, in an attempt to alight, fell exhausted into the sea: it was, however, rescued; and in a short time both recruited, and arrived in New York in good condition. They were fed with meal, fish, bread, and various articles of diet from the table. They were also furnished with water for bathing, of which they made free use. They appeared to be quite contented in their confinement, and for several months seemed to enjoy perfect health, when the female was suddenly taken with cramps and died, the male surviving her but a few days. About the time of the severe revolving southerly gale of the 30th of January, 1870, an individual of this species was driven into the harbor of Halifax, and was secured. Mr. J. Matthew Jones, of that city, states that this is the only individual of the species known to have been taken in Nova Scotia. Mr. C. W. Wyatt met with this bird near Lake Paturia, in Colombia, South America, and Mr. Leyland found it in the lagoons near Peten, in Central America. Mr. E. C. Taylor states that it is abundant in suitable localities in Trinidad, and that he afterward met with it in great numbers at Porto Rico. Léotaud also states that he found it very abundant in Trinidad, where it keeps mostly among the rushes and reeds that cover the inundated meadows. At certain parts of the day, especially in the early morning, and still more frequently in the afternoon, it comes out from these hiding-places to the banks of the rivers or the borders of the waves, as if to display the exquisite grace of its movements and the brilliancy of its colors. Ever on the lookout for any danger that may menace it, at the least noise it takes to flight and hides among the rushes. It is only when its place of retreat is inaccessible that flight is attempted, its movement in the air being heavy, and not well sustained. Its voice is loud and strong, but has in it nothing remarkable. Worms, mollusks, and the fruit of various kinds of aquatic plants are its food. It gathers seeds and carries them to its beak with its claws, and it also makes use of them in clinging to the rushes where the water is very deep. It is not often kept in captivity, but when thus confined endures its lot contentedly. Its flesh is not considered good.

In Jamaica this bird is known as the "Sultana," and is said by Mr. Gosse to be not uncommon in some of the lowland ponds and marshy rivers. This author states that once, in riding from Savanna la Mar to Negril, he saw one of this species walking in the middle of the road. On his approach the bird took no more notice of him than a Common Fowl would have done, but sauntered about, picking here and there, and allowing him to come within three or four feet. At length he made a noise and a sudden motion with his hand; the bird only half opened its wing and gave a little start, as a Chicken would have done, but neither flew nor ran. The vast morass in that neighborhood abounded with these birds, and their presence in this highway was a matter of daily occurrence. Although he did not see another quite so fearless as this one, they were all very bold, coming out from the rushes and strolling across the road in sight of passers-by.

He adds that it has little of the aspect of a Gallinule, but stands higher, and has its legs more forward. As it walks, the neck is alternately bridled up or thrown forward, and its short black-and-white tail is changed from a semi-erect to a perpendicular position, with a flirting motion. As this bird walks over the tangled leaves and stems of aquatic plants resting on the surface of water, it moves with great deliberation, frequently standing still and looking leisurely on either side. When kept in confinement it soon becomes quite tame, and feeds eagerly on the seeds of the *Holcus sorghum*, or Guinea corn. It is sometimes spoken of as the "Plantain Coot," from its fondness for that fruit, and the "Carpenter Coot," from the noise the bird makes when it breaks the shells of water-snails against pieces of timber, which is supposed to resemble that of a carpenter at work.

On the Mississippi, according to Audubon, this species is rarely found above Memphis, and even there it is rare; but between Natchez and the mouth of the river it is decidedly abundant. As soon as its young are hatched, it retires with them to the tall grass of the savannas bordering the lakes and bayous, where it remains until September; and at this time it has a delicate whistling note, resembling that of the Blue-winged Teal. At the approach of winter this bird returns to the borders of ponds and rivers, and becomes more shy and vigilant, usually moving in the night-time and feeding by day. It breeds at a remarkably early period of the year — according to Audubon, as early as February. The calls of the parent bird to its young are almost incessant during the entire night, and are elicited by any unusual noise; indeed, so intent is it on the welfare of its progeny, that it will allow itself to be caught while thus occupied.

The nest, according to Audubon's observations, is generally placed among a species of rush which is green at all seasons, round, very pithy, rarely more than five feet high, and which grows along the margins of ponds. The birds gather many of these rushes, fastening them at the height of two or three feet, and placing the nest upon them. This is built of the finest rushes, both green and withered, and is quite as loosely made as that of the Common Gallinule, it being flat, and having an internal diameter of eight or ten inches, and an entire breadth of about fifteen. The eggs are said to be from five to seven in number — rarely more — and to resemble those of *G. galeata*. This resemblance is not very marked, however, and the eggs of the two species may always be readily distinguished one from the other by the delicacy of the shell of the egg of this species, and the more pinkish hue of the ground. Audubon describes the eggs as of a light yellowish gray, spotted with blackish brown. The young are at first quite black, and covered with down, and are fully fledged by the 1st of June.

The ground-color of the eggs, both in the collection of the Smithsonian Institution and in my own, is of a light pinkish buff, covered with scattered markings of a purplish slate, and these are, for the most part, small roundish spots. Two eggs (No. 79) in my collection, from Matamoras, collected by Dr. Berlandier, measure, one 1.75 inches by 1.20; the other, 1.58 by 1.25. Two other eggs, from Louisiana (No. 670), measure, one, 1.75 by 1.20 inches; the other, 1.70 by 1.28. The ground-color of the latter is of a deeper shade than usual of the pinkish buff so characteristic of the eggs of the genus *Porphyrio*.

Genus **GALLINULA**, Brisson.

Gallinula, Briss. Orn. VI. 1760, 3 (type, *Fulica chloropus*, Linn.).

Char. Bill shorter than head, compressed, its vertical outlines convex terminally, straight or slightly concave opposite the nostril; nostril elongated, longitudinal, slit-like; forehead covered by an extension of the horny covering of the bill (rudimentary in the young). Middle toe longer than the tarsus; toes with a slight lateral membrane or margin.

The above characters will serve readily to distinguish the species of this genus from the allied American genera, *Ionornis* and *Porphyriops*, the former having the nostril small and oval, the middle

G. galeata.

toe shorter than the tarsus, and the toes without trace of lateral membrane, while the latter (an exclusively South American genus) has the frontal shield small and conical, and is, moreover, composed of birds of small size. Two American species of *Gallinula* are known, both more nearly allied to the *G. chloropus* of Europe than to any another species, but very distinct from that, as well as from each other. Their distinctive characters may be expressed thus: —

Com. Char. Plain dark plumbeous, clearer plumbeous beneath, usually tinged with dark olive or sepia-brown above ; broad longitudinal stripes on the flanks, lateral feathers of the crissum, and border of the wing, white. Bill and frontal shield (in adult) bright red, the end of the former yellowish green ; legs and feet green (in life), the upper part of the tibia scarlet.

A. Frontal shield rounded or pointed posteriorly.

1. **G. chloropus.**[1] Wing, 6.60–7.00 inches ; culmen, including frontal shield, 1.50–1.75 ; tarsus, 1.90–2.00 ; middle toe, 2.25. Back greenish olive. *Hab.* Palæarctic Region.

B. Frontal shield truncate posteriorly.

2. **G. galeata.** Wing, 6.85–7.25 inches ; bill, from end of frontal shield, 1.70–1.85 ; tarsus, 2.10–2.30 ; middle toe, 2.50–2.60. Back, scapulars, and rump, dark sepia-brown (more olivaceous anteriorly), distinctly different from the clear plumbeous of the lower parts ; lateral feathers of the crissum entirely pure white. *Hab.* North and Middle, and much of South, America, and West Indies.
3. **G. Garmani.**[2] Wing, 9.10 inches ; bill, from end of frontal shield, 1.90 ; tarsus, 2.60 ; middle toe, 2.80. Back dark slate, slightly tinged with dark sooty brown, not distinctly different from the dark slaty plumbeous of the lower parts ; lateral feathers of the crissum bordered with blackish slate. *Hab.* Vicinity of Lake Titicaca, Peru.

Gallinula galeata.

THE FLORIDA GALLINULE.

Crex galeata, LICHT. Verz. Doubl. 1823, 80, no. 826.

Gallinula galeata, BONAP. Am. Orn. IV. 1832, 128. — NUTT. Man. II. 1834, 221. — CASS. in Baird's B. N. Am. 1858, 752. — BAIRD, B. N. Am. 1859, no. 560. — COUES, Key, 1872, 275 ; Check List, 1873, no. 472 ; 2d ed. 1882, no. 684 ; Birds N. W. 1874, 540. — RIDGW. Nom. N. Am. B. 1881, no. 579.

Gallinula chloropus, BONAP. Synop. 1828, 336 (nec LATH.). — AUD. Orn. Biog. III. 1835, 330, pl. 224 ; Synop. 1839, 210 ; B. Am. V. 1842, 132, pl. 304.

HAB. The whole of tropical and temperate America, north to Canada, south to Brazil and Chili.

SP. CHAR. *Adult:* Frontal plate large, obovate, truncated or slightly convex posteriorly, flat and smooth, or tumid and corrugated. Bill shorter than the head, rather thick, compressed. Head, neck, and entire lower parts dark plumbeous, with a bluish cinereous cast, frequently nearly black on the head and neck, and generally lighter (in autumnal and winter specimens quite white) on the abdomen. Crissum white, the middle feathers black ; feathers of the flanks widely edged with white, producing broad stripes ; edge of the wing and edge of outer primary white. Upper parts dark russet-, or sepia-brown, darker on the rump. Bill and frontal shield bright scarlet in life, the end of the former greenish yellow or bright yellow ; iris brown ; legs and feet yellowish green, the joints ashy blue ; upper part of the naked tibiæ scarlet. *Young:* Similar, but frontal shield rudimentary, the bill brownish, paler at the tip ; the whole lower parts suffused with whitish, and the head mixed with the same, particularly the throat, which is sometimes wholly

[1] GALLINULA CHLOROPUS. The European Gallinule or Moor-hen.

Fulica chloropus, LINN. S. N. ed. 10, 1758, 152 ; ed. 12, 1766, 258.

Gallinula chloropus, LATH. Ind. Orn. II. 1790, 770. — NAUM. Vög. Deutschl. IX. 1838, 587, pl. 240. — BONAP. Comp. List, 1838, 53. — KEYS. & BLAS. Wirb. Eur. 1840, 68. — MACGILL. Man. II. 117. — GRAY, Gen. B. III. 1849, 599 ; Cat. Brit. B. 1863, 180.

Stagnicola septentrionalis, BREHM, Vög. Deutschl. 1831, 704.

Fulica fusca, GMEL. S. N. I. 1788, 697.

Fulica maculata, GMEL. t. c. 701.

Fulica flavipes and *F. fistulans*, GMEL. t. c. 702.

Common Gallinule, PENN. Brit. Zool. II. 1812, 121, pl. 22, up. fig. ; et AUCT.

Moor-hen, YARR. BRIT. B. ed. 2, III. 114, fig. ; ed. 3, III. 129, fig. ; et AUCT.

[2] GALLINULA GARMANI. Garman's Gallinule.

Gallinula Garmani, ALLEN, Bull. Mus. Comp. Zool. III. July, 1876, 357 (Lake Titicaca).

white. Stripes on the flanks less distinct or nearly obsolete. *Downy young:* Glossy black, the medial lower parts fuliginous; throat and cheeks interspersed with silvery white hairs; bill yellowish (red in life?) crossed about the middle by a dusky bar.

Total length, about 12.00 to 13.00 inches; extent, 20.00 to 21.00; wing, 6.85–7.25; culmen (to end of frontal shield) 1.70–1.85; tarsus, 2.10–2.30; middle toe, 2.50–2.60.

This species much resembles the Moor-hen, Water-hen, or Gallinule of Europe (*G. chloropus*), but is larger, has the frontal shield truncated instead of pointed posteriorly, and is otherwise different. It likewise resembles other exotic species, particularly *G. Garmani* of the Peruvian Andes, but is quite distinct. Specimens vary a great deal in the size and shape of the frontal shield, and in the amount of white on the abdomen. These variations are by no means dependent on locality, however, but upon the individual, having doubtless some connection with age and season, the white on the abdomen being more marked on winter specimens.

The habits and the distribution of this species, more especially the latter, have been very imperfectly known, and very incorrectly given. Wilson appears to have been unaware of its existence. Audubon regarded it as identical with the European Moor-hen, and as an exclusively southern species — a few migrating to Carolina on the east — and thought that those found on the fresh waters of the middle districts were only stragglers. It was said not to ascend the Mississippi above Natchez, and not to be seen in the western country. Nuttall, while recognizing its distinctness as a species from *G. chloropus* of Europe, calls it the Florida Gallinule — a name calculated to perpetuate the wrong impression existing as to its distribution — and speaks of it as "unknown in Canada." Even Mr. Cassin, in the ninth volume of the "Pacific Railroad Reports," assigns to it a habitat exclusively southern, and considers it as only accidental in the Middle and Northern States — making no mention of its abundant presence both in the Northwestern States and on the coast of California. Instead of being known as the Florida Gallinule, it deserves the more comprehensive title of American Gallinule. It is abundant in South America from Panama to the region of the La Plata, in the West India Islands, in Central America, in the Southern Gulf States from South Carolina to the Mississippi, and probably to Mexico, on the California coast, and in the region of the Great Lakes, both on the American and the Canadian shores.

Professor Newton found it a common and resident species in St. Croix. While it closely resembles the European *chloropus* in its appearance, and while the habits of the two birds appear to be identically the same, their eggs even being undistinguishable from each other, the notes of the two birds are very different. This Gallinule breeds in St. Croix in April, and also in Cuba, where it is abundant. Mr. March and Mr. Gosse call it the Scarlet-fronted Gallinule. It is common in Jamaica, and nests in January, and even earlier. In February Mr. March obtained unfledged young in a pond near Spanishtown. It is said to lay eight eggs, and these are described as having a clayish-white ground splashed sparsely with small spots of sepia-brown. By contact with the damp nest the ground-color is not infrequently changed to different shades of drab. Major Wedderburn found it breeding and not uncommon in Bermuda, and obtained a number of specimens during his stay. Mr. Hurdis speaks of it as one of the native birds of the Bermudas, rearing its young in pools and swamps, where the dense growth of flags and sedge renders its pursuit almost impossible. It is more common in October than at any other time, appearing all at once in marshes and ponds, where for months previously it had been unknown — owing, probably, to an influx of migratory individuals from the American shore.

It is said by Léotaud to be quite common in Trinidad, where both in its abode and in its manners it does not appear to be different from the *martinica*, though a much more social bird than the latter. It hides itself in the rushes or takes to flight at the least danger, sometimes seeking shelter in the branches of the mangrove-trees which overhang the water. It can run among these branches with astonishing rapidity, occasionally extending its wings, as if to preserve its equilibrium or to avoid losing its footing. Its flight, which is almost always accompanied by a harsh cry, is heavy and not well sustained, being apparently retarded by its claws, which are always hanging down. Its flesh is eaten, but is not regarded as good.

Mr. G. C. Taylor met with this species at the Lake of Yojoye, and has no doubt that it is common throughout Honduras; and Mr. Salvin names it as among the birds which frequent the Lake of Dueñas, Guatemala — where, however, it is not common.

It is an occasional visitant along the Atlantic coast, as far to the eastward, at least, as Calais; and a few occasionally breed in Massachusetts. Mr. George A. Boardman obtained a single specimen of this bird near Calais, Me., in the spring of 1871. An immature example of this species was shot at Fresh Pond, Mass., Sept. 3, 1868, and two other individuals were seen. The specimen obtained had without doubt been hatched in that locality. On the 9th of October, in the same year, Mr. Brewster shot another example, and wounded a third in the same place. He also met with an adult bird there on the 3d of June. It is more than probable that straggling pairs of this bird occur in favorable situations in Massachusetts and breed there.

Giraud speaks of this species as a bird seldom observed on Long Island, a few only having been known to occur on its south shore, while one example is recorded as having been taken on Staten Island. Mr. Giraud refers to information received by letter from Professor Baird to the effect that this bird has been occasionally observed on the Susquehanna River and its tributaries, where it was usually noticed in the vicinity of fresh-water streams and ponds. It appeared to be exceedingly timid, to conceal itself among the rank grass, and, like the Rails, seldom to take wing except when performing its migratory flight. When surprised it runs nimbly, and if hard pressed takes to the water and swims and dives well. Its food consists of worms, insects, and various vegetable productions which grow in low wet grounds. It was found abundant by Dr. Bannister on the Parana, among the reeds of the lagoons.

Mr. Ridgway frequently met with it at Sacramento, in the tule sloughs, in company with the Coot, and mingling its own guttural noises with the clucking, boisterous notes of the latter species. In the interior it was not seen, although the Coot was abundant in all the large marshes. According to Dr. Heermann this species is not rare in the marshes in the interior of California, and Dr. Newberry mentions finding it at San Francisco. Dr. Cooper did not meet with it near the sea-coast.

Mr. Audubon states that when he was at Spring Garden Springs, in East Florida, in the early part of January, this Gallinule was seen in great numbers on every bayou leading toward the waters of the St. John. He describes the nest as formed with more labor than art, and as composed of a quantity of withered rushes and plants woven into a circular form. It was frequently from two to three inches thick in the centre, and surrounded by an edge or brim four or five inches high. If not disturbed this bird will raise at least two broods in a season, using the same nest, which each time is refitted. In Lower Louisiana the nest is usually five or six feet from the water, along the bayous and ponds, among the rank weeds which are so abundant there. The number of eggs seldom exceeds nine. When the Gallinule leaves its nest it covers the eggs, to protect them from its numerous enemies. Both sexes incubate, and the young follow the parent as soon as they are hatched, the mother being assiduous in her attentions to them. Their food consists of grass-seeds, water insects, worms, and snails, together with which they swallow a good deal of fine gravel. They run over the broad leaves of the lilies as if on land, and can dive readily when necessary. On land this bird walks like a Chicken, and may frequently be seen searching for worms and insects among the grass, which it nips in the manner of the common Domestic Fowl.

According to Mr. Gosse, the Gallinule in Jamaica is known as the Coot, while the latter is called the Water-hen. He found it scarcely distinguishable from the European Moor-hen, either in appearance or manner, delighting in water where there is cover, sometimes a swiftly running stream, but usually large ponds where tall thick bulrushes and masses of the ginger fern surround the banks. In such a piece of water, early in the morning, or if the place is unfrequented, at any hour of the day, the Gallinule may be seen playing on the surface, and uttering a loud cluck at short intervals as it swims to and fro. When alarmed each bird sounds the note, but in a higher key, and the whole flock seeks concealment. There they continue to call to one another, and if much pressed conceal themselves by keeping under water, holding on the roots of the rushes. If the observer remains silent and concealed, in about half an hour the cluck is again raised, and the bird begins cautiously to re-emerge, and resumes its occupation at the margin of the reeds. One of this species which had been slightly wounded was fastened with a cord attached to one foot, and allowed to swim in the pools of Bluefield's River. Its first impulse was to dive, and then to swim along about a foot beneath the surface, striking out both with the feet and with the expanded wings. When thus immersed in the water, its whole plumage was coated with a pellicle of air, which had a singular effect. When it swam at the surface only the head, neck, and a part of the back was exposed. When permitted to do so, it would creep in among the weeds and grass at the margin and remain motionless. It was unwilling to walk on boards, and when on the turf, was only capable of maintaining a walking posture as long as its motion was rapid. It is said to be abundant in the neighborhood of Hamilton, on Lake Ontario, where — as Mr. McIlwraith states — it is only less common than the Coot. It breeds abundantly on the Canadian side opposite Detroit, from which locality I have received its eggs. It breeds commonly in the Calumet marshes in Northern Illinois, on Lake Michigan, and is also abundant in the vicinity of Lake Koskonong in Southern Wisconsin.

Mr. B. F. Goss informs me that this bird breeds abundantly in the shallow muddy flats which border the lakes and streams of Wisconsin, and which, being covered with a thick growth of flags, rushes, and aquatic grasses, furnish a suitable home to the Gallinules. There they build their nests, rear their young, and spend the entire season. The nest is not very elaborately constructed, being raised but a few inches above the shallow water, and slightly hollowed. The leaves of the cat-tail flag seem to be the favorite material used in its construction. From six to eight is the usual number of eggs, and these are light yellowish brown, spotted and splashed with dark brown, and varying in length from 1.67 to 1.80 inches, and in breadth from 1.17 to 1.25 inches. When driven from her nest, the female bird skulks a short distance through the herbage, and then with head erect and expanded tail she walks slowly away.

Mr. Moore found this species nesting in Florida on the 20th of April. One nest, containing ten eggs, was in a tussock of grass a few inches above the water, quite exposed from above and on all sides, and was made of blades of grass and lined with the same. The eggs were taken, and on the second day the nest was found to contain another egg, just laid; and a day or two later a second one was discovered on a tussock near by. It is possible that two birds together laid these twelve eggs.

Another nest — only just begun when found — was visited daily till the young were seen to leave it; this was on the 20th of May. Before this nest was finished an egg was laid in it, and material was added after as many as three eggs had been laid, the total being six. The first was laid on the 22d of April, and the sixth on the 30th. This nest was quite unlike the other. It was placed in a close collection of *Pontederias*, and was formed almost entirely of their leaves. Some were bent down to form the bed of the nest; others were bent in a like manner for a rude canopy over it; others were divided, and used to raise the sides of the nest and to finish it. Most of the materials were used in a green state. The leaves of this plant are spongy, and on losing their vitality shrink to a mere trifle of their living bulk; and this may have occasioned the additions made to the nest.

The ground-color of the eggs varies from a dark cream to a light buff, the depth of the coloring being affected by the influence of the materials of the nest. When first laid, and unstained, the ground-color is a creamy white. The markings are usually scattered, small, and rounded, of bright reddish brown, and lighter and fainter stains of purplish slate. Two specimens of the egg of this bird (No. 1278) collected in Minnesota by Mr. B. F. Goss, are of oval shape, one end but very slightly larger than the other; one measures 1.80 inches in length by 1.25 inches in breadth, the other 1.70 by 1.30 inches.

GENUS **FULICA**, LINNÆUS.

Fulica, LINN. S. N. ed. 10, 1758, 152; ed. 12, I 1766, 257 (type, *F. atra*, LINN.).

CHAR. Very similar to *Gallinula*, but the toes margined by a broad, deeply scalloped lateral membrane. Bill shorter than the head, straight, strong, compressed, and advancing into the feathers of the forehead, where it frequently forms a wide and somewhat projecting frontal plate; nostrils in a groove, with a large membrane, near the middle of the bill. Wings rather short, second and third quills usually longest; tail very short; tarsus robust, shorter than the middle toe, with very distinct transverse scales; toes long, each having semicircular lobes, larger on the inner side; hind toe rather long, lobed.

Almost the only difference between *Fulica* and *Gallinula* consists in the single character of the toes, as pointed out above. The two genera are, however, quite distinct, since there appears to be no species known that is intermediate in the character of the feet.

Leaving out the remarkable *F. cornuta*, BONAP., which has been made the type of a distinct genus[1] — and we think properly so — there are known six American species of *Fulica*, whose char-

[1] *Lycornis*, BONAP. Ann. Sc. Nat. ser. 4, Zool. I. 46 (1854).

acters, translated from Messrs. SCLATER & SALVIN'S "*Clavis specierum*" (P. Z. S. 1868, p. 462), are as follows: —

a'. Crissum black centrally, mixed with white laterally.
 Large: Bend of the wing black . . . . *F. gigantea.*
 Small: Bend of the wing white . . . . *F. ardesiaca.*
b'. Crissum wholly white.
 a''. Secondaries concolored.
  Margin of the wing white . . . . *F. armillata.*
  Margin of the wing concolored . . . . *F. leucopyga.*
 b''. Secondaries tipped with white.
  Large: Bill yellow . . . . *F. leucoptera.*
  Small: Bill spotted with red . . . . *F. americana.*

F. americana.

The two species occurring (one of them accidentally) in North America differ in the following characters: —

1. **F. americana.** Lateral and posterior feathers of crissum, edge of wing, and tips of secondaries white; bill with a dark-brownish spot near end of each mandible, the frontal shield dark brown. Wing, 7.25–7.60; tarsus, 2.00–2.20; middle toe, 2.45–2.65. *Hab.* Whole of North and Middle America, and West Indies.
2. **F. atra.** Only the edge of the wing and very narrow edge to outer primary white; bill without dark spots near end, and frontal shield not conspicuously different in color from the bill. Wing, 7.70–8.80; tarsus, 2.25–2.35; middle toe, 2.85–3.15. *Hab.* Palæarctic Region; accidental in Greenland.

Fulica americana.

THE AMERICAN COOT.

Fulica americana, GMEL. S. N. I. ii. 1788, 704. — SW. & RICH. F. B. A. II. 1831, 404. — NUTT. Man. II. 1834, 229. — AUD. Orn. Biog. III. 1835, 291; V. 1839, 568; Synop. 1839, 212; B. Am. V. 1842, 138, pl. 305. — CASS. in Baird's B. N. Am. 1858, 751. — BAIRD, Cat. N. Am. B. 1859, no. 559. — COUES, Key, 1872, 275; Check List, 1873, no. 474; 2d ed, 1882, no. 686; Birds N. W. 1874, 541. — RIDGW. Nom. N. Am. B. 1881, no. 580.

Fulica Wilsoni, STEPHENS, Shaw's Gen. Zool. XII. 1824, 236.

Fulica atra, WILS. Am. Orn. IX. 1825, 61, pl. 73, fig. 1 (nec LINN.).

Hab. The whole of North America, Middle America, and West Indies; north to Greenland and Alaska, south to Veragua and Trinidad.

Sp. Char. *Adult:* General color uniform slate-color or slaty plumbeous, the head and neck and anterior central portion of the crissum black; lateral and posterior portions of the crissum, edge of wing, and tips of secondaries white. (In winter, the belly suffused with whitish.) Bill milk-white, more bluish terminally, each mandible with a spot of dark brown near the end, bordered anteriorly with a more or less distinct bar of reddish chestnut; frontal shield dark chestnut- or liver-brown, the culmen just in front of this tinged with greenish yellow; iris bright crimson; legs bright yellowish green, the tibiæ tinged behind and above with orange-red; toes light bluish

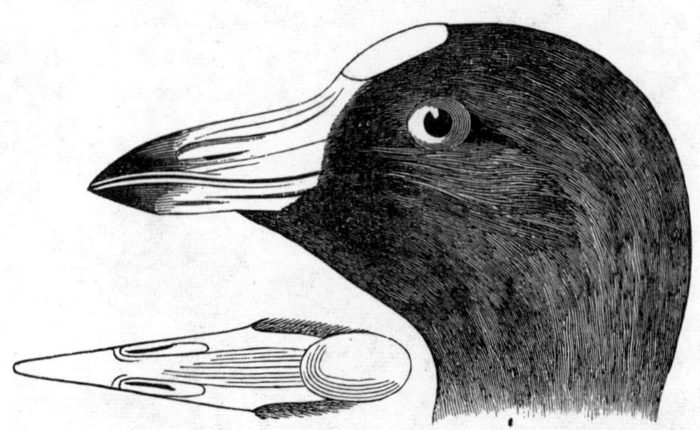

gray, tinged with yellowish green on scutellæ of basal phalanges.[1] *Young:* Similar, but lower parts more gray, and much suffused with whitish, especially on the throat and belly; bill dull flesh-color, tinged with olive-greenish, the frontal shield rudimentary; iris brown. *Downy young:* Prevailing color blackish plumbeous; head, neck, and upper parts relieved by numerous crisp, elongated, somewhat filamentous bristles, these sparse, light orange-buff and white, on the upper parts, but dense and deep salmon-orange on the head and neck, where the dark plumbeous down is almost or quite concealed; these colored filaments entirely absent from the whole pileum, which is mostly bald toward the occiput, elsewhere covered with closely appressed black bristles; lores densely covered with short, stamen-like, orange-red papillæ. Bill orange-red, the tip of the maxilla black; feet dusky (in skin).

Total length, about 14 inches; wing, 7.25–7.60; culmen (to commencement of frontal shield), 1.25–1.50; tarsus, 2.00–2.20; middle toe, 2.45–2.65.

The Common Coot of the North American fauna has a very widely extended distribution. It is found present and breeding in a large part of Northern South America, in Jamaica, Cuba, and other West India Islands, in many of the Southern States, in the Northwestern States, in the interior between the Missouri and the Western Mountains, on the Pacific coast, and on the Saskatchewan and the Mackenzie as far to the north as the 55th parallel, and even farther. It is not so common on the Atlantic coast, and is met with chiefly, or wholly, in its migrations — usually in September. It is very abundant in Mexico in the winter. Two instances are cited by Reinhardt of its having been taken in Greenland: one was in 1854, by Mr. Olric, the governor of North Greenland, in the harbor of Christianshaab; the other in the same year, by Holböll, at Godthaab. It is an occasional visitant of Bermuda. Richardson, who met with it in the Fur Country, states that its habits exactly resemble those of the closely allied European Coot. The small grassy lakes which skirt the Saskatchewan Plains are much frequented by this species. It was not met with near

[1] Fresh colors of an adult male killed at Wheatland, Ind., April 15, 1881.

Hudson's Bay, nor farther north than the 55th parallel. In the Fur Country it was always observed to arrive in the night-time. The crops of those that were killed were found to be filled with fine sand. Captain Blakiston also mentions that he met with this bird in large numbers on the reedy lakes of the Saskatchewan Valley, in the prairies of which it arrives about the end of April. He noticed that it has the habit of making a sharp rattling noise at night, and he was told that it migrates only by night. Its eggs are collected in great numbers by the fur-traders; and on one occasion Captain Blakiston went out on such an excursion in a canoe, and obtained a hundred and fifty in a few hours — even this was considered a poor day's work. This species was found in the neighborhood of Fort Carlton and on the Mackenzie, but was not met with on Hudson's Bay. It was procured at Fort Resolution, Fort Simpson, Big Island, Lake Manitoba, and in the Gens de Large Mountains.

Mr. Boardman informs me that it is not uncommon about Calais, Me., being seen in the fall and spring; but it is not known to breed there, and its presence is presumed to occur only in its migrations from more northern regions. It is found in Massachusetts, on the coast only as a migrant, so far as I am aware. It is said by Mr. Allen to breed near Springfield.

According to the observations of Mr. Giraud, this bird is nowhere plentiful in the middle Atlantic districts. Throughout the sea-coast of New Jersey, as well as on that of Long Island, it is sufficiently frequent to be known to the hunters, by whom it is called the "Mud-hen." When it does occur it is usually to be seen on low wet marshes and on the necks of land along the margins of creeks, which are thickly covered with rank grass and weeds, that afford it shelter in the intervals between the tides. It is then seldom seen, and when noticed disappears so quickly through the close cover that it is impossible to pursue it. At high-tide it sits on the drift grass, or retreats to higher places on the embankment, awaiting the fall of the tide to resume its opportunity of feeding on the worms, crustacea, insects, or seeds of the various plants which abound on the muddy places it frequents. In its habits it is sedentary, and, like the Rails and Gallinules, to which in many respects it has a strong resemblance, is averse to taking wing. Except when alarmed or suspicious of danger, it moves very leisurely along in pursuit of its food. When not thus employed its attitude is drowsy and listless. If pursued, it can run very fast and swim and dive very well, and if in danger, with great rapidity, making use of both wings and feet in swimming, like the Gallinule. It has not been ascertained to breed on Long Island.

Mr. Dresser found this bird abundant near Matamoras and Brownville during the time he was in that region; near San Antonio, late in the autumn of 1863, he also procured several specimens of it. Mr. J. A. Allen found it common in May in Eastern Kansas, where it was seen in large numbers in the lagoons. Mr. Ridgway speaks of it as excessively abundant and resident in all the marshes of California, as well as throughout the interior. It is also mentioned by Mr. R. Browne as one of the birds of Vancouver Island. Dr. Cooper states that it abounds in the marshy neighborhood of nearly every pond and stream in California, and it is probably equally numerous in Oregon and Washington Territory. South of San Francisco it is known only as a winter visitor. Being but rarely shot at by hunters, it is remarkably tame, collecting in flocks of hundreds in the marshes about San Francisco and other cities, as well as near remote mountain-lakes, walking awkwardly about on their shores, and scarcely getting out of the way to escape the sportsman, who thinks it an unworthy object of his skill, as its flesh is dark and unpalatable. The young bird, however, is said to be good eating.

The Coot can swim and dive with great ease; but when starting to fly seems to have great difficulty in rising, at first flapping the water and almost walking upon it for some distance. When once fairly up it can move with considerable swiftness, resembling in this a Grebe much more than a Rail. In the spring it becomes quite noisy, the flocks making a kind of chattering chorus, but becoming silent again after they have separated in pairs for the breeding-season. A few breed as far south as Santa Barbara, where Dr. Cooper saw young on the 10th of May, while at Puget Sound they appear early in June. Dr. Cooper did not meet with the nest of this species, but he was informed by Dr. Lieb that it is composed of dry rushes, without lining, loosely constructed, and several inches thick at the bottom. It is five inches deep and nearly two feet wide, and sometimes floats among the rushes. The eggs are said to be from ten to fifteen in number, greenish yellow in ground-color, sprinkled with small brown specks, and measure 2.00 by 1.25 inches.

This bird resembles the Rail in having a compressed body, and can make its way through the dense reeds where Ducks cannot pass, and where the water is too deep for Rails. In such situations it spends most of its time, feeding on grass-seeds, leaves of aquatic plants, small shells, and insects, collecting much of its food under the water. On the land it can sometimes be caught by hand before it is able to rise.

Examples were obtained by Mr. Skinner in Central America, and others were observed in abundance on the Lake of Dueñas by Mr. Salvin, which, from specimens afterward obtained, were ascertained with certainty to be of this species. It is given by Léotaud as rare in Trinidad.

Mr. March describes the eggs of this species, found by him in Jamaica, as being eight or more in number, oval, pointed at one end, grayish stone-color, splashed all over with small bistre-brown spots and dots. The ground-color is at first very pale, but becomes darker by exposure.

Mr. Gosse states that it may be seen at all hours of the day in the immense morass of Savanna la Mar, there being hundreds congregated within an acre. There they are wary to an excess, the distant sight of a man or the snapping of a dry twig alarming the whole flock, though the noise of cattle walking on the shore has no such effect.

A few specimens of this bird are recorded by Major Wedderburn and Mr. Hurdis as having been obtained at Bermuda, usually in November and December, and in one instance on the 28th of May.

Mr. Say observed it in the lower part of Missouri Territory; and in Long's Expedition it was seen in Lake Winnipique on the 7th of June. Mr. Swainson also obtained specimens on the Plateau of Mexico. Mr. Nuttall mentions that about the 15th of April, 1833, a pair took up their residence in Fresh Pond, Mass., and in the following June were occasionally seen, accompanied by their young. It is probable that similar occurrences are more common than is generally supposed. Bartram informed Wilson that this bird is resident and abundant in Florida. Audubon, however, controverts this statement, believing that the Coot is found in either Louisiana or Florida from November to the middle of April only, that none remain there after that period, and that none breed there. So sweeping a conclusion from merely negative evidence is somewhat rash, in view of the fact that the Coot is known to breed in large numbers in the Island of Cuba on the one hand, and in Texas, and Tamaulipas, Mexico, on the other. In one instance, at least, it has been found breeding at Monticello, West Florida, from which place its egg was sent me by Mr. Samuel Pasco, a citizen of that place.

Mr. Audubon mentions having once encountered a large flock of these birds, several hundreds in number, on the Mississippi on the 22d of March. They were feeding on the grass of a savanna bordering the river. He plainly saw them nibble the tender grass in the same manner as poultry. When he fired into the flock, the survivors, after running a few steps, rose and flew off toward the river, their legs hanging behind, their wings producing a constant whirr. While swimming they flew with ease, although not with much speed, and moved the head and neck in unison with their feet.

Mr. Moore states that Mr. Audubon was in error in supposing that this bird never dives. It is not in the habit of immersing its entire body; yet he has occasionally seen one or two birds, in a squad of four or six, plunge and remain so long beneath the surface that this had become smooth before they emerged. This is frequently done by one individual while others by its side are engaged in picking from the surface. In like manner the common *Fulica atra* of Europe dives and brings up its food from the bottom in a very skilful manner.

Mr. Moore is of the opinion that this bird rarely breeds in Florida. It comes in flocks about the 20th of September, and often remains in the same pond until its departure, which takes place between the last of March and the 10th of April. At the approach of danger the Coot does not sink its body in the water, but, like the Gallinule, hurries to a covert by striking the water with its feet and flying. The forward stroke of its wing is performed when swimming slowly in search of food. When moving with its highest speed, it uses its feet only, its head and neck being carried as steadily as those of a Duck.

Two eggs in my collection (No. 1275) — collected in Minnesota by Mr. B. F. Goss — have a ground-color of a light grayish buff, sprinkled uniformly with very minute specks and round dots of purplish black. In shape these eggs are of an oblong oval, tapering at one end and rounded slightly at the other; these measure, one 1.85 inches by 1.35, the other 1.90 inches by 1.30. A third, from Lake Koskonong, Wis., is oval in shape, the smaller end being hardly perceptibly less than the other; its ground-color is a deep buff, with a decided reddish tinge; the spots, though small, are larger, deeper, and more uniformly rounded, but still sparsely scattered. This egg (No. 78) measures 1.82 inches by 1.25.

A nest of this species obtained from a reedy swamp at Marysville, Utah, is composed entirely of coarse reeds. It is eight inches high, thirteen inches wide, and has a cavity four inches deep. It contained ten eggs. Dr. J. C. Merrill mentions having found as many as fourteen eggs in a single nest. Mr. B. F. Goss writes me that it is very abundant in Wisconsin in early spring, and that later in the season it congregates in flocks, frequenting more open water. Its preference is for shallow water, muddy bottoms, the vicinity of reeds and rushes, and during its breeding-season it is rarely found far from such situations. Its nest is built about the last of May, in some thick cover, where the old growth is broken down, forming a platform just above the mud or shallow water. It is built with some care, rather deeply hollowed, and composed of rushes, flag-leaves, etc. Eleven eggs have been found in a nest, but the usual number is eight or nine. The eggs vary in length from 1.75 to 2.10 inches, and in breadth from 1.17 to 1.42 inches. The ground-color is dark grayish cream, thickly covered with fine spots of different shades of dark brown, lilac, etc. Its nest is usually so carefully concealed that it is usually much more difficult to find than that of the Gallinule.

Fulica atra.

THE EUROPEAN COOT.

Fulica atra, LINN. S. N. ed. 10, I. 1758, 152; ed. 12, I. 1766, 257. — KEYS. & BLAS. Wirb. Eur. 1840, 68. — NAUM. Vög. Deutschl. IX. 1838, 635, pl. 241. — SCHLEG. Rev. Crit. 1844, 102. — MACGILL. Man. Orn. II. 118; Hist. Brit. B. IV. 1852, 560. — RIDGW. Nom. N. Am. B. 1881, no. 580 (Greenland, *fide* Prof. J. REINHARDT). — COUES, Check List, 2d ed. 1882, no. 885.
Fulica aterrima, RETZ. Faun. Suec. 1800, 199. — BREHM, Vög. Deutschl. 1831, 710, pl. 36, fig. 4.
Fulica leucoryx, GMEL. S. N. I. 1788, 703.
Fulica æthiops, GMEL. t. c. 704.
Fulica platyuros, BREHM, Vög. Deutschl. 711.

HAB. Palæarctic Region in general; accidental in Greenland (Prof. J. REINHARDT).

SP. CHAR. *Adult:* Head and neck black, this changing gradually into very dark plumbeous-slate on the upper parts, and to lighter, more grayish, slate on the lower surface; rump, posterior scapulars, and hind part of back more or less tinged with dark olivaceous; under surface of primaries silvery gray; edge of wing and very narrow margin to outer web of outer primary, white. Bill (in life) pale red at the base, the tip white; frontal plate bluish white; iris crimson; feet bluish gray tinged with olive; the bare part of the tibia orange; claws olivaceous (MACGILLIVRAY). *Young:* Similar to the adult, but more grayish; the bill and frontal plate dull greenish; the iris brown, etc. *Downy young:* Sooty blackish above, dark sooty gray below; neck, back, and wings ornamented with fine dull-white filaments, the forehead and lores with peculiar small, thickened, and somewhat curled horny attachments to the down, of a pale dull orange-color (perhaps bright orange or reddish in life); basal half of bill pale brownish (reddish or orange in life?), the terminal half porcelain-white, tipped with jet-black.

Total length, about 16.00 inches; extent of wings, 22.00; wing, 7.70–8.80; culmen (including frontal plate), 1.70–2.00; tarsus, 2.25–2.35; middle toe, 2.85–3.15.

FAMILY ARAMIDÆ. — THE COURLANS.

Aramidæ, BONAP. Consp. II. 1855, 103.

CHAR. Large Rail-like birds, differing from the true Rails (*Rallidæ*) in the outer primary being shorter than the seventh, its inner web greatly narrowed, as if cut away, except at end; the elongated bill (about equal to the tarsus) slightly curved to one side at the tip; the inner secondaries well developed, broad, their webs slightly decomposed; the rectrices well developed, firm, and very distinct from the coverts.

The Courlans are very closely related to the true Rails, and so far as the external structure is concerned, scarcely differ except in the peculiarities pointed out above, none of which, however, seem to be shared by any of the *Rallidæ* proper. But one genus is known, the characters of which are as follows: —

GENUS **ARAMUS**, VIEILLOT.

Aramus, VIEILL. Analyse, 1816, 58 (type, *Courliri*, BUFF., = *Ardea scolopacea*, GMEL.). — BAIRD, B. N. Am. 1858, 657.

CHAR. Bill elongated, much compressed, both mandibles decurved and turned slightly to one side at tip. Gonys very long. Bill of equal width nearly from base to tip; nostrils pervious, in the basal fourth of the bill. Head feathered to bill, only the eyelids naked. Legs lengthened; tibia half bare; tarsus longer than middle toe; toes without basal membrane: outer lateral rather longer than inner; middle claw not pectinated. The tarsi are broadly scutellate anteriorly.

The wings are broad and rounded; the tertials equal to the primaries. The first quill is scarcely longer than the tenth, and subfalcate. The tail is composed of twelve feathers.

A. scolopaceus.

Two species are at present known to naturalists, formerly supposed to be one. Cabanis was the first to point out the differences between them, and to insist that they were distinct, and not merely adult and young. They differ as follows: —

COM. CHAR. Prevailing color dark brown, varying from a chocolate to an olivaceous shade; head and neck, and sometimes (in *A. pictus*) the back, wing-coverts, and lower parts longitudinally spotted or striped with white; remiges and rectrices glossed with purple.

1. **A. scolopaceus.**[1] White markings confined to the head and neck (concealed or altogether wanting on other portions). Wing, 12.50–14.20 inches; tail, 7.60; culmen, 4.30–4.70; tarsus, 4.60–5.20. *Hab.* Eastern South America.
2. **A. pictus.** White stripes extending over back, wing-coverts, and entire lower parts, except crissum. Wing, 11.00–13.00; tail, 5.90; culmen, 3.50–4.80; tarsus, 3.50–5.20. *Hab.* West Indies, Florida, and Central America.

[1] ARAMUS SCOLOPACEUS. The Scolopaceous Courlan; Brazilian Courlan.
Courlan, ou Courliri, BUFF. Hist. Nat. Ois. VII. 442.
Le Courlan, de Cayenne, BUFF. Pl. Enl. 1770–1784, pl. 848.
Scolopaceous Heron, LATH. Synop. III. i. 1785, 102 (ex Pl. Enl. 848).
Ardea scolopacea, GMEL. S. N. I. ii. 1788, 647, no. 87 (ex BUFF. & LATH. l. c.).
Aramus scolopaceus, VIEILL. Nouv. Dict. VIII. 1817, 301; Gal. Ois. II. 134, pl. 252. — AUD. Orn. Biog. IV. 1838, pl. 377 (not the descr.); B. Am. V. 1842, pl. 312 (not the descr.). — BAIRD, B. N. Am. 1858, 657 (footnote).
Carau, AZARA, Apunt. III. 1805, 202, no. 366.
Aramus carau, VIEILL. N. D. VIII. 1817, 300.
Rallus ardeoides, SPIX, Av. Bras. II. 1824, 72, pl. xci.
Rallus gigas, LICHT. Verz. Doubl. 1823, 79.
Notherodius guarauna, WAGL. Syst. Av. 1827 (not *Scolopax guarauna*, LINN.).

Aramus pictus.

FLORIDA COURLAN; LIMPKIN.

Tantalus pictus (*Ephouskyka Indian*), *the Crying Bird, beautifully speckled*, BARTRAM, Travels, 1792, 293.

Aramus pictus, COUES, Pr. Ac. Nat. Sci. Philad. 1875, 354 (ex BARTR. l. c.); Check List, 2d ed. 1882, no. 671. — RIDGW. Nom. N. Am. B. 1881, no. 581.

Rallus giganteus, BONAP. Jour. Ac. Nat. Sci. Philad. V. 1825, 31 (Florida).

Aramus giganteus, BAIRD, B. N. Am. 1858, 657; Cat. N. Am. B. 1859, no. 481.

Aramus scolopaceus, var. *giganteus*, COUES, Key, 1872, 271; Check List, 1873, no. 464.

Aramus scolopaceus, BONAP. Am. Orn. III. 1828, 111, pl. xxvi. (nec VIEILL.). — NUTT. Man. II. 1834, 68. — AUD. Orn. Biog. IV. 1838, 543 (not pl. 377, which is true *A. scolopaceus*); Synop. 1839, 219; B. Am. V. 1842, 181 (not pl. 312, which is *A. scolopaceus*).

Notherodius holostictus, CAB. J. f. O. 1856, 426 (Cuba).

Aramus holostictus, SCL. & SALV. Ibis, I. 1859, 227 (Belize and Omoa, Honduras).

HAB. Greater Antilles, Florida, and Atlantic coast of Central America, to Honduras and Costa Rica (Pacific coast).

SP. CHAR. *Adult:* General color olivaceous umber-brown, each feather marked centrally with a stripe of white, these markings linear on the head and neck, but much broader and more or less cuneate and ovate on the lower parts, upper part of the back, scapulars, and wing-coverts; sides, flanks, and crissum uniform chocolate-brown, without streaks; primaries and tail uniform rich purplish chocolate, with purplish reflections; upper parts generally more or less glossed with

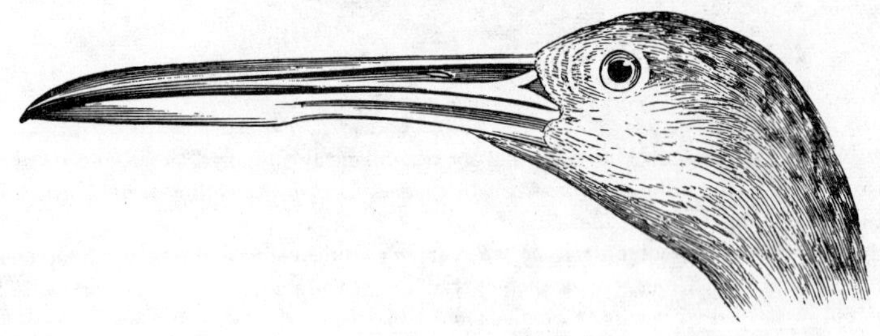

purplish bronze. Lores, malar region, chin, and throat dull white, faintly streaked with brown. "Bill greenish yellow, dusky toward the end of both mandibles, but especially the upper; iris hazel; feet lead-gray; claws dusky"[1] (AUDUBON). *Young:* Similar to the adult, but the brown duller, the white markings much narrower, and less sharply defined. *Downy young:* "Covered with coarse tufty feathers of a black color" (AUDUBON).

Total length, about 25.00–27.00 inches; extent, 40.00–42.00; wing, 11.00–13.00; culmen, 3.50–4.75; tarsus, 3.50–5.20; middle toe, 3.30–3.50.

Among more than fifty specimens of this bird examined, we find great variations of size and proportions; and if the labels are to be credited, this variation seems quite independent of sex. Young birds resemble adults, but are duller colored, with the white markings much narrower and less distinct. Several examples from Porto Rico have shorter and deeper bills, and are smaller generally, than any we have seen from Florida. In a larger series, however, these differences may prove not constant. An example from La Palma, Costa Rica (Pacific side), collected by Mr. C. C. Nutting, is not essentially different from some Floridan specimens, although rather more richly colored than most of them.

[1] In the dried skin, the bill is mainly dusky, the mandible light brownish on the basal half, the terminal half horn-color, dusky, or even glaucous; the legs and feet black.

The Courlan, in the North American fauna, has a restricted distribution, being confined exclusively to the peninsula of Florida, and not being known to exist in any other portion of the United States. It occurs in Cuba and Jamaica, and probably in others of the West India Islands, and in portions of Central America. It is not mentioned by Léotaud as occurring in Trinidad.

In Florida, according to Audubon, it appears to be entirely confined to that section of the peninsula of Florida known as the Everglades, and the swampy borders of the bayous and lagoons issuing therefrom. In one instance it is said to have been procured among the Florida Keys by Titian Peale. It was not met with by Audubon on any of those islands, nor did he notice it on any part of the coast between Florida and Texas. Audubon describes its flight as heavy and of short duration, the concavity and shortness of the wings, with the nature of the places which it inhabits, rendering it slow to remove from one spot to another on wing, it being found chiefly among tall plants, the roots of which are frequently under water. When it rises of its own accord, it passes through the air at a short distance above the weeds, with regular beats of the wings, its neck extended to its full length, and its long legs dangling beneath, until it suddenly drops to the ground. If pursued, few birds excel it in speed. It proceeds by long strides, first in a direct course, and afterward diverging, so as to insure its safety even when chased by the best dogs. When accidentally surprised, it rises obliquely out of its recess, with the neck greatly bent downward; and although its legs dangle for a while, they are afterward extended behind in the manner of Herons. At such times it is easily shot. If only wounded, it is vain to pursue it. By the great length and expansion of its toes it is enabled, although of considerable size, to walk on the broad leaves of the *Nymphea*. It can swim with all the buoyancy of the Coot and the Gallinule.

Its nest is composed of rank weeds matted together and forming a large mass with a depression in the centre. This is placed among the larger tufts of the tallest grasses which grow at short distances from the bayous, some of them influenced by the low tides of the Gulf; it is fastened to the stems of these plants in the same manner as that of the Clapper Rail, and is generally secure from inundation. The eggs are usually six in number, and are large for the bird. The young are hatched out early in May, are covered with a rather coarse black down, and follow their parents soon after their appearance. This bird is said to feed, in Florida, chiefly on a large greenish snail which is abundant in the Everglades. While on the wing it utters a note said to be a sort of cackle, like that of the Common Hen; but when on the ground this cry is much louder, especially during the pairing-season, or when startled by the report of a gun. Its flesh is regarded as good eating. The statements as to its ever alighting on trees Audubon was inclined to discredit.

Dr. Bryant (Proc. Boston Nat. Hist. Soc. VII. p. 11) does not consider Audubon as being quite accurate in regarding the Everglades as the headquarters of this species. In his visits to that portion situated near Fort Dallas, he did not meet with an individual. He never found it either on the shallow ponds or the wet savannas so numerous in the neighborhood of Indian River. The part of Florida in which he saw it was on the St. John's and the waters connected with it, between Lake Harney and Lake George. He first noticed it at Wikiva, and from there found it in great numbers as he descended the river, wherever the locality was suited to its habits, until he arrived at Spring Garden Lake, where it was more numerous than at any locality previously visited. It was generally seen standing on the edge of the shore, or else on the *Nymphea* or other broad-leaved plants able to support its weight. He found it very tame and unsuspicious for so large a bird, allowing itself to be approached within gunshot, standing in the same place, bobbing its head up and down like a Sandpiper. On taking wing it utters a loud cluck, and if a tree is in the neighborhood generally alights on it, or, if not, usually alights in some thick part of the marsh, and is not easily started again. On the St. John's it feeds principally on a species of *Natica*, which is extremely abundant, and also on the small unios. Its ordinary note — which this bird seems to be very fond of uttering — is said to be very disagreeable, and to resemble that of the Peacock. Besides this it makes a number of other sounds, all of the most unharmonious description. Incubation is said to begin in February. The few nests Dr. Bryant saw were made on low willows. In Spring Garden Lake he saw four on one small island. The number of eggs is unusually large, fifteen having been taken from one nest. From the unsuspicious nature of this bird, and the fact that it betrays its whereabouts by loud cries, Dr. Bryant predicts its extermination as soon as that part of Florida is settled.

Mr. Boardman informs me that this bird is more generally known in Florida as the "Limpkin," and it is so called from the peculiarity of its walking, its movements resembling the motions of a lame person. It is a very tame and unsuspicious bird, and will not infrequently answer a call, and thus betray its position to the sportsman. It is of nocturnal habit, moving about in the night-time, and during the hours of darkness is much more noisy than in the daytime.

In Jamaica, according to Gosse, this bird is generally known as the "Clucking-hen," from its ordinary note when undisturbed in its solitudes. He mentions meeting one in August, in a wood on Bluefields Peak, where it was walking at a little distance from him, and clucking deliberately, with a voice exactly resembling that of a sauntering Fowl. A precipitous gully behind the Bluefields abounded with this species, and in February, a parching drought having wasted the mountain pools, this bird was driven in numbers to the springs gushing out at the foot of the mountain. He was informed that it was in the habit of roosting in the high trees in that neighborhood, and went one evening to the spot to observe. Just as the twilight was fading into darkness, he began to hear them screaming and flying around. Their notes were sometimes a series of shrill screams uttered in succession, then a harsh cry, like *krau, krau, krau, kreaow.* All were loud, sudden, and startling. Several alighted on a large tree not far from him, but were too wary for him to approach within gunshot; one, however, was secured by his servant.

During the drought several of these birds frequented the morasses near Paradise River, and from the summit of a matted mass of convolvulus covering a large bush, he had an opportunity to see and to watch their singular movements. The tangled creepers afforded a support for their broad feet, and they stood boldly erect, as if watching, in an attitude exactly like that of an Ibis, though flirting their tails in the manner of a Rail. At brief intervals they uttered a short, sharp sound, and sometimes loud, harsh screams of *krēaow.* When alarmed they flew heavily and slowly, with their long legs hanging down, and with outstretched neck, making a very awkward appearance. Gosse was informed that they scratch and pick in the manner of a Common Fowl. The stomach of one that he examined was stuffed with small water-snails, divested of the shells and filling the œsophagus almost to the fauces. The piercing cries uttered at the approach of night were not heard at any other time, and during the day this bird commonly emits only its deliberate clucking. Gosse did not regard it as a nocturnal bird, but considered these cries as only indicative of preparations for repose, as they soon relapse into silence.

Being so swift of foot, this bird, in Jamaica, does not confine itself merely to a few localities, but ranges the lonely woods from the mangrove morasses of the sea-shore to the very tops of the wooded mountains. Gosse esteemed it the best wild-fowl of the country.

Mr. W. T. March, of Spanishtown, Jamaica, furnishes the following full and particular account of its habits: —

"The Clucking-hen appears more closely allied to the Land than it is to the Water Birds. It is found in all parts of the island, and is now very common in the lowland districts of the South Midland parishes, along gully courses, and near wet, marshy lands. It is often seen and heard in the driest seasons about the gullies in the vicinity of Spanishtown. It roosts on trees and breeds on the ground, like the Common Fowl — in the lowlands, usually in Penguin fences. It lays eight or more eggs, and these measure $2\frac{1}{4}$ by $1\frac{5}{8}$ of an inch; the ground-color rufous, splashed at the large end with small burnt-ochre spots; and I have had eggs taken from April to November. The flesh is tender and well flavored, but a strong prejudice exists against it from the prevailing, though I believe erroneous, opinion that it feeds on snakes and lizards. I have never found in its stomach any other food than snails, slugs, portions of small crabs, and wood-worms (*Hullandia palmaria*). The junks of snakes referred to by Robinson were probably large slugs. One of my collectors, however, assures me that he has found a young snake and lizards in them; and a young sportsman lately told me, in support of his assertion that it does not confine itself to the food I have mentioned, that whilst beating up a gully-course he shot a White-belly Dove, and that as soon as the bird fell to the ground, and notwithstanding the report of the gun, a Clucking-hen deliberately came down the bank and endeavored to carry off the Dove. It feeds late and early, and has been considered a night-feeder. I have often heard that the *Arami* are to be seen on moonlight nights stalking about the water-flashes at Papage Fort and Great Salt Pond, feeding on the small crabs and snails abounding at certain seasons in those localities; but from my own observations I believe the birds thus seen were Night Herons. Another opinion which I believe to be erroneous is, that it broods like the Barn-door Fowl. The foot of this bird does not, however, seem to be very well adapted to scratching the ground, the bill appearing more useful in securing and preparing the food it lives on."

An egg of this species in the Smithsonian Collection (No. 8521) has a rounded oval shape, one end being only very slightly less rounded than the other. It measures 2.20 inches in length by 1.55 in breadth. Its ground-color is a dark grayish white with a light wash of sepia, and marked with a few scattered blotches of a darker sepia. Over the extreme of the larger end these are more marked and numerous, and nearly cover it. This egg was procured in Cuba by Dr. Gundlach.

FAMILY GRUIDÆ. — THE CRANES.

THE diagnosis of this family has already been given on page 350. The species are all of very large size, and inhabit grassy plains as well as marshes. The bill is moderately long; the nostrils broad and pervious, the nasal groove extending but little beyond them. The legs are long, but the toes are short; the hind toe is very short and much elevated, the claw scarcely touching the ground.

The genera are few in number, but one, *Grus*, belonging to North America.

GENUS **GRUS**, PALLAS.

Grus, PALL. Misc. Zool. 1766, 66 (type, *Ardea grus*, L.).

CHAR. Bill lengthened, straight, the upper mandible only slightly decurved at the extreme tip; the commissure and other outlines straight. Nasal groove very large and open, extending over the basal two thirds of the bill. Nostrils broadly open, pervious; the anterior extremity half way from the tip of bill to eye. The upper half of the head naked, warty, but with short hairs.

Legs much lengthened; toes short, hardly more than one third the tarsus. Inner toe rather longer, its claw much larger than the outer. Hind toe elevated, short. Toes connected at base by membrane. Tarsi broadly scutellate anteriorly. Tertials longer than primaries, decurved ; first quill not much shorter than second. Tail of twelve feathers.

Synopsis of Species.

A. Adult plumage white, the primaries black ; cheeks naked.

1. **G. americana.** Bill very thick, the gonys strongly convex.

B. Adult plumage grayish or plumbeous, the primaries slate-color ; cheeks always feathered.

2. **G. canadensis.** Bill slender, longer than middle toe ; gonys straight.

a. canadensis. Wing, 17.75–19.00 inches ; culmen, 2.90–3.70 ; tarsus, 6.70–8.00 ; middle toe, 2.80–2.95. *Hab.* Alaska to New Mexico and Texas, breeding (exclusively ?) far northward.

β. mexicana. Wing, 22.00 inches ; culmen, 5.00–6.00 inches ; tarsus, 10.00 ; middle toe, 3.50 or more. *Hab.* Western United States and Gulf States from Washington Territory to Florida.

G. canadensis mexicana.

Grus americana.

THE WHOOPING CRANE.

Ardea americana, LINN. S. N. I. 1766, 234 (based on EDW. pl. 132 ; CATESB. pl. 75 ; BRISS. V. 382). — WILS. Am. Orn. VIII. 1814, 20, pl. 64, fig. 3.

Grus americana, SW. & RICH. F. B. A. II. 1831, 372. — NUTT. Man. II. 1834, 34. — AUD. Orn. Biog. III. 1835, 202, pl. 226 ; Synop. 1839, 219 ; B. Am. V. 1842, 188, pl. 313. — BAIRD, B. N. Am. 1858, 654 ; Cat. N. Am. B. 1859, no. 478. — COUES, Key, 1872, 271 ; Check List, 1873, no. 462 ; ed. 2, 1882, no. 668 ; Birds N. W. 1874, 530. — RIDGW. Nom. N. Am. B. 1881, no. 582.

Grus clamator, BARTR. Trav. 1791, 292.

Grus struthio, WAGL. Syst. Av. 1827, Grus, no. 6.

Grus Hoyanus, DUDLEY, Pr. Ac. Nat. Sci. Philad. VII. 1854, 64 (young). — STIMPSON, Mem. Chicago Acad. I. 1868, 129, pl. 19.

La Grue d'Amérique, BUFF. Pl. Enl. 1770–1784, pl. 889 (adult).

Hooping Crane, FORSTER, Philos. Trans. LXII. 1772, 409, no. 37. — PENN. Arct. Zool. II. 1785, 442.

HAB. The interior of North America from Texas and Florida to the Fur Countries, and from Colorado to Ohio; south to Guanajuato, Central Mexico?[1] Formerly found, casually, in the Atlantic States.

SP. CHAR. *Adult:* Whole crown and occiput covered by a warty or granulated skin, almost bare on the occiput, but covered anteriorly by black hair-like bristles; the color of this skin reddish in life. Lores and malar region, including a narrow angular strip extending from the latter down each side of the throat, also naked, and similarly bristled, the bristles denser anteriorly. Color entirely pure white, excepting the primaries and their coverts, which are uniform slate-black, and a patch of plumbeous on the upper part of the nape, adjoining the bare skin of the occiput and extending downward for the distance of about two inches. "Bill wax-yellow; iris gamboge-yellow; bare skin of head dull orange-color; legs blue-black." (SW. & RICH. l. c.) *Young:* Head completely feathered. General color white, with large patches here and there, especially above, of light cinnamon, the head and neck almost continuously of this color. The primaries and their coverts uniform dull black, as in the adult. Bill dull wax-yellow, the terminal portion blackish; legs and feet blackish. *Immature:* Bare portions of the head indicated by feathers of a harsher texture and darker color than elsewhere, occupying the areas which are naked in the fully adult. Plumage much stained with pale cinnamon, as in the first plumage.

Total length, about 52.00 inches; extent, 92.00; wing, 24.00; culmen, 5.35; tarsus, 12.00; middle toe, 4.25.

The Great White or Whooping Crane is nearly confined to the central portion of North America, passing the winter months in the swamps of Florida and Texas, and breeding in the more northern portions of the continent. It breeds in favorable localities in the region north of the 43d parallel, some, however, nesting in the prairies of Central Illinois, Iowa, Minnesota, and Dakota. Captain Blakiston ("Ibis," 1863, p. 128) mentions meeting with this species at different times during his travels in the interior, though he was not able to procure specimens. Mr. Ross records the capture of a single specimen on Mackenzie River — where, however, the bird was quite rare. Specimens in the Smithsonian Institution were procured at Fort Resolution, Big Island, Fort Rae, and at Salt River, near the Great Slave Lake.

Hearne, in the Appendix to his "Journey to the Northern Ocean," published in 1795, states that the Whooping Crane visits Hudson's Bay in the spring, though not in great numbers. It was generally seen only in pairs, but not very often, and was usually observed to frequent the open swamps, the sides of rivers, and the margins of lakes and ponds, and to feed on frogs and small fishes. It was esteemed very good eating. In breeding it seldom had more than two young, and it retired southward early in the fall. He adds that its wing-bones are so long and large that he has known them made successfully into flutes.

Richardson states that he found this species frequenting every part of the Fur Country, though nowhere in such numbers as the Brown Crane. It migrates in flocks, and performs its journeys in the night, and at such an altitude that its passage is known only by the peculiarly shrill screams which it utters. It rises from the ground with great difficulty, flying for a time quite low, and affording a fair mark for the sportsman; but if the bird is not entirely disabled by the shot, it will fight with great determination, and can inflict a very severe wound with its formidable bill. Richardson knew of several instances in which the wounded bird had put the fowler to flight and fairly driven him off the field. When fat its flesh is good eating, but is very inferior to that of the Brown Crane (*Grus canadensis*).

Mr. Dresser states that on his first visit to the town lagoon at Matamoras, in June, 1863, he saw a pair of these Cranes, and subsequently met with a small flock of seven

[1] *Fide* Professor A. DUGÈS, in epist.

or eight; but these were so wary that he only succeeded in shooting two. He inquired of the Mexicans as to where they bred, and was informed that their eggs could be procured at a lagoon some distance to the west of Bagdad, Boca del Rio Grande. Mr. Dresser was not able to go there, and was thus unable to test the accuracy of this very doubtful information. On his return to Matamoras, in 1864, he saw none at the lagoons there. During his rambles in Texas he saw this bird on only two or three occasions near San Antonio, and once at Point Isabel. He was told that it is occasionally seen on Galveston Island, and at the mouth of the Brazos River. Mr. J. A. Allen was informed that it is tolerably common in the valley of Great Salt Lake, both in the spring and in the fall.

Mr. Boardman writes me that, so far as he is aware, this species is wholly unknown on the coast of Maine; and I can find no certain evidence that it has ever been seen in any part of New England. It is not given by Giraud as a bird of Long Island, and is very rare on any part of the coast north of the Chesapeake, though Mr. Turnbull states that, in 1857, while at Beasley's Point, he saw three of this species off the inlet. They were very wary, and could not be approached. In Wilson's day a few appeared in the marshes of Cape May in December, particularly on and near Egg Island, and lingered in those marshes during the whole of the winter, setting out northward about the time the ice broke up. During their stay they wandered about the marshes and muddy flats near the sea-shore, occasionally sailing from place to place with a low and heavy flight, just above the surface, at times uttering a loud, clear, and piercing cry, which might be heard to the distance of two miles. This singular cry — to which the Whooping Crane owes its name — is uttered with various modulations.

As Wilson considered the *G. canadensis* to be but the immature bird of this species, we cannot with certainty separate his statements and assign each where it belongs. He states that he frequently met with it in the low grounds and rice plantations of the Southern States, noticing it near the Waccamaw River, in South Carolina, on the 10th of February, and in a pond near Louisville on the 20th of March. The birds seen were extremely shy and vigilant. They would sometimes rise spirally in the air to a great height, the mingled noise of the screaming, even when the flock was almost beyond the reach of sight, resembling that of a pack of hounds in full cry. On these occasions they flew around in large circles, as if reconnoitring the country to a vast extent for fresh quarters to feed in. His information in regard to their breeding must be rejected as agreeing in no respect with the present reality. Audubon also regarded the *canadensis* as identical with the young of this species, and he gives the time of its arrival in the western country as about the middle of October or first of November, in flocks of twenty or thirty, and even thrice that number, spreading from the Northwestern States to the Carolinas and Florida, on the southeast to Louisiana and the countries bordering on Mexico, in all of which this Crane spends the winter, returning north about the beginning of May. He found it on the edges of large ponds, in swampy woods, and in extensive morasses. In its migrations it travels both by night and day. He states that in the fall, while the water is low in the ponds, this bird works with its bill in the mud to uncover the roots of the great water-lily, which when reached it greedily devours. While intent upon this the bird may be easily approached. As soon as the heavy rains fill these pools it abandons them, and resorts to other places. It is said to frequent fields in which corn, peas, sweet potatoes, etc., have been planted, feeding on the grain and peas, and digging up and devouring the potatoes. It also feeds on water insects, frogs, reptiles, moles, and field-mice. Audubon once found a garter-snake fifteen inches long in the stomach of one of this species. He describes the cries uttered by this bird as loud and piercing — so loud that they might be heard at the distance of three miles. The flesh of the young bird he speaks of as being tender and juicy, while in the old birds it becomes very dark and tough, and is unfit for the table. In captivity this Crane is extremely gentle, and will feed freely on grain and other vegetable substances.

Mr. Audubon kept one, while he was in Boston, which had been taken, while young, on the Florida coast, a wing having been fractured and afterward amputated. This bird was very gentle, and would suffer him to caress it with the hand. It searched the wood-pile for worms and grubs, watched with the patience of a cat for mice, and would swallow them whole. It also fed on corn and garbage from the kitchen. At times it would look upward, and, as if calling to some acquaintance passing high in the air, would cry aloud. It was naturally suspicious of some lurking danger; and sometimes, on very slight occasion, would manifest a sudden and causeless alarm, as if some dreaded enemy were at hand.

This bird has never been detected on the Pacific coast, or west of the Great Plains; and as *G. canadensis mexicana* is common there, this of itself is sufficient evidence of the difference of the two species. Mr. Kennicott met with it at Fort Resolution, May 20, and procured a specimen. A nest of this species, containing two eggs, was found near Salt River, not far from Fort Resolution, Great Slave Lake, in 1864. The eggs (Smithsonian Institution, No. 9288) measure, one 3.80 inches by 2.60, the other 3.70 inches by 2.50. Their ground-color is a deep grayish white, with a washing of sepia, marked sparsely, except at the larger end, with bold patches of dark rusty sepia-brown, and more obscure blotches of an opaque sepia. These last are thinly scattered over nearly the whole egg. At the extreme portion of the obtuse end these markings are far more numerous, become confluent, and form an irregular crown. The eggs are oval in shape, and a little more rounded at one end than at the other.

Grus canadensis.

a. canadensis. THE LITTLE BROWN CRANE.

Ardea canadensis, Linn. ed. 10, I. 1758, 141 ; ed. 12, 1766, 234 (based on Edwards, I. 33 ; Briss. V. 385). — Forst. Philos. Jour. LXII. 1772, 409 (Severn R.).

Grus canadensis, Temm. Man. I. 1820, p. c. — Sabine, Franklin's Jour. 685. — Richards, Parry's Second Voy. 353. — Sw. & Rich. F. B. A. II. 1831, 373. — Bonap. Consp. I. 1850, 98. — Scl. Ibis, 1860, 418 (Hudson's Bay). — Blakist. Ibis, 1863, 128 (int. Brit. Am.). — Dall & Bannist. Trans. Chicago Acad. I. 1869, 289 (St. Michael's, Alaska). — Tacz. J. f. O. 1873, 112 (N. E. Siberia). — Coues, Check List, 2d ed. 1882, no. 669.

Grus fusca (part), Vieill. Nouv. Dict. XIII. 1817, 558 (includes both forms).

Grus poliophœa, Wagl. Syst. Av. 1827, Grus, sp. 7 (based on Edwards).

Grus fraterculus, Cass. in Baird's B. N. Am. 1858, 656 (=*juv.* ; New Mexico !). — Baird, Cat. N. Am. B. 1859, no. 480. — Allen, Bull. N. O. C., V. 1880, 123. — Ridgw. ib. 187 ; Nom. N. Am. B. 1881, no. 584.

Grus fratercula, Tacz. Bull. Soc. Zool. France, 1876, 246.

Blue Crane, Forst. l. c.

Brown Crane, Penn. Arct. Zool. II. 1785, 443. — Lath. Synop. III. 1785, 43.

Little Brown Crane, Ridgw. l. c.

Northern Sandhill Crane, Coues, l. c.

β. mexicana. THE SANDHILL CRANE.

Ardea (grus) mexicana, Müller, S. N. Suppl. 1776, 110 (ex Briss. V. 380).

Ardea canadensis, var. *β*, Lath. Ind. Orn. II. 1790, 676 (Mexico).

Grus pratensis, Bartr. Travels, 1791, 144, 218 (descr.). — Coues, Check List, 2d ed. 1882, no. 670.

Grus fusca (part), VIEILL. Nouv. Dict. XIII. 1817, 558 (= "*Ardea canadensis*, LATH.," and refers to both forms).

Grus canadensis (nec TEMM. ex LINN.), NUTT. Man. II. 1834, 38.—BAIRD, B. N. Am. 1858, 655; Cat. N. Am. B. 1859, no. 479.—COUES, Key, 1872, 271; Check List, 1873, no. 463; Birds N. W. 1874, 532.—RIDGW. Nom. N. Am. B. 1881, no. 583.

Grus americana (supposed young), AUD. Orn. Biog. III. 1835, 441, pl. 261!; Synop. 1839, 219; B. Am. V. 1842, 188, pl. 314.

HAB. The true *G. canadensis*, Arctic and Subarctic America, migrating south in winter. Breeds in Alaska to the coast at St. Michael's, in the Mackenzie River district, along the whole of the Arctic coast, and other parts of the high north, where entirely replacing the larger *G. mexicana*. The latter, southern half of North America in general, excepting the Atlantic seaboard north of Florida (and the extreme north ?); Cuba; Mexico. Formerly found throughout the east also.

SP. CHAR. *Adult:* Entire pileum, including lores, covered with a bare, granulated skin (reddish in life), interspersed with scattered fine blackish hairs; the posterior margin of this bare skin

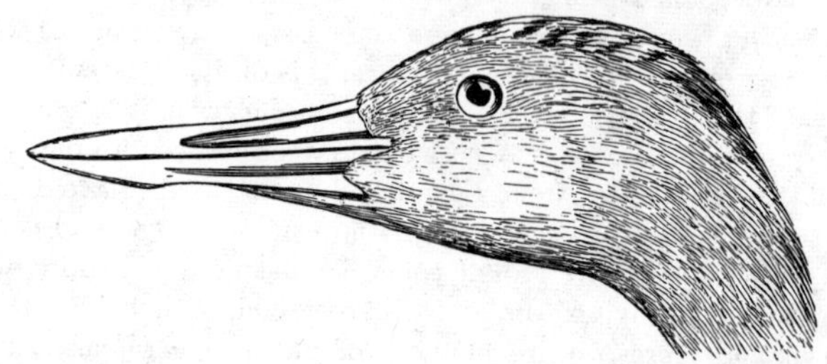

divided medially, on the occiput, by an angular projection of the feathers on the upper part of the nape. General color of the plumage continuous and nearly uniform plumbeous-gray, this frequently stained or overlain in places by a rusty wash, the primaries slate-colored, with whitish shafts. Cheeks and throat sometimes distinctly whitish. Legs and feet blackish; bill blackish, paler at tip; iris crimson? *Young:* Head entirely feathered. Plumage much as in the adult, but of a lighter and more brownish gray, and always conspicuously stained, especially on upper parts, with tawny cinnamon or ferruginous.

α. canadensis.

Wing, 17.50–19.00 inches; culmen, 2.90–3.70; tarsus, 6.70–8.00; middle toe, 2.80–2.95.

β. mexicana.

Wing, 20.00–22.00 inches; culmen, 5.00–6.00; tarsus, 10.00; middle toe, 3.50–4.10.

In this species there is a vast amount of individual variation in both proportions and colors, especially the former, scarcely two specimens being approximately alike in all their measurements. As to colors, the cheeks and throat are usually grayish or light ash-gray; but sometimes they are distinctly white, in very marked contrast to the plumbeous-gray of the nape—a peculiarity we are inclined to ascribe to probable greater maturity of the individual. Besides this variation, the plumage is frequently almost entirely devoid of any rusty stain, while again it is very highly tinged with that color.

The shape of the bill also varies greatly, as does also the appearance of the naked part of the head; the latter is sometimes roughly granulated or almost papillose, with few hairs (as in No. 8914, Nebraska, in which it is also scarcely divided by the occipital feathers), while again (as in No. 13440, Utah) it is densely covered, especially on the lores, with black hairs, while the occipital feathers form a deep angle projecting far into the naked skin of the crown.

Although we have as yet not been able to find specimens which were not positively the one form or the other, we consider it very probable that the two races distinguished above as *canadensis* and *mexicana* will yet be found to intergrade, since we have been wholly unable to discover any differences between them except in size. In this connection, however, the reader is referred to the "Bulletin of the Nuttall Ornithological Club" for April, 1880, p. 123, and for July, 1880, p. 187, where Mr. J. A. Allen and Mr. Ridgway, respectively, consider them distinct species.

The larger and better-known race of the Sandhill Crane (here called *mexicana*) while having, to a large extent, the same distribution as the *americana*, is found to extend its movements over a somewhat larger territory, breeding much farther south than the Whooping Crane, and being distributed as far west as the Pacific coast, where *G. americana* is unknown. Where the two are found together this is ever the more abundant species. It is an occasional straggler to New England, and is also known to breed in Cuba, and possibly in others of the West India Islands.

In Southeastern Oregon Captain Bendire found this a common summer resident, breeding abundantly on the lowlands as well as in the highest mountain valleys. Its hoarse cries could be heard almost everywhere in the vicinity of water so long as the locality remained quiet. Each pair appeared to have a certain district during the breeding-season, and he never found two pairs breeding within half a mile of each other.

Dr. Cooper speaks of this species as descending from the mountains into the San Joaquin Valley, California, about September 15th, when the low water enables it to obtain an abundance of fish and other food.

He also mentions meeting with two individuals of this species among the mountains of Montana, but none elsewhere, excepting a tame one near Fort Colville. This bird would follow their horses for some distance, apparently for the pleasure of the race, running with outspread wings until it had been passed, then flying ahead and circling around to meet them again.

Elsewhere Dr. Cooper speaks of this as being an abundant species in California during the colder months, some remaining throughout the summer among the summits of the Sierra Nevada. They arrive from the north in flocks about the last week in September, and in the interior apparently go south of the limits of California, as he has seen returning flocks passing to the north, over the Colorado Valley, about the 13th of March. At this season they rise from the ground by laborious flappings, circling around higher and higher, until they get so far up as to seem like flocks of butterflies, and then gradually move northward; but most of these migrations are done at night. Their cry, almost constantly heard when they are flying, Dr. Cooper states, is a rattling sound exactly like that made by the blocks and ropes when hoisting sail on a vessel. They also at times have a loud whooping cry. He adds that this bird builds its nest on the ground, in May, on some elevated spot, among ferns, where it may be partly concealed, and yet whence the approach of danger can be perceived. The young of this species are often raised from the nest, becoming very familiar and amusing, showing much sagacity and a disposition to join in play with their friends. But as pets they sometimes become dangerous, from a propensity to use their sharp bills too freely, even pecking at the eyes of the children with whom they are playing.

The Sandhill Crane feeds on all the small animals it can catch, such as mice, frogs, grasshoppers, etc., and probably on young birds. In a state of domestication it is omnivorous, eating bread and vegetables also. It does not usually frequent the sea-shore, nor is it often found in wet places, but prefers dry prairies, ploughed fields, sandy hills, and like places, and in this respect is unlike the Heron family. It is a very wary bird, and difficult of approach within shooting distance, and can be reached only by stratagem. As food Dr. Cooper regards it as nearly equal to the Turkey, especially when young; and it is constantly brought to the San Francisco market during the cooler months.

Dr. Bryant ascertained positively that this species breeds in Florida. His first impression was that it began to breed about the 1st of March, but he afterward ascertained that some breed much earlier than this. On the 11th of March a young bird was brought to him which was already two feet in height, and was covered with down of a ferruginous color above and cinereous below. The eyes were large and projecting, and the bird looked like a miniature ostrich. The young remain with their parents till they are fully grown, and are fed for a long time by regurgitation. They do not fly until they are as large as their parents, but run with great speed, and hide like young partridges. A nest found by him on the 11th of March contained two eggs in which incubation had just commenced; another found on the 15th contained two fresh eggs, and a third on the same day had two nearly hatched. It is a very singular feature in the history of this bird that it should be thus found breeding in Cuba, through all the lower parts of the peninsula of Florida, and thence only seen in its migrations between there and the Northwestern States.

The observations of Mr. Moore have led him to the conclusion that the migrating individuals of this species do not visit Florida during their southern sojourn, as there is no increase in the numbers which are seen there during the winter, and no movements take place among them to favor this idea. The Florida birds are never seen to soar high in the air in flocks at any time of the year, as the migrating individuals may frequently be seen to do in their southern winter homes in Louisiana, Texas, and other States. One, or at most a pair, has been seen moving in this manner, not intent on travel, but as if to take an airing. When flushed it runs three or four steps, and then rises and soars away, but without mounting to the height of the pines. Its notes are uttered on the ground in sight of apprehended danger. It can alight on trees, but does so very rarely.

Mr. Moore states, also, that nests of this species are generally placed in the shallow ponds with which Florida abounds, among aquatic plants, of which they are formed. In one instance a large mass of these plants was heaped up, constituting a nest, which, when found, March 2, was six or eight inches above the water in its highest parts. It was about a hundred yards from dry ground, and in the midst of mud and water. It was within two hundred yards of a travelled road, and in full view. The sitting bird had lowered her head, and so remained until Mr. Moore was within sixty yards, when she flew off, and dropped down among some plants not far distant. The mate soon appeared, and continued to fly around, but did not come near. The two eggs in the nest lay with their longitudinal diameter in a line parallel with the spinal cord of the bird as she sat on them, and were six inches apart. The eggs measured, one 3.75 by 2.33, the other 3.87 by 2.37 inches. Other nests were placed on the dryest ground, among the saw-palmettos, and formed of pliable materials, herbs, grasses, and the like, but never with stiff material or sticks. In one instance the nest was composed of grasses plucked up by the roots, with much sand attached. The entire nest, lining and all, was thus made up.

The young birds run as soon as they are hatched, and may be seen, when not larger than a week-old Turkey, moving about with their parents, with whom they remain till they are nearly a year old. Sometimes they are run down and taken before they are able to fly, the parents remaining at a distance, expressing their anxiety by the utterance of loud and peculiar notes, and by moving about, but at such times never attacking the enemy.

In the stomachs of those Mr. Moore dissected he was never able to discover any animal food; but in those of two that were killed feeding together in three inches of water, he found masses composed of the roots of a small species of *Sagittaria*. Another contained seeds of an unknown plant as large as coffee-beans. All contained more or less sand, bits of quartz, and small brown pebbles. When dry these materials would weigh two ounces. Excavations, such as Audubon saw these birds making in Kentucky, where they rooted like hogs, have never been noticed in Florida, although the same lily roots are common and abundant. The largest excavations seen were not larger than a coffee-cup.

Incubation takes place from the last or the middle of February to the middle of May, or later.

Mr. Moore describes a peculiar use by this bird of the wing in its flight. There is an upward lift or jerk made suddenly. The wing is now laid on the air gently, and suffered to dip slowly down; then, having reached the proper point, it is suddenly flirted upwards, and again laid upon the air — just, it would seem, at that critical moment when it is necessary to prevent the bird from declining in its chosen line of flight.

Mr. Ridgway speaks of finding this species very abundant in the marshes of Ruby Valley, where it was seen daily. It was also quite common in the wet meadows of Carson Valley, where a tame Crane, caught when young in the neighboring meadows, was a remarkable and amusing pet. As he was entering the gate, the bird's eye quickly detected a *Junco oregonus* that had been partially thrust into his coat pocket; and walking boldly up to him, the Crane snatched it out and deliberately beat it upon the ground until nearly denuded of feathers, when it was swallowed with apparent relish. The Crane then again approached, and carefully examined his person for more birds; but failing to find any, marched away across the yard with a stately step. This pet would frequently walk upon the porch, go up to the window, and watch with curiosity and apparent interest the sports of the children in the house; and if any of them approached the window it would evince its pleasure by amusing gesticulations.

Mr. Dresser did not meet with this species near Matamoras; but on his journey from Brownville to San Antonio in September, 1863, he saw birds of this species every day. During the winter they were quite common near San Antonio; but all disappeared toward spring. He was told that they breed near Galveston and in Matagordo Bay; but this statement requires confirmation.

It is probable that much of the description of habits applied by Audubon to the Whooping Crane is equally referable to the present species. At any rate in one instance it is very evident that he must have had this bird in view. This was in December, 1833, when his son went to Spring Island, on the coast of Georgia, and where the only specimen obtained was evidently a *G. mexicana*. He found the Cranes plentiful, resorting to the sweet-potato fields, digging up their produce as expertly as a troop of negroes would have done. The birds would walk over the little heaps, probing them in various parts in the manner of a Woodcock; and whenever a potato was found, removing the soil, and taking out and devouring the root. In this manner the flock searched over the whole field, gleaning all the potatoes which had escaped the gatherers.

An egg in my cabinet (No. 652) measures — as nearly as can be estimated, the smaller end being wanting — 4.00 inches in length by 2.40 inches in breadth. The ground-color is a deep washing of sepia-brown, over which are distributed large blotches, a few rounded in shape, but chiefly longitudinal, of dark sepia. A few of the larger blotches are fainter, and have a slight tinge of purplish. This egg was obtained near Lake Koskonong, Wis. Mr. Kumlien received it on the 1st of May; but it had been taken three weeks previously, or about April 10, 1851, and contained at the time a young bird nearly ready to be hatched out. Mr. Kumlien wrote me in October, 1851: "This Crane, called here the Sandhill Crane, is larger than the *Grus cinerea* of Europe, but resembles that bird very much. It is quite common here, but is the only Grus we have. It has both the color and the notes of the European *cinerea*. It is very shy. The people here — that is, the Americans — consider it good to eat. It nests in the marshes late in March and early in April."

Another egg (No. 653), laid in confinement in a private garden at Niagara Falls, in 1852, has a light gray ground. The markings are of sepia, few, faint, and scattered, except about the larger end, where they form a confluent patch. A few blotches are of a faint purplish tint. This egg measures 3.80 by 2.40 inches.

A third from Cuba — sent me by Dr. Gundlach — was found by him among the mountain marshes of that island. It closely resembles No. 653, except that the spots are all quite small and rounded in shape, and nowhere confluent. This egg measures 3.72 by 2.39 inches.

The smaller northern form (*Grus canadensis*) has a history so blended with that of the more common and larger races of the south, that it is now somewhat difficult to separate that which pertains especially to each species. This bird was first described by Mr. Cassin from a single young specimen that had been obtained in October, 1853, near Albuquerque by Dr. H. B. Mollhausen. It was next mentioned by Mr. B. R. Ross, on the authority of Captain Blakiston, as an inhabitant in the summer of the west side of the Rocky Mountains.

Mr. Dresser was confident that he had noticed this species several times near San Antonio and once near the Rio Nueces, and he regarded it as a species of not uncommon occurrence in Southern Texas. He also claims to have secured a single example which had been shot near San Antonio, and preserved for him by Dr. Heermann. It was the only specimen that could be procured, as the birds were very wary and difficult of approach.

Both Mr. Bannister and Mr. Dall met with and refer to individuals belonging to this species which, at the time, they supposed to belong to the *canadensis*. Mr. Bannister found it common in the marshes of the Island of St. Michael's and the neighboring mainland; and Mr. Dall, always supposing it to be the *canadensis*, states that it is a common bird at St. Michael's, as well as at the mouth of the Yukon River, but that it is rare in the interior, and not often seen at Nulato. It is called by the Indians "Teltintla;" and by them the young of this species is often domesticated, as these birds become very tame, and eat up the vermin and insects, as well as scraps of food about their camps. Mr. Dall adds that the young are downy until their first moult, when the red appears very much as it does in the young Turkey. Mr. Dall obtained the eggs of this species June 17th on the Yukon River. They had been laid in a small depression in the sandy beach, without any attempt at a nest. The flesh when well cooked is eatable, but to Mr. Dall's taste is rather strong. The fibula of this bird is among the Indians and trappers a favorite substitute for a pipe-stem.

Mr. E. Adams ("Ibis," 1878) mentions the arrival of this Crane on the shores of Norton Sound, Alaska, with the earliest of the Geese in the beginning of May; and by the middle of the month the whole of the marshes were alive with these birds, and their noisy croakings were to be heard in every direction, especially about the extensive marshes on both sides of the river. Their nests were placed about the dry knolls in the marshes, and they had eggs before the end of May.

Captain Blakiston states that this species arrives on the Saskatchewan Plains in large numbers in April from the south, and in the beginning of May he met with its eggs. He found it as far west as the Rocky Mountains. Mr. Murray met with it on Hudson's Bay, and Mr. Ross found it common along the banks of the Mackenzie River as far north as the Arctic coast.

Hearne, in his "Journey to the Northern Ocean" (p. 423), refers to this species as the Brown Crane, speaking of it as greatly inferior in size to the Whooping Crane, and as being seldom more than three and a half feet in length, and not weighing on an average more than seven pounds. Its haunts and manner of life are, he adds, nearly the same as those of the larger species, each pair never having more than two young, and these being seldom able to fly before September. This species is found much farther north than the larger one, several having been killed by him on Marble Island; and he has also met with it on the continent as high at least as latitude 65°. It is generally esteemed good eating, and goes by the name of the "Northwest Turkey." He states that the gizzard of this species is larger than that of the Trumpeter Swan, and is especially large in the young bird. In hot calm days the Brown Crane may be frequently seen soaring to an amazing height, always flying in circles, until by degrees it passes almost out of sight. Yet its note is so very loud that the sportsman, before he sees its situation, will often imagine the bird is very near him. This species visits Hudson's Bay in far greater numbers than the larger one. Richardson also states that it is found in all parts of the Fur Country in summer, even as far as the shores of the Arctic Sea. Its flesh is regarded by him as excellent, resembling that of the Trumpeter Swan in its flavor. It breeds throughout the Arctic regions.

Mr. Kennicott met with this species at Fort Resolution, May 30, where he procured two examples. Mr. MacFarlane obtained a skin, in the autumn of 1863, from the Eskimos on the Lower Anderson River, and an egg in June, 1864, from an island in Franklin Bay. The nest is said to have been a hole scooped in the sand, and lined with a considerable quantity of withered grasses. A few more birds of the same species evidently had nests on the same island, but they could not be discovered. Dr. Walker met with a single specimen of this bird at Pond's Bay, in latitude 72°, on the west coast of Baffin's Bay; but it has been very rarely seen so far north as that coast.

An egg of this species (S. I. No. 15731) obtained by Mr. MacFarlane in Liverpool Bay, on the Arctic coast, measures 3.65 inches in length by 2.30 in breadth, is oval in shape, and very nearly equally obtuse at either end. Its ground-color is a faint washing of sepia-brown, and it is marked, over the entire egg, with patches of pronounced sepia, which become more and more deep until about the larger end they form a ring of darker and still more distinct sepia.

Order PHŒNICOPTERI.

LAMELLIROSTRAL GRALLATORES.

Char. Lamellirostral and Præcocial Grallatores, with the neck and legs excessively elongated, the anterior toes fully webbed, the hallux very small, elevated, or sometimes altogether wanting, the bill abruptly bent in the middle portion, the mandible much deeper in the middle portion than the maxilla. Eggs few in number (one or two), pure white, with a soft calcareous shell.

The Flamingoes are Lamellirostral Waders, and possess so many peculiarities of structure, that they may very properly be considered as constituting by themselves a distinct Order, for which Professor Huxley has proposed the term *Amphimorphæ*. This Order comprises a single family, which is represented throughout the warmer parts of the globe, with the exception of the Australian and Malayan Regions.

Family PHŒNICOPTERIDÆ. — The Flamingoes.

Char. Same as those of the Order.

The Flamingoes constitute a strongly marked and very peculiar family of birds, resembling somewhat the Cranes, Herons, and Storks in general appearance, but much more nearly related to the *Anatidæ* (Ducks, Geese, and Swans) in their structure, while in the peculiar form of the bill and excessive elongation of the neck and legs they are entirely unique. There appear to be only two well-marked genera, *Phœnicopterus* and *Phœnicoparrus*,[1] the latter, distinguished by the absence of the hind toe and a peculiar form of bill, being represented by a single species, found in the Peruvian Andes.

Genus **PHŒNICOPTERUS**, Linnæus.

Phœnicopterus, Linn. S. N. ed. 10, 1758, 139; ed. 12, I. 1766, 230 (type, *P. ruber*, Linn.).
Phœniconaias, Gray, Ibis, 1869, 442 (type, *Phœnicopterus rubidus*, Feilden).
Phœnicorodias, Gray, Ibis, 1869, 443 (type, *Phœnicopterus ruber*, Linn.).

Char. Neck and legs excessively elongated, the lower two thirds of the tibia bare, the anterior two thirds of both tibia and tarsus enveloped by one continuous series of broad transverse scutellæ, the circumference completed by a smaller posterior series. All the anterior toes completely webbed, the longest about one fourth the tarsus; hind toe present, but small and elevated; claws short, broad, and blunt, scarcely extending beyond the underlying pad forming the end of

[1] Phœnicoparrus, "Bp. 185" (Gray), (type, *Phœnicopterus andinus*, Philippi; cf. "Ibis," 1869, p. 441, pl. 15, figs. 9, 10).

the toes. Maxilla much depressed, especially for the terminal half, everywhere narrower than the mandible, which is greatly thickened in the middle portion, its sides roughened or slightly corrugated, the end with numerous deep longitudinal sulcations; maxilla with a distinct lateral groove from the nostril to the tip; both maxillary and mandibular laminæ exposed.

P. ruber.

The above characters are drawn from *P. ruber*, but they apply equally well to the other species of the genus, of which about six are known, only two of which are American, one, *P. ruber*, belonging to the West Indies and shores of the Gulf of Mexico, and the Galapagos, the other, *P. ignipalliatus*, peculiar to Southern South America.

Phœnicopterus ruber.

THE AMERICAN FLAMINGO.

Phœnicopterus ruber, LINN. S. N. ed. 10, I. 1758, 139 (part); ed. 12, I. 1766, 230 (part). — WILS. Am. Orn. VIII. 1814, 45, pl. 66. — NUTT. Man. II. 1834, 70. — AUD. Orn. Biog. V. 1839, 255, pl. 431; Synop. 1839, 269; B. Am. VI. 1843, 169, pl. 375. — CASS. in Baird's B. N. Am. 1858, 687. — BAIRD, Cat. N. Am. B. 1859, no. 502. — COUES, Key, 1872, 278; Check List, 1873, no. 475; 2d ed. 1882, no. 687. — RIDGW. Nom. N. Am. B. 1881, no. 585.

? *Phœnicopterus glyphorhynchus*, GRAY, Ibis, 1869, pl. 14, fig. 5 (Galapagos).

HAB Atlantic coasts of tropical and subtropical America from Florida Keys to Northern South America; Bermudas; Galapagos? (= "*glyphorhynchus*," GRAY.)

SP. CHAR. *Adult:* Prevailing color pure vermilion-scarlet, most intense on the wings, elsewhere inclining to vermilion-pink; flanks rosy carmine; primaries and secondaries uniform deep black. Terminal third of the bill (portion beyond the bend) black; basal portion orange, becoming pure yellow at the extreme base and on the lores; iris blue; legs and feet lake-red (AUDUBON).

Length, about 42.00–48.00 inches; extent, 64.00–66.00; wing, 15.30–16.50; culmen, about 5.20; bare portion of tibia, 10.00; tarsus, 12.00–14.50; middle toe, 3.20.

Perfectly adult examples are almost uniform fine vermilion-scarlet, as described above; less mature individuals are paler, the neck and body light vermilion-pink, the wings light vermilion-scarlet. The very young birds are said to be covered with a white cottony down.

The American Flamingo has small claim to be ranked as a bird of the North American fauna, being found only in the extreme portion of Florida; and, even there, the constant persecutions to which it is subjected must, by the resulting extermination of the species within a very few years, put an end to even this limited claim. This Flamingo is more or less abundant in several of the West India Islands, most especially Cuba and the Bahama Islands; and a single specimen has been noticed in the Bermudas.

The late Dr. Gustavus Würdemann visited Florida in 1857, and made some interesting observations relative to this species, which were published, after his death, in the "Annual Report of the Smithsonian Institution" for 1860. He speaks of the Flamingo as being known to but few of the inhabitants of Florida, and as being confined to the immediate neighborhood of the most southern portion of that peninsula — Cape Sable and the Keys in its vicinity. It existed formerly near Indian River, but had been driven from that region. On the west coast of Florida it ranges as far north as Cape Romano, where it was seen every year, but was not known to breed there, and was supposed to nest among the fresh-water lakes near Cape Sable.

Having been told that Flamingoes were taken during the latter part of June and early in July, when moulting, in large numbers by wreckers, Dr. Würdemann sought for an opportunity to witness their capture, and with this view accompanied a small party early in August. We give Dr. Würdemann's account, only abridging his narrative somewhat. After a while the Captain shouted, "The Flamingoes!" But it was not until an advance of another mile had been made that the Doctor was able to perceive two red spots, apparently under two distant Keys; these proved to be large flocks of this bird, which started up when the party came within half a mile of them, leaving six of their number behind, which were moulting, and unable to follow. Paddling as fast as they could, the men soon came up with these birds, which employed both wings and legs in endeavoring to escape. The Captain seized one after another and threw them into the boat, taking the whole six. They afterward overtook other flocks of the Flamingoes in a similar manner, until the small canoe was loaded down with more than a hundred of these unfortunate birds, packed away without the smallest regard either for their comfort or their lives. On the return of the party to Indian Key the dead birds, which were all in a very fat condition, were distributed, and the living ones confined in a ten-pin alley.

Dr. Würdemann states that there must have been not less than five hundred Flamingoes assembled where the last were captured. They appeared to congregate in these shallow waters, feeding on a small shellfish having the form of a clam, which they fished up from the muddy banks. No other food was found in their stomachs. They were always seen in flocks, and their notes sounded at a distance like those of Wild Geese. When captured, they uttered a single low note like that of a Crane when suddenly started.

While in confinement one Flamingo would utter a cry like that of the Domestic Goose calling for its mate, and this cry would be answered by another bird in notes similar to those of a Gander. The captives were fed on rice and fresh water, but would not eat so long as they were watched. Of eight birds dissected by Dr. Würdemann only one was found to be a female, and he inferred that the females moult earlier than the males. The helpless condition to which the Flamingo is reduced when moulting makes it an easy prey to its enemies, and must eventually lead to its extermination. In confinement it becomes so tame as to feed from the hand of its captor.

Wilson, copying from Dr. Latham's "Synopsis," gives an account of the breeding of this bird which, though long considered as trustworthy, is now known to be erroneous. The Flamingo does not build up a small hillock-like nest, hollowed at the top, on which it can sit, resting either foot on the ground. The nest is raised but slightly above the surface, and only just enough to protect it from the danger of being overflowed by the water of the marshes in which it is placed.

Mr. J. L. Hurdis states that a party from Bermuda, in July, 1850, visited the Bahamas, where they found the Flamingoes in great numbers. This party visited Lake Rosa and waded to some of the islands, the water being only knee-deep. On one of these islands there were at least two hundred of these birds, too shy to admit of a near approach. Many young Flamingoes were discovered, some of which were run down and captured. These had an awkward gait, but scuttled along at a good pace. They were in the gray plumage, of different stages of growth. Mr. Hollis — one of the party — stated that he saw several of the nests of these birds, and obtained some of their eggs. These all proved to be addled, and to have been thrown out by the parent birds. He speaks of them as being white, and about the size of the egg of the Common Goose. The nests were composed of mud and sticks, more or less raised, on account of the surrounding water. The highest was not more than nine inches above the ground, while many others were nearly level with it. The surface was hollowed out, and only capable of holding two eggs.

Mr. Audubon mentions meeting, May 7, 1832, while sailing from Indian Key, a flock of Flamingoes advancing in "Indian file," with spread wings, outstretched necks, and long legs directed backward. These birds were very shy, and kept at a distance, so that he was not able, during his stay in Florida, to procure a single specimen. He states that these Flamingoes have been met with along the eastern coast to as far as Charleston, S. C., where some were procured as late as 1830. None have ever been seen about the Mississippi or in Texas.

This bird is said to be common in Cuba, especially among the small islands on the southern shore not far from the mainland. Its flight is like that of an Ibis, usually in lines, with neck and legs extended, alternately flapping and sailing at brief intervals. It usually sails round a locality several times before it alights, doing this for the most part in shallow water, and rarely on the land. Its walk is slow and stiff; and it moves with great caution, its height enabling it to watch for the approach of enemies. In flying over water it rarely rises higher than ten feet; but in crossing land it always increases its elevation.

Mr. A. Mallory — as quoted by Mr. Audubon — writes, in 1837, that the Flamingoes were then breeding on the Keys near Matanzas. He describes the nests as being built on the ground, and as irregular masses of earth placed in salt ponds, surrounded by water and two or three feet above it, their tops being hollowed out, and without lining.

The number of eggs is always two, and they are described as being white, about the size of those of a Goose, showing, when scraped, a bluish tinge within. The young are said to be white at first, and not to attain their full scarlet color until they are two years old. They take at once to the water, and cannot walk until two weeks after they are hatched. Mr. Audubon describes an egg procured from Cuba by Dr. Bachman as measuring $3\frac{3}{8}$ inches in length by $2\frac{1}{8}$ in breadth, of an elongated shape, pure white externally, and of a bluish tint where the surface has been scraped. The shell is described as being rough, granulated, and rather thick.

Dr. Bryant found the Bahamas a favorite resort of the Flamingo, and saw immense numbers of them at different localities. He heard of three breeding-places, but was unable to visit them, owing to ill health; these were the Bight of Bahama, Andros Island, and Inagua. The same observer had seen it stated in the "Naturalist in Bermuda" that this bird does not sit on its nest with its legs hanging down on each side; but all the persons he questioned in regard to this statement — and they were quite a number, there being among them several very intelligent persons — gave him the same account of its nesting; namely, that the nest is built of clay or marl, and that it is raised gradually, the bird waiting for one layer to dry before applying another, and that when completed the nest has a conical form, resembling a sugar-loaf in shape, and being slightly excavated at the top; also that the bird sits on it with its legs hanging down on each side. The breeding-places are in shallow lagoons, at a distance from the shore; and as the bottom is a tenacious clay, they can only be approached with great exertion. The eggs, when fresh, are pure white, have a smooth feeling to the touch even when the surface exhibits numerous slight depressions, and resemble plaster models rather than eggs. They are of an extremely elongated shape, and taper at one end, varying greatly in size. One taken by Dr. Bachman at Matanzas, Cuba, measures 3.40 inches by 2.00; another, also from Cuba, 3.80 inches by 2.11. Two procured in the Bahamas measure, one 3.55 inches by 2.08, the other 3.63 inches by 2.20.

Order ANSERES.

THE LAMELLIROSTRAL SWIMMERS.

Char. Lamellirostral Swimming Birds, with straight bills, short legs (always shorter than the wing), the tibiæ usually completely feathered, and scarcely free from the body; hallux well developed, though usually small, never absent. Reproduction præcocial, and young ptilopædic; eggs numerous and unmarked, with a hard, usually very smooth, shell.

Like the *Phœnicopteri*, the Order *Anseres* is composed of a single family, which, however, includes very numerous genera and species. The Order is represented in every portion of the globe, but most numerously in the northern hemisphere.

Family ANATIDÆ. — The Swans, Geese, and Ducks.

Char. The same as those of the Order.

The Family *Anatidæ*, which includes all the known *Anseres* proper, or Lamellirostral Swimmers, constitutes so well-marked and natural a group of birds as to need no further definition than that given above. The *Anatidæ* are allied most nearly to the *Phœnicopteridæ*, or Flamingoes, which, however, are trenchantly separated by many striking peculiarities of structure. The species being very numerous, naturally fall into several more or less well-defined groups, which have been accorded the rank of sub-families. These, however, grade so insensibly into one another, that it is extremely doubtful whether this rank can be maintained for them.[1] Birds of this family are found in every known part of the world; but they abound most in the northern hemisphere, particularly in boreal regions. The North American representatives may, for convenience of classification, be divided into three tolerably well-defined groups, as follows: —

Cygninæ. Neck extremely long (as long as or longer than the body); size very large; bill longer than the head, the edges parallel, the nail small; tarsi shorter than middle toe; lores naked; tail-feathers 20–24; color chiefly or entirely white (except in *Chenopis atrata*, the Black Swan of Australia).

[1] "The whole family *Anatidæ* forms, as to structural features, a very homogeneous group, and intermediate links are everywhere to be found. Thus it is very difficult to define the sub-families anatomically, and to give the structural differences by which they are to be separated, so that I find it not improbable that an exact investigation, based on a more abundant material than I can at present procure, will reduce the sub-families to groups of lower rank." — Stejneger, in Proc. U. S. Nat. Mus., Vol. 5, 1882, pp. 174, 175.

Anserinæ. Neck moderately long (shorter than the body); size variable (usually medium, never very large); bill not longer than the head, tapering to the end, which is chiefly occupied by the large, broad nail; tarsus longer than the middle toe; lores feathered; tail-feathers 14–20; color extremely variable.

Anatinæ. Neck moderately long (shorter than the body); size variable (usually small or medium); bill extremely variable; tarsus shorter than the middle toe; lores usually feathered; tail-feathers 14–18; color extremely variable.

SUB-FAMILY CYGNINÆ, BONAPARTE. — THE SWANS.*

"1838. — *Cygninæ*, BP. Comp. List, p. 55.
1850. — *Cygnidæ*, KAUP (*fide* GRAY).
1852. — *Olörinæ*, REICHB. Syst. Av. p. x.
1860. — *Cycnidæ*, DES MURS, Tr. Ool. Ornith. p. 537.

"DIAGN. *Anatidæ having the hind toe without web and the lores naked, coincident with reticulate tarsi, the latter shorter than the middle with the claw.*

"Neck very long, as long as, or longer than, the body. Bill longer than the head, broad, and of nearly equal breadth for the whole length, rounded at the end, culmen high, depressed at the tip; nail rather large, only slightly arched; lamellæ of upper mandible vertical, in one row; nostrils situated nearly at the middle of the bill, in the fore part of the oblong nasal sinus. Lores naked in the adults; in all species, except one, thinly covered with small down or feathers in the young. Legs short, stout; lower part of tibia naked; tarsi compressed, much shorter than the middle toe with the claw, and covered with small hexagonal plates, the size of which diminishes laterally and posteriorly; the anterior toes reticulate as far as the second joint, then scutellate; middle toe longest, longer than the tarsus, the outer longer than the inner, which has a broad margin; hind toe short, elevated, and without web, the claws strong, arched, compressed, except the middle, which is only compressed on the one side, the claw of the inner toe in old birds the largest and most arched. Wings long, ample, the inner remiges highly developed, with about 32 quills. Tail composed of 20–24 rectrices, short, rounded, or cuneate.

"Sexes similar.

"The preceding marks combined appear to express the essential characters of the *Cygninæ*. By this diagnosis I follow Mr. Sundevall in excluding the genus *Coscoroba*, REICHB., which has the lores feathered at all ages. . . . The removal of *Coscoroba* to the *Anatinæ* will be discussed more explicitly below. The criterion 'tarsi reticulate' further excludes the genera *Cairina*, FLEM., and *Plectropterus*, LEACH, which, it is true, have the lores naked, but the tarsi of which are scutellate instead of reticulate. *Anseranas*, LESS., has certainly both naked lores and reticulate tarsi, but differs in having the tarsus longer than the middle toe with claw.

"*Anatidæ* which do not at once unite all the above characters consequently belong to one of the other sub-families."

"Synopsis of the Genera.

a^1. Predominant color of the adults white; young with downy or feathered lores; tertiaries and scapulars normal, not crisp; tail longer than the middle toe with claw.

b^1. Tail cuneate; the young with the down on the sides of the bill not forming loral antiæ.†

c^1. Inner webs of outer four primaries and outer webs of the second, third, fourth, and fifth sinuated; the young with the down on the sides of the bill reaching almost to the nostrils; webs of the feet scalloped.

* In the preparation of this article on the *Cygninæ* much use has been made of the very valuable "Outlines of a Monograph of the *Cygninæ*," by Dr. Leonhard Stejneger, published in Vol. 5 of the "Proceedings of the U. S. National Museum," pp. 174–221. The matter taken directly therefrom is inclosed in quotation marks.

† This term denotes the projecting angle of the loral feathering at the base of the bill.

1. **Sthenelus**, Stejneger, 1882.

c^2. Inner webs of outer three primaries and outer webs of the second, third, and fourth sinuated; the young with the down on the sides of the bill terminating far back of the nostrils; webs of the feet straight, not scalloped.

2. **Cygnus**, Bechst., 1803.

b^2. Tail rounded; the young with the down on the sides of the bill forming very distinct loral antiæ.

3. **Olor**, Wagl., 1832.

a^2. Predominant color of the adults blackish; the young with naked lores; tertiaries and scapulars crisp; tail shorter than the middle toe with claw.

4. **Chenopis**, Wagl. 1832.

" *Geographical Distribution.*

" The *Cygninæ* appear both in the northern and the southern hemispheres as extra-tropical birds, no representatives of these large *Lamellirostres* being found within the tropics. They are consequently wanting both in the Indo-African Tropical — they do not at all breed in Africa — and in the American Tropical Region, only one species being met with in the South American Temperate and one in the Australian Region. The remaining seven species occur in the Arctic and the North Temperate Regions, the greatest number, viz., five, being found in the Old World, and here they only extend their winter migrations to the two southern provinces, the Mediterranean and the Manchurian, without breeding there. The two North American species only breed within the American division of the Arctic Region.

" The following table gives a synopsis of their distribution: —

Name of species.	Arctic reg.		North temp. reg.		Amer. trop. reg.	Indo-Afr. trop. reg.	South Amer. temp. reg.	African temp. reg.	Antarctic reg.	Australian reg.
	Old World.	New World.	Old World.	New World.						
Sthenelus melancorypha	—	—	—	—	—	—	×	—	—	—
Cygnus gibbus	—	—	×	—	—	—	—	—	—	—
immutabilis	—	—	×	—	—	—	—	—	—	—
Unwini	—	—	×	—	—	—	—	—	—	—
Olor cygnus	×	—	×	—	—	—	—	—	—	—
Bewickii	×	—	—	—	—	—	—	—	—	—
columbianus	—	×	—	×	—	—	—	—	—	—
buccinator	—	×	—	×	—	—	—	—	—	—
Chenopis atratus	—	—	—	—	—	—	—	—	—	×

Of the genera, as defined above, only the third (*Olor*) belongs to North America, the remainder being distributed as follows: —

The first, *Sthenelus* (new genus, Pr. U. S. Nat. Mus., Vol. 5, July 25, 1882, p. 183), includes only the Black-necked Swan (*Anas melancorypha*, Mol., *Cygnus nigricollis*, Auct. ex Gmel.) of Chili and other parts of Southern South America; *Cygnus* proper contains three species (one of them the common domestic species), all of them peculiar to the Palæarctic Region; *Chenopis*, including only the Black Swan of Australia (*Anas atrata*, Lath., *Cygnus atratus*, Auct.), is confined to Southern Australia.

As before remarked, the Coscoroba Swan (*Anas coscoroba*, Mol., *Cygnus coscoroba*, Auct., *Anser candidus*, Vieill., *Coscoroba candida*, Stejn.) of South America, while resembling the true Swans in its large size and pure white color, agrees in structure with the Ducks, and can properly be considered only as a gigantic member of that sub-family.

GENUS **OLOR**, WAGLER.

Olor, WAGL. Isis, 1832, 1234 (type, *Anas cygnus*, LINN.).

CHAR.* Neck very long (longer than the body), bill longer than the head (commissure longer than the tarsus), widening slightly to the end, the edges straight; basal portion of the bill covered by a soft skin extending over the lores to the eye, the upper outline running nearly straight back from the forehead to the upper eyelid, the lower running from the eye obliquely downward, in a nearly straight line, to the rictus. Nostrils situated a little posterior to the middle of the maxilla,

O. buccinator.

and quite near the culmen; no trace of a knob or caruncle at base of the bill. Lower portion of the tibia bare; tarsus much shorter than the middle toe (but little longer than the inner), much compressed, covered with hexagonal scales which become smaller on the sides and behind. Hind toe small, much elevated, the lobe narrow. Tail very short, rounded, or graduated, of 20 to 24 feathers. Wings rounded, the second and third quills longest; primaries scarcely reaching beyond the ends of the secondaries. Color entirely white, the sexes alike; young pale grayish.

"Synopsis of the Species.

a^1. The distance from the anterior angle of the eye to the hind border of the nostrils much longer than the distance from the latter to the tip of the bill.

b^1. The yellow color at the base of the bill extending beyond the nostrils.

* "DIAGN. Predominant color of the adults white; the young with downy or feathered lores, the down on the sides of the bill terminating far back of the nostrils, and forming very distinct loral antiæ; tertiaries and scapulars normal, not crisp; tail longer than the middle toe with claw, rounded; inner webs of outer three primaries, and outer webs of the second, third, and fourth, sinuated; webs of the feet not scalloped" (STEJNEGER, *tom. cit.* pp. 197, 198).

1. **Cygnus** (LINN.), 1758.

b^2. The yellow color at the base of the bill not extending to the nostrils.

c^1 Smaller: Total length about 1,150 mm; middle toe with claw about 125 mm; the yellow spot at the base of the bill making at least one third of the surface of the bill and lores.

2. **Bewickii** (YARR.), 1830.

c^2. Larger: Total length about 1,400 mm; middle toe with claw about 140 mm; the yellow spot at the base of the bill making, at most, one fifteenth of the surface of the bill and lores.

3. **Columbianus** (ORD.), 1815.

a^2. The distance from the anterior angle of the eye to the hind border of the nostrils equal to the distance from the latter to the tip of the bill.

4. **Buccinator** (RICH.), 1831."

The North American species of *Olor* may be readily distinguished by the following characters: —

1. **O. columbianus.** Tail-feathers usually 20; bill not longer than the head, the anterior end of the nostrils considerably anterior to the middle of the maxilla; naked loral skin usually with a yellow oblong spot.
2. **O. buccinator.** Tail-feathers usually 24; bill longer than the head, the anterior end of the nostrils reaching to about the middle of the maxilla; naked loral skin entirely black. Size considerably larger.

Through a misconception of statements made on p. 465 of the "Fauna Boreali-Americana," Vol. II., the author of a "Nomenclature of North American Birds" (Bull. U. S. Nat. Mus. No. 21) included Bewick's Swan in the North American fauna. In this, however, it seems that he was in error, as pointed out on pp. 210 and 211 of Dr. Stejneger's Monograph, before referred to. In view, however, of the possibility that this species may yet be found within our limits, we quote below, from Dr. Stejneger's paper, its chief synonymy and principal characters: —

"**Olor Bewickii**, YARR. (BEWICK'S SWAN)."

"DIAGN. The distance from the anterior angle of the eye to the hind border of the nostrils is much longer than the distance from the latter to the tip of the bill; the yellow color at the base of the bill does not extend to the nostrils, making at least one third of the surface of the bill and lores. Smaller: Total length about 1150 mm; middle toe with claw about 125 mm."

Syn. — 1830. — *Cygnus Bewickii*, YARRELL, Trans. Linn. Soc. XVI. p. 453 (nec RICH. 1831 quæ *O. columbianus*, ORD).

1838. — *Cygnus islandicus*, NAUM., WIEGM. Archiv IV. 1838, p. 364 (nec BREHM, 1830, quæ *Olor cygnus*, LINN.).

1838. — *Cygnus Berwickii*, EYTON, Monogr. Anat. Pl. 18 (*err. typ.*).

1840. — *Cygnus minor*, KEYS. & BLAS. Wirbelth. Europ. p. LXXXII.

1842. — *Cygnus melanorhinus*, NAUM. Vög. Deutschl. XI. p. 497.

1851. — *Cygnus musicus*, KJÆRBÖLL. Orn. Dan. Pl. XLIV. (nec BECHST. quæ *O. cygnus*, LINN.).

1854. — *Cygnus americanus*, HARTL. Naumannia, 1864, p. 327 (nec SHARPL. quæ *columbianus*, ORD).

1856. — '*Cygnus Altumi*, HOMEYER,' BP. Cat. PARZUD., p. 15.

1866. — '*Cygnus Altumii*, BÄDEKER,' SCHLEGEL, Mus. P. B. VI. *Anseres*, p. 82.

1880. — *Cygnus Bewicki*, DRESSER, Birds of Eur. pt. lxxvii.–lxxix."

Olor cygnus.

THE HOOPER SWAN.

Anas cygnus, LINN. S. N. ed. 10, I. 1758, 122; ed. 12, I. 1766, 194.

Olor cygnus, "BONAP." RIDGW. Proc. U. S. Nat. Mus. Vol. 3, 1880, 202, 222; Nom. N. Am. B. 1881, no. 586. — STEJN. Proc. U. S. Nat. Mus. Vol. 5, 1882, 198.

Cygnus ferus, LEACH, Syst. Cat. 1816, 37. — STEPH. Gen. Zool. XII. 10, pl. 37. — GRAY, Gen. B. III. 610; Cat. Brit. B. 1863, 188. — REINH. Ibis, 1861, 13 (Greenland).
Cygnus musicus, BECHST. Naturg. Deutschl. IV. 1809, 830. — BONAP. Comp. List, 1838, 55. — KEYS. & BLAS. Wirb. Eur. 82. — MACGILL. Man. II. 158. — COUES, Check List, 2d ed. 1882, no. 690.
Olor musicus, WAGL. Isis, 1832, 1234.
Cygnus olor, PALL. Zoogr. Rosso-As. II. 1826, 211.
Cygnus xanthorhinus, NAUM. Vög. Deutschl. XI. 1842, 478, pl. 296.
Whistling or *Wild Swan*, AUCT.
The Hooper, Elk, or *Whistling Swan*, YARR. Brit. B. ed. 2, III. 187, fig.; ed. 3, III. 191, fig.

HAB. Palæarctic Region. Accidental in Greenland (REINH. "Ibis," 1861, 13).

SP. CHAR. "The distance from the anterior angle of the eye to the hind border of the nostrils is much longer than the distance from the latter to the tip of the bill; the yellow color at the base of the bill extending beyond the nostrils, making two thirds of the surface of the bill and lore" (STEJN. *tom. cit*).

Adult: Pure white, the head sometimes tinged with rusty; lores and basal portion of bill to beyond the nostril yellow, the terminal portion black; iris brown; legs and feet black. *Young:* Grayish brown, the bill flesh-color basally, dusky terminally; legs and feet grayish. Total length about 5 feet; extent about 7.00–8.00 feet; wing, 23.00–26.00 inches, culmen (to frontal feathers) 4.00–4.75; tarsus, 4.00; middle toe, 5.00–6.00.

The Wild Swan of the Old World has no other claim to be classed as a North American bird than its supposed presence in Greenland. Dr. Reinhardt states that, according to the accounts received from the Eskimos, it formerly bred on several places near Godthaab, but was long ago totally exterminated by persecutions at the time of its moulting. During the fifteen years preceding the year 1861, according to that author, this bird had again made its appearance in Greenland; and Holböll states that several individuals were observed at Julianehaab in 1846. Dr. Reinhardt saw two specimens which had been sent from South Greenland in 1852; and in June, 1859, a fine one was shot at Atanink, nearly ten miles north of Godthaab. If undisturbed this may again acquire a claim to be mentioned as one of the birds of Greenland.

Called in Europe the "Hooper," "Elk," or "Whistling Swan," this species is found throughout Europe, breeding in the more secluded parts of the north, and appearing in the winter in the more southern regions. Its very peculiar note, said to resemble the word *hoop*, gives it the name by which it is most generally known.

This bird is a winter visitant of the more southern portions of the British Islands, where it arrives in flocks about the middle of December, and in greater numbers as the weather becomes more severe. It is found throughout the year in the Orkneys, where a few pairs breed, and where large flocks appear from the north in October, a portion of these remaining all winter. In December these birds are seen flying in compact bodies along the coast-lines, at which time the London markets are sometimes supplied with them to profusion.

They also visit Holland, France, Spain, and Italy, and a few go as far south as Barbary, or even Egypt; in severe winters they are found in Corfu and Sicily.

Linnæus, in his account of his travels in Lapland, mentions meeting with this Swan on several occasions; he saw three at the residence of the Governor of the province which were as tame as Domestic Geese. This bird is said to appear in Lapland with the first breaking-up of the ice, and to be the earliest of the *Anatidæ* in its northern migrations. It frequents the most secluded swamps and lakes in the wooded districts, and in the northeastern portions of the country is reported to be very numerous.

According to Bechstein this species is more frequently domesticated than the Mute Swan, and there are several instances on record of its having produced young when in confinement in England.

Mr. Yarrell states that a pair of these Swans bred on one of the islands at the Gardens of the Zoological Society, in the summer of 1839. As the Cygnets, when only a few days old, were sunning themselves on the margin of an island close to deep water, a Carrion Crow made a descent and struck at one of them. The male bird came to the rescue in an instant, and seizing the Crow with his beak, pulled it into the water, and in spite of its resistance held it there until it was drowned.

In the eastern parts of Europe this species ranges from the lakes of Siberia in summer to the Caspian Sea in winter. It is said to fly, in the manner of the Wild Goose, in wedge-shaped flocks, uttering, as it moves, a fine melodious clang; and this is all which can be put forward on its behalf to support its claim to having a musical voice. Its weight varies, in different individuals of this species, from thirteen to twenty-one pounds.

The Wild Swan builds on the ground in secluded and marshy places, the nest being large, and composed of rushes and coarse herbage. The egg is described by Yarrell as being of a uniform pale brownish white, and measuring four inches and one line in length by two inches and eight lines in breadth. The incubation of this Swan lasts forty-two days. Its food consists of grasses, weeds, roots, and the seeds of plants.

According to Wheelwright this bird is only seen during the periods of migration in the southern and midland districts of Scandinavia. It breeds up in Lapland, generally in the retired Fell lakes. The eggs are seven in number, in color a brown yellow, rather shorter and thicker than those of the common tame Swan. Many birds of this species remain in the Sound, off the southern coast of Sweden, during mild winters; but none are seen at this season off the north coast of Finland. An egg in my cabinet, taken by Proctor in Iceland in 1841, is of a dark ivory color, and measures 4.30 by 2.90 inches.

Olor columbianus.

THE WHISTLING SWAN.

? *Cygnus ferus*, BARTR. Trav. 1791, 294 (may be *O. buccinator*).

Cygnus musicus, BONAP. Synop. 1828, 379 (nec BECHST. 1809).

Cygnus Bewicki, SW. & RICH. F. B. A. II. 1831, 465 (nec YARR.). — NUTT. Man. II. 1834, 372.

Cygnus ferus, NUTT. Man. II. 1834, 366 (nec LEACH, 1816).

Cygnus americanus, SHARPLESS, Doughty's Cab. N. H. I. 1830, 185, pl. 16. — AUD. Orn. Biog. V. 1839, 133, pl. 411; Synop. 1839, 274; B. Am. VI. 1843, 226, pl. 384. — BAIRD, B. N. Am. 1858, 758; Cat. N. Am. B. 1859, no. 561 *a*. — COUES, Key, 1872, 281; Check List, 1873, no. 477; B. N. W. 1874, 545.

Olor americanus, GRAY, Cat. Brit. Mus. 1844, 131. — BONAP. Compt. Rend. XLIII. 1856. — RIDGW. Nom. N. Am. B. 1881, no. 588.

Anas columbianus, ORD, Guthrie's Geog. 2d Am. ed. 1815, 319.

Cygnus columbianus, COUES, Bull. U. S. Geol. & Geogr. Surv. Terr. 2d series, no. 6, 1876, 444; Check List, 2d ed. 1882, no. 689.

Olor columbianus, STEJN. Proc. U. S. Nat. Mus. Vol. 5, 1882, 210.

HAB. The whole of North America, breeding far north; accidental in Scotland.

SP. CHAR. Tail usually of twenty feathers; bill not longer than the head. *Adult:* Entire plumage pure white, the head, sometimes the neck, or even entire under parts, tinged with rusty. Bill, tarsi, and feet deep black, the bare loral skin usually marked by an oblong spot of orange or yellow (dull pale reddish, yellowish, or whitish in the skin); iris brown. *Young:* Light plumbeous, paler beneath, the fore part and top of the head tinged with reddish brown. Bill reddish flesh-color, dusky at the tip; feet dull yellowish flesh-color, or grayish.

Total length, about 53.00–55.50 inches; extent about 7.00 feet; wing, 21.50–22.00 inches; culmen, 3.82–4.20; tarsus, 4.06–4.32; middle toe, 5.40–5.90.

"The principal anatomical character of this species is the disposition of the trachea in the sternum, it making but one horizontal turn upon itself at the point farthest from its entrance in the front of the enlarged carina. We have not had the opportunity of examining full skeletons or perfect skulls of the other North American species of Swan (*O. buccinator*), but it probably agrees with this in the particulars differing from the other *Anserinæ*. The general form of the skull is

much more slender; its height is less in proportion to its length; the occipital condyle is deeper and more rounded; the descending process of the lachrymal shows a widely expanded quadrate external surface, which is wanting in the Geese. The development of the frontal sinuses, and the obliteration of the retreating angle between the anterior portions of the frontal bones, which is sometimes to be observed, appear to be merely evidences of full maturity." (H. M. BANNISTER, MS.)

The smaller of the North American Swans, known among authors as the "American Swan," is found throughout the more northern portions of the continent from the Atlantic to the Pacific. It is not, however, abundant on either coast near the sea. In the summer it frequents the high interior, and breeds on islands in inland lakes and along the shores of the Arctic Ocean. It is very rare in New England, though probably some of this species do pass over this region each year in their autumnal migrations; in fact, specimens are occasionally secured. One was taken at Nahant, and is now in the museum of the Boston Society of Natural History. I am not aware, however, that any have been observed in New England in the spring. Mr. Giraud includes this bird among the winter visitants of Long Island, and it is the only Swan known to occur in that neighborhood.

On the Pacific coast large flocks of these Swans were seen by Dr. Cooper on the Columbia River, in the Cascade Cañon, in 1860, as early as October 29, and their migrations southward appeared to be generally quite early. Dr. Cooper had previously — in 1853 — seen them in the lakes of the Columbia Plain, about the same time. He also states that this bird appears to be less common in California than the *buccinator*. During the entire winter it is abundant on the Columbia River and the fresh-water lakes toward the north, so long as these are not frozen. At such times it occasionally — but very rarely — appears on salt water. These birds arrive on the Columbia in October, flying in long V-shaped lines, and uttering loud whooping cries. They feed almost altogether on vegetable food, such as the roots of the *Sagittaria*, and on grasses and various water-plants. In searching for these, as well as for snails, their long necks become quite useful in deep water.

Hearne, in his "Arctic Voyage" (p. 435), writing nearly a century ago, states that both this species and the *O. buccinator* visit Hudson's Bay in the summer, and that there appeared to be no perceptible difference between them except in size. *O. Columbianus* was then the more common one near the sea-coast, but was by no means abundant, being seen only in pairs, or occasionally singly, where the mate had been shot on the passage north. The weight of this bird he gives as varying from nineteen to twenty-four pounds.

According to Richardson, this Swan arrives in the Arctic Regions later than the Geese, and breeds on the small lakes of the coast and islands of the Arctic Sea. Its nest is generally placed on a small island, and is constructed of any loose materials which happen to be in the immediate vicinity. These are heaped together until a large mound is formed. This bird is very shy, and can usually be killed only at a long shot with a ball. In its migrations some flocks are said to cross the interior, but the greater part follow the coast-line of Hudson's Bay. Richardson states further that it is only seen in the interior of the Fur Countries on its passage. He mentions that Captain Lyon describes its nest as being built of moss-peat, and as having a length of nearly six feet, a width of four and three quarters, and a height on the outside of two feet, the cavity being a foot and a half in diameter. The eggs are said by the same authority to be brownish white, or white slightly clouded with a brownish tint.

Mr. George Barnston states that at present, except in a few particular localities, this Swan has become scarce on the shores of Hudson's Bay. It is seen at the same time as the other migratory birds, winging its way to more secluded recesses in the north, nesting throughout the interior. In the scarcity of its favorite food, the roots of the *Sagittaria sagittifolia*, it has recourse to those of the *Equisetaceæ* and the tender underground runners of certain grasses peculiar to northern latitudes. A few of these birds are said by him to stop to breed in the interior, and not to reach the Arctic coast. Mr. Barnston had two eggs brought to him from a nest on the banks of a lake near Norway House; but these eggs were probably those of *O. buccinator.* A considerable number of this species hatch near Eastman's Fort, in James Bay. As an article of food Mr. Barnston regards this bird as being decidedly inferior to Geese of every description — differing in this respect from most writers.

From November to March this Swan is abundant in the waters of the Chesapeake and in all the inlets of North Carolina. In the latter it is now said to be more common than formerly, having been partially driven from Chesapeake Bay by the severity of the warfare waged upon it. An occasional specimen, according to Major Wedderburn, is seen in the Bermuda Islands.

An experienced sportsman who contributed an account of this species to "Doughty's Cabinet" states that, unless the weather at the north has been unusually severe, this species rarely appears in the Chesapeake until the middle of November. He adds that this Swan, when less than five years old, is by far the finest eating of any of the Waterfowl found on that bay. It possesses the flavor of the finest Goose, and is far more tender. The length of time that its flesh can be preserved untainted is also mentioned as remarkable, this same writer having seen one still perfectly sweet four weeks after its death, no other method of preservation than an exposure to the air having been employed.

The age of this Swan may be known by the color of the feathers, the yearling being of a deep leaden tint, with a delicate red bill. In the second year it has a lighter color, and a white bill. In the third season the bill has become jet black, and about one third of the plumage is still tipped with gray; and until it is fully five years old an occasional feather will present this tint of youth. This bird is supposed to live to a great age, and its flesh becomes exceedingly tough and tasteless. In consequence of this, the more experienced hunters of the Chesapeake usually allow the patriarchs of the flock, who lead in their flight, to pass unharmed. These old leaders have a note thought to resemble in a remarkable degree the sound of a common tin horn; and the unmusical character of their cries increases in intensity with their age.

In the autumn of 1829 the writer was, with another person, on Abby Island, when seven Swans were approaching the Point in one line, and three others were a short distance behind them. The small group endeavored to pass the larger, and as they doubled the Point, at about sixty yards' distance, the three formed with the second birds of the larger flock a square of less than three feet. At this moment both guns were discharged and three Swans were killed, and the fourth so much injured that it left the flock. These were all less than five years old, and averaged eighteen pounds in weight.

These Swans rarely, if ever, leave the open shores of the bay for the side streams, and few, after their regular settlement, are found above Spesutic Island; but they are seen in flocks, varying from fifty to five hundred in number, along the western shores as far down as the mouth of the Potomac. Since these observations were made, however, the number of these birds frequenting that region has been greatly reduced.

During a still night a few Swans could often be seen asleep in the middle of the bay, surrounded by a group of far more watchful Geese; and the writer from whose account this information is derived was paddled, one morning at daybreak, within ten feet of a sleeping Swan. The food to which this bird seems to be most partial on the Chesapeake is the canvass-back grass, worms, insects, and small shellfish. It rarely actually flies, even when pursued by a boat, unless very closely followed; and when it does rise, it is generally with a scream. On alighting in the water, particularly if any other birds of the same species are near, there is usually an interchange of noisy greetings. Even when one of the wings of this bird has been broken, it can swim with great rapidity, and if not otherwise hurt a single oarsman is rarely able to overtake it.

Dr. Sharpless, of Philadelphia, states that he has known unwounded birds to collect around a crippled companion and urge it to escape, pushing it forward and placing themselves on each side, supporting the broken wing, and almost lifting the object of their affectionate care out of the water. The same writer — probably also the author of the article referred to as having appeared in "Doughty's Cabinet" — furnished Mr. Audubon with a full account of the habits of this species, as observed by him in winter, in the waters of the Chesapeake. He states that in its migrations southward it collects in flocks of twenty or thirty, and moves only when the wind is not opposed to the direction of its flight. It mounts high in the air, forms an elongated wedge, and utters loud screams as it departs, these cries being occasionally repeated as the bird moves on its way. When flying, the wings seem almost without movement, and their sweep is very unlike the semicircular movements of Geese. Dr. Sharpless estimates that this bird travels at the rate of at least a hundred miles an hour when at a high elevation and with a moderate wind in its favor. Its flight is estimated to be twice as rapid as that of the Wild Goose.

In travelling from its summer abode to its winter residence, this bird keeps far inland, mounted above the highest peaks of the Alleghany, and rarely follows the watercourses. It usually arrives at its regular feeding-grounds at night, and signalizes its coming by loud and vociferous screaming, with which the shores ring for several hours. In the spring these birds again assemble, as early as March, and after many preparations by incessant washings and dressings, meanwhile disturbing the neighborhood with their noise, they depart for the north with a general clamor of unmusical screams. In the Chesapeake they collect in flocks of from one to five hundred on the flats near the western shores, from the mouth of the Susquehanna almost to the Rip Raps. When alarmed they become instantly silent, and they depend much more on swimming than on flying for effecting an escape. When feeding, or dressing their plumage, this Swan is usually very noisy, and at night these clamors may be heard to the distance of several miles. Their notes are varied, some resembling the lower ones made by the common tin horn, others running through the various modulations of the notes of the clarinet. These differences are presumed to be dependent upon age.

In shooting at a flying Swan, Dr. Sharpless states that the bill should be aimed at, or, if going with a breeze, a foot before the bill. A Swan can rarely be killed unless struck in the neck, and large masses of feathers may be shot away without impeding the bird's progress for a moment. When wounded in the wing only, these Swans will readily beat off a dog, or even a man. They are sometimes brought within shooting range by sailing down upon them while feeding, as they rise to disadvantage against the wind. In winter, by means of white dresses and boats covered with ice, sportsmen paddle or float by night into the centre of a flock, and numbers may thus be killed by blows of a pole.

This species admits of being tamed and partially domesticated. A pair belonging to the cemetery at Milford, Mass., were exhibited at the poultry show in Boston in 1874. They were perfectly tame, permitted themselves to be touched without resistance, and fed readily from the hands of entire strangers.

Mr. MacFarlane mentions this Swan as breeding in considerable numbers in the vicinity of Fort Anderson. The eggs were found from the middle of June to the last of July. The nests were on the ground, and generally lined with hay, or occasionally with down and feathers. The maximum number of eggs was four. Other nests were seen on islands in Franklin Bay and in other portions of the Arctic Sea. The eggs taken in July usually contained embryos.

According to Mr. Dall, this Swan is common all along the Yukon, arriving with the Geese about May 1, but in a contrary direction, coming down instead of going up the river, and breeding in the great marshes near the mouth of that river. The eggs are usually on a tussock quite surrounded with water, and so near it that the female sometimes sits with her feet in the water. The Indian name of the species is "Tohwâh." At Nulato the eggs are laid about May 21, but later at the mouth of the Yukon. These birds moult in July, and cannot fly; at that time the Indians spear them with bone tridents. They are very shy. Mr. Bannister found them common at St. Michael's. They flew in small flocks of ten or twelve, in a single line, advancing obliquely.

Captain Bendire, in a letter written Nov. 14, 1874, mentions the capture of birds of this species on Lake Harney, in Eastern Oregon, where it was very numerous. The stomach of one contained about twenty small shells, half an inch in length, and identical in kind with shells common on the beach near Los Angeles, Cal., a quantity of gravel, and a few black seeds. He found the meat excellent — much superior to that of the Wild Goose. On the 18th of April, 1875, he wrote, mentioning the arrival of a large flock, all of this species, there not being a *buccinator* among them. He afterward noticed them as being very common on the borders of Lake Malheur during the migrations, a few remaining until April 24. In the Upper

Sylvie's valley, in the Blue Mountains, their trumpetings were heard as late as May 29. They feed on the small bulbous roots of a water-plant growing near the shores of the lake. He thinks that none breed there, and that only disabled ones remain on the Oregon lakes in the summer.

Specimens of this Swan were procured by Mr. Kennicott on the Porcupine River, and others by Mr. J. Reid on Big Island. They were obtained on the Anderson and Swan rivers, as also on the Barren Grounds and the islands in Franklin Bay, in the Arctic Ocean, by Mr. MacFarlane.

The eggs of this species — those from Anderson River as well as those from the Yukon — are all alike, and vary but little in size or color. They are of a uniform unspotted buffy white color, becoming yellowish when exposed to the weather. Three of these eggs furnish the following measurements: 4.05 inches by 2.55, 4.25 by 2.80, and 4.25 by 2.65.

Olor buccinator.

THE TRUMPETER SWAN.

Cygnus buccinator, RICH. F. B. A. II. 1831, 464 (Hudson's Bay). — NUTT. Man. II. 1834, 370. — AUD. Orn. Biog. IV. 1838, 536; V. 1839, 114, pls. 406, 376; Synop. 1839, 74; B. Am. VI. 1843, 219, pl. 382, 383. — BAIRD, B. N. Am. 1858, 758; Cat. N. Am. B. 1859, no. 562. — COUES, Key, 1872, 281; Check List, 1873, no. 476; 2d ed. 1882, no. 688; Birds N. W. 1874, 544.

Olor buccinator, WAGL. Isis, 1832, 1234. — RIDGW. Nom. N. Am. B. 1881, no. 589. — STEJN. Proc. U. S. Nat. Mus. Vol. 3, 1882, 216.

Cygnus Pasmorei, HINCKS, Pr. Linn. Soc. VIII. 1864, 1 (Toronto); P. Z. S. 1868, 211. — MOORE, P. Z. S. 1867, 8 (critical).

HAB. Chiefly the interior of North America, from the Gulf coast to the Fur Countries, breeding from Iowa and Dakota northward; west to the Pacific coast, but rare or casual on the Atlantic. Accidental in England.

SP. CHAR. Tail of usually 24 feathers; bill longer than the head. *Adult:* Plumage entirely pure white, the head, sometimes the neck also, or even the entire lower parts, tinged with rusty.

Bill, naked lores, legs, and feet, uniform deep black; iris brown. *Young:* "In winter the young has the bill black, with the middle portion of the ridge, to the length of an inch and a half, light flesh-color, and a large elongated patch of light dull purple on each side; the edge of the lower mandible and the tongue dull yellowish flesh-color. The eye is dark brown. The feet are dull yellowish brown, tinged with olive; the claws brownish black, the webs blackish brown. The upper part of the head and the cheeks are light reddish brown, each feather having toward its extremity a small oblong whitish spot, narrowly margined with dusky; the throat nearly white, as well as the edge of the lower eyelid. The general color of the other parts is grayish white, slightly tinged with yellow; the upper part of the neck marked with spots similar to those on the head" (AUDUBON).

Total length, about 58.50 to 68.00 inches; extent, about 8.00 to nearly 10.00 feet; wing, 21.00–27.25 inches; culmen (from frontal feathers) 4.34–4.70; tarsus, 4.54–4.92; middle toe, 6.00–6.50.

The arrangement of the trachea in this species is very different from that in *O. columbianus*, in having, besides the horizontal bend, a vertical flexure, occupying a prominent protuberance on the anterior portion of the dorsal aspect of the sternum.

The Trumpeter Swan is almost exclusively found in the interior during the breeding-season, is common in all the valley of the Mississippi, and is found from Southern California in the winter to the highest Arctic regions in the summer. It breeds in the interior as far north at least as the 70th parallel, and as far south as latitude 42°. A few of this species breed in Central and Northern Iowa, and thence northward.

On the Pacific coast, according to Dr. Cooper, this is the prevailing species, as it also is throughout the interior of the continent, being found in Minnesota and Nebraska in June, July, and August, where some undoubtedly breed. It is present in California in the middle of the winter only in small numbers, frequenting, as usual, the inland fresh-waters. Its habits are said to be much the same as those of the Whooper, but its cry is very different, resembling the notes of a French horn, and being very sonorous. These peculiar tones are dependent on the form of the windpipe, which is very long, and bent in various S-shaped turns through hollows of the breast-bone — the differences corresponding to the different cries, as well as other distinctions of the species. A flock of what Dr. Cooper supposed to be this species wintered at Fort Mojave, in latitude 35°, Colorado Valley; but Dr. Cooper saw none near the southern coast of California.

According to Sir John Richardson, the Trumpeter Swan arrives in the spring in the Arctic Regions several days in advance of the Goose, and remains later in the season. He found it breeding in the interior from the 60th to the 68th parallel. It frequents only the fresh water, swims with great rapidity and elegance, aiding itself by raising its wings when going before the wind. If attacked when swimming, it can strike severely with its wings. This Swan flies very high, and usually alights in the water. It is the Common Swan of the interior of the Fur Countries, and was found breeding as far south as latitude 61° N. With the exception of the Eagles, it is the earliest of all the migratory birds.

Hearne states that at his time this species visited Hudson's Bay in large numbers in the summer months, and bred on the islands in the fresh-water ponds and lakes. The eggs he speaks of as so large that one of them would be a sufficient meal for a moderate man, without bread or any other additions. In the interior parts of the country this species precedes every other kind of waterfowl, and in some years arrives as early as the month of March, and long before the ice of the rivers is broken up. At those times these birds always frequent the open waters of falls and rapids, where they are shot by the Indians in considerable numbers. This Swan is said frequently to weigh as much as thirty pounds. Its flesh is regarded as excellent eating, and when roasted equals in flavor the beef of a young heifer. The Cygnets are also very delicate. Hearne states that notwithstanding its size this Swan is so swift on the wing that it is, in his opinion, more difficult to shoot than any other bird. Indeed, in order to hit it at all, the hunter must take sight at a point several feet in advance of the bill. Hearne thinks that its speed, when flying before the wind in a brisk gale, cannot be less than a hundred miles an hour. When moving against or across the wind, however, it makes slow progress, and is more easily shot.

Captain Blakiston mentions procuring a specimen at Fort Carlton, on the Saskatchewan, on the 30th of March. It was the first of the spring migration; it was a male bird, and weighed twenty-three pounds. Mr. Bernard Ross found this species common on the Mackenzie River, and Mr. R. Browne includes it in his list of the birds of Vancouver Island.

The Journal of Major Long's Expedition to the Rocky Mountains refers to Swans, which were probably this species, seen passing northward as early as the 22d of February. This bird is among the first of the migratory ones to reach Hudson's Bay, where it appears in flocks of from twenty to a hundred. It is strictly monogamous, and breeds in the islands and in low grounds among the reeds and sedges, making its nest of leaves and dry grasses. It lays from five to seven eggs of a dirty-white color. The young are hatched in July, and in August the moulting season commences, when, for a while this Swan is unable to fly. It begins to move southward about the 1st of September, resorting to the lakes and rivers about the 60th parallel, where it remains until October. Its manner of migration is said to be almost identical with that of the *americanus*, the birds collecting in flocks of considerable size, and, availing themselves of favorable winds, when they mount high in the air, forming an elongated wedge, and departing with loud sonorous screams. They reach their places of winter resort late in October or early in November, and their arrival is marked by the same outbursts which attend the coming of the smaller species, under similar circumstances.

Although not able to fly when moulting, this bird cannot be readily taken in that condition, as its large feet, powerful leg, and vigorous wings enable it to run on the surface of the water faster than an Indian can paddle his canoe; and to capture it by hand is rendered almost impossible, by the circumstance that resort is had to diving and other skilful manœuvres to facilitate escape.

A nest of this species was found by Mr. W. C. Rice at Oakland Valley, Ia., in the spring of 1871, and the Cygnets taken from it. Three of these were successfully raised, and were purchased for the Mount Auburn Cemetery, where they were received in December. They bore their transportation, in a week of unparalleled severity for the season, without injury, and were remarkably docile and tame. In the summer months when at large they would leave their pond and seek the companionship of their keeper, whose occupation as painter occasionally required his presence on the grounds near their place of abode. If permitted they would spend the day in his company rather than remain in their pond. They were perfectly and completely domesticated, and showed no fear of any person, feeding from the hands of any stranger. This Swan has also been domesticated in the cemetery in Cincinnati, a pair of the progeny having been sent to the London Zoological Gardens, and another to Mount Auburn.

Mr. Audubon states that these Swans appear on the lower waters of the Ohio about the end of October, in the larger ponds and lakes at no great distance from the river, preferring such as are closely surrounded by dense and tall cane-brakes. There they remain until the water is frozen, when they move southward. During mild winters a few remain in these ponds until March. Mr. Audubon traced the winter migrations of this species as far south as Texas, where at times it is quite abundant. He met with a pair there that had been taken alive in the winter of 1836, and had been domesticated. In New Orleans examples are frequently exposed for sale in the markets, having been procured on the ponds in the interior. The waters of the Arkansas and its tributaries are well supplied each winter with this species, and the largest specimen Mr. Audubon ever saw was shot on a lake near the junction of that river with the Mississippi; it weighed thirty-eight pounds.

This Swan is said to feed chiefly by partially immersing the body and extending the neck under water in the manner of the fresh-water Ducks, with its feet in the air, thus preserving its balance. Occasionally it resorts to the land, where it feeds, more in the manner of the Duck than in that of the Goose. Its food consists of the roots of various plants, leaves, seeds, aquatic insects, land-snails, small reptiles, etc.

Mr. Audubon once kept a male Swan alive two years. At first extremely shy, it soon became accustomed to the servants, and after a time came at the call of its name, "Trumpeter," and ate bread from the hand. It at last became quite bold, and would drive before it the Turkey-Cock, as well as the dogs and servants.

Mr. MacFarlane saw the Trumpeter Swan breeding on the Barren Grounds, on islands in Franklin Bay, and near the Arctic coast. In one instance a nest containing six eggs was found near the beach on a rising ground. It was composed of hay, down, and feathers intermixed. This was the general character as regards structure and situation of the nests of this species. Those in the Barrens were usually placed on elevated ground; others were found near the banks of the Lower Anderson River. The usual number of eggs was four.

The Trumpeter was also met with on the head-waters of the Frazer River by Mr. Elliot; as also near Fort Yukon, where it was ascertained to breed, and where examples of its eggs were procured. Specimens were also taken both by Mr. Kennicott and by Mr. Lockhart in the same region; by Mr. L. Clark and Mr. B. R. Ross at Fort Rae; and on Big Island by Mr. J. Reid.

This was the only Swan observed by Mr. E. Adams on Norton Sound, where it appeared by the 30th of May. It was at no time abundant, but associated itself with others of the species, so as to form flocks of from two to eight or ten in number. A few were said to breed in that locality, but the greater part of them went farther north.

The eggs of the Trumpeter are of a uniform chalky white color, and rough and granulated on the surface. They measure from 4.35 inches in length to 4.65, and from 2.65 to 2.90 inches in breadth.

Sub-family ANSERINÆ. — The Geese.

The chief characters of the *Anserinæ*, as distinguished from the *Cygninæ* and *Anatinæ*, consist in the more elevated body, with the lengthened legs, fitting the species for a more terrestrial life, although equally able to swim. Their necks are very much shorter than in the Swans, and usually longer than those of the Ducks. From the latter, all the Geese are distinguished by the character of the covering of the anterior part of the tarsus, which consists of small hexagonal scales, but in the Ducks of narrow transverse scutellæ. Including the genus *Dendrocycna*, which, notwithstanding its close superficial resemblance to the Ducks, seems to belong rather to this sub-family, the *Anserinæ* of North America may be divided into two groups, as follows: —

Ansereæ. Bill tapering to the tip, not longer than the head (frequently shorter); nostrils situated near the middle of the maxilla; only the lower end of the tibia bare.

Dendrocycneæ. Bill depressed and broad at the end, longer than the head, the edges nearly parallel; nostrils situated far posterior to the middle of the maxilla; lower half of the tibia bare.

The Geese of the Northern Hemisphere vary so much in the details of form, that the genera usually recognized are far more artificial than natural, their definition being of the utmost difficulty, scarcely two species being exactly alike in the minutiæ of external anatomy. No great violence would be done their true relationship, were all the North American Geese, except *Philacte* and *Dendrocycna*, referred to a single genus, *Anser;* but for convenience of classification it may serve the purpose best to admit a limited number of genera, defined as follows: —

ANSEREÆ.

A. Bill variable, the nasal cavity [1] situated near the middle of the maxilla, elongated, and indistinctly defined; "nails" of the bill rather small, occupying much less than the terminal third of the bill.

a. Colors variable, but head and neck with little, if any, black. Bill and feet light colored (usually reddish) in adult.

1. **Chen.** Bill very robust, the culmen slightly, the lower outline of the mandible decidedly, convex; very slightly depressed immediately behind the thickened nails; commissure widely gaping (except in *C. Rossi*). Head and neck of adult white; some species entirely white in adult dress, except primaries. Bill and feet reddish in the adult.

2. **Anser.** Bill more slender, the culmen gently concave, the lower outline of the mandible slightly concave anteriorly; decidedly depressed immediately behind the rather thin nails; commissure nearly or quite closed, by the close approximation of the tomia. Head and neck never white, and no species entirely white (normally). Bill and feet light colored in the adult.

b. Colors dark, with the head and neck chiefly black; bill and feet deep black at all ages.

3. **Bernicla.** Bill usually much as in *Anser;* all the characters, except those defined above, exceedingly variable.

B. Bill depressed and broad, the nasal cavity situated in the basal half of the maxilla (its posterior end nearly or quite touching the frontal feathers), broadly ovate, and distinctly defined; nails of the bill very large, occupying nearly the terminal third of the bill.

4. **Philacte.** Color bluish, variegated with whitish borders to the feathers and subterminal dusky crescentic bars; exposed portion of the tail white. Adult with the head and nape white, the bill and feet light colored; young with the head plumbeous, the bill and feet dusky.

DENDROCYCNEÆ.

5. **Dendrocycna.** Bill longer than the head, the edges nearly parallel, the lamellæ entirely concealed by the overhanging edge of the maxilla. Lower part of the tibia bare for a considerable distance. Tarsus shorter than the middle toe with claw, but longer than the middle toe without claw.

Besides the species properly considered to be American, another has been recorded as occurring within our limits, on the strength of a single specimen shot on Long Island, N. Y. This is the Egyptian Goose, *Chenalopex ægyptiacus*, of South Europe and Northern Africa — a common species in aviaries; so that it is altogether probable that the example in question was one escaped from confinement. The genus *Chenalopex* differs from all the North American Geese in its style of coloration, the wing-coverts being white, and the secondaries metallic purplish; the maxillary tomium hangs over the mandible so as almost to conceal it terminally, the bill being much depressed at the end, and very deep through the base; the legs are lengthened, the tarsus considerably exceeding the middle toe in length; the hallux well developed. The colors of *C. ægyptiacus* are as follows: Head whitish, with an elongated patch surrounding the eye, and a collar encircling the lower part of the neck, chestnut rufous; neck light brownish gray; breast, back, scapulars, sides, and flanks pale fulvous, finely undulated with dusky; outer webs of tertials (inner secondaries) plain chestnut-rufous; abdomen, anal region, and wing-coverts white, the greater coverts barred near the end with black, forming a single narrow bar across the wing; secondaries dark metallic purplish; primaries, primary-coverts, and alulæ, rump, upper tail-coverts, and tail plain

[1] By "nasal cavity" is here meant not the opening of the external nostrils, but the opening in the maxillary bone, chiefly covered by the overlying membrane.

greenish black, scarcely glossy; breast with a large central irregular patch of dark chestnut; crissum ochraceous buff. Bill, legs, and feet red in life. Wing, 14.75 inches; culmen, 1.90; depth of bill at base, 1.00; tarsus, 2.95; middle toe, 2.50.

The following is the principal synonymy of the species: —

Chenalopex[1] **ægyptiaca.** — Egyptian Goose.

Anas ægyptiaca, Linn. S. N. ed. 12, I. 1766, 197.
Chenalopex ægyptiaca, Steph. Gen. Zool. XII. 1824, 43, pl. 42. — Bonap. Comp. List, 1838, 56. — Keys. & Blas. Wirb. Eur. 1840, 84. — Macgill. Man. II. 153. — Gray, Gen. B. III. 1849, 605; Cat. Brit. B. 1863, 183 (England; two instances). — Akhurst, Bull. N. O. C. II. Apr. 1877, 52 (Carnarsie, Long Island, N. Y. Jan. 3, 1877!).
Anas varia, Bechst. Orn. Taschenb. II. 1803, 454.
Egyptian Goose, Yarr. Brit. B. ed. 2, III. 173, fig.; ed. 3, III. 177, fig.

Genus CHEN, Boie.

Chen, Boie, Isis, 1822 (type, *Anser hyperboreus*, Pallas).
Exanthemops, Elliot, Pr. Philad. Acad. 1868, (type, *Anser Rossii*, Baird).

Of the three North American species of this genus, two, *C. hyperboreus*, the type, and *C. cærulescens*, are precisely alike in the details of form, the only difference being the coloration, which is

C. hyperboreus.

very distinct in the two; the third species, *C. Rossi*, while agreeing strictly with *A. hyperboreus* in plumage, both in the adult and young stages, differs decidedly in the form of the bill, which is quite peculiar. It seems unnecessary, however, to adopt the generic term *Exanthemops*, proposed for

[1] *Chenalopex*, Stephens, Shaw's Gen. Zool. XII. ii. 1824, 41 (type, *Anser jubatus*, Spix. — Scl. & Salv. P. Z. S. 1876, 360). [The Egyptian Goose seems hardly strictly congeneric with the South American species upon which this genus was based, and may require another generic name.]

it by Mr. D. G. Elliot, since the difference in the character of the bill from that of the typical species of the genus is hardly of generic value. The species may be distinguished as follows:—

Synopsis of Species.

A. Plumage never chiefly white; the adult mainly grayish brown, with bluish-gray rump and wing-coverts, the head and part of the neck white. Young almost wholly grayish brown, including head and neck.

1. **C. cærulescens.** Bill very robust, the posterior lateral outline of the maxilla decidedly concave; commissure widely gaping, and lower outline of the mandible decidedly convex. Wing, about 15.00–17.00 inches; culmen, 2.10–2.30; tarsus, 3.00–3.30; middle toe, 2.15–2.50. *Hab.* Interior of North America; Mississippi Valley, chiefly in winter.

B. Plumage of the adult pure white, the primaries black, more grayish toward the base; young grayish white, the centres of the feathers darker gray.

2. **C. hyperboreus.** Bill robust, and shaped like that of *C. cærulescens.* Wing, 15.00–18.50 inches; culmen, 1.95–2.80; depth of maxilla at base, 1.15–1.50; tarsus, 2.80–3.50; middle toe, 2.10–2.90. *Hab.* The whole of North America.
3. **C. Rossi.** Bill small, the posterior lateral outline of the maxilla almost perfectly straight, the tomia closely approximated, and the lower outline of the mandible scarcely convex; in older specimens the base of the maxilla corrugated or warty. Wing, 13.75–15.50 inches; culmen, 1.50–1.70; depth of maxilla at base, .85–.95; tarsus, 2.30–3.00; middle toe, 1.80–2.05. *Hab.* Northwestern North America.

Chen cærulescens.

THE BLUE-WINGED GOOSE.

Anas cærulescens, LINN. S. N. ed. 10, I. 1758, 124; ed. 12, I. 1766, 198. — GMEL. S. N. I. 1788, 513. — LATH. Ind. Orn. II. 1790, 836.

Anser cærulescens, VIEILL. Enc. Méth. I. 1823, 115. — BAIRD, Cat. N. Am. B. 1859, no. 564. — COUES, Key, 1872, 282; Check List, 1873, no. 479; Birds N. W. 1874, 553.

Chen cærulescens, RIDGW. Proc. U. S. Nat. Mus. Vol. 3, 1880, 202; Nom. N. Am. B. 1881, no. 590. — COUES, Check List, 2d ed. 1882, no. 694.

Anser hyperboreus (supposed young), STEPHENS, Shaw's Gen. Zool. XII. ii. 1824, 33. — BAIRD, B. N. Am. 1858, 760.

HAB. North America in general, but chiefly the interior.

SP. CHAR. *Adult:* Head and upper half of the neck white, or mostly white, the former frequently washed with orange-rufous anteriorly; lower neck and body grayish brown, the feathers bordered terminally with paler, these pale edgings, however, nearly obsolete on the neck, where the tint is darker, inclining to plumbeous-umber, which joins irregularly against the white above it. Rump and wings plain pearl-gray or bluish cinereous (the former sometimes white), in striking contrast to the deep grayish brown of the scapulars, sides, etc.; that of the rump fading into white on the upper tail-coverts, and that of the greater coverts edged externally with the same. Primaries black, fading basally into hoary gray; secondaries deep black, narrowly skirted with white; tail deep cinereous, the feathers distinctly bordered with white. Bill reddish, the commissural space black; feet reddish. *Young:* Very similar, but the chin, only, white, the rest of the head and neck being uniform plumbeous-umber or brownish plumbeous, like the breast, only darker in shade; body more cinereous than in the adult, the pale tips to the nearly truncated contour-feathers being obsolete. Rump, wings, and tail as in the adult. Bill and feet blackish. *Downy young*, not seen.

Total length, about 30.00 inches; wing, 15.00–17.00; culmen, 2.10–2.30; tarsus, 3.00–3.30; middle toe, 2.15–2.50.

The chief variation in the plumage of adults of this species consists in the extent and continuity of the white of the neck. This is usually more or less broken, the dusky of the lower portion running upwards in irregular spots or projections; it extends highest on the nape, where it sometimes reaches to the crown. The bright orange-rufous tinge to the anterior portion of the head, being an artificial stain, is frequently entirely absent. The color of the abdomen also varies from nearly pure white to a tint hardly paler than the breast; the rump is also sometimes, but rarely, entirely white, while occasionally white feathers are irregularly interspersed among the dark feathers of the body.

In both the adult and young stages of this Goose the plumage is so very distinct from that of *C. hyperboreus* that there is no occasion for confounding the two when the points of distinction are understood. We are unable, however, to find the slightest difference in the details of form or in proportions — a fact which suggests the mere possibility of their being white and colored phases of the same species, as in some Herons; but we do not consider this as at all probable, although in view of their similarity of form and size, and that the chief variations are a tendency toward partial albinism,[1] the possibility of such a relationship should be borne in mind.

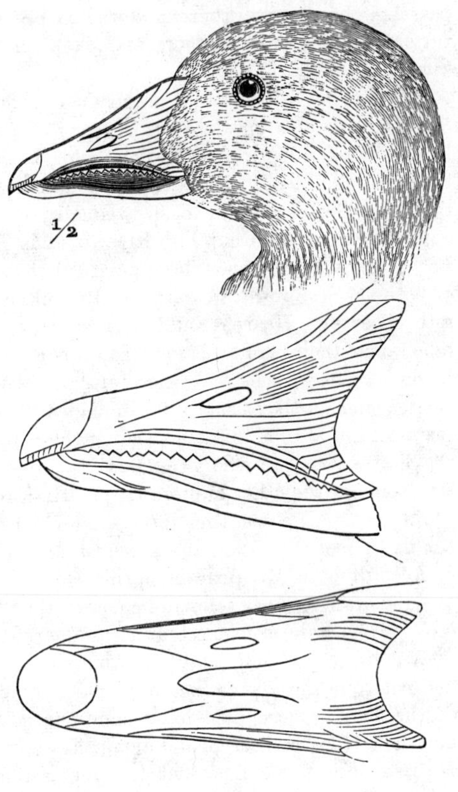

This form, once supposed to be the young of the Snow Goose, is now regarded as an entirely good and distinct species. Mr. G. Barnston, in his valuable paper on the Geese of Hudson's Bay, referring to the prevalent supposition that this species and the *A. hyperboreus* are mere varieties, because of the friendly intercourse that exists between them, is positive that this belief is not well founded. The young of the *hyperboreus* arrive from the north with their parents without any intermixture of other Geese in their flocks. They have the same white garb as the old birds, but with their heads as if soiled with iron-rust, and with a bill, tender, soft, and compressible. On the other hand, the *cœrulescens* comes down upon the eastern coast also in perfectly distinct flocks, the young birds having a more

[1] A specimen figured in the "Transactions" of the Chicago Academy of Sciences, Vol. I. 1869, pl. 18, has the whole under parts, posterior to the jugulum, pure white. We have also seen examples in which not only the abdomen, but also the rump, was white; while, as noted above, white feathers are sometimes interspersed irregularly in the dark plumage of the body. There is also something very "unsatisfactory" or suspicious in the irregular, variable, and undecided way in which the white of the neck joins upon the dark color below it.

Mr. E. W. Nelson, of Chicago, who has enjoyed the advantage of inspecting very numerous specimens in the markets of that great game centre, writes as follows (Bull. "Nutt. Orn. Club," VIII. 1876, p. 137) with regard to the changes of plumage in this species: —

"The adults of this species invariably possess the white head and upper part of the neck, which in the younger specimens is more or less variegated with dark feathers. These disappear as the bird becomes older; and in many the head is a pure snowy white, in sharp contrast to the dark plumage of the rest of

diffused and darker blue color, and being also of a smaller size. In the spring James Bay is frequently crossed by both species at Cape Jones and at Cape Henrietta Maria. Occasionally two or three of the *cœrulescens* may be seen in a flock of the Snow Geese on the Albany shore, while two or three of the latter may also be seen accompanying full flocks of the *cœrulescens* on the east main shore. This may be accounted for by the similarity of their cry.

By Indian report the great breeding-ground of the *cœrulescens* is the country lying in the interior from the northeast point of Labrador. Extensive swamps and impassable bogs prevail there, and the Geese incubate on the more solid and driest tufts, dispersed over the morasses, safe from the approach of man or any other than a winged enemy.

Mr. Hearne, who wrote a century ago, refers to this as a species distinct from the Snow Goose. He speaks of it as being of the same size as the latter, and, like it, having bill and legs of a deep flesh-color, but with the entire plumage of a dirty blue, resembling old lead. Its skin, stripped of its feathers, is of the same color as that of the Snow Goose, and the flesh is equally good eating. This species, he adds, is seldom seen north of Churchill River, and is not very common at Fort York; but at Fort Albany it was much more plentiful than the Snow Goose. The breeding-places of both species, however, were equally unknown, even to the most careful and accurate observer. Hearne could not ascertain that any of their eggs had ever been taken, and their winter haunts had, up to his time, remained wholly undiscovered. Birds of this species were not infrequently observed to lead a flock of the Snow Geese; and as they usually fly in angles, it was sometimes quite a striking thing to see a bird of a different color leading the van. The leader is generally the object of the first sportsman who fires, as this throws the whole flock into such confusion that some of the other hunters frequently kill six or seven at a shot.

So far as is known, this species does not occur on the Pacific coast; Dr. Cooper has never met with it on any part of that coast.

According to Mr. Boardman, this Goose occurs occasionally in the neighborhood of Calais, where it is even more common than the White-fronted species (*Anser Gambeli*). He also informs me that a specimen has been taken at Grand Menan.

It is quite probable that Mr. Audubon, to whom the existence of this species as distinct from the *hyperboreus* was unknown, may have referred to it as the gray state of the Snow Goose, which he mentions as so very common in winter about the mouths of the Mississippi and along the shores of the Gulf of Mexico as far as Texas. He also notices the fact that the young remain for several years of a dark-bluish color, and mentions that a friend kept one four years without any change being noticed.

the upper parts. The young would appear at first sight to be a distinct species, so different is the pattern of coloration. The white of the head, neck, abdomen, and tail-coverts is entirely absent, and the bird is of an almost uniform ashy plumbeous, slightly darker about the head, and lighter on the abdomen. This plumage is retained until the second year at least, as many specimens are procured in spring with the dark head, neck, and abdomen still immaculate; and these, I think, are young of the preceding year. At the same time specimens are found with the dark feathers about the head well mixed with white, representing the second year. In birds of the third year the white predominates; but not until the fourth or fifth year does the plumage become perfect."

Chen hyperboreus.

THE SNOW GOOSE.

Anser hyperboreus, PALL. Spic. Zool. VIII. 1767, 80, 25, pl. 65 ; (Eastern Siberia) Zoog. Rossô-As. II. 1826, 227. — SW. & RICH. F. B. A. II. 1831, 467. — NUTT. Man. II. 1834, 344. — AUD. Orn. Biog. IV. 1838, 562, pl. 381 ; Synop. 1839, 273 ; B. Am. VI. 1843, 212, pl. 381. — BAIRD, B. N. Am. 1858, 760 ; Cat. N. Am. B. 1859, no. 563. — COUES, Key, 1872, 282 ; Check List, 1873, no. 480 ; B. N. W. 1874, 548.

Anas hyperboreus, GMEL. S. N. I. ii. 1788, 504. — WILS. Am. Orn. VIII. 1814, 76, pl. 68, f. 3.

Chen hyperboreus, BOIE, Isis, 1822, 563. — RIDGW. Nom. N. Am. B. 1881, no. 591. — COUES, Check List, 2d ed. 1882, no. 695.

Anas nivalis, FORST. Philos. Trans. LXII. 1772, 413 (Severn R.).

Tadorna nivea, BREHM, Vög. Deutschl. 1831, 854.

White Brant, LAWSON, Carol. 147.

Snow Goose, PENN. Arct. Zool. II. 1790, 479. — LATH. Synop. VI. 1785, 445.

Anser albatus, CASS. Pr. Philad. Acad. 1856, 41. — BAIRD, B. N. Am. 1858, 925.

Chen albatus, ELLIOT, Illustr. Am. B. II. 1869, pl. 42.

Anser hyperboreus, var. *albatus*, COUES, Key, 1872, 282 ; Check List, 1873, no. 480*a*.

Anser hyperboreus, b. *albatus*, COUES, Birds N. W. 1874, 549.

Chen hyperboreus albatus, RIDGW. Pr. U. S. Nat. Mus. 1880, 202 ; Nom. N. Am. B. 1881, no. 591*a*. — COUES, Check List, 2d ed. 1882, no. 696.

HAB. The whole of North America, breeding far north ; more rare on Atlantic coast than westward. Greenland ; casual in Europe. South to Cuba.

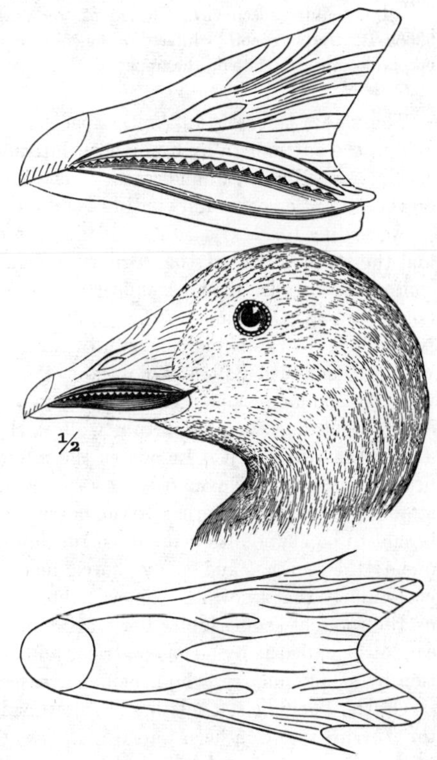

SP. CHAR. *Adult:* Entire plumage, except the primaries, snow-white, the head sometimes stained with orange-rufous anteriorly ; primaries deep black, fading basally into grayish, the primary coverts and alula being hoary ash. Bill purplish red, the nail whitish, and the intertomial space black ; iris dark brown ; eyelids whitish ; feet purple- or orange-red, the soles dingy yellowish. *Young:* Above, including the head and neck, pale cinereous, the feathers of the dorsal region more whitish on their edges ; wing-coverts and tertials dark cinereous centrally, their edges broadly pure white ; secondaries mottled cinereous, skirted with white ; primaries as in the adult. Rump, upper tail-coverts, tail, and lower parts, immaculate snowy white, the tail and breast tinged with pale ash. Head usually more or less tinged with orange-rufous, this deepest anteriorly. Bill and feet dusky. *Downy young* not seen.

Total length, about 30.00 inches ; wing, 15.00–18.50 ; culmen, 1.95–2.80 ; depth of maxilla, at base, 1.15–1.50 ; tarsus, 2.80–3.50 ; middle toe, 2.10–2.90.

There can be little question that two forms of the Snow Goose exist in North America, distinguished by their size and also their geographical distribution. The smaller, to which the name *hyperboreus* properly belongs, and of which *albatus*, CASS., is a pure synonyme, occurs throughout the northwestern portions of the continent (being the only one known to breed in Alaska), and in winter migrates over the whole of the country from the Pacific coast to the Mississippi Valley. The other, with larger general size and disproportionately heavier bill, breeds in the region about Hudson's Bay, and in winter migrates southward chiefly along the Atlantic coast. This bird is the *Anas nivalis* of Forster (1772), and if it is to be recognized as a race, as we think it ought, it should be called *Chen* (or *Anser*) *hyperboreus nivalis*.

Among the specimens examined is a young bird (No. 84698, U. S. Nat. Mus., S. Turner, coll.) obtained at Mount Carmel, Ill. (in winter), which is exceptionally small, measuring, wing, 14.50; culmen, 2.05; depth of maxilla, at base, 1.20; tarsus, 3.00; middle toe, 2.00. Of the fifteen examined altogether, all possessed sixteen rectrices except one, an adult from Alaska, which had eighteen tail-feathers.

An adult male killed at Mount Carmel, Ill., Oct. 6, 1873 (No. 84696, R. RIDGWAY, coll.), measured, when fresh, 27.00 inches in length and 57.00 in extent, and weighed 5¼ lbs. The fresh colors of the unfeathered portions were as follows: Bill bright salmon-pink, becoming brighter flesh-color around the nostril, and more dilute purplish on the lower mandible; ungui yellowish white, and commissural space deep black; iris dark brown; eyelids greenish white; feet dilute purple-lake, the soles of the toes dull light naples-yellow. An adult male collected at Pyramid Lake, Nev., Dec. 28, 1867 (No. 53690, U. S. Nat. Mus., R. RIDGWAY, coll.), weighed 5 lbs.; length, 28.00 inches. Bill dull light salmon-purple, becoming white on the ungui; the salmon-color purest on the culmen, and most purplish basally; the black of the commissural space separated from the purple by a backward extension of the white of the nail; *eyelids flesh-color;* iris vandyke-brown; tarsi and toes deep salmon-purple; claws black.

An immature specimen, collected at the Sink of the Humboldt, Nev., Oct. 31, 1867 (No. 53689, R. RIDGWAY, coll.), differed in the color of the bill and feet as follows: Bill blackish dusky, becoming greenish slate on the upper basal portion; tarsi and toes greenish slate.

The Snow Goose is an Arctic species, common to both continents, and occurring during the summer in high northern latitudes. It is found in its migrations on both coasts, as well as on inland water in the interior, is abundant on the Pacific, but rare on the Atlantic coast, and visiting even Japan, where its local name is *Hakugan*.

According to Mr. Boardman, it is by no means uncommon on the coast of Maine; and the same is true of the region adjacent to the St. Croix River. It is, however, comparatively rare in Massachusetts. On Long Island, according to Giraud, it is also not common. Occasionally the young of this species are seen exposed for sale in the New York markets, but the adults rarely. In some seasons small flocks are met with on the South Bay, and now and then stragglers are noticed flying in company with the common Canada Goose. The whiteness of their plumage renders them very conspicuous, and when opportunity offers they are singled out by the hunters. On the Jersey coast this bird is known as the "Red Goose," and it there usually makes its first appearance in November. As the winter progresses it proceeds farther south, stopping again on its return to the north, late in winter or early in spring. At times it is said to be abundant on the coast of New Jersey and in Delaware Bay. It there frequents the marshes and reedy shores, feeding upon the roots of various marine plants, particularly that known as the sea-cabbage. Its bill is very strong, enabling it to pull up the roots of sedges and other marine plants with great ease. The flesh — while it cannot be called fishy — has a strong and peculiar taste, but is held in high estimation by some epicures, who consider it superior to that of the tame Goose.

On the Pacific coast this bird is more or less abundant from Alaska and Washington Territory to Southern California. Dr. Cooper mentions having seen large flocks of this species at Los Angeles in December, 1860. It occurs in great numbers in the middle and western portions of California in winter, frequenting especially the marshes and plains near the sea, sometimes appearing on the sandy bars about the shore. It arrives from the north in October, and remains until March, when it joins its kindred of other species, and together they depart for more northern regions. While in California this bird feeds chiefly on grass, and is very shy and watchful. It is generally silent, but at times, chiefly when flying, utters a shrill *howk*. It is hunted and shot, and many are brought to market, being considered, when young, better than the common Wild Goose.

This bird occurs in the interior of the continent on all the large lakes, as well as on the smaller collections of water. Mr. J. A. Allen met with it in Salt Lake Valley, where it begins to arrive in considerable numbers about October 1st, being known there as the White Brant. Mr. Ridgway also found it a more or less common winter resident or visitant on all the larger lakes of the Great Basin. Captain Bendire mentions it as common during the migrations in Eastern Oregon. It is of accidental occurrence in the Bermudas, two examples, according to Major Wedderburn, having been shot at Riddle's Bay in October, 1848.

Hearne, in his Account of his Journey to the Northern Ocean, speaks of the White or Snow Goose as being the most numerous of all the species of birds frequenting the northern part of Hudson's Bay, and says that it makes its appearance about a week or ten days after the common Wild Goose. In the first part of the season it arrives in small parties; but in the middle and toward the latter end comes in such amazing numbers, that when they settle in the marshes, the ground for a considerable distance appears like a field of snow. When feeding in the same marsh with *A. canadensis*, the two species never mingle. Like the latter, it will fly to a call resembling its own note; and in some years it has been killed and salted in great numbers for winter consumption, it being almost universally regarded as good eating. If proper care be taken in the curing it will continue good for two years. The Indians at Hudson's Bay are said to be far more expert than the Europeans in killing this bird, some of them having been known to obtain upward of a hundred in a single day, a single Indian commonly killing from a thousand to twelve hundred in a season; but at the time Hearne wrote he was reckoned a good hunter who could kill three hundred, as these Geese did not then frequent that region in as great numbers as they formerly did.

Hearne adds that the general breeding-place of this species was not known to the Indians of Hudson's Bay, nor to the Eskimos that frequent the extreme north. The general route they take in their return to the south in the fall of the year was equally unknown.

About Hudson's Bay this bird is said to be the shyest and most watchful of all the species of Geese, never suffering an open approach, not even to within two or three gunshots. Yet on some of the rivers near Cumberland House, and at Basquian, the Indians would occasionally kill twenty at a shot. This was done on moonlight nights, when the Geese were sitting in the mud, and the sportsmen were concealed from view.

According to the observations of Dr. Richardson, the Snow Goose in summer feeds chiefly on berries, and is seldom seen on the water except during the night or when moulting. It frequents the shores of rivers and lakes, and visits both the interior and the coasts in its migrations, but resorts in great numbers to the Barren Grounds to breed. The eggs are of a yellowish white color, and of a regular ovate form, their length being three inches, and their breadth two. The young fly in the middle of August, and by the end of September have all departed south. Their food in the summer consists of rushes and insects, and in the autumn of berries, particularly those of the *Empetrum nigrum*. When in good condition — as Richardson says —

this bird is very excellent eating, and far superior to the Canada Goose in juiciness and flavor. The young do not attain to the full plumage of the old bird before their fourth year; and until that period they keep in separate flocks. They are said to have been numerous at Fort Albany, in the southern portion of Hudson's Bay, where the old birds were rarely seen; and, on the other hand, the old birds in their migrations visit York Factory in great numbers, but always unaccompanied by their young. They appear in the spring a few days later than the Canada Geese, and pass in large flocks both on the coast and through the interior.

According to the observations of Mr. Barnston, this species — known among the Indians as the *Wevois* or *Wavies* — is less conspicuous in the interior than some other kinds of Geese. It seldom alights except along the margins of large lakes and streams, and the grassy ponds of the prairies. Owing to its arrival in such great numbers, it becomes the first object of sport in James Bay, and the havoc made there is often very great. In the fall, when flocks of the young birds are passing southward, it is no uncommon thing for a good shot to kill a hundred in a single day. This bird still forms the staple article of food for natives at the Albany Factory. This is the last of the Geese to leave for the south, its migration taking place in the latter part of September.

These birds are deliberate and judicious, Mr. Barnston adds, in their preparations for flight, and make their arrangements in a business-like manner. They cease to feed in the marshes, keeping out with the retreating tide, and at its flow retiring step by step, continually dressing their feathers with their fatty oil. They are then ready for the first northerly wind which blows; and in twenty-four hours the coast so lately resonant with their incessant cries, and covered, patch-like, with their whitening squadrons, is entirely deserted.

Reinhardt states that this species is known as a bird of Greenland by the occurrence there of a few stragglers only in immature plumage. It is not known to breed in any part of that coast occupied by the Danish settlements, and probably does not breed in any part of the island.

Captain Blakiston speaks of this Goose as being late in its arrival in spring, and as delaying behind the others of its family in going south in the autumn. He found it quite numerous both on Hudson's Bay and in the west, tracing it as far as the Rocky Mountains. Mr. Ross speaks of it as equally abundant on the Mackenzie. He was informed by Mr. Pruden, a fur-trader, that the father of the latter, living at the Red River Settlement, had domesticated a pair of these birds, one of which, after a time, died. The next fall, as a flock of this species was passing over, one of them separated itself from the others, descended, and took up its quarters with the tame Goose, remaining there all winter. The following spring, however, it joined its brethren as they came by, and proceeded north. In the fall it again returned, rejoining and living with its mate of the former winter: this is said to have been repeated for several years.

Mr. Audubon's observations enabled him to ascertain that this species regularly visits the valley of the Mississippi in October, individuals appearing in the immature plumage a fortnight or more before the adult birds arrive. As a general thing the flocks of old and young kept apart and did not mingle. This Goose was especially abundant in the gray plumage about the mouth of the Mississippi, as well as on all the muddy or grassy shores of the bays and inlets of the Gulf of Mexico. During the rainy seasons it abounds among the large prairies of Louisiana, feeding on the roots of plants. It is said to be more silent than any other species, rarely emitting any cry except when pursued after being wounded. Dr. Bachman kept for several years a tame Snow Goose, which mated with a common tame bird; but the eggs were unproductive.

According to Middendorff the Snow Goose occurs in Siberia, whence it extends its movements to the extreme north. Mr. Dresser also states that this bird is found quite regularly in the eastern portion of European Russia. It has also been met with in Japan; but is not known to have been seen either in Great Britain or in Scandinavia. It is believed to have been taken on several occasions in Germany. According to Naumann, considerable flocks have been known to pass through Silesia. Bechstein mentions the occurrence of a large flock on the 13th of January, 1792, passing over the Thüringerwald. A single specimen is reported to have been taken in France in 1829. It is also said to occur in Greece.

Dr. Degland — as quoted by Mr. Dresser — states that Snow Geese are common in Cuba from October to April. In October, 1845, two of these birds came to a pond on which some tame Geese were swimming, and were shot. He adds that when the Cienaga de Zapata begins to dry up, portions are covered with Snow Geese, and that he had killed at least thirty of them in one season. Dr. Merrill mentions this species as quite common during winter on the western coast of Texas.

Mr. MacFarlane describes these Geese as being very numerous at Fort Anderson about May 25, flying northward, but being afterward driven back by the severity of the weather. The nests of these birds were discovered on a small island in a lake near Liverpool Bay. They were in holes in the sandy soil, and were well lined with down. Mr. Dall found these birds common on the Yukon in the spring. Their Indian name is *Hohkol*, or Great White Bird. They arrive about May 9, flying from the south up the river, but only stop to feed in the marshes during the night. They do not breed in the vicinity of the Yukon, nor do they return in the fall by the same route by which they came. They have all gone by May 30.

Examples of this species were also procured at Fort Resolution by Mr. Kennicott, near Fort Simpson by Mr. B. R. Ross, and at Fort Rae by Mr. Clarke.

In a paper of the late Mr. E. Adams on the Birds of Michalaski, Alaska ("Ibis," 1878), the first arrival of the Snow Goose on Norton Sound is noted as having taken place on the 9th of May. During the two following days this bird was constantly passing over in large flocks of from one hundred to three hundred, an immense number thus arriving. After that time only a few stragglers were seen. The flocks followed one another with great rapidity, and as soon as one large body disappeared, another was seen advancing. In this manner — as he was assured — they pass every year, and all return about the end of September; at each season, with the exception of a few stragglers, being seen for only three days. None of the other kinds of Geese were seen in such numbers as this was, nor was any other species so regular in its flight. This bird generally passes over at a considerable height, and seldom alights except at night; but the stragglers flew exceptionally low, and were easily shot. Every bird seemed to be in full plumage and in good condition, but none remained to breed.

The smaller form probably does not differ as to its general habits and other characteristics from the larger. But little is known as to its distribution and history. According to Dr. Cooper it appears to be rather common in California in the winter. In company with the Snow Goose it frequents the plains, and is said to have very similar habits; at least nothing distinctive has been observed. This bird is much less abundant than the Snow Goose; but a considerable number are brought to market every winter, and they are known in the markets of San Francisco as the "White Brant," on account of their smaller size.

Cassin, who described this species in 1856, regarded it as being very rare, but not unknown on the Atlantic coast. He had seen but five specimens, one of which was from Oregon; and the other four — which occurred in pairs — were found in the market in Philadelphia, and are now in the collection of the Academy of that city. Two were adults, and two were in immature plumage.

Two examples of the smaller form were obtained in Ireland in November, 1871. Mr. Howard Saunders chronicled their occurrence at a meeting of the Zoological Society in 1872. He states that on the 9th of November his attention was attracted to two Geese hanging up in Leadenhall Market, London. By diligent inquiry he subsequently ascertained that they had been shot near Wexford, on the lake of Tacumshin, on the south coast, by a boy. They were the only ones that had appeared there; but there was a third one subsequently shot in Wexford Harbor. They had been swimming about on the lake for some days before they were shot. The lake adjoins the sea, from which it is separated by only a narrow ridge of sand; and it probably would be one of the first places birds would make if coming from the sea.

Under the name of *Anser hyperboreus,* Mr. Peale writes that it is impossible to convey any idea of the incessant clatter of sounds emitted by this and the White-fronted Goose when disturbed at night by some prowling wolf, as they all roost on the ground in wet prairies. The old Geese of this species generally keep together; and their white plumage, contrasted with the dark ground, presents the appearance of snow-banks. Rarely seen in the water, they remain all winter in California and the southern parts of Oregon. When they first arrive from the north they are very tame, allowing persons to approach very near, and a skilful rider on a horse is enabled to catch them with a lasso. Mr. Peale saw four that had been taken in this way in one afternoon.

Two examples of this Goose were obtained at Fort Resolution on the 26th of May by Mr. Kennicott.

The egg of the Snow Goose is quite large as compared with the size of the bird, is oval in shape, the two ends being of unequal size, and the color is a uniform dirty chalky white. They average 3.40 by 2.20 inches.

Chen Rossi.

ROSS'S SNOW GOOSE.

Anser Rossi, BAIRD, MS. CASS. Pr. Philad. Acad. 1861, 73. — COUES, Key, 1872, 282; Check List, 1873, no. 481; Birds N. W. 1874, 553.

Exanthemops Rossi, ELLIOT, Illustr. Am. B. IV. 1869, pl. 44.

Chen Rossi, RIDGW. Pr. U. S. Nat. Mus. 1880, 203; Nom. N. Am. B. 1881, no. 592. — COUES, Check List, 2d ed. 1882, no. 697.

HAB. Arctic America in summer, Pacific coast to Southern California in winter.

SP. CHAR. *Adult:* Colors exactly as in *A. hyperboreus.* Entirely snowy white, the primaries black, fading into hoary ash basally. Bill and feet dull reddish, the nails of the former white. Tomia of the bill closely approximated, the intervening space scarcely exposed. Latero-basal outline of the bill straight; base of the bill frequently warted or corrugated. *Young:* White, tinged with grayish, the centres of the feathers of upper parts deeper grayish; bill and feet dusky.

Wing, 13.75–15.50 inches; culmen, 1.50–1.70; depth of maxilla at base, .85–.95; width, .70–.80; tarsus, 2.30–3.00; middle toe, 1.80–2.05; tail-feathers, 16.00.

In adults obtained at the same season (winter or summer) there is great variation in the roughness of the base of the maxilla; in many (perhaps a majority of specimens) the base is simply slightly rugose, with longitudinal sulcations, little if any more distinct than in *C. hyperboreus*. (See accompanying cuts.)

Specimen No. 41705, from Great Slave Lake, probably an immature individual, is exceptional in having the secondary quills deep black, tipped with white, the plumage of the nape and anal region slightly verging toward ashy, the nail of the bill black, tipped with white. In all other respects than those mentioned, the appearance is that of an adult bird; and these differences would seem to indicate a rather different transition plumage from youth to maturity than in the *A. hyperboreus*.

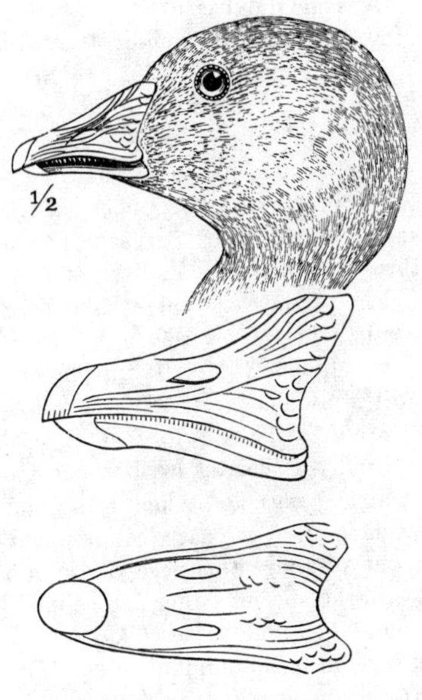

Hearne, in his "Journey to the Northern Ocean," refers to a small Goose which was undoubtedly this species. He calls it the "Horned Wavey," probably from the caruncles at the base of the bill; and he describes it as follows: "This delicate and diminutive species of the Goose is not much larger than the Mallard Duck. Its plumage is delicately white, except the quill-feathers, which are black. The bill is not more than an inch long, and at the base is studded round with little knobs about the size of peas, but more remarkably so in the male. Both the bill and the feet are of the same color with those of the Snow Goose. This species is very scarce at Churchill River, and I believe are never found at any of the southern settlements; but about two or three hundred miles to the northwest of Churchill I have seen them in as large flocks as the Common Wavey or Snow Goose. The flesh of this is exceedingly delicate, but they are so small that when I was on my journey to the north I ate two of them one night for supper." Hearne adds that this species was

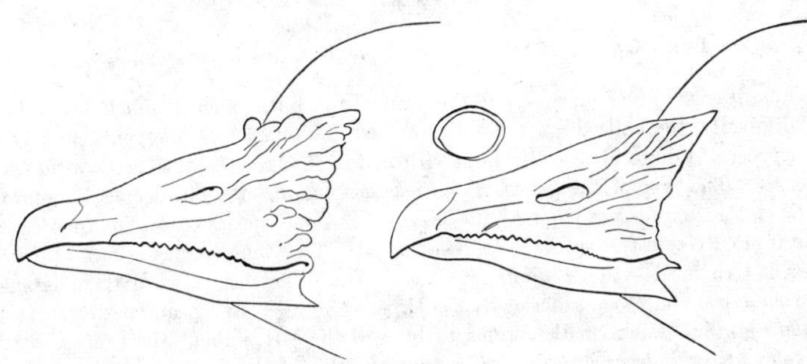

not described by Pennant in his "Arctic Zoology"—probably for the reason that the person who presided at Fort Prince of Wales at the time the collection was making, did not pay any attention to its completeness. According to Hearne, the Indians had never met with any of the eggs of this species, and he conjectured that these birds retired to North Greenland to breed. Their route in the fall of the year, as they return south, was also unknown. They were rarely seen on the coast of Hudson's Bay south of 59° north.

Mr. Bernard H. Ross mentions the fact that the Slave Lake Indians recognize the difference between this species and both the *albatus* and the *hyperboreus*, it being said to arrive from the south later than the former, and earlier than the latter.

A large number of individuals of this species were taken at Fort Resolution in May, 1860, by Mr. Kennicott, and in May, 1863 and 1865, by Mr. J. Lockhart.

Mr. Blakiston ("Ibis," 1878) refers to a smaller White Goose mixed with the flocks of *A. hyperboreus* in Japan, which he refers to "*A. albatus*," but which may have been this species. Its local name was Ko-hakugan.

Captain Bendire mentions the procuring a single specimen of this Goose on Silver River in Eastern Oregon, April 12, 1876, but considered it a very rare species there. It had been shot by Sergeant Kennedy out of a flock of twelve, and weighed two and three fourths pounds. Its note was said to be quite different from that of the Snow Goose. Other examples have been taken in Marin Co. and in other parts of California, where its presence, however, is exceptional and rare.

Dr. James C. Merrill informs me that this Goose is by no means uncommon about Fort Missoula, in Montana Territory.

Mr. L. Belding, of Stockton, Cal., writes us as follows concerning this species: "Usually associates with other Geese when in the San Joaquin Valley, especially *C. hyperboreus*, and when flying individuals are sometimes scattered through a flock, or, as is often the case, congregated on one side or other portions of it. I once saw about a hundred of these Geese in a separate flock, flying very high, and going northward, the species being determined by its cry, which somewhat resembles that of the small 'Cackling Goose' (*B. canadensis leucopareia*). In November and December, 1880, it was quite as abundant in the Stockton market as *C. hyperboreus* — owing, I suppose, to its tameness." Specimens of *C. Rossi* were observed at Stockton by Mr. Belding as early as Oct. 6, 1880, and by the 15th they became common. Mr. Belding further remarks that "the flesh of *C. Rossi*, unlike that of Geese generally, is excellent food."

Genus **ANSER**, Brisson.

Anser, Briss. Orn. I. 1760 (type, *Anas anser*, Linn., = *A. cinereus*, Meyer).

This genus differs from *Chen* chiefly in the form of the bill, which is much less robust, more depressed terminally, the nails thinner and less arched, the tomia less divergent, etc. In fact, the bill of some species is quite identical in form with that of the larger species of *Bernicla* (*canadensis* and *Hutchinsi*). The type of the genus, *A. cinereus*, Meyer, has the bill decidedly approximating to that of *Chen*, the commissure gaping quite widely. But one species occurs in America, the common White-fronted Goose (*Anser Gambeli*, Hartlaub). The same species occurs also in Europe in a representative form — the *A. albifrons*, Gmel. The difference between them is chiefly one of size, the American bird being decidedly the larger. Another European species or race resembling *A. albifrons*, but much smaller, seems to bear to the latter about the same relation which *Bernicla Hutchinsi* or *B. leucoparia* do to *B. canadensis*. The following measurements from a considerable series of specimens will serve to show the comparative size of the three birds: —

	Wing.	Culmen.	Depth of max. at base.	Width of max. at base.	Tarsus.	Middle toe.
1. *A. Gambeli*,	14.25–17.50	1.80–2.35	.90–1.20	.85–1.05	2.60–3.20	2.35–3.00
2. *A. albifrons*,	14.75–16.00	1.60–1.75	.90	.80–0.85	2.25–2.80	2.20–2.50
3. *A. minutus*,	13.25–15.00	1.15–1.35	.65–0.70	.70–0.75	2.00–2.50	2.00–2.15

From these measurements it may be readily seen that the three forms intergrade as to general size, the bill being the only member in which there is a constant difference; and as we are not aware of any positive characters of coloration, it seems very probable that they constitute merely races of one species. At any rate, we shall so here regard the American form and its nearest European ally (*A. albifrons*), leaving the final determination of the question (if determinable it be) to future investigators.

Another species of true *Anser* — the Bean Goose (*A. segetum*) — has been credited to North America by NUTTALL ("Man." ii. 1832, p. 348; "Canada and Hudson's Bay"); but apparently without good authority for so doing. Considering the possibility of its occurrence, however, its principal synonymy and characters are herewith given: —

ANSER SEGETUM (GM.) BP. The Bean Goose.
Anas segetum, GM. S. N. I. 1788, 512.
Anser segetum, MEYER, Tasch. II. 554, et AUCT.
Anser arvensis, BREHM, Vög. Deutschl. 838.
? Anser rufescens, } BREHM, t. c. pp. 837, 838.
Anser platyuros, }

SP. CHAR. "Male thirty inches long; bill moderately thick, nearly as long as the head, two inches and a third in length, and an inch and two twelfths in height at the base, nine twelfths in

A. albifrons.

height behind the circular unguis, yellowish orange, with the base and unguis black; tarsus three inches long, dull orange-yellow; the wings longer than the tail; feathers of the neck linear-oblong, disposed in ridges; head and neck grayish brown; upper parts dark brown and gray, barred with the whitish terminal margins of the feathers; hind part of back blackish brown; lower parts pale brownish gray, becoming white behind. *Female* similar, but smaller. *Young* with the upper parts darker, the head and neck of a lighter brown, three small patches of white feathers at the base of the bill" (MACGILLIVRAY, "Hist. Brit. B." IV. 1852, p. 595).

Anser albifrons.

a. albifrons. THE EUROPEAN WHITE-FRONTED GOOSE.

Anas albifrons, GMEL. S. N. I. ii. 1788, 509.

Anser albifrons, BECHST. Naturg. IV. 1809, 898. — MACGILL. Man. II. 1842, 149. — SCHLEG. Rev. Crit. 1844, 110. — NEWT. P. Z. S. 1860, 339 (critical). — REINH. Ibis, 1861, 12 (Greenland). — RIDGW. Nom. N. Am. B. 1881, no. 593. — COUES, Check List, 2d ed. 1882, no. 692.

Anser erythropus, FLEM. Br. An. 1828, 127 (nec LINN., = *Temminckii*, BOIE, = *minutus*, NAUM.). — GRAY, Gen. B. III. 1849, 607. — SCHLEG. Mus. P.-B. Anseres, 110.

Anas casarca, S. G. GM. Reise, II. pl. 13.

(?) *Anser intermedius*, NAUM. Nat. Vög. Deutschl. XI. p. 340, pl. 288.

(?) *Anser medius*, TEMM. Man. Orn. II. p. 519.

(?) *Anser pallipes*, SELYS. Naumannia, 1855, 264.

A. albifrons Gambeli (adult). *A. albifrons Gambeli (young).*

b. Gambeli. THE AMERICAN WHITE-FRONTED GOOSE.

Anser albifrons, BONAP. Synop. 1828, 376. — SW. & RICH. F. B. A. II. 1831, 466. — NUTT. Man. II. 1834, 346. — AUD. Orn. Biog. III. 1835, 568, pl. 286; Synop. 1839, 272; B. Am. VI. 1843, 209, pl. 380.

Anser Gambeli, HARTLAUB, R. M. Z. 1852, 7. — BAIRD, B. N. Am. 1858, 761; Cat. N. Am. B. 1859, no. 565.

Anser albifrons, var. *Gambeli*, COUES, Key, 1872, 282; Check List, 1873, no. 478; B. N. W. 1874, 546.

Anser albifrons Gambeli, Ridgw. Pr. U. S. Nat. Mus. 1880, 203 ; Nom. N. Am. B. 1881, no. 593 *a*. — Coues, Check List, 2d ed. 1882, no. 693.

Anser erythropus, Baird, Stansbury's Rep. 1852, 321 (nec Linn.).

Anser frontalis, Baird, B. N. Am. 1858, 562 (= young ; New Mexico) ; Cat. N. Am. B. 1859, no. 566.

Hab. The whole of North America, breeding far northward ; Cuba. The true *A. albifrons*, restricted to the Palæarctic Region and Greenland.

a. Gambeli.

Sp. Char. *Adult:* Prevailing color brownish gray, this uniform on the head and neck, and becoming much darker on the flanks ; feathers of the mantle, wings, sides, and flanks distinctly bordered terminally with pale brownish ash (sometimes approaching grayish white) ; upper edges of the upper layer of flank-feathers pure white, producing a conspicuous white stripe when the feathers are properly adjusted. Breast and abdomen grayish white, mixed more or less with irregular spots and patches of black, sometimes scattered and isolated, but oftener more or less confluent. Anal region, crissum, and upper tail-coverts immaculate pure white ; rump brownish-slate ; greater wing-coverts glaucous-gray tipped with white ; secondaries black, their edges narrowly white ; primaries slaty black, growing ashy basally ; primary-coverts glaucous-gray. Tail brownish slate, broadly tipped with white, the feathers narrowly skirted with the same. Front of the head, from the base of the bill to about half way across the lores and forehead, including the anterior border of the chin, white, bordered behind by brownish black, which gradually fades into the grayish brown of the head and neck. Bill reddish (wax-yellow, *fide* Nelson), the nail white ; feet reddish. *Young* (= *A. frontalis*, Baird) : Nearly similar to the adult, but the anterior portion of the head dark brown, instead of white ; wing-coverts less glaucous ; black blotches of the under surface absent. Nail of the bill black. *Downy young:* Above, olive-green ; beneath, dingy greenish yellow, deepest yellow on the abdomen. (Hardly distinguishable from young of *Bernicla canadensis*, but apparently more deeply colored, and with greater contrast between color of upper and lower surfaces.)

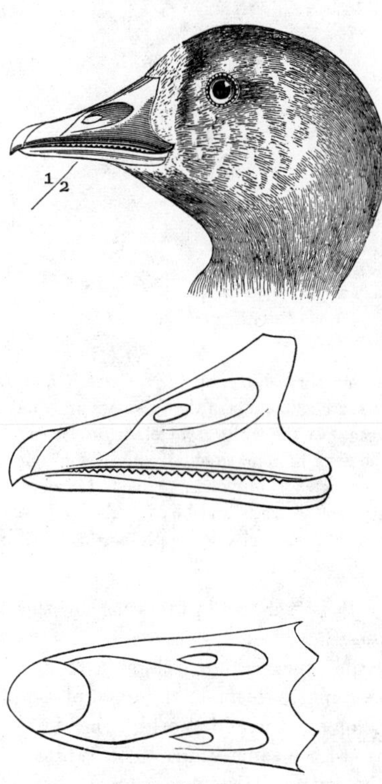

A. albifrons.

Wing, 14.50–17.25 inches ; culmen, 1.40–2.35 ; tarsus, 2.60–3.10 ; middle toe, 2.35–2.70. Tail-feathers 16 to 18, usually the former.

b. albifrons.

Sp. Char. Exactly like *A. Gambeli*, but smaller. Wing, 15.00–15.75 inches; culmen, 1.65–1.75 ; depth of maxilla at base, .90, width, .80–.85 ; tarsus, 2.25–2.80 ; middle toe, 2.20–2.45.

The principal variation among individuals of this species is in the amount of the black blotching on the lower parts. In some specimens (as No. 10463, Frontera, Texas) there are only two or three small spots, while in others (as No. 16788, Hudson's Bay Territory) the black predominates over the lower parts, being continuous on the abdomen, and only broken on the breast by the admixture of a few pale cinereous feathers. In No. 4517, Washington, D. C., the whitish gray of the lower parts is strongly tinged with ochraceous-rufous — without doubt merely an accidental stain from ferruginous clay. There is also a slight range of variation in the shade of the brownish tints of the body, some specimens inclining to cinereous and others approaching dark umber. The smallest specimen (see measurements above) is No. 10463, Frontera, Texas; the largest is No. 16788, Washington, D. C. In No. 20138, Fort Resolution, the white of the forehead is more extended than in any others, reaching as far as the middle of the eye, and sending back a stripe over the eye to its posterior angle, and another on each side the throat.

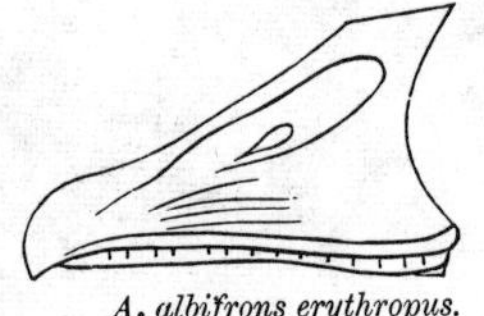

A. albifrons erythropus.

The variations of plumage in this species are thus discussed by Mr. E. W. Nelson, in the "Bulletin of the Essex Institute," Vol. VIII. (1876), pp. 136, 137: —

"The individual variation in this species is very great. A large majority have the ordinary white frontal band and the under parts plentifully mottled with black. In others the black gradually decreases, until some specimens do not show the least trace of dark on the abdomen; in such instances the frontal white band is usually present. The young exhibit a dark brown frontal band in place of white, but with more or less dark spots on the abdomen. In very high plumage the abdomen becomes almost entirely black, only a few rusty-colored feathers being interspersed through the black. The white nail on the bill is generally crossed by one or more longitudinal stripes of dark horn-color. In spring, as the breeding-season approaches, the bill becomes a clear waxy yellow. There is also much variation in size among adults of this species. I have examined a number of specimens, which by correct comparison were at least *one fourth* smaller than the average."

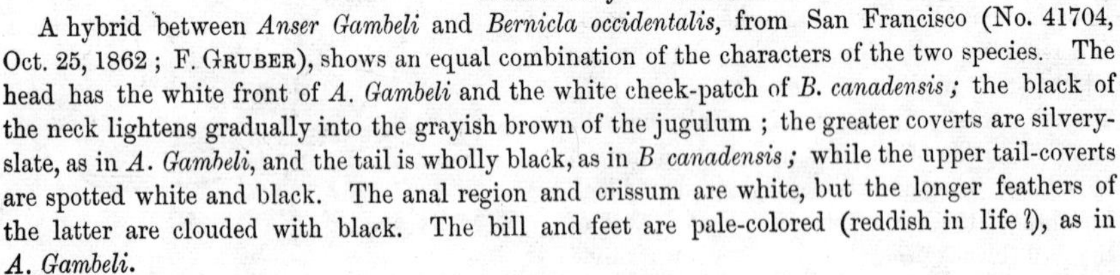

A hybrid between *Anser Gambeli* and *Bernicla occidentalis,* from San Francisco (No. 41704, Oct. 25, 1862; F. GRUBER), shows an equal combination of the characters of the two species. The head has the white front of *A. Gambeli* and the white cheek-patch of *B. canadensis;* the black of the neck lightens gradually into the grayish brown of the jugulum; the greater coverts are silvery-slate, as in *A. Gambeli,* and the tail is wholly black, as in *B canadensis;* while the upper tail-coverts are spotted white and black. The anal region and crissum are white, but the longer feathers of the latter are clouded with black. The bill and feet are pale-colored (reddish in life ?), as in *A. Gambeli.*

It is very doubtful whether the White-fronted Goose of Greenland belongs to the European species or to the larger American form. Professor Newton appears rather inclined to assign it to the latter; but as the true *albifrons* is a regular visitant to Iceland, the examples taken on the east coast of Greenland may perhaps belong to the Old World form; but it does not follow that those of the west coast are of the same kind. The White-fronted Goose is pretty generally distributed over the entire Palæarctic Region, breeding near the coast-line of the Arctic Ocean, in both Europe and Asia, and also on the larger rivers, bays, and inlets. In its migrations it is variously and unequally distributed, but is more abundant in Eastern Europe than in West, extending its migrations into Central Africa almost as far as the Equator. It is usually found in Great Britain and Ireland, and is a tolerably regular visitant, although more common in the severest winters.

This bird is abundant in Northeastern Africa during the cold season, and at that time is the most common Goose in Egypt, where it may be met with in flocks. It leaves that region in March. It is also a winter visitant to India, and is also quite frequently seen in the northern districts of Siberia, where Middendorff speaks of it as the most common species found breeding on the Taimyr. It also occurs in China and Japan.

In its general habits this Goose appears to be in no wise different from our common Nearctic form, *A. Gambeli.* It flies in wedge-shaped flocks, frequently uttering a loud and harsh cry, which may be heard at a considerable distance. These flocks are said to be generally on the wing just before sunrise and sunset, and they are very regular in their movements, taking the same line of flight, and feeding at the same spot each day; they may in consequence be readily obtained by lying in wait for them. When once fired upon, the flock usually leaves the neighborhood. This bird prefers low damp districts to the uplands, and may more frequently be found in localities where aquatic plants grow than in cultivated fields. Mr. St. John states that it is frequently seen off the coasts of England and Scotland in severe weather, and also in marshy districts and grass-fields. It arrives in Morayshire earlier than the other species of Geese, but is never seen there in flocks of more than eight or ten individuals. This Goose feeds almost exclusively on vegetable matters; and Mr. Macgillivray states that a specimen sent to him from Northumberland had its stomach filled with the tender shoots and leaves of the common clover, on which it had been feeding after a severe snow-storm. Like the other species, it breeds near fresh-water or salt pools not immediately on the coast, and makes a large nest on the ground, warmly lined with down. The eggs are from four to six in number, are yellowish white in color, and measure about 3.12 inches in length by 2.13 in breadth.

The American "White-fronted," or "Laughing, Goose" is a resident, during the summer months, in high Arctic regions, migratory in the spring and fall, and in the winter diffused over all the southern portions of North America, being more abundant in the central and western regions, and comparatively rare on the Atlantic coast.

According to Mr. Boardman, it is of occasional occurrence near Calais. One was procured at St. Stephen that had flown against the flag-staff, and had thus become disabled. It is rarely seen in Massachusetts, although individuals are occasionally brought to the markets which have been taken on Cape Cod. Mr. Giraud speaks of this bird as being exceedingly rare on Long Island. A single specimen is mentioned as having been shot near Babylon, and given to the New York Lyceum.

On the Pacific coast it is more abundant. Dr. Cooper mentions having seen flocks of this species at Los Angeles in December, 1860. It is also given by Mr. R. Browne as one of the birds of Vancouver Island. Captain Bendire mentions it as abundant in Oregon during migrations, and the first to arrive in the fall.

Dr. Pickering, in his Notes taken when naturalist of the Wilkes Expedition, mentions the occurrence of immense numbers of Geese of various species on the coast of California and Oregon, in the month of April, and subsequently in October. He calls particular attention to the abundance of this species in that region, and says that the Geese are usually seen either flying in lines — generally bifurcating from a point, but frequently irregular — or walking on the ground in search of food.

Mr. Peale, referring to this species, states that about the middle of October vast numbers of White-fronted or Laughing Geese arrive in Oregon and California from the north. They are generally found on moist prairies, and feed almost entirely on grass. None were seen that were black anywhere, except in patches on the breast.

Mr. E. Adams, in his Notes on the Birds observed on the Coast of Norton Sound ("Ibis," 1878), speaks of this Goose as arriving there as early as the 23d of April, but not becoming abundant until the first week in May. They did not congregate in large flocks, but were more often met with singly or in small parties. A few remained to breed in company with the *Bernicla nigricans*, but by far the greater number went farther north.

Dr. J. C. Merrill mentions this species as the first to arrive in the autumn in Southwestern Texas, usually about the first week in October. Comparatively few remained throughout the winter, but during the migrations it was only exceeded in numbers by the Snow Goose. In their spring migrations he has seen flocks of at least two hundred pass over Fort Brown as late as the 18th of April.

Dr. Cooper mentions it as very abundant during the wet season in California, some arriving as early as the second week in September, frequenting the plains almost exclusively, rarely appearing on the sea-shore or in the water. Of all the Geese that are found in California, this is regarded as by far the best for the table; and near the Columbia River it was found a very easy bird to shoot. The hunter could walk in the long grass where the birds were, and shoot them down as they rose singly or in pairs. In California they are more suspicious and wild, and it requires considerable artifice to obtain a shot at them. This is done by means of brush hiding-places, over which they fly, or by driving an ox that has been trained for the purpose toward them, keeping concealed behind it until close to the birds. In this way most of these Geese are now shot for market.

Mr. Grayson met with this species on the western coast of Mexico, near Mazatlan, where, from the month of September until February, it occurs in considerable flocks, appearing to migrate up and down the southern Gulf shores.

It is said to feed chiefly on berries, and is seldom seen on the water, except at night or when moulting. It frequents the sandy shores of rivers and lakes in flocks, one of their number performing the duty of sentinel. They breed in great numbers in Arctic America and on the islands of the Polar Sea, but are more rarely seen on the coast of Hudson's Bay. This bird migrates over the interior, and its breeding-places are always chosen in the vicinity of wooded tracts. It passes north in large flocks at the same time with, or a little later than, the Snow Goose, through the interior of the Fur Country to the breeding-places, which are in the woody districts skirting the Mackenzie to the north of the sixty-seventh parallel, and also to the islands in the Arctic seas. The Indians imitate its call by patting the mouth with the hand while they repeat the syllable *wah*. The resemblance of the note of this species to the laugh of a man has given to the bird the common name of "Laughing Goose."

Mr. Hearne, in his "Journey" (p. 443), refers to this species as the "Laughing Goose." In size, he says, it is the equal of the Snow Goose, but its skin, when stripped of its feathers, is delicately white, and the flesh excellent. It visits Churchill River in very small numbers; but about two hundred miles to the northwest of that River he has seen it fly in large flocks, like the common Snow Goose. Near Cumberland House and Basquian this bird is found in such numbers that the Indians, in the moonlight, frequently kill upwards of twenty at a shot. Like the "Horned Wavey" (*Anser Rossi*), it never flies with the lead of the shore, but is always seen arriving from the westward. The general breeding-places of this species were not known to Mr. Hearne, although a few of their eggs had been occasionally found north of Churchill River. Captain Blakiston speaks of this Goose as being a common bird on the Saskatchewan in the spring and autumn, especially in the latter season, when it is found in immense numbers. Mr. Ross also found it abundant on the Mackenzie, as far north as the Arctic coast. The marshy country bordering the lower parts of the Saskatchewan River, in the neighborhood of Fort Cumberland, is a great resort of this species.

According to Mr. G. Barnston, the Laughing Goose is seldom seen in the southern portion of Hudson's Bay. At Fort York it is less rare, and at Fort Churchill quite abundant. He regards it as being an inhabitant of Central and Western America in the winter months, rather than of the eastern side. Therefore in its progress northward it strikes upon the coast westward of James Bay, where it is seldom seen. On the Lower Columbia and in Oregon, or in the Willamette Valley, it abounds with other wild fowl, when, as frequently happens, the winter is mild and there is no snow on the ground. It is included by Holböll among the birds of Greenland.

Mr. Audubon states that during his residence in Kentucky not a winter passed without his noticing a large number of these birds, and says that they are frequently offered for sale at that season in the market of New Orleans. From the numbers seen high on the Arkansas River, he presumed that many winter beyond the southern limits of the United States. In Kentucky birds of this species generally arrive before the Canada Goose, betaking themselves to the grassy ponds; and of the different Geese which visit that country, these are by far the least shy. The flocks seldom exceed from thirty to fifty individuals. The flight of this bird is firm and well-sustained, and resembles that of *Bernicla canadensis*. In its migrations it passes at a considerable height, arranged in a flock of an angular shape, an old Gander leading. On the ground it walks with ease, and when wounded runs with considerable speed. While in Kentucky it feeds on beechnuts and acorns, and gleans in the cornfields for grains of maize. It also nibbles young grain and blades of grass. In its stomach the broken shells of snails are also found. It leaves Kentucky a fortnight sooner than the Canada Goose, starting at the same time with the Snow Goose; but the two species do not mingle with each other.

Mr. Dall mentions finding the White-fronted Goose extremely common in Alaska. It arrives at Nulato about May 6th to 10th, and breeds all along the river gregariously, laying from six to ten eggs in a depression in the sand, without any kind of nest or lining. He found its eggs all along the river, from Fort Yukon to the sea, and thence to St. Michael's. The Indian name of the bird is *Tutsanáh*. Mr. Bannister speaks of it as one of the first of the Geese to arrive in the spring, when it soon becomes abundant. He found it nesting on Stuart's Island, and probably also on St. Michael's.

Mr. MacFarlane found this species breeding abundantly on the Lower Anderson River, on the Arctic coast, and among the islands in the Arctic Sea. He has furnished notes as to their nesting, and from these it appears that the maximum number of eggs is seven, and that in nearly every instance observed by him the eggs were not deposited in a mere depression without lining, but that there was a plentiful supply of hay, down, and feathers, although in some instances this lining was more scanty than in others. The eggs were found in June and July. Those obtained as late as June 20 usually contained large embryos, but in a few instances they were found to be fresh as late as July 6. When the nest was approached the parent bird would exhibit signs of fear, flying off without noise at a low elevation. Mr. MacFarlane found this bird breeding about the Lower Anderson River, in the vicinity of fresh-water lakes. The nests were generally in wooded districts, and were a mere depression in the ground, but well lined with feathers and down.

The White-fronted Goose was also taken in the neighborhood of Fort Resolution by Mr. Kennicott, May 24 and 26, 1860.

Dr. Berlandier's manuscript notes seem to show that this Goose, in the winter, inhabits only the wooded marshes formed by the overflowing of the Rio Bravo del Norte, in the vicinity of Matamoras.

The eggs of this species, in shape and general appearance, are undistinguishable from those of the Snow Goose. They are of a uniform dull-white color, and measure about 2.80 by 2.00 inches.

GENUS **BERNICLA**, STEPHENS.

Bernicla, STEPHENS, Gen. Zool. XII. ii. 1824, 45 (type, *Anas bernicla*, LINN.).
Leucopareia, REICH. Syst. Av. 1853, pl. ix. (type, *Anser leucopsis*, BECHST.).
Leucoblepharon, BAIRD, B. N. Am. 1858, 763 (type, *Anas canadensis*, LINN.).

With much the same form throughout as the species of *Anser*, those belonging to the genus *Bernicla* are distinguished by the darker plumage, with the head and neck chiefly black, and the bill and feet entirely deep black, at all ages. All the known species of *Bernicla* (as properly restricted) occur in North America, and may be defined as follows: —

B. canadensis.

A. Head and neck black, with a somewhat triangular patch of white on each cheek, usually confluent underneath the head, but sometimes separated by a black stripe or "isthmus" along the throat; in some specimens a white collar around the lower neck.

1. **B. canadensis**. Tail-feathers 14 to 20 inches; wing, 13.60–21.00; culmen, .95–2.70; tarsus, 2.10–3.70; middle toe, 1.80–3.40. Tail, rump, and primaries brownish black; upper tail-coverts, crissum, and anal region white; rest of the plumage grayish brown, lighter below, the feathers tipped with paler *Hab.* Whole of North America, south to Mexico.

B. Head, neck, and jugulum black, the middle of the neck with a white patch on each side, or a wide collar of the same, interrupted behind.

2. **B. bernicla.** Wing, 12.30–13.60 inches ; culmen, 1.20–1.50 ; tarsus, 2.10–2.40 ; middle toe 1.70–2.10. White of the neck confined to two broken (streaked) patches on each side. Above, brownish gray, the feathers narrowly tipped with grayish white ; wing-coverts nearly uniform, more bluish gray ; remiges, rump, middle upper tail-coverts, and rectrices, brownish black ; terminal and lateral upper tail-coverts, crissum, and anal region white ; lower parts pale gray, the feathers tipped with grayish white, abruptly and strongly contrasted with the black of the jugulum, and fading insensibly into the white of the anal region. *Hab.* Sea-coasts of Europe and Eastern North America ; rare inland.

3. **B. nigricans.** Wing, 12.70–13.50 inches ; culmen, 1.20–1.35 ; tarsus, 2.20–2.50; middle toe, 1.80–2.00. White of the neck forming a distinct collar, interrupted only behind. Above, nearly uniform dark sooty brown ; tail-coverts, etc., white, and remiges, etc., black, as in *B. brenta ;* lower parts dark sooty plumbeous (much like the upper parts in *brenta*), nearly as dark as, but abruptly defined against, the black of the jugulum, as well as the white of the crissum ; feathers of the sides and flanks tipped with grayish white. *Hab.* Western districts of Arctic America, south in winter to Lower California ; accidental on Atlantic coast.

C. Head mostly white, the lores, occiput, neck, and jugulum black.

4. **B. leucopsis.** Wing, 14.90–16.90 inches ; culmen, 1.10–1.45 ; tarsus, 2.50-3.00 ; middle toe, 1.90–2.10. Above, silvery gray, the feathers marked with a broad subterminal bar of black and narrow tip of white ; remiges, rump, and tail black ; upper tail-coverts, anal region, and crissum white ; lower parts grayish white, darker on the sides and flanks. *Hab.* Sea-coasts of Northern Europe, but occasional along Atlantic coast of North America (Hudson's Bay, Long Island, Currituck Sound, N. C., etc.).

Bernicla canadensis.

a. Canadensis. THE CANADA GOOSE.

Anas canadensis, LINN. S. N. I. 1766, 198. — WILS. Am. Orn. VIII. 1814, 52, pl. 67, f. 4.

Anser canadensis, VIEILL. Enc. Méth. 1823, 114. — SW. & RICH. F. B. A. II. 1831, 468. — NUTT. Man. II. 1834, 349. — AUD. Orn. Biog. III. 1835, 1; V. 1839, 607, pl. 201; Synop. 1839, 270 ; B. Am. VI. 1843, 178, pl. 376.

Bernicla canadensis, BOIE, Isis, 1826, 921. — BAIRD, B. N. Am. 1858, xlix. 764 ; Cat. N. Am. B. 1859, no. 567. — RIDGW. Nom. N. Am. B. 1881, no. 594. — COUES, Check List, 2d ed. 1882, no. 702.

Branta canadensis, BANNIST. Pr. Ac. Nat. Sci. Philad. 1870, 131. — COUES, Key, 1872, 283 ; Check List, 1873, no. 485 ; Birds N. W. 1874, 554.

? *Bernicla Barnstoni,* ROSS, Canad. Nat. VII. Apr. 1862, 152.

β. Occidentalis. THE WESTERN GOOSE.

Bernicla occidentalis, BAIRD, B. N. Am. 1858, 766 (in text); Cat. N. Am. B. 1859, no. 567 *a.*

Bernicla canadensis, var. *occidentalis,* DALL. & BANNIST. Tr. Chicago Acad. I. 1869, 295.

Bernicla canadensis occidentalis, RIDGW. Pr. U. S. Nat. Mus. Vol. 3, 1880, 203 ; Nom. N. Am. B. 1881, no. 594 *c.*

γ. Hutchinsi. HUTCHINS'S GOOSE.

Anas bernicla, var. *b.* RICH. App. Parry's Vog. 368.

Anser Hutchinsi, SW. & RICH. F. B. A. II. 1831, 470. — NUTT. Man. II. 1834, 362. — Orn. Biog. III. 1835, 226, pl. 277 ; Synop. 1839, 271 ; B. Am. VI. 1843, 198, pl. 377.

Bernicla Hutchinsi, WOODH. Sitgr. Exp. 1853, 102. — BAIRD, B. N. Am. 1858, pp. xlix. 766 ; Cat. N. Am. B. 1859, no. 569.

Branta Hutchinsi, BANNIST. Pr. Ac. Nat. Sci. Philad. 1870, 131.

Branta canadensis, var. *Hutchinsi,* COUES, Key, 1872, 284.

Branta canadensis, c. *Hutchinsi,* COUES, B. N. W. 1874, 554.

Bernicla canadensis Hutchinsi, RIDGW. Pr. U. S. Nat. Mus. Vol. 3, 1880, 203 ; Nom. N. Am. B. 1881, no. 594 *a.* — COUES, Check List, 2d ed. 1882, no. 704.

δ. Leucopareia. THE WHITE-CHEEKED GOOSE.

Anser canadensis, PALL. Zoog. R.-A. II. 1826, 230 (nec LINN.).
Anser leucopareius, BRANDT, Bull. Sc. Ac. St. Petersb. I. 1836, 37.
Bernicla leucopareia, CASS. Illustr. B. Cal. Tex. etc. 1853, 272, pl. 45. — BAIRD, B. N. Am. 1858, xlix. 765; Cat. N. Am. B. 1859, no. 568.
Branta canadensis, var. *leucopareia*, COUES, Key, 1872, 284; Check List, 1873, no. 485 *a*.
Branta canadensis, b. *leucopareia*, COUES, B. N. W. 1874, 554.
Bernicla canadensis leucoparia, RIDGW. Pr. U. S. Nat. Mus. Vol. 3, 1880, 203; Nom. N. Am. B. 1882, no. 594 *b*. — COUES, Check List. 2d ed. 1882, no. 703 (part).

HAB. Of *canadensis* proper, temperate North America in general, breeding in the United States and British Provinces; casual in Europe; *occidentalis*, the northwest coast (California to Sitka); *Hutchinsi*, breeding in the Arctic districts, migrating south, chiefly through the Mississippi Valley and westward; *leucopareia*, Pacific coast chiefly, breeding along the coast of Alaska, but frequently straying inland during migrations.

SP. CHAR. *Adult:* Head and neck deep black, the former with a white patch covering the throat and extending up over the cheeks to behind the eyes, growing gradually narrower above, the upper outline usually more or less truncated, this white patch, however, sometimes interrupted on the throat by a narrow black stripe or isthmus. Very rarely, a broad white band, more or less distinctly indicated, crosses the forehead between the eyes. Black of neck frequently bordered below by a white collar, more or less distinct. Upper surface grayish brown, varying from almost cinereous to umber, each feather bordered terminally by a paler shade; lower parts with the exposed surface of about the same shade as the tips of the feathers of the upper parts, the concealed portion of the feathers of the shade of the prevailing color above — this much exposed along the sides and on the flanks. Primaries and their coverts plain dusky, the former growing nearly black terminally. Anal region, crissum, and lower tail-coverts immaculate pure white. Tail plain deep black; rump plain blackish slate. Bill and feet deep black. *Young:* Similar to the adult, but the colors duller, the markings less sharply defined; black of the neck passing gradually below into the grayish of the jugulum; white cheek patches usually finely speckled with dusky; light-colored tips to the contour-feathers broader. *Downy young:* Above, including an occipital patch, golden olive-green; beneath, pale-greenish ochre, the head rather deeper.

Total length, about 20 to upwards of 40 inches; wing, 13.60–21.00; culmen, .95–2.70; depth of maxilla at base, .60–1.20; width, .52–1.20; tarsus, 2.10–3.70; middle toe, 1.80–3.40. Tail-feathers, 13 to 20.

If, as seems to be the case, all the North American Wild Geese similar to *Bernicla canadensis* in color are of one species, there is probably no feral bird and few domesticated kinds, which vary to such great extremes of size. A series of upwards of fifty specimens, carefully measured at the same time, gives the above results, the variation amounting to the following percentums of the maximum measurements, only adult birds being measured: Wing, 35.24 per cent; culmen, 64.81 per cent; tarsus, 43.25 per cent; middle toe, 47.06 per cent.

The only character which seems to approach constancy is the number of tail-feathers, the smaller specimens usually possessing 13 or 14 to 16, and the larger 18 to 20; but the number varies with the individual, some examples, referable to *Hutchinsi* on account of size, possessing 18 or more, and *vice versa*. After a very careful consideration of all the facts involved, we feel constrained to look upon all the North American Wild Geese resembling *B. canadensis* in coloration as of one species, no matter what their size may be, it being scarcely possible to define the line between even geographical races. The following, however, is an attempt at a subdivision of the species such as seems warranted by the material in hand; but it may be premised that examples not infrequently occur which are as properly referable to one as to the other: —

A. Tail-feathers usually 18 to 20; size usually large.

1. **Canadensis.** Lower parts much paler than the upper, the light brownish gray sometimes fading gradually into the white of the anal region; white cheek-patches usually confluent on the throat, and white collar round lower neck in the winter plumage very indistinct or obsolete on account of the light color of the jugulum. Wing, 15.60–21.00

inches; culmen, 1.55–2.70; depth of mandible at base, .80–1.20; width, .75–1.20; tarsus, 2.45–3.70; middle toe, 2.25–3.30. (Ten specimens measured.) *Hab.* United States generally, and British Provinces, breeding chiefly north of 40°.

2. **Occidentalis.** Whole plumage more brown than in *canadensis*, the lower parts only slightly paler than the upper, the deep brown of the abdomen contrasted abruptly with the white of the anal region; white cheek-patches frequently separated by a black throat-stripe, and white collar round lower neck usually very distinct in winter plumage. Wing, 16.25–18.00 inches; culmen, 1.40–1.65; depth of maxilla at base, .80–.95; width, .70–1.00; tarsus, 3.05–3.25; middle toe, 2.50–2.75. (Two specimens measured.) *Hab.* Northwest coast, south to California in winter; north to Sitka.

B. Tail-feathers usually 13 to 16; size usually small.

3. **Hutchinsi.** Exactly like *canadensis* in plumage, but averaging slightly darker; size smaller. Wing, 14.75–17.75 inches; culmen, 1.20–1.90; depth of maxilla at base, .70–1.00; width, .60–.85; tarsus, 2.25–3.20; middle toe, 2.05–2.80. (Seventeen specimens measured.) *Hab.* Breeding in the Arctic Regions, migrating south in winter, chiefly through the Western United States and Mississippi Valley.

4. **Leucopareia.** Exactly like *occidentalis* in colors, but averaging still darker, the size much smaller. Wing, 13.60–16.35 inches; culmen, .95–1.35; depth of maxilla at base, .60–.75; width, .52–.70; tarsus, 2.10–3.10; middle toe, 1.80–2.45. (Ten specimens measured.) *Hab.* Breeding in the Western Arctic Regions (coast of Alaska, etc.), migrating southward into Western United States, though occasionally straying eastward to the Mississippi Valley.

It is barely possible that the several forms defined above really represent as many distinct species, and the intermediate specimens which occur are the result of extensive hybridization; or there may be two species, a larger and smaller (*B. canadensis* and *B. Hutchinsi*), distinguished also by a difference in the number of rectrices, and each having a darker western representative race. Indeed we are inclined to regard the latter view with considerable favor. At present, however, we can do no more than to describe each form in detail, and present the history of each as known at the present time.[1]

A. canadensis.

a. **canadensis.** — THE LARGE CANADA GOOSE.

Adult (No. 10402, Salt Lake, Utah; Captain STANSBURY): Size very large, the bill lengthened and depressed, the lower parts pale gray in color, fading insensibly into the white of the anal region. White gular patch immaculate. Wing, 20.00 inches; culmen, 2.10; tarsus, 3.30; middle toe, 3.20. Tail-feathers, 17.

[1] Since the above was written many additional specimens of *B. leucopareia* have been received at the National Museum. These are so uniform in all their characters as to leave no doubt in my mind that the species is distinct from *B. canadensis.* The relationship of *B. Hutchinsi* is still uncertain, but the probability is that it represents a lighter-colored inland race of *leucopareia;* though, on the other hand, it may be a small northern form of *canadensis,* bearing the same relation to the latter that *Grus canadensis* does to *G. mexicana.* — R. R.

The specimen described above is an average representative of the typical form of *Bernicla canadensis*, known to hunters usually as the "Big Wild Goose." The distribution of this form is somewhat uncertain, but it apparently prevails in the region around Hudson's Bay, and the United States generally, breeding as far south at least as the parallel of 40°, but now rare, except during the migrations, east of the Mississippi Valley.

Two specimens in the collection (Nos. 20116, Fort Simpson, May, 1860; B. R. Ross — "*B. Barnstonii*" on original label — and 53691, Truckee Meadows, Nev., Nov. 5, 1867; R. RIDGWAY) have a well-defined band across the forehead, between the eyes, of speckled white and dusky. A specimen formerly in the collection, but destroyed by insects, somewhere from the high north, had this band unspotted white! No. 9954, Rio Rita Laguna, New Mexico, has the entire lower parts stained with reddish ochraceous, this being perhaps merely a discoloration from contact with ferruginous clay. Among the variations of this large race of the Canada Goose are perhaps to be ranged the *Bernicla leucolæma*, or White-frilled Goose of Murray, and the *B. Barnstoni*, or Barnston's Goose of Ross, descriptions of which are given farther on (see p. 460).

β. occidentalis. — LARGER WHITE-CHEEKED GOOSE.

Adult (No. 5994, Port Townsend, Washington Territory; Dr. SUCKLEY): Throat speckled with black medially, indicating an isthmus, not complete enough, however, to separate the white of the opposite cheeks; black of the neck bordered below and in front by a collar of pure white, abruptly defined against the dark grayish brown of the jugulum. Plumage generally, dark grayish umber, the paler terminal borders to the feathers very inconspicuous, the lower parts scarcely paler than the upper, and abruptly defined against the pure white of the crissum. Wing, 18.00 inches; culmen, 1.65; tarsus, 3.05; middle toe, 2.75. Tail-feathers, 18.

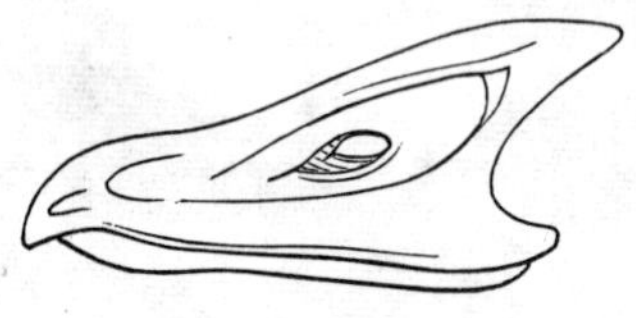

B. Hutchinsii.

No. 66615, Puget Sound, Dr. KENNERLY, differs in lacking the white collar; No. 46228, Sitka, May, 1866, F. BISCHOFF, is like the last, but preserves a trace of the white collar. No. 23238, San Francisco, Cal., April, 1861, F. GRUBER, is considerably smaller, measuring, wing, 16.25 inches; culmen, 1.40; tarsus, 3.25; and middle toe, 2.50. In coloration it is quite peculiar: the very broad and continuous white collar extends entirely around the neck, though it is somewhat interrupted behind; while below, it is bordered by a very dark-brown collar, which is nearly black at the edge of the white, but fading off gradually into the ash of the jugulum, which is considerably paler than in the foregoing examples. The feathers of the neck all appear to be white below the surface.

As in the *leucopareia*, the seasonal differences of plumage are well marked in this race. The white collar belongs only to fall and winter birds, in which the brown tints are darker and more of an umber cast. As spring advances, the white gradually disappears, and in midsummer is entirely obsolete, *this change taking place without moulting of the feathers.*

γ. Hutchinsi. — HUTCHINS'S GOOSE.

Adult (No. 49829, ♂, Nulato, Lower Yukon, Alaska, May 9, 1867; W. H. DALL): Exactly like typical *canadensis* in colors. Wing, 16.35 inches; culmen, 1.20; tarsus, 2.90; middle toe, 2.10. Tail feathers, 15.

In a large series of specimens, the following variations are noted: The ashy beneath varies from the pale tint of *canadensis* to the dark shades of *leucopareia* and *occidentalis*, but is usually about intermediate between the two extremes; the white collar round the neck, at the lower edge of the black, is seen only in autumnal or winter specimens. The white of the head is usually uninterrupted on the throat, even in very dark-plumaged examples, but occasionally separated into two patches by a black throat-stripe, as in *leucopareia* and *occidentalis*, the plumage otherwise being light colored.

δ. **leucopareia.** — LITTLE WHITE-CHEEKED GOOSE.

Adult (No. 62526, ♂ ad., St. Paul's Island, Alaska, May 14, 1872; H. W. ELLIOTT): Throat with a black "isthmus" .75 of an inch broad, separating widely the white cheek-patches. A distinct white collar between the black of the neck and dark brownish gray of the jugulum, this about .75 of an inch wide in front, and extending completely around, though much narrower, and somewhat interrupted, behind. Lower parts dark brownish gray, abruptly defined against the white of the crissum. Wing, 14.25 inches; culmen, 1.30; depth of maxilla at base, .75; width, .65; tarsus, 2.55; middle toe, 2.30. Tail feathers, 14.

Other specimens in the collection are chiefly in summer plumage, having paler lower parts and less conspicuous white collar; but nearly all have the two cheek-patches completely separated by a broad black isthmus on the throat.

With only two exceptions, the specimens are from the Pacific coast, chiefly the northern portion.

No. 9956, North Red River (September; R. KENNICOTT), is one of the smallest in the series, and is otherwise peculiar. It is apparently a young bird, as its plumage presents some features indicative of immaturity. The black of the neck fades gradually into the smoky gray of the jugu-

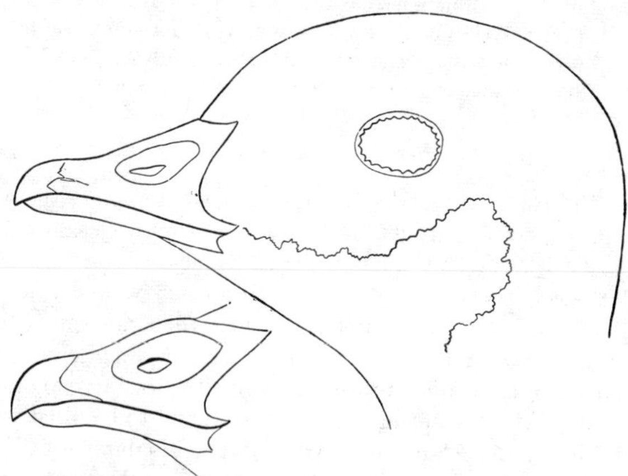

Washoe Lake, Nev. (adult). St. Michael's, Alaska. (♂ ad.)

lum, without being separated by the usual white collar; the white cheek-patches are thickly, though minutely, speckled with black; the feathers of the lower parts, and also the upper tail-coverts, have blackish shafts. It measures as follows: Wing, 13.70 inches; culmen, 1.25; tarsus, 2.60; middle toe, 2.10. The smallest examples we have seen are the following:—

No.	Locality.	Date.	Wing.	Culmen.	Depth of bill at base.	Width of bill at base.	Tarsus.	Middle toe.	Number of rectrices.
——,	Fort Klamath, Or.		14.20	.95	.60	.55	2.50	1.90	16
77164,	Stockton, Cal.	December	13.60	1.10	.60	.52	2.60	1.90	15
70066,	Andalusia, Ill.		14.25	1.25	.70	.65	2.10	1.80	16
73136,	St. Michael's, Alaska,	Sept. 13	14.15	1.05	.60	.55	2.60	1.90	15
72744,	Washoe Lake, Nev.	Nov. 12	14.25	1.12	.70	.55	2.40	1.95	16

There are others but slightly larger. Any of the above could stand, in a natural attitude, beneath the breast of some of the larger examples of *canadensis* or *occidentalis*; still, other specimens, having 13 to 16 rectrices, vary in size, so as to lead directly up to the smaller examples, possessing 18 to 20 rectrices, : being wholly impossible to separate specimens by size alone.

The accompanying figures, which are life-size, are intended to show extreme variations in the shape of the bill in this diminutive race.

There appear to be other variations of this species, which are hardly to be classed as geographical races, but which seem to owe their characteristics to hybridization with other species, or to an abnormal degree of individual variation. Among these may be classed the —

Bernicla leucolæma, Murray, White-Frilled Goose, Ed. New Phi. Jour. IX. April, 1859, 226.

Sp. Char. Similar to the common Canada Goose of the United States in markings, but larger. Chin from rami of lower mandible, cravat on sides and beneath the jaws, and extending along under side of neck nearly to end of black portion, white, becoming narrower and spotted with black ; under eyelid broadly white ; lower part of neck pale dirty lavender, upper part of breast paler ; lower part and belly almost white ; or breast and belly pale lavender, with a broad white band across breast ; legs brown ; web bright yellow. Length 40.00 inches ; upper mandible, above 2.50 ; wing, 19.25 ; tarsus, 3.00 ; first phalanx of middle toe, 1.50.

Differs from *B. canadensis* in larger size, and plumage paler throughout ; brown replacing black, etc. The white of head is more extended, reaching along nearly the whole throat and to lower jaw ; the interdigital spaces yellow, not black, etc.

Bernicla Barnstonii, Ross, Canad. Nat. VII. 1862, 152 ; Nat. Hist. Review, 1862, p. 28.

"This bird was shot at Fort Simpson (on the Mackenzie). It is of very large size, with the breast of a bright fawn-color. The delta of feathers running up into the lower mandible is white, instead of black, as in *B. canadensis*. The tail is of sixteen feathers. The Indians consider it a distinct species from the Canada Goose. It seldom flies in parties of more than five or six."

Bernicla Canadensis.

Our common Wild Goose has a very extended range throughout the whole of North America, occurring from the Gulf of Mexico to the Arctic Ocean, and from the Atlantic to the Pacific. Abundant upon nearly all the interior waters, it breeds in various parts of the country as far south as latitude 42° N., and even farther south than this parallel in favorable localities, and throughout all the regions north.

Richardson found it abundant, in pairs, throughout the Fur Countries up to a high parallel of latitude. It associates in flocks only on its first arrival, and feeds on all kinds of berries. Early in the spring its crops are found to be filled with the farinaceous astringent fruit of the *Elæagnus argentea*. The inhabitants of the wooded and swampy districts depend principally upon this Goose for subsistence during the summer. It makes its first appearance in flocks of twenty or thirty, and is readily decoyed within gunshot by the hunters, who imitate its call. About three weeks after its first appearance it disperses in pairs throughout the country to breed, retiring at the same time from the shores of Hudson's Bay. It was found nesting as far north as Fort Anderson and the Lower Anderson River ; but the statement of Dr. Richardson, that it is not known to breed on the Arctic coast, remains unchallenged.

In July, after the young birds are hatched, the parents moult, and vast numbers are killed in the rivers and small lakes before they are able to fly. When chased by a canoe and obliged to dive frequently, this bird soon becomes fatigued, and makes for the shore to hide, thus falling an easy prey to its pursuers. In the autumn it assembles in flocks on the shores of Hudson's Bay for a month previous to its departure for the south. In its migrations it annually resorts to certain resting-places, some of which are frequented both in the spring and autumn, and others only in the spring. While on the Saskatchewan it generally builds its nest on the ground; some pairs were found breeding in trees, depositing their eggs in the deserted nests of Ravens and Fish-hawks. Its call is imitated by a prolonged nasal pronunciation of the syllable *wook* frequently repeated.

Mr. George Barnston states that this species — the largest of any of the Geese visiting Hudson's Bay — is almost always the earliest in its arrival. At first only a single straggler appears; then two or three together, soon to be followed by a continuous flock of fresh immigrants. These are the advance-guard of the serried legions of other Waterfowl, and they soon spread themselves over the whole breadth of the continent. In its disposition this species has less of wildness than the Snow Goose. It hatches in quiet corners, where there is still water, and grass and rushes to afford it sustenance. It is at home in the wooded country as well as in the extensive marshes of the sea-coast, and on the Barrens of the Eskimo lands. During the winter it takes refuge in the open water of more southern regions, although Mr. Barnston saw a small flock of this species in the open current of water above Lachine, near Montreal, in the month of January or February. Before Oregon was settled, the Post at Fort Vancouver was supplied with these Geese in immense numbers.

Captain Blakiston gives as the range of this species in the territory of the Hudson's Bay Company, from the Bay to the Rocky Mountains, as far north as the Arctic Ocean. He found that it was the earliest of the Geese, appearing at Fort Carlton as early as March 28, and remaining there as late as November 3. It is not restricted in its breeding-grounds to the Far North, as he discovered a nest with four eggs between the north and south branches of the Saskatchewan on the 4th of May. It also occurs west of the Rocky Mountains, and Mr. R. Browne gives it as one of the common birds of Vancouver Island.

Hearne, in the "Narrative of his Journey to the Northern Ocean" (p. 437), designates this species as the common Gray Goose, while he gives the name of Canada Goose to the *Bernicla Hutchinsi*. He also states that this bird precedes every other in the Hudson's Bay region, and that in some early springs it is seen on Churchill River as soon as the latter end of April, although more commonly arriving between the 11th and the 16th of May. In one year it did not make its appearance until the 26th of May. At their first arrival these birds generally come in pairs, and are readily decoyed by cries imitating their notes, so that they are easily shot. They breed in great numbers in the plains and marshes near Churchill River; and in some years the young ones are taken in considerable numbers, and are easily tamed; they will, however, never learn to eat corn unless some of the old ones are taken with them.

Mr. Hearne adds that on the 9th of August, 1781, when residing at Fort Prince of Wales, he sent a party of Indians in canoes up Churchill River to procure some of these Geese. In the afternoon they were seen coming down the river driving a large flock before them, the young ones not more than half grown, and the old ones so far advanced in moulting as to be incapable of flying. The whole flock, to the number of forty-one, was driven within the stockade which incloses the fort, where they were fattened for winter use. Wild Geese fattened in this way are preferable, in his opinion, to any others. When full grown, and in good condition, this bird often weighs twelve pounds.

According to Dr. Cooper this is not a very common Goose in California, though some are sold in the market every winter. He met with a few in January near Fort Mojave, but saw none at San Diego. By its large size and sonorous *honk-honk*, uttered as it flies, this bird may readily be distinguished from other species, even at a considerable distance. It is much more southern in its range than the other

Geese, some remaining to breed about Klamath Lake, and others in the Cascade Range, if not farther south.

Mr. Ridgway mentions it as breeding in the interior, about all the large lakes of the Great Basin. Its young were caught in May at Pyramid Lake, and the old birds were shot there. It is resident in the Truckee meadows, specimens having been procured there in November; but it was not so abundant there at that time as *B. Hutchinsi* was. Mr. J. A. Allen found it already present in great numbers in the valley of Great Salt Lake.

Dr. Cooper states that he noticed a large number of this species breeding along the Missouri, where every day he met with broods, from Fort Leavenworth up to Fort Benton. They were said to lay in nests, on trees, probably the deserted nests of some other large bird. He also saw two at Spokane River, in Washington Territory, Septemher 25, which had passed the summer there.

Many interesting and striking evidences of the sagacity of this bird are narrated, having reference to the manner in which its migrations are managed, and its safety provided for on its feeding-grounds.

In the migrations of these Geese, families assemble in flocks, and many of them unite in forming a vast column, each band having its chosen leader. They generally continue flying during the night, but occasionally alight and await the day. Before doing so the pioneers survey the ground below, and select a spot favorable for food and safety. Sentinels are appointed from among the Ganders to sound the alarm, should an enemy appear. Mr. Giraud states that he has seen these Geese adopt the same precautions when in large flocks in the daytime. The sentinels separate from the main body, move about with heads erect, ready to detect the first indications of intruders. After an interval these outposts would return to the main body, their places being immediately supplied by others.

The hoarse *honk* of the Gander is a cry so familiar to the inhabitants, that it is impossible for the birds to arrive without their visits becoming known. The practised bay-hunter watches their flight, discovers their favorite sanding-place, and, on gaining the desired point, puts out his decoys, sinks a box in the sand, and there conceals himself; and as the Geese approach he carefully prepares for their reception. When wounded this bird is able to sink itself in the water, leaving only its bill above the surface, and can remain in that situation for a considerable time. During storms it flies low; and also when the weather is very foggy it becomes confused, and alights on the ground. Wild Geese remain on Long Island in the fall until the bays are frozen, and return on the disappearance of the ice in the spring; but at that season their stay is short. Early in April they collect in large flocks, and move off almost simultaneously. Their food consists of sedge roots, marine plants, berries, and herbage of various kinds. In the winter they are common on the lakes in the neighborhood of the Lower Mississippi. There — as Mr. Giraud was informed — a few stragglers are wont to remain all summer. The Wild Geese are said to arrive in the waters of Chesapeake Bay about the last of October, when they immediately distribute themselves over the entire bay, rarely leaving its shores for the smaller streams, although often retiring to the smaller inlets to roost, or to feed, at night.

According to Mr. Lewis this bird sometimes makes its first appearance in the Delaware and in the Chesapeake in October, this early arrival being considered a certain prognostic of a long and hard winter. On return of the Wild Goose to the north it passes through the Eastern States in April — earlier or later, according to the weather. When in the southern waters it feeds on the leaves, blades, and seeds of maritime plants, and the roots of sedges.

Its flight is heavy and laborious, the flock forming a triangle, and being always led by an old gander. When wounded the Wild Goose can swim and dive with great facility, going long distances under the water. When taken alive it is easily domesticated, and mixes readily with the common tame Goose. Yet even after it has become quite domesticated, and even after it has reared a brood or two, it will exhibit symptoms of uneasiness as the periods of migration approach, and will sometimes fly off and join the wild ones passing within hearing overhead. On the other hand, whole flocks of Wild Geese have been known to be decoyed by domesticated ones, and induced to alight among them.

Mr. Audubon found this Goose on the Magdalen Islands, sitting on its eggs, early in June, and in Labrador nesting in every suitable marshy plain. According to his observations, all the birds of this species unite together before departing on their spring migrations. He has noted preparatory symptoms of meeting as early as January. In his opinion these Geese are far more abundant, during the winter, on the interior waters than they are near the sea-coast. He observed them in immense flocks in Kentucky, and was informed that before the settlement of the country the Wild Goose bred abundantly in all the temperate parts of North America. As late as 1819 Mr. Audubon met with the nest, eggs, and young of this species near Henderson, on the Ohio. It usually builds its nest on the ground, in some retired place not far from the water, preferably among the rankest grass. The nest is carefully formed of dry plants of various kinds, and is of large size, flat, and raised to the height of several inches. In one instance Audubon found a nest elevated above the ground on the high stump of a large tree in the centre of a pond. The greatest number of eggs found in the nest of this bird when in a wild state is nine; but six is the more common number. The domesticated Goose, however, lays as many as eleven. The eggs average 3.50 inches in length by 2.50 in breadth, and are thick-shelled, smooth, and of a dull yellowish-green color. The period of incubation is twenty-eight days, and there is but one brood in a season. The young follow their parents to the water within a day or two after they are hatched, and remain with them until the following spring, being the objects of their devoted care.

Mr. Audubon gives an interesting account of a pair of this species which he captured at the mouth of Green River, Kentucky. Their young were taken with them, and these he succeeded in raising by feeding them with locusts. They mated and bred in confinement, but the old ones were only partially domesticated, and would not mate. These birds were all especially inimical to dogs, but evinced a still greater dislike of an old Swan and an old Turkey-Cock. They proved very useful in clearing the garden of slugs and snails.

The flight of this species is firm, rapid, and protracted, the bird moving with great steadiness and regularity. Before rising it usually runs a few feet with outspread wings, but when surprised can rise with a sudden spring. In its migrations it is liable to be thrown into confusion by passing into a fog-bank, or over a city or a place where there is much shipping. Severe snow-storms also disturb it; so much so, that individuals have been known to dash themselves against the walls of lighthouses and other buildings in the daytime. In the spring migrations flocks not infrequently alight in fields of young grain, and commit great havoc in the course of a single night. Both keenness of sight and quickness of hearing are remarkable in this bird, and it is always vigilant and suspicious; so that it is with great difficulty taken by surprise.

Mr. MacFarlane found this species breeding in the vicinity of Fort Anderson, the nests being placed near small inland lakes; they appeared as early as May 17. In one instance five eggs of this species were found in a deserted Hawk's nest warmly lined with down, which had apparently been plucked by the female from her own body. In other instances nests were found by him in similar positions. When built on the ground the nests appear to have been variously composed — in one instance of decayed leaves, down, and hay; in another of dry willow sticks and moss, lined with feathers and down. Eggs found after the middle of June contained embryos, which were more or less developed. In one instance a nest was composed of a quantity of turf and decayed vegetable matter lined with down, feathers, and moss.

Mr. Dall found this bird not uncommon at Fort Yukon, where its eggs were also obtained, and it was also taken at Sitka by Bischoff.

It was found breeding by Mr. Kennicott on Lake Winnipeg in June, at Fort Resolution as early as April 5, and at Fort Yukon, May 29; by Mr. L. Clarke at Fort Rae in May, at Fort Simpson by Mr. B. R. Ross, on the Anderson River by Mr. MacFarlane, among the mountains west of the Lower Mackenzie by Mr. R. M'Donald, at Port Elder by Mr. Minot, and at Sitka by Bischoff.

Dr. Berlandier, in his manuscript notes, speaks of it as inhabiting during the winter the great plains of Tamaulipas, Mexico. He has seen it in flocks of several hundreds in the grassy marshes between San Fernando and Matamoras, in the vicinity of Soto Le Nanine, etc. It is commonly called *Patotriguero.* He also met with it in December on the central plateau between the Hacienda of Encarnacion and Aguas Nuevas, near Saltillo.

Its eggs are of a uniform bright ivory white, of an oval shape; but vary both in size and shape. Specimens in the Smithsonian Collection exhibit the following measurements: (No. 9455, Anderson River, MacFarlane) 3.25 by 2.15, and 3.10 by 2.25 inches; (No. 1994) 3.45 by 2.40, and 3.10 by 2.30 inches; (Smithsonian Institution, No. 9434½) Fort Yukon, 3.45 by 2.10.

The form called *Bernicla occidentalis* is apparently the Pacific coast representative of the common Canada Goose. Examples of it were taken at Sitka by Mr. Bischoff, but no mention was made of any specific variations in habit. Since then it is said to have been found in great abundance by Mr. Grayson in Western Mexico, where, as he states, he saw it in large flocks while on the road to Durango, between the Sierra Madre Mountains and that city. This was in the months of February and March. He did not, however, see or hear of any west of the Cordilleras.

Bernicla Hutchinsi.

Although the Hutchins's Goose was first distinctively named by Dr. Richardson in the "Fauna Boreali-Americana," its existence as a well-marked race or species, distinct from the *canadensis,* was well known to Mr. Hearne nearly a century ago. Under the name of the Canada Goose, he refers to it as quite distinct from our *canadensis,* which he calls the common Gray Goose. At the time he wrote it was well known to the Indians, as well as to the English, in Hudson's Bay as the *Pisk-a-fisl.* While it does not differ in plumage from the common Wild Goose, it is much inferior in size, the bill is much smaller in proportion to the size of the body, and the flesh, which is much whiter, is more highly esteemed as food. It is by no means so abundant at Hudson's Bay as the common species; and as a general thing it goes much farther north to breed. A few pairs were, however, known to have bred near Churchill River. It was seldom that either this or the true Canada Goose was known to lay more than four eggs, all of which, if the nests were not robbed, the birds usually succeeded in hatching.

This Goose breeds on the shores of the Arctic Sea; but in its migrations keeps near the sea-coast, and is seldom seen in the interior.

Although closely resembling the Canada Goose in most respects, except its smaller size, its habits are said to be quite different from those of that bird. While the *canadensis* frequents the fresh-water lakes and rivers of the interior, and feeds chiefly on herbage, the *Hutchinsi* is always found on the sea-coast, feeding on the marine plants and the mollusca which adhere to them — whence its flesh derives a strong fishy taste. In form, size, and general colors of the plumage it more nearly resembles the Brant than the Canada Goose.

According to Mr. Barnston, Hutchins's Goose arrives at Hudson's Bay later in the season than *B. canadensis*, and at about the same time as the Snow Goose. It is shot in considerable quantities at Albany and elsewhere along the coast of James Bay. This bird does not incubate in scattered or detached parties throughout the wooded country, but proceeds in large and united flocks to the extreme north, reaching Hudson's Bay about the beginning of May, and at once beginning to feed in the salt-marshes among the soft white-rooted grasses, remaining a fortnight or three weeks, in company with the "Waveys," or Snow Geese. By this time the Geese are in good plight, and they then take their departure, not reappearing until they return with their young broods in the month of September. They are killed in less numbers on their passage to Hudson's Bay than the *canadensis*, which may be accounted for by their habits; but when once the birds have settled upon their feeding-grounds, the slaughter of them is immense.

Captain James Clark Ross, as quoted by Audubon, states that this species arrives in flocks, in the neighborhood of Felix Harbor, about the middle of June, and soon disperses in pairs to its breeding-places. At Igloolik, the only place where he had previously met with them, their nests were found in the marshes near the sea. But on this occasion several pairs constructed their nests on a ledge of rocks near the foot of a high precipice; immediately above them the Dovekies, Loons, and several species of Gulls, and near its summit the Gyrfalcon and Raven, had also built their nests. From three to four eggs were found in each nest, of a pure white color and of an oval form, measuring 3.10 inches in length by 2.10 inches in breadth. Its flesh Mr. Ross pronounces of a most exquisite flavor.

In Texas, both on the coast and inland, Mr. Dresser found these birds quite common. During the winter he shot several on Mitchell's Pond. The shore hunters there are well aware of the difference between this species and the *canadensis*, calling the latter the "Bay Goose," and the former the "Prairie Goose." Dr. Merrill also mentions this form as being more common than the *canadensis*.

Dr. Cooper states that this bird is altogether the most common of the Brant family of Geese along the Pacific coast, where it arrives about the first of October, and frequents both the inland plains and the salt-marshes that border the coast. He thinks it goes as far south as San Diego, though he met with none there. It usually feeds on the plains early in the morning, and toward noon returns to the water, where it rests during the middle of the day and night. Large numbers are shot, both while feeding and resting, but the mode of pursuit varies according to circumstances. The brush shed and the trained ox are used on the plains; but in the water a boat is required, with which the Geese may be approached very closely under cover of the tall weeds. With a large gun twenty or thirty are often killed in two shots, one fired while the birds are sitting, the other as they rise. After feeding again in the afternoon, the greater part of those in the interior are said to assemble at favorite roosts in the wide creeks and sloughs, though many are seen in scattered flocks about the marshes. Dr. Cooper is confident he saw this species in the San Joaquin Valley as early as September 10, and on the 15th he met with a large flock there. Mr. Ridgway saw many of this species in November on the Truckee meadows, where it is a fall and winter visitant.

This species is of irregular occurrence on the Atlantic coast. At some seasons it has been found not uncommon in the vicinity of Boston; and numbers have been brought to market from the Cape. On the eastern extremity of Long Island, according to Dr. Giraud, it is also not uncommon. It is well known to hunters as the "Mud Goose" at Montauk Point, where it is frequently observed in company with the *canadensis*. The sportsmen of the south side of Long Island are not acquainted with it, although there is no reason to doubt that it is frequently procured there. At some seasons it has been known to be quite abundant in the Chesapeake Bay.

Mr. Dall found this bird to be the most common of all the Geese, both in the Alaskan islands and all along the Yukon River as high up as Nulato. It was breeding on St. Michael's and Pastolik, as well as on the river. In the latter place it takes the place of the *leucopareia*, which is comparatively rare there. The nests were depressions in the sand-beaches, similar to those of the *A. Gambeli*. It arrives in company with the latter species, and leaves about the end of September. The number of its eggs varies from six to eight.

Mr. MacFarlane found it nesting in great numbers on the Lower Anderson, and on the shores and islands of the Arctic Sea. Some nests were on low, small islets in fresh-water lakes; these were constructed of a quantity of down placed in a depression in the ground. The number of eggs was six. The old birds were generally quite tame. Other nests were found on islands in the Anderson River, and also in the Arctic Sea. In all instances there was more or less down and feathers, and in some cases these were mingled with dry grasses or leaves. In one instance four eggs of this species were found in the deserted nest of a Crow or Hawk, built on the fork of a pine-tree, and at the height of nine feet. The parent bird was shot while on her eggs. The ground in the vicinity was at that time covered with snow and water, and this was probably the reason the bird nested in so unusual a place.

Mr. Adams notes the arrival of these birds on the shores of Norton Sound on the 8th of May; and a considerable number remained to breed in the marshes. They came in small flocks as well as by twos and threes, and were all in good condition, but varying greatly in their weight — one being less than three pounds in weight, while others were nearly six. They were not numerous in the immediate vicinity of Michalaski, the greater number remaining in the marshes thirty miles south.

Specimens of this Goose were secured by Mr. Kennicott at Fort Resolution and Fort Yukon, in May, 1860; by Mr. B. R. Ross at Big Island and Fort Simpson; by Mr. MacFarlane on the Anderson, on islands in the Arctic Sea east of that river, also in Franklin Bay and at other points in that region.

The eggs of Hutchins's Goose are of a dull ivory-white color, and oval in shape. Two from Fort Yukon (Smithsonian Institution, No. 14583) measure, one 3.00 inches in length by 2.00 in breadth, the other 2.95 inches in length by 2.05 in breadth.

Bernicla leucopareia.

The form known as *Bernicla leucopareia* was first described by Brandt, in 1836, and afterward by Professor Baird from a specimen obtained in Puget Sound by Dr. Suckley, in January. Mr. R. Browne claims to have obtained this bird on Vancouver Island, and mentions it as common there. Mr. Kennicott procured specimens of this form on the Yukon, but noted nothing specifically distinct as to its habits. Mr. Bannister speaks of it as common in the early spring at St. Michael's; and Mr. Dall cites it as abundant on the sea-coast, near the mouth of the River Yukon, where it breeds. It was rare at Nulato, or farther inland, on the Yukon. Its eggs were taken by him at Pastolik.

According to the observations of Mr. Elliott, it is of occasional occurrence on the Prybilof Islands, where from time to time it straggles in small squads of from ten to thirty, evidently driven by the high winds from their customary line of emigration along the mainland. Although not breeding there, this bird spends occasionally weeks at a time on the lakelets and uplands before taking flight.

Several specimens were taken on the Yukon River by Mr. Kennicott, in May, 1861; at Fort Yukon by Mr. S. Jones; on St. Michael's Island by Mr. Bannister; and at Fort Kenai by Mr. Bischoff.

Mr. L. Belding (*in epist.*) considers the *B. leucopareia* "a strongly-marked species," and says that it is abundant in winter in California, where it is known to hunters as the "Cackler," or "Cackling Goose," on account of its peculiar cry. His first fall record of its occurrence at Stockton is October 12, and the latest spring record, April 25.

Bernicla brenta.

THE BRANT GOOSE.

Anas bernicla, LINN. S. N. I. 1766, 198. — WILS. Am. Orn. VIII. 1814, pl. 72, fig. 1.
Branta bernicla, BANNIST. Pr. Ac. Nat. Sci. Philad. 1870, 131 (nec SCOPOLI). — COUES, Key, 1872, 284; Check List, 1873, no. 484; B. N. W. 1874, 556.
Anser bernicla, ILLIG. Prodr. 1811, 277. — SW. & RICH. F. B. A. II. 1831, 469. — NUTT. Man. II. 1834, 359. — AUD. Orn. Biog. V. 1839, 24, 610, pl. 391; Synop. 1839, 272; B. Am. VI. 1843, 203, pl. 379.
Anser brenta, PALL. Zoog. R.-A. II. 1826, 223.
Bernicla brenta, STEPHENS, Gen. Zool. XII. pt. ii. 1824, 46. — BAIRD, B. N. Am. 1858, 767; Cat. N. Am. B. 1859, no. 570. — RIDGW. Nom. N. Am. B. 1881, no. 595. — COUES, Check List, 2d ed. 1882, no. 700.
Anser torquata, FRISCH, Vög. Deutschl. II. pl. 156.
Bernicla melanopsis, MACGILL. Man. Orn. II. 1842, 151.

HAB. Eastern North America in general, but chiefly the Atlantic coast; rare in the interior, or away from salt water; Palæarctic Region.

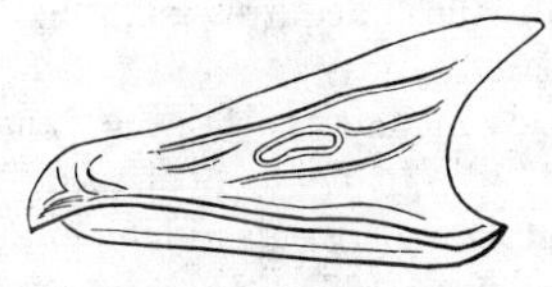

SP. CHAR. *Adult* (No. 63616, New York market, J. H. BATTY): Head, neck, and jugulum continuous black, the anterior portion of the head having a brownish cast; posterior outline of the black on the jugulum very regular and sharply-defined against the brownish gray of the breast. Middle of the neck with a transverse crescentic patch of white on each side, formed of white tips and sub-tips of the feathers, the black showing through in places so as to form oblique lines. Above, smoky-plumbeous, the feathers distinctly bordered terminally with a much paler and more brownish shade. Wings like the back, but with a somewhat plumbeous cast, the paler margins nearly obsolete. Secondaries blackish brown; primaries brownish black. Tail uniform black, but almost concealed by the snow-white lengthened coverts, the upper of which, however, are invaded by a medial stripe of blackish plumbeous-brown from the rump. Breast, abdomen, sides, and flanks much like the upper parts, but the light tips to the feathers whiter, broader, and more conspicuous; anal region and crissum immaculate snow-white. Wing, 12.30 inches; culmen, 1.20; tarsus, 2.05; middle toe, 1.70. *Young* (No. 12786, Washington, D. C., December, 1858; C. DREXLER): Similar to the adult, but the wing-coverts and secondaries broadly tipped with pure white, forming very conspicuous bars. Lower parts paler and more uniform; white on middle of the neck reduced to small specks.

Two adult specimens from Europe differ from any in a series of four American skins (adults), in larger size and slightly paler colors; the differences are so slight, however, that they probably would not prove constant, if more examples were compared. Indeed, a third European specimen, labelled (by SCHLÜTER) "hoher Norden," is nearly as dark everywhere as *B. nigricans*, and would be instantly referred to that species, were it not for the white neck-patches, which are exactly as in typical *brenta* — that is, widely separated in front, as well as behind. It may be a hybrid between the two.

The Common Brant Goose has an almost cosmopolitan distribution. In the summer it retires to very high northern latitudes to breed, and in the autumn and winter wanders over large portions of both the Old and the New World. It is found in all the high Arctic regions of Asia and Europe, and in North America east of the Rocky Mountains. In the western portions of America it is replaced by *B. nigricans*, a closely allied form. It is almost unknown in the interior. A single example taken on Lake Michigan, near Racine, by Dr. Hoy, is the only exception, so far as I know.

Hearne was convinced that this bird must breed in the remote north, as it seldom appeared at Churchill River until September. Its route in the spring was unknown, nor did any of the Hudson's Bay Indians know of its breeding-place. It always came from the north in its visits to Churchill River, flew near the margin of the coast, and was never seen in the interior. Its flesh, although delicate to the eye, was not much esteemed as food. In some years birds of this species passed the mouth of Churchill River in incredible numbers. In their movements south they usually availed themselves of a strong northerly or northwesterly wind; and this made their flight so swift, that once, when Mr. Hearne killed four or five at a single shot, they all fell from twenty to fifty yards beyond the place where they were hit. When in large flocks they are known to fly, in the manner of the Snow Goose, in the form of a wedge, and to make a great noise. Their flight is irregular, sometimes being forty or fifty yards above the water, and yet, an instant later, they may be seen skimming close to its surface, then again they will rise to a considerable height; so that by some they are said to "fly in festoons."

According to Richardson, this species breeds on the shores and among the islands of the Arctic Sea, and keeps near the sea-coast in its migrations. It is rarely, if ever, seen in the interior. As no mention is made among the records of the Smithsonian Institution of this Goose being known to breed on the coast of the Arctic Sea, Richardson may have been mistaken in this supposition. He mentions its feeding on mollusca, the *Ulva lactuca*, and other marine plants — chiefly upon the latter, from which its flesh acquires a strong flavor. It is said to leave its breeding-quarters in September.

Dr. Bessels includes this species among the birds procured on the "Polaris" Expedition ("Bulletin de la Société de Géographie," March, 1875); and Mr. Feilden ("Ibis," October, 1877) also includes it among the birds procured in the British Arctic Expedition of 1875–1876, and supplies the following interesting note: "During the first week of June, parties of these birds arrived in the vicinity of our winter-quarters (lat. 82° 27′ N.); for some days they continued flying up and down the coast-line, evidently looking out for places bare of snow to feed on. They were very wary, and kept well out of gunshot range. On the 21st of June I found the first nest with eggs in lat. 82° 33′ N.; subsequently many were found. When the young are hatched the parent birds and broods congregate on the lakes, or in open water-spaces near the shore, in large flocks; by the end of July the old birds were moulting, and unable to fly, so that they were easily secured. . . . The flesh of this bird is most excellent. The gander remains in the vicinity of the nest while the goose is sitting, and accompanies the young brood. In one instance, where I killed a female as she left her nest, the gander came hissing at me."

Dr. Walker met with this Goose on the coast of Greenland, near Godthaab, and afterward, in the mouth of Bellot's Strait, saw it moving northward in May. Some of these birds constructed nests on the cliffs which form the sides of the Strait.

According to Mr. Barnston, this Goose is the *Callewapimaw* of the Cree Indians; and is still but little cared for at Hudson's Bay. He speaks of it as keeping out to sea, on the shoals, near low-water mark. It arrives the latest of all the birds of its family.

According to Professor Reinhardt, it is one of the common birds of Greenland, where, on the entire coast occupied by the Danish settlements, it appears only on its passage to or from its breeding-places, which must be in very high latitude — at the least north of the seventy-third parallel.

Professor Alfred Newton states ("Ibis," 1865) that on Parry's Expedition one of its nests, containing two eggs, was obtained at Ross Inlet, latitude 80° 48′ N., on the 16th of June, which was at that time probably the most northern land ever visited by man. It was then also seen in large flocks about Walden and Little Table Islands. Dr. Malmgren found it breeding on the Depot Holme, Spitzbergen, and also on the shore of the mainland and in Treurenberg Bay, showing that Professor Torell was in error in stating that it only breeds on islets.

Sir James Ross states that the Brant Goose did not remain near Felix Harbor to breed, but went still farther north; and that during the summer months it was only seen in the highest northern latitudes that were visited. It was found breeding on Parry's Islands, in latitude 74° and 75°. Captain Scoresby reported that it was not common at Spitzbergen; but Messrs. Evans and Sturge, in their visit to that group of islands, found it breeding in immense numbers, and reported the ground covered with its nests. These were constructed on the beach, and were perfect masses of down and feathers, in which three or four eggs were buried. This was on the South Cape Islands.

Mr. G. Gillett found this species quite common in Matthew's Strait, Nova Zembla; Von Heuglin also saw it in large flocks at the same place; and Von Baer mentions its occurrence on Nova Zembla, and adds that it is not considered by the Russians to be a Goose. It collects in much greater numbers upon the Island of Kolgujew, where expeditions are sent to kill and salt these birds. A merchant of Archangel informed Von Baer that on one occasion fifteen thousand Geese were killed there in two hunts. Middendorff enumerates it as one of the birds of Arctic Siberia, occurring only in the extreme north.

Mr. Boardman informs me that this bird is common in the fall about Macey's Bay, in the Bay of Fundy. It occurs in varying numbers on the New England coast, both in the spring and fall, and is especially abundant on Cape Cod in the spring, or from March to May.

Mr. W. Hapgood, in a very full account of the habits of this species ("Forest and Stream," Sept. 2, 1875), states that in ordinary seasons Brant begin to be common at Cape Cod early in March, and continue coming and going until the end of April. At times they are present on the feeding-grounds in immense numbers. They never migrate against a northeast wind, but await a breeze from the southwest. Their course is first east-northeast, but afterward so deflected as to bring them into the Bay of Fundy, up which they pass, rising over the narrow neck of land to Northumberland Straits, where they find shoal-water and good feeding-grounds, and where they remain until the end of May. Leaving the Gulf of St. Lawrence, their course is said to be westward of Anticosti, and in a northwesterly direction, toward the Arctic Ocean. Their exact route is partly conjectured. They are known to arrive in the vicinity of Melville Island in immense numbers, and to pass along Wellington Channel to more northern regions. That they also reach Smith's Sound, and breed in large numbers at the junction of its waters with the Arctic Sea, has recently been ascertained by Mr. Feilden's observations.

Mr. Hapgood mentions as a noteworthy peculiarity of the Brant, when in confinement, that it pecks at and eats decayed wood, and suggests that this seems to indicate that driftwood may be no inconsiderable portion of its food in Arctic regions, which in some regions is quite abundant. In their southern migrations the Brant are said to make no stop at Cape Cod, unless compelled by stress of weather, but spend their winter months along shore from Barnegat to Florida. Dr. Kane regarded the presence of this bird in large numbers as clearly indicative of open water.

On Long Island, where it is familiarly known as the Brant, according to Dr. Giraud it makes its appearance about the 15th of October. In the spring and autumn it is very numerous on the coast, exceeding in number both the Canada Goose and the Dusky Duck. Its manner of flight is very different from that of *B. canadensis.* It moves in more compact bodies, less rapidly, and without seeming to have any chosen leader. While in the bays of Long Island it seems to be inactive, seldom taking to wing, unless disturbed by a passing boat or the near approach of a gun.

It rises slowly, and when on the wing moves sluggishly for a short distance, and, unless attracted by a distant flock, frequently returns to the place just left. Its food there consists largely of the *Zostera marina*, or eel-grass. At low water it may be seen industriously at work tearing up its favorite plant. When the tide has risen to such a height as to compel it to relinquish its work, it then drifts with the current, feeding on the fruits of its labor.

The Brant is very fond of what is known to hunters as "sanding," and resorts to sandbars for that purpose, where it is killed in great numbers by men who secrete themselves in excavations made in the sand. The locality known as Fire Island Bar, on the south side of Long Island, is a celebrated point for procuring this species. Giraud was informed in 1840 that the lessees of this island sent to the New York market annually from this bar several hundred dollars' worth of birds — chiefly Brant. In passing over the Long Island bays, these birds avoid as much as possible the points of land and the tussocks of grass, and this makes them difficult to obtain, except in the manner described, or by shooting them from batteries anchored in the shallow parts of the bays. These batteries are constructed by taking a box six feet long, two and a half wide, and one foot deep, with sides and ends shelving, on which sand is placed, to imitate a bar. The upper edges of these boxes are even with the surface of the water, and in them the hunters lie concealed, having a number of decoys around. By means of this arrangement one man can often discharge, with deadly effect, two double-barrelled guns into a flock. A statute was passed in 1838 prohibiting the use of this method of killing birds; but this law was defied and openly violated, and becoming a dead letter, was at last repealed.

While the Brant is not known to dive for its food, it not infrequently endeavors to escape by doing this when it has been wounded, although it rarely succeeds in accomplishing its purpose. While by many this bird is not considered as being desirable as food, Giraud speaks of it as excellent, even the adult birds being tender and juicy, and free from any fishy flavor. Its flesh has the most desirable taste in the spring; but at times it acquires a disagreeable sedgy flavor.

Owing to its apparent unwillingness to give up its wandering habits, this bird cannot be fully domesticated. Giraud tried the experiment with young birds, but without success. Even where the attempt has seemed partially successful, the Brant could not be made to breed.

Mr. Audubon did not meet with this species in Texas, and could not obtain any evidence of its having ever been seen there; but Mr. Dresser mentions it as common on that coast during the winter.

According to Yarrell, the Brant is a regular winter visitor to the shores of all the maritime counties of England, remaining through all the cold months of the year. It is a marine species, never seen in fresh water, passing the greater portion of the time out at sea, frequenting extensive muddy flats, or such sand-bars as are exposed at every ebb-tide. It makes its appearance at these feeding-places a short time before the water leaves the ground exposed, and remains there, unless disturbed, until this is again covered by the tide. In such situations the flocks of Brant are often of extraordinary size.

Colonel Hawker states that these birds are always wild, except in very severe weather, and that their cautious instincts prompt them to leave their feeding-grounds as soon as the tide flows high enough to bear an enemy. To kill Brant by day it is necessary to get out of sight in a small punt at low water, and keep as near as possible to the edge of the sea. The cry of a flock as it approaches is said to resemble that of a pack of hounds. When they come near to a boat, if the hunter springs up suddenly, the Brant in their fright hover together and present a fine mark. Other writers also speak of the resemblance of the notes of a flock of these birds to those of a pack of hounds in full cry. On the British coast these birds feed chiefly on the fronds of several algæ, especially *Ulva latissima.*

Yarrell states that the eggs brought home by the northern voyagers were of a uniform grayish white, measuring 2.75 inches in length by 1.75 in breadth. The birds kept in confinement in St. James's Park and at the Zoological Gardens have never manifested any disposition to mate. In confinement they are exclusive and reserved, never consort with other birds, but hiss when they are approached, as do other geese; and their cries are described as resembling the syllables *ruck-ruck, r-r-ronk, r-r-ronk.*

Bernicla nigricans.

THE BLACK BRANT.

Anser nigricans, LAWR. Ann. Lyc. N. Y. IV. 1846, 171, plate.
Bernicla nigricans, CASS. Illustr. B. Cal. Tex. etc. 1853, 52, pl. 10. — BAIRD, B. N. Am. 1858, 767; Cat. N. Am. B. 1859, no. 571. — RIDGW. Nom. N. Am. B. 1882, no. 596.
Branta nigricans, BANNIST. Pr. Ac. Nat. Sci. Philad. 1870, 131.
Branta bernicla, var. *nigricans,* COUES, Key, 1872, 284.
Branta bernicla, b. *nigricans,* COUES, B. N. W. 1874, 557.
Bernicla brenta nigricans, COUES, Check List, 2d ed. 1882, no. 701.

HAB. Arctic and Western North America; rare or casual in the Atlantic States.

SP. CHAR. *Adult* (No. 12787, Simiahmoo, Washington Territory; Dr. KENNERLY): Head, neck, and jugulum uniform deep black; middle of the neck with a conspicuous collar of pure white, interrupted only on the nape, and with oblique streaks running upward for an inch outside the ring. Upper parts, breast, and abdomen uniform dark brownish plumbeous, the rump, primaries, and secondaries approaching black. Anal region, crissum, sides of the rump, and upper tail-coverts immaculate snow-white. Tail uniform black. Feathers of the sides and flanks with very

Bernicla nigricans.

broad white tips, these almost concealing the dusky of the basal portion. Bill and feet deep black; tarsi dark reddish (black in life?). Wing, 13.40 inches; culmen, 1.35; tarsus, 2.50; middle toe, 2.00. *Young* (No. 61963, ♀, Unalakleet, Alaska, Sept. 28, 1867; W. H. Dall): Similar to the adult, but collar obsolete, greater wing-coverts and secondaries broadly tipped with pure white, and feathers of the sides and flanks uniform brownish gray, without white tips.

A very curious specimen from Northern Europe (No. 57167, "hoher Norden;" Schlüter Coll.) is exactly intermediate between this species and *B. brenta*, and is probably a hybrid. It has the uniform colors of the body characteristic of the *B. nigricans;* but the shade is rather lighter, presenting a more appreciable demarcation of the black of the jugulum, and has a more bluish cast — the wing-coverts in strong and abrupt contrast with the black secondaries. The white of the neck is in two opposite isolated crescents, as in *bernicla*. It measures as follows: Wing, 12.85 inches; culmen, 1.25; tarsus, 2.30; middle toe, 1.75.

This form is very closely allied to the common Brant Goose, and takes its place on the Pacific coast, where the latter does not seem to occur. The present species is quite rare on the eastern coast. Mr. Henshaw informed me that he has seen a single specimen of it in the Boston market; and there is, Mr. Lawrence informs me, a fine specimen in the museum of the Long Island Historical Society which was obtained on that island. It is rare in the interior, but Captain Bendire mentions its occasional occurrence in Eastern Oregon.

Mr. R. Browne includes it in his list of the birds of Vancouver Island. He mentions having seen one of these Geese, apparently quite tame, stalking about the Unchaltaw Indian village in Discovery Passage, in March, 1866. It is known as the *Nulla* by the Quakwolths, who also had a tame one in the village at Fort Rupert.

According to Dr. Cooper, this species appears to resort, in winter, only to salt-water bays. Dr. Suckley found it exceedingly abundant near the Straits of Fuca at that season, and occurring more sparingly about the mouths of other bays as far south as San Diego, where, in the winter of 1861–1862, Dr. Cooper saw these birds in large numbers. They appeared in October, and remained until April 20, the spring being much more backward, and their departure taking place probably as much as two weeks later than usual. He saw no other species in company with them during the whole winter, though others were common on the prairies at some distance inland. They appeared to feed almost entirely on the leaves and roots of the marine grass (*zostera*) which abounds in that bay. Dr. Cooper supposes that they also feed on small fish and shells, as they acquire a somewhat fishy, though not a disagreeable, flavor. They were exceedingly wild, and flew so high that he only succeeded in procuring a single specimen. Their note is said to be a croaking cry, much less strong than that of the other species. Dr. Cooper never saw any in the San Francisco market, but he met with them about and outside of the Bay, in 1863, as late as the 24th of April; and he has every reason to believe that large numbers frequent the fields of kelp which line the coast and extend out some miles from the shore.

Mr. Kennicott, in a note dated Fort Yukon, May 19, refers to procuring three specimens of this bird, known in that region as the "Eskimo Goose." He states that it arrives there the latest of all the birds, and after nearly all the other Geese have passed. It flies in large flocks, and very rapidly. The three specimens were the first noticed that season, and the only ones killed, although two dozen or more flocks of from twenty-five to fifty were seen in all; but in no comparison, in point of numbers, with the other four species. This bird is said to pass La Pierre House in immense numbers both in spring and fall.

Mr. Dall states that this Goose arrives in immense flocks in the spring along the sea-coast, and he shot one at Nulato, May 29, 1868; but it was regarded as being a very rare visitor on the Yukon. It passes Fort Yukon in the spring, as it does St. Michael's, being present only a few days, and breeding only on the shores of the Arctic Sea. Mr. Dall was informed that this species is not found at Fort Yukon in the fall. He killed one at Unalaktak, Sept. 28, 1867, on the edge of the ice in a small stream; and mentions that he uniformly found this Goose lean, tough, and of a disagreeable flavor. It is also very shy. The few that appear in Norton Sound in the fall are the last of the Geese, except the "Emperor Goose" (*Philacte canagica*).

Mr. Bannister mentions that he was told that this bird was far less abundant than usual at St. Michael's the season he was there, when only a few were killed. It arrived there the 12th of May, almost the last of all the migratory birds; and was observed Sept. 23, 1865, on its return. It is said to come usually in immense flocks, and to afford more profitable sport for a few days than all the other species put together. The flight of the main body of these migratory birds is along the western edge of St. Michael's Island, touching Stewart's Island, and then proceeding directly northward, across the open sea toward Golovin Sound.

It was seen breeding abundantly by Mr. MacFarlane near the Arctic Ocean. Some of the nests were found on small islets in fresh-water ponds; others on islands in the Anderson, near its mouth; and many others either on the shore or on islands in Franklin Bay, or other parts of the Arctic Sea. In some cases the nest was nothing more than a mere depression lined with down; but in some the quantity of down was quite large. The number of eggs in a nest was generally five; but in one case as many as seven were seen, and in six or seven instances six.

On the coast of Norton Sound, Alaska, as observed by Mr. E. Adams ("Ibis," 1878), these Geese were observed to arrive in the middle of May in great numbers. They were first noticed on the 12th. They keep much more to the sea than the other Geese, and large flocks are only seen inland near their breeding-places. They keep along the coast, out of shot, and in the spring their line of flight is directly north. They breed in the southern marshes with the Hutchins's Goose, the natives collecting their eggs at the end of June, and bringing them by boat-loads to Michalaski. Mr. Adams regards the eggs as being by no means good eating, since they are rank and fishy; but the Russians consider them excellent.

Examples were taken in large numbers on the Yukon by Mr. Kennicott, and afterward by Mr. T. Lockhart. Mr. MacFarlane found it breeding in abundance on islands northeast of the mouth of Anderson River, in Liverpool Bay on the Arctic coast, on Franklin Bay, on various other parts of the coast, and especially in regions west of Anderson River.

Eggs of this species from Liverpool Bay (Smithsonian Institution, No. 9483) are of a dull ivory-white, or a grayish-white color, and range in length from 2.75 to 2.90 inches, and in breadth from 1.80 to 1.85 inches.

Branta leucopsis.

THE BARNACLE GOOSE.

Anser leucopsis, BECHST. Taschb. 1803, 424. — NUTT. Man. II. 1834, 355. — AUD. Orn. Biog. III. 1835, 609, pl. 296; Synop. 1839, 271; B. Am. VI. 1843, 200, pl. 378.

Anas leucopsis, TEMM. Man. 1815, 531.

Bernicla leucopsis, BOIE, Isis, 1822, 563. — BAIRD, B. N. Am. 1858, 768; Cat N. Am. B. 1859, no. 572. — RIDGW. Nom. N. Am. B. 1882, no. 597. — COUES, Check List, 2d ed. 1882, no. 699.

Branta leucopsis, BANNIST. Pr. Ac. Nat. Sci. Philad. 1870, 131. — COUES, Key, 1872, 283; Check List, 1873, no. 483; Birds N. W. 1874, 558.

HAB. Palæarctic Region; casual in Eastern North America (Hudson's Bay and Jamaica Bay, Long Island, specimens in U. S. National Museum; Currituck Sound, N. C.; cf. LAWR. Am. Nat. V. 1871, 10).

SP. CHAR. *Adult* (No. 49788, Hudson's Bay Territory; B. R. Ross): Anterior portion of the back, jugulum, neck, and occiput, to nearly above the eyes, uniform deep black, the posterior outline of which on the jugulum is very regular and sharply defined. Head mostly white, with a black stripe from the upper basal angle of the bill to the eye. Lower parts grayish white, becoming dark cinereous on the sides and flanks, where the feathers are broadly tipped with grayish white. Anal region, crissum, and upper tail-coverts immaculate pure white. Interscapulars, rump, and tail uniform black; scapulars black, their concealed bases slate-color. Wing-coverts glaucous-ash, broadly tipped (for about .65 of an inch) with black, the last row ("greater coverts") conspicuously tipped with white. Secondaries and primaries brownish slate-black, fading basally into slaty ash. Bill and feet deep black. Wing, 16.50 inches; tail, 6.00; culmen, 1.20; bill .80 wide and deep at base; tarsus, 2.75; middle toe, 1.90.

Two European specimens in the National Collection differ from that described above — which is the only American example of the species we have seen — in the much lighter color of the upper parts, all the feathers of the back, the scapulars, and the larger wing-coverts being distinctly, though narrowly, tipped with pale ash, while the more bluish gray at the base of the feathers is everywhere more or less distinctly exposed. It is not likely, however, that these differences will prove constant.[1] These European skins measure as follows: Wing, 14.90–16.90 inches; culmen, 1.10–1.45; tarsus, 2.50–3.00; middle toe, 1.90–2.10.

The claim of the Barnacle Goose to be included in the North American fauna is based upon its probable constant occurrence in Greenland, and occasional capture along the Atlantic coast. The individual instances of its being taken at long intervals and in distant localities may possibly be accounted for by considering them as birds escaped from confinement. In a few instances the occurrence of this bird in this country can be proved to have been caused in the manner suggested; other cases are, and will perhaps remain, doubtful.

Holböll states that this Goose in autumn regularly visits the southern part of Greenland; but he does not believe that it breeds anywhere in that country. Professor Reinhardt, however, considers these two statements inconsistent with each other — and indeed he has been told that a few of the eggs of this Goose have been actually taken in Greenland; though he is not positive as to the truth of this statement.

One specimen was obtained by Mr. B. R. Ross near Rupert House, on James's Bay, at the southern end of Hudson's Bay, and is presumed to be the first North American specimen ever procured, or at least known to have been taken. Another was shot on the coast of Nova Scotia; but there is no doubt that it was one of several that a short time before had escaped from the grounds of Mr. A. Downs, near Halifax.

No mention is made of the Barnacle Goose by Dr. Richardson, and it was not noticed either by himself or by any of his party. Hearne, however, refers to the occurrence, on Hudson's Bay, of a single specimen of what he styles the Bean Goose. He speaks also of seeing this Goose at least three several times; and it is quite possible that the bird he refers to under this name may be the Barnacle.

A second specimen has more recently been taken in Currituck Sound, N. C. It was killed on the 31st of October, 1870, from a blind where there were fifteen or twenty live Geese as decoys, toward whom it was attracted. It was unaccompanied by any other bird. It is not improbable that this may have been a bird escaped from confinement.

Both Nuttall and Bonaparte refer to this species as being rare and accidental in America; but unfortunately mention no authority for the statement, and refer to no

[1] Since the above was written there has been received at the National Museum a fine mounted example of the Barnacle Goose, obtained at Jamaica Bay, Long Island, on Oct. 18, 1876, by Mr. J. Kendall, by whom it was kindly presented to the Museum. This example is even more different from the Hudson's Bay one than the European specimens above mentioned, the whole back being distinctly marked with broad bars of bluish gray. In size it is intermediate, in all its measurements, between the extremes as given in the diagnosis on p. 455.

instance of its actual occurrence. Audubon himself never met with it; but single specimens have more recently been secured in Vermont, and near New York City.

Mr. Selby speaks of it as a regular winter visitant of Great Britain, and says that it comes, upon the approach of autumn, in vast numbers to the western shores of that country, and to the north of Ireland. It is very abundant on the coast of Lancashire, frequenting the marshy grounds that are occasionally covered by the spring tides, and such sands as produce the sea-grasses and plants upon which it feeds. It is a very wary bird, and can be approached only by the most cautious manœuvres. It may be shot by moonlight, when it comes upon the sands to feed, by persons crouching on the ground, or from behind some shelter, in such places as the flocks are known to frequent. Its flesh is said to be sweet and tender, and is highly esteemed for the table. On the approach of spring it departs for more northern countries, and by the middle of March none are left behind. When made captive it soon becomes as familiar as the Domestic Goose, adapting itself to confinement, and breeding readily. It has been known to mate with the White-fronted Goose, and to hatch out a brood. Small flocks have been kept for several seasons in St. James's Park; and young broods were hatched in 1844, and again in 1845. Broods have also been raised on the grounds of Mr. A. W. Austin, near Boston, in Lincolnshire. Mr. Yarrell states that the eggs laid in St. James's Park were white, and measured 2.75 inches in length by 1.87 inches in breadth.

Mr. Dunn states that this Goose migrates in vast numbers along the western coast of Norway, from the Naze of Norway northward, where it generally seems to make the land after leaving the Danish coast. The shores of the White Sea are its supposed breeding-place. It appears in vast numbers on the coast of Scona, in October and November, and is reported as visiting the Faröe Islands and Iceland. During its migrations it is said to be abundant in Holland, France, and Germany.

Mr. Audubon describes its eggs, from specimens in the Museum of the University of Edinburgh, as measuring 2.87 inches in length, by 1.87 inches in breadth, and as being of a uniform yellowish cream-color.

Professor Malmgren states ("Ibis," 1869) that this species is certainly an inhabitant of Spitzbergen. Many were seen in Advent Bay, and one was killed in the beginning of August.

Middendorff gives it as occurring, during the breeding-season, in Siberia, in the northern *Tundras*, or Barrens. Mr. H. Saunders met with a single specimen of this species in Spain, near Seville. It was shot in the "marisma" (lagoon), in the southern part of the kingdom.

Mr. Wheelwright states it to be only a bird of passage through Scandinavia, going to and from its breeding haunts. The eggs in his collection, he mentions, bear a very close resemblance to those of the *Anser minutus*, but are smaller. It does not breed in any part of Scandinavia.

Genus **PHILACTE**, Bannister.

"*Chlœphaga*," Baird, B. N. Am. 1858, 768 (not of Eyton, 1838).
Philacte, Bannist. Pr. Philad. Acad. 1870, 131 (type, *Anas canagica*, Sevast.).

Char. This genus, the most distinct among the North American *Anseres*, differs from all other of our Geese in the peculiar form of the bill. This member is unusually short, with very large, broad, and thick nails, which occupy nearly the terminal third of the bill. The nasal cavity is very large, broadly ovate, and distinctly defined, its posterior end nearly or quite touching the frontal feathers. The feet are also somewhat peculiar, the tarsus being proportionally shorter, and the toes longer, than in other genera. From the South American genus *Chlœphaga*, with which it has been associated, it is as far removed structurally as geographically.

The only known species is the beautiful Painted, or Emperor Goose of Alaska, said to have been found also on the Caspian Sea.

Philacte canagica.

Philacte canagica.

THE EMPEROR GOOSE.

Anas canagica, SEVAST. N. Act. Petrop. XIII. 1800, 346, pl. x.
Anser canagicus, BRANDT, Bull. Acad. St. Petersb. I. 1836, 37. — SCHLEG. Mus. P.-B. Anseres, 1865, 113.
Bernicla canagica, GRAY, Genera B. III. 1849, 607.
Chlœphaga canagica, BONAP. Compt. Rend. XLIII. 1856, 648. — BAIRD, B. N. Am. 1858, 768 ; Cat. N. Am. B. 1859, no. 573. — ELLIOT, Illustr. Am. B. III. 1860, pl. 45. — COUES, Check List, 2d ed. 1882, no. 698.
Philacte canagica, BANNIST. Pr. Ac. Nat. Sci. Philad. 1870, 131. — COUES, Key, 1872, 283 ; Check List, 1873, no. 482 ; B. N. W. 1874, 558. — RIDGW. Nom. N. Am. B. 1882, no. 598.
Anser pictus, PALL. Zoog. Rosso-As. II. 1826, 233.

HAB. Coast and islands of Alaska ; Caspian Sea (?).

SP. CHAR. *Adult:* Head and nape white, the former frequently stained, especially anteriorly, with orange-rufous ; throat, and neck frontally and laterally, brownish black, or dusky grayish brown. Tail slaty on basal, and white on terminal, half. Prevailing color of rest of plumage bluish ash, with a glaucous cast, each feather handsomely variegated by a narrow terminal bar of white and a broader subterminal crescent-shaped one of black ; these markings very sharply defined on the upper surface, breast, and sides, but nearly obsolete on the abdomen and crissum. Greater coverts and secondaries slate-black, conspicuously margined with white ; anterior lesser coverts, primaries, and primary coverts plain slaty gray. "Lower mandible dark horn-color, with a white spot on each side of branching rami ; membrane about nares livid blue ; rest of upper mandible pale purplish, with a fleshy white wash ; edge of nail dark horn-color, rest of the nail horn-white ; iris hazel ; legs and feet bright rich orange-yellow" (E. W. NELSON, MS.). *Young:* Nearly similar to the adult, but the head and neck plumbeous, the former speckled with white, especially on top; the transverse barring of the feathers less distinct than in the adult. Bill and feet dusky.

Wing, 14.30–15.70 inches; culmen, 1.40–1.65; tarsus, 2.60–2.85; middle toe, 2.40–2.50.

In a very large series of fine adult specimens before us there is little appreciable variation in colors, except in regard to the orange-rufous stain on the head, which is entirely wanting in some, but in others very deep, and covering nearly the whole head.

This species was introduced as a probable bird of North America by Professor Baird, in the ninth volume of the "Pacific Railroad Reports." It had been said to be common among the Aleutian Islands; but according to the observations of Mr. Dall, it was not seen in any of the regions visited by him. He was at some pains to make inquiries in regard to it, and the existence of such a bird appeared to be unknown to the natives of the islands visited by him. It has been found, however, by Mr. Bannister on the Island of St. Michael's and on the Lower Yukon, and about its mouth by Mr. Pease and others. Mr. Dall speaks of it as a magnificent bird, and states that it abounds in profusion in the Kusilvak Slough, or mouth of the Yukon River, to the exclusion of all other species. His endeavors to reach that point being unavailing, he was obliged to obtain specimens elsewhere. It was quite scarce about the Kwichpak Slough and on the sea-coast. By means of a large reward, Mr. Dall obtained four fine specimens from the marshes around Kutlik. This is the largest of the Geese of that region; and the delicate colors of the body, with the head and nape snow-white, tipped with rich amber-yellow, have a very beautiful effect. Its eye is dark brown, and the feet are flesh-color. The eggs are said to be larger and longer than those of *Anser Gambeli,* and rather brown fulvous, the color being in minute dots. This bird rests on the ground in the manner of the other Geese. The Eskimo name of this Goose is *Machówthiluk.* The raw flesh and skin, Mr. Dall states, have an intolerable odor of garlic, which renders skinning it a very disagreeable task; but on cooking this passes away, and he found the flesh tender and good eating.

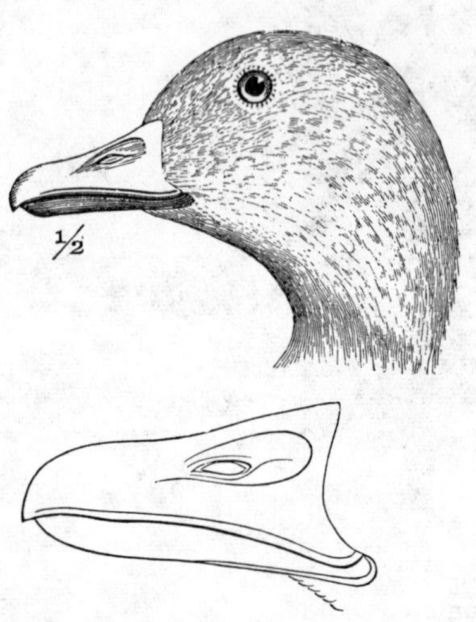

This species arrives at Alaska about the first of June, or earlier, according to the season. As soon as the eggs are hatched the old birds begin to moult. Mr. Dall saw half-moulted individuals at Pastolik, July 29, 1867. This Goose remains longer than any other, lingering until the whole sea-coast is fringed with ice, feeding on *Mytilus edilis* and other shellfish. It has been observed as late as November 1 by the Russians. It usually goes in pairs, or four or five together, rather than in large flocks. Its note is shriller and clearer than that of *A. Gambeli* or of *B. Hutchinsi,* and it is shyer than any of the Geese, except the Black Brant.

Mr. Bannister states that two of this species were shot at St. Michael's during the period of his stay there, both of them young, and not in the best of plumage. This bird cannot be regarded as common at that particular point; but Mr. Pease reported having seen it in June in large numbers on the Lower Yukon while descending that river. Mr. Bannister also speaks of the strongly offensive odor of its flesh, stating that skinning it leaves a taint upon the hands which can hardly be removed by washing. He considers the flesh so strong as to be wholly unfit for food, though the Indians and the Eskimos eat it.

According to the observations of Mr. Elliott, this species visits the Prybilof Islands, but only as a straggler, and sometimes landing in such an exhausted condition that the natives capture whole flocks in open chase over the grass, the birds being unable to use their wings for flight. He adds that he found the flesh of this bird — contrary to report — free from any unpleasant flavor, and in fact very good. The objectionable quality is only skin-deep, and may be got rid of by due care in the preparation of the bird for the table.

Mr. E. Adams ("Ibis," 1878), in his Notes on the Birds observed by him on Norton Sound, near the mouth of the Yukon, refers to this bird as the "White-headed Goose," its name in the Eski dialect being *Nud-jár-lik*. He first met with it at Port Clarence, and was told by an old hunter that it came in very small numbers every year, and was excellent eating. Coming suddenly upon a flock of eight, on the 16th of May, he could not get near them, but was able to examine them through a glass as they were standing in the water, just at the edge of a lake, dressing their feathers. They reminded him very much of the Barnacle Goose, but were larger, had more white, and no black on their neck, and had red bills and feet. Their local name is supposed to be derived from an Indian word signifying a cap.

The eggs of this species taken by Mr. Dall, June 20, 1873, in Kusilvak Slough, at the mouth of the Yukon, vary in length from 3.33 inches to 3.40, and in breadth from 2.90 to 3.10. In shape they are of an unusually elongated form, nearly equal at both ends; in color white, but with a general dirty brown aspect, caused by minute discolorations.

Genus **DENDROCYCNA**, Swainson.

Dendronessa, Wagl. Isis, 1832, 281 (type, *Anas arcuata*, Cuv. nec Swainson, 1831).
Dendrocygna, Swains. Classif. B. II. 1837, 365 (same type).
? *Leptotarsis*, Eyton, Monog. Anat. 1838, 29 (type, *L. Eytoni*, Gould).

Char. Bill longer than the head, the edges nearly parallel, deep through the base, depressed terminally, the nail large and much hooked; mandible almost wholly concealed behind the overhanging edge of the maxilla; neck and legs long, the tarsus nearly equal to or longer than the middle toe, and reticulated in front (as in the Swans and true Geese); wings rather short, rounded, the primaries not projecting beyond the ends of the inner secondaries; second to fourth quills longest, and nearly equal; tail short, almost hidden by the coverts. Habits, arboreal.

The Tree Ducks appear to be more nearly related structurally to the Sheldrakes (*Tadorna*, *Casarca*, etc.) and the Goose-like genus *Chenalopex*, than to the true Ducks on the one hand or Geese proper on the other; and with these forms perhaps constitute a distinct group.

The genus *Dendrocycna* is distributed throughout the tropical and subtropical regions of the earth, some of the species having a very anomalous range; for instance, the *D. fulva* is common in Mexico and the southern border of the United States, and in the southern part of tropical South America (South Brazil, Buenos Ayres, etc.), but is apparently absent from the entire intervening territory; but what is still more remarkable, the same species is said to be found in Madagascar and Southern India. The *D. viduata* of South America is also a common bird of Western Africa.[1]

The American species of *Dendrocycna* may be distinguished as follows:—

[1] See Scl. & Salv. P. Z. S. 1864, p. 299.

A. Crissum white, spotted with black.

1. **D. arborea.**[1] Above, dull brown, the feathers tipped with lighter; neck streaked with pale fulvous and dusky; lower parts dull whitish, irregularly spotted with black. *Hab.* West Indies (Jamaica and St. Croix).
2. **D. autumnalis.** Above, reddish brown, the rump and upper tail-coverts black; abdomen, flanks, sides, and under side of wing, black.

a. autumnalis. Lower part of neck all round, including breast, reddish brown, like the back. Wing, 9.20–9.70 inches; culmen, 1.90–2.15; tarsus, 2.25–2.60; middle toe, 2.25–2.70. *Hab.* Middle America, including Rio Grande valley of Texas.

β. discolor.[2] Lower part of neck all round, including breast, brownish gray, abruptly contrasted above with the chestnut-brown of the back. *Hab.* South America.

D. fulva.

B. Crissum plain white.

3. **D. fulva.** Lower parts plain light cinnamon, the flanks striped with paler; back and scapulars black, the feathers tipped with fulvous; upper tail-coverts white. Wing. 8.10–8.90 inches; culmen, 1.65–1.95; tarsus, 2.10–2.40; middle toe, 2.30–2.80. *Hab.* Middle America, north to California, Nevada, and Louisiana; South Brazil, Buenos Ayres, and Paraguay.

[1] DENDROCYCNA ARBOREA.

Black-billed Whistling Duck, EDWARDS, Glean. t. 193.
Canard siffleur, de la Jamaique, BUFF. Pl. Enl. 804.
Anas arborea, LINN. S. N. I. 1766, 207 (ex EDW. l. c.).
Dendrocygna arborea, EYTON, Monog. Anat. 1838, 110. — SCL. & SALV. Nom. Neotr. 1873, 73; P. Z. S. 1876, 376 (monographic). — COUES, B. N. W. 1874, 558 (synonymy).
? *Anas Jacquini*, GMEL. S. N. I. ii. 1788, 536 (ex JACQ. Beitr. p. 5, no. 3).
HAB. Bahamas, Cuba, Santo Domingo, Jamaica, and St. Croix.

[2] DENDROCYCNA AUTUMNALIS DISCOLOR.

Canard siffleur, de Cayenne, BUFF. Pl. Enl. 826.
"*Dendrocygna autumnalis*," AUCT. (all quotations from South America).
Dendrocygna discolor, SCL. & SALV. Nom. Neotr. 1873, 161; P. Z. S. 1876, 375.

C. Crissum black.

4. **D. viduata.**[1] Breast and lower neck (all round), rich chestnut; sides pale fulvous or yellowish white, barred with blackish; abdomen black; forepart of head white; rest of head and upper part of neck black, with a white patch on the foreneck. *Hab.* Southern South America.

Dendrocycna autumnalis.

THE BLACK-BELLIED TREE DUCK.

Anas autumnalis, LINN. S. N. I. 1766, 205 (based on the *Red-billed Whistling Duck*, EDWARDS, pl. 194; West Indies).

Dendrocygna autumnalis, EYTON, Monog. Anat. 1838, 109. — BAIRD, B. N. Am. 1858, 770; Cat. N. Am. B. 1859, no. 574. — COUES, Key, 1872, 284; Check List, 1873, no. 487; 2d ed. 1882, no. 706; Birds N. W. 1874, 558. — SCL. & SALV. P. Z. S. 1876, 374 (monographic).

Dendrocycna autumnalis, RIDGW. Nom. N. Am. B. 1881, no. 599.

HAB. Middle America and southwestern border of United States; West Indies. Replaced in South America by the *D. autumnalis discolor*.

SP. CHAR. *Adult:* Pileum, neck, back, scapulars, jugulum, and breast cinnamon-brown; the forehead paler, the occiput passing posteriorly into black (which is continued in a narrow stripe

D. autumnalis.

down the nape), and the dorsal region more ferruginous. Head and upper part of the neck, except as described, pale ochraceous-ashy. Abdomen, flanks, rump, and lining of the wing deep black, abruptly defined against the cinnamon of the breast; crissum white, spotted with black. Lesser wing-coverts light cinereous, overlaid by an ochraceous-olive wash; middle coverts purer ash; greater and primary coverts pure white, the lower feathers of the latter dusky; secondaries, pri-

[1] DENDROCYCNA VIDUATA.

Anas viduata, LINN. S. N. I. 1766, 205.

Dendrocygna viduata, EYTON, Monog. Anat. 1838, 110. — SCL. & SALV. Nom. Neotr. 1873, 129; P. Z. S. 1876, 376 (monographic). — COUES, B. N. W. 1874, 559 (synonymy).

Canard du maragnon, BUFF. Pl. Enl. 808.

Pato caro blanco, AZARA, Apunt. III. 1805, no. 435.

HAB. South America in general; Cuba.

maries, and tail deep black, the rectrices pure white basally. Bill and feet bright flesh-color, the former yellow near the nostrils and black on the nail; iris brown.[1] Sexes alike. *Young:* Much like the adult, but with the pattern less distinct and the colors duller. Cinnamon replaced by dingy gray, more or less tinged with rusty ochraceous. Abdomen, flanks, and crissum grayish white, tinged with deeper gray. Bill dusky; feet dark reddish. *Downy young:* Above, blackish brown, varied by large areas of sulphury buff, as follows: a supraloral streak extending over the eye; a wide stripe from the bill under the eye and extending across the occiput, the blackish below it extending forward only about as far as directly beneath the eye, and confluent posteriorly with the nuchal longitudinal stripe of the same color; a pair of sulphury buff patches on each side of the back, and another on each side the rump; posterior half of the wing whitish buff, the end of the wing blackish; the black of the upper parts sends off two lateral projections on each side, the first on each side the crop, the second over the flanks to the tibiæ; the buff of the abdomen extending upward in front of this last stripe as far as the middle portion of the buff spot on the side of the back. Lower parts wholly whitish buff, paler and less yellowish along the middle. [Described from a specimen "about four days old," obtained by Dr. J. C. Merrill, U. S. A., at Fort Brown, Texas, Aug. 14, 1877. "Bill bluish above, yellow below; legs olive."]

Wing, 9.20–9.70 inches; culmen, 1.90–2.15; tarsus, 2.25–2.60; middle toe, 2.30–2.70.

The cinnamon-color of the breast varies, in this species, from a vinaceous to a rich rufous cast, but that of the lower neck is always continuous with that of the back; the white of the wing-coverts is sometimes clouded with pale ash. The South American representative, *D. discolor*, Scl. & Salv., differs conspicuously, in the lower neck and breast being fulvous-gray, strongly and abruptly contrasted against the dark chestnut-brown of the back, the black instead of whitish tibiæ, and different proportions. It is perhaps specifically distinct; but in the absence of specimens from the region in which intergradation, if existing, would occur, we for the present consider it a geographical race of the same species. Three examples in the collection measure as follows: wing, 9.10–9.30 inches; culmen, 1.80–1.90; width of bill across middle, .70–.75; tarsus, 2.20–2.25; middle toe, 2.25–2.35.

This species of Tree Duck obtains a place in the North American fauna from its occurrence on the Rio Grande and in Southern California. It is found throughout Mexico, Central America, the northern portions of South America, and many of the West India Islands.

In Texas it is known as the "Long-legged Duck." Mr. Dresser mentions it as being found occasionally near Matamoras during the summer; and he was assured by a person residing in Monterey — one well acquainted with the bird — that it breeds in the neighborhood of that place. At Galveston a German hunter informed Mr. Dresser that it is quite common there during the winter, arriving in November and departing in March.

In regard to its presence in Southern California, nothing more is known beyond

[1] "The soft parts in a full-plumaged living male were as follow: iris brown; bill coral red, orange above; nail of bill bluish; legs and feet pinkish white." — Merrill, Proc. U. S. Nat. Mus. Vol. I. p. 170.

the procuring of a single specimen at Fort Tejon by Mr. Xantus, who regarded it as of rare and unusual occurrence.

Specimens were obtained by Mr. G. C. Taylor on the Lake of Tojoa, in Honduras. The birds were very plentiful, easy of approach, and were very good eating. Mr. E. C. Taylor found this species abundant in the Island of Porto Rico, where it was breeding.

Mr. Salvin mentions having met with a flock on the Pacific coast of Guatemala. He could plainly distinguish the clear whistling note which this bird utters as it flies. According to Léotaud it is a permanent resident of Trinidad. It certainly is known to breed there, and it is also to be met with at all seasons of the year, but generally in very limited numbers. In the course of July and August it regularly visits Trinidad in large numbers. The swamps then contain but very little water, and certain aquatic plants which grow on the edges of pools produce seeds of which this Duck is very fond. This undoubtedly is what attracts these birds, for it cannot be that they are driven by cold from the neighboring portions of the South American continent, where they abound. On the other hand, there seems to be some evident necessity for this movement, for at that period hardly an individual remains behind. This Duck is always seen in flocks more or less considerable in size. It utters a very peculiar whistling sound, said to resemble the syllables *oui-ki-ki;* and by this name the bird is known in Trinidad. It is not infrequently known to perch on the limbs of trees. In captivity it will freely mingle with the other inhabitants of the barnyard, appearing to be quite contented with its lot; but it will not breed. Its flesh, like that of all the Ducks of South America, is deservedly considered a great delicacy by epicures.

Colonel A. J. Grayson, quoted by Mr. Lawrence in his paper on the Birds of Western Mexico, states that the history of the habits of this species would be almost identical with that of its near ally, *D. fulva.* It is, however, more nocturnal in pursuit of subsistence, visiting the dry cornfields during the night in great numbers, and doing considerable damage there. Colonel Grayson adds that he has also met with these birds in the night-time, as they were walking along the road, far from any water, picking up the grains of corn which had been dropped by the packers.

This species is said to be more abundant in the vicinity of Mazatlan in the latter part of the dry season than the *D. fulva,* but in April and May it migrates during the night toward Sonora. Many, however, remain and breed in the neighborhood of Mazatlan during the summer, where they are seen during every month of the year, breeding in the hollows of large trees, and laying from twelve to fifteen eggs. The young are lowered to the ground, one at a time, in the mouth of the mother: after all are safely landed, she cautiously leads her young brood to the nearest water.

This Duck perches with facility on the branches of trees, and when in the cornfields, upon the stalks, in order to reach the ears of corn. Large flocks spend the day on the bank of some secluded lagoon, densely bordered with woods or water-flags, also sitting amongst the branches of trees, not often feeding or stirring about during the day. When upon the wing this bird constantly utters its peculiar whistle of *pe-che-che-ne,* from which its native name is derived. Colonel Grayson noticed that it seldom alights in deep water, always preferring the shallow edges or the ground; the cause of this may be the fear of the numerous alligators that usually infest the lagoons.

When this Duck is taken young, or when its eggs are hatched under the common Barnyard Hen, it becomes very tame, and does not require to be confined; it is very watchful during the night, and, like the Goose, gives the alarm by a shrill whistle when any strange animal or person comes about the house. A lady of

Colonel Grayson's acquaintance possessed a pair of these Ducks, which she said were as good as the best watch-dog; he himself had a pair which were equally vigilant, and very docile.

Dr. J. C. Merrill writes me that this large and handsome Duck arrives from the South, in the vicinity of Fort Brown, in April, and soon thereafter becomes abundant on the river-banks and lagoons. Migrating at night, it continually utters a very peculiar chattering whistle, which at once indicates its presence. The Mexicans call it *Pato maizal*, or Cornfield Duck, from its habit of frequenting those localities. It is by no means shy, and large numbers are offered for sale in the Brownsville market. It is easily domesticated, and becomes very tame, roosting at night in the trees with the Chickens and Turkeys. When the females begin to lay, the males leave them and gather in large flocks on sandbars in the river. Dr. S. M. Finley, U. S. A., who had had ample opportunity of observing these birds at Hidalgo, informed Dr. Merrill that the eggs are deposited in hollow trees and branches, often at the considerable distance of two miles or more from water, and from eight to thirty feet above the ground. They are placed on the bare wood, and are from twelve to sixteen in number. Two broods are raised in a season, and the parent carries the young to water in her bill. Twelve eggs received from Dr. Finley average 2.11 inches by 1.53, with but little variation in size; they are of the usual Duck-shape, and in color are a rather clear yellowish white. The birds usually depart in September, but a few very late broods are seen even in November.

The eggs of this species from the Berlandier Collection, from Tamaulipas, Mexico (Smithsonian Institution, No. 743), are of an ivory-white color, with a greenish tinge. In their shape they are of a rounded oval. Three eggs have the following measurements: 2.00 by 1.50 inches; 2.30 by 1.60; 2.10 by 1.60.

Dendrocycna fulva.

THE FULVOUS-BELLIED TREE DUCK.

Penelope mexicana, BRISS. Orn. VI. 1760, 390 (Mexico).

Anas fulva, GMEL. S. N. I. ii. 1788, 530 (ex BRISS. l. c.).

Dendrocygna fulva, BURM. Reise La Plata, 1856, 515. — BAIRD, B. N. Am. 1858, 770; ed. 1860, pl. 60; Cat. N. Am. B. 1859, no. 575. — COUES, Key, 1872, 284; Check List, 1873, no. 486; 2d ed. 1882, no. 705; B. N. W. 1874, 558.

Dendrocycna fulva, RIDGW. Nom. N. Am. B. 1881, no. 600.

Anas virgata, MAX. Reise Bras. I. 1820, 322.

Pato roxo y negro, AZARA, Apunt. III. 1805, no. 436.

Anas bicolor, VIEILL. Nouv. Dict. V. 136 (ex AZARA, l. c.).

Anas collaris, MERREM, in Ersch u. Grub. Enc. Sct. i. Vol. XXXV. 31.

? *Dendrocygna major*, JERDON, Birds India, III. 790 (India !). — SCL. P. Z. S. 1866, 148 (Madagascar !).

HAB. Southern border of the United States, north to Central California and Western Nevada (Washoe Lake), east to Louisiana. Mexico; Southern South America. India? Madagascar? Not recorded from Northern South America (except Trinidad), Central America, or the West Indies.

SP. CHAR. *Adult:* Head, neck, and lower parts deep reddish ochraceous, passing into cinnamon on the flanks, where the longer feathers have a broad medial stripe of pale ochraceous, bordered by dusky. Crown inclining to ferruginous; nape with a distinct black stripe, commencing at the occiput. Middle of the neck dirty whitish, minutely streaked with dusky, beneath the surface. Prevailing color above brownish black, the dorsal and scapular feathers broadly tipped with the color of the lower parts; lesser wing-coverts tinged with rusty chestnut. Upper tail-coverts immaculate white; crissum yellowish white. Bill and feet black, in the dried skin; in life, "bill bluish black, legs light slaty blue" (MERRILL). Sexes alike. *Young* not seen.

Wing, 8.10–8.90 inches; culmen, 1.65–1.95; tarsus, 2.10–2.40; middle toe, 2.30–2.80.

The chief variation noticed in this species is a slight one in the precise shade of the tints. Specimens from Buenos Ayres are larger than those from Mexico, but are otherwise similar.

The Brown Tree Duck has a very different geographical distribution from that of the *D. autumnalis,* as it is not known to occur in the northern portions of South America (excepting Trinidad), Central America, or the West India Islands. It is found, however, in Mexico, and extends northward near the Pacific coast of the United States through portions of California and Nevada, and has also been met with in Texas and Louisiana.

Mr. J. Hepburn met with this species breeding in the extensive marshes near the junction of the Sacramento and the San Joaquin rivers, in the summer of 1864; Dr. Cooper also mentions seeing a flock of this species flying over the Sacramento east-

ward, in June, 1865; and Mr. H. D. Morse procured an example near San Francisco, which is now in the museum of the Boston Natural History Society.

A single individual of this species was killed near New Orleans on the 22d of January, 1870, by Mr. N. B. Moore, and was by him presented to the Smithsonian Institution. This is the first, and at present the only, recorded instance of the occurrence of this species so far to the east, although it has been known for some time as an inhabitant of California. The first instance on record of its occurrence in that State was the capture of a specimen near Fort Tejon by Mr. Hunter.

Mr. Dresser refers to this as the "Rufous Long-legged Duck," stating that he observed it occasionally near Brownville, in Texas. In June he found it in great abundance on Galveston Island. A German whom he saw carrying one told him that birds of this species were found there, and afterward took him to their chief place of resort, a lake in the middle of the island, and told him also that it bred there, but very late in the season. This was in the month of June, and breeding had not then begun. Dr. J. C. Merrill states that this Duck is about as common as the *D. autumnalis* in the vicinity of Fort Brown, Texas. Like that species, it is only a summer visitor, and both species frequent the same localities; but their notes while flying are quite different. Dr. Finley did not meet with this species at Hidalgo.

This Duck is spoken of as occurring sparingly in Southern South America. Burmeister cites it as having been noticed in varying numbers in all the easterly and northerly regions of La Plata, on the Rio Uruguay, and on the Parana as far up as Tucuran. This Duck — supposed by Léotaud to be the *bicolor* of Vieillot — is said by the former to occur in Trinidad, but to be found there chiefly as a bird of passage, visiting that island very irregularly. Occasionally it comes in considerable numbers, nests in the island, rears its young, and even has a second and sometimes a third brood before it departs. It then abandons the island, and is gone for several years without repeating its visit. Its habits, so far as Léotaud observed them, are precisely the same as those of the *autumnalis*, and its flesh — like that — is also very highly esteemed by epicures.

Colonel Grayson — quoted by Mr. Lawrence — gives very full notes of the habits both of this species and of the *autumnalis*, as observed by him in Western Mexico. Both species much resemble each other in their general appearance, as well as in their habits; and both are quite abundant in Western Mexico as far north as Sonora. The present species is the most numerous in that region.

At the end of the rainy season, or in the month of October, this bird makes its appearance in the vicinity of Mazatlan in large flocks, inhabiting the fresh-water lakes and ponds in the coast region, or *tierra caliente*, during the entire winter, or dry months, subsisting principally upon the seeds of grass and weeds, and often, at night, visiting the corn-fields for grain. During these months Colonel Grayson has found it in the shallow grass-grown ponds in very large numbers, affording excellent sport to the hunter and delicious game for the table. Its flesh is white and juicy, and also free from the strong or rank flavor which Ducks not feeding exclusively on grain and seeds usually have. This bird is large and heavy, and often very fat.

It is more easy of approach than our northern Ducks ; and Colonel Grayson states that he has often shot as many as fifteen with two discharges of his double-barrelled gun. When only winged, it is almost sure to make its escape, which its long and stout legs enable it to do by running and springing with extraordinary agility, ultimately eluding pursuit by dodging into the grass or nearest thicket. If the water is deep, it dives, and when it rises to breathe, raises only the head above the water, remaining concealed among the aquatic vegetation, where it baffles the hunter's efforts to find it.

Although its geographical range is almost entirely within the tropics, yet this species has its seasons of periodical migration from one part of the country to the other. During the month of April its well-known peculiar whistle may be heard nightly as northward-bound flocks are passing in apparently large numbers over Mazatlan. At first Colonel Grayson was not a little puzzled by this movement, especially as he had been assured that this bird is not seen north of the tropic, except as an occasional straggler; but by frequent inquiries of the natives he was enlightened as to the point of destination of these Ducks, and was satisfied that they go no farther north than the Mayo and Taqui rivers, in Sonora, and the adjacent lakes and lagoons, and that they breed there. Some, however, remain and breed in Sinaloa and in the adjacent region; and Colonel Grayson found, as late as November, young broods near San Blas which were unable to fly. They doubtless raise two or more broods during the season; but he was never able to discover whether they nest in hollow trees, as the *autumnalis* does, or on the ground, among the grass. He was informed by the natives, however, that the latter is the case; and they assured him that this bird lays from ten to fifteen pure white eggs. Though it inhabits the region near the sea-coast, this Duck is never met with on the sea, and very seldom in the estero, or salt-water lagoon, it being an exclusively fresh-water bird.

Mr. L. Belding informs us that this species arrives in the vicinity of Stockton, Cal., from April 1 to May 9; his latest fall record of its occurrence there being November 1, "when two immature birds or young of the year were noticed in the market."

Sub-family ANATINÆ. — The Ducks.

The *Anatinæ* differ from the *Anserinæ* in having the tarsus shorter than the middle toe, instead of longer, and scutellate, instead of reticulate, in front. Most of the Ducks are of smaller size than the Geese ; in many species the males are adorned with a very beautiful plumage, with a metallic wing-speculum, the sexual difference in plumage being usually well marked. The North American genera may be defined as follows [1] : —

A. Hind toe without a membraneous lobe (*Anateæ*).

1. **Anas**. Bill broad, about as long as the head, the edges parallel, the middle of the culmen concave, the terminal part (behind the nail) convex ; lamellæ scarcely exposed ; scapulars, tertials, and rectrices broad, not acuminate ; speculum brilliant.
2. **Chaulelasmus**. Bill rather narrow, shorter than the head, the edges nearly parallel, culmen gently concave in the middle, straight before and behind ; lamellæ distinctly exposed ; scapulars, etc., as in *Anas ;* speculum dull-colored — black and white.
3. **Mareca**. Bill as in *Chaulelasmus*, but lamellæ scarcely exposed ; scapulars, etc., lanceolate, the middle rectrices slightly elongated ; speculum chiefly black ; a white patch on the lesser wing-covert region.
4. **Dafila**. Similar to *Mareca*, but neck very long, bill longer than the head, narrow, the edges nearly parallel, the terminal two-thirds of the culmen quite straight and nearly horizontal, the basal portion rapidly ascending. In the adult male, scapulars, etc., elongated and lanceolate, and the middle rectrices projecting far beyond the rest.
5. **Nettion**. Size very small (wing less than six inches) ; in form much like *Dafila*, but neck much shorter, scapulars and middle rectrices broader and less elongated, bill shorter than the head, the lamellæ completely concealed ; nape with a small mane-like tuft.
6. **Querquedula**. Small, like *Nettion*, but bill longer (longer than the head), broader, less depressed, the culmen decidedly convex anteriorly ; lesser wing-coverts pale dull blue (in North American species) ; nape without a tuft.
7. **Spatula**. Bill much longer than the head, compressed at the base, very broad toward the

[1] Some South American genera of Ducks, which for present purposes it is unnecessary to include in the above synopsis, are the following : —

1. Genus Heteronetta, Salvadori.
Heteronetta, Salvad. Atti de la Soc. Ital. d. Sci. Nat. VIII. 1865, 574 (type, *Anas melanocephala*, Vieill.). — Scl. & Salv. P. Z. S. 1876, 382.

2. Genus Metopiana, Bonaparte.
Metopiana, Bonap. Compt. Rend. XLIII. 1856, 146 (type, *Anas peposaca*, Vieill.). — Scl. & Salv. P. Z. S. 1876, 398.

3. Genus Cairina, Fleming.
Cairina, Fleming, Phil. of Zool. 1822, 260 (type, *Anas moschata*, Linn.).
Moschata, Less. Traité, I. 1831, 633 (same type).
Gymnathus, Nutt. Man. II. 1834, 403 (same type).

4. Genus Tachyeres, Owen.
"*Micropterus*," Less. Traité, II. 1831, 630 (type, *Anas cinerea*, Gmel.). (Preoccupied in Ichthyology.)
Tachyeres, Owen, Trans. Zool. Soc. IX. 1875, 254 (same type).

5. Genus Merganetta, Gould.
Merganetta, Gould, P. Z. S. 1841, 95 (type, *M. armata*, Gould).
Raphipterus, Gay, Fauna Chil. 1848, 459 (type, "*R. chilensis*, Gay," = *M. armata*, Gould).

end, where the edge of the maxilla overhangs the mandible on each side; behind this, the fine lamellæ completely exposed. Otherwise much like *Querquedula* (the wings colored exactly the same), but larger.

8. **Aix.** Bill much shorter than the head, deep through the base, depressed terminally, the edges gently convex, and converging terminally; nail very large; base of the maxilla produced backward and upward into an elongated angle, extending on each side the forehead nearly half-way to the eye. Tail lengthened, composed of broad, rounded feathers. Male with a full, elegant pendant crest of silky feathers.

B. Hind toe furnished with a membraneous lobe.

a. Bill broad, depressed terminally; tail short, the feathers moderately rigid, rounded at ends, and more than half concealed by the coverts (*Fuligulæ*).

9. **Fuligula.** Bill decidedly broadest at base, much depressed terminally, the vertical thickness just behind the nail being only about one fourth that at the base; nail large and very broad. Adult male with the head rufous, the pileum ornamented by a full and very soft, bushy, rounded crest.

10. **Fulix.** Bill about as long as the inner toe (with claw), the nail small and narrow. Head and neck black in adult males.

11. **Æythyia.** Bill longer than inner toe, with claw. Head and neck reddish in adult males.

b. Bill shorter than the head, rather compressed, the depth through the base considerably exceeding the width near the end; terminal portion of the bill not at all depressed. Tail as in *Fuligulæ* (the central pair of rectrices much elongated in *Harelda*). (*Clangulæ.*)

12. **Clangula.** Bill much shorter than the head, compressed, and tapering, both laterally and vertically, to the end, the nail small and narrow. Plumage chiefly black and white in the male; grayish and white, with brown head, in the female.

13. **Histrionicus.** Bill as in *Clangula*, but the nail very large and broad, forming the end of the bill, the rictus overhung by a small wrinkled membrane. Color plumbeous, with white collar and other bands and markings, in the male; dull grayish brown, with white spots on head, in female.

14. **Harelda.** Bill much shorter than the head, nearly as broad as deep, the nail large and broad, the feathering at the base forming a nearly straight line running obliquely from the base of the culmen to the rictus.[1] Middle pair of rectrices and posterior scapulars much elongated and lanceolate in the male. Colors variable.

15. **Eniconetta.** Bill shorter than the head, much compressed, the edges of the maxilla inflexed so as partly to inclose the mandible; nail very large and broad, forming the end of the bill, which is not at all "hooked." Male with the feathers of the lores and occiput stiff and bristly, the tertials strongly falcate, the plumage beautifully variegated; female dull chestnut-brownish, variegated with black.

16. **Camptolæmus.** Bill nearly as long as the head, the edges of the maxilla furnished terminally with a thickened membraneous appendage, the base of the maxilla encased with overlying skin, including the nostrils. Feathers of the cheeks stiffened and bristly. Color black and white (head, neck, jugulum, and wings chiefly white, under parts, ring round lower neck, and other parts black) in the male; nearly uniform brownish-plumbeous in the female.

c. Bill shorter than the head, tapering both laterally and vertically toward the end; the base of the maxilla continued in a lengthened angle or broad lobe on each side of the forehead, or else (in *Arctonetta*) densely feathered as far forward as the nostril. Males with areas of stiff, bristly, greenish feathers about the head, the tertials strongly falcate, the plumage chiefly white and black, or plumbeous. Females brownish, barred with black (*Somateriæ*).

17. **Arctonetta.** Feathering at base of the maxilla extending as far forward as the nostril, and forming a continuous oblique line from the culmen to the rictus; feathers of the lores dense and velvety; eyes surrounded by a dense roundish "cushion" of short, soft, velvety feathers.

[1] In some specimens there is a distinct feathered angle projecting toward the nostril, the bare skin of the bill forming an obtuse angle above it.

18. **Somateria.** Feathering at base of maxilla exceedingly irregular, the frontal and loral regions being separated by a backward extension of the bare skin of the maxilla in the form of an elongated angle or broad lobe.

d. Bill more or less gibbous at the base, much depressed at the end, which is formed entirely by the broad, flat nail; nostrils usually anterior to the middle of the maxilla. Color black, with or without white on the head or wing, in the male; dusky grayish brown in the female (*Œdemiæ*).

19. **Œdemia.** Feathering on forehead extending only slightly in advance of that on the lores, or only to the base of the gibbosity; nostrils linear, about the middle of the maxilla. No white in the plumage of either sex.

20. **Melanetta.** Feathering on the lores advancing as far forward as that on the forehead (nearly to the nostrils). Bill extremely broad and depressed at the end. Wing with a white speculum.

21. **Pelionetta.** Feathering on the forehead extending forward almost or quite to the nostril (an inch or more in advance of that on the lores); sides of the maxilla greatly swollen in the adult male; end of bill rather pointed, much narrower than the middle portion. No white on the wing, but head with white patches (indistinct or obsolete in the female).

e. Bill very broad and depressed terminally, as in the *Fuliguleæ*. Tail rather long, graduated, the feathers narrow and very rigid, their shafts grooved on the under surface; tail-coverts very short, scarcely covering the base of the tail (*Erismatureæ*).

22. **Erismatura.** Nail of the maxilla very small, narrow, and linear, the terminal half bent abruptly downward and backward, so as to be invisible from above.

23. **Nomonyx.** Nail of the maxilla large and broad, gradually bent downward terminally, and wholly visible from above.

f. Bill narrow, sub-cylindrical, terminated by a conspicuous hooked nail, the edges serrated (*Mergeæ*).

f'. Bill as long as, or longer than, the head, its depth through the base much less than half its length, the serrations prominent.

24. **Mergus.** Bill much longer than the head, the serrations acute, curved; tarsus nearly three fourths the middle toe (with claw); crest depressed, or pointed.

25. **Lophodytes.** Bill about as long as the head (without crest), the serrations short and conical (viewed laterally); tarsus about two thirds the middle toe (with claw); crest compressed, with a semicircular posterior outline (when erected).

f''. Bill much shorter than the head, its depth through the base equal to about half its length, the serrations small and inconspicuous.

26. **Mergellus.** Serrations of the bill very fine, conical; tarsus about two thirds the middle toe; crest somewhat as in *Lophodytes*, but very much smaller.

Genus **ANAS**, Linnæus.

Anas, Linn. S. N. ed. 10, I. 1758, 122; ed. 12, I. 1766, 194 (type, by elimination, *A. boschas*, Linn.).

Char. Usually rather large-sized Ducks, with the bill a little longer than the head or foot, rather broad, depressed, the edges parallel, the end rounded; speculum metallic green, blue, or violet, in both sexes, usually bordered posteriorly by a black band, this generally succeeded by a white one.

Only four species of true *Anas* are found in America, these being easily distinguished by the following characters: —

A. Size large (wing not less than 10 inches).

a. Adult male, except in breeding-season, very different from the female, the plumage varied and brilliant; secondaries tipped with white, and greater coverts crossed by a subterminal bar of the same.

1. **A. boschas.** *Adult male in winter:* Four middle tail-feathers strongly recurved or curled; head and neck brilliant velvety green; jugulum rich chestnut, with a white collar between it and the green of the neck; speculum rich metallic violet, bounded anteriorly by a black bar, this preceded by a white one, and posteriorly by a black subterminal and white terminal band. *Adult female and male in breeding season:* Wings as in the above; elsewhere, variegated with dusky and ochraceous, the former on the centres of the feathers, and predominating on the upper parts, the latter on the borders, and prevailing beneath. Wing, 10.25–12.00 inches; culmen, 2.00–2.40; tarsus, 1.50–1.80; middle toe, 1.90–2.15. *Hab.* Whole northern hemisphere.

A. boschas.

b. Sexes alike, at all ages and seasons; no white on the outer surface of the wing.

2. **A. obscura.** Prevailing color dusky, the feathers bordered with dull ochraceous; head and neck dull buff, everywhere streaked with dusky; no black at base of the bill; speculum usually deep violet. Wing, 10.50–11.50 inches; culmen, 2.00–2.35; tarsus, 1.70–1.80; middle toe, 1.90–2.10. *Hab.* Eastern North America.

3. **A. fulvigula.** Prevailing color ochraceous, the feathers marked centrally with dusky; entire chin and throat immaculate creamy ochraceous or buff; base of the maxilla, especially below, black; speculum usually green. Wing, 10.00–10.50 inches; culmen, 2.05–2.35; tarsus, 1.70–1.80; middle toe, 1.90–2.00. *Hab.* Florida.

B. Size small (wing, 8.50).

4. **A. Aberti**[1] ♀. Prevailing color ochraceous, spotted above and streaked beneath with

[1] Anas Aberti, Ridgway.

?*Anas obscura*, Lawr. Mem. Boston Soc. II. pt. iii. no. ii. 1874, 314 (Tepic, W. Mexico).

Anas Aberti, Ridgw. Proc. U. S. Nat. Mus. Vol. I. 1878, 250 (Mazatlan).

Sp. Char. *Adult female:* Size of *Querquedula discors* and *cyanoptera*, but in coloration closely resembling *A. fulvigula.* Prevailing color ochraceous-buff, but this everywhere relieved by brownish-black spots or streaks. Head, neck, and lower parts streaked, the streaks finest on the neck and sides of the head, broadest on the jugulum and crissum, which is somewhat tinged with rusty, and assuming the form of oblong spots on the abdomen, thighs, and anal region; throat immaculate. Back, scapulars, and rump with the blackish predominating; the feathers bordered with ochraceous; those of the back and the scapulars with irregular indentations and occasional bars of the same. Lesser wing-coverts brownish slate, bordered with dull earthy brown; middle coverts with their exposed portion velvety black, forming a distinct bar. Secondaries widely tipped with pure white (forming a conspicuous band about .35 of an inch wide), this preceded by a velvety black bar of about equal width, the basal half or more (of the exposed brownish black, the throat immaculate; bill light yellowish brown, darker on culmen; speculum dark grass-green, changing to blue and violet, followed, successively, by a velvety black subterminal and a pure white terminal bar, each about .35 of an inch wide. Wing, 8.50 inches; culmen, 1.65; tarsus, 1.30; middle toe, 1.70. *Hab.* Western Mexico (Mazatlan).

Anas boschas.[1]

THE MALLARD.

Anas boschas, LINN. S. N. ed. 12, I. 1766, 205. — WILS. Am. Orn. VIII. 1814, 112, pl. 70, f. 7. — AUD. Orn. Biog. III. 1835, 164, pl. 221; Synop. 1839, 276; B. Am. VI. 1843, 236, pl. 385. — BAIRD, B. N. Am. 1858, 774; Cat. N. Am. B. 1859, no. 576. — COUES, Key, 1872, 285; Check List, 1873, no. 488; B. N. W. 1874, 559.

Anas boscas, WHARTON, Ibis, 1879, 453. — RIDGW. Nom. N. Am. B. 1881, no. 601. — COUES, Check List, 2d ed. 1882, no. 707.

Anas domestica, GMEL. S. N. I. ii. 1788, 538.

Anas (*Boschas*) *domestica*, SW. & RICH. F. B. A. II. 1831, 442. — NUTT. Man. II. 1834, 378.

Anas fera, "BRISS." — LEACH, Cat. Brit. Mus. 1816, 30.

Anas adunca, LINN. S. N. ed. 12, I. 1766, 206. — GMEL. S. N. I. ii. 1788, 538.

HAB. North America in general, south to Panama; Cuba; Bahamas; Greenland. Palæarctic Region.

SP. CHAR. *Adult male in fall, winter, and spring:* Head and neck continuous soft brilliant metallic green, showing purple and golden-bronze reflections in different lights. A ring of pure white round the lower part of the neck interrupted on the nape; jugulum and upper part of the breast rich dark chestnut. Interscapulars brownish gray, finely waved with grayish white; scapulars and lower parts grayish white, delicately waved with dark ash. Outer webs of tertials dark

portion) consisting of a metallic speculum of dark grass-green, varying to blue and violet in certain lights. Tertials opaque velvety black exteriorly, the inner webs brownish slate; primary-coverts and primaries brownish slate, the latter edged with lighter. Tail brownish gray, the feathers edged and coarsely spotted with light buff. Bill light yellowish brown, darker on the culmen, the unguis dusky; feet light yellowish (probably orange in life). Wing, 8.50 inches; tail, 3.25; culmen, 1.65; greatest width of the bill, .60; depth of maxilla through the base, .50; tarsus, 1.30; middle toe, 1.70.

Type, No. 12,789, U. S. Nat. Mus.; Mazatlan, Mexico; Colonel ABERT.

REMARKS. This remarkable little Duck is very different from any other known species. In its small size, and, to a certain extent, the narrow bill, it is like the species of *Querquedula*, but its coloration calls instantly to mind the *Anas fulvigula* from Florida, and the species (*A. Wyvilliana*) from the Sandwich Islands recently described by Mr. Sclater. The specimen is marked as being a female, so it is possible that the male may be more brilliant in plumage.

In addition to the characters given above, it may be mentioned that there is a distinct indication of a narrow, dusky, postocular streak, and of a wider and less distinct loral stripe, thus separating a light superciliary stripe from the light color of the cheeks. The lining of the wing and the axillars are pure white, the latter with a segregation of dusky spots near the carpo-metacarpal joint.

[1] The following names also have been referred to this species, as designating varieties or hybrids with other species: —

"*Anas curvirostra*, PALL." (GRAY.)
"*Anas Freycineti*, BONAP." (GRAY.)
Anas archiboschas, subboschas, conboschas, BREHM, Vög. Deutschl. 862, 864, 865.
Anas purpureoviridis, SCHINZ.
Anas maxima, GOSSE, Birds Jam. 1847, 399 (= hybrid with *Cairina moschata*).
Anas bicolor, DONOVAN, Br. Birds, IX. pl. 212.
Anas Breweri, AUD. Orn. Biog. IV. 1838, 302, pl. 338 ("*glocitans*"); Synop. 1839, 277; B. Am. VI. 1843, 252, pl. 387. [Perhaps adult ♂ of *A. boschas* in changing plumage.]
Anas Auduboni, BONAP. List, 1838, 56 ("*bimaculata*"). (Same as *Breweri*.)
Fuligula viola, BELL. Ann. Lyc. N. Y. V. 1852, 219.
Anas iopareia, PHIL. Wiegm. Archiv, I. 1860, 25; P. Z. S. 1866, 531.

umber-brown, this also tinging the adjoining scapulars ; wing-coverts uniform deep brownish gray, the last row tipped with opaque velvety black, and with a subterminal bar of pure white ; speculum rich metallic violet, with a subterminal velvety black, and terminal pure white bar; primaries plain brownish gray. Rump, upper tail-coverts, and crissum, intense velvety black, showing faint reflections of bluish green. Tail white, the feathers grayish centrally. Two middle feathers black, slightly recurved ; the two longer upper tail-coverts greatly recurved. Bill olive-yellow or ochraceous-olive (in life), the nail black ; iris hazel ; tarsi and toes fine rich orange-red (changing to yellowish in dried skin). Length, about 24.00 inches ; extent, 38.00 ; wing, 11.00–11.85 ; culmen, 2.10–2.40 ; tarsus, 1.60–1.80 ; middle toe, 2.00–2.15. *Adult male in summer:* "Closely resembling the female, being merely somewhat darker in color. This plumage is donned by degrees early in June ; and in August the full rich winter dress is again resumed" (SHARPE & DRESSER). *Adult female:* Wing as in the male. Above, brownish dusky, much variegated by broad pale ochraceous edges to the feathers ; beneath pale ochraceous, the feathers dusky centrally, producing a thickly spotted or striped appearance. On the top of the head the dusky predominates, as it also does in a loral and auricular line, forming a lighter superciliary stripe between this and the crown. Wing, 10.25–11.50 ; culmen, 2.00–2.35 ; tarsus, 1.50–1.80 ; middle toe, 1.90–2.05.

Male.

Downy young:[1] Above, deep olivaceous, relieved by two pairs of yellowish buff spots, the first pair on the back, just behind the wings, the second at the base of the tail, the first not confluent with the buff of the lower parts ; wings deep olivaceous, varied on both edges with dull greenish yellow ; pileum and nape olivaceous, darker on the occiput, lighter on the forehead ; a broad superciliary stripe, including the sides of the forehead, sides of the head and neck, and entire lower parts, yellowish buff, deepest on the head, paler on the anal region and crissum ; sides more grayish, and crossed, between the wings and thighs, by two wide patches of dark olive projecting from that of the back. Side of the head marked by a narrow but very distinct stripe of dark brown from the upper basal angle of the maxilla to the eye, thence back to and confluent with the olivaceous of the occiput ; beneath the latter, almost directly over the ear, an isolated spot of the same.

The adult males in winter plumage vary chiefly in the extent and richness of the chestnut of the jugulum. Sometimes this is restricted to the jugulum, but occasionally it spreads over the

[1] Described from No. 77546, Washoe Lake, Nev., May 22, 1877 : H. W. HENSHAW. This specimen represents the youngest stage, not long from the egg, and is less than 6 inches in total length, the bill about half an inch long. Older specimens are larger, the size, of course, proportioned to the age, while as they increase in size the bright yellowish tints become gradually replaced with pale dingy grayish ; the olivaceous of the upper parts also becomes more gray.

breast, as in No. 12718, Washington, D. C. (December), in which the entire lower parts, except the sides, are tinged with rich cream-color.

The single European specimen in the collection differs from all the North American males in its considerably smaller size. It measures: Wing, 10.20 inches; culmen, 2.00; tarsus, 1.50; middle toe, 1.80. The smallest North American male, among a large series of specimens, measures: Wing, 11.00 inches; culmen, 2.10; tarsus, 1.60; middle toe, 2.00; while the average is considerably larger. The European specimen differs also in markings, the speculum being much narrower (the violet less than 1.00 inch wide, instead of 1.50 or more), while black and white bars on each side of it are not nearly so broad. There is no difference, however, in color. Two females from Europe measure: Wing, 9.70–10.00 inches; culmen, 2.00–2.10; tarsus, 1.65–1.70; middle toe, 1.80–1.85.[1] The only tangible difference in pattern of coloration consists in the narrower bars of the speculum, the terminal white one being reduced to a narrow line, instead of a quite broad bar.

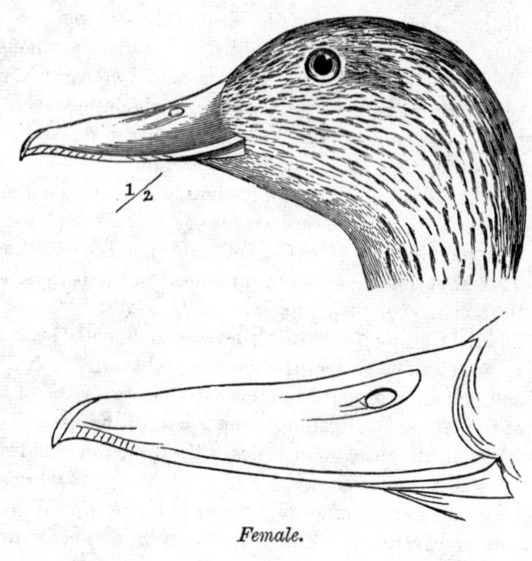

Female.

Even in its feral state, the Mallard varies greatly in size and markings, although the proportionate number of "abnormal" examples is of course small. Many of these variations are due to hybridism with other species; but very many examples occur in which no connection with another species can be traced. The latter are usually considerably larger than the ordinary wild bird, and the colors wholly indeterminate, the range of variation in this respect being fully equal to that in the domesticated bird. Such examples are frequently killed during the migrations, either mixed singly with flocks of the ordinary bird, or in companies by themselves. Without going into further details in regard to these feral varieties, we will proceed to describe a few of the more remarkable specimens and hybrids which are now before us: —

(1.) An autumnal female from Mount Carmel, Ill., is so different from all other specimens examined that there is some doubt whether it is pure *A. boschas;* the differences from the normal female of *A. boschas* involve the proportions as well as the colors. The bill is very broad, measuring 1.00 inch in width near the end, and .95 at the base; its length along the culmen being 2.00 inches, and its height through the base .95. Its color is black, except the terminal third, which is bright orange, the nail jet black; the feet are bright orange-red. The ground-color of the entire plumage, except the wings, is a deep and very uniform ochraceous; the head and neck are very finely streaked with narrow lines of black, except on the chin and throat, which are immaculate; this streaking is so uniform, that *there is no indication of a darker loral stripe or lighter one above it*, the post-orbital light stripe alone being perceptible. Each feather of the lower parts has a medial stripe of black, *these markings being of uniform size and shape throughout the entire lower surface.* The back and scapulars are more irregularly variegated, the black being nearly in the form of V-shaped markings, though they vary on different feathers. The rump and upper tail-coverts are almost cinnamon-color, each feather being broadly black medially, *these black markings having a bright green reflection.* The wings are normal in coloration, except that the coverts are more conspicuously bordered with white than is usual. The measurements of this specimen are as follows: Wing, 10.90 inches; culmen, 2.00; tarsus, 1.95; middle toe, 2.30.

[1] Messrs. Sharpe & Dresser, however, in their "History of the Birds of Europe" (part xvii.) give the measurements of European *A. boschas* as follows: "Total length, 23.00 inches; culmen, 2.60; wing, 10.50; tail, 4.00; tarsus, 1.85."

(2.) A melanotic variety of the domesticated race is propagated at Mount Auburn, Mass., and in other localities in the Northern States. A fine adult male from the former place, presented by Dr. Brewer to the National Museum (No. 66231), has the following characters : Entire plumage intense coal-black, with an irregular patch of pure white on the breast, and a smaller one on the middle of the foreneck. Lower surface opaque, and with a slight brownish cast ; but entire upper surface (except primaries and rectrices), including the head and neck, glossed with a brilliant green reflection, changing to violet in certain lights ; the speculum is of the same changeable green or violet as the wing-coverts, but is broadly tipped with opaque black ; the head and neck are more brilliant green than the other portions. This specimen measures, wing, 11.25 inches ; culmen, 2.10 ; tarsus, 1.90 ; middle toe, 2.15. The bill is blackish olive, and the feet black. The latter are much stouter than those of the wild bird ; but this is said to be a peculiarity of the Domestic Mallard as distinguished from the wild bird. The size and proportions of this specimen prove it to be a true Mallard, and not a hybrid with another species, though the prevalence of the metallic reflections over the whole of the upper parts caused an early comparison with *Cairina moschata*, on suspicion that it might be part " Muscovy " — which, however, proves to be not the case. The curled upper tail-coverts and middle tail-feathers are precisely as in the ordinary Mallard. The characters of this variety are said to be very constant.

(3.) Among the undoubted hybrids between the Mallard and other species of Ducks, there are three before us, represented by four examples. That of most common occurrence is a cross with the Muscovy (*Cairina moschata* [1]), a Tropical American species, but common in domestication. These hybrids are no doubt produced in the barnyard ; but it is said that such birds do not inherit the tameness of their progenitors, but revert to the original wildness of both species, and escape by flight. Certain it is, that they are frequently shot by gunners along our coast. The two specimens before us possess the following characters : No. 17142, ♂ ad. has the large, broad speculum, and broad, lengthened tail specially characteristic of the Muscovy, and lacks the recurved feathers of the Mallard. Head and upper half of the neck black, with a dull green reflection, mixed with white on the throat and beneath the eye ; lower half of the neck, except behind, white ; breast and sides deep rufous-chestnut ; rest of lower parts white, the flanks and post-tibial region undulated with slate-color ; crissum brownish black, tinged with rufous. Above, brownish black, grizzled with transverse sprinkling of grayish brown, becoming uniform black on the rump and upper tail-coverts, which have a rich dark-green reflection. Wing-coverts uniform slate-color ; speculum uniform bottle-green, narrowly tipped with white ; primaries entirely immaculate pure white ; tail uniform dark slate. Bill yellow (pink in life ?), mottled with black ; feet orange. Head completely feathered. Wing, 13.20 ; culmen, 2.30 ; tarsus, 2.20 ; middle toe, 2.60.

No. 66617, ♂ ad., with the same general appearance, differs in some important particulars. It is destitute of the albinotic indication seen in the white primaries and neck-patch. The head and neck are continuous greenish bronze of a peculiar tint, intermediate between the purplish of *C. moschata* and the pure green of *A. boschas*. The lower portion of the neck, the breast, and sides

[1] Cairina moschata.

Anas moschata, Linn. S. N. ed. 10, I. 1758, 124 ; ed. 12, I. 1766, 199. — Nutt. Man. Water Birds, 1834, 403 (Lower Mississippi and Gulf Coast of U. S. !).

Cairina moschata, Flem. Phil. Zool. 1822, 260 ; Br. Anim. 1828, 122. — Scl. & Salv. Nom. Neotr. 1873, 129 ; P. Z. S. 1876, 378 (monographic). — Coues, Birds N. W. 1874, 559 (synonymy).

Cairina sylvestris, Stephens, Shaw's Gen. Zool. XII. ii. 1824, 69.

Le Canard Musque, Buff. Pl. Enl. 986.

El Pato grande o Real, Azara, Apunt. III. 1805, no. 437.

? *Anas Marianæ*, Shaw, Nat. Misc. II. t. 69.

Hab. The whole of tropical America, except West Indies.

This species is most likely yet to be detected in the wild state along our southern border — in fact, Nuttall, as quoted above, says that it is "occasionally seen along the coasts of the Mexican Gulf, in the lower part of Mississippi, and stragglers are frequently observed along the coasts of the warmer parts of the Union." In its habits it much resembles the common Wood Duck (*Aix sponsa*), its favorite haunts being swampy woods and the forest-border of streams, where it nests in hollows of the trees, and perches on the branches in true arboreal fashion.

are chestnut-rufous, the feathers having narrow white borders, and those in front with a central black dot on each; the crissum is black, tinged with chestnut; remaining lower parts white, slightly grizzled laterally. Dorsal region black, the feathers bordered terminally with white, and grizzled basally with the same, some of them tinged with rufous; rump and upper tail-coverts continuous intense greenish black; tail uniform dark slate, with a violet reflection. Wing-coverts white, mottled transversely with black, the last row dusky, sharply bordered with white; speculum bright bottle-green, narrowly tipped with white; primaries dusky, the outer webs white. Bill and feet deep black. Head normally feathered. Wing, 13.00 inches; culmen, 2.35; tarsus, 2.10; middle toe, 2.50.

A beautiful hybrid between the Mallard and the Pintail (*Dafila acuta*) was sent to the National Museum (No. 66618) by Dr. J. W. Velie, from Chicago. It corresponds very closely with that figured and described by Professor Newton, in the "Proceedings" of the London Zoological Society, June, 1860, pl. clxviii., and in both form and coloration is throughout a perfect combination of both species. The head and neck are continuous brownish green, ranging from the brown of *D. acuta* on the anterior part of the head to the brilliant green of *A. boschas* on the back of the neck. The white collar is broader than in *A. boschas*, and posteriorly sends upward on each side of the nape a short arm, corresponding to the lengthened stripe of *D. acuta*. The jugulum is pale cinnamon; the wings are those of *D. acuta*, except the tertials, which are those of *A. boschas;* the upper tail-coverts are purplish-black, edged with pale fulvous; the two middle tail-feathers are elongated about half as much as in *D. acuta*, and curled half as tightly as in *A. boschas!* The bill is dark lead-color, and the feet are dark reddish. Wing, 11.00 inches; culmen, 2.20; tarsus, 1.55; middle toe, 1.90.

The remaining supposed hybrid is an adult male, intermediate between *A. boschas* and *A. obscura*, purchased by Professor Baird in the Washington market, Jan. 25, 1871, and is apparently much like the bird described by Audubon as *Anas Breweri*. With the prevalent aspect of *A. obscura*, it has the side of the occiput and nape brilliant green, and the jugulum and breast strongly tinged with chestnut. The lateral upper tail-coverts are black with a violet reflection, as are also the terminal and lateral lower coverts; while the middle tail-feathers curl upward, though not so much so as in pure *A. boschas*. The white bar anterior to the speculum of *boschas* is obsolete, or very faintly indicated, and the white collar round the neck is wanting. It measures, wing, 10.75 inches; culmen, 2.05; tarsus, 1.55; middle toe, 1.95; and before skinning was 23.50 inches in total length, and 48.50 in extent of wings. The bill was grayish olive-green on terminal half and along culmen, greenish olive-yellow basally; nail and most of lower mandible black; iris brown; legs and feet dull salmon-orange, the webs purplish.

Probably no Duck has a wider distribution, or is found in greater numbers where it occurs, than the Common Mallard, the undoubted origin of the domesticated inmates of our poultry-yards. It is found throughout North America, from Mexico to the Arctic Ocean, and from the Atlantic to the Pacific. It occurs in every part of Europe, breeding from Southern Spain to Lapland on the west, and from Greece to Siberia on the east. No part of Asia, except the more southern portions of India, is supposed to be without it, and it is more or less abundant in all the northern portions of Africa. And wherever found, the birds of this species are more or less resident, some remaining all winter as far north as they can find open inland water, and breeding, in limited numbers, in localities where the larger proportion spend their winter.

This Duck is cited by Professor Reinhardt as among the birds which breed in Greenland. Captain Blakiston found it on the Saskatchewan, and abundant throughout the interior. Mr. Ross met with it along the entire course of the Mackenzie, even as far north as the shores of the Arctic Sea. It is abundant in Vancouver Island; and Dr. Cooper found it very common in the Rocky Mountains in Montana, where it breeds.

In Hearne's time (1790) flocks of this Duck visited Hudson's Bay in great numbers, and were distributed over the region extending from the sea-coast to the remotest west. Near Cumberland House these birds were found in vast multitudes. At their first arrival on the sea-coast their flesh was good; but when the bird was moulting, it became so rank that few Europeans could eat it. This peculiarity, however, was confined to those Ducks which bred near the sea-coast.

This species is not common in Eastern North America. Mr. Boardman has seen it in New Brunswick and Eastern Maine, but it is only an occasional and rare visitor to that region, and is by no means common in Massachusetts. It is found in small numbers on Cape Cod, and may possibly breed there. I am not aware that it has been seen there in winter. Only a single specimen is reported as having been met with in Bermuda. Dr. Bryant speaks of it as being very common, during the winter, in the Bahamas.

Dr. Kennerly, in March, 1855, found this Duck abundant along the Conalitos and Janos rivers, occurring generally in flocks, but sometimes singly. It was also common along the Rio San Pedro of Sonora.

Professor Kumlien finds the Mallard quite common in Southern Wisconsin, where it breeds in the marshes. The males gather in flocks in Lake Koskonong, while the females take the entire charge of the nest, eggs, and young. In some cases these Ducks remain during mild winters, gathering around open spring-holes. They are much more abundant in the fall than at any other time, when they visit the cornfields of the prairies in large numbers, and commit great depredations on the crops.

Mr. J. A. Allen found this bird very common in the valley of Great Salt Lake. In California, according to Dr. Cooper, it abounds during the wet season on all the fresh waters of that region, but rarely appearing on those that are salt. It is supposed to breed in nearly all parts of that State. It also breeds along the inland lakes and streams up to the very summits of the mountains, and northward up to and beyond the sixty-eighth parallel. This remarkable power of adaptation to life in various climates and conditions seems to fit this species for domestication. Moreover its flesh is not surpassed by that of any other species; fed with the same food, even the renowned Canvas-back is not its superior.

Mr. Dall found it to be one of the most abundant winter visitants at Unalashka, where it occurred in large numbers as early as October 12, remaining until the succeeding month of April, when it migrated northward. It was seen near Mazatlan, in Western Mexico, by Colonel Grayson, but was not abundant, and was met with only during the winter months.

According to Mr. Ridgway, this is the most common Duck throughout the interior, where it breeds abundantly in all suitable localities, and where it is also a winter resident. Mr. Osbert Salvin found this species common at Zane, in Northeastern Africa. It was noticed in the Sahara Region by Mr. Tristram, and was seen by Mr. E. C. Taylor in Egypt. Captain E. G. Shelley states ("Ibis," 1871) that he found it very abundant in Egypt and Nubia, and frequently remaining there to breed. According to Mr. T. L. Powys, the marshes of Epirus and Albania swarm with it throughout the winter; and Mr. H. Saunders describes it as breeding in the "Marisma," or salt-water lagoons, in Spain. Mr. C. W. Shepard observed it breeding in the north of Iceland, on the shores of Lake Mý-vatn. It was wild and unsociable, and nested in quiet, swampy places on the shore of the lake, or on the islands not frequented by other species. Mr. Swinhoe adds this Duck to the fauna of Formosa, and also states that he found it near Amoy, in China. Mr. Godwin notes its presence in all the lakes throughout all the islands of the Azores group, and found it breeding among the mountain lakes and marshes in Flores. Middendorff includes this species among the birds of Siberia, where he found it breeding in the wooded districts and forests. It is also given by Wheelwright as the most common of all the Ducks throughout the whole of Scandinavia.

In no portion of Eastern North America is it a common species in the summer. Even on Long Island Giraud saw but a single pair — in July, 1837 — and was unable to find their nest. He met with this bird in large numbers, however, in North Carolina, where it frequents the rice-fields; and also found it common in the bayous of the Lower Mississippi, and still more numerous in Alabama. The voice of the Wild Mallard is not distinguishable from that of the domesticated bird.

While more or less common on all our rivers, fresh-water ponds, and lakes, it is seldom met with near the sea-coast. In the winter it is found in large numbers in all the Southern waters, and especially in the rice-fields, where it becomes very fat, and acquires a delicate flavor. It prefers vegetable matter to any other kind of food, and its flesh is almost universally excellent. It is easily brought within gunshot by means of decoys. At certain seasons it is abundant on the Delaware, where it feeds on the seeds of the wild oats, of which it is very fond, and which contribute greatly to the delicacy of its flavor.

It is abundant in all parts of Great Britain and Ireland; and in many parts of Scotland, where it is protected, it exhibits great fearlessness, and even familiarity. Mr. Robert Gray mentions that in walking through the policies of Duff House, in Banffshire, he saw many hundreds of Mallards, in a particular pool in the Deveron, which were so tame, that on being approached they merely swam to the other side of the river. He also witnessed a remarkable assemblage of Mallards, in the spring of 1870, on a pond at Douglas Castle, Lanarkshire, which were so unsuspicious as to allow even strangers to approach within six or eight yards of the bank where they sat preening their feathers.

Mr. Gray was also informed by Mr. D. Macdonald that he has seen hundreds of Mallards, on a mill-dam in Aberdeenshire, so tame as to come at the call of the miller who fed them. This man no sooner appeared and uttered a peculiar whistle, than the Ducks came flying from all parts of the pond and alighted within a few yards of where he stood. But no stranger could prevail upon them to approach.

Mr. H. E. Dresser, who enjoyed favorable opportunities for studying the habits of the Mallard in Northern Finland, noticed certain peculiarities that have escaped other observers. Like its very near relative, the *Anas obscura*, it was observed to feed chiefly, if not entirely, by night. When found in the marshy lowlands during the daytime, it was resting, and not feeding; but began to move as soon as evening approached. Mr. Macgillivray states that around Edinburgh it resorts at night, from October to April, to open ditches and brooks to feed. As it discovers its food by means of the sense of touch rather than of sight, it can feed equally well by night or day; but in populous districts it is compelled to feed in the dark.

Marshy places, the margins of ponds and streams, pools and ditches, are its favorite resorts. It walks with ease, and can even run with considerable speed, or dive, if forced to do so; but never dives in order to feed. Its food consists chiefly of the seeds of grasses, fibrous roots of plants, worms, mollusks, and insects. In feeding in shallow water it keeps the hind part of its body erect, while it searches the muddy bottom with its bill. When alarmed and made to fly, it utters a loud *quack*, the cry of the female being the louder. It feeds silently; but after hunger is appeased, it amuses itself with various jabberings, swims about, moves its head backward and forward, throws the water over its back, shoots along the surface, half flying, half running, and seems quite playful. If alarmed, it springs up at once with a bound, rises obliquely to a considerable height, and flies off with great speed, the wings producing a whistling sound. It flies by repeated flaps, without sailing or undulations; and when in full flight its speed is hardly less than a hundred miles in an hour.

The Mallard pairs early in the spring, and soon disperses, each pair seeking its breeding-place, and nesting on the ground, in the midst of marshes or among water-plants, occasionally on higher ground, but always in the vicinity of water. Its nest is usually large, and rudely constructed of sedges and coarse grasses, rarely lined with down or feathers. It has been known in rare instances to nest in a tree; in such cases occupying the deserted nest of a Hawk, Crow, or other large bird. The eggs, usually six or eight in number, are pale dull green or greenish white, and measure 2.25 inches by 1.60 inches.

The female alone incubates, the male leaving her to undergo his annual moult. The female sits very closely, and will sometimes even allow herself to be taken on the nest, or permit the eggs to be removed while she is sitting. When she leaves the nest she conceals the eggs with hay, down, or any convenient material. The period of incubation is four weeks. The young, when hatched, immediately follow their mother to the water, where she attends them devotedly, aids them in procuring food, and warns them of the approach of danger. While they are attempting to escape, she feigns lameness, to attract to herself the attention of the enemy. The young are extremely active, dive with surprising celerity, and remain under the water with only the bill above the surface. When the young are full-grown, the male rejoins the brood; and several families unite to form a small flock.

The breeding-season lasts from April to June, though few nest south of 40° north latitude after the middle of May. Dr. E. Rey, of Leipzig, informed Mr. Dresser that he has known as many as fifteen eggs in a nest.

The Mallard, both in the wild and in the domesticated state, readily hybridizes with other species. The *Anas maxima* of Gosse is a hybrid between this species and the Muscovy Duck. A highly esteemed race of Domestic Duck, known to fanciers as the Cayuga Duck, is unquestionably the product of a union between a male Mallard and a female Muscovy. Hybridisms between the Mallard and the Godwell, the Shoveller and the Dusky Duck, and other species, are on record.

The following statements in regard to this species are abridged from the very full Arctic notes of the late Mr. Robert Kennicott: —

The Mallard is found as far north as the shores of the Arctic Ocean. Being a strictly fresh-water Duck, it does not breed immediately upon the sea-coast, but prefers the inland rivers and lakes. Nor does it frequent the great lakes and rivers as much as it does the smaller streams and grassy lakes and marshes. It breeds sparingly as far south as Mexico, and its nests are not rare in the Northern United States, but occur in greatest abundance between the Northern United States and the Arctic Circle. In summer this is the most common Duck from the United States northward to Great Slave Lake. It is also abundant on the Yukon and at Peel's River, and Mr. MacFarlane also found it common at Fort Anderson, north of Bear Lake.

At Great Slave Lake and on the Yukon it arrives among the first of the Water Birds, the earliest comers being seen in the latter part of April, though the greater number do not appear until early in May. At Fort Good Hope it arrives a little later. When it reaches Slave Lake, about the 10th of May, it is already paired. A few begin to nest before the middle of May; but there and on the Yukon the greater number nest early in June, the young hatching about the 1st of July. It leaves its northern breeding-grounds for the south, without collecting in large flocks, about the last of September.

At the north its nest is always found among trees, and within two or three rods of the water — never in moist places among marshes unprotected by trees, nor at any considerable distance from water. The nest is large, the base very unartificial, consisting usually of a simple depression among the leaves, but warmly lined with down and feathers. In Northern Illinois it was frequently found nesting on the prairie at the edges of sloughs.

At the north the old males moult while the females are incubating, the females moulting some two weeks later, after the young are hatched. The males remain near the nest some time after the females begin to incubate; but before the young leave the nest they collect in small parties of three or four, and go off by themselves. He rarely observed them accompanying the mother and her young. The young broods seek the protection of the reeds and grass, and are rarely seen, like the Sea Ducks, on open rivers or lakes. In summer, the young, before they can fly, and while the old birds are moulting, are very fat, and are killed in great numbers by the Indians. The hunter stands erect in his canoe, paddling silently along the lakes they frequent. Upon his approach they seek the grassy edges, where they cannot so readily dive, and the movement of the grass betraying their course, they are easily killed with arrows, or even with the paddle. At Fort Yukon he saw an Indian kill thirty young Ducks in two or three hours.

In the United States this Duck ranks among the first as an article of food, and when fattened on wild rice, in autumn, is superior even to the Canvas-back fed on *vallisneria;* but in the far north it loses its fine flavor. In the spring it is lean and tough; and in summer, until after it leaves for the south, its flavor is spoiled by the stagnant marshy water in which it feeds.

The northern Indians acknowledge this species as the type of all Ducks, simply calling it, in their various languages, "Big Duck." The Canadians and French half-breeds call it the "*Canard français;*" while the English call it the "Stock Duck."

Mr. Dall states that its Indian name at Nulato is *Nintála;* it is one of the first of the Ducks to arrive in spring, it generally appearing, about the 1st of May, in company with *Bucephala albeola.* It is common both on the sea-coast and in the interior. He found its eggs, eight in number, in a rotten stump about six inches above the level of the ground, laid directly on the wood, and covered with dead leaves and a few feathers.

The eggs of the Mallard are usually grayish white, with a more or less decided tinge of green; in some the green is quite prominent. Three eggs from Dubuque, Ia. (Smithsonian Institution, No. 9834), measure respectively, 2.35 by 1.70 inches; 2.20 by 1.70; 2.40 by 1.70; two from the Yukon (Smithsonian Institution, No. 6570) measure 2.45 by 1.75, and 2.55 by 1.80. The least length is 2.10 inches, and the smallest breadth 1.50.

Anas obscura.

THE BLACK MALLARD; DUSKY DUCK.

Anas obscura, Gmel. S. N. I. ii. 1788, 541. — Wils. Am. Orn. VIII. 1814, 141; pl. 72, f. 5. — Nutt. Man. II. 1834, 392. — Aud. Orn. Biog. IV. 1838, 15, pl. 302; Synop. 1839, 276; B. Am. VI. 1843, 244, pl. 386. — Baird, B. N. Am. 1858, 775; Cat. N. Am. B. 1859, no. 577. — Coues, Key, 1872, 285; Check List, 1873, no. 489; 2d ed. 1882, no. 708; B. N. W. 1874, 560. — Ridgw. Nom. N. Am. B. 1881, no. 602.

Hab. Eastern North America, west to Utah and Texas, north to Labrador. Cuba?

Sp. Char. *Adult:* Prevailing color brownish black or dusky, the feathers edged, more or less distinctly, with pale grayish fulvous. Head and neck about equally streaked with grayish white (more ochraceous near the bill) and dusky; pileum nearly uniform dusky, and a dusky stripe back from the eye. Speculum violet, changing to green in some lights, narrowly tipped with white, and with a broad subterminal bar of velvety black; last row of coverts dusky brownish, broadly tipped with black. Sexes alike. "Bill yellowish green, the unguis dusky; iris dark brown; feet orange-red, the webs dusky" (AUDUBON).

Downy young:[1] Above, olivaceous-brown, faintly relieved by six inconspicuous markings of light brownish buff, situated as follows: one on the posterior border of each arm-wing; one (small, and sometimes nearly obsolete) on each side of the back, behind the wings, and one, more distinct,

A. obscura.

on each side the rump, near the base of the tail. Pileum and nape (longitudinally), brown, like the back; rest of the head and neck, with lower parts, light dingy brownish buff, paler on the abdomen; side of the head marked with a narrow dusky stripe running from the upper basal angle of the maxilla to the eye, thence back toward the occiput, but scarcely confluent with the brown on the latter; an indistinct spot on the auricular region, with a still less distinct dusky mark extending back from this to the nape.

Wing, 10.50–11.50 inches; culmen, 2.00–2.35; tarsus, 1.70–1.80; middle toe, 1.90–2.10.

A summer specimen from Moose Factory, Hudson's Bay Territory No. 17971, (JOHN MCKENZIE), differs from United States (fall, winter, and spring) examples in having the pale edges of the feathers nearly all worn off, so that the plumage appears to be nearly uniform black, while the lower parts are strongly tinged with rusty, this approaching a bright ferruginous tint on the breast. Some examples have a slight tinge of metallic green on the sides of the head, behind the eye.

The Dusky Duck appears to be confined to the eastern portions of North America. It is found from the Atlantic coast to the western parts of the Mississippi Valley, occurring along the tributary streams to an extent not fully ascertained. It is abundant throughout the British Provinces of Canada, New Brunswick, and Nova Scotia, and individuals have been occasionally taken farther north. It is also more or less abundant during the winter months in all the Eastern and Southern States, including South Carolina, Florida, and Texas. It has been taken near Fort Anderson in June, where the species was reported as being tolerably numerous. This is the most northern point to which it has been traced.

[1] Described from No. 52392, Calais, Me.; G. A. BOARDMAN.

It has not been taken on the Pacific coast, so far as I am aware, nor is it known west of the Mississippi Valley. A single specimen is reported by Blakiston as having been taken near York Factory, on Hudson's Bay. That the species occurs in Labrador and breeds there, is attested by a set of eggs in my cabinet collected there by a correspondent of Mr. Möschaler, of Herrnhut, Saxony.

It is very abundant in Nova Scotia, especially in the vicinity of Halifax, where it has been successfully reared in confinement, and domesticated by Mr. Andrew Downes. Mr. Boardman informs me that it is very numerous in the summer near Calais, breeding there in great abundance. It is more or less common in all parts of New England, and is present in Massachusetts all the year. The birds found in winter are said to be of a smaller and different race from the summer visitants; but I can find no evidence of the correctness of this statement. In severe winter weather they are driven to the open sea, and their numbers are then greatly reduced. This bird is known to our hunters only as the "Black Duck."

According to Giraud, it is only partially migratory on Long Island, but is more abundant in winter than in summer. In the latter season it is rarely seen, as it keeps concealed in the tall grass, which grows luxuriantly in the places it selects for its abode. As it subsists on roots and small shellfish, so abundant on the salt-marshes during the season of reproduction, it has no occasion to leave its secluded retreats in quest of food, either for itself or its young. In the selection of its summer residence it so carefully avoids places visited by man, that its nest is seldom met with. A friend of Mr. Giraud is stated to have found on the 19th of May, on the south side of the island, two nests, both made of very coarse materials. One contained seven, the other nine eggs, all of a dull white color. They were placed under a hen, and eleven of the sixteen were hatched. Their foster-mother could not restrain them from their prolonged visits to the creek, and it became necessary to confine them in a pen. There they were very uneasy, and refused to eat any kind of grain, but eagerly devoured clams and all kinds of shellfish. When seven weeks old they were given to another gentleman, who succeeded in domesticating them. In their wild state, however, this species is not infrequently "baited" with corn and other kinds of grain.

Mr. Giraud states that the most successful mode of procuring this species on Long Island is what is there known as "dusking." This is practised on moonlight evenings by lying concealed in places it is in the habit of frequenting. Perfect silence must be observed, as the slightest noise will frighten it away. By this method of hunting large numbers are frequently killed. Two celebrated hunters residing at South Oyster Bay informed Mr. Giraud that while dusking one evening they killed ninety-nine birds, and would have killed more, but for the want of ammunition.

This Duck keeps continually moving about in small parties all night. When wounded it frequently escapes by diving, and often flies a great distance before falling, even when fatally hit, and not infrequently strikes the water at least half a mile from where it was shot. In stormy or very severe weather this species seldom ventures out to sea, and at such times flies low, affording a good opportunity to the hunter.

In mild winters, when food is easily procured, it is in fine condition, and is highly esteemed. It does not, like other Ducks, always rise against the wind, but will spring up in any direction, and continue to ascend until out of reach. Its voice generally resembles that of the common Domestic Duck, but at times it gives utterance to a loud whistling note.

Mr. Giraud mentions that when he was at Niagara Falls, Oct. 16, 1840, eighty-three Dusky Ducks were killed by flying into the Falls, and were picked up by the boatmen in attendance a short distance below. This is said to be a not unusual occurrence in foggy weather, when many Ducks lose their lives by alighting a short distance from the precipice, being carried over and killed before they can rise.

Mr. Lewis states ("American Sportsman") that this Duck is brought in innumerable quantities into the New York and Philadelphia markets, where it meets with a ready sale; though he regards its flesh as inferior to that of most other wild species of Ducks. In this, however, I cannot agree with him; as when brought to market from fresh-water regions, during the fall, it is usually excellent. In severer weather, when it feeds in the salt water, and in the spring, when vegetable food is not procurable, the character of its flesh is changed, and it is then less desirable.

Many are shot in the salt-marshes of the Delaware; here, however, they become very wary, and cannot be decoyed. They feed on small bivalves, so abundant in these waters. They swim and fly with great velocity. Their notes are not distinguishable from those of the Mallard; but their flesh, owing to the character of their food, is at times inferior. On the Delaware, as on Long Island, they are killed, on moonlight nights, by hunters who lie in wait for them as they return from the sea to the marshes to feed.

Major Wedderburn states that this Duck occasionally visits the Bermudas in the fall and winter, making its appearance about the middle of September, and being last seen in December. Mr. Robert Kennicott met with a few individuals of this species in Northern Minnesota, where they were feeding on wild rice in company with Mallards.

In Southern Wisconsin, where nearly all the other fresh-water Ducks are so abundant, Professor Kumlien informs me that this species is by no means common. It is more frequently met with in the fall than in the spring. He has never seen it there in the summer, and he does not believe that it breeds in that region. Mr. Audubon found it breeding in the Bay of Fundy on the 10th of May, 1833, where he met with young birds apparently not more than a week old.

The flight of this Duck is similar to that of the Mallard, but is even more powerful and rapid, and equally well sustained. It may always be readily distinguished from that species by the whiteness of its lower wing-coverts, which strongly contrasts with the dark tints of its general plumage.

The eggs of this species are of a deep grayish white, usually with a slight tinge of green. Three eggs obtained north of Rupert House (Smithsonian Institution, No. 4348) have the following measurements: 2.50 inches by 1.75; 2.35 by 1.75; and 2.50 by 1.85.

Anas fulvigula.

THE FLORIDA DUSKY DUCK.

Anas obscura, var. *fulvigula*, RIDGW. Am. Nat. VIII. Feb. 1874, 111 (St. John's R. Fla.).
Anas obscura, b. *fulvigula*, COUES, Birds N. W. 1874, 561.
Anas obscura fulvigula, COUES, Check List, 2d ed. 1882, no. 709.
Anas fulvigula, RIDGW. Proc. U. S. Nat. Mus. Vol. I. 1878, 251 ; Nom. N. Am. B. 1881, no. 603.

HAB. Florida (resident) ; Cuba?

SP. CHAR. *Adult:* Colors brownish black and ochraceous in nearly equal amount, the former in the centre and the latter on the margin of the feathers ; many of the feathers, especially the scapulars and long feathers of the sides and flanks, with a second V-shaped mark of ochraceous inside the marginal one. Entire throat and chin immaculate delicate ochraceous, or deep cream-color. Speculum deep metallic green (rarely purplish), with a faint purple or blue tinge in some lights, tipped broadly with velvety black ; last row of coverts brownish black, broadly tipped with velvety black and with a subterminal bar of deep ochraceous. Bill olive-yellow, the margin and base of the maxilla, especially below, black ; feet deep orange-red. Wing, 10.00–10.50 inches; tail, 5.00 ; culmen, 2.05–2.35 ; width of the bill, .90 ; tarsus, 1.70–1.80 ; middle toe, 1.90–2.00.

This well-marked and apparently very local species resembles *A. obscura* in general appearance, particularly in the absence of white bars on the wing, but is very much lighter in color, the entire chin and throat, as well as the greater part of the foreneck, being immaculate creamy buff, whereas these parts in *A. obscura* are thickly streaked with dusky ; the speculum is more often green than violet, the contrary being the case in *A. obscura*. An apparently constant point of distinction is to be found in the bill, the maxilla in *A. obscura* being olivaceous to the extreme base, while in *A. fulvigula* the base is margined by a narrow black line which widens out into a triangular space near the rictus or beneath the feathering of the lores.

Specimens vary chiefly in the color of the speculum, which ranges from bright grass-green to violet, the former being the usual color. As in the Dusky Duck, the under wing-coverts and axillars are pure white.

What has been supposed to be only a smaller southern race of the common Dusky Duck has for some time been known to exist in Florida. It is now recognized as a distinct and valid resident form, confined to southern regions exclusively. It is also probable that the Dusky Ducks known to be resident in South Carolina may also be referable to this species rather than to *A. obscura*.

For the history of its peculiar habits I am indebted to Mr. N. B. Moore; its existence being first made known to him, in 1869, by his killing several adults and meeting with a brood of nine young. An informant of Mr. Moore, who has lived sixty-six years in Florida — and for twenty-five years on Sarasota Bay — informed him that it was unknown to him until within the last six years, when he killed a few on the Sarasota. This Duck hatches in Florida from the first to the last of April, only one set of eggs being laid in a season, unless it fails in raising its first brood. The nest is always placed on the ground, and the number of eggs is usually nine or ten. In one instance a nest was discovered which was nearly three hundred yards from water, and other nests were met with still farther from water. The one first referred to was cautiously concealed in a thick mass of dead grass held upright by green palmettoes, about two feet high. Mr. Moore once noticed a pair of Ducks fly from a pond, near which he was seated, and pass over the pine-barrens. One of them dropped among the grass ; the other returned to the water. Suspecting that the birds might have a nest, he visited the locality the next day, when the birds behaved as before. He soon made his way to the spot where the female alighted, and found her in a somewhat open space. On her return to the pond he soon discovered her nest. It was carefully screened from view on all sides, and so canopied by the standing grass that the eggs were not visible from above. There was a rim of soft down, from the mother's breast, around the eggs, partly covering those in the outer circle. On viewing the nest the next day this down was found to have been drawn over all the eggs. Mr. Moore took them and placed them under a hen; and six days after they were hatched. This was early in April. It would appear, therefore, that the statement that the male forsakes his mate during incubation is not well founded; for in this instance the male bird, about the twenty-fourth day of incubation, still kept in the vicinity of the nest. It is, however, the universal belief that he does not assist in rearing the young.

Mr. Moore also informs me that in August, September, and the first part of October, parties of from five to twenty of this species leave the fresh ponds and fly across the bay to sand-bars on the inner sides of the Keys, where they spend the night in the pools or coves near the mangroves, and return at sunrise the next morning. Those shot at this time were all males; but in January, February, and March mated birds, flying in pairs, spend their nights in the same places. In one instance Mr. Moore came suddenly on a flock of three old birds and nine young; the latter were only a few days old. Two of the old birds flew off; but the mother remained, and led the Ducklings from the shallow pond over a dry and bare bed into a tangled mass of palmettoes and grass.

Mr. Moore has no doubt that this Duck would be a much more common bird in Florida but for the sweeping fires that are set to burn off this coarse growth of grass, to allow a fresher growth to spring up for the cattle. In these fires a great many of the birds must be destroyed. Mr. Moore has not succeeded in inducing this Duck to breed in confinement, although in 1874 he was in possession of nine of this species, in their third summer, all of which had been hatched out under a hen.

Mr. Audubon mentions finding the nest of a Dusky Duck, probably this species, on the 30th of April, 1837, on Galveston Island, Texas, formed of grass and feathers, and containing eight eggs. These were surrounded and partially covered with down. On the same island others were seen that evidently had nests. Mr. Audubon was informed that those which breed in Texas are resident there throughout the year. In South Carolina he was informed by the Rev. Dr. Bachman that this species, once rare, was becoming more and more abundant, attracted probably by the rice-fields; and farther inland it was even more plentiful. Hybrids between this and the Domestic Duck had been reared, and their eggs were productive, the offspring being larger than either parent. The young of this species, in the opinion of Mr. Audubon, afford delicious eating, and are said to be far superior to the more celebrated Canvas-back.

An egg of the Florida Dusky Duck, collected by Mr. Maynard, measures 2.33 inches in length by 1.70 in breadth. It has a general resemblance to the eggs of the common *A. obscura*, but is of a lighter shade of greenish white.

Genus **CHAULELASMUS**, Gray.

Chaulelasmus, Gray, 1838 (type, *Anas strepera*, Linn.).
Chauliodus, Swains. F. B. A. II. 1831, 440 (type, *Anas strepera*, Linn.). (Not of Bloch, 1801.)
Chauliodes, Eyton, Mon. Anat. 1838, 43 (same type). (Not of Latreille, 1798.)

But two species of this genus are known, the common and widely diffused *C. streperus*, and the more recently discovered *C. Couesi*, Streets, of Washington Island, in the South Pacific Ocean. The latter is very similar to *C. streperus*, having the same form and essentially the same coloration, but is much smaller, with several differences in plumage. The sides are white, coarsely spotted with grayish, instead of finely undulated with the same, as is the case with the adult male of

C. streperus; but this may very possibly be owing to a difference of age, as the type of *Couesi* is immature.

C. Couesi is very distinct, however, and much smaller, the measurements being as follows: Wing, 8.20 inches; culmen, 1.40; width of bill, .55; depth at base, .60; tarsus, 1.40; middle toe, 1.60.[1]

C. streperus.

1 CHAULELASMUS COUESI, Streets.

Chaulelasmus Couesi, STREETS, Bull. Nutt. Orn. Club, I. no. 2, July, 1876, 46 (Washington and New York islands, Fanning Group); Bull. U. S. Nat. Mus. no. 7, 1877, 21 (do.).

"Bill nearly as long as the head, about as deep as broad at the base, depressed anteriorly, sides nearly parallel, but converging slightly toward the base, tip rounded, and unguis abruptly curved; frontal angle short and obtuse; dorsal line at first sloping, rather more so than in *C. streperus,* anterior portion broad, straight, and flattened. Internal lamellæ numerous, small, and closely packed, about seventy-five in number — in *streperus* only about fifty. Nostrils sub-basal, lateral, large, and oblong.

"*Plumage* (*immature*): Head above dark brown, the feathers tipped with a lighter shade; frontal feathers with the central portion black, and edged with brownish white; throat and sides of head brownish white, shafts of the feathers brown, a small brown spot at the extremity of each; lower portion of the neck and breast all around with the feathers marked with concentric bars of black and light reddish brown; under surface of the body white, each feather with a broad dark band near the extremity, which gives to this region a mottled aspect; toward the tail the white of the abdomen assumes a dull reddish-brown tinge; the brownish-red color becomes more decided on the flanks and sides of the body where covered by the wings. On the back the plumage is more mature. Color dark brown marked transversely by fine wavy lines of black and white; scapulars dark brown and fringed with a narrow rim of reddish brown. Middle wing-coverts chestnut; greater, velvet black; speculum pure white, the inner web of the white feathers grayish brown; in the third feather in the speculum, counting from within, the white gives place to a hoary gray with a black outer margin; the primaries light brown, the portion of both webs nearest the shaft lighter; shaft light brown. Tail containing fourteen feathers, hoary plumbeous gray, under surface lighter and shining; under tail-coverts crossed by transverse bars of black and white; upper coverts composed of dark-brown and black feathers mingled. Under wing-coverts and axillars pure white. Bill and feet black, somewhat lighter on the inner side of the tarsus. Tibia bare for about half an inch. Length, 17 inches; wing, 8; tarsus, 1.40; commissure, 1.65; culmen, 1.45; height and breadth of bill at base, .55; average width of bill, .55; first toe, .30; second, 1.48, including claw, shorter than third toe without claw; third toe, 1.88, without claw, longer than outer toe without claw; outer toe, 1.75.

"A female is similar, but with little trace of the peculiar wing markings, both the chestnut and black being wanting, and the speculum being hoary gray instead of white. Both the specimens before me are immature; the adults, it is presumed, will show the peculiar vermiculated appearance of *C. streperus.* They resemble the immature condition of *C. streperus* so closely that one description of the coloration

Chaulelasmus streperus.

THE GADWALL; GRAY DUCK.

Anas strepera, LINN. S. N. ed. 10, I. 1758, 125; ed. 12, I. 1766, 200. — WILS. Am. Orn. VIII. 1814, 120, pl. 71. — NUTT. Man. II. 1834, 383. — AUD. Orn. Biog. IV. 1838, 353, pl. 348; Synop. 1839, 378; B. Am. VI. 1843, 254, pl. 388.
Anas (Chauliodus) streperus, SW. & RICH. F. B. A. II. 1831, 440.
Chaulelasmus streperus, "GRAY, 1838;" List B. Br. Mus. 1844, 139. — BAIRD, B. N. Am. 1858, 782; Cat. N. Am. B. 1859, no. 584. — COUES, Key, 1872, 286; Check List, 1873, no. 491; 2d ed. 1882, no. 711; Birds N. W. 1874, 563. — RIDGW. Nom. N. Am. B. 1881, no. 604.
Anas strepera americana, MAX. Jour. für Orn. II. 1842, 169.
"*Chaulelasmus americana*, BP." (GRAY).
"*Anas cinerea* et *subulata*, S. G. GMELIN." (GRAY).
Anas kekuschka, GMEL. S. N. I. ii. 1788, 531.
"*Anas mail*, HODGSON" (GRAY).
"*Anas capensis*, SWAINSON" (GRAY).

HAB. Nearly cosmopolitan (Europe, Asia, Africa, and North America). Temperate North America in general, breeding chiefly within the United States; West Indies (SCL. & SALV.).

SP. CHAR. *Adult male in fall, winter, and spring:* Ground-color of the head and neck pale brown, or brownish white, thickly speckled with black; on the pileum the brown deeper and more uniform, and the specks obsolete; on the occiput, when present, they incline to the form of transverse bars. Jugulum marked with greatly curved bars, or crescents, of white and black, the bars of the latter wider. Lateral portions of the body beneath, back, and scapulars finely undulated, in curved transverse lines, with slate-color and white. Many of the longer scapulars plain brownish gray, broadly edged with a lighter, more fulvous tint. Rump plain dull slate. Tail-coverts, above and below, intense opaque velvety black. Tail cinereous, faintly edged with white. Middle rows of wing-coverts bright chestnut, the anterior coverts brownish gray, and the posterior ones deep black; last row deep velvety black. Speculum immaculate pure white, the lower feathers cinereous (some with black on outer webs), narrowly tipped with white; tertials plain pale ash, the primaries a darker shade of the same. "Bill bluish black. Iris reddish hazel. Feet dull orange-yellow, claws brownish black, webs dusky" (AUDUBON). *Adult male, in summer:* "Crown brownish black, with a greenish tinge; an indistinct streak through the eye, dark brown; rest of the head and neck dull brownish white, marked with blackish brown, as in the previously described bird [adult male in spring]; back, rump, and upper tail-coverts dark blackish brown, each feather margined with rusty red; wings and tail as in the bird above described; breast dull rusty red, each feather with a central black spot; flanks dark brown, broadly marked and margined with dull rufous; the rest of the under parts dull white, each feather having a central blackish brown-drop-shaped mark" (SHARPE & DRESSER).

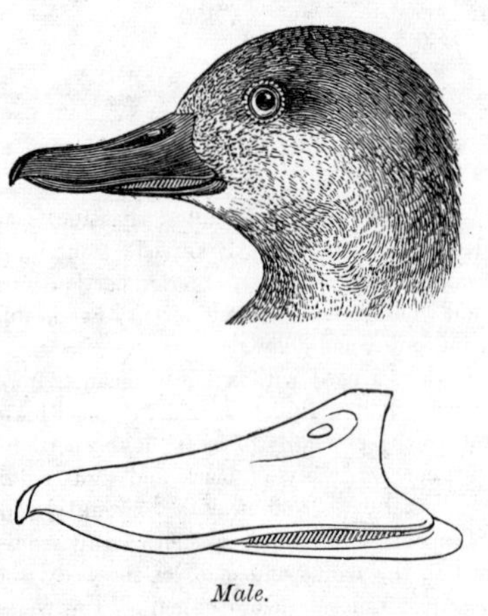
Male.

Adult female: Colors chiefly brownish dusky and brownish white, in longitudinal streaks on

would answer for both species; but the *C. Couesi* is immediately distinguished by its greatly inferior size, which hardly exceeds that of a Teal, the different color of the bill and feet, and the singular discrepancy in the lamellæ of the bill, which are much smaller, and *one third* more numerous.

"*Habitat:* Washington Island, one of the Fanning Group, situated about latitude 6° N. and longitude 160° W."

the head and neck, and in irregular transverse spots and bars on other portions. On the upper surface the dusky prevails, and on the lower parts the whitish predominates. Wing nearly as in the male, but the chestnut usually absent, the black less extended, and the gray of the coverts generally more or less barred and tipped with white. Abdomen and lower part of the breast pure white; throat finely streaked with dusky. *Downy young:* "Covered with soft short down; head, nape, back, and rump, dark dull brown, on each side of the rump and back of each wing-joint a sulphur-yellow spot, the wing-joints being marked with that color; forehead, space round the eye, throat, and chest pale sulphur-yellow; abdomen white, shaded with sulphur-yellow, on the lower part sooty gray" (SHARPE & DRESSER).

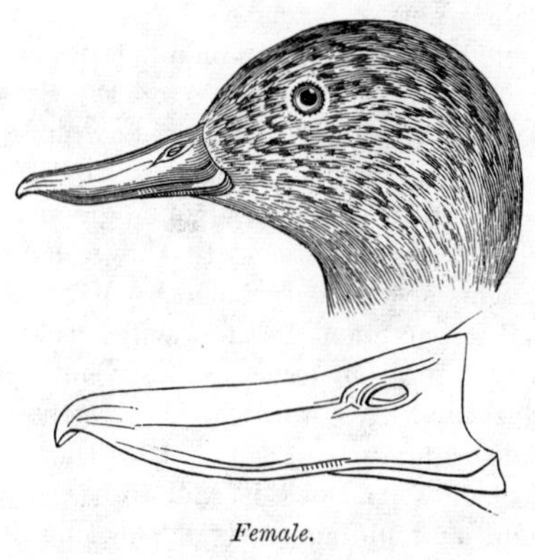

Female.

Male, wing, 10.25–11.00 inches; culmen, 1.60–1.75; width of bill, .60–.75; tarsus, 1.45–1.70; middle toe, 1.80–1.90. *Female,* wing, 10.00–10.10; culmen, 1.55–1.65; width of bill, .60–.70; tarsus, 1.60; middle toe, 1.75–1.80.

Although one of the above diagnoses will fit almost any example of this species, there is yet a very considerable extent of individual variation noticeable in a large series. Thus, No. 17040 (Washington, D. C., Feb. 25, 1860; C. DREXLER) has the uniform brown of the pileum coming down over the side of the head to a line on a level with the lower eyelid, the whole upper half of the head being thus nearly free from specks; while that portion behind the eye has a faint, but very perceptible, rose-purple reflection — this part of the head calling strongly to mind the head-pattern of *Nettion* and *Mareca americana.* On the other hand, an adult male from Philadelphia (No. 46658, J. KRIDER) has even the top of the head spotted. No. 9791, ♂ ad., Fort Steilacoom, W. T. (DR. GEORGE SUCKLEY), has the pileum almost chestnut, the brown having there such a deeply reddish cast; the lower neck is nearly plain pale ochraceous, abruptly defined against the darkly colored jugulum. Specimens from Cape St. Lucas and Utah present no unusual features.

All American specimens differ uniformly, from the single European pair before us, in several very tangible respects. The European male has the neck quite deeply ochraceous, while in the American ones there is seldom more than a mere tinge of this color; the jugulum is also pervaded by a wash of a more pinkish tinge of the same, while there is appreciably less regularity and clearness in the markings of that region. The longer scapulars are more deeply tinged with fulvous, and the finely undulated portions are pervaded with a brownish wash, entirely wanting in the American series. The measurements of this specimen (No. 57187, Europe; Schlüter Collection) are as follows: Wing, 10.80 inches; culmen, 1.65; width of bill, .70; tarsus, 1.55; middle toe, 1.85. The female specimen from Europe is very similar to North American examples, but is rather more deeply colored, the dark centres to the feathers being nearly deep black. The whole throat is immaculate white. The measurements are as follows: Wing, 9.50 inches; culmen, 1.50; tarsus, 1.35; middle toe, 1.60.

The Gadwall, or Gray Duck, like the Mallard, the Pintail, the Shoveller, and one or two other fresh-water Ducks, has a general distribution, nearly or quite throughout the northern hemisphere. It is more or less common in nearly all parts of North America, from the Fur Region to Central America, and from Maine to the Pacific. Its presence in several extended districts, however, remains to be confirmed. It is found in all parts of Europe, from Iceland to Gibraltar, occurs throughout North Africa, and is distributed over the larger portion of Asia.

Mr. Robert Kennicott, in his manuscript notes on the *Anatidæ* of North America, states that this Duck, like the *Aythya americana* and some other birds, though extending west of the mountains within the United States, apparently passes in its migrations to the north wholly to the eastward of Slave Lake. He was unable to detect it in either the Yukon or Mackenzie Region. If occurring at all, even at Slave Lake, he believes he should at least have heard of it from the Indians, for, unobservant as they are of the smaller birds, they pay attention to anything that affords them food, and the Opippewayans of Slave Lake shoot large numbers of Ducks. The Gadwall is not, so far as he knew, an abundant species in any part of North America, though it is not uncommon in October in Northern Illinois; and Richardson mentions it as common in summer on the Saskatchewan. Mr. Merrill found it breeding at Anticosti, in the Gulf of St. Lawrence. Dr. Suckley observed it in summer in Minnesota, and Captain Bendire found it breeding in Eastern Oregon.

According to Mr. Dall, a single specimen was procured in British Columbia by Mr. Elliott, and he believes that its range extends as far as the vicinity of Sitka.

This species is included by Mr. R. Browne among the birds of Vancouver Island; and it was found on the Pacific coast of Mexico by Colonel Grayson, who speaks of it as being abundant from November until late in the spring in the neighborhood of Mazatlan. According to Dr. Cooper, it is also common in the winter throughout California, in company with other fresh-water Ducks, and sometimes in distinct flocks. This Duck is said to be generally shy and quiet, feeding mostly in the twilight, and hiding much of the time among the reeds and bushes. It has, however, considerable power of voice, and in the spring is at times quite noisy.

Dr. Heermann states that it breeds in small numbers in the marshes of the Sacramento Valley, and Dr. Cooper found two nests at San Pedro on the 20th of July. These were constructed chiefly of feathers, and one contained nine eggs. As a rule, however, this species breeds in the more northern parts of the United States, especially about the lakes of Minnesota, and beyond latitude 68° N. Mr. J. A. Allen met with a solitary individual on the Platte River, in South Park, Colorado; he afterward found it very abundant in the valley of Salt Lake, Utah. It is also included by Mr. H. W. Parker in his List of the Birds of Iowa, and given as occurring in the counties of Polk and Clinton.

A female of this species was obtained in Bermuda in December, 1849. She was kept in confinement, became quite tame, associated with the domesticated Ducks, and laid quite a number of eggs. Although a persistent sitter, none of her eggs ever hatched.

According to the experience of Mr. Boardman, this Duck is not uncommon in the fall in the vicinity of Calais, Me. It is occasionally found on the ponds and streams of Massachusetts, but is rare, and of irregular appearance.

Mr. Giraud considered it as quite rare on Long Island, where it was very shy, seldom came to the decoys, and was very difficult of approach, unless the hunters advanced under cover of reeds and rushes. At Egg Harbor, New Jersey, a few of this species are seen every fall and spring, and are there known as the "Welch Drake" and the "German Duck." This Duck is said to be one of the most active of its tribe, flying swiftly, and being an excellent diver. It is exceedingly timid, and the superior quality of its flesh would seem to show that its food must be chiefly vegetable.

Throughout Europe and in all the countries of Northern Africa the Gadwall appears to have a very general distribution, especially during its migrations. Mr. Salvin mentions finding it common near Zara, in Northeastern Africa; it was also noticed in the Sahara by Mr. Tristram; and Captain E. G. Shelley met with it in Egypt and Nubia — where, however, it was not abundant. The latter saw one small flock of these birds near El-Kab on February 26, and obtained a single specimen.

Mr. T. L. Powys found the Gadwall common in the winter in the Ionian Islands. Unlike most other writers, he speaks of it as the easiest to approach of all the European Ducks, and he also regarded it as the best for the table. It is given by Mr. H. Saunders in his List of the Birds of Southern Spain, where it was abundant throughout the winter until April, and he adds that it certainly breeds at Santa Olaga.

According to Middendorff, it is found in the forest regions of Siberia. Its presence in Iceland was first positively announced by Professor Newton, Mr. G. C. Fowler having obtained a pair, with their nest and eggs, in 1862, and Mr. Proctor having received skins from there. More recently Mr. C. W. Shepard has found it breeding in the northern part of that island, on the shores of the Mý-vatn Lake. It was shy and unsociable, and its nests were found only in quiet swampy places on the shores of the lake or on islands not frequented by any other species of Duck.

In Ireland and Great Britain this Duck is comparatively rare, occurring in winter, but more frequently in spring, and then only in very limited numbers. In Holland, on the other hand, in the months of September and October, it is the most common Duck in the markets.

Mr. Dresser did not meet with this bird in Finland, though it is supposed to occur in the southeastern part of that country. It has been procured in the neighborhood of Archangel, but is rare in the northern part of Russia. It is more numerous in Southeastern Russia, inhabiting large marshy localities, where reeds and rushes abound, and also frequenting the swampy banks of rivers. In the autumn, during the evening and in the night, it flies about the fields. It nests in swamps or on the banks of lakes and rivers, and the usual number of its eggs is from eight to twelve.

In Asia it has been obtained as far east as China and Japan. Throughout India, during the whole of the cold season, according to Mr. Hume, it is the most plentiful species of Duck.

Like all the Ducks with long-pointed wings, the Gadwall has a strong and rapid flight. It is generally regarded as a shy species, disliking exposure, and hiding itself among thick reeds and aquatic plants. This, Mr. Yarrell states, was observed to be the habit of a pair in the Garden of the Zoological Society, which concealed themselves in the long grass of the islands. These birds bred there in the season of 1839, and again in 1841, laying seven or eight eggs. They fed on vegetable matter, aquatic insects, and small fish.

In general habits this species very closely resembles the Mallard. It is essentially a fresh-water Duck, frequenting streams, lakes, and ponds where suitable food is to be found, this consisting chiefly of the leaves, buds, and roots of water-plants. While feeding this bird sometimes utters a low quacking. In confinement it readily eats oats, bread, pieces of cabbage, turnip, potatoes, and various other vegetables. A pair kept at Mount Auburn, Mass., ate greedily the roots of the common celery.

It breeds throughout Central and Southern Europe, making a nest, like that of the Mallard, close to the water's edge, on the borders of fresh-water lakes and streams. The nest is a mere depression in the ground, lined with dry leaves or hay and down. The eggs are from nine to thirteen in number, of a pale creamy yellow. Those in Mr. Dresser's collection averaged 2.10 inches in length and 1.50 inches in breadth.

Dr. Bachman informed Mr. Audubon that in the year 1812 he saw in Dutchess Co., New York, about thirty of these Ducks in a single flock. He was informed that three years previously a pair of Gadwalls had been captured alive in a mill-pond. They were kept in the poultry-yard, and were easily tamed, one joint of the wing having been broken, to prevent their flying away. In the following spring they were suffered to go into the pond, but returned daily to the house to be fed. They built their nest on the edge of the pond, and reared a large brood. The young were perfectly domesticated, and made no attempt to fly away, even though their wings were perfect.

This species, as Professor Kumlien informs me, occurs both in the spring and fall at Lake Koskonong, but is rather rare. He has a mounted specimen shot Nov. 14th, 1874. He has never seen it there in summer, but has met with it in spring in marshes covered with water, and in the fall on the mud-bars and among the wild rice. It is very seldom seen far from the shore. Mr. B. F. Goss, of Pewaukee, Wis., writes me that it breeds rarely in his vicinity. About May 24, 1868, he spent several days on an island in Horicon Lake, where the Gadwall had just begun to lay. He found three nests, two containing one, and one three eggs. The nests did not differ in their construction from the Mallard's, but were more concealed, all of them being in thick cover, one perhaps ten feet from the water, the farthest about three rods. The eggs were smaller and lighter colored than the Mallard's. It was found breeding on Shoal Lake in 1865 by Mr. Donald Gunn, and at New Westminster by Mr. H. W. Elliott. Dr. Kennerly speaks of finding it very common in April in the vicinity of Janos River, Chihuahua, going in large flocks. Beyond that point it was not observed.

Eggs of this species in the collection of the Smithsonian Institution (No. 12723) from Shoal Lake are of a uniform cream-color, and range from 2.05 inches in length to 2.20 inches, and from 1.45 to 1.55 inches in breadth.

Genus **DAFILA**, Stephens.

Dafila, Stephens, Shaw's Gen. Zool. XII. ii. 1824, 126 (type, *Anas acuta*, Linn.).
Phasianurus, Wagl. Isis, 1832, 1235 (same type).

Char. Bill longer than the head, narrow, the edges parallel, deep through the base, but otherwise much depressed, the basal portion of the culmen much ascending. In the male, the scapulars, tertials, and middle rectrices lanceolate, the latter elongated considerably beyond the other tail-feathers. The adult male in winter plumage very different from the adult female, but the sexes much alike in summer.

D. acuta.

As defined above, the genus *Dafila* includes but a single species, the *D. acuta*, or Common Pintail, of the northern hemisphere. Several South American species have been referred to it; but they all differ in having the sexes alike, in the dull (much spotted) coloration, and in the very slight elongation of the middle rectrices. They constitute a group somewhat intermediate between *Dafila* and *Nettion*, and are again directly connected with the latter by several small Ducks of the southern hemisphere, usually referred to the genus *Querquedula* (e. g. *Q. flavirostris*, of South America, and *Q. Eatoni*, of Kerguelen Island). The genus *Pœcilonetta* (type, *Anas bahamensis*, LINN.) was proposed for this group by Kaup, and should probably be retained for it.

Dafila acuta.

THE PIN-TAIL; SPRIG-TAIL.

Anas acuta, LINN. S. N. I. 1766, 202. — WILS. Am. Orn. VIII. 1814, pl. 68, fig. 3. — NUTT. Man. II. 1834, 386. — AUD. Orn. Biog. III. 1835, 214; V. 1839, 615, pl. 227; Synop. 1839, 279; Birds Am. VI. 1843, 266, pl. 390.

Dafila acuta, BONAP. Comp. List, 1838, 56. — BAIRD, B. N. Am. 1858, 776; Cat. N. Am. B. 1859, no. 578; COUES, Key, 1872, 286; Check List, 1873, no. 490; 2d ed. 1882, no. 710; Birds N. W. 1874, 561. — RIDGW. Nom. N. Am. B. 1881, no. 605.

Anas alandica, SPARRM. Mus. Carls. III. , pl. 60.

Anas Sparrmanni, LATH. Ind. Orn. II. 1790, 876.

Anas caudacuta, PALL. Zoog. Rosso-As. II. 1826, 280.

Anas longicauda, BRISS. Orn. VI. 1760, 366, pl. 34, figs. 1, 2.

Anas caudata, BREHM, Vög. Deutschl. 869.

Dafila acuta, var. *americana*, BONAP. Compt. Rend. XLII. 1856.

HAB. The whole of North America; Europe. Breeding chiefly far north, migrating south in winter as far as Panama; Cuba.

SP. CHAR. *Adult male in winter:* Head and upper half of the neck hair-brown or grayish umber, the upper surface darker, often inclining to deep burnt-umber; all the feathers (usually) appreciably darker centrally, producing an indistinctly and minutely speckled appearance; on each side of the occiput the brown has a metallic gloss of dull green, showing a faint purple reflection in some lights. Upper half of the nape opaque intense black, separated from the brown by an upward extension of the white of the lower neck nearly to the occiput. Stripe on each side of the nape (as described above), lower half of the neck frontally and laterally, jugulum, breast, and abdomen immaculate white. Lower half of the nape, with entire dorsal region and lateral lower parts, finely waved with transverse, rather zigzag, lines of white and black, of nearly equal width. Longer scapulars opaque velvety black centrally, edged broadly with grayish white; outer scapulars with exposed ends of their outer webs entirely velvety black. Tertials silvery ash, with a medial stripe of intense velvety black. Speculum dull green, varying to dull bronzy purple, with a subterminal bar of velvety black and a tip of white. Wing-coverts very uniform brownish gray, the last row broadly tipped with cinnamon-rufous. Primaries dull slaty.

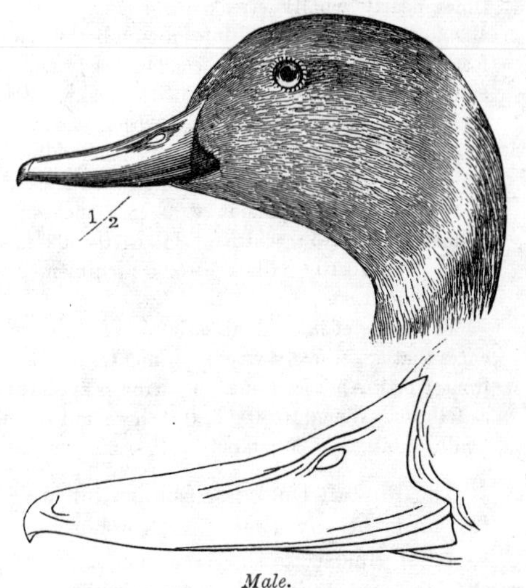

Male.

Upper tail-coverts with outer webs black, the inner ones grayish white; lower coverts deep opaque velvety black, the exterior row with their outer webs white; post-femoral space delicate cream-color. Tail-feathers dark cinereous edged with white, the elongated middle pair uniform deep black. Bill plumbeous-blue, the ungui, base, and strip along culmen, black; iris brown; feet dusky. *Adult male in summer:* "Head, neck, and under parts generally as in the adult female, except that the abdomen is duller in color and less marked; back dull dark brown, each feather having one or two irregular dirty-white bars, and some being irregularly vermiculated with that color; rump washed with gray; tail similar in color to that of the bird last described [*i.e.* adult male in winter], but the two central feathers are but slightly elongated; wings also as in the last-described stage of plumage, but the elongated secondaries and scapulars are shorter and blunter, and in color dark gray, black along the centre, some of the latter being marked like the back; flanks grayish brown, every feather having broad yellowish-white bars; under tail-coverts as in the female" (SHARPE & DRESSER). *Adult female:* Above, plumbeous-dusky, variegated transversely with yellowish white or pale ochraceous; these markings sometimes irregularly bar-like, but oftener of U-shaped form, one on the edge, and one in the middle portion of each feather. Wing much as in the male, but metallic color of the speculum duller, the ochraceous bar anterior to it paler, and the white terminal bar tinged with buff; wing-coverts narrowly tipped with whitish. Upper tail-coverts broadly edged with whitish, and more or less marked with irregular — usually V-shaped — lines of the same. Tail-feathers dusky, edged with whitish, and with more or less distinct indications of distant bars of the same. Head and neck dingy whitish, tinged with brown on the superior surface, which is heavily streaked with blackish, the other portions more finely and thinly streaked, the throat being nearly immaculate. Rest of the lower parts dingy white, the feathers more grayish beneath the surface; crissum and flanks streaked with dusky, but abdomen, etc., usually immaculate. *Young male:* Similar to the female, but markings on upper parts more bar-like, and lower parts sometimes nearly wholly streaked. *Young female* (No. 54633, Kadiak, Alaska, Aug. 1, 1868; F. BISCHOFF): Speculum dilute raw-umber, marbled toward base of feathers with dusky. All the feathers of the upper parts conspicuously and broadly bordered with buffy white; lower parts everywhere densely streaked with dusky. *Downy young:* Above, grayish raw-umber, with a white stripe along each side of the back, a white space on the wing, and a white superciliary stripe. Beneath, grayish white, with a very faint yellowish tinge; an umber-brown stripe behind the eye, and an indistinct space of the same over the ears.

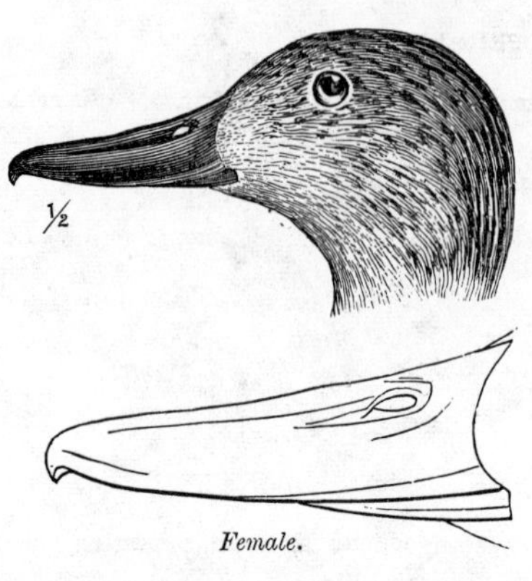

Female.

Male, total length, about 26.00–28.00 inches; extent, 36.00; wing, 10.25–11.10; tail, 7.25–9.50; culmen, 1.85–2.15; width of bill, .70–.80; tarsus, 1.55–1.85; middle toe, 1.70–2.10. *Female,* wing, 9.60–10.10; tail, 4.50–5.00; culmen, 1.80–2.10; width of bill, .65–.75; tarsus, 1.65; middle toe, 1.80.

The range of individual variation of the colors in this species is very slight, consisting of differences that are scarcely worthy of mention. European specimens differ, however, very appreciably from North American ones in narrower speculum, but not in other respects. Two males measure as follows: Wing, 10.30–11.00 inches; tail (elongated middle feathers), 8.50; culmen, 1.85–1.95; width of bill, .70–.75; tarsus, 1.40–1.60; middle toe, 1.85–1.90.[1]

The Pin-tail Duck is cosmopolitan, and enjoys a distribution exceeded in extent by few birds of any kind. In North America it is found from Greenland and the Arctic coast almost to the Isthmus of Panama. Less abundant, wherever found, than the Mallard, its distribution appears to be quite as extensive. In the Old World it is found throughout Europe, in Asia as far south as Ceylon, in Japan, in different portions of China, and in Northern Africa.

[1] Sharpe & Dresser ("History of the Birds of Europe," Part XIX.) give the dimensions of the European Pin-tail as follows: "Total length, 2 feet; culmen, 2.2 inches; wing, 11.2; tail, 7.5; tarsus, 1.6."

Mr. Salvin obtained it at Balize, and found it common throughout the winter in the Lake of Dueñas. It is given by Mr. R. Browne in his List of the Birds of Vancouver Island; and Mr. J. A. Allen found it in abundance in the valley of Great Salt Lake. Major Wedderburn mentions the occurrence, in November, 1847, of several specimens — all young birds — in Bermuda.

According to Dr. Cooper, the Pin-tail migrates in winter to the extreme southern limits of California, being then numerous along the Colorado, and at San Diego. He found it frequenting fresh-water ponds and inundated meadows, rarely appearing on the salt water. Being one of the best for the table of all the wild Ducks, it is much hunted; and although very vigilant, great numbers are killed for the market. When associated with other species, it is the first to give the alarm. Unlike most writers, Dr. Cooper speaks of it as very noisy, quacking much like the Mallard, but not so loudly, diving but little, and feeding chiefly on vegetable food. In April it departs for the far north, where it breeds about the lakes in latitude 50°, and farther north, laying eight or nine bluish-green eggs. It returns southward in October, and winters in large numbers in Puget Sound and on the Columbia River.

It was found in winter near Mazatlan, Western Mexico, by Colonel Grayson, where, during that season, it is common. It was also found at Coahuana by Mr. John Xantus.

In Dakota, Idaho, and Montana it is said to breed in all the reedy prairie sloughs, and to be more abundant in that region than any other of the Ducks. By the 1st of July nearly all the broods are hatched, and some of the young are nearly ready to fly.

Dr. Walker met with this species on the coast of Greenland, near Godthaab; and Professor Reinhardt mentions it as accidental, but not rare, being found in North as well as in South Greenland. Captain Blakiston found it inhabiting the Saskatchewan, and the Red River to Hudson's Bay. It was also met with on the Mackenzie by Mr. Ross. Dr. Richardson found it frequenting chiefly the clear lakes of the northern districts, and breeding in the Barren Grounds, being found, in spring and autumn only, in large numbers in the more southern wooded districts.

The evidence of its almost universal presence in Asia, Europe, and Northern Africa is very abundant, and so voluminous, that one is embarrassed in selecting from the many authorities. Mr. Swinhoe found it both in Formosa and at Amoy. It was found in Egypt by Mr. E. C. Taylor; and Captain E. G. Shelley afterward met with it in considerable numbers both in Egypt and in Nubia ("Ibis," 1871). It was noticed in the Sahara by Mr. Tristram, and Mr. T. L. Powys found it common in winter in Greece. Mr. H. Whitely mentions meeting with it at Hakodadi, in Japan. It was also procured by the Perry Expedition on the Island of Niphon, near Yeddo, and Middendorff found it abundant in Siberia, chiefly in the wooded regions. Mr. H. Saunders records it as a not uncommon winter visitant in Spain.

Mr. C. W. Shepard found it breeding in the vicinity of Lake Mý-vatn, in the northern part of Iceland. The birds were seen in considerable numbers; but their nests were not so easily found, being placed singly at some distance from the lake, in lava-streams that were overgrown with bushes and grass.

In Great Britain and Ireland, though occurring every winter, the Pin-tail is no longer an abundant species. It is found mostly on the eastern coast of Scotland, and in Ireland is a regular visitant, both on the coast and the inland waters. It breeds in various parts of Norway, up to and within the Polar Circle; and some remain all winter on the southern coast. It also breeds throughout Sweden, Lapland, Finland, and Northern Russia, in Poland, the northern parts of Germany, Denmark, and other countries. During its migrations it is found in every portion of Europe.

In general habits it differs little from the Mallard, but is found more commonly on open water, and is more wary. Its slender and graceful figure renders it conspicuously easier in its movements. It swims high out of the water, and more in the manner of a Swan. Its food is essentially the same as the Mallard's. According to Montagu, its note is soft, and it is less noisy than other fresh-water Ducks, being rather a silent bird. It is said generally to breed later than the Mallard.

According to Mr. Dresser, the nests found by him in Finland were mere depressions in the soil, often under the shelter of a bush, usually not far from the water, and lined with small flags and grass-bents. Within, down and feathers form a soft bed, on which the eggs are deposited. These were from seven to nine in number, colored like those of the Mallard, but more elongated in shape, and smaller in size. The eggs obtained by Mr. Dresser in Finland average 2.00 by 1.50 inches.

Mr. Boardman informs me that this Duck occurs in the vicinity of Calais in the fall, but is not found there in the spring. In Massachusetts it is not very common, but is not at all rare, and is met with both in the spring and the fall. A fine male was shot in Cambridge, Mass., in April, 1873, which had alighted in a pool of water in a small yard near a dwelling, apparently unconscious of danger.

In Long Island it is well known to hunters as the "Sprig-tail" and the "Spindle-tail." Although shy and timid, it is often brought within reach of the fowler's gun by decoys. When surprised by the hunter's rising to fire, the birds crowd close together, presenting what is called a "doublet;" and many fall by a single discharge. Though not known to dive for its food, it will attempt to escape in this way when wounded. When finally compelled to rise to the surface, it will try to hide under the bow of a boat, or will skulk in the grass of the marsh, often concealing itself so well as to escape detection. Its flesh is always sweet, and highly esteemed. Mr. N. B. Moore, who met with it in abundance in Florida, writes me that he has frequently seen it, when in confinement, plunge into the water to the depth of two feet, when dressing its plumage.

Mr. Bannister found it common on the small ponds on the Island of St. Michael's and the adjacent mainland. Mr. Dall speaks of it as extremely common on all parts of the Yukon, and on the marshes near the sea-coast. In the early spring, arriving at Nulato about May 1, it is gregarious; but about May 20, when it begins to breed, it is generally found solitary or in pairs. Its nest is said to be usually in the sedge, lined with dry grass; and when both parents are absent, the eggs are covered with dry leaves and feathers.

The Pin-tail is said to fly more swiftly than any other Duck, and is very hard to shoot on the wing. It lays from six to ten, and even twelve, eggs. As soon as the young are hatched, it withdraws from the river into the small creeks and rivulets, where it remains until the Ducklings are fully able to fly. Then they all repair to the great marshes, where, on the roots of the *Equisetum*, they become exceedingly fat. They all leave about the end of September. This species was also obtained at Sitka and at Kadiak by Bischoff.

The following valuable notes relative to the summer distribution and breeding of this Duck are abridged from the papers of my late esteemed friend, Robert Kennicott: In America the summer home of the Pin-tail is within the Arctic regions, farther to the northward than that of any other of our fresh-water Ducks, comparatively few breeding south of Great Slave Lake. In their spring migrations to the northward they move in immense flocks, which only disperse upon their arrival at their breeding-grounds. A few reach that lake about May 1; but the main body arrive about a week or so later, and mostly pass directly on across the lake to the northward. On the Yukon the first specimens were seen in the latter part of April; and before the 10th of May they had arrived in immense flocks, which remained some time together in that vicinity before passing farther north or separating to breed. At this time the birds were fat, and their flesh delicious, much superior to that of any other Duck, except the Widgeon. At the Yukon the Pin-tails are the latest in nesting of any of the fresh-water Ducks, and generally hatch a week or two after the Mallard. He found them breeding in the same grounds, and at about the same time, with *Fulix affinis*, though they do not associate with that species. He always found their nest in low but dry ground, under the shelter of trees or bushes, though never among thick large trees, and not more than two or three rods from water. They never build on hummocks in the water, nor on high land, but always just upon the edge of a marsh or lake.

The nest is usually placed at the foot of a willow, among grass, rather than leaves or moss, and is extremely simple, being composed of merely a few bits of broken dry grass and sticks, but well lined with down.

In observing the breeding-habits of these Ducks, Mr. Kennicott was struck with the remarkable persistence in the individuals of each species in always choosing precisely similar localities for their nests, so far as was possible; and he was therefore somewhat particular in describing minutely the peculiar nesting-place chosen by each.

The eggs are from seven to nine in number, and rather small in size. At the Yukon the young are mostly hatched in the early part of July. The old males moult before this time, and the females somewhat later. During the summer and fall, as in the spring, the flesh of this species is superior to that of any other Duck in that region. It leaves the Yukon and the Mackenzie River Region a little later than the other fresh-water Ducks, except the Widgeon. It does not collect in such large flocks in autumn as on its arrival in the spring.

Mr. Kennicott found but few Pin-tails feeding on the wild rice in Northern Minnesota, where Mallards, Widgeons, and Green-winged Teals were plentiful. He saw the young of this Duck in considerable numbers as early as June 14.

Mr. MacFarlane found it breeding in large numbers in the neighborhood of Fort Anderson, and furnishes notes in regard to many nests with their eggs, identified by him. The nests were invariably upon the ground, usually near the water, rarely more than thirty or forty yards therefrom. The nest was usually a mere depression in the ground, lined with down, with a few decayed feathers under the eggs. The female sits very closely. In one case he approached within four feet before she flew off. The eggs were usually from six to eight in number; and the male bird was frequently found in the vicinity of the nest. Mr. MacFarlane states that the Pin-tail is an abundant Duck in that quarter, and among the first to arrive in spring. It deserts its nest almost immediately after the young are hatched, and takes to the water with them. From personal observations he was convinced that this species, as well as the *Harelda glacialis*, invariably selects land-locked sheets of water for the purpose of rearing its young; while other species give the preference to small streams of running water.

Mr. L. Kumlien informs me that this is one of the first of the Ducks to arrive in the spring in Southern Wisconsin, and is then quite common. Some remain all summer; but he has never found them breeding, nor seen any very young birds — as would in all probability be the case if any bred in that neighborhood.

The points in the Arctic Regions from which this Duck was reported to the Smithsonian Institution, are Fort Resolution and the Yukon, by Mr. Kennicott; mouth of the Porcupine River, by Mr. Jones; Fort Yukon, by Mr. J. S. Ibbiston and Mr. Lockhart; Anderson River, Fort Anderson, the Lower Anderson, Rendezvous Lake, the Barren Grounds, etc., by Mr. MacFarlane; Kadiak and Fort Kenai, by Mr. Bischoff; and New Westminster, by Mr. H. W. Elliott.

They are mentioned by Mr. Adams as the first Ducks to arrive — April 28 — in Alaska ("Ibis," 1878), and the only fresh-water species there that was numerous. They frequent all parts of the marshes in groups of three or four, are very wary, and can only be procured by ambush in the lines of its flight. The nests were placed in the rough grass of the marshes, and very carefully concealed; the eggs, nine in number, were of a pale green, almost white.

The eggs of this species are oval in shape, and of a pale grayish-green color. Three eggs in the Smithsonian Collection (No. 4242), from St. George's Island, in St. James's Bay, measure 2.30 by 1.55 inches; 2.25 by 1.55; 2.20 by 1.55.

Genus **MARECA**, Stephens.

Mareca, Stephens, Shaw's Gen. Zoöl. XII. ii. 1824, 130 (type, *Anas penelope*, Linn.).

Char. Bill small, shorter than the head, rather narrow, the edges parallel to near the end, where they gradually converge to a rounded tip; culmen gently concave; lamellæ of the maxillæ almost concealed; feet small, the tarsus about as long as the bill; sexes very different in winter, much alike in summer. Adult male in winter with the scapulars and tertials (in the North American species the tail-coverts and rectrices also) lanceolate.

M. penelope.

The three known species of *Mareca* (all American, but one peculiar to the southern continent) may be distinguished as follows: —

Com. Char. (adult males in winter dress). Forehead white; posterior half of the middle wing-covert regions white, forming a large patch of this color; sides and flanks reddish; abdomen immaculate white; speculum velvety black, with or without green.

A. Speculum metallic green anteriorly; jugulum plain pinkish vinaceous; sides, flanks, scapulars, and back, delicately undulated with dusky upon a lighter ground; crissum black. Tail-feathers acuminate, the middle pair projecting considerably beyond the rest.

1. **M. penelope.** Head and neck plain rufous, the forehead and part of the crown white;

ground-color of the dorsal region, sides, and flanks, whitish. Wing, 10.00–11.00 inches; culmen, 1.35–1.45; tarsus, 1.45–1.60; middle toe, 1.65–1.75. *Hab.* Palæarctic Region; occasional in Eastern North America, more frequent in Alaska.

2. **M. americana.** Head and neck whitish, speckled with black, and with a dark metallic-green space on the side of the occiput (sometimes continued down the nape); ground-color of the dorsal region, sides, and flanks, vinaceous or pinkish cinnamon. Wing, 10.25–10.75 inches; culmen, 1.30–1.50; tarsus, 1.45–1.65; middle toe, 1.65–1.85. *Hab.* North America.

B. Speculum wholly velvety black; jugulum and anterior part of back black, irregularly barred with white; sides and flanks light rufous; scapulars and back black, the feathers widely bordered with white; crissum white, tinged with rufous. Tail-feathers not acuminate, the middle pair scarcely projecting.

3. **M. sibilatrix.**[1] Forehead, lores, and cheeks white, the latter finely barred with dusky; posterior part of the crown and middle of the occiput (longitudinally) brownish dusky; a space of metallic green, varying to violet-purple on each side the occiput, from the eye to the middle of the neck; neck, including throat, dusky black. Wing, 10.40 inches; culmen, 1.50; tarsus, 1.60; middle toe, 1.80.[2] *Hab.* Southern South America.

Mareca penelope.

THE EUROPEAN WIDGEON.

Anas penelope, LINN. S. N. ed. 10, I. 1758, 126; ed. 12, I. 1766, 202 (*penelope*). — NAUM. Vög. Deutschl. XI. 1842, 724, pl. 305. — REINH. Ibis, III. 1861, 13 (Greenland).

Mareca penelope, SELBY, Br. Orn. II. 324. — BAIRD, B. N. Am. 1858, 784; Cat. N. Am. B. 1859, no. 586. — COUES, Pr. Essex Inst. V. 1868, 299 (New England); Key, 1872, 268; Check List, 1873, no. 492; 2d ed. 1882, no. 712; B. N. W. 1874, 564 (footnote). — RIDGW. Nom. N. Am. B. 1881, no. 606.

Anas cagolca, S. G. GMEL. Reise, I. 1770, 77.

Mareca fistularis, STEPHENS, Shaw's Gen. Zool. XII. ii. 1824, 131, pl. 50.

Wigeon, YARR. Brit. B. ed. 2, III. 286, fig.; ed. 3, III. 287, fig.; et AUCT.

HAB. Palæarctic Region in general, and occasional in Eastern North America (several records — New York, Pennsylvania, Maryland, Virginia, Florida, Wisconsin, etc.); breeding in the Aleutian Islands, Alaska.

[1] MARECA SIBILATRIX. The Chilian Widgeon.

Anas sibilatrix, POEPPIG, Fror. Not. 1829, 10, no. 539 (Chili).

Mareca sibilatrix, SCL. & SALV. P. Z. S. Apr. 4, 1876, 395 (monographic).

Anas chilœnsis, KING, P. Z. S. 1830–1831, 15.

Mareca chilœnsis, EYTON, Monog. Anat. 1838, 117, pl. 21. — CASS. U. S. Astr. Exp. II. 1856, 201. — SCL. & SALV. Nom. Neotr. 1873, 130.

Pato pico pequeño, AZARA, Apunt. III. 1805, no. 432 (Buenos Ayres).

Anas parvirostris, MERREM, Ersch. u. Grub. Enc. sect. i. xxxv. 1841, 43 (ex AZARA, l. c.).

HAB. South America.

This species differs from both *M. penelope* and *M. americana* in details of form and color, which, however, are merely of specific importance. The bill is quite similar, though the commissure it more elevated basally and more depressed in the middle, and its greatest width is through the base. The middle tail-feathers are not more elongated than the rest, and the upper tail-coverts are less lanceolate. The coloration is yet more different, the only similarity being in the white wing-covert patch, as in both *M. americana* and *M. penelope*, and the green space on the side of the occiput, as in the former. The forehead, but also the lores and cheeks, are white. In other respects it differs totally from the two northern species as follows: Neck black; jugulum with broad transverse bars of black and white; sides and flanks plain rufous; upper tail-coverts immaculate white; speculum plain opaque black; crissum rusty. An adult male measures as follows: wing, 10.30 inches; tail, 4.50; culmen, 1.50; tarsus, 1.60; middle toe, 1.80; width of bill, .70 — the size being thus about the same as that of *M. penelope* and *M. americana*.

[2] Only one example measured.

SP. CHAR. *Adult male in winter:* Head and neck plain bright rufous, abruptly defined below, and becoming paler next the bill; forehead and pileum medially immaculate white; a few blackish feathers around the eyelids. Jugulum and sides of the breast pinkish vinaceous, the tips of the feathers paler. Sides, flanks, and entire dorsal surface delicately undulated with transverse, zig-zag bars of black and pure white, the bars of the latter rather the narrower. Wing-coverts immaculate pure white, except the anterior portion of the lesser-covert region, which is deep cinereous; last row of coverts tipped with velvety black; tertials velvety black, shafted and edged with pure white; the lower one with the entire lower web pure white. Speculum soft metallic green on the anterior half or two thirds, the terminal portion velvety black. Primaries plain cinereous. Tail-coverts (both upper and lower) deep black, with a very faint bluish gloss; rest of the lower parts immaculate white. Tail-feathers dark cinereous, edged with ashy white. Bill "light grayish blue, with the tip, including the unguis, black;" iris "hazel brown;" legs and feet "light grayish blue" (MACGILLIVRAY).

Male.

Wing, 10.00–11.00 inches; culmen, 1.35–1.45; tarsus, 1.45–1.60; middle toe, 1.65–1.75.

Adult female: "Much smaller and differently colored. The bill, iris, and feet, however are as in the male. The head and upper neck are yellowish red, with small greenish black spots, the feathers being barred with that color, of which there is more on the upper part of the head. The feathers of the upper parts in general are dusky brown, edged with brownish red or whitish, and barred with the same. The wings are dusky gray; the coverts in the part which is white in the male tipped with that color, the secondary coverts with an indication of a dark terminal bar; the speculum grayish, without lustre; the inner secondaries marked somewhat as in the male, but with dark gray in place of black. The tail-feathers brownish gray, edged with brownish white. On the lower forepart and sides of the neck the feathers are obscurely barred with reddish brown and brownish gray; the sides are similar; the breast and abdomen white; the feathers under the tail white, barred with brown, as are the smaller lower wing-coverts; the larger pale gray" (MACGILLIVRAY). Length, about 19.25 inches; extent, 32.50; wing, 10.00; tail, 4.00; culmen, 1.50; tarsus, 1.50; middle toe, 1.25. *Young male:* Head, neck, jugulum, sides, and flanks, umber-brown, varying to a cinnamon shade, the head and neck thickly streaked with black, and the feathers of the jugulum, sides, etc., centred with dusky. Back and scapulars dusky, the feathers broadly bordered with dull fulvous; crissum irregularly streaked and spotted with dusky; rump and upper tail-coverts slaty brown, bordered with dull whitish. Wing as in the adult, except that the coverts are dull cinereous broadly bordered with white. Lower parts, except as described, pure white.

An adult male from Alexandria, Va. (No. 29519), has the rufous of the head perfectly uniform, with only a few blackish feathers immediately around the eye, and a suffusion of the same on the chin; while the pinkish of the jugulum joins the rufous of the neck. No. 1271, New York market, has the sides of the head speckled minutely with greenish black, the nape and entire throat clouded with the same, and the pinkish of the jugulum separated from the rufous of the neck by a narrow indistinct collar of whitish, undulated with blackish. No. 10376, from Florida, approaches still more closely to *M. americana* in having also the occiput spotted with black, the eye more broadly surrounded with greenish, the ground-color of the cheeks nearly white, and the sides pervaded by a tinge of the pinkish of the jugulum. No. 62525, from St. Paul's Island, Alaska, is most like the Alexandria specimen.

A young male (No. 57119, Europe) has the brown of the head, neck, sides, and flanks, almost chestnut; the wing as in the adult, and the dorsal region mostly clothed with feathers of the adult dress.

The Common Widgeon of the Palæarctic Region is entitled to a place in the fauna of North America on rather more than the ordinary grounds of an occasional straggler. It has been found on different occasions in Greenland, has been taken on Long Island, is not infrequently seen exposed in the New York markets, and comes within our fauna on the Pacific coast. Two instances are on record of its occurrence in Illinois. Holböll mentions its presence in Greenland — a young male procured in 1851, and sent to the Royal Museum of Copenhagen. Besides this, Professor Reinhardt mentions having seen two other specimens — young birds obtained in South Greenland.

Mr. Giraud refers to an individual shot in the Bay of Long Island in December, 1842. This is now in the collection of Mr. George N. Lawrence, of New York. Richardson was confident that this species occurs in the wooded districts of the Fur Country, and that it breeds northward to latitude 68° N.

According to Dr. Cooper this bird is a not infrequent visitor to California. He has seen quite a number in the collections of Mr. F. Gruber and of Mr. Lorquin in San Francisco, where they are frequently sold in the market. Their habits are said to be similar to those of the *M. americana.*

According to Mr. Dall, this species is not uncommon among the Ducks brought in by the native hunters of Unalashka. One was obtained there Oct. 12, 1871. It is a winter visitor, and migrates about May 1. It was also met with by Mr. Elliott on the Prybilof Islands, where, as he states, it is seldom seen, never in pairs, does not breed, the few individuals observed being apparently wind-bound or astray.

In the Palæarctic Region it has a very extended distribution, occurring throughout Europe and Asia, from Iceland and Siberia southward, and as far eastward as China and Japan. It was found in Formosa by Mr. Swinhoe, and at Hakodadi in Japan by Mr. H. Whitely ("Ibis," 1867). In Siberia, according to Middendorff, it occurs in the wooded or forest regions. Mr. C. W. Shepard met with a few breeding in the north of Iceland and in the neighborhood of Lake Mý-vatn, where it was the rarest of the birds found breeding in that locality. Occasionally one or two were seen, but they were very shy, and it was impossible to say in what numbers they existed there. Only one bird with its nest was obtained; but during the night the shrill whistle of this Duck could be heard above the general chorus of cooings and quackings.

Captain G. E. Shelley includes it among the birds of Egypt ("Ibis," 1871). He met with it on Lake Menzaleh, while stopping at Port Said, and frequently saw specimens in the market at Alexandria.

Mr. Wheelwright found it one of the most common of all the northern Ducks in Scandinavia, breeding in almost all the still waters to far up within the Polar Circle. The eggs are described as being of a clear yellowish-white color, about 2.25 inches in length and 1.50 in breadth.

According to Yarrell the Widgeon visits Great Britain in immense numbers during the winter season. It frequents the shores all around the coast, as well as the rivers, lakes, and fens of the interior, and is held in great esteem for the table; but from its great abundance generally sells for a moderate price. Its habits in some respects resemble those of the Common Mallard, and great numbers are taken with that bird, by means of decoys. For coast night-shooting Colonel Hawker thinks this Duck furnishes the finest sport in Great Britain.

It makes its first appearance on the coast of that country about the end of September or the beginning of October, and flocks continue to arrive until the weather becomes severe. It differs from nearly all its congeners in the nature of its food, and in the time when this is procured. While the other species obtain nearly the whole of their nourishment during the night, the Widgeon procures its food — consisting of grass — in the daytime; and while the Mallard and the Teal are sporting on the water or reposing on the banks, the Widgeon is devouring with avidity the same kind of short grass on which the Geese are found to feed. Though many flocks of Widgeons are known to accompany the other Waterfowl in their nocturnal wanderings, the larger number of them pass the whole night where they have spent the day. This is shown by their singular whistling noise, which is heard at all hours.

In March and April the Widgeons again move northward for the breeding-season, a small number remaining in the northern part of Scotland to breed about the lakes of Sutherlandshire. Mr. Selby, in his paper on the birds of that region, writes that he was much pleased to observe several pairs of this species upon the smaller lochs near Lairg. They probably had their nests among the reeds and other herbage which grew in their vicinity. Mr. Selby was not so fortunate as to find any of them, but afterward, upon one of the islands of Lake Laoghall, he shot a female upon a nest of seven eggs. This was placed in the midst of a large collection of rushes, and was made of decayed rushes and reeds, with a lining of warm down from the bird's body. The eggs are described as being smaller than those of the Mallard, and of a rich creamy white color. They measure 2.13 inches in length and 1.50 in breadth.

The note of the Widgeon is a shrill whistle, and on this account it is known in some parts of England as the Whew Duck, and in France as the *Canard Siffleur.*

According to the observations of Mr. Richard Dunn, the Widgeon is the most abundant of all the Duck tribe in Lapland, frequenting the grassy swamps, lakes, and rivers, appearing in pairs with the first breaking-up of the ice. As soon as the female begins to lay, the male loses his beautiful plumage, and secretes himself in the swamps and inaccessible morasses. The female lays from five to eight eggs. The young keep among the rushes and reeds in the lakes, the old birds betaking themselves to the shallows on the coast. The Widgeon leaves for the south early in September, appearing in great flocks on the coast of Norway and Sweden; it entirely leaves Sweden in the winter.

Mareca americana.

THE AMERICAN WIDGEON; BALD-PATE.

Anas americana, GMEL. S. N. I. ii. 1788, 526. — WILS. Am. Orn. VIII. 1814, 86, pl. 69, f. 1. — AUD. Orn. Biog. IV. 1838, 337, pl. 345; Synop. 1839, 279; B. Am. VI. 1843, 259, pl. 389.

Mareca americana, STEPHENS, Shaw's Gen. Zool. XII. ii. 1824, 135. — SW. & RICH. F. B. A. II. 1831, 445. — BAIRD, B. N. Am. 1858, 783; Cat. N. Am. B. 1859, no. 585. — COUES, Key, 1872, 286; Check List, 1873, no. 493; 2d ed. 1882, no. 713; Birds N. W. 1874, 564. — RIDGW. Nom. N. Am. B. 1882, no. 607.

Mareca penelope, b., BLASIUS, B. Eur. 1862, 21.

HAB. North America in general, north to Arctic Ocean, south to Guatemala and Cuba. Accidental in Europe. Breeds nearly throughout its range.

SP. CHAR. *Adult male in winter:* Forehead and middle of crown (longitudinally) white, generally immaculate; ground-color of head and neck white, sometimes more or less soiled with grayish or brown, and thickly speckled with black; a broad space of metallic blackish green on the side of the occiput, running forward to the eye, and sometimes down the nape, where the two spaces are confluent. Jugulum plain pinkish vinaceous; sides and flanks the same, delicately undulated with black; lower tail-coverts velvety black; rest of lower parts pure white. Back and scapulars grayish white, more or less tinged with the color of the sides, and similarly undulated with black. Wing-coverts immaculate pure white, the anterior portion of the lesser-covert region cinereous, and the last row tipped with velvety black; speculum soft metallic green anteriorly, velvety black posteriorly; tertials velvety black, sharply edged with white, the lower one with its lower edge entirely pure white; primaries plain dark cinereous. Rump cinereous, minutely undulated on the edges of the feathers; upper tail-coverts velvety black, the inner webs mostly grayish; tail hoary cinereous. Bill light grayish blue, the end black; iris brown; legs and feet light bluish. Wing, 10.25–10.75 inches; culmen, 1.30–1.50; tarsus, 1.45–1.65; middle toe, 1.65–

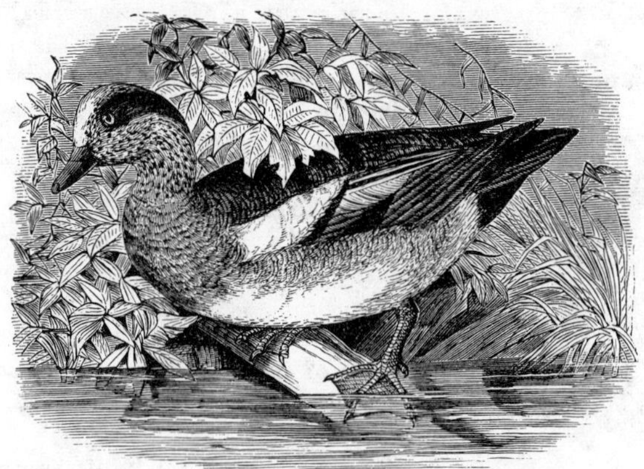

M. americana.

1.85. *Adult female:* Above, dusky grayish brown, with transverse, rather distant, bars of dull white or light ochraceous. Wing-coverts dark dull cinereous, broadly tipped and bordered with white; speculum dull black. Head and neck streaked with blackish upon a dull whitish ground, the former color prevailing on the nape and behind the eye. Jugulum pale grayish vinaceous, the feathers darker beneath the surface; sides and flanks deeper vinaceous; lower tail-coverts transversely spotted with brown; rest of lower parts pure white. *Young male:* Similar to the adult female, but the colors more pronounced and the pattern better defined, especially on the wing. *Downy young:* Above, dark olive, with a sepia tinge; a spot of pale greenish fulvous on the posterior half of the wing, one on each side of the back, and one on each side of the rump. Lower parts, including head and neck, pale fulvous; a distinct blackish olive stripe from bill to and back from the eye, with a wide and conspicuous superciliary stripe of fulvous above it.

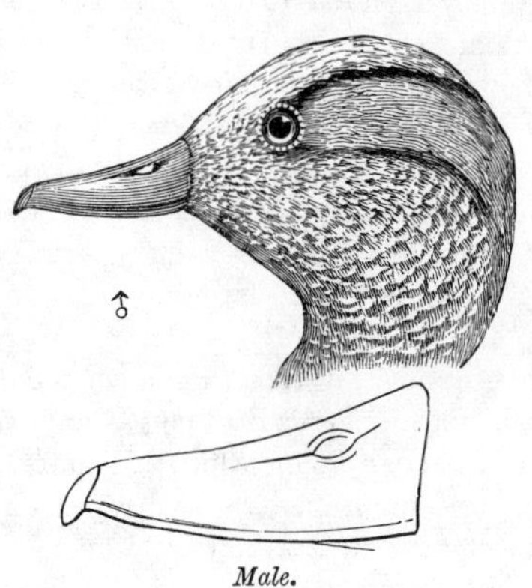

Male.

The chief variation in the plumage of adult males of this species consists in the extent of the green patch and the amount of black spotting on the head, the pureness of the white on the forehead, and the extent of the white patch on the wing-coverts. The green patch on the side of the occiput is usually poorly defined, and broken up by lighter spotting; but in No. 21426, Washington, D. C., and No. 84712, from Southern Ohio (Dr. F. W. LANGDON), it is as conspicuous as in the adult male of *Nettion carolinensis*, and of very similar extent and form. Anteriorly, it surrounds the eye, and posteriorly it passes down the nape (where the two opposite spaces are confluent for the entire length of the neck); its outlines are firm throughout, and its surface is entirely unbroken by admixture of white. In the former specimen the black spotting is so aggregated on the throat that the gular region is almost uniformly dusky, while the spots at the lower end of the white portion of the neck are so large as almost to blend into a collar, uniting the green of the nape with the black of the throat. All the other characters of the species are very much exaggerated in this specimen. Younger specimens, just possessed of the adult dress, are usually distinguished by having the white wing-covert patch clouded with ash, the green of the head poorly defined, and the white of the forehead more or less speckled.

The Bald-pate, or American Widgeon, is distributed nearly throughout North America, is found in winter as far to the south as Central America, and in summer goes to high northern latitudes to breed. It is a straggler to Europe, specimens having been taken in the London markets. In its migrations it passes through the interior as well as along the coast. At Lake Koskonong, Wis., Mr. Kumlien has found it abundant both in the spring and fall. A few remain in the lake during the summer, but these are always in flocks, unmated, and in immature plumage. No broods of young have been met with.

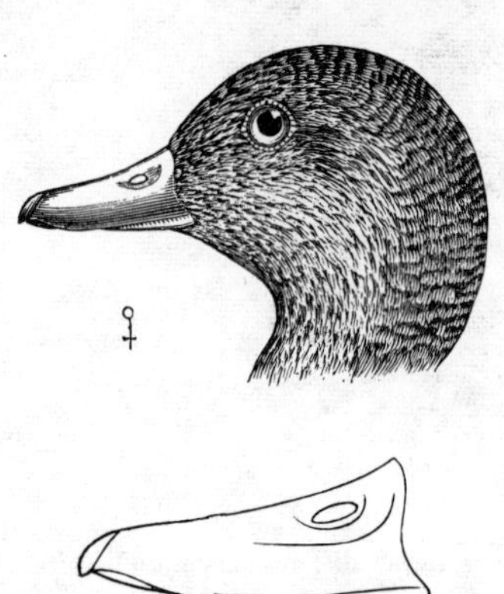

Female.

Mr. Salvin found this Duck common on the Lake of Atitlan, where it was seen in May, 1858; and it was also observed near the village of Laguna, about a day's journey from Guatemala. Mr. Salvin afterward met with it also among the lagoons on the Pacific coast. It was found abundant on the eastern coast of Mexico and on the southern coast of Texas by Mr. Dresser; and Colonel Grayson found it abundant on the coast of Western Mexico, near Mazatlan, from November until late in spring. It occurs more or less numerously in most of the West India Islands, having been noted in St. Thomas, Cuba, Jamaica, and Trinidad. In the last-named island it is said by Léotaud to arrive in December and January, leaving for the north in April; but in some years is not met with. Its flesh is held in high esteem, especially when the birds are young, and after they have been for some time on the island.

Mr. Hearne states that this Duck was, a century ago, a very uncommon visitor to Hudson's Bay. It usually kept in pairs, being rarely seen in flocks, and was most frequently observed in rivers and marshes near the sea-coast. Mr. Ross found it common on the Mackenzie; and Captain Blakiston also met with it in Hudson's Bay, and saw it in large numbers on the Saskatchewan. It occurs in the spring and fall near Calais, Me. — where, however, Mr. Boardman regards it as rather rare. It is an occasional, rather than a common, visitor to New England. According to Giraud, it is not numerous on Long Island, though so abundant farther south.

Mr. Allen found this bird quite common in the valley of the Salt Lake; Mr. R. Browne mentions its occurrence on Vancouver Island; and Mr. Dall found it not uncommon near Nulato and on the Yukon, but rare at St. Michael's. Its eggs and nests were not distinguishable from those of the *Dafila acuta*, but the bird is less active than that species, and slower in flight.

On the coast of Norton Sound — according to Mr. Adams — the Widgeon does not arrive until the 12th of May; but later a considerable number were always to be met with about the inland marshes. It appeared to live very much upon insects, which it captures on the water and about the rushes. The small inland lakes were its principal places of resort, and its nests were generally upon the grassy banks. The eggs are described as being small, much elongated, generally larger at one end, and of a pale sea-green color.

According to Dr. Cooper, this species is one of the most abundant fresh-water Ducks found during the winter in California, and, being easily shot, is one of the most common kinds in the market. It is, unlike the European species, very rarely seen on salt water; but, like the Teals, resorts to every little pool and swamp. It is generally supposed to keep a sentinel on guard while feeding, but may be decoyed within easy gunshot by imitating its notes. It has been found, during the summer, among the Rocky Mountains, in latitude 42° N., and is said by Dr. Suckley to breed among the inland lakes of Oregon. At that season it usually ranges from latitude 50° to 68°.

During the violent revolving gale which visited the Bermudas, Oct. 22, 1854 — as Mr. Hurdis states — a large number of Ducks, including this species, took refuge in the creeks and marshes of the islands, where several Bald-pates were shot by different persons and brought to him for inspection. In November of the same year a single example — a female — was shot. These were the only ones taken on the Islands during his residence there.

From the full and interesting notes of the late Mr. Robert Kennicott relative to this species we gather the following observations: A Bald-pate's nest was taken near Fort Yukon, June 7, some thirty rods from the river, on high, dry ground, among large spruces and poplars. This species always nests on high, dry ground, among trees or bushes, at a considerable distance from water. The *Dafila acuta* nests in somewhat similar situations — though not generally so far from water — and sometimes in dry spots in grassy meadows. *Spatula clypeata* breeds in the woods; *Bucephala albeola* in holes in trees; *Querquedula discors* and *Nettion carolinensis* in high, dry ground among trees; *Fulix affinis* and *F. marila* in grassy edges of lakes, in water, but never in deep water, unless the nest be on a tussock. *Æthyia vallisneria* nests in rather deep water, among grass. *Melanetta velvetina* and *Pelionetta perspicillata* breed here — the former very abundantly — nesting among large spruces close to the water. Thus it will be seen that the River Ducks nest generally on dry land, and the Sea Ducks in water, or just on the edge of water. *Melanetta* nests the latest of all the Ducks, and the Mallard the earliest. Mr. Kennicott adds that the Bald-pate is generally known to the *voyageurs* throughout the Fur Countries by the name of "Smoking-Duck," or by its Cree name of *Nimimipikhtwan*, which signifies a smoker; and its soft, gentle whistle may be easily imagined to resemble the Cree words.

The Widgeon breeds rather abundantly throughout the whole of British America, as far north as the Arctic Ocean, but only rarely in the extreme northern parts of the United States, both east and west of the Rocky Mountains. In October and April it visits in large numbers the rivers and marshes, as well as both sea-coasts, of Northern United States, and is much sought by hunters, its flesh being excellent, and the bird generally in good condition. It winters in the Southern States, Mexico, and the West Indies. Though in winter the Widgeon collects in very large flocks, it passes over the northern parts of the Mississippi Valley in small bands, and usually arrives at the Mackenzie and the Yukon in pairs, or in small parties of three or four together. It reaches Slave Lake and the Yukon early in May, and begins to nest about the middle of that month, though some do not do so till the early part of June. It is rather more common west of the mountains than in the Mackenzie Region, and considerable numbers are found in the breeding-season on Lake Winnipeg, where several were obtained by Mr. Donald Gunn. In the north the Widgeon exhibits a greater preference for rivers and open lakes than most of the other fresh-water Ducks, which prefer the grassy lakes and marshes. Most of the nests which Mr. Kennicott observed were near rivers in places not frequented by other Ducks, except sometimes by the Mallard. The favorite situation for the nest is remarkable; for while the other Ducks — except, perhaps, the Teal — choose the immediate vicinity of water, he found the Widgeon always breeding at some considerable distance from it. Several of the nests obtained on the Yukon were fully half a mile from the river — the nearest water. He invariably found the nest among dry leaves, upon high, dry ground, either under large trees or in thick groves of small ones — frequently among thick spruces. The nest is rather small — simply a depression among the leaves — but thickly lined with down, with which, after incubation is begun, the eggs are covered when left by the parent. The nest is usually placed at the foot of a tree or bush, with generally no attempt at concealment. The female, when started from her nest, rises silently into the air, and usually flies to the nearest water, though sometimes she will alight on the ground a few rods distant. The males remain more or less in the vicinity for some time after the females begin to incubate; but when the time of moulting arrives they retire to the grassy marshes and edges of lakes for concealment, leading a solitary life. The young, while unable to fly, are frequently found seeking the shelter of grassy lakes. As soon, however, as they can fly they return to their favorite river-shores and open feeding-places, where they obtain aquatic insects, a few small shells, and the seeds and roots of various plants. In the fall the broods often separate before leaving for the south; this they do about the middle of September. Mr. Kennicott several times found perfect eggs of this species — though never of any other Duck — dropped along the shores of rivers, at their feeding-places. This bird is said to make its first appearance on the Chesapeake about the last of October.

While the Canvas-backs and the Black-heads dive and pull up by the roots the *vallisneria* grass, the Bald-pates manage to obtain their full share of it, and at times succeed in robbing them of the whole. At this time the flavor of the Bald-pate is considered preferable to that of even the far-famed Canvas-backs. Of all the ducks that are found in the Chesapeake, the Widgeon is said to be one of the most difficult to attract to the shore by the process known as "toling." In wing-shooting it is regarded by the hunters as a great nuisance. It is not only so shy that it avoids the points of land, but by its whistling and confused manner of flight it alarms the other species. During its stay in those waters it is the constant companion of the Canvas-backs, upon whose superiority in diving it depends in a large degree for its food, stealing from them, as they rise to the surface of the water, the tender roots of the plant of which both are so fond. When in good condition the flesh of the Bald-pate cannot easily be distinguished from that of the Canvas-back. It is also thought that birds killed on other waters, though excellent eating, are far inferior to those from the flats of the Chesapeake. The Bald-pate is said to visit the rice-fields of the South during the winter in considerable numbers.

The places in the northern regions from which this Duck has been reported in its breeding-season are the Yukon River and Fort Yukon, by Mr. J. Lockhart and Mr. S. Jones; Fort Resolution, by Mr. Kennicott; Fort Anderson, Anderson River, the Lower Anderson, Swan River, etc., by Mr. MacFarlane; Selkirk Settlement, by Mr. Donald Gunn; Nulato and the Lower Yukon, by Mr. Dall; New Westminster, by Mr. H. W. Elliott.

The eggs of this species are of a creamy ivory white color, and vary in length from 2.15 to 2.20 inches, and from 1.45 to 1.50 in breadth.

Genus **SPATULA**, Boie.

Spatula, Boie, Isis, 1822, 564 (type, *Anas clypeata*, Linn.).
Rhynchaspis, "Leach," Stephens, Shaw's Gen. Zool. XII. ii. 1824, 114 (same type).

Char. Bill longer than the head, much expanded, or almost spatulate, terminally, where about twice as wide as at the compressed base; maxillary lamellæ very thin, lengthened, almost completely exposed posteriorly, where resembling the teeth of a fine comb. Tail short, the feathers acute.

Of this very curious and well-marked genus, in which, however, there is little that is peculiar except in the form of the bill, about five species are known — one occurring throughout the northern hemisphere, the others peculiar to South America, South Africa, Australia, and New Zealand. In the two American species and that from Australia there is a very close resemblance in the coloration of the wing to certain species of *Querquedula* (e. g. *discors* and *cyanoptera*); while in the Australian species (*S. rhynchotis*) this curious analogy is carried still farther, the coloration of the head, including the white crescentic bar across the lores, being almost exactly as in *Q. discors*.

The characters of the two American and the Australian species are as follows: —

S. clypeata.

Com. Char. (adult males). Lesser wing-coverts pale dull blue; middle coverts broadly tipped with white; speculum bronze-green; tertials striped centrally with white; lower parts chestnut-rufous; a white patch at the base of the tail, on each side.

A. Culmen nearly straight, slightly depressed in the middle; feathering at base of maxilla, on each side extending forward as far as that on the forehead.

1. **S. clypeata.** Head and neck dull dark green; jugulum white. *Hab.* Northern hemisphere.
2. **S. rhynchotis.** Head and neck dull brownish gray, faintly glossed with glaucous-green on the nape; the anterior part of the head marked on each side by a white crescentic bar across the lore; jugulum dusky, marked with buff. *Hab.* Australia.

B. Culmen decidedly concave in the middle portion; feathering at the base of the maxilla on each side, forming a straight vertical line.

3. **S. platalea.** Head and neck buff, speckled with dusky; jugulum light cinnamon, spotted with black. *Hab.* Southern South America.

The genus *Spatula* has a near relative in the curious *Malacorhynchus membranaceus* of Australia, which has a somewhat similar but still more remarkable bill, and differs further in the following particulars: The maxilla is less expanded terminally, the edges being nearly parallel; but on each side, near the end, is a membraneous, somewhat angular lobe, the end of the mandible being nearly truncated, and the nail much smaller and narrower than in *Spatula;* the nostrils are much smaller, and near the base of the bill; the tertials and rectrices are broad and rounded, instead of acute.

The two American species of *Spatula* differ more particularly as follows: —

1. **S. clypeata.** *Male:* Head and neck dark metallic green; jugulum white; abdomen and sides chestnut, unspotted; back and inner scapulars dusky; outer scapulars white. *Female:* Back and scapulars nearly uniform dusky; bill brown, the mandible dull orange.
2. **S. platalea.**[1] *Male:* Head and neck buff, streaked with black; jugulum, back, and scapulars (outer as well as inner) deep cinnamon-buff, thickly marked with roundish spots of black; abdomen and sides chestnut, speckled with black. *Female:* Back and scapulars dusky, the feathers broadly bordered and otherwise variegated with buff; bill wholly black.

The female and young male of *S. platalea* may also be readily distinguished from those of *S. clypeata* by the much longer, more cuneate tail, the rectrices being almost, if not quite, as acuminate as in the species of *Pœcilonetta;* thus, while the middle rectrices in a female of *S. clypeata* measure about 3.75 inches, those of an example of *S. platalea* measure 4.25, or half an inch longer.

Spatula clypeata.

THE SHOVELLER; SPOON-BILL DUCK.

Anas clypeata, LINN. S. N. ed. 10, I. 1758, 124; ed, 12, I. 1766, 200. — WILS. Am. Orn. VIII. 1814, 65, pl. 67, fig. 7. — SW. & RICH. F. B. A. II. 1831, 439. — NUTT. Man. II. 1834, 375. — AUD. Orn. Biog. IV. 1838, 241, pl. 327; Synop. 1839, 283; B. Am. VI. 1843, 293, pl. 394.

Spatula clypeata, BOIE, Isis, 1822, 564. — BAIRD, B. N. Am. 1858, 781; Cat. N. Am. B. 1859, no. 583. — COUES, Key, 1872, 288; Check List, 1873, no. 498; 2d ed. 1881, no. 718; B. N. W. 1874, 570. — RIDGW. Nom. N. Am. B. 1881, no. 608.

Anas rubens, GMEL. S. N. I. ii. 1788, 419.

? *Anas mexicana*, LATH. Ind. Orn. II. 1790, 857.

Clypeata macrorhynchos, platyrhynchos, pomarina, brachyrhynchos, BREHM, Vög. Deutschl. 876, 877, 878, 879.

HAB. The whole of the Northern Hemisphere; Australia. Breeding from Texas to Alaska; wintering as far south as Guatemala, Cuba, and Jamaica.

SP. CHAR. *Adult male, in winter:* Head and neck dark metallic bluish green, much duller than in *Anas boschas;* breast and outer scapulars white, the former sometimes spotted with dusky; entire abdomen and sides uniform chestnut; crissum dark metallic bluish green, bounded anteriorly by a band of finely undulated grayish white. Back and inner scapulars dusky, the feathers sometimes bordered with white; longer, lanceolate scapulars marked with a mesial lanceolate stripe of white; wing-coverts light grayish blue, the last row tipped with white, forming a narrow band across the wing; speculum bright metallic green, very narrowly tipped with white; tertials dusky black, with faint green reflections, and marked toward the end with an indistinct mesial stripe of grayish white; primaries and their coverts dull slate-gray; rump and upper tail-coverts black, the former with faint, the latter with bright, green reflections; rectrices chiefly grayish white, the middle

[1] SPATULA PLATALEA.

Pato espatulato, AZARA, Apunt. III. 1805, 431 (Buenos Ayres).

Anas platalea, VIEILL. Nouv. Dict. V. 1816, 157 (ex AZARA, l. c.).

Spatula platalea, HARTL. Ind. Azara, 1847, 27. — SCL. & SALV. Nom. Neotr. 1873, 130; P. Z. S. 1876, 396 (monographic).

Rhynchaspis maculatus, "GOULD, MS." JARD. & SELBY, Illustr. Orn. pl. 147.

Dafila cæsio-scapulata, REICHENB. Natat. pl. 51, fig. 180.

ones dark gray, edged with white. Bill deep black; iris bright yellow; legs and feet beautiful orange-red. *Adult female:* Wings as in the male, but colors rather duller. Other parts grayish brown above, varied with brownish white; brownish white below, the head and neck streaked, the breast, abdomen, etc., spotted, with grayish brown. Bill brown, mandible orange; iris yellow and feet orange-red, as in the male. *Young male:* Similar to the adult female, but lower parts (always ?) tinged with chestnut. *Young female:* Similar to the adult, but wing-coverts dull slate, with little, if any, blue tinge, the speculum dusky, with a very faint green reflection, and rather broadly tipped with brownish white. *Downy young:* Above, grayish brown, with a brownish-white spot on each side of the back, and a corresponding pair on the rump; pileum darker than the back and nape; head (except pileum) and entire lower parts pale grayish fulvous, or dirty grayish buffy white, shaded with brownish gray across the jugulum; a narrow stripe of dark brown from the upper angle of the base of the bill to the eye, and continued posteriorly about half way to the occiput; another similar stripe beneath the last, beginning a little behind the posterior border of the eye, and extending farther back than the one above it. [Described from No. 65561, Souris R., Dakota, Aug. 10, 1873; Dr. E. Coues, U. S. A.]

Male.

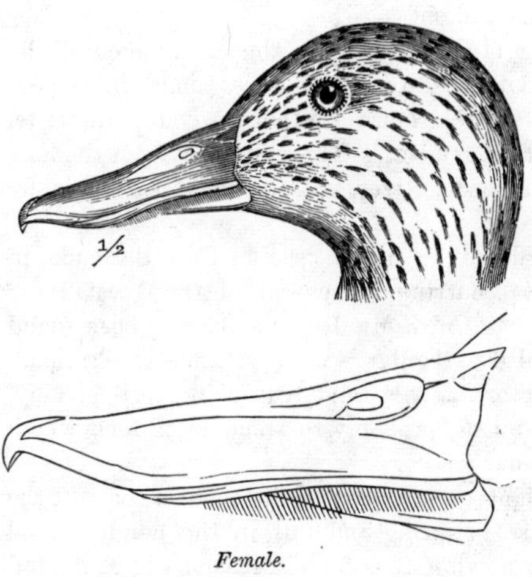

Female.

Total length, about 20.00 inches; extent, 31.00 to 33.00 inches; wing, 9.00–10.00; culmen, 2.60–2.90; width of bill at end, 1.10–1.20, at base, .60; tarsus, 1.40–1.50; middle toe, 1.65–1.75. Specimens vary considerably in colors: usually the white of the chest and scapulars is nearly or quite immaculate; but not infrequently these portions are more or less spotted with dusky. The chestnut of the abdomen is sometimes immaculate, sometimes barred with dusky.

The Shoveller Duck, while nowhere conspicuously numerous, appears to have the most extended distribution of any species of the Duck tribe. It is found throughout North and Central America as far to the south as Panama; is more or less common in every portion of Europe and Asia, except in the extreme north; is found in Northern and Central Africa; and is said to have been taken even in South Africa and in Australia; but the evidence in this regard is not wholly satisfactory.

Mr. Salvin found it inhabiting the Lake of Dueñas during the winter, where it remained until about the end of March. Colonel Grayson met with it on the western coast of Mexico, and Dr. Palmer obtained it at Guaymas. The former speaks of it as very common about Mazatlan from November to May. According to Dr. Cooper, the Shoveller, or, as there called, the "Spoon-bill Duck," is common in winter along the entire coast of California and throughout the interior, as far north as the Columbia, wherever the fresh water to which it resorts is not frozen over. It arrives from the north about the 1st of October, and remains until March or April, associating with other fresh-water Ducks. It is generally silent, and has at all times but a feeble voice. Its food consists of the same vegetable and animal substances as those eaten by the allied species; but this bird has the advantage of a more expanded and sensitive bill as a help in finding them, and consequently becomes very fat; its flesh is also considered well flavored.

From the late Mr. Robert Kennicott's manuscripts we take the following: "Though the Shoveller goes in summer nearly or quite as far to the north as *Dafila acuta*, a larger proportion nest farther south. A few breed within the United States; and Dr. Hoy mentions it as sometimes nesting in Southern Wisconsin. At Slave Lake I first observed it about the middle of May, when they had already paired. It is highly probable that they arrived earlier, but from their small numbers escape attention. A pair commenced nesting at the Yukon about the 20th of May. I found it rather rare at the north, though less so west of the mountains than in the Mackenzie Region. I did not see more than a pair of old birds together at any time. The few specimens observed were usually feeding in shallow water near the shore; though they appeared to seek the grassy spots less than the other fresh-water Ducks."

Mr. Bannister states that this species was frequently seen by him among the birds brought in by the hunters of the Fort, during the month of May, at St. Michael's. Mr. Dall was informed that it breeds at one point in the strait between St. Michael's and the mainland. He obtained only a single skin at Unalaklik; and thinks this bird cannot be abundant anywhere near the Yukon.

Dr. Richardson states that this species chiefly frequents the clear lakes of the northern districts, and breeds in the Barren Grounds; but is found in considerable numbers, in spring and autumn, in the more southern wooded districts. Captain Blakiston procured specimens from Hudson's Bay, and also from the Saskatchewan; and it was found on the Mackenzie River, within the Arctic Circle, by Mr. Bernard Ross.

Major Wedderburn mentions the capture of a single specimen in Bermuda in December, 1844. It is also recorded as occurring in several of the West India Islands, Dr. Gundlach noting it as a visitor to Cuba, Mr. Rüsse as having been found in St. Thomas, and Léotaud as being quite a regular winter visitant to Trinidad. In the latter place it arrives in December or January, and leaves in April or May. It occurs rarely in flocks; and its flesh, owing probably to some local food which impairs its flavor, is not favorably regarded.

It does not appear to be at all abundant on any part of the eastern coast of the United States. It occurs in small numbers, in spring and fall, in the neighborhood of Calais, but is not recorded from farther north. It is found occasionally in the fall in Massachusetts, but is not recorded as occurring there in the spring. Two were shot at Rye Beach in August, 1872.

According to Giraud, it is met with in small numbers on Long Island, where it is known to hunters by the name of the "Spoon-bill." It is occasionally met with along the sea-coast; but is much more generally found in the lakes and fresh-water streams, although never abundant in any part of Long Island. Its flesh is tender and juicy, and is deservedly held in high esteem. Mr. J. A. Allen met with this species in the valley of Salt Lake, in Utah, where he found it common.

Our space would not suffice to enumerate the various records of its presence in different parts of the Old World, where it seems to have an almost universal distribution. Mr. Salvin met with it in small numbers near Zara, in Northeastern Africa. Mr. Saunders found it not uncommon in Southern Spain, where it was supposed to be resident, and to breed. Captain G. E. Shelley ("Ibis," 1871) found it one of the most abundant of the Ducks throughout Egypt, where also some remained to breed. Mr. E. C. Taylor met with it in Egypt; Mr. Tristram in Southern Palestine on the Jordan, and in the region of the Sahara. Mr. T. L. Powys records it as common in the winter in Greece. It was observed in Japan by Mr. H. Whitely ("Ibis," 1867); and also in Japan and China by other authorities.

According to Yarrell, it is chiefly a winter visitant in Great Britain, inhabiting marshes, lakes, rivers, and muddy shores, gathering its food in shallow water. It is most plentiful on the eastern parts of England, and breeds in various places, from Essex to Lincolnshire. Various attempts have been made to rear this bird from the egg, but generally without much success. During the summer of 1841 a pair of Shovellers made a nest and brought out their young on one of the islands in the Garden of the Zoological Society. The bills of these ducklings were as narrow and the sides as parallel as the bills of some young Gadwalls hatched at the same time. The egg of the Shoveller is described as buffy-white, tinged with green, 2.17 inches long, and 1.50 wide.

Yarrell says that this bird is not common in Scandinavia, where it is chiefly confined to the south of Sweden, and that it is found in Russia and Germany, is abundant in Holland, and breeds regularly in the marshes of France. It also occurs in various parts of India, and nearly throughout Asia. Mr. Dresser states that it has not been found in Southern Africa; but Mr. Yarrell refers to specimens brought from there by Mr. Andrew Smith. Von Heuglin speaks of it as a permanent resident in Abyssinia. In Nubia, according to Captain Shelley, it seemed to prefer the smaller pools and the banks of lakes and rivers, and to be less shy than other species of Water-Fowl. He speaks of its flesh as "very inferior eating." Dr. Jerdon, in recording its occurrence in India, speaks of it as feeding, near the edges of tanks, in shallow water, among weeds, chiefly on minute worms and larvæ, which it sifts from the mud.

Although a fresh-water Duck, it is not infrequently met with on the coast; but its favorite resort is fresh waters overgrown with aquatic plants. It is not particularly shy, and is generally seen in flocks. It feeds on the seeds of various water-plants, grain, and minute water-insects, for which last its fringed mandibles are especially useful, enabling it to expel the water, and yet retain the minutest insects gathered in at the same time. On account of its fondness for insects one author has named the species *muscaria*.

In Europe it breeds in May, June, and July. Its nest — placed close to some fresh-water pond or lake — is a hole scratched in the soil, lined with a few grasses and a considerable quantity of down plucked from the bird itself. In Denmark it breeds near the coast, and on islands in the fiords. The nests are usually concealed in the high grass or under low bushes, and contain from nine to fourteen eggs. Eggs have been found as early as the 2d of May and as late as the 24th of July.

They are described as paler than those of the Mallard, and of very fine texture; the color is greenish gray of a very pale, soft tone; in shape they are oblong oval, tapering slightly at one end, and measure from 1.97 by 1.30 to 2.03 by 1.40 inches. The color sometimes varies to grayish cream.

Professor Kumlien informs me that these Ducks are common in Southern Wisconsin, where they arrive quite late in the spring, and a few remain to breed. He has met with several broods of young; but has found only one nest, which was placed in the midst of a high bog. It resembled that of the Mallard, but was less bulky, and was plentifully supplied with down. A great many old males are seen in the early part of summer, in flocks; from which he naturally conjectures that their females breed somewhere in the extensive marshes that surround Lake Koskonong.

Near Pewaukee, in the same State, this Duck has been found breeding by Mr. B. F. Goss, who writes me that on May 24, in Horicon Lake, near the highest part of a small island, some five feet above the water, a single "Spoon-bill" had made her nest. The Mallards were all around within a few feet. As the ground was quite bare, with merely a few rocks scattered about, the birds could be seen from the water sitting on their nests. On his first approach he noticed the Spoon-bill rising with the rest; and after examining the nests, selected one that was somewhat smaller than the others, with smaller eggs, and lined with feathers of a little different shade, as the Spoon-bill's nest. He set a small stake to mark the place, and retired until the birds returned to their eggs, when he again approached, watching carefully the indicated spot, and had the good fortune to kill the bird as she rose. The nest contained ten eggs, quite fresh, a little smaller than the Mallard's, from which they differed somewhat in color and in shape.

The localities in the Fur Region from which this Duck has been reported as breeding are Fort Resolution, on Great Slave Lake, the Yukon River, Fort Rae, Big Island, Lake Winnipeg, Anderson River, the Lower Anderson, Shoal Lake, Unalakleet, Red River, etc.

Eggs from the Yukon River in the Smithsonian Collection (No. 6612) are of a greenish-white color, and measure from 2.05 to 2.10 inches in length, and from 1.40 to 1.50 in breadth.

Genus **QUERQUEDULA**, Stephens.

Querquedula, Stephens, Shaw's Gen. Zool. XII. ii. 1824, 142 (type, *Anas querquedula*, Linn.).
Cyanopterus, Eyton, Mon. Anat. 1838, 38 (type ?). (Not of Halliday, 1835.)
Pterocyanea, Bp. Cat. Met. 1842, 71 (type).

Char. Size small (wing less than 8 inches). Bill slightly longer than the head, the edges nearly parallel, the maxillary tomium sinuated, so as to distinctly expose the lamellæ for the basal half, and the terminal half of the culmen slightly but distinctly arched. Otherwise much like *Nettion.*

The two North American species of *Querquedula* agree very closely in the details of form, in which respect they scarcely differ from the type of the genus, the *Q. circia* (L.) of Europe. The coloration of the wing, which is almost exactly that of *Spatula*, is also essentially the same in these three species. The females are very different from the males, except in the colors of the wing, being much duller. The following are the main differential characters of the North American species :—

1. **Q. discors.** *Adult male:* Head and neck dull plumbeous, with a faint lavender-purple gloss on the sides of the occiput; pileum blackish; a large white, somewhat crescent-shaped, mark before the eye, entirely across fore part of the head; lower parts pale

reddish, spotted with black. *Hab.* North America generally, but chiefly the Eastern Province.

2. **Q. cyanoptera**. *Adult male:* Head, neck, and lower parts rich uniform chestnut, the abdomen duller (sometimes dusky), the pileum blackish. *Hab.* Western America, from Chili to Washington Territory.

Q. discors.

Querquedula discors.

THE BLUE-WINGED TEAL.

Anas discors, LINN. S. N. ed. 12, I. 1766, 205 (based on *Querq. americ. variegata*, CATESB. 100; BRISS. VI. 452. — *Querq. americ. fusca*, CATESB. 99. — *Querq. virginiana*, BRISS. VI. 455). — WILS. Am. Orn. VIII. 1814, 74, pl. 68, fig. 4. — AUD. Orn. Biog. IV. 1838, 111, pl. 313 ; Synop. 1839, 282 ; B. Am. VI. 1843, 287, pl. 393.

Anas (*Boschas*) *discors*, SW. & RICH. F. B. A. II. 1831, 444. — NUTT. Man. II. 1834, 397.

Querquedula discors, STEPHENS, Shaw's Gen. Zool. XII. ii. 1824, 149. — BAIRD, B. N. Am. 1858, 779 ; Cat. N. Am. B. 1859, no. 581. — COUES, Key, 1872, 287 ; Check List, 1873, no. 496 ; 2d ed. 1882, no. 716 ; Birds N. W. 1874, 566. — RIDGW. Nom. N. Am. B. 1881, no. 609.

Sarcelle mâle de Cayenne, dite le Soucrourou, BUFF. Pl. Enl. 966 (♂ ad.).

HAB. North America in general, but chiefly the Eastern Province ; north to Alaska, south to Ecuador, and throughout West Indies. Accidental in Europe.

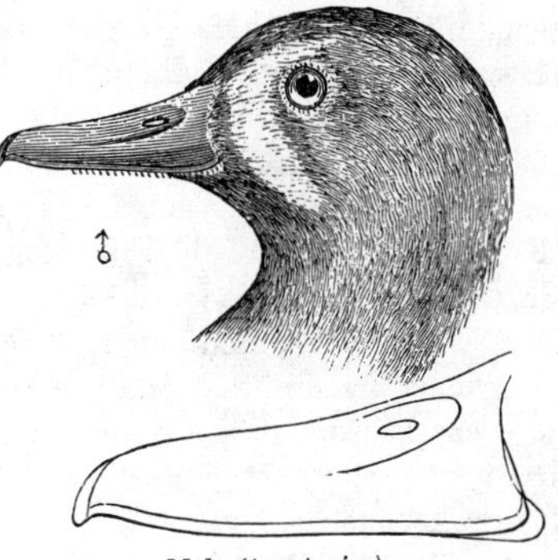

Male (½ nat. size).

SP. CHAR. *Adult male:* Head and neck dull plumbeous, slightly glossed with lavender-purple on the side of the occiput and nape, and marked in front of the eyes by a large, somewhat crescentic, patch of white, extending entirely across the anterior portion of the head ; pileum, chin, and feathers bordering the white patches, blackish ; lower parts pale reddish, thickly spotted with black, the crissum uniform black. Back and anterior scapulars dusky, marked with concentric or U-shaped bars of pale reddish buff ; lesser wing-coverts and outer webs of some of the longer scapulars pale blue ; middle coverts white for the exposed portion, forming a bar across the wing ; speculum bronzy green, dusky terminally, with a very narrow white tip ; tertials black, with a central stripe of buff ; a white patch at the base of the tail on each side ; axillars immaculate pure white. Bill uniform black ; iris brown ; feet yellowish. *Adult female:* Wings, only, as in the male ; upper parts dusky, the feathers bordered with dull buff, the pileum and nape finely streaked; rest of head and neck, and lower parts generally, brownish white, the head and neck streaked with dusky, except on the chin and upper part of the throat, the streaks more dense immediately before and behind the eye, thus forming an indistinct stripe on the side of the head; feathers of the lower parts generally with dusky grayish brown centres, forming spots when exposed, less distinct on the abdomen, where sometimes obsolete.

Total length, about 16 inches; extent, about 25; wing, 7.00–7.50; culmen, 1.40–1.65; tarsus, 1.20–1.30; middle toe, 1.40–1.45.

The Blue-winged Teal has a more restricted distribution than the Green-winged, and is also a much more southern species. It is rarely to be met with north of 60°

Female (nat. size).

N. latitude, and, so far as is positively known, is not found on the Pacific coast between the Gulf of California and Vancouver Island, although occurring on the Pacific coast of Mexico and Central America, as well as, more sparingly, on the coast of Alaska. It is supposed to breed in various favorable localities from Florida to Labrador, and from Mazatlan to the Saskatchewan, but principally between latitudes 42° and 58° N., and most abundantly in the Mississippi Valley. It occurs sparingly at Fort Resolution, Lake Winnipeg, Shoal Lake, and even at Fort Yukon.

Mr. Salvin found it common in the winter on Lake Dueñas, in Guatemala, but not remaining through March. Dr. Bryant gives it as common in winter at Bahamas. It was also seen at Sultana Mixtlan, in the Pacific coast region. Mr. G. C. Taylor found it in Honduras, both at Tigre Island and on Lake Yojoya.

It was met with in Western Mexico, near Mazatlan, by Colonel Grayson, in which region he speaks of it as being a very common species, a few remaining throughout the summer, and probably breeding there. Mr. Dresser found it common throughout Northern Mexico and Southern Texas, where, as supposed by Dr. Heermann, it breeds. Mr. N. B. Moore found Ducks of this species abundant in Florida, and believes that some must breed in that State, as he has seen them in fresh ponds near Sarasota Lake at every season of the year, and has killed the young in September on Miska Lake. He thinks it probable that they breed on the islands, or about the shores of Lake Okeechobee.

Mr. Bernard Ross found this species abundant in the vicinity of Great Slave Lake, where it was much more abundant than the Green-wing. Mr. Kennicott met with it east of the Rocky Mountains only, where he found it nesting in rather open ground;

but found none on the Yukon, nor north of Slave Lake. In Illinois and Wisconsin he found it nesting in the prairie sloughs. Mr. Dall, however, speaks of having met with it sparingly both at Fort Yukon and at the mouth of Yukon River, but it was not seen at Nulato. Captain Smith obtained its eggs from near Cape Romanzoff. Mr. Bannister reports it as not uncommon at St. Michael's.

It is a visitor to Cuba and other West India Islands. Léotaud states that it arrives in Trinidad about the 1st of November, and remains there until April. It is quite regular and constant in its visits — with, however, occasional intermissions. It is much sought after by epicures, and in the opinion of Léotaud, the flesh of no other Duck can be compared with that of this Teal after it has been one or two months on the island.

It breeds in the neighborhood of Calais, Me. — as Mr. Boardman informs me — but is not common there. It is a regular fall and spring visitor in Massachusetts, but I am not aware that it stops to breed. At Fort Pond, near Montauk Point, Long Island, it is said to breed every season.

In the fall of the year this is one of the first of the Duck tribe to leave its more northern quarters. Subsisting chiefly on insects and tender plants, it is compelled to seek a milder climate early, and usually arrives in the Middle States in the month of September, selecting for its abode the small streams and mill-ponds, where an abundant supply of its favorite food is found. In a short time, however, it leaves for more southern regions. It is the first Duck, in the fall, to visit the shores of the Delaware and the Chesapeake bays, where it begins to arrive in September, and remains until driven farther south by the approach of winter, being found in winter only where the weather is mild. It is not timid, being easily approached in a boat or under cover of any simple device. Large numbers are killed among the reeds, on the Delaware, by means of what are termed "stool Ducks," set out in the mud. The birds are more readily attracted by these decoys if they are set in the mud than if placed in the water.

This Duck is fond of the seeds of wild oats, and becomes very fat after feeding on them for a short time, and it is caught in great numbers in the Southern rice-fields by means of traps set by the negroes. It flies with great rapidity and considerable noise; and is said at times to drop suddenly among the reeds in the manner of the Woodcock.

Although Dr. Newberry mentions this species in his Report as a bird of California, Dr. Cooper is confident that he is in error, and thinks that he probably mistook the female and young of the *Q. cyanoptera* for it, as they greatly resemble each other. Dr. Richardson found this species very plentiful on the Saskatchewan, but did not observe it farther north than the 58th parallel. It is occasionally met with in the autumn and winter in the Bermudas, and again in April, according to Major Wedderburn. Mr. Hurdis adds that it not infrequently visits these islands in its southern migrations. It is first seen about the 20th of September, and is met with at intervals until the 24th of December. It is most numerous, however, in the month of October, particularly when a storm is raging or has passed between those islands and the American coast. A large number were shot during the occurrence of the great gale of Nov. 22, 1854. It is very rarely seen in spring, and then usually about the end of March.

The mouths of the Mississippi, according to Mr. Audubon, are a great rendezvous of this species in autumn and during the greater part of winter, where those arriving coastways meet other multitudes that have come across the interior from the north and west. These Ducks are the first to arrive in that part of the country, frequently making their appearance in large flocks by the middle of September, when they are exceedingly fat. They depart, however, when the weather becomes so cold that ice forms. Toward the end of February they again become abundant; but this time they are lean, though in their summer garb, in which the male is very beautiful. During their stay they are seen in the bayous and ponds, along the banks of the Mississippi, and on the large and muddy sand-bars, feeding on grasses and their seeds, particularly in autumn, when they are very fond of the wild pimento. In the spring some remain as late as the 15th of May.

On the 26th of April, 1837, in his visit to Texas, Audubon found them on all the ponds and salt bayous or inlets of Galveston Island, as well as on the watercourses of the interior, where, he was assured, they breed in great numbers.

The flight of this Duck is extremely rapid, fully as swift as that of the Passenger Pigeon. When advancing against a stiff breeze it shows alternately its upper and lower surface. During its flight it utters a soft, lisping note, which it also emits when apprehensive of danger. It swims buoyantly, and when in a flock so closely together that the individuals nearly touch each other. In consequence of this habit hunters are able to make a frightful havoc among these birds on their first appearance in the fall, when they are easily approached. Audubon has seen as many as eighty-four killed by a single discharge of a double-barrelled gun.

It may readily be kept in confinement, soon becomes very docile, feeds readily on coarse corn-meal, and might easily be domesticated. Professor Kumlien, however, has made several unsuccessful attempts to raise this Duck by placing its eggs under a Domestic Hen. He informs me that this species is the latest Duck to arrive in the spring. It is very common, and breeds abundantly in Southern Wisconsin, especially on the borders of Lake Koskonong. It nests on the ground among the reeds and coarse herbage, generally near the water, but he has met with its nest at least half a mile from the nearest water, though always on low land. The nest is simply an accumulation of reeds and rushes lined in the middle with down and feathers. This Duck prefers the dryer marshes near creeks. He has always found its nests well lined with down, and when the female leaves her nest she always covers her eggs with down, and draws the grass, of which the outside of the nest is composed, over the top. He does not think that she ever lays more than twelve eggs, the usual number being eight to twelve. These are of a clear ivory white, without even the slightest tinge of green. They range from 1.80 to 1.95 inches in length, and from 1.25 to 1.35 in breadth.

Querquedula cyanoptera.

THE CINNAMON TEAL.

Anas cyanoptera, VIEILL. Nouv. Dict. V. 1816, 104.

Querquedula cyanoptera, CASS. U. S. Astr. Exp. II. 1856, 202 (Chili); Illustr. B. Cal. Tex. etc. 1855, 82, pl. 15. — BAIRD, B. N. Am. 1858, 780; Cat. N. Am. B. 1859, no. 582. — COUES, Key, 1872, 288; Check List, 1873, no. 497; 2d ed. 1882, no. 717; B. N. W. 1874, 567. — RIDGW. Nom. N. Am. B. 1881, no. 610.

Anas Rafflesi, KING, Zool. Jour. IV. 1828, 87; Suppl. pl. 29 (Straits of Magellan).

Pterocyanea cæruleata, "LICHT." GRAY, Gen. B. III. 1849, 617.

HAB. Western America, from the Columbia River to Chili, Buenos Ayres, and Falkland Islands. Casual in Eastern North America (Louisiana, Illinois, Florida?)

SP. CHAR. *Adult male:* Head, neck, and lower parts rich purplish chestnut, duller — sometimes quite dusky — on the abdomen; pileum and crissum black; scapulars and part of the back chestnut, marked with U-shaped bars of black, the middle of the back more dusky; tertials black, with a central stripe of buff; longer scapulars similar, the outermost feathers with the outer webs light blue; lesser wing-coverts plain light blue; middle coverts dusky, tipped with white; speculum uniform green, varying from metallic grass-green to bronze; primaries and primary-coverts dusky; upper tail-coverts dusky, edged with pale fulvous; rectrices dusky, edged with brownish white or pale brownish gray; axillars immaculate pure white. Bill deep black; iris orange; feet orange, joints and webs blackish. *Adult female:* Similar to that of *Q. discors*, but larger and

Q. cyanoptera.

deeper colored, only the upper part of the throat (sometimes only the chin) unstreaked, the abdomen usually distinctly spotted; jugulum deeply tinged with light brown. *Young male:* Similar to the adult female, but markings on the lower parts all distinctly longitudinal, or streak-like. *Downy young:*[1] Above, dark olivaceous, relieved by a longitudinal oblong oblique spot of deep greenish buff on each side the back (behind the wings), and a similar spot of clearer yellowish on each side of the base of the tail; the anterior spots confluent with the yellow of the sides, the posterior ones isolated by the extension beneath them of the olivaceous of the tail. Pileum and nape similar to the back, but darker; forehead, broad superciliary stripe, and rest of the head and neck, except as described, with entire lower parts, deep yellowish buff, the side of the head marked with a distinct narrow stripe of dark brown extending from the upper base of the maxilla to the eye, thence back to the occiput.

Male (½ nat. size).

Total length (adult), about 15.50–16.50 inches; extent, 24.00–24.50; wing, 7.20–7.75; culmen, 1.65–1.85; tarsus, 1.25–1.35; middle toe, 1.40–1.50.

Examples from Chili and Buenos Ayres are larger and more richly colored than those from the Western United States; the white bar across the end of the middle coverts narrower, and nearly concealed by the overlying last row of lesser coverts. These differences, however, may not prove constant.

The female of this species is very difficult to distinguish from that of *Q. discors*, and it is probably not possible always to separate them with certainty. The present species averages considerably larger, however; the wing in the adult female ranging from 7.20 to 7.50 inches, the culmen 1.70 to 1.75, against 6.70 to 7.00, and 1.40 to 1.50, as in *Q. discors*. The colors are also deeper,

[1] Described from No. 77549, Washoe Lake, Nev., June 2, 1877; H. W. HENSHAW.

nearly the whole throat being streaked, the breast deeply tinged with light brown, and the abdomen almost always distinctly spotted.

The Red-breasted Teal, so characteristic of California, is almost exclusively a western species, and is found along the Pacific coast from Puget Sound to Chili, and even, at certain seasons, to the Falkland Islands. It occurs eastward to the Rocky Mountains, and stragglers have been taken in Louisiana, in Florida, and — as I am assured by friends who have met with it there — in the inlets of North Carolina.

Colonel Grayson met with it at Mazatlan, where it was rather common, but where it occurred only during the winter and spring months, and never in large numbers.

Female (nat. size).

Mr. J. A. Allen mentions finding it in great abundance in the valley of Great Salt Lake. Captain Abbott speaks of meeting with it at Mare Harbor, in East Falkland, where he obtained seven examples in one day. It was generally very wild, and far from common. Although he was unable to find its nest, he had no doubt that it was breeding on the island, he having noticed it in pairs during the summer months. Mr. H. Durnford mentions it as resident, but rare, in Central Patagonia, where he met with it at the mouth of the Sengel.

According to Dr. Cooper, this western analogue of the Blue-winged Teal of the east is common in winter throughout the lower portion of California, assembling in considerable flocks, though everywhere less abundant than the Green-winged species. It associates with that and other species on all the fresh waters, and has similar habits in respect to its manner of flight and mode of feeding. It is also easily shot, and very good for the table. In summer it is found in nearly all parts of the State, and also migrates north through the open country east of the Cascade Mountains to the Upper Columbia, it having been obtained by Dr. Suckley at Fort Dalles in May. Dr. Cooper has also shot it in October near the Spokane River in Washington Territory. Dr. Heermann was of the opinion that this species leaves the central portions of California in winter; but examples were found there at that season by Dr. Kennerly, and Dr. Cooper also saw it in small numbers near the Colorado, in latitude 35°.

Captain Bendire found it more common than either of the other two species of Teal in Eastern Oregon, where it breeds in large numbers. It begins laying about May 15, and not infrequently he found its nest placed a hundred yards or more from the nearest water. Dr. Merrill states that it passes through Texas in its migrations, but is more abundant there in the spring than in the autumn.

Its nest is composed of coarse grass lined with feathers from the breast of the mother, and is placed in the marshes, usually near ponds and still water. The eggs are from twelve to fourteen in number, and are described by some writers as of a pale green color; but I have never seen any to which this description applies.

Dr. Cooper obtained an egg, just ready for exclusion, from a female killed on the 22d of June, at a pond close to the sea-beach near San Diego. He describes it as bluish white, and as measuring 1.66 inches in length and 1.32 inches in breadth. After the egg is laid the color becomes somewhat different. Eggs of this species from Fort Crook, Cal. (Smithsonian Institution, No. 5252), are of an ivory-white color, with a deep creamy tinge. Three eggs present the following measurements: 1.85 by 1.40 inches, 1.75 by 1.35 inches, 1.90 by 1.35 inches.

University Press: John Wilson & Son, Cambridge.

THE WATER BIRDS

OF

NORTH AMERICA.

VOL. II.

Memoirs of the Museum of Comparative Zoölogy
AT HARVARD COLLEGE.
VOL. XIII.

THE WATER BIRDS OF NORTH AMERICA.

BY

S. F. BAIRD, T. M. BREWER,
AND
R. RIDGWAY.

ISSUED IN CONTINUATION OF THE

PUBLICATIONS OF THE GEOLOGICAL SURVEY OF CALIFORNIA.

J. D. WHITNEY, STATE GEOLOGIST.

VOLUME II.

BOSTON:
LITTLE, BROWN, AND COMPANY.
1884.

JOHN WILSON & SON
UNIVERSITY PRESS
1639
CAMBRIDGE, MASS.

CONTENTS.

THE

WATER BIRDS

OF

NORTH AMERICA.

ORDER ANSERES.

THE LAMELLIROSTRAL SWIMMERS.

(*Continued.*)

GENUS **NETTION**, KAUP.

Nettion, KAUP, Entwick. 1829, 95, 196 (type, *Anas crecca*, LINN.).

Querquedula, BONAP. Comp. List, 1838, et AUCT. var. (not of STEPHENS, 1824, and subsequent authors).

CHAR. Bill shorter than the head, narrow, depressed (except at base), the edges parallel; tarsus shorter than the bill or middle toe; nape with a small mane-like tuft; rectrices more or less acuminate, the middle pair longest.

This genus is very readily distinguished from *Querquedula* by the very different form of the bill,

N. carolinensis.

which is more like that of *Dafila*, but much smaller, being much more depressed terminally, and proportionally deeper through the base than in *Querquedula;* while the lower edge or maxillary tomium is either gently convex throughout (as in the southern species), or straight anteriorly and decidedly convex posteriorly (as in the northern forms); the lamellæ being thus completely hidden. In *Querquedula,* on the other hand, the terminal portion of the tomium is strongly convex, and the posterior half cut away, as it were, so as to fully expose the lamellæ. Through the forms occurring in the southern hemisphere,[1] this genus leads directly to *Pœcilonetta,* which in turn is intermediate between *Nettion* and *Dafila.*

The two species of *Nettion* occurring in the northern hemisphere are much alike, the males being very handsome in plumage; they may be distinguished as follows:—

COM. CHAR. *Adult males:* Head and upper half of the neck chestnut-rufous, marked with a large patch of metallic green on each side the head, behind the eye; chin and upper part of throat

N. crecca.

dull black; nuchal tuft blue-black; lower part of the neck, upper part of the back, scapulars, and lateral parts of the body beneath, beautifully undulated with black and white; outer scapulars marked with black and white; speculum bright metallic green, the lower feathers black, tipped with white; crissum black centrally, creamy buff laterally. *Adult females:* Wing, only, as in the males; elsewhere varied with dusky and brownish white, the former prevailing above, the latter beneath; the abdomen nearly or quite immaculate.

1. **N. carolinensis.** A broad white bar across side of breast, before the wing; inner webs of outer scapulars vermiculated with dusky and brownish white, the outer webs marked with a longitudinal lanceolate spot of black, bordered internally with a white line. *Hab.* North America generally.
2. **N. crecca.** No white bar on side of breast; inner web of outer scapulars wholly, and outer web partly, white; exposed surface of outer webs almost entirely black; undulations of sides, etc., much coarser than in *N. carolinensis.* *Hab.* Palæarctic Region, occasional in Eastern North America.

Nettion carolinensis.

THE AMERICAN GREEN-WINGED TEAL.

Anas crecca, var. FORST. Philos. Trans. LXII. 1772, 383, 419.
Anas (*Boschas*) *crecca,* var. SW. & RICH. F. B. A. II. 1831, 443. — NUTT. Man. II. 1834, 400.
Anas crecca, "LINN." WILS. Am. Orn. VIII. 1814, 101, pl. 60, fig. 1 (not of LINN.). — AUD. Orn. Biog. III. 1835, 218; V. 1839, 616, pl. 228.
Anas carolinensis, GMEL. S. N. I. ii. 1788, 533. — AUD. Synop. 1839, 281; B. Am. VI. 1843, 281, pl. 392.

[1] Among these may be mentioned, as very close to true *Nettion,* but approaching *Pœcilonetta* in the form of the bill and the greater elongation and acumination of the scapulars, tertials, and rectrices, *Anas flavirostris,* VIEILL., of South America, and "*Querquedula*" *Eatoni,* SHARPE, of Kerguelen Island.

Querquedula carolinensis, STEPHENS, Shaw's Gen. Zool. XII. ii. 1824, 128. — COUES, Key, 1872, 287, Check List, 1873, no. 495; 2d ed. 1882, no. 715; B. N. W. 1874, 565.
Nettion carolinensis, BAIRD, B. N. Am. 1858, 777; Cat. N. Am. B. 1859, no. 579. — RIDGW. Nom N. Am. B. 1881, no. 612.
Anas americana, VIEILL. Enc. Méth. 1823, 155.
"*Anas sylvatica*, VIEILL. ?"

HAB. North America in general, breeding chiefly north of the United States, migrating south as far as Honduras and Cuba. Greenland.

Adult male: Head and neck rich chestnut-rufous, inclosing a broad patch of soft dark metallic green on each side of the occiput, from the eye (which it surrounds) down the sides of the nape, where the two areas of the opposite sides touch a short nuchal crest of bluish-black. The green patch bordered anteriorly and beneath by a yellowish white line, and a less distinct line of the

same bordering the base of the upper mandible, extending thence back to, and indistinctly following, for a short distance, the upper anterior portion of the green patch. Chin and upper part of the throat dull black. Front of the jugulum deep pinkish cream-color, with roundish and transversely ovate spots of black. Collar round the lower neck, sides of the jugulum, sides, and flanks, very delicately and beautifully undulated with black upon a white ground; outer scapulars similarly waved. Sides of the breast with a large transverse bar of plain white. Crissum rich deep cream-color, bounded anteriorly, and divided medially, with velvety black; post-femoral region waved like the flanks; rest of lower parts plain white, sometimes tinged with cream-color. Back, scapulars, rump, wing-coverts, primaries, and tail, plain cinereous. Outer row of scapulars with their outer webs about half velvety black bordered interiorly with a white line. Last row of coverts broadly tipped with deep ochraceous; speculum opaque black, narrowly tipped with white, the four or five upper feathers with their outer webs richly brilliant soft metallic green, varying from golden to violaceous, according to the light. Bill black; iris brown; feet light fleshy (horn-color when dried). *Adult female:* Wing as in the male, but duller. Above, cinereous-dusky, variegated with edgings and transverse bars of ochraceous-white. Ground-color of the head, neck, and lower parts, dingy whitish, more or less tinged with ochraceous; head and neck speckled with dusky, the spots enlarged and aggregated on the pileum, so as to form the prevailing color, and also along the upper border of the ear-coverts, producing a stripe from the eye back. Jugulum, sides, and flanks more heavily spotted with dusky. Abdomen sometimes plain, but usually speckled. Bill brownish ; iris brown ; feet pale brown (fleshy in life).

Young male: Similar to the adult female, but entire abdomen and sides immaculate white. *Downy young:* Above, grayish brown, with a light grayish-buff spot on each side the back, and a similar pair on the rump ; wings crossed near the end by a light grayish-buff bar. Head, neck, and

lower parts light dull buff ; crown and occiput covered by an elongated patch of grayish brown (darker than the back), this scarcely reaching the forehead, but continued down the nape to the brown of the back ; a dusky streak behind the eye, not reaching to the occiput ; below the posterior end of this, an oblong spot of grayish brown.

Total length, about 14 inches ; extent 20.00 to 24.50 ; wing, 6.25–7.40 ; culmen, 1.40–1.60 ; tarsus, 1.25 ; middle toe, 1.30–1.35.

Many specimens, both males and females, have the lower parts tinged with ferruginous-orange, like the stain on the head of the Swans and White Geese. Sometimes this tinge pervades the whole under surface, and is occasionally so deep as to give the lower parts a uniform ferruginous aspect. Adult females usually have the abdomen and sides thickly spotted or flecked with brown, being thereby readily distinguished from the young males, which have the whole abdomen, etc., immaculate white.

The common Green-winged Teal, so closely allied with the Teal of Europe, has an extended distribution throughout North America. During the summer it is found in the extreme northern portions from Greenland to Alaska, and in the winter it extends its migrations to Mexico, Central America, and the West India Islands.

Mr. Leyland met with individuals of this species on the Ulua River in Honduras. Mr. Dresser found it in Southern Texas, but it was not very common. In Western Mexico, according to the observations of Colonel Grayson, it is abundant from November to March. It was seen in flocks, although rarely, by Dr. Kennerly, in Chihuahua. It breeds at least as far south as latitude 42° N., as its nest has been taken in Southern Wisconsin, and it is said to breed in Western Iowa, and thence northward, in favorable situations, throughout the continent, as far north as the Arctic Ocean.

Captain Bendire found this species a common summer resident in Eastern Oregon, where also it breeds, seeming to be more partial to the smaller mountain streams than to the large bodies of water in the valleys — at least during the seasons of reproduction.

In the Aleutian Islands Mr. Dall states that he found it to be abundant in the winter, and to breed occasionally in Unalashka. The greater number of individuals migrate northward about the 1st of May. Mr. Bannister found this bird very common at St. Michael's and at Nulato, as well as on the Yukon River generally. According to Mr. Dall, it is one of the earliest comers to that region, and one of the first to lay. He obtained its eggs from a nest of dry grass in a sedge tussock about May 20. Except while migrating this bird appeared to be solitary in its habits. Mr. Dall regards it as far superior to any other Duck for the table. It was obtained from Sitka and Kadiak by Mr. Bischoff, and is nowhere rare in any part of the Yukon Region. Richardson speaks of it as being abundant even as far north as the extremity of the continent, both in the wooded and in the barren districts. Captain Blakiston obtained it on the Saskatchewan, as well as Hudson's Bay; and it was found by Mr. Bernard Ross common on the Mackenzie, to the Arctic Circle. Hearne states that it is found at Hudson's Bay in considerable numbers near the sea-coast, and is still more plentiful in the interior parts of that region, flying in such large flocks that he has often killed from twelve to fourteen of these birds at a single shot, and has seen both Indians and English kill a much larger number of them. At their first arrival they are usually quite poor, although even then they are generally esteemed good eating. He adds that this species is far more prolific than any of the Ducks resorting to Hudson's Bay, and that he has seen the old ones swimming at the head of seventeen young when the latter were not much larger than walnuts. This Duck remains in that region as long as the season will permit, and some were killed by Hearne, in 1775, on the way from Cumberland House to York Fort, in the rivers he and his party passed through, as late as the 20th of October. At that time the birds were a perfect mass of fat, and their delicate white flesh was regarded as a great luxury.

The Green-winged Teal is found in even greater abundance on the Pacific than on the Atlantic coast. Mr. R. Browne gives it as one of the common birds of Vancouver Island.

Mr. E. Adams ("Ibis," 1878) mentions that this species was present, but not numerous, about St. Michael's. A few pairs were generally to be found near the most grassy of the lakes, where they were continually playing about, ducking their heads, and catching insects from the surface of the water. They were late in arriving, none coming before the 20th of May, but remained to breed. Their name in the Eski dialect is *Ting-a-zo-meók*.

According to Dr. Cooper, during the wet season it migrates throughout the entire State of California, appearing on every little pool and stream in large flocks, especially toward the north. It remains throughout the winter as far north as Puget Sound, and also occurs all the way from there to Mexico. It is much less timid than the larger species, and, congregating closely together, often furnishes to the sportsman a fine supply of game, while its flesh is as good as that of most other kinds, and is, indeed, by some preferred to all others.

According to Dr. Newberry this Duck breeds in the mountains of Oregon, although he did not succeed in finding its nest.

Mr. J. A. Allen met with it near Fort Hays, in Western Kansas, in May. He afterward noticed it in great numbers in the valley of Salt Lake. Dr. Cooper also found it common in St. Mary's Valley, Montana, in August. It probably breeds among the neighboring mountains.

In its migrations, both in the fall and spring, it is abundant throughout New England. In the fall it is common on the coast, and on the inland waters late in October. In open winters a few of these birds remain nearly throughout the season.

In Long Island, according to Giraud, many postpone their departure until quite late in the winter. Associated usually in flocks, they frequent the streams and ponds, where they feed on insects and tender plants. In the earlier parts of the season they sometimes visit the ponds on the beach, although they more generally confine themselves to creeks and mill-ponds. At the South — where during the winter they are very abundant — they resort to the rice-fields in company with the Mallard. Their flesh is very highly esteemed, being tender and juicy, and always commands a high price in the markets of large cities.

This Duck is an occasional autumnal visitant in Bermuda, where, however, it is much more common in some years than in others. It is also spoken of by Dr. Bryant as being common in the Bahamas.

It feeds much at night, as indeed most of the fresh-water Ducks do when they cannot with safety seek their food along the shores by day. They live on plants, seeds, and insects. In autumn the males usually keep in separate flocks from the females and young. Their notes are rather faint and piping, and their wings make a loud whistling during flight.

Mr. MacFarlane found this species breeding near Fort Anderson. The nest was composed of feathers and down, and placed in a depression on a dry piece of ground.

Mr. Robert Kennicott, in his notes on this species, states that it is very rare on the Upper Yukon River, although he found it abundant in Oregon and in Washington Territory, and throughout British America as far north as latitude 70°; but he did not see it anywhere in the Mackenzie Region in any considerable abundance. As it is more common in the Atlantic States than in the valley of the Mississippi, the main body breed more toward the northeast, and breed beyond the limits of the United States in the region of Hudson's Bay. Though arriving in this country among the earliest of the migrating Ducks, this species is quite late in leaving the Yukon and the Mackenzie. Mr. Kennicott saw it October 2 at Fort Liard. The nests found by him were in nearly open ground, among moss, and generally far from water. In one instance he saw the nest of this Duck at the foot of a small spruce in a mossy, half-barren, small dry plain, and at least forty rods from water. This nest was a simple depression in the moss, but thickly lined with down, and well protected by the overhanging branches of the spruce. The female fluttered slowly off along the ground at his approach, and the nest was found to contain eight eggs. According to Mr. Dall nests of this species frequently have from sixteen to eighteen eggs.

Audubon says that the food of the Green-winged Teal consists principally of the seeds of grasses — which are collected when floating, or while still adhering to their stalks — small acorns, fallen grapes or berries, as well as aquatic insects, worms, and small snails. It is much more particular in the selection of its food than are most Ducks, and its flesh is therefore delicious, and probably better than that of any other of the Duck tribe. Audubon adds that when this bird has fed on wild oats at Green Bay, or soaked rice in the fields of Georgia or Carolina, it is much superior to the Canvas-back in tenderness, juiciness, and flavor.

On land it moves with more grace and ease than any other species except the Wood Duck, and it can run with considerable speed without its feet becoming entangled. In the water also it moves with great ease and rapidity, and on the wing it is one of the swiftest of its tribe. It rises from the water with a single spring, and so swiftly that it can only be hit by a very expert marksman; and it also dives readily when wounded. This is a fresh-water bird, and it is very rarely met with near the sea. Its migrations are over the land, and not along the sea-shore.

This Duck moves northward from Louisiana early in March, but remains nearly a month later in the Carolinas, a few lingering on the Delaware until the first week in May. Mr. Audubon met with none of this species in Labrador. It is quite common in Southern Wisconsin, according to Mr. Kumlien, arriving there early in the spring, and a few undoubtedly remaining to breed. He has never with certainty met with its nest, but has found one which he supposed must have belonged to this species.

The Green-winged Teal was found in abundance about Fort Resolution and Fort Yukon by Mr. Kennicott; at Fort Rae by Mr. L. Clarke; on the Yukon River and in the Mackenzie River district by Mr. J. Lockhart; on the Porcupine River by Mr. Jones; at La Pierre House by Mr. Iibbiston; on Big Island by Mr. Reid, etc.

Eggs of this species from Fort Simpson (Smithsonian Institution, No. 5034) are of a pure ivory white color. Three of these measure respectively, 1.80 by 1.30 inches, 1.85 by 1.35, and 1.75 by 1.30.

Nettion crecca.

THE EUROPEAN GREEN-WINGED TEAL.

Anas crecca, LINN. S. N. ed. 10, I. 1758, 126; ed. 12, I. 1766, 204.

Querquedula crecca, STEPHENS, Shaw's Gen. Zool. XII. ii. 1824, 146. — COUES, Key, 1872, 287; Check List, 1873, no. 494; ed. 2, 1882, no. 714; B. N. W. 1874, 566.

Nettion crecca, BAIRD, B. N. Am. 1858, 778; Cat. N. Am. B. 1859, no. 580. — RIDGW. Nom. N. Am. B. 1881, no. 611.

Querquedula subcrecca et creccoides, BREHM, V. D. 1831, 885, 886.

Teal, YARR. Brit. B. ed. 2, III. 281, fig.; ed. 3, III. 282, fig.

HAB. Palæarctic Region; occasional in Eastern North America.

SP. CHAR. *Adult male:* Similar to *N. carolinensis,* but side of the breast without any white bar; the outer scapulars with their inner webs creamy white, the forehead bordered on each side

by a pale-buff line; and the sides, back, etc., much more coarsely undulated. *Adult female:* Not distinguishable with certainty from that of *N. carolinensis?*

Total length, about 14.00 inches; wing, 7.00–7.30; culmen, 1.45–1.50; tarsus, 1.10–1.25; middle toe, 1.25–1.30.

While unquestionably distinct from *N. carolinensis*, the male being very easily separated, we have not been able, with our limited material, to discover tangible differences between the females of the two species.

The Common Teal of the Old World fauna is of irregular occurrence in Eastern North America. Several specimens have from time to time been taken in the vicinity of New York city, and others have been found in the New York market by Mr. J. G. Bell. It has also been taken occasionally in different parts of Greenland, according to the testimony of the elder Reinhardt and of Holböll. It is also very common in Iceland.

In the Palæarctic Region it is widely distributed, occurring, at different seasons, over nearly or quite every portion of that country. In Great Britain and in Ireland it is an early and a constant winter visitant, making its appearance about the end of September, and remaining until late in the spring, its numbers being recruited through the winter by additional arrivals from the northern parts of Europe. In the spring many remain in both islands, and breed in various places — some as far south as Suffolk in England, and others in Wales. In Northumberland, according to Mr. Selby, the indigenous broods of the Teal seldom quit the immediate neighborhood of the place in which they were bred. This bird is quite abundant in Scotland, but less so on the Orkney and Shetland Islands.

It is widely and numerously dispersed all over Sweden and Norway, but is most plentiful in the northern portions during the breeding-season. It breeds in abundance all over Lapland and Northern Russia; and in the migrations is more or less common in all the countries of Europe, as well as of Northern Africa. It is included in the list of the birds of Asia, and is found in various parts of India, China, and Japan.

According to Yarrell, the Teal bears confinement well; and in the gardens of the Zoological Society of London, though restricted to a very small pond, with a margin of high and thick grass and some low shrubs, it has bred regularly for several seasons in succession. The eggs are white, tinged with buff, measuring 1.75 inches in length by 1.34 in breadth.

The food of the Teal in its wild state consists of seeds, grasses, roots, water-plants, and various insects; but in confinement it is best fed with grain. It breeds in the long rushy herbage about the edges of lakes, or in the boggy parts of the upland moors; its nest, according to Selby, being formed of a large mass of decayed vegetable matter, with a lining of down and feathers, upon which eight or ten eggs usually rest — these in some instances, however, numbering as many as fifteen. In the cultivated regions of Lapland, where the Teal is very common, it breeds in all the mossy fields and bogs.

Mr. Vernon Harcourt found it in Madeira; and in the Azores Mr. Godman reports it as quite common, a few pairs breeding in the Island of Flores. It also occurs at Teneriffe and in the Canaries. A few of this species are supposed to breed in France and in the northern portions of Greece; and Captain Shelley is confident that this bird breeds even in Egypt and Nubia. It occurs in Siberia as far to the east as Kamtschatka.

According to the observations of Mr. Dresser, the Teal is more especially a fresh-water Duck, its presence on the salt water being something exceptional. In the daytime it frequents ponds, pools, or sheets of water in marshy countries, where the rank growth of flags or rushes affords it a shelter, and either sits motionless on the banks, or floats on the surface of the water. Toward the close of the day it becomes restless, and with the first shades of evening goes in quest of food, being essentially a night-feeding bird. In disposition it is gentle and affectionate, often evincing a fatal unwillingness to leave its wounded mate. The parent birds are always very solicitous about the safety of their young. Mr. St. John once overtook an old Teal with eight newly-hatched young ones crossing his path; he got off his horse, lifted the little ones up, and carried them a short distance down the road to a ditch, the old bird constantly fluttering about him, within reach of his riding-whip.

According to Naumann, the Teal visits during the day the shallow shores among the weeds, in morasses or shallow pools, the bottoms of which it can reach without diving, frequenting in preference small pools, flooded meadows, marshes, and marshy ponds, and the swampy green shores of small streams. Toward evening it flies restlessly from pool to pool, hunting after worms or grain, and feeding on barley, oats, or the seeds of several species of *Panicum.* This bird is particularly fond of the seeds of certain rushes and grasses, and it visits the places where these grow in abundance, remaining there all night, and fattening on this nourishing food, so that its flesh becomes very delicate. While swimming on the water it may often be seen carefully picking up small articles of food, with neck and head held down or pushed forward. It feeds on all sorts of small worms, larvæ, water-insects, small fresh-water shellfish, shoots of tender plants, seeds of many water-plants, and, very rarely, on spawn or tadpoles.

Mr. Dresser repeatedly procured the nests of this species in Northern Finland, where he found them on the ground, among the grass and usually under some low bush, by which they were concealed, often at a considerable distance from the water. The eggs — usually from eight to ten in number — are described as being oval in shape, measuring 1.77 inches in length by 1.30 in breadth, and pale yellowish-white in color. Only the females incubate; but during the breeding-season the males are never very far distant from the sitting female. When the young are hatched, both male and female appear to be equally unremitting in their attention to them.

Genus **AIX**, Boie.

Aix, Boie, Isis, 1828, 329 (type, *Anas galericulata*, Linn.).
Dendronessa, Swains. F. B. A. II. 1831, 446 (type, *Anas sponsa*, Linn.).
Lampronessa, Wagl. Isis, 1832, 282 (type, *Anas sponsa*, Linn.).

Char. Bill small, much shorter than the head, all the lateral outlines gradually converging toward the end, the nail very large, broad, and prominent, forming the tip of the bill; lamellæ completely hidden. Adult male with the head crested, the colors rich and varied, and the markings elegant, tertials exceedingly broad, truncate.

The above characters are framed so as to include the Chinese Mandarin Duck (*Aix galericulata*),[1] the only species closely related to our Wood Duck (*A. sponsa*). This Duck is quite similar to the American species in style of coloration and in general appearance, but differs in so many points of external anatomy as to render it extremely doubtful whether the two species should be kept together in the same genus. They differ in form as follows: —

A. galericulata. Feathering at the base of the maxilla extending farther forward on the side of the forehead than at the rictus, and forming a straight line between these two points; depth of the bill through the base about equal to its width. Feathers of the sides of the

[1] Aix galericulata. The Mandarin Duck.
Anas galericulata, Linn. S. N. ed. 10, I. 1758, 128; ed. 12, I. 1766, 206.
Aix galericulata, Boie, Isis, 1828, 329. — Gray, Handl. III. 1871, 80, no. 10627.

neck much elongated, forming a conspicuous ruff of soft, narrow feathers; inner tertial with the shaft much bent, giving to the outer web a falcate form, the inner web widened into an excessively broad, fan-like, or sail-like ornament. Tail short; the rectrices shorter than the lower coverts, much longer than the upper. (*Aix*, BOIE.)

A. sponsa. Feathering at the base of the maxilla extending much farther forward at the rictus than at the sides of the forehead, and forming a gently curved (convex) line between these points; depth of the bill at the base much greater than the width, the upper base of the maxilla forming a deep angle extending a considerable distance on each side of the forehead; feathers of the side of the head and neck short and velvety; inner tertial of normal form, the shaft straight. Tail long (half as long as the wing), vaulted, graduated, the feathers very broad, and extending far beyond the coverts. (*Dendronessa*, SWAINSON.)

The nearest ally of *Aix*, so far as structure is concerned, in America, is the genus *Cairina*, represented by the well-known Muscovy Duck (*C. moschata*); but this differs in many important

A. sponsa.

particulars, chief among which are the very large stature and marked discrepancy in size between the sexes, and the brownish fleshy caruncles on the forehead and lores. The points of similarity are numerous, however, the tail being long, broad, graduated, and somewhat vaulted, the nail of the bill very large and broad, the nostrils large and open, the head crested, etc. Among the peculiarities of *Cairina*, as distinguished from other American genera, are the naked and caruncled face, the extremely lengthened secondaries, and relatively short greater wing-coverts.

Aix sponsa.

THE WOOD DUCK; SUMMER DUCK.

Anas sponsa, LINN. S. N. ed. 10, I. 1758, 128; ed. 12, I. 1766, 207. — WILS. Am. Orn. VIII. 1814, 97, pl. 70, f. 3. — NUTT. Man. II. 1834, 394. — AUD. Orn. Biog. III. 1835, 52; V. 1839, 618, pl. 206; Synop. 1839, 280; B. Am. VI. 1843, 271, pl. 391.

Aix sponsa, BOIE, Isis, 1826, 329. — BAIRD, B. N. Am. 1858, 785; Cat. N. Am. B. 1859, no. 587. — COUES, Key, 1872, 288; Check List, 1873, no. 499; 2d ed. 1882, no. 719; B. N. W. 1874, 571. — RIDGW. Nom. N. Am. B. 1881, no. 613.

Dendronessa sponsa, SW. & RICH. F. B. A. II. 1831, 446.

HAB. Whole of temperate North America, north to the Fur Countries; breeding throughout its range. Cuba. Accidental in Europe.

SP. CHAR. *Adult male:* Chin, throat, and foreneck pure white, sending off laterally two branches, — the first across the cheeks, back of, and nearly to, the posterior angle of the eye, the second across the lower part of the neck, almost to the nape; both bars tapering toward the end, and somewhat curved or falcate in shape; a narrow white line begins at the point of the maxillary angle, and is continued back on each side of the crown, widening considerably on the side of the crest; a second white line commences about half an inch behind the eye, and nearly the same distance above the end of the white cheek-bar, and follows the lower edge of the crest, where considerably wider than anteriorly; remainder of the head silky metallic green, violet, and purple, as follows: cheeks and space behind the white cheek bar soft violaceous-black, in the latter region extending up to the lower white stripe, but in the anterior area bounded above and anteriorly by dark metallic green, the orbital region and anterior half of the crest between the white lines metallic-reddish purple; forehead, crown, and posterior portion of the crest metallic green; terminal portion of the crest, above, laterally, and beneath, dark metallic violet. Jugulum rich purplish chestnut, with a metallic-purple gloss laterally, the front and lower part marked with deltoid spots of white, growing larger toward the breast; breast and abdomen immaculate white; sides of the breast with a broad white transverse bar, and a wide black one immediately behind it; sides and flanks pale fulvous buff, delicately undulated with black, the broad feathers forming the upper border each beautifully marked with two black crescentic bars, inclosing a white one; crissum dull black, fading gradually into dull rusty fulvous on the anal region. Back, lesser wing-coverts, and rump dark slaty brownish, very faintly glossed with bronze, the wing-coverts more slaty, the rump much darker, and gradually deepening into black toward the upper tail-coverts, which, with the tail, are deep black, the latter with bronze-green reflection in certain lights; a somewhat ovate patch (pointed posteriorly) of rich dark metallic maroon-purple on each side of the rump, immediately behind the flanks; just behind this, the two or three elongated lateral upper tail-coverts

Male.

are marked with a central stripe of deep fulvous, falling gracefully over the sides of the crissum. Tertials and posterior scapulars intense black, with rich velvety reflections of blue, green, and purple (chiefly the first), in certain lights; the longest tertial tipped with a wide bar of white, the next black to the end, the third much shorter, much narrower than the rest, pointed, and of a dull greenish-bronze color;[1] middle and greater wing-coverts steel-blue, narrowly tipped with black; secondaries ("speculum") purplish steel-blue, narrowly tipped with white, and with a narrow subterminal black bar; primary coverts slate-color; primaries with the exposed ends of the inner webs steel-blue, the ends of the outer webs grayish or glaucous-white, becoming slate-color basally; lining of the wing spotted with slate-color and white. Sagittate longitudinal space on the culmen and terminal "nail" of the bill deep polished black; an oblong space of milk-white from nostril to the "nail;" a line or border of gamboge-yellow following the basal outline of the bill; rest of bill dark purplish red, deepening into scarlet just behind the nostril. Iris bright orange-red; eyelids deep vermilion; legs and feet dull chrome-yellow, the webs and joints dusky.[2] Total length, about 19.00 inches; extent, 29.00; wing, 9.00-9.50; culmen, 1.40; tarsus, 1.40; middle toe, 1.70. *Adult female:* Feathers bordering the base of the bill all round, a space on side of the head surrounding the eyes and extending back in a point toward the occiput, chin, and whole throat white; remainder of the head plumbeous-gray, the crown and slight occipital crest glossed with metallic green; jugulum brownish, the feathers marked centrally with fulvous-buff, those toward the breast tipped with white; remaining lower parts white, the crissum freckled with dusky grayish, the sides and flanks raw-umber brown, spotted with brownish-white; back, rump, and upper tail-coverts hair-brown, glossed, in certain lights, with bronze and reddish purple; tail brightly glossed with greenish bronze; scapulars and tertials olivaceous-umber, richly glossed with reddish purple and bronze; wings as in the adult male, but secondaries more widely tipped with white, and the four upper greater-coverts rich metallic reddish purple, more bluish in the centre, bronzy toward the edge and base, and narrowly tipped with velvety black. Bill dark plumbeous, the nail and longitudinal space on the culmen black; eyelids chrome-yellow; iris raw-sienna; legs and feet yellowish brown.[3] Total length, about 17.75 inches; extent, 28.00; wing, 8.50; culmen, 1.30; tarsus, 1.35; middle toe, 1.60. *Downy young:* Above, deep hair-brown, darker, or clove-brown, on the pileum and tail; a dingy whitish bar along the posterior border of the arm-wing, and a roundish spot of the same on each side of the rump. Lores, superciliary stripe extending back nearly to the occiput, with lateral and under parts of the head generally, bright sulphury-buff, crossed by a wide stripe of blackish brown extending from the occiput forward to the eye; remaining lower parts dingy white, the sides brownish, this crossed on the flanks by an indistinct whitish bar.[4]

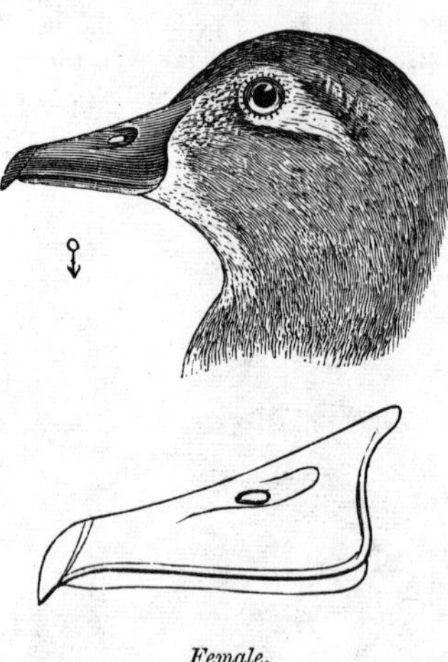

Female.

[1] There is in this species a very strange and probably altogether peculiar arrangement of the tertials, longer scapulars, and inner secondaries, both as to form and colors. The exposed surface of the first appears continuously intense black, as described above; but upon lifting the feathers it is seen that between each two there is a concealed one of different form and color — narrow and pointed, instead of broad and nearly truncated, and dull bronzy, instead of deep black. Of these bronzy feathers, only the last (or the longest scapular) has its tip exposed; the innermost secondary is the longest, and is entirely intense black to the tip; the next is very much (nearly an inch) shorter, entirely concealed, and also wholly black; the third is little, if any, shorter than the first, but is marked at the end by a broad bar of pure white; the fourth is a little shorter, without any white at the tip, and the outer web chiefly reddish purple; this, like the third, has the outer web much widened terminally.

[2] Fresh colors of a specimen killed October 19, at Mount Carmel, Ill.

[3] Fresh colors of a specimen killed October 14, at Mount Carmel, Ill.

[4] Described from No. 84725, obtained at Mount Carmel, Ill., July 17, 1871; R. RIDGWAY, coll.

The Wood or Summer Duck is by far the most beautiful and graceful of all the North American *Anatidæ*, and indeed has no superior in any water. It is widely distributed over the North American continent from Southern Mexico to Hudson's Bay, and from the Atlantic to the Pacific coast. It breeds abundantly from Texas to the British Provinces.

Richardson states that the Wood Duck is quite rare in the Fur Countries, and is never found farther north than the 54th parallel. Mr. Murray, however, mentions finding it on the western side of Hudson's Bay, in a locality some six degrees farther north than this limit. It is, however, very rare north of latitude 50°. Mr. Kennicott mentions meeting with several small flocks of this species, in the latter part of September, north of the Red River, in Minnesota. They were feeding on the wild rice, in company with immense flocks of Mallards, Widgeon, and Teal. Mr. J. A. Allen met with this species in Northwestern Kansas, in May, in the neighborhood of Fort Hays, and he afterward found it quite numerous in the valley of Salt Lake in Utah. A single specimen only — a female — is recorded by Major Wedderburn as having been taken in Bermuda, in December, 1846.

According to the observations of Dr. Cooper, the Wood Duck is abundant in California, and is a resident throughout the winter in the lower districts. It migrates, in April, toward the north, and returns southward in October. Dr. Cooper is not sure that any go to the extreme southern part of that State, having never met with any there, but infers it as probable, inasmuch as they extend their migrations on the eastern coast as far south as the Gulf of Mexico. According to Mr. Dresser, the Wood Duck is not merely a migratory visitor to Southern Texas, but is a resident, and not uncommon, near San Antonio during the summer. He obtained a fine male on the San Pedro, April 23, 1864, and one at Fort Stockton, April 19. According to Mr. Lawrence, Colonel Abert met with this species near Mazatlan, in Western Mexico. It is quite common in all the British Provinces, in New England, and probably in nearly all parts of the Union, even to Florida. It is given by Dr. Gundlach as resident in and breeding in Cuba. Mr. McIlwraith speaks of it as abundant near Hamilton, C. W., and in the West generally, and breeding all over the country.

In Long Island, according to Giraud, the Wood Duck is very seldom seen on the open bay, preferring the still ponds and shady creeks, where it finds an abundant supply of its favorite food, which consists chiefly of insects, seeds, and leaves of plants. In the fall it feeds freely on acorns, with which its stomach is often found to be stuffed full. It is known as the Summer Duck from its remaining through that season, and the Wood Duck by others, because it frequents wooded regions, and breeds in the hollow of trees. Its beautiful plumage and its quiet and gentle character make it quite a favorite in many parts of the country; and it is not unusual for persons residing in suitable situations to invite its presence by preparing boxes and other convenient places for it to nest in. The Wood Duck usually keeps in small parties, and moves about in pairs. It was formerly frequently taken in nets, and sent to market; but this exterminating process is now discouraged, and in many States is forbidden by law.

According to Wilson, the Wood Duck winters as far north as Virginia, and he states that he has met with individuals near Petersburg in January. In Pennsylvania the female is said to begin to lay late in April, almost invariably in the hollows of trees, sometimes on a broken branch. Wilson says that this bird occasionally constructs its own nest of sticks — a statement not accepted by Audubon. It is not improbable that — like some other Ducks — this species may make use of the deserted nest of a Crow or a Hawk.

Wilson narrates that on the 18th of May he visited a tree containing a nest of a Summer Duck, on the banks of Tuckahoe River, New Jersey. This tree stood on a declivity twenty yards from the water; and in its hollow and broken top, about six feet down, on the soft decayed wood, were thirteen eggs covered with down from the mother's breast. The eggs were of an exact oval shape, the surface finely polished and fine grained, of a yellowish color, resembling old polished ivory, and measured 2.12 by 1.50 inches. This tree had been occupied by the same pair, during the breeding-time, for four successive years. Wilson's informant, who lived within twenty yards of the tree, had seen the female, the spring preceding, carry down thirteen young, one by one, in less than ten minutes. She caught them in her bill by the wing or the back of the neck, and landed them safely at the foot of the tree, and finally led them to the water. In evidence of the unwillingness of this species to abandon its breeding-place, Wilson mentions that under this tree a large sloop lay on the stocks, its deck not more than ten feet distant from the nest. Notwithstanding the presence and noise of the workmen, the Ducks would not abandon their old home, but continued to pass out and in, as if no person were near. While the female was laying, and afterward, when she was sitting, the male usually perched on an adjoining limb, and kept watch. The common note of the drake was *peet-peet*, and when, standing sentinel, he apprehended danger, he made a noise not unlike the crowing of a young cock, *oe-eek*.

The Wood Duck has been repeatedly tamed and partially domesticated, and of this statement there are many well-attested cases on record. My own attempts to effect this, however, have been unsuccessful, the old birds remaining wild, and not breeding. Wilson was informed of an instance where a resident near Gunpowder Creek had a yard swarming with Wood Ducks which were completely domesticated. Audubon also gives an interesting account of his attempts to tame and domesticate this Duck, in which he so far succeeded that the birds bred within his grounds, in boxes. The wild ducklings when taken were put in the bottom of empty flour-barrels; but he soon found that they could raise themselves from the bottom to the brim by moving a few inches at a time up the side, lifting foot after foot, by means of their diminutive hooked claws, when they would tumble over, and run in every direction. They fed freely on corn-meal soaked in water, and, as they grew, caught flies with great expertness.

The Wood Duck is conspicuous for the swiftness, ease, and elegance of its flight. It can pass through woods, and among the branches of trees, with as much facility as the Wild Pigeon. While flying it is rarely ever heard to utter any cry.

Audubon states that this Duck usually pairs about the first of March in Louisiana, but sometimes a fortnight earlier. He has never known one to nest either on the ground or in the branches of trees. For three successive years a pair near Henderson, Ky., occupied the abandoned hole of an Ivory-billed Woodpecker. The eggs were from six to fifteen in number, according to the age of the bird, and were placed on dry plants, feathers, and a scanty portion of down from the breast of the female. He also states that the latter is abandoned by the male as soon as she begins to incubate. This, however, is not in accordance with the statement of Wilson, and probably is not correct. In most of the nests examined by Audubon there were found quantities of feathers belonging to other species, including the Domestic Fowl, Wild Geese, and Turkeys. At an early age the young answer to the call of their parent with a mellow *pee-pee-pee*, often repeated. The cry of the mother is soft, low, and prolonged, resembling the syllables *pē̄ē-ēē*.

In the summer of 1867 Mr. Boardman, of St. Stephen — as he informs me — was told of some Ducks which had a nest in a hollow in a high tree, and which were continually fighting. This having been noticed for several days, his curiosity was aroused, and he visited the locality, and became an eye-witness of a singular contest between a female Wood Duck and a Hooded Merganser. They were evidently contending for the possession of this nest, and neither would allow the other peaceful possession. The nest was found to contain eighteen eggs, two thirds of which were those of the Wood Duck. They were all fresh, as neither had been able to sit. Which was the original occupant and which the intruder, it was not possible to ascertain.

Professor Kumlien informs me that this species, still common in Wisconsin, occasionally breeds at a considerable distance from the water. One pair nested for a number of years in a burr-oak in a thicket about three quarters of a mile from the nearest water. The tree was very high, and the nest was also far from the ground. According to his observations, this Duck uses plenty of down in its nest.

The eggs of the Wood Duck are of a rounded oval shape, of a clear ivory-white color when unsoiled, and measure from 2.05 to 2.10 inches in length by 1.55 in breadth.

GENUS **FULIGULA**, STEPHENS.[1]

Branta, BOIE, Isis, 1822, 564 (type, *Anas rufina*, PALL.) ; not of SCOPOLI, 1769.
Fuligula, STEPHENS, Gen. Zool. XII. 1824, 187 (type, *Anas rufina*, PALL.).
Netta, KAUP, Nat. Syst. 1829, 102 (same type).
Callichen, BREHM, Vög. Deutschl. 1831, 921 (same type).
Mergoides, EYTON, Cat. Brit. B. 1836, 57 (same type).

CHAR. Similar to *Fulix*, but the bill decidedly broader at the base than at any other part, gradually narrowing toward the end, which has a large and very broad nail ; maxilla very much depressed terminally, its depth at the base of the nail being only about one fourth that at the extreme base. Male with the head rufous, the pileum ornamented with a very full, soft tuft or bushy crest, occupying the whole top of the head.

Fuligula rufina.

THE RUFOUS-CRESTED DUCK.

Anas rufina, PALL. It. II. App. 1773, 731, no. 28. — GMEL. S. N. I. 1788, 541.
Branta rufina, BOIE, Isis, 1822, 564. — GRAY, Cat. Brit. B. 1863, 198.
Fuligula rufina, STEPH. Gen. Zool. XII. 1824, 188. — DRESSER, B. Eur. Pt. XXII. Oct. 1873.
Netta rufina, KAUP, Nat. Syst. 1829, 102.
Platypus rufinus, BREHM, Vög. Deutschl. 1831, 922.
Callichen rufinus, BREHM, t. c. 924.
Mergoides rufina, EYT. Rar. Brit. B. 1836, 57.
Aythya rufina, MACGILL. Man. Brit. B. 1846, 191.
Callichen ruficeps, BREHM, t. c. 922.

[1] Some recent authorities have used the generic term *Fuligula* for the entire group of lobe-halluxed River-Ducks, or those which have usually been assigned to the genera *Fuligula*, *Fulix*, and *Æthyia*. But *Anas rufina*, PALL., upon which the genus *Fuligula* of Stephens was based, is quite a different type from *Fulix* (formally restricted to *F. marila* and its allies by Professor Baird, in 1858) and *Æthyia*, and should, in our opinion, be separated generically. The first use of the term *Branta* in a generic sense was by Scopoli in 1769 (for *Anser bernicla*, L., *A. moschata*, L., *A. torrita*, L., *A. albifrons*, L. — a very heterogeneous assemblage), which invalidates its subsequent employment, unless restricted to one or another of the species named by Scopoli not already supplied with a generic name — with which, however, there appears to be none not provided.

Callichen subrufinus, BREHM, t. c. 924.
Callichen micropus, BREHM, t. c. 925.
Callichen rufescens, BREHM, Vogelfang, 1855, 379.
Red-crested Pochard, SELBY, Brit. Orn. II. 350. — DRESSER, *l. c.*
Red-crested Whistling Duck, YARRELL, Brit. B. ed. 2, III. 327, fig. ; ed. 3. III. 329, fig. — GRAY, *l. c.*

HAB. Southern and Eastern Europe, Northern Africa, and India ; occasional in Northern and Central Europe, and casual in the British Islands ; accidental in Eastern U. S. (New York market, BOARDMAN ; spec. in U. S. Nat. Mus.).

SP. CHAR. *Adult* ♂ (57207, U. S. Nat. Mus. ; Hungary, W. SCHLÜTER) : Head and upper half of the neck delicate pinkish cinnamon, or vinaceous-rufous, the full, soft crest (occupying the entire pileum) paler and less reddish, the feathers light buff at tips ; lower half of the neck (including a narrow stripe which extends up the nape to the occiput), jugulum, breast, abdomen, anal region, crissum, upper tail-coverts, and rump brownish black, deepest on the neck and jugulum, and with a decided dark-green gloss on the upper tail-coverts. Back and scapulars uniform light umber-drab or isabella-color ; wing-coverts and tertials brownish gray ; speculum white basally, changing gradually into pale grayish, then succeeded by a rather broad subterminal bar of dusky, the tip narrowly and abruptly white ; four outer primaries with exterior tips dusky ; inner quills pale ashy, with broad dusky ends ; tail dull dark grayish. A broad bar or transverse patch across anterior scapular region, anterior border of the wing, lining of the wing, axillars, and a very large patch covering the flanks and posterior half of the sides, pure white. "Bill bright vermilion-red, the tip white ; irides reddish brown ; legs orange-red. Total length, 21 inches." (DRESSER, B. Eur. Pt. XXII.) Wing, 10.20 inches ; culmen, 2.00 ; tarsus, 1.50 ; middle toe, 2.25.

Adult ♀ (57209, U. S. Nat. Mus. ; Hungary, W. SCHLÜTER) : Crest much less developed than in the male, light hair-brown, this color descending to the level of the lower border of the eye, and posteriorly continuing in a narrow stripe down the nape ; rest of the head and neck very pale ashy, as are also the lower parts in general ; jugulum, sides, and flanks light raw-umber brown, the tips of the feathers lighter ; anal region and crissum uniform light drab, the latter whitish terminally. Upper parts in general umber-drab (the wings being more brownish than in the ♂), darker on the rump ; white patch at base of scapular region wholly obsolete, and white border to the wing indistinct ; speculum pale ashy, becoming gradually dull white basally, and brownish dusky subterminally, and with a narrow white terminal margin as in the ♂. "Eyes hazel ; beak blackish, with a pink tip, a portion of the lower mandible being yellowish pink ; legs and feet pinkish, webs blackish." (DRESSER, *l. c.*) Wing, 9.90 ; culmen, 1.90 ; tarsus, 1.50 ; middle toe, 2.20.

Immature ♂ (61957, U. S. Nat. Mus. ; vicinity of New York City, February, 1872, G. A. BOARDMAN) : Similar in general appearance to the adult ♀, as described above, but crest much less developed (the tips of the feathers much worn) and decidedly more reddish in color ; sides and under parts of head thickly interspersed with cinnamon-colored feathers (new moult) ; the jugulum, breast, and posterior under parts also mixed with black feathers, indicating the approaching adult livery ; white patch at base of scapular region plainly indicated, and broad white border to anterior portion of the wing very distinct ; speculum much as in the ♀, lacking the distinct subterminal dusky bar of the adult ♂. Wing, 9.80 inches ; culmen, 1.80 ; tarsus, 1.50 ; middle toe, 2.15.

"*Young in down* (*fide* BALDAMUS, Cab. Journ. 1870, 280) : Differs from every other Duck in this plumage that I know in having a double olive-gray stripe from the lores, dividing before the eye, and bordering the yellowish-gray eyebrow above and the cheeks and auriculars below ; upper parts, crown from the base of the bill, nape, back, and wings dull olive-gray, excepting the spot on the shoulder, which, with the rest of the body, is pale yellowish gray ; iris dark brown ; bill reddish brown, with the nail white ; feet ash-gray, with a greenish tinge, webs and toes narrowly edged with yellowish white." (DRESSER, *l. c.*)

The only claim which this handsome species has to a place among North American birds rests on a single individual having been obtained in Fulton Market, New York, the 2d of February, 1872, by Mr. George A. Boardman. The specimen in question, a young male, was undoubtedly shot near New York City, probably on Long Island Sound, and is now preserved in the U. S. National Museum. (Cf. Proc. U. S. Nat. Mus., Vol. IV., 1881, pp. 22–24.)

Genus FULIX, Sundevall.

Fulix, Sundev. Kong. Vet. Ak. Hand. 1835, 129. (No type designated, but restricted to the group of which *Anas marila*, Linn., is typical, by Professor Baird in B. N. Am. 1858, 790.)
Fuligula, Auct. (nec Stephens, 1824).
Marila, Bonap. Compt. Rend. XLIII. Sept. 1856, 651. (Not of Reichenbach, 1852.)
Nettarion, Baird, B. N. Am. 1858, 790 (in text), (type, *Anas marila*, Linn.).

Char. Bill longer than the tarsus (about as long as the head), very broad and much depressed for the terminal half, the edges nearly parallel or slightly divergent terminally; lower edge of the maxilla strongly convex, concealing all of the mandible except the basal portion. Colors chiefly black and white (the head, neck, and jugulum black, lower parts white) in the adult male the black replaced by brownish in the female.

F. marila, male.

This genus, as restricted, embraces three North American and one European species, whose characters are as follows: —

A. Speculum white, tipped with black; sides and flanks plain white, or very minutely undulated with grayish.

1. **F. marila.** Occiput not crested; back and scapulars grayish white in the male, undulated with black. Wing, 8.25–9.00 inches;[1] bill, 1.85–2.20 × .85–1.05 × .70–.90; tarsus, 1.40–1.60; middle toe, 2.25–2.45. *Hab.* North America.
2. **F. affinis.** Similar to *F. marila*, but smaller. Wing, 7.60–8.25 inches; bill, 1.58–1.90 × .80–.95 × .60–.80; tarsus, 1.15–1.50; middle toe, 2.00–2.25. *Hab.* North America.

[1] The *average* dimensions of the two are as follows: —

F. marila: Wing, 8.59 inches; culmen, 2.02; width of bill, near end, .97, at base, .79; tarsus, 1.51; middle toe, 2.32. (17 specimens.)

F. affinis: Wing, 7.80 inches; culmen, 1.75; width of bill, near end, .88, at base, .69; tarsus, 1.38; middle toe. 2.14. (20 specimens.)

3. **F. fuligula.**[1] Occiput with a long, pendant, but closely appressed, crest; back and scapulars plain black. Wing, 7.60–8.10 inches; bill, 1.85–1.90 × .75–.85 × .55–.65; tarsus, 1.25–1.30; middle toe, 2.05–2.10; *Hab.* Palæarctic Region; accidental in Greenland?

B. Speculum bluish gray, narrowly tipped with white; sides and flanks grayish white, very distinctly undulated with blackish.

4. **F. collaris.** Occiput without crest; back and scapulars plain black; lower neck with a more or less distinct collar of chestnut or dark reddish brown; chin with a triangular white spot.

Fulix marila.

THE SCAUP DUCK; BIG BLACK-HEAD OR BLUE-BILL.

Le Millouinan, BUFF. Pl. Enl. 1002 (♂ ad.).

Anas marila, LINN. Faun. Suec. 2d ed. 1761, 39; S. N. ed. 12, I. 1766, 196. — ? WILS. Am. Orn. VIII. 1814, 84, pl. 69, fig. 3 (may be *F. affinis*).

Fuligula marila, STEPHENS, Shaw's Gen. Zool. XII. ii. 1824, 198. — SW. & RICH. F. B. A. II. 1831, 453 (part; includes *F. affinis*). — NUTT. Man. II. 1834, 437 (do.). — AUD. B. Am. VII. 1843, 355, pl. 498 (not of VI. 1843, 316, pl. 397, nor of his earlier works, which = *F. affinis*). — COUES, Key, 1872, 289; Check List, 1873, no. 500; 2d ed. 1882, no. 720; Birds N. W. 1874, 573.

Fulix marila, BAIRD, B. N. Am. 1858, 791; Cat. N. Am. B. 1859, no. 588. — RIDGW. Nom. N. Am. B. 1881, no. 614.

Anas frenata, SPARRM. Mus. Carls. 1786, pl. 38.

Fuligula Gesneri, EYTON, Cat. Br. B. 1836, 58.

HAB. Entire northern hemisphere; in America, breeding far north.

SP. CHAR. Head, neck, and jugulum black, the first with a greenish gloss; back and scapulars white, irregularly undulated with zigzag lines of black; wing-coverts dusky, finely grizzled with grayish white; secondaries white, tipped, and sometimes narrowly edged with black; tertials black, with a very faint bottle-green reflection; primary-coverts dusky black; primaries similar, but the inner quills pale grayish on outer webs, except at ends, the gray growing whiter on the shorter feathers; rump, upper tail-coverts, tail, and crissum, dull black. Lower parts between the jugulum and crissum white, the posterior portion (and sometimes the sides and flanks), zigzagged with dusky. Bill pale blue (or bluish white) in life, the nail black; iris bright yellow; legs and feet pale slate. *Adult female:* Head and neck sepia-brown, the anterior portion of the former, all round the base of the bill, white; jugulum, anal region, and crissum, pale grayish brown, fading gradually into the white of the breast and abdomen; sides and flanks deeper brown; above, brownish dusky, the back and scapulars but faintly or not at all grizzled with white; wings much as in the male.

Total length, about 18 to 20 inches; extent, 29.50 to 35.00; wing, 8.25–9.00; culmen, 1.85–2.20; width of bill near end, .85–1.05, at base, .70–.90; tarsus, 1.40–1.60; middle toe, 2.25–2.45.

[1] FULIX FULIGULA. The European Crested Duck.

Le Morillon, BUFF. Pl. Enl. 1001 (♂ ad.).

Anas fuligula, LINN. S. N. ed. 10, I. 1758, 128; ed. 12, I. 1766, 202. — NAUM. Vög. Deutschl. XII. 1844, 64, pl. 310.

Anas scandiaca, GMEL. S. N. I. 1788, 520.

Anas cristata, LEACH, Syst. Cat. 1816, 39.

Fuligula cristata, STEPH. Gen. Zool. XII. 1824, 190. — BONAP. Comp. List. 1838, 58. — KEYS. & BLAS. Wirb. Eur. 87. — MACGILL. Man. II. 189. — GRAY, Gen. B. III. 621; Cat. Brit. B. 1863, 199.

Anas colymbis, PALL. Zoog. Rosso-As. II. 1826, 266.

Tufted Duck, YARR. Brit. B. ed. 2, III. 351, fig.; ed. 3, III. 353, fig.; et AUCT.

SP. CHAR. *Adult male:* Head and neck glossy black, showing purple and green reflections in certain lights; pendant occipital crest, and lower part of neck (forming indistinct collar) brownish; upper parts in general, jugulum, breast, and crissum brownish black, the back and scapulars minutely freckled with grayish. Speculum white, widely tipped with black; primaries light brownish gray, their ends, with entire outer web of two outer quills, blackish. Entire abdomen, sides, and flanks, immaculate white.

The "Scaup Duck" of Great Britain — the "Blue-bill" of New England, the "Black-head" of Long Island and Chesapeake Bay — is one of the most abundant and one of the most widely distributed of its tribe. In North America it occurs on the Atlantic coast, the interior waters, and on the Pacific. In the latter it is found from Alaska to Central America, in the interior from the Barren Grounds to the Gulf of Mexico, and on the east from Greenland and Hudson's Bay to Florida and the West India Islands. It is found throughout Europe and Asia as far east as China and Japan. It does not appear to move farther south than the north shore of the Mediterranean, and is more northern than most of the fresh-water Ducks.

Male.

Dr. Walker mentions having obtained several specimens of this Duck near Godthaab, on the coast of Greenland, and Professor Reinhardt states that two adult males and a female of this species were sent to Denmark from Nenortalik in 1860. Mr. Ross met with this bird on Great Slave Lake, and Captain Blakiston obtained specimens of it on Hudson's Bay. In the territory of the Hudson's Bay Company, as Mr. Kennicott states, it is known by the *voyageurs* as the "Big Fall Duck" (*Gros Canard d'Automne*). It was rather rare on the Yukon, but more common about the Slave Lake. Although abundant on the west coast, the main body appears to pass to the northeastward, although not going so far east as the Dusky Duck and the Red-head. It was supposed by Mr. Kennicott to breed more toward Hudson's Bay; and he found its general habits to be very similar to those of the *Fulix affinis*, with which it associates. It was ascertained to be abundant at Sitka, where it was obtained by Mr. Bischoff. Mr. Dall found it common on the Lower Yukon and on the sea-coast, where it was one of the first of the Ducks to arrive in the spring; and he obtained its eggs near the mouth of the Yukon in the early part of June. He speaks of its nest as being very rude — a mere excavation, with a few straws about it — and of the bird as usually tough and lean, and but poor eating. This Duck was found by Mr. R. Browne on the coast of Vancouver Island, and Richardson states that it breeds in all parts of the Fur Countries, from the 50th parallel to the most northern limits.

According to Dr. Cooper, this Duck, variously known as the "Broad-bill," the "Blue-bill," and the "Shuffler," is common during the winter along the entire coast of California, frequenting the salt bays and creeks, and occasionally going a short distance up the more open rivers, in fresh water. It is said to feed on small shell-fish, crustacea, etc., for which it dives a good deal in very deep water, both by night and day. Its stay in California is from October until April, when it leaves for the Arctic Regions to breed. It utters a grunting noise, and occasionally a guttural quack.

This Duck has been tamed and made to feed on barley; but in California it is deemed an inferior bird for the table.

Colonel Grayson mentions meeting with it in Western Mexico, near Mazatlan, during the winter months. Mr. Dresser found it common throughout the winter in Southwestern Texas and Northern Mexico. It occurs in several of the West India Islands; in Cuba, according to Dr. Gundlach; and in Trinidad, on the authority of Léotaud. In the latter place it is a frequent but not a very regular visitant, arriving usually in November, and departing in April, generally in small flocks of five or six individuals only. Its flesh is not of the first quality.

Dr. Bryant states that this species is common during the winter in the Bahamas, and that it is sometimes seen in immense flocks, acres in extent.

Mr. Swinhoe includes it in his List of the Birds of Formosa, and met with it near Amoy, in China. It was also observed in Japan by Mr. H. Whitely, who met with it in May near Hakodadi.

In Europe it is regarded as a decidedly northern species, not breeding south of Lapland. Mr. Wheelwright found it very common at Quickiock, in the lowlands and fell meadows. The eggs were said greatly to resemble those of the Pintail in color, but to be larger and thicker. In Iceland Mr. C. W. Shepard found it on an island in the Lake of Mý-vatn, in the northern part. Although a great many other Ducks were breeding in and about this lake, only one other, the *Harelda glacialis,* occupied this island. Most of the birds left their nests as soon as the boat touched the shore, but a few remained, and would not leave until they were driven away. He found two Ducks, one of them of this species, the other a *Harelda,* sitting on the same nest, which contained several eggs of both species, very easily distinguished by the differences in their color, shape, and size.

The Blue-bill is not uncommon in the fall, and also in the spring, near Calais, Me., but it is not found there in the winter. It winters on the coast of Massachusetts in mild seasons, and is especially common on the southern coast of Cape Cod. It is also occasional during winter in Bermuda.

Professor Kumlien informs me that this species occurs on Lake Koskonong, Wis., both in its spring and in its fall migrations. It is not common, and is more frequently found in the lake than in the creek.

Mr. J. A. Allen found it quite common in the fall in the valley of Great Salt Lake.

According to Giraud it is known to the hunters of Long Island as the "Broad-bill," and also as the "Blue-bill." It arrives on the southern coast of that island between the 10th and the 20th of October, associating in large flocks. On its first appearance it is easily decoyed, but after having been frequently shot at it becomes more shy. In the stormy weather it takes shelter in the coves, and is frequently decoyed to within gunshot from the shore by having a dog trained to swim between it and the land, and also by the rapid waving of a red handkerchief, the party keeping concealed. It is supposed, from the impetuous manner in which the bird approaches, that it is angered by this manœuvre; and the effect is said to be very amusing. The Blue-bill remains on the coast of Long Island all the winter, unless compelled by the severity of the weather to seek a better supply of food elsewhere. Even when the bays are frozen it may be killed at the "air openings." When wounded it avoids pursuit by diving, and is celebrated for skulking under banks. But little advantage can be derived from the fact that the flock is a large one, if the hunter shows himself. The birds all scatter, and it is rarely possible to get even two in a range. Greater havoc is made if the flock swims up to the hunter when in position.

Birds of this species usually pass the nights on the flats in large flocks, seldom roosting on the marshes or meadows; and they readily discover the best feeding-grounds.

When in good condition this Duck is very highly esteemed for the table. In flying it rarely utters any note, but when swimming leisurely about in calm weather it is said to give utterance to a quick rattling or rolling sound. In its migrations its flight is high and rapid. It is common in the winter on the Ohio and Mississippi rivers and their tributaries.

In Chesapeake Bay, where it is very abundant, it is more generally known as the "Black-head," and in Virginia it is called the "Raft Duck." A writer in "Doughty's Cabinet" (I. 41) says the Black-heads arrive on the Chesapeake about the last of October, and rapidly distribute themselves over the Bay. This is one of the very few Ducks that are able to dive and pull up by the roots the *Vallisneria* plants on which it feeds. Other Ducks share in the spoils, especially the Baldpate, which, though of inferior size, is able, by its address and boldness, to rob both this species and the Canvas-back of the fruits of their labors. On the Chesapeake, where the Blue-bill feeds exclusively on the *Vallisneria* or other aquatic plants, it becomes very fat. Its flesh is tender and juicy, and entirely free from the strong fishy taste acquired in other localities. This bird feeds chiefly by night.

According to Yarrell, the Scaup Duck is a very late winter visitor to Great Britain, seldom appearing until the beginning of November, and arriving, in small flocks, on various parts of the coast, and at the mouths of rivers, but rarely visiting inland waters. It prefers low flat muddy shores, where it is pursued by the wild-fowl shooters in gun-punts, and is occasionally caught by fishermen in upright nets, fixed in curving lines on stakes in shallow bays. It feeds on small fish, mollusca, aquatic insects, and marine plants, and is not in request for the table, as its flesh becomes coarse, dark in color, and fishy in flavor. Being very expert in diving, it obtains the greater part of its food in this way. It rises slowly from the surface of the water, and usually against the wind, and flies at a moderate speed.

Colonel Montague kept Ducks of this species in confinement many years. They held apart from the other Ducks, and both sexes made the same grunting noise, and had the same singular toss of the head, in performing which they at the same time open the bill.

In spring this Duck departs to countries north of the Orkneys to breed, and there is only a single instance recorded of its breeding in Scotland. This was in Sutherlandshire, in June, 1834, and was observed by Sir W. Jardine.

Mr. Proctor, who found this bird breeding in Iceland, states that it lays its eggs either among the aquatic herbage or the large stones near the edge of fresh water, making little or no nest. A quantity of down usually covers the eggs, which are from five to eight in number. An egg brought from Iceland by Mr. Proctor is described by Yarrell as being of a uniform clay-brown color, 2.37 inches in length by 1.63 in breadth.

This species was found breeding on the Yukon River by Mr. J. Lockhart; on Big Island in Slave Lake by Mr. J. Reid; at Fort Rae by Mr. L. Clarke; at Lake Winnipeg by Mr. Donald Gunn; at Pastolik, Kutleet, Nulato, and on the Island of St. Michael's by Mr. Dall; and at Sitka by Mr. F. Bischoff.

Eggs in the Smithsonian Collection from the Yukon (No. 6617) are of a pale olive-gray, varying in length from 2.55 to 2.60 inches, and have an average breadth of 1.70 inches.

Fulix affinis.

THE LESSER SCAUP DUCK; LITTLE BLACK-HEAD, OR BLUE-BILL.

Fuligula marila, AUD. Orn. Biog. III. 1835, 226; V. 1839, 614, pl. 229; Synop. 1839, 286; B. Am. VI. 1843, 316, pl. 397.

Fuligula affinis, EYTON, Mon. Anat. 1838, 157. — COUES, Key, 1872, 289; Check List, 1873, no. 501; 2d ed. 1882, no. 721; B. N. W. 1874, 573.

Fulix affinis, BAIRD, B. N. Am. 1858, 791; Cat. N. Am. B. 1859, no. 589. — RIDGW. Nom. N. Am. B. 1881, no. 615.

Fuligula mariloides, VIG. Zool. Blossom, 1839, 31.

Fuligula minor, BELL, Pr. Ac. Nat. Sci. Philad. I. 1842, 141. — GIRAUD, B. Long. I. 1844, 323.

HAB. The whole of North America, south to Guatemala and the West Indies; breeds chiefly north of the United States.

SP. CHAR. Entirely similar to *F. marila*, but smaller. Total length, about 16.00 inches; extent, 25.00–30.00; wing, 7.60–8.25; culmen, 1.58–1.90; width of bill near end, .80–.95, at base, .60–.80; tarsus, 1.15–1.50; middle toe, 2.00–2.25.

Male (reduced).

Beyond the decidedly smaller size, we can perceive no difference between this bird and *F. marila* which seems to be constant. In most of the specimens before us, however, the green gloss of the head is much less distinct, in fact wanting entirely, or in many replaced by faint purplish; while the lower part of the neck is usually dull brownish and quite lustreless, in many examples forming quite as distinct a collar as in some specimens of *F. collaris*, though the color is never so rufescent as in the latter species. The zigzag markings on the back and scapular appear to be, as a rule, somewhat coarser than in *F. marila*. As in the larger species, the sides and flanks may be either marked with dusky, or quite immaculate.

A larger series of specimens may prove the intergradation of this form with *F. marila*.

A full and complete history of this species cannot be given, in consequence of the confusion that has existed between it and the better-known *Fulix marila*, which, in appearance, and probably in habits, it so closely resembles. So far as my own observations go, I am inclined to agree with Dr. Cooper in regarding this species as a much more decided frequenter of the land than is the larger Black-head; and it is quite probable that much that has been written by Audubon and others in regard to the Scaup Duck, as seen on our rivers and lakes, may have had reference only to this species. In April, 1872, the markets of Detroit were abundantly and almost exclusively supplied with this Duck, brought from the marshes of Lake St. Clair; and both in the spring and in the fall it is abundant on Lake Koskonong, in Southern Wisconsin. It is found over the whole North American continent, both on the eastern and western coasts, is common in the interior waters, reaching the farthest north during its breeding-season, and in the winter wanders to the shores of the Gulf of Mexico, to Central America, and to Mexico. Mr. Dall found it not uncommon at the mouth of the Yukon River, and on the upper waters of that river. Mr. Kennicott mentions it as by far the most abundant Duck, and much more numerous there than on Slave Lake, not arriving early, but being the last to depart. Large flocks were also seen on the Porcupine River. They collect in large bands as soon as the young can fly; and these flocks are more numerous in the fall than in the spring.

Mr. Salvin found this Duck exceedingly abundant on the Lake of Dueñas during the winter months; and it was seen on Lake Atitlan as late as the month of May. Colonel Grayson found it in Western Mexico, in the neighborhood of Mazatlan, during the winter; and Dr. Heermann informed Mr. Dresser that it was common on the coast of Texas during the whole of that season.

Mr. Murray obtained it at Hudson's Bay, and Captain Blakiston also received examples from the same region. Mr. Ross found it abundant along the Mackenzie River, as far north as the Arctic Ocean. According to Mr. Hurdis it is occasionally obtained in the Bermudas.

Dr. Cooper found it less common on the Pacific coast than the *marila,* and he suggests, as the probable explanation, that it is more partial to the interior than it is to

Female (natural size).

the sea-coast. In Eastern Oregon Captain Bendire found these Ducks common during the migrations, and thinks a few breed in the higher valleys of the Blue Mountains, where they remained into June.

Mr. George A. Boardman informs me that this species occurs both in the spring and in the fall in the neighborhood of Calais, and that it is by no means uncommon there. It is also found on the coast of Massachusetts at the same times, but to what extent is not certainly known. Its distinctness from the larger Black-head is not generally recognized by hunters, nor always by taxidermists. Mr. Maynard regards it as rare, and only found in its migrations.

Mr. Giraud was one of the first to recognize it as a species distinct from the *marila,* calling it the "Lesser Scaup Duck." He states that it had long been known to the Bay hunters, and by them was called the "Creek Broad-bill," from its habit of frequenting the small streams; while the *Fulix marila* is usually observed in the open bays. The Scaup Duck is said be a very abundant species; and during the autumn and the early part of spring it is quite common along the Middle Atlantic districts, as well as on the streams in the interior. In its choice of food, in its migrations, and in its breeding-range, its habits are presumed to be similar to those of the larger species. It is said to be of accidental occurrence in Europe.

Mr. Kennicott and Mr. MacFarlane both found it breeding in large numbers on the Yukon River, and have furnished interesting notes as to the general character, position, and locality of the nests. One of these, described by Mr. Kennicott, was found, June 19, at Fort Yukon; it was placed among grassy tussocks, surrounded by water, at the edge of a lake. The nest of this species is never built literally in the water, as is the case with the Canvas-back. This particular nest, as is usual with this species, was made of dry grasses, the bottom two inches above the water, and it contained nine eggs. Another nest was at the edge of a marsh, among long grass, and contained but a single egg. This nest was very incomplete; and Mr. Kennicott remarks that in all the nests of this species which he has found, in which the number of eggs is not nearly completed, the nest is only partially made, and is, in fact, only a pile of grass with the sides not built up, and without any feathers or down. A third nest with only two eggs, and incomplete, was found, June 18, upon and between two tussocks of grass, on the edge of a large lake, and in from one to two feet of water.

A nest found by Mr. MacFarlane, June 23, was in the midst of a swamp, and was a mere hole or depression in the centre of a tuft of grass; it was lined on its sides with a dark-colored down, and contained three eggs. Another, found in June, 1864, was in a swampy tract on the borders of the wooded country, was made of a quantity of down placed in the midst of a tuft of grassy turf, commonly called a *tête de femme.* The female was snared on the nest; and the eggs, six in number, contained partially developed embryos. A third nest, taken July 14, contained eight eggs with embryos well developed; it was situated in a clump of willows in the midst of a swamp, and close to a small lake, and was made of hay and down. Mr. MacFarlane also found this Duck breeding in the neighborhood of Fort Anderson and on the Lower Anderson River. His notes, describing twelve nests taken in this region, indicate a general uniformity in their situation and characteristics. The general number of eggs in a nest was nine, and this appears to be the usual complement. In several instances the male bird was found in company with his mate, and in one instance was shot in close proximity to the nest, even when the eggs contained embryos.

A careful examination of Audubon's account of the habits of the Scaup Duck clearly indicates that nearly all he says of it belongs in reality to this species; and this supposition is strengthened by the fact that he figures and describes the *affinis* rather than the larger Black-head. He speaks of observing the Scaup Duck by the thousand on the Ohio, the Missouri, and the Mississippi, from Pittsburg to New Orleans, where it occurred in such large bands that it was generally known as the "Flocking Fowl." These Ducks were seldom seen close together, and rarely associated with birds of other species. They seemed fond of large eddies below projecting points of land, frequently diving to a considerable distance in search of food. In such situations they might easily be approached and shot; and when danger was near they seemed to prefer to escape by swimming and diving rather than by flight, and they rose with some difficulty from the water. Audubon noted that these Ducks differed greatly in size, but does not seem to have been led from this to suspect that they really belonged to two distinct species.

Professor Kumlien informs me that this Duck is quite common in Southern Wisconsin both in the spring and in the fall. Some of these birds are to be found on Lake

Koskonong all the summer, and perhaps breed there; they have not, however, been found doing this, nor have any broods of young birds been noticed.

Eggs of this Duck from the Yukon River (Smithsonian Institution, Nos. 5637 and 6626) are of a pale grayish buff with a tinge of olive; their usual breadth is 1.50 inches, and their length varies from 2.20 to 2.50 inches.

Fulix collaris.

THE RING-NECKED SCAUP DUCK; RING-BILL.

Anas collaris, DONOVAN, Br. Birds, VI. 1809, pl. 147 (England).
Fuligula collaris, BONAP. List B. Eur. 1842, 73. — COUES, Key, 1872, 289; Check List, 1873, no. 502; 2d ed. 1882, no. 722; B. N. W. 1874, 574.
Fulix collaris, BAIRD, B. N. Am. 1858, 792; Cat. N. Am. B. 1859, no. 590. — RIDGW. Nom. N. Am. B. 1881, no. 616.
Anas fuligula, WILS. Am. Orn. VIII. 1814, 66, pl. 67, fig. 5 (not of LINN. 1766).
Anas (*Fuligula*) *rufitorques*, BONAP. Jour. Philad. Acad. III. 1824, 381.
Fuligula rufitorques, BONAP. Synop. 1828, 393. — SW. & RICH. F. B. A. II. 1831, 454. — NUTT. Man. II. 1834, 439. — AUD. Orn. Biog. III. 1835, 259, pl. 234; Synop. 1839, 287; B. Am. VI. 1843, 320, pl. 398.

HAB. The whole of North America, south to Guatemala and the West Indies; breeding chiefly in the high north. Accidental in Europe.

SP. CHAR. *Adult male:* Head, neck, jugulum, crissum, and upper parts generally, black, the head and neck with a faint violet gloss, the wing-coverts inclining to slate; secondaries ("speculum") bluish gray, darker subterminally, and very narrowly tipped with white; primaries slate-gray, the outer quills and ends of the others dusky. A triangular spot of white on the chin, and

F. collaris, male.

a more or less distinct collar of chestnut round the lower neck; breast and abdomen white, abruptly defined anteriorly against the black of the jugulum, but changing insensibly into the black on the crissum, through a graduated barring or transverse mottling of white and dusky; sides white, delicately undulated with grayish dusky. Axillars and lining of the wing immaculate white. Bill lead-color, with a narrow basal and broad subterminal band of bluish white, the end black; iris bright yellow; legs and feet pale slaty. *Adult female:* Crown and nape dull dark brown, becoming gradually lighter below; rest of the head paler and grayer, the anterior half of the lores, the chin, throat, and foreneck nearly or quite white; jugulum, sides, and flanks, deep fulvous or raw-umber brown ; breast and abdomen white ; anal region dull brown, longer feathers of the crissum whitish ; wings as in the male ; remaining upper parts dull dark brown, the feathers of the back narrowly tipped with fulvous. Bands on the bill narrower and less distinct than in the male ; iris yellow ; feet slaty.

Total length, about 16 to 18 inches, extent, 24 to 27 ; culmen, 1.75–2.00 ; tarsus, 1.30–1.45 ; middle toe, 2.00–2.15.

Downy young :[1] Above, grayish umber-brown, relieved by seven spots of light buff, as follows : a small and inconspicuous spot in the middle of the back, between, and a little anterior to, the wings ; a large patch on each side the back, another on each side the rump, at the base of the tail, and a bar across the posterior border of each wing. Crown, occiput, and nape crossed longitudinally by a wide stripe of deep grayish umber ; a roundish isolated spot of light grayish brown directly over the ears ; remainder of the head, including the forehead, and lower parts generally, light dingy buff, the flanks crossed by a brown transverse stripe from the rump to the tibia. *Side of the head without any longitudinal stripes.*

Male.

The chief variation in the plumage of this species consists in the distinctness of the chestnut collar in the male. In some examples this is scarcely more conspicuous than in *F. affinis*, being dull brown instead of reddish ; but usually the color is a well-defined chestnut, particularly in front.

The female Ring-neck resembles very closely indeed that of the Red-head (*Æthyia americana*) ; but may be distinguished by the character to which attention is called under the latter species (see p. 36).

Female.

The Ring-necked Duck, as compared with other species, does not appear to be anywhere an abundant bird, although found nearly throughout America. It breeds as far south as Calais, near the eastern coast, in Southern Wisconsin, and in Minnesota. It is said to breed as far to the north as Fort Simpson, where it was found by Mr. B. Ross. In the winter it extends its migrations to the Gulf of Mexico, to the Pacific coast of Mexico, and to Central America. It is also found in the winter in Cuba, and probably in most, if not all, the other West India islands. Dr. Bryant speaks of finding it in immense flocks in winter in the Bahamas.

This Duck was taken by Mr. Salvin at Coban, Vera Paz, November, 1859, when it was found frequenting the river in considerable numbers. Colonel Grayson also

[1] Described from No. 60550, Calais, Me. ; G. A. Boardman. This example is pretty well grown, being nearly 8 inches in total length, the bill nearly 1 inch ; younger individuals would doubtless be more highly colored — probably deep buff beneath and on the head.

obtained it at Mazatlan in Western Mexico, and Mr. John Xantus on the Rio de Coahuano in the same region. Mr. Dresser, in his journey from San Antonio to Eagle Pass, in Western Texas, in December, shot one of this species on the Nueces River, and saw several others at the same time and place.

This Duck occurs on the Pacific coast at least as far north as Vancouver Island, where it was taken by Mr. R. Browne. Dr. Cooper mentions that a single specimen of this species was obtained near the Straits of Fuca by Dr. Kennerly, when with the Northwestern Boundary Expedition in 1857. It was shot September 14; and from its occurrence so early in the season in that latitude the inference may be drawn that it occasionally comes into California in the winter, unless only an accidental visitor to the Pacific coast. Dr. Cooper does not regard it as common there, but states that it may be found to the south as far as Mexico, and that it is usually seen in localities similar to those in which the Blue-bill occurs.

Mr. George A. Boardman informs me that this Duck is seen every summer in the vicinity of Calais, and that it breeds there. The same gentleman states in the "Naturalist" (V. 121) that in the spring of 1870 he found several flocks of the Ring-necked Duck breeding on the river near Calais, and that in one instance he secured the old birds and the young ducklings. In the summer of 1874 Mr. Boardman was so fortunate as to meet with the nest and eggs of this species. The nest, containing eleven eggs, was placed among the reeds and thick grass on the banks of the St. Croix River, and was made of dry grasses, but without any down.

This Duck is of not infrequent occurrence in Eastern Massachusetts, where it is usually seen on the larger streams near their mouths; but it has been taken in several instances in the Merrimack just below Haverhill. Mr. William Brewster shot a specimen near Belmont, Mass., November, 1867; and several other instances of its capture in this region are recorded.

This Duck is mentioned by Giraud as of occasional occurrence on Long Island. By the hunters of that locality it is generally considered as a hybrid, and is familiarly known as the "Bastard Broad-bill." Along the sea-coast it is not abundant, but a few of this species are observed almost every spring and autumn on the south shore of Long Island, and at Egg Harbor, New Jersey. On the streams of the interior it is quite common during the winter. Mr. Giraud met with it on the Ohio in various localities, and also on the Mississippi as far south as New Orleans. It associates with others of the same species in small flocks, and is usually observed flying but a short distance above the water. The largest flock Mr. Giraud ever noticed consisted of from nine to twelve individuals. These he saw at the mouth of the Licking River. They were not so plentiful in the vicinity of Cincinnati as they were farther down the Ohio.

A single specimen was obtained at Bermuda by Mr. Hurdis in November. It was a young bird in the plumage of the first season which had been taken alive, and an attempt was made to keep it.

Richardson states that this species breeds in all parts of the Fur Country, from the 50th parallel to its most northern limits. Whether this is given on his own knowledge or on the authority of others does not appear. There has been no farther evidence confirmatory of his statement, which quite possibly is not correct.

Audubon speaks of this Duck as being abundant on all the western waters during the autumn and winter. It is also met with along our Atlantic coast, but by no means in such numbers as in the interior. He says that its flesh is excellent, being fat, tender, and juicy, and having none of the fishy flavor of those species which are in the habit of diving deep for their food. This Duck arrives in the region between

Kentucky and New Orleans from the 20th of September to the middle of October; and at this period it may also be found from Massachusetts to Louisiana. It is said to move in flocks of from fifteen to twenty, keeping rather scattered, flying with rapidity, and at a considerable height. It is also described as swimming with lightness and ease, and experiencing no difficulty in rising on wing, either from land or water. Like *F. marila*, it is said to have the almost constant practice of raising its head in a curved manner, erecting its occipital feathers, and emitting a note resembling the sound produced by a person blowing through a tube. Ducks of this species feed by diving and by dabbling with their bills among the roots of grasses — eating seeds, as well as snails and aquatic insects. A male which Mr. Audubon shot near Louisville, in the beginning of May, was found to contain a frog, the body of which was nearly two inches long, and by which the bird had been almost choked.

This Duck is found nearly throughout the year in Southern Wisconsin, where it breeds to some extent, and from which region it is only absent during the severity of the winter. It has also been found breeding in Minnesota by Mr. Goss, who obtained several nests with their eggs.

Professor Kumlien informs me that this species is quite common in Southern Wisconsin, but that it is not so abundant in the spring and fall as the *F. affinis*. Both of these two species are found all summer in Rice and Koskonong lakes in pairs, and he thinks that this species undoubtedly breeds in both places, though its eggs have not been identified with certainty. Several years ago a nest supposed to be of this bird was found in Rice Lake, which is also known as Bunting's Lake.

Mr. B. F. Goss, of Pewaukee, Wis., writes me that several years ago he found a nest of the Ring-necked Duck, containing ten eggs, on a bog in thick cover close to the water. He has since met with several pairs of these Ducks, which were evidently breeding; but he could not find their nests. The one referred to was found on the 20th of May, 1867, near Pewaukee Lake, about three feet from the edge, in thick cover. It was made of old grasses very neatly put together and slightly lined with feathers. Every year since, several pairs have remained all summer in the lake, but he has not been able to discover their nests.

Dr. Kennerly, in his Notes on the Birds of the Mexican Boundary Survey, mentions procuring his first specimen of this bird at Boca Grande, Chihuahua. It was quite tame, and was easily approached. Another was taken on Janos River in April, where this Duck was seen in very large flocks.

The eggs of this species are of a grayish ivory-white, a buffy tinge occasionally replacing the gray. They measure 2.10 inches in length by 1.65 in breadth.

Genus **ÆTHYIA**, Boie.

Aythya, Boie, Isis, 1822, 564 (type, *Anas ferina*, Linn.).
Aristonetta, Baird, B. N. Am. Aug. 19, 1858, 793 (type, *Anas vallisneria*, Wils.).

Char. Very similar to *Fulix*, but bill longer and narrower, the head and neck chestnut-red instead of black, in the males. Otherwise quite of the same form and style of coloration.

As stated in "Birds of North America" (p. 793), it is exceedingly questionable whether this so-called genus should be separated from *Fulix*. It is true that *Æ. vallisneria* is very different in the shape of the bill from the typical species of *Fulix*, but other species, belonging chiefly to the Old World, are more or less intermediate.

The two American species and their European analogue may be distinguished by the following characters: —

COM. CHAR. Secondaries bluish gray, the upper feathers narrowly edged with black. *Adult male:* Head and neck reddish brown; jugulum and anterior part of back, lower part of rump, upper tail-coverts, and crissum black; back, scapulars, flanks, anal region, and sometimes (in *Æ. ferina*) whole abdomen, white, finely vermiculated with dusky.

Æ. americana.

A. Bill as long as middle toe (without claw), its greatest width not more than one third the length of the culmen, much depressed at the end, the nail scarcely hooked (*Aristonetta*, BAIRD).

1. **Æ. vallisneria.** Head and neck reddish cinnamon or rusty brown in the male, the former dusky on top and anteriorly; jugulum, anterior portion of back, rump, upper tail-coverts, tail, and crissum black; remainder of the body white, the upper surface, sides, flanks, and anal region finely vermiculated with dusky. Bill entirely black. Wing, 8.75–9.25 inches; culmen, 2.10–2.50; greatest width of bill, .75–.80; tarsus, 1.70; middle toe, 2.60–2.65. *Hab.* North America.

B. Bill much shorter than middle toe (without claw), its greatest width nearly half the length of the culmen, the end moderately depressed, and the nail decidedly hooked (*Æthyia*).

2. **Æ. americana.** Head and neck rich reddish chestnut, the latter glossed with reddish purple; back, scapulars, sides, and flanks vermiculated with white and dusky in nearly equal quantity; abdomen immaculate white. Bill pale blue, the end black. Wing, 8.50–9.25 inches; culmen, 2.05–2.25; greatest width of bill, .75–.85; tarsus, 1.60–1.65; middle toe, 2.30–2.40. *Hab.* North America.

3. **Æ. ferina.**[1] Head and neck chestnut-rufous, the latter without decided purplish gloss; back, scapulars, sides, flanks, and abdomen white, everywhere finely vermiculated with dusky. Bill black, crossed, a little anterior to the middle, by a wide band of pale blue. Wing, 8.00–8.50 inches; culmen, 2.20–2.40; greatest width of bill, .70–.78; tarsus, 1.30–1.55; middle toe, 2.30–2.50. *Hab.* Europe.

[1] ÆTHYIA FERINA.

Anas ferina, LINN. S. N. ed. 10, I. 1758, 126; ed. 12, I. 1766, 203. — NAUM. Vög. Deutschl. XII. 1844, 21, pl. 308.
Fuligula ferina, KEYS. & BLAS. Wirb. Eur. 87.
Nyroca ferina, FLEM. Phil. of Zool. II. 260. — GRAY, Gen. III. 621; Cat. Brit. B. 1863, 200.
Aythya ferina, BOIE, Isis, 1822, 564. — BONAP. Comp. List, 1838, 58. — MACGILL. Man. II. 191.
Anas rufa, GMEL. S. N., I. 1788, 515.
Anas erythrocephala, S. G. GMEL. Reise, I. 1770, 71.
Aythya erythrocephala, BREHM, Vög. Deutschl. 919.
Pochard, YARR. Brit. B. ed. 2, III. 332, fig.; ed. 3, III. 334, fig.

HAB. Palæarctic Region.

Æthyia vallisneria.

THE CANVAS-BACK DUCK.

Anas vallisneria, WILS. Am. Orn. VIII. 1814, 103, pl. 7, fig. 3.

Fuligula vallisneria, STEPHENS, Shaw's Gen. Zool. XII. ii. 1824, 196. — SW. & RICH. F. B. A. II. 1831, 451. — NUTT. Man. II. 1834, 430. — AUD. Orn. Biog. IV. 1838, 1, pl. 301; Synop. 1839, 285; B. Am. VI. 1843, 299, pl. 395. — COUES, Key, 1872, 290; Check List, 1873, no. 504; ed. 2, 1882, no. 724; B. N. W. 1874, 575.

Aythya vallisneria, BOIE, Isis, 1826, 980. — BAIRD, B. N. Am. 1858, 794; Cat. N. Am. B. 1859, no. 592.

Æthyia vallisneria, SCL. & SALV. Nom. Neotr. 1873. — RIDGW. Nom. N. Am. B. 1881, no. 617.

Aristonetta vallisneria, BAIRD, B. N. Am. 1858, 793 (in text).

HAB. Nearly the whole of North America, breeding from the Northwestern States northward to Alaska; south in winter to Guatemala.

SP. CHAR. Bill long and narrow, the end much depressed, with the nail scarcely decurved, the base high, with the culmen gradually sloping and scarcely concave; culmen nearly as long as

Æ. vallisneria.

the middle toe (without claw), and about three times the greatest width of the maxilla. *Adult male:* Head and neck chestnut-rufous, the former brownish dusky (sometimes quite blackish) anteriorly and on top; jugulum and anterior part of back, lower part of rump, upper tail-coverts, and posterior part of crissum black; back, scapulars, flanks, sides, and anal region white, finely and delicately vermiculated with dusky; breast and abdomen immaculate white. Wing-coverts deep ash-gray, finely sprinkled with white; secondaries ("speculum") lighter, more bluish gray, the upper feathers edged with black; tertials like the longer scapulars; primaries slate-color, the inner quills more cinereous, except at ends, where dusky; tail dusky. Bill entirely greenish black; iris carmine-red; feet bluish gray. *Adult female:* Head, neck, jugulum, and anterior part of back raw-umber brown, a post-ocular space and the foreneck whitish, the chin, throat, and cheeks tinged with fulvous; wings as in the male, but coverts almost or quite uniform gray; back, scapulars, sides, and flanks with only the exposed ends of the feathers vermiculated with white and dusky, the remainder being grayish brown. Bill greenish black; iris brownish red; feet plumbeous.

Total length, about 20.00 to 22.00 inches; extent, 30.00 to 33.00; wing, 8.75–9.25; culmen, 2.10–2.50; greatest width of bill, .75–.80; tarsus, 1.70; middle toe, 2.60–2.65.

The far-famed Canvas-back Duck is an exclusively North American species. Closely resembling, in appearance, habits, and in very many of its general characteristics, the Pochard of Europe and the Red-head of America, it is still quite distinct from, and superior to, both these species in the reputation and the intrinsic excellence of its flesh. It is found throughout North America, from the Arctic Ocean to Central America, on the interior waters, and on both shores. It is not found on either shore of the more northern portions of the continent, unless as an exceptional occurrence. It breeds on the interior ponds, rivers, and lakes, from Oregon to the more extreme northern portions of the continent.

Male.

Only a single specimen was obtained by Mr. Salvin from the Lake of Dueñas, in Guatemala. Mr. Dresser met with it in Texas — killing two on the Nueces, and seeing others on Turkey Creek.

Mr. Dall speaks of it as occurring at Fort Yukon, where it was breeding in abundance; but none were seen on the Yukon River to the southwest of that point, nor is there any evidence that this species is known on the Pacific coast north of Vancouver Island, where its presence was noticed by Mr. R. Browne.

According to Dr. Cooper this Duck is very common along the Pacific coast, wintering from Puget Sound to San Diego. It is also found on the interior rivers, being quite abundant along the Colorado at that season, arriving in October and remaining until April, when it departs for its northern breeding-places. Dr. Newberry found it more abundant than any other Duck in the lakes and streams of the Cascade Range, in whose deep solitudes he obtained satisfactory evidence that this bird nests, and rears its young, as he frequently met with broods of this Duck.

The *Vallisneria*, on which plant the Canvas-back feeds in the Chesapeake and other waters east of the mountains, is not found on the Pacific coast; and this species, being there obliged to live on grass, seeds, and the other usual food of the Duck family, is not considered superior to the Mallard, or even as good as that bird. The Canvas-backs assemble in great flocks in the bays, especially at night; they sleep on the open water, at which time many are shot by the hunters, who pursue them in boats, concealed by means of branches and other disguises, and row silently down into the midst of the flock. On the Pacific coast, however, they are not hunted so much as some other kinds held in higher esteem.

This species of Duck extends its winter migrations on the Pacific farther south than California, reaching Mazatlan, in Western Mexico, where Colonel Grayson found it not uncommon during the winter months.

Richardson states that in the interior this Duck breeds from the fiftieth parallel to the most northern limit of the Fur Country. Mr. Ross met with it on Great Slave Lake, but did not observe it any farther north. Captain Blakiston obtained a single specimen at Fort Carlton, in the valley of the Saskatchewan.

Mr. Boardman informs me that examples of this species are occasionally taken near Calais, but that its appearance there is very irregular. This bird is also extremely rare on the coast of Massachusetts; yet hardly a year passes that some specimens of it are not brought into the Boston market, chiefly from the county of Barnstable, in the southeastern portion of the State. In November, 1874, a small flock was found off that coast, and seven individuals were brought to the stall of Mr. David A. Dunham, in Quincy Market.

Those Canvas-backs which frequent the shores of Long Island, according to Giraud, return from their breeding-places at the north about the first of November; and in the winter some are occasionally shot in the eastern part of Great South Bay. They are also sometimes taken in Long Island Sound, both on the southern and on the Connecticut shore. Dr. Woods has obtained them on the Connecticut, a few miles above its mouth. Canvas-backs from the vicinity of New York are much inferior to those taken in the Chesapeake and its tributaries, owing to the difference in the quality of their food. This Duck feeds in preference on the root of the *Vallisneria spiralis,* called by some tape-grass, and by others, incorrectly, wild celery. This plant grows both in fresh and in brackish water. Where this favorite food cannot be obtained, this Duck feeds on various marine plants and small shellfish, which abound on the coast, and furnish an abundant supply of food to other Ducks of less note. Where this tape-grass cannot be procured, the flesh loses in a great degree that delicacy of flavor for which the Canvas-back is so celebrated. This bird is in the best condition for the table in the latter part of the autumn.

These Ducks associate in large flocks; and when they all rise together from the water the noise made may be heard to a great distance. They are very vigilant, and difficult of approach, except in severe weather, when they may be easily killed at air-openings in the ice. This bird is an excellent diver, and when only wounded can with difficulty be secured. Miller's Island, about fifteen miles from Baltimore, was formerly a famous place for shooting Canvas-backs, as well as other Ducks; and points on this island, and on others in the vicinity, were rented for large sums.

A writer in "Doughty's Cabinet" (I. 41) states that unless the weather at the north has been very severe, the Canvas-back rarely appears in large numbers in Chesapeake Bay before the middle of November. When first arrived these birds are thin and tasteless, and need several days of undisturbed repose to give them that peculiar flavor for which they are so celebrated. During the low tides succeeding their arrival they sit on the flats far from the shore, and rarely rise to the wing unless disturbed. When the spring-tides render the water too deep for feeding, they pass down the bay in the morning, and return in the evening.

By the middle of December, particularly if the weather has been severe, the fowl of every kind have become so fat that Canvas-backs have been known to burst open in the breast in falling on the water. They now spend less time in feeding, pass up and down the Bay, from river to river, in their morning and evening flights, and offer at certain localities great opportunities for their destruction. They pursue, even in their short passages, very much the order of their migratory movements, flying in two lines diverging from a centre; and when the wind blows on the points which lie in their course, the sportsman has great chances of success. The birds avoid, if possible, an approach to the shore; but when a strong breeze sets them in that direction, they are compelled to pass near the projecting points of land within gunshot. In the Susquehanna and Elk rivers there are few of these points, and success depends on shooting the Ducks on their feeding-grounds. After passing the eastern point at the mouth of the Susquehanna, and Turkey Point on the western side of the Elk, the first place of much celebrity is the "Narrows," between Spesutic Island and the western shore, about three miles in length, and from three to five hundred yards in breadth; and here the Canvas-backs feed. A few miles down the western shore is Taylor's Island, at the mouth of the Rumney, and also Abby Island, at the mouth of the Bush — both celebrated localities for Ducks, Geese, and Swans. The south point of Bush River, and Robbins's and Rickett's Points, near Gunpowder, are also famous. When disturbed on their feeding-grounds, the birds forsake those haunts and seek others; therefore in the rivers leading to the Bay, near shooting-points, they should not be annoyed by being shot at from boats, either by night or day, as a repetition of such visits would soon drive the Ducks from their favorite haunts.

The best grounds are found on the western side; and there southerly winds are the most favorable ones. If a high tide is attended with a smart frost and mild south winds, the number of birds set in motion is inconceivable; and they approach the points so closely, that even a moderately good shot can procure from fifty to a hundred Ducks in a day. This was once quite a common occurrence; and the writer quoted has known eight Canvas-backs to be killed at one discharge. The usual mode of taking these Ducks was either by shooting them from the point during flight, or by "toling" — an operation by which the birds are sometimes induced to approach within a few feet of the shore from a distance of several hundred yards. A favorable spot is selected, where the Ducks are feeding a few hundred yards from the shore, and where they can easily approach it closely by swimming. The higher the tides and the calmer the day, the better the chance of success. A kind of poodle-dog, of the breed familiarly known as the "toler," is trained to run along the shore in sight of the Ducks. The dog soon becomes quite expert at the business, and learns, as the Ducks approach, gradually to conceal himself. The nearest Ducks notice this strange appearance, raise their heads, gaze intently, and approach the shore. The rest follow; and in some cases several thousand Ducks of various kinds have been seen to swim in solid mass direct to the object of their curiosity. By removing the dog farther into the grass they have been attracted to within fifteen feet of the bank. Black-heads can be toled the most readily, then Red-heads, and next the Canvas-back.

Another method of killing Canvas-backs, described by Lewis, is to boat them on their feeding-grounds in small skiffs, either during the daytime or at night — the latter being the most destructive method. A large swivel, carrying several ounces of powder and a pound or more of shot, is placed on the bows of a light boat, and by means of muffled oars, and under cover of the darkness, this is carried into the very midst of the sleeping Ducks; and on firing into their thick columns, great numbers are crippled or killed. This mode of slaughter is considered very disreputable, and has been forbidden by legislative enactments. Boating Ducks on their feeding-grounds, even with small guns and by daylight, will soon drive them from their accustomed haunts, and should be condemned by the true sportsman.

Another ingenious, but very objectionable, way of taking this Duck, known as "netting," was once resorted to. This consisted in sinking gill-nets a short distance below the surface of the water, so that the Ducks, in diving, would get entangled in the meshes; and great numbers were secured in this way. But this has the effect of completely driving the Ducks away; and it was found that when taken in this manner they were hardly fit to eat.

Another successful mode of killing Ducks, and one that once was much in vogue, is the use of what are known as "dugouts." These are small boats moored over the flats, concealed from observation as far as possible by quantities of eel-grass thrown over and about them, and surrounded by large numbers of decoys anchored near the vessel. The occupant of the dugout patiently awaits the arrival of the Wild Ducks, which are attracted by the decoys. When the weather is favorable and the Ducks are flying, this plan is very successful; but it is not successful in cold or boisterous weather. More recently the old-fashioned dugout has been superseded by the "surface-boat," or "battery," as it is called. This contrivance is anchored on the feeding-ground, and surrounded by decoys. Its construction is such that when anchored out the water is on a level with the deck of the box, the occupant, when reclining, being entirely concealed from observation, so that nothing can be seen even at a distance of only a few hundred feet. Several double-barrelled guns are usually in readiness; and this battery is accompanied by a companion in a sail or row boat, who keeps at a distance, ready to pick up the dead Ducks, or to render such aid as may be required. The number of Ducks killed in this manner is said to be incredible.

A very ingenious contrivance for Duck-shooting was seen by Mr. Lewis on Elk River. This ambush was prepared by taking advantage of low tides, and driving four strong posts in a square into the soft mud, in the centre of a wide expanse of feeding-ground, in the path of the Ducks as they fly up and down the river. The upper portions of these posts are perforated with large holes, permitting the introduction of long hickory pins, which pass through and project several inches; from these pins is suspended a light frame, strong enough to bear the weight of the hunter, who is concealed from observation by a pile of cedar-brush or eel-grass — the framework being raised or lowered according to the condition of the tide. This particular kind of blind is well adapted for this river, where the feeding-grounds are quite extensive; and immense flocks of wild-fowl are occasionally thus attracted.

Another, and often very successful, device for shooting the Canvas-back is by taking advantage of the severity of the weather, which drives the bird from its favorite feeding-grounds, and then enticing them within reach of an ambush on shore, by cutting a large hole in the ice directly over some choice feeding-shoal. Large numbers may be killed in this manner.

This species, in and around Chesapeake Bay, has long been regarded as pre-eminent for the richness and delicacy of the flavor of its flesh; and it is claimed by many that no wild-fowl in any part of the world can vie in this respect with the Canvas-back of these waters. It has been hunted on the Chesapeake and its tributaries with unrelenting greed, until its numbers have been greatly reduced, and many have been driven to more southern regions. This bird always commands a ready sale; and even when sent to the market by thousands, always brings a high price. While a few Canvas-backs are met with in the waters of the Hudson, the Delaware, and in other eastern rivers, by far the larger portion of them resort to Chesapeake Bay and the adjacent waters. Of late years its numbers have greatly increased along the short rivers of North Carolina. It is also found in abundance on the western lakes, and is particularly numerous on Lake Koskonong, in Southern Wisconsin. In March I have seen the markets of Chicago well supplied with this Duck; and although there in no wise superior to the Mallard, the Pin-tail, the Teals, and other Ducks, yet commanding twice the market-price of any other species.

The Canvas-back extends its migrations to Florida, Louisiana, and Texas. In New Orleans it is called the *Canard Cheval*, and is much esteemed in that city for its delicacy, though far inferior to birds of this species killed on the Chesapeake. It is occasionally found in the markets of Charleston and Savannah; but it is not there esteemed so highly as are many other kinds. This Duck is also very abundant at times near Galveston, Texas, where it feeds on the seeds of the wild oats, the water-lily, and other plants, and is said to become delicious eating.

Messrs. Lockhart and Kennicott have supplied interesting notes in relation to the nesting of this Duck, which was found breeding on the Yukon in great numbers. The eggs were from seven to ten in number, and incubation began about the middle of June.

In Eastern Oregon, in the neighborhood of Lake Malheur and Camp Harney, Captain Bendire found this an abundant species during its migrations, and breeding in the higher mountain valleys of the Blue Mountains, where he found it nesting on Bear Creek, at an altitude of six thousand feet. In the spring and fall it frequents the shallow portions of the lakes in immense flocks; but its flesh is not so well flavored as at the east.

The Canvas-back was found breeding at Fort Resolution, as well as on the Yukon River, by Mr. Kennicott; on the Yukon also by Mr. J. Lockhart; at Fort Simpson by Mr. B. Ross; at Fort Rae by Mr. L. Clarke; at Fort Yukon by Mr. S. Jones; on Anderson River by Mr. MacFarlane; at Nulato by Mr. Dall; at Sitka by Mr. Bischoff; and near the mouth of Frazer River by Mr. H. W. Elliott.

Mr. Lockhart describes the nest of No. 27808 as being formed of rushes and grass, in water, and built from the bottom, large and deep; but less thickly lined with down and feathers than the nests of Ducks usually are. It contained seven eggs. All the nests found, with a single exception, resembled this one, and were similarly situated. They are constructed gradually, as the Duck continues to lay, and are entirely finished when incubation begins. The exception referred to was on the ground in an open place, which had been left dry as the river fell; the nest in this case was at the foot of a few small willows, and about twenty yards from the water. It was built of down and feathers, and had small sticks on the sides, but little or nothing on the bottom. The feathers in the nest were gray, tipped with chestnut, similar to those on the breast of the Canvas-back. This nest contained eight eggs.

Mr. Kennicott describes nest No. 6669 as built from the ground, in water a foot deep, in the grassy edge of a lake. The base was large, and formed of a pile of grass, the nest proper being placed on top. The cavity was large, the sides well built up, and thoroughly lined with down. For the construction of this large base the bird had pulled up or broken off all the dry grass within a yard or two of the nest, thus leaving it in a clear place. The shell of the egg is remarkably hard and brittle. From the same nest was taken a second lot of eggs, the female having again made use of it. When first found, in June, it was not complete; as among all the Ducks the nest is not finished until incubation begins.

Eggs of this species from Fort Yukon (Smithsonian Institution, Nos. 6669 and 6660) are of a uniform pale grayish-green color. Four eggs have the following measurements: 2.50 by 1.80 inches; 2.55 by 1.75; 2.60 by 1.80; 2.40 by 1.75.

Æthyia americana.

THE RED-HEADED DUCK.

Anas ferina, WILS. Am. Orn. VIII. 1814, 110, pl. 70, fig. 6 (not of LINN.).

Fuligula ferina, BONAP. Synop. 1828, 392. — SW. & RICH. F. B. A. II. 1831, 452. — NUTT. Man. II. 1834, 434. — AUD. Orn. Biog. IV. 1838, 198, pl. 322; Synop. 1839, 287; B. Am. VI. 1843, 311, pl. 396.

Fuligula americana, EYTON, Mon. Anat. 1838, 155.

Aythya ferina, δ, *americana*, BONAP. Compt. Rend. XLIII. Sept. 1856, 651.

Aythya americana, BAIRD, B. N. Am. 1858, 793; Cat. N. Am. B. 1859, no. 591.

Æthyia americana, SCL. & SALV. Nom. Neotr. 1873. — RIDGW. Nom. N. Am. B. 1881, no. 618.

Aythya ferina, var. *americana*, ALLEN, Bull. M. C. Z. III. 1872, 183.

Fuligula ferina, var. *americana*, COUES, Key, 1872, 289; Check List, 1873, no. 503; B. N. W. 1874, 575.

Fuligula ferina americana, COUES, Check List, 2d ed. 1882, no. 723.

Aythya erythrocephala, BONAP. Comp. List, 1838, 58.

HAB. The whole of North America, breeding from Central California and Maine, to the Fur Countries; Bahamas.

SP. CHAR. Bill much shorter than the middle toe (without claw), broad, the end moderately depressed, and with the nail decidedly decurved, the culmen about two and a half times the greatest width of the maxilla, and decidedly concave. *Adult male:* Head and upper half, or more, of the neck rich reddish chestnut, the latter glossed with reddish purple; lower part of the neck, jugulum, anterior part of the back, lower part of the rump, upper tail-coverts, and crissum, black; back, scapulars, sides, and flanks, densely vermiculated with white and dusky in about equal proportion; anal region similarly, but more faintly, marked; entire abdomen immaculate white; wing-coverts deep plumbeous-gray, faintly and minutely sprinkled with white; secondaries ("speculum") pale bluish gray, the upper feathers edged with black, the others narrowly tipped with white; primaries dusky, the inner quills slate-gray, except at ends; tail dusky. Bill pale blue, the end black; iris red; feet bluish gray. *Adult female:* Head and neck grayish brown, darkest above; the anterior part of the head lighter, almost white on the chin and upper part of the throat; jugulum, sides, and flanks dull grayish brown, the feathers tipped with fulvous; wings as in the male, but the coverts plain slate-color; back and scapulars grayish brown, the feathers with paler tips; rump, upper tail-coverts, and tail dusky grayish brown; anal region paler; longer lower tail-coverts whitish. Bill plumbeous, the end black; iris yellow; feet plumbeous. *Downy young* (No. 82481, St. Clair Flats, Mich., June 29, 1880; W. H. COLLINS): Above, ochreous olive-brown, indistinctly relieved by an olive-yellow spot back of each wing, one on the hind border of each arm-wing, and one on each side of the rump; entire head and neck (except pileum and nape), with whole lower parts deep, buff yellow, paler and less yellow on abdomen and anal region. No dark markings whatever on side of head. Bill and feet light colored (brownish in dried skin).

Male.

Total length, about, 20.00–21.00 inches; extent, 33.00; wing, about 8.50; culmen, 2.05–2.25; greatest width of bill, .75–.85; tarsus, 1.60–1.65; middle toe, 2.30–2.40.

The American Red-head Duck is quite distinct from the Pochard of Europe, though resembling it very closely. The latter has the bill narrower and longer, in fact nearly intermediate in shape between that of *Æ. americana* and *Æ. vallisneria;* its color is also different, being black, crossed by a band of pale blue, instead of pale blue with the end black; the entire abdomen is undulated with gray, like the sides and flanks, only more delicately, while the back, scapulars, and sides are much whiter than in *Æ. americana.* The rich chestnut-red of the neck is destitute of the metallic reddish-purple gloss, while it involves the entire neck, even tinging the anterior part of the back, instead of being confined to about the upper half of the neck; the wing-coverts are also much lighter colored, and, in most specimens, very distinctly vermiculated with white, instead of nearly plain slaty gray. In general size the European species is decidedly inferior; the tarsus is considerably shorter, while the middle toe is decidedly longer.

Female.

The female of the Red-head resembles that of the Ring-neck, or Ring-billed Black-head (*Fulix collaris*), so closely as to be distinguished with difficulty, except on direct comparison. The latter has all the colors darker, however, the fore part of the head and the throat more decidedly white, and the bill much shorter and broader. The different proportions, however, afford the surest means of distinguishing them, the two species comparing about as follows: —

Æ. americana. Wing, 8.50 inches; culmen, 1.90; greatest width of bill, .85, least width, .75; tarsus, 1.60; middle toe, 2.30.

F. collaris. Wing, 7.50 inches; culmen, 1.80; greatest width of bill, .85, least width, .65; tarsus, 1.35; middle toe, 2.00.

The Red-head Duck has a distribution more or less general throughout North America, breeding in high northern latitudes down to about 44°, and frequenting in the winter the southern portions of the continent as far as Mexico. It is found both on the Atlantic and the Pacific coasts.

It was met with on the western coast of Mexico, near Mazatlan, by Colonel Grayson, and in Northeastern Mexico and Southern Texas by Mr. Dresser. It is given as occurring on the Pacific coast at Vancouver Island by Mr. R. Browne. On the coast of California, according to Dr. Cooper, the Red-head is not so common as the Canvas-back, but it has been obtained from San Francisco to San Diego, and throughout the interior in the winter. Dr. Heermann believes that some of these Ducks breed in the marshes of the Sacramento Valley; and he mentions obtaining several females there in June with their breasts denuded of feathers, as is usually the case with Ducks when sitting on their eggs. Mr. J. A. Allen found this species in great abundance in the valley of Great Salt Lake, Utah.

Richardson states that this species breeds in all parts of the Fur Countries, from the fiftieth parallel to their most northern limits. Mr. Boardman informs me that in the summer of 1871 he found a pair of Red-heads which were evidently breeding in the vicinity of Calais, Me. This statement, coupled with that of Dr. Heermann, goes to show that this species, on both the eastern and the western shores, breeds much farther south than the limit assigned by Dr. Richardson. Its nest and eggs were afterward, in the summer of 1874, actually found by Mr. William Bryant about thirty miles north of Calais. The presence of this bird about Calais had been previously noted by Mr. Boardman during each summer, and he had not doubted that a few pair remain about there for the purpose of rearing their young. They have not been seen there in any large number, and they are rare in Massachusetts, a few only being occasionally obtained in the late fall on the southern shores of Cape Cod.

The Red-head is somewhat abundant on Long Island — where, however, according to Giraud, it is not so common as many other species. It is seldom seen in any considerable numbers west of Babylon, being chiefly limited to the eastern part of South Bay, where it is sometimes seen in company with the Canvas-back. Both species not infrequently feed on the same plant, the former eating the stems, and the latter the roots; these are tender and juicy, and it is to them that the delicate flavor of the flesh of the Canvas-back is due. The Red-headed Duck is also excellent eating, and commands a high price in the New York market — indeed, it is not infrequently sold to the inexperienced as the genuine Canvas-back, which it so strongly resembles.

About Egg Harbor, N. J., this Duck is more common than it is on Long Island; but it is not so abundant there as it is on Chesapeake Bay. Mr. Giraud states that frequent attempts have been made to domesticate this species, and in one instance, at least, with considerable success. A Red-headed Duck in the possession of Mr. Edmund Powell, of Westbury, L. I., became as completely reconciled to its new home as if it had never known any other course of life. The Red-headed Duck makes its appearance on the Long Island coast usually about the first of November, and leaves for its northern breeding-places early in March.

A writer in "Doughty's Cabinet" (I. 41) gives the last of October as being nearly the date of its first arrival in the waters of the Chesapeake. These birds from that time on appear in large flocks, and very rapidly distribute themselves over the Bay. Much difference of opinion has been expressed as to the excellence of the flesh of this species; but the writer quoted believes that this diversity of view is due — in part, at least — to the difference of the food of the bird in different localities. On the Chesapeake, where it feeds in company with the Canvas-back, it is said to be hardly second even to that Duck in the delicacy of its flavor. It is not so restricted to a few localities in Eastern North America as is the Canvas-back; and while abundant in Chesapeake Bay, is also found in considerable numbers in many other regions. It feeds on the blades of the *Vallisneria* grass when unable to obtain the roots. It is frequently shot in the waters of the Hudson, the Delaware, and, later in the winter, in the streams of the Southern States. Dr. Bryant found it very common in winter at the Bahamas, where it was the most abundant of all the Ducks, occurring in large flocks, acres in extent.

At New Orleans, where this Duck was then commonly known as the *Dos gris*, or Gray-back, Audubon states that it arrives in great flocks early in November, and departs late in April. It is very abundant on lakes St. John, Pontchartrain, and Borgne, keeping in large flocks, and not mingling with any other species. There its food seems to consist of small fishes, for which it is continually diving. It is caught in nets in great numbers, and is easily kept in confinement, as it feeds greedily on crushed Indian corn. In 1816 these and other Ducks were thus taken by the thousand by a Frenchman, who used to send them to market alive in cages.

Audubon saw none of these birds during the spring and summer he spent in Labrador, nor did he hear of any in Newfoundland; and on his excursion to Kansas none were seen to the west of the Southwest Pass. In this, however, others have been more successful; and this bird has been found on the Texan coast. He mentions it as abundant in November, and afterward in December, in the marshes near St. Augustine, in East Florida. It was shy, and kept in company with the Mallards and other Ducks in shallow fresh-water ponds, at some distance from the sea-shore. In South Carolina he was informed that this species had latterly become much more abundant than it was twenty years before, especially on the Santee River. It is an expert diver when in deep bays and estuaries; but in shallow ponds in the interior it dabbles in the mud in the manner of the Mallard, and its stomach is filled with tadpoles, small water-lizards, and blades of grass. At other times Audubon found acorns and beechnuts, as well as snails and fragments of the shells of unios, together with much gravel. The notes of this Duck are said to be rough and coarse, and not to have as much resemblance to those of species peculiar to fresh water, as the cries of birds of this family generally have. Its flight is hurried, the bird rising from the water in a confused manner, but being able to continue long on the wing. This bird produces with its wings, when in motion, a clear whistling sound. Audubon regarded this species as identical with the Pochard (*Æ. ferina*) of Europe.

According to the observations of Professor Kumlien, this species is quite common in the waters of Southern Wisconsin, both in the spring and fall. It is not known to occur there in the summer, and is later in its arrival in the fall than the Canvas-back. Mr. B. F. Goss, however, writes me that he has known this species to breed occasionally, but rarely, in his neighborhood — Pewaukee, Wis. On the 24th of May, 1868, he camped on an island in Horicon Lake, and remained there four days. This lake is twelve miles long and two broad, with numerous islands and grassy bogs; these were covered to the water's edge with a scattering growth of trees, with thick bushes and weeds. Here various Ducks were breeding in great numbers. On one island, containing about half an acre, the nests were only a few feet apart; and as he approached, the Ducks rose from their nests in a great flock, and it was difficult to identify the few nests of other species among the great multitude of Mallards. He found eight nests of the Red-head, which were almost always in thick grass or weeds, and near the water, none being more than twenty feet distant. The nests were sometimes slightly elevated, made of any convenient loose material, rather small, and not very neatly finished. They contained from one to five eggs; but their full complement was probably nine or ten.

This Duck was found breeding in great numbers on Manitoba Lake, on Shoal Lake, and in the Selkirk Settlement by Mr. Donald Gunn.

Dr. Kennerly observed it at Boca Grande, in Chihuahua, in March, 1855. It was also found on the Janos and Conalitos rivers, at various points, at this season, generally going in pairs, rarely in large flocks, and being very shy.

Eggs of this species, procured by Mr. Goss, and now in the Smithsonian Museum (No. 15176), are of a grayish white with a slight tinge of cream-color. They vary in breadth from 1.70 to 1.75 inches, and from 2.35 to 2.40 in length. Those from the Selkirk Settlement (Smithsonian Institution, No. 14190), measure 1.70 by 1.35.

GENUS **CLANGULA**, BOIE.

Clangula, BOIE, Isis, 1822, 564. — "FLEMING, Philos. Zool. II. 1822, 260" (type, *Anas clangula*, LINN.). (Cf. DRESSER, B. Eur. Pt. XLVI. Dec. 1875; COUES, Bull. Nutt. Orn. Club, April, 1880, 101.)

Glaucion, KAUP, Ent. Europ. Thierw. 1829, 53 (same type; preoccupied in *Mollusca*; OKEN, 1816).

Bucephala, BAIRD, B. N. Am. Aug. 19, 1858, 795 (type, *Anas albeola*, LINN.).

CHAR. Bill much shorter than the head, deep through the base, the lateral outlines converging toward the tip, which is rather pointed than rounded; lamellæ completely hidden by the over-hanging edge of the maxilla; nostrils situated near the middle of the bill; tarsus longer than the culmen; tail rather long (about half the wing), of sixteen feathers. Colors, pied white and black in the male, brown and white in the female.

This genus comes nearest in its characters to *Histrionicus*, but is quite distinct. Three species are known, their special characters being as follows: —

COM. CHAR. *Adult:* Head and upper part of the neck black, with metallic reflections, and with a patch of white, varying in form with the species; lower part of the neck, all round, entire lower

C. glaucion.

parts, part of scapulars, wing-coverts, and secondaries white; other upper parts black. *Female:* The black replaced by brown, the white absent from the head (except in *B. albeola*), and more restricted elsewhere.

A. Size rather large (wing, 7.40 inches or more); male with a white spot before the eye; female without white on the head.

1. **C. islandica.** *Male:* White patch on lores wedge-shaped, the head glossed with bluish violet; a broad black bar between the white of the middle and greater wing-coverts. *Female:* Head dark sepia or purplish snuff-brown; a distinct black bar across the ends of the greater wing-coverts. Wing, 8.25-9.40 inches; length of bill to point of basal angle, 1.40–1.80; tarsus, 1.30–1.60; middle toe, 2.15–2.50. *Hab.* Northern North America, breeding far southward (at least to Colorado) in higher portions of Rocky Mountains; Greenland; Iceland; accidental in Europe.

2. **C. glaucion.** *Male:* White patch on lores roundish; white patch of wings not interrupted by a black bar. *Female:* Head grayish umber-brown; white wing-patch usually continuous.

a. Glaucion.[1] *Male adult:* Wing, 8.50 inches; bill from tip to basal angle, 1.70–1.80; tarsus, 1.30; middle toe, 2.20. *Hab.* Palæarctic Region.

[1] CLANGULA GLAUCION, Linn. The Golden-eye.

Anas clangula, LINN. S. N. ed. 10, I. 1758, 125; ed. 12, I. 1766, 201. — NAUM. Vög. Deutschl. XII. 1844, 162, pl. 316.

Glaucion clangula, KAUP, Naturl. Syst. 53. — KEYS. & BLAS. Wirb. Eur. 1840, lxxxvi.

Anas glaucion, LINN. S. N. ed. 10, I. 1758, 126; ed. 12, I. 1766, 201.

Clangula glaucion, BREHM, Vög. Deutschl. 929. — GRAY, Gen. B. III. 622; Cat. Brit. B. 1863, 202.

Anas hyemalis, PALL. Zoog. Rosso. As. II. 1826, 270.

Clangula chrysopthalmos, STEPH. Gen. Zool. XII. pt. ii. 182, pl. 56. — BONAP. Comp. List, 1838, 58. — MACGILL. Man. II. 183.

Clangula vulgaris, FLEM. Brit. Anim. 1828, 120.

Clangula leucomelas and *C. peregrina*, BREHM, Vög. Deutschl. 1831, 927.

Golden-eye, YARR. Brit. B. ed. 2, III. 368, fig.; ed. 3, III. 371, fig.

β. *Americana.* *Male adult:* Wing, 9.25 inches; bill to basal angle, 1.85; tarsus, 1.60; middle toe, 2.50. *Hab.* North America.

B. Size small (wing less than 7.00 inches); male with a large white patch on each side of the occiput (confluent behind); female with a white spot on the auricular region.

3. **C. albeola.** Wing, 6.00–6.75 inches; bill from tip to end of basal angle, 1.15–1.25; depth at base, .55–.70; width, .45–.60; tarsus, 1.15–1.25; middle toe, 1.80–2.00. *Hab.* North America.

Clangula islandica.

BARROW'S GOLDEN-EYE.

Anas islandica, GMEL. S. N. I. ii. 1788, 541.

Bucephala islandica, BAIRD, B. N Am. 1858, 796; Cat. N. Am. B. 1859, no. 594.—COUES, Key, 1872, 290; Check List, 1873, no. 506; Birds N. W. 1874, 577.

Clangula islandica, BONAP. Cat. Met. Ucc. Eur. 1842, 74.—RIDGW. Nom. N. Am. B. 1881, no. 619.—COUES, Check List, 2d ed. 1882, no. 726.

Clangula Barrovii, SW. & RICH. F. B. A. II. 1831, 456, pl. 70 (♂).

Fuligula Barrovii, NUTT. Man. II. 1834, 444.

Clangula scapularis, BREHM, Vög. Deutschl. 1831, 932.

Fuligula clangula, var., AUD. Orn. Biog. V. 1839, 105, pl. 403; Synop. 1839, 292 (part); B. Am. VII. 1843, 362 (part; describes the species as supposed summer plumage of *B. clangula*).

HAB. Northern North America, south in winter to New York, Illinois, Utah, etc.; breeding in the high north, and south in the Rocky Mountains to Colorado. Greenland; Iceland; accidental in Europe.

SP. CHAR. *Adult male:* Head and upper half of the neck glossy blue-black, with reflections of green, blue, and violet, according to the light; a somewhat wedge-shaped vertical patch of white

C. islandica.

across the anterior half of the lores, bordering the lateral base of the bill, the upper part forming an acute angle on each side of the forehead, the lower part rounded. Upper parts velvety black, with a soft bluish-violet tinge; outer row of scapulars marked with a mesial cuneate stripe of satiny white, the greater portion of the stripes concealed, so that the exposed portion forms roundish or oblong spots; middle wing-coverts white, producing a broad bar; exposed terminal half of greater coverts, with the whole of the exposed portion of the five or six inner secondaries, white, forming a large, somewhat cuneate, patch. Outer feathers of the sides and flanks widely edged exteriorly with deep black; femoral region and sides of crissum dull black. Lower half of neck (all round) and entire lower parts (except as described) pure white. Bill black (in skin); iris bright yellow; legs and feet pale. *Adult female:* Head and upper half of the neck dark sepia-brown, considerably darker and somewhat more purplish than in the female of *C. glaucion;* lower part of the neck, all round, white, sometimes tinged with gray on the nape. Upper parts dark grayish-brown, the scapulars, interscapulars, and smaller wing-coverts tipped with lighter ash-gray; last two or three rows of middle wing-coverts tipped with white, forming a broken, rather narrow, transverse patch; greater coverts with the terminal half of their exposed portion white, as in the male, but distinctly tipped with blackish, forming a conspicuous dusky bar between the white of the coverts and that of the inner secondaries. Jugulum and sides ash-gray, the feathers darker and more brown beneath the surface, the breast lighter and more uniform, the flanks darker; other lower parts pure white. Bill usually party-colored (black and yellow), but sometimes wholly black.

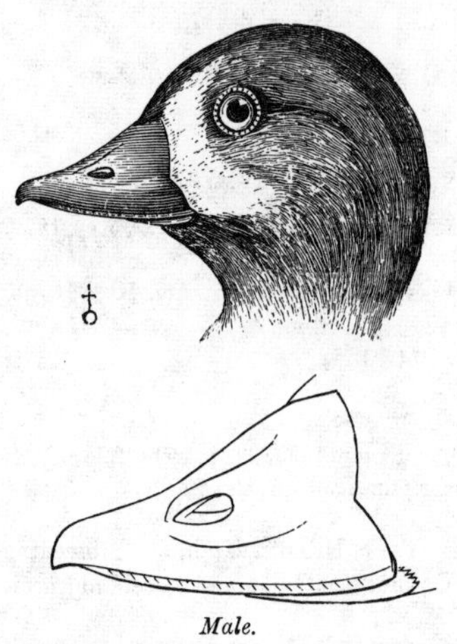

Male.

Adult male: Wing, 9.00–9.40 inches; culmen, 1.65–1.80; depth of bill at base, .95–1.10, width .75–.85; tarsus, 1.50–1.60; middle toe, 2.45–2.50. *Adult female:* Wing, 8.25–8.75 inches; culmen, 1.40–1.60; depth of bill, .85–.90; width, .70; tarsus, 1.30–1.60; middle toe, 2.15–2.20.

Bearing in mind the salient points of difference, as given on p. 40, there need never be any difficulty in distinguishing the adult male of this very distinct species from that of *C. glaucion.* With the female, however, the case is very different; the two species being so much alike that, with the series at our command (about twenty specimens, including six unquestionably referable to *C. islandica*), we must acknowledge our inability to give infallible points of distinction. The examples which are known to represent *C. islandica* differ from the positively determined females of *C. glaucion* in the following respects: (1) The color of the head and upper half of the neck is considerably darker, being a rich sepia- or snuff-brown, rather than grayish brown; (2) the greater wing-coverts are distinctly tipped with black, forming a conspicuous dusky stripe between the two larger white areas of the wing, which in *C. glaucion* are (usually, at least) merged into one continuous space. Further than these we find no distinction, while indeed some examples are so decidedly intermediate in both respects as to render it quite uncertain to which species they belong. Of the two characters named, however, the color of the head is far the more constant, and may, perhaps, be found quite distinctive.

Barrow's Golden-eye, or the Rocky Mountain Golden-eye, as it was very appropriately called by Nuttall, is almost exclusively a North American species, occurring in the interior among the mountains, from Southern Colorado, and probably even farther south, to the Yukon on the northwest, and Greenland on the east. It is also a resident in Iceland, and in a very few instances straggles into Europe. A single individual was taken in Spain by Mr. Howard Saunders, and four individuals are recorded as having been taken on the coast of Norway at different times and places. With these exceptions, it is not known to be a European species.

Up to the present time this species has been strangely overlooked by some writers, while the nature of its geographical distribution has been entirely misunderstood. It was unknown to Wilson, and it escaped the notice of Audubon; and, more recently, Dr. Coues refers to it in different works as belonging to Arctic America and to Northern Europe, mentioning it as being the most northerly of the genus, and as having apparently a Circumpolar distribution, while I can find no evidence that it is either of Arctic or Circumpolar occurrence. It has not been found east of Iceland, either in Europe or Asia; neither is it known to nest anywhere within the Arctic Circle.

It is both a northern and a mountain species, breeding in Greenland, Iceland, and Alaska up to 64° 30′ north latitude, and occurring throughout the Rocky Mountains from high northern regions at least as far to the south as 38° north latitude. It is also seen during the breeding-season in Maine and New Brunswick, and probably throughout the British Provinces generally. It is found on the Atlantic coast in winter as far south at least as Southern Massachusetts, and on the Pacific up to a limit not yet ascertained.

Its presence in the more northerly portion of the Rocky Mountains, among the valleys, was first noted in 1831 by Dr. Richardson, who describes its habits as being very similar to those of the Common Golden-eye; and, three years later, Mr. Nuttall ("Water Birds," p. 444) mentions it as occurring in the Rocky Mountains; but whether on the authority of his own observations or of those of Dr. Richardson, he does not state. More recently, Dr. Cooper was the first of our naturalists to recall the fact of its being found among the mountains of the United States. (See "Fauna of Montana," Am. Nat. III., p. 83.)

Holböll and Reinhardt have also recorded it as being a bird of Greenland, in the southern part of which country it breeds; and it has been procured in the neighborhood of Godthaab and Nenortalik. Its range is there restricted to a narrow belt between 63° 45′ and 64° 30′. North of this the natives have no knowledge of its occurrence.

Mr. Boardman informs me that a few birds of this species are seen each summer in the neighborhood of Calais, Me., and that they undoubtedly breed there, but that as yet he has not been able to discover their nests. They are somewhat rare in the region at that season, but become much more common on the St. Croix River in the winter, and also in the Bay of Fundy.

Mr. William Brewster, of Cambridge, obtained an adult female in the flesh from Cape Cod, Mass., Dec. 7, 1871. Since then he has met with several females and two adult males in the Boston Market, most of which were shot within the limits of Massachusetts. It is now thought to be more common on that coast in the winter than had been previously supposed.

Mr. Nelson states that Barrow's Golden-eye is a winter resident on Lake Michigan, and that it is found at that season irregularly throughout the State of Illinois. This bird was obtained on the Wabash, at Mount Carmel, in December, 1874, by Professor Stein; and Mr. Nelson has observed it at Chicago. Dr. Hoy procured a specimen at Racine in 1860. It is probably not uncommon on Lake Michigan; but the winter season is unfavorable for procuring it, or even for ascertaining its numbers.

This species has been procured by Dr. Hayden in the interior of the United States, and subsequently, in 1872, by Mr. Henshaw, who is inclined to regard this as a species occurring regularly and in considerable numbers on Utah Lake, where two specimens were taken by him, and where — as he was assured by the hunters — some are shot every winter, although this species is less abundant than the common Golden-eye, from which it is easily distinguished.

Mr. Edwin Carter, of Colorado, was probably the first person actually to secure the nest and eggs of this species, whose presence in the mountains of that region had been well known to him for several years. A set of seven eggs obtained by him is now in the Museum of Comparative Zoology of Cambridge. Mr. Carter writes me that "the usual nest complement of Barrow's Golden-eye is from six to ten, varying with the age and vigor of the parents." In 1876 he took a nest of ten eggs, which contained large embryos, and also another set of six; another clutch (that sent to the Museum) consisted of seven. He writes that he has met with several young broods numbering from six to eight, and one of ten. These birds nest in hollow trees; and it is surprising to see in what small cavities they in some instances can accommodate themselves. The following season he examined a great many trees, and every one that had a suitable opening either contained an occupant or indicated former nesting by egg-shells and other marks.

This species is not known to occur in California; but Dr. Cooper has no doubt that it will yet be found among the mountains of the northeastern portion of the State. Mr. Dall speaks of it as present, but rare, on the Yukon River; and specimens were obtained by Bischoff at Sitka. An individual was taken by Mr. M. McLeod in the vicinity of Fort Anderson, June 29, 1863. On the 14th of June, 1864, Mr. MacFarlane obtained a male example at Fort Anderson. It had been in the habit of flying over the fort for several evenings in succession, and was at length shot on a small lake. The female, without doubt, had her nest somewhere in the vicinity, but she eluded his endeavors to discover the place. Mr. MacFarlane adds that this species may be classed among the rarest of the Ducks visiting that region.

Mr. C. W. Sheperd, in his visit to Iceland, found this Duck breeding on a small island in the Lake of Mý-vatn, in the northern part of that island. This islet was occupied almost exclusively by two species — the Golden-eye and the *Mergus serrator*. The soil was composed of broken lava, and both species were breeding in holes, some of their nests being entirely out of reach, in the cracks and crevices of the lava. The two species were found to live together in the most familiar manner, and upon the best of terms. A female Merganser was found sitting on a nest evidently not her own, but which contained four eggs belonging to *B. islandicus;* the difference between the eggs of the two species being so strongly marked as to admit of no possibility of confounding them.

Two eggs of this species from the Yukon (Smithsonian Institution, No. 9547) measure 2.40 by 1.60 inches, and 2.40 by 1.70; two from Iceland (Smithsonian Institution, No. 13409), 2.55 by 1.80, and 2.45 by 1.80. They are of a uniform deep grayish pea-green color.

Clangula glaucion americana.

THE AMERICAN GOLDEN-EYE.

Anas clangula, Wils. Am. Orn. VIII. 1814, 62, pl. 67, fig. 5.

Fuligula clangula, Bonap. Synop. 1828, 393. — Nutt. Man. II. 1834, 441. — Aud. Orn. Biog. IV. 1838, 318, pl. 342; Synop. 1839, 292; B. Am. VI. 1843, 362, pl. 406 (includes *islandica*).

Bucephala clangula, Coues, Key, 1872, 290; Check List, 1873, no. 505; B. N. W. 1874,576.

Clangula glaucium, Coues, Check List, 2d ed. 1882, no. 725.

Clangula vulgaris, Sw. & Rich. F. B. A. II. 1831, 456.

Clangula americana, Bonap. Comp. List, 1838, 58.

Bucephala americana, Baird, B. N. Am. 1858, 796; Cat. N. Am. B. 1859, no. 593.

Clangula glaucium americana, Ridgw. Pr. U. S. Nat. Mus. Vol. 3, 1880, 204; Nom. N. Am. B. 1881, no. 620.

Hab. The whole of North America, breeding from Maine and the British Provinces, northward; south to Cuba in winter.

Sp. Char. *Adult male:* Head and upper half of neck black, glossed with dark green, varying to violet; a roundish white spot between the rictus and the eye, but not reaching to the latter; back, inner scapulars, tertials, rump, and upper tail-coverts, deep black; lower half of the neck (all round), lower parts, outer scapulars, posterior lesser, middle and greater wing-coverts, and secondaries, pure white ; anterior lesser wing-coverts, and outer edges of scapulars and flank feathers, and concealed portion of greater coverts, deep black ; primaries blackish dusky ; tail dull slate ; sides of the anal region behind the flanks clouded with grayish. Bill deep black; iris bright yellow ; feet orange-yellow, with dusky webs. *Adult female :* Similar to that of *C. islandica*, but head and neck hair-brown or grayish brown, rather than purplish sepia or snuff-brown, and white on the wing usually not interrupted by a distinct black bar.

Downy young :[1] Upper parts generally, including the whole upper half of the head, to the rictus, and considerably below the eyes, the jugulum, sides, and thighs, deep sooty brown, lighter and more grayish on the jugulum ; the brown of the upper parts relieved by about eight spots of grayish white, as follows : one on the posterior border (secondary region) of each wing ; one on each side the back ; one on each side the rump, at the base of the tail, and one on each flank just before the brown of the thighs. Chin, throat, and cheeks pure white, in abrupt and decided contrast to the brown, which entirely surrounds it ; remaining lower parts grayish white. Bill brownish ; nail yellowish.

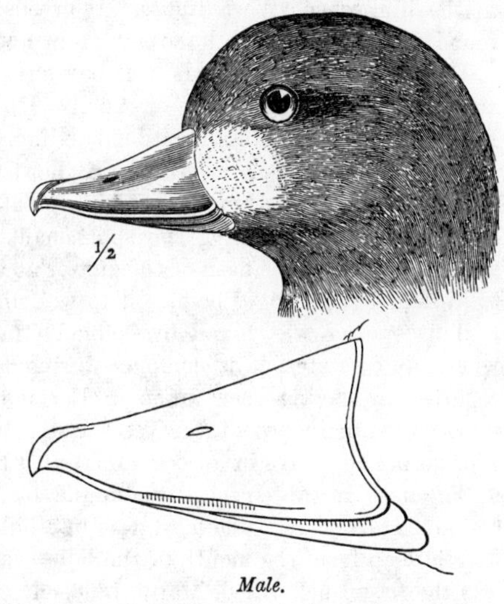

Male.

Adult male : Total length, about 18.50 to 20.00 inches ; extent, 31.00 ; wing, about 9.25 ; length of bill, from tip to end of basal angle, 1.85 ; depth at base, 1.00 ; width, .85 ; tarsus, 1.60 ; middle toe, 2.50. *Adult female :* Total length, 16.50 ; extent, 26.75 ; wing, 8.25 ; culmen, 1.60 ; depth of bill at base, .90, width, .70 ; tarsus, 1.40 ; middle toe, 2.20.

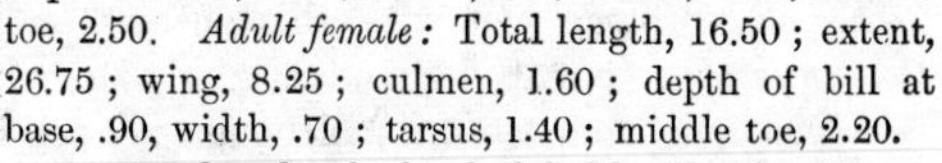

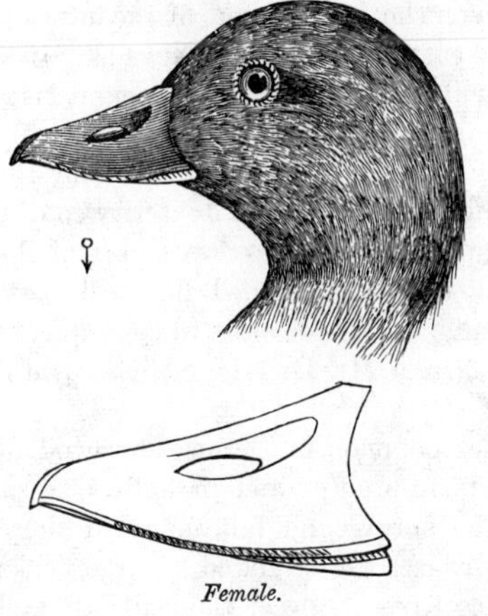

Female.

As stated under the head of *C. islandica* (p. 42), we are unable to discover, in the material at our command (consisting of upward of twenty specimens, including six unquestionable *C. islandica* and many more equally undoubted *C. glaucion*) positive points of distinction between the female of the common and of that of Barrow's Golden-eye. All specimens, however, possessing no dusky bar across the ends of the greater wing-coverts, thus interrupting the white wing-patch, should probably be referred to the present species. The females of both species are so variable in every character we have tested that it is quite impossible to say to which some examples should be referred.[2]

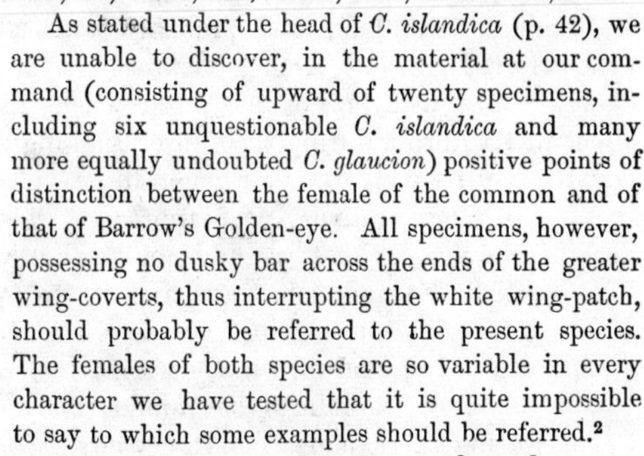

Upon comparing a series of two males and as many females of the European Golden-eye (*B. clangula*) with a very large number of American specimens, we are unable to detect any difference in coloration. The difference in size, however, is so great, and moreover constant, as fully to justify their separation as distinct races.

[1] Described from No. 23261, New Brunswick ; G. A. Boardman.

[2] In a paper entitled "On the Golden-eyes, or Garrots, in Nova Scotia," Mr. J. Bernard Gilpin arrives at the same conclusion, after careful study of specimens in the flesh (see pp. 398, 399). This paper, which, in its way, is quite a monograph, is evidently an extract from some larger publication, the title of

The American Golden-eye, "Whistler," and "Great Head," as it is variously known in different parts of the United States, has a very extended distribution, being found as far south as Florida and Mexico during the winter, and in summer to the highest northern limits. It breeds from the 42d parallel northward, and is found in winter on both coasts from about the same parallel southward.

Captain Blakiston records it as having been first seen by him on the Saskatchewan, at Fort Carlton, on the 10th of April. He also received specimens from Hudson's Bay. Mr. Bernard Ross mentions finding it along the Mackenzie River as far north as the Arctic coast. According to Richardson, it frequents the rivers and fresh-water lakes throughout the Fur Countries in great numbers. In that region it appears to be by no means shy, allowing the sportsman to approach sufficiently near; but it dives so dexterously at the flash of the gun or at the twanging of the bow, and is so difficult to kill, that the natives believe it to be endowed with a supernatural power.

This species was found by Colonel Grayson near Mazatlan, in Western Mexico, where, as he states, it is common during the winter months. A single specimen is reported as having been taken in Bermuda in April, 1854. I can find no record of its occurrence in any of the West India Islands, though its presence in Southern Florida is suggestive of an occasional visit to Cuba.

The nest of this species was found by Mr. Lockhart on the Yukon, June 18. It contained six eggs. The nest was in a hole high up in a poplar-tree, about an arm's length deep from the mouth of the hole. Mr. Dall met with it at Nulato, where it was the first Duck killed, May 3, 1868. It is always early in arriving, and is common both on the Yukon and on the Pacific coast, near the mouth of that river. Its eggs were obtained from near Pastolik from the marshes. The skin of this Duck, which, after being stuffed and decorated with beads, had been used as an ornament in the lodge, was bought from some Indians on the Yukon, near the Mission.

Mr. R. Browne met with this species on the Pacific at Vancouver Island. Dr. Cooper states that it is abundant along the whole Pacific coast from Puget Sound to San Diego, and beyond; and although not common on the fresh waters of the interior, it frequents Salt Lake, and probably other lakes east of the Sierra Nevada. It is generally recognizable from a distance by the shrill noise which it makes as it rises slowly from the surface of the water when starting to fly. It seems to be perfectly silent in California during the winter, making no noise, except that produced by the whistling of its wings. It is generally shy; though, trusting to its dexterity in diving, it will allow of a very near approach. This species dives so very quickly at the flash of the powder that it could not be shot with the old-fashioned flint-lock. Its food consists of small fish, crabs, and marine plants, and its flesh is in consequence rather fishy, and inferior for the table. At Unalashka Mr. Dall found it a winter visitor, migrating landward in the spring.

Mr. George A. Boardman has found this species common in the neighborhood of Calais during the summer months, where it breeds in stumps and in hollow trees. In Massachusetts it is quite abundant both in the spring and fall, many of these Ducks wintering in the State at places where open water can be found. Large flocks often spend each winter in the open parts of Charles River, between the Mill-dam and Cambridge Bridge. In very severe weather, if that portion of the river is obstructed by ice, the birds are temporarily driven to the open harbor, but invariably return when the ice is broken up. They are excessively shy, and unapproachable when

which we are unable to quote, since no clew is given in the extra edition of the paper in question. Dr. Coues (see "Key to North American Birds," p. 290) also admits his inability to distinguish the females of the two species.

disturbed, but generally appear as much at home in this land-locked basin as if in their wild retreats, swimming up to within a few rods of the dwellings in Beacon Street, or diving under the much-frequented bridges.

On Long Island, as Mr. Giraud states, the Golden-eye is better known among the hunters as the "Whistler," from the peculiar noise produced by its wings when flying. By others it is also called the "Great-Head," from its beautifully rich and thickly crested head. On that island it is said to be a not very abundant species, arriving there in company with other migratory Ducks. He met with it in the fall and spring on the Delaware and in Chesapeake Bay, as well as at Egg Harbor and on Long Island. In the interior it is said to be much more common. Its food seemed to consist of small shell and other fish, which it procures by diving. In the fall its flesh is said to be about equal or even superior to that of the Scaup Duck. It is very shy, and is decoyed with great difficulty. In stormy weather it often takes shelter in the coves with the Scaup Duck, and there it may be more readily killed. It usually flies very high, and the whistling sound produced by the action of its wings is the only noise that it makes as it proceeds.

Audubon found the Golden-eye abundant in South Carolina during the winter, where at times it frequented the preserves of the rice-planters. He also met with it at that season on the watercourses of Florida. In the Ohio River he found it preferring the eddies and rapids, and there it was in the habit of diving for its food. Naturally the Golden-eye is chiefly seen in company with the Buffle-head, the Merganser, and other species that are expert divers like itself. When wounded, unless badly hurt, its power of diving and of remaining under water is so remarkable that it cannot be taken. In 1842 Mr. Jonathan Johnson, of Nahant, shot a male of this species, wounding it in the head and stunning it. The back part of the skull had been shot away, and the bird was supposed to be mortally wounded. It, however, appeared to recover, fed readily on corn, and became quite tame. It was purchased by the late Thomas Lee, Esq., and kept by him in an enclosure. But the cover of its enclosure being one day incautiously opened, the bird, which had seemed reconciled to confinement, suddenly bounded upward through the open space, and disappeared.

The flight of the Whistler is powerful, rapid, and protracted. On rising from the water it proceeds at first very low, and does not ascend to its usual height until it has gone a considerable distance. Although generally a very silent bird, yet just before it leaves for its breeding-places in the spring, the male has a rough croaking note; and this note may also be heard if, having fallen wounded to the ground, it is taken alive.

Audubon pronounces the flesh of this Duck fishy and unfit for food. This may be true where it has been rendered rank and strong by some peculiar kind of food, but birds of this species taken near Boston that I have eaten were far from being unpalatable. It feeds on shellfish, mollusca, marine vegetables, and seeds, and in confinement will readily eat corn and grain.

In Southern Wisconsin, according to the observations of Professor Kumlien, Ducks of this species are found sparingly in the spring, but are more abundant in the fall, a few being known to pass the winter in that locality, wherever they can find deep and open water. They do not, however, remain there during the summer.

Eggs of this species closely resemble those of the *islandica*, being uniformly of a pale grayish pea-green color. Two from Moose River, Southern Hudson Bay (Smithsonian Institution, No. 4338), measure 2.55 by 1.70 inches, and 2.50 by 1.70. Three from Fort Rae (No. 5032), Great Slave Lake, are of a deeper green, and measure, two, 2.35 by 1.70 inches, and one 2.30 by 1.70.

Clangula albeola.

THE BUFFLE-HEADED DUCK; BUTTER-BALL.

Anas albeola, LINN. S. N. ed. 10, I. 1758, 124; ed. 12, I. 1766, 199. — WILS. Am. Orn. VIII. 1814, 51, pl. 62, figs. 2, 3.
Fuligula albeola, BONAP. Synop. 1828, 394. — NUTT. Man. II. 1834, 445. — AUD. Orn. Biog. IV. 1838, 217, pl. 225; Synop. 1839, 293; B. Am. VI. 1843, 369, pl. 408.
Clangula albeola, STEPHENS, Shaw's Gen. Zool. XII. ii. 1824, 184. — SW. & RICH. F. B. A. II. 1831, 458. — RIDGW. Nom. N. Am. B. 1881, no. 621. — COUES, Check List, 2d ed. 1882, no. 727.
Bucephala albeola, BAIRD, B. N. Am. 1858, 797; Cat. N. Am. B. 1859, no. 595. — COUES, Key, 1872, 290; Check List, 1873, no. 507; Birds N. W. 1874, 577.
Anas bucephala, LINN. S. N. ed. 10, I. 1758, 125; ed. 12, I. 1766, 200 (♂).
Anas rustica, LINN. tt. c. 125, 201 (♀).

HAB. North America, breeding northerly; migrating south in winter to Cuba and Mexico.

SP. CHAR. *Adult male:* Head and upper half of the neck rich silky metallic green, violet-

C. albeola.

purple and greenish bronze, the last prevailing on the lower part of the neck, the green on the anterior part of the head, the purple on the cheeks and crown; a large patch of pure white on the side of the head, extending from the eye back to and around the occiput; lower half of the neck, lower parts generally, wing-coverts, secondaries, and outer scapulars pure white, the latter narrowly, and the feathers of the flanks more widely, edged with black; posterior parts of the body beneath tinged with pale ash-gray; upper tail-coverts light hoary gray; tail slate-gray, the shafts black. Bill bluish plumbeous, dusky on the nail and at base; iris very dark brown; legs and feet pinkish, or lilaceous, white. Total length, about 14.50 inches; extent, 24.50; wing, 6.75–6.90; culmen, 1.10–1.15; tarsus, 1.30; middle toe, 1.90–2.00. *Adult female:* Head, neck, and upper parts generally dusky grayish brown; an oblong or somewhat ovate white longitudinal patch on the auricular region, and the inner secondaries (sometimes also the greater wing-coverts, except at ends), white; lower parts white, tinged with brownish gray posteriorly, anteriorly, and laterally. Bill dusky, inclining to plumbeous at end and along commissure; iris very dark brown; legs and toes dilute lilac-pink, the webs and joints darker. Length, about 12.50 inches; extent, 21.00; wing, 5.90–6.00; culmen, .95–1.00; tarsus, 1.15–1.20; middle toe, 1.75.

Male.

There is very little variation among the males of this species. The females vary in the markings of the wing, some having the greater coverts white, tipped with dusky; while in others only the inner secondaries are white.

This species, peculiar to this continent, but of accidental or occasional occurrence in Europe, has an extended distribution throughout North America, being found in winter in the more southern States, in the West India Islands, and on both coasts of Mexico. It goes as far north as Greenland on the northeast, and Alaska on the northwest, coast.

An adult female specimen was obtained at Godthaab, in Greenland, by the elder Reinhardt. Mr. Bernard Ross met with it throughout the whole valley of the Mackenzie, to the very mouth of that river. It was taken on the Saskatchewan by Captain Blakiston, who also received it from Hudson's Bay.

Female (natural size).

This species is said by Dr. Richardson to frequent the rivers and fresh-water lakes throughout the Fur Countries in great numbers. It is very far from being shy, will allow the sportsman to approach quite near, and then dives so dexterously at the flash of the gun, and is so very difficult to kill, that the natives believe it to possess supernatural powers, and call it the "Spirit Duck."

Mr. Dall mentions it as not uncommon on the Yukon, where it breeds. It is abundant at the mouth of the Yukon River, where there are no trees except scrubby willows and alders, and it probably breeds there. Specimens were obtained by Mr. Bischoff at Sitka. It was found on Vancouver Island by Mr. R. Browne.

Dr. Cooper writes that he has found this little Duck very abundant throughout California, and that he has traced it as far north as latitude 49° during the colder months. It arrives in California about October, and remains as far south as San Diego as late as April 20. It is known to frequent both fresh and salt water; and seems to obtain an abundance of food everywhere, becoming so very fat as to acquire the general appellation of "Butter-ball." Its expertness in diving enables it to obtain food in deep water more readily than most other Ducks.

Dr. Gundlach mentions this species as a visitant to Cuba; and Major Wedderburn states that it is occasionally observed in Bermuda in the winter. Mr. Dresser received the skin of a male bird which had been taken at Fort Stockton; and he was informed that specimens were occasionally found at the Boca del Rio, in Southwestern Texas.

Mr. Boardman informs me that this Duck is occasionally found in the neighborhood of Calais, where a few remain and breed, nesting in trees. It is rare, however, and he has not met with its nest. In Massachusetts it is more or less common from September to April, being absent only during the severest weather, and in mild winters remaining throughout the season.

This species is variously known as the "Dipper," from its dexterity in diving, the "Buffle-head," from the apparently disproportionate size of its neck and head, as well as "Butter-box" or "Butter-ball," and "Spirit Duck." Mr. Giraud states that he has met with it in various parts of the United States, and has found it during the spring and autumn dispersed throughout the Union, visiting the interior as well as the sea-coast. It dives so dexterously that it can be shot only with the greatest difficulty when sitting on the water. It is an excellent swimmer, and flies swiftly, when on the wing uttering a deep guttural note. Its food consists chiefly of small fish. It is generally in fine condition, but is not considered a superior bird for the table. It is generally met with in pairs until the appearance of spring, when it is seen in small flocks. It arrives in Long Island in October, and remains until the latter part of April, when it leaves for the north. On the coast of New Jersey it is most generally known either as the "Butter-box," or "Butter-ball." A writer in "Doughty's Cabinet" (I. 41), who claims to have studied the habits of this Duck on the waters of Chesapeake Bay and its tributaries, states that it makes its first appearance in the upper part of that bay as early as the first or second week in October. It is said to be one of the very first Ducks to make its appearance in those waters. The taste of its flesh varies greatly, according to the different conditions under which the bird has lived, being at times very fishy, but occasionally having a very fine flavor.

Mr. Lockhart met with this Duck on the Yukon River, where, by a mere accident, he found its nest, concealed in the hollow of a rotten stump of a tree near the bank of that stream, and containing nine eggs. The female was supposed to have been killed, incubation not having begun. This was presumed to have been her second nest, the eggs having been taken from the first. Another nest was met with by Mr. Lockhart in the hollow of a poplar-tree about twenty feet from the ground; it was found near the Black River on the 7th of July. The hole was dug out in the same manner as a Woodpecker's, and was an arm's length in depth, containing ten eggs. A third nest was in the hollow of a dead tree near a lake, and only five feet from the ground. These nests had no other lining than down. The number of eggs was usually nine or ten; in one instance only six.

Audubon met with this species on the 11th of May, 1833, near Eastport, in Maine. During the period of its movement toward the north he found it exceedingly abundant on the waters of the Bay of Fundy. The males in flocks, and in their full summer dress, preceded the females about a fortnight. In the vicinity of New Orleans this species is known as the "Marionette." He met with it, during extremely cold weather, on the Ohio, when the river was thickly covered with floating ice, among which it was seen diving, almost constantly, in search of food. When the river was frozen over, these birds sought the head-waters of rapid streams, and in their turbulent eddies found an abundance of food. Apparently feeling secure in the rapidity with which they can dive, they allow a very near approach; but at the first snap of the gun dive with the quickness of thought, and often as quickly rise again within a few yards of the same spot. Their flight is usually low, and made by regularly repeated beats of the wings; and it is surprisingly rapid — equalling in rapidity that of the Hooded Merganser. Its note is a mere croak, resembling that of the Golden-eye, but feebler. Its food is varied, according to the situation. On the sea-coast and on the estuaries it obtains, by diving, small fry, shrimps, bivalve-shells, and mollusks; in fresh water, small crayfish, leeches, snails, grasses, and other water-plants.

Professor Kumlien informs me that this species is abundant in Southern Wisconsin both in the fall and in the spring, but that none remain there during the summer. Eggs taken in Iowa, and purporting to be of this species, have been widely distributed; but this is a more southern locality, and they are, therefore, not so likely to be authentic as those from farther north; and all that I have seen of these are the eggs of *Q. discors,* bearing but slight resemblance in shade or size to those of *B. albeola.* Mr. B. F. Goss, of Pewaukee, Wis., informs me that the young of this species, still unable to fly, have been killed in Pewaukee Lake — this being the only instance of its being there in the breeding-season which has come to his knowledge.

The Buffle-head was found breeding at Fort Resolution by Mr. Kennicott, May 19; the nest was in a hollow tree. The following year, May 8, 1861, Mr. Kennicott also found it breeding on the Yukon River, in which locality its nests were obtained by Mr. Lockhart, who also procured them on Porcupine River. This species was found breeding at Fort Simpson by Mr. B. R. Ross; at Fort Rae by the younger Mr. Clarke; and at Fort Yukon by Mr. Lockhart.

Dr. Berlandier, in his manuscript notes, speaks of this species as occurring in winter on the borders of the rivers and marshes in the State of Tamaulipas, Mexico. In the spring it retires to the north, and reappears at the beginning of winter.

In March, 1855 — as Dr. Kennerly, in his Notes on the Birds observed on the Mexican Boundary Survey, mentions — this Duck was found in abundance at the Boca Grande, in Chihuahua, in flocks; and also at other points on the Conalitos and Janos rivers.

Eggs of this species from the Yukon River (Smithsonian Institution, No. 9550) are of a grayish ivory-white color, with a quite distinct tinge of green. They vary considerably in size; and in some specimens this greenish tinge is much deeper than in others. The smaller-sized eggs of this species, with only very faint tintings of green, approach in appearance the eggs of the Blue-winged Teal; and in collecting, the latter egg has been substituted for the rarer one of the Buffle-head. The following are the measurements of four specimens: 2.00 by 1.45 inches; 2.05 by 1.50; 1.95 by 1.35; 1.95 by 1.45.

GENUS **HISTRIONICUS**, LESSON.

Histrionicus, LESS. Man. II. 1828, 415 (type, *Anas histrionica,* LINN.).
Cosmonessa, KAUP, Entw. Europ. Thierw. 1829, 46 (same type).
Cosmonetta, KAUP, t. c., 196.
Phlyaconetta, BRANDT, Mem. Ac. St. Petersb. VI. 1849, 4 (same type).
"*Phylaconetta,* BRANDT," BAIRD et COUES.

CHAR. Most like *Clangula.* Bill very small (shorter than the tarsus), the lateral outlines converging rapidly to the tip, which is occupied entirely by the very large nail; depth of the maxilla at the base about equal to its width; lamellæ entirely hidden by the overhanging maxillary tomium; upper basal portion of the maxilla forming a decided angle, inserted between the feathering of the forehead and that of the lores, the former reaching rather farther forward; a slight membraneous lobe at the lower base of the maxilla, overhanging the rictus. Tail rather long (more than half the wing), much graduated, consisting of fourteen feathers. Plumage of the sexes very different, the male very handsomely marked, the female very sombre.

H. minutus.

But a single species of this well-marked genus is known. This, the well-known Harlequin Duck, is common to both continents of the northern hemisphere, where it inhabits chiefly high latitudes.

Histrionicus minutus.

THE HARLEQUIN DUCK.

Anas histrionica, LINN. S. N. ed. 10, I. 1758, 127 ; ed. 12, I. 1766, 204. — WILS. Am. Orn. VIII. 1814, 139, pl. 72, fig. 4.

Fuligula (Clangula) histrionica, BONAP. Synop. 1828, 394. — NUTT. Man. II. 1834, 448.

Fuligula histrionica, AUD. Orn. Biog. III. 1835, 612 ; V. 1839, 617 ; Synop. 1839, 617 ; B. Am. VI. 1843, 374, pl. 409.

Clangula torquata, BREHM, Vogelf. 1855, 385.

Histrionicus torquatus, BONAP. Compt. Rend. XLIII. 1856. — BAIRD, B. N. Am. 1858, 798 ; Cat. N. Am. B. 1859, no. 596. — COUES, Key, 1872, 291 ; Check List, 1873, no. 510 ; B. N. W. 1874, 578.

Anas minuta, LINN. S. N. ed. 10, I. 1758, 127 ; ed. 12, I. 1766, 204 (♀).

Histrionicus minutus, DRESSER, Birds of Europe (in text). — COUES, Bull. Nutt. Orn. Club, V. Apr. 1880, 101; Check List, 2d ed. 1882, no. 730. — RIDGW. Nom. N. Am. B. 1881, no. 622.

HAB. Northern North America ; south in winter to the Middle States and California ; breeding south to Newfoundland, the Northern Rocky Mountains, and in the Sierra Nevada to lat. 38° or farther.

SP. CHAR. *Adult male:* Entire loral region, continued back, from its upper part, in a stripe on each side of the crown, an oval spot over the ears, a stripe of a little more than an inch in length down each side of the nape, a narrow collar completely encircling the lower neck, a broad bar across each side of the breast, the middle portion (longitudinally) of the outer scapulars, the greater part of the tertials, a spot near the tip of the greater wing-coverts, and a small spot on each side of the crissum, at the base of the tail, white. A broad longitudinal stripe on each side of the crown and occiput, with entire sides and flanks, bright rufous. Head and neck, except as described, dark plumbeous, with a faint violaceous cast, becoming gradually black along the border of the white markings ; pileum with a mesial stripe of blue-black extending from the base of the culmen to the occiput. Back, jugulum, and sides of the breast bluish plumbeous, the white collar and the white bar on the sides of the breast bordered on each side by deep blue-black; rump, upper tail-coverts, and crissum deep blue-black; abdomen dark sooty grayish, blending insensibly into the plumbeous of the breast and the black of the crissum, but distinctly defined against the rufous of the sides and flanks; wing-coverts plumbeous-slate; primaries and rectrices dusky black; secondaries ("speculum") metallic dark violet-blue; tertials white, the outer webs edged with

Female (natural size).

black, the inner with dark plumbeous. Bill light yellowish olive, the extreme tip paler; iris reddish brown; feet pale-bluish, the webs dusky, the claws whitish. *Immature male (2d year?):* Pattern of the head-markings same as in the preceding, but the plumbeous much duller, the black stripe of the pileum dusky, the rufous on the sides of the crown and occiput wanting, or but faintly indicated. Upper parts in general nearly uniform dusky grayish brown, without well-defined white anywhere, no blue-black, and the speculum dull dusky brownish gray, with little, if any, gloss. Lower parts grayish white, each feather marked with a subterminal transverse spot of grayish brown, the sides, flanks, and crissum nearly uniform grayish brown; no rufous on sides or flanks, and collar round the lower neck imperfect, or only slightly indicated. *Adult female:* Somewhat similar to the male, but the head, neck, and jugulum grayish brown, with a distinct white spot on the auricular region, and the lores and sides of the forehead inclining to white. Jugulum, sides, flanks, and crissum entirely uniform grayish brown. "Bill and feet dull bluish gray; iris brown" (AUDUBON). *Young:* Similar to the adult female, but above browner and more uniform, the jugulum, sides, flanks, and crissum tinged with umber.

Male.

Total length, about 17.50 inches; extent, 27.00; wing, 7.40 to nearly 8.00; culmen, 1.05–1.10; tarsus, 1.50; middle toe, 2.00. Female slightly smaller.

The Harlequin Duck seems to be nowhere a common species, but to be found chiefly in the more northern or mountainous regions of both continents during the summer, appearing only occasionally here and there on the sea-coasts, and upon open interior waters at very irregular periods, and usually only singly or in pairs. In reference to the geographical range of this species in the Palæarctic Region, Professor Alfred Newton is of the opinion that, with the exception of Iceland and Eastern Asia, it occurs only as an accidental straggler on that continent. It is not known as a bird of Lapland; it has not been ascertained to occur in European Russia, but is simply accidental on the Caspian Sea and on the Sea of Aral. It is also said to be met with about Lake Baikal, and it was found by Middendorff only in the extreme eastern portion of Siberia. It is also a regular visitor to Japan.

Dr. Walker mentions having obtained specimens of this Duck near Godthaab, on the coast of Greenland; and it is also given by Professor Reinhardt as a resident species of that island. Mr. Bernard Ross found it on the Mackenzie River. Captain Blakiston met with it also at York Factory, on Hudson's Bay. It was found at Vancouver by Mr. R. Browne. It occurs occasionally upon Lake Michigan in winter, but it is not frequently observed there.

Sir John Richardson states that this Duck is found, although very rarely, in the Fur Region, where it haunts the eddies below waterfalls and similar localities in rapid streams. It is a very vigilant bird, taking wing at once on being disturbed; and it has never been found associating with any other species of Duck.

Mr. Dall states that the Harlequin Duck was obtained both at Sitka and at Kadiak by Mr. Bischoff, and that it was found to be rather rare in the vicinity of the Yukon River. He speaks of it as an essentially solitary species, found either alone or in pairs, and only in the most retired spots, on the small rivers flowing into the Yukon; localities of this kind being those in which it breeds. It was never found on the main river, except apparently by accident. Mr. Dall afterward met with it at Unalashka, where it appeared to be rather common as a winter visitant, remaining there later than most of the Ducks; and some individuals of this species seemed to reside and breed there. He also speaks of it as not rare at the Shumagins in summer.

Specimens were obtained near Fort Resolution, in May and June, by Mr. Kennicott; at Fort Simpson and the St. Pierre House, by Mr. B. R. Ross; near Fort Halkett, by Mr. Lockhart; at Fort Rae and on the Barren Lands, by Mr. Clarke; at Nulato and on the Lower Yukon, by Mr. Dall; and at Kadiak, by Mr. Bischoff.

According to the observations of Dr. Suckley, the Harlequin Duck was found sparingly on the waters of Puget Sound, not going far inland, but remaining near the Straits of Fuca. As individuals have been taken there in May and September, it is not unlikely that some of this species wander down the coast, during the colder months, as far as California.

This Duck is common, as Mr. Boardman informs me, in the neighborhood of Eastport, Me., during the winter months, but is not supposed to breed anywhere in that vicinity. It was formerly not uncommon in winter on the coast of Massachusetts, and specimens were occasionally seen in the Boston markets from 1835 to 1840. Since then it has been comparatively rare.

On the coast of Long Island, as stated by Mr. Giraud, the Harlequin Duck is very rarely seen. Indeed, he never met with other than immature specimens in that vicinity. He was, however, informed by several of the more experienced of the Bay hunters that, a number of years before, the appearance of adults of this species was not an uncommon event. The flesh of this Duck was said to be very excellent eating.

Professor Newton's conjecture that this Duck would be found to be a native of Japan was verified by Mr. H. Whitely, who obtained a specimen in the Harbor of Hakodadi, December 23.

Mr. C. W. Shepard, in his interesting account of his journey in Iceland, makes mention of his finding the Harlequin Duck breeding in that island. So far as his observations went, this bird seemed to confine itself to the River Laxa, where it was found by him breeding in holes in trees on the banks. He met with it in great numbers in the northwestern portion of Iceland, but found it only on the most rapid streams and rivers.

According to Yarrell, it is a rare and occasional visitor to the British coast. Two specimens were shot, in 1802, on the coast of Scotland; another was afterward taken on the Orkneys — where, however, it is very rare. According to Vieillot, it has been taken on the coasts of France and Germany; Nilsson says it visits Sweden.

Mr. Hewitson figures an egg of this species brought from Iceland by Mr. G. C. Atkinson, of Newcastle, who is said to have found a nest containing seven or eight eggs, deposited in a bed of the bird's down, upon the grass bordering the margin of a shallow lake — a position quite different from that of the nests seen by Mr. Shepard. The egg is described as being of a pale buff tinged with green, and 2.13 inches long, by 1.63 in breadth.

In the "Zoologist" for 1850 Mr. J. J. Briggs publishes an interesting account of the breeding of a pair of this species in confinement in the Melbourne Gardens in Derbyshire. Although they had been kept there for several years, they did not breed until 1849. In these grounds, at a considerable distance from the pool, where the birds had usually lived, and in a retired part, was an ice-house, against which some thatch-sheaves had been placed. Upon these, sheltered from wet and sun, at a height of three feet, the pair formed a nest. This was simply a depression in the thatch, made very soft and warm by being lined with down plucked from the parent bird. The nest contained eight eggs, which were hatched about the middle of June. These eggs are described as being similar in color to those of the European Partridge. When the female left them to feed, she carefully covered them up with down. After feeding, she was always escorted back to her nest by the male bird — who, however, took no share in sitting on the eggs. Several of the young Ducks were reared, but the female died.

I am constrained to believe that Audubon's account of this bird and of its presence on our Atlantic coast is full of error. That it breeds, or has ever bred, on Seal, Grand Menan, or White-head islands, is contrary to all the information I have been able to obtain, after the most careful scrutiny. The gentleman who had Audubon's party in charge assured me that during nearly fifty years' experience he has never seen the "Lord and Lady Ducks," as these are there called, except in winter. He was sure that none were seen when Audubon was there, and that the nests taken at White-head Islands were those of the Red-breasted Merganser. My informant also assured me that he had never met with this Duck on the coast of Labrador, but that he had been told by trappers who had penetrated into the interior that it is found only on the edge of mountain-streams or of elevated ponds and lakes, and even then rarely. Its nest was unknown to him, nor had he ever heard of its having been met with by others.

Several years since, Dr. Hayden captured in the Rocky Mountains a female Harlequin Duck having a fully formed egg in her oviduct — proving that this species probably breeds somewhere within our limits.

In the summer of 1874 Dr. Coues found several pairs of these Ducks, with the young still following the mother, in the Rocky Mountains, near Chief Mountain Lake, in the northwestern corner of Montana, lat. 49°. He saw them on some small pools about the lakes, and also on a brawling mountain-brook — these being just such places as would be inhabited by a Dipper. This was in the latter part of August. One old bird, and several young ones still unable to fly, were secured. Some were killed with stones by the soldiers. The nest itself was not discovered. The birds noticed on the mountain-brook, when alarmed, dived and swam entirely under water, or with only the head exposed, — much like a Grebe. In one instance a bird took refuge in a quiet spot behind a sheet of water that formed a little cascade.

Mr. Edwin Carter informs me that this species breeds in Colorado, though its eggs or nest have not been seen. In the summer of 1876 he met with a pair with young just from the shell.

Mr. Henry W. Elliott mentions finding these Ducks common on and around the shores of the Prybilof Islands, where they were idly floating amid the surf in flocks of fifty or sixty, or basking and preening their feathers on the beaches and outlying rocks. They were to be seen all the year round, excepting only when forced away by the ice-floes. Their nests, however, eluded his search; and although he was quite confident that they bred either on the rocky beaches or on the high ridges inland, the natives themselves were entirely unacquainted with their eggs. Mr. Elliott's experience in relation to this bird differs, it will be observed, from that of most naturalists who have met with it, since these represent it as essentially solitary, and as being generally found either alone or in pairs. Those birds seen by Mr. Elliott were not particularly wild or shy, and numbers were killed by the natives every fall and spring. This species is said to be remarkably silent; he heard from it no cry whatever during the entire year. It seemed to be decidedly gregarious, solitary pairs never straying away from the flock: the females apparently outnumbered the males two to one.

Professor Kumlien informs me that hunters have repeatedly given him descriptions of a Duck corresponding in the peculiarities of its plumage with no other species than this, and said to occur in the lakes of Southern Wisconsin; but he had never met with it himself. He mentions seeing three examples of this species, one of which was secured at Annaanaatook. This was not an uncommon bird in the Godthaab district, on the Greenland coast.

According to Mr. L. Belding, "several pairs of this Duck breed every summer on the Stanislaus River, Calaveras Co., Cal., as low down as four thousand feet altitude, and perhaps lower." At this locality Mr. Belding saw, on June 30, 1881, two flocks, consisting of young birds with their parents, the former at least a month old; July 5, 1881, five flocks, also consisting of young and old, were seen; and July 20, another flock. Mr. Belding further remarks that this is the only species of Duck he has seen in that part of the country in summer, while he also favors us with the following notes: "These birds, young and old, tumble over and through rapids and cascades in an astonishing manner. The crop and gizzard of one I dissected were full of insects, partly, if not principally, the Caddis Fly; and I could not ascertain that it had been eating fish, although shot in a trout-stream. The flesh, while not a luxury, is not offensive to taste or smell. Wilson praises it; but as he also praises the flesh of the Ruddy Duck (*Erismatura rubida*) and that of the Shoveller (*Spatula clypeata*), I am reminded not only that tastes differ, but also that birds may vary in the flavor of their flesh, according to food or other causes; for certain it is that the two last-mentioned Ducks are considered very inferior food on the Pacific coast."

The eggs of this Duck are of a rounded oval form, measure 2.20 inches by 1.70, and are of a dark brownish-gray color.

Genus **HARELDA**, Leach.

Harelda, Leach, Steph. Gen. Zool. XII. 1824, 174 (type, *Anas glacialis*, Linn.).
Pagonetta, Kaup, Ent. Europ. Thierw. 1829, 66 (same type).
Crymonessa, Macg. Man. Brit. Orn. II. 1842, 185 (same type).
Melonetta, Sund. Teut. 1872, 149 (same type).

CHAR. Bill small (much shorter than the tarsus), all its outlines tapering rapidly to the end, which is occupied entirely by the very large broad nail; lower edge of the maxilla nearly straight for the basal half, then suddenly rising to the prominently decurved nail; lamellæ slightly exposed along the straight basal portion of the maxillary tomium; feathering at the base of the bill forming a nearly straight oblique line, advancing farthest forward on the forehead, and scarcely interrupted by any re-entrant angle, so prominent in most Ducks. Adult male with the longer scapulars elongated and lanceolate, the rectrices (14 in number) acute, the middle pair slender and greatly lengthened.

H. hyemalis (winter plumage).

The most important peculiarity of structure in this well-marked genus consists in the almost unique outline of the feathering at the base of the bill, this outline advancing gradually farther forward from the rictus to the base of the culmen, the continuity of the slightly curved line interrupted by only a very faint, sometimes scarcely perceptible, indentation at the place of the deep angle seen in most Ducks. The only other genus showing an approach to this character is *Camptolæmus*, which, however, has the bill and other features very different.

But a single species is known, which, like *Histrionicus*, is circumpolar in its distribution, but descending to lower latitudes in winter.

Harelda hyemalis.

THE LONG-TAILED DUCK; OLD SQUAW.

Anas hyemalis, LINN. S. N. ed. 10, I. 1758, 126; ed. 12, I. 1766, 202.
Anas hiemalis, BRÜNN. Orn. Bor. 1764, 17.
Anas glacialis, LINN. S. N. ed. 12, I. 1766, 203. — WILS. Am. Orn. VIII. 1814, 93, 96, pl. 70.
Harelda glacialis, "LEACH," STEPHENS, Shaw's Gen. Zool. XII. ii. 1824, 175, pl. 58. — SW. & RICH. F. B. A. II. 1831, 460. — BAIRD, B. N. Am. 1858, 800; Cat. N. Am. B. 1859, no. 597. — COUES, Key, 1872, 291; Check List, 1873, no. 508; 2d ed. 1882, no. 728; B. N. W. 1874, 579. — RIDGW. Nom. N. Am. B. 1881, no. 623.
Fuligula (Harelda) glacialis, NUTT. Man. II. 1834, 453.
Fuligula glacialis, AUD. Orn. Biog. IV. 1838, 403, pl. 312; Synop. 1839, 295; B. Am. VI. 1843, 379, pl. 410.
Anas miclonia, BODD. Tabl. P. E. 1783, 58.
Anas longicauda, LEACH, Syst. Cat. Mam. and Birds, Brit. Mus. 1816, 37.
Anas brachyrhynchos, BESEKE, Vög. Kurl. 1792, 50.
Platypus Faberi, BREHM, Lerb. Eur. Vög. II. 1824, 1004.
Clangula Faberi, meguaros, musica, brachyrhynchos, BREHM, V. D. 1831, 935, 936, 937, 938.

HAB. Northern hemisphere; in America, south to the Potomac River and the Ohio; chiefly littoral.

Sp. Char. *Adult male, in winter:* Forehead, crown, occiput, nape, chin, throat, lower part of the neck (all round), and upper part of the jugulum and back, white; lores, cheeks, and orbital region light mouse-gray, the eyelids white; a large oblong space covering the sides of the neck, black, becoming light grayish brown in its lower portion. Middle of the back, rump, upper tail-coverts, tail, wings, lower part of the jugulum, whole breast, and upper part of the abdomen, black; the pectoral area very abruptly defined both anteriorly and posteriorly — the latter with a strongly convex outline. Scapulars glaucous-white or very pale pearl-gray; posterior lower parts white, the sides strongly shaded with pearl-gray. Basal half of the bill black, the terminal portion orange-yellow, with the nail bluish gray; iris bright carmine; feet light plumbeous, the webs dusky, and claws black. "The outer half of the bill rich orange-yellow, that color extending to the base along the ridge, the unguis and the basal half black, as well as the unguis and edges of the lower mandible" (Audubon). *Adult male, in summer:* Lores, cheeks, and sides of the forehead, pale mouse-gray; eyelids, and a postocular longitudinal space, white; rest of the head, whole neck, and upper parts generally sooty-black; upper part of the back more or less variegated with fulvous; scapulars widely edged with the same, varying on some feathers to ochraceous and pale buff. Breast and upper part of the abdomen dark sooty-grayish, abruptly defined behind with a semicircular outline, as in the winter plumage; remaining lower parts white, shaded on the sides with pale pearl-gray. Bill black, crossed, in front of the nostrils, by a wide band of orange; iris yellowish brown; feet bluish black, the joints and under surface of the webs black.[1]

Male, winter plumage.

Adult female, in winter: Head, neck, and lower parts, chiefly white; forehead, medially, and crown, dusky; auricular region, chin, and throat, tinged with the same; jugulum light dingy gray. Upper parts dusky brown, the scapulars bordered with grayish fulvous or light raw-umber brown, some of the feathers tipped with pale ashy. *Adult female, in summer:* Head and neck dark grayish brown, with a large space surrounding the eye, and another on the side of the neck, grayish white; upper parts as in the winter plumage, but upper part of the back variegated with light brown, the scapulars chiefly of this color, with the central portion dusky. "Bill and feet dusky green; iris yellow" (Audubon). *Young:* Somewhat similar to the winter female, but much more uniform above, with scarcely any lighter borders to the scapulars, the head and neck light brownish gray, darker on the pileum, and indistinctly whitish before and behind the eye.

Male, summer plumage.

Downy young:[2] Above, uniform dark hair-brown, relieved only on side of head by a grayish white space on lower eyelid, a similar but smaller spot immediately above the eye, a light brownish

[1] Fresh colors of No. 67837, ♂ ad., St. Michael's, Alaska; L. M. Turner. Audubon describes the fresh colors of bill, etc., in the summer ♂ of this species as follows: "Bill black in its basal half, orange-yellow toward the end, the unguis bluish-gray. Iris bright carmine. Feet light bluish-gray, the webs dusky, claws black."

[2] Described from specimens obtained at Point Barrow, Alaska (Arctic coast), by Messrs. Murdoch

gray loral stripe, and a light brownish gray postocular spot; brown on side of head forming a broad stripe from the rictus back to occiput. Lower parts white, interrupted only by a distinct jugular collar of sooty hair-brown. Bill and feet dusky (in dried skins).

Adult male: Total length, about 23 inches; extent, 30.00; wing, 8.50–9.00; tail, 8.00–8.50; culmen, 1.10; tarsus, 1.35; middle toe, 1.90. *Female,* smaller, the total length considerably less, owing chiefly to the abbreviation of the middle rectrices.

This bird, variously known as the "Long-tailed Duck" of authors, the "Old Wife" and the "Old Squaw" of hunters, the "South-south Southerly" of some localities — the last name being derived from its peculiar jabbering note — is an Arctic species of universal distribution in all the northern portion of the globe. It is Arctic in its summer abode, and in the winter is found on the sea-coasts of America, Europe, and Asia as far south as latitude 35° N.

According to Dr. Bessels, this Duck was seen in the "Polaris" Expedition, under Captain Hall; and Mr. Fielden, in his enumeration of the birds obtained by him in 1875–1876, mentions observing a flock in the pools of water between the floes on the 1st of September, 1875, near Floeberg Beach (lat. 82° 27′ N.). During the summer of 1876 a few of these birds visited the northern shores of Grinnell Land, where they were found in pairs on lakes and ponds, and were evidently breeding.

Dr. Walker met with this species on the coast of Greenland, near Godthaab; and afterward — early in June — noticed it assembling in the pools of water near the shore at Bellot's Strait. Professor Reinhardt also gives it as one of the resident species of Greenland. Mr. Murray met with it at Hudson's Bay, and Captain Blakiston also received it from the same region. Mr. Bernard Ross found it abundant along the whole course of the Mackenzie River.

Professor Newton did not meet with it on Spitzbergen, though this species is known to occur there as a regular visitant — not, however, in great numbers. It is found there as far north as Depot Holm, latitude 80° N., where Dr. Malmgren saw a female bird. He also noticed a pair in Kobbe Bay, May 28, 1861; and, Aug. 1, 1864, he met with a group of five on a small pool of fresh water on one of the islands in Horn Sound. Mr. Gillett found it common in Matthews' Strait, Nova Zembla, but did not meet with it elsewhere. In the same region Von Heuglin found it quite common everywhere. It was especially abundant in shallow places, under the cliffs, on the sea, on fresh-water pools, and at the mouths of rivers. The stomachs of those captured were found to contain chiefly univalve shells — a species of *Natica.*

Mr. C. W. Shepard found this species breeding in great abundance in different parts of Iceland. In one instance he met with quite a number nesting on a small island in the Lake of Mý-vatn. This island was only about sixty yards in circumference, was quite flat, and covered with a long brown grass, and on it he counted more than twenty nests. The Long-tailed Ducks and the Scaup Ducks (*F. marila*) alone

and Smith. A specimen labelled *H. glacialis,* collected by R. MacFarlane on the Arctic coast, July 12, 1864, is quite different, and probably belongs to another species. Its characters are as follows: —

Downy young: (No. 44138, U. S. Nat. Mus., Arctic America, "B. W. C.," July 12, 1864; R. MacFarlane): Above, hair-brown or grayish umber, relieved by a longitudinal oblong spot of dull grayish white on each side the back (behind the wings), and a much smaller spot of the same on each side of the base of the tail; wings brown, like the back, with a small, inconspicuous, spot of dull light grayish on the bend, and one on the posterior border. Pileum and nape like the back, but darker; remainder of the head and neck, with entire lower parts, dull light grayish, the breast and abdomen nearly white; lores and cheeks strongly tinged with hair-brown; a narrow stripe of darker brown before and behind the eye.

According to Audubon, the "young when newly excluded are covered with stiffish down. Bill and feet greenish dusky; the upper parts chocolate-brown, a small spot of white under the eye; throat and lower parts whitish, as well as an oblong patch on the cheeks."

occupied this island. Nearly all these birds forsook their nests as soon as the boat touched the shore; but a few would not stir until actually driven away. Among the latter were two Ducks — a Scaup and a Long-tail; these were sitting together on the same nest, in which were several eggs of the two species, readily distinguishable from each other by their difference in color, size, and shape. All the nests of the Long-tailed Duck were filled with down, which appeared but little inferior to that of the Eider.

Mr. Dall found this Duck extremely abundant on the sea-coast of Alaska. It was very common in the fall of 1865 at St. Michael's, where it was one of the last Ducks to leave. It was, however, rare on the Yukon River. A single specimen was killed, June 1, 1868, at Nulato, when the river was full of floating ice. Mr. Dall describes this bird as being an expert diver, and hard to shoot, except on the wing. He noticed it breeding abundantly on every beach, in a very simple nest without any lining. He also found it in large numbers resident in the Aleutian Islands, and exhibiting a great variety in the colors of its plumage; the same thing was noticed on the Yukon. Although this Duck is mentioned by Dr. Newberry as being a rare visitor on the coast of California, Dr. Cooper thinks that probably it is never met with there at all. It is, however, quite common on the Columbia River in the winter, and probably goes much farther south. Rarely appearing on fresh water, it frequents the most open bays, and feeds upon shellfish and marine plants.

On Norton Sound, Alaska, according to Mr. Adams ("Ibis," 1878), it makes its first appearance about the 7th of May, but by no means in large numbers, and generally only in pairs. It breeds about the inland marshes, its nest resembling that of other Sea-Ducks; the eggs being nine in number, and of a dark olive-green color. The name of this bird in the Eski dialect is *Ad-le-guk-lú-luk.*

Sir John Richardson speaks of finding this Duck abundant in the Arctic Sea, associating with the *Oidemiæ*, remaining in the north as long as it can find open water, and assembling in very large flocks previous to migrating. During its progress south it halts both on the shores of Hudson's Bay and among the inland lakes, and is one of the last of the birds of passage to quit the Fur Countries. In the latter part of August, when a thin crust of ice forms during the night on the Arctic Sea, the female may often be seen breaking a way with her wings for her young brood. This bird is called by the Canadians the "*Cacca-wee,*" and is by far the most noisy of all the Ducks.

Mr. Hearne, writing about a century ago, speaks of the birds of this species as visiting Hudson's Bay in great numbers, and as extending their range from the sea-coast to the remotest West. They were found in vast multitudes near Cumberland House. At their first arrival they are excellent eating; but when they are moulting, though very fat, they are generally so rank that few Europeans can tolerate them.

This species is very abundant during the winter off the coast of Maine, and indeed on all the New England sea-shore, and occurs in great numbers in all the bays and estuaries between Eastport and Long Island. It leaves the northern regions in large flocks, which gradually separate into smaller parties, and in the course of the winter are distributed along the entire Atlantic region. It is a watchful and vigilant bird, very difficult of approach, and quite expert in diving, passing so rapidly under the water that shooting it is almost impossible. It can be best approached by sailing down upon it or by gradually drifting among the flock in a boat unpropelled by oars, the occupants keeping concealed. On the wing it is one of the swiftest of its tribe, and one of those birds most difficult to shoot. As a general thing its flesh is tough and fishy.

It is known in the region of the Chesapeake as the "South-southerly," and it usually arrives in those waters between the middle and the last of October.

Audubon mentions that on the borders of a large fresh-water lake in Labrador, July 28, he met with several young broods of this species, carefully attended by their mothers. The lake was two miles from the sea, and not a male bird was in sight. He found several of the deserted nests, and all still contained the down which the mother had plucked from her breast to protect the eggs in her absence. The nests were under low bushes, among rank weeds, and not more than ten feet from the water. They were formed of coarse grass, with an upper layer of finer weeds, and lined with down. In one of them were two unhatched eggs. These measured 2.13 inches by 1.56. Audubon pursued, and at last caught, several of the young, which kept diving before him like so many water-witches, the mothers keeping aloof, but sounding their notes of alarm and admonition. The old birds did not dive, but seemed constantly to urge their young to do so; and he adds, the little things so profited by the advice of their parents, that had they remained in the water instead of making for the land, it would have been impossible for him, with all his exertions, to capture a single one.

The young remain in the ponds until the end of August, by which time they are able to fly, when they remove to the sea, and soon after leave the coast.

In Europe the Long-tailed Duck is chiefly known as an inhabitant of the more northern countries. To Great Britain it is only a winter visitant, coming in small numbers, except when the weather is unusually severe; and the birds arriving at such times are chiefly immature ones. This Duck appears rather often on the coast of Holland, occasionally visits the lakes of Germany, is rare on the coast of France, and is an irregular or accidental visitor in Italy. In the Orkneys it is known as the "*Calloo*," from a supposed resemblance of this word to the musical cry it utters when on the wing.

Mr. G. C. Atkinson describes a nest of this species, found by him in Iceland, as placed on the margin of a small lake, lined with down, which contained six eggs. Mr. Proctor found several nests in the same locality. They were generally among low bushes, by the edge of the fresh water, constructed of a few stems of grass, and lined with down. The number of eggs varied from six to twelve. These are described as of a pale greenish white, with a tinge of buff color.

The abundance of this species on our great lakes during the winter, especially on Michigan and such others as are free from ice, is a new and interesting point in its history. Mr. Nelson found it an exceedingly abundant winter resident in Michigan, and sparingly dispersed throughout Illinois during that season. A few stragglers come about the last of October; but the great body did not arrive before the 1st of December, departing on the 1st of April, although a few lingered until the last of that month. Professor Kumlien informs me that this Duck is frequently met with in winter as a straggler in the streams and lakes of Southern Wisconsin.

The food of this species varies with its feeding-grounds. In shallow water near the coast it collects mollusca, crustacea, fish, and marine insects. In a few instances the remains of the common mussel and shrimp are found. In the summer its stomach is usually filled with fresh-water insects.

The note of this species is one of its great peculiarities, and is very distinct from that of any other of the Ducks, being really musical when heard from a distance, especially if there are a large number of individuals joining in the refrain. The words *south-south southerly*, to my ear, do not in the least resemble the sounds this bird makes; they cannot be represented, or even imitated. The terms "Old Wives" and "Old Squaws," as applied to these Ducks, are not wholly inappropriate; since their gabble has an effect on the ear not very unlike that produced by the incoherent flow of words coming from many old women talking at once.

Mr. MacFarlane found this Duck breeding in immense numbers in the neighborhood of Fort Anderson, on the Lower Anderson River, on the Barren Grounds, and on the shores of the Arctic Sea. By far the greater proportion of the nests were in the vicinity of fresh water; but several were found on small islands, in Franklin, Liverpool, and Langdon bays, on the Arctic coast. They were all on the ground. In a few instances no down was seen in them, but only hay; and in these cases the eggs were invariably quite fresh. The eggs were generally found covered over with the down; but where this was wanting, with the hay. The eggs varied from five to seven, the latter being the largest number recorded in any one nest. The female was usually reluctant to leave her nest, and only rose when nearly approached. From his own personal observations, Mr. MacFarlane came to the conclusion that the usual quantity of down necessary for a Duck's nest is seldom met with before a full set of eggs has been deposited, and that the process of lining with down, which is plucked off from her body by the female, goes on simultaneously with their laying.

Mr. H. W. Elliott found this a very common resident species on the Prybilof Islands, and breeding in limited numbers on the lakelets of St. Paul's. He speaks of it as being a very noisy bird, particularly in spring, when, with the breaking-up of the ice, it comes into the open reaches of water with its peculiar sonorous and reiterated cry — resembling the syllables *ah-naah-naah-yah* — which rings cheerfully upon the ear after the silence and desolation of an Arctic ice-bound winter.

This Duck is of accidental occurrence in the interior of the United States in its autumnal migrations. On one occasion Professor Kumlien procured a specimen at Lake Koskonong, in Southern Wisconsin; and in December, 1874, Mr. R. Ridgway obtained one on the Wabash River, in Southern Illinois. Its occurrence in such localities is quite uncommon, and undoubtedly originates in some disturbing cause.

The eggs of this species are usually of a pale grayish-green; some are paler, and with less green mingled with the gray. They vary in length from 2.00 to 2.10 inches, and in breadth from 1.40 to 1.45.

GENUS **CAMPTOLÆMUS**, GRAY.

Kamptorhynchus, EYTON, Monog. Anat. 1838, 57 (type, *Anas labradoria*, GMEL.); not of CUVIER.
Camptolaimus, GRAY, List Genera, 1841, 95 (same type).

CHAR. Bill nearly as long as the head, much longer than the tarsus, its depth at the base nearly equal to the width, the edges nearly parallel, and furnished near the end with a membraneous lobe, causing a slight expansion; end of the bill gently convex or nearly truncated, the nail broad and slightly hooked; maxillary tomium gently, but very decidedly, convex basally, the lamellæ entirely concealed; basal portion of the maxilla furnished with a sort of cere, or overlying thin plate, covering nearly the posterior half of the bill, and extending considerably anterior to the nostrils; basal outline of the bill much as in *Harelda*, but the angles on each side the forehead more distinct. Feathers of the cheeks stiffened and bristly. Tail rather short, rounded, of fourteen rather pointed feathers. Tertials straight.

This genus stands quite alone, no other being very closely related. In the form of the bill it is entirely unique, the only resemblance to any other consisting in an approximation to *Harelda* in the basal outline, while the membraneous appendage to the edge of the maxilla, near the end, calls to mind the genus *Malacorhynchus* of Australia (see Vol. I. p. 525). There is, however, a decided approximation to the same character in *Eniconetta*.

Camptolæmus labradorius.

THE PIED DUCK.

Anas labradoria, GMEL. S. N. I. ii. 1788, 537. — WILS. Am. Orn. VIII. 1814, 91, pl. 69.
Fuligula labradora, BONAP. Synop. 1828, 391. — NUTT. Man. II. 1834, 428. — AUD. Orn. Biog. IV. 1838, 271, pl. 332; Synop. 1839, 288; B. Am. VI. 1843, 329, pl. 400.
Camptolaimus labradorus, GRAY, List Gen. 1841.
Camptolæmus labradorius, BAIRD, B. N. Am. 1858, 803; Cat. N. Am. B. 1859, no. 600. — COUES, Key, 1872, 291; Check List, 1873, no. 509; 2d ed. 1882, no. 729; B. N. W. 1874, 579. — RIDGW. Nom. N. Am. B. 1881, no. 624.
Fuligula grisea, LEIB, Jour. Phil. Ac. VIII. 1840, 170 (young).

HAB. Formerly, northern Atlantic coast of North America, south in winter to New Jersey and New York; Michigan? Supposed to be now nearly, if not quite, extinct.

SP. CHAR. *Adult male:* Head, neck, jugulum, scapulars, and wings (except primaries) white; longitudinal stripe on the crown and occiput, collar round lower part of neck, back, primaries, rump, upper tail-coverts, tail, and entire lower parts black, the tail and lower surface, except

C. labradorius.

laterally and anteriorly, decidedly more grayish — almost brownish-slate; the ring round the neck composed of soft velvety feathers, and having a dark brownish-purple tinge. Stiff feathers of the cheeks brownish white; tertials edged with black. "Bill with the basal space between the nostrils running into a rounded point in the middle, pale grayish blue; the sides of the base and the edges of both mandibles for two thirds of their length dull pale-orange; the rest of the bill black. Iris reddish hazel; feet light grayish blue, webs and claws dusky" (AUDUBON). *Adult female:* Uniform brownish gray, the wings more plumbeous; tertials silvery gray, edged with blackish; secondaries white; primaries dusky. *Young male:* Similar to the adult female, but chin and throat white, and the white of the jugulum strongly indicated; greater wing-coverts, as well as secondaries, white. Bill as in adult male and female.

Total length, about 18.00 to 20.00 inches; extent, 30.00; wing, 8.50–8.90; culmen, 1.60–1-70; width of bill at base, .82–.90; tarsus, 1.50–1.60; middle toe, 2.25–2.40.

Very little is known as to the history of this Duck. It has always been a somewhat rare species on the Atlantic coast, and within the past ten or twelve years its visits have very nearly ceased. Occasional specimens have been taken about the Island of Grand Menan, near Eastport, Me. The last of which we have any record was obtained by Mr. H. Herrick; it was a female, and had been shot by Mr. Cheney in April, 1871.

Audubon's account of it is apparently in part conjectural, and in part from hearsay testimony, and must be received with caution. He did not meet with any when in Labrador; but his son, John W. Audubon, on a visit to Blanc Sablon, July 28, 1833, found several deserted nests on the top of low tangled fir-bushes, and was told by the English clerk of the fishing establishment there that these belonged to the Pied Duck — the present species. The nests had much the appearance of those of the Eider, were very large, formed externally of fir-twigs, internally of dried grasses, and lined with down. From this Audubon inferred that the Pied Duck breeds earlier than most of its tribe. It is a hardy bird, and at the time Audubon wrote was seen during the most severe cold of winter along the coasts of Nova Scotia, Maine, and Massachusetts. Professor Maccullock, of Pictou, procured several of this species in that neighborhood; and the pair figured by Audubon, and now in the collection of the Smithsonian Institution, were killed by Daniel Webster on Vineyard Island, on the coast of Massachusetts, and by him given to Audubon. The bird which the latter figured as a female is now believed to have been a young male.

Male.

Audubon states that this Duck ranged as far south as the Chesapeake, near the influx of the James River; that he found them in the Baltimore market, and that it was met with every winter along the coasts of Long Island and New Jersey; that it entered the Delaware River, and ascended as far as Philadelphia; and that a bird-stuffer of Camden caught many fine specimens of this species with fish-hooks baited with mussels.

Mr. P. Turnbull, in his List of the Birds of East Pennsylvania and New Jersey, published in 1869, gives this Duck as being rare, but states that it is seen in small numbers every season.

A writer in the "Naturalist," for August, 1868, states that a single individual of this species had been shot the winter before on Long Island.

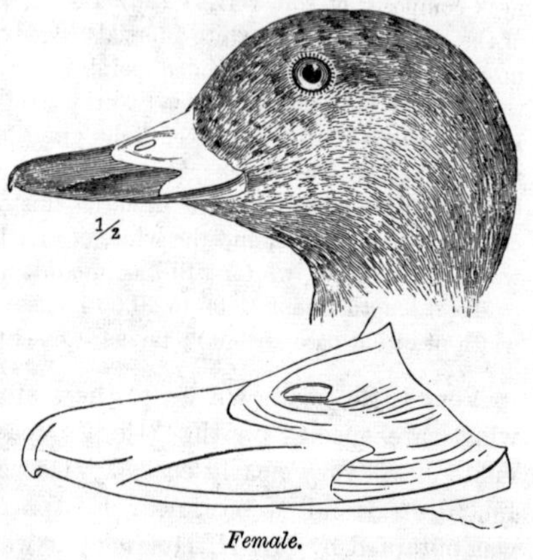

Female.

Mr. Giraud, in 1843, speaks of this Duck as being then very rare on Long Island, where it was known to hunters as the "Skunk

Duck" — so called from the similarity of its markings to those of that animal. On the coast of New Jersey it was known as the "Sand-shoal Duck." It is said to subsist on small shells and other fish, which it procures by diving. Its flesh is not considered a delicacy, although this bird is said to be seen from time to time in the New York markets during every season.

Mr. George A. Boardman, writing to the "Naturalist" (III. 383), states that not many years ago this was a common bird all along our coasts from Delaware to Labrador; and that in the New York market there would at times be dozens of them, and then not one for several years. It would, he adds, be very interesting to know where they have gone. So good a flier and diver cannot, like the clumsy *Alca impennis,* have become extinct. That it has not entirely disappeared Mr. Boardman has himself received evidence, single individuals of this species having been occasionally procured in the Bay of Fundy.

Genus **ENICONETTA**, Gray.

Macropus, Nutt. Man. II. 1834, 450 (nec Spix, 1824).

Polysticta, Eyton, Brit. Birds, 1836 (type, *Anas Stelleri,* Gmel.); antedated by *Polysticte,* Smith, 1835.

Stellaria, Bonap. Comp. List, 1838, 57 (same type); err. typ. for *Stelleria,* preoccupied in Zoology.

Stelleria, Bonap. Cat. Met. 1842, 74.

Eniconetta, Gray, Genera B. 1840, 75 (same type).

Heniconetta, Agass. Ind. Univ. 1846, 178 (nom. emend.).

Char. Bill a little longer than the tarsus, and about intermediate in form between that of *Camptolœmus* and that of *Histrionicus,* compressed, and tapering toward the end, with a broad, depressed, and indistinctly defined nail, as in the latter, but with the maxillary tomium very convex basally and sinuated terminally, as in the latter; edges of the maxilla turned *inward*

E. Stelleri.

against, and partly enclosing, the mandible; feathers of the head and neck peculiarly soft and velvety, except on the lores and occiput, where stiffened, on the latter elongated, and forming a short transverse, crescent-shaped tuft. Tertials greatly decurved or falcate, but broad to the tip. Tail graduated, of fourteen pointed feathers. Colors of the male beautifully varied.

This genus is quite intermediate between *Camptolœmus* and *Histrionicus* in the form of the bill and in other characters, but is altogether peculiar in many respects. The turning inward of the edges of the maxilla, so as partly to cover the mandible, in the enclosed bill, is not found in any other genus. The falcate tertials and the general style of coloration approximate it to the Eiders — which, however, are very different in the form of the bill, and in other respects.

Eniconetta Stelleri.

STELLER'S DUCK.

Anas Stelleri, PALL. Spic. Zool. VI. 1765, 35, pl. 5.
Fuligula (Macropus) Stelleri, NUTT. Man. II. 1834, 451.
Fuligula (Polysticta) Stelleri, BRANDT, Mem. Acad. St. Petersb. VI. 1849, 7.
Polysticta Stelleri, EYTON, Cat. Br. Mus. 58; Mon. Anat. 1838, 150. — BAIRD, B. N. Am. 1858, 801; Cat. N. Am. B. 1859, 598.
Somateria Stelleri, JARD. Brit. B. IV. 1839, 73. — COUES, Key, 1872, 291; Check List, 1873, no. 511; 2d ed. 1882, no. 731; B. N. W. 1874, 580.
Anas dispar, SPARRM. Mus. Carls. 1786, pls. 7, 8.
Stellaria dispar, BONAP. Comp. List, 1838, 57.
Anas occidua, BONN. Tabl. Orn. I. 1790, 130. — SHAW, Nat. Misc. pl. 34.

HAB. Arctic and Subarctic coasts of the Northern Hemisphere.

SP. CHAR. *Adult male:* Greater part of the head, and upper portion of the neck, satiny white; lores, and crescentic tuft across occiput, dark dull greenish; space surrounding the eye (widest behind), chin, throat (narrowing greatly below), lower part of the neck (all round), middle of the back (longitudinally), scapulars, tertials, and secondaries glossy blue-black or dark steel-blue; rump, upper tail-coverts, and tail duller blue-black; scapulars marked with a mesial lanceolate stripe of satiny white, widest on the inner webs; tertials with their inner webs wholly satiny white, this invading the inner portion of the outer webs; secondaries tipped with white. All the wing-coverts, anterior scapulars, and sides of the back pure white; primaries dull black. Lower parts dull ferruginous, becoming gradually dusky on the middle of the abdomen, fading into buff on the sides, flanks, and jugulum, the buff changing insensibly to white next to the blue-black of the neck and on the upper border of the flanks; the dusky of the abdomen gradually darkening posteriorly, the whole anal region and crissum being dull black. A small spot of blue-black on the anterior part of the sides, beneath the bend of the wing; lining of the wing entirely white. "Bill dull grayish blue, as are the feet, the claws yellowish gray" (AUDUBON). *Adult female, in summer:* Above, dusky, more or less relieved by pale fulvous or light-brown edgings to the feathers, the anterior portion of the back more spotted, but the rump sometimes uniform blackish, though the feathers are usually narrowly tipped with light brownish; head and neck pale-brown, freckled or transversely speckled with dusky, this forming more distinct bars on the pileum; jugulum and breast light rusty brown, spotted or irregularly barred with dusky; feathers of sides and flanks dusky, bordered with light brown; abdomen, anal region, and crissum nearly plain sooty blackish. Wing-coverts dusky, broadly tipped with brownish gray; speculum dull metallic blue or violet, bounded on each side by a white bar, as in the male; falcate

Male.

tertials mostly dusky. *Young male:* Similar to the adult female, but speculum dusky grayish brown, with little, if any, metallic gloss, the tertials but slightly curved, and with little or no white.

Total length, about 18.00 inches; extent, 27.00 to 30.00; wing, 8.00–8.50; culmen, 1.40–1.45; tarsus, 1.50; middle toe, 1.95.

A supposed young male from Northern Europe (No. 57266) corresponds with the description given above, except that the throat is black, the occipital feathers stiffened, while white feathers appear on the sides of the breast.

This species was first described from specimens obtained by Steller in Kamtschatka, where it was said to breed upon rocks inaccessible to man. It appears to be most abundant in the northern portions of Western America and Eastern Asia, and in the intermediate islands. It is of occasional or accidental occurrence in Great Britain, where one was taken at Caistor, Feb. 10, 1830, and another near Scarborough, Aug. 15, 1835. The former of these was figured by Audubon. Three or four were procured in Sweden, and another in Denmark. Temminck states that this Duck visits the eastern parts of Northern Europe, and that it has occasionally wandered into Germany. Professor Blasius records the capture of one on the Island of Heligoland. It is also given by Middendorff as having been found by him in the Barrens of Northern Siberia. Mr. Wheelwright states that it appears to remain during the whole year off Varanger Fiord, near North Cape, where it most probably breeds. It is only accidental in the other parts of Scandinavia. A single specimen was taken on the coast of France, between Calais and Boulogne, in February, 1855.

Female.

Mr. Robert Collett writes to Mr. Dresser that this Duck occurs annually on the Lapland coast, where it is still to be seen during the summer, at the mouths of the rivers, close to the sea, feeding on shellfish. In the "Proceedings of the Zoological Society" for 1861, Professor Newton figures an egg of this species, obtained by Middendorff on the *tundras* of the Taimyr. On the 27th of June nests were found containing from seven to nine newly laid eggs. Professor Newton also states that in June and July, 1855, in East Finmark, he saw several small flocks of this species at various places along the Varanger Fiord. Though he made unceasing inquiries, he could not ascertain that it breeds in any part of Norway, or in the adjoining districts of Russia. In its habits it resembles the Common Eider. It was generally seen swimming near the shore, or sitting, at low water, on the rocks covered by seaweed, or flying near the surface from point to point.

Since Professor Newton published this account, Mr. Schancke found Steller's Duck breeding on the Varanger Fiord, and sent to the British Museum two of its eggs with the down from a nest taken near Vardö. Pastor Sommerfeldt states that this species is found on the Varanger Fiord throughout the year, particularly toward the spring; and he was informed that it breeds to the eastward in Russian Finmark.

Middendorff found it breeding and in abundance on the Taimyr River, although not so common as the King Eider. On the 25th of June its nests, containing fresh eggs, were found placed in the moss on the flat barrens; they were cup-shaped, and well lined with down. The male remains in the neighborhood of the sitting female; and the latter leaves the nest unwillingly, uttering a cry resembling that of the Common Teal, but harsher. The eggs were said to vary from 2.20 to 2.41 inches in length, and from 1.53 to 1.61 in breadth.

Specimens of this Duck were taken by Mr. Bischoff at Kadiak; and Mr. Dall found it abundant at Unalashka, where he speaks of it as one of the most common, as well as one of the most beautiful, of the birds of that region. It is resident there throughout the year, as well as at Shumagins; but in the latter place it is much less frequently seen. Unalashka appears to be the headquarters of this species in the Alaskan Region. It is more or less gregarious in the winter, and is to be found in small flocks, which are sometimes joined by a single individual of *Somateria spectabilis;* but it was not observed associating with any other species. The pairing is said to begin about the first of May, and this Duck is never seen with more than one companion during the breeding-season. It also at that period becomes very shy, and if its nest is visited by any one, this is immediately abandoned — a habit not noticed in any other species of Duck. On the 18th of May, 1872, Mr. Dall found a nest on the flat portion of Amaknak Island, Unalashka; it was built between two tussocks of dry grass, and the depression was carefully lined with the same material. Above the nest the standing grass was pressed together so as entirely to conceal it; and it would have escaped notice had not the bird flown out from under his feet. The nest contained a single egg, of a pale olivaceous cast. There was no down or feathers; but had the nest remained undisturbed, these would probably have been added later in the season. This bird was also observed in the Shumagins in March, and also during the summer months, although not in great numbers.

A few of these Ducks were observed by Mr. H. W. Elliott on St. Paul's, one of the Prybilof Islands, in the spring of 1872. Two were shot at St. George's the same year. It is only a straggler on these islands.

Mr. A. G. Nordvi ("Cabanis's Journal," 1871, p. 208) places on record the evidence of the occurrence of this species, and its breeding, in Northern Europe, citing two instances. In the first he received some eggs obtained in Russian Finmark, on the Arctic coast; among these was one undoubtedly of this species. There was no down with it, and of course the identification was not complete. This nest was taken June 14, 1859. There were more eggs, but these were eaten. The other instance was the obtaining, with their down, of three undoubted eggs of this species in the summer of 1870, near Petschinka, in Northern Russia.[1] These facts confirm the conjectures of Mr. Wheelwright and of Professor Newton, that this Duck passes the summer, and probably breeds, in Northeastern Norway and in Northern Russia in Europe, as well as in Siberia.

Mr. L. Kumlien mentions that a beautiful adult male of this species was shot in Disko Fiord, in August, 1878; he also saw three or four while in his winter harbor, Cumberland.

Mr. Dall, in his paper on the birds found west of Unalashka, states that this species was reported to him by Mr. Thompson as wintering in large numbers at Sannakh Island, in lat. 54° 28′ N., long. 162° 52′ W. As illustrative of the irregularities noticed in the migrations of birds at different seasons, he mentions that in May,

[1] Mr. Robert Collett has more recently had the opportunity of examining the eggs and down from the same locality, and considers that they belong undoubtedly to this species. (Cf. N. Mag. Naturvid. (1881), XXVI. 376.)

1872, this species was very abundant at Unalashka, but that in the same month of the next year not a single one was seen.

An egg, said to be of this species, obtained in Alaska by Mr. Dall (No. 15571), is, like that of the Eider, of a pale grayish-green color, measuring 2.20 by 1.60 inches. Its identification may, however, be considered as very doubtful.

Genus **ARCTONETTA**, Gray.

Lampronetta, Brandt, Mém. Acad. St. Petersb. 6th Ser. Sc. Nat. VI. 1849 (published 1847?), 5 (type, *L. Fischeri*, Brandt); nec *Lampronessa*, Wagl. 1832.

Arctonetta, Gray, P. Z. S. 1855, 212 (same type).

Char. Bill shorter than the head, the basal portion densely covered with soft velvety feathers on the sides quite to the nostrils, and on the culmen to their anterior end; outline of the feathering extending backward and downward in a straight line from the point on the culmen to the rictus; culmen descending in a straight line to the nail, which is broad and slightly arched; maxillary tomium very straight and regular, the lamellæ very slightly exposed along the middle portion. Feathers of the lores and forehead dense, much stiffened, pointing directly outward; those of the occiput bristle-like, lengthened, and pendulous; orbital region covered by a subcircular or subquadrate mat of very soft, short, dense, and satin-like feathers; below this a longitudinal stripe of short, stiff, bristly feathers directed backward. Tertials falcate. Tail short, graduated, of fourteen feathers.

A. Fischeri.

Arctonetta Fischeri.

FISCHER'S EIDER; SPECTACLED EIDER.

Fuligula (Lampronetta) Fischeri, Brandt, Mém. Acad. St. Petersb. VI. 1849, 6, 10, 14, pl. 1, figs. 1–4.

Lampronetta Fischeri, Baird, B. N. Am. 1858, 803; Cat. N. Am. B. 1859, no. 599. — Elliot, Illustr. B. Am. V. pl. 47. — Ridgw. Nom. N. Am. B. 1881, no. 626.

Arctonetta Fischeri, Blakist. Ibis, 1863, 150.

Somateria Fischeri, Coues, Key, 1872, 292; Check List, 1873, no. 512; 2d ed. 1882, no. 732; Birds N. W. 1874, 580.

Hab. Coasts of Alaska, chiefly in the vicinity of Norton Sound, north to Point Barrow.

Sp. Char. *Adult male:* Orbital region silky white, bordered anteriorly and posteriorly by a vertical line of velvety black; lores and forehead white anteriorly, then olive-green, this passing gradually into light greenish buff next to the black bar bounding the orbital region anteriorly; middle of the crown, whole occiput, and upper part of the nape light olive-green; a broad stripe beneath the white orbital space, extending back to the nape, deep silky dull green, abruptly defined except posteriorly; remainder of the head and neck white. Entire lower parts, including the breast and jugulum, rump, upper tail-coverts, tail, remiges, greater and primary wing-coverts, and alulæ plain plumbeous-drab; entire back, scapulars, wing-coverts (except the greater), falcate tertials, and patch on each side the rump plain yellowish white; axillars pure white. Bill light reddish in the skin (orange in life); iris pale bluish; feet brownish. *Adult female, in summer:* Above, light fulvous, barred with black; jugulum, sides, flanks, and upper tail-coverts similar; rump darker; head and neck light grayish buff, finely streaked with dusky, the throat nearly immaculate; abdomen and anal region plain grayish brown; greater wing-coverts, remiges, and rectrices grayish brown, the first, with the secondaries, indistinctly tipped with white.

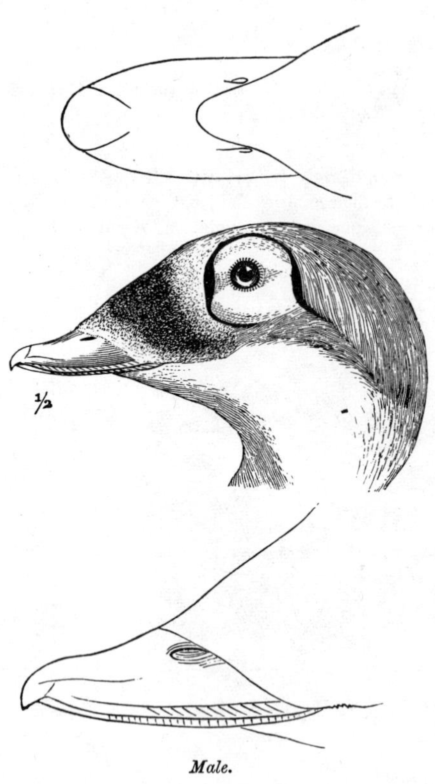

Male.

Total length, about 21.50 inches; wing, 10.00; tarsus, 1.70; commissure, 2.20.

The female and young birds of this beautiful species may be distinguished from the other Eiders (of the genus *Somateria*) by the peculiar feathering over the base of the bill (extending to the nostril, as in the adult male), and by the distinctly indicated circumorbital ring.

We are indebted to Mr. Dall for the little we know in reference to the history and distribution of this very rare and, unfortunately, little known species. He met with it in 1867 in and around the Island of St. Michael's, and at a later period in the Aleutian Islands. It was introduced by Mr. Cassin in the ninth volume of the Pacific Railroad Reports, on the supposition that in severe winters it would ultimately be found on our coast; although it at that time was only known from the descriptions and figures of Brandt and Gray, and had only been obtained in Norton's Sound, in Russian America, 63° 30′ north latitude. Mr. Dall informs us that, so far as he then knew, it breeds only in the marshes which lie between the Island of St. Michael's and the mainland, and are intersected by a narrow channel called the Canal. It was not seen near the mouth of the Yukon, nor even a few miles south of the Canal, nor, according to the repeated assertions of the natives, is it found on any point of Norton's Sound to the north of St. Michael's. Its winter habitat was then unknown, but was supposed to be possibly Cook's Inlet or Bristol Bay. It is not abundant, even at St. Michael's. Several specimens which had been reported to have come from other localities have all been definitely traced to that point.

The Russian name for all Eiders is *Pistrik*, and this species is known as the "Small Pistrik."

A nest belonging to a bird of this species was discovered by Mr. Dall in the centre of a small pool in a marsh, built on a tussock just above the surface of the water; it was oval, lined with dry grass, and contained two eggs, which were surrounded and covered with down — evidently from the breast of the parent. The eggs were small as compared in size with the bird, and of an olivaceous brown. There were a number of other Ducks of this species breeding in the vicinity, and also several of the *Somateria V-nigrum;* and some eggs were obtained which, from their resemblance to identified specimens, were probably those of *S. spectabilis*, although the parent was not fully identified. The eye of this species, Mr. Dall adds, is dark brown or hazel, and not blue, as has been asserted. The fall plumage of male and female is nearly identical — a dark brown with black pencillings; only the faintest indications of the spring markings remaining. This bird usually flies in flocks. The last one killed in 1867 was obtained September 27; but some of these Ducks probably remain a short time longer than this.

Female.

Mr. Dall, in a later paper, states that although no birds of this species were actually killed at Unalashka, some were observed on several occasions, and were reported by the natives — who perfectly distinguish between the different kinds of Eiders. Those seen were very shy, and but one or two individuals were observed at a time. This bird is a winter visitant, migrating early in May to its breeding-grounds on Norton Sound.

The late Mr. E. Adams, in his Notes on the Birds observed by him at Michalaski, on Norton Sound, mentions procuring three specimens of this Duck, which he calls the Blue-eyed — in the Eski dialect, *Ong-óo.* They had been shot out of a flock on the 28th of May. He does not seem to have met with this species on any other occasion, and was unable to give any information as to its habits.

Mr. Bannister speaks of it as moderately common near Fort St. Michael's, some fifteen or eighteen individuals having been shot during the spring of 1866. This species and the *Somateria V-nigrum* are said to arrive a little later than most of the other Ducks and some of the Geese, making their appearance about the 6th of May. In their habits the two species are apparently very much alike, and both breed in that vicinity. This species is the more shy of the two, and on that account the more difficult to observe.

In July and August, during the moulting period, this bird is said to be unable to fly. It is reported that on Stewart's Island, just west of St. Michael's Island, numbers have been killed by the Eskimos with sticks and clubs. The skin of this species, prepared in a certain way, is used by these natives for caps, and is by them considered as of some little value. The scalps, also, with their silky bright-green plumage, are sometimes used for adorning the skin dresses worn by the natives.

The flight of this Duck is rapid — more so than that of most other Ducks — being generally low, and very near the surface of the water. In all the specimens seen the iris was of a dark hazel.

Eggs of this species from the Canal of St. Michael's Island are of a pale olive-gray color (Smithsonian Institution, No. 14596). Five specimens measure as follows: 2.50 by 1.85 inches; 2.50 by 1.65; 2.40 by 1.65; 2.35 by 1.55; and 2.40 by 1.70.

Genus **SOMATERIA**, Leach.

Somateria, "Leach," Boie, Isis, 564 (type, *Anas mollissima*, Linn.).

Char. Bill about as long as the head, narrower than deep, the tip formed by the very broad, large nail; feathers of the forehead advancing forward in a long, narrow pointed strip, between two backward extensions of the maxilla, which, intervening between the frontal feathers and those of the cheeks, form a distinct basal angle or lobe; maxillary tomium regular and nearly straight,

S. mollissima.

the lamellæ completely concealed. Head with some portions bristly-feathered (in males); tertials falcate; tail small, short, and pointed, composed of fourteen pointed feathers. Plumage of the males varied and handsome.

The four species which compose this genus differ very considerably from one another in form, but they all possess the characters defined above, Like the more or less nearly related genera *Arctonetta*, *Eniconetta*, *Histrionicus*, and *Camptolæmus*, they are birds of high northern latitudes, barely entering the warm-temperate zone in winter.

They may be defined as follows: —

A. Frontal feathers reaching about half way from the base of the maxillary angle to the nostril; feathering of the lores extending forward to beneath the middle of the nostril. Males with white scapulars and tertials, the top of the head chiefly black.

1. **S. mollissima.** *Male*, with the throat entirely white. Basal angle of the maxilla narrow (.25–.35 of an inch wide across widest part), and ending in a point. *Hab.* Palæarctic

Region, Greenland, and west shores of Cumberland Gulf. *Female:* Wing, 10.75–11.60 inches; length of bill, from end of basal angle, 2.45–2.85.

2. **S. Dresseri.** Similar to *S. mollissima*, but basal angle of the maxilla broad (.38–.50 of an inch wide at widest part), and terminating in a broad convex end. *Hab.* Eastern North America, from Maine northward to Labrador; Newfoundland.

3. **S. V-nigrum.** *Male*, with a large V-shaped mark of black on the throat. *Female:* Wing, 11.75–12.50 inches; length of bill, from tip to end of basal angle, 2.50–2.65. *Hab.* Northwestern North America, and portions of Eastern Siberia.

B. Frontal feathers reaching forward as far as the nostrils; feathering of the lores extending only about half way to the nostrils. Male with the scapulars and tertials black, the top of the head light grayish blue.

4. **S. spectabilis.** *Male*, with a large V-shaped mark of black on the throat, as in *S. V-nigrum*. *Female:* Wing, 10.50–11.25 inches; bill, to end of basal angle, 1.20–1.30. *Hab.* Circumpolar regions.

Somateria mollissima.

COMMON EIDER.

Anas mollissima, LINN. S. N. ed. 10, I. 1758, 124; ed. 12, I. 1766, 198.

Somateria mollissima, BOIE, Isis, 1822, 564, et AUCT. (all quotations from Europe). — RIDGW. Proc. U. S. Nat. Mus. Vol. 3, 1880, 204; Nom. N. Am. B. 1881, no. 627. — COUES, Check List, 2d ed. 1882, no. 733.

Anas Cuthberti, PALL. Zoog. Rosso-As. II. 1826, 235.

Somateria St. Cuthberti, EYT. Cat. Br. B. 1836, 58; Mon. Anat. 1838, 149.

"*Anser lanuginosus*, LEACH, Cat. 1816, 37" (GRAY).

Platypus borealis, BREHM, Lehrb. Eur. Vög. 1824, 813 (shores of Baffin's Bay and Davis' Strait).

? *Somateria thulensis*, MALMG. Kongl. Vet. Ak. Ofv. 1864, 380 (Spitzbergen).

Somateria danica, norwegica, platyuros, faeroeensis, megauros, islandica, borealis, Leisleri, planifrons, BREHM, V. D. 890, 891, 892, 893, 894, 895, 896, 897.

HAB. Northern part of the Palæarctic Region; Greenland; breeding abundantly on western shores of Cumberland Gulf (L. Kumlien, Bull. U. S. Nat. Mus. No. 15, 1879, p. 89.).

SP. CHAR. *Adult male:* Pileum deep blue-black, divided medially for the posterior half by a stripe of white or greenish white, and extending anteriorly along the upper edge of the lores almost to the limit of feathering on the latter; upper part of the nape, and posterior part of the auricular region, pale sea-green, this color sometimes extending anteriorly along the lower edge of the black as far as the middle of the lores; remainder of the head and neck, with entire back and scapulars, tertials, all the wing-coverts, sides of the rump, and jugulum, white, tinged, except on head and neck (most deeply on back, scapulars, and jugulum), with yellowish cream-color; breast pinkish cream-color; remaining lower parts, greater wing-coverts, secondaries, middle of the rump (longitudinally), and upper tail-coverts, deep black; primaries and rectrices brownish black. Lining of the wing pure white. Bill dull olivaceous in the skin, orange-yellow with greenish yellow nail in life; iris dark brown; legs and feet dusky grayish in skin, dusky orange in life.[1]

Adult female: Prevailing color brownish buff, everywhere, except on the head, neck, abdomen, remiges, rectrices, and larger wing-coverts, barred with black, the bars broadest on the upper surface; head and neck streaked with blackish, the streaks finer and less distinct toward the throat, which is almost immaculate; larger wing-coverts, remiges, and rectrices plain grayish brown, the first narrowly tipped with white; abdomen and anal region plain, rather dark, grayish brown [No. 76180, Cumberland Gulf, June 6, 1878; L. KUMLIEN]. *Young (full plumage, both sexes):* Above, dusky, the feathers bordered (but not barred) with rusty brown or dull ochraceous, except the greater wing-coverts, remiges, and rectrices, which are plain dusky, the first not tipped with white; head and neck dull grayish fulvous, streaked with dusky, the latter predominating on the pileum; lower parts barred with dull fulvous and dusky, the abdomen sometimes plain dusky.

[1] Fresh colors, *fide* L. Kumlien, MS.

Downy young: Plain grayish brown, lighter beneath and over the eyes, the abdomen sometimes, but rarely, almost dirty whitish; the light superciliary stripe usually distinct and continuous.

Total length, about 22 inches; wing, 10.50–11.60; culmen, 1.75–2.20; length of bill from tip to end of basal angle, 2.45–3.00; greatest width of angle, .25–.35; tarsus, 1.90–2.20; middle toe, 2.35–2.70.[1]

With the single exception of the Common Mallard, no Duck is more generally known to the world at large than this species. The value of its down, as an article of luxury and of commerce for several centuries, has given it an intrinsic value, and to its history an interest, beyond that belonging to any of its tribe. The importance of this bird has been increased by the pains and success with which its cultivation has been carried on in Iceland, Norway, and in other parts of Europe. In America, where it is equally common, no corresponding attempts have been made to protect it in the breeding-season.

The Eider Duck is an Arctic species, common to the Atlantic shores of Europe and America, but nowhere seen on the Pacific coast of Asia or America. It is found in the Arctic Ocean as far west as the Coppermine River in North America, and as far east as Nova Zembla and the islands north of Siberia.

Messrs. Evans and Sturge found Ducks of this species breeding in immense numbers on the beach of West Spitzbergen. Their nests were mere hollows scooped in the pebbly ground, very scantily lined with down, mixed with seaweed. Subsequently Professor Newton saw it numerous all around Spitzbergen, but less abundant toward the north. Yet on the 15th of July, 1861, flocks of hundreds of male birds were observed at Shoal Point, latitude 80° 10′ N., which seemed to be on their way still farther north.

Mr. Gillette speaks of finding this species tolerably common all along the coast of Nova Zembla; but he nowhere saw it in large flocks. Von Heuglin also met with it in the same locality. He found it everywhere on rocky islands, but not so common as in Spitzbergen. As late as August 8 he met with breeding females, but saw no old males.

Middendorff enumerates the Eider among the birds of Siberia, and includes it in the list of those which penetrate to the extremest northern points.

Mr. C. W. Shepard, in his interesting sketch of his explorations in the northwestern peninsula of Iceland, gives a graphic account of his visit to an island on the northern coast of Iceland, and of the wonderful tameness of the Eider. "The islands of Vigr and Oedey are their headquarters in the northwest of Iceland. In these they live in undisturbed tranquillity. They have become almost domesticated, and are found in vast multitudes, as the young remain and breed in the place of their birth. As the island [Vigr] was approached we could see flocks upon flocks of the sacred birds, and could hear their cooing at a great distance. We landed on a rocky, wave-worn shore. It was the most wonderful ornithological sight conceivable. The Ducks and their nests were everywhere. Great brown Ducks sat upon their nests in masses, and at every step started from under our feet. It was with difficulty that we avoided treading on some of the nests. On the coast of the opposite shore was a wall built of large stones, just above the high-water level, about three feet in height, and of considerable thickness. At the bottom, on both sides of it, alternate stones had been left out, so as to form a series of square compartments for the Ducks to nest in. Almost every compartment was occupied, and as we walked along the shore, a long line of Ducks flew out, one after the other. The surface of the water also was per-

[1] Ten examples.

fectly white with drakes, who welcomed their brown wives with loud and clamorous cooing. The house itself was a marvel. The earthen walls that surrounded it and the window embrasures were occupied by Ducks. On the ground the house was fringed with Ducks. On the turf slopes of its roof we could see Ducks, and a Duck sat on the door-scraper. The grassy banks had been cut into square patches, about eighteen inches having been removed, and each hollow had been filled with Ducks. A windmill was infested, and so were all the outhouses, mounds, rocks, and crevices. The Ducks were everywhere. Many were so tame that we could stroke them on their nests; and the good lady told us that there was scarcely a Duck on the island that would not allow her to take its eggs without flight or fear. Our hostess told us that when she first became possessor of the island the produce of down from the Ducks was not more than fifteen pounds in a year; but that under her careful nurture of twenty years, it had risen to nearly a hundred pounds annually. Most of the eggs are taken and pickled for winter consumption, one or two only being left in each nest to hatch."

The Eider is indigenous to the northern portions of Great Britain; but is only a winter visitor, and in very limited numbers, to the southern portions, and is rarely met with in Ireland. It is of rare occurrence on the coast of France.

On the Farn Islands, off the northeastern coast of England, the Eider formerly bred regularly. Mr. Selby visited these islands, and has given an interesting account of his observations. In April these birds assembled in groups along the shores of the mainland, and crossed over to the islands early in May. The females began to lay about the 20th, when the males all deserted them, returning to the adjoining coast. The nests were made of fine seaweed; and as incubation proceeded, a lining of down plucked by the bird from her own body was added. This increased from day to day, and became so considerable in quantity as to envelop and entirely conceal the eggs from view. Incubation lasted about a month, and the young as soon as hatched were conducted to the water; and, in many instances, this could only be done by the parent carrying them in her bill. The food of the Eider consists of the different mussels and other kinds of bivalves, with which the rocks are covered. This bird can be reared with difficulty in confinement, and does not walk on the land readily. It dives with great facility, and remains submerged a long while.

The Messrs. Godman found this the most common Duck about Bodo, in Norway, and mention finding several pairs that were breeding on a marsh, near a fresh-water lake, several miles from the sea.

Dr. Walker met with Ducks of this species on the coast of Greenland, near Godthaab; and at Bellot's Strait he saw them beginning to assemble, in the pools of water, early in June. This is also cited by Professor Reinhardt as a resident species of Greenland. Hearne states that it was known, in his day, as the "Dunter Goose" in the Hudson's Bay Region. It was common about the mouth of the Churchill River as soon as the ice broke up; but generally flew farther north to breed, the few that did remain about the settlement there being so scattered among small islands and sea-girt rocks and shoals as to render it not worth while to gather their down. Their eggs were exceedingly good eating; and in the fall of the year their flesh was by no means unpleasant, although this bird is known to feed on fish.

Mr. Kumlien mentions this as the most abundant Duck at Cumberland. The old males, separating from the females and young as soon as the breeding-season is over, assemble in large flocks and migrate southward much earlier than the latter. This Duck can endure any temperature where it can find open water. On one occasion an adult male was seen in the tide rifts in January, with the thermometer at $-50°$; but he was too lively to be secured. Young unable to fly were seen as late as the middle of October. Their food in autumn consists almost wholly of mollusks. On one occasion Mr. Kumlien disturbed a large colony of them, and the Ducks all left their nests. He sent his Eskimos to another island while he remained behind to see how the birds would behave. As soon as the boat left, both males and females returned to their nests. One male alighted by the side of a nest and settled down on the eggs with a well-satisfied air, when suddenly a female appeared, and seemed to inform him that he had made a mistake, and that it was not his nest; he thereupon withdrew with an awkward bow. The Ducks all seemed very noisy and communicative; but when Mr. Kumlien crept out into full view from his hiding-place, there was a general look of disgust and astonishment among them. Many would not even leave their nests, but hissed and squaked at him, after the manner of Geese. He mentions also seeing large flocks of immature birds, both male and female, that do not breed.

Dr. Bessels includes the Eider among the birds taken by the "Polaris" Expedition, under Captain Hall, in Polaris Bay. Mr. Feilden, in the British Arctic Expedition of 1875–1876, found it breeding in great numbers in the neighborhood of Fort Foulke, but decreasing in numbers as it passed northward. It became rare after passing Cape Frazer, the meeting-place of the Polar and Baffin's Bay tides. He did not meet with one north of Cape Union; but Dr. Coppinger procured both this species and the *spectabilis* at Thank-God Harbor (lat. 81° 38′ N.) in the month of July, 1876.

Sir John Richardson regarded this as an exclusively marine species, and was not aware that it is ever seen in fresh water. Its food is said to consist almost wholly of the soft mollusca so common in northern waters. It is only partially migratory, the older birds rarely moving farther south in winter than to permanent open water.

Somateria Dresseri.

THE AMERICAN EIDER.

Anas mollissima, Wils. Am. Orn. VIII. 1814, 122, pl. 71.

Fuligula (*Somateria*) *mollissima*, Nutt. Man. II. 1834, 407.

Fuligula mollissima, Aud. Orn. Biog. III. 1835, 344; V. 1839, 611, pl. 246; Synop. 1839, 291; B. Am. VI. 1843, 349, pl. 405.

Somateria mollissima, Bonap. Comp. List, 1838, 57 (part). — Baird, B. N. Am. 1858, 809; Cat. N. Am. B. 1859, no. 606. — Coues, Key, 1872, 293; Check List, 1873, no. 513.

Somateria Dresseri, Sharpe, Ann. Mag. N. H. July, 1871, 51, figs. 1, 2.

Somateria mollissima, var. (?) *Dresseri*, Coues, Birds N. W. 1874, 580.

Somateria mollissima Dresseri, Ridgw. Pr. U. S. Nat. Mus. vol. 3, 1880, 205, 222; Nom. N. Am. B. 1881, no. 627 *a*. —Coues, Check List, 2d ed. 1882, no. 734.

Hab. American coasts of the North Atlantic, from Maine, etc., to Labrador.

Sp. Char. *Adult male:* Similar to *S. mollissima*, but the "cere" very much broader (.38 to .50 of an inch wide anteriorly), much corrugated, the posterior extremity broad and rounded; green of the head rather more extended, usually following along underneath the black almost or quite to the bill. "Bill pale grayish yellow, the unguis lighter, the soft tumid part pale flesh-color; iris brown; feet dingy light green, the webs dusky" (Audubon). *Adult female:* Scarcely distinguishable from that of *mollissima*, but basal angles of the maxilla deeper and broader. "Bill pale grayish green; iris and feet as in the male" (Audubon). *Downy young:* Not distinguishable from that of *mollissima*.

Total length, about 24.00 to 26.00 inches; extent, 39.00 to 42.00; wing, 11.15–11.50; culmen, 1.95–2.40; from tip of bill to end of basal angle, 2.75–3.35; greatest width of angle, .38–.50; tarsus, 2.00–2.20; middle toe, 2.50–2.70 (six examples).

After a close direct comparison of six males of *S. mollissima* with five of *S. Dresseri*, we have been unable to verify the points of distinction given by Messrs. Sharpe & Dresser ("Birds of

Europe," Pt. IV., p. 14), other than those defined above. We find the falcate tertials equally developed in specimens of both forms, while the extent of the green of the head is quite variable, according to the individual.

The accompanying outline figures will serve to show the great difference in the form of the bill, especially its basal portion, in the two species.

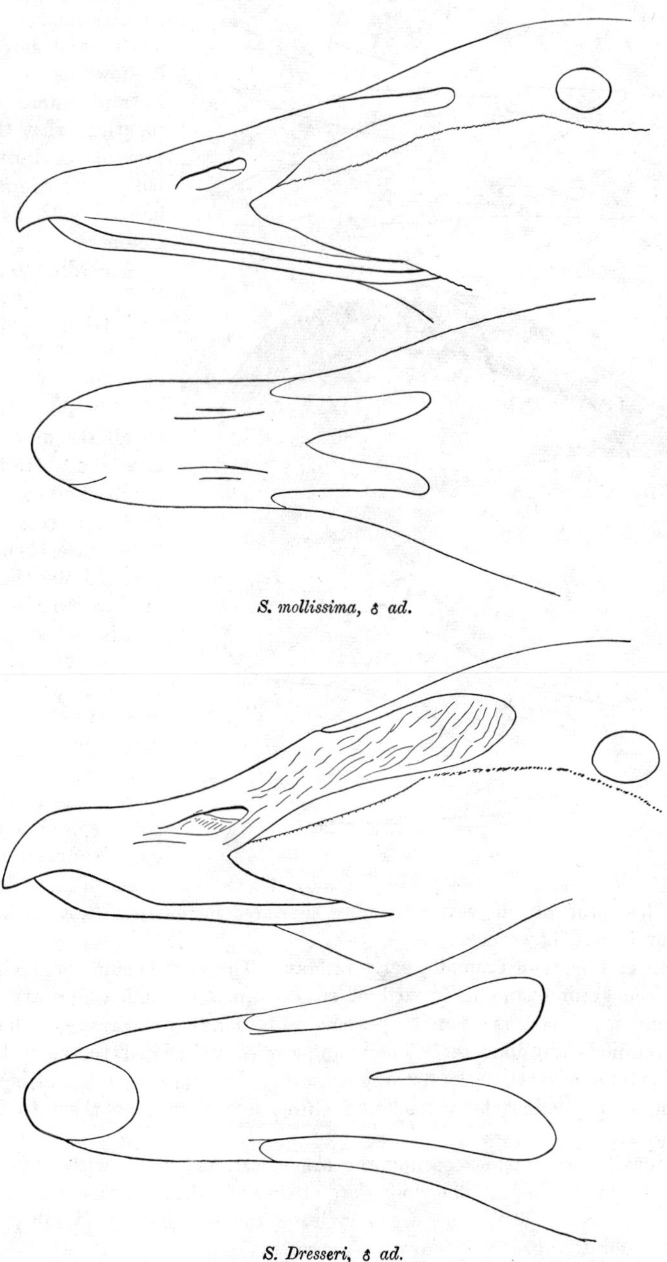

S. mollissima, ♂ *ad.*

S. Dresseri, ♂ *ad.*

The Eider breeds on the extreme eastern coast of Maine and in the Bay of Fundy, and would, no doubt, do so in considerable numbers were it not so constantly robbed of its eggs and down. It is found in the winter along the whole Atlantic coast as far south as the Delaware. Ducks of this species are brought to the Boston market every winter, but in much smaller numbers than formerly; and they are rarely now met with except in midwinter. Audubon mentions that they were present in Boston Harbor in considerable numbers in 1832, as early as October.

Male.

According to Audubon, this Duck breeds along the Atlantic coast from the Bay of Fundy to the extreme northern points of Labrador, and thence on all the more northern headlands. He found the number of eggs to vary from five to ten; in the latter case they are supposed to be the product of two females. If the nest is robbed in the early part of the season, the female seeks her mate once more, and lays another and smaller set; but if the eggs are taken late in the season, the nest is forsaken. Early in August Audubon found the Eider in Labrador moving southward, — probably, however, to more sheltered havens, and not farther to the south than the St. Lawrence.

This species nests in Labrador early in May. The nest is sunk as much as possible into the ground, and is formed of seaweed, mosses, and a few dry twigs, so matted and interlaced as often to present quite a neat appearance. The cavity is about seven inches in diameter. The young are led, or carried, to the water by the mother, and for several weeks nothing can exceed the care she takes of her brood — defending them against the attacks of Gulls, and prompting them to dive when necessary.

Occasionally two females occupy the same nest, and share with each other the care of the young flock. The young are at first of a dark mouse-color, and covered with a soft down. Their feet are very large, and they are remarkably expert in swimming and diving. They grow with great rapidity.

The Eider can easily be domesticated, especially when raised from the egg, becoming accustomed to feed on corn and meal, and is as tame and contented in confinement as the Mallard. It is necessary, however, that the bird be provided with an abundant supply of gravel and of varied food. The cry of the female when startled from her nest is described as being a hoarse rolling croak. The food of this species consists largely of shellfish, the shells of which are broken in pieces by the muscular gizzards of the birds, aided by coarse gravel.

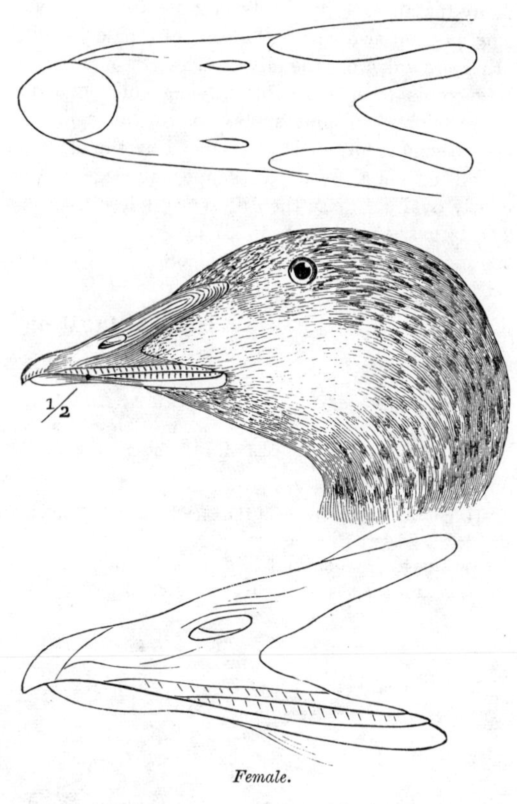

Female.

Dr. Henry Bryant, who visited Labrador in the summer of 1860, gives an interesting account of his observations on the breeding of the Eider on that coast. We copy substantially his narrative. He found it still breeding in great abundance along the whole extent of the shore, some nests being placed under the shelter of the dwarf-firs and junipers, although the favorite breeding-places were the little grassy islands found in bays, and particularly those where small spots of turf were protected by a rock from the prevailing wind. On many islands an umbelliferous plant grows abundantly, the shelter of whose thick foliage these birds seemed to prefer. It was not often that many nests were found on one island — from one to a dozen being the ordinary number; but on Greenlet Island he found over sixty; and this was probably not a quarter of the whole number. This island was peculiarly well adapted to the wants of this Duck, being covered with a thick growth of this umbelliferous plant, but slightly elevated above the water, and at a distance from the mainland. He found on this island a nest in a small stone hut made for the purpose of concealing the hunters in the spring. Many nests were seen in which the down was quite clean, and he believed that it is always so if the bird is undisturbed; but after the nest has been frequently robbed, the supply of this material is not sufficient, and whatever substitute is most convenient has to be taken in its place: so that, late in the season, nests are found without any down. Some contained fresh eggs, and others were only just finished, as late as the middle of July. Audubon states that the eggs are deposited on the grass, etc., of which the nest is principally composed; Dr. Bryant, however, did not see a single instance in which this had been done, provided there was any down; and nearly every day, during the first week or two, he found nests containing freshly laid eggs lying on a bed of down so exquisitely soft and warm that, in that almost painfully barren and frigid region, the nest seemed to be the ideal of comfort, and almost of beauty. When the bird leaves her nest without being suddenly disturbed, the eggs are generally covered with down, and always so when the full complement has been laid. The largest number found in a nest was six; and this happened in so many instances that Dr. Bryant regarded six as the normal number. In color the eggs present two varieties — one of a pale greenish-olive or oil-green color, and the other brownish or true olive. The first-mentioned variety is frequently marked with large spots, or splashes, of the same color, of much greater intensity; the other kind is invariably without spots. After the eggs have been incubated for some time they become more or less scratched by the claws of the parent while sitting on them or rolling them over. In shape the eggs present but little variety, being always nearly oval. In size the difference is less than is the case in the majority of birds. The largest egg measured 3.27 by 2.16 inches; the most elongated, 2.95 by 1.85; and the most broadly oval, 2.79 by 2.08.

Somateria V-nigrum.

THE PACIFIC EIDER.

Somateria V-nigra, GRAY, P. Z. S. 1855, 212, pl. 107. — BAIRD, B. N. Am. 1858, 810; Cat. N. Am. B. 1859, no. 607. — ELLIOT, Illustr. Am. B. pl. 48. — COUES, Key, 1872, 293; Check List, 1873, no. 514; 2d ed. 1882, no. 735; B. N. W. 1874, 581. — RIDGW. Nom. N. Am. B. 1881, no. 628.

HAB. American coasts of the North Pacific; Yukon Valley, Mackenzie River, and Slave Lake districts; Eastern Siberia.

SP. CHAR. Similar to *S. mollissima*, but decidedly larger, the bill broader, and deeper through the base, the angles of the maxilla proportionally shorter and much more acute; *male* with a

S. V-nigrum.

large V-shaped black mark on the throat, as in *S. spectabilis*. *Adult male:* Top of the head velvety black, with a slight violet gloss, divided mesially, from the middle of the crown back, by a narrow stripe of greenish white; the black extending forward in a rather wide stripe along the upper edge of the lores, underneath the basal angle of the maxilla, but not extending anteriorly as far as the nostril; greater wing-coverts, secondaries, middle line of the rump, upper tail-coverts, and entire lower parts from the breast back, deep black; primary coverts, primaries, and tail blackish dusky; rest of the plumage, including the falcate tertials, continuous white, the breast tinged with creamy buff (much less deeply than in *S. mollissima*), the upper half of the nape, the auricular region, and the upper border of the cheeks deeply stained with yellowish green; throat with a large V-shaped mark of velvety black. Bill orange red, paler terminally (light reddish in the dried skin), the nail yellowish white; iris dark brown; feet yellow. *Adult female:* Light fulvous, barred with black, the bars widest on the scapulars; head and neck finely streaked with black, the throat nearly immaculate; abdomen usually plain grayish brown; greater wing-coverts, primary coverts, remiges, and rectrices plain grayish dusky, the greater coverts and secondaries distinctly tipped with white. *Young:* Similar to the adult female, but upper parts dusky, the feathers bordered with rusty fulvous, the greater coverts and secondaries not tipped with white.

Wing, 11.75–12.75 inches; culmen, 1.80–2.20; from tip of bill to end of basal angle, 2.50–3.10; greatest width of angle, .20–.30; tarsus, 2.00–2.30; middle toe, 2.50–2.85.[1]

Male.

This species — essentially an Eider in all respects, not only in habits, appearance, but in all the peculiar characteristics of this well-marked form — replaces the *mollissima* on the northwestern coast of America, and on the Arctic Ocean, at least as far to the east as the mouth of the Coppermine River. Mr. Bernard Ross records it as occurring at Great Slave Lake, lat. 61° north, and long. 114° west; but it was rare in that locality, only two specimens having been obtained.

Mr. Dall mentions finding this Duck common in the Island of St. Michael's in the month of July, at which time his observations began. It was known to the Russians as the Large Pistrik. So far as he was able to observe, it appeared to have a very limited range — as much so as that of *Arctonetta Fischeri.* Individuals were much more numerous, and large flocks of males were frequently seen near the Fort. By September all had assumed a uniform brown color, with dark pencillings. The eye is said to be hazel. They all left in a body about the first of October.

Mr. Bannister also speaks of this Duck as breeding in abundance in and around St. Michael's. In the early spring, when it first made its appearance, the sexes

[1] Nine examples measured.

seemed to be present in about equal numbers, and were generally found together. In June, however, he noticed numerous small flocks composed entirely of males; and still later in the season — in the latter part of July, and in August — the flocks were apparently all females, though perhaps partly composed of males in their autumnal plumage. Throughout the month of July, however, solitary males could often be started on the small outlying rocky islands, apparently in full spring colors, though generally unable to fly. They escaped by rapid swimming and diving, and they could only be shot or followed in a *kyak* when circumstances were very favorable. Mr. Bannister's observations of this species led him to believe that these birds dislike swimming in rough water. On windy days he has generally seen them in small flocks squatting along the upper edge of the beach or swimming in the more sheltered coves and inlets. The noise made by these Ducks in spring is said to be very peculiar; and when many are heard together — as is generally the case — it can only be described as a continuous grunting.

Female.

Mr. MacFarlane found this species breeding in great numbers on the Arctic coast, near the mouth of Anderson River. The nests were seen in various situations — some on a rising band near the sea-shore, others on sloping ground three hundred feet or more from the water. Some were on the coast, and others on islands in the bays. All the nests were on the ground, and, for the most part, mere depressions in the soil, but plentifully lined with down. Those found after the middle of June contained more or less developed embryos. By the last of June the males appeared to have left their mates, as Mr. MacFarlane noticed that the two sexes kept apart, although they were occasionally seen in pairs. In some cases Mr. MacFarlane found what he believed to be eggs of the *spectabilis* in the same nest with those of the *V-nigrum*, for which fact he could only account on the supposition that the former had dispossessed the latter, who were the original and rightful owners. He also noticed that the number of females seemed to be always in excess of that of the males; and it may be that this Eider is also to some extent polygamous — as is also the *mollissima*, two females sometimes using the same nest.

The largest number of eggs recorded by Mr. MacFarlane as having been found in any one nest is apparently six — and this in only one instance; the general number was five. Mr. Dall, in his second paper, states that this Duck is apparently a resident in the Aleutian Islands. Wintering abundantly at Unalashka, it seeks its breeding-grounds in the islands to the westward; and it is certain that the large flocks which winter in Captain's Bay do not breed in the immediate vicinity, while this is the most common Duck among the western islands throughout the summer.

The Pacific Eider was found in large numbers on the coast of Norton Sound by Mr. E. Adams ("Ibis," 1878, p. 434). Its Eskimo name is *Mit-kok.* The first noticed near the redoubt of St. Michael's was on the 10th of May; and soon after these birds became quite numerous. They frequented all the marshes, but were generally flying about; they seldom alighted on a lake, but came straight in from the sea, following the course of the rivers; and after taking a few turns about the marshes, they again went out to sea. They soon fixed upon their breeding-places, and their nests were scattered over the whole of the marshes. One nest was within thirty yards of the fort, in the midst of children and dogs — the parent bird having built her nest and laid four eggs before she was discovered. Yet these Ducks are very wary, and difficult to approach. On the wing they fly in a straight line, appearing stupid, and often approaching within a few yards of the hunter. They are very swift on the wing, and can carry off a great quantity of shot. One pair built their nest in a swampy hollow between two small lakes, and about twenty yards from one of them; this nest was placed in the midst of tall grass, and built of rushes and grass, and well lined with feathers and down. By the latter end of May this pair had laid six eggs; and the female then began to sit. The male assisted in building the nest, but not in the process of incubation. While building they worked only very early in the morning. When the female began to lay, both of them came in from seaward a little before noon, and after a few turns round, as if to see that all was right, both alighted in the lake. There they remained some little time, and then the female walked off to her nest; and very soon after her mate went out to sea. In about an hour he came back to the lake, and his mate then joined him; but she was never known to leave her nest until she heard him cooing on the lake. They remained there a short time, playing about and cooing, and then again went out to sea, and did not return until the next day. When the female began to sit, her mate came in every day and took her out to sea, and again accompanied her to the lake; but was never seen to approach the nest. The eggs had not been hatched at the time Mr. Adams left the place.

The principal food of this Eider is mussels and other small shellfish, for which it dives in from three to six fathoms of water. On one day Mr. Adams counted from the fort two hundred and six of these birds feeding along the edge of the water in the Bay; and of the whole number only four were females. Their note very much resembles the cooing of the European Wood-Pigeon.

This Duck is said seldom to weigh less than four pounds, and sometimes as much as six. The eggs are generally six or seven in number, of a pale sea-green color, with a tinge of olive. Eggs in the Smithsonian Collection, from Anderson River (No. 9571), are of a uniform light grayish-green color, with an olive shade, and measure from 2.95 to 3.20 inches in length, and from 1.95 to 2.10 in breadth.

Somateria spectabilis.

THE KING EIDER.

Anas spectabilis, LINN. S. N. ed. 10, I. 1758, 123; ed. 12, I. 1766, 195.

Somateria spectabilis, BOIE, Isis, 1822, 564. — SW. & RICH. F. B. A. II. 1831, 447. — BAIRD, B. N. Am. 1858, 810; Cat. N. Am. B. 1859, no. 608. — COUES, Key, 1872, 293; Check List, 1873, no. 515; 2d ed. 1882, no. 736; B. N. W. 1874, 581. — RIDGW. Nom. N. Am. B. 1881, no. 629.

Fuligula (Somateria) spectabilis, BONAP. Synop. 1828, 389. — NUTT. Man. II. 1834, 414.

Fuligula spectabilis, AUD. Orn. Biog. III. 1835, 523, pl. 276; Synop. 1839, 291; B. Am. VI. 1843, 347, pl. 404.

Anas Beringii, GM. S. N. I. 1788, 508.

Anas superba, LEACH, Syst. Cat. 1816.

HAB. Northern part of the northern hemisphere; in America, south, casually, in winter, to New Jersey and the Great Lakes.

S. spectabilis.

SP. CHAR. *Adult male:* Feathers bordering the base of the maxilla all round, a spot beneath and behind the eye, and a large V-shaped mark on the throat, black; entire top of the head and upper part of the nape delicate pearl-gray, or glaucous-blue, growing gradually deeper behind, where sometimes bordered by an indistinct blackish line; upper and anterior portion of the cheeks, below the eye and immediately behind the black bordering the side of the bill, and an oblique patch on the auricular region delicate sea-green, the auricular patch abruptly defined anteriorly, but above gradually fading into white, along the edge of the bluish-gray of the occiput and nape; remainder of the head, neck, middle of the back, wing-coverts (except greater coverts and exterior border of lesser coverts), lining of the wing, and a patch on each side of the rump white; breast and jugulum deep creamy buff. Remainder of the plumage dull black, the falcate tertials with a narrow and rather indistinct central stripe of dull brownish. "Bill flesh-colored, the sides of the upper mandible and soft frontal lobes bright orange; iris bright yellow; feet dull orange, the webs dusky, the claws brownish black" (AUDUBON). *Adult female, in summer:* Pale fulvous, varied with black, the latter occupying the central portion of the feathers on the dorsal region, forming streaks on the head and neck, and bars on the jugulum, sides, flanks, and upper tail-coverts; abdomen and anal region nearly plain grayish

Male.

brown; wing-coverts, remiges, and rectrices plain grayish dusky, the primaries darker; greater coverts and secondaries scarcely, if at all, tipped with white; rump nearly plain dusky. *Adult female, in autumn:* Rich cinnamon-rufous, varied with black much as in the summer plumage; abdomen and anal region plain brown; greater coverts and secondaries distinctly tipped with white. *Young male:* Head and neck plain umber-brown; upper parts dusky, the feathers bordered with fulvous, especially the scapulars; rump, greater wing-coverts, remiges, and tail plain dusky; upper tail-coverts and lower parts barred with pale fulvous and dusky, the abdomen nearly plain grayish-brown. "Bill pale greenish gray; iris dull yellow; feet dull ochre" (AUDUBON). *Young female:* Similar to the young male, but head and neck grayish-buff, finely streaked with dusky.

Total length, about 20.00–25.00 inches; wing, 10.50–11.25; bill, from base of frontal lobe to tip, in the male, 1.20–1.30; tarsus, 1.80–1.86; middle toe, 2.20.

The female of this species may be easily distinguished from that of the Common and Pacific Eiders (*S. mollissima* and *S. V-nigrum*) by the very different outline of the feathering at the base of the bill, as explained in the diagnostic table on page 73.

Female.

The King Eider is an Arctic bird very closely resembling in its general habits the two other species of the genus *Somateria,* but nowhere so abundant as they are, although more generally distributed, since it is found on the Pacific shores of America and Asia, where the Common Eider does not occur, as well as on the Atlantic coasts of Europe and America.

Dr. Bessels mentions the King Duck as one of the species secured in the northern waters of Smith's Sound by the "Polaris" Expedition, under Captain Hall; and Mr. W. H. Feilden, in his notes on the birds procured in the Arctic Expedition of 1875–1876, states that in the end of June, 1876, several flocks of males and females, numbering from ten to twenty individuals, were seen near Floeberg Beach, lat. 82° 27′. Most of them fell a prey to the hunters, but those that escaped settled down to breed along the coast; and several nests were found with fresh eggs between the 9th and the middle of July.

Mr. Kumlien mentions the arrival of Ducks of this species at Cumberland by the 20th of June; but they were much less abundant than *S. mollissima.* They keep apart from all other kinds during the breeding-season. He was told by the Eskimos that in some seasons they are much more abundant than in others, and that they came later and left earlier than the Eider. A large proportion of those seen were evidently immature or barren birds, and were not breeding. These Ducks were very common about Disco — breeding, however, farther north.

Professor Reinhardt gives this Duck as a resident species in Greenland. Dr. Walker met with it on the coast near the settlement of Godthaab. In the following June he noted its arrival early in that month at its supposed breeding-grounds, where it assembled in the pools of melted water, in the neighborhood of Bellot's Straits. A few of these Ducks annually breed as far to the south as the Bay of Fundy, where Mr. Cheney has several times during the summer found its nest, and has procured specimens for Mr. Boardman.

This bird is seen every winter on the coast of Massachusetts; but only as an occasional visitor, and never in any considerable numbers, except about Nantucket. Some four or five — usually young males — are seen almost every winter in the Boston market.

The Eiders are generally supposed to be exclusively Sea-Ducks — by which name they are universally known on the coast of New England; and it is not infrequently stated that they are not known to occur in fresh water. However rare these exceptions may be, the Common Eider, both in Labrador and on the coast of Norway, has been found spending the breeding-season in inland fresh-water marshes, or on the borders of lakes, several miles from the sea. This species furnishes also a noticeable exception to the general rule of its occurrence, in that it has been found in flocks on the waters of Lake Erie, above the Falls of Niagara, several hundred miles from the sea-coast.

Mr. Charles Linden, of Buffalo, in a letter bearing date of Nov. 21, 1874, writes: "In regard to the occurrence of the King Duck (*Somateria spectabilis*) on Lake Erie, I saw the bird in question, and it proves to be a young male, with the well-marked characteristics of the species clearly and unmistakably developed. Two flocks of these birds, numbering from five to eight each, have been observed this month on Niagara River. Two specimens, male and female, both young, and with very immature plumage, were shot two years ago within five miles of Buffalo, and these were found also to belong to the same species — *spectabilis*. Both were mounted by myself, and are now in the collection of the Buffalo Society of Natural Science."

Mr. Nelson cites this species also as being a rare winter visitant to Lake Michigan and to other parts of Illinois and Wisconsin. There are also in the Smithsonian Collection specimens of young female King Eiders shot in the winter of 1874–1875 on Lake Erie, and of others secured on the Illinois River the same season.

Mr. Hearne makes mention of this species as being quite common in Hudson's Bay. So far as he had noticed, it visits only the sea-coast, and there feeds on fish and fish-spawn. It breeds in that locality, as he speaks of its eggs as being excellent eating, though the flesh is said not by any means to be held in high esteem.

Sir John Richardson speaks of this species as a Sea Duck, and as having never been known by him to occur in fresh water. Its food — he says — is principally the soft mollusca so common in northern waters. This Duck is said to be only partially migratory, rarely moving farther south than is necessary to enable it to get access to open water. The older birds, in the mature plumage, are supposed to be very rarely met with south of the 59th parallel. However true Richardson's statement may be as a general rule, it is not without a considerable number of exceptions.

Although rarely taken within the limits of the United States, the King Duck has occasionally been seen as far south as New York. Mr. Giraud mentions having had the good fortune to procure an adult male of this species in perfect plumage, which had been shot on Long Island Sound in the winter of 1839. He also states that, during the winter, at Egg Harbor, N. J., as well as on the shores of Long Island, young King Eiders are occasionally observed; but the adult specimen in his possession, and one other, were the only individuals in full and mature plumage he had ever known to be procured in the vicinity of New York.

In the Appendix to Sir Edward Parry's First Voyage Colonel Sabine states that this species was seen in great numbers in the North Georgian Islands, the birds having their nests on the ground in the neighborhood of fresh-water ponds, and feeding on the aquatic vegetation.

Sir James C. Ross, also, in the Appendix to his work, says in reference to this species: "Vast numbers of this beautiful Duck resort annually to the shores and islands of the Arctic Regions in the breeding-season, and have on many occasions afforded a valuable and salutary supply of fresh provision to the crews of the vessels employed on those seas. On our late voyage comparatively few were obtained, although seen in very great numbers. They do not retire far to the south during the winter, but assemble in large flocks. The males by themselves and the females with their young brood are often met with in the Atlantic Ocean, far distant from any land, where the numerous crustaceans and other marine animals afford them abundance of food."

Mr. Dall found a single specimen of this species lying dead on the beach near the Rapids on the Yukon. It is known to the Russians as the Pistrik. A series of eggs from St. Michael's, of which the parent was not identified, appeared to belong to this species. Mr. Bannister did not meet with it, and regards it as being extremely uncommon in that region. Mr. Dall afterward observed this species among the winter Ducks at Unalashka, where it was somewhat abundant; but he did not notice any in the Shumagins. There seems to be no evidence of its occurrence on any portion of the west of Oregon or California.

Middendorff includes this species in his list of the birds found in the extreme north of Siberia; and Professor Newton states that it has been several times noticed in Spitzbergen, as also by Loven in Ice Sound in 1857, by Sundevall in Bell Sound the ensuing year, and by Nordenskjöld, who killed two specimens on the northeast coast in 1858; but the latter does not regard it as being of common occurrence, and doubts if it breeds in that region. It has not been met with farther north than lat. 76° 14′. Dr. Malmgren shot one out from a small flock early in July in Safe Haven. Another flock was observed by him in August on Horn Sound Islands. In the Southeast Harbor, Bear Island, July 18, he also saw a very large flock, consisting of hundreds of Ducks and young drakes, with only one or two old drakes among them; but they did not appear to have been breeding there.

Mr. Gillett, in his account of the birds of Nova Zembla, mentions meeting with this Duck in Matthews Strait on the 6th of August. There were several in a small flock, all being apparently immature males; but as their wings were entirely destitute of quill-feathers, they could not fly, but could dive in a wonderful manner, so that they could not be procured without great difficulty. Von Heuglin also met with this species in the same locality.

According to Yarrell, the King Duck is very rare on the British coast. Mr. Bullock found it breeding on Papa Westray, one of the Orkney Islands, in the latter part of June. There were six eggs, covered with the down of the parent, the nest being on a rock which overhung the sea. An egg in Yarrell's collection is described as being 2.50 inches long by 1.75 wide, and of a pale green color.

According to Vieillot, specimens of this bird have been taken in France. Professor Nilsson states that it frequents the most northern parts of the Baltic, of Denmark, and of Norway, and that a few breed in the Faröe Islands and in Iceland. Some of these birds were seen by Audubon in his journey to Labrador; but he did not succeed in finding their nests.

Mr. MacFarlane observed the King Duck breeding on the coast of the Arctic Ocean, in the neighborhood of Franklin Bay; and he writes that when on Island

Point, as he was walking along the sea-beach, a female of this species got up and flew violently away to a short distance, where she alighted on the ground. He at once discovered her nest, which was a mere hole or depression in the ground, about fifty yards from the beach, wholly composed of Eider down, and containing six eggs. Other nests were found on the coast during several seasons, and also among the islands of the Arctic Sea. All appear to have been similar to the one described, and six is the largest number of eggs mentioned as having been found in any one nest.

The eggs of this species are in color of a light shade of olive gray, some being grayish green. They vary considerably in size, ranging from 3.10 to 3.15 inches in length, and from 1.75 to 2.05 in breadth.

Genus **ŒDEMIA**, Fleming.

Oidemia, Fleming, Philos. Zool. II. 1822, 260 (type, *Anas nigra*, Linn.).

Char. Feathers at the base of the maxilla forming a nearly straight oblique line from the forehead back to the rictus, advancing scarcely, if at all, on the forehead; bill very deep through the base, where sometimes elevated into a roundish knob, and much depressed toward the end. No white whatever on the plumage.

Two species only of this genus are known, one European, the other American. They are much alike, but may be distinguished as follows: —

Com. Char. Entire plumage deep black, the bill partly orange, in the males; dull grayish brown (lighter below), the bill wholly black, in the females.

1. **Œ. nigra.**[1] Bill black, the middle portion on top yellow or orange; nail much depressed, scarcely hooked; base of the maxilla much swollen, entirely black. Wing, 8.00–9.20 inches; culmen, 1.90; depth of maxilla at base, .98–1.00, width, .85; tarsus, 1.50–1.60; middle toe, 2.50. *Hab.* Palæarctic Region.
2. **Œ. americana.** Bill with the basal half of the maxilla, except a stripe along the tomium, yellow or orange, the terminal portion and tomial stripe, only, black; nail arched, decidedly hooked; base of the maxilla slightly or not at all swollen, entirely yellow, or orange. Wing, 8.75–9.50 inches; culmen, 1.65–1.80; depth of maxilla at base, .85–.95, width, .90–1.00; tarsus, 1.65–2.00; middle toe, 2.50–2.80.[2] *Hab.* Northern North America.

[1] Œdemia nigra.

Anas nigra, Linn. S. N. I. ed. 10, I. 1758, 123; ed. 12, 1766, 196. — Naum. Vög. Deutschl. XII. 1844, 108, pl. 312.

Oidemia nigra, Flem. Phil. of Zool. II. 1822, 260. — Bonap. Comp. List, 1838, 38. — Keys. & Blas. Wirb. Eur. 1840, 86. — Macgill. Man. II. 181.

Fuligula nigra, Nutt. Man. II. 1832, 423 ("Coast of the United States").

Anas atra, Pall. Zoogr. Rosso-As. II. 1826, 247.

Melanitta nigripes, M. megauros, and *M. gibbera*, Brehm, Vög. Deutschl. 1831, 901, 902.

Oidemia leucocephala, Flem. Brit. An. 1828, 119.

Common Scoter, Yarr. Brit. B. ed. 2, III. 317, fig.; ed. 3, IV. 319, fig.

[2] Only one adult male of *Œ. nigra* is accessible to us for measurement, while of *Œ. americana* we have measured eight examples; a larger series of the former would of course alter the results given above to some extent, but would most likely verify the constancy of the difference in proportions indicated by the above figures.

Œdemia americana.

THE AMERICAN BLACK SCOTER.

Anas nigra, WILS. Am. Orn. VIII. 1814, 135, pl. 72 (not of LINN.).

Oidemia americana, SW. & RICH. F. B. A. II. 1831, 450. — BAIRD, B. N. Am. 1858, 807; Cat. N. Am. B. 1859, no. 604.

Œdemia americana, COUES, Key, 1872, 293; Check List, 1873, no. 516; 2d ed. 1882, no. 737; B. N. W. 1874, 581. — RIDGW. Nom. N. Am. B. 1881, no. 630.

Fuligula (*Oidemia*) *americana*, NUTT. Man. II. 1834, 422.

Fuligula americana, AUD. Orn. Biog. V. 1839, 117, pl. 408; Synop. 1839, 290; B. Am. VI. 1843, 343, pl. 403.

HAB. Coasts and larger inland waters of Northern North America, south to the Great Lakes, New Jersey, and California. Mountains of Colorado (Boulder Co., June!; Mrs. M. A. MAXWELL).

SP. CHAR. *Adult male:* Entire plumage uniform deep black, the neck very faintly glossed with dull violaceous, the feathers somewhat distinctly defined; basal half of the maxilla, except a

Œ. americana.

stripe along the tomium, bright orange (yellowish in the dried skin), the remainder of the bill black; iris hazel; legs and feet dull black. "The bulging part of the upper mandible is bright orange, paler above, that color extending to a little before the nostrils; the rest of the upper mandible, including its basal margin to the breadth of from three to two twelfths of an inch, black, as is the lower mandible. Iris brown. Feet brownish black" (AUDUBON). *Adult female:* Above, dull dark grayish brown, the feathers of the back and scapulars tipped with lighter; lower parts lighter, the pale tips broader, though lacking on the posterior portions; lateral and lower parts of the head and neck nearly uniform very pale grayish brown, quite abruptly defined against the uniform dark brown of the pileum and nape. Bill entirely black. *Young:* Upper parts, jugulum, sides, and flanks, uniform dark grayish brown; sides of head and neck, chin and throat, dirty whitish, tinged with brownish gray, quite abruptly defined against the dark brown of the pileum and nape; abdomen whitish, each feather marked with a dusky grayish brown bar just beneath the surface, some of these bars exposed; anal region and crissum grayish brown, the feathers tipped with white. Bill and feet black.

Total length, about 17 to 19 inches ; extent, 29 to 34. *Male:* Wing, 8.75–9.50 ; culmen, 1.65–1.80 ; tarsus, 1.65–2.00 ; middle toe, 2.50–2.80. *Female*, slightly smaller.

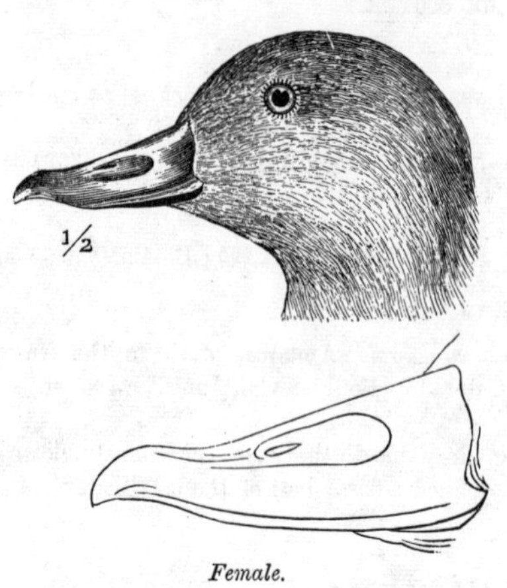

Female.

Having only three European examples of *Œdemia* before us, the material at our command for a satisfactory comparison with *Œ. americana* is not as extensive as could be desired. Two of these specimens, a male and a female received from Schlüter, appear to be the genuine *Œ. nigra*, since they differ very decidedly from all American specimens ; but the third, an adult male (No. 15584, Feb. 8, 1844), from Baron von Müller, is entirely identical with the American bird, and may be an American specimen. Setting aside this latter example, the differences between the two species are very obvious, consisting of the following points : The male of *Œ. nigra* has the bill black, including the basal knob, the culmen having a shield-shaped patch of yellow, extending back to the base of the knob, and reaching forward nearly to the nail ; the end of the bill is altogether more depressed than in *Œ. americana*, the top of the nail being nearly flat, instead of very strongly convex. The female also has the bill conspicuously flattened terminally, as in the male, and also at the base, the maxilla being only about .55 instead of .70 deep. (See accompanying outline figures of the maxillæ of the females of the two species.) There is scarcely any difference in plumage, in either sex, between the two species.

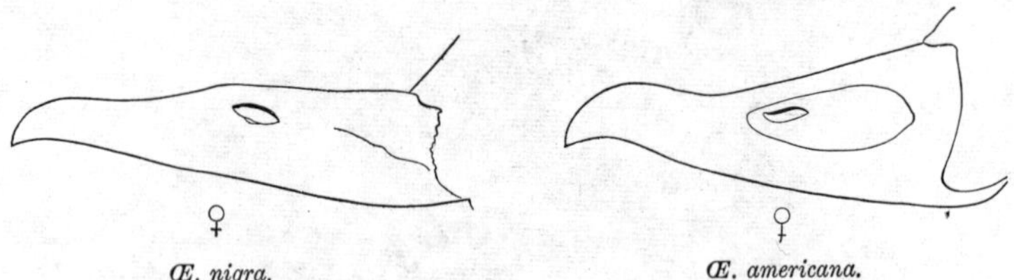

Œ. nigra. *Œ. americana.*

Except the differences of form and plumage, there is very little in the history of this bird to distinguish it from its common associates, the Velvet and the Surf Ducks, the habits, movements, and distribution of these different species appearing to be substantially the same. This Duck is common in the winter on both the Pacific and the Atlantic coasts, and along their entire length, at different portions of the year. It is perhaps a trifle earlier in its migrations southward, and it may linger later in the spring. During September and October, and again in March and April, it is especially common on the coast of New England, and is found present to a greater or less extent during the whole winter. It breeds in the extreme north, but does not appear to have been found by Mr. MacFarlane at such times in company with the Surf and Velvet Ducks in the neighborhood of Fort Anderson. It visits the Great Lakes, and is especially common in the winter upon Lake Michigan.

Sir John Richardson says, in regard to this Duck, that it feeds almost exclusively in the open sea, that its flesh is always oily and strongly flavored, and that it frequents the shores of Hudson's Bay, breeding there between the 50th and the 60th parallels of latitude. He also states that he never saw it at any season of the year in the interior of the country.

Hearne writes that at his time — 1780 — this Duck was one of the most common in Hudson's Bay, where it visited the sea-coast exclusively, and was never found in the interior, feeding chiefly on fish and their spawn. Its flesh was by no means held in esteem, but the eggs were quite palatable. Mr. Murray and Captain Blakiston both cite this species as still being abundant in the region adjacent to Hudson's Bay.

On the Pacific coast its presence has been noted from Alaska to Southern California, and Mr. Bannister found it common on the Island of St. Michael's; and he states that, except on one occasion, he has never seen it in any of the small fresh-water ponds of that island. Ordinarily it kept to the salt-water, even flying round points of land rather than directly across them.

Male.

The name of this Duck in the Eskimo dialect, according to Mr. E. Adams ("Ibis," 1878), is *Too-tár-lik*; and it is spoken of by him as being rather late in its arrival on the shores of Norton Sound, none of this species coming until the 19th of May. Toward the end of the month several pairs had taken possession of the larger lakes near St. Michael's, where they remained to breed, seldom going out to sea, but keeping together in small flocks in the middle of the lake. Their nests were carefully secreted in the clefts and hollows about the steep banks of the lakes, close to the water, and were built of coarse grass, well lined with feathers and down. The females had their eggs at the time of his leaving, which was in June.

Mr. Dall speaks of this as being a salt-water Duck, abundant at the mouth of the Yukon, but not going up that river for any distance. He was so fortunate as to find it breeding near Pastolik, June 17, discovering a nest which contained two eggs. These he describes as being quite white, and large as compared with the size of the bird. The nest was placed on the ground, on a small island, in a clump of willows, and was well supplied with dry grass, feathers, leaves, and moss. Since that Mr. Dall has met with this species on the Aleutian Islands, where he found it not uncommon during the winter, but migrating with the other Ducks in the spring. It was noticed both at Unalashka and on the Shumagins, and it was also seen on the coast of Vancouver Island by Mr. R. Browne. Dr. Cooper speaks of finding it less abundant along the entire coast of California than the other Surf Ducks, but associating with them, and with habits almost exactly similar to theirs.

Mr. Giraud speaks of this Duck as being common in winter on the Atlantic side of Long Island. It is there also one of that class of Ducks known to fishermen and hunters as "Coots." By some it is called the "Butter-billed Coot" — a name by which it is also generally known to sportsmen in New England. It is also there called the "Hollow-billed Coot" — a designation applied in New England exclusively to the Surf Duck. On the Long Island shore this bird passes its time in the open sea in company with the Velvet and the Surf Ducks. Like other diving Ducks, it is occasionally taken by being entangled in the fishermen's nets.

According to Audubon the Scoter Duck ranges along our entire southern coast, even as far as New Orleans — or rather, the mouth of the Mississippi River. He also states that a few of this species remain in Labrador to breed, and that some of his young companions met with their nests on the 11th of July; but he is either in error in the description he gives of the eggs found, or else they were not those of this Duck. The nest, he says, was placed at the distance of about two yards from the margin of a large fresh-water pond, about a mile from the shore of the Gulf of St. Lawrence, under a low fir, in the manner often adopted by the Eider Duck, whose nest it somewhat resembled, although much smaller. It was composed externally of sticks, moss, and grasses, and was lined with down mixed with feathers. The eggs — eight in number — were nearly ready to be hatched. Audubon describes them as being 2.00 inches in length and 1.63 in breadth, of an oval form, and of a pale yellowish color. The identified eggs of this species — so far as I know — are uniformly white. Audubon afterward found a female with seven young ones, of which she took such affectionate care that none of them fell into his hands. When they had become fatigued by diving she received all of them on her back, and, swimming very fast, carried them to the shore, where they escaped by hiding among the tall grass.

Eggs of this species (Smithsonian Institution, No. 14602), obtained by Mr. Dall at Pastolik, are of a pinkish ivory-white, varying in length from 2.65 to 2.70 inches, and with a breadth of 1.60.

Genus **MELANETTA**, Boie.

Melanitta, Boie, Isis, 1822, 564 (type, by elimination, *Anas fusca*, Linn.).
Melanetta, Gray, 1840; List Gen. 1841, 95. — Baird, B. N. Am. 1858, 805.
Maceranas, Less. Man. II. 1828, 414 (same type).

Char. Feathers at the base of the bill extending forward almost to the nostril in two prominent angles — one on the side of the maxilla, the other on top, at the base of the culmen; sides of

M. velvetina.

the maxilla rather sunken or compressed above the tomium. Colors uniform black or brown, with a white speculum on the wings, the adult male with a white spot immediately beneath the eye.

This genus differs from *Œdemia* and *Pelionetta*—to which it is otherwise nearly allied—in the form of the bill, particularly in the outline of the feathering at the base, as defined above. Two species only are known, one peculiar to Northern North America, the other to the Palæarctic Region, but occurring also in Greenland and Alaska. Their differential characters are as follows: —

1. **M. fusca.** Maxilla much swollen near the rictus, the base of the culmen only slightly elevated ; reddish color of the maxilla crossed on each side by a black line, running obliquely from the black above the nostril to that on each side of the nail. *Adult male:* Wing, 10.80–11.40 inches ; culmen, 1.80–1.70 ; depth of maxilla at base, 1.10 ; tarsus, 1.70–1.80 ; middle toe, 2.75 (two examples). *Hab.* Palæarctic Region, Greenland, and Alaska.
2. **M. velvetina.** Maxilla deeply sunken near the rictus, the base of the culmen elevated into a prominent knob ; reddish color of the maxilla not crossed by a black line. *Adult male:* Wing, 10.65–11.40 inches ; culmen, 1.40–1.70 ; depth of maxilla at base, 1.10–1.30 ; tarsus, 1.80–2.10 ; middle toe, 2.70–2.90 (eleven examples[1]). *Hab.* Northern North America.

Melanetta velvetina.

THE VELVET SCOTER.

Anas fusca, WILS. Am. Orn. VIII. 1814, 137, pl. 72 (not of LINN.).
Fuligula (Oidemia) fusca, BONAP. Synop. 1828, 390. — NUTT. Man. II. 1834, 419.
Oidemia fusca, SW. & RICH. F. B. A. II. 1831, 449.
Œdemia fusca, COUES, Check List, 2d ed. 1882, no. 738.
Fuligula fusca, AUD. Orn. Biog. III. 1835, 454, pl. 247 ; Synop. 1839, 280 ; B. Am. VI. 1843, 332, pl. 401.
? *Fuligula bimaculata*, HERBERT, Field Sports, 2d ed. II. 1848, 366, fig. (young).
Oidemia (Pelionetta) bimaculata, BAIRD, B. N. Am. 1858, 808.
Oidemia velvetina, CASS. Pr. Ac. Nat. Sci. Philad. V. 1850, 126.
Melanetta velvetina, BAIRD, B. N. Am. 1858, 805 ; Cat. N. Am. B. 1859, no. 601. — RIDGW. Nom. N. Am. B. 1881, no. 632.
Œdemia fusca, var. (?), COUES, Key, 1872, 294 ; Check List, 1873, no. 517.
Œdemia fusca, b. (?) *velvetina*, COUES, Birds N. W. 1874, 582.
Oidemia Deglandii, BONAP. Rev. Crit. Degland, 1850, 108.

HAB. Northern North America ; chiefly maritime, but occurring on various inland waters ; south in winter to the Middle States, Great Lakes, Mississippi River near St. Louis, Illinois River, and Southern California.

SP. CHAR. *Adult male:* Base of the culmen elevated into a prominent knob ; lateral base of the maxilla sunken beneath the feathering of the lores. Plumage uniform brownish black. A crescentic spot beneath the eye, and extending backward for half an inch or more, secondaries, and greater wing-coverts, white. Knob of the bill, with base, and margin of the maxilla, black ; "sides of the bill red-lead, fading into orange ;" "nail vermilion, the anterior flat portion of the upper mandible whitish ;" iris "white tinged with straw-yellow ; legs scarlet, with black webs, and a tinge of black on the joints" (NUTTALL).[2] *Young male:* Dark sooty-brown, the head and neck sooty-black ; white on wings as in the adult, but no white spot beneath the eye. *Adult female:* Uniform grayish fuliginous, the wings darker ; white speculum as in the male, but no white about the head, or with faint indication of white spot at base of maxilla and behind the eye.

[1] With the exception of the culmen, which in only one of eleven specimens reaches the *minimum* of the same in *M. fusca*, the *average* measurements of this series would approximate much more nearly to the maximum than to the minimum.

[2] Audubon's description of the Velvet Scoter refers wholly to the European species (*M. fusca*), which has the bill and feet colored very differently from the American bird.

In summer, feathers of the back, scapular region, and jugulum narrowly tipped with light brownish gray. Bill uniform dusky; iris yellow; feet as in the male, but duller in color.

Total length, about 19.75 to 22.50 inches; extent, 36.00 to 40.00; wing, 10.75–12.00; commissure, 2.82; tarsus, 2.08.

This well-known North American form — the Velvet Duck — is an Arctic species during the breeding-season; and in the fall, winter, and spring is distributed along the entire Atlantic and the Pacific coasts, to an extent varying with the severity of the season and the abundance of the food. It is eminently a Sea-Duck, resorting to inland waters chiefly during the brief season of reproduction. It is also a winter visitant to the Great Lakes — especially Michigan — and to the rivers of Illinois. It is also said to occur on the Pacific coasts of Asia. Captain Blakiston is very sure that he obtained this species at Chin-Kiang, on the Yang-tse River, in China, the specimens there procured being identical with those he saw on the Pacific coast of North America; and he also mentions finding this Duck on Hudson's Bay. Mr. Murray also reports it as occurring between Hudson's Bay and Lake Winnipeg; and Mr. Ross met with it on the Mackenzie River as far north as the Arctic Ocean.

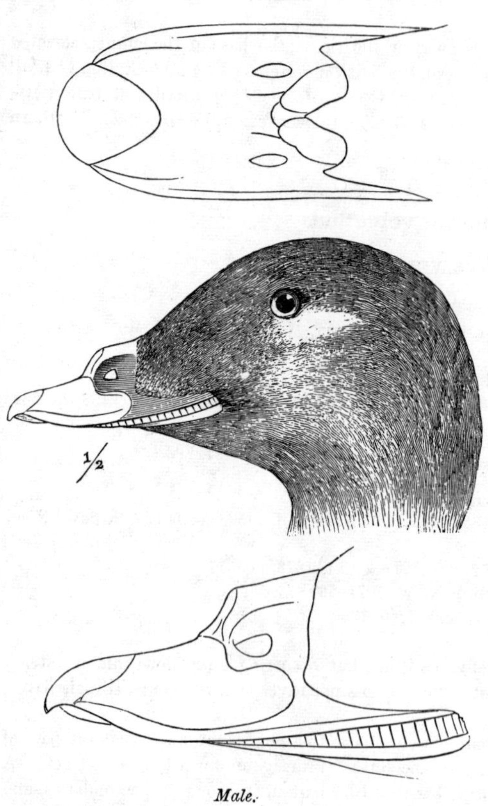

Male.

On the New England coast this species makes its appearance in the fall from the middle to the last of September, coming in flocks of moderate size, the old birds often preceding the young by several weeks. It is universally known from Eastport to the Chesapeake as the "White-winged Coot." It is much hunted; and although its flesh is dark, coarse, and strongly flavored, it is esteemed by those who have become accustomed to its flavor. In its flight, except when the weather is stormy, this bird passes very high; and when it is thus out of their reach hunters resort to the expedient of shooting, in order to alarm the flock. This often has the desired effect; the foolish birds, alarmed at the unusual noise, make a sudden plunge in the direction of the water, as if that element alone could give them safety, and in their descent present the opportunity desired by the hunter. This habit is peculiar to the Velvet Duck, and has not been noticed either in the Scoter or the Surf-Ducks.

On Long Island, according to Giraud, large flocks of this Duck keep outside of the beach, and are seen along the entire Atlantic district, where they subsist by fishing.

They seldom visit the small bays, unless driven by the storms, when they are also sometimes seen passing over the land. During their long migrations they fly high, performing in silence extended journeys from their northern breeding-places. They arrive off the coast of Long Island about the middle of October, and remain there until about the middle of April. This bird, when well supplied with down and in full plumage, can only be brought down by a gun heavily charged with powder and shot. When this Duck is present in large numbers on the south shore of Long Island, the hunters watch for a favorable opportunity when the surf is down, and form a line with fifteen or twenty boats about two or three gunshots apart; by adopting this method of attack it becomes difficult for a flock to escape entirely. The boats used for this purpose are light skiffs, each containing but a single person, in order that the waves may be ridden with safety. But this mode of shooting can be practised only by experienced hunters; for if the wind rises suddenly from the south, a dangerous surf is created, in which even the most skilful boatmen are occasionally drowned. According to Mr. Giraud, the flesh of the Velvet Duck is not held in high esteem, but is dark-colored and fishy; yet a large number of these birds find a ready sale in the New York market. Richardson speaks of this species as feeding principally in the open sea, and as having strong and oily flesh. This bird is said to breed on the Arctic coast, and to move southwardly in company with the Surf and the Long-tailed Ducks. On its way it stops on the lakes of the interior so long as they remain open, and again on the shores of Hudson's Bay, feeding on tender shellfish and mollusca.

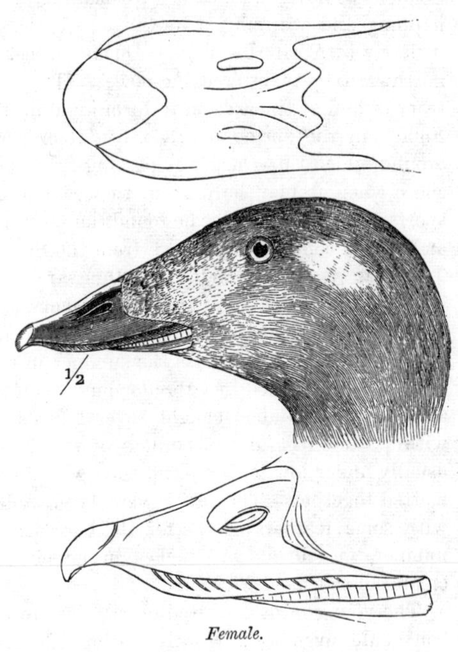

Female.

On the Pacific coast it is met with, according to the season, from Alaska to Southern California. Mr. Dall found it not uncommon on the Lower Yukon; and he obtained a female fifty miles below the fort. Shortly afterward — June 23, 1866 — he secured several of the young ducklings, still in their downy coat. Mr. Bannister thinks that this species occurs at St. Michael's; but he did not identify it with certainty. Mr. Bischoff obtained it in great abundance at Sitka. Mr. Dall also speaks of it as having been killed by him, Oct. 27, 1871, at Unalashka; and he noticed its presence there at intervals throughout the winter. It was not seen on the Shumagins, though it may, and probably does, occur there. It is only a winter visitor in that region.

Mr. R. Browne found this species a winter visitor on Vancouver Island.

Dr. Cooper informs me that on the coast of California this species is often called the Black Surf Duck. It is common in winter along the entire sea-coast of California, and a few superannuated individuals remain throughout the summer. It frequents almost exclusively the salt water in the open bays and the outer beaches, very rarely appearing on the fresh ponds, and only on those near the beach. The main body of these Ducks arrive about the first of October, and remain until April, together with the other Surf Ducks with which they associate. Their food consists of small fish, mollusca, crabs, and the like; and for these they dive in deep water. Their habits are to some extent nocturnal, and during the day they often float out in the centre of the Bay, remaining asleep for hours. At such times they may be approached; but usually they are very vigilant, flying out of gunshot, or diving. Dr. Cooper has never heard this bird making any other noise than that produced by the flapping and whizzing of its wings as it rises with difficulty from the water.

Early in April the Velvet Ducks collect in large flocks preparatory to moving northward to their breeding-places. They pass along the shore, at a short distance from it, and at times seem to form an almost continuous line. While in the Bay of Fundy, in the spring of 1833, Audubon went with his party to a projecting cape, around which this Duck was passing from daylight until evening — approaching the shore when it blew hard from the sea, and affording abundant opportunities for the sportsman. In Labrador he found the waters covered with dense flocks of this species, and others continued to arrive from the St. Lawrence for several days in succession. This was about the middle of June, and the season was an unusually late one, the fishermen informing him that these Ducks usually passed a fortnight earlier. A few of them remained to breed on the southern coast of Labrador; and a large number of sterile individuals also pass the summer in the Bay of Fundy.

Those which bred in Labrador built their nests from the 1st to the 10th of June; and July 28 Audubon caught several birds a few days old. The nests were placed within a few feet of the borders of small lakes distant a mile or two from the sea, usually under low bushes; and they were formed of twigs, mosses, and various plants matted together. The nests were large, and almost flat, several inches thick, lined with some feathers of the female, but without down. The eggs were usually six in number, measuring 2.75 inches in length and 1.88 in breadth, of a uniform pale cream-color, tinged with green.

The young-birds procured on the 28th of July were about a week old; and Audubon could even then readily distinguish the males from the females — the former having a white spot under the eye. The down with which they were covered was stiff and hair-like, of a black color, except under the chin, which was white. The ducklings swam with so much ease that it was impossible to catch them while in the water, as they would dive with great dexterity, the mother in the meanwhile manifesting the greatest anxiety, calling to her brood with short squeaking notes — which, however, were by no means unpleasant to the ear.

The Velvet Duck dives with great agility, and when wounded can only be taken with difficulty.

Mr. MacFarlane met with this bird breeding in considerable numbers on the Lower Anderson River, in the neighborhood of the Fort, on the Barren Grounds; and also quite as frequently in the wooded country. The nests were always on the ground, near fresh water, and all contained more or less down. The number of eggs ranged from five to eight. One nest, taken June 14, was on the ground in a small clump of woods near Fort Anderson, and was made of feathers, down, etc. Another one, found July 3, contained seven eggs, and was in a clump of small spruce, where it was entirely concealed. A third, taken June 22, was found at the foot of a low pine, shaded by its branches, and almost entirely hidden; it was made of down, with the addition of a few feathers. All the other nests were essentially similar in character to these — being invariably depressions made in the ground, at the foot of small trees, and lined almost entirely with down and feathers.

Specimens of this bird were taken by Mr. Kennicott near Fort Resolution, June 5, 1860; and, a little later, on the Yukon River. In this neighborhood it was also found by Mr. Lockhart in June, 1861 and 1862.

This Duck is very rarely seen on any of the interior waters of the United States. A male in very shabby plumage was shot near Black-hawk Island, in Lake Koskonong, Wisconsin, Oct. 12, 1860; and this specimen is still in Professor Kumlien's collection.

Eggs of this species are of a uniform pale pinkish cream-color. Examples in the Smithsonian Collection from the Yukon (Nos. 6679 and 6678) measure 2.70 by 1.90 inches, and 2.75 by 1.80.

Melanetta fusca.

THE EUROPEAN VELVET SCOTER.

Anas fusca, LINN. S. N. ed. 10, I. 1758, 123; ed. 12, I. 1766, 196. — NAUM. Vög. Deutschl. XII. 1844, 123, pl. 313.

Melanitta fusca, BOIE, Isis, 1822, 564.

Melanetta fusca, RIDGW. Pr. U. S. Nat. Mus. Vol. 3, 1880, 205, 222; Nom. N. Am. B. 1881, no. 631.

Oidemia fusca, STEPHENS, Shaw's Gen. Zool. XII. pt. ii. 1824, 216. — BONAP. Comp. List, 1838, 57. — KEYS. & BLAS. Wirb. Eur. 86. — MACGILL. Man. II. 180. — GRAY, Gen. III. 625; Cat. Brit. B. 1863, 206.

Anas carbo, PALL. Zoog. Rosso-As. II. 1826, 244.

Anas fuliginosa, BECHST. Naturg. IV. 962, pl. 36.

Melanitta Hornschuchii, *M. megapus*, and *M. platyrhynchos*, BREHM. Vög. Deutschl. 1831, pp. 904, 906, 907.

Velvet Scoter, YARR. Brit. B. ed. 2, III. 312, fig.; ed. 3, III. 314, fig.; et AUCT.

HAB. Palæarctic Region; accidental in Southern Greenland (REINHARDT, Vid. Med. Nat. For. Kjöbenhavn, 1879, 1); Alloknagik Lake, Alaska, July 20, 1883; C. L. MCKAY (spec. in Nat. Mus. Coll.).

SP. CHAR. *Adult male:* Maxilla much swollen near the rictus, the base of the culmen only slightly elevated, orange or reddish of the maxilla crossed on each side by a black line running obliquely from the black above the nostril to that on each side of the nail. General color brownish black, relieved by a white, somewhat crescentic, patch beneath the eye, and extending somewhat behind it, and a white speculum on the wings (involving the secondary quills). "The upper basal prominence of the bill, the nostrils, part of the lateral prominences, the margins of the upper mandible, and a streak on each side of the unguis black; the sides rich orange, the unguis and part of the ridge reddish flesh-color; the basal half of the lower mandible black, the rest lake-red. The iris is grayish white, with an external dusky ring. The inner side of the tarsus, of the hind toe and its web, as well as of the other toes, with the whole loose web of the inner orpiment-orange; the outer side of the tarsus, hind toe and its web, as well as of the other toes, bluish carmine, or lake; the sole of the toes and the webs above brownish black; the claws black" (MACGILLIVRAY). *Adult female:* Sooty grayish, or grayish dusky, darker above; wing with a white speculum, but no white spot on side of head. Bill entirely dusky; feet as in the male, but colors duller.

Wing, 10.65–11.40 inches; culmen, 1.40–1.70; depth of maxilla at base, 1.10–1.30; tarsus, 1.80–2.10; middle toe, 2.70–2.90.

GENUS **PELIONETTA**, KAUP.

Pelionetta, KAUP, Entw. Europ. Thierw. 1829, 107 (type, *Anas perspicillata*, LINN.).

CHAR. Feathers on the forehead extending in a broad strip nearly or quite as far as the posterior end of the nostrils, but those of the lores not advancing forward of the rictus, the lateral base of the maxilla in the adult male greatly swollen, and with the basal outline convex, nail very

P. perspicillata.

large and broad, but narrowed terminally. No white on the wing, but the head with large white patches (indistinct in the female and young).

Except in the form of the bill, as described above, this genus very closely resembles *Melanetta* and *Œdemia*, but is sufficiently distinct. Only one species is known.

Pelionetta perspicillata.

THE SURF DUCK.

Anas perspicillata, LINN. S. N. ed. 10, I. 1758, 125; ed. 12, I. 1766, 201. — WILS. Am. Orn. VIII. 1824, 49, pl. 67.

Fuligula (*Oidemia*) *perspicillata*, BONAP. Synop. 1828, 389. — NUTT. Man. II. 1834, 416.

Oidemia perspicillata, STEPHENS, Gen. Zool. XII. ii. 1824, 219. — SW. & RICH. F. B. A. II. 1831, 449.

Œdemia perspicillata, COUES, Key, 1872, 294; Check List, 1873, no. 518; 2d ed. 1882, no. 739; B. N. W. 1874, 582.

Pelionetta perspicillata, REICH. Syst. Av. 1852, p. viii. — BAIRD, B. N. Am. 1858, 806; Cat. N. Am. B. 1859, no. 602. — RIDGW. Nom. N. Am. B. 1881, no. 633.

Fuligula perspicillata, AUD. Orn. Biog. IV. 1838, 161, pl. 317; Synop. 1839, 289; B. Am. VI. 1843, 337, pl. 402.

Pelionetta Trowbridgii, BAIRD, B. N. Am. 1858, 806; Cat. N. Am. B. 1859, no. 603.

Œdemia perspicillata, var. *Trowbridgii*, COUES, Key, 1872, 295; Check List, 1873, no. 518*a*.

Œdemia perspicillata, b. *Trowbridgii*, COUES, B. N. W. 1874, 582.

Œdemia perspicillata Trowbridgii, COUES, Check List, 2d ed. 1882, no. 740.

HAB. Coasts and larger inland waters of Northern North America, south in winter to Atlantic coast of the United States, to the Ohio in the interior, and Lower California, on the Pacific side; accidental in Europe. Jamaica (and other West India islands?) in winter.

SP. CHAR. *Adult male:* General color deep black, very intense above, more sooty on the lower surface; a white patch on the forehead, the anterior outline semicircular or somewhat angular, and reaching forward a little in advance of the lateral base of the bill, the posterior outline almost directly transverse, and extending back to a little past the middle of the eye; nape with a somewhat shield-shaped, or cuneate, longitudinal patch of pure white, having the upper outline almost directly transverse. Bill chiefly orange-red, deeper (intense red in some specimens) above the nostrils; swollen base of the maxilla with a large, irregularly roundish, somewhat quadrate, or trapezoidal, spot of deep black, with a light-colored space (bluish white in life) in front, as far as the nostrils; nails duller orange, or dingy grayish; iris yellowish white; feet orange-red, the webs greenish dusky; claws black. "Upper mandible with a nearly square black patch at the base, margined with orange, except in front, where there is a patch of bluish white extending to near the nostrils, prominent part over the nostrils deep reddish orange, becoming lighter toward the unguis, and shaded into rich yellow toward the margins; the unguis dingy grayish yellow; lower mandible flesh-colored, unguis darker. Iris bright yellowish white. Tarsi and toes orange-red, the webs dusky, tinged with green; claws black" (AUDUBON). *Adult female:* Pileum and nape brownish black; rest of the head ashy brown, with an indistinct whitish patch (not always indicated) on the lower anterior portion of the lores, bordering the lateral base of the bill; upper parts brownish dusky, the contour feathers sometimes showing paler tips; lower parts grayish brown, becoming nearly white on the abdomen, the feathers of the breast and sides tipped with the same, the anal region and crissum uniform dusky. Bill greenish black, scarcely swollen at the base, where the black spot of the male is slightly, if at all, indicated; iris yellowish white; "feet yellowish orange, webs grayish dusky, claws black" (AUDUBON). *Young:* Similar to the adult female, but head with two quite distinct whitish patches, one against the lateral base of the bill, the other over the auriculars, behind and below the eye; plumage above, more uniform than in the adult female, and feathers everywhere of a softer texture.

Male.

Total length, about 19.00–20.00 inches; extent, 31.00–34.00; wing, 9.25–9.75; culmen, 1.30–1.60; from tip of bill to lateral base, 2.35–2.60; distance through base of bill horizontally, between most prominent point of lateral swellings, 1.10–1.40; tarsus, 1.55–1.85; middle toe, 2.15–2.55 (twenty examples).

There is considerable variation among individuals of this species, but we find no constant difference between specimens from the Atlantic coast and those from the Pacific. Occasionally, in specimens which appear to be fully adult (as No. 12727, ♂, Washington, D. C.; C. Drexler), the white patch on the crown is entirely absent, that on the nape being present, as usual. An example from Sitka (No. 46266; F. Bischoff) has, in addition to the usual white patches (on crown and nape), a white bar across the lower part of the foreneck, and a longitudinal streak of the same on the chin. The bill, in fully adult examples, occasionally has other black markings besides the large black spot near the base. Thus, No. 31727, Yukon River, Alaska, has a black spot at the base of the culmen; in some others there is a small black spot on each side of the maxilla, near the end. Dr. Otto Finsch has sent to Professor Baird drawings of the head of a Scoter from Alaska, which is quite different in many respects from any example we have seen of *P. perspicillata.* The bill is very different in shape from that of the common species, being in every way more slender, the greatest breadth of the maxilla anteriorly being but .75 of an inch, while the transverse diameter through the base, which is but slightly swollen, is only 1.00 inch; the length from the culmen is about 1.35, to the loral feathers, 2.10; the culmen is much less elevated above the nostrils, and the tip of the bill less depressed. The prevailing color of the bill is black, the nail lighter, but across the culmen, just behind the nail, and continued back in a narrow stripe, between the nostrils and the tomium, almost to the base, is a mark (having somewhat this form, W) of salmon-color or orange, becoming yellow posteriorly. The head and neck are deep black, with a longitudinal, cuneate, nuchal patch of white, as in *P. perspicillata,* and the frontal spot is also distinctly indicated, though somewhat broken by the admixture of black feathers; but in addition to these markings, the lores are covered by a large subquadrate white patch extending from the lateral base of the bill, for its entire length, back about .75 of an inch, almost touching the eye above; there is also a white ovate spot immediately above and behind the eye, and another of crescentic form on the lower eyelid. The differences in the markings of the head would not alone be sufficient to indicate more than a variation of plumage of the common species; but the form and coloration of the bill is so different as to suggest the possibility of the specimen being a hybrid between *P. perspicillata* and *Melanetta fusca* or *velvetina.* The wing, however, is said to lack the white speculum of *Melanetta.*

Female.

The three examples (from San Diego, Cal.) upon which the *P. Trowbridgii* was based, differ but little from some eastern specimens of *P. perspicillata,* while other Pacific coast specimens, including examples from as far south as the coast of Lower California, are unquestionably identical with the eastern bird.

The Surf Duck is a peculiarly North American species, nearly identical, both as to its habits and its distribution, with the Velvet Duck, both species being known on the Atlantic coast to hunters and fishermen as Coots; this term being used there as a synonyme of the name "Sea Duck." The Surf Duck is generally known in New England as the "Skunk-head Coot," and also to some persons as the "Hollow-billed Coot." Its young and female, as well as the young and female of the Scoter (*Œdemia americana*), are indiscriminately called "Gray Coots;" but some persons apply the term Gray Coot to the young and females of the Surf Duck only.

In Europe this species appears to have been found only as an occasional and accidental visitor. According to Mr. Selby, specimens of this Duck have been taken on the Shetland and Orkney islands. Others have been secured in different parts of Scotland and England. Vieillot states that it sometimes appears on the coast of France. A single example was taken in 1818 in Switzerland, and others are recorded as coming from Germany and Scandinavia; but these instances are few in number, and the appearance of this species in any part of Europe is decidedly an uncommon occurrence.

It is cited by Professor Reinhardt as being a visitant in Greenland — where, however, only a few individuals are known to have been taken. It was found abundant on the Mackenzie River by Mr. Ross; Captain Blakiston received a number of specimens from York Factory, on Hudson's Bay; and Mr. Murray also obtained it in the same locality, where it appears only occasionally as a migrant.

From September to April the Surf Duck is common on the whole Atlantic coast, from Nova Scotia to North Carolina, its presence apparently being regulated as much by the abundance of its food as by the severity of the weather. Until midwinter the flocks gradually move southward, their food being more abundant in warmer waters, and after February as gradually find their way back. In April a general migration northward becomes very perceptible, and by the end of that month the immense procession of this very abundant species has passed, beyond the Bay of Fundy, toward its breeding-places, only the crippled, immature, or superannuated individuals having been left behind; and these remain unmated in the more southern latitudes through the whole summer.

Mr. Giraud states that by the hunters of Long Island this species is known as the "Spectacled Coot," and also as the "Surf Coot." It associates with the Velvet Duck, and its habits are substantially the same as those of that species. He relates that when at Montauk Point, in the autumn of 1834, on walking out in the morning, after a very stormy night, and looking up at the lighthouse, he was surprised to see a bird suspended from the wire frame by which the glass is protected. On taking it down, he found it to be a Surf Duck. The wind having been very high the night before, and the water having doubtless become so rough that the bird was obliged to take wing, it was attracted by the light, and flying with great force, thrust its head through the wires, and in this situation was strangled. The flesh of the Surf Duck Giraud found to be dark-colored and fishy.

Sir John Richardson states that this bird seeks its food principally in the sea; that its flesh is oily and highly flavored; and that he found it breeding on the Arctic coast, from whence it migrated southward, in company with the Velvet and the Long-tailed Ducks. In these migrations southward it stops both on the shores of Hudson's Bay and on the lakes of the interior — at least as long as these remain open — feeding on mollusca and shellfish. It is rare in Bermuda, there being only two instances on record of its occurrence there — one in Hamilton Harbor, in January, 1847, and another in the Pembroke Marshes, October, 1854.

This species is as abundant on the Pacific as on the Atlantic coast. It was obtained, with the eggs, at Sitka, by Bischoff, and Mr. Dall — although he did not fully identify it — thinks that it is found at the mouth of the Yukon River. Mr. R. Browne also met with it on the coast of Vancouver Island.

Mr. Nelson mentions the Surf Duck as being a common winter resident upon Lake Michigan, and says that it also occurs throughout the State of Illinois during that season. A large number of examples of this species were taken near the Calumet Marshes during the fall of 1875, and many others were seen, arriving the last of October and departing toward the end of March. A single specimen of this bird, in immature plumage, was procured on the Wabash by Professor Stein, in October, 1875.

It is said to be abundant on the Pacific coast near San Pedro; but it was not found inland, nor on any of the interior lagoons, apparently never leaving the sea and its estuaries. Dr. Cooper also writes that this is an abundant species in the winter along the entire Pacific coast, associating with the other Surf Ducks, and having habits similar to theirs. Being but little hunted, and having but few enemies among the wild animals, many of this species become very old, and linger along the southern coast in large flocks — some of them finally dying of old age. The long rainy seasons are frequently fatal to them, as at that time they seem to be very delicate, and are peculiarly subject to the influences of the weather. Many become very thin, and even blind, at the time of assuming their spring plumage, and swim, unconscious of danger, near the wharves and shores, or after storms are found dead along the beaches.

Audubon states that in his visit to Labrador, in the spring of 1833, he found this species not the least numerous of the various kinds of Ducks with which the waters of that region seemed to be alive. The numbers of this species that passed the shores of Labrador bound for the far north exceeded all his previous conceptions. He noticed that a few pairs had remained in the neighborhood of Little Macatina, and on examining a fresh-water marsh he suddenly started a female Surf Duck from her nest. This was snugly placed among the tall leaves of a bunch of grass, and raised a few inches above the roots. It was entirely made of withered and rotten weeds, the former being circularly arranged over the latter, producing a well-rounded cavity 6.00 inches in diameter, and 2.50 deep. The borders of the inner cup were lined with the down of the bird, and in it there were five eggs. These were 2.31 inches in length, by 1.63 in breadth, and about equally rounded at both ends. The shell was perfectly smooth, and of a pale yellowish or cream color.

Audubon states that Dr. Bachman met with this Duck in the winter as far south as Charleston, S. C. He speaks of it as being a powerful swimmer and an expert diver, but as rising from the water with some difficulty, and, when once under way, flying with great rapidity. The female, as she rises from her nest, utters a rough guttural cry; but this Duck is generally a very silent bird. Audubon was assured that in Newfoundland this species breeds in considerable numbers in the lakes and ponds of the interior. Its stomach was found to contain fish of different kinds, several species of shellfish, and quantities of coarse gravel.

Mr. Lockhart observed this species breeding near the Arctic Sea. The nest was on the edge of a small portage between two lakes, and concealed under the spreading branches of a stunted pine-tree.

Mr. MacFarlane found the Surf Duck breeding in considerable numbers in the neighborhood of Fort Anderson and on the Lower Anderson River, and a nest containing six eggs was obtained July 5 on the margin of a small lake. It was not distinguishable from the nests of the Velvet Duck. Another nest, containing eight eggs, was found, June 25, on a ridge of ground at the foot of a dry stunted pine, and was made of dark-colored down, being entirely concealed from view by the lower branches of the pine-tree. This species of Duck was very numerous in the wooded country, but the nests were found only with great difficulty. It was afterward ascertained to be very abundant on the sea-coast about Franklin's Bay. All the nests found appear to have been of the same style and pattern, and nothing is said of any other material than down being used in building them. The number of eggs varied from five to eight; but the latter number was found in only a single instance.

This Duck was seen breeding near Fort Resolution by Mr. Kennicott in June, 1860, and on the Yukon River both by him and Mr. Lockhart. It was found near Fort Simpson by Mr. B. R. Ross and Mr. McDonald; near Fort Rae by Mr. L. Clarke; and at La Pierre House by Mr. J. Flett.

We have no data in reference to any peculiarly distinctive habits of the so-called *P. Trowbridgii* that would enable us to state whether these exhibit anything of a specific character. The individuals upon which this supposed species was founded were taken by Lieutenants Trowbridge and Williamson at San Diego in the winter of 1853. Two other specimens have since been obtained by Mr. Bischoff at Sitka.

Dr. Cooper writes that although he was constantly on the lookout for Ducks of this species while on the southern coast of California, he never succeeded in finding one. If any do occur, he thinks that they must have come as stragglers from the coast of Asia.

Eggs of the Surf Duck obtained on the Arctic coast east of Anderson River by Mr. MacFarlane (Smithsonian Institution, No. 9566) are of a uniform ivory-white color, with a slight pinkish tinge, ranging from 2.25 to 2.30 inches in length, and averaging about 1.60 in breadth.

Genus **ERISMATURA**, Bonaparte.

Oxyura, Bonap. Synop. 1828, 390 (type, *Anas rubida*, Wils.); nec *Oxyurus*, Sw. 1827.
Erismatura, Bonap. Saggio Distr. Met. 1832, 143 (same type).
Gymnura, Nutt. Man. II. 1834, 426 (same type).
Undina, Gould, Birds Eur. V. 1836, pl. 383 (type, *Anas mersa*).
Cerconectes, Wagl. Isis, 1832, 282 (same type).
Bythonessa, Gloger, Handb. 1842, 472 (same type).

Char. Bill about as long as the head (much longer than the tarsus), very broad, widened toward the end, elevated at the base, the nostrils very small, and situated very near the culmen;

E. rubida.

maxillary unguis very small, narrow, and linear, the terminal half bent abruptly downward and backward, so as to be invisible from above; tail more than half as long as the wings, much graduated, consisting of eighteen very stiff, narrow feathers, with the shafts strong and rigid, and grooved underneath, toward the base; the tail-coverts extremely short, scarcely covering the base of the tail; wings very short, and very concave beneath, the primaries scarcely or not at all extending beyond the tertials; tarsus very short, much less than one half as long as the longest toe.

In the characters defined above, all the known species which we have examined [1] agree strictly, with the exception of *Anas dominica*, LINN., which has usually been referred to this genus, but which differs radically in the character of the nail of the bill, this being broad and gradually curved, as in other Ducks. This difference is so great that *A. dominica* should undoubtedly be separated generically from the true *Erismaturæ*,[2] among which the only important deviation in structure is seen in *E. leucocephala*, of Europe, which has the base of the maxilla much swollen both vertically and laterally.

The two American species of *Erismatura* may be distinguished as follows: —

1. **E. rubida**. Bill, .90–.95 of an inch broad near the end. *Adult male:* Above, bright reddish ferruginous, including the whole neck, except upper part of the nape; pileum and upper part of the nape black; entire side of head, below the eyes, white; lower parts whitish (dark brownish gray beneath the surface, the breast tinged with buff). *Adult female* and *young male:* Above, grayish brown, finely mottled, and sometimes indistinctly barred, with grayish buff; pileum darker brown, finely mottled with reddish; rest of head grayish white, crossed longitudinally by a stripe of mottled brownish, from the rictus back over the auriculars, and parallel with the lower edge of the brown of the top of the head; neck pale brownish gray; lower parts as in the adult male. *Hab.* North America, south to Guatemala and West Indies.
2. **E. ferruginea.**[3] Bill, .70–.85 of an inch broad near end. *Adult male:* Head and neck, except lower half of the latter in front, uniform black; jugulum and upper parts deep ferruginous, as in *E. rubida;* lower parts as in *E. rubida. Adult female:* Similar to *E. rubida* but darker, and very distinctly barred on the sides and upper parts with fulvous-buff. *Hab.* Southern South America.

Erismatura rubida.

THE RUDDY DUCK; SPINE-TAILED DUCK.

Anas rubida, WILS. Am. Orn. VIII. 1814, 128, pl. 71, figs. 5, 6.
Fuligula (Gymnura) rubida, NUTT. Man. II. 1834, 426.
Fuligula rubida, SW. & RICH. F. B. A. II. 1831, 455. — AUD. Orn. Biog. IV. 1838, 326, pl. 343; Synop. 1839, 288; B. Am. VI. 1843, 324, pl. 399.
Erismatura rubida, BONAP. Comp. List, 1838, 59. — BAIRD, B. N. Am. 1858, 811; Cat. N. Am. B. 1859, no. 609. — COUES, Key, 1872, 295; Check List, 1873, no. 519, 2d ed. 1882, no. 741; Birds N. W. 1874, 583. — RIDGW. Nom. N. Am. B. 1881, no. 634.
Anas jamaicensis, ORD, ed. Wils. VIII. 1825, 138.

HAB. The whole of North America, breeding throughout its range, which extends south to Guatemala and New Grenada; Cuba.

SP. CHAR. *Adult male, full plumage:* Pileum and upper half of the nape uniform black; entire

[1] *E. rubida* (WILS.), *E. ferruginea* (EYTON), of Chili, *E. australis* (GOULD), of Australia, and *E. leucocephala* (SCOP.), of Europe. There remains only *E. moccoa*, SMITH, of South Africa.

[2] For "*E.*" *dominica* we have already proposed the generic name *Nomonyx* (cf. Proc. U. S. Nat. Mus. II. March 27, 1880, p. 15).

[3] ERISMATURA FERRUGINEA.

Erismatura ferruginea, EYTON, Monog. Anat. 1838, 170 (Chili). — GRAY & MITCH. Gen. B. I. 1844, pl. 169. — CASS. U. S. Astr. Exp. II. 1856, 204. — SCL. & SALV. P. Z. S. 1876, 404 (monographic); Nom. Neotr. 1873, 138.
Erismatura vittata, PHIL. & LANDB. Weigm. Archiv, 1860, 26 (Chili).

The Australian *E. australis* closely resembles the South American species, but is rather larger and deeper colored.

side of the head, below the eyes, including the malar region and chin, pure white; rest of neck, entire upper parts, sides, and flanks, rich chestnut-rufous or purplish-ferruginous; wing-coverts and middle of the rump dusky grayish brown, minutely mottled with paler; remiges dull brownish dusky; rectrices brownish black, the shafts deep black; lower parts white on the surface, but the

Male.

concealed portion of all the feathers dark brownish gray, showing when the feathers are disarranged, and in midsummer specimens completely exposed by abrasion of the tips of the feathers; jugulum strongly washed with fulvous-buff, this sometimes invading the abdomen. Lower tail-coverts entirely white, to the roots of the feathers. "Bill and edges of the eyelids grayish blue; iris

Female.

hazel; feet dull grayish blue, webs inclining to dusky; claws grayish brown" (AUDUBON). *Adult female:* Top of the head, down to below the eyes, and upper parts generally, dusky grayish brown, minutely freckled with pale grayish fulvous (more reddish on the head); remainder of the head dirty grayish white, crossed longitudinally by a stripe of speckled dusky, running from the rictus back across the auriculars, parallel with the lower edge of the brown of the top of the head; neck pale brownish gray, fading gradually into the white of the chin; lower parts, except sides and flanks (which are similar to the abdomen, but darker), as on the adult male. *Young:* Similar to the adult female. *Downy young:* Above, dark smoky brown, darker on the head; a whitish spot on each side the back; a brownish white stripe beneath the eye, from the bill to near the occiput; beneath this, a narrower dusky brown one, confluent with the brown of the nape, reaching almost or quite to the rictus. Lower parts grayish white, strongly shaded with sooty brown across the jugulum. [Described from a specimen obtained by Dr. E. Coues, U. S. A., at Turtle Mountain, Dakota, July 28, 1873.]

Although the collection of the National Museum contains numerous examples of this species, only a small proportion of them have the sex indicated, while on a still smaller number is the date noted. It is therefore difficult to determine satisfactorily, from the material at hand, the seasonal and sexual differences of plumage. Certain it is, however, that specimens in the plumage described above as that of the adult male in full plumage occur both in summer and winter. Audubon says that the "adult female in summer" "presents the same characters as in the male;" but although this may very likely be true, the series under examination affords no indication of it. He describes the "male one year old" as having "a similar white patch on the side of the head; upper part of head and hind neck dull blackish brown; throat and sides of neck grayish brown, lower part of neck dull reddish brown, waved with dusky; upper parts as in the adult, but of a duller tint; lower parts grayish white."

The Ruddy Duck is an exclusively American species, and, so far as I am aware, has never been met with, even as a straggler, in Europe. It is found throughout North America from high northern latitudes to Central America, and even the northern portion of South America, in all of which places it also undoubtedly breeds; though in the country intermediate between Guatemala and the Arctic Regions it is of rare occurrence.

Mr. Salvin states that it was the only resident Duck found by him on the Lake of Dueñas. Its numbers diminish during the period of the spring migration, the immature birds at that time seeking other quarters. He found this species more easily procurable than any other of the Ducks frequenting that lake, as a peculiarity in its powers of flight renders its escape less easy than it would otherwise be. This bird, namely, can fly as well as any other when it is once fairly started, but it rises with great difficulty from the water; and, in consequence of this, it can be approached within easy gunshot by sailing down upon it before the wind. Sometimes, however, this Duck seeks safety by diving; and when it does this, so rapid are its motions that it is almost certain to escape. Mr. Salvin found this species building its nest in May among the reeds on the margin of the lake, using for this purpose the stones and leaves of the dead flags, together with a little down. The eggs are like those of the European *Erismatura leucocephala*, and very rough in texture, although not quite as much so as the eggs of that species. He describes them as being of a dirty cream-white color, measuring 2.37 inches in length, and 1.83 in breadth. The eggs were sometimes rather more elongated than this, as some measured 2.56 by 1.77 inches. It was found by Dr. Kennerly in large flocks on a small lake, near Janos, Mexico, in April, and on the Petataro River.

Captain Blakiston mentions the occurrence of this species at York Factory on Hudson's Bay, and Mr. Ross met with it in the region of Great Slave Lake.

According to the observations of Sir John Richardson, it frequents the small lakes of the interior up to the 58th parallel. He speaks of it as being very unwilling to take to wing, but as diving remarkably well. In swimming it carries its tail erect, and, in consequence of the shortness of its neck, nearly as high as the head: this peculiarity causes the bird to appear as if it had two heads, and makes it very easy of recognition, even at a distance. Dr. Bryant found this species very common in winter in the Bahamas.

According to the observations of Dr. Cooper, it is present in all parts of California during the winter, both on fresh and on salt water. The young are very tame, and may readily be approached; but the adult bird is more shy, and full-plumaged specimens are not easily procured. Dr. Cooper met with a number of these Ducks at Santa Barbara, in a marshy pond, as late as the middle of May, and he thinks that probably a few remain to breed within the limits of that State, though their chief resort appears to be in regions farther north. This conjecture has since been verified, as I have in my cabinet a set of the eggs of this bird taken by Mr. William A. Cooper near Santa Cruz.

Colonel Grayson mentions meeting with this species at Tepic, in Western Mexico, and also at Mazatlan — where, however, it was rarely seen. Mr. Boardman speaks of its occurrence in the vicinity of Calais as occasional, both in the spring and in the fall; but he does not think that it remains there to breed.

It is frequently met with in Massachusetts, being much more common there in the fall than in the spring, especially on ponds of fresh water; and Mr. William Brewster informs me that he has shot as many as thirteen of these Ducks in a single morning. They arrive in quite large flocks of from thirty to forty, are very tame, and permit a boat to be rowed close up to them; and, as they rise very slowly from the water, they may be very readily shot.

Mr. Giraud found this species comparatively rare in the vicinity of New York; it is, however, quite common on Chesapeake Bay, where it is known to hunters as the Salt-water Teal. It is said to frequent the salt-ponds along the sea-coast, and to procure its food by diving, subsisting chiefly on marine plants. A writer in "Doughty's Cabinet" calls this species the Heavy-tailed Duck, and states that it arrives on the waters of the Upper Chesapeake Bay as early as the first or second week of October.

Mr. Nelson speaks of it as being very common in Northern Illinois during its migrations; it is a summer resident in that State, and occasionally breeds there. The spring migrations begin about the middle of April and continue until the 5th of May. A few of this species return early in October; but the main migration takes place a month later than that. Mr. T. H. Douglas, of Waukegan, is cited as having met with a pair of these birds, with eight or ten young, in a small lake near that place, and as saying that there is good reason to suppose the young had been hatched in the vicinity. Mr. Nelson several times started females while incubating: the nests, however, he was never able to find. These occurrences took place about the middle of June; and the circumstances were such as to leave no doubt that the birds were actually breeding in the neighborhood.

Mr. J. A. Allen met with this Duck in September in the valley of Great Salt Lake, where it was very common. It is also more or less abundant on the waters of most of the interior rivers and ponds.

Audubon noticed it in large numbers during the winter months in Florida, sometimes shooting upwards of forty in a single morning; and he was informed by Dr. Bachman that this species had been becoming more and more abundant in South Carolina; yet he had never met with an example in full summer plumage. This Duck seemed to be equally fond of salt, brackish, and fresh water. In the Southern States it congregates in great flocks. Its flight is rapid, with a whirring sound, occasioned by the concave form of the wings. It rises from the water with considerable difficulty, being obliged to assist itself with its broad webbed feet, and for that purpose to run on the surface for several yards. From the ground, however, it can spring up at once. This Duck swims with ease and grace and deeply immersed. It is also extremely expert at diving; and when wounded, often escapes by doing this, and then hiding in the grass, if there is any accessible. This bird is generally regarded as being excellent eating, as its food consists chiefly of the roots and leaves of plants found at the bottoms of ponds.

In Southern Wisconsin — as Professor Kumlien informs me — this species is a regular visitant in spring and in fall. It is not abundant, but is by no means rare. A few of these birds — mostly those whose plumage is immature — remain all summer about Lake Koskonong — where, however, this species is not known to breed; but I am assured by Mr. Goss that it does this — in limited numbers — in the neighborhood of Pewaukee.

This Duck was found breeding near Fort Resolution by Mr. Kennicott in June. It was taken in July, with its eggs, in the same neighborhood, by Mr. J. Lockhart; and also at Shoal Lake, in the summer of 1865, by Mr. Donald Gunn, who states that he has sometimes seen as many as twenty eggs in a single nest.

Eggs of this species from Guatemala and from Shoal Lake are in the Smithsonian Collection. The latter (No. 12727) — collected by Mr. Gunn — are of a dull white, with a slight shade of cream-color. They vary in their length from 2.35 to 2.55 inches, and in their breadth from 1.80 to 1.85. The specimen from Dueñas, obtained by Mr. Salvin (No. 13434), measures 2.55 by 1.85.

Genus **NOMONYX**, Ridgway.

Erismatura, Auct. nec Bonaparte.
Nomonyx, Ridgw. Proc. U. S. Nat. Mus. II. Mar. 27, 1880, p. 15 (type, *Anas dominica*, Linn.).

Char. Similar to *Erismatura*, but differing from all the species of that genus in the form of the maxillary unguis, which is similar to that of *Fulix* and allied genera, the same being in *Erismatura* the most peculiar and important generic character.

Altogether the most distinctive feature of the genus *Erismatura* consists in the remarkably peculiar conformation of the maxillary unguis, or nail of the upper mandible. This, viewed from

N. dominicus.

above, is extremely small, narrow, and linear, the broader terminal half being bent very abruptly downward and backward, so as to be visible only from in front or below. With the sole exception of *Anas dominica*, Linn., all the species usually referred to this genus agree strictly with the type, *Anas leucocephala*, Scop., notwithstanding other characters are more or less variable. *Anas dominica*, Linn., has the nail of normal form, or very much like that prevailing among the Ducks generally, and on this account should be separated generically from *Erismatura*.

Nomonyx dominicus.

THE MASKED DUCK.

Anas querquedula dominicensis, BRISS. Orn. VI. 1760, 472 (St. Domingo).
Anas dominica, LINN. S. N. ed. 12, I. 1766, 201 (ex BRISS. l. c.).
Erismatura dominica, EYTON, Mon. Anat. 1838, 172. — BAIRD, B. N. Am. 1858, 925; ed. 1860, pl. 92; Cat. N. Am. B. 1859, no. 610. — COUES, Key, 1872, 295; Check List, 1873, no. 520; B. N. W. 1874, p. 583 (foot-note). — SCL. & SALV. P. Z. S. 1876, 405 (monographic).
Nomonyx dominicus, RIDGW. Proc. U. S. Nat. Mus. Vol. 2, 1880, 15; Nom. N. Am. B. 1881, no. 635. — COUES, Check List, 2d ed. 1882, no. 742.
Sarcelle, de la Guadeloupe, BUFF. Pl. Enl. 1770–1784, pl. 967 (female).
Anas spinosa, GMEL. S. N. I. ii. 1788, 522 (ex BUFF. l. c.).
Erismatura ortygoides, "HILL," GOSSE, Birds Jam. 1847, 406; Illustr. B. Jam. pl. 113.

HAB. Tropical America at large; accidental in Eastern North America (Wisconsin, KUMLIEN; Lake Champlain, CABOT).

SP. CHAR. *Adult male, in full plumage:* Neck all round, back, and sides dark cinnamon-brown, the two latter with the feathers streaked centrally, broadly, and conspicuously, with black. Lower parts yellowish rusty, the feathers occasionally showing their brownish centres. Entire fore part

of the head, including the chin, cheeks, and pileum, black, the eye being about mid way between the bill and the posterior edge of the black; the occiput, however, like the neck. Wings brown, with a conspicuous white speculum on the greater coverts. Tail brown; lining of wings gray, the axillars white. Length, about 14.50 inches; wing, 5.75; tail, 4.25; culmen, 1.37; commissure, 1.60; tarsus, 1.10; middle toe and claw, 2.10.[1] *Adult male (in second year?)* (No. 42014, Spanish Town, Jamaica, April, 1866; W. T. MARCH): Pileum, two stripes along side of the head, and general color of the upper parts, black; spaces between the black stripes of the head, including cheeks and chin, dull white; neck and jugulum ferruginous, with a purplish-chestnut tinge; rest of lower parts dull ochraceous, stained with ferruginous, the feathers with concealed central dusky spot. Middle and greater wing-coverts, basal portion of lower secondaries, and axillars uniform pure white. Dorsal region transversely barred and bordered with ferruginous. "Bill black, under mandible fleshy; tail twenty-two feathers." Wing, 5.50 inches; tail, 3.90; culmen, 1.30; tarsus, 1.00; middle toe, 1.80. *Adult female* (Sumner, Wis., summer, 1870; T. KUMLIEN; Coll. Boston Society): Similar to the male, but black less deep and not so uniform, the ferruginous paler, or replaced by ochraceous and spotted with black; abdomen dull ochraceous-white; wing-speculum smaller. Wing, 5.50 inches; tail, 3.50; culmen, 1.30; tarsus, .90; middle toe, 1.75.

[1] Described from the specimen obtained on Lake Champlain by Dr. Cabot, now in the Museum of the Boston Society of Natural History.

The markings of the head are the same in both sexes, the black stripes being duller, and the light ones approaching nearer to white in the female. The upper light stripe is a superciliary one, extending from the upper basal angle of the bill to the side of the occiput; the next is a suborbital one, beginning at the lower half of the basal outline of the maxilla, and extending back to a little farther than the upper stripe; this is bounded below by a dusky stripe of about equal width, beginning at the lower or basal angle of the maxilla, and reaching back as far as the light stripe.

Different individuals vary more or less in the shade of colors: the male from Lake Champlain, described above, is the most deeply colored specimen in the whole series. The Wisconsin specimen is exactly like one (No. 52856) from Tepic, Western Mexico; both are unlike Jamaican females, which differ from the male described merely in paler colors. An adult male from Tepic (No. 58818; A. J. Grayson) also differs from the Jamaican male in very noticeable points of coloration. The ferruginous borders to the feathers of the dorsal region are much broader and more regular, and the transverse bars of this color seen in the other specimen are entirely absent; the neck and jugulum are paler ferruginous than the back markings, instead of deeper; the lower parts are nearly white. The white speculum on the wing also appears to be much larger. It measures as follows: Wing, 5.10 inches; tail, 4.20; culmen, 1.35; tarsus, .90; middle toe, 1.90.

Should these differences hold good through a large series of specimens, the birds from the two regions would be separable as geographical races.

The *Nomonyx dominicus* is a West Indian and South American species, and accidental only in North America. Two instances are on record of the occurrence of this bird within the limits of the United States. The first was on the Vermont shore of Lake Champlain, where an adult male was obtained; the other took place several years afterward, in Jefferson Co., Wis. The specimen then taken was a female, and was procured by Mr. L. Kumlien, of Bussyville. We have no record of the circumstances attending the capture of either specimen.

This species is found in several of the West India Islands, and in the northeastern portions of South America. Professor A. Newton was confident that he met with this species in St. Croix; stating that in 1857 he found a large lagoon in that island, situated near its eastern end, frequented by a small flock of what he had no doubt were birds of this species. He first saw them on the 9th of March, sitting motionless on the water; and he again met with the same kind in May. On this occasion the birds were present in considerable numbers, swimming quite low, so that the hinder part of the back appeared to be beneath the surface. On the 15th of June he again had a good view of these Ducks; but did not succeed in procuring any specimens, by means of which he could make sure of their being of this species.

Léotaud mentions this Duck as being one of the birds of Trinidad, where it is by no means rare. While to a certain extent it seems to be migratory, some are always present on that island. It is social in its habits, and seems more disposed than any other Duck to keep to the water. Its flight is rapid, but is not so well sustained as that of most of the other kinds. When it is on the land it keeps in an upright position, its tail resting on the ground. Its movements on dry land are embarrassed by its claws, which are placed so far back as to disturb its equilibrium. Its flesh is excellent, and is held in high esteem in that island.

Mr. William B. Lee ("Ibis," April, 1873) mentions obtaining a single specimen on the banks of the Gato River, in the Argentine Republic. He found it a very expert diver, and watched its movements in a deep part of the river, in which it was diving, and where, on each occasion, it remained under the water for a long time.

Colonel Grayson states that he met with a number of pairs of this species — about fifty in all — in Western Mexico, in the neighborhood of Tepic, where they were frequenting a small lake, or rather lagoon, as late as the month of June. They were evidently preparing to breed in that locality; and the females he shot were found to have enlarged ovaries. He did not, however, meet with any of this species in the neighborhood of Mazatlan.

The specimen procured in Wisconsin was taken on Rock River, November, 1870. Mr. L. Kumlien is confident that he has since met with one of these birds on Lake Koskonong; but he was not able to secure it.

Genus **MERGUS**, Linnæus.

Mergus, Linn. S. N. ed. 10, I. 1758, 129; ed. 12, I. 1766, 207 (type, *Mergus merganser*, Linn.).

Char. Bill longer than the head, the breadth uniformly about equal to the depth, the serrations conical, acute, and pointed backward; crest occipital, pointed, or scarcely developed and

M. merganser.

depressed. Tarsus nearly three fourths the middle toe, with claw. Tail about half the length of the wings. Bill mostly reddish.

The two North American species of this genus may be readily distinguished as follows, the females alone resembling one another: —

1. **M. merganser.** Nostril situated near the middle of the maxilla; frontal feathers extending farther forward than those on lateral base of bill. *Adult male:* Head and most of the neck greenish black; head scarcely crested; jugulum and other lower parts creamy white, or pale salmon-color. *Adult female:* Head and neck reddish (chin and throat white), the occiput with a full crest of lengthened feathers. Above, chiefly bluish gray.
   a. Merganser.[1] Black bases of the greater wing-coverts entirely concealed by the over-

[1] Mergus merganser.

Mergus merganser, Linn. S. N. ed. 10, I. 1758, 129; ed. 12, I. 1766, 208. — Naum. Vög. Deutschl. XII. 1844, 356, pl. 326.
Mergus rubricapilla, Brünn. Orn. Bor. 1764, 22.
Mergus castor, Linn. S. N. I. 1766, 209. — Keys. & Blas. Wirb. Eur. 88. — Gray, Gen. B. III. 629; Cat. Brit. B. 1863, 208.
Merganser castor, Bonap. Comp. List, 1838, 59. — Macgill. Man. II. 194.
Merganser Raii, Leach, Syst. Cat. 1816, 36. — Steph. Gen. Zool. XII. 1824, 161, pl. 53.
Mergus gulo, Scop. Ann. I. N. H. 1769, 69.
Goosander, Yarr. Brit. B. ed. 2, III. 395, fig.; ed. 3, III. 398, fig.
Hab. Palæarctic Region.

lying feathers. *Male:* Wing, 10.70–11.00 inches; culmen, 2.05–2.30; tarsus, 1.90–2.00; middle toe, 2.35–2.60. *Female:* Wing, 9.75–10.25 inches; culmen, 1.80–1.90; tarsus, 1.65–1.80; middle toe, 2.35. *Hab.* Palæarctic Region.

β. *Americanus.* Black bases of the greater wing-coverts exposed, so as to form a distinct bar about half way across the wing. *Male:* Wing, 10.50–11.25 inches; culmen, 1.90–2.20; tarsus, 1.90–2.00; middle toe, 2.40–2.50. *Female:* Wing, 9.60–9.75 inches; culmen, 1.80–2.00; tarsus, 1.85–1.90; middle toe, 2.25–2.40. *Hab.* North America.

2. **M. serrator.** Nostril situated near the base of the maxilla; feathers on lateral base of bill extending farther forward than those on the forehead. *Adult male:* Head dull greenish black, the occiput with a long pointed crest of narrow feathers; neck and sides of the jugulum dull buff, or light cinnamon, streaked with black; other lower parts mainly white. *Adult female:* Very similar in color to that of *M. merganser*, but distinguished by different position of the nostrils, and different outline of the feathering at base of the bill. Size also smaller. *Hab.* North America and Palæarctic Region.

Mergus merganser americanus.

THE BUFF-BREASTED SHELDRAKE.

Mergus merganser, Wils. Am. Orn. VIII. 1814, 68, pl. 68.—Sw. & Rich. F. B. A. II. 1831, 461.—Nutt. Man. II. 1834, 460.—Aud. Orn. Biog. IV. 1838, 261, pl. 331; Synop. 1839, 297; B. Am. VI. 1843, 387, pl. 411.—Coues, Key, 1872, 296; Check List, 1873, no. 521; 2d ed. 1882, no. 743; B. N. W. 1874, 583.

Mergus americanus, Cass. Pr. Ac. Nat. Sci. Philad. 1853, 187.—Baird, B. N. Am. 1858, 813; Cat. N. Am. B. 1859, no. 611.

Mergus castor, a. *americanus*, Bonap. Compt. Rend. XLIII, 1856, 652.

Mergus merganser americanus, Ridgw. Proc. U. S. Nat. Vol. 3, 1880, 205; Nom. N. Am. B. 1881, no. 636.

Hab. The whole of North America, breeding south to the Northern United States. No extralimital record except Bermudas.

Adult male: Head and upper half (or more) of the neck deep black, the elongated feathers of the pileum and nape distinctly, other portions faintly, glossed with greenish; whole back and inner scapulars, deep black; rump, upper tail-coverts, and tail, plain cinereous; sides of the crissum (anteriorly) and femoral region, whitish, narrowly barred with slate-color; primary-coverts, primaries, and outer secondaries, plain blackish dusky. Remainder of the plumage fine light salmon-buff in life, fading to buffy white in dried skins; inner secondaries narrowly skirted with black; base of the greater coverts deep black, forming a distinct bar about half way across the wing; anterior border of the wing dusky grayish, or blackish. Bill deep vermilion-red, the culmen and nail black; feet deep red; iris carmine. *Adult female:* Head and upper half of the neck reddish cinnamon, the pileum and occipital crest

Male.

(the latter much longer than in the male) more brown, the lores grayish ; chin, throat, and malar region, white ; upper parts, sides, and flanks, bluish gray, the inner secondaries white, the exposed portion of the lower greater coverts white, tipped with dusky ; outer secondaries, primary coverts, and primaries, uniform slate-color. Lower parts, except laterally, pale creamy salmon-color, fading to nearly white in dried specimens, the feathers of the jugulum ash-gray beneath the surface. Bill, eyes, and feet, as in the male, but less brilliant in color.

Female.

Downy young :[1] Upper half of the head, with nape, reddish brown, more reddish on the nape, where encroaching on the sides of the neck ; remaining upper parts hair-brown or grayish umber, relieved by four white spots, one on the posterior border of each wing, and one on each side the rump ; lower parts white ; a stripe on the lower half of the lores, running back beneath the eye, white ; below this a narrower stripe of deep brown, from the rictus back to the auricular region ; a wide stripe, occupying the upper half of the lore, from the bill to the eye, blackish brown, this separated from the umber of the forehead by a very indistinct streak of brownish white or pale brown.

Adult male : Total length, about 27 inches, extent, 36 ; wing, 10.50–11.25 ; culmen, 1.90–2.20 ; tarsus, 1.90–2.00 ; middle toe, 2.40–2.50. *Adult female :* Total length, about 24 inches, extent, 34 ; wing, 9.60–9.75 ; culmen, 1.80–2.00 ; tarsus, 1.85–1.90 ; middle toe, 2.25–2.40.

We can perceive no difference of coloration between American and European specimens of this species, further than that adult males of the former have the black at the base of the greater wing-coverts exposed, so as to form a very distinct band about half way across the wing, while in those of the latter this black is entirely concealed by the overlying middle coverts. There is, however, a difference in the proportions of the bill in the two forms which may prove of specific importance. In the females, this difference in the bill is the only obvious distinguishing character.

The North American Goosander bears very close resemblance to the European form, and by most writers the two are regarded as being the same species. It is generally known in all parts of the country as the "Sheldrake," and is not infrequently confounded with the Red-breasted Merganser — from which it differs, however, in its larger size, as well as in certain peculiarities of its habits and distribution ; moreover, while the Red-breasted Merganser is a more maritime species, the Goosander prefers inland lakes and rivers.

The last-named species is found nearly throughout North America, breeding from about latitude 42° N. to the extreme points of the Fur Country, and in the winter months occurring throughout the continent.

Sir John Richardson describes this bird as making a nest of withered grass and feathers in the manner of Ducks in unfrequented places ; but in this he may have been misinformed, or may have confounded the *serrator* with this species. Or it may be true of Ducks that breed in regions where there are few hollow trees to nest in. This Duck is said to be one of the last of the *Anatidæ* to move south in the fall.

Mr. Hearne, in his Arctic journey, makes mention of the Goosander — which is

[1] Described from No. 5783, Bridger's Pass, Rocky Mountains, Aug. 13, 1856 ; W. S. Wood. Distinguishable with certainty from the young of *M. serrator* by the different position of the nostril.

usually called, on Hudson's Bay, the Sheldrake — and speaks of it as very common on the sea-coast and in the interior parts of the country, flying in very large flocks. He describes it as being an excellent diver, and as devouring fish in such great quantities that it is frequently obliged to disgorge several before it can rise from the water. It frequently swallows fish six or seven inches in length and proportionally thick. Birds of this species frequenting the interior parts of the Fur Country feed chiefly on crawfish, which are very numerous in some of the stony shallow rivers. In the fall of the year they became very fat, and though they feed principally upon fish, yet their flesh at that season is very good. They are said to remain in the Arctic Regions as long as the frost does not prevent their obtaining a subsistence.

Captain Blakiston mentions meeting with this species in the Saskatchewan Region, as far west as the Rocky Mountains. He also received specimens from Hudson's Bay.

The Goosander is found on the Pacific coast from Alaska to Southern California. It was taken at Sitka by Mr. Bischoff, and a single specimen was obtained at Fort Yukon by Mr. Lockhart; but it was not observed by any of Mr. Dall's party during their three years' explorations on the Yukon River and its vicinity. In his account of the birds of the Aleutian Islands, Mr. Dall states that several extremely fat examples of this species were killed, December 20, after a norther, in the outer bay, at Unalashka, — where, however, it seemed to be only an accidental visitor. It was not observed at the Shumagins, although reported as common in the winter near the Prybilof Islands.

Dr. Cooper obtained a female bird of this species at the highest encampment on the Little Black-foot River, where it had doubtless raised a brood, as this species is known to seek such clear rapid streams in the Cascade Mountains for breeding. *M. serrator* — the female of which so much resembles this species — is not known to occur so far from the coast.

Mr. J. A. Allen met with a pair of these birds on Mount Lincoln, in Colorado Territory; and he afterward, in September, found them very common in the valley of Great Salt Lake.

This Merganser has been found on the coast of Vancouver Island by Mr. R. Browne. According to Dr. Cooper, it is common in some parts of California, but not so abundant as in regions farther north, where it occurs along the sea-coast, in the bays, and in the larger rivers, from October to April. In all probability some individuals of this species remain to breed in that region along the mountain streams and upon the lakes, but none have been seen doing this.

Major Wedderburn states that this bird has been met with in the Bermudas. It occurs in large numbers in the neighborhood of Calais, where it is found throughout the summer months, as well as early in the spring and late in the fall. Mr. Boardman informs me that many of this species breed there, always resorting for that purpose to hollow trees, and that the nests are composed of dry and fine grasses, feathers, and down. In Massachusetts it is common in its vernal and autumnal migrations, and is then found almost exclusively in fresh water; a few of these birds being supposed to breed there.

This species — also known to the sportsmen of Long Island as the Sheldrake — arrives on the Long Island coast late in the fall, and continues its occupation of fishing until compelled to leave for a milder climate in search of food with others of its tribe. On its first appearance it is seen in large flocks; but it soon scatters, forming smaller parties of from five to twelve, and frequently associating with the Scaup Duck. It is said by Mr. Giraud to be decoyed without much difficulty. When wounded this bird dives so dexterously that only with the greatest difficulty can it be secured.

When badly wounded it has been known to dive to the bottom and cling to the grass. In the spring it again assembles in large flocks, preparatory to leaving for its summer residence. At that season it generally flies along the bottom land, at a short distance from the shore, and may be readily killed by hunters concealed in holes cut in the bank for that purpose.

The Merganser is very tenacious of life. Even when fairly shot down, if the lead has not reached a vital part, the next moment the bird will be gone. Giraud mentions a striking instance in which a young male Goosander had been shot, and picked up apparently lifeless, and then thrown into the bottom of a boat. There it remained apparently dead until he had sailed about two miles, when, to his great surprise, the bird flew off as if nothing had happened, leaving a pool of blood in the place where it had been lying. Although this species feeds almost exclusively on fish, yet in the fall of the year its flesh is quite tolerable; but in the spring it is oily, and has a rancid taste. In calm weather the Goosander has been known to collect in large parties for the purpose of diving for amusement. When thus engaged, at a given signal they all pass under the water, and some minutes elapse before any of them rise to the surface. In this way these birds will spend whole hours, apparently much delighted with the frolic. In overcast and in blustering weather they keep moving about all the day, and in heavy storms they shelter themselves in coves, and are occasionally seen steering up the small creeks to take refuge in the swamps.

Mr. Dresser met with this Goosander in Southwestern Texas in the winter, and three specimens were procured near Fort Stockton. Audubon also obtained birds of this species in Texas, in April, 1837. They are rarely, if ever, seen in South Carolina or Florida.

According to the observations of Messrs. G. A. Boardman, J. Elliot Cabot, and others, who have found this species breeding, it invariably nests in the hollows of trees. Audubon was either mistaken in his account of the nesting of this Merganser, or else he met with a very exceptional instance, since he describes it as nesting on the ground among rushes, in the manner of the *serrator*, having a large nest raised seven or eight inches above the surface.

Mr. Nuttall, in May, 1832, saw in the Susquehanna River, near Duntown, a female Merganser with a brood of eight young; but it required the utmost exertion on his part to overtake them. When the young, becoming fatigued, crowded round their parent, she took them on her back, and thus bore them along. The young Mergansers, though not larger than the egg of a Goose, were already elegant epitomes of the female parent, being generally gray, with rufous head and neck, and having the rudiments of a growing crest.

In Southern Wisconsin — as Professor Kumlien tells me — this species is quite common early in the spring and late in the fall, and on Rock River, wherever that stream is not closed by ice, it is found all the winter.

Dr. Kennerly mentions frequently observing this species at Boca Grande, in Chihuahua, and elsewhere along the Conalitos River, in large flocks. He found the birds exceedingly fat and heavy, but not at all palatable. One specimen when caught had in its throat several fish three or four inches in length.

The eggs of this species are of a buffy ivory white, usually from ten to twelve in number, and measure 2.55 inches in length by 1.75 in breadth.

Mergus serrator.

THE RED-BREASTED SHELDRAKE.

Mergus serrator, LINN. S. N. ed. 10, I. 1758, 129; ed. 12, I. 1766, 208. — WILS. Am. Orn. VIII. 1814, 81, pl. 69. — SW. & RICH. F. B. A. II. 1831, 462. — NUTT. Man. II. 1834, 463. — AUD. Orn. Biog. V. 1839, 92, pl. 401; Synop. 1839, 298; B. Am. VI. 1843, 395, pl. 412. — BAIRD, B. N. Am. 1858, 814; Cat. N. Am. B. 1859, no. 612. — COUES, Key, 1872, 296; Check List, 1873, no. 522; 2d ed. 1882, no. 744; B. N. W. 1874, 584. — RIDGW. Nom. N. Am. B. 1881, no. 637.
Mergus cristatus, BRÜNN. Orn. Bor. 1764, 23.
Mergus niger, GMEL. S. N. I. ii. 1788, 546.
Mergus leucomelas, GMEL. tom. cit.

HAB. Northern portion of northern hemisphere; in America migrating south, in winter, throughout the United States. No extralimital record.

SP. CHAR. *Adult male:* Head dull greenish black, duller and more brownish on the forehead and throat, the crest faintly glossed with purplish; neck and sides of the jugulum pale fawn-color or

M. serrator.

dull buff, indistinctly streaked with black, the streaks being on the edges of the feathers; a white collar round upper part of the neck, just below the black. Lower parts pure creamy white, the sides and flanks undulated with narrow zigzag bars of black. Back and scapulars uniform black; shoulders overhung by a tuft of broad feathers, broadly margined with black, the central space being white. Anterior and outer lesser wing-coverts dark slate-gray, darker centrally; posterior lesser coverts and middle coverts wholly white; greater coverts with the terminal half white, the basal half black, partly exposed, thus forming a narrow band or bar across the wing; two inner tertials wholly black, the rest white, edged with black; inner secondaries entirely white; outer secondaries, primary-coverts, and primaries black. Rump and upper tail-coverts dark ash-gray, with black shafts

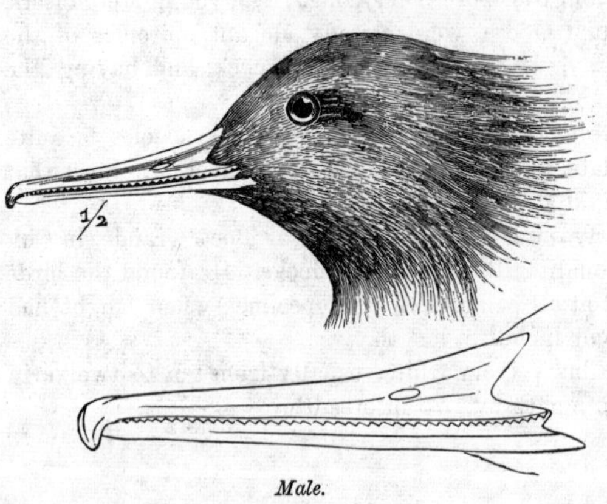

Male.

centrally, finely mottled laterally with white-and-black zigzags. Tail slate-gray, with black shafts. Bill deep carmine, the culmen black, the nail yellowish; iris carmine; feet bright red. *Adult female:* Head and neck cinnamon-brown, duller or more grayish on the pileum and nape, the crest shorter than in the male; throat and lower parts white, the sides and flanks ash-gray. Upper parts dark ash-gray, the feathers with darker shafts; exposed portion of greater coverts and secondaries white, the base of the latter black, but seldom showing as a narrow bar; primaries black. Bill, eyes, and feet as in the male, but less intense in color. *Young:* Similar to the adult female, but chin and throat pale reddish, instead of pure white, the lower part of the neck, and jugulum, brownish white, with the feathers mouse-gray beneath the surface; black at base of the secondaries exposed, forming a narrow bar between two white areas. *Downy young:* Above, hair-brown, the posterior border of each wing, and a large spot on each side of the rump, yellowish-white; lower parts, including the malar region, yellowish white; side of head and neck reddish cinnamon, paler on the lores, which are bordered above by a dusky stripe running back to the anterior angle of the eye, and below by a dark brown, rather indistinct, rictal stripe; lower eyelid white.

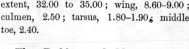

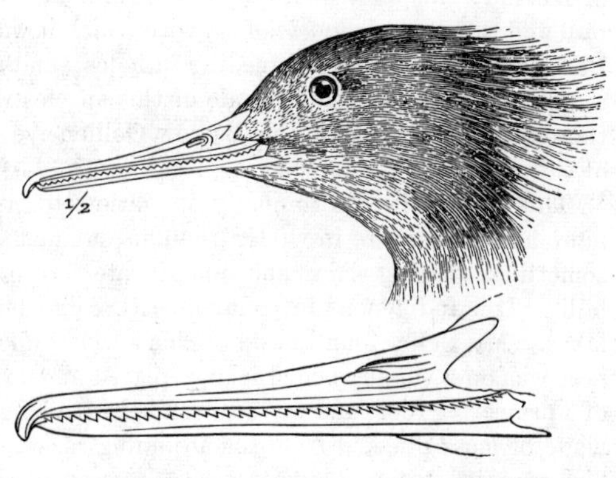

Female.

Total length, about 20.00 to 25.00 inches; extent, 32.00 to 35.00; wing, 8.60–9.00; culmen, 2.50; tarsus, 1.80–1.90; middle toe, 2.40.

Pullus.

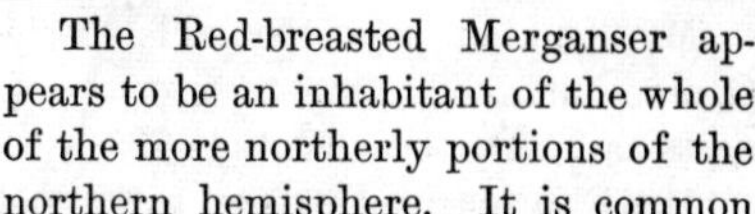

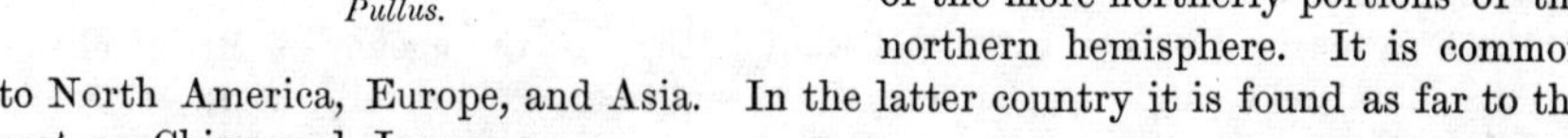

The Red-breasted Merganser appears to be an inhabitant of the whole of the more northerly portions of the northern hemisphere. It is common to North America, Europe, and Asia. In the latter country it is found as far to the east as China and Japan.

This is far more marine than the larger species, and is principally, but not wholly, confined to the sea-coast, breeding as far south as latitude 45° north, and thence northward to an uncertain extent, varying with the conditions and peculiarities of the localities. It certainly breeds as far north as Alaska, on the Pacific, and Greenland, on the Atlantic coasts, as well as in Iceland and in other extremely northern latitudes.

This bird is included by Mr. Swinhoe in the fauna of Formosa, and is also given by him as having been found at Amoy, China. Temminck mentions it as occurring in Japan. It is given by Mr. T. L. Powys as not uncommon in winter in Epirus, Albania, and Corfu; and Mr. C. A. Wright ("Ibis," 1864) speaks of this as being a common species at Malta — as much rarer, however, in some years than in others. It arrives there in November, but is present in much larger numbers in December and January, immature birds being more abundant than adults. It is also said by Mr. H. Saunders to occur in Southern Spain in winter, especially on Lake Albufera.

It was met with on Nova Zembla by Von Heuglin; and was found, mingled with flocks of *Harelda glacialis* and *Œdemia nigra*, on Waigatsch Island. A male shot in the middle of September was changing its smaller plumage. This species is mentioned by Middendorff as occurring in the forest region of Siberia; and Mr. C. W. Shepard found it breeding on a small island in the Lake of Mý-vatn, in the northwestern part of Iceland; this islet was composed of broken lava, and was inhabited chiefly by this bird and the *Bucephala islandica*, with which it was living on the most familiar terms. Both of these birds were breeding in holes; and some of their nests were beyond his reach. In one instance a female of this species was found sitting on a nest in which there were four eggs of the Barrow Golden-eye — which eggs are very unlike those of this species.

This species breeds annually in various parts of the British Islands, but is far more abundant there in winter than in summer; preferring bogs and estuaries, but sometimes visiting rivers and inland waters. In some parts it is known as the "Saw-bill." It is indigenous in Ireland, nesting on islets both of marine and of fresh-water lakes. Mr. Selby found nests of this species upon Loch Awe, in Argyllshire. One nest was on a small wooded island, placed among thick brushwood, under the shelter of a projecting rock, and was surrounded with long grasses and ferns. It was carefully made of moss plucked from the adjoining rocks, mixed with the down of the parent bird, and in structure and materials resembled the nests of the Eider. It contained nine eggs of a rich fawn-color, measuring 2.50 by 1.75 inches. The female was remarkably tame, and remained sitting until nearly taken in a hand-net.

Mr. Hewitson, in his excursion to the west coast of Norway, found this species abundant on most of the lakes and rivers; and the eggs were laid under shelter, either on their margins, or in the interior of the numerous wooded islands. It breeds in the mountains of Lapland, as high up as the birch-trees grow.

The Red-breasted Merganser is given by Professor Reinhardt as one of the resident species of Greenland. It was found common on the Mackenzie River by Mr. Ross. It was met with by Mr. Murray on Hudson's Bay; and from that region specimens were also received by Captain Blakiston.

Mr. Kumlien says that this species is a regular, but not very common, breeder in Cumberland, beginning to nest about the first of July. On the Greenland coast it nests as far north as latitude 73°.

Mr. Dall received it from Sitka and Kadiak, through the agency of Mr. Bischoff; and also obtained a single specimen in May near Nulato, and several at St. Michael's in July. It was not a very common bird in any locality. On a small island in the Yukon, near its mouth, he found six nests of this species, all carefully concealed under dry leaves; most of them were under a log of driftwood in a small hollow, and were lined with down from the breast of the parent. The nests contained from six to ten eggs of a rich cream-color. The parents flew round and round the island, but out of range. Mr. MacFarlane found a few of this species breeding in the neighborhood of Fort Anderson and on the Lower Anderson River, in the wooded country. One of the nests obtained by him contained ten eggs.

This bird is very common about Eastport and Calais; and breeds both among the islands in the Bay and on the margins of the inland ponds. Its nest was hardly distinguishable from that of the Dusky Duck, and was placed on the ground, concealed under shelter of some projecting object — bank, rock, or branch. There were generally ten eggs; but the number varied from nine to twelve.

On Long Island, according to Giraud, this bird is known to the hunters as the Pied Sheldrake; it is not so abundant there as is the larger species. It feeds exclusively on fish, and its flesh is not esteemed as a delicacy.

Richardson appears to have confounded the habits of this species with those of the larger one; thus rendering it difficult to determine how far his account of either bird is correct. He states that the Merganser frequents the lakes and rivers in all parts of the Fur Countries, making its nest, in uninhabited places, of withered grass and feathers. It passes most of its time in the water, swimming with great rapidity, and with the body immersed. Upon the appearance of danger it immediately dives, and remains under the water for a long time. It flies rapidly, and for long distances; but moves on the land with great awkwardness and difficulty.

In California, according to Dr. Cooper, this bird is more abundant in the winter than the larger species, but has habits very similar to those of that bird. It is found as far south as San Diego. Dr. Cooper is of opinion that the female of this species may be seen in the Sierra Nevada in summer, and that it is then also common in the Rocky Mountains, as also in the Cascade Range. Possibly, however, the larger species is the one found in those localities; nevertheless Dr. Cooper may be correct, inasmuch as Captain Bendire has since found it common in Eastern Oregon.

It was seen breeding in considerable numbers in the neighborhood of Fort Anderson, on the borders of the wooded country, by Mr. MacFarlane. The nests were on the ground, near the edges of fresh-water lakes and ponds, under the shelter of fallen timber or of projecting banks, and were generally composed almost exclusively of down. A nest with six eggs was found July 4, the eggs containing partially developed embryos. The largest number seen in any one nest was eight. Mr. MacFarlane mentions that when descending Lockhart River in a canoe, in September, 1864, the party met with a small flock of this Merganser; the birds appeared to be occupied in hunting fish, and were found to be exceedingly fat and heavy. At first they suffered him to approach near enough for a shot; but when he missed his mark they would dive, and remain a considerable time under the water, and then appear a long way ahead or astern of the canoe. After being once missed, they became exceedingly shy and wary, and would dive while they were still too far off to be shot at with effect. They were very nearly as active, and as wary in the water, as is the Loon; but he managed to secure four specimens.

Mr. W. E. Barry, of Kennebunk, Me. ("Am. Nat.," II. 660), gives an interesting paper on the migratory movements of this species, from which we here present a few facts. Before the river has begun to open in spring this bird makes its appearance in the morning, but rarely before sunrise. It flies from the sea up the stream. Sometimes the birds file along one after the other; but more often preserve no regular order. When anything alarms them they sometimes croak. If attracted, they turn at a distance, retrace their flight, scale low over the water, throw out their webbed feet, and stop with a splash. They croak, dive with vigor, and return to the surface in a moment. No noise is heard from their wings, be their flight ever so rapid. The Mergansers seen on the breaking up of the ice are said to be as nothing in numbers compared with the quantity following a little later, when they come in flocks of from twelve to seventy-five, all going east. Most of the flocks in spring appeared to be made up of males. The females came later, and in large flocks. These birds are not only among the first to appear in the early spring, but also are among those which form the rear of the great migratory flight.

This species is of regular occurrence, both in spring and in fall, at Lake Koskonong, where, according to Professor Kumlien, it is not very common.

Mr. Dall met with it at Amchitka, lat. 51° 23′ north, long. 179° 12′ west — the only locality in the Aleutian Islands where it has yet been observed. It was rare there, was evidently only a summer visitor, and was apparently breeding.

Eggs of this species collected on Hudson's Bay by Mr. Drexler (Smithsonian Institution, No. 4350) vary from 2.45 to 2.50 inches in length, and from 1.75 to 1.80 in breadth, and are of a uniform pale-drab color. Mr. Dresser describes the color of this egg as being a dull stone-drab, or creamy buff, with a greenish-gray tinge, and as measuring from 2.55 inches by 1.75, and 2.55 by 1.85, to 2.75 by 1.80, and 2.65 by 1.70. The down with which the nest of this bird is lined is light gray, with a bluish tinge, the centres being white, and the tips grayish white. Mr. Dresser thinks none of this species remain to breed in New Brunswick; but in this he is certainly mistaken, as I have met with its nests in the more southern portions. It is probably more or less common in that province and in Nova Scotia.

Genus **LOPHODYTES**, Reichenbach.

Lophodytes, Reichenb. Syst. Av. 1852, p. ix. (type, *Mergus cucullatus*, Linn.).

Char. Bill shorter than the head, black; serrations compressed, low, short, inserted obliquely on the edge of the bill. Tail more than half as long as the wings. Tarsus about two thirds as long as the longest toe (with claw). Head with a full, semicircular, compressed crest of hair-like feathers.

L. cucullatus

The genus *Lophodytes* is quite distinct from *Mergus* in the possession of the above characters. The bill is also much more depressed terminally, and, in proportion to its length, deeper through the base. The nostrils are situated far back, as in *M. serrator.* But one species is known, unless the *Mergus octosetaceus* of Vieillot,[1] a South American bird (which we have not seen), be referable to this genus rather than to *Mergus.*

[1] Mergus octosetaceus.

Mergus octosetaceus, Vieill. Nouv. Dict. XIV. 1817, 222. — Scl. & Salv. P. Z. S. 1876, 409 (monographic).

Mergus brasilianus, Vieill. Gal. Ois. II. 1834, 209, pl. 283. — Pelz. Orn. Bras. 1870, 322. — Scl. & Salv. Nom. Neotr. 1873, 131.

Mergus fuscus, Licht. Verz. Doubl. 1823, 85.

"*Mergus lophotes*, Cuv. MS." (Schlegel.)

Lophodytes cucullatus.

THE HOODED SHELDRAKE.

Mergus cucullatus, LINN. S. N. ed. 10, I. 1758, 129; ed. 12, I. 1766, 207. — WILS. Am. Orn. VIII. 1814, pl. lxix. fig. 1 — SW. & RICH. F. B. A. II. 1831, 463. — NUTT. Man. II. 1834, 465. — AUD. Orn. Biog. III. 1835, 246, pl. 233; Synop. 1839, 299; B. Am. VI. 1843, 402, pl. 413. — COUES, Key, 1872, 296; Check List, 1873, no. 523; 2d ed. 1882, no. 745; B. N. W. 1874, 584.
Lophodytes cucullatus, REICHENB. Syst. Av. 1852, p. ix. — BAIRD, B. N. Am. 1858, 816; Cat. N. Am. B. 1859, no. 613. — RIDGW. Nom. N. Am. B. 1881, no. 638.

HAB. All of North America, south to Mexico and Cuba, north to Alaska, and accidentally to Greenland; breeds nearly throughout its range; Bermudas, in autumn; casual in Europe.

SP. CHAR. *Adult male:* Head, neck, back, and scapulars black; crest chiefly pure white, but bordered by a distinct "rim" of black; forehead, and feathers round base of the bill, dark fuliginous, but this blending insensibly into the deep black. Wing-coverts dark gray, lighter and more ashy posteriorly; greater coverts broadly tipped with white, the base black, this exposed sufficiently to show a distinct band; inner secondaries with their exposed surface (in closed wing) white, the basal portion black, showing narrowly beyond the end of the greater coverts; tertials with a central stripe of white. Primaries, primary coverts, rump, upper tail-coverts, and tail brownish dusky. Sides of the breast crossed by two black crescents, projecting from the black of the back, these interdigitating with two white ones, the last crescent being black. Sides and flanks rusty cinnamon (more grayish anteriorly), narrowly undulated with black; remaining lower parts white, the posterior part of the crissum mottled with grayish brown. Bill deep black; iris bright yellow; legs and feet yellowish brown, the claws dusky. *Adult female:* Head, neck, jugulum, and upper parts generally, grayish brown, darker above, the crest reddish hair-brown, or dull cinnamon, smaller and of looser texture than in the male; chin, upper part of the throat, and lower parts, except sides, and posterior part of the crissum, white; middle feathers of the greater wing-coverts tipped with white; inner secondaries with their exposed surface white, except at the base. Maxilla black, edged with orange; mandible orange; iris hazel; feet dusky. *Young:* Similar to the adult female, but crest rudimentary, or wanting, the sides and posterior part of the crissum more distinctly brown. *Downy young:*[1] Above, deep hair-brown, darkest on the back and rump; posterior border of the arm-wing, a small spot on each side of the back (nearly concealed by the closed wing), and a larger one on each side of the rump grayish white. Lower half

Male.

[1] Described from No. 12730, "Northwest Coast of America;" T. R. PEALE.

of the head (from about on a line with the eye) brownish buff, paler on the chin and throat; jugulum light dingy brownish; remaining lower parts dingy white, the sides brown, like the upper parts.

Total length, about 17.50–19.00 inches; extent, 24.00–26.00; wing, 7.50–7.90; culmen, 1.50; tarsus, 1.25–1.30; middle toe, 1.90–1.95.

Young female.

The Hooded Merganser is an exclusively North American species, found nearly throughout the continent, from the Southern States, in which it spends the winter months, to the more northern portions of the wooded regions, where it breeds. It is found both on the Pacific and the Atlantic coasts, and is only a straggler in Europe, especially in Great Britain.

Mr. Dall states that it was not obtained by any of his party in Alaska, and believes that, if found at all in that region, it must be very rare. Mr. Bannister, however, thinks that he observed a large flock of this species in October, 1865, only a short time before the harbor at St. Michael's had become frozen over. He shot one of the birds; but having no boat, could not secure it. He did not notice this species at any other time. It was seen on Vancouver Island by Mr. R. Browne; and Dr. Cooper found it common, in winter, along the whole Pacific coast, and thinks that it very probably breeds within the limits of Washington Territory, as its unfledged young were found by Dr. Suckley on Puget Sound. This species appears to prefer clear fresh water in the forests and along mountain streams, where it can obtain plenty of young trout and insects.

It was found on the Mackenzie River by Mr. Ross, and on Hudson's Bay by Mr. Murray; and by Captain Blakiston. Sir John Richardson speaks of meeting with it in all parts of the Fur Countries, where he found it frequenting the lakes and rivers.

Major Wedderburn states that a single specimen of this bird was taken alive near Ireland Island, in Bermuda, in January, 1849, by a sailor; and Mr. Hurdis adds that another was shot in 1850.

It is found along the Atlantic coast, from the St. Lawrence to Florida. In winter it is especially abundant in the Carolinas; and during the breeding-season it is common in Northern Maine and in the provinces of New Brunswick and Nova Scotia. It is equally abundant in the forests of Oregon and Washington Territory, and is found, without doubt, throughout the interior in all suitable localities.

Mr. Dresser states that he noticed this species on the Nueces, Leona, and Medina rivers, although it was not very common in that region; and he thinks that it probably occurs on most of the larger streams of Texas.

It is found in the neighborhood of Calais, Me., where it spends the summer, and where it breeds in considerable numbers. Mr. George A. Boardman informs me that he has repeatedly noticed it breeding in the neighborhood of the St. Croix River, where it always nests in the hollows of trees, lining the cavity with fine dry grasses, leaves, and down; the eggs are from five to eight in number. Several years ago, Mr. Boardman's attention was called to a singular contest between a female Wood Duck and a female of the Hooded Merganser for the possession of a hollow tree. The two birds had been observed for several days contesting for the nest, neither permitting the other to remain in peaceful occupancy. The nest was found to contain eighteen fresh eggs, of which about a third belonged to the Merganser; and as the nest was lined with her own dark-colored down, it appeared probable that this bird was the rightful owner of the premises.

This species is quite common in the fall in Massachusetts. It comes in flocks, and is at times abundant. Mr. William Brewster informs me that he has shot several of these birds in each season, and that he has frequently seen as many as thirty or forty in a single flock. It is a difficult bird to shoot, as it is very shy, and flies rapidly. It is the swiftest in flight of the whole Duck family. On Long Island — according to Giraud — this bird is known as the "Water Pheasant," and also as the "Hairy-head;" but it is rather rare on that coast. It is a very active diver, subsists by fishing, and its flesh is not held in high esteem.

Audubon describes this species as being conspicuous for the activity of its motions and the rapidity of its flight, as well as for other habits which render it a pleasing object to the student of nature. On the waters of the Western and Southern States it is said to arrive from the north early in October, to be a most expert diver, and so vigilant that at times it escapes even from the best percussion gun. Even on wing it is not easily shot; and when wounded, it cannot be secured without the aid of a good dog. The young birds are carefully conveyed, one by one, to the water by the mother in her bill, who is thenceforth devoted in her attentions to the care and protection of her brood.

According to Audubon's observations, this species breeds in Kentucky, and also in Ohio and Indiana, and probably in other Western States. Dr. Bachman also found evidence of its breeding even as far south as South Carolina. He informed Audubon that on the 19th of April, 1838, he obtained an old female and her five young ones on the Santee River, the young being about three weeks old. As he approached them the female sank deep in the water, exhibiting only a small portion of her back above the surface, and swimming, with neck outstretched, close to the surface of the water. The young dived in various directions, in the manner of Grebes. On the following day Dr. Bachman met two other broods, each numbering five; and a cypress-tree was pointed out, in the hollow of which a pair had been breeding that season.

The Hooded Merganser is common during the spring and fall on the lakes and rivers of Southern Wisconsin, where, in the opinion of Professor Kumlien, some of this species undoubtedly remain and breed. He has never succeeded in finding their nests, but he has several times met with the young broods, and has shot a number of the birds when scarcely half grown.

The notes of Dr. Berlandier show that this species during the winter months inhabits the fresh-water marshes caused by the overflowing of the Rio Bravo del Norte near Matamoras.

Captain Bendire found this to be the most common of the three species of Merganser in Eastern Oregon. He could not ascertain positively whether it bred there, but had no doubt that it did so. It was seen in larger numbers on the lakes than on the small creeks, and was especially abundant during the season of its migrations. Two examples were taken in September, 1862, near Fort Resolution by Mr. J. Lockhart.

The eggs of this species are of a pure ivory-white, stained occasionally with a neutral tint, and are of a rounded oval, almost globular, form. They measure 2.05 inches by 1.70 (Smithsonian Institution, No. 15,560; RICKSECKER, Iowa); 2.15 inches by 1.75 (No. 8745; SAMUELS, Maine); 2.05 inches by 1.75 (No. 9785; BOARDMAN, New Brunswick).

NOTE. — The Smew (*Mergellus albellus*) has been attributed to North America by Wilson, Audubon, and Nuttall, but apparently upon erroneous data. In view, however, of the possibility of its occurrence in this country, it may not be amiss to give here the characters of the genus and species, with the principal synonymatic references: —

GENUS **MERGELLUS**, SELBY.

Mergellus, "SELBY, 1840," GRAY (type, *Mergus albellus*, LINN.).

CHAR. The peculiarities of the genus *Mergellus* consist in the very short bill (the culmen being shorter than the tarsus), which has the serrations much like those of *Lophodytes*, only finer and more numerous; the bill is very deep through the base, its greatest depth being equal to about half the length of the culmen; the nostril very large, broadly oval, and situated near the middle of the maxilla. The tarsus is about two thirds as long as the middle toe, with claw. The coloration and crest remind one strongly of *Lophodytes;* but the latter is smaller and less compressed, while there is much more white in the plumage.

Mergellus albellus.

THE SMEW.

Mergus albellus, LINN. S. N. ed. 10, I. 1758, 129; ed. 12, I. 1766, 209. — WILS. Am. Orn. VIII, 1814, 126, pl. 69. — BONAP. Obs. Wils. 1825, 250. — NUTTALL, Man. II. 1834, 467. — AUD. Orn. Biog. IV. 1838, 350, pl. 347 (♀ fig'd from specimen said to have been obtained at New Orleans; ♂, from a European skin); Synop. 1839; B. Am. VI. 1843, 408, pl. 414.

Mergellus albellus, SELBY, Brit. Orn. 1840. — BAIRD, B. N. Am. 1858, 817; Cat. N. Am. B. 1859, no. 614.

Mergus minutus, LINN. S. N. ed. 12, I. 1758, 129; ed. 12, I. 1766, 209 (= young).

Mergus albulus and *pannonicus*, SCOPOLI, Ann. I. Hist. Nat. 1769, 71, 72.

Mergus glacialis, BRÜNN. Orn. Bor. 1764, 24.

HAB. Palæarctic Region; accidental in Eastern North America ("New Orleans;" AUDUBON)?

Adult male: Prevailing color pure white. A patch covering the lores, and narrowly surrounding the eyes, deep black, with a greenish reflection; under portion of the crest glossy greenish black; back, rump, anterior and inner lesser wing-coverts, greater coverts, secondaries, two narrow bars across the side of the jugulum and breast (the posterior one strongly curved, in crescent form), deep black; upper tail-coverts and tail, ash-gray; tertials silvery gray; primaries blackish dusky; sides and flanks finely undulated with dark grayish. Bill and feet dusky (in skin), plumbeous in life; iris deep red. Wing, about 7.75 inches; culmen, 1.10; tarsus, 1.30; middle toe, 1.90. *Adult female:* Upper part of the head, including whole lores, reddish brown; rest of head, with neck (except nape), breast, abdomen, and crissum, pure white; upper parts generally, sides, and flanks, cinereous, darker on the back; wings much as in the male; jugulum tinged with pale cinereous. Size a little smaller than the male.

This species — known in Great Britain as the Smew, and as the *Harle Piette* in France — has small claim to a place in the fauna of North America. The only instance on record, so far as I am aware, of its occurrence, is the claim of Audubon to have obtained a single specimen, and that a female, on Lake Barataria, near New Orleans, in 1817. Wilson, indeed, speaks of it as being common on the coast of New

England, and in the ponds of New England and of New York. But he was misinformed; and probably mistook the common Buffle-head for this species. Its occurrence on any portion of the Atlantic coast, even in Greenland, has not the support of any well-attested evidence.

This species is exclusively migratory to Great Britain, and is there one of the most common species of its genus, frequenting the rivers and the larger sheets of fresh water, as well as most parts of the coast. The appearance of the adult male is said to be very striking; but it is the contrast rather than the variety of the colors of its plumage which makes it so. The immature birds — known as Red-headed Smews — are more common than the adults. The birds of this species are shy and vigilant, feeding on small fish, crustacea, and aquatic insects. These they obtain without difficulty, as they are excellent divers. They move on land awkwardly, owing to the backward position of their legs. They are not known to breed in Great Britain, but leave early in spring for localities farther to the northeast.

According to Mr. Dann, this bird is very common on the Elbe in winter, and is present in the Stockholm Fiord in November. It is not found on the west coast of Norway, in the Faröe Islands, in Iceland, or in Greenland, and it has not been observed by Arctic explorers in any part of the North American continent. During the winter months it is of occasional and irregular occurrence in Holland, Germany, France, and Switzerland, and has been met with even as far south as the Grecian Archipelago. It has also been obtained in Northwestern India and in Japan. The Zoological Society of London has received specimens of this bird from Trebizond.

Mr. John Wolley ("Ibis," 1859, p. 69) mentions procuring the eggs of this species in Lapland in 1853. It is there known by the name of *Ungilo*. It was said by the natives to breed in the cavities of trees, and also in nest-boxes prepared for its use. Although smaller than the Golden-eyed Duck, it is said to be able to turn that bird out of its hole, if desirous of taking possession. A nest of this bird was found by a native in an old hollow beech-tree, which, though greatly decayed, was still standing. It contained seven eggs in all. The female Smew was taken on the nest. The eggs were hardly distinguishable from those of the common European Widgeon (*Mareca penelope*), and were about the same size as the eggs of that bird, though rather below the average; but were a little more flattened at the smaller end, and had a little less of a yellowish tinge. There is said also to be a decided difference of texture. These eggs varied in length from 2.05 to 2.04 inches, and in breadth from 1.42 to 1.52. Mr. Wolley was informed by Hoffmansegg, a German naturalist, that the Smew occurs in his neighborhood, which is more southerly than the district where the former was staying; and as Mr. Wolley did not hear of it on the north or northeast coast of Norway, and as it is not known to breed in Sweden, he infers that it is an eastern as well as a northern bird.

The Smew is given by Middendorff as occurring in the wooded regions of Siberia.

Mr. Wheelwright says of this species: "It is never seen on the southwestern or eastern coast of Scandinavia, except in winter. It breeds sparingly in the far north, but the egg is more difficult to obtain than that of any other Scandinavian bird." The egg in his collection was taken out of a hole in a tree between Joakmock and Junàkiok, in Lulea, Lapland. The year before, a Golden-eye had bred in the same hole. The egg is so like that of *Mareca penelope* in shape, size, and coloring, that it is difficult to distinguish one from the other.

Mr. T. L. Powys found the Smew common in Epirus in February and March, chiefly in immature plumage. It was also found in Southern Spain during the winter by Mr. H. Saunders; and it was especially common at the Albufera.

ORDER STEGANOPODES.

THE TOTIPALMATE SWIMMERS.

CHAR. Hallux united by a web with the inner toe; bill longer than the head, with sharp cutting edges, and usually with a curved maxillary unguis or terminal hook (wanting in *Plotidæ* and *Phaëthontidæ*). Throat usually with a more or less distensible pouch of naked skin, situated between the mandibular rami (wanting in *Phaëthontidæ*).

Leaving out the genus *Phaëthon*, which, if truly belonging to this Order, is at least an aberrant form, the Steganopodes constitute a very natural group of birds, the main characters of which are as given above. So far as its external appearance goes, *Phaëthon* is very similar to the larger Terns, the most obvious difference being in the character of the feet.

Synopsis of the American Families of Steganopodes.

A. Bill terminated by a conspicuous, strongly curved hook.

a. Tarsus excessively short, scarcely equal to the hallux, including its claw.

1. **Fregatidæ.** Wings and tail excessively elongated, the latter deeply forked; middle toe much longer than the outer, its claw flattened and pectinated on the inner edge; webs very small, occupying less than half the space between the toes.

b. Tarsus moderately lengthened, much longer than the hallux, including its claw (nearly, sometimes more than, twice as long).

2. **Pelecanidæ.** Bill excessively elongated (much longer than the tarsus and middle toe), greatly depressed, the gular pouch very large, and greatly distensible. Middle toe longer than the outer.

3. **Phalacrocoracidæ.** Bill moderately elongated, or rather short (shorter than the middle toe), compressed; gular pouch small, scarcely distensible. Outer toe much longer than the middle.

B. Bill tapering to the point, which is without a terminal hook or unguis (very faintly indicated in *Sulidæ*).

a. Nostrils obliterated; outer and middle toes nearly equal in length, and much longer than the inner; lores, orbital region, lower jaw, chin, and throat, naked.

4. **Plotidæ.** Bill slender, heron-like, the outlines nearly straight (the culmen perfectly so); head very small, neck extremely long and slender. Tail long and fan-shaped (nearly as long as the wing), rounded, the feathers very broad, the middle rectrices transversely corrugated in the adult.

5. **Sulidæ.** Bill very thick through the base, but tapering rapidly to the tip, which is very slightly curved, with the maxillary unguis faintly indicated. Tail short (about half the wing), cuneate, the feathers narrowed toward the end.

b. Nostrils distinct (as in the *Laridæ*); lateral toes nearly equal, and nearly as long as the middle; whole head normally feathered.

6. **Phaëthontidæ.** Bill conical, much compressed, the culmen curved; maxillary tomium very concave. Tail short, graduated, the central pair of rectrices linear and excessively elongated.

FAMILY FREGATIDÆ. — THE FRIGATE PELICANS.

CHAR. Bill longer than the head, thick, but broader than deep, the culmen gently concave, and the terminal ungui strongly decurved; nostrils obliterated. Gular pouch naked, but rest of the head scantily feathered except on top, where densely clothed. Wings and tail excessively elongated, the latter deeply forked. Tarsi excessively abbreviated, wholly concealed by feathers; toes weak and slender, the middle much longer than the outer, which again greatly exceeds the inner; middle claw with its inner edge flattened and pectinated; webs occupying less than half the space between the toes.

A single genus only is known, which includes two closely allied species, or perhaps more properly, geographical races. They inhabit the sea-coasts of intertropical countries.

GENUS **FREGATA**, CUVIER.

Atagen, "MOERHING, Gen. Av. 1752."
Fregata, CUV. Leç. d'Anat. Comp. I. tabl. ii. 1799–1800.
Halieus, ILLIG. Prodr. 1811, 279.
Tachypetes, VIEILL. Analyse, 1816, 63 (type, *Pelecanus aquilus*, LINN.).

CHAR. Same as those of the family; see above.

F. aquila.

Fregata aquila.

THE FRIGATE PELICAN; MAN-O'-WAR HAWK.

Pelecanus aquilus, LINN. S. N. ed. 10, I. 1758, 133; ed. 12, I. 1766, 216.
Tachypetes aquilus, VIEILL. Gal. Ois. 1825, pl. 274. — BONAP. Consp. II. 1855, 166. — NUTT. Man. II. 1834, 491. — AUD. Orn. Biog. III. 1835, 495; V. 1839, 634; Synop. 1839, 307; B. Am. VII. 1844, 10, pl. 421. — LAWR. in Baird's B. N. Am. 1858, 873.
Tachypetes aquila, BAIRD, Cat. N. Am. B. 1859, no. 619. — COUES, Key, 1872, 306; Check List, 1873, no. 537; 2d ed. 1882, no. 761.
Attagen aquila, GRAY, Genera B. III. 1845.
Fregata aquila, REICH. Syst. Av. 1852, p. vi.

HAB. Coasts of tropical and subtropical America, north, casually, to Long Island, regularly to Florida, Texas, and California.

SP. CHAR. *Adult male:* Entirely black, the lanceolate feathers of the back and scapulars glossed with dull bottle-green and reddish purple. "Bill light purplish blue, white in the middle, the curved tips dusky; inside of mouth carmine; gular sac orange; bare space about the eye purplish blue; iris deep brown; feet light carmine above, orange beneath" (AUDUBON). *Adult female:* Dull black, the central area of the lesser wing-covert region light grayish brown; back and scapulars only faintly glossed, the feathers not lanceolate. Breast with a large white patch, extending downward along each side nearly or quite to the flanks, and upward on the sides of the

Young.

jugulum (sometimes extending round the hind neck). "Iris dark brown; orbits and gular skin dark plumbeous, with a tinge of violaceus; feet carmine" (SUMICHRAST, MS.). *Young* (second year?): Upper parts as in the adult female. Head, neck, breast, and abdomen white. "Iris dull dark blue; bill horn-color, darker at base; legs and feet pale pinkish blue" (GREENE SMITH, MS.). *Nestling:* Covered with very fluffy white cottony down.

Total length, about 41 inches; wing, 22.00–27.10 (24.90); tail, 14.25–19.25 (17.73); culmen, 4.25–5.15 (4.62); longest toe, 1.95–2.20 (2.08). [Eleven specimens measured.]

Some specimens in the young (white-headed) plumage have the jugulum and foreneck strongly tinged with light cinnamon. The stage described above as the young seems not to be that of the youngest individuals, since two nestlings of the South Pacific race (*F. minor*) show quite well-developed scapular feathers which are uniform grayish brown.

The *F. minor* [1] differs, so far as we can see, only in smaller size, and seems to be merely a small

[1] FREGATA MINOR.
Pelecanus minor, GMEL. S. N. I. 1788, 572 (*Fregata minor*, BRISS. Orn. VI. 1760, 509, sp. 7).
Tachypetes minor, STREETS, Bull. U. S. Nat. Mus. no. 7, 1877, 25 (Christmas Islands).
Pelecanus Palmerstoni, GMEL. t. c. 573.
Attagen ariel, "GOULD," GRAY & MITCH. Genera of Birds, III. 1845, pl. 185. — GOULD, B. Austr. VII. 1848, t. 72.

race of the same species. Four adult examples in the National Museum measure as follows: Wing, 21.25–25.25 (22.56) inches; tail, 15.75–17.10 (16.27); culmen, 3.65–4.10 (3.90); longest toe, 1.65–2.10 (1.92).

The "Frigate-bird," "Frigate Pelican," and "Man-of-War's Bird," as this species is variously called, has a tropical habitat both on the Pacific and Atlantic shores of Southern North America, Mexico, Central and South America, and all the islands in both oceans between the parallels of 30° north and south. Beyond these limits it wanders occasionally; but its area of reproduction is chiefly limited to the region between the tropics.

Mr. Salvin met with this species both on the Pacific and on the Atlantic coast of Central America; and Mr. G. C. Taylor obtained its eggs, in 1858, in the Bay of Fonseca, on the Pacific coast of Honduras. The island which he visited was about an acre in extent; and its surface, which had an elevation of forty feet above the sea-level, was covered with long grass, scattered trees, and low shrubs, with a belt of mangroves growing at about high-water mark. This whole island was appropriated by the Frigate-birds; and nearly every tree and bush — both high and low — was covered with their nests, which were made by laying a few sticks crossways. Each nest contained a single egg, of a chalky whiteness, measuring 2.75 inches in length, by 1.35 in breadth. At the time of his visit — January 1 — some of the eggs were quite fresh, while others had been incubated for several days. Many of the nests were on the mangrove-bushes growing just above high-water mark. Some of the birds were sitting on their nests, and others were perched upon the branches. It was found nearly impossible to induce the birds to leave their nests. Shouting and throwing stones at them, discharging guns, and even poking them with the gun, had little effect; the birds merely snapped their bills in token of their indignation. Mr. G. C. Taylor subsequently found these birds very plentiful in Fonseca Bay, as also on the coast, in all parts of the western tropics. They have been said to fish in the same manner as the Pelicans; but according to his observations, instead of entering the water, they stop short on reaching its edge, and seize their prey with the beak, almost without causing the slightest ripple, ascending again with a heavy flapping of their long wings. In their flight and in their general appearance they resemble large Black Terns. They soar to an immense height, often appearing as mere specks in the sky.

Three different kinds of plumage were noticed; namely, the male, the female, and the immature dress. The males had a bright scarlet pouch, which the bird when on the wing inflates to the size of an ostrich egg.

Individuals of this species were observed by Professor Newton about St. Croix, soaring at a great height. It was a beautiful sight to watch one or more of these birds suspended in the sky above, with no perceptible motion of the wings. At one time the deeply forked tail was seen to be open; at another it was folded into a wedge-like shape; but the bird seemed to remain immovable. Before a gale they are said to fly quite low, and even to settle on the ground; and hence is derived the name "Hurricane Bird," which is one of the appellations by which they are commonly known in the West Indies, their appearance being regarded as a prognostic of bad weather.

Mr. E. C. Taylor, in his visit to the Windward Islands, repeatedly enjoyed opportunities of observing this species. He describes it as being very graceful, soaring high up in the air. He did not see it attack other birds, for the purpose of robbing them of their prey; but, on the other hand, he did see it plunging into the sea, as if fishing on its own account.

Mr. Salvin visited one of the breeding-places of this species, among some islands, on the coast of Honduras, called "Man-of-War Keys." On his approach the birds rose up in a cloud, and hung over the Key, like Rooks over a rookery. He describes their manner of hovering as being apparently unattended by any effort, and declares that no Eagle flies with the same ease as the Frigate-bird. He found this bird nesting on the highest mangroves on the island. Three fourths of the nests contained young of various ages, the youngest looking like puff-balls of pure white; while those which had just escaped from the shell were lying helpless on the frail structure of sticks composing the nests. These are so slightly built that the young, in their earliest infancy, must be in great peril. Where the eggs were still unhatched, the birds could hardly be driven from them. This reluctance on the part of such birds as build an open nest to leave their eggs exposed to the direct rays of a tropical sun, Mr. Salvin had previously noticed; but on cloudy days the same solicitude is not manifested; and it always seemed to be in proportion to the age of the offspring, or the degree of development of the embryo.

The Frigate Pelican is a great wanderer, and has been met with on the southern coasts of Europe and on those of Africa. Mr. J. C. Melliss ("Ibis," 1870) states that this species is known formerly to have frequented the landing-steps at Jamestown, on the Island of St. Helena, and to have bred on a portion of the southwest coast of that island, at a locality known as the Man-of-War's Roost. It is now seldom met with in that region. Mr. E. L. Layard, in a letter to the "Ibis" (1871), also mentions that in his voyage to South Africa, while steaming from St. Helena to Ascension, a Frigate-bird paid great attention to the dog-vane of the foremast head, and succeeded in tearing away half the bunting. It being Sunday, the bird was not interfered with.

In the Atlantic this bird occasionally wanders to the Bermudas. Major Wedderburn mentions the occurrence of an individual there, Sept. 27, 1848. A large Frigate-bird had been observed soaring about in the dock-yard at Ireland Island, and it finally flew into one of the barrack-rooms of the Royal Artillery, thus making its escape for the time. But it was shot eventually; and three days later another was secured. This was when a strong easterly gale had been blowing for some time. Two other instances of its capture in Bermuda are on record.

This species also occurs, as an irregular visitor, on the Pacific coast, as far north as San Francisco. Dr. Cooper was informed of a single example shot at San Diego. It had entered the Bay, and alighted on the mast of an old hulk anchored there. He was also told by others that this bird is common at some seasons outside of the Bay. The skull of an individual of this species was obtained at the Farallones by Mr. Gruber.

Both Colonel Grayson and Mr. Bischoff met with the Frigate-bird off Mazatlan, in Western Mexico; and the former found it breeding in large numbers on the Island of Isabella. There was only one egg in each nest, and that was pure white, and nearly the size of that of the Common Goose.

Mr. Gosse visited a large roosting-place of this species near Bluefields, Jamaica. At most hours of the day the birds might be seen resting, in large numbers, on lofty trees, or else soaring and circling round and round over the place. In their size and color, in the graceful freedom of their motions, and in the sublimity of the elevation attained by them in their flight, they might be confounded with the Turkey Vulture, but for the curvature of their wings, their long-pointed tail, often opened and closed, and the superior elegance of their form. When about to alight, the Frigate-bird sometimes cackles; but it is generally silent. Mr. Gosse never saw it attack the Booby for the purpose of compelling this bird to disgorge; but the fishermen assured him that this often happened. Dr. Chamberlaine states positively that when the various sea-birds have secured their prey, by watching the drawing of the fishermen's nets, they are often pounced upon with violence by the Frigate-bird, and forced to yield their hard-earned booty to this formidable assailant, from whose rapacious attacks they would otherwise have been entirely unable to escape.

The egg of this species, according to Colonel Grayson, measures 2.87 inches in length by 2.00 in breadth, is of an elongate form, and has a thick smooth shell of a greenish-white color. The young are fed by regurgitation, but grow slowly, and do not leave their nests until able to fly. He describes this bird as being generally silent, the only note to which it gives utterance being a rough croak. It devours the young of the Brown Pelican when these are quite small, as well as the young of such other birds as have nests which are flat, when these are exposed by the absence of the parents. Audubon, however, questions the ability of the Frigate-bird to compel either the Pelican or the Booby to disgorge or drop its prey.

Dr. Bryant found a few birds of this species breeding at the Biminis (Bahamas). Their nests were placed upon the mangroves, amidst those of the Brown Pelican and the Florida Cormorant. On the central, and highest, part of Booby Key a colony of about two hundred pairs was breeding. The nests were on the bare rock, and closely grouped together; the whole not occupying a space more than forty feet square. There were no Boobies among them. The largest breeding-place visited by Dr. Bryant was on one of the Ragged Island Keys, having an area of six acres. The nests were on the tops of the prickly-pear, and were crowded very thickly together. By the 8th of April the young in half the nests were hatched, the largest being about one third grown. The other nests contained eggs more or less incubated, and out of many hundreds which were procured only seven were fresh. He speaks of the breeding-place as the most interesting he had ever visited. The birds covered the whole surface of the prickly-pears in thousands as they sat on their nests, or darkened the air as they hovered over them, and were so tame that they would hardly move when touched. On firing a gun the whole colony rose at once, and the noise made by their long and powerful wings was almost deafening. Incubation was carried on by both male and female. The young were fed at first by regurgitation. The food was principally obtained by robbing the Boobies; but why the latter, being by far the more powerful birds, should submit to this treatment, Dr. Bryant was unable to explain.

The young are at first nearly naked; later they are covered with a white down; and by the time they are of the size of a Pigeon they have the bronzed-black scapulars so developed that they look, while sitting on their nests, erect on their tarsi, as if they had on cloaks. He speaks of their eggs as being single, white in color, large for the size of the bird, and uniform in shape.

Eggs of this species in the Smithsonian Collection (No. 1711), collected in the Bahamas by Dr. Bryant and others (No. 15516), taken near Mazatlan, Mexico, by Colonel Grayson, are all of a uniform chalky white color, oval in shape, and of a nearly uniform size. They vary in length from 2.75 inches to 2.50, and in breadth from 1.80 to 1.70.

Family PELECANIDÆ: The Pelicans.

Char. Bill greatly elongated and excessively depressed, the terminal unguis very prominent and strongly hooked; gular pouch exceedingly large and greatly distensible; lores and orbital region — sometimes other parts of the head also — naked. Toes fully webbed, the outer almost as long as the middle, the inner much shorter. Tail very short, nearly even, or slightly rounded. Size usually very large.

The Pelicans include about ten species, which are found mostly in the warmer parts of the world, although two of them — the common American *P. erythrorhynchos* and the Palæarctic *P. crispus* — extend in summer to high northern latitudes. As may be seen from the synonymy of the genus *Pelecanus* as given below, these birds have been divided into several genera by authors; but each species possesses so many peculiarities of external structure that it is doubtful whether the differences between the supposed genera are of more than subgeneric importance.[1]

Genus **PELECANUS**, Linnæus.

Pelecanus, Linn. S. N. ed. 10, I. 1758, 132; ed. 12, I. 1766, 215 (type, *P. onocrotalus*, Linn.).
Onocrotalus, Briss. Orn. VI. 1760, 519 (type, *Pelecanus onocrotalus*, Linn.).
Cyrtopelicanus, Reich. Syst. Av. 1853, p. vii. (type, *Pelecanus erythrorhynchos*, Gmel.).
Leptopelicanus, Reich. l. c. (type, *Pelecanus fuscus*, Linn.).
Catoptropelicanus, Reich. l. c. (type, *Pelecanus conspicillatus*, Temm.).

The characters of this genus having been sufficiently indicated above, it is unnecessary to repeat them here. It is quite likely that the genus as here used in a comprehensive sense should be subdivided, as indicated by the above synonymy.

The species of this genus which occur in North America may be thus distinguished: —

A. Lower jaw densely feathered to the base of the mandible. Tail-feathers, 24. (*Cyrtopelicanus*.)

1. **P. erythrorhynchos.** Color white, the primaries blackish. Bill and feet yellowish, deepening to red in the breeding-season. Wing, 22.00–25.25 inches; culmen, 11.30–13.85. *Hab.* North America generally, but rare along Atlantic coast; north in the interior to about 61°, south to Central America.

B. Lower jaw wholly naked. Tail-feathers, 22. (*Leptopelicanus*.)

2. **P. fuscus.** Prevailing color dusky, the upper parts silvery-striped in adults, grayish brown in the young; bill dull grayish, or purplish brown, stained with red toward end (in breeding-season); pouch greenish brown, grayish, or dusky. Wing, 19.00–21.00 inches; culmen, 9.40–12.20. *Hab.* Coasts of Gulf of Mexico and Caribbean Sea, including West Indies; Atlantic coast of South America?
3. **P. californicus.** Similar to *P. fuscus*, but larger, and with the pouch red in the breeding-season. Wing, 20.50–23.25 inches; culmen, 12.25–14.75. *Hab.* Coast of California, from San Francisco Bay to Cape St. Lucas. Pacific coast of Mexico and Central America?

[1] For a more comprehensive review of the Pelicans, the reader is referred to the "Proceedings of the Zoological Society of London," 1868, p. 264, pls. 25, 26; 1869, p. 571, pl. 44; 1871, p. 631, pl. 51.

Pelecanus erythrorhynchos.

THE AMERICAN WHITE PELICAN.

Pelecanus erythrorhynchos, GMEL. S. N. I. ii. 1788, 571. — BAIRD, B. N. Am. 1858, 868; Cat. N. Am. B. 1859, no. 615. — ELLIOT, P. Z. S. 1869, 588 (monographic).

Pelecanus trachyrhynchos, LATH. Ind. Orn. II. 1790, 884 (based on Rough-billed Pelican, Synop. VI. 1790, 586). — COUES, Key, 1872, 300; Check List, 1873, no. 526; 2d ed. 1882, no. 748; B. N. W. 1874, 586 (synonomy).

Pelecanus onocrotalus ("A variety"), FORSTER, Philos. Trans. LXII. 1772, 419.

Pelecanus thagus (nec MOL.), STEPHENS, Gen. Zool. XIII. 1826, 117 (Mexico).

Pelecanus onocrotalus, BONAP. Synop. 1828, 400 (not of LINN.). — SW. & RICH. F. B. A. II. 1831, 472. — NUTT. Man. II. 1834, 471.

Pelecanus Hernandezii, WAGL. Isis, 1832, p. 1233 (Mexico).

Pelecanus americanus, AUD. Orn. Biog. IV. 1838, 88, pl. 311; Synop. 1839, 309; B. Am. VII. 1844, 20, pl. 422.

Pelecanus occipitalis, RIDGW. Am. Sportsman, IV. 1874, 297 (Nevada).

HAB. Temperate North America, north in the interior to about lat. 61°, south to Central America; rare or casual in the North Atlantic States, abundant in the Middle Province and along the Gulf coast.

SP. CHAR. Tail-feathers, 24. Malar region completely feathered; color chiefly white; bill, pouch, and feet light-yellowish or reddish. *Adult, in full breeding-plumage:* Culmen with a

P. erythrorhynchos.

narrow median horny excrescence, situated a little anterior to the middle of the culmen, the upper outline more or less convex, the fibres vertical, the size and exact shape variable. Plumage white, sometimes tinged with pale pinkish, the narrow lesser wing-coverts and jugular plumes straw yellow or (rarely) purplish buff; primaries dull black, their shafts white toward the base; secondaries dusky, edged both externally and internally with ashy-white. Upper part of the nape with a pendant crest of long, narrow, silky, pure white or pale straw-colored feathers.

Bill chiefly orange, paler on the culmen, the nails and edges of the maxilla and mandible more reddish; mandible deeper red than the maxilla, growing almost brick-red basally; pouch dirty-whitish anteriorly, where suffused with blackish, passing successively through yellow and orange into intense dragon's-blood, or brick-red, at the base; lower edge of the mandible sometimes black-

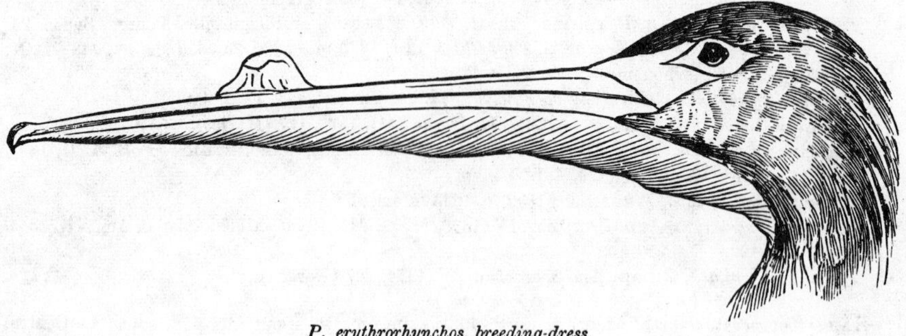

P. erythrorhynchos, breeding-dress.

ish, and side of the mandible sometimes marked, nearly opposite the maxillary crest, with a somewhat quadrate black spot; bare skin of the lores and orbital region rich orange-yellow; eyelids dark-reddish; iris pearl-white; legs and feet intense orange-red.[1] *Adult, during latter part of the breeding-season:* Similar to the above, but maxillary excrescence wanting (having been cast), and the nuchal crest replaced by a patch of brownish gray. *Adult, in fall and winter:* Similar to the last, but no grayish patch on the occiput (crest also absent), the bill and feet clear yellow. *Young:* Similar to the winter adult, but lesser wing-coverts brownish gray centrally, the pileum similarly marked; jugular feathers short and broad, and pure white, like the other feathers of the lower surface; bill, pouch, and feet pale yellow.

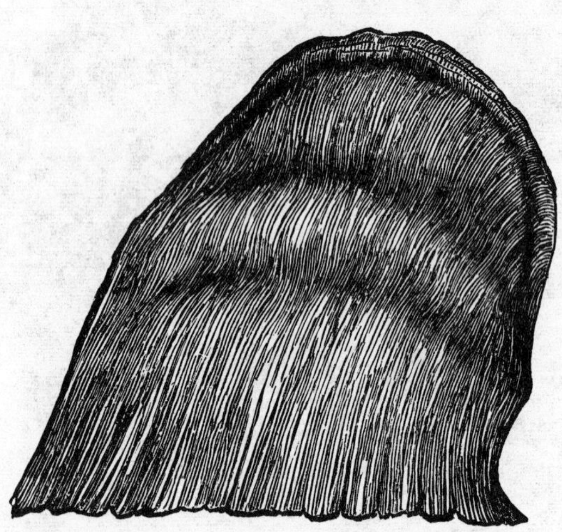

A maxillary crest of rather exceptional regularity.

Total length, about 62.00 inches; extent, 8.50–9.00 feet; wing, 22.25–25.25 inches; culmen, 11.30–13.85; tarsus, 4.30–4.65; middle toe, 3.70–4.25.[2] Weight of adult, about 17 pounds.

Individual variation, both in size and in the details of coloration, is very considerable in this species. Most descriptions of the perfectly adult bird say that the plumage is tinged with peach-blossom pink; but in only a single example among the very large number examined by us (including both skins and freshly killed birds) was the faintest trace of this color visible, and that confined to a few feathers of the back. The straw-yellow color of the narrow jugular feathers and lesser wing-coverts, however, seems to be always a characteristic of the

[1] Taken from specimens freshly killed, in May, at Pyramid Lake, Nevada; the iris is said to be sometimes hazel.

[2] The average of a series of eight adult examples is as follows: Wing, 23.55 inches; culmen, 12.62; tarsus, 4.50; middle toe, 3.98.

adult birds, both in winter and summer, though much paler in the former season. The black along the lower edge of the mandible and the squarish spot on its side are not infrequently entirely absent. The maxillary excrescence varies greatly both in size and shape. Frequently it consists of a single piece, nearly as high as long, its vertical outlines almost parallel, and the upper outline quite regularly convex, the largest specimen seen being about three inches high, by as many in length. More frequently, however, it is very irregular in shape, usually less elevated, and not infrequently with ragged anterior, or even posterior, continuations. This excrescence, which is assumed gradually in the spring, reaches its perfect development in the pairing season, and is dropped before or soon after the young are hatched; simultaneously with the shedding of this appendage the nuchal crest falls off, and in its place a patch of short brownish gray feathers appears; this disappears with the fall moult, when the occiput is entirely unadorned, there being neither crest nor colored patch.

The American White Pelican occurs nearly throughout North America, from Panama to the more extreme northern regions. Although found in large numbers in the Fur Country, as well as in the region beyond the Rocky Mountains, it is quite rare on the eastern coast, as well as in the interior between the Atlantic and the Rocky Mountains. Only a few stragglers are met with — and that irregularly and by accident — except on the Ohio and the Mississippi, where their visits, though irregular, are more frequent.

Captain Blakiston met with this species on the Saskatchewan, and Mr. Murray reports having received one specimen from the Hudson's Bay Region. The former states that the Grand Rapid, at the mouth of the Saskatchewan, is a favorite resort. Mr. Bernard Ross also found it frequenting the Mackenzie River.

Hearne ("Journey to the Northern Ocean," p. 433) speaks of this species as being numerous in the interior part of the country, but never appearing near the sea-coast. It is said generally to frequent large lakes, and always to make its nest on islands. These birds are so provident for their young that great quantities of fish lie rotting near their nests, and emit such a stench as to be noticed at a considerable distance. The young are frequently eaten by the Indians; and great quantities of their fat are melted down and preserved in bladders for winter use, to be mixed with pounded flesh; but this in time becomes very rank. The skin of this bird, which is thick and tough, is frequently dressed by the Indians, and converted into bags, but never into clothing.

This species is mentioned by Sir John Richardson as being numerous in the interior of the Fur Country, up to lat. 61°; but he says that it seldom comes within two hundred miles of Hudson's Bay. It usually deposits its eggs on small rocky islands on the brink of cascades, where it is almost entirely secure from approach; but otherwise it is by no means shy. It flies low and heavily, usually in flocks of from six to fourteen, sometimes abreast, at other times in an oblique line. It is often known to pass close over a building, or within a few yards of a party of men, without exhibiting any signs of fear. It haunts eddies under waterfalls, and devours great quantities of fish. When gorged with food it dozes on the water, and may then be easily captured, as it takes wing at such times only with great difficulty. It may be most generally seen either on the wing or swimming.

There are quite a number of well-attested instances of the occurrence of this species in different parts of the Provinces, of New England, and of the interior of New York. W. J. Beal ("Naturalist," I. 323) states that in the spring of 1874 a pair of these birds visited the marshes of Cayuga Lake, one of which — a female — was killed. The hunters had never seen anything of the kind about there before. In the stomach were found two of the common *Pomotis* and the remains of two Bull-heads, that must have been ten inches long; but no small fish. Two specimens were seen about ten years ago in the Bay of Fundy, near St. John. One was killed, mounted, and placed in the collection of that city. A flock of seven is reported as having been seen in the St. Croix River in August, 1874, by Captain Worcester, of St. Stephens, N. B. Mr. J. A. Allen informs me that thirteen White Pelicans were seen a few years ago on Nantucket, near Brant Point Lighthouse, one of them having been killed; and Mr. Maynard states that about the same time several of these birds were seen near Ipswich, Mass. This species is now of irregular appearance on the New England coast, although it is said to have been formerly not uncommon.

Henry Gillman, of Detroit, records ("Naturalist," X. 758) the capture, June 15, 1870, of a remarkably fine specimen which was shot in a marsh near Sarnia, Ontario, by Captain Oliver Maisonville. It was a male of unusually large size, weighing thirty-three pounds. It had been very active, wandering over the marsh all day, swimming about, or only rising for a short flight, and then alighting again in the water. No fish were found in its pouch, and only a few small worms and insects in its stomach.

Dr. Cooper speaks of this species as being common on the coast of California in winter, though few reach San Diego. It was found in the Gulf of California; and on the 5th of April, 1861, he saw a large flock of two hundred or more passing northward over Fort Mojave, the motion of their wings sounding like the rush of a meteor through the air. They stopped, and circled around the fort, their white plumage glistening in the sunshine, all moving simultaneously, as if under military orders, and occasionally uttering a croaking sound; then forming a wedge-shaped column, with skirmishers on their flanks, they moved on toward the north, flapping and sailing alternately, and as uniformly as if by word of command. When at Lake Tahoe, over six thousand feet above the level of the sea, Sept. 12, 1863, Dr. Cooper saw a flock of these birds, apparently a mile above the lake, flying directly on an air-line course from Great Salt Lake to San Francisco, showing that their residence in the interior lasts about five months, although it may probably continue longer when their fishing resorts are not frozen over. He did not notice this bird at Lake Tahoe, although Dr. Newberry mentions having seen one in summer at Klamath Lake. On Sept. 12, 1865, Dr. Cooper found immense flocks of this species in the lagoons along the coast, twenty-six miles south of Stockton. They arose from their resting-places among the groves with a sound like that of the distant surf, and circled about in a majestic manner, performing various evolutions in the air with the accuracy of a regiment moving under command. The attraction at that season was the low state of the waters, which afforded them an opportunity of obtaining an abundance of the cyprinoids inhabiting those lagoons.

Colonel Grayson mentions this Pelican as being occasionally seen in large flocks on Rio Mazatlan, in Western Mexico; but it is not resident there, being seen only in the winter months, and not remaining long in that locality.

According to Mr. Salvin, this bird was obtained by Mr. Skinner on the Pacific coast of Guatemala. Mr. Salvin afterward himself visited the west coast of Central America, where he found the lagoons frequented by large flocks of White Pelicans. When first seen they were feeding in the lagoon, and he tried in vain to obtain a specimen. He noticed that this bird soars much more than the Brown species; and he frequently observed it doing this after the manner of the Vulture, and mounting in gyrations until almost out of sight. After a while, gradually descending, it would fly off to a lagoon to feed. He estimates that there must have been nearly a thousand individuals in the flock which he saw; and the noise they made by dashing into the water while feeding, could be heard to a great distance. They never flew more than twenty or thirty yards in pursuit of fish. When they all plunged into the water together, it would be lashed into foam. After several disappointments, Mr. Salvin managed to secure some specimens of this Pelican by getting into a canoe with some fishermen, and gradually approaching them.

Mr. Charles H. Nauman informs me that he found birds of this species breeding abundantly on the sandbars opposite to New Found Harbor, in Indian River, Florida. They laid their eggs about the middle of May, on the bare sand, making no nest whatever. Audubon did not meet with any of their eggs in Florida, but states that about 1810 they were frequently seen on the sandbars of the Ohio. In April, 1837, he met with the White Pelican in great abundance near the southwest mouth of the Mississippi; and afterward, in the course of the same season, he saw it in almost every inlet, bay, or river in Texas.

Mr. Peale mentions procuring specimens of this Pelican at Council Bluff as early as April 8. He also records the killing of a pair of birds of this species on the Delaware, a few miles below Philadelphia. On the western rivers this species has been observed as high as lat. 42°. Mr. Peale found it in company with *P. fuscus*, breeding in vast numbers on the Mangrove Islands, in Mosquito River, East Florida. He visited these islands in the winter. The birds collected there at night, although it was not their breeding-season. They gathered there to roost, apparently coming from a great distance. The inhabitants of the surrounding country collected the young in great numbers, in June, for the sake of their oil, which is said to burn freely and to emit a clear light.

The great peculiarity of the Pelicans, as a family, consist in their possession of a pouch attached to the lower mandible, which they have the power of contracting, when empty, into a small compass, so that it hardly hangs below the bill, though when fully expanded it is of great size. This pouch serves all the purposes of a crop, and also enables the bird to retain its food unaltered for a considerable time. The food as fast as collected is stowed away in the pouch; and when the bird returns to the shore it devours at its leisure that which has thus been laid aside for future use. From the same receptacle, also, the female feeds her young. The membrane of this pouch may be prepared so as to be of silky softness, and is made into work-bags, purses, tobacco-pouches, and shot-bags.

This species flies well, and can remain on the wing for a long time. It swims and dives with great celerity. The young are fed with fish that have been for some time macerated in the pouch of the mother. The Pelican can be easily tamed, and trained to fish for its owner. According to Faber, a Pelican (*P. onocrotalus*) in the collection of the King of Bavaria was kept over forty years, and showed evidences of great sagacity. Other instances are also on record of birds of this family attaining a wonderful longevity.

Mr. Ridgway met with the White Pelican on the Truckee River, about fifteen miles above Pyramid Lake. At first only a few of these birds were seen. In August he accompanied a small party to explore the lake, and visit the abode of the Pelicans upon the islands therein. The number increased as the party descended the river, and many were seen as they reached the open sheet of water. They were very unsuspicious, and took little notice of the approach of the party. When at last he reached the lake, and encamped about three quarters of a mile from the mouth of the Truckee, thousands of Pelicans could be seen scattered over the surface of the lake. In the morning, at sunrise, lines of these birds in hundreds could be observed flying from the island to their feeding-grounds at the mouth of the river, in single lines, one behind the other; their manner of flight being a succession of slow, regular flappings of the wings, which at intervals are extended to their full length, the birds sailing thus for a few rods, and the flapping being then resumed. The flock preserves the utmost method and order in its flight. The leader is always the first to extend or flap his wings, and is followed in these movements by each one in the line in succession. Occasionally individuals break the ranks, and alight upon the water, where they often remain for hours.

Mr. Ridgway visited the island at midnight when there was a bright moonlight. The arrival of the party startled the thousands of Pelicans slumbering on the beach, and they all flew away, making, as they rose, a great and confused noise with their wings. When he landed, all the birds had gone, except a few old or sick ones; but they were plainly seen, like a floating mass, some distance out upon the water. As the party moved away, the birds began to swim slowly toward the beach. Their roosting-place was very offensive, and the party was obliged to spread their blankets at some distance from it. In the morning the shore was covered with a dense mass of these birds, who at first scarcely noticed the intruders; but as these approached, the Pelicans pushed one another awkwardly into the water, or rose heavily from the ground and flew out into the lake. Of the thousands of birds seen at that time not one was found possessed of the horny appendage to the upper mandible, so characteristic of this species at certain seasons. On Mr. Ridgway's visit to the lake in December not one of these Pelicans was to be found; all had migrated. About the 20th of March immense flocks were seen returning, and moving in the direction of the lake, but deviating from a regular course, as if uncertain of their way.

In May the lake was again visited, and the Pelicans found to be in as great abundance as before, more active, flying up and down the river quite near the ground, by pairs, in small companies, or singly. Many were easily distinguished by their conspicuous process, known as their "centre-board," the others having already lost these appendages. At this time both sexes were very highly colored, the naked skin of the face and feet being fiery orange-red instead of pale straw-yellow, as in August. On his first visit to the island all the eggs had been destroyed by the Gulls (*L. californicus*), which were breeding in immense numbers on another portion of the island. Returning a few days later, he found one corner of the island covered with a dense body of Pelicans. The place where they had been was covered with their nests, upon which the females had been sitting, the males standing beside them. Each nest was merely a heap of earth and gravel raked into a pile about six or eight inches high, and about twenty inches broad on the top, which was only very slightly hollowed. In no instance was there more than one egg in a nest; but Mr. Ridgway was informed that the usual number is two, and that three are not infrequently present. The Pelicans had evidently laid twice before during the season, and each time upon a different part of the island, as there were two other areas — each of an acre or more — covered by their nests and strewn with fragments of eggs destroyed by the Gulls. Soon after his arrival he found that the number of birds possessing the "centre-boards" began daily to decrease, while a corresponding number of these which had been cast off were found on the ground. Some were quite fresh, others dry, and warped by the sun. By the 25th of May not a bird was to be seen with one of these appendages; but these were scattered over the ground in all directions. The use of these processes is not easily determined. One hundred and nine eggs were taken from as many nests, which were on a narrow point of the island, only a few feet above the water.

The Lyons (Nevada) "Sentinel" mentions that the eggs of this bird were brought into market in large numbers in the spring of 1870, and sold at the low rate of seventy-five cents per dozen. One egg was said to be equal to three Hen's eggs, and to be quite as palatable.

Professor Kumlien informs me that this Pelican visits Lake Koskonong, in Southern Wisconsin, nearly every spring, arriving and departing in the month of April, none ever remaining into May. He has never noticed any birds of this species on their return in the fall. If they pass by that route southward, their passage is supposed to be by night.

The eggs of the White Pelican have a very uneven surface, with a tendency to granulations in spots, and corrugations. Their color is a uniform dull chalky white, marked in some instances with conspicuous blood-stains. Specimens in the Smithsonian Institution collections (No. 13692) are of a rounded oval shape, and present the following measurements: 3.40 inches by 2.30; 3.15 by 2.15; 3.05 by 2.15; 3.45 by 2.25.

Captain Charles Bendire, who enjoyed unusual opportunities for observing the breeding-habits of this species in Eastern Oregon, has furnished additional and valuable notes in regard to them. He found it a very common summer resident in that region, making its appearance early in spring, before the lakes were free from ice, and moving south early in November. He observed it breeding in large numbers on several of the small islands in the eastern part of Malheur Lake, beginning as early as April 12; the nest being a mere depression scraped in the sand. The number of eggs in a nest was usually two, but occasionally three. In rare instances five were found in the same nest; but these were perhaps the product of more than one female. The birds breed in communities, the nests being about a yard apart. Eggs of this species placed under a Hen were hatched out in twenty-nine days. The eggs were all of a dull chalky white color, and their average measurement — obtained from a large number of examples — was found to be 3.45 inches by 2.30. The following are the measurements of nine eggs selected as representing the extremes (*e. g.* the largest, the smallest, and the most spherical): 3.72 inches by 2.40; 3.86 by 2.35; 3.87 by 2.32; 3.62 by 2.40; 3.60 by 2.40; 3.57 by 2.35; 3.17 by 2.23; 3.20 by 2.21; 3.20 by 2.50. The last is exceptional in shape and appearance, resembling the egg of a very large Bald Eagle.

Pelecanus fuscus.

THE BROWN PELICAN.

Pelecanus fuscus, LINN. S. N. I. 1766, 215. — NUTT. Man. II. 1834, 476. — AUD. Orn. Biog. III. 1835, 376; V. 1839, 212; Synop. 1839, 212; B. Am. VII. 1844, 32, pls. 423, 424. — LAWR. in Baird's B. N. Am. 1858, 870. — BAIRD, Cat. N. Am. B. 1859, no. 616. — COUES, Key, 1872, 300; Check List, 1873, no. 527; 2d ed. 1882, no. 749.

Leptopelicanus fuscus, REICHENB. Syst. Av. 1852, p. vii.

Onocrotalus fuscus, BONAP. Consp. II. 1855, 163.

HAB. Atlantic coast of tropical and subtropical America, north in the United States to North Carolina. Accidental in Illinois (C. K. WORTHEN; cf. Bull. Nutt. Orn. Club, January, 1880, p. 32).

SP. CHAR. Tail of twenty-two feathers. Malar region entirely naked: color silvery gray above and dusky beneath in the adult, brown or grayish above and white beneath in the young; bill grayish; pouch and feet dusky. *Adult, in full breeding-plumage:* Head, and feathers of the neck bordering the base of the gular pouch, white, the forehead sometimes tinged with straw-yellow; rest of the neck rich chestnut or seal-brown, the upper part of the nape with a narrow crest of lighter reddish. Upper parts nearly uniform velvety light ash-gray, the feathers of the upper part of the back, the smaller lesser wing-coverts, the rump, and upper tail-coverts edged with dark snuff-brown. Lower parts uniform dark brownish gray, the feathers of the sides, flanks, and crissum streaked centrally with silvery white. Lining of the wing, and exterior border, snuff-brown, streaked with silvery white. "Bill grayish white, tinged with brown, and marked with irregular spots of pale carmine; upper mandible dusky toward the end, lower blackish from the middle to near the end; bare space between the bill and eye deep blue; eyelids pink; iris white; feet black; gular pouch greenish black, the ridges of its wrinkles lighter" (AUDUBON). *Adult, in winter:* Similar to the above, but head and neck wholly white, the head and lower part of the

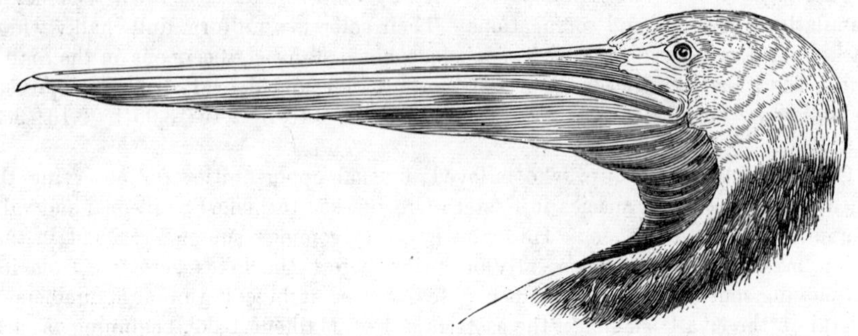

P. fuscus, summer plumage.

foreneck usually tinged with straw-yellow. *Young, first plumage:* Head and neck light brownish gray, lighter on the nape, the tips of the feathers paler; back, scapulars, and wing-coverts dull brown, the feathers tipped with light fulvous; secondaries, tertials, and rectrices silvery gray, edged with paler; rump and upper tail-coverts similar. Lower parts white, the sides, flanks, and crissum tinged with brownish gray. "Bill grayish blue, its edges and unguis grayish yellow; gular pouch dull grayish blue; iris brownish yellow; bare space around the eye dusky bluish; feet and claws dull lead-color" (AUDUBON). *Young, in autumn:* Similar to the adult, but head and neck dull light ash-gray, the feathers bordering the base of the gular pouch white, the occiput dark plumbeous or slaty, the feathers streaked centrally, or tipped with white. Upper parts less uniform and more tinged with brownish than in the adult.

Total length, about 44.00 to 56.00 inches; extent 6.50 to 7.00 feet; wing, 19.00–21.00 inches; culmen, 9.40–12.20; tarsus, 2.60–3.05; middle toe, 3.40–3.95. (Average of seven specimens, 19.79, 11.12, 2.84, 3.70.)

It was supposed by Audubon and other earlier writers that the white-necked plumage, described above as the winter dress of both sexes, represented the peculiar garb of the female. It is now known, however, that both sexes assume this plumage after the breeding-season, there being at no time any obvious difference between the male and female. (Cf. SCLATER, Proc. Zool. Soc. Lond., 1868, p. 268.)

The Brown Pelican is more tropical in its residence and general distribution than the white, and is chiefly restricted to the Southern Atlantic and Gulf States; the southern portion of California, Mexico, and Central America; and South America. It is accidental on the Atlantic coast farther north than the Carolinas. It has been said to occur as far north as Nantucket; but this has not been positively ascertained.

This species was met with on the Atlantic coast of Guatemala by Mr. Salvin; and was found breeding on the Pacific coast,[1] in the Bay of Fonseca, by Mr. G. C. Taylor, who also found it very abundant both on the Atlantic and on the Pacific coast of

[1] Accounts of the habits of Brown Pelicans found on the Pacific coast probably refer wholly to the succeeding species or race, *P. californicus*, the description of which was not written until this article had been put in type.

Honduras — and, indeed, wherever he went in the western tropics. These birds have quite a large breeding-place near Fonseca Bay; and it was quite an interesting, as well as a beautiful, sight to watch them when engaged in fishing. They fly at a considerable height, with slowly flapping wings; on seeing a shoal of fish beneath them they round to and fall like a stone in the water, causing the spray to dash up to a height of several feet. If successful, they sit on the water and dispose of their prey. The spray caused by the dashing into the water may be seen far away — much farther than the bird itself is visible.

Mr. Salvin subsequently visited Saddle Bay, on the coast of Honduras, where there was a settlement of this species, and found some forty or fifty birds, both old and immature, but could discover no trace of a nest. He was informed by his boatman that this bird breeds in November; and that as soon as the young can fly, the old birds destroy the nests. A bird less adapted than the Brown Pelican for perching on trees he could hardly imagine; yet he found it sitting on mangrove boughs for hours together, preening its feathers with its long hooked bills, all the time keeping its balance with ease — even when a strong wind tried the security of its footing. A portion were resting on a spit of sand that ran out from one end of the island, and others were fishing in the shallows.

According to Professor Newton, the Brown Pelican is one of the first birds to meet the eye of a stranger arriving at St. Croix. No shooting of any kind is allowed in the roadstead or harbor of Christiansted; and there it is very tame, and takes no heed of what is going on — often flying within a few yards of the landing-stages or boats. In all other places it was much more wary. A few of these birds might almost always be seen in a rill along the shores of the island, either resting lazily on a stump in the water, or with a clumsy activity diving for fish. When engaged in fishing they fly over the shallows until they find a promising spot; there they alight, begin diving incessantly, and always seem to rise to the surface with their heads turned in a direction contrary to that which they had at the moment of diving. These birds were said to breed near the Island of Tortola, or on some rocks adjacent to it.

Dr. Cooper states that the Brown Pelican is very abundant along the whole southern coast of the Pacific during winter, even as far as Panama, where he has seen it in May. It also extends its migrations northward in summer. He could find no traces of its nesting in the more southern islands, but was informed that a few of these birds breed on the Island of Anacapa — a locality which he was unable to visit. He saw none at the Farallones in June, although there were then many about the mouth of the Bay of San Francisco. At San Diego, in February, they were already assuming their mature plumage.

Birds of this species are said to feed chiefly during the rising tide, wandering in extended trains along the shore, and diving occasionally, one after the other, when they meet with a shoal of fish. They are very regular in their motions when flying, keeping at uniform distances, alternately flapping and sailing, in imitation of their leader. They usually fly very close to the surface of the water, and then merely plunge obliquely, holding the bill so as to scoop up the small fish sideways; then, closing their wings, they hold up the head with the bill down, so as to allow the water to run out. This permits the escape of some of the fish, and gives the parasitic Gull a chance to obtain a share of the plunder, without in the least offending the dignified Pelican. Sometimes this bird dives from a considerable height, plunging downward with a spiral motion, although scarcely ever going beneath the surface, but immediately raising its bill from the water — usually with a stock of young fish in it. As a general rule this Pelican does not catch fish more than six inches long; but occasionally one weighing more than two pounds and a half may be found in its pouch. Like most fish-eaters, the Pelican is a stupid bird, seeming to have no ideas beyond the supplying of its immediate wants. It seems to be a very silent bird; and at times prefers feeding in the twilight.

Colonel Grayson found this species very abundant at all seasons near Mazatlan, and also near Socorro, on the coast of Western Mexico. Léotaud states that this Pelican is common about the Island of Trinidad, where it is always found on the shores, except during the time of its breeding-season. Dr. Gundlach observed this bird breeding in Cuba, where he obtained its eggs. Mr. Gosse also found it abundant about Jamaica, in the neighborhood of Bluefield Bay. The latter mentions, as a matter worthy of observation, that the Pelican invariably performs a somerset under the surface of the water; for, descending diagonally, the head emerges turned in the opposite direction from that in which it was looking before diving. In alighting on the water to swim, the Pelican brings its feet into a standing position, and slides along the surface for several yards before it swims. Its pouch is said to hold seventeen pints of water.

Mr. Dresser found this bird common in Southwestern Texas in June, July, and August, and abundant in Galveston in June.

Major Wedderburn records the capture of two specimens of this species in Bermuda. Mr. J. A. Allen also mentions ("Naturalist," IV. 58) that a flock of five of these birds came in from the sea in a storm, apparently much fatigued, and alighted on the beach near Sankaty Head Lighthouse, Nantucket, where they remained until they were driven away by being fired at. This is the only instance, so far as I am aware, of the occurrence of this Pelican in New England.

Mr. N. B. Moore, of Sarasota, Fla., writes me that he has known this bird capture its prey without plunging into the water, by thrusting its bill forward among the shoal of small fry.

In Florida, where the Brown Pelican is a constant resident, Audubon has never known it to enter fresh-water streams in the manner of the White Pelican. He states that it is rarely seen north of Cape Hatteras. It was formerly quite common at Charleston, S. C., but is now comparatively rare there; and is not known to breed north of the salt-water inlets fifty miles south of St. Augustine. On the ground the Pelican walks heavily, and when it attempts to run, does so very clumsily, stretching out its neck, partially extending its wings, and reeling from side to side. It usually keeps in flocks of about fifty individuals, of both sexes, and of different ages. Audubon found it nesting on the tops of the mangroves — usually on the southwest side. The nests were composed of sticks laid crossways until a strong platform is constructed; the inner nest, a shallow basin, being made with fine roots and withered plants; these nests were often placed side by side, covering the top of the tree. The eggs are usually three in number, elliptical in shape, and averaging 3.13 inches in length by 2.13 in breadth; the shell is thick and rough, and of a chalky-white color. When fresh the eggs have a rosy tint, and are usually more or less stained and discolored.

Eggs in the Smithsonian Collection, from the Tortugas, Fla. (No. 2955), are of a uniform pinkish chalky-white color. Three present the following measurements: 2.95 by 1.90 inches, 2.90 by 2.00; 2.85 by 2.00.

Pelecanus (fuscus?) californicus.

THE CALIFORNIAN BROWN PELICAN.

?? *Pelecanus Molinæ*, GRAY, Gen. B. III. 1845 (*Nomen nudum!*).

?? *Pelecanus Molinæ*, "GRAY," SCL. P. Z. S. 1868, 269. — ELLIOT, P. Z. S. 1869, 588, pl. 44 (young?).

Pelecanus fuscus, AUCT. (all citations from the Pacific coast of the United States and Mexico, south, at least, to Cape St. Lucas).

HAB. Pacific coast, from San Francisco to Cape St. Lucas. (Also probably Pacific coast of Mexico and Central America.)

SP. CHAR. Similar to *P. fuscus*, but decidedly larger, the gular sac, in breeding-plumage, reddish instead of greenish, and the chestnut of the nape usually much darker (often nearly black). "Bare skin around eye, brown; base and much of pouch deep red" (fresh colors of an adult male "in breeding-plumage and condition" shot Feb. 24, 1882, at La Paz, Lower California; cf. BELDING, Proc. U. S. Nat. Mus. Vol. 5, 1883, p. 545). Culmen, 12.25–14.75 inches; wing, 20.50–23.25.

In Volume V. of the "Proceedings" of the United States National Museum, p. 545, the following comments occur concerning a specimen of Brown Pelican from La Paz, Lower California, collected by Mr. L. Belding: "In the . . . specimen sent, the back of the neck is a rich brownish black, quite different from the seal-brown or chestnut of all eastern specimens I have seen. Audubon describes the color of the naked orbits [of *P. fuscus*] as pink, the naked skin about the base of the bill as deep blue, and the pouch greenish black. Thus it would seem that the soft parts are very differently colored. Should this difference prove constant, the western bird would have to be separated as a race."

In dried skins it is unfortunately not possible to detect the original color of the soft parts; but a second example received from Mr. Belding (No. 90035, U. S. National Museum, ♀ ad., San José, Lower California, Feb. 8, 1882), agrees closely with the male, the red color of the pouch being at this date (April 25, 1884) very perceptible. Both these specimens are decidedly larger than any we have seen from Florida, the West Indies, or other localities on the Atlantic side; and on comparing three adults from San Francisco Bay (the only additional ones from the Pacific side that we have been able to examine), we find them to agree in larger size. Only one of them is in summer plumage, however, and this (No. 9958, U. S. Nat. Mus., ♂ ad.) has the nape light chestnut, as in some of the lighter colored eastern examples; but the feathers of this part of the plumage appear worn and faded. It may be that the supposed difference in the color of the nape will not prove sufficiently constant to serve as a diagnostic character; but even if this should be the case the difference in dimensions [2] and in the color of the soft parts is of itself, in our opinion, sufficient to justify the recognition of two species or races.

It may be that this bird is the "*Pelecanus Molinæ*, GRAY," of Messrs. Sclater and Elliot, as cited in the synonymy; but from the very meagre descriptions given it is unfortunately quite impossible to tell with certainty.

The account of the habits of Californian specimens given under the head of *P. fuscus* of course refer to the present form.

[1] No. 86384, U. S. Nat. Mus.; La Paz, Feb. 24, 1882.

[2] The five adult examples of *P. californicus* compared with seven adults of *P. fuscus* as follows, the extreme and average measurements being given:—

	Wing.	Bill, from base of culmen.
P. californicus,	20.50–23.25 (21.75)	12.25–14.75 (12.90)
P. fuscus,	18.50–21.00 (19.79)	9.40–12.20 (11.12)

FAMILY PHALACROCORACIDÆ. — THE CORMORANTS.

CHAR. Bill small (shorter than the middle toe), variable in outline, but the maxillary unguis always prominent and strongly hooked; nostrils obliterated; lores, orbital region, lower jaw, chin, and upper part of throat naked. Middle toe longer than, or about equal to, the tarsus, the outer toe much longer, and the inner about as much shorter. Wings rather short, concave, reaching but little beyond the base of the tail; tail variable as to length, usually rounded or graduated, the feathers stiff, with very rigid shafts, which are exposed almost to the base of the tail, on account of the much abbreviated coverts. Plumage very compact, usually dark-colored and glossy.

GENUS **PHALACROCORAX**, BRISSON.

Pelecanus, LINN. S. N. 1758 and 1766 (part).
Phalacrocorax, BRISS. Orn. VI. 1760, 511 (type, *Pelecanus carbo*, LINN.).
Carbo, LACÉP. Mem. de l'Inst. 1800–1801.
Urile, BONAP. Consp. II. 1856, 175 (type, *Pelecanus urile*, GMEL.).
Halieus, ILLIG. Prodr. 1811, 279. — BONAP. Consp. II. 1856, 177 (type, *Hydrocorax melanoleucus*, VIEILL.).
Hydrocorax, VIEILL. Analyse, 1816, 63.
Graucalus, GRAY, List Gen. 1841, 101.
Graculus, GRAY, Gen. B. III. 1845, 667.
Hypoleucus, REICH. 1853 (type, *Pelecanus varius*, GMEL.). — BONAP. Consp. II. 1856, 173.
Stictocarbo, BONAP. "1854," Consp. II. 1856, 174 (type, *Pelecanus punctatus*, GMEL.).
Microcarbo, "BONAP. 1856" (type, *Phalacrocorax pygmæus*, PALL.).

CHAR. Same as those of the family.

NOTE. — As in the case of the genus *Pelecanus*, it is quite likely that a systematic investigation of the Cormorants will eventually require a subdivision of the genus *Phalacrocorax*, as here defined.

Synopsis of North American Cormorants.

A. Bill robust, the maxillary unguis arched and strongly hooked, the culmen slightly concave in the middle portion, and gently ascending basally. (*Phalacrocorax.*)

a. Tail-feathers fourteen.

1. **P. carbo.** Size large (largest of the genus). *Adult*, with white patch adjoining base of the gular pouch; rest of head, neck, and lower parts blue-black; back and wing-coverts grayish brown, feathers bordered with black. *In breeding-season*, head covered with white filaments, occiput with a short mane-like black crest, and flanks with a large white patch. *Hab.* Europe, and Northeastern North America.

b. Tail-feathers twelve.

2. **P. dilophus.** Usually smaller than *P. carbo*. *Adult*, greenish blue-black, the back and wings slaty brown, feathers bordered with black. *In breeding-season*, crown with a tuft on each side (behind eye) of lengthened, curved, narrow black or white feathers. *Hab.* Whole of North America.

3. **P. mexicanus.** Very small (wing less than 10.50 inches). *Adult*, brownish black, with a white line bordering the base of the gular pouch; mantle dull brownish slate, the feathers narrowly bordered with black. *In the breeding-season*, head, neck, and anal region ornamented with scattered small white filaments. *Hab.* Mexico, Cuba, and southern border of United States, north to Kansas and Southern Illinois.

B. Bill robust, compressed, the culmen straight, the maxillary unguis slender and not arched. Tail-feathers fourteen, very short (less than half the wing). (*Compsohalieus.*[1])

4. **P. penicillatus.** *Adult,* glossy blue-black, with a patch of pale fawn-color or brownish white adjoining base of the gular sac. *In the breeding-season,* sides of the neck and upper scapulars ornamented by long, stiff, bristly white or pale straw-colored filaments. *Hab.* Western coast of North America.

C. Bill slender (more robust in *P. perspicillatus*), nearly cylindrical, the maxilla much broader than deep, its unguis abruptly hooked and not arched, that of the mandible strongly convex below. Tail-feathers twelve. (*Urile.*)

5. **P. pelagicus.** Feathers of the forehead advancing to the base of the culmen. *Adult,* head and neck rich silky violet; lower parts and rump silky dark green; scapulars and wings bottle-green, tinged with purple. *In the breeding-season,* neck and rump ornamented by narrow pure-white filaments, and flanks covered with a pure-white patch. *Hab.* Pacific coast of North America.
6. **P. urile.** Feathers of the forehead separated from the base of the culmen by a strip of bare skin connecting the naked lores. *Adult,* similar to *pelagicus,* but neck less purplish, the scapulars rich purplish violet. Nuptial ornaments same as in *P. pelagicus. Hab.* Coast and islands of Alaska, north of Kadiak.
7. **P. perspicillatus.** Similar to *pelagicus* and *urile,* but much larger (length, 36.00 inches, bill 4.00, tail 9.00, tarsus 3.00), with straw-colored filaments on head and upper neck, the eyes encircled with a broad white ring of naked skin, like spectacles. Otherwise much like *urile* in plumage. *Hab.* Behring Island, Kamtschatka; "Russian America." (Probably now extinct!)

Phalacrocorax carbo.

THE COMMON CORMORANT.

Pelecanus carbo, LINN. S. N. ed. 10, I. 1758, 133; ed. 12, I. 1766, 216.
Phalacrocorax carbo, BONAP. Synop. 1828, no. 353. — NUTT. Man. II. 1834, 479. — AUD. Orn. Biog. III. 1835, 458; Synop. 1839, 302; B. Am. VI. 1843, 412, pl. 415. — RIDGW. Nom. N. Am. B. 1881, no. 642. — COUES, Check List, 2d ed. 1882, no. 750.
Graculus carbo, GRAY, Gen. B. 1845. — LAWR. in Baird's B. N. Am. 1858, 876. — BAIRD, Cat. N. Am. B. 1859, no. 620. — COUES, Key, 1872, 302; Check List, 1873, no. 528.
Carbo macrorhynchus, LESS. Traité, 1831, 604 (Newfoundland).
Phalacrocorax carbo, var. *macrorhynchus,* BONAP. Consp. II. 1855, 168.
Phalacrocorax macrorhynchus, BONAP. Compt. Rend. XLII. 1856, 766.
Pelecanus phalacrocorax, BRÜNN. Orn. Bor. 1764, 31.
Carbo cormoranus, MEYER, Taschenb. II. 1810, 576.
Carbo glacialis, arboreus, and *subcormoranus,* BREHM. Vög. Deutschl. 1831, 817, 818, 819.
Phalacrocorax americanus, REICH. Syst. Av. 1850, t. 47.

HAB. Coasts of the North Atlantic; south, in America, to New Jersey in winter.

SP. CHAR. Tail of fourteen feathers; bill strong, the culmen slightly concave in the middle portion, ascending basally, the nail arched and strongly hooked; maxilla broader than high. Outline of the feathering behind the orbits rounded, extending thence backward and downward to behind the rictus (where the bare skin forms an obtuse angle), then straight downward across the lower jaw, and finally curving gradually forward, forming an acute angle on the middle of the gular pouch. *Adult, in full breeding-plumage:* Occiput with a narrow mane-like pendant crest of soft feathers. Head, neck, rump, and lower parts soft glossy blue-black; back, scapulars, and wing-coverts bronzy slate-brown, each feather broadly and sharply bordered with blue-black; primaries and tail deep dull black, the shafts of the latter growing milky white toward the base. A broad crescentic patch of white adjoining the posterior part of the gular pouch, its posterior outline

[1] *Compsohalieus,* RIDGW.; type, *Carbo penicillatus,* BRANDT (κομψός = *comptus,* and ἁλιεύς = *piscator*).

nearly parallel in its curvature with the anterior; but the patch becomes narrower upward, where it extends on each side to immediately behind the orbit. A large white patch on each flank, at the insertion of the leg. Entire top and sides of the head (except the occipital crest), down nearly to the middle of the neck, covered with narrow white filamentous feathers. "Upper mandible

P. carbo.

grayish black, along the edges yellowish white; lower yellowish white at the base, dusky toward the end; iris light bluish green, margins of eyelids dusky; bare space about the eye dull olive, below it bright red, the gular sac yellow; feet and claws grayish black"[1] (AUDUBON). *Adult, in winter:* Similar to the above, but white flank-patch and filamentous feathers of the head absent.

No red in the bare skin of the head. *Young, first plumage:* Above, dull brownish gray, the feathers bordered with dull black (much less sharply than in the adult); rump and upper tail-

[1] According to Audubon, the "soft parts" of an adult female obtained in July were colored as follows: "The bill, eyes, and feet are colored as in the male [see above], as are the bare parts about the base of the bill; only the part under the eye, which is bright red in the male, is bright yellow in the female."

coverts black, slightly glossy; primaries and tail dusky, the shafts of the rectrices dull light ashy, paler basally. Head, neck, and jugulum dull grayish brown, the pileum and nape blackish dusky, the upper part of the throat brownish white; remaining lower parts brownish dusky, mixed with white along the median line. *Young, in winter:* Similar to the above, but upper part of throat, jugulum, breast, and middle of the abdomen white, streaked, except on the first, with grayish brown; pileum, nape, sides of the neck, and middle of the foreneck grayish brown.[1] *Nestling:* "The inside of the mouth and the gular sac flesh-colored; the bill dusky, at the base flesh-colored; the eyes bluish gray. The general color of their skin is dull livid; the feet purplish dusky, the webs yellowish brown" (AUDUBON).

Total length, about 37.00 inches; extent, 40.00; wing, 12.90–14.00; tail, 7.25–7.75; culmen, 2.30–2.85; tarsus, 2.51; outer toe, 3.47. (Average of four specimens, 13.84, 7.50, 2.57, 2.51, 3.47.)

We have not been able to examine sufficient material to enable us to decide whether, to our mind, American examples of this species are separable from European.

The Common Cormorant appears to be a bird of very general distribution throughout nearly the whole northern hemisphere — breeding in high northern regions, wandering southward in the winter, and occurring also irregularly in places distant from its usual resort. It is found in Greenland and Labrador, in North America, in summer, and along the Atlantic coast in winter. It breeds in Northern Europe and Asia, and wanders in winter to the Mediterranean, to India, to China, to Japan, and even to Australia. Though met with on the eastern shores of Asia, I cannot find that any are reported from the western coast of North America.

The Cormorant is almost exclusively confined to the sea-coast and large rivers, and is only occasionally seen on inland waters. Like the Pelican, the Gannet, and the Booby, it is a fisher, and lives exclusively upon the food it thus catches. Its plumage, its general structure, and its powerful hooked bill are admirably adapted for this mode of life.

It is given by Reinhardt as a regular resident of Greenland, breeding on its coast, and continuing there the greater part of the year. It was also met with by Dr. Walker on the same coast, near Godthaab. Audubon and Dr. Bryant found it breeding in considerable numbers in the Gulf of St. Lawrence and on the coast of Labrador.

The Messrs. Godman found this bird abundant on all the islands off the coast of Norway, where it was breeding indiscriminately in company with the common Crested Shag. It is also given by Middendorff as occurring in Siberia, in the northern barrens, or *tundras*.

Lieutenant Sperling mentions finding this species abundant in the Mediterranean. On the morning of December 6, when shooting Ducks on the coast of Greece, he saw a large flock of Cormorants — not less than two thousand in number — passing close over his head as he was lying concealed; they appeared to be flying in a southeast direction. Mr. Saunders found this species common in Southern Spain, where, during the winter, it was very generally distributed along the coast and on the principal rivers. Captain G. E. Shelley found it abundant throughout Egypt during the winter; but did not observe any in Nubia, nor did he meet with any after March. Dr. A. L. Adams speaks of finding this bird in large numbers below Thebes,

[1] These two descriptions of the young are taken from two European examples without dates on their labels. They may be of the same age, and the differences of coloration due to individual variation; but judging from analogy in the case of *P. dilophus*, the whiter the lower parts, the greater the age of the individual — the black of the adult dress appearing in spots the following, or possibly not until the third, year.

and thence northward, in which region it was seen roosting in flocks on the date-trees. He thinks it was breeding near Manfloot.

Mr. R. Swinhoe states that he found this Cormorant somewhat abundant on the rocks about Formosa, and also in Southern China, during the winter. Early in the spring it assembled in flocks, and seemed to be moving southward. He also states that birds of this species are tamed by the Chinese, and taught to catch fish for the benefit of their owners. In this state of domestication they become subject to great variations in their plumage. Mr. Swinhoe also found them common during the winter at Amoy. They assembled there also in large flocks, preparatory to leaving to pass the summer months elsewhere. Mr. H. Whitely mentions procuring two examples of this species at Hakodadi, in Japan, in December. Messrs. Blakiston and Pryer also speak ("Ibis," 1878, p. 216) of seeing great numbers roosting in some trees at Babasaka, in the centre of Tokio. They were seen flying over that city to their roosting-place in immense V-shaped lines, three, and even four, hundred yards long. This species was also found far inland in Yamoto, on the mountain streams, feeding on trout. It was seen on the coast of Yezo, and also at Yokohama.

A single specimen was obtained by Captain Hutton ("Ibis," 1871) among the Chatham Islands, about five hundred miles east of New Zealand.

This species is not mentioned by Gosse as having been found in Jamaica, nor by Dr. Gundlach as occurring in Cuba. Léotaud, however, states — but doubtless erroneously — that it is a migratory visitant of Trinidad, coming each year at the close of July.

In Great Britain, according to Yarrell, this bird is known as the Great Cormorant, or Black Cormorant; and is there found in considerable numbers on the rocky portions of the entire coast. For their breeding-stations they seem to prefer the higher parts of rocky cliffs, where many individuals of this species congregate harmoniously together. There they make large nests composed of sticks, with a mass of seaweed and long coarse grass. They lay from four to six eggs, which are small compared with the size of the bird. The eggs are oblong in shape, alike at both ends, rough externally in texture, and of a chalky-white color, varied with pale blue; they are 2.75 inches in length, and 1.63 inches in their breadth. Upon an island near Castle Martyr, belonging to the Earl of Shannon, in Ireland, the nests of more than eighty Cormorants are said to have been counted in a single season, on Scotch fir-trees not under sixty feet in height, where they securely raised their young. Rev. Dr. Lubbock also states that this bird in some seasons has been known to nest in trees near Fritton, in Norfolk. Mr. Malherbe also states that it breeds in the marshes in Sicily, in trees. This mode of nesting is probably abnormal, having been caused by persecution.

According to Selby, the young bird of this species, when first excluded, is blind, and covered with a bluish-black skin. In a few days it acquires a thick covering of black down, and in the space of three weeks, though still unable to fly, it is sufficiently fledged to take to the water.

The Cormorant flies with great rapidity and vigor, usually near the surface of the water. It can swim with great rapidity, and has no superior in diving. It can catch its food — which consists of fish — with great ease, and which it holds securely with the sharp hooked horny points of its upper mandible. Its throat admits of being greatly dilated, so that it is able to swallow a fish of large size. It stations itself on a post, a projecting rock, or a leafless branch near the water, in a position where its powers of vision enable it to discover a passing fish, upon which it pounces with a never-failing aim.

As evidence that the Cormorant possesses considerable intelligence, and that it is easily reconciled to confinement, Montagu gives an account of one which soon became so tame and attached to its owner that it seemed never to be so happy as when permitted to remain by his side. Sir Robert S. Adair informed Yarrell that he was eye-witness to a pair of Cormorants feeding and bringing up a nest of Ravens — whose natural parents had been killed — and he noticed that they kept the young birds well supplied with fish.

This species formerly bred at several points on the New England coast, from Nahant northward; but it has long since been driven away, although a few of these birds still breed on rocky cliffs in Frenchman's Bay and in the Bay of Fundy. During the winter and in the fall they are met with in their migrations along the sea-coast from Maine to the Delaware, and even still farther south.

Audubon found this Cormorant breeding on the rocky coast of Labrador. The nests were placed on the highest shelves of the precipitous rocks fronting the water, and were formed of a quantity of small sticks, matted in a rude way with a quantity of weeds and mosses, having a thickness of from four to twelve or more inches. The same nests were evidently occupied for several years in succession. These nests varied greatly in their size, and some were crowded close together on the same shelf; but they were generally placed at some distance from each other. The eggs were usually three or four in number.

In the summer of 1860 — twenty-seven years after Audubon's visit — Dr. Bryant examined the same cliffs, on the south side of the rocky wall which bounds the Gulf of St. Lawrence, at Wapitaguan, where he found the nests built precisely as described by Audubon, and placed wherever room could be found for them. On the 26th of June some contained half-grown young, and others were but just completed. The full number of eggs was four. In shape they were more regular than the Florida, but less so than the Double-crested, Cormorants. The calcareous coating of the egg is softer than in the *floridanus*, and can readily be rubbed off with the fingers. In some specimens this is quite thick, and is deposited in irregular sheets or lumps. The birds were very tame, and returned to their nests as soon as he moved from the spot. On alighting on the sides of the precipice they cling to it with their tail and claws, in the manner of Swifts or Woodpeckers; and before alighting they almost always swooped down to very near the surface of the water, and then rose in a curved line to the surface of the cliff, without moving their wings, and almost with the regularity of a pendulum. He estimated the number of this species breeding on these cliffs at from four to five thousand. Dr. Bryant gives the measurement of four eggs, as characteristic of their general size and shape, as follows: 2.65 by 1.49 inches; 2.39 by 1.49; 2.35 by 1.60; 2.52 by 1.29.

Phalacrocorax dilophus.

a. Dilophus. THE COMMON DOUBLE-CRESTED CORMORANT.

Pelecanus (*Carbo*) *dilophus*, Sw. & Rich. F. B. A. II. 1831, 473.

Phalacrocorax dilophus, Nutt. Man. II. 1834, 483. — Aud. Orn. Biog. III. 1835, 420; V. 1839, 629, pl. 257; Synop. 1839, 302; B. Am. VI. 1844, 423, pl. 416. — Ridgw. Nom. N. Am. B. 1881, no. 643. — Coues, 2d Check List, 1882, no. 751.

Graculus dilophus, Gray, Gen. B. III. 1849. — Baird, B. N. Am. 1858, 877; Cat. N. Am. B. 1859, no. 623. — Coues, Key, 1872, 303; Check List, 1873, no. 530.

Graculus dilophus a. *dilophus*, Coues, B. N. W. 1874, 587.

b. Floridanus. THE SOUTHERN DOUBLE-CRESTED CORMORANT.

Phalacrocorax floridanus, AUD. Orn. Biog. III. 1835, 387 ; V. 1839, 632, pl. 251 ; Synop. 1839, 303 ; B. Am. VI. 1843, 430, pl. 417.

Graculus floridanus, BONAP. Consp. II. 1855, 172. — LAWR. in Baird's B. N. Am. 1858, 879. — BAIRD, Cat. N. Am. B. 1859, no. 624.

Graculus dilophus, var. *floridanus*, COUES, Key, 1872, 303 ; Check List, 1873, no. 530*a*.

Graculus dilophus, b. *floridanus*, COUES, B. N. W. 1874, 587.

Phalacrocorax dilophus floridanus, RIDGW. Nom. N. Am. B. 1881, no. 643*a*. — COUES, 2d Check List, 1882, no. 753.

c. Cincinnatus. THE WHITE-TUFTED CORMORANT.

Carbo cincinnatus, BRANDT, Bull. Sc. Ac. St. Petersb. III. 1838, 55.

Graculus cincinnatus, GRAY, Gen. B. 1845. — LAWR. in Baird's B. N. Am. 1858, 877. — BAIRD, Cat. N. Am. B. 1859, no. 622.

Phalacrocorax cincinnatus, BONAP. Consp. II. 1855, 168 ; Compt. Rend. XLII. 1856, 766.

Phalacrocorax dilophus cincinnatus, RIDGW. N. Am. B. 1881, no. 643*b*. — COUES, 2d Check List, 1882, no. 752.

Graculus dilophus, DALL & BANNIST. Trans. Chicago Acad. I. 1869, 302 (Sitka).

d. Albociliatus. THE LESSER WHITE-TUFTED CORMORANT.

Phalacrocorax dilophus albociliatus, RIDGW. Cat. Aquat. and Fish-eating Birds, 1883, 27 (no description) ; Proc. Biol. Soc. Washington, II. Apr. 10, 1884, 94.

HAB. Of true *dilophus*, the whole of Eastern North America, breeding chiefly north of the United States ; of *floridanus*, South Atlantic and Gulf States, and Lower Mississippi Valley, to Southern Illinois ; of *cincinnatus*, the Pacific coast of North America, south in winter, to California, north to coast of Norton Sound, Alaska ; of *albociliatus*, coast of California, south to Cape St. Lucas and Revillegigedo Islands.

SP. CHAR. Basal outline of the gular pouch extending straight across the throat or projecting slightly back along the median line. *Adult, in full breeding-plumage:* Head, neck, rump, and entire lower parts, glossy black, with a faint lustre of dull bluish green ; back, scapulars, and wings, dull grayish brown, each feather conspicuously and broadly bordered with black ; tail uniform dull black. A tuft of narrow, lengthened, curved feathers on each side the crown, springing from behind and above the eye, these feathers either wholly black (in eastern specimens), mixed black and white (in specimens from the interior), or wholly pure white (in Pacific coast examples); neck sometimes, but rarely, with a few scattered white filamentous feathers. Maxilla black, mottled with grayish or dull yellowish along the sides ; mandible yellowish or pale bluish, mottled with dusky ; loral region and gular sac deep orange ; eyelids and whole interior of the mouth bright cobalt-blue, the former sometimes dotted with white iris bright grass-green ; legs and feet deep black.[1] *Adult, in winter:*

P. dilophus floridanus, nuptial dress.

[1] Audubon gives the fresh colors of the larger eastern form (or true *dilophus*) as follows : — "*Adult male, at commencement of the breeding-season:* Upper mandible dusky, along the edges grayish-yellow ; lower yellow, irregularly marked with dusky toward the edges. Iris bright green, margin of eyelids,

Similar to the above, but tufts of the head wanting, and the bare skin of the lores, gular pouch, etc., deep yellow instead of orange, and the blue of the mouth and eyelids absent. *Young, first plumage:* Head and neck grayish brown, lighter next to the gular sac, darker on the crown and nape; back, scapulars, and wings, dull brownish gray, the feathers bordered with dusky brown; rump dusky brown; primaries and tail dull grayish black; lower parts light fawn-color, darker on the sides, anal-region, and crissum. Bill dull brownish yellow, nearly black on the culmen; gular sac deep chrome yellow; iris greenish gray; legs and feet deep black. *Young, in winter:* Similar to the above, but throat, jugulum, and breast paler, sometimes quite white.

P. dilophus, nuptial dress.

Total length, about 29 to 33 inches; extent, 45 to 55; wing, 11.20–14.00; tail, 5.60–8.50; culmen, 1.90–2.55; tarsus, 2.05–2.90; longest toe, 3.05–3.75. (A marked increase of size to the northward.)

A very careful examination and comparison of more than fifty examples of these birds, very clearly proves the identity of the three supposed species respectively called by authors *P. dilophus*, *P. floridanus*, and *P. cincinnatus*, the latter representing a very marked geographical modification of color; the so-called *floridanus*, on the other hand, representing merely a slight modification of size. The examination in question shows the geographical variation in this species to be of two kinds, viz.: (1) A more or less marked increase of size to the northward, and (2) a gradual change from uniform glossy black nuptial crests, in eastern birds, to crests entirely pure white, or with merely a slight admixture of black,

P. dilophus cincinnatus, nuptial dress.

bare space on the head, and gular sac, rich orange. Feet and claws black." "*P. floridanus:*" — "*Adult male, in spring:* Upper mandible black, along the basal margins bright blue; lower bright blue, curiously spotted with white. Iris light green, margins of eyelids light blue, spotted with white. Bare space on the head and gular sac rich orange. Feet and claws grayish black."

in Pacific coast examples; specimens from the interior of the continent having the tufts mixed black and white. The question of whether a subspecies *floridanus* should be recognized involves the expediency of recognizing a fourth race in the resident bird of the Californian (including the Lower Californian) coast, which differs from the true *P. cincinnatus* of the northern Pacific coast in exactly the same characters that distinguish the so-called *floridanus* from *dilophus* proper; *i. e.*, in smaller size, with relatively weaker bill, the difference in the two cases being apparently greater in the case of the western forms. Regarding the small Californian bird with white crests as being much more entitled to recognition as a race than *floridanus*, Mr. Ridgway has already separated it as such under the name of *albociliatus*.

The following measurements of specimens from various localities will convey an idea of the geographical variation in size in this species: —

a. Five specimens from Northeastern North America.

	Wing.	Tail.	Culmen.
Maximum,	12.90	7.50	2.45
Average,	12.46	7.15	2.36
Minimum,	12.20	6.50	2.10

b. Ten specimens from Florida.

	Wing.	Tail.	Culmen.
Maximum,	12.50	7.75	2.40
Average,	11.77	7.00	2.17
Minimum,	11.20	6.50	2.00

c. Six specimens from Southern Illinois and Iowa.

	Wing.	Tail.	Culmen.
Maximum,	13.00	8.00	2.35
Average,	12.34	7.29	2.10
Minimum,	12.00	7.00	2.00

d. Two specimens from Great Salt Lake, Utah.

	Wing.	Tail.	Culmen.
Maximum,	12.60	7.50	2.20
Average,	12.55	7.37	2.17
Minimum,	12.50	7.25	2.15

e. Twelve specimens from coast of California and Lower California.

	Wing.	Tail.	Culmen.
Maximum,	13.00	7.75	2.35
Average,	12.23	6.89	2.15
Minimum,	11.75	6.00	1.90

f. Seven specimens from Northwest coast (including one each from Nevada and Oregon).

	Wing.	Tail.	Culmen.
Maximum,	14.00	8.50	2.55
Average,	13.70	7.75	2.40
Minimum,	12.50	7.50	2.25

Summary of averages.

	Wing.	Tail.	Culmen.	
Northeastern specimens,	12.46	7.15	2.36	Five specimens.
Florida "	11.77	7.00	2.17	Ten "
Mississippi Valley "	12.34	7.29	2.10	Six "
Utah "	12.55	7.37	2.17	Two "
California "	12.23	6.89	2.15	Twelve "
Northwestern "	13.70	7.75	2.40	Seven "

The above figures would of course be somewhat changed were an equal number of specimens from each region measured. The general result, however, would in all probability be the same, showing a gradual diminution in size to the southward.

The Double-crested Cormorant is an exclusively North American species; it is found both on the Atlantic and on the Pacific coast, and is also not uncommon on our inland waters; differing essentially in this respect from the *carbo*. Mr. Bernard Ross met with it in the neighborhood of Great Slave Lake, where he saw no other form of Cormorant. Two examples were obtained at Sitka by Mr. Bischoff. It was also found on Vancouver Island by Mr. R. Browne. It is an unsuspicious species, and may be easily approached and shot.

Dr. Cooper describes this species as common along the Pacific coast; and, as he also states, he has met with it on the Colorado, in small numbers, in winter — although, like all other fishing birds, the Cormorant inclines to avoid that river, on account of the muddiness of its waters. This bird is said to be a permanent resident along the whole of the Pacific coast; and north of the Columbia River it is found on clear inland waters. It nests on the steep ridges and cliffs of the islands, and occasionally on the main shores. The nests are composed entirely of sticks, neatly piled up in a conical form, about one foot high, with a depression in the middle. The eggs are said to be three or four in number, and to have an average measurement of 2.25 inches in length by 1.40 in breadth. They are of a greenish-white color, with more or less of calcareous incrustations. The birds lay from the first of May to July; and if they are robbed they will lay several times. The eggs have a very strong and disagreeable flavor, and they cannot be made to coagulate by boiling; yet, as Dr. Cooper states, there are persons who can eat them.

Like the common Black Cormorant, this bird lives entirely on fish, which it catches by pursuing them under the water, diving only from the surface, and never when flying. Its power of swimming is very great, and it can remain under the water for a long time, so that when only wounded its pursuit in a boat is useless. Individuals of this species occasionally seem to prefer inland waters during the summer, while others breed on the islands at sea and along the large rivers. They may often be seen sitting on snags or on rocks; but are so shy that they cannot be approached in a boat, although in flying they often pass very near the hunter, and thus afford an opportunity for a shot. In winter they associate in small numbers with the more marine species. This seems to be an altogether silent species. In flying it proceeds by constant and laborious flappings, and moves with great rapidity. Occasionally it sails for a short distance.

Mr. Henshaw states that it nests on the Farallon Islands and upon the Santa Barbara Group; and that it is common along the coast and on the interior waters. Mr. Hepburn also states that it breeds along the Sacramento River, where in the spring he found these birds already having their peculiar crests.

Mr. J. A. Allen mentions meeting with this species in considerable numbers in the valley of Great Salt Lake, where it bears the singular name of Black Brant. It also occurs in small numbers, in the spring and fall, in the vicinity of Lake Koskonong, in Southern Wisconsin, where a few mature specimens have been obtained by Professor Kumlien, who informs me that this has of late years been found to be by no means an uncommon bird in that region. It is met with there only in the spring, collecting, about sunset at that time of the year, in a grove of dead trees, at the mouth of Koskonong Creek, as well as at other points near the lake, where, at the present time, the larger trees have been killed by the unusual prevalence of high water. When Mr. Kumlien first came to that region these trees were living, and these birds either did not frequent that locality in such large numbers as now, or their presence was not noticed.

Major Wedderburn mentions the taking of two examples of this species on Bermuda: one was shot in October, 1847; the other in February, 1848.

This is a common bird in the spring and fall in the neighborhood of Calais and in all parts of the Bay of Fundy; it also visits the sea-coast of the United States as far south as Maryland, and is believed once to have been resident on the northern shores of Massachusetts, but long since to have been driven away.

Audubon states that he saw it breeding on the Seal Islands, off the Bay of Fundy, and that it was also found by his son nesting on a low flat island a few miles from the entrance of the harbor of Wapitaguan, where some of the nests contained eggs, the others young of all sizes. None of the latter attempted to gain the water, but they all hid themselves in the fissures of the rocks. The nests were formed of a few sticks, together with seaweeds, moss, and clods of earth. These were piled in a solid mass three feet high, and having a diameter of from fifteen to eighteen inches at the top, and two and a half feet at the base. The eggs — three or four in number — averaged 2.50 by 1.56 inches, were of an elongated form, and were covered with a white calcareous coating, showing when removed a fine light greenish blue tint underneath. The young when just hatched are of a bluish black color tinged with purple, and are blind for several days. In this condition they are fed by the parents, with the greatest care, with prepared food, regurgitated into their open throats. Afterward they become covered with long down of a brownish black. Their eggs are not deemed fit to eat, and are never gathered by the fishermen.

Dr. Bryant found this Cormorant breeding in company with *P. carbo* on the rocks at Wapitaguan; but not by any means present in such large numbers as was the last-named species, with the nests of which the northern part of the breeding-place was exclusively occupied. Though early in the season, there was hardly a trace of the crest remaining on any of the birds. Their nests were as bulky as those of the common species, and it was probably not uncommon for the old nest of the one species to be occupied by the other during a later season. As a general thing this Cormorant preferred the lowest ledges, although the highest nest of all was of this species. Where the ledge was long enough to admit of several nests, it was generally occupied by one and the same species. In one or two places near the summit, where the rock was broken in such a way as to present a series of little niches, the two species seemed to alternate in position, as if intentionally, they being evidently on terms of perfect friendship, while no differences could be detected in their habits or movements. The eggs — four in number — were of a more regular oval than those of *P. carbo*, but otherwise similar to them in appearance, the difference in size of the eggs of the two species being by no means proportioned to the difference in size of the birds themselves. At the time of Audubon's visit, none of the present species were seen at Wapitaguan, and he says that he found them breeding only on flat rocks. Four eggs selected by Dr. Bryant as typical of their variations in length and breadth give the following measurements: 2.26 by 1.36 inches; 2.13 by 1.51; 2.09 by 1.42; 2.20 by 1.45.

Captain Bendire in his visits to Lake Malheur, in Eastern Oregon, met with a large breeding-place of this Cormorant. Most of the nests were on the ground; about one third were on bushes not over three feet high; and the remainder on rubbish piles not more than six inches above the ground. The young birds when about two weeks old were still devoid of down or feathers, their skin being of a deep glossy black, and altogether presenting a very curious appearance. The eggs — usually five in number — are described as being of an elongated oval, pale green with chalky coatings, their average size being 2.42 by 1.48 inches. The nests were composed of coarse sticks, about fifteen inches in diameter, shallow, and lined with a few strips of bark and pieces of *tule*, and were usually raised a few inches above the ground, and placed close to the water. The birds began to lay about the 20th of April.

Eggs of this species (Smithsonian Institution, No. 12718) are of the usual glaucous-white color of eggs of this family, and measure from 2.30 to 2.55 inches in length, and from 1.40 to 1.45 in breadth. These were obtained by Mr. Donald Gunn at Shoal Lake. This Cormorant was also found breeding in the Selkirk Settlement by Mr. Gunn, and at Sitka by Mr. Bischoff.

Birds of this species which are resident in Florida were considered by Audubon to be specifically distinct from *dilophus;* but beyond a slight difference of size, they bear so close a resemblance to the more northern birds as to render it somewhat doubtful whether they can be separated even as a race. There are probably no very noticeable differences in the habits and movements of the two forms, other than what may be occasioned by the differences of conditions resulting from living in a partially tropical and a subarctic region. In the United States this bird is chiefly confined to the peninsula of Florida; a few are found on the Atlantic coast as far east as South Carolina, and along the coast of the Mexican Gulf as far west as the mouths of the Mississippi. On the southwest it seems to be replaced by *Phalacrocorax mexicanus*. It also occurs in Cuba, where it breeds, and probably in some others of the West India islands. It is also found on the Atlantic sea-coast of Central America. Mr. Salvin gives an account of having visited one of its breeding-places on the coast of Honduras. The nests were built on the outer boughs of the mangrove-bushes, some twelve feet above the water. These were very strongly constructed of sticks, hollowed considerably on the inside, and partly lined with freshly picked mangrove-leaves. The birds, at the time of his visit, were just depositing their eggs, and some nests had in them what appeared to be their full complement of four, while others had two or three, or only one. Mr. H. E. Dresser obtained examples of this species at Man-of-War Bay, on the Belize coast.

According to Audubon's observations in Florida, it is chiefly found about the shore, in bays, inlets, and large rivers, and was not seen far out to sea. It is at all seasons gregarious. So far as he noticed, it only nested on trees or bushes, and never on the ground. He visited its breeding-places, April 26, on several small Keys. On the branches of the mangroves a large colony, numbering several thousand pairs, had already built their nests, and were sitting on their eggs; and sometimes as many as ten nests were on a single tree.

The nest of this species is of a rather small size, it being only about nine inches in diameter, and it is formed of sticks crossing each other. The eggs varied greatly in dimensions, averaging 2.25 inches in length, and 1.42 in breadth. They are rendered rough by a coating of calcareous matter. The young at first are blind, and of a black color; and if approached when about a month old, they throw themselves into the water. When undisturbed, however, they remain in their nest until they are able to fly. As soon as the birds are old enough to take care of themselves large numbers go to the inland streams and ponds for food. At this season some wander up the shore, going as far north as the Carolina coast, and others ascend the Mississippi to the Ohio, where individuals have been seen in October. It is, however, quite possible that Audubon may have confounded the *dilophus* with this form, especially as he was not aware of the fact that the former is frequently met with in the interior.

The flesh of *P. floridanus* is dark colored, of a rank taste, tough, and of a very fishy flavor. The young are eaten by the Indians and negroes, and are sold in the New Orleans market, and used by the poorer people for gumbo soup.

Eggs of this species in the Smithsonian Collection (No. 2949), obtained in Florida, at the Island of St. George's, by Dr. Bryant, have the chalky glaucous whiteness peculiar to all the eggs of this genus. Three specimens measure, 2.30 by 1.45 inches; 2.20 by 1.50; and 2.20 by 1.45.

Phalacrocorax mexicanus.

THE MEXICAN CORMORANT.

Carbo mexicanus, Brandt, Bull. Sc. Acad. St. Petersb. III. 1838, 55.

Graculus mexicanus, Bonap. Consp. II. 1855, 173. — Coues, Key, 1872, 203; Check List, 1873, no. 531; B. N. W. 1874, 588. — Snow, Cat. B. Kansas, 1873, 12 (Lawrence, Kan., April 2, 1872; one specimen). — Ridgw. Bull. N. O. C. V. 1880, 31 (Cairo, Ill.).

Phalacrocorax mexicanus, Ridgw. Nom. N. Am. B. 1881, no. 644. — Coues, 2d Check List, 1882, no. 754.

Phalacrocorax lacustris, GUNDL. MSS. (LAWRENCE.)
Phalacrocorax resplendens, LEMB. Aves de Cuba. (Adult; not of AUDUBON.)
Phalacrocorax Townsendii, LEMB. t. c. (Young; not of AUDUBON.)

HAB. Mexico, Cuba, and Southern United States, north, in the Mississippi Valley, to Kansas and Southern Illinois, south to Honduras.

SP. CHAR. Smallest American species of the genus. Tail-feathers, 12. Bill moderately robust, the unguis arched and strongly hooked, the culmen slightly concave in the middle portion, and gently ascending basally. Bare skin of the face extending farthest back on the side of the head, forming quite an angle behind the rictus; feathers of the throat advancing forward to a little anterior to the rictus, the middle portion sometimes slightly indented by an obtuse angle of the naked skin of the gular sac. Scapulars and wing-coverts rather narrow and tapering, and nearly or quite pointed. *Adult (in full breeding-plumage?):* Gular sac bordered posteriorly by a line of white reaching upward nearly or quite to the eye. Head, neck, rump, and entire lower parts deep silky

brownish black, with a very faint purplish-brown gloss in some lights; back, scapulars, and wings dark brownish-slaty, each feather narrowly bordered with black; primaries slate-black; tail uniform deep dull black, the shafts black. Superciliary region, sides of the neck, and anal region ornamented by a few short and narrow white filamentous feathers. Bill light colored (in skin), mottled with darker, the culmen dusky; gular sac brownish (orange-red in life?); iris green; legs and feet deep black. *Adult, in winter:* Similar to the above, but without the white filaments. *Young, first plumage:* Head, neck, and lower parts grayish umber-brown, becoming gradually darker, or nearly black, on the nape, sides, flanks, anal region, and crissum, and whitish on the upper part of the throat, next the gular pouch. Upper parts as in the adult. "Iris green; bill dark fleshy, culmen and upper part of lower mandible dusky; gular sac brownish; feet deep black" (SUMICHRAST, MS.). *Young, in winter:* Similar to the above, but throat, foreneck, jugulum, and breast much lighter colored — sometimes almost white.

Total length, 23.00–28.75 inches; extent, 38.00–42.75; wing, 9.95–10.40; tail, 6.75–8.30; culmen, 1.70–2.00; tarsus, 1.85–2.10; middle toe, 2.15–2.85.

This species does not in the least resemble the South American *P. brasilianus*,[1] which occurs as

[1] PHALACROCORAX BRASILIANUS.
Procellaria brasiliana, GMEL. S. N. I. ii. 1788, 564 (based on *Puffinus brasilianus*, BRISS. Orn. VI. 1760, 138, sp. 4).
Haliæus brasilianus, LICHT. Verz. Doubl. 1823, 86, 908.
Graculus brasilianus, GRAY, Gen. B.
Carbo brasilianus, SPIX, Av. Bras. II. 1824, t. 106.
Zaramagullon negro, AZARA, Apunt. III. 1805, 395, 423.
Pelecanus vigna, VIEILL. Enc. Méth. I. 1823, 342.
"*Phalacrocorax graculus*, GOULD, B. Eur. t. 408" (STREETS).
Phalacrocorax niger, KING, Zool. Journ. IV. 1828, 101, sp. 63.
Carbo mystacalis, LESS. Traité, 1831, 604.

far north as Nicaragua. The latter is somewhat similar to *P. dilophus*, but is decidedly smaller than even southern specimens, and has the gular sac divided posteriorly along the middle line by an angular extension of the feathering of the throat.

The Mexican Cormorant is a tropical species, and has but a limited claim to be counted as belonging to the North American fauna. It is common only on the southwestern portion of the coast of Texas, and also probably in the extreme southern portion of California; and is also of accidental occurrence within the interior portions of the United States. It is found on both coasts of Mexico, and is abundant on that of Yucatan, Honduras, Central America, and South America; it is also occasionally met with in the waters of the interior.

This species was taken on Lake Peten, in Honduras, by Mr. Layard; and Mr. G. C. Taylor met with it in the Lake of Yojoya, in the same region. Mr. Salvin, in his explorations among the creeks on the Pacific coast of Guatemala, observed individuals that were nesting on the branches of trees, while others were swimming in the muddy waters. Colonel Grayson mentions finding it everywhere common on the Pacific coast in the neighborhood of Mazatlan, in Western Mexico, but does not give any description of its habits. Dr. Burmeister appears to have met with it in large numbers throughout nearly all the La Plata Regions, and he speaks of seeing it everywhere, on the Rio Parana, and farther inland, on the lagoons and large ponds of the interior. Dr. J. W. Viele informs me that he found it abundant on the coast of Yucatan, where he met with it in large breeding communities, and obtained its eggs. He did not notice any specific peculiarities of habit by which it might be distinguished from the common *P. floridanus*. A single specimen was secured by Professor Frank H. Snow, of Lawrence, Kan.; it was taken four miles south of that city, April 2, 1872.

Mr. F. Germain ("Proc. Boston Nat. Hist. Soc." VII. 315) mentions this as one of the birds breeding in Chili, where its common name is *Yeco Cuervo*. It chooses as a place for its nest the rocks on the sea-coast, or trees which border certain lakes or pools, depositing its eggs in October and November, at which time birds of this species collect in great numbers. Their nests are made of marine or aquatic plants, which after a few days give forth an offensive smell; the number of eggs in each nest is three or four.

The observations of Mr. H. Durnford ("Ibis," 1878) confirm the fact of the distribution of this species over all South America. He met with it on the Sengel and Sengelen rivers, as well as on the Chupat, in Patagonia, where it was both resident and common. Every evening he observed large flocks ascending the River Chupat for a distance of many miles, the birds flying in from the sea to fish in the river during the night.

Mr. Dresser mentions finding this Cormorant common near Matamoras during the summer months; and he also saw at Galveston several birds which he recognized as being Cormorants, and which, as he thought, must belong to this species; but he did not succeed in procuring any specimens from that locality, although he received two from Fort Stockton. Both Dr. Merrill and Mr. Sennett mention the Mexican Cormorant as being a common summer resident near Fort Brown. The latter states that it was seen near the fresh-water lagoons up the river, as well as about the adjacent salt-ponds and marshes. He did not notice any as high up as Hidalgo; and although it undoubtedly breeds along the coast, none of its nests were found. The manuscript notes of the late Dr. Berlandier, of Matamoras, mention it as being common on the lakes or lagoons of the Gulf coast, and also as having been found on those of Tamiagua, Tuxpan, Puebla, Chairael del Carpentero, etc., and in the marshy places on the borders of the Rio Bravo del Norte, in the vicinity of Matamoras, and also along the coast of Texas.

Eggs in the Smithsonian Collection, procured in Cuba by Professor Poey, are, in all respects of color and shape, like those of all the species of this genus, the color being a glaucous white, with cretaceous incrustations. These eggs measure from 2.15 to 2.25 inches in length, by from 1.35 to 1.40 in breadth.

Phalacrocorax penicillatus.

BRANDT'S CORMORANT.

Carbo penicillatus, BRANDT, Bull. Sc. Acad. St. Petersb. III. 1838, 55 (*patria ignota*).
Phalacrocorax penicillatus, HEERM. Pr. Philad. Acad. VII. 1854, 178. — RIDGW. Nom. N. Am. B. 1881, no. 645. — COUES, 2d Check List, 1882, no. 754.
Urile penicillatus, BONAP. Consp. II. 1855, 175 (part).
Graculus penicillatus, GRAY, Gen. B. III. 1845, 668. — LAWR. in Baird's B. N. Am. 1858, 880. — BAIRD, Cat. N. Am. B. 1859, no. 626. — COUES, Key, 1872, 304; Check List, 1873, no. 532.
Phalacrocorax Townsendi, AUD. Orn. Biog. V. 1839, 149; Synop. 1839, 304; B. Am. VI. 1843, 438, pl. 418 (=young).

HAB. Pacific coast of North America, from Cape St. Lucas to Washington Territory.

SP. CHAR. Tail-feathers, 12. Feathers of the throat forming an acute angle anteriorly, those on the malar region forming a shorter angle, extending nearly to the base of the mandible; bill narrower than deep, the maxillary unguis not arched, but slender and decidedly hooked, the culmen gently ascending basally; both maxilla and mandible marked with numerous fine longitudinal sulcations. *Adult, in full breeding-plumage:* Head, neck, and rump soft glossy blue-black, or dark indigo-blue, passing insensibly into soft dark bottle-green on the lower parts; forehead less lustrous and more brownish; scapulars and wing-coverts dark dull greenish, each feather narrowly and rather indistinctly bordered with black. Feathers adjoining the base of the gular sac pale fawn- or isabella-color (sometimes brownish white), forming a somewhat crescentic patch on the upper part of the throat, extending up on each side to the rictus. On each side of the neck, commencing behind the brownish gorget, and continued downward for a greater or less distance, long, rather rigid, hair-like filamentous feathers of brownish white or pale straw-color; anterior part of the scapular region adorned with similar but broader filaments. Bill grayish dusky; gular sac

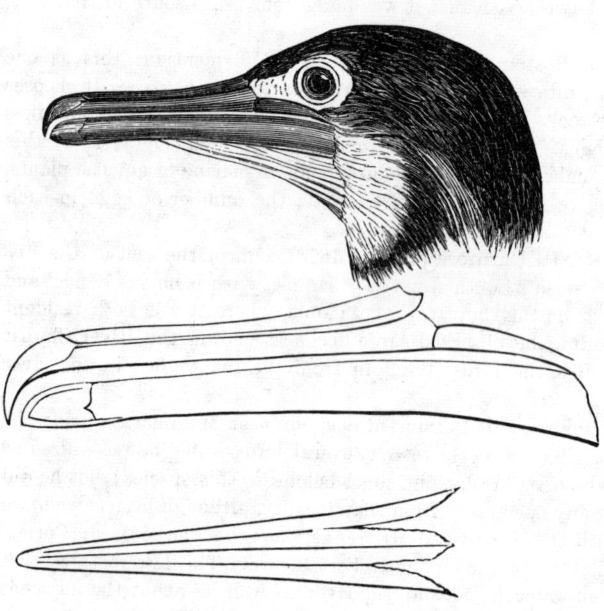

blue; iris green; legs and feet deep black. *Adult, in winter:* Similar to the above, but white filamentous feathers entirely absent. *Young, first plumage:* Head, neck, and rump dark silky fuliginous, nearly black on the nape; back, scapulars, and wing-coverts blackish dusky, the feathers bordered with light grayish brown; upper part of the throat and median lower parts pale fawn-color; jugulum, breast, sides, and flanks raw-umber brown. "Bill yellow, with the edge brown; gular sac and bare skin about the eyes orange" (AUDUBON).

Seven specimens examined, the measurements being as follows: Wing, 10.50–11.75 inches (average, 11.28); tail, 5.50–6.50 (5.93); culmen, 2.60–2.95 (2.80); tarsus, 2.40–2.75 (2.58); middle toe, 3.50–3.80 (3.63).

This species, described by Audubon under the name of Townsend's Cormorant, had previously been given by Gray as Brandt's Cormorant, and is, so far as we are aware, confined to the Pacific coast of North America. We have no descriptions of its habits or movements warranting us in supposing that these differ in any essential respect from the habits of the other birds of this well-characterized genus, the various species of which conform in all cases very closely to a certain uniform mode of living and nesting, and which agree in all other respects except specific in their markings and their geographical distribution. It appears to be restricted to the coast of California, Oregon, and Washington Territory. The examples described by Audubon were given him by Mr. Townsend, who obtained them at Cape Disappointment, in October, 1836.

Mr. Henshaw states that this Cormorant is found upon the Farallon Islands in the summer, and that it undoubtedly breeds also in the Santa Barbara Group, although he was not quite positive in regard to its presence on Santa Cruz in June. A number of birds of this species were also taken on San Miguel Island by Captain Forney.

Dr. Cooper's observations enable him to state that this is by far the most abundant species on the coast of California, and that it is supposed to extend very far to the north, beyond San Francisco, and also to an unknown distance in the opposite direction. He found it abundant at San Diego during the winter, and in flocks of several hundreds, which sometimes frequented the Bay, and at other times flew off to the outside waters to fish, moving in long straggling companies. This bird is also met with in abundance all the year round at San Francisco, and about the mouth of the Columbia River. Dr. Cooper saw a few of this species among the Southern Islands during the summer months; but he did not find any of their nests. They build in large numbers on the Farallon Islands, their nests and eggs being much like those of the other species of this genus; the principal difference being that the eggs of this species are rather more incrusted with a calcareous coating. Dr. Cooper gives as their average measurements 2.45 inches in length, and 1.52 in breadth. This bird has nothing peculiar in its mode of fishing, except that it is rather more gregarious than the others are. It is said to have its full share of the stupidity supposed to be common to this family. Hence it is not infrequently found flying on board steamboats and other vessels, although at times it appears to be very suspicious. At San Diego large numbers of this Cormorant were found putting on their mature plumage; and this process appeared to be dependent on a change in the color of their feathers, rather than one resulting from the usual process of moulting.

Eggs of this species in the Smithsonian Institution collection (No. 10055), from the Farallon Islands, collected by Mr. Hepburn, measure from 2.20 inches to 2.45 in length, and from 1.45 to 1.55 in breadth.

Phalacrocorax pelagicus.

a. Pelagicus. THE ALEUTIAN VIOLET-GREEN CORMORANT.

Phalacrocorax pelagicus, PALL. Zoog. Rosso-As. II. 1826, 303, pl. 76.
Graculus Bairdii, DALL, Avifauna Aleutian Islands from Unalashka westward, 1874, p. 6 (not of COOPER).

b. Robustus. THE ALASKAN VIOLET-GREEN CORMORANT.

Graculus violaceus (part), LAWR. in Baird's B. N. Am. 1858, 881. — BAIRD, Cat. N. Am. B. 1859, no. 627. — COUES, Key, 1872, 305 ; Check List, 1873, no. 535.
Phalacrocorax violaceus, RIDGW. Nom. N. Am. B. 1881, no. 646. — COUES, 2d Check List, 1882, no. 758.
Phalacrocorax pelagicus robustus, RIDGW. MS.

c. Resplendens. THE VIOLET-GREEN CORMORANT; BAIRD'S CORMORANT.

Phalacrocorax resplendens, AUD. Orn. Biog. V. 1839, 148 ; Synop. 1839, 304 ; B. Am. VI. 1843, 430, pl. 419.
Phalacrocorax violaceus resplendens, RIDGW. Nom. N. Am. B. 1881, no 646 *a*. — COUES, 2d Check List, 1882, no. 759.
Graculus Bairdii, "GRUBER, MSS." COOPER, Pr. Ac. Nat. Sci. Philad. Jan. 1865, 5 (Farallon Islands, coast of California).
Graculus violaceus, var. *Bairdii*, HENSHAW, Orn. Wheeler's Exp. 1876, 276 (Santa Cruz I., Cal. ; June).
White-patch Cormorant, COOPER, l. c.

HAB. Pacific coast of North America, from Alaska to California. True *pelagicus* restricted to the Aleutian Islands, Kamtschatka, Kuriles, and (in winter) Japan ; *robustus* to the coast of Alaska, from Norton Sound to Sitka ; and *resplendens* to Washington Territory, and southward as far as Cape St. Lucas and Mazatlan.

SP. CHAR. Tail-feathers twelve. Forehead feathered down to the base of the culmen. *Adult:* Head and neck rich silky metallic violet, the pileum and lower part of the neck more blue ; back, rump, and entire lower parts rich silky metallic bottle-green ; scapulars and wing-coverts similar, but tinged with purplish-bronze ; primaries and tail dull black. *In the breeding-season*, the neck, lower back, and rump adorned with narrow white filamentous feathers, and the flanks covered with a large patch of pure white ; pileum with two erectile flattened tufts of broad, rather loose-webbed feathers — one tuft on the forehead, the other on the occiput. Bill dusky ; gular sac and naked lores reddish brown or coral-red ; iris light green ; legs and feet deep black. *In winter*, the white filamentous feathers of the neck and rump, and the white flank-patches entirely absent ; the tufts of the head absent, or but slightly developed. *Young:* Uniform brownish dusky, lighter (nearly brownish gray) on the head, the upper parts darker and glossy, with a faint bottle-green reflection, the scapulars with indistinct dull black borders. Iris brown. *Downy young:* Uniform dark sooty brown.

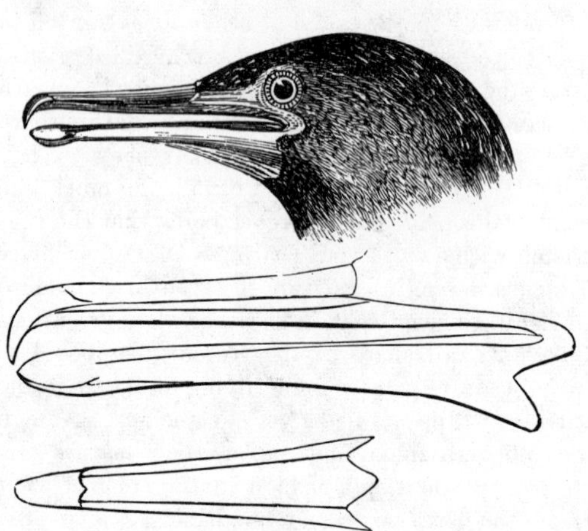

P. pelagicus resplendens, ♂ *ad., in winter.*

a. Pelagicus: Total length, about 26.50–29.50 inches ; wing, 9.50–10.60 (average, 10.10) ; tail, 6.00–6.75 (6.30) ; culmen, 1.70–2.00 (1.85) ; tarsus, 1.90–2.15 (2.02) ; outer toe, 2.80–3.30 (3.05). [Eight specimens.]

b. Robustus: Wing, 10.00–11.40 inches (average, 10.80); tail, 6.25–8.50 (7.00); culmen, 1.70–2.10 (1.95); tarsus, 1.95–2.45 (2.16); outer toe, 3.00–3.50 (3.26). [Eleven specimens.]

c. Resplendens: Total length, 25.50–29.00 inches; extent, 39.10–43.50; wing, 9.30–10.50 (average, 9.79); tail, 5.80–7.00 (6.30); culmen, 1.65–2.00 (1.81); tarsus, 1.80–2.15 (1.95); outer toe, 2.90–3.40 (3.04). [Fifteen specimens.]

The Violet-green Cormorant was first described as a North American bird by Audubon from a specimen obtained by Mr. Townsend at Cape Disappointment, near the mouth of Columbia River. It is said to be the most beautiful of the family found within the limits of the United States. This species appears to have very nearly the same distribution as *G. penicillatus;* but it is a somewhat more northern species. Mr. Dall speaks of it as being very common at Sitka and at Kadiak, where specimens were obtained by Mr. Bischoff. It is also said to be abundant at St. George's Island, in Behring's Sea, where Captain Smith obtained several examples. It was also found on the coast of Vancouver Island by Mr. R. Browne.

P. pelagicus resplendens: Female adult, summer plumage.

Dr. Cooper writes that the original locality where this beautiful species was first discovered — namely, Cape Disappointment, near the mouth of the Columbia — was also the place where he first met with it, in 1854. The locality is very difficult of approach, on account of the heavy surf constantly breaking upon the rocky shore, and it was not without danger that he secured his specimen. At the same time he also noticed there the *penicillatus* and another Cormorant, which he supposed to be the adult of *P. pelagicus,* and which had its flanks marked with a large patch of white. This, he thinks, must have been the same bird referred to by Townsend and Audubon as *P. leuconotis,* and seen by the former at Cape Disappointment.

Mr. Dall refers to this species as being resident in the Aleutian Islands. It was common on the rocks in the outer bay at Unalashka, but seldom approached the harbor. He describes it as occurring in large flocks, and appearing to be of a very inquisitive disposition — flying around the boat when the party was employed in sounding, and uttering at intervals a shrill cry. He also found this species abundant at the Shumagins.

Eggs of this Cormorant in the Smithsonian Collection (No. 12858), obtained at Sitka by Mr. Bischoff, measure 2.25 by 1.45 inches, and are in all respects undistinguishable from the eggs of the other species of this peculiar genus.

Mr. Dall, in his Report on the Avifauna of the Aleutian Islands west of Unalashka, mentions this species as a resident of the Aleutian Islands. Specimens from Kyska, procured July 8 — females — had the iris brown, and naked membrane somewhat carunculated and of a coral-red; the mandible nearly black. Others from Amchitka, July 26, had a dark-green iris and a similarly-colored gular sac. One obtained in 1872, at Unalashka, had a dark, nearly black, iris, with the gular sac flesh-colored, passing into ashy gray above. All the birds seen appeared to possess small white feathers scattered through the plumage in the breeding-season; but Mr. Dall is not sure that the white thigh-patches are always of this character. There appears to be some variation in the shade of green of the plumage: in some specimens it is much more rusty than in others.

Mr. H. W. Henshaw states that this bird occurs in large numbers all along the coast of Southern California, and that it probably extends its range northward into Oregon. He saw many of this species in May in San Francisco Bay, and found them congregated in great numbers on the islands in Santa Barbara Channel — most of the places selected as nesting-sites being inaccessible. At low tide he succeeded in entering one of the gloomy caverns, where a dozen pair had established themselves. The nests were merely collections of weeds and sticks matted together, and placed upon the rocky shelves sufficiently high to be out of the reach of the tide. This was on the 4th of June, and all the nests contained young in a downy state. The old birds all forsook the place, and flew wildly about the entrance, but without attempting to re-enter, though the young birds kept up a continuous vociferous calling. In flying about the island the old birds passed within easy gunshot of the rocky points, but never ventured over the land. The constant habit of this species is to spend the morning in fishing; and then, having appeased its hunger, to sit in groups on the cliffs which immediately overhang the sea — often in such numbers as to blacken the rocks. When disturbed, those nearest to the edge drop into the water; while those in the rear scramble forward in the most awkward manner, and having made the plunge, swim beneath the surface until they have gained a safe distance.

Eggs of this bird in the Smithsonian Collection (No. 2035, obtained by Dr. Canfield on the coast of California; and No. 6156, taken on the Farallones by Mr. Gruber) vary from 2.20 to 2.25 inches in length, and from 1.35 to 1.45 in breadth; and are not distinguishable by any specific characteristics from the eggs of any other species of Cormorants.

Phalacrocorax urile.

THE RED-FACED CORMORANT.

Red-faced Cormorant, or *Shag*, PENN. Arct. Zool. II. 1785, 584 (Kamtschatka). — LATH. Synop. VI. 1785, 601.

Pelecanus urile, GMEL. S. N. I. 1788, 575. — LATH. Ind. Orn. II. 1790, 888.

Phalacrocorax urile, BONAP. Compt. Rend. XLII. 1856, 766 (part).

Phalacrocorax bicristatus, PALL. Zoog. Rosso-As. II. 1826, 301, pl. 75, fig. 2. — RIDGW. Nom. N. Am. B. 1881, no. 647. — COUES, 2d Check List, 1882, no. 757.

Graculus bicristatus, GRAY, Gen. B. III. 1845. — BAIRD, Tr. Chicago Ac. I. 1869, 321, pl. 33. — COUES, Key, 1872, 304; Check List, 1873, no. 534; in Elliott's Alaska, 1875, 192 (Pribylof Islands).

Urile bicristatus, BONAP. Consp. II. 1855, 175 (part).

HAB. Prybilof, Aleutian, and Curile Islands, and coast of Kamtschatka. (Said to occur also in Japan and Formosa.)

SP. CHAR. Similar to *P. pelagicus*, but slightly larger, and the base of the culmen crossed by a strip of naked skin, connecting that of the lores. *Adult, in full breeding-plumage:* Head and neck deep silky steel-blue (much less purplish than in *pelagicus*), the tufts dull silky brownish bottle-green or bronzy-purplish; lower parts silky metallic bottle-green; scapulars and sides of the back silky dark metallic violet-purple (much more purple than in *pelagicus*); middle of the back (longitudinally), dark bronzy green; rump and upper tail-coverts similar to the lower parts; wings similar to the scapulars, but duller, the lesser coverts more bronzy. Primaries brownish black; tail deep dull black. Flanks covered by a large patch of silky white filamentous feathers. Neck and rump with scattered, linear, filamentous pure white feathers (soon cast). Maxilla dusky, the base, as well as that of the mandible (which is light-colored) bright blue (in life); bare skin round base of bill, light scarlet; legs and feet deep black; iris light green. *Adult, in winter:* Similar, but without the white flank patches or filamentous feathers on neck and rump. *Young:* Uniform brownish dusky, with a faint purplish cast, the upper parts darker and more glossy. "Base of mandibles dull ashy blue, with a narrow orange stripe around it, but the borders of the naked membrane ill-defined" (W. H. Dall, MS.); iris brown; legs and feet black. *Downy young:* Uniform sooty grayish brown.

Total length, about 33 to 35 inches; extent, 48; wing, 10.50–11.60 (10.94); tail, 6.30–8.00 (7.25); culmen, 2.05–2.30 (2.16); tarsus, 1.75–2.50 (2.17); outer toe, 3.10–3.70 (3.44). [Fifteen specimens measured.]

This species is very similar to *P. pelagicus,* but may be readily distinguished, at all ages, by the strip of naked skin across the base of the culmen, the same region being covered by the frontal feathers in *P. pelagicus.* The colors of the adult are also quite appreciably different, the neck being less purple, while the scapulars are decidedly more so; the lower parts are rather more bronzy than in *pelagicus.*

This appears to be a species peculiar to the North Pacific region, occurring on the Asiatic coast from Kamtschatka to Formosa, and Japan. On the American shore it has not been met with south of Alaska; but it is said to be abundant on the coast of Japan, where specimens were obtained in March, 1865, by Mr. H. Whitely near Hakodadi ("Ibis," 1867).

Mr. Dall found it abundant on the Island of St. George, where he obtained specimens, and whence its eggs have since been procured. The colors reflected from its feathers during life are said to be very brilliant, and the skin near the eye passes from bright crimson, near the bill, to a bright bluish purple toward the feathers.

Mr. Henry W. Elliott met with this species in great abundance through the whole year on the Prybilof Islands, it being — as he states — the only one of its tribe visiting that group of islands. The terrible storms occurring in February and March are not sufficient to drive it away from the sheltered cliffs, while all other species — even the Great Northern Gull (*L. glaucus*) — depart for the open water south. This species resorts to the cliffs to make its nest, and is the earliest of the sea-birds to appear in that region. Two eggs were taken from a nest on the reef at St. Paul's Island, June 1, 1872 — a date over three weeks in advance of the breeding of almost all the other Water Fowl. The nests were large, carefully rounded up, and built upon some jutting point, or on a narrow shelf, along the face of a cliff or bluff. In their construction sea-ferns (*Sertularidæ*), grass, etc., are used, together with a cement made largely of the excrements of the bird itself.

The eggs are usually three in number — sometimes four — and very small, as compared with the size of the bird. They are oval, of a dirty whitish-gray green and blue color, but soon become soiled; for although its plumage is sleek and bright, the bird itself is exceedingly slovenly, and filthy about its nest. The young come from the shell after three weeks' incubation, without feathers, and almost bare even of down. They grow rapidly, being fed by the old birds, who in doing this eject the contents of their stomachs — such as small fish, crabs, and shrimps — all over and around the nest. In about six weeks the young Cormorant can take to its wings, being then as large and heavy as are the parent birds; but it is not until the beginning of its second year that it has the bright plumage and metallic gloss of the adult, wearing during the first year a dull drab-brown coat, with the brilliant colors of the base of the bill and gular sac subdued.

The Red-faced Cormorant is said to be a very bold and inquisitive bird, uttering no sound whatever, except when flying over and around a boat or ship — objects which seem to have a magnetic power of attraction for this bird. When it is hovering and circling around in this way, it is occasionally heard to utter a low droning croak. This cannot be called a bird of graceful action, either on the wing or on the shore. Its flight is performed by means of a quick beating of the usually more or less ragged wings, the neck and head being stretched out horizontally to their full length. This is an exceedingly inquisitive bird; as it flies around a boat or ship again and again in order to satisfy its curiosity, but never alights, although sometimes coming close enough to them to be touched by the hand. In the brilliancy and beauty of its plumage this species cannot be surpassed, or even equalled, by any bird found in the Behring Sea. It fairly shimmers, when in the sunlight, with deep bronze and purple reflections as though clothed in steel armor. In its stomach are found invariably, together with the remains of small fish, a coil of worms (*Nematoda*).

As, however severe the weather may be, this Red-faced Cormorant may be seen during the whole winter perched on the sheltered bluffs, the natives regard it with a species of affection, since it furnishes the only source of supply which they can draw upon at that season for fresh meat, soups, and stews, always wanted by the sick; and were these Cormorants sought after throughout the year as they are during the short spell of intensely bitter weather that occurs in severe winters, when the other Water Fowl are driven away, this species would be certainly and speedily exterminated. It is seldom shot, however, when anything else can be obtained. Quite a large number of its eggs were brought to Washington in the collections of Mr. Elliott. They, like all other eggs of the birds of the genus, are covered with white chalky incrustations of a varying thickness, and with great irregularity of surface, the underlying shell having a pale bluish or greenish tinge. The eggs also vary somewhat in size and in shape; but all are very much elongated, measuring 2.50 inches in average length, and 1.50 in breadth. They are of very nearly equal size at either end, and are more or less stained — a natural result of the filthy condition of the nest.

Eggs of this species in the Smithsonian Collection (No. 16324, obtained by Mr. H. W. Elliott on St. Paul's Island) are of a glaucous white color, with incrustations of a chalky whiteness. Five eggs selected as typical of the variations in size and shape present the following measurements: 2.30 by 1.55 inches; 2.35 by 1.55; 2.45 by 1.55; 2.50 by 1.50; 2.55 by 1.50.

Phalacrocorax perspicillatus.

PALLAS'S CORMORANT.

Phalacrocorax perspicillatus, Pall. Zoog. Rosso-As. II. 1826, 305. — Gould, Zool. Voy. Sulphur, 1844, 49, pl. 32. — Bonap. Consp. II. 1855, 167 — Ridgw. Nom. N. Am. B. 1881, no. 648. — Coues, 2d Check List, 1882, no. 756.

Graculus perspicillatus, Lawr. in Baird's B. N. Am. 1858, 877. — Baird, Cat. N. Am. B. 1859, no. 621. — Coues, Key, 1872, 304; Check List, 1873, no. 533.

Hab. Behring's Island; possibly in some of the westernmost islands of the Aleutian chain.

Sp. Char. Somewhat like *P. urile*, but very much larger, and the nuptial plumes scattered over entire head and upper neck. *Adult, in perfect breeding-dress:* "Face and crest deep rich shining purple; neck deep greenish blue; the face and upper part of the neck ornamented with some thinly-dispersed, long, narrow, hair-like, straw-colored feathers; body above and beneath deep glossy green; scapulars and wings deep purple, primaries and tail black, the latter with white shafts; on each side of the abdomen, at the insertion of the leg, a large patch of white; bill blackish hair-color, lighter at the tip; naked part of the throat, corners of the mouth, and naked skin of the orbits apparently rich orange.

"Total length, 36.00 inches; bill, 4.00; tail, 9.00; tarsi, 3.00.

"*Hab.* Russian America.

"Nearly allied to, if not identical with, but differs from, the *Pelecanus urile* of LATHAM in its much larger size, and in the ornamental plumes being dispersed over the face and sides of the neck, instead of on the front of the latter only" (GOULD).

This species still remains unknown in American collections. It evidently belongs to the same group as *P. urile* and *P. pelagicus*, but is very much larger even than the former, and otherwise different.

Pallas's description, in some respects more precise than the preceding, is as follows: —

"Size of the largest Goose. Form of the preceding [*P. pelagicus*], which also has pure white spots on the flanks. Body entirely black. Thin white, rather long, and narrow feathers hanging about the neck, as in *Ardea*. Occiput with an enormous erectile tuft. Around the base of the bill a naked skin varied with vermilion, blue, and white, as in the Turkey. About the eyes a kind of 'spectacles' of thick white skin, six lines broad. Weight, twelve to fourteen pounds. Female smaller, without the crest and spectacles.

"This species Steller observed nowhere but in the island named after the unfortunate Bering, where he lived shipwrecked. There they are very common; but never go to the shores of Camtschatka. As it exceeds its relatives in size, it also exceeds them in stupidity. It is a very ridiculous-looking bird, on account of the eye-rings, which, so to speak, represent spectacles, and its habit of making clown-like contortions of the neck and head."

It seems probable that this fine bird must now be ranked among the extinct species. Dr. Leonhard Stejneger, who spent two years on Behring Island, and made diligent search for it, writes thus concerning it (cf. Proc. U. S. Nat. Mus. vol. 6, 1883, p. 65): "It is not to be doubted that the *Phalacrocorax perspicillatus* does not occur on the islands at present. The natives, however, remember very well the time when it was plentiful on the rocks, especially on the outlying islet, Are-Kamen. About thirty years ago, they say, the last ones were seen; and the reason they give why this bird has become exterminated here on the island is, that it was killed in great numbers for food. They unanimously assert that it has not been seen since; and they only laughed when I offered a very high reward for a specimen."

We know of only three examples of this bird in museums — one in St. Petersburg, one in the British Museum, and one in Leyden.

Family PLOTIDÆ. — The Anhingas.

Char. Bill slender, pointed, compressed, and very Heron-like in shape, the culmen and commissure almost straight, the gonys slightly ascending; terminal half of the tomia finely serrated, the serrations directed backward, and forming a series of close-set, sharp-pointed, fine bristly teeth; nostrils obliterated. Head small, neck slender and greatly elongated (nearly as long as the wing); outer toe about as long as the middle, or slightly shorter. Tail very long, fan-shaped, rounded, the feathers widened toward the ends, the outer webs of the intermediæ in fully adult birds transversely corrugated or "fluted."

This singular family consists of but one genus, *Plotus*, which has a representative in the warmer parts of each of the great divisions of the earth.

Genus **PLOTUS**, Linnæus.

Plotus, Linn. S. N. I. 1766, 218 (type, *P. anhinga*, Linn.).

Char. The same as those of the family (see above).

Only one species of this genus occurs in America. This is represented in Africa by the *P. Levaillantii*, Licht.; in India by *P. melanogaster*, Gmel.; and in Australia by *P. novæ-hollandiæ*, Gould. They all closely resemble *P. anhinga*, but are quite distinct.

Plotus anhinga.

THE AMERICAN ANHINGA; SNAKE-BIRD.

Plotus anhinga, Linn. S. N. I. 1766, 580. — Nutt. Man. II. 1834, 507. — Bonap. Consp. II. 1855, 180. — Aud. Orn. Biog. IV. 1838, 136; Synop. 1839, 306; B. Am. VI. 1843, 443, pl. 420. — Lawr. in Baird's B. N. Am. 1858, 883. — Baird, Cat. N. Am. B. 1859, no. 628. — Coues, Key, 1872, 306; Check List, 1873, no. 536; 2d ed. 1882, no. 760. — Ridgw. Nom. N. Am. B. 1881, no. 649.

Plotus melanogaster, Wils. Am. Orn. IX. 1824, 79, 82, pl. 74 (not of Gmel.).

Hab. Tropical and Subtropical America; Gulf States and Lower Mississippi Valley, north to the mouth of the Ohio.

Sp. Char. *Adult male, in full breeding-plumage:* Plumage of the neck and body deep glossy black, with a faint greenish gloss; scapulars and lesser wing-coverts marked centrally (longitudinally) with light hoary ash, these markings elliptical on the upper part of the scapular region, linear or nearly acicular on the longer scapulars, and broadly ovate on the wing-coverts; exposed surface of the middle and greater wing-coverts light hoary ash; remainder of the wings, with the tail, deep black, the latter less glossy, and broadly tipped with pale brown, passing into dirty whitish terminally. Sides of the occiput and neck ornamented by lengthened, loose-webbed, hair-like feathers of dirty white or pale grayish lilac; nuchal feathers elongated, hair-like, forming a sort of loose mane. "Upper mandible dusky-olive, the edges yellow; lower mandible bright yellow, the edges and tip greenish; bare space about the eye bluish green; gular sac bright orange; iris bright carmine; tarsi and toes anteriorly dusky-olive, the hind parts and webs yellow, claws brownish black" (AUDUBON). *Adult male, in winter:* Similar to the above, but destitute of the

P. anhinga.

whitish feathers of the head and neck. *Adult female, in full breeding-plumage:* Head, neck, and breast grayish buff, becoming grayish brown (sometimes quite dusky) on the pileum and nape, the breast lighter, and bounded below by a narrow band of dark chestnut, bordering the upper edge of the black of the abdomen; sides of the upper part of the neck adorned with an inconspicuous longitudinal stripe of short white loose-webbed feathers. Rest of the plumage as in the male. Bill, etc., colored much as in the male, but iris paler red (pinkish). *Young, in first winter:* Similar to the adult female, but lower parts duller black (the feathers usually indistinctly tipped with grayish brown), the chestnut pectoral band entirely absent; upper parts much duller black (the back

decidedly brownish), the light markings much smaller and more indistinct. *Young, first plumage:* Similar to the above, but entire lower parts light grayish buff, darker posteriorly. Transverse corrugations of the middle rectrices quite obsolete. *Nestling:* Covered with buff-colored down (AUDUBON).

Total length, about 34.00 to 36.00 inches; extent, 43.00 to 44.00; wing, 14.00; tail, 11.00; bill, 3.25; tarsus, 1.35.

The Australian *P. novæ-hollandiæ* resembles very closely the American species in the details of form, in size, and in general coloration. The chief difference between the adult males of the two species consists in the possession of a white stripe on the side of the head in *P. novæ-hollandiæ*, commencing near the rictus and extending backward, growing gradually narrower, and terminating in a point on the upper part of the neck; the gular sac is likewise bordered with a white line. In *P. anhinga* the head is wholly deep black, excepting, of course, the nuptial plumes, which are present only during a portion of the breeding-season. In the Australian bird the front part of the neck is light brownish, and the light-grayish markings of the wings narrower and less handsome.

The "Snake Bird," or "Darter," is found occupying a somewhat restricted area within the limits of the United States. It occurs in South Carolina and in all the States bordering the Gulf of Mexico, from Georgia and Florida to the Rio Grande. I am not aware that it has ever been seen on the Pacific coast within the limits of the United States, although it is found in Mexico and in Central America, on the Atlantic as well as on the Pacific coast. It also occurs in all the northern portions of South America, wherever there are rivers of considerable size.

Mr. Dresser found it common on all the large streams of Texas, having obtained specimens from Fort Stockton and from the Medina River. It is equally abundant on all the rivers of Tamaulipas and the other Gulf regions of Eastern Mexico, as well as on the western side of that country. Mr. Bischoff obtained examples of this species near Mazatlan; and Colonel Grayson found it common on the fresh-water lagoons, and on the Mazatlan and Santiago rivers. It was also seen in large numbers in the small river of Tepic and on Lake Chapala, near Guadalajara. In that region it is a constant resident, and builds its nests in trees near, or over, fresh-water lagoons or streams. It is found in nearly all the principal islands of the West Indies, although Mr. Gosse does not include it among the birds of Jamaica. It is abundant and a resident in Cuba, where Dr. Gundlach saw it breeding, and obtained its eggs. Léotaud includes this species among the birds of Trinidad — where, however, it is not very common, and where it keeps in the trees bordering the streams which flow through the low swampy meadows. It lives principally upon fish, which it seizes by rapidly darting upon them with its sharply pointed and slightly toothed beak. In this movement its neck, which is very long, is thrust forward with the force of a spring, aided by the muscles, that are large and well developed in the lower and anterior portion of the neck. These muscles are said to be white, tender, and of an agreeable flavor; while those of the body are of a dark color, and have a disagreeable taste. When fishing, the Anhinga stands with only its head and neck above the water. When it makes a plunge it remains a long while beneath the surface; and when it rises again, the long and undulating neck has somewhat the appearance of a serpent. Léotaud was unable to state with certainty whether the Anhinga is or is not a resident species in Trinidad, or whether it occurs there only in its migrations.

This bird was found at Lake Peten, Honduras, by Mr. Leyland; and Mr. G. C. Taylor met with several individuals of this species on the Lake of Yojoya, in the same region. Mr. E. C. Taylor mentions seeing a number of them on the Orinoco. He generally found them perched on the stump of a tree overhanging the river, ready at the shortest notice to plunge into the water.

Mr. C. Barrington Brown speaks of meeting with this bird in his descent of the Paruni River, in British Guiana, where its local name is "Duckler."

Mr. N. B. Moore studied the movements of this species in Florida, and ascertained that it does not fish exclusively in fresh water. He repeatedly saw it diving in the waters of a bay or creek between two oyster-bars, where the tide ebbed and flowed daily. He never knew it to fly with its wings directly extended, or with its neck stretched to its full length, but always with the neck folded upon itself, as is the case with the Herons; but in the Anhinga the folds are shorter, so that a greater length of the neck is extended in front of them. There is a moment during the expansion of the wings when the neck may be seen fully extended; this is when the bird quits its perch. So suddenly is the neck folded in this movement, and so unlike is this action to that of Herons when getting on wing, that a wrong inference has been drawn in regard to the position of the Anhinga's neck when that bird is on the wing.

In a subsequent letter Mr. Moore again repeats his observations as to the fishing of this species in salt water in localities where there is a constant ebb and flow of the tide. The bird seemed to him to delight to forage in water of an obstructed nature, no matter whether fresh or salt, as it very rarely resorted to the open water of the bay or to the mouths of creeks, to obtain its prey by a clear chase, instead of taking it by surprise.

Audubon states that he has known a few birds of this species extend their migrations in spring as far to the north as North Carolina, where they breed near the coasts. They go up the Mississippi to Natchez; and are there known to the Creoles by the name of *Bec à Lancette*. At the mouth of that river they are called by the fishermen the "Water Crow," and in Florida the "Grecian Lady." To some persons this bird is known as a Cormorant. In Carolina it is the "Snake-bird," and the male is termed the "Black-bellied Darter."

It was found by Mr. Kennicott to be common in the vicinity of Cairo, Ill., in 1855, and was also seen in the same locality by Mr. Nelson in 1875.

These birds, in their migrations, move northward in April, and return to the borders of the Gulf in November, where many are resident throughout the year. Audubon never happened to meet with this bird when it was feeding in salt water, but has generally found it in still water, and in such secluded places as were abundantly supplied with fish.

Audubon never saw the Anhinga plunge or dive for its prey from an eminence. It is more or less gregarious by habit, the number seen together varying with the attractions of the locality, and ranging from eight or ten to thirty, or even several hundred. In the breeding-season it moves in pairs. It is a diurnal bird, and if unmolested, returns each night to the same roosting-place. When asleep it is said to stand with its body almost erect. In rainy weather it often spends the greater part of the day standing erect, with its neck and head stretched upward, remaining perfectly motionless, so that the water may glide off its plumage. The roosting-place of the Anhinga is generally over water, often in the midst of some stagnant pool.

This is said to be the very first among fresh-water divers, disappearing beneath the surface with the quickness of thought, leaving scarcely a ripple on the spot, and reappearing, perhaps with its head only above the water for a moment, at a place several hundred yards distant. If hit, and only wounded, this bird readily baffles all the endeavors of the sportsman to secure it. When swimming, and unmolested, it is buoyant, and moves with its whole body above the water; but when in danger it sinks its body, leaving only the head and neck out of the water, presenting the appearance of a portion of a large snake.

Rev. Dr. Bachman, of Charleston, S. C., kept one in confinement until it became quite tame. This bird had the curious habit of diving under any substance floating on the surface of the water, such as rice-chaff. When swimming beneath the surface of the water, the Anhinga spreads its wings partially, keeps its tail expanded, and uses the feet as paddles either simultaneously or alternately. When taken young it is content in its state of domestication; and even though left at full liberty to fish for itself, returns to its home at night to roost.

The nests of the Anhinga are variously placed — sometimes in a low bush; on the common smilax, at an elevation of only a few feet; or on the upper branches of a high tree; but always over the water. They are sometimes alone, at other times surrounded by hundreds of nests of various species of Herons. The nest of the Anhinga is about two feet in diameter, and of a flattened shape. The foundation is made of dry sticks laid crossways, so as to enclose a circular space. The inner part of the nest — which is solid and compact — is made up with branches and leaves of the common myrtle, Spanish moss, and slender roots. The number of eggs is usually four, and never more than this number. The same nest is frequently used several seasons in succession.

Audubon describes the eggs as measuring 2.63 inches in length by 1.25 in breadth, as being of an elongated oval form, of a dull uniform whitish color externally, and as covered with a chalky substance, beneath which the shell is of a light blue, resembling the eggs of the different species of Cormorants. The young are covered with buff-colored down, resembling young Cormorants, though of a different color. They are fed by regurgitation of prepared food, and the act of feeding is said to be done at great inconvenience and in an awkward manner. Both parents sit on the eggs, and take part in feeding the young.

The manuscript notes of Dr. Berlandier, of Matamoras, mention this species as being found in the swamps and marshes of Texas and Tamaulipas, where it feeds on fish, and is called the *garza* — a name somewhat indiscriminately given by the Mexicans to a great variety of Herons and other birds.

Eggs of this species, collected in Florida by Dr. Bryant (No. 3838), present the same chalky appearance as do the eggs of the Cormorants, and are of a uniform bluish chalky-white color, of an oblong oval shape, ranging from 2.00 to 2.30 inches in length, and from 1.30 to 1.40 in breadth.

FAMILY SULIDÆ. — THE GANNETS.

CHAR. Bill somewhat conical, very thick through the base, but rapidly tapering to the tip, the maxillary unguis being only faintly indicated, and but slightly curved; basal portion of the maxillary tomium covered by a supernumerary wedge-shaped piece, distinctly separated from the anterior portion; nostrils obsolete; lores, malar region, chin, and more or less of the throat naked; outer toe about equal to the middle, or very slightly longer; inner edge of middle claw distinctly pectinated. Tail about half as long as the wing, cuneate, the feathers tapering toward the tips.

The Gannets are perhaps properly separable into two genera — *Sula* and *Dysporus;* the latter including only the *S. bassana.* But in considering the small number of American species, no great violence will be done in referring them to a single genus.

GENUS **SULA**, BRISSON.

Sula, BRISS. Orn. VI. 1760, 495 (type, by elimination, *Pelecanus leucogaster*, BODD.).
Dysporus, ILLIG. Prodr. 1811, 279 (type, by elimination, *Pelecanus bassanus*, LINN.).
Piscatrix, REICH. Av. Syst. 1852, p. vi (type, *Pelecanus piscator*, LINN.).
Plancus, REICH. l. c. (type, *Pelecanus parvus*, GM. ?).

CHAR. Same as those of the family.

The four North American species of this genus may be distinguished as follows: —

A. Malar region, with sides of chin and throat, feathered; a narrow strip of naked skin down the middle line of the throat. (*Dysporus.*)

1. **S. bassana.** Legs and feet blackish (in the dried skin). *Adult:* White, the remiges brownish dusky, the head and neck above washed with buff. *Young:* Dusky, streaked or speckled with white. Wing, 19.50 inches; tail, 10.00; culmen, 4.00; tarsus, 2.35. *Hab.* Atlantic coast of North America, south, in winter, to the Gulf of Mexico; Europe.

B. Malar region, with whole chin and upper part of throat naked. (*Sula.*)

2. **S. cyanops.** Legs and feet reddish. *Adult:* White, the greater wing-coverts, alulæ, primary coverts, and remiges dark sooty brown; tail sooty brown, the middle feathers and bases of the others whitish. *Young:* Head, neck, and upper parts dusky; lower parts white, the flanks streaked with grayish; middle of the back and upper part of the rump streaked with white. Wing, 16.53 inches; tail, 8.42; culmen, 3.96; depth of bill through base, 1.44; tarsus, 2.02; middle toe, 2.88 (average dimensions). *Hab.* Coasts and islands of the South Pacific and various intertropical seas; Bahamas and Florida.
3. **S. leucogastra.** Feet greenish or yellowish. *Adult:* Head, neck, breast, and upper parts dark sooty brown; the head and neck hoary grayish in older specimens, sometimes nearly white anteriorly; lower parts posterior to the breast white. *Young:* Nearly uniform sooty brown, lighter beneath. Wing, 15.72 inches; tail, 8.23; culmen, 3.74; depth of bill through base, 1.24; tarsus, 1.71; middle toe, 2.59 (average measurements). *Hab.* Coasts of tropical and subtropical America, north to Georgia.
4. **S. piscator.** Legs and feet always reddish. *Adult:* White, the head and neck tinged with buff, the shafts of the tail-feathers straw- or cream-colored, and the remiges hoary slate. *Young:* Above, sooty brown, the remiges and rectrices more hoary; head, neck, and lower parts light smoky gray. (Colors extremely variable, scarcely two specimens being exactly alike.) Wing, 15.04 inches; tail, 8.93; culmen, 3.26; depth of bill through base, 1.07; tarsus, 1.34; middle toe, 2.25 (average measurements). *Hab.* Intertropical seas and coasts north to Florida.

Sula bassana.

THE COMMON GANNET.

Pelecanus bassanus, LINN. S. N. I. 1758, 133; ed. 12, I. 1766, 217.

Sula bassana, BRISS. Orn. VI. 1760, 503. — BONAP. Synop. 1828, no. 359; Consp. II. 1857, 165. — NUTT. Man. II. 1834, 495. — AUD. Orn. Biog. IV. 1838, 222; Synop. 1839, 311; B. Am. VII. 1844, 44, pl. 425. — LAWR. in Baird's B. N. Am. 1858, 871. — BAIRD, Cat. N. Am. B. 1859, no. 617. — COUES, Key, 1872, 298; Check List, 1873, no. 524; 2d ed. 1882, no. 746. — RIDGW. Nom. N. Am. B. 1881, no. 650.

Sula americana, BONAP. Comp. List, 1838, 60.

Pelecanus maculatus, GMEL. S. N. I. 1788, 579 (young).

Sula alba, MEYER, Taschenb. II. 1810, 582 (adult).

Sula major, BREHM, Vög. Deutschl. 1831, 812.

HAB. Coasts of the North Atlantic; in America, south, in winter, to the Gulf of Mexico.

SP. CHAR. *Adult:* Prevailing color white, the head and neck, except underneath, more or less deeply buff; remiges brownish dusky. "Bill pale bluish gray, tinged with green toward the base; the lines on the upper mandible blackish blue; the bare space about the eye and that on the throat blackish blue; iris white; tarsi, toes, and webs brownish black, the bands of narrow scutellæ on the tarsus and toes light greenish blue; claws grayish white" (AUDUBON).[1] *Young, first plumage:* Head, neck, and upper parts dark grayish brown, relieved by small wedge-shaped white spots on the tips of the feathers, except the remiges and tail-feathers, these markings partaking more of the character of streaks on the head and neck; lower parts whitish, the feathers edged with grayish

[1] The following are the fresh colors of a fine adult killed in Chesapeake Bay, and sent in the flesh to the National Museum: Bill pale glaucous gray, with sulcus, edges of mandibles, lores, etc., dull blue-black; iris pale yellow; eyelids dull light blue; feet dull slate, with a sharply-defined narrow stripe of apple-green along top of each toe, and following the course of each tendon along the front of the tarsus.

brown, this color sometimes overlying the whole lower surface, the white being mostly concealed. "Bill light grayish brown; the bare space around the eye pale grayish blue; iris green; feet dusky, the narrow bands of scutellæ pale grayish blue; claws grayish white" (AUDUBON). *Nestling:* Entirely covered with very fluffy yellowish white down.

S. bassana.

Total length, 37.00–39.00 inches; extent, 68.50–74.00; wing, about 19.50; tail, 10.00; culmen, 4.00; tarsus, 2.25.

Adult specimens in the collection of the National Museum vary greatly in the extent of the strip of bare skin on the throat. In a male, not quite adult, from the Straits of Gibraltar, it reaches almost to the jugulum; but in others it does not extend beyond the throat. Perfectly adult individuals have the tail entirely white, only the remiges being dusky. In less mature examples, the tail, as well as the larger wing-coverts, are dusky. Still more immature specimens have the back and scapulars mixed with dusky feathers. A young bird from Europe is very much darker-colored than an American specimen, the lower surface being nearly uniform brownish gray, only the concealed portion of the feathers white; the white markings are almost entirely wanting on the back and scapulars, and very minute elsewhere.

The Soland Goose, or Gannet, is a bird peculiar to the Northern Atlantic Ocean, and is found both on its eastern and western shores, ranging in America as far south as the New England States, and in Europe to the coasts of Great Britain. Farther south than this its appearance is comparatively rare. This is a northern species, and is more or less resident wherever it is found.

The Gannet is generally given as a resident of Greenland; but Professor Reinhardt states that it is very rare there, and only accidental. It is common in winter off the coast of Maine, and formerly bred on Gannet Rock, near Grand Menan. From time to time specimens are obtained on the coast of Massachusetts; but this is not of frequent occurrence, and examples thus seen are usually immature birds. Its appearance in the bays and inlets of Long Island is so very rare that, according to Giraud, it is not generally known to the hunters; but he received a fine specimen that had been shot on the South Bay, opposite Bellport, and he had also known of several others being procured in the vicinity of New York. Audubon has observed the Gannet as far south as the Gulf of Mexico.

On the opposite side of the Atlantic, Mr. H. Saunders met with this species in considerable numbers, fishing off Cape Trafalgar, in December; and Yarrell mentions its appearance at Madeira, and even as far south as Southern Africa.

Dr. Robert O. Cunningham, in the "Ibis" of January, 1866, gives a very complete account of the history, distribution, and habits of this species, as gathered from the accounts given by the earlier writers, whose works date as far back even as the year 975 A. D. The name of Gannet is an Old English one (Anglo-Saxon, *ganot;* Old English, *gante*); but the origin of the word Soland cannot be satisfactorily made out. There was formerly an idea prevalent that this bird had the habit of hatching out its egg by covering this with its feet; and by some the name is associated with this belief. The Gannet appears to be widely distributed throughout the North Atlantic, on the western shores of Europe, and in the eastern waters of North America. Its breeding-places are not numerous; but in these the birds collect in immense numbers. In the waters of Great Britain and Ireland some of them continue throughout the year; and the same is probably true in regard to the mouth of the St. Lawrence River. There are but six places known in the British waters where this species breeds, but it is also numerous in various portions where it has never been known to breed. It also breeds in the Faröe Islands and in islands on the coast of Iceland. It migrates to the shores of Holland, France, Spain, Portugal, the Mediterranean, and Madeira. In America it has but few breeding-places, is common on the coast, and though found as far north as Greenland, is not known to breed there.

One of the most celebrated breeding-places of the Gannet is the Bass Rock, at the mouth of the Firth of Forth, near the old town of North Berwick. This island is a huge mass of greenstone trap, over four hundred feet in height, and with sides mostly bold and perpendicular. It has on the southeast its only landing-place. *Uriæ*, Gulls, Cormorants, Razor-bills, and Puffins breed on this rock, in common with the Gannet. The latter are met with in great numbers on all the several faces of the rock, and even in the immediate neighborhood of the landing-place. Macgillivray, who visited this rock in 1831, estimated the number of *Sulæ* at about twenty thousand; and Dr. Cunningham, whose visit was made in 1862, estimated their number then at about the same. These birds make their appearance at the island from the middle of February to the first of March, and take their departure in October, though a few remain there all winter.

The earlier writers speak of the nests of the Gannet as being made of sticks; but all now agree that at present no other materials are used in their construction than the common *Fucus digitatus* and other fucoids. They are built in the form of a flattened cone, with a base twenty inches in diameter, and with a shallow terminal cavity. The birds are said to exhibit great industry in collecting the materials, tearing up grass and turf with their powerful bills, and in the process engaging in frequent conflicts. The Gannet lays but a single egg; and if this be removed it is replaced by another. It is described as being elliptical in form, with a rough, dull-white surface — originally white, but almost always more or less patched and stained with a yellowish brown.

It is said that the albumen of this egg does not become white when it is boiled, but remains clear and colorless. The egg is subject to rough usage; for the bird, in alighting, or when disturbed by human visitors, tosses it about or stands upon it. This habit has given rise to the assertion that the egg is hatched by the bird's feet. At the time of Macgillivray's visit the Gannets would allow a person to approach within three feet, and sometimes so near that they could be touched. When any one approached they merely opened their bills and uttered their usual cry, or rose to their feet, expressing some degree of resentment, but none of alarm. Dr. Cunningham, however, had a very different experience when he visited the island. The old birds manifested every symptom of displeasure. Even a young one, only a few weeks old, squeaked angrily, and made impotent demonstrations of self-defence with its soft bill.

Professor Jones, in a note to the St. John's "Natural History and Sport," in Moray, mentions an instance wherein a man, who had ventured to meddle with a young Gannet in the downy state, was attacked by the infuriated parent, who made a swoop at his face, and caught him violently by the nose. This bird is capable of inflicting a very severe bite with the razor-like edges of its mandibles.

In descending from the cliffs into the water, the Gannet usually utters a single plaintive cry, performs a curve, shakes its tail or the whole plumage, and draws the feet backward. When it flies, the body, tail, neck, and bill are nearly in a straight line; the wings are extended, and never brought close to the body, and it moves by regular flappings, alternating with regular sailings. In alighting, it ascends in a long curve, keeps the feet spread, and comes down rather heavily. It has considerable difficulty, when on low ground, in taking wing; and when found inland, in places unfavorable for flight, is occasionally taken alive.

The great power of dilatation possessed by its œsophagus enables this bird to swallow fish of very considerable dimensions. Its food consists of fish of various kinds — chiefly herring. Its power of digestion is very great. It is very greedy, and occasionally becomes so gorged with food as to be unable to rise from the surface of the water, and may then be easily captured.

The old bird feeds her offspring with partially digested fish, which is prepared in her stomach, and introduced little by little into the throat of the young bird; and when the latter is well advanced in growth, it inserts its own bill within the parent's mouth, and receives the fragments the latter disgorges. The cry of the young bird is a shrill squeak, while that of the old bird is hoarse, and resembles the words *kuma, kuma*, repeated rapidly.

Dr. Cunningham states that from one to two thousand of the young birds of this species are annually killed for sale; although they are not now held in such high value as formerly, when they figured at the tables of even the Scottish monarchs. Their consumption is now confined to the lower classes.

Ailsa Craig, an island composed of columnar trap, of a conical form, and eleven hundred feet in height, in the Firth of Clyde, is an important breeding-place of the

Gannet, where it builds in great numbers. St. Kilda, the outermost of the Hebrides, the sides of which are precipitous cliffs fourteen hundred feet high, is another place where the Gannet breeds in large numbers, and where it forms one of the principal sources of the sustenance of the inhabitants.

Gannets also abound on several of the islands on the south of Iceland. There they arrive early in April, and build large and conspicuous nests of seaweed, which they often bring from a great distance. The eggs are deposited in May, and hatched in July. The Gannets leave for the south in October.

This is said to be a very long-lived species. Selby was informed by the keeper of the Bass Rock lighthouse that he could recognize certain individuals that for upwards of forty years had returned to the same spot to breed. This bird is also very long in arriving at maturity, the time required being estimated at from four to five years.

The late Dr. Henry Bryant visited the "Bird Rocks," in the Gulf of St. Lawrence, in the summer of 1860, reaching them on the 23d of June. These rocks are two in number, and are known as the Great Gannet Rock and the Little, or North Bird. On these rocky islands he found the Gannets breeding in large numbers. The highest half of the summit of Gannet Rock and the ledges on its sides, and the whole upper part of the pillar-like portion of Little Bird, and the greater part of the remaining portion of this rock, were covered with the nests of the Gannet. On the ledges these were arranged in single lines, nearly or quite touching one another; and at the summit they were placed at regular distances one from the other of about three feet. Those on the ledges were built entirely of seaweed and other floating substances; on the summit of the rock they were raised on cones, formed of earth or small stones, about ten inches in height and eighteen in diameter when first constructed, presenting at a short distance the appearance of a well-hilled potato-field. He saw no nests built of *Zostera*, or grass, or sods; the materials were almost entirely *Fuci;* though anything available was probably used. In one case the whole nest was composed of straw; and in another, the chief article used was manila rope-yarn. The nests on the summit of Gannet Rock were never scattered, but ended abruptly in as regular a line as a military encampment. Through the midst of the nests were several open spaces, like lanes, made quite smooth by the continued trampling of the birds, which spaces seemed to be used for play-grounds, and generally extended to the brink of the precipice.

The birds were feeding principally on herring, but also on capelin filled with spawn, some fine-looking mackerel, a few squids, and in one instance a codfish weighing at least two pounds. The surface was swarming with a species of *Staphylinus*, that subsisted on the fish dropped by the birds. Occasionally a nest could be seen in which the single egg had not been deposited, and perhaps one in two or three hundred with a newly laid one. On all the rest the Gannets were already sitting; and though none of the eggs were as yet hatched, many of them contained fully formed chicks. On being approached the birds manifested but slight symptoms of fear, and could hardly be driven from their nests; occasionally one more bold would actually attack the intruder. Their number on the summit could be easily determined by measuring the surface occupied by them. By a rough computation it was made to be about fifty thousand pairs. Probably half as many more were breeding upon the remaining portion of the rock and on the Little Bird. All the birds were in adult plumage; differing in this respect from those breeding in the Bay of Fundy, where there were many young ones.

In shape and general appearance the eggs obtained by Dr. Bryant are more like those of the Brown Pelican than of any other North American bird; and they are sometimes stained with blood, as that also commonly is. The calcareous coating is thicker than it is on the eggs of other birds, with few exceptions, and it is very generally marked with scratches and furrows, as if deposited in a soft state. In one specimen this coating was two millimetres in thickness, or nearly one twelfth of an inch; so that the eggshell, though emptied of its contents, is nearly as heavy as an ordinary one that has not been blown. In shape there is a greater tendency to elongation or flattening of the ellipse than in the Pelicans. The color of the egg when it is first laid is chalky-white, which soon becomes a dirty drab. Four eggs selected by Dr. Bryant from many hundreds gave the following measurements: 3.50 inches by 1.79; 3.30 by 2.04; 3.25 by 1.88; 3.26 by 1.65.

Sula cyanops.

THE BLUE-FACED GANNET.

Dysporus cyanops, SUNDEV. Phys. Tidskr. Lund. 1837, pt. 5; Ann. & Mag. N. H. 1847, XIX. 236 P. Z. S. 1871, 125.

Sula cyanops, SUNDEV. Isis, 1842, 858. — SALV. Trans. Zool. Soc. IX. ix. 1875, 496 (Galapagos; critical). — STREETS, Bull. U. S. Nat. Mus. no. 7, 1877, 24 (Christmas I.). — LAWR. Pr. Boston Soc. 1871 (Socorro I. W. Mexico).

Sula personata, GRAY, P. Z. S. 1846, 21.

Sula piscator, PEALE, U. S. Expl. Exp. Orn. 1848, 273 (not of LINN. 1766).

Revillagigedo Gannet, LAWR. l. c.

HAB. Coasts and islands of the South Pacific; Bahamas (breeding; BRYANT), and other West India islands; Southern Florida.

SP. CHAR. Larger than *S. leucogastra* and *S. piscator*, the bill much thicker through the base; feet reddish. *Adult, perfect plumage:* (No. 11953, Bahamas, April, 1859; Dr. H. BRYANT[1]):

Prevailing color white, the greater wing-coverts, alulæ, primary-coverts, and remiges, dark sooty brown; middle rectrices hoary white, becoming gradually sooty brown at ends; other tail-feathers hoary white basally, the exposed portion dark sooty brown. Bill (in skin) grayish yellow; bare skin of face, and gular sac blackish (blue in life); feet light reddish. Wing, 16.15 inches; tail, 7.75; culmen, 3.95; depth of bill through base, 1.40; tarsus, 1.80; middle toe, 2.85.[2] *Young*

[1] Labelled "*S. parva*" and "*S. chrysops.*"

[2] The average dimensions of this species are considerably greater than those given above, six examples averaging as follows; 16.53 inches, 8.42, 3.96, 1.44, 2.02, 2.88. The maximum in this series is 17.80,

(No. 67316, Christmas I.; Dr. T. H. STREETS): Head, neck, and upper parts generally, dark grayish brown; lower neck and entire lower parts white, the flanks streaked with grayish; middle of the back, and upper part of rump, streaked with white. *Older* (No. 68361, Callao, Peru, July 15, 1870; Dr. L. REDTENBACHER): Head, neck, and lower parts, white; upper parts dark grayish brown, the feathers (except remiges and rectrices) narrowly tipped with white; middle tail-feathers hoary white toward base. Bill purplish, the maxilla pale grayish horn-color; feet dusky (in dried skin). Wing, 14.60 inches; tail, 7.75; culmen, 3.60; depth of bill through base, 1.20; tarsus, 1.75; middle toe, 2.35.

In the adult plumage this species presents a quite close resemblance to the mature stage of *S. bassana*; but the very different form of the bill and bare skin about the face will serve readily to distinguish it. The coloration seems to be much more constant in this species than in either *S. leucogastra* or *S. piscator*, the four adults before us not presenting any appreciable differences.

The immature specimen from Callao, Peru, described above, differs slightly from others in the bill being more slender, and of a more purplish hue. It is labelled "*S. variegata*, TSCH.;" but whether really *variegata* or not, there can be little doubt that it is referable to *S. cyanops*.

This species was procured by Dr. Bryant at the Bahamas. It was about the size of the *Sula leucogastra*, but was heavier, and more muscular. He found about twenty pairs breeding at Santo Domingo Key. They apparently lay their eggs later than the Booby; and the largest of the young, found early in April, were not more than half grown, and the eggs of several had been freshly laid. As in the case of the Booby, the number of the eggs is always two. The eggs are whiter than those of the Booby, the chalky covering being much thicker, and do not differ much in size and proportions, the two extremes measuring 2.60 by 1.67 inches, and 2.45 by 1.73. These Gannets did not associate with the other species. The young birds and eggs were all in one part of the island. When half fledged they were very pretty, the snowy white down with which they were covered forming a striking contrast to the dark brown of the tail and wings, then just appearing. Their habits were precisely the same as those of the Boobies, and their internal structure presented no appreciable difference.

The *Sula personata* of Gould is identical with the Bahama species. It was noticed at sea by Dr. Pickering, between the Sandwich Islands and our western coast, in long. 167° 30′ W. As this locality is the nearest to the coast of North America of any given by the naturalists of the Wilkes Expedition, this species may be looked for as an inhabitant of the Pacific coast of the United States. It was also observed in other localities in large numbers by the naturalists of that Expedition. It was found most abundant at Honden Island and Enderby's Island, in both of which it was engaged in the duties of incubation. So far as is known, it inhabits the Pacific Ocean as far to the southwest as Northern Australia, and is more abundant in the northern and eastern portion of its range during the season devoted to the rearing of its young.

Mr. Peale states that these birds were first seen on the 20th of July, lat. 13° 30′ 28″ S., long. 89° 25′ W. One month afterward they were found in great numbers at Honden Island, one of the Paumotu Group, where they were sitting on a single egg each, one bird having only two eggs. They had no nest whatever, not even a cavity scratched in the sand. Flat dry sandy beaches were selected on the shores of the lagoons, the female laying her egg on the bare ground, the male assisting in the duties of incubation. They remained very gravely at their stations, regardless even of man. Many were pushed off their nests with the muzzles of the guns; they

9.10, 4.15, 1.60, 2.15, 3.10 — a specimen from the Paumotu Islands being the largest. The smallest is the Peruvian specimen described above.

fought and scuffled with the offensive weapon, but returned the moment it was withdrawn. A few had the sense to bite at the hands in place of the gun-barrel. They hissed like the Domestic Goose, and had a very hoarse, croaking voice.

The egg is said to measure 2.60 by 1.80 inches, some being equally rounded at both ends, while others are a little pointed at one end. The color is a bluish green inside, but covered outside with a dry rough white coating, showing the color of the interior through it. The young were at first covered with a fine white down, but the feathers afterward came out of an ash-color. The seasons of incubation did not appear to be regular. At Enderby's Island these birds were hatching in January, and at other places in intermediate seasons. This species is also referred to by Dr. Pickering as being abundant at Gardner's Island, and in other places.

Eggs of this bird, obtained in the Bahamas by Dr. Bryant, are now in the Smithsonian Collection (No. 1712). They are of a uniform dull white color, and measure 2.45 by 1.70 inches; one egg (No. 2438) measures 2.55 by 1.75.

Sula leucogastra.

THE BOOBY GANNET.

Petit Fou, BUFF. Pl. Enl. 973.
Pelecanus leucogaster, BODD. Tabl. P. E. 1783, 57 (ex Pl. Enl. 973).
Dysporus leucogaster, SUNDEV. P. Z. S. 1871, 125.
Sula leucogastra, SALV. Trans. Zool. Soc. IX. ix. 1875, 496 (Galapagos; critical). — STREETS, Bull. U. S. Nat. Mus. no. 7, 1877, 22 (Gulf of California). — RIDGW. Nom. N. Am. B. 1881, no. 652. — COUES, 2d Check List, 1882, no. 747.
Sula fusca, AUD. B. Am. VII. 1844, 57, pl. 426 (not *Pelecanus fuscus*, LINN.).
Sula fiber, LAWR. in Baird's B. N. Am. 1858, 872 (not *Pelecanus fiber*, of LINN. 1766). —BAIRD, Cat. N. Am. B. 1859, no. 618. — COUES, Key, 1872, 298; Check List, 1873, no. 525. — SCL. & SALV. Nom. Neotr. 1873, 124.

HAB. Coasts of tropical and subtropical America, north to Georgia.

SP. CHAR. Feet greenish or yellowish. *Adult male, full breeding-plumage?* (No. 58805, Isabella Island, Western Mexico, April, 27, 1869; Colonel A. J. GRAYSON): Head, throat, and nape, grayish white, the feathers edged with grayish brown, especially toward bases; foreneck, jugulum, and entire lower parts, pure white, this color extending in a broad collar round lower part of the nape, the foreneck and jugulum strongly tinged with delicate peach-blossom pink. Upper parts in general grayish brown, the remiges darker, the larger scapulars tipped with grayish white; upper tail-coverts and middle tail-feathers white, the latter passing into light brownish gray terminally, along the edges; outer rectrices grayish brown, paler basally, the shaft white, except near the end; other rectrices intermediate in color between the middle and outer. Wing, 16.30 inches; tail, 6.50; culmen 3.95; depth of bill through base, 1.30; tarsus, 1.85; middle toe, 2.65.[1] Bill (in dried skin) pale purplish gray, nearly white in middle portion; feet dusky greenish. *Adult, usual plumage:* Head, neck, and breast, dark sooty brown; upper parts in general similar, but lighter, the remiges and rectrices more dusky, especially the former. Lower parts, posterior to the breast, uniform white. Bill greenish gray or dirty yellowish, in skin (said to be "bright yellow, pale flesh-colored toward the end," in life), the naked lores and gular sac darker; iris white (AUDUBON); feet greenish in dried skin, said to be pale yellow, in life. *Young:* Plumage nearly uniform grayish brown, or sooty gray, lighter beneath. "Bill and claws dusky; tarsi and toes with their membranes dusky" (AUDUBON).

The changes of plumage in this species are, as is the case with *S. piscator* and *S. cyanops,* very perplexing. The greenish or yellowish feet afford the most obvious specific character, the feet being reddish in both the species named above. The size is about intermediate between the two. The

[1] The average dimensions of fifteen specimens are as follows, the measurements being in the same sequence as given above: 15.72 inches, 8.23, 3.74, 1.24, 1.71. 2.59.

change from the first plumage to the perfect adult dress must be a very gradual one, since scarcely two individuals are exactly alike. In the youngest specimens the head and neck are light smoky grayish, like the lower parts, considerably paler than the wings, the remiges having a slight glaucous cast. The first change toward maturity is seen in the darkening of the head and neck (or lightening of the abdomen), so that the difference in color between the lower parts and the neck is more or less distinctly marked. It is quite possible that this species sometimes becomes almost wholly white, like *S. piscator,* since the specimen described above as being probably the adult in full breeding-dress corresponds quite closely with some specimens of *S. piscator* which have nearly

assumed the white dress of the perfect adult. This stage is represented in the collection by a single specimen. A phase intermediate between this and the plumage generally considered the adult (dusky head, neck, and breast, and white under parts), is represented by two examples, one from Isabella Island, the other from Manzanillo Bay (both Western Mexico). This phase is similar to the plumage usually considered the adult, but the brown of the breast passes gradually into grayish white on the head.

The Booby Gannet has only a limited claim to a place in the fauna of North America, where its appearance is chiefly accidental on the southern coast from Georgia southward, and along the shores of the Gulf of Mexico. It is more common about the Tortugas and among the Florida Keys, and is said to breed in some of the islands about the extreme southern end of Florida. It is found in the West India Islands, on the northeast coast of South America, and in Central America; and being a great wanderer, is of accidental occurrence in various parts of the ocean.

Mr. Salvin mentions that one of this species came on board the steamer in which he was a passenger, when off the coast of San Salvador; and Mr. G. C. Taylor speaks of this bird as not uncommon along the coast of Honduras. He saw an individual of this species in Fonseca Bay; and one flew on board the steamer, on the passage from Panama to La Union, which had kept company with the vessel for some time, and finally, after repeated attempts to alight, had perched in the rigging, where it was caught by a boy.

Professor Alfred Newton states that this species was occasionally met with in the Island of St. Croix; but he is quite sure that it does not breed in that vicinity, as it evinced altogether too great a partiality for the deep-sea fishery to be seen often on land. One was brought alive to Mr. Edward Newton in September, 1858, which had been taken asleep by a negro. It was of an exceedingly fierce disposition, refused all food, and at last died; at no time, however, exhibiting anything like fear. When between St. Croix and St. Thomas, one of this species flew within a few yards of the schooner on which Mr. Newton was; and he was informed of another that flew so close to the deck of one of the Royal Mail Company's steamers that it was caught on the wing by one of the passengers.

Mr. E. C. Taylor states that he occasionally met with this species among the Windward Islands; but he afterward found it much more abundant on the coast of Venezuela.

A Booby Gannet was taken in Bermuda, which had flown into one of the soldiers' barrack-rooms at Fort Catharine, Oct. 3, 1847. This species is given by Mr. G. R. Gray as being entitled to a place in the fauna of New Zealand. Captain Beavan ("Ibis," 1868) also mentions meeting with it on the 3d of July in the Bay of Bengal. The birds were quite numerous, and were flying low and very fast, skimming along the surface of the water, and paying no attention to the vessel.

Audubon met with this species near the Tortugas, and he found one of its places of resort on a small sandy island eight miles from the lighthouse, obtaining there a number of specimens. The wounded birds that fell on the land made immediately for the water, moving with considerable ease. Those which fell on the water swam off with great buoyancy and such rapidity that it was difficult to overtake them, and those which had only a wing broken escaped altogether. On another island, covered with bushes and low trees, he found a number of Boobies breeding in company with the *Anous stolidus*. He found them perched on the top branches of the trees in which they had nests. As they flew about overhead they made no noise, except at the moment they rose from their perches; their cry at that time was a single harsh and guttural sound, resembling the syllables *hork-hork*. He found the nest placed on the tops of the bushes at a height of from four to ten feet, large and flat, formed of a few dry sticks, covered and matted with seaweeds in great quantities. The bird evidently returns to the same nest for years in succession, repairing it as occasion requires. In all the nests which he examined, only one egg was found; and as most of the birds were sitting, and some of the eggs had the chick nearly ready for exclusion, it is probable that this bird raises but a single young one at a time.

Audubon describes the egg as being of a dull white color, without spots, about the size of the egg of a Common Hen, but more elongated, being 2.38 inches in length, and 1.75 in breadth. In some nests the eggs were more or less incrusted with the filth of the parent. The young were covered with down, and had an uncouth appearance. Their bills and feet were of a deep livid blue. They were evidently abundantly supplied with food, as a great quantity lay under the trees in a state of putrefaction, and a constant succession of birds were coming from the sea with food for their young. This consisted chiefly of flying-fish and small mullets, which they disgorged in a half macerated state into the open throats of their young. No birds having an immature plumage were found breeding.

Audubon describes the flight of this species as being graceful and sustained for a great length of time. The Gannet passes swiftly at a height varying from two feet to twenty yards above the surface, its wings being distended at right angles to the body. When overloaded with food it alights on the water, where it will remain for hours at a time. Its range extends along our coast not farther than Cape Hatteras. This bird has a sufficient power of wing to enable it to brave the tempest; and in fair weather it ventures far out to sea, and is often seen one or two hundred miles from the land..

In the bodies of those Gannets which Audubon examined, he found mullets weighing more than half a pound each. The old birds drive away from their neighborhood those in immature plumage during the periods of incubation. This species apparently requires several years to arrive at maturity. Like the Common Gannet, it may be secured by fastening fish to a soft plank and sinking it in the water. The Booby plunges headlong upon the plank, and drives its bill into the wood.

Mr. Gosse met with this species in Jamaica. He found it not infrequently taking shelter from the attacks of the Frigate Bird in trees near Bluefield Bay. The birds huddled there in little groups, sitting closely side by side, so that four or five might be brought down at a shot. He invariably found the stomachs of those which were thus obtained entirely empty, the birds having probably been obliged to disgorge their prey by the attacks of the Frigate-birds. As they sit they frequently utter a loud croaking cackle. One Gannet which had been disabled manifested great ferocity, striking forcibly with its open beak, endeavoring to pierce with its very acute points, as well as to cut with its keen, saw-like edges. It had sufficient sagacity to pay no attention to a stick, but struck at the hand of Mr. Gosse, by whom the instrument of attack was held.

Dr. Bryant, in his paper on the birds of East Florida ("Proc. Boston Soc. Nat. Hist." VII. 5), states that he found the Booby quite numerous at the Tortugas, but did not find any breeding there; and he was informed by the keeper of the light that, so far as he knew, none had bred there for eighteen years, and Dr. Bryant could find no one that had ever known it to breed in that locality.

Afterward, in his paper on the birds seen at the Bahamas, in the same volume (p. 123), he is positive that Audubon was mistaken in saying that this species breeds at the Tortugas. The time at which it lays its eggs, and the absence of any nest, are circumstances quite at variance with his account; and he evidently mistook the nests of the Brown Pelican for those of the Booby. Dr. Bryant found the eggs laid in most cases by the first of February, the bird making no nest, not even an excavation in the soil. The eggs were deposited indifferently on sand, grass, or bare rock. His first visit to one of their breeding-places was made on the 10th of April at Santo Domingo Key, thirty-three miles south of Great Ragged Island, at the extremity of the southern point of the bank, and rarely visited. It is four acres in extent, and so low that in storms it is entirely washed by the waves. At the time of his visit it was covered with Boobies, mostly young, the greater part fully fledged, but still dependent upon the parent birds for food. The latter kept by themselves, and were perched on the rocks all around the edge of the Key. The young were sprinkled over the Key, wherever there was room, and were of all ages, from those almost able to fly, to such as had just been hatched. He found the eggs of twenty pairs, most of them on the point of hatching. The number in every case was two. In appearance they resembled those of the family generally, being a greenish white covered with a chalky substance. In size they varied considerably, as also in form. The most elongated one measured 2.64 by 1.50 inches, the broadest 2.16 by 1.57 inches; the others varying between these two extremes, but averaging more nearly like the latter.

The young were entirely naked when first hatched, and of a livid blue color. They soon become covered with a white down; then the quills and tail-feathers, of a cinereous brown, make their appearance; then the feathers of the body, neck, and head; and lastly those of the throat. The old birds did not trouble themselves to get out of his way, but on being approached too nearly, darted at him with their powerful bills in a most savage manner. They were very quarrelsome, continually striking at one another, not at all in an amicable manner, but as if they intended to do all the mischief in their power. It was difficult to understand how the different birds recognized their own young, as they did not continue in the same place after the young had attained any size.

Dr. Bryant considers the Booby the most expert diver with which he is acquainted.

In whatever position this bird may be — whether flying in a straight line, sailing in a circle, just rising from the water, or swimming on the surface — the instant it sees its prey it plunges into the water. He has frequently seen one dive while on the wing, rise to the surface, and dive in rapid succession five or six times; and on taking flight again dive before it had risen more than two or three feet from the surface, and catch a dozen fish in the space of a minute. But there is nothing graceful in its movements. The stomachs of the Boobies examined contained a great many varieties of fish; their principal food seemed to be flying-fish and a species of *Hemirhamphus*.

In the Report on the Birds of the Wilkes Exploring Expedition the Booby is referred to as one of the most extensively diffused of aquatic birds, being equally abundant both on the Atlantic and Pacific coast of the southern portion of the continent of America, and throughout the Pacific Ocean to the coasts of Asia. Mr. Peale found it breeding on nearly all the coral islands visited by the Expedition. The nests were constructed of sticks and weeds, on bushes and low trees, and were generally found to contain but one egg, which was of a bluish-white color.

Mr. Peale relates that while exploring Enderby's Island — which is of coral formation — he found, at least a quarter of a mile from the shore, a bird of this species in full plumage, having a white breast, which indicated that it was several years old. On picking it up he was surprised to find that it had but one wing, the other having been, by some accident, taken off close to the body. The wound was perfectly healed, and the bird in excellent health, and very fat! It was fed by its comrades, which were younger birds — as was indicated by the brown plumage of their breasts; and they continued while Mr. Peale was near to display toward their injured companion all the careful anxiety of parents for their young.

This species was noticed by Dr. Pickering in the Bay of Rio de Janeiro, where it was common. He also saw it at various other localities, and found it particularly abundant at Aurora Island in September.

Eggs of this species in the Smithsonian Collection (No. 1713), obtained in the Bahamas by Dr. Bryant, are of a uniform dull chalky white color. Two examples measure, one 2.30 by 1.55 inches, the other 2.20 by 1.60.

Sula piscator.

THE RED-FOOTED BOOBY.

Pelecanus piscator, LINN. S. N. ed. 10, I. 1758, 134; ed. 12, I. 1766, 217.

Sula piscator, BONAP. Consp. II. 1857, 166. — LAWR. Pr. Boston Soc. 1871, 302 (Socorro I., W. Mexico; common). — STREETS, Bull. U. S. Nat. Mus. no. 7, 1877, 23 (Fanning Islands, N. Pacific).

Sula candida, "BRISS." STEPHENS, Shaw's Gen. Zool. XIII. 1826, 103.

Sula erythrorhyncha, LESS. Traité, I. 1831, 601.

Sula rubripes, GOULD, P. Z. S. 1837, 156.

Sula rubripeda, PEALE, U. S. Expl. Exp. Orn. 1848, 274.

HAB. Coasts and islands of the intertropical regions. Florida (Mus. Philad. Acad.).

SP. CHAR. Feet reddish. *Adult male, perfect plumage* (No. 15611, Pacific Ocean; T. R. PEALE): Plumage white, the head and neck tinged with buff, the shafts of the tail-feathers deep straw-yellow; remiges, greater and primary wing-coverts, and alulæ hoary slate-gray. *Adult female (perfect plumage?)*, (No. 50866, Socorro Island, Western Mexico; Colonel A. J. GRAYSON): Similar to the above, but the tail hoary brownish gray, with whitish shafts, the white of the entire upper parts strongly tinged with buff-yellow. "Iris brown; bare space on chin and throat jet-black; bill pale violet, bare space on forehead, and base of lower mandible, purplish red; bare space round eye violet-blue;" feet coral-red. Length, 29.50 inches; extent,

60.00 ; wing, 15.80 ; tail, 9.00 ; culmen, 3.50 ; depth of bill through base, 1.10 ; tarsus, 1.50 ; middle toe, 2.40.[1] *Younger:* Upper tail-coverts and tail as in the preceding ; rest of the plumage sooty gray, the head and neck paler, sometimes nearly white. "Bill lead-color, with a band of yellow across the forehead and two yellow patches at the base of the lower mandible ; feet and legs red" (W. T. MARCH, manuscript). *Young, first plumage* (77905, Dominica, West Indies, April, 1879 ; Dr. H. A. NICHOLLS) : Above, sooty grayish brown, the remiges and rectrices hoary slate ; head, neck, and lower parts light smoky gray. Bill blackish. *Older?:* Similar, but lower parts, posterior to the breast, dirty white, the head and neck sooty grayish brown ; bill blackish.

The plumage of this species is so exceedingly variable as to render it quite doubtful whether the various phases noted (scarcely two examples in a series of fourteen specimens being alike) are wholly dependent on age or sex. Some examples in the immature dress have the head, neck, and jugulum (!) nearly white, the remaining lower parts light sooty gray ; while others (apparently younger) have the head, neck, and jugulum dark sooty brown, and the lower parts whitish — just the reverse. At all stages it may be distinguished from *S. eucogastra* by the red feet and, usually, the smaller size, especially of the bill and feet.

In all adult examples, and in most young ones, the red color of the feet is sufficient to distinguish this species from *S. leucogastra*, independent of the shorter bill and difference of plumage. There are two young specimens[2] in the collection, however, which, although *apparently* having reddish feet (it being, of course, impossible to tell what the color was originally), agree best with *S. leucogastra* in the size and shape of the bill, and in colors. In every respect they agree quite closely with a specimen of unquestionable *S. leucogastra* from Jamaica, in which the feet seem to be reddish, but which *in life* (so we learn from the label) had them "horny yellow."

The claims of this species to a place in the North American fauna rest upon a specimen, examined by Professor Baird, in the collection of the Philadelphia Academy, labelled as from Florida, and presented by Mr. Audubon, by whom it was considered as the *Sula fusca* (= *leucogastra*). It is smaller than *S. leucogastra*, but of much the same shape and general appearance. The head, neck, and whole under parts are white, the feathers of the sides tinged with brown. The back, wings, and tail are dusky brown, the feathers of the back and the wing-coverts edged with whitish, those of the rump and upper tail-coverts less distinctly. The middle tail-feathers are hoary gray at the base, with whitish shafts ; the rest become darker, the shafts browner toward the exterior of the tail. The colors of the naked parts are not distinguishable ; the legs and feet appear to have been greenish dusky.[3]

Length, about 27.00 inches ; wing, 14.00 ; tail, 8.00 ; tarsus, 2.00 ; middle toe and claw, 3.00 ; bill, about 3.25.

[1] The average measurements, given in the same sequence as above, of a series of fourteen specimens, are as follows : 15.04 inches, 8.93, 3.26, 1.07, 1.34, 2.25. Upon comparing these figures with those on p. 178, it will be seen that while the wing and tail are about the same average length as in *S. leucogastra*, the bill is decidedly shorter and more slender, and the tarsus and middle toe also much shorter.

[2] Nos. 1963 (no locality), J. J. AUDUBON ; labelled "*Sula fusca*, L.," and 21279, "off Meia-co-shima Islands."

[3] If the specimen is really *S. piscator*, the feet must have been red in life ; otherwise it must be *S. leucogastra*.

Mr. Richard Hill has identified this species as one of three or four kinds of Boobies which frequent the Pedro Keys of Jamaica, and are also seen on the coast near Kingston. It is known as the Black-and-white Booby. Mr. Hill had in his possession a pair of this species alive, of whose habits in confinement Mr. Gosse has published some interesting notes. The sympathy manifested by most gregarious birds for their wounded companions is very strongly shown by this species. It makes extraordinary efforts to assist a wounded bird when fluttering in the water. An accident which happened to one of the two Boobies in Mr. Hill's yard gave an opportunity of witnessing these traits of feeling and the attendant emotions. Mr. Hill's little nephew, in chasing with a whip one of the birds, entangled the lash about its wing and snapped the arm-bone. Mr. Hill adds: The one bird not only showed sympathy for the other, but exhibited curiosity about the nature of the accident. The wounded bird withdrew into a lonely part of the yard, and stood there drooping. The female sought him as soon as she heard his cry; and after ascertaining that the injury was in the wing, proceeded to prevail on him to move the limb, that she might see if he was disabled beyond the power of using it for flight. After a quacking *honk* or two, as a call to do something required of him, the female stretched out one of her wings; the wounded male imitated her, and making an effort, moved out in some sort of way the wounded member to its full length. He was now required, by a corresponding movement, to raise it; he raised the broken arm, but the wing could not be elevated. Her wounded companion was next persuaded to make another trial at imitation, and to give the wing some three or four good flaps. He followed the given signal, and gave the required beats; but twirled the broken wing quite round, and turned it inside out. As by this the mischief was greatly increased, Mr. Hill deemed it necessary to put a stop to this process of investigation of the one bird into the misfortune of the other. Taking up the bird with the twisted wing and setting the limb, he restrained him from any farther gratification of his mate's curiosity by tying the wing into place, and keeping it so tied until the bone united. She continued to attend him, carefully examined day after day the broken limb, and occasionally called upon him to make an effort to raise his disabled member, using ineffectual endeavors to persuade him to lift it by lifting her own from time to time.

This species is said to have a predilection for elevated spots as perching-places. If a single stone is higher than the others, the fact is quickly noticed, and the bird, after having partaken of a satisfactory meal, takes its stand on the elevated spot. If a log or pile of wood is at hand, the bird perches on that to sun itself, extending its wings over its tail, and erecting its dorsal feathers for the admission of the sun's rays. It roosts upon similar elevated places. It has great prehensile power with its foot, and its serrated middle toe is frequently applied to scratch the naked skin about its eyes and face. Mr. Hill's birds were more fond of flesh meat, such as beef and pork, than of fish. They disliked fat, and would reject it when given separately from the lean. They never drank, and were as regardless of the water about the yard as if they were unadapted for it. Mr. Hill also states that the anatomy of this species exhibits in a remarkably interesting manner its fine adaptation for the purpose of giving the bird buoyancy: the muscles show air-vessels interspersed among them in a manner altogether surprising.

Family PHAËTHONTIDÆ. — The Tropic Birds.

Char. Bill conical, much compressed, the maxillary tomium exceedingly concave in the middle portion, descending, convex, and bulging outward at the base; culmen gently curved; nostrils very distinct, linear; head normally feathered. Primaries much elongated in proportion to the secondaries; tail very short, graduated, the central pair of rectrices linear and excessively elongated (longer than the wing) in the adult. Lateral toes nearly equal (outer longest), and but little shorter than the middle. Plumage very compact, satiny. Color chiefly white.

This family is composed of the single genus *Phaëthon*, of tropicopolitan range, and represented in America by two of the three known species.

Genus **PHAËTHON**, Linnæus.

Lepturus, Briss. Orn. VI. 1760, p. 479.
Phaëthon, Linn. S. N. ed. 10, I. 1758, 134; ed. 12, I. 1766, 219 (type, *P. æthereus*, Linn.). — Lawr. in Baird's B. N. Am. 1858, 885.
" *Tropicophilus*, Leach," Steph. Gen. Zool. XIII. i. 1826, 124.
Phœnicurus, Bonap. Consp. II. 1857, 183 (type, *Phaëton phoenicuros*, Gmel.).

P. flavirostris.

Char. Same as those of the family.

The three known species of this genus are very well marked, and may be easily distinguished by the following characters: —

A. Elongated middle rectrices, with their webs very much broader than the moderately rigid shaft.

1. **P. flavirostris.** Bill yellow; middle tail-feathers pinkish, with black shafts; wing about 11.00 inches; culmen 2.00 or less. *Hab.* Intertropical seas, north to Florida.
2. **P. æthereus.** Bill deep coral red; middle tail-feathers pure white, with white shafts; wing about 12.00 inches; culmen about 2.50. *Hab.* Intertropical seas, north to Lower California.

B. Elongated middle rectrices with their webs much narrower than the very rigid shaft.

3. **P. rubricaudus.**[1] Bill yellowish ; middle tail-feathers dull reddish, with black shafts ; wing 13.00 inches or more ; culmen about 2.50. *Hab.* South Pacific Ocean.

Phaëthon flavirostris.

THE YELLOW-BILLED TROPIC BIRD.

Lepturus candidus, BRISS. Orn. VI. 1760, 485.

Phaeton candidus, GRAY, Gen. B. 1847, pl. 183.

Phaeton aethereus, BODD. Tabl. P. E. 1783, 22 (ex Pl. Enl. 369 ; nec LINN., 1758). — BONAP. Synop. 1828, no. 361 ; Consp. II. 1855, 183. — NUTT. Man. II. 1834, 503. — AUD. Orn. Biog. III. 1835, 442 ; Synop. 1839, 312 ; B. Am. VII. 1844, 64, pl. 427.

Phaethon flavirostris, BRANDT, Bull. Sc. Acad. St. Petersb. II. 1837, 349. — SCL. P. Z. S. 1856, 144. — LAWR. in Baird's B. N. Am. 1858, 885. — BAIRD, Cat. N. Am. B. 1859, no. 629. — COUES, Key, 1872, 307 ; Check List, 1873, no. 538 ; 2d ed. 1882, no. 763. — RIDGW. Nom. N. Am. B. 1881, no. 654.

? *Phæton flavo-aurantius*, LAWR. Ann. Lyc. N. Y. VII. April, 1860, 143 (hab. ignot.).

" *Phaeton Edwardi*, BRANDT."

The Tropic Bird, EDWARDS, Nat. Hist. B. 1749, pl. 149.

HAB. Atlantic coasts of Central America, north to Florida ; West Indies ; Samoan Islands.

SP. CHAR. Bill yellow. *Adult:* General color satiny white, usually tinged more or less with salmon-pink ; a broad crescent before the eye and a stripe behind it, exposed portion of the posterior scapulars, inner tertials, a broad stripe across the middle of the middle wing-covert region, and outer webs of four to six outer primaries deep black. Shafts of the tail-feathers, and of all the primaries toward the base, and a broad stripe on the inner web of the outer primaries next the shaft also black ; edge of longer scapulars and ends of outer webs of outer primaries white ; flanks longitudinally striped with black ; elongated middle rectrices delicate pinkish salmon-color, sometimes nearly white. Bill deep chrome- or wax-yellow ;[2] iris brown ; tarsi and extreme base of the toes yellow, rest of feet black. *Young:* General color white ; black of the wings and that behind the eye indicated by spots ; back, scapulars, rump, upper tail-coverts, nape, and crown irregularly barred with black ; tail-feathers marked with a black spot near the end, the middle rectrices not elongated.

Total length, about 25.00 to 32.00 inches ; extent, about 38.00 ; wing, 11.00 ; elongated middle tail-feathers sometimes 20.00 ; culmen, 2.25.

[1] PHAËTHON RUBRICAUDUS.

Phaeton rubricauda, BODD. Tabl. P. E. 1783, 57 (ex BUFF. Pl. Enl. 979).

Phaëthon rubricaudus, STREETS, Bull. U. S. Nat. Mus. no. 7, 1877, 25 (Christmas I.).

Phœnicurus rubricauda, BONAP. Consp. II. 1857, 183.

Phaëton phoenicuros, GMEL. S. N. I. ii. 1788, 583. — JARD. Contr. Orn. 1852, pl. 84, fig. 3.

Phaëthon æthereus, BLOXH. Voy. Blonde, 1826, 251 (not of LINN., 1766).

[2] Audubon describes the bill of the male as " orange-red," and that of the female as yellow ; but he seems to have had *P. æthereus* in mind in the former case, though his description otherwise applies exclusively to *P. flavirostris*. He says that both sexes have the " iris brown ; tarsi and base of toes yellow, the rest and the webs black, as are the claws " (" Birds of America," Vol. 7, p. 65).

The Yellow-billed Tropic-bird — intertropical in its distribution, and nomadic in its general character, breeding in different parts of the globe on islands placed in mid-ocean, thousands of miles apart — is entitled to a place in the fauna of North America as an occasional visitor to the Atlantic coast. Under the name of *ætherius* Audubon figured and described an individual which had been taken on the Tortugas, in the summer of 1832, by Mr. Robert Day, of the United States revenue-cutter "Marion." Two specimens were shot out of a flock of eight or ten.

The description of this species given by Mr. Cassin was from a specimen obtained on the south side of Cuba, where — as Dr. Guudlach has informed me — it is resident throughout the year; and from this its breeding in that neighborhood may naturally be inferred.

Mr. Gosse, in his Birds of Jamaica, refers to the manuscript of Mr. Robinson, in which reference is evidently made to this species. The bird described was an immature example. Its habits are indicated as being similar to those of the Terns. It was brought to him alive, having been knocked off a fish-pot buoy, and he kept it alive for nearly a week, feeding it with the offal of fish, which it ate greedily. When this bird attempted to walk, it spread its wings and waddled along with great difficulty — a result due not only to the position of its legs, but also to their shortness and weakness. Sometimes it made a chattering noise, like that of the Belted Kingfisher; and at other times it had another cry not unlike that of a Gull. It would, when provoked, bite severely. Mr. Gosse was informed that this species is one of the constant frequenters of the Pedro Keys.

Professor Alfred Newton describes the flight of the Phaëton as something having no resemblance to that of any other sea-bird with which he is acquainted. The chief peculiarity of its motion is the regularity and rapidity with which the strokes of the wing are given.

In the islands of Bermuda, according to Major Wedderburn, this species is very common. It arrives regularly every year from the south in March and April. In 1848 it was seen as early as the 10th of March, and as late as September 25. In 1850 eight were seen near the lighthouse as early as March 1. One was seen Nov. 19, 1849, twenty miles out at sea.

The Tropic-bird breeds about the beginning of May, in holes in the rocks in the Bermuda islands — particularly about the South Shore and Garnet-head Rock. The parent-bird sits so close that it will allow itself to be caught in the hand. It shows some disposition to fight, however, and will seize an intruding hand in its powerful serrated bill, occasionally biting severely. The young birds are marked on the back and wings with transverse bracket-shaped bars, but want the two elongated centre tail-feathers. It is a very curious fact that the young birds are never seen after they leave the holes in which they were reared; and it is supposed that they at once go to sea with their parents. The Phaëton lays one egg only, and this is of a chocolate color, with large brown patches, and spotted with black and brown — exactly resembling in color the eggs of the European Kestrel, but being larger and more oval.

The account of the breeding-habits of this species here given, Mr. Hurdis supplements by the statement that the favorite resort of this interesting bird is among the small islands at the entrance of Castle Harbor, on the shores of Harrington Sound, and along the south coast, from the lighthouse to the northwest extremity of Somerset. There, conspicuous by the glittering whiteness of the plumage, and by the two long slender feathers of the tail, numbers of this species may be seen, busy on the wing, wheeling occasionally in their flight, and dashing perpendicularly into the blue waves to secure their prey, in the manner of the Terns.

On the 10th of May Mr. Hurdis explored for miles the rugged coast frequented by these birds, and found it to all appearance deserted, not only by them, but by every other species of sea-bird; but on a careful examination the rocky cliffs were discovered to abound with the Phaëton in the act of incubation. Those not thus employed were seeking food at a distance in the ocean.

This bird makes no nest; but having selected a hole or cavity in the rock — sometimes elevated, at other times merely beyond the reach of the waves — it invariably lays a single egg. Some of these holes are superficial; others, in the softer rock, appear like a rabbit's burrow; and in a few instances he found the entrance barely large enough to admit the arm, and too deep to allow the egg to be reached with the hand. In one instance he could only ascertain the presence of the old bird by touching it with the end of the ramrod, and thus causing it to give utterance to its well-known grating cry.

When the breeding-place is intruded upon, the sitting bird makes no effort to escape, but allows itself to be taken by the hand — not, however, without some resistance from its strong and sharp-pointed bill; both male and female may be captured in this manner. According to Mr. Hurdis, the egg varies considerably in color. Some specimens are of a reddish gray, thickly covered with streaks and blotches of Indian-red, deepest at the larger end; others are drab, finely speckled with the same deep red. The young remain in the nest, or breeding-place, until capable of flight. They are at first covered with a long white down, which gradually disappears as the bird advances in growth.

From the diminutive size and backward position of the feet, this bird is unable to walk in the ordinary mode; but, resting its breast on the ground, and partially spreading its wings, it shuffles from place to place in a peculiar and awkward manner.

Mr. E. L. Layard states that this species breeds in Mauritius, in the inaccessible sides of the ravines, where, from a curious projection called the "World's End," he often saw them entering the crevices of the rocks on either side. This bird also breeds in hollow trees, and it could frequently be seen flying over the forest and darting into the holes caused by the fall of rotten branches. The first pair he obtained had for several years frequented a large tree, on striking which the birds flew out and were shot. The season was too far advanced to admit of his procuring any of their eggs.

Mr. Edward Newton, in his visit to the Seychelles Archipelago, near Mauritius, in ascending a mountain, observed this species — the local name of which is *Paille en queue* — soaring overhead. In his ascent he had seen one enter a hole in the stump of a dead capuchin-tree about a quarter of a mile off, and on his return he sought the place. The hole was about fifteen feet from the ground; and his assistant ascended to it, finding only a young bird, which Mr. Newton took home and tried to rear, but without success.

This species is frequently mentioned as occurring at various localities visited during the voyage of the Wilkes Expedition, and is thus shown to be a widely distributed species. Mr. Peale states that it has been occasionally seen on the southern sea-coast of the United States. Soon after the Expedition left Chesapeake Bay, and when in lat. 38° 13′ N., long. 60° 35′ W., this bird was met with; which is probably the northern limit of its range. He expresses a belief that a few of this species breed on that part of our coast; as he has known young birds, just fledged, to be killed on the Potomac in the month of October. It was also frequently seen in the Pacific Ocean, but never so far to the north. It was always seen in the greatest abundance near high islands, breeding in holes made in the face of rocky precipices. In the mountainous regions of Tahiti it is quite numerous.

Dr. Henry Bryant found the Tropic-bird breeding in the Bahamas, where he visited three breeding-places. At Long Rock, near Exuma, it breeds in holes in the horizontal surface of the rock, as also at Water Key, one of the Ragged Island Keys; at Cayo Verde — which is about thirty miles east of Great Ragged Island — in holes in the perpendicular faces of the cliffs, and also in the horizontal surface of the rock. Before the depositing of the egg the pair occupy the same hole; but afterward only one bird is found. Both sexes incubate. On the 20th of April about half had begun to lay, and only a few eggs had been sat on three or four days; most of them had been freshly laid. The birds feed from early daylight until about nine o'clock, when they return to their holes, in which they pass the hotter part of the day, again leaving them toward sunset in search of food. The holes chosen are seldom shallow, and are often so winding that, though its harsh note can be heard within, the bird can only be procured by demolishing the rock. In their habits the Phaëtons closely resemble the Terns, as they do also in their mode of flight and external appearance. When flying, the long feathers of the tail do not separate. If their breeding-places are approached when the parent birds are out of their holes, they hover over the intruder, screaming and darting at him in the manner of the Terns. The single egg is large for the size of the bird, whitish, covered almost entirely with reddish chocolate-colored spots, finely dotted over the surface; and these marks may be easily rubbed off. They measure 2.09 inches in length by 1.65 in breadth. The egg was sometimes deposited on the bare rock, and sometimes on a few twigs — which may, however, have accidentally fallen into the hole.

Eggs of this species in the Smithsonian Collection (No. 1859), obtained in the Bermudas by Mr. J. H. Darrell, have a ground-color of a purplish brownish white, marked with fine spots and sprinkled with deep claret-brown — in some so dark as to approach blackness. They are 2.10 inches long, and from 1.45 to 1.55 inches in breadth.

Phaëthon æthereus.

THE RED-BILLED TROPIC BIRD.

Phaëthon æthereus, LINN. S. N. I. 1758, 134; ed. 12, 1766, 219. — BODD. Tabl. P. E. 1783, 58 (ex Pl. Enl. 998). — SEMPER, P. Z. S. 1872, 653 (St. Lucia, W. I.). — SALVIN, Trans. Zool. Soc. Lond. IX. ix. 1875, 497 (Tower I. Galapagos). — RIDGW. Nom. N. Am. B. 1881, no. 655. — COUES, 2d Check List, 1882, no. 762.

Phaëton Catesbyi, BRANDT, Mem. Ac. St. Petersb. 1840, Sc. Nat. III. 270.

? *Phaëton melanorhynchas*, GMEL. S. N. I. ii. 1788.

HAB. Coasts of tropical America. Socorro Island, Western Mexico, and Gulf of California; casual near Newfoundland Banks.

SP. CHAR. Bill deep coral-red. *Adult:* Prevailing color satiny white; a broad crescent immediately in front of the eye, and a stripe behind it, extending back to the occiput (sometimes meeting behind), longer scapulars (except edges), greater portion of the primary-coverts, and outer webs of four to six outer primaries (except at ends), deep black; nape, back, scapulars, rump, and upper tail-coverts, narrowly and rather irregularly barred with blackish plumbeous; flanks broadly striped with plumbeous. Elongated central rectrices pure white, the shafts blackish toward the base. Bill deep coral-red; iris brown; tarsi and base of feet, to first joint of toes, including nearly the whole of the web between inner and hind toes, yellow (orange in life?); remainder of feet black.

Total length about 30 to 35 inches; wing, 11.75–12.50; elongated middle rectrices, sometimes 22.00; culmen, about 2.50.

This species occurs along the Pacific coast of South America, and in the West Indies, though it has not — so far as I am aware — been taken within our waters. It occurs, however, in the vicinity of Cape St. Lucas, and is therefore entitled to a place in the present work. Mr. Xantus found it on the coast of Michoacan. Colonel

Grayson met with it in the Gulf of California, and also far out at sea, and he subsequently found it breeding on Isabella Island, near San Blas, where he obtained its eggs (National Museum, No. 15513). Their ground-color is a creamy white, with a purplish tinge, minutely sprinkled with dots of neutral tint and claret brown. Three specimens gave the following measurements: 2.35 by 1.55 inches; 2.40 by 1.70; 2.30 by 1.70.

ORDER LONGIPENNES.

THE LONG-WINGED SWIMMERS.

CHAR. Nostrils lateral and perforate, never tubular; covering of the bill simple, or broken only by a sort of imperfect cere (in *Stercorariidæ*). Tip of the maxilla never strongly hooked, often straight. Hallux generally well developed, but small and elevated, sometimes rudimentary. Basipterygoid bones absent. Eggs several, colored. Habit highly volucral.

The following groups, which it seems to us should rank as families, have usually had only the value of sub-families assigned them. They are so very strongly marked, however, that no intermediate forms are known.

A. *Covering of the bill simple.*

1. **Rhynchopidæ.** Bill much longer than the head, excessively compressed, except at the extreme base, the mandible much longer than the maxilla, both broad and nearly truncate. Tail much shorter than the wing, forked. Legs and feet extremely small.
2. **Laridæ.** Bill rarely longer than the head (usually shorter), moderately compressed, or sometimes nearly cylindrical, pointed, the maxilla always longer than the mandible. Tail variable in length and shape. Legs and feet of proportionate size.

B. *Covering of the bill compound.*

3. **Stercorariidæ.** Bill shorter than the head, the terminal half of the culmen strongly curved, the basal half consisting of a horny cere, beneath the overhanging edge of which the nostrils are situated. Feet rather strong, the claws well developed, rather strongly curved. Tail nearly even, but the intermediæ more or less prolonged beyond the other rectrices, their tips rounded or pointed, according to the species.

FAMILY RHYNCHOPIDÆ. — THE SKIMMERS.

CHAR. Bill compressed to knife-like thinness, except at the extreme base, the mandible much longer than the maxilla, the latter freely movable. Nostrils basal, inferior. Wings extremely lengthened. Tail about one third the wing, slightly forked. Legs and feet extremely small.

The peculiarities of form expressed in the characters given above render this very remarkable type worthy, according to our views, of family rank, as distinguished from the Gulls and Terns, the most widely different forms of which are perfectly united by the interposition of a graduated series of intermediate forms, while between *Rhynchops* and any of the *Laridæ* there exists a very wide gap. The family is composed of the single genus *Rhynchops*.

Genus **RHYNCHOPS**, Linnæus.

Rynchops, Linn. S. N. ed. 10, I. 1758, 228; ed. 12, I. 1766, 228 (type, *R. nigra*, Linn.).
Rhynchops, Lath. Ind. Orn. II. 1790, 802.

Char. Same as those of the family.

The genus *Rhynchops* contains only three species, so far as known; the *R. nigra*, peculiar to America; *R. flavirostris*, Vieill., of the Red Sea, and *R. albicollis*, Swains., of India. We have not been able to examine either of the exotic species, but upon examining an excellent colored

R. nigra.

plate of *R. albicollis* in Gray and Mitchell's "Genera of Birds" (Vol. III. pl. clxxxi.), we are unable to appreciate any point wherein it differs from the winter plumage of *R. nigra*.

Rhynchops nigra.

THE BLACK SKIMMER.

Rynchops nigra, Linn. S. N. ed. 10, I. 1758, 228; ed. 12, I. 1766, 228.
Rhynchops nigra, Lath. Ind. Orn. II. 1790, 802. — Lawr. in Baird's B. N. Am. 1858, 866. — Baird, Cat. N. Am. B. 1859, no. 697. — Coues, Key, 1872, 324; Check List, 1873, no. 577; 2d ed. 1882, no. 809; Birds N. W. 1874, 715. — Ridgw. Nom. N. Am. B. 1881, no. 656.
Rynchops fulva, Linn. S. N. I. 1766, 229 (young?).
Rhynchops cinerascens, Spix, Av. Bras. 1826, pl. 102 (young).
Rhynchops brevirostris, Spix, Av. Bras. 1826, pl. 103 (young).
? *Rhynchops melanurus*, "Boie," Swains. Anim. in Menag. 1838, 340 (Demerara).
Rhynchops borealis, Swains. l. c.

Hab. Warmer parts of America, south to 45° S., north, along the Atlantic coast, to New Jersey (regularly), or even Maine (casually). Both coasts of Central America.

Sp. Char. *Adult:* Forehead, lores, cheeks, and entire lower parts, from chin to crissum, inclusive, with axillars, lining of the wing, lateral upper tail-coverts, and ends of secondaries and inner primaries (broadly), pure white; rest of the plumage, including upper parts in general, with auriculars, dusky black. Tail white, the shafts of the feathers brownish on the upper surface, the intermediæ grayish brown edged with white, the other rectrices more or less tinged at ends with the same. Basal half (approximately) of the bill bright vermilion, the mandible more scarlet, shading into yellowish on the tomium ; terminal portion black ; iris dark brown ; legs and feet rich orange-vermilion, claws black. *Adult, in winter:* Similar, but the black more brownish, and interrupted by a broad nuchal collar of white. *Young, first plumage:* Upper parts light buff, each feather with a central spot of black, these spots largest on the scapulars ; lores and suborbital region uniform pale buff ; a space immediately before and behind the eyes, dusky. Greater wing-

coverts slate-black, tipped with white ; secondaries pure white for nearly the whole of the exposed portion ; primaries black, the fourth, fifth, and sixth bordered terminally with light buff, the four inner quills dusky, passing gradually into white at the ends. Lower parts entirely pure white. Bill and feet reddish dusky. *Downy young:* Above, very pale grayish buff, irregularly and sparsely mottled with blackish ; below, immaculate white.

Adult male: Total length, about 17.00 to 20.00 inches ; extent, 48.00 ; wing, 14.75–15.75 ; tail, 5.50, its fork, about 1.20 ; culmen, 2.55–2.80 ; gonys, 3.40–4.70 ; tarsus, 1.30 ; middle toe, .80–.85. *Adult female:* 15.25 to 16.75, 44.50, 13.50–14.25, 4.40–5.00, 2.00–2.30, 2.45–3.00, 1.15–1.20, .75.

As a rule, South American specimens are larger than those from North America, the bill especially being much longer. Thus, in a series of eight adult examples from northern localities, the mandible measures from 2.90 to 4.10 inches in length (measuring from the chin), while in three skins from South America, and one each from Guatemala and Nicaragua, the same measurement ranges from 4.50 to 4.70 inches. In an adult male from Conchitas, Buenos Ayres, however, the mandible is only 3.25 in length ; while in another from Peru (No. 15511 ; Captain WILKES) it measures 3.60, and is remarkably narrow. This specimen has the tail wholly uniform dusky. We have not been able to discover any constant differences of coloration between northern and southern birds of this species. There is much variation as regards the color of the tail, which in some is wholly a uniform dusky-brown color ; in others (older birds ?) the tail is white, only the intermediæ being brownish, and these with a broad edging of white. Other specimens are variously intermediate in this respect, so that this variation is probably due to age.[1] Audubon ("Birds of America," VII. 73) says that in the young, "after the first autumnal moult, there is on the hind part of the neck a broad band of white, mottled with grayish black ;" the upper parts of

[1] According to M. Taczanowski, in "Proc. Zool. Soc. Lond ," 1874, pp. 562, 563, Peruvian specimens differ constantly in several respects from North American examples, and to such an extent that he considers them specifically distinct. He says : "These birds are so different from *R. nigra* that it is impossible to confound them. The length of the wing presents the greatest difference : that of the Peruvian species exceeds the wing of *R. nigra* by sixty millim. The bill is much larger and stronger. The coloring also presents several differences ; the principal consists in the complete absence of the white speculum on the wing, which in the North American bird occupies the terminal half of the secondary quills. The white demi-collar on the neck also is wanting in our bird, being indicated only by a little paler color than that of the surrounding parts. The under wing-coverts are not white, but brownish gray ; the forehead, sides of the face, and front part of the throat are more or less clouded with gray. The whole tail is blackish brown, the rectrices with a clear border.

"M. Jelski has indicated on the labels that the pupil is not round, but vertical, as in the cat. Dimensions of a male :—

	Millim.		Millim.
Length of folded wing	415	Length of maxilla	105
" the tail	136	" tarsus	35
" the bill from the gape .	135	" middle toe with claw .	30"

a duller black, and the bill and feet less richly colored than in the adult. A specimen from Matamoras (No. 4167), evidently a young bird, in much worn and apparently faded plumage, has the black replaced by brownish gray (this very pale on the head above), while all the wing-coverts are conspicuously tipped with white.

The females are uniformly much smaller than the males, but exactly the same in colors, the fresh tints of the bill and feet being equally bright.

This unique and very peculiar species, variously known as the "Razor-bill," the "Cut-water," the "Shearwater," and the "Black Skimmer," is found on our Atlantic coast from Long Island to Southern Brazil, and also on the Pacific coast; but to what extent I am not able to state. Dr. Burmeister speaks of it as being common on the Rio Parana, especially among the lagoons near the river, where this singular bird, in the manner so well described by Azara, fishes for its prey, making long furrows through the water — a peculiarity which causes it to be generally known by the name of *El Rayador*. Mr. Xantus procured this species on the Zacatula River, in Western Mexico; and Colonel Grayson noticed it during the summer months near San Blas. He speaks of it as not being abundant, and as partly nocturnal in its habits.

Mr. C. B. Brown met with it in the rivers of British Guiana, especially on the Essequibo, where, as he states, the "Scissor-billed Gulls," or "Sea-dogs," were frequently seen flying swiftly along in small parties, with their long sharp flat beaks dipping in the water. Their cries resembled somewhat the barking of a dog; hence they have received the name of Sea-dogs.

According to the observations of Mr. Giraud, this is one of the regular visitants of Long Island — where, however it is not very common. At Egg Harbor, on the coast of New Jersey, it is much more abundant, and has been known to breed there.

Birds of this species associate in small parties, and pass most of their time on the wing — flying very low at a short distance from the shore. Giraud has never known them to alight on the water; but they may usually be seen skimming over its surface, ploughing it with their long bills, seemingly in pursuit of small fish, on which they feed. They are never known to dive, and they apparently only take their prey when this comes to the surface of the water.

The voice of this Gull is a harsh scream, somewhat resembling the cry of the Tern, but is stronger. When fishing this bird flies steadily and slowly, flapping its long wings. At other times its flight is exceedingly swift. It is not known to breed on Long Island, where it is rarely seen except at midsummer.

Its nest is a mere hollow formed in the sand, without the addition of any materials. The female lays three eggs, almost exactly oval, of a dirty white, marked with large spots of brownish black intermixed with others of a pale India-ink. These measure 1.75 inches in length by 1.25 in breadth. It is said that half a bushel and more of these eggs have sometimes been collected from one sandbar within the compass of half an acre. Giraud states that he found them to have something of a fishy taste; yet they are eaten by many people on the coast. The female sits on them only during the night, or in wet and stormy weather. The young remain unable to fly for several weeks after they are hatched; and during this time they are fed by both parents with remarkable assiduity — seeming to delight in lying with half-opened wings flat on the sand, as if enjoying its invigorating warmth. This bird breeds but once in a season, and is much later in depositing its eggs than are other water birds. In my visit to Cape Charles, in June, 1852, while these birds were present in considerable numbers, they showed no signs of breeding, although their companions of various kinds had all full complements of eggs.

Mr. N. B. Moore, living near Sarasota Bay, Fla., writes me that he has seen small and scattered parties of this species skimming over the quiet waters of the lagoons and flooded flats, at high tide, in the middle of the day, near the sea-shore, procuring food; while a flock of from fifty to a hundred were basking in the sunshine on an island sandflat near by. One of these birds was observed to take a fish which seemed too large to be readily swallowed, and which it carried to a sandbar, and then perched among its fellows.

In the autumn the Razor-bills are seen to quit their basking-grounds a little after sunset, and all fly off in a southerly direction. They skim low over the water; and if the surface is smooth when they come upon a shoal of small fry, they settle down a little, lower the long under-jaw into the water, and at the same moment cease to beat the air, but elevate the open wings, and thus move on for a considerable distance. They only carry their bill in the water when there is an immediate prospect of abundant prey. They return in the morning from their roosting-places, flying in the same manner as in the evening, but higher, and seem to be less inclined to feed while on their way. They are said to proceed to Charlotte Harbor to pass the night and to feed; this is distant fifty miles or more. But these statements have not been positively verified. Mr. Moore has never known them to fly over the land, as Gulls and Terns are often seen to do.

Mr. Salvin met with this species at the lagoon of Acapam, on the Pacific coast of Guatemala; and Professor Newton mentions seeing a single example, on the 14th of June, 1838, between St. Thomas and St. Croix; it passed close to the vessel on the deck of which he was standing at the time.

Mr. C. W. Wyatt, in an account of the birds of Colombia, South America, states that while he was waiting at the Digue, on the banks of the Magdalena River, he had several opportunities of watching this curious bird as it flew over the shallows by the sandbanks, or ploughed the water and the mud with its scissor-shaped bill. It was not seen by him on the lower portion of the Magdalena.

Léotaud cites this species as an irregular visitant of the Island of Trinidad, there being frequent intervals during which it is not seen there; and when it does come it is regarded as the sure herald of the wintry rains. It is preceded in its migrations by all the other birds visiting that island at that season.

Audubon regarded this bird as being largely nocturnal in its feeding; and says that it sometimes spends the whole night on the wing, diligently searching for food. Although silent when beginning this occupation, it becomes more and more noisy as darkness draws on; its call-notes resemble the syllables *hurk-hurk*, repeated at short intervals. The same writer states that while at Galveston Island he saw three Razor-bills pursue a Night Heron several hundred yards, as if intent on overtaking it; their cries during the chase resembling the barking of a very small dog.

The flight of this bird is remarkable for its elegance, and for the vigor with which it is maintained against even the most violent gale. It is never known to be driven astray by any storm, however violent.

The Notes of Dr. Berlandier, of Matamoras, show that he regarded this as being a rare species on the Mexican coast; he met with only a single example in the neighborhood of Tampico. He states that it inhabits the salt lakes and the shores of the Gulf of Mexico between the Tropics, delighting in lonely shoals and marshy places. It is known to the French as *Le Bec en Ciseau*, and to the Spaniards as the *Pescador*. It does not feed solely upon shellfish and mollusks, but is found on the edge of lakes around Matamoras, where there are very few mollusks, and where it hunts for fishes.

Dr. Bachman informed Audubon that this bird is very abundant and breeds in great numbers on the sea-islands at Ball's Bay, S. C., where twenty thousand nests could be seen at one time. The sailors collected enormous numbers of their eggs, the birds screaming unceasingly. Whenever a Pelican or a Turkey Buzzard passed near they assailed the intruder by hundreds, and drove it fairly out of sight. The Razor-bill forms no other nest than a slight hollow in the sand. The eggs are always three, having a pure-white ground, largely blotched and patched with very dark umber, with here and there a large spot of an obscure purplish tint. The young are at first of the same color as is the sand on which they lie; and are not able to fly until five or six weeks after being hatched.

If this bird is shot at and wounded, and then falls into the water, it is easily secured, as it cannot dive. At such a time its cries excite the sympathy of its fellows, who crowd around it as Terns do under similar circumstances.

Specimens of the egg of the Razor-bill in the Smithsonian collection, from Hog Island, Va., and from Florida, vary in their length from 1.70 to 1.80 inches, and in their breadth from 1.30 to 1.40. Their ground-color is a pale buff or buffy white; the markings are large, longitudinal, and of a conspicuous blackish brown, intermingled with subdued spots of umber and lavender-gray. The ground-color of South American examples is a very deep drab.

Family LARIDÆ. — The Gulls and Terns.

Char. Bill moderately compressed, or sometimes nearly cylindrical, its covering entire; the tip of the maxilla overhanging, or at least meeting, that of the mandible; the culmen more or less curved, but never arched terminally — sometimes nearly straight throughout; symphysis of the mandible usually forming more or less of an angle, this, in most cases, prominent in proportion to the relative depth of the bill; nostrils sub-basal, perforate; legs and feet of proportionate size. Tail extremely variable in form and length.

Although including among its very numerous members great extremes of size and form, the family *Laridæ* as here restricted is not divisible into more than two sub-families; and these are so nearly united through certain forms as to be really more artificial than natural. They may, with considerable difficulty, be defined as follows: —

Larinæ. Depth of the bill through the angle decidedly greater than through the middle of the nostrils; terminal portion of the culmen decidedly curved; mandibular angle frequently prominent, always distinct. Tail even, except in *Xema* (forked) and *Rhodostethia* (wedge-shaped). Size extremely variable, but usually medium or large; sometimes very large.

Sterninæ. Depth of the bill through the angle (symphysis of the lower jaw) less than through the middle of the nostrils; terminal portion of the culmen slightly curved, or nearly straight; mandibular angle seldom prominent. Tail forked, except in *Anous* (graduated). Size extremely variable, but usually small; never very large.

In probably no other group of birds are there so many and great extremes of form connected by imperceptible transitions, as among the *Laridæ*. Owing to this fact, the genera are exceedingly difficult of definition, unless restricted to the smallest possible number, some of those thus comprehended containing a considerable number of "sub-genera," many of which are almost, if not quite, sufficiently different in form or size to be of generic distinctness. The genus *Larus*, for instance, in its most comprehensive sense includes both the gigantic *L. marinus* and the pigmy *L. minutus;* the latter smaller than many Terns, the former approaching an Albatross in size; while the difference in form is not less striking than that of size. The genus *Sterna* offers scarcely less of a contrast between the large, Gull-like *S. caspia* and the minute *S. antillarum.* In order to separate the more marked variations of form in either of these genera, however, it would be necessary to name a larger number of subdivisions than most authors would recognize as distinct genera. Notwithstanding this fact, we are convinced that, while such a procedure undoubtedly simplifies the nomenclature, it by no means expresses the true relationship of the forms so designated to call all the square-tailed Gulls (excepting *Pagophila* and *Rissa*) *Larus*, and all the fork-tailed Terns with fully webbed-feet *Sterna.* In fact it is only from want of suitable material that we have not attempted a subdivision of the genera *Larus* and *Sterna* in their comprehensive sense. Allowing, therefore, each the fullest possible scope, we submit the following analysis of the North American genera of *Laridæ*: —

Larinæ.

1. **Pagophila.** Tail even; hind toe perfectly developed, though small; tarsus shorter than the middle toe and claw, serrate behind. Color entirely white, the young sparsely spotted with dusky. Size medium.
2. **Rissa.** Tail even, or slightly emarginate; hind toe rudimentary, or altogether absent; tarsus much shorter than the middle toe without its claw, not serrate behind. Above, pearl-blue, beneath white; young similar, but with a black nuchal patch (and in one species a black shoulder-patch). Size medium.
3. **Larus.** Tail even; hind toe always well developed; tarsus always longer than the middle toe with its claw, not serrate behind. Size and coloration extremely variable, but young always very different from the adults.
4. **Rhodostethia.** Tail graduated, or wedge-shaped. Size small. Adult pearl-blue above, rosy white beneath and on head and neck, the latter encircled by a black collar.
5. **Xema.** Tail forked. Size small. Adult pearl-gray above, white beneath, including the neck all round, the head dusky.

Sterninæ.

6. **Sterna.** Tail decidedly forked; webs of the toes filling the greater part of the interdigital spaces, but both with a concave or scalloped anterior outline. Size extremely variable.
7. **Hydrochelidon.** Tail emarginate; webs of the toes very deeply scalloped, occupying much less than half the interdigital space. Size small.
8. **Anous.** Tail graduated, or wedge-shaped; webs of the toes completely filling the interdigital spaces, and scarcely or not at all scalloped in front.

Genus PAGOPHILA, Kaup.

Gavia, Boie, Isis, 1822, 563 (type, *Larus eburneus*, Phipps).[1]
Pagophila, Kaup, Nat. Syst. Eur. Thierw. 1829, 69 (type, *Larus eburneus*, Phipps).
Cetosparactes, Macgill. Man. Brit. Orn. II. 1842, 251.

Char. Size medium; tail even; hind toe well developed, though small, the nail relatively large; tarsus shorter than the middle toe and claw, roughly granular or almost serrate behind; color entirely white in the summer adult; white, sparsely spotted with dusky, in the winter plumage (and young?).

The genus *Pagophila* contains but one well established species, although several nominal ones have been recognized, all of which were probably based upon special stages, or somewhat abnormal individuals, of *P. eburnea.*

[1] It is quite probable that a proper adherence to the rules of nomenclature will require the use of *Gavia* for this genus instead of *Pagophila*; but at present we are unwilling to make the change. (Cf. Stejneger, "Proc. U. S. Nat. Mus." Vol. 5, p. 39.)

Pagophila eburnea.

THE IVORY GULL.

Larus albus, GUNN. in Leem, Beskr. Finm. Lapp. 1767, 285. — SCHÄFF. Mus. Orn. 1789, 65, tab. 42.

Gavia alba, STEJN. Pr. U. S. N. M. Vol. 5, 1882, p. 39.[1]

Larus eburneus, PHIPPS, Voy. N. Pole, App. 1774, 187. — NUTT. Man. II. 1834, 301. — AUD. Orn. Biog. III. 1835, 571; Synop. 1839, 326; B. Am. VII. 1844, 150, pl. 445. — COUES, Key, 1872, 313; Check List, 1873, no. 550.

Pagophila eburnea, GRAY, App. List, Gen. B. 1842, 15. — LAWR. in Baird's B. N. Am. 1858, 836. — BAIRD, Cat. N. Am. B. 1859, no. 676. — SAUNDERS, P. Z. S. 1878, 162 (synonymy, etc.).

Larus (*Pagophila*) *eburneus*, BRUCH, J. f. O. 1853, 106. — COUES, B. N. W. 1874, 648.

Larus candidus, MÜLLER, Prod. Zool. Dan. 1776, p. viii.

Larus niveus, BODD. Tabl. P. E. 1783, 58, no. 994.

Larus brachytarsus, HOLBÖLL, Fn. Grœnl. 1846, 52.

Larus (*Pagophila*) *brachytarsus*, BRUCH, J. f. O. 1853, 106. — LAWR. in Baird's B. N. Am. 1858, 856. — BAIRD, Cat. N. Am. B. 1859, no. 677.

HAB. Circumpolar seas, south in winter on the Atlantic coast of America to Labrador, Newfoundland, and (rarely?) New Brunswick. No Pacific coast record.

SP. CHAR. *Adult:* Entirely pure white, the shafts of the primaries pale yellowish. Bill yellowish green, the terminal third yellow; iris brown; eyelids vermilion-red; legs and feet black.

P. eburnea.

Young: Similar, but anterior part of the head tinged more or less with brownish gray,[2] the remiges, rectrices, primary coverts, and longer scapulars marked terminally by a spot of dusky, the lesser wing-coverts marked centrally by smaller spots of the same. "Bill black, clouded with pale yellow; legs and feet black" (L. KUMLIEN, MS.).

Total length, about 17.00–19.50 inches; wing, 13.25; culmen, 1.40; depth of bill through nostrils, .45; tarsus, 1.45; middle toe (with claw), 1.75.

Audubon mentions this species as occasional on the coasts of the United States, and was also informed that it is not uncommon on the coasts of Labrador and Newfoundland during the winter. During the summer months it is found only in high northern latitudes, and generally only far out to sea.

According to Yarrell, several individuals of this species have been taken from time to time on the coasts of Great Britain and Ireland. The first known instance of this kind occurred in Balta Sound, Shetland, in 1822; and another happened soon

[1] The same remarks apply to this as to the name of the genus, as explained in footnote on p. 197.

[2] This perhaps an accidental stain.

after in the Firth of Clyde. In 1834 a similar occurrence was noted by Mr. Sabine on the western coast of Ireland; and another has since been recorded near Galway. More recently there have been several of these birds obtained in Great Britain. Temminck with his own hands shot one on the coast of Holland. Vieillot records this species as having appeared on the coast of France. Nilsson states that it is seen occasionally in winter both in Sweden and in the northern part of Scandinavia. It is given by Middendorff as one of the birds of Siberia, where it is said to be found only in the extreme north.

Messrs. Evans and Sturge, in their paper on the Birds of Western Spitzbergen, state that of the beautiful snow-white Ivory Gull they saw only six or seven individuals; and although both of the examples that they killed had their bellies bare of feathers, as is the case with sitting birds, all endeavors to find where they were breeding failed. The sailors asserted that this bird was never seen excepting upon ice; and in only one instance was this statement proved to be incorrect.

Professor Alfred Newton, in his Notes on the Birds of Spitzbergen, referring to this species, remarks: —

"The Ivory Gull is, of all others, the bird of which every visitor to Spitzbergen will carry away the keenest recollection. One can only wish that a creature so fair to look upon was not so foul a feeder. Contrary to the experience of all other observers, I once saw an Ivory Gull, of its own accord, deliberately settle on the water and swim. This was in the Stor Fjord. There is a very great variation in the size of different examples, which is not to be attributed to sex nor to age; but I do not for one moment countenance the belief in a second species, which some ornithologists have endeavored to establish under the name of *P. brachytarsa.*"

The Swedish expedition to Spitzbergen in 1861 obtained some eggs of this species; and these were the first well-authenticated specimens taken to Europe. I transcribe what Dr. Malmgren says about them: —

"On the 7th of July, 1861, I found on the north shore of Murchison Bay, lat. 80° N., a number of Ivory Gulls established on the side of a steep limestone precipice, some hundred feet high, in company with the *Rissa tridactyla* and *Larus glaucus.* The last-named occupied the higher zones of the precipice. The *Larus eburneus,* on the other hand, occupied the niches and clefts lower down, at a height of from fifty to a hundred feet. I could plainly see that the hen birds were sitting on their nests; but these were inaccessible. Circumstances did not permit, before the 30th of July, my making the attempt, with the help of a long rope and some necessary assistance, to get at the eggs. With the assistance of three men I succeeded in reaching two of the lowest in situation; and each contained one egg. The nest was artless and without connection, and consisted of a shallow depression eight or nine inches broad, in a loose clay or mould, on a sublayer of limestone. Inside, the nest was carefully lined with dry plants, moss, grasses, and the like, and a few feathers. The eggs were much incubated, and already contained down-clad young. Both of the hen-birds were shot upon their nests, and are now in the National Museum. The male birds were at first observable, but disappeared when we began the work of reaching their nests."

Professor Newton believes that the Ivory Gull breeds sporadically on many other parts of Spitzbergen proper. Several of the birds shot in Ice Sound and the Stor Fjord had their bellies bared of feathers, as is the case with sitting birds; and his pilot informed him that a ship's boat, which in 1857 succeeded in reaching Gilies Land, found the nests of many Ivory Gulls on its lonely shore. This bird probably does not always breed in colonies; and as it selects the inaccessible places, an occasional nest here and there on the mountains or crags might well escape notice.

Professor E. Percival Wright ("Ibis" 1866, p. 216) states that Commodore McClintock, on his return from the Arctic expedition of 1852–1853, among the very few specimens of natural history he was able to retain, brought home with him one egg of the Ivory Gull. An extract from McClintock's Diary is given, from which it appears that from the 12th to the 15th of June he examined the Polynia Islands, lat. 78°, which are composed entirely of gravel, none of them being more than sixty feet above the sea. Upon one he saw two old nests of this species. They were chiefly made of moss, and a larger quantity of this material had been used in their construction than he had seen growing upon the whole group. The broken pieces of eggshells which the nests contained were of a pale olive color, with irregular dark-brown blotches. On the 18th of June, as he was rounding Cape Krabbe, on the east shore of Prince Patrick's Island, he saw an Ivory Gull sitting on her nest, on a bare patch of gravel near the beach. There was a single egg in the nest, which was exactly like those seen on the Polynia Islands; only, in addition to the moss, there was a little white down, and also a few feathers in it. This egg is now in the Museum of the Royal Society of Dublin.

Mr. G. Gillett found this species in abundance on Nova Zembla wherever there was ice. He did not see any of its breeding-places, nor could he detect any other than adult birds. He mentions having frequently seen them settle on the water. Von Heuglin reports this bird as being present, but in small numbers, in Matthews Strait and along the west coast of Nova Zembla.

Dr. Alexander Carte contributed to the Dublin Royal Society a paper relative to the nidification of this species, in which this bird is mentioned as being almost exclusively resident in the Arctic Regions of both hemispheres, seldom visiting more temperate climes. In addition to those instances of its occurrence in England and elsewhere which have already been mentioned, Dr. Carte cites eight others of its being taken in other parts of Great Britain, and still others of its capture in Ireland. Captain Scoresby is quoted as characterizing it as being quite as ravenous as the Fulmar, and as little nice in the choice of its food. It is, however, somewhat more cautious than that bird; and while it is a constant attendant on the operations of the whale-fishers, it generally seizes its portion on the wing. It rarely alights on the water, but often sits on the ice, preferring the most elevated situations. Its cry is a loud and disagreeable scream. Captain McClintock, in his Diary, mentions that, in lat. 77° N., long. 116° W., he discovered around a nest of this bird the remains of the bleached bones of the *Myodes hudsonius*, and also fresh pellets consisting of their hair and bones, showing that this bird preys upon that animal.

Sir John Richardson saw this Gull breeding in great numbers on the high perforated cliffs that form the extremity of Cape Parry, in latitude 70°; but he was unable to obtain any specimens of its eggs. A quotation is given from the Diary of Captain McClintock, in which he mentions meeting with three species of Gull in the Arctic Regions, the Ivory Gull appearing the earliest of all, and being found the farthest north. The first seen and shot was on the 12th of June, in lat. 77° 45′ N., long. 116° W. Eight were noticed, all of them on Prince Patrick's Land.

Mr. Kumlien states that this Gull was very common in Kingwah Fiord and its vicinity, just before the closing of the ice, for a few days only; none were seen in the spring. It is by no means common on the Greenland coast. The stomachs of all the examples which were secured contained small crustaceans; these Gulls do not, however, restrict themselves to this food, but are very fond of meat, and especially of the flesh of the seal and whale.

Dr. Walker mentions meeting with this species about Godthaab; and it is given by Professor Reinhardt as being included among the resident species of Greenland. Mr. Proctor informed Professor Alfred Newton ("Ibis," 1864) that he had on two occasions received specimens of it from Iceland. It is known to frequent Davis Straits, Baffin's Bay, and various parts of the northern shores of the continent, where it is a constant attendant upon the whale-fishers, and preys upon the blubber.

Mr. H. W. Feilden ("Ibis," Oct. 1877) speaks of this Gull as being one of the birds most frequently observed in Smith's Sound, but as not met with beyond latitude 82° 20′. He found a pair of them nesting in a lofty and inaccessible cliff near Cape Hayes on the 16th of August, 1875. On the 1st of September a single example flew around the "Alert" as she lay moored in the ice in Lincoln Bay, latitude 82° 6′. On the 2d of August, 1876, he observed one near Cape Union; and on the 12th of August they were common in Discovery Bay, and from there southward to the north water of Baffin's Bay. This species is also enumerated by Dr. Bessels among the birds taken in the Polaris Expedition, under Captain Hall — probably in Polaris Bay.

The egg of this Gull obtained by Captain McClintock is represented in a colored plate in the "Proceedings of the Royal Society of Dublin." It is 2.45 inches in length and 1.70 in breadth, of an oblong-oval shape, and slightly more obtuse at one end than at the other. It has a ground color of a light yellowish olive, marked over its entire surface with small blotches of a dark brown, intermingled with others of a lighter and more obscure brown, and with larger cloudings of a faint lilac.

GENUS **RISSA**, LEACH.

Rissa, LEACH, Stephen's Gen. Zool. XIII. 1825, 180 (type, *Larus rissa*, BRÜNN. = *L. tridactylus*, LINN.).

CHAR. Size medium; tail even, or very faintly emarginate; hind toe rudimentary, or entirely absent, the nail usually obsolete; tarsus much shorter than the middle toe without its claw, not rough or serrate behind. Above, pearl-blue, beneath, white, the young with a black nuchal patch (and in *R. tridactyla* a black shoulder-patch).

Only two species of *Rissa* are known, both of which belong to the North American fauna. They may readily be distinguished by the following characters: —

1. **R. tridactyla.** Legs and feet black; wing, about 12.25 inches; culmen, 1.40–1.50; depth of bill at base, .59; tarsus, 1.30; middle toe with claw, 1.80. *Hab.* Northern portion of northern hemisphere.
2. **R. brevirostris.** Legs and feet deep coral- or vermilion-red (drying yellowish); wing, about 13.00 inches; culmen, 1.20; depth of bill through base, .50; tarsus, 1.25; middle toe with claw, nearly 2.00. *Hab.* North Pacific, particularly the American side.

Rissa tridactyla.

THE KITTIWAKE GULL.

a. **Tridactyla.**

Larus tridactylus, LINN. S. N. ed. 10, I. 1758, 136 ; ed. 12, I. 1766, 224. — Sw. & RICH. II. 1831, 423. — NUTT. Man. II. 1834, 298. — AUD. Orn. Biog. III. 1835, 186, pl. 224 ; Synop. 1839, 326 ; B. Am. VII. 1844, 146, pl. 444. — COUES, Key, 1872, 314 ; Check List, 1873, no. 552.
Rissa tridactyla, BONAP. Comp. List, 1838, 62. — LAWR. in Baird's B. N. Am. 1858, 854. — BAIRD, Cat. N. Am. B. 1859, no. 672. — SAUNDERS, P. Z. S. 1878, 163 (synonymy, etc.). — RIDGW. Nom. N. Am. B. 1881, no. 658. — COUES, 2d Check List, 1882, no. 782.
Larus (*Rissa*) *tridactyla*, COUES, B. N. W. 1874, 644.
Larus rissa, BRÜNN. Orn. Bor. 1764, 42. — LINN. S. N. ed. 12, I. 1766, 224.
Larus albus, MÜLLER, Natursyst. 1776, 108 (based on Buffon's *Mouette cendrée tachetée*).
Larus cinerarius, FABR. Fauna Grœnl. 1780, 101 (not of LINN. 1766. — Winter plumage).
Larus nævius, SCHÄFF. Mus. Orn. 1789, 64 (not of LINN.).
Larus torquatus, PALL. Zoog. Rosso-As. II. 1826, 328.
Larus canus, PALL. t. c. 330 (not of LINN.).
Larus gavia, PALL. t. c. 329.
Larus riga, GMEL. S. N. I. ii. 1788, 594 (misprint).
Rissa Brunnichii, LEACH, Stephen's Gen. Zool. XIII. i. 1826, 181, pl. 21.
Rissa cinerea, EYTON, Cat. Br. B. 1836, 52.
Laroides minor, BREHM, Vög. Deutschl. 1831, 756.
Rissa borealis, BREHM, Naum. 1855, 294 (not *Larus borealis*, BRUCH).
Rissa gregaria, BREHM, l. c.

b. **Pollicaris.**

Larus rissa, PALL. Zoog. Rosso-As. II. 1826, 321 (not of BRÜNN.).
Larus tridactylus, KITTL. Isis, 1832, 1104 (not of LINN.).
Larus (*Rissa*) *brachyrhynchus*, BRUCH, J. f. O. 1853, 103, sp. 31 (nec RICHARDSON, 1831, nec GOULD, 1843).
Rissa nivea, BP. Naum. 1854, 212 (*nomen nudum ;* not of GRAY, 1845).
Rissa Kotzebui, BONAP. Consp. II. 1856, 226 (not of 1854 ! . — ELLIOT, Illustr. B. Am. pl. 54.
Larus tridactylus, var. *Kotzebui*, COUES, Key, 1872, 314 ; Check List, 1873, no. 552 *a* ; B. N. W. 1874, 646 ; Elliott's Alaska, 1875, 199.
Rissa tridactyla Kotzbuei, RIDGW. Nom. N. Am. B. 1881, no. 658 *a*.
Rissa tridactyla Kotzebuii, COUES, 2d Check List, 1882, no. 783.
Rissa tridactyla pollicaris, STEJN. MS.

R. tridactyla.

Hab. Circumpolar Regions in summer, coming south in winter to the Middle States and Great Lakes; no Pacific coast record south of Alaska.

Sp. Char. *Adult, in summer:* Mantle deep pearl-gray (about the same shade as in *Larus brachyrhynchus* and *L. californicus*), the secondaries passing into white terminally. Primaries paler pearl-blue, the five outer quills with their terminal portion black, this color extending for about 3.25 inches on the outer and .75 of an inch, more or less, on the fifth, and of intermediate extent on those between; outer web of the exterior quill almost wholly black; inner quills pale pearl-blue, scarcely paler terminally, the sixth sometimes marked with a black spot near the end of the outer web; fifth quill tipped with white, and fourth with a minute apical spot (when not worn off). Rest of the plumage snow-white. Bill pale yellow, sometimes tinged with greenish; inside of mouth vermilion-red; eyelids red; iris brown; legs and feet black or dusky brown. *Adult, in winter:* Similar, but nape and occiput washed with the color of the back, the auricular region, and immediately in front of the eye, with a dark plumbeous suffusion, sometimes extending across the occiput. *Young, first plumage:* Somewhat similar to the winter adult, but lower part of nape covered by a large transverse patch of black, the anterior lesser wing-coverts also more or less black, as are the centres of the inner longer coverts and tertials; primary coverts and outer webs of four or five outer primaries also black. Tail crossed at the end (except lateral pair of feathers) by a broad black band, widest on the intermediæ. Bill wholly black; "edge of eyelids and iris as in the adult" (Audubon); legs and feet dusky brownish. *Downy young:* Head, neck, wings, and lower parts, immaculate white, the nape and base of the wings more or less tinged with buff; back, rump, and flanks, yellowish gray, the down darker at the base.

Wing, about 12.25 inches; culmen, 1.40–1.50; depth of bill at base, .59, through angle, .40; tarsus, 1.30; middle toe (with claw), 1.80.

The Common Kittiwake is a northern species, found both in Europe and America, in the waters of the Atlantic, and represented on the Pacific by an allied form so essentially similar to it that the two cannot be specifically distinguished from each other. It is more or less abundant in the northern portions of Asia and Europe, and occurs on both the eastern and western shores of North America in northern latitudes. During the winter it wanders south in an irregular manner.

Mr. Godman met with a few individuals about the harbor of Punta Delgada, in the Azores, on his arrival there, and was informed by the master of one of the fruit schooners that these birds frequently followed his vessel through the whole of the voyage from England. Mr. Godman was led to believe that this species breeds about the coast of Teneriffe. He is confident that he saw either this bird or *L. canus* at Teneriffe in the middle of May, but he was not able to secure any specimens. Mr. Saunders found the Kittiwake abundant on the outside of the Straits of Gibraltar in the winter, but it was more rare to the eastward.

The Kittiwake is given by Middendorff as a bird of Siberia, where it extends its movements to the farthest north. Mr. Gillett mentions his having found it common along the entire coast of Nova Zembla. Von Heuglin found it one of the most common species on the west coast of Nova Zembla. It was not seen in Matthews' Strait, nor on Waigatsch Island.

Professor Alfred Newton found it a very common bird in Spitzbergen, where it frequented the whole coast. In Parry's Expedition it was observed feeding on *Merlangus polaris* and *Alpheus polaris* as far to the north as was reached; namely, lat. 82° 45′ N. Dr. Malmgren saw it occupying a middle station on the cliffs where the Gulls were breeding, and found its stomach filled with the *Limacina arctica* and the *Clio borealis*. In his last voyage he noticed it breeding on Beacon Island.

Mr. Wheelwright states that this Gull is only an occasional visitant of the Scandinavian coasts, and appears to be limited exclusively to the Polar seas.

According to Yarrell, the Kittiwake is far from being a rare bird on the coast of England, and is decidedly a rock-breeder; and very common in the breeding-season on all the rocky parts of the coasts of Hampshire, Dorsetshire, Devonshire, and Cornwall. It is only a summer visitor to Ireland; but is found in considerable numbers on the coast of England in winter, and is also resident on the coast of France. It is said to breed on many of the high ranges of cliffs along the southern shore of England, and also on the high rocky promontories on the eastern coast, such as Flamborough Head, Scarborough, the Farne Islands, St. Abb's Head, the Bass Rock, Aberdeen, and the Orkney and Shetland Islands. Mr. Proctor found it very plentiful in Iceland. In the winter it is said to wander to Genoa, Madeira, Tripoli, and the Caspian Sea.

This bird is given by Professor Reinhardt as one of the most common and abundant of the resident species of Greenland. According to the observations of Sir James Ross, it inhabits nearly all parts of the Arctic Regions, having been met with in the highest latitudes then attained by man. It is extremely numerous during the summer season along the west coast of Prince Regent's Inlet, where, in several places peculiarly well fitted for breeding stations, it congregates in inconceivable numbers. The party under the command of Ross killed enough to supply themselves with several meals, and found it excellent eating, and the flesh free from any unpleasant flavor. Except in the fall, winter, and early spring, this species is not found south of the St. Lawrence; but it is numerous after September and until April in the Bay of Fundy, and along the New England coast; it even extends its visits to Long Island and New Jersey, but is not common there.

According to information obtained by Sir John Richardson, the Kittiwake abounds in the interior of the Fur Countries, on the coasts of the Pacific, and also on the shores of the Arctic Seas, where it breeds. The young appear in considerable numbers in the autumn on the muddy shores of Hudson's Bay, after which they retire to the southward. The food of this species consists chiefly of small fish and marine and fresh-water insects. This bird is mentioned by Dr. Bessels among those secured in Captain Hall's expedition in the "Polaris." Mr. H. W. Feilden also states that he saw a few Kittiwakes flying over the open water in the vicinity of Port Foulke, July 28, 1875, but did not observe any to the northward after entering the ice of Smith's Sound; and in 1876, as the Expedition returned south, none of these birds were seen until the north water of Baffin's Bay was reached.

The Kittiwake was met with constantly by Mr. Kumlien from the Straits of Belle Isle northward; and from September until the ice covered the water it was seen in very great numbers. Where the tide ran strongly, these birds followed the stream for many miles in regular order, half the number constantly dipping into the water, the rest flying on a few feet farther.

The Kittiwake is occasionally taken at Bermuda in the winter. Mr. Hurdis states that its presence there is usually in consequence of the violent westerly gales prevailing at that season.

Audubon found it breeding on the Gannet Rocks of the St. Lawrence, where it continues to do so in large numbers; and this is probably its most southern breeding-place on the Atlantic. Dr. Bryant did not meet with any on the coasts of Maine, New Brunswick, or Nova Scotia.

In England the young and the old Kittiwakes are popularly regarded as being two distinct species. The former is known as the "Tarrock," and the latter as the "Kittiwake," from the cry of this Gull when disturbed at its breeding-stations, as its three notes, uttered in quick succession, resemble this word. Yarrell quotes an interesting account of a young Kittiwake which had been reared from its nest, and which became quite domesticated, and so strongly attached to its benefactors that although left at full liberty, it would mate during the summer, inhabiting the cliffs on the coast of the Isle of Wight, and in the winter returning to live with its friends. It was so familiar with those persons it knew, that it would enter their cottages and eat from their hands; but would not permit the approach of a stranger.

The nests of this species — found on Gannet Rock, in the St. Lawrence — are described by Audubon as placed on narrow ledges, and composed of eel-grass and other coarse grasses from the upper portions of the island. The surfaces of the nests were quite flat, although some were several inches in thickness, and appeared to have been added to from year to year. The sitting birds remained persistently on their eggs, seldom flying off, but merely moving to one side. The male birds were exceedingly clamorous, flew around the party in great concern, and showed much courage. The eggs are described as being of a light olive-green color, marked with numerous irregular spots of dark brown. Their average length was 2.25 inches, and their breadth 1.87.

The form found on the Pacific shores, and known to some writers as the *Rissa Kotzebui*, differs so little from the common *R. tridactyla* that it can only be regarded as a very proximate variety. Its habits and general peculiarities are not in any wise different, but it appears to be confined exclusively to the waters of the North Pacific, where it is chiefly found in the Aleutian Islands and on the northeastern coast of Asia. Mr. Dall states that this variety was found by him frequenting the regions about the peninsula of Aliaska at all seasons, but was seldom known to come into the harbor except during storms. A pair came into Ilinliak Harbor, in Unalashka, whenever in the course of the winter a severe gale was blowing on the outside, but were not seen under any different circumstances. They were considered by Mr. Dall as presenting well-marked differences in their appearance from the Common Kittiwake, as well as from the *R. brevirostris*, which is so very common in the Prybilof Islands.

According to the observations of Mr. Elliott, these birds breed in the Prybilof Group, by tens of thousands, in company with the *brevirostris*, coming at the same time, but laying a week or ten days earlier. In all other respects the two correspond in habits, and are present in just about the same numbers.

Two examples of this species were obtained at Sitka by Bischoff. The young were shot at Amak Island, north of Aliaska, by Captain Smith. This bird is abundant at Sitka, and also at Plover Bay, Siberia.

Mr. Dall, in his Notes on the Aleutian Islands, mentions his obtaining its nests, eggs, and young about July 11, 1872, at Round Island, Coal Harbor, Unga Island, Shumagins. It was also common at Delaroff Harbor, Unga, and was seen at Kadiak. On entering Coal Harbor he was struck with a peculiar white line which wound round the precipitous cliffs of Round Island, that was found to be caused by the presence of these birds. The nests in their position were unlike anything he had ever seen before. They appeared as if fastened to the perpendicular face of the rock; but a close examination showed that two parallel strata of sandstone projected irregularly from the face of the cliff for a distance of from one to four inches, and that the nests were built where these broken ledges afforded a partial support, although the shelf thus originated was seldom more than half as wide as the nest. The line of nests followed the winding projections of these ledges, the material used being dry grasses agglutinated together, and also secured in the same way to the rock. Each nest had a very shallow depression at the top, in which were two eggs. The whole had an intolerable odor, and the nests were very filthy. The birds hardly moved at the approach of an intruder; only those within a distance of a few yards left their posts. Mr. Dall took away a nest containing two young ones, and the parent bird, coming back soon after, was astonished at their mysterious disappearance, and evidently suspecting foul play on the part of her nearest neighbor, began a furious assault upon the latter. A few eggs were obtained in a moderately fresh condition, but most of those seen were far advanced toward hatching.

Mr. Dall adds that the Kittiwake manifests great curiosity, sending out scouts whenever any unusual object approaches. If not molested, these scouts soon return to the flock, and the whole then proceed to investigate the phenomenon. This bird is described as having a shrill, harsh cry as well as a low whistle, the former being the one generally uttered when it is alarmed, and the latter being addressed to their young, or used in communication with each other. After the young are fully fledged the parent birds leave the harbors, and are found during winter off shore, except in heavy storms.

At Delaroff Harbor Mr. Dall found the nests attached to the sides of the bare rocks and pinnacles of scoriaceous lava near the entrance. The slight ledges and projections being so small as to be invisible at a short distance, the nests appeared to be fastened, like those of the Swallow, to the perpendicular faces of the rocks; and the appearance they presented was very remarkable.

In building its nest — as Mr. Elliott states — this species uses more grass and less mud than the *brevirostris*, and its eggs are more pointed at the small end than those of the last-named bird, the ground-color being also lighter, with numerous spots and blotches of dark brown. The chicks cannot with certainty be distinguished from those of the *brevirostris* until two or three weeks have elapsed after they have been hatched.

The eggs of the Pacific variety — collected from Round Island, Alaska, by Mr. Dall, and from the Prybilof Islands by Mr. Elliott — vary in length from 2.20 to 2.35 inches, and in breadth from 1.60 to 1.65. The ground-color of some is a pale brownish gray, that of others is a pale greenish gray. The markings are more or less scattered, are rather faint, slightly longitudinal and zigzag in their shape, of lilac-gray, mingled with other markings of a dilute umber. The eggs are somewhat uniform in their appearance, and do not exactly correspond with any of the common *R. tridactyla* which I have ever met with. But this variation, although thus constant, is not greater than that which has been found to occur in other instances in eggs of the same species taken at different localities which were at some distance from each other.

Rissa brevirostris.

THE RED-LEGGED KITTIWAKE.

Rissa nivea, GRAY, Gen. B. III. 1845 (not of PALLAS, 1826). — LAWR. in Baird's B. N. Am. 1858 855. — ELLIOT, Illustr. Am. B. pl. 54.
Larus brachyrhynchus, GOULD, P. Z. S. 1843, 106; Zool. Voy. Sulph. 50, pl. 34 (not of RICHARDSON, 1831).
Larus (*Rissa*) *brevirostris*, "BRANDT," BRUCH, J. f. O. 1853, 285. — COUES, B. N. W. 1874, 647.
Rissa brevirostris, LAWR. in Baird's B. N. Am. 1858, 855. — BAIRD, Cat. N. Am. B. 1859, no. 674. — RIDGW. Nom. N. Am. B. 1881, no. 659. — COUES, 2d Check List, 1882, no. 784.
Larus brevirostris, COUES, Key, 1872, 315; Check List, 1873, no. 553; in Elliott's Alaska, 1875, 199.
Larus Warneckii, COINDE, Rev. et Mag. Zool. 1860, 401.

HAB. Coasts and islands of the North Pacific, south to the Prybilof Group and Aleutians.

SP. CHAR. Feet deep coral-red or vermilion in the adult. *Adult, in summer:* Mantle deep bluish plumbeous (decidedly darker than in *R. tridactyla*, nearly the same shade as in *Larus atricilla*), the secondaries broadly and somewhat abruptly tipped with white. Primaries not lighter than the back, the exterior quill with the outer web black, the next nearly (sometimes quite) so, the next three with a large subterminal space of black extending from about 2.50 inches on the third to about .75 of an inch (more or less) on the fifth, these three quills tipped with plumbeous; remaining quills bluish plumbeous, the inner webs broadly edged and the outer tipped with white; sixth quill usually with a black spot near the end of the outer web. Remainder of the plumage snow-white. Bill yellow, sometimes tinged with greenish; rictus and inside of mouth orange-red; naked eyelids vermilion; iris dark brown (STEJNEGER, MS.). *Adult, in winter:* Similar, but nape tinged transversely with pale pearl-blue, the auriculars crossed by a bar of plumbeous. *Young, first plumage:* Similar to the adult, but nape crossed by a band of blackish plumbeous, another across the auriculars, and a suffusion of the same in front of the eyes. Primary coverts and outer webs of three or four exterior primaries black, but no other black or dusky on wings or on tail. Bill black or dusky; feet brownish. *Downy young:* Not distinguishable from that of *R. tridactyla*.

Wing, about 13.00 inches; culmen, 1.20; depth of bill through base, .50; through angle, .42; tarsus, 1.25; middle toe (with claw) nearly 2.00.

Our knowledge of the habits and geographical distribution of this species is somewhat limited, though considerably increased by the investigations of Mr. H. W. Elliott in the Prybilof Islands, where it is abundant. Its peculiar habits do not appear to be essentially different from those of the common Kittiwake. It is probably more or less common both to these islands and to the sea-coast of both shores of the North Pacific Ocean and of the Behring Sea.

Mr. Dall, in his Notes on the Birds of the Aleutian Islands, speaks of it as very common in the Prybilof Islands; and in his paper on the Birds of Alaska mentions it as occurring by thousands over a small lake on St. George's Island, where it was very conspicuous from its coral-red legs and feet — this rendering clear to him that it must be the true form originally described by Brandt. The specimens in the collection of the Smithsonian Institution, which while differing from this in no other respect were found to have yellowish legs, and were at first an occasion of doubt, prove to be identical with this, the yellow color having been found to be the result of drying. Mr. Dall rightly conjectured that this is the same species as that since described by Gould as *Larus brachyrhynchus,* from Kamtschatka. Examples of the present species were obtained by Captain Smith, Aug. 15, 1868.

Mr. Henry W. Elliott makes the following remarks in regard to this species as observed by him in the Prybilof Islands: —

"This beautiful Gull, one of the most elegant of birds while on the wing, seems to favor these islands with its presence to the exclusion of other lands, coming by tens of thousands to breed. It is especially abundant on St. George's Island. It is certainly by far the most attractive of all the Gulls, its short, symmetrical bill, large hazel eye, with crimson lids, and bright red feet, contrasting richly with the snowy-white plumage of the head, neck, and under parts. Like the *Larus glaucus,* it remains about the islands the whole season, coming on the cliffs for the purpose of nest-building, breeding by the 9th of May, and deserting the bluffs when the young are fully fledged and ready for flight, early in October.

"It is much more cautious and prudent than the 'Avrie,' for its nests are placed on almost inaccessible shelves and points, so that seldom can a nest be reached unless a person is lowered down to it by a rope passed over the cliff. Nest-building is commenced by this bird early in May, and not usually completed much before the 1st of July. It uses dry grass and moss, cemented with mud, which it gathers at the margins of the small fresh-water sloughs and ponds scattered over the islands. The nest is solidly and neatly put up, the parent birds working in the most diligent and amiable manner.

"Two eggs are the usual number, although occasionally three will be found in the nest. If these eggs are removed, the female will renew them in the course of another week or ten days. The eggs are of the size and shape of those of the common Hen, colored with a dark gray ground, spotted and blotched with sepia-brown patches and dots. Once in a while an egg will have on its smaller end a large number of suffused blood-red spots.

"Both parents assist in the labor of incubation, which lasts from twenty-four to twenty-six days. The chick comes out with a pure white downy coat, and pale whitish-gray bill and feet, resting helpless in the nest while its feathers grow. During this period it is a comical-looking object. At this age the natives capture them and pet them, leaving a number every year scattered through the village, where they become very tame; and it is not until fall, when cold weather sets in, and makes them restless, that they leave their captors and fly away to sea."

Mr. Elliott further states that this bird is very constant in its specific characters. Among thousands of them he has never observed any variation in the coloration of the bills, feet, or plumage of the mature bird, with one exception. There is a variety, seldom seen, in which the feet are nearly yellow, or more yellow than red, and the edge of the eyelid is black instead of scarlet; there is also a dark patch back of each eye. The color of the feet may be only an accidental individual peculiarity; the dark eye-patch and absence of bright color from the eyelids may depend upon the season.

Eggs of this species (Smithsonian Institution, No. 16326) collected by Mr. Elliott from St. Paul's Island, in the Behring Sea, have an average length of 2.20 inches, and a breadth of 1.55. Their ground-color is a dull brownish white, varying to a light drab, with intermediate shades of grayish buff, marked with blotches of a sepia-brown color and of raw umber; these are underlain by two shades of cloudings of a lilac-gray. Three eggs in my own collection measure 2.10 inches by 1.62; 2.22 by 1.68; 2.25 by 1.66. The ground-color of two is tinged with greenish, and that of the other with a reddish hue.

Genus **LARUS**, Linnæus.

Larus, Linn. S. N. ed. 10, I. 1758, 136; ed. 12, I. 1766, 224 (no particular type indicated).
Leucus, Kaup, Nat. Syst. Eur. Thierw. 1829, 86 ("includes *L. marinus, glaucus*, and *fuscus*").
Laroides, Brehm, Vög. Deutschl. 1831, 738 ("includes most of the European hoodless Gulls").
Gavina, Bonap. Naum. 1854, 212 ("For *L. canus* and allies and for *L. adouini*." — Saunders).
Chroicocephalus, Eyton, Brit. B. 1836, 53 (type, *Larus capistratus*, Temm. ?).
Atricilla, Bonap. Naum. 1854, 212 (type, *A. Catesbœi*, Bp. = *Larus atricilla*, Linn.).
Dominicanus, Bruch, t. c. 100 (type, *Larus marinus*, Linn.).
Glaucus, Bruch, J. f. O. 1853, 101 (type, *Larus glaucus*, Linn.).
Blasipus, "Bp." Bruch, J. f. O. 1853, 108 (type, *Larus modestus*, Tschudi).
Melagavia, Bonap. Naum. 1854, 213 (type, *Larus Franklini*, Sw. & Rich.).

Char. Size exceedingly variable, ranging from that of the smaller Albatrosses down to that of the medium-sized Terns; tail even; tarsus always longer than the middle toe with its claw (except in *L. minutus*), and smoothish behind; colors extremely variable, but young always widely different from the adult.

The genus *Larus*, in the comprehensive sense in which we have here, for reasons stated on p. 196, adopted it, includes many very dissimilar forms, which probably represent distinct genera. The North American species may be defined as follows: —

A. *Adult with the entire head, neck, lower parts, and tail pure white.* (**Larus**, Linn.)

a. Mantle very pale pearl-blue; primaries the same, fading into white toward the ends.

1. **L. glaucus**. Wing, 16.75–18.60 inches; culmen, 2.15–2.65; depth of bill through the angle, .75–1.00; tarsus, 2.30–3.00; middle toe, 1.95–2.50. Eyelids in summer adult, reddish purple; feet flesh-color. *Hab.* Circumpolar Regions, south, in winter, to Long Island, the Great Lakes, and North Pacific.

2. **L. leucopterus**. Wing, 15.40–16.50 inches; culmen, 1.65–1.90; depth of bill through angle, .60–.70; tarsus, 2.05–2.20; middle toe, 1.70–1.95. Eyelids in summer adult, flesh-color; feet inclining to orange-red. *Hab.* Same as *L. glaucus*.

b. Mantle pale pearl-blue; primaries similar, but abruptly tipped with white.

3. **L. Kumlieni**. Five outer primaries marked with slate-gray spaces immediately before the white tips; color of the mantle as in *L. leucopterus*, and size about the same. Eyelids in summer adult reddish purple, or purplish flesh-color; feet flesh-color. Wing, 15.00–17.00 inches; culmen, 1.60–1.90; depth of bill through angle, .55–.66; tarsus, 2.10–2.40. *Hab.* North Atlantic coast, breeding in Cumberland Sound, and migrating south in winter to Nova Scotia, New Brunswick, and New York.

4. **L. Nelsoni**. Similar in plumage to *L. Kumlieni*, but much larger. Wing, 18 25 inches; culmen, 2.35; depth of bill through angle, .80; tarsus, 3.05; middle toe, 2.40. *Hab.* Norton Sound, Alaska.

5. **L. glaucescens**. Five outer primaries without slate-gray spaces before the white tips. Wing, 16.25–17.30 inches; culmen, 2.20–2.60; depth of bill, .80–.90; tarsus, 2.35–2.90; middle toe, 2.05–2.45. *Hab.* North Pacific coast of North America, south to Washington Territory; Cumberland Gulf.

c. Mantle dark slate, dark plumbeous, or blackish; primaries similar, marked at and near the ends with white.

6. **L. marinus**. Mantle dark slate, or blackish slate, without blue shade. Wing, 17.60–19.50 inches; culmen, 2.40–2.60; depth of bill through angle, .98–1.05; tarsus, 2.70–3.10; middle toe, 2.10–2.50. *Hab.* Coasts of the North Atlantic; in America, south to Long Island and Great Lakes.

7. **L. schistisagus**. Mantle deep dark plumbeous, or dark bluish slate. Eyelids in summer adults, reddish violet-gray; iris light yellow; feet pinkish flesh-color. Wing, 18.10 inches; culmen, 2.35; depth of bill through angle, .90; tarsus, 2.75; middle toe, 2.40. *Hab.* North Pacific, chiefly on the Asiatic side, but also occasionally along the coast of Alaska (Port Clarence; Bean).

d. Mantle some shade of bluish gray; primaries marked with black and white at and near the ends.

8. **L. occidentalis.** Mantle deep plumbeous. Wing, 15.25–17.00 inches; culmen, 2.00–2.35; depth of bill at angle, .85–.95; tarsus, 2.45–2.65; middle toe, 2.00–2.45. Bill deep yellow, the mandible with a red subterminal spot; eyelids red; iris brown; legs and feet pale flesh-color.[1] *Hab.* Pacific coast of North America.

9. **L. affinis.** Mantle deep plumbeous. Wing, 16.60–17.20 inches; culmen, 1.92–2.10; depth of bill through angle, .76; tarsus, 2.24–2.50; middle toe with claw, 2.24. Bill yellow, with a red spot near the end of the mandible and a red tinge to the maxilla in front of the nostril; iris yellow; eyelids orange-red or vermilion; legs and feet yellow.[2] *Hab.* Northern part of Palæarctic Region; Greenland.

10. **L. argentatus.** Wing, 15.75–17.50 inches; culmen, 1.95–2.50; depth of bill through angle, .70–.85; tarsus, 2.30-2.80; middle toe, 1.85–2.25. Mantle pale pearl-blue. Bill deep yellow, the mandible with red subterminal spot; eyelids yellowish; iris silvery white or pale yellow; legs and feet flesh-color. *Hab.* North America in general, but rare on the Pacific coast; Europe.

11. **L. cachinnans.** Mantle deep cinereous-blue. Wing, 15.15–18.30 inches; culmen, 1.90–2.20; depth of bill through angle, .60–.80; tarsus, 2.15–2.50; middle toe, 1.60–2.15. Bill deep yellow, the mandible with a red subterminal spot; eyelids orange-red; iris pale yellow; legs and feet bright yellow. *Hab.* Northern Asia and North Pacific coast of North America, south, in winter, to California.

12. **L. californicus.** Mantle deep cinereous-blue (precisely as in *L. cachinnans*). Wing, 15.00–16 75 inches; culmen, 1.65–2.15; depth of bill through angle, .60–.75; tarsus, 2.00–2.60; middle toe, 1.70–1.95. Bill deep yellow, the mandible with a red subterminal spot enclosing a dusky one, with a corresponding dusky spot near end of the maxilla; eyelids vermilion-red; iris deep brown; legs and feet pale grayish pea-green. *Hab.* Western North America, from Western Mexico to Alaska (interior waters chiefly).

13. **L. delawarensis.** Mantle pale pearl-blue (much as in *L. argentatus*). Wing, 13.60–15.75 inches; culmen, 1.55–1.75; depth of bill through angle, .50–.65; tarsus, 1.90–2.45; middle toe, 1.30–1.60. Bill greenish yellow, crossed near the end by a blackish band, the tip sometimes tinged with orange; eyelids vermilion-red; iris clear pale yellow; legs and feet pale yellow, sometimes tinged with greenish. *Hab.* North America in general.

14. **L. brachyrhynchus.** Mantle pale ashy blue (intermediate in shade between *L. argentatus* and *L. californicus*). Wing, 13.20–14.50 inches; culmen, 1.25–1.70; depth of bill through angle, .40–.50; tarsus, 1.70–2.10; middle toe, 1.30–1.55. Bill yellowish green, somewhat glaucous, the tip and cutting edges yellow; eyelids orange-yellow; iris brown; legs and feet bluish green, the webs yellowish. *Hab.* Interior of Arctic America; Pacific coast, south to Washington Territory.

15. **L. canus.** Mantle pale ashy blue (as in *L. brachyrhynchus*). Wing, 13.90–14.50 inches; culmen, 1.35–1.60; depth of bill through angle, .45–.50; tarsus, 1.90–2.25; middle toe, 1.35–1.45. Bill greenish olivaceous (in the dried skin), the terminal third yellow; eyelids vermilion-red; iris grayish brown; legs and feet yellowish green. *Hab.* Palæarctic region; casual in Labrador.

B. *Adult with the lower parts plumbeous or dusky, like the upper; tail wholly or chiefly black or dusky; bill red.* (**Blasipus**, Bonap.)

16. **L. Heermanni.** *Adult:* Ash-gray below, and plumbeous-slate above; head white in summer, dusky in winter. Secondaries broadly tipped with white; tail dusky black, tipped with white; bill red, usually tipped with black; eyelids red; legs and feet black. *Young:* Sooty grayish brown, the feathers of the upper parts bordered with grayish

[1] An adult obtained by Mr. L. Belding at La Paz, Lower California, in February, appears to have had bright yellow legs and feet!

[2] We are unfortunately not able to give a satisfactory diagnosis of this form, which is admitted by good authorities to be a quite distinct species.

white; bill brownish, black terminally. Wing, about 13.15 inches. *Hab.* Pacific coast, from British Columbia to Panama.

C. *Adult with the head and upper part of the neck black in summer, forming a well-defined "hood;" plumage of the lower parts rose-tinted; size medium to very small; the bill slender.* (**Chroicocephalus,** EYTON.)

a. Tarsus longer than the middle toe and claw.

17. **L. atricilla.** Bill and feet dark brownish red, the former sometimes tipped with brighter red; eyelids dull red; iris dark brown; hood dark sooty-slate; mantle deep plumbeous-slate. Wing, about 13.00 inches. *Hab.* Atlantic coast of America, south to the Lower Amazon, north, casually, to Maine; Pacific coast of Central America; casual in Europe.

b. Tarsus shorter than the middle toe and claw.

18. **L. Franklini.** Bill and feet carmine-red; iris dark brown; hood plumbeous-black; mantle deep bluish-plumbeous. Wing, about 11.25 inches. *Hab.* Interior of North America, migrating south over the most of Central and South America, and breeding chiefly north of the United States.

19. **L. philadelphiæ.** Bill uniform deep black; legs and feet fine orange-red in summer, flesh-color in winter; iris dark brown; hood dark plumbeous; mantle delicate pearl-blue. Wing, about 10.25 inches. *Hab.* North America in general, but not south of the United States, except in Bermudas; breeding far northward.

[**L. minutus.** Bill reddish dusky; legs and feet vermilion- or coral-red; hood deep black; mantle delicate pearl-gray; primaries without any black markings. Wing, about 8.75–9.00 inches. *Hab.* Palæarctic Region.[1]]

Larus glaucus.

THE GLAUCOUS GULL.

Larus glaucus, BRÜNN. Orn. Bor. 1764, 44. — FABR. Faun. Grœnl. 1780, 100. — GMEL. S. N. I. ii. 1788, 600. — NUTT. Man. II. 1834, 306. — AUD. Orn. Biog. V. 1839, 59, pl. 396; Synop. 1839, 329; B. Am. VII. 1844, 170, pl. 449. — LAWR. in Baird's B. N. Am. 1858, 842. — BAIRD, Cat. N. Am. B. 1859, no. 656. — COUES, Key, 1872, 311; Check List, 1873, no. 543; 2d ed. 1882, no. 768; B. N. W. 1874, 620. — SAUNDERS, P. Z. S. 1878, 165. — RIDGW. Nom. N. Am. B. 1881, no. 660.

Larus hyperboreus, GUNN. in Leem's Lapp. Beskr. 1767, 283. — STEJN. Proc. U. S. Nat. Mus. V. 1882, 39.

Larus glacialis, "BENICKE," MACGILL. Mem. Wern. Soc. V. pt. i. 1824, 270.

Larus giganteus, "TEMM." BENICKE, Ann. Wetterau. Gesellsch. III. 1814, 140.

"*Larus consul,* BOIE, Wiedemann's Zool. Mag. I. 126" (SAUNDERS).

Larus leuceretes, SCHLEEP, N. Ann. Wetterau. Gesellsch. I. 1819, 314.

Larus islandicus, EDMONST. Mem. Wern. Soc. IV. 1822, 185 (nec EDMONST. op. cit. p. 506 = *L. leucopterus*).

Larus Hutchinsii, RICH. F. B. A. II. 1831, 419 (note). — COUES, Pr. Acad. Nat. Sci. 1862, 294. — ELLIOT, Illustr. Am. B. II. pl. 53.

HAB. Circumpolar Regions, south in winter to Long Island, the Great Lakes, and North Pacific.

SP. CHAR. *Adult, in summer:* Mantle very pale pearl-blue; primaries still paler pearl-blue, or bluish white, fading gradually into white at ends, their shafts yellowish white or pale straw-color. "Iris golden yellow; eyelids orange-yellow; bill lemon-yellow, greenish toward tip, crimson spot on lower mandible; tarsi and toes flesh-color" (L. KUMLIEN, MS.[2]). *Adult,*

[1] The characters of this species are given on account of its possible occurrence in North America.

[2] According to Audubon, the adult male has the bill, etc., colored as follows: "Bill gamboge-yellow, with a carmine patch toward the end of the lower mandible, and the edges of both mandibles at the base of the same color. Edges of eyelids red, iris yellow. Feet flesh-colored, claws yellowish." The young are described as having the bill yellow to beyond the nostrils, the end black; the feet flesh-colored, with dusky claws; and the iris brown.

in winter: Similar to the summer plumage, but head and neck streaked with pale brownish gray. "The bill is wine-yellow, the lower mandible with an orpiment patch near the end; the edges of the eyelids pale yellow; the feet flesh-colored, the claws bluish black" (MACGILLIVRAY). *Young, first plumage:* Ashy white, more or less tinged with pale brownish ash below, the upper parts more or less mottled transversely with the same; head and neck faintly streaked with the same. Terminal third of bill dusky, basal portion flesh-color; legs and feet flesh-color; "iris yellowish brown" (KUMLIEN, MS.).[1] *Young, in second winter:* Wholly pure *white*, the bill and feet colored as above. *Downy young* (No. 76217, Kingwah Fiord, Cumberland Gulf, June 24, 1878; L. KUMLIEN): Grayish white, paler below; head and neck irregularly marked with scattered large spots of dusky; back, wings, and rump irregularly clouded with dark grayish. Bill brownish, crossed by a broad dusky band; feet light brown.

Adult.

Total length, 28.50 to 32.00 inches; extent, 57.00 to 65.00; wing, 16.75–18.60 (17.93); culmen, 2.15–2.65 (2.44); depth of bill through angle, .75–1.00 (.85); tarsus, 2.30–3.00 (2.70); middle toe, 1.95–2.50 (2.26). [Fourteen specimens.]

There is a very great amount of individual variation in this species, some specimens being hardly distinguishable from *L. leucopterus*, while others are larger than the average of *L. marinus*. We have found it exceedingly difficult, with a series of eighteen examples of both species before us, to define the limit between *glaucus* and *leucopterus*, the coloration being quite the same in the adult stage, and the individual variation in each so great that they very nearly intergrade, notwithstanding the vast difference in size between the largest specimens of the former and the smallest of the latter. The variation in size seems to be individual and sexual rather than local.

The Burgomaster Gull appears to be confined, during the summer, to the northern shores of the Atlantic and Pacific oceans, and to the connecting portions of the Arctic Sea. It is peculiarly a high northern species, being found in the Arctic Regions of Europe and Asia, and in the more northern portions of North America. In the Pacific it appears to be to a large extent replaced, on the American shore, by the *glaucescens*.

Messrs. Evans and Sturge, in their visit to Spitzbergen, found it breeding in im-

[1] Macgillivray ("Hist. Brit. B." V. 563, 564) describes the fresh colors of the bill, etc., in the young as follows: "*Young:* The bill is horn-color, or pale yellowish gray; the upper mandible brownish black beyond the nostrils; the lower beyond the angle. The feet are flesh-color; the claws lightish brown. *Young, in third winter:* The bill is yellowish flesh-color, with only a dusky spot on each mandible toward the end; iris dull gray; the edges of the eyelids yellow; the feet flesh-color; the claws light grayish black."

mense numbers. They speak of its nest as being large and untidy, formed of seaweed, and usually containing three eggs. The nests were found on the shore, or, more often, on the low rocks, and in one or two instances were even built on masses of ice. This Gull was observed to act in a very tyrannical manner toward the weaker birds in its vicinity. Its plumage was so very dense that it could only with the greatest difficulty be penetrated by shot. Its eggs were hardly distinguishable from those of *Larus marinus*.

Young.

Professor Alfred Newton, in his paper on the Ornithology of Spitzbergen, speaks of finding this Gull far less numerous than the Kittiwakes, but probably extending its range along the entire coast of the country.

Sir James Ross refers to this species as being abundant on the shores of Low Island, although it was not seen north of latitude 81°. Professor Newton's friend, who went to the eastward from the Thousand Islands, met with many young Burgomaster Gulls about half-fledged; and he was informed by his pilot that they had been found breeding, in the summer of 1859, on Gilies Land. Dr. Malmgren reported this species as breeding in incredible numbers on Bear Island; he also remarked that it chooses the highest parts of the cliffs for nidification. He likewise found it breeding high up on the mountain sides, apart from any other species. When in Loon Bay he saw one of these Gulls swoop down like a Falcon upon a young *Uria grylle*, seize it in its beak, and devour it on the projecting point of the nearest rocky cliff, where the numerous skeletons bore witness to its rapacity at previous times.

Middendorff includes this species among the birds of Siberia, and places it in the list of those which penetrate to the most northern portions of that country. Mr. G. Gillett, in his Notes on the Birds of Nova Zembla, mentions finding it abundant everywhere in that region. It was noticed all along the coast, both on the eastern and on the western sides, and did not confine itself to the ice as much as do some of the other species. In this same locality Von Heuglin reports it as pretty common southward as far as Jugors Strait. Mr. R. Swinhoe ("Ibis," April, 1874) reports this species as having been seen at Hakodadi, Japan, in March.

Mr. Wheelwright was informed that the Glaucous Gull breeds occasionally on the coast of East Finland. The eggs are two — seldom three — in number, and are rather smaller than those of the *marinus* — which, however, they closely resemble, although their ground-color is lighter, and the markings are smaller.

In Great Britain this Gull is a winter visitor only; and is a winter resident in the more northern of the Shetland Islands, where it arrives late in the autumn and leaves late in the spring. It is also of occasional occurrence in the winter on the coast of England and of Ireland. A single specimen of this bird was killed in the interior of Scotland, on Loch Lomond.

In Iceland, according to Faber, this species is present through the year — keeping to the open sea in the winter, and breeding, in the summer, on the rocks of the southern and western coast, in company with *Larus marinus* — these two species being much alike in nest, eggs, and habits. This Gull attacks smaller birds, and robs their nests of eggs and young; it feeds also on crabs, shellfish, and the *Cyclopterus lumpus*, or Lump Sucking-fish. It is said to be more numerous than *L. marinus.*

In North America this bird is of rare occurrence in winter on any part of the coast, except about the Bay of Passamaquoddy, where, as well as in the Bay of Fundy, it is not uncommon. It is of occasional occurrence as far west as Long Island; but those seen are nearly all in immature plumage, an adult individual being rarely taken. Mr. Giraud was not aware that a single specimen of this Gull in adult plumage had ever been observed on Long Island; and it is very seldom seen even in its immature dress.

Dr. Walker mentions having met with it on the coast of Greenland, in the vicinity of the port of Frederikshaab, and afterward in Melville Bay, near Cape York. In May, 1859, while he was in Bellot's Bay, Dr. Walker noticed it evidently moving to the northward. He afterward met with it building its nest on the high cliffs which form the sides of Bellot's Strait. This bird is also mentioned by Professor Reinhardt as being one of the residents of Greenland.

Hearne, in his account of his journey to the Arctic Sea, notes the occurrence of what is without doubt this species, which he speaks of as the White Gull. He mentions its visiting Hudson's Bay in great numbers, both on the sea-coast and in the interior; and thinks its range must extend across the continent. It makes its first appearance about Churchill River about the middle of May, builds its nests on the islands in the lakes and rivers, lays two speckled eggs, and hatches its young in June. The eggs are said to be good eating; and the same is true of the flesh of those birds found in the interior, notwithstanding the fact that they feed on fish and carrion. This Gull prolongs its stay on Hudson's Bay as late into the fall as the frost will permit of its procuring a livelihood.

Sir John Richardson states that during the summer this species inhabits Greenland, the Polar Sea, Baffin's Bay, and the adjoining coasts and straits in considerable numbers. It is notoriously greedy and voracious, preying on fish, young birds, and carrion. A specimen killed on Ross's expedition, when struck, disgorged a Little Auk entire, and was found on dissection to have another in its stomach. It is described as being a shy and inactive bird, except when impelled by hunger; and it has none of the clamorousness of other Gulls. Richardson describes its eggs as being of a pale purplish gray, with scattered spots of umber-brown and subdued lavender-purple.

Though of rare occurrence, occasional instances are known of the appearance of this Gull in midwinter on Lake Michigan.

As described by writers who have enjoyed favorable opportunities for studying its peculiarities, the habits of this bird are strongly marked, and differ in many respects from those of most of the genus. Its favorite resorts are the entrances of the more exposed bays, or the open ocean a few miles off the land. There it assiduously attends the fishing-boats for the purpose of picking up any offal which may be thrown overboard. This Gull may without difficulty be taken by a hook and line, fish being used as bait. It is ordinarily shy; but when allured by carrion ceases to be so, and even appears to be indifferent to danger. It will then venture to enter the bays, and even inland waters. When feeding in company with other species, its appearance is peculiar and striking. Its bearing is grave, dignified, and silent, this bird exhibiting none of the liveliness so characteristic of its tribe. When it flies it extends its wings more than most of the genus do, and its flight is more buoyant. When not in quest of food it is shy and retiring, soars out of reach of the fowling-piece, and at intervals is heard to utter a hoarse scream — making a noise unlike that of any other species. This bird has none of the social affections so characteristic of most Gulls and Terns, prompting them to hazard their own lives when their kindred are in trouble; but when once alarmed it instantly flies off. Rev. W. Scoresby, in his account of the Arctic Regions, refers to the Burgomaster as being the chief magistrate of the feathered tribe in the Spitzbergen Region, where none of its class dare dispute its authority. It attends the whale-fishers, hovers over the scene of action; and on its descent, the most dainty pieces must be relinquished, even if already in the grasp of Fulmar Petrel, Ivory Gull, or Kittiwake. This bird seldom alights on the water; and when it rests on the ice it selects a hummock and fixes itself on the highest point. Its eggs were found by Mr. Scoresby on the beach of Spitzbergen, deposited in the same manner as those of a Tern, in depressions in the shingle just above high-water mark, and exposed to the full rays of the sun.

Mr. MacFarlane found the Glaucous Gull breeding on islands in the Arctic Sea. In the sixteen nests in regard to which information is given, the eggs were three in number in three instances, and two in nearly all the others. In no case were more than three found. The nest was generally a mere depression scantily lined with decayed reeds or grasses. In one instance two eggs of this Gull and one egg of the Black Brant were seen in the same nest, which was being incubated by one of this species. The egg of the Goose contained an embryo in a more advanced state than those of the Gull. Both parents were seen, and both were very noisy; making a stout resistance, and trying to drive the intruders off. The female was shot. In another instance both birds were said to be very bold, and several times very nearly struck the man who took the eggs.

Mr. E. Adams mentions this Gull as being among the first to arrive at Norton Sound ("Ibis," 1878); several were seen about the edge of the ice May 2. They bred in the cliffs of some small islands near St. Michael's. The natives value them for their quills — using the back of the shaft for attaching their fishing-lines to the hooks.

Mr. R. Kennicott secured an example of this species, September 17, in the Hudson's Bay Territory. It was seen by Mr. MacFarlane at various localities on the Arctic coast east of Anderson River, in July, 1863; at Liverpool Bay, on islands in Franklin Bay, June and July, 1864; on islands in Liverpool Bay, July, 1874; on islands in the Lower Anderson River; also on the Yukon River by Mr. Dall; and at St. Michael's by Messrs. C. Pease, R. D. Cotter, and H. M. Bannister. It is given by Dr. Bessels as among the birds secured by Captain Hall's party in the Polaris Expedition. The British expedition of 1875 did not find it breeding north of Cape Sabine, but stray individuals were observed as far north as lat. 82° 34′. It was not noticed after Sept. 1, 1875; and did not reappear until the middle of June in lat. 82° 27′ N.

Mr. H. W. Elliott found this species abundant in the Prybilof group, where it appeared to be restricted by its own choice to Walrus Island; although it was seen sailing over and around all the islands in easy graceful flight at every hour of the day; and frequently, late in the fall, would settle down by hundreds upon the carcases on the killing-grounds of the fur-seal. At Walrus Island it is resident throughout the season, and lays its eggs in neat nests built of sea-ferns and dry grass, placed among the grassy tussocks on the centre of the island. Though it is sometimes driven by the ice to the open water fifty to a hundred miles south, it returns immediately after the floe disappears. It lays as early as the first of June, depositing three eggs usually within a week or ten days. These eggs are large, spherically oval, having a dark grayish-brown ground, with irregular patches of darker brownish black. They vary somewhat in size, but the shape and pattern of coloring is quite constant.

The young Burgomaster comes from its shell, after an incubation of three weeks, in a pure-white thick coat of down, which is speedily supplanted by a brownish-black and gray plumage, with which the bird takes flight — having at that time nearly the size of the parent-bird. This dark coat becomes within the next three months nearly white, with the lavender-gray back of the adult. The legs change from a pale grayish tone to the rich yellow of the mature condition; and the bill also passes from a dull-brown color to a bright yellow, with red spots on the lower mandible.

This Gull has a loud shrill cry, which soon becomes very monotonous from its constant repetition. It also utters a low chattering croak while sailing around the islands. It is a very neat bird about its nest, and keeps its plumage in a condition of snowy purity. It is not seen in such large numbers as are several other species. In 1872, when Mr. Elliott visited Walrus Island, he estimated that there were not more than five or six hundred nests.

The egg of this species exhibits the same variations as to the shades of its ground-coloring as does that of the *argentatus* — being of a deep brown clay-color, a pale ash, a light pale clay, or a pearly white. The markings, which are small, and not very numerous, are deep bistre — almost black. The breadth of the egg is usually relatively greater than in other species.

Larus leucopterus.

THE WHITE-WINGED GULL.

Larus argentatus, SABINE, Trans. Linn. Soc. XII. 1818, 546 (not of BRÜNN. 1764).

Larus leucopterus, FABER, Prodr. Isl. Orn. 1822, 91. — SW. & RICH. F. B. A. II. 1831, 418. — NUTT. Man. II. 1834, 305. — AUD. Orn. Biog. III. 1835, 553, pl. 282; Synop. 1839, 327; B. Am. VII. 1844, 159, pl. 447. — LAWR. in Baird's B. N. Am. 1858, 843. — BAIRD, Cat. N. Am. B. 1859, no. 658. — COUES, Key, 1872, 311; Check List, 1873, no. 544; 2d ed. 1882, no. 769; B. N. W. 1874, 622. — RIDGW. Nom. N. Am. B. 1881, no. 661.

Larus arcticus, MACGILL. Mem. Wern. Soc. V. 1824, 268.

Larus glaucoides, "TEMM." MEYER, Taschenb. Vög. Deutschl. IV. 1822, 197. — TEMM. Pl. Col. 77e livr. Introd. Larus, 1828.

Larus islandicus, EDMONST. Mem. Wern. Soc. IV. 1823, 506 (nec *op. cit.* p. 185 = *L. glaucus*).

Larus minor, BREHM, Vög. Deutschl. 1831, 736.

Laroides subleucopterus, BREHM, t. c. 746.

Larus (*Glaucus*) *glacialis*, BRUCH, J. f. O. 1853, 101 (nec MACGILL. 1824).

HAB. Range about the same as that of *L. glaucus*. South in winter to coast of Massachusetts.

SP. CHAR. Similar to *L. glaucus*, but much smaller, the young darker colored. *Adult, in summer:* Mantle pale pearl-blue (a shade darker than in *L. glaucus*); remiges similar, but slightly paler, passing terminally into pure white. Rest of the plumage snow-white. "Bill bright orange-yellow, tipped with yellowish green; vermilion spot on lower mandible; tarsi and toes flesh-color; iris cream-color" (L. KUMLIEN, MS.[1]). *Adult, in winter:* Similar, but head and neck

[1] "Bill gamboge-yellow, with a spot of orange-red near the end of lower mandible; the angle of the mouth and the edges of the eyelids are also orange-red. Iris pale yellow. Feet pale flesh-color; claws grayish brown" (AUDUBON).

streaked with dusky grayish. "The bill is wine-yellow, the lower mandible with an orpiment patch near the end; the edges of the eyelids yellow; the feet pale flesh-colored, the claws grayish brown; the iris pale yellow" (MACGILLIVRAY). *Young, first plumage:* Grayish white, the head and neck broadly streaked, the upper parts coarsely spotted with brownish ash-gray; lower parts nearly uniform light brownish ash, the chin and throat white; bill wholly blackish; feet brownish. "The bill is very pale flesh-colored as far as the anterior extremity of the nostrils, beyond which both mandibles are brownish black. The feet are pale flesh-colored, the claws brownish black" (MACGILLIVRAY).[1]

Wing, 15.40–16.50 (15.76) inches; culmen, 1.65–1.90 (1.75); depth of bill through angle, .60–.70 (.66); tarsus, 2.05–2.20 (2.14); middle toe, 1.70–1.95 (1.81). [Four adults.]

This bird is so close an ally of *L. glaucus* that we must confess our inability to give characters whereby it may invariably be distinguished. There appears to be a nearly complete intergradation in size, or at least some of the larger males of *leucopterus* are equal to the smaller females of *glaucus*. A series collected at Point Barrow, Alaska, by Messrs. Murdoch and Smith, seems to include a form which is intermediate between the two; and we are quite in doubt as to which form some specimens should be referred. Mr. Kumlien ("Bull. U. S. Nat. Mus.," No. 15, p. 98), however, gives the following as characters which appeared to be constant in the living and freshly killed birds which came under his notice: —

"My opportunities for studying *leucopterus* were not very extensive, and my conclusions may be too hasty; but still it is worth while for others, that may get better opportunities, to observe if the following points of difference are constant: —

"First. *Leucopterus*, 24 inches or less; *glaucus*, 27 to 32 inches.

"Second. Tarsus and toes of *leucopterus* in fully adult birds often orange-red, and not flesh-colored, as in *glaucus*.

"Third. Ring around the eye in *leucopterus* flesh-colored; in *glaucus* reddish purple.

"Fourth. Young of *glaucus* in first plumage as light as the bird of the second year; the young of *leucopterus* nearly as dark as the young of *glaucescens*. The bill is also weaker and thinner than in *glaucus*."

The particulars of the history of this species and of the extent of its distribution are not so well known as they probably would be if its resemblance to *Larus glaucus* were not so close; the two species differing chiefly in that the latter is of larger size than the former. It is difficult, however, if not impossible, to distinguish the two when seen at some distance; and it is hence not always safe to apply to either species statements as to its actual presence, except only where the identification has been rendered positive by obtaining a specimen of the bird seen.

The Lesser White-winged Gull is an Arctic species, and its distribution is very nearly identical with that of the Burgomaster. It is found in the northern portions of Asia, Europe, and North America. Middendorff mentions it as one of the birds of Siberia, and includes it in his list of those which penetrate to the farthest north. Mr. Wheelwright was informed that this species breeds on the coast of East Finland,

[1] "Bill yellow, the tips black. Edges of eyelids pale reddish-orange; iris brown. Feet yellowish flesh-color; claws grayish brown" (AUDUBON).

and that it is only an occasional visitor, generally in the winter, to the other portions of the Scandinavian coast.

This Gull is occasionally seen in the winter on the coast of Great Britain and Ireland, where it was for a long while confounded with the larger Glaucous Gull. It is also found on the Faröe Islands and in Iceland — where, however, it is not known to breed. According to Faber, this is the only Gull which passes the winter in that island without also breeding there in the summer.

Sir James C. Ross, in his last Appendix, states that he found this species breeding on the face of the same precipices with *L. glaucus,* but at a much less height, and in greater numbers. He met with it in Greenland, and afterward in the Shetland Islands. During the first voyages of Ross, and also in those of Sir Edward Parry, many specimens were obtained in Davis Straits, Baffin's Bay, and on Melville Island. Through an error of Temminck, these birds were regarded as being an Arctic variety of *L. argentatus,* and were so described. This Gull is also mentioned by Dr. Walker as having been met with by him near Godthaab, in Greenland. Afterward, while at the mouth of Bellot's Strait, he noted its arrival in May. It was building its nest on the high cliffs which fringe the shores of that strait. It is also named by Professor Reinhardt as a resident species of Greenland, where it breeds, and where it is more or less common at all seasons. Mr. L. Kumlien found it in Cumberland far less common than the *glaucus;* while on the coast of Greenland it was, next to the Kittiwake, the most abundant Gull.

This species is occasional along the entire Atlantic coast in the winter, but is said to be rare near New York. Those individuals which are occasionally met with are chiefly immature birds. This Gull is more abundant in the Bay of Fundy, but is rare there in summer. An occasional pair has been known to breed among the outer islands. In the summer of 1850 I found a pair nesting on one of the Green Islands. The nest was placed on the ground, on the highest point of the land, on the top of a small hillock. This was the only Gull nesting on that island, although on all the others the nests of the *L. Smithsonianus* were quite abundant. The birds were not shy; but they kept out of gunshot, and watched our movements very closely. Unlike the Herring Gulls, they were very quiet, and uttered no sound or cry whatever. There were three eggs in the nest, which was very slightly made.

Mr. E. W. Nelson states that the White-winged Gull is a regular and not uncommon winter resident on Lake Michigan.

Faber was confident that none of this species breed in Iceland. Not an individual was to be seen on the rocks of Faxe and Bredebugt, where *L. glaucus* was breeding in large colonies. Just after the middle of September the first specimens, both old and young, make their appearance on the coast of Iceland, confining themselves to the northern part, among the small inlets, where great numbers pass the winter. Toward the end of April their numbers decreased, and by the end of May nearly all had disappeared. These birds were Faber's daily guests. They came on land to his winter dwelling, and snapped up the entrails thrown to them, fighting fiercely for them with the Ravens. One was so tame that it presented itself at his door every morning at a certain time, that it might be fed, and always gave notice of its arrival by a cry. This Gull would indicate to the seal-shooters in the fiord where the seals were to be looked for, by following their track to the sea, and hovering over them in flocks, with incessant cries. It is said to follow, in the same manner, the track of the codfish in the sea, in order to feed upon the booty hunted up by this fish. Faber further states that in the winter (1821) he passed at Debratte, on the southern coast, not a single bird of this species was to be seen. On the 1st of March the shore was free of Sea-Gulls; but early on the 2d the air was filled with numbers of this species which had arrived during the night. The Icelanders concluded from the sudden appearance of the birds that shoals of codfish must have arrived on the coast, and it was soon found that this conjecture was correct. And there, where but a short time before an ornithological quiet had reigned, everything became enlivened by the coming of these birds, which hovered over the nets without intermission, and with incessant cries. Faber afterward heard that this particular species of Gull had been very scarce during that winter on the northern coast, owing to the prevalence of ice. The birds seen by him remained on the southern coast until the middle of May, when they all departed northward to their breeding-places.

During the winter these Gulls were Faber's weather-guide. If they swam near the shore with their feathers puffed out, then on the following day storms and snow were to be expected. In fine weather the birds soared high in the air. These Gulls often sat by hundreds on a piece of ice, and in this way were drifted many miles. Their habits differ from those of the Glaucous Gull, which moves with more energy, while the *leucopterus* in its flight and deportment is the more graceful of the two. The latter is said to hover over its prey, to be somewhat greedy, always active, and never afraid to fight for its food with antagonists of equal or even superior strength.

Mr. Wolley kept one of these Gulls alive for several weeks when in Iceland. It had been caught with a fish-hook, and in a day or two became so tame as to eat in his presence.

Audubon observed but few birds of this species on the coast of Labrador, nor did he think that any were breeding there at the time of his visit. Their flight he speaks of as being similar to that of the Herring Gull, while the *leucopterus* is less shy, proceeds farther up rivers and creeks, and its notes are neither so loud nor so often heard as those of the other species.

Yarrell describes the egg of this Gull as being 2.50 inches in length by 1.75 in breadth, and of a pale greenish-white color, with numerous spots, and speaks of two shades of brown, with other spots of a bluish gray scattered generally over the surface.

Mr. MacFarlane procured several sets of the eggs of this species on the Arctic coast in July, 1863, and again in July, 1865.

Larus Kumlieni.

KUMLIEN'S GULL.

? *Larus* (*Glaucus*) *glaucescens*, Bruch, J. f. O. 1853, 101 (part?; nec *L. glaucescens*, Naum. 1840).
? *Larus* (*Laroides*) *chalcopterus*, Bruch, J. f. O. 1855, 22 (part?).
? *Larus chalcopterus*, Lawr. in Baird's B. N. Am. 1858, 843. — Coues, Pr. Phil. Ac. 1862, 295.
Larus glaucescens, Kuml. Bull. U. S. Nat. Mus. no. 15, 1879, 98 (nec Naum. 1840). — Brewst. Bull. N. O. C. VIII. no. 2, April, 1883, 125.
Larus Kumlieni, Brewst. Bull. N. O. C. VIII. no. 4, Oct. 1883, 216. — Park, The Auk, Vol. I. April, 1884, 196.

Hab. North Atlantic coast of North America; breeding in Cumberland Gulf (Kumlien), and visiting the northern Atlantic coast of the United States in winter. Grand Menan and Bay of Fundy (Brewster); mouth of Mohawk River, New York, Jan. 27, 1884 (Park).

Sp. Char. *Adult* ♂, *in summer* (No. 76225, U. S. Nat. Mus., Cumberland Sound, June 14, 1878; L. Kumlien): Head, neck, lower rump, upper tail-coverts, tail, and entire lower parts pure white; mantle and wings delicate pale pearl-blue, exactly as in *L. leucopterus* (and in the paler specimens of *L. argentatus*). Secondaries very broadly and very abruptly tipped with pure white.

Primaries pale pearl-blue, like the mantle, but the five outer primaries marked with deep ash-gray, as follows : the first quill has the outer web ash-gray to within three inches of the tip, measured along the shaft, and an inch farther along the edge ; the inner web has a paler ash-gray stripe about .25 of an inch wide next the shaft, and extending to within 2.75 inches of the tip ; the remainder, also the terminal portion of the outer web, being pure white. The second quill has no ash-gray on the inner web, which is very pale pearl-blue basally, and changing very gradually into pure white toward the end ; the outer web is pure white for the space of 2.50 inches from the

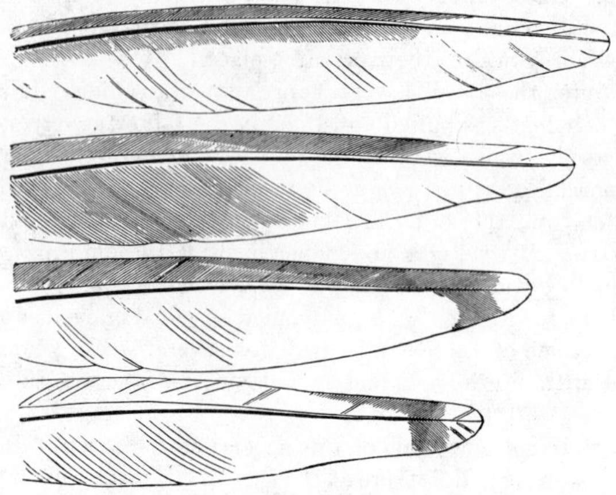

Larus Kumlieni.

tip (measured along the shaft), whence begins an elongated space of ash-gray, occupying the full width of the web for about 1.25 inches, then gradually narrowing toward the edge, and finally disappearing at a point a little more than six inches from the tip of the quill. The third quill has an abruptly defined white tip about half an inch in extent, this being immediately preceded by an ash-gray bar, more than half an inch wide, entirely across the inner web, and confluent with the space of the same color on the outer web, which extends toward the base of the feather for the distance of five inches from the tip, though occupying the full width of the web for only about two inches. The *fourth quill* is similarly marked, except that the ash-gray is fainter and less extended, especially on the outer web, where it follows the shaft for only the width of the bar on the inner web, while along the edge it reaches to a distance of less than 2.50 inches from the tip ; anterior to these gray spaces both webs are pure white for about 1.25 inches, when this color gradually changes to the prevailing pale pearl-blue. The *fifth quill* has the terminal two inches white, but this slightly relieved by a nearly obsolete small spot of light gray on each web, about .60 of an inch from the tip. The remaining primaries are uniform pale pearl-blue, with broad white tips, the two colors passing gradually together. "Iris cream-color ; bill yellow, with vermilion spot on lower mandible ; orbital ring reddish purple ; legs and feet flesh-color" (KUMLIEN, MS.). Total length (before skinning), 24.00 inches ; wing, 16.00 ; tail, 6.60 ; culmen, 1.90 ; depth of bill at base, .70, through angle, .65 ; tarsus, 2.40 ; middle toe, 1.95.

Adult ♀, *in summer* (No. 76229, U. S. Nat. Mus., Annanactook Harbor, head of Cumberland Gulf, June 20, 1824 ; L. KUMLIEN) : Similar to the adult ♂, as described above, but only four outer primaries marked with ash-gray, and the pattern of these markings somewhat different, as follows : On the outer web of the *first quill* the gray color is darker, inclining to slate-color ; on the *second quill* the spot near the end of the inner web is larger and more rounded ; the *third quill* has the subterminal gray band quite interrupted, the portion indicated being, in fact, very faint and badly defined ; and the *fourth quill* on one side is immaculate, while on the other there is a just perceptible indication of a spot near the tip of the inner web, while on the outer the gray space is much broken by a white freckling posteriorly. "Iris cream-color ; bill bright orange-yellow, tipped with yellowish green, and with vermilion spot on lower mandible ; ring round eye purplish flesh-color ; tarsi and toes flesh-color" (Kumlien, MS.). Total length (before skinning), 22.00 inches; wing, 15.00; tail, 6.40; culmen, 1.60; depth of bill through base, .60; through angle, .55; tarsus, 2.15.

In his original description of this species, Mr. Brewster gives the following measurements of additional specimens, which we have not had the opportunity of examining: —

(1) *Adult*, from Bay of Fundy (obtained about Nov. 1, 1881), mentioned by Mr. Brewster in "Bull. Nutt. Orn. Club," April, 1883, p. 125: "Wing, 16.00 inches; culmen, 1.88; bill from nostril, .88; gape, 2.75; height at nostril, .66; do. at angle, .66; tarsus, 2.25; middle toe and claw, 2.30; tail, 6.50."

(2) *Adult* ♂, Grand Menan, New Brunswick, Jan. 21, 1883: "'Length, 23.75 inches;' wing, 17.00; culmen, 1.85; bill from nostril, .89; gape, 2.75; height at nostril, .65; do. at angle, .65; tarsus, 2.30; middle toe and claw, 2.28; tail, 7.22."

(3) *Immature*, Bay of Fundy, February, 1883: "'Length, 23.50 inches; extent, 50.00;' wing, 15.50; culmen, 1.65; bill from nostril, .89; gape, 2.50; height at nostril, .56; do. at angle, .60; tarsus, 2.10; middle toe and claw, 2.15; tail, 6.90."

Another specimen, a female, apparently not quite in mature plumage, shot Jan. 27, 1884, on the Mohawk River, near its junction with the Hudson, and mentioned by Mr. Austin F. Park in "The Auk" for April, 1884, p. 196, measured as follows: "Length, 23.00 inches; extent, 51.75; wing, 15.75; bill, 1.60; from nostril, .80; from gape, 2.60; height at nostril, .60; at angle, .63; tarsus, 2.20; middle toe and claw, 2.25; tail, 7.00." Color of irides, one day after death, "pale grayish brown; of its bill, light watery yellow, with a greenish shade near the base, and a small red spot in a little cloud of dusky on each side of the lower mandible above the angle." Legs and feet flesh-color.

According to Mr. Brewster ("Bull. Nutt. Orn. Club," October, 1883, p. 218), the characteristics of this species "are pretty uniformly maintained" among the four specimens examined; "but there is some individual as well as seasonal variation. Thus Mr. Merrill's bird differs from the type in having a more decided approach to a subterminal bar on the second primary, where a transverse spot of gray on the inner web is continued across to the shaft, but fails to connect with a smaller corresponding spot on the edge of the outer web. It also has a dusky spot in front of the eye, and some obscure mottling on the crown and nape — probably seasonal (winter) characteristics.

"Mr. Smith's specimen is evidently immature. Its entire head and neck, and even the breast, are mottled with dusky, and the bill is greenish at the base. The mantle, however, is perfectly pure, and the wings show no traces of immaturity. The bill is much weaker and more depressed than in the other examples. The pattern of the primaries is essentially the same, but there is a greater extension of gray, especially on the first two feathers, where it occupies a longer space on the outer webs, and on the second primary forms a complete subterminal bar.

"In Mr. Welch's example the fifth as well as the second primary has a perfect subterminal bar, and the sixth shows an interrupted one; while the slate spreads over the greater part of the webs of the first three feathers, except terminally. This extension of the dark color restricts the white spaces at the ends of the second, third, fourth, and fifth primaries to rounded apical spots which resemble those of *glaucescens*. There is a further approach to *glaucescens* in the unusually deep shade of the mantle and the bluish cast of many of the light areas on the primaries; but the mantle is still much lighter than in any specimen of *glaucescens* which I have seen."

Mr. Park's specimen, according to Mr. Brewster ("The Auk," April, 1884, p. 196), is most nearly like Mr. Welch's among those he had previously examined. "The blue of the mantle is similarly deep, and the slate-gray of the primaries perhaps even more extended, the first three feathers having their outer webs almost wholly dark, except terminally, where the white apical spots, although present, are unusually restricted. . . . I may add that Mr. Park's specimen has an unusually short stout bill, which is further peculiar in having the superior outline of the maxilla almost perfectly straight from the base to the angle."

Larus Kumlieni is apparently a distinct species, having its nearest ally in *L. argentatus*, but related somewhat to *L. leucopterus*, and perhaps, as Mr. Brewster has suggested, also to *L. glaucescens*. From the latter, however, it seems to us to differ rather materially in size, in the form of the bill, and in the pronounced pattern of the quill-markings. The latter character, however, is, according to Mr. Brewster, somewhat variable.

In case the present bird should prove to be not a distinct species, only two possible explanations of its characters occur to us; namely: (1) That it may be a hybrid between *L. argentatus* and *L. leucopterus*; or (2) that it may represent extreme old age of the former. The first of these hypotheses is rendered extremely improbable from the fact that Mr. Kumlien found this bird breeding in considerable numbers near the head of Cumberland Gulf; while the second is disposed of by the circumstance that at least one of the known specimens is in immature plumage, but still possessing gray instead of black quill-markings, while specimens in the first plumage were also obtained by Mr. Kumlien.

Mr. Kumlien's account of this species (which he erroneously identified with *L. glaucescens*) is as follows: —

"So far as I am aware, this is the first instance on record of this bird being taken on the Atlantic coast. They are quite common in the upper Cumberland waters, where they breed. Arrived with the opening of the water, and soon began nesting. The nest was placed on the shelving rocks on high cliffs. Two pairs nested very near our harbor; but the Ravens tore the nest down and destroyed the eggs. Only a single well-identified egg was secured. This Gull is unknown to Governor Fencker on the Greenland coast. They remained about the harbor a great deal, and were often observed making away with such scraps as the cook had thrown overboard; were shy, and difficult to shoot. Full-grown young of this species were shot in the first days of September; these were even darker than the young of *L. argentatus*, the primaries and tail being *very nearly black*." [1]

Larus Nelsoni.

NELSON'S GULL.

Larus Nelsoni, HENSH. The Auk, Vol. I. July, 1884, 250.

SP. CHAR. *Adult* (No. 97253, U. S. Nat. Mus., St. Michael's, Alaska, June 20, 1880; E. W. NELSON): Mantle pale pearl-blue, exactly as in *L. argentatus*. Primaries same color as the mantle, but broadly tipped with white, and the outer five marked with deep brownish gray, as follows: First quill with the outer web deep brownish gray to within three inches of the tip (next to the shaft), the inner web rather lighter, more ashy, gray, for about the same distance, but broadly edged with white (the gray about .40 and the white .80 of an inch in width), this white confluent with that of the terminal portion. On the second quill the white tip is 2.40 inches long, the deep brownish gray space being 2.30 inches long next the shaft, but much more (some 4.50 inches) along the edge, the very oblique anterior outline being very sharply defined against the pale pearl-blue of the basal portion. The third quill has the tip white for .90 of an inch (measured along the shaft), the outer web then deep brownish gray for 2.70 inches; the inner web is pale pearl-gray, like the basal portion of the outer web, but at about 2.50 inches from the tip it fades gradually into white — which color, however, is interrupted near the end of the quill by an indistinct broad spot of mottled grayish, extending quite across the web. The fourth quill is white for about the terminal inch, the outer web then brownish gray for 1.10 inches along the shaft and 2.50 inches along the edge, the pearl-gray of the remaining portion perceptibly paler next the brownish gray space; the inner web has a very indistinct spot of brownish gray about opposite the end of the dark space on the outer web, the succeeding 1.40 inches being nearly white, but changing gradually into the light pearl-gray of the remaining portion. The fifth quill fades terminally into white at about 1.80 inches from the tip, but the white portion marked on both webs by a spot of brownish gray; that on the outer web 1.80 inches long on the edge of the quill, but less than half as much along the inner margin; that on the inner web about .50 of an inch broad, and much more distinctly defined than the corresponding spots on the third and fourth quills; neither spot touches the shaft. The remaining primaries are pale pearl-gray, fading gradually to white at the ends. The head, neck, rump, upper tail-coverts, tail, and entire lower parts are pure white. Bill deep wax-yellow, the tip whitish, the mandible with a large bright red spot at the angle. Wing, 18.25 inches; tail, 7.75; culmen, 2.35; depth of bill at base, .80, through angle, .80; tarsus, 3.05; middle toe, 2.40.

Although at first sight this bird has some resemblance to *L. glaucescens*, it may readily be

[1] "Bull. U. S. Nat. Mus." No. 15, pp. 98, 99.

distinguished by the very differently shaped bill, the paler color of the mantle, and the totally different markings of the primaries. It is, in fact, much more closely allied to the larger race of *L. argentatus*, the principal difference consisting in the brownish gray, and much more restricted, instead of black, spaces on the primaries. In all examples of *L. argentatus* we have been able to examine, the black portion of the primaries involves a considerable portion of the inner webs ; but in the present bird the darker color is confined almost entirely to the outer web, the inner webs being pale pearl-gray, like the mantle, and fading into white at the end of the quills.

It is barely possible that this specimen may represent a very old *argentatus* with the black faded to brownish gray, and unusually restricted on account of great age ; but until this can be proven we prefer to keep it separate. At any rate, *Larus Nelsoni* apparently holds exactly the same relation to *Larus argentatus Smithsonianus* that *L. Kumlieni* does to the smaller race of the Herring Gull.

Larus glaucescens.

THE GLAUCOUS-WINGED GULL.

Larus glaucescens, NAUM. Naturg. Vög. Deutschl. X. 1840, 351. — LAWR. in Baird's B. N. Am. 1858, 842. — BAIRD, Cat. N. Am. B. 1859, no. 657. — COUES, Pr. Ac. Nat. Sci. Philad. 1862, 295 ; Key, 1872, 311; Check List, 1873, no. 545 ; 2d ed. 1882, no. 770 ; B. N. W. 1874, 623. — SAUNDERS, P. Z. S. 1878, 167. — RIDGW. Nom. N. Am. B. 1881, no. 662.

Larus (*Glaucus*) *glaucopterus*, "KITTLITZ," BRUCH, J. f. O. 1853, 101.

"*Larus chalcopterus*," LAWR. in Baird's B. N. Am. 1858, 843 (not of LICHT. 1854). — BAIRD, Cat. N. Am. B. 1859, no. 659. — COUES, Pr. Ac. Nat. Sci. Philad. 1862, 295.

HAB. North Pacific coast of North America, from Washington Territory to Alaska.

SP. CHAR. *Adult, in summer:* Mantle delicate pearl-blue (deeper than in *leucopterus*); primaries similar, becoming slightly darker (the fourth and fifth abruptly) terminally, all abruptly tipped with white ; the outer quill with the tip and a space of an inch or more in extent anterior to a subterminal deep ashy spot white ; the sixth with a broad subterminal bar of deep ash, preceded and followed by white spaces. Rest of the plumage, including almost all the exposed portion of the secondaries, snow-white. *Adult, in winter:* Similar, but head and neck clouded (!) with sooty grayish. *Young, first plumage:* Prevailing color deep ash-gray, nearly uniform below, relieved above by a coarse irregular spotting of grayish white, or pale dull buff, the head and neck indistinctly streaked. Primaries and rectrices pale brownish gray, with somewhat of a glaucous cast. Bill wholly dusky, brownish basally ; legs and feet brownish. *Young, first winter:* Mantle mixed brownish ash and pearl-blue ; primaries and tail uniform brownish ash-gray ; head, neck, and lower parts grayish white, clouded with brownish gray, the lower surface nearly uniform brownish gray. Bill yellowish on basal half and tip, the intermediate portion dusky black ; legs and feet pale brownish (in skin).

Wing, 16.25–17.30 (average, 16.92) inches ; tail, 7.50–8.25 (7.81) ; culmen, 2.20–2.60 (2.42) ; depth of bill through angle, .80–.90 (.82) ; tarsus, 2.35–2.90 (2.62) ; middle toe, 2.05–2.45 (2.25). (Six adults.)

In this species the form of the bill approaches decidedly to that so characteristic of *L. occidentalis* and *L. dominicanus*, the angle being very prominent and the depth through the base proportionally narrow.

This large and handsome Gull bears a very close resemblance to, and is very nearly as large as, the Burgomaster Gull of the Atlantic coasts. It appears to replace that species in the southern portions of the Pacific waters. It is found on the northeastern coasts of Asia, and on the entire Pacific coast of North America almost as far south as the Mexican line. In most respects its habits appear to bear a very close resemblance to those of the *glaucus*, but it is not so exclusively northern as that species. It is abundant along the Arctic Ocean as far to the west as the Mackenzie River, along the banks of which it was found by Mr. Ross. It was met with on the shores of Vancouver Island by Mr. R. Browne; and Mr. Bischoff obtained a large number of specimens at Sitka, and others at Kadiak. Mr. Dall mentions it as being a common species on the west coast, from California northward. It also occurs as far east as Cumberland, where Mr. L. Kumlien found it quite common in the upper Cumberland waters, and where it was breeding. These Gulls came as soon as there was open water. Their nests were placed on the shelving rocks, on high cliffs. They are not known to occur on the coast of Greenland.[1]

Dr. Cooper mentions this as being an exclusively winter bird in California, where it makes its appearance in October in large numbers, wandering along the coast as far south as San Diego, and even farther, remaining until May. A few individuals in immature plumage occur all the year round.

This Gull feeds on dead animal matter of all kinds, as well as on fish and crustaceans; but it is very rarely seen in the interior, or far inland. Its voice is rather high, yet not loud or querulous, being very different from that of the noisy *occidentalis*, which in many other respects it very closely resembles. Dr. Cooper is quite sure that it does not breed on any island south of San Francisco, or on any part of the coast as far north as latitude 49°.

Mr. Dall found this species resident on all the Aleutian Islands which he visited, and by far the most abundant and prevalent, others being only occasionally observed. The habit of this and of other species of breeding on isolated rocks and small islands is attributed by him to their appreciation of the immunity thus obtained from the attacks of foxes on the eggs and the young broods. On the 2d of June, 1872, many eggs in a pretty fresh condition were obtained on the Chica Rocks and islets in the Akutan Pass. The eggs were very abundant, not more than three being usually found together, and they were laid in almost any small depression of the ground, with little or no attempt at a lining. About the 18th of July, in the Shumagins, at Coal Harbor, on a peculiar high round island, an abundance of eggs were obtained; but most of them had been incubated for some time. In this case, the island being covered with tall, rank grass, the nests were almost concealed; and either from the dead grass naturally occurring in the depression, or for some other reason, the nests all had more or less of this material in and about them. The Gulls built solely on the top of the highest part of the island, in the grass, and never in the lower portion near the shore, or on the shelves of the rocky and precipitous sides. Mr. Dall also states that this species is a resident of the Aleutian Islands throughout the year. The young of this bird were obtained in the down, about the middle of July; and the iris of these, as well as their bill and feet, was of a black color.

The late Mr. James Hepburn found this Gull breeding on Williamson's Rock, not far from Smith's Island, and near to and south of San Juan, in the Straits of San Juan de Fuca.

Eggs of this species in the Smithsonian Collection (No. 12852), obtained at Sitka, have a ground-color of a pale grayish drab, with markings of a pale lilac-gray and a rich dark sepia. The ground-color in various specimens varies from a pale blue to a brownish clay-color. Four eggs present the following measurements: 2.70 inches by 1.85; 2.80 by 1.90; 2.85 by 1.95; 2.75 by 1.95.

[1] Mr. Kumlien's observations here quoted relate to what has since been described by Mr. Brewster as *Larus Kumlieni*. — J. A. A.

Larus marinus.

THE BLACK-BACKED GULL.

Larus marinus, LINN. S. N. ed. 10, i. 1758, 136 ; ed. 12, I. 1766, 225. — NUTT. Man. II. 1834, 308. — AUD. Orn. Biog. III. 1835, 305 ; V. 1839, 636, pl. 241 ; Synop. 1839, 329 ; B. Am. VII. 1844, 172, pl. 450. — LAWR. in Baird's B. N. Am. 1858, 844. — BAIRD, Cat. N. Am. B. 1859, no. 660. — COUES, Key, 1872, 312 ; Check List, 1873, no. 546; 2d ed. 1882, no. 771; B. N. W. 1874, 624. — RIDGW. Nom. N. Am. B. 1881, no. 663.

Larus niger, BRISS. Orn. VI. 1760, 158.

Larus nævius, LINN. S. N. I. 1766, 225.

Larus maculatus, BODD. Tabl. P. E. 1783, 16 (nec BRÜNN. 1764).

Larus maximus, LEACH, Cat. 1816, 40.

Larus Mülleri, BREHM, Vög. Deutschl. 1831, 729.

Larus Fabricii, BREHM, t. c. 730.

HAB. Coasts of the North Atlantic ; in America, south in winter to Long Island and the Great Lakes?

SP. CHAR. Size very large (about equal to *L. glaucus*). *Adult, summer plumage:* Mantle dark brownish slate, the secondaries and tertials broadly (the former abruptly) tipped with white ; first primary black, with the end for a distance of about 2.50 inches, white ; second similar, but the white tip marked near the end by a broad black bar on one or both webs; fourth quill black, tipped with white ; fifth and sixth quills more slaty, tipped with white, and with a wide black subterminal space, preceded by an irregular white bar ; shorter quills lighter slate, widely tipped with white. Rest of the plumage pure white. "Bill gamboge-yellow, the lower mandible bright carmine toward the end ; edges of eyelids bright carmine ; iris silvery ; feet yellow ;[1] claws black" (AUDUBON). *Adult, in winter:* Similar to the summer plumage, but head and neck, superiorly and posteriorly, streaked with dusky. *Young, first plumage:* Above, dark slate-brown, the feathers broadly bordered with pale dull buff ; remiges uniform brownish dusky, with narrow whitish tips ; rectrices dusky, tipped with white and crossed near the end by a narrow band of grayish or brownish white. Head, neck, and lower parts dirty white, the head and neck, superiorly and posteriorly, streaked, and the lateral lower parts clouded or irregularly spotted, with grayish brown. Bill dusky, black terminally and brownish at the base ; iris dark brown ; legs and feet "dusky whitish" (COUES, MS.). *Downy young:* Prevailing color grayish white, the upper parts marbled or irregularly spotted with dull grayish. Head marked with numerous irregular spots of dull black, somewhat as follows : forehead with a narrow mesial streak ; crown with two spots, one behind the

[1] Other authorities give the color of the feet as flesh-color ; and it seems that Audubon made a mistake in calling them yellow. Macgillivray describes the fresh colors of the adult male in winter as follows : "The bill is light yellow, the lower mandible with an orange-red patch near the end; the edges of the eyelids orange-red, the iris pale yellow ; the feet flesh-colored, the claws dusky."

other, with a minute spot on each side, opposite the space between the two larger spots; occiput with four large spots arranged in a transverse series; below these, three others, their position corresponding to the spaces between the spots of the series above; below these three spots a ragged band across each side of the nape, the two separated by a considerable interval; then follow two or three spots across the lower part of the nape, their form and arrangement being rather indefinite. On the lores are three small spots arranged longitudinally; a spot over each eye; there are also several irregular large spots on the lower part of the head, rather less distinctly defined than the others. Total length, about 10.00 inches; bill (from culmen), 1.00 inch.[1]

Total length, about 30.00 inches; wing, 17.60–19.50 (average, 18.48); culmen, 2.40–2.60 (2.49); depth of bill through angle, .98–1.05 (1.01); tarsus, 2.70–3.10 (2.83); middle toe, 2.10–2.50 (2.34). (Five adults.)

The Great Black-backed Gull — or Saddle-back, as it is more commonly called on the American coast — is a North Atlantic species, common to both the European and the American coasts, and found as far north as the Arctic Circle. It also occurs in the Pacific, as Mr. Swinhoe met with it in Japan in May ("Ibis," 1874). It is found along the entire coast of Europe and North Africa, from Norway to Madeira; and it breeds from the northern coast of France and Great Britain northward.[2]

The Messrs. Godman found this species breeding in large numbers on all the islands off the coast of Norway; and Mr. Wheelwright also affirms that it breeds along the coast of Scandinavia as far as North Cape; but states that in the southern portion of that country it is more common on the Baltic shore than along the Cattegat and the North Sea. It also breeds sparingly on Lake Wener.

Mr. Godman, in his paper on the Birds of Madeira and the Canary Islands ("Ibis," 1871), states that several birds of this species followed his vessel from Lisbon until they were nearly in sight of the Canaries, although he did not afterward meet with any in that group of islands. He was informed, however, that these birds breed on the Island of Alegranza. Mr. Saunders found them not uncommon, in their immature plumage, on the coast of Spain; adults were comparatively rare.

According to Yarrell, this species is found throughout the year on various parts of the British coast. It does not, however, generally occur in large numbers, and is most frequently seen in pairs. It remains all the year on the flat shores at the mouth of the Thames, where it is a marsh-breeder; both male and female birds assisting in building their grassy nests, and driving other birds away.

According to Thompson, it is a resident species in Ireland. It is found in Wales in abundance on the extensive sandy flats of the coast; and it also breeds in Scotland in considerable numbers on Bass Rock, in the Firth of Forth, and in the firths of Sunderlandshire.

According to Mr. Hewitson, this Gull breeds in abundance on some of the islands of the Orkney and Shetland groups. There it selects with care a place surrounded by

[1] Described from No. 84765, from Labrador. It may be remarked with regard to the markings of the head, that while in the main those of the two sides correspond in position, some of them are asymmetrical; thus, the left lore has the three spots near together and roundish in form, the middle one above the others; the other lore has these spots much farther apart, in a line with one another, the middle one much elongated; there is but one spot over the right eye, two over the left.

[2] The bird found in the North Pacific is the closely allied *L. schistisagus*, recently described by Dr. Stejneger. — J. A. A.

the waters of some inland lake, on some spot difficult of access. The eggs, which are excellent food, are a valuable acquisition to the owners of the islands, and the birds are allowed to sit upon their third set only. One gentleman informed Mr. Hewitson that in a single season he had secured for winter use sixty dozen of the eggs of this bird on one island, although its extent scarcely exceeds half an acre.

This species is observed on the coasts of Germany, Holland, and France, is occasional in Italy, and was found by the Russian naturalists in the vicinity of the Caspian Sea.

On the American coast it appears to be present during the breeding-season from the Bay of Fundy to the coast of Greenland, and in the winter it wanders south as far as the coast of New Jersey. A few in immature plumage, according to Audubon, wander even to Florida.

According to Professor Reinhardt, it is a resident species of Greenland. It is rare in the summer in the Bay of Fundy. All that I met with there were in the immature plumage, and were apparently solitary and unmated birds. I saw none in the mature plumage; but was assured, however, that they do so occur, and that a few of them breed there. This species becomes quite abundant in that locality in the winter; and it is known as the "Farmer Gull" — a name indiscriminately given to the immature forms of two or three species, and hence having no specific significance.

According to the observations of Giraud, it is not, as a general rule, abundant on the coast of Long Island, although in certain exceptional seasons it has been seen there in considerable numbers.

This species is of rare occurrence at Bermuda, where a living specimen was taken Dec. 24, 1851. It is a not uncommon visitor to the Great Lakes during the winter, especially to Lake Michigan.

Audubon states that the shores of Labrador for an extent of three hundred miles afford stations to which this species resorts during spring and summer, where it is abundant, and breeds in large numbers. Its nest was usually found placed on the bare rock of some low island, sometimes beneath a projecting shelf, sometimes in a wide fissure. It is formed of moss and seaweed carefully arranged, has a diameter of about two feet, being raised on the edges to the height of five or six inches, and is seldom more than two inches thick in the centre, where feathers, dry grass, and other materials are added. The eggs — three in number — are described as 2.87 inches in length by 2.13 in breadth, broadly ovate, rough, but not granulated, of a pale earthy greenish gray color, irregularly blotched and spotted with brownish black, dark umber, and dull purple. The eggs are deposited from the middle of May to the last of June. The old birds do not leave their nests for any considerable length of time until after the young are hatched. Both sexes incubate, and supply each other with food. During the first week the young are fed with materials macerated by the parent bird; but afterward the supply is laid by their side. On being approached, the young endeavor to hide themselves; if as much as four or five weeks old, they escape to the water, and swim with great buoyancy. Their cry resembles that of their parents. Several young birds were kept alive by Audubon; these walked the deck with ease, and picked up the food thrown to them, and soon became quite tame and familiar, behaving themselves very much as vultures do.

This bird appears to feed indiscriminately on fish and on other productions of the sea. It is extremely ravenous, and when pressed by hunger it will attack the smaller Gulls. It is also accused of making murderous attacks upon various small land animals. When other food could not be obtained it has been known to frequent the sea-shore and to feed upon dead fish and such substances as are thrown up by the sea. It is exceedingly wary and difficult of approach. Its cry is loud and hoarse.

The flight of the mature bird of this species is firm and steady, rather than long protracted, and at times quite swift, and majestic when executed in extended circles. It usually proceeds in a direct course, with easy, regulated flappings, and in calm weather is fond of soaring to a great height. It is noisy during the breeding-season, but at all other times is comparatively silent. It swims lightly, but slowly; and if wounded may be readily overtaken, as it has no power of diving. The eggs and the young of this species are excellent eating; but the old birds are tough, strong, and unpalatable.

Dr. Sundström, of Stockholm — as quoted by Mr. Dresser — states that this Gull is regarded as a great pest in Sweden, and is destroyed wherever it can be approached, which is not often. It is very destructive of the eggs and young of the Eider and other wild Ducks, and destroys and devours quite large birds.

Mr. N. W. Johnson describes a nest observed by him in Shetland as placed on the ground, among the grass, large in size, and loosely put together. It covered a circle of two and a half feet in diameter, was deeply hollowed, and the materials used in its formation were dry tufts of grass, sheep's wool, heather-moss, and large feathers. When its nest is being robbed the great Black-backed Gull sails over head, occasionally making swoops at the intruder, and uttering loud, indignant croaks.

Dr. Bryant, in his visit to Labrador in 1860, mentions having found it breeding on almost all the grassy islands north of Romaine, and in greater abundance as he approached the Straits. He is quite sure that it is by no means so rapacious and tyrannical as it has been represented as being. On Greenlet Island — the abode of a great number of Eider Ducks — he found twenty-two nests of this bird, one of them not a foot from the nest of an Eider, both containing eggs. He did not see a single eggshell, or any appearance of eggs having been destroyed by the Gulls. This species is found in greater or less numbers on all the islands where the Herring Gulls breed, apparently on as good terms with them as with those of its own species. Dr. Bryant saw no peculiarity in the flight of this species to distinguish it from other Gulls. Its nest is oftener placed on the bare rock than is that of the Herring Gull, and is not infrequently found singly on some small rocky island — which is never the case with the other species. The eggs are three in number, and are generally easily distinguished from those of the Herring Gull by the color as well as the size. The spots are fewer and larger; and this difference is almost a specific character. A light clay is the prevailing ground-color, but it varies to a brownish gray or a brownish white. The markings are the same in respect to color as in the other species of this genus; but in size are smaller, and more rounded and regular.

Mr. Dresser describes the egg of this species as olive-brown in color, sometimes darker, and sometimes lighter, spotted, and blotched with dark brown. As compared with the eggs of *Larus glaucus*, it is darker, and has not the greenish tinge which usually pervades the eggs of the latter species. Dr. E. Rey, of Halle, gives as the average size of twenty-three eggs of this species: 2.83 inches in length, by 2.02 in breadth. The largest measured 3.21 inches by 2.05, and the smallest 2.71 by 1.94.

Larus schistisagus.

THE SLATY-BACKED GULL.

? *Larus* (*Dominicanus*) *fuscescens*, BRUCH, J. f. O. 1853, 100 (part).
Larus cachinnans, KITTL. Denkw. I. 1858, 336 (nec PALL. 1826). — STEJN. Naturen, 1884, 6.
Larus argentatus, var. *cachinnans*, SCHRENCK, Reise, Amurl. I. 1860, 504.
Larus marinus, SWINH. Ibis, 1874, 165 (nec LINN.). — SAUNDERS, P. Z. S. 1878, 180. — BLAKIST. & PRYER, Ibis, 1878, 217; Trans. Ass. Soc. Jap. VIII. 1880, 189; ib. X. 1882, 104. — SEEB. Ibis, 1879, 24. — RIDGW. Bull. Nutt. Orn. Club, 1882, 60. — BEAN, Pr. U. S. Nat. Mus. 1882, 168. — NELSON, Cruise of the Corwin, 1883, 107. — BLAKIST. Amend. List B. Jap. 1884, 20.
Larus pelagicus, TACZAN. Bull. Soc. Zool. France, 1876, 263 (nec BRUCH); Orn. Faun. Vost. Sibir. 1877.
? *Larus affinus*, NELSON, Cruise of the Corwin, 1883, 107 (Plover Bay).
Larus schistisagus, STEJNEGER, The Auk, Vol. I. July, 1884, 231.

HAB. North Pacific, chiefly on the Asiatic side. Japan (BLAKISTON & PRYER, SAUNDERS, and SEEBOHM, ll. c.); Amoor River (SCHRENCK); Behring Island and Petropaulski, Kamtschatka (STEJNEGER); Plover Bay? (NELSON); Unalashka (BEAN); Herald Island, Arctic Ocean, and Port Clarence, Alaska (RIDGWAY, l. c.).

SP. CHAR. *Adult* ♂ (No. 92825, U. S. Nat. Mus., Behring Island, Kamtschatka, May 5, 1883): Head, neck, rump, upper tail-coverts, tail, and entire lower parts pure white; mantle and wings deep plumbeous, or bluish slate-gray, much darker than in *L. occidentalis*, and altogether more bluish than in *L. marinus*. Four outer primaries slaty black, more grayish basally and on the inner webs, the latter fading into bluish gray toward the edge; outer quill with the terminal 2.10 inches (measured along the shaft) white, both webs with a small blackish spot on the edge, about .40 of an inch from the tip; second quill with the terminal white spot only .40 of an inch in extent, but the inner web with a large oval spot of white, .90 of an inch long, and extending entirely across, and situated .50 of an inch anterior to the terminal white spot; third quill with the terminal white spot about the same size as that on the second, the inner web with a grayish white space, beginning about 1.60 inches from the tip, abruptly defined, with a deeply convex outline, against the black subterminal portion, but not distinctly contrasted with the plumbeous-gray of the remaining portion of the web; fourth quill similar to the third, but the white spot rather more distinct, and beginning only 1.30 inches from the tip; fifth quill similar, but with the white spot on the inner web still larger and still nearer the tip (only 1.00 inch), and the outer web dark plumbeous-gray to within about 1.50 inches of the end, the extremity of this grayish portion obtusely wedge-shaped, and fading into white at the extremity; sixth quill without any distinct black spot on the inner web, which is white for about 1.80 inches (measured next the shaft) from the tip, the white rather abruptly defined against the plumbeous of the anterior portion; outer web white for .60 of an inch, then slaty black for about .70 of an inch (measured along the edge), the anterior outline deeply concave, and enclosing a rather indistinct grayish white space, which deepens gradually into the dark plumbeous-gray preceding it. Remaining primaries without any black, being uniform deep plumbeous, with very broad and rather abrupt white tips. "Iris clear naples yellow, or rather a yellowish cream-color; bill deep gamboge-yellow, with whitish tip and tomia; an orange-red spot on each side of the lower mandible; angle of the mouth yellowish flesh-color; naked eye-ring reddish violet gray; feet pinkish flesh-color, nails horny black, with whitish tips" (Colors of freshly killed bird, *fide* STEJNEGER, MSS.).

Wing, 18.10 inches; tail, 7.50; culmen, 2.35; depth of bill through base, .80, at angle, .90; tarsus, 2.75; middle toe, 2.40.

This species is apparently the North Pacific representative of *L. marinus*, from which it may easily be distinguished by the different color of the mantle, which is of a deep bluish slate, or plumbeous, without any of the brown tinge that is always seen in *marinus*. The latter has no gray "wedge" on the inner web of the first primary, and has on the second quill a subapical white crossbar. The white subapical spot on the third primary of *schistisagus* is altogether wanting in *marinus*.

From *L. cachinnans* the present bird differs in having a very much darker mantle (*cachinnans* being decidedly paler than *occidentalis*, while *schistisagus* is much darker), flesh-colored instead of yellow feet, in being of larger size, and in possessing other marked characters.

Little is known of the habits of this bird, which has been confounded by authors with various other species, as is indicated by the above synonymy. The only complete specimen which I have been able to examine is the type described above, and which I have been kindly allowed the privilege of describing in advance of the publication of Dr. Stejneger's description intended for the next number of the "The Auk." A much fuller account than that herein given will be published with Dr. Stejneger's important report upon the birds of the Commander Islands, now in course of preparation.

Larus occidentalis.

THE WESTERN GULL.

Larus occidentalis, AUD. Orn. Biog. V. 1839, 320; Synop. 1839, 328; B. Am. VII. 1844, 161. — LAWR. in Baird's B. N. Am. 1858, 845. — BAIRD, Cat. N. Am. 1859, no. 662. — ELLIOT. Illustr. Am. B. II. pl. 52. — COUES, Pr. Ac. Nat. Sci. Philad. 1862, 296; 2d Check List, 1882, no. 774. — SAUNDERS, P. Z. S. 1878, 172. — RIDGW. Nom. N. Am. B. 1881, no. 664.
Larus argentatus, var. *occidentalis*, COUES, Key, 1872, 312; Check List, 1873, no. 547 *b*.
Larus argentatus, c. *occidentalis*, COUES, B. N. W. 1874, 626.
"*Larus fuscus?*" SAUNDERS, P. Z. S. 1875, 158 (L. Calif.).

HAB. Pacific coast of North America, breeding from Southern California, northward.

SP. CHAR. Rather smaller than *L. argentatus*, except the bill, which is proportionally larger, with the angle of the mandible much more prominent; colors much darker. *Adult, in summer:* Mantle deep plumbeous, the secondaries and tertials very broadly (for one inch or more), and abruptly tipped with pure white. Four outer primaries black, more slaty basally, especially the fourth; outer quill with about two inches of its terminal portion white, crossed near the tip by a wide black bar, on one or both webs; second to fifth quills tipped with white, the fifth abruptly plumbeous for its basal (exposed) two thirds; sixth quill plumbeous, tipped with white, and with a broad subterminal bar of black; remaining shorter quills lighter plumbeous, more broadly and less abruptly tipped with white. Remainder of the plumage snow-white. Bill deep chrome- or wax-yellow, the broad part of the mandible marked by a spot of bright red; iris brown; feet yellow?[1] *Adult, in winter:* Similar, but the head and neck, superiorly and posteriorly, streaked with dusky. *Young, first plumage:* Above, brownish slate, irregularly spotted with grayish white; remiges, rectrices, and primary coverts uniform dull black, narrowly tipped with white; lower parts brownish gray, clouded or irregularly spotted with grayish white — the breast and abdomen sometimes nearly uniform grayish. Bill dusky black terminally, flesh-colored basally; iris brown; legs and feet flesh-color (pale brownish in skin). *Downy young:*[2] Grayish buffy white, the head marked with well-defined black blotches, of indefinite arrangement; upper parts clouded or irregularly blotched with brownish dusky. Lower parts (except throat) immaculate.

[1] Audubon gives the color of the feet in this species as flesh-color; but in recently prepared skins which we have examined the feet appear to have been rich yellow.

[2] Scarcely distinguishable from young of *argentatus*, but spots about the head blacker and more distinctly defined, the markings of the upper parts also darker.

Wing, 15.25–17.00 (16.10) inches; culmen, 2.00–2.35 (2.24); depth of bill through angle, .85–.95 (.88); tarsus, 2.45–2.75 (2.61); middle toe, without claw, 2.00–2.45 (2.26). [Eight adults.]

This species, both common on and confined to our northwest Pacific coast, was first described by Audubon from two specimens procured by Mr. Townsend in October, 1836, near Cape Disappointment. He furnished no account of its habits.

Mr. Henshaw mentions it as very numerous in all the bays and inlets of the Pacific coast, where its numbers are greater all the year round than those of any other species. Free from molestation, it has become almost semi-domesticated, and flies about the wharves and over the vessels with a fearlessness of long immunity from molestation. The rocky islets along the coast furnish these birds with safe breeding-grounds. At Santa Cruz thousands had congregated, and were nesting in early June. On one of the small adjoining islets, and the only one accessible, a few pair had nested. The nests were made of a generous supply of seaweed and similar materials, well matted together, the cavity being quite deep. It is probable that this species is also found on the Pacific shores of Asia, as Mr. H. Whitely states ("Ibis," 1867) that he procured several specimens at Hakodadi, in Japan, in December and January.

Dr. Cooper regards the *L. occidentalis* as at once the most abundant and the most characteristic species of the Californian coast. It is everywhere resident, and appears never to leave its home, unless possibly some of these birds residing in summer far to the north come down to California in the winter. Yet he noticed but little diminution in their number in winter north of the Columbia, although he found them in December common as far as the end of the peninsula of Lower California, which is about their southern limit. They breed through all the immense range from Cape Flattery to San Diego, and probably even farther in each direction. Dr. E. Palmer informs me that during his visit to San Diego he was surprised to witness the tameness and familiarity of this species. It wanders about the gardens, door-yards, and streets of that town in great numbers, mixing with the domestic Fowls, and gathers up and eats almost everything, not refusing even potato-parings. It is very tame notwithstanding the rough usage it receives from boys. Dr. Palmer saw numbers perched on the tops of buildings in rows intermingled with the domestic Pigeons. On the coast of California its chief breeding-places are the Farallones, Santa Barbara Island, and the Coronados, just south of the Mexican boundary line. Some of these birds, however, make their nests on isolated rocks and cliffs along the entire coast. On Santa Barbara Island there are great numbers of eggs laid; but fewer than formerly, on account of the depredations of the sealers and eggers, who rob these birds so often that few are able to hatch out any young, and then only very late in the season, or after the middle of June, although they begin to lay about the first of May — the time varying, however, considerably with the season and the locality. At the Farallones, in 1863, this species began to lay about the 6th of May; and in 1864, May 13, as Dr. Cooper was informed by Mr. Tasker, the keeper of the lighthouse.

The nest is constructed of pliable stalks of seaweeds and other vegetation, neatly matted together around a slight depression scooped in the ground. The eggs are two or three in number, and are described by Dr. Cooper as having in some instances a ground of pale gray, and in others an olive-brown hue, thickly blotched with dark brown of two shades, or of black. They measure from 2.70 to 2.90 inches in length, and from 1.80 to 2.00 in breadth. For about three weeks in May these eggs are carried in large quantities from the Farallones to San Francisco. After this time the Gulls are no longer molested, and only the eggs of the Murre are gathered. During Dr. Cooper's visit there in June he found numerous Gulls sitting, and saw the first eggs hatched on the 28th of that month — probably a month later than they would have been if the birds had not been disturbed. He saw young fledged Gulls at San Pedro as early as July 12 the previous year.

This species builds its nest both on the soft ground and on the bare rocks; but in the latter position the nest is much thicker than if built on the ground. There are certain localities on Santa Barbara Island which this bird prefers, and these are chiefly such as afford a good opportunity to see the approach of danger. There these birds sit in great flocks, the males and females taking turns on the nests; and when an intruder comes near, they all rise with deafening screams, circling round his head and darting toward him, although never daring to strike him, but snapping their bills sharply, and cackling as if in defiance. Their ordinary cry is a loud scream, which has an enlivening sound, and is uttered on all occasions, but especially when they find food; their first impulse apparently being to call their companions before beginning to eat. They are said to swim around the whale and the seal fishing places, and become so impudent as to steal the scraps almost from the try-pot; it is necessary, therefore, to shoot one occasionally as an example — a warning the meaning of which they are very quick to understand, soon appreciating the danger of having a gun pointed at them.

This bird is, in fact, very sagacious and amusing; and its habits often furnished Dr. Cooper with matter for interesting study on the most lifeless and dreary part of the coast. It deserves, in his opinion, to be regarded as the Raven of the sea; and its reputation for stupidity is not merited; although, unlike the Raven, it is not always as cautious and as distrustful of mankind as its safety demands. It is the Raven's superior in generosity and sociability, always sharing its food with its fellows, and congregating harmoniously in large flocks. It is very nearly omnivorous, although it probably never eats grain in an uncooked condition. Its flight is slow, being made by laborious flappings; although in windy weather it sometimes soars to a great height, circling around, and sometimes wandering far inland. This behavior is considered the sure forerunner of a storm.

When this bird depends chiefly upon small marine animals for its food, it feeds principally at low water, both by night and by day, its white eyes apparently enabling it to see at night; as is the case with many other nocturnal marine birds. No sooner does the tide begin to ebb, than hundreds of Gulls that have been dozing for hours on the beach, or, if the weather is calm, floating quietly on the water at a little distance, join the long train of screaming Godwits, Sandpipers, and Curlews flying to the sandbanks, river-shores, and mussel-beds, to feast until the returning tide drives them off. If a Gull finds a hard-shelled clam which it cannot break, it flies to some well-known hard sandbank or rock, and rising, by a circling flight, fifty feet or more, drops the shell. If it is not broken at the first fall, the operation is repeated until successful, the bird each time rising higher, or flying to a harder place, and as the shell falls, descending by short oblique turns to pick it up. Crabs, sea-worms, small fish, and even dead rats, this bird swallows whole, if possible, and its throat can be greatly distended. While resting, and digesting its food, it frequently remains asleep on the sand until floated off by the rising tide. But it is not easily approached if aware that it is being pursued, although at times it flies close to a person or a boat, screaming, and watching for some stray bits of food. It occasionally, but not often, dives for fish, catching them close to the surface like other Gulls; but can usually procure its food by easier modes, such as watching for fish at the edge of the rising tide. It also follows vessels, easily keeping up with the fastest steamers, which flocks of them always accompany, to pick up the scraps thrown overboard. It always keeps itself remarkably clean, and though not a brilliant, is always a beautiful bird.

The eggs of *L. occidentalis* do not differ much either in shape or size from those of *L. argentatus.* Their most common ground-color is a pale clay; but they vary from pearly white to grayish green, pale ash, or even deep brownish clay-color. The markings of the eggs of the former species are more numerous, and of a darker shade than those of the latter.

Larus affinis.

THE SIBERIAN HERRING GULL.

Larus affinis, REINH. Vid. Med. 1853, 78 (Greenland); Ibis, 1861, 17. — SEEBOHM & BROWN, Ibis, 1876, 452. — SAUNDERS, P. Z. S. 1878, 171.
Larus cachinnans, MEVES, Öfv. K. Vetensk. Ak. Förh. 1871, 786 (not of PALLAS, 1826).
Larus fuscus, JERDON, B. India, II. 1864, 830 (not of LINN. 1758).
Larus occidentalis, HUME, Stray Feathers, 1873, 273 (not of AUD. 1839).
Larus Heuglini, BREE, B. Eur. 2d ed. V. 1876, 58.

HAB. Northern part of Palæarctic Region; Greenland.

SP. CHAR. Similar in general appearance to *L. occidentalis,* but of quite different proportions, and the bill with the red spot continued, though more faintly, on to the upper mandible. Legs and feet yellow; eyelids orange-red or vermilion at all seasons.

There being, to our knowledge, no example of this species in American collections, and no more satisfactory description being at present accessible to us, we give below a translation of the original description by Dr. Reinhardt: —

"In the year 1851 the Royal Museum received from Nenortalik, in the district of Julianehaab, a remarkable Gull belonging to the *Glaucus* group of Bruch, which probably accidentally strayed to the Greenland coast; it is a full-plumaged bird, which has already the spotted head of the winter dress, but has not entirely completed its shedding, as the first three quills are not yet changed. In its plumage it shows considerable resemblance to *Larus argentatus;* but the back and the wings have a remarkably darker grayish blue color, which is even considerably deeper than in *Larus tridactylus;* besides, the head and throat are more densely and darkly spotted than ever appears to be the case in the first-named species. The quill-feathers resemble in the main those of *L. argentatus;* the first is brownish black [1] in the greatest part of its length, with the exception of a quite little slate-colored area on its inner surface nearest to the root, and ends in a white point two inches [2] long, which again a little before the end of the feather is furnished with a small black cross-band. On the other quill-feather the slate-gray spot is somewhat more extended on the inner surface, and the feather has indeed a white point, but wants a round spot of the same color, which in *L. argentatus* is found on the inner surface of this feather a little in advance of the tip. The remaining quill-feathers also have white points; but the grayish-blue color, which on the other quill-feathers has already begun to show itself also on the outer surface, spreads in these places more and more, until finally, on the sixth quill-feather, the black color is limited to a small cross-band just in front of the white tip. The shoulder-feathers also have white tips. The feet appear to have been of the same color as in *L. argentatus,* and the beak is yellow, with a bright red spot in front of the angle of the lower jaw, and a lighter tint of the same color on the upper jaw in front of the nostrils, which is likewise a continuation of the spot on the lower jaw.

"In size it is considerably smaller than the adult *Larus argentatus,* and agrees in this respect closely with the young of the latter species; but . . . it has the beak considerably larger, higher, and at the same time more powerfully constructed, than is the case in the young *argentatus.*

Total length	520 Mill.	Height of beak at angle of lower jaw	19 Mill.
Length of folded wing	420 "	Tarsus (foot-root)	56 "
Distance from forehead to tip of beak	48 "	Middle toe with claw	56 "
Distance from corner of mouth to tip of beak	74 "		

[1] "The brownish-black color of the first three quill-feathers is to a great extent only a result of fading, and will in the newly-grown feathers be deeper and purer."

[2] 2.00 Danish inches = about 2.06 English inches. — TRANSLATOR.

"That this Gull may already be considered a sufficiently established species is not my opinion; but, on the other hand, I could not well avoid designating it by a separate name, — partly because the differences from *L. argentatus* seem to me too great to suppose that it is an accidental variety of one of the races of this species, and partly because it has been impossible for me to refer it with any certainty to any other known Gull. In some respects it resembles Audubon's *L. occidentalis* from the west coast of North America; and I should be inclined to consider it this, did not Audubon expressly say of his species that it is just as large as *L. marinus* ('Orn. Biogr.' V. 320). Bruch, to be sure, attributes ('Journal für Ornithologie,' I. 101) a size to this species which agrees better with the Gull here mentioned; but how can this discrepancy be reconciled with the size of the two examples whose measurements Audubon gives, and on which he has established the species?"

In the "Ibis" for 1878, p. 489, are the following remarks by H. Gätke, on a specimen of this Gull obtained in Heligoland on the 20th of August of that year: —

"The coloration of the back and outer wing-coverts forms an exact middle shade between the slaty black of *L. fuscus* and the light gray of *L. argentatus*. The specimen being in the moult for its winter-dress, the marks on the feathers of the neck appear darker than those of any Gull I know of; in fact these arrow-shaped marks may be termed pure black.

"About the identity of the species no doubt whatever exists, as I have been able to compare the specimen with one of *L. affinis* in my possession, obtained by Dr. Otto Finsch on the Ob during his recent Siberian excursion."

The Siberian Herring Gull claims a place in the fauna of North America as a bird of Greenland — in which place, however, it is presumed to be only a rare and occasional visitor. It was first described by Reinhardt in 1853, from an immature specimen that had straggled to Greenland.

Middendorff met with this species, which he described as a variety of *L. argentatus*, on the southern shores of the Sea of Okotsk. Immature specimens had previously been taken on the Red Sea and on the Beloochistan coast; but the true specific relations of these birds had remained unexplained until they had been proved to belong to this species. The same is true of birds taken by Hume about Kurrachee, which he mistook for *L. occidentalis.*

We know as yet but little of the distinctive habits of this species. Its centre of distribution during the summer appears to be on the Petchora River, while in the winter it wanders to Southern Asia and Northern Africa; but how much farther is not known.

Messrs. Henry Seebohm and J. A. Harvie-Brown met with this species on the Petchora. It arrives in its spring migration at Ust-Zylma about the 11th of May, and breeds on the shores of the delta and the lagoons of the Petchora. Several of its eggs were procured; but these did not differ from those of the Herring Gull. Nearly all the birds met with on the Petchora were in the adult plumage.

Wherever a party of fishermen was stationed there were sure to be plenty of these Gulls. They hovered over the nets as they were being dragged in, and frequently secured the small fish as these attempted to escape.

Mr. Seebohm, in his paper on the Ornithology of Siberia ("Ibis," 1879, p. 162), mentions that they did not find this Gull breeding until after the party had reached latitude 69°. Its geographical distribution, as studied in the Museum of St. Petersburg, appears to show that it breeds in the extreme north of Europe and in Kamtschatka. It has been obtained, in the breeding-season, on Bear Island, south of Solovetsk, in the White Sea, on the Petchora, on the Ob, on the Yenesei, on the Boganida and the Taimyr, near Northeast Cape, and in Kamtschatka. In its spring and autumn migrations it has been found in the Caspian Sea, and at Ayan, in the Sea of Okotsk. Seebohm states that it is described as not being uncommon at St. Michael's, in Alaska; but this requires confirmation.

The eggs were found to vary somewhat in size and color, and were not distinguishable from those of *L. fuscus* or *L. argentatus*. Nor were the notes of this species distinguishable from those of *L. cachinnans* or *L. argentatus*.

Larus argentatus.

THE HERRING GULL.

a. Argentatus.

Larus cinereus, BRISS. Orn. VI. 1760, 160, pl. 14.

Larus argentatus, BRÜNN. Orn. Bor. 1764, 44. — GMEL. S. N. I. ii. 1788, 600, et AUCT. — SAUNDERS, P. Z. S. 1878, 167 (part). — COUES, Check List, 1873, no. 547; 2d ed. 1882, no. 772. — RIDGW. Nom. N. Am. B. 1881, no. 666.

Larus argentatus, a. *argentatus*, COUES, B. N. W. 1874, 625.

Larus marinus, var. *β*, LATH. Ind. Orn. II. 1790, 814.

Larus glaucus, RETZ. Fn. Suec. I. 1800, 156 (not of BRÜNN. 1764).

Larus argenteus, BREHM, Beitr. Vög. III. 1822, 781, 799 (part).

Larus argentatoides, BREHM, t. c. 791, 799 (part).

Laroides major, BREHM, Vög. Deutschl. 1831, 738.

Laroides argentaceus, BREHM, t. c. 742.

? Laroides americanus, BREHM, Vög. Deutschl. 1831, 743.

Goëland à manteau gris, BUFF. Hist. Nat. Ois. VIII. 1781, 406, pl. 32; Pl. Enl. 253.

β. Smithsonianus.

Larus argentatoides, BREHM, Beitr. Vög. III. 1822, 791, 799 (part). — SW. & RICH. F. B. A. II. 1831, 417 (?).

Larus argentatus, BONAP. Synop. 1828, 360, no. 300. — NUTT. Man. II. 1834, 304. — AUD. Orn. Biog. III. 1835, 588; V. 1839, 638; Synop. 1839, 328; B. Am. VII. 1844, 163, pl. 448. — LAWR. in Baird's B. N. Am. 1858, 844. — BAIRD, Cat. N. Am. B. 1859, no. 661. — COUES, Key, 1872, 312. — SAUNDERS, P. Z. S. 1878, 167 (part).

Larus Smithsonianus, COUES, Pr. Ac. Nat. Sci. Philad. 1862, 296.

Larus argentatus, var. *Smithsonianus*, COUES, Check List, 1873, no. 547 *b*.

Larus argentatus, b. *Smithsonianus*, COUES, B. N. W. 1874, 625.

Larus argentatus Smithsonianus, RIDGW. Nom. N. Am. B. 1881, no. 666 *a*. — COUES, 2d Check List, 1882, no. 773.

L. argentatus.

HAB. The var. *Smithsonianus*, North America in general, more especially the Atlantic coast, where extending from Labrador to Cuba; breeding from Eastern Maine northward; frequent throughout the interior, on the larger inland waters, and occasional on the Pacific coast. True *L. argentatus*, chiefly Palæarctic, but occasional, or casual, in Eastern North America, though apparently the predominant, if not exclusive, form in the region of Cumberland Sound.

SP. CHAR. *Adult, in summer:* Mantle pale pearl-blue (a shade darker than in *L. glaucescens*), the secondaries and tertials passing terminally into white. Outer primary black, more slaty basally, the tip white, and a large white spot across the inner, and sometimes the outer, web; next quill black, tipped with white, and usually without any white except the apical spot; third, fourth, and fifth quills similar, but the basal half or more light pearl-gray (this extending farther on the inner web), the line of demarcation sharply defined; sixth quill light pearl-gray, broadly tipped with white, this preceded by a broad subterminal space of black, widest on the outer web; seventh quill similar, but the black much more restricted, and confined to the outer web; remaining primaries pale pearl-gray, passing gradually into white at ends. Remainder of the plumage snow-white. Bill deep chrome or wax-yellow, with a large spot of bright red near the end of the mandible; eyelids bright yellow; iris silvery white or pale yellow; legs and feet flesh-color, claws brownish black. *Adult, in winter:* Similar, but head and neck, except underneath, streaked with dusky grayish. Bill pale grayish yellow, deepest on anterior half of maxilla, and inclining to flesh-color on basal portion of mandible, except along upper edge; angle of mandible with a large spot of dull orange-red, becoming dusky toward gonys; iris dull light yellow; eyelids dusky yellowish; legs and feet very pale grayish flesh-color. (Fresh colors of a specimen killed at Washington, D. C., Nov. 11, 1880.) *Young, first plumage:* Prevailing color brownish ash, nearly uniform below, the head and neck streaked with white; upper parts variegated by borders to the feathers and irregular spots of pale grayish buff; primary coverts, remiges, and rectrices blackish dusky. Bill dusky black, more brownish basally; iris brown; legs and feet purplish flesh-color in life, brownish in the dried skin. *Downy young:* Grayish white, the lower parts (except throat) immaculate; head marked with irregular spots of black, indefinitely distributed; back, wings, and rump clouded with dusky grayish. Bill black, the end yellowish; feet brownish.[1]

The fresh colors of the European bird (British specimens) are given as follows by Macgillivray ("Hist. Brit. B." V. 546, 551, 552): *Adult male, in winter:* "The bill is pure yellow, the lower mandible with an orange-red patch toward the end; the edges of the eyelids yellow; the iris pale yellow; the feet flesh-colored; the claws brownish black." *Young, in first winter:* "The bill is bluish black, the base of the lower mandible flesh-colored; the iris brown; the feet purplish flesh-colored." *After next moult:* "The bill is dull yellow, with a dusky patch on each mandible, and a little red on the lower; the iris yellow; the feet flesh-colored."

Wing, 16.25–17.50 (average, 17.15) inches; culmen, 1.95–2.50 (2.24); depth of bill through angle, .70–.85 (.80); tarsus, 2.30–2.80 (2.57); middle toe, 1.85–2.25 (2.10). (Twelve adults.)

[1] "Bill brownish black, paler at the base of the lower mandible. Edges of eyelids greenish gray; iris hazel. Feet purplish flesh-color; claws brownish black" (AUDUBON).

We find, upon the comparison of eleven adult American specimens with four adults of the European Herring Gull,[1] that the differences between the two, as stated by Dr. Coues, are quite constant, particularly as regards size, as may be seen from the following averages of each series: —

American specimens.

	Wing.	Culmen.	Depth of bill.	Tarsus.	Middle toe.
Average,	17.24	2.26	.80	2.57	2.10
Smallest,	17.00	1.95	.70	2.30	1.85
Largest,	17.50	2.50	.85	2.80	2.25

European specimens.

	Wing.	Culmen.	Depth of bill.	Tarsus.	Middle toe.
Average,	16.07	2.05	.76	2.38	2.00
Smallest,	15.75	1.95	.75	2.30	1.90
Largest,	16.25	2.15	.80	2.55	2.15

An adult female from Cumberland Sound (No. 76222; L. Kumlien) measures as follows: Wing, 16.25 inches; culmen, 1.95; depth of bill at angle, .75; the dimensions thus agreeing very closely with those of European specimens.

Assuming as one and the same species the Herring Gulls of the Atlantic coasts of Europe and America, we find for this species quite an extended range. The recent discoveries of Mr. Saunders, showing that on the Mediterranean this species is nearly or quite replaced by the *cachinnans;* and the more recent investigations of Mr. Ridgway, proving that the same replacement occurs on our Pacific coast — compel us greatly to diminish the area of distribution once attributed to this bird.

According to Mr. Ridgway, only a single example of this species has been detected on the Pacific shores; this came from British Columbia. Its area of range as given by Mr. Saunders is the northwest of Europe from the Varanger Fiord, the Baltic, and the western coast generally, down to North Africa, the Azores, Madeira, and the Canaries. It is in Greenland a rare straggler, but has been obtained at Winter Islands, near Melville Peninsula; it also occurs in the Hudson's Bay Territory, as far as Mackenzie River, and thence probably to the Pacific coast; since there is a specimen of this bird in the St. Petersburg Museum collected at Kadiak by Wosnessensky. Several specimens from the west coast of Mexico are in Mr. Saunders's collection. It also ranges down the American coast as far as Texas; and even visits Cuba and the Bermudas.

This is a common species in Great Britain, where it remains on the southern coast through the whole year, and in the summer breeds on all the sea-coasts and islands where these are bordered by high cliffs. It is everywhere a bold and familiar bird, fearlessly approaching the boats and nets of the fishermen. It is especially abundant on the islands of the Outer Hebrides, breeding on the coast, but not in the interior. The cliffs of Sumburgh Head — the southern termination of Shetland — is another point where it is very abundant. It is also very numerous in the Orkneys, in the Faröe Islands, and in Iceland. It is resident throughout the year on the coast of Holland and France; and during the winter on that of Spain.

It is one of the most common Gulls on the coast of Scandinavia, even extending its range as far as the North Cape; but it is not known to breed in the southern portion of the country, with the exception of the province of Gotland. The Isle of Sylt, in Denmark, is one of its great breeding-places; and here, according to Kjarbölling, from thirty to forty thousand of their eggs are annually collected for exportation.

[1] From Denmark, Germany, and the Orkneys.

Mr. Godman mentions finding this species common everywhere about the sea-coast and mountain-lakes of the Azores. It remains there throughout the year, but appears to be more abundant in the summer than in the winter. It breeds about the coast, and particularly on a small island near the southwest point of Fayal, which in June is covered with its nests. Mr. Godman also mentions finding this Gull the most common of its family about Madeira, and in all the islands of the Canary group. According to Mr. Saunders, it is abundant in winter on the coast of Spain, especially outside of the Straits of Gibraltar.

In North America this Gull is found throughout nearly its whole extent, being abundant on the Atlantic side during the winter, and in the summer breeding from Frenchman's Bay, on the coast of Maine, to Labrador. On the interior lakes it breeds from Superior to Slave, and northward of these almost or quite to the Arctic shores. Although Professor Reinhardt regards it as a rare, and even accidental, species in Greenland, it is mentioned by Dr. Walker, of the "Fox," as having been seen by him flying about in abundance at Frederikshaab.

Captain Blakiston received an example of this bird taken at York Factory; and Mr. Murray makes record of others received from Severn House, which is still farther north. Mr. Bernard Ross procured it on the Mackenzie River; and Mr. MacFarlane found it breeding on the Arctic coast between the Mackenzie and the Anderson rivers.

J. Elliot Cabot found it breeding on the shores and among the islands of Lake Superior; and Mr. Giraud has observed it on Lakes Ontario, Erie, Huron, and Michigan, as well as on the larger streams of the interior. It is more or less abundant on all our inland lakes and rivers during its periods of migration. In Southern Wisconsin it is quite common in the spring, arriving, as soon as the ice begins to loosen, along the shores, in the latter part of March. The full-plumaged old birds come first, and the immature ones — which appear to surpass the mature in number — arrive later, some not appearing until the first of June. None remain to breed. In fall they are not so abundant as in the spring.

This species was found breeding in great numbers at Fort Resolution by Mr. Kennicott; at Fort Simpson by Mr. B. R. Ross; at Fort Rae by Mr. Clarke; on Big Island by Mr. Reid; at Lake Winnipeg by Mr. Gunn; on islands in the Lower Anderson River, in June, 1863, by Mr. MacFarlane; also at Horton River and at Fort Anderson by the same; and at Fort Simpson by Rev. Dr. Kirkby.

Dr. Berlandier, of Matamoras, in his manuscript Notes of the Birds of the Lower Rio Grande, states that this Gull during the winter inhabits the marshes on the eastern coast of Mexico, but that it is seldom found in the swampy localities produced by the overflowing of the Rio Bravo del Norte in the vicinity of Matamoras.

The Herring Gull has been given by Mr. Bischoff as occurring at Plover Bay, in Eastern Siberia; by Mr. Bannister at St. Michael's; and is said by Mr. Dall to have been found on the Upper Yukon. But this last statement is an error, the species found having been *Larus cachinnans*, which replaces this bird on the Pacific coast. Only a single individual is recorded from British Columbia.

On Long Island this bird is common in the winter months from November to March, and resorts at low water, with the other species, to the bars and shoals, congregating in such large numbers as to line the shore for a considerable distance. At the influx of the tide it passes most of its time in the air, flying around in wide circles, and at times rising to a very great height. At other times it is observed to follow the shoals of fry, on which it depends for the greater portion of its support. It is incapable of diving, and can only secure its prey when this is near the surface of the water, in doing which it immerses only its head and neck. Major Wedderburn mentions the taking of a number of examples in Bermuda, Feb. 23, 1848.

Richardson states that this species — called by him *argentoides* — breeds on Melville Peninsula. He describes the eggs as having an oil-green color, and being marked with spots and blotches of blackish brown and subdued purplish gray. This bird is noted at Hudson's Bay for robbing the nets set in the fresh-water lakes.

In the summers of 1850 and 1851, spending several weeks on Grand Menan, in the Bay of Fundy — a locality visited by Audubon in May, 1833 — I found this species more or less abundant, and breeding on the ground on most of the uninhabited islands, and on the largest one breeding on the high, inaccessible cliffs, or very generally constructing nests high up in tall and almost inaccessible spruce-trees. Audubon was informed by Mr. Frankland, who lived on Whitehead — a part of Grand Menan, but insulated at high tide — that the remarkable habit of these birds of constructing their nests in trees had been acquired by them within his recollection; and that when he first settled there — many years before — these birds all built their nests on the moss of the open ground. They were induced thus to conceal their eggs and young in consequence of the depredations committed upon their nests; and they gradually began to put these on the trees in the thickest part of the woods. At the time I visited these islands an attempt had been made to arrest or limit these depredations; and persons were prohibited by the proprietors from taking any eggs after the 20th of June. The sparseness of the population, however, and the distance of most of these resorts from the oversight of those interested in enforcing these rules, rendered them almost inoperative.

A nest of one of this species, built near the top of a tall spruce, and at least sixty feet above the ground, was brought to me with its contents. It was composed entirely of long, fine, flexible grasses, evidently gathered, when green, from the salt marshes, and carefully woven into a circular fabric. Taking into consideration the clumsy web-feet and the hardly less unwieldy bill of the bird, it was certainly a remarkable structure. The materials were strongly interwoven and compacted, and the nest could be handled without coming to pieces; indeed it had been thrown to me from a height of fifty or sixty feet, and remained uninjured. It contained three eggs, nearly fresh, whose large size indicated that the parent bird was very old. The nest measured about eighteen inches in diameter, its sides being three or four inches thick, and its cavity at the centre at least four inches deep. The bird remained upon her eggs until she had been nearly reached, and flew over our heads, screaming, when we were despoiling her of her treasures.

The nests found upon the ground varied exceedingly, some being merely a shallow depression with a slight lining, and others large, and elaborately built of mosses and fine bent. The eggs were never more than three in number; and when there were less, they were almost invariably fresh. The Gulls were shy; and without exception flew from their nests on the ground on our approach while we were still at a distance from them. Several years later I found these Gulls very abundant on all the rocky islands and among the high cliffs of the upper parts of the Bay of Fundy, on the Isle of Hant, at Cape Split, and at Porsboro. In almost all cases they were in inaccessible places, where they must have been in nearly complete security. In such situations and in their nests in trees the young remain until they can fly. Those that hatch on the ground leave their nests to hide in the crevices of rocks and under any other convenient shelter, and resort to the water long before they can fly.

Mr. R. Kennicott found this species breeding on the southern shores of Great

Slave Lake. The nests were in great numbers and close together, on a point of a large wooded island, and are said to have been made, with considerable art, of sticks, leaves, and feathers; not being placed in unsheltered positions, but generally hidden among low bushes or beside drift-logs, and often under willows. The nests were deep and large.

Dr. Bryant mentions finding the Herring Gull, in 1860, one of the most common birds on the coast of Labrador, where it was breeding on nearly all the grassy islands; and he was assured by the inhabitants that it had always been abundant there. He visited thirty of its breeding-places between Romaine and Château Beau, at all of which there were also Black-backed Gulls in greater or less abundance. As the eggs and young are both favorite articles of food, the birds are much harassed by the inhabitants. The eggs were found to be subject to greater variations in form and color than those of most of the species of this genus. The large spots, which form so marked a feature in the eggs of the *marinus*, were seldom seen. He gives the measurement of four typical specimens as follows: 2.73 inches by 1.64; 2.84 by 1.83; 2.05 by 1.79; 2.91 by 1.94.

In the various examples of the eggs of this species which I have examined, the ground-color has been found to vary from a pearly-white, or a pale drab, or a grayish green, to a brownish clay-color. The markings are more usually of a violet-gray, blended with the more conspicuous blotches of a deep sepia-brown.

Larus cachinnans.

PALLAS'S HERRING GULL.

Larus cachinnans, PALL. Zoog. Rosso-As. II. 1826, 318. — SAUNDERS, P. Z. S. 1878, 119.
Larus argentatus, AUCT. ex Siberia (part).
Larus (*Glaucus*) *leucophæus*, "LICHT." BRUCH, J. f. O. 1853, 101 (Red Sea).
Larus leucophæus, SHARPE & DRESSER, Birds Eur. Pt. XXII. 1873.
Larus (*Glaucus*) *Michahellesii*, BRUCH, l. c.
Larus (*Glaucus*) *borealis*, "BRANDT," BRUCH, l. c.
Larus borealis, DALL & BANNIST. Tr. Chicago Acad. I. 1869, 305 (St. Michael's, Alaska). — BAIRD, l. c.
Larus argentatus d. *borealis*, COUES, B. N. W. 1874, 626.
Larus epargyrus, LICHT. Nomencl. 1854, 99.
Larus fuscescens, "LICHT." BRUCH, J. f. O. 1853, 100 (part).

HAB. Northern Asia, from the Red Sea, Kashmir, etc., to Kamtschatka and the Arctic Ocean; coast of Alaska (common at St. Michael's, DALL & BANNISTER, l. c.), and south, in winter, to California.

SP. CHAR. Similar to *L. californicus*, but larger, the bill more robust, without the black spots, and the feet yellow (SAUNDERS). *Adult, in summer:* Mantle deep cinereous-blue, precisely as in *L. californicus*, the secondaries and tertials broadly and abruptly tipped with white. Outer primary brownish black, the terminal portion, for the space of about 2.25 inches, white, marked by a subterminal spot or broad bar of black;[1] second quill brownish black, tipped with white, the inner web marked near the end by a large oval spot of white; third, similar, but becoming bluish gray basally, the tip only white, the inner web paler gray than the outer, becoming lighter terminally, where sharply defined against the black, and reaching to within about 2.50–2.75 inches of the end of the feather; fourth similar, but the black more restricted, the inner web decidedly white posteriorly, next the black; fifth similar, with the black still more restricted, the gray of the outer web lighter; sixth quill pale grayish blue, passing into white terminally, crossed near the end by a broad bar or band of black; seventh similar, but with the black band incomplete or scarcely indicated; rest of the quills pale grayish blue, passing gradually into white on ends.

[1] In some specimens the white tip is worn off, thus causing the black to appear terminal.

Remainder of the plumage pure white. Bill deep chrome-yellow, the mandible red subterminally, near the angle; eyelids orange-red (SAUNDERS); legs and feet yellow (SAUNDERS); iris pale yellow. *Adult, in winter:* Similar, but head and neck, above and posteriorly, streaked with brownish gray.[1] *Young:* "The young have always flesh-colored legs, and cannot possibly, I believe, be distinguished from the young of *L. argentatus*" (GIGLIOLI, "Ibis," 1881, p. 219).

Total length, about 26.00 inches; wing, 15.15–18.30 (average 16.39); culmen, 1.90–2.20 (2.05); depth of bill through angle, .60–.80 (.72); tarsus, 2.15–2.50 (2.41); middle toe, 1.60–2.15 (1.95). [Six adults.]

This easily recognized species more nearly resembles, except in size, *L. californicus* than *L. argentatus*, with which it has generally been compared, the color of the mantle being precisely similar, while the eyelids are red, as in that species, and not yellow, as in *argentatus.* The bill, however, is similar in shape, size, and color to that of *argentatus*, being destitute of the black spots always present in *californicus.* The feet are stated to be yellow (cf. SAUNDERS, P. Z. S., 1878, p. 170), while those of *californicus* are pea-green, and those of *argentatus* flesh-colored. It would be interesting to know the color of the iris in this species, since its true relationship might thus be more easily determined. *L. argentatus* and *L. californicus* are very different in this respect, the former having pale yellow or silvery-white, the latter dark brown, irides.

This species has been only quite recently ascertained by Mr. Ridgway to be the common Gull of the Northern Pacific coast from San Francisco northward to Alaska. While closely resembling the *argentatus*, Mr. Howard Saunders thinks that it may properly be considered as being distinct from that bird. Owing to the great confusion that has existed in regard to the identity of this species, very little can be given with certainty descriptive of its specific peculiarity of habits; and even its area of distribution must remain for the present largely conjectural. Mr. Saunders, who was not then aware of its presence on our Pacific coast, mentions it as straggling up the French coast as far north as Havre, as replacing the *argentatus* in the Mediterranean, ranging throughout that inland sea, and breeding on its shores and islands; thence it extends up the Black Sea, across the steppes and low-lying marshy and salt-lake districts of Russia, from the mouths of the Volga and the shores of the Caspian as far as Vologola; across the Ural River and the Kirgish steppes to the Irtich, and as far as Lake Baikal. It goes down the Red Sea; and in winter visits the Persian Gulf and the Mekran coast as far as Kurrachee. It is also found at that season along the coasts of China and Japan; and is the species recorded under the names of *L. cachinnans* and *L. occidentalis* by Swinhoe — who, however, did not meet with the true *occidentalis*, which has never been obtained on the Asiatic shore. All the notes we have which can properly be referred to this species as existing on our own coasts have been given under the supposition that the species spoken of were the *argentatus.* Both Mr. Bischoff and Mr. Dall refer to what is presumed to have been this bird as occurring at Plover Bay, in Eastern Siberia; and he also met with it on the Upper Yukon, where he found it replacing the *leucopterus* of the Lower Yukon. It arrives in that region about the 2d of May, breeds on the islands of that river, where he obtained examples of its eggs. These were laid on the bare ground in slight depressions.

According to Dr. Cooper's observations, this species is not so common on the Pacific coast as is the *argentatus* on that of the Atlantic. It occurs in considerable numbers about the large rivers and lakes of the interior of California, and is not uncommon in the winter on the coast. In the severe winter of 1861–1862 Dr. Cooper

[1] According to Professor Giglioli (cf. "Ibis," April, 1881, p. 219), "the adults in all seasons have the head and neck pure white, without any trace of brown specks, and the legs and feet of a bright yellow." Specimens in the National Museum, however, from Japan and the Pacific coast of North America, are marked as described above.

found it nearly as abundant about San Diego as *L. occidentalis.* He speaks of its habits as being very similar to those of that species; but adds that its screams are not nearly so loud, its voice seeming to be rather faint for so large a bird. It entirely disappears from the Pacific coast during the summer.

Larus californicus.

THE CALIFORNIA GULL.

Larus californicus, LAWR. Ann. Lyc. N. Y. VI. 1854, 79; in Baird's B. N. Am. 1858, 846.— BAIRD, Cat. N. Am. B. 1859, no. 663. — COUES, B. N. W. 1874, 634; 2d Check List, 1882, no. 777. — SAUNDERS, P. Z. S. 1878, 175. — RIDGW. Nom. N. Am. B. 1881, no. 668.

Larus delawarensis, var. *californicus*, COUES, Key, 1872, 313; Check List, 1873, no. 548 *a*.

HAB. Western Province of North America; abundant on the larger inland waters as well as on the coast; north to Alaska, south to Rio de Coahuyana, Western Mexico.

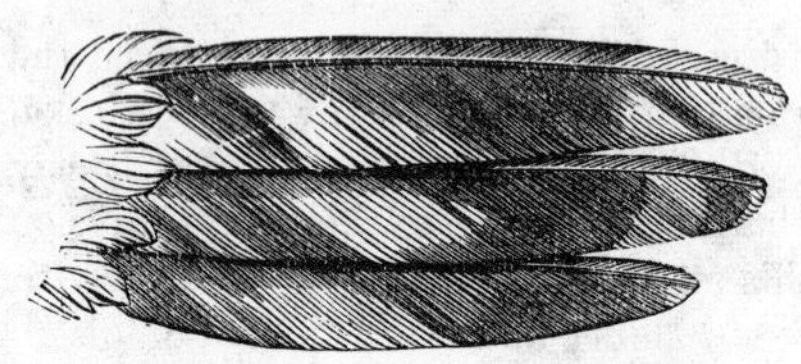

SP. CHAR. Slightly smaller than *L. occidentalis*, with much weaker bill and lighter mantle. *Adult, in summer:* Mantle deep bluish cinereous, intermediate in shade between the plumbeous of *occidentalis* and the pearl-blue of *argentatus*,[1] the secondaries and tertials broadly (for about one inch) tipped with white. Outer primary black, its terminal portion white for about two inches, with or without a black subterminal spot; second quill also black, the tip white, and usually (though not always) marked by a white spot (sometimes one inch long) near the end; third quill black, tipped with white, the base plumbeous; fourth, with the basal half plumbeous-blue, the terminal half black, tipped with white; fifth similar, but the black more restricted, and the line of demarcation between the black and blue still more sharply defined; sixth, lighter plumbeous-blue, passing into white toward the end, and crossed by a wide subterminal band of black; remaining quills cinereous-blue, broadly tipped with white. Remainder of the plumage snow-white. Bill yellow, varying from greenish-lemon to chrome, the terminal third of the mandible bright red (varying from orange-red to carmine), the tip again yellow; a more or less distinct dusky spot in or immediately in front of the red, and one directly above it on the maxilla, the tip of which is sometimes grayish white; rictus and eyelids vermilion red; *iris dark hazel or vandyke-brown; legs and feet pale pea-green, sometimes tinged with grayish.*[2] *Adult, in winter:* Similar, but head and neck (except underneath) broadly streaked with grayish brown. *Young, first plumage:* Above, coarsely spotted, in nearly

[1] Exactly as in *L. cachinnans*, PALLAS!

[2] Notes from upward of fifty freshly-killed specimens! (Cf. RIDGWAY, "Orn, Fortieth Par." 1877, p. 637.)

equal quantities, with brownish slate and grayish buffy white, the latter bordering the feathers, and forming broad irregular bars, mostly beneath the surface; primary coverts, remiges, and rectrices dusky black, the inner primaries more grayish, the primary-coverts narrowly tipped with white and the outer tail-feathers with irregular broken bars of the same. Head, neck, and lower parts mottled or clouded with grayish white and brownish gray, the latter prevailing on the head and neck — nearly uniform on the nape. Bill dusky, black at the tip and brownish basally; iris brown; legs and feet brownish (in the dried skin). *Downy young:* Grayish white, purer white centrally beneath, where immaculate; head marked by irregular dusky black spots, of indefinite arrangement, but most numerous above; upper parts clouded with dusky grayish. Bill black, tipped with pale yellowish brown.

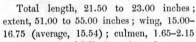

Total length, 21.50 to 23.00 inches; extent, 51.00 to 55.00 inches; wing, 15.00–16.75 (average, 15.54); culmen, 1.65–2.15 (1.83); depth of bill through angle, .60–.75 (.64); tarsus, 2.00–2.60 (2.25); middle toe, 1.70–1.95 (1.88). [Fifteen adults.]

The salient points distinguishing this well-marked species from others occurring in the same regions consist in the peculiar shade of the mantle, which is a deep cinereous-blue, intermediate between the plumbeous of *occidentalis* and the pearl-blue of *argentatus*, and exactly as in *L. cachinnans*, Pallas, of the Palæarctic Region and Northwestern America; the red mandibular spot of *argentatus*, etc., combined with a more or less complete black band near the end of the bill, as in *delawarensis*, although there is rarely, if ever, a complete band, as in the latter species. The dark-brown irides and pea-green feet of the perfect adult distinguish it at once from all its allies, which, except *L. occidentalis*,[1] have, when adult, yellow or whitish irides and flesh-colored feet.

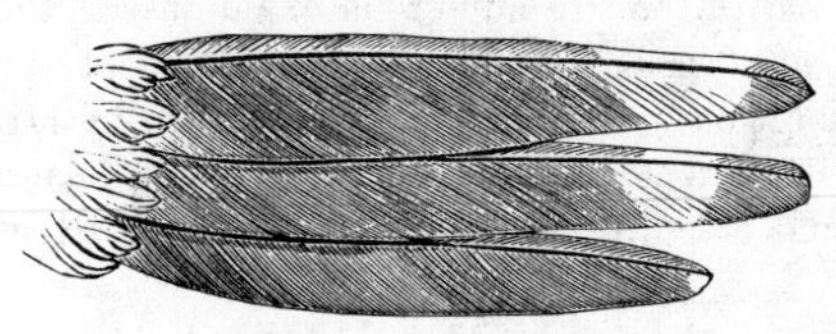

As in other species of this group, the white *picturæ* of the primaries increase in size with the age of the bird; as coincident with this change, it may be mentioned that in the older individuals the black spots of the bill are sometimes almost obsolete, being most distinct in younger specimens.

This is an exclusively northwestern and northern species, and is found on the Pacific coast in the winter; but retires to its breeding-places in the summer. Mr. Bernard Ross claims to have met with it on the Mackenzie River. Dr. Cooper writes that he found this Gull not rare on the Pacific coast in the neighborhood of San Diego during the winter; and he also states that it winters along the entire coast as far north as Puget's Sound; but that it retires in the summer to its breeding-places in more northern regions. He describes this species as being less vigorous in flight than *L. occidentalis,* more inclined to dive for fish, and not so varied in its mode of obtaining its subsistence. He thinks it probable that this species is one of those Gulls which breed on Mono Lake and on other salt bodies of water in the interior basin.

1 *L. occidentalis* has brown irides, and yellow, though, according to the labels of some collectors, flesh-colored feet!

Captain Bendire mentions finding this a very common species on Lake Malheur, in Eastern Oregon, where it breeds abundantly.

Mr. Ridgway found it in large numbers on Pyramid Lake, as well as on Great Salt Lake. It nested in immense numbers upon the islands in both of these lakes, and fed chiefly about the mouths of the streams flowing into them — often ascending the large rivers for some distance. The birds were found there only in summer, during which season no other species of Gull was seen in the same localities; while in winter this species was entirely replaced by *L. delawarensis.* In Great Salt Lake it nested almost, if not quite, exclusively on Carrington Island; and in Pyramid Lake, on the main island. It was on the latter that Mr. Ridgway became best acquainted with the species; for during his several visits in the month of May, 1868, he found it exceedingly abundant on the northwest side, which was occupied by this Gull as its breeding-ground. An area of several acres was thickly crowded with the nests, which were mere heaps of dirt and gravel, mingled with rubbish of sticks, bones, and feathers, raised a few inches above the surface, and with a slight depression on the top. By far the larger number of these nests were placed upon rocks; but some on the tops of stunted sage or on greasewood bushes.

The eggs were from one to five in number, but usually three or four. When the nesting-ground was invaded, the Gulls flew reluctantly from their nests — some circling about overhead, and others perching upon the ledges of rock, all uttering deafening cries. The eggs were used for food during the stay of the party at the lake, and were highly esteemed by all, being very rich, and entirely free from the disagreeable musky odor and toughness of the eggs of some Geese and Ducks.

This colony of Gulls was a great pest to the Pelicans, and their eggs had been twice destroyed by the latter during the season.

In the collection of the Smithsonian Institution are numerous examples of the eggs of this species from the neighborhood of Great Slave Lake. Specimens of the birds and eggs were secured near Fort Resolution by Mr. Kennicott, and also by Mr. Mackenzie; and others were taken by Mr. B. Ross at Fort Simpson, and at Big Island by Mr. J. Reid. These Gulls were also found breeding on the Lower Anderson River by Mr. MacFarlane.

Six eggs (Smithsonian Collection, No. 4226), collected by Mr. Ridgway at Pyramid Lake, present the following variations in their measurement: 2.50 inches by 1.90; 2.55 by 1.65; 2.60 by 1.95; 2.65 by 1.85; and 2.70 by 1.75. The ground-colors of these eggs vary from a bluish white, without any markings whatever, to a deep brownish clay-color, with numerous spots of brownish slate and dark clove-brown. In a few examples the subdued spots of lilac and slate predominate; in others they are overlain with the darker brown: some of these are in blotches, others are in zigzag lines.

Larus delawarensis.

THE RING-BILLED GULL.

Larus delawarensis, Ord, Guthrie's Geog. 2d Am. ed. 1815, 319. — Lawr. in Baird's B. N. Am. 1858, 846. — Baird, Cat. N. Am. B. 1859, no. 664. — Coues, Key, 1872, 313; Check List, 1873, no. 548; 2d ed. 1882, no. 778; B. N. W. 1874, 636. — Saunders, P. Z. S. 1878, 176. — Ridgw. Nom. N. Am. B. 1881, no. 669.

Larus canus, Bonap. Specc. Comp. 1827, 69 (not of Linn. 1758).

? Larus argentatoides, "Brehm," Bonap. Synop. 1828, 360 (not of Brehm, 1822).

Larus zonorhynchus, Richardson, F. B. A. II. 1831, 421. — Aud. Orn. Biog. III. 1835, 98; V. 1839, 638, pl. 212; Synop. 1839, 327; B. Am. VII. 1844, 152, pl. 446.

Gavina Bruchii, Bonap. Naum. IV. 1854, 212.

Larus zonórhynchus, var. *mexicanus*, Bonap. Consp. II. 1857, 224.

HAB. The whole of North America; south (in winter) to Mexico and Cuba.

SP. CHAR. Smaller than *L. californicus*, the bill more slender, and without red spot, the mantle much paler, the iris yellow, and feet greenish yellow in the adult. *Adult, in summer:* Mantle pale pearl-blue (much as in *L. argentatus*, much paler than in *L. brachyrhynchus* or *L. canus*), the secondaries and tertials passing terminally into pure white. Outer primary black, with a white space 1.25 to 1.50 inches long near the end, involving both webs, the shaft, however, black; second quill similar, but with the white space smaller, and the extreme tip also white; third, with the basal half pale pearl-gray, and the apical white spot larger; next, similar, but the subterminal black more restricted, the line of demarcation between it and the pale pearl-gray still more sharply defined; fifth, pale pearl-gray, passing terminally into white, but crossed near the end by a wide band of black, about .75 of an inch wide; sixth quill pale pearl-gray, passing into white terminally, and marked near the end by a more or less imperfect black spot; remaining quills pale pearl-blue, passing terminally into white, and without a trace of black. Bill greenish yellow, crossed near the end by a blackish band, the tip sometimes tinged with orange; rictus and eyelids vermilion-red; interior of mouth rich orange-red, more intense posteriorly; iris clear pale yellow; feet pale yellow, sometimes tinged with greenish; claws black.[1] *Adult, in winter:* Similar, but the head and neck, except beneath, streaked with brownish gray. *Young, first plumage:* Above, brownish dusky, the feathers bordered with pale grayish buff; primaries blackish dusky, the inner quills bluish gray basally, and tipped with white; secondaries bluish gray on basal half, dusky black terminally where edged with white; basal two thirds of the tail pale gray, more whitish basally, mottled with deeper grayish; terminal third dusky black, narrowly tipped with white. Lower parts white, spotted laterally with grayish brown. "Bill black, base of lower mandible and edges of the upper toward the base, livid flesh-color; edges of eyelids livid blue; iris hazel; feet purplish gray, claws brownish black" (AUDUBON).

Larger form (= *Bruchi*, Bp?.)

Adult, in summer.

Wing, 13.60–15.75 (average, 14.45) inches; culmen, 1.55–1.75 (1.64); depth of bill through angle, .50–.65 (.56); tarsus, 1.90–2.45 (2.14); middle toe, 1.30–1.60 (1.46). [Sixteen adults.]

This species appears to be found nearly throughout North America, though quite irregularly. It breeds in high northern latitudes, on the coast of Labrador, and in the interior; it occurs in winter both on the Atlantic and on the Pacific coast, on the latter as far to the south as Mazatlan, and in the interior as far to the north in summer as Lake Winnipeg.

Sir John Richardson refers to it as *Larus canus*, and also as *L. zonorhynchus*. In

1 "*Adult male, in summer:* Bill marked opposite the angle with a broad transverse band of brownish black, between which and the base it is light greenish yellow, the tips orange-yellow. Edges of eyelids greenish yellow; iris bright yellow. Feet greenish yellow, the webs tinged with orange, claws black" (AUDUBON).

speaking of it under the former name, he states that it breeds in Arctic America, but that it retires to the south when winter sets in; referring to it as *zonorhynchus*, he adds that he found it breeding in considerable numbers in swampy places on the banks of the Saskatchewan. Captain Blakiston also mentions meeting with it on the lower portions of the Saskatchewan.

Colonel Grayson states that he found this species common during the winter months in the neighborhood of Mazatlan.

It breeds on the northern coast of Labrador, and in the summer of 1850 I obtained in Halifax specimens of the birds and eggs that had been procured the previous summer in the neighborhood of Cape Harrison. This bird is said to be not at all shy, and to permit a near approach. Dr. Bryant did not meet with it either on the Gannet Rocks, in the St. Lawrence, where Audubon states that he found it breeding, or in Labrador. On the latter coast, on the 18th of July, on a low rocky island near the harbor of Little Macatina, Audubon found a large colony of these birds breeding. All the eggs contained chicks in a more or less advanced condition. The number of eggs in each nest was generally three, and they were said to resemble those of the *marinus* in form and color, and to measure 2.75 inches in length by 1.68 in breadth. There was considerable diversity both in the tint of their ground-color and in the number and size of their spots. Generally they were of a dull dark cream-color, thickly blotched, and sprinkled with different shades of purple, umber, and black. The nests, formed of seaweed, were all placed on the bare rock, were well constructed, and were about twelve inches in their greatest diameter. The whole place had the appearance of having been resorted to for several years in succession. The birds were very shy.

Mr. Boardman informs me that this species is quite common both in spring and fall in Passamaquoddy Bay, and also in the Bay of Fundy; but he thinks that it does not breed in that neighborhood now, whatever may have been the case when Audubon visited Eastport. It is common in the winter along the Atlantic coast as far south as Maryland at least, and probably immature birds wander still farther.

It is of occasional occurrence in Bermuda, where Major Wedderburn speaks of it as rare, one specimen only, so far as he knew, having been met with there, in January, 1849. It is, according to Giraud, common off the coast of Long Island throughout the winter, from November to April.

In its migrations, both in the spring and fall, this species appears to be more or less abundant in the valley of the Mississippi, and also farther west. It is of frequent occurrence throughout Colorado, especially in the spring. Professor Frank H. Snow, of the Lawrence (Kan.) University, obtained a specimen near that city, April 2, 1872. Professor Kumlien writes me that this Gull is common about Lake Koskonong, in Southern Wisconsin, where it is found in much larger flocks than the *argentatus*. Immature birds are often seen in small flocks of from eight to twenty in the lake in June; and occasionally a few have been noticed there all summer. They are not known to breed there; although once on the sandy shore the fragment of an egg was found which may have belonged to this species, as it was very much like the egg of *Larus canus* of Europe. This Gull arrives later than *argentatus*, about the middle or latter part of April, and remains as late in the fall as November 7.

Mr. J. A. Allen states that he found this species, or its western representative, a common summer resident in Salt Lake Valley; it was breeding on the islands in great numbers. At the period of his visit these birds spent much of their time on the sandbars of Weber River, and at certain hours of the day rose in the air to feast on the grasshoppers, on which they seemed at this time almost wholly to subsist.

The stomachs of those Gulls that were killed were not only filled with grasshoppers, but some birds had stuffed themselves so full that these could be seen when the birds opened their mouths. And it was a curious fact that the Gulls captured the grasshoppers in the air, and not by walking over the ground, as they have been said to do. Sailing around in broad circles, as though soaring merely for pleasure, the birds seized the flying grasshoppers as easily, if not as gracefully, as a swallow while in rapid flight secures its prey of smaller insects.

Mr. Henshaw regards this Gull as being common throughout Utah on all the larger bodies of water. It was seen in large numbers on Provo River late in November, when the lake was frozen over, and he had no doubt that it was a winter resident there.

Dr. Cooper refers to this species as being rare in California, and as visiting the Lower Pacific coast only in winter, and usually in small numbers. He met with a few of these Gulls near San Diego between November and February, but found them common in Puget Sound during the winter. They appeared to subsist almost entirely by fishing; and for this purpose they follow the rivers far into the interior. At San Diego neither this species nor the *californicus* was known to feed on dead whales — a diet which formed the chief subsistence of the two larger species, and to some extent of the *argentatus*. Dr. Cooper also met with this species near Lake Tahoe in September.

It was seen by Captain Stansbury during his expedition to Salt Lake, April 9; and he mentions in his Journal that while rounding the northern point of Antelope Island he came upon a rocky islet covered with innumerable flocks of Gulls which had congregated there to build their nests. It is also mentioned by Captain Bendire as being a summer resident of Eastern Oregon, and as breeding there abundantly.

Four eggs in my collection — two from Labrador, and two from Great Slave Lake — present the following measurements: 2.20 by 1.60 inches; 2.20 by 1.65; 2.23 by 1.60; 2.40 by 1.60. Their ground-color varies from a pale grayish green to a deep drab. These are spotted, in varying proportions, but chiefly about the larger end, with subdued markings of lilac and slate, and larger blotches of a dark clove-brown.

Larus brachyrhynchus.

THE SHORT-BILLED GULL.

Larus canus, Rich. F. B. A. II. 1831, 420 (=adult; not of Linn. 1758). — Nutt. Man. II. 1834, 301.

Larus brachyrhynchus, Rich. F. B. A. II. 1831, 421 (=young). — Nutt. Man. II. 1834, 301. — Coues, Pr. Ac. Nat. Sci. Philad. 1862, 302; 2d Check List, 1882, no. 780. — Elliot, Illustr. Am. B. II. pl. 53. — Ridgw. Nom. N. Am. B. 1881, no. 670.

Larus canus, var. *brachyrhynchus*, Coues, Key, 1872, 313; Check List, 1873, no. 549; B. N. W. 1874, 639.

Larus Suckleyi, Lawr. Ann. Lyc. N. Y. 1854, 264 (= young); in Baird's B. N. Am. 1858, 847. — Baird, Cat. N. Am. B. 1859, no. 665.

Rissa septentrionalis, Lawr. Ann. Lyc. N. Y. 1854, 266 (= adult); in Baird's B. N. Am. 1858, 854. — Baird, Cat. N. Am. B. 1859, no. 673.

Hab. The interior of Arctic America, and Pacific coast, south to Washington Territory.

Sp. Char. Similar to *L. canus*, but bill proportionally shorter and deeper, middle toe longer in proportion to the tarsus, and pattern of the primaries quite different. Size small (wing about 14.00 inches); bill small, the culmen about as long as the middle toe, which is much shorter than the tarsus. *Adult, in summer:* Mantle light pearl-blue, the shade *averaging* exactly as in *L. canus*,[1] the secondaries and tertials broadly (the former rather abruptly) tipped with white.

[1] On this point cf. Howard Saunders, P. Z. S., 1878, p. 179.

Outer primary slate-black, about 2.50 inches of the subterminal portion (including the shaft) white, the tip again black; inner web more slaty than the outer, the basal half sometimes ashy white, minutely freckled with darker, but usually uniform slaty gray, paler basally; second quill with the basal half of the outer web and much more of the inner pale bluish gray (much like the mantle), a large space of white, about 1.75 inches in extent, near the end, the intervening space black, abruptly contrasted with the basal pale bluish gray; a small apical spot of white, preceded by a broad subterminal one of black, about .70 of an inch in length; third quill tipped with white, the subterminal portion black for about 1.00 inch on the inner, and more than 2.00 inches on the outer web (next the shaft), the remaining portion pale grayish blue, becoming nearly or quite white on the inner web where adjoining the black; fourth quill similar, but the black more restricted, and the outer web becoming white posteriorly; fifth, similar, but with the black space more restricted, forming a subterminal band about .75 of an inch wide, the white preceding it still more extensive than on the fourth quill; sixth with a still narrower black band (seldom more, generally less, than .50 of an inch wide); remaining quills pale pearl-blue, passing gradually, but broadly, into white, terminally, the seventh sometimes with a small black bar near the end of the outer web. Rest of the plumage snow-white. "Bill bluish green, its terminal third bright yellow; legs and feet dusky bluish green, the webs yellowish" (COUES).[1] *Adult, in winter:* Similar, but the head and neck, sometimes also the jugulum, longitudinally spotted with light grayish brown. *Nearly adult:* Similar, but the white of the primaries more restricted and the black more extended, the latter color more brownish; quills without white apical spots; bill more or less dusky terminally; tail sometimes (in younger individuals) more or less blotched with dusky terminally, and upper tail-coverts sometimes (rarely) faintly barred with grayish brown. Head, etc., spotted or immaculate, according to the season. *Young, first plumage:* Above, grayish brown, the feathers widely and distinctly bordered with pale grayish buff; rump and upper tail-coverts grayish buffy white, marked more or less distinctly with irregularly sagittate spots of grayish brown; basal half of the tail grayish white or pale grayish, transversely mottled with darker; terminal portion dusky grayish brown, forming a well-defined broad zone, the tip whitish. Head, neck, and lower parts nearly uniform light brownish gray. Primaries uniform dusky grayish brown, the terminal margin paler. Bill dusky, more brownish at base; feet (in skin) light brown. *Older:* Similar, but the light borders to the feathers of back, etc., purer white; basal half of the tail uniform bluish white; lower parts white, the breast and sides spotted with light grayish brown; basal half (or less) of the bill light colored. Upper parts more or less tinged with the pale blue of the adult plumage.

Total length, about 17.50 to 18.00 inches; extent 43; wing, 13.20–14.50 (average, 13.93); culmen, 1.25–1.70 (1.45); depth of bill, .40–.50 (.45); tarsus, 1.70–2.10 (1.94); middle toe, 1.30–1.55 (1.44). [Twenty-six adults.]

This species, while agreeing closely with *L. canus* in size and general appearance, may be very easily distinguished when adult by the dissimilar pattern of the primaries, and the somewhat different proportions, as shown in the diagnosis on p. 210. In many specimens (chiefly younger individuals), the dark portion of the primaries is dusky brownish, instead of black. In one (No. 70299, St. Michael's, Alaska; L. M. TURNER), a perfectly adult, though probably not a very old, bird, this color is quite a light grayish brown, as though the color had been washed out, the pattern being the same as in most adult specimens.

[1] "*Adult, high breeding-plumage:* Eyelids, ocular region, and gape of mouth, bright orange-yellow, which color extends over the tip and cutting edges of the bill; the green of the bill with a peculiar hoary glaucescence. Legs and feet bluish green, the webs bright gamboge-yellow" (COUES).

Adult male (No. 70299, U. S. Nat. Mus., St. Michael's, Alaska, May 31, 1875): "Iris dark hazel; bill, feet, and toes dark greenish yellow, webs yellowish; eyelids crimson" (L. M. TURNER, MS.).

Sir John Richardson first refers to this bird as a distinct species on the strength of an individual obtained at Great Bear Lake. This example was a female that had been killed on the 23d of May, 1826. Mr. Murray states that he met with this species on Hudson's Bay; and Mr. Bernard Ross also saw it on the Mackenzie River.

Dr. Cooper mentions having also met with it, during its migrations, near the Columbia River. He found it passing only during the spring and fall; but specimens are said to have been obtained by others near the Straits of Fuca, both in December and in July. He is of opinion that in all probability these birds proceed south only as far as the extreme northern limits of California, and only during the extremity of winter. Dr. Cooper found them in flocks that were constantly fluttering over shoal water, rapidly diving for fish, and keeping up a constant chattering. In their flight their movements were rapid and easy. They were rather shy.

Mr. Bannister found this species abundant on the marshes and ponds along the canal or channel which separates the Island of St. Michael's from the mainland. It was not so abundant on the more open water near the fort.

Mr. Dall speaks of it as being eminently a river Gull, and as abundant from Fort Yukon to the sea; but it was not seen by him on the sea-coast. He states that he obtained its eggs in great abundance about the mouth of the Yukon — where a variety was noticed having a bright yellow bill — and also the young Gulls in their downy plumage near Fort Yukon. The black-and-white pattern on the wings of this species is said to vary a good deal; not so much in itself, as in relation to the different feathers, as if it had been carelessly stamped on with the hand by a die. These birds were eaten by the old Indians.

Mr. MacFarlane found this species breeding at various points, near the Arctic Sea, between the Mackenzie Valley and the Anderson, and from there to the Yukon. One nest, which was merely a small cavity in the sand, and which contained two eggs, was found on Lockhart River on the 28th of May; another was seen, June 3, on the ground near a small lake in the neighborhood of Fort Anderson; and a third, obtained on the 10th of June near Fort Anderson, contained three eggs. This last nest was made of hay, and was placed on a stump, four feet from the ground, near a small lake; the parent bird was secured. A fourth, also containing three eggs, was found on the following day in a precisely similar situation. On the 21st of June a nest of this species, which was built on a tree at least ten feet from the ground, was seen near Rendezvous Lake. It was composed of sticks and twigs, and was lined with mosses and hay. Both parents were near the spot, and the male was secured. Another nest was taken on Swan River, in the Barren Grounds; it also was built on a tree, in the same situation as the last mentioned, and was similar in its construction.

Specimens of this Gull were also secured during the breeding-season on Slave River, at Fort Resolution, and on the Yukon, by Mr. Kennicott; at Big Island by Mr. Reid and by Mr. Ross; at Fort Rae by Mr. Clarke; and at various places by Mr. MacFarlane.

The eggs in the Smithsonian Collection were taken from Great Slave Lake, the Yukon, Anderson River, Fort Rae, Fort Resolution, and Peale's River. Six eggs present the following measurements: 2.00 by 1.45 inches; 2.00 by 1.60; 2.05 by 1.50; 2.25 by 1.70; 2.30 by 1.70; and 2.35 by 1.60. Their ground-color is a greenish olive-brown, the olive tending to green in some, and to brown in others. The markings are of various forms, but are chiefly small spots of a dark buffy umber, larger and more numerous towards the more rounded portion of the egg.

Larus canus.

THE MEW GULL.

Larus canus, LINN. S. N. ed. 10, I. 1758, 136; ed. 12, I. 1766, 224. — SHARPE & DRESSER, B. Eur. pt. xvii. (1873). — SAUNDERS, P. Z. S. 1878, 177. — RIDGW. Nom. N. Am. B. 1881, no. 671. — COUES, 2d Check List, 1882, no. 779.
Larus canus, a. *canus*, COUES, B. N. W. 1874, 638.
Larus cinereus, SCOP. Ann. i. Hist. Nat. 1769, 80.
Larus hybernus, GMEL. S. N. I. ii. 1788, 596.
Larus procellosus, BECHST. Orn. Tasch. 1802, 373.
Larus cyanorhynchus, MEYER, Tasch. Vög. Deutschl. II. 1810, 480.
Laroides canescens, BREHM, Vög. Deutschl. 1831, 753.
Larus canus, var. *major*, MIDDEND. Sibir. Reise, II. 1853, 243.
Larus Heinei, HOMEYER, Naum. 1853, 129.
Larus (*Glaucus*) *lachrymosus*, "LICHT.," BRUCH, J. f. O. 1853, 102.
Larus delawarensis (part), COUES, Pr. Ac. Nat. Sci. Philad. 1861, 246 (Labrador).
Larus Audouini, TRISTRAM, Ibis, 1868, 330 (not of PAYR. 1826).

HAB. Palæarctic Region; accidental or casual in Labrador.

SP. CHAR. *Adult, in summer:* Mantle pale ashy blue (intermediate in shade between that of *L. cachinnans* and *L. argentatus*), the secondaries and tertials broadly, but not abruptly, white terminally. Outer primary black, with a white subterminal space, including both webs and the shaft, of about 2.00–2.25 inches in length; second quill similar, but the white space smaller (about 1.00–1.25 inches in length), the base of the feather more distinctly slaty; third usually[1] without any white, except at the tip, the basal portion abruptly bluish gray; fourth, similar, but the bluish gray occupying about the basal half of exposed portion of the quill, and more sharply defined against the black; fifth grayish blue, tipped with white, and with a large subterminal space of black, an inch or more in length (running anteriorly along the edges for about .75 of an inch, the pale bluish almost or quite white where joining the anterior border of the black on inner web; sixth quill with a much smaller (about .50 wide) subterminal black bar; remaining quills grayish blue, passing into white terminally. Remainder of the plumage snow-white. Bill greenish olivaceous (in skin — greenish yellow in life), the terminal third yellow; iris grayish brown; eyelids vermilion-red; legs and feet yellowish green.[2] *Adult, in winter:* Similar, but occiput and nape longitudinally spotted with grayish brown. *Young, first plumage* (No. 18221, Henley Harbor, Labrador, Aug. 21; E. COUES): Above, grayish brown, the feathers irregularly but broadly bordered with pale dull buff; greater wing-coverts and secondaries pale bluish gray, bordered with pale buff, and with a subterminal border of brownish dusky; tertials grayish brown, bordered with buffy white; primary coverts and primaries dusky black, very narrowly tipped with white; rump and upper tail-coverts white, marked with irregular sagittate spots of brownish dusky; basal two-thirds of the tail bluish white (fading into pure white basally); terminal portion dusky, narrowly tipped with white, the grayish white of the lateral feathers finely mottled with dusky posteriorly. Lower parts grayish white, the jugulum and sides thickly spotted with light grayish brown. "Bill white, tip black; mouth white; legs dusky white" (MS. on label).

Wing, 14.00–14.50 (average, 14.23) inches; culmen, 1.35–1.60 (1.50); depth of bill through angle, .45–.50 (.47); tarsus, 1.90–2.25 (2.03); middle toe, 1.35–1.45 (1.39). (Five specimens.)

[1] In some examples — probably very old birds — there is a roundish spot of white on the inner web about 1.50 inches from the tip of the feather.

[2] The fresh colors of the soft parts in this species are given by Macgillivray as follows: *Adult male, in summer:* "The bill is greenish yellow, purer toward the end; the margins of the eyelids vermilion. *Young:* The bill is black, at the base livid flesh-color; the iris dusky; the edges of the eyelids brown; the feet flesh-color, tinged with yellow." *Adult male, in winter:* "The bill is of a uniform grayish-green tint, shaded at the end with ochre-yellow; the basal margins and mouth orange; the edges of the eyelids dull reddish; the iris brown. The feet deep greenish-gray; the claws black." *Young, in second winter:* "Bill yellowish green, with the end dusky; feet livid yellowish green."

The Common Gull of Europe — more generally known in England and Scotland as the Sea-mew and the Sea-mall — is of rare and accidental occurrence in North America. One was taken by Dr. Coues, Aug. 21, 1860, at Henley Harbor, Labrador (SAUNDERS, "Proc. Zool. Soc.," 1878, p. 178); and this is the only authentic instance of its capture on this continent. Its habitat is throughout the Palæarctic Region, but it is very rare in Iceland.

In its general habits this Gull differs but very little from most of its congeners; and in one respect — namely, its partiality for open cultivated fields — strikingly resembles our own *Larus delawarensis*. Macgillivray states that in the fall or winter, when the fields have been cleared of their produce, and are being prepared for another crop, the Sea-mew deserts the coast and appears in large flocks, finding subsistence in picking up worms and larvæ which the farmers' labors have exposed. These flocks may be met with in all the agricultural districts, both near the sea and in parts quite remote from it. They are more numerous in stormy weather, but also in the finest days of winter they may be seen in close attendance upon the plough. Should the country become covered with snow, this bird retreats to the shore; but returns as soon as a thaw partially exposes the ground.

This bird is said to have a light, buoyant flight, during which it often inclines to one side; it walks and runs prettily, with short steps, patting the sands at the edge of the water with its feet, emitting a shrill, somewhat harsh cry, and often on the approach of the sportsman giving the alarm to other birds. It is not, however, so sensible of danger as are the larger Gulls; and both in the fields and on the sea-shore will often allow a person to come within gunshot. It never molests any other species, nor is it quarrelsome among its fellows. Its food consists of small fishes, such as sand-eels and young herring, which it picks from the water. It also feeds on stranded fish, star-fishes, mollusca, shrimp, and small crustacea. It will sometimes pick up grain in the fields, and when domesticated will eat bread. It is easily tamed, but will not long survive confinement.

This species is much more abundant in Great Britain in winter than in summer, while it breeds more or less along the entire coast. An immense colony occupies a small island in the Hebrides. It breeds alike on the grassy summits of precipitous rocks near the sea, on moorland lochs at some distance inland, and even on the highest mountain ranges. It is a common resident all along the Norwegian coast, and large numbers breed between Stavanger and the North Cape. It also breeds in large numbers on the rivers and fresh-water lakes in the interior of Scandinavia. This Gull is also a common species, and breeds through almost the whole of Central and Northern Russia; and it is abundant on the Prussian coast, and on the northern coast of France. It is an irregular winter visitant of most parts of Southern Europe, as well as of Asia Minor and other parts of Western Asia. In Eastern Asia it is replaced by a larger variety, from which, however, it does not specifically differ.

The Sea-mew breeds on the sea-coast, occasionally also on inland lakes, making a carefully constructed nest among the drift-stuff on the shore. Its usual number of eggs is said to be three. The nests are composed generally of fuci, occasionally of grass, bits of turf, and various vegetable substances. The eggs are described as being of a broadly ovate form, olive-brown, yellowish brown, oil-green, greenish gray, or greenish white, irregularly marked with dark brown and purplish gray, these markings being generally larger and more numerous on eggs having the deepest ground-color. The eggs vary in length from 2.08 to 2.25 inches, and have an average breadth of 1.50.

Mr. Robert Collett found this species breeding in Norway on fresh-water lakes, four thousand feet above the sea. In one instance a pair was found by Dr. Ludwig Holtz occupying the deserted nest of a Hooded Crow, built on a bush near the shore, ten feet from the ground. The same pair was said to have nested there during several successive years. In another instance Mr. Collett observed a pair near Trondhjem, in the summer of 1868, which had taken possession of the nest of an old Crow, on the top of a fir-tree. The eggs when removed were replaced by another set.

Dr. Rey informed Mr. Dresser that a careful measurement of fifty specimens gave as the average size of the egg of this bird, 2.30 by 1.63 inches, the largest measuring 2.55 by 1.62, and the smallest 2.11 by 1.60.

Larus Heermanni.

HEERMANN'S GULL.

Larus Heermanni, CASS. Pr. Ac. Nat. Sci. Philad. VI. 1852, 187 ; Illustr. B. Tex. Cal. etc. 1853, 28, pl. 5 (adult and young). — SAUNDERS, P. Z. S. 1878, 182. — RIDGW. Nom. N. Am. B. 1881, no. 672. — COUES, 2d Check List, 1882, no. 781.

Blasipus Heermanni, BONAP. Consp. II. 1857, 211. — LAWR. in Baird's B. N. Am. 1858, 848. — BAIRD, Cat. N. Am. B. 1859, no. 666. — COUES, Pr. Ac. Nat. Sci. Philad. 1862, 304.

Larus (Blasipus) Heermanni, SCL. & SALV. P. Z. S. 1871, 574 (figure). — COUES, B. N. W. 1874, 641.

Larus Belcheri, SCHLEG. Mus. P.-B. Lari, 1863, 9 (part ; excl. syn. ; not of VIGORS, 1829).

Larus (Blasipus) Belcheri, COUES, Key, 1872, 314 (excl. syn. *fuliginosus*) ; Check List, 1873, no. 551.

HAB. Pacific coast of America, from British Columbia to Panama.

SP. CHAR. *Adult, summer plumage:* Head and upper part of the neck white, changing gradually into ash-gray on the lower parts and plumbeous-slate on the upper surface, the wings rather darker than the back, and with a slight brownish tinge ; secondaries dusky slate, broadly tipped

L. Heermanni, summer adult.

with white ; tertials like the coverts, but passing terminally into white, like the secondaries ; primaries dusky black, the shorter quills narrowly tipped with white. Upper tail-coverts light ash-gray, like the medial lower parts. Tail dusky black, tipped with white. Bill bright red, tipped with black (sometimes wholly red) ; eyelids red ; iris "brownish gray ;" legs and feet black.

Adult, in winter: Similar, but the head and upper parts of the neck dusky grayish brown. *Young, first plumage:* Sooty grayish brown, lighter and more grayish beneath; wing-coverts, scapulars, rump feathers, and upper tail-coverts, bordered terminally with grayish white; remiges dusky black; tail blackish dusky, very narrowly tipped with white. Bill brownish, the terminal third black; legs and feet brownish black. *Young (second year?):* Similar to the preceding, but without light margins to wing-coverts, etc., the general color rather darker, and the tail without white tip. Bill light reddish for basal two thirds, the end black; legs and feet brownish black.

Total length, about 17.50 inches; wing, 13.50; tail, 5.50; bill, from gape, 2.50.

Heermann's Gull — or the White-headed Gull, as this species is called by Mr. Cassin — was first made known by him as a North American bird in 1852, and is said to be one of the handsomest of the large family to which it belongs. It was first noticed by Dr. A. L. Heermann, who found it of frequent occurrence on the coast of California, and most numerous in the harbor of San Diego in the month of March, at which time, although a few of these birds were in mature plumage, yet a large proportion of them were evidently in an immature dress. This Gull was usually observed to be flying in company with *L. occidentalis*, and to be engaged in the capture of small fishes, of which there were many species in the harbor of San Diego. It also appeared to feed on the small maritime animals of various kinds which inhabit the immense beds of kelp (*Macrocystis*) occurring on that coast, and which are so extensive off the harbor of San Diego. The nests and eggs of this bird were found by Dr. Heermann on the Coronados, a group of islands lying a short distance outside the entrance of this harbor.

Mr. Salvin met with this species on the Pacific coast of Guatemala, several specimens having been taken near Chiapam, all in their immature plumage. The Gulls were usually noticed along the shore, and not in the lagoons.

Mr. Henshaw speaks of this species as being common all along the coast of California, and as breeding upon many of the adjacent islands. A very large flock were pursuing their way along the shore near Santa Barbara, and later in the day he came upon them where they had settled on a rocky point that jutted out into the water. Many were fishing, hovering over the half-submerged kelp-covered rocks, the shallow water surrounding which abounded in the smaller kinds of fish. At the discharge of his gun the mass of birds flew wildly about, and it was some time before they left the place. The flock was composed of old males; and it was evident that the journey was one between their breeding-grounds and the fishing-place, where there was probably an unusual abundance of food fitted for their young. Mr. R. Browne met with this species on the coast of Vancouver Island.

Dr. Cooper writes that he has noticed this Gull along the entire Pacific coast, and that it was abundant in winter; but that he found it rather rare in summer, and saw none of this species between April and the end of June, at which latter date he saw some of the young of that year about the islands, though he could find no evidence of their having been hatched there. Referring to the statement of Dr. Heermann that this species breeds on the Coronados Islands, Dr. Cooper remarks that it probably breeds on other island groups on the coast south of San Francisco.

These birds are common as far north in the summer as the Straits of Fuca, but come south to the Columbia in winter. The young-plumaged birds are very constant attendants on the flocks of Pelicans, and rob the latter of a portion of the fish which these bring up in their scoop-like pouches, seizing upon those which fall out or hang outside, the Pelicans never resenting this treatment. Audubon ascribes the same habit to the Black-headed Gull in Florida.

At San Diego Dr. Cooper did not observe that this species followed the Pelicans so much as it does at the north. It is almost exclusively a fish-eater, and is known to dive for this food. It is also very much given to frequenting the fields of kelp which fringe the shores, at a distance of from one to three miles, where it finds small crustacea and mollusca. In one instance only did he see one of this species feeding on the carcase of a bird, and this was a bird which he himself had thrown away. This Gull also follows vessels in or near the bays, but never accompanies them far to sea, although its flight is very rapid. Dr. Heermann mentions having once seen this species feeding on a dead seal.

According to Dr. Newberry, this species is common as far up the Sacramento as Feather River; but Dr. Cooper never saw it far from the salt water. Its voice is said to be faint, and rather querulous; and it is rarely heard except when the bird is fishing.

Colonel Grayson met with this species on the Pacific coast near Mazatlan, in Western Mexico, and also on the Island of Isabella; but it was not common there. In the neighborhood of Mazatlan it occurred chiefly as a winter visitor. Specimens were shot on the sea-beach near that city in February and March. An egg of this species collected by Colonel Grayson on an island near Mazatlan (Smithsonian Institution, No. 15519) is of a rather oblong oval form, tapering toward one end, and rounded at the other. It measures 2.35 inches in length by 1.65 in breadth. Its ground-color is a light clayish-drab, over which it is marked with bold spots of lilac-gray and two different shades of sepia-brown. Another egg in my collection — procured from the Farallones by Mr. George F. Faulkner — measures 2.27 inches in length by 1.55 in breadth. Its ground-color is a deep drab, and the markings are large blotches of dark bistre, approaching to blackness. These are scattered over the surface of the egg, and are of rounded shape about the smaller end, and more irregular in shape, and more confluently grouped together, about the larger end. The obscure shell-marks of lilac are few and scattered.

Larus atricilla.

THE LAUGHING GULL.

Larus atricilla, LINN. S. N. ed. 10, I. 1758, 136; ed. 12, I. 1766, 225 (based on *Larus major*, Catesb. I. 89, but also includes the European species, *L. ridibundus*, LINN.). — NUTT. Man. II. 1834, 291. — AUD. Orn. Biog. IV. 1838, 118, pl. 314; Synop. 1839, 324; B. Am. VII. 1844, 136, pl. 443. — COUES, Key, 1872, 315; Check List, 1873, no. 554. — SAUNDERS, P. Z. S. 1878, 194. — RIDGW. Nom. N. Am. B. 1881, no. 673.

Larus (*Chroicocephalus*) *atricilla*, BRUCH, J. f. O. 1853, 106. — COUES, B. N. W. 1874, 650.

Chroicocephalus atricilla, LAWR. in Baird's B. N. Am. 1858, 850. — BAIRD, Cat. N. Am. B. 1859, no. 667. — COUES, Pr. Ac. Nat. Sci. Philad. 1862, 310; 2d Check List, 1882, no. 786.

Larus ridibundus, WILS. Am. Orn. IX. 1814, 89, pl. 74, fig. 4 (not of LINN.).

Larus plumbiceps, BREHM, Lehrb. 722 (GRAY).

Larus (*Atricilla*) *megalopterus*, BRUCH, J. f. O. 1855, 287.

Atricilla Catesbœi, BONAP. Naumannia, 1854, 212.
Atricilla minor, BONAP. l. c.
Atricilla macroptera, BONAP. l. c.
Larus (*Atricilla*) *micropterus*, BRUCH, t. c. 288.

HAB. Tropical and Warm-temperate America, north to Maine, Ohio, Illinois, etc., but chiefly along the sea-coast; south to the Lower Amazon; both coasts of Central America. Casual in Europe.

SP. CHAR. *Adult, in summer:* Head and upper half of the neck (extending farther down in front than on the nape) dark slate-color, with a slight brownish tinge, darkest on the neck; an elongated white spot on each eyelid; lower half of the neck, all round, entire lower parts, upper tail-coverts, and tail, pure white, the under surface with a delicate roseate tinge in fresh specimens; mantle deep plumbeous, the secondaries and tertials broadly tipped with white. Outer five primaries black, with or without a small white apical spot, the bases of the third, fourth, and fifth slaty for a greater or less distance, this sometimes abruptly defined against the black, but oftener grading insensibly into it; remaining quills hoary plumbeous, tipped with white, the sixth sometimes with a subterminal black spot. Bill dark brownish red, the terminal third of the culmen and the gonys blood-red or carmine; eyelids dull dark red; rictus and interior of mouth fleshy red; iris dark grayish brown; legs and feet dark reddish brown, the webs darker; claws black. *Adult, in winter:* Similar, but head and neck white, the occiput and auricular region spotted or mottled with brownish gray, and the eyes more or less surrounded by the same. Bill and feet more dusky. *Young, first plumage:* Interscapulars, scapulars, and wing-coverts, grayish brown centrally, broadly bordered with pale grayish buff or clay-color; greater wing-coverts ash-gray, tinged on terminal edges with pale grayish buff; secondaries dusky, abruptly tipped with white; primary coverts and primaries black, the latter narrowly tipped with white. Central portion of the rump light brownish ash; lateral and posterior portion of the rump, upper tail-coverts, and posterior lower parts, white. Basal half of the tail light ash-gray; terminal portion black, narrowly tipped with white. Head, neck, breast, and sides, nearly uniform brownish gray, darker on the occiput and nape, and more or less tinged with pale buffy beneath, especially in younger individuals; abdomen grayish white or pale brownish gray. Bill and feet dusky brownish (in skin). *Downy young:* Above, grayish fulvous, the head irregularly striped or spotted, the back, wings, and rump irregularly marbled with dusky. Lower parts light grayish fulvous, inclining to ochraceous on the breast and middle of the abdomen, which are immaculate; lateral and under parts of the head marked with several large and distinct spots of black; foreneck, sides, flanks, and anal region dull fulvous-grayish, faintly mottled with darker. Bill dull light brown; legs and feet dull dusky brown.

Total length, about 16.50 inches; wing, 13.00; tail, 5.00; culmen, 1.75; depth of bill through nostrils, .45; tarsus, 2.00; middle toe with claw, 1.50.

The Black-headed, or Laughing, Gull is found at different seasons along the whole Atlantic coast of the United States. It breeds as far to the northeast as Tennant's Harbor, in Maine, near the western extremity of Penobscot Bay, and during the latter part of the summer extends its migrations as far as the Bay of Fundy; but none of these birds are to be seen north of Florida after the early part of October. This is an abundant and a resident species on both coasts of Florida, along the whole extent of the Gulf of Mexico, and both on the Atlantic and on the Pacific coast of Central America. It is not found on the Pacific coast of the United States.

This Gull is more or less abundant in nearly all the West India Islands, where it breeds, and is probably resident throughout the year. Léotaud cites it as being a somewhat uncommon visitant of Trinidad, where it is known to occur only from July to October. It is a bird that is easily tamed, and will live apparently perfectly contented and domesticated in the courtyards of dwellings.

Professor Alfred Newton obtained examples of this species at St. Thomas, and often saw small birds of this family, with a dark hood, about St. Croix, which he had no hesitation in referring to this species. They generally kept in small flocks at no great distance from the shore. Professor Newton also states that the only trustworthy instance on record of the occurrence of this Gull in Europe is that mentioned by Colonel Montagu, which took place August, 1774. The other supposed instances, mentioned by other writers, are now presumed to have reference to individuals of *Larus Audouini.*

Mr. E. C. Taylor mentions this species as being the only Gull he saw in the West India Islands, and he did not meet with it south of the Island of St. Thomas. There, however, and at Porto Rico it was very abundant, especially in the harbor of St. Thomas and at San Juan de Porto Rico.

On the authority of Mr. Hill, Mr. Gosse includes this species among the birds of Jamaica; it is found about the San Pedro Keys.

Mr. Salvin found it quite common about the Belize, and thinks that it breeds on the Keys along the coast. He subsequently met with it both on the Atlantic and on the Pacific coast of Guatemala. Individuals from the eastern coast were in the plumage of summer; while those from Chiapam were either in their winter or in their immature plumage.

Mr. Dresser speaks of this Gull as being abundant on the sea-coast of Texas during the summer, and he saw great numbers off Bagdad from June to August; when at Galveston in June, 1864, he found it breeding abundantly, making a very slight nest of straws and drift-stuff, in which it lays four eggs. The nest was generally placed on the ground or in a tussock of grass.

Dr. Bryant found it abundant, resident, and breeding, at New Providence, in the Bahamas. It is of rare occurrence in Bermuda, where Major Wedderburn reports the capture of a single specimen taken alive in the winter of 1851.

This species arrives on the coast of Long Island in the latter part of April, is quite common, and is well known to sportsmen as the "Laughing Gull" — a name it evidently well deserves, as its notes resemble in the most striking manner a loud burst of derisive laughter. This is more especially the case when the bird has eggs or young, and these are threatened by intruders. Its cries of deep distress strangely resemble shouts of laughter, and seem expressive of sentiments quite unlike what they really are intended to convey. This is a courageous bird, and willingly exposes itself to almost certain death in defence of its young. I have found it breeding in large numbers on the Island of Muskegat, near Nantucket, and again on small islands near the entrance of the Chesapeake. In both these places the birds were much harassed, and their eggs and young were taken by the fishermen. In the former place, where I found them so abundant in 1842, I am told they have already become extinct.

This Gull breeds in considerable abundance on the coast of Long Island, and its eggs are said to be three in number, rarely more. On the low islands in South Bay, eggs were found by Giraud which had been dropped on the grass with little or no preparations for a nest. He speaks of this bird as being watchful and timid, like the rest of the Gulls, and yet very courageous in defence of its young. He frequently observed it when fishing, and when making aërial excursions in company with the common Tern, *Sterna hirundo.*

Colonel Grayson found this species on the Pacific coast, near Mazatlan, on the west coast of Mexico.

Audubon regarded it as a resident all the year round on the Southern coast, from South Carolina to Mexico, and as being more especially abundant at all times on the shores and Keys of Florida. None were observed on the Mississippi above New Orleans — at which place, however, it is plentiful during winter. He thinks that none of these Gulls ever travel beyond tide-water in any stream. This is perhaps true as a general rule; and there is, at all events, no positive evidence that this species has ever been actually taken in the interior. On Lake Koskonong in the summer, some twenty-five years ago, Professor Kumlien shot a Gull which he thinks must have been of this species.

Audubon found it breeding as early as the first of March; although in Massachusetts it breeds as late as the middle of June. He speaks of its nest as being somewhat elaborately made of dry seaweed and land plants, and as sometimes being three inches high. All the nests which I have seen were slight depressions in the soil, scantily and loosely lined with dry grass. Audubon mentions having once found a nest of nearly double the ordinary size, formed by two pairs, where during the rainy weather the two birds sat close to each other, but each on its own three eggs. The males as well as the females concerned in this singular partnership manifested great fondness for each other. The eggs, which were never more than three in number, he found to average 2.06 inches in length, and a little more than 1.50 in breadth, varying in their general tint, but being usually of a light earthy olive, blotched and spotted with dull reddish brown and black, the markings being more abundant toward the larger end of the egg. These eggs are excellent as an article of food.

The Laughing Gull is eminently social and sympathetic. It associates and breeds in large companies. If one is wounded and falls into the water its cries of distress are sure to attract its companions, who soar above it and plunge toward it as if desirous of affording aid. Audubon states that off the coast of Florida this Gull watches the movements of the Brown Pelican, and when the latter dives flies toward it, alights on its head as it rises from the water, and snatches at such fish as may escape from the Pelican's pouch when the water is allowed to drain off.

Eggs of this species (Smithsonian Institution, No. 2369) from Sand Shoal Island, Va., vary from 2.20 to 2.25 inches in length, and from 1.55 to 1.60 in breadth. Their ground-color is a brownish olive; but this varies greatly, sometimes becoming a brownish white. One specimen from the Tortugas, Fla. (Smithsonian Institution, No. 4794), measures 2.45 by 1.45 inches. The Smithsonian Collection also contains eggs from Cape May and from Cuba.

Larus Franklini.

FRANKLIN'S ROSY GULL.

Larus atricilla, SABINE, App. Franklin's Polar Sea, 1823, 695 (not of LINN. 1758).
Larus Franklinii, SW. & RICH. F. B. A. II. 1831, 424, pl. 71. — AUD. Orn. Biog. V. 1839, 324; Synop. 1839, 325; B. Am. VII. 1844, 145. — COUES, Key, 1872, 316; Check List, 1873, no. 555. — SAUNDERS, P. Z. S. 1878, 195. — RIDGW. Nom. N. Am. B. 1881, no. 674.
Larus (Chroicocephalus) Franklinii, BRUCH, J. f. O. 1855, 289. — COUES, B. N. W. 1874, 653.
Chroicocephalus Franklinii, LAWR. in Baird's B. N. Am. 1858, 851. — BAIRD, Cat. N. Am. B. 1859, no. 668. — COUES, 2d Check List, 1882, no. 787.
Larus pipixcan, WAGL. Isis, 1831, 515.
Larus cucullatus, LICHT. Nomencl. 1854, 98 (no description). (Mexico.)
Larus (Chroicocephalus) cucullatus, BRUCH, J. f. O. 1855, 290. — LAWR. in Baird's B. N. Am. 1858, 851. — BAIRD, B. N. Am. 1859, no. 669.
Larus cinereo-caudatus, PHIL. & LANDB. Wiegm. Archiv, 1861, 293 (Chili).
? *Larus (Chroicocephalus) Kittlitzii,* BRUCH, J. f. O. 1853, 104.
Chroicocephalus Schimperi, BRUCH, l. c. (not of SCHLEG. 1863, which = *L. Saundersi,* SWINHOE).

HAB. The interior of North America, chiefly the Mississippi Valley and northward, but breeding mostly north of the United States; Central and South America, during migrations, as far as Chili; part of the West Indies.

Adult, summer plumage.

SP. CHAR. *Adult, in summer:* Head and upper part of the neck plumbeous-black (more plumbeous anteriorly); an elongated white spot on each eyelid; lower part of the neck (all round), entire lower parts, lower part of the rump, and upper tail-coverts snow-white, the neck and lower parts with a deep tinge of delicate rose-pink in fresh specimens. Mantle deep bluish plumbeous, a little lighter than in *L. atricilla,* the secondaries and tertials broadly tipped with white. Tail white, the four to six central feathers tinged with pale grayish blue, deepest on the intermediæ. Primaries bluish gray, the shafts white, the five outer quills marked with a subterminal space of black, varying in extent from nearly 2.00 inches long on the second quill to about .50 on the fifth, each quill broadly tipped with white, this occupying on the outer about 1.50 inches of the terminal portion, on the rest less than .50 of an inch; the bluish gray of the basal portion

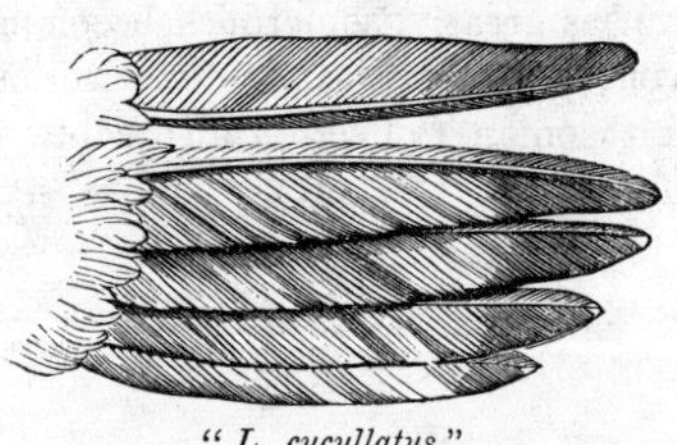

" L. cucullatus."

of the quills becoming nearly or quite white where joining the black, and the shaft of the black portion also black; remaining quills light grayish blue, broadly, but not abruptly, tipped with white, the sixth sometimes marked with a subterminal black spot or bar. Bill deep red, with a more or less distinct darker subterminal band; eyelids red; feet deep red. *Adult, in winter:* Similar, but head and neck white, the occiput, with orbital and auricular regions, grayish dusky. Bill and feet brownish, the former tipped with orange-reddish. *Young, first plumage:* Top and sides of the head (except forehead and lores), back, and scapulars grayish brown, the longer scapulars bordered terminally with pale grayish buff; wing-coverts bluish gray, tinged with grayish

Not quite adult (= "L. cucullatus"), summer plumage.

brown; secondaries dusky, edged with pale grayish blue, and broadly tipped with white; primaries dusky, the inner more plumbeous, all rather broadly tipped with white. Central portion of the rump uniform light bluish gray; lateral and posterior portions of the rump, upper tail-coverts, entire lower parts, forehead, lores, and eyelids white. Bill brownish, dusky terminally; feet brown (in skin).

Total length, about 14.00 inches; extent, 35.00; wing, 11.25; culmen, 1.30; depth of bill through nostrils, .35; tarsus, 1.60; middle toe, with claw, 1.60.

We still know comparatively little of the specific habits of Franklin's Rosy Gull; nor can we give with any exactness its geographical distribution. It appears to be common throughout the Fur Countries during the summer from about the 50th to the 65th parallel, and perhaps farther north. It is a great wanderer in its migrations, and probably passes the winter in Central and South America. Unlike *L. atricilla*, it appears to confine itself in the summer to fresh water, and is not to be found on the margin of the ocean, excepting in its migrations. It was first described by Sir John Richardson from a specimen obtained in June, 1827, on the Saskatchewan. It was found to be a very common species in the interior of the Fur Countries, where it frequents the shores of the larger lakes. It was almost exclusively found in flocks, and was observed to be a very noisy bird. It breeds chiefly in marshy places.

Captain Blakiston met with this species in the region of the Saskatchewan, where he found it rather abundant. It was breeding on the lakes of the Buffalo Plains in the summer.

In a letter dated May 21, 1860, Dr. J. G. Cooper wrote me that he found this Gull not uncommon in the neighborhood of Sioux City; and though he had no positive evidence to that effect, he had no doubt that it was breeding in that region.

Dr. Giraud is authority for the occurrence of this species in immature plumage on Long Island; but as no other observer has made mention of its presence on the Atlantic coast, this is perhaps an error. He speaks of it as a very handsome and strongly marked species, and as occasionally uttering, as it flies, a peculiarly shrill and plaintive cry.

Colonel Grayson met with this bird in and about Mazatlan, and procured specimens in December. A few other birds of this species were seen during the same month, but they were not common in that locality.

Mr. Salvin obtained a single specimen of this Gull in the plumage, which has been described with the name of *C. cucullatus*, at Chiapam, on the Pacific coast of Guatemala, in January, 1863.

Mr. Donald Gunn, in his Notes and Journal of his visits to Shoal and other lakes, mentions his having met with this species. We copy from his Journal: —

"We passed from Shoal Lake to Manitoba. The Franklin Gulls had forsaken the marsh at the south end of that lake — which movement of theirs reduced us to the necessity of following them to the north as far as Swan Creek. Here we found them in considerable force. Their nests were among the bulrushes — flat on the water, and composed of these rushes. We had a hard run for the eggs, as lots of fellows from the Oak Point followed us, and began an active competition. However, we secured one hundred and sixty-five of their eggs, and thirteen specimens of the Gulls themselves."

This Gull was found breeding at Selkirk Settlement and in the Red River Settlement, as well as on Lake Manitoba, by Mr. Gunn.

The Smithsonian Collection contains a specimen which I received from Professor Kumlien in 1871; it was shot on the 29th of October. He writes me that but few others have been noticed in that neighborhood.

The ground-color of the eggs of this Gull varies from a pale grayish green to a light drab, and even to an olive. The markings vary greatly in shape and size. Some are rounded, others are zigzag; some are large, and others are small; and all are of a very dark olive-brown. Those in the Smithsonian Collection were brought by Mr. Gunn from Shoal Lake. Five eggs present the following measurements: 2.00 by 1.40 inches; 2.00 by 1.45; 2.05 by 1.50; 2.15 by 1.45; 2.25 by 1.50.

Larus philadelphia.

BONAPARTE'S GULL.

Sterna philadelphia, ORD, Guthrie's Geog. 2d Am. ed. II. 1815, 319.

Chroicocephalus philadelphia, LAWR. in Baird's B. N. Am. 1858, 852. — BAIRD, Cat. N. Am. B. 1859, no. 670. — NEWTON, P. Z. S. 1871, 57, pl. 4, fig. 6 (egg). — COUES, Pr. Ac. Nat. Sci. Philad. 1862, 310; 2d Check List, 1882, no. 788.

Larus philadelphia, GRAY, List Brit. B. 1863, 235 (Great Britain). — COUES, Key, 1872, 316; Check List, 1873, no. 556.

Larus philadelphiæ, SAUNDERS, P. Z. S. 1878, 206. — RIDGW. Nom. N. Am. B. 1881, no. 675.

Larus (*Chrœcocephalus*) *philadelphia*, COUES, B. N. W. 1874, 655.

Larus minutus, SABINE, App. Franklin's Voy. 1823, 696. — SW. & RICH. F. B. A. II. 1831, 426 (not of PALL. 1776).

Larus capistratus, BONAP. Specc. Comp. 1828, 69 (not of TEMM. 1820).

? *Larus melanorhynchus*, TEMM. Pl. Col. livr. 85, pl. 504 (1830; Chili).

Larus Bonapartii, SW. & RICH. F. B. A. II. 1831, 425, pl. 72. — NUTT. Man. II. 1834, 294. — AUD. Orn. Biog. IV. 1838, 212, pl. 324; Synop. 1839, 323; B. Am. VII. 1844, 131, pl. 452.

Larus (*Chroicocephalus*) *subulirostris*, "BP." BRUCH, J. f. O. 1853, 105 (type in Mus. Mainz).

HAB. The whole of North America, but no valid record of its occurrence south of the United States, except Bermudas (HURDIS).

SP. CHAR. *Adult, in summer:* Head and upper part of the neck dark plumbeous, the eyelids marked by an elongated white spot. Lower part of the neck, entire lower parts, tail, upper tail-coverts, lower and lateral portions of the rump, border of the wing, alulæ, primary coverts, and greater portion of the primaries snow-white, the neck and lower parts with a delicate rose-pink blush in fresh specimens. Mantle, including upper and middle portions of rump, delicate light pearl-blue. Three outer primaries chiefly white, the outer web of the exterior quill, and the terminal portion of all, deep black ; fourth quill similar to the third, but the inner web pale gray-

L. philadelphia, summer plumage.

ish blue ; fifth and sixth quills pale grayish blue, with a large subterminal black space, and tipped with white (third and fourth quills also marked with a small white apical spot) ; remaining quills pale grayish blue, without white tips, but marked near the end, usually on inner web only, with a black spot. Bill deep black ; iris dark brown ; interior of mouth, with legs and feet, rich clear orange-red ;[1] claws black. *Adult, in winter:* Similar, but head and neck white, the occiput tinged with grayish, and the auricular region marked by a spot of dusky gray. Legs and feet flesh-color.

Summer adult.

Young, first plumage: Sides and under part of head and neck, entire lower parts, upper tail-coverts, and basal three fourths of the tail pure white ; crown, occiput, and upper part of the back brownish gray ; a dusky grayish spot on the auricular region ; scapulars and posterior interscapulars grayish umber, tipped with pale buff ; central area of lesser wing-covert region dusky brownish gray ; rest of wing-coverts, edges of secondaries, greater portion of inner primaries, with upper and central portions of the rump, light grayish blue ; band across end of tail black or dusky, the tip narrowly

[1] In some very high-colored specimens the *feathers* surrounding the naked rim of the eyelids are fine orange-red.

whitish. Outer primary with the entire outer web, and a stripe along the inner next the shaft, with the end, black, the remaining portion white; second and third quills similar, but the white successively more restricted; fourth, bluish white on both webs (inner web more bluish), the subterminal portion black for more than an inch, the tip with a small white spot; remaining quills similar, but deeper bluish gray. Bill dusky; feet pale brownish (in skin). *Young, second year:* Similar to the adult in winter plumage, but central lesser wing-coverts dusky, tail crossed by a subterminal band of dusky brown, and primaries marked as in the first plumage.

Total length, about 14.00 inches; extent, 32.00; wing, 10.25; culmen, 1.20; depth of bill through nostrils, .25; tarsus, 1.40; middle toe with claw, 1.40.

This is a widely distributed species, found throughout North America at different seasons, being common both to the Atlantic and the Pacific coasts, and breeding from about latitude 45° or 50° north nearly or quite to the Arctic Ocean. It winters in the southern portions of the United States, on both shores, and also, to a certain extent — not well ascertained — in Mexico and in Central America. It is found in the interior as well as on the sea-coast, but chiefly in its migrations. It is abundant in the waters of the St. Croix and on Passamaquoddy Bay, and is quite common in the summer. Richardson states in regard to it, that he found it in large numbers in all parts of the Fur Countries, where it associates with the Terns, and is distinguished by its peculiar shrill and plaintive cry. Captain Blakiston mentions that he met with this species at the mouth of Hayes River, on the west coast of Hudson's Bay; and Mr. Murray received specimens from the same locality. This Gull was also found on the Mackenzie River by Mr. Bernard Ross.

Mr. J. A. Allen obtained three specimens in Great Salt Lake Valley; these were all in the adult plumage, and differed from the eastern specimens of this Gull in having thicker, much shorter, and less decurved bills.

Birds of this species occur as occasional stragglers in various parts of New England; and they are quite common in spring and fall in the neighborhood of Calais, on the St. Croix River, and in Passamaquoddy Bay. They are less abundant in the summer; but many remain, and are supposed to breed somewhere in that neighborhood in trees. In my visits to Eastport, the Bay of Fundy, and its islands, I have noticed them in large numbers in the months of June and July. I could obtain, however, no evidence in any quarter of their nesting in that vicinity. If they do breed there, it has entirely escaped the notice of those who live in that region. The Gulls were all in flocks, and mostly in mature plumage; but all appeared to be unmated. I found them on the water at all hours of the day and night, and as they were very rarely molested, exceedingly tame and unsuspicious.

Dr. Cooper speaks of finding birds of this species common at Puget Sound at all seasons of the year; and the same statement is made by Dr. Suckley. They appear about San Francisco only from September to May; and do not seem to migrate as far south as San Diego, although Dr. Cooper met with some at San Pedro, late in May, in their immature plumage. They were almost constantly on the wing, diving actively for fish, and were rather shy. Their notes consisted of sharp, but rather faint, squeaks. They are considered good eating.

This Gull occurs in small numbers in spring and fall in Southern Wisconsin, on Lake Koskonong, where examples are each season procured by Professor Kumlien, who writes me that this is the most common Gull of Southern Wisconsin — arriving there in April, when the young grass begins to start, passing northward in large scattered flocks, flying leisurely and low, as if they intended carefully to examine the country they pass over. These are all old ones in their best spring plumage. The immature young birds come in May, and are not uncommon in the lake in June;

and in some summers single immature birds may be seen throughout the season; no old ones are seen in summer. Specimens have been secured in the fall as late as November 7; these vary greatly in size, differing in length from twelve inches to fourteen and one half.

Audubon met with this Gull in the neighborhood of Cincinnati in August, 1819. After the female had been shot, another bird, evidently her mate, alighted immediately by her side to share her fate. Audubon afterward met with the same species on the Mississippi. In May, 1833, he observed this bird in great numbers in the Passamaquoddy, at Eastport. At low water they covered all the sand and mud bars in the neighborhood. They were very gentle, scarcely heeding his near presence; and his son shot seventeen at a single discharge of his double-barrelled gun. They were all young birds of the preceding year. There were no indications in either sex that they would probably breed that season. He found their stomachs filled with coleopterous insects which they had caught on the wing or picked up from the water. On the 24th of August, 1831, he shot ten others in the same locality. In their stomachs were shrimps and small fish. None were observed by Audubon in any part of the Gulf of St. Lawrence, on the coast of Labrador, or of Newfoundland. In the winter he found these Gulls common in the harbor of Charleston; but never saw any at that season about the mouths of the Mississippi. The flight of this bird he describes as being light, elevated, and rapid, more resembling that of Terns than is usually the case with Gulls. Audubon, as well as Yarrell, refers this bird to Greenland; but Professor Reinhardt thinks this reference incorrect.

Individuals of this species have been shot in various parts of Europe. One was taken near Belfast in 1848, and another was shot on the coast. In 1851 one was shot on Loch Lomond, in Scotland, and another on a lake in the North of England; and since that time several others have been taken in that district.

Mr. Donald Gunn found a few of this species breeding in the marshes of Swan Creek, not far from Shoal Lake, in company with the Franklin Gull.

Mr. Dall found these birds not uncommon in the marshes near the Yukon, but rare near the main river. They were most numerous on the Kaigul River, where they were breeding, not far from Nulato. Their eggs have been obtained near Fort Yukon; and the birds themselves are not very rare at Sitka, where Bischoff obtained several specimens.

Mr. MacFarlane found this species breeding in the wooded regions in the neighborhood of Fort Anderson. All the nests were placed either in bushes or on trees, at various heights from the ground — none less than four feet, and others from fifteen to twenty feet. One, found June 23, 1864, was on a tree and at a height of from twelve to fourteen feet; it was between two small ponds of water about a hundred feet from either. The eggs were fresh, indicating that this pair must have nested unusually late. Another nest, found on the following day, was on the dry branch of a pine-tree, and was about ten feet from the ground. There were no sticks in this nest, but it was composed of dark velvety pine-leaves and fine down. He mentions meeting with this Gull in that season much more frequently on his line of travel than on any other occasion; while it was much later than usual in nesting.

Mr. Kennicott found this Gull nesting in the neighborhood of Fort Yukon, and describes the nest as being of about the size of that of *Zenaidura carolinensis*, but the cavity is rather deeper. It was placed on the side-branch of a green spruce, several feet from the trunk, and about twenty feet from the ground, near a lake. Mr. Kennicott saw several nests near this one, all alike and in similar positions, except that some were not over ten feet from the ground, and were on smaller trees; but all were on spruce-trees. One nest which he examined contained three young birds of a dirty yellowish color, thickly spotted with dark brown. He saw between twenty-five and fifty Gulls about that breeding-place, but he found only a few of their nests. These birds were said by the Indians always to breed in similar situations.

In regard to twenty-two other nests described by Mr. MacFarlane, we gather that the usual maximum number of eggs in a nest is three — very rarely four; that all are placed in elevated situations, on high stumps, or bushes, or trees; that the nests are made of sticks, and lined with hay and other soft substances; and that the parents are fearless when they have young, flying about in close proximity, and screaming vehemently. The nests were found with eggs from June 10 to the 10th of July; and in some cases mosses and lichens from the pines and spruces had been largely used in their construction. They were usually placed flat on horizontal branches at some distance from the trunk. The eggs procured by Mr. MacFarlane vary in length from 1.90 to 2.05 inches, and in breadth from 1.35 to 1.45. Their ground-color is a grayish olive, passing into a greenish tint; while the markings consist of small spots of clove-brown, and are chiefly gathered around the larger end of the egg.

Specimens of this Gull and of its eggs were also procured at Fort Resolution, on the Yukon; at Fort Simpson, at Big Island, at Fort Rae, and at Peel's River Fort; at Fort Good Hope, Fort Anderson, on the Lower Anderson; and at various other points.

Larus minutus.

LITTLE GULL.

Larus albus, SCOP. Ann. I. Hist. Nat. 1769, 106 (not of GUNN., 1767).
Larus minutus, PALL. Reise, Russ. Reichs, III. App. no. 35 (1776); Zoog. Rosso-As. II. 1826, 331. — GMEL. S. N. I. ii. 1788, 595. — SAUNDERS, P. Z. S. 1878, 206.
Chroicocephalus minutus, EYTON, Cat. Brit. B. 1836, 61.
Larus atricilloides, FALK, Itin. III. p. 355, t. 24 (fide GMEL. S. N. I. ii. 1788, 601).
Larus d'Orbignyi, AUDOUIN, Hist. Nat. de l'Egypte, 1825, pl. 9, fig. 3, Expl. p. 271.
Larus nigrotis, LESS. Traité, II. 1831, 619.

SP. CHAR. *Adult, in summer:* Head and extreme upper part of the neck uniform deep black; middle and lower part of the neck (all round), entire lower parts, upper tail-coverts, tail, and ends of the remiges (broadly) snow-white. Mantle, including remiges, except their ends, delicate pale

Winter adult.

pearl-blue. "Bill blackish red, gape dark red: legs bright vermilion or coral; iris deep brown" (SHARPE & DRESSER). *Adult, in winter:* Similar, but head and neck white, the occiput washed with brownish gray, and the auricular region marked by a spot of dusky black. "Feet yellowish red" (SHARPE & DRESSER). *Young, first plumage:* Forehead, lores, cheeks, entire lower parts, upper tail-coverts, and greater portion of the tail, pure white; occiput, auricular region, lower part of the nape, lesser and middle wing-coverts, scapulars, tertials, and terminal third of the tail (except lateral feathers) blackish fuliginous, the feathers (except on head and neck) bordered terminally with white or pale buff; greater wing-coverts and secondaries delicate pale pearl-blue;

primaries with outer webs mostly blackish (more slaty basally), the inner webs mostly white, except next the shaft and toward ends; primary-coverts uniform black. "Bill horn-black; feet flesh-colored."[1]

Wing, about 8.75–9.00 inches; tail, 4.30; culmen, .90; tarsus, 1.00; middle toe, .90.

The claim of this bird to be included in the fauna of North America rests upon somewhat questionable grounds. Richardson states that a single individual of this species was obtained on Sir John Franklin's first expedition to the Arctic Regions, and that this specimen was a young bird in its first year. According to Major Wedderburn, this species is an occasional winter visitant in Bermuda, occurring there only in midwinter. Major Wedderburn procured a specimen on the 22d of January, 1849, during a strong northerly gale, and another one was killed in the following month.

This Gull was noticed, and a specimen obtained, on the western coast of Mexico by Colonel Grayson, in the neighborhood of Mazatlan. He states that a few individuals were seen, and that specimens were procured in a fresh-water lagoon near the sea-shore, March 27, 1868. He did not meet with any others afterward.

According to Wheelwright, this species breeds in Gotland, but is not known to do so in any other part of Scandinavia. It is far more common around Novaya Ladoga and Archangel in Russia. Its habits are said greatly to resemble those of the *Larus ridibundus* of Europe; and its eggs are described by Mr. Wheelwright as being of much the same shape and color, but smaller than those of that bird, and measuring 1.66 inches by 1.25.

According to Yarrell, this species is only a winter visitant to Great Britain, where, though not abundant it is of by no means infrequent occurrence. He mentions twenty-three instances in which the time and place of capture of this Gull have been put on record in various parts of Ireland, England, and Scotland, stating that in nearly all these the birds were in immature plumage. In only one or two instances have the individuals been in the adult plumage, and these were taken in Ireland.

The egg of the *L. minutus*, as figured by Mr. Hewitson, is 1.63 inches in length, and 1.25 in breadth; the ground-color is olive-brown, and this is spotted and blotched with two shades of reddish brown.

Mr. Temminck killed two specimens of this Gull and procured several others in Holland, and Messrs. Necker and Schinz record five instances of its having been taken about the lakes of Switzerland. Savi includes it among the birds of Italy; and it is said to be found every winter on the shores of the Adriatic, the Mediterranean, and also on the Caspian Sea.

[1] The fresh colors are given by Macgillivray as follows: "*Adult, in winter:* Bill and iris blackish brown; feet of a very bright vermilion. *Adult, in summer:* Bill of a very deep lake-red, iris deep brown; feet crimson. *Young:* Bill blackish brown; feet livid flesh-color."

According to Temminck it feeds on insects and worms; and on several occasions where it was shot in Great Britain it was found in company with different species of Terns.

Genus RHODOSTETHIA, Macgillivray.

Rossia, Bonap. Comp. List, 1838, 62 (type, *Larus roseus*, Macgill.; not of Owen, 1838).
Rhodostethia, Macgill. Man. Brit. Orn. II. 1842, 253 (same type).

Gen. Char. "Body moderate; neck rather short; head ovate; bill short, rather slender; upper mandible with its dorsal outline nearly straight for half its length, arcuate-decurvate toward the end; lower mandible with the intercrural space narrow, the knot slight, the dorsal line concave, the tip narrow; legs short; tibiæ bare for a very short space; tarsus rather stout, anteriorly

R. rosea, summer adult.

scutellate, rough behind; first toe short, with a large curved claw; anterior toes moderate, with their webs entire; claws rather large, arched, compressed, acute; plumage soft and full; wings long, rather narrow, pointed; tail cuneate, of twelve feathers, of which the central are much larger than the lateral" (Macgillivray).

A single species only is known, this being one of the rarest of the family; no specimen having until very recently come to any American collection.

Rhodostethia rosea.

ROSS'S GULL; WEDGE-TAILED GULL.

Larus roseus, Macgill. Mem. Wern. Soc. V. 1824, 249. — Jard. & Selby, Illustr. Orn. 1828, pl. 14.
Larus (*Rhodostethia*) *roseus*, Bruch, J. f. O. 1853, 106.
Rhodostethia rosea, Lawr. in Baird's B. N. Am. 1858, 856. —Baird, Cat. N. Am. B. 1859, no. 678. — Coues, Pr. Ac. Nat. Sci. Philad. 1862, 311; Key, 1872, 316; Check List, 1873, no. 557; 2d ed. 1882, no. 789; B. N. W. 1874, 659. — Saunders, Ibis, 1875, 484; P. Z. S. 1878, 208. — Ridgw. Nom. N. Am. B. 1881, no. 676.
Larus Rossii, Rich. App. Parry's 2d Voy. 1825, 359 (Melville Peninsula); F. B. A. II. 1831, 427. — Nutt. Man. II. 1834, 295. — Aud. Orn. Biog. V. 1839, 324; Synop. 1839, 323; B. Am. VII. 1844, 130.
Rhodostethia Rossii, Macgill. Man. Orn. II. 1842, 253.

Hab. Region of Melville Peninsula, chiefly. Disco Bay; Heligoland; Faröes; Yorkshire, England; Point Barrow, Alaska, and Arctic Ocean north of Siberia;[1] Kamtschatka?

Sp. Char. *Adult, in summer:* "*Color.* Scapulars, interscapulars, and both surfaces of the

[1] For full list of the specimens (eleven in number) known to exist in collections to that date, see the "Ibis," 1875, p. 487.

wings clear pearl-gray; outer web of the first quill blackish brown to its tip, which is gray; tips of the scapulars and lesser quills whitish; some small feathers near the eye and a collar round the middle of the neck pitch-black, rest of the plumage white; the neck above and the whole under plumage deeply tinged with peach-blossom red in recent specimens. Bill black; its rictus and the edges of the eyelids reddish orange; legs and feet vermilion-red; nails blackish.

"*Form.* Bill slender, weak, with a scarcely perceptible salient angle beneath; the upper mandible slightly arched and compressed toward the point; the commissure slightly curved at the tip. Wings an inch longer than the decidedly cuneiform tail; the central feathers of which are an inch longer than the outer ones. Tarsi rather stout; the thumb very distinct, armed with a nail as large as that of the outer toe.

"*Dimensions.* Length, 14.00 inches; wing, 10.50; tail, 5.50; bill above, .75, along gape, 1.25; tarsus, $1\frac{1}{12}$" (RICHARDSON, Faun. Bor. Am. II. 427).

Adult male, in winter (No. 87230, U. S. Nat. Mus., lat. 71° 50′ N., Arctic Ocean, north of Siberia, Oct. 7, 1879; R. L. NEWCOMB): Head, neck, and lower parts pure white, the pileum tinged with pale pearl-gray, the breast and most of other lower parts tinged with a very fine delicate rose-pink; no trace of black collar, but a distinct blackish patch or bar immediately in front of eye. Mantle and wings delicate pale pearl-gray, the secondaries very broadly tipped with pinkish white, the two inner primaries becoming gradually white terminally, and the outer web of the outer primary chiefly black. Lower part of rump, upper tail-coverts, and tail white, faintly tinged with delicate rose-pink. Bill black; iris brown; legs and feet pale brownish in dried skin.[1] Wing, 10.00 inches; tail, 4.50, the lateral feathers .75 shorter; culmen, .75; tarsus, 1.25; middle toe, 1.00.

Young male, in second summer (No. 87232, U. S. Nat. Mus., Arctic Ocean, north of Siberia, June 23; R. L. NEWCOMB): Head, neck, lower parts, lower part of rump, and upper tail-coverts pale, delicate rose-pink, this deepest beneath the surface of the feathers, the head and neck, except underneath, nearly pure white; upper part of neck encircled by a narrow black collar, broadest on the throat, only the tips of the feathers being black. Mantle and wings delicate pale pearl-gray, the lesser and middle wing-coverts dusky black on the surface (only the concealed portion being pearl-gray); inner secondaries, primary coverts, alulæ, and adjacent small feathers, with three outer primaries, blackish dusky, the inner webs of the latter, however, with the marginal half pearl-gray; remaining primaries pearl-gray, becoming white on the innermost quills, all of them broadly tipped with black; under surface of wing pale pearl-gray, like the mantle. Tail white, the third, fourth, and fifth feathers broadly tipped with black (this .75 of an inch in extent on fifth or next to the middle feather). Bill black; iris brown; legs and feet bright red, claws black. Wing, about 9.75 (quills much abraded) inches; tail, 4.80, the lateral feathers 1.50 shorter; culmen, .70; tarsus, 1.20; middle toe, 1.00.

Another young male in second summer, also collected by Mr. Newcomb (No. 87231, June 30, 1880), differs in having the rosy tint almost entirely absent, the black necklace much less distinct, and the tail wholly white. It measures: Wing, 9.50 inches; tail, 5.10, the lateral feathers 1.20 shorter; culmen, .65; tarsus, 1.25; middle toe, 1.05.

Young, in first plumage (No. 81224, St. Michael's, Alaska, Oct. 10, 1879; E. W. NELSON): General color of pileum, nape, and mantle very pale pearl-gray, but this only on the surface, all the underlying portion of the feathers being pure white; all the parts described heavily clouded with dark fuliginous, or blackish dusky, there being many feathers with the tip very broadly of this color; these dark markings prevail on the upper portion of the rump, where the feathers have dull buffy tips. Lower part of rump, upper tail-coverts, and greater part of tail immaculate pure white; middle pair of tail-feathers with the end sooty-black for about .85 of an inch, the next feather on each side black for a much less distance, the third with merely a slight mottling of dusky at the extreme tip. Lesser and middle wing-coverts, tertials, and most of the scapulars dark sooty or brownish black, each feather distinctly bordered terminally with pale grayish buff; greater wing-coverts

[1] Professor J. Murdoch has kindly furnished us with the following description of the fresh colors of an adult male in winter plumage obtained by him at Point Barrow, Alaska: "Feet terra-cotta red, with brown webs and knuckles. White everywhere tinged with red, except rectrices; rose-color somewhat blotchy and approaching salmon-color, especially on crissum. Mantle pearly blue, extending as mottlings to the back of the head. Edge of wing, from shoulder to wrist, bright rosy."

immaculate, very pale pearl-gray, fading gradually into white terminally ; secondaries and two inner primaries pure white ; next two primaries with pure white inner webs and shafts, the outer webs very pale pearl-gray, the first quill having the inner web narrowly margined at end with black, the next with a somewhat oblong spot of black near end of each web ; next two quills with inner web bluish white, the outer web pearl-gray, both very broadly tipped with black, and the shaft dusky ; next quill similar, but with the central portion grayish dusky, forming a longitudinal lanceolate stripe, divided medially by the shaft ; three outer quills with outer webs wholly blackish, and the inner web with a broad stripe of the same next the shaft ; alulæ, carpal region, and primary coverts plain sooty black, the latter narrowly tipped with pale grayish buff. Lateral and under sides of head and neck white, with rather indistinct transverse bars of dusky, except on chin and throat ; a dusky suffusion immediately before the eye. Lower parts, from jugulum back, including axillars, entirely immaculate pure white ; lining of wing and under surface of primaries light silvery gray. Bill black, brownish basally ; "iris hazel ; legs and feet dull fleshy purple" (Nelson, MS.). Wing, 9.55 inches ; tail, 4.00, the lateral feathers .70 shorter ; culmen, .65 ; tarsus, 1.25 ; middle toe, 1.00.

Herr J. C. H. Fischer, in "Kröyer's Natural History Journal" for 1864, records the occurrence of this extremely rare Gull in the Faröe Islands. It is there spoken of as the "Cuneate-tailed Gull." The example in this instance had been taken in Suderoe in February, 1863 ; it is now in a private collection in Copenhagen. The "Ibis" (1865, p. 104) makes the statement that only five other examples of this species are known to exist. One of these, obtained June, 1823, on Melville Peninsula, is in the Edinburgh Museum ; another, from the same place, is now in the Derby Museum of Liverpool ; the third specimen, from Kamtschatka, is in the Museum at Mainz ; the fourth, in a private collection in England, is said to have been killed in Yorkshire ; and the other, killed on the Island of Heligoland, is in the collection of Herr Gätke.

Richardson states that two specimens were killed on the coast of Melville Peninsula, during Sir Edward Parry's second voyage. Ross, in his Zoological Appendix to Parry's narrative of his boat voyage toward the Pole, states that several individuals were seen during the journey over the ice north of Spitzbergen, and that Lieutenant Forster also found it in Waygatsch Straits, which is presumed to be one of its breeding-places. In regard to any of its specific peculiarities of habits, or the places of its retreat in the winter, no information has been obtained.

Mr. Charlesworth published a paper in the first part of the first volume of the "Proceedings of the Yorkshire Philosophical Society," giving the particulars of the capture of this example in Yorkshire. It was killed, in 1847, by a Mr. Horner, in February, in a ploughed field near the hamlet of Milford. Its flight is said to have been similar to that of any other Gull, and the bird did not appear at all shy.

Mr. Macgillivray states, in his edition of 1842, that it has once occurred in Ireland ; but the statement is unsupported by evidence, and Mr. Yarrell thinks that Ireland is wrongly printed instead of Iceland. It is not accepted as a bird of Ireland either by Thompson or Walter.

It has not been met with in Smith's Sound by any of the exploring expeditions. Its entire absence, so far as is known, from Spitzbergen, Nova Zembla, Franz-Josef Land, and Siberia, and its not having been seen by any of the Franklin search expeditions that have entered Lancaster Sound or skirted the northern shores of America from Behring's Straits, and its not having been noticed in Alaska, has led Captain Fielden to conclude that it must be a bird of limited distribution, and that it probably has its breeding-haunts north of Hudson's Bay.

Genus XEMA, Leach.

Xema, "Leach," Ross's Voy. App. 1819, p. lvii (type, *Larus Sabinei*, Sab.).
?? *Creagrus*, Bonap. Naum. 1854, 213 (type, *Larus furcatus*, Neboux).

Char. Size small or medium; tail forked; tarsus equal to or rather shorter than the middle toe, with claw; adult with a dark hood, the plumage otherwise pearl-gray above and white beneath.

It is very doubtful whether the *Larus furcatus*, Neboux, should be referred to the genus *Xema*. Mr. Salvin, who has had the opportunity of examining a specimen, remarks as follows on this question: "*Creagrus*, as a genus, differs but slightly from *Xema*, both having a deeply forked tail.

X. Sabini, summer adult.

The former, however, is a more robust form, and has the nostril situated rather nearer the point of the bill. In coloration, *Creagrus* wants the black ring which encircles the hood of *Xema*. I doubt whether in a well-considered classification of the *Laridæ* the two genera could be maintained as distinct" (Trans. Zool. Soc. Lond. IX. 1876, p. 506). It might also have been added, that the tail of *Creagrus* is much more deeply forked, and that the coloration of the bill and feet is radically different.

Assuming, however, that they may be referred to the same genus, their differential characters may be stated as follows: —

1. **X. Sabini.** Wing, 11.00 inches or less; tail slightly forked; hood plumbeous, bounded below by a well-defined black collar; bill black, tipped with yellow; feet black. *Hab.* Circumpolar Regions.
2. **X. furcata.** Wing, 16.00 inches or more; tail deeply forked; hood sooty black, with a white frontal bar, but no dark collar; bill and feet red. *Hab.* Galapagos; coast of Peru; coast of California (?).

Xema Sabini.

THE FORK-TAILED GULL.

Larus Sabini, J. Sabine, Tr. Linn. Soc. XII. 1818, 520, pl. 29.
Larus Sabinii, Rich. App. Parry's 2d Voy. 1825, 360. — Sw. & Rich. F. B. A. II. 1831, 428 — Nutt. Man. II. 1834, 295. — Aud. Orn. Biog. III. 1835, 561, pl. 285; Synop. 1839, 323; B. Am. VII. 1844, 127, pl. 441.
Xema Sabini, Edw. & Beverley, App. Ross's Voy. Baf. Bay, 4to ed. 1819, lvii.
Larus (Xema) Sabini, Bruch, J. f. O. 1853, 103.

Xema Sabinii, LAWR. in Baird's B. N. Am. 1858, 857. — BAIRD, Cat. N. Am. B. 1859, no. 680. — SAUNDERS, P. Z. S. 1878, 209. — COUES, 2d Check List, 1882, no. 790.

Xema Sabinei, COUES, Pr. Philad. Acad. 1862, 311 ; Key, 1872, 317 ; Check List, 1873, no. 558 ; B. N. W. 1874, 66. — RIDGW. Nom. N. Am. B. 1881, no. 677.

Xema collaris, "SCHREIBERS," ROSS, in App. Ross's Voy. Baf. Bay, II. 8vo ed. 1819, 164 (nec SCHREIBERS, = *Rhodostethia rosea!* Cf. SAUNDERS, P. Z. S. 1878, p. 209).

HAB. Circumpolar Regions ; in winter migrating south, in America, to Maine, New York, the Great Lakes, and Great Salt Lake, Utah. Very abundant in Alaska. Bermudas, one instance (SAUNDERS). Macabi Island, coast of Peru, lat. 8° S. (one specimen, *fide* SAUNDERS, P. Z. S. 1878, p. 210).

SP. CHAR. *Adult, in summer:* Head and upper part of the neck plumbeous, bounded below by a well-defined collar of black, widest behind ; lower part of the neck, entire lower parts, tail, upper tail-coverts, and lower part of rump snow-white, the lower parts faintly tinged with delicate rose-pink in some freshly killed specimens. Mantle deep bluish gray (nearly the same shade as in

Larus Franklini), the secondaries pure white, becoming gradually pale grayish blue toward bases ; most of the exposed portion of the greater coverts also white, forming, together with the secondaries, a conspicuous longitudinal white stripe on the closed wing. Four outer primaries black, broadly tipped with white, the inner webs broadly margined with the same ; fifth quill with the greater part of the inner web, and about 1.75 inches of the terminal portion of the outer, white, the remainder black; remaining quills white; outer border of the wing, from the carpal joint back to the primary coverts, including the latter and the alulæ, uniform black. Bill black, tipped with yellow ; eyelids red ; iris brown ; "feet dull lead-color, claws black" (L. M. TURNER, MS.). *Adult in winter:* Similar to the summer plumage, but head and neck white, except occiput, nape, and auricular region, which are dull dusky plumbeous. *Young, first plumage:* Crown, nape, back, scapulars, wing-coverts, and rump brownish gray, each feather bordered terminally with light fulvous or pale grayish buff, this fulvous border preceded on the tertials, longer scapulars, etc., by a dusky internal sub-border ; greater wing-coverts and secondaries white, as in the adult ; primaries much as in the adult. Tail white, with a broad subterminal band of black, the tip narrowly white or pale fulvous ; upper tail-coverts and entire lower parts white. Bill dusky, brownish toward the base ; feet light brownish (in the skin).

Wing, about 10.75 inches ; culmen, 1.00 ; depth of bill through angle, .30 ; tarsus, 1.25 ; middle toe and claw, 1.25.

The Fork-tailed Gull is an almost exclusively Arctic species. It is found in the breeding-season in the extreme northern portions of America and Asia, but is of only occasional occurrence in Europe. So far as is now known, it breeds exclusively in North America and in portions of Asia. In the winter it wanders south of the Arctic Circle; but at all times the larger portion of the birds of this species remain in high northern latitudes, only a very small number wandering as far south as the United States.

This Gull is of occasional occurrence in New England, and is probably found there more frequently than the present scanty records would seem to indicate. One was shot in September, 1874, in Boston Harbor, and is now in the collection of Mr. William Brewster; and early in June, 1878, Mr. Boardman procured a fine example on the St. Croix. This gentleman had become aware that this species was present in that region every spring, but had never before been able to secure an example. He had often noticed it among the numerous Bonaparte Gulls, of which a "cartload" had to be sacrificed before the desired *Sabini* could be secured.

Mr. Howard Saunders, referring to its autumnal movements southward, mentions the procuring of many examples of this species on the British coast, and on that of the continent of Europe, as far south as Holstein and France; these were mostly immature birds. One adult was taken on the coast of Brittany, Aug. 25, 1872. In America he cites the range of this Gull as extending to New York on the east, and Great Salt Lake in the interior. In the Museum of the University of Michigan there is said to be an example procured near Tumbez, one of the Macabi Islands, on the coast of Peru, in latitude 8° south.

This species was first described by Sabine from specimens obtained by his brother, Colonel Edward, a member of the Northwest Expedition of 1818. The account of its capture is to the effect that this bird was seen and killed on the 25th of July, 1818, on a group of three rocky islands, each about a mile in diameter, on the west coast of Greenland, twenty miles from the mainland, in lat. 75° 29′ N. It was in company with Arctic Terns, both species breeding on those islands, and their nests being intermingled. This Gull was said to lay two eggs on the bare ground, which were hatched the last week in July. The young at first are mottled with brown, and of a dull yellow. The eggs are described as being an inch and a half in length, of regular shape, and not much pointed; the color is olive, blotched with brown. The parent birds flew with great impetuosity toward persons approaching their nest and young; and when one bird of a pair was killed, its mate, although frequently shot at, continued on the wing close to the spot where its dead mate lay. These birds appeared to get their food on the sea-beach, standing near the water's edge and picking up marine insects cast on the shore.

During the second Arctic voyage, a Gull of this species was seen in Prince Regent's Inlet; and afterward many specimens were obtained on Melville Peninsula. This bird has also been met with at Spitzbergen, Igloolik, Behring's Straits, Cape Garry, and Felix Harbor. The Eskimos informed Sir James C. Ross that it breeds in great numbers west of Neitgelli. It is said to arrive in high northern latitudes in June, and to move southward in August. When recently killed, its under plumage is of a delicate pink blush-color.

In the course of a voyage from Pictou, in Nova Scotia, to Hull, in England, Mr. Thomas Macullock saw great numbers of this species when more than a hundred miles off Newfoundland. They flew around the ship in company with an almost equal number of Ross's Gull.

This bird is mentioned by Reinhardt as being very rare in the Danish settlements of Greenland, and as breeding only to the north of Upernavik. Professor Blasius also describes it as occurring in Heligoland. According to Middendorff, Sabine's Gull is a bird of Siberia; and it is included in his list of those that penetrate to the farthest north. He also states ("Sib. Reise," p. 244) that this Gull appeared on the Taimyr River (lat. 73° 45′ N.) on the 5th of June; but soon left, and was not seen again until he reached the ponds in the Barrens (*tundras*) and the small alluvial islands in the river and lake of Taimyr, in about 74° north latitude; there it was common, breeding in company with the Arctic Tern. The same writer, quoted by Dresser, states that he found this bird breeding in Northern Siberia, and that on the 10th of July the eggs were much incubated. They were deposited in depressions in the moss, lined with dry grass-bents of the previous year, and there were two in each nest. On the 19th of July most of the young birds seen had only just been hatched out; but a few were of considerable size. On the 15th of August he saw full-grown, though not full-feathered, young. They dived with ease, while the parents were flying overhead — every now and then darting down, uttering a harsh note somewhat resembling that of *Turdus pilaris*. He found the crops of the old birds and the stomachs of the young filled with the larvæ of dipterous insects.

Richardson, in his "Journal of a Boat-voyage," refers to an island off Cape Dalhousie, on which he encamped, as being one of the breeding-places of this bird, and states that the eggs were deposited in hollows in the short and mossy turf.

Mr. Giraud mentions that a single individual of this species was shot at Raynor South, on Long Island, in July, 1837, and states that, so far as he was aware, this was the only one ever procured on the island.

Mr. J. A. Allen obtained a single specimen of Sabine's Gull at Salt Lake Valley in September, and one is said also to have been taken in Bermuda — shot by Colonel Drummond near St. George; but in this case there was no record of the date.

According to Yarrell, there are several instances on record of the shooting of this Gull in the British Islands. The first specimen, so far as known, was shot in Belfast Bay in September, 1822; the second, now in the Museum of the Royal Dublin Society, was shot in Dublin Bay by Mr. Wall. Both of these birds were in the plumage of the first autumn. Other specimens have since been obtained in Cambridgeshire, at Milford Haven, at Newhaven, near Dublin, and in several other places. Temminck mentions three instances of the occurrence of this species which had become known to him — one was a young bird on the coast of Holland; a second was killed on the Rhine; a third in France, not far from Rouen; and still another near Dunkirk.

Captain MacFarlane found this Gull breeding in the islands of the Arctic Ocean. He mentions that the under plumage of a male shot by him early in July was deeply tinged with crimson. The first nest found was by itself on an island near a small lake, and contained three eggs. In June, 1865, Mr. MacFarlane found a number of these birds breeding on the "large island" in Franklin Bay — a place often referred to in his notes as such, which, however, was ascertained not to be an island, but an extensive neck or point of land. The nests were on an islet in a small lake.

Mr. Dall mentions finding the Fork-tailed Gull abundant in the marshes about Pastolik and St. Michael's, where it breeds. He also states that this species is not rare at Plover Bay, in Eastern Siberia. Mr. Dall has never observed it far inland, in strictly fresh water, and is certain that it is not found at Nulato.

Mr. Bannister states that in the early part of July he observed large flocks of these birds in the Canal at St. Michael's, and that at about the same time two specimens were shot by Mr. Pease in the same locality. They did not observe this species at any other point near the redoubt. But Mr. E. Adams mentions ("Ibis," 1878) having met with this species at St. Michael's, where a few individuals made their appearance about the salt-marshes on the 7th of May, and a few pairs bred there. They were often feeding about the mud of the lakes, but he did not see any of them on the sea-shore. Their food consisted of worms and insects. They were very bold, dashing like the Kittiwakes at the head of any intruder upon their domain; at other times they were rather shy and wary.

Eggs of this species, procured on the Arctic coast by Mr. MacFarlane, exhibit the following measurements: 1.75 by 1.20 inches; 1.70 by 1.25; and 1.76 by 1.20. They are of nearly uniform appearance, size, and shape. Their ground-color is a deep olive-brown, varying to greenish in some, to a deeper olive in others, and spotted with markings of a deep sepia, with no obscure cloudings of slate or lilac.

Xema furcata.

THE SWALLOW-TAILED GULL.

Mouette à queue fourchue, NEBOUX, Rev. Zool. 1840, 290.

Larus furcatus, NEBOUX, Voy. "Vénus," Atlas, pl. x. (1846). — PRÉVOST & DES MURS, Voy. "Vénus," V. Ois. 1855, 277.

Larus (*Xema*) *furcatus*, BRUCH, J. f. O. 1853, 103.

Xema furcatum, COUES, Key, 1872, 317; Check List, 1873, no. 559; Birds N. W. 1874, 661. — SAUNDERS, P. Z. S. 1878, 210; 1882, 523, pl. 34 (adult and young; Peru).

Xema furcata, COUES, 2d Check List, 1882, no. 791.

Creagrus furcatus, BONAP. Naumannia, 1854, 213. — LAWR. in Baird's B. N. Am. 1858, 857. — BAIRD, Cat. N. Am. B. 1859, no. 679. — SALVIN, Trans. Zool. Soc. IX. 1876, 506 (Galapagos). — RIDGW. Nom. N. Am. B. 1881, no. 678.

HAB. Coast of California? ; Galapagos; Paracas Bay, Peru (SAUNDERS).

SP. CHAR. *Adult* (*summer plumage?*): Above, cinereous; entire head, with anterior half of the neck, sooty black; frontal bar, exterior margin of the scapulars, under wing-coverts, tail, and entire lower parts, white; first to fourth quills, with the whole of the outer and the terminal portion of the inner webs, black, the third and fourth gray at the base; fifth and sixth gray

X. furcata, summer adult.

exteriorly, black terminally; fourth, fifth, and sixth with a white apical bar. Bill and feet red. Total length, 23.00 inches; wing, 16.00; middle rectrices, 4.70; exterior rectrices, 8.00; tarsus, 1.90; middle toe, with claw, 2.00.[1]

[1] Translation of Salvin's Latin diagnosis in Trans. Zool. Soc. Lond. IX. 1876, p. 506.

The first known example of the young of this excessively rare species has very recently been described by Mr. Saunders (Proc. Zool. Soc. Lond. 1882, pp. 523, 524, pl. 34), who gives the following information respecting the specimens known to date:—

"The third known example of this rarest of Gulls, the history of which may here be briefly recapitulated. The Paris Museum possesses one, in somewhat immature plumage, said to have been obtained by Dr. Neboux, of the French frigate 'Vénus,' at Monterey, Cal., in the month of November. The British Museum has an adult in full breeding-plumage obtained during the voyage of H.M. SS. 'Herald' and 'Pandora,' at Dalrymple Rock, Chatham Island, Galapagos Group, nearly on the equator, between the 11th and 16th of January. It is a medium-sized Gull, with long wings (16 inches), a dark slate-colored hood, and a forked tail; indeed were it not that the hood is separated from the base of the bill by a band of white feathers, and that there is no black neck-ring at the base of the hood, *Xema furcatum* might be described as a gigantic Sabine's Gull. In the young, now figured, the resemblance to the young of *Xema Sabinii* is very marked. The entire head is white, with dark markings in front of and surrounding the eyes, and a brown auricular patch as in most of the immature hooded Gulls; neck and mantle ashy brown, the tips of the feathers margined with white; upper wing-coverts and secondaries white; primaries 1–5 black, with greater part of inner web white, 6 and 7 white barred with dusky, 8–10 pure white. Tail much forked, the outer feathers nearly white, the others banded with brown and tipped with white; rump white, slightly mottled with brown. Under parts white. Bill horn-black; tarsi and feet livid brown. The bill is proportionately longer, slenderer, and more curved than in *X. Sabinii,* from which it also differs in having a considerable bare space between the base of the feathers and the nares. The first primary which shows the slightest tip of white is the 5th, and there is less white at the tips of the upper ones than in the young of *X. Sabinii.*

"The feathers are all quite fresh; and, reasoning from analogy, I should think that this example cannot have been more than three or four months old. Where, then, are the headquarters of this mysterious Gull? It would seem by this specimen that its breeding-time corresponds to that of the northern hemisphere, and that, like some other Gulls, it passes southward to escape the northern winter; but as yet nothing is known. It is, however, somewhat remarkable that American naturalists who have devoted so much attention to the exploration of the coast of the Pacific, from Vancouver Island down to Mexico, have discovered no trace of it; nor have repeated visits to the Galapagos produced more than the isolated adult specimen above noticed. Captain Markham's valuable acquisition has now made us acquainted with the first plumage of this extremely rare bird; and the proof of the existence of this long-lost species may be expected to awaken an interest which will probably in a few years lead to the discovery of its real habitat."

The Fork-tailed Gull was originally described from a specimen said to have been taken at sea off the coast of California. There has been no subsequent confirmation of the claim of this species to a place in the fauna of North America. Dr. Cooper writes me that he has never seen any individual answering to the description of this species along the Pacific coast of California, nor has it been obtained there by any one else. Nothing is known as to its distribution or its general habits. It is now positively ascertained that of the three specimens — all that have ever been procured

— one was certainly obtained in the Galapagos, and not within our limits; and as the expedition that procured the supposed Californian example visited the same group, Mr. Salvin is of the opinion that this was the locality from which both specimens came, and that this bird does not belong to the fauna of the United States.

GENUS **STERNA**, LINNÆUS.

Sterna, LINN. S. N. ed. 10, I. 1758, 137, ed. 12, I. 1766, 227 (type, by elim., *Sterna hirundo*, LINN.).
Sternula, BOIE, Isis, 1822, 563 (type, *Sterna minuta*, LINN.).
Thalasseus, BOIE, Isis, 1822, 563 (type, *Sterna caspia*, PALL.).
Thalassea, KAUP, Sk. Entw. Eur. Thierw. 1829, 97 (type, *Sterna paradisea*, BRÜNN.).
Sylochelidon, BREHM, Vög. Deutschl. 1830, 767 (type, *Sterna caspia*, LINN.).
Actochelidon, KAUP, Sk. Ent. Eur. Thierw. 1829, 31 (type, *Sterna cantiaca*, GMEL.).
Gelochelidon, BREHM, Naturg. Vög. Deutschl. 1831, 774 (type, *G. meridionalis*, BREHM, *Sterna anglica*, MONT.).
Haliplana, WAGL. Isis, 1832, 1224 (type, *Sterna fuliginosa*, GMEL.).

CHAR. Size exceedingly variable, the form and colors less so; tail always decidedly forked, and toes almost fully webbed, but the webs concave, or "scalloped out," anteriorly.

Synopsis of North American Species.

A. Size medium (wing about 11.75–12.25 inches); tail emarginate; occipital feathers soft and blended; inner webs of primaries bicolored (a blackish stripe next the shaft, the inner border broadly white); bill wholly black, short and thick, its upper and lower outlines strongly convex, the depth through the base about one third the length of the culmen; pileum entirely black in summer, uniform ashy white in winter. (*Gelochelidon*, BREHM.)

1. **S. anglica.** Bill and feet black: above, pale pearl-blue, including the rump, upper tail-coverts, and tail; beneath, entirely white. Wing, 11.75–12.25 inches; tail, 5.50; culmen, 1.40; tarsus, 1.30; middle toe, 1.10. *Hab.* Eastern coast of North America, and various parts of the Old World.

B. Size very large (wing 15.00 inches or more); tail emarginate; occipital feathers soft and blended, not forming a crest; inner webs of primaries concolored (dusky grayish); adult, above, pale pearl-gray, beneath, white; hood wholly black in summer, wholly streaked or speckled with white in winter. (*Thalasseus*, BOIE.)

2. **S. caspia.** Bill very robust (the depth through the base a little less than one third the length of the culmen), deep red. *Hab.* North America in general, and various parts of the Old World.

C. Size large or medium (wing 12.50–15.00 inches); tail deeply forked; occipital feathers pointed and somewhat lengthened, forming a short but distinct crest; inner webs of primaries bicolored (dusky in a well-defined stripe next the shaft, the inner edge broadly and abruptly white); adult, pale pearl-gray above, white beneath; pileum wholly black in spring, the forehead, lores, and centre of the crown white in breeding-season. (*Actochelidon*, KAUP.)

3. **S. maxima.** Bill stout (depth through the base much less than one third the length of the culmen), deep orange; wing, 14.00–15.00 inches. *Hab.* Coasts and inland waters of Middle and Southern North America, north to about 40°.
4. **S. elegans.** Bill very slender (depth through the base about one fifth the length of the culmen), deep orange-red; occipital feathers much elongated, and lower parts deeply tinged with peach-blossom pink. Wing, about 12.50 inches. *Hab.* Pacific coast of Middle America, north to California.
5. **S. sandvicensis.** Bill very slender, as in *S. elegans*, but deep black, tipped with yellow; occipital feathers less elongated, and lower parts without pink tinge. Wing, about 12.50 inches. *Hab.* Atlantic coast of North, and both coasts of Middle, America; Palæarctic Region.

D. Size small (wing less than 11.00 inches, and more than 8.00); tail excessively forked, the lateral rectrices attenuated;[1] occipital feathers soft, blended, not forming a crest; inner webs of primaries bicolored; adult pearl-blue above, white, pale pink, or grayish beneath; pileum wholly deep black in summer, except in *Trudeaui* (whole head white, with a lateral dusky bar) and *aleutica* (white frontal lunule). (*Sterna*, LINN.)

a. Pileum entirely white in summer.

6. **S. Trudeaui.** Bill black, tipped with yellowish; head white, with a dusky lateral bar; upper and lower parts pale pearl-gray; rump, tail-coverts, and tail white, slightly silvered. Wing, 9.70–10.60 inches; tail, 4.60–6.00; culmen, 1.50–1.70; tarsus, .92–.96; middle toe, .75–.80. *Hab.* Coasts of South America, and casual along the Atlantic coast of the United States.

b. Pileum entirely black in summer.

7. **S. Forsteri.** Bill dull orange, dusky at the tip; feet rich orange-red (in life); outer web of lateral rectrices pure white throughout, the inner web usually dusky or grayish toward the end, in more or less marked contrast;[2] lower parts entirely white. Wing, 9.50–10.30 inches; tail, 5.00–7.70; culmen, 1.50–1.65; tarsus, .90–.99; middle toe, 1.05–1.15. *Hab.* Temperate North America in general, south in winter to Brazil.

8. **S. hirundo.** Bill vermilion, the tip dusky; feet rich vermilion (in life); outer web of lateral rectrices grayish or dusky, the inner pure white throughout, in abrupt contrast; lower parts usually pale grayish, rarely nearly white. Wing, 9.75–11.75 inches; tail, 5.00–7.00; culmen, 1.25–1.50; tarsus, .66–.87; middle toe, .75. *Hab.* Eastern North America; Palæarctic Region.

9. **S. paradisæa.** Bill rich carmine, with or without black tip; feet intense red (in life); outer rectrices as in *fluviatilis,* but usually more elongated; lower parts deep, somewhat smoky, pearl-gray, almost as dark as the upper parts. Wing, 10.00–10.75 inches; tail, 6.50–8.50; culmen, 1.08–1.40; tarsus, .55–.65; middle toe, with claw, .80–.85. *Hab.* Northern parts of northern hemisphere.

10. **S. Dougalli.** Bill black, usually reddish basally; feet bright red (in life); lateral rectrices wholly white, sometimes very faintly silvered; lower parts delicate peach-blossom-pink in life, fading to pinkish white or even pure white in the dried skin. Wing, 9.25–9.75 inches; tail, 7.25–7.75; culmen, 1.50; tarsus, .85; middle toe, .75. *Hab.* Atlantic coast of North America; West Indies; Palæarctic Region.

c. Forehead white, this color extending back along the sides of the crown to the eyes.

11. **S. aleutica.** Bill and feet wholly deep black; upper parts pearly plumbeous, the upper tail-coverts and tail abruptly pure white; lower parts paler plumbeous, fading into white on the chin and crissum. Wing, 9.75–10.75 inches; tail, 6.50–7.00; culmen, 1.25–1.40; tarsus, .60–.75; middle toe, .80–.85. *Hab.* Coasts and islands of Alaska.

E. Size extremely small (wing less than 8.00 inches); tail moderately forked, the lateral feathers not much attenuated; occipital feathers soft and blended. Adult pale pearl-blue above, the rump and tail sometimes white; white beneath; the pileum with a white frontal lunule, as in *Sterna aleutica* and in *Haliplana*. (*Sternula*, BOIE.)

12. **S. antillarum.** Bill yellow, usually tipped with black; upper parts entirely pale pearl-blue, including the tail; lower parts white; wing less than 7.00 inches; culmen less than 1.25; the bill usually black-tipped. *Hab.* Warm-temperate North America and Middle America; West Indies.

F. Size small (wing about 10.50 to 12.00 inches); bill very straight, the culmen sometimes even slightly depressed in the middle portion; nasal groove long and deep, the nostrils more anterior than in *Sterna;* tail deeply forked, but the feathers relatively broader and stiffer; color, dusky above, sometimes interrupted by a whitish nuchal band; beneath, entirely white; pileum black, with a white frontal lunule as in *Sternula* and in *Sterna aleutica*. (*Haliplana*, WAGLER.)

13. **S. fuliginosa.** Above, entirely brownish black, uninterrupted on the nape; wing, about 12.00 inches. *Hab.* Sea-coasts throughout the warmer parts of the world; in North

[1] When fully developed, and not abraded.

[2] This latter feature by no means constant, however.

America, known only from the Gulf and South Atlantic coasts, north, casually, to Pennsylvania.

14. **S. anæstheta.** Above, sooty plumbeous, lightening gradually on the upper back into ashy, this gradually fading into whitish on the nape, the black of the pileum being strongly contrasted. Wing, about 10.50 inches. *Hab.* Sea-coasts throughout the warmer parts of the world; casual on the coast of Florida.

Sterna anglica.

THE GULL-BILLED TERN.

Sterna anglica, MONTAGUE, Orn. Dict. Suppl. 1813. — NUTT. Man. II. 1834, 269. — AUD. Orn. Biog. V. 1839, 127, pl. 410; Synop. 1839, 316; B. Am. VII. 1844, 81, pl. 430. — COUES, Key, 1872, 319; Check List, 1873, no. 560; 2d ed. 1882, no. 792. — RIDGW. Nom. N. Am. B. 1881, no. 679.

Gelochelidon anglica, BONAP. Comp. List, 1838, 61. — COUES, Pr. Ac. Nat. Sci. Philad. 1862, 536 (critical).

Sterna (*Gelochelidon*) *anglica*, COUES, B. N. W. 1874, 664.

Sterna aranea, WILS. Am. Orn. VIII. 1814, 143, pl. 72, f. 6. — LAWR. in Baird's B. N. Am. 1858, 859. — BAIRD, Cat. N. Am. B. 1859, no. 681.

Sterna risoria, BREHM, Lehrb. 1823, 683; Beitr. III. 650.

? *Sterna macrotarsa*, GOULD, Proc. Zool. Soc. Lond. pt. v. 1837, 26; B. Austr. Suppl., pl.

Sterna affinis, HORSF. (*fide* BLAS.)

Gelochelidon palustris, MACGILL. Man. II. 1842, 237.

Gelochelidon balthica, *agraria*, *meridionalis*, BREHM, Vög. Deutschl. 1831, 772, 773, 774.

HAB. Nearly cosmopolitan, but in North America confined to the Eastern Province, and rare away from the coast; the greater part of tropical America, south to Brazil; both coasts of Central America; Bermuda?

SP. CHAR. *Adult, in summer:* Pileum and nape deep black; upper parts, including the rump, upper tail-coverts, and tail, delicate pale pearl-gray, the primaries more hoary, and usually darker; inner webs of primaries ash-gray, with a broad white space from the edge more than half way to the shaft, but not extending to the ends of the quills. Rest of the plumage pure white. Bill wholly deep black; interior of mouth flesh-color; iris dark brown; legs and feet dark walnut-brown, the soles pale pinkish brown; claws black. *Adult, in winter:* Similar, but whole head and neck white, the nape tinged with grayish, the auriculars darker grayish, as is also a crescentic space immediately in front of the eyes. *Young, first plumage:* Above, pale pearl-blue, the feathers

more or less tipped with light clay-color, this sometimes almost uniform over the back and scapulars, where the feathers are bluish only beneath the surface; a blackish crescentic spot immediately in front of the eye, and a dusky grayish suffusion on the auriculars, forming a more or less distinct postocular stripe. Lower parts entirely pure white. Rump, upper tail-coverts, tail, and wing-coverts nearly uniform pale pearl-blue; remiges deeper silvery gray, the secondaries and inner primaries tipped with white; rectrices darker subterminally, and tipped with white or pale ochraceous-buff. Pileum, back, and scapulars sometimes streaked with dusky, oftener immaculate. Bill dusky brownish, the mandible dull orange-brown, except terminally; legs and feet varying from dull reddish brown to dusky brown, the soles more reddish. *Downy young:* Above, light grayish buff, with several large and tolerably well-defined dusky spots on the hind half of the head, most distinct on the latero-occipital region; a distinct longitudinal stripe of dusky down each side of the lower nape and upper back; wings, rump, and flanks, with large, rather distinct, spots of dusky. Lower parts white, the sides of the throat faintly tinged with grayish. Bill dull brownish, the mandible more orange; legs and feet dull brownish orange.

Total length, about 13.00 to 14.50 inches; extent, 33.00 to 35.00; wing, 11.75–12.25; tail, 5.50; depth of fork, 1.50–1.75; culmen, 1.40; depth of bill through base, .45; tarsus, 1.30; middle toe, with claw, 1.10.

Much light has been thrown within a few years upon the distribution of the Gull-billed Tern — Marsh Tern it is hardly entitled to be called. Recent records show it to be much more cosmopolitan than was formerly supposed. It is characteristic of no particular region, but breeds alike in the Indian Ocean and in the Gulf of Mexico, in Denmark, and in Patagonia. Its range — as given by Mr. Howard Saunders — is from Western Europe to the China Seas, throughout India, Ceylon, and the Malay Region, to Australia, and along the east coast of America as far as Patagonia. It is recorded by Salvin as being found on the Pacific coast of Guatemala; but the statement of M. F. Germain in regard to its abundance on the coast of Chili ("Proc. Boston Nat. Hist. Soc." VII. 314) lacks confirmation. North of Western Mexico it is unknown on the Pacific coast; nor has it been recorded from South Africa. It was first described by Montagu from an example procured in England, and hence its inappropriate specific name, *anglica;* but it is of very rare occurrence in England, and should not be known as the English Tern.

In America, until quite recently, this species was supposed to breed only in a restricted region on the sea-coast of Delaware, New Jersey, Maryland, and Virginia; but it is now known to nest abundantly in various localities in Texas, Cuba, the Bahamas, and Mexico; and may be presumed to breed in various other regions where its presence has thus far escaped detection.

Mr. Ridgway — who in company with Mr. Henshaw visited Cobb's Island, Va., in the latter part of July, 1879 — informs me that he found this the most numerous species, nesting on the dry sand, just beyond the surf, and on the higher parts of the island, and there at least not a *Marsh* Tern. Its note he describes as being a harsh chattering laugh; and he thinks that this bird might with propriety be called the Laughing Tern. Mr. Ridgway describes this as being much bolder than the other Terns in its attempts to protect its breeding-place. It darts downward, from directly overhead, with such impetuosity as almost to strike the intruder, the noise which the bird makes in opening its wings to check its downward course being similar to, and sometimes almost as loud as, the "boom" of the Night-hawk.

Mr. Salvin met with this Tern in February on the Pacific coast of Guatemala, and procured several specimens. It did not congregate in any numbers; two or three, at the most, being all that flew in company. Léotaud states that at times this Tern is quite common about the Island of Trinidad, where it appears to be a migratory species. Dr. Gundlach has informed me that it breeds in Cuba, where he has obtained both eggs and young.

Mr. N. B. Moore records the procuring of a single example on Long Island (one of the Bahamas) Aug. 6, 1876. Mr. Lawrence notes the capture of specimens in Southwestern Mexico, by Sumichrast, in August and February. Dr. James C. Merrill and Mr. G. B. Sennett found a large colony of these Terns breeding in company with the *Sterna Forsteri*, on a salt prairie, near Fort Brown, Texas, May 16, 1877. The latter mentions having also observed this species, March 1, at Galveston, and afterward at Nueces Bay and Corpus Christi Pass. Near Fort Brown the two Terns were breeding at adjacent but separate localities.

Mr. Dresser also found it breeding on the coast of Texas, near Galveston. He also states that he found it not uncommon near Matamoras in July and August. On the 2d of June, 1864, he observed it breeding on Galveston Island, the eggs being then incubated. The nest was generally merely a hole scratched in the sand; but in some instances an attempt had been made to form a bed of straw and drift-stuff. The eggs were generally three, but sometimes four, in number.

A single specimen of this Tern was obtained on Ipswich beach, in September, 1871, by Mr. C. J. Maynard; with this exception I am not aware of any having been taken in New England. Giraud speaks of this Tern as being very rare about Long Island, where he never met with it in any of his excursions. Mr. Lawrence includes it in his list of birds found about New York.

Wilson met with it in the neighborhood of Cape May, particularly in the salt-marshes, where it was found to feed largely on a kind of black spider, plentiful in such places, and which seemed to constitute its principal food, as in several of these birds which he opened the stomach was crammed with a mass of spiders and nothing else. The voice of this species he describes as being stronger and sharper than that of the common Tern. This bird did not associate with others, but kept in small parties by itself. He found it breeding on the marshes, the female dropping her eggs — which were three or four in number — on the dry drift grass, without the slightest appearance of a nest. He describes them as being of a greenish olive, spotted with brown.

According to Audubon, this Tern is abundant in the beginning of April about the salt-marshes at the mouth of the Mississippi, making its appearance along the coast in small flocks, there being seldom more than half-a-dozen individuals together, and often only two. He speaks of its flight as being remarkable for its power, as well as for its elegance. Its usual cry is rough and sharp, distinguishable at a considerable distance, and often repeated. It swims buoyantly, but not swiftly, and when wounded does not attempt to dive; but if taken in the hand bites severely, without uttering any cry. Audubon is inclined to the belief that this Tern rarely eats fish. In a large number of individuals of this species, obtained in various localities, he never found any other food in their stomachs than insects of various kinds. In many instances he observed them catching insects on the wing, both over pools of water and over dry land.

Audubon also states that they deposit three eggs, on such dry rushes as are commonly found in salt-marshes, and at a short distance from the water, but carefully placed, so as to be beyond the reach of the tides. Like the eggs of all Terns, these differ considerably in their markings. They are said to measure 1.75 inches in length, and 1.07 in breadth, and have a greenish-olivaceous ground-color, marked with irregular splashes of dark umber, almost black, disposed around the larger end. The parents sit more closely than is usual with Terns; and in cloudy weather they never leave their charge.

Temminck mentions that Boie procured a number of examples of this bird from the eastern coast of Jutland, where the latter was assured that it breeds; and Mr. Dresser cites numerous instances of its breeding in various parts of Denmark. It formerly bred on the Island of Lips, in the Baltic, and is now a rare visitant to the northern coast of Germany. A few birds of this species have been taken on the coast of France; and it is mentioned as being common in Hungary, Turkey, and also in Greece and Asia Minor, breeding abundantly in the lagoons of Missolonghi, and near Smyrna. It breeds in various other portions of Southern Europe, as well as in North Africa, where Canon Tristram met with it in the Sahara; other writers also mention it as being abundant in Egypt.

This species occurs throughout Asia, from the eastern coast of the Mediterranean to the China Seas. It is abundant all over India, where it feeds on aquatic food in the marshes, and occasionally hunts for grasshoppers in cultivated fields. It is common in Ceylon and in China, and has been seen throughout the Malay Archipelago, as far south as Australia; in that country, however, it is very rare. It is also quite common on the shores of the Red Sea, breeding along the coast of India, and in other portions of Southern Asia. Mr. Blyth obtained examples of this species near Calcutta, and it is said to be abundant about the Island of Sunda. The Tern taken by Horsfield on the Island of Java, and described by him under the name of *Sterna affinis*, is now recognized as being identical with this species. I am indebted to Mr. Howard Saunders for an example of its egg taken by Captain Butler from the Island of Warraba, in the Persian Gulf. It is not distinguishable from eggs of this species taken on the coast of Virginia, and the examples of this bird shot by Prince Neuwied on the coast of Brazil, and sent by him to Temminck, are described by the latter as being identical with those taken on the lakes of Hungary.

The ground-color of the eggs of the Marsh Tern varies from a pale greenish buff to a light olive-drab. They are of a rounded oval shape, less oblong than the eggs of most Terns, and more gull-like both in shape and general appearance. Three eggs from Hogg Island, Va., measure 1.85 by 1.30 inches; 1.90 by 1.35; and 1.95 by 1.35. Mr. Seebohm describes an egg taken by him in Greece as measuring 2.36 inches in length, and others as ranging from that to 1.70 inches. He describes their ground-color as yellow ochre or stone-color, varying from a grayish white to a brownish citron. The spots are a mixture of greenish brown and reddish brown. The underlying spots are of a lighter color, but are quite distinct. The egg from the Island of Warraba measures 1.92 by 1.36 inches, has a ground-color of a yellowish drab, and is boldly but sparingly spotted with rounded splashes of deep purplish brown, the underlying spots being similar, but of a lighter shade. Mingled with these are a few smaller blotches of yellowish brown.

An egg taken by Mr. Sennett, near Fort Brown, measures 1.88 by 1.34 inches, and may be described in the same words as the egg from the Gulf of Arabia, except that the blotches are of a smaller size.

Sterna caspia.

THE CASPIAN TERN.

Old World references.

Sterna caspia, PALL. Nov. Comm. Petrop. XIV. 1770, 582. — GMEL. S. N. I. ii. 1788, 603.
Sterna caspica, SPARRM. Mus. Carls. III. 1788, pl. 62.
Thalasseus caspius, BOIE, Isis, 1822, 563.
Sterna Tschegrava, LEPECH. Nov. Comm. Petrop. XIV. 1770, 500, pl. 13, fig. 2.
Sterna megarhynchos, MEYER, Tasch. Deutsch. Vög. II. 1810, 457.
Sylochelidon strennuus, GOULD, P. Z. S. 1846, 21; B. Austr. VII. 1848, pl. 22 (Australia).
Thalassites melanotis, SW. B. W. Afr. 1837, 253 (type in Cambridge Mus.; examined by H. S.).
Sylochelidon balthica et *Schillingii*, BREHM, V. D. 1831, 769, 770.
Sterna major, ELLMAN, Zool. 1861, 7472.

American references.

Sterna caspia, LAWR. in Baird's B. N. Am. 1858, 859. — BAIRD, Cat. N. Am. B. 1858, no. 682. — COUES, Key, 1872, 319 ; Check List, no. 561 ; 2d ed. 1882, no. 793. — RIDGW. Nom. N. Am. B. 1881, no. 680.

Thalasseus caspius, COUES, Pr. Ac. Nat. Sci. Philad. 1862, 537 (part). — ELLIOT, Illustr. Am. B. pl. 56.

Sterna (Thalasseus) caspia, COUES, B. N. W. 1874, 667 (part).

Thalasseus imperator, COUES, Pr. Ac. Nat. Sci. Philad. 1862, 538 (in text ; Labrador).

Sterna caspia, var. *imperator*, RIDGW. Ann. Lyc. N. Y. X. 1874, 391.

HAB. Palæarctic Region. North America in general, but very irregularly distributed ; breeding in Labrador, along the Arctic coast, on islands in Lake Michigan and along coast of Virginia and Texas ! ? Humboldt Marshes, Nevada, numerous ; coast of California.

SP. CHAR. Largest of the Terns (wing not less than 15.00 inches). Bill very robust, reddish ; tail short and but slightly forked ; inner webs of primaries wholly dark slaty. *Adult, in summer :* Entire pileum, including occipital crest and upper half of lores, deep black, the lower eyelid with a white crescentic spot. Upper parts very pale pearl-gray, fading insensibly to white on the upper tail-coverts, the tail bluish white ; outer surface of the primaries light hoary ash, their inner webs uniform slate or dark hoary gray. Rest of the plumage snow-white. Bill deep coral-red, with a

dusky suffusion subterminally, the tip orange or yellowish ; iris dark brown ; legs and feet deep black. *Adult, in winter :* Similar, but the black of the head streaked with white. *Young, first plumage :* Similar to the adult, but with the following differences : Pileum (including occiput and upper two thirds of lores) grayish white, thickly streaked with dull black ; side of head with a uniform dull black bar, beginning before and beneath the eye and extending back over upper portion of auriculars ; lower portion of lores and auriculars grayish white, mottled with darker grayish. Mantle pale pearl-gray, sparsely marked with irregular spots, mostly inclining to crescentic or V-shaped form, of brownish dusky, the wing-coverts, however, nearly immaculate ; the markings largest on longer scapulars and terminal portion of tertials ; primaries hoary gray, with white shafts, the shorter ones margined with white ; rump and upper tail-coverts immaculate pearly white ; rectrices hoary gray, distinctly spotted with blackish toward tips. Rest of plumage plain white. Bill dull orange (in dried skin), dusky subterminally ; feet brownish (in skin). (No. 93033, ♀, Warsaw, Ill., Sept. 21, 1883 ; CHARLES K. WORTHEN.) *Downy young:* Above, grayish white, the down of the head dusky grayish at the base ; back and rump finely and indistinctly mottled with grayish; throat and foreneck uniform pale grayish; remaining lower parts, including the chin, immaculate white. Bill, legs, and feet dull orange, the former with the tip blackish.

Total length, about 21.50 inches; extent, 51.00; wing, 15.00–17.40; tail, 5.30–6.75, depth of its forking, .75–1.60; culmen, 2.48–3.10; depth of bill through base, .75–.95; tarsus, 1.60–1.95; middle toe, 1.15–1.40.

The difference in size between examples of this species from North America and those from Europe seems scarcely sufficient to warrant the recognition of a var. *imperator*. We have examined fourteen adult examples; but of these only two were European, one being from Australia, the others from various parts of North America, including the coast of California. The smallest of this series is from Denmark, the wing of which measures only 15.00 inches, the culmen 2.48; but a Californian specimen is scarcely larger, measuring only 15.15 and 2.50 respectively. The bill is narrower in the latter specimen than in any other, measuring only .75 of an inch deep at the base, instead of from .80 to .95. The largest specimen is one from Western Australia, which measures: Wing, 17.00 inches; tail, 6.50; culmen, 3.10; depth of bill, .90; tarsus, 1.75; middle toe, 1.30. A Canadian specimen (No. 70316, ♀, Detroit River, near Sandwich, Ontario, May 2) is scarcely smaller, however, while the wing is actually longer, the measurements, as above, being 17.40, 6.05, 2.65, .86, 1.60, 1.22 inches. There are two American specimens in the collection which are decidedly smaller than an adult male from Europe, one being the example from California, noted above, the other from Wapitugan, Labrador. The latter measures 16.00, 6.00, 2.55, .80, 1.65, 1.15 inches; the European specimen in question being 16.00, 6.25, 2.75, .85, 1.65, 1.20. It is therefore evident that while we may perhaps concede to the American birds of this species a larger average size, the difference is not sufficiently constant to warrant the formal recognition of a var. *imperator* based upon difference of size alone.

The Caspian Tern is somewhat cosmopolitan in its distribution. It is of irregular and comparatively limited occurrence, so far as we know, in North America. Mr. Lawrence has received specimens that had been procured on the southern coast of Long Island. Dr. Turnbull mentions the taking of examples on the coast of New Jersey. Mr. Boardman informs me that individuals have been occasionally taken in the Bay of Fundy. Mr. William Brewster met with a flock at Ipswich, Mass., Sept. 15, 1871, one of which was secured. There were about half a dozen others flying about at the time. Mr. Sennett saw this Tern on the coast of Texas, and Dr. Merrill found it breeding on Padre Island, near Fort Brown. It has been found by Mr. B. F. Goss breeding on islands in Lake Michigan.

Professor Kumlien, to whom this species was once familiar, informs me that he has occasionally seen a large Tern in Lake Koskonong, Wis., which he is very confident can be none other than this bird. He has seen it near enough to know that it is a Tern, but has never been so fortunate as to secure one. He has met with it in May and in June; but has never noticed more than three at a time, and generally not more than one.

Messrs. Ridgway and Henshaw found this species breeding on Cobb's Island, Va., in the summers of 1879 and 1880. Late in July Mr. Henshaw procured one pair with their downy young, and others were positively identified; and there may have been still other individuals among the large Terns seen at too great a distance to be identified as not being the *regia*. These two Terns are not distinguished by the residents, both species being confounded under the local name of "Gannet-Strikers," or "Gannets." The Caspian Tern is supposed to breed in considerable numbers on certain islands in the vicinity of Cobb's.

Mr. Ridgway now regards it as probable that the large red-billed Terns which he saw at the Humboldt Marshes in September, 1867, at Washoe Lake in May, 1868, and at Great Salt Lake in June and July, 1869, were of this species, and not *S. maxima*, as he had supposed ("Ornithology of the Fortieth Parallel," p. 639).

Audubon when in Labrador was surprised to find a Tern — which he supposed to be what he called the Cayenne (*S. maxima*) — breeding on that coast. It is not probable that the birds he saw, but was unfortunately unable to secure, were of the species to which he referred them. He obtained an egg — now in my possession — marked as that of the Cayenne Tern; but it certainly is not an egg of a *Sterna maxima*, nor hardly one of the present species. Mr. Howard Saunders thinks the bird seen by Audubon was the Kittiwake Gull; but it does not seem likely that this ornithologist could have mistaken it for a Tern — a bird with which he was so familiar.

Mr. Bernard Ross met with the Caspian Tern on the Mackenzie River; and the Smithsonian Institution has examples from the Hudson's Bay Region. Several individuals of this species have been both observed and procured in various portions of the Arctic Regions. Mr. Robert Kennicott secured three near Fort Resolution, in 1860; Mr. Clarke, Jr., several near Fort Rae, in 1863; Mr. J. Lockhart, others at Fort Resolution, in 1864; Mr. J. Reid, several on Big Island, May 20, 1864; and Mr. McKenzie, a single specimen near Moose Factory.

The Caspian Tern was described by Pallas, who first met with it on the shores of the Caspian Sea — from which circumstance it received its name; more recently other Russian naturalists have seen it in that region, though it has never been found in abundance there.

Mr. Wheelwright met with it in Scandinavia, where it is a very local bird. A few pairs breed yearly on the Wener, and it has been killed as far north as Tornea; but it is rare in Sweden. It seems to breed commonly on the Isle of Sylt, in Denmark. Its eggs — three in number — are described as considerably larger than those of the *Larus canus*, smooth, and of a light drab ground-color, with large and small purple-brown spots scattered over the whole surface of the egg. The spots are wide apart, leaving the ground-color very apparent, and giving to the egg a lighter appearance than is common in the egg of a bird of this family.

Nilsson states that this species also visits the mouth of the Baltic, and is seen in the vicinity of the Elbe. Mr. E. L. Layard mentions having observed it on the sea-coast of New Zealand.

Mr. H. Saunders, in his Notes on the Birds of Southern Spain ("Ibis," 1871), states that it was occasionally obtained at the mouth of the Guadalquivir, in Spain, but that according to Guirao it is more abundant on the eastern coast.

The Caspian Tern is said by Mr. R. Swinhoe to visit the coast of Formosa in its migrations from more northern latitudes, in winter, more especially after severe northeasterly winds. It is also a winter visitor at Amoy. The same observing naturalist also mentions his finding it plentiful about the harbor of Hoenow, on the Island of Hainan, in February and until the beginning of April. These birds were often seen sitting in large parties on the sand-flats.

Individuals were met with by Mr. Tristram on the shore near Jaffa; and Dr. Heuglin found it in pairs throughout the whole year in the Red Sea and in the Gulf of Aden. It is also stated by Mr. T. L. Powys to occur sparingly in winter at Corfu and on the coast of Epirus; and Lord Sperling found it very abundant near Missolonghi, in Greece, where hundreds of this species could be seen at a time floating over the lagoons on the lookout for their prey. Dr. A. L. Adams ("Ibis," 1864) speaks of finding this species common in Lower Egypt. Dr. Kirk, in his Notes on the Birds of the Zambesi Region, in Eastern and Tropical Africa, also mentions ("Ibis," 1864) finding these birds, in the month of January, breeding in company with the *Sterna velox*, on the low sand-islands off the mouth of the main stream of the Zambesi. There were two or three eggs in each nest, and these are described as being of a dirty gray, with black spots. The nests consisted of slight hollows in the sand, with a few sticks gathered round.

Mr. C. A. Wright, in his List of the Birds of Malta ("Ibis," 1870), mentions having observed one of this species, on the 21st of May, at Fort Mandel Island, which was quite fearless, and repeatedly approached close to the soldiers on guard, who threw pieces of bread to it, which were immediately pounced upon and swallowed. This bird was afterward shot, and ascertained to be a female, with eggs in the ovary in an advanced stage of development.

According to Yarrell, the Caspian Tern is an occasional visitant of the British coast. Seven instances of its occurrence there are named, one of which was in October, 1825, one in June, 1849, and one in August, 1851. It is also known to have been taken at different times in Germany, Holland, Switzerland, France, Italy, Corsica, and Sicily. It has also been obtained at Senegal, at the Cape of Good Hope, and near Calcutta.

Eggs in Yarrell's collection — from the vicinity of Hamburg — are described by him as being 2.50 inches in length, and 1.65 in breadth; of a yellowish stone ground-color, spotted with ash-gray and dark red-brown. The ground-color of the egg of this species in my cabinet is a light grayish drab. The markings are scattered and rather small, of a subdued lavender and raw-umber, of different shades, in some cases being more nearly black. Two eggs — procured at Great Slave Lake by Mr. L. Clarke — measure, one, 2.70 by 1.70 inches; the other, 2.55 by 1.80. An egg marked as having been taken in Turkey has a ground of a light but distinct drab, with very nearly black scattered and rounded spots. This egg measures 2.44 by 1.80 inches. Other eggs from Scandinavia measure as follows: 2.48 by 1.73; 2.55 by 1.72; 2.59 by 1.76; 2.60 by 1.80.

Sterna maxima.

THE ROYAL TERN.

La Grande Hirondelle de Mer, de Cayenne, BUFF. Ois. VIII. 346.

Hirondelle de Mer, de Cayenne, BUFF. Pl. Enl. 988.

Sterna maxima, BODD. Tabl. P. E. 58 (ex Pl. Enl. 988). — SCL. & SALV. P. Z. S. 1871, 567 (critical). — SAUNDERS, P. Z. S. 1878, 655 (do.). — COUES, 2d Check List, 1882, no. 794.

Sterna cayennensis, GMEL. S. N. I. ii. 1788, 604.

Sterna cayana, LATH. Ind. Orn. II. 1790, 804, no. 2. — NUTT. Man. II. 1834, 268. — AUD. Orn. Biog. III. 1835, 505; V. 1839, 639, pl. 273; Synop. 1839, 316; B. Am. VII. 1844, 76, pl. 429.

Sterna galericulata, LICHT. Verz. Doubl. 1823, 81 (type in Berlin Mus.; determined by H. S.).

Sterna erythrorhynchus, WIED, Beitr. IV. 1833, 857.

Sterna cristata, SWAINS. B. W. Afr. II. 1837, 247, pl. 30 (type in Cambridge Mus.; examined by H. S.).

Sterna regia, GAMB. Pr. Acad. Nat. Sci. Philad. 1848, 228. — COUES, Key, 1872, 319; Check List, 1873, no. 562. — LAWR. in Baird's B. N. Am. 1858, 859. — BAIRD, Cat. N. Am. B. 1859, no. 683. — RIDGW. Nom. N. Am. B. 1881, no. 681.

Thalasseus regius, GAMB. Journ. Philad. Acad. I. 2d ser. 1849, 228. — COUES, Pr. Philad. Acad. 1862, 539 (critical).

Sterna (Thalasseus) regia, COUES, B. N. W. 1874, 669.

"*Sterna Bergii*," IRBY, Orn. Str. Gibr. 1875, 209 (specimen examined by H. S.). Not *S. Bergii*, LICHT. 1823.

HAB. Tropical and warm-temperate parts of America, north to Long Island, Massachusetts, Great Lakes, Utah (?), Nevada (?), and coast of California; south to Brazil and Peru. West coast of Africa, north to Tangiers (DALGLEISH, "Auk," January, 1884, p. 97).

SP. CHAR. Nearly as large as *S. caspia*. Bill deep orange-red or orange. Tail quite deeply forked. *Adult, in spring:* Entire pileum, including occipital crest and upper half of the lores, deep black. Upper parts pale pearl-gray (about as in *S. caspia*), becoming white on the rump and upper tail-coverts. Tail grayish white, tinged with pearl-gray. Outer webs of primaries pale silvery gray, the outer quill darker; inner webs slaty in a broad stripe next the shaft, the inner portion abruptly white, the dusky extending anteriorly near the inner edge of the web, except on the outer quill. Bill deep orange-red; iris dark brown; legs and feet deep black. *Adult, in summer:* Similar, but the forehead, lores, and fore part of crown white. Bill uniform deep orange-chrome, paler at tip; edges of eyelids black; iris dark brown; legs and feet deep black. *Adult, in winter:* Similar to summer dress, but feathers of the occipital crest more or less bordered with white; tail-feathers more decidedly tinged with gray, the outer rectrices sometimes quite dark ash terminally. "*Young of the year, in August:* Bill considerably smaller and shorter than in the adult, its tip less acute, and its angles and ridges less sharply defined, mostly reddish yellow, but light yellowish at tip. Crown much as in the adults in winter, but the occipital crest scarcely recognizable as such. Upper parts mostly white, but the pearl-gray of the adult appearing in irregular patches, and the whole back marked with small irregularly shaped, but well-defined spots of brown. On the tertials the brown occupies nearly the whole of each feather, a narrow edge only remaining white. Lesser wing-coverts dusky-plumbeous. Primaries much as in the adults, but the line of demarcation of the black and white wanting sharpness of definition. Tail basally white, but soon becoming plumbeous, then decidedly brownish, the extreme tips of the feathers again markedly white. Otherwise as in the adults" (Coues.)

Total length, about 18.00 to 20.00 inches; extent, 42.00 to 44.00; wing, 14.00–15.00; tail, 6.00–8.00; the depth of its fork, about 3.00–4.00; culmen, 2.50–2.75; depth of bill through base, .70; tarsus, 1.37; middle toe, with claw, 1.40.

It is very questionable whether the bird with entirely black pileum can be regarded as in full breeding-plumage. In July, 1880, Mr. Ridgway found a colony consisting of several thousands of this species breeding on Cobb's Island, Va. Dozens were shot as they flew from their eggs, and *not one* could be secured, or even observed, which did not have the forehead and fore part of the crown white. All the eggs were quite fresh; but it is barely possible that the birds may have previously laid in some other place, and their eggs have been taken by fishermen. It seems, therefore, most probable that the wholly black pileum represents the full spring, or perhaps pairing, dress, rather than the livery of the breeding-season.

This handsome Tern, so far as we now know, has a somewhat restricted residence. Breeding in small numbers on the Atlantic coast as far north as Chesapeake Bay, it becomes more common in Florida, and is probably found more or less abundant along the entire coast of the Gulf of Mexico, as well as on the Pacific coast of Central America, Mexico, and Southern California.

Mr. Dresser found it common about the mouth of the Rio Grande during the summer months; and both Dr. Merrill and Mr. Sennett have met with it in the same locality. Mr. Salvin procured examples among the Keys on the coast of Honduras, in May, 1862. Numerous other specimens, both adult and young, of this bird were afterward obtained in the same locality.

According to Dr. Cooper, this Tern wanders in midsummer along the Pacific coast as far north as the Columbia River. On the Atlantic it occasionally visits Long Island and, more rarely, the islands of Southeastern Massachusetts, where a pair was obtained in the summer of 1874 by Mr. C. J. Maynard and Mr. William Brewster. A few breed as far north as Southern Maryland, on its eastern shore.

Late in July, 1879, Messrs. Ridgway and Henshaw met with this Tern in considerable numbers at Cobb's Island, on the eastern shore of Virginia. It was in company with *S. caspia;* and the two species were confounded by the residents of the island under the common name of "Gannet-strikers," or "Gannets." This species appeared to be much the more numerous of the two. Mr. Ridgway visited the same locality the following season (July, 1880), and found a colony numbering several thousands breeding near the northern end of the island, their eggs covering thickly an area of less than an acre in extent.

This species occurs in several of the West India islands. It was found breeding in Cuba by Dr. Gundlach. In 1854 Professor Alfred Newton received from St. Croix an example of this bird which had been killed on that island; and he afterward not infrequently saw Terns in that vicinity which he judged to be the same species. Léotaud mentions this bird as being an occasional visitant of Trinidad; the Terns which are seen are chiefly in their immature plumage, appearing to be migratory only, coming in August during the period of the wintry rains. They are also common in Jamaica, where, according to Mr. Gosse, this is the most abundant species about the Bay of Bluefields.

Giraud states that this Tern, though rare on Long Island, is yet not entirely unknown in that locality; and he mentions the existence in private cabinets of two specimens, shot at Islip. He also states that Mr. Bell has from time to time received other specimens procured at various points of the southern coast, near Raynor South, and Moriches, and in that vicinity.

Dr. Cooper mentions this as the only species of Tern seen by him on the coast of California, where it is abundant at all seasons. He did not, however, ascertain where it breeds, and saw no locality which would seem favorable for this purpose. Even San Nicolas, the only island lying far south to which it resorts, is too much infested by foxes; and there seemed to be no Terns on Santa Barbara, which is such a favorite nesting-place for several other species.

Mr. Henshaw does not think that the range of this Tern extends any farther north than the coast of California, where it is of rather common occurrence. He saw it near San Francisco, and received from Captain Forney a specimen which had been obtained on the Island of San Miguel, where it is known to breed.

This bird is usually observed flying in straight lines along the shores, or up and down the bays, occasionally uttering a squealing cry, and often darting directly down into the water as if shot, but generally emerging with a fish, which is immediately swallowed, or, if too large, divided by its sharp cutting bill. This Tern is generally a very shy and suspicious bird; but if wounded, will strike boldly with its bill — being much more pugnacious than are the tamer Gulls. Though it usually fishes singly, yet it will associate in large flocks on its resting-place; and when one of these birds is wounded, all its companions will fly anxiously around in such proximity as to be easily shot.

In the autumn months Mr. Gosse used frequently to see individuals of this species engaged in fishing on a reef about a quarter of a mile from the Jamaican shore. The birds were solitary in their habits, and did not associate with others of their kind. They would fly rapidly around in large circles high above the water, flapping their wings rapidly and without intermission; then all at once they would descend perpendicularly, at the same time turning the body in a jerky, irregular manner. On touching the water the birds would disappear with a sudden splash, but reappear a moment later, struggling as if it were not an easy thing to rise again; then all at once they would utter plaintive cries, as if alarmed, and fly off along the coast; but would return again, and calmly resume their wonted occupation. When satisfied, this bird betakes itself to some buoy marking a sunken fishpot, and there reposes. The fishermen, on returning to their pots at early day, often find it sitting on their buoys, so fearless that the canoe will almost touch it before it will fly. Though web-footed, it is rarely known to swim; and, when wounded, struggles in the water as a land bird would do.

In Florida Audubon found this Tern surprisingly shy. At first the birds were in great flocks, resorting at low water to a large flat sandbar, where they reposed awaiting the return of the tide. For several days he was unable to procure a specimen, and only succeeded by employing several boats to join in the pursuit. After one had been wounded there was no difficulty in procuring others. He found this Tern on the St. John's River, at a distance of several miles from the sea. When disturbed at its breeding-place, it manifests the noisy displeasure so characteristic of its tribe, uttering loud cries that may be heard to the distance of half a mile or more.

On the 11th of May, 1832, Audubon saw it breeding on one of the Tortugas. The eggs had been dropped on the bare sand a few yards from high-water mark, and during the heat of the day none of the birds paid much attention to them. The number of eggs was usually two, but sometimes only one. They are described as being 2.75 inches in length, and 1.80 in breadth. They have a pale-yellowish ground-color, spotted with dark umber and faint purple.

The eggs of this species are remarkably uniform in their general characteristics. Their ground-color is a buffy white, varying only in the intensity of the tinge. The markings are black, suffused with sepia-brown, with dark shades of the same deepening into blackness. Four eggs in the Smithsonian Collection, from the Tortugas, present the following measurements: 2.45 by 1.75 inches; 2.45 by 1.85; 2.55 by 1.75; and 2.65 by 1.75.

Sterna elegans.

THE ELEGANT TERN.

Sterna elegans, GAMB. Pr. Philad. Acad. IV. 1848, 129 (Mazatlan). — LAWR. in Baird's B. N. Am. 1858, 860; ed. 1860, pl. 94. — BAIRD, Cat. N. Am. B. 1859, no. 684. — SAUNDERS, P. Z. S. 1876, 653 (critical). — RIDGW. Nom. N. Am. B. 1881, no. 682. — COUES, 2d Check List, 1882, no. 795.

Thalasseus elegans, GAMB. Journ. Philad. Acad. ser. 2, I. 1849, 228. — COUES, ib. 1862, 540 (critical).

Sterna comata, PHIL. & LANDB. Wiegm. Archiv, 1868 (?), 1863, pt. 1, 126.

Sterna galericulata, FINSCH, Abh. Nat. 1870, 359 (Mazatlan; not of LICHT. 1823, which = *S. maxima*, BODD.). — SCL. & SALV. P. Z. S. 1871, 568. — COUES, Key, 1872, 319; Check List, 1873, no. 563.

Sterna (*Thalasseus*) *galericulata*, COUES, B. N. W. 1874, 671.

HAB. Pacific coast of America, from Chili to California. No valid reference from the Atlantic coast.

SP. CHAR. Smaller than *S. maxima*, and decidedly more slender. Bill more reddish orange. Tail more deeply forked. *Adult, in spring:* Pileum, including occipital crest and upper half of lores, deep black. Upper parts pale pearl-gray (about the same shade as in *caspia* and *maxima*), becoming pure white on the lower part of the rump, upper tail-coverts, and tail; outer surface of primaries light silvery gray, the inner webs edged with white; inner webs of primaries marked next the shaft with a broad stripe of dark gray, this color, except on the outer quill, extending anteriorly in a point near the end of the feather. Rest of the plumage, including nape, pure white, the lower parts tinged with delicate rose-pink in fresh specimens. Bill red (yellowish or orange in dried skins); iris brown; legs and feet black. *Adult, in winter:* Similar, but forehead and lores white; crown white, spotted with dusky; occipital crest and side of head to in front of the eyes, deep black. *Young (first plumage)*: Pileum dull brownish black, nearly uniform on the occiput, where the feathers are not elongated, but short and blended; whole crown streaked with white; forehead and lores white, finely streaked with black. Nape, upper tail-coverts, and lower parts, white, the lower part of the first with sparse roundish spots; back, scapulars, and wing-coverts dirty whitish, coarsely and irregularly spotted with dusky brown, this color almost uniform near the anterior portion of the lesser wing-covert region, the anterior border of which is white; secondaries dusky, bordered terminally with white; primaries hoary slate, with a narrow terminal border of white, the inner webs mostly white, with a broad dusky stripe next the shaft. Tail-feathers brownish slate, becoming grayish basally, the ends conspicuously bordered with white. Bill reddish; feet dusky.

Wing, 12.40–12.50 inches; tail, 6.60–7.30, the depth of its fork, 2.60–3.50; culmen, 2.25–2.55; depth of bill through base, .45–.50; tarsus, 1.05–1.25; middle toe, .80–.86.

This species has only a limited claim to a place in the fauna of North America. It is a Mexican and Central American species, and occurs on the coast of California only occasionally, irregularly, and very rarely. It was procured on the Pacific coast of Mexico by Dr. Gambel, and was particularly common near Mazatlan. Dr. Cooper could procure no evidence that this species ever occurs so far north as San Diego, in California. Mr. Salvin obtained, at San Salvador, in Central America, a specimen of this Tern, which he regarded as being absolutely identical with the typical *S. elegans* from the Gulf of California. It was taken in December, 1862.

A specimen of the egg of this Tern — obtained at Guaymas, west of Sonora, Mexico, by Captain Stone (Smithsonian Institution, No. 579) — measures 2.20 inches in length by 1.45 in breadth. It has a ground-color of white with a pinkish tinge. Its markings are quite bold and distinct, and are of a deep black and burnt sienna color, with subdued shell-markings of lavender-gray.

Sterna sandvicensis acuflavida.

CABOT'S TERN.

Sterna cantiaca, Aud. Orn. Biog. III. 1835, 531, pl. 279 (not of Gmel. 1788); Synop. 1839, 317; B. Am. VII. 1844, 87, pl. 431. — Coues, Key, 1872, 320; Check List, 1873, no. 564; 2d ed. 1882, no. 796.

Sterna (Thalasseus) cantiaca, Coues, B. N. W. 1874, 673.

Sterna Boysii, Nutt. Man. II. 1834, 276 (not of Lath. 1790, = *cantiaca*, Gmel.).

Sterna acuflavida, Cabot, Pr. Boston Soc. II. 1847, 257. — Lawr. in Baird's B. N. Am. 1858, 860. — Baird, Cat. N. Am. B. 1859, no. 685.

Thalasseus acuflavidus, Coues, Pr. Philad. Acad. 1862, 540 (critical).

Sterna cantiaca acuflavida, Ridgw. Nom. N. Am. B. 1881, no. 683.

HAB. Atlantic coast of North America, north, irregularly, to Southern New England, breeding south to Honduras; West Indies in general; both coasts of Central America. South to Brazil.

SP. CHAR. Very similar in size and form to *S. elegans*, but bill black, usually tipped with yellowish or whitish. *Adult, in spring:* Pileum, including occipital crest and upper half of lores, deep black; upper parts pale pearl-gray, a shade lighter than in *elegans;* outer surface of primaries slightly darker, with a silvery or hoary cast; inner webs of primaries white, with a broad stripe of dark grayish along the shaft. Rest of the plumage, including the nape, rump, upper tail-coverts, and tail, snow-white. Bill deep black, tipped with yellow or whitish; iris dark brown; legs and feet black. *Adult, in winter:* Similar, but the forehead and lores white, the crown streaked with white and black, and the black feathers of the occiput faintly tipped with white. *Young, first plumage:* Upper half of the head, including nearly the whole of the lores, with upper part of the nape, dusky black, irregularly mixed with dull whitish, especially on the crown, which is coarsely spotted; occipital feathers short and blended. Upper parts, including the rump, upper tail-coverts, and tail, pale pearl-gray, coarsely and irregularly spotted with brownish black; wings, except smaller coverts, as in the adult; rectrices growing darker grayish terminally, where irregularly spotted, or with irregular hastate marks of dusky black. Lower parts immaculate white. Bill dusky blackish, scarcely paler at the tip; iris dark brown; legs and feet black.

Total length, about 15.00 to 16.00 inches; wing, 12.50; tail, 6.00, the depth of its fork, 2.35; culmen, 2.25; depth of bill through base, .48; tarsus, 1.00; middle toe, about 1.00.

As remarked by Dr. Coues ("Birds of the Northwest," p. 674), there appear to be constant though slight differences between American and European birds of this species, which are quite sufficient, if they prove really constant, to separate them as geographical races. These differences are thus expressed by Dr. Coues:—

"*European:* White margin of inner web of outer three or four primaries wide, extending quite to tip, which it wholly occupies. Breadth of white portion one and a half inches from tip of first primary, .25 of an inch."[1]

"*American:* White margin of inner web of three or four outer primaries narrow, falling short of tip, which is wholly occupied by the black portion. Breadth of white margin one and a half inches, from tip of first primary, .10 of an inch."[1]

The American examples of the Sandwich Tern, claimed by some to be a distinct species, bear so strong a resemblance to the *S. sandvicensis* of Europe that the two are no longer separated by some who have examined into the alleged differences in their plumage. The European bird, so far as we know, is more nearly exclusively northern in its area of reproduction. It was first observed in Great Britain in 1784, and has since been ascertained to be a regular summer visitor, appearing in spring, and departing in autumn after rearing its brood. It also visits Ireland, where its breeding-haunts are not known. It is not abundant in England; but it is known to breed in various parts of that country, particularly on the Farne Islands and the Croquet Islands, where — as Selby states — the nests are so close to each other that it is difficult to cross the ground without breaking the eggs or injuring the unfledged young It is there known as the "Tern" *par excellence,* all others of its kind being called Sea-Swallows. Its flight is strong and rapid; and, except when engaged in incubation, it is almost constantly on the wing, uttering at intervals a hoarse and discordant cry, which may be heard to a great distance. The eggs — three or four in number — are

[1] STERNA SANDVICENSIS SANDVICENSIS. — The Sandwich Tern.
Sterna sandvicensis, LATH. Synop. Suppl. I. 1787, 296.
Sterna cantiaca, GMEL. S. N. I. ii. 1788, 606 (exactly = *S. sandvicensis,* LATH.). — SAUNDERS, P. Z. S. 1876, 653.
Sterna africana, GMEL. t. c. 605 (young).
Sterna Boysii, LATH. Ind. Orn. II. 1790, 804 (= *cantiaca,* GMEL.).
Sterna canescens, MEYER & WOLF. Tasch. Deutsch. Vög. II. 1810, 458.
Thalasseus candicans, BREHM, Vög. Deutschl. 1831, 777.

placed in shallow holes scratched in the ground, and are 2.00 inches long by 1.63 broad, of a yellowish stone-color, thickly spotted with ash-gray, orange-brown, and deep red-brown, but subject to considerable variations in their markings. This bird is said to breed in Scotland, Sweden, Germany, and North Holland, and on islands off Ushant. It is also said to occur in its migrations in various parts of Africa.

This species was first introduced as a bird of our fauna by Audubon, who met with it in Florida in 1832. It was not then known to occur in any other part of the United States. In August, 1865, a single stray specimen of this Tern was secured in Chatham, Mass., by Mr. Vickary. I am not aware that there is any other instance on record of its occurrence north of the southern portion of Florida. Mr. Salvin found this bird very common both on the Atlantic and on the Pacific coast of Guatemala, and he obtained several specimens at Chiapam, on the Pacific coast of Guatemala, in January, 1863. These were all in immature plumage, and somewhat smaller than the average North American bird, but were undoubtedly specifically identical with it.

A flock of these birds was first met with by Audubon among the Florida Keys May 26; and in their flight and appearance they reminded him of the Marsh Tern, though in their power of flight they are said to surpass that bird. Their cries were loud, sharp, and grating, and were heard half a mile or more. These cries are kept up at intervals when the bird is in motion, and they are repeated incessantly when an intruder trespasses on its breeding-grounds, on which occasion it will dash close to the intruder's head with loud and disagreeable outcries.

When Audubon visited the Key on which this species was breeding many were still depositing their eggs, and none were sitting. Three eggs seemed to be the full complement to a nest. They were dropped on the sand at short intervals, with scarcely any appearance of a hollow for their reception. All were fully exposed to the heat of the sun, which seemed almost sufficient to cook them. Mr. Audubon gives as their average measurement 2.12 inches in length by 1.42 in breadth. The ground-color is said to be yellowish gray, varying in depth, and all more or less spotted, blotched, or marked with different tints of umber, pale brown, and reddish. He was informed by the wreckers that they were in the habit of watching the birds, and that these spend the entire winter near and upon the Keys, the young keeping apart from the old birds.

Eggs of this species in the Smithsonian Collection are from Charlotte Harbor, in the Tortugas. The ground-color of these varies from a grayish white to a deep buff, with intermediate shadings. The markings vary both as to size and shape, and in color from a light burnt sienna to black, intermingled with lavender-gray; they also vary from rounded spots to long zigzag lines. Four eggs, selected as typical, present the following measurements: 1.95 by 1.40 inches; 2.05 by 1.35; 2.05 by 1.45; and 2.35 by 1.40.

Sterna Trudeaui.

TRUDEAU'S TERN.

Sterna Trudeaui, AUD. Orn. Biog. V. 1839, 125, pl. 409; Synop. 1839, 319; B. Am. VII. 1844, 105, pl. 435. — LAWR. in Baird's B. N. Am. 1858, 861. — BAIRD, Cat. N. Am. B. 1859, no. 687. — COUES, Key, 1872, 322; Check List, 1873, no. 571; 2d ed. 1882, no. 802; B. N. W. 1874, 675. — RIDGW. Nom. N. Am. B. 1881, no. 684.

Sterna Frobceni, PHIL. & LANDB. Wiegm. Arch. 1863, 125 (Chili).

HAB. Southern South America (Chili, Buenos Ayres, South Brazil, etc.). Casual on Atlantic coast of North America (New Jersey and Long Island; AUDUBON & TRUDEAU).

Sp. Char. *Adult, in summer* (?): Head, axillars, entire lining of the wing, and tail-coverts (above and below) silky white; a blackish or dusky stripe on each side of the head, entirely surrounding the eye, and extending back over the auriculars. Rest of the plumage very pale pearl-gray (the lower surface uniform with the upper), the outer surface of the primaries and their coverts inclining to silvery white; inner web of outer quill chiefly white, with a stripe of plumbeous-gray next the shaft; second quill with the gray stripe paler and less sharply defined, and the inner side of the web slate-gray, the edge itself narrowly white; third quill similar, but with the inner dusky stripe still more distinct, the grayish next the shaft still paler, and blended gradually into the white, which is more restricted; fourth, fifth, and sixth quills with the dusky equally distinct, and the white (except that along the edge) obsolete; remaining quills uniform silvery white. Tail uniform silvery white. Basal half of the bill brownish yellow (in the dried skin),

the terminal half black, the tip pale yellow for about .25 of an inch; feet pale yellowish brown (in dried skin).[1] *Adult, in winter:* Similar, but the entire lower parts and neck pure white, the primaries more dusky, with the white on the inner webs more sharply defined. Bill dusky, the tip yellowish.

Wing, 9.70–10.60 inches; tail, 4.60–6.00, the depth of its fork, 1.60–2.60; culmen, 1.50–1.70; depth of bill through base, .35–.46; tarsus, .92–.96; middle toe, .75–.80.

This species in winter plumage is so similar to the same stage of *S. Forsteri* (= "*Havelli,*" Aud.) as to be not easily distinguished. The most obvious difference consists in the shorter and less deeply forked tail, with the outer pair of rectrices broader and less elongated, their color being uniform pale silvery gray or ashy white on both webs — the inner web in *S. Forsteri* being always more or less darker than on the outer web, toward the terminal portion. The bill is also stouter than in *S. Forsteri*, especially at the base, and the tip distinctly yellowish; although this latter feature may not prove constant.

It is now generally believed that this species is exclusively South American, and only of accidental occurrence on the southern coast of Long Island, and on that of New Jersey in the neighborhood of Absecom Beach. I am not aware that any specimens have been observed within the United States since it was first described by Audubon. It was first noticed within our limits by Dr. Trudeau, who is said to have obtained several examples at the above-named beach, in the southern part of New Jersey. It is stated by Giraud as having been observed on Long Island in the adult form, but never in the immature. The bird obtained by Dr. Trudeau in the vicinity of Great Egg Harbor was in the company of a few others of the same kind.

We have no information in regard to its specific peculiarities of habits.

1 "Bill black, with part of the base of the lower mandible, the edges of both mandibles, and their tips to the length of about five-twelfths of an inch, yellow; iris brown; feet orange-yellow, claws dusky yellow" (Audubon).

Sterna Forsteri.

FORSTER'S TERN.

Sterna hirundo, Sw. & Rich. F. B. A. II. 1831, 412 (not of Linn.).

Sterna Forsteri, Nutt. Man. II. 1834, 274 (footnote). — Lawr. in Baird's B. N. Am. 1858, 862. — Baird, Cat. N. Am. B. 1859, no. 691. — Coues, Key, 1872, 321 ; Check List, 1873, no. 566 ; 2d ed. 1882, no. 798 ; Birds N. W. 1874, 676. — Ridgw. Nom. N. Am. B. 1881, no. 685.

Sterna Havelli, Aud. Orn. Biog. V. 1839, 122, pl. 409, fig. 1 (young in winter) ; Synop. 1839, 318 ; B. Am. VIII. 1844, 103, pl. 434. — Lawr. in Baird's B. N. Am. 1858,861. — Baird, Cat. N. Am. B. 1859, no. 686.

Hab. North America generally, breeding from interior of British America south to the Potomac River, Illinois, Southern Texas, Nevada, California, etc. ; migrating south to Brazil.

Sp. Char. *Adult, in summer:* Pileum and nape deep black. Upper parts, including rump and tail, light pearl-gray, the primaries and tail paler and more silvery, the inner webs of the outer pair of rectrices usually darker (sometimes quite dusky) for that portion beyond the tip of the next feather. Inner webs of primaries without any well-defined white space, except on two outer quills, but the edge usually more or less dusky. Tips of secondaries, anterior upper tail-coverts, sides and under part of head and neck, and entire lower parts pure white. Bill dull waxy orange, the terminal third or more blackish, with the tip usually paler ; mouth orange ; edges of eyelids black ; iris dark brown ; legs and feet very fine orange-red, the claws black. *Adult, in winter:* Similar, but the head and neck white, the occiput and nape more or less tinged with grayish, the sides of the head marked by a broad space of black surrounding the eyes and extending

Adult, in summer.

Adult in winter.

back over the auriculars. Tail less deeply forked than in summer, the outer rectrices broader and less elongated. *Young, first plumage:* Similar to the winter plumage, but the pileum, nape, back, scapulars, tertials, and wing-coverts overlaid by a wash of raw-umber brown, chiefly on the ends of the feathers, but appearing nearly uniform on the back and crown; sides of the breast tinged with the same. Rectrices all distinctly dusky terminally, especially on inner webs (the outer web of the lateral feather hoary white to the tip), the middle feathers tipped with raw-umber. Bill dusky, more brownish on basal portion of the mandible; legs and feet light brown in the dried skin. *Downy young:* Prevailing color light brownish buff, the breast and abdomen white; lower surface entirely immaculate, but upper parts coarsely and irregularly marbled with black, the sides of the head with a few scattered irregular minute markings of the same. Length, about 3.50 inches, the culmen .35 of an inch.[1]

Total length, about 12.00 to 15.00 inches; extent, 30.00; wing, 9.50–10.30; tail, 5.00–7.70; depth of its fork, 2.30–5.00; culmen, 1.50–1.65; depth of bill through base, .35–.49; tarsus, .90–.99; middle toe, 1.05–1.15.

This species, in the immature form, was described by Mr. Audubon as Havell's Tern, from specimens obtained by him near New Orleans in 1820. The flock from which these individuals were shot was congregated on the broad eddies of the river opposite to the city. They were engaged in picking up coleopterous insects. He afterward obtained two other specimens in Texas in the spring of 1837; and supposing it to be a southern species, gave its habitat as extending from Texas to South Carolina. Richardson met with it in the Arctic Regions, and confounded it with *Sterna hirundo,* to which it so closely conforms in its habits that the two species are with difficulty distinguished from each other.

Recent investigations have greatly extended the known area of distribution of this bird. While it has been ascertained by Mr. Ridgway to breed on our Atlantic sea-coast, near the Chesapeake, it has been also found to be an abundant species throughout our western territory, where it is found from the Mississippi Valley to California, breeding in the summer as far south as Southern Texas, and thence northward to extreme northern regions.

It was first specifically distinguished as *S. Forsteri* by Nuttall, in a note to *Sterna hirundo,* in his edition of 1834 (p. 274).

A single example of this species, in the plumage figured by Audubon as *S. Havelli,* was taken by Mr. Salvin on Lake Dueñas, Guatemala, Oct. 28, 1862, and was the only Tern seen by him on that lake. Colonel Grayson met with this bird near Mazatlan, in Western Mexico, where, as he states, it is quite abundant along the shores and *esteros* from October until April.

Dr. Cooper writes me, that while he has never met with this Tern within the limits of California, it has been obtained by others in different parts of the State, and especially by Dr. Heermann, who found it breeding in the valley of the Sacramento.

Although this species appears to be so largely a resident of the interior, and to be most numerous west of the Mississippi, and although it was supposed to be comparatively rare both on the Pacific and the Atlantic coast, recent discoveries show it to be less rare on the latter than has been generally supposed. A single example in immature plumage was taken by Mr. Maynard on Ipswich Beach, September, 1870; and since then several others have been secured on the sea-coast of Massachusetts. During the winter this is said to be one of the most common birds in the open water of the Patapsco, near Baltimore, and to be also a winter resident on the coast of the Carolinas. Examples have also been taken in Florida. During the months of

[1] Described from a very young individual (No. 84780, U. S. Nat. Mus.) from Grass Lake, Ill., June 15, 1876; E. W. Nelson, coll.

October and November it is one of the most common of the Terns seen in the harbor of Beaufort, N. C.

In the summers of 1879 and 1880 Mr. Ridgway met with this species breeding in considerable abundance about Cobb's Island, Va. It was only less abundant than the *anglica*, and quite as numerous as the *hirundo*, but always found in different situations from either — frequenting especially grassy marshes, in which it nests. He found it pre-eminently a *marsh* Tern. It nested in company with, or in close proximity to, colonies of the Black-headed Gull. It could be readily distinguished from the Common Tern, which it closely resembles when on the wing, by its grating, monotonous note, which very closely resembles one frequently uttered by the Loggerhead Shrike.

In May, 1877, Dr. J. C. Merrill and Mr. Geo. B. Sennett found a colony of these Terns nesting on a nearly submerged grassy island among lagoons and marshes near Fort Brown, Texas. The birds had but just begun to lay; the nests were in depressions in the short grass, and the eggs were frequently wet. Mr. Henshaw found this species quite common at Utah Lake in the summer, where, as he also states, it breeds along the shore.

It has been taken at Lake Winnipeg by Mr. Donald Gunn, and also on Shoal Lake, in Selkirk Settlement, and in Manitoba; and it may be found even farther to the north than this; but we have thus far no evidence to this effect; and the fact that this species breeds in large numbers near the mouth of the Rio Grande, in Texas, seems to demonstrate that it is a bird of the interior, and not particularly northern.

Sir John Richardson — who in his account of what he presumed to be *S. hirundo* evidently had this bird in view — states that it does not breed farther north than the fifty-seventh parallel. Its eggs — two, sometimes three, in number — are deposited on a tuft of dry grass, upon sand, or among stones, and are hatched principally by the heat of the sun, the bird sitting upon them only during the night, or in very cold, cloudy, or stormy weather. This Tern is described as being very clamorous when any one approaches the spot where it nests, flying toward the intruder, plunging close to his head, then rising again with great velocity. In these evolutions the bird's forked tail is sometimes spread out, but is more generally closed, so as to appear pointed. It feeds principally upon small fish, which it picks up from shallow water on the wing. The length of its wings and tail and the shortness of its legs much impede its movements on the ground. It is supposed by Richardson to pass its winters south of the limits of the United States. It appears, so far as is known, to breed exclusively in the neighborhood of inland water, in the marshes bordering small lakes, ponds, and sluggish streams.

Mr. Gunn, who found it breeding in large numbers on the borders of Lake Winnipeg in the latter part of May, and afterward on the border of Shoal Lake, at Selkirk Settlement, and at Manitoba, in his notes relative to Shoal Lake makes no other mention of it than what is contained in these words: "Saw Forster's Terns in considerable numbers; their nests were among the reeds."

In the spring and summer of 1873 Mr. Thure Kumlien found this species breeding in considerable numbers on the borders of Lake Koskonong, in Southern Wisconsin. The nests were built among the thick reeds which cover its marshy shores, and were constructed, with considerable care, of coarse flags and stems of water-plants, and lined with finer reeds. The nests were raised above the ground — evidently to avoid the danger of being flooded by a rise of the lake. The eggs were three in number, and similar in size, shape, and general appearance to those of the common *S. hirundo*. Mr. Kumlien informs me that this species is much more common than the *hirundo* during the breeding-season, though by no means so common as the smaller Black Tern. It breeds in the same places with the common *hirundo*, several nests being often placed in a small space. Some of their nests are very bulky. They breed in the latter part of June, chiefly in the large muddy reedy marshes of Blackhawk Island, in Lake Koskonong. When his son Ludwig first discovered their breeding-place, their young were generally hatched, and as he approached, the old birds gave the alarm, and all the young birds deserted their nests and hid among the reeds.

Eggs of this species in the collection of the Smithsonian Institution are from Minnesota, Illinois, Cobb's Island, and from Shoal Lake in British America. The ground-color is a pale buffy drab, varying to a pale grayish green. The markings are of blackish brown, mingling with fainter markings of lilac-gray. They vary in length from 1.55 to 1.80 inches, and in breadth from 1.20 to 1.15 inches.

Sterna hirundo.

THE COMMON TERN.

Sterna hirundo,[1] LINN. S. N. ed. 10, I. 1758, 137 ; ed. 12, I. 1766, 227. — WILS. Am. Orn. VII. 1813, 76, pl. 60, fig. 1. — NUTT. Man. II. 1834, 271. — AUD. Orn. Biog. IV. 1838, 74, pl. 309 ; Synop. 1839, 318 ; B. Am. VII. 1844, 97, pl. 433. — COUES, Key, 1872, 320 ; Check List, 1873, no. 565 ; 2d ed. 1882, no. 797 ; B. N. W. 1874, 680.

Sterna fluviatilis, NAUM. Isis, 1819, p. 1847-48. — SHARPE & DRESSER, B. Eur. Pt. XI. (1872). — SAUNDERS, P. Z. S. 1876, 649.

Sterna senegalensis, SWAINS. B. W. Afr. II. 1837, 250.

Sterna Wilsoni, BONAP. Comp. List, 1838, 61. — LAWR. in Baird's B. N. Am. 1858, 861. — BAIRD, Cat. N. Am. B. 1859, no. 689.

S. hirundo.

HAB. Palæarctic Region and Eastern North America, chiefly near the coast. Winters north to about 37° ; breeds irregularly nearly throughout its range. Arizona (HENSHAW) ; Bermudas (summer resident).

SP. CHAR. *Adult, in summer:* Pileum and nape, including upper half of the lores, uniform deep black. Upper parts deep pearl-gray (much the same shade as in *paradisæa*), the border of the

[1] We cannot at all share in Mr. Saunders's doubts ("Proceedings" of the Zoological Society of London for 1876, pp. 650, 651) as to the general, or even exclusive, pertinence of Linnæus's descriptions of his *Sterna hirundo* to the present species.

wing, tips of secondaries, lower part of rump, upper tail-coverts, and greater portion of the tail pure white. Lower parts pale pearl-gray or grayish white (much lighter than the upper parts), becoming gradually white on the under part and sides of the head, and pure white on the crissum. Outer web of lateral tail-feather ash-gray, darker terminally, in abrupt contrast with the pure white of the inner web; outer webs of remaining rectrices, except the intermediæ, paler grayish. Outer web of outer primary blackish slate; outer surface of other primaries light silvery gray, slightly paler than the back; inner webs chiefly white, with a stripe of grayish next the shaft, this stripe abruptly defined on the first five quills, but growing gradually broader and paler toward the fifth, and extending, near the end of the feathers, a greater or less distance toward the base, but the edge itself narrowly white; five inner quills pale silvery gray, the inner webs edged with white. Bill bright vermilion blackish terminally, except on the tomia; inside of mouth orange-vermilion; edges of eyelids black; iris very dark brown; legs and feet orange-vermilion, lighter than the bill; claws black. *Adult, in winter:* Similar, but forehead, crown, and anterior part of lores white, the vertex mixed with black; entire lower parts pure white. *Young, first plumage:* Orbital region, occiput, and nape dull black; crown mixed black and grayish white; forehead and lores, with

entire lower parts, upper tail-coverts, inner webs of rectrices, and tips of secondaries, white. Upper parts pale bluish gray, the scapulars, interscapulars, and tertials tipped with pale buff, and marked with an indistinct subterminal lunule of dusky brown; anterior lesser wing-coverts dusky, forming a broad bar across the wing; primaries much as in the adult, but darker; wing-coverts paler than the back, and bordered indistinctly with white. Outer webs of rectrices grayish, deepening on outer feathers into slate. Bill dusky brownish, the base of the mandible paler and more reddish; feet pale yellowish (in the dried skin). *Downy young:* Not distinguishable with certainty from that of *S. paradisæa* (?).

Total length, 13.00–16.00 (14.50) inches; extent, 29.00–32.00 (31.00); wing, 9.75–11.75 (10.50); tail, 5.00–7.00 (6.00); depth of its fork, about 3.50 (average); culmen, 1.25–1.50 (1.35); depth of bill through base, about .33; tarsus, .66–.87; middle toe, .75.

Assuming *Sterna hirundo* and *S. Wilsoni* to be specifically the same, we must consider it as having an extent of distribution throughout the entire globe hardly surpassed by that of any other species. At different seasons it is found in all parts of Europe and Western Asia, and has also been taken at Madeira, on the Canary Islands, in Senegal, and in Southern Africa. It is found on the Atlantic coast of North America, from Texas and Florida, as far as the St. Lawrence, breeding sporadically, often in company with the Laughing Gull and the Roseate Tern, from Florida to New Hampshire, and with the Arctic Tern, from Muskegat, Mass., northward. Sometimes the colonies of these different species are harmoniously mingled; but more generally, even when on the same island, they keep somewhat apart. This Tern is also common in the interior, nesting on islands in fresh-water lakes and ponds, but usually in smaller numbers than on the sea-shore — probably on account of the less abundant supply of food.

Occasional pairs of this species were observed in the Fur Region, even as far as the Arctic coast. An example was taken by Mr. Kennicott, June 6, 1859, on Lake Winnipeg; another at Fort Rae, by Mr. L. Clarke; one on the Arctic coast below Anderson River, in June, 1863, by Mr. MacFarlane; and three on Big Island, in Great Slave Lake, by Mr. J. Reid.

In Europe, according to Yarrell, it is found to be less common than it was once supposed to be, when it was confounded with two other distinct species, on account of their general resemblance to each other when on the wing, and the fact that their habits are almost identical.

Mr. Wheelwright states that this species is the most common Tern on the coast of Scandinavia, and that it breeds far inland, on Lake Wener, and even goes up into Lapland. In the winter it visits Germany, Holland, France, Spain, Italy, and the Mediterranean.

In England it breeds occasionally on rocks or on banks of shingle above the sea-beach; but generally seems to prefer building on the ground, in marshes, or on small, low, and sandy islands.

It is not common — if indeed it breeds at all — on the Pacific coast; but throughout California — according to Dr. Heermann — it is very abundant along the rivers in the interior during the summer, retiring southward in the winter. Dr. Cooper never met with it on the sea-coast of California, and has never visited its summer resorts, except during the cold weather; nor did he see it on the Columbia River.

This Tern breeds on the islands of Bermuda in the summer, but is not very abundant there. Mr. Hurdis states that in August Gannet-head Rock teems with it and its young. It is known at Bermuda as the "Red-shank;" on the coast of Massachusetts it is called the "Mackerel Gull;" and on Long Island and the coast of New Jersey it is the "Summer Gull." In common with the Arctic Tern, and one or two others of the smaller kinds, it is known as a "Sea Swallow" in England.

Mr. Bernard Ross met with it on the Mackenzie River; the Smithsonian Institution has specimens received from Nelson's River; and Mr. Murray obtained specimens that were taken at Hudson's Bay. Mr. MacFarlane found it breeding on the Lower Anderson River, and it is also known to breed on the shores of Franklin Bay and of the Arctic Ocean.

Mr. Dresser obtained one specimen at San Antonio in May, 1864, and in June he found numbers breeding in Galveston Bay, the eggs being either just hatched out, or hatching. The nests were made in the high piles of drift stuff, and the eggs were three, in some instances four, in number. Mr. Audubon also mentions finding it breeding on Galveston Island; and on his voyage to Labrador he met with this same species nesting on the Magdalen Islands; and afterward in the neighborhood of American Harbor, on the coast of Labrador.

According to Giraud, this Tern arrives on the coast of Long Island and in New Jersey in the latter part of the month of April, and begins to lay early in May, depositing three eggs. It continues on that coast in great numbers until the approach of winter, when they all appear to retire beyond the limits of the United States. Dr. Bryant found it breeding as far south as Florida.

On the Island of Muskegat — a low, irregular collection of shifting sandbars, less than three miles in length, and hardly half a mile in its greatest breadth — lying between the islands of Nantucket and Martha's Vineyard, this Tern formerly bred in great numbers, in company with the Roseate and Arctic Terns and the Laughing Gull, this species in 1842 being by far the most abundant.

Spending a week, in August, 1873, on the Island of Penikese, one of the smallest of the Elizabeth Islands, I had an excellent opportunity of observing its habits. Inclusive of the young birds, it was estimated that there were about one thousand of these birds on the southern portions of that island. They nested on the uplands, from a few yards to a hundred rods or more from the water, and their nests varied from a mere depression in the ground, with scanty and loose linings, to quite an elaborate interweaving of flags. The usual number of eggs was two; but frequently there was only one, and more rarely three. This may have been owing to the lateness of the season. In one or two instances there were five eggs in the same depression; but these I presume to have been laid by at least two females, and they were watched over by several birds, which vied with each other in resenting any intrusion near their common treasures. There were many young birds of various ages about the breeding-grounds, and these were abundantly supplied with young fry of the mackerel. I had no doubt that other birds than their parents aided in this supply. The number of old birds was at least ten times that of the young; and nearly all seemed to join in the task of fishing and feeding the young birds, who were kept perfectly stuffed, and grew in size surprisingly fast.

This appears to be a very restless and a very noisy bird. It passes most of its time, from early morning until late in the evening, in the air, flying about over the beach, or marsh, as if in pursuit of insects, or skimming swiftly over the surface of the water in pursuit of small fish, which it seizes without pausing in its flight. At other times it may be seen hovering over a shoal of fish; and the instant these come to the surface it dashes headlong upon its prey, partially submerging itself in its effort. It is very buoyant on the water, and swims lightly, but never dives, other than by a partial plunge in fishing, and is seldom seen on the surface of the water. It may often be seen, at low water, resorting to sandbars and shoals, in company with smaller Gulls, picking up marine insects, small shell-fish, and other forms that abound in such places. Like several other species, it is eminently social in its disposition, moving about in large companies, and keeping up a continuous interchange of cries. It is often found associating with, and breeding in the same locality with, the *Larus atricilla,* with which it is always on good terms. Like its associate, even when not pursued by the hunter, it is timid and watchful. When one of its kind is wounded and falls into the water, those within hearing of its shrill outcries collect around the spot, where, as they hover over their stricken companion, they afford an easy mark to any disposed to continue the work of destruction.

In some localities — as on the south side of Long Island, and where their breeding-places are mere collections of sand — their eggs are laid on the bare ground, without any preparation of a nest other than a slight excavation made loosely in it, and are hatched chiefly by the heat of the sun's rays and by that of the sand itself, which retains its elevated temperature until late in the evening. The females usually sit upon their eggs only at night and during unpleasant weather. They are not, however, neglectful of their charge, but remain near at hand, and make their presence manifest if their nest is approached. If the eggs are incubated, both parents hover directly above their nest, so that where there are several species breeding together, each can easily be referred to its proper nest. If the young are hatched out, the parent bird is all the more clamorous, and plunges in the direction of the head of the intruder, occasionally striking at him with its wing, or letting fall fœcal matter upon the object of its displeasure.

A few birds of this species breed every summer in the marshes bordering Lake Koskonong, in Southern Wisconsin, from which locality I have received both nests and eggs. The former, made of coarse water-plants, are remarkably elaborate structures, evidently so constructed as to protect the eggs from the water naturally to be expected in a marshy site. Professor Kumlien writes me that this bird visits the lake in varying numbers, according to the season, arriving about the end of April. The prevalence of high winds, floods, and other adverse circumstances has a tendency to make it less abundant in some years.

The eggs in the Smithsonian Collection are from Great Slave Lake, in the extreme north, and from Hog Island, Va., in the extreme southeast. How far north on our Atlantic coast this species breeds I cannot say. I have never observed it breeding farther north than Massachusetts; but it probably ranges in the summer much farther. The eggs vary in length from 1.50 to 1.75 inches, and in breadth from 1.15 to 1.30; but 1.20 is their average breadth. Their ground-color varies from a pale greenish buff to a brownish drab. Their markings are chiefly of a dark clove-brown color, intermingled with fewer shell-markings of an obscure lavender-gray.

Sterna paradisæa.

THE ARCTIC TERN.

Sterna paradisæa, BRÜNN. Orn. Bor. 1764, 46 (not of KEYS. & BLAS. 1840,= *S. Dougalli*).

Sterna hirundo, PHIPPS, Zool. Voy. N. Pole, 1774, 188. — SHARPE & DRESSER, Birds Eur. pt. xii. (1872).

Sterna macrura, NAUM. Isis, 1819, p. 1847. — LAWR. in Baird's B. N. Am. 1858, 862. — BAIRD, Cat. N. Am. B. 1859, no. 690. — COUES, Key, 1872, 321; Check List, 1873, no. 567; B. N. W. 1874, 685. — SAUNDERS, P. Z. S. 1876, 650.

Sterna arctica, TEMM. Man. II. 1820, 742. — SW. & RICH. F. B. A. II. 1831, 414. — NUTT. Man. II. 1834, 275. — AUD. Orn. Biog. III. 1835, 366, pl. 250; Synop. 1839, 319; B. Am. VII. 1844, 107, pl. 424.

Sterna brachytarsa, GRABA, Reise. n. Färoe, 1830, 218.

Sterna brachypus, SWAINS. B. W. Afr. II. 1837, 252.

Sterna Pikei, LAWR. Ann. Lyc. N. Y. VI. 1853, 3; in Baird's B. N. Am. 1858, 853, pl. 95. — BAIRD, Cat. N. Am. B. 1859, no. 693.

Sterna portlandica, RIDGW. Am. Nat. VIII. 1874, 433. — COUES, B. N. W. 1874, 691.

Sterna longipennis, COUES, Check List, 1873, no. 568 (= *S. Pikei*, LAWR.); nec *longipennis*, NORDM.!

HAB. Northern hemisphere in general; in America, south to the Middle States and California, breeding from the Northern States to about latitude 81° 50′ (Smith's Sound; FEILDEN, "Ibis," 1877, p. 408). No valid Central American, South American, or West Indian record.

SP. CHAR. *Adult, in summer:* Pileum and nape, including upper two thirds of the lores, deep black. Prevailing color pearl-gray, paler on the lower surface, still paler on the throat and chin, the side of the head, bordering the black of the hood, distinctly white. Tips of the secondaries and tertials, upper and under tail-coverts, greater portion of the tail, and entire lining of the wing pure white; outer web of lateral pair of tail-feathers deep ash-gray, darker terminally, in strong and abrupt contrast with the pure white of the inner web; outer web of next feather pale pearl-gray. Outer web of outer primary dark slate; inner webs of all the quills chiefly white, with a narrow stripe of silvery gray next the shaft; this stripe gradually widening on the inner feathers, where, near the end of each quill, it runs anteriorly near the inner edge; three or four inner quills uniform silvery gray, the inner web edged with white. Bill and feet deep carmine-red in life, the former usually without a black tip; iris brown. *Adult, in winter:* Similar, but forehead, anterior part of the lores, and crown white, the latter streaked with black; lower parts white, sometimes with a slight wash of plumbeous. Bill and feet duller red. *Young, first plumage:* Orbital region, occiput, and posterior part of the crown dull black; forehead and anterior portion of lores and crown white, the crown mixed with blackish and stained with brownish. Back, scapulars, and wings pearl-gray, as in the adult, but feathers tipped with pale buff, and marked with a subterminal lunule of dusky brown, these markings most distinct on the tertials and longer scapulars, fainter on the back; primaries and secondaries much as in the adult; lower part of rump, upper tail-coverts, and entire lower parts white, the sides of the jugulum and breast, as well as the chin and throat, stained with pale dull brownish. Outer webs of rectrices slate-color, paler on middle feathers; all the rectrices marked at the ends in the same manner as the tertials, but less distinctly. Basal half of bill orange-red, terminal half blackish; feet pale reddish. *Downy young:* Upper surface pale fulvous or grayish buff (the shade very variable), coarsely and very irregularly marbled with dusky, except on the forehead; lower parts whitish, distinctly buffy or fulvous on the sides and flanks, the throat and cheeks distinctly uniform dusky or sooty brown.

Total length, 14.00–17.00 inches; extent, 29.00–33.00; wing, 10.00–10.75; tail, 6.50–8.50, the depth of the fork, 4.00–5.00; culmen, 1.08–1.40; depth of bill at base, .30; tarsus, .55–.65; middle toe, with claw, .80–.85.

The Arctic Tern very closely resembles the common *hirundo* both in its general appearance and in its habits; so that nearly all that may be said in regard to the mode of nesting of the latter, its manner of flight, its cries and restlessness, its social characteristics, its solicitude for its young, and other traits, will apply with equal force to this species. As its name would imply, the Arctic Tern is by far the more northern, in its distribution, of the two species, and is found breeding to the highest point of northern latitude, where the other is found — if at all — only in limited numbers. It may be met with in all the Arctic Regions of America and the Old World.

It has been seen occurring in abundance by Mr. Kennicott at Fort Resolution and Fort Yukon; by others at Fort Rae, Anderson River, Slave River, Slave Lake, Buffalo River, Mackenzie River, Fort Simpson, Big Island, and Peel's River; by Mr. MacFarlane on the Arctic coast; by Mr. Dall at Franklin Bay, Fort Anderson, Rendezvous Lake, Swan Islands, the Lower Anderson, and Nulato; by Mr. Bischoff at Kadiak.

On the eastern coast of America it breeds from Southeastern Massachusetts to the most extreme points of Greenland, in latitude 82° 34′, and on the western coast of Europe from Great Britain to Iceland.

Captain H. W. Feilden ("Ibis," October, 1877) found this species breeding in Smith's Sound at all the localities visited on the route of the expedition. On a small islet off the north end of Bellot's Island (latitude 81° 44′) he saw several pair breeding, August 21. The land at that time was covered with snow, and on that islet it was three inches deep. In one nest he found a newly hatched Tern, which seemed quite well and lively in its snowy cradle. The parent birds had thrown the snow, as it fell, out of the nest, which was surrounded by a border of snow marked by their feet and raised two inches above the general level. Birds were seen as early as June 16 in 1876, and by the end of that month pairs were scattered at intervals along the coast. A nest scraped in the gravel, containing two eggs, was found June 27; and during the first week in August a pair of young birds, nearly ready to fly, were seen in latitude 81° 50′. This Tern is included by Dr. Bessels in his list of the birds procured at Polaris Bay.

The Messrs. Godman found the Arctic Tern breeding along the whole of the northwest coast of Norway. In Iceland, according to Professor Newton, it has many breeding-places in various parts of that island. According to Faber, it arrives there about the middle of May, and departs about the end of August; although generally a few young ones remain a month longer on the southern coast. Professor Newton also states ("Ibis," 1865) that the Arctic Tern is common in Spitzbergen, breeding as far north as latitude 80°, where Dr. Malmgren found it in countless numbers in July. It was not abundant in Ice Sound, but it was quite common among the Thousand Islands, where its eggs are much sought after by the walrus-hunters who resort thither. Martin mentions the excellence of these eggs as food; and since his time visitors to Spitzbergen have not failed to appreciate this fact. Dr. Malmgren first observed this bird on the 10th of June in Treurenberg Bay, feeding principally on surface-swimmers, as crustaceans, mollusks, and the like. Messrs. Evans and Sturge mention meeting with a few Arctic Terns in Western Spitzbergen late in June; but the birds did not appear to be breeding, nor were any eggs of this species seen.

According to Middendorff, this species occurs in the tundras of the northern portions of Siberia. Mr. G. Gillett found it numerous both on the western and on the eastern coasts of Nova Zembla; and Von Heuglin also observed it along the same coast in small flocks.

Mr. Wheelwright speaks of this species as being the commonest of the Terns in the heart of Lapland; and this is the only species of Tern mentioned by Sommerfeldt in his list of the birds of Vardö, near the North Cape, who did not find it on the west or northwest coast of Scandinavia.

Dr. Walker found it on the coast of Greenland, near Godthaab; and it is also given by Professor Reinhardt as being a resident species of that island. Mr. Bernard Ross met with it on Great Bear Lake; and Mr. Murray received it from Hudson's Bay, from which region Captain Blakiston also procured specimens.

Mr. Boardman informs me that this species breeds abundantly on the coast of Maine, near Calais; and it is also said to breed on islands in the fresh-water lakes and ponds in the interior both of Maine and New Brunswick. Giraud did not recognize it as one of the Terns which breed in and about the sea-coast of Long Island, and it probably is not found south of Muskegat.

Captain Elmes ("Ibis," 1869) mentions finding this Tern breeding on a small rock among the Outer Hebrides, called Hysker, although it was at a considerable distance from their feeding-grounds; and he noticed that none of the nests contained more than two eggs. This was the case at all the other points he visited; while the common Tern (*S. hirundo*), which he states to be also abundant in the Hebrides, usually lays three.

Yarrell regards this species as being more common than the bird usually known as the common Tern, particularly in high northern latitudes. It is found in large numbers in the Faröes, and is the Tern described by Graba under the name of *S. brachytarsa*, and said to frequent that group of islands. Mr. Dunn states that it is abundant in the summer in the Orkney and Shetland Islands, as well as in the Outer Hebrides — where, according to Macgillivray, it is much more common than *S. hirundo*. Mr. Thompson states that it occurs in large numbers, and is widely distributed through Ireland.

The several Arctic voyagers have found this species in great abundance at all the points which they have visited. It was found breeding on Melville Peninsula, and generally on the islands and beaches of the Arctic Sea.

Generally this Tern is found in colonies by itself, Muskegat being the only instance where I have seen it mingling with other species. In 1842 I there found this species in company with the *hirundo* and the *Dougalli*. In 1869, when Mr. Allen visited this island, the breeding-place of this species seemed to be apart from the others. On the Island of Damariscotta, on the coast of Maine, and on a small island near Bristol, I found this species breeding in distinct colonies, no other bird being in the neighborhood.

Richardson found this Tern breeding generally on the shores and islands of the Arctic Ocean, and in great abundance. He describes its eggs as being obtuse at one end and tapering at the other, varying in ground-color from a light yellowish brown to a bluish gray, and marked with many irregular brown spots of different degrees of intensity. They are said to be deposited upon a gravelly beach or upon sand; and the parents show great anxiety for their safety, and are very bold in their endeavors to defend them.

Mr. Hearne refers to this species as the "Black-head," and speaks of it as being the smallest Gull met with by him. It is said to visit the coast of Hudson's Bay in such vast numbers that it is frequently seen in flocks of several hundred; and he has known their eggs to be gathered by bushels on a very small island. These eggs are very delicate eating, the yolks being equal to those of a young pullet, and the whites of a semi-transparent azure; but the bird itself has always a fishy taste, and is unsuitable for food. The affection of this species for its young is so strong that when any person attempts to rob its nest it will fly at him, and approach so near as to touch his head with its pinions; and will frequently follow the plunderer to a considerable distance, with unusual screams and noisy outcries. This species was found in the farthest northern localities visited by Hearne, and was observed to leave the Arctic Regions early in the fall.

Mr. Dall found this species abundant in the Shumagins, in certain localities, and especially on a small island in Popoff Strait, called Range Island. There a large number of the eggs, mostly in an incubated condition, were obtained in the months of June and July. He did not notice any of these birds at Unalashka; but he speaks of them as being abundant on the marshes near the sea-coast and also everywhere on the Yukon, where they were seen in large flocks hovering over the water, and often appearing as if suspended in the air, the birds remaining in the same place, almost motionless, for ten or fifteen minutes. At other times they were sitting on sticks of driftwood, chattering to one another, or gathering around a shoal of young minnows, diving, eating, and screaming with equal vivacity. They are perfectly fearless, especially when a companion has been wounded, or when their young are menaced. They gather in large numbers around a wounded companion, cry to it, and endeavor to assist it to rise. Their note, when not disturbed, is between a hiss and a whistle; when alarmed, it is a sharp cry, like the scream of a Gull; and when at rest, they keep up a kind of chatter. They are extremely inquisitive, and will follow a boat for miles, keeping a short distance from it. The young were obtained in the down, June 22, near Fort Yukon, and had from the first coral-red legs and bills. The eggs were found, June 14, at the mouth of the Yukon River.

Mr. MacFarlane, Mr. Lockhart, and Mr. Kennicott found this species abundant in all parts of the Arctic Regions, breeding in various situations on the ground, usually in large companies, but occasionally in single pairs, some on the bare prairie, others on the beach, or on islets in a lake, or in the sea.

Some writers speak of the number of eggs in a nest as never more than two. Mr. Dunn, writing of the Orkneys, speaks of it as three or four, and adds that this bird is seldom seen except when on the wing, in pursuit of the small coal-fish which abound in the harbors and inlets of that region. It darts down upon them with great rapidity as they swim on the surface.

Mr. Macgillivray, writing of the Hebrides, says that on several of the smaller and less frequented islands many hundred eggs of this bird were taken in a few minutes, and that it was difficult to move without treading on them. A scattered band of Terns hovered about the party, uttering incessant cries, and darting down to within a few feet of the invaders of their peaceful territory.

In May, 1842, during the prevalence of high winds, the coast in the neighborhood of Bristol, England, was visited by an extraordinary flight of this Tern. They were in such vast numbers that three hundred and more were killed with stones and other missiles, and many were taken alive. Flocks were also observed at other places along the Channel coast, and a simultaneous appearance of this bird took place over a large extent of country in that vicinity. The wind had been blowing hard for several days from the east and northeast, but suddenly changed to the westward, the gale still continuing. The birds were evidently on their route to their northern summer quarters, and their intended course was thus interfered with by the prevalence of unusually strong winds.

Audubon found this species breeding in large numbers at several different points on the coast of Labrador, and always in colonies unmixed with any other species. He found them sitting closely upon their eggs at all times.

The eggs of this Tern are represented in the Smithsonian Collection by specimens from the Yukon River, the Arctic coast, Sable Island, Fort Anderson and the region east, Range Island, Alaska, Kutleet, Great Whale River, and Greenland. In my own collection are eggs from Muskegat Island and Beverly, Mass., and from the coast of Maine. These eggs vary extraordinarily, some being unspotted, and having a ground-color of a grayish white, others being profusely blotched and spotted, while the ground-color is either a tawny drab, a grayish green, or an olive-brown. The markings are generally of a dark brown, inclining to black. Five eggs, taken as typical of their variations in size and shape, present the following measurements: 1.50 by 1.10 inches; 1.55 by 1.20; 1.60 by 1.15; 1.65 by 1.15; 1.75 by 1.25.

Sterna Dougalli.

THE ROSEATE TERN.

Sterna Dougalli, MONTAGUE, Orn. Dict. Suppl. 1813. — NUTT. Man. II. 1834, 278. — AUD. Orn. Biog. III. 1835, 296, pl. 240; Synop. 1839, 320; B. Am. VII. 1844, 112, pl. 437. — COUES, B. N. W. 1874, 688; 2d Check List, 1882, no. 800. — SAUNDERS, P. Z. S. 1876, 652. — RIDGW. Nom. N. Am. B. 1881, no. 688.

Sterna paradisea, KEYS. & BLAS. Wirb. Eur. II. 1840, 97 (not of BRÜNN, 1764). — LAWR. in Baird's B. N. Am. 1858, 863. — BAIRD, Cat. N. Am. B. 1859, no. 692. — COUES, Key, 1872, 321; Check List, 1873, no. 569.

Sterna gracilis, GOULD, P. Z. S. 1847, 222 (Australia); B. Austr. VII. 1848, pl. 27.

HAB. More southern portions of Palæarctic Region, Australia, and Atlantic coast of North America, north to Massachusetts, south, in winter, nearly throughout the West Indies and Central America; both coasts of the latter region. Bermuda (breeding).

SP. CHAR. *Adult in summer:* Entire pileum and nape, down to the lower edge of the eyes uniform deep black. Above, delicate pale pearl-gray, becoming gradually silvery white on the upper tail-coverts and tail; tips of the secondaries, and edges of inner webs of primaries, pure white. Outer primary with the outer web dark slate; inner webs of three outer primaries white, with a stripe of silvery gray next the shaft, the white extending to the extreme tip of the feathers;

remaining quills light silvery gray, the inner web broadly edged with white. Lateral and lower part of head and neck (including lower half of the lores and extreme lower part of the nape), with entire lower parts, pure white, strongly tinged in fresh specimens with delicate rose-pink. Bill black (reddish basally, in life) ; iris brown ; legs and feet bright red (in life). *Adult in winter:* Similar, but forehead and anterior part of crown white, the latter shaded with grayish and indistinctly streaked with darker ; orbital region, occiput, and upper part of nape uniform black. *Young, first plumage:* Pileum and nape pale buffy grayish, finely mottled or sprinkled with darker, and streaked, especially on the crown, with dusky ; orbital and auricular regions dusky blackish ; remainder of the head, extreme lower part of the nape, and entire lower parts, white, the nape, and sometimes the sides of the breast, finely mottled with buffy gray. Back, scapulars, wing-coverts, rump, upper tail-coverts, and tail, pale pearl-blue, the back and scapulars overlaid with pale buff, irregularly mottled with dusky, each feather with a submarginal dusky V-shaped mark ; primary coverts and primaries darker bluish gray, edged with paler, the inner webs of the latter broadly edged with white. Tail-feathers marked near their ends much like the longer scapulars, their outer webs rather dark grayish. Bill brownish dusky ; feet dusky.

Summer plumage.

Winter plumage.

Total length, about 14.00 to 15.50 inches ; extent, 30.00 ; wing, 9.25–9.75 ; tail, 7.25–7.75, the depth of its fork, 3.50–4.50 ; culmen, 1.50 ; depth of bill at base, .35 ; tarsus, .85 ; middle toe, .75.

The beautiful Roseate Tern is almost cosmopolitan in its widely extended geographical distribution; but in North America it appears to be confined to the Atlantic Region, as I find no reference to its existence on any part of the Pacific coast; nor does any writer mention meeting with it in the interior. It is also exclusively maritime in its residence.

Mr. Salvin found a few birds of this species breeding among the Keys on the coast of Honduras late in April, but makes no mention of it as occurring on the west coast. Léotaud refers to it as being a common bird in Trinidad, and as having habits nearly identical with those of *S. maxima.* It is not mentioned by Dr. Gundlach as occurring in Cuba; yet it seems hardly possible that it should not be one of the common birds of that island, since it is so abundant in Florida at all seasons of the year. Neither is it included by Mr. Gosse among the birds of Jamaica. Dr. Bryant did not meet with it breeding either in Florida or in the Bahamas. In the Bermudas, according to Major Wedderburn, this species breeds in considerable numbers, appearing there about the end of April. It is very common at Spanish Point and in Castle Harbor. Its eggs were procured on Gurnet-head Rock June 17, 1848, and others were taken as late as the 1st of August; from which it was inferred that this bird rears two broods in a season. It is not seen at Bermuda during the winter.

This species is found along the Atlantic coast as far east, probably, as Maine, and thence to Florida, and probably along the coast of the Gulf of Mexico to Central America. A few once bred on a small island near Tennant's Harbor, St. George, Me., and at the Isles of Shoals. Mr. Allen has found it breeding off Ipswich, and Dr. Samuel Cabot off Beverly. In 1840 I obtained its eggs on Egg Rock, Nahant; and it still breeds in considerable colonies on Muskegat, on the Elizabeth Islands, on the coasts of Connecticut and New Jersey, on islands near Cape Charles, and at other points on the coast from the Chesapeake to Key West. On Long Island, N. Y., Giraud mentioned it as not common. He regarded it as rare, and as being only occasionally seen in company with the common *hirundo.*

In Great Britain — where this was formerly regarded as being a comparatively rare species — it seems to have increased in numbers, as it is found to be more abundant than it once was. This bird was first recognized as a British species by Montagu in 1813; and since then it has been found breeding at various stations frequented by other Terns, and has been ascertained to be a regular summer visitant, though not in very large numbers. It breeds on a small rocky islet near the entrance to Belfast Bay, Ireland, on islands in the Firth of Solway, and on the Farne Islands, on the east coast of England. At the latter place, according to Selby, its advent as a new species was noted by the lighthouse-keeper, and afterward confirmed by the writer. Since then the colony has greatly increased, and has now become quite numerous; and a second colony has been formed upon another island — one of the Walmseys. Mr. Selby says that the old birds may be easily recognized among hundreds of those of the other species by their peculiar and buoyant flight, long tail, and by their note, which may be expressed by the word *crake,* uttered in a hoarse grating key. The eggs are larger than those of the Arctic Tern; and the young differ from those of that bird in their downy as well as in their feathered stage.

The Roseate Tern is included among the birds of Germany, and was found by Temminck in August and September on the coast of Holland, breeding also on several small islands on the coast of Picardy and Brittany. Savi includes this species among the birds of Italy; and specimens of it have been received from Madeira and from the Cape of Good Hope. Mr. Gould has skins brought from the Malabar coast.

According to Audubon, the Roseate Tern spends the breeding-season in considerable numbers along the southern shores of Florida; where, at different times, he met with flocks of thirty or more pairs breeding on small detached islands. Their full number of eggs he found to be three. These differ considerably in size and marking, and are of an oblong oval shape, narrowed at the smaller end, of a dull buff or clay-color, sprinkled and spotted with different tints of umber and light purple. He found them deposited on the bare rocks, among the roots of the grasses, and in bright weather left exposed to the rays of the sun. Toward night the parent sat upon her eggs.

Audubon describes this Tern as being a noisy, restless bird, emitting a sharp shrill cry whenever its breeding-place is approached; and adds that it is buoyant and graceful in its movements, but unsteady and flickering in its flight. It will make a dash in one direction, and be off in another, with the quickness of thought. When fishing, it plunges perpendicularly downward like a shot, immersing part of its body — and immediately reascending. Its food consists of small fish and mollusks. In the spring it returns to those islands regularly about the 10th of April, and departs southward early in September.

In 1842 I found this species breeding in a large colony on the low sandy Island of Muskegat, where they shared its large area with the common species and the Arctic, as well as with the Laughing Gull. There did not then appear to be any separation of the different species, but all were intermingled. The larger number were of the roseate species. In 1852 I visited a small island of about fifty acres near Cape Charles, and about eighteen miles northeast from Old Point. It was occupied by about thirty pairs of this species, but by no other Tern. And in the summer of 1873 I had an opportunity of observing another small colony on the Island of Penikese. In the last-named instance the larger part of the island was in the exclusive occupation of the *hirundo;* the low marshy portion was occupied by the Least Tern; and a small high promontory by the Roseate Tern. It was the month of August, and this species, having been uninterrupted in its breeding, had ceased laying, nearly all its young having left their nests, but being still cared for by the parent birds.

There is a noticeable difference between this and both the *hirundo* and the *paradisœa,* which, having been once carefully studied, will not be lost sight of. The present species is easily distinguished in its flight by its long and graceful tail-feathers, its more brilliant under parts, and its more regular and even motions in flight. Its voice is different, less sharp, more hoarse, and its cry of *crēēk* is more prolonged and less frequently enunciated, than is the case with the other species named. It is less clamorous when its nest is approached, hovers overhead at a higher point, and rarely makes a rush at one's head, as does the impetuous *paradisœa.* At Cape Charles, where the eggs were fresh, all the birds kept at a respectful distance, and none could be procured. At Muskegat, where the eggs were incubated, the birds could easily be obtained; but it soon ceased to be necessary, as they could readily be identified. At Penikese, where they occupied the part of the island most remote from the dwellings, they were much less disturbed by the presence of intruders; and only when their young were handled, or made to utter an outcry, did they change their calm inspection of our proceedings for an excited and clamorous utterance of their displeasure — rarely making, however, any attempt to attack the intruder or swoop down toward his head.

Captain O. N. Brooks, of Guilford, Conn., who is the proprietor of Faulkner's Island, in the Sound, where a large colony of this Tern breed, has furnished me, through Dr. Wood, of Windsor Hill, some interesting notes on its habits, which are here given in substance. It makes its appearance about the 15th of May, seldom varying three days from this date. At first six or eight of these birds are seen well up in the air. These hover over the island a while, and then disappear. The next day the same individuals return, with an addition of twelve or more to their number; but none of them alight on the island until the third or fourth day. After this, if nothing disturbs them, their number increases very fast. They begin to lay about the 1st of June, never varying three days from that time. While some gather a few dry weeds or a little dry seaweed, others make only a hollow in the sand; and some deposit their eggs on the stones without any nest at all. They usually lay two eggs, though some nests are found to have three, and some four, eggs. When four are found they are never alike; when three, they are sometimes alike, and sometimes one of them differs both in shape and color. Where there are only two, they are usually very much alike.

The male feeds its mate while she is sitting, and may frequently be seen carrying fish to the island, which is often found deposited near their nests. The young bird begins to run soon after it is hatched, and when disturbed, it leaves its nest and hides among the stones, or in grass and weeds. When the young one is large enough to fly, the parent takes it out alone to practise flying. At first it ventures only a few rods, but soon is able to fly a mile or more, but always accompanied by the old bird; the latter never taking more than one of her young out with her at the same time. The islet on which these birds breed contains a quarter of an acre of upland covered with grass and weeds; and while they were thus engaged they were not disturbed. During the month of June only the eggs laid on the stones and sand below the upland — averaging in number a hundred or more a day — were collected, and they are said to be much nicer in flavor than those of the domestic Fowl. The young birds reach their growth by the 20th of August, and their stay after September 1 depends upon the abundance of their food. When fish is plentiful they remain until the first of October. They feed entirely on fish, which they catch by diving. They are greatly troubled by the depredations of Hawks, and in one year — 1863 — the birds were driven away before their young were ready to fly. The Duck Hawk seems to be their most troublesome enemy.

The eggs of this species have a ground-color of a pale buffy drab, varying to a pale grayish green. The spottings are of a lilac-gray and blackish brown. Five eggs from New England present the following variations in measurement: 1.55 by 1.15 inches; 1.60 by 1.15; 1.70 by 1.25; 1.75 by 1.20; 1.75 by 1.10.

Sterna aleutica.

THE ALEUTIAN TERN.

Sterna aleutica, BAIRD, Trans. Chicago Acad. Nat. Sci. I. 1869, 321, pl. 31, fig. 1 (Kadiak). — DALL & BANN. ib. 307. — COUES, Key, 1872, 322; Check List, 1873, no. 572; 2d ed. 1882, no. 803; Birds N. W. 1874, 696. — SAUNDERS, P. Z. S. 1876, 664. — RIDGW. Nom. N. Am. B. 1881, no. 689.

Sterna Camtschatica, "PALL.," FINSCH, Abh. Nat. III. 1872, 85 (not of PALLAS).

HAB. Coast of Alaska from Kadiak to Norton Sound.

SP. CHAR. *Adult, in summer:* Upper half of head and nape deep black, the forehead white, this color extending back about .50 of an inch medially, and about twice as far, or to the posterior angle of the eye, laterally, the black forming a stripe across the lores, from the eye to the bill. Upper parts deep plumbeous-gray, the primaries slightly darker, with white shafts, the inner webs mostly white, with a broad stripe next the shaft, and a narrow edging, of plumbeous. Tips of secondaries, upper and lower tail-coverts, tail, cheeks, malar region, chin, and entire lining of the wing, including maxillars, pure white; remaining lower parts pale pearl-gray, fading insensibly into the white of the chin and crissum; plumbeous of the rump very abruptly defined against the white of the upper tail-coverts. Bill and feet deep black; iris brown. *Downy young* (No. 97160, St. Michael's, Alaska, July 29, 1880; E. W. NELSON): Above, rather light sooty brown, confusedly marbled or mottled with dusky, the head with the light brown predominating, and the dusky markings more distinct. Forehead, chin, entire throat, and sides of the neck, uniform sooty slate; jugulum and breast pure white; sides, flanks, abdomen, and anal region, sooty gray. Bill pale yellowish brown (flesh-color in life), with black tip; legs and feet pale yellowish brown (flesh-color in life?). No. 97162, same locality and date, differs in having the ground-color of the upper parts decidedly more buffy, the dark marblings coarser and more distinct; the whole anterior portion of the crown, for the space of about half an inch, together with the superciliary region, is immaculate brownish buff; the throat is rather lighter sooty, the sides, etc., paler grayish. From the downy young of *S. paradisœa*, the above described specimens may be distinguished by the much less fulvous coloring of the upper parts, and much darker as well as decidedly more gray color of the sides and posterior lower parts. In short, while the general coloration is bright tawny buff in *paradisœa*, the general aspect is decidedly sooty in *aleutica*. *Young, first plumage:* Forehead, lores, crown, and entire nape smoky grayish brown, darkening on the occiput into fuliginous-dusky, this color extending anteriorly on each side nearly or quite to the eye; the smoke-color of the nape extending over the sides of the neck to the sides of the breast, sometimes even tinging the jugulum and foreneck. Back, scapulars, inner wing-coverts, and tertials dull slate-black, broadly and sharply bordered, especially terminally, with deep yellowish ochraceous; remainder of the wing plumbeous, the greater coverts and secondaries tipped with white; primaries as in the adult; upper part of the rump dark brownish slate, the feathers narrowly tipped

with pale fulvous, this preceded by a dusky subterminal bar; lower part of rump and upper tail-coverts plumbeous-gray, the lateral coverts nearly white, and the longer tipped with buff; tail pale bluish gray, the feathers growing dusky subterminally, and tipped with deep ochraceous-buff; inner webs of the rectrices paler than the outer, or nearly white; outer web of exterior feather almost entirely pure white. Lower parts entirely white, the under side of the head and neck, as well as the sides of the breast, more or less stained or clouded with smoke-brown. Maxilla dusky; mandible light reddish (brownish in dried skin), the terminal third or fourth black; *legs and feet clear light reddish.*

Total length, 13.25 to 14.75 inches; extent, 30.00 to 31.00; wing, 9.75–10.75; tail, 6.50–7.00; depth of its fork, 2.40–3.75; culmen, 1.25–1.40; depth of bill through base, .38; tarsus, .60–.75; middle toe, without claw, .80–.85.

The young of *Sterna aleutica* may be very easily distinguished from that of *S. paradisœa* — the only other Tern found in any part of Alaska — by the following differences of coloration: (1) The distinctly cinereous rump and upper tail-coverts; (2) the pure white, instead of uniform blackish, outer webs of the lateral rectrices; (3) the deep smoke-brown hue of the forehead, crown, nape, and sides of the breast; (4) the broad white anterior border to the forearm; (5) the dusky stripe near the edge of the inner webs of the primaries; and (6) the much darker general coloration, and especially the blackish dorsal region, with wide deep ochraceous borders to the feathers.

The adult needs no comparison with any other species of the genus.

Our information in regard to the specific habits of this newly discovered species and the extent of its geographical distribution is still quite meagre. It is not probable that its habits vary greatly from those of other Terns, which in all the members of this family are quite similar. The species was first met with, and its eggs procured at the same time, by Mr. Bischoff at Kadiak; and examples of the birds and eggs have since been obtained from different parts of Alaska. Mr. Dall was informed that it was common in the Aleutian Islands, and expected to meet with it there; but none were seen.

Four eggs of the Aleutian Tern (Smithsonian Institution, No. 1347), procured by Mr. Bischoff on the Island of Kadiak, have the following measurements: 1.65 by 1.15 inches; 1.75 by 1.15; 1.85 by 1.10; 1.85 by 1.15. They all have a ground-color of a brownish and a greenish olive; the markings are large, partly longitudinal, confluent, and in patches, and of a dark clove-brown.

Sterna antillarum.

THE LEAST TERN.

Sterna minuta, Wils. Am. Orn. VII. 1813, 80, pl. 70, fig. 2 (not of Linn.). — Aud. Orn. Biog. IV. 1838, 175, pl. 319; Synop. 1839, 321; B. Am. VI. 1844, 119, 439.

Sterna argentea, Nutt. Man. II. 1834, 280 (not of Max. 1820).

Sternula antillarum, Less. Descr. Mam. et Ois. 1847, 256.

Sterna antillarum, Coues, Pr. Acad. Nat. Sci. Philad. 1862, 552. — Scl. & Salv. P. Z. S. 1871, 571. — Saunders, P. Z. S. 1876, 661. — Ridgw. Nom. N. Am. B. 1881, no. 690.

Sterna superciliaris, b. *antillarum*, Coues, B. N. W. 1874, 692.

Sterna superciliaris antillarum, Coues, 2d Check List, 1882, no. 801.

Sterna frenata, Gamb. Pr. Acad. Nat. Sci. Philad. 1848, 128. — Lawr. in Baird's B. N. Am. 1858, 864. — Baird, Cat. N. Am. B. 1859, no. 694.

Sterna superciliaris, Gundl. & Caban. J. f. O. V. 1857, 232 (not of Vieill.). — Coues, Key, 1872, 332; Check List, 1873, no. 570.

Hab. Temperate and tropical North America in general; south to Trinidad. Both coasts of Central America; on the Atlantic coast north, casually, to Labrador; on the Pacific side, north to California.

Sp. Char. Smallest of the Terns (wing less than seven inches). *Adult in summer:* Pileum and nape deep black, the forehead covered by a broad lunule of white extending back laterally to the eyes, the lores being crossed by a black line or narrow stripe extending from the eye to the lateral base of the maxilla, immediately behind the nostril. Entire upper parts, including lower part of the nape, upper tail-coverts, and tail pale pearl-gray, deepest on the dorsal region and wings. Two to three outer primaries dusky slate, the inner webs broadly edged with white; remaining quills pale pearl-gray, like the coverts, the edge of the inner webs white. Entire lower parts pure white. Bill bright yellow, usually (but not always) tipped with black; iris dark

brown; legs and feet bright orange-yellow. *Adult, in winter:* Similar, but lores, forehead, and crown grayish white (purer white anteriorly), an occipital crescent and a stripe forward from this to and surrounding the eye blackish. Bill dusky; legs and feet dull yellowish. *Young, first plumage:* Somewhat similar to the winter plumage, but humeral region marked by a wide space of dusky slate, the scapulars and interscapulars with submarginal V- or U-shaped marks of dusky, the crown streaked and the occiput mottled with dusky, and the primaries darker than in the adult. Bill dusky, brownish toward the base; feet brownish. *Downy young:* Above, grayish white, finely mottled with dusky grayish, the head distinctly marked with irregular dots of dusky black; lower parts entirely immaculate white. Bill dull yellow, tipped with dusky; legs and feet clear pale yellow.

Total length, about 9.00 inches; extent, 20.00; wing, 6.60; tail, 3.50, its fork, 1.75; culmen, 1.20; depth of bill at base, .28; tarsus, .60; middle toe, with claw, .72.

This little Tern has several near allies in different parts of the world. The differential characters of the American species and their European representative are as follows: —

A. *Lower parts white.*

a. Rump and tail white. 1. *S. minuta.*[1]

b. Rump and tail pearl-gray.

b′. Bill more or less black tipped. Wing less than 7.00 inches. Feet bright yellow . . . . 2. *S. antillarum.*

b″. Bill without black tip. Wing 7.00 inches or longer. Feet olivaceous yellow. Upper parts darker gray. Bill larger and much stouter, and lateral rectrices more elongated . . . . 3. *S. superciliaris.*[2]

B. *Lower parts gray* . . . . 4. *S. exilis.*[3]

The Least Tern of North America appears to be restricted to the Atlantic coast; occurring occasionally in the interior, along the banks of our larger rivers. I have never met with it north of Southern Massachusetts; but Mr. Boardman informs me that it is occasionally seen in midsummer as far east as the St. Croix River and the Passamaquoddy — where, however, it is very rare. Audubon claims to have found this species breeding off Labrador, in June, 1833, and to have again observed it on Newfoundland on the 14th of August; but I can find no corroboration of its presence beyond the Bay of Fundy.

This species is supposed to leave the United States in the month of October, and to return here in the following April. It is more or less common in several of the West India Islands. In Cuba it is undoubtedly a resident, and breeds there. In

[1] Sterna minuta.

Sterna minuta, Linn. S. N. I. 1766, 228. — Keys. & Blas. Wirb. Eur. 97. — Naum. Vög. Deutschl. X. 1840, 145, pl. 254. — Macgill. Man. II. 1840, 234.

Sterna metopoleucus, S. G. Gmel. Nov. Comm. Petrop. XV. 475, pl. 22.

Sterna fissipes, Brehm, Vög. Deutschl. 790 (not of Linn.).

Sterna pomarina and *danica,* Brehm, t. c. 791.

Lesser Tern, Yarr. Brit. B. ed. 2, III. 519, fig.; ed. 3, III. 524, fig.; et Auct.

Hab. Palæarctic Region, to India and Cape of Good Hope.

[2] Sterna superciliaris.

Sterna superciliaris, Vieill. Nouv. Dict. XXXII. 1819, 126. — Scl. & Salv. P. Z. S. 1871, 571. — Saunders, P. Z. S. 1878, 662.

Sterna superciliaris, a. *superciliaris,* Coues, Birds N. W. 1874, 692.

Sterna maculata, Vieill. Enc. Méth. 1823, 350.

Sterna argentea, Max. Voy. I. 1820, 67; Beitr. IV. 1833, 871. — Pelz. Orn. Bras. 1870, 325.

Hab. Eastern South America, west to the headwaters of the Amazonian tributaries.

[3] Sterna exilis.

Sterna exilis, Tschudi, Faun. Per. Aves, 1846, 306. — Scl. & Salv., P. Z. S. 1871, 572. — Saunders, ib. 1878, 663.

Sterna lorata, Ph. & Landb. Wiegm. Archiv, 1863, pt. I. 124.

Sternula loricata, Gray, Handl. III. 1871, 121.

Hab. Coast of Peru and Chili.

There are, in addition to these, *S. sinensis,* Gm. (China to Australia); *S. sumatrana,* Raffl. (Ceylon to the Red Sea); *S. nereis,* Gould (Australia and New Zealand); and *S. balænarum,* Strickl. (from the Cape of Good Hope).

Jamaica it is not common, and Mr. Gosse only met with a single chance individual. It is resident in Central America.

Mr. Salvin obtained a skin of this Tern at Coban, in Guatemala, but was not able to ascertain just where it had been procured. He afterward found this species breeding on the coast of Honduras in the latter part of April. As he approached Gassey Key, the Terns rose from the land in a cloud. On this key about a hundred pairs had assembled to lay, and numbers of nests were already occupied, each containing one, two, or three eggs — nearly all of the nests being mere depressions in the sand.

Léotaud mentions this species as being one of the resident birds of Trinidad, living in company with the other Terns, and having, in all essential respects, the same habits.

Mr. Dresser mentions it as being common on the coast of Southern Texas during the summer. He often met with it about the lagoon near Matamoras, and also found it abundant about the mouth of the Rio Grande. In June, 1864, it was breeding in West Galveston Bay, on the small shell-bars or sand islets, but not on the mainland. The eggs were fresh, and he was told that it breeds late in the season. Mr. Ridgway found it very abundant on Cobb's Island, Va., where it was nesting on the dry sand in isolated colonies. Its usual note was a sharp squeak, much like the cry of a very young pig following its mother.

According to Giraud, this is a common species on Long Island, and thence southward, having a very extended range; returning to that locality early in May, and departing southward early in the autumn. It feeds on various kinds of insects, as well as on small fish. About the 25th of May or the 1st of June the female begins to lay. The eggs are dropped on the dry and warm sand, the temperature of which during the day is fully sufficient for the purposes of incubation; as the sand is sometimes so hot that one can scarcely bear the hand in it for a few moments without inconvenience. The wonder would therefore be greater should the bird sit on her eggs during the day, when her warmth is altogether unnecessary, and perhaps injurious; it seems perfectly reasonable that she should cover them only at night, or in wet and stormy weather. Giraud states that the eggs are generally four in number, and placed on the flat sand, safe beyond the reach of the highest summer tide. They are described by him as being of a yellowish-brown color, blotched with rufous. Giraud and Wilson give the length of the egg as 1.75 inches; but this is a mistake.

In 1842 I visited a small sandy island called Tuckernuk, lying between Muskegat and Nantucket Point, which was then supposed to be the most northerly locality in which this species bred in any considerable numbers. This colony, which was then one of considerable size, is now nearly or quite exterminated; and at the time of my visit it was very evident that constant spoliation would ere long result in its extermination. In the summer of 1842, and again in the following year, as we approached the shore the birds all rose and hovered over the land, resembling a small white cloud. They were quite as fearless as the Arctic Terns; and a stronger comparison could hardly be used. For when either of these birds has young or incubated eggs, it seems to fear nothing. The Terns dashed about in rapid flight, now this way, now that, plunging at our heads, but always turning to one side just before touching us. A few of the most interested made these demonstrations, while their companions hovered about us like a moving cloud of witnesses, all of them joining in the clamor of indignant and plaintive cries. The eggs were in slight depressions made in the sand, with no lining whatever.

In the Smithsonian Collection there are eggs of this species from Ipswich, Mass.;

New Jersey; North Carolina; Georgia; the Tortugas; and San Diego, Cal. The number found in a nest varies from one to four; but the last number is rarely found, and probably the same parent never deposits more than three eggs — perhaps not more than two. The ground-color is a very uniform shade of light buff, becoming paler with age. The spots are for the most part small, evenly distributed, colored a lavender-gray and burnt umber. Four eggs in my own collection, from Tuckernuk, measure 1.20 by .96 inches; 1.25 by .96; 1.24 by .91; 1.23 by .94. A few in the Smithsonian Collection measure 1.30 by 1.00. The smallest length is 1.20, and the least breadth .91. In some descriptions the ground-color of these eggs is spoken of as being a greenish white; but I have never found any with the least tinge of that color. In most examples the spots are small and evenly distributed; occasionally they are in large blotches, and in a few instances they form a confluent ring.

Sterna fuliginosa.

THE SOOTY TERN.

Sterna fuliginosa, GMEL. S. N. I. ii. 1788, 605. — WILS. Am. Orn. VIII. 1814, 145, pl. 72, fig. 7. — NUTT. Man. II. 1834, 284. — AUD. Orn. Biog. III. 1835, 263; V. 1839, 641, pl. 235; Synop. 1839, 317; B. Am. VII. 1844, 90, pl. 432. — LAWR. in Baird's B. N. Am. 1858, 861. — BAIRD, Cat. N. Am. B. 1859, no. 688. — COUES, Check List, 1873, no. 573; 2d ed. 1882, no. 804. — SAUNDERS, P. Z. S. 1876, 666. — RIDGW. Nom. N. Am. B. 1881, no. 691.

Sterna (*Haliplana*) *fuliginosa*, COUES, Key, 1872, 322; B. N. W. 1874, 698.

Sterna serrata, FORST. Descr. An. ed. Licht. 1844, 276.

Sterna guttata, FORST. t. c. 211 (young).

Anous l'Hermenieri, LESS. Descr. Mam. et Ois. 1847, 255 (young).

Sterna Gouldii, REICH. (*fide* GRAY).

Sterna luctuosa, PHIL. & LANDB. Wiegm. Archiv, 1866, 126.

Sterna fuliginosa, var. *crissalis*, "BAIRD," LAWR. Pr. Bost. Soc. 1871, 285 (Socorro I.).

HAB. Intertropical and subtropical coast-regions, completely round the globe. In America, south to Chili, north, regularly to the Carolinas and Western Mexico; casually to Pennsylvania, Massachusetts, and Vermont.

SP. CHAR. *Adult:* Forehead and upper part of the lores white, this color extending back laterally to the middle of the upper eyelid; a broad stripe across the lores (growing gradually

narrower anteriorly), auricular region, crown, occiput, nape (broadly), and entire upper parts, fuliginous black, the outer pair of rectrices white, with the inner webs growing gradually blackish terminally. Entire lower parts, including axillars and lining of the wing, white, sometimes faintly tinged posteriorly with pale bluish gray. Bill deep black; "iris chestnut" (AUDUBON); feet black. *Young, first plumage:* Dark fuliginous, more dusky grayish below; lining of the wing, and anal region, white; crissum pale smoky gray. Scapulars and wing-coverts distinctly but narrowly tipped with white. Lateral tail-feathers entirely blackish.

Average total length, about 16.50 inches; extent, 33.00 to 35.00; wing, 12.00; tail, 7.00–7.50, its fork, 3.00–3.50; culmen, 1.80; depth of bill at base, .50; tarsus, 1.00; middle toe, with claw, 1.20.

The series before us exhibits a marked difference between specimens from certain localities — quite sufficient, if constant, to characterize definable local races. Thus, examples from Florida and other parts of the Atlantic coast have the exterior pair of rectrices pure white, growing grayish-dusky terminally, the entire abdomen, anal region, and crissum being pure white. Those from Western Mexico (Socorro and Isabella islands) are the same as regards the rectrices; but the lower part of the abdomen, the anal region, and crissum, are light pearl-gray, in decided contrast to the white of the breast, etc. These constitute the var. *crissalis*, BAIRD. A specimen from the Hondou Islands, and another from Dog Island, South Pacific Ocean, are very similar to Florida examples; but the outer rectrices are pale gray to the extreme base, the terminal portion of the inner web dusky grayish for the extent of 2.50 inches. The posterior lower parts are also quite distinctly tinged with pale grayish. Three specimens from Palmyra Island (Dr. STREETS) resemble the last in the coloration of the lower parts; but the lateral rectrices are deep brownish gray throughout, the terminal portion dusky — this, in two examples, extending quite to the base of the outer web! The blackish of the nape is much narrower than in specimens from any other locality, and is much interrupted by the exposure of the whitish bases of the feathers.

The Sooty Tern is an intertropical species found in all parts of the globe, sporadically, between the 30th degree of north latitude and the same degree south. It is especially abundant in the islands off the southern coast of Florida and in various points in the West Indies. It is a great wanderer, and has occasionally been met with at a considerable distance from its usual residence.

According to Yarrell, a single specimen was shot, October, 1852, in England; and Naumann states that one was taken near Magdeburg, in Germany. During Captain Cook's voyage this species is said to have been met with several hundred miles from land. It is abundant about Ascension and Christmas islands, and appears to be common on some of the island groups of the South Seas. Mr. Gould includes it among the birds of Australia.

Mr. Salvin met with a few solitary birds of this species on the coast of Honduras in the latter part of April; but was told that they were much more abundant, and that they bred in large numbers at Cape Gracias a Dios. Mr. Dresser procured two specimens on the southern coast of Texas, but he did not meet with any breeding-place. In a voyage from England to Cape Town, Mr. Layard saw a flock of these Terns passing directly over the vessel, early in the morning, in lat. 10° 35′ S. Mr. J. C. Melliss ("Ibis," 1870) speaks of this species as occurring, although not very abundantly, at St. Helena. It inhabits the rocky islets off the coast, known as George's and Spury Island, in considerable numbers. It does not remain there all the year, but arrives about the end of December, and breeds during the months of January, February, and March. Much risk of life is run to obtain its eggs, which are brought to the market, and are regarded by some as a great delicacy. It seldom comes near the inhabited portion of the Island of St. Helena.

Mr. Edward Newton mentions ("Ibis," 1865) finding this species breeding on the Island of Rodriguez, near Mauritius. Von Heuglin met with it in pairs or in small flocks in the Red Sea, south of 14° north latitude, and on the Somali coast. It is also found — although rarely — on the guano island of Bur-da-Rebschi.

Captain Sperling ("Ibis," 1868, p. 286) gives an account of his visit to the breeding-place of this species on Ascension Island; the spot where these birds gather together for nesting purposes being called by the sailors "Wide-awake Fair." As he approached the place he noticed flocks of Terns converging from various parts of the ocean to a spot apparently about a mile in front of him, and toward which he proceeded; and on surmounting a low ridge the whole scene was disclosed. A gradual incline of a quarter of a mile terminated in a plain of ten or fifteen acres in extent, which was literally covered with these birds. This plain was surrounded by low mountains, except toward the side on which he stood. No description could convey an adequate idea of the effect produced by the thousands upon thousands of these wild sea-birds, hovering and screaming over this arid cinder-bed — the eggs and the young being scattered so thickly on the ground that in some instances it was impossible to avoid treading upon them. During the short walk down the slope, large flocks of parent birds hovered over their heads, and saluted the party with plaintive cries. On arriving within the precinct of the breeding-grounds the numbers of the birds increased. Large flocks were arriving in endless succession from seaward; others rose in clouds from the ground, and joining them, the whole assemblage wheeled around until he was almost made giddy by their gyrations. He sat down on a lump of cinder; and the birds being at length convinced that he was not there with hostile purposes, went on with their ordinary routine of incubation. There were young of all sizes, from the little callow nestlings, just hatched, to the newly fledged birds that fluttered and crawled like young Pigeons. There were also numbers of eggs exposed on the bare ground. In most instances the old birds sat, each on its own solitary treasure, hissing defiance as he approached, and fighting manfully if he attempted to remove it. The young were of a very light sooty color, both above and beneath, the ends of most of the feathers having a white spot the size of a pea, which gives to them a speckled appearance. Captain Sperling was informed that all these Terns leave the Island of Ascension as soon as the young can fly.

Colonel Grayson met with this species (variety *crissalis*) in the vicinity of the Tres Marias Islands, and also found it breeding on the small island of Isabella, near San Blas. It was not observed near the main shore, but usually far out to sea. It seemed to be semi-nocturnal in its habits, and to be a constant resident in the localities cited.

Examples from the Pacific, taken in the Wilkes Exploring Expedition, are identical with those found on the coast of the United States. This species was observed by Mr. Peale throughout all the islands of the Dangerous Archipelago, and on most of the coral islands of the Pacific. At Honden Island it was found in great numbers on the 21st of August, when the young were just able to fly. The nests were mere cavities in the coral sand, under low bushes. Their number was so great, and they were so near each other, that great care was required in walking to avoid crushing both young and old birds.

Oct. 7, 1839, Dr. Pickering visited Cora Island, an annular coral reef, inundated at high water, with the exception of two banks, one of which was covered by a grove of trees. Great numbers of birds were flying over and about the grove. The Terns, and especially *Sterna fuliginosa*, came out from under the low branches in vast numbers. There were three species of *Sterna*, one of *Fregata*, and three of *Sula* observed on this island; and nearly all of them were engaged in rearing their young. The Sooty Tern was present in larger numbers than all the others combined, its breeding-place occupying the weather side of the grove, or that most exposed to the sea. Here the trees presented a dense growth of branches, reaching almost to the ground; and beneath these the birds were obliged to force themselves out before they could take to flight. The eggs of this species were laid on the ground, under the thicket, without any nest, but with some regularity, and at a distance of about two and a half feet apart. In two instances only, out of at least a thousand nests examined, were there two eggs together. The birds, after having once risen, kept flying around the grove, and their cries might have been heard at a considerable distance. On the discharge of a gun, or a loud shout, there was complete stillness for a few moments, and then the noise recommenced.

The Sooty Tern is mentioned in Dr. Pickering's Journal as occurring at nearly all the points in the Pacific Ocean visited by the United States Exploring Expedition; and is shown to be one of the most extensively diffused of all the aquatic birds, being found both in temperate and tropical regions almost everywhere throughout the world.

Professor Alfred Newton, toward the end of May, 1857, saw several individuals of this species about midway between St. Thomas and Santa Cruz; and Mr. Osbert Salvin, on the 29th of May, 1859, when passing along the south side of Tortole and St. John's, also saw numbers of them. They came close to the ship, and he could make them out quite well. This species is of occasional occurrence in Bermuda. Two instances are mentioned by Major Wedderburn, and one is also furnished by Mr. Hurdis. Its presence there seemed generally to be due to the occurrence of a severe gale, by which it had been driven upon the shore.

This bird occurs at Jamaica, and its eggs constitute an article of considerable commercial importance. The Pedro Keys are the resort of this species, as also of the *Anous stolidus* and of other sea-fowl. This Tern is the "Egg-bird" of Jamaica. On the 9th of May, 1832, Audubon visited a low island among the Tortugas on which large numbers of this species were breeding. On landing it seemed to him for a moment, as he says, as if the birds would raise him from the ground, so thickly were they crowded around him, and so rapid were the motions of their wings; while their cries were deafening. The birds might easily have been caught while they were sitting, or when scrambling through the bushes to escape from the intruders. The sailors, provided with sticks, knocked down the Terns as they flew over them; and in less than half an hour more than a hundred were killed, and several baskets of eggs collected. The latter proved to be delicious eating, in whatever way cooked. During each night, or between 2 and 4 A. M., a large number of these Terns went out to sea to feed, being able to do this by night as well as by day. This species is said rarely to alight on the water, and never to dive headlong in pursuit of fish, as the smaller Terns are wont to do, but passes over its prey in a curved line and picks it up. This Tern may often be seen following in the wake of a porpoise, capturing some of the fish thus brought within reach. Its flight is firm and steady, rather than light and buoyant, and it hovers close to the surface of the water, in the manner of a Gull, to pick up floating objects.

Audubon states that the Sooty Tern always lays three eggs, and that he never found more than this number. When wounded, and seized by the hand, this bird bites severely and utters a plaintive cry; this cry differs from its usual note, which is loud and shrill, resembling the syllables *oo-ee, oo-ee.* The nests were scooped near the stems of the bushes, under the shade of the boughs, and were within a few inches of one another. The egg measured 2.13 inches in length by 1.50 in breadth; it has a pale cream-colored ground, is marked with various tints of light umber, and has lighter marks of purple, which appear as if within the shell. The eggs in the Smithsonian Collection from the Tortugas have the ground-color of a light pinkish cream, and are marked with blotches of a rich reddish chestnut, with cloudings of lavender of two shades. In some specimens the reddish chestnut-color of the markings deepens almost to blackness.

Sterna anosthæta.

THE BRIDLED TERN.

Sterna anosthæta, SCOP. Del. Faun. et Flor. Ins. I. 1786, no. 72 (ex Sonn. Voy. 125, pl. 84). — COUES, Check List, 1873, no. 574.
Sterna (*Haliplana*) *anosthæta*, COUES, Key, 1872, 322.
Sterna (*Haliplana*) *anæstheta*, COUES, Birds N. W. 1874, 701.
Sterna anæstheta, SAUNDERS, P. Z. S. 1876, 664 (fig. of foot on p. 665). — RIDGW. Nom. N. Am. B. 1881, no. 692.
Sterna anæsthetica, COUES, 2d Check List, 1882, no. 805.
Sterna oahuensis, BLOX. Voy. "Blonde," 1826, 251.
Sterna panayensis, GMEL. S. N. I. ii. 1788, 607.
Sterna panaya, LATH. Ind. Orn. II. 1790, 808.
Sterna antarctica, "CUV." LESS. Traité, 1831, 621.
Sterna infuscata, HEUGL. Ibis, 1859, 351.
Haliplana discolor, COUES, Ibis, 1864, 392. — ELLIOT, Illustr. Am. B. II. 1869, pl. 57.
? *Hydrochelidon somalensis*, HEUGL. Orn. N.-O. Afr. 1873, p. ccvii.
Sterna melanoptera, SWAINS. B. N. W. Afr. 1837, 249.

HAB. Nearly the same range as *S. fuliginosa*, but not ranging so far from the tropics. Florida (only North American record).

SP. CHAR. *Adult:* Lores, crown, occiput, and upper part of nape deep black; forehead and superciliary region, entire lower parts, and under surface of the wing pure white. Lower part of nape and extreme upper part of the back ashy white; remaining upper parts brownish slate, more plumbeous on the back, where shading gradually into the whitish of the nape; primaries, primary

coverts, and alulæ blackish slate. Rump and six middle tail-feathers brownish ashy, like the back, the two outer rectrices on each side white, shading into grayish terminally, most extensively on the second feather, the outer web of the first being wholly white. Bill and feet black; iris dark brown. *Young, first plumage:* Entire lower parts, with cheeks, forehead, and sides of the crown, white, as in the adult; middle of the crown, with occiput and nape, brownish dusky, the first streaked with grayish white. Upper parts grayish brown, the scapulars, interscapulars, and tertials bordered terminally with grayish white.

Total length, 14.00 to 15.00 inches; wing, 10.50; tail, 6.00–7.00; culmen, 1.40-1.60; depth of bill at base, .35–.40; tarsus, .85; middle toe, .85.

There can be very little doubt that this species is an occasional visitant of Florida, both on the Atlantic and on the Gulf coast. There is now in the collection of Mr. George N. Lawrence, of New York, an example labelled as having been taken in Florida; it was formerly in the Audubon collection; and Mr. Charles B. Cory, of Boston, in the summer of 1879 found it abundant in June on Long Island, one of the Bahamas. In the West India Islands, where it is especially numerous, it is "the egg-bird" *par excellence*, and is more or less confounded with the *S. fuliginosa*. Mr. Lawrence, in his paper on the Birds of Sombrero — a rocky islet near St. Martin's — quotes Mr. Julien as believing that the number of individuals of this species which visited that place was at one time equalled only by those of *S. maxima* and *Anous stolidus*. It is said to be remarkable for its social peculiarities — almost always associating with the Noddies; and in however great numbers it may be present on any Key, it is found to be almost always more or less mixed with flocks of that Tern. It arrives at Sombrero in March, and departs in August. Its nest is said to be similar to that of the Noddy, and it lays but one egg. It often flies high, and with a peculiarly quick darting motion, keeping up a noisy chattering very different from the discordant "caw-caw" of *Anous stolidus*. Mr. Julien never observed the two species to quarrel with each other, although individuals of the same species often engaged in long and obstinate combats.

The eggs of this bird found at Sombrero are described by Mr. Lawrence as measuring 1.88 inches in length by 1.25 in breadth, as having a ground-color of a creamy white, and as being marked with blotches of deep rusty brown, most abundant on the larger end. Eggs collected in British Honduras by Mr. Osbert Salvin vary in length from 1.90 inches to 1.85, and in breadth from 1.35 to 1.30. Their ground-color is pale brownish cream, and the markings are small spots of burnt-sienna and lavender-gray.

Mr. Cory found birds of this species breeding in large numbers at Clarence Harbor. They were in company with the Sooty and the Roseate Tern; and eggs procured as late as June 8 were quite fresh. In their breeding habits Mr. Cory found them very similar to the *fuliginosa*. Their eggs were found deposited in sheltered clefts in ledges of rocks, or in cavities among the loose bowlders which lined the sea-shore. The egg in all instances was single, and resembled that of the *fuliginosa*, but was more spotted about the larger end, while the reddish tinge of the ground-color was much fainter. The egg taken by Mr. Cory measures 2.00 inches in length by 1.42 in breadth; the ground-color is a rich cream, strongly washed with a rufous tint; around the larger end is a ring of large and confluent blotches of reddish brown; smaller spots of the same are diffused in a scattered manner over the whole egg, with obscure shell-markings of lilac and slate.

An egg in my collection, taken by Mr. Godeffroy on the coast of New Guinea, measures 2.05 inches by 1.45. The ground-color is pure cream, without a tinge of any other shade. Grouped around the larger end, covering nearly the entire portion, are numerous spots of light brown, and others of much deeper shade, interspersed, and occasionally confluent. Smaller ones are sparingly scattered over the entire surface, and there are also a few shell-markings of a faint purple.

Genus **HYDROCHELIDON**, Boie.

Hydrochelidon, Boie, Isis, 1822, 563 (type, *Sterna nigra*, Linn.).

Char. Similar to the smaller species of *Sterna*, but tail only very slightly forked or emarginate, the rectrices not attenuated at ends, and the webs of the toes filling less than half the interdigital spaces. Adults gray or blackish beneath, as dark as, or darker than, the color of the upper surface.

The three known species of this genus may be defined as follows — *H. leucoparia* being included, partly for comparison, but more especially on account of having been obtained in the West Indies, and therefore entitled to a place in the American fauna: —

A. Smaller (wing 8.50 inches or less); head wholly dusky or black.

1. **H. nigra.** Upper tail-coverts and tail plumbeous, like the back; wings uniform plumbeous.
   - *a.* Lower parts plumbeous, scarcely, if at all, darker than the upper surface. *Hab.* Europe. . . . . *nigra.*[1]
   - *β.* Lower parts black, much darker than the upper parts, which are decidedly darker than in *H. nigra.* *Hab.* America . . . . *surinamensis.*
2. **H. leucoptera.** Upper tail-coverts and tail white, sometimes shaded with pearl-gray; anterior lesser wing-coverts white, lower parts black, as in *H. surinamensis.* *Hab.* Palæarctic Region; accidental in North America (Wisconsin; KUMLIEN).

B. Larger (wing 9.50 inches); a broad white stripe on side of the head, below the eye.

3. **H. leucopareia.**[2] Entire pileum, including lores and nape, uniform black; a wide stripe on the side of the head, from the chin and rictus back to the nape, beneath the eyes, also the crissum and lining of the wing, white; rest of the plumage uniform light bluish plumbeous. *Hab.* Palæarctic Region; accidental in West Indies.

Hydrochelidon nigra surinamensis.

THE BLACK TERN.

Sterna surinamensis, GMEL. S. N. I. 1788, 604.
Hydrochelidon surinamensis, BONAP. Compt. Rend. 1856, 773.
Hydrochelidon lariformis surinamensis, RIDGW. Nom. N. Am. B. 1881, no. 693.
Hydrochelidon nigra surinamensis, STEJN. Proc. U. S. Nat. Mus. Vol. 5, 1882, 40.
Sterna plumbea, WILS. Am. Orn. VII. 1813, 83, pl. 83 (= young).
Hydrochelidon plumbea, LAWR. in Baird's B. N. Am. 1858, 864. — BAIRD, Cat. N. Am. B. 1859, no. 695.
Sterna nigra, SW. & RICH. F. B. A. II. 1831, 415 (nec LINN.). — NUTT. Man. II. 1834, 282. — AUD. Orn. Biog. III. 1835, 593; V. 1839, 642, pl. 180; Synop. 1839, 320; B. Am. VII. 1844, 116, pl. 438.
Hydrochelidon nigra (part), SAUNDERS, P. Z. S. 1878, 642.
Hydrochelidon fissipes (part), COUES, Pr. Philad. Acad. 1862, 554 (nec *Sterna fissipes*, LINN.); Key, 1872, 323; Check List, 1873, no. 575.
Hydrochelidon lariformis (part), COUES, B. N. W. 1874, 704 (nec *Rallus lariformis*, LINN.); 2d Check List, 1882, no. 806.

HAB. The whole of temperate North America, and portions of tropical America; north to Alaska, south to Chili; breeds throughout its range, except toward the extreme south.

SP. CHAR. *Adult, in summer:* Head, neck, and lower parts sooty black, the head and neck, especially above, nearly pure black; anal region and crissum pure white. Entire upper parts

[1] HYDROCHELIDON NIGRA.
Sterna nigra, LINN. S. N. ed. 10, I. 1758, 137; ed. 12, I. 1766, 227.
Hydrochelidon nigra, BOIE, Isis, 1822, 563.
Rallus lariformis, LINN. S. N. ed. 10, I. 1758, 153.
Hydrochelidon lariformis, COUES, B. N. W. 1874, 704 (part).
Sterna nævia, LINN. S. N. I. 1766, 228 (ex BRISS.; = *Rallus lariformis* of ed. 10).

[2] HYDROCHELIDON LEUCOPAREIA.
Sterna leucopareia, NATTERER, in Temm. Man. 1820, 726.
Hydrochelidon leucopareia, GOULD, Handb. to B. Austr. II. 1865, 406.
Sterna javanica, HORSF. Trans. Linn. Soc. XIII. 1820, 198.
Sterna grisea, HORSF. t. c. 199.
Sterna hybrida, PALL. Zoog. Rosso-As. II. 1826, 338.
Hydrochelidon hybrida, GRAY, Gen. B. III. 1846, 660. — SAUNDERS, P. Z. S. 1876, 640.
Sterna Delamottei, VIEILL. Faun. Fr. 1828, 402.
Sterna similis, GRAY & HARDW. Illustr. Ind. Zool. I. 1882, pl. 70, fig. 2.
Hydrochelidon fluviatilis, GOULD, P. Z. S. 1842, 140.
Hydrochelidon Delalandii, BONAP. Compt. Rend. XLII. 1856, 773.
Sterna innotata, BEAVAN, Ibis, 1868, 404 (young).

uniform plumbeous, the border of the wing, from the shoulders to the carpo-metacarpal joint, white. Lining of the wing light plumbeous-gray. Bill deep black, the rictus lake-red, the interior of the mouth pinkish ; iris dark brown ; legs and feet purplish dusky. *Adult, in winter:* Head, neck, and lower parts pure white ; orbital and auricular regions dusky ; crown and occiput dark grayish, the feathers bordered with paler. Upper parts as in the summer plumage, but rather paler plumbeous. *Young, first plumage:* Very similar to the winter plumage, but scapulars, interscapulars,

H. nigra, adult in summer.

and tertials tipped with raw-umber brown, the anterior lesser wing-coverts dusky, the crown, occiput, and upper part of the nape dusky, and the entire sides washed with plumbeous. *Downy young:* Above, deep, soft umber-brown, with a few coarse, irregular marblings of black ; forehead, crown, throat, and jugulum more sooty brown, without markings ; side of the head (including lores) dull whitish ; abdomen white centrally, pale sooty grayish exteriorly.[1]

Total length, about 9.25 inches ; extent, 24.00–25.00 ; wing, 8.25 ; tail, 3.75, its fork, .90 ; culmen, 1.10 ; depth of bill at base, .25 ; tarsus, .68 ; middle toe (with claw), .90.

Summer plumage.

With a series before us of five adult specimens of the European bird in summer plumage, we are much surprised that authors maintain the absolute identity of the American Black Tern with the true *H. nigra.* Not one of these five specimens can be matched among a series of over fifty examples of the American bird in corresponding dress, while three of them are in a plumage never approached by the American form. These three examples are bluish plumbeous beneath, the shade being exactly that of the upper parts, which are very decidedly lighter than in any American examples. All of these three specimens have the feathers of the throat white beneath the surface, while one of them (No. 57088, ♀) has the chin and upper part of the throat uniform grayish white, in

[1] From No. 77564, Cold Springs, Cal., July 27, 1877 ; H. W. Henshaw, collector.

abrupt and marked contrast with the sooty black of the lores and orbital region. Only the upper half of the head is blackish, this color forming a well-defined "hood," as in the species of *Sterna*, its lower edge on a line with the rictus, and including the auriculars; the lower eyelid being marked by a whitish crescent. Only one example in the very large series of American specimens approaches the darkest-colored individual from Europe, and even in this instance the difference is very decided. In his paper on the *Sterninæ* (P. Z. S. 1876, p. 643), published subsequently to Dr. Coues's mono-

Winter plumage.

graph in "Birds of the Northwest," Mr. Howard Saunders remarks as follows concerning the differences between the American and the European birds of this species: —

"In almost all the adult American specimens which I have examined — about a dozen in number — the black of the under parts is of a deeper and more sooty brown tint than in any European examples out of upwards of a hundred from various localities, the black being as dark as in *H. leucoptera* — an intensity of hue which our form never possesses. In two or three examples, however, all females, the lightest colored American birds approach more closely to very dark specimens from Europe; and in the young and winter plumage the two forms are absolutely undistinguishable; so that any specific separation is out of the question."

The geographical difference in coloration as exhibited in the series before us, which in proportionate numbers of the two forms is just the reverse of that examined by Mr. Saunders, is so very marked that it is only in view of the possible intergradation through the lighter American and the darker European examples that we consider them as specifically identical. The extreme and average measurements of five adults of the European form are as follows: Wing, 8.40–8.75 inches (average, 8.56); tail, 3.50–3.70 (3.60); culmen, 1.05–1.10 (1.09); depth of bill through base, .20–.25 (.22); tarsus, .60–.68 (.62); middle toe, .55–.65 (.58).

The Black Tern is a cosmopolitan species, common to both continents. It is distributed, at different seasons, in nearly all parts of North America; regularly and abundantly in some regions, occasionally and in small numbers in others. It is found throughout Central America and Mexico, and in South America as far south at least as Chili, and north to the Fur Regions and Hudson's Bay. Examples of this bird were taken near Fort Resolution, Fort Yukon, and Moose Fort, and it is abundant in the Red River and Selkirk settlements.

In Great Britain this bird is only a summer visitor, differing from all the other Terns in some of its habits, seldom associating with any other species, and being rarely seen on the sea-coast, and then only in the spring, at the time of its arrival, or in the fall, when about to leave for the winter. Preferring fresh-water marshes, the vicinity of rivers, and reedy pools, it is found in the summer only in the interior. It is rare in the north of England, and makes its appearance in the southern part by the end of April or the beginning of May, and leaves early in October, being very rarely seen as late as November.

This is said to be a common bird in Sweden; it is also abundant in Holland and in Germany, as well as in the extensive marshes of Hungary. It visits several districts in France and Switzerland. In its migrations it passes through Italy, Corfu, Crete, Sicily, Asia Minor, and is found in the regions of the Caucasus. It is to be met with during the winter in Madeira and on the African coast of the Mediterranean. Kalm — as quoted by Pennant — saw flocks of hundreds of this species in the Atlantic Ocean, midway between England and America.

Mr. C. A. Wright, in a paper on the birds of Malta, states in reference to this species that in July, 1870, a large number of these Terns visited the harbors of Malta, and remained until September; but none of them were in their summer plumage. It was exceedingly interesting to watch their light and rapid movements, as they dropped suddenly from a great height, splashing the water like a falling stone, or coursed through the air, as if imitating the Swallow. One of these Terns, perched on a floating cork, allowed the boat to drift down toward it, and did not move until almost near enough to be touched with the hand. Occasionally one would exchange calls with a passing companion; the note was a shrill scream.

Mr. Salvin, late in April, met with a large flock of this species on the coast of Honduras, and obtained several examples. Mr. Grayson found it at Mazatlan, where it makes its appearance in September and October, and where it remains through the winter months. Mr. Dresser mentions it as being common at the mouth of the Rio Grande during the summer; but he noticed none at Galveston. At the lagoons near Matamoras he often saw twenty or thirty of these birds at one time.

Mr. N. B. Moore writes from Sarasota Bay, Fla., that he was surprised to see, on the last day of June, 1873, two groups of this species, of five each, in a strong gale from the southwest, scudding toward the south. They were in their young plumage, and passed quite near him. After this none were seen until August 6. He inferred that some breed in that neighborhood.

This species is present on the coast of the Carolinas, for a few days only, after the second week in May, reappearing in August.

Captain Blakiston obtained a specimen of this bird on the Saskatchewan; Mr. Bernard Ross met with it on the Mackenzie, and Mr. Murray procured it on Hudson's Bay. Richardson states that it is common in the interior of the Fur Countries, on the borders of lakes. It breeds chiefly in the swamps, and is said to feed principally upon winged insects.

Giraud mentions the fact that the young of this species were found by Mr. Brasher in the extensive meadows between the Passaic and the Hackensack rivers, in August, 1843, but neither its nest nor its eggs have ever been detected; yet Giraud was confident that a few of these birds breed along the rush-covered margins of the streams and ponds of Long Island. This Tern, he adds, is very strong and muscular, and possesses great power of wing. It is very active in pursuit of its prey, but displays the timidity of disposition peculiar to its race, except when defending its young.

This bird is of occasional occurrence in Massachusetts after the breeding season. Mr. George O. Welch has procured specimens in the marshes near the sea, in Lynn, late in the fall; and Mr. Maynard has obtained specimens at Ipswich. Mr. William Brewster informs me that one was procured in his presence at Rye Beach, N. H.; and it has also been taken at Nantucket.

Dr. Cooper states that this Tern migrates through the interior valleys of California, and that some probably breed about the marshes within the State, especially in the mountains, as he met with it on the head-waters of the Mohave River as late as the 7th of June. It is also common along clear water throughout the Rocky Mountains, especially in the cooler months, where it fishes pretty much in the same manner as the larger Terns, also feeding on insects, in pursuit of which it flies in the manner of Swallows. It is rarely seen on the Pacific sea-coast, and only in spring and fall.

Mr. B. F. Goss found this Tern breeding in large numbers in the marshes bordering small inland lakes and ponds in Minnesota. The late Mr. R. Kennicott mentioned its breeding in the Calumet marshes, on the southeastern margin of Lake Michigan; and it also breeds in large numbers in the marshes adjacent to Lake Koskonong, in Southern Wisconsin, where its eggs have been taken, at different times, in considerable numbers.

Its nest is usually placed near water — sometimes over shallows — on tufts of reeds or rushes. More commonly than otherwise it builds in very wet localities, and not infrequently the nest is but little raised above the level of the water. It is made of coarse flags, reeds, and grasses, and lined with slender bits of the same materials. The eggs — usually three — are occasionally four in number, average 1.42 inches in length by 1.00 inch in breadth, and have a ground-color of a dark olive-brown, blotched and spotted with bistre so deep as to have the effect of blackness. The markings are in most cases quite bold, and are principally at the larger end.

This Tern is quite celebrated for the ease and certainty with which it pursues and captures, on the wing, the larger insects, such as dragon-flies and beetles. Its flight is rapid, and it can stop, turn, and alter its course with all the ease of a Swallow.

It is said to arrive in Louisiana, coming across the water from the Mexican territories, about the middle of April, and to continue passing through until into May. It reappears, in the course of its southern migrations, in the months of September and October. Many pairs breed in the intermediate range between the Southern States and the Great Lakes. Audubon found it breeding on the margins of ponds near the Ohio River in Kentucky, and also in the neighborhood of Vincennes, Ind.

Professor Kumlien informs me that the Black Tern is very abundant not only near Lake Koskonong, but also wherever there are suitable situations, such as muddy marshes, with water here and there with a depth of from a few inches to three or four feet. In the large marshes, at some distance from the lake, or in a shallow bay, it makes its nest of broken pieces of reeds, the nest being one large mass of reeds, more or less rotten, heaped together, the whole raised from one to four inches above the water. But the nests appear to vary very considerably, there being sometimes hardly anything more than a simple depression, and at other times quite an elaborate structure. The chick (beautifully mottled with different shades of brown) swims and dives when but a few hours old. By far the greater number of the Black Terns seen in the lake during the early part of summer have their nests in the adjoining marshes, and only visit the lake for foraging purposes. This bird arrives in May, and departs so gradually that it is impossible to say anything more definite about the time of its leaving than that by September these Terns have gone. Among the immense numbers of Black Terns seen there in June comparatively few are immature birds.

Captain Bendire found this a common summer resident in Eastern Oregon, breeding in colonies in several of the sloughs in the vicinity of Silver River. He obtained a large number of their eggs, nearly fresh, June 1, 1876.

Eggs of this species in the Smithsonian Collection, from California and from Pewaukee, Wis., have a ground-color varying from a deep drab, or a brownish olive, to a light drab, and also to a light greenish drab. The spots are numerous, evenly distributed, and are of a dull lavender-gray, brownish black, and umber-brown, intensified to blackness. Specimens in my own collection, from Lake Koskonong, have the following average measurements: 1.21 by .96 inches; 1.42 by 1.00; 1.37 by 1.00; 1.36 by .90.

Hydrochelidon leucoptera.

THE WHITE-WINGED BLACK TERN.

Sterna leucoptera, MEISNER & SCHINZ, Vög. Schweiz, 1815, 264.

Hydrochelidon leucoptera, BOIE, Isis, 1822, 563. — SAUNDERS, P. Z. S. 1876, 641. — RIDGW. Nom. N. Am. B. 1881, no. 694. — COUES, 2d Check List, 1882, no. 807.

Hydrochelidon nigra, GRAY, Gen. B. III. 1849, 660 (not *Sterna nigra*, LINN.). — COUES, B. N. W. 1874, 709.

Hydrochelidon subleucoptera, BREHM, Vogelfang, 1855, 350.

HAB. Palæarctic Region, Africa, Australia, and New Zealand. Casual or accidental in Eastern North America (Wisconsin; KUMLIEN).

SP. CHAR. *Adult, in summer:* Head, neck, and lower parts, except anal region and crissum, uniform sooty black, deeper black on the head and neck; back, scapulars, tertials, and upper part of rump plumbeous; wings silvery gray, becoming gradually white on the anterior lesser coverts. Lower part of rump, and upper tail-coverts, white, sometimes tinged with bluish gray; tail grayish white or pale grayish, the feathers tinged with deeper grayish toward ends. Anal region and lower tail-coverts pure white. Lining of the wing, and axillars, dark plumbeous. Bill dark brownish; iris dark brown; legs and feet pale brownish, in the dried skin.

Wing, 7.60–8.20 inches (average, 7.99); tail, 2.80–3.25 (3.06); culmen, .90–.95 (.94); depth of bill through base, .20; tarsus, .70–.75 (.71); middle toe, .60–.65 (.61). [Four specimens.]

The single American specimen examined (the only one known — No. 66213, ♀ ad., Lake Koskonong, Wis.; TH. KUMLIEN), has the wing and tail much shorter than either of the three European specimens, measuring, respectively, only 7.60 and 2.80 inches against 8.00 and 3.00 — the minimum of the same measurements in the European examples.

The occurrence of a single specimen of this well-known European species within the limits of the United States is an interesting incident of comparatively recent occurrence. It was taken by Ludwig Kumlien, the son of the well-known ornithologist, Professor Thure Kumlien, on Black-hawk Island, Koskonong Lake, July 5, 1873. It was a female, apparently breeding, and flying in company with a flock of the common Black Tern. The eggs in its ovaries were as large as No. 6 shot.

In Europe this species is a common companion of *H. nigra*, and rather a southern species than a northern one. It is of only occasional occurrence in Great Britain, and is merely accidental in Sweden, in both of which countries the Black Tern is comparatively common. Mr. Wheelwright states that only a single example of this species has been seen in South Sweden. A solitary specimen was shot on the Shannon River in 1841; this was supposed to be a form of the Black Tern, and was for a while so labelled in the museum of the Dublin Natural History Society. Another specimen was shot near Yarmouth, England, May 17, 1853. According to Temminck, this Tern inhabits the bays and inlets of the shores of the Mediterranean, and is very common about Gibraltar. It visits also the lakes, rivers, and marshes of the countries in the vicinity of the Alps. It is said to be very common about the lakes of Lucamo, Lugano, Como, Iseo, and Garda, and is occasionally seen on the Lake of Geneva. It is included by Dr. Schinz among the birds of Switzerland, and has also been procured in France and Belgium. Brehm includes it in his work on the Birds of Germany, and Nilsson in his Fauna of Scandinavia, as a very rare straggler; and Savi and Malherbe give it as a bird of Italy. Mr. Drummond met with it in Northern Africa, near Tunis. It is said to be common in spring in Dalmatia. Its habits do not appear to differ essentially from those of its near relative, *H. nigra*.

Its occurrence in the Transvaal, in Africa, renders it probable that this species may be more or less generally distributed over the whole of that continent. Mr. T.

Ayres mentions seeing several of these birds hawking for insects over a swamp some eight miles from Potchefstroom. He speaks of their flight as being slow, uncertain, and wavy. Their stomachs were found to contain insects.

GENUS **ANOUS**, LEACH.

Anous, LEACH, Stephens' Gen. Zool. XIII. 1826, 139 (type, *Sterna stolida*, LINN.).

CHAR. Size rather small; tail graduated or wedge-shaped; webs of the toes completely filling the interdigital spaces, and not at all scalloped out anteriorly. Color uniform dusky, becoming hoary on the forehead.

A. stolidus.

The genus *Anous* embraces but one North American species — the *A. stolidus*, LINN. In other portions of the world, more especially in the several regions of the South Pacific Ocean, several other more or less nearly related species occur, only one of which (*A. melanogenys*) reaches the American coast. Their characters are as follows: —

A. Lores dusky, in abrupt and marked contrast with the hoary of the forehead.

a. Forehead only distinctly whitish.

1. **A. stolidus.** Plumage sooty brown, gradually lightening into hoary gray on the nape and pileum.

b. Entire pileum distinctly whitish.

2. **A. melanogenys.**[1] White of the pileum changing gradually into ashy on the nape; plumage of the body sooty brown.
3. **A. leucocapillus.**[2] White of the pileum abruptly defined posteriorly against the sooty brown of the nape; plumage of the body sooty black

B. Lores hoary whitish, like the forehead.

4. **A. tenuirostris.**[3] Hoary ash of occiput and nape changing gradually into sooty brown on the chin and throat, the cheeks also being grayish brown.

[1] ANOUS MELANOGENYS, Gray.

Anous melanogenys, GRAY, Gen. B. III 1849, 661, pl. 182; Handl. III. 1871, 123. — SAUNDERS, P. Z. S. 1876, 670, pl. 61, fig. 2.

Anous tenuirostris, SCL. & SALV. P. Z. S. 1871, 566. — COUES, B. N. W. 1874, 710, footnote.

Hab. Intertropical seas and coasts, from Australia, Africa, and throughout Polynesia, to Central America, breeding in immense numbers along the coast of Honduras, and undoubtedly to be detected along the Gulf Coast of the United States.

[2] ANOUS LEUCOCAPILLUS, Gould.

Anous leucocapillus, GOULD, P. Z. S. 1845, 103; Birds Austr. pt. vii. 1848, pl. 35. — SAUNDERS, P. Z. S. 1876, 670, pl. lxi. fig. 3.

Hab. Raines Islet, Australia; Bristow Island, south coast New Guinea; Paumotu Islands.

[3] ANOUS TENUIROSTRIS, Temm.

Sterna tenuirostris, TEMM. Pl. Col. 202 (1838).

Anous tenuirostris, SAUNDERS, P. Z. S. 1876, 670, pl. lxi. fig. 1.

Anous melanops, GOULD, P. Z. S. 1845, 103; B. Austr. pt. vii. 1848, pl. 34.

Hab. Senegal; Rodriguez and Mauritius; Houtmann's Abrolhos, west coast Australia.

Anous stolidus.

THE NODDY TERN.

Sterna stolida, LINN. S. N. ed. 10, I. 1758, 137 ; ed. 12, I. 1766, 227. — NUTT. Man. II. 1834, 285. — AUD. Orn. Biog. III. 1835, 516 ; V. 1839, 642, pl. 275 ; Synop. 1839, 322 ; B. Am. VII. 1844, 153, pl. 440.

Anous stolidus, GRAY, List Gen. B. III. 1841, 100. — LAWR. in Baird's B. N. Am. 1858, 865. — BAIRD, Cat. N. Am. B. 1859, no. 696. — COUES, Key, 1872, 323; Check List, 1873, no. 576 ; 2d ed. 1882, no. 808 ; Birds N. W. 1874, 710. — SAUNDERS, P. Z. S. 1876, 669. — RIDGW. Nom. N. Am. B. 1881, no. 695.

Sterna fuscata, LINN. S. N. I. 1766, 228.

Sterna pileata, SCOPOLI, Del. Faun. et Flor. Ins. I. 1786, 92, no. 73 (ex Sonn. Voy. 125, pl. 85).

Anous niger, STEPHENS, Gen. Zool. XIII. 1826, 140, pl. 17.

Anous spadicea, STEPHENS, in Shaw's Gen. Zool. XIII. 1826, 143 (young).

Sterna unicolor, NORDM. in Erm. Verz. v. Thier. & Pfl. 1835, 17.

Anous Rousseauii, HARTL. Beitr. Orn. Madagasc. 1860, 86.

Anous frater, COUES, Pr. Phil. Acad. 1862, 558 (Pacific Ocean).

Anous stolidus, var. *frater*, COUES, B. N. W. 1874, 712 (in text).

A. stolidus.

HAB. Intertropical regions in general. In America, north to the Gulf and South Atlantic States, south to Brazil and Chili ; both coasts of Central America.

SP. CHAR. *Adult:* Prevailing color uniform sooty brown, becoming gradually grayer on the neck and head, laterally and underneath, but lightening on the nape and pileum into pale ashy,

A. melanogenys.

which grows gradually lighter anteriorly, the forehead being quite white ; lores dark sooty plumbeous, in abrupt and marked contrast with the white or pale ashy of the forehead. Remiges, primary-coverts, and tail dusky brown, the primaries nearly black. Bill deep black ; iris brown ; "feet dull brownish red, the webs dusky, the claws black" (AUDUBON). *Young?* (No. 67323,

Palmyra Island; T. H. Streets): Similar, but head uniform grayish brown, the frontlet hoary grayish.

Total length, about 16.00 inches; extent, 31.00; wing, 10.00–10.50; tail, 6.00; culmen, 1.75; depth of bill at base, .38; tarsus, 1.00; middle toe, with claw, 1.45.

There is considerable variation among different specimens in regard to the color of the pileum, which is frequently grayish, the extreme anterior part of the forehead only white. In some examples the head and neck are decidedly plumbeous.

The common Noddy Tern appears to be an intertropical species, and to be found round the entire surface of the globe, both north and south of the equator, at a distance from it of rarely exceeding thirty degrees north or south. While the specimens from the shores and islands of the Pacific Ocean differ, with considerable uniformity, in certain respects from those obtained on the Atlantic coast, these differences are small and unimportant, and apparently not sufficient to warrant us in separating specifically the birds of the Atlantic from those of the Pacific. This being the case, it is evident that this bird has a very extended range.

It is mentioned by the naturalists connected with the Wilkes Expedition as having been observed at widely distant points in the Pacific Ocean. One specimen having been attracted by the ship's light at night, was obtained by Mr. Peale on the equator, in longitude 17° 44′, in the Atlantic Ocean. It was not distinguishable from others obtained at the Dangerous Archipelago or New Zealand. Unlike the Sooty Tern, the presence of this bird does not indicate the vicinity of land. On the islands of the Pacific Mr. Peale found it building its nests of sticks, on trees; the eggs being brownish white, spotted with reddish brown, 2.20 inches long and 1.50 inches in breadth.

Dr. Pickering mentions this species as of common occurrence at Gardner's Island, August 19. Its nest was built in the fork of a tree, with much more care than is usual in this family. The egg or young was single in all instances noticed. Subsequently at sea, September 4, he states that one of this species alighted on the taffrail, and was taken by hand. It had very limited power of perching, and preferred walking. At first it seemed awkward and confused, but in an hour became accustomed to confinement, and very carefully adjusted its feathers. It was set at liberty in the afternoon, but would not leave the ship for some time. The occurrence of this bird at nearly all the points visited by the Expedition in the Southern Pacific Ocean is mentioned by Dr. Pickering.

Mr. J. C. Melliss ("Ibis," 1870) speaks of this species as being a common bird on the Island of St. Helena. It is described as a less shy and retiring species than the other sea-birds, frequenting the roadstead, where, in the neighborhood of ships riding at anchor, it may be seen sitting on the surface of the water, or in close proximity to a boat. It inhabits principally the cliffs of the islets — as, for instance, Egg Island — where it breeds in swarms. It does not associate there with any other birds, but is one of the most abundant species.

Mr. Stoltenhoff states that he found this bird breeding on Inaccessible Island, one of the Tristan d'Acunha group, where it is called the "Wood Pigeon." It arrives about the middle of September, and nests about the middle of November, building a nest of sticks, leaves, etc., in the branches of trees. One egg only is laid, and this is hatched in January. It builds all over the island, which it leaves the third week in April.

It also breeds on Ascension Island — where it is not numerous — in company with a few Gannets, on small rocky islets off the northwest corner of the main island.

This species is also included by Mr. G. R. Gray in his List of the Birds of New Zealand and of the Adjacent Islands. Mr. Edward Newton found it breeding on the

Island of Rodriguez, near Mauritius. Mr. R. Swinhoe states that in the harbor of Sawo, on the northeast side of Formosa, a few of these Terns were found breeding on the cliffs. One individual flew into his boat, and was knocked down by a sailor. Another was brought to him alive. In the voyage round the island he frequently noticed these birds crossing and recrossing his wake, as if searching for food in the troubled waters stirred up by the steamer's paddles. They always kept a long distance in the rear, and made no attempt to come on board.

This Tern was observed on the Pacific coast of Guatemala by Mr. Salvin. In May, 1859, he also met with it near the Island of St. John's; and presumes that it probably occurs about St. Croix. On the coast of Honduras he visited its breeding-place, where it was nesting, in company with the *A. melanogenys*. Its nest was a large loose structure made of sticks heaped together at the top of a cocoanut-tree, or on the outer branches of a mangrove. The bird was as tame as possible, and was not at all disturbed when Mr. Salvin climbed the tree on which it was nesting. The eggs had all been hatched.

Mr. Grayson found it breeding on Isabella Island, on the north end of which, as he states, these birds were present in large communities, their nests being built upon shelving rocks beneath the overhanging cliffs, like those of the Mud-Swallow. In one particular locality there were a great many of these birds, and when they were fired at they came down in swarm over the canoe, circling around like Swallows. The nests were all placed close together, and were inaccessible.

A single individual of this species is stated by Major Wedderburn to have been taken in Bermuda, September, 1854.

Audubon found the Noddies on one of the Tortugas, called Noddy Key. There they formed regular nests of twigs and dry grass, which they placed on low trees or bushes, but in no instance on the ground. On the 11th of May, 1832, he found many repairing and augmenting old nests, while others were constructing new ones. Some were already sitting on their eggs. Some of the nests were two feet in height; yet in all there was only a slight depression on the top.

Audubon — disagreeing with most observers — states that the Noddy lays three eggs; while others say that it never has more than one. He describes the eggs as of a reddish-yellow color, spotted and patched with dull red and faint purple, and gives their measurement as 2.00 inches in length and 1.37 in breadth — which is considerably less than the average. They are said to be excellent eating. This bird was observed to go far out to sea to collect its food, which consisted of fish caught on the floating seaweed by skimming close over the surface, in the manner of Gulls. When seized by the hand it is said to utter a rough cawing cry, not unlike that of a young Crow.

Mr. Richard Hill, of Jamaica, quoted by Mr. Gosse, speaks of its breeding on the Pedro Keys. The only vegetation is a low stunted kind of tree known as saffron-wood — the "tea-shrub" of the Bahama Islands. Among their branches, at a very small elevation from the ground, the Noddies build nests which grow larger by accumulations of materials; these nests being repaired and used again in successive seasons. They are exceedingly shallow, with scarcely any hollowing at all, and are generally embellished with an addition of broken sea-shells — such being selected as are spotted and speckled, like the eggs. The object of this curious feature in their construction is not at all understood.

The eggs of this species have a white ground, with a well-marked creamy tinge, and some have a distinctly cream-color, almost buffy. The spots are few and small, and are chiefly about the larger end. In a few instances they are larger. The color is usually a dark chestnut, with subdued shell-markings of lavender gray.

FAMILY STERCORARIIDÆ. — THE SKUAS AND JAEGERS.

CHAR. Covering of the maxilla not entire, as in the *Laridæ*, the basal half being furnished with a horny cere, the lower edge of which overhangs the nostrils; toes fully webbed; claws strongly curved; tail more or less graduated, the central pair of rectrices projecting a greater or less distance beyond the rest.

The Family *Stercorariidæ* is separable from the *Laridæ* chiefly on account of the peculiar bill, which shows a not distant approach in character to that of some forms of the *Raptores*. The species are all predatory in their nature, the smaller kinds pirating upon the Gulls and other sea-fowl, the larger ones beating along the shores, or even over the land, and preying upon various birds, much in the manner of the *Falconidæ*. Indeed it is said that at Kerguelen Island the *Megalestris antarcticus* is seldom seen near the water, but keeps strictly to the land, where it is very destructive to Ducks and other water-fowl.

The two North American genera may be thus defined: —

Megalestris. Size large (about equal to *Larus argentatus*), form robust and powerful; depth of the bill through the base equal to one half or more of the length of the mandible measured along the side; tarsus shorter than the middle toe and claw; tail short, the middle rectrices scarcely projecting beyond the rest.

Stercorarius. Size medium (about that of the medium-sized Gulls, *Larus delawarensis* and *canus*), form more graceful and slender; depth of bill through the base less than one half the length of the mandible, measured as above; tarsus decidedly longer than the middle toe and claw; middle rectrices (in full adult birds) projecting far beyond the rest.

GENUS **MEGALESTRIS**, BONAPARTE.

Catharacta, BRÜNN. Orn. Bor. 1764, 32 (type, *C. skua*, BRÜNN.); nec *Catharactes*, BRISS. 1760.
Megalestris, BONAP. Cat. Parzudaki, 1856, 11 (type, *Larus catarractes*, LINN. = *Catharacta skua*, BRÜNN.).
Buphagus, "MOEHR.," COUES, Pr. Phil. Acad. 1863, 124 (same type).

The characters of this genus have been sufficiently indicated above. Only three species (perhaps more properly geographical races) are known, but one of which (*M. skua*) belongs to the North American fauna; the other two belonging, one to Chili, the other to the Antarctic seas.

Megalestris skua.

THE SKUA GULL.

Catharacta skua, BRÜNN. Orn. Bor. 1764, 33.
Buphagus skua, COUES, Pr. Acad. Nat. Sci. Philad. 1863, 125; B. N. W. 1874, 604.
Stercorarius (Buphagus) skua, COUES, Key, 1872, 309.
Stercorarius skua, COUES, Check List, 1873, no. 539; ed. 2, 1882, no. 764.
Megalestris skua, RIDGW. Nom. N. Am. B. 1881, no. 696.
Larus catarractes, LINN. S. N. I. 1766, 226.
Lestris catarractes, ILLIG. Prodr. 1811, 272. — NUTT. Man. II. 1834, 312.
Stercorarius catarractes, BONAP. Consp. II. 1856, 206. — LAWR. in Baird's B. N. Am. 1858, 838. — BAIRD, Cat. N. Am. B. 1859, no. 652. — ELLIOT, Illustr. B. Am. II. pl. 56. — SAUNDERS, P. Z. S. 1856, 319.
Catarracta fusca, LEACH, Syst. Cat. 1816, 40.

HAB. Coasts and islands of the North Atlantic, chiefly northward. In America, south to coast of New England (Massachusetts; spec. in U. S. Nat. Mus.).

SP. CHAR. *Adult:* Prevailing color dull brownish, the interscapulars, scapulars, and wing-coverts striped centrally with pale cinnamon; feathers of the head and neck marked with narrow

M. skua.

mesial streaks of the same; lower parts mixed reddish cinnamon and grayish brown, in ill-defined stripes laterally, but nearly uniform on the breast and abdomen. Remiges, primary coverts, and alulæ brownish dusky, the former white basally; this white concealed on the secondaries, but forming an extensive exposed patch on the primaries. Tail uniform dusky brown. Bill dusky; iris brown; legs and feet black. *Young:* Head, neck, and lower parts uniform grayish brown, the lower surface tinged with cinnamon; upper parts darker grayish brown, lightest on the back and lesser wing-coverts, where very indistinctly spotted with rusty cinnamon. Bill and feet brownish.

Wing, 15.75–16.15 inches (average, 15.95); culmen, 2.05; depth of bill through base, .80; tarsus, 2.40–2.70 (2.55); middle toe, 2.15–2.45 (2.32). (Three specimens.)

Megalestris skua.

Having six specimens before us for comparison, we find the Antarctic representative[1] of this species to be easily distinguishable, the colors being appreciably different in all, and the measurements all much greater. The series in question gives the following as the results of careful measurements: Wing, 16.05–16.90 inches (average, 16.28); culmen, 2.20–2.85 (2.37); depth of bill through base, .95–1.00 (.98);

[1] MEGALESTRIS SKUA ANTARCTICA. — Antarctic Skua.
Lestris antarcticus, LESS. Traité, 1831, 606.
Stercorarius antarcticus, BONAP. Consp. II. 1856, 207.
Buphagus antarcticus, COUES, Pr. Ac. Nat. Sci. Philad. 1863, 127.
Buphagus skua, b. *antarcticus*, COUES, B. N. W. 1874, 605.
Hab. Antarctic seas.

tarsus, 2.70–3.20 (2.96); middle toe, 2.55–2.80 (2.67). The differences pointed out by Mr. Saunders, in his paper on the "Stercorariinæ" (P. Z. S. 1876, pp. 321, 322), are perfectly constant in the series we have examined.

This is another species that has had, until quite recently, very doubtful claims to a place in the fauna of North America; since the only ground for such a claim was its occurrence at Greenland, upon the coast of which it is said by Professor Reinhardt to be an occasional visitant. Mr. Bernard Ross, however, believes that he met with it on the Mackenzie River.

On the coast of California, as Dr. Cooper informs me, it certainly occurs very rarely — if at all — as he has never seen it, nor met with it in local collections; nor does he know of its having been identified on that coast by any one.

Mr. Kumlien procured a single specimen of this species at sea, lat. 41° N., 66° W.; and others were seen at the time. It is of frequent occurrence on the George's and other banks in the winter. He met with it near Lady Franklin Island, north of Hudson Strait, in September. The birds then were with their young on the rocks.

A single specimen was procured off the coast of Massachusetts in the summer of 1878. It was taken alive by Captain Daniel Carroll, of Gloucester, on George's Bank, early in July, with the aid of a fish-hook, and was kept by him on his fishing-schooner a number of days. As it refused food it was thrown overboard; but fortunately was found and preserved by Professor Baird, and is now in the National Museum at Washington. It is mentioned by Mr. G. R. Gray as having a habitat at Campbell Island, Norfolk Island, and Macaulay Island.

Mr. C. A. Wright ("Ibis," 1864) records the capture of a single specimen of this species on the 9th of June, 1860, at Salini, on the north coast of Malta.

Mr. A. G. More ("Ibis," 1865) states that the Great Skua only breeds, within the limits of Great Britain, in the Shetland Islands, where its nesting has long been known. There the birds extend to the Island of Uist, a little beyond lat. 61° N. It is said by Mr. Wheelwright to be rare in the south of Scandinavia — never being seen in the Baltic or in the Sound — but more common on the west coast of Norway.[1]

This bird is said to be common off the coast of Spain in the winter, outside of the Straits of Gibraltar.

Professor Alfred Newton speaks of it as abundant off the coast of Iceland, and occasionally breeding some distance inland. According to Faber it is resident there all the year; he names four places in the southern part of that island where he has known it to breed. Dr. Krüper saw it in the north of Iceland in the summer time, so that it probably breeds there also. It is known to inhabit the Faröe Islands.

In the Island of Uist it is strictly preserved by the proprietors, the belief being general that this bird will defend the flocks from the attacks of the Golden Eagle. It is known to attack and drive off an Eagle if the latter approaches the nest of the Skua, Mr. Dunn having been eyewitness to an occurrence of this kind at Rona's Hill. It is also a great favorite with the fishermen, who consider its accompanying their boats to the fishing-grounds as being a favorable omen, and in return give it the refuse of the fish they catch. This bird does not associate in flocks, and two or more pairs are rarely seen together.

In the autumn and winter this Skua visits the coasts of Ireland, England, France, Holland, and Germany. It is noted for its courage and daring, and for the predatory attacks with which it harasses the Gulls, and compels them to disgorge the fish

[1] According to later authorities, this species is of rare and rather sporadic occurrence along the Norwegian coast.

which they have swallowed. As soon as the fish has been disgorged, the Skua swoops down upon it with so rapid a movement and so sure an aim as frequently to seize the prize before it reaches the water. This bird is on this account known to some as the "Parasitic Gull." It is supposed to be a bird of great longevity. Yarrell states that a specimen brought alive to Dr. Neill in the summer of 1820 — then a nestling — was alive at the Cannon-mills in October, 1843. Its plumage in its twenty-fourth year had become very pale, and its head was grayish white. Another bird was kept alive by Mr. G. T. Fox for ten years, undergoing no change of color at any of its moultings.

This bird lays two or three eggs, olive-brown in color, blotched with darker brown, 2.75 inches in length and 2.00 in breadth. An egg in the Smithsonian Collection, from Greenland (No. 2658), measures 2.90 by 1.95 inches, has a ground-color of a dark grayish drab, with irregular spots of raw-umber and sepia. Another specimen, measuring 2.55 by 1.95 inches, has markings much deeper in color and more distinct.

Genus **STERCORARIUS**, Brisson.

Stercorarius, Briss. Orn. V. 1760, 149 (type, *Larus parasiticus*, Linn.).
Lestris, Illig. Prod. 1811, 272 (same type).

The difference between this genus and *Megalestris* consists chiefly in the smaller size and more slender, graceful form of *Stercorarius*, the increased slenderness extending to all parts of the organization. One of the three known species differs considerably in form from the other two, which are so much alike that they are sometimes with difficulty distinguished from each other.

S. parasiticus.

Synopsis of Species.

A. Middle rectrices broad and rounded at ends.

1. **S. pomarinus.** Wing, about 13.50–14.00 inches; middle tail-feathers, 8.00–9.00; culmen, 1.45–1.55; tarsus, 2.10; middle toe (without claw), 1.60–1.75.

B. Middle rectrices attenuated and pointed at ends.

2. **S. parasiticus.** Wing, 11.80–13.15 inches (average, 12.67); central rectrices, 7.70–10.25 (8.66); culmen, 1.15–1.40 (1.27); tarsus, 1.50–1.85 (1.70); middle toe, 1.20–1.45 (1.34). Tarsi black in adult; nasal shield longer than the distance from the anterior edge of the nostril to the tip of the bill.

3. **S. longicaudus.** Wing, 11.55–12.85 inches (average, 12.25); central rectrices, 10.50–14.50 (12.89); culmen, 1.10–1.30 (1.19); tarsus, 1.50–1.80 (1.66); middle toe, 1.08–1.30 (1.20). Tarsi light bluish in adult; nasal shield not longer than the distance from anterior end of nostril to tip of bill.

Stercorarius pomarinus.

THE POMARINE JAEGER.

Larus pomarinus, TEMM. Man. Orn. 1815, 514.— SW. & RICH. F. B. A. II. 1831, 429.— NUTT. Man. II. 1834, 315.— AUD. Orn. Biog. III. 1835, 396; Synop. 1839, 332; B. Am. VII. 1844, 186, pl. 451.

Stercorarius pomarinus, VIEILL. Nouv. Dict. XXXII. 1819, 158.— LAWR. in Baird's B. N. Am. 1858, 838.— BAIRD, Cat. N. Am. B. 1859, no. 653.

Stercorarius pomatorhinus, NEWTON, Ibis, 1865, 509.— COUES, Key, 1872, 309; Check List, 1873, no. 540; ed. 2, 1882, no. 765; B. N. W. 1874, 607.— RIDGW. Nom. N. Am. B. 1881, no. 697.

HAB. Northern portion of northern hemisphere, on the seas and larger inland waters, but chiefly maritime. South, in North America, to New Jersey and the Great Lakes.

SP. CHAR. *Adult, lightest phase:* Pileum, lores, and malar region, with entire upper surface, except the nape, uniform dark sooty slate, with a slight plumbeous tinge in certain lights; anal region and crissum uniform plumbeous-slate, sometimes mixed with whitish. Rest of the head and neck (including entire nape), and lower parts, except as described, immaculate white, the auricular region more or less deeply tinged with straw-yellow. Bill brownish white (dull brownish in the dried skin), the terminal third black; iris dark brown; legs and feet black, sometimes clouded with bluish.[1] *Adult, usual plumage:* Similar to the above, but jugulum and nape barred or transversely spotted with dusky, and the sides irregularly barred with the same. *Adult, melanotic phase:* Entirely dark sooty slate, with a plumbeous cast in certain lights. *Young, light phase:* Head, neck, and lower parts dull buff, everywhere barred with dusky; the bars broad and sharply defined on the crissum and flanks, faint or nearly obsolete on the head and neck. Upper parts brownish dusky, the scapulars and interscapulars tipped with buff, the rump and upper tail-coverts spotted with the same. *Young, dark phase:* Whole plumage sooty slate, the breast, abdomen, and sides narrowly and rather indistinctly, the crissum and upper tail-coverts broadly and sharply, barred with deep buff.

S. pomarinus.

Total length, about 20.00 inches; extent, 48.00; wing, 13.50–14.00; tail, 8.00–9.00; culmen, 1.45–1.75; tarsus, 2.00–2.10; middle toe (without claw), 1.60–1.75.

In the above diagnosis we have described the light and dark extremes of coloration, with an intermediate phase which characterizes perhaps a majority of individuals of this species. Scarcely two specimens are exactly alike, however, in the details of coloration, every condition between the light and dark extremes existing in a large series.

The Pomarine Skua, or Gull Hunter, is an eminently Arctic species, resident during the summer in high northern regions, chiefly within the Arctic Circle, and extending from Siberia, in Eastern Asia, entirely around the zone. It breeds so exclusively in remote and inaccessible places that but little is comparatively known of its habits at that season. In the fall and in winter it is a great wanderer, and

[1] *Adult male:* "Bill blackish brown at the end, dingy yellow toward the base; iris brown; tibia, toes, webs, and lower half of tarsus black; the upper half light blue; claws black" (AUDUBON).

is occasionally seen in the interior, on the Great Lakes, and on both of the Atlantic shores, and is found far down the southern coast, to Africa on the east, and to Florida on the west.

It is abundant during the winter on the coasts of Maine and Massachusetts, and is the common Gull Hunter of our fishermen. Single examples have been taken on Lake Michigan in midwinter.

A single example of this species was procured by Mr. MacFarlane on the Lower Anderson River, near the Arctic Ocean; it was shot in June, 1863. It was not noted by Mr. Dall as occurring in Alaska, and no specimen was secured; but Mr. Bannister refers to a *Stercorarius* with an apparently even tail, which he frequently observed at St. Michael's.

Mr. Kumlien states that this bird was observed by him at Bourne Bay, Newfoundland, August 16; and he met with it from that point to latitude 71°. It was abundant in many localities. He nowhere found it so common as on the southern shores of Disco Island, where it was breeding on inaccessible cliffs. This bird lives chiefly by plundering the Kittiwake; but will also attack other species — even the *glaucus*. It is also very destructive of young birds and eggs.

Specimens of this bird were secured at Fort Simpson by Mr. B. Ross; at Fort Rae by Mr. Clarke; at Fort Resolution by Mr. McKenzie; at Big Island by Mr. Reid; and it is said by Richardson to be a not uncommon species in the Arctic Seas and in the northern outlet of Hudson's Bay, where it subsists on putrid fish and other substances thrown up by the sea, and also on the matters disgorged by the Gulls which it pursues. It retires from the north in the winter, and makes its first appearance in Hudson's Bay in May, coming in from seaward. The Indians of the Hudson's Bay region look upon it as the companion of the Eskimos, and as partaking of all the evil qualities ascribed to that hated race, and therefore hold it in abhorrence. It is given by Professor Reinhardt as being a resident species in Greenland; and Mr. Bernard Ross met with it on the Mackenzie.

Professor Alfred Newton refers to Scoresby as having observed two species of Skua in Spitzbergen, but thinks it doubtful whether one of them was this bird or the *longicaudus*. Ross speaks positively as to a single example of this species having been seen in Parry's voyage; this flew past his boats, in latitude 82°. Professor Newton adds that some of his party saw a bird in Sassen Bay which Mr. Wagstaffe described as having the form of the tail unmistakably characteristic of the adult of this species. No specimen has, however, been actually secured at Spitzbergen.

An immature bird of this species is mentioned by Giraud as having been shot on the south shore of Long Island. Its occurrence on that coast he regarded as exceedingly rare. An example is recorded as having been obtained, July 4, 1869, on the Susquehanna, in Lancaster County, Pa., by Mr. Vincent Barnard; and an adult bird was secured by Professor Baird, during the summer of 1840, at Harrisburg, on the same river. Such occurrences, of course, can only be regarded as accidental, and cannot be readily accounted for.

J. Matthew Jones records ("Am. Nat." IV. 253) that, Oct. 4, 1869, a fine example of this species was shot at Digby, N. S.

Professor Newton states that on his voyage to Madeira the steamer in which he was a passenger was followed by a company of about thirty birds of this species, which kept in close attendance while the vessel was weather-bound at Torbay; and about as many more were around each of two other craft detained in like manner. The birds were very tame, coming close alongside the quarter-deck in quest of food; and dire was the strife and loud the contention as one lucky bird after another seized upon some choice morsel and conveyed it far astern to be devoured. A single specimen is recorded by Schembri, a naturalist of Malta, as having been captured at sea about twenty miles north of that island.

According to the observations of Mr. H. Saunders, made at Malaga, this species is the most abundant of the three kinds of Skuas occurring on the coast of Spain in winter, and chiefly on the Atlantic side.

It is given by Middendorff as occurring on the tundras of Northern Siberia, and is included in the list of those most Arctic in their distribution.

It was met with by Mr. G. Gillett on the coast of Nova Zembla; and Von Heuglin also states that it is by far the most common species in that island, as well as on Waigatsch. He found it feeding principally on lemmings (*Myodes*); and it was not unfrequently seen in flocks, especially on the ice-fields.

According to the observations of Mr. Wheelwright, it is rarely seen in the summer on the Scandinavian coast below the Arctic Circle. It is not known with certainty to breed on the coast of Norway, and is nowhere so common as is the *parasiticus*. It is occasionally seen, late in autumn, in the Cattegat and the Baltic. He adds that, so far as his experience goes, the eggs of all the Skuas have much the same appearance; they have a pale olive-green or yellowish-gray ground-color, and are irregularly blotched and spotted with two shades of reddish brown. The eggs of *Megalestris skua* are easily recognized by their size; those of the other three species are with difficulty distinguished from each other. They all vary in size, shape, and color. The egg of the *pomarinus* is usually thinner and more pointed at the smaller end than are the other two; but there is hardly any difference between the eggs of *parasiticus* and *longicaudus*, except, perhaps, that the egg of the latter species is thicker and a little blunter at the larger end, and usually greener in color, especially when first taken. Sommerfeldt states erroneously that the Pomarine Skua breeds inland, a little way from the coast.

The Pomarine Skua does not breed in any part of Great Britain, and is only a winter visitor there, coming down the lines both of the eastern and the western coast in the autumn — some remaining on the southern shores all winter. It also visits the shores of Germany, Holland, and France; and several young birds appear almost every year on the lakes of Switzerland.

Professor Newton speaks of this species — which he calls the Pomatorrhine Skua — as having been observed by several travellers in Iceland, but as not being common there. He saw but a single individual — on the day of his arrival at Reykjavik, April 27. This bird is also found on the Faröe Islands.

In the several Arctic voyages it has been observed on the coast of Greenland, at Whale-fish Island, in Prince Regent's Inlet, at Melville Island, and at Igloolik. A nest, containing two eggs, was found near Fury Point by Sir James C. Ross, on the margin of a small lake. This bird is said to form a rude nest of grass and moss, placed on a tuft in the marshes, or on a small rock. The eggs are two or three in number.

Audubon, when within a few miles of the coast of Labrador, observed one of these Skuas approaching his vessel. It resembled, in its manner of flight, the Pigeon-hawk, alighting on the water like a Gull, and it fed on some codfish-liver thrown to it. On the 30th of July a fine adult female was shot by one of the party. During the prevalence of a severe gale, while they were lying in the harbor of Bras d'Or, quite a number came about their vessel, but none within gunshot. They flew wildly about, with much grace, moving rapidly to and fro, at one time struggling with the blast, and at another drifting with it, and chasing with success the smaller species of Gulls, but never approaching the *Larus marinus.* They remained in the harbor until the gale had abated, when they all went to sea.

A single example of this species was procured on the Prybilof Group by Mr. Elliott, and was the only one seen by him. It is a rare visitor to those islands.

An egg of this species, procured by Mr. Kumlien in Greenland, measures 2.25 inches in length and 1.70 in breadth. Its shape is a rounded ovoid; its ground-color a deep olive drab, sparingly spotted with slate-colored markings, and others of both a light and a dark raw-umber color. These are chiefly at the larger end, where they become confluent. There are also a very few scattered dots of black.

Stercorarius parasiticus.

PARASITIC JAEGER; RICHARDSON'S JAEGER.

Larus parasiticus, LINN. S. N. ed. 10, I. 1758, 136; ed. 12, I. 1766, 226.

Stercorarius parasiticus, SCHÄFF. Mus. Orn. 1779, 62, pl. 37. — LAWR. in Baird's B. N. Am. 1858, 839. — BAIRD, Cat. N. Am. B. 1859, no. 654. — COUES, Key, 1872, 309; Check List, 1873, no. 541; ed. 2, 1882, no. 766; B. N. W. 1874, 611.

Catarractes parasita, PALL. Zoog. Rosso-As. II. 1826, 310.

? *Catharacta coprotheres*, BRÜNN. Orn. Bor. 1764, 38.

Catharacta cepphus, BRÜNN. Orn. Bor. 1764, 36. — LEACH, Syst. Cat. 1816, 39.

Larus crepidatus, BANKS, Hawkesworth's Voy. II. 1773, 15. — GM. S. N. II. 1788, 602.

Stercorarius crepidatus, VIEILL. Nouv. Dict. 1819, 155. — SAUNDERS, P. Z. S. 1876, 326. — RIDGW. Nom. N. Am. B. 1881, no. 698.

Lestris Richardsoni, SW. & RICH. F. B. A. II. 1831, 433, pl. 73. — NUTT. Man. II. 1834, 319. — AUD. Orn. Biog. III. 1835, 503; Synop, 1839, 332; B. Am. VII. 1844, 190, pl. 452.

Lestris Boji, Schleepii, Benickii, BREHM, Lehrb. Eur. Vög. 1824, 991, 993, 996.

Lestris thuliaca, PREYER, Reise n. Island, 1862.

Lestris spinicaudus, HARDY, Rev. et Mag. Zool. 1854, 657.

Stercorarius tephras, MALMGR. J. f. O. 1865, 392.

Stercorarius asiaticus, HUME, Stray Feath. 1873, 269.

HAB. Northern part of northern hemisphere; south in America to New York, Illinois, and Colorado, and even to Brazil (Rio de Janeiro; *fide* SAUNDERS, Jour. Linn. Soc. XIV. 392). Breeds in the Barren Grounds of Arctic America.

SP. CHAR. *Adult, light phase:* Entire pileum, with lores, grayish brown; rest of the head, with entire neck and lower parts as far as the crissum, white, the head and neck more or less

Adult, dark phase.

tinged with straw-yellow. Upper parts uniform brownish slate, becoming gradually darker on the primaries and tail. Crissum uniform brownish gray. "Bill grayish black, the upper part bluish; iris brown; legs and feet black" (AUDUBON). *Adult, dark phase:* Entirely uniform dark fuliginous-slate, the remiges darker, nearly black terminally. *Young, light phase:* Head and neck streaked with dusky brown and fulvous-buff, the latter usually predominating; lower parts more or less distinctly barred, or spotted transversely, with the same. Upper parts brownish dusky, all the feathers bordered terminally with fulvous-buff. *Young, dark phase:* Prevailing color dark brownish slate, the wings and tail darker. Middle of the neck, all round, indistinctly streaked with grayish white; lower parts, except jugulum and upper part of breast, barred with grayish white, the bars broad and sharply defined on the crissum. Scapulars, interscapulars, wing-coverts, upper tail-coverts, and feathers of the rump narrowly tipped with pale dull buff. "Bill light blue, dusky at the end; iris brown; tarsi and basal portion of the toes and webs light blue, the rest black" (AUDUBON). *Downy young:* Entirely silky grayish brown, lighter on the under surface.

Adult, light phase.

Total length, about 18.50 inches; extent, 40.00; wing, 11.80–13.15 (average, 12.67); middle tail-feathers, 7.70–10.25 (8.66), the lateral rectrices, 4.90–6.25 (5.40); culmen, 1.15–1.40 (1.27); tarsus, 1.50–1.85 (1.70); middle toe, 1.20–1.45 (1.34).[1]

This species is almost if not quite as variable in plumage as the *S. pomarinus*, there being so much individual variation in this respect that we have described only the light and dark extremes of coloration.

As may be found noted under the head of that species, specimens occur which in every character of plumage, including length of the middle rectrices, are intermediate between the present bird and *S. longicaudus*. But there are two excellent characters, to which our attention has been directed by Dr. L. Stejneger, which may always be relied on. These consist (1) in the color of the tarsi, which in adult *parasiticus* are always black, but in *longicaudus* light bluish (or, in dried skins, more or less olivaceous); and (2) in the different proportions of the bill, *parasiticus* having the nasal shield much longer, measured along the culmen, than the distance from the anterior border of the nostril to the tip of the bill, these measurements being equal in *longicaudus*.

The Parasitic Jaëger is a northern species, although not as exclusively boreal as are the *pomarinus* and the *longicaudus*. It is common both to Arctic America and to the more northern portions of Asia and of Europe. Messrs. Evans and Sturge mention meeting with it on Spitzbergen. They saw it tormenting — as is its manner — almost every flock of Kittiwake Gulls and Terns, but they met with neither its nest, nor its eggs or young. Pennant narrates that the Arctic Skua — as he calls this species — was breeding, at his time, on the islands of Islay, Jura, and Rona; and Mr. A. G. More ("Ibis," 1865) thinks it highly probable that a few pairs still linger in some of the numerous islands of the Hebrides. It is said to be extinct at Jura.

Thompson, in his "Birds of Ireland," states that a pair was shot in 1837 on the Island of Rona. He further states that they still breed in Sutherland and in

[1] Extreme and average measurements of twenty-two adults.

Caithness, and in all the three groups of the Scottish islands. Professor Newton mentions it as quite as common in Spitzbergen as anywhere that he has met with it, except the Lofoden Islands, off the coast of Norway. Parry's Expedition met with it in their journey over the ice, but north of 82° 2'. Dr. Malmgren found it breeding on the small islets near the coast, and once on the main island. It was also very common on Bear Island. Wheelwright mentions it as the most common of the Skuas off the coast of Norway, but he does not believe that either this bird or the Pomarine Jaëger goes far inland to breed, as does the *Stercorarius longicaudus*. It is given by Dr. Bessels as one of the birds taken in the "Polaris" Expedition.

It is included by Middendorff among the birds of Eastern Siberia, and is also mentioned as one of those that go to the farthest north. It is given by Mr. G. Gillett as having been met with by him in Nova Zembla, and is also mentioned by Von Heuglin as having been found in the same locality by his party. It was less common there than were the other Skuas.

In Iceland — according to Professor Newton — this species is common enough throughout the island, and was known to breed on the moors far inland. Faber says that it arrives in Iceland about the 25th of April, and remains until the middle of September. It inhabits the Arctic sea-coast of America as well as of Asia and Europe during the summer months, or from May to September, migrating in winter to more temperate regions. Numerous examples of this species were procured in the various Arctic expeditions on the Melville Peninsula, the North Georgian Islands, Baffin's Bay, and Spitzbergen. In its habits, so far as these are known, it does not appear to be different from the Pomarine. Dr. Reinhardt gives it as one of the resident species of Greenland; and Dr. Walker, in his Notes on the Voyage of the "Fox," mentions having met with it in entering the Danish port of Frederikshaab. Captain Blakiston received specimens from Hudson's Bay; and it is said to have been found on the Mackenzie by Mr. Bernard Ross.

Hearne refers to what is most probably this species as the "Black Gull," and usually known in the Hudson's Bay region as the "Man-of-War," from its pursuing and taking its prey from the smaller species of Gull known there as the "Black-Head" (Arctic Tern). In size it is said to be much inferior to the Glaucous Gull, and like the latter always makes its nest on islands, or on the margins of lakes and ponds. It is said to lay only two eggs, and its nest to be found at a considerable distance from the sea-coast. The length of its wings is given as very great in proportion to that of the body; the tail is uniform, and the two middle feathers are four or five inches longer than the rest. The eggs are sought for and eaten both by the Indians and the English; but the bird is generally rejected. It is quite common both in the spring and fall in the Bay of Fundy and along the coast of Maine. In the winter it is found off the coast of Massachusetts, and thence to the Chesapeake, occurring near the land chiefly in stormy weather. An adult specimen, a female, was shot at Oyster Bay South, and another example, a young male, was shot in October, 1842, on Gowannus Bay, Long Island. The latter was flying about near the surface of the water as if in pursuit of fish, though upon dissection nothing of the kind was found. Mr. Giraud does not regard it as at all common on the coast of Long Island, though of more frequent occurrence than the *pomarinus*.

Audubon found it more shy and difficult of approach than the *pomarinus*, its flight equally rapid and protracted, and its habits, in harassing the Terns and smaller Gulls, the same. Dr. Richardson speaks of its breeding in considerable numbers on the Barren Grounds at a distance from the coast, and of its feeding upon the small mollusca, so plentiful in the small lakes of the Fur Countries.

Mr. Bannister mentions this species as being quite common at St. Michael's, though less abundant, and, according to his observations, more shy, than *S. longicaudus*. Specimens were also obtained at Kadiak by Mr. Bischoff. Mr. Dall speaks of it as being common on the Yukon, as high up as Nulato, and also as abundant at the mouth of that river. The Indians and the Russians call it *razboinik*, or "the robber," and have many absurd notions in regard to it. Mr. Dall has never known it to alight except on the water or on a smooth beach. It is said to nest on the beach in the manner of the Gulls; but he was unable to obtain its eggs. The long feathers of the tail differ greatly even in the same individual. It is wonderfully swift on the wing.

Mr. MacFarlane found it breeding on the Barren Grounds, at some distance from the Arctic Sea. One nest was on the ground, found June 27. Both parents were near, and when closely pursued would fly a short distance and alight on the ground; and this they continued to do for some time. The nest contained two eggs, in one of which the embryo was much larger than it was in the other. Another nest, found July 8, was about a hundred yards from the sea-beach, and was a mere depression in the ground, lined with a few withered leaves. It contained one egg and one young bird in the down. The eggs so much resemble the surrounding soil in color that they are difficult to find. The nests were all mere depressions in the ground, lined scantily either with a few dried grasses or leaves, or with both. Specimens were taken by other Arctic explorers at Fort Resolution, Fort Simpson, Fort Rae, Fort Anderson, etc.

In Shetland these birds seem to breed in society, from fifty to sixty being met with at the same place. In Norway, however — as Mr. Hewitson states — they breed most commonly apart from each other, each pair taking possession of its separate island, upon the highest point of which they are almost constantly seen perching, and upon which they place their nests. The eggs are usually two in number, and are olive-brown in color, spotted with darker brown, 2.33 inches in length, and 1.66 in breadth. At the time Mr. Drosier visited Shetland the young were already hatched, and were discovered hiding in the long grass. They were covered only with down, their blue legs and black toes being already very distinct. The more advanced were of a beautiful light brownish color, distinctly barred and spotted with black; but as they grew older the brown color gradually disappeared. This species is occasional on the shores of Belgium and Holland. Mr. H. W. Elliott found it an infrequent visitor at the Prybilof Islands, where it was not known to breed, and where but four or five of these birds in all were seen. These would occasionally alight on the grassy uplands, and stand dozing for hours in an indolent attitude.

The numerous eggs of this species collected from the Arctic coast and the Anderson River Region ranged in their length from 2.00 to 2.40 inches, and from 1.50 to 1.70 in breadth. The ground-color is an olive-drab, but varies greatly, in some tending more to a green, in others to a gray, or even to a brown. The markings are equally various in their shades, and differ also in shape, size, and number. They exhibit a combination of sepia-brown, dark chocolate, and bistre, with obscure markings of stone-gray. In some the markings are all small, and are distributed with great uniformity over the whole egg.

Stercorarius longicaudus.

THE ARCTIC JAEGER; LONG-TAILED JAEGER.

Stercorarius longicaudus, VIEILL. Nouv. Dict. XXXII. 1819, 157. — STEJNEGER, Proc. U. S. Nat. Mus. Vol. 5, pp. 40–42.

Stercorarius longicaudatus, DE SELYS, Faune Belg. 1842, 156.

Lestris parasitica, ILLIG. Prodr. 1811, 273. — LESS. Man. II. 1828, 288 (nec LINN.). — SW. & RICH. F. B. A. II. 1831, 430. — NUTT. Man. II. 1834, 317.

Lestris parasiticus, TEMM. Man. Orn. ed. 1815, 512. — AUD. Orn. Biog. III. 1835, 470; B. Am. VII. 1844, 192, pl. 452; Synop. 1839, 333.

Stercorarius parasiticus, SAUNDERS, P. Z. S. 1876, 330. — RIDGW. Nom. N. Am. B. 1881, no. 699.

Lestris crepidata, BREHM & SCHILL. Beitr. z. Vög. III. 1822, 861 (not of BANKS, 1713).

Lestris Buffoni, BOIE, Meyer's Tasch. III. 1822, 212. — DE KAY, N. Y. Zool. II. 1844, 315, pl. 133, fig. 291.

Stercorarius Buffoni, COUES, Pr. Phil. Ac. 1863, 136; Key, 1872, 309; Check List, 1873, 542; ed. 2, 1882, no. 767; B. N. W. 1874, 615.

Stercorarius cepphus, STEPH. Shaw's Zool. XIII. 1826, 211, pl. 23. — LAWR. Baird's B. N. Am. 1858, 840. — BAIRD, Cat. N. Am. B. 1859, no. 655.

Lestris microrhynchus, BREHM, Handb. Vög. Deutschl. 1831, 725.

Lestris Lessoni, DEGL. Mém. Ac. R. Lille, 1838, 108.

Lestris brachyrhynchus, BREHM, Vogelf. 1855, 337.

Lestris Hardyi, BONAP. Tabl. d. Longipenn. Compt. Rend. 1856, 770; Consp. II. 1857, 210.

Lestris Brissoni, "BOIE," DEGL. & GERBE, Orn. Eur. II. 1867, 400.

HAB. Northern part of northern hemisphere, breeding in Arctic districts, and migrating south in winter to the Northern United States.

SP. CHAR. *Adult, light phase:* Entire pileum and upper part of nape, including lores, malar region, and orbital region, sooty black; rest of the head and neck, including lower portion of the nape, straw-yellow, paler on the chin and throat. Remaining upper parts rather dark brownish cinereous or slate-color (more ashy on the back, where lighter anteriorly), the remiges and rec-

trices darker, especially toward ends, where nearly dusky blackish. Jugulum (sometimes the breast also, or, rarely, even the abdomen) white, shading gradually into grayish, the entire crissum, flanks, sides, and usually the abdomen being uniform deep ash-gray, becoming gradually lighter anteriorly. "Bill grayish black, the upper part bluish; iris brown; feet black, but with the greater part of the tarsus yellow"[1] (AUDUBON).

Total length, about 23.00 inches; extent, 45.00; wing, 11.55–12.85 (average, 12.25); central

[1] *In life*, the color of the tarsi is light grayish blue, which in *dried skins* sometimes changes to yellow.

rectrices, 10.50–14.50 (12.89); lateral rectrices, 4.75–6.00 (5.25); culmen, 1.10–1.30 (1.19); tarsus, 1.50–1.80 (1.66); middle toe, 1.08–1.30 (1.20).[1]

It is somewhat curious that in the entire series of eighteen examples of this species contained in the collection of the National Museum there is not a single young bird, nor one representing a melanotic phase, all being in the plumage described above. The only notable variation in this series consists in the extent of the plumbeous of the under surface of the body, a very few specimens having this confined to the posterior portions, the abdomen being white, just as in *S. parasiticus.* Usually, the two species may be readily distinguished by this restriction of the plumbeous underneath, in *S. parasiticus*, and its extension forward over the abdomen, almost or quite to the breast, in *S. longicaudus.* It is sometimes, though very rarely, difficult to distinguish the two even by the length of the central rectrices; one example of *S. parasiticus* having these feathers 10.25 inches long, and narrower than usual, while an individual of *S. longicaudus* has them only 10.50 long, and broader than in most examples of that species. Upon the whole, there is sometimes a very close resemblance between these two forms in their normal phase of coloration (the only one in which we have seen *S. longicaudus*).

In fact, there can be no question that in every character of plumage or coloration, including the length and breadth of the middle rectrices, the number of primaries having white shafts, the relative extent of gray and white on the lower parts, etc., the two species do, in some specimens, completely intergrade, notwithstanding the fact that typical examples may be very readily distinguished. The shape of the bill and the color of the tarsi in the adults, however, it is believed are constantly different in the two species, as stated under the head of *S. parasiticus* and in the synopsis of the species.

These intermediate specimens may, of course, be hybrids; but it seems more reasonable to suppose that the two forms represent merely extreme modifications of one species.

Buffon's Skua partakes of all the peculiarities of this strongly characterized genus, especially in its Arctic distribution. It appears to be the most northern of its family, and to have, during the season when it is not breeding, a somewhat wider range of migration than the others. In the summer it is found in all parts of the region near the Arctic Circle, breeding from Siberia around the circuit, including Northern Asia, Europe, and America, and the Arctic islands.

It is a resident species in Greenland, and is also found in Iceland, although not given by Faber, who confounded it with the *parasiticus.* In 1858 Mr. Wolley and Professor Newton met with it several times near Kyrkjnvogn; and others are mentioned as having been obtained elsewhere. Mr. Bernard Ross procured specimens of this bird at various points on the Mackenzie; Mr. Murray mentions having seen it on Hudson's Bay; and Captain Blakiston received specimens from that region.

According to Sir John Richardson, it inhabits the Arctic sea-coasts of America as well as of Europe, in the summer, migrating in winter to more temperate localities. Numerous specimens of this Gull were brought back by the Arctic expeditions from Melville Peninsula and the North Georgian Islands.

Mr. A. G. More states ("Ibis," 1865), on the authority of Mr. R. G. Shearer, of Ulbster House-wick, that some seven or eight years before that time a few pairs of the Long-tailed Skua could always be found breeding at that place, together with the more common species, on a large inland flat studded with small dark lochs. In 1860 a pair of these Skuas was shot on this ground during the breeding-season; and in June, 1862, a pair was obtained on one of the Outer Hebrides, where these birds were probably breeding.

Captain W. H. Feilden ("Ibis," October, 1877) states that this was the only species of Skua Gull which the Expedition of 1875–1876 saw in Smith's Sound, where it arrived in considerable numbers in the neighborhood of the winter quarters of the party during

[1] Extreme and average measurements of eighteen adults.

the first week in June; after that date it was to be seen at every hour of the day, searching for lemmings. It lays its two eggs in hollows in the ground, and defends them with great bravery. On several occasions Captain Feilden had to strike at the old birds with his gun-barrel to defend himself against their attacks as he was robbing their nests. He could always easily distinguish this species from the *parasiticus* by the mottled color of its tarsus and the webs of the feet, which in the latter are black.

Mr. Kumlien mentions meeting with a few on the Upper Cumberland waters in June; but none breed so far south. It is one of the first birds to come in the spring; and — as he has no doubt — its range is more northerly than that of any other bird of this genus.

According to Middendorff this is one of the common species of Eastern Siberia, where it is found to the extreme northern parts of the main land and also on the islands north of Asia. Mr. G. Gillett gives it as quite abundant on Nova Zembla, especially on the west coast and in the Kara Sea, where it was found in all stages of plumage. Every flock of Kittiwakes was attended by a number of the Skuas, which swooped down upon them in the manner of Hawks, and obliged them to disgorge their prey. Von Heuglin also found these birds very numerous in the same locality, generally in pairs.

Professor Newton mentions having seen a specimen of this Skua obtained by Professor Malmgren on the 12th of July near the Russian Hut, in Advent Bay, Spitzbergen, who also observed it on two other occasions in Ice Sound; but that it breeds in that region has not been, as yet, definitely ascertained.

According to Mr. Wheelwright, although it is occasionally seen in other parts of Scandinavia, its peculiar breeding-home is on the Lapland fells. There it is not always seen in the same numbers every year. The first eggs he obtained were found on the 3d of June; and never but once did he find more than two eggs in a nest. The nest is nothing more than a few pieces of dry hay scratched together on the ground, generally near the water, never on the real snow-fells. Although it breeds in colonies, he never found two nests close together. In the young bird just ready to fly, the plumage greatly resembles that of the common Skua, and the tail is perfectly even.

Richardson found this species breeding in considerable numbers in the Barren Grounds, at a distance from the Arctic coast. It feeds on the shelly mollusca so plentiful in the small lakes of the Fur Countries, and harasses the Gulls just as others of this genus do.

It is common in the Bay of Fundy and on the coast of Maine in the fall, and again in the spring, and is occasionally seen off Cape Ann and Cape Cod during the winter; and occasionally in very severe weather a few of these birds are driven upon the coast. A single specimen is recorded by Mr. Giraud as having been taken on Long Island, shot in the vicinity of Islip.

During the winter — according to Audubon — this species ranges along our southern coast as far as the Gulf of Mexico, usually singly or in pairs. In April he observed it congregating in flocks of from ten to fifteen, as if for the purpose of returning north to breed.

According to Selby, it breeds on several of the Orkney and Shetland Islands, and is gregarious during that period; the situations selected for its nests being unfrequented heaths at some distance from the shores. The nest is composed of dry grass and mosses, and its eggs are said to be of a dark oil-green, with irregular blotches of liver-brown. It is very courageous at this season, and attacks every intruder within the limits of its territory by pouncing and striking at the head with bill and wings.

The young, when ready to leave the nest, are deep gray on the top of the head; neck light gray, with longitudinal streaks of brown, with a mixture of umber-brown, yellowish brown, and reddish in the residue of their plumage.

This species was procured by Mr. Dall at the mouth of the Yukon River, and by Mr. E. K. Laborne at Anadyr Gulf, in Eastern Siberia. Mr. Bannister found it common at St. Michael's. All the specimens that he obtained were shot on the ground, they having apparently a habit of sitting on the mossy *tundras*, or heaths; and not infrequently he has followed one for more than a mile at a time, the bird flying short distances, and alighting just out of range. This habit is explained by some by the statement that it feeds on the berries that abound in these situations; by others, that it is in quest of the eggs of some other species, which it is accused of devouring. Mr. Bannister was not able to verify either explanation.

Mr. E. Adams ("Ibis," 1878) mentions the arrival of this species on Norton Sound, Alaska, on the 7th of May; after which several were always to be found near the stages for drying fish, by plundering which they seemed chiefly to subsist. Some of them frequented the marshes, hunting about for eggs, and robbing the Terns and small Gulls. They bred about the dry knolls in the marshes.

Mr. MacFarlane found it abundant throughout the Barren Grounds, as well as in the neighborhood of Fort Anderson, and also on the shores of Franklin Bay and the Arctic Ocean. The nests were all mere depressions in the soil, scantily lined with dry hay, leaves, and the like, and the number of eggs was never more than two. One nest is mentioned as having been discovered in a very thinly wooded plain, June 28. The eggs contained well-developed embryos. The parents were both present, but did not make so much noise as usual, and when closely approached flew off to a tree in the vicinity. One nest was near a small lake, and it was lined with a few withered leaves of grasses. Another was some distance from a lake, and both parents flew and screamed over the heads of the intruders while these were searching for the nest. One egg was only slightly advanced, while the other was nearly ready to hatch. In another instance the parents made an unprecedented disturbance, flying close overhead, and were easily secured. In some instances the birds examined were found to have partaken of a quantity of last year's berries, thus confirming the statements to that effect made by the natives to Mr. Dall. Another memorandum states that a nest with two eggs was found, June 27, on a dry turfy piece of ground, about fifty yards from the beach, on Franklin Bay. There really was no nest, and the eggs were extremely difficult to find, owing partly to their color being exactly similar to that of the soil, and partly to the efforts of both parents to mislead those searching for the nest — to effect which they scream and fly over the head of the intruder; and if their treasure seems on the point of being discovered, the parent birds — especially the female — become so savage that there is danger of actual injury resulting from their attacks. In another instance, where a nest was being sought for on the Barren Grounds, June 26, 1863, the parents endeavored by various stratagems to lead the intruder away from the place; and when the eggs were finally discovered, they began a furious attack upon his head, so that it was necessary to shoot them in self-defence. In another instance, on the same day, a female sitting on her nest fluttered off when discovered, as if with a broken wing, much as a Plover would do in a similar case.

In a note made June 28, 1863, Mr. MacFarlane says: "At midnight the sun is several degrees above the horizon, and there is, of course, no night. During the period answering to it, however, as many as twenty or thirty birds of the genus *Stercorarius* are sometimes seen sitting or standing on the ground, each bird at the distance of a few yards from its fellow. They probably repose at such times, as they never move, except when closely approached. No eggs have ever been obtained by us in the vicinity of such resting-places. During the day, also, we have frequently observed two or more birds quietly reposing, or moving very slowly along the ground; and this, too, where no nest actually existed."

Examples of this species were also secured at Fort Peel's River by Mr. C. P. Gaudet, and at Fort Yukon by Mr. McDougal.

Mr. H. W. Elliott reports this species as being seldom seen in the Prybilof Group. The single specimen in his collection is one of the only two he observed while in that locality. When he came upon them — July 29, 1872 — they were apparently feeding upon insects, and upon a small black berry that ripens on the high lands — the fruit of the *Empetrum nigrum.*

The eggs of this species are not always distinguishable from those of the *parasiticus,* although they are smaller than those of that species, on the average; but exceptionally large specimens of the egg of *S. longicaudus* are sometimes as large as exceptionally small ones of *S. parasiticus.* They range from 2.10 to 1.90 inches in length, and from 1.50 to 1.40 in breadth.

Order TUBINARES.

THE TUBE-NOSED SWIMMERS.

Char. Swimming birds with tubular nostrils, the horny covering of the bill consisting of several distinct pieces, separated by more or less marked grooves. Terminal portion of maxilla produced into a strongly hooked unguis. Feet fully webbed, anteriorly. Hallux rudimentary, consisting of an elevated sessile, often minute, claw, sometimes wholly absent. Wings usually very long. Basipterygoids usually absent? Egg single, white.

The number of families into which the Order Tubinares is properly divisible is an unsettled question. In a "Report on the Anatomy of the Petrels (*Tubinares*)," which forms the leading article of Vol. IV. of the Zoological Reports of H.M.S. "Challenger," the late Professor W. A. Forbes divides the Tubinares into two families as follows: (1) *Procellariidæ*, including as sub-families *Procellariinæ* and *Diomedeinæ;* and (2) *Oceanitidæ*, composed of the genera *Fregetta, Pelagodroma, Oceanites,* and *Garrodia.* According to this arrangement, the Albatrosses are held to be much more nearly related to the genera *Procellaria, Cymochorea,* and *Halocyptena* than are *Oceanites* and the other *Oceanitidæ*[1] — a proposition which, notwithstanding the reasons advanced,[2] we are not prepared to accept.

The arrangement we have to propose is not supposed to be a perfectly natural one, but there can be no question as to the naturalness of the groups defined below:—

1. **Diomedeidæ.** Wings very long and narrow, on account of the extreme development of the humerus and ulna. Remiges 39–50 (the largest number in any known bird). Nasal tubes lateral, widely and completely separated by the intervening "culminicorn." No hind toe. Size very large.
2. **Procellariidæ.** Wings lengthened, but of different structure from the preceding (remiges 20–39, usually about 30). Nasal tubes near together, laid side by side upon the culmen, the nostrils opening anteriorly. Hind toe present, though sometimes minute. Size extremely variable.

[1] ". . . In spite of the general superficial resemblance of the *Oceanitidæ* to the smaller forms of *Procellariidæ*, with which all ornithologists previous to Garrod had confounded them, the differences between the two families are, it will be seen, numerous and important. The special points of resemblance which the *Oceanitidæ* have with such Procellarian genera as *Procellaria* and *Cymochorea* — such as the general small size, style of coloration, form of skull, comparative simplicity of the *tensor patagii* arrangement, simple sternum and syrinx (the last three peculiarities being also common to *Pelecanoides*) — may best be explained by supposing that these small Procellarian forms are on the whole less specialized than the larger ones (Fulmars, Albatrosses, Shearwaters, etc.), and so retain more of the characters possessed by the primitive and now extinct common form from which both the *Procellariidæ* and *Oceanitidæ* must have been derived" (Forbes, t. c. p. 56).

[2] "According to modern ideas, the object of a classification is not so much to represent morphological facts as to indicate the phylogenetic relations of the different forms concerned" (Forbes, t. c. p. 58).

3. **Pelecanoididæ.** Wings short, and general appearance decidedly Auk-like. Nasal tubes vertical, the nostrils opening superiorly.

The *Pelecanoididæ* are not represented in the North American fauna; and both the other families are known mainly as irregular though often abundant visitors to the coast, and are even occasionally driven by gales far inland.

Family DIOMEDEIDÆ. — The Albatrosses.

The three known genera of this family may readily be distinguished by the following characters: —

A. Sides of the mandible without longitudinal groove. Wing three or more times as long as the short rounded tail.

1. **Diomedea.** "Culminicorn" much broadest at the base, where joined closely to the "latericorn."
2. **Thalassogeron** (*gen. nov.*).[1] "Culminicorn" narrow, and of equal width from the middle of the culmen to the base, where widely separated from the "latericorn" by the interposition of a strip of naked skin extending from the nasal tubes to the forehead. Bill much more compressed.

B. Sides of the mandible with a deep longitudinal groove, extending the entire length of the lateral lamina. Wing only about twice as long as the graduated or cuneate tail.

3. **Phœbetria.** In his "Report on the Anatomy of the Petrels" (Zoology of H.M.S. "Challenger," Vol. IV. p. 57), the late Professor W. A. Forbes says that these "three good genera of Albatrosses . . . may be distinguished, independently of external characters, as follows: —

"**Diomedea.** Tongue very short; uncinate bones more or less styliform (*Diomedea exulans* and *brachyura*).

"**Thalassiarche** [= **Thalassogeron**]. Tongue intermediate; uncinate bones styliform (*Thalassiarche culminata*).

"**Phœbetria.** Tongue much longer; uncinate bones flattened; hallux better developed than in the other forms, and with an external claw (*Phœbetria fuliginosa*)."

The type of *Thalassarche*, Reichenbach, being the *Diomedea melanophrys* — a true *Diomedea* — it unfortunately becomes necessary to give a new name for the genus represented by *T. culminata*, and we have selected *Thalassogeron* as being an appropriate one.

Genus **DIOMEDEA**, Linnæus.

Diomedea, Linn. S. N. ed. 10, I. 1758, 132; ed. 12, I. 1766, 214 (type, *D. exulans*, Linn.).
Albatrus, Briss. Orn. VI. 1760, 125 (same type).
Phœbastria, Reichenb. Syst. Av. 1852, v (type, *Diomedea brachyura*, Temm.).
Thalassarche, Reichenb. t. c. v (type, *Diomedea melanophrys*, Boie).

Char. Size very large (one species perhaps the largest bird of flight); wings extremely long, through very narrow; sides of the mandible smooth, without a longitudinal groove; bill moderately or slightly compressed, the culmen broad and rounded; tail rounded, one third as long as the tail, or less.

The Albatrosses are strictly oceanic birds, which rarely visit the land, except at their breeding-grounds, which are usually remote islands or isolated rocks. The species which have been obtained in North American waters are the following: —

[1] *Thalassogeron* (*gen. nov.*), *θάλασσα* = *mare*; ὁ *γέρων* = *senex*.

A. Culmen very concave ; feathers at base of maxilla extending in an angle nearly or quite to the base of the nasal tube, that on the mandible forming a still more decided angle. (*Diomedea.*)

1. **D. exulans.** Wing, 26.50–29.00 inches. *Adult:* White, the remiges blackish. *Young:* Dusky, with fore part of head whitish (older individuals with more white).

D. albatrus, adult.

B. Culmen slightly concave, the bill more compressed ; feathering at base of maxilla extending obliquely in a nearly straight line far back of the nasal tube, that of the mandible also nearly straight.

a. Latericorn narrower at base than in middle portion. (*Phœbastria.*)

2. **D. albatrus.** Wing, 22.00–23.00 inches ; culmen, 5.50–5.60 ; depth of bill at base, 1.95–2.05 ; tarsus, 3.80–4.00 ; middle toe, 4.65–4.90. *Adult:* White, the pileum and nape bright straw-yellow ; tail, remiges, etc., slaty brown, the shafts of the quills bright straw-yellow ; bill grayish white, more yellowish on the unguis, and purple brownish on the mandible ; legs and feet grayish dusky. *Young:* Uniform sooty, the pileum and nape blackish ; shafts of primaries bright straw-yellow ; bill pale horn-yellow ; legs and feet grayish brown. *Hab.* Off the Pacific coast of North America (especially of Alaska).

3. **D. nigripes.** Wing, 18.50–20.50 inches ; culmen, 4.00–4.25 ; depth of bill at base, 1.45–1.60 ; tarsus, 3.50–3.70 ; middle toe, 4.05–4.40. Uniform dusky (more grayish below), the crissum, upper tail-coverts, and base of the tail white in the adult ; anterior portion of the head whitish ; bill dusky purplish brown ; legs and feet black. *Hab.* Pacific coast of North America.

b. Latericorn much broader at base than in middle portion. (*Thalassarche.*)

4. **D. melanophrys.** Wing, 19.50–20.00 inches ; tail, 8.00–8.50 ; culmen, 4.30–4.70 ; tarsus, 3.00–3.25 ; middle toe, 4.00–4.30. *Adult:* Head, neck, rump, upper tail-coverts, and entire lower parts white, the side of the head with a more or less distinct grayish stripe, darkest immediately before and behind the eye ; back and scapulars brownish slate, more ashy anteriorly ; wings uniform dark brownish slate ; tail brownish gray, the shafts of the feathers yellowish white. Bill yellowish, the ungui and base of culmen sometimes (in younger individuals ?) tinged or clouded with grayish ; legs and feet "pearly slate." *Hab.* Southern oceans ; casual (?) off coast of California.

Diomedea exulans.

THE WANDERING ALBATROSS.

Diomedea exulans, LINN. S. N. ed. 10, I. 1758, 132; ed. 12, I. 1766, 214. — NUTT. Man. W. B. 1834, 340. — GOULD, B. Austr. VII. 1848, pl. 38. — LAWR. in Baird's B. N. Am. 1858, 821. — BAIRD, Cat. N. Am. B. 1859, no. 630. — COUES, Pr. Philad. Acad. 1866, 175. — KIDDER, Bull. U. S. Nat. Mus. no. 2, 1875, 19; no. 3, 1876, 11. — SCL. Rep. "Challenger," Zool. II. 1881, 147.
Diomedea spadicea, GMEL. S. N. I. ii. 1788, 568 (= young).
? *Diomedea adusta*, TSCHUDI, J. f. O. 1856, 157, no. 7.

HAB. Southern oceans in general, but occasionally wandering north of the equator. Near Dieppe, France, and near Antwerp, Belgium, September, 1833 (BOIE, "Isis," 1835, p. 259); three specimens near Chaumont, France, November, 1758 (DEGL. & GERBE, "Orn. Eur." 2d ed. 1867, p. 368); ? coast of Norway, one specimen (BRÜNN. "Orn. Bor." 1764, p. 31). "Rare and accidental in the Middle States" (BONAPARTE); "Accidental to the coasts of the central part of the Union" (NUTTALL). Tampa Bay, Florida?[1]

SP. CHAR. *Adult:* Prevailing color yellowish white, the remiges dusky, and, except in very old birds, the larger wing-coverts and dorsal region more or less barred irregularly with blackish. Bill white (KIDDER), or "delicate pinky white, inclining to yellow at the tip" (GOULD); iris "very dark blue to purple" (KIDDER), or "very dark brown" (GOULD); feet "white, with a pale-blue tint" (KIDDER), or "pinky white" (GOULD); "eyelash bare, fleshy, and of a pale green" (GOULD). *Young:* Prevailing color dark fuliginous or blackish brown, older individuals varied with white according to age, the fore-part of the head and lining of the wings always more or less white. Bill "pinkish white" (KIDDER).

Total length, 47.00–55.00 inches; extent, about 10–12 feet (average, 10 feet 1 inch, *fide* GOULD); average weight, 17 lbs., maximum weight about 20 lbs.

The Wandering Albatross of the Southern Pacific and Atlantic oceans has probably but little claim to a place in the fauna of North America. I am unable to find any well-authenticated instance where this bird is known to have been taken in the vicinity either of the Atlantic or of the Pacific coast of the United States. Numerous specimens were collected in the Wilkes Exploring Expedition, both from the Atlantic and the Pacific oceans; and from the numerous and careful records of Dr. Pickering it is evidently both the most numerous and the most widely diffused of its family. It was first met with in the Atlantic January 22, in lat. 40° S., on the passage from Rio de Janeiro to the Rio Negro, occasionally afterward to Cape Horn, and as far south as the cruise extended. It seemed much more common in the Pacific, especially on the passage to Callao. On the 4th of April, in lat. 42° S., numbers of these birds were taken with hooks and lines, their abundance being in all probability due to the fact that the ship was then passing over whaling-ground.

Mr. E. L. Layard mentions meeting with them in great numbers in the Antarctic Ocean, lat. 44° S.; they were chiefly young birds. This species is given by Mr. G. R. Gray as one of those occurring in New Zealand.

Captain F. W. Hutton ("Ibis," 1865) states that the food of this Albatross consists entirely of the oceanic mollusca, small crustaceans, medusæ, and the refuse thrown overboard from ships. No remains of fish were found in its stomach. It always settles down slowly to eat, and can only be caught with the hook when the vessel is

[1] I have recently been informed, on what I consider reliable authority, of the capture of a specimen of this species in Tampa Bay, Florida, my informant having the head in his possession. Up to this writing, however, he has been unable to get the specimen from a box which had been placed in storage during his absence from the city. — R. R.

moving slowly through the water, and when plenty of line can be paid out. The best bait is a piece of the rind of raw salt pork, as this is so tough that other birds cannot get it off the hook, which usually catches in the curved end of the upper mandible. The habits of the Albatross are diurnal, both on land and at sea; and it is never known to fly by night. It was rarely seen north of 30° south latitude. In April, 1854, Captain Hutton met with a single bird in lat. 26° S.; but from the manner in which it was hastening directly south it was supposed to be a released prisoner. This Albatross was found very common south of lat. 40° S. — monopolizing nearly the whole of Prince Edward's Island and the southeastern portions of Kerguelen Island, where it retires to breed in October. The nest is always placed on high table-land, and is in the shape of a frustum of a cone, with a slightly hollow top; it is made of grass and mud, which the birds obtain by digging a circular ditch about two yards in diameter, and pushing the earth toward the centre until it is about eighteen inches high. In this nest the female lays one white egg, which is not hatched until January.

At a certain time of the year — between February and June — the old birds leave their young, going to sea, and not returning until the following October, when they arrive in large numbers. Each pair goes at once to its old nest, and after a little fondling of the young one, which has remained near the nest the whole time, they turn it out, and prepare the nest for incubation. The deserted young ones are usually found in good condition and lively. When the old birds return, the young ones usually keep about the parents, and nibble at their heads until the feathers between the beak and the eyes are removed and the skin made quite sore. The young birds do not go far from the land until the following year, and then accompany the old ones to sea. How the young birds obtain their food has not been explained; but it is positively averred that no old birds are seen near the islands for several months together. Captain Hutton is of the opinion that the young birds are of nocturnal habit, and feed by night; but in this he is not confirmed by the observations of his friend Mr. Harris — an engineer in the Royal Navy — who is also quite certain that each bird revisits its own nest, and uses it again for its next brood. The instinct which thus guides the Albatross, after its long wanderings, to return to its own nest, cannot but be regarded as extremely remarkable.

The flight of the Albatross, as with outstretched, motionless wings it sails over the surface of the sea, is described as being truly majestic. At one time the bird rises high in the air, and then with a bold sweep, inclined at an angle with the horizon, descends until the tip of its wings just touches the crests of the waves as it skims over them. When it sees something floating on the water, and prepares to alight, the whole appearance of the bird is changed. Its wings are raised, its head thrown back, its back drawn in, while its enormous feet are thrust out to their full extent; and with a hoarse croak it drops upon the water, where it floats like a cork on the surface. In order to rise again, it stretches out its neck, and with great exertion of the wings runs along the top of the water, until, having obtained a sufficient impetus, it launches once more into the air.

The Albatross is never seen to dive. When on deck it is unable to stand, and cannot rise unless a strong wind is blowing, but lies helpless on its breast. When first caught it ejects a quantity of oil.

Mr. Howard Saunders ("Ibis," January, 1866) states that he has observed this Albatross fly at night, both by moonlight, and afterward, in the summer twilight of the Antarctic seas; he has watched these birds come sweeping out of space, wheel over the main truck, and then disappear, without so much as one flap of their huge wings.

Captain Hutton ("Ibis," 1867, p. 185) mentions that on his voyage in 1866 from London to New Zealand, he first met this Albatross April 5, in lat. 34° 15′ S., and saw birds of this species afterwards all the way to New Zealand. One that was caught — a male — measured ten feet across the wings, and weighed sixteen pounds. The fat on its breast was half an inch thick. It was taken in the morning, and its stomach was empty.

Captain E. L. Layard, who received several fine eggs of this species from Captain Armson, collected by the latter on the Crozette Islands, states ("Ibis," 1867) that the egg bears a marked similarity in form and color to that of *Phœbetria fuliginosa*, measuring 5.00 by 3.30 inches. Captain Armson also brought nestlings of several ages, and a young bird only about six days old, which was covered with a pure white silky down. The bill was the most remarkable feature, the tips of the mandible being armed for about three quarters of an inch with obtuse tumid sheaths, hard, white, and shining, like china. Mr. Layard was informed by the sealers that the Albatross feeds its young, all the time it is in the nest, with squids. The young birds remain until driven away by the old ones when these need the nest again. The young are in the nest growing very slowly, but are very fat, and not at all fishy. The sealers ridicule the suggestions of Captain Hutton that the young Albatross can subsist without food any length of time.

Captain Sperling ("Ibis," 1868) is of opinion that this Albatross is seldom seen near land. He has never met with it north of the twenty-seventh parallel of south latitude, and does not believe that it ever visits the northern hemisphere. He discredits the statements in regard to the examples said to have been taken in Europe, and thinks this species has no more right in a northern avifauna than an escaped Cockatoo would have. The statement of Nuttall, that the Albatross flies near the water, watching for flying-fish, is purely imaginative. It never takes food while on the wing, nor could this bird possibly do this. In regard to its powers of flight, the Captain remarks: "Having attentively watched the flight of the Albatross, I have failed to detect the mysterious and wonderful power of wing ascribed to it by observers who have perhaps been more highly favored. None can regard without admiration the beautiful picture presented by this bird, cleaving its way in graceful curves and sweeps over the wild troubled waves of the Atlantic; but its immense pectoral muscles and light hollow bones, added to its surface of wings, amply account for all."

Captain Sperling visited, in September, 1868, the Island of Tristan d'Acunha, and communicated in a letter to the "Ibis" (1872, p. 75) some additional information in regard to this bird. He found it nesting on the highest ledges of the cliffs, at so great an altitude as to present the appearance of a mere speck. The inhabitants stated most positively that the Albatrosses remained about the island throughout the year, laying their eggs in January, and the young flying in November; and that consequently there is almost always on the island a supply of young birds. These are consumed for food in great quantities, and appear to be considered a delicacy. The northern range of this species is given as from 27° to 25° south on the Atlantic coast of Africa, and at 27° on the eastern. On the Atlantic coast of South America it is 24° south.

Frederick Stoltenhof, who resided two years in the same group, in his account of the birds visiting Inaccessible Island, mentions this Albatross. In the latter part of November it appears singly, and alights on the highest portion of the island — avoiding the high tussock-grass, from which it with difficulty rises. It builds a circular nest, slightly concave at the top, about eight feet high, and broader at the bottom than at the top. This nest is made of earth and grass, the bird availing itself of rainy weather, when the soil is soft, and a natural mortar provided. In shaping it the earth is hammered down with the flat side of the beak; and the rows of nests are like a lot of round forts with, in wet weather, the surrounding fosse. Both birds work at their nest; and about the middle of January a solitary egg is deposited, which requires nine weeks for incubation. During their stay at the island one or the other of each pair goes to the sea in search of food each day. Not more than two hundred pairs of this species visit the island. They leave at the beginning of July, and are not seen again until November. The egg is good to eat; but when cooked, the white portion becomes grisly and hard. The young bird is eaten, and is regarded as excellent food.

The following interesting account of this species, by Dr. J. H. Kidder, U. S. N., is from that gentleman's "Contributions to the Natural History of Kerguelen Island,"[1] pp. 19–21: —

"None of these birds had shown themselves in the neighborhood of our camp until December 17, when Mr. Train captured and brought in the specimen No. 181, which he had carried more than two miles. It was found near an old nest, seemingly about to rebuild it; but no egg was found until December 30. On the 2d of January the steam-launch of the 'Monongahela' carried me several miles down the beach to the low strip which connects Prince of Wales Foreland with the mainland. Here I saw very many Albatrosses nesting upon hillocks, built up some two feet, or more, from the ground. The nests are composed mostly of grass, and, being of different heights, seemed to have been used again, and added to, year after year. I counted twenty-three birds in sight at one time, each perched upon its nest. Being conspicuous by the whiteness of their plumage, and rarely very near together, they rather remind one of the whitewashed cairns set up by surveyors. Driven from the nests, and compelled to walk, they look not unlike overgrown geese. The distribution of their weight compels them to stretch out their necks horizontally, and to walk with a widely-swaying gait. Two approached each other as I was watching them, and went through with some very odd manœuvres. One raised its head and spread out its wings as if to embrace the other, which remained with wings folded. Both then clattered their bills, and touched them together, first on one side and then on the other. This manœuvre was repeated several times. *Phœbetria fuliginosa* has the same trick of touching bills with its mate, and clattering the mandibles, about pairing-time; but I have never seen them approach one another with outspread wings. All of the nesting Albatrosses that I saw, without exception, showed a slight pinkish discoloration of the neck, as if a blood-stain had been washed out, usually on the left side, and extending downward from the region of the ear.

"They are dull birds, making but little attempt to defend their eggs beyond loudly clattering their bills. The sound thus produced is louder than would be expected, owing to the resonance of the considerable cavity included by the mandibles. It is very like the sound of a tin pan beaten with a stick. I knocked several off with my heavy overcoat twisted up like a rope, and secured their eggs before they recovered sufficiently to approach the nests. They climbed on to the empty nests again, however, and sat as contentedly, to all appearance, as before. I believe that they do not lay a second time. Certainly, the nest robbed December 30 was still empty January 2, although occupied by the old bird; and the whalers, who are very fond of the eggs, assert that they never find a second one in a nest that has been once robbed.

[1] Bulletin of the United States National Museum, No. 2, 1875.

"I have read somewhere that Albatrosses and Penguins nest together, but cannot see how it is possible. The King Penguin is the only one nesting in low land (as I am told); but none were found in this neighborhood. The eggs would be frequently immersed in water, unless raised on similar pedestals to those which the Albatrosses build."

Six eggs obtained by Dr. Kidder, and described by him on page 12 of "Bulletin No. 3 of the United States National Museum," measured 4.80–5.21 inches in length by 3.08–3.25 in width, the larger and smaller circumferences being respectively 12.80–13.80 and 9.60–10.50 inches. They are described as follows: "The shell is white, of loose granular texture, and roughly mammillated surface. There are no markings beneath the superficial calcareous layer, and the spots which appear on this seem to be adventitious stains from the secretions of the oviduct, or accidental soiling after extrusion. Some specimens show a reddish stain upon the larger end, probably dried blood, since it is readily washed off."

Diomedea albatrus.

THE SHORT-TAILED ALBATROSS.

Diomedea albatrus, PALL. Spic. Zool. V. 1769, 28.
Diomedea spadicea, var. B. LATH. Gen. Hist. X. 1824, 52, no. 2, var. B. (cites Pl. Enl. 963).
Diomedea brachiura, TEMM. Pl. Col. 554 (1828), *Adult.*
Diomedea brachyura, LAWR. in Baird's B. N. Am. 1858, 822. — BAIRD, Cat. N. Am. B. 1859, no. 631. — COUES, Pr. Ac. Nat. Sci. Philad. 1866, 177; Key, 1872, 325; Check List, 1873, no. 578; ed. 2, 1882, no. 810. — RIDGW. Nom. N. Am. B. 1881, no. 701.
Diomedea epomophora, LESS. Man. II. 1828, 351.
Diomedea chinensis, TEMMINCK, Man. d'Orn. I. 1820, cx.

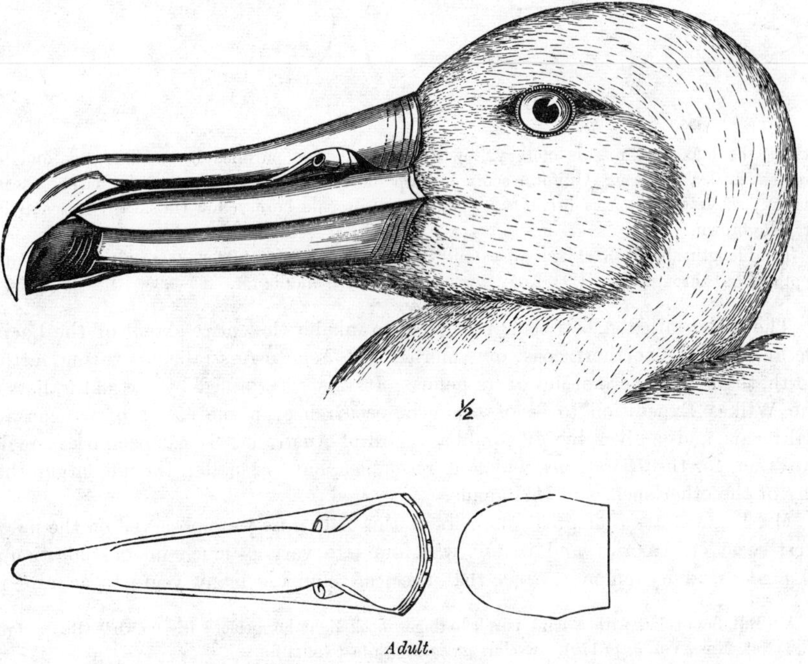

Adult.

HAB. Pacific Ocean, including the western coast of America, especially northward to Aleutian and Prybilof Islands, and Behring's Sea.

SP. CHAR. *Adult:* Prevailing color white, the top and sides of the head, with nape, strongly tinged with bright straw-yellow. Longer scapulars, tertials, primaries, and tail-feathers slaty brown, the shafts of the primaries bright straw-yellow; anterior and lower lesser wing-coverts, lower middle and greater coverts, with secondaries, hoary brownish gray. Bill grayish white (in

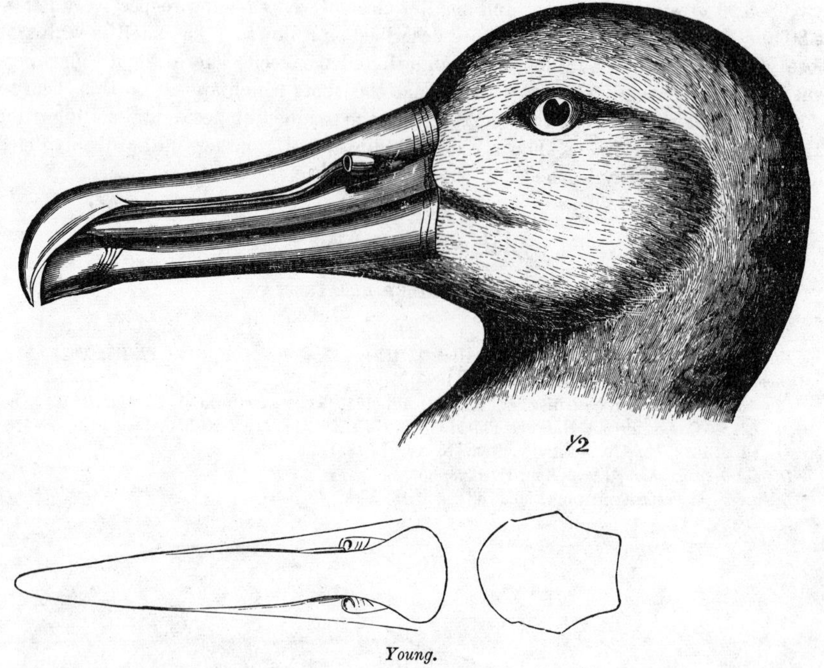

Young.

skins), the maxillary unguis more yellowish, the mandible purplish brownish;[1] legs and feet grayish dusky. *Young:* Uniform sooty grayish brown, the pileum and nape darker (nearly black); shafts of primaries bright straw-yellow. Bill pale horn-yellow (in skin); legs and feet grayish brown.

Total length, about 33.00 inches; extent, 84.00–88.00; wing, 21.00–23.00; culmen, 5.19–5.60; depth of bill through base, 1.95–2.05; tarsus, 3.80–4.00; middle toe, 4.65–4.90.

The Short-tailed Albatross is presumed to inhabit the entire extent of the Pacific Ocean, from the northern coast of America and Asia to Australia, venturing farther north than any other species of its genus. It was ascertained by the naturalists of the Wilkes Expedition to be of frequent occurrence on the coasts of Oregon and California, and is given by Mr. Gould as a bird of Australia. It has been occasionally mistaken for the *D. exulans,* which it resembles, but is smaller, though larger than any of the other species of this genus.

Mr. Peale states that great numbers of this Albatross were observed on the northwest coast of America, and that it was found to vary as much in its coloration as *D. exulans,* and even more than that species, requiring many years to acquire its

[1] "Bill flesh-color, with a faint purplish tinge; hook light horn-color; iris brown" (BEAN, Proc. U. S. Nat. Mus., Vol. 5, p. 170). Eyelids greenish white (GOULD).

perfect plumage. Confounding its young with *D. nigripes* — a distinct species — he states that until its second year its plumage remains of a dark sooty brown, and that in this dress it pairs, and raises young. But all this is now supposed to have reference to *D. nigripes* and not to *D. albatrus*. In the course of several years the plumage of the body changes from nearly black to a pure snow-like white.

Mr. Peale adds that birds of this species are usually silent; but that they sometimes quarrel over the offal thrown from the ship, and then they utter a sound like the braying of an ass. They are easily caught with hook and line, but, owing to their thick plumage and tenacity of life, they are with difficulty killed with shot.

On the 20th of December this bird was found breeding on Wake's Island. The single egg of each pair was laid on the ground, in a slight concavity, without any lining. Both sexes take turns in the labors of incubation, and neither the male nor the female parent abandons the vicinity of the nest when approached, but both walk around the intruders in a very dignified manner, making but few attempts to defend themselves, even if taken up. The egg is white, of an oblong shape, with both ends nearly alike; it measures 4.20 inches in length, and 2.60 in breadth. The two sexes are alike in plumage, and do not vary much in size, the male being rather the larger.

Dr. Pickering mentions this species as occurring on the coast of Oregon, and as being particularly abundant at sea north of the Sandwich Islands. Under date of April 10, 1841, he speaks of finding it skimming over the surface of the water, and bending its long wings, but not at so great an angle as is usual among birds. The rate at which it flies is surprising, though at the same time its wings are without perceptible motion. It alights on the water rather awkwardly, and seems to take particular care to adjust its long wings without wetting them. It swims with considerable rapidity.

Dr. Pickering mentions that on the 16th of April (lat. 30° 15′ N.) birds of this species alighted in the wake of the vessel, picking up such substances suitable for food as had been thrown overboard; and that in doing this they uttered faint cries, intermediate in character between the honk of a Goose and the bleating of a sheep. At ordinary times, however, this bird seems for the most part remarkably silent.

Mr. R. Swinhoe, in his remarks on the Formosan ornithology ("Ibis," 1863), speaks of this species as being the large Albatross of the Chinese seas, seen in more or less abundance on every voyage. It goes as far north as Japan. He was not able to discover its breeding-place, though, from its being found at Formosa at all seasons, he suspected the islands on which it nests to be not far from the south coast of China. He was of opinion that the Albatross is never figured correctly while on the wing. When flying, the wings are curved like the head of a pickaxe. It skims the surface, rising and falling with every trough of the sea, with scarcely any perceptible motion of the wings, except at their tips. It often sails upward, and continues in its flight, throwing first one shoulder forward, and then the other. This species is also mentioned by Mr. Swinhoe as having been seen by him at Amoy, China, and again off the Island of Hainan, at sea, where it was noticed on various occasions during his cruise.

Messrs. Blakiston and Pryer mention this bird as being common about Oshima, in Japan, and as present at Yezo, but not so common. The young, which resembles *D. derogata*, is figured in the "Fauna Japonica."

Dr. Cooper, while staying at Monterey, Cal., in May, 1861, noted the near presence to the shore of immature birds of this species. They had been attracted by the whale-fishers, and were busily engaged in picking up scraps of blubber in company with *Ossifraga gigantea*. He regards this as being the characteristic species of the North

Pacific Ocean, and the only one common on the Californian coast, all others being mere stragglers, or found so far from land as to be rarely seen, and hardly belonging to our fauna. He mentions finding young specimens of this Albatross as far south as San Nicolas Island, lat. 33° N., on the 1st of July, but was assured that none breed on any of the more southern islands; and it is very unlikely that they do this on any of those within our limits. These birds had apparently followed some vessel from the far north. They were extremely familiar, alighting within a few yards of his craft, and evidently expecting to be fed, as they followed the vessel for some distance, and caught at the pieces of meat thrown to them. They are often taken with a hook when following vessels along the coast, especially when young. He saw it off Monterey in April; but whether it leaves the coast entirely between that month and July he cannot state with certainty, but presumes that the few birds noticed at that time are immature or unmated. Of the old birds in the white plumage he met with but a single specimen, and that was found dead on the beach at San Diego. This species very rarely shows itself within sight of land.

Dr. Cooper also mentions that at San Diego he saw none of these birds until about December 15, when the whale-fishery commenced. They usually kept outside of the bay; but in stormy weather came a short distance in, sailing rapidly about over the surface, in an oblique position, in search of scraps, and if they found a quantity near together, settling down and swimming about after them. At such times he found no difficulty in approaching the birds in a skiff, and one morning he shot two on the water very near together. Though killed instantly, they disgorged the oily contents of their stomachs, as they do when taken alive. He has seen seven or eight together near the mouth of the bay, all in the sooty plumage. One of the three obtained was a female, and did not differ in size from the largest male. When caught with a hook, as it follows a vessel, and taken on board, this bird is unable to rise from the deck, as it requires a long range of surface on which to flap its wings.

Mr. H. W. Elliott states that the Short-tailed Albatross was often seen about the Prybilof Islands some twenty or thirty years ago, when whaling vessels were reaping their rich harvests in the Behring and Arctic seas, thus affording the birds an opportunity to feed upon any refuse of the whales which might drift on shore. With the decrease of the fishery, the Albatross has almost entirely disappeared; and only a single individual was seen by Mr. Elliott during his two years' residence in that locality. This bird is common around Unalashka Island, where he saw a large number on his way to San Francisco, in August, 1873.

Mr. Dall speaks of this species as being very abundant off shore throughout the Aleutian Islands, where it takes the place of *D. nigripes*, which seldom ventures north of lat. 50° N. It probably breeds in the islands, as he saw the remains of a young bird at Atka. Its bones were abundant in the ancient Aleutian shell-heaps. It is much larger than *D. nigripes,* and is apparently a resident in the Aleutian Islands from Atka eastward.

An egg of this species (Smithsonian Institution, No. 949 — taken by Mr. Titian R. Peale in the Pacific islands) is of an oval shape, with rounded ends, and of a dull white color, measuring 4.00 inches in length by 2.60 in breadth.

Diomedea nigripes.

THE BLACK-FOOTED ALBATROSS.

Diomedea nigripes, AUD. Orn. Biog. V. 1839, 327; B. Am. VII. 1842, 198. — CASS. Illustr. B. Cal. Tex. etc. 1853, 210, pl. 35. — COUES, Pr. Ac. Nat. Sci. Philad. 1866, 178; Key, 1872, 326; Check List, 1873, no. 579; ed. 2, 1882, no. 811. — RIDGW. Nom. N. Am. B. 1881, no. 700.

Diomedea brachyura (supposed young), CASS. Illustr. B. Cal. Tex. etc. 1853, 291. — LAWR. in Baird's B. N. Am. 1858, 822.

HAB. North Pacific Ocean, including the west coast of North America.

SP. CHAR. *Adult:* Above, brownish dusky, the scapulars indistinctly margined terminally with paler; primaries nearly black, their shafts clear straw-yellow; upper tail-coverts and concealed base of the tail white. Anterior portion of the head and auricular region dirty whitish, shading gradually into brownish gray, except behind the eyes, where very abruptly defined against

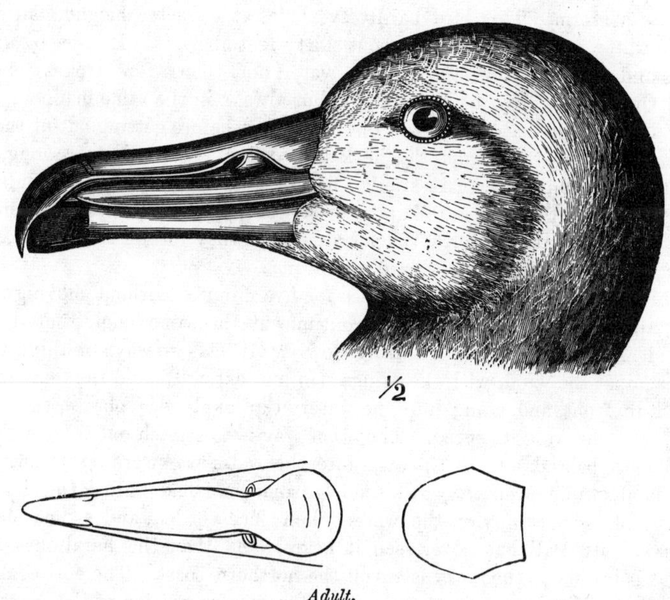

Adult.

the blackish dusky of the sides of the occiput; lower parts fuliginous-gray, deepest on the neck, sides, and flanks, fading gradually into white on the crissum and middle portion of the abdomen. Bill dusky purplish brown; legs and feet black.[1] *Young:* Similar, but head darker, showing whitish only against the base of the bill, the lower parts entirely uniform smoky gray (darker than in the adult), the upper tail-coverts dusky, like the rump.

Total length, 28.50–32.50 inches; extent, 79.50; wing, 18.50–21.50; culmen, 3.75–4.31; depth of bill at base, 1.45–1.60; tarsus, 3.50–3.70; middle toe, 4.05–4.40.

This species was first described by Audubon from a specimen obtained by Mr. Townsend, Dec. 25, 1834, on the Pacific Ocean, in latitude 50°. Nothing was then known in regard to its habits, and it was supposed by Mr. Cassin to be an immature

[1] "Iris umber; tarsus, foot, base and tip of bill, black; remainder of bill plumbeous;" of another specimen, "iris umber or golden brown" (BEAN, Proc. U. S. Nat. Mus. Vol. 5. pp. 169, 170).

specimen of *D. albatrus;* but the young of the latter species, though somewhat similar in plumage, is very distinct in form and dimensions.

Mr. Dall speaks of this bird as being very common in the North Pacific, and as accompanying the ships for weeks. It is not found in Behring's Sea; but as soon as the party had passed the islands, coming south, their vessel was several times joined and followed to San Francisco by a company of this species. They were generally dusky; but the old males had more or less white on the head. They are described as very greedy, swallowing all sorts of scraps thrown overboard; and fishing for them with a hook and line baited with pork, is a favorite amusement for the passengers when becalmed. With the exception of the small Petrels, these were the only birds met with off soundings in the North Pacific. They will follow a ship for hundreds of miles, and will feed upon all manner of refuse. They are indefatigable on the wing; but are dirty, ugly, awkward, and cruel to wounded birds of their kind. They have an angry note, which is only uttered when some more fortunate bird has secured the coveted morsel; and a croaking whine, in which they give vent to their apprehensions just before a storm. This bird hardly ever flies at a greater height than fifty feet above the water, and usually keeps about thirty feet above it. It rises by unfolding its wings and running a few steps in the water, and then a few strokes send it into the air. On a rough day it rises quickly, but always in the same manner; while in a dead calm it often has to run ten or twenty feet before getting out of the water; and it cannot rise at all from the deck of a vessel. Its wings are long, and the movement in unfolding them is similar to that made in opening a carpenter's rule. In rising or falling, the wings are kept perfectly stiff; and they are folded only when the bird is settled in the water. When half folded they form a triangular arch over the back, and present a very awkward appearance.

This bird remains in the air sometimes for five minutes without moving its wings in flight, although it does not always continue at the same height, but slides from side to side, like a sheet of paper falling slowly. It has two ways of alighting — one is to fly against the wind, with the wings stiff and extended, and the feet spread and stuck out in front, and going into the water at an angle very obtuse, the outspread web-feet soon checking its speed. The other way is to stretch out the legs stiff and at full length behind, and to tip over into the water backward on its posteriors — exactly as if, while preparing to sit down, some one had pulled the chair away. This bird rests very calmly on the water when once settled, and swims slowly and laboriously. Mr. Dall has never seen it nearer land than the Farallones, and supposes that it breeds on the rocky islets off the northern coast. The entire absence of birds of all kinds, except only Petrels, from the eastern portion of the North Pacific Ocean, is a fact quite remarkable.

Mr. Dall, in his paper on the Eastern Aleutian Islands, remarks in regard to the flight of this species, that its ordinary method of support, when there was a breeze, consisted in rising against the wind and falling with it; this being sometimes kept up for hours with hardly a stroke of the wings. It rises only against the wind, except in rare cases, when its descending momentum is sufficient to raise it slightly for a short distance, or when the reflex eddy from the high surge is strong enough to give it a slight lift. It uses its strong webbed feet to some extent in balancing itself when turning with the wind; also, by extending them downward at a right angle with the body, to check its course, especially when alighting on the water. Generally, when flying, the feet are stretched out behind, with the webs extended, and assist the bird materially in guiding itself, the tail being shorter than the extended feet. It rises by running against the wind over the water, until sufficiently raised above the surface to use its wings without wetting them. Its eyesight is exceedingly acute; it can distinguish a discolored spot in the water a yard in diameter from a distance of at least five miles, and even much farther than our unaided eyes can see the bird itself. Its flight, in calm weather, consists of a series of five or six short, sharp strokes, made at intervals of a second, or more, apart, followed by a short period of comparative quiet. It appears to subsist mainly on a pelagic crab and the refuse from vessels. It usually flies in flocks of six or eight, but often smaller; and on one occasion a solitary individual followed the vessel for hundreds of miles without a companion.

Mr. Dall, in his Notes on the Avifauna of the Aleutian Islands west of Unalashka, referring to the question as to where this species breeds, states, on the authority of Mr. George Holder, that it nests on the coral island of Gaspar Rico, near the equator, in the winter season. This gentleman, who is said to be an intelligent and trustworthy observer, informed Mr. Dall that, on a voyage in quest of new guano islands, he touched at Gaspar Rico, and found this bird, together with a species of Petrel, and a Tern, breeding abundantly in a low scrubby growth of bushes, which are the only representatives of trees on that island. His impression was that it laid but one moderately-sized white egg in a depression in the soil, around which a little sea-weed or dry herbage was gathered. It is not known to breed anywhere on the northwest coast of America, or on the northern Pacific islands.

Diomedea melanophrys.

THE SPECTACLED ALBATROSS.

Diomedea melanophrys, "BOIE," TEMM. Pl. Col. no. 456 (1838). — GOULD, Birds Australia, VII. pl. 43. — COUES, Proc. Philad. Acad. 1866, 181. — BEAN, Proc. U. S. Nat. Mus. Vol. 5, 1882, 170 (off coast of California, long. 142° 23′ W., lat. 40° 30′ N.).

HAB. Southern oceans generally, north to at least 40° 30′ north latitude, and east nearly to coast of California (BEAN, l. c.).

SP. CHAR. *Adult:* Back and scapulars brownish slate, becoming more ashy anteriorly; wings uniform dark brownish slate; tail brownish gray, the shafts of the feathers yellowish white; shafts of primaries deep yellow basally, dark brownish terminally. Head, neck, rump, upper tail-coverts, and entire lower parts white; an indistinct grayish stripe through eye, darkest immediately before and behind the eye. Bill yellowish, the ungui and base of culmen tinged with horn-color;[1] legs and feet "pearly slate" (light brownish in dried skin). Wing, 19.50–20.00 inches; tail, 8.00–8.50; tarsus, 3.00–3.25; middle toe, 4.00–4.30; culmen, 4.30–4.70.

GENUS **THALASSOGERON**, RIDGWAY.

Thalassiarche, FORBES, Zool. Challenger Exp. IV. 1882, 57 (not *Thalassarche*, REICH. 1852).
Thalassogeron, RIDGW. MS. (type, *Diomedea culminata*, GOULD).

CHAR. Similar to *Diomedea*, but culminicorn widely separated from the latericorn by the interposition of a strip of naked skin behind the nostril. Bill much compressed.

[1] "No difference whatever is observable in the plumage of the sexes, neither is there any visible variation in this respect between youth and maturity; a never-failing mark, however, exists, by which these latter may be distinguished — the young bird has the bill dark brown, while in the adult that organ is of a bright buffy yellow; and individuals in the same flight may frequently be seen in which the bill varies from dark horn-brown to the most delicate yellow" (GOULD, Birds of Australia, pt. vii.).

A male from Valparaiso, Chili, had the "bill gray, with dark tips; feet light gray; iris dark brown" (SHARPE, P. Z. S. 1881, p. 12).

Thalassogeron culminatus.

THE YELLOW-NOSED ALBATROSS.

Diomedea culminata, GOULD, P. Z. S. July 25, 1843, 107; Birds Austral. VII. pl. 41. — GRAY, Gen. B. 1849, pl. 179. — COUES, Pr. Philad. Acad. 1866, 183. — STREETS, Bull. U. S. Nat. Mus. no. 7, 1877, 31. — RIDGW. Nom. N. Am. B. 1881, no. 702.

Diomedea chlororhynchos, AUD. Orn. Biog. V. 1839, 326; B. Am. VII. 1844, 196. — LAWR. in Baird's B. N. Am. 1858, 822 (excl. syn.). — BAIRD, Cat. N. Am. B. 1859, no. 632.

HAB. "Southern, Indian, and South Pacific Oceans" (GOULD, l. c.); casual off the coast of Oregon (AUDUBON).

SP. CHAR. *Adult:* Head and neck light ash-gray, darker immediately in front of the eyes, paler on the throat, and fading into white on the lower surface of the body; lower eyelid white. Back brownish plumbeous, fading gradually into the light ashy of the nape, growing gradually darker

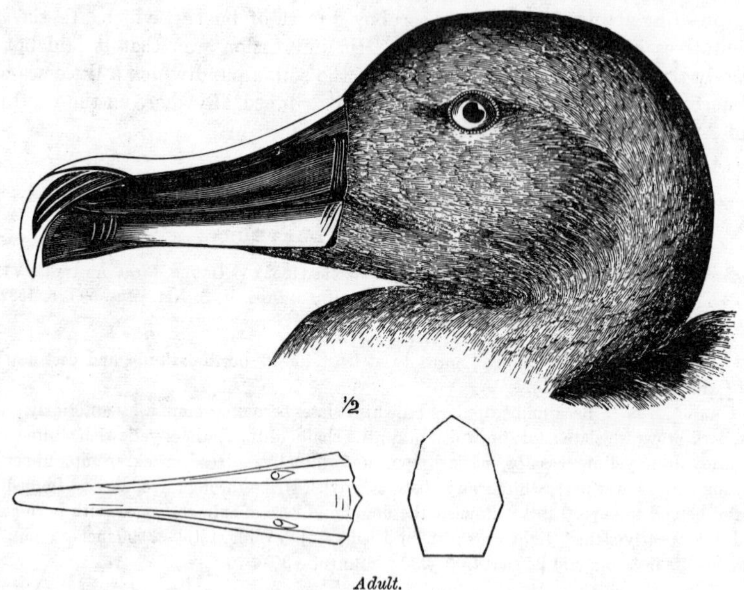

Adult.

toward the scapulars, which, with the entire wings, are uniform dark brownish slate, or dusky; rump and upper tail-coverts white; tail hoary slate-gray, the shafts yellowish white. Shafts of primaries straw-yellow, changing to brown terminally. Bill grayish black, the culmen (abruptly) and the lower part of the mandible yellowish white; legs and feet dull brownish.[1] *Young:* "Head and neck dark gray;" the bill "almost uniform brownish black, with only an indication of the lighter color of the culmen" (GOULD).

Wing, 21.00 inches; culmen, 4.50; depth of bill at base, 1.75; tarsus, 3.25; middle toe, 5.00.

The individual described by Audubon as the Yellow-nosed Albatross (*D. chlororhynchos*), and said to have been procured by Mr. Townsend near the mouth of the

[1] "Bill black, the culmen horn-color, and the edge of the basal two thirds of the under mandible orange" (GOULD, Birds of Australia, pt. vii.).

"Bill black, with the ridge in its entire length and breadth, the tip of the upper mandible, and the crura of the lower along their inferior edges yellow. Feet yellow, claws yellowish gray" (AUDUBON).

Columbia River, has been ascertained by Professor Baird to belong, not to that, but to the present species. It is exceedingly problematical whether this bird is really entitled to a place in the avifauna of North America. In regard to its history and distribution generally I have no information.

Dr. Cooper expresses his conviction that this is a rare visitant on the Pacific coast north of the equator, though said to have been obtained in 1836 off the mouth of the Columbia River by Mr. Townsend. Dr. Cooper has, however, seen a skull answering to the description of that of this species in the collection of the Academy of Natural Sciences in San Francisco. It was taken by Dr. W. O. Ayres from a dead specimen found on the outer beach near the Golden Gate.

Genus **PHŒBETRIA**, Reichenbach.

Phœbetria, Reichenb. Syst. Av. 1852, p. v (type, *Diomedea fuliginosa*, Gmel.).

Char. Similar to *Thalassogeron*, but bill much more compressed, with sharper culmen, and a deep longitudinal sulcus or groove along the side of the lower mandible; base of the culmen forming a deep angle into the feathering of the forehead, and feathers of the malar region extending forward as an acute angle on the lateral base of the mandible; tail lengthened, cuneate.

Only one species of this genus is known, this (*P. fuliginosa*) ranging over the greater part of the Pacific and Southern oceans.

Phœbetria fuliginosa.

THE SOOTY ALBATROSS.

Diomedea fuliginosa, Gmel. S. N. I. ii. 1788, 568. — Temm. Pl. Col. 469. — Lawr. in Baird's B. N. Am. 1858, 823. — Baird, Cat. N. Am. B. 1859, no. 633. — Coues, Key, 1872, 326; Check List, 1873, no. 580.

Diomedea (Phœbetria) fuliginosa, Bonap. Consp. II. 1855, 186.

Phœbetria fuliginosa, Coues, Pr. Ac. Nat. Sci. Philad. 1866, 186; 2d Check List, 1882, no. 812. — Ridgw. Nom. N. Am. B. 1881, 703.

Diomedea palpebrata, Forst. "ic. ined. no. 102."

Diomedea fusca, Aud. Orn. Biog. V. 1839, 116; B. Am. VII. 1844, 200, pl. 444.

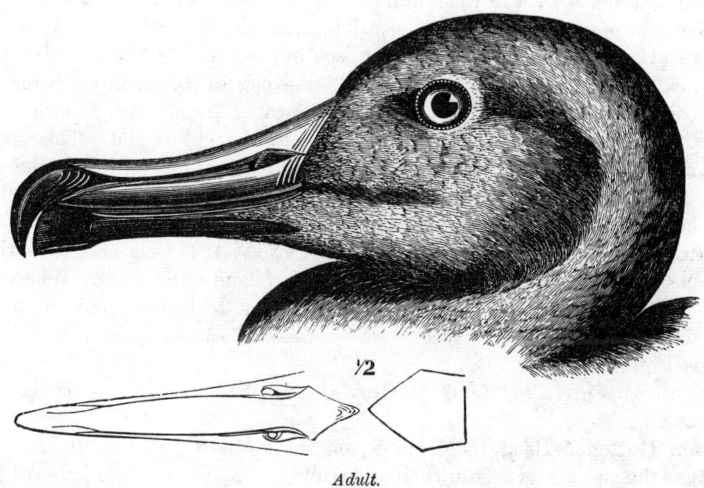

Adult.

HAB. Oceans of the southern hemisphere, northeastward to the coast of Oregon. (AUDUBON.)

SP. CHAR. *Adult* (?) : Neck, back, and entire lower parts pale smoky ash, lightest on the neck and anterior portion of the back, where the tips of the feathers are nearly white ; pileum clouded with pale yellowish ash and dusky ; sides of the head, including lores, orbital and malar regions, chin, and throat, deep fuliginous, darkest around the eyes, where nearly black. Eyelids whitish. Wings and tail dark slaty fuliginous, the shafts of the primaries and rectrices yellowish, except terminally ; scapulars and rump intermediate in color between the wings and back. Bill black, except the sulci, which are light colored ; legs and feet pale reddish. *Young:* Entire head deep fuliginous, fading gradually into the uniform smoky gray of the lower surface of the body, the back, rump, and upper tail-coverts ; scapulars sooty gray, considerably darker than the back ; wings and tail sooty slate, the inner lesser coverts faintly tipped with dull ferruginous, the shafts of the primaries and rectrices yellowish white. Eyelids conspicuously white, except anteriorly. Bill and feet colored as in the adult.

Wing, 20.00–21.50 inches; tail, 10.50–13.00, the lateral feathers 3.00–5.50 shorter; culmen, 4.00–4.25 ; depth of bill at base, 1.40–1.55 ; tarsus, 3.25 ; middle toe, 4.00–4.50.

This species was introduced into the North American fauna by Audubon, who figured and described it as *D. fusca* — supposing it to be a new species — from an individual procured by Dr. Townsend near the mouth of the Columbia River. It is a bird of the Pacific Ocean, a great wanderer, more common in the South than in the North Pacific Regions, and with very doubtful claims to be regarded as even a visitor of the North American coast at any point.

Mr. R. Swinhoe speaks of it as being abundant at all seasons in the Formosan Channel. He kept several birds of this species, as well as of *D. albatrus*, alive for several days in his veranda at Amoy; but he could not induce any of them to feed. For a few days they walked about in a clumsy manner, but soon became too weak. He kept one alive, in order to ascertain how long it was possible for this bird to exist without food. It had been kept a week or more when he received it, and it remained alive twenty-nine days after that; so that it must have lived in all at least five weeks without swallowing anything.

It was also found about Amoy, China, where it was caught, in company with *D. albatrus*, by the fishermen, and brought into the market for sale — the flesh, all musk-flavored as it is, being devoured by the omnivorous Chinamen. There it goes by the name of *A-haieau-gong*, or Booby of Hainan.

Mr. Layard met with it in the Antarctic Ocean, in lat. 41° S. It was in company with *Ossifraga gigantea.* The same gentleman, in the "Ibis" (1867), describes an egg that had been obtained by Captain Armson in the Crozette Islands. It measured 4.20 inches by 2.60, and resembled generally the egg of *D. exulans* — being chalky white, coarse to the touch, and of a squarely truncated form. It was also minutely pitted with reddish dots in an indistinct band at the obtuse end. This species is called the "Blue Bird" by the sealers, who readily distinguish it from the equally sooty Giant Petrel by its white eyelids and the white mark along the bill. The female lays but a single egg, which is said to be very good eating.

Captain P. P. King writes ("Zoologist," XXXIV. 128) that he met with birds of this species in the greatest abundance near the Island of St. Paul. Wherever one species of *Diomedea* abounded, the others were found to be less common; and from this he inferred that the three species, *D. spadicea*, *D. chlororhynchos*, and *P. fuliginosa*, breed in different haunts.

This species is given by Mr. G. R. Gray as one of the birds found on the coast of New Zealand.

Captain Hutton ("Ibis," 1865) states, on the authority of Mr. Richard Harris, R. N., that this species breeds in the inaccessible cliffs of the Prince Edward Islands and Kerguelen Island — where, however, he was never able to secure a nest. This bird had an unpleasant habit of screeching at night, and was called by the sealers the *Pee-u.* Sir John Ross mentions seeing young birds of this species, fully fledged and ready to go to sea, in May, at Kerguelen Island. This Albatross was so very shy that Mr. Harris was not able to make any observations as to its habits. It is described by Mr. Gould as being very wary, seldom caught, and the only one of all the Petrel tribe which is wont to fly directly over a ship.

The unrivalled flight of the Albatross has been the admiration of voyagers from the earliest time; and this species, as Captain Hutton contends, carries off the palm from all its competitors. "Never," he states, "have I seen anything to equal the ease and grace of this bird as it sweeps past, often within a few yards, every part of its body perfectly motionless, except the head and eye, which turns slowly, and seems to take notice of everything. I have sometimes watched narrowly one of these birds sailing and wheeling about in all directions for more than an hour, without seeing the slightest movement of its wings."

In a subsequent voyage, in 1866, from London to New Zealand, as Captain Hutton again states, he saw a large number around the ship on the 8th of April, and also when off the Island of Tristan d'Acunha. After that he met with none until the 28th, in latitude 38°; but from that time forward they continued to be seen until the 20th of May.

Dr. J. H. Kidder, in his Notes on the Birds of Kerguelen Island, mentions the capture of two specimens of the Sooty Albatross, October 16, at the entrance of a shallow cave in the face of a rock some distance inland. The birds kept about the huts several days, showing no disposition to escape; but very unexpectedly one of them walked to the edge of a rock and flew off. October 24, two had been found to have made a nest on a shelf formed by a considerable tuft of cabbage and azarella at the entrance of a small cavity in the perpendicular face of a lofty rock, some two miles distant. Their screams were very loud, and not unlike the call of a cat. The name of *Pee-aw* has been given it as descriptive of this call, which is presumed to be peculiar to the breeding-season. November 2, an egg and both parents were secured. The nest was a conical mound, seven or eight inches high, hollowed into a cup at the top, and rudely lined with grass. The male was sitting on the egg when captured, and the female standing on an old nest not far away. Both — especially the male — showed fight when approached, clattering their large bills with an odd noise, and biting viciously. In captivity both birds ate freely of fresh meat. The egg was single, white, and very long in proportion to its thickness. Other eggs were met with as late as November 21.

In Dr. Kidder's Notes on the Oology of Kerguelen, he describes the eggs of this species as being broadly ovoidal, generally white, and marked by a collection of spots about the larger end. The shell is said to be compact in structure, thin for its size, and smooth to the touch. Examined by the lens, it is found to be marked by minute pits and linear depressions. Both eggs measured 3.95 inches in length, and one 2.60, the other 2.64, in breadth.

FAMILY PROCELLARIIDÆ. — THE PETRELS.

The North American genera of this family are numerous, and may be distinguished as follows: —

PROCELLARIINÆ. Secondaries 13 or more; tarsi covered with small hexagonal scutellæ; claws sharp, curved, more or less compressed. Leg-bones shorter than wing-bones; cervico-dorsal vertebræ not less than 22; basal phalanx of middle toe shorter than the next two joints, together.

A. Size very large (wing, 17.00 inches or more). Bill longer than tarsus.

3. **Ossifraga.** Tail of sixteen feathers; bill longer than the tarsus, very stout; nasal tube much longer than the maxillary unguis, the nasal orifice single at the entrance, the septum being hidden.

B. Size medium (wing less than 14.00 inches, and more than 7.00). Bill shorter than tarsus.

4. **Fulmarus.** Tail of twelve to fourteen feathers; bill very stout; nasal tube much shorter than the unguis, straight on top; maxillary unguis separated from the nasal tube by a very narrow space.
5. **Priocella.** Similar to *Fulmarus*, but bill much more slender, the nasal tube concave on top, and separated from the unguis by a very wide space.
6. **Priofinus.** Tail-feathers twelve; nasal tubes about half as long as the unguis, and separated from the latter by a space equal in length to about two thirds the length of the unguis; nostrils opening directly anteriorly.
7. **Puffinus.** Tail-feathers twelve; nasal tubes about half as long as the unguis, and separated from the latter by a space nearly equal to the length of the unguis; nostrils opening obliquely upward.
8. **Œstrelata.** Bill much compressed and very deep, the ungui very large, occupying nearly the terminal half of the bill; nasal tubes short and very prominent, about one third to one half as long as the maxillary unguis, the nostrils opening directly in front.
9. **Bulweria.** Similar to *Œstrelata*, but smaller and more slender, the tail longer (about half the wing) and more graduated. Myological formula said to be very different.
10. **Daption.** Tail of fourteen feathers; bill broad and depressed, except terminally, the unguis occupying less than one third its length; nasal tubes depressed and concave in the middle, nearly as long as the unguis, and separated from the latter by a space equal to about two thirds its length; maxillary rami separated below from the angle back, bowed slightly outward, the intervening space occupied with bare skin; tarsus much longer than the bill, but shorter than the middle toe.

C. Size very small (wing less than 7.00 inches).

11. **Halocyptena.** Tail much rounded, or slightly graduated; tarsus decidedly longer than the middle claw (about twice the culmen); no white on the rump.
12. **Procellaria.** Tail even or slightly rounded; tarsus about equal to the middle toe and claw (about twice the culmen); a white patch on the rump.
13. **Cymochorea.** Tail much forked; tarsus about as long as, or a little shorter than, the middle toe and claw (about one and a half times as long as the culmen); with or without a white rump patch.
14. **Oceanodroma.** Tail forked, the feathers scalloped at the end, the lateral rectrices narrowed terminally; tarsus about equal to, or very little shorter than, the middle toe and claw (not quite twice as long as the culmen); no white on the rump.

OCEANITINÆ. Secondaries 10; tarsi ocreate, or else covered in front with large obliquely transverse scutes; claws flat and broad. Leg-bones longer than wing-bones; cervico-dorsal vertebræ 21; basal phalanx of middle toe longer than the next two together. Nasal aperture single, circular.

15. **Oceanites.** Tail forked, the feathers broad and nearly truncate at the end; tarsus much longer than the middle toe and claw (about two and a half times the length of the culmen); a white rump patch.

16. **Cymodroma** (*gen. nov.*). Tail even, the feathers exceedingly broad, with truncated tips; tarsus about twice as long as the middle toe without the claw (more than two and a half times as long as the culmen).

Genus OSSIFRAGA, Hombron & Jacquinot.

Ossifraga, Homb. & Jacq. Compt. Rend. XVIII. 1844, 356 (type, *Procellaria gigantea*, Gmel.).

Char. Size very large (equal to the smaller *Diomedeæ*); bill very robust, longer than the tarsus; nasal tubes very large and long, occupying the greater part of the culmen, the external orifice of the nostrils simple, the septum commencing far back. Tail-feathers 16.

O. gigantea, dark phase.

Only a single species of this genus is known. It much resembles in size and general appearance the smaller Albatrosses, but may be at once distinguished by the very different form of the bill.

Ossifraga gigantea.

THE GIANT FULMAR.

Procellaria gigantea, Gmel. S. N. I. ii. 1788, 563. — Nutt. Man. II. 1834, 329. — Aud. Orn. Biog. V. 1849, 330; B. Am. VII. 1844, 202. — Lawr. in Baird's B. N. Am. 1858, 825. — Baird, Cat. N. Am. B. 1859, no. 634.

Ossifraga gigantea, Reichenb. Syst. Av. 185, pl. 20, fig. 332. — Bonap. Consp. II. 1856, 186. — Coues, Pr. Ac. Nat. Sci. Phil. 1866, 32; 2d Check List, 1882, no. 813. — Ridgw. Nom. N. Am. B. 1881, no. 704.

Fulmarus giganteus, Coues, Key, 1872, 327; Check List, 1873, no. 581.

? Procellaria brasiliana, Lath. Ind. Orn. II. 1790, 821, no. 2.

HAB. Southern oceans ; casual off the coast of Oregon.

SP. CHAR. *Adult:* Head, neck, and lower parts, white ;[1] upper parts plain fuliginous-slate, the feathers, particularly the scapulars, sometimes indistinctly tipped with lighter. Bill yellow ; legs and feet yellowish or dusky. *Young?:* Uniform dark fuliginous-slate, sometimes with whitish feathers around base of the bill. Bill more olivaceous.[2]

Dark phase.

Total length, about 3 feet ; extent, about 7 ; wing, 17.00 to 21.00 inches ; culmen, 3.50–4.00 ; tarsus, 3.50 ; middle toe, without claw, 4.50–4.70.

Audubon states that a specimen of this enormous Petrel was shot at some distance from the mouth of Columbia River, and sent to him by Mr. Townsend. Its great size gave to it, at first sight, the appearance of an Albatross. By some sailors it is said to be known by the name of "Mother Carey's Goose." In the Report of the Wilkes Expedition it is spoken of as the "Giant Petrel." It was frequently observed during the voyage of that Expedition, and its claim to be regarded as one of the birds of North America is confirmed by the collection of specimens on the coast of Oregon. Since this species is much larger than its immediate relatives in this group, it would seem as if it was more nearly allied to the Albatrosses than to the Fulmars. So far, however, as its manners and habits are known, they vary but little from those of the Fulmars.

The occurrence of this bird is frequently referred to by Dr. Pickering in his Journal of the Events of the United States Exploring Expedition. On the morning of Feb. 13, 1839, an example of this large Fulmar was captured ; but the locality is not given. He states that an individual of this species had been seen occasionally since the 15th of January, when the Expedition was in latitude 39° 5′, in the Atlantic Ocean ; but at first it was mistaken for an Albatross. In size it was equal to a Goose, its total length being two feet, five inches, and its expanse of wing six feet. Its iris was lake-brown. It was captured alive ; and when placed on deck, could run or stand for a few moments without expanding its wings, but was apparently very soon fatigued with such exertion, and almost immediately assumed a sitting position, like that

[1] According to Dr. Coues (see Pr. Philad. Acad. 1866, p. 32) some specimens are "pure white all over, even to the wings and tail ; the continuity of the white only interrupted by a few isolated brown feathers sparsely scattered at irregular intervals over the body."

[2] Audubon describes the bill and feet of a specimen in the uniform dark-brown plumage as yellow ; while a male (age not stated) from Tom Bay, Patagonia, is thus described by Mr. Sharpe (Proc. Zool. Soc. Lond., 1881, p. 11) : "Bill light gray ; iris dark brown ; eyelids black ; legs and feet dark gray."

of *Thalassidromæ.* Its wings were, like those of an Albatross, long and narrow, and in flying were extended almost in a straight line, at right angles from the body. Its flight was chiefly sailing, which, though long continued, was performed with great rapidity and apparent ease. The bird was called a "Molly-Mawk" by the seamen, some of whom recognized in it an old acquaintance. It was frequently seen alighting and resting on the water.

Dr. Cooper mentions ("Am. Nat." X. 758) having observed this enormous Petrel — known to whalers as the "Gong" — off the coast, at Monterey, Cal. The whale-fishery had attracted it nearer the land than was usual, and it could be seen swimming lazily near the try-works, in order to pick up scraps of blubber. According to his experience, it usually keeps very far from land, as he has never seen any bird answering its description nearer to the Californian coast, though Steller refers to it as having been seen by him in great numbers feeding on a dead whale, two hundred versts from the land off the northwest coast.

Captain Sperling speaks of the Giant Petrel as not uncommon from the Cape of Good Hope as far south as latitude 27°; beyond that he saw no more of it. At night, when hovering over the ship, this bird would emit the most diabolical cry — between a croak and a scream — often startling the sailors, who could hardly imagine to what cause these sounds were to be attributed.

Captain C. C. Abbott mentions finding this species common along the shores of the East Falkland Islands. It was generally seen on the wing, though occasionally it was resting on the water. He was told that it breeds on many of the adjacent islets; and as a proof of the correctness of the statement, he mentions that the eggs were frequently brought to him.

This species is included by Mr. G. R. Gray in his list of the birds of New Zealand and of the adjacent islands.

Captain Hutton ("Ibis," 1865) states that it breeds on the cliffs of Prince Edward's Island and of Kerguelen Island, in localities which are not entirely inaccessible. The nestlings are at first covered with a beautiful long light-gray down; and when fledged they are dark brown, mottled with white. When a person approaches the nest, the old birds remain a short distance away, while the young ones squirt a horribly smelling oil out of their nostrils, to a distance of six or eight feet. This Fulmar is remarkable for its voracity, hovering over the sealers when they are cutting up a seal, and devouring the carcase the moment it is abandoned. This bird was known to the sailors as the "Melly." It will occasionally chase the smaller sea-birds, but it is not known ever to kill them; and as these are swift on the wing, it is doubtful if they could be overtaken by this bird. Captain Hutton entirely discredits the statements of Lord Macartney, that this species is in the habit of killing other birds, and then only feeding upon the heart and liver of its victims.

Mr. Layard ("Ibis," 1862) mentions his first meeting with it in the Antarctic Ocean, in latitude 41° S., in company with the Black Albatross — *D. fuliginosa.* Many of this species took the hook freely, when the vessel was not going through the water. They were all unusually lean, and it was presumed that their breeding-season was already over, and that they were feeding their young birds — or this was the only way in which their poor condition could be accounted for.

Mr. Layard afterward ("Ibis," 1867) describes the egg of this species obtained in the Crozette Islands by Captain Armson. It measures 4.25 inches in length by 2.66 in breadth, is of a dirty white, and very rough to the touch, reminding one of the egg of a *Crax.* In shape it is like that of a common Goose, and is rather pointed at each end. It retains the strong musky odor of the parents, which is called

"Glutton Bird" by the sealers, who cannot eat the egg on account of its odor. This bird lays but a single egg. These birds are said to be so fearless that they congregate on the carcasses of the seals that are being cut up, and rival the men in the flensing process.

Dr. Kidder did not meet with any egg of this species, but found the nest on elevated ground, at the distance of half a mile from the sea. When the young were first seen, January 2, there was no vestige of any artificial nest, and the nestlings were nearly fledged, and as large and heavy as the adults. They were found in natural hollows between mounds of *Azorella*. Dr. Kidder describes these birds as being exceedingly filthy, ejecting the contents of their stomachs for two or three feet from their bodies, with an almost unlimited supply from which to draw. When disturbed they soon surrounded themselves with a puddle of vomited matters, among which were noticed many Penguins' feathers. In the same neighborhood was a young bird of an earlier brood, fully fledged, but still unable to fly. These data prove that this Petrel is among the earliest of the birds of Kerguelen in breeding, and that it is destructive of other species of birds. The down of the young bird is entirely gray, and the head is partly naked.

GENUS **FULMARUS**, LEACH.

Fulmarus, LEACH, Stephens' Gen. Zool. XIII. 1825, 233 (type, *Procellaria glacialis*, LINN.).

CHAR. Similar to *Ossifraga*, but much smaller, the bill shorter than the tarsus, the nasal tubes shorter and smaller (decidedly shorter than the maxillary unguis), the nasal septum extending almost to the orifice. Tail-feathers 12–14.

Of this genus there appears to be but a single species, which varies greatly in plumage, even in the same locality.

Fulmarus glacialis.

a. Glacialis. THE ARCTIC FULMAR.

Procellaria glacialis, LINN. Faun. Suec. 2d ed. 1761, 51; S. N. I. 1766, 213. — NUTT. Man. II. 1834, 331. — AUD. Orn. Biog. III. 1835, 446; B. Am. VII. 1844, 204, pl. 355. — LAWR. in Baird's B. N. Am. 1858, 825. — BAIRD, Cat. N. Am. B. 1859, no. 635.

Fulmarus glacialis, STEPHENS, Gen. Zool. XIII. 1826, 234, pl. 27. — BONAP. Consp. II. 1856, 187. — COUES, Pr. Ac. Nat. Sci. Philad. 1866, 27; Key, 1872, 327; Check List, 1873, no. 582; ed. 2, 1882, no. 814. — RIDGW. Nom. N. Am. B. 1881, no. 705.

Fulmarus glacialis, a. *Auduboni*, BONAP. Consp. II. 1856, 187.

Fulmarus glacialis, b. *minor*, BONAP. l. c.

Procellaria grönlandica, GUNN. in Lœm. Fenm. Lapp. 1767, 273.

Procellaria minor, KJÆRB. Danm. Fugle, 1052, 324.

Procellaria hiemalis, BREHM, Vög. Deutschl. 1831, 800.

b. Glupischa. THE PACIFIC FULMAR.

Procellaria pacifica, AUD. Orn. Biog. V. 1839, 331; B. Am. VII. 1844, 208 (not of GMEL. 1788). — LAWR. in Baird's B. N. Am. 1858, 826. — BAIRD, Cat. N. Am. B. 1859, no. 636.

Fulmarus glacialis, c. *pacifica*, BONAP. Consp. II. 1856, 187.

Fulmarus glacialis, var. *pacificus*, COUES, Key, 1872, 327; Check List, 1873, no. 582 *a*.

Fulmarus glacialis pacificus, RIDGW. Proc. U. S. Nat. Mus. II. 1880, 209; Nom. N. Am. B. 1881, no. 705 *a*. — COUES, 2d Check List, 1882, no. 815.

Fulmarus pacificus, COUES, Pr. Ac. Nat. Sci. Philad. 1866, 28.

Fulmarus glacialis glupischa, STEJN. The Auk, I. No. 3, July, 1884, 234.

c. Rodgersi. RODGERS' FULMAR.

Fulmarus Rodgersii, CASS. Pr. Ac. Nat. Sci. Philad. 1862, 290. — COUES, ib. 1866, 29. — BAIRD, Trans. Chicago Ac. I. 1869, 323, pl. 34, fig. 1.

Fulmarus glacialis, var. *Rodgersi*, COUES, Key, 1872, 327 ; Check List, 1873, no. 582 *b*.

Fulmarus glacialis Rodgersi, RIDGW. Pr. U. S. Nat. Mus. Vol. 2, 1880, 209 ; Nom. N. Am. B. 1881, no. 705 *b*.

HAB. True *glacialis*, North Atlantic Ocean, south in America to coast of New England (Massachusetts specimens in U. S. Nat. Mus.) ; *F. glacialis glupischa*, North Pacific Ocean, south to Western Mexico ; *Rodgersi*, restricted to the North Pacific.

SP. CHAR. *Adult* (?) : Head, neck, and lower parts, white ; upper surface bluish gray, the primaries darker, the wing-coverts and tertials sometimes partly white. Bill, legs, and feet, greenish yellow ; iris yellow. *Young* (?) : Uniform cinereous or sooty gray. " Bill dusky brown, blotched and streaked with pale yellowish green ; inner side of tarsus, with feet, very pale yellowish white ; outer side of tarsus dark brown ; iris dark brown " (L. KUMLIEN, MS.).

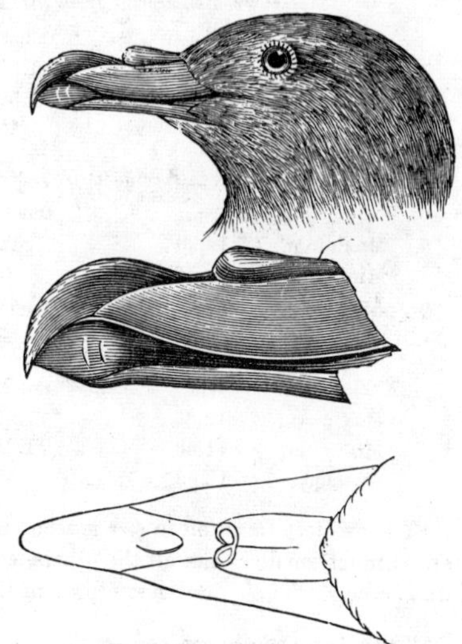

F. glacialis : dark phase.

Total length, about 18.00 to 20.00 inches ; wing, 11.80–13.75 ; culmen, 1.30–1.65 ; depth of bill through base, .60–.80 ; tarsus, 1.65–2.15 ; middle toe, 2.05–2.60.

With a considerable series of specimens before us, we are unable to detect constant differences between Fulmars from the North Pacific Ocean and those from the North Atlantic. In fact there is much more of individual than local variation in this species, as regards size and proportions, while the color-variation is also chiefly individual. The few and slight differences in coloration which appear to be at all suggestive of local difference in this respect are as follows : In all stages of plumage, specimens from the North Atlantic

F. glacialis : light phase.

F. glacialis Rodgersi.

are of an appreciably, and in a majority decidedly, more bluish or " pearly " gray than those from the North Pacific, and have, without exception, a dusky space immediately in front of the eye. Not one of the three "adult" specimens shows any white on the wings. In all specimens from the North Pacific the gray is much darker, of a more smoky hue ; some have no trace of dusky in front of the eye, while others have a greater or less amount of white on the wing ; the type of

F. "*Rodgersi*," CASS., having the wing almost entirely white, as are also the rump and upper tail-coverts. There is, however, absolutely no constancy in regard to the continuity of the gray, the shade of which varies from a pale smoky cinereous to a deep, almost slate-, gray. In order to test the question of local *versus* individual variation in size and proportions, careful measurements have been made of the twenty-four specimens examined, and the following summary is presented as the result : —

Seven specimens from the North Atlantic (=*glacialis et* "*minor*").

	Wing.	Culmen.	Depth of bill through base.	Tarsus.	Middle toe.
Maximum,	13.75	1.58	.80	2.15	2.60
Minimum,	11.80	1.30	.60	1.65	2.05
Average,	12.69	1.45	.71	1.88	2.30

Seven specimens from the North Pacific, labelled "*F. Rodgersi.*"

	Wing.	Culmen.	Depth of bill at base.	Tarsus.	Middle toe.
Maximum,	12.90	1.60	.75	2.05	2.50
Minimum,	12.10	1.40	.65	1.75	2.20
Average,	12.46	1.49	.72	1.90	2.32

Seven specimens from the North Pacific, labelled "*F. pacificus.*"

	Wing.	Culmen.	Depth of bill at base.	Tarsus.	Middle toe.
Maximum,	12.35	1.65	.70	2.00	2.35
Minimum,	11.90	1.35	.65	1.75	2.10
Average,	12.06	1.48	.68	1.88	2.25

The greatest variation in size is seen among specimens from the North Atlantic, three of which are so much smaller than all the others, especially in regard to the bill, as almost to suggest specific distinctness. These doubtless represent the *P. minor*, KJÆRB.[1]

These three specimens, compared with seven others from various localities in the North Atlantic measure as follows : —

F. glacialis minor.

No.			Wing.	Culmen.	Depth of bill at base.	Tarsus.	Middle toe.
76293,*	Ovifak, Greenland,	Aug. 10,	11.90	1.30	.70	1.90	2.20
76289,*	Cumberland Gulf,	Oct. 13,	11.80	1.30	.60	1.65	2.05
77114,†	Coast New England,		12.00	1.38	.60	1.75	2.15
Average,			11.90	1.38	.63	1.77	2.13

F. glacialis glacialis.

No.			Wing.	Culmen.	Depth of bill at base.	Tarsus.	Middle toe.
71021,	Niantilik, Cumberland Gulf,	Aug. 7,	13.75	1.50	.80		
71022,	" "	" 7,	12.80	1.50	.75		
	" "	" 10,	12.90	1.55	.78	2.15	2.45
71020,	" "	" 10,	12.70	1.45	.75	1.95	2.20
76290,	Quickstep Harbor, "	July 11,	13.40	1.45	.75	1.85	2.45
57136,	Greenland,		13.20	1.58	.75	2.00	2.60
78012,	Lat. 45° 10′, long. 55° 21′ W.,	Mar. 14,	12.50	1.45	.65	1.80	2.30
Average,			13.04	1.50	.75	1.95	2.40

* L. Kumlien. † [U. S. Fish Commission.]

The colors of the small specimens mentioned above are in no way peculiar, except that the bill is darker, or almost blackish.

With a few rare and occasional exceptions, the typical Fulmar, or Fulmar Petrel, as it is more generally called, is a northern and Arctic species, confined to the Northern Atlantic and to the Arctic oceans, to the northern portions of America,

[1] See Coues, Pr. Philad. Acad. 1866, p. 28.

Europe, and Asia, being best known and probably most numerous in the waters north and northwest of Europe. It is a very abundant species, and yet the localities where it has been ascertained to breed are but few in number.

Messrs. Evans and Sturge met with it in abundance in the waters around Spitzbergen, where they were attracted toward the vessel in a large flock by the carcass of a seal. At first the birds were very timid, only skimming over it, and settling on the water at some distance, to reconnoitre. At last one ventured to alight upon it, and began to feed, but was soon interrupted by the arrival of others, among whom a lively contest ensued for the best positions. By the time they had been left far in the wake of the vessel, they had assembled in a vast crowd. At other times they were seen skimming swiftly over the water, after the manner of a European Kestrel, and as noiselessly as an owl. One of the lofty peaks of the mountains, known as the Alkenfels, that stood out like an immense horn, was literally alive with swarms of Fulmars, Brunnich's Guillemot, Black Guillemots, and Kittiwake Gulls. These had their nests in its inaccessible fastnesses, secure from the depredations of man or beast.

This bird was found abundant all around Spitzbergen, and was also met with at the very northernmost point attained by Parry's Expedition. Dr. Malmgren found it breeding by the thousands on the north side of Brandywine Bay, lat. 80° 24′ N. It was also found breeding, but in smaller numbers, on the Alkenhorn, where Professor Newton obtained its eggs. Dr. Malmgren also found it breeding plentifully on Bear Island. Professor Newton adds, in a note, that the very limited number of breeding-places of the Fulmar forms a curious contrast to the extraordinary abundance of the species. Among the British Islands, St. Kilda is said to be its only place of abode. About the year 1839 it was first found breeding about the Faröe Islands, where it has since much increased, and now occupies several spots in that group of islands. In Iceland it has four or five stations.

Captain Elmes, who visited the breeding-place above referred to — St. Kilda — ("Ibis," 1869) gives a full account of it. Soon after landing he started with some of the best cragsmen for the cliffs at the north side of the island. On reaching the summit of Conachan, the highest point, he came suddenly on a precipice not less than 1220 feet in height. The whole of this immense face of rock was so crowded with birds that the water was seen far below as if through a heavy snow-storm, and the birds, which were flying in front of the cliff, almost obscured the view. All the ledges near the top were covered with short turf, full of holes, in which the Fulmars were sitting on their eggs, with their heads and part of their bodies exposed outside. In some cases they were quite concealed; but generally the soil was too thin for them to make more than a slight excavation. Thousands of Fulmars were flying backward and forward, with a quiet, owl-like flight; and although the air was full of them, hardly one ever came over the top of the cliff.

After admiring the scene for some time the Captain prepared to descend; and on arriving at the first ledge, where the Fulmars were, he had no difficulty in collecting the eggs, which were laid in small holes among the stones, or in the turf on a few bits of grass, or on the stems of the sea-pink, and so slightly built as hardly to suffice to keep the eggs from the bare ground. The birds were very tame, and sometimes allowed themselves to be caught with the hand. The eggs were quite fresh; and all that he took on that part of the cliff were distinctly marked with reddish-brown dots and freckles. All the eggs from other places were spotless.

The young Fulmars, as soon as fledged, are eagerly sought for as food by the St. Kildians; and even the old birds — as Mr. Scoresby states — when cleared of the skin and every particle of fat, are tolerably good eating. He further says that this bird is remarkably light and swift on the wing, and that it can fly to windward in the severest gales, and rest on the water with complete composure in the most tremendous seas. In heavy gales it flies quite low, skimming over the surface of the water.

The Fulmar when caught vomits from its mouth nearly a wine-glassful of clear yellow oil, with minute green particles floating in it, of which oil the St. Kildians collect large quantities. All the birds taken on their nests were females, and their eyes were not yellow, but black or dark brown. The feathers of the breast were unusually thick and close, and there was a bare hollow place on the stomach of the size and shape of the egg.

Mr. Wheelwright states that the Fulmar is not seen on the Swedish coast in summer, but that it is occasionally met with there in winter and in the autumn, and never farther south on the Norwegian coast than Trondhjem. It breeds in the far north, in the islands off Nordland, and Finland; but Iceland appears to be its principal breeding-place. The female lays but one white egg, said to be three inches in length, and two in breadth.

Mr. Gillett saw the Fulmar in the waters around Nova Zembla, where it was a constant attendant on ships in the Arctic Sea, and was easily caught with a baited hook. When placed on deck it was quite unable to rise, or even to stand upright, but shuffled along with the help of its wings. It would, as soon as caught, readily eat blubber; and if thrown overboard would come again to the hook without the least hesitation. This bird never settles on the flat ice; but on one occasion was seen on the sloping side of an iceberg. It was usually either on the wing, or sitting on the water.

Von Heuglin did not find this species anywhere about on the shores of Nova Zembla, but on the high sea he saw it everywhere between that island and the Norwegian coast.

Mr. E. L. Layard mentions meeting with a single example of this species in the Antarctic Ocean, in latitude 44° S. Afterward, on the 16th of September, when sailing along the southern coast of Tasmania, he again saw a single specimen of this bird, which came close under the stern of the vessel, and was several times very nearly taken.

Dr. Walker mentions that, in the voyage of the "Fox," upon approaching the coast of Greenland, the Fulmars first made their appearance, and were thence met with as far as the Expedition sailed. This species is given by Professor Reinhardt as one of the resident birds of Greenland.

These birds were first noticed by Mr. Kumlien off Belle Isle August 20; and from this point northward they increased in numbers, and were seen everywhere, both close in shore and far out to sea, at all times and in all weathers. They were very common in Cumberland until the middle of October, and were especially abundant off the shore at Cape Chidly, Resolution Island, Grinnell Bay, and Frobisher's Straits. On Blue Mountain, Ovifak, Greenland, they were breeding in myriads to its very summit, at the height of two thousand feet. Their abundance near Cape Searle is also spoken of as something extraordinary, and they were so tame about their nesting-places that they could be killed with a stick. In their greediness they are quite equal to Vultures. This Fulmar possesses extraordinary powers of flight, and is very graceful when on the wing.

This is given by Dr. Bessels as being one of the species secured by the "Polaris" Expedition, and Captain Feilden ("Ibis," October, 1877) mentions it as being quite common in the north water of Baffin's Bay; these birds following the ships until they entered the pack off Cape Sabine. On the 26th of June, 1876, on the coast of Grinnell Land (lat. 82° 30′ N.), a single Fulmar was seen; and a few days later another was picked up dead on the shore, some two miles farther north. This species was not again observed until the return of the Expedition to Baffin's Bay in September, 1876.

Mr. George C. Taylor states that, in a voyage from Liverpool to New York, he saw, on the 22d of May, large flocks of these birds near the coast of Newfoundland. Mr. Boardman informs me that the fishermen represent this bird — known to them as the White Hagdon — as being quite common off the coast of Labrador, where it is said to breed.

Neither Mr. Lawrence nor Mr. Giraud mentions this bird as being known in the waters of Long Island or New York; but Audubon cites that region as its southern limit, and in August, on a voyage from England to New York, he procured several examples of this species. They were quite fearless, and floated on the water very buoyantly, some swimming about with great ease. He did not meet with any on the coast of Labrador, though he was told that they are regularly observed in spring to move northward in files opposite the entrance of the Straits of Belle Isle; and Captain Sabine states that while the ships were detained by the ice in Jacob's Bay, latitude 71°, from the 24th of June to the 23d of July, Fulmars were passing in a continual stream to the northward, in numbers inferior only to those seen in the flights of the Passenger Pigeon.

The Fulmar is extremely greedy of the fat of the whale. As soon as the flensing process begins, these birds flock in from all quarters, and sometimes accumulate to the number of several thousands, fearlessly advancing within a few yards of the men employed in cutting up the carcass; even approaching near enough to be knocked down with the boat-hook, or taken alive, and frequently glutting themselves so completely as to be unable to fly.

Mr. Macgillivray describes the egg of the Fulmar as being pure white in color, when clean, and varying in size from 2.63 inches to 3.12 in length by 2.00 inches in its average breadth. On the 30th of June, having descended a nearly perpendicular precipice six hundred feet in height, the whole face of which was covered with nests of the Fulmar, he enjoyed an opportunity of watching its habits. The nests had all been robbed about a month before by the natives, who esteem the eggs of this bird above all others. Many of the nests contained each a young bird a day or two old at farthest, thickly covered with long white down. The young ones were very clamorous on being handled, and vomited a quantity of clear oil, with which he observed the parent birds feeding them by disgorging. The old birds, when taken hold of, vomit a quantity of clear, amber-colored oil, which imparts to the whole bird, its nest, and young, and even to the rock which it frequents, a peculiar and very disagreeable odor. This oil is one of the most valuable productions of St. Kilda.

This bird, called *pacifica*, was described by Mr. Audubon from a specimen obtained by Mr. Townsend on the Pacific coast. It chiefly differed from the common Fulmar in the shape and size of its bill. Dr. Cooper ("Am. Nat." Vol. IV.) met with birds of this species in close proximity to the coast of Monterey, attracted thither by the whale-fishery. They were called by the whalers "Tagers" and "Haglets," were quite common off the shore, and were seen at times feeding on the flesh of the whale, but were more frequently observed chasing the Gulls to make them disgorge. This was in May. A specimen supposed to belong to this species — as Dr. Cooper states — was found by Mr. Lorquin dead on the beach near San Francisco in winter, and is now in the collection of the Academy. Dr. Cooper has since seen many other dead specimens on the beach both there and at San Diego, but not in a condition to be preserved. He has also seen them along the whole southern coast, and at all seasons of the year, but always too far from the land to be shot, and very shy. They very rarely enter bays, and when they do, are so constantly in motion that only by chance do they come within range; and it is useless to pursue them. They are usually seen in chase of the Gulls, obliging the latter to disgorge, when the Fulmars seize the morsel before it reaches the water. Dr. Cooper has also seen this bird picking up scraps in the neighborhood of whale-ships, near San Diego.

Dr. Pickering mentions, in his Journal, that on the 29th of April, 1841, on the coast of Oregon, several specimens were taken with hook and line. They were in an ashy and somewhat mottled plumage, and were all young birds. One set at liberty was quite unable to rise from the deck, and was destitute of the power of standing, though it could run with the aid of its wings. In alighting in the water, it takes the same care in folding and adjusting its wings, without wetting them, as the Albatross. One was observed to seize a *Thalassidroma* violently, and to hold it under the water as if for the purpose of drowning it; but whether the attempt succeeded or not was not noticed. The small Petrel did not appear to be afraid of this species.

Rodgers' Fulmar Petrel, or *Lupus*, as it is called by the natives, is an inhabitant of the Prybilof Islands, where it was found by Mr. H. W. Elliott. He states that it is the only representative of the *Procellarinæ* that he saw on or about the islands. It repairs to the cliffs, on the south and east shores of Saint George's, in great numbers, coming up early in the season, and selecting some rocky shelf, secure from all enemies save man, where, making no nest whatever, it lays a single large, white, oblong-oval egg, and immediately begins sitting upon it. Of all the water fowls, this is the one most devoted to its charge, for it cannot be scared from the egg by any demonstration that may be made in the way of throwing stones or shouting, and it will rather die as it sits than take to flight. The Fulmar lays between the 1st and the 5th of June; the eggs are very palatable, being fully equal to those of the domestic Duck, and even better. The natives lower themselves over the cliffs, and gather a large number of them every season.

This species of Fulmar never flies in flocks, and pairs early. It is then exceedingly quiet, and is never heard to utter any sound, save a low droning croak when it is disgorging food for its young. The chick comes out from the shell a perfect puff-ball of white down, gaining its first plumage in about six weeks. This is a dull gray, black at first, but by the end of the season it becomes like the parents' in coloration, only much darker on the back and scapularies. Its egg is naturally very similar to that of *Fulmarus glacialis*. As a general rule it is more elongated than the egg of the eastern bird; but this difference is not very striking. The shell of the egg is rougher, and filled with innumerable raised granulations and minute depressions. Its average measurement is 2.90 inches in length, and 1.90 in breadth. The color is white, but liable to be stained, and soiled from various causes, with dirty yellow or brown discolorations.

Specimens of the eggs of this bird were also obtained at St. George's by Captain Smith and by Mr. Dall. Their extreme length was 3.00 inches, and the least breadth 1.85.

Genus PRIOCELLA, Hombron and Jacquinot.

Priocella, Homb. & Jacq. Compt. Rend. XVIII. 1844, 357 (type, *P. Garnoti*, Homb. & Jacq., =*Procellaria glacialoides*, Smith).

Char. Similar to *Fulmarus*, but bill much slenderer, the nasal tubes shorter, more depressed, concave on top, and separated by a wide space from the maxillary unguis.

P. glacialoides.

The generic name *Thalassoica*, Reich. ("Syst. Av." 1852, p. iv) has usually been employed for this species. But, aside from any question of priority (*Thalassoica* dating 1852, and *Priocella* 1844), the type of *Thalassoica* is explicitly stated to be the *Procellaria antarctica* (Gmel.), a bird which the late Professor W. A. Forbes has recently ("Zool. 'Challenger,'" Vol. IV. 1882, p. 59) made the type of a new genus, *Aeipetes*, and which is certainly perfectly distinct generically from the type of the genus *Priocella*. *Aeipetes*, however, is clearly a synonyme of *Thalassoica*.

Priocella glacialoides.

THE SLENDER-BILLED FULMAR.

Procellaria tenuirostris, Aud. Orn. Biog. V. 1839, 333; B. Am. VII. 1844, 210 (not of Temm. 1828). — Lawr. in Baird's B. N. Am. 1858, 826. — Baird, Cat. N. Am. B. 1859, no. 637.

Thalassoica glacialoides, b. *tenuirostris*, Bonap. Consp. II. 1856, 192.

Fulmarus tenuirostris, Coues, Check List, 1873, no. 583.

Priocella tenuirostris, Ridgw. Pr. U. S. Nat. Mus. Vol. 2, 1880, 209; Nom. N. Am. B. 1881, no. 706. — Coues, 2d Check List, 1882, no. 817.

Procellaria glacialoides, Smith, Illustr. S. Afr. B. 1849 (?), t. 51.

Thalassoica glacialoides, Reichenb. Syst. Av. 1852, p. iv. — Bonap. Consp. II. 1856, 192. — Coues, Pr. Ac. Nat. Sci. Phil. 1866, 30.

Thalassoica glacialoides, a. *polaris*, Bonap. Consp. II. 1856, 192.

Procellaria Smithi, Schleg. Mus. P.-B. Proc. 1863, 22.

Priocella Garnoti, Homb. et Jacq. Voy. Pole Sud. III. 1853, pl. 32, fig. 42 (*fide* Gray).

Hab. Seas throughout the southern hemisphere; also, whole Pacific coast of North America (common off the Columbia River). Apparently absent from the North Atlantic.

Sp. Char. *Adult:* Head, neck, and lower parts white; upper parts pale pearl-gray, fading gradually into the white of the head; remiges dark slate, the inner webs of the primaries chiefly white. "Irides brownish black; nostrils, culmen, and a portion of the base of the upper mandible bluish lead-color; tips of both mandibles fleshy horn-color, deepening into black at their points; remainder of the bill pinky flesh-color; legs and feet gray, washed with pink on the tarsi, and blotched with slaty black on the joints" (Gould).[1]

[1] Male killed at Valparaiso, Chili, Aug. 4, 1879: "Legs gray, with blue stains; bill gray, with blue patches" (Sharpe, P. Z. S. 1881, p. 11).

Total length, about 18.50 inches; wing, 13.00–13.50; tail, 5.00; culmen, 2.10; tarsus, 1.90.

A specimen from South Africa has a much slenderer bill than have two examples from Oregon; the bill is also differently colored, the dusky of the basal portion of the maxilla being almost or quite absent, and that at the tip more restricted.

This species was first described by Audubon from a specimen procured near the Pacific coast by Dr. Townsend, which was said to have been taken at sea, not far from the mouth of the Columbia River. The only information in regard to it, as furnished by Mr. Townsend, is derived from a brief manuscript note appended to the bird, and quoted by Audubon, to the effect that it was first observed when about a day's sail from the mouth of the Columbia. Its habits are spoken of as almost precisely the same as those of *Daption capensis*, both keeping constantly around the vessel, and frequently alighting in her wake, for the purpose of feeding. It was easily taken with a hook baited with pork, and at times — particularly during a gale — was so tame as almost to allow itself to be taken with the hand. The stomachs of most of the birds that Dr. Townsend captured were found to contain a species of sepia and some oil.

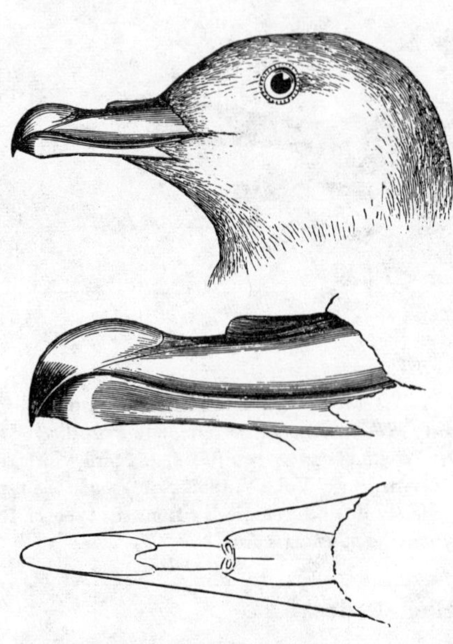

According to Mr. Cassin, it has a most extensive range of locality, being known to frequent the southern points of both of the great divisions of the globe, and those of Australia, and many other localities in the Pacific Ocean. Only a single specimen was found among the collection brought home by the Wilkes Exploring Expedition, which was labelled as having been obtained on the coast of Oregon.

According to Dr. Cooper, the only more recent evidence of the appearance of this species on our Pacific coast, and of its claim to be classed as a bird of California, is founded upon a supposed skeleton of a bird of this species obtained on the beach of Catalina Island in June, 1863.

Genus **PRIOFINUS**, Hombron and Jacquinot.

Priofinus, Homb. & Jacq. Compt. Rend. XVIII. 1844, 355 (type, *Procellaria cinerea*, Gmel.).
Adamastor, Bonap. Consp. II. 1856, 187 (type, *A. typus*, Bp. = *Procellaria cinerea*, Gmel.).

Char. Size medium; rectrices, twelve; bill moderately stout, the culmen much shorter than the tarsus, and about three times the greatest depth of the bill near the base; nasal tubes short, and separated from the maxillary unguis by a space equal in extent to about two thirds the length of the unguis, which is more than twice as long as the nasal tubes; nostrils nearly circular, opening directly forward.

Priofinus cinereus.

THE BLACK-TAILED SHEARWATER.

Procellaria cinerea, GMEL. S. N. I. 1788, 563.
Priofinus cinereus, HOMB. & JACQ. Compt. Rend. XVIII. 1844, 355.
Puffinus cinereus, LAWR. in Birds N. Am. 1858, 835. — BAIRD, Cat. N. Am. B. 1859, no. 651.
Adamastor cinereus, COUES, Pr. Philad. Acad. 1864, 119. — STREETS, Bull. U. S. Nat. Mus. no. 7, 1877, 29.
? *Procellaria melanura*, BONN. "Enc. Méth. 1790, 79."
Adamastor melanurus, COUES, Check List, 1873, no. 595.
Priofinus melanurus, RIDGW. Pr. U. S. Nat. Mus. Vol. 2, 1880, 209; Nom. N. Am. B. 1881, no. 707. — COUES, 2d Check List, 1882, no. 830.
Procellaria hæsitata, LICHT. ed. FORST. Descr. An. 1844, 208. — GOULD, B. Austr. VII. 1848, pl. 67 (not of KUHL, Beitr. Zool. 1820, 142; Tem. Pl. Col. 1820, 416, = *Œstrelata hæsitata* !).
Adamastor typus, BONAP. Consp. II. 1856, 187.
Procellaria adamastor, SCHLEG. Mus. P.-B. Procell. 1863, 25.
Puffinus Kuhlii, CASS. Pr. Philad. Acad. 1862, 327 (not of BOIE).

HAB. South Pacific Ocean; accidental off coast of California (Monterey; LAWRENCE).

SP. CHAR. *Adult:* Head, neck, and back silky cinereous, fading insensibly into whitish on the chin, throat, and foreneck; wings, rump, and upper tail-coverts darker and more brownish than the back; primaries and tail dusky. Lower parts white, the crissum and whole under surface of the wing brownish gray, the flanks, and sometimes the sides, tinged with the same. Bill dull light horn-yellow, the nasal tubes, culmen as far as the unguis, and the maxillary sulcus blackish; legs and feet light brownish, in the dried skin.[1]

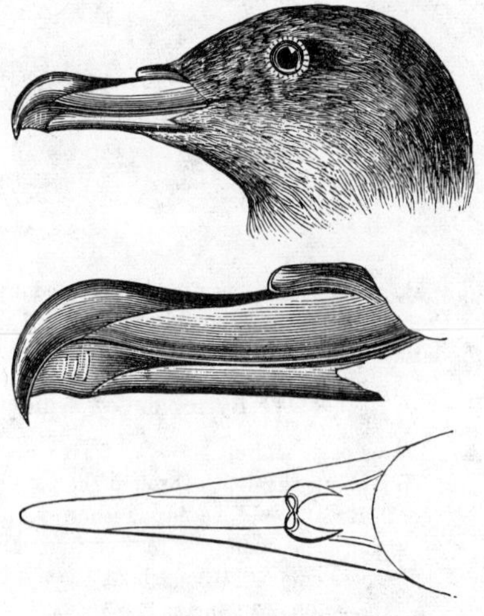

Wing, 12.25–13.50 inches; culmen, 1.75–1.85; depth of bill through base, .70–.75; tarsus, 2.25–2.30; middle toe, 2.50–2.60.

The history of the manners and our knowledge of the distribution of this species is wanting. All that is known in regard to it is that it was first referred to as one of our Western coast-birds by Mr. Lawrence, under the name of *Procellaria hæsitata*, based upon an example said to have been killed off the coast near Monterey, and found in the collection of N. Pike, Esq. Afterward, in the "Pacific Railroad Reports," Vol. IX., it was given as *Puffinus cinereus*.

In the "Proceedings of the Philadelphia Academy," 1862, Mr. Cassin describes as *P. Kuhlii* certain examples that had been taken, Sept. 11, 1853, by Professor F. H. Storer, of the Rogers Exploring Expedition, about fifty miles off the Cape of Good Hope. These are regarded as identical with the Monterey example; and these two instances of the occurrence of this species in widely separated localities constitute the sum of our scanty knowledge of its distribution.

[1] "Irides dark brown; culmen and nostrils black; tip of upper mandible blackish horn-color; tomia whitish horn-color; lower part of under mandible blackish horn-color; feet white, tinged with blue, the outer toe brownish black" (GOULD).

Genus PUFFINUS, Brisson.

Puffinus, Briss. Orn. VI. 1760, 131 (type, *Procellaria puffinus*, Brünn., = *P. anglorum*, Temm.).
Nectris, Bonap. (ex Forst.), Consp. II. 1856, 201 (type, *Puffinus brevicaudus*, Brandt).

Char. Similar to *Priofinus*, but bill much slenderer, the nasal tubes not more than half as long as the maxillary unguis, depressed anteriorly, ascending basally, the nostrils opening obliquely

P. Stricklandi.

upward, usually narrower, and separated by a thick septum; culmen much shorter than the tarsus; space between the nasal tubes and the unguis equal to about three fourths the length of the latter.

Synopsis of American Species of Puffinus.

A. Lower parts white.

a. Bill stout, the depth through the base equal to one third its length; nostrils circular.

1. **P. Kuhlii.** Above, brownish gray, the dorsal feathers tipped with paler; sides of the head and neck, along the line of junction of the gray and white, transversely undulated with these colors. Wing, about 13.00–14.00 inches; culmen, 1.80–2.00; depth of bill through base, .65–.75; tarsus, 1.85–2.00; middle toe, 2.10–2.25. *Hab.* Middle Atlantic, chiefly the eastern side.

2. **P. borealis.** Similar to *P. Kuhli*, but much larger. Wing, 14.50 inches; tail, 6.50; culmen, 2.25; depth of bill through base, .75; tarsus, 2.20; middle toe, 2.30. *Hab.* Off coast of Massachusetts.

b. Bill slender, the depth through the base decidedly less than one third the total length; nostrils longitudinally oval, more horizontal.

3. **P. major.** Above, sooty grayish brown, the dorsal feathers with paler tips; longer upper tail-coverts mostly white; abdomen more or less clouded with smoky gray or grayish brown; flanks and crissum chiefly grayish brown; bill dusky. Wing, 11.50–13.00 inches; culmen, 1.80–1.85; depth of bill at base, .60–.65; tarsus, 2.20–2.25; middle toe, 2.40–2.50. *Hab.* Atlantic Ocean generally.

4. **P. creatopus.** Above, sooty slate, the dorsal feathers with paler tips; no white on upper tail-coverts; malar region, sides of the throat, and sometimes the anal region, indistinctly barred, or transversely spotted, with grayish; flanks and crissum sooty grayish; bill pale

horny or buffy, the culmen darker, the ungui grayish. Wing, 12.50–13.25 inches; culmen, 1.60–1.70; depth of bill through base, .65–.75; tarsus, 2.05–2.12; middle toe, 2.15–2.40. *Hab.* Pacific coast from California to Chili.

5. **P. anglorum.** Above, uniform blackish, the dorsal feathers without lighter tips; lower eyelid and crissum white. Wing, 8.50–9.25 inches; culmen, 1.35–1.40; depth of bill at base, .40–.45; tarsus, 1.70–1.80; middle toe, 1.65–1.70. *Hab.* North Atlantic, particularly the eastern side.

6. **P. Auduboni.** Similar in color to *P. anglorum*, but black of the head not extending below the eyes; crissum dusky, except near anal region. Wing, 7.60–8.00 inches; culmen, 1.20–1.25; depth of bill at base, .35; tarsus, 1.50–1.60; middle toe, 1.45–1.50. *Hab.* Warmer parts of the Atlantic Ocean, north to New Jersey.

[**P. obscurus.** Similar to *P. Auduboni*, but with the lower tail-coverts entirely white. *Hab.* Southern Pacific Ocean; accidental on Pacific coast of North America? [1]]

7. **P. gavia.** Similar in color to *P. anglorum* and *P. Auduboni*, but no white about the eye, and the crissum fuliginous. Wing, 9.00 inches; culmen, 1.30–1.40; depth of bill through base, .35; tarsus, 1.75; middle toe, 1.70–175. *Hab.* Coast of Lower California to New Zealand.

B. Lower parts uniform fuliginous or smoky gray, like the upper.

8. **P. Stricklandi.** Uniform fuliginous-dusky, much lighter and more grayish below; bill uniform dusky. Wing, 11.15–12.00 inches; culmen, 1.60–1.75; depth of bill through base, .50–.55; tarsus, 2.05–2.15; middle toe, 2.05–2.20. *Hab.* North Atlantic.

9. **P. griseus.** Similar in color to *P. Stricklandi*, but chin and throat paler, the under wing-coverts grayish white, with dusky shaft-streaks. Wing, 11.15–11.50 inches; culmen, 1.55–1.65; depth of bill through base, .45–.55; tarsus, 2.12–2.25; middle toe, 2.05–2.25. *Hab.* South Pacific, north to Lower California.

10. **P. tenuirostris.** Similar to the last in color, but darker; more blackish above and more gray beneath. Wing, 10.00–10.10 inches; culmen, 1.20; depth of bill at base, .40; tarsus, 1.90–1.95; middle toe, 1.90–1.95. *Hab.* North Pacific.

Puffinus Kuhlii.

THE CINEREOUS SHEARWATER.

Procellaria puffinus, LINN. TEMM. Man. II. 1820, 805 (not of LINN. 1766).
Puffinus cinereus, CUV. Règ. An. I. 1817, 554. — TEMM. Man. IV. 1840, 506 (not of AUDUBON).
Procellaria cinerea, KUHL, Beitr. Zool. 1820, 148, pl. 9, fig. 12 (nec GMEL. 1788).
Procellaria Kuhlii, BOIE, Isis, 1835, 257, sp. 25.
Puffinus Kuhlii, BONAP. Consp. II. 1856, 202. — COUES, Pr. Ac. Nat. Sci. Philad. 1864, 128; Key, 1872, 331; Check List, 1873, no. 596; ed. 2, 1882, no. 596. — RIDGW. Nom. N. Am. B. 1881, no. 708.

HAB. Eastern Atlantic, particularly in the vicinity of Madeira, and the Mediterranean Sea; casual on the coast of North America (?).

SP. CHAR. *Adult:* Pileum, nape, back, scapulars and rump light brownish cinereous, the feathers of the dorsal region with lighter terminal borders; wings much darker slaty-fuliginous, the primaries and tail uniform dark slate; upper tail-coverts mottled with white terminally. Lower parts entirely white, the anterior under wing-coverts marked with narrow dusky shaft-streaks; malar region and sides of the neck and breast, along the junction of the white and gray, transversely undulated with white and cinereous. Bill dull yellowish, dusky on the base of the ungui; legs and feet light brownish in the dried skin.

Wing, about 13.00 inches; culmen, 1.80–2.00; depth of bill through base, .65–.75; tarsus, 1.85–2.00; middle toe, 2.10–2.25.

The biography of the common Cinereous Shearwater of Western Europe is one of some little difficulty, as the name *cinereus*, by which it has been long known to

[1] King George's Sound, *fide* LATHAM, Synop. III. pt. ii. p. 417 (under "Dusky Petrel").

some writers, has been given by others to entirely different species. In speaking of one we are liable to quote accounts of habits or residence that belong to another. This species is of rare and even doubtful occurrence in the United States.

Mr. E. L. Layard ("Ibis," 1863) mentions procuring the eggs of what I presume to be this species, on islands north of Mauritius. The birds were breeding in holes in the cliffs. Their eggs are said to have measured 2.50 inches in length and 1.50 in breadth, and their color to be of a dull white.

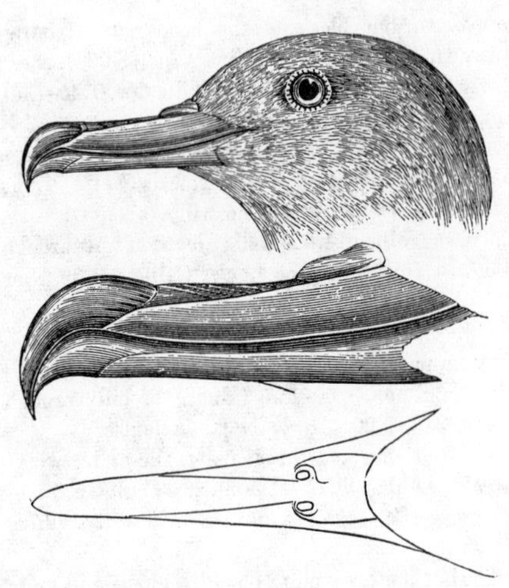

This species, referred to as *P. cinereus*, is stated to have been met with by Mr. T. L. Powys among the Ionian Islands. Mr. C. A. Wright, in his Notes on the Birds of Malta ("Ibis," 1864), speaks of it as resident and breeding on the southern coast of Malta and Gozo, and also on the small islands of Filfa and Comino. It is said to lay a single unspotted egg of pure white, rather large, and to deposit it on the bare ground, in a crevice, or under a fragment of rock. While it is sitting on its egg it allows itself to be taken, without making any attempt to escape, merely snapping with its strong sharp bill. Both the old and the young birds, when handled, are apt to eject, in a very disagreeable manner, a greenish fluid formed by their feeding on the *Inula crithmoides*, one of the few plants which grow on those rocky islets.

Lieutenant Sperling also mentions finding these birds breeding in considerable numbers among the rocks of a small precipitous uninhabited island near Malta. He also noticed them at sea sitting on the water, where they were easily approached.

Mr. Godman met with this species in all the archipelagoes of Madeira and the Canaries, and thinks that it must breed on the Desertas or some of the neighboring islands, as he saw it there in the month of June in considerable numbers. Mr. E. C. Taylor ("Ibis," 1878) mentions the capture of a single individual in Alexandria, Egypt, in April, 1877.

Mr. Howard Saunders found this bird very abundant on the Mediterranean coast of Spain. It appeared to be much less nocturnal than the *P. anglorum*, and could be found in great numbers in the daytime. Both species are said to breed on the Island of Dragonena; but, to his great surprise, he found that he was too late for their eggs on the 20th of May.

Degland and Gerbe state that this species inhabits the Mediterranean and certain points in the Atlantic Ocean. It is found off the coast of Provence, Corsica, Sardinia, Sicily, in the Adriatic, in the Grecian Archipelago, and on the coast of Barbary, etc. It is said to wander to Greenland, and to be found thence to the Canary Islands; but Mr. L. Kumlien, while he speaks of it as common from Belle Isle to Grinnell Bay, did not observe any either on Cumberland Island or on the Greenland coast.

It breeds on the islands near the harbors of Marseilles, Toulon, and Hyères, nesting in holes in the rocks, laying upon the ground, without any preparations for a nest.

The egg is large, and somewhat rounded in shape, pure white in color, and without spots, or sometimes white, washed with gray; it measures 2.75 inches in its greater diameter, and 1.85 in its smaller. The female alone performs the duties of incubation; and as soon as the young bird is hatched, abandons her nest and hides the nestling in some other retreat in the neighborhood, and visits it only during the night to bring its food.

This bird feeds principally on fish, mollusks, and crustaceans, which it collects from the surface of the water. It is most commonly seen on the approach of a tempest, or during the morning or evening twilight. The young, when they first appear, are covered with a thick downy coat of a bright ashy gray.

Puffinus borealis.

THE NORTHERN SHEARWATER.

Puffinus borealis, CORY, Bull. Nutt. Orn. Club, VI. no. 2, April, 1881, 84 (coast of Massachusetts). — JOB, ib. VIII. Oct. 1883, 244 (off Cape Cod, in August).

SP. CHAR. "Above, brownish ash, the feathers of the back becoming pale at the tips, those on the nape and sides of the neck narrowly tipped with white; on the sides of the neck and head the ash and white gradually mingling, as in *P. Kuhlii.* Tips of the upper tail-coverts white. Under eyelid white, showing clearly in contrast with the ashy gray of the head. The first three primaries are light ash on the inner webs. Wings and tail brownish gray. Under parts white, slightly touched with ash on the flanks; lining of wings white. Under tail-coverts white, the longest tinged with ash near the ends, which extend nearly to the tips of the longest tail-feathers. Outside of foot greenish black, inside and webs dull orange; bill pale yellowish at the base, shading into greenish black, but again becoming pale near the tip.

"Length, 20.50 inches; wing, 14.50; bill (straight line to tip), 2.25, depth at base, .75; tail, 6.50; tarsus, 2.20.

"The type specimen of this Shearwater was killed near Chatham Island, Cape Cod, Mass., on the 11th of October last. Being unacquainted with it, I showed it to some fishermen, and requested them to procure any birds they might meet with resembling it. During the afternoon one of the boats returned bringing a number of birds of this species. The men stated that they had met with a flock a short distance from shore, and had shot several and knocked others down with their oars. According to their statement, after firing the first shot the birds flew about them in a dazed manner, often passing within a few feet of the boat" (CORY, *l. c.*).

This Shearwater, of which the National Museum has received two specimens since the above was written, is a near ally of *P. Kuhlii*, but is decidedly larger, and somewhat different in coloration. The coloration of the bill and other soft parts are in particular supposed to differ much in life and in freshly killed examples of the two species. The two examples in the National Collection measure as follows: —

No. 82488, male adult, Chatham, Mass., Oct. 11, 1880. Wing, 13.75 inches; tail, 5.60; culmen, 2.10; depth of bill through base, .80; tarsus, 2.25; middle toe, 2.45.

No. 93040, adult (sex not given), same locality, Oct. 12, 1880. Wing, 14.00 inches; tail, 5.70; culmen, 2.25; depth of bill through base, .80; tarsus, 2.15; middle toe, 2.30.

The habits and distribution of this recently discovered species are little known, the following, by Mr. Herbert K. Job, in the "Nuttall Bulletin" (VIII. 244), comprising nearly all there is on record: —

"On the 2d of last August I was out in a yacht collecting sea-birds, about thirty miles eastward from the southeast end of Cape Cod. Wilson's Petrels, Pomarine Skuas, and Greater and Sooty Shearwaters were abundant. Both these Shearwaters were often seen sitting on the water in flocks, associating freely with one another, and were easily approached.

"On one occasion I sailed up to quite a large flock, and shot a *P. fuliginosus.* As the rest rose, I suddenly perceived amongst them a Shearwater entirely new to me; and my other barrel soon brought it down. The yacht was put about, and I was on the point of laying hands on the prize, when it suddenly started up, and was gone — much to my chagrin. Soon, however, I saw a similar one flying about in company with several of the common Shearwaters. It presently came near, and was shot, proving to be a Cory's Shearwater. This was enough to keep me on the lookout for more; and when about half way in to land, another came scaling along over the water, and was also secured. These were all that I saw. One of the fishermen to whom I showed the birds reported having seen a few others the next day. This, however, may be open to some doubt.

"In habits they perfectly resemble the other species, but are readily distinguished from *P. major* by their lighter colors and conspicuously large yellow bill. They are very tame, and when engaged in feeding may almost be run down by a boat. Considerable effort is shown in rising from the water; but when once a-wing, they fly with great swiftness.

"Nothing is known of them by the fishermen, who perhaps overlook them among the thousands of the other commoner varieties. Specimens were first taken by Mr. Charles B. Cory in nearly the same locality where mine were captured, and were described by him in the 'Bulletin' of April, 1881."

Puffinus major.

THE GREATER SHEARWATER.

Procellaria puffinus, KUHL, Beitr. Zool. 1820, 146, pl. 11, fig. 10 (not of BRÜNN, 1764).

Puffinus major, FABER, Prodr. Isl. Orn. 1822, 56. — BONAP. Consp. II. 1856, 203. — LAWR. in Baird's B. N. Am. 1858, 833. — BAIRD, Cat. N. Am. B. 1859, no. 647. — COUES, Key, 1872, 331; Check List, 1873, no. 597; ed. 2, 1882, no. 832. — RIDGW. Nom. N. Am. B. 1881, no. 709.

Puffinus cinereus, BONAP. Synop. 1828, 370, no. 311 (not of CUVIER, ex KUHL). — NUTT. Man. II. 1834, 334. — AUD. Orn. Biog. III. 1835, 555; B. Am. VII. 1844, 212, pl. 456.

HAB. Atlantic Ocean generally, but more particularly north of the equator; south to Cape of Good Hope and Cape Horn.

SP. CHAR. *Adult:* Pileum, down to below the eyes, and upper parts generally, sooty grayish brown, the first uniform, but the feathers of the back, rump, the scapulars, wing-coverts, and upper tail-coverts with considerably lighter terminal margins; nape lighter grayish brown than the pileum; primaries and tail uniform dusky; longer upper tail-coverts mostly white, their bases irregularly marked with grayish brown. Lower parts white, the abdomen more or less clouded with light grayish brown, the sides irregularly, but sparsely, marked with a darker shade of the same, the flanks and crissum nearly uniform grayish brown (sometimes much mixed with white). Bill brownish dusky; legs and feet pale brownish, in the dried skin, the outer side of the tarsus and outer toe dusky.[1]

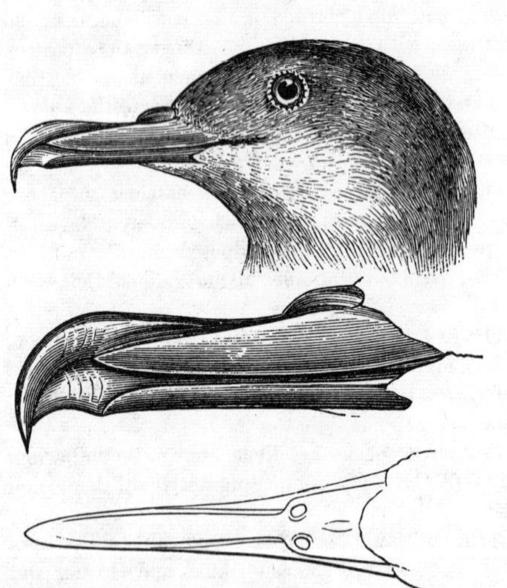

Wing, 11.50–13.00 inches; culmen, 1.80–1.85; depth of bill through base, .60–.65; tarsus, 2.20–2.25; middle toe, 2.40–2.50.

Specimens from both sides of the North Atlantic are quite identical, and we can discover nothing peculiar in an example (No. 15541; T. R. PEALE) from Tierra del Fuego.

[1] "Bill yellowish green, the tips brownish black, tinged with green. Edges of eyelids dark gray; iris brown. Feet light greenish gray, webs and claws yellowish flesh-color" (AUDUBON).

The Greater Shearwater is a North Atlantic species, passing the greater part of its life in mid-ocean, and rarely approaching either shore. It belongs only as a rare visitor either to the European or to the American coast.

The first example known to have been seen in Great Britain was obtained by Mr. Arthur Strickland, and was shot in August, 1828, on a very stormy day, near the mouth of the Tees. It was seen early in the morning, sitting on the water like a duck, and was shot as it rose. A second specimen was obtained several years afterward. Other specimens have since been procured on various parts of the English seacoast; and it is now supposed that individuals of this species had been previously met with, but confounded with the *Puffinus anglorum.*

Mr. Yarrell's figures and descriptions are taken from birds procured by Mr. D. W. Mitchell on the coast of Cornwall. Mr. Mitchell states that, in November, 1837, a man brought him one of these birds alive. He had found it asleep in his boat, about three o'clock in the afternoon, and the bird had probably taken up its quarters there by daylight. The boat was moored about two hundred yards from the shore. At that time there were a great many more of this species off Mount Bay, and two others were brought in that had been taken by hooks. He also states that this bird, in the adult plumage, appears pretty regularly every autumn, but not always in equal numbers. It had long been in several collections in Plymouth, England, where it was confounded with *P. anglorum;* but the latter is not common there, and hence the error. It is also quite abundant about the Scilly Isles, where it is known as the Hackbolt. It is a constant visitor there in the latter part of autumn, and its movements are said to be undistinguishable from those of the Manx Shearwater. Mr. Mitchell also informed Mr. Yarrell that the previous year, late in an afternoon, when the wind was blowing hard from the S.S.W., he saw through his telescope four of these birds in Mount's Bay. The weather was probably the cause of their being so far in shore, as they are generally deep-sea-goers. They had exactly the flight of *P. anglorum,* and they kept so close to the water as almost to skim the tops of the waves. He was informed that these birds appear some autumns in thousands off the islands of Love and Polpezzo.

Mr. Thompson records the occurrence of birds of this species in the south of Ireland in the autumn. Mr. Davis, of Clonmel, mentions keeping one alive about a week. It was quite lively, and ran along very rapidly with its breast about an inch and a half from the ground. Having put it on a sloping roof, the bird seemed more at its ease than it was on a level surface, and mounted rapidly to the top; though when it came to the edge it made no attempt to fly, but fell heavily to the ground. It rarely stirred during the day, but kept itself as much concealed as possible; and if it could not hide its body, would endeavor to conceal its head. The fishermen sometimes keep these birds for weeks about their houses; and in some instances they become quite tame, and do not attempt to fly. It is rarely, if ever, shot, but is usually taken with a hook. It is commonly known by the name of Hagdown. Mr. Thompson also states that Dr. R. Bell, dredging off Bundoran, on the west coast of Ireland, July 16, 1840, saw three Petrels of this species, on the wing, near him. There are specimens in the British Museum said to be from South Africa.

Yarrell does not mention how or where this bird breeds, but states that the egg is very large for the size of the bird, and that only a single one is laid. It is said to measure 2.75 inches in length by 1.87 in breadth. Its color is pure white when deposited, becoming soiled as incubation progresses.

Audubon mentions finding this species ranging from the Gulf of St. Lawrence to that of Mexico; but he very rarely met with it near the coast. In sailing to

Labrador, when off the coast of Nova Scotia, one evening in June, about sunset, he observed a great number flying from the rocky shore, and believed they were breeding there. In this belief he was confirmed by the fact that hardly one was to be seen there by day, that being the time when these birds are in the habit of remaining about their nests. In September they are to be seen far from land, both by day and by night; and in calm weather they alight on the water, and may then be easily approached. They swim buoyantly, and when sporting on the water present a very graceful appearance. Two that had been caught with hooks walked about as well as Ducks. On being approached they would open their bills, raise their feathers, and eject through their nostrils an oily substance. When held in the hand they would continue to do this, at the same time scratching with their sharp claws and bills. They refused all sorts of food, and being very unpleasant pets, were soon set at liberty; when, instead of flying away directly, they plunged into the water, dived about, then splashed and washed themselves, before they took to their wings, flying with their usual ease and grace. In the stomachs of those he opened Audubon found portions of fish, crabs, seaweeds, and oily substances. He was of the opinion that this bird does not go farther to the north than Newfoundland; but Dr. Walker in his notes on the birds observed in the voyage of the "Fox," mentions that as the vessel approached Cape Farewell large numbers of this species were observed; Professor Reinhardt speaks of it as being a resident of Greenland; and I have its eggs taken in Greenland. Mr. Kumlien found this species abundant from Belle Isle to Resolution Island, but it was not observed by him in Greenland. Faber mentions it as of rare occurrence in Iceland, as only seen on the most southern portions, and as not known to breed there.

Dr. Henry Bryant ("Proc. Boston Soc. Nat. Hist.," VIII. 72) refers to a species of *Puffinus* as very numerous in the Straits of Belle Isle; and as at that time (July) they must have been feeding their young, their breeding-places were probably at no great distance. None of the inhabitants questioned by him had ever found the egg, or knew anything about their breeding-places. It may be that — like *P. Kuhlii* — it breeds earlier than most water birds. It occurs off the coast of Massachusetts early in August, if not before.

Mr. Godman states that this species is found throughout the Azores, and that it breeds there about the end of May, in holes in the cliffs. One bird that he shot contained an egg just ready for exclusion; but the bird he refers to, Mr. Dresser states, has been ascertained to be *P. Kuhlii*, and the presence of *P. major* in that region is discredited. But according to Mr. Dresser it has been obtained off the coast of Guinea by Pel, at the Cape of Good Hope by Smith and Dr. Van Horstock, and near Tierra del Fuego by Mr. T. R. Peale.

Mr. George C. Taylor, in a voyage from Liverpool to New York, met with large flocks of this species on the 22d of May, when nearing the coast of Newfoundland. On the following day, passing the longitude of Cape Race about ten miles from shore, there were again large flocks of this Shearwater. As the ship approached, the birds would rise, not in mass, but in succession, fly half a mile or so forward, and alight until the vessel again came near them. Toward evening they were not so numerous; but throughout the day he could see flocks or companies from twenty to a hundred sitting here and there on the sea. On the return voyage, leaving New York July 15, Mr. Taylor again fell in with this species on the 21st, two days after passing Cape Race. Mr. Boardman also informs me that he has found it quite common in September off the coast of Maine and Nova Scotia.

Its occurrence on the coast of Long Island is spoken of by Giraud as very rare.

A fine specimen in the collection of Mr. Brasher is mentioned as having been procured near the Narrows. It was taken by a fisherman, who noticed it feeding on the offal of the fish that he was cleaning. Not having any gun, and being desirous of capturing this rare bird, he resorted to the ingenious stratagem of attaching to the end of a line a fish-hook; and by letting this drift among the offal upon which the bird was feeding, it became fastened to the web, and was thus secured alive. It proved to be a fine adult male. Its stomach contained a few particles of shells, and its boldness had evidently been produced by extreme hunger.

Mr. Hurdis mentions two instances of the capture of this species in Bermuda. One specimen, alive, was given him by Mr. Downes. It had been found lying on the high road, on the opposite side of Hamilton Water, June 2, 1851. It was uninjured, and in perfect plumage. On the same day a second specimen was brought to him by a man who had observed it swimming near the shore; this also was captured alive. These were the only specimens then known to have been taken in Bermuda.

Mr. Dresser states that there is no authentic account of the breeding-habits of this Shearwater, and that the eggs which do duty for it in the cabinets of collectors are almost always those of *P. Kuhlii.* But I think he is mistaken, and that eggs taken by Moravian collectors in Greenland and referred to this species are authentic.

One example given me by Mr. Wilmot, collected on an island of South Greenland, measures 2.88 inches in length by 2.00 in breadth, is nearly oval in shape, has a ground originally white, but which has been soiled by the peaty black earth from which it was excavated. Another egg, collected by a different person at the same locality, is of smaller size, and of a yellowish white; it measures 2.75 inches by 1.85.

Puffinus creatopus.

THE PINK-FOOTED SHEARWATER.

Puffinus creatopus, "Cooper (MSS.)," Coues, Pr. Ac. Nat. Sci. Philad. April, 1864, 131 (Lower California); Key, 1872, 331; Check List, 1873, no. 598; ed. 2, 1882, no. 833. — Salvin, Ibis, 1875, 377 (Juan Fernandez). — Ridgw. Nom. N. Am. B. 1881, no. 710.

Hab. Coast of Lower California (San Nicolas), south to the Juan Fernandez group of islands.

Sp. Char. *Adult:* Above, sooty slate, the feathers of the dorsal and scapular regions, with distinct terminal margins of paler grayish; wings darker than the back, the remiges nearly black, as is also the tail. Lower parts white, the malar region, sides of the throat, and sometimes the anal region indistinctly barred, or transversely spotted, with grayish. Flanks and crissum sooty grayish. Lining of the wing white, the feathers with dusky shaft-streaks. Bill pale yellowish horn-color or buffy, the ungui horn-gray, and the culmen dusky; legs and feet flesh-color in life, light brownish in the dried skin.

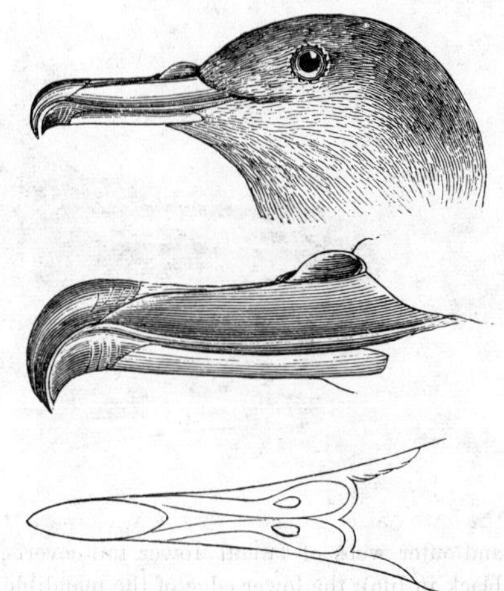

Total length, about 19 inches; extent, 45; wing, 12.50–13.25; culmen, 1.60–1.70; depth of bill through base, .65–.75; tarsus, 2.05–2.12; middle toe, 2.15–2.40.

Nothing is known as to the habits or habitat of this form, whose specific validity is not free from doubts. A single individual was procured on San Nicolas Island, in California, said to be about the size of *P. major.* It is not referable to any other known species, and Dr. Cooper has no doubts as to its validity. He thinks that its habits and those of *Priocella glacialoides* are very similar. He states that they associate together along the coast from San Francisco south. Dr. Cooper has seen and observed both species during the six warmer months of the year, but was unable to learn anything in regard to their breeding on any part of our coast. He considers it quite probable that they may breed on some of the distant Pacific islands in the winter. They are generally seen in flocks several miles off the shore, flying, like the Albatross, by rapid flappings, alternating with sailings. They congregate quickly around shoals of fish, and dive to a short distance beneath the water in pursuit of them. They often rest on the water, swimming very lightly, but not rapidly, and appear to be the most active when the wind roughens the surface of the water, enabling them to scoop up small fish from the agitated tops of the waves. Dr. Cooper further states that he found this species most abundant and most approachable about San Nicolas Island, where the water is shoal and small fish are numerous. The birds were moulting about the first of July.

Puffinus anglorum.

THE MANX SHEARWATER.

Procellaria puffinus, Brünn. Orn. Bor. 1764, 29, sp. 119. — Linn. S. N. I. 1766, 213.
Procellaria anglorum, Temm. Man. II. 1820, 806.
Puffinus anglorum, Temm. Man. IV. 1840, 509. — Nutt. Man. II. 1834, 336. — Aud. Orn. Biog. III. 1835, 604 ; B. Am. VII. 1844, 214, pl. 457. — Lawr. in Baird's B. N. Am. 1858, 834. — Baird, Cat. N. Am. B. 1859, no. 649. — Reinhardt, Ibis, 1861, 16 (Greenland). — Coues, Pr. Ac. Nat. Sci. Philad. 1864, 134 ; Key, 1872, 331 ; Check List, 1873, no. 599 ; ed. 2, 1882, no. 834. — Ridgw. Nom. N. Am. B. 1881, no. 711.
Puffinus arcticus, Faber, Prodr. Isl. Orn. 1822, 56, sp. 1.

Hab. North Atlantic generally, chiefly the eastern side; rare or casual off the American coast?

Sp. Char. *Adult:* Above, uniform fuliginous-dusky, this color occupying the sides of the head and neck. Lower parts, including the under surface of the wing and the malar region, white,

the latter, also the sides of the neck, sometimes transversely spotted with plumbeous ; femorals and outer webs of lateral lower tail-coverts, fuliginous-dusky or grayish. Bill dusky (greenish black in life), the lower edge of the mandible paler ; iris dark brown ; "inner and middle of outer side of tibia [*i. e.* tarsus] dingy orange, the rest greenish black, as is the fourth toe and outer side of the third, the inside of the latter and the whole of the second dingy orange; the webs much paler; claws brownish black" (AUDUBON).

Total length, about 15.00 inches; extent, 32.00; wing, 8.50–9.25; culmen, 1.35–1.40; depth of bill through base, .40–.45; tarsus, 1.70–1.80; middle toe, 1.65–1.70.

Although some writers speak of this species as being common on the North Atlantic coast of America, I am disposed to question the correctness of this statement. At most, so far as I can ascertain, it is possibly of very occasional and rare occurrence, and only to be met with after a violent storm; but even of this we have no evidence. So far as I can learn, this bird does not breed on any part of our coast, nor has it been noticed on any of our Arctic exploring expeditions. Except at sea, several hundred miles from our coast, it was not seen by Audubon, and is given by Professor Reinhardt as being only an occasional visitor in Greenland. Mr. Boardman informs me that a single individual of this species has from time to time been met with at sea off the coast of Maine and Nova Scotia; but he regards such an occurrence as something extremely uncommon, and as purely accidental. This bird is also mentioned as being only an accidental and very rare visitor on the coast of Long Island. It is exclusively aquatic, and never visits land except for purposes of incubation, generally selecting islands remote from the mainland, the rocky nature of which offers favorable opportunities for seclusion and safety. It is found in such situations along the western shore of Europe, from Iceland to the Mediterranean, and is more common in the latter sea than in its more northern breeding-places.

In Iceland, according to Faber, it remains all the winter, occurring only in its neighboring water. It is more common in the south, especially on the Vestmannaeyjar, than in the north.

According to Mr. Howard Saunders, it is quite abundant on the Mediterranean coast of Spain; but from the nocturnal character of its habits, it does not appear to be so common as it really is. But, he adds, pass a night at sea in a fishing-boat, and as the sun goes down, and the last rosy tint fades from the mountains, the air suddenly becomes alive with dark, sharp-winged Manx Shearwaters, dashing hither and thither in the gloom, and justifying the name the Malaga fishermen give to them of *Animas* and *Diablos*. They breed on the Island of Dragonera; but, to Mr. Saunders's great surprise, he was too late to procure their eggs, for all had been hatched out before the 20th of May.

Mr. Godman found this species at the Azores, but not so abundant as was a larger one (*P. Kuhlii?*). Like the latter, it was found to be breeding in holes in the cliffs, in May. It is highly esteemed by the inhabitants as an article of food. The specimens obtained were all very fat, and two of the females were found to contain eggs ready for exclusion.

In his account of the birds of Madeira and the Canary Islands, Mr. Godman refers to this species as occurring in all the islands of those groups, and thinks that it must breed on the Desertas and on other neighboring islands, as he saw it there in considerable numbers in the month of June.

Mr. C. A. Wright ("Ibis," 1864) speaks of it as a resident species, breeding in company with *P. cinereus* (*P. Kuhlii*) on the southern coast of Malta, and on several small rocky islands in the neighborhood. He states that he has frequently visited Filfla in June and July, and taken the eggs, as well as the young and the old birds. This species lays a single egg, of pure white color, which it deposits in a crevice or under a fragment of rock, and which is said to be smaller and more elliptical than the egg of the larger species, to which he refers under the name of *P. cinereus*.

Captain Sperling also mentions finding these birds breeding on a small rocky island near Malta. The fishermen take them in large numbers in nets, and make use of their flesh as bait.

Mr. A. G. More ("Ibis," 1865) states that this Shearwater breeds on the Scilly Islands, and also on Lundy Island, in the Bristol Channel. It was formerly abundant on the Calf of Man, but has become extinct there, its extermination being supposed to have been caused by rats. It is also said to breed on the Island of Staffa, the Outer Hebrides, in Orkney, and in Shetland.

Captain Elmes found this species breeding on the Island of Mingalay, one of the Hebrides. He was told that it was once much more common than it is now, and that the young birds were formerly very highly regarded as an article of food. Of late this Shearwater has been very nearly driven away by the intrusions of the *Fratercula arctica*.

Mr. D. W. Mitchell furnished Yarrell with an interesting sketch of his visit to the Scilly Islands. There, on a barren island called Annet, the northern shore of which is abrupt and craggy, and gradually sloping toward the south, where it narrows into a sandy peninsula, is the headquarters of this Shearwater. Yet a visitor to this spot may wait an entire day in June without seeing one of these birds, either on land or water. There are many of them near all the time, as is easily perceived by the odor that comes from their burrows. As soon as the sun is down, the birds themselves begin to issue in small parties. One evening he encountered a great gathering of not less than three hundred of them in Smith's Sound, in the middle of the tideway, washing, dipping, preening their feathers, and stretching their wings, evidently having just been roused from sleep. They are said to sit low on the water, and when disturbed there to make no noise; but in their holes they are noisy enough, the fishermen's names of *Crew* and *Cockothodon* being derived from the guttural sounds the bird pours forth as the spade approaches its nest.

The egg is frequently deposited on the fine sandy soil without any preparation, although generally there is a slight accumulation of fern-leaves and old stems. The bird lays but one egg, which when fresh is of the most dazzling whiteness, and of peculiarly beautiful texture. It is said to measure 2.42 inches in length by 1.75 in breadth, and to be very large in comparison with the size of the bird.

This Shearwater when handled vomits a very offensive oil, which is apparently of a green color, although the stain which it leaves is yellow. The quantity of this fluid discharged is often enormous. The young bird when just hatched is covered with a grayish black down, except a stripe along the centre of the breast and belly, which is white.

This species is also found on the coast of Norway, on the Faröe Islands, and about Cape Farewell. It is rare on the east coast of England. Mr. Strickland procured it from Smyrna.

Puffinus Auduboni.

AUDUBON'S DUSKY SHEARWATER.

Puffinus obscurus, BONAP. Synop. 1828, 371; Consp. II. 1856, 204 (nec *Procellaria obscura*, GMEL.). — NUTT. Man. II. 1834, 337. — AUD. Orn. Biog. III. 1835, 620; B. Am. VII. 1844, 216, pl. 458. — LAWR. in Baird's B. N. Am. 1858, 835. — BAIRD, Cat. N. Am. B. 1859, no. 650. — COUES, Pr. Ac. Nat. Sci. Philad. 1864, 137; Key, 1872, 331; Check List, 1873, no. 600; ed. 2, 1882, no. 835.

? *Puffinus Lherminieri*, LESSON, Rev. Zool. 1839, 102 (Antilles).

Puffinus Auduboni, FINSCH, P. Z. S. 1872, 111. — RIDGW. Nom. N. Am. B. 1881, no. 712.

HAB. Warmer parts of the Atlantic Ocean; north, casually, to New Jersey; accidental in Europe.

SP. CHAR. *Adult:* Above, uniform fuliginous-dusky; lower parts, including lower half of the lores, suborbital region, auriculars, sides of the neck, and under surface of the wing white, the auricular region clouded with grayish dusky; sides of the breast dusky grayish; femorals and outer webs of lateral lower tail-coverts (sometimes nearly whole crissum) fuliginous-dusky. "Bill light blue, the tips black, mouth light blue; edges of eyelids light blue, iris bluish black; outside

of tarsus and toes indigo-black, inside and webs pale-yellowish flesh-color, claws bluish black" (AUDUBON). *Downy young:* Side of head and neck, with throat and chin, naked, or with very minute and scant downy flecks, these more conspicuous along the middle line of the throat. Rest of the head, neck, and body covered with a smoky-gray down, this shorter and denser on the lower parts, where paler or grayish white along the middle line; looser and longer on the head and neck above, and back. Bill and feet colored as in the adult. (Described from No. 80980, Saba, W. I.; F. A. OBER.)

Total length, about 11.00 inches; extent, 26.00; wing, 7.60–8.00; culmen, 1.20–1.25; depth of bill through base, .35; tarsus, 1.50–1.60; middle toe, 1.45–1.50.

According to Dr. Finsch (l. c.), the *Puffinus obscurus* (GMEL.) is a Pacific Ocean species, distinguished by its white under tail-coverts, larger size, and by the white on the side of the head, covering the loral and auricular regions. It is not unlikely that true *P. obscurus* occurs as an accidental or occasional visitor, since Latham ("Synop." III. pt. 2, p. 417) mentions a specimen "in the Leverian Museum, said to have come from King George's Sound, on the American coast."

The Dusky Shearwater is an Atlantic species, found on the eastern coast of the United States from New Jersey to Florida. It also occurs among the West India Islands, and breeds in the Bermudas and the Bahamas. It extends its wanderings to the coast of Africa, and is said to breed in several of the groups of islands lying west of that coast. The area over which it is distributed is probably large, although not yet fully made out.

Mr. Godman was informed by some of the inhabitants of the Island of Flores that a bird which from the description given, he considers as undoubtedly belonging to this species, visits that island, arriving early in March, and nesting in the holes in the cliffs. These birds had reared their young, and had again left, before Mr. Godman arrived; and he was unable either to see them or to procure a specimen. The inhabitants frequently tame and rear the young of this species; and they are said to afford great amusement from the grotesque manner in which they waddle about. In a visit subsequently made by this gentleman to Madeira and the Canaries, he states that he succeeded in identifying this species, and found it abundant all over that group of islands; and has no doubt that it breeds on the Desertas and on other neighboring islands, as he saw it there in considerable numbers, though he failed to procure examples.

This species was ascertained by Major Wedderburn to breed on Gurnet-head Rock; and is supposed to be the same as the bird described as the "Cahow" by Captain Smith, in his account of Bermuda, in 1629. It was found breeding by Captains Orde and McLeod, and specimens of the bird, together with its eggs and young, were procured in May, 1849. To this statement Mr. Hurdis adds that this species is still known in Bermuda by the name of "Cahow," which is said to be an imitation of its peculiarly guttural note, described as sounding like the syllables *cao-hoo.* Mr. Salton Smith, of St. George, informed Mr. Hurdis that he visited Black Rock, at the entrance to Castle Harbor, where he obtained two young birds of this species and a dozen or more of their eggs. Unfortunately his boat was upset, and all the specimens lost. The two young birds were both found in the same hole, but the old ones were not seen. On the 17th of May, 1849, Captains Orde and McLeod visited Black Rock, landed without difficulty, and on a ledge half way from the summit captured two fine examples of this species. One was sitting on a single white egg; the other had nothing under it. Both were found in holes in the rock, and allowed themselves to be captured by the hand. A young bird of the same species, covered with black down, was also found upon the rock. The egg is described as about the size of that of the Common Fowl, and more finely polished on the surface.

Audubon mentions that on the 26th of June, 1826, when becalmed in the Gulf of Mexico, off the western coast of Florida, he noticed that birds of this species were quite numerous. They were skimming along near the surface of the water, and in doing this would flap their wings six or seven times in succession, and then sail for three or four seconds with great ease, having their tail much spread and their long wings extended at right angles with the body. On approaching a mass of seaweed they would raise their wings obliquely, drop their legs and feet, and appear to run on the water, and at length to alight. They were able to swim and dive with all the ease of a Duck. Their wings are strong and muscular. The stomach of a specimen examined resembled a leather purse, and was found much distended with fish of various kinds, partially digested or entire, some of which were two and a half inches long. Audubon also states that he has met with this species as far north as Sandy Hook; and it is said by Giraud to visit the coast of Long Island occasionally as a straggler.

Dr. Bryant, on his visit to the Bahamas, was repeatedly told of a singular bird called the Pimlico, which had a hooked bill, and only flew by night, and which bred in the Keys. This bird proved to be the present species. It was very abundant, and was found on all the uninhabited Keys which were near the channel and not frequently visited. The birds were breeding in holes in the rocks. He first met with them near Nassau, in the Ship-channel Keys. Incubation had already begun on the 24th of March. The nest consisted of a few dry twigs, and was always placed in a hole or under a projecting portion of the rock — seldom more than a foot from the surface, and never out of reach of the hand. On being caught, the bird made no noise and offered no resistance. The egg does not in the least resemble that of a Hen, being much more fragile, and more highly polished. A number of eggs were broken in endeavoring to remove the bird from the nest; they varied a good deal in size and form, some being quite rounded, and others elongated. Three of them are said to have had the following measurements: 2.32 inches by 1.41; 2.04 by 1.30; 2.01 by 1.45. Both sexes incubate.

The mournful note of these birds could be heard at all hours of the night by those anchored in the night-time near one of the Keys on which they were breeding. During the day they could be seen feeding in large flocks, generally out of sight of land.

They did not fly round much, but remained quiet on the surface of the water. Dr. Bryant did not see one of them on the banks; and his observations were in conflict with those of Audubon, as he never saw them dive, or apparently catch any fish, though they were often in company with Boobies and different species of Terns, all of which were actively employed in fishing. Between Andros and the Bank he saw on the 26th of April a large flock of this species covering the surface of the water, or hovering over it, for an extent of a square mile. Their number must have been enormous. In the stomachs of all those he examined — nine in number — he found a mass largely composed of the scales of small fish and the mandibles of squids and cuttle-fish.

Four eggs of this species (Smithsonian Institution, No. 1714), obtained by Dr. Bryant, are of a clear chalky-white color, exactly oval in shape, and have the following measurements: 2.10 by 1.45 inches; 2.05 by 1.40; 2.00 by 1.40; 2.00 by 1.40.

Puffinus gavia.

THE BLACK-VENTED SHEARWATER.

Procellaria gavia, FORST. Descr. Anim. 1844, 148. — HUTTON, Ibis, 1872, 84.
Æstrelata gavia, GIGL. & SALVAD. Ibis, 1869, 66.
Cookilaria gavia, GRAY, Handl. III. 1871, 107.
Puffinus gavia, FINSCH, J. f. O. 1872, 256. — RIDGW. Nom. N. Am. B. 1881, no. 713.
Puffinus opisthomelas, COUES, Pr. Ac. Nat. Sci. Philad. April, 1864, 139 (Cape St. Lucas); Key, 1872, 331; Check List, 1873, no. 601; ed. 2, 1882, no. 836.

HAB Coast of Lower California (Cape St. Lucas), and across the Pacific to New Zealand.

SP. CHAR. *Adult:* Above, uniform fuliginous-dusky, the feathers without distinct lighter terminal margins; lower parts, including entire under surface of the wings, white, the sides of the neck and suborbital region faintly and indistinctly undulated with dusky grayish; crissum and

posterior portion of the flanks grayish fuliginous. Bill brownish (much like the color of the back), the unguis and lower edge of both mandibles paler; iris dark brown; legs and feet pale colored in the dried skin, the outer side of the tarsus and outer toe dusky.

Total length, 12.25 to 15.00 inches; extent, about 26.00 to 32.00; wing, 9.00; culmen, 1.30–1.40; depth of bill through base, .35; tarsus, 1.75; middle toe, 1.70–1.75.[1]

[1] Captain F. W. Hutton (in the "Ibis," January, 1872, p. 84), gives the average measurements of New Zealand specimens as follows: —
"Expanse, 26; length, 12¼ to 13¼; bill along culmen, 1½, to gap, 2; tail, 3.5 to 2.75."

I am not aware that anything is known in regard to the habits or specific peculiarities of this recent addition to our fauna. It was first met with on our Pacific coast by Mr. John Xantus at Cape St. Lucas, in Lower California, where he procured two fine specimens. It is supposed to occur along the whole of our Pacific coast as far north at least as Oregon. Some eggs have been received by the Smithsonian Institution from the sea-coast of Northern California. From their size and their close resemblance to the eggs of other members of this family, there can be but little doubt that they are eggs of birds of this species.

Puffinus Stricklandi.

THE SOOTY SHEARWATER.

Puffinus fuliginosus, STRICKL. P. Z. S. 1832, 129 (not *Procellaria fuliginosa* of KUHL, 1820). — LAWR. in Baird's B. N. Am. 1858, 834. — BAIRD, Cat. N. Am. B. 1859, no. 648. — COUES, Key, 1872, 332 ; Check List, 1873, no. 602 ; ed. 2, 1882, no. 837. — RIDGW. Nom. N. Am. B. 1881, no. 714.

Nectris fuliginosa, KEYS. & BLAS. Wirb. Eur. 1840, p. xciv.

Nectris fuliginosus, COUES, Pr. Ac. Nat. Sci. Philad. 1864, 123.

Puffinus cinereus, DEKAY, Zool. N. Y. Birds, 1844, 287, pl. 136, fig. 298.

Procellaria tristis, LICHT. ed. FORST. Descr. An. 1844, 23.

Puffinus tristis, GRAY, Ibis, 1862, 44. — BULLER, B. N. Zeal. 1873, 317.

Puffinus Stricklandi, RIDGW. MS.

HAB. North Atlantic Ocean ; south to the coast of New England.

SP. CHAR. *Adult:* Uniform fuliginous-dusky, much lighter and more grayish underneath ; scapulars, interscapulars, and wing-coverts sometimes indistinctly paler on their terminal margins. Bill uniform dusky, sometimes with a brownish tinge ; legs and feet dusky brownish (in the dried skin), the outer side of the tarsus and outer toe blackish.

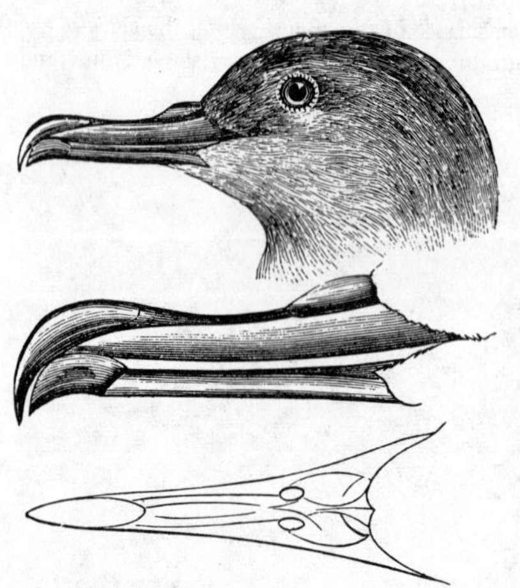

Wing, 11.15–12.00 inches ; culmen, 1.60–1.75 ; depth of bill through base, .50–.55 ; tarsus, 2.05–2.15 ; middle toe, 2.05–2.20.

This species is of very nearly the same size and form as *P. major*, but is slightly smaller in all its measurements, has the bill decidedly more slender, and the tarsus and middle toe more nearly of the same length.

The history, habits, and distribution of the Sooty Shearwater have been little known. On our eastern coast it is abundant from the waters of the North Atlantic as far south as South Carolina. It escaped the notice of our earlier ornithologists, and no reference is made to it either by Wilson, Nuttall, or Audubon. Indeed all the information we have in regard to this species is very vague and unsatisfactory. Its breeding-places and its manner of reproduction have remained entirely unknown. It is at times very abundant during the month of August off the coast of Massachusetts, and in the latter part of that month in 1871, during the prevalence of stormy weather, a large number of birds of this species were driven by the storm into Wood's Hole. This Shearwater is stated — on not entirely trustworthy authority — to be especially abundant off the coast of Newfoundland, but to be much more rare on the opposite shores of Europe. Dekay, in his Report on the Birds of New York, mentions this bird as having been occasionally captured on the coast of New York, and speaks of it as occurring from the Gulf of Mexico to Newfoundland. Degland and Gerbe assign to it the same habitat, and regard its appearance on the European coast as purely accidental, and as limited chiefly to the coast of the British Islands. It has been several times observed off the coast of Normandy, in the neighborhood of Dieppe.

By some writers the Fuliginous Shearwater has been regarded as only an immature form of *Puffinus major*. The accounts of its capture indicate that it is more abundant on the eastern coast of England than on the southern or western.

Captain Feilden informed Mr. Dresser that he observed this species, in company with *Puffinus major*, sixty miles south of Cape Farewell on the 22d of June, 1875, and was informed that it was common off the coast of Labrador. It is abundant in the Bay of Fundy and off the coast of Nova Scotia and New Brunswick. It has been found in the Atlantic as far south as the Cape of Good Hope, where Mr. Smith states it to be common.

Puffinus griseus.

THE DARK-BODIED SHEARWATER.

Procellaria grisea, GMEL. S. N. I. 1788, 564 (nec KUHL, 1820).
Puffinus griseus, FINSCH, J. f. O. 1874, 209. — SALVIN, Rowley's Orn. Misc. IV. 1876, 236. — RIDGW. Nom. N. Am. B. 1881, no. 715.
"*Procellaria tristis*, J. R. FORST. Descr. Anim. 1844, 23" (SALVIN). — HUTTON, Ibis, 1872, 83.
Nectris amaurosoma, COUES, Pr. Ac. Nat. Sci. Philad. April, 1864, 124 (Cape St. Lucas).
Puffinus amaurosoma, GRAY, Handl. III. 1871, 102. — COUES, Key, 1872, 332; Check List, 1873, no. 603; ed. 2, 1882, no. 838.
Nectris fuliginosus, a. *chilensis*, BONAP. Consp. II. 1856, 202.
"*Puffinus chilensis*, PH. & LANDB."[1]
Gray Petrel, LATH. Synop. III. pt. 2, p. 399.

HAB. Coast of Lower California (Cape St. Lucas); thence to the South Pacific (New Zealand, etc.).

SP. CHAR. *Adult:* Above, uniform fuliginous-dusky, the tips of some of the feathers indistinctly lighter; lower surface much paler, or smoky grayish; lining of the wing grayish white, mottled with smoky gray. Bill dusky grayish brown, sometimes tinged with grayish white; legs and feet brownish (reddish in life ?).[2]

Wing, 11.15–11.50 inches; culmen, 1.55–1.65; depth of bill through base, .45–.55; tarsus, 2.12–2.25; middle toe, 2.05–2.25.

Having compared the type of *Nectris amaurosoma*, COUES, and a Chilian example of what is unquestionably the same species, with specimens of the Atlantic *P. Stricklandi*, NOBIS (*P. fuliginosus*, AUCT., nec KUHL, nec GMEL.), we can see no reason for uniting them; on the other hand, they appear to be very distinct. Furthermore, the Pacific specimens correspond very exactly with Latham's description of his "Grey Petrel," upon which the *Procellaria grisea* of Gmelin is based.

P. griseus is smaller in all its measurements than *P. Stricklandi;* has the under wing-coverts white, faintly mottled with pale gray, and with very distinct shaft-streaks of darker gray; while in *P. Stricklandi* these feathers are smoky gray, mottled with white (the latter, however, prevailing near the bend of the wing), and without conspicuous dark shaft-streaks. In *P. griseus* the chin and upper part of throat are lighter gray than in *P. Stricklandi.*

1 On labels of specimens in Coll. U. S. Nat. Mus., from Museo Nacional of Chili.

2 According to Captain F. W. Hutton ("Ibis," January, 1872, p. 83), the fresh colors are as follows: "The bill is bluish white, passing into black on the culmen and gonys; feet and legs bluish white; in the young birds the bill, legs, and feet are brownish black."

The type specimen of the *Puffinus amaurosoma* of Coues was taken off the coast of Cape San Lucas. The National Museum also possesses specimens from the coast of Chili. According to Buller, it is extremely abundant in the neighborhood of Stewart's Island and along the adjacent coast of New Zealand.

The only accounts I can find touching the nidification of this bird are — the statement of Mr. Buller that its egg is white, with reddish-brown stains, and measures 3.25 inches in length and 2.00 in breadth; and the Notes of Mr. Travers, quoted by Mr. Dresser, that this Shearwater is common all around the coasts of the Chatham Group, where it burrows in peaty ground a horizontal hole, from three to four feet deep, and turning slightly to the right or left. At the end of this hole it forms a rude nest of twigs and dead leaves. Only one egg is laid, and the male is said to assist in incubation; and the parent birds are very savage while on the nest, biting and scratching those who molest them. The old birds roost on the shore, and the noise they make during the whole night is described as being something absolutely frightful. Taken out of their holes, they fluttered about on the ground for some time in a confused manner before they made for the sea.

Puffinus tenuirostris.

THE SLENDER-BILLED SHEARWATER.

Procellaria tenuirostris, Temm. Pl. Col. 1828, 587. — Schleg. Mus. P.-B. Proc. 1863, 26.
Puffinus tenuirostris, Temm. & Schleg. Fauna Jap. Aves, 1849, 131, pl. 86. — Coues, Key, 1872, 332; Check List, 1873, no. 604; ed. 2, 1882, no. 839. — Ridgw. Nom. N. Am. B. 1881, no. 716.
Nectris tenuirostris, Bonap. Consp. II. 1856, 202. — Coues, Pr. Ac. Nat. Sci. Philad. 1864, 126.
Priocella tenuirostris, Nels. Cruise Corwin, 1883, 152 (not of authors !).
Puffinus curilicus, Licht. Nomencl. Mus. Berol. 1854, 100.

Hab. North Pacific, including the coast of Northwestern America (Sitka, Kadiak, Unalashka, Kotzebue Sound, etc.).

Sp. Char. *Adult:* Above, uniform fuliginous-dusky; beneath, light smoky gray, darker on the flanks and crissum, lighter on the chin. Bill dusky brownish; legs and feet pale-colored, the outer side of the tarsus and outer toe dusky.

Wing, 10.00–10.10 inches; culmen, 1.20; depth of bill at base, .40; tarsus, 1.90–1.95; middle toe, 1.90–1.95.

This species quite closely resembles the *P. nativitatis*, Streets,[1] from Christmas Island, Pacific

[1] Puffinus (Nectris) nativitatis, Streets, Bull. U. S. Nat. Mus. no. 7, 1877, 29.
Uniform dusky-fuliginous, slightly paler beneath. Bill deep black; legs and feet dusky. Wing, 9.75 inches; culmen, 1.25; depth of bill through base, .45; tarsus, 1.75; middle toe, 1.70.

Ocean, but is much lighter colored beneath, *P. nativitatis* being dark fuliginous below, only a few shades paler than the upper parts. The proportions are also quite different.

This species appears to be exclusively an inhabitant of the North Pacific coasts. Mr. Dall refers to it as the "Seal Bird," and states that a specimen, a perfect skin, was bought of Isaac Koliak, an Eskimo of great intelligence, who informed him that he had bought it at Kotzebue Sound, when on a visit, having never himself seen such a bird on Norton's Sound. The man of whom this bird was purchased said that it was called *Minklok tingmynk*, or "Seal-bird," as it is only found with the seals, and follows them in their migrations.

Examples of this species are stated by Mr. Cassin to have been taken off the coast of Japan, near the eastern shore of Niphon, in lat. 36° N.; and Messrs. Blakiston and Pryer mention another example obtained after a typhoon at Yoshino, Tamato, the nearest sea being forty miles distant. It had been struck down by a Hawk. It agreed with the figure in the "Fauna Japonica." Its local name is given as *Umikamome*. Nothing is known in regard to its distribution, numbers, habits, or breeding-place.

Genus **ŒSTRELATA**, Bonaparte.

Aestrelata, Bonap. Consp. II. 1856, 188 (type, *Procellaria hæsitata*, Kuhl).
Cookilaria, Bonap. Consp. II. 1856, 190 (type, *Procellaria Cookii*, Gray).
Pterodroma, Bonap. Consp. II. 1856, 191 (type, *Procellaria macroptera*, Smith).

Char. Bill about as long as, or shorter than, the tarsus, very deep, and much compressed; ungui very large, occupying nearly the terminal half of the bill; nasal case very short (less than one third as long as the unguis).

The species of *Œstrelata* are very numerous (about twenty being known at the present time), but only three of them are recorded from North American waters. They are the following: —

1. **Œ. hæsitata.** *Adult* (?): Forehead, sides of head, neck (all round), entire lower parts, upper tail-coverts, and base of tail white; upper parts and patch on top of head dusky, and side of head with a blackish bar. *Young* (?): White much more restricted, immaculate only on forehead, lores, and median lower parts (the latter even sometimes more or less mixed with dusky); nape and sides of neck, with upper tail-coverts, white only beneath the surface. Bill black; iris brown; tarsi and basal third, or more, of toes, with webs, yellowish in dried skins (flesh-color in life?). Wing, 11.70–12.00 inches; tail, 5.50–5.75, graduated for about 1.50–2.30; culmen, 1.20–1.45; depth of bill at base, .52–.68; tarsus, 1.35–1.40; middle toe, 1.50, or more. *Hab.* Warmer parts of Atlantic Ocean, straying north to Florida, France, and England. Sandwich Islands?
2. **Œ. Fisheri.** *Adult:* Above, silvery plumbeous, with a distinctly darker (blackish slate) area on lesser wing-covert region; greater and middle wing-coverts and tertials plumbeous-gray, very distinctly edged with white; outer primaries and their coverts blackish slate, the inner ones gradually more plumbeous; tail-feathers transversely vermiculated with white and gray, the middle feathers uniform plumbeous-gray. Lores, chin, throat, jugulum, and crissum immaculate white; forehead and crown white, spotted with dusky; abdomen, flanks, and breast smoky plumbeous on the surface, but pure white immediately beneath, this white showing through in places; a distinct dusky spot immediately before and beneath the eye; middle portion of wing-lining and inner webs of primaries pure white, the latter with a distinct blackish stripe next the shaft. Bill black; iris brown; legs flesh-color (?), pale brownish in dried skin; toes dusky, the basal third of inner web and basal phalanx of inner and middle toes pale-colored. Wing, 10.15 inches; tail, 4.00, its graduation, .75; culmen, 1.00; depth of bill at base, .40; tarsus, 1.35; middle toe, with claw, 1.70. *Hab.* Off coast of Alaska (Kadiak).

3. **Œ. gularis.** *Adult* (?) : Above, quite uniform dark sooty grayish, the concealed bases of all the feathers, however, white ; greater and middle wing-coverts lighter and less sooty grayish, but without distinct light edges ; upper tail-coverts and tail uniform rather light sooty gray, the inner webs of the latter paler, on the outer finely mottled ; chin, throat, and crissum immaculate white ; other lower parts white beneath the surface, but this overlaid by sooty gray, nearly uniform over abdomen and flanks. Under side of wings mainly white, the anterior and outer border dusky. Wing, 9.88–10.00 inches ; tail, 3.95–4.00, its graduation about .90 ; culmen, 1.02–1.03 ; depth of bill at base, .46–.50 ; tarsus, 1.20–1.37 ; middle toe, with claw, 1.55–1.70. *Hab.* South Pacific Ocean.

4. **Œ. jamaicensis.**[1] *Adult :* Uniform sooty brown, lighter beneath, darkest on occiput and sides of head ; upper tail-coverts pale lavender-gray, sometimes tinged with buff. Bill, legs, and feet entirely black ; iris (?). Wing, 11.00 inches ; tail, 5.00, its graduation, 1.30–1.50 ; culmen, 1.15–1.20 ; depth of bill at base, .60 ; tarsus, 1.40 ; middle toe, 1.70–1.80. *Hab.* Jamaica (breeding in Blue Mountains).

Œstrelata hæsitata.

THE BLACK-CAPPED PETREL.

Procellaria hasitata, KUHL, Mon. Proc. Beitr. Zool. 1820, 142, no. 11 (excl. syn.). — TEMM. Pl. Col. 416. — NEWTON, Zoologist, X. 1852, 3691.

Æstrelata hæsitata, COUES, Pr. Ac. Nat. Sci. Philad. 1866, 139 ; Key, 1872, 328 ; Check List, 1873, no. 585.

Œstrelata hæsitata, RIDGW. Nom. N. Am. B. 1881, no. 717. — COUES, 2d Check List, 1882, no. 819.

Æstrelata diabolica, BONAP. Consp. II. 1856, 189 (ex "*Procellaria diabolica*, L'HERMINIER").

Procellaria meridionalis, LAWR. Ann. Lyc. N. Y. IV. 1848, 475 ; in Baird's B. N. Am. 1858, 827.

HAB. Warmer parts of the Atlantic Ocean, straying to Florida, England, and France. Sandwich Islands ?

SP. CHAR. *Adult :* "Forehead, sides of head, neck all round, upper tail-coverts, base of tail, and all under parts white ; back clear bistre-brown (nearly uniform, but the feathers often with paler or ashy edges), deepening on the quills and terminal half of tail ; crown with an isolated blackish cap, and sides of head with a black bar (younger birds with the white of the head and neck behind restricted, so that these dark areas run together) ; bill black ; tarsi and base of toes and webs flesh-colored (drying yellowish) ; rest of toes and webs black. *Young :* Extensively dark below ?" (COUES).

Total length, about 16.00 inches ; "wing, 12 ; tail, $5\frac{1}{4}$, cuneate, its graduation, $1\frac{1}{2}$; tarsus, $1\frac{3}{8}$; middle toe and claw, $2\frac{1}{8}$; bill, $1\frac{3}{8}$, $\frac{2}{3}$ deep at base, $\frac{3}{8}$ wide ; tube, $\frac{1}{3}$" (COUES).

A specimen from the Sandwich Islands (No. 61259 ; V. KNUDSEN, coll.), labelled "*Puffinus meridionalis*," differs from the above diagnosis in several particulars, and may possibly be distinct. The entire upper parts, except forehead, are continuously uniform dusky, nearly black on the head, the nape, back, and scapulars more grayish brown ; this dark color even covers uniformly the entire side of the head and neck, except that portion of the former before the eye, and thence downward and backward across the malar region. The feathers of the nape and side of the neck, however, are white immediately beneath the surface, this color showing conspicuously wherever

[1] ŒSTRELATA JAMAICENSIS (Bancroft) Newton.
Procellaria jamaicensis, BANCR. Zool. Jour. V. 1828, 81.
Œstrelata jamaicensis, A. & E. NEWTON, Handb. Jam. 1881, 117.
Pterodroma caribbæa, CARTE, P. Z. S. 1866, 93, pl. x.
Œstrelata caribæa, AUCT.
Blue Mountain Duck, GOSSE.

This species is introduced into the synopsis on account of the possibility of its occasional occurrence off the South Atlantic coast of the United States.

the feathers may be disturbed. There is likewise no exposed white on the upper tail-coverts or base of the tail; the former are, however, very abruptly white beneath the surface, but the latter is white only at the extreme base; and the outer rectrices have a considerable amount of white on their inner webs. The lower parts are almost entirely white, there being merely a few plumbeous irregular bars on the flanks. The measurements are as follows: Wing, 11.80 inches (less than the average of *Œ. hæsitata* as given by Dr. Coues); tail, 5.75, its graduation, 2.40; culmen, 1.22; depth of bill at base, .55; tarsus, 1.40; middle toe (without claw), 1.55. In view of the differences of coloration, much more graduated tail, and smaller dimensions — and especially in view of its different habitat, no specimens of *Œ. hæsitata* having to our knowledge been reported from any part of the Pacific Ocean — the specimen in question may be really distinct. Should such prove to be the case, the name *Œ. sandwichensis* is proposed as a suitable designation.[1]

Hardly anything is known of the history, habits, and distribution of this rare species. Its claim to be counted into our fauna rests only on accident, and nothing has been ascertained in regard to either the places or the periods of its reproductive season. It is a great wanderer, or more probably, under the influences of continued storms, is occasionally driven to regions quite remote from its natural habitat. Its usual abode is said by Degland and Gerbe to be the Indian Ocean; and its occurrence in Europe and elsewhere is considered by them as only occasional and accidental.

The museum of Boulogne-sur-Mer possesses a specimen procured in that neighborhood; and it has been elsewhere observed on the coasts of France and England. Yarrell records an instance where one was taken on a heath at Southacre, Norfolk, by a boy. It was alive when captured, and greatly exhausted, but had strength enough to bite violently the hand of its captor, who thereupon killed it. This occurred in the spring of 1850. The specimen is in the private collection of Mr. Newcome, of Hockwold Hall, Brandon. A specimen of this bird from the Indian Ocean is in the Museum at Leyden. Yarrell states that one has also been taken in Australia; and one obtained in the South Seas was in Mr. Bullock's museum. A specimen brought from Hayti by John Hearne is now in the British Museum.

Mr. George N. Lawrence, in Vol. IV. "Pacific Railroad Reports," cites this species under the name of the "Tropical Fulmar," and mentions its distribution on our coast as extending from New York southward to Florida, referring to two specimens, one taken off the coast of Florida, the other on that of New York. The first of these was given to Mr. Lawrence by Dr. C. H. Stillwell, of Brooklyn, N. Y., who had obtained it in Florida in the winter of 1846. It had been wounded, and was floating in the salt lagoon, opposite Indian River Inlet, on the east coast of Florida, two hundred and forty miles from St. John River. The other specimen had been shot in the bay at Quoque, Long Island, after a severe storm, in July, 1850. No other specimens are on record.

[1] In pattern of coloration, this specimen agrees exactly with an example of *Œ. Cooki*, but has the back, scapulars, rump, and tail decidedly less ashy.

Œstrelata Fisheri.

FISHER'S PETREL.

Œstrelata Fisheri, RIDGW. Pr. U. S. Nat. Mus. Vol. 5, June 26, 1883, 656 (Kadiak, Alaska).

SP. CHAR. *Adult?* (type of the species, No. 89431, U. S. Nat. Mus. Kadiak Island, Alaska, June 11, 1882; WILLIAM J. FISHER): Head, neck, and lower parts pure white, but this unvaried only on sides of forehead, lores, malar region, chin, throat, jugulum, and crissum; feathers of middle of forehead (longitudinally) and fore part of crown, marked with a central spot of slate-color, the feathers of the hinder part of crown and occiput similarly marked, but the spots becoming gradually more transverse posteriorly, and, at the same time, the lighter borders of the feathers more grayish; a blackish spot immediately before and beneath the eye; sides of breast washed with grayish, and belly and flanks overlaid by a nearly uniform wash of smoky plumbeous, all the feathers being very pure snow-white immediately beneath the surface; many of the feathers of the sides barred with plumbeous-gray; anterior under wing-coverts dark sooty gray or slate-color, the coverts along the outer margin of the under side of the wing mainly of the same color; rest of wing-lining, with inner webs of primaries, uniform pure white, the quills having merely a narrow, but abruptly defined, dusky stripe next the shaft, the white portion being margined for a short distance along the terminal portion with grayish; axillars mainly plumbeous, or barred with the same. Nape, back, scapulars, rump, and upper tail-coverts plumbeous, darkest on the lower part of the rump, the feathers with distinct dusky shaft-streaks, except on the nape. Tail white, with very irregular zigzag bars of plumbeous-gray, the middle rectrices mainly gray (the central pair, however, are wanting). Lesser wing-coverts dark slate (many shades darker than the back); greater coverts, secondaries, and tertials plumbeous-gray, more silvery toward edge of wing, very distinctly edged with pure white; three outer primaries and primary coverts slate-black, the inner quills gradually more grayish, and narrowly bordered with white. Bill wholly deep black; tarsi, most of basal phalanx of inner toe, and basal portion of webs, light brownish (flesh-color in life?), rest of feet dusky. Wing, 10.15 inches; tail, 4.00, slightly graduated; culmen, 1.00; depth of bill at base, .40, width at base, .40; tarsus, 1.35; middle toe, 1.40.

This elegant Petrel, probably the handsomest of the genus, belongs to the delicately formed, slender-billed group containing *Œ. Cooki*, GRAY, *Œ. gavia*, FORST., *Œ. desolata*, GMEL., and *Œ. Defilippiana*, GIGL. & SALVAD. It differs from all the allied species, however, in so many marked peculiarities of dimensions and of coloration, that comparison is scarcely needed with any. To *Œ. Defilippiana* there is some resemblance, but the differences are many and striking, as follows: —

Œ. Defilippiana. Lower parts pure white, merely tinged laterally with cinereous; greater wing-coverts, secondaries, and tertials dusky, edged terminally with grayish; six middle rectrices uniform cinereous, the outer pair with exterior webs uniform white (?). Tarsi pale bluish. Wing, 9.00 inches; tail, 3.80; culmen, 1.04; tarsus, 1.07; middle toe, with claw, 1.40. *Hab.* Eastern South Pacific Ocean (off coast of Peru).

Œ. Fisheri. Lower parts overlaid by a wash of smoky plumbeous, nearly uniform on abdomen and flanks; greater wing-coverts, secondaries, and tertials, silvery plumbeous, broadly edged with pure white; only the two middle tail-feathers uniform cinereous, the outer webs of *all* the rest white zigzagly barred, or transversely vermiculated with cinereous. Tarsi pale brownish (flesh-colored in life?). Wing, 10.15 inches; tail, 4.00; culmen, 1.00; tarsus, 1.35; middle toe, with claw, 1.70. *Hab.* Eastern North Pacific Ocean (off coast of Alaska).

The most nearly related species with which we have been able to compare the present bird is *Œ. gularis*, PEALE. The latter, however, is very distinct in coloration (agreeing only in the color of the under surface of the wing), has the bill much stouter, and the tarsi and toes decidedly shorter.

Œstrelata gularis.

PEALE'S PETREL.

Procellaria gularis, PEALE, Zool. U. S. Expl. 1848, 299.
Œstrelata gularis, BREWST. Bull. Nutt. Orn. Club, IV. 1881, 94 (Livingston Co., N. Y.).
Procellaria mollis, "GOULD," CASS. U. S. Expl. Exp. 1858, 410 (not of GOULD, 1844).
Æstrelata mollis,[1] COUES, Pr. Philad. Acad. 1866, 150 (part).

HAB. Antarctic Ocean; accidental in Western New York (Livingston Co., *fide* BREWSTER, l. c.)?

SP. CHAR. *Adult?* (type specimen, No. 15706, Antarctic Ocean; T. R. PEALE): Above, nearly uniform brownish slate, more plumbeous on the secondaries and greater wing-coverts, which have very narrow (barely visible) whitish margins; paler, and with the basal white shining through on the occiput and nape. Lores, cheeks, chin, and throat white, the two latter immaculate; frontal feather slightly margined with whitish, and superciliary region mixed with white (only the tips of the feathers being dusky), forming a broken superciliary stripe extending nearly to the occiput; ante- and sub-orbital regions nearly uniform dusky, but feathers with white bases. Lower parts white, but this overlaid on breast, abdomen, flanks, and anal region with smoky plumbeous, appearing almost uniformly of this color where the feathers are undisturbed; jugulum transversely mottled or vermiculated with dusky; crissum immaculate white. Lining of wing pure white, except anteriorly and exteriorly, where the color is uniformly dusky; inner webs of primaries pure white, with an abruptly defined grayish stripe next the shaft. Tail uniform brownish gray, the inner web of the exterior feather white, mottled, or irregularly speckled, with gray. Bill uniform black; tarsi and base of toes, with webs, pale colored (pinkish or flesh-colored in life), the terminal portion of the feet blackish.

Wing, 10.00 inches; tail, 4.00; culmen, 1.05; nasal tubes, .30; length of mandible, measured from malar apex, .85; gonys, .25; tarsus, 1.30; middle toe, without claw, 1.25.

Although Mr. Cassin (l. c.) says that the specimen described above, and which is unquestionably the type of *Procellaria gularis*, PEALE, "is quite identical with the type of *P. mollis*, of which there are numerous specimens, including those of Mr. Gould, in the museum of the Philadelphia Academy," he evidently overlooked the radical difference in the coloration of the under surface of the wing. Dr. Coues, who examined the Philadelphia Academy series, says (l. c.) that in all of these "the under surface of the wing is chiefly dusky brownish; but there is an illy-defined and interrupted area of whitish, particularly toward the base of the primaries." *Œ. gularis*, then, must be considered as more nearly related to *Œ. Fisheri*, *Œ. Defilippiana*, *Œ. gavia*, and *Œ. desolata*, all of which have the under surface of the wing mainly or largely white.

A Petrel described by Mr. Brewster, in the "Bulletin of the Nuttall Ornithological Club" for April, 1881, from a specimen obtained in Livingston Co., N. Y., in April, 1880, is supposed to belong to this species. Mr. Brewster's description is as follows: —

"*Adult (?) plumage* (No. 5224, author's collection, Mount Morris, Livingston Co., N. Y., April, 1880): Upper parts, including tail-coverts and exposed surfaces of rectrices, pure cinereous, which deepens to plumbeous only on the occiput, rump, and wings, the latter having the middle and greater coverts of the same tint as the back. The feathers of the back (but not those of the rump or occiput), with the greater and middle wing-coverts, broadly tipped with ashy white, giving these parts a scaled appearance. The throat, jugulum, upper part of breast, and under tail-coverts, pure silky white. The cinereous of the upper parts comes down along the sides of the neck, encroaching more and more, and deepening in tint as it extends backward, until it throws across the abdomen a broad band of nearly pure plumbeous. Around this colored tract there is nowhere a definite line of demarcation; the cinereous of the neck fades imperceptibly into the white of the throat, and the edges of the abdominal bar become mingled with white, until the dark

[1] ŒSTRELATA MOLLIS, Gould.
Procellaria mollis, GOULD, Ann. & Mag. N. H. XIII. 1844, 363; B. Austr. VII. pl. 50. — COUES, Pr. Philad. Acad. 1866, 150.
Procellaria inexpectata, LICHT. ed. Först. Descr. An. 1844, 204.
? *Œstrelata Kidderi*, COUES, Bull. U. S. Nat. Mus. no. 2, 1875, 28 (= whole-colored phase?).

color is entirely lost along the sides under the wings and at the beginning of the under tail-coverts; while forward, on the lower part of the breast, and over the ventral region generally, the feathers are spotted, barred, or finely vermiculated, in varying shades of color. The sides of the head backward to behind the eye (where the band of color already described begins) are essentially white, but the feathers immediately below the eye are obscurely banded, and there is a narrow but distinct transocular fascia of a dark color, which barely interrupts a broad and pure white superciliary line passing from the bill to a short distance behind the eye. The forehead and crown are much mixed with white. On the forehead the white forms a broad edging to the feathers, and extending more narrowly around their tips, confines the plumbeous ashy to triangular central patches; but toward the crown it becomes restricted to the edges alone, and when the occiput is reached gives way entirely to the uniform plumbeous of that part.

"The peculiar color and marking of the wings, alike in both specimens, has already been so well treated by Dr. Coues that I will save repeating these details by referring the reader to his description, previously quoted in the present article. But in this connection it is necessary to call attention to two points which are not there noticed. The first is, that the *secondaries*, as well as the primaries, have the white areas on their inner webs. The second, that each successive primary, beginning with the first, is lighter and more plumbeous than the preceding one; but with the first *secondary*, the color abruptly darkens again, becoming on the exposed portion nearly black, and continuing uniformly so to the tertials, which are of an equally dark cast.

"The bill is black; the tarsus, obscure flesh-color with a bluish tinge. The basal third of toes, with contained webs, pale yellowish; the terminal portion black.

"*Dimensions:* Bill (chord of culmen), 1.03 inches; height at base, .46, width, .42; tarsus, 1.37; outer toe and claw, 1.65; middle, 1.70; inner, 1.43; wing, 9.88; tail, 3.95; the graduation of the rectrices, .90."

Genus **BULWERIA**, Bonaparte.

Bulweria, Bonap. Cat. Met. Ucc. Eur. 1842, 81 (type, *Procellaria Bulweri*, Jard. & Selby); Consp. II. 1856, 194.

Char. Very similar to the smaller species of *Œstrelata* (*Œ. Cooki*, etc.), but tail longer and more graduated, bill less compressed, and feet smaller. Myological formula said to be very different.

The type of this species is so much like the smaller *Œstrelatæ* (as, for example, *Œ. Cooki*) that we should hesitate to separate it generically, were it not for important anatomical differences which are said to exist. The late Professor Forbes says (Zool. "Challenger" Expedition, Vol. IV. p. 60) that "*Bulweria* is a peculiar form, with no very close ally, and must be regarded as a highly specialized form, as shown by its myological formula . . . and its peculiar cuneate tail." The tail is decidedly more graduated than in *Œstrelata Cooki* (which among the true *Œstrelatæ* approaches most nearly in this and other features), and the feet are relatively smaller; but beyond these differences we are unable to appreciate any external characters of importance.

Besides *B. Bulweri* there is said to be another species, the *B. Macgillivrayi*, Gray, from the Fiji Islands.[1]

Bulweria Bulwerii.

BULWER'S PETREL.

Procellaria Bulwerii, Jard. & Selby, Illustr. Orn. pl. 65.

Thalassidroma Bulweri, Gould, B. Eur. pl. 448. — Keys. & Blas. Wirb. Eur. 93. — Schleg. Rev. Crit. 134. — Macgill. Man. II. 264. — Gray, Gen. B. III. 648; Cat. Brit. B. 1863, 224. — Newton, Man. N. H. Greenl. 1875, 108.

Æstrelata Bulweri, Coues, Pr. Philad. Acad. 1866, 158.

Œstrelata Bulweri, Ridgw. Pr. U. S. Nat. Mus. 1880, 209; Nom. N. Am. B. 1881, no. 718. — Coues, 2d Check List, 1882, no. 820.

[1] *Thalassidroma* (*Bulweria*) *Macgillivrayi*, Gray, Cat. B. Isl. Pacif. 1859, 56.

? *Procellaria anjinho*, HEINEKEN, Edinb. Jour. Sci. Oct. 1829.
Puffinus columbinus, MOQUIN-TANDON, in Webb & Berth. Nat. Hist. Canar. II. 1841, 44, pl. 4. fig. 2 (*Procellaria columbina* on plate).
Bulweria columbina, DRESSER, B. Eur. VIII. 1871, 551.
Bulwer's Petrel, YARR. Brit. B. ed. 2, III. 636, fig.; ed. 3, III. 664, fig.

HAB. Eastern Atlantic, including coasts of Europe and Africa. Accidental in Greenland.

SP. CHAR. *Adult:* Uniform fuliginous-dusky, lighter, more grayish brown underneath, the wings blackish, except the greater coverts, which are light grayish brown, like the lower parts. Bill black; legs and feet brownish (in dried skin).

Wing, 8.00 inches; tail, 4.75, its graduation, 1.45–1.75; culmen, .85; tarsus, .90–1.00; middle toe, .95.

This bird is said to be an occasional visitor to the Bermudas; but its occurrence there must be very rare, and due to accidental circumstances; and its claim to be received into the North American fauna appears to me to be very doubtful. The first published mention of Bulwer's Petrel was made by Selby and Jardine, in the second volume of their Illustrations; and it was there described from specimens procured by Mr. Bulwer, a gentleman who had been living for several years in Madeira, where this bird was ascertained to be resident during its breeding-season, chiefly on the small adjacent islets.

Dr. Schlegel also claims to possess an example of this Petrel procured in Greenland. Gould, in the twenty-second number of his "British Birds," mentions a single instance of its occurrence in England; this was on the banks of the Ure, near Tanfield, in Yorkshire, May 8, 1837, where a specimen of this bird was found which had been dead but a short time; and Mr. Dresser records another, taken off Scarborough in the spring of 1849.

It is not known to breed elsewhere than in the Canaries and Madeira. Moquin-Tandon speaks of it as very common on the small Island of Alegranza, where it breeds in the holes in the rocks. It has a cry resembling that of a puppy, from which it receives the local name of Perrito. Mr. Godman ("Ibis," 1872) mentions finding it breeding in considerable numbers on the small Island of Deserta. It was nocturnal in its habits, and was not seen flying about in the daytime, although there were plenty of a smaller species. The nests were low down at the foot of the cliffs, under the fallen rocks, where the birds were easily caught with the hand while sitting on their eggs.

Dr. Heineken ("Edinburgh Journal of Science," October, 1829) refers probably to this Petrel as found on the uninhabited islands near Madeira and Porto Santo. He states that it first appears in February and March, begins to lay in June, hatches out its young in July, and that none are seen after September until the following spring. It is never seen in flocks, nor in the Bay, but keeps out to sea, and is in a great measure nocturnal in its habits.

In 1850 a correspondent of mine — Dr. Frere, of London — sent me a number of fine specimens of the eggs of this species procured on the group of small islands near Madeira known as the Desertas. He informed me that they had been taken in burrows màde by the bird in the soft earth under overlying bowlder-rocks, and in deep crevices in the cliffs. The eggs are of an oblong oval shape, of nearly equal size at either end, pure white in color, and measure about 1.65 inches in length by 1.20 in breadth. They are variable in size, differing in length from 1.59 to 1.76 inches, and in breadth from 1.17 to 1.23.

GENUS **DAPTION**, STEPHENS.

Daption, STEPHENS, Shaw's Gen. Zool. XIII. 1825, 239 (type, *Procellaria capensis*, LINN.).

CHAR. Size medium; bill shorter than the tarsus, depressed, its lateral outlines somewhat convex, the mandibular rami widely separated and bowed outward, the intervening space occupied by a naked, somewhat distensible skin; nasal case about three fourths as long as the unguis, depressed, except anteriorly, its upper outline gently but decidedly concave; separated from the unguis by a space equal to about two thirds the length of the case. Plumage spotted with white and dusky above, immaculate white below.

A single species, the well-known "Cape Pigeon," or "Pintado," constitutes this very distinct genus.

Daption capensis.

THE PINTADO PETREL; CAPE PIGEON.

Procellaria capensis, LINN. S. N. ed. 10, I. 1758, 132; ed. 12, I. 1766, 213.
Daption capensis, STEPHENS, Shaw's Gen. Zool. XIII. 1825, 241. — BONAP. Consp. II. 1856, 188. — LAWR. in Baird's B. N. Am. 1858, 828. — BAIRD, Cat. N. Am. B. 1859, no. 639. — COUES, Pr. Ac. Nat. Sci. Philad. 1866, 162; Key, 1872, 328; Check List, 1873, no. 584. — RIDGW. Nom. N. Am. B. 1881, no. 719.
Daptium capense, COUES, 2d Check List, 1882, no. 818.
Procellaria nævia, BRISS. Orn. VI. 1760, 146, no. 3.
Procellaria punctata, ELLMAN, Zool. 1861, 7473.

HAB. Oceans of the southern hemisphere; accidental on coast of California?

SP. CHAR. *Adult:* Lower parts (except sides of throat and chin), rump, upper tail-coverts, basal two thirds of the tail, the greater portion of the scapulars and secondaries, white; the back, rump, upper tail-coverts, and scapulars marked with deltoid spots of dark sooty plumbeous. Head and neck (except middle of the throat), uniform dark sooty plumbeous; wings chiefly sooty plumbeous, the inner primary coverts and inner webs of the primaries chiefly white, and the coverts, with much white at their bases, chiefly concealed; terminal third of the tail uniform sooty plumbeous, forming a wide, sharply defined terminal zone. Bill uniform deep black; legs and feet dusky in the dried skin, the inner and middle toes apparently varied with flesh-color or yellowish in life.

Wing, 10.25–11.00 inches; culmen, about 1.25; tarsus, 1.75; middle toe, 1.85.

The Pintado Petrel is, without much doubt, entirely accidental on the Pacific coast, if it occurs there at all, and its usual residence is the South Pacific, South Atlantic oceans, and the Antarctic seas. It was added to our fauna by Mr. George

N. Lawrence, in 1853, on the strength of a single specimen said to have been obtained on the coast of California, and now in the cabinet of that gentleman. Numerous specimens were obtained by the naturalists connected with the Wilkes Exploring Expedition, and its presence, at various places visited by their vessels, is noted in the Journal of Dr. Pickering. He first observed it on the 19th day of January, 1839, in latitude 39° south, in the Atlantic Ocean. It is subsequently mentioned by him at various points, and for the last time on the 14th of July, the same year, on the western coast of South America, the day after sailing from the harbor of Callao, in about 12° south latitude.

Mr. E. L. Layard, in his account of the sea-birds observed by him during a voyage in the Antarctic Sea, makes repeated mention of this species, which he first observed soon after leaving Capetown, August 15. He speaks particularly of its habit of alighting on the water. Between latitudes 37° and 41° south he mentions it as being very abundant, so that many were caught by letting a strong thread trail with a cork at the end of it. The birds fouled the line, which became entangled with their wings, rendering them helpless. As soon as one was thus entangled it fell into the water, and the rest immediately clustered around it.

This bird dives readily, dropping suddenly into the water, and instantly disappearing. It will also throw up its tail into the air in the manner of a Duck, and fish up bits of food from a slight depth. On the 16th of September, when running along the southern coast of Tasmania, this species was seen in vast numbers, there being frequently as many as two hundred of these birds around the vessel at one time. This Petrel is also included ("Ibis," 1862) in Mr. G. R. Gray's List of the Birds of New Zealand and of the Adjacent Islands.

Captain Hutton ("Ibis," 1865) states that the "Cape Pigeon" — as it is also called by the sailors — when caught and hauled upon the deck of a vessel, throws up from its mouth or ejects from its nostrils, like the rest of its family, a quantity of reddish, strongly offensive oil. This it does not for purposes of defence, but apparently from fright. It is never known, in moments of irritation, to eject an oily fluid from its nostrils in the manner described by Mr. Gould. When placed on deck it is unable to rise directly, but runs along with outstretched wings.

Its cry resembles the sound produced by drawing a piece of iron across a large toothed comb, and may be represented nearly by the syllables *cac-cac-cac-cac-cac.*

The breeding-place of this species was not positively known until quite recently. Gould states that it breeds in Tristan d'Acunha; but this is disputed by Captain Hutton. Darwin was informed that it resorts to the islands of South Georgia. It was not found on the Prince Edward's Islands, nor on Kerguelen Island. Sir J. Ross saw large flocks of young birds of this species in January, 1841, in lat. 71° 50′ S., near South Victoria. It seems, therefore, probable that this Petrel breeds in islands in the Antarctic Ocean. According to Captain Hutton, its usual northern limit appears to be lat. 27° S., although in one instance it was seen as far as 17° S. It was most readily caught by a thread attached to a bit of wood, with which the bird in flying becomes entangled. The power of flight of this species seems almost without any limit. Lieutenant Weld, R. N., informed Captain Hutton that a Cape Pigeon, with a piece of red ribbon around its neck, once followed the ship on board of which he was for more than fifteen hundred miles.

Captain Hutton mentions, in a subsequent voyage, his meeting with this bird, April 19, in southern latitude; but it did not become common until the 26th. From this he infers that it does not return from its breeding-grounds until the end of April. He was informed by a sailor that on a voyage to Australia, where he arrived about the middle of March, he did not see one of these birds. The same man once took seven of this species alive, and released them in the English Channel. They had been kept in a large tub, and fed with soft pork.

Mr. Layard mentions meeting with this bird, in November, in his voyage from England to Capetown, in lat. 3° 2′ N. Neither he nor any one of the officers of the ship had ever before seen it so far to the north.

Captain Hutton, in a subsequent reference to this species ("Ibis," 1871), mentions his finding it common on the Chatham Islands — a group lying five hundred miles east of New Zealand.

Mr. R. M. Sperling gives as the northern range of this species from 27° to 25° S., on the western coast of Africa, and from 26° to 25° on the eastern, and 24° on the eastern coast of South America. Captain P. R. King ("Proc. Zool. Soc.," 1834) writes that on his voyage from the meridian of the Island of Tristan d'Acunha to that of the Island of St. Paul, in about 40° south latitude, he was daily surrounded by a multitude of oceanic birds of the Petrel tribe, this species being the most abundant.

Genus **HALOCYPTENA**, Coues.

Halocyptena, Coues, Pr. Ac. Nat. Sci. Philad. March, 1864, 78 (type, *H. microsoma*, Coues).

Char. Size very small; tail a little more than half as long as the wing, graduated; tarsus a little longer than the middle toe and claw (not quite twice the culmen); plumage uniform dusky.

This genus embraces but a single species, *H. microsoma*, Coues, which is, with one exception, the smallest of the family.

Halocyptena microsoma.

WEDGE-TAILED PETREL; LEAST PETREL.

Halocyptena microsoma, Coues, Pr. Ac. Nat. Sci. Philad. March, 1864, 79 (Lower California); Key, 1872, 328; Check List, 1873, no. 586; ed. 2, 1882, no. 821. — Ridgw. Nom. N. Am. B. 1881, no. 720.

Hab. Coast of Lower California.

Sp. Char. *Adult:* Fuliginous-black, lighter and more brown on the lower parts, middle and greater wing-coverts, and anterior portion of the head. Bill and feet uniform black.

Wing, 4.80 inches; tail, 2.50, its graduation, .40; culmen, .45; tarsus, .85; middle toe, .60.

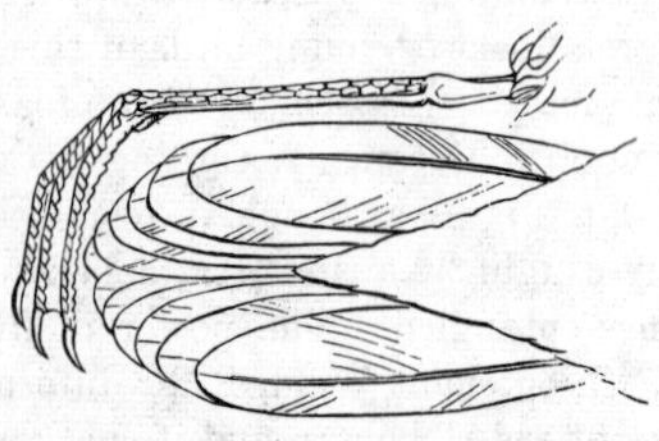

I have no information in regard to the general habits of this species, nor am I aware that the extent of its distribution is known. It is assigned to the Pacific fauna of North America in consideration of the capture of a single example, taken in May, 1861, near San Jose del Cabo, in Lower California. This specimen, an adult female, is in the collection of the Smithsonian Institution (No. 11420).

Genus PROCELLARIA, Linnæus.

Procellaria, Linn. S. N. ed. 10, I. 1758, 131 ; ed. 12, I. 1766, 212 ; (type, *P. pelagica*, Linn.).
Hydrobates, Boie, Isis, 1822, 562 (part ; same type).
Thalassidroma, Vig. Zool. Journ. II. 1825, 105 (same type).

Char. Size very small ; tail about half the wing, even, or very slightly rounded ; tarsus a little longer than the middle toe and claw (about twice as long as the culmen) ; plumage dusky, with a white rump-patch.

Although composed of several distinct species, the genus *Procellaria* has but one representative in North America.

P. pelagica.

Procellaria pelagica.[1]

THE STORMY PETREL; MOTHER CAREY'S CHICKEN.

Procellaria pelagica, Linn. S. N. ed. 10, I. 1758, 131 ; ed. 12, I. 1766, 212. — Bonap. Consp. I. 1856, 196. — Coues, Pr. Ac. Nat. Sci. Philad. 1864, 80 ; Key, 1872, 328 ; Check List, 1873, no. 587 ; ed. 2, 1882, no. 822. — Ridgw. Nom. N. Am. B. 1881, no. 721.
Thalassidroma pelagica, Vig. Zool. Journ. II. 1825, 405. — Nutt. Man. II. 1834, 327. — Aud. Orn. Biog. IV. 1838, 310 ; B. Am. VII. 1844, 228, pl. 461. — Lawr. in Baird's B. N. Am. 1858, 831. — Baird, Cat. N. Am. B. 1859, no. 645.

Hab. North Atlantic Ocean, south to the Newfoundland Banks.

[1] The following names are said to belong here or to very closely allied species or races : —
Procellaria lugubris, Natterer, Act. Ital. Med. 1844, —. — Coues, Pr. Ac. Nat. Sci. Philad. 1864, 80.
Procellaria melitensis, Schembri, Cat. Orn. del Grupp. di Malta, 1843, 118. — Coues, Pr. Ac. Nat. Sci. Philad. 1864, 81.

Sp. Char. *Adult:* Above, sooty-black or dusky-fuliginous, the upper tail-coverts, except the ends of the longer feathers, with the sides of the crissum, white. Lower parts, with anterior portion of the head, grayish-fuliginous. Bill deep black; feet blackish, the legs sometimes more brown.

Wing, 4.50–4.90 inches; tail, 2.40–2.60; culmen, .40–.45; tarsus, .90; middle toe, .60–.65.

The Least Petrel — supposed to be the original "Mother Carey's Chicken" of the sailors — appears to be an exclusively Atlantic species. Common nearly all the year in various portions of the Northern Atlantic, it is rarely found near the land, or only when breeding, or during the prevalence of severe storms. At certain seasons of the year, especially during the latter part of summer, it is found just outside of the coast of Maine and Nova Scotia, and in the Bay of Fundy. So far as I am aware, it breeds only on different portions of the Atlantic coast of Europe and in the Mediterranean, and is not known to breed on any part of the American coast. It has also been met with on the eastern coast of Africa. It is found in Iceland; but, according to Professor Newton, it is evidently of infrequent occurrence there. It is more common on the Faröe Islands during the breeding-season, its principal stations being the northern islands of Fugloe and Naalsoe, near Thorslaon. Small flocks are seen in autumn on the coast of Norway, and occasional stragglers are driven into the fiords. It has not been found breeding on the Scandinavian coasts. It is occasionally seen near the coast of Sweden, but is not known to occur in any part of Finland. It is quite common in the breeding-season on the coast of Scotland, and breeds in considerable numbers on several of the islands, being met with more or less abundantly in all three groups of the western and northern islands, in Skye, Staffa, Iona, etc. It is common in the Hebrides, and its breeding-places are numerous around most of the larger islands of that group. Its most southern breeding-place on the coast of Scotland is Ailsa Craig. It also breeds on certain parts of the coast of England and of Ireland — as off the Isle of Man, Lundy Island, the Scilly Islands, the Channel Islands, and many other islets.

Mr. T. L. Powys met with it in the Ionian Sea, near Pagania, in December, 1857. Mr. C. A. Wright ("Ibis," 1864) mentions finding it resident all the year about Malta, and very common on the south side of the island; breeding also on the neighboring Island of Filfola, where he found it laying a single white egg, without any nest.

Mr. A. G. More speaks of having found it breeding on the Scilly Islands, on Iona, Staffa, in Skye, and in all the several groups of the western and northern islands. Sir William Jardine is quoted as having seen it apparently breeding on the Isle of Man.

Captain Sperling ("Ibis," 1868) states that he met with it on the eastern coast of Africa, where, between the latitudes of Zambesi and Zanzibar, it appears to replace the *melanogaster*. The mouth of the Zambesi nearly marks its most southern range in that region.

Mr. Howard Saunders ("Ibis," 1871) states that it, or a variety of it, breeds in great abundance on the Hormigas, Isla Grossa, and other islands just outside the entrance to the Mar Menor.

In other parts of Europe, in the interior, stragglers of this species have been met with; but in all instances their appearance has been fortuitous, and owing to their inability to resist the violence of storms. In this way specimens have been obtained in Denmark, North Germany, Belgium, Holland, etc.

This bird is said also to breed on islands on the coast of Brittany, on others near Marseilles, on the small islands near Sardinia, and in various other localities, both on the Atlantic coast and in the Mediterranean Sea. It is also resident on and about the coast of Northwestern Africa — breeding on rocky islets on the coast of Algeria, where Major Locke found it nesting from the beginning of May till September, and where young birds were found from the end of May until October. It has also been taken on the Canaries, at Madeira, at Fantee in Walfisch Bay, and in other places on the southwest coast of Africa.

Mr. George A. Boardman informs me that this species occurs during the latter part of the summer — more especially in August — off the coast of Eastern Maine, Southern New Brunswick, and along the entire Atlantic coast of Nova Scotia. It is also found off the coast of Newfoundland at the same time. Audubon mentions that in August, 1830, when becalmed on the Banks of Newfoundland, he obtained several individuals of this species. In their general manner, while feeding and moving around his boat, he noticed no points in which they differed from the Wilson's and the Leach's Petrels, in whose company he found them.

We learn from an interesting sketch given by Mr. Hewitson, in his British Oology, that on an excursion through the Shetland Islands he found this bird breeding on several of the small islets in the Bay of Scalloway. These he visited on the 31st of May, in hopes of finding the eggs; but in this he was disappointed. The "Swallows," as the fishermen called them, had not yet "come up from the sea." June 16, and the three following days, he was at Foxla, but was then equally unsuccessful. The birds had arrived, although they had not yet begun laying their eggs; but numbers were already in their holes, and were easily caught; and two of them were kept alive in his room for several days. During the day they were mostly inactive; and after pacing about the floor, and poking their heads into every hole, they hid themselves between the feet of the table and the wall. He could not prevail upon them to eat anything. Their manner of walking is described as being graceful and easy, but differing from that of every other bird he had seen — this Petrel carrying its body so far forward and so nearly in a straight line, as to have the appearance of being out of equilibrium. In the evening, toward sunset, the captives left their hiding place, and for hours never ceased in their endeavors to regain their liberty — flying round the room, or fluttering against the windows. In flying, their length of wing and white rumps gave them the appearance of the European House Martin.

On the 30th of June Mr. Hewitson again visited Oxna, and found these birds only just beginning to lay. In Foxla they were breeding in the holes in the cliffs, at a great height above the sea. In Oxna, they go down under the stones with which the beach is lined, to a distance of three or four feet, or more, according to the depth to which the stones are sunk, and beneath these they deposit their eggs. On walking over the surface he could hear the birds very distinctly singing, in a sort of warbling chatter a good deal like that of Swallows, but in a harsher tone. By listening attentively he was readily guided to their retreats; and by lifting out the stones he seldom failed of capturing the birds on their nests. These latter were constructed of much the same material as that of the ground on which they were placed, and seemed to have been made with care; small bits of stalks of plants and pieces of hard dry earth were chiefly used. This Petrel never lays more than one egg. During the daytime these birds remain within their holes, and are then seldom heard. Toward night they become extremely querulous, and issue forth in great numbers, spreading far over the surface of the sea, and surround the fishermen, who attract them by throwing bits of fish overboard. The egg is described as measuring 1.13 inches in length and .80 in breadth, and as being of nearly the same size at both ends, thick-shelled, pure white, with numerous minute dots of dull red at the larger end, in a circular band.

According to Macgillivray, this bird has the same habit as Leach's Petrel, of ejecting, when handled, a quantity of pure oil, which is carefully preserved by the fowlers. This Petrel may be kept alive in confinement by smearing its breast with oil, which it will suck from the feathers, drawing each feather singly through each mandible.

This Petrel is often met with far out at sea; and will follow vessels for the sake of shelter as well as for food. When the latter is thrown to them they will very gracefully hover over the surface of the water with upraised wings, presenting very much of the appearance and movements of a large butterfly hovering over a flower. In this manner they pick up whatever is thrown to them, feeding on any fatty substance, small crustaceans, minute fishes, and almost any refuse.

Mr. Macgillivray thus describes the movements of these Petrels in a storm: "When the waves are high and the wind fierce, it is pleasant, even midst the noise of the storm and the heaving of the vessel, to watch the little creatures as they advance against the gale, at the height of scarcely a foot above the surface of the water, which they follow in all its undulations — mounting to the top of the wave, there quivering in the blast, and making good their way by repeated strokes of their long narrow wings; then sliding down the slope, resting a moment in the advancing mass of water, gliding up its side, and again meeting on its summit the force of the rude wind that scatters abroad its foam-bells. I have seen them thus advancing, apparently with little labor; and in such cases less effort must be required than when they have to encounter a gale before it has blown long enough to raise the waves, which afford them partial shelter."

Mr. Robert Gray states that in the Island of Soa he found this species having its holes in the soft earth. The entrances were about as large as rabbit-burrows. From these, other smaller galleries branch off, so that one external aperture serves as a kind of lobby for a number of pairs.

Genus **CYMOCHOREA**, Coues.

Thalassidroma, Bp. Comp. List, 1838, 64 (part; not of Vigors).
Cymochorea, Coues, Pr. Ac. Nat. Sci. Philad. March, 1864, 75 (type, *Procellaria leucorhoa*, Vieill).

Char. Size small, but larger than the preceding genera; tail much more than half the wings, forked, the feathers very broad at the ends; tarsus scarcely longer than the middle toe and claw (about one and a half times as long as the culmen); plumage dusky, with or without a white rump-patch.

The following species belong to the North American fauna, and are the only ones known: —

A. A white rump-patch.

1. **C. leucorhoa.** Uniform dusky, more fuliginous below; upper tail-coverts white, usually mixed with grayish. Wing, 6.00–6.30 inches; tail, 3.50–4.00, forked for .80–.90; culmen, .60–.65; tarsus, .90–.95; middle toe, .80–.85. *Hab.* Northern Atlantic and Pacific oceans.
2. **C. cryptoleucura.**[1] Uniform fuliginous, the head and upper parts more slaty, greater wing-coverts and tertials paler, inclining to dull grayish; remiges and rectrices dull black, the latter (except middle pair) white at base; upper tail-coverts white, the longer broadly tipped with black (as in *Procellaria pelagica*). Bill, legs, and feet (including webs) black. Wing, 5.80–6.30 inches; tail, 3.00–3.15, forked for .20–.30; culmen, .60; tarsus, .85–.90; middle toe (with claw), .85–.90. *Hab.* Sandwich Islands.

[1] *Cymochorea cryptoleucura*, Ridgw. Proc. U. S. Nat. Mus. Vol. 4, 1882, 337 (types in Nat. Mus. Coll.).

B. No white on the rump.

3. **C. melania.** Uniform fuliginous-dusky, lighter and browner beneath, the greater wing-coverts and outer webs of tertials light grayish brown. Wing, 6.80 inches; tail, 3.90, forked for 1.20; culmen, .60; tarsus, 1.20; middle toe, 1.00. *Hab.* South Pacific Ocean, north to Lower California.
4. **C. homochroa.** Smoky plumbeous, the wing-coverts lighter and more brown, remiges and tail dusky, rump and upper tail-coverts ashy plumbeous. Wing, 5.30–5.40 inches; tail, 3.30–3.50, forked for .70–.90; culmen, .50–.55; tarsus, .80–.90; middle toe, .75–.80. *Hab.* Farallone Islands, coast of California.

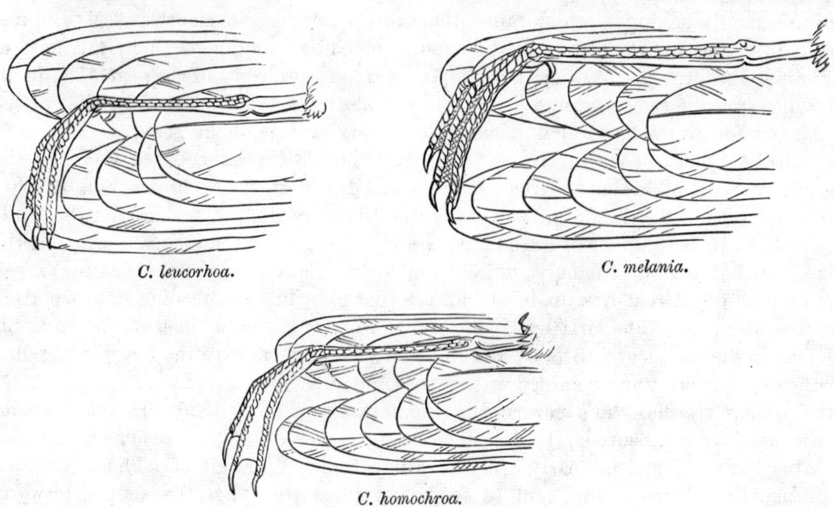

C. leucorhoa. *C. melania.*

C. homochroa.

Cymochorea leucorhoa.

LEACH'S PETREL.

Procellaria leucorhoa, VIEILL. Nouv. Dict. XXV. 1817, 422.
Cymochorea leucorrhoa, COUES, Pr. Ac. Nat. Sci. Philad. 1864, 76; Key, 1872, 329; Check List, 1873, no. 588; ed. 2, 1882, no. 823. — RIDGW. Nom. N. Am. B. 1881, no. 723.
Procellaria Leachii, TEMM. Man. II. 1820, 812.
Thalassidroma Leachii, BONAP. Synop. 1828, no. 309; Consp. II. 1856, 193. — NUTT. Man. II. 1834, 326. — AUD. Orn. Biog. III. 1835, 424; B. Am. VII. 1844, 219, pl. 459. — LAWRENCE, in Baird's B. N. Am. 1858, 830. — BAIRD, Cat. N. Am. B. 1859, no. 642.
Procellaria Bullockii, FLEMING, Brit. An. 1828, 136, no. 219.

HAB. North Atlantic and Pacific oceans, south to Virginia (Petersburg, Va., and Potomac River, near Washington, D. C. !), and Aleutian Islands; breeds from the coast of Maine northward.

Sp. Char. *Adult:* Sooty plumbeous, the head and neck clearer plumbeous, the former lighter anteriorly; lower parts decidedly fuliginous; middle and greater wing-coverts light smoky gray; remiges and tail nearly black; upper tail-coverts white, usually more or less clouded with sooty gray. Bill deep black; iris dark brown; legs and feet entirely dusky. *Downy young:* Covered with a very fluffy down of a uniform smoky gray color, the anterior half of the head almost naked.

Wing, 6.00–6.30 inches; tail, 3.50–4.00, the depth of the fork, .80–.90; culmen, .60–.65; tarsus, .90–.95; middle toe, .80–.85.

Leach's Fork-tailed Petrel — the common Mother Carey's Chicken of the Northern and Eastern New England coast — has a very extended distribution, but few birds of this family having a wider range than this. During the months of May, June, and July, and a part of August, it is found breeding in high northern latitudes in Europe, Eastern and Western North America, and probably in Eastern Asia, in all instances on the sea-coast, and never in the interior. During the remainder of the year it wanders over a large portion of the watery surface of the globe.

On the Atlantic coast of North America it breeds from the Casco Bay and the southern coast of Maine to Greenland. It breeds also in the Hebrides, and on other islands north of Scotland, but is not mentioned as breeding in Iceland, on the Faröe Islands, or in any portion of Scandinavia; and although Nilsson includes it among the birds of that region, it is only an accidental visitor there. It is mentioned by Yarrell as occurring in Great Britain, but is not referred to by him as breeding in any portion of the kingdom. The first specimen known to have been obtained was taken at St. Kilda, in the summer of 1818, by Mr. Bullock, and this is now in the British Museum. Other specimens were obtained in France, and preserved as great rarities. After the violent storms which occurred in the autumns of 1823, 1825, and 1831, several specimens were procured. It has since been taken on several occasions in various parts of Ireland, and in nearly every maritime county of England. Those captured are usually exhausted for want of food, and if secured alive die soon afterward. This species is mentioned by Professor Blasius as one of the birds which visit the shores of Heligoland.

Mr. A. G. More ("Ibis," 1865) states that the only breeding-place of this species known to exist within the British Islands is St. Kilda, one of the Outer Hebrides. Mr. J. H. Dunn mentions that it formerly nested within the Orkneys; and it is given by Mr. Dunbar in his List of the Birds of Ross-shire. Captain Elwes, who visited the Hebrides at a later date, mentions ("Ibis," 1869) finding this Petrel, in company with *Procellaria pelagica*, breeding on Mirigatay, a small islet near St. Kilda. He did not procure any of the eggs, but he had no doubt whatever that the birds were either actually breeding, or preparing so to do, in the dry peat on the tops of the cliffs.

According to Reinhardt, this Petrel is a common resident species of Greenland, breeding in all favorable localities from that region southward to the coast of Maine. The most southern and western point on which I have found it breeding is Damariscotta Island, a few miles east of the Kennebec; but it has been taken breeding on islands near Portland. Except during the breeding-season it is rare on the New England coast, and is only known in Massachusetts when driven inland by violent easterly storms. Giraud states that this species is of very rare occurrence on the coast of Long Island. He quotes a letter from Professor Baird in reference to the appearance of a large number of these birds inland, after the violent gale of August, 1842. Six or more specimens were procured in the neighborhood of Washington. Others were killed in the vicinity of Petersburg, Va., and at other points, hundreds of miles from the open sea. One was picked up near Springfield, Mass., nearly a hundred miles from the Atlantic.

Mr. Dall, in his paper on the Birds of the Eastern Aleutian Islands, states that though this species was often seen in the region south of lat. 50° N., it was not noticed by him in the region east of Unalashka. In his subsequent paper upon the Western Aleutians, he further states that though not noticed east of Amchitka, this bird breeds abundantly on the rocky islets off Atta and on the highlands of Kyska and Amchitka. As is also noticed in regard to the habits of *O. furcata*, the male seems to do a large proportion of the incubation. As a rule, the female was found to lay only one white egg, in a burrow from six inches to a foot in horizontal length. This burrow was usually in the side of a turfy bank, and often curved considerably to one side; and he never met with one absolutely straight. When handled, this bird disgorges a reddish oily fluid of a strong and disagreeable musky smell; and if the burrow was tenanted, this could be easily recognized by its smell. On the coast of Mendocino Co., Cal., this bird is known as the "Musk Bird." While breeding it is largely nocturnal in its habits. Fresh eggs were found from June 10th to the end of July. The specimens of this bird taken on the Western Aleutians are said to be darker than those from Sitka. They are summer residents only, going south in winter, and arriving at the islands in May. It was found abundant at Sitka by Bischoff, the specimens taken being more rusty-colored than is usual with birds of this species.

The appearance of Leach's Petrel in different parts of Europe has been found in all instances to have been caused by severe storms, the birds, exhausted by inability to procure food, and overpowered by the wind, having been dashed upon the shore, or even driven far into the interior. Since attention has been drawn to the subject, the records of their appearance in this manner in England, France, Portugal, and other places have become more frequent. Dr. L. von Schrenck obtained examples of this species at the Kurile Islands, and Mr. Wosnessensky procured others on the Island of Schauschu.

In the summers of 1850 and 1851 I found this species breeding on a number of small islands in the Bay of Fundy, on the coast of New Brunswick; and since then Dr. Bryant has several times met with it, also breeding in large numbers, on the low islands on the opposite shore of Nova Scotia. I first noticed it at sea, off the coast of Maine, about the middle of June, 1850. Our steamer had been overtaken by a violent northeasterly gale, and for eight hours was unable to make any headway. The sea had been lashed by the tempest into a violent commotion, and the Petrels were about in countless numbers, and seemed to be totally unmindful of the storm. They flew singly, and in no instance did I see two together. I was doubtful whether they succeeded in procuring any food; yet they appeared to be very busy, and whereever a wave broke and its crest descended in foam, the Petrel might be seen skimming its surface. Whether the sea was full of Petrels, as it appeared to be, or whether the same birds were constantly reappearing, it was impossible to tell; but not more than three or four were in sight at any one moment. I first found this species breeding on Great Duck Island, a large and inhabited island near Grand Menan, a considerable portion of which was covered by a thick growth of spruce and birch trees. The birds nested in holes among the thick network of roots, where they were nearly inaccessible. It was only with the aid of an axe and with considerable hard work that we could get to their retreats. Although it was already the 24th of June, in only one of the nests we opened was there an egg, the male bird being present; in all the other nests both birds were found, but no egg. I have since observed that during the daytime, except when the weather is lowering, the pair may always, preceding the deposition of the egg, be found in their hole. In all instances we were guided to the nest by its strong odor; otherwise it would have been impossible to distinguish which among the many hollows between the roots of the trees were thus made use of. Here, as the birds could not make any excavations, we found the nests very shallow, not more than fifteen inches in depth; there was, in fact, no proper nest, and the egg was lying on the bare soil.

The following summer I visited the Green Islands and other small islands lower down the Bay. All of these were bare of trees, and were covered with grass, and the surface consisted of soft black mould, easily penetrated. Here the whole surface of the islands, where this favorable soil was found, was honeycombed with the burrows of this Petrel. These were winding, and turned in various directions. Several after winding a few inches below the grass-roots, to the extent longitudinally of thirty inches, would again descend about four inches more, and then turn directly back toward the opening, making the excavation directly under the first, and the terminus or nest-place would be about ten inches below, and directly under, the entrance. In all there would be fully sixty inches of devious passage to reach the nest. In every instance we found the male bird alone, sitting upon the solitary egg. The female was not to be seen. The inference seems to be, that after the deposition of the egg the duties of incubation — certainly during the daytime — are performed by the male. Whether the female supplies him with food or takes his place at night-time, I am not able to state. Mr. H. B. W. Milner, as quoted by Mr. Dresser, mentions being drawn to the nest of this bird by its twittering notes, which are said to resemble those of the European Swallow. In no instance that I can recall did these birds utter a sound, not even when taken in the hand.

When their retreat was uncovered, they made no effort to escape; and the only indication of being annoyed which they gave was the ejecting, sometimes with considerable force, through their nostrils of a strong, pungent, musky oil, of a reddish-yellow color, the odor of which was very disagreeable, scenting woollen cloth for several days when thrown upon it. In one instance this oil was squirted directly into both the eyes of one of my companions, producing temporary blindness and sharp pains. A thorough ablution in sea-water, however, soon gave complete relief.

The tenacity of life possessed by this species is remarkable. One of my specimens, supposed to be dead, was closely wrapped in paper, stowed away in my trunk, and not taken out for nearly a week. It proved to have remained alive, and on being released and thrown up into the air, it flew away.

On the ground this bird is nearly helpless, and can rise on the wing only with the greatest difficulty. At first it appears to be unable to stand, but rests on the ground, its feet bent under its body. If undisturbed it partially raises itself, appears to run forward, partly on its toes, and partly by aid of its wings, and rises very gradually, not flying with any degree of speed until it has attained a height of several feet above the ground. This bird is nocturnal in its habits, keeping close during the day, except in very cloudy weather. At night it could be heard in all directions, both over the water and over the land. Arriving late one night at the wharf of Duck Island, the effect produced by these birds flying backward and forward, and all uttering their sad twittering notes, was almost startling, and strongly suggestive of unearthly sights and sounds.

The young when first hatched are covered with long loose down, neither wings nor bill being visible, and they resemble some nondescript quadruped rather than a bird in the down.

The egg — and there is never more than one — is oval in shape, but slightly more pointed at one end than at the other; the color is a dull or creamy white. Around the larger circumference is a faint ring, almost always apparent, of fine reddish dottings. These eggs are quite fragile and delicate, and measure from 1.25 to 1.40 inches in length, and from .92 to .95 of an inch in their greatest breadth. The egg of this species is an almost exact miniature of that of *Diomedea exulans.*

Cymochorea melania.

THE BLACK PETREL.

Procellaria melania, BONAP. Compt. Rend. XXVIII. 1854, 662.
Thalassidroma melania, BONAP. Consp. II. 1856, 196.
Cymochorea melania, COUES, Pr. Ac. Nat. Sci. Philad. 1864, 76 ; Key, 1872, 329 ; Check List, 1873, no. 589.
Cymochorea melæna, RIDGW. Nom. N. Am. B. 1881, no. 724. — COUES, 2d Check List, 1882, no. 824.

HAB. South Pacific Ocean, including the coast of Lower California.

SP. CHAR. *Adult:* Fuliginous-dusky, lighter and browner beneath ; middle and greater wing-coverts and outer webs of tertials light grayish brown ; remiges, larger scapulars, and tail, blackish dusky ; upper tail-coverts fuliginous, like the back. Bill, legs, and feet, entirely black.

Length, about 7.50 inches ; wing, 6.80 ; tail, 3.90, depth of its fork, 1.20 ; culmen, .60 ; tarsus, 1.20 ; middle toe, 1.00.

I can find no account of the general habits of this species, nor any indication of the area of its distribution or resort. It is said to be a visitor of the coasts of California, Oregon, and Washington Territory ; but so far as can be ascertained, there is no positive evidence of the capture of a single specimen in that region ; certainly not since 1854. Prince Bonaparte, in his Notes on the Birds collected by M. A. Delattse in his Voyage between Nicaragua and California, and in which he first describes this bird as a new species, assumes, apparently without any evidence, that it belongs to the Californian fauna, and expresses some surprise that it should have escaped previous explorers on that coast. That it should not since have been met with is a strong indication that it does not belong to our fauna.

Cymochorea homochroa.

THE ASHY PETREL.

Cymochorea homochroa, COUES, Pr. Ac. Nat. Sci. Philad. March, 1864, 77 (Farallone Islands, coast of California) ; Key, 1872, 329 ; Check List, 1873, no. 590, ed. 2, 1882, no. 825. — RIDGW. Nom. N. Am. B. 1881, no. 725.
Thalassidroma melania, LAWR. in Baird's B. N. Am. 1858, 830 (not of BONAP. 1857). — BAIRD, Cat. N. Am. B. 1859, no. 643.

HAB. Farallon Islands, coast of California.

SP. CHAR. *Adult:* Smoky plumbeous, the wing-coverts lighter and more brown, the remiges and tail dusky; rump and upper tail-coverts ashy plumbeous; anterior portion of the head inclining to ashy. Bill deep black; legs and feet brownish black.

Wing, 5.30–5.40 inches; tail, 3.30–3.50, depth of its fork, .70–.90; culmen, .50–.55; tarsus, .80–.90; middle toe, .75–.80.

This has been one of the species doubtfully attributed to the Californian coast, the occurrence of which has only recently received verification. It had not been met with there by Dr. Cooper, and until identified by Mr. Henshaw, there was no satisfactory evidence in support of its claim to a place in the fauna of North America. But little is known as to its habits, its distribution, or the places to which it resorts for breeding. Mr. Henshaw states that Petrels appear to be quite numerous along the entire coast of California. He received an example of this species from Captain Forney, who had procured it on San Miguel, where it was said to be breeding in great numbers. As usual with this family, it was nesting in burrows.

GENUS **OCEANODROMA**, REICHENBACH.

Oceanodroma, REICHENB. Av. Syst. 1852, p. iv (type, *Procellaria furcata*, GMEL.).

O. furcata.

CHAR. Size of *Cymochorea;* tail more than half as long as the wing, forked, the feathers narrowed and scalloped out toward ends; tarsus scarcely longer than the middle toe and claw (less than twice the culmen); plumage ashy, with or without white collar and lower parts.

Two species of this genus are known, distinguished by the following characters: —

1. **O. furcata.** Bluish ashy, the orbital region and wings (except greater coverts) dusky. *Hab.* North Pacific.
2. **O. Hornbyi.** Forehead, cheeks, nuchal collar, and lower parts white; quills black; rest of plumage dark gray, including a jugular band. *Hab.* North Pacific.

Oceanodroma furcata.

THE FORK-TAILED PETREL.

Procellaria furcata, GMEL. S. N. I. ii. 1788, 561.

Thalassidroma furcata, GOULD, Voy. Sulphur, Birds, 1844, 50, pl. 33. — CASSIN, Illustr. B. Cal. Tex. etc. 1855, 274, pl. 47. — LAWR. in Baird's B. N. Am. 1858, 829. — BAIRD, Cat. N. Am. B. 1859, no. 640.

Oceanodroma furcata, BONAP. Consp. II. 1856, 194. — COUES, Pr. Ac. Nat. Sci. Philad. 1864, 74; Key, 1872, 329; Check List, 1873, no. 591; ed. 2, 1882, no. 826. — RIDGW. Nom. N. Am. B. 1881, no. 726.

Procellaria orientalis, PALLAS, Zoog. Rosso-As. II. 1826, 315.

" *Thalassidroma cinerea*, GOULD." (BONAP.)

Thalassidroma plumbea, PEALE, Zool. Expl. Exp. Birds, 1848, 292.

HAB. North Pacific Ocean, south to coast of Oregon.

SP. CHAR. *Adult:* Fine light cinereous, fading gradually to white on the chin and throat, anal region, and crissum; orbital region, longer scapulars, inner wing-coverts, anterior and outer lesser coverts, alulæ, primary coverts, and remiges grayish dusky; central lesser, middle, and inner greater coverts, and tertials broadly edged with ashy white. Lining of the wing clouded

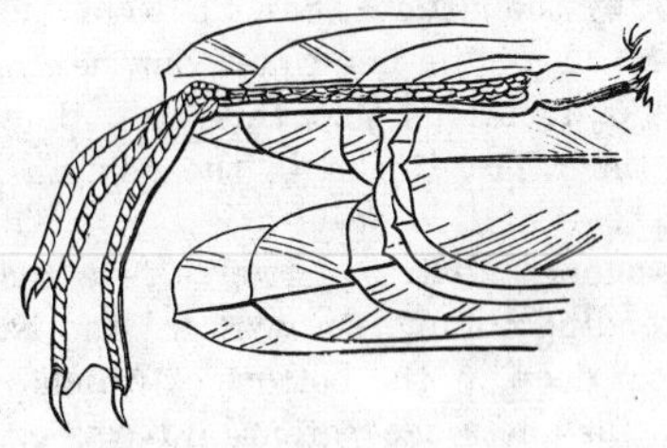

with grayish dusky and ashy white, the former predominating. Bill wholly deep black; iris dark brown; legs and feet dusky brown. *Younger:* Similar, but colors much more dingy, with little if any of a bluish cast.

Length, about 8.50 to 9.00 inches; extent, 18.25 to 19.00; wing, 5.95–6.40; tail, 3.75–4.00, forked for about 1.00; culmen, .55–.60; tarsus, 1.00–1.10; middle toe .90–95.

This species appears to be less of a wanderer than are most of its family, and to be exclusively an inhabitant of the Northern Pacific Ocean. It is an interesting addition to the fauna of the United States made by the naturalists in the Wilkes Exploring Expedition — having been previously known only as a bird of the Asiatic coast, of the islands of the North Pacific, and of Russian America. It was found in large numbers by this Expedition on the southern coast of Oregon.

This bird was first noticed by Pennant in his "Arctic Zoology," and called by him the "Fork-tailed Petrel." The only account given of it was, that it had been taken among the ice between Asia and America. Subsequently Pallas referred to it as an inhabitant of the coasts of Unalashka and the Kurile Islands.

We next find it mentioned in the Zoology of the Voyage of the "Sulphur," 1844, where it is said to have been taken at Sitka; although nothing is added in regard to its history.

Dr. Pickering, in his Journal, first records its occurrence at sea, on the 20th of April, 1840, the coast of Oregon being about two hundred miles distant. Three days later, when in sight of that coast, great numbers of this species were noticed flitting around in the track of the vessel, actively engaged in searching for particles of food thrown overboard. Generally they reminded him of Wilson's Petrel, but their wings seemed longer and their movements appeared to be more rapid; in fact, they appeared to resemble the larger *Procellariæ.* Occasionally this bird sailed in its flight; but during the greater part of the time it moved by very rapidly flexing its wings in the same manner as Wilson's Petrel. It proved to be not difficult to capture, and several specimens were taken with hook and line. The birds would dive a foot or two after the bait, and made use of their wings in and under the water, from which they evidently had not the difficulty in rising which is observable in the Albatross. Their power of swimming seemed rather feeble, yet they alighted in the water without any apparent hesitation. The dead body of one of their companions having been thrown overboard, the other birds clustered about it with as much avidity as around any other food. This bird uttered a faint cry when it was taken on board.

In addition to these notes of Dr. Pickering, Mr. Peale farther states that this species was observed in considerable numbers on the northwest coast of America, in the most northerly regions visited by the Expedition, but not farther south than the thirty-eighth degree of north latitude.

Dr. Cooper states that although he has never met with it on the coast of California, he has received a specimen obtained by Mr. E. Lorquin, of San Francisco, and shot by the latter at San Pedro in August.

Mr. Dall, in his Notes on the Avifauna of the Aleutian Islands, east of Unalashka, mentions that this bird, though not observed anywhere at sea, was found on the Chica Rocks, in the Akutan Pass, near Unalashka, breeding, June 2, 1872. The eye of this species is black. The nests were on the edge of a steep bank near the shore, and ten or twelve feet above it; and each structure was placed in a hole extending obliquely downward and backward from the face of the bank, and about a foot deep, at the bottom of which a little dry grass or fine roots were placed. In two instances the parent-bird was caught on the nest alive. Each nest contained only one small white egg, perfectly fresh — though others might have been laid afterward, had the bird not been disturbed.

Mr. Dall states, in his second paper on the Aleutian Islands, that the male of this species appears to do a large part of the work of incubation. This species, as well as Leach's Petrel, has the habit, when handled, of disgorging a reddish oily fluid of a strong and disagreeable musky smell; and one can tell by the odor of the burrow alone whether it is tenanted by a Petrel or by one of the *Alcidæ.* It was found by Mr. Dall breeding on all the less populated islands as far east as Unalashka. Unlike the reported habits of the North Atlantic Petrels, this species is never seen in stormy weather at sea, nor does it ever follow in a vessel's wake, so far as his observations go. It is occasionally seen flying about in calm, fine weather, throughout the North Pacific.

Eggs of this species in the Smithsonian Collection, obtained by Mr. Dall and by Mr. Bischoff at Sitka, Alaska (12854), are of a dirty chalky-white color, oval in shape, with rounded ends; and four present the following measurements: 1.35 by 1.00 inches; 1.30 by 1.00; 1.40 by 1.00; 1.35 by 1.00.

Oceanodroma Hornbyi.

HORNBY'S PETREL.

Thalassidroma Hornbyi, GRAY, P. Z. S. 1853, 62. — LAWR. in Baird's B. N. Am. 1858, 829. — BAIRD, Cat. N. Am. B. 1859, no. 641.

Oceanodroma Hornbyi, BONAP. Consp. II. 1856, 195. — COUES, Pr. Ac. Nat. Sci. Philad. 1864, 75; Key, 1872, 329; Check List, 1873, no. 592; ed. 2, 1882, no. 827. — RIDGW. Nom. N. Am. B. 1881, no. 727.

HAB. North Pacific Ocean (coast of Alaska).

SP. CHAR. *Adult:* "Front, cheeks, throat, collar round hind part of the neck, breast, and abdomen, pure white; crown, hind-head, a broad band in front of neck, bend of wing and lesser

wing-coverts, sooty gray; upper part of back gray; lower part of back and tail ashy gray; greater wing-coverts brownish gray; tertiaries and quills deep black.

"Total length, $8\frac{1}{4}''$; bill from gape, $10\frac{1}{2}'''$, from front, $8\frac{1}{2}'''$; tail (outer feather), $3\frac{3}{4}''$; tarsus, $1''$; middle toe, $1''$" (GRAY).

This rare species continues unknown to American collections.

This species was described by G. R. Gray, and the example from which its description was taken had been procured on the northwest coast of North America. In its general appearance and peculiarities it is said to correspond most nearly with *O. furcata.* We know nothing in regard to its specific habits or distribution. It has not been met with by any of the parties who have visited or explored the regions whence this species is said to have been obtained.

GENUS **OCEANITES**, KEYSERLING AND BLASIUS.

Oceanites, KEYS. & BLAS. Wirb. Eur. I. 1844, p. xciii (type, *Thalassidroma Wilsoni*, BP., = *Procellaria oceanica*, KUHL).

CHAR. Size very small; tail more than half the wing, forked, the feathers very broad at the ends; tarsus much longer than the middle toe and claw (about two and a half times as long as the culmen); plumage dusky, with a white rump-patch.

This genus is represented by a single species — the well-known Wilson's Stormy Petrel (*O. oceanicus*).

Oceanites oceanicus.

WILSON'S PETREL.

Procellaria pelagica, WILS. Am. Orn. VI. 1808, 90, pl. 60 (not of LINN.).
Procellaria oceanica, KUHL, Beitr. Zool. 1820, Monog. Proc. 136, pl. 10, fig. 1.
Thalassidroma oceanica, GRAY, Gen. B. III. 1849.
Oceanites oceanica, COUES, Pr. Ac. Nat. Sci. Philad. 1864, 82; Key, 1872, 329; Check List, 1873, no. 593. — RIDGW. Nom. N. Am. B. 1881, no. 722.
Oceanites oceanicus, COUES, 2d Check List, 1882, no. 828.
Thalassidroma Wilsoni, BONAP. Journ. Ac. Nat. Sci. Philad. III. 1823, 231, pl. 9. — NUTT. Man. II. 1834, 324. — AUD. Orn. Biog. III. 1835, 486; V. 1839, 645; B. Am. VII. 1844, 223, pl. 460. — LAWR. in Baird's B. N. Am. 1858, 831. — BAIRD, Cat. N. Am. B. 1859, no. 644.

HAB. Atlantic Ocean in general; Australian seas.

SP. CHAR. *Adult:* Above, fuliginous-dusky, becoming black on the remiges and tail, and fading into light brownish gray on the outer surface of the greater coverts and secondaries. Upper

tail-coverts (including their extreme tips) and sides of the crissum pure white. Lower parts plain fuliginous. Bill deep black; legs and feet black, the webs marked with an oblong central space of yellow.

Wing, 5.70–6.20 inches; tail, 3.00–3.25; culmen, .45–.50; tarsus, 1.30–1.35; middle toe, .95–1.00.

The species generally known in the books as Wilson's Petrel is emphatically a cosmopolite, and seems to be found very nearly over the whole watery expanse of the globe, in south latitude and in north latitude, and in regions so far remote as almost to warrant the conclusion that it must occur in the intervening spaces, and that the absence of evidence of its presence can by no means be held to be conclusive proof to the contrary. Its breeding-places have been, and to some extent remain, in doubt. It is especially common throughout the month of August — but at no other time, so far as I am aware — off the coast of North America from Newfoundland to New Jersey, and probably farther south. It keeps close to the shore, comes into the more open bays and harbors, and is readily attracted to the vicinity of vessels in quest of food. Eggs purporting to belong to this species, said to have been taken near Madeira, were received by Mr. Frere, of London.

According to Mr. Godman, this species is abundant and resident about the Azores, where its local name is *Alma de Mestre.* On his return from Flores to Fayal, being becalmed for several hours, and there being a great many Petrels flying about, Mr. Godman went out in a boat and shot several. They proved to be all of this species. In flying, these birds carried their legs stretched out behind them, and their feet protruding an inch beyond their tail — producing the effect of two long feathers. He could not ascertain with positive certainty that this species breeds in this group of islands, but as it is abundant there throughout the year, he has no doubt that this is the case.

Mr. E. L. Layard mentions meeting with it in the Southern Ocean in lat. 23° 30′ S., long. 72° E.; and subsequently, when in lat. 24° S., long. 75° 30′ E., he again met with it. When in lat. 32° 50′ S., long. 29° 50′ E., near the mouth of Great Fish River, these birds were most abundant; at least three hundred were in sight at one time. At no other time did he see so many together, except in his voyage out to Canada, in 1843, when they appeared off Anticosti in similar flocks. In his opinion these birds very rarely alight upon the water, for he repeatedly watched them far into the night, and still they kept on their unwearied flight; and even after the moon had set, and their tiny forms were no longer visible, he could distinguish their querulous cries.

Captain F. W. Hutton, in his voyage from London to New Zealand ("Ibis," 1867), states that he met with this species several times in the northern temperate zone, but saw none while in the tropics. It reappeared in lat. 33° S., and continued common until May 2, lat. 39° S. It was then seen occasionally until May 18, lat. 40° 40′ S., after which none were met with.

Mr. L. Kumlien in the Arctic expedition found it far more abundant than Leach's Petrel, and traced it as far north as Resolution Island. On the return voyage it was first met with a hundred miles south of Cape Farewell. It has been observed in the Pacific, and is given by Mr. Gould as a bird of Australia.

Dr. Pickering met with this species Oct. 24, 1838 (the latitude and longitude not given, but the nearest land was the coast of Africa), and a specimen was taken alive. It was found to be not only entirely incapable of perching, but even of standing upright, except by aid of its wings. It sat rather than stood, and the whole of the tarsus rested on the ground; and it walked in the same awkward position, being frequently obliged to balance itself with the aid of its wings, with a more powerful exertion of which it was enabled to run along on its toes, as it does on the surface of the water. Birds of this species continued abundant about the vessel for several days, and their coursing over the water with flitting wings reminded him of the movement of butterflies about a pool. Only in one instance was this bird seen to rest on the surface of the water. This Petrel does not sail in the continued manner of Gulls and other sea-birds, but moves by rapidly flexing its wings, somewhat after the manner of a Bat. It was continually coursing around and in the wake of the vessel, generally in considerable numbers, during the greater part of the time the expedition was in the Atlantic Ocean. It was taken in the Atlantic in lat. 35° S., and was seen occasionally as far as Cape Horn. In the Pacific it occurred at times until within a day's sail of Callao. Specimens were procured by the Expedition from various and widely remote localities.

It is often met with flying about the North Rock, Bermuda, in stormy weather; and Mr. Hurdis records the capture of a very fine specimen, shot by Mr. Harford on the 30th of June, 1853, killed some miles from shore, the date being suggestive of its breeding in that vicinity.

This species is not uncommon off Sandy Hook, within sight of land, and occasionally stragglers are seen coasting along the shores of Long Island. Mr. Giraud states that he had a favorable opportunity of observing the manners of these birds when he was making an excursion in a pilot-boat. The vessel being low, by throwing over small pieces of fat, which they seized with avidity, he was enabled to keep them very near. He observed that they were capable of a very rapid as well as a very protracted flight, at times shooting past the boat, which, under full sail, was moving at a very rapid rate, but which seemed, by comparison with the birds, to be lying at anchor. When wearied, this Petrel rests on the water; and at such times it stands with outspread wings, or runs upon its surface with facility and ease. The lightness of its body is rendered even more buoyant by the action of its wings. Its note, usually low and feeble, becomes louder and harsher during boisterous weather, and at such times is more frequently repeated.

Audubon was entirely mistaken in his supposition that this species breeds in the Mud Islands off the coast of Nova Scotia.

I have had frequent opportunities of observing it in the outer harbor of Boston, where it is generally present in abundance from the last week in July to the first week in September.

In the latter part of August, 1871, in company with Professor Baird, on the small Government steamer "Moccasin," when off the southern shore of Martha's Vineyard, we saw a large number of these birds. They were readily attracted about our craft by fragments of biscuit, scraps of meat, and almost any kind of food, and were evidently possessed of very keen vision; for while at first only an occasional bird was in sight, as soon as we began to throw out food they came flocking in from all directions, until we could count seventy or more of them. They hovered about the water, preparatory to seizing their scraps of food, in a manner that reminded us at once of the action of butterflies. The uplifted wings, the feet thrown forward as if patting the water, and then rising from it, the bill inclined forward and downward — all this recalled the movements of the butterfly, and seemed more like those of an insect than of a bird. It rarely, and only for a moment, rested on the water.

Dr. J. H. Kidder found this Petrel present about Kerguelen Island, and noted its crepuscular habits when near the shore. This species became much more common after its first appearance, December 8. He had previously met with it at sea east of the Cape of Good Hope, and, December 14, saw it about by day feeding on the oily matters floating away from the carcass of a sea-elephant. The birds frequented the rocky parts of the hillsides, flitting about like Swallows, apparently in pursuit of insects, though there seemed to be none flying on the island other than minute gnats. Dr. Kidder did not succeed in finding any eggs, but was informed that Rev. Mr. Eaton, of the English Expedition, found one on Thumb Mountain, some fifteen miles from the American station; there was only one on the nest, which had been made under a large rock not far from the beach. The egg, which was white, was found December 8; and Dr. Kidder had no doubt that this bird nests habitually among and under rocks, and at a considerable elevation above the sea.

Genus **CYMODROMA**, Ridgway.

Fregetta, Bonap. Consp. II. 1856, 197 (type, *Procellaria tropica*, Gould; not *Fregata*, Briss. 1760).

Char. Size small; inner toe about equal to or slightly longer than the middle, which is decidedly shorter than the outer; claws very broad and flat, somewhat <> shaped; tarsus nearly twice as long as the middle toe without the claw (about two and a half times as long as the culmen); tail more than half as long as the wing, even, the feathers extremely broad, and truncated at the tip; plumage party-colored.

Only one species of this very peculiar genus belongs to the North American fauna, and this on account of its accidental occurrence on the coast of Florida.

Cymodroma grallaria.

THE WHITE-BELLIED PETREL.

Procellaria grallaria, VIEILL. Nouv. Dict. XXVI. 1817, 418.

Fregetta grallaria, BONAP. Consp. II. 1856, 197. — COUES, Pr. Ac. Nat. Sci. Philad. 1864, 86; Key, 1872, 330; Check List, 1873, no. 594; ed. 2, 1882, no. 829. — RIDGW. Nom. N. Am. B. 1881, no. 728.

Procellaria fregatta, "BANKS," KUHL, Mon. Proc. 1820, 138, pl. 10, fig. 3 (not *P. fregata*, LINN. 1766.)

Thalassidroma fregetta, LAWR. Ann. Lyc. N. Y. 1851, 117.

Fregetta Laurencii, BONAP. Consp. II. 1856, 198.

Fregetta Lawrencii, LAWR. in Baird's B. N. Am. 1858, 832. — BAIRD, Cat. N. Am. B. 1859, no. 646.

Thalassidroma leucogastra, GOULD, Ann. Mag. N. H. XIII. 367; B. Austr. VII. 1848, pl. 63.

HAB. Tropical oceans in general. Accidental on Florida coast?

SP. CHAR. *Adult;* Grayish dusky, lighter on the larger wing-coverts; remiges and rectrices dull black, the latter white at the extreme base, except the middle pair; lower parts from the breast back, a large portion of the under surface of the wing, with upper tail-coverts, white. Bill, legs, and feet black.

Wing, 6.00–6.50 inches; tail, 3.00–3.30; culmen, .50; tarsus, 1.40; middle toe without claw, .80.

So far as we are aware, the Black-and-White Stormy Petrel is only known to have been taken in a single instance within our waters, and its claim to a place in the fauna of North America rests entirely on the capture of these specimens on the Gulf coast of Florida. Seven examples of this bird are said to have been captured with a hook and line by the captain of a vessel while at anchor in the harbor of St. Mark's, Fla. One of these was secured by Mr. John Hooper, of Brooklyn, N. Y. They were observed about the vessel two days; after which none were met with. In regard to their distribution in other parts of the world, and habits generally, I have no information.

Order PYGOPODES.

THE DIVING BIRDS.

The Pygopodes include three very distinct families of birds, all of which are well represented in North America. Some authors include in this Order the Penguins (*Spheniscidæ*); but they possess so many peculiar features as unquestionably to entitle them to the rank of a distinct Order (*Sphenisci*).

The families of Pygopodes which come within the scope of the present work be defined as follows: —

A. *Hallux present.*

1. **Podicipidæ.** Toes lobed, the nails flat, broad, and rounded at tips; tail rudi- bare loral stripe extending from the bill to the eye; bill variable in for- more or less elongated.
2. **Urinatoridæ.** Toes fully webbed, the nails curved, acute, claw-like; t- completely and compactly feathered; bill elongated, acute, compressed

B. *Hallux absent.*

3. **Alcidæ.** Toes fully webbed, the claws curved and acute; tail no- bill excessively variable in form.

FAMILY PODICIPIDÆ. — The Grebes.

Char. Swimmers resembling the Loons in the posterior inser- legs, but the toes lobate and semipalmate, instead of completely we- claws broad, flat, and nail-like, instead of normally narrow and curved. Bill variable in shape; nostrils variable, but without an overhanging lobe; wings very short and concave, the primaries covered by the secondaries in the closed wing; tail rudimentary, consisting of a mere tuft of downy, loose-webbed feathers, without perfectly formed rectrices; plumage of the lower surface remarkably silky and lustrous, usually white.

The Grebes have by many authors been included in a single genus — *Podiceps* (= *Colymbus*) — while a majority of writers admit but two — *Podiceps* and *Podilymbus*. The former, however, in this comprehensive sense, contains many extremely dissimilar forms, and should, it appears to us, be subdivided, as has been done by Dr. Coues in his monograph of the family ("Pr. Philad. Acad." 1862, p. 230). The following North American genera appear to be rather well characterized. *Colymbus*, it may be remarked, approaches *Æchmophorus* through the South American *C. major*, Bodd., a species having the bill of *Æchmophorus*, but the coloration and shorter neck of a true *Colymbus*.

A. Bill slender, the length of the culmen from $2\frac{1}{2}$ to 6 times greater than the basal depth.

a. Size large (wing, 6.45–9.00 inches ; culmen, 1.50–3.05).

1. **Æchmophorus.** Neck extremely long (almost equal to the body in length); bill longer than the head, very slender and acute (the culmen 5 to 6 times longer than the depth through the base), straight, or even slightly recurved; tarsus equal to the middle toe and claw ; no colored tufts, ruffs, or patches about the head, and plumage the same at all stages and seasons.

2. **Colymbus.** Neck much shorter than the body ; bill about equal to the head, stout (culmen about $3\frac{1}{2}$ times the basal depth), the tip obtuse, and the outlines more or less curved ; tarsus shorter than the middle toe with claw ; adult in the breeding-season ornamented by colored ruffs, tufts, or patches about the head, the winter plumage and the young very different.

b. Size small (wing, about 5.00–6.00 inches ; culmen, .95–1.10).

3. **Dytes.** Neck much shorter than the body ; bill much shorter than the head, the culmen equal to about 3 to $3\frac{1}{2}$ times the basal depth ; tarsus about equal to the middle toe without the claw ; adult in breeding-plumage with colored tufts or patches about the head ; young and winter adult very different from the breeding-plumage.

c. Size very small (wing, 3.50–4.00 inches ; culmen, less than 1.00).

4. **Podiceps.** Neck much shorter than the body ; bill shorter than the head, the culmen less than 3 times the basal depth ; tarsus decidedly shorter than the middle toe without claw ; in the American species, adult in breeding-plumage without ornamental tufts or patches.

[illegible] very stout, the length of the culmen less than twice as great as the basal depth.

[illegible]odilymbus. Size rather small (wing, about 4.50–5.00 inches) ; bill much shorter than [illegible]d, the culmen much curved terminally ; tarsus shorter than middle toe without claw. [illegible] tufts in summer plumage, but bill crossed by a broad black bar, and throat covered [illegible] black patch.

Genus **ÆCHMOPHORUS**, Coues.

[illegible]s, Pr. Ac. Nat. Sci. Philad. April, 1862, 229 (type, *Podiceps occidentalis*, Lawr.).

[illegible]k extremely lo[illegible] (almost as long as the body), the bill longer than the head, very [illegible] (the length of t[illegible]e culmen 5 to 6 times greater than the depth through the base), [illegible]lightly recurved ; tarsus equal to the middle toe and claw. Plumage plain plum[illegible]ckish above, pure white beneath, including the whole under side of head and [illegible] same at all seasons and stages.

[illegible]ecies of t[illegible]is genus is known ; this, however, represented by two supposed races, [illegible]ist[illegible] [illegible]ainly, if not entirely, by their dimensions. They differ as follows : —

1. **Occi[illegible]ntalis.** Wing, 7.45–8.50 inches (average, 8.07) ; culmen, 2.60–3.05 (2.78). *Hab.* Western North America in general, but chiefly the interior.
2. **Clarki.** Wing, 6.70–7.75 inches (average, 7.31) ; culmen, 2.10–2.48 (2.25).[1] *Hab.* Pacific coast of North America.

Æchmophorus occidentalis.

THE WESTERN GREBE.

Podiceps occidentalis, Lawr. in Baird's B. N. Am. 1858, 894. — Baird, Cat. N. Am. B. 1859, no. 704. — Coop. & Suck. N. H. Wash. Terr. 1860, 281, pl. 38. — Coues, Key, 1872, 336 ; Check List, 1873, no. 608.

Æchmophorus occidentalis, Coues, Pr. Ac. Nat. Sci. Philad. 1862, 229 ; 2d Check List, 1882, no. 846. — Ridgw. Nom. N. Am. B. 1881, no. 729.

Podiceps (*Æchmophorus*) *occidentalis*, Coues, Birds N. W. 1874, 727.

[1] The above measurements are from specimens in the National Museum collection. That the two forms intergrade, however, not only in measurements, but also other supposed distinctive characters, is, we believe, clearly demonstrated by Mr. Henshaw in Bull. Nutt. Orn. Club, October, 1881, pp. 214-218.

HAB. Western Province of North America, breeding nearly throughout its range; extending from Southern California on the southwest to the Red River Region (Shoal Lake, breeding abundantly) at the northeast.

SP. CHAR. *Adult, full breeding-plumage:* Pileum and nape slaty black; remaining upper parts brownish slate, the remiges paler and more grayish, with the inner webs chiefly white; concealed bases of primaries and outer webs of secondaries next the shaft also white. Entire lower parts satiny white, abruptly defined against the black of the pileum and nape; sides, beneath the the wings, clouded with grayish; lores usually brownish gray, sometimes white. Bill olivaceous, becoming clear yellowish terminally and along the commissure; iris bright clear rose-red; legs

and feet greenish olive in the dried skin. *Adult (and Young) in winter:* Similar, but p[illegible] nape brownish slate, like the back. "Bill dull, rather light yellow, the lower mandible [illegible] into orange terminally; culmen and broad longitudinal space on the side of the basal [illegible] of the lower mandible dark olive-green, the former nearly black; iris pure carmine (h[illegible] the appearance of a red currant), growing narrowly whitish around the pupil; tarsi [illegible] olivaceous yellow, the outer side of the tarsus and joints of the toes nearly black."[1] [illegible] Above, uniform brownish gray, the nape and pileum lighter; lower parts uniform [illegible] blackish. No streaks or other markings whatever about the plumage.

Total length, about 26.00 inches; extent, 40.00; wing, 7.45–8.50 (average, 8.07); cu[illegible] 3.05 (2.78); depth of bill through base, .45–.56 (.54); tarsus, 2.75–3.10 (2.94); oute[illegible] 3.20 (2.67). (Fourteen adults.)

This large and conspicuous species was first made known in the "Report of the Pacific Railroad Explorations," from specimens collected by Drs. Kennerly, Cooper, and Suckley, at Bodega, Cal., in Shoalwater Bay, Fort Steilacoom, and on Puget Sound. Since that time this bird has been ascertained to have an extended distribution from the Pacific coast of Southern California to Shoal Lake, in the Fur Regions.

Mr. Donald Gunn, referring to this species, states that the large Grebes were only met with by him on the shores of Shoal Lake. Although he had travelled over a large portion of what is known as Rupert's Land, he is quite positive that he has never seen this bird anywhere before. He met with it in vast numbers at Shoal Lake. There he found them breeding, making their nests of bulrushes fixed to other rushes that were standing. The nest floats on the water, but is kept by the stems of the rooted plants, to which it is fastened, from drifting away from its moorings. All the other Grebes, so far as he has seen, make their nests of the same materials and in the same manner.

[1] Fresh colors of an adult male killed January 13. (See Ridgway, Orn. Fortieth Parallel, p. 641.)

This species has been described as being a fine-looking bird as it sits on the water, riding very lightly, its long neck erect, its bill pointing horizontally forward. Its length of neck makes the motion, during the act of diving, a very peculiar one. When it flies, both its feet and its neck are outstretched. The colors of certain parts, which are very beautiful in life, change and fade after death.

This species is included by Mr. R. Browne in his list of the birds found on Vancouver Island. Dr. Cooper met with it among the alkaline lakes of the Great Plain of the Columbia, in October, 1860; and it was about the same time of the year that he obtained at Walla-walla, in 1853, the first known example of this species. In all probability it breeds on the shores of those lakes. Dr. Cooper also mentions that in his visit, in 1862, to Monterey, on the sea-coast of California, he noted its first arrival in that neighborhood about the 25th of September.

According to the observations of the same accurate and observant naturalist, this bird winters along the Pacific coast from Puget Sound to San Francisco, but does not, so far as he is aware, occur farther south. He remarks that this Grebe greatly resembles the Loon in its habits, so far as could be ascertained from observations made in the winter; but he was not able to obtain any information in regard to its habits in the breeding-season. This species can dive, and swim under the water, with the greatest ease; and when once raised above the surface, can fly with rapidity. About dusk it is often heard to make a loud bleating sound, especially in the spring. Dr. Cooper thinks it quite probable that birds of this species never obtain the elongated feathers on the head that decorate the other species of this family in the spring, since he has procured examples late in April without their exhibiting any signs of this adornment.

Captain Bendire found this Grebe an abundant summer resident in Lake Malheur, in Eastern Oregon, where it undoubtedly breeds. Mr. Henshaw regards the waters of Utah as the eastern limit of this peculiarly western species. It is common in Utah Lake in summer, and breeds there. In the fall its numbers are increased by arrivals from the north. It is less timid than others of this family, and very little difficulty is found in killing it with a shot-gun. The fishermen informed him that when they draw their seines this bird will often swim up to the edges, in close proximity to the boats, and not infrequently allows itself to be inclosed in the meshes. A single individual was shot in the Gila River, N. M., in November.

Æchmophorus occidentalis Clarkii.

CLARK'S GREBE.

Podiceps Clarkii, Lawr. in Baird's B. N. Am. 1858, 895. — Baird, Cat. N. Am. B. 1859, no. 705.
Æchmophorus Clarkii, Coues, Pr. Ac. Nat. Sci. Philad. 1862, 229. — Ridgw. Nom. N. Am. B. 1881, no. 730.
Podiceps occidentalis, var. *Clarkii*, Coues, Key, 1872, 336; Check List, 1873, no. 608 *a*.
Æchmophorus occidentalis Clarki, Coues, 2d Check List, 1882, no. 846.
Podiceps (*Æchmophorus*) *occidentalis*, b. *Clarkii*, Coues, Birds N. W. 1874, 727.

Hab. Range nearly coextensive with that of the preceding, but chiefly confined to the Pacific coast district.

Sp. Char. Exactly like *occidentalis*, but much smaller, with the bill more slender, and more or less recurved; lores usually white. Wing, 6.70–7.75 inches (average, 7.31); culmen, 2.10–2.48 (2.25); depth of bill through base, .45–.50 (.46); tarsus, 2.45–2.85 (2.67); outer toe, 2.35–2.75 (2.65). (Nine adults.)

While bearing much the same relation that *Urinator pacificus* does to *U. arcticus*, this "species" appears to be still in the "incipient stage," the measurements of the larger individuals inosculating with those of the smaller specimens of *occidentalis.* In fact, examples occasionally occur which may with equal propriety be referred to either species; a majority, however, are typically one or the other, the incompletely differentiated individuals forming a small minority. There is appar-

ently no constant difference of coloration between the two, but *Clarkii* seems to have the lores more often distinctly whitish than *occidentalis.* (See Henshaw, "Bull. Nutt. Orn. Club," Vol. VI. Oct. 1881, pp. 214–218.)

It is not unlikely that the present bird may yet prove to be simply the female of *Æ. occidentalis.*

This form, which bears a very strong resemblance to *Æ. occidentalis,* was regarded by Mr. Lawrence as being a distinct species, but is now considered as only a variety. While it thus strongly resembles the *occidentalis* in size and in some of its markings, it constantly differs. The two seem to have nearly the same habitat; and as it is not usual for two races of the same species to dwell in exactly the same area, it seems more probable either that the differences are specific, or that they possess some sexual or other significance, unless the present form should be found to have a more southern range. The first known specimen of this form was taken by Mr. J. H. Clark in Chihuahua, Mexico, and other specimens were procured from the sea-coast of California at Santa Barbara and on San Pueblo Bay.

Dr. Cooper writes that near San Pedro, Cal., in July, 1863, he saw two large Grebes, which he had no doubt were of this variety, frequenting the creeks and bays for some months; but they were so very shy, and seemed to know so well the range of his gun, that he did not succeed in shooting one. He also saw large Grebes at Monterey, after the 25th of September; and as that is much earlier than the *Æ. occidentalis* is seen near the Columbia River, he thinks that these also may have belonged to this species. He observed nothing peculiar either in their habits or cries. Dr. Heermann obtained one of these birds at Santa Barbara, which he referred to as *C. cristatus.*

This bird, as well as all the other species of Grebes, and also the Loons, have a habit of gradually sinking into the water, until they entirely disappear, without leaving a ripple on the surface. They can also swim with the head or the bill only just above the water, and thus pass over a long distance without once being seen. One of these birds was shot near San Francisco by Mr. Hepburn. Subsequently to having made the above cited observations, Dr. Cooper writes that after a careful examination of some specimens obtained by himself at San Pedro in 1865, it appears to him doubtful whether the *Æ. occidentalis* is not identical with *Æ. Clarkii.*

Eggs of this species from Shoal Lake, in British America, vary from 2.15 inches to 2.60 in their length, and from 1.45 to 1.50 in their breadth. They are unspotted, and in all essential respects resemble the eggs of all the members of the entire genus.

Genus **COLYMBUS**, Linnæus.

Colymbus, Linn. S. N. ed. 10, I. 1758, 135; ed. 12, I. 1766, 220 (type, by elimination, *Colymbus cristatus*, Linn.).[1]

Podiceps, Lath. Ind. Orn. II. 1790, 780 (part; but, type, by elimination and restriction, *Colymbus fluviatilis*, Tunst.).

Char. Neck much shorter than the body; bill about equal to the head, stout (length of the culmen about three and a half times the depth through the base), the tip blunt, and the outlines more or less convex; tarsus shorter than middle toe with claw. Breeding plumage ornamented by colored tufts or patches about the head, the winter plumage and the young very different.

C. cristatus.

Only one species of this genus, as here restricted, belongs to North America, the occurrence of *C. cristatus* — which for half a century or more has been included in most works on North American ornithology, and generally considered a common bird of this country — being so very doubtful that there is not a single reliable record of its having been taken on this continent. For convenience of identification, however, in case it should be found in America, the characters of this species are given along with those of *C. Holbœllii* and the European representative of the latter, *C. grisegena*.

1. **C. Holbœllii.** Wing, 7.30–8.10 inches (average, 7.65); culmen, 1.65–2.40 (2.02); depth of bill at base, .52–.60 (.57); tarsus, 2.25–2.60 (2.53); outer toe, 2.50–3.05 (2.76). No

[1] Notwithstanding the extreme dislike we have to this harsh transfer of the name *Colymbus* from the Loons to the Grebes, we unfortunately can see no help for it. Sundevall has clearly shown (Met. Av. Nat. 1872, p. xxix) that it should never have been retained for the former, and most other authorities are pretty well agreed as to the incorrectness of its use in that connection. It is a case in which the facts are clear, and the rules of procedure so explicit that there is no alternative if we would be consistent in our efforts to assist toward reaching a fixed or stable nomenclature.

distinct tufts about head in breeding-plumage; neck bright rufous, sides of head ash-gray, pileum and nape glossy black. *Hab.* North America.

2. **C. grisegena.**[1] Wing, 6.45–7.00 inches (average, 6.63); culmen, 1.50–1.55 (1.53); depth of bill through base, .45–.50 (.48); tarsus, 1.98–2.15 (2.06); outer toe, 2.30–2.40 (2.35). Colors of *C. Holbœllii*. *Hab.* Palæarctic Region.

3. **C. cristatus.**[2] Wing, 6.80–7.75 inches (average, 7.10); culmen, 1.75–2.30 (1.96); depth

[1] COLYMBUS GRISEGENA, Bodd. Red-necked Grebe.
Colymbus grisegena, BODD. Tabl. P. E. 1783, 55 (ex Pl. Enl. 404, fig. 1).
Podiceps griseigena, GRAY, Genera B. III. 633.
Colymbus parotis, SPARRM. Mus. Carls. 1786, pl. 9. — GMEL. S. N. I. ii. 1788, 592.
Colymbus subcristatus, JACQ. Beitr. 1784, 37, pl. 18.
Podiceps subscristatus, BECHST. Taschb. Vög. Deutschl. 1803, 351.
Podiceps rubricollis, LATH. Ind. Orn. II. 1790, 783.
Colymbus cucullatus et *nævius*, PALL. Zoog. R.-A. II. 1826, 355, 356.
Podiceps canogularis, BREHM, Vög. Deutschl. 1831, 958.

SP. CHAR. Exactly like *C. Holbœllii*, but much smaller. Wing, 6.45–7.00 inches; culmen, 1.50–1.55; depth of bill through base, .45–.50; tarsus, 1.98–2.15; outer toe, 2.30–2.40.

Following is a description of an example of this species in the down:— *Downy Young:* Head and neck longitudinally striped with dusky and dull white, the dusky stripes widest (except underneath the head), and about six in number; the crown is divided medially by a narrow stripe of white, which, however, does not extend anteriorly to the white of the forehead; the dusky stripe, extending back from the lower eyelid, terminates just behind the ears, but that extending from above the eye is continued down the side of the neck, there being between this and its fellow of the opposite side three dusky stripes down the back of the neck; there is a broad but short rictal streak, with three narrower streaks on the chin; there are also three dusky streaks on the throat — one on each side, and one between. The plumage of the body is dull grayish-fuliginous, lighter beneath, where fading into dull grayish white on the abdomen. (No. 57307, Europe.)

C. grisegena.

From the corresponding stage of *C. cristatus*, this may be distinguished most readily by the much darker lower parts, the abdomen only being light colored, and this dull grayish white, while in the young of *C. cristatus* the entire lower parts, except the sides, are nearly pure white. There are also some differences in the markings of the head and neck, the most obvious of which consist in the absence of streaks on the throat in *C. cristatus*.

[2] COLYMBUS CRISTATUS. The Crested Grebe.
Colymbus cristatus, LINN. S. N. ed. 10, I. 1758, 135; ed. 12, I. 1766, 222.
Podiceps cristatus, LATH. Ind. Orn. II. 1790, 780. — SW. & RICH. F. B. A. II. 1831, 410. — NUTT. Man. II. 1834, 250. — AUD. Orn. Biog. III. 1835, 598, pl. 292; Synop. 1839, 356; B. Am. VII. 1844, 308, pl. 479. — LAWR. in Baird's B. N. Am. 1858, 893. — BAIRD, Cat. N. Am. B. 1859, no. 703. — COUES, Key, 1872, 336; Check List, 1873, no. 609; Birds N. W. 1874, 729.
Colymbus urinator, LINN. S. N. ed. 12, I. 1766, 223.
Podiceps australis, GOULD, P. Z. S. 1844, 135.
Podiceps Hectori, BULLER, Essay on New Zealand Orn. 1865, 19.

HAB. Northern part of the Palæarctic Region; also, New Zealand and Australia. *No valid North American record!*

SP. CHAR. *Adult, breeding-plumage:* Pileum, including an elongated tuft on each side of the occiput, and outer margin (broadly) of the frill, black; lores, postocular region, malar region, chin, and upper part of of bill through base, .45–.55 (.51); tarsus, 2.25–2.70 (2.48); outer toe, 2.50–2.85 (2.63). *Breeding-plumage:* Throat and chin buffy white, passing posteriorly into rich ferruginous on the prominent auricular "frill," which is tipped with black; pileum and elongated tuft on each side of occiput, black. *Hab.* Palæarctic Region.

the throat, buffy white, succeeded posteriorly by ferruginous, on the basal portion of the frill. Upper parts dark brownish gray, sometimes nearly or quite black; secondaries, anterior border of the wing, and inner tertials, entirely white; lower parts white, the sides and flanks grayish brown, tinged with ferruginous. "Bill blackish brown, tinged with carmine [in the female "dusky green"]; bare loral space dusky green, as is the edge of the eyelids; iris bright carmine; feet greenish black, the webs grayish blue" (AUDUBON). *Winter plumage:* Similar to the summer dress, except the plumage of the head, the occipital tufts and the frill being entirely absent; pileum and nape sooty grayish brown, fading gradually into grayish white on the lower part of the head and neck, the foreneck pale grayish; sides and flanks without any reddish tinge. *Downy young:* Neck with six longitudinal dusky stripes alternating with as many stripes of white; that on the foreneck fainter than the rest, and bifurcating below, each branch extending toward the side of the breast; head with six dusky stripes, the four upper ones being continuations of the neck-stripes, the fifth and sixth running across the cheek (one on each side of the head) from beneath the eye back to beneath the ears; a dusky spot on the lower jaw, beneath the rictus; chin and throat entirely white. Upper parts sooty grayish brown, lower parts white.

C. cristatus.

Total length, about 19.00–24.00 inches; extent, 30.00–33.00; wing, 6.80–7.75; culmen, 1.75–2.30; depth of bill at base, .45–.55; tarsus, 2.25–2.70; outer toe, 2.50–2.85.

A specimen in summer dress, said to have been obtained in Greenland, is similar to European examples, but has the wing shorter and the bill narrower than any of the five European skins we have examined. An example from New South Wales is not distinguishable in colors from European ones, but is much larger; while two from Lake Wakatipa, New Zealand, besides being even larger than the Australian specimen, have much longer bills and tarsi, and are altogether richer colored than any others, the upper parts being deep brownish black, and the basal portion of the frills rich chestnut, while the crown and occipital tufts are glossy greenish black.

The following measurements exhibit the apparent geographical variations in size: —

	Wing.	Culmen.	Depth of bill at base.	Tarsus.	Outer toe.
Average of 5 European specimens,	7.25	1.54	.53	2.30	2.58
One specimen said to be from Greenland,	6.80	1.80	.45	2.30	2.50
Average of 2 New Zealand specimens,	7.47	2.25	.55	2.70	2.76
One specimen from New South Wales,	7.30	2.23	.52	2.62	2.70

Colymbus Holbœllii.

THE AMERICAN RED-NECKED GREBE.

Podiceps rubricollis, "LATH." BONAP. Synop. 1828, 417. — SW. & RICH. F. B. A. II. 1831, 411. — NUTT. Man. II. 1834, 253. — AUD. Orn. Biog. III. 1835, 617, pl. 298; Synop. 1839, 357; B. Am. VII. 1844, 312, pl. 480.

Podiceps rubricollis major, TEMM. & SCHLEG. Faun. Jap. 1849, pl. 78, B (not *Colymbus major*, BODD. 1783).

Podiceps griseigena, "BODD." LAWR. in Baird's B. N. Am. 1858, 892. — BAIRD, Cat. N. Am. B. 1859, no. 702.

Podiceps Holbœllii, REINH. Vid. Meddel. 1853, 76; Ibis, 1861, 14 (Greenland). — COUES, Pr. Ac. Nat. Sci. Philad. 1862, 231. — RIDGW. Nom. N. Am. B. 1881, no. 731.

Podiceps griseigena, var. *Hölbolli*, COUES, Key, 1872, 337; Check List, 1873, no. 610; Birds N. W. 1874, 730.

Podicipes griseigena Holbœlli, COUES, 2d Check List, 1882, no. 847.

Podiceps Cooperi, LAWR. in Baird's B. N. Am. 1858, 893 (in text; winter adult).

Podiceps subcristatus, KITTL. Denkw. II. 1858, 313 (not of JACQ. 1784).

Podiceps affinis, SALVADORI, Atti Soc. Ital. VIII. 1866, 45.

Podiceps cucullatus, TACZ. J. f. O. 1874, 336 (not of PALL. 1826).

HAB. North America in general, including Greenland; breeding far north, migrating south, in winter, quite across the United States. Eastern Siberia, and south to Japan.

SP. CHAR. *Adult, breeding-plumage:* Pileum (including lores and depressed occipital tuft) and nape glossy dull black; rest of the head light ash-gray, bordered above and below by whitish, this most distinct along the upper border, from the eyes back; neck (except nape) rich rufous, abruptly defined above against the ashy of the throat, but below gradually merging into the whitish of the breast. Upper parts blackish dusky, the feathers sometimes with paler margins; secondaries chiefly white. Lower parts grayish white, faintly spotted, except on the abdomen, with dusky grayish; sides and flanks nearly uniform grayish. "Bill brownish black, bright yellow at the base; iris carmine; tarsi and toes greenish black externally, yellow on the inner side, the edges of the lobes dusky" (AUDUBON). *Winter plumage:* Pileum dusky, the occiput without elongated feathers; neck smoky grayish brown, lighter in front, dusky on the nape; chin, throat, and malar region whitish. Otherwise as in the summer plumage. *Young:* Pileum and sides of the head dusky, marked with several white stripes — one originating at the sides of the forehead, and passing over and behind the eye, another extending from the eye backward over the auriculars, and another dividing the cheeks; a short whitish stripe on each side of the upper part of the nape; fore part and sides of the neck light ferruginous. Otherwise as in the adult.

Summer adult.

Total length, about 18.00 to 19.50 inches; extent, about 32.00; wing, 7.30–8.10 (average, 7.65); culmen, 1.65–2.40 (2.02); depth of bill at base, .52–.60 (.57); tarsus, 2.25–2.60 (2.53); outer toe, 2.50–3.05 (2.76). (Seventeen specimens.)

The American Red-necked Grebe is a counterpart of the European *C. grisegena* [1] in plumage,

[1] See p. 426, footnote.

but is a very much larger bird, the difference in size being moreover entirely constant, as will appear from the following measurements: —

	Wing.	Culmen.	Depth of bill.	Tarsus.	Outer toe.
Average of 17 specimens of *C. Holbœllii* . .	7.65	2.02	.57	2.53	2.76
" 4 " *C. grisegena* . .	6.63	1.53	.48	2.06	2.35
Minimum of *C Holbœllii*	7.30	1.65	.52	2.25	2.50
Maximum of *C. grisegena*	7.00	1.55	.50	2.15	2.40

Examples from Eastern Asia appear to agree closely with those from North America. For the former the name "*cucullatus*, PALL.," has generally been used; but upon turning to p. 355 of the

Winter adult (*type of P. Cooperi, Lawr.*).

"Zoographia Rosso-Asiatica," we find that Pallas did not know the bird from Eastern Siberia, but described, under the name *cucullatus*, a specimen of the ordinary European species (*C. grisegena*, BODD.).

The Red-necked Grebe of North America, though probably not identical specifically with the European species, is closely allied to it both in appearance, markings, and habits; but it is said to differ from that species in size, being larger and stouter. It is distributed from the Middle States northward; being most common in the Fur Countries, where it breeds, and from which region it straggles southward in the winter as far as the Chesapeake. So far as known, it does not breed to the south of Calais, Me. In Northern Maine and New Brunswick — especially in the region of the St. Croix River, as far south as St. Andrew — this species is found in considerable numbers, and is much more common in the spring and in the fall than it is in the summer, many of these birds remaining in that region throughout the winter. A few of them stay during the summer and breed; but at that time they are present in much fewer numbers than in winter. This Grebe has been observed to have the same interesting peculiarities as the Horned Grebe and the Loon in regard to the management of its young. As soon as these are hatched the mother takes them upon her back, swims with them in this position, as if to sun them, and takes them with her under the water when diving for their food — feeding them with small fishes and vegetable substances.

This species is found as far west as the Pacific coast, and at least as far south as Vancouver Island, where Mr. R. Browne obtained specimens. Mr. Bernard Ross met with it on the Mackenzie River; and specimens have been received by the Smithsonian Institution from the Red River Settlement.

A single specimen was obtained by Mr. Elliott on the Prybilof Islands; it was the only one seen during his residence there. It had been observed before by the natives, who, however, affirmed that it was quite uncommon. Eggs of this species obtained from the Yukon and other interior Arctic localities, are rough and white, some inclining to pale greenish, others with buff-colored stains, and all of the usual elongated shape so peculiar to the family. They measure in length from 2.10 inches to 2.35, and in breadth from 1.25 to 1.45.

Professor Kumlien writes me that in October, 1873, his son Ludwig saw in the middle of Lake Koskonong five large Grebes, which were not *cristatus*, but which agreed perfectly with *C. grisegena* in their markings. Unfortunately he was unable to obtain one of them.

This Grebe is more or less common along the whole New England coast at different periods; and in the winter of 1838 I procured a number of examples in immature plumage in the Boston market, which were sent in the flesh to Mr. Audubon. Early in September, 1867, Mr. William Brewster procured a fine specimen in Plymouth, Mass., which had been shot as it was diving among the breakers. This bird is still found more or less frequently during the fall and winter in the markets of Boston.

According to Giraud, it occasionally extends its migrations along the coasts of Long Island and New Jersey. The specimens procured in that vicinity are nearly all young birds, the adult being a great rarity.

Mr. Donald Gunn, writes in regard to the presence of this species in the Red River Region, that it is a comparatively rare bird there, living in unfrequented and solitary places, feeding on small fish and fresh-water shells. He is not able to state the usual number of eggs that this bird lays, but from its general scarcity he is inclined to the opinion that it cannot be large. The flesh of this Grebe is black and unpalatable, and is never eaten by the whites.

Mr. Robert Kennicott, who found this species breeding in the neighborhood of Fort Yukon, states that the nest found June 14 was floating on the water among the grass on the borders of the lake. It was nearly flat on the top, and very little above the surface of the water, and contained three eggs. He saw the female, but only at a distance; both this species and *Dytes auritus* being seldom or never seen to leave their nests, as they quietly slip into the water and dive at once. After incubation has begun, the female, when she leaves her nest, covers up her eggs with wet grass taken from the bottom of her nest, unless compelled to depart on the instant. In several cases Mr. Kennicott found the eggs quite warm when thus hidden; and he was convinced that the bird could only have just left the nest on his approach, but that she had stopped long enough to conceal her eggs. The top of the nest is always more or less wet, and this causes the discoloration of the eggs.

This Grebe appears to have been found in considerable numbers at Fort Rae and on the Yukon by Mr. Kennicott and Mr. Lockhart; at Fort Rae also by Mr. S. Clarke; at Fort Simpson by Mr. Ross; on Peal's River by Mr. C. P. Gaudet; at Fort Yukon by Mr. S. Jones and Mr. J. Sibbiston; among the mountains west of the Lower Mackenzie, at Fort Anderson, by Mr. MacFarlane; and at Shoal Lake by Mr. D. Gunn.

Mr. Bischoff collected specimens of this Grebe at Sitka; and Mr. Dall found it not uncommon in the marshes on the banks of the Yukon River as far up as Fort Yukon, where Mr. Kennicott had previously obtained its eggs. Sir John Richardson speaks of this Grebe as being very common in the Fur Countries, where it was found in nearly every lake having grassy borders.

Eggs of this species from Yukon, Peal's River, and Fort Simpson, resemble those of this genus generally, and vary greatly in size; namely, from 2.05 inches to 2.55 in length, and from 1.20 to 1.50 in breadth.

Genus **DYTES**, Kaup.

Dytes, Kaup, Sk. Ent. Eur. Thierw. 1829, 49 (type, *Colymbus cornutus*, Gmel. = *C. auritus*, Linn.).
Proctopus, Kaup, l. c. (type, *Podiceps nigricollis*, Brehm).
Otodytes, Reich. Syst. Nat. 1853, p. iii (same type).

Char. Size small (wing 5.00 to 6.00 inches) ; neck much shorter than the body ; bill much shorter than the head, the culmen equal to about three to three and a half times the basal depth ; tarsus about as long as the middle toe without the claw. Breeding-plumage ornamented with colored tufts and patches about the head.

D. auritus.

Two well-marked species of this genus occur in North America, their characters being as follows : —

1. **D. auritus.** Bill compressed (deeper than wide at the base). *Breeding-plumage :* Lower neck and jugulum rufous; sides of occiput with very full tuft of dense, soft, blended ochraceous feathers. *Hab.* Northern hemisphere.
2. **D. nigricollis.** Bill depressed (wider than deep at the base). *Breeding-plumage :* Lower neck and jugulum black ; sides of head behind eyes with a tuft-like patch of slender acicular ochraceous feathers.
   a. Three or four inner primaries mostly or entirely white. *Hab.* Palæarctic Region, and Greenland. *Nigricollis.*
   β. Inner primaries with inner webs wholly dusky ; colors decidedly duller, and bill slenderer. *Hab.* Western North America. *Californicus.*

Dytes auritus.

THE HORNED GREBE.

Colymbus auritus, LINN. S. N. ed. 10, I. 1758, 135; ed. 12, I. 1766, 222.
Dytes auritus, RIDGW. Nom. N. Am. B. 1881, no. 732.
Colymbus cornutus, GMEL. S. N. I. ii. 1788, 591.
Podiceps cornutus, LATH. Ind. Orn. II. 1790, 783. — SW. & RICH. F. B. A. II. 1831, 411. — NUTT. Man. II. 1834, 254. — AUD. Orn. Biog. III. 1835, 429, pl. 259; Synop. 1839, 357; B. Am. VII. 1844, 316, pl. 481. — LAWR. in Baird's B. N. Am. 1858, 895. — BAIRD, Cat. N. Am. B. 1859, no. 706. — COUES, Key, 1872, 337; Check List, 1873, no. 611; ed. 2, 1882, no. 848; Birds N. W. 1874, 731.
Colymbus obscurus, GMEL. S. N. I. ii. 1788, 592.
Colymbus caspicus, S. G. GMEL. Reise, IV. 1774–1784, 137. — GMEL. S. N. I. ii. 1788, 593.
Podiceps bicornis, BREHM, Vög. Deutschl. 1831, 96, pl. 44, fig. 4.

HAB. Northern hemisphere in general. Breeds in the Northern United States and northward.

SP. CHAR. *Adult, breeding-plumage:* Head generally, including the fluffy tufts on each side of the upper neck, slightly glossy dull greenish black, becoming gradually dull sooty slate on the forehead; lores dull ochraceous-rufous, communicating with a broad superciliary stripe of bright ochraceous, which continues, gradually widening, to the sides of the occiput; foreneck rich rufous. Upper parts dusky, the feathers sometimes with indistinctly paler margins; secondaries chiefly or entirely white. Lower parts white, the sides mixed chestnut-rufous and grayish dusky. "Bill bluish black, its tip yellow; short loral space bright carmine, as is the iris, its inner margin white; edges of eyelids grayish blue; feet dusky externally, internally, and on anterior and posterior ridges of the tarsus dull yellow; claws dusky" (AUDUBON). *Winter plumage:* Pileum, nape, and sides of the jugulum smoky slate; under part and sides of the head, lores, and lower parts generally, white; jugulum faintly shaded with pale grayish, and sides clouded with dark grayish. Upper parts as in the summer plumage, but more slaty. "Bill bluish gray, as is the bare loral space; the eye bright carmine, with an inner white edge; the feet bluish gray" (AUDUBON). *Downy young (half-grown):* Pileum and nape dusky; sides of the head with two dusky stripes and several irregular spots of the same color; throat with a dusky streak on each side. Otherwise similar in color to the winter plumage.

Total length, about 14.75 inches; extent, 25.50; wing, 5.75; culmen, 1.00; tarsus, 1.75.

This species, variously known among authors as the "Horned Grebe," the "Dusky Grebe," and the "Sclavonian Grebe," is common to the northern portions of both continents, and is found on the Pacific coast as far north at least as Vancouver, and to Greenland on the eastern. It is equally common in the northern portions of Europe and Asia in the summer, wandering in the winter farther south. It is rather a rare bird in Great Britain during the summer, but is of more frequent appearance in the winter, frequenting the coast and the marshy districts; and is not uncommon in Ireland during the same season. It has been said to be resident in Scotland all the year, but there is no recent evidence of the fact. Mr. Dunn found it extremely rare in the Orkney and Shetland Islands, only noticing seven or eight. He describes it as being a very shy bird and a most expert diver — frequenting the sea, but always remaining close to the rocks. When alarmed it dives to a great distance, and on coming to the surface immediately takes wing.

Mr. Proctor, who visited Iceland in 1837, found this Grebe there frequenting the fresh water, and breeding among the reeds and the ranker herbage. The nest is large, and floats on the surface of the water, with which it rises and falls, being composed of a mass of reeds and other aquatic plants. The eggs vary from two to four in number, and when just laid are of a bluish-white color; but they soon become stained by the materials of which the nest is composed, and changed to a dirty yellowish brown. In size the egg is 1.75 inches long by 1.25 in breadth. The young birds when first hatched are covered with gray-colored down. When the old bird is alarmed by the approach of an intruder, she instantly dives, but reappears at the distance of about thirty yards. Mr. Proctor mentions that, having observed one of these birds dive from the nest, which he killed as it arose, he was surprised to see two young birds, that had been concealed beneath the wings of the parent, drop upon the water. In several other instances he found these birds diving with their young under their wings, these being placed with their heads toward the tail, and their bills resting upon the back of the parent bird.

Mr. George A. Boardman informs me that he has noticed similar habits in the birds of this species, which are not uncommon in the summer in the vicinity of Milltown, N. B. In the summer of 1873 he obtained a female with a brood of chicks. In swimming about in the lake the parent carried her young about with her on her back, the purpose of this being apparently to enable the young birds to have an opportunity of sunning themselves, as has been observed to be the habit of the common Loon in reference to its young. This species of Grebe is common near Calais, Me., throughout the year, occurring in the winter where there is open water.

In Scandinavia Mr. Wheelwright found this species sparingly distributed over the whole country, from Gottenburg up to East Finland and far into Norway. It is not very common in Sweden, but breeds there in the reedy parts of shallow water. Middendorff includes it in his List of the Birds of Siberia, where it is found in the wooded districts.

Professor Reinhardt mentions the occurrence of a single bird of this species, in immature plumage, in the southern part of Greenland. Captain Blakiston obtained specimens of it on the Plains of the Saskatchewan, and also about Hudson's Bay. Mr. Bernard Ross met with it on the Mackenzie River; Mr. Murray cites it as occurring on Lake Winnipeg and Hudson's Bay; and Mr. Kennicott obtained it on the Red River of the North. Mr. Dall killed a number of this species at Nulato, in May, 1868; but it was not very common in that region. One specimen obtained was a female with one egg well developed in the ovary. He obtained a parent with her two eggs from an Indian at Fort Yukon, in June, 1867. It is not otherwise referred to in the notes of explorers in the Arctic Regions, though Sir John Richardson states that it is very common in the Fur Countries, frequenting every grass-bordered lake. Its shy and retiring habits render it a bird not readily noticed. It is given by Mr. R. Browne as one of the birds of Vancouver Island.

This Grebe is quite common in the fall in the Boston market, the specimens being usually in an immature plumage.

According to Giraud, it is quite common in and about Long Island. It is well known to the hunters of that region under the name of the "Hell-diver" — an emphatic mode of indicating its wonderful powers of disappearance under water. It is usually found in the submerged meadows; and when surprised, avoids pursuit by diving. Its food is chiefly fish, and its flesh is said to be very unpalatable.

Mr. J. A. Allen met with this Grebe in the valley of Great Salt Lake, in the month of September.

A single specimen of this bird is recorded by Major Wedderburn as having been taken in Bermuda in 1846; and Mr. Hurdis mentions that a fine specimen in the spring plumage was shot in February, 1855.

Professor Kumlien informs me that this Grebe arrives in Southern Wisconsin in April, and is not rare in Lake Koskonong in May. It keeps within a few rods of the shore, where the water is not too shallow, but is rarely, if ever, seen far out in the lake. It is not known to breed there, and is not seen in the summer.

In 1842, when collecting on the Island of Gottland, in the Baltic, July 14, Mr. Kumlien procured seven adult specimens and four young chicks. The old birds were quite tame, and would not take to wing, or did so very reluctantly. When startled they flew very sharply, but low. They were great divers; but the water being less than two feet deep, and clear, he could easily see them under the water, and caught two of the old birds while they were diving. He has never met with this species in the fall.

This Grebe probably breeds from New Brunswick to Oregon in all suitable places, and north of those regions. In the neighborhood of Pembina its eggs are found by the middle of June, on nests essentially similar to all those of this family, being floating masses of reeds. The young are nearly full-grown by the last of July or the first of August. Examples of this species were secured in large numbers, during the breeding-season, at Fort Resolution, on the Yukon, by Mr. Kennicott; by Mr. Ross on the Anderson, near Fort Simpson, Fort Rae, and Fort Resolution; on Big Island by Mr. Reid; and on the Lower Mackenzie by Mr. Sibbiston.

The eggs of this species are usually four in number. They are very nearly oval, with little difference in either end, and have quite a smooth surface. The ground-color, like that of the eggs of all the Grebes, is originally of a bluish chalky-white, but more or less incrusted. They almost always become discolored, and are thus changed to various shades of buff, brown, and even, in some instances, to orange. Eggs from Great Slave Lake and from the Yukon River, in the National Museum, vary in length from 1.60 to 1.80 and 1.85 inches, and in breadth from 1.10 to 1.15 and 1.20. The longest eggs have usually the smallest breadth.

Dytes nigricollis.

THE EARED GREBE.

a. Nigricollis.

Colymbus auritus, LINN. Faun. Suec. ed. 2, 1761, 53 (part; not of 1758).
Podiceps nigricollis, BREHM, Vög. Deutschl. 1831, 963.
Dytes nigricollis, RIDGW. Nom. N. Am. B. 1881, no. 733.
Eared Grebe, YARR. Brit. B. ed. 2, III. 417; ed. 3, III. 420, fig.; *et* AUCT.

b. Californicus.

Podiceps auritus, NUTT. Man. II. 1834, 256. — AUD. Orn. Biog. V. 1839, 108, pl. 404; Synop. 1839, 358; B. Am. VII. 1844, 322, pl. 482. — LAWR. in Baird's B. N. Am. 1858, 897.
Podiceps californicus, HEERM. Pr. Ac. Nat. Sci. Philad. 1854, 179; Pacific R. R. Rep. X. 1859, 76, pl. 8 (young). — LAWR. in Baird's B. N. Am. 1858, 896. — BAIRD, Cat. N. Am. B. 1859, no. 707.
Podiceps (*Proctopus*) *californicus*, COUES, Pr. Ac. Nat. Sci. Philad. 1862, 231, 404.
Podiceps auritus, var. *californicus*, COUES, Key, 1872, 337; Check List, 1873, no. 612; Birds N. W. 1874, 733.
Podicipes auritus californicus, COUES, 2d Check List, 1882, no. 850.
Dytes nigricollis californicus, RIDGW. Nom. N. Am. B. 1881, no. 733 *a*.

Hab. The typical form restricted to the Palæarctic Region and Greenland; var. *californicus* distributed over Northern and Western North America, north to Great Slave Lake, south to Guatemala, and east to the Mississippi Valley. Breeds nearly throughout its North American range.

Sp. Char. *Adult, breeding-plumage:* Head, neck, and upper parts dull black; on each side of the head, behind the eyes, and occupying the whole of the postocular and auricular regions, a flattened tuft of elongated, narrow, and pointed feathers of an ochraceous color, those of the lower part of the tuft inclining to rufous or ferruginous, those along the upper edge straw-yellow or buff, sometimes, but rarely, forming a rather well-defined streak; fore part of the head sometimes inclining to grayish or smoky dusky. Upper parts blackish dusky, the secondaries — sometimes also the inner primaries — mostly or entirely white. Lower parts satiny white, the sides mixed chestnut-rufous and dusky. Bill deep black; iris bright carmine, with an inner whitish ring; legs and feet "dusky gray externally, greenish gray on the inner side" (Audubon). *Winter plumage:* Pileum, nape, and upper parts fuliginous-slate or plumbeous-dusky; malar region, chin, and throat white; auricular region white, sometimes tinged pale grayish buff or light grayish; fore part and sides of the neck pale dull grayish; lower parts satiny white, the sides plumbeous-dusky. "Upper mandible greenish black, growing pale ashy olive-green on basal third of the commissure (broadly) and on the culmen; lower mandible ashy olive-green, paler below, and more yellowish basally; iris bright orange-red, more scarlet outwardly, and with a fine thread-like white ring around the pupil; tarsi and toes dull blackish on the outer side, passing on the edges into olive-green; inner side dull light yellowish green; inner toe apple green."[1] *Young, first plumage:* Similar to the winter adult, but colors more brownish. *Downy young:* Top of the head, as far down as the auriculars, dusky, the forehead divided medially by a white line, which soon separates into two, each of which again bifurcates on the side of the crown (over the eye), one branch running obliquely downward and backward to the sides of the nape, the other continued straight back to the occiput; middle of the crown with a small oblong or elliptical spot of bare reddish skin. Suborbital, auricular, and malar regions, chin, and throat immaculate white; foreneck pale grayish; lower parts white, becoming grayish laterally and posteriorly; upper parts dusky grayish.

Total length, about 13.00 inches; extent, 21.00; wing, about 5.20–5.50; culmen, .95–1.10.

With four adults and two young birds of true *nigricollis*, and a very large series of American specimens (*P.* "*californicus*," Lawr.), we notice certain differences, already pointed out by Dr. Coues ("Pr. Philad. Acad." 1862, p. 231), which distinguish the birds of the two continents, with the very notable exception of a single specimen of the American series, from California, in which the chief supposed peculiarity of the European form is vastly exaggerated. Were it not for this solitary exception to the rule, we should have little hesitation in separating the American birds as a distinct species. It should be borne in mind in this connection that the series of European specimens is very small, so that a conclusion based upon their comparison with the American series would hardly be a fair one. All the European examples we have seen, both old and young, have stouter bills, with the gonys more decidedly ascending; and the latter are more darkly colored than the young of the American form.

The main difference supposed to distinguish the American from the European birds of this species is stated by Dr. Coues to be as follows: "In the American Eared Grebe all the primaries are throughout their whole extent dark chocolate-brown, with a more or less notable amount of dull reddish in the adult. The two first secondaries are of the color of its primaries, and bordered with white; and the basal portions and shafts of all, for the greater part of their length, are of the same chocolate-brown. In all the specimens of the European type examined, the characters of the wing are very different. The four inner primaries are wholly pure white; the next is white, with a sprinkling of brown on the outer web; the next is white, its outer vane brown; and all

[1] Orn. Fortieth Parallel, p. 642; from a male killed, December 21, at Pyramid Lake, Nev.

the secondaries, except the three innermost, are entirely pure white, and their shafts are white to the very base. The three innermost have a dusky spot near the end of the outer web. These differences, so far as we can discover, are entirely constant; and if so, quite sufficient to separate the two."

Since the writing of Dr. Coues's admirable synopsis of the Grebes, the number of specimens of these birds, and especially of the American Eared Grebe, in the collection of the National Museum has very greatly increased, so that we have now probably more than double the amount of material which came under Dr. Coues's inspection. We have examined this material very carefully, and find in the American series but the one specimen mentioned above which does not confirm the difference pointed out. The specimen in question (No. 74461, Stockton, Cal., May 9: L. BELDING) has *all* the primaries white, except their terminal portion, less than half of the exposed portion of the quills being brown! Although in every other respect the coloration of this example is entirely normal, the amount of white on the quills is so very unusual, even for a European specimen, that there is much probability of its being an indication of partial albinism.

On the other hand, an adult male, in breeding-plumage, from Europe (not seen by Dr. Coues), has the outer web of all but *two* of the inner quills entirely brown, except the extreme tip of the seventh, eighth, and ninth quills, the tenth and eleventh[1] having much brown near the end of the outer web, while the tenth has a brown spot near the end of the inner web also. It is therefore evident that the amount of white on the inner quills varies to some extent in the European bird; but we have yet to see a specimen in which there is not more or less of white on the inner webs of all the quills, with the outer webs of two or more of the inner quills white also. The difference in the form and size of the bill, and the darker color of the young, of the European bird, is apparently constant, so that, upon the whole, we can hardly do otherwise than separate the birds of the two continents as tolerably well-defined races.

Both American and European specimens vary considerably in the quantity of rufous along the sides, some examples having the entire sides and flanks a nearly continuous chestnut-rufous, while others have only a slight tinge of this color; a nearly equal admixture of rufous and dusky is, however, more usual. There is also much variation in the brightness of the elongated feathers on the sides of the head, some having these tufts a nearly uniform dull buff or ochraceous, while in others they are rich rusty rufous, those along the upper border being bright ochraceous, in marked contrast. This latter condition, or a brighter plumage generally, seems more common among European specimens, and may prove characteristic of that form.

A very fine adult in summer plumage, from Northern Europe, in the collection of the Boston Society of Natural History (No. 8164, Lafresnaye Collection), is remarkable for the great amount of rufous on the lesser wing-coverts, where this color prevails anteriorly; the middle, and even the greater, coverts being spotted with this color. The sides and flanks are almost continuously rich chestnut-rufous. We have not been able to detect a trace of rufous on the lesser wing-coverts in any other of the numerous specimens examined, either European or North American. The five inner primaries all have the inner webs white, except at the tip; but there is not a trace of white on the outer webs, except of the last two.

The Californian Grebe is a form very closely allied with *Dytes nigricollis* of the Palæarctic Region; and it was probably one of this latter species which was figured and described by Audubon as *Podiceps auritus*, and said to have been received from Western America. The present form appears to have an area of distribution bounded, approximately, by the Missouri River Region on the east, and extending westward to the Pacific, and northward to an indefinite extent.

Dr. Heermann mentions finding this Grebe abundant in California, both on the sea-shore and on the inland fresh-water ponds; Dr. Palmer met with it in the neighborhood of Guayamas, in Western Mexico; and Mr. Salvin mentions finding it common on the Lake of Dueñas, in Guatemala, where it was in its immature and winter plumage. A single specimen in its summer dress was shot near Cubalco, in the Guatemala province of Vera Paz.

[1] The Grebes have eleven primary quills!

Dr. Cooper, while at Monterey, on the coast of California, saw, about the middle of September, some small Grebes which proved to be of this species, and which had apparently only recently come from their breeding-station. By the 18th of the month families of about five each had become common. Dr. Cooper gives as the habitat of this species California, and thence northward and eastward to the head waters of the Missouri River. At Monterey, about the middle of September, 1861, he met with flocks of four or five just arrived from the mountains, and swimming very tamely close to the shores; and he found them very numerous during the ensuing winter along the southern coast. They were generally very fearless, unless they had been repeatedly shot at, swimming and diving actively near the shore, and rarely taking wing, though able to fly rapidly when startled. Most of this species go north in April; but at Santa Barbara, on the 5th of May, he shot a female — probably an immature or sickly bird. He met with individuals of what he supposed to be this species in the Colorado Valley, on a small pond; and Dr. Heermann mentions his having frequently met with them on fresh water. Dr. Suckley, in 1853, shot one on the west side of the Rocky Mountains in about lat. 47° N.; and they have been obtained by Dr. Hayden on the Upper Missouri River in September. On one occasion Dr. Cooper found an individual in a deep ravine, into which it had probably been blown in a fog, and where it had been unable to rise from the ground.

The Californian form of the Eared Grebe was found quite numerous about Denver, Col., by Mr. Henshaw as late as the 15th of May. The birds were seen occasionally in the river, but resorted mostly to certain small ponds not well adapted as breeding-grounds, and they were apparently still migrating. Later, on the 23d of June, they were found breeding in the alkali ponds of Southern Colorado, where he noticed them in several of these ponds, and presumed that small colonies had been formed in each. In the only instance in which he was able to inspect their nests a community of a dozen pairs had selected a bed of reeds in the middle of the pond, isolated from the land by a considerable interval of water. The nests are described as being slightly hollowed piles of decaying reeds and rushes, just raised above the surface of the water, upon which they float. Each nest contained three eggs, most of them being fresh, a few only being in a somewhat advanced stage of incubation. In every instance the eggs were entirely covered by a pile of vegetable material; and as in no case were the birds found incubating, even where the eggs contained slight embryos, it seems highly probable that their hatching is dependent more or less upon the heat derived from the sun's rays.

The eggs are said to vary little in shape, being considerably elongated, and one end slightly more pointed than the other, and in size varying from 1.70 to 1.80 inches in length, and from 1.18 to 1.33 in breadth. The color is a faint yellowish white, usually much stained by contact with the nest. The texture is generally quite smooth, but in some cases roughened by a chalky deposit.

Captain Bendire noted this species as being a common summer resident in Eastern Oregon, breeding in colonies in several localities in the neighborhood of Camp Harney. He found in the summer of 1876 quite a number of its nests, containing from three to five eggs. It was seen by Mr. Gunn breeding in great numbers at Shoal Lake.

Eggs of this species from California, and from Shoal Lake, in British America, resemble in size and shape, as well as in their ground-colors, those of the Horned Grebe. The measurements of four, taken as typical, are: 1.70 by 1.10 inches; 1.70 by 1.25; 1.75 by 1.15; and 1.80 by 1.25.

Genus PODICEPS, Latham.

Podiceps, Lath. Ind. Orn. II. 1790, 780 (part; type, by elimination and restriction, *Colymbus fluviatilis*, Tunst.).

Tachybaptus, Reichenb. Syst. Av. 1852, p. iii (type, *Colymbus minor*, Gmel., = *C. fluviatilis*, Tunst.).

Char. Very small (wing not more than 4.00 inches). Neck much smaller than the body; bill shorter than the head, the culmen less than 3 times the basal depth; tarsus decidedly shorter than the middle toe without claw; adult in breeding-plumage without ornamental tufts (or, in the American species, colored patches).

Although quite different in its coloration from the type of the genus (*P. fluviatilis*), which has the head brightly colored in the breeding-season, the American species which we place here agrees very minutely in the details of form.

Podiceps dominicus.

THE LEAST GREBE.

Colymbus dominicus, Linn. S. N. I. 1766, 223 (based on *Colymbus fluviatilis dominicensis*, Briss. Orn. VI. 1760, 64, pl. 5, fig. 2).

Podiceps dominicus, Lath. Ind. Orn. II. 1790, 785. — Baird, Rep. U. S. & Mex. Bound. Survey, II. 1859, pt. ii. Birds, 28; Birds N. Am. ed. 1860, pl. 99, fig. 1; Cat. N. Am. B. 1859, no. 708 *a*. — Coues, Key, 1872, 338; Check List, 1873, no. 613; ed. 2, 1882, no. 851.

Sylbeocyclus dominicus, Coues, Pr. Ac. Nat. Sci. Philad. 1862, 232.

Podiceps (Tachybaptes) dominicus, Coues, Birds N. W. 1874, 736.

Tachybaptes dominicus, Ridgw. Nom. N. Am. B. 1881, no. 734.

Hab. The whole of tropical America, both continental and Antillean; south to Paraguay, north to Texas and Lower California.

Sp. Char. *Adult, breeding-plumage:* Head and neck dark grayish or dull plumbeous, the pileum slightly glossy greenish black, the chin and throat dull black; remaining upper parts dusky brown, the remiges light brownish gray, with their inner webs chiefly white. Lower parts white, clouded, chiefly beneath the surface, with grayish dusky, the sides and crissum uniform grayish

brown, the jugulum similar, sometimes tinged with ferruginous. Bill deep black, the tip paler; iris orange; legs and feet blackish. *Winter plumage:* Similar to the preceding, but chin and throat white, and the lower parts more uniformly white. *Downy young:* Head and neck marked with white and dusky black lines; upper parts uniform dusky, lower grayish white.[1]

Total length, about 9.00 inches; wing, 4.00; culmen, .90; depth of bill at base, .35; tarsus, 1.30; middle toe, without claw, 1.50.

[1] The downy young are thus described by M. Taczanowski, in Proc. Zool. Soc. Lond. 1882, p. 49:— "The young ones in down, collected in July, have the top of the head black, with a rufous spot in the middle and a series of white stripes disposed in the following manner: a median stripe in front of the

This diminutive Grebe is a West Indian, Mexican, Central American, and South American species, coming within our fauna only in Southwestern Texas and in the valley of the Colorado.

In the Berlandier Collection, purchased by Lieutenant Couch and presented to the Smithsonian Institution, there were a number of the eggs of this Grebe, showing that this bird must be not uncommon in the valley of the Rio Grande, especially on its western side.

Mr. Salvin met with this species on the Lake of Dueñas on the 15th of October, 1859. Mr. G. C. Taylor saw several individuals on the lagoon in Tigre Island, Honduras. Mr. E. C. Taylor mentions his meeting with it in Porto Rico. There he once came upon several of these birds swimming about in a deep broad ditch, and succeeded in obtaining one. He found that it differs from the true Grebe in having the feet semipalmated as well as lobated. Léotaud includes it among the birds of Trinidad, where it is frequently to be met with. He regards it as a true Grebe in its habits, and as passing all its life in the water. Its plumage thickly matted, and thoroughly impregnated with oil, is utterly impervious to moisture. The anatomical formation of its respiratory organs is such that there is not the usual necessity for frequent renewals of respiration. When, therefore, it plunges in alarm under the water, to escape the danger that menaces, it will exhaust the patience of the hunter before it reappears. Sometimes it will go to the bottom, and there remain a long time, moving about all the while as if it were on the land. Whenever it chances to be upon the land, and attempts to move, its awkwardness clearly indicates that the bird is entirely out of its element. When it is at rest it keeps itself nearly upright, supporting itself on its tarsi and rump. Léotaud also mentions that he has heard of persons who maintain the excellence of the flesh of this Grebe, but that he is decidedly not one of that number. He is not able to state with positive certainty whether this species is a resident of Trinidad, or only a visitant.

Dr. Burmeister mentions that this species is found everywhere throughout the whole region of the La Plata, upon the lakes, ponds, and streams in the pampas, and in the lagoons near the larger rivers, preferring always still water.

Colonel Grayson speaks of the Santo Domingo Grebe as being an abundant and common species near Mazatlan, in Western Mexico. It is found in all the fresh-water ponds and lakelets of that locality, and may be met with near Tepic through the entire year.

Dr. Berlandier, in his manuscript notes, speaks of a Grebe, corresponding in size to this species, as inhabiting the lakes produced by the overflowing of the Rio Bravo del Norte, in the vicinity of Matamoras.

Dr. Merrill — the first positively to confirm the claim of this Grebe to belong to our fauna — found it a rather common resident in Southwestern Texas. Several nests, undoubtedly belonging to this species, were found by him May 16, 1877, in a salt-marsh a few miles from Fort Brown. These nests were made of water-plants and pieces of reeds slightly fastened to one or two *tulé* stalks, forming a wet floating mass. No eggs were obtained.

rufous spot, an eyebrow over each eye; a postocular stripe, an oblique cervical stripe extending along the whole length of the neck, and a nuchal stripe also passing on to the neck; cheeks, throat, and foreneck are white, varied with blackish lines, one of which extends from the chin along the whole length of the throat and neck; two others on each side of the neck, one on the sides of the throat, and the other the whole length of the lower part of the cheeks. Back blackish gray, interspersed with white hairs; breast and sides deep gray, mixed with whitish hairs; middle of the under part largely white. Iris nearly black."

The eggs of the Least Grebe are of a pale chalky greenish white, varying from discolorations, and are unspotted. Those in the Smithsonian Collection are from Matamoras, Mazatlan, Cuba, and Jamaica. They vary from 1.25 inches to 1.50 in length, and from .85 to 1.00 in breadth.[1]

GENUS **PODILYMBUS**, LESSON.

Podilymbus, LESSON, Traité, I. 1831, 595 (type, *Podiceps carolinensis*, LATH., = *Colymbus podiceps*, LINN.).

Sylbeocyclus, BONAP. Saggio, 1832, 144 (same type; cf. SCL. Ibis, 1874, p. 98).

CHAR. Size medium (wing about 4.50–5.00 inches); bill very stout, the length of the culmen less than twice the basal depth; bill much shorter than the head, the culmen much curved termi-

P. podiceps.

nally; tarsus shorter than the middle toe without claw. No tufts in summer plumage, but bill parti-colored, and throat ornamented by a black patch.

Podilymbus podiceps.

THICK-BILLED GREBE; CAROLINA GREBE.

Colymbus podiceps, LINN. S. N. ed. 10, I. 1758, 136; ed. 12, I. 1766, 223 (based on *Podiceps minor rostro vario*, CATESBY, Car. 91. — *Colymbus fluviatilis carolinensis*, BRISS. Orn. VI. 1760, 63).

Podilymbus podiceps, LAWR. in Baird's B. N. Am. 1858, 898. — BAIRD, Cat. N. Am. B. 1859, no. 709. — COUES, Key, 1872, 338; Check List, 1873, no. 614; Birds N. W. 1874, 737. — RIDGW. Nom. N. Am. B. 1881, no. 735.

Podilymbus podiceps, COUES, 2d Check List, 1882, no. 852.

Podiceps ludovicianus, LATH. Ind. Orn. II. 1790, 785.

Podiceps carolinensis, LATH. l. c. — SW. & RICH. F. B. A. II. 1831, 412. — NUTT. Man. II. 1834, 259. — AUD. Orn. Biog. III. 1835, 359; Synop. 1839, 358; B. Am. VII. 1844, 324, pl. 483.

Podilymbus lineatus, HEERM. Pr. Ac. Nat. Sci. Philad. 1854, 179; Pacific R. R. Rep. X. 1859, 77, pl. 9 (young).

Podiceps antarcticus, LESS. Rev. Zool. 1842, 209.

Podilymbus antarcticus, GRAY, Hand-l. III. 1871, 95, no. 10771.

Podilymbus podiceps, b. *antarcticus*, COUES, Birds N. W. 1874, 737.

Podiceps brevirostris, GRAY, Gen. B. III. 1839, pl. 172.

[1] "The eggs of the two layings resemble those of the *P. minor* of Europe, and are in general a little smaller. Dimensions: 36 × 25; 35.5 × 27.8; 36.3 × 27.8; 35 × 25; 37.3 × 25.7 millim." (TACZANOWSKI, Proc. Zool. Soc. Lond. 1882, p. 49).

HAB. Greater part of South America, whole of Middle America, West Indies, and temperate North America, breeding nearly throughout its range. South to Brazil, Buenos Ayres, and Chili, north to British Provinces. Bermudas.

SP. CHAR. *Adult, breeding-plumage:* Chin, throat, and a spot at the base of the mandible, black; rest of the head and neck brownish gray, darker on the pileum and nape, lighter on the sides of the head, the malar region light ashy, streaked with dusky. Upper parts uniform dusky grayish brown, the remiges paler, the inner webs of the secondaries tipped with white; lower parts grayish white, everywhere spotted with dusky grayish. Bill milk-white, crossed past the middle

Summer adult.

by a black band, the terminal portion more bluish; eyelids white; naked lores bluish; iris rich dark brown, with a narrow outer ring of ochraceous-white, and an inner thread-like ring of pure white; tarsi and toes greenish slate-black on the outer, and plumbeous on the inner side.[1] *Winter plumage:* Head and neck dull brownish, darker on the pileum and nape, and becoming white on the chin and throat (sometimes also on the malar region); lower parts silvery white, brownish laterally and posteriorly; upper parts as in the summer plumage. Bill horn-color, becoming blackish basally and on the culmen; lower mandible more lilaceous, with a dusky lateral stripe; iris of three distinct colors, disposed in concentric rings, the first (around the pupil) clear milk-white, the next dark olive-brown, the outer pale ochraceous-brown, the dark ring reticulated into the lighter; tarsi and toes greenish slate, the joints darker.[2] *Young, first plumage:* Similar to the winter dress, but side and under part of the head white, indefinitely striped with brown, the throat sometimes immaculate. *Downy young:* Head and neck distinctly striped with white and black; a spot of rufous on the middle of the crown, one on each side the occiput, and one on the upper part of the nape; the latter confluent with two white stripes running down the nape, the others entirely surrounded with black; upper parts blackish dusky, marked with four longitudinal stripes or lines of grayish white running the whole length of the body; lower parts immaculate white medially, dusky grayish anteriorly, laterally, and posteriorly.

Total length, about 13.25 to 15.00 inches; extent, 20.00–23.00; wing, 4.50–5.00; culmen, .75; depth of bill at base, .45; tarsus, 1.40; middle toe without claw, 1.80.

We are entirely unable to discover any tangible difference between several South American examples, in different stages of plumage, and North American specimens, and can therefore see no reason for admitting the so-called *P. antarcticus*.

The "Pied-billed" or "Carolina Grebe" is an exclusively American species, and is widely distributed. It is found throughout South and North America from Cape Horn to the Mackenzie River, and occurs on the Pacific as well as on the Atlantic coast. It is resident in Santo Domingo, Cuba, Jamaica, Trinidad, and probably in most of the West India Islands, is also resident in Central America, and probably in Mexico. To what extent it is anywhere resident, or only a visitor, is with

[1] Fresh colors of an adult female killed March 24 at Carson City, Nev.

[2] From a specimen killed November 18 at Truckee Meadows, Nev.

difficulty determined, since this is not a bird whose presence is easily detected, owing to its quiet and secretive habits.

Mr. Salvin found this Grebe a resident in Dueñas, Guatemala, where it breeds in May, making a nest among the reeds of the lake, of a pile of flags, heaped up so as just to raise the edge of the structure above the surface of the water. The eggs were generally half immersed. These were from two to five in number, and of a chalky exterior on an under surface of bluish green, measuring 1.55 inches in length by 1.08 in breadth. A specimen was taken by Dr. Cunningham near the Island of Chiloe, in the Straits of Magellan, on the 20th of March.

Mr. Bernard Ross met with it as far to the north as the valley of the Mackenzie. Mr. H. E. Dresser found it not uncommon near San Antonio, Texas, in the winter. He observed several on a pond near Matamoras in August, 1864. Another specimen — a young bird — was obtained from Fort Stockton.

Dr. Gundlach informs me by letter that he has found this Grebe breeding in Cuba, and he has sent me specimens of its eggs. I have also received its eggs from Jamaica. Mr. Gosse frequently met with it in the marshes on the banks of the Rio Cobre. When taken alive it soon becomes reconciled to confinement, and feeds readily on raw chopped fish. A bird of this species, which Mr. Richard Hill kept alive a few weeks, apparently felt great pleasure in lying on the weeds placed for him by the side of a bowl of water, from which he drank. He would there repose hour after hour, doubled up on the grass. The food given to this bird was Guinea-corn, which he ate readily after it had been softened in the water. Léotaud mentions this species as being one of the common birds of Trinidad. Its habits are precisely similar to those of *P. dominicus.* Three examples are recorded by Major Wedderburn as having been taken in Bermuda in 1849 and 1850. This Grebe is abundant in the neighborhood of Calais, Me., where it breeds.

Mr. J. A. Allen met with it in September in the valley of Great Salt Lake, Utah.

Mr. N. B. Moore, writing from Sarasota Bay, Fla., states that in the spring of 1870 he killed a bird of this species in which he found an egg of nearly full size; and in a day or two afterward found her nest, containing one egg. In April, 1873, he found another nest on the same pond. The young, five in number, stood in the nest uttering a faint peep, something like the cry of a very young duckling. They all toddled overboard on his approach. The terrified mother in the meanwhile was swimming rapidly about, frequently diving and uttering sad notes of alarm, with scarcely a feather of her back above the water. The nest was composed of broken stems of dog-fennel, matted together with a large portion of decayed and withered aquatic plants, presenting, when found, a wet, black, and soggy bed, to all appearances as uncomfortable a nest as ever fell to the lot of delicate and beautiful downy creatures such as these were. The nest was ten yards from the shore, within the pond, and situated in a thick clump of erect dead stems of the fennel where it rested on the bottom of the pond, the water being about eight inches deep. The part above the water was circular, twelve inches in breadth, the central depression being rather shallow, and an inch in depth and five or six in breadth. There was no lining, and the whole presented an appearance of solidity resembling masonry. The upper part of the rim was only about two and a half inches above the surface of the pond, and could not possibly have floated had the water risen to any height. When about three weeks old the young dive for their own food, though the mother feeds them long afterward. The young have been caught as late as September 15th, and it is probable that this bird has two or three broods in a season. This Grebe winters as far north as Puget Sound, where also it is by no means rare during the summer. Dr. Heermann states that it is found in winter about marshy lakes throughout California, and that it also breeds there. The nest is built near the edge of the water. One of the nests which Dr. Cooper found was floating in water over two feet deep, but was held in its place by the stalks of living plants, to which it was fastened by the aid of the rushes of which it was composed. Its shape was conical, and it was a foot wide at the bottom and nine inches at the top, where it was slightly hollowed out. The eggs — four in number — were white, with brownish incrustations, and of nearly equal size at both ends. The eggs found on the 11th of June at Puget Sound were just ready to hatch.

These birds are usually perfectly fearless, swimming quite near to the spectator, and trusting to their power of diving to escape from danger. They become suspicious, however, after having been shot at. They can swim to a long distance under water, merely raising the bill above the surface occasionally, and they are somewhat nocturnal in habit. In the spring they make a loud and sonorous braying noise. They feed on small fish and insects, and prefer to hunt for them in places covered with dense aquatic vegetation, being chiefly fresh-water birds, though seeking the bays in the winter. This bird has the singular habit, in common with all the other Grebes, of sinking down gradually and backwards into the water until it entirely disappears, not leaving a ripple on the surface. This it does in order to escape, when not compelled to dive quickly.

Mr. John Xantus found this Grebe at Manzanilla Bay, in Western Mexico, where it was not abundant.

In Southern Wisconsin this species goes by the name — more emphatic than euphonious — of "Hell-diver." Mr. Kumlien informs me that it breeds there both in the lake and in the mill-pond, the nest being very bulky. Of these birds in the full plumage he has seen only a single specimen, although he has obtained a great many individuals. They exhibit greater variations in size than any bird with which he is acquainted. They are found from April 13 to October 20.

Mr. B. F. Goss writes me that he has found this bird common on the lakes of Wisconsin, nesting about the 20th of May, on rushes of the previous year, in water from one to three feet deep. In such situations the old rushes are piled upon each other until the fabric rises to the top of the water; a nest formed of moss and weeds gathered from the bottom is raised but little, and is always wet except when the water has receded and left it higher than it was originally built. It appears like a circular mass of weeds and moss, about the size of a dinner plate, floating on the water, and when filled with eggs and carefully covered, it resembles a floating ball, and would be passed without notice by one unacquainted with its peculiarity. It does not, however, really float, as its foundations rest more or less perfectly on the bottom. The eggs — five in number — are white at first; but are soon stained by contact with the wet nest. Sometimes the shell is quite rough, and has a calcareous incrustation. In the absence of the bird the eggs are usually carefully covered. This is done with surprising quickness when the nest is approached, the bird always escaping unseen. The many nests Mr. Goss has examined were always alike, always in shallow water, and constructed of rushes, never of flags, grass, or weeds, however abundant these might be. The bird is very shy in the breeding-season, keeping out of sight; and even where abundant its presence may remain unsuspected. He spent several days among its haunts, and found numerous nests without seeing a single bird; and it was only by concealing himself, and watching the nest with a field-glass, that he was able to identify the species.

Eggs of this species from Cuba, Jamaica, Great Slave Lake, Michigan, Illinois, and

Wisconsin are in the museum of the Smithsonian Institution. They are essentially like all the eggs of this genus in shape and colors, and vary greatly in size. Two eggs in my own collection, from Wisconsin, measure, one 1.92 inches in length by 1.20 in breadth, the other 1.68 by 1.20; while one from Dueñas, Guatemala, measures 1.63 by 1.18.

Family URINATORIDÆ. — The Loons.

Char. Swimming birds, with the feet situated far back, a well developed hallux, the anterior toes completely webbed and normally clawed; the bill straight, acute, compressed, the nostrils linear, overhung by a membraneous lobe; tail normal, but short. Nature præcocial; eggs two or three, dark-colored, and more or less spotted.

The Family includes a single genus, *Urinator*, usually, but wrongly, called *Colymbus*.

Genus **URINATOR**, Cuvier.

Colymbus, Linn. S. N. ed. 10, I. 1758, 135; ed. 12, I. 1766, 220 (part).
Mergus, Briss. Orn. VI. 1760, 104 (not of Linn. 1758).
Uria, Scop. Introd. 1777, 473 (not of Briss. 1760).
Urinator, Cuv. Anat. Comp. I. 1799, tabl. ii. (types, *Colymbi arcticus, glacialis, et septentrionalis*, Linn.).
Eudytes, Illig. Prodr. 1811, 282 (same types).

Char. The same as those of the Family.

We cannot allow our aversion for violent or otherwise distasteful changes to overrule the obvious necessities of the present case. There can be no question that the name *Colymbus*, so long

U. immer, adult.

used by many authors for this genus, belongs properly to the Grebes. This fact has long ago been clearly demonstrated by Sundeval and other competent authorities, and more recently by Dr. L.

Stejneger in the "Proceedings" of the United States National Museum, Vol. 5, pp. 42, 43, as follows: —

"Linnæus united the Grebes and the Loons or Divers in the same genus, *Colymbus;* but in 1760 Brisson had already separated the Loons from the Grebes, retaining the name *Colymbus* for the latter. In 1777 Scopoli followed his example. Ten years later Latham applied the name *Podiceps* to the same group, this consequently being a mere synonyme of *Colymbus* as restricted by Brisson. As the name given by the latter author to the Loons was preoccupied, the next name, which is Cuvier's *Urinator*, is to be used. The name *Eudytes* (ILLIGER), although twelve years younger, has been generally adopted, but it must give way to the older name, for the suppression of which I see no reason."

The North American species (there are none extralimital) may be distinguished as follows: —

Synopsis of Species.

1. **U. immer.** *Adult:* Head, neck, and upper parts black, the head and neck faintly glossed with dull greenish; middle of the foreneck, and sides of the lower neck, crossed by a bar of longitudinal white streaks; upper parts handsomely dotted with white, these markings largest, and quite quadrate, on the scapulars; lower parts white. Bill black, the extreme tip only light colored. *Young:* Upper parts dusky, many of the feathers tipped or edged with plumbeous; lower parts, including under side of head and neck, white. Wing, 13.00–15.25 inches (average, 14.06); culmen, 2.75–3.50 (3.07); depth of bill through base, .90–1.05 (.96); tarsus, 2.75–3.85 (3.35); outer toe, 3.85–4.65. *Hab.* Northern part of northern hemisphere.
2. **U. Adamsii.** Similar to *immer*, but much larger, the bill very differently shaped, the head and neck glossed with violet-blue, instead of greenish, the white spots of the scapulars decidedly longer than broad, and the bill light colored. Wing, 14.85–15.45 inches (average, 15.11); culmen, 3.50–3.65 (3.59); depth of bill through base, 1.00–1.20 (1.09); tarsus, 3.25–3.55 (3.41); outer toe, 4.15–4.65 (4.34). *Hab.* Western Arctic America.
3. **U. arcticus.** *Adult:* Under side of head, with foreneck, velvety purplish black, with purplish violet gloss; upper part of head and nape smoky ash; sides of the neck with several longitudinal rows of white streaks; upper parts black, the back and scapulars with three longitudinal series of broad white bars; lower parts white. *Young:* Similar in colors to the same stage of *immer* and *Adamsii.* Wing, 12.15–13.20 inches (average, 12.55); culmen, 2.50–2.85 (2.60); depth of bill through base, .75–.80 (.78); tarsus, 2.90–3.30 (3.11); outer toe, 3.45–3.95 (3.76). *Hab.* Northern part of northern hemisphere, chiefly the Palæarctic Region and Northeastern America.
4. **U. pacificus.** Similar to *arcticus*, but decidedly smaller, with much smaller and more slender bill; occiput and nape much paler ashy — almost smoky white; black of the foreneck rather greenish than purplish. Wing, 11.20–12.25 inches (average, 11.54); culmen, 2.00–2.35 (2.15); depth of bill through base, .55–.65 (.62); tarsus, 2.70–3.00 (2.86); outer toe, 3.30–3.70 (3.47). *Hab.* Pacific coast of North America.
5. **U. lumme.** *Adult:* Head and neck ashy, the crown and nape streaked with dusky and white; foreneck with a longitudinal wedge-shaped patch of rich chestnut; upper parts dusky slate, speckled with white; lower parts white. *Young:* Similar, but lower half of head and whole foreneck white, like the under parts. Wing, 10.00–11.50 inches; culmen, 2.25; tarsus, 2.75. *Hab.* Northern portion of northern hemisphere.

Urinator immer.

THE GREAT NORTHERN DIVER.

Colymbus imber,[1] GUNN. Trond. Selsk. Skr. I. 1761, pl. iii.
Colymbus immer, BRÜNN. Orn. Bor. 1764, 34 (young). — LINN. S. N. ed. 12, I. 1766, 222.
Urinator immer, STEJN. Pr. U. S. Nat. Mus. Vol. 5, 1882, 43.
Colymbus torquatus, BRÜNN. Orn. Bor. 1764, 41. — LAWR. in Baird's B. N. Am. 1858, 888. — BAIRD, Cat. N. Am. B. 1859, no. 698. — COUES, Pr. Ac. Nat. Sci. Philad. 1862, 227 ; Key, 1872, 334 ; Check List, 1873, no. 605 ; ed. 2, 1882, no. 840. — RIDGW. Nom. N. Am. B. 1881, no. 736.
Colymbus glacialis, LINN. S. N. I. 1766, 221. — WILS. Am. Orn. IX. 1824, 84, pl. 74. — RICH. & Sw. F. B. A. II. 1831, 474. — NUTT. Man. II. 1834, 513. — AUD. Orn. Biog. IV. 1838, 43, pl. 306 ; B. Am. VII. 1844, 282, pl. 476.
Colymbus maximus, GUNN. Tr. Selsk. Skr. III. 1765, 125.
Mergus nævius, BONNAT. Enc. Méth. Orn. I. 1790, 73.
Colymbus atrogularis, MEYER & WOLF, Tasch. Vög. Deutschl. II. 1810, 449 (part).
Colymbus hyemalis, BREHM, Lehrb. Eur. Vög. II. 1824, 883.

HAB. Northern part of northern hemisphere. In America, breeding from the Northern States northward, wintering south to the Gulf of Mexico; no extralimital American record.

SP. CHAR. *Adult:* Head and neck dull black, with a greenish reflection, this brightest on the lower part of the neck; foreneck crossed by a narrow bar of white longitudinal oblong dots or

short streaks; sides of the neck some distance below this crossed by a broad bar of longitudinal white streaks; upper parts black, beautifully variegated with white dots, these largest, and nearly quadrate in form, on the scapulars, minute and dot-like on the rump. Lower parts immaculate white, the sides of the jugulum narrowly streaked with black, the sides and flanks black, dotted

[1] The preference is here given to *Colymbus immer*, BRÜNN., over *C. imber*, GUNN., only for the reason that there may be a question as to whether Gunnerus is acceptable as a binomialist. He is unquestionably as much so as Bartram, whose *identifiable* names are not challenged, and furthermore describes his species much more accurately and scientifically than did Bartram; while his diagnoses are accompanied by perfectly recognizable plates. (See STEJNEGER, Proc. U. S. Nat. Mus. Vol. 5, p. 37, and The Auk, April, 1884, p. 119.) Our reasons for preferring *immer* to *torquatus* are that the latter does not occur in the twelfth edition of Linnæus's Systema Naturæ, while the former does, and may therefore be taken by those ornithologists who do not recognize names dating earlier than 1766.

with white. Bill black, paler at the tip; iris carmine; legs and feet "livid grayish blue, their inner sides tinged with pale yellowish flesh-color; claws black, lighter at the base; webs brownish black, lighter in the middle" (AUDUBON). *Young:* Upper parts dusky, the scapulars, interscapulars, and upper tail-coverts bordered terminally with plumbeous-gray; lower parts, including malar region, chin, throat, and foreneck, white, the sides and flanks dusky brown, squamated with grayish. "Bill pale yellowish green, the ridge and tip of uppper mandible dusky; iris brown; feet dusky externally, pale yellowish flesh-color internally, webs dusky, but yellow in the middle" (AUDUBON). *Downy young:* Uniform dark fuliginous, lighter and more slaty on the throat, foreneck, jugulum, and sides, the entire abdomen velvety yellowish white, shaded with pale ash-gray exteriorly. The down short and very dense, very similar to the fur of an otter or other fur-bearing mammal.

Total length, 32.00 to 36.00 inches; extent, 52.00 to 57.50; wing, 13.05–15.25 (average, 14.06); culmen, 2.75–3.50 (3.07); depth of bill through base, .90–1.05 (.96); tarsus, 2.75–3.85 (3.35); outer toe, 3.85–4.65 (4.22). (Thirteen adults.)

Two examples from Iceland are identical with American specimens.

The Loon, or Great Northern Diver, of North America has a high northern distribution during its season of reproduction. It is found from the Atlantic to the Pacific, and breeds from about latitude 42° to within the Arctic Circle. During the winter it is found on both the western and eastern sea-coasts, from lat. 48° N. to San Diego on the Pacific, and from Maine to Florida and Texas on the Atlantic and Gulf coast. In the interior it is found as far north as it can procure food and find open water.

According to Professor Reinhardt it is a resident species in Greenland. It is common throughout the interior of the Fur Countries in the summer season, frequenting lakes and ponds. Mr. Ross procured specimens on the Mackenzie, and Mr. Murray received them from the Hudson's Bay Region. Mr. Bannister mentions this bird as common on the Island of St. Michael's, and Mr. Dall as not uncommon on the Yukon, particularly near the sea. It was obtained by Mr. Kennicott at Fort Yukon. It breeds at Kyska, and is abundant at Amchitka in July; but was not seen elsewhere among the Aleutian Islands, except at the Shumagins, where it is a summer resident, according to Mr. Dall.

Dr. Cooper states that it is abundant during the winter in San Diego Bay, and along the whole coast up to the forty-eighth degree of north latitude, and in all open fresh waters. He saw it about San Diego as late as May, where the birds were in pairs. They are found in the summer about every lake and pond in the Cascade Mountains and the Sierra Nevada. They build on the borders of these lakes, and, north of the Columbia, down nearly to the level of the sea. As soon as the young have been hatched, the males desert their mates, and repair to the salt water. Soon after this they moult, and become so bare of feathers as to be unable to rise from the water.

A specimen was taken by Dr. Holden in the Colorado River; and a single individual was secured by Mr. Dresser in Southwestern Texas.

Mr. N. B. Moore states that in Florida, in winter — usually in December — he has occasionally seen as many as eight of this species, in immature plumage, swimming in company. It does not always swallow its fish when under the water. He has frequently seen the Loon bring the fish to the surface, if large, and there attempt to swallow it. He has known this bird to be taken in a common cast-net thrown by the hand.

Mr. George A. Boardman informs me that the Loon breeds abundantly in the ponds of the neighborhood of Calais; and he has ascertained that the number of its young is invariably two. These, as soon as they are hatched, are taken by the old bird upon her back, and in this position they are carried about with her wherever she moves upon the water; they are thus kept in the rays of the sun. This she continues to do for several days, and until they have grown to a considerable size.

The Loon very rarely associates in flocks, and then only apparently from necessity — as when a limited surface of open water compels them to crowd together. During the winter, either singly or in pairs, or in small parties, they are dispersed throughout the United States. Knowing that man is its mortal enemy, this bird is constantly on the watch. When it meets a passing boat it widens the distance by immediately steering off, is active in diving, and when sitting, defies the keenest sportsman. It is a very hardy bird, and is said to live to an incredible old age. Giraud states that in 1843 an individual was killed on the eastern end of Long Island, in which was found the head of an Indian file, confined in the back of the neck, between the bone and the skin. The wound was completely healed over, and had the appearance of having been made a long time before; and it was supposed by some that the wound must have been received before the settlement of the country.

The flesh of this bird is tough, hard, and unpalatable; but it is not infrequently eaten by the fishermen.

The Loon subsists almost entirely on fish, is an excellent diver, and when alarmed, eludes pursuit by passing swiftly to a considerable distance under the water. Its habits are strictly aquatic. When, in its migrations, it passes over the land, it flies at a great height and very rapidly. In stormy weather it takes shelter in coves and creeks, and occasionally in mill-ponds.

Hearne, in his "Journey to the Northern Ocean," speaks of the Loon as being common in Hudson's Bay. It is very seldom found there near the sea-coast, but more frequently in fresh-water lakes, and usually in pairs. It makes its nest on the edge of a small island or on the margins of lakes or ponds, laying only two eggs; and it is very common to find that a sheet of water is in exclusive possession of one pair and their young.

This bird is universally known near Hudson's Bay as the Loon; and it is sometimes found so large as to weigh fifteen or sixteen pounds. The flesh, though black, hard, and fishy, is generally eaten by the Indians. It can swim with great swiftness to a considerable distance under water, and when it comes to the surface rarely exposes more than the neck. It takes wing with difficulty, flies heavily, though swiftly, and frequently in a circle round those that intrude on its haunts. Richardson speaks of its cry as being loud and melancholy — not unlike the howl of a wolf, or, at other times, the distant scream of a man in distress. He caught several in nets, in which they had entangled themselves when in pursuit of fish.

Mr. B. F. Goss, of Southern Wisconsin, writes me that this bird begins to arrive early in the spring, as soon as the ice first breaks up around the shores of the lakes and streams. During their spring migrations they are sometimes seen in large flocks; but most of these pass to the northward, only a few remaining through the season to breed. The Loon is formed for swimming and diving — the conformation of its legs being such that for it to stand on the land is nearly impossible; but in its home on the water it is a graceful and beautiful bird, swimming with the greatest ease, and diving in the most surprising manner. It can swim to a great distance under the water, sinking silently and without apparent effort; and its reappearance will be looked for in vain, even on one of our large lakes, where the view is unobstructed and the water smooth. It builds its nest about the 20th of May. This is sometimes constructed on a musk-rat's mound, but usually on a small bog, close to the edge, where the bird can slip directly into the water; it is composed of mud, moss, and aquatic plants, and though quite bulky, is seldom raised more than six inches above the water. Sometimes this elevation is barely large enough to contain the nest. There is no attempt at concealment; on the contrary, the most open situation is chosen, where the view is unobstructed in all directions. If a boat approaches, the bird glides silently into the water, rising only at a great distance, and unless closely watched, is rarely seen. Two eggs is the usual number, measuring 3.40 by 2.33 inches, the ground-color yellowish brown, covered more or less thickly over the whole egg with spots, and sometimes large blotches, of black. The shell is very hard; and when two are struck together they rattle like stones. They are never covered in the absence of the bird. The young leave the nest as soon as hatched, are expert divers, and difficult to catch, even when very small. The old bird is often very brave in their defence; on one occasion approaching close to the boat and dashing water over Mr. Goss with her wings.

Audubon states that, in Labrador, in a number of instances he found the nest of this bird several yards from the water; and where this was the case, a well-beaten path was found leading from it to the water. The nests were fifteen inches in diameter and seven inches high. He claims to have more frequently found three than two eggs — a statement that leads me to think he may have sometimes mistaken the nest of the *septentrionalis* (= *lumme*) for that of this bird. Certainly I have never seen, nor have I ever heard of, more than two eggs in a nest of this species. He gives 3.75 inches by 2.25 as the average size of its egg; ground-color a dull greenish ochrey, marked with spots of dark umber. The young, when just from the shell, is covered with a stiff black down.

In regard to the number of eggs in a nest, two is the unvarying number, so far as I know. Nuttall mentions having received three from a nest in Sebago Pond; but as he did not take them himself, it is quite possible he inferred rather than knew that they were all taken from one nest. The only apparent exception to there being but two eggs to a nest is one mentioned by Mr. Thomas B. Stearns, who, in the summers of 1877 and 1878, carefully observed the habits of this species among the lakes of Northern Maine. He collected the eggs of twelve pairs; in each instance the number in the nest was two; but in one case a third egg was in the water, and had evidently rolled out of the nest. This was fresh, and possibly its loss was supplemented, and not that there are ever at any one time three eggs in a nest. Mr. Stearns informs me that he found great differences in the structures used as nests, some being quite elaborate, others a mere scooped-out cavity in the bog or sandbank. In hardly any two cases was the behavior of the parent bird the same. In one instance she remained on her nest until the boat had approached within fifty feet, only at first lowering and trying to hide her head. In other cases the parents were very shy, and did not permit themselves to be seen. In another instance the parents kept closely about his boat, uttering mournful cries, and only removed to a safer distance after having been several times shot at. Mr. Stearns found in some cases one egg much incubated, the other quite fresh. One nest was the mere surface of a muddy bog that was floating on the surface of the water, but only partially detatched. These eggs were visible some thirty feet distant, and the hollow in which they lay was so damp that their under side was wet. Another nest had two distinct paths leading in different directions, thus furnishing two avenues of escape. In one instance the water was too shoal for the bird to dive, and she was captured alive just after her leaving her nest.

The Loon moves with difficulty on the land; but locomotion is not impossible, and when stimulated by fear it can flounder over the ground with considerable rapidity.

When kept in confinement, and crippled in wing, it will wander to quite a distance from its pond by night, and seek to escape or hide itself. If, when wounded, it falls upon the land, it will, if pursued, attempt to escape in a very rapid, though a very clumsy, manner.

In the spring the Loon may be attracted to the shore by the waving of a bright-colored handkerchief, as I have several times witnessed. On such occasions the bird seems to lay aside all its caution, and swims up to almost sure death. One person waves the attractive lure, while another keeps a steady aim, and fires when the bird is in short range and can make no successful effort to dive. In one instance my companion in the boat, Mr. Jonathan Johnson, of Nahant, shot a very old bird that behaved in a manner at first unaccountable. Its attention was fixed upon another boat, from which it moved away and directly toward us, apparently taking no notice of us, and not diving at the flash of Mr. Johnson's gun. We found that it had been blinded of one eye — which explained its not seeing us, especially when its attention was fixed elsewhere. It had evidently long before received a ghastly wound on the side and top of the head, that, strangely enough, had not proved mortal; this had partially healed over; though a portion of the skull had been shot away, and one eye was shrunken and useless. That it could have survived such a wound, and lived, as it evidently had, for months — if not years — after the injury was inflicted, showed the wonderful tenacity of life of this bird.

On another occasion a number of Loons became hemmed in by drift-ice in a small opening in Lynn Harbor. The space was too limited to permit them to escape by flying, and they did not succeed by diving in passing out into the open sea, although the distance was not more than a quarter of a mile. They seemed to have lost all presence of mind, and to be panic-stricken; and allowed themselves to be shot one after the other, though escape by diving was evidently within their reach.

Mr. MacFarlane found this species breeding in considerable numbers in the vicinity of Fort Anderson. A nest, found in June on the edge of a pond of water, was a tolerably large mass of turf, and was partially screened from observation by grass and reeds growing in its vicinity. Another nest, found in July, was composed of a large mass of decayed vegetable matter, situated on the edge of a small lake. There was a depression made by the female in the centre of this mass, on which the eggs lay. In no instance were more than two eggs found in a nest.

The specimens of the eggs of this species in the collection of the Smithsonian Institution are from Maine, Nova Scotia, Alexandria Bay, N. Y., and from Minnesota. The ground-color of this egg varies from a deep raw-umber to an olivaceous-drab. The markings are small in size, sparsely distributed, and brownish black. Three typical specimens measure 3.30 by 2.25 inches; 3.50 by 2.15; and 3.55 by 2.40.

Urinator Adamsii.

THE WHITE-BILLED LOON.

Colymbus Adamsii, Gray, P. Z. S. 1859, 167. — Coues, Pr. Ac. Nat. Sci. Philad. 1862, 227. — Ridgw. Nom. N. Am. B. 1881, no. 737.
Colymbus torquatus, var. *Adamsii*, Coues, Key, 1872, 334; Check List, 1873, no. 605 *a*.
Colymbus torquatus, b. *Adamsii*, Coues, Birds N. W. 1874, 720.
Colymbus torquatus Adamsi, Coues, 2d Check List, 1882, no. 841.
Urinator Adamsii, Stejn. Proc. U. S. Nat. Mus. Vol. 5, 1882, 43.

Hab. Arctic America, west of Hudson's Bay; casual in Northern Europe and Asia (?).

Sp. Char. Similar to *U. immer*, but much larger, the bill very different in shape and color, the plumage also slightly different. Bill very large, much compressed, the terminal half tapering rapidly from the well-defined or even prominent angle at the base of the gonys ; culmen almost perfectly straight ; feathering on sides of maxilla reaching nearly to anterior end of the nostrils. *Adult:* Upper half of the head (including loral, orbital, and auricular regions), with nape, dull black, with slight brownish green reflections ; lower half of head (including malar region, chin, and throat), with foreneck and lower neck, all round, blue-black, with violet-blue reflections ; foreneck crossed by a bar of white longitudinal spots, these much broader than in *U. immer ;* sides of the neck, below this bar, with a transverse broad patch of similar markings. Upper parts black, variegated by white dots, as in *U. immer*, but those of the scapulars much longer than broad, instead of nearly square ; lower parts white, the sides of the jugulum streaked with black ; sides and flanks

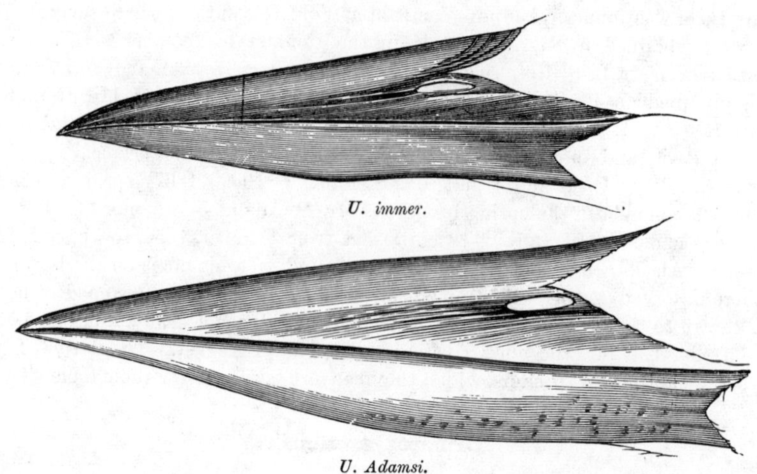

U. immer.

U. Adamsi.

blue-black, variegated by small round dots of white. Bill dull yellowish, dusky basally, inclining to ivory-white terminally ; iris " light reddish brown ; legs and feet olivaceous." *Young:* Similar to that of *U. immer*, but larger, the bill larger, deeper, more compressed, and with a decided gonydeal angle ; under side of head and neck grayish white, clouded with sooty grayish brown.

Wing, 14.85–15.45 inches (average, 15.11); culmen, 3.50–3.65 (3.59); depth of bill through base, 1.00–1.20 (1.09); tarsus, 3.25–3.55 (3.41); outer toe, 4.15–4.65 (4.34). (Six adults.)

So far as American specimens are concerned, this species appears to be perfectly distinct from *U. immer*, no examples at all intermediate occurring in large series of the two. It is a much larger bird in all its measurements, the bill is very differently shaped, and the plumage quite distinct in the points referred to above.

In "Birds of America," Vol. VII. p. 291, Audubon proposes a name, *Colymbus Richardsoni*, which some writers have considered as belonging to the present bird ; but although specimens of what were unquestionably *U. Adamsii*, collected by Captain Ross, are mentioned in the same paragraph, the name *Colymbus Richardsoni* was clearly based upon "a very large and *handsomely crested* Diver" which Dr. Richardson saw during one of his northern journeys, and which, "although somewhat prematurely," Audubon proposed " honoring with the name of *Colymbus Richardsoni*."

Mr. Audubon ("Birds of America," VII. 291) refers to a specimen of a Loon given to him by Captain James Clark Ross which had been procured in a very high latitude, and which, upon inspection, he found to differ from the common Northern Diver in having the point of the bill slightly recurved, and of a fine yellow tint; and Dr. Richardson also informed him that he had met with a very large and handsomely crested Diver. Regarding the latter as a new and undescribed species, Audubon proposed for it the name of *Colymbus Richardsoni*. This, however, could scarcely have been identical with the form since described as *Colymbus Adamsii.* It is common in the northwestern parts of North America, and said to be also of occasional occurrence in England, Asia, and perhaps elsewhere. We have no notes touching its specific peculiarities; and, indeed, it is not probable that these differ in any respect from those of the common Loon.

Mr. Bernard Ross mentions his having met with it in considerable numbers in Great Slave Lake. Mr. MacFarlane found it breeding, and obtained two eggs and several specimens of the bird, in the vicinity of Fort Anderson and on the shores of the Arctic Ocean. Specimens were also taken by Mr. Ross at Fort Simpson, by Mr. Clarke at Fort Rae, by Mr. J. Reid on Big Island, and by Bischoff at Kadiak.

This Loon was found to be quite common at Fort Resolution, where several specimens were obtained by Mr. Kennicott in the summer of 1860, as well as on the Yukon River. Mr. B. R. Ross secured specimens at Fort Norman and Fort Simpson. It was obtained on Peal's River by Mr. Gaudet, on Big Island by Mr. John Reid, at Fort Rae by Mr. L. Clarke, at Fort Resolution by Mr. J. Lockhart, and on the Anderson River and in its neighborhood generally by Mr. MacFarlane.

Mr. Whitely ("Ibis," 1867) and Mr. Swinhoe ("Ibis," 1867) speak of finding this species common in the spring in Yezo. Mr. E. Adams — in honor of whom this species was named by Mr. Gray — was present from October, 1850, to June, 1851, at Michalaski, Alaska, on the shores of Norton's Sound. In his notes on the birds then and there observed ("Ibis," 1878), mention is made of what is presumed to be this form, known to the natives as the *Too-oo-slik.* He did not see any himself, but he was told that this bird did not arrive before the end of August. The natives had in their possession plenty of skins, which they convert into bags for their tools.

Urinator arcticus.

THE ARCTIC LOON.

Colymbus arcticus, LINN. S. N. I. ed. 10, 1758, 135; ed. 12, 1766, 221. — RICH. & SW. F. B. A. II. 1831, 475. — NUTT. Man. II. 1834, 517. — AUD. Orn. Biog. IV. 1838, 345; B. Am. VII. 1844, 295, pl. 477. — LAWR. in Baird's B. N. Am. 1858, 888. — BAIRD, Cat. N. Am. B. 1859, no. 699. — COUES, Pr. Ac. Nat. Sci. Philad. 1862, 228; Key, 1872, 334; Check List, 1873, no. 606; ed. 2, 1882, no. 842; Birds N. W. 1874, 721. — RIDGW. Nom. N. Am. B. 1881, no. 738.

Urinator arcticus, STEJN. Proc. U. S. Nat. Mus. Vol. 5, 1882, 43.

Colymbus macrorhynchos, BREHM, Vög. Deutschl. 1831, 974.

Colymbus megarhynchos, BREHM, Naum. V. 1855, 300.

Colymbus ignotus, BECHST. Gemein. Naturg. Deutschl. II. 1791, 782.

Colymbus leucopus, BECHST. Naturg. IV. 1809, 625.

HAB. Northern part of northern hemisphere. In America, migrating south in winter, through the Eastern Province, to the Northern United States.

SP. CHAR. *Adult:* Chin, throat, and foreneck velvety purplish black, with a purplish violet reflection, this black bounded sharply below, but on the sides of the head blending gradually into the color of the cheeks and lores, which are smoky slate, this color gradually fading into a rather light smoky cinereous, which occupies the whole upper part of the head and the entire nape; across the foreneck, just below the throat, a bar of white streaks; on the sides of the neck, between the purplish black of the foreneck and the ash of the nape, several longitudinal rows of black and white streaks, the latter narrowest. Upper parts deep black, the upper part of the back with two parallel longitudinal series of broad white bars, the inner scapulars with a single series of much larger but otherwise similar bars, and the wing-coverts marked with small ovate spots of white. Lower parts white, the sides of the jugulum streaked with black; entire sides uniform intense black. Bill black, the tip lighter; iris bright carmine; legs and feet "grayish blue, their inner sides tinged with yellow; claws black, that of the inner toe yellowish at the base" (AUDUBON).

Young: Similar to that of *U. immer*, but usually much smaller, the angle of the mandible less prominent.

Total length, about 29.00 inches; extent 39.50; wing, 12.15–13.20 (average, 12.55); culmen, 2.50–2.85 (2.60); depth of bill through base, .75–.80 (.78); tarsus, 2.90–3.30 (3.11); outer toe, 3.45–3.95 (3.76). (Five adults.)

The only North American examples of this species in the National Museum collection are from Alaska; several localities in that country being represented, as the Prybilof Islands and St. Michael's.

Summer adult.

The young of this species, particularly full-grown specimens, are sometimes difficult to distinguish from immature specimens of *U. immer;* but the measurements will in most cases determine the species, *U. arcticus* being decidedly smaller; the two comparing about as follows: —

	Wing.	Culmen.	Gonys.	Tip of bill to nostril.	Depth of bill at nostril.	Tarsus.
U. arcticus, juv.	12.00	2.53	1.18	1.85	.67	3.10
U. immer, juv.	13.00 or more	3.20	1.43	2.43	.94	2.75–3.85

This species appears to be common to the Northern and Arctic Regions of the globe, though more so in some parts of the high northern regions than in others. It is very rare, and not even positively known to occur, in the United States. It is more common in the regions of Hudson's Bay, and thence westward. On the Pacific it is replaced by the *pacificus*, similar, but of smaller size and weaker bill.

Mr. Murray procured specimens on Hudson's Bay, and Hearne ("Journey," p. 430) refers to the presence of this Diver in the same region, and speaks of it as being about the same size as *U. immer*, and more beautiful than that bird. It is extremely watchful, diving at the flash of a gun, and being of course very rarely killed, except when on the wing. Its flesh is quite as dark and fishy as that of the common Loon, but it is always eaten by the Indians. The skin of this bird is very thick and strong, and is frequently dressed with the feathers on, and made into caps for the Indian men. This Loon is also spoken of by Dr. Richardson as being common on the shores of Hudson's Bay, but very rarely seen in the interior. He mentions the fact that the skins both of the common Loon and of this species are tough and impervious to wet, and says that they are used both by the Indians and the Eskimos as materials for dress.

According to Mr. Kumlien, this species breeds, but is not common in Kingwah Fiord, where it was first seen June 24. A few individuals were seen in autumn near Grinnell Bay. He was informed by Governor Fencker that it is not found in North Greenland. Only a single individual is known to have been taken so far south as Point Lepreau, in the Bay of Fundy.

The Messrs. Godman met with this species in Norway, but did not regard it as common there. They found one nest on a small island close to the shore of an inland lake. Mr. Wheelwright states that it breeds commonly all over Scandinavia from the north of Scania to far up into Lapland and Finland, but principally in the interior of those regions. Sommerfeldt mentions that every winter the Black-throated Divers are seen off the north coast in Varanger Fiord. They are met with also on the Bohus-län coast all through the year.

This bird was found in the Barrens (*Tundras*) of Northern Siberia by Middendorff; and Von Heuglin, while he did not meet with it about Nova Zembla, states that he saw examples not infrequently, in pairs, in Jugor Straits and the Kara Sea.

Mr. H. Whitely found it common in the harbor of Hakodadi, Japan; it was very shy and difficult of approach.

Audubon speaks of having found the young of this species scattered over the United States as far as Texas; but as this species is not now found anywhere, and is unknown within our limits, we naturally infer that he was mistaken, and that he must have confounded with it immature birds of another species. He certainly was in error in quoting Mr. Townsend as including it in his List of Birds found on the Columbia, in which list it is not given. Audubon met with a few pairs of these birds in Labrador, but procured no specimens, and did not find them nesting. This Loon has almost as powerful a flight as the Great Northern Diver, and flies with even greater velocity.

In the British Islands the Black-throated Diver is given by Mr. Yarrell as being the rarest of the Loons, occurring but seldom on the southern shores. Young birds are the more common, and are occasionally brought to the London market. Birds in the mature plumage have been taken in the summer, but very rarely.

Mr. Selby states that the Black-throated Diver dives with the same ease and as perseveringly as do the other species, and can remain long submerged, traversing a great distance in its submarine flight; as was experienced by himself and Sir William Jardine when in chase of one of these birds, in a light boat on Loch Awe. Their utmost exertions could not bring the Loon within range, and they were often foiled by its returning on its former track and reappearing in a direction contrary to that in which it had seemed to dive. It was frequently lost for several minutes, and would then come up a quarter of a mile ahead. Its progress under the water was estimated to have been not less than eight miles an hour. He saw a pair toward the end of June, but did not succeed in detecting their place of nidification. Their food seemed to be fish, aquatic insects, and such other articles as they could procure on or under the water.

In Sutherlandshire Mr. Selby found this species on most of the lochs of the interior. At the foot of Loch Shin he found its nest, or rather the two eggs on the bare ground, on a small islet, removed about ten or twelve feet from the water's edge. The female was in the act of incubation, sitting horizontally, and not in upright position on the eggs. When shot at she immediately dived off to her mate, who was at a short distance. His pursuit of them was quite ineffectual. Their submersion continued two minutes at a time. They came up fully a quarter of a mile distant from the spot where they went down; and where they would reappear it was impossible to calculate. In no instance did they attempt to escape by taking wing. A visible track from the water to the eggs was made by the female, whose progress upon the land is effected by shuffling along upon her belly, while being propelled by her legs behind.

A pair, attended by their young, did not attempt to dive on being approached, but kept swimming around their young, which were of tender age, and were easily approached and shot. The egg is described as measuring 2.75 inches in length by 1.83 in breadth, and as having a ground of a dark olive-brown, thinly spotted with a dark umber-brown.

This species breeds in the Hebrides, and is found at all seasons in the sounds and bays of the Orkneys. Mr. Richard Dann states that it makes its first appearance in the spring with the breaking-up of the ice on the lakes, never failing to show itself within twelve hours of the appearance of open water. After the young are hatched, both male and female are very assiduous in bringing them food, are then much on the wing, and may often be seen to fly at a vast height, with fish in their beaks, from one lake to another, and in alighting, to descend very suddenly in an oblique direction. The cries of this species during the breeding-season are said to be very peculiar. On the approach of winter it retires to the west coast of Norway; and the young birds, migrating to more temperate climates, are found on the open parts of the Baltic, in the Elbe, and on the coast of Holland.

A single specimen was obtained by Mr. Elliott on the Prybilof Islands. It was found dead on the sea-beach at Zapadnee, St. George's Island, and brought to him by the natives, who differed in opinion as to whether it had ever been seen before about the islands or not. It was the typical *U. arcticus*, and not *U. pacificus.*

Mr. Nelson speaks of the Black-throated Loon as being a rare winter visitant upon Lake Michigan. One specimen, secured near Racine, is in the collection of Dr. Hoy; and a second specimen was taken near Milwaukee, and is also preserved in the museum of that city.

Urinator pacificus.

THE PACIFIC DIVER.

Colymbus pacificus, LAWR. in Baird's B. N. Am. Sept. 23, 1858, 889 (California; Puget's Sound). — BAIRD, Cat. N. Am B. 1859, no. 700. — COUES, Pr. Ac. Nat. Sci. Philad. 1862, 228. — RIDGW. Nom. N. Am. B. 1881, no. 739.

Colymbus arcticus, var. *pacificus*, COUES, Key, 1872, 335; Check List, 1873, no. 606 *a*.

Colymbus arcticus, b. *pacificus*, COUES, Birds N. W. 1874, 721.

Colymbus arcticus pacificus, COUES, Key, 1882, no. 843.

Urinator pacificus, STEJN. Proc. U. S. Nat. Mus. Vol. 5, 1882, 43.

HAB. Pacific coast of North America, south in winter to the extremity of Lower California and Guadalupe Island.

SP. CHAR. Similar to *U. arcticus*, but smaller, the bill much smaller, straighter, slenderer, and more pointed, and the colors somewhat different. *Adult:* Occiput and nape very pale ashy, or almost smoky white, much paler than in *U. arcticus;* white bars on the scapulars proportionately broader, black streaks on the sides of the jugulum narrower, and black of the foreneck less purplish, than in *U. arcticus.*

Wing, 11.20–12.25 inches (average, 11.54); culmen, 2.00–2.35 (2.15); depth of bill through base, .55–.65 (.62); tarsus, 2.70–3.00 (2.86); outer toe, 3.30–3.70 (3.47). [Fourteen adults.]

Although closely resembling *U. arcticus*, and unquestionably from the same parent stock, the characters of this form are so constant as apparently to warrant our considering it in the light of a species which has passed the "incipient stage." Careful measurements of the two show that, so far as the large series examined is concerned, their dimensions scarcely inosculate (those of the bill not at all), while the peculiarities of color pointed out above are constant throughout the series, which includes, besides five perfect specimens, a large number of heads and necks, which all show the grayish white coloration of the occiput and nape characteristic of this species. The comparative measurements of *arcticus* and *pacificus* may be best shown by the following figures: —

	Wing.	Culmen.	Depth of bill at base.	Tarsus.	Longest toe.
Maximum of *U. pacificus*,	12.25	2.35	.65	3.00	3.70
Minimum of *U. arcticus*,	12.15	2.50	.75	2.90	3.45
Average of *U. pacificus*,	11.54	2.15	.62	2.86	3.47
Average of *U. arcticus*,	12.55	2.60	.78	3.11	3.76

Young.

Mr. Kennicott met with the Pacific form of the Black-throated Diver breeding on the edges of lakes, and mentions finding a nest in water about eighteen inches deep, in grass at the edge of a long, narrow lake. It consisted of a mere pile of hay, like the nest of a Grebe, with the top very little above the surface of the water. Another was in the grass at the edge of a lake, built like a Grebe's nest, but larger.

Mr. Bannister speaks of this bird as being common at the Island of St. Michael's. Mr. Dall states that the skins are much sought for by the natives, and are obtained while the birds are breeding in the shallow lagoons, where they cannot dive, and where they are netted in great numbers; the eggs were obtained at Fort Yukon. Mr. Ross mentions finding a few birds of this species on the Mackenzie River.

Dr. Cooper speaks of this form as quite common in the winter as far south as San Diego. From the fact of his having killed a female in May, he thinks that it may breed in the mountain lakes, though not yet observed there, in summer. In its habits it closely resembles the *U. immer;* but he has never known it to scream or to utter any sound. This silence may be attributable to the season.

Mr. MacFarlane found it breeding in considerable numbers in the vicinity of Fort Anderson. The nests were usually on the borders of small lakes, sometimes a mere hole in the turf with a slight sprinkling of feathers therein, or a mere piece of turf without lining, hardly above the level of the water, or a mass of decayed vegetable matter with a slight depression in the centre, on the edge of and in the water. In another instance the nest was composed of a piece of turf about two feet square, on the border of a small lake, and nearly four feet from the shore. A hole had been scooped in the centre of the turf, in which the eggs were found lying on a very few withered reeds. In the record, of one hundred and five nests, made by Mr. MacFarlane, in no instance were there more than two eggs in a nest.

Mr. Adams ("Ibis," 1878) mentions this species as always to be met with, after the first week in June, in the shallow bays along the coast of Norton Sound, where these birds kept up a continual screaming throughout the day. They were said to breed there; but he was not able to verify the truth of the statement.

The localities in the northern regions in which this Diver has been procured are as follows: Fort Rae, Great Slave Lake, Fort Yukon, and the Yukon River generally, by Mr. Kennicott; Fort Rae, by Mr. B. R. Ross and Mr. L. Clarke; Fort Yukon, by Mr. J. Sibbiston and Mr. S. Jones; Anderson River, Fort Anderson, the Barren Grounds, Arctic coast, Rendezvous Lake, etc., by Mr. MacFarlane; on the islands in Liverpool Bay, islands in Franklin Bay, on Stuart's Island, by Mr. Pease; at Sitka, by Mr. Bischoff; among the Gens de Large Mountains, by Mr. McDougall.

The eggs of this species have a ground-color varying from a deep umber to a pale greenish gray. The markings, like those of the *torquatus* (= *immer*) and the *septentrionalis* (= *lumme*), are of a deep brownish black. Three eggs from the Yukon have these measurements: 2.95 by 2.00 inches; 3.00 by 2.00; 3.25 by 1.85.

Urinator lumme.

THE RED-THROATED LOON.

Colymbus lumme, GUNNER. Trond. Selsk. Skr. I. 1761, pl. ii. fig. 2. — BRÜNN. Orn. Bor. 1764, 39 (adult).

Urinator lumme, STEJN. Pr. U. S. Nat. Mus. Vol. 5, 1882, 43.

Colymbus septentrionalis, LINN. S. N. I. 1766, 220 (adult). — SW. & RICH. F. B. A. II. 1831, 476. — NUTT. Man. II. 1834, 519. — AUD. Orn. Biog. III. 1835, 20, pl. 202; Synop. 1839, 354; B. Am. VII. 1844, 299, pl. 478. — LAWR. in Baird's B. N. Am. 1858, 890. — BAIRD, Cat. N. Am. B. 1859, no. 701. — COUES, Key, 1872, 335; Check List, 1873, no. 607; ed. 2, 1882, no. 844; B. N. W. 1874, 724. — RIDGW. Nom. N. Am. B. 1881, no. 740.

Colymbus stellatus, BRÜNN. t. c. no. 130 (young).

Colymbus borealis, BRÜNN. t. c. no. 131.

Colymbus striatus, GMEL. S. N. I. ii. 1788, 586 (young).

Colymbus rufogularis, MEYER, Tasch. Deutsch. Vög. II. 453 (adult).

Colymbus microrhynchos, BREHM, Naum. V. 1855, 300.

Adult, summer plumage.

HAB. Northern part of the northern hemisphere, south in winter nearly across the United States.

SP. CHAR. *Adult, summer plumage:* Head and neck soft velvety cinereous, the crown streaked with dusky; nape dusky, streaked with white; a longitudinal, wedge-shaped patch of rich chestnut covering the foreneck, the lower, truncated, edge adjoining the white of the jugulum, the upper point reaching to the lower part of the throat. Upper parts dusky slate, more or less speckled with white. Lower parts entirely pure white, except along the sides, beneath the wings, and on the crissum, where more or less mixed with slate-color. Bill deep black, the extreme point yellowish, and the culmen sometimes bluish; iris carmine; "tarsi and toes bluish white, each joint of the latter, and the whole of the outer toe, black" (L. M. TURNER, MS.). *Winter plumage:* Similar to the above, but the whole lower half of the head, with entire foreneck, white, the nape and upper half of the head uniformly marked with broad streaks of dusky and narrower ones of white, and the upper parts more uniformly and distinctly speckled with white. Bill brownish or grayish. *Downy young:* "The young are at first covered with a dense elastic down of a grayish black color, tinged with brown. The bill is bluish black, its basal edges yellow; the iris reddish brown" (AUDUBON).

Total length, 23.00–26.00 inches; extent, 38.50–43.00; wing, 10.00–11.50; culmen, 2.25; tarsus, 2.75.

The Red-throated Diver is an Arctic species common to all parts of the northern hemisphere, found in equal abundance in Asia, Europe, and America, in summer breeding to the highest extent of available lands, and in winter wandering southward to a varying and indefinite extent.

According to Professor Reinhardt, this is a resident species in Greenland. Captain Blakiston cites it as procured from Hudson's Bay; Mr. Bernard Ross, as abundant on the Mackenzie River. Hearne ("Journey," p. 430) states that it is also known as a Loon in Hudson's Bay, but that it is far inferior in size to the other species of Loon, seldom weighing more than three or four pounds. This bird, as well as the other species, is an excellent diver. It always feeds on fish; and while in pursuit of its prey, frequently becomes entangled in the fishing-nets set at the mouths of creeks and small rivers. It is the most numerous species, and frequently flies in considerable flocks. Like the other Loons, it makes its nests at the edge of the water, and lays two eggs, which, though very rank and fishy, are always eaten, as well by the English residents as by the Indians.

Mr. Kumlien found this Loon very common in all the localities visited by him, beginning to nest on the Upper Cumberland waters about the last of June, the eggs being placed on the bare rocks, with very little grass or moss beneath them. The birds were very noisy during the mating-season, and remained as long as the water was open.

Sir John Richardson states that the Red-throated Diver frequents the shores of Hudson's Bay up to the most northern extremity of Melville Peninsula, and that it is also abundant on the interior lakes. It is said to lay two eggs, by the margin of the water. The eggs brought home by Parry were 2.92 inches in length and 1.75 in breadth, and of a pale oil-green color, blotched with umber.

This species is found on the Atlantic coast only as a migrating visitor in spring and fall. At the latter season the visitors are principally young birds. Giraud states that it rarely occurs on the coast of Long Island except in the immature plumage. Dr. Wood states ("American Naturalist," III. 518) that immature birds of this species are very common in Long Island Sound, but that the adult is never, so far as he knows, seen there.

According to Dr. Cooper, it is found on the Pacific coast as far south as San Diego. It is more rare than are the two other species of Loons. Dr. Heerman obtained one example at San Diego; and Dr. Cooper procured another — a fine male — at Santa Barbara, in 1863, as late as April 27.

Mr. E. Adams found it quite common on the shores of Norton Sound ("Ibis," 1878). The first example arrived there May 21, and soon afterward most of the larger lakes had at least one pair of them as tenants. They seldom went out to sea — and then apparently only for the purpose of feeding — but were continually flying about the marshes, and diving and screaming upon the lakes. He describes this Loon as being a "complete Mocking-bird" in its imitation of harsh sounds, its cry resembling by turns the squalling of a cat, the barking of a dog, the shrill laugh of a man, or the quacking of a Duck; and sometimes all these sounds are united in one loud scream, as the bird dives into the lake in play. The nests were numerous, and generally placed quite close to the water, on the banks of the lake. They consisted merely of a little loose grass in a hollow; a few were more carefully formed, though none were lined with feathers or down. The eggs were two in number, of an olive-greenish color, thinly spotted with dark brown.

Mr. Bannister found this species abundant on the Island of St. Michael's. Mr. Dall speaks of it also as being common at the mouth of the Yukon. A single specimen was procured on the rapids of the Yukon in July, 1867. Mr. Dall also found it very abundant at Amchitka, in July, where it was breeding. It was seen nowhere else in the Aleutian chain, and there it is only a summer resident. Six or eight were observed at a time in the harbor of Amchitka, quite bold, and usually appearing in the early morning or the dusk of evening. Crossing the island, Mr. Dall observed a female with one young bird swimming in a pool of fresh water. Alarmed at his approach, the mother settled down into the water until only her neck appeared above the surface, when the little one immediately took up its position on her back. Wishing to procure the plumage of the fledgling, he shot the young bird and picked it up. Just then the male arrived from the coast with a small fish in his mouth, intended for the young bird. Not seeing it, he uttered a mournful cry, which was replied to by the female, who had remained in the pool without attempting to escape. For some minutes these cries were kept up, when both birds took wing and disappeared, still uttering low moaning cries.

According to Mr. Swinhoe, several of these birds wander down during the winter to the coast of Formosa from the north; but very few show any indications of the Red-throat, nearly all being in their winter plumage.

Mr. H. Whitely obtained a single example of this species at Hakodadi, Japan, in January; and Mr. Swinhoe has since met with it there in May ("Ibis," April, 1874). It is given by Mr. T. L. Powys as occurring sparingly on the coast of Epirus and Albania in winter.

Mr. C. A. Wright ("Ibis," 1864) mentions it as occasional at Malta. Schembri saw one in 1839, and another in 1841; and four birds in immature plumage were taken at Gozo in the winter of 1858–1859.

Mr. Wheelwright states that it is common in Lapland during the summer, but not nearly as much so as the Black-throated species, in the midland districts. Both of these Divers are said to cover up their eggs when they leave their nests, in the manner of the Grebes; but this cannot be always the case, as in every instance Mr. Wheelwright found the eggs uncovered. The Messrs. Godman also speak of it as being abundant in Norway during the summer months. Almost every pond and small lake had its pair, and many eggs were collected.

Professor Newton states that this species breeds in Spitzbergen as far north as the Seven Islands, lat. 80° 45′. Eggs from Depot Holm and other places were obtained by the Swedes. A young bird was found on one of the Thousand Islands; and Professor Newton saw a pair of old ones on Russö, which evidently had a nest not far off. It seemed to be pretty generally, but sparingly, distributed throughout the whole region. It is said by Dr. Malmgren to feed its young on a species of *Apus* which he found in plenty in the fresh-water pools on the Star Fiord.

This species was found by Middendorff inhabiting the *tundras* of Northern Siberia; and Von Heuglin, in his account of the birds of Nova Zembla ("Ibis," 1872), states that he found it breeding in Matthews' Straits.

According to Yarrell, it is only a winter visitant of England and Ireland, occurring on all parts of the coast. A few breed in the Orkney and Shetland Islands, and probably in other of the northern islands. Rev. Mr. Low, in his "Natural History of the Orkneys," accuses it of making a vast howling, and sometimes a croaking noise, which is believed to prognosticate rain; and hence its name of "Rain-goose."

Mr. Robert Dunn states that these Loons lay their eggs so close to the water's edge that the bird can touch the water with its bill while sitting. He has invariably found the egg not more than three inches from the water's edge, and usually deposited among a few loose stones.

Mr. Hewitson speaks of the cry of this bird as being a loud and singular scream; Mr. Richard Dann characterizes it as very mournful and melancholy. During the breeding-season, while on the wing, the birds frequently utter a sound like the word *kakera-kakera;* and by this name they are known in many parts of Scandinavia.

Mr. Yarrell describes its eggs in his cabinet as averaging 2.66 inches in length by 1.82 in breadth. The ground-color is of a dark greenish brown when fresh, but changes a little, and becomes a chestnut or dark reddish brown when the egg has been long incubated. It is rather thickly spotted with dark umber-brown.

According to Audubon, this species begins to breed in Labrador in the beginning of June. The nests consist of a few blades of grass loosely put together, and quite flat, and without any down. The male incubates as well as the female. The young birds dive beautifully, and swim with great buoyancy. By the hunters and fishermen on the New England coast this bird is called the "Cape Racer."

Mr. MacFarlane observed it breeding in the neighborhood of Fort Anderson and on the Arctic coast. Two eggs found July 2 were on a very small island, about two feet square, and so small that one of the eggs was found at the bottom of the lake on the borders of which the nest was situated. This was simply a slight depression in the turf of which the island was composed; and others were found almost identical in character with this. This species was not very numerous in the neighborhood of Fort Anderson. Sixteen nests are described by Mr. MacFarlane, in all of which the maximum number of eggs is two.

It is of occasional occurrence in the interior, on the great lakes, and more rarely on smaller ones. These are usually noticed in the fall, are immature specimens, and occur singly. Professor Kumlien procured one in October, 1873, on Lake Koskonong, in Southern Wisconsin.

It was met with, and examples secured, on the Liard River and at Fort Resolution by Mr. Robert Kennicott; on the Anderson River, on Bear Lake, at Fort Simpson, and on Big Island by Mr. B. R. Ross; at Fort Rae by Mr. L. Clarke; on Big Island by Mr. John Reid; on Anderson River and the Arctic coast near its mouth, on the Barren Grounds, Franklin Bay, and at Fort Anderson, by Mr. MacFarlane; at Sitka and St. Michael's by Mr. H. M. Bannister and Mr. Charles Pease; on the Yukon River by Mr. Dall; and at Fort Kenai by Mr. Bischoff.

The eggs of this species in the Smithsonian collection are from Great Slave Lake, the Yukon River, Sitka, Anderson River, and Greenland. The ground-color varies from a deep reddish umber, or a deep raw umber, to a grayish green. The markings are usually small, sparse, and of a brownish black. The eggs vary in their length from 2.65 to 3.00 inches, and in their breadth from 1.70 to 1.85.

FAMILY ALCIDÆ. — THE AUKS.

CHAR. Swimming birds with the feet situated far back, the anterior toes fully webbed, and armed with strong claws, the hallux entirely absent. Lores feathered; tail normal, always short; nostrils without overhanging membrane. Bill excessively variable in form.

The above diagnosis, though brief, is quite sufficient to distinguish this family from that most nearly related — the *Urinatoridæ* — which differs essentially in the possession of a well-developed hind toe, and in the nostrils being overhung by a membrane. The different genera exhibit remarkable extremes of form, especially of the bill (the variation of other parts being comparatively trifling), and, to a less extent, of size.

All the genera, and most, if not all, of the species, are American, the family being of circumpolar distribution, with few, if any, forms peculiar to either continent, the chief difference being between the North Pacific and North Atlantic representatives.

Following is an arrangement of the genera which is believed to express very nearly the natural affinities of the various forms: —

A. Inner claw normal (not larger or more curved than the others). No tumid "rosette" at angle of mouth.

a^1. Mental apex much nearer to tip of bill than to nostril; carotid single (double in all other *Alcidæ*, so far as known).

Sub-family ALLINÆ.

1. **Alle.** Bill short and very broad, the width at the base about equal to the depth and to the distance from the nostril to the tip. Nasal operculum completely exposed. Gonys very short, being less than the width of the space between the mandibular rami at a point immediately beneath the nostril. Size small (wing less than 5.00 inches).

a^2. Mental apex much nearer to nostril than to tip of bill.

b^1. Sub-family ALCINÆ. Nasal fossæ completely filled with dense velvety feathering, extending to or beyond anterior end of nostrils.

c^1. Bill very deep, the culmen very strongly convex, the maxilla (sometimes mandible also) with very distinct obliquely transverse grooves. Tail graduated, the feathers pointed. (*Alceæ.*)

2. **Plautus.** Largest of the *Alcidæ*. Wings rudimentary, not admitting of flight. Bill equal to the head in length, the mandible with numerous transverse sulcations.

3. **Alca.** Size medium. Wings well developed, admitting of sustained flight. Bill much shorter than head, the mandible with but one or two well-defined sulci (or none).

c^2. Bill more slender, the culmen slightly or gently convex, both mandibles destitute of transverse grooves. Tail rounded, the feathers not pointed. (*Urieæ.*)

4. **Uria.** Size of *Alca*.

b^2. Sub-family PHALERINÆ. Nasal fossæ only partly feathered, the feathering never reaching anterior end of nostrils, the nasal operculum always completely exposed.

c^1. Bill slender, compressed, nearly as long as the head, the culmen straight to near the tip, where abruptly decurved; gonys nearly straight, ascending to the tip from the angle, which is situated nearer the tip than the base of the mandible. Loral apex forming an acute angle. (*Cepphеæ.*)

5. **Cepphus.** Size medium (wing about 6.50 to 7.50).

c^2. Bill exceedingly variable in form, but never curved abruptly at the tip, always (except in *Cerorhyncha*) much shorter than the head, the gonydeal angle much nearer the base than the tip of the mandible (except in *Synthliboramphus*).

d^1. Distance from anterior border of nasal fossæ to nearest feathering one fourth, or less than one fourth, of the distance from the same point to the tip of the maxilla. (*Brachyramphœ.*)

6. **Brachyramphus.** Tarsi reticulate in front, not longer than the maxillary tomium (measured to base of horny portion); bill moderately compressed, the depth through the base decidedly less than one half the culmen. Size small (wing less than 6.00 inches).

7. **Synthliboramphus.** Tarsi scutellate in front, much longer than the maxillary tomium; bill much compressed, the depth through the base much more than half the culmen. Size of *Brachyramphus.*

d^2. Distance from anterior border of nasal fossæ to nearest feathering one half, or more, the distance from the same point to the tip of the maxilla. (*Phalereœ.*)

8. **Ciceronia.** Bill small, without accessory pieces, except a small compressed knob at the base of the culmen in the breeding-season. Head without crests, but ornamented (in the adult) with white acicular feathers over frontal and loral regions. Size smallest of the *Alcidæ* (wing less than 4.00 inches)

9. **Phaleris.** Similar to *Ciceronia*, but culmen destitute of knob, even in breeding-season, the head ornamented with a long, slender, recurved crest on the fore part of the crown, several long, slender, whitish filaments springing from above the eye, a postocular series of long, slender, pointed, white feathers, and a similar series crossing the cheeks. Size a little larger than *Ciceronia* (wing about 4.50 inches).

10. **Simorhynchus.** *In the breeding-season:* Covering of the bill complicated by the following accessory pieces, all of which are shed before winter: base of mandibular rami developed into a prominent broad plate, curving upward to the rictus; base of maxillary tomia developed into a large semicircular concave plate. A frontal recurved crest, as in *Phaleris*, but no other ornaments except a postocular line of narrow, pointed, white feathers. *In winter:* Bill simple, as in *Phaleris.* Size larger (wing 5.00 inches or more).

11. **Cyclorhynchus.** Bill without accessory pieces; much compressed, very deep, with rounded outlines, the depth through the base equal to the chord of the culmen; the latter decidedly convex; mandible falcate, or strongly recurved, and sharp-pointed. A single line of pointed white feathers behind the eye. Size of *Simorhynchus.*

12. **Ptychoramphus.** Bill without supernumerary pieces, and head without ornamental feathers. Bill elongate-conical, the maxilla much broader than deep at the base; culmen nearly straight, and gonys likewise little curved, but decidedly ascending from the mental angle. Nasal fossæ very large (occupying nearly the basal half of the mandible). Size small (wing about 5.00 inches).

13. **Cerorhyncha.** Bill large and much compressed, nearly as long as the head, height nearly half the length, the culmen strongly curved, the gonys slightly concave, the mental angle being very prominent. Cere surmounted in the breeding-season by a prominent vertical compressed knob or horn. Adult with a postocular and mystacial series of narrow, pointed white feathers. Size large (wing about 7.00 inches).

B. Inner claw much larger and more strongly curved than the others. A tumid "rosette" at the angle of the mouth.

Sub-family FRATERCULINÆ. Bill excessively compressed, its depth at the base nearly or quite equal to the chord of the culmen, the terminal half transversely grooved, the basal portion ornamented in the breeding-season by a greater or less number of supernumerary deciduous pieces.

14. **Fratercula.** Deciduous nasal shield, rapidly diminishing in width toward the top; basal outline of the mandible concave; maxillary sulci and anterior outline of the nasal shield with the concave sides posterior; terminal half of mandible obliquely sulcate; eyelids furnished with deciduous horny plates; head not tufted.

15. **Lunda**. Deciduous nasal shield rapidly increasing in width toward the top, where forming an arched and much thickened ridge ; basal outline of the mandible convex ; maxillary sulci and anterior outline of the nasal shield with the concave sides anterior; terminal half of mandible perfectly smooth ; eyelids without horny plates ; adult furnished with elongated, pendent, silky, ornamental supra-auricular tufts.

GENUS **ALLE**, LINK.

Alle, LINK, Beschr. Nat.-Samml. Univ. Rostock, I. 1806, 17 (type, *A. nigricans*, LINK, = *Alca alle*, LINN.). — COUES, Bull. Nutt. Orn. Club, IV. Oct. 1879, 244.
Mergulus, VIEILL. Analyse, 1816, 66 (type, *Alca alle*, LINN.).

CHAR. Size small (wing about four and a half inches). Bill very short and thick, the culmen strongly convex, the gonys exceedingly short (less than one third the culmen) and straight; mandibular rami widely separated, the interval filled by a very broad, densely feathered area,

A. nigricans, summer dress.

extending nearly to the tip of the bill ; nasal fossæ semicircular, the lower third occupied by the nostril. Head, neck, and upper parts black, the under side of the head and neck white in winter ; lower parts white, and scapulars streaked with white, at all stages.

The single species of this genus is the well-known Sea Dove, or Dovekie, abundant along the coast of New England in winter, but breeding much farther north.

Alle nigricans.

THE SEA-DOVE; DOVEKIE.

Alca alle, LINN. S. N. ed. 10, I. 1758, 131, no. 6 ; ed. 12, I. 1766, 211, no. 5. — WILS. Am. Orn. IX. pl. 74, fig. 5.
Uria alle, PALL. Zoog. Rosso-As. II. 1826, 369. — AUD. Orn. Biog. V. 1838, 304, pl. 339.
Mergulus alle, VIEILL. Analyse, 1816, 66 ; Gal. Ois. 1825, 236, pl. 295. — GOULD, B. Eur. V. 1837, pl. 402. — CASS. in Baird's B. N. Am. 1858, 918. — BAIRD, Cat. N. Am. B. 1859, no. 738. — COUES, Pr. Ac. Nat. Sci. Philad. 1868, 54 ; Key, 1872, 343 ; Check List, 1873, no. 626.
A'ca candida, BRÜNN. Orn. Bor. 1764, 26, no. 107 (albino ?).
Alca alce, GMEL. S. N. I. 1788, 554.
Mergulus melanoleucus, LEACH, Syst. Cat. 1816, 42.
Mergulus arcticus, BREHM, Vög. Deutschl. 1831, 994.
Alle nigricans, LINK, Beschr. Nat.-Samml. Univ. Rostock, I. 1806, 17. — COUES, Bull. Nutt. Orn. Club, IV. 1879, 244 ; 2d Check List, 1882, no. 863. — RIDGW. Nom. N. Am. B. 1881, no. 752.

HAB. Coasts and islands of the North Atlantic, south in America to New Jersey in winter; breeds far northward.

SP. CHAR. *Adult, in summer:* Head, neck, and jugulum uniform fuliginous-brown, growing gradually darker on the pileum and nape; remaining upper parts fuliginous-black, the secondaries tipped with white, and posterior scapulars edged with the same. Lower parts, from the jugulum back, immaculate white, the upper flank-feathers striped with dusky. Bill black; iris dark brown; "feet pale flesh-colored, webs dusky, claws black; inside of mouth light yellow" (AUDUBON). *Winter plumage:* Chin, throat, jugulum, malar region, and sides of the upper part of the nape white, the latter mottled with grayish, and the jugular feathers with dusky bases; otherwise like the summer plumage. "*Young, first winter:* Recognizable by its smaller and weaker bill, by the duller and more brownish black of the upper parts, almost wanting in gloss, and by the greater extension of the white upon the sides of the hind head and neck. The scapulars and coverts are conspicuously marked with white, as in the adult. The feet are mostly dusky" (COUES). *Downy young:* Uniform dark grayish fuliginous, somewhat paler beneath; bill black; legs and feet brownish (in dried skins).

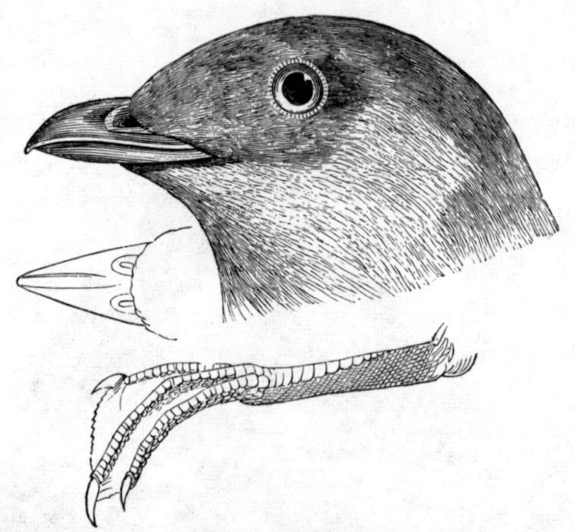

Winter plumage.

Total length, about 8.50 inches; wing, 4.50–4.75; culmen, .50; tarsus, .80; middle toe, with claw, 1.20.

The Little Auk is the most decidedly oceanic, and also one of the most Arctic, of the family of *Alcidæ.* It lives and spends most of its time on the open sea, and very rarely resorts to the land — never doing so voluntarily, except during the breeding-season. It breeds exclusively in high northern regions — chiefly on islands — and always in places near the ocean.

It is found in the Arctic regions of America and Europe, and the islands in the Arctic Ocean, and in the northwestern portions of Asia, on the islands of Nova Zembla and Spitzbergen. In the last-named place Messrs. Evans and Sturge met with these birds in immense flocks. In one locality a great number of them were seen by these naturalists flying in and out of the cliffs; and one of the party was let down into close proximity with the nests by means of a wire rope. But it was found that this bird builds in such deep and narrow crevices that it was only after much hard labor, and by breaking the rock with a hammer, that the hand could be inserted so that the nests could be reached; and even then only three eggs were procured. Professor Newton also found this species numerous almost beyond belief on the greater part of the coast of Spitzbergen. Parry's Expedition met with it as far to the north as that party travelled. On their return, in August, they found it in great numbers between latitudes 82° and 81°. It was not met with in the Stor Fjord. Its breeding-places, though at a less height than those of its kindred, are very far from being easily accessible.

Mr. Gillett found this species numerous in Nova Zembla, especially in the northern portion. Its wild and peculiar cry is said to have a very startling effect in the calm light nights of the Arctic summer, especially when heard at the same time with the hoarse bellowing of the walruses. Von Heuglin found this Auk abundant wherever he went in the northern regions; and he speaks of it as more abundant farther north than it is in the more southern regions. In the Kara Sea all the birds of this species that he noticed were seen on floating ice.

Dr. Walker, in his "Ornithological Notes of the Voyage of the Fox," mentions that in passing up Baffin's Bay, and again in Melville Bay, he encountered myriads of birds of this species. In the summer of 1858, when in the last-named locality, great numbers were shot. They were found breeding near Cape York, and a number of their eggs were procured. In that locality they were found in vast numbers flying in and out of the stones, which formed a talus along the cliffs of primary rock. The bird lays a single egg in the hollows between the stones, where foxes and Gulls cannot reach them.

According to Professor Reinhardt, this Auk is a common resident species in Greenland.

It is occasionally found wandering along the coast of Europe and Africa to Spain, Madeira, and to the Azores. A single example was found by Mr. Godwin in a private collection of native birds at Terceira, in the Azores; it had been killed on the island several years previous to his visit. Mr. Layard, in his voyage in 1867 from England to Cape Town, when off Finisterre, on the coast of France, in November, met with a large number of these birds. They appeared to be chiefly in pairs. Mr. Godman also includes this species in his List of the Migratory Birds of Madeira and the Canaries. It is more numerous among the eastern islands of the latter group, although found occasionally among the others. It is also of occasional occurrence in Bermuda, where one was taken alive, Jan. 28, 1850, four or five having been driven on to a piece of grass-land near the house of Rev. J. N. Campbell.

This Auk is common during the winter off the New England coast, and was especially abundant during the winter of 1871–1872. In a long and violent northeast storm which prevailed on the coast in the latter part of November, 1871, thousands of these birds were driven upon the shore, and large numbers of them perished. They were utterly powerless to resist the wind and waves, and were forced into creeks, inlets, bays, harbors, and upon open beaches. Many were driven into the harbor of Boston, and, at high tide, forced upon the wharves and under the bridges, where hundreds were ruthlessly knocked on the head. This occurred also along the entire extent of coast; and some were even carried far inland, and were picked up near Middletown, Conn., and other interior towns, a hundred miles or more from the ocean. The birds, when found alive, appeared to be utterly exhausted, and a large number were already dead.

According to Giraud, this species is occasionally seen by the fishermen of Egg Harbor, N. J., when hauling their nets outside of the beach. It is an excellent diver, can fly well, subsists on small fish, and, not being timid, is easily secured.

According to Professor Newton, it occurs in Iceland all the year round. It is only known to breed on Grimsey, where Faber found it in 1820, and Proctor in 1837.

According to Yarrell, the "Rotches," as these birds are there called, are only winter visitors to the British Islands, where they seldom make their appearance on the coasts except during, or after, very stormy weather, when they are forced by violent and long-continuing winds to leave the rough sea and take shelter in land-locked bays. In the same manner they are sometimes driven upon the coasts of France and Holland.

Captain James C. Ross obtained a specimen of this Auk as far north as latitude 81°; and its only food appeared to be small thin-skinned crustaceans. Colonel Sabine found it abundant in Baffin's Bay and Davis Straits; and in latitude 76° it was so numerous in the channels of water separating fields of ice, that many hundreds were killed daily, and the ship's company supplied with them. All these birds in the breeding-season had the under part of the neck sooty black, terminating abruptly and in an even line against the white of the belly. The young ones, in all stages from the egg, as soon as they were feathered, were marked exactly like the mature birds; but in the third week in September every specimen, old or young, was observed to be undergoing a change, and in the course of a few days the feathers of the throat and cheeks and the under part of the neck had become white.

Mr. Kumlien found this Auk common on the north coast of Labrador, off Resolution Island, Grinnell Bay, and Frobisher's Straits, but did not meet with any in Cumberland. It was abundant off Exeter Sound and to the northward, on the west coast of Baffin's Bay, nesting as far north as latitude 78°, and perhaps farther. It was very abundant on the pack ice in Davis Straits during July, and was so unsuspicious that it could be caught from the schooner's deck with a net on the end of a pole.

Eggs of this species from Greenland in the Smithsonian collection are of a rounded shape — one end being less rounded than the other — and of a pale glaucous-white color, without spots. Three eggs measure 1.80 inches by 1.30; 1.85 by 1.25; and 1.90 by 1.25.

Genus **PLAUTUS**, Brünnich.

Alca, Linn. S. N. ed. 10, I. 1758, 130; ed. 12, I. 1766, 210 (part).
Plautus, Brünn. Zool. Fund. 1772, 78 (type, *Alca impennis*, Linn.). — Brandt, Bull. Ac. St. Petersb. VII. 1869, 203.
Pinguinus, Bonnat. Enc. Méth. 1790, 28 (same type; not of Brünn. 1772).
Torda, Duméril, Zool. Anal. 1806, 72 (same type).
Chenalopex, Vieill. Nouv. Dict. XXIV. 1818, 132 (same type).
Matæoptera, Gloger, Handb. 1842, (same type).
Gyralca, Steenstrup, Vid. Med. Nat. For. Kjöb. 1855, 114 (same type).

Char. Largest of the family. Form heavy and robust, the wings disproportionately small, not admitting of flight; tail short, pointed; bill about as long as the head, much compressed, its greatest depth equal to about half the culmen; culmen straight, and parallel with the commissure for the basal half, then regularly curved to the gently declinate tip; terminal half of the maxilla with about six to ten obliquely transverse faintly curved grooves; terminal half of the mandible with about the same number of vertical grooves; lores completely and densely feathered, the nostrils hidden beneath the lower edge of the feathered area; legs short and stout, the tarsi compressed and transversely scutellate anteriorly; web of the feet full and broad.

Only a single species of this genus is known, and this is supposed to be now entirely extinct, although a considerable number of examples are preserved in museums.

Plautus impennis.

THE GREAT AUK.

Alca impennis, LINN. S. N. ed. 10, 1758, 130, no. 2; ed. 12, I. 1766, 210, no. 2. — AUD. Orn. Biog. IV. 1838, 316; B. Am. pl. 341; oct. ed. VII. pl. 465. — CASS. in Baird's B. N. Am. 1858, 900. — BAIRD, Cat. N. Am. B. 1859, no. 710. — COUES, Pr. Ac. Nat. Sci. Philad. 1868, 14; Key, 1872, 339; Check List, 1873, no. 615; ed. 2, 1882, no. 878. — RIDGW. Nom. N. Am. B. 1881, no. 741.

Plautus impennis, STEENSTR. Vid. Med. Nat. For. Kjöb. 1855, 114.

Alca borealis, FORST. Synop. Cat. Brit. B. 1817, 29.

HAB. Believed to be now extinct. Formerly (previous to 1844) inhabited the islands of the North Atlantic, south to the coast of New England (Nahant and islands in Boston Bay); probably did not occur north of the Arctic circle (WOLLEY).

P. impennis, summer adult.

SP. CHAR. *Adult, in summer:* Head, neck, and upper parts, blackish, the throat and sides of the head and neck inclining to a clear snuff-brown shade; lower parts, a large oval space covering the greater part of the loral region, and the tips of the secondaries, white; the white of the jugulum extending upward in a point into the snuff-brown of the middle portion of the throat. "Bill black, with the grooves between the transverse ridges white; iris hazel; feet and claws black" (AUDUBON).

Total length, about 29.00 to 30.00 inches; extent, 27.25 (AUDUBON); wings, 5.75; tail, about 3.00; bill along gape, 4.25–4.50; culmen, 3.15–3.50; greatest depth of closed bill, about 1.50; tarsus, 1.66; middle toe with claw, 3.25.

We have seen no description of this species in young or winter plumage; the latter, however,

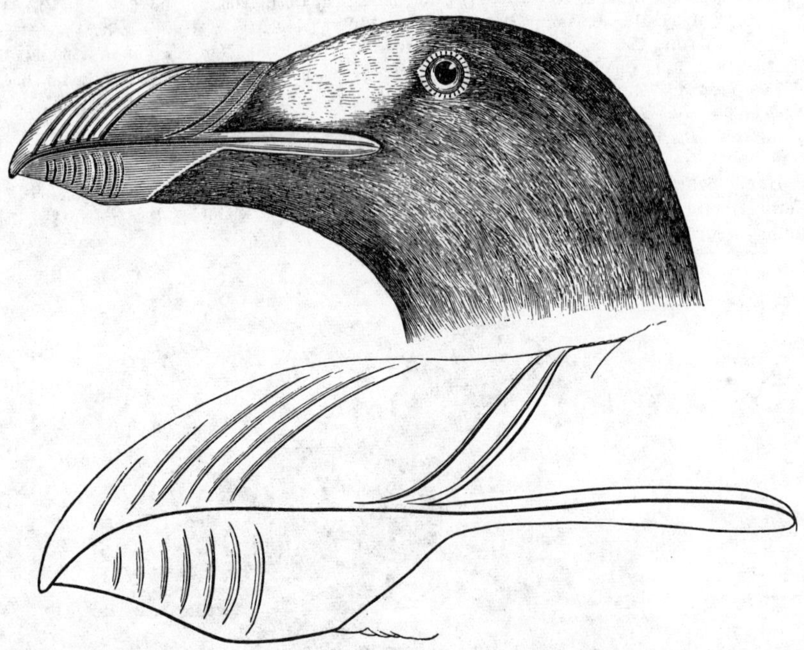

judging from the seasonal changes in *Alca torda* and other members of the family, would doubtless have the under side of the head white, the maxilla destitute of the basal lamina, and perhaps the loral white patch absent.

The researches of the late Mr. John Wolley into the history of this probably extinct species, as presented by Professor Alfred Newton ("Ibis," 1861, pp. 374–399), have thrown much light upon their closing existence in Iceland, and have preserved the records of many interesting facts that would otherwise have passed into oblivion. This author calls attention to the very general misconception that has prevailed, to the effect that the Great Auk was a bird of the Far North, and belonged to Polar Regions. This error — as he supposes — originated in the inadvertence of naturalists, who have confounded localities quite distinct and remote from one another. There is hardly a single reliable instance on record of the capture of the Great Auk within the limits of the Arctic circle. Even the statement, quoted by Reinhardt, that this bird has been taken on Disco Island ("Ibis," 1861, p. 15) is not free from doubt, and possibly it may have been confounded with the specimen obtained at Fiskernaes in 1815; and Professor Newton is evidently inclined to the belief that there is no trustworthy evidence that this bird ever existed within the Arctic circle.

Mr. Wolley could find no traces of the recent presence of the Great Auk about Iceland, except among a small chain of volcanic islets, known as the Fuglasker, lying off the southwestern point of that island. These islets are from thirteen to thirty miles distant from the shore, widely separated from each other, and, owing to currents and the tempestuous character of the locality, of dangerous approach. The outer island of all, and the one on which these birds are supposed to have chiefly abounded, was formerly one of the most considerable of the chain; but in 1830, after a series of submarine disturbances, it entirely disappeared. Other rocky islets exist in this chain more distant from the shore. Professor Newton found in the public library of Reykjavik a manuscript account of this outer island — the former habitation of this Auk — in which, in one of the accompanying notes, a very accurate description is given of the bird itself and of its peculiarities, as also of its egg. This manuscript is supposed to have been written somewhere about the year 1760. Three authors are cited, who refer to the former abundance of this bird on these islets, one of them stating that the people had often filled their boats with the eggs. There was also abundant evidence derived from parties still living as to the existence of these birds during the present century. In 1807, during the hostilities between England and Denmark, a privateer that had plundered the Faröes and Reykjavik visited these islands and made the most wholesale slaughter of the Auks. Again in 1810, the inhabitants of the Faröes, being reduced almost to starvation by the war, made an excursion to Iceland, on which occasion these islands were again invaded, and this bird subjected to a murderous attack. It is probable that these two wholesale massacres so very nearly exterminated the Auks that they never recovered from their effects. Faber mentions that seven of these birds were killed in 1814 on a more northern islet. In 1821 the same writer visited their usual breeding-place, but met with none of them; and it was supposed that they all had been destroyed by a party of French sailors who had recently visited the islands. The birds had not then, however, been quite exterminated, as that very season others were seen and killed, proof of these statements having been obtained by Professor Newton. There was also reliable evidence of the capture of an example of this Auk in 1828.

In 1830, the year in which the main islet disappeared beneath the waves, an inhabitant of Kyrkjuvogr visited the high rock which stands between the sunken island and the cape, and in two excursions obtained about twenty specimens of this bird; and in the following year as many as twenty-four of them were taken, one of which was brought off alive. Again in 1833, and also in 1834, more of these birds were captured on the same rocky islet, as well as several eggs, most of which were sold to a dealer in Hamburg. A few more were afterward taken in 1840 or in 1841. The last of these birds known to have been procured in Iceland were two killed in 1844. A drawing of one of these was made by a French artist, which in 1860 was hanging in the shop of an apothecary in Reykjavik.

These last specimens of the Auk were taken by a party of fourteen men in an excursion to one of these rocky islets, now known as Eldey. This island is a precipitous stack, perpendicular nearly everywhere, and seventy fathoms in height at its loftiest point, but with a gradual slope on one side from the sea to a considerable elevation. Here is the only landing-place, and farther up is the spot where the birds made their home. Two Auks were seen among the numberless other rock-fowl, and were at once pursued. They did not show the slightest disposition to repel the invaders, but immediately ran along under the high cliff, with their heads erect and their little wings extended. They uttered no cry of alarm, but moved with short steps about as fast as the usual gait of a man. One bird was driven into a corner, and there captured; the other secured just on the edge of the precipice, over the water. Both were strangled; and their bodies are now in the Museum of the University of Copenhagen. One egg was found, but it was broken.

Professor Newton was informed that within the recollection of many persons now living, the "Gare-fowls" — as they were called in Iceland — were so constantly observed in the sea by the fishermen that their appearance hardly attracted any attention. They were said to swim with their heads much lifted up and their necks drawn in. They never made any attempt to flap along the water, but dived as soon as they were alarmed. On the rocks they sat more upright than do either the Guillemots or Razor-bills, and their stations were usually farther removed from the sea than are those of these birds. They were easily frightened by loud noises, but not by anything seen, and they would sometimes utter a few low croaks. They were not known ever to attempt to make any defence of their eggs or young, but when caught would bite fiercely. They walked or ran with short steps, and went straight on, in the manner of a man. They have been known to drop from a rock into the water some two fathoms below.

To this account of the Great Auk Professor Newton adds the information — received from Sir William Milner — of the possession by the latter of a fine specimen of this bird that had been killed in the Hebrides. It has been stated by Professor Reinhardt — although this is not fully credited by Professor Newton — that some time before the extinction of this species, and when it was still numerous at its breeding-places, it appears to have visited Greenland, but only during the winter months. The birds were all in immature plumage, and appeared only in limited numbers. He adds that at some time during the present century — probably about 1821 — a specimen is known to have been killed on Disco Island, and one other is supposed to have been captured some years earlier. But none of the other instances in which this bird is said to have been captured in Greenland are credited by Professor Reinhardt.

In the "Ibis" of January, 1865, mention is made of the fact that among a set of bird bones from a place of ancient interment on the coast of Caithness, some remains of this species were identified by Professor Owen. Mr. J. M. Jones, of Halifax, presented to the British Museum an almost perfect skeleton of this bird, which had been found on Funk Island, off the northeast coast of Newfoundland. In connection with this interesting discovery, Mr. George A. Boardman, of Milltown, N. B., informs me that he was told by Rev. Mr. Wilson that this species, to his certain knowledge, was still in existence about Newfoundland between 1814 and 1818.

Audubon was told that the "Gare-fowl" was once plentiful about Nahant and islands in Massachusetts Bay; and although Professor Orton doubts the truth of the statement made by the old hunters of Chelsea, it is probably true. The Auk was not an Arctic bird, as Professor Orton states — certainly not exclusively so; and the frequency with which fragments of its bones have been found in the shell-heaps along the coast of Massachusetts is strong confirmatory evidence of the probable truth of the statement given above. Bones of this species have been taken from shell-heaps in Marblehead, from Eagle Hill, Ipswich, and from Plum Island, Newburyport.

Mr. J. E. Cabot was informed by an old fisherman living in Ipswich that a bird which must have been one of this species was captured by his father in that place many years ago; Mr. Cabot has no doubt that the bird then taken was the Great Auk. Professor Wyman discovered the remains of this bird at Mount Desert; and Professor Baird obtained a humerus of this species in a shell-heap in Ipswich in August, 1868.

Audubon also states that Mr. Henry Havell, when on his passage from New York to England, hooked a Great Auk, on the Banks of Newfoundland, in extremely boisterous weather. This bird was left at liberty on deck, where it walked very awkwardly, often tumbling over, biting every one that came within reach of its powerful bill, and entirely refusing food. When in Labrador, Audubon was informed that this Auk was then living on rocky islands off the southeastern end of Newfoundland; but he was not able to obtain further confirmatory evidence on this point. But as a few of these birds are known to have been alive at the time this statement was made, it may have been true, as we have no data as to the exact time of the disappearance of this bird from American waters.

This Auk is said to have been an unrivalled swimmer and diver. One that was pursued by Mr. Bullock, among the Orkney Islands, north of Scotland, near Papa Westra, distanced a six-oared boat. Buffon mentions, in regard to this bird, that it was rarely if ever seen out of soundings, and that its presence was regarded as an infallible indication of the near presence of land.

Dr. Fleming refers to a bird of this species as having been obtained at St. Kilda — one of the Outer Hebrides — in the winter of 1822; another was taken alive there in 1829, but managed to escape from its captors. Mr. Macgillivray visited these islands in 1840, and was informed by the inhabitants that the Great Auk was of not infrequent occurrence about St. Kilda; but that it had not been known to breed there for many years back. A specimen of this bird was picked up dead near Lundy Island, off the coast of Devonshire, in 1829. In 1834 one was taken off the coast of Waterford, Ireland, and is now in the collection of Trinity College, Dublin. This is the last specimen known to have been obtained in British waters; that referred to by Mr. Edwards having been captured at sea, over a fishing-bank, about three hundred miles from Newfoundland.

There is more or less disagreement in regard to some of the habits of this bird. Yarrell states that it was rarely seen out of water; but if this had been true, how it came to be exterminated would be hard to explain. That "the female lays her single large egg close above sea-tide mark" is not confirmed by information obtained by Professor Newton, according to which this bird appeared to have nested farther from the water than do most of its class of divers. Most writers agree that it laid but a single egg, and that when attacked it made no resistance, unless taken in the hand; but Yarrell states that in 1829 a pair — male and female — were killed on the Geirfugle-Skjœr whilst courageously defending their two eggs.

In a work descriptive of "Newfoundland and its Missionaries," printed in Halifax by Dakin & Metcalf, and published by the Wesleyan Book-room in 1866, the following reference is made to the Great Auk: "Half a century ago the Penguin was very plenty. It is a handsome bird, about the size of a Goose, with a coal-black head and back, a white belly, and a milk-white spot under the right eye. They cannot fly well, their wings are more like fins. They have on their bodies short feathers and down. The Penguin is now but seldom seen; such destruction of the bird was made for the sake of its feathers, that it is now all but extinct" (p. 64).

Mr. George A. Boardman having seen the above paragraph, and meeting its author, questioned him more particularly about the Penguin, and obtained a few further details. At the time of his residence in Newfoundland he was a Methodist missionary stationed on the coast, not far from the Funk or Fogo Island, between the years 1818 and 1823. He saw the Penguins during the whole of his stay in the island in considerable number, and frequently lectured the inhabitants for their cruelty in destroying them merely for their feathers. It was quite common for the boys to keep them tied by the leg as pets.

In a work on "New England Rarities," by John Josselyn, Gent., London, 1672, occurs the following reference to the Auk: "The Wobble is an ill shaped Fowl, having no long Feathers in their Pinions, which is the reason they cannot fly, not much unlike the *Pengwin;* they are in the Spring very fat, or rather oyly, but pull'd and garbidg'd, and laid to the Fire to roast, they yield not one drop." This author lived eight years in Scarborough, a hundred leagues east of Boston. This renders it highly probable that the Auk was then common in Casco Bay, where its bones are now found in shell-heaps.

In *Il Gazettiere Americano,* published in Leghorn, in 1763 (Vol. III. p. 158), under the head of Newfoundland, is the following paragraph: "The bird which is represented in the annexed plate [a very good figure of *P. impennis*] is found more frequently here than elsewhere. Although commonly called the Penguin of the north, it is quite different from the true Penguin of the south, with which by some it is wrongly confounded. In size it is equal to the common domestic Goose; and the better to judge of this in the plate the head and bill are given the size of life."

In "A Discovrse and Discovery of Nevv-fovnd-land," etc., by Captain Richard Whitbourne, of Exmouth, in the county of Devon, imprinted at London by Felix Kingston, 1622 (p. 9), is the following: "These Penguins are as bigge as Geese, and flye not, for they haue but a little short wing; and they multiplie so infinitely, vpon a certain flat Iland, that men driue them from thence vpon a boord, into their boats by hundreds at a time; as if God had made the innocency of so poore a creature, to become such an admirable instrument for the sustentation of man."

In a description of Greenland by Hans Egede, translated and published at London (2d ed.), 1818 [author's date, Copenhagen, July 20, 1718], we find: "There is another sea-bird, which the Norway-men call Alkes, which in the winter season contributes much to the maintenance of the Greenlanders. Sometimes there are such numbers of them that they drive them in large flocks to the shore, where they catch them with their hands" (pp. 95–98).

In "New Voyages to North America," from 1683 to 1694, by the Baron Lahontan, Lord Lieutenant, etc., translated from the French, London, 1735 (Vol. I. p. 241), occurs the following: "The *Moyacks* are a sort of Fowl, as big as a Goose, having a short Neck and a broad Foot; and which is very strange, their Eggs are half as big again as a Swan's, and yet they are all Yelk, and that so thick, that they must be diluted with Water before they can be us'd as Pancakes."

GENUS **ALCA**, LINNÆUS.

Alca, LINN. S. N. ed. 10, I. 1758, 130; ed. 12, I. 1766, 210 (type, *A. torda,* LINN.).
Utamania, LEACH, Syst. Cat. Brit. Mus. 1816 (same type).

CHAR. Similar to *Plautus,* but smaller, the wings well developed, so as to admit of long-sustained flight; bill much shorter than the head, the culmen much arched from the base, the maxilla with only three to five sulci, the mandible with but two or three, and these indistinct.

There is but one species of this genus, the well-known Razor-bill Auk (*A. torda*), common to both sides of the North Atlantic.

Alca torda.

THE RAZOR-BILLED AUK.

Alca torda, LINN. S. N. I. 1758, 130 (adult); ed. 12, I. 1766, 210. — AUD. Orn. Biog. III. 1835, 112; V. 1839, 428, pl. 214. — CASS. in Baird's B. N. Am. 1858, 901. — BAIRD, Cat. N. Am. B. 1859, no. 711. — COUES, Check List, 1873, no. 616.

Utamania torda, LEACH, Stephens's Gen. Zool. XIII. 1825, 27. — COUES, Pr. Ac. Nat. Sci. Philad. 1868, 18; Key, 1872, 340; 2d Check List, 1882, no. 877. — RIDGW. Nom. N. Am. B. 1881, no. 742.

Alca pica, LINN. S. N. I. 1766, 210 (young, or winter plumage).

Alca balthica, BRÜNN. Orn. Bor. 1764, 25, no. 101 (immature, without white line from bill to eye).
Alca unisulcata, BRÜNN. t. c. no. 102 (young).
Alca glacialis, BREHM, Vög. Deutschl. 1831, 1004.
Alca islandica, BREHM, t. c. 1005.
Alca microrhynchus, BREHM, Vogelf. 1855, 410.

HAB. Coasts and islands of the North Atlantic, down to about latitude 40° in winter. Japan? (*fide* SCHLEGEL).

A. torda.

SP. CHAR. *Adult, in summer:* Head, neck, and upper parts black, the head and neck more fuliginous, and changing to soft, velvety snuff-brown on the under portion of the head and fore-neck; secondaries narrowly tipped with white; a narrow white line running from the base of the culmen to the eye. Lower parts, including jugulum, axillars, and lining of the wing, immaculate white. Bill black, both mandibles crossed about the middle by a white line; "inside of mouth gamboge-yellow; iris deep hazel; feet black" (AUDUBON). *Adult, in winter:* Whole under portion of the head, fore-neck, and post-auricular region white; no white line from eye to bill; bill without basal lamina. Otherwise like the summer plumage. *Young:* Similar to the winter plumage, but bill smaller, perfectly smooth, and without the white bar across the middle portion.

Summer adult.

Total length, about 17.00 inches; wing, 8.00 to 8.50; tail, 3.50; culmen, 1.25; greatest depth of bill, .90; tarsus, 1.25; middle toe, 1.55.

This is a northern and Arctic species, abundant throughout the eastern shores of North America from the highest latitudes to Maine in summer and to New Jersey in winter. It is found on the western coast of Europe in the winter as far south as the Mediterranean. It is present on the Arctic coast of Asia; but so far as I am aware has never been taken on the Pacific shores of Asia or America, with the exception of the single Japanese record of Schlegel.

According to Professor Reinhardt, the Razor-bill is a resident of Greenland. It is also given by Middendorff as being found in the extreme northern portions of Siberia. It was met with on the coast of Spain, as well as on the shores of the Mediterranean, by Mr. Saunders, but it was very rare. This is still a not uncommon species at Grand Menan and on other rocky islands in the Bay of Fundy. During the winter it wanders down along the Atlantic sea-coast as far as Long Island, where, according to Giraud, it has been occasionally observed, but is not common. During the winter months an occasional bird of this species is exposed for sale in the Boston and New York markets, but it is nearly valueless for food.

The Razor-bill is an oceanic bird, having in many of its habits considerable resemblance to the Divers. It swims and dives with wonderful ease, and feeds upon small fish and crustaceans. In most respects, also, its habits are identical with those of the Guillemots and Mormons. Except during the breeding-season, when congregating in immense numbers on its breeding-grounds, it is generally seen singly. It is said to venture out farther from the shore, and to be able to dive in deeper water to collect its food, than can any of its family.

Audubon, in his voyage to Labrador, saw the Razor-bill constantly, and observed it fishing on banks where the water was eighteen fathoms deep. From the length of time the bird remained under water he had no doubt that it dived to the bottom and fed there. He was told that these birds arrive at the Madeleine Islands — where many of them breed — about the middle of April, while the Gulf of St. Lawrence is still covered with ice. On his way to Labrador he noticed these birds every now and then passing in long files, and flying, at the height of a few yards above the water, in an undulating manner and with regular beat of the wing. They often flew within musket-shot of the vessel.

He afterwards found this bird breeding in immense numbers on a small rocky island in the harbor of Wapatiguan, in deep and narrow fissures of the rocks. In order to reach both the birds and their eggs, long poles, with hooks at their extremities, were made use of. In a small horizontal cavern about two feet in height, where many were nesting, he found their eggs scattered at the distance of a few inches from each other; and where they were in fissures of the rock, they lay close together, small pebbles and broken stones being heaped up to the height of several inches so as to allow the water to flow off beneath them. In such localities this Auk sits flat upon its egg, in the manner of a Duck. When the single egg is deposited on an exposed rock, each bird stands almost upright upon it. Audubon also states that in several instances, where the parent bird was in a sheltered situation, he found her sitting on two eggs. It is, however, probable that in such cases the eggs were the product of different birds nesting near each other. He also states that these birds begin early in May to deposit their eggs; but as their period of incubation is four weeks, and as it was not until July that he found any young birds, all of which were yet small, it is probable he named too early a period for the beginning of the time of incubation. The young have tender unformed bills, are covered with down, and have a lisping note. Their parents supplied them plentifully with shrimps and small bits of fish. They were on good terms one with the other, and did not quarrel, as do the Puffins. When a finger was placed within their reach, they seized hold of it with their bills, showing thus early their desire to bite, so characteristic of their parents when these are taken in the hand. The old birds, when wounded, throw themselves on their backs, in the manner of Hawks, and fight desperately with their bills and claws. They walk on the rocks with considerable celerity and apparent ease; when intruded upon, they take to wing as soon as possible, and fly around the spot several times before they will again descend; or alight on the water and await the departure of the intruder before they venture to return.

Most writers speak of the Razor-bill as having but a single egg at a time; but Audubon thinks it occasionally lays two. The eggs are said to average 3.12 inches in length by 2.13 in breadth. They are generally of a pure white color, much blotched with dark reddish brown or blackish spots, which are usually confluent about the larger end. The yolk is orange-yellow, and the white tinged with a pale blue. Owing to the difficulty of procuring these eggs — most of them being secreted in deep crevices — these birds are rarely disturbed by the eggers, who plunder the Guillemots much more successfully.

This species feeds on the roe of fish, on shrimps, on various small marine animals, and on the smaller fishes. Its flesh is dark, and not prepossessing in appearance; but it is considered good by the fishermen, and according to Audubon was found tolerable when cooked in a stew. The bird is said to be two years in acquiring its full size and the mature form of its bill. When full grown its weight is about a pound and a half. After breeding the birds moult, and are then unable to fly before the beginning of October, when they move southward or into the open sea.

According to Yarrell, this bird has occasionally appeared on the shores of Italy and Sicily; and the London Zoological Society has received an immature specimen from Tangier.

Dr. Henry Bryant found it breeding on the northern shores of the Gulf of St. Lawrence. Though abundant, it was less numerous than the Foolish Guillemot, but much more generally distributed, breeding in greater or less numbers on almost all the rocky islands, even on those at some distance from the open waters of the Gulf; this the *Uria* never does.

Generally its eggs can be easily distinguished from those of the Guillemot; but it occasionally happens that an egg of the latter is so much like that of the Razor-bill that a mistake may be made. Dr. Bryant doubts the correctness of Naumann's statement that the egg of this species may be distinguished by the spots being always shaded on their edges with reddish brown, as he has found eggs of the Guillemot similarly shaded. In regard to the number of the eggs of the Razor-bill, Dr. Bryant states that though he has found hundreds of them, he never knew more than one to be laid by the same bird, and in no instance did he ever find anything like a nest. Four eggs selected by Dr. Bryant as average representatives of size and shape varied from 2.80 to 3.29 inches in length, and from 1.71 to 1.93 in breadth. The following are the measurements of each: 2.80 by 1.71 inches; 2.97 by 1.93; 3.29 by 1.87; 3.17 by 1.93. About 3.00 inches appears to be their average length, and about 2.00 the average breadth.

Dr. Coues, who visited Labrador in 1860, sent me, on his return, September 20, some interesting notes in regard to this species. He found it breeding at the first place at which he landed — Sloop Harbor — and procured its eggs at Eskimo Bay, the farthest point north visited. They were called "Backalaw birds," from their having formerly bred on the island of that name; but are more commonly known as "Trikers." They do not form such large colonies as the Murres and Puffins, but breed in greater or less numbers wherever there is a suitable island — often together with other birds. At Puffin Island they were in great abundance, laying in deserted

Puffins' holes and crevices of the rocks. When he passed the Murre Rocks, a large proportion of the myriads of birds flying around the ship were Auks, easily distinguished, even at a long distance, by their bill. As the two species thus breed indiscriminately together, many of the eggs coming from the rocks where the Murre nests are in reality those of the Auk. There is no difficulty, however, in distinguishing them from each other. The egg of the Auk never has a green or a blue ground-color, but is always white, spotted and blotched with dark umber, and seldom or never streaked. It is also more elliptical, much less pointed, and somewhat smaller. The Razor-bill lays by preference in the cracks and crevices of rocks, but also in company with the Murres on the bare rock, and with the Puffins in their deserted holes. He found young, that had been hatched out but a short time, on the 26th of July. On being wounded, or taken in the hand alive, this bird utters a loud hoarse cry, and fights and scratches most furiously, biting with great force, its strong hooked bill enabling it to inflict a severe wound. Dr. Coues found the flesh of this bird well flavored, and not possessing the slightest rank or fishy taste when thoroughly stewed. He never noticed more than a single egg. The eggs, though differing in their markings, are comparatively uniform in their size and shape, about 3.00 inches in length by a little less than 2.00 in breadth; the ground-color is either pure white or with a creamy tinge, and the spots are of different shades of umber-brown.

Eggs of this species have a ground-color varying from a dull buffy white to a pale greenish buff, or a buffy white with a greenish tinge. They are usually boldly marked with large blotches of blackish brown, burnt-umber, and lavender-gray. They do not usually vary much in their general appearance or size, and their shape is almost always exactly oval. Typical eggs in my collection from Labrador measure: 2.92 by 1.80 inches; 3.00 by 1.90; 2.85 by 1.92.

Genus **URIA**, Brisson.

Uria, Briss. Orn. VI. 1760, 70 (part).
Lomvia, Brandt, Bull. Ac. St. Petersb. II. 1837, 345 (type, *Colymbus troile*, Linn.).
Cataractes, Gray, List Gen. and Subgen. 1841, 98 (same type).

Char. Much larger than *Cepphus*. Bill much longer than the tarsus, much compressed, the gonys concave, and nearly as long as the culmen; maxilla notched near the tip, its tomia much inflected; nasal fossæ completely and densely feathered; a distinct longitudinal furrow in the feathering behind the eyes; plumage white beneath at all seasons.

Key to the Species.

1. **U. troile.** Depth of bill through angle less than one third the length of the culmen; head and neck uniform smoky brown, scarcely, never conspicuously, darker on pileum and nape.

   a. Troile. Wing, 7.75–8.30 inches (average, 7.99); culmen, 1.70–1.90 (1.81); gonys, 1.05–1.20 (1.14); depth of bill through angle, .50–.60 (.52); tarsus, 1.40–1.60 (1.51); middle toe, 1.60–1.75 (1.70). *Hab.* North Atlantic, south, in winter, to New England.

   β. Californica. Wing, 7.85–8.80 inches (average, 8.30); culmen, 1.60–2.50 (1.86); gonys, 1.15–1.40 (1.27); depth of bill through base, .55–.62 (.57); tarsus, 1.35–1.60 (1.50); middle toe, 1.65–1.85 (1.74). *Hab.* Pacific coast of North America, south to California (breeding).

2. **U. lomvia.** Depth of bill through angle more than one third the length of the culmen; pileum and nape black, like the back, in more or less conspicuous contrast with the deep snuff-brown of other portions of the head and neck.

a. Lomvia. Wing, 7.45–8.80 inches (average, 8.24); culmen, 1.40–1.50 (1.45); gonys, .75–.90 (.83); depth of bill through angle, .52–.58 (.55); tarsus, 1.40–1.55 (1.45); middle toe, 1.65–1.75 (1.70). *Hab.* North Atlantic, south to New Jersey; Arctic Ocean.

β. Arra. Wing, 8.15–9.25 inches (average, 8.71); culmen, 1.45–1.75 (1.65); gonys, .85–1.00 (.92); depth of bill through angle, .55–.60 (.58); tarsus, 1.45–1.60 (1.51); middle toe, 1.70–1.90 (1.81). *Hab.* North Pacific.

Uria troile.

THE COMMON GUILLEMOT.

U. troile (summer and winter plumages).

Colymbus troile, LINN. Faun. Suec. ed. 1761, 52; S. N. I. 1766, 220.
Uria troile, LATH. Ind. Orn. II. 1790, 796, no. 1. — DE KAY, N. Y. Zool. II. 1844, Birds, 279.
Catarractes troille, BRYANT, Pr. Boston Soc. 1861, 6, fig. 2 *a*.
Uria (Lomvia) troile, BRANDT, Bull. Ac. St. Petersb. II. 1837, 345.
Lomvia troile, COUES, Pr. Ac. Nat. Sci. Philad. 1868, 75; Key, 1872, 346; Check List, 1873, no. 634; ed. 2, 1882, no. 874. — RIDGW. Nom. N. Am. B. 1881, no. 763.
Uria lomvia, BRÜNN. Orn. Bor. 1764, 27, no. 108. — CASS. in Baird's B. N. Am. 1858, 913. — BAIRD, Cat. N. Am. B. 1859, no. 729.
Colymbus minor, GMEL. S. N. I. ii. 1788, 585 (part).
?[1] *Uria ringvia*, BRÜNN. Orn. Bor. 1764, p. 28, no. 111. — BAIRD, Cat. N. Am. B. 1858, no. 730.
? *Uria (Lomvia) ringvia*, BRANDT, Bull. Ac. St. Petersb. II. 1837, 345.
? *Lomvia ringvia*, COUES, Pr. Philad. Acad. 1868, 77.
Uria ringvia, CASS. in Birds N. Am. 1858, 914 (description and part of specimens enumerated).
? *Catarractes ringvia*, BRYANT, Pr. Boston Soc. 1861, 8.
Uria alga, BRÜNN. l. c. no. 112.

[1] The names preceded by an interrogation point refer to the form known as *Uria ringvia*.

"*Columbus langvia*, OLAFF, Reise n. Isl. p. 562" (BRYANT).[1]
Colymbus troile, var. *β*, DONNDORFF, Beytr. Zool. II. pt. i. 1794, 875.
Colymbus troile, var. *γ*, DONNDORFF, t. c. p. 876.
? *Uria lachrymans*, VALENC. in Choris, Voyages Pitt. autour du Monde, Aléout, 1822, 27, pl. 23.
? *Uria troile leucophthalmos*, FABER, Prodr. Isl. Orn. 1822, 42; Isis, 1824, 146.
? *Uria leucopsis*, BREHM, Beitr. Vogelk. III. 1823, p. 880; Isis, 1826, 888.

HAB. Coasts and islands of the North Atlantic, north to at least 80°, south, in America, to Southern New England in winter; breeding from Nova Scotia northward.

SP. CHAR. *Adult, summer plumage:* Head and neck, *including the pileum and nape*, uniform smoky brown, scarcely — never conspicuously — darker above; in some specimens (= *U.* "*ringvia*"), the edge of the eyelids, forming a ring completely round the eye, and a narrow postocular line, white. Upper parts uniform dusky, sometimes nearly black, the secondaries narrowly tipped with white. Lower parts, including the jugulum, white, this color anteriorly forming more or less of an angle on the foreneck; exterior feathers of the sides and flanks broadly edged on both webs with smoky gray or fuliginous-dusky. "Bill black; inside of mouth gamboge-yellow; feet black" (AUDUBON). *Winter plumage:* Similar to the above, but whole throat, cheeks, auricular region, and a broad stripe on each side of the occiput white, the latero-occipital stripe separated from the white below it, except posteriorly, by a narrow stripe of dark smoky brown along the upper edge of the auriculars. Stripes along the sides and flanks indistinct. Bill and feet dull brownish. *Young:* Similar to the winter plumage, but no white on the sides of the occiput, and that of the foreneck faintly mottled with dusky. *Downy young:* Head, neck, and upper parts smoky grayish brown, the head and neck finely streaked with dingy whitish; lower parts dingy white centrally.

"*U. ringvia*," *summer dress.*

Total length, about 17.00 inches; extent, 30.00; wing, 7.75–8.30 (average, 7.99); culmen, 1.70–1.90 (1.81); gonys, 1.05–1.20 (1.14); depth of bill through angle, .50–.60; tarsus, 1.40–1.60 (1.51); middle toe, 1.60–1.75 (1.70).[2]

U. troile, summer dress.

With regard to the perplexing form with white eyelids and postocular streak, we must confess ourselves undecided. The theory that it is an individual variation of *troile* seems the only one which can be adopted, in view of the asserted fact that the feature in question is not seasonal or sexual, and that the two forms "are known to copulate with each other" (cf. COUES, Pr. Philad. Acad., 1868, 78). There may be some mistake, however, as to these supposed facts; at any rate, were they true, it seems very strange that the same phase is never assumed by the western form of the species (*californica*).

[1] By typographical error printed "Plaff." in original. The correct quotation is probably *Colymbus langvigia*, OLAFFS. Reise, p. 562.

[2] Extremes and average of nine adults.

Uria troile.

The Foolish Guillemot may be taken as eminently typical of those diving-birds which are at once oceanic and Arctic. It occurs throughout the northern hemisphere, although rare in the North Pacific Ocean. On the American coast it breeds from the mouth of the Bay of Fundy — where it is comparatively rare — northward as far as the land extends. In midwinter it is found in the open sea as far south as the

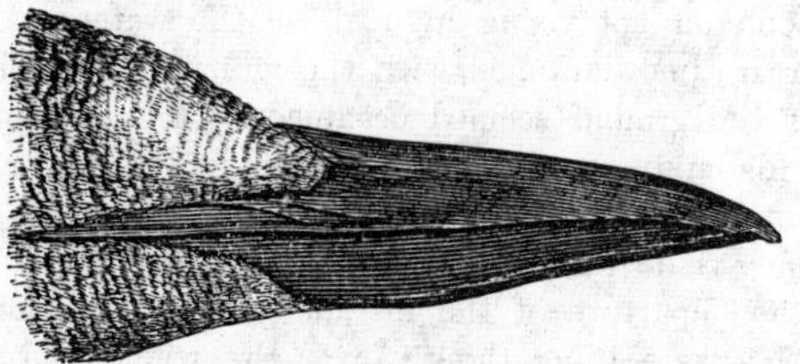

U. troile californica, summer adult.

lower waters of the Chesapeake. It is very rarely met with in bays or land-locked inlets, unless driven there by severe storms and against its own will.

In Europe it wanders in winter to the Mediterranean, and breeds from the British Islands northward. It is found throughout the Arctic Ocean, and breeds on nearly all the islands north of Asia, Europe, and America. It was found by Bischoff present, but not abundant, at Kadiak.

It is given by Professor Reinhardt as being one of the resident species of Greenland. In the summer of 1858 Dr. Walker, in the Expedition of the "Fox," encountered thousands of this species on the coast of Greenland, and afterward in Melville Bay.

According to Giraud, this bird is to be met with in winter off the coasts of Long Island and New Jersey. Professor Newton states that Dr. Malmgren found it breeding on Bear Island, Spitzbergen, in almost incredible numbers; and there he found intermingled with it occasional specimens of *Uria ringvia,* which he regards rather as a variety of this bird than as entitled to specific rank.

Middendorff met with this species on the Siberian coast, on the margins of the tundras of that desolate region.

Mr. Howard Saunders states that it is found on the Mediterranean coast of Spain, but that it is of very rare occurrence there. Three specimens only were obtained by him during the winter. Near Gibraltar it was more numerous. Mr. Layard ("Ibis," 1867, p. 249) mentions that in his voyage from England to Cape Town, when off Cape Finisterre he fell in with flocks of these birds. Mr. Wright mentions that a single example of this species was taken, about 1852, at Malta, and that in 1864 it was still preserved in the museum of Professor Delicatu.

During the breeding-season these birds assemble by hundreds, or, more frequently, by thousands, at certain localities, generally on extensive rocky islands, or on cliffs, or bold shores. Toward these points they usually converge early in the month of May. Notwithstanding the immense numbers that sometimes resort to the same rock, and although we often find these birds breeding in company with those of several other species, except when disturbed by the intrusion of man, there is a freedom from confusion and a prevalence of order and system in their operations that is quite remarkable. As if by mutual and common consent, not only do the different species keep apart, and occupy separate portions of their common breeding-ground, but each individual bird apparently knows its place and keeps to it, going at once to its own chosen spot to renew its egg when the nest has been despoiled of its treasure. It is very rare to find two distinct species breeding side by side, although Audubon speaks of having found the Razor-bill breeding in company with this species on the coast of Labrador.

When Audubon visited Labrador in 1832 he found this bird breeding by thousands on the Masse Rocks, near Great Macatina Harbor. These were several low islands, destitute of vegetation, and not rising high above the water. As he approached these islands the air became darkened with the multitudes of birds flying about. Every square foot of the ground seemed occupied by a Guillemot sitting erect on its solitary egg. On his landing, each affrighted bird left its egg hastily, ran a few steps, and launched into the air in silence, flying rapidly around as if to discover the object of the unwelcome visit; and then all alighted in the water at some distance, anxiously awaiting the departure of the intruder. Eggs — green and white, and of almost every color — were lying thickly over the whole rock; and these were collected by the eggers in astonishing quantities and taken to distant markets.

These wholesale depredations have been followed by the inevitable consequences; and when Dr. Bryant visited these same islands twenty-eight years later, he found them almost abandoned.

According to the last-named authority, this species breeds at various points from the extremity of Nova Scotia to Hudson's Bay, and is the most common bird on the Labrador coast. The extent to which these birds are persecuted may be imagined from the fact that though on the 23d of June young birds were common at the Gannet Rock — where they are but little, if at all, disturbed — Dr. Bryant had seen, up to the 20th of July, but one young bird on the Labrador coast. At the Masse Rock not more than a hundred eggs could be collected on the 2d of July; and the number of Guillemots breeding there was probably not a hundredth of what it was in Audubon's time.

When undisturbed, this bird lays but a single egg in a season; and this is of large size in proportiön to that of the bird, and very variable in color, hardly any two being exactly alike. The ground-color, which is even more variable than are the shades of the markings, may be white, or bluish green, white tinged with reddish, with just a slight tinge of green, or with the latter color very deep and bright. The markings are generally a dark reddish brown, deepening in some almost to black. In a few instances the eggs are unmarked, some being entirely green or wholly white. Their extreme length is 3.31 inches, and their minimum length about 2.81; the breadth varies from 1.77 to 2.00. Their form is elongated pear-shape.

The Guillemot makes no nest; and sits in an upright position on her single egg, incubation lasting four weeks. The young bird is at first covered with a brownish-black, bristly, hairlike down, and is fed for a short time by the parent with pieces of fish. Mr. Waterton, on his visit to Flamborough Head, was assured by the men there that when the young bird reaches a certain size, it climbs upon the back of the old bird, and is conveyed by the latter to the ocean. Through a good telescope he saw numbers of the young Guillemots, still unable to fly, sporting in the sea, and others on the edges of the cliffs in such situations that had they attempted to fall into the water they would inevitably have been killed by striking upon the intervening rocks; and he therefore accepted the information of the rock-climbers as being the only probable explanation of the fact that the young bird reaches the water at so early an age.

Yarrell states that he has seen in the water at the base of high cliffs, in the Isle of Wight, young Guillemots so small that they could not have made the descent from the lofty site of their birthplace without having been killed. Yet these little birds knew perfectly well how to take care of themselves, and on the approach of a boat would swim and dive in various directions. Early in September these birds, young and old, quit the foot of the rocks near their breeding-places for the open ocean, where they remain until the following May.

This bird is said to remain about the rocks and bays of Orkney and Shetland all the year; and also on the coast of Iceland and among the Farne Islands. It was found by Sir Edward Parry and Sir James C. Ross, in their journey over the ice, as high as latitude 81°.

Uria ringvia.

The claim of this form, which so closely resembles the common Guillemot, to be ranked as of specific significance, is generally challenged by writers. Certainly there is no difference noticeable in the habits, and but little in the distribution, of the two birds. When found at all, it is almost invariably in company with the *troile;* but the latter is usually present in much the larger numbers. According to Gould, the *ringvia* is particularly common on the coast of Wales, where, as he was informed, the Bridled Guillemot is quite as numerous as the other form. It was first described in 1822, from a specimen obtained at Newfoundland by A. Valenciennes. It is considered a distinct species from the *troile* by Temminck, Thienemann, and other naturalists, both French and German. Degland and Gerbe give it as being only a variety of the common species. Temminck (IV. 577) remarks that Faber and Graba, who have resided both in Iceland and the Faröe Islands, are positive that both this form and the Thick-billed are only varieties of the common species. While allowing due weight to the opinions of two such competent judges, based upon observations made on the spot, he is unconvinced, especially as Brünnich's Guillemot is also reduced to a mere variety of *troile*, and not regarded a good species.

Audubon figures the *ringvia* as the male of the *troile*, evidently not appreciating the fact that the difference is not one of sex.

Dr. Bryant, who met with this bird on Gannet Rock, says in regard to it: "As this bird was unfortunately confounded by Audubon with the preceding species [*troile*], it is at present impossible to ascertain what were its limits or numbers at the time of his visit. There can be little doubt, however, that it was not at all rare on the Labrador shore. None of these birds were seen by me at any place, except on Gannet Rock, though I think it must breed at other points on the coast. The eggs are said by Naumann to be larger than those of the Foolish Guillemot, the shell to be smooth, and the spots to be seldom large, etc. The largest Guillemot egg found by me was one of the present species; but in respect to coloration I notice no particular mark by which they could be distinguished from the others. The largest and handsomest egg procured is one of the green variety, and marked over the whole surface with lines presenting very much the appearance of Chinese characters; it resembles, however, specimens of the eggs of *Uria troile*, and I see no character by which it could be distinguished from them."

Degland and Gerbe, while treating this form as a variety, state that it inhabits the Arctic regions generally, including Iceland, the Faröes, and Newfoundland; and is a migratory visitor on the coast of France, individuals having been found dead on the shores of the English Channel, and others killed along the French coast. On the 7th of June, 1846, a male and two females were shot — so M. Degland was informed by letter — at Aiguilles d'Étretat. This species, to the knowledge of the writer, M. Hardy, has twice been found breeding in the last-named locality. It was nesting in holes in the rocks on the border of the sea, in company with the *troile.* It laid a single egg, very pyriform, of a brownish white, with a few spots of ashy-gray and sinuous zigzag lines of mingled red and brownish black. In other respects the egg of this species varies as much as do those of the *troile.* They vary in length from 3.15 to 3.35 inches, and in breadth from 1.94 to 2.04. These measurements differ from those of Dr. Bryant, who gives 3.10 as the maximum length, and 1.96 as the greatest breadth. M. Gerbe, in a note, referring to the views of Faber and Graba as to the specific unity of *troile, ringvia,* and *lomvia,* adds that Thienemann, who also visited the same countries, is of an entirely different opinion. He considers these three forms as three distinct species; and while, on this point, the opinions of ornithologists remain very much divided, M. Gerbe states that — so far as this form is concerned — if it is not a good species, it is certainly a well-marked race. Thienemann founded his belief in the diversity of these species on the constant differences in their eggs; and Mr. Proctor, of Durham, England, who has visited the breeding-places of these birds in Iceland, agrees with Thienemann entirely. He visited Grimsey, an island forty miles north of Iceland, where he found these three forms breeding on the rocks. They were regarded by all the inhabitants as three entirely distinct birds. Brünnich's Guillemot was the most numerous, and was called *Stutnefia.* The *troile* was next in point of numbers, and was known as *Langnefia.* The Ringed Guillemot was the least numerous, and was called *Hring langnefia.* The eggs of all three kinds were obtained; and the distinctions between them were well known to the fishermen, who separated them, when put together, without difficulty or hesitation. The eggs of the *ringvia* were the most rare, less from the smaller number of the parent birds than from the circumstances of their breeding away from the others, far lower down on the precipitous ledges, where they were inaccessible from below, and more difficult to obtain by those lowered down from above. The Common Guillemot and the Ringed do not breed together, but each keeps by itself.

I attach far more importance to the fact that these forms, in nesting, appear thus to keep exclusively by themselves, than to the supposed differences in eggs, on which, as evidence of specific separation, we cannot safely rely. Like the eggs of the Arctic, Common, and Roseate Terns, those of the three forms vary so much, and appear to run into such corresponding variations, that no certain rule, in my judgment, is yet possible. On the other hand, the careful separation of breeding-places is a more sure sign of specific demarcation. All the eggs that I have ever seen of this variety (*ringvia*) are uniformly large, have a constant white ground, and are marked with red and brown lines, long, slender, and irregular. Dr. Bryant's experience was, however, different, as we have seen.

According to Professor Reinhardt, the *Uria ringvia* is found in Greenland, but is a very rare bird there. Captain Elmes found it breeding on the Island of Berneray, one of the outer Hebrides. It was in company with the more abundant *Uria troile,* and was, in proportion to the latter, as one to ten or twelve, which corresponds with the observations of other persons on Handa Island and Ailsa Craig. He took several of the eggs on each of which he actually saw one of the Ringed Guillemots sitting, and found that they vary as much as the others, though more were marked with streaks than with blotches.

This bird is comparatively rare on the New England coast, but has been met with in winter, and is more abundant off the more easterly portions of the coast of Maine than elsewhere.

Examples of this species obtained by Dr. Bryant on Gannet Rock, in the Gulf of St. Lawrence, have a ground of cream-color, and the markings are black. They measure 3.25 inches in length, and from 2.00 to 2.05 in breadth.

Uria troile californica.

THE CALIFORNIAN GUILLEMOT.

Uria troile, NEWB. Pacific R.R. Rep. VI. iv. 1857, 110 (not *Colymbus troile*, LINN.).
Uria Brünnichii, HEERM. Ib. X. 1859, Birds, 75 (not of SABINE, 1818).
Catarractes californicus, BRYANT, Pr. Boston Soc. 1861, 11, figs. 3, 5 (Farallon Islands, coast of California).
Lomvia californica, COUES, Pr. Ac. Nat. Sci. Philad. 1862, 79, fig. 16.
Lomvia troile, var. *californica*, COUES, Key, 1872, 346; Elliott's Alaska, 1875, 210.
Lomvia troile californica, RIDGW. Pr. U. S. Nat. Mus. Vol. 3, 1880, 212; Nom. N. Am. B. 1881, no. 763 *a*. — COUES, 2d Check List, 1882, no. 875.

HAB. Pacific coast of North America, breeding from California (Farallones) north to the Prybilof Islands, and across Aleutian chain to Kamtschatka.

SP. CHAR. Similar in colors, in all stages, to typical *troile*, but averaging larger in all its measurements, except the length of the tarsus, which is slightly shorter; all the outlines of the bill usually less curved than in *troile*.

Total length, about 16.00 inches; extent, 27.00; wing, 7.85–8.80 (average, 8.30); culmen, 1.60–2.05 (1.86); gonys, 1.15–1.40 (1.27); depth of bill through angle, .55–.62 (.57); tarsus, 1.35–1.60 (1.50); middle toe, 1.65–1.90 (1.74).[1]

The characters adduced by authors for distinguishing this race from true *troile* of the North Atlantic we find exceedingly variable, and practically entirely inconstant, the individual variation in the contour of the bill being very great, as may be seen by the measurements given above. All the dimensions, however, are almost constantly and decidedly larger.

This appears to be the Pacific representative of *U. troile*, and is, so far as America is concerned, confined to the Pacific coast, from Southern California to Alaska. Mr. Dall states that it was obtained, with its eggs, both at Sitka and at Kadiak. He afterward found it at Unalashka, in company with *Simorhynchus cristatellus*, but much less common than that species. In his Notes on the Birds of the Aleutian Islands west of Unalashka he speaks of this species as being abundant, and apparently a resident all through the islands. It is less common and more shy than the *Cepphus columba*, but, unlike that species, congregating in immense flocks a few miles off shore. He has never met with the *columba* in large flocks — never more than two or three individuals together.

Dr. Cooper, when at Monterey in May, 1862, noticed these birds in the open bay. Their presence there at that season seemed strange, and rendered it probable that they were breeding in the vicinity. Dr. Cooper also remarks that the chief locality — indeed the only one known to him — to which this species resorts during the breeding-season is the Farallones. There these birds swarm, clustering like bees on every ledge and slope of the ragged peaks which constitute these islands, and depositing their eggs on the bare rock. Each bird, if undisturbed, lays but a single egg, which it incubates in a standing position. It is able to walk tolerably well when standing nearly erect.

The abundance and the large size of the eggs of this species have made them a valuable article of import to San Francisco. The Farallones, twenty-five miles from the mouth of the bay of San Francisco, are admirably situated for furnishing this

[1] Average measurements of thirteen adults.

supply, as they are too far to be easily reached, and the birds are consequently free from being wantonly and unnecessarily disturbed. They begin to lay from the 17th to the 27th of May — so Dr. Cooper was informed by Mr. Tasker, of the lighthouse — and eggs can be found as late as August, since the many robberies to which the birds are subjected oblige them to lay several times. As the eggs are laid on the bare rock, and often on narrow ledges which are sloping and slippery, there are also numerous chances of breakage; and the birds have many enemies besides man, so that Nature has provided them with the ability to lay many successive times in order that some, at least, of the eggs may be hatched. Yet as each female lays but one egg at a time, and as the birds are robbed of many thousands, the wonder is that so many birds are successfully raised as must be in order to form the enormous flocks that are still seen together. Probably if they were scattered over a more extensive surface, or along the whole coast, their numbers would not seem so great. Even now, the oldest eggers begin to see a diminution in the numbers; and probably as the old birds die off there will be much fewer raised to supply their places. There is, however, one fact in their favor; namely, that the market value of their eggs has decreased so much with the increase in the product of eggs of the domestic Hen, that they are now worth little more than one third of the price of the latter; and consequently the gathering of them is no longer profitable after they begin to be a little scarce. This occurs about the first of July, or after the gathering season has lasted about six weeks; and the birds are then left to themselves. The mode of gathering the eggs is as follows: The island is divided into two parts, and each is hunted over every other day. After noon, the eggers having previously broken every egg they can find, so as to secure freshness for the next lot, start out with large baskets, which they leave at convenient points. The men then scatter, and collect the eggs from the ledges, carrying them down in a bag suspended in front, from which they are transferred to the baskets; and when these are full, a covering of dry seaweed is put over them to protect them from the Gulls, and they are carried to the storehouse, and thence shipped to San Francisco.

On the approach of the men the Murres reluctantly flutter off, and often drag with them the precious eggs, which are dashed to pieces on the rocks, while the birds fly to some distant point on the rocks or the water, making only a faint croaking sound, the only note with which they seem to be gifted. At this time the Gulls, which have been following the eggers with loud screams, watching their opportunity, sometimes seize an egg by sticking their open bill into it, and fly off to eat its contents at their leisure. Dr. Heermann relates an instance in which two Gulls made a feint of attacking the Murre in front, while another stole up behind and seized the egg, when the three flew off together to devour it.

Specimens of the eggs of this Murre from the Farallones show, according to Dr. Cooper, the following differences: The ground-color is white, greenish, blue-green, sea-green, yellowish, or cinnamon, and they are either unspotted, or blotched, speckled, or variously streaked with different shades of brown or black. They measure generally from 3.30 to 3.53 inches in length, by from 1.90 to 2.05 in width. Occasionally very small ones — which are possibly abortive — measure only 2.05 by 1.45 inches.

Limited numbers of this species were found by Mr. H. W. Elliott on the Prybilof Islands, perched on the cliffs with the "Arrie," the two resembling each other so closely, and being so much alike in their habits, that it requires a practised eye to distinguish them, unless the observer is very near. The largest gathering of these birds seen at any place on these islands was a flock of about fifty, at the high bluffs on St. George's. They are generally scattered, by ones, twos, and threes, among thousands and tens of thousands of the *arra*.

The following extracts from a letter written by Dr. W. O. Ayres are interesting as showing the early history of the traffic in the eggs of this species. It is dated San Francisco, Oct. 13, 1854: The "Farallones de los Frayles" are a group of small islands lying a little over twenty miles west of the entrance to the Bay of San Francisco. They are almost inaccessible, entirely uninhabited — with a single exception — and afford therefore very naturally a resort for great multitudes of birds. Some time since, a company was organized in this city for the purpose of bringing the eggs of these birds to market. An imperfect idea of the number of the birds may be formed from the fact that this company sold here during the last season — a period of less than two months, in June, July, and August — more than five hundred thousand eggs; that all these were gathered on a single one of the islands; and that in the opinion of the eggers, not more than one egg in six of those deposited on that island was gathered. The eggs were gathered in only one limited portion of the island known as the Great Farallon, called the Rookery, in which one species of bird they called the Murre swarmed in myriads, there being no other species among them. The eggs vary to a greater degree than I have known in any other instance.

Accompanying this letter are outlines of seven eggs (two of them evidently those of *Cepphus columba*) and the measurements of twelve others. The broadest measures 3.60 by 2.23 inches, while two others measure, one 3.66 by 1.87, and the other 3.64 by 1.77. One very pointed egg measures 3.43 by 1.81 inches. The least length is 3.07 inches. The ground-color of this egg is usually a pure white; but quite frequently a bluish-white, greenish-white, cream-white, buffy white, blue, green, dilute rufous, etc., constitute the ground. The markings are combinations of subdued lavender, pale brown, and deep brownish black. In some these are sparse; others are thickly covered by them.

Uria lomvia.

a. Lomvia. BRÜNNICH'S GUILLEMOT.

Alca lomvia, LINN. S. N. ed. 10, I. 1758, 130, no. 4.
Cataractes lomvia, BRYANT, Pr. Boston Soc. 1861, 9, figs. 1, 4.
Uria svarbag, BRUNN. Orn. Bor. 1764, 27, no. 110 (winter pl.).
Lomvia svarbag, COUES, Pr. Ac. Nat. Sci. Philad. 1868, 80.
Uria Brünnichii, SABINE, Trans. Linn. Soc. XII. 1818, 538. — SW. & RICH. F. B. A. II. 1831, 477. NUTT. Man. II. 1834, 529. — GOULD, B. Eur. V. 1837, pl. 398. — AUD. Orn. Biog. III. 1835, 336, pl. 345; B. Am. oct. ed. VII. 1844, pl. 472.
Lomvia arra Brünnichi, RIDGW. Nom. N. Am. B. 1881, no. 764 *a*.
Uria arra, CASS. in Baird's B. N. Am. 1858, 914 (not of PALL. 1826). — BAIRD, B. N. Am. 1859, no. 731.
Lomvia arra, (pt.) COUES, Key, 1872, 346; 2d Check List, 1882, no. 876.
Uria Francesii, LEACH, Trans. Linn. Soc. XII. 1818, 588. — DE KAY, N. Y. Zool. Birds, 1844, 280.
Uria polaris, BREHM, Handb. Vög. Deutschl. 1831, 984.

b. Arra. THE THICK-BILLED GUILLEMOT.

Cepphus arra, PALL. Zoog. Rosso-As. II. 1826, 347.
Uria arra, CASS. Pr. Philad. Acad. 1864, 324.
Lomvia arra, COUES, Key, 1872, 346 (part); Elliott's Alaska, 1875, 211; 2d Check List, 1882, no. 876 (part). — RIDGW. Nom. N. Am. B. 1881, no. 764.
Uria Brünnichii, of authors referring to the Thick-billed Guillemot of the North Pacific.

HAB. Coasts and islands of the North Atlantic, Arctic, and Pacific oceans; on the Atlantic coast of North America, south in winter to New Jersey, breeding from the Gulf of St. Lawrence northward. On the Pacific side the typical form replaced by the *arra* (Prybilof Islands, Kadiak, Aleutians, Kamtschatka, etc.).

a. **Lomvia.**

Sp. Char. *Adult, breeding-plumage:* Entire upper parts, *including pileum and nape,* glossy fuliginous-black, the secondaries narrowly tipped with white; sides and under part of head and neck rich velvety dark snuff-brown, shading gradually into the black above it. Lower parts continuous white, ending anteriorly, on the jugulum, in an obtuse angle, extending a greater or less distance into the dark brown of the foreneck; outer webs of exterior feathers of the sides and flanks broadly edged with sooty black. Bill uniform deep black, the basal half of the maxillary tomium plumbeous, sometimes conspicuously light colored; iris brown; legs and feet dusky brown in the dried skin. *Winter plumage:* Whole throat, foreneck, auricular region, and sides of the occiput white, the upper border of the auriculars crossed by a narrow blackish stripe; white latero-occipital space and lower part of foreneck, faintly mottled transversely with dusky. Upper parts as in the summer plumage. *Young:* Similar to the winter plumage, but without white on the sides of the occiput. *Downy young:* Fuliginous-dusky, the lower parts white centrally, shading exteriorly into smoky grayish; head and neck variegated with irregular pale smoky buff streaks and filamentous downy tufts of the same color.

U. lomvia, summer plumage.

Total length, about 18.50 inches; extent, 30.00 to 32.00; wing, 7.45–8.80 (average,[1] 8.24); culmen, 1.40–1.50 (1.45); gonys, .75–.90 (.83); depth of bill, through angle, .52–.58 (.55); tarsus, 1.40–1.55 (1.45); middle toe, without claw, 1.65–1.75 (1.70).

b. **Arra.**

Sp. Char. Precisely similar in colors, in all stages of plumage, to typical *lomvia,* but decidedly larger in all its measurements, and with the maxillary tomium less distinctly light colored toward the base.

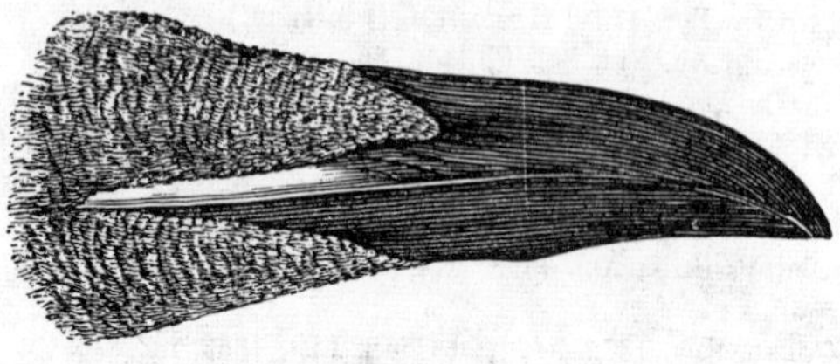

U. lomvia arra.

Wing, 8.15–9.25 inches (average, 8.71); culmen, 1.45–1.75 (1.65); gonys, .85–1.00 (.92); depth of bill through angle, .55–.60 (.58); tarsus, 1.45–1.60 (1.51); middle toe, without claw, 1.70–1.90 (1.81).

Though by many the Brünnich's Guillemot has been regarded as merely a local race of the common species, it has of late become generally regarded as having good claims to be considered a distinct species. It appears to have to a large degree the same distribution as has the *troile,* and so far as it has been observed, the same habits.

[1] Of eight adult examples.

It is alleged by Thienemann and others that there are always distinctive differences to be found between its eggs and those of either *troile* or *ringvia.* But of this I am not able to find any satisfactory evidence. This is, if anything, the more Arctic species; and where found in more northern latitudes appears to be much more abundant than the *troile.*

Near Horn Sound, Spitzbergen, Messrs. Evans and Sturge met with it in immense numbers. The birds were in company with the Little Auk, and flew about in large flocks, settling close around the vessel, playing and diving in all directions, and seeming to be quite regardless of the presence of intruders, keeping up all the while a shrill chattering.

It is also much more abundant in the North Pacific and Behring Sea, where the *ringvia* has not been observed, and where the *troile* has been rarely met with. Mr. Dall mentions it as not uncommon at Kadiak, and abundant at St. George's, where it breeds in immense numbers on the perpendicular cliffs. It is not given as occurring in the Aleutian Islands.

Mr. Henry W. Elliott states that this species — the great Egg-bird of the North Pacific — frequents the Prybilof Islands by millions. This *Uria* and one other, the *U. californica,* are the only birds of this genus found there. They appear very early in the season, but do not begin to lay until the 18th or 25th of June; and in open, mild winters these birds are said to be seen in straggling flocks all around the islands. He considers it certain that the birds of this species do not all migrate from that sea and the vicinity of the Aleutian Islands. They lay their eggs upon the points and narrow shelves on the faces of the cliff-fronts to the islands, making no nests, but standing over the eggs, side by side, as thickly as they can be crowded together. They quarrel desperately, and so earnestly that all along the high bluffs on the north shore of St. George's hundreds of dead birds are lying, having been killed by falling on to the rocks while clinched in combat with rivals in mid-air. The birds lay but a single egg on the bare rock. The egg is large and very fancifully colored, having a bluish green ground with dark-brown mottlings and patches; but it is exceedingly variable in size and coloring. The outline of the egg is pyriform, and sometimes more acute. This is the most palatable of all the varieties found on the islands, having no disagreeable flavor, and when perfectly fresh being fully as good as a Hen's egg. Incubation lasts nearly twenty-eight days, and the young come out with a dark thick coat of down, which within six weeks from hatching is supplanted by the plumage and color of the old birds. They are fed by the disgorging of the parents, apparently without intermission, and utter all the while a harsh, rough, and decidedly lugubrious croak.

On St. George's Island, while the females begin to sit, toward the end of June and first of July, the males go flying around, at regular hours in the morning and evening, in great files and platoons, always circling against or quartering on the wind, forming a dark girdle of birds more than a quarter of a mile broad and thirty miles long, whirling round and round the island. The flight of the "Arrie" is straight, steady, and rapid, the wings beating quickly and powerfully. It makes no noise, and utters no cry, save a low, hoarse, grunting croak, and that only when quarrelling or mating.

Captain W. H. Feilden ("Ibis," October, 1877) observed two individuals of this species in August as far north as Buchanan's Strait (lat. 79° N.), but it was not seen again until the return of the Expedition southward in September, 1876, after regaining navigable waters south of Cape Sabine. The north waters of Baffin's Bay appeared to be the northern limits of the species in this direction, nor were there any breeding-places north of Cape Alexander.

Dr. Walker, in the Voyage of the "Fox," mentions finding this species in thousands on the coast of Greenland, and Professor Reinhardt gives it as a common resident species of that island. Professor Newton found this the most common, with perhaps one exception, of the birds of Spitzbergen. Dr. Malmgren regarded it as altogether the most numerous, even more so than the *Mergulus alle* (= *Alle nigricans*). It was breeding as far to the north as Walden Island, in lat. 80° 38′ N. Its food, according to Professor Newton, is chiefly crustaceans; and according to the observations of Professor Malmgren, it also lives a good deal on fish. By the end of August all the breeding-places on the north coast had been deserted, and about the same time the birds that had previously thronged the Alkenhorn in such countless numbers were rapidly quitting it. Eastward of the South Cape he did not meet with this species at all. It is given by Middendorff as one of the birds of Siberia, occurring in the most northern portions, on the coast of the Arctic Ocean. Mr. Gillett met with it on Nova Zembla, where it was abundant along the coast, breeding in all the cliffs. Von Heuglin in his subsequent visit to the same region makes a very similar statement.

In winter this bird is quite common along the entire New England coast, and is especially abundant in the lower portions of the Bay of Fundy, where a few still breed every summer. Dr. Henry Bryant found it breeding abundantly on Gannet Rock, in the Gulf of St. Lawrence, and only a little inferior in numbers to the *troile.* He noticed nothing peculiar in the habits of this species differing from what is already known in reference to the genus. He states that though the shape of the eggs of this species is generally more ovate than that of the *troile* or *ringvia,* he was not able to find any character by which they can be with certainty distinguished. Their maximum length he gives as 3.11 inches, their minimum 2.75; their breadth varying from 1.77 to 1.89.

According to Mr. W. Thompson, this species is found, and probably breeds, on the coast of Kerry, Ireland. Sir James C. Ross met with it at Uist, the most northern of the Shetland Islands, and in several parts of Scotland; and Macgillivray received specimens from the Orkneys. A single accidental specimen is recorded as having been taken near Naples, where it is still preserved.

Mr. Proctor found this bird breeding in great abundance on the Island of Grimsey, north of Iceland, where it was the most numerous of the *Uriæ,* and where it is known to the inhabitants by the name of *Stutnefia.*

Mr. Kumlien mentions large breeding-places of this bird about Capes Mercy and Walsingham, and on the islands in Exeter Sound. They are also very abundant on the Greenland coast, breeding by thousands in many localities.

In the winter it usually keeps well off the coast, but is occasionally forced into the bays by violent or long-continued easterly winds. It becomes confused by heavy falls of snow, and in its attempts to escape by flight loses its way, and is driven inward upon the land, where it perishes with cold. I received one in 1839 that had been picked up in a field in Hingham Centre. It was uninjured, and no other cause could be assigned for its death than cold.

Eggs of this species in the Smithsonian collection are from Gannet Rock in the Gulf of St. Lawrence, the Arctic coast, and the Prybilof Islands. The ground-color of these eggs varies remarkably, some being white, others of a deep buff, a bright grass-green, a pale blue, a deep blue, intermediate tints of blue, etc. The markings of some are in lines, others in blotches and spots varying from a light umber-brown to a deep black. Four eggs selected as typical of their varying size and shape measure: 3.10 by 1.95 inches; 3.30 by 1.95; 3.05 by 2.05; 3.00 by 1.90.

Genus **CEPPHUS**, Pallas.

Uria, Briss. Orn. VI. 1760, 70 (part), et Auct.
Cepphus, Pall. Spic. Zool. V. 1769, 33 (type, *C. lacteolus*, Pall., = *C. grylle, albino*).
Grylle, Leach, in Ross's Voy. Disc. N. W. Pass. App. 1819, p. li (type, *G. scapularis*, Leach, = *Uria grylle*, Brünn., + *U. Mandti*, Licht.). — Brandt, Bull. Ac. St. Petersb. II. 1837, 346 (type, *U. grylle*, Brünn.).

Char. Size medium. Bill decidedly shorter than head, about equal in length to the tarsus, moderately compressed; upper and lower outlines straight and nearly parallel for about the basal half (or more), the terminal portion of the culmen gently decurved, the gonys (which is less than half as long as the culmen) gently ascending, straight, or slightly convex; nasal fossæ only partly feathered, occupied chiefly by membrane, the nostrils narrow, slit-like, in the lower edge of the fossæ; no furrow in the plumage behind the eye. Color in summer uniform blackish, with or without a white wing-patch.

C. Mandtii, summer dress.

The characters given above are merely the more prominent ones distinguishing this genus from its allies, more especially *Uria*, which by many authors has not been considered as distinct from *Cepphus*.

Five species are known, all but one of them being certainly North American; they differ as follows: —

A. A large white patch on the outer surface of the wing.

a. Lining of wing pure white.

1. **C. Mandtii.** Greater wing-coverts white to the extreme base, sometimes with a little dusky along the basal portion of the shafts. Wing, about 6.50 inches; culmen, 1.00–1.10; gonys, .50; depth of bill through middle of nostril, .35; tarsus, about 1.30; middle toe, with claw, 1.60–1.65. *Hab.* Circumpolar Regions and Northern North America, south in winter to New Jersey and Norton Sound, Alaska.

2. **C. grylle.** Greater wing-coverts with at least their basal half black, this often showing as a narrow bar beyond tips of anterior row of coverts. About the same dimensions as *Mandtii*, but bill larger and stouter. Culmen, 1.20–1.30; gonys, .55–.60; depth of bill through middle of nostril, .40–.45. *Hab.* Coasts of Northern Europe, south to Denmark and northern parts of British Islands; coast of Newfoundland (?); Eastport, Me.; south in winter to Philadelphia.

b. Lining of wing smoky gray.

3. **C. columba.** Greater wing-coverts black basally, this increasing in extent toward edge of wing, where occupying almost the whole of the outermost feather, thus producing a broad black "wedge" between the two white areas. Wing, about 7.00 inches; culmen, 1.20; gonys, . ; depth of bill, . ; tarsus, 1.25; middle toe, with claw, 1.90. *Hab.* Pacific coast of North America, from California to the Aleutian Islands, and across to Kamtschatka and Northern Japan.

B. No white on outer surface of wing.

4. **C. carbo.** A whitish patch surrounding the eye. Wing, about 7.75 inches; culmen, 1.55–1.70; gonys, .75–.80; depth of bill through nostril, .50; tarsus, about, 1.36; middle toe, with claw, 2.10. *Hab.* Coasts of Northeastern Asia, from Northern Japan and Kuriles to the Okotsk Sea; Behring Island, Kamtschatka, accidental? (STEJNEGER); Unalashka ?? (PALLAS).

5. **C. Motzfeldi.** No white on side of head. Culmen, 1 inch 9 lines; commissure, 2 inches 3 lines; bill from nostril, 1 inch; tarsus, 1 inch 6 lines. *Hab.* High North Atlantic (west side of Cumberland Gulf, Greenland, and Iceland).

Cepphus Mandtii.

MANDT'S GUILLEMOT.

Colymbus grylle, PHIPPS, Voy. N. P. 1774, 186 (not of LINN.).

Uria grylle, CASS. in Baird's B. N. Am. 1858, 911; Phil. Acad. 1862, 323. — BAIRD, Cat. N. Am. B. 1859, no. 726. — NELSON, Cruise Corwin, 1883, 117. — COUES, Key, 1872, 345 (part); Check List, 1873, no. 631; 2d ed. 1882, no. 871. — RIDGW. Nom. N. Am. B. 1881, no. 760.

Cepphus grylle, NEWTON, P. Z. S. 1864, 495.

Grylle scapularis, LEACH, Ross's Voy. N. W. Pass. App. 1819, p. li, in Thoms. Ann. Philos. XIII. 1819, 60 (part).

Uria scapularis, STEPH. Gen. Zool. XII. 1824, 250, pl. 64.

Uria Mandtii, LICHT. in Mandt's Obs. Itin. Dissert. 1822, 30; VERZ. Doubl. 1823, 88. — FABER, Isis, 1824, 980. — KEYS. & BLAS. Wirb. Eur. I. 1840, p. xcii. — NAUM. Nat. Deutsch. XII. 1844, 462.

Cepphus Mandtii, NEWTON, Ibis, 1865, p. 517. — STEJN. Tr. U. S. Nat. Mus. 1884.

Uria grylle Mandtii, SCHLEG. Rev. Crit. 1844, p. cvii.

Uria glacialis, BREHM, Lehrb. Vög. Eur. 1824, 924, 1008.

Uria Meisneri, BREHM, t. c. 1006.

Uria grylle, var. *glacialis*, SUNDEV. Voy. Scand. Atl. 1847, Livr. IV. pl.

HAB. Circumpolar Regions; on the western coasts of the Atlantic, breeding south to Hudson's Bay and coast of Labrador, and in winter migrating as far as the coast of New Jersey; in Western Arctic America passing through Behring's Straits in winter as far as Norton Sound.

SP. CHAR. *Adult, in summer:* Uniform black (more sooty below), showing a faint gloss of "invisible" green in certain lights. Wings with a large unbroken patch of white, including the greater, middle, and posterior lesser coverts, *these feathers all white to the base.* Axillars, entire lining of the wing, and basal half (or more) of inner webs of the primaries, unbroken pure white. Bill deep black; interior of mouth, with legs and feet, deep vermilion-red; claws black; iris dark brown. *Winter plumage:* Wings and tail as in the summer plumage; rest of the plumage pure white, the pileum, back, scapulars, and upper part of rump varied with black, the whole of the concealed, and part of the exposed, portion of the feathers being of the latter color. Feet dull red. *Young, first plumage:* Similar to the winter plumage, but white wing-patch broken by blackish tips to all the feathers (their bases still white, however), the secondaries and primary coverts with terminal spots of white, and rump and lower parts indistinctly barred with grayish dusky. Pileum showing very little concealed dusky. *Downy young:* Uniform blackish-fuliginous, paler and more grayish below.

Total length, about 12.50 to 13.50 inches; extent, 22.00 to 23.00; wing, 6.25–7.20; culmen, 1.00–1.20; gonys, .45–.55; depth of bill through middle of nostril, .35–.40; tarsus, 1.20–1.30; middle toe, without claw, 1.25–1.35.[1]

Specimens from various localities agree very closely in coloration. The only one sufficiently abnormal to call for special mention is No. 76318, Kingwah Fiord, Cumberland Sound, June 9, 1878; L. Kumlien, collector. This has the seven outer primaries marked with a small white terminal spot, anterior to which are several grayish transverse bars, like "water-marks." The claws, instead of being jet black, are pale brownish yellow ("light pink" in life).

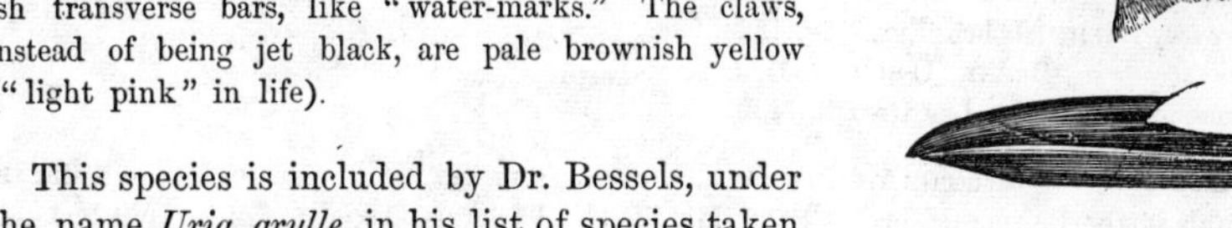

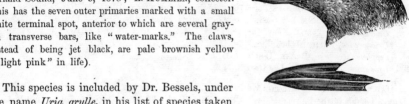

This species is included by Dr. Bessels, under the name *Uria grylle,* in his list of species taken by the "Polaris" Expedition in Smith's Sound; and Captain Feilden found it breeding at various points along the shores of Smith's Sound and northward, especially at Washington Irving Island, Dobbin Bay, Cape Hayes, and Bessels Bay. It was not ascertained to breed north of Cape Union. Two or three of these birds were seen feeding in pools on the floe as far north as lat. 82° 33′ N.; but these were evidently stragglers.

Dr. Walker, in his Notes upon the Birds observed in the Voyage of the "Fox," mentions his having procured this species in midwinter in 1858 and 1859; and the Black Guillemot is also included by Professor Reinhardt among the birds of Greenland, resident throughout the year.

Richardson states that this Guillemot abounds throughout the Arctic seas and straits, from Melville Island to Hudson's Bay, and that it remains — though in diminished numbers — throughout the winter in the pools of open water that occur among the ice-floes even in the highest latitudes.

Mr. Hearne, in his "Journey to the Northern Ocean" (p. 428), states that this bird is known in the Hudson's Bay Region as the "Sea Pigeon." It is said to frequent the shores both of the Bay and of the connecting straits in considerable numbers, but more particularly the northern parts, where it flies in large flocks; to the southward it is seen only in pairs. In weight it is said to be fully equal to a Widgeon, though to appearance not so large. It usually makes its nest in holes of rocks, and lays two eggs that are justly regarded as a great delicacy, being excellent eating. Referring to the statement of Mr. Pennant, that this Guillemot braves the coldest winters in that region, he states that it is never known to makes its appearance near the land after the frost becomes severe.

This is eminently a resident species, occupying one locality continuously, provided it finds there constant supplies of food. In localities that become ice-bound, or where in winter food is not abundant, we find it shifting its quarters to more attractive regions.

[1] Ten adults. The largest in the series are a specimen in summer plumage from Herald Island, and one in winter dress from St. Michael's, Alaska.

Cepphus grylle.

THE BLACK GUILLEMOT.

Alca grylle, LINN. Syst. Nat. ed. 10, I. 1758, 130.
Uria grylle, BRÜNN. Orn. Bor. 1764, 28. — FABER, Isis, 1827, 635. — MACG. Hist. Brit. B. V. 1852, 331. — DEGL. & GERBE, Orn. Eur. II. 1867, 603.
Colymbus grylle, LINN. S. N. ed. 12, I. 1766, 220.
Cepphus grylle, BREHM, Handb. Vög. Deutschl. 1831, 987. — NAUM. Naturg. Vög. Deutschl. XII. 1844, 461. — NEWTON, Ibis, 1865. 519.
Uria grylloides, BRÜNN. Orn. Bor. 1764, 28 (= changing plumage).
Uria balthica, BRÜNN. l. c. (= immature or winter plumage).
Uria leucoptera, VIEILL. Nouv. Dict. XIV. 1817, 35.
Uria arctica, BREHM, Lehrb. Eur. Vög. 1824, 988.
Cepphus faeroeensis, BREHM, Handb. 1831, 990.
Uria grœnlandica, GRAY, List Gen. B. 1840, 98.

HAB. Coasts of Northern and Northwestern Europe, from the White Sea to Finland and the Danish islands in the Baltic; Hebrides, St. Kilda, Shetland Islands, Orkneys, Faröes, and Iceland; in North America, found in summer from Eastport, Me. (specimen in National Museum), to Newfoundland, and probably Southern Labrador; also in Southern Greenland.

SP. CHAR. *Adult, in summer:* Similar to *C. Mandtii*, but greater wing-coverts with at least the basal half black, this seldom quite concealed by the overlying row of coverts, and often showing distinctly as a narrow band. *Winter plumage:* Similar to corresponding stage of *C. Mandtii*, but plumage much darker, the back, scapulars, and rump being black barred with white, only the extreme lower part of the rump being uniform white; white of lower parts more distinctly clouded or barred with grayish dusky, and pileum with dusky prevailing. Wing-coverts with basal half, or more, abruptly dusky, and secondaries and primary coverts without white terminal spots. *Young, first plumage:* Similar to the winter plumage, but white wing-coverts distinctly tipped with brownish black. *Downy young:* Uniform sooty blackish, lighter and grayer below (hardly, or not at all, distinguishable from corresponding stage of *C. Mandtii*).

Wing, 6.00–6.80 inches; culmen, 1.20–1.30; gonys, .50–.60; depth of bill through middle of nostril, .40–.45; tarsus, 1.20–1.35; middle toe, without claw, 1.30–1.40. (Six summer adults.) Bill deep black; interior of mouth, with legs and feet, intense vermilion-red (in life); iris dark brown.

This species may be readily distinguished in any stage, except the downy young, from *C. Mandtii* by the characters given above. A fine adult from Eastport, Me., collected by Professor Baird, July 1, 1872 (No. 62381, U. S. Nat. Mus.), agrees minutely with Scandinavian examples.

In this species, as well as in *C. Mandtii* and *C. columba*, there is a remarkable difference in the intensity of the black, according to the length of time which has elapsed since the specimen was prepared. Examples of the present species killed in April, 1884, are now (July 2, 1884) deep coal-black beneath, there being scarcely any difference in color between the upper and lower parts. On the other hand, skins several years old are without exception decidedly fuliginous, with the lower parts very appreciably browner than the upper. The difference is indeed very striking when recently prepared and older specimens are placed side by side. The downy young differ in the same manner, freshly prepared birds being decidedly slaty, while those which have been prepared several years are smoky brown.

Like all the members of this very remarkable family, the Black Guillemot is an inhabitant of the open sea, never frequenting or resorting to the land except for purposes of reproduction; keeping off from the shore, even in midwinter, and seeking safety in the open ocean from the fury of tempestuous wintry weather, rather than in sheltered bays that are ice-bound and inaccessible at that season. On the European coast it breeds from the northern part of Great Britain to the Arctic Ocean.

Along the coast of Eastern Maine and in the Bay of Fundy an inconsiderable number breed and pass the year. In the winter they are joined by a much larger number driven out by the ice from more northern places, where this barricade compels them to move to more open water. Among these, Mr. Boardman informs me, it is no uncommon thing to find individuals of this species in their full black plumage in midwinter.

Off the coast of Norway the Messrs. Godman found this bird wintering in the latitude of Bodö. During the summer it was everywhere common along the entire coast of Norway, where its eggs are much sought for, and esteemed as a great delicacy by the natives.

In the British Islands it is more abundant in the more northern portions. It is a resident species in the north of Ireland, and among the Hebrides and other Scottish islands it breeds more or less commonly; Mr. Macgillivray met with it among the Hebrides. Mr. Salmon found it among the Orkneys in 1831, where it is called the "Tyste." He found it breeding on a small holm eastward of Papa-Westra, where it was very numerous, and would scarcely move off the rocks when approached. In every instance two eggs were found together, deposited on the bare ground. He describes the egg as white, slightly tinged with green, blotched, spotted, and speckled with ash-gray, reddish brown, and very dark brown. The length is 2.25 inches; the breadth 1.50. The first covering of the young birds is a grayish-black down; and the feathers, which soon appear, are mottled with black and white. The young of this species do not leave the nest until perfectly fledged, and able to provide for themselves. Then the care of the parents ceases, and they do not even keep company with their young. Their food is chiefly crustaceans and small fishes.

In the summers of 1850 and 1851 I found the Black Guillemot breeding in the Duck Islands, Grand Menan. Their eggs were never more than two in number, and appeared to be placed on the bare rock, without any preparation, even of pebbles, to keep them dry. They were placed under loose overlying rocks, the broken surfaces of which left room for the ingress and egress of the bird. They were usually where they could not be reached by the arm, and could only be secured with the aid of a short pole with a forked end. The birds were shy, and not infrequently betrayed the locality of their nests by flying from under the rocks at our approach; which, had they not done, they might have escaped observation. The eggs were all fresh; and it is possible that a little later more than two might have been found in a nest.

In the spring of 1836, in the months of April and May, this bird was still present off Nahant, and specimens were procured, one of which is referred to by Audubon. They were obtained without difficulty from an open boat; for, though the birds are expert divers, they would always rise within a short distance of the place where they disappeared, and could be shot before they had time to dive a second time.

Giraud does not include this species among the birds of Long Island; but Mr. Lawrence gives it as found in the neighborhood of New York. It is quite common in the outer waters of Massachusetts Bay as far as Provincetown. South of the Cape it is said to be much less common.

Audubon states that this species always lays three eggs; but I think that he must be mistaken — at least I never met with more than two eggs under one bird; and this I was universally assured was the prevailing number. Dr. Bryant, in his paper on the Birds that breed in the Gulf of St. Lawrence, where he found it breeding everywhere in abundance, also states that he never found more than two eggs laid by the same bird. This was noticed on a small island where there was nothing indicating that the bird had been disturbed, where the greater number had but just begun to incubate, and none of the eggs had been hatched.

Four eggs, selected by Dr. Bryant as characteristic of their general size and shape, measure 2.24 by 1.42 inches; 2.16 by 1.50; 2.01 by 1.46; 2.28 by 1.51.

The Smithsonian Institution has eggs of this species from the Bay of Fundy, Gulf of St. Lawrence, and Newfoundland. In some the ground-color is a glaucous-white; in others a deep buff; the markings are of a rich brown intensified into blackness. Their average size is 2.30 by 1.85 inches.

Cepphus columba.

THE PIGEON GUILLEMOT.

Uria grylle, β, LATH. Ind. Orn. II. 1790, 797.

Cepphus columba, PALL. Zoog. Rosso-As. II. 1826, 348 (part).

Uria columba, KEYS. & BLAS. Wirb. Eur. 1840, p. xcii. — CASS. U. S. Expl. Exp. Orn. 1858, 346, pl. 38, fig. 1; in Baird's B. N. Am. 1858, 912; ed. 1860, pl. 96, fig. 1. — BAIRD, Cat. N. Am. B. 1859, no. 727. — COUES, Key, 1872, 345; Check List, 1873, no. 632; 2d ed. 1882, no. 872. — RIDGW. Nom. N. Am. B. 1881, no. 761.

HAB. Coasts and islands of the North Pacific, from Southern California (breeding) to Aleutian Islands, and across to Kamtschatka; thence southward to Northern Japan. Wholly replaced north of Behring's Straits by *C. Mandtii*.

C. columba, summer dress.

SP. CHAR. Similar to *C. grylle*, but the bill stouter and more obtuse at the tip, the under surface of the wings without any distinct white, and with the white patch on outer surface of the

Summer adult.

Downy young.

wings divided for the lower half by a black V-shaped bar. *Adult, in summer:* Uniform sooty slate-black, slightly glossed with "invisible" green; wing with two white patches, one covering the middle and posterior lesser coverts, the other, the end of the greater coverts ; the latter patch completely separated from the other for the lower half, being very narrow near the outer edge of the wing, but gradually widening above (where overlain by the ends of the middle coverts), so as to blend the two white patches ; under wing-coverts pale smoky grayish. Bill black ; mouth, legs, and feet bright red in life ; claws black ; iris dark brown. *Winter plumage:* Similar to the same stage of *C. grylle*, but the white wing-patch divided, as above. *Young:* Distinguishable from the corresponding stage of *C. grylle* by the absence of white on the under surface of the wing; otherwise very similar. *Downy young:* Scarcely distinguishable from that of *C. grylle.*

Total length, about 13.00 inches ; extent, 23.00 ; wing, 6.90–7.30 (average about 7.00); culmen, 1.20–1.40 ; gonys, .55–.60 ; depth of bill through middle of nostril, .40–.42 ; tarsus, 1.35–1.50 ; middle toe, without claw, 1.45–1.55. (Six summer adults.)

This species, closely resembling the *Cepphus grylle*, though differing slightly in size and in certain specific markings, replaces that species on the Pacific coast of North America, and on the eastern coast of Asia also. It is quite common in the neighborhood of Sitka, where Bischoff obtained twenty specimens. It was found abundant at Kadiak, where its eggs were also procured. Mr. Dall did not meet with it about Unalashka, but it was very common at the Shumagins. He speaks of it as being a very expert diver, very quick in its motions, and very hard to kill. Its eggs were obtained June 24, 1872, at Popoff Island, one of the Shumagins ; they were two in number. The nest was in a burrow or hole under rocks near the water's edge.

Several birds of this species were caught alive on their nests at Coal Harbor, Unga. The young in down were also obtained there July 16, 1872. All the eggs were more or less developed. It is presumed to be a summer visitor, yet, like the *C. grylle*, it may be to some extent a resident wherever found. In the Aleutian Islands, west of Unalashka, Mr. Dall noticed it as being abundant everywhere from Attu to the Shumagins ; but it was not seen in winter. It is named by Mr. R. Browne as one of the birds of Vancouver Island.

Dr. Cooper speaks of this species as being a handsome bird, and as one abundant north of California ; but he did not meet with it in summer south of Santa Barbara and San Nicolas Island, where he saw it, but not in large numbers. It is more common about the Farallones, and breeds there, laying its eggs in slight burrows which are hollowed out among the rocks. The eggs are white, blotched with dark and light brown, chiefly in a ring about the larger end, and measure in length 2.50 inches, in breadth 1.66.

About the shores of Puget Sound however — as Dr. Cooper states — this species burrows two or three feet deep in the softer banks, making an entrance where the cliff is steep and overhangs the water, and at a distance of a few feet below the top, the burrow winding so as to be difficult to follow. From this habit the bird has the local name of the Bank Duck. On the water it swims and dives with so much skill as to make its capture difficult. If swiftly pursued, it sometimes utters a shrill but not loud whistling cry, not unlike that of the Western Oyster-catcher. Its flight is strong and rapid, not unlike that of a Pigeon ; but this is the only point in which it resembles the bird from which it derives its name. It can walk quite easily on the land, and resorts there to rest. When thus perched on the rock, Dr. Cooper has heard it utter a low, rather musical song, which he at first mistook for that of some sparrow. It is, therefore, like *Ptycoramphus aleuticus*, a kind of aquatic song-bird. At Santa Cruz Dr. Cooper found pairs of this species in June on various points of the beach where there are high bluffs of sandstone soft enough for them to burrow in ; and he has no doubt that a few breed as far south as this, if not as far as the southern islands, of which San Nicolas is the only one suited for this purpose.

Mr. Henshaw is also of the opinion that the Santa Barbara Islands are the southern limit of this species during the breeding-season. Among these islands it is quite numerous, breeding in the caves and hollows of the generally inaccessible cliffs. Noticing, early one morning, many of these birds, frightened by the report of his gun, issuing out of a ravine hemmed in by high rocky cliffs and terminating in a low, narrow cave, Mr. Henshaw gained access to the latter, and succeeded in finding their eggs. No nest at all had been prepared for these, but they had been deposited on the sandy floor of the cavern, and at its farther end, where it was so dark that he could not see them without the aid of a light. Other pairs had availed themselves of the nooks and fissures in the face of the wall, laying their two eggs on the bare rock. He was able to find but a few of the many eggs that must have been there, as the shelves of the rocks were in most instances too high to be reached. The birds submitted to this pillage without a murmur, though not without solicitude, as was evinced by the anxious manner in which they swam back and forth at the entrance to the ravine, keeping well out of gunshot. He describes their eggs, when fresh, as having a faint greenish white ground, spotted, mostly at the larger end, with irregular blotches.

Eggs of this species are in the Smithsonian collection from Coal Harbor, Alaska, Puget Sound, Kadiak, and the Farallones. The ground-color varies from a glaucous white to a deep buff. The markings are a deep warm tint of claret-brown, deepening into blackness, in bold, large blotches intermingled with smaller, subdued cloudings of a faint lavender and purplish slate. Two eggs in my own collection, from the Farallones, measure: 2.30 by 1.70 inches; 2.45 by 1.65.

Cepphus carbo.

THE SOOTY GUILLEMOT.

Cepphus carbo, PALL. Zoogr. Rosso-As. II. 1826, 350. — NEWT. Ibis, 1865, 519.
Uria carbo, BRANDT, Bull. Sci. II. 1837, 346. — CASS. Pr. Philad. Acad. 1862, 323; in Baird's B. N. Am. 1858, 913; ed. 1860, pl. xcvii. — BAIRD, Cat. N. Am. B. 1859, no. 728. — COUES, Key, 1872, 345; Check List, 1873, no. 633; 2d ed. 1882, no. 873. — RIDGW. Nom. N. Am. B. 1881, no. 762.

HAB. Shores of the Okotsk Sea, Kurile Islands, and Northern Japan; Behring's Island (accidental? STEJNEGER); ?? Unalashka (PALLAS).

SP. CHAR. A little larger and more robust than *C. columba*. Bill black, very robust, in thickness and length superior to that of that species, rather obtuse, very straight, with the back rounded and convex. Nasal fossæ as in *C. columba;* linear nostrils longer. Small feathers at the frontal angle as far as the nostril and around the base of the lower mandible are white. Orbital region white, broader below the eyes and posteriorly drawn out into a thin point. Body entirely brownish black, the shoulders more grayish, but no white wing-spot. Feet intense red, also the webs, more robust than in *C. columba;* claws black, stronger, shorter, less pointed.

Comparative proportions.	*C. columbæ.*	*C. carbonis.*
Length of the bill to the frontal angle,	1″ 2‴	1″ 5‴
Length of the bill to the rictus,	1 4	1 8

Comparative proportions.	*C. columbæ.*	*C. carbonis.*
Length of the bill to the nostrils,	0″ 11‴	1″ $1\frac{3}{5}$‴
Length of wing,	6 7	7 6
Length of tarsus,	1 3	1 4
Length of middle toe, with claw,	1 9	1 11
Length of the claw,	0 5	0 $4\frac{1}{5}$
Length of the rectrices,	2 0	2 0

(PALLAS, l. c., translation.)

According to Von Schrenck ("Reis. Amurl." I. 1860, p. 497), there is some variation in the amount of the white on the head, especially around the base of the bill, where in some specimens there is scarcely any trace whatever of this color. The single example in the National Museum collection (a head from Japan, collected by Dr. W. Stimpson) agrees exactly with Pallas's description, as above, in having the feathers all round the base of the bill distinctly white. The measurements of this specimen are as follows: Culmen, 1.70; commissure, 2.10; gonys, .80; side of mandible to malar apex, 1.55; depth at base, .50; width, .38. This head is of a dull grayish-fuliginous, darker on the pileum and lower part of neck, and becoming dull white at the base of the bill all round), as well as around the eyes, and thence backward, as an ill-defined streak, along the upper edge of the auriculars. The under side of the head, as well as the greater extent of the lateral portions, is dull smoky grayish, this color fading rather gradually into the white, which is abruptly defined only above the eyes, where the dusky color of the crown forms a marked contrast.

I can find no mention of the living presence of this species either on any portion of the American coast or in the Aleutian Islands; nor is there any evidence that it has a claim to be retained in the avi-fauna of North America. Its habits — in regard to which I have no notes — are probably nearly identical with those of *C. grylle* and *C. columba.* This bird is not uncommon in the summer in Yezo, Japan (Swinhoe, "Ibis," 1875).

Cepphus Motzfeldi.

MOTZFELD'S GUILLEMOT.

Uria Motzfeldi, BENICKEN, Isis, Aug. 1824, 889.
Cepphus Motzfeldi, STEJN. Pr. U. S. Nat. Mus. 1884.
Uria unicolor, FABER, Isis, Sept. 1824, 981. — BREHM, Isis, 1826, 988; Handb. Vög. Deutschl. 1831, 985. — SCHLEG. Rev. Crit. 1844, 106. — BP. Compt. Rend. XLII. 1856, 774; Cat. Parzud. 1856, 12.
Grylle carbo, BP. Cat. Met. Ucc. Eur. 1842, 82 (not of PALL. 1826).
"*Uria carbo* (Brit. Mus. ex Iceland)," NEWT. Ibis, 1865, 518 (part).
Alca grylle, SCHLEG. Mus. P.-B. Urinat. 1867, 20 (part).
Uria grylle, KUML. Bull. U. S. Nat. Mus. No. 15, p. 104 (part).

HAB. High North Atlantic (west shores of Cumberland Sound, Greenland, and Iceland).

SP. CHAR. Similar to *C. carbo*, but without any white or light grayish about the head. *Adult:* Entire plumage uniform sooty black or dark sooty brown, the abdomen somewhat more grayish. "Bill black, very compressed, with very prominent gonydeal protuberance, bent tip, and feathered as far as above the nostrils" (BENICKEN, *l. c.*, translation). Total length, 16 inches 9 lines (Hamburg measure); culmen, 1 inch 9 lines; bill from angle of mouth, 2 inches 3 lines; from nostril, 1 inch; tarsus, 1 inch 6 lines. Feet yellowish brown (in dried skin), the webs whitish.

This bird, which evidently is a distinct, but little known, species, was first described by Benicken from a specimen received by him in 1820 from Greenland. A month afterward the same specimen was re-described by Faber as *Uria unicolor*, under the supposition that it had not yet received a name. To his description he adds the information that the owner of the bird-rookery on Draugœ, Iceland, had occasionally observed a pair of uniformly dusky Guillemots breeding on the rocks at that place. A specimen similar to Benicken's type was received at the Leyden Museum from Greenland, and is mentioned by Schlegel in his "Revue critique," as cited above. A third specimen, in the British Museum, is recorded by Professor Newton in "The Ibis" for 1865, p. 518 — said to have come from Iceland; and in the "Arctic Manual" (1875), p. 109, he remarks that Holböll says that he has seen in Greenland an "entirely black example," which is probably the same species. The latest testimony that we have is that of Mr. L. Kumlien, who accompanied the Howgate Polar Expedition in 1877–1878, and who saw "three entirely black specimens," which were considered to be *C. carbo.* "One was procured in Cumberland, but was lost."

It will thus be seen that we have abundant and incontrovertible evidence of the existence in the higher latitudes of the North Atlantic of a uniformly black or dusky Guillemot. Some authors have referred it to *C. carbo,* but it is evidently distinct from that species, which seems to be strictly confined to the Asiatic coast of the North Pacific. Others have considered it a melanism of *C. grylle;* but the larger size and very different proportions preclude the likelihood of such relationship. Upon the whole, there can be little doubt that it is a distinct species, probably most nearly related to *C. carbo,* and representing the latter in the North Atlantic. At any rate, it should be kept in mind by those who have the opportunity of investigating the avian fauna of the northern waters of the Atlantic.[1]

Genus **BRACHYRAMPHUS**, Brandt.

Brachyramphus, Brandt, Bull. Ac. St. Petersb. II. 1837 (type, *Colymbus marmoratus,* Gmel.).
Apobapton, Brandt, l. c. (same type).

Char. Size small (wing less than 5.50 inches). Bill small and slender, much shorter than the head (not longer than the short tarsus), compressed, and acute; culmen gently curved, gonys nearly straight; mandibular tomium notched near the tip, and greatly inflected toward the base;

B. marmoratus, summer dress.

nasal fossæ small, shallow, mostly filled with feathers, which nearly conceal the very small nostrils; head without ornamental plumes.

The exact number of species composing this genus is a matter of some doubt. The following key includes those whose validity is established, and also another (*B. brevirostris*), which, if not identical with *B. Kittlitzi,* must also be a well-marked species.

[1] A much more detailed history of this bird, by Dr. L. Stejneger, in an article entitled Remarks on the Species of the Genus *Cepphus,* will soon be published in the Proceedings of the United States National Museum. We have been kindly permitted by Dr. Stejneger to compile the information given in the present article from his manuscript.

A. Tarsus much shorter than the middle toe without its claw.

1. **B. marmoratus.** Wing, 5.00 inches; culmen, .60–.70; depth of bill at anterior end of nostril, .24; width at same point, .15; tarsus, .70; middle toe, .92–1.00. *Summer plumage:* Dusky above, barred with rusty; below, mixed white and fuliginous. *Winter plumage:* Above, dusky, interrupted by a white nuchal collar; feathers of back, etc., tipped with plumbeous. Entire lower parts white. *Hab.* Pacific coast, south to Santa Cruz, Cal.
2. **B. Kittlitzi.** Wing, 5.10–5.80 inches; culmen, .40–.45; depth of bill at anterior end of nostril, .20–.22; width at same point, .15; tarsus, .60–.65; middle toe, .85–.95. *Summer plumage:* Above, plumbeous, with indistinct narrow bars of black and very irregular (mostly longitudinal) spots of creamy buff; lower parts chiefly white, the jugulum and entire sides strongly overlaid by creamy buff, and heavily, but irregularly, barred and spotted with blackish; other lower parts (except anal region and crissum) more faintly marked with bars (mostly crescentic) of grayish dusky. *Winter plumage:* Above, plumbeous, the back and rump indistinctly and narrowly barred with white; entire side of head (including whole of lores and superciliary region), narrow but distinct nuchal collar, and entire lower parts immaculate pure white; sides of breast crossed by a broad band of grayish slate, narrowing toward middle of jugulum. Bill black; iris brown; feet light brown in dried skin (livid purplish gray in life?). *Hab.* From Northern Japan and Kamtschatka to Unalashka.

[3? **B. brevirostris.**[1] Wing, 5.25 inches; culmen, .50; tarsus, .50. *Adult, summer plumage:* Above, grayish brown, the head and back spotted with white; below, white, waved and spotted with brown; bill black; feet yellow, the webs and claws brown. *Hab.* San Blas, W. Mexico.]

B. Tarsus equal to the middle toe, without claw.

4. **B. hypoleucus.** Wing, 4.50–5.25; culmen, .70–.80; tarsus, .90–.95; middle toe, .85. Lining of wings white; above, plain dark slaty; below, wholly pure white. *Hab.* San Diego to Cape St. Lucas.
5. **B. Craverii.** Wing, 4.60; culmen, .78–.80; tarsus, .88–.90; middle toe, .80–.88. Lining of wings smoky gray or slaty. Otherwise similar to *B. hypoleucus.* *Hab.* Lower California.

Brachyramphus marmoratus.

THE MARBLED GUILLEMOT.

Colymbus marmoratus, GMEL. S. N. I. ii. 1788, 583, no. 12.

Brachyramphus (Apobapton) marmoratus, BRANDT, Bull. Ac. St. Petersb. II. 1837, 346.

Brachyrhamphus marmoratus, GRAY, Gen. B. III. 1849, 644. — CASS. in Baird's B. N. Am. 1858, 915. — BAIRD, Cat. N. Am. B. 1859, no. 732. — COUES, Pr. Ac. Nat. Sci. Philad. 1868, 61; Key, 1872, 344; Check List, 1873, no. 629; ed. 2, 1882, no. 866. — RIDGW. Nom. N. Am. B. 1881, no. 755.

Cepphus perdix, PALL. Zoog. Rosso-As. II. 1826, 351, pl. 80.

Brachyramphus Wrangeli, BRANDT, Bull. Ac. St. Petersb. II. 1837, 344. — CASS. in Baird's B. N. Am. 1858, 917. — BAIRD, Cat. N. Am. B. 1859, no. 733. — COUES, Pr. Ac. Nat. Sci. Philad. 1868, 63.

Uria Townsendii, AUD. Orn. Biog. V. 1839, 251, pl. 430; B. Am. oct. ed. VII. 1844, pl. 475.

HAB. Coasts and islands of the North Pacific, south, on the American side, to San Diego, Cal.; breeds at least as far south as Vancouver's Island.

SP. CHAR. *Adult, full breeding-plumage:* Above, dusky, the back, scapulars, rump, and upper tail-coverts barred with rusty, the tips of the feathers being of this color. Lower parts fuliginous, more or less mixed with white, the underlying portion of the feathers being of the latter color; the lower parts never uniform fuliginous, but usually with this color largely predominating.

[1] BRACHYRHAMPHUS BREVIROSTRIS. — Short-billed Guillemot.
Uria brevirostris, VIG. Zool. Jour. IV. 1828, 357; Zool. Beechey's Voy. 1839, Orn. p. 32 (San Blas). (This is possibly the same as *B. Kittlitzi.*)

Lining of the wing deep smoky gray. Bill uniform black, the extreme tip a little paler; iris dark brown; legs and feet pale colored in the dried skin (flesh-color in life[1]), the webs and claws dusky. *Midsummer plumage:* Similar to the above, but more uniformly dusky, the rusty bars of the rump, etc., wanting, owing to abrasion of the tips of the feathers. *Winter plumage* (= *B. Wrangeli,*

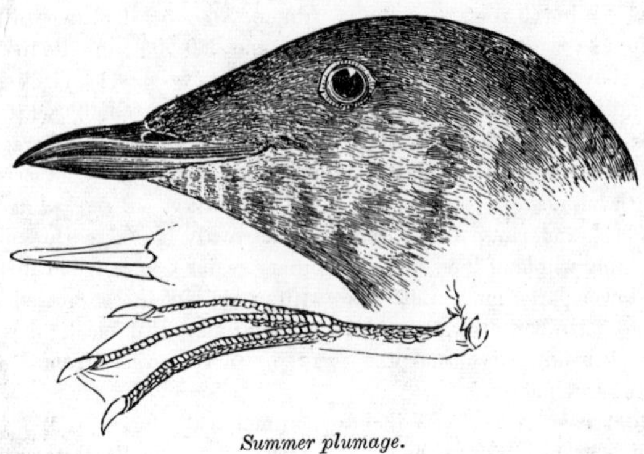

Summer plumage.

Brandt): Above, dusky, interrupted by a narrow white band across the upper part of the nape; interscapulars, feathers of the rump, and upper tail-coverts tipped with plumbeous; scapulars chiefly white, especially the inner ones, forming a conspicuous longitudinal patch on each side of the back. Entire lower parts, including the lower half of the lores and the whole side of the head, except the orbital region, pure white. the exterior feathers of the sides and flanks striped with

Winter plumage.

plumbeous or dusky grayish. Lining of the wing smoky gray, as in the summer plumage. *Young, first plumage:* Above, uniform blackish (without plumbeous tips to any of the feathers), the occipital band of the winter plumage slightly indicated or interrupted; scapular patch less distinct than in the winter plumage. Lores almost wholly dusky. Lower parts white nearly everywhere, but more especially on the jugulum, breast, and sides, transversely mottled with fuliginous-dusky. Bill much smaller and weaker than in the adult.

Total length, about 9.50 to 10.00 inches; extent, 18.00; wing, 5.00; culmen, .60–.70; tarsus, .70; middle toe, without claw, .90–1.00.

This also is an oceanic and a Pacific species, occurring from the coast of California northward. To what extent this bird is to be found on the opposite coasts of Asia,

[1] According to Audubon (l. c.) the feet are yellow.

or if at all, has not been satisfactorily ascertained. According to the observations of Mr. R. Browne, it occurs on the western sea-coast of Vancouver Island. Dr. Cooper, in his Report on the Birds of Washington Territory, mentions finding it common in winter about the mouth of the Columbia River, and was induced to express the belief that it does not occur farther south — which opinion he was afterward led to modify, having met with a number of these birds in the open water off Monterey in May, 1862. Their presence there at that season indicated the probability that they might be breeding in that neighborhood. He had previously to this obtained on the coast, at the mouth of the Columbia, two specimens that had been killed by the storms; and he had observed, on his way down the coast, birds which he supposed to be of this species, flying from under the steamer. He could obtain no information as to their habits or place of summer residence. The dead specimen found on the beach at Santa Cruz in January was taken at the most southern point where, so far as he knew, this species had been noticed.

Under the name of *B. Wrangeli* Mr. Dall mentions the procuring of several specimens of this bird by Bischoff at Sitka; where also many others in the normal plumage were taken. And again referring to this species under that name, Mr. Dall mentions it as being quite common in the Aleutian Islands east of Unalashka. He did not meet with any at the Shumagins, but thinks that it probably abounds there. He does not refer to it in his Notes on the Birds of the Western Aleutian Islands.

Brachyramphus Kittlitzii.

KITTLITZ'S GUILLEMOT.

Brachyramphus Kittlitzii, BRANDT, Bull. Ac. St. Petersb. II. 1837, 346 (young). — CASS. in Baird's B. N. Am. 1858, 917. — BAIRD, Cat. N. Am. B. 1859, no. 735. — COUES, Key, 1872, 344; Check List, 1873, no. 630; ed. 2, 1882, no. 867. — RIDGW. Nom. N. Am. B. 1881, no. 756.

"*Uria antiqua*" (supposed young), AUD. B. Am. VII. 1844, 263, pl. 470, fig. 2.

?? *Uria brevirostris*, VIG. Zool. Journ. IV. 1828, 357 ("San Blas"); Zool. Beechey's Voy. 1839, Orn. p. 32.

?? *Brachyrhamphus brevirostris*, AUCT. (See foot-note on p. 499.)

HAB. Kamtschatka and Aleutian Islands, east to Unalashka, Point Ebolin, and Nushagak Bay.

SP. CHAR. *Adult, breeding-plumage:* Above, glossy plumbeous-black, everywhere, except on the wings and tail, thickly spotted with creamy buff, the spots generally having a longitudinal tendency; wings dusky slate, the middle and greater coverts narrowly bordered with ashy, the inner webs of the secondaries tipped with white; tail slate-color, the tips of all the feathers, and the inner webs of all except the intermediæ, white. Sides of the head and neck, jugulum, sides, and flanks, creamy buff, thickly spotted transversely, except on the head and neck, with dusky, the spots on the jugulum partaking more or less of the form of lunulate bars; other lower parts white with scattered and less distinct lunulate bars of dusky, the crissum and anal region immaculate. Lining of the wing uniform smoky slate, rather darker than in *B. marmoratus*. Bill uniform black; legs and feet light brownish in the skin, the webs and claws blackish. *Adult, winter plumage:* Pileum, crescentic bar immediately in front of eye, a broad bar extending across the sides of the jugulum (nearly meeting anteriorly), with upper parts generally, plumbeous-slate with a silky gloss; the feathers of the back and rump narrowly tipped with white, many of them showing a darker shade beneath the surface; scapulars mostly white, with plumbeous prevailing on the outer webs; wings much darker than the back, the greater coverts and secondaries distinctly, the remiges and primary coverts very indistinctly, bordered with pale grayish. Lining of the wing and axillars uniform slate-gray. Entire lower parts, and all of the head and neck except as described, including a collar around the nape, immaculate pure white. Bill uniform black; feet brownish (in the skin), the webs darker.

Wing, 5.10–5.80 inches; culmen, .35–.45; depth of bill near base (at anterior end of nostril), 20–.22, width at same point, .15; tarsus, .60–.65; middle toe, .85–.95.

Brachyramphus hypoleucus.

XANTUS'S GUILLEMOT.

Brachyrhamphus hypoleucus, XANTUS, Pr. Ac. Nat. Sci. Philad. Nov. 1859, 299 (Cape St. Lucas). — COUES, Ib. 1868, 64 ; 2d Check List, 1882, no. 868. — RIDGW. Nom. N. Am. B. 1881, no. 757.

HAB. Coast of Southern California, from San Diego to Cape St. Lucas.

SP. CHAR. *Adult, summer (breeding ?) plumage:* Above, uniform dark slaty, the feathers nearly black just beneath the surface, but pale grayish basally ; entire lower parts, including greater part of the lores, orbital region, except above the eye, and auriculars, continuous white. Lining of the wing pure white, the anterior and exterior lesser under coverts with concealed spots of grayish ;

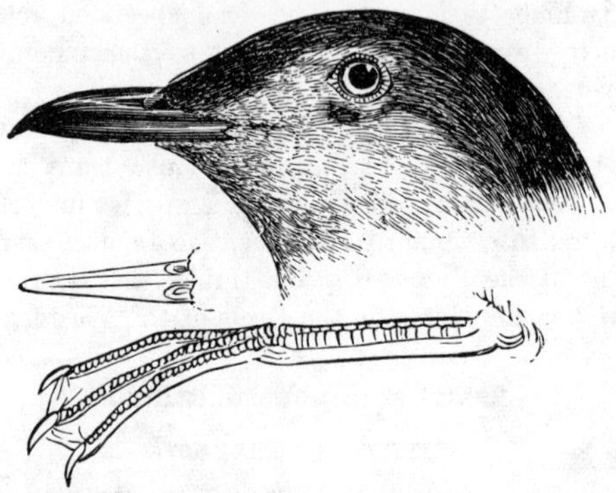

inner webs of primaries chiefly grayish white. Sides and flanks, beneath the wings, plumbeous-slate, some of the feathers tipped with white. Bill black, the mandible brownish basally ; iris "pale blue" (XANTUS, MS.); legs and feet pale brownish gray in the dried skin. *Winter plumage:* Similar to the above, but nearly the whole of the lores and orbital-region plumbeous. Bill black, the base of the mandible whitish ; "feet whitish blue, black below" (COOPER, MS.).

Total length, 10.00 to 10.50 inches ; extent, 15.80 to 19.50 ; wing, 4.50–5.25 ; culmen, .70–.80 ; tarsus, .90–.95 ; middle toe, .85.

Brachyramphus Craverii.

CRAVERI'S GUILLEMOT.

Uria Craverii, SALVADORI, Descriz. di altre Nuove Specie di Ucc. Mus. di Torino, 1867, 17 (Lower California).

Brachyrhamphus Craverii, COUES, Pr. Ac. Nat. Sci. Philad. 1868, 66 ; 2d Check List, 1882, no. 869. — STREETS, Bull. U. S. Nat. Mus. no. 7, 1877, 32 (critical ; habits). — RIDGW. Nom. N. Am. B. 1881, no. 758.

HAB. Coast of the Gulf of California ; Island of Natividad, near the western coast of Lower California.

SP. CHAR. *Adult, summer and winter:* Above, including the entire lores and orbital region, with upper part of the auriculars, blackish slate ; a longitudinal whitish space on each eyelid. Entire lower parts, except sides and flanks, continuous white ; sides and flanks uniform dull slate or sooty plumbeous. Lining of the wing smoky gray or slaty, the greater under coverts and the tips of some of the smaller coverts, white ; inner webs of primaries grayish white only toward the base. "Bill black ; iris dark brown ; feet green" (XANTUS, MS.).[1]

Total length, about 10.25 inches ; extent, 16.00 ; wing, 4.60 ; culmen, .78–.80 ; tarsus, .88–.90 ; middle toe, .80–.88.

[1] One specimen is marked as above ; on the label of another the color of the iris is recorded as "pale blue, nearly white."

There is apparently something not yet understood in the relationship between this bird and *B. hypoleucus*, and it would not be at all surprising if the two should prove to be different phases of one species. Dr. Coues ("Pr. Philad. Acad." 1868, p. 65) suggests the possibility of *Craverii* being the young of *hypoleucus;* but Dr. T. H. Streets ("Bull. U. S. Nat. Mus." No. 7, 1877, pp. 32, 33) proves this not to be the case, and substitutes the theory of the latter being the *winter*, the former

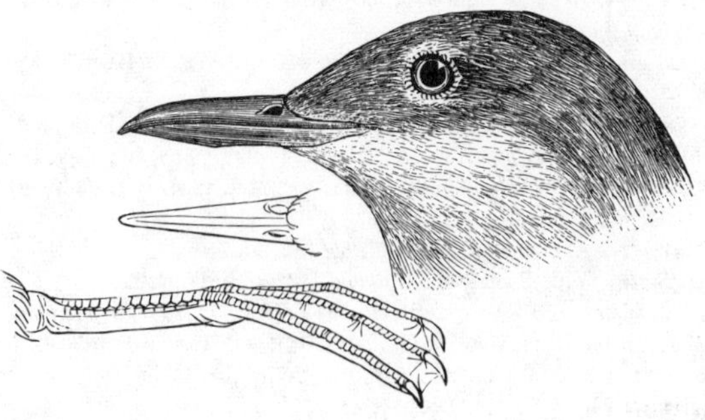

the *summer*, plumage of the same species. His remarks are as follows: "Dr. Coues alludes to the 'bare possibility' that *Craverii* was the young of *hypoleucus* — a supposition disproved by finding it breeding. *B. Craverii* can only be referred to *hypoleucus* now upon the assumption that the latter is the winter plumage of the former, as all specimens which have come to hand thus far with pure white lining of the wings were taken in winter, as far as known. Such an assumption would not be widely at variance with the known characters of the seasonal changes of plumage in some members of this family, but remains to be proven. Pending this determination, *Craverii* should be recognized as a good species."

To the above we have to say that although no date is given on the label of the type specimen of *B. hypoleucus*, it is apparently a midsummer bird, the plumage being exceedingly worn or weather-beaten, which would hardly be the case had it been killed in winter.

Genus **SYNTHLIBORAMPHUS**, Brandt.

Synthliboramphus, Brandt, Bull. Ac. St. Petersb. II. 1837, 347 (type, *Alca antiqua*, Gmel.).

Char. Size rather small (wing about 5.50 inches). Bill much shorter than the head, very compressed, but the culmen comparatively broad; culmen regularly convex; gonys lengthened (more than half as long as the culmen), nearly straight; nasal fossæ very small, the oval nostrils situated near their centre; color chiefly plumbeous above and white beneath, the head and neck pied black and white.

Com. Char. Above plumbeous, beneath white. *Summer plumage:* Chin and part or whole of the throat dusky; top of the head with a broad white stripe on each side; entire sides, from neck to flanks, sooty blackish. *Winter plumage:* Similar, but whole throat white, the chin plumbeous; white stripes on top of head absent; sides and flanks white, striped with slaty.

Of this genus two species are known, distinguished as follows: —

1. **S. antiquus**. Never crested. *Summer plumage:* Chin and whole throat sooty black, with a convex lower outline. *Winter plumage:* Auricular region crossed by a horizontal broad bar of dusky.
2. **S. wumizusume**. Crested in the breeding-season. *Summer plumage:* Forehead with a loose crest of several narrow, much elongated, nearly straight feathers, extending back toward the occiput; lores, orbital region, cheeks, chin, and upper half of the throat, velvety plumbeous, with a truncated lower outline. *Winter plumage:* Auricular region entirely white.

Synthliboramphus antiquus.

THE BLACK-THROATED GUILLEMOT.

Alca antiqua, GMEL. S. N. I. ii. 1788, 554, no. 11.

Uria antiqua, TEMM. & SCHLEG. Fauna Jap. 1845, pl. 80. —AUD. Orn. Biog. V. 1839, 100, pl. 402, fig. 12 ; B. Am. VII. 1844, 263, pl. 470, fig. 1 (but not fig. 2, which = *Brachyramphus Kittlitzi*, summer plumage).

Brachyramphus antiquus, GRAY, Gen. B. III. 1849, 644.— CASS. in Baird's B. N. Am. 1858, 916. — BAIRD, Cat. N. Am. B. 1859, no. 736.

Brachyramphus (*Synthliboramphus*) *antiquus*, BRANDT, Bull. Ac. St. Petersb. II. 1837, 347.

Synthliborhamphus antiquus, COUES, Pr. Ac. Nat. Sci. Philad. 1868, 56 ; Key, 1872, 344 ; Check List, 1873, no. 627 ; 2d ed. 1882, no. 864. — BRANDT, Mel. Biol. VII. 1869, 217. — RIDGW. Nom. N. Am. B. 1881, no. 753.

Uria senicula, PALL. Zoog. Rosso-As. II. 1826, 369, pl. 85.

Mergulus cirrhocephalus, VIG. Zool. Voy. Blossom, 1839, Birds, p. 32.

Brachyramphus brachypterus, BRANDT, Bull. Ac. St.-Petersb. II. 1837, 346 (quotes "*Uria brachyptera*, KITTLITZ, MSS."). — GRAY, Gen. B. III. 1849, 644. — CASS. in Baird's B. N. Am. 1858, 917. — BAIRD, Cat. N. Am. B. 1859, no. 734.— COUES, Pr. Philad. Acad. 1868, 66 ; 2d Check List, 1882, no. 870. — RIDGW. Nom. N. Am. B. 1881, no. 759.

HAB. Coasts and islands of the North Pacific, from Japan to Kamtschatka, across the Aleutian chain, and south to Sitka.

SP. CHAR. *Adult, breeding-plumage :* Head and neck chiefly black, duller and more fuliginous anteriorly and on the throat ; on each side of the occiput, from above the middle of the eyes to the nape, a series of white streaks, blended so as to form a broad stripe, those of opposite sides sometimes meeting across the lower part of the occiput ; black of the throat separated from that of the

Summer plumage.

nape by a broad intervening space of white, which extends upward on each side of the neck to the auricular region. Lower parts continuous white, the sides and flanks, beneath the wings, sooty black. Upper parts uniform plumbeous, the anterior lesser coverts and the remiges darker ; sides of the upper back, between the deep black of the nape and the dull black on the sides of the breast, black, marked with numerous broad white streaks. Bill yellowish, the basal half blackish ; iris brown ; legs and feet dull yellowish (in the skin), the webs dusky. *Winter plumage :* Similar to the above, but whole throat white (the chin, sometimes upper throat also, plumbeous), the broad white latero-occipital stripes and the streaks on the upper back absent ; the sides and flanks white, the outermost feathers striped with slaty.

Total length, about 9.50–10.50 inches ; extent, 16.75–18.25 ; wing, 5.25–5.50 ; culmen, .60 ; tarsus, .95–1.00 ; middle toe, without claw, 1.00–1.05.

The Black-throated Guillemot is another of the strikingly peculiar forms of deep-sea-going birds found exclusively in the Pacific Ocean, visiting the islands and the coasts of both the American and the Asiatic mainland. They occur with some irregularity in their distribution, and being probably, like most of their family, of nocturnal habits, we know but little of their specific peculiarities of manner. They are found as far south as Japan, and as far north as Sitka and the Island of Amak.

Several specimens were taken by Mr. H. Whitely in Hakodadi Harbor, Japan, in May. Most of them had lost either their right or their left foot; these had been apparently bitten off some time previously, as the place was healed and the skin grown over it. Mr. Blakiston speaks of it as common in the game market of Yokohama in winter, and Swinhoe found it common in Yezo from October to May.

Mr. Dall states that this species, called by the Russians "Starik," is common at St. George's, and also at Amak Island, north of the peninsula of Aliaska. Specimens were also obtained at Sitka by Bischoff.

In his Notes on the Avifauna of the Aleutian Islands, lying east of Unalashka, Mr. Dall states that this species was obtained breeding, with the eggs, at the Chica Islets, Akutau Pass, near Unalashka, June 2, 1872. They were caught sitting on their nests, which are in holes in the bank, similar to those of the Petrels — *Oceanodroma furcata.* There were two eggs in each nest, and in several cases the male bird was sitting on the eggs. He did not meet with this species in any other place, yet it may be abundant, notwithstanding.

Afterward, in his Notes on the Birds of the Islands west of Unalashka, Mr. Dall speaks of finding it abundant throughout the islands, especially in certain localities. He obtained it from Kyska eastward. While it congregates off shore in very great numbers, it also frequents the bays and harbors much more than any of the other small Auks. The iris of this bird is white.

Among other specimens of the young form, Mr. Dall obtained one at Amchitka with a malformation of the lower mandible, which was nearly one half shorter than the upper one. The bird was fat and healthy.

Specimens of the eggs of this species are in the Smithsonian collection, obtained from Chico Island, Sitka, and Aliaska. Their ground-color is a pale buff; over this are very generally and equally distributed small longitudinal markings, somewhat subdued, of lavender-gray and a light brown. Four eggs measure as follows: 2.15 by 1.45 inches; 2.35 by 1.55; 2.45 by 1.55; 2.50 by 1.40.

Synthliboramphus wumizusume.

TEMMINCK'S GUILLEMOT.

Uria wumizusume, TEMM. Pl. Col. 579 (1838). — TEMM. & SCHLEG. Fauna Jap. 1845, pl. 79.

Anobapton (*Synthliboramphus*) *wumizusume*, BONAP. Compt. Rend. XLII. 1856, 774.

Synthliborhamphus wurmizusume, COUES, Pr. Ac. Nat. Sci. Philad. 1868, 58; Key, 1872, 344; Check List, 1873, no. 628. — RIDGW. Nom. N. Am. B. 1881, no. 754.

Synthliborhamphus umizusume, COUES, 2d Check List, 1882, no. 865.

Synthliboramphus Temminckii, BRANDT, Bull. Ac. St. Petersb. II. 1837, 347.

Brachyramphus Temminckii, CASS. in Baird's B. N. Am. 1858, 916. — BAIRD, Cat. N. Am. B. 1859, no. 737.

HAB. Coasts and islands of the North Pacific, from Washington Territory to Japan.

SP. CHAR. *Adult, breeding-plumage:* Forehead, centre of crown, nape, and sides of neck black, this color continued down the sides to the flanks; nape sometimes marked with scattered short white streaks; fore part of crown with a loose crest of slender, much elongated feathers, slightly curved, or nearly straight, and inclining backward toward the occiput; top of head with a broad white stripe, originating on each side of the crest and extending back to and including the occiput; loral, orbital, and malar regions, chin, and upper half of the throat, with orbital and auricular regions, uniform velvety plumbeous, with a truncated lower outline; remaining lower parts con-

Summer plumage.

tinuous white, except along the sides, which are sooty blackish. Upper parts, except as described, plumbeous, the anterior lesser wing-coverts, remiges, and tail dusky. Bill yellowish, the culmen black; iris blackish; legs and feet dusky yellowish (in the dried skin). *Winter plumage:* Similar to the above, but whole throat white, chin light plumbeous, crest and white stripes of the crown absent, and the sides and flanks white, striped with slate-gray. *Downy young:* Above, brownish

Winter plumage.

gray, the whole back and rump indistinctly streaked with grayish white; lower parts entirely pure white, including chin and throat. Bill dusky, legs and feet pale brownish (in dried skins), the webs dusky.

Total length, about 10.50–11.00 inches; extent, 18.00–18.50; wing, 5.10–5.50; culmen, .70; tarsus, 1.00; middle toe, .90–1.00.

Temminck's Guillemot appears to have been first described, by the distinguished ornithologist whose name it bears, from a Japanese specimen. It has since been collected by Mr. W. Heine, in Commodore Perry's Expedition, at Simoda, and also in Yedo Bay. Dr. Cooper obtained specimens at Port Gamble, Washington Territory, and on Shoal-water Bay. In regard to its breeding-habits and its other specific peculiarities, we have no information. Dr. Suckley only states in regard to it that it is found in summer at Puget Sound; while Dr. Cooper presumes that it has about the same range as the *Brachyramphus marmoratus,* and so far as he has observed has similar habits. It is said to be common at Hakodadi in October.

Genus **CICERONIA**, Reichenbach.

Ciceronia, Reichenb. Syst. Avium, 1852, p. iii (type, *Phaleris microceros*, Brandt, = *Uria pusilla*, Pall.).

Ciceronia pusilla.

THE KNOB-BILLED AUK; LEAST AUK.

Uria pusilla, Pall. Zoog. Rosso-As. II. 1826, 373, pl. 70 (excl. syn.).
Phaleris pusilla, Cass. Pr. Ac. Nat. Sci. Philad. 1862, 324; in Baird's B. N. Am. 1858, 909. — Baird, Cat. N. Am. B. 1859, no. 723.
Simorhynchus pusillus, Coues, Pr. Ac. Nat. Sci. Philad. 1868, 48, fig. 12, figs. 227, 228; Key, 1872, 343; Check List, 1873, no. 624; ed. 2, 1882, no. 861; Elliott's Alaska, 1875, 208.
Ciceronia pusilla, Ridgw. Nom. N. Am. B. 1881, no. 750.
Phaleris corniculata, Eschsch. Zool. Atl. IV. 1831, 4, pl. 16 (= summer adult).
Phaleris microceros, Brandt, Bull. Ac. St. Petersb. II. 1837, 346 (= summer adult). — Cass. in Baird's B. N. Am. 1858, 908. — Baird, Cat. N. Am. B. 1859, no. 722.
Simorhynchus microceros, Coues, Pr. Philad. Acad. 1868, 46, fig. 11.
Phaleris pygmæa, Brandt, Bull. Ac. St. Petersb. II. 1837, 347 (not *Alca pygmæa*, Gmel. 1788).
Phaleris nodirostra, Bonap. Comp. List, 1838, 66 (= summer adult). — Aud. Orn. Biog. V. 1839, 101, pl. 402; B. Am. VII. 1844, pl. 468.

Hab. Coasts and islands of the North Pacific, south to Japan and Sitka, north to the Prybilof Group.

Sp. Char. *Adult, breeding-plumage:* Bill very short, the depth and width through the base about equal to the length of the culmen, which is decidedly arched; gonys slightly convex; top of the cere furnished with a small semicircular compressed tubercle. Upper parts almost wholly deep slate-black, inclining to glossy black in some specimens; inner scapulars usually white, form-

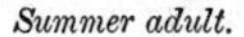
Summer adult.

Winter adult.

ing more or less of a longitudinal patch on each side of the back; inner greater coverts and secondaries also usually tipped with white. Forehead and lores more or less conspicuously ornamented with delicate acuminate white feathers, a few of which, narrower and more thread-like, extend backward in a narrow streak from the rictus across the cheeks, while a more conspicuous line of similar acicular feathers crosses the auricular region, from behind the lower eyelid. Lower parts chiefly white, the breast and sides more or less spotted with dark slate, this frequently forming a distinct and uninterrupted collar across the jugulum, usually in abrupt and marked contrast to the white of the throat; chin and malar region plumbeous, this usually fading gradually into the white below it. Bill dark reddish; iris white; legs and feet dusky in the dried skin. *Adult, in winter* (= *Uria pusilla*, Pallas): Bill smaller, more compressed, and destitute of the tubercle at the base of the culmen; lower parts, including the sides of the neck, continuously white, the chin plumbeous, as in the summer plumage; white ornamental feathers of the forehead, etc., usually less developed, or, in younger specimens, altogether wanting. *Young, first plumage:* Similar to the winter adult, but bill still smaller, no trace of the ornamental plumes about the head, and white scapular patches larger and more distinct. *Downy young:* Uniform sooty slate, paler and more grayish on the lower parts.

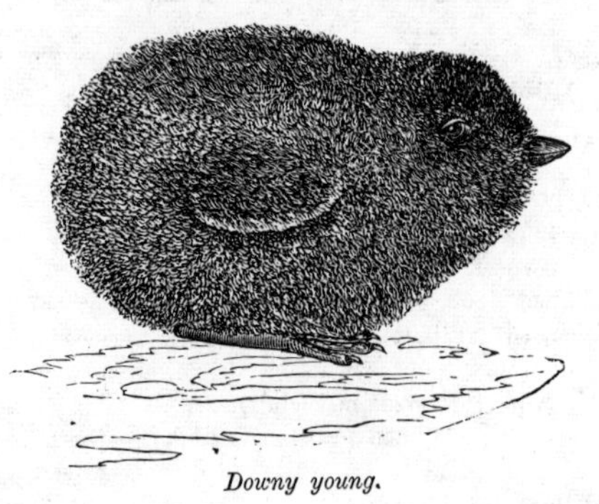

Downy young.

Wing, 3.50–4.00 inches; culmen, .35–.40; depth of bill (in summer adult), about .30, in winter adult and young, about .20; tarsus, .65; middle toe, .80.

A series of nearly seventy specimens obtained on the breeding-grounds in June and July on St. Paul's and St. George's Islands, Alaska, by Mr. H. W. Elliott, affords ample material for studying the individual variations of this species, which, as shown by this immense series, is very considerable. The principal variation consists in the degree to which the white of the lower parts is broken by dark spotting. In none is the white perfectly continuous, as in the winter plumage, although in a few it is very nearly so; there being in all more or less dark spotting across the jugulum and along the sides. The most highly plumaged specimens have a broad and uninterrupted collar of dark slaty across the jugulum, abruptly defined against the immaculate white of the throat, but below broken up into coarse spots, which continue along the entire sides, and often over the breast and abdomen also; in none, however, is there more than an approach to a segregation of the spots on the breast, and the lower parts are probably never uniformly dark, except the jugular collar. There is also much variation in the distinctness and extent of the white scapular areas, the majority of specimens having these well defined, while in some they are nearly obsolete. In one example (No. 62624), in which the upper parts are a particularly deep and glossy black, there is no trace of them; this specimen being also wholly destitute of the ornamental filaments of the head, and having the knob on the bill very slightly developed.

Mr. H. W. Elliott met with this species — the Least, or Knob-billed, Auk — on the Prybilof Islands. He speaks of it as the most characteristic of the waterfowl frequenting these islands, to which it repairs every summer by millions to breed with its allies, *Simorhynchus cristatellus* (Canooskie) and the *Cyclorrhynchus psittaculus*. It is said to be comically indifferent to the proximity of man, and can be approached almost within arm's length before taking flight, sitting upright, and eying one with an air of great wisdom combined with profound astonishment. Usually about the 1st or 4th of May every year the Choochkie — as this bird is called — makes its first appearance around the islands, for the season, in small flocks of a few hundreds or thousands, hovering over, and now and then alighting, upon the water, sporting, one with another, in apparent high glee, and making an incessant low chattering sound. By the 1st to the 6th of June they have arrived in great numbers, and then begin to lay. They frequent the loose stony reefs and bowlder-bars on St. Paul's, together with the cliffs on both islands, and an area of over five square miles of basaltic shingle on St. George's. On the last island they hover in the greatest number. There are millions of them. They make no nests, but lay a single egg each, far down below among loose rocks, or they deposit it deep within the crevices or chinks in the faces of the cliffs. Although, owing to their immense numbers, they seem to be in a state of great confusion, yet they pair off, under the rocks, upon the spot selected for incubation, making during this interesting period a singular grunting or croaking sound, more like a "devil's fiddle" than anything he ever heard outside of city limits. A walk over their breeding-grounds at this season is exceedingly interesting and amusing, as the noise of hundreds of these little birds directly under foot gives rise to an endless variation of sound as it comes up from the stony holes and caverns below, while the birds come and go, in and out, with bewildering rapidity, comically blinking and fluttering. The male birds, and many of the females, regularly leave the breeding-grounds in the morning, and go off to sea, where they feed on small water-shrimps and sea-fleas (*Amphipoda*), returning to their nests and sitting partners in the evening.

The Choochkie lays a single pure white egg, exceedingly variable in size and shape, usually oblong oval, with the smaller end somewhat pointed. Several specimens almost spherical were obtained, and others drawn out into an elongated ellipse; but the oblong-oval with the pointed smaller end is the prevailing type. The egg is very large, compared with the size and weight of the parent; average length, 1.55 inches; width, 1.12. The general aspect is much like that of a Pigeon's egg, excepting the roughness of the shell.

The chick is covered with a thick uniform dark grayish black down, which is speedily succeeded by feathers, all darker than those of the parent are six months later, at the time it takes its flight from the island for the year. The parents feed their young by disgorging, and when the young birds leave they are as large and heavy as the old ones. Mr. Elliott is strongly inclined to the opinion that the male bird feeds the female when incubating, but was not able to verify this supposition by observation, as the birds are always hidden from sight at that time.

Mr. Dall states that he obtained specimens of this bird from the peninsula of Aliaska, where it was abundant; from Plover Bay, in Eastern Siberia, where he collected it in person, and where the specimens were found to have the bill wider and deeper than usual; and also from St. George, one of the Prybilof Islands.

Eggs of this species from St. Paul's Island, Behring Sea — procured by Mr. H. W. Elliott — are of a pure chalky white color, one end more tapering than the other. They measure about 1.63 inches in length by 1.13 in breadth.

Genus **PHALERIS**, Temminck.

Phaleris, Temm. Man. Orn. 1820, p. cxii (type, *Alca pygmæa*, Gmel.).

Char. Similar to *Simorhynchus*, but bill simple, without accessory deciduous pieces at any season. Head ornamented by several series of lengthened ornamental filamentous feathers.

The single species belonging to this genus resembles both *Simorhynchus* and *Ciceronia*, being, in fact, somewhat intermediate. It must be considered generically distinct, however, unless all three are merged into one genus — a proposition which we cannot indorse.

Phaleris pygmæus.

THE WHISKERED AUK.

Alca pygmæa, GMEL. S. N. I. ii. 1788, 555 (= young; based on *Pygmy Auk*, PENN. Arct. Zool. no. 431).

Simorhynchus pygmæus, BRANDT, Mel. Zool. vii. 1869, 228. — RIDGW. Pr. U. S. Nat. Mus. 1880, 211; Nom. N. Am. B. 1881, no. 749. — COUES, 2d Check List, 1882, no. 860.

Alca Kamtschatica, LEPÉCHIN, Nova Acta Petrop. XII. 1801, 369, pl. 8 (= *adult*).

Phaleris camtschatica, BRANDT, Bull. Ac. St. Petersb. II. 1837, 347. — CASSIN, in Baird's B. N. Am. 1858, 908. — BAIRD, Cat. N. Am. B. 1859, no. 721.

Simorhynchus camtschaticus, SCHLEG. Mus. P.-B. Urin. 1867, livr. ix. p. 25. — COUES, Pr. Ac. Nat. Sci. Philad. 1868, 41; Key, 1872, 342; Check List, 1873, no. 623.

Uria mystacca, PALL. Zoog. Rosso-As. II. 1826, 372, pl. 89.

Phaleris cristatella, TEMM. Pl. Col. 200 (not of authors).

Mormon superciliosum, LICHT. Verz. Doubl. 1823, 89.

Simorhynchus Cassini, COUES, Pr. Philad. Acad. 1868, 44 (Ounimak Pass, Aleutian Islands; = *young*).

HAB. Coasts and islands of the North Pacific, from Unalashka through the Aleutian chain to Kamtschatka.

Adult ♂, *nuptial plumage* (85617, Atkha Island, Aleutian chain, June, 1879; L. M. TURNER): Above, glossy blackish slate, appearing more plumbeous in certain lights, especially on the rump; wings and tail dull brownish black. Lower parts sooty plumbeous, darker anteriorly, and nearly white posteriorly, the crissum being quite white; entire sides and flanks uniform deep, slightly smoky, plumbeous, like the breast. Head ornamented by an erect, gracefully recurved crest of narrow plumes of dull black, about 1.50 inches long (when straightened out); anterior half of the lores covered with a triangular patch of pure white pointed feather-tips, this patch bifurcating posteriorly, and continued in one branch downward and backward across the cheeks, the white

Summer adult.

Young.

filamentous tips becoming very long and lanceolate or acicular posteriorly; the upper branch extending to each side of the crown, where spring three very narrow dull white, slightly recurved filaments, nearly as long as the crest, and originating on the same transverse line as the latter; another series of yellowish white filaments originates immediately beneath the eye, and extends backward along the upper border of the auriculars, the posterior ones extending about an inch beyond the terminal portion of the auricular region. Bill in dried skin dull, rather dark, coral-red, the tip first dark grayish, then white; in life, "deep vermilion, with bluish tip" (TURNER); "iris blackish blue" (TURNER) or white (STEJNEGER); feet "dusky" in life, dark brown in dried skin. Wing, 4.20 inches; culmen, .35; greatest depth of bill, .30, width at base, .28; tarsus, .80; middle toe, .85.

(Another adult male from the same locality, and collected about the same date, is similar, except that the superciliary filaments are pure white, while the crest is light brownish gray. Wing, 4.10 inches; culmen .30; greatest depth of bill, .30; tarsus, .85; middle toe, .90.)

Young (= *Alca pygmæa*, GMEL., and *Simorhynchus Cassini*, COUES; No. 65436, Constantine Harbor, Amchitka Island, Aleutians, July 26, 1873, W. H. DALL): Above, entirely uniform glossy plumbeous-black, including the whole loral, orbital, and upper part of the malar regions; lower part of auricular region, throat, and chin deep smoky gray, the lower part of the throat with a mixed hoary white and dusky suffusion, forming a somewhat triangular transverse patch; foreneck, jugulum, and entire sides, deep uniform slaty plumbeous, gradually lightening on the breast, and changing insensibly to white on the lower part of the abdomen, anal region, and crissum; lining of the wing deep smoky plumbeous or slate. On each side of the forehead, from the base of the culmen back to above the eye, a series of indistinct, small, narrow white feathers, and from the same origin another series of similar feathers running obliquely downward across the lores, thence horizontally backward on a line with the commissure, about as far as the posterior angle of the eye. A whitish streak behind the eye. Maxilla black, more brownish below the nostril; mandible brownish, paler basally; "iris white" (DALL); legs and feet brownish in the dried skin. Wing, 4.10 inches; culmen, .40; depth of bill at base, .30, width, .25; tarsus, .85; middle toe, without claw, .90. *Another specimen* (type of "*S. Cassini*," COUES, No. 46564, ♂, Ouninak Pass, Aleutians, Aug. 3, 1866; W. H. DALL) is similar to the preceding, but has no trace of ornamental filaments about the head, and the whole throat is smoky gray, not distinctly defined against the plumbeous-slate of the foreneck. Wing, 4.25 inches; culmen, .35; depth of bill at base, .25, width, .20; tarsus, .85; middle toe, .85. *Downy young:* Uniform grayish fuliginous, lighter below.

There can be no question that the *Simorhynchus Cassini*, COUES, is the young of *S. camtschaticus*, PALLAS; and it is equally certain that the *Alca pygmæa*, GMEL., is the same stage of this species. Gmelin's description [1] fits the young plumage (= "*Cassini*") in every particular, while it does not answer at all to any other known member of the family.

There are several fine adults in breeding-plumage of this species in the National Museum collection, collected in the Aleutian Islands by Mr. Lucien M. Turner, and in the Commander Islands by Dr. Leonhard Stejneger. Of the immature plumage there are, besides the type of "*S. Cassini*," also many specimens, besides several in the down. Two of the latter, with feathers just appearing beneath the surface of the down on the lateral lower parts, as well as on the wings, scapular region, and fore part of the head, were obtained by Mr. W. H. Dall at Kyska Harbor, Aleutians, July 3, 1873. There are also two specimens in the collection from Constantine Harbor, besides the one described above, and one (No. 67399, ♂) from Akootan Island, collected Sept. 10, 1874, by Mr. H. W. Elliott.

We have no notes or information in regard to the habits of this species. It was met with by Mr. Dall on several of the Aleutian Islands. It was originally described by Lepéchin as having come from Kamtschatka.

Messrs. Blakiston and Pryer ("Ibis," 1878, p. 210) state that this bird was obtained from the Kurile Islands (Chigima) in summer by Mr. N. Fukusi. Mr. H. Whitely procured two specimens off the east coast of Japan ("Ibis," 1867, p. 209); and in Commodore Perry's Expedition examples were secured at Simoda and Tokio Bay.

GENUS **SIMORHYNCHUS**, MERREM.

Simorhynchus, MERREM, 1819 (type, *Alca cristatella*, PALL. *fide* G. R. GRAY). — COUES, Pr. Philad. Acad. 1868, p. 34 (part).
Tyloramphus, BRANDT, Bull. Acad. St. Petersb. II. 1837, 348 (same type).

CHAR. Mandibles triangular, the lower nearly as deep as the upper, with the gonys very straight, forming a more or less decided, and sometimes prominent, angle at the base; *in the breeding season* the base of the bill furnished with several accessory corneous pieces, most conspicuous of

[1] "Rostro nigro, vertice, cervice, dorso, alis, caudâ pedibusque obscuris, jugulo et pectore glaucis, abdomine sordide albo . . . alce minor, 7 poll. longa" (GMELIN).

which are a rictal plate and a broad, curved, posteriorly truncate shield covering the lateral base of the mandible. Forehead ornamented by an upright recurved tuft of slender feathers, the tips of

S. cristatellus.

which overhang the bill; head farther ornamented by a postocular series of slender white filamentous feathers. Plumage plain — uniform dusky above, gray below.

A single species (*S. cristatellus*) belongs to this genus, as here restricted.

Simorhynchus cristatellus.

THE CRESTED AUK.

Alca cristatella, PALL. Spic. Zool. V. 1769, 20, pl. 3 and pl. 5, figs. 7, 8, 9. — GMEL. S. N. I. ii. 1788, 552, no. 7.

Simorhynchus cristatellus, "MERREM," BONAP. Compt. Rend. XLII. 1856, 774. — COUES, Pr. Ac. Nat. Sci. Philad. 1868, 37; Key, 1872, 342; Check List, 1873, no. 622; ed. 2, 1882, no. 859; Elliott's Alaska, 1875, 206. — RIDGW. Nom. N. Am. B. 1881, no. 748.

Phaleris cristatellus, STEPHENS, Gen. Zool. XIII. 1825, 47, pl. 5. — CASS. in Baird's B. N. Am. 1858, 906. — BAIRD, Cat. N. Am. B. 1859, no. 719.

Phaleris superciliata, AUD. Orn. Biog. pl. 402; B. Am. VII. 1844, pl. 437 (not *Mormon superciliosa*, LICHT., = *Alca pygmæa*, GM.).

Uria dubia, PALL. Zoog. Rosso-As. II. 1826, 371, pl. 87 (= young).

Simorhynchus dubius, COUES, Pr. Ac. Nat. Sci. Philad. 1868, 40.

Alca tetracula, PALL. Spic. Zool. V. 1769, 23, pl. 4, and pl. 5, figs. 10, 11, 12. — GMEL. S. N.I. ii. 1788, 552, no. 8.

Phaleris tetracula, CASS. in Baird's B. N. Am. 1858, 907. — BAIRD, Cat. N. Am. B. 1859, no. 720.

Simorhynchus tetraculus, COUES, Pr. Ac. Nat. Sci. Philad. 1868, 43, fig. 9; Key, 1872, 342.

HAB. Coasts and islands of the North Pacific, from Kadiak and Unalashka through the Aleutian chain to Kamtschatka and Northern Japan; north to Prybilof Islands.

SP. CHAR. *Adult, breeding-dress:* Basal portion of the bill covered with complicated supernumerary pieces, the most conspicuous of which is a detached semicircular concave plate situated just above the rictus. Upper parts dusky blackish; lower parts uniform smoky gray, shading insensibly into the blackish of the upper parts. On the forehead a curled crest of narrow dusky brown feathers, curved forward in the greater part of a circle; behind the eye, extending thence back over the auriculars, a streak of narrow acicular white feathers. Bill bright orange-red, the end pale horn-color; iris white; legs and feet dusky in the dried skin. *Adult, in winter* (= *Alca tetracula*, PALLAS): Similar in plumage, even to the crest and white auricular filaments; but bill very different, owing to the loss of the supernumerary basal pieces, being much smaller, smooth, and destitute of the rictal shield, the broad expansion of the mandibular rami and nasal shield;

color of bill dull brownish. *Young* (= *Uria dubia*, PALLAS) : Bill simple and smooth as in the winter adult, but smaller ; plumage as in the adult, but crest and auricular filaments absent or but

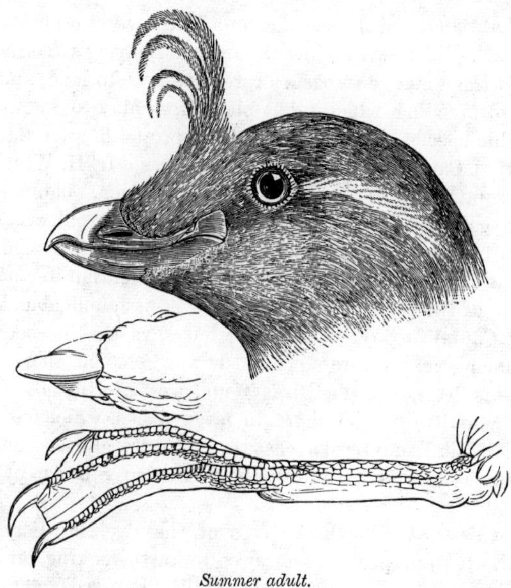

Summer adult.

slightly developed. Bill dull brownish. Total length, about 9.00 inches ; wing, 5.25 ; culmen, .45 ; tarsus, 1.00 ; middle toe, with claw, 1.35.

Judging from the very extensive series of specimens before us, it appears that the young gradually assume both the frontal crest and the white auricular filaments during the latter part of their

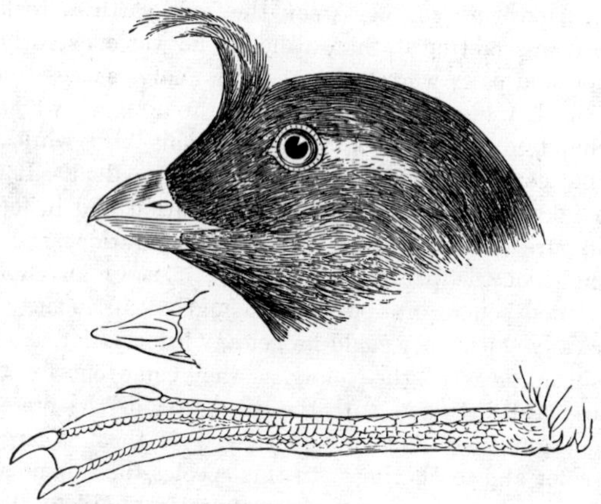

Winter adult.

first year, the peculiar character of the bill being gradually assumed at the approach of the breeding-season. Perfectly adult birds apparently retain as *permanent* ornaments the curled frontal crest and line of white acicular feathers across the auricular region ; but after the close of the breeding-season the basal horny parts of the bill (perhaps also of the *entire* bill, since the terminal portion becomes much smaller than in the breeding-season) are shed, giving that member a totally different appearance. In this stage the bird is the *Alca tetracula* of Pallas; while before reaching maturity it is the *Uria dubia* of the same author.

The Crested Auk is eminently oceanic, and, like several others of this remarkable group, peculiar to the Northern Pacific Ocean and Behring's Sea, and common both to the Asiatic and the American coasts; rarely resorts to land, and apparently only for the purposes of breeding, which takes place from May to August.

Examples of this species were taken at Simoda and in the Bay of Yedo, Japan, by the naturalists of Captain Perry's Expedition; and Mr. H. Whitely ("Ibis," 1867) mentions having captured two others in a voyage between Yokohama and Hakodadi. It was blowing a gale off the land at the time, and several others were observed. Specimens of this bird were also procured at Kadiak by Mr. Bischoff.

Mr. Dall, in his Notes on the Avifauna of the Aleutian Islands eastward from Unalashka, speaks of the Crested Auk as having been found abundant in very large flocks outside of Captain's Bay, Unalashka; but says that it was rarely seen inside the Bay except during very severe storms. It was resident there, as well as at the Shumagins. In his Notes on the Birds found west of Unalashka, he refers to this species as being abundant off the shore in large flocks, which covered acres. It is a resident species; but from Kyska eastward it is rarely seen in bays or harbors. Several specimens were shot at Plover Bay, Eastern Siberia, by Captain Everett Smith.

It is called the *Canooskie* by the natives of the Prybilof Islands, where it was found by Mr. Elliott, who speaks of it as a fantastic-looking bird, conspicuous by reason of its curling crest and bright crimson bill. It breeds there in company with the *Ciceronia pusilla*, but is present in small numbers as compared with the latter, there being only a few thousand pairs at St. Paul's, and relatively more on St. George's.

It makes its appearance early in May, and repairs to chinks and holes in the rocky cliffs, or deep down under large bowlders and rough basaltic shingle, to lay — making no nest whatever, depositing the egg upon the bare earth or rock. But so well do these birds succeed in secreting it, that, although he was constantly upon the ground where several thousand pairs were laying, he was unable successfully to overturn the rocks under which they hide, or get more than four eggs; which number was the result of over a hundred attempts. The note of this bird while mating is a loud clanging, honk-like sound; at all other seasons it is silent. It lays but one egg, and the parents take turns in the labor of incubation and in feeding their young. The egg is rough, pure white, but with frequent discolorations, and, as compared with the size and weight of the parents, very large; it is of an elongated oblong-oval shape, the smaller end being quite pointed. Length, 2.10 inches; width, 1.40. Mr. Elliott did not see any chicks, nor could he get any information as to their appearance from the natives; but he shot the young as they came out for the first time from their hiding-places, fully fledged with the exception of the crest. The time was from the 10th to the 15th of August, and they were then as large as the old birds, and of the same color and feathering. In this species there is no sexual variation in size or plumage, males and females appearing precisely alike. The bright crimson bill varies considerably in its relative strength and curve, the slenderer bill not being confined to the young birds, some old ones having the light and more pointed beak.

Mr. Adams mentions ("Ibis," 1878) obtaining two specimens that had been picked up at sea by a native, June 14, in Norton Sound, Alaska. They were weak and half starved; these were the only birds of this species which he saw. The Eskimos about Kotzebue Sound and Port Clarence make so much use of the small orange-colored plates at the base of the bill of this bird for ornamenting their water-proof frocks, that it was evident that it must have extensive breeding-places in that vicinity.

Eggs of this species from St. Paul's Island, in the Behring Sea, collected by Mr. Elliott, are of a pure chalky-white color, and of an oblong oval shape, with rounded ends. They measure 2.10 inches in length by 1.45 in breadth.

Genus CYCLORRHYNCHUS, Kaup.

Phaleris, Temm. Man. Orn. II. 1820, 929 (part).
Cyclorrhynchus, Kaup. Entw. Eur. Thierw. 1829, 15 (type, *Alca psittacula*, Pall.).
Ombria, Eschscholtz, Zool. Atl. pt. iv. 1831, 3 (same type).

Char. Bill much compressed, the maxilla blunt at the end, and with the culmen and tomium both decidedly convex; mandible strongly falcate, both gonys and tomium being greatly curved upward toward the tip, which is very acute; nasal shield not extending to the culmen, and bill destitute of accessory deciduous appendages. Plumage dull (dusky above and white below), ornamented only by a single longitudinal postocular series of slender white filamentous feathers.

C. psittaculus.

The form of the bill in this genus is unique, separating it trenchantly from *Simorhynchus*, its nearest ally. But one species is known.

Cyclorrhynchus psittaculus.

THE PARROT AUK.

Alca psittacula, Pall. Spic. Zool. V. 1760, 13, pl. 2, and pl. 5, figs. 4, 5, 6.
Phaleris psittacula, Temm. Man. II. 1820, 929. — Coues, Key, 1872, 342; Check List, 1873, no. 621; Elliott's Alaska, 1875, 204. — Ridgw. Nom. N. Am. B. 1881, no. 747.
Ombria psittacula, Eschsch. Zool. Atl. IV. 1831, 3, pl. 17. — Cass. in Baird's B. N. Am. 1858, 410. — Baird, Cat. N. Am. B. 1859, no. 725. — Elliot, Illustr. Am. B. I. 1869, pl. 70.
Simorhynchus psittaculus, Schleg. Mus. P.-B. IX. 1867, 24. — Coues, Pr. Ac. Nat. Sci. Philad. 1868, 36, fig. 6 (bill); 2d Check List, 1882, no. 858.

HAB. Coasts and islands of the North Pacific (Kamtschatka, Prybilof Islands, Aleutians, etc.). Japan. Accidental in Sweden!

SP. CHAR. *Adult, breeding-plumage:* Head (all round), sides of neck, sides, and entire upper parts slate-dusky or dull black, more plumbeous on the throat, which is usually more or less mixed with whitish. Lower parts, except as described, plain white. A line of narrow acicular white feathers beginning just beneath the eye and extending back over the auriculars. Bill wholly orange-red; iris white; feet brownish in the dried skin. *Adult, in winter* (?): "Upper parts as described above, but no whitish feathers below and behind the eye. Entire under parts white, marbled on the throat, breast, and sides with dusky or blackish; this color usually occupying chiefly or wholly the tips of the feathers, whose bases are white. The mottling is thickest on the breast, most sparse on the abdomen; but it varies in degree with almost every specimen" (COUES). *Young* (?): "A state of plumage is described as that of the young, in which the white occupies almost the whole under parts, and is scarcely mixed with dusky, even on the throat and breast" (COUES).

Wing, about 5.40–6.00 inches; culmen, about .60; greatest depth of the bill nearly the same; tarsus, 1.00; middle toe, 1.10.

In his "Monograph of the *Alcidæ*," Dr. Coues describes the adult as having the "chin, throat, breast, and flanks fuliginous or brownish black, lighter or grayer below than above;" but in a series of nearly fifty examples, including thirty-nine collected on the breeding-grounds in June and July, not one has the breast uniform dusky, the greater number having not only the breast, but the jugulum also, white, the latter, however, clouded with dusky.[1] In many even the chin and throat are mottled with grayish white. All these specimens, it may be remarked, possess the streak of white filaments across the auricular region.

This is an oceanic and a North Pacific species, resident in the open sea, and only visiting land for the purposes of breeding. It is found in the Aleutian Islands, and also at the Prybilof Group, and is distributed irregularly throughout the Northern Pacific and Behring's Sea.

It is of accidental occurrence in Sweden. M. Olphe-Galliard records in the "Revue et Magasin de Zoologie" (1868, pp. 95, 96) the occurrence in Sweden of an individual of this species. It was taken alive near Jönköping about the middle of December, 1860; and the "Ibis" of 1869 (p. 221), gives from Professor Sundeval some further particulars of this extraordinary fact. The bird had crept, through a fence set along the edge of the water by the side of Lake Vetter, into the courtyard of a weaving manufactory, where it was caught by two men, and soon after died. Its species was determined by Professor Fredrik Malmgren, of the University of Lund.

Mr. Dall, in his Notes on the Avifauna of the Aleutian Islands west of Unalashka, speaks of it as resident and not uncommon at Amchitka, but not seen anywhere else. He thinks that Brandt is mistaken in supposing that the peculiarly shaped bill is used for opening bivalve shells. He has never found anything in its crop except fragments of crustacea, and thinks that the bird uses its sharp, recurved lower mandible in tearing out the softer parts of the larger Isopods, and in picking them out of crevices in the rocks and from under round stones.

Mr. H. W. Elliott states that this quaintly beaked bird is quite common on the Prybilof Group, and that it can be obtained at St. George's in considerable numbers. It comes here early in May, and selects a deep chink or crevice of some inaccessible cliff, where it lays its single egg and rears its young. It is very quiet and undemonstrative during the pairing-season, its only note being a low, sonorous, vibrating whistle. Like the *Simorhynchus cristatellus*, it will breed in company with the

[1] Since the above was written, several specimens from Behring's Island, collected by Dr. L. Stejneger in May, 1882, have been received at the National Museum. These have the throat and *upper part* of the jugulum uniform dusky; but the whole breast is pure white, like the abdomen.

Choochkie, but will not follow it upon the uplands, being found only on the shore-line. It is the *Baillie Brushkie* of the natives, the Paroquet Auk of authors.

The egg — which is laid upon the bare earth or rock — is pure white, oblong-ovate, measuring 2.50 by 1.50 inches. It is exceedingly difficult to obtain, owing to the bird's great caution in hiding it, and care in selecting for that purpose some deep and winding crevice in the face of the cliff. At the entrance to this nesting-cavern the parent will sometimes squat down and sit silently for hours at a time, if undisturbed. This bird does not fly about in flocks, but seems to lead a quiet, independent life by itself, apparently not caring to associate with its kind. The young, by the 10th to the 15th of August, may be observed for the first time coming out from their secure retreat and taking to wing, being then as fully fledged and as large as their parents. They take their departure from the 20th of August to the 1st of September, and go out upon the North Pacific for the winter, where they find their food, which consists of *Amphipoda* and fish-fry. Mr. Elliott has never seen one, among the thousands that were around him, opening bivalve shells, as this bird has been said by Professor Brandt to do. It feeds at sea, flying out every morning, returning in the afternoon.

The shape of its egg is extremely variable. One measures 2.25 inches by 1.50, and another 2.35 by 1.45, the latter example being remarkably narrow, elongate, and pointed. The shell is minutely granular, and rough to the touch; it is white, unmarked, but often found variously soiled and discolored — sometimes by mechanical effect, and sometimes by the fluids of the cloaca. So effectually did these birds secrete their eggs in the deep crevices of the cliffs, that Mr. Elliott was unable to obtain more than four perfect specimens, although several hundreds were breeding on the cliffs near the village at St. George's Island, each pair having been watched closely by him during the summer of 1873. Nothing save blasting-powder, or some similar agency, could open the basaltic crevices in which this bird hides; and if this were done the egg would be destroyed.

An egg of this species in the Smithsonian Museum is of a dirty chalky-white color unspotted, of an oblong-oval shape, with rounded ends, and measures 2.25 inches in length by 1.60 in breadth. It was taken on St. George's Island, in Behring's Sea, by Mr. H. W. Elliott.

Genus **PTYCHORAMPHUS**, Brandt.

Ptychoramphus, Brandt, Bull. Ac. St. Petersb. II. 1837, 347 (type, *Uria aleutica*, Pall.).

Char. Bill elongate-conical, and somewhat depressed, the maxilla being much broader than deep at the base; culmen straight for the basal half, then gently curved; gonys straight and rapidly ascending terminally; nostrils overhung by the prominent, flaring edge of the nasal membrane, or shield, which in the breeding-season is more or less corrugated above. Head entirely destitute of any ornamental plumes or crest; plumage plain slaty above, whitish beneath.

Ptychoramphus aleuticus.

THE ALEUTIAN AUK.

Uria aleutica, Pall. Zoog. Rosso-As. II. 1826, 370.

Ptychoramphus aleuticus, Brandt, Bull. Ac. St. Petersb. II. 1837, 347. — Cass. in Baird's B. N. Am. 1858, 910. — Baird, Cat. N. Am. B. 1859, no. 724. — Coues, Pr. Ac. Nat. Sci. Philad. 1868, 52; Key, 1872, 343; Check List, 1873, no. 625; ed. 2, 1882, no. 862. — Ridgw. Nom. N. Am. B. 1881, no. 751.

Mergulus Cassinii, Gambel, Pr. Ac. Nat. Sci. Philad. 1845, 266 (coast of California); Journ. Ac. Nat. Sci. Philad. II. 1850, pl. 6.

Hab. Whole Pacific coast of North America, from the Aleutian Islands south to San Diego, Cal.; breeding as far south as the Farallones.

Sp. Char. *Adult:* Above, entirely uniform plumbeous black; under part and sides of the head, with fore part and sides of the neck, plumbeous, blending gradually into the blackish of

P. aleuticus.

the pileum and nape; a white spot on the lower eyelid. Lower parts, from the jugulum back, immaculate white, the sides, beneath the wings, and the femoral region plumbeous. Bill black, the basal third of the mandible yellowish or pale colored; iris white; legs and feet bluish and dusky in life, brownish dusky in the dried skin. *Young:* Apparently similar to the adult.

Total length, 8.00–9.50 inches; extent, 16.00–18.50; wing, 4.75–5.25; tail, 1.50–1.75; culmen, .75; depth of bill at base, .40; tarsus, 1.00; middle toe, with claw, 1.40.

The only seasonal changes in this very plainly colored species consist apparently in the wrinkling or corrugation of the nasal shield, especially on top, in the breeding-season.

The Aleutian Auk was not met with by Mr. Dall among the Aleutian Islands, nor by Mr. Elliott among the Prybilof Islands. It is an oceanic species, and is presumed to be an inhabitant of both shores of the Pacific Ocean.

Dr. Cooper informs me that all the specimens of this bird which he has obtained are considerably larger than the measurements given by Mr. Cassin. He found two of this species at San Diego, on the shore, after a severe storm, in January, both being dead. These birds are usually to be met with a long distance off the shore, but within sight of land, often rising almost from under the paddle-wheels of the steamers. In May, 1863, he found them very numerous on Santa Barbara Island, where they had undermined almost every part of the soft earthy surface with their burrows. These are about four feet long, horizontal, and run at about the depth of a foot beneath the surface, though often so near it as to be broken in by the weight of a man stepping on them. On examining about a dozen burrows he found in most of them young in every stage of growth, showing that they must have begun about the first of May to deposit their eggs. Where hatching had not taken place there was one egg in each burrow, on which either the male or the female was sitting. These are pure white, and measure 1.70 inches in length by 1.25 in breadth, the ends being very nearly of equal size.

These birds are also found in the Farallones, where, however, they are not very abundant, the rocky soil being unsuited for their burrows, so that their nests can only be made in accidental cavities. Mr. Gruber, however, obtained an egg there in 1862, and dead birds are not infrequently to be found, many dying from accidents or from blows inflicted by other and stronger birds. An egg from the Farallones measured 1.78 by 1.30 inches, and was of an unusually oval form. During the day most of the birds go off far from the islands, and are seen swimming about, occasionally diving for fish, etc., or perhaps asleep the greater part of the time, their most active period being the earlier part of the night. At that time they fly to their burrows; and though so very short-winged, when fairly started go like bullets, often killing themselves by flying against the ground; and if there is a camp-fire on the island, many fly directly into it, being dazzled and perplexed by its light. The male birds, alighting near their burrows, make the night melodious with their cries, being really musical for a sea-bird, and reminding one of the Whip-poor-will. As nearly as this cry can be expressed in words, it is *whit-cheer*, *whit-cheer*, etc., repeated about five times, faint at first, gradually dying, and then falling with a peculiar ringing sound. To some ears the cry sounds like *too-near;* and this name has been given to the bird by the sealers.

Dr. Cooper found the birds of this species most abundant during the day about San Nicolas Island, where the shoal waters furnish them with excellent feeding, and whence they probably fly every night to Santa Barbara Island — a distance of about thirty miles. Three eggs in the collection of the Smithsonian Institution range from 1.80 to 1.95 inches in length, and from 1.25 to 1.30 in breadth. They are of oblong-oval shape, and of a pure chalky white color.

Genus **CERORHYNCHA**, Bonaparte.

Cerorhinca, Bonap. Ann. Lyc. N. Y. 1828, 427 (type, *C. occidentalis*, Bp., = *Alca monocerata*, Pall.).
Ceratorhynchus, Sundev. Orn. Syst. 1836, 130.
Ceratorhyncha, Bonap. Comp. List, 1838, 66. — Coues, Pr. Philad. Ac. 1868, 28.
Cerorhina, Brandt, Bull. Sc. St. Petersb. II. 1837, 348. — Cass. in Baird's B. N. Am. 1858, 904.
Ceratorrhina, Bonap. Oss. Règ. An. 1830, 134; Saggio, 1831, 62.
Ceratorhina, Aud. Orn. Biog. V. 1839, 104.
Chimerina, Eschscholtz, Zool. Atl. 1829, 2 (type, *C. cornuta*, Eschs., = *Alca monocerata*, Pall.).

Char. Culmen regularly and decidedly convex; gonys straight, or slightly concave, with an accessory corneous piece at the base, interposed longitudinally between the rami of the mandible from their symphesis back to the feathers of the chin; this deciduous, however, and, like the compressed vertical process of the nasal shield, characteristic of the breeding-season. When the latter is cast, the upper outline of the cere is nearly straight, and depressed decidedly below the level of the base of the culmen. Head ornamented by four (two on each side) longitudinal series of filamentous white feathers. Plumage dull-grayish dusky above, whitish below, the under side of the head and neck brownish gray.

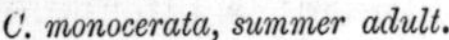

C. monocerata, summer adult.

C. monocerata, winter adult.

Of this remarkable genus but one species is known; this having given ornithologists much trouble before the deciduous character of the nasal horn and mandibular process was fully understood; the same species in winter plumage, with these appendages absent, being referred to a different genus ("*Sagmatorhina*").

Cerorhyncha monocerata.

THE HORN-BILLED AUK.

Alca monocerata, PALL. Zoog. Rosso-As. II. 1826, 362, no. 414.

Cerorhina monocerata, CASS. in Baird's B. N. Am. 1858, 905. — BAIRD, Cat. N. Am. B. 1859, no. 717.

Ceratorhyncha monocerata, COUES, Pr. Ac. Nat. Sci. Philad. 1868, 28, figs. 1, 2.

Ceratorhina monocerata, COUES, Key, 1872, 341; Check List, 1873, no. 620; ed. 2, 1882, no. 857. — RIDGW. Nom. N. Am. B. 1881, no. 620.

Phaleris cerorhynca, BONAP. Zool. Journ. 1827, 53.

Cerorhinca occidentalis, BONAP. Ann. Lyc. N. Y. (Synop. N. Am. B.) IV. 1828, 428. — NUTT. Man. II. 1834, 538.

Ceratorhina occidentalis, AUD. Orn. Biog. V. 1839, 104, pl. 402, fig. 5.

Uria occidentalis, AUD. B. Am. VII. 1844, 364, pl. 471.

Cerorhina orientalis, BRANDT, Bull. Ac. St. Petersb. II. 1837, 348 (*lapsus calami* for *occidentalis* ?).

Chimerina cornuta, ESCHSCHOLTZ, Zool. Atl. III. 1829, 2, pl. 12.

Cerorhina Suckleyi, CASS. in Baird's B. N. Am. 1858, 906 (adult without knob on bill). — BAIRD, Cat. N. Am. B. 1859, no. 718.

Sagmatorhina Suckleyi, COUES, Pr. Ac. Nat. Sci. Philad. 1868, 32, figs. 4, 5 (bill).

The Horn-billed Guillemot, CASS. & BAIRD, ll. c.

HAB. Coasts and islands of the North Pacific, breeding as far south as California (Farallon Islands) and Northern Japan; in winter, as far as Lower California.

SP. CHAR. *Adult, breeding plumage:* Entire upper parts dull brownish black, the feathers sometimes with paler or grayish brown tips; lateral and under parts of head and neck, jugulum, and sides smoky plumbeous; lower parts white, usually faintly clouded with smoky gray. A row of straight white filamentous feathers along each side of the occiput, originating just behind and above the eye; another row of similar but larger feathers across the cheeks, from the rictus back. Bill dull orange, the culmen, with anterior and posterior edges of the horn, black; legs and feet pale

Summer adult.

yellowish brown (in skin), the webs and claws dusky; iris hazel (W. A. COOPER, MS.). *Adult, in winter* (= "*Cerrohina Suckleyi*," CASS., "*Sagmatorhina Suckleyi*," COUES): Exactly like the summer plumage, but breast more uniformly smoky gray, the abdomen more uniform white; horn-like process of the nasal shield and mandibular process entirely absent. *Young, first plumage:* Similar to the adult, but white filamentous feathers of the head entirely absent, maxillary horn wanting

Winter adult.

or imperfectly developed, the bill smaller and of a dusky brown color. *Downy young:* Uniform sooty grayish brown, lighter than the corresponding stage of *Lunda cirrhata*, and with slenderer bill, but otherwise very similar.

Total length, about 14.00–15.50 inches; wing, 7.25; culmen, from cere or anterior edge of horn, 1.00; height of horn from nostril, .75; tarsus, 1.10–1.20; middle toe, with claw, 1.80–1.90.

The Horn-billed Guillemot, once supposed to be a very rare species, has been found by recent explorations to be quite common, not only on our western coast, but in various parts of the Pacific. It may be regarded as an oceanic species of the Pacific, breeding on the islands of the western coast of America, and probably on the eastern side of Asia. It was procured at Hakodadi, Japan, by Mr. R. Swinhoe, in the months of March and April ("Ibis," 1874); and others were obtained by the United States Expedition under Commodore Perry, as also by Mr. Whitely, at the same place on the 11th of May, the dates indicating that it probably breeds there. The last found it by no means rare; and it could be very easily shot, as should it dive on the approach of a boat it will rise to the surface again in a very short time. How far north on the Asiatic coast it extends we have no data to show; but as it is found on the American as far north as Sitka, it is also, very probably, common along the entire Pacific coast of Asia. Mr. Bischoff collected a number of specimens at Sitka; and Mr. R. Browne, in his List of the Birds of Vancouver Island, mentions finding it common in the neighborhood of Fort Rupert, and states that it was seen as far north as Fort Simpson.

At San Diego, during the stormy winter of 1861–1862, Dr. Cooper obtained many specimens of this Guillemot, most of them picked up dead on shore, where they had apparently perished on account of the severity of the weather at the time of their change of plumage, as happens with the Pelicans and the Cormorants. They were usually seen swimming near the shore. On no other occasion did he meet with any of these birds, though they are probably common along the whole coast from the Straits of Fuca to Margarita Bay. Dr. Heermann states that the Horn-billed Guillemot is nocturnal in its habits in the summer, inhabiting burrows among the rocks in the Farallones; and that — although he met with none there — he thinks they also burrow on Santa Barbara Island, and perhaps on others, lying concealed during the day, and going out to fish at night. Dr. Heermann saw one toward night fly ashore with a fish in its mouth, and plunge into a hole. Dr. Cooper conjectures that, like the *Ptychoramphus aleuticus*, this bird may remain at sea during the day, and come on shore at night in order to feed its young.

An egg of this species — obtained on the Farallones by Mr. Gruber for Dr. Cooper in May, 1862 — measures 2.60 inches in length by 1.80 in breadth, is of a dirty white color, and in shape resembles the egg of the common Hen.

The late Mr. James Hepburn obtained birds of this species in abundance on Smith's Island, south of San Juan, Washington Territory. They were breeding in the most astonishing numbers, so that the light soil of the island was perfectly honeycombed with their burrows. The lighthouse-keepers were feeding their dogs and pigs with the eggs and with the old birds. The eggs are of a dull chalky white, with discolorations and faint shell-markings of obscure purplish gray, and are very similar to the eggs of *Fratercula corniculata*. They range from 2.65 inches to 2.90 in length, and in breadth from 1.80 to 1.90.

Genus **FRATERCULA**, Brisson.

Fratercula, Briss. Orn. VI. 1760, 81 (type, *Alca arctica*, Linn.).
Mormon, Illiger, Prodr. 1811, 283 (same type).
Larva, Vieill. Analyse, 1816, 67 (same type).
Ceratoblepharum, Brandt, Bull. Sc. St. Petersb. II. 1837, 348 (same type).

Char. Bill extremely deep and excessively compressed, the basal portion covered in the breeding-season by a greater or less number of deciduous horny laminæ. Basal depth of the closed bill nearly or quite equal to the length of the gonys; culmen arched, sometimes even to the extreme base; gonys convex toward the base, straight, or even sometimes slightly concave, for the terminal half, or more; deciduous nasal shield becoming rapidly narrower toward the top; terminal portion of the bill transversely sulcate; base of the maxilla surrounded by a deciduous thickened horny rim, and rictus ornamented by a deciduous tumid rosette; eyelids furnished with deciduous horny plates. No tufts about the head in the breeding-season.

F. arctica.

The deciduous accessory pieces of the bill, together with the rictal and palpebral ornaments, are cast at the close of the breeding-season.[1]

Following is a key to the known species.

1. **F. arctica.** Horny process of upper eyelid short, subconical; grooves of the bill very oblique, broad, and distinct, the deciduous shields occupying not more than the basal half of the bill. Chin and whole throat grayish.
   a. arctica. Bill and general size smaller. Culmen, 1.60–1.90 inches; gonys, 1.40–1.50; depth of maxilla at base, .75–.90; of mandible, .40–.50; tarsus, 1.00–1.10; middle toe, without claw, 1.25–1.40. Wing, 6.00–6.50. *Hab.* Coasts of the North Atlantic, from Southern Greenland southward.
   β. glacialis. Bill and general size larger. Culmen, 2.00–2.30 inches; gonys, 1.40–1.60; depth of maxilla at base, .85–1.00; of mandible, .70–.80; tarsus, 1.10–1.35; middle toe, without claw, 1.45–1.60. *Hab.* Arctic Ocean, from Spitzbergen to northern and western Greenland; probably also western shores of Baffin's Bay, and Northern Labrador.
2. **F. corniculata.** Horny process of upper eyelid narrow, elongated, horn-like; grooves of bill nearly vertical, narrow, and less distinct; deciduous shields occupying much more than the basal half of the bill. Whole throat blackish, only the chin gray. *Hab.* Coasts and islands of the North Pacific and Behring's Sea.

[1] See Dr. Louis Bureau: De la Mue du Bec et des Ornements Palpébraux du Macaroux arctique, *Fratercula arctica* (Lin.), Steph., après la Saison des Amours (Bull. Soc. Zool. de France, 1878, pp. 1–21, pls. iv. v.).

Fraternula arctica.

THE COMMON PUFFIN.

Alca arctica, LINN. S. N. I. 1758, 13, no. 3; ed. 12, I. 1766, 211, no. 3.

Fratercula arctica, STEPHENS, Shaw's Gen. Zool. XIII. 1825, 37. — COUES, Pr. Philad. Acad. 1868, 21; Key, 1872, 340; Check List, 1873, no. 618; ed. 2, 1882, no. 854. — BUREAU, Bull. Soc. Zool. France, 1878, pl. iv. figs. 1-5. — RIDGW. Nom. N. Am. B. 1881, no. 743.

Mormon arctica, NAUM. Isis, 1821, 783, pl. 7, figs. 5-7. — NUTT. Man. II. 1834, 548. — AUD. Orn. Biog. III. 1835, 105, pl. 213; oct. ed. VII. 184, pl. 464. — CASS. in Baird's B. N. Am. 1858, 903. — BAIRD, Cat. N. Am. B. 1859, no. 715.

Mormon fratercula, TEMM. Man. 1820, 933. — GOULD, B. Eur. V. 1837, pl. 403.

Alca deleta, BRÜNN, Orn. Bor. 1764, 25, no. 104 (= young).

Alca labradoria, GMEL. S. N. I. ii. 1788, 550, no. 6 (= young).

Mormon polaris, BREHM, Isis, 1826, 985.

Mormon Grabæ, BREHM, Vög. Deutschl. 1831, 999.

HAB. Coasts and islands of the North Atlantic, as far as Southern Greenland; south in winter to Atlantic States, and breeding as far south as France and the Bay of Fundy.

SP. CHAR. *Adult, in breeding-season:* Pileum fuliginous-dusky, inclining to brownish slate, darker along the lateral margin, lighter anteriorly, the forehead sometimes almost ashy; rest of the head, including chin and throat, light ashy, the throat with a darker suffusion on each side; broad collar across foreneck fuliginous-dusky, growing gradually black on sides of neck, the nape

F. arctica, winter adult.

and entire upper parts uniform deep black. Lower parts white, the sides (beneath wings) grayish fuliginous; lining of wings light smoky gray. "Bill with the basal rim and the first ridge of the upper mandible dull yellow, the intervening space grayish blue; basal margin of lower mandible bright red; first ridge and intervening space as in the upper, the rest bright red (carmine tinged with vermilion); membrane at the base of the gape gamboge-yellow, inside of mouth, and tongue, yellow; edges of eyelids vermilion, horny appendages of eyelids grayish blue; iris light blue; feet vermilion, claws black"[1] (AUDUBON). *Adult, winter plumage:* Similar to

[1] "*Adult* (*breeding-plumage*). — Iris hazel-brown. Eyelids vermilion-red, fleshy callosities bluish ash. Base of bill and first ridge dull yellowish, the contained space bluish, rest of bill vermilion-red, the tip of the lower mandible and the two terminal grooves yellowish. Legs and feet coral-red, claws black" (COUES).

the above, but the basal shields of the bill wanting, and replaced by a soft skin of a brownish-black color, the horny appendages to the eyelids wanting, the rictal "rosette" much reduced in size, of a dull purplish red color; sides of head darker gray, the loral and orbital regions quite blackish.

Total length, about 11.75 inches; extent, 23.00; wing, 6.00–6.50; culmen, 1.60–1.90; gonys, 1.40–1.50; depth of maxilla at base, .75–.90; of mandible, .40–.50; tarsus, 1.00–1.10; middle toe, without claw, 1.25–1.40.

We are unable to appreciate sufficiently decided or constant differences between specimens of corresponding sex, age, and season from Labrador, Southern Greenland, Norway, and the Orkneys. Examples from the Faröes appear to have slenderer bills, and those from the coast of France smaller bills, than any others in the collection examined; but these apparent differences may not prove constant in a larger series.

The "Sea Parrot," the "Puffin," or "Coulternet," as this bird is called in various localities, is an oceanic bird, found exclusively in the waters of the Atlantic, and breeding on the eastern coast of North America from Eastern Maine to Greenland, and in Europe from Great Britain to the North Cape. A few of this species breed in the islands off the coast of Portugal, and it also extends its movements into the Arctic Sea north of Europe.

According to Reinhardt it is a resident species of Greenland. It also visits the Faröe Islands, Iceland, and Nova Zembla, and other northern regions. According to the observations of Mr. Howard Saunders, this species, though not abundant, is found not uncommon on the east coast of Spain. It was also found by the fishermen on the Island of Dragonena — where, however, it does not breed. Mr. Saunders was informed that it is abundant, occurring in flocks, off the coast of Morocco, near Mogador. The most southern breeding-place of this bird with which Mr. Saunders is acquainted is at the Berlengas, or Farallones, a group of rocks in the Atlantic, a little north of the latitude of Lisbon. The Puffin in the winter also visits the shores of Holland and France. A single specimen was taken at Genoa in the winter of 1823; and M. Savi includes it in his "History of the Birds of Italy." Accidental specimens wander occasionally to Sicily and to Malta; in the latter place Schembri obtained a single specimen in 1832 ("Ibis, 1864).

In Great Britain, according to Yarrell, it is only a summer visitor, appearing early in April, and departing about the last of August. There it breeds in the crevices of high rocks or cliffs on the sea-coast, or in the short turf on the table-lands above. Early in May it deposits its single large egg, sometimes in the fissures on the perpendicular surface of the cliffs, to the depth of three or four feet from the front; sometimes in rabbit-warrens, which are common on that coast; and sometimes, selecting islands that are covered with a stratum of vegetable mould, the birds dig their own burrows. This hole is generally excavated to the depth of three feet, often in a curving direction, and occasionally has two entrances. The digging is principally performed by the male; and he is at times so intent upon his work as to suffer himself to be taken by the hand. This happens also with the female when incubating. They can be handled, however, only at the risk of receiving a severe bite from their sharp and powerful bill. The egg is laid at the farthest end of the burrow. It is 2.75 inches long and 1.63 broad, pure white when deposited, sometimes spotted with pale cinereous, and often becoming soiled and dirty from contact with the earth, as no materials are ever collected for the nest. The young are hatched after a month's incubation; these are covered at first with a long blackish down, which is soon replaced by their feather-plumage; and at the end of a month or five weeks they are able to quit their burrow and follow their parents to the open sea. When the time for migration comes, those birds which are not able to follow their parents are deserted.

On the land the Sea Parrot rests on the whole length of the foot and heel, and walks with a waddling gait. It flies rapidly for a short distance, and can swim and dive well.

On the American coast this bird formerly bred abundantly on the rocky islands near the mouth of the Bay of Fundy. This it still does, but in greatly diminished numbers. It becomes quite abundant off the coast in the latter part of the fall and during winter and early spring, and extends along the coast as far as Long Island, where, according to Giraud, it is of occasional but rare occurrence. Audubon has known it to wander as far south as the Savannah River. This happened only once; namely, in the winter of 1831–1832.

In his excursion to Labrador Audubon visited several of the breeding-places of this bird. In one, where the soil was light, many of the burrows extended to the depth of five or six feet. The ground was everywhere perforated like a rabbit-warren. On the 28th of June none of the eggs were found to have been hatched. On the 12th of August he visited Perroket Island, about two miles from the harbor of Bras d'Or, where these birds were breeding in thousands. This time he found the burrows inhabited by young birds of different ages. Clouds of Puffins were flying overhead, having fish in their mouths, with which to feed their young. The fish were about five inches in length, and are known as the "Lint." As they flew the birds uttered a loud croaking noise, but did not drop their fish, even when brought down by a shot. They manifested great affection for each other; and when one was shot, its companions would alight by its side, swim around it, push it with the bill, as if urging it to fly or dive. Those that were wounded and fell on the land immediately ran into a hole, where it was not safe to meddle with them. Those which were caught alive bit so severely, and scratched so desperately with their claws, that their captors were only too happy to let them go. The burrows communicated in various ways with each other, and the whole island was so perforated that there was danger of falling in at every step. The birds did not leave during his visit, but attended to their duties. Here one rose from under his feet; there, within a few yards, another would alight with a fish and dive into its burrow, or feed the young that stood waiting at the entrance. The young birds were continually fighting, and their cries, which resembled the wailing of young whelps, came up from under the ground with sepulchral effect. In some instances two birds were found sitting, each on its egg, in the same hole. He found great variation both in the shape and size of the eggs, some being much more rounded than others. When boiled, the whites of the eggs became of a livid-blue color. He found them unfit for food, and they are never collected by the eggers.

The flight of these birds is direct and firm. They can rise either from the water or the land; and can do this, if necessary, without running to gain impetus. Some that he kept on board his vessel fed freely, and were very amusing; but they were continually uttering an unpleasant grunting noise, and were never quiet during the night.

In the young the bills do not begin to acquire their peculiar form for several weeks, and it is several years before the change is complete.

Dr. Coues, in September, 1860, after his visit to Labrador, wrote me in reference to this species, that they were breeding on the Puffin Island, so called, on the northern side of the mouth of Groswater Bay. In several respects his statements are in conflict with those of Audubon. At the place where the birds live which he visited, the soil is of a kind in which the birds can easily dig. The holes were just about deep enough to be reached with the arm, and generally straight, though some were quite tortuous. The entrances were worn perfectly smooth and slippery. Many of the holes were only passages from one nest to another. The nest itself consisted of only a few dried grasses laid at the end of the hole. Only one egg is laid; and this is obscurely and often almost imperceptibly blotched with light bluish ash. He heard not the slightest sound from one of these birds; but as he climbed the side of the island they started out from their holes all around him. Each bird would generally stop for a moment at the mouth of its hole to see what was going on, and then scramble and flutter down to the water, diving immediately. When taken in the hand it struggles and bites furiously, at the same time uttering a hoarse croaking cry. Its inner nail is very strong, sharp, and curved. When the bird is standing, this lies flat; but when scratching or digging, it is held upright. There was no evidence of any sympathy between the survivors and those wounded or dead, who were not noticed in any way by those which had escaped injury. The flight of this bird, when once on the wing, is well sustained and firm, and is performed with short, quick beats. When it throws itself into the air from a rock it launches out with ease; but it rises from the water with difficulty, flapping along over its surface before it can rise well on the wing. When standing at the entrance of its burrow it presents a peculiarly grotesque appearance, its short, thick-set body, enormous head and bill, with its contrast of colors, giving it an air, the comicality of which its upright position and its odd movements contribute not a little to enhance.

This species was observed by Mr. Kumlien in abundance from the Gulf of St. Lawrence to Hudson's Straits. It was unknown in Cumberland, but was common on the Greenland coast as far north as 70°. They breed abundantly on the islands in Disco Bay.

M. Bureau has recently published ("Bull. Soc. Zool. France," 1878) a very interesting account of the moulting of portions of the beak of this species after their breeding-season. Certain portions of its beak at the base of the maxilla and of the mandible, as well as the horny excrescences above and below the eye, are regularly shed every year, and as regularly assumed as the breeding-season approaches. The number of deciduous pieces is thirteen. It is quite probable that similar changes take place in the other species of this genus.

Eggs of this species in the Smithsonian Collection, collected in Labrador, have a ground of a dull chalky white, with faint shell-markings about the larger end of a lavender-gray. Four specimens present the following variations in their respective measurements: 2.40 by 1.85 inches; 2.55 by 1.75; 2.60 by 1.65; 2.65 by 1.70.

Fratercula arctica glacialis.

THE LARGE-BILLED PUFFIN.

Mormon glacialis, "LEACH," NAUM. Isis, 1821, 782, pl. 7. fig. 2. — CASS. in Baird's B. N. Am. 1858, 903. — BAIRD, Cat. N. Am. B. 1859, no. 714.

Fratercula glacialis, LEACH, Steph. Gen. Zool. XIII. 1825, 40, pl. 4, fig. 2. — COUES, Pr. Philad. Acad. 1868, 23. — BUREAU, Bull. Soc. Zool. France, 1878, pl. v. figs. 1, 2.

Fratercula arctica, var. *glacialis*, COUES, Key, 1872, 340; Check List, 1873, no. 618 *a*.

Fratercula arctica glacialis, RIDGW. Nom. N. Am. B. 1881, no. 743 *a*. — COUES, 2d Check List, 1882, no. 855.

HAB. Coasts and islands of the Arctic Ocean, from Spitzbergen to Northern and Western Greenland; also probably west shores of Baffin's Bay and Northern Labrador.

SUB-SP. CHAR. Exactly like *F. arctica*, but bill much larger, and general size also greater. Wing, 6.80–7.40 inches; culmen, 2.00–2.30; gonys, 1.40–1.60; depth of maxilla at base, .75–.90, of mandible, .70–.80; tarsus, 1.10–1.35; middle toe, without claw, 1.45–1.60.

This bird is apparently a larger hyperborean race of *F. arctica*, since there appear to be no differences from the latter except larger size. The material at our command is, however, very small, embracing only three examples. It may not be more worthy of separation from the true *F. arctica* than is the very small-billed form breeding on the coast of France, which seems to represent the opposite extreme of size.

F. arctica glacialis, summer adult.

By most writers this is regarded as being a mere variety of the *arcticus*. Bonaparte speaks of it in his Synopsis as not uncommon in winter on our coast. Audubon only met with it once, and even then was not certain of its identity. This was at the outer side of Grand Menan, in the Bay of Fundy. None were seen by him in Labrador. The bird which he figures for the *glacialis* was probably *corniculata.*

Professor Newton was informed by Mr. Proctor that two specimens of this Puffin had been received by the latter from Iceland. Professor Newton also states that he found this form of Puffin the least common of the *Alcidæ* in the waters about Spitzbergen. Ross, however, states that it was found in considerable numbers on Walden and Little Table islands; but Dr. Malmgren states that such was not his experience. The latter, however, mentions that he saw several near Norway and Amsterdam islands, and in June some were shot in Treurenberg Bay. He also found them on Bear Island, but not in great numbers. He observed them several times at a considerable distance from land. They were most plentiful in Sassen Bay, forty miles from the open sea. No mention is made of their breeding, and I have no information in regard to this or as to any of their distinctive breeding habits. Even if this bird is specifically distinct from *arcticus*, there is every reason to suppose its habits to be nearly identical with those of that and of other kindred species.

Two eggs in the Smithsonian Museum from Greenland (Drouet) purporting to be of this species are not distinguishable from those of the *arcticus*, and measure, one 2.65 by 1.85 inches, the other 2.70 by 1.85.

Fratercula corniculata.

THE HORNED PUFFIN.

Mormon corniculatum, NAUM. Isis, 1821, 782, pl. 7, figs. 3, 4 (Kamtschatka). — CASS. in Baird's B. N. Am. 1858, 902. — BAIRD, Cat. N. Am. B. 1859, no. 713. — DALL & BANNIST. Tr. Chicago Ac. I. 1869, 308.

Lunda arctica, PALL. Zoog. Rosso-As. II. 1826, 365 (part).

Fratercula corniculata, GRAY, Gen. B. III. 1849, 637, pl. 174. — COUES, Pr. Ac. Nat. Sci. Philad. 1868, 24; Key, 1872, 340; Check List, 1873, no. 617; ed. 2, 1882, no. 853; Elliott's Alaska, 1875, 202. — RIDGW. Nom. N. Am. B. 1881, no. 744.

Mormon glacialis, AUD. Orn. Biog. III. 1835, 599, pl. 293, fig. 1; B. Am. VII. 1844, 236, pl. 463 (not of LEACH). — GOULD, B. Eur. V. 1837, pl. 404.

HAB. Coasts and islands of the North Pacific, from Kamtschatka to Sitka.

SP. CHAR. *Adult, breeding-plumage:* Pileum uniform drab or grayish brown; entire side of the head, including a broad superciliary stripe, white; lower part of neck (all round), with entire upper parts, uniform deep black, the throat more fuliginous, and changing to smoky gray toward the base of the mandible. Entire lower parts, except as described, plain white, the lining of the wing uniform smoky gray. Soft eye-horns brownish black, with a delicate silky gloss; naked eye-ring vermilion; tip of bill, to between 2d and 3d groove, salmon-red along culmen and gonys,

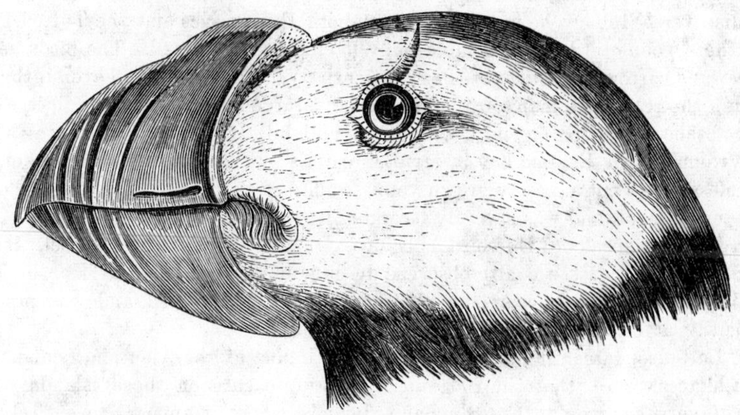

F. corniculata, summer adult.

elsewhere brownish red; base of bill very light and bright chrome-yellow, the tumid rosette at the corner of the mouth bright orange, as is also the interior of the mouth and the tongue; iris brownish gray; feet intense vermilion-red during height of breeding-season, but much paler both before a[illegible] after.[1] *Adult, in winter:* Bill much broader through the middle portion than at the base, the culmen being more or less arched just behind the middle portion; destitute of the basal shields; the gonys horizontal and nearly straight for the basal half, then perfectly straight, and forming a decided upward angle to the tip; rictal rosette nearly obsolete, pale yellow, and superciliary horn absent. Color of bill dark brownish, the terminal portion lighter, and tinged more or less with orange-reddish. Side of head ash-gray, becoming sooty blackish on lores and orbital

[1] The Authors are under obligations to Dr. L. Stejneger for the privilege of consulting his notes and colored drawings made from freshly killed specimens, and for his kind permission to make use of them here. They are also indebted to him for much information concerning the perplexing transitions of plumage and other particulars regarding various *Alcidæ* which could only be known from a study of these remarkable birds in their natural haunts.

region. Plumage otherwise as in summer, but pileum darker or blackish brown. Eyelids brownish gray, feet pale reddish. *Young:* Similar in plumage to the winter adult, but bill very different, being much narrower, the culmen not at all arched, and the terminal portion of both maxilla and mandible destitute of any trace of transverse grooves. *Downy young:* Uniform fuliginous-black or dusky, the abdomen abruptly white.

Downy young.

Total length, about 13.00 inches; extent, 24.50; wing, 7.00–7.25; culmen (chord), 2.00–2.25; gonys, 1.60–1.70; depth of maxilla at base, 1.15–1.25; of mandible, .70–.80; tarsus, 1.15–1.25; middle toe, 1.55–1.65.

This species is common to the Northern Pacific Ocean, and is found along the Alaskan coast and on nearly all the islands in Behring's Sea. It also occurs on the eastern shore of Asia, and was taken in the Sea of Ochotsk by the naturalists connected with the Rogers Exploring Expedition.

Mr. Bannister mentions this species as being common on Whale Island, north of St. Michael's. This island is steep and rocky, and landing on it except in very favorable weather is difficult. Upon the only occasion on which it was visited no nests were discovered, though he is confident that both this species and the Tufted Puffin breed there, young birds scarcely able to fly having been captured. The birds nest in the deep and narrow interstices of the rocks, entirely out of reach; and even if the nest is within the reach of a man's arm, it would be hazardous to attempt to rob it, except in the absence of the parent bird, whose powerful bill is capable of inflicting a very severe wound. An Eskimo boy in Mr. Bannister's service, not having a pocket, was so careless as to put a nearly grown young Puffin of this species for security under his upper garment, and was severely lacerated by the bird.

Mr. Dall also speaks of this bird as being extremely abundant on the rocky islands near St. Michael's. It was also observed by him at Plover Bay, Coal Harbor, Unga Island, and Aliaska. It has been obtained at Kotzebue Sound, and was procured abundantly at Sitka and Kadiak by Mr. Bischoff.

Mr. Dall also states, in his Notes on the Avifauna of the Aleutian Islands from Unalashka eastward, that the *F. corniculata* is quite rare on those islands. It is, however, very common in the Shumagin Islands, where it appears to entirely take the place of the *Lunda cirrhata*. It is resident there throughout the year, and breeds in holes and crevices in the cliffs of Round Island, Coal Harbor, and Unga. The eggs of this species were obtained there; and though the parent bird, which was caught on the nest, managed to escape, they were well identified. The eggs which were then taken were single, one in each nest, and were of a mottled rusty color with dark spots, though he had expected to have found them white. These eggs, as it now appears, must have been discolored by the soil on the rock on which they were laid, as the color of the egg when fresh is white.

To this Mr. Dall adds, in his Notes on the Birds of the Islands west of Unalashka, that he there found it resident and abundant from Attu to the Shumagins, and with habits similar to those of the *L. cirrhata*.

Mr. H. W. Elliott found this species common in the Prybilof Islands, and states in reference to it, that the eye never fails to be arrested by this odd-looking bird, with its great shovel-like, lemon-yellow and red bill, as it sits squatted in glum silence on the rocky cliff-perches, regarding approach with an air of stolid wonder, seemingly fashioned with especial regard to the fantastic and the comical. In common with the *cirrhata,* it comes up from the sea, from the south, to the cliffs of the islands about the 10th of May, always in pairs, never coming or going in flocks. It makes a nest of dried sea-ferns, grass, moss, etc., far back or down in some deep rocky crevice, where the egg when laid is generally inaccessible. It lays but a single egg, large, oblong-oval, pure white; and, contrary to the custom of Gulls, Arries, Choochkies, etc., when the egg is removed the Sea Parrot does not renew it, but deserts the nest, probably locating elsewhere. The young chick Mr. Elliott was not able to get until it emerged fully fledged and ready for flight, in August, when it does not differ materially from its parent; it leaves the islands about the 10th of September. This bird is said to be very quiet and unobtrusive, and not to come to the islands in large numbers, and to breed everywhere else in Behring's Sea. Its flight is performed with quick and rapid wing-beats, in a straight and steady course. There is no difference between the sexes as to size, shape, or plumage.

The egg is noticeably more elongate than are those of *Fratercula arctica* or *Lunda cirrhata,* though not more pointed. The shell is rough and of a dead white, and, so far as known, without any obscure or obsolete marking of the other species. The specimens measure about 2.75 inches in length, and 1.75 in their larger breadth.

Genus **LUNDA**, Pallas.

Lunda, Pall. Zoog. Rosso-As. II. 1826, 363 (type, *Alca cirrhata,* Pall.).
Sagmatorhina, Bonap. P. Z. S. 1851, 252 (type, *S. Lathami,* Bp., = *Lunda cirrhata,* juv.!).
Gymnoblepharum, Brandt, Bull. Sc. St. Petersb. II. 1837, 349 (type, *Alca cirrhata,* Pall.).
Cheniscus, Gray, Cat. Gen. & Subgen. B. Brit. Mus. 1855, 127 (same type; not of Eyton, 1838).

Char. Similar to *Fratercula,* but nasal shield rapidly increasing in width toward the top, where forming a thickened, slightly arched ridge nearly equal in length to the culmen; mandible

L. cirrhata, summer adult.

smooth, without grooves; eyelids without horny appendages; head ornamented by a decurved superciliary tuft of long, silky, straw-colored feathers. Lower parts dusky.

Lunda cirrhata.

THE TUFTED PUFFIN.

Alca cirrhata, PALL. Spic. Zoöl. V. 1769, 7, pl. 1 and pl. 2, figs. 1, 2, 3.

Lunda cirrhata, PALL. Zoog. Rosso-As. II. 1826, 363, pl. 82. — COUES, Pr. Ac. Nat. Sci. Philad. 1868, 26. — RIDGW. Nom. N. Am. B. 1881, no. 745.

Mormon cirrhata, BONAP. Synop. 1828, 429. — AUD. Orn. Biog. III. 1835, 36, pl. 249, figs. 1, 2; B. Am. VII. 1844, 234, pl. 462. — CASS. in Baird's B. N. Am. 1858, 902. — BAIRD, Cat. N. Am. B. 1859, no. 712. — DALL & BANNIST. Tr. Chicago Ac. Sci. I. 1869, 308.

Fratercula cirrhata, STEPHENS, Gen. Zool. XIII. 1825, 40. — COUES, Key, 1872, 341; Check List, 1873, no. 716; Elliot's Alaska, 1875, 203.

Fratercula cirrata, COUES, 2d Check List, 1882, no. 856.

Sagmatorhina Lathami, BONAP. P. Z. S. 1851, 202, pl. 44 (young). — COUES, Pr. Ac. Nat. Sci. Philad. 1868, 31, fig. 3.

Sagmatorhina labradoria, CASS. in Baird's B. N. Am. 1858, 904 (not of GMEL.). — BAIRD, Cat. N. Am. B. 1859, no. 716.

Fratercula carinata, VIG. Zool. Journ. IV. 358.

HAB. Coasts and islands of the North Pacific, from California (south of San Francisco Bay) to Alaska, and across, through Aleutian chain, to Kamtschatka and Japan; also coasts and islands of Behring's Sea. Occurrence in the Arctic Ocean far from Behring's Straits doubtful, but examples said to have been taken on the Kennebec River, Me. (AUDUBON), and in the Bay of Fundy

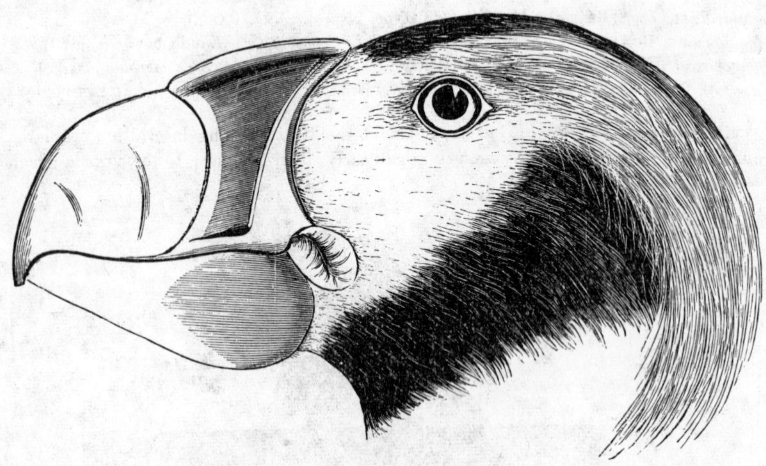

Summer adult.

(VERRILL). On the Pacific coast breeding at least as far south as the Farallon Islands, coast of California.

SP. CHAR. *Adult, breeding-plumage:* Upper parts uniform deep black; lower surface fuliginous-dusky, sometimes with the feathers on the breast and abdomen grayish white beneath the surface, but the entire sides, with whole under and lateral portions of head and neck, always uniform dark fuliginous. Feathers bordering the bill, all round, with entire loral and orbital regions, dull white; on each side the crown, above and behind the eyes, a tuft of much elongated, narrow, filamentous feathers of a straw-yellow or pale buff color. Terminal portion of bill bright salmon-red (more or less tinged with brownish posteriorly), the basal part light olive-green, the deciduous culminal ridge more apple-green; narrow rim of naked skin around base of bill, together with rosette at corner of mouth and naked eyelids, vermilion-red; iris creamy white, dirty white, or light grayish cream-color; feet vivid salmon-red (STEJNEGER, MS.). *Adult, in winter:* Supra-auricular tufts wanting; basal shields of the bill wanting, and replaced by a soft skin of a dusky brown color; terminal portion of the bill exactly as in summer, the grooves varying in distinctness according to age. Otherwise exactly as in summer, but feet pale, dirty flesh-color (STEJNEGER, MS.). *Young, about seven months old:* Much like the winter adult, but terminal portion of bill without trace of grooves, and of a much duller red or brownish orange color; distinct supra-auricular tufts of a deep isabella-brown or fawn-color, but smaller than in the adult; plumage of the lower parts grayish white beneath the surface; feet fleshy white, the webs deeper dull flesh-color. *Young, about five or six months old* (= *Sagmatorhina Lathami*, BP.): Differing from the preceding in absence of the supra-auricular tufts and more slender bill. *Downy young:* Uniform fuliginous-dusky.

Total length, about 15.00 inches; extent, 22.50; wing, 7.75; culmen, 1.30–1.45; nasal shield (on top), 1.00–1.10; greatest depth of closed bill, 1.75–2.00; tarsus, 1.20–1.35; middle toe, 1.75–1.90.

The Tufted Puffin belongs to the Pacific waters, but is said to be of occasional occurrence on the Atlantic coast. One example is alleged to have been received from Greenland by Pastor Möschler in 1846; and Audubon states that the specimen from which he drew the figure of his representation of this species was procured near the mouth of the Kennebec, and that it had been shot in the winter of 1831–1832 by a fisherman while it was standing on some floating ice. It was a male in adult plumage, and no other example was seen.

On the Pacific this species occurs from the latitude of San Francisco northward, and breeds wherever found. It is included by Mr. R. Browne in his List of the Birds of Vancouver Island, and is said to be found as far north as Fort Simpson, where the Indians trim their dancing leggings with its beaks. So far as Dr. Cooper has observed, it seems to be confined to the islands north of the latitude of San Francisco, as he has never seen or heard of any south of the Farallones, nor has he ever heard of its occurrence along the main shore, although it may be found on some islands very near the land, especially about the Straits of Fuca; and it perhaps occasionally visits the main shore. It seems to be a constant resident wherever it does inhabit, finding a very uniform climate and abundance of food at all seasons about the islands.

This bird has in general a striking resemblance to the Parrot, especially in its heavy, plump body, its short legs, its rather short and broad wings, its manner of flight, even in its breeding in holes, and the color of its eggs.

On the Farallones these Puffins are numerous, and during Dr. Cooper's visit in June he found them laying, having begun about the 15th. Their burrows were scratched among the crevices of the granite rocks, and were so shallow that, by protecting the hand so that it would not suffer from a severe bite, both birds and eggs could easily be obtained. He saw no appearance of any nest, the dry earthy bottom of the burrow not requiring any. The egg is single, larger than that of the common Hen, white, somewhat blotched with pale brown, and its ends nearly alike. It measures 2.80 inches in length by 2.00 in breadth. Dr. Cooper never heard this bird utter any sound, although there were several of them perched on the rocks very near him during his visit; they seemed to be at rest during most of the day, and, like all birds with white eyes, somewhat nocturnal in their habits. This Puffin feeds about the rocky shores, swimming and diving well; and by some is supposed to force off limpets and other shells from the rocks with its knife-like bill, though no shells are found in its stomach. These birds eat small fish, and perhaps seaweed also.

Mr. Bannister states that though this bird is by no means scarce in some situations at St. Michael's, it is very much less abundant than the *corniculata*. Its tufts are said to be indicative of maturity; young individuals, though otherwise nearly fully fledged, and able to fly, having them very imperfectly developed. Both this species and the *corniculata* are used as food by the Eskimos, and their skins are made into winter dresses by the Magemuts and the Southern Unaleets. Mr. Dall adds that this bird is abundant on Besborough Island, and that it was plentifully obtained by Mr. Bischoff at Sitka and Kadiak. It is seen abundantly at Unalashka, on the outer rocks and cliffs, where it breeds in inaccessible situations, but never in the harbor, where it is resident. None were seen on the Shumagins. Mr. Dall also found it abundant west of Unalashka, throughout the islands, more especially the unfrequented ones. It was more rare east of Unalashka. Mr. Dall states that it lays two eggs. He found fresh eggs of this species and of the *corniculata* from May to the end of July. The skins are used by the Western Aleuts for making hunting-shirts.

The Tufted Puffin of authors — the Tawpawkie of the natives of the Prybilof Islands, according to Mr. H. W. Elliott — comes to those islands at the same time with the *corniculata*, and resembles that species in its habits generally. It lays a single large white egg, of a rounded oval shape. He was not able to see a newly hatched chick, owing to the retired and inaccessible nature of the breeding-places. Could Walrus Island be visited frequently during the season, interesting observations might be made there, for the nests are more easy of access. The young when six weeks old resemble the parents exactly, only the bill is lighter-colored, and the plumes on the head incipient. He took eggs from over thirty nests in July. The natives say that it is very quarrelsome when mating, its cries sounding like the growling of a bear, as heard far down under the rocks that cover its nest. The egg is much thicker and more capacious than that of *corniculata*, though no longer. The shell is rough, dead white, and, besides the frequent discolorations, shows in several specimens very pale obsolete shell-markings of purplish gray. Several of Mr. Elliott's specimens measured: 2.85 by 1.95 inches; 2.80 by 1.92; 2.75 by 2.00; 2.65 by 1.95.

A few specimens of this bird were obtained from the Kurile Islands in summer by Mr. N. Fukusi, where its common name is *Etopirika* ("Ibis," 1878).

INDEXES.

INDEX OF SCIENTIFIC NAMES.

INDEX OF POPULAR NAMES.

University Press: John Wilson and Son, Cambridge.

NATURAL SCIENCES IN AMERICA

An Arno Press Collection

Allen, J[oel] A[saph]. **The American Bisons,** Living and Extinct. 1876

Allen, Joel Asaph. **History of the North American Pinnipeds:** A Monograph of the Walruses, Sea-Lions, Sea-Bears and Seals of North America. 1880

American Natural History Studies: The Bairdian Period. 1974

American Ornithological Bibliography. 1974

Anker, Jean. **Bird Books and Bird Art.** 1938

Audubon, John James and John Bachman. **The Quadrupeds of North America.** Three vols. 1854

Baird, Spencer F[ullerton]. **Mammals of North America.** 1859

Baird, S[pencer] F[ullerton], T[homas] M. Brewer and R[obert] Ridgway. **A History of North American Birds:** Land Birds. Three vols., 1874

Baird, Spencer F[ullerton], John Cassin and George N. Lawrence. **The Birds of North America.** 1860. Two vols. in one.

Baird, S[pencer] F[ullerton], T[homas] M. Brewer, and R[obert] Ridgway. **The Water Birds of North America.** 1884. Two vols. in one.

Barton, Benjamin Smith. **Notes on the Animals of North America.** Edited, with an Introduction by Keir B. Sterling. 1792

Bendire, Charles [Emil]. **Life Histories of North American Birds** With Special Reference to Their Breeding Habits and Eggs. 1892/1895. Two vols. in one.

Bonaparte, Charles Lucian [Jules Laurent]. **American Ornithology:** Or The Natural History of Birds Inhabiting the United States, Not Given by Wilson. 1825/1828/1833. Four vols. in one.

Cameron, Jenks. **The Bureau of Biological Survey:** Its History, Activities, and Organization. 1929

Caton, John Dean. **The Antelope and Deer of America:** A Comprehensive Scientific Treatise Upon the Natural History, Including the Characteristics, Habits, Affinities, and Capacity for Domestication of the Antilocapra and Cervidae of North America. 1877

Contributions to American Systematics. 1974

Contributions to the Bibliographical Literature of American Mammals. 1974

Contributions to the History of American Natural History. 1974

Contributions to the History of American Ornithology. 1974

Cooper, J[ames] G[raham]. **Ornithology.** Volume I, Land Birds. 1870

Cope, E[dward] D[rinker]. **The Origin of the Fittest:** Essays on Evolution and **The Primary Factors of Organic Evolution.** 1887/1896. Two vols. in one.

Coues, Elliott. **Birds of the Colorado Valley.** 1878

Coues, Elliott. **Birds of the Northwest.** 1874

Coues, Elliott. **Key To North American Birds.** Two vols. 1903

Early Nineteenth-Century Studies and Surveys. 1974

Emmons, Ebenezer. **American Geology:** Containing a Statement of the Principles of the Science. 1855. Two vols. in one.

Fauna Americana. 1825-1826

Fisher, A[lbert] K[enrick]. **The Hawks and Owls of the United States in Their Relation to Agriculture.** 1893

Godman, John D. **American Natural History:** Part I — Mastology and **Rambles of a Naturalist.** 1826-28/1833. Three vols. in one.

Gregory, William King. **Evolution Emerging:** A Survey of Changing Patterns from Primeval Life to Man. Two vols. 1951

Hay, Oliver Perry. **Bibliography and Catalogue of the Fossil Vertebrata of North America.** 1902

Heilprin, Angelo. **The Geographical and Geological Distribution of Animals.** 1887

Hitchcock, Edward. **A Report on the Sandstone of the Connecticut Valley,** Especially Its Fossil Footmarks. 1858

Hubbs, Carl L., editor. **Zoogeography.** 1958

[Kessel, Edward L., editor]. **A Century of Progress in the Natural Sciences: 1853-1953.** 1955

Leidy, Joseph. **The Extinct Mammalian Fauna of Dakota and Nebraska,** Including an Account of Some Allied Forms from Other Localities, Together with a Synopsis of the Mammalian Remains of North America. 1869

Lyon, Marcus Ward, Jr. **Mammals of Indiana.** 1936

Matthew, W[illiam] D[iller]. **Climate and Evolution.** 1915

Mayr, Ernst, editor. **The Species Problem.** 1957

Mearns, Edgar Alexander. **Mammals of the Mexican Boundary of the United States.** Part I: Families Didelphiidae to Muridae. 1907

Merriam, Clinton Hart. **The Mammals of the Adirondack Region,** Northeastern New York. 1884

Nuttall, Thomas. **A Manual of the Ornithology of the United States and of Canada.** Two vols. 1832-1834

Nuttall Ornithological Club. **Bulletin of the Nuttall Ornithological Club:** A Quarterly Journal of Ornithology. 1876-1883. Eight vols. in three.

[Pennant, Thomas]. **Arctic Zoology. 1784-1787.** Two vols. in one.

Richardson, John. **Fauna Boreali-Americana;** Or the Zoology of the Northern Parts of British America, Containing Descriptions of the Objects of Natural History Collected on the Late Northern Land Expeditions Under Command of Captain Sir John Franklin, R. N. Part I: Quadrupeds. 1829

Richardson, John and William Swainson. **Fauna Boreali-Americana:** Or the Zoology of the Northern Parts of British America, Containing Descriptions of the Objects of Natural History Collected by the Late Northern Land Expeditions Under Command of Captain Sir John Franklin, R. N. Part II: The Birds. 1831

Ridgway, Robert. **Ornithology.** 1877

Selected Works By Eighteenth-Century Naturalists and Travellers. 1974

Selected Works in Nineteenth-Century North American Paleontology. 1974

Selected Works of Clinton Hart Merriam. 1974

Selected Works of Joel Asaph Allen. 1974

Selections From the Literature of American Biogeography. 1974

Seton, Ernest Thompson. **Life-Histories of Northern Animals: An Account of the Mammals of Manitoba.** Two vols. 1909

Sterling, Keir Brooks. **Last of the Naturalists:** The Career of C. Hart Merriam. 1974

Vieillot, L. P. **Histoire Naturelle Des Oiseaux de L'Amerique Septentrionale,** Contenant Un Grand Nombre D'Especes Decrites ou Figurees Pour La Premiere Fois. 1807. Two vols. in one.

Wilson, Scott B., assisted by A. H. Evans. **Aves Hawaiienses:** The Birds of the Sandwich Islands. 1890-99

Wood, Casey A., editor. **An Introduction to the Literature of Vertebrate Zoology.** 1931

Zimmer, John Todd. **Catalogue of the Edward E. Ayer Ornithological Library.** 1926